Augsburg College
George Sverdrup Library
Minneapolis, Minnesota 55404

*The American
Immigration Collection*

Reports of the Industrial Commission on Immigration:
Including Testimony with Review and Digest

U. S. Industrial Commission

Arno Press and The New York Times

NEW YORK 1970

Reprint Edition 1970 by Arno Press Inc.

Reprinted from a copy in
The University of Illinois Library

LC# 70-129417
ISBN 0-405-00571-7

The American Immigration Collection—Series II
ISBN for complete set 0-405-00543-1

Manufactured in the United States of America

REPORTS

OF THE

INDUSTRIAL COMMISSION

ON

IMMIGRATION,

INCLUDING TESTIMONY, WITH REVIEW AND DIGEST, AND SPECIAL REPORTS.

AND ON

EDUCATION,

INCLUDING TESTIMONY, WITH REVIEW AND DIGEST.

VOLUME XV

OF THE COMMISSION'S REPORTS.

WASHINGTON:
GOVERNMENT PRINTING OFFICE.
1901.

MEMBERS OF THE INDUSTRIAL COMMISSION.

Mr. ALBERT CLARKE, *Chairman.*

Senator BOIES PENROSE.
Senator STEPHEN R. MALLORY.
Senator JOHN W. DANIEL.
Senator THOMAS R. BARD.
Representative JOHN J. GARDNER.
Representative L. F. LIVINGSTON.
Representative JOHN C. BELL.
Representative THEOBALD OTJEN.
Mr. WILLIAM LORIMER.

Mr. ANDREW L. HARRIS.
Mr. JOHN M. FARQUHAR.
Mr. EUGENE D. CONGER.
Mr. THOMAS W. PHILLIPS.
Mr. CHARLES J. HARRIS.
Mr. JOHN L. KENNEDY.
Mr. CHARLES H. LITCHMAN.
Mr. D. A. TOMPKINS.

E. DANA DURAND, *Secretary.*

[Extract from act of Congress of June 18, 1898, defining the duties of the Industrial Commission and showing the scope of its inquiries.]

SEC. 2. That it shall be the duty of this commission to investigate questions pertaining to immigration, to labor, to agriculture, to manufacturing, and to business, and to report to Congress and to suggest such legislation as it may deem best upon these subjects.

SEC. 3. That it shall furnish such information and suggest such laws as may be made a basis for uniform legislation by the various States of the Union, in order to harmonize conflicting interests and to be equitable to the laborer, the employer, the producer, and the consumer.

IMMIGRATION.

INDUSTRIAL COMMISSION,
December 5, 1901.

To the Fifty-seventh Congress:

I have the honor to transmit herewith, on behalf of the Industrial Commission, a report to Congress on the subject of Immigration, prepared in conformity with an act of Congress of June 18, 1898.

The conclusions and recommendations of the Commission on this subject will be presented in its final report.

Respectfully,

ALBERT CLARKE, *Chairman.*

CONTENTS OF REPORT ON IMMIGRATION.

INTRODUCTORY REVIEW AND DIGEST OF TESTIMONY.

REVIEW OF EVIDENCE: Page.
- A. Statistics of immigration... IX
- B. Social character and effects of immigration......................... IX
- C. Economic effects of immigration XI
- D. Distribution and employment of immigrants.......................... XII
- E. Causes inducing immigration XIII
- F. Assisted immigration... XIV
- G. Existing legislation restricting immigration XV

REVIEW OF SPECIAL REPORTS:
- Statistics and social effects of immigration............................ XIX
- Economic effects of immigration XXII
- Foreign immigrant in New York City.................................... XLII
- Agricultural distribution XLVIII
- Immigration legislation LVII

TOPICAL DIGEST OF EVIDENCE:
- I. STATISTICS OF IMMIGRATION... LXV
  - A. Defective statistics LXV
  - B. Nationality and race... LXVI
- II. SOCIAL CHARACTER AND EFFECTS OF IMMIGRATION....................... LXVII
  - A. Illiteracy of immigrants LXVII
  - B. Tendency of foreign born toward cities LXVII
  - C. Citizenship and naturalization LXIX
  - D. Criminality... LXIX
  - E. Pauperism and insanity LXX
  - F. Contagious diseases.. LXXIII
  - G. Religious faith LXXIV
- III. ECONOMIC EFFECTS OF IMMIGRATION................................... LXXIV
  - A. Money sent out of the country LXXIV
  - B. Standards of living LXXV
  - C. Demand for immigrant labor....................................... LXXVI
  - D. Occupation of immigrants... LXXVI
  - E. Effects on native labor LXXVII
  - F. Distribution and employment of immigrants LXXXIII
  - G. Legislation governing employment agencies in New York... LXXXV
- IV. CAUSES INDUCING IMMIGRATION LXXXIX
  - A. In general LXXXIX
  - B. Prosperity of country.. XIXXXL
  - C. Advertising in Europe.. XC
  - D. Steamship companies.. XC
  - E. Assisted immigration... XCI

V

CONTENTS.

TOPICAL DIGEST OF EVIDENCE:—Continued. Page.
  V. EXISTING LEGISLATION RESTRICTING IMMIGRATION XCIV
      A. History of legislation... XCIV
      B. Inspection and registration....................................... XCV
      C. Chinese immigration.. C
      D. Contract labor... C
      E. Criminals... CII
      F. Immigration through Canada...................................... CIII
      G. Hardships of deportation.. CIII
      H. Steamship companies... CIII
  VI. PROPOSED AMENDMENTS TO IMMIGRATION LAW CV
      A. Need of further restriction..................................... CV
      B. Proposed administrative amendments.............................. CVII
      C. Distribution of immigrants...................................... CXII
      D. Extension of period for deportation............................. CXIII
      E. Bonds regarding immigrants...................................... CXIII
      F. Head tax.. CXIV
      G. Educational test.. CXIV
INDEX TO DIGEST OF EVIDENCE... CXVII

PART I.

HEARINGS ON THE SUBJECT OF IMMIGRATION 1–255

PART II.

SPECIAL REPORT ON GENERAL STATISTICS OF IMMIGRATION AND FOREIGN-BORN POPULATION 257
  CHAP. I.—THE FOREIGN BORN IN RELATION TO TOTAL POPULATION.. 259
     II.—FOREIGN-BORN POPULATION ACCORDING TO COUNTRY OF BIRTH 261
     III.—STATISTICS OF IMMIGRATION............................. 267
     IV.—TENDENCY OF FOREIGN BORN TOWARD CITIES 278
     V.—ILLITERACY AMONG FOREIGN BORN 280
     VI.—PAUPERISM AND CRIMINALITY AMONG THE FOREIGN BORN 285

PART III.

SPECIAL REPORT ON IMMIGRATION AND ITS ECONOMIC EFFECTS 293
  CHAP. I.—OCCUPATIONS OF IMMIGRANTS 295
     II.—RELATION OF IMMIGRATION TO OTHER CAUSES AFFECTING WAGES AND EMPLOYMENT.............. 304
        I. Cycles of prosperity and depression.................... 305
        II. Standard of living................................... 309
        III. Unequal distribution of immigrants.................. 311
        IV. Labor organization................................. 312
        V. Machinery and division of labor..................... 313
        VI. Competition of women and children................. 314
        VII. Country competition............................... 316
     III.—FOREIGN-BORN LABOR IN THE CLOTHING TRADE... 316
        I. Number of foreign born employed.................... 316
        II. The sweating system 319
        III. Position of various nationalities.................. 324
        IV. Labor organizations in the clothing trade 327
        V. Wage statistics in the clothing trade 335
        VI. Modes of production and relation to nationalities..... 343

CONTENTS.

IMMIGRATION AND ITS ECONOMIC EFFECTS—Continued.   Page.
CHAP. III—Continued.
- VII. The task system... 345
- VIII. The factory system... 348
- IX. Conclusions as to clothing trades.......................... 368
- X. Tenement-house work and legislation regarding it..... 369
- IV.—EFFECT OF FOREIGN-BORN ON CIGARMAKING TRADE 385
- V.—THE FOREIGN-BORN IN THE COAL MINES................ 389
  - I. Distribution of foreign-born and of nationalities........ 389
  - II. Effects on unemployment.................................. 393
  - III. Machine mining... 398
  - IV. Labor organizations in coal mining...................... 405
  - V. Wage statistics.. 411
  - VI. Accidents in relation to the foreign-born............... 416
- VI.—MISCELLANEOUS TRADES...................................... 420
  - Shoe trade... 422
  - Woodworkers... 423
  - Iron, steel, and machinery trades............................ 424
  - Machinists... 425
  - Iron and tin workers... 425
  - Glass workers—Flint-glass workers........................... 425
  - Glass-bottle blowers.. 426
  - The building trades... 427
  - Granite cutters... 427
  - Stonecutters... 428
  - Bricklayers... 428
  - Plumbers... 428
  - Longshoremen.. 428
  - Bakers... 428
  - Investigation made by New York bureau of labor statistics.. 428
- VII.—THE PADRONE SYSTEM AND COMMON LABOR......... 430
- VIII.—IMMIGRATION FROM CANADA................................ 446
- IX.—THE FOREIGN IMMIGRANT IN NEW YORK CITY...... 449
- X.—AGRICULTURAL DISTRIBUTION OF IMMIGRANTS....... 492
  - I. Introductory.. 492
  - II. Nationalities in agriculture................................ 495
    - Italians.. 495
    - Bohemians... 507
    - Finnish colonization.. 510
    - Distribution of Jewish immigrants........................ 510
  - III. Immigration and agriculture in the separate States... 517
    - North Atlantic States... 517
    - North Central States.. 528
    - Southern States... 550
    - Western States.. 575
  - IV. Statistical tables... 583
- XI.—IMMIGRATION LEGISLATION AND ITS WORKINGS.. 617
  - A. The alien contract-labor law.............................. 617
  - B. Excepted classes of alien contract laborers........... 648
  - C. Prosecution of the importer................................ 655
  - D. Deportation of contract laborers c....................... 658
  - E. The Bureau of Immigration................................ 659
  - F. Cases showing the operation of the contract-labor laws... 666
  - G. Chinese-exclusion laws and treaties..................... 671
  - H. Immigration through Canada.............................. 681

CONTENTS.

IMMIGRATION AND ITS ECONOMIC EFFECTS—Continued.

	Page.
CHAP. XII.—LEGISLATION OF FOREIGN COUNTRIES AFFECTING EMIGRATION AND IMMIGRATION	695

APPENDIX:
Philadelphia clothing trade ... 723

PART IV.

SPECIAL REPORT ON CHINESE AND JAPANESE LABOR IN THE MOUNTAIN AND PACIFIC COAST STATES ... 745
Manufacturing in San Francisco ... 747
Laborers upon railway lines ... 749
Laborers in mines ... 753
Agricultural industries ... 754
Smuggling over Canadian and Mexican frontiers ... 758
Highbinders and highbinderism ... 762

EXHIBITS:
A. Statement of Mr. Frank Schuyler, Chinese importer, San Francisco ... 765
B. Affidavit of Hon. Cleveland L. Dam ... 767
C. Statement of Dr. John Endicott Gardner, with exhibits attached thereto ... 768
D. Statement of William Price, lieutenant of police, San Francisco ... 775
E. Statement of Chun Ho, Chinese slave girl ... 783
F. Statement of Miss Donaldina Cameron ... 786
G. Statement of rescued Chinese slave girls ... 789
H. Statement of Hon. Ho Yow, H. I. C. consul-general at San Francisco ... 791
I. Statement of Chinese merchant ... 792
J. Statement of Hon. John P. Jackson, collector of customs, San Francisco ... 795
K. Statement of John D. Putnam, Chinese inspector, Los Angeles ... 797
L. Statement of Mr. Fred Wadham, deputy revenue collector, San Diego, Cal ... 800
M. Affidavit of Hon. P. H. McCarthy, president of Federated Trades of the Pacific Coast ... 801

REVIEW OF EVIDENCE AND SPECIAL REPORTS.

I. REVIEW OF EVIDENCE.

A.—STATISTICS OF IMMIGRATION.

It was not until after the enactment of the law of 1893 providing for a set of questions to be answered upon the ships' manifests, that statistics relating to social and economic characteristics of immigration were obtained. Even since that date doubt has been expressed by witnesses as to the reliability of statistics—especially those which concern the occupations and destination of immigrants are of little or no value.[1] Immigrants who state themselves to be farmers are usually mere farm laborers, and a large proportion of those who give their destination as New York City do not actually remain there. One witness maintains that even the United States census statistics are inaccurate. He claims that the number of Italians in the country in 1890 was placed at 182,000, whereas it was estimated by Italian authorities at 500,000.[2]

The most important improvement since 1893 in the method of compiling statistics of immigration was introduced in 1899, when, instead of the preceding classification of immigrants according to the countries or political divisions from which they came, they were classified according to the races to which they belonged. This makes an important difference in comparing statistics for all years preceding 1899 with those for 1899 and succeeding years. For example, it appeared that, in 1898, 40,000 Russians came to the United States, whereas the great majority of these were Poles or Jews, probably not over 200 being actually Russians. Likewise there are very few Austrians and comparatively few Huns or Magyars, the immigrants from Austro-Hungary since 1899 appearing as mostly Slovaks, Slavonians, Croatians, and Poles.[1]

Lack of caution in observing this change in classification has led to many misleading statements,[3] yet comparisons can be made with the statistics prior to 1899, since the original method of classification by political divisions is still followed, the new method being simply added to the old.[4] Protests against this classification by races were made by leading Jews on the ground that they were not a nationality but a religious body, and ought no more to be separately classified than Presbyterians or Catholics. On the other hand it is maintained that the classification does not discriminate against Jews, but it gives what it pretends to do—information not regarding nationality, but regarding races of immigrants.

B.—SOCIAL CHARACTER AND EFFECTS OF IMMIGRATION.

Illiteracy.—It has been pointed out by witnesses and by special report that there is a marked distinction in the illiteracy of immigrants from western Europe and those from eastern and southern Europe. Those from western Europe, including Scandinavians, Finns, Irish, Germans, Scotch, British, and northern Italians showed an illiteracy of 2.8 per cent in 1899, and 4 per cent in 1900, of those over 14 years of age, whereas illiteracy of immigrants from eastern Europe, including Hebrews, Slovaks,

---

[1] McSweeney, 82–83.   [3] Senner, 187.
[2] Schulteis, 27, 28, 30.   [4] Safford, 131–132.

Poles, Croatians, and southern Italians, was 38.4 per cent in 1899 and 36.6 per cent in 1900.[1] It has been pointed out that the amount of money brought in by immigrants varies on the whole inversely with their illiteracy; thus the Portuguese, with 60 per cent illiteracy, brought in 1900 $10.47 per capita, and the southern Italians, 54.5 per cent illiteracy, brought with them to this country $8.84 per capita.[2]

Tendency of foreign born toward cities.—The tendency of the foreign born to congregate in the larger cities of the country is noted by witnesses, and is considered in the special report. These immigrants are found mainly in those districts which are recognized as slums, and the immigrants from southern Europe furnish 19 times as many of the slum population of New York as immigrants from northwestern Europe, and so on for other cities.[3] The reasons for settlement in cities are stated to be the desire to live among their own people which develops in colonization in the slum district.[4] While certain nationalities, especially the Scandinavians, settle in foreign colonies,[5] others, like the Irish, Poles, and Hebrews, have more than one-half of their numbers in this country dwelling in large cities. The Jewish colonies in New Jersey are stated by one authority to have made success at farming,[6] but in another place it is shown that only by the aid of industrial occupations, especially clothing factories, have the colonies been able to survive.[7] This establishment of factories in these Jewish colonies, aided by the Baron de Hirsch fund, is claimed by another witness to work hardship upon the clothing workers in the cities, owing to the fact that the deficits being met out of charity enable the product to be placed upon the market below cost.[8]

Citizenship and naturalization.—It is represented by one witness that the immigrants from the southwestern countries of Europe are much less inclined to become citizens than those from the northwestern countries, the average proportion of the southeastern immigrants who were aliens, being 32 per cent as against 9.9 per cent of those from the northwestern countries. Sixteen States of the Union permit aliens to vote without naturalization.[9] Two or 3 witnesses maintain that a distinction should be made between the illiteracy test for immigrants and the one for naturalization, and that while immigrants should be admitted to the country on economic grounds, they should be admitted to citizenship only on educational grounds.[10]

Criminality of immigrants.—One witness maintains that persons of foreign birth furnish a much larger proportion of criminals than their general proportion of the general population.[11] These statistics are shown in the special report to be based upon a fallacy in that they fail to take account of the different distribution of ages as between the foreign born and the native born.[12]

As regards nationality, various statistics are presented showing alleged preeminence of certain nationalities over others, but since these neglect the element of age they are not conclusive, and especially inconclusive is the comparison of commitments with the total immigration of a given race.[13]

One witness denies the general impression that Italians are disorderly, and another notes that the Jews are a temperate people and not prone to drunkenness.[14]

Pauperism and insanity.—It is asserted by a witness that the census of 1890 shows the foreign-born population, constituting one-seventh of the population, furnish one-third of the total number of insane persons. This is ascribed in part to the evasion of the law by which immigrants are assisted from abroad and are able to enter the country through loopholes in the law, especially at the Canadian entrances, and as second-cabin passengers, a class who are not inspected.[15]

---

[1] Hall, 50–54; Stump, 6–7.
[2] Hall, 87.
[3] Hall, pp. 54, 56; Special report, pp. 277, 281.
[4] Rosendale, p. 195.
[5] Hall, pp. 55, 56.
[6] Wolf, p. 246.
[7] P. 512.
[8] Rosendale, p. 194.
[9] Hall, pp. 57, 62.
[10] Powderly, p. 45; Stump, p. 22; Schwab, p. 108.
[11] Hall, 51.
[12] p. 287, 288.
[13] Senner, p. 171, 175.
[14] Senner, 170; Rosendale, 194.
[15] Dobler, 147.

There are 15 different charitable societies or missionary organizations which meet the immigrants on their landing in New York.[1] The United Hebrew societies are the most extensive in their operations, and it is claimed that through the efforts of these societies the Jews help their own poor and keep them out of the almshouses.[2] These societies are not merely charities, but are educational in the largest sense, dealing almost exclusively with Russian refugees and endeavoring to assimilate them and equip them to earn a living. The Educational Alliance has an attendance that averages more than 5,000 persons a day, and there are Jewish manual training schools in Cleveland, Philadelphia, and Atlanta.[3]

Contagious diseases.—The courts have held that the steamship companies can not be fined for bringing persons with contagious and loathsome diseases into this country unless they are actually landed, and since the inspectors are required to deport such cases, the steamship is not liable.[4] There is a great increase in two contagious diseases, namely, trachona, or granulated eyelids, and favus, or scald head, owing to the increased immigration of Italians and Syrians. The medical inspection is final in such cases, and the other immigrant inspectors have no authority except to order deportation, but where medical inspection reveals only some physical defect in immigrants it is optional with the board to admit or deport.[5]

C.—ECONOMIC EFFECTS OF IMMIGRATION.[6]

Witnesses who discuss the effects of immigration on industry take two opposing standpoints. On the one side, it is held that they add to the productive energy of the country, and that immigrants of low intelligence are desirable to do the rough work. On the other side, it is claimed that the rapid influx of low-standard population, especially those of southern and eastern Europe, depresses wages and lessens the amount of employment available for American labor. While it is admitted that the Irish and Germans who came to this country before 1875 added materially to its growth and prosperity, witnesses hold that those who have come recently from southern and eastern Europe have had an injurious social effect, and have been exceedingly injurious to American labor.[7] It was not necessary nor desirable 10 or 12 years ago to apply an educational test, but this changing character of immigration makes such a test now desirable.[8]

On the other hand, it is stated that the American workingmen do not appreciate that it is industrial depression rather than immigration which affects their wages,[9] and that a population of 70,000,000 can at the present time more easily absorb 300,000 immigrants than the smaller population of forty or fifty millions in 1880 could absorb the five to seven hundred thousand immigrants who came at that time.[10] Statistics are offered going to show that with continuous immigration wages have risen during the past 30 years.[11]

One peculiar effect of immigration is that of the so-called "birds of passage," of whom it is estimated that 70,000 come annually from Canada to work during the busy season and return to that country.[12] This class of immigrants is also very extensive amongst the Italians, of whom it is asserted that an examination in April, 1896, of 3,174 of that nationality landed at New York showed that 27.7 per cent had been in this country before. When these people return to Italy they take with them $200 to $1,000, with the intention of purchasing a home and remaining in their own country in comparative prosperity.[13]

---

[1] McSweeney, 85.
[2] Rosendale, 195, 201.
[3] Wolf, 248, 249.
[4] Fitchie, 71.
[5] Williams, 127, 129.
[6] See also Special Report, p. 295 ff.
[7] Schulteis, 435, 436.
[8] Hall, 58, 59.
[9] Senner, 180.
[10] Senner, 173.
[11] Senner, 176, 184.
[12] McSweeney, 92. 93.
[13] Hall, 53; Quinlan, 122.

On the other hand, it is maintained that the reason why Italians return to Italy in the winter is because they can not find employment here and that Italian immigration is becoming more and more permanent;[1] that the number of women and children who accompany Italian immigrants is increasing proportionately to the total immigration.[2] Formerly one-half of the Italians who came to this country returned, but now the proportion does not exceed one-fourth.[3]

The padrone system has been particularly reported upon by various witnesses, and it is shown, both by their testimony and by the special report upon this subject, that the system, as it existed in the early days of Italian immigration, has ceased, and that the Italians are now coming in such large numbers that it is no longer necessary for contractors to go abroad and import them into this country. The padrone system, as it exists at the present time, is simply the mode of oppression which Italians who are acquainted with the language are able to exercise upon newcomers through their ignorance and poverty. As a remedy for this new form of padrone system, which is not a violation of the contract-labor law, it is proposed that any immigrant who comes on the invitation of any person whatever except a relative should be deported.[4]

The Armenian and Greek immigration also presents resemblances to the Italian padrone system. These immigrants are believed to be under the control of a central organization which sends them out as notion peddlers.[5]

D.—DISTRIBUTION AND EMPLOYMENT OF IMMIGRANTS.

The Governments of Italy and Austria-Hungary furnish subventions to bureaus of those respective nationalities designed to assist immigrants upon landing at New York. The Italian bureau formerly was granted a location at Ellis Island, but this privilege has been revoked. This bureau was created in order to counteract the evils of the padrone system, and the chief, Dr. Rossi, considers that it has been of considerable success.[6] The revocation of the permit was owing to the allegation that the bureau assisted immigrants to evade the law and was practically an agent of the padrones,[7] but this is denied by the chief, who asserts that the officers of the bureau did not come in contact with immigrants until after they had passed the inspection officers.[8] No other country has as great need of a bureau of this sort as Italy for the protection of its immigrants. The Germans, English, and Irish, when they arrive here, are practically arriving at home.

The Austro-Hungarian Home, supported by the Austrian Government and by Austrian and Hungarian societies in New York, furnishes intelligence for immigrants as to the labor market, and attempts to place them throughout the country. The demand for women as servants is so great that no trouble is found in this direction. Most of the single men are provided with employment in the neighborhood of New York.[9]

Various witnesses have emphasized the need of a better distribution of immigrants throughout the country by means of a comprehensive system of employment agencies, and with this in view the Industrial Commission has listened to testimony from the superintendent of the free employment bureau of the State of New York, located in New York City, and from the deputy chief of the bureau of licenses of New York, whose official duty is the supervision of private agencies, and from a representative of private agencies. Mr. Bealin, of the State free employment bureau, complains that the law governing employment agencies in New York gives no effective power of supervision; that there is evidence to show that servants have

---

[1] Rossi, 160.
[2] Senner, 175.
[3] Ter. Kuile, 115.
[4] Powderly, 33, 43, 44.
[5] McSweeney, 83, 88.
[6] Rossi, 154, 156, 159.
[7] Powderly, 43.
[8] Rossi, 155, 157.
[9] Ritter, 219, 222.

repeatedly found places in families on the recommendation of employment agents and have carried on a regular system of robbing their employers.[1] Furthermore, the employment agencies are sometimes connected with saloons and boarding houses which make a practice of exploiting the laborer. Women are sometimes treated coarsely and brutally, contrary to law. It is in the protection of this class of women that the Austro-Hungarian Home considers its most useful work to have been done.[2]

Mr. Bealin states that, contrary to law, fees paid to employment agencies are not returned when work is not found. On the other hand, those who represent the private employment agencies and the bureau of licenses maintain that very few complaints are made; that the supervision is thorough; that licenses are revoked or suspended on the proof of charges; that a fee for the use of the office, whether or not employment is found, is a proper mode of payment, provided a larger fee be charged when employment is found. Very few frauds are known to exist, and the public knowledge of the same is largely based on hearsay.[3]

The proposed law in New York advocated by the State free employment agency and charitable bodies is designed to bring about a better class of private employment agencies. It places the fees in New York City at $50 the first year and $25 the second year; prohibits saloon keepers from keeping an employment agency; requires a registry of the name and address of every applicant and his last employer, which registers must be open to inspection; provides for punishing those who publish false advertisements or give false information; prohibits sending female help to any place of bad repute, and requires the fee to be returned on demand if employment is not found,[4] as is required by the law of Massachusetts.[5]

E.—CAUSES INDUCING IMMIGRATION.

In general people coming to this country do so from a desire for better opportunities. A few come on account of the republican principles of our Government, but this is not usually an important motive. One witness attributes the increase of immigration from southern Italy and eastern Europe largely to the desire to anticipate the enactment of educational restrictions.[6]

The most important influence affecting immigration is the prosperity of the country. The highest number coming to this country in one year was in the exceptionally prosperous year of 1882, when it reached 778,000, after which it declined, and again in 1892 reached 580,000. The immigrants in 1874, immediately following the panic, were only 261,000, a decline from 438,000 of the preceding year. The fluctuations of immigration according to the prosperity of the country are largely accounted for by the fact that immigrants come in many, if not most cases, by inducements of friends and relatives who have come before.[7] It is stated by representatives of steamship companies that 40 to 55 per cent of those who come have their passage prepaid by friends in this country.[8] If to this be added those to whom money is sent from this side for purchase of tickets abroad, the proportion coming on prepaid transportation would amount to 65 per cent.[9] This class of immigration is claimed to be desirable, but there are many tickets sold by peddlers on the installment plan, and the chances are that those coming on such tickets would be of a more undesirable class. For the sake of checking this practice a provision has been suggested prohibiting the sale of tickets except by authorized agents of steamship companies.[10]

Mr. Ritter, manager of the Austro-Hungarian Home of New York, an institution receiving subvention from the Austro-Hungarian Government, says that nearly all

---

[1] Bealin, 227, 228.
[2] Ritter, 222.
[3] Hotchkiss, 237; Brown, 231, 233.
[4] Bealin, 225, 226.
[5] Hotchkiss, 242.
[6] Senner, 167, 168, 179.
[7] Hall, 49.
[8] Ter Kuile, 115; Lederer, 118.
[9] McSweeney, 95.
[10] McSweeney 95.

the Hungarian and Slavonic immigrants get their tickets from agents who induce them to come here. He believes, however, these agents work merely for the commission they get on the transportation tickets, and are not employed by persons or corporations in this country.[1]

Another witness alleges that the steamship lines have their agents in the little European villages to induce men to come to America as miners. He has been told by men who would be glad to go back if they could that they have been enticed by circulars scattered in their villages by the steamship agents. Steamship agents also work among the people in this country and entice them to buy tickets on the installment plan for their relatives and friends. The agents drum up custom like life-insurance agents.[2] Another witness speaks of extensive advertising in Europe of free public lands and high wages.[3]

Representatives of steamship companies deny the attempt to induce immigrants to come to the United States. This is prohibited by stringent laws in most of the European countries, for the reason that those countries desire for military service all the young men who are likely to emigrate. Only agents licensed by the Governments are permitted to sell tickets, and in the case of one company numbers of agents have had their licenses revoked because they have sent circulars to persons whom they thought likely to emigrate. Similarly the agents who sell prepaid tickets in this country do not attempt to stimulate immigration or to induce the sale of tickets. It would hardly be possible for them to do so if they tried, and the small commission on tickets, $2, takes away the motive.[4]

The influence of changes in steerage rates is commented on by one or two witnesses. The existing rate of $28 from Naples to New York, and $36.50 from Bremen to New York, $29.50 from Antwerp to New York, are about double the rates which were charged in 1880, and are based upon combinations or "conferences" between the steamship lines.[5] Difference of opinion is expressed regarding the influence of steerage rates on immigration. While it is agreed that the rates now are about one-half the rates of 20 years ago, when the enormous immigration came from western Europe, yet it is claimed by several witnesses representing the steamship companies that this has but little influence, and that the prosperity of the country is the main cause of changes in migration. At the same time the rates could not profitably be advanced beyond the present figures, since to do so would tend to reduce traffic.[6]

F.—ASSISTED IMMIGRATION.

In times past several governments, local and national, as well as private charitable societies, in Europe engaged more or less in the assistance of paupers and criminals to emigrate to colonial countries and to the United States. Owing to the representations of our Government these countries have officially restricted or prohibited such assistance, and in so far as it exists at the present time it is without the official knowledge of the governments concerned.[7] It is asserted, however, that a large proportion of immigration is at present of the assisted character, and that the chief source of such migration is Great Britain, the immigrants coming largely by the way of Canada. This assistance is granted by various local authorities seeking to pass on paupers from their own jurisdiction.[8] It is both asserted and denied that the policy of the Italian Government is to encourage emigration, especially temporary migration, of those who return and bring money to Italy.[9] The Italian Government continues to treat as Italian citizens, whom it designates as "colonists," such persons as come to this country and, not having taken out naturalization papers, are subject to

---

[1] Ritter, 221.
[2] Rosendale, 189, 200.
[3] Schulteis, 24, 25.
[4] Schwab, 103, 107.
[5] Schwab, 107, 109.
[6] Schwab, 107, 108.
[7] McSweeney, 87, 88; Hall, 60; Rossi, 154, 160; Ritter, 221.
[8] McSweeney, 87, 88.
[9] McSweeney, 89; Rossi, 154 160.

military service in Italy. (See also text of recent Italian Law on Emigration, p. 000.) The Government requires that every Italian who is deported from New York shall be given by the Italian bureau at that port a card stating why he has been deported, and under the Italian laws he is then enittled to prosecute the agent who sold him his ticket. The Italian Government has, on the complaint of the bureau at New York, withdrawn the licenses from various steamship agencies in Italy and has punished others. The Government also adopted the practice of giving to convicts who emigrate to the United States a certificate stating the cause of imprisonment, etc. In only one case does the agent of the Italian bureau know of a convict who came to the United States from Italy with a passport but without such a certificate.[1]

The Austro-Hungarian Government does not desire emigration to this country, but would prefer to keep its people at home, and Mr. Ritter, the agent of the Austro-Hungarian Home, which receives a subvention from that Government, does not think that any undesirable person has received public aid in emigrating to this country.[2]

The immigration of Jews from Austro-Hungary, Russia, and Roumania has been directly owing to persecution and the growth of anti-Semitism in those countries. The earliest persecution which drove Jews abroad began in Russia in 1880, and the exodus which, after continuing a year or two, diminished for 7 or 8 years, was renewed in 1891, when the persecutions were again revived.[3] The Jews from Roumania began to migrate within the last 2 or 3 years as a result of the Dreyfus agitation which spread to that country. During 3 months of 1900, more than 20,000 Jews left Roumania, but owing to a resulting industrial disturbance and commercial crisis, this persecution was discontinued. The thousands of Jews thus expatriated were without means for emigration, and at this juncture the Baron de Hirsch fund was provided, by which they have been assisted to migrate in large numbers. But it is claimed that this fund was never used to any considerable extent except in the way of helping families to go together.[4] Other countries besides the United States received large contingencies of Jews through the assistance of this fund. American Jews have always discouraged immigration of European Jews, and are in full accord with the laws to prevent the immigration of paupers and diseased persons and all who are unfitted to enjoy the franchise.[5] Those who come from Roumania are largely capable of self-support, but the American Jews, with the help of the Baron de Hirsch fund, endeavor to furnish employment and to distribute their beneficiaries throughout the country, and thus remove them from the congestion in New York City.

G.—EXISTING LEGISLATION RESTRICTING IMMIGRATION.

The early immigration laws sought to regulate immigration rather than to restrict it, and provided a head tax to defray the expense. It declared that no convict, lunatic, idiot, or person likely to become a public charge should be permitted to land, but there was no provision for returning such persons to their homes. The contract-labor laws were enacted between 1882 and 1891. The law of 1891 defined more strictly the persons to be excluded, and the act of 1893 added a large number of ineligibles, so that it is estimated as a result of this law that fully 50,000 persons were refused the sale of tickets within a year after it was passed.[6] The immigration laws, thus added one to another, are not clear at many points, and they have afforded many opportunities for evasion.[7]

Regarding the efficiency of the existing laws there is a difference of opinion. One witness testifying in 1899 held that the recent decrease in immigration is largely due

---

[1] Rossi, 154, 160.
[2] Ritter, 221.
[3] Wolf, 245, 247.
[4] Senner, 171.
[5] Wolf, 245.
[6] McSweeney, 77, 78.
[7] Ullo, 141.

to the restrictive effect of the law of 1893, but his conclusion seems to be unwarranted in view of the increase which followed in the 2 years since his testimony was given.[1] This witness lays emphasis on the annoyance and vexation to which immigrants are exposed. On the other hand, the larger number of witnesses considers the laws and the inspection of immigrants as unsatisfactory, and that only a very small proportion of the undesirable immigrants are excluded. The actual number deported is from one-half of one to one per cent of the total number of immigrants. The question as to whether a person is likely to become a public charge is indefinite. The inspectors are hurried and can not ask questions in sufficient detail to elicit the facts. The procedure before the board of special inquiry is cumbrous and not frequently resorted to.[2]

The methods of inspection are described at length by various witnesses connected with the inspection service at New York. When a vessel approaches the harbor it is boarded by 1 or 2 inspectors, who examine the cabin passengers. These men are confronted with 100 or 150 passengers at a time, and they have an hour and a half for an examination covering the period of time from touching at quarantine and landing at the dock. Cabin passengers are asked questions calculated to ascertain whether they are likely to become a public charge or whether they are under contract to perform labor. If one is suspected he is brought to Ellis Island for further investigation. No one is allowed to mingle with the steerage passengers until they have passed through the inspection office at the island.[3]

After landing at Ellis Island immigrants pass before the medical officers of the Marine-Hospital Service. The rigidity of the medical inspection depends on the general appearance and character of the immigrants. In many shiploads only a casual inspection is necessary. The greatest difficulty is found in the fact that Italians and Syrians are especially subject to trachoma and favus.[4] The medical examination of emigrants before embarkation is insufficient. The most effective examination of this kind is at Liverpool, but even there a physician views them at the rate of 2,000 an hour, even without uncovering their heads.[5] The surgeons in Europe do not recognize two of the diseases which are grounds for exclusion, viz, trachoma and favus.

After medical inspection the immigrants file in lines of 30 each, according to the manifests furnished by the steamship company, before the immigration inspectors. These inspectors are registry clerks, who speak the several languages of the immigrants. Each registry clerk has a steamship manifest before him and examines each applicant to ascertain if there is any discrepancy. Sometimes as many as 4,000 persons pass through the office in a day, but the verification is correct, at least so far as the count of the immigrants goes.[6] Two or three witnesses complain that the immigration officers at present are scarcely qualified for the satisfactory performance of their duties. An inspector ought to be able to judge each individual according to his merits upon the basis of many considerations. The inspectors are poorly paid, and the interpreters are often incompetent to secure correct information.[7] It is contended by the commissioner of immigration at the port of New York that the application of the civil-service examination to the position of immigration inspector is disadvantageous to the service. The system may be satisfactory for clerical positions, but no academic examination based on book learning or linguistic knowledge can be a guaranty that the person will have the necessary common sense and honesty to decide whether an immigrant is desirable or not. The bureau at New York has had difficulty with men who have been chosen under the civil-service rules. The law, moreover, protects men who have never taken an examination.[8]

---

[1] Senner, 168, 179.
[2] Hall, 58.
[3] Dobler, 147, 150.
[4] Williams, 126, 128.
[5] Powderly, 35, 38.
[6] McSweeney, 81, 84, 85.
[7] Senner, 169, 170.
[8] Fitchie, 72, 75.

The immigration inspectors are required to detain for special inquiry all who are not plainly and unquestionably entitled to admission. Under this rule they detain about 13 to 15 per cent of the immigrants. These amounted in 1898–99 to about 25,000 persons examined before boards of special inquiry. The proportion of those who require such examination varies greatly in the case of different vessels. Since the steamship companies are required to provide for immigrants during their detention, the amounts paid by the different companies is a fair index to the character of the immigrants. These amounts vary from 2 cents per capita for the passengers on board to 50 cents per capita. On some vessels only 3 or 4 may be detained, while a ship bringing immigrants from Italy may have three-fourths to three-fifths of the passengers detained.[1] The board of special inquiry consists of 4 inspectors especially designated. An affirmative vote of 3 of the members is required for admission. Any member dissenting has a right to appeal to the Secretary of the Treasury, and the immigrant has the same right. The decisions of the board, however, are seldom overruled.[2] If the immigrant is excluded, the steamship company bears the expense of deportation.

Contract laborers often come as cabin passengers, and it is here that the greatest difficulty in their detection occurs. If the alleged contract laborer is detained by the inspector, he is then brought before the board of special inquiry for examination, the same as other immigrants who are detained. The authority of the immigration inspectors, on approval by the Secretary of the Treasury, in ordering the deportation of an immigrant whom they deem ineligible is final. It is so recognized by the courts, who will refuse to review their action.

Besides the deportation of the contract laborer, the law provides for the punishment of an importer who contracts for his employment in this country. There have been but few cases of conviction, although there have been in 6 years some 4,000 contract laborers deported.[3] This is because the law requires that the contract be proven and does not provide punishment for the mere inducement, request, or solicitation, or for the offer of employment.[4] The contract must also be made in a foreign country in order to convict the importer.[5] At the present time very few such contracts are made. The more common practice is for the foreman to inquire of his foreign workmen whether they have any friends or relatives whom they would like to bring to the United States. In this way large numbers of immigrants reach this country with the object of replacing Americans at lower wages.[6] It is asserted that the wholesale importation of contract labor has practically been stopped, although the person making the contract is not convicted.[7]

Criminals.—The immigration law provides only for the exclusion of persons convicted of crime, but not for those charged with crime or those deemed to be immoral.[8] Although it provides for the exclusion of polygamists, it is impossible to prove such a charge, and consequently a constant stream of Mormon converts, of whom 90 to 95 per cent are women, are continually coming to this country.[9]

Immigration through Canada.—The law does not provide for restriction of immigration from Canada, and the inspection of those who come from Europe through Canada is wholly inadequate. The United States Commissioner made an agreement with the Canadian steamship companies allowing them to board the ships at Canadian ports and to pay the United States head tax for those destined to this country. The railroads through Canada agree to transport none who are not granted a certificate of inspection by these inspectors entitling them to enter at the frontier.[10]

Notwithstanding these agreements, a large number of immigrants from Europe evade the law by giving some place in Canada as their destination, which relieves them of

---

[1] McSweeney, 90, 96, 101.
[2] Holman, 134.
[3] Quinlan, 120, 123, 125.
[4] Quinlan, 121, 122.
[5] Quinlan, 121, 123.
[6] Quinlan, 123.
[7] Stump, 5.
[8] Ullo, 141, 142.
[9] McSweeney, 90.
[10] Stump, 15–18.

inspection by the United States officers, and then after remaining there only a short time they cross over to the American side. This is affirmed to be the greatest loophole in the restriction of legislation, and as a remedy it is proposed that inspectors should be placed along the Canadian border.[1]

Steamship companies.—Prior to 1893 steamship agents in Europe were very little restricted as to persons to whom they sold tickets. The result was an indiscriminate emigration to the United States. The act of 1893, compelling the steamship companies to deport those of their passengers who might be rejected by the inspectors, has had the effect of making the European agents of the companies the most effective inspectors under the law.[2] Indeed, the steamship representatives maintain that this class of inspection is much superior to that of consular officers or direct representatives of the United States Government.[3] The reasons given are that the companies hold their agents responsible for immigrants to whom tickets have been sold in case these immigrants are deported. These agents are fully informed of all the details of American legislation, and are furnished with minute instructions regarding the classes of immigrants who are ineligible.[4]

---

[1] Schulteis, 28; McSweeney, 92, 93.
[2] Stump, 9, 20.
[3] Schwab, 102.
[4] Schwab, 102, 104, 109–114; Floyd, 117; Lederer, 118, 119; Ter Kuile, 115.

II. REVIEW OF SPECIAL REPORTS.

STATISTICS AND SOCIAL EFFECTS OF IMMIGRATION.

Part II of this volume, prepared under the direction of the Commission by E. Dana Durand, secretary, presents statistical exhibits based upon the several censuses and upon the reports of the Bureau of Immigration, showing the general effect of immigration upon population and social conditions. It appears that from the year 1850 to 1890 the proportion of foreign born increased from about one-tenth to one-seventh of the total population. This increase has gone chiefly to the States already having the largest proportion, the New England States and Illinois, however, showing the principal increase. From 1880 to 1890 the great manufacturing urban States of New England, New York, New Jersey, Pennsylvania, and Illinois received the largest accession of foreigners.[1]

Interesting and significant changes have occurred in the past 50 years in the distribution of immigrants according to the country of birth. These statistics are shown in two ways—first, by the foreign-born population at the date of each census, and, secondly, by the annual immigration. Considering the latter feature, the immigration by decades indicates that the largest absolute number of immigrants, exceeding 5,000,000, came to this country from 1881 to 1890. The preceding three decades show a remarkable uniformity, the total immigration for each ranging from 2,300,000 to 2,800,000. From 1891 to 1900 the aggregate was 3,687,564.[2]

While the aggregate numbers of immigrants changed in the order indicated, the composition by country of birth gives an entirely different aspect to the statistics. The Irish were the first to appear in large proportions, and from 1840 to 1850 constituted 46 per cent of the total immigration. Their proportion has greatly diminished until the present time. The Germans followed close upon the Irish in the early days of immigration and reached their largest proportion in the period 1880 to 1884, when they constituted 30 per cent of the entire number of immigrants. In that period of 5 years nearly 1,000,000 Germans came to our shores, but in the 5 years from 1895 to 1899 only 125,000, constituting but 9 per cent of the total immigration. The proportion of Scandinavians reached its highest point in 1885 to 1889, constituting 11 per cent, but their decline has been less rapid than the Germans, their proportion amounting to 7.8 per cent in the past 5 years.[3]

Thus the decade from 1880 to 1890 marks a turning point in the character of immigration. Up to that time it was mainly the inhabitants of western Europe, including England, Scotland, Wales, Ireland, Germany, Sweden and Norway, who furnished nearly two-thirds of the immigrants. Since that time immigration from eastern and southern Europe has rapidly increased, and in the 5-year period from 1895 to 1899 constituted 54 per cent of the immigration. Italy shows the most striking increase of all; numbering only 20,000 immigrants from 1875 to 1879, they rose to 307,000 from 1890 to 1894 and 300,000 from 1895 to 1899—15 times greater than from 1875 to 1879. It will be seen that the immigration from the northern and western countries of Europe reached its maximum during the decade 1880 to 1889, when it

---

[1] P. 260.   [2] P. 267.   [3] P. 271.

represented a little more than two-thirds of the total influx. For the past 5 years, on the other hand, the absolute number of immigrants from these countries has been barely one-third the number for the 5 years from 1885 to 1889, while the proportion to the total immigration has fallen to 39.9 per cent. The immigration from the southern and eastern countries of Europe began to increase in 1880–1884, but reached its maximum in absolute numbers from 1890 to 1894, when it was more than 10 times greater than from 1875 to 1879, and had risen from 9.4 to 38.6 of the total. The proportion borne by the immigration from these countries to the total for the period 1895 to 1899 is still greater, amounting to no less than 54.1 per cent.[1]

The enormous influx of immigrants may lead to the hasty conclusion that immigration has been the leading factor in the rapid increase of the aggregate population of the United States, but this conclusion was objected to by the late Francis A. Walker, superintendent of the censuses of 1870 to 1880, who maintained that foreign immigration into this country, from the time when it first assumed large proportions, amounted, not to a reenforcement of our population, but to a replacement of native by foreign stock. The ingenious estimates made by President Walker, based upon the predictions of Elkanah Watson in 1815, give plausibility to this estimate, since it appears that the growth of population from 1790 to 1840, when there was very little immigration, was as great in proportion to numbers as from 1840 to 1860, when there was a large foreign immigration, and that since 1860 the growth of population has been at a lower rate of increase than during the 50 years prior to the large influx. President Walker's explanation is based on the economic ground that the American shrank from the industrial competition imposed upon him by the low standards of the incoming foreigners, and was unwilling either to handicap himself by family ties in his efforts to rise above them or to bring sons and daughters into the world to enter into that competition.[2]

The tendency of the foreign born to congregate in the larger cities of the country has been frequently noticed and commented upon. While the foreign born constitute only 14.4 per cent of the total population of our country, they constitute more than twice as large proportion, namely, 29.18 per cent, of the population of cities over 25,000. In rural districts only a little over one-tenth of the total number of inhabitants are of foreign birth. The three cities possessing the largest proportion of foreign-born population are New York, San Francisco, and Chicago, each exceeding 40 per cent. Eighteen of the 28 great cities have more than one-fourth of their population of foreign birth.[3]

Great differences exist as to the relative tendency of different nationalities toward city life. There is marked aptitude for urban life among the Hebrews, Poles, and Irish, each of which nationalities has more than one-half of its numbers in this country dwelling in large cities. The Irish and Germans, owing to their great absolute numbers, constitute together more than one-half of the total foreign-born population in the cities of the country as a whole, the Irish furnishing 20 per cent and the Germans 30 per cent. The Germans are the predominant foreign nationality in most of the cities individually as well as in the urban population as a whole. They constitute more than two-thirds of the total foreign-born population in Milwaukee and Cincinnati. The Irish constitute 47 per cent of the foreign-born population in Providence, 45 per cent in Boston, 41 per cent in Jersey City, and 41 per cent in Philadelphia.[3]

Bearing upon the question of American citizenship and the proposed educational test for immigrants, the question of literacy and illiteracy among the foreign born is important. For the United States as a whole 6.2 per cent of the native whites are illiterate, while more than twice that proportion, 13 per cent, of the foreign-born whites are unable to read and write. The disparity is greatest in those States with

---

[1] P. 272 ff. [2] P. 277. [3] P. 279.

the most advanced systems of education. In the North Atlantic States only 2.3 per cent of the native whites are illiterate, against 15.6 per cent of the foreign-born whites. In the great cities, on the whole, the efficiency of the common school system is especially indicated by the fact that the illiteracy is scarcely greater among native whites of foreign parentage than among those having native parents. The illiteracy among the foreign-born city dwellers, on the other hand, is very much greater than among the natives. Thus, in New York the per cent of illiteracy among the native whites of native parentage is 0.52; among the native whites of foreign parentage, 0.66; while among the foreign whites it is 14.6.[1]

From the reports of the Bureau of Immigration it appears that the proportion of illiteracy among those landing in this country, of 14 years of age and over, varies by years from 20 to 24 per cent. Comparing the countries of their origin, the illiteracy of immigrants 14 years of age and over from the countries of western Europe, including Scandinavians, the Finnish, the Irish, the Germans, and the northern Italians, was only 2.8 per cent in 1899 and 4 per cent in 1900; whereas the illiteracy of those who came from eastern Europe, including Hebrews, Slovaks, Poles, Croatians, and southern Italians, was 38.4 in 1899 and 36.6 in 1900. The nationality showing the highest illiteracy is the Turkish, being 78.7 per cent; but the absolute number arriving is so small—namely, 184—that this high percentage loses social significance. Of those nationalities having heavy immigration the southern Italians, out of 84,346 immigrants in 1900, had an illiteracy of 54.5 per cent; the Poles, with 46,938 immigrants, had an illiteracy of 31.6 per cent; the Slovaks, with 29,243 immigrants, had an illiteracy of 28 per cent; and the Hebrews, with 60,764 immigrants, had an illiteracy of 22.8 per cent. The lowest illiteracy in the entire list of nationalities is that of the Scandinavians, who, numbering 32,952 immigrants in 1900, had an illiteracy of only 0.8 per cent; the English, with 10,897 immigrants, had an illiteracy of 2 per cent; the Finns, with more than 12,000 immigrants, had an illiteracy of 2.7 per cent; the Irish, with 35,607 immigrants, had 3.2 per cent illiteracy; and the Germans, with 29,682 immigrants, had 5.8 per cent illiteracy.[2]

The financial condition of immigrants by nationalities varies, on the whole, inversely with their illiteracy. Thus the Portuguese, with 60 per cent illiteracy, brought in 1900 $10.47 per capita, and the southern Italians, with 54.5 per cent of illiterates, brought with them to this country $8.84; on the other hand, the Germans, with 5.8 per cent of illiterates, brought $28.53 per capita; and the English and Scotch, with 2 per cent illiterates, brought $38.90 and $41.51 per capita, respectively.[3]

The effect of immigration upon the amount of pauperism and criminality in the United States is of leading importance, and the immigration laws of this country have from their earliest inception been directed mainly to the diminishing of these effects. The census statistics comparing the tendency to pauperism and criminality of the foreign born with the native born should be accepted with caution.[4] These statistics present the serious defect of failing to take account of the different distribution of ages as between the foreign born and the native born. Immigrants come to this country mainly after they have reached the criminal age, and consequently when the census writer for 1890 states that 16.39 per cent of the whole population furnishes 30.24 per cent of the institution population, the conclusion, in so far as it includes prisoners, is misleading. Persons under the age of 20 seldom commit crimes; the immense number of persons of native birth below that age contribute very little to the number of prisoners in the country. If, on the other hand, the number of males of the ages of 20 to 45 of native birth and of foreign birth be compared with the number of criminals of native birth and foreign birth, the showing is quite different. On this basis it appears that the whites of foreign birth show a trifle less criminality than the total number of whites of native birth.[5]

---

[1] Pp. 280, 281.   [2] Pp. 282, 283.   [3] P. 284.   [4] P. 285.   [5] Pp. 287, 288.

At the same time the full effect of immigration on the prison population of the country can not be measured by simply the number of foreigners. Account must also be taken of the children of foreigners. The excessively large proportion of prisoners among the latter class—namely, 7,435 per million voters, compared with 2,517 of native parentage and 3,269 of foreign born—constitute nearly as strong an argument as to the injurious effects of immigration as would the high proportion among the foreign born themselves. The second generation of the foreign element break readily away from the control of their parents, whom they learn to look down upon as ignorant and out of date. They become more familiar with the criminal ways of this country, and so they present an excessively high proportion of criminality. This appears from the census tables showing the birthplaces of the parents of white prisoners by specific crimes, wherein it appears that 38 per cent of the total male population of militia age—namely, 18 to 44 years—being the children of foreigners, whether themselves born in this country or born abroad, furnish more than half the prisoners, and that this proportion, in the case of intoxication and disorderly conduct, amounts to two-fifths of the population producing nearly four-fifths of the punished offenses.[1]

ECONOMIC EFFECTS OF IMMIGRATION.

Part III, prepared by John R. Commons, special agent of the Industrial Commission, deals with the economic effects of immigration, with legislation affecting immigration in this and other countries and with the agricultural distribution of immigrants.

The effect of immigration on industry, looked at from the standpoint of the productive energy of the country, can not be measured by the aggregate numbers, but by the predominance of males among immigrants and by the predominant age periods at which they migrate. The proportion of males among the native born in the census of 1890 was 51.21 per cent, while among the foreign born it was 54.9 per cent. The immigration statistics show an even greater disproportion. In 1881 to 1890 males numbered 61 per cent of the total influx. When we consider that the most productive ages for labor are those from the ages of 20 to 45, it is significant that while the proportion of native-born population falling within these years is only 34 per cent, the proportion of foreign-born population is 51 per cent; and when we examine the statistics of immigrants as presented by the Bureau of Immigration, we find that the immigrants belonging to the productive years, 15 to 40, constitute not less than 68 per cent of the total number. From these facts it follows, seeing that it is the male population above 15 years of age that predominate in competitive industry, that the effect of immigrants upon industry and wages is proportionately greater than the effect of the corresponding number of native born.[2]

Equally important with the gross proportion of immigrants is the unequal distribution of immigration throughout the several occupations. Whereas the foreign-born whites constituted in 1890 14.40 per cent of the total population, those engaged in gainful occupations constituted no less than 22.45 per cent of the total number in such occupations. In the manufacturing and mechanical industries, and in domestic and personal service the number was 31 per cent, whereas, on the other hand, in agriculture the number was only 14.49 per cent.[3]

The unskilled occupations, those of domestic and personal service, receive the largest access of immigrants. Only 16 per cent of the male immigrants declare themselves as belonging to the skilled occupations, while 57 per cent are rated unskilled,

---

[1] P. 298.   [2] Pp. 295, 296.   [3] P. 297.

and 23 per cent, including women and children, as without occupation. The industries in which one-fourth of the total number of employees are foreign born present the following occupations conspicuously: Tailors, bakers, boot and shoe makers, brick and tile makers, butchers, cabinetmakers and upholsterers, textile and mill operatives, leather dressers and tanners, marble and stone cutters.[1]

Of peculiar interest in enforcing the statements already made concerning the tendency of foreigners to city life are the figures showing the proportion of foreign born and their descendants in agriculture. While nearly one-half of the native whites of native parents are engaged in agriculture, less than one-fourth of the foreign whites are so engaged. The second generation of foreign classes shows a slightly greater inclination to agricultural life than the first generation.[2] Nationalities differ widely in this regard. Those which show the greatest inclination toward agriculture are the Scandinavians, Germans, and Bohemians, numbering 27, 21, and 28 per cent of the total population of these respective nationalities in this country. The Irish have but 14 per cent of those engaged in gainful occupations on the farm. The lowest proportions are found among the Italians and Hungarians, numbering 4 per cent each.[3]

The races having the largest proportion of unskilled and miscellaneous laborers are the Chinese, Japanese, Croatians, Russians, Greeks, Italians, Lithuanians, Magyar, Poles, Portuguese, Ruthenians, Scandinavians, and Slovaks. The immigrants with the largest proportion of skilled laborers are the Hebrews, Scotch, English, French, and Cubans.[4]

Owing to a conflict of various causes it is impossible to determine precisely the effect of immigration on wages. The cycles of business prosperity and depression are the principal conflicting factor.[5] The low standard of living of immigrants, especially from eastern and southern Europe, is shown in a table on page 310, and it appears that the wages in American cities are 4 to 5 times the wages of farm laborers in those sections of Europe, but the immigrant who attempts to enter American industry is not able to keep up the pace, owing to his low standard. In the course of time he is compelled to organize for the mere purpose of finding the adequate food, shelter, and clothing to continue at work. This point was reached by the bituminous coal miners in 1897 and the anthracite coal miners in 1900, and the remarkable labor organization in that occupation at the present time is the result of the direst poverty to which a large class of labor in this country has probably ever been reduced. Immigrants from southern and eastern Europe displace those from the British Isles, and, having competed among themselves, are at last compelled to organize for protection. In the clothing trade a similar condition has been reached, but in that trade the continuous influx of immigrants has not yet afforded a breathing spell for organization.[6]

Labor organizations are handicapped by the mixed nationalities, languages, and religions which make it impossible even to bring them together on a mutual understanding.[7]

One of the factors which conceals the effect of immigration and at the same time cooperates with it is machinery and division of labor. This, by displacing the skilled mechanic, makes room for the unskilled immigrant. The fact that machinery has been introduced so largely in this country is a part of the results of immigration, since, by breaking down the traditions and organization of the trade unions, their resistance to machinery and new methods has been overcome; but at the same time the lower and lower standards of living which have come into machine industries illustrate the cooperation between machinery and immigration in depressing the condition of labor. If, however, they are able to organize, they may recover their position. This, as already stated, is difficult until the immigrants have experienced a period of extreme poverty.

---

[1] Pp. 298, 299. [3] P. 301. [5] P. 305. [7] P. 312.
[2] P. 300. [4] P. 304. [6] P. 311.

XXIV   THE INDUSTRIAL COMMISSION:—IMMIGRATION.

The competition of women and children is a contributing factor in depressing wages, but it is noticeable that the women and children who work in factories are usually the wives and daughters of immigrants. Furthermore, the fact that the complaints against immigrants proceed from cities, where the cost of living is high, makes it important to note that the country competition of native Americans where the cost of living is low often acts as a depressing effect on wages in the same occupation in cities.

In contrasting these various causes it appears that the effect of immigration tends to cumulate upon the same industry where the other causes are in operation, and that the relative effect of immigration depends upon the rapidity of the influx, while a moderate amount of immigration would be assimilated. A rapid influx into particular trades by breaking down organization subjects workingmen to an unfair competition.

THE CLOTHING TRADE.

According to the census of 1890, that branch of the clothing trade known as custom work shows the largest proportion of foreigners of all occupations in the United States—namely, 71 per cent. This was 11½ per cent higher than the occupation next in order—namely, the bakers. The other branch of the clothing trade, the so-called factory product, is not presented in the census tables upon the basis of the nationality of the operatives; but it is probably true that the proportion of foreign born is as large, if not larger, in this branch than in that of the custom tailors.

The immigration of tailors into the United States at the present time is mainly Hebrews, numbering 7,031, and Italians, numbering 1,312. This is a marked change in the character of immigration, since in 1882 it was the German element, numbering 1,935, that contributed the largest proportion of the total number of immigrants stating that to be their trade. The German immigration in 1900 was only 270. The indirect effect of immigration on the tailoring trade is even greater than the direct effect. The division of labor has advanced to such a stage of minuteness that in the ready-made or factory work less than 1 man in 4 is a tailor. The majority, instead of requiring 4 or 5 years to learn the trade of a custom tailor, require only 2 or 3 months to learn such simple work as operating, pressing, sewing buttons, felling, and so on, although a longer time is required to develop speed and endurance. It is this minute subdivision of labor which opens the way for the serious effects of immigration.

The manufacture of clothing is largely centered in New York City, and it is in this place that immigration plays its weightiest part. In lieu of the census of 1900, which at the time of writing has not yet presented the statistics for that year, it may be stated that, in the opinion of those best versed in the trade, fully one-half of the ready-made clothing in the United States is manufactured in New York City. In this way immigration in this trade holds a peculiarly strategic position. Organizations of employees in other cities throughout the country are met continually with the threat that their demands for improved conditions will result simply in transferring the work to New York. On this account a careful examination of the conditions in that city is important.[1]

The characteristic feature of the clothing trade is the so-called sweating system.[2] The definition of the sweating system by different parties varies widely, and a committee of the House of Lords, which in 1888 investigated the subject in Great Britain, was unable to decide upon a precise definition. Their conclusions are summed up in a description of what they consider to be the conditions attending the sweating system—namely, first, a rate of wages inadequate to the necessities of the workman, or disproportionate to the work done; second, excessive hours of labor; third, the insanitary state of the houses in which work is carried on.

It will be seen that this description does not in any way state a method of work, but rather the condition of the operatives employed. In general the sweating sys-

[1] Pp. 316–319.   [2] P. 319 ff.

tem is one in which the work is done by a middleman or contractor, who takes the cloth from the manufacturer at a competitive price, and then, employing his own labor at such wages as he can force them to accept, makes such a profit as his attention to details and his oppression of employees can secure. We have, therefore, in this trade three classes of people concerned—namely, the manufacturer, the contractor, and the workman. The term "manufacturer" does not exactly describe the position of this member of the joint production. The manufacturer (so-called) is more properly a wholesale merchant or warehouseman who may employ his own help directly in the manufacture of garments, or may let it out to contractors. In case the manufacturer employs his help direct, the shop which he conducts is technically known as an "inside shop;" whereas the shops operated by contractors are called "outside shops." The opposition to the contractor on the part of the workmen consists in the demand that the manufacturers substitute inside shops for outside shops. But here a peculiar distinction is necessary. An inside shop, it would be assumed, is one in which the workmen are employed under the direction of a foreman, the latter being a representative of the manufacturer, the wages being paid directly to the workman by the manufacturer and not by the foreman; but the labor organizations which attempt to secure inside shops do not go as far as this. They consider that the evil of the contracting system consists in the fact of a number of competing contractors bidding against each other for the work of the manufacturer, this competition continually reducing the price which they receive for making the garment and the wages of the workers. If, however, the manufacturer would agree to dispense with this system of competing contractors, and would substitute, not a foreman, but a noncompetitive contractor, who has a regular employment with the manufacturer and is not subject to underbidding from other contractors, they would be willing still to content themselves with this modification of the contracting system.

The contractor at the present time in New York and Chicago occupies the peculiar position of an organizer and employer of immigrants. The man best fitted to be a contractor is the man who is well acquainted with his neighbors, who is able to speak the languages of several classes of immigrants, and who can easily persuade them or their wives and children to work for him, and in this way can secure the cheapest help. So irregular is the business and unsteady the employment that in the busy season when the work doubles it is to the advantage of the manufacturer to rely upon contractors who have this ability to increase the number of employees quickly and in proportion to the amount of work. The ability to become a contracting employer depends also upon the small amount of capital invested. Probably $50, under the system of renting the sewing machines, is enough to enable an employee to become a contractor on his own account. He has no investment in goods and runs no risk. Little managing ability is required, because the number of employees is small. He locates in the midst of the districts occupied by immigrants, and contributes to their clannishness by making it possible for them to earn a living without mingling with other nationalities. There is always competition among contractors. The contractor feels more dependent than any of his employees. His profits are often less than the wages of his better-paid workmen.

It must not be inferred, however, that the contractor is the cause of the sweating system. Both the contractor and the sweating system are the product of a disorganized and crowded labor market.

That the contracting system is not essential to the sweating system is shown by the fact that in one branch of the clothing trade, namely, that of the manufacture of ladies' ready-made suits, these small contractors have become manufacturers; that is to say, they have opened up their shops and have begun to sell their ready-made garments direct to the wholesale trade—the clothing houses, cloak jobbers, country merchants, or "mail-order houses." They do not send out traveling salesmen, but wait for buyers to call and see the samples and leave their orders. They manufacture only on order, and frequently, with the help of a banking house, by depositing the order as a guaranty, they are able to secure the cloth necessary to make up the garments. It is in this way that the development of this branch of clothing manufacture in New York City presents exactly the opposite development to that which has occurred in other large industries. Instead of the large manufacturer successfully underbidding and driving out the small manufacturer, leading ultimately to the greater consolidation in the so-called trusts, in this business the small manufacturer has driven out the large manufacturer. The small man does not need to pay a high-priced designer, since he designs his own patterns; he does not have to pay a superintendent, since he manages his own business; he does not pay high rent, since he locates in the poor quarter of the city; he can get labor as cheap as any contractor; the shop is open day and night; the people can work as long hours as they wish. The wages which these small manufacturers pay to their employees vary widely in the different seasons of the trade. In the busy season they are sometimes double the wages paid in the dull season. It has been the effort of the unions to compel the manufacturers to agree upon a scale of prices which shall be unchanged through the year; but as soon as the dull season comes and the large numbers of unskilled and poverty-stricken workmen, pushed on by the influx of immigrants, are crowding for employment, the uniform scale is abandoned, and every manufacturer or contractor is able to command labor at wages barely covering cost of living.

New York and Chicago are the largest centers of the ready-made clothing trade.[1] The industry in New York is practically in the hands of the Russian Jews, who have displaced the earlier Germans and Irish. One branch of the work, that of the finishing or hand sewing on coats and trousers, has within the past 10 years fallen into the hands of the Italian women who work in tenement houses. It is a mistake, however, to infer that tenement-house work is increasing. Contractors no longer have their machines in tenement houses to any material extent. Legislation on this subject and the agitation of the unions has caused them to move into buildings especially erected for their purposes; but in this branch of the work, the so-called home finishing, the Italian women, owing to the fact that they work at prices 25 to 50 per cent less than those formerly received by other nationalities, have absorbed 95 per cent of the work. In Chicago the clothing workers are distributed more equally throughout the different nationalities; the Swedes, Bohemians, and Jews represent probably 25 per cent each of the total number, the Poles 15 per cent, the Germans 5 per cent.

The Jew occupies a unique position in the clothing trade. His physical strength does not fit him for manual labor; his instincts lead him to speculation and trade; his individualism unsuits him for the life of a wage earner, and especially for the discipline of labor organization. For these reasons when a Jew first lands in this country he enters such light occupations as sewing, cigar making, and shoemaking. Jewish women are employed to a much less extent than women of other nationalities, and their children are kept in school until 15 or 16 years of age. The Jew's conception of a labor organization is that of a tradesman rather than that of a workman. Whenever a real abuse arises among the Jewish workmen they all come together to form a giant union and at once engage in a strike. They bring in 95 per cent of the trade. They hold out a long time, even under the greatest suffering. They usually win their case, but when once a strike is settled they are contented, and that usually ends the union, since they do not see any practical use for organization where there is no cause to fight for; consequently the membership of the Jewish union is wholly uncertain. The Jew is also exceedingly abstract and metaphysical and greatly interested in general principles; for this reason the socialistic element acquires control and the practical problems and serious conditions of the trade are neglected.

---

[1] P. 324 ff.

The Italian tailor in his own country receives only about one-half the wages received by the Jews in the country of their European origin and about one-fourth of the wages paid for the same grades of work in western Europe, consequently, in the United States the Italian is able successfully to compete with the newly arrived Russian Jew, and far more able to compete with the German or Englishman. The Italian has usually been a farmer or a farm hand, and his standard of living is even lower than that of the Italian tailor. While as yet the Italians have not gone into the trade in very large numbers, since they have sought mainly outdoor employment, yet, considering the large numbers and their readiness in taking up this branch of work, it seems probable that the future clothing workers of New York are not likely to be Jews, but Italians. One point in which the Italians have the advantage is in the employment of their wives and sisters. The Italian and his wife work in a shop together. In the case of the Jews, a Jewish woman after she is married will not go to work in a shop. The Italian, like the Jew, has a very elastic character; he is energetic and thrifty and will work hard, with little regard for the number of hours.

The Polish clothing workers are mainly women, since the former Polish farmer when coming to this country clings to common work requiring hard labor. He can compete successfully in factory work where hard automatic labor is needed, and consequently in Chicago, where large numbers of Poles are employed in this class of work, the Polish women and girls are employed in the clothing shops. Owing to the opposition of their priests they have never made any attempt to join the labor organizations. During the strike in Chicago in 1896 it was the Polish shops that continued at work and defeated the strike. They are a submissive people while working, and it is in their shops that the hardest driving is done. Their children begin to work early.

The best people in the clothing trade in Chicago are the Scandinavians, including Swedes, Norwegians, and Danes. They are engaged in the manufacture of pants and vests under contractors of their own nationalities. They do not work more than 10 hours a day, as a rule, usually in large shops with steam power. The standard of living is high, and many of them are fairly well educated. The proportion of women who work is large; there are about 5 women to 1 man in the Swedish shops, about 2 women to 1 man in the Polish and Bohemian coat shops, about equal numbers of men and women in the Jewish shops, although the women are mainly of other nationalities.

Unquestionably the standard of living of all nationalities has been raised greatly after their immigration to this country. The Poles and Italians adhere to a lower standard for a longer time than the others; at the same time the low standard of living on the part of those immigrants who are continuously coming into the trade is always a successful check on the efforts others are making to better their condition. The Jews have been especially successful in escaping from the trade, since they change their standard of living soonest and are most energetic in finding employment in other trades or in advancing to the position of contractor or merchant.

Estimating the effect of immigration on the wages in the clothing trade,[1] it will be seen a variety of factors enter to confuse the judgment. In the first place, a change in the character of the trade has occurred in the past 50 years, consisting in the introduction of ready-made clothing, first for men, then for children, and finally for women. These new branches of work, whereby a product, which when formerly made by the custom tailor, the dressmaker, or the housewife cost higher prices than the most of the people could afford, is now made in the latest styles, enables all classes of people to be better dressed and to spend much more money every year for clothing. Herein the immigrant has created his own employment and cultivated a

---
[1] Pp. 368, 369.

market for his product. The journeyman tailor who in former times made the entire coat continues to do so only for the wealthier classes of the public, and for that reason he can earn higher wages than formerly. But, owing to the increasing subdivision of labor in the manufacture of ready-made garments, such important changes have occurred in the several occupations involved that it is a difficult problem to identify any one occupation over a period of years. The first important advance in the subdivision of journeyman tailor's work was introduced by the Jews some 20 years ago in New York City and has been known as the "task" system. This remarkable system, by which perhaps nine-tenths of the ready-made coats in New York are manufactured, exists in no other city of this or other country. Its peculiarity is found in the fact that the 3 men who make the greater part of the coat work in a team or "set," and in their agreement with the contractor they undertake to turn out a certain number of coats per day. This results in what is practically a piece-price system with unrestricted work. Whereas the journeyman tailor formerly filled in his dull season by making coats at half price, which were later sold as ready-made garments, the task system made it possible to manufacture the same coat at one-half the journeyman's price in the dull season. Since this task system has continued unchanged for 20 years, it is possible to measure precisely the changes in wages during that period. The wages per week of male operators and basters have fallen one-sixth; their hours increased one-fifth; their weekly output has increased two-thirds; the piece price for their product has decreased one-half, without any change in machinery or subdivision of labor. Formerly 1 woman was a member of the team, but so intense has become their exertion that women have been replaced by male immigrants at wages per week about 50 per cent higher than those which the women formerly received, but per piece the same, owing to the greater speed and endurance of the men. It can not, however, be said that the low wages, long hours, and overexertion in the task shops of New York are owing solely to immigration, since in recent years a new form of production, which may be called the factory or large-shop method, has entered, and those Jews who adhere to the task system are operating under an antiquated system of production in competition with a modern system.

This factory system carries the subdivision of labor far beyond that of the task system, so that a coat passes through the hands of 40 or 50, or more, work people, whereas in the task system it passed through the hands of only 8 or 10. This increasing subdivision of labor has substituted simple operations for complex operations and has increased the speed and exertion of the workmen. While wages by the hour, day, or week on factory products have decreased in most cases, and remained constant in the cases of the more highly skilled and indispensable workers, yet the increased overexertion and overtime are much more exhausting to the employee than they were 20 years ago. The cost of manufacture, owing to this subdivision of labor, is 40 per cent below that of the task system, so that, altogether, the cost of making a coat in 20 years has been reduced 70 per cent below the price received by the journeyman tailor in the dull season.

The amount of wages in the clothing trade is directly affected by the fate of labor organizations. With the continual influx of immigrants, with the subdivision of labor, with the employment of women and children, and with the prevalence of home work, the problem of organization is indeed serious.

After male immigrants have been here 2 or 3 years they are willing to organize, but are prevented from bettering their condition by the new arrivals, whose necessities compel them to accept low pay. The most successful organization is that of the Swedish Pants and Vest Makers of Chicago, who, owing to peculiar advantages in the nature of their trade, have greatly increased their wages in recent years; in nearly all other occupations of the trade the influx of immigrants is a constant menace to organization, and the conclusion is inevitable that such restriction of immigration as would lessen the number of those nationalities now coming into this trade would enable the clothing workers to organize and secure generally shorter hours and higher pay.

TENEMENT-HOUSE MANUFACTURE.[1]

The so-called sweat-shop legislation of American States is legislation directed against tenement-house work. In this legislation the American States are dealing practically with the subject of immigration in its most urgent and threatening aspect. Practically all the work in tenements governed by these laws is carried on by foreign-born men and women, and by the latest arrivals and lowest conditioned of the foreign born. Two races are the ones mainly affected—the Hebrew and the Italian. The Italian woman working in her tenement has absorbed 95 per cent of the so-called "home finishing" in New York City. Home finishing is that remnant of work in the former home shop where the entire garment was made at home; since through legislation and economic development the regular shop has largely taken the place of the home, this "finishing" is that portion which has not been carried over to the shop. In New York coats and trousers are finished at home; in other cities, only trousers. Finishing amounts to about one-fourth of the work on a garment, but owing to the low wages paid in this class of work, the price is about one-seventh of the price for the entire garment. The Italian home finisher works for about two-thirds of the price which other nationalities formerly received for the same work, and, where formerly 10 to 14 cents was paid for finishing, the Italian does the same work for 5 to 7 cents. By means of this kind of work done at home by his wife and children the Italian laborer is able to bid at much cheaper rates for employment in other occupations; so that home work not only has a damaging effect on the shop work in the trade, but it also affects the people engaged in the same calling as the Italian laborers.

Other classes of clothing workers who are employed at home to more or less extent are the custom tailor, who is a skilled mechanic, making the entire coat; also married women or widows of American birth who, in this way, earn small amounts of "pin money." These women take up this work in emergency, or when they are partly dependent upon charity or upon the help of friends, and on this account they accept wages considerably below the cost of living for a girl working in a shop who has this as her only means of livelihood.

Subcontracting is the rule in this business. Manufacturers dislike the administration of the small lots of work distributed in secluded places where they are unable to keep oversight, and consequently the clothing contractor who takes work from the manufacturer, and who is in closer connection with the home workers, sublets the finishing to them. The objections made to home work are not only the low wages, but the low standard of living which is consequent upon the crowded condition of the home, with pieces of cloth and rags lying about, and pressing irons and sewing machines crowding upon the space. The man who works at home has irregular hours, and usually works all the time he can spare, day and night. He employs his wife and children as helpers, and thus in open competition is able to underbid the man or woman who works in the factory. Home work is depressing upon the intelligence and personal initiative of the tailors. Since it affords but little opportunity for improved machinery or subdivision of labor, the workman makes up in long hours what he loses in economy of manufacture. Labor organization is especially difficult with this class of workers. The journeyman tailors' organizations in this country direct their agitation more vigorously against the home work of their numbers than they do against accepting low prices for work. Scattered over the city, the

---

[1] P. 369 ff.

home workers have no opportunity of meeting together and organizing. They do not learn the English language and are slow to become Americanized. With the abolition or restriction of home work organization becomes more effective, the wages are increased, and hours diminished.

But the legislation of American States directed against tenement-house work has been undertaken not on behalf of the workers, but on behalf of the consumers. It is the protection of the public against contagious and infectious diseases which has induced the States of Massachusetts, New York, Pennsylvania, Illinois, and others, to deal in a rigid manner with this class of employment. In no State does the legislature take the legal step of prohibiting outright tenement-house work; the statute simply restricts the number of persons who shall be employed in a room or tenement, usually to the immediate members of the family living therein. Legislation covers wearing apparel and includes, in some cases, also, cigars and cigarettes.

As regards the administrative details of this legislation, it is noticeable that in those States most directly affected by immigration, namely, New York, Massachusetts, and Pennsylvania, the legislation has been most radical and even despotic. In the first place, a register is required to be kept by the contractor or manufacturer of all home workers in his employment. This register, unfortunately, is not treated as a public record, and hence does not afford opportunity for trade unions, consumers' leagues, and charity societies to carry on effective agitation which will reach the manufacturers.

But the despotic feature of the legislation appears in the provisions requiring a license or permit in order to work at home. In the enforcement of ordinary factory and workshop laws the factory inspector is required to come into court and prove the alleged violation of the law. The defendant enjoys the benefit of the doubt, and the inspector and prosecuting attorney are held to a strict interpretation of the statute. By the license feature, however, the inspector is not dependent upon the courts; his action is summary and decisive; he grants or revokes the license upon his own discretion and judgment, and the penalty thus imposed, since it deprives the workman of his entire living, is far heavier than the imposition of a fine by the court. The inspector, under this provision of the law, calls upon the courts not to punish the material violation of the law, but to punish the workman who works without a license. Both the prosecution and the punishment of the offender are therefore practically in the hands of the administrative officer without recourse to the court. There remains, indeed, the judicial remedy by mandamus or injunction, but in the case of the poverty-stricken workers of the tenement house this is not a substantial remedy.

Massachusetts was the first State to introduce the license feature as a part of its factory legislation. New York, Pennsylvania, New Jersey, Indiana, and Michigan within the last 2 or 3 years have followed the example of Massachusetts. In Pennsylvania the law goes much farther than in other States, and requires a license not only for tenement-house work, but for any "building or parts of building" where wearing apparel is manufactured, and in New York it applies to any building in the rear of a tenement building.

While the law lays down conditions under which the inspector shall grant or revoke a license the decision is in the judgment of the inspector. The law in no case attempts to deal with wages or hours of labor, but, in harmony with its purpose of protecting the consumer, provides only that work shall be conducted under clean and proper sanitary conditions. In New York it provides for absolute cleanliness, and it is conceivable that with inspectors whose standards of cleanliness are high very few licenses would be long outstanding and tenement-house work would be practically abolished.

An interesting feature of the legislation of Massachusetts and New York is the so-called "tenement-made" tag. The inspector is empowered when he discovers garments manufactured under unsanitary conditions or in violation of the law to affix this label to the garment, and any person removing the label is subject to a fine or imprisonment. It is often assumed that the tenement-made label is designed to reach the manufacturer or wholesale merchant and to be kept upon the garments until they have been placed upon the market. This may have been the intention of the legislator, but in no case do the inspectors go so far as to enforce such a penalty upon the manufacturer. They consider the purpose of the tag accomplished when the home worker or the contractor is punished or when the goods have been disinfected. They then remove the tag and the goods are placed upon the market.

Whether garments which have been subject to contagion can be fully disinfected is a matter of dispute, but it is certain that did such goods carry a label at the time when the consumer makes his purchases they could not be sold. In Pennsylvania the law does not provide for a tag, but requires that goods subject to contagion shall be destroyed.

The penalties imposed by the law apply only to home workers and contractors and do not affect the wholesale manufacturer. On this account they are defective. The home worker is an obscure person, and a slight penalty is a heavy burden. The contractor also is unknown, but the manufacturer's position before the community is a responsible one; the sale of his goods depends upon the reputation of his house. Now, the existing laws do not make the manufacturer responsible for tenement-house work unless he gives this work out directly to the home workers; he is not responsible for work given out by his contractors. In this way the contract system shows its advantage, not merely as a cheap method of manufacture, but also as a method of shifting legal responsibility from the manufacturer to the middleman. Were the law to make the manufacturer responsible for all tenement work, whether given out directly by himself or through a contractor, both tenement work and the contractor would quickly disappear.

The results of legislation on tenement-house work in the States of Massachusetts, New York, and Pennsylvania, in so far as they have been satisfactory, have depended not so much on the terms of the law as on the efficiency and integrity of the inspectors. With their enormous powers and wide discretion legislation has created opportunities for bribery and political favoritism unusually tempting. The law of Massachusetts, although inferior to that of other States, has yet accomplished far better results, owing to the civil-service regulations and the permanent tenure of the inspectors. Although not directed to the improvement of wages, nevertheless, by restricting the amount of tenement work, the wages for this class of employment in Boston are 40 to 50 per cent higher than the wages in New York for the same work. The depressing effects of immigration on wages, therefore, are partly counteracted by the restriction of tenement-house work.

This class of legislation is, on the whole, superior to the proposed total abolition of tenement-house manufacture, since it makes it possible to abolish the work in the majority of cases, but also makes it possible to grant exceptions in those emergency cases where hardship would be caused by its prohibition.[1]

While neither the Federal Government nor any State government has undertaken to abolish tenement-house work where the work is sold to private purchasers, yet, where the Federal Government is itself a purchaser of clothing, it has undertaken to establish this condition. Since the Spanish-American war, when it seemed to be clearly demonstrated that the contagion of measles and other diseases in the army camps was owing directly to tenement-house manufacture, the War Department has inserted in its contracts with the manufacturers of military garments that all work must be done in a regularly organized factory, and no part of the work shall be sublet to contractors. In the several States clothing for the National Guard is usually purchased from the War Department, and is therefore protected by the specifications

---

[1] P. 380.

XXXII   THE INDUSTRIAL COMMISSION:—IMMIGRATION.

of that Department; but in those States where clothing is manufactured by the State authorities there exist at present but few restrictions. These are in Massachusetts, which provides that military clothing shall be made in the city of Boston, and not in sweat shops; in California, that it shall not be made by convict or Chinese labor; and in New York, that it shall be made under the conditions prescribed by the factory and sweat-shop legislation of the State. In one State, Pennsylvania, clothing for the National Guard is made in the manufacturing department of the State arsenal, and in the case of the United States Navy, clothing is manufactured by the naval clothing factory, navy-yard, Brooklyn.[1]

The legislation of Great Britain and Canada and the ordinances of the London county council go further than the legislation of American States, in that their object is not merely the protection of the public, but also the protection of the workers in securing a "fair rate of wages." In Canada this object is thought to be secured by prohibiting subcontracting.

The wish of the purchaser to know the conditions under which his garments are manufactured is the basis of the Consumers' League, organized in May, 1899. This league adopts an official label to be attached to the garments of those manufacturers who abide by the conditions imposed upon them—that they obey the State factory laws, that they manufacture the goods on their premises, that they employ no children under 16 years of age, and that they use no overtime work. More than two-thirds of the labels granted to manufacturers by this league are in the State of Massachusetts, owing to the excellent factory legislation in that State and especially the thorough manner in which it is enforced.

Besides the label of the Consumers' League, the organization of the garment workers has adopted a label based on slightly different principles. This label is granted only to those manufacturers or contractors who employ solely union help. Hitherto the garment workers' label has been somewhat misleading, since it has been granted to contractors and has not stood for the absence of sweatshop conditions; but by a resolution adopted in May, 1901, the label henceforth is to be furnished only to those manufacturers who maintain exclusively their own shops.[2]

An appendix to this chapter, dealing with the Philadelphia trade, prepared by Helen Marot and Caroline L. Pratt, is added at pages 723–743.

CIGAR MAKERS.[3]

The problem of the effect of immigration on the wages and employment of cigar makers can not be separated from the effects of machinery, division of labor, country competition, and the competition of women and girls. The machinery which has been introduced in recent years, known as the "suction table," is exceedingly limited in character, but it is such that less skilled workmen and girls can take the place of the skilled mechanic. With this new condition, girls working at $4.50 per 1,000 cigars, where the union scale is $7.50 to $8.50 per 1,000, can earn wages amounting to $7.50 per week. The large establishments in New York and Philadelphia which have in recent years extended the sale of advertised cigars employ almost exclusively girls and women. But it must be noted that these are the American-born daughters of immigrant parents.

Of similar effect upon the wages of city cigar makers is the remarkable development of country shops. This is especially true in Pennsylvania where, in the counties of Berks, Bucks, Montgomery, York, and Lancaster, Philadelphia manufacturers have located their annexes, and, in place of the very low union scale of $7.50 in Philadelphia, they can have the same cigar made for $5.50. This rate is so low that the suction table is not profitable. The advantages of country employment to the

[1] P. 382, 383.   [2] P. 384.   [3] P. 385 ff.

manufacturer consist often in the favorable inducements—in the exemption from taxes, even in donations of ground and subscriptions for buildings—offered by the citizens, but mainly in the low cost of living. Much of the work, however, is crude, and the 10-cent cigars are not made in these localities on a large scale.

Contrasted with country competition and the employment of women and girls are the efforts of the labor organization, which includes about 40 per cent of the workmen in the trade. The union, through its strong organization, has effected a continuous increase in wages paid to its members, so that it is estimated that on the class of work where sweat-shop and nonunion labor earn $6 to $9 a week union labor earns $12 to $18. But the union scale is based largely upon the union label, which, being in effect a substitute for the expensive advertising of the large manufacturers, enables the members of the union to distribute among themselves the $4 or $5 per 1,000 which the manufacturer usually invests in advertising. In this way the union maintains a high scale of wages, keeps immigrants out of its ranks, and prohibits the use of machinery, but at the same time loses control of the large establishments employing 200 to 2,000 working people. The immigrants crowding into the cheaper lines of work and the unorganized branches of employment have forced down the prices to a very low point, so that in the Jewish sweat shops of New York and Chicago cigars are manufactured at $4.50 per 1,000 equal in quality to those which are made at the union scale of $8.50 and $9.50.

On account of these several peculiar conditions in the trade it may be asserted that at the present time the effect of immigration is less than the effect of country competition or of the employment of women and girls; and that, were it not for the label, these three factors cooperating would depress wages, except in the highest grades of work, below the point at which the members of the union could afford to work longer at the trade.

COAL MINERS.[1]

The coal mining industry of the United States has from its earliest days been a field peculiarly affected by the influx of fresh immigrants. In the earlier days they were mainly from the British Isles—Englishmen, Scotchmen, Welshmen, and Irishmen. Within the past 20 years these earlier nationalities have been displaced by immigrants from Austria-Hungary, Italy, and Russia. According to the census of 1890 the foreign-born miners constituted 58.1 per cent of the total in Pennsylvania, 57.4 per cent in Illinois, and 59 per cent in Ohio. In the mines of the Philadelphia and Reading Coal and Iron Company in 1896 one-fourth were Polish, one-fifth were Irish, one-fifth Americans, and one-tenth were, respectively, Germans and Hungarians. In the mines of Illinois in 1899 the foreign-born miners in the order of precedence were Germans, English, Italians, Polish, Irish, Scotch, Austrians, Bohemians, and Hungarians.

The principal complaint arising from the presence of foreigners is the alleged oversupply of labor. This is shown in the diminished number of days for which employment is obtainable in the course of the year. The fact that there is a seasonal character in the mining of coal is exaggerated by the presence of an oversupply of labor. Relying upon such oversupply, the operator is content to mine his coal only on the receipt of orders, or with the orders in view, and does not endeavor to distribute employment throughout the year. Bituminous coal can not economically be stored, as it disintegrates with exposure; but, on the other hand, since bituminous coal is used mainly for manufactures and railroads, while anthracite coal is used for domestic purposes, the demand for bituminous is more continuous throughout the year, and the number of days of employment is greater. Coupled with this consideration is the fact that the anthracite coal mines lie nearer the Atlantic coast and are

[1] P. 389 ff

more accessible to the inroads of immigrants, and consequently the oversupply of labor is greater than in the bituminous mines which lie at farther distance from the ports. These influences appear in the aggregate number of days employed in the different fields. In 1892 anthracite coal miners worked 206.6 days out of a possible 310, but in 1898 they worked only 148 days. On the other hand, bituminous coal miners in Pennsylvania, in 1892, worked 208.6 days, and in 1898, 208.5 days. Comparing these industries with 47 manufacturing industries in the State of Pennsylvania, it appears that for bituminous coal mining there is employment for 68 per cent of the possible working days; in anthracite coal mining for 48.5 per cent of the working days, and in 47 leading industries for 97.3 per cent of the working days. On an average the workers in iron, steel, cotton, woolen, and general manufactures have an opportunity to work from 35 to 50 per cent more of the total time per year than the coal miners in the anthracite field, and from 30 to 40 per cent more than the bituminous miners. The increase in the number of employees in the anthracite region has meant not so much an increase in the amount of the resulting product as a decrease in the number of days worked per man.

Closely connected with the influx of immigrants is the introduction of machinery. This applies only to bituminous coal mining, since anthracite coal is more refractory and has not yet been submitted to machine cutting. At the same time it is doubtful, in the opinion of many operators, whether machinery could have been introduced in the bituminous coal mines had it not been for the introduction of foreign labor. The English, Scotch, Welsh, and Irish miners in earlier days successfully resisted the machine, and it was their displacement by Slavs and Italians that permitted the introduction of machinery.

Machinery has had a twofold effect—it has greatly reduced the cost of mining coal and has displaced skilled labor by unskilled labor. The reduction in the cost appears in the investigations of the United States Department of Labor, which shows that one mine, where formerly the cost per ton by hand mining was 71.2 cents, was able to mine the same coal by machinery for 42.3 cents, and that another was able to reduce the cost from 77.6 to 42.4 cents.

The effect of machinery on skilled labor is shown in two establishments reported by the bureau of statistics of Illinois, in one of which, mined by hand, the miners numbered 71.2 per cent of the men employed, and in the other, operated by machinery, the cutters, blasters, and timbermen who took the places of the miners were only 9.37 per cent of employees. The machine has greatly subdivided the work, so that 7 or 8 men are required on various operations which formerly were performed by the individual miner. The smaller proportion of skilled laborers following the introduction of the machine has required even greater skill and endurance on their part, and the larger proportion of laborers who follow the machine and load the cars must have greater endurance and physical strength than formerly; consequently, the wages have not, in all cases, been reduced on the substitution of machine production, but the exhaustion and overexertion of the workmen have increased.

The most important circumstance which determines whether the mine worker shall gain an increase in wages with the introduction of machinery is the state of his labor organization. This is shown by the fact that with the introduction of machinery wages were continually declining until the year 1897, but in that year, after the organization of the union, wages increased 30 to 40 per cent, and in Illinois, where the union is strongest, the average gain in wages in machine mines was 36.3 per cent, whereas the average for all mines, including machine mines, was 26.4 per cent. Through this organization in Illinois the union fixes the price of machine mining at only 7 cents less per ton than the price for pick mining, whereas in Pennsylvania and Ohio, where the union has less strength, the differential is 19.2 cents. It is needless to say that this narrow differential in Illinois, while giving the miner a share in the advantages of machinery, is at the same time a discouragement to the mine operator in the introduction of machinery.

Labor organization among the coal miners has passed through extraordinary vicissitudes. The Welsh, Scotch, English, and Irish miners were well organized and maintained high wages, but in 1875, not owing to the presence of immigrants, but as a result of a strike against a falling market, their organization was entirely broken and their wages greatly reduced. Not until 1897, in the bituminous field, and 1900, in the anthracite field, was a reorganization affected, this time not of the original British stock alone, but also of the mixed nationalities from eastern and southeastern Europe. These new immigrants began displacing the earlier ones following the strike of 1875, and their numbers increased so rapidly that the general strike in 1887 for a restoration of the conditions of 12 years before was utterly defeated. The same was true of the strike in 1894. Owing to these disasters of the union the rates of wages were continually declining for more than 20 years. In Illinois, from 1881 to 1886, they fell 33 per cent; from 1890 to 1896 there was an additional decline of 17 per cent, but following 1897, when the union secured influence, wages rose the first year 26.42 per cent, and in the 2 years following they had increased 49 per cent for hand mining and 42 per cent for machine mining.

The problem of organizing the diverse races and languages of the mine workers has been more serious than that which has confronted any other labor organization in this or other conntries. Not only have these races been divided by language, but equally or more by the antagonisms of religion, which usually have accompanied race divisions and have been played upon by the operators. In the earlier form of local organization it was the custom to organize each nationality separately in its own branch in order that it might conduct its business in its own language and then meet the other branches through its chosen representatives. This method was soon abandoned, first, because the non-English miners themselves wished to be in a better position to learn the English language, and, second, because the organization by nationalities brought together workmen in different mines whose legislative problems were different. At the present time the local unions are organized as English-speaking unions for each mine or district. The non-English members are represented in the executive board by one of their own race and in their business meetings the motions and speeches are translated by interpreters.

Naturally and necessarily the leaders of the Miners' Union are English-speaking persons, but it is a notable fact that the predominant race of leaders and officers is Irish. The Irishman possesses peculiar gifts in bringing together and organizing conflicting nationalities, races, and religions.

While there have been serious problems in the organization of mixed nationalities, an equally serious problem which has confronted the organization of these immigrants has been the competition of the unorganized Americans of native stock. This was fully shown in the experience of the miners prior to 1897, when their organizations in northern Illinois were defeated by the native Americans in southern Illinois. In the first mining district of Illinois the per cent of Americans is only 11, and in the seventh, in the southern part of the State, it is 80. Yet it was these American miners in the thick and more easily mined veins of the southern section whose competition reduced wages so low that they were actually earning less than in the northern districts. The success of the strike in 1897 consisted mainly in the fact that the southern American-born miners were brought into the union and placed on a basis of equal competition with the northern foreign-born miners.

A similar condition at the present time confronts the mining organization of the 4 great States of the bituminous field in the competition of West Virginia, where the native whites of native parents number 57½ per cent and the colored miners number 21 per cent of the total number of miners, compared with 20 to 48 per cent native whites of both native and foreign parentage in the other States. Prices and wages in West Virginia are 30 to 70 per cent below those under similar conditions in the other States. Colored miners of themselves present no greater difficulties than do the native whites, since, in other Southern States, like Alabama, where they number one-half the miners, they are well organized and receive equal pay with the whites. Alabama coal, however, does not enter into competition with Northern coal, and the low pay of both whites and blacks is not threatening as it is in West Virginia. As far as the great northern central field is concerned the result of conditions in West Virginia has been that while the output of the other States has increased somewhat the output of West Virginia has leaped forward by bounds, and the organization of 150,000 bituminous mine workers, over one-half of whom are foreign born of diverse races, is menaced more by the unorganized Americans of native stock than by their own internal divisions.

TEXTILE TRADES.[1]

The textile trades exhibit in a remarkable way the combination of machinery, immigration, employment of women and children, and country competition. Weavers have more than doubled their capacity in the last 30 years, and, with the introduction of the Northrop loom, they are able to produce 5 times as much as they produced 40 years ago. The ring-spindle machine does twice the work of the mule spindle. With the increase of machinery the intensity of exertion of the weaver has greatly increased. Formerly, when both machine and thread were in an imperfect state, the machines ran slower and there were more frequent breaks, but now, with better machines and better cotton, there is greater speeding and no cessation. In the spindle room, where formerly a hard-working spinner earned $12 to $14, the woman attending the ring-spinning machine earns only $6 to $8, and the work is not as hard.

With these improvements unskilled labor takes the place of skilled labor, since only a week or two is needed to learn to operate the ring-spinning machine and 3 or 4 weeks to run 4 looms and earn some money. This has been the opportunity for the immigrant. The succession of nationalities in the cotton-textile trade is well known by the public. The Americans 50 years ago were the only employees; then came the English, Irish, and Scotch. Owing to the high prices at the time of the war, wages rose, but the French Canadians, beginning to come in 1866, coupled with the decline in markets, brought a rapid decline in wages. This continued with variations until 1897, when earnings which 30 years ago were $12 to $13 a week had been reduced to $8 and $10 a week. Since that time there has been a slight increase, but this increase is again checked and a reduction is again in prospect owing to a new factor—the competition of Southern mills working 66 hours a week with low fixed charges, improved machinery, and exceedingly cheap labor.

The French Canadians brought a remarkably low standard of living. They were willing to work for almost any wages, but gradually their standard has improved and they copy the living of their English, Irish, and American fellow laborers. At the same time they look upon American employment as more or less temporary. The French farmers in Canada send their families to Fall River and other New England towns to earn a little money and then return. When the price for labor rises they come in large numbers, and when the price falls large numbers return, but more of them remain than was formerly the case. On account of their temporary residence they do not seriously strive to raise their standard of living, but consider themselves able to endure privation in view of the savings which they may take with them to their Canadian homes. Formerly they placed their children at work at very low ages, but now legislation has stopped this practice. Again, in the earlier days they worked unlimited hours, but since the law of Massachusetts fixes the hours at 58 per week their competition in this direction has been restricted. In these two ways, through legislation, by prohibiting child labor and by reducing the hours of employment of women, the State of Massachusetts has dealt directly with the evil factors of

---

[1] Pp. 420 ff.

French-Canadian immigration, and has to a certain extent protected the American standard of living.

Labor organization is exceedingly difficult, owing to the variety of nationalities. In the card-picking and ring-spinning branches at Fall River, whereas 55 per cent of the employees are Irish, English, and Scotch, these races constitute 75 per cent of the union; the French, with 30 per cent employees, are 20 per cent of the union; Portuguese, Poles, and others, with 15 per cent employees, are 5 per cent of the union. Proportionate to their numbers the French, Poles, and Portuguese are poorly organized. In the more highly skilled occupations, as that of mule spinners, where they have been in the country for a longer time and have become Americanized, they are more eager to maintain union principles. But the mule spinners are being displaced by the cheaper ring spinners. While it is doubtless true that the French Canadians, with their low standard and their incapacity for organization, have greatly reduced the earnings of textile workers, it is also true that now, when they show a readiness to improve their condition, they are handicapped by a new factor not connected with immigration—the competition of native labor in the cheaper districts of the South.

BOOT AND SHOE WORKERS.[1]

In recent years immigration has played a minor part in this trade, except where in certain isolated cases Armenians and Italians have been introduced in order to break a strike. Probably 85 per cent of the workers throughout the country are native born. The difference in wages which has occurred has been owing to the introduction of machinery and the employment of women and girls in country districts. These are generally the children of immigrants, so that taking into account the 15 per cent of foreign born and the 85 per cent of native born, it is probably true that immigration, both of the first and second generation, plays a leading part in the industry.

WOODWORKERS.[2]

The enormous development in recent years of the factory product in this industry has been accompanied by a corresponding influx of immigrants. Work which the carpenter formerly executed at the place of building is now prepared beforehand in factories, and these factories are manned to the extent of 50 to 75 per cent by foreigners. The wood-working factory is essentially a machine industry with unskilled labor. The majority are located in Chicago, Michigan, and Wisconsin. In the furniture factory out of 75 men perhaps only 5 are skilled mechanics, the rest being only feeders. In this way a large number of immigrants are employed, and often children and women find places. In cabinetmaking 50 per cent are Germans, who are considered the best men in the trade, and 25 per cent are foreigners of all other nationalities, and 25 per cent are native born. In furniture factories in country districts in Wisconsin the Germans have worked recently at as low as 50 cents a day and their women were doing carpenter work at the bench.

The organization of woodworkers relies to a large extent on outside help. For example, in Chicago they control 60 per cent of the sash and door employees, the union being supported prior to 1900 by the building trades of Chicago. After the defeat of the building trades council in the strike of 1900, the hours of labor in the building material factories were increased from 8 to 9, owing to the loss of this support. The unions control 95 per cent of the office and saloon factories, but none of the regular furniture factories, and only 1 desk factory. In the box-making trade the union shops are those which have probably 90 per cent skilled labor, while the nonunion shops have 90 per cent unskilled labor, thus showing the success of organizing skilled mechanics, but the difficulty in organizing machine shops with their large proportion of immigrants, women, and boys. In these shops the union scale runs from $2 to $2.50 dozen and the nonunion scale runs from $1 to $1.75.

---

[1] P. 422 ff.   [2] P. 423 ff.

IRON, STEEL, AND MACHINERY.[1]

The iron, steel, and machinery trades illustrate the fact that skilled occupations, affected only by immigration from western Europe, have far less complaint to make at the present time than those unskilled trades affected by immigration from southern and eastern Europe. The machinists who come from Great Britain or Sweden have been accustomed to organization, and, bringing their "cards" with them, do not enter into strong competition with those already here. The iron, steel, and tin workers, whose immigrant competitors come from Belgium and Alsace-Lorraine, have been affected somewhat by alleged evasions of the alien contract-labor laws, and their disastrous defeat at Homestead is ascribed partly to the importation of aliens. In the branch of the trade thus affected wages have been reduced and have not recovered their former standard.

The steel industry offers examples of the effect of immigration on the speed and exertion of the workmen. Formerly there were rigid restrictions imposed by the union on the amount of work which the team of men should be permitted to accomplish in the 8 hours' employment. This output has been doubled in the past 7 years, mainly because immigrants, with only a temporary interest in their residence here, would not submit to the restrictions.

More serious than immigration for the skilled workman of the iron and steel trades is the introduction of machinery. This is a means for introducing low-grade labor from southern and eastern Europe, but so rapid has been the growth of the industry that, although the skilled workmen are a continually smaller proportion of the number employed, they are continually increasing in absolute numbers, thus being able to maintain the standard of earnings, but yielding a larger and larger proportion of their work to machinery and immigrant labor.

GLASS WORKERS.[2]

The glass workers illustrate in certain branches the way in which immigration has compelled the removal of restrictions on output. In some departments of the flint-glass trade there is the limited system, and in others the unlimited. In the unlimited branches of the work there are scarcely any foreigners, since the skill is of a very high degree and the speed is so great that immigrants can not endure it. The men work in teams, earning $6 and $8 a day, paid by the piece, and the trade longevity of the men, owing to the severe exertion, is seriously reduced. In other branches of the work, where formerly there were agreements with other groups of employers, the quantity of output was limited; immigrants found ingress to nonunion establishments and, working on an unlimited system, in the course of time compelled the union, in order to protect itself, to remove the restrictions on its own members. In one branch the increased production, with the removal of the union limitations, amounted to 100 per cent, and the increase in earnings about 15 per cent.

The flint-glass workers protect themselves against immigration by a discriminating initiation fee, charging $3 for Americans and $100 to foreigners, recently reduced to $50. This discriminating fee depends for its success on union monopoly of the business, since immigrants unable to pay the fee are forced to enter nonunion establishments. Glass-bottle blowers prohibit the admission of foreign blowers, but the president of the union is given authority to make exceptions if the executive board thinks necessary. The union does not think foreigners should come here, because whenever the trade needs more workmen the union, through its annual agreement with the manufacturers, increases the apprentices accordingly, and when trade is dull and there are plenty of idle members the manufacturers agree to take no apprentices, or to take a smaller proportion. The initiation fee is normally $100 for foreigners, compared with $5 for Americans, but this high fee has been levied but once in 5 years. Foreigners usually pay $50, but when they are taken in from a nonunion factory, which is usually the case, they are charged nothing.

---

[1] Pp. 424, 425.   [2] P. 425, 426.

BUILDING TRADES.[1]

The strong organization of the building trades in American cities, and the rapid growth of the cities themselves have contributed to maintaining high standards of wages. The branch most seriously affected is that of the carpenters, and in this case the competition of country and suburban carpenters in the interior cities is more important than the competition of immigrants. On the other hand, along the Canadian border the competition of Canadians who come from country districts and small villages of Canada contributes to a lower scale of wages than those maintained at interior points. The granite workers in the cities complain of work done at the quarries, where mainly immigrant labor is employed and the wages are very low, but they are able to maintain the high standard in the cities themselves. Stonecutters have complained in times past of so-called "harvesters" who come from abroad during the busy season, but by the discriminatory initiation fee of $50, compared with the American fee of $10, this form of competition has been checked.

The bricklayers, one of the strongest organizations in the building trade, has successfully protected itself in New York against immigrants by requiring its members to be citizens of the United States, and by requiring a second initiation fee of those who absent themselves for more than 1 month from the locality. Plumbers receive competition only from England and Scotland, where the immigrants have strong unions of their own, and they readily abide by the union rules when they migrate. Hod carriers and building laborers are naturally the branches of the building trade most affected by immigration, but owing to their association with the other stronger trades, based sometimes on sympathetic strikes, they have been able to maintain standards of wages higher than those received by common laborers.

LONGSHOREMEN.[2]

The organization of longshoremen on the Great Lakes is one of the most striking instances of the way in which organization overcomes the disadvantages of race competition. Formerly, under a system which was substantially that of subcontracting or sweating, a man received very low pay for very irregular work, but since the organization of their international union in 1897, in which they have become their own contractors, their year's earnings have doubled. Their local branches are often organized by races, each with its own representation in the central council, which conducts business in English and has jurisdiction over the several branches. The same arrangement exists at Newport News between the white and colored races.

PADRONE SYSTEM.[3]

The so-called padrone system of the Italian immigrants differs at the present time essentially from the original system as first introduced in this country. The term itself in Italy, as well as in the early stages of Italian immigration, applied in general to the employment of children in the roving professions, such as strolling musicians, performers on the harp and hand organ, and street acrobats. These children were collected by the padrone, the "little father," from the hillsides of Italy, and, practically in the condition of slaves, were carried from Europe to America. This practice was prohibited by law, and does not now exist except in irregular and surreptitious ways.

But it was respecting adult Italian labor that the padrone system acquired its earliest and its present ill reputation. In the early days of Italian immigration the apprehension of change, the fear of going to a strange and unknown land had to be counteracted by a guaranty of some kind. The padrone therefore was an importer of contract labor. He engaged with the American manufacturer or contractor to furnish cheap labor, and then in order to secure this labor himself went to Italy,

---

[1] Pp. 426–428. [2] P. 428. [3] Pp. 430–442.

entered into contracts at 40, 50, or 60 cents a day, and furnished labor to the manufacturer at $1 to $1.50 a day. Sometimes he would act upon his own initiative, and enter into a contract with an Italian at, say, $40 a year for 2 years, and then would take his chances after importing the Italian laborer of finding employment at wages three or four times as high. This form of the padrone system has, however, at the present time entirely disappeared. The immigration of Italians has reached such enormous bulk, and the communications of those already in the country attract their fellow-countrymen so successfully, that it is necessary no longer to employ the system of contracting in order to induce immigration. The padrone system at present is strictly a system of "bossism," and the so-called padrone is known by the Italians themselves not as padrone but as "the boss." This padrone thrives simply on the ignorance, illiteracy, and distrust of the green immigrant. His revenues are, in the words of Dr. Rossi, "the forced tribute which the newly arrived pays to those of his own race who are acquainted with the ways and language of the country." The padrone's methods are analogous to those of an employment agency, though he does not have an employment-agency license. He often goes to a regular employment agency in search of work for his fellows. His business is to accompany his gang, and to continue with them at their place of work, but he is not their foreman and not their contractor. He acts, perhaps, as interpreter, but mainly as the proprietor of the shanty or boarding house in which they crowd together for the time being. His profit is partly in the commission which he receives from the employer, but mainly in the prices which he charges for food and lodging. The food which he furnishes has a monopoly value, because his subjects are prohibited from purchasing elsewhere on pain of discharge. For this reason he is able to charge 10 cents for macaroni which in the market costs 3 cents, or 15 cents for beer which can be purchased for 4 cents, and so on. He has this strong hold largely because the Italians suffer more than any other race from irregular employment. In the winter there is no employment at all. The laborers must therefore board with the contractor, a dozen or more in one room, under the most unsanitary conditions.

The padrone is usually in combination with an Italian banker, who, out of the deposits of the laborers themselves who distrust the post-office and the American bankers, furnishes capital for the padrone to establish his shanty and pay the transportation of his help. The profits are shared by the padrone with the banker.

Laborers working under this system cost the contractor in Eastern States as low as $1 per day during the period of depression, and at the present time as high as $1.35 to $1.75 per day. On the Erie Canal in 1898, of 15,000 common laborers employed, only 1,000 were American citizens, 13,500 were Italian aliens, 350 were Poles, and 150 were Hungarians. The local laborers of the State were deprived of the wages they might have earned on this great public improvement, the merchants lost the benefit of their purchases, and at the close of the employment many of the Italians were left on the local authorities for support.

In the small country towns the padrone stands ready to furnish skilled help, such as masons, carpenters, stonecutters, and machinists, but in the larger cities he is confined to work upon sewers, railroads, waterworks, construction, and similar common employment. In public employment of the leading cities of the country at the present time the padrone system is not known to exist to any great extent. In Eastern cities rules are quite generally adopted either by the city council or by the State legislature intended to exclude this class of employment. In Philadelphia only those who are citizens of the United States can be employed upon work paid from the general tax levy, but aliens may be employed on work paid from assessments of benefits.

Italian labor has very largely displaced all other kinds of labor in railway construction in the Eastern States. The same is true of the Chinese and Japanese on the Pacific coast. The Italians in the Eastern States work from $1 to $1.25 per day, point that it is no longer a practical means of restricting immigration. The cheap labor from eastern and southern Europe does not come under contract, and so evades the law, while skilled laborers, who naturally would be more likely to enter into contracts, are by this decision exempted from the law.

Turning to the second aspect of the alien contract labor law, the deportation of immigrants, we find the conditions entirely different from those which pertain to the prosecution of the importer. By an amendment to the law adopted in 1894, the decisions of the inspectors, upon appeal to the Secretary of the Treasury, are final in the case of all aliens, whether immigrants or former residents. There is no appeal to the courts. The courts will refuse to interfere on habeas corpus, even when they see that what they consider serious injustice is being done; they affirm that the statute does not require inspectors even to take testimony, and that they can exclude an immigrant on whatever inspection and examination they choose to undertake. Of course the decision of the inspectors and the Secretary is not binding upon the court in the prosecution of the importer.

Such being the large discretion in the hands of the Treasury Department, the efficiency of the law in respect to the exclusion of obnoxious immigrants depends partly upon the opinions and convictions of the official, and partly upon the administrative machinery. The latter may be briefly stated. Excluded classes whom the Bureau of Immigration is authorized to debar, without appeal to the courts, are those who are likely to become a public charge on account of idiocy, insanity, and pauperism; those who suffer from loathsome or contagious diseases; those who have been convicted of a felony, or even a misdemeanor involving moral turpitude; polygamists and contract laborers. In order that the inspectors may properly execute their duties, they require in the first place as complete information as possible regarding the thousands of immigrants who pass under their examination. The methods devised for this purpose do not include consular or medical examination at the foreign port of debarkation. The principal reliance to prevent debarkation of the ineligible classes is placed upon the agents of the steamship companies. It is reasoned that if the steamship companies are compelled to bear the burden of deporting the passengers who have been excluded from landing, they will take careful precautions in prohibiting their agents from selling tickets to those liable to be debarred. The better class of steamship companies, indeed, carry out this theory, since they make their agents responsible even for the expense of the passage back to the country of debarkation. The steamship companies are required to fill out, for the use of inspectors at the United States ports, a manifest or list of names of all alien immigrants before they embark on the steamer, giving certain information specified by law. These manifests are verified by the master and surgeon of the vessel before the United States consul at the port of embarkation.

Upon arrival at the American port the immigrants are passed in file, first before the medical inspectors detailed from the Marine-Hospital Service for this work, then before the immigration inspectors who, with the ship's manifest in their presence, make inquiries relative to their eligibility to land. Should the immigration inspector entertain any doubt whatever as to eligibility, he is required by law to hold the immigrant for further inquiry before a board of inspectors. This board is known as the board of special inquiry, and in framing it the legislators contemplated an administrative court which should be free as much as possible from the personal motives of the individual inspector, and able to establish standards for admission and rejection. It is found that on an average the immigration inspectors admit 80 or 90 per cent of all immigrants, and retain 10 to 20 per cent for special inquiry. The board of special inquiry in turn admits some 85 per cent of those examined by it, and rejects 10 or 15 per cent. As a result the total number debarred each year is about 1 per cent of the total number of the immigrants.

XLII   THE INDUSTRIAL COMMISSION:—IMMIGRATION.

The institution is, curiously enough, one of the great anticipated advantages of immigration to America. He recognizes it as "the college," a term which he has applied in his own land to the charity institutions of the missionaries; and as soon as the law and the administration permit the Syrian brings his children to "the college," to be supported by the public until old enough to assist him in earning a living.

At the same time the standard of living is improving. A cooking stove is the first new necessity added to the room; next comes a bed as a substitute for the rug or blanket. As to citizenship, probably there are 300 fully naturalized Syrian-Americans in New York City.

THE FOREIGN IMMIGRANT IN NEW YORK CITY.[1]

Of all the great cities, New York is perhaps the most intimately concerned with the problem of immigration, since of the nineteen millions and odd foreign immigrants who have landed in this country between 1820 and 1900, approximately 13,500,000, or about 71 per cent, have entered at this port. On account of this preeminent importance of New York in the problems of immigration, considerable space has been given in the report on the economic effects of immigration to a chapter prepared by Kate Holladay Claghorn, Ph. D.

Down to 1870 immigration was mainly British, Irish, and German. Since that period there has been a rapid decrease in the proportion furnished by these races in successive years, and a rapid increase in the proportion of immigrants from Italy, Austria-Hungary, and Russia, until in the year 1899–1900 British made up only 2.8 per cent, Irish 8 per cent, Germans 4.1 per cent, and Scandinavians 7 per cent of the total immigration, while immigrants from Italy made up 22.3 per cent, those from Austria-Hungary 25.6 per cent, and those from Russia and Poland 20.2 per cent.

The immigration problem was felt as a serious one in New York City as early as 1819. In that year the managers of the Society for the Prevention of Pauperism, in their second annual report, outlined the problem much as we know it to-day, complaining of the pauperism and the general social and moral evils that were likely to follow the influx of immigration.

The complaint was made as early as 1817, while the country was as yet sparsely settled, that immigrants were lingering in crowded cities instead of proceeding to the interior, where there was need of their services.

An evil especially felt, and ascribed to the foreign immigrant, was an increase in sickness and of the death rate in the city. Hospital accommodation had to be provided for "diseased emigrants" as early as 1769. Newly arrived immigrants were the principal victims of the yellow-fever epidemic of 1795. The city inspector for the year 1816 ascribed the great mortality of that year to the "constant influx of immigrants." From this time on city inspectors called attention again and again to immigration as a cause of disease, their reports showing in especial a great increase in consumption of the lungs, typhoid and typhus fever, and smallpox, coincident with increase in immigration.

Much of the disease brought in by immigrants was due to bad conditions on shipboard, to neglect by shipmasters of the simplest sanitary precautions, to their failure to provide for proper food, ventilation, or cleanliness.

Various Government regulations made for the purpose of doing away with these evils worked to reduce them, until in 1864 it could be said that the diseases engendered by "confined air, filthy habits, bad fare, and long voyages," were no longer a source of serious apprehension.

Another more important cause of ill health among foreign immigrants in New York was bad housing.

In the course of the city's growth business pressed into residence districts, driving out the well-to-do residents who objected to the noise and bustle of a business quarter. The old private residences left behind were, in part, pulled down to give place

[1] Pp. 449–492.

to business houses; in part were turned over to occupancy by the poor, who crowded into them—4, 5, and 6 families to a house originally built for the uses of 1 family only. In such quarters foreign immigrants found their first homes.

By 1834 overcrowding was recognized as a serious evil, the city inspector of that year stating that the great increase in the death rate was caused, largely, by bad housing.

Former good residence districts gradually being changed into tenement quarters were, at this time, the lower west side of the city from the Battery up toward Greenwich village and the Fourth Ward. The Sixth Ward, never so good a residence district as the others named, was now known as a long-settled Irish neighborhood and a center of crime and disorder. Housing was especially bad here and disease flourished..

As the poor population of the city increased, largely from foreign immigration, in addition to the old private residences turned over to their use, large barrack buildings, especially built for their accommodation, were provided for them. From the use of the older type of tenement house, the abandoned family residence, had come the great crowding of the poor into cellars and attics, which was an especial evil of the time. The newer barrack type, by housing more people in its greater number of stories, to some extent did away with the necessity for cellar dwellings, but as they were built to a greater height than the old dwellings and covered every available foot of ground space along narrow "courts" and "alleys," the light and ventilation they could receive was reduced far below the limits of health. It was said in 1842 that occupancy of these courts and the cellars of the old type of dwellings was the cause of the high death rate from consumption shown by the foreign born. By 1864 it was noted that the poor population of New York had become more and more concentrated in given areas, and the rate of crowding, by houses, far exceeded that of other cities. The total number of tenant houses was 15,309; the average number of families to each was $7\frac{1}{4}$. The number of persons residing in tenant houses and cellars was 495,592. Tenements were built to a greater height in stories than before, and courts, alleys, and yard spaces were smaller and narrower, consequently affording less light and air.

It was noticed at this time that poor people were not only concentrated in certain districts, but segregated according to nationalities, with their own theaters, military and national organizations, schools, churches, trades unions, and newspapers.

The lower west side had become a crowded tenement district, mainly inhabited by Irish.

Farther up on the west side the foreign tenement-house population pressed upon the native-born population up to Fourteenth street. From Fourteenth to Fortieth streets the two elements occupied the district side by side, the foreigners in the western part of the district, the well-to-do natives in the eastern part, the center of the city.

As the foreigners were coming into a district not thickly built up, there were comparatively few old residences used as tenements; nearly all were of the barrack type. Sanitary conditions were extremely bad.

Above Fortieth street the foreigners had outstripped the natives in the race uptown, occupying large tracts of otherwise vacant land as a squatter population in little shanties, which were kept in as uncleanly a condition as the tenements, but were, on the whole, more healthy, as each was occupied by one family only and admitted more light and air. The squatter population of the upper west side was largely German.

In the center of the city the Fourth, Sixth, and Fourteenth wards had increased in crowding and offensiveness and were largely occupied by Irish.

The east side below Fourteenth street was rapidly filling up with a tenant-house population, largely Irish. The Tenth Ward was at this time the one distinctively

German district in the city. Many new tenement houses of a pretty good character were found here. On the upper east side, as on the upper west side, foreigners in tenements were to be found along the half of the district nearest the river, the native born in private residences in the center of the city, while above the thickly settled part of the city was a squatter population of foreigners. Irish were scattered pretty well over the city; Germans were seen to be gathered more closely into colonies.

In all quarters tenement conditions were bad. Besides the general lack of light and ventilation were other especially bad sanitary conditions. Closets and privies were badly constructed and always foul. Yards and courts overflowed with sewage and other drainage. Owing to the bad condition of closets much offense was committed in the houses themselves, which reeked with foul odors. All of these bad conditions led to physical decay and this to moral degeneracy, which was, furthermore, directly brought about by a degree of overcrowding which made ordinary decency practically impossible. The connection between bad housing conditions and "filthiness, indecency, and lawlessness" was remarked by students of social matters again and again.

For these bad housing conditions the immigrants themselves were partly responsible. It is plainly evident that the tenement houses came into being in response to the demand caused by rapid immigration. The numbers and poverty of the immigrants naturally led to overcrowding, and their habits of life were such as not to improve bad conditions where such already existed. But the landlords were mainly responsible, as they had it in their power to determine special conditions of housing, and they chose, for the sake of exorbitant profit, to violate every law of health and decency in providing shelter for the poor.

In considering the problem of immigration as it affects the city, special race characteristics, as well as general housing conditions, etc., have to be taken into account.

The Irish came here in especially bad physical condition, and their sickness and death rate in the city was higher than that of other peoples. They were notably hard drinkers, and of violent, quarrelsome dispositions. The worst tenement conditions were found in Irish neighborhoods, as contrasted with German neighborhoods.

The Germans came here in good physical condition from healthy country districts, and were industrious, hard working, and orderly.

With respect to pauperism and crime, it was stated in 1860 that while the native born made up 48 per cent of the population, 14.2 per cent of the paupers, and 23 per cent of the criminals, the Irish, making up only 28 per cent of the population, were 69 per cent of the paupers and 55 per cent of the criminals; and the Germans, 15 per cent of the population, were 10.8 per cent of the paupers and 10 per cent of the criminals.

An interesting type among the Germans was the ragpickers or "chiffoniers," as they were then called. They lived in crowded and filthy quarters, but were industrious, orderly, and ambitious enough, many of them, to invest their savings, often considerable, in Western lands, to which they migrated. They afford a curious and interesting parallel as to habits and general character with the Italian ragpicking class which followed them many years later.

Migration to country districts was early thought of as a remedy for bad city conditions, and many schemes for the ruralization of immigrants and other poor people were tried one after the other.

These schemes, however, were none of them successful. The main reasons seemed to be that those who could make use of the opportunities for labor afforded in the interior could either get there themselves or find work in the city, while those who made up the bulk of the pauper class either would not go or would not be able to care for themselves if they did go. It is to be noted that the Germans largely fell within the former class, while the latter was mainly made up of Irish. The Germans in large proportion went of their own accord to the country, either directly upon arrival or after having saved enough to purchase land, while the Irish persistently lingered in the cities.

On the whole, however, there was a fairly rapid dispersion of immigrants from the city up to 1860, the rate of dispersion, somewhat contrary to expectation, increasing with the increase of immigration.

PERIOD II, 1871–1900.

By 1890 foreigners from Italy, Austria-Hungary, and Russia, who were noted as coming in increasing numbers from 1870 on, had become a considerable element in the city's population. Although Germans and Irish still predominated, the total foreign born were at that time 42.23 per cent of the total population. Of the foreign born, regarded as 100 per cent, Germans made up 32.93 per cent; Irish, 29.76 per cent; Russians (Hebrews), 7.62 per cent; Italians, 6.24 per cent, and Austro-Hungarians, 6.16 per cent.

At this time, while the foreign born were 42 per cent of the population, native whites of foreign parentage were 38 per cent and colored 2 per cent of the population, leaving only 18 per cent of the strictly native element—native whites of native parentage. Females predominated in all of the above classes (except the colored, which is not taken into account); but dividing the city at Fourteenth street it is found that males predominate in all three classes below that line; females above it.

Comparing the foreign born to the native born of foreign parents, the first to the second generation of the "foreign element," the Hungarians, Scandinavians, Italians, and Russians show the highest proportion of the first to the second generation in the order named, the foreign born making up over 70 per cent of the total group of the first and second generations for each race for all four.

Of the second generation by far the greater proportion for all races had both parents foreign of the same race. The highest proportion is shown by the Bohemians.

Of the second generation born of one native and one foreign parent many more of all races have native mothers and foreign fathers than have native fathers and foreign mothers.

Examining the distribution of population over the city by wards, it is found that native whites of native parentage are distributed over the city with great evenness at a low degree of density. It is something of a surprise to find that in the down-town districts from which they were supposed to be entirely driven out they are as numerous to the acre as anywhere uptown. These are, however, in many cases third-generation Irish and Germans.

The Irish are also distributed quite evenly through the city, but more densely than the native population; while the Germans are gathered in some parts of the city into highly congested districts, from others they are almost entirely absent.

The Irish and Germans have pressed farther up the east and west sides than they were found in 1864—the former largely on the west, the latter on the east. On the other hand, the Irish are less thickly settled in their old districts—the Sixth, Fourteenth, and Fourth wards—than are some other peoples, and the Germans have pressed out of their old district—the Tenth Ward—into the territory to the north.

Italians by 1890 had come into the old Irish neighborhoods, and Russians and Poles (practically all Hebrews) into old German neighborhoods, driving out the older occupants. Italians were found in 1890 massed to the west of the Bowery, in the Sixth and Fourteenth wards; they were also found in the Fourth, the Eighth, the Ninth wards, and in Harlem. Russian and Polish Hebrews were massed to the east of the Bowery, with the Tenth Ward as their center, and were scattered along up the east side of the city to Harlem. Hungarians (a considerable proportion of whom were Hebrews) were gathered in a considerable colony east of avenue B, about

Houston street, and Bohemians on the upper east side, near the river, from about Fiftieth to Seventy-sixth streets.

Of the newer peoples coming in the Italians and Hebrews are the most important as affecting city conditions, both on account of their absolute numbers and their tendency to remain in the cities.

The few Italians noted in the city's population at an earlier period were mainly a vagabond but harmless class—ragpickers or organ grinders. These were noted in the Sixth Ward as early as 1864. A colony of Italian ragpickers was found in the upper part of the Fourteenth Ward, a few years later, where they were described as to filth and overcrowding in terms that would have applied equally well to the German ragpickers of 30 years before, but were said to be "peaceable, thrifty, and orderly," never begging or stealing, and keeping generally out of trouble.

Later came the class of unskilled day-laborers—steady, industrious peasantry in the home country—who now make up the bulk of our immigration. The men at first come alone, and return to Italy after a season or two of work, with their earnings, but later bring wives and children to this country and settle down here. Besides the day-laborers are now to be found in the city many Italian tradesmen—barbers, bootblacks, fruiterers, shoemakers, etc. These, in the main, come from cities in Italy, as the day-laborers come from the country. They are ambitious and generally successful in business, the more successful of them moving to the suburbs and becoming property owners. There are also many skilled workmen from the north of Italy employed in the city. All classes, except the most prosperous, live in crowded quarters, in bad air, and more or less dirty surroundings, but they are highly industrious, thrifty, and saving. Some are ambitious, but as a whole they are slower than some other peoples to take up American habits and customs. Italian children, however, are rapidly Americanized. Coming under the influence of the public schools they are generally satisfactory pupils, mainly in the line of manual work and the arts, however, rather than in bookwork, and on leaving the schools try to take up occupations of a higher grade than those their parents are engaged in.

Even the adults feel more or less of the Americanizing influence of the schools. Evening classes are held for them, which, while giving instruction primarily in the English language, incidentally teach something of American citizenship in an informal way.

Hebrew immigrants in the city have passed far beyond the narrow boundaries within which they were found in 1890. They have pretty well filled the east side below Fourteenth street, the former German inhabitants being almost entirely dispersed, and a large Hebrew colony in Harlem has been formed.

These immigrant Hebrews are found in conditions of extreme filth and overcrowding, but, unlike the adult Italians, they have definite aspirations toward social, economic, and educational advancement. Economic prosperity comes to them with surprising rapidity. Much tenement property is owned by Russian Hebrews, who, a few years before, were themselves living in crowded tenement quarters. The poorest among them will make great sacrifices to keep his children in school, and the children themselves are considered as perhaps the most satisfactory and successful class of scholars the schools have to deal with. They fill the high schools and colleges and are especially anxious to get into the professions or into the higher class of commercial pursuits.

Like the Italians, the Hebrews are, in general, a quiet, orderly, industrious people; but for both peoples tenement-house life tends to their physical and moral deterioration.

The Jews have shown a low death rate even in tenement districts, but tuberculosis, a disease fostered by tenement conditions, is gaining a great hold on them. The Italians, too, are subject to tuberculosis, and there is considerable general sickness among them, especially among the children.

REVIEW OF SPECIAL REPORTS. XLVII

The moral surroundings also are bad for them. In tenement districts the unsophisticated Italian peasant or the quiet, inoffensive Hebrew is thrown in contact with the degenerate remnants of former immigrant populations, who bring every influence to bear to rob, persecute, and corrupt the newcomers.

Both Italians and Hebrews are accredited with a tendency to pauperism from their practice of turning their children over to institutions as far as possible. In doing this, however, they are mainly trying to secure what they consider a legitimate educational advantage, as well as support, reasoning imperfectly from the analogy of the free day schools. The parents themselves are not paupers. They work unremittingly and are rarely found as charges upon public or private charity. The census of 1890 shows that the Irish still lead the list of paupers, as they did 50 years ago, the proportion of paupers to the thousand of population of the same race element for the whole country being $7\frac{1}{2}$ for the Irish, $2\frac{1}{2}$ for the Germans, a little over 2 for the English, $1\frac{1}{2}$ for the Bohemians, eight-tenths for the Italians, and six-tenths for the Russians (Hebrews).

As to criminality, the census of 1890 showed that while Italians were 1.98 per cent of the general population, Italian prisoners were 3.7 per cent of the foreign prison population, Irish were 20.23 per cent of the total population and 35 per cent of the prison population, English in like manner, 9.82 per cent and 12 per cent; Russians, 1.97 per cent and 1 per cent; and Germans, 30 per cent and 19 per cent.

The crime rate for the Italians as compared with the Irish should be modified by the consideration that their general population is so much more largely made up of adult males than is that of the Irish, for whom the large proportion of women and children reduces the crime rate. The crime rate of Italians here will naturally be reduced by the incoming of women and children in increasing proportions, and by changes going on in the home country itself, such as the growth of education, intercommunication, etc.; that seem to be reducing the crime rate there.

Many attempts have been made to reduce tenement-house evils by legislation affecting tenement houses. The most important pieces of legislation enacted in New York State dealing with this matter were, up to the present year, the laws of 1867, 1879, 1887, and 1895. These laws effected some improvement of the most glaring sanitary evils, such as arose from lack of sewerage, plumbing, etc., but under all of them overcrowding was not simply unchecked, but increased, and conditions of light and ventilation were not bettered. The "double-decker" tenement house, invented and introduced in 1879 as a "model tenement," kept quite within the provisions of all of these laws, but proved to be the worst type of tenement yet used. It was built to a still greater height than the "barrack" had been and covered, for all practical purposes, a greater per cent of the ground space. Thus light and ventilation were still further reduced, and crowding of population under one roof—with all its consequent evils—still further increased.

A tenement-house law passed in the present year, 1901, promises definite improvement as to light and ventilation in tenement houses hereafter to be built, by more stringent provisions as to yard and court spaces, height of buildings, etc., and for tenements of the old barrack type by provisions regarding windows in interior rooms. But nothing has been done to help the "double-decker," of which type are about 60 per cent of the tenements now in existence on Manhattan Island, in this regard. Sanitary evils still remaining will be materially improved by the new law; and in it social evils are for the first time touched upon directly in a tenement-house law, by provisions dealing with prostitution in tenement houses, providing in a practical way for the punishment of the prostitute, the landlord, and the lessee, in cases where the law is violated.

A serious hindrance to the effectiveness of former laws has been the difficulty of enforcing them, either through the disinclination or inability of the administrative officers to act. Provision has been made for the better enforcement of the new law, by the establishment of a special tenement-house department, which shall stand in public view as wholly responsible for the enforcement of the law, and shall have an adequate staff for that purpose.

But no radical reduction of overcrowding, the great evil of the tenement, may be looked for under the new law. Owing to high ground rents in the city a law that should effect this would involve so great a reduction of income from a given ground area to owners, at the rates of rental possible to the poor, as to put a stop to the erection of new tenements, and to drive those already occupied as such out of use. Such a law, indeed, could never be passed; but if it were it would practically deprive the poor of housing accommodations in the city altogether. On the whole, the newer immigration does not seem to offer any more serious problems than the old, except as they add to the total numbers, and increase overcrowding.

In the newer period sickness and death rates have fallen, the immigrants themselves are of fully as good a type as those who preceded them and in some cases they have brought positive improvement to the neighborhoods they have entered.

Migration is urged, as in the earlier period, to relieve the overcrowding which remains as a serious evil, but still there are difficulties in the way. Agriculture, the special industry of country districts, is probably the least remunerative of any of the great classes of industry. At least it is thought to be so. The large city is the great center for manufacturing and mechanical industries, and the great market for labor in these lines. In the cities, too, are found the hospitals, dispensaries, charities, libraries, and schools. These are great and substantial advantages to the immigrant, and he is not quickly ready to give them up.

AGRICULTURAL DISTRIBUTION OF IMMIGRANTS.[1]

The foreign peoples now coming among us are, on the whole, especially skillful in intensive methods in farming; consequently room may be found for them not only in the sparsely settled districts (such as those of the Northwest and portions of the South) adapted to extensive agriculture, but in parts of the country now regarded as about full, where, however, intensive farming is needed to provide for the wants of the growing community, and will support a population of a density of indefinite limit.

Among the immigrant peoples noted for their success in intensive agriculture are the Scandinavians, Germans, Dutch, Bohemians, and Italians.

ITALIANS.[2]

The Italians who come to this country would naturally be expected to go directly into agricultural pursuits, as at least 80 per cent of the Italian immigrants now coming here were agricultural laborers at home. They do not do this to any extent, however, partly because in following this occupation they were at so great a social and economic disadvantage at home and can not imagine anything better here, partly because most of the Italians now coming here—those from the South—are unfamiliar with country life as we know it. In the home country they worked in the fields by day, it is true, but returned at night to crowded towns, in which they huddled themselves for protection against the dangers of the open country, such as brigands and malaria.

Italian immigrants have already formed centers of Italian population in the cities, which attract other immigrants. If some could be established in country districts, these settlements also would become centers of attraction and draw the Italian peasant away from the cities and out of reach of the camp followers of their own race, who gather in cities simply to prey upon them.

In other respects, too, city conditions are bad for the Italian immigrant. The bad housing causes disease in them and their children; the food they have to buy is poor. During the long idle winter that the common day laborer has to spend in the

---

[1] Pp. 492–646.   [2] Pp. 495–507.

city, because there is no work for him to do, he falls into habits of drinking and gambling that are bad for his health and waste his money.

The Italian Government has interested itself in the welfare of the Italian emigrant, and various laws have been passed to improve his condition, but the proper remedy has never been strongly enough urged, viz, to induce migration of the Italians from the city to the country.

Something, however, has been done in this way. Signor Secchi de Casale founded an Italian agricultural colony at Vineland, N. J., in 1878, which has been successful and has grown greatly, comprising now about 5,000 Italians, engaged in truck farming mainly. An agricultural colony was founded about the year 1880 at Bryan, Brazos County, Tex., by some Sicilians who were working on the Houston and Texas Railway. They are mainly engaged in cotton farming, have been successful, and now number about 500 persons.

In 1881 some well-to-do Italians in San Francisco made plans for a colony to engage in the raising of grapes and the making of wine. The enterprise was started as a strictly cooperative association. Funds were raised by monthly payments from shareholders, and land was bought at Asti, Sonoma County. It was planned that all permanent laborers employed on the estate should be members of the association, but as they declined to enter into this scheme, city business men remained the sole owners and managers of the concern. Many difficulties were met with in the early years of the colony, but it is now in a highly prosperous condition. For the past 20 years the industries carried on—grape raising and wine making—have given employment to over 200 laborers daily. The Italians in this colony were mainly from the Italian-Swiss cantons and from Piedmont.

Besides these colonists at Asti there are many other Swiss-Italians in California, successful as truck farmers, ranchmen, and dairymen.

Italians are found in large numbers in Louisiana and Mississippi on the sugar plantations, from which, it is said, they are driving out the negroes. They are mostly Sicilians.

Agricultural colonies of Italians were established by Sig. A. Mastro-Valerio, who contributes the chapter on Italian colonists in this report—one at Daphne, Baldwin County, Ala., in 1890; the other at Lamberth, Mobile County, Ala., in 1893. The first colony is quite successful. The colonists carry on general and truck farming under intensive methods. The second colony now consists of about 12 families of very prosperous people, engaged in viticulture and truck farming.

At Sunnyside, Ark., an island in the Mississippi River, a colony of about 500 families, brought directly from Italy—from Romagna and the Marche—was established by Mr. Austin Corbin in 1895. Mr. Corbin provided everything needed for the use of an agricultural colony—teams, tools and seed, means of transportation, houses and allotments of land for each family, etc. Malaria, however, killed off large numbers of the colony. This circumstance and the death of Mr. Corbin in 1896, which put an end to improvements that might have reduced the disease, caused the abandonment of the colony. Many of the families went back to Italy, others went to South America, to Alabama, New Orleans, and to Northern States.

The remaining families went to form the colonies of Tontitown, Ark.; Montebello and Verdella, Mo., which are small, but fairly successful.

BOHEMIANS.[1]

The Bohemians are fond of the soil, and have always been considered a rural people, but in this country the majority are found in cities. This is due partly to lack of capital to start on a farm, partly to the loneliness of life on American farms as contrasted with farm life in Bohemia.

---

[1] Pp. 507-510.

Several attempts have been made to start agricultural colonies of Bohemians, but all have failed. Individually, however, Bohemian farmers have done well. The most prosperous are found in Iowa, Nebraska, Texas, and Wisconsin. Some in Minnesota and Nebraska have started cooperative mills and cheese factories. Few of the Bohemian farmers came in as farm laborers; most of them brought money enough to buy land at once. The Bohemian farmers settled mostly in groups, mingling little with other nationalities, and retaining their Bohemian habits. Where they are near other nationalities, however, they Americanize very rapidly.

Bohemian farmers are hard workers; their farms prosper, and they grow rich.

FINNS.[1]

A large proportion of the Finns driven here in recent years by political troubles and economic hardships at home go directly to the country. Many are found in the Northwest, where they are regarded as excellent farmers.

They are going also to the South. A colony of these people was established about 2 years ago in Hickman County, Tenn., which promises to be quite successful, and another is planned for South Carolina.

JEWS.[2]

The Jews are not generally regarded as an agricultural people, and, as a matter of fact, a larger proportion of this class of immigrants than of any other settle down in cities.

Not a little has been done, however, in the way of agricultural settlement by Jews.

In 1880 a group of these people from Odessa formed a communistic agricultural colony near Glendale Station, Oregon. They received some outside financial aid, and made encouraging progress, but finding themselves too isolated, they disbanded.

In 1881 a colony of 25 families located in South Carolina, removing after a year to North Dakota. After 4 years this colony was disbanded. Other colonies established at various points in the Western States about this time met the same fate.

In 1882 the first of the now well-known Jewish colonies in southern New Jersey was founded. This was Alliance, and was followed by settlements at Rosenhayn and at Carmel. All of these colonies received more or less aid from the start, but in a few years came to a crisis in which they had to be helped by the Baron de Hirsch fund. With this assistance they are still continued, and are in a fairly prosperous condition.

The Baron de Hirsch fund established in 1891 the best known and largest of the Jewish colonies, Woodbine, also in southern New Jersey. All possible assistance was given to make this, as well as the other three, purely agricultural colonies; but the attempt failed. Industrial pursuits had to be introduced into all four. It is said that practically none of the Jewish farmers in this region are gaining their entire living from farming.

The Baron de Hirsch fund has also assisted individuals by giving information about farm property and financial aid for its purchase. Many of the "abandoned farms" of New England have been purchased by Jews in this way, and the farmers have been quite successful. Purchasers were seldom new immigrants, but persons who had made some money in business—usually tailoring—in the city. This work has somewhat slackened up for the present, owing to the fact that business has been so good in the city as to keep persons there who might otherwise wish to buy farms.

So many difficulties have been found in the way of agricultural removal that plans of industrial removal are now being tried. A branch of the Baron de Hirsch fund, known as the Industrial Removal Society, is finding employment out of the city, in such occupations as they can follow, for Russian and Roumanian Jews. From

---

[1] P. 510.   [2] Pp. 510–517.

August, 1900, to the spring of 1901, about 2,500 persons have been assisted in this way, and are scattered to almost every State in the Union.

At present plans are being made to induce the removal of factories that employ Hebrew immigrants out of New York City. This plan, if successful, will do much to relieve the congestion there.

In Chicago the Jewish Agriculturists' Aid Society has been, for the past 13 years, engaged in establishing poor Jews on farms. They have so far placed 76 families— 71 in the Middle West. The society believes in individualism rather than the colony principle.

That so few Jews, after all such efforts, are found in farming is not to be taken as an indication that they are generally unfit to carry on that pursuit. In most of the many cases reported of Jews giving up their farms, they have not been unsuccessful as farmers; they have simply seen an opportunity of doing even better in some other pursuit.

IMMIGRATION AND AGRICULTURE IN THE SEPARATE STATES.

NORTH ATLANTIC STATES.[1]

Maine.—There are said to be greater opportunities at present in this State for immigrants than at any time in the past, in farming, lumbering, and general manufacture. Swedes, Canadian French, and Finns have proved the most effective as farmers and farm laborers. The farmers of this State, however, do not generally welcome a further influx of immigrants. In the State is a colony of Swedes at New Sweden, and one of Finns at South Thomaston.

New Hampshire.—Representative farmers heard from do not generally encourage the incoming of foreign immigrants. Where Swedes and Poles are employed, however, they seem to be liked. Good opportunities in the many "abandoned farms" offered for sale in this State are afforded to foreign immigrants with a little money to purchase land.

Vermont.—Farmers as a class would not favor the further influx of foreigners into the State. There are, however, opportunities for immigrants as farm laborers, as labor is very scarce. Many farm laborers now employed are Canadian French, Swedes, Norwegians, and Poles, the last three in increasing proportions of late years. Scandinavians do not settle down in colonies, nor do they seem to care to migrate to the northwest. Scandinavians seem to be regarded as the best farm help, but Poles are quite satisfactory. The State secretary of agriculture says that the French, Irish, and Norwegians, of the foreigners, make the best farmers, but Americans are more successful than any.

Massachusetts.—There are greater opportunities for immigrants than in past years. Poles are numerous as farm laborers and considered satisfactory. Many French Canadians are also employed. Many Portuguese are abandoning fishing and going on to farms. Farmers favor the coming in of the better class of foreigners.

Rhode Island.—Farmers would probably favor the influx of foreigners, as they might not be able to cultivate their farms without them. Of the foreigners, Swedes are found most effective as farmers and farm laborers. Considerable opportunity to purchase is given the immigrant in the many "abandoned farms" offered for sale at low prices.

Connecticut.—Most of the Irish of the second generation are farming for themselves or have gone into other employment, so that Italians, Swedes, and Poles are coming in to perform field labor. The Swedes and Poles and better class of Italians are satisfactory. Farmers do not object to the incoming of foreigners of the right sort. Besides the nationalities above mentioned as farm laborers, are Danes, Swiss, and Portuguese. Russian Jews are found in Salem and in other towns.

---

[1] Pp. 517–528, 583–594.

New York.—Irish and Germans prevail, of the foreigners, as farm laborers. German and Dutch settlers have made good farmers and good citizens, although somewhat clannish. They are said to be more thorough farmers than the Americans. Poles, Swedes, Russians, and Hungarians are found in some counties. Italians are also found as farm laborers and as farmers. Italians have been employed in sugar-beet culture. This industry in general affords especially good opportunities to foreign farmers and farm laborers, as they are willing to do the work required and Americans generally are not.

New Jersey.—Germans and Danes are said to be the best farm laborers. Hungarians and Italians are also employed. Foreign farmers are no more successful than Americans. Farmers would not object to the incoming of a good class of immigrants. Foreign laborers are becoming proprietors, especially near the cities, where they go into market gardening. There is considerable opportunity for immigrants who do not speak English.

Pennsylvania.—The State secretary of agriculture says that very few immigrants come to take up land for agricultural purposes –land is too dear, but farmers would not oppose the incoming of any person who wished to become a citizen and buy land. As to immigrants going into farming, however, representative farmers speak of foreign farmers in many parts of the State, largely Irish and German, and a few French, Belgians, and Poles. They also say that there is considerable opportunity for immigrants who do not speak English. Among farm laborers are already many Germans, some Irish and Swedes, and a few Welsh and Poles.

NORTH CENTRAL STATES.[1]

Ohio.—Germans are found most effective as farmers and farm laborers, and their success is greater than that of the native born, owing to greater industry and frugality. Farmers as a class would probably favor further immigration, especially of Germans, who are already numerous in central and northern counties. Few foreigners are found in the southern part of the State.

Indiana.—There are many foreign farm laborers, mostly Swedes and Germans. They have a tendency to colonize, and where they settle the price of land advances. They make desirable citizens. There is little call for further immigration, however.

Illinois.—Foreign farm laborers through the central part of the State are mainly Germans, Danes, and Swedes, and an intelligent class of people. They show a tendency to colonize. Germans, French, Danes, Swedes, Scotch, and Irish are found as farmers in southwestern and central counties, and as laborers, except the French, in the same localities. Germans and Swedes are liked as farm laborers, and the call for immigrants is general.

Michigan.—Opportunities for foreign immigrants are good, as agricultural labor is very scarce. Farmers would favor further immigration.

There are many colonies of foreigners in the State. One in Ottawa and Allegan counties, of Hollanders, now numbers about 40,000. They were established in 1847, and have been very successful as farmers. An offshoot of this colony is located in and about Rudyard, Chippewa County, and consists of about 5,000 persons. Finns, Danes, and Norwegians are also located at Rudyard, and thought well of. Germans are scattered over the State.

There are also many French Canadians, especially in Menominee and Delta counties. They came in originally as lumbermen. They are not clannish.

The sugar-beet industry gives good opportunity for foreign laborers. Germans, Poles and Russians are found most effective as laborers in the sugar-beet fields.

Wisconsin.—Good opportunities are offered for immigrants, and farmers would favor further immigration to the State. Germans and Scandinavians are found most effective as farmers and farm laborers. Foreign farmers, if German or Scandinavian, succeed better than the native born, owing to greater industry and thrift.

Especial opportunities for immigrants to settle on farms of their own are afforded in the "cut-over" lands, of which there are some 8,000,000 acres in the State, and which are to be had on favorable terms. One land company has been settling Poles on such lands for the past 14 years, selling land in that time to about 1,000 of them. Another land company is forming a colony of Russians, from Odessa, and brings Germans and Norwegians from Europe and from other States to their land. Many private and railroad land companies are engaged in the work of getting settlers, including foreign immigrants. Two companies heard from maintain agents in European countries for the purpose of securing settlers.

"Wisconsin probably contains a greater variety of foreign groups than any American State." (Professor Thwaites.) The principal nationalities colonized here rank in numbers as follows: Germans, Scandinavians, Irish, British, Canadians, Bohemians, and Dutch. There are, besides, Belgians, Poles (many), Italians, Russians (Slavs and Hebrews, mostly in Milwaukee), Swiss (very prosperous), Finns, and Austrians. Many of these foreign groups occupy entire townships and control within them all political, educational, and religious affairs. In considerable districts, especially among Germans and Welsh, English is seldom spoken, and public schools are conducted in the foreign tongue. But as a rule the foreign-born people of the States desire to become Americanized. The second generation invariably drops foreign customs and habits.

Minnesota.—There are generally good opportunities for immigrants in this State. Scandinavians, Germans, Poles, Bohemians, English, Irish, and Canadians are found as farmers and farm laborers. Germans, Scandinavians, and Canadians are preferred. Foreigners are found in colonies and also scattered. A railway company with land to dispose of states that their customers have been mostly Scandinavians, Finns, and Poles.

Iowa.—There are good opportunities for immigrants, but farmers as a class would oppose a further influx of foreigners. Germans are found most effective as farmers and farm laborers, but the success of foreign farmers is no greater than that of the native born. English, Scotch, Irish, Welsh, Germans, Dutch, Bohemians, Poles, Slovaks, and Belgians are found as farmers and farm laborers.

Missouri.—Returns received from representative farmers in 13 counties of the State show diversity of opinion as to opportunity for immigrants. Foreign farmers—Germans, Irish, Scandinavians, and French—are found in every county. They seem to be more frequent than foreign laborers.

North Dakota.—Population in this State is still very sparse, affording good opportunity for new settlers. Farmers would decidedly favor the incoming of foreign immigrants. Germans, Scandinavians, German-Russians, Austrians, Dutch, Belgians, Bohemians, Poles, Irish, Canadians, English, Scotch, French, and Icelanders are found here as farmers' and farm laborers.

South Dakota.—There is abundant room here for immigrants, and farmers favor their coming to the eastern farming counties. There are also opportunities for them in the western stock-raising counties. Germans, Scandinavians, Russians, Bohemians, Belgians, Dutch, Finns, Irish, and Scotch are found as farmers and farm laborers.

Kansas.—Foreign farmers and farm laborers are found throughout the State. Germans are most prevalent, closely followed by Swedes. There are also some Danes. Russians are found in various parts of the State and are prosperous. They are not Hebrews. The Union Pacific Railroad has land for sale in the State, and the land commissioner of the road says that a large proportion of their sales have been to foreigners, particularly to English, Swedes, Germans, and Russians.

THE INDUSTRIAL COMMISSION:—IMMIGRATION.

Nebraska.—There are good opportunities for immigrants, and farmers would make them welcome. The nationalities found most effective in farming are Germans, Bohemians, Swedes, Norwegians, and Danes. The success of foreign farmers, as a rule, is greater than that of the native born, owing to their lower standard of life and greater thrift. The State encourages immigration through publication of information regarding the resources of the State. Besides the nationalities above mentioned, English, Irish, Scotch, Russian, and French farmers and laborers are found. Foreign farmers have been, as a rule, very prosperous. The land commissioner of the Burlington road, which has land to sell in the State, says that the class of immigrants arriving of late years are not profitable customers. The road now prefers to get renters or other people who want cheaper land from other States.

The sugar-beet industry is opening up opportunities for immigrants. One large corporation is making special efforts to get farm laborers either from rural districts or from cities. Russians, although backward, ignorant, and under the control of leaders, are much sought after, as the best of them are quite satisfactory, and all know something already of beet culture. Men with large families are so greatly desired that the company above mentioned refuses employment to those with small families. About 50 per cent of the laborers on the farm of the company are native born; the rest are Bohemians, Germans, Russians, Scandinavians, Irish, English, and Canadians. Probably Germans are preferred.

SOUTHERN STATES.[1]

In these States the enforced change from a system of agriculture based on slave labor is resulting in: (1) A decline of old kinds of farming; (2) a growth of manufacturing interests; (3) a beginning of new forms of agriculture and a demand for farmers and farm laborers able to carry these on. Extensive farming of staple crops by the aid of cheap labor is growing less profitable. Negro labor has deteriorated since the war. "Cropping" and renting, the usual methods of arranging for the working of the land, are bad for the land, wasting its fertility and not securing the best yield from a given area. These methods are in vogue, partly on account of the necessities of planters, partly from the peculiar characteristics of the negro, who does not care to be bound down to continuous daily work as he would be under a wage system.

A remedy for this state of things is proposed in diversified or intensive farming. For this sort of farming the negro is generally considered unsuitable. The prevalence of negro labor is at once an inducement to go into diversified farming as a relief from cotton farming, which depends upon the negro, and a drawback to making the change as "the laborer must be worked some way, and cotton is all that they know how to make."

Diversified and intensive farming will, however, gain ground in the South, as the advantages offered by these forms of culture are better known. Such farming will restore fertility, reduce the labor cost of crops by the use of machinery, and help out cotton farming itself by supplying the general needs of the plantation. Such farming, too, is more and more in demand with the growth of manufacturing industries in the South, which afford a better market at home, and with the improvement of transportation facilities which bring the markets of the North nearer. These circumstances are peculiarly favorable to the introduction of European farmers and farm laborers with their special skill at intensive and diversified farming.

Delaware.—Farm laborers here are mostly negroes, but Irish, Germans, Swedes, and Poles are also found. Germans, Swedes, and Poles are liked. Germans, English, and Canadians are found as independent farmers. Many of the Germans began as farm laborers. There are said to be good opportunities for newly arrived immigrants who do not speak English.

---

[1] Pp. 550–575, 615–634.

Maryland.—A State bureau of immigration, established in 1896, is at work to bring settlers to the State. Dutch and Germans are especially desired. As a result of their work many families of Germans, Dutch, and Swedes have been settled in the State. Up to November, 1899, from 400 to 500 families had settled in the State and bought over 25,000 acres of land. Most of the foreign settlers have come from the Western States. For the year ending April 30, 1901, 249 immigrants came to the State through the State board of immigration, and bought 4,577 acres of land. Ninety-six were from the United States or Canada, 74 from Germany, 12 from the Netherlands, 23 from Switzerland, 41 from Austria-Hungary, 1 from Denmark, and 2 from South Africa.

Virginia.—There are good opportunities for immigrants in this State; farmers gladly welcome them. Germans are found to be the best farmers. They are especially successful in the use of intensive methods. Farmers from the Blue Ridge region only were heard from in response to a circular letter addressed to farmers in all parts of the State. In this region practically no foreigners are found, but some dissatisfaction with negro labor is expressed, and one farmer heard from thought that Germans would probably suit better.

West Virginia.—In all of the counties heard from (too few and scattering to represent the State as a whole) there are almost no foreign farmers or farm laborers, no desire is expressed for their coming, and there are said to be no opportunities for English-speaking immigrants.

North Carolina.—There has been but little foreign immigration to this State, but there are growing opportunities for foreign immigrants on farms deprived of native labor by the cotton mills and other manufactories. Farmers as a class would welcome foreign farmers who came to buy homes.

The State encourages immigration through the agency of a special subdepartment of the State department of agriculture. This department wishes only such immigrants as have money to invest in land. They are especially desirous of attracting the small German farmers who usually go to the Northwest, and to this end distribute descriptions of the country, etc., in the German language in Germany.

There is now a German colony of about 25 persons at Ridgeway, established 17 years ago and very successful, and also a Waldensian colony at Valdese of about 40 families (250 persons) from the Italian Alps, established 7 years ago.

South Carolina.—From reports of representative farmers there appear to be practically no foreign farmers or farm laborers in the State. Laborers are exclusively negroes and poor whites. Some dissatisfaction with negro labor is expressed, and truck and dairy farming is coming into greater prominence, so that foreign labor may before long find some opportunity in the State.

Georgia.—There are good opportunities to buy so-called worn-out lands, which can be restored by careful cultivation at the hands of thrifty foreign purchasers who are familiar with intensive methods. There are a few foreign farmers and farm laborers already in the State—English, Scotch, Irish, Dutch, and Germans. The Central of Georgia Railway is encouraging the better element of foreign immigrants to locate in their territory. They especially desire Germans and Swedes.

Florida.—Some foreign farmers and farm laborers have found their way to this State. Italians have come in to engage in orange culture. English, Scotch Irish, Germans, Swedes, Russians, French, and Spanish are found as independent farmers, and English, Germans, and Swedes as farm laborers. Germans and Swedes are liked.

Kentucky.—Farmers favor the influx of the right kind of foreigners into the State. Foreign farmers on the whole are more successful than the natives, owing to skill in intensive methods. Germans are found most effective as farmers and farm laborers, especially in market gardening. The Germans come as individuals, not in colonies. There is a Swiss colony at Bernstadt doing well after 12 years of settlement. There are, on the whole, few foreign farmers and farm laborers in the State.

LVI   THE INDUSTRIAL COMMISSION:—IMMIGRATION.

Tennessee.—The Nashville and Chattanooga Railway is interested in getting settlers into the State, and would be glad to have Germans to engage in fruit and vegetable culture for the Northern markets. There is a Swiss colony at Hohenwald and another at Belvidere, accounted very good farmers. Most of them came from the Northwest. A colony of Finns in Hickman County and colonies of Italians have already been noted.

Alabama.—Within the last few years Scandinavians and other northern Europeans have shown a disposition to locate south of the Tennessee River. These are mostly such as have been in the United States for some years. A Scandinavian settlement has been started at Thorsby, and a large and prosperous colony of Germans is found at Cullman. Italian settlers have already been noted.

Mississippi.—Quite a number of foreign farmers are found in the State. These are mainly Germans and Swedes, with a few Irish. Farm labor is exclusively negro labor, and this seems fairly acceptable, but some desire is expressed for Germans and Swedes. Six out of 15 farmers heard from consider that there are good opportunities for non-English speaking immigrants in their neighborhoods. A few Italians were engaged in cotton farming in Delta County as renters. They soon left off, however, having made enough money to engage in some other more profitable line of business.

Louisiana.—There are better opportunities for immigrants at present than a few years ago, and farmers as a class do not oppose the influx of honest and industrious foreigners. Of the foreign farmers, Swedes, Germans, and Dutch are found to be the best. The foreign farmers, after they become familiar with the soil, crops, etc., are as successful as the native born. The State encourages immigration to the State by means of a State immigration department in connection with the bureau of agriculture. There are as yet only a few foreign farmers in the State—Germans, Irish, Swedes, and Italians. Italians are found as laborers on large sugar plantations.

Texas.—Representative farmers from the Brazos River region say that chances for foreign immigrants are good. No foreign farm laborers are reported from these counties, but foreign farmers are found. These are Germans, Scandinavians, Bohemians, Poles, and Italians. The Southern Pacific and Houston and Texas Railways maintain joint agencies in Hamburg, Antwerp, Rotterdam, London, and Liverpool, to secure foreign settlers on their lands. Their commissioner speaks of a German colony in the State, near New Braunfels, and a Scandinavian colony in Travis and Williamson counties which have been remarkably successful. Other railways maintain immigration and land agencies, but reach only those foreigners who have already settled in the United States. Bohemian and Italian settlers in the State have been referred to above in the separate accounts of these peoples.

Arkansas.—There are capital opportunities for immigrants, and farmers favor their incoming. Germans are the most effective farmers, surpassing the native born, owing to their use of intensive methods. Many colonies of German farmers have been established here. A Hungarian colony, which afterwards removed, was established near Searcy. In Arkansas County a colony of Slovaks is said to be located. Another colony of Slovaks was established near Little Rock, but failed; only about 60 families remaining.

The State encourages immigration through its department of mines, manufactures, and agriculture.

WESTERN STATES.[1]

General.—There is not much European immigration direct to the Pacific coast, on account of the distance and expense. Railway land agencies have not tried to secure foreign settlers, especially, but some foreign colonies have settled along their lines. The Northern Pacific colonized some Hollanders in the Gallatin Valley in Montana,

[1] Pp 575–582, 635–646.

and the Yakima Valley in Washington. These were principally persons who were already located in other States, principally Michigan, Iowa, and South Dakota.

Montana.—There are some openings for non-English speaking immigrants, and many foreign farmers and farm laborers are already found in the State. These are Germans, Scandinavians, British, Irish, Canadians, French, Austrians, and Italians.

Colorado.—There are better opportunities for immigrants than ever before. Farmers do not oppose the influx of foreigners. As general farmers or farm laborers Germans are more effective. For truck gardening Italians seem to take the lead. Foreign farmers, by their thrift, economy, and use of intensive methods, succeed in many cases where the native born fail.

The beet-sugar industry affords good openings for immigrants, the large companies being especially desirous of securing foreigners to raise the beets.

Arizona.—Representative farmers from 3 counties are divided as to opportunities for immigrants in the State. In none of the 3 counties were foreign laborers spoken of. There were said to be many Scandinavian farmers, some quite wealthy, in Maricopa County, and in Yuma a few German farmers.

Utah.—Farming is mostly on small farms, worked by owners and their families. Many of these small farmers are foreigners—English, German, Scandinavian, Swiss, and Dutch. There are also some farm laborers of these nationalities. Italian truck farmers are found near Salt Lake City. There are said to be no chances for non-English speaking immigrants.

Washington.—There are many foreign farmers and farm laborers in this State. These are English, Irish, Scotch, Germans, Scandinavians, Finns, German-Russians, Italians, and French. There are excellent chances for newly arrived immigrants.

Oregon.—Representative farmers report good chances for immigrants. Many foreign farmers have settled here. Most of them are Germans. There are also Scandinavians, Swiss, Dutch, English, Scotch, and Irish. Many of them started as poor men.

California.—Representative farmers from 9 counties speak of Germans, Swedes, Danes, English, Scotch, and Swiss as farmers. There are also Mexicans and many Portuguese. Italians are found in many parts of the State, as before noted. Further immigration of foreigners is not generally encouraged.

IMMIGRATION LEGISLATION.[1]

The Federal legislation restricting immigration is a series of acts added one to another during the past 25 years, and, since portions of the earlier laws without being repealed were given a new construction by later laws, the result is a system ambiguous and conflicting at many points. Not only are the laws conflicting in their terms, but also they have grown out of conflicting views as to the principles and objects to be attained. The earlier laws, those of 1875 and 1882, were designed to exclude the vicious, the criminals, and the paupers, those who could not or would not support themselves. The later laws, the anti-contract labor laws of 1885, 1887, and 1888, sought to exclude those who had the ability and forethought to provide means of supporting themselves, namely, a definite contract for work in this country. The earlier laws excluded the worst; the later laws often exclude the best, though they have also another important bearing. The consequence is that both the immigrant and the inspector must summon all their ingenuity to steer between the two extremes. If an immigrant is sound in body and mind, and therefore able to compete with American workmen, he is admitted, but if he has the certain prospect of competing with American workmen as shown in the possession of a contract, they exclude him. On the face of the law, the contradiction seems inexplicable. But an examination of the principles underlying the two phases of the law explains the contradiction. On the one side it is sought to protect the American public generally by

---
[1] P. 647.

excluding those classes who threaten the property or lives or morals of the people, and whose presence increases the expenses of Government. On the other hand, it is sought to protect a single class of the community—the working class. In this respect the alien contract labor law is analogous to the protective tariff, whereby it is intended, by protecting one class of the community against the cheap manufactures of foreign countries, to promote industry and indirectly to benefit the entire community. The object of the contract labor law is, through protecting a single class, the largest class in the community, to raise the standards of living and benefit the whole community. But the analogy is not precise, since the immigration laws impose no general restrictive head tax but are limited only to one class of immigrants, namely, those who come under that kind of special inducement and solicitation involved in a contract to work in this country. Moreover, employers have sometimes made it a practice to import large bodies of men, often mere unskilled laborers, for the purpose of combating labor organizations or of breaking a strike. These forms of inducement are especially characteristic of the earlier immigration from a given country, preceding such time as the workingmen of that country have learned to look upon immigration as a means of improving their industrial condition. After immigration reaches the magnitude of a flood, and foreigners are thenceforth attracted by letters and prepaid tickets of their friends already here, the earlier protection of the alien contract labor law loses much of its efficacy, and additional restrictions more analogous to a protective tariff find favor. In the case of the Chinese, the protective theory has been carried to its extreme limit, and workingmen of this race are absolutely prohibited from stopping in this country. But in the case of the Europeans, foreign competition has not been considered so menacing. The great majority up until quite a recent period came from countries related to the people already here in race, language, literature, religion, and representative government. Any restriction against immigrants from these countries must be a specific protection against a definite recognized evil. This evil appeared at first chiefly in the artificial immigration induced by employers for the purpose of breaking labor organizations. Immigrants who came on their own initiative or on the representation of friends and relatives are especially exempt. This difference in the treatment of the Chinese and the European immigrant, however, loses its force in proportion as European immigration extends its recruiting area more and more toward the Orient, as it has done in recent years. The question now uppermost is that of the direct restriction of immigrants who are considered undesirable on general economic and social grounds and not merely on the ground of contract labor.

In addition to these new characteristics of immigration itself, which render the principle of the alien contract labor law relatively less important, the law does not accomplish the results originally expected by its advocates, and the successive interpretations of the courts, coupled with an administration at some points less strict and a growing acquaintance with its loopholes on the part of the immigrants themselves, have rendered the law practically a nullity.

This appears plainly in a review of the legislation itself as affected by the decisions of the courts and by an examination of the practices of the inspectors and the administrative authorities.

The alien contract labor law, as originally enacted in 1885, applied only to the importer of contract laborers and not to the immigrant. This defect was partially corrected in 1887 by a clause which commanded the officers to send back to the nation to which they belong all contract laborers. In so far as the law has been effective it has been due mainly to the latter clause. There have been very few cases in which the importer was fined, but there have been over 8,000 contract laborers, or those deemed to be such, sent back by the contract labor inspectors. The reasons for the difference are plain. The conviction of the importer depends upon a prosecution in court, but the deportation of an immigrant turns upon the views of administrative authorities who are not strictly bound by the letter of the law. This feature was definitely provided for by the law of 1894 which makes the decision of the immigration officers, if adverse to the admission of an alien of the excluded classes, final, with an appeal only to the Secretary of the Treasury and not to the courts.

There are therefore two broad divisions in the application of the alien contract labor law: First, the interpretation placed upon the law by the courts, affecting mainly the importer; second, the administration of the law by the Treasury Department, affecting mainly the exclusion of contract laborers.

In the prosecution of importers very few judgments have been secured. The courts hold the law to be highly penal, since it provides a fine to be imposed upon the importer, and on this account he is given the benefit of every doubt. With this in view the courts hold strictly to the letter of the law in defining a contract, but hold to the so-called spirit of the law in exempting from its penalties all those laborers who could not be shown to be specifically and unquestionably excluded by its terms from the country. In other words, if the contract reveals any flaw whatever the importer is released, and if an imported laborer can possibly be admitted the importer is also released.

The strict interpretation in the case of the contract is shown in the holding of the courts that in order to convict the importer the contract must have the following elements:

1. It must designate the time during which employment is to continue and the rate of wages to be paid. This practically exempts in nearly every case the importer, since a labor contract seldom specifies the duration of employment, and even often the amount of wages is left indefinite.

2. The importer can not be convicted unless the contract is completed. This completion requires the actual migration of the laborer to the United States and his landing upon American soil. Now the law in another place requires the immigration officials to deport before landing all aliens coming under a labor contract. Therefore they are required not only to send back their only witness to the contract, but also to prevent the completion of the illegal contract itself.

3. The importer can not be convicted for encouraging or soliciting immigration, or prepaying the passage of the immigrant unless when he did so he knew the existence of the illegal contract.

Taking these three strict interpretations into consideration, the immigration officials and the district attorneys have been able in only an insignificant number of cases to secure conviction of the importer. Conviction, however, is sometimes secured under another clause which prohibits advertisements published in a foreign country promising employment to aliens when they come to the United States. In this case actual immigration need not take place, and the proof of a contract is not required in order to convict the importer. The advertisement is looked upon simply as a form of solicitation and is punished as such. This, however, is the only form of solicitation for whose punishment the law provides.

The foregoing statement shows the strict interpretation of the courts as applied to a contract. The following shows the liberal interpretation as applied to the exempted classes of laborers—that is, those classes with whom the importer may contract for employment without laying himself liable to the violation of the law.

The general law applies in terms only to "alien immigrants," and the courts have distinguished, on the one hand, aliens who are immigrants and, on the other hand, aliens who are only temporary visitors and aliens who are residents. It has been held that all persons who come across the border from Canada to perform daily labor and return at night, even though they be under contract, do not furnish ground for the conviction of the importer, since they are not immigrants, because they do not come here intending to acquire permanent or temporary home.

Also it has been held that aliens who have once been in the country have thereby become residents, even though unnaturalized, and when, having returned to their own land, they enter the United States a second time, they are no longer "alien immigrants," but they are alien residents. Thus the importer who brings in the alien residents under contract is not liable to penalty. Congress amended the law in 1894 so as to give the Secretary of the Treasury final authority in deporting aliens whether they were immigrants or residents, but this does not apply to a prosecution of an importer, who may continue to import aliens under contract, provided they formerly resided in this country.

There are certain classes of aliens who are immigrants who may be admitted, even though they come under contract. These are personal or domestic servants, including coachmen, but not including farm hands or dairymen. There are also relatives or friends of persons in this country who have been assisted by the latter to come. When it is considered that 65 per cent of the immigrants come on tickets that have been bought or paid for in this country it will be seen that this exemption is a large one, and, moreover, it is the principal means by which, at the present time, employers desiring to import laborers secure their immigration. They simply speak to their friends, advising them of the opportunities for employment, and the latter attend to the correspondence and solicitation necessary to bring the foreigner to these shores. This exemption, however, does not permit an immigrant to come if he belongs to one of the excluded classes, or if he can be shown to be under contract. In other words, when an immigrant comes with his own money the burden is on the Government to show that he belongs to the excluded classes, but when he comes assisted by a relative or friend the burden is on the immigrant to prove that he is not of the excluded classes.

The act of 1885, through an oversight, had not specifically exempted from its prohibition ministers and college professors. When, therefore, the corporation of Trinity Church in 1888 engaged a minister in England to come here and take charge of its church as a pastor, a suit was brought in a Federal court charging violation of the alien contract-labor law. Judge Wallace, of the lower court, maintained that Congress had prohibited the importation of all aliens under contract to perform, not only labor, but any service of any kind; but that Congress had made certain specific exceptions, such as actors, lecturers, artists, and so on. Therefore the law applied to all kinds of service not specifically exempted. Now, there was no specific exemption of ministers. Consequently the law applied to ministers, and their importation under contract is a violation of the law. He surmised that this was an oversight in the enactment of the law, but he held that the courts are not at liberty to go outside of the language of a statute to search for a meaning which it does not reasonably bear. When this case came before the Supreme Court of the United States, the ruling of Judge Wallace was overthrown, and the Supreme Court maintained the right of the courts to inquire into the debates of Congress, the reports of Senate and House committees, in order to ascertain the intention of the lawmakers. In doing this the court inferred that Congress intended to exclude only those whose labor or service s manual in character, and that all other classes could be admitted even under contract without imposing a penalty upon the importer.

The decision in the Trinity case furnished a precedent for exemptions on the part of the lower courts, which grew wider and wider year by year, until by a decision in the circuit court of appeals in the seventh circuit in 1899 not only were professional classes exempted from the prohibition of the law, but even all skilled labor. It was held in this decision that the "law does not exclude such professional classes as surgeons and physicians or such skilled occupations as those of engineer, bookkeeper, stenographer, typewriter, clerk, saleswoman, draper, or window dresser;" indeed, that "Congress never intended to include in the act skilled labor of any kind;" that it was the intention of Congress merely to "stay the influx of cheap, unskilled manual labor," and to shut out "only the cheaper, grosser sort of unskilled and unhoused manual labor." This decision of the appellate court, accepted as it has been by other courts and by the administrative authorities, has reduced the law to such a which is 25 cents less than the wages paid to other nationalities. In Maine the construction of large works was done by Americans and then by the Irish, then by the French Canadians, and now by the Italians brought over from New York and Boston. In North Dakota the railroads have imported Italians from Chicago at $1.40 per day, considerably less than that which American laborers receive.

SYRIANS.[1]

The changing character of immigration and the rapid extension of its recruiting area toward the Orient is strikingly indicated in the case of Syrians. Beginning in small numbers some 10 years ago, their immigration amounted in 1900 to nearly 3,000 persons. This immigration is similar to the beginnings of all immigration from a newly contributing country, being, in the first place, stimulated by outside influences, in this case primarily by the American missionaries, and secondly, having a patriarchial or padrone character. Unlike the padrone system, the Syrian immigrants bring with them the primitive clan organization of the family, so that it is not strange that a score, or even a hundred, may claim relationship. The authority of their superiors, owing to this relationship, plays an important part in their migration, but more significant is the fact that they come mainly from the cities and towns of Syria, and that they number only a small proportion of peasants or workingmen. Their characteristics are those of the business man or trader. In New York a score or more of Syrians are reputed to be worth from $10,000 to $40,000. These are the most enterprising of the Syrian population. In their business activities in this country—mainly peddling—they rely to a considerable extent upon the help of their wives and daughters, and these women extend their enterprise to many parts of the United States.

As far as the Syrian is a wage-earner his field of occupation is mainly in the old First Ward of New York City, where probably 6,000 of the estimated 25,000 Syrians in the country at present reside. In this locality the products manufactured are mainly those which their fellow-countrymen afterwards peddle upon the streets; they are combs, brushes, hat pins, razor strops, bibs, tuckers, aprons, wrappers, garters, suspenders, toothpicks, and lace. As a factory operative, the Syrian is as yet an experiment. Probably 15 to 20 per cent are employed in the textile mills, especially in the silk mills of New Jersey. They are found in Lawrence and Worcester, Mass., and in Scranton, Pa. Silk mill owners have used Syrian help a times in attempting to break a strike, but only rarely. As a worker, although entirely docile, he is limited by his fatalism, which leads him to abandon a job when once he is driven. At the same time he has an instinct for weaving, and learns it rapidly, and is preferred by certain proprietors to the Armenian or Italian. It may be stated in general that the competition of the Syrian does not bear directly upon native or earlier immigrant labor, but that he is displacing the Italian who had in turn already displaced the natives. In the silk mills, partly through the introduction of Syrians and Armenians, the price for weaving in the last 4 years has declined one-third.

The problem of labor organization is especially difficult with the Syrian. Other nationalities distrust him. He has not yet been brought into any organization, but quite recently unrestricted competition has so lowered the price of his labor that he himself is dissatisfied, and is making the first overtures to get into line with the other nationalities.

In the Syrian quarter in New York the tenements occupied are old and in bad condition. The poor Syrian contracts to pay $5 to $7 for two rooms; sometimes he is able to get one room for $4 a month, and proceeds to crowd his family of 7 persons into it. It is not extraordinary to find 6 or 8 women making their headquarters in such a garret; their husbands away peddling and their children in institutions.

[1] Pp. 442–448.

The leading cause for exclusion in point of numbers is that of pauperism or liability to become a public charge. The next in order is that of contract labor; following is that of loathsome and contagious diseases.

CONTRACT-LABOR INSPECTION.

The inspection of contract laborers is distinguished from that of the general inspection in the contemplation of the law. The contract-labor inspectors receive higher salaries than others and are selected with a special view to the peculiar nature of their employment. Owing to a change made in the spring of 1899 at the port of New York in the assignment of duties to the contract-labor inspectors, there has been a marked falling off in the number of deportations. Prior to that date these inspectors did not take charge of a line of immigrants when engaged in a regular inspection, but limited themselves to observation of immigrants as they passed before the immigrant inspector. Since that time the various classes of inspectors have been placed on the same line of duty, with the falling off already noted in the deportation. The justification advanced by the commissioner at New York for this change in method is the need of uniformity in inspection and securing the advantages of these highly paid inspectors in cooperation with the other less skilled immigrant inspectors. This justification, however, is denied by other officers of the Bureau of Immigration, who contend that the change in method has practically defeated the purpose of the law. (p. 662–665.)

It is, of course, impossible that of the thousands of immigrants landing each year none should be admitted who should not have been excluded. In view of this condition, the law since 1888 provides that the Secretary of the Treasury may, within 1 year after landing, arrest and deport any immigrant who has landed contrary to the prohibition of the law. The expense of such deportation is borne by the importing vessel if the causes originated prior to migration, or by the immigrant fund if the causes originated after migration. The importance of this provision is shown in the fact that in the year 1900 the number of immigrants deported within 1 year after landing was 356 out of a total of 4,603. The 1-year period is peculiarly valuable in the case of contract laborers who, coming as they do to this country admirably coached in the answers to be given to inspectors, are able to effect a landing and to fulfill their contracts for employment. The discretion of the Secretary in arresting and deporting such cases without the delay and formality of legal procedure, after investigation by agents of the Bureau at the locality of employment, is an effective feature in the law. Whether the period of 1 year is long enough may be questioned. The extension of the period to 2 years, especially in the case of those who become public charges or those who become insane, would increase the efficiency of the law.

IMMIGRATION THROUGH CANADA.

Apart from the defects of the alien contract-labor law, unquestionably the most serious defect in immigration legislation is found in the failure to protect the border lines between Canada and Mexico. In proportion to the efficiency of the inspection and deportation of immigrants at the seaports of the United States, those classes liable to be debarred naturally seek these back entrances. In 1893 and in 1896 the Commissioner of Immigration entered into agreements with the steamship companies entering Canadian ports, and with the railroad companies carrying passengers from those ports to the American border, by which the United States inspectors were permitted to examine immigrants on landing. This agreement was not officially recognized by the Canadian government, and its standing is maintained only as a voluntary arrangement, without power of enforcement by the American Government in case of violation. The agreement applies only to those immigrants from Europe or Asia manifested to the United States, and of course does not apply to

REVIEW OF SPECIAL REPORTS. LXIII

those manifested to interior points of Canada, who might intend thereafter to cross over to the American side. The railroad companies agree not to sell tickets to those who are rejected by the American inspectors, and the steamship companies agree to carry them back to the port whence they came. The agreement has proved unsatisfactory, mainly because the American Government lacks the power of legal enforcement.

More serious, however, is the evasion of the law which is practiced by manifesting immigrants to Canadian interior points. These, of course, being ostensibly immigrants to Canada, can not be subjected to inspection by officials of the United States, and it is an easy matter for them, having once reached their Canadian destination, to cross to the American side. The commissioners at the American border have power only to send them back to the Canadian side and not to conduct them to the ships which brought them. Consequently they find it an easy matter to return at unguarded points along the 3,000 miles of the frontier. The only method which has been adopted to meet this evasion has been the attempt to inspect immigrants at Liverpool, but as this also depends on the consent of the steamship companies and has no binding force, it is found that many undesirable immigrants are carried by the companies even after having been rejected by the representatives of the American Government. (pp. 684-692.)

LEGISLATION OF GERMANY AND ITALY.

The legislation of European countries in general has during the past fifty years permitted free and voluntary emigration, except in case of attempt to escape military duties. The German Government, however, in 1897, adopted a law which marks an important innovation. In addition to the design of the law to protect the emigrant in the purchase of his ticket and in his transportation, the law provides for additional protection on the part of the fatherland in the country of his settlement, and endeavors also to maintain German institutions among the emigrants by diverting their migration away from North America, where they are rapidly assimilated, to South America, where they continue commercial and even political relations with the home country. This is brought about by granting to the chancellor of the Empire the power to license contractors or companies, who are permitted to solicit emigrants and to settle them in colonies. These licenses are not granted to companies operating in the United States, but solely to those who conduct emigration to South America and the German colonies. (p. 695.)

The Italian legislation of 1901 is modeled somewhat after the German legislation of 1897, but does not carry to the same extent the attempt to discriminate between countries to which emigrants shall be encouraged to migrate. The law provides for the establishment of employment agencies in the countries of settlement, for protection to emigrants in the purchase of tickets and their transportation, and creates the office of commissioner of immigration, with assistants nominated by cooperative societies and trade organizations, for supervision of emigration. (p. 699.)

Other countries, outside of the United States, receiving immigrants, which have legislated especially upon the subject, are the British colonies of Canada, Australia, and South Africa. Canada has, with one exception, adopted legislation of various kinds for the promotion of immigratiom, especially that of desirable immigrants for the agricultural sections of the country. The several British colonies have agencies in Great Britain, and certain colonies of Australia provide free and assisted passages for laborers and domestic servants and for small farmers. They also provide "nominated passages"—that is, assistance to immigrants who are named by the residents of the colony, for whom they have contracted to furnish employment after immigration. These colonies make special effort to secure only the best immigrants from the British Isles, and have severe restrictions against pauper, criminal, and diseased

LXIV   THE INDUSTRIAL COMMISSION:—IMMIGRATION.

immigrants of all classes. Natal, New Zealand, and South Wales have in the last three or four years adopted educational tests. The legislation of the Australasian colonies restricting Chinese immigration is prohibitive in the form of a high head tax, ranging from $50 to $150, and limiting the number who can be brought to a certain ratio of the tonnage of the vessel, usually 1 immigrant for every 100 or 500 tons, and imposing heavy penalties upon the shipowner for all Chinese carried in excess of this proportion. This legislation also extends to the Japanese and the inhabitants of the Malay Islands (pp. 709–719).

The exception to the liberal policy of Canada, noted above, is found in the contract labor law of 1897, modeled after similar legislation in the United States, with the important addition that a private citizen, as well as the attorney-general, is authorized to institute prosecution of the importer of the laborer. This exception to the general character of Canadian legislation can not, however, be considered as really an exception, since it applies only to immigrants from the United States, and may be considered as in the nature of a retaliatory enactment (p. 719).

TOPICAL DIGEST OF EVIDENCE.

I. STATISTICS OF IMMIGRATION.

A. Defective statistics.—Dr. SENNER, former commissioner of immigration at New York, declares that the statistics of immigration were exceedingly defective before the new law of 1893 went into effect, especially under the administration of the State of New York. Many old records showed whole pages blank so far as the answers to the questions concerning nationality, destination, and age were concerned. About half of the immigrants stated their destination as New York, though comparatively few actually remained there. The officials freely admitted that the statistics on these subjects had been largely guesswork. This was necessarily the case on account of the very small number of inspectors. Even the count of immigrants could not always be accurate and complete. A comparison of the statistics of immigration with the census figures shows great inaccuracy in the former, especially arising from the failure to ascertain whether the immigrant had been in the United States before.

The statistics as to nationality have up to the latest period been unsatisfactory, partly on account of the ignorance of the inspectors as to the many and complex nationalities of Europe, and partly on account of the changes in the methods of preparing the tables. Nevertheless the statistics generally are greatly improved since 1893.

Dr. Senner suggests that the immigration authorities would be greatly assisted in preparing statistics if the ticket agent in Europe who sells the ticket should require answers to interrogatories as to the points covered by the statistics and should enter these replies with the signature of the immigrant, the schedule thus prepared to be submitted to the inspectors. (173, 179.)

Mr. SCHULTEIS, a special commissioner who visited Europe in 1891 to investigate immigration, declares that the methods of counting immigrants and ascertaining their nationality have been and are still very unsatisfactory. Only at New York are immigrants counted by immigration officers; at the other ports they are reported by steamship companies merely. Statistics of immigration from Canada have been entirely dropped. Formerly it was the practice to count two children as equal to one person. Steamship companies often land immigrants under guise of employees, thus evading the head tax. Statistics of nationality are based entirely on port from which immigrant sailed, an undue number thus being assigned to Germany and England (an erroneous statement). Italian and German statistics show larger numbers of emigrants than our statistics of immigration. Even the census statistics are inaccurate. The number of Italians in the country in 1890 was placed at 182,000. It was estimated by Italian authorities at 500,000. (27, 28, 30.)

Mr. EICHLER, chief of the statistical and record division of the bureau of immigration at New York, testifies that nearly all of the early records of the New York State inspection bureau, as well as those of the first years of the United States service at New York City, were destroyed by fire at Ellis Island. He thinks that the loss was a very serious one, since the only duplicates of these records are to be found at the United States custom-house.

Mr. Eichler states further, that the United States authorities followed the statistical methods of the State bureau up to the time of the recent adoption of the race classification of immigrants in place of that by political divisions. He considers that the statistical methods at present are very satisfactory, being much superior to those existing before, but adds that more careful statistics concerning cabin passengers are desirable. (133.)

Occupations of immigrants.—Mr. MCSWEENEY, assistant commissioner of immigration at New York, believes that the statistics concerning the occupations of individuals are of no value whatever. Especially those who state themselves to be farmers are usually mere farm laborers, who are ready to drift into any unskilled labor which presents itself.

The statements of the immigrants concerning their destination in this country also give very little information as to the actual distribution of immigrants. (82, 83.)

Destination of immigrants.—Mr. McSWEENEY says that the statements concerning destination of immigrants in their manifests are usually exceedingly misleading. A much larger proportion give their destination as New York City than actually remain there. This is partly owing to the fact that the immigrants know no other place to put down, but sometimes there is willful falsification. The effect of such falsification is not merely to make the statistics unsatisfactory, but persons are sometimes admitted on the strength of having a certain amount of money, practically all of which is immediately taken from them in paying railway fare, so that they are likely to become paupers when reaching their actual destination. For this reason the witness thinks that a fine for willful falsification as to destination would be desirable.

B. Nationality and race.—Mr. McSWEENEY believes that the statistics concerning the nationality of immigrants have been of little value prior to 1899. Regard has been given hitherto only to the political divisions from which the immigrants came and not to their nationality. Thus it appeared that 40,000 Russians came to the United States during 1898, whereas the great majority of these were Poles or Jews, probably not over 200 being actual Russians. Austria-Hungary furnishes a large proportion of our immigrants, yet there are very few who can be called Austrians and comparatively few "Huns" or Magyars. The immigrants from Austria-Hungary are mostly Slovaks, Slavonians, and Croatians, etc. Although Poland has been divided among different countries the Poles are as distinguished a race as ever. The witness greatly approves the change in methods adopted in 1899 by which the attempt is made to ascertain the race of the immigrants. (82, 83.)

Dr. SENNER points out the danger of misunderstanding on the part of the general public as the result of the change in the method of classifying immigrants from the basis of nationality to that of race. He quotes from a recent editorial in the New York Times, which makes entirely misleading statements as to the number of Swiss and Hungarians coming into the United States, as compared with the previous year, these errors arising from the change in classification. To avoid these difficulties the old statistics by nationality should be continued with the others. Moreover, there are a number of ethnological errors in the new classification, and the system is exceedingly difficult to carry out with accuracy. (187.)

Mr. McSweeney says that the purposes of the new classification of immigrants according to race rather than nationality is to afford a fairer basis for judging the industrial character and effects of immigration. The system is not intended to discriminate against the Jews or against those of any other faith, although in order to secure accurate information as to nationality inquiries concerning religious faith are often necessary.

Under the former practice the immigration bureau trusted primarily to the statements made by the immigrants upon their manifests for ascertaining the place from which the immigrants had come. It is easy for these statements to be made incorrectly or dishonestly. The present method of investigation on the basis of language and race thus reduces the statistical errors. (91, 82.)

Dr. SAFFORD, who was a member on the committee, with Mr. McSweeney, Mr. Campbell, and Mr. Rogers, which recommended the adoption of the new method of statistics, first adopted in 1898–99, which substitutes classification according to language or race for that according to territory, believes that the new system is a great improvement on the old. At the same time he considers that the former statistics were essentially accurate as regards the number of persons coming from each political division, and that the conclusions which have been based upon these statistics were by no means misleading. Statistics based on political divisions are still compiled, the new method being in addition to the old. (131, 132.)

Mr. WOLF, vice-president of the B'nai B'rith, states that he and others have protested against the separate classification of Jews in the statistics of immigration, on the ground that they are not a nationality but a religious body, and ought no more to be separately classified than Presbyterians or Catholics. (250.)

Mr. HALL, secretary of the Immigration Restriction League, submitted statements and diagrams showing the changes in the nationality of immigrants in recent years. In 1869 the immigrants from southeastern Europe, including Austria-Hungary, Italy, Russia, and Poland, furnished only nine-tenths of 1 per cent of the total number of immigrants; while those from northwestern Europe, including Great Britain, France, Germany, and the Scandinavian countries, furnished 74 per cent. In 1880 southeastern Europe furnished 8 per cent and northwestern Europe 64 per cent. In 1896 the proportion from southeastern Europe had risen to 52 per cent and that from northwestern Europe had fallen to but 39 per cent; while the respective proportions in 1898 were 57 per cent and 33 per cent. (50.)

Mr. WOLF presents an estimate showing that for the year ending November 1, 1899, the number of Jewish immigrants to the United States was about 37,000, and for the year ending November 1, 1900, about 63,000. Jews are estimated to have furnished about 12 per cent of the total immigration in the fiscal years 1898, 1899, 1900. (252.)

II. SOCIAL CHARACTER AND EFFECTS OF IMMIGRATION.

A. Illiteracy of immigrants.—Mr. STUMP, ex-commissioner-general of immigration, says that at present the asking by the immigration bureau of the question as to ability to read and write is not specially authorized by law. Even among steerage passengers the proportion of illiterate Swiss, Germans, Swedes, Norwegians, English, and Irish is less than the proportion for the entire population of the United States. But the southern countries of Europe, and Russia, have inferior educational facilities, and the proportion of illiteracy is high. In Portugal 77 per cent of the population are illiterate; Italy, 54 per cent; Hungary, 46 per cent; Russia, 41 per cent. The average for the entire United States is 13.43 per cent. The illiteracy of immigrants was less in 1897 than in 1896. (6, 7.)

Mr. HALL points out that the immigrants from the southeastern countries of Europe, who have been increasing greatly in proportion, are much more illiterate than those from northwestern Europe. In 1896 only 4.5 per cent of the immigrants from Great Britain, France, Germany, and the Scandinavian countries were illiterate, while 47 per cent of those from Italy, Austria-Hungary, Russia, and Poland were illiterate. The females, as a rule, are more illiterate than the males. The fact that a large proportion of the immigrants are above the school age and not likely to attend schools in this country has an important bearing not only upon their future standard of intelligence, but also upon their assimilation. (50, 54.)

Mr. Hall calls attention to the fact that the immigration from Italy has increased from less than 1 per cent of the total in 1869 to nearly one-fourth of the total in 1899. Of the 76,489 Italians who landed in New York in the latter year 83 per cent were from southern Italy, Sicily, and Sardinia. The southern Italians are a very undesirable class. The average illiteracy of southern Italians is 57.4 per cent, as compared with 11.2 per cent for northern Italians. The average amount of money brought by southern Italians was $8; by northern, $21. Of southern Italians 2.1 per cent were debarred from entrance; of northern Italians, only 0.7 per cent. (67.)

Out of 50 anthracite miners whom Mr. ROSENDALE, special agent of the department of agriculture of the State of Pennsylvania, interviewed in 1897, 8 could read and write English, 20 their own language, and 22 were illiterate. Very few of the children—not 1 out of 50—attended the public schools. The boys were mostly at work as helpers, pickers, etc., in the mines, and the girls did the housework. (190, 191.)

B. Tendency of foreign born toward cities.—Mr. HALL refers to the well-known tendency of the foreign born to settle largely in cities rather than in small towns or in the rural districts. In 1890, 44 per cent of all foreign born in the United States were found in the 124 principal cities. The proportion of Norwegians in these cities was 20 per cent; English, 41 per cent; Germans, 48 per cent; Russians, 55 per cent; Poles, 57 per cent; Italians, 59 per cent. In other words, the more illiterate races tend to the cities in a greater degree than the others. This fact is attributed by the witness to the lack of enterprise and energy on the part of these races. There are plenty of unsettled regions in the country to which Italians could go if they would, but they have not the disposition. They do not even go South where they might seem to be invited by the climate.

The immigrants are found in especially large numbers in those districts or cities which are recognized as being slums. The less advanced races furnish a much larger proportion of the inhabitants of these slums than the more advanced. Thus immigrants from southern Europe furnish 19 times as many of the slum population of New York as immigrants from northwestern Europe, 20 times as many in the slums of Chicago, and 71 times as many in the slums of Philadelphia. The average of illiteracy of the immigrants from northwestern Europe in the slums of these 4 cities is 25 per cent, of those from southeastern Europe 54 per cent, while the average illiteracy of the native Americans in the slums is only 7 per cent.

Efforts to induce immigrants to leave the cities and settle in the country have usually proved to be unsuccessful. Thus the Hebrew Aid Society of New York spent about $600 per family in carrying a number of families into the country, but within 2 years most of them were back again. (54-56.)

Distribution of immigrants—Mr. HALL points out that most immigrants to this country settle in the Northeastern States. This is attributed largely to the fact that New York is the chief landing place, and that the immigrants do not know of opportunities elsewhere. In the South the colored race furnishes all the unskilled labor that is required. The reports of the Commissioner of Immigration say that in 1896 72 per cent of all the immigrants stated that their destination was either Illinois, Massachusetts, New York, or Pennsylvania, while only 11 per cent were destined for States south of the Potomac and west of the Mississippi. The Scandinavians have to a considerable extent settled in colonies in Minnesota and other Northwestern States, but the immigrants from the southeastern countries of Europe are especially prone to locate in the Northeastern States. (55, 56.)

Mr. STUMP speaks of the marked tendency of people of same nationality to settle together, especially in cities. The Scandinavians to some extent form farm colonies in the West, and the Huns and Poles in the mining regions of Pennsylvania. In these latter cases the native language is retained in places of worship and schools. (22.)

Mr. SCHULTEIS says that there is a natural tendency of persons of same nationality to group together, but that this has an injurious effect in the case of our immigrants, preventing assimilation. The second generation, however, usually learn to read and write English. (31.)

Dr. SENNER declares that the settlement of immigrants in colonies of their own nationality is to a certain extent necessary and unavoidable at the outset. Such colonies, however, do not stick together very long in most cases. The desire of the foreign born to become Americanized is usually intense. The second generation, in any case, can no longer be held to the old customs or language. There is indeed considerable complaint on this latter score among Germans in this country. Even the Jews in New York are rapidly becoming assimilated and Americanized. The colonies of Poles and Hungarians in Pennsylvania are to be sure still far from being assimilated, but this is accounted for in part by opposition to them on the part of Americans which makes them social outcasts. Many of them, especially of the second generation, would be glad to mingle more with Americans. The witness does not think that the public school facilities offered to these people in Pennsylvania are sufficient or that proper compulsion is exercised to bring children into the schools.

Dr. Senner says further that these classes in Pennsylvania are not "Huns," as they are frequently called, but are Poles, Polacks, and Croats chiefly from Austria. Most of them came to this country under contract between 1881 and 1885. They are a tractable and peaceful people if left alone and not maltreated. At any rate, the cause of their nonassimilation is an exceptional one and it will not long continue. (183, 185, 186.)

Mr. ROSENDALE gives as reasons for the tendency of the Jews to settle in colonies in the cities, first, that by this means they are able to live among their own people. They have their synagogues and their theaters. They can understand their neighbors and their neighbors can understand them. In the country they would be isolated. In the second place, the other races about them despise them, ridicule them, call names after them in the streets, and moreover, object to living among them, and remove from their neighborhood. The solidity of the race colonies is due partly to the voluntary withdrawal of other races, as well as to the exclusiveness of the race itself. (195, 196.)

Mr. BROWN, deputy chief of the bureau of licenses of New York, considers that the great number of unemployed and of paupers in New York City is due to the fact that many people had rather live in the city in the most abject poverty than earn a fairly comfortable living in other places. Mr. Brown would not favor an attempt to make it certain by law that every person could get a job in New York. If it were certain that a job would be provided for everyone who should come, the whole population of the United States would gather there. (235.)

Jewish colonies in New Jersey.—Mr. WOLF gives statistics of population, wealth, and pursuits of a part of the Jewish colonies in New Jersey. Those at Alliance, Norma, and Carmel contain altogether 185 Jewish families, of which 52 are said to be devoted exclusively to farming, 26 to farming and tailoring, 59 to farming and other workshop occupations, and 48 to tailoring exclusively. These families own 2,529 acres of land, of which 643 are under fruit, 1,081 under truck, and the remainder uncultivated. Their holdings are valued at $196,000, and there is an indebtedness on them of $70,000. Some statistics for the colony at Rosenhayn are also given. (246.)

Mr. POWDERLY says there is an increasing immigration of Russian Jews. They are very undesirable, being in poor physical condition and largely paupers. Their settlements in Tennessee and New Jersey are not successful. An educational test would exclude such Jews only temporarily, for they would soon learn to read some passage. (36, 42.)

C. Citizenship and naturalization of immigrants.—Mr. HALL says that the immigrants from the southeastern countries of Europe, the Slav and Latin races, are much less inclined to become citizens than those from the northwestern countries. The average proportion of the southeastern immigrants in this country who are still aliens is about 32 per cent, as against 9.9 per c nt for those from the northwestern countries. The fact that the immigrants from the southeastern countries have, in many cases, not been in this country as long as the others does not explain all of this difference. There are comparatively few applications for naturalization even among those who have been here for some time, although in many cases Italians take out the first papers in order to facilitate the passage of inspection in case they return to this country for a second time. Mr. Hall points out further that there are 16 States in the Union which permit aliens to vote without naturalization. (57, 62.)

Mr. POWDERLY, Commissioner-General of Immigration, says that the naturalization laws are frequently violated, both for the purpose of securing the franchise and of evading immigration laws. International questions have been precipitated by the arrest of persons abroad who claimed, fraudulently, to be United States citizens. The educational test for naturalization should be established. It is also desirable to give a landing certificate for each immigrant, to be presented on applying for naturalization. (45.)

Mr. ROSENDALE found that out of 50 anthracite miners whom he interviewed in 1897, 2 had applied for citizenship and 4 were naturalized. (188.)

Mr. STUMP says that opposition to immigration comes largely from those who fear its political effects. The question of immigration should be clearly distinguished from that of naturalization and the franchise. Stricter laws on the latter subject are perhaps desirable without restricting immigration. (22.)

Mr. SCHWAB, of the North-German Lloyd Company, favors a requirement of ability to read and understand the Constitution of the United States as a condition of naturalization. (108.)

D. Criminality of immigrants.—Mr. HALL asserts that the foreign born and the children of the foreign born are much more criminal in their tendencies than the native-born population. The census of 1890 showed that while persons of foreign birth or foreign parentage represented two-fifths of the total white population they furnished three-fifths of the white criminals in the country. In Massachusetts, in 1894, 85 per cent of the commitments to prisons were of persons of foreign parentage, 30 per cent being of foreign birth, while the proportion of the foreign born to the total population was 29 per cent. From this Mr. Hall draws the conclusion that 100 persons of foreign birth in Massachusetts furnish ten times as many criminals as 100 persons of native birth and parentage (a conclusion incorrectly drawn). The witness has compared the criminality of the different nationalities in Massachusetts, leaving out of account commitments for drunkenness as perhaps not fairly to be compared. He finds that immigrants from Germany furnished 3.6 criminals per thousand of their number in the State. Scandinavia, Scotland, France, and Ireland follow in the order named. Next came English immigrants, showing 7.2 criminals per thousand population; Russia, 7.9; Austria, 10.4; Hungary, 15.4; Poland, 16; Italy, 18.2. The average number of commitments of the native born was only 2.7 per thousand. The progression among the foreign born is exactly parallel to the proportion of illiteracy. (51.)

Dr. SENNER denies that there is any close connection between illiteracy and crime. He presents statistics concerning the nationality of immigrants in the State prisons of Massachusetts, New York, Illinois, Pennsylvania, New Jersey, Connecticut, Ohio, Indiana, Missouri, Wisconsin, Minnesota, and Michigan (house of correction). The figures also include the number of inmates of local jails and the number of commitments for drunkenness in Massachusetts, and statistics for reformatories and other institutions in Illinois, Connecticut, and Ohio. He compares these figures with the total immigration of the respective nationalities during the years from 1886 to 1897. The prisoners of Polish birth have been evenly

LXX   THE INDUSTRIAL COMMISSION:—IMMIGRATION.

distributed between Russia and Austria. By bringing together the figures for
these different States the witness has prepared the following table, which he
declares shows that Italy, Austria, and Russia furnish a much smaller proportion
of commitments than the more literate States of North Europe. (This method
of comparison is, of course, an exceedingly rough one.) (171-175.)

	Total commitments.	Immigration 1886-1897.	Percentage.
England	3,199	530,872	0.60
Ireland	15,819	605,968	2.61
Scotland	1,027	124,494	.82
Germany	1,214	945,008	.13
Italy	733	613,531	.12
Austria	253	642,642	.04
Russia	445	537,201	.08
Sweden and Norway	745	518,602	.12

Italians.—Dr. SENNER declares that the Italians are an orderly and law-fearing
class, the cases of the too free use of the knife being too rare exceptions to prove
the contrary. Although their standard of life upon arriving in this country is
relatively low, it rises rapidly. Italian labor is certainly welcome to do the
rough work on railroads, sewers, etc., which American laborers are unwilling to
undertake. (170, 171.)

Jews.—Mr. ROSENDALE says that the Jews are a temperate people. Even
among the lowest Polish Jews there is not so much drunkenness as among others.
There is not much crime among them, though there is much more than there
used to be. Their crimes are largely in the way of fraud; swindling, buying
goods under false pretenses, setting their stores on fire. But in sanitary conditions the Russian and Polish Jews are far below other immigrants. They seem
to prefer to live in dirt. (194, 195.)

Mrs. STUCKLEN, matron of the Immigration Bureau at New York, believes that
the law should be amended so that immoral women coming to this country may
be excluded. She thinks that it would often be possible to get proof of their character by questioning in the board of special inquiry. The witness refers to one
instance in particular where a woman of this character came nominally as the
wife of an immigrant. (146, 147.)

Mr. RITTER, manager of the Austro-Hungarian Home, says that one reason for
the establishment of this home was the fact that immigrant women were getting
into bad habits and even sometimes into disorderly houses. The percentage
going astray is practically nothing in comparison with what it formerly was.
(222.)

Dr. SENNER thinks that the existing laws sufficiently prevent immigration of
criminals to the United States, although, of course, there are exceptional cases in
which they are admitted. (185.)

E. Pauperism and insanity.—Mr. HALL refers to the census of 1890 as
showing that the foreign-born population, constituting about one-seventh of the
total population, furnished one-third of the total number of insane persons in
the country. The foreign-born whites, one-sixth of the total number of whites,
furnished one-half of the paupers supported in public institutions. It was found
in Boston in 1897 that 66 per cent of those who were aided by the Industrial Aid
Society, the chief form of public charity, were foreign born, although the foreign born were only 30 per cent of the population.

In conclusion the witness states that there were supported at the public expense
in 1899 about 80,000 criminals, insane, and paupers of foreign birth. The average
cost of supporting them may be estimated at $150 yearly, making the total
expense $12,000,000. (51, 52.)

Mr. SCHULTEIS affirms that 40 per cent of inmates of our eleemosynary institutes are foreigners or of foreign descent. (26, 27.)

Mr. DOBLER, inspector Immigration Bureau, New York, says that in his opinion
a considerable number of immigrants who come in the second cabin of vessels,
bringing with them very little money, are likely to become public charges soon
after landing. Thus clerks, bookkeepers, and others who have been used to the
less profitable professions in Europe are likely to be unable to support themselves
here. (147.)

Nationality of insane.—Mr. GOODWIN BROWN, counsel for the New York State
Commission in Lunacy, says that a fraction over 50 per cent of the insane in the

SOCIAL CHARACTER AND EFFECTS OF IMMIGRATION.   LXXI

hospitals in the State of New York are foreign born, although the foreign population of the State of New York constitutes only 25 per cent of the total population. The conclusion is inevitable that the defective classes of immigrants have not been successfully excluded from this country. The proportion of foreign-born insane during the last 10 years has varied from 40 to 50 per cent of the total number of insane.

As the net increase in the number of insane in the State of New York is now about 700 per year, the net increase in the number of foreign-born insane may be taken to be 350 a year. The estimates show that the entire average cost to the State for each insane person is $3,000. On this basis, the yearly increase in the cost to the State from the foreign-born insane is more than $1,000,000. What is true in regard to the insane, in respect to the large proportion of foreign born, is true in respect to the inmates of the prisons, reformatories, houses of refuge, and all other public institutions. A larger percentage of the foreign-born insane come from Ireland than from any other country. It is probably true that it is the least thrifty of the Irish who come over here. They come because of the hard conditions at home, and are, therefore, largely people who have lived on a low diet. This is, perhaps, in part an explanation of the large percentage of foreign born among the insane in the New York institutions. (204, 205, 207, 213.)

Proportion of insane.—Mr. GOODWIN BROWN says that in the Eastern States the ratio of insane persons to the whole population is pretty nearly constant, and that there is about 1 insane person in every 300 of the population. As one goes farther west the proportion runs less, and in the far Western States there is only 1 insane person to every 1,500 of the population. It seems to be the hardy persons who go to the Western States. The feeble and defective ones are left behind. It is impossible to estimate what the proportion of insane is in foreign countries. There is no centralized administration, and things are in a confused state. Furthermore, those countries permit a far greater number of defective persons to roam at large than is the case in this country. (213, 214.)

Increase in number of insane.—Mr. GOODWIN BROWN says it is very questionable whether the insane are actually increasing. Apparently the insane increase much faster proportionately than the population. That, however, may be largely attributed to the fact that more of the insane are now being given public care and treatment than was formerly the case. The management of the institutions in the State of New York to-day is so satisfactory that relatives and friends are no longer unwilling, as they were formerly, to commit insane persons to public institutions. Up to 1890 the insane were increasing in New York State at the rate of about 1,000 a year, net increase. In the last few years the annual net increase has averaged between 600 and 700. (203.)

State care of insane.—Mr. GOODWIN BROWN says that the abuses in the care of the insane by local authorities were so great that, in 1890, an act was passed by the New York legislature providing for the care of all the insane by the State. Certain counties were exempted, but the act provided that those counties might turn over their insane to the State on certain terms, and, as a matter of fact, by 1896 all of those counties had turned over their insane to the care of the State. Since 1896 therefore all the insane in the State of New York have been under the care of the State, and the care of the insane had ceased to be a local affair in any sense, with the exception that the local authorities are obliged to provide the clothing and pay the expenses of commitment for the insane from their localities. The cost of caring for the insane has increased the expenses of the State, but, on the other hand, the expenses of the municipalities have been relieved from that tax. It is better to care for the insane in public institutions than to have them cared for at home, or to allow them to wander about the country. If allowed to go at large they constantly commit acts of violence or depredation. The policy of the State of New York has been to take under its charge every person properly committed.

Since the care of the insane has been put under a centralized management the average cost of caring for them has been reduced, and a material saving made to the State. The purchase of supplies on joint account has been extensively introduced under centralized management, and a saving has been made in that way. It is impossible to estimate with any degree of accuracy what the cost of caring for the insane was under local management. The figures in New York and Kings counties were juggled, and in the case of other counties it was found that frequently the books were not kept so as to show the separate cost of caring for paupers and for the insane. (202, 204, 205, 206, 218.)

New York State Commission in Lunacy.—Mr. GOODWIN BROWN says that when the insane were, by the act of the legislature, put under the care of the State, a State commission in lunacy, consisting of three members, was established. The commission has sole and exclusive jurisdiction over the insane. It does not have jurisdiction over idiots and epileptics. The separation of these classes of defectives has proved to be a satisfactory thing. The powers of the commission have been constantly extended, and now it has control over all expenditures whatsoever connected with the care of the insane. It also has authority over the removal of the insane from the State and their deportation to other States and countries. The commission has established a uniform system of accounts, a uniform system of commitment, a uniform system of dietary, of wages, of salaries, etc. It has spared no reasonable expenditure in effort to discover the causes of insanity, and in the employment of the most skillful physicians, nurses, and attendants. (202, 203.)

Cost of caring for the insane.—Mr. GOODWIN BROWN says that last year the average cost of caring for each insane person in the State of New York was $165. The average length of time which an insane person lives after commitment to an institution is from 10 to 12 years. The cost of buildings for the care of the insane is now limited to $550 per capita. According to the estimate of the National Fire Underwriters, the life of a brick store building is 20 years. On that basis, the cost of buildings for each lunatic is $275. Adding interest to the cost of maintenance and the cost of buildings, a conservative estimate would be that each lunatic costs the State a total of $3,000.

The cost of maintenance for the insane in the State of New York is about $4,000,000 per year. Of this amount the friends and relatives of the insane contribute about one-sixteenth. The law in the State of New York makes all the relatives of an insane person liable for his maintenance, in the order of their relationship. Practically, however, cousins are never called upon to pay, though brothers and sisters have been compelled to pay for the maintenance of the insane. (204, 205, 206, 214.)

Charitable societies.—Mr. MCSWEENEY says that representatives of more than 15 different charitable societies or missionary organizations meet the immigrants on their landing in New York. Thus the united Hebrew societies have an agent and an assistant at the barge office. There is a society especially for the protection of Irish girls. There are also a German society, a Russian society, a Methodist woman's mission society, and others. (85.)

Mr. STUMP says that Italians and Jews are almost never found in almshouses. Their friends care for them when in need. The immigration bureau pays expenses of such immigrants as become paupers within 1 year after landing. From $20,000 to $40,000 a year are thus expended, but the amount is amply covered by the receipts from the head tax. (11.)

Mr. ROSENDALE states that the Italians furnish a large proportion of the inmates of the almshouses, but few Jews go there. The Jews of Philadelphia,'through the United Hebrew Charity Association, help their own poor and keep them out of the almshouses. The poor exist, however, under wretched sanitary conditions. (195, 201.)

Mr. HALL says that there are few Jews in jails or in poorhouses, although many of them are relieved by private charity. It is believed that a certain class of Russian Jews are incorrigible paupers, although the care of them falls almost altogether upon their own race. (63.)

Mr. MCSWEENEY says that the Russian Jews, although not of such large stature as the French immigrants, are much less subject to tubercular diseases. Those who are paupers upon landing, and who temporarily receive assistance from the various organizations of their own race, are not permanently pauperized by such a system, but within a few years themselves contribute toward aiding others. The Russian Jews have practically driven out all other nationalities from the clothing trade in New York, although there is some competition from Italians. The witness refers to the practice of these Russian Jews in establishing colonies, especially on the East Side in New York and at Brownsville. (94.)

Mr. WOLF declares that the Hebrew charitable and educational organizations throughout the country have as their work almost exclusively the dealing with the refugees from Russia. The Roumanian and other refugees are in a very large degree able to establish and maintain themselves. (248.)

B'nai B'rith.—Mr. WOLF states that the B'nai B'rith is nearly 60 years old. It was founded by a number of earnest-minded men, mostly German Jews, who had come here under normal conditions, as other immigrants came in those times. It was the revolution of 1848 that brought the first notable number of Jews to this country, chiefly from Germany.

The object of the order is the education and Americanization of its members. The membership is now about 20,000. It has 7 districts in the United States and 3 in Europe. There are lodges in Austria, Germany, Roumania, and the Holy

Land, and efforts are now making to start one in France. Besides its educational work, it maintains hospitals, orphan asylums, homes for the aged, and free libraries. It supports a national hospital for consumptives at Denver, which takes no pay patients whatever, and which, though established for Jewish consumptives, is open to the world without reference to creed or nationality. In Philadelphia there is a hospital originally established by the order and open to all people irrespective of faith. (248, 249.)

Mr. Wolf says that while the B'nai B'rith is a very important agency of Jewish charitable and educational work, it is by no means the only one. In New York there is a vast network of affiliated organizations, which are ramifications from the central body of the United Hebrew Charities. Besides the relief of physical necessities by hospitals, orphan asylums, and similar institutions, there is centered in the Educational Alliance a system of day schools, night schools, and manual training schools, which give instruction to thousands of pupils of all ages and of both sexes. A college in Cincinnati is maintained by the Union of American Hebrew Congregations. In every large city and in many of the minor towns charities have been organized and have worked earnestly to further the assimilation of Jewish immigrants. All of these societies have to deal almost exclusively with the Russian refugees. (248, 249.)

Mr. Wolf says that the American Jews have given special attention to educating and Americanizing the European refugees and immigrants of their faith. The great Educational Alliance in New York has an attendance which averages more than 5,000 persons a day. There is also the Hebrew Technical Institute, which educates Jewish boys in mechanical and scientific pursuits. The duties of patriotism are carefully inculcated, the Constitution of the United States and the Declaration of Independence are made part of the educational system, and a tiny United States flag is on the desk of every child. There are Jewish manual training schools in Cleveland, in Philadelphia, and in Atlanta. At the Hebrew Orphan Home in Atlanta the girls are taught to be housemaids and cooks, and the boys to be mechanics, artisans, stenographers, and typewriters. (246, 250.)

F. Contagious diseases.—Mr. FITCHIE, commissioner of immigration at New York, declares that although the present law requires all immigrants to be examined by the surgeon of the vessel before sailing and a sworn statement as to their health to be entered upon the manifest, nevertheless large numbers of persons with contagious and loathsome diseases are allowed to embark and have to be debarred, under the law, from landing in this country. The contagious diseases of trachoma and favus are especially increasing. The courts have held that the steamship companies can not be fined for bringing such persons unless they are actually landed. The law should be changed so as to make attempting to land such persons an offense, and a fine should be imposed sufficiently large to make the steamship companies more strict. (71.)

Dr. WILLIAMS, surgeon of the Marine-Hospital Service, detailed to inspect immigrants at the port of New York, submitted the following statement showing the number of cases of contagious diseases, etc., detected by the medical inspection service at New York:

Number of hospital cases for past year ... 1,862
Number of landed cases applying for relief for past year ... 235
Number of arriving immigrants certified to during past year ... 1,244
Number of cases certified loathsome or dangerous contagious diseases:
  Favus ... 48
  Trachoma ... 312
Number of contagious cases deported:
  Trachoma ... 298
  Favus ... 36

Dr. Williams states that such dangerous diseases as smallpox are reached by the quarantine inspection. Mild contagious diseases like scarlet fever and measles are treated in the isolation hospital connected with the immigration department; such cases as these develop on board vessel and, being only temporary, the immigrants are not returned. Practically the only forms of contagious diseases which call for deportation are trachoma, or granulated eyelids, and favus, or scaldhead, which are especially common among Italians and Syrians. Where these diseases are discovered, the board of special inquiry has practically no discretion, but must return the person afflicted. Where, however, the medical inspection reveals some physical defect in the immigrants, it is optional with the board to admit him or deport him. (127-129.)

Dr. Williams thinks that there would be less immigration of persons with contagious diseases if it were left to the discretion of the commissioner of immigration whether the immigrant should be immediately deported or should be kept in the hospital until cured, at the expense of the steamship company. The companies would dread more the cost of maintaining the immigrant in the hospital than that of deportation. Moreover, such a provision would be advantageous from the standpoint of humanity. It often involves hardship to debar a person with a contagious disease who is a member of a family. (127.)

Mr. POWDERLY says that favus is a disease of the scalp, originating in filth, which ultimately destroys the hair. Where children are afflicted, it seems more humane to return them with one of the parents than to allow the spread of the disease. (35.)

G. Religious faith of foreign-born.—Mr. ROSENDALE, investigating the condition of anthracite miners in Shickshinny in 1897, found in the neighborhood 5 Roman Catholic churches, presided over by Italian and Polish priests; 1 Greek Catholic church; 2 Polish-Jewish synagogues; 1 Methodist meetinghouse, and another meetinghouse the use of which was divided between the Presbyterians and the Episcopalians. (188.)

Mr. Rosendale refers to the superstition of the lower classes of immigrant Jews—they depend upon the rabbis for charms against evil spirits, etc. He believes that the rabbis try to maintain these superstitious opinions in order to keep control over the people. An ignorant man, Mr. Rosendale thinks, can be much more easily controlled by the rabbis and priests than one who can read. This is one ground of Mr. Rosendale's belief in a restriction of immigration by an educational test. (193, 197.)

III. ECONOMIC EFFECTS OF IMMIGRATION.

A. Money sent out of the country.—Mr. HALL says that in 1892, according to the statistics of the Bureau of Immigration, each immigrant from France brought, on an average, $55 into this country; from Germany, $35; England, $26; Sweden, $21; Russia; $22; Austria, $14; Poland, $12; Italy and Hungary, $11. Roughly speaking, the more illiterate the race the smaller the proportion of money brought.

Mr. Hall says, further, that immigrants to this country send out a very large amount of money to their homes in Europe. The amount is not definitely known, but an estimate made by the New York Herald in 1892 that $25,000,000 went back to Europe every winter is believed to be too low. Italians send back large sums through their bankers, storing them in the old country until they can accumulate a sufficient amount to establish themselves comfortably at home. (52.)

Mr. ALLEN, a representative of the Advanced Labor Club of Brooklyn, presents an argument in favor of restricting the immigration of those who come to the United States temporarily, returning to their native countries after accumulating money. He declares that the movement in favor of such restriction is based on economic reasons, and race prejudice has nothing to do with it. The witness believes that immigrants who do not intend to stay in the United States are more dangerous than those who are uneducated.

Mr. Allen insists that the proportion of temporary immigrants is constantly increasing. He says that the number of immigrants who arrived in the United States during the 10 years ending June 30, 1891, was 5,246,613. Besides these there were probably 950,000 coming from Canada who were not enumerated. There were only 2,569,604 more foreign-born persons in the United States according to the census of 1890 than there were according to the census of 1880. Since only part of the immigrants remain in this country, an allowance of 10 per cent of those who arrive for deaths is a fair one. With this allowance it appears that 3,007,348 of foreign-born persons must have returned home from the United States during that decade. (161, 162.)

Mr. Allen declares that the loss of money sent or taken away by immigrants is a serious menace to the finances of the United States.

In 1892 the New York Herald, on the basis of testimony of padrones, steamship agents, and others, concluded that the average amount taken back to Europe by returning Italians was $250 each. The witness considers this estimate too low, especially for skilled laborers, but accepting it as a basis he declares that the amount of money taken back by returning immigrants would be fully $118,000,000 yearly, aside from the cost of passage both ways.

Mr. Allen thinks that the exportation of money in this way was the chief cause of the financial panic of 1893. He shows that the export movement of gold averaged only $54,000,000 from the years 1885 to 1893, which is less than the amount which aliens must have taken with them. Moreover, the outflow began before the passage of the Sherman Act and continued after its repeal, so that it can not be attributed to that act. Most of the gold that went abroad during those 4 years

ECONOMIC EFFECTS OF IMMIGRATION. LXXV

was shipped to France and Germany and thence largely reshipped to Austria, as stated by the Director of the Mint. Austria held no American stocks at that time to constitute a claim for money, nor would the Rothschilds, who were then negotiating a loan for Austria, have been likely to borrow gold in the United States, where it was scarce and dear, while it was plentiful and cheap in England. An Italian banker testified before a Senate committee in 1893 that his firm alone had sent away $2,000,000 the year before and that there were about 80 other Italian banking firms in New York, some of which had sent away even larger amounts.

Mr. Allen declares further that our present financial condition is not sufficiently assured so that we can afford to lose the gold which aliens are continually taking away from us. In 1898-99 the balance of trade in our favor was $530,000,000, while our net imports of gold and silver were only $25,000,000. This great difference can not be altogether accounted for by the return and sale of American stocks held abroad, for there is reason to believe that fully as many stocks were bought by Europeans during that year as were sold. The witness thinks that the amount of money paid as interest on foreign investments is underestimated, but that the chief mistake of those who seek to explain the difference between the balance of trade and the imports of gold and silver arises from the disregard of the money taken out by temporary immigrants.

The witness says, further, that for the last financial year the balance of trade in favor of the United States as against Canada was $52,000,000, but that we received only $13,500,000 in cash from Canada, the balance having gone as the hoardings of the Canadian laborers who come to the United States. (161-164.)

B. Standards of living.—Mr. ROSENDALE describes in detail several cases which he investigated during his study of the slum districts in 1899. In one 2-story frame building, formerly a dwelling house, he found a grocery store in the front room; the back room used as a workshop for making shirt waists, and occupied by 6 working girls; and the second story, containing 4 bedrooms, occupied by 3 different families. Twenty-two people lived in the house. All were Russian Jews. Only 2 adults could speak English, and they very poorly. There were 8 children, none of whom attended the public schools. They were sent to the Hebrew school to learn to read Hebrew—not to translate it, but only so that they could read their prayers. The children sold matches and newspapers. Everything was very filthy, and there was no sanitary regulation. In another case a Jewish woman whose husband had left her had got a divorce from the rabbi, not from the courts, and had married again. In another case a man displayed a sign consisting of 3 Hebrew words. The first indicated that he was a killer of animals according to the Jewish rites. The second indicated that he was licensed by the chief rabbi to perform the rite of circumcision. The third indicated that he was licensed by the rabbi to perform marriages and grant divorces. Several other cases are described. (192, 193.)

Mr. Rosendale says that the rising generation of Jews, Italians, and Hungarians mean to live for the most part in the same surroundings as their parents. His impression is that they are growing up to be unskilled laborers. (196.)

Anthracite miners.—In 1897 Mr. ROSENDALE found the children of the miners not in the schools but mostly working as helpers, pickers, etc., in the mines. He found a great many women working in the mines as helpers, leaving their infant children in the shade of trees. In 1884 he had seen an entirely different class of people, contented, living in clean dwellings. He was told that many of those Welsh and Irish miners could not stand the competition of the newcomers, with their low standard of living. They had gone West to try to find employment in other mines, where the influx of the foreign element was not so strong. (189, 190.)

Mr. Rosendale found the social conditions of the anthracite miners in 1897 deplorable. Fights and quarrels were very frequent among them. They lived huddled together like cattle in dilapidated shanties. Mr. Rosendale found 20 Hungarians living in one shanty and hiring one woman to cook for them. (188.)

Poles.—Dr. SENNER quotes from a letter by the collector of customs at Buffalo regarding the Polish colony in that city. The population of the Polish colony in 1893 was about 55,000 and Poles owned about 3,000 city lots valued at $6,181,100. They had 5 large churches and 4 schoolhouses. They appear more anxious than any other class of foreigners to secure their own homes. They pay taxes more promptly than any other nationality and take a great interest in informing themselves as to American politics. They are better educated than many other immigrants and are industrious, frugal, and law-abiding. (170, 171.)

Roumanian Jews.—Mr. WOLF declares that the majority of the Jewish refugees who have recently come from Roumania possess means enough to establish themselves in the United States and require no assistance. The report of an inspector of the United States Immigration Bureau sent to Roumania to investigate the conditions is quoted, to the effect the Roumanian refugees are people who had acquired a competence by signal abilities in spite of the unfavorable conditions under which they lived, and that they will be a desirable acquisition to the population of America. (247, 254.)

Enforcement of sanitary regulations.—Mr. ROSENDALE asserts that in Berlin if a building is found to be in an insanitary condition the landlord or owner is notified to put it in sanitary condition and keep it so. If this is not done the city removes the inhabitants of the house to the suburbs, keeps them there under police surveillance, and forces them to keep themselves clean and to keep their house clean. It keeps them there until they become used to that kind of living, and keeps them under watch when they go back to the city. If such regulations could be enforced in our cities, the improvement would be vast; the herding of 20 people in one house would be stopped; the people would be forced to a higher standard of living. But such things could not be done in our cities; the cost would be too enormous. Just as soon as a district was cleaned out, 2,000, or 3,000, or 20,000 more would come from the landing places, and the whole work would have to be done over again. The trouble is the constant influx of new immigrants who perpetuate here conditions they have been accustomed to in Europe. (196, 201.)

Compulsory education.—Mr. ROSENDALE says that there is a compulsory education law in Pennsylvania, but it is a dead letter in the mining regions, so far as he knows, and also in the slum districts of Philadelphia; though in Philadelphia they are trying to enforce it. (191.)

C. Demand for immigrant labor.—Mr. STUMP, former Commissioner-General of Immigration, says that the commission appointed by the Secretary of the Treasury in 1895 addressed questions to trades unions and similar organizations and to governors of States as to the conditions of immigrants, desirable changes in law or in methods of enforcement, and as to the desire for further immigration. (4.)

Mr. HALL refers to this investigation. He says that 52 replies were received from governors of States, commissioners of labor, and similar authorities as to whether immigrants were desired. Of these 15 expressed a preference for German immigrants, 12 for English, Scotch, and Irish, 3 for French, and 2 for Swiss. Only two desired Italian immigration, and one of those did not want unskilled labor, and the other only wanted farmers with money and families. Ten States did not want any immigrants at all. There seems to be practically no demand for common laborers and unskilled farm laborers, while, on the other hand, the labor unions oppose the coming of skilled labor. (57, 65.)

D. Occupation of immigrants.—Mr. HALL presents statistics for the year 1896 showing that only an exceedingly small proportion of the male immigrants belong to the professional occupations, while the proportion of skilled laborers is also small, these two classes together being less than one-fifth of the total number of male immigrants. Much the largest proportion of immigrants state that they are laborers, servants, or farmers, the latter term usually meaning that they are farm laborers or peasants, who, in fact, usually stop in the cities; while one-sixth of the total number have no occupation.

The proportion of the skilled laborers varies in roughly inverse proportion to the illiteracy of the immigrants of the respective nationalities. Thus, of the immigrants from Scotland, 1 in 4 is skilled; from England and Wales, 1 in 5; Belgium, 1 in 9; Germany and Norway, 1 in 10; Italy, 1 in 14; Russia, 1 in 18; Ireland, 1 in 19; Poland, 1 in 27; Austria-Hungary, 1 in 29. (50, 54.)

Mr. POWDERLY says that a comparatively small proportion of immigrants class themselves as farmers, and most of these are destined to States containing large cities. (41.)

Mr. ROSENDALE states that he knows very few instances of Jews following agriculture for a living. That is not the fault of the Jews; it is the fault of the Christians, who have prevented them from following agriculture and have restricted them to trade. But the fact remains that the attempts to get the Jews into agriculture, as by the Baron Hirsch colony at Woodbine and the colonies in the Argentine Republic, have all been failures. These philanthropic efforts have been a detriment to the workingmen at large; for the Jews brought to those colonies all end in factories in competition with American workmen. Mr. Rosendale thinks that now that the Jews have in this country an equal chance with others, they ought to try to work on different lines, and not pursue the occupations which in the old country they have been forced to pursue. He condemns them for persisting in the lines of barter and trade. As a matter of fact, there are among the Jews of Philadelphia a large proportion of manual workers; the professions of law and medicine, and even of mechanical arts, are well represented. The ratio of Jews in the mechanical department of the University of Pennsylvania is showing a good increase. (194, 195.)

E. Effects on native labor.—1. *In general.*—Mr. POWDERLY says that there is no satisfactory statistical information as to the effect of immigration. Trade unions believe the effect injurious in depressing wages and standard of living, and in increasing unemployment.

Mr. SCHULTEIS does not admit that immigrants of low intelligence are desirable to do rough work, since we already have several millions of idle and unskilled workmen in this country, especially the 3,000,000 colored men in the South. If the lowest grade of labor is badly paid on account of the competition of the foreign born, higher grades suffer correspondingly. Southern Europeans are especially undesirable. (23, 24.)

Mr. SCHONFARBER, of the Knights of Labor, believes that the Irish and Germans who came to this country before 1875 added materially to its growth and prosperity. On the other hand, the lower classes who have been coming since that time, especially from southern and eastern Europe, have had not only an injurious social effect, but have been exceedingly injurious to American labor. The unskilled labor of the country has suffered especially. Miners have perhaps been more seriously affected by the importation of unskilled labor than any other class. At the same time many skilled immigrants have been imported, largely under contract, and have displaced skilled labor by working at lower wages. The witness thinks that the proportion of skilled immigrants is likely to decrease, but that at the same time the effect of the immigration of unskilled labor will become more and more widespread, because machinery is tending constantly to decrease the proportion of skilled workers in this country, reducing all to the ranks of common laborers. (435, 436.)

Mr. HALL admits that the earlier immigration to this country has had a beneficial effect in building up States and cities. In Chicago, Buffalo, Pittsburg, Cincinnati, and other cities the comparatively recent immigrants and their descendants have largely built up the State and paid the most of the taxes. Even Italians have become a large and valuable element of the population in some cases. The witness would not have considered an education necessary or desirable 10 or 12 years ago. It then cost more to come here and immigrants were of the better class. At present, however, immigrants are not desired. (58, 59.)

Dr. SENNER says that immigrants, especially on account of their inability to speak our language, often fail to receive full recognition of their merits. He declares that very soon immigrants become effective consumers and that without them the United States could never have built up its unparalleled home market. Immigrants improve rapidly under contact with our civilization, as is seen in the contrast between new arrivals and friends who meet them at the pier. (170.)

Dr. Senner says that he can understand how the laboring classes in times of industrial depression and enforced idleness should feel jealous of immigrants, but while there may be a sentiment in favor of restriction on the part of a great many people, there are also many who oppose it, as the witness has found out in connection with his work as secretary of the Immigration Protective League. The representatives of labor who favor restriction are usually sadly misinformed as to the effects of immigration. Most of the evils of which they complain arise from the presence of immigrants who have been here a long time, and would be little affected by present restrictions. (180, 181, 184.)

Dr. Senner thinks that whatever political or economic dangers formerly existed from immigration will more and more decrease. The country with a population of 70,000,000 is naturally better able to absorb 300,000 immigrants yearly than it was able to absorb from five to seven hundred thousand when the population was only forty or fifty millions. Moreover the European countries are rapidly advancing so that the character of immigrants is bound to improve. (173.)

1. *Immigration and wages.*—Dr. SENNER declares that the influences affecting wages are so exceedingly complex that it is impossible to determine the effect of immigration alone has had upon them. He denies emphatically, however, that wages have fallen since the great tide of immigration. In 1891 a Senate committee declared that wages had been highest during the years of heaviest immigration, which naturally coincide with periods of prosperity, and that there has been a steady increase of wages during the past 3 decades. A table prepared by the department of labor in 1898 compares the average daily wages of men in certain occupations in 12 of the largest cities in the United States for the years 1870 and 1898. The summary of these tables by trades shows an increase in every case, ranging from 1 to 20 per cent, the average increase being between 5 and 10

per cent. The following table, also submitted by the witness on the same authority, shows the average wages in these occupations for each year since 1870, together with the annual immigration:

Year.	Average wages.	Increase as compared with 1870.	Immigration into the United States.	Year.	Average wages.	Increase as compared with 1870.	Immigration into the United States.
		Per cent.				*Per cent.*	
1870	$2.20½	....	387,203	1884	2.49	12.9	518,592
1871	2.39¼	8.5	321,350	1885	2.47¼	12.1	395,346
1872	2.45	11.1	404,806	1886	2.47¼	12.1	334,203
1873	2.35½	6.8	459,803	1887	2.49¼	13	490,109
1874	2.30¼	4.4	313.339	1888	2.50¾	13.7	546,889
1875	2.24¼	1.7	227,498	1889	2.51½	14.1	444,427
1876	2.18	1.1	169,986	1890	2.52¾	14.6	455,302
1877	2.24½	1.8	141,857	1891	2.54½	15.4	560,319
1878	2.30¾	4.6	138,469	1892	2.56	16.1	623,084
1879	2.32	5.2	172,826	1893	2.54¼	15.3	502,917
1880	2.34	6.1	457,257	1894	2.49¼	13	314,467
1881	2.40¾	9.2	669,431	1895	2.47¼	12.1	279,948
1882	2.44¾	11	788,992	1896	2.45¾	11.5	343,267
1883	2.47	12	603,322	1897	2.44½	10.9	230,823

Dr. Senner declares further that wages have a much higher purchasing power at present than 20 or 30 years ago. He submits tables prepared by the Massachusetts bureau of statistics of labor comparing the average retail prices of the leading articles of household consumption in Massachusetts for the years 1872 and 1897. These articles are the chief standard food products, with a limited number of items of fuel, cloths, rents, etc. A corresponding table shows the amount of these different commodities that $1 would purchase in 1872 and 1897, together with the percentage of the increase in purchasing power for the latter year. This table shows an increase in purchasing power as regards all but two of the commodities enumerated, the increase in most cases being more than 30 per cent, reaching 124 per cent in the case of wheat and 117 in the case of sugar, while the increase as regards shirting, sheeting, and other cheap grades of cloths has averaged more than 100 per cent.

Dr. Senner also denies that a decrease in the wages of unskilled labor tends to bring about in the course of time a decrease in the wages of skilled labor. (170, 176–178, 184.)

2. "*Birds of passage.*"—Mr. McSweeney says that a very large number of native Canadians come yearly into the United States to work during the busy season, returning to Canada during the winter. This number has been estimated at as many as 50,000 or 70,000 annually. The competition of these Canadians is felt most severely in the neighborhood of Boston, where it has affected especially the building trades. This temporary immigration is alike injurious to Canada and to the United States, and the witness believes that the Canadian government disapproves of it. Canada loses the benefit of the labor of these persons in developing its industries, since she has need of labor; and while the United States gets value for their work, it loses because they do not spend the money they earn largely in this country and also because they lower the wages of citizens of the United States. (92, 93.)

Mr. Powderly declares that Canadian labor is not necessary to keep the cotton mills running. It has depressed wages and has checked increase of native population, since young men can no longer afford to marry. (39.)

Mr. Powderly and Mr. Schulties refer to the large temporary immigration of Canadian labor. Along the border many even cross daily into this country to work, returning at night. (18, 28.)

Mr. Hall says that a large proportion of Italians who come to this country have no intention of remaining longer than is necessary to accumulate sufficient money to make themselves responsible at home. A great many come to this country several times. An examination of the 3,174 Italians who landed at New York in April, 1896, showed that 27.7 per cent had been in this country before, some of them two or three times, according to their own statements. These men do not usually bring their families, the proportion of women among the immigrants being very low. So far as Italian women do come to this country, however, the witness thinks that the conjugal morality is comparatively high. (53.)

Mr. Quinlan, contract labor inspector, says that he has personally investigated at least 1,000 cases, chiefly of Italians, who have come to this country for a second

ECONOMIC EFFECTS OF IMMIGRATION. LXXIX

time. Each of these brought to the United States only a small sum of money, but on his previous return to Italy had taken with him from $200 to $1,000. With this money they often bought homes in Italy, and returned to this country to earn money to lift the mortgage which had been given for part payment. While in this country they buy nothing except what they eat and drink. In the fall the steerage of many of the lines is crowded with persons of this class returning to Italy.

The immigration department has no power to exclude these "birds of passage," but if they be found with a very small sum of money they are debarred as likely to become paupers.

There are also a considerable number of skilled laborers, carpenters, bricklayers, and others who come to this country from Ireland, Scotland, and England during the summer, returning for the winter. Some of these hold international union cards, but that is not the rule. (122, 123.)

Dr. ROSSI declares that Italians who come to this country in the spring to work return to Italy in the winter only because the enterprises on which they are employed are suspended and they can not find work here. They are not to be blamed for returning under these circumstances. Many Americans go to Europe yearly and spend millions of dollars there, far more than Italians take back with them. Moreover, Italian immigration is becoming more and more permanent. (160.)

Dr. SENNER says that, although many Italians for some years keep up the habit of returning to Italy in the winter, they are very apt on their second or third return to bring their families and become permanent residents. The increasing permanency of the immigrants is shown by the growing proportion of women and children who are coming. While in 1883, of the Italians who arrived, 28,217 were males, 3,567 females, and 2,528 under 15 years of age, the proportion in 1890 was 40,717 males, 11,082 females, and 8,759 children, while in 1898 there were 40,248 males, 18,365 females, and 11,935 children. (170.)

Mr. STUMP says that large numbers of steerage passengers annually return to Europe. These are often persons who work here during the season and spend the winter in Europe because living is cheaper. There has been great confusion of immigration statistics because of repeated entries of such persons. Many thus returning to Europe are, however, bona fide residents of this country, going to visit friends and relatives. (8.)

Mr. TER KUILE thinks that the number of Italians who return from this country in the fall is relatively decreasing. Formerly fully one-half of those coming each year return, but now the proportion does not exceed one-fourth. Those who do return a single time are apt on their second coming to settle permanently in the United States. (115.)

3. *Unskilled labor.*—Mr. SCHWAB, agent of the North-German Lloyd Company, declares that the immigrants who come to this country are absolutely needed to do the rough work, such as construction of railways, sewers, etc., which Americans are unwilling to do. The influx of immigration has not depressed wages; as a matter of fact, wages have risen during the past 25 years, while at the same time there has been a great decrease in the cost of living. The witness does not even think that the country is injured by those who come here for a short time merely, since they contribute to advance our industry during their stay. (103, 108.)

Mr. McSWEENEY, testifying in July, 1899, expresses the opinion that, owing to the general revival of business, there was at that time a demand for all the unskilled labor which was likely to arrive in this country. There have been many inquiries at the immigration office for unskilled labor, although the department has no power to assist in securing employment for immigrants. (96.)

Mr. POWDERLY says agriculture is little affected, and skilled trades much less than unskilled. Most immigrants are ordinary laborers, though many are tailors. In the shoe trade, for example, subdivision of labor and use of machinery has made the employment of cheap labor possible, and this tends to depress the wages of all trades. (32–34, 39, 42.)

4. *Padrone sytem.*—Mr. STUMP declares that the padrone system formerly existed extensively among Italians. Italian bankers in New York had arrangements with steamship companies or had agents of their own in Europe. Money was advanced to pay for the passage of the immigrant on agreement to work for the contractor in the United States. These bankers would send gangs of laborers to railways, etc., under charge of a boss. He would put up a cheap shanty, charge laborers $1 a month or more for bunks, furnish them with all food and clothing, and account for their wages to the padrone. The laborer thus found himself a debtor and slave for years. This practice is now largely broken up by the contract-labor

LXXX   THE INDUSTRIAL COMMIISION:—IMMIGRATION.

law, but has started afresh among Assyrians, Arabs, Turks, Greeks, and Armenians, who are being brought here to peddle goods, black boots, and often to beg. (7, 8.)

Mr. SCHULTEIS says that the padrone system still flourishes to a limited degree. There are about 80 Italian banks in New York City which still maintain the system, and can furnish men in lots of 50 to 100. They care for the immigrants' money, write their letters, and save their earnings until they amount to perhaps $400, which is a sufficient capital to enable Italians at home to cease manual labor. The system of importing contract labor has been largely broken up, partly through the effect of law, but largely through the sentiment of the people affected themselves. (30, 31.)

Mr. MCSWEENEY believes that while the practice among bankers and padrones of making contracts in Italy to furnish labor to immigrants has been largely abandoned, the immigrants are still aware that they are practically certain to find employment through the padrones on reaching this country, and a large proportion of them put themselves under the control of the padrones on reaching here. The system still flourishes and the immigrants themselves prefer that it should continue. (88.)

Mr. POWDERLY says that the padrone system still exists in Pennsylvania coal mines in a form hard to detect. An active Italian or other foreigner, who knows English, is asked to write to his friends, warning them against disclosing the fact of agreement for employment. The law should be amended so that fact of coming in response to invitation of any kind, except from relatives, should debar. Instances exist where workmen thus brought over are compelled to work practically 2 years before being able to repay the passage money advanced, and are then discharged to make room for other victims. Such employees live in the rudest fashion, and if killed in an accident will not be received by their associates, but must be buried at public expense. Nearly everyone of the Italian banks is employed in the padrone business. (33, 43, 44.)

Dr. ROSSI declares that the padrone system was formerly a very great evil in this country, but asserts that it has been considerably mitigated by the efforts of the Italian bureau. The recent failure of some of the Italian bankers has also weakened the system. The witness admits, however, that Italian laborers in the United States are still to some extent under the control of padrones. There is an element of slavery in the employment of many Italians, but the control of the padrones is not as complete as before. (155, 156, 159.)

Dr. Rossi says that through the efforts of the Italian bureau correspondence of padrones in Italy—ticket agents and others—have often been discovered and punished by the home Government, especially by the withdrawal of licenses from agents of steamship companies. (159.)

Dr. Rossi says that there have been a considerable number of failures among Italian bankers in recent years; that these have occasioned discredit among all of the bankers, so that many of the immigrants prefer to keep their savings in their own hands. There are, however, some honest and straightforward Italian bankers.

The witness is unwilling to give any estimate as to the amount of money sent back to Italy from the United States. (156.)

Mr. TER KUILE thinks that the padrone system no longer exists. Years ago Italian immigrants preferred to put themselves under the care of padrones, and the system became a great evil. At present the Italians no longer feel as helpless as before, and they need little assistance from the padrone. The Italian bankers with whom the immigrants still continue to do business are often responsible persons or corporations, although some of them are not responsible. (115, 116.)

Armenian and Greek immigration.—Mr. MCSWEENEY says that there is a considerable immigration of Syrians, Armenians, and Greeks. Armenians have gone to Minnesota to a considerable degree. The Syrians are mostly peddlers There is to a considerable extent something similar to the Italian padrone system among this class. It is also believed that the immigrants are largely under the control of a central organization which sends them out as notion peddlers, although information as to this practice is not definite. (83, 88.)

Mr. STUMP also refers to the development of the padrone system among these nationalities. (8.)

5. *Coal mines.*—Mr. POWDERLY says that American labor and that of early Irish, Scotch, English, Welsh, and German immigrants, whose standard of living was high, has been largely displaced by importation or immigration of less desirable foreigners, especially Italians, Hungarians, and Poles. The number of Hungarians and Italians in the mines is now about equal. These foreigners were first brought about 1869 to replace men on strike. At present few English-speak-

ECONOMIC EFFECTS OF IMMIGRATION.   LXXXI

ing miners remain, and a large number of miners are out of employment. Wages have been reduced and business injured. Though many Italians, Hungarians, and Poles remain in this country, others, especially from south Italy, come here only temporarily and save most of their wages. They live in exceedingly crowded houses and spend barely 15 cents of their daily wage of $1. Other causes have contributed to the reduction of wages, but immigration is the chief cause. (32–34, 44.)

Mr. ROSENDALE understands that the first Italians who came to the anthracite region were brought by the wife of a coal man in Wilkesbarre, who was traveling in Italy, and who sent them over at her own expense, because she took pity on them. Though Mr. Rosendale considers the result deplorable, he thinks the act was one of pure philanthropy. (189.)

Mr. Rosendale doubts whether 2 per cent of the anthracite miners were Italians, Hungarians, or Polish Jews up to 1882, or possibly up to 1884 or 1885. It was in 1884 that they began to come in small numbers, and they came in alarming numbers from 1888 on. There was a slight decrease in 1894 on account of the panic, but a rapid increase at the time of Mr. Rosendale's testimony, January, 1900. (191, 200.)

Mr. Rosendale says that he was in the anthracite region in the years immediately following the war as a mining engineer, and found the miners Welsh, Irish, Americans, Germans, and Scandinavians. In 1897 he made a study of the conditions there and found Italians and Hungarians in the majority. A report of a legislative committee at that time said 60 per cent were foreigners. (188.)

Mr. Rosendale states that a Pennsylvania legislative committee made an investigation in 1897 of the condition of the miners both in the anthracite region and in the bituminous region. The report on the bituminous region was printed, but that on the anthracite, for some reason, was not. (188, 192.)

Earnings.—Mr. ROSENDALE, in 1897, investigating the condition of the anthracite miners, found that earnings ranged from $4 to $5 a week for adults, and from $1.50 to $2.50 for boys and girls. (188.)

Relation of wages to price of coal.—Mr. ROSENDALE does not think there has been a fall in the price of coal commensurate with the lowering of the wages of the anthracite miners. The wages have fallen not so much by a lowering of rates as by the restriction of production, so that a man is permitted to work only 6 months, or perhaps only 3. (190.)

Unemployment.—Mr. ROSENDALE states that in 1897 if the anthracite mines were worked to their full capacity they could not give employment to all the miners for more than 6 months. (189.)

Company stores.—Mr. ROSENDALE states that when he investigated the condition of the miners in the parts of the anthracite regions in 1897 he found nothing but company stores. The only other source of supply was Polish Jews, who carried packs upon their backs from house to house. The small grocery stores and dry goods stores that existed 20 or 30 years ago were broken up. Mr. Rosendale found the prices in company stores higher than elsewhere. He says that Mr. George Chance, president of the United Labor League, of Philadelphia, made a special study of this question and found a difference in prices of 20 or 25 per cent. Mr. Rosendale has seen slips marked with circles and red crosses, which he was informed by the recipients were warnings that if they did not buy more at the company stores they could have no work. The Pennsylvania legislature passed a bill a few years ago taxing the scrip of company stores 10 per cent, but it was vetoed by the governor. (188, 192.)

Independent anthracite operators and railroads.—Mr. ROSENDALE says that when he was in the anthracite regions in 1880, the great difficulty of the individual owners of mines was discrimination by the railroad companies in not giving them cars to take their coal to market. "In 1894 I heard very little complaint of that; but it seems to me there are no more individual operators. I think that is the reason I did not hear any more complaints." (190.)

6. *Sweat shops.*—Mr. ROSENDALE says that there is not now the misery and starvation in the clothing manufacture and cap manufacture that existed in 1894 and 1895 and up to 1897; but if new immigrants continue to flock, the same result must reappear—a surplus supply of labor; "and it is getting worse and worse." (196.)

Mr. Rosendale states that in 1894, at the request of the factory inspector, he undertook an investigation of the sweat shops of Philadelphia. He stuck to it for two days and gave it up. He found the conditions too hard—such filth, vice, and immorality, such suffering and actual starvation. (192.)

Mr. Rosendale declares that it is impossible for the factory inspectors to keep track of the sweat shops. The law requires that every such place be registered and take out a license, but he himself stumbled by chance on a room back of a grocery store where 6 girls were engaged in making shirt waists. The place was not registered and the factory inspector could not be expected to find it. (192, 194.)

Mr. WOLF asserts that the popular idea of the prevalence of sweat-shop work among the Jews is exaggerated. Nearly all who are in the work are Russian Jews. The Jew is innately individualistic and ambitious, and, while he makes the struggle of competition keen even among his own people, the low wages are to him only the stepping stone to higher wages. The economic question involved in the presence of the Russian Jews would quickly solve itself if the conditions out of which it has grown were put an end to, so that the stream of refugees could cease to flow. (251.)

7. *Cigar makers.*—Mr. PERKINS, president of the International Cigar Makers' Union, says his organization has twice declared, by a general vote of the members, in favor of laws restricting immigration, although not for absolute prohibition. The trade has suffered severely from immigration. Many of the immigrants, especially Jews, have been given some training in the cigar trade in schools of a charitable nature and have then begun competing with American workmen. Many of these immigrants were assisted to come here. In New York City, where they are most numerous, only about 6,000 out of 20,000 cigar makers belong to the unions.

The following is a resolution adopted by the Cigar Makers' Union in 1893: "*Resolved*, That the convention of the C. M. I. U. of America recommend to the executive officers of the A. F. of L., the various States' Federation of Labor, and the executive officers of all trades and labor unions to cooperate and demand of Congress and the Federal officers of the United States the absolute necessity of placing more restriction upon the present influx of such immigration."

In 1896 or 1897 the American Federation of Labor submitted 7 questions for vote by trade unions, inquiring whether their members favored (1) restriction of immigration further than at present, (2) exclusion of criminal and pauper elements, (3) increasing the power of the consular and immigration service to enforce the laws, (4) making employers punishable by imprisonment for violating the alien contract labor law, (5) holding steamship companies responsible for a term of years regarding character of their passengers, (6) requiring stricter civil and educational tests for nataralization, (7) requiring every immigrant to declare his intention of becoming a citizen. On all these questions the vote of the Cigar Makers' Union was affirmative by about 4 to 1. (Perkins, Vol. VII, Reports of Industrial Commission, 179, 180.)

8. *Boot and shoe trade.*—Mr. EATON, of the Boot and Shoe Workers' Union, thinks that fully 85 per cent of the workers in the boot and shoe trade are still native-born, although there are persons of various foreign nationalities also in the industry. In addition to the Irish, Germans, and French Canadians, a considerable number of Italians and Armenians have come into the trade within the past few years. They come to this country in destitute circumstances, knowing nothing of the customs and standards of living here, and they have had a very bad effect on the trade. These immigrants have also been an important factor in breaking strikes, having been especially imported for that purpose in certain cases. (Reports of Industrial Commission, Vol. VII, 369.)

9. *Iron and steel trades.*—Mr. SCHAFFER, president of the Amalgamated Association of Iron, Steel, and Tin Workers, says that the introduction of the lower class of foreign labor to the steel mills has done much to reduce wages, increase hours, compel Sunday work, and to lower the standard of the people. A large number of Poles, Hungarians, and Slavs have displaced unskilled American labor in steel mills. The proportion of foreign-born skilled laborers is comparatively small, since they are usually much less competent. They lack in knowledge, intelligence, and skill. It is found, however, that the second generation of the foreign classes are creeping up into the skilled work, having been educated by contact with American civilization.

In the tin industry foreign labor has competed very extensively, even in the skilled work. This industry being new in the country, it was perhaps natural that foreigners should be imported, although at about the time of the introduction of the tin manufacture there had been a considerable displacement of men in the boiling of iron and in the sheet-iron mills, and these men had, in considerable numbers, entered the tin mills. Many of the foreign laborers who have come into the trade have joined the unions and have become citizens; but some of them do not intend to remain, and they work excessively hard, without regard to the evil effect upon themselves and upon the trade. While the output per man has been raised gradually, according to the official agreements, from about 3,900 pounds in 1895 to 5,750 pounds in 1899 (on 30 gauge), the witness has recently known of a foreigner who has made as much as 7,500 pounds in 8 hours, defending this excessive work on the ground that he was making his money to go back to the old country. (Reports of Industrial Commission, Vol. VII, 392, 393.)

10. *Granite cutters.*—Mr. DUNCAN, of the Granite Cutters' National Union, says the granite cutters have not been materially affected by the importation of labor from abroad or from other States, but the quarrymen and paving cutters have suffered seriously by this practice. In fact, it has been the means of destroying in Maine and Massachusetts the prosperity of an industry which was a staple in both States a few years ago. It was then rare to find a paving cutter receiving less than from $2.75 to $3.50 per day. Italians and Finlanders have largely been brought in. Instead of being hired by the day, a part of the quarry is assigned to some 2 or 3 Finnish families, who work together, employing the boys of the families, supplying their own tools, and receiving so much per ton or thousand for the blocks cut, at rates so low that wages have been driven down to about $1.20 per day. The paving cutters' union has been destroyed. These low-paid men are shifted from one locality to another, according to the interests of the employers, being often used to fill the places of men on strike.

The witness attributes the riots among the foreign-born in Pennsylvania to this practice of importation of labor. He considers the protection which the authorities of various States have given to employers bringing in labor from other States unjustifiable, and believes that workingmen generally approve the position taken by Governor Tanner, of Illinois, Governor Jones, of Arkansas, and Governor Waite, of Colorado, in refusing to place the militia of the State at the disposal of the moneyed interests in this way. He does not approve of violation of law, however, nor do trade unionists generally so. The granite cutters have recently had a very unfortunate experience with the padrone system upon public works in New York. The law of that State requires that mechanics employed on public buildings shall be paid prevailing wages and work the prevailing hours. These in New York are $4 for 8 hours. It has recently been proved in court that contractors on public buildings have arranged with padrones to furnish Italian workmen in large numbers. These workmen pay the padrones $6 per week commission, which he turns over to the contractor, so that the real wage paid is only $3 per day instead of $4. The padrones manage the workers like so many sheep or horses. They are cautioned so that they may evade the law. Often they assume new names and falsely declare their intention to become citizens.

In the case of the particular padrone concerned in the transaction just described it was proved that he often gave to applicants for work, in case they refused to pay the required commissions, letters of apparent recommendation to contractors, which, because lacking some private mark, really indicated that the men were not to be employed, so that they would be put off with excuses.

Padrones sometimes endeavor to evade the law by not charging cash commissions, but by furnishing goods, renting tools, etc., to workmen at excessive rates.

Mr. Duncan advocates making it a criminal offense to act as an agent in such proceedings. He would also favor annulling the contracts for public works in case the contractor connived in such a padrone system. The licensing of employment offices by the State would also be advantageous. (See Reports of Industrial Commission, Vol. VII, Duncan, 206, 207, 212, 213.)

F. Distribution and employment of immigrants.—*Italian bureau.*—Dr. ROSSI, chief of the Italian bureau at New York, testifies that that bureau was established in 1894 and is supported by the Italian Government. Its first object was to restrict the evils of the padrone system by giving information to the Italian immigrant to protect him from the padrone and to render the padrone's services unnecessary. A second object was to find employment directly for Italian immigrants, scattering them throughout the States, especially in the agricultural districts. This latter part of the programme has not yet been carried out, as it would require large expenditure. The witness believes, however, that the existence of the bureau has mitigated to a considerable degree the evils of the padrone system. A great many immigrants bring with them a letter of introduction from some steamship agent or other person in Italy addressed to a banker or hotel keeper who is in connection with a padrone. Such immigrants are required to state to the Italian bureau the person to whom they are going and the reason for going there. In many cases the bureau informs the immigrant that the banker upon whom he has a draft can be compelled to bring the money to the bureau to cash it. Frequently Italians whose destination is to some distant point are assisted to go there directly without coming into contact with the middleman or labor speculator at New York. The bureau has also in various cases called the attention of the Italian consul to abuses of Italian subjects by padrones. (154–156, 159.)

Mr. POWDERLY states that this bureau was established about 1895. It met the immigrants at Ellis Island, nominally to give them information. The immigration commissioner became convinced that it assisted immigrants to evade the law and was practically an agent of the padrones. It was abolished, but later, on request of a representative of the Italian Government, was allowed to be reestablished. (43.)

Mr. MCSWEENEY says that by an arrangement between Secretary Carlisle and Baron Fava, the Italian ambassador, the Italian Government was permitted in 1894 to establish an agency at the immigration office in New York, primarily for the purpose of protecting Italian immigrants against imposition by padrones. It was understood that the arrangement was an experimental one, and the witness thinks that it has proved disadvantageous. The Italian bureau is supposed to be restricted in its action to the examination of passports and the aiding of immigrants who give their destination as New York. Those who are destined to railroad points are not reached by the bureau. The witness believes that at times the bureau has sought to fix the decision as to the admission of immigrants, and has otherwise interfered with the American officers, although there has been less difficulty in this regard during the past year than before. Moreover, the fact that Italians believe they will be protected on arriving in the United States tends to encourage undesirable immigration. The witness thinks also that the arrangement has proved ineffective as regards the breaking up of the padrone system.

The Government of Austria-Hungary also has a bureau at New York for aiding the immigrants from that country. It is carried on in an entirely different manner, however. The bureau has no office directly at the immigration office, but its purpose is to protect Austrians of all classes, furnishing them temporarily with lodging if necessary, and assisting them to secure labor. It is conducted by a private society for a subvention from the Government. (86–89.)

Mr. HOLMAN, secretary of the board of special inquiry at New York, says that although the board has never recognized the right of the Italian bureau to interfere in its proceedings, the bureau formerly did try to interfere. The head of the bureau, Dr. Rossi, disclaimed knowledge of this interference and took steps to prevent it. The witness thinks that there is no necessity or advantage in the maintenance of such a bureau at the immigration office itself. (135.)

Dr. ROSSI, chief of the bureau, specifically denies that the Italian bureau has ever sought to interfere with the United States immigration authorities. He declares that it is absolutely impossible for anyone to come in contact with the immigrants at all until after they have passed the inspection officers, although those who are temporarily detained for some reason, not being under the jurisdiction of the board of special inquiry, may be approached by representatives of the Italian bureau, as they are by steamship agents, representatives of benevolent societies, and others. No illegal means of reaching immigrants have been employed by the bureau.

Dr. Rossi declares, however, that there is great need for the existence of the bureau, especially for the sake of preventing impositions upon immigrants by padrones. The work of the bureau can not be attended to satisfactorily outside of the barge office, since it consists largely in warning immigrants against those who meet them immediately after leaving that office. Most of the immigrants could not be reached at all after they once fell into the clutches of their countrymen who are awaiting them. The witness, with his 3 clerks, is able to give information to such as are in special need of assistance, or to investigate the cases of those who arrive under suspicious circumstances and who are evidently likely to be defrauded by padrones. No other country, except Italy, has such need of a bureau of this sort for the protection of its immigrants. The Germans, English, and Irish when they arrive here are practically arriving at home. Italian immigrants arrive without even the most elementary knowledge of American customs and language. The bureau gives much important information. (155–157, 160.)

Mr. HALL thinks that the special agency of the Italian Government, the main purpose of which is to prevent immigrants from falling into the clutches of the padrones, has been, on the whole, beneficial. There have been charges made that the bureau has been in collusion with evasions of the law. (64.)

Austro-Hungarian Home.—Mr. RITTER, manager of the Austro-Hungarian Home and Free Employment Bureau, says that this institution is supported in part by the Austrian Government, and for the rest by the Austrian Society of New York and the Hungarian Relief Society. The Austrian consulate has supervision of it. Its work is to receive newly landed immigrants from the Austro-Hungarian Empire, to help them to reach relatives, when they have relatives, and otherwise to find employment for them. Its agent has a permit to go to Ellis Island and take out immigrants from the Austro-Hungarian monarchy. Immigrants are investigated as to their eligibility to land before being delivered into the care of the society, and the home, while it gives no bond, is regarded as responsible for the self-support of the immigrants. It undertakes to watch them for a year, with a view to the provisions of the law, to see that they do not become public charges within that time. Mr. Ritter thinks that the home handles about one-half of the Austro-Hungarian immigrants. The immigrants were afraid of the home at first, but now they have confidence in it. It has existed about 3 years. The men are put into positions as laborers in factories, and sometimes as porters in hotels or restaurants. Even intelligent men have to work as laborers, because of their ignorance of the English language. The women are largely provided with places as servants. Most of the single men settle down near New York. The labor market is greatly overcrowded there, and the agency is trying to disperse the immigrants over the country. A record is kept of every immigrant who comes to the home, his name, the place he comes from, his language, how much money he brings, the ship by which he came, his occupation, his destination, and, in the case of girls, the address of relatives: (219–222.)

G. Legislation governing employment agencies in New York.—Mr. BEALIN, superintendent of the Free Employment Bureau of the State of New York, says there is a law governing employment agencies in Buffalo, and one covering Brooklyn and one for New York; but there is no effective power of supervision in any officer. Moreover, there are persons who act as employment agents without a license. There is evidence to show that servants have repeatedly found places in families on the recommendation of employment agencies and have carried on a regular system of robbing their employers. The employment agencies in such cases are at least guilty of criminal negligence. (227, 228.)

Mr. Bealin states that the law requires the State Free Employment Bureau to keep a register of all applicants for employment, showing address, occupation, nativity, name of last employer, character, and duration of employment, cause for being unemployed, and whether they would be willing to go to the country. A reference blank is sent in each case to the last employer. Occasionally a fictitious address is given, as that of the last employer. There are very few applicants whose last employers do not speak of them as competent, sober, honest, willing, and obliging. The bureau has been in operation since July 20, 1896. It now averages a little more than 5,000 applicants for work in the year. In 1899 it found employment for 45.4 per cent of the applicants; in 1900, for 51.7 per cent. (223.)

In illustration of the need of State employment bureaus Mr. Bealin refers to the case of a woman of 50 whose husband and children were dead and who came to his bureau for employment and found it. If, he says, the State had not found her an opportunity to support herself it would have had to support her in the almshouse. (229.)

Mr. Bealin says that in the fall of 1896 the commissioner of labor made an investigation of the methods of employment agencies in New York. It was found that women were sometimes treated very coarsely and brutally, and that, contrary to law, fees paid to employment agencies were not returned when work was not found. Reports of similar conditions still come to Mr. Bealin's office, and he believes that matters are not much changed. He reports such cases to the commissioner, but the commissioner has no authority to act. A law like that which came near passage a year ago, giving the commissioner of labor supervision over the employment agencies, would go far to remedy these evils. (224.)

Mr. Bealin says that there are many respectable employment agencies in New York which recognize the wrongs which exist in the system and which favor a law to limit the possibility of these wrongs. (228.)

Mr. Bealin refers to the freight handlers' strike in Buffalo, which was caused, he says, by the necessity of going to a certain employment agency kept by a liquor dealer in order to get a place as a grain shoveler. The men who spent the most money at the bar were given the preference. In consequence of the strike that particular evil was cured, but similar conditions exist all over the State. (224.)

Mr. BROWN, deputy chief of the bureau of licenses of New York, considers that the fact that so few intelligence offices are complained against shows that the existing license law is a good one, and that as a rule the people in the business are reputable. There are offices which have been doing business under licenses for 18 or 20 years continuously without any complaint against them. There have been instances, however, in which a number of persons have paid fees to an intelligence office and the proprietor has then disappeared. He has got as many fees as possible and left the town. Statements have occasionally been made to the bureau about the sending of persons to places of ill repute, but the bureau has never been able to find that such things had been done. (232-234.)

Mr. HOTCHKISS, manager of the St. Bartholomew's Employment Bureau, New York City, states that this bureau is divided into 4 distinct departments—domestic, professional, mercantile, and labor and mechanical trades. The so-called professional department is chiefly for matrons for institutions, housekeepers, nurses, trained and untrained attendants, and similar workers. A fee of 10 per cent of the first month's wages is charged in the domestic and the labor department and 15 per cent in the mechanical and the professional. Until very recently a registration fee was charged, whether employment was obtained or not, of 25 cents for the domestic department and 50 cents for the other three. This has now been abolished, and no fee is charged except that contingent upon employment.

The number of applications from employers in all departments during the year ending October 31, 1900, was 3,713, and the number of applications from workers was 5,169. Employment was found for 2,592 persons, or almost exactly half the applicants. In the domestic department 72 per cent of the applicants obtained employment—20 per cent in the mercantile, 11 per cent in the professional, and 36 per cent in the labor department.

The expenses of conducting the office for the year were $5,759.93, or $2.22 for each person placed in a position. The average per capita expense in the last 5 years has been $2.15. Mr. Hotchkiss declares that the office is operated as economically as an office could possibly be. The bureau has hitherto been self-supporting, but since the abolition of the registration fee it has operated at a loss. Mr. Hotchkiss hopes, however, that it will be possible to cut down the expenses and bring them within the income. It is desired to make the agency self-supporting, chiefly in order that those who apply to it may know that they are not applying to a charitable institution. (240, 241, 243.)

Regulation of fees.—Mr. BROWN says that the New York law requires that if a fee is paid by an employer the employer must be supplied with a servant, who shall stay at least 1 month. A fee paid by an employee, with the understanding that he shall be provided with a place, must be returned unless a place is actually found for him. According to Mr. Brown's interpretation of the law it is permitted to divide a fee into two parts, one of which shall be a fee for registration and for the privileges of the office and the other a fee for procuring employment. If such a division is made, or if any fee is paid with the distinct understanding that it is paid for the privileges of the office, such fee need not be returned, even if employment is not found. This seems to Mr. Brown just, because the keeper of the office pays rent and hires clerical help and furnishes a place where employer and employee may meet. He performs an actual service, even if a given individual does not get employment. As a matter of fact, some intelligence offices charge a fee for registration and a further fee if employment is obtained. Some charge a fee only to the employee, and some charge both him and the employer. There is no legal limit on the fee that may be charged. Some intelligence offices, if they get hold of a man who is very anxious for work, will extort a large fee from him, if he has a little money, in consideration, perhaps, of a very poor place. Others deal fairly and even generously. Places are often found for servant girls without their making any payment, the keeper of the office trusting to their honesty to pay out of their wages. In many cases such debts are not paid. (231-233.)

Mr. HOTCHKISS, counsel of the Protective Association of Employment Agencies of New York State, considers that an employment agency is entitled to reimbursement for services rendered, even though no employment results. Even if no service were rendered beyond that of keeping a registry of names in a public office, applicants for employment might reasonably be expected to pay a fee for the maintenance of such registry. But an employment office is an active agency, requiring intelligent conduct of the search for employment by agent, and subject to expense for advertising, stationery, postage, etc., as well as rent. There are only two State laws which require that the agent shall receive no fee unless a position is obtained. One of these is that of Massachusetts. In Maine a fee of not over $1 may be retained when no position is secured. The ordinance of the city of Buffalo is similar. Mr. Hotchkiss considers such a fee fair for domestic and hotel agencies and for those which place workers at labor and mechanical trades. It would be inadequate for teachers' agencies. In addition to this registration fee, there should be a fee contingent upon employment, and preferably based upon the rate of pay. In New York city fees of from 10 to 15 per cent of the first month's salary, according to the character of the employment, are usual, though there are wide differences between those of different agencies. (240-242.)

ECONOMIC EFFECTS OF IMMIGRATION. LXXXVII

Frauds.—Mr. HOTCHKISS says that his knowledge of frauds perpetrated by employment agencies rests altogether upon hearsay. He quotes a passage from an article by Professor Bogart, enumerating certain frauds which are said to be common. The least of the abuses, says Professor Bogart, is " the universal practice of accepting a fee whether there is a prospect of finding a position or not, and of refusing to refund it when a position is not secured." More strictly fraudulent practices are the sending of laborers to distant cities, after accepting their fee, to fill purely fictitious positions; the maintenance of an agreement between an agency and a foreman, under which laborers, having paid their fees, are given employment for a few days and then discharged to make room for others; sometimes, in addition to this collusion between agency and employer or foreman, the sending of applicants to a guaranty agency which is also in the league, and which exacts another fee for looking up the references. " It is a not uncommon plan to have the employment agency located in the rear of a dramshop, which the men, who are purposely kept waiting in the hope of securing a position, will unfailingly patronize."

Mr. Hotchkiss, while he quotes Professor Bogart's statements without marked dissent, suggests that a person who is out of employment may easily persuade himself that he is a victim of fraud; not to speak of the possibility of consciously false accusations. In many cases, says Mr. Hotchkiss, allegations of fraud have been made when the proof was not forthcoming. (237.)

Mr. BROWN, deputy chief of the bureau of licenses of New York, states that during 1900 his bureau issued 91 new licenses and 335 renewals to intelligence offices in the city of New York, showing a total of 426 licensed offices. Seventy-two of the licenses and 276 of the renewals were issued for the boroughs of Manhattan and the Bronx, comprising the territory of the old city of New York. In the old city 39 new licenses and 152 renewals were issued in 1890. The growth has been gradual and fairly uniform. Some licenses are issued to church and charitable organizations, and many are issued to individuals who are held responsible for the business, although others are associated with them in the actual conduct of it. The fee is $25 for new licenses and $12.50 for renewals.

The law does not define an intelligence office. It simply provides that no person shall engage in the business of keeping an "intelligence office, employment bureau, or other agency," except under specified conditions. In practice, the licensed offices are chiefly for furnishing domestic help. A few restrict themselves to the furnishing of female help only, or of male help only, but most furnish help of both sexes. Some are accustomed to supply only help of particular nationalities. Some restrict themselves to certain kinds of service; for instance, cooks, or waiters, or barbers. (230, 231, 234.)

Mr. Brown says that the bureau of licenses of New York City has attached to it as a part of the police department a squad called the "ordinance squad," and one or two men are usually charged with seeing that the licensed employment agencies comply with the law, and that no employment agencies do business without licenses. The bureau has power to hear complaints and to revoke licenses for violation of law. The commonest complaints relate to the retention of fees, without furnishing employment, if the fee has been paid by an employee, or without furnishing a servant, if the fee has been paid by an employer. In such cases the usual course of the bureau is, after a hearing, to order that the fee be returned, or if it has been paid by an employer, that the agreed service be rendered. Mr. Brown declares that out of 426 licensed employment agencies he thinks the complaints are confined to perhaps 10 or 15. Yet he says, speaking of the number of complaints, "some days we have quite a number and other days none at all."

The present law does not require the keeping of registration books by employment offices, but the bureau is in the habit of requiring them to keep records, on the ground that proper records are implied in proper conduct of the business. Some agencies invariably investigate the references given by servants, and give employers the benefit of the results. (231, 232.)

Employment and politics.—Mr. BEALIN, superintendent of the free employment bureau of New York, says that the common laborer in New York, outside of the labor organizations, if he wants to get a job, for instance, on sewer digging or on the subway, must go to his district leader. If he is vouched for as faithful to the political organization which is locally dominant, he gets employment for a time, until he is displaced to make room for another. (224.)

Proposed law.—Mr. Bealin quotes in full the bill which was presented in the New York legislature, with the sanction of the university settlements, the Society of St. Vincent de Paul, the Bureau of Labor Statistics, and the better class of private employment agencies. It provided that no person should keep an employment agency in a city of the first or the second class without a license from the

LXXXVIII   THE INDUSTRIAL COMMISSION:—IMMIGRATION.

State controller, costing in cities of the first class $50 for the first year and $25 for each succeeding year, and in cities of the second class $25 for the first year and $12.50 for each succeeding year. No saloon keeper might conduct an employment agency in any building where liquor was sold or offered for sale. Every employment agency must enter in the register the name and address of every applicant for employment, the name and address of his last employer, and the name and address of the person who should employ him. The name and address of every person who applied for help, with the name and nature of the employment, must also be registered. These registers must be open to the inspection of the commissioner of labor or his agents. The bill forbade publishing any false or fraudulent notices or advertisements, giving any false information, making any false promise as to work or employment, or making any false entry in the registers. Mr. Bealin explains that these provisions would make it possible for the agents of the commissioner of labor, by comparing advertisements with the registers, to determine whether fraudulent advertisements had been published. The bill also forbade the sending of any female help to any place of bad repute. It required giving a receipt for every fee, and provided that if employment was not found, or was not accepted through the agency, within one month, the fee must be returned on demand. This bill was passed by the assembly and finally died in the senate committee merely for lack of time. (225, 226.)

Mr. HOTCHKISS, counsel of the Protective Association of Employment Agencies of New York State, presents the objections of that association to the Ford-Kelsey bill, which failed to pass the legislature of New York, and which Mr. Bealin quotes in his testimony and regrets the loss of. In the first place, it is regarded as an unjust discrimination to exempt teachers' agencies and agencies for actors from the operation of the law. Second, the bill, as first presented, required an annual license fee of $200. This would be not a license fee but a tax, and would wipe many agencies out of existence. Indeed, the provision was advocated on the ground that the lessening of the number would make inspection easier, as well as on the ground that the surplus receipts of the tax would enable the department of labor to establish free employment bureaus in various parts of the State. Such taxation of the city in order to establish free bureaus elsewhere is an added injustice, and the suppression by excessive taxation of many agencies which are performing valuable services, both for employers and for employees, is unfair to the agencies and detrimental to the public good. Mr. Hotchkiss believes, on the basis of a North Carolina case which he refers to, that the suppression of such businesses by law, directly or indirectly, is unconstitutional. The Protective Association of Employment Agencies, however, assented to a fee of $100 for the first year and $50 annually thereafter. This is regarded as sufficient to pay for the administration of the law, including all expenses of inspection.

The Protective Association favors a bond of $2,000, with responsible sureties, but Mr. Hotchkiss's individual opinion is that such a bond should run not to the municipality, but to the party aggrieved by any fraudulent practice, so that he might receive compensation.

The Protective Association favors the requirement of the keeping of certain books and the entering of certain information in these books, so that proper officers may make a proper inspection and the police may be aided in tracing thieves who may have registered at employment agencies. The association does not think, however, that the Ford-Kelsey bill outlined a proper system of books. Moreover, while the association believes in a system of inspection, it holds that inspections should take place only on the sworn complaint of an applicant for employment or an employer. This would avoid unnecessary disclosure of confidential communications, and would avoid the possibility of making lists of unemployed workers for partisan election purposes.

Finally, the bill is held to be unconstitutional as to the section which forbids that any fee be retained in the case of an applicant for employment who shall not obtain or accept a situation. Mr. Hotchkiss quotes an opinion of Mr. Carl L. Schurz to this effect. Mr. Schurz points out that the conduct of an employment agency requires outlays of labor and money, and that to command, as the bill in question does, that persons be permitted to make use of the facilities of the agency without payment is to take from the licensed person his time and his money without reimbursement. It is admitted that the prices to be charged in certain kinds of business affected with a public interest may be regulated by law. This bill does not propose to regulate prices, but orders that certain work be done without any payment whatever. The phrase "or accept" is especially objectionable, since it leaves to the option of the applicant to take from the employment agent the entire fruits of his labors, however faithful and successful they may have been. Finally, it is even questionable whether this business is one so affected with a public interest that legal regulation of its charges is admissible. All the cases in the United States which have sustained such regulations relate to commercial carriers, ferrymen, hackmen, etc. (237–239.)

Mr. BROWN dislikes paternal government and thinks the less legislation we have changing the existing laws about employment agencies the better. For instance, to require a bond of the keeper of such an office would be very hard upon many married women on the east side, who add to the family income by keeping intelligence offices and who keep entirely reputable places. Mr. Brown would, however, approve a law which should provide a small fee for registration and a further fee to be paid when the place was found, and to be graduated according to the value of the place. (234, 235.)

Employment agencies—Field of work.—Mr. HOTCHKISS, manager of St. Bartholomew's Employment Bureau, New York City, says that the bulk of the work of hiring labor and seeking employment will continue to be done directly between workmen and employers, and that the labor bureaus can not serve the workmen of organized trades so efficiently as well-managed trade unions. The organized workers look out for themselves. The chief field of usefulness of labor bureaus is likely to be found, not necessarily in the less skilled employments, but in those which are unorganized. (241.)

Organized labor—Care for unemployed.—Mr. BEALIN says that the labor organizations find work for their own unemployed. Some unions have places where men out of employment are taken care of. Some, as the printers, have a regular system of publishing information as to opportunities for employment. It is the business of the walking delegate to find work for the members of his union. (223, 224, 229.)

Age as a cause of unemployment.—Mr. BEALIN says that the average woman who earns her living as a domestic can find no place after she is 45 years old. The average man can find no place as a common laborer after he is 50 if he shows his age. (223.)

IV. CAUSES INDUCING IMMIGRATION.

A. In general.—Dr. SENNER says that the causes affecting immigration are very complicated, partly local, partly individual, partly national, partly economic. It is impossible to regulate the amount of immigration by statute, since the causes acting in foreign countries are beyond our control. Dr. Senner does not think that overpopulation of European countries is the chief cause of immigration from them. People who come to this country largely do so from a desire for better opportunities; they are ambitious. A few come on account of the republican principles of our Government, as in the case of the Mennonites, but this is not usually an important motive. (167, 183.)

Dr. Senner attributes the increase of immigration from southern Italy and other countries of southern Europe largely to the desire to anticipate the enactment of educational restrictions. He says that only three years ago a new steamship line was started exclusively in view of the restriction agitation in this country. On the other hand the decrease in immigration from Germany and other northern countries of Europe, in spite of the prosperity of the United States, is chiefly due to the restrictive effect of the existing immigration law, with its inconvenience and vexations, even to those not coming under the excluded classes. The decrease in immigration from these countries can not be altogether explained by the development of their own industries or by the thorough settlement of the United States. (167, 168, 179.)

B. Prosperity of country.—The most important influence affecting immigration, says Mr. HALL, is the degree of prosperity in this country. Thus there was a great falling off in immigration immediately after the panic of 1837, and again in 1844. In 1854, during a period of great prosperity, the immigration was 427,000, a number increased by the Irish famine and the revolution in Germany. In 1860 the outbreak of the war reduced the immigration to 90,000. The immigrants numbered 438,000 in 1872 and only 261,000 in 1874, after the panic. A maximum was reached in 1882, during a period of general prosperity, which was followed by a decrease during a period of depression. The immigration then increased gradually up to 1892, when it reached 580,000. Since that time the hard times have kept the immigration low, but the history of the past leads to the opinion that as soon as industrial conditions are favorable the tide of immigration will again rise.

The fluctuations of immigration according to the prosperity of the country are largely accounted for by the fact that immigrants come in many, if not most cases, by the inducements of friends and relatives who have come before. The reports of the immigration bureau for 1896 show that, of 263,000 persons arriving, 95,000 were going to join their immediate families, mostly having had their tickets prepaid. (49.)

Dr. SENNER also says that immigration tends to fall off in times of industrial depression. This effect would be seen the more clearly if the character of the immigrants who arrive during periods of depression should be carefully studied. A large proportion of them would be found to be members of the immediate families of former immigrants or persons who had already been in this country before. (182.)

C. Advertising in Europe.—Dr. SENNER declares that the effect of advertising by the land-grant railroads, immigration associations, etc., has been greatly exaggerated. Though such advertising is being done continually, the people have become accustomed to make much allowance in considering it. Several of the States—Michigan, Wisconsin, and others—have permanent colonization bureaus in Europe, but their effect is very small. Comparatively few colonies are established in this country by immigrants. (182.)

D. Steamship companies. (See also *Existing legislation*, p. CIII.)—Mr. SCHULTEIS declares that steamship companies use all means to procure steerage passengers, because of the high profit. The average steerage passage fee $22.50; the cost to the company only $1.70. Over $118,000,000 is invested in steamship lines; practically all owned by foreigners. Dividends as high as 17 per cent are paid by some lines. The companies sell prepaid tickets largely. They advertise that free public land can readily be obtained in the West. Some advertisements state that each family can get 160 acres, an additional 160 acres by timber culture, and 160 acres more for each adult in the family. (24, 25.)

Steerage rates.—Mr. HALL says that the reduction in steerage rates on ocean vessels has been a material factor in increasing the number of immigrants. At times of rate wars the immigration has been especially heavy. The advertisements of opportunities in the United States by railroad and steamship lines and by steamship agents has had an important influence. The antisemitic agitation has had the effect of driving Jews to this country. (49.)

Mr. ROSENDALE understands that the steamboat lines have their agents in the little European villages to entice men to come to America as miners. He has been told by men, who would be glad to go back if they could, that they were enticed by circulars scattered in their villages by the steamship agents. These circulars stated that a miner could earn $2.50 to $3.50 per day, a fabulous sum to those people.

The steamship agents also work among the people in this country and entice them to buy tickets on the installment plan for their relatives and friends. The agents drum up custom like life-insurance agents. (189, 200.)

Mr. RITTER, manager of the Austro-Hungarian Home, of New York, says that nearly all the Hungarian and Slavic immigrants get their tickets from agents who induce them to come over. He believes, however, that these agents work simply for the commission they get on the transportation tickets and are not employed by persons or corporations in this country. (221.)

Mr. SCHWAB, agent of the North-German Lloyd Company, declares that the carrying of immigrants is relatively a less important part of the business of steamship companies now than in former years. The cabin business has increased with great rapidity. It is not true that the revenues of steamship lines are excessive. The North-German Lloyd Company during the past 20 years has paid 5 per cent dividends on the average. (103, 105.)

Mr. Schwab states that the steerage rate on the express steamers of the North-German Lloyd Company is $38.50 from Bremen to New York, and on the slower steamers $36.50. (104.)

Mr. TER KUILE, agent of the Fabre Steamship Company at New York, states that the fare from Naples to New York by that line is $28. He thinks it was about $25 in 1881 when the company commenced operation. (115.)

Mr. FLOYD, of the Cunard Steamship Company, says that the steerage rate from Liverpool to New York on that line is $25 on some tickets and $27.50 on others. He thinks the present rate is a reasonable one, but that the former low rates probably had some effect in stimulating immigration. (117.)

Mr. LEDERER, of the American and Red Star lines, says that the steerage passage from Antwerp to New York is $29.50. He does not think that the increase in the rate has affected immigration. (119.)

Messrs. Schwab, Floyd, and Lederer agree in thinking that the steerage rates at present are about 50 per cent higher than in 1880.

Mr. SCHWAB testifies that the increase in steerage rates has been due to an

CAUSES INDUCING IMMIGRATION.   XCI

agreement between the steamship lines made in Europe. There are three "conferences" of transatlantic lines—the North Atlantic, the Mediterranean, and the Continental. The lines of the Mediterranean conference have the exclusive right to book American passengers from Italy. There is no combination of agencies by the different lines, but simply an agreement concerning rates. The rates could not profitably be advanced beyond the present figures, since to do so would tend to reduce traffic. (107–109.)

Mr. FLOYD also refers to this agreement concerning rates, as well as to the consultations held by agents of different lines on this side of the ocean. (118.)

Mr. SCHWAB, of the North-German Lloyd Company, believes that 60 per cent of all immigrants come on tickets bought in this country or with money sent from this country. He declares, however, that this is assisted immigration of the right kind. Immigrants come under these circumstances only when their friends and relatives in this country know of openings for them. When the country is prosperous the number of persons coming in this way increases. (104.)

Mr. TER KUILE, of the Fabre Steamship Line, says that about half of the immigrants by that line in 1898 came on prepaid tickets. (115.)

Mr. LEDERER, of the American and Red Star lines, states that about 40 or 45 per cent of the immigrants on those lines come on prepaid tickets. (118.)

Mr. SCHWAB declares that no reputable steamship company is guilty of attempting to induce immigrants to come to the United States. Moreover, this is prohibited by stringent laws in most of the European countries, for the reason that these countries depend for military service on the young men who are likely to emigrate. Only agents licensed by the government are permitted to sell tickets, and Mr. Schwab declares that numbers of agents of the North-German Lloyd have had their licenses revoked because they have sent circulars to persons whom they thought would emigrate.

Similarly the agents who sell prepaid tickets in this country do not attempt to stimulate immigration or to solicit the sale of tickets. It would hardly be possible for them to do so if they tried, and the small commission on tickets, $2, takes away the motive. (103, 107.)

Mr. Ter Kuile, of the Fabre Steamship Company, believes that the class of immigrants from Italy has decidedly improved during the past 5 or 6 ye rs. Most immigrants come from the agricultural districts. The number who come in defiance of law is constantly decreasing. The Italian Government aids in rejecting those immigrants who might be rejected in this country. One of the regulations of law prohibits agents of steamship companies from procuring "the departure or embarkation of persons whose immigration is not permitted to the countries to which they are directed." Immigration generally is discouraged by the Italian Government. (115, 116.)

Prepaid tickets.—Mr. MCSWEENEY believes that, while the proportion of immigrants who come to this country upon tickets actually bought for them by friends on this side may not be more than from 40 to 55 per cent, yet if those persons be also included whose tickets are paid for by money sent from this side the proportion whose passage is prepaid would be about 65 per cent. The witness believes that the majority of persons coming on prepaid tickets are a desirable class. But there are many tickets sold by peddlers on the installment plan, and the chances are that those coming on such tickets will be of a more undesirable class. For the sake of checking this practice a provision has been suggested prohibiting the sale of tickets except by authorized agents of steamship companies. Mr. McSweeney thinks that the reputable steamship companies would favor such a statute. (95.)

Mr. LEDERER does not think that the agents of the steamship companies in the United States solicit the fellow-countrymen of possible immigrants to buy tickets. Such a practice would not be successful even if tried. A man who wishes to bring over one of his friends or relatives seeks the ticket agent.

Mr. Lederer also declares that European countries prohibit the solicitation of emigration. (119.)

E. Assisted immigration.—*Attitude of British Government.*—Mr. MCSWEENEY says that at present the chief source of assisted immigration is Great Britain, and such immigrants come largely by way of Canada. The practice on the part of the British Government itself of giving wholesale assistance to criminals and paupers to emigrate has been largely discontinued, but the various local authorities seek to pass on paupers from their own jurisdiction, and finally they are apt to reach Liverpool and be given passage to Canada. It is a common boast among steamship officers that such immigrants can easily find their way to the United States. (87, 88.)

Mr. HALL says that the laws and the actions of the courts in foreign countries to some extent tend to aid the emigration of undesirable persons to the United States. It was formerly the case that certain British societies made a business of aiding discharged convicts to emigrate, but this is scarcely done at present. (60.)

Mr. SCHULTEIS says that the law prohibiting the landing of convicts is laxly administered. European countries largely send criminals here to get rid of them. There are 160 societies organized in England for this purpose. Evidence as to such action is obtained from statements of societies themselves, from money orders cashed here, etc. Judges in England encourage emigration by giving short sentences in prison with long periods of surveillance after discharge. Crime increases in years when immigration is high and in localities where immigrants chiefly settle. (26, 27.)

Mr. STUMP says that not more than 2 or 3 persons are returned yearly on ground of being criminals. The local governments of Europe sometimes pay the passage money of criminals, but the steamship companies do not connive knowingly with evasion of our law. Previous to 1893 the Prisoners' Aid Society, of London, sent ticket-of-leave men to the United States, but since the act of 1893 it has ceased to do so, and believes that none are sent from England. An isolated case of a habitual drunkard sent to this country by local authorities in Switzerland was also mentioned by this witness. (12, 13.)

Attitude of Italian Government.—Mr. STUMP says the Italian Government is entirely willing to have its subjects come to the United States, since they usually save money and return to Italy to spend it. The Government does not desire that United States laws be violated, but desires that they be fairly enforced, so as not to prevent those really eligible from immigration. (14.)

Mr. McSWEENEY says that it is the policy of the Italian Government to encourage emigration, especially temporary emigration, of those who return and bring money to Italy. On the other hand, during the war with Spain and the depression of industry about that time, the Italian Government instructed the local officers to discourage emigration. During 1898, however, as stated in the letter from the American embassy at Rome, the Government reduced the railway fare to the seaboard for all emigrants by 50 per cent. (89.)

Dr. ROSSI denies that the Italian Government seeks to encourage emigration to the United States. He admits that emigrants frequently return with money or send back money which is invested in property from which the Government collects taxes, but does not think that the Government gains especially by this fact. The Government continues to treat as Italian citizens, designated as "colonists," such persons as come to this country but have not taken out naturalization papers and are subject to military service in Italy.

Dr. ROSSI states, further, that every Italian who is deported from New York is given by the Italian bureau at that port a card stating why he has been deported. Under the Italian emigration laws the immigrant is then entitled to prosecute the agent who has sold him the ticket. The Italian Government has, on the complaint of the bureau at New York, withdrawn the licenses from various steamship agents in Italy and punished others. The witness states, also, that the Italian Government has adopted the practice of giving to convicts who emigrate to the United States a certificate, stating the causes of imprisonment, the length of the term, etc. The witness knows of only one case where a convict has come to the United States from Italy with a passport, but without such a certificate. Italian criminals sometimes come to this country from ports in other countries of Europe and over which the Italian Government has no control. (154-160.)

Dr. ROSSI, chief of the Italian Immigration Bureau at New York, says that the circular referred to was issued by the Italian Government at the suggestion of the Italian bureau at New York in view of the fact that many immigrants had landed at that port without the proper address of relatives or without sufficient money. The circular simply urged the various local officers to see to it that no emigrant should be given a passport unless he could meet the conditions required by the United States law, and added that this was the more to be recommended since the United States was then engaged in war with Spain, which would naturally reduce the demand for labor. After the war ceased emigration to the United States naturally increased. (158.)

Attitude of Austro-Hungarian Government.—Mr. RITTER, manager of the Austro-Hungarian Home, says that the Austro-Hungarian Government does not desire emigration to this country, but would prefer to keep its people at home. Neither the Government nor provinces or municipalities encourage emigration, and Mr. Ritter does not think that any undesirable person has received public aid in emigrating to this country. (221.)

Hebrews.—Mr. WOLF estimates that there are between 9,000,000 and 10,000,000 Jewish people in the world, of whom 5,000,000 or 6,000,000 live in Russia. The

CAUSES INDUCING IMMIGRATION. XCIII

ancestors of the Russian Jews moved eastward from the Rhineland under the persecutions during the middle ages, and were welcomed by the Kings of Bohemia and Poland. They lived there in peace until Bohemia was conquered by Austria and Poland by Austria and Russia. Investigations made by Mr. Wolf and others in 1876 indicated that at that time there were only 150,000 Jews in the United States. Recent estimates show between 800,000 and 900,000. These estimates are based upon the returns of the synagogues.

Mr. Wolf asserts that there were more Jews in both the Northern and the Southern army during the civil war in proportion to population than men of any other faith. (250.)

Mr. SCHULTEIS says that various European countries have laws restricting immigration, which, though general in scope, really apply only to Jews. Wealthy Jews, especially the Hirsch Immigration Society, aim to bring all pauper Jews to the United States or elsewhere. At present they are paying fully $30,000,000 a year to sustain 3,000,000 paupers within Russia itself. Jews entering this country do not join labor unions. They monopolize the tailoring business and similar light work, but will not do heavy manual labor. They increase the number of middlemen also. (28, 29.)

Mr. STUMP says that emigration of Jews from Europe has been largely assisted by the Baron Hirsch fund, which is managed by an incorporated company with a capital of $10,000,000. This company does not now aid emigration to the United States, but rather to the Argentine Republic. Many Russian Jews, however, come to this country, chiefly from Libeau. The German steamship companies have secured a law of Germany to inspect persons entering Germany from Russia, which largely restricts the coming of Jews. Russia has some excuse for severe measures against the Jews, since they often claim to be subjects of Turkey and refuse to pay taxes or render military service. (13, 14, 22.)

Mr. WOLF declares that there is scarcely any Jewish immigration from countries where the Jew is recognized as a citizen and treated with equality. Of the Jewish immigrants who entered Philadelphia in the year ending November 1, 1900, more than 99 per cent were registered as coming from the Slavic countries of Central Europe. It is in those regions, Russia, Roumania, and parts of Austria-Hungary, that the violent persecution of the Jews has existed. Of the immigration to the United States from Austria-Hungary during the fiscal year 1900, 16,920 out of a total of 114,847 were Jews; of the 6,459 immigrants from Roumania, 6,183 were Jews; of the 90,787 immigrants from Russia, 37,011 were Jews. On the other hand, there were only 17 Jews among 1,739 immigrants from France, 337 among 18,507 from Germany, 4 out of 1,190 from Belgium, 2 out of 735 from Holland, 114 out of 4,247 from the Turkish Empire, 133 out of 48,237 from the United Kingdom, and only 2 out of more than 100,000 from Italy. In the most of these countries there are many Jews. There are Jews in the Parliament of Italy, in its army, and in all the walks of civilized life; but in all these countries the Jews are free to live like other citizens, and they cling to the lands of their birth. Among the 31,151 immigrants within the year from Denmark, Sweden, and Norway there was not a single Jew, though these countries contain a considerable number of Jewish inhabitants. (247, 252, 253.)

Dr. SENNER says that at one time the Russian edicts against Jews greatly increased the emigration from that country to the United States, and that a considerable proportion of those then coming were assisted immigrants. The effect of those edicts has now ceased. The Baron Hirsch fund was never used to any considerable extent in assisting immigration, except in the way of helping families to come together. It was largely applied to more or less unsuccessful agricultural experiments, but principally to educational purposes. (171.)

Mr. WOLF calls attention to the fact that the political rights of the Jews of Roumania were guaranteed by the treaty of Berlin. That treaty has, however, practically, though not formally, been repudiated. The provisions of equality of rights for the Jews have been evaded. The Jewish inhabitants have been placed by gradual encroachments in the legal status of foreigners, and naturalization laws have been so framed as to make the acquisition of citizenship by Jews practically impossible. The Jewish children have been excluded from the schools; private schools established by the Jewish people have been harried and taxed into insignificance, and the existence of the Jewish community has been made impossible, except on condition of unbearable burdens of taxation. Within the last 2 or 3 years, as a result of the Dreyfus agitation, antisemitism has broken out afresh in Roumania. In May, June, and July, of 1900, a veritable panic arose among the Roumanian Jews. During those 3 months more than 20,000 of them left their country. Some went to Turkey, some to Cyprus, and the rest turned westward toward England and America. The resultant industrial disturbance brought on a commercial crisis in Roumania, which resulted in the overturning

XCIV   THE INDUSTRIAL COMMISSION:—IMMIGRATION.

of the antisemitic cabinet, and in an improvement, at least for the time being, of the condition of the Jews. (247, 253.)

Mr. Wolf states that the American Jews have always discouraged the immigration of European Jews, and that they are in full accord with the laws to prevent the immigration of criminals, paupers, and diseased persons, and all persons who are unfitted to enjoy the franchise. Yet Mr. Wolf declares that the vast majority of the immigrants of all nationalities who have come in the last 50 or 60 years, and who are now the bone and sinew of American citizenship, came in practically the same condition of poverty in which the majority of immigrants now come, and which is often made the pretext for projects of exclusion. (245, 246, 249.)

Mr. Wolf says that the first organized effort of American Jews to care for Jewish immigrants was made at the time of the Russian persecution in 1882, and the consequent exodus. The American Jews at that time undertook to care for such Russian Jews as found their way to America, distributed them in various parts of the country, cared for their necessities, and provided them with means of work as well as means of subsistence. At the same time they took measures to discourage the movement to this country. They appointed representative men to go to Europe and confer with leading Jews in London, Berlin, Frankfort, Vienna, Paris, and other centers. to divert as much as possible the stream of refugees. Notices were published in the Jewish press of the disturbed districts, warning the people against precipitate flight from their homes, and especially against indiscriminated immigration to America. A great deal was accomplished by this means, and only a fraction of the immense number of expatriated Russian Jews came here.

After continuing for a year or two, the exodus diminished for 7 or 8 years, until 1891. Then the same conditions, or worse, broke out again. The neighboring States of Austria and Germany tried to stem the tide of refugees. The condition of the poor people became most deplorable. Despite efforts to prevent it, a considerable number came to the United States, and a large proportion of them settled in New York.

There has never been among the Jews of the United States any organization which has encouraged or desired the wholesale influx of European Jews. Since the immemorial traditions of the Jewish people require that they care for their own, such immigration places a heavy burden upon the American Jews, and one which they by no means desire to take up. There is no fund available in this country for paying the transportation hither of any of these refugees or immigrants. (245–247, 249.)

A paper quoted by Mr. Wolf asserts that while the value of the Zionists' hope can hardly be appreciated by the Jews who live under American conditions, the way of Palestine is the nearest way to the redemption for the Jews who live in the shadow of the Middle Ages in Russia, Roumania, and Austria, and its goal is nearest to their hearts. (254.)

V. EXISTING LEGISLATION RESTRICTING IMMIGRATION.

A. History of legislation.—Mr. McSweeney states that the first immigration law, passed in 1882, sought to regulate immigration rather than to restrict it. It provided for a head tax to defray the expense of regulation and the relief of immigrants who fell into distress. The law declared that no convict, lunatic, idiot, or person unable to take care of himself without becoming a public charge, should be admitted to land. But there was no provision for returning such persons to their homes. Between 1882 and 1891 Congress sought to restrict the immigration of contract labor. In 1891 the law was amended by more strictly defining the persons to be excluded and the methods of excluding them. This act was amended in 1893. The new law excluded a still larger number of persons, it being estimated that as a result of the law fully 50,000 persons were refused the sale of tickets within a year after it was passed. Various administrative changes were also made, such as the requirement that immigrants shall be manifested by the steamship company in groups of 30, and the establishment of a board of special inquiry to investigate doubtful cases.

The excluded classes as at present defined are as follows:

"All idiots, insane persons, paupers, or persons likely to become a public charge, persons suffering from a loathsome or a dangerous contagious disease, persons who have been convicted of a felony or other infamous crime or misdemeanor involving moral turpitude, polygamists, and also any persons whose ticket or passage is paid for with the money of another, or who is assisted by others to come, unless it is affirmatively and satisfactorily shown in special inquiry that such person does not belong to one of the foregoing excluded classes, or to the class of contract laborers excluded by the act of February 26, 1885." (77, 78.)

Mr. McSweeney states that the supervision of immigration at that port was under the control of State commissioners appointed by the governor of New York up to 1890, when it passed to the United States Government. In January 18, 1892, the station at Ellis Island was first occupied. At present, that station having been destroyed by fire, the inspection is carried on at the Barge Office, on the Batery, in New York. The witness believes that the administration has been much more efficient under the United States than under the State. (76.)

Application of immigration laws.—Dr. ULLO, counsel of the immigration bureau at New York, states that the United States immigration laws sometimes use the word "alien" and sometimes the words "alien immigrants." Some of the courts have held that the law applies only to alien immigrants and not to aliens generally. Many immigrants formerly declared that they were coming to visit or as tourists. Moreover, the courts have held that a person who has been in this country before is not to be considered an immigrant, so that there was no way for the time being of applying the law to "birds of passage." In 1894, in connection with the appropriation for enforcing the Chinese exclusion act, Congress enacted that the examination of aliens by the immigration department should be final unless appeal should be taken to the Secretary of the Treasury. This has been held to apply to all aliens, not merely to Chinese, but at the time of the testimony of the witness, July, 1899, a case involving the application of this provision was pending. (141.)

B. Inspection and registration.—Dr. SENNER declares that the recent decrease in immigration is largely due to the restrictive effect of the law of 1893. This is shown conclusively by the failure of immigration to increase during the past year of great prosperity. The steamship companies and their agents, being financially responsible for debarred immigrants, exercise extreme caution, rejecting large numbers of applications for tickets, while a still larger number of would-be immigrants are deterred by the annoyances of the minute inquiry made by the agents. On landing in the United States the immigrant is scarcely ever delayed less than 24 hours, and if his admission is doubtful he may be held for 1 or more weeks, during all of which time he is subject to constant vexations and is treated as a prisoner. The steerage passengers are not allowed to leave the ship until after every cabin passenger has left. There are only 4 or 5 lines of persons passing through the inspection office at the same time. When there are 800 or more immigrants on a vessel the progress is very slow, and a large proportion have at least to be detained until the next day. One of the chief objections to the educational test arises from the necessary increase in these delays and inconveniences. (168–179, 180.)

Although Mr. HALL believes that the methods of inspecting immigrants are at present fairly satisfactory, he asserts that under the present law only a very small proportion of the undesirable immigrants are excluded. The actual number debarred varies from one-half of 1 to 1 per cent of the total number of immigrants. The question whether a person is likely to become a public charge is by no means a definite one. The inspector is frequently hurried and can not ask a question in sufficient detail to learn the facts. In case of appeal or reference to a board of special inquiry, the procedure is so cumbrous that it is not frequently resorted to. (58.)

Mr. MCSWEENEY states that each emigrant on buying his ticket is required to answer a list of questions identical with those on the manifest list of the steamer and with those asked by the inspection departments in this country. His answers to these questions are forwarded to the captain of the vessel at the port of embarkation, and the names are made up into lists of 30. These lists are sworn to by the captain of the ship and attested by the United States consul. (77.)

Mr. McSweeney says that it is possible for immigrants to make misstatements concerning the questions asked in the manifests prepared by the steamship companies. The last 4 or 5 questions on the manifests especially are usually answered without special thought. Moreover, the character of the paper and writing materials used in the manifests is so poor that they are likely to become valueless as records within a very short time. (92, 101.)

Mr. FITCHIE, commissioner of immigration at the port of New York, describes the organization of the immigration bureau at that port and its methods of work. The department is divided into several branches—the contract labor bureau, Marine-Hospital Service, registry division, board of special inquiry, statistical division, boarding division, matron's division, and law department.

Certain officers of the department go down New York Harbor to meet incoming vessels. They examine first and second cabin passengers on the vessel itself unless it is necessary to land certain ones at the office for further investigation. The steerage passengers are brought to the Barge Office in New York City. There they are first examined by the marine-hospital surgeon, and those suffering from contagious and other diseases are excluded. Passengers are then examined by the registry clerks, being asked the same questions which appear upon the manifests prepared by the steamship companies. If there is any doubt in the mind of a registry clerk as to the desirability of an immigrant, he is referred to the board of special inquiry for further examination. This board consists of 4 of the inspectors specially designated by the commissioner. One hearing is held by the board with no one but the immigrant present; at a second hearing his friends and others are admitted. The finding of this board is final unless appeal is taken to the Treasury Department at Washington. The decisions of the board are usually sustained by the Department. (70–72.)

Mr. STUMP says that when a vessel arrives at New York an immigration officer boards her and examines the manifests. Passengers in the first and second class cabins are also examined to prevent evasion of the contract-labor law. When immigrants are landed they are passed before a registry clerk and are required to answer again the same interrogatories as appear on the manifests. Doubtful cases are referred to a board of 4 inspectors. All immigrants are specially examined by a surgeon. Matrons examine women as to health and pregnancy. (9, 10.)

Mr. DOBLER, an inspector at New York, states that no person is permitted to mingle with the steerage passengers while or after reaching quarantine until they have passed through the inspection office. He believes, however, that if immigrants are detained at the office the steamship agent or near relatives are permitted to communicate with them in the presence of an inspector. There are cases where railroad agents and others attempt to communicate with passengers, but it is always detected and prevented. (149, 150.)

Mr. MCSWEENEY says that the first examination of immigrants is by the medical department. As the immigrants pass in line on their way to the registry or inspection clerks the doctors draw to one side all whose appearance is suspicious and they are specially examined. The immigrants then pass to the inspectors in several lines, each containing 30 persons who have been entered together upon the manifest prepared by the steamship company. The registry clerks almost all speak German, Italian, and Yiddish, and there are some who speak the Slavonic languages, and at least one who speaks the Oriental languages. The immigrants are questioned in their own language. Each registry clerk has the steamship manifest before him and examines each applicant to ascertain if there is any discrepancy. If there is any doubt as to whether an immigrant is entitled to admission, he is referred to the board of special inquiry.

Although sometimes as many as 4,000 persons pass through the office in a day the witness believes that the verification of the manifests is quite correct, at least so far as the counting of the immigrants goes. Occasionally there is a discrepancy between the number of names on the manifest and the actual number of immigrants on board. Some passengers may have decided not to embark at the last moment, or others may have come on board too late to be entered in the manifest, which is prepared at the head office of the steamship company. Occasionally an immigrant who is entered upon the manifest escapes inspection, but this is not common. (81, 84, 85.)

Dr. SENNER declares that there is great inconvenience and delay under the present methods of inspection. There should be a larger number of inspectors, so that at least 10 different lines of immigrants shall be undergoing inspection at the same time. Great difficulty also arises from the inability of the inspectors to speak the language of the immigrants. Speaking through an interpreter requires double the time, besides involving great uncertainty as to the correctness of the replies. The interpreters at New York are paid only $1,000 per year, whereas court interpreters are paid about $2,000. During Dr. Senner's administration, 1893–1897, there were no permanent interpreters for the Portuguese language or for some of the Asiatic languages or for some of the Slavonic dialects. There should be more permanent interpreters employed with provisions for securing interpreters temporarily for rarer languages. The inspectors themselves, especially those belonging to the board of special inquiry, ought to have a large command of languages. (180, 181.)

Qualifications of immigration inspectors.—Dr. SENNER thinks that the immigration officers at present are scarcely qualified for the satisfactory performance of their duties, however honest they may be and however well determined to carry out the law. An immigration inspector ought to be able to judge each individual according to his merits on the basis of many considerations. For this purpose he needs especially knowledge of the language of the immigrant. To rely upon a few poorly paid and incompetent interpreters is to secure incorrect information. It is also necessary that the inspector understand the peculiarities of the various races and nationalities. It would doubtless be advisable to send immigrant inspectors to foreign ports that they might mingle with immigrants and detect attempts to evade the law by direct observation; but this is impossible since the inspectors can scarcely, if at all, speak the language of the immigrants. (169, 170.)

Mr. FITCHIE testifies that all of the appointments in the immigration department, except those of laborers, are protected by the civil-service regulations. As a result there have been few changes in the staff at New York when the commissioner has been changed. Practically the same force has been employed during the 2 years of Mr. Fitchie's administration as during the 4 years preceding.

Mr. Fitchie does not think that the application of the civil-service examination to the position of immigration inspector is desirable. The system is satisfactory enough for clerical positions, but no academic examination based on book learning or linguistic knowledge can be a guaranty that the person will have the necessary common sense and honesty to decide whether an immigrant is desirable or not. The bureau at New York has had difficulty with men who have been chosen under the civil-service rules. The law moreover protects men who have never taken an examination. The witness refers especially to an instance of the appointment of an assistant engineer for a period of 4 months during the winter. A man having long experience in steam and electrical engineering was appointed by the commissioner, but the Civil Service Commissioners sought to supplant him, recommending men who had passed an examination but who had had little or no experience. It was finally decided, however, to allow the first appointee to remain. In another case a man who had been rejected by the chief engineer as unfit for the position appeared at the head of the next list of eligible candidates sent from Washington.

Mr. Fitchie does not think that the protection of a civil-service law is necessary to prevent the displacement of competent men. The appointing power can refuse to recommend the dismissal of men who are essential to the work. Moreover, civil-service laws throughout the country often fail to prevent the displacement of good men, evasions being winked at in many cases. (72-75.)

Inspection of cabin passengers.—Mr. DOBLER, an inspector at New York, testifies that he has charge of the inspectors who board the incoming steamers at quarantine for the purpose of examining cabin passengers. He has under his direction 3 contract labor inspectors and 6 assistants. The passengers are examined during the hour or hour and a half between touching at quarantine and landing at the dock. This scarcely gives sufficient time for thorough examination. Whereas each registry clerk at the Barge Office meets only 30 immigrants at a time, usually in the second cabin of the steamer 2 men are confronted with 100 or 150 passengers, and the procedure is necessarily less systematic. Nevertheless, most of the immigrants are questioned, although sometimes passengers, especially those in the first cabin, are permitted to go without examination rather than to detain them. Sometimes, however, passengers are detained temporarily on shipboard until examined.

Cabin passengers are asked questions calculated to ascertain whether they are likely to become a public charge or whether they come under contract to perform labor in the United States. To ascertain these facts they are asked concerning their occupations, their intentions in coming here, their destination, etc. If a person is found who has no occupation or who has little means, or who is suspected to be a contract laborer, he is brought to the Barge Office for further investigation. The boarding division also sees to it that unprotected women who have no one to meet them are taken to the Barge Office while awaiting their friends.

Mr. Dobler says further that officers of the foreign consulates or other persons are sometimes permitted by the customs authorities to board the steamers at quarantine, and in that case they have free access to the cabin passengers, but no one is allowed to mingle with the steerage passengers until they have passed through the inspection office. (147-150.)

Medical inspection.—Dr. WILLIAMS, of the Marine-Hospital Service, detailed to inspect immigrants at New York, testifies that the law requires that the medical inspection of immigrants shall be made by a medical officer of the Marine-Hospital Service. Some of the medical inspectors under Dr. Williams board the vessels at quarantine and examine the first and second class passengers. The steerage passengers are examined by the witness and an assistant, and to some extent by the chemist of the department at the Barge Office. The witness thinks that the force is fairly sufficient.

The rigidity of the inspection depends upon the general appearance and character of the immigrants. There are many shiploads in which passengers are so obviously in good health that only casual inspection is necessary. The greatest difficulty is found with the Italians and Syrians, especially the latter, who are peculiarly subject to trachoma. These are usually stopped and their eyelids examined. (126–128.)

Dr. SAFFORD, a surgeon in the immigration service in New York, testifies that the medical inspection of steerage passengers is usually conducted by 2 and sometimes by 3 inspectors. The first inspector looks chiefly at the hands, head, and eyes of the immigrant. The second looks for other matters, while the third checks the other two. Suspicious persons are taken from the line and examined more thoroughly. Sometimes such persons are required to remove their clothing or are sent to the hospital for inspection. Immigrants needing treatment are sent to the hospital. The medical inspectors report those who are afflicted with dangerous contagious diseases to the commissioner, who attends to their deportation. A record is also kept of physical defects, incipient blindness, heart disease, etc., and these circumstances are taken into consideration in the decision of the board of special inquiry as to whether the immigrant is likely to become a public charge.

Dr. Safford states further that the medical department has occasion sometimes to examine those who have been landed for some time in whom a contagious disease afterwards develops. Such persons are sometimes returned to Europe, the evidence of their affidavits as to the disease being checked by the records of the original inspection and by the evidence of the diseased condition itself.

During the month of May, 1899, out of 44,754 examined, 178 immigrants were deported on account of contagious diseases, while in addition record was made of 1,224 cases of minor defects. (130–132.)

Mr. POWDERLY declares that the present medical examinations of emigrants before embarkation are insufficient. If examined in England, the inspection is exceedingly hasty, passengers passing the physician at the rate of about 2,000 an hour, often without even uncovering their heads. The English physician is under no obligation to the United States, but acts only under British laws to protect the health of the emigrant while on ship. The United States should have its own physicians to examine before embarkation. (35, 38.)

Dr. WILLIAMS, of the immigration bureau at New York, does not consider the medical inspection of emigrants at European ports very efficient in most cases. The inspection at Liverpool is better than anywhere else. The ship surgeon there examines all passengers, sometimes on shore, but sometimes necessarily on board. In addition the Government has 2 medical inspectors, who examine the steerage and second-cabin passengers on board, with a view to excluding those having contagious diseases.

The witness believes that some cases of contagious diseases are rejected by the ship surgeons in Europe. The surgeons, however, practically do not recognize the existence of trachoma (granulated eyelids) or favus (scaldhead), which are not so readily observable as some other contagious diseases. There is no attempt to isolate those having trachoma or favus while on board the ship.

Dr. Williams says that at present there is no requirement of law that all emigrants shall be bathed and disinfected before going on board, except in case the United States, under the quarantine law of 1893, sends a medical officer to some foreign port to inspect passengers where there is special danger of contagious diseases. The witness thinks that it would be desirable to require bathing and disinfection, although the steamship companies would object to it on the ground of the delay after the emigrant arrives at the port of embarkation. The requirement is more necessary because of the crowded condition of the steerage. (129, 130.)

Inspection of women.—Mrs. STUCKLEN, matron of the immigration bureau at New York, states that it is her duty, together with her assistant, to inspect the women as they pass in line with a view to ascertaining whether they are pregnant. Those who are believed from a superficial examination to be in that condition are taken to one side for further inspection. Those who are with their husbands, or are going to their husbands, are allowed to pass. If a pregnant woman is unmarried, but is going to her intended husband, an attempt is made to bring him to the Barge Office and get him married to the woman. On an average there is 1 marriage at the office every day, frequently under these circumstances. There are many other marriages of persons who have come together on the steamship and have been cohabiting there or before embarkation. During the fiscal year 1898–99 52 unmarried women who were pregnant were deported. In some cases—24 during that year—relatives of such women receive them in this country.

The matron's department also detains and cares for women and children awaiting the arrival of relatives, or assists them to take passage on trains for their destination. Sometimes children as young as 2 or 3 years of age are sent in charge of the steamship officers to be forwarded to relatives in this country. The matron's department sees to it that such children are sent on the proper trains and that their relatives are duly notified, or they are held until their relatives come to New York. (145, 146.)

Mr. POWDERLY says that there is frequent evasion of the law as to the entrance of women. Steamship companies or friends arrange with some man on this side to meet a woman coming alone and claim her as wife to avoid difficulty. Frequently a man and woman becoming acquainted on steamer claim to be married purely for this purpose. An instance is cited. (42, 43.)

Board of special inquiry.—Mr. MCSWEENEY says that on the average from 85 to 87 per cent of the immigrants were passed by the registry clerks directly. The remainder, amounting in 1898–99 to about 25,000 persons, were examined before boards of special inquiry. The proportion of those who require special examination varies greatly in the case of different vessels. The amounts paid by the different steamship companies for feeding and caring for immigrants during their detention afford a fair index of the character of the immigrants. These amounts vary from 2 cents per capita for the passengers on board to 50 cents. On some vessels only 3 or 4 may be detained for further examination, while a ship bringing immigrants from Italy may have one-half or three-fifths of its passengers detained. In such a case the work of the immigration bureau extends over many days, and sometimes there are several boards of special inquiry sitting at the time. Delay is not caused by ignorance of the language, since most of the inspectors have a smattering of a number of different languages, and there are competent interpreters as to practically all. (90, 96, 101.)

Mr. HOLMAN, secretary of the board of special inquiry at New York, testifies that that board consists of 4 inspectors specially designated. It examines cases referred to it by the registry clerks or by the medical department. After taking the testimony of the immigrant or of others a vote is taken as to permitting him to land. An affirmative vote of 3 members is required for admission. Any member dissenting has the right to appeal to the Secretary of the Treasury, and the immigrant has the same right. The decisions of the board, however, are seldom overruled.

The board usually examines during the busy season about 100 cases per day, the time for each case sometimes being insufficient. Some cases require more investigation than others; this is especially true of contract-labor cases. Sometimes 3 or 4 boards are in session at the same time, although usually 1 is sufficient. (134.)

Mr. WEIHE, a member of the board of special inquiry at New York, says that from 75 to 125 persons are usually examined by the board daily. Families will be questioned as to their destination, as to who paid their passage, where they obtained their money, etc. If they have relatives in the United States or have sufficient means they are admitted. Sometimes they are held until it can be learned whether the persons to whom they are going are able to care for them. Sometimes the evidence of such persons and of friends is awaited. Questions are asked of immigrants as to whether they have been guilty of crime. Questions also concerning contracts for labor, although this matter has been previously investigated by the contract-labor bureau. Sometimes persons suspected of coming as contract laborers are held for several days to await further information. The longest period of detention is perhaps 3 or 4 weeks. (150, 151.)

Care during detention.—Mr. MCSWEENEY says that while they are being detained in the building the immigrants are fed at the cost of the steamship company. The meals are furnished by a contractor under competitive bids. It is in the power of the commissioner to supervise the character of the food, and Mr. McSweeney believes that it is entirely satisfactory. (85, 86.)

Mr. STUMP also says that the expense of maintaining immigrants during investigation is now met by the steamship companies, although there was some dispute as to it at first. The companies also bear expense of deportation. They usually cheerfully comply with all laws and regulations. It is the duty of the companies also to communicate with the friends of the immigrant. (10, 20.)

Dr. ULLO, counsel of the immigration bureau at New York, says that the inspection system has been greatly improved under the United States administration. The methods were formerly mere chaotic. The system of preliminary examinations with ultimate decisions by a board of special inquiry is particularly advantageous. The steamship companies seldom complain as to the judgments passed concerning immigrants, but they do complain of the fact that immigrants prolong their detention by appeals to the Secretary of the Treasury, thus increasing the expense of the steamship company for maintenance. (139.)

C. Chinese immigration.—Mr. ALLEN, a representative of the Advance Labor Club of Brooklyn, believes that the number of Chinese in the United States is constantly and rapidly increasing. He refers to a report of the House Committee on Immigration of 1892, stating that Chinese were being smuggled into the United States at the rate of 20,000 per year. He says that while the census of 1890 put the Chinese population at 107,000 the secretary of the Chinese Equal Rights League, in his petition against the Geary law, claimed that there were 150,000 Chinese in that organization in this country. There is a steady expansion in the Chinese quarters of New York and other cities. The witness quotes from an article from the New York Herald of November 28, 1896, in which it was stated that the Chinese-inspector stationed at New York had submitted an elaborate report to the Secretary of the Treasury specifically charging collusion on the part of the officials at Malone, N. Y., in admitting Chinese laborers brought by the Canadian Pacific Railroad. This report also charged that many Chinese landed at New York from Cuba, either falsely claiming to be merchants and thus not subject to exclusion or else giving their destination as some point in Canada and being permitted to land under bond that they would continue passage to that country, a stipulation which was evaded in various ways. (162, 165.)

D. Contract labor.—*Inspection methods.*—Mr. QUINLAN, supervising inspector of the contract-labor bureau at New York, states that there are in his department about 30 employees, 15 being regular inspectors. The officers of the quarantine division of the department board the vessels not belonging to the regular lines; those of the boarding division meet incoming steamers at quarantine and examine cabin passengers, while those of the contract-labor bureau proper examine steerage passengers at the Barge Office in order to detect violations of the contract-labor law and to work up cases in shape for presentation to the board of special inquiry. The inspectors of the contract-labor bureau usually stand beside the registry or inspection clerks and listen to their questions and answers, which sometimes serve to bring out suspicious circumstances, and if any case attracts attention the immigrant is taken to one side and subjected to special examination. There is a considerable degree of cooperation between the registry clerks and the contract-labor inspectors. Occasionally the bureau is notified in advance that some person is expected to arrive who has been sent for to take the place of an American workman. On the whole, however, the bureau receives little assistance from organized labor.

Mr. Quinlan thinks that the contract-labor bureau should have a larger force and that it should receive greater appropriation than that of $100,000 which Congress now gives it. There should be at least 10 more inspectors. In the rush of work at present, through the shortness of the force, many suspicious persons must be permitted to slip through. For example, the fact may be noticed that a group of immigrants are all destined to the same place and that each has a small sum with him. Nothing can be proved without detailed investigation. If the bureau had a larger force, a man might be sent to follow such groups and to obtain evidence. About 4,000 contract laborers have been deported during the 6 years in which Mr. Quinlan has been connected with the department, but he believes that many contract laborers have come in in spite of all possible vigilance. (120, 123-125.)

Mr. DOBLER, an inspector of the division whose duty it is to examine cabin passengers on board vessels, states that in his opinion many persons coming to perform labor under contract take passage in the cabins, especially in the second cabin, with a view to escaping the stricter examination to which steerage passengers are subjected. The inspectors on shipboard do all they can to discover such persons and to bring them to the Barge Office for further investigation. The witness states further that passengers sometimes declare that they are coming to take employment in the belief that they will be more likely to be permitted to land on that account, since they would thus be less apt to become public charges. In examining cabin passengers, persons making such statements are sometimes found on second examination not really to be under contract and are permitted to enter without detention at the Barge Office. (149, 150.)

Mr. HOLMAN, secretary of the board of special inquiry at New York, states that in the case of persons suspected of coming to labor under contract the immigration inspector reduces the result of his examination to an affidavit, which the immigrant signs. This affidavit is presented to the board of special inquiry and the immigrant is further examined. Usually such cases are given prompt attention, since if the immigrant finds that he is to be deported he may change his mind and claim that he is not under contract. Some immigrants have the idea that if they do not have work promised they may be sent back as likely to become public charges, but the board usually warns them that this is not the

EXISTING LEGISLATION RESTRICTING IMMIGRATION.   CI

case and simply urges them to tell the plain truth. After this first hearing the person who has promised the work or other persons often appear, frequently with the means to employ a lawyer.

The witness thinks that the law should be amended to make it more possible to punish the persons who offer inducements to immigrants. (135, 137.)

Deportation of contract laborers—Penalties, prosecutions, etc.—Dr. ULLO says that there is no very specific provision of the laws giving authority to the immigration department to debar contract laborers. The title of the original law of 1885 implied this power, while the law of 1887, which in its terms referred only to the persons who make contracts in this country, nevertheless states that persons included under the prohibition of the act shall not be permitted to land, but shall be sent back. The law of 1891 also mentions contract laborers under the list of undesirable aliens who may be deported. (140, 141.)

Mr. WEIHE, an inspector, of New York, declares that it is not the intention of those who proposed the contract-labor law that persons coming under contract should be deported, as is the present custom. The main purpose was to punish the contractor in this country rather than the immigrant, but it has been found impossible to convict the contractor as the statute now stands. (154.)

Interpretation of contract—Relatives, etc.—Dr. ULLO says that the courts have held that where an immigrant coming under contract is debarred and deported the person making the contract in this country can not be held, since the immigrant has not been actually imported. (140.)

Further difficulty, Dr. Ullo states, is occasioned with regard to the interpretation in the provision in the contract-labor law which excepts aliens coming to perform work in a "new industry not at present established." It is very difficult to determine what is a new industry, as was found in a case relating to diamond cutters. Moreover, it is uncertain whether the law refers to industries not established in 1885, when the original statute was passed, or to those not established at the time of the importation. (140.)

Dr. Ullo refers to the case of the importation of a minister for service at Trinity Church in New York. The lower court decided that, being under contract, he was to be excluded, since ministers were not provided for by the specific exceptions in the law. The Supreme Court of the United States, however, decided that this was not within the spirit of the law. Since then the law of 1891 has made an exception for ministers and for persons belonging to any recognized profession. But this last exception is held not to apply, for instance, to managers of great business enterprises or to newspaper men. Sometimes a house which has business both in the United States and in Europe may wish to bring one of its managers from Europe to this country, and there is doubt as to whether he is entitled to enter under the law. (144, 145.)

Dr. Ullo testifies that the contract-labor law especially provides that no person in the United States is prevented from sending for a relative or friend who does not belong to the excluded classes. The witness does not think it advisable to hinder efforts of immigrants in this country to help their friends to find positions. (143.)

Mr. WEIHE refers to one particular case in which a company, through its manager, wrote to Wales for men, promising them a certain wage. The department of immigration was told that the case could not be prosecuted because the company was not criminally responsible for the acts of its manager, who had written a letter making the contract. (151, 152, 154.)

Mr. STUMP says that fines as high as $30,000 or $50,000 have been imposed; e. g., against Phillips Hosiery Company in Rhode Island, but cases are usually compromised. (19.)

Evidence of contract.—Mr. QUINLAN says that it is usually difficult to prove that the head of any enterprise has formally made a contract for bringing laborers from other countries. The more common practice is for the foreman of a mine, for example, to inquire of his foreign workmen whether they have any friends or relatives whom they would like to bring to the United States. The object in each case is to replace Americans by those who are willing to work for less money.

The witness also refers especially to the recent case where about 15 Croatians came to this country, destined for Rathbun, Iowa. They stated that they were farmers, but immediately on arriving went to work in a coal mine. They were about to be deported, but it had been impossible to prove that their coming had been due to formal contract. (123.)

Mr. Quinlan declares that the requirement of the courts that it must be proved that a contract has been made in a foreign country in order to convict the person making the contract makes it practically impossible to secure the necessary evidence. There have been thousands of deportations by the department on evidence sufficient to convince the inspectors, but there have been very few convictions of those importing the labor. Most cases which have actually been brought have been compromised. The only recent case of conviction was that of John Wanamaker, who imported a salesman from London.

The witness refers especially to one recent instance of the importation of a number of stevedores. These persons came to New York on the inducement of a letter, but the counsel of the department declared that it would be impossible to convince a judge that this constituted a violation of the law. In another case two cigar makers came from Habana on the strength of a letter which stated: "If you come over here you can go to work in my factory on Murray street at $20 per week." This was a contract, but the judge charged the jury that the contract was not made in foreign lands, so that there was no case.

In view of this condition Mr. Quinlan advocates an amendment to the contract-labor law, authorizing the exclusion of any alien who comes to this country on the strength of any inducement, request, or suggestion that work can be secured, and also the punishment of persons who shall make such inducements, requests, or suggestions, whether in this country or elsewhere. (121, 122.)

Mr. WEIHE declares that it is very difficult to get accurate information as to contract labor. Most of the evidence comes through the confession of immigrants themselves. Before those who confess are deported, however, evidence is often taken from the alleged contractor, who usually denies that a contract has been made. The authorities believe that persons have often secured work for the immigrants who swear that they have simply invited the immigrants to come to the country and sent passage money as friends. The witness believes that laborers are often coached as to what they shall say in order to avoid detection. The usual way in which such immigrants come is by invitation from some one of their own countrymen who has been made foreman of a gang in this country.

Mr. QUINLAN says that the immigration authorities use some discretion in their application of the law excluding contract labor. If a man comes to this country to work with his brother he will not be interfered with. On the other hand if a tailor or a person in a skilled trade should write to his first cousin or other relative saying, "If you come over here I can get you a job," the witness thinks the immigrant ought to be sent back. The inspectors have not so far excluded farm laborers. It is possible to make the law ridiculous by being too stringent. What the witness desires is to protect the laboring man in established industries against the foreigner who is willing to work for less money. Just at present there is a demand for additional labor in this country, but for the most part imported labor is simply destined to take the place of American labor. (124.)

Working of the law.—Mr. STUMP, while believing that wholesale importation of contract laborers has practically been stopped, also refers to the difficulty of securing the punishment of the person making contract in this country, since the chief witness, the laborer himself, is promptly deported. The law is also evaded by making promises to make a contract upon arrival. It is desirable to pass an amendment to reach this practice. (5.)

Mr. WEIHE says that there are still many cases in which groups of from 5 to 100 laborers come to the United States under some sort of an arrangement amounting to a contract, even where it is impossible to prove the contract definitely. The witness refers especially to a recent case in which a number of Italians each claimed to be going to join a cousin in Wampum, Pa. In another case, about 20 Dalmatians and Croatians arrived.. They denied that they had been promised work, but were all destined for Rathbun, Iowa. Investigation showed that when they arrived at Rathbun they were immediately put to work in the mines. It appears that some of their relatives or friends had secured this work for them, and at the time of the witness's testimony they were about to be deported as being contract laborers. The witness believes that in most such cases the men are induced to come to this country because they will work for lower wages, and that they accordingly displace American labor. American labor organizations have no particular objection to immigrants coming to this country without previous contract and taking their chances in the same way as American laborers. (151-153.)

E. Criminals.—Dr. ULLO refers to the fact that the immigration law provides only for the exclusion of persons convicted of crime. Cases have arisen where immigrants have landed who were charged with murder and who were confronted with witnesses against them, but in the absence of action by the Government of the country from which they come the Immigration Bureau has no power to debar them. In one case the American courts held that there was sufficient evidence to justify the extradition of a criminal, but it was only on the ground that he had no money that the Immigration Bureau was able to order him

EXISTING LEGISLATION RESTRICTING IMMIGRATION. CIII

deported. The statute also gives no power to deport immoral persons generally. (141, 142.)

Exclusion of polygamists.—Mr. McSWEENEY testifies that there is a constant stream of Mormon converts coming to this country. These usually come in the charge of a Mormon elder and travel in the second cabin of the vessels. The great majority of them are women; the witness has been told that from 90 to 95 per cent are usually women. They will deny that they are polygamists or intend to become such, and the Immigration Bureau has been unable to prove anything against them that would warrant exclusion. (90.)

F. Immigration through Canada and its inspection.—Mr. McSWEENEY refers to an address made in the Canadian parliament in 1890, in which it was stated that from 1870 to 1880 341 675 persons landed in Canada from Europe. By comparing the total number of foreign-born persons in the country, according to the censuses of 1870 and 1880, making allowances for deaths, it appeared that 184,820 of these had been lost, doubtless chiefly by emigration to the United States. Similarly while 653,510 immigrants came into Canada during the period from 1881 to 1890, more than one-half have gone into the United States. The Canadian people apparently do not wish thus to lose a large proportion of their immigrants. (92, 93.)

Mr. STUMP states that the law does not provide for restriction of immigration from Canada. An attempt was made to secure the cooperation of the Canadian Government in restricting immigration of Europeans through Canada to the United States, but it was opposed by the Canadian people. Finally the United States Commissioner made an agreement with the Canadian steamship companies which were anxious to secure immigration business to aid in inspection, allowing United States officials to board ships. Finally they agreed to pay the United States head tax as to those destined to this country. The railways agreed to transport none without a certificate of inspection. The companies even pay the head tax on persons who remain some time in Canada before entering the United States. Canadians themselves not restricted. (15–18.)

Mr. SCHULTEIS says that a large number of immigrants evade the head tax by giving some place in Canada as their destination, and remaining there a short time only before entering the United States. Canadian workingmen themselves protest against British policy of allowing free immigration to Canada. Inspectors should be placed along the Canadian border. (28.)

G. Hardships of deportation.—Mr. McSWEENEY states that hardships often arise in the enforcement of the exclusion provisions. Thus the law is peremptory in excluding idiots, insane persons, and those suffering from trachoma or dangerous contageous diseases. Cases sometimes arise where a child is brought by its parents who must under the statute be excluded, and no power is given to the Commissioner to consider the fact that the parents are able to care for the child, and he is in doubt whether to allow the parents to land, sending back the child, or whether to send the family back. A regulation of the Treasury Department that one parent should be returned in such cases has been held invalid by the courts. On the other hand, the provision of the law that persons shall be excluded who are likely to become a public charge can not be effectively applied to children coming with their parents who are likely to be supported for the time being, and yet who may be miserable degenerates, and sooner or later very apt to become burdens to the community. (78.)

Mr. STUMP says that the rigid terms of the law often work hardship, separating families and preventing single individuals from making arrangements with friends, relatives, and others in order that they may not land without anything to do. An amendment is recommended that the law shall not prevent near relatives from aiding each other to immigrate, whether by pecuniary aid, maintenance, or promise of employment in connection with the business of such relative. (5, 21.)

Mr. POWDERLY says that usually when persons send for their relatives and promise employment in their own establishments, this is not treated as a violation of law. No restriction should be placed on assistance in any form to near relatives (43.)

H. Steamship companies.—*Inspection before embarkation.*—Mr. STUMP says that previous to 1893 steamship agents in Europe were little restricted as to persons to whom they sold tickets. The result was an indiscriminate emigration to the United States. The act of 1893 requires captains of vessels to prepare lists of passengers, and to swear that they know of none prohibited entry by United States law. The steamship surgeon is also required to swear that no passenger is unfitted for labor, or afflicted with prohibited diseases. The companies have accordingly instructed agents to exhibit the United States laws, and not to sell tickets to persons prohibited, holding agents responsible for the expense of returning rejected immigrants to their homes. Agents thus become the most effective inspectors under the law. (9, 20.)

Dr. SENNER, declares that the examination of immigrants by the ticket agents of steamship companies who are officially responsible for those who are debarred is the most efficient means of excluding undesirable classes. (180.)

Dr. ULLO thinks that there are instances in which steamship companies willfully bring persons who belong to the classes excluded by United States law. Instances have been proven in which the companies have taken deposits from passengers in order to protect themselves in case of nonadmission. The witness thinks that steamship companies should be subject to punishment if such willful action can be proved, and would favor giving the passengers who have been induced to come over the right to prosecute the companies. Dr. Ullo thinks also that the steamship companies, or the company rather than the officer or individual, should be held responsible for violation of the law. (142, 143.)

Mr. SCHWAB believes that the present practice of holding steamship companies responsible for immigrants brought is just in principle and highly effective in practice. The agents who sell tickets in Europe are compelled to exercise careful scrutiny of every passenger, since it is for the interest of the company that no passenger shall be subject to debarment. The North German Lloyd Company, at any rate, has carefully instructed its agents, giving them full statements of the laws and holding them responsible for the expense of returning debarred immigrants. The witness believes that this inspection by the agents of the company is much more effective than inspection by consular officers or through direct representatives of the United States Government. The steamship companies wish always to be on the safe side and are, if anything, excessively cautious. Agents of the North German Lloyd Company in Europe frequently cable to the representatives of the company in the United States inquiring whether it would be wise to accept certain passengers, and the reply is usually in the negative. Circulars issued to agents selling prepaid tickets in this country also contain careful statements concerning the class who are excluded under the law.

In support of these general statements, Mr. Schwab submitted a number of circulars addressed by the North German Lloyd Company to its agents in different parts of Europe, together with the notice which is appended to the printed letter sent to applicants for steerage passage, the question blank attached to each ticket, which must be filled out before it is sold, and translations of the American immigration laws into various foreign languages for posting in the offices of agents in Europe. These various documents seem to show clearly that the most explicit instructions concerning the excluded classes are given to all agents, and that they are warned to exercise great caution in accepting passengers and are held responsible for those who are debarred. (102, 104, 109-114.)

Mr. STUMP says that the rules of the American Line state in detail the classes excluded, inform agents that the law is strictly enforced, and request them to use the utmost care in accepting immigrants and to consult the head office in doubtful cases. Agents are held responsible where they have failed to exercise due care in excluding prohibited persons. (20.)

Mr. SCHWAB says that all immigrants sailing from Germany by that line are subject to medical inspection by a doctor or doctors in the employ of the company. This inspection is held at Bremen, 30 miles from the actual point of embarkation.

Since most of the dangerous diseases are found among passengers coming from the south of Russia, the North German Lloyd Company has established 7 "control stations" on the frontier between Prussia and Russia, for the examination of emigrants from that country. At each of these there is a practicing physician and a force of attendants. The other steamship companies sailing from Germany and Holland contribute toward maintaining these control stations and make use of them.

The regulations of the steamship company also require careful inspection of the passengers on board of the vessel daily. On the larger vessels there are two physicians, and on the smaller, one. These must have passed the rigid German medical examination. The purpose of this inspection, which is not required by law, is to avoid danger of contagious diseases, which might result in long delay of the vessel at quarantine. The inspection is scarcely as effective in stormy weather as at other times. (105-107.)

Mr. FLOYD, of the Cunard Steamship Line, says that all passengers of the Cunard Line are examined at the port of embarkation, and if there is any doubt as to their admission into this country under our immigration laws they are rejected.

Moreover, the ticket agents are very careful to inquire as to the character of immigrants, since they are held accountable for those who are rejected. (117.)

Mr. Floyd, of the Cunard Steamship Line, says that as regards Scandinavia that company has a system of detaining and inspecting emigrants in the interior of the country. British and Irish passengers, who have to come but a short distance from their homes to the port, are examined at the port of embarkation. (177.)

Mr. LEDERER, of the American and Red Star lines, testifies that the agents of those lines in Europe are furnished with verbatim translations of the United States immigration laws and are given explicit instructions to refuse tickets to those who would be excluded under the laws. Similar circulars are sent to agents in the United States engaged in the sale of prepaid tickets. These two companies do not seek to take passengers who are likely to be returned. Immigrants must be at the port of departure for inspection 48 hours before the vessel sails. (118, 119.)

Mr. Lederer says that immigrants are required to be at the port 48 hours before the vessel sails for the purpose of medical and other inspection. (119.)

Mr. TER KUILE, of the Fabre Steamship Company, thinks that the inspection of immigrants by that company at Naples is very rigid, having been materially improved since the report of an American commission as to the inefficiency of the examination at that port. (115.)

Mr. HALL, of the Immigration Restriction League, admits that the steamship companies make some efforts to prevent undesirable emigrants from taking passage for fear that they may be compelled to return them to Europe. On the other hand, a company sometimes takes a doubtful person and charges him double the passage money in order to protect itself. (61.)

Return of deported persons.—Dr. WILLIAMS mentioned several specific instances where persons who had been deported on the ground of being afflicted with loathsome and dangerous contagious diseases had returned again within a short time on the same vessel or upon other vessels or other lines. He states that the agents of steamship companies are informed of the deportation of any immigrant, so that they are put on their guard against bringing him back again. (128.)

Dr. ULLO says that cases have been proved in which immigrants, after being deported, have been brought back to this country by another steamer. Immigrants have stated that the officers and agents of the steamship company told them that they could come back, and have put them in the first or second cabin for the sake of evading inspection. (142.)

Dr. SAFFORD also mentions instances in which persons who had been rejected and deported on account of contagious diseases or for other reasons have afterwards returned to the United States. (131.)

Mr. TER KUILE, of the Fabre Steamship Company; Mr. FLOYD, of the Cunard Line, and Mr. LEDERER, of the American and Red Star lines, all deny knowledge of any case in which a person who has been deported from the United States has subsequently returned to this country by the same line. They declare that the companies have no desire to incur the risk of a second rejection. (114, 117, 119.)

Sailors—Kidnapped by crimps.—Mr. ROSENDALE tells of a case in which a Jewish immigrant, 4 months in this country, was enticed by crimps, made drunk, and shipped as a sailor. He worked for 4 months and when he landed again in Philadelphia his wages were $3.75. (193.)

VI. PROPOSED AMENDMENTS TO IMMIGRATION LAW.

A. Need of further restriction.—Mr. SCHONFARBER, of the Knights of Labor, says that organized workingmen throughout the country, even those who are unskilled, believe that some restriction of immigration is absolutely necessary. Even men, like the witness himself, who are sons of foreigners believe in some restriction. The witness thinks that statements concerning the opposition of the Germans and Irish in this country to restriction of immigration must be taken with a grain of salt. The Knights of Labor have at various times demanded that Congress should enact restriction laws. The organization believes that only those foreigners should be admitted who will add something to the material welfare of the country by bringing a certain amount of money and giving assurance of ability to earn a living. The witness himself, however, does not believe in the property qualification for immigration, nor does he think that the Knights of Labor lay much stress upon it. A mechanic or laborer of intelligence and ability will add more to the wealth of the country than a rich man. The Knights of Labor have also expressed themselves in favor of the educational restriction under the Lodge bill. Mr. Schonfarber doubts whether the people of the United States generally understand that proposed measure sufficiently well to know what they think about it. He does not believe that an educational restriction will be altogether effective in protecting American labor, so long as capitalists are able to import skilled workmen to take the places of native labor. (435-437.)

Mr. SCHAFFER, of the Amalgamated Association, would favor the exclusion, if possible, of certain undesirable classes of immigrants, especially those from southeastern Europe, the Hungarians, Poles, Russians, and Italians. He suggests as a possible means of accomplishing this end an increase of the head tax to $25 or even $100. This would compel skilled laborers to contribute more to the revenue of the Government and would shut out unskilled laborers. The witness has known of skilled men who have earned as much as $12 or $15 per day in the steel mills, but who have never become citizens. A prohibition upon the entrance of "birds of passage" would be desirable if practicable. At any rate, it would be well to require all immigrants on landing to take oath of allegiance to this country, making them subject to our laws and to taxation, but not conferring full citizenship. (394, 395.)

Mr. EATON, of the Boot and Shoe Workers' Union, says that the rank and file of trade unionists favor a restriction of immigration. His own organization has voted for restriction. Restriction is advocated even by some of the foreign born themselves, although their tendency is usually against it.

The witness doubts the advisability of an educational test. Its restrictive effect at any rate would be slight, since investigation shows that only a comparatively small percentage of immigrants would be unable to read in some language. Moreover, strong capable men would sometimes be shut out by this requirement. The witness sees no gain to be obtained by requiring an oath of allegiance from the immigrant immediately upon landing.

Mr. Eaton considers the present inspection system little more than a farce. He has himself observed its working at Ellis Island. He thinks that there is too close an affiliation between immigration and the transportation interests. The system of consular inspection would probably be advantageous in stopping immigrants before taking passage. (370, 371.)

Mr. ROSENDALE declares that the leaders of organized labor, so far as he has come in contact with them, whether native born or foreign born, are all in favor of restricting immigration. It is true that men who come from abroad with union cards are often admitted at once to labor organizations in this country and to places in their workshops. Such men, members of labor unions, would almost invariably be admitted under an educational qualification. They are the better class of workmen. In Germany there is not a member of a labor organization who can not read and write his language. Even in London, if a man is a member of a union, he becomes more intelligent. There are no labor unions in Italy, and in Russia, Poland, and Austria they are not tolerated. (197, 198.)

Mr. Rosendale says that our present immigration law has not kept out many immigrants. They are admitted, to a certain extent indiscriminately. Only a few formal questions are asked. It is not possible to subject such crowds to any proper inspection, especially with so small a force. It is true that the more rigid enforcement of the laws by Mr. Powderly will have a more beneficial effect, not only by sending back some, but by discouraging others from coming, but the laws are not strict enough. (200, 201.)

Restriction of immigration and protection.—Mr. ROSENDALE says: "While we have a protective tariff—and I am in favor of protection to the manufacturer—the manufacturer can scour the markets of Europe where he can get the cheapest labor and import it free of duty. I think if protection is given to the manufacturer, protection should be given to the workingman; and the only protection he needs is not too much competition in the labor market."

He thinks that many of the manufacturers are not willing to give equal opportunities to the workingmen. They want all the protection themselves. (197, 200.)

Importation of labor.—Mr. ROSENDALE states that a committee of the State legislature of Pennsylvania, after investigating the condition of the coal regions in 1897, recommended that the State prohibit the importation of pauper labor. Nothing, however, was done. (191.)

Past advantages to this country.—Mr. ROSENDALE declares that we should never have come to our present condition except through immigration, and that American manufacturers ought still to have the right the right to bring men over to teach new arts and new industries to American workmen. The success of the American manufacturer has been greatly promoted by the employment of men who have seen different methods in other countries and by the selection of the best methods. But the immigrants who have built up our industries were an intelligent class. It is a very different class that we now wish to keep out by restrictions upon immigration. (198, 199.)

PROPOSED AMENDMENTS TO IMMIGRATION LAW. CVII

Immigration Protective League.—Dr. SENNER, secretary of the Immigration Protective League, says that its object is "to oppose any further restriction of immigration to the United States and to protect and advance the interests of persons immigrating to this country." He declares that the league represents a large body of citizens. (185, 187.)

General argument against restriction.—Dr. SENNER thinks that it is impracticable to restrict the absolute number of immigrants. It is only possible to exclude undesirable classes, and opinions differ as to those who are undesirable. The only policy which can be recommended is one which will be for the best for the whole country. In many parts of the country immigration is still desired. The witness does not believe that the country is by any means thoroughly settled; much of the land is certainly not thoroughly cultivated. Moreover, the evils which are specially complained of—the driving out of native labor from certain sections or trades—are accomplished facts, and can not be remedied by restrictions on future immigration. If naturalization be restricted, the country will soon be able to assimilate immigrants and the problems arising from immigration will be solved. (167, 169, 182, 184.)

Dr. Senner declares that there is no ground for apprehension as to an increase in immigration. Notwithstanding the almost unprecedented prosperity of the United States, the number of immigrants in 1898–99 (311,707) is more than 10 per cent less than in 1896, and much less than in any year from 1880 to 1893. Immigration is largely coming from countries which are not densely populated. The witness attributes the decrease in immigration largely to the restrictive effect of the laws. (167, 168.)

Ambiguity of existing laws.—Dr. ULLO points out various respects in which the immigration laws are inconsistent or vague. He states that the later laws have not expressly repealed the law of 1882, and that there is considerable doubt as to what is the existing statute in various points. For this reason he thinks that a general revision of the immigration laws is highly desirable. (140, 141.)

Dr. SENNER admits that the existing immigration laws are ambiguous and defective, but thinks that the existing difficulties can be solved by court decisions and administrative regulations. On the other hand, a recodification of the laws would introduce new complications and would reopen many settled questions. (169.)

Exclusion of unskilled immigrants.—Mr. HALL thinks that, although immigration of unskilled labor is in few cases desirable, it would nevertheless be impossible to attempt to make a law of exclusion on the basis of skill. Not only would the application of the test be unsatisfactory, but some desirable elements would be shut out. The proportion of the unskilled among the total number of immigrants is very great. Moreover, the labor unions object quite as much to the coming of skilled as of unskilled labor. (65.)

Race restrictions.—Mr. HALL does not think it would be feasible, especially in view of political opposition from foreign countries, to attempt to restrict immigration by races in the same way as is done regarding the Chinese. (62.)

B. Proposed administrative amendments to immigration law.—*Report of immigration investigation commission of 1895.*—Mr. MCSWEENEY summarizes the recommendations made by the immigration investigation commission, consisting of Dr. Senner, Mr. Stump, and Mr. McSweeney, which was appointed by the Treasury Department in 1895. The proposed amendments were as follows:

(1) That steamship companies should be required to make manifests as to each outgoing alien passenger, giving his name, age, nationality, and occupation, and stating whether he had declared his intention to become a citizen and whether he intends to return to the United States.

(2) That the sale of prepaid ocean tickets be prohibited, except by duly authorized agents of the steamship companies.

(3) That there be added to the excluded classes persons imported for the purpose of prostitution.

(4) That power be given to the Secretary of the Treasury to arrest any immigrant who has entered unlawfully, at any time within 2 years after arrival, and to deport him after due hearing. Any alien who becomes a public charge within 1 year shall be deported and the company bringing him to the United States shall be subject to fine as in other cases.

(5) That the contract-labor law be made broader by adding the words "by any undertaking or promise of employment upon arrival in the United States."

(6) That immigration officials be empowered to administer oaths.

(7) That aliens who come unlawfully shall be sent back upon a vessel of the company bringing them, where possible, but in other cases shall be returned upon

some other vessel at the expense of the company bringing them, such company to be subject to fine for refusal to return the alien or to pay for the passage.

(8) That money received from fines, penalties, and other sources be paid into the immigration fund.

(9) That in order to ascertain those who come to this country repeatedly, additional questions be inserted in the manifests prepared by the steamship companies. These should inquire whether the immigrant has been in the United States before, how many times, how much money he brought each time, how much money he carried back each time, and also various facts concerning his family and his property.

(10) At present the immigration authorities are authorized to inquire how much money the immigrant has, provided it does not exceed $30. It is recommended that they be empowered to demand information as to the actual amount in every case.

(11) Strike out the provision in the existing law that no more money shall be spent in maintaining the immigration department at any port than is collected at that port.

(12) That greater care shall be taken by steamship companies in preparing and verifying manifests.

(13) That debarred immigrants shall be returned to the country whence they came, provided that those who come in transit to contiguous territory shall be returned to the country in which they were last resident.

(14) That transportation lines shall not be permitted to collect from the debarred immigrant any charge for returning him or his belongings.

(15) That transportation companies shall be subject to a fine of $10 for each person concerning whom the required information is not given in the manifests.

(16) That false testimony before the board of special inquiry, or false affidavit as to the financial responsibility of a security on a bond, shall be punished as perjury.

(17) That the commissioners of immigration be empowered to temporarily suspend the execution of the decision of boards of special inquiry, subject to appeal to the Secretary of the Treasury.

(18) That persons assisting immigrants to evade or falsely answer inquiries shall be deemed guilty of a misdemeanor.

(19) That members of the board of special inquiry shall be empowered to exclude such aliens as appear to them suspicious or disreputable characters, unless they shall establish a good reputation.

(20) That when, under the contract-labor law, a person is ordered debarred, his testimony may be taken, after short but reasonable notice to the person charged with inducing him to immigrate, and that this testimony may be used as evidence against such person.

(21) That the boards of special inquiry may admit conditionally such persons as intend to settle in the United States, and later to bring their families, and within 1 year thereafter may reopen the case and take into consideration the admission of the whole family as if all had arrived at the same time. A person thus received would perhaps be required to return with his family in case it should be found that the family contained an idiot or other debarred person.

Finally, Mr. McSweeney declares that the immigration laws as a whole need to be codified for the sake of clearness and simplicity. (97–100.)

Discretionary powers of immigration commissioner.—Mr. FITCHIE, commissioner of immigration at New York, thinks that the commissioners of immigration at the respective ports, being the officers directly appointed by the President and responsible to him, should be given greater control over the acts of their subordinates. At present the law gives to each inspector the power to pass any who are, in his judgment, clearly and beyond doubt entitled to admission. If the inspector admits any person regardless of the facts in his case the commissioner has no definite right to reverse his decision. Similarly the commissioner has no control over the boards of special inquiry, whose decision is final unless appeal is taken to the commissioner-general of immigration. (75.)

Mr. McSWEENEY believes that the commissioners of immigration at the various ports should be given plenary power to act according to their discretion in cases where no precise provision of law exists, or to modify the requirement of the law in certain cases where injustice would clearly be done otherwise. (80.)

Discretionary powers of inspectors.—Mr. HOLMAN, secretary of the board of special inquiry at New York, also thinks that great discretionary power should be given to the commissioner of immigration and the board of special inquiry at each port, with a view to preventing hardship arising from the too strict application of the tests of exclusion, as well as to enable these officers to exclude those not

PROPOSED AMENDMENTS TO IMMIGRATION LAW.   CIX

coming under any specific provision. In this connection the witness expresses the opinion that to make ability to read and write an absolute requirement would result in injustice and hardship, but that such ability might well be made one of the considerations on which the board of special inquiry should base its decisions. That board should approach as nearly as possible to a jury in its character and powers, so that a person whom it considers unfit for admission could safely be excluded. (136, 137.)

Mr. McSWEENEY says that although the law at present provides for excluding persons convicted of felony or other infamous crime or misdemeanor involving moral turpitude, there is no provision for excluding other immoral persons, such as, for example, those who are fleeing from justice. The law excludes polygamists but does not exclude married men who run away with women or women not the wives of the person with whom they come. Such immoral persons usually have a sufficient supply of money and can not be excluded on the ground that they are likely to become a public charge.

The witness thinks that the law should be amended so as to give the immigration authorities greater discretion as to excluding such persons not coming under the precise provisions of the law. (79, 80.)

Inspection by consuls.—Mr. HALL says that the plan of requiring United States consuls to examine emigrants and grant them certificates looks attractive since the consuls have apparently better opportunities for information than inspectors on this side. But the system would necessitate a large increase in the consular force. The inspection would often be made by some clerk on a small salary subject to the temptation to accept bribes, especially if he were a native. The number of immigrants from a single port is often very great, and careful inspection would be impossible. The services of the consuls are already required and the witness has seen manifests sworn to in blank without any actual investigation. The system also would divide the responsibility, the inspector in Europe trusting that the one in America would detect any one not entitled to entrance, while the American inspector would rely upon the European one.

It would be still more undesirable to rely upon the governments of the foreign countries themselves to inspect the emigrants. They would have no motive to act as efficient agents in enforcing United States laws and might even wish to get rid of undesirable population.

The system of consular inspection would constitute a direct notice to the foreign governments to ascertain in connection with it whether persons who might be available for army service were seeking to leave the country. The military laws of Europe have made it difficult for the United States to secure a good class of immigrants.

The proposed system might also encounter political difficulties. It would be practically to establish an extraterritorial court and would require treaty stipulations. (59–62.)

Mr. STUMP says that European countries, especially Germany, are now passing laws to prevent emigration of their citizens, which has proved injurious to them. Consequently there is less need for inspection by American consuls. (22.)

Deportation of immigrants.—Dr. ULLO, counsel of the immigration bureau at New York, states that the immigration laws are indefinite as to the place to which persons who are deported must be returned. With regard to convicts, the statute declares that they must be sent to the nation to which they belong and from which they come. The port from which the immigrant has come may not be in the nation to which he belongs. The United States has no power to force a steamship company to transport a passenger by land from the European port to his own country. Indeed, while the United States has complete jurisdiction over steamship companies so far as their vessels are within the limit of 3 miles from our shores, it has no power to compel performance of its orders outside of that limit, and could have no such power in Europe, except by treaty with European countries. At present it is the custom of the immigration department to order persons debarred to be returned to the ports from which they come. In fact, the law does not consider that an immigrant has been landed at all, the examination being supposed to take place on board the vessel, even when it is actually made on land.

Dr. Ullo thinks that the form of order concerning the debarred immigrants should be simply "Not permitted to land." The steamship company would then do as it saw fit with regard to the contract with the immigrant or to the payment of damages for nonexecution, and would take such steps as it found necessary with regard to the return of the immigrant. (138, 139.)

Deportation of the insane.—Mr. GOODWIN BROWN, counsel for the New York State Commission in Lunacy, says that about 168 insane persons are sent out of the State of New York in the course of a year. About 100 of these are sent to foreign countries. A trained attendant is always sent with the lunatic and arrangements are made beforehand with friends and relatives to take care of him. These arrangements must be made, for there is no way in which a lunatic can be compelled to go. No lunatic is ever sent into a State until careful investigation has shown that he should be sent there. There is great difficulty in sending insane persons to foreign countries, as the steamship companies object to having a lunatic on board. There ought to be some provision whereby, in case a State wishes to return lunatics or other dependent persons to a foreign country, the steamship companies could be obliged to take them if they were properly accompanied. In cases where the insane are sent back in accordance with the provision of the immigration law which compels a steamship company bringing them over to return them, when insanity, due to causes arising prior to their coming to this country, develops within a year from their coming, the lunatics are simply delivered to the steamship company. Probably much suffering and hardship is endured by these people when they are taken back under those circumstances.

The steamship company when it returns them simply deposits them at the point of departure and leaves them. There ought to be some provision made so that they should be sent back to the place from which they come. (207, 208, 209, 215.)

Proposed amendment to the immigration laws.—Mr. GOODWIN BROWN, referring to the section of the immigration law providing that when an immigrant becomes insane within one year from the time of his arrival in this country from causes which arose prior to his departure for this country he shall be shipped back at the expense of the steamship company, says that a period of one year is altogether too short a time, and that the time should be extended to two years at least. The clause "from causes existing prior to his landing" should be stricken out, because it is practically impossible to prove that the causes of insanity existed prior to the coming of the immigrant to this country without a very elaborate investigation. The law also should be amended so as to exclude idiots, epileptics, and imbeciles, and to exclude persons who have been insane within ten years previous to their coming to this country. The United States, and even the State of New York, could better afford to keep at every port one or two trained alienists to examine immigrants for insanity than to allow these people to come in and become a public charge. In May, 1898, a bill was introduced into the United States Senate by Senator Fairbanks at the solicitation of the lunacy commission providing for an amendment to the immigration law along the lines suggested. It is not known to a certainty that foreign countries deliberately deport many of their insane and imbeciles to this country, but there are certain facts which indicate that the thing is being done. (208, 209, 210, 211, 212.)

Contract-labor law.—Dr. ULLO, who has had charge of the preparation of testimony in nearly all contract-labor cases, declares that under the existing provisions of the law scarcely 1 in 1,000 can be brought to conviction. The law makes it unlawful to import into the United States any person under contract made previous to the importation. The courts hold that this contract must be of such a character that it could have been enforced at law. It is very rare that any one makes such formal contract before coming to this country, and it is practically impossible to prove the existence of a contract made on the other side.

Where the immigration officers decide to refuse admission to an immigrant under the contract-labor law, it is possible to take his testimony *de bene esse* before he is deported. But since the person thus taking the testimony does not know what the defense on the other side will be, the testimony thus taken in written form is of little value as compared with the oral testimony of the defendant in court. Although the law permits a contract-labor case to be taken up at any time within 1 year after the landing of the immigrant, it is naturally difficult to get testimony from the person who is at work for the defendant in the case.

The witness accordingly advocates an amendment to the law making it unlawful to offer inducements to any person to bring him to this country. The decision as to what constitutes an inducement will then be left to the jury under proper instructions from the court. (140, 143, 144.)

Dr. Ullo thinks that the immigrant brought to the United States under contract should be given a right to sue the person who has made the contract and to collect part or all of the fine. The immigrant is frequently an innocent man. He does not know the law of this country and is not presumed to know it. He has disposed of his property and broken up his home, and on being debarred has to build up a home again. To grant to private parties generally the power to sue for violation of the contract-labor law would tend to make the enforcement of the law much more effective. (143.)

Mr. McSWEENEY believes that the contract-labor law should be amended to make it less difficult to prove violations. The courts have construed the law strictly, declaring that it must be proved that the contract made is such a one as would entitle the contracting parties to enforce it. Evidence of contract can be secured in only 3 ways: (1) Through parties present at the making of the contract. Since the contract is made outside of the United States in most cases the witnesses to the contract are outside and can not be secured. (2) By the confession of the alien contracting for admission. But he knows that he will be punished by deportation. Moreover, if once he is allowed to land he presumably goes straight to work for the person importing him and is not likely to betray him. (3) Through the person importing the alien, who will certainly seek to conceal the fact since he is threatened with a fine.

For these reasons very few fines have been imposed under the act, although a considerable number of persons have been deported. The administrative officers value evidence in a different way from judicial officers, and are willing to take the responsibility of excluding men where the evidence is not sufficient to secure a legal conviction. As a matter of fact, this deportation is done without any specific authorization by statute.

Mr. McSweeney thinks that the contract-labor law should be amended so that evidence that any inducement or allurement has been held out to aliens to come to this country for the performance of labor should be sufficient to make the importer subject to fine. (77–80.)

Mr. POWDERLY speaks of the difficulty of proving contract, and especially of proving that it was made abroad. The law should be amended so that the fact of coming in response to invitation of any kind should be sufficient for debarment. (33.)

Mr. FITCHIE, commissioner of immigration at the port of New York, thinks that the contract labor law should be amended so as to make it an offense on the part of the steamship companies to attempt to land persons brought under contract. The penalties also should be made more severe than at present. (71.)

Mr. SCHWAB, agent of the North German Lloyd Company, thinks that the law should be amended so as to punish the person who sends for the contract laborer rather than the unfortunate laborer himself, who comes to the United States ignorant of its law on the subject. (102.)

Mr. QUINLAN advocates an amendment by which any attorney who declares that he has evidence as to a violation of the contract labor law may go before a United States district attorney, and in case the district attorney does not see fit to take up the case may himself prosecute the alleged offender and on conviction receive one-half of the penalty, the court to have power to award the other half of the penalty to the witnesses. Mr. Quinlan believes that such a provision would make every labor organization a contract labor inspector and that many more convictions would be secured. At present only the district attorney may bring action. It is objected that the change would tend to further blackmail. (121, 122.)

Mr. ROSENDALE favors the bill which was once passed by Congress and vetoed by President Cleveland, providing that no male alien who has not in good faith declared his intention to become a citizen may be employed on any public work of the United States or may come regularly or habitually into the United States to engage in any mechanical trade or manual labor for wages or salary, returning from time to time to a foreign country. (198.)

Temporary immigration.—Mr. McSWEENEY says that there are many aliens who come to this country during the labor season and return to their homes during the winter, so-called "birds of passage." The witness thinks that the immigration authorities should be given discretionary power to exclude this class, since they are usually undesirable and displace the laborers of this country. The status of aliens who have acquired a residence here and who return to their native land should be more carefully defined in the law. (80, 81.)

Mr. POWDERLY thinks it is necessary to establish inspectors along the border between Canada and the United States. The present Canadian inspectors can not examine immigrants destined for Canada, and many really coming to the United States are manifested as going to some point near the United States border, whence they enter this country. When such are later discovered, the law only allows deportation to Canada as the country whence they last came. It should be amended to allow return to their original country. Such immigrants frequently change their names to avoid detection. The greater part of those who become public charges come by way of Canada. (38.)

Steamship companies.—Mr. POWDERLY states that the law requires the master of each vessel to prepare a manifest containing answers to numerous questions as to each alien passenger. Formerly this was required only as to steerage passengers, but many persons prohibited entrance evaded the law by coming in the first or second cabin, so that the requirement was recently extended by the Immigration Bureau to these. American citizens are not manifested, and aliens sometimes evade the law by claiming to be citizens. The examination in preparation of manifests is hasty and insufficient, and should be replaced by more thorough examination on board ship by an immigration agent or by the purser, or by examination by United States agents before embarkation. (37, 38.)

Mr. SCHULTEIS declares that the steamship companies have used strong influence against the Lodge bill and other restrictive measures. The efforts of Dr. Senner and Dr. Glavis were especially vigorous. This influence was largely exerted to keep the press silent or favorable to immigration. The companies have furnished free excursions to New York and entertainments on steamers, have advertised largely in papers, etc. Many German-Americans who really favor the educational test were led through Dr. Senner's bureau to sign petitions against the bill without knowing their contents. (24, 25.)

Mr. SCHWAB declares that the statement that the steamship companies have maintained a powerful lobby in Washington to oppose immigration legislation is an absolute untruth. The late Dr. Glavis did represent steamship companies in Washington, but not as a lobbyist, and since his death the companies have had no representatives except ordinary passenger agents.

Mr. Schwab also declares that it is the policy of the steamship lines to comply with the laws of the United States and to forward the interests of this country. The witness believes that the existing statutes represent the right principle in holding the steamship lines themselves responsible for the passenger.

Mr. Schwab believes that the present inspection of immigrants by agents of the steamship companies is much more efficient and effective than inspection by consular agents would be likely to be. We have very few consuls in the countries from which most of the immigrants come. It would be necessary practically to have an agent of the United States at the side of every one of the agents of the steamship companies. The steamship companies would not object to the system of consular inspection. (102, 105, 107.)

Condition of steerage.—Dr. WILLIAMS thinks that in most ships there is now sufficient provision of air space in the steerage for the ordinary needs of passengers during the trip across the Atlantic. The steerage often appears exceedingly dirty, even filthy, upon the arrival of the ship in port, but this is not always the fault of the company, since the passengers are often very filthy in their habits. Moreover most dirt is more repulsive than dangerous. (130.)

Protection of immigrants at sea.—Mr. MCSWEENEY does not think that there is an adequate supply of life preservers and other means for protecting the lives of immigrants at sea. The Commissioner-General of Immigration should be given supervisory power in this matter. (94.)

C. Distribution of immigrants.—"*Immigrant clearing house.*"—Dr. SENNER, former commissioner of immigration at New York, declares that there is great need of facilities for distributing newly arrived immigrants throughout the country in the sections where they are especially needed, and that means should also be taken, if possible, to distribute more satisfactorily the foreign-born already in this country. For this purpose the witness approves the suggestion that the heads of the various State bureaus of labor statistics should be made agents of the Federal Government for collecting information as to the conditions of trade and labor in the various States.

Dr. Senner especially advocates the establishment of "an immigrant clearing house" at Ellis Island. At this establishment there should be a permanent exhibition showing the products and resources of the various States. Each State should be represented by a permanent bureau with agents, subject to rigid examination as to their honesty and reliability, to give information concerning conditions of labor. Representatives of railroads and other bodies could also be admitted. In this way the immigrant could learn what sections he would find best adapted to his abilities and desires. At present the immigrant does not know in one case out of a hundred what he is going to do in the United States. (174, 185, 186.)

Mr. STUMP thinks that as a remedy for congestion in large cities and in particular sections there should be a system of cooperation among officers of different States for furnishing information, at a central office at Ellis Island, as to opportunities for employment and local conditions throughout the country. An exhibition hall should be erected for displaying the products of different States and presenting inducements for immigration. (5.)

PROPOSED AMENDMENTS TO IMMIGRATION LAW. CXIII

Mr. McSWEENEY is disposed to question the desirability of attempting to establish an exhibition hall on Ellis Island in which the States should show their products with a view to attracting immigrants. (96.)
Information regarding labor market.—Mr. POWDERLY believes that State bureaus of immigration and of labor should be designated agents of the Federal Government to collect information as to conditions of trade and employment for the guidance of immigrants. Post-office and other Federal authorities could also be employed to gather statistics as to local conditions. (39.)

Mr. PERKINS, president of the Cigar Makers' International Union, favors cooperation between the immigration authorities, the bureaus of labor statistics, and labor organizations to ascertain the proportion of men employed and of men needed in the various trades, with a view to limiting immigration of men skilled in each trade to a certain proportion of the number engaged in the trade, varying according to the conditions of employment. (180.)

D. Extension of period for deportation.—Dr. ULLO refers to the provision of the immigration law which permits the arrest and deportation of any person who has come in violation of law at any time within 1 year after landing. The law further declares that any alien who becomes a public charge within 1 year after landing from causes existing prior to his landing shall be deemed to have come in violation of law. This throws the burden upon the Government of proving that the causes existed before landing, and the law should be amended to make the fact of becoming a public charge sufficient ground for deportation. (144.)

Mr. SCHULTEIS also thinks the time limit within which immigrants found to be illegally admitted may be returned should be extended to 5 years. Where a person has been pauperized abroad by heavy taxation and low wages and is sent here to get rid of him, this country should have the privilege of returning him if he becomes a public charge. The same argument applies to criminals. European countries frequently send paupers to this country to get rid of them. The English Government pays its superannuated employees their pension in a lump sum if they will emigrate. Paupers are much more numerous in England than in the United States. (26, 27.)

Mr. STUMP says that much less than 1 per cent of immigrants are deported. Hardships are sometimes caused by separation of families and otherwise. Immigrants found within 1 year after arrival to have come contrary to law may be deported, but there is difficulty because the law gives no one formal authority to arrest such persons. So far as contract labor law is concerned, the suggested extension of this time limit to 5 years is scarcely necessary, but it would be of advantage where persons are discovered to be criminals or insane after the first year has expired. (11, 19.)

E. Bonds regarding immigrants.—Mr. POWDERLY says that the immigration authorities often require a bond that the immigrant shall not become a public charge. Such bonds are often given by mistaken charity or by collusion. The immigrant frequently evades liability by changing his name and giving a different port of entry other than the real one. It is desirable to furnish a landing certificate to each immigrant, requiring its presentation when applying for naturalization or for public relief. A record of the same facts should be preserved by the Bureau of Immigration as an immigration directory. (45.)

Mr. POWDERLY declares that the limit of 1 year within which immigrant may be returned is insufficient. It should be extended until naturalization. A guaranty from steamship companies, or a bond of $500 with 2 sufficient sureties, binding for 5 years, would be a great advantage. (40, 41.)

Mr. MCSWEENEY believes that the period for which immigrants are bonded should be extended to at least 2 years. He does not think that responsible steamship companies would oppose such an extension. (84.)

Mr. FITCHIE thinks that the provision permitting immigrants to be admitted on giving bond that they shall not become public charge needs to be carefully revised. It has been decided by one of the law officers of the Government that under certain conditions even members of the classes specifically excluded by the statute can be admitted on giving bond. Moreover the bond does not constitute a lien on the property of the persons giving the guarantee. By change of names and other methods the bond is often evaded, and the witness is sure that there are persons now supported in public institutions who have given bond not to become a public charge. The bond should be made a matter of record, and the immigrant giving it should be required to appear for inspection semiannually or annually. (75, 76.)

Mr. HALL declares that the attempt to prevent immigrants from becoming a burden upon the public by requiring bonds from steamship companies to support them in case of need has proved ineffective. From 1799 to 1872 Massachusetts required a bond good for 5 years, but the law was repealed as being absolutely unworkable. Immigrants frequently change their names for convenience, and in case they become public charges they are especially apt to deceive as to their names, as to the date of immigration, etc. During 1896 out of 372 cases of sick poor in Massachusetts only 133 could be identified to such an extent as to be turned over to the United States authorities for deportation. During 2 months there were 35 persons relieved from the Boston City Hospital as to whom too little information could be gained to satisfy the United States. These persons were all Russians, Hungarians, and Italians, and all illiterate except 2.

Mr. Hall thinks there might be some advantage in a requirement that immigrants should secure certificates identifying them and giving the facts concerning their landing, but it would furnish protection more in regard to naturalization than in regard to other questions. (63, 64.)

Mr. SCHWAB says that if it seem wise and necessary to extend the period during which the steamship companies are liable for immigrants to 2 years, the companies would consider it a hardship, but would not especially oppose the change. To extend the period to 5 years, however, would be unduly severe. The witness thinks there is no especial hardship in the law of this country to support alien paupers since it is benefiting by the labor of the great body of alien immigrants. (108.)

Dr. SENNER thinks that the United States is sufficiently protected by the present laws against the immigration of pauper immigrants. Although there are some recently arrived immigrants who become inmates of charitable institutions, often changing their names to avoid detection, these cases are rare. Most foreigners who are public charges came to this country some time ago. The existing law is effective in preventing wholesale immigration of undesirable elements. (184, 185.)

F. Head tax.—Mr. STUMP says that the original tax of 50 cents levied in 1882 has been increased to $1 for each alien passenger, whether in the steerage or otherwise. This sum is paid to the collector of the port by the captain or owner of the vessel, and usually added by the steamship companies to the passage money of the immigrant. This sum has been sufficient to defray all expenses of the immigration bureau and care of immigrants who become dependent after arrival. The former buildings at Ellis Island were also constructed out of this fund. This tax is also paid by special arrangement by Canadian steamship lines upon passengers destined for the United States, or upon those who come to this country within a certain number of months after landing. (12, 18.)

Mr. POWDERLY favors an increase of the tax to $2 for the purpose of furnishing sufficient revenue to establish inspectors at foreign ports and along the land borders of the United States. Such a tax would not be restrictive. Nor would a higher rate of $10 or $20 probably have much beneficial effect. Many persons who could not pay $5 would be more desirable than others who could pay $100.

Mr. MCSWEENEY believes that the head tax should be doubled, especially for the purpose of avoiding all danger that the immigration service will be crippled for lack of funds as it was in 1892. (84.)

Mr. SCHULTEIS advocates an increase of the tax to at least $10. Tickets to the United States cost $8 less than to South American countries, and the difference brings many immigrants here. A large number would be excluded by such increase. (24.)

Mr. SCHWAB declares that the steamship lines are willing to accept whatever changes in the immigration laws are deemed necessary for effective enforcement. They would prefer that the head money remain unchanged, but would not oppose a reasonable increase. The tax is paid in the first instance by the steamship company but is, of course, reckoned as one of the items of cost in fixing the price of tickets. To increase the tax to an unduly high figure, such as $5 or $10, would exclude many immigrants. The character of the immigrant as a citizen depends very little upon his ability to pay such a tax. (102, 105.)

Property test.—Mr. SCHWAB declares that the amount of money which an immigrant brings to the United States is comparatively little indication as to his desirability as a citizen. (102.)

G. Educational test.—Mr. HALL, secretary of the Immigration Restrictive League, testifies that that body favors an educational test for admission to this country. The organization was formed in 1894 and includes about 700 persons as active members, while about 5,000 others assist the league and receive its documents. The league does not advocate the exclusion of laborers or other immigrants of such character as to fit them for good citizens, but only the exclusion of undesirable elements. For this it considers the educational test the most effective. The league was instrumental in drafting the bill which was introduced in the Fifty-fourth Congress by Senator Lodge.

The league does not believe that an educational test is necessary evidence of moral worth, but an examination of the illiteracy of immigrants from different nations and a comparison of their criminality indicates that the more illiterate nationalities furnish proportionately the greater number of criminals. Similarly, the greatest proportion of paupers and of unskilled laborers are found in the most illiterate nationalities. The proportion of money brought into this country is smallest among the most illiterate, while the tendency to congregate densely in the cities is also most marked among them. (See Mr. Hall's statistics on these points, p. 56.) In view of the increase in the proportion of illiteracy, and especially in view of the constantly increasing proportion of the immigrants who come from the southeastern countries of Europe as compared with the northwestern countries, the league believes that the educational test is especially desirable. (46, 50–54.)

Mr. Hall admits that the educational test is not an ideal one, but thinks that on the whole it would tend to exclude the more undesirable classes. Moreover, if we make public-school education the basis of citizenship in this country, we can scarcely consider the immigration of illiterate persons very advantageous even if they be morally upright. There must be some sort of test, more or less rigid. To attempt to ascertain directly by question or otherwise whether a person is of criminal character or whether he is unskilled or otherwise undesirable is very difficult. There must be hardship in individual cases through the application of any test. Mr. Hall does not believe that treaties with foreign countries stand in the way of an educational restriction of immigration.

The educational test, Mr. Hall declares, is very generally favored throughout the country. The Immigration Restriction League has ascertained by correspondence and otherwise the opinions of many organizations, a large number of chambers of commerce, of labor organizations, including the American Federation of Labor and Knights of Labor, of State legislatures and officers, and of factory inspectors. These mostly favor the educational test. Even in the Northwestern States, where there is the most room for a new population, and where offices and associations have been established for the purpose of promoting immigration, those classes of immigrants who would be excluded by an educational test are not desired. Although the advocacy of restriction is perhaps most marked near the Canadian border, it is by no means confined to that section.

The objections which have been raised to restriction of immigration have come either from theoretical economists, who have considered that the economic advantages from immigration offset any social disadvantages, or who have felt that it was against the rights of the individual to shut out anyone; or it has come from certain classes of the foreign population in this country. The opposition of this latter class, Mr. Hall asserts, has been largely developed by the actions of the steamship lines, which have sent out circulars misrepresenting facts and which have sought to stir up race prejudice. Mr. Hall quotes from such a circular, addressed to the Germans, in which it is intimated that the effect of the proposed legislation would be to completely cut off German immigration, and that there will afterwards be a tendency to oppress Germans already in this country. A certain amount of opposition has also been raised by Roman Catholic societies, who think that the measure is directed chiefly against immigration from Roman Catholic countries. (58, 61, 66.)

Mr. SCHULTEIS says that the educational test, as proposed in original draft of Lodge bill, would have excluded the Russian Jews, since the "native language" of such Jews is Russian, which most can not read or write. They can read and write Jewish, and thus would not be affected by amended bill. (29.)

Mr. Schulteis considers this the best method of excluding the undesirable element. Practically only those from southern European countries would be affected. At present those coming from Italy are chiefly from the southern part, the most undesirable of all. Practically one-fourth of the immigrants would be excluded by such a test. (23, 24.)

Mr. DUNCAN says the Granite Cutters' National Union is in favor of the Lodge bill. It believes that where a man is able to read his own language he soon becomes familiar with the facts regarding the relations of labor and capital and can readily be brought into trade-union movements. Uneducated men, on the other hand, discredit the well-meant advice of the unions. (Vol. VII, 207.)

Mr. ROSENDALE favors the Lodge bill for restricting immigration by an educational test. He states that such a test would keep out Italians as a class, and Hungarians, because they do not read their own language. He declares that it would keep out two-thirds of the Jews; but this seems to be connected with his statement that he would not recognize the Hebrew jargon as a language. He admits that a large per cent of the Jews can read that; but he says they are barely able to read their prayers in Hebrew, without understanding the language. (196, 197.)

Mr. Rosendale admits that the educational test does not directly gauge the ability of a workman. A workman may have high mechanical skill without being able to read or write. But all good workmen coming from such countries as Germany are, in fact, able to read and write, and some degree of education may be found among the better class of workmen generally. An educational test would, as a matter of fact, separate the higher classes of workmen in a great degree from those who could do nothing but common manual labor. (199.)

Dr. SENNER opposes the educational test on various grounds. He declares that its application would involve a doubling of the time required for examining immigrants and would greatly increase the vexations of the inspection system. The test, if applied to women, would result in injustice, and would especially hinder the obtaining of required servant girls from Europe. It would have no effect in protecting American labor, since skilled laborers, whose competition is most feared, could pass the examination. The United States still needs immigrants to perform its unskilled labor. The time to apply an educational test is at naturalization. (169.)

Dr. Senner thinks that the educational test should be strictly applied as a condition of naturalization. He deprecates exceedingly the fact that many States permit aliens to vote before naturalization, after a residence of six months or one year. He declares that it is his desire that the foreign-born population should become Americanized as rapidly as possible. (183, 184.)

Mr. SCHWAB thinks that an educational test would exclude many immigrants who are necessary for the development of the natural resources of this country. He declares also that illiteracy has nothing to do with criminality; that those countries whose immigrants are the most literate often show the largest percentage of criminals. (102, 103.)

Mr. STUMP thinks that the educational test would prove an efficient mode of restricting immigration, especially from southern Europe, but it would exclude a class of immigrants very beneficial to this country. American workmen are the most skillful in the world, and themselves perform the higher classes of labor; a cheaper grade of labor must be imported to do rougher manual work on roads, railways, sewers, etc. Such a test would exclude few from the northern countries of Europe, where education is as far advanced as in the United States. Educated rascals could not be excluded by such a method. (6, 21.)

Mr. HOLMAN, secretary of the board of special inquiry at New York, is disposed to doubt the wisdom of establishing an absolute educational test. Often it is more desirable to exclude certain persons who are well educated than others, young, able-bodied, and industrious, who have not been blessed with the opportunity of getting an education. Many persons of the latter class can easily overcome their lack of education and become good citizens. It is true that the educational test would exclude many undesirable immigrants, especially from certain countries, but it seems better to assign the real reason why these immigrants are undesirable rather than to assign illiteracy as the chief reason. The witness thinks that it would be legitimate to make ability to read and write one of the tests to be considered by the immigration officers if they were given discretionary power as to the admission of immigrants.

Mr. Holman believes, further, that the application of the educational test for naturalization is desirable. (136, 137.)

Mr. POWDERLY thinks it doubtful if the educational test is desirable as a condition of immigration, though highly desirable for naturalization. It would not check Chinese or Japanese immigration, and would have little effect on Russian Jews, who would soon learn to read a passage. (42.)

INDEX OF REVIEWS AND TOPICAL DIGEST.

[For index of Testimony and of Special Reports see end of Immigration Report, pp. 803.]

	Page.
Agricultural colonies:	
Finns	L
Italians	XLIX
Jews	L
Agricultural distribution of immigrants (see *Distribution*)	XLVIII–LVII
Agriculture:	
Bohemians, success in	XLIX, L
Finns, success in	L
Foreign-born, local distribution of	LI–LVII
Small percentage engaged in	XXIII
Italians, work in	XLVIII, XLIX
Jewish colonies engaged in	L
Jews, conditions in	L, LI
Nationalities, comparative inclination of different, toward	XXIII
South, conditions in	LIV
Alabama, foreign-born as agriculturists	LVI
Anthracite coal mines:	
Church affiliations of miners	LXXIV
Company stores in connection with	LXXXI
Earnings of miners	LXXXI
Nationality of miners	LXXXI
Standard of living of miners	LXXV
Arizona, foreign-born as agriculturists	LVII
Arkansas, foreign-born as agriculturists	LVI
Armenians, immigration of	LXXX
Army clothing, contracts for	XXXI
Assistance to immigrants:	
Effect in inducing immigration	XIV, XV, XCI–XCIII
Paupers and criminals	XCI, XCII
Austria-Hungary, Government, emigration, attitude toward	XCII
Austro-Hungarian Home, objects, work, etc	LXXXIV, LXXXV
"Birds of passage:"	
Exclusion advocated	CXI
Italians and Canadians	XI, LXXVIII, LXXIX
B'nai B'rith, objects, work	LXXIII
Boards of special inquiry, work of	XCIX
Bohemians, agriculturists, success as	L
Bonding of immigrants:	
Modification of privilege discussed	CXIII, CXIV
Boot and shoe trade:	
Foreign-born employees, percentage	XXXVII
Nationality of workers	LXXXII
Bricklaying trade, labor organizations, discriminations against aliens	XXXIX
British colonies, immigration legislation	LXIII, LXIV
Building trades, Canadian competition	XXXIV
California, foreign-born as agriculturists	LVII
Canada:	
Evasion of laws by immigration through	XVII, XVIII, LXII, LXIII
Immigration legislation	LXIII, LXIV
Immigration through, inadequate inspection	XVII, XVIII, CIII
Canadians:	
"Birds of passage"	XI, LXXVIII
Building trades, competition in	XXXIX
French, in textile trades	XXXVI
Care of immigrants, charitable societies	LXXII, LXXIII

CXVII

INDEX OF REVIEWS AND TOPICAL DIGEST.

	Page.
Causes inducing immigration	XIII–XV
Ambition of immigrants	LXXXIX
Assistance, outside	XIV, XV, XCI–XCIII
Efforts of railroads and steamship companies	XC, XCI
Oppression abroad	XV, XCIII
Prosperity of the country	XIII, LXXXIX
Steamship companies, efforts of	XIV
Transportation rates, low, influence of	XIV, XC

Charitable societies:
B'nai B'rith	LXXII
Foreign-born, work for	XI
Immigrants, aid furnished to	LXXII
Jewish	L, LI
Attitude toward immigration	XCIII

Children:
Competition, effect in depressing wages	XXIV
Criminality among foreign and native born	XXII
Inspection of immigrants	XCVIII, XCIX

Chinese immigration, evasion of exclusion laws	C
Cigar Makers' International Union, restriction of immigration advocated by	LXXXIII

Cigar-making trade:
Immigration, effect of	XXXIII, LXXXII
Machinery, effect	XXXII
Wages, rates of	XXXII, XXXIII
Country competition, effect	XXXII, XXXIII
Labor organization, effect of	XXXIII
Women, employment of	XXXII

Cities, tendency of foreign-born toward	X, XX, LXVII, LXVIII
Citizenship, voting not a necessary qualification for, in certain States	LXIX

Classification of immigrants:
By race, discussed	LXVI
Law of 1893	IX
1899	IX

Clearing houses for immigrants, establishment advocated	CXII

Clothing trade:
Army contracts	XXXI–XXXII
Consumers' League, work of	XXXII
Cost of manufacture, reduction in	XXVIII
Employment, irregularity of	XXV
Factory system, working and conditions	XXVIII
Foreign-born, employment	XXIV
Labor, subdivision	XXVIII
Labor organizations, work of	XXVIII, XXIX
Nationality of workers	XXVI, XXVII
New York City, center of manufacture	XXIV
State inspection	XXX, XXXI
Subcontracting	XXIX
Sweating system, described	XXIV, XXV, XXIX
Task system, working, conditions, etc	XXVIII
Tenement-house manufacture—	
Conditions in	XXIX
Amount of work not increasing	XXVI
Inspection by State	XXX, XXXI
Union label, effect of	XXXII
Wages, effect of immigration discussed	XXVII, XXVIII

Coal mines (see also *Anthracite coal mines*):
Foreign-born, effect of employment of	XXXIII, LXXX, LXXXI
Labor, oversupply due to immigration	XXXIII, XXXIV
Labor organizations—	
Difficulty of organizing	XXXIV, XXXVI
Wages, effect on	XXXIV, XXXV
Machinery, effect of introduction	XXXIV
Unemployment, amount	XXXIV
Wages, lowering, effect of immigration	XXXIII, LXXXI

Colonies of foreign-born:
Finns	L
Italians	XLIX

INDEX OF REVIEWS AND TOPICAL DIGEST. CXIX

Page.
Colonies of foreign-born—Continued.
  Jewish .... L, LXVIII, LXIX
    Temporary duration LXVIII
Colorado, foreign-born as agriculturists LVII
Commissioners of Immigration, proposed increase of powers .... CVIII, CIX
Company stores, anthracite coal regions LXXXI
Connecticut, foreign-born as agriculturists LI
Consuls, inspection of immigrants by, advocated CIX
Consumers' League, work of XXXII
Contagious diseases:
  Deportation of immigrants having XI
  Immigrants, number of cases detected LXXIII
  Increase among immigrants XI
  Proposed amendment to existing laws .... LXXIII, LXXIV
Contract labor (see also *Padrone system*):
  General discussion of law and its working .... LVII–LXI
  Deportation of laborers .... XVII, LXI, CI
  Evidence of contract, difficulty of securing .... CI, CII
  Excepted classes of laborers .... LX, CI
  Inspection, methods .... XVII, LXI, IC
  Inspectors, insufficiency of force for C
  Proposed amendments to law .... CII, CX, CXI
  Prosecution of employer LXIX
Contract system. (See *Padrone system; Contract labor*.)
Criminality of foreign-born:
  Children of XXII
    Comparison with criminality of native-born XXI
  Percentage of criminals, various nationalities .... XLIV, XLVII, LXIX, LXX
  Statistics discussed X
Criminals:
  Exclusion, applies only to convicts .... CII, CIII
  Immigration of, assisted .... XCI, XCII
Delaware, foreign-born as agriculturists LIV
Deportation of immigrants:
  Contract laborers .... XVII, LXI, CI
  Defects of present law CIX
  Diseased persons XI
  Extension of period for, advocated CXIII
  Hardships of CIII
  Insane, difficulties of .... CIX, CX
  Legislative provisions LXII
  Steamship companies, liability for CXIX
Destination of immigrants, statistics inaccurate .... LXV, LXVI
Detention of immigrants, care during XCIX
Diseases:
  Contagious—
    Deportation of immigrants having XI
    Cases detected LXXIII
    Increase among immigrants XI
    Proposed amendments to laws LXXIII
  Increase due to immigration XLII
Distribution of immigrants (see also *Employment bureaus*):
  Agricultural—
    Nationalities engaged in agriculture .... XLVIII, LI
    Difficulties .... XLIV, XLVIII
    Separate States, conditions and opportunities (see specific states) . LI–LVII
  Austro-Hungarian Home, influence of .... LXXXIV, LXXXV
  Charitable societies, efforts toward .... LXXII, LXXIII
  Cities, tendency of foreign-born toward .... X, XX, LXVII, LXVIII
    An early manifestation XLII
  Colonies .... LXVIII, LXIX
  Demand for labor of .... LXXVI, LXXIX
  Destinations stated, inaccuracy of .... LXV, LXVI
  Dissemination of information concerning labor conditions, proposed .. CXIII
  Immigration clearing house, establishment of, proposed CXII
  Industrial .... XXII, XXIII
  Italian bureau .... LXXXIII, LXXXIV
  Local .... XIX, XX

CXX   INDEX OF REVIEWS AND TOPICAL DIGEST.

Page.

Distribution of immigrants—Continued.
  Nationalities, changes, 1840 to 1890.. XIX, XX
  New York City .... XLV, XLVI
  Northern States, settlement in LXVIII
  Ruralization, difficulties XLVIII
    Early efforts unsuccessful.. XLIV
Drunkenness:
  Rare among Jewish immigrants LXX
Economic effects of immigration. (See *Effects of immigration*.)
Educational test:
  Discussed .... CXIV, CXVI
  Naturalization, requirement for, advocated LXIX
Effects of immigration:
  Economic—
    General discussion... LXXVII
    Boot and shoe trade... LXXXII
    Building trades... XXXIX
    Cigar-making trade LXXXII
    Clothing trade... XXIX
    Coal mines LXXXI
    Diversity of opinion regarding XI
    Facts to be considered in making estimate......................... XXII
    Glass trades XXXVIII
    Granite and paving cutting trade .... XXXIX, LXXXVI
    Iron and steel trades XXXVIII
    Labor organizations, destruction of paving-cutting LXXXVI
    Machinery, introduction of XXIII
    Money sent out of the country LXXIV
    Textile trades.. XXXVI
    Tin industry LXXXII
    Wages, effect on, general discussion .... XXXIII, LXXVII, LXXVIII
    Woodworking trade .... XXV, XXVII
  Social—
    Cities, tendency of foreign-born toward............................. X, XX, XLII, LXVII
    Criminality among foreign-born .... X, XXI
      Different nationalities .... XLIV, XLVII
    Illiteracy of immigrants .... IX, X, XXI, LXVII, LXVIII
    Insanity among foreign-born... X, LXX
    Pauperism, prevalence among foreign-born .... XXI, LXX
      Different nationalities .... XLIV, XLVII
    Poverty of foreign-born.. XXI
    Standard of living, effect on .... LXXV, LXXVI
Emigration:
  Austria-Hungary, attitude of Government toward................. XCII
  Foreign countries, attitude toward... XCII
  Legislation of foreign countries regarding............................. LXIII, LXIV
Employment:
  Age a cause of unemployment... LXXXIX
  Coal miners, decreased by influx of immigration .... XXXIV, LXXXI
Employment bureaus:
  Austro-Hungarian Home.. LXXXIV, LXXXV
  Fees, regulation of.. LXXXVI
  Fraudulent practices of certain .... LXXXV, LXXXVI, LXXXVII
  Foreign governments, maintenance of XII
  Italian bureau.. LXXXIII, LXXXIV
  Legislation proposed .... LXXXVII–LXXXIX
  Licensing of LXXXXII
  St. Bartholomew's Employment Bureau, New York City ... LXXXVI
  State free bureau, New York... LXXXV
  Private .... XII, XIII
Europe. (See *Foreign countries*, and names of separate countries.)
Factory inspection:
  Legislative provisions... XXX, XXXI
  Sweat shops, impossibility of effective.................................... LXXXI, LXXXII
  Wages, effect on XXXI
Financial condition of immigrants:
  Illiteracy, relation to XXI
Finns, agriculturists, success as L
Florida, foreign-born as agriculturists... LV

INDEX OF REVIEWS AND TOPICAL DIGEST.

	Page.
Foreign-born (see also *Effects of immigration, Nationality of immigrants, Statistics of immigration*):	
Proportion of total population	XIX
Charitable societies, work for	XI
Foreign countries:	
Emigration, attitude toward	XCII
Legislation regarding	LXIII, LXIV
Employment bureaus, governmental	XII
Oppression, effect in causing immigration	XV, XCIII
French Canadians, textile trades, employment in	XXXVI
Georgia, foreign-born as agriculturists	LV
Germany, emigration legislation	LXIII
Glass trades:	
Labor organizations, discriminations against aliens	XXXVIII
Productiveness, effect of immigration	XXXVIII
Wages	XXXVIII
Granite cutting:	
Foreign labor, effects of	LXXXIII
Labor organizations, discriminations against aliens	XXXIX
Padrone system in New York	LXXXIII
Wages, effect of immigration	XXXIX
Head tax on immigrants, increase advocated	CXIV
Home work, clothing trade (see *Clothing trade*)	XXIX–XXXII
Hours of labor, iron and steel trades, increased through immigration	LXXXII
Housing of immigrants. (See *Tenement houses*.)	
Illinois, foreign-born as agriculturists	LII
Illiteracy of foreign-born:	
Eastern Europe	IX, X
Educational test discussed	CXIV, CXVI
Financial condition, relation to	XXI
Nationalities compared	XXI, LXVII
Percentage of	XX
Southern Europe	X
Western Europe	IX
Immigration Investigation Commission, legislation proposed by	CVII, CVIII
Immigration Protective League, objects	CVII
Indiana, foreign-born as agriculturists	LII
Industrial Removal Society, work of	L, LI
Insane immigrants, deportation of, difficult	CIX
Insanity:	
Cost of caring for insane, per capita	LXXII
New York	LXXI
Foreign-born, prevalence among	X, LXX
Increase of, questioned	LXI
Proportion of, in Eastern and Western States	LXXI
State care of insane in New York	LXXI
Inspection of immigrants	XCV–CIII
Board of special inquiry	XCIX
Cabin passengers, methods	XCVII
Canada, evasion of law by immigration through	LXII, LXIII
Inadequacy	CIII
Care of, during detention	XCIX
Consuls, inspection by, discussed	CIX
Contract laborers—	
Discussed	C
Methods of	XVII
Criminals, exclusion of	CII, CIII
Detention	XCIX
Medical	XVI, XCVII
Methods followed	XVI, XVII, LXI
Previous to embarkation, character	CIII–CV
Qualifications of inspectors	XVI, XCVI
Steamship companies, inspection by	XVIII, CIII, CV
Steerage passengers, methods	XCV, XCVI
Women and children, methods	XCVIII, XCIX
Inspection of sweat shops (see also *Factory inspection*):	
Discussed	XXX, XXXI
Effective, impossible	LXXXI, LXXXII

INDEX OF REVIEWS AND TOPICAL DIGEST.

	Page.
Iowa:	
Foreign-born as agriculturists	LIII
Immigration opposed by farmers	LIII
Iron and steel trades:	
Foreign labor, competition of, not a serious factor	XXXVIII
Effects of	LXXXII
Machinery a means of introducing foreign labor	XXXVIII
Productiveness, effect of immigration	XXXVIII
Italian bureau, objects, work, etc	LXXXIII, LXXXIV
Italians:	
Agricultural colonies	XLIX
"Birds of passage"	XI, LXXVIII
New York City, characteristics and standard of living	XLVI
Occupations	XXVII
Padrone system among	XII
Italy:	
Emigration legislation	LXIII
Government, emigration, attitude toward	XCII
Jewish Agricultural Aid Society, work of	LI
Jews:	
Agricultural colonies of	L, LXVIII
Charitable societies	L, LI
Attitude toward immigration	XCIII, XCIV
Colonies of	L, LXVIII, LXIX
Drunkenness rare	LXX
Immigration due to persecution abroad	XV, XCIII
Labor unions among	XXVI
New York City, characteristics and standard of living	XLVI
Number of immigrants	XCIII
Occupations	XXVI
Purchasers of abandoned farms in New England	L
Standard of living	LXX, LXXV
Sweat shops, employment in	LXXXII
Kansas, foreign-born as agriculturists	LIII
Kentucky:	
Foreign-born as agriculturists	LV
Immigration favored by farmers	LV
Labor (see also *Effects of immigration; Wages*, etc.):	
Immigrants, demand for	LXXVI, LXXIX
Immigration, effect of, on	LXXVII–LXXXIII
Skilled and unskilled, among immigrants, proportion of	LXXVI
Labor organizations:	
Aliens, discriminations against	XXXVIII, XXXIX
Clothing trades	XXVIII, XXIX
Coal miners—	
Difficulty of forming, among	XXXIV, XXXVI
Effect on wages	XXXIV, XXXV
Foreign-born—	
Necessary for protection	XXIII
Obstacles to formation among	XXIII
Glass trades	XXXVIII
Granite cutters, aliens, discrimination against	XXXIX
Immigration, effect on	XXVIII, XXIX
Jewish unions	XXVI
Longshoremen, effects of	XXXIX
Syrians, difficulty of forming, among	XLI
Textile trades	XXVI, XXXVII
Unemployed members, care of	LXXXIX
Union labels, clothing trade	XXXII
Wages, effect on	XXVIII, XXXIII, XXXIV
Woodworking trades	XXXVII
Laboring classes, effect of immigration, diversity of opinion among	XI
Legislation (see also *Restriction of immigration*):	
British colonies, described	LXIII, LXIV
Classification of immigrants, laws of 1893 and 1899	IX
Consuls, inspection by	CIX
Contract-labor law—	
Discussion	LVII–LXI, CII, CX, CXI
Inspection methods	XVII, LXII
Deportation law discussed	CIII, CIX, CX, CXIII

INDEX OF REVIEWS AND TOPICAL DIGEST. CXXIII

	Page.
Legislation—Continued.	
Distribution of immigrants, methods discussed	CXII, CXIII
Emigration, foreign countries	LXIII, XCII
Excluded classes of immigrants under present laws	LXI, XCIV, XCV
Existing laws, defects in	LXII
Foreign countries	LXIII, LXIV
History of	LVII, XCIV
Proposed amendments to immigration laws—	
Bonding privilege, modification of	CXIII, CXIV
Commissioners of Immigration, increase of powers of	CVIII, CIX
Contract-labor law, proposed amendments to	CII, CX, CXI
Deportation, extension of period for	CXIII
Educational test, general discussion	CXIV, CXVI
Exclusion of "birds of passage"	CXI
Head tax, increase of	CXIV
"Immigration clearing house," establishment of	CXII
Immigration Investigation Commission of 1895, proposals by	CVII, CVIII
New York State commission in lunacy, proposed by	CX
Protection of immigrants at sea	CXII
Tenement house regulations—	
Early laws in New York	XLVII
Inefficient enforcement of laws	XLVII
Law of 1901, New York	XLVII, XLVIII
Longshoremen, race competition, disadvantages overcome by organization	XXXIX
Louisiana, foreign-born as agriculturists	LVI
Machinery:	
Coal mines—	
Effect of introduction	XXXIV
Introduction due to employment of foreign labor	XXXIV
Extensive introduction due to immigration	XXIII
Iron and steel trades, effect of introduction	XXXVIII
Textile trades, effect on wages	XXXVI
Maine:	
Foreign-born as agriculturists	LI
Immigration opposed by farmers	LI
Maryland, foreign-born as agriculturists	LV
Massachusetts:	
Foreign-born as agriculturists	LI
Immigration favored by farmers	LI
Medical inspection of immigrants	XVI, XCVII
Michigan:	
Foreign-born as agriculturists	LII
Immigration favored by farmers	LII
Mines. (See *Coal mines, Anthracite coal mines.*)	
Minnesota, foreign-born as agriculturists	LIII
Mississippi, foreign-born as agriculturists	LVI
Missouri, foreign-born as agriculturists	LIII
Money (see also *Financial condition*):	
Amount brought by immigrants	XXI
Large amounts sent out of the country by immigrants	LXXIV
Montana, foreign-born as agriculturists	LVII
Nationality of immigrants:	
Changes in recent years	LXVI, LXVII
1840 to 1900	XIX, XX
Distribution according to, changes in	XIX, XX
Statistics inaccurate	LXV, LXVI
Successive, 1870 to 1900	XLII
Naturalization:	
Educational test advocated	LXIX
Syrians	XLII
Unnaturalized immigrants, percentage of	X, LXIX
Violation of laws	LXIX
Voting not necesssary for, in certain States	LXIX
Nebraska:	
Foreign-born as agriculturists	LIV
Immigration favored by farmers	LIV
New Hampshire, foreign-born as agriculturists	LI
New Jersey, foreign-born as agriculturists	LII
Jewish colonies in	LXVIII, LXIX

New York: Page.
  Free employment bureau LXXXV
  Foreign born as agriculturists LI
  State-care of insane .... LXI, LXXI
  Tenement-house legislation .... XLVII, XLVIII
New York City:
  Distribution of immigrants in .... XLV, XLVI
  Foreign-born, 1890, percentage of XLV
  Housing of immigrants, conditions .... XLII–XLIV
New York commission in lunacy:
  Constitution and powers .... LXXI, LXXII
  Proposed amendments to immigration laws CX
North Carolina:
  Foreign-born as agriculturists LV
  Immigration favored by farmers LV
North Dakota:
  Foreign-born as agriculturists LIII
  Immigration favored by farmers LIII
Number of immigrants. (See *Statistics of Immigration*.)
Occupations of immigrants:
  Italians XXVII
  Jews .... XXVI, LXXVI
  Poles XXVII
  Skilled and unskilled labor, proportion of LXXVI
  Statistics inaccurate .... LXV–LXVI
  Syrians XLI
Ohio:
  Foreign-born as agriculturists LII
  Immigration favored by farmers LII
Oregon, foreign-born as agriculturists LVII
Padrone system .... XII, XXXIX, XLI, LXXIX, LXXX, LXXXIII, LXXXIV
Paupers, immigration assisted .... XCI, XCII
Pauperism:
  Foreign-born, prevalence among .... XXI, LXX
  Percentage of, by nationalities .... XLIV, XLVII
Paving cutting, foreign labor, injurious effects of LXXXIII
Pennsylvania, foreign-born as agriculturists LII
Poles:
  Occupations of XXVII
  Standard of living LXXV
Population:
  Foreign-born, percentage of total population XIX
  Increase of, relation of immigration to XX
Productiveness of labor:
  Immigration, effect of—
    Glass trades XXXVIII
    Iron and steel trades XXXVIII
Promotion of immigration, British colonies LXIII
Prosperity, effect of condition on immigration .... XIII, LXXXIX
Races (see also *Nationality of immigrants*):
  Classification of immigrants by LXVI
Railroads, immigration, efforts in inducing .... XC, XCI
Religious affiliations of foreign-born anthracite miners LXXIV
Restriction of immigration (see also *Legislation*):
  Additional restrictions—
    Advocated .... CV, CVI
    Deprecated CVII
    Trade unions, attitude toward .... CV, CVI
  Cigar Makers' Union, advocated by LXXXII
  Early legislation XV
  Economic effects, clothing trade XXIX
  Educational test discussed .... CXIV, CXVI
  Evasion of laws by immigration through Canada .... XVII, CIII
  Excluded classes under existing laws .... LXI, XCIV, XCV
  Existing legislation .... XV–XVIII
    Defectiveness of CVII
    Efficiency, diversity of opinion .... XV, XVI
  Foreign countries .... LXIII, LXIV
  Inspection of immigrants. (See *Inspection*.)

INDEX OF REVIEWS AND TOPICAL DIGEST. CXXV

	Page.
Restriction of immigration—Continued.	
Legislation, history of existing	XCIV
Proposed	CV–CXII
Temporary immigration, restriction of, advocated	LXXIV
Rhode Island:	
Agricultural opportunities for immigrants	LI
Immigration favored by farmers	LI
Roumanian Jews, standard of living	LXXV
Russian Jews (see also *Jews*):	
Standard of living	LXXV
St. Bartholomew's Employment Bureau, work described	LXXXVI
Skilled laborers, immigrants, number among	LXXVI
Slum districts, immigrants, largely populated by	LXVII, LXVIII
South Carolina, foreign-born as agriculturists	LV
South Dakota:	
Foreign-born as agriculturists	LIII
Immigration favored by farmers	LIII
Southern Europe:	
Illiteracy of immigrants from	X
Immigration from	LXXX
Southern States, agricultural conditions in	LIV
Standard of living:	
Anthracite miners	LXXV
Effect of immigration	LXXV, LXXVI
Foreign-born, raised by immigration	XXVII
Jews	LXX, LXXV, LXXVI
Poles	LXXV
Roumanian Jews	LXXV, LXXVI
Russian and Polish Jews	LXX, LXXV
Syrians	XLI, XLII
Textile trades, effect of immigration	XXXVI
Statistics of immigration:	
Accuracy questioned	IX, LXV, LXVI
1870–1897	LXXVIII
Methods of securing and presenting discussed	LXV
Steamship companies:	
Efforts to induce immigration	XIV, XC, XCI
Immigration legislation, attitude toward	CXI, CXII
Inspection of immigrants	XVIII, CIII–CV
Liability for—	
Care of detained immigrants	XCIX
Transportation of deported immigrants	XCIX
Protection of immigrants at sea, proposed legislation	CXII
Rates, low, effect on immigration	XIV, XC
Sunday labor, introduction due to immigration, iron and steel trade	LXXXII
Sweat shops (see also *Clothing trade*):	
Evil conditions	LXXXI
Inspection, impossibility of	LXXXI, LXXXII
Jews, employment of	LXXXII
Tenement houses, amount of clothing produced in, discussed	XXIX, XXXI, XXXVI
Sweating system:	
Causes of existence	XXV
Existing conditions	XXIV–XXVI
Subcontract system	XXIV–XXVI
Syrians:	
Clan organization	XLI
Immigration of	LXXX
Labor organizations, difficulty of forming	XLI
Naturalization	XLII
Number of immigrants	XLI
Occupations	XLI
Standard of living	XLI, XLII
Task system, clothing trade	XXVIII
Tax, head, on immigrants, increase advocated	CXIV
Temporary immigration (see also "*Birds of passage*"):	
Restriction discussed	LXXIV
Tenement-house manufacture: Clothing trade. (See *Clothing trade*.)	

Tenement houses: Page.
    Clothing trade, work in, conditions XXIX
    Laws, inefficient enforcement of XLVII
    New York City—
        Conditions .... XLII–XLIV
        Responsibility for bad conditions XLIV
    New York State—
        Early legislation XLVII
        Law of 1901 .... XLVII, XLVIII
Tennessee, foreign-born as agriculturists LVI
Texas, foreign-born as agriculturists LXI
Textile trades:
    French Canadians, employment of, effects XXXVI
    Labor organizations, difficulty in forming XXXVII
    Machinery, skill and wages, effect on XXXVI
Tin industry, foreign-born, employment of .... LXXXII, LXXXIII
Transportation:
    Rates, low—
        Effect on immigration .... XIV, XC
Unemployment:
    Age as a cause LXXXIX
    Coal miners, effect of immigration .... XXXIV, LXXXI
Union labels, effect of, clothing trade XXXII
Utah, foreign-born as agriculturists LVII
Vermont:
    Foreign-born as agriculturists LI
    Immigration opposed by farmers LI
Virginia, foreign-born as agriculturists LV
Wages:
    Anthracite-coal miners LXXXI
    Cigar-making trade—
        Country competition, effect of .... XXXII, XXXIII
        Immigration, effect of XXXIII
        Organization, effect of XXXIII
        Rates of .... XXXII, XXXIII
    Clothing trade—
        Effect of immigration discussed .... XXVII, XXVIII
        Fluctuation XXVI
        Increase through factory inspection XXXI
        Tenement-house work XXIX
    Coal miners, effects of immigration LXXXI
    Country competition, factor in depressing XXIV
    Factors tending to depress XXIV
    Granite-cutting trade, effect of immigration XXXIX
    Immigration, effect of, discussed .... XXIII, XXVII, XXXIII, XXXIX, LXXXI
    Increase, continuous tendency .... LXXVII, LXXVIII
    Iron and steel trades, lowered through immigration LXXXII
    Labor organizations, effect on .... XXVIII, XXXIII, XXXIV, XXXVII
    Machinery, effect on .... XXXII, XXXIV, XXXVI, XXXVIII
    Textile trades, effect of immigration XXXVI
    Wood-working trades XXXVII
    Women and children, competition of, effect on XXIV
Washington, foreign-born as agriculturists LVII
West Virginia, foreign-born as agriculturists LV
Wisconsin:
    Foreign-born as agriculturists .... LII, LIII
    Immigration favored by farmers LII
Wood-working trades:
    Foreign-born employees, percentage of XXXVII
    Labor organizations XXXVII
    Wages XXXVII
Women:
    Competition, effect in depressing wages XXIV
    Inspection of immigrants .... XCVIII, XCIX

PART I.

HEARINGS BEFORE THE INDUSTRIAL COMMISSION ON THE SUBJECT OF IMMIGRATION.

INDUSTRIAL COMMISSION.

IMMIGRATION.

WASHINGTON, D. C., *January 10, 1899.*

TESTIMONY OF HON. HERMAN STUMP,

Ex-Commissioner-General of Immigration.

The commission met at 11 a. m. January 10, 1899. Vice-Chairman Phillips presided, and introducing the witness said, Mr. Stump, who was formerly Commissioner-General of Immigration, had been invited to appear before the commission and give testimony upon the subject of immigration.

Q. (By Mr. SMYTH.) Please state whether you were a member of Congress and had anything to do with the Chinese exclusion act.—A. I became a member of Congress on the 4th of March, 1889, when Harrison was inaugurated. I was placed on the Committee on Immigration at that time, and two years subsequently I was made chairman of the Immigration Committee. Upon my retirement from Congress I was appointed Commissioner-General of Immigration, and served four years, and until August of the McKinley Administration.

Q. Did you have anything to do with preparing the draft of the Chinese exclusion act?—A. I did. While a member of a joint committee of the House and Senate of the Fifty-first Congress, in company with Mr. Owen and Mr. Lehlbach, of New Jersey, I traveled extensively, collecting information in regard to immigration, and visited Detroit, Chicago, St. Louis, Cincinnati, and several other cities. That report was made to Congress by Mr. Owen, and you will find it on file. Subsequently we were directed to go to the Pacific coast, and with Senator Watson C. Squire we made investigations in regard to Chinese immigration. We visited Spokane Falls, Seattle, Port Townsend, Portland, San Francisco, San Diego, etc., and we made a report to Congress (House Doc. No. 4048, second session Fifty-first Congress), and subsequently I introduced a bill for the exclusion of the Chinese, which, with some modifications, was the same as what was called the "Geary Act," the present law relating to Chinese immigration.

Q. Did you later, as a member of Congress, prepare the present immigration law?—A. Yes. Mr. Owen, Mr. Chandler, and myself prepared the act of 1891. When I became chairman of the House committee, Mr. Chandler and myself drafted the act of 1893, but he was kind enough to say that it was the "Stump Act."

Q. How long were you Commissioner of Immigration?—A. Four years and some months.

Q. Was that act successful in limiting the immigration to this country?—A. Eminently so, I think, and, with very slight modifications, I doubt whether it should be changed for some time.

Q. Is immigration to this country affected by the degree of our prosperity?—A. Undoubtedly it is. Immigration to this country. I believe, is promoted very much by letters written by people here inviting their friends and relatives to come. They know the state of the country, and whether their friends can secure employment when they arrive. and they write to them when to come and when not to come. In that way I think immigration indicates the prosperity of the country.

Q. Did your Bureau take any cognizance of the number of immigrants who returned to foreign lands?—A. No, there is no law requiring these statistics to be furnished. I have urged Congress to pass such a law. We had to depend entirely upon the courtesy of the steamship companies, which would furnish us the number of steerage passengers leaving the country. We knew, of course, the number that came in.

Q. Will you tell us whether the present law can be amended to make it more satisfactory?—A. I think amendments should be principally in relation to minor details relating to the administration of that law. Its main features should not be altered. There are quite a number of minor suggestions which we have made both to the Secretary of the Treasury and to Congress. They were reported to the Secretary under the commission which Mr. Carlisle appointed, consisting of Dr. J. H. Senner, then commissioner of the port of New York, Mr. Edward F. McSweeney, then assistant commissioner, and myself. Under that commission we did considerable work, which was reported to the Secretary in the report of the Immigration Investigation Commission. You will find that that commission was directed to inquire and report upon the following interrogatories:

"1. What changes, if any, in the rules and regulations now in force are necessary in order to secure a more efficient execution of existing laws relating to immigration and the laws prohibiting the importation of alien laborers under contract?

"2. Whether said laws are defective in any particular, and what practical difficulties, if any, have been encountered in their execution?

"3. What effect, if any, immigration has had upon the wages of labor or opportunities for employment in the United States, and whether or not the existing industrial condition of the country is attributable in any degree to the influx of laborers from abroad?

"4. Whether any measures, and if so what, can be adopted under existing legislation to discourage the concentration of immigrant laborers in particular localities and to secure a better distribution of immigrants whose admission to the country is not prohibited by law?

"5. Whether the 'padrone' system exists in this country, and if so, to what extent and among what classes of immigrants, and what measures can be taken under existing laws to break it up and protect American laborers against its evil effects upon wages, and at the same time improve the social and economic condition of the immigrants?"

The commission was also directed to procure and report such information, from all available sources, as would enable the Department to employ its official force in the most effective manner for the enforcement of the immigration and alien contract-labor laws according to their true intent and purpose, and to suggest such amendments as experience may have shown to be necessary to adapt them to existing conditions.

That commission was organized, I being made chairman. The first step we took was to address a circular letter to all the labor organizations of the United States of which we knew, and Mr. McSweeney had the assistance of Mr. Gompers and Mr. Sovereign and others. He was given lists of the organizations to which letters were directed. The circular letter first stated the scope of the commission, as given you, and then asked for such replies as they considered proper. The replies are contained in this book. The next step we took was to address the following letter to the various governors of States:

"1. Does your State, or any portion thereof, desire immigration? If only portions, what portions?

"2. What are the resources that need development? If agricultural, what character of products are to be cultivated, etc.? If mineral, what kinds of mines are to be worked? If artisans are required, please state the trades and occupations in which employment can be found. If unskilled labor is wanted, please indicate the kind of work for which it is needed.

"3. What wages are usually paid in each of the occupations referred to? Please also give any other information you think will be useful in guiding desirable immigrants to your section.

"4. State what nationalities are preferred, and the order of preference, numerically."

We received replies to this letter from probably half or maybe three-fourths of the governors of the States of the Union. You will find those replies in the report of the Immigration Investigation Commission.

With regard to the distribution of immigration, the commission recommended a plan which had not been thought of before, and the more I consider it the more I am convinced it would be wise to have it adopted. I will now speak of the port of New York, where nearly three-fourths of the emigrants to the United States are landed. Many of them have a fixed destination and go there. Many of them arrive in New York, where they remain an indefinite time in order to determine where they should go. Some would go to Chicago, some to Cincinnati, etc. We found that the larger cities of the United States were being congested with immigrants who really desired to find employment elsewhere. It is a known fact that two, three, or four hundred thousand immigrants come into New York yearly. In ten years that would be a vast number of newly arrived immigrants, but most of them find employment elsewhere after they have expended what little means they had and have become impoverished. For that reason we suggested to the Secretary that we should have erected on Ellis Island, by private enterprise, a large exhibition hall, where the various State immigration bureaus or authorities could have rooms and an opportunity for displaying the products of their State, informing the immigrant what inducements they could offer him and giving him all other information which it would be necessary for him to obtain. He would also ascertain there that in certain States and portions of States, take New York and Pennsylvania, for instance, no immigrants were desired. In that way the immigrant would have an intelligent idea where he could locate. He would be informed regarding the prices of land and labor, adaptability of the soil, mines, the working of railroads, and all places where labor is desired throughout the United States, and before leaving the station could make an intelligent selection of locality for settlement. We regarded it as a large distributing center for immigration, and of course States that did not desire immigration would not be represented there. Railroads that wanted laborers would be represented, and it would be a clearing-house for immigrants. Bills were introduced by Mr. Lodge and by Mr. Chandler to carry out that intention, when the buildings on Ellis Island were burned down, and I suppose the project is now in abeyance.

Q. How did the law forbidding the importation of contract labor operate?—A. I found, when I came into office, that that law was exceedingly defective. I administered it to the best of my ability and, I think, quite successfully, meeting the approval of the labor men. At the time that law was passed there were various strikes in the country, and employers imported directly all kind of immigrants with the view of giving them the places of American workingmen. That law was so successfully administered, that the wholesale importation of contract laborers was stopped. We found sometimes that four or five, or maybe eight or ten men, would come under promises from mining people to take the place of American labor. Those men we sent back, to the best of our ability, upon information we received from labor organizations, and we had the privilege of doing so until after they had been here for a year. We found many isolated cases in which a brother would write to his brother saying if he would come out to his farm he would give him employment until he could find another place. I do not believe that when this law was enacted it was intended to reach a case like that. But we rigidly enforced the law and separated families in that way. I think it was a hardship and that that feature of the law should be modified. It is perfectly natural for a man who has his family over there to promise aid and assistance to his relatives until they can find something to do; but the law, as it stands, compels us to send them back. If an employer could go to his workman and say, "Have you not a brother in Germany? We are in need of a man; write to your brother to come"—in that case there is no hardship at all. Those people were sent back.

Q. Do you think that phase of the law is successfully enforced?—A. I think so. It was during my administration in many cases which I thought entailed great hardship. The difficulty of sending these men back is, that in the law which was drawn, I have been told by Mr. Powderly, there is this language:

(Mr. Stump here read the first section of the act of February 26, 1885, known as the "Contract Labor Law.")

"*Be it enacted by the Senate and House of Representatives of the United States of America in Congress assembled,* That from and after the passage of this act it shall be unlawful for any person, company, partnership, or corporation, in any manner whatsoever, to prepay the transportation, or in any way assist or encourage the importation or migration of any alien or aliens, any foreigner or foreigners, into the United States, its Territories, or the District of Columbia, under contract or agreement, parol or special, express or implied, made previous to the mportation or migration of such alien or aliens, foreigner or foreigners, to perform labor or service of any kind in the United States, its Territories, or the District of Columbia."

The courts have uniformly held that there must be an express or implied contract entered into abroad, which must be proved before the party can be deported. That is almost an impossibility. The prosecution of the contractor is almost invariably impossible. The immigrant comes here and we examine him and ask him: "What induced you to come to America?" He replies: "Such and such a party told me if I came here he would give me certain wages." We sent that fellow back. We can not prosecute the employer because, in the first place, what little testimony we had we banished to the other side of the water. But his testimony would not be sufficient because the courts have held that that contract must be made abroad; and he has merely said: "If you will come here, we will do so and so." We could not prosecute the contractor, but sent back the person who had sold out all his little possessions and become separated from the land of his birth, and the guilty man escaped. In order to rectify that I suggested that the law be amended by inserting one or two words which I thought would cover the difficulty. Some twenty suggestions were made. I will show you one which I think is most important. The amendment I suggested to section 1 of the act of 1885 was by adding thereto, after the words "United States, the Territories, or the District of Columbia," on the seventh line and wherever else it may be necessary, the words "or by undertaking or promise of employment upon arrival in the United States, or under any contract," etc., expressed or implied. That made the party guilty who, by any offer to the foreigner, induced his immigration into the United States. Of course it was not necessary to have the contract made abroad, but if he was induced to leave home upon a promise to make a contract on his arrival it would be sufficient to procure conviction, and I think that would go far toward breaking up this induced immigration by persons who desire to employ workmen to take the place of American labor.

Q. If you deported the immigrant, would you have lost your witness?—A. We would not deport that person, but we deported the immigrant before because we knew it was useless to hold him to convict the principal. We sent the immigrant back, but could do nothing with the party who made the contract. Here, if he testifies that this party induced him to come over by letter or otherwise (frequently they have the letter inducing them to come over), we would hold that party as a witness, because he would be of service then, but would not be of service unless the law was changed.

Q. Was there not an act passed in the last Congress amending the immigration laws which failed because Mr. Cleveland did not sign it?—A. That was what was called the "educational bill."

Q. Did it provide an educational test affecting immigration?—A. Yes; and it has been pending since in the present Congress.

Q. What are your views in regard to that?—A. I have not seen the bill as it is now presented, but my views on the educational test are fully set forth in the report of the Immigration Investigating Committee. We reported on the educational test. If you desire to get the most efficient mode of restricting immigration, I would take the educational bill with some amendments, but if you desire to get a class of immigrants here who would be most beneficial to our country I think the educational bill does not reach it. My idea of immigration is this: We have, in my mind, the most skillful and the best laboring class in the world. I think American workingmen are superior to others. It may be in some of the finer arts, where it takes long years to acquire the skill that is required, it is not so, but for the production of work, with our improved machinery, we can beat the world. We are also an educated people. We find that Americans are performing higher classes of labor. We want our sons to become our clerks, accountants, and business men and find employment in the higher walks and occupations. We must necessarily have a certain other class to do our manual work—not menial exactly, but work which is honorable but at the same time of a lower order, which requires no skill or education at all. We want laborers upon our roads, upon our railroads, to clean our sewers and streets, and everything of that kind, and when you look around I think you will find that Americans are getting beyond that. I think the importation of good, able-bodied workmen into the United States has tended to elevate our own people. A young able-bodied man who comes from a foreign land to settle here, with energy and willingness to work, is an acquisition to the country, and while we do not want him to occupy the positions which education would enable him to occupy, we want him to occupy the positions where it does not much matter whether he knows his A B C's or the single rule of three or anything else; but as a rule, with few exceptions, I think you will find that even the steerage passengers coming over here are as well and better educated, as a class, than the Americans. Take the Swiss, German, Swede, Norwegian, Englishman, and Irishman, and the percentage of those unable to read and write is much less than the United States census gives as the percentage in the United States. It will astonish you, but such is the fact. On the other hand, if you go into the southern countries of Europe, you will find that education has been woefully neglected. From the last report I made, at the end of the fiscal year, June 30, 1897, page 6, I state that—

"Under the present laws ability to read and write is not essential to the admission of the immigrant, and the question of illiteracy has only been taken up for statistical purposes.

"The educational attainments of the immigrants who came during this fiscal year show a marked improvement over those who came in 1895-96. For instance, the percentage of illiteracy was in those who came from—

Country.	1896.	1897.	Country.	1896.	1897.
Austria-Hungary	0.39	0.29	Sweden	0.0116	0.0087
Russia	.41	.28	Denmark	.0095	.0048
Italy	.54	.50	Switzerland	.079	.011
Germany	.0296	.019	France	.0488	.042

By the United States census of 1890 the illiteracy of the whole United States was 0.1334 per cent. As I say in my reports, illiteracy and undesirability of immigrants seem to go hand in hand because we find that while the people of the north of Italy are good people and desirable immigrants those coming from Naples, from Palermo and Messina (all of whom ship from Naples) are objectionable, as a rule. Undesirable immigration comes from the south of Europe, and in these countries the greatest illiteracy prevails. Below a line drawn, say, south of France, running through the Pyrenees, which would leave Spain and Portugal south, thence to Naples, thence northward toward Vienna, thence toward St. Petersburg, illiteracy is dense.

Q. (By Mr. KENNEDY.) Do you refer to the immigrants coming into this country?—A. Yes, sir.

Portugal is 0.7769 per cent illiterate. Of the southern countries Italy will come next. Italy is 0.5459 per cent. Austria-Hungary is divided up into several provinces, and there we get the Poles and Slavs. Take Hungary, it is 0.4651, and Gallacia is 0.6037. Russia is about the next. Russia proper is 0.4114. I say that south of a line between France and Spain and running a little north into Hungary and Poland the education of Europe seems to be very much neglected, while in the northern portion the educational facilities are far superior to those in our own country, where the percentage of educated people is very much less. We have 0.1343 per cent of illiteracy. It is hardly generous to treat the comparison in that way, for this reason: The census gives the percentage looking at the educated and uneducated of the whole country; but here we have only investigated the educational qualifications of the steerage passengers; and we find that education in Europe is carried to much greater extent than it is really in America. I suppose in our country the negro population would add very much to the illiteracy and percentage. Taking our New England States as an example, and although I have had no occasion to look into that, I imagine that the percentage of illiteracy there is as low as in any portion of Europe; and for that reason, I dare say, you could draw a line in the United States in the same way between the northern and southern portions. There is a highly educated class in the South, but they have at the same time the most ignorant negro class.

Q. (By Mr. C. J. HARRIS.) Is the effect of these ocean steamship companies bringing immigrants here good or bad?—A. Well, the ocean steamship lines are only the means of transportation. If you will read carefully the act of 1893, you will find that it does not add another class to the excluded people, but is an administrative act and is directed to secure a proper examination of immigrants before embarkation. It has led to a very great restriction of immigration, as my reports will show throughout. Steamship lines have agents throughout the whole of Europe. They are located in almost every little town, and are more numerous in places from which immigration comes. They had a system by which they gave a commission to their agents for every ticket sold, so that their agents were interested in selling as many tickets as possible, totally regardless of the character of people that bought them. The result was an indiscriminate flow of all classes to the United States, and largely of the most undesirable classes. There were "padrones," Italian bankers, and so on, who were largely interested in bringing these people over, and they were probably associated with, and maybe were, steamship agents. I know Italian bankers in New York who are really "padrones," who furnish money to immigrants in Italy. I went over there to look into it myself. The agent abroad would approach a man and say: "Would you like to go to America?" and he would say: "Yes; but I have no money." "Well, if I give you a ticket, will you work for me for wages in America," and so on. The consequence was he made that agreement, and when he arrived in New York he became body and soul the slave of that "padrone." The Italians are a quiet, peaceable, genial, hard-working race. They work on little lots of land. They are exceedingly good cultivators of the soil. They are the best masons, I suppose, you can find anywhere, and always ready and willing to work; but when they arrive, say in New York, and go to their banker to whom they belong, he puts them in gangs and sells their labor out to corporations, railroad corporations, or various employments, and he sends with them what is called a "boss." Take 500 or 1,000 men, contracted to go out to some of your States to work on a railroad. They arrive there under the charge of this boss, they speak no English, and will have nothing to do with anybody but that boss. The boss will buy $100 worth of lumber, will rig up a shanty, and will charge those Italians each $1 a month for sleeping bunks. If he lodges some 500 in that shanty, it is paying him $500 a month. He has the supplying of all they eat and wear. When pay day comes the boss receives the wages, and he accounts to the "padrone," and the poor Italian finds himself a debtor and slave for years under that system, and it is the slavery which I, under the directions of the Administration, tried to eradicate. I think the success with which we have met must be admitted. The "padrones" lately call themselves bankers. They say they have got enough Italians in this country now, and that they do not want any more. The last case I investigated, I think, was in Brunswick, Ga., in connection with the building of sewers or something else. You will find a report of it in the report of the Immigration Investigating Committee.

Q. (By Mr. KENNEDY.) Is that system now broken up?—A. Yes, sir; you may say it is pretty well broken up; but I will tell you where it has broken out afresh, and it will need a very great surgical operation to cut it out. It is among the Assyrians, Arabs, Turks, Greeks, and Armenians coming into this country. They are all under the bosses that I spoke of in relation to the Italian immigrants, and they are brought here generally to peddle goods, to black boots, to be scissors grinders, and actual beggars on the streets. These men will import and pay well to get a woman to come here with a child in her arms to shed tears on the streets and solicit alms, which she gives to her employer. These things may astonish you. Forty of them were arrested at Ellis Island some days ago. They were going down to one of the Southern States. I think they were ticketed for New Orleans. They serve their master for so much a day, and are obliged to turn in every evening what they collect. You will find them with push-carts in the streets of New York. My experience is that they have an idea that they require $25 to get in. They arrive at Ellis Island, and almost every one of them will have $25 in American gold, and the mystery is where they get it. It is the impression of immigration officials that the gold they have on their persons at the time they arrive is immediately taken from them and shipped back to the country from which they came, to be returned with others. That money goes backward and forward.

Q. (By Mr. FARQUHAR.) What is the percentage of this class of people you are speaking of in relation to the whole immigration of a year?—A. We can give you the exact figures.

Q. I mean the class owned by "padrones."—A. I do not think there are so many. I think they are nearly all that class of people that come from the countries I named. From those countries it is almost all induced immigration.

Q. Has the alien contract-labor law really partly stopped all padroning?—A. That is not due so much to the alien contract-labor law as it is to the immigration law. They are entirely distinct, but both operate in this case.

Q. I think in your last report you mention the fact that the immigration of 1896 and 1897 had been smaller than it had been from 1870, and in the returns of the steamship companies on the steerage passenger lists returning to Europe and elsewhere, that same fiscal year, there were nearly 112,000. Does the padroning system exist among those people who were returning?—A. I suppose a great many thousands went back to visit their friends in Europe, because the season for labor had expired, and to come again another year. It is cheaper to live in Europe in their own homes and pay their passage back at the winter rate, than it is to live in America idle.

Those returning over the steerage may be bona fide residents of our country. They are sons who live in the West and have their parents in Europe. They make visits to their parents, and probably in the spring bring their parents, and sisters, and brothers with them. A great many have gone back because it is hard to procure labor, because of hard times, in the United States. I must call your attention to the fact that no money is required of an immigrant to land in America—not a cent. A man, under our present law, who is able-bodied, ready and willing to work, is entitled to admission whether he has a dollar in his pocket or not. Now, that is lost sight of for the reason that under the act of 1893, Mr. Chandler and myself desired, as far as we were able, to ascertain, only for statistical purposes, how much money immigrants brought into the United States. It was not a sine qua non as to their landing, and we arrived at the conclusion that we would ask them whether they had as much as $30, and if they had $30 only, we required them to show it, not that it was necessary for them to have any money, but we wanted that as statistics to show how many came with $30 or less. Then we said it would not do to ask them how much money they had over $30, because we would make them the objects of designing men, and probably they would be robbed or deprived of their funds if they were required to disclose it upon our records. Therefore, we said, "Have you got $30 or less?" and if they said less, we said, "How much?" If they said they had $30 or more, no other question was ever asked. It was not for the purpose of admission.

Q. In the decade before 1894 the average of the immigration into America was about 472,063, and the average in 1894 to 1897, during your administration, was only 279,000. How do you account for that difference of nearly 50 per cent?—A. We can not claim all the credit of the decrease in immigration for the act of 1893, because there was great depression throughout this country and it was not as desirable for immigrants to come to America as it had been; but, fortunately, we had administered this law so rigidly that we sent back, maybe, three or four persons to every little hamlet where they were coming from before, and they carried the news to those who purposed coming, and they were thus deterred from coming, and that restricted immigration.

Something carried me away from what I was going to tell you in regard to the purchase and sale of tickets and the inspection of immigrants abroad, and the purposes of the act of 1893. I said that these steamships had their agents in all the various little towns and places, and paid a commission for the sale of tickets. The act of 1893 required that before the embarkation of any immigrants upon any vessel the manifest should be sworn to by the captain of the vessel before the consul of the United States, stating that he had no (designating the prohibited class) aboard his ship; then the surgeon was required also to make an affidavit that there was no immigrant aboard that ship who was not physically able to work, and that there were no diseases aboard that ship that were prohibited. When the steamship companies found that agents throughout the country had sold tickets and the immigrants had arrived at the port of embarkation, and that many upon being examined were not allowed to go aboard the ship, they immediately gave instructions to all their agents, who became the best inspectors of immigrants we had. These agents were located in towns and villages, and had the opportunity of knowing and coming into personal contact with the people to whom those tickets were sold. By that law, wherever a ticket was sold, the man selling it had to have exhibited all the laws of the United States with regard to immigration, showing who were prohibited and who were not, and they called their attention to them. The steamship companies said: "If you sell a ticket to a man or woman who is rejected at the point of embarkation we will not only take away your commission, but we will charge you with the expenses of returning that immigrant to his home." So that the very ticket seller himself became one of the inspectors for the benefit of the United States. That was the first inspection, and I found it the best inspection of all, because they punished their ticket agents if they sold to a person who was rejected at the point of embarkation or when he arrived in the United States.

Q. Were the medical inspector and agent at these foreign ports of embarkation under the employ of the steamship companies or the Government?—A. In all the foreign countries I visited they have a health officer, who is a Government employee, and he makes an inspection. We have also our consuls at every point. The shipmaster and surgeon, though, are the men who make the affidavit.

Q. He is a medical inspector, then, of the immigrant?—A. Yes; and he is required to make a daily report of the condition of those immigrants, which is brought with the quarantine guard and exhibited to the immigrant officials at the time of landing, when they come to be inspected on arrival.

Upon the arrival of a ship at quarantine, at New York, for instance, officers of the immigration service board that vessel, with the health and customs officers, and they examine the manifests. They examine the first and second class cabins. If they have any information as to any person who is in the first or second class cabins that they are either contract laborers or trying to evade the laws, they inspect those two cabins especially. We generally get such information from labor organizations. Diamond cutters and glass blowers slip in in the second-class cabins, and we generally get onto them. If any persons are found in there whom we want to examine further, we direct the captain of the vessel to send them with the steerage passengers to Ellis Island. Then they are arranged in groups, and the manifest that has been made in Europe, which has the oath of the captain and of the surgeon of the vessel and certificate of our consul attached to it, is placed on the register's desk, and these men are grouped according to the lists. When the immigrant appears the registry clerk has exactly what is stated by the captain, the company, and the surgeon in regard to his case, and the immigrant has to answer all those interrogatories, and the clerk goes over that again to see whether there is any variance between the two and if, to all appearances, the immigrant is entitled to land he is immediately passed by that registry clerk, and he goes where he pleases. When a person appears whom the registry clerk has any suspicion of, or who does not show sufficient ability to work, who is aged, poor, etc., he is detained to go before a special board of inquiry, and those cases are tried just as you would try any case before any other tribunal. There are four inspectors detailed for that duty, and it requires the vote of three of them to land anybody. In the meantime all women have been examined by a matron with regard to possible pregnancy, and all immigrants are especially examined by a surgeon of the United States Marine-Hospital Service, and if they appear weakly or diseased they are put in another room for a special examination. If the surgeon certifies that a man, in his opinion, is not capable of earning his living in the United States or is suffering from disease, mental or physical, he sends his certificate, with his report, to the board of examiners. He is rejected by the board and deported. They make this examination. They send for witnesses. If a woman comes over and says her husband is in this country, and shows no money, she is detained. A telegram is sent to where she says her husband is, and unless that husband reports, in all probability she is sent back. Pregnant unmarried females and lewd women are returned. In the same way, if a boy comes and no one turns up to take care of him, and he is not otherwise capable of landing, he is sent back.

Q. (By Mr. SMYTH.) Are they kept at the expense of the Government?—A. No, sir; they are kept at the expense of the steamship company. The law is that they are quasi aboard ship until they have been examined and passed. Ellis Island and the immigration station are for the accommodation of the steamship companies. A vessel coming into New York with a thousand immigrants can not unload or do anything until she gets rid of those immigrants, and they are sent to the island and fed at the expense of the steamship companies and treated exactly as if they were aboard a ship. The steamship companies have their agents there, and when a man or woman is detained they telegraph and bring the case to the attention of the immigrant's friends and furnish desired information to this board of special inspectors, so that the Government is not at any expense in regard to the matter. If they are rejected they are returned to the country from which they came, at the steamship company's expense, and for that reason their agents in Europe are exceedingly particular to whom they sell a ticket, because the expense which has been incurred by reason of the sale of that ticket is deducted from their earnings.

Q. (By Mr. FARQUHAR.) Is there any penalty attached to the steamship companies for bringing this undesirable class of passengers?—A. If they do it designedly they are liable to quite a heavy penalty. You will find that in the act of 1891. It is always better to go to the law. I can not recollect those items.

Q. Are there many cases involving steamship companies that bring immigrants under the contract-labor law that go into court now?—A. No, sir; I am afraid I am responsible for that. When I went to California, looking into the Chinese question, I found that United States officers there had pending three or four thousand habeas corpus cases relating to the Chinese. A Chinaman would, as a general thing, come to the United States and in two or three years accumulate one, two, or three hundred dollars, which was a fortune to him, and go home. He would arrive, and immediately he would be detained. A writ of habeas corpus would be obtained for him, straw bond would be given, and that case would not be heard for years. The Chinaman would go back in the interim, and the result was the Government had to pay costs and was out an enormous amount for habeas corpus proceedings. What was called the "Japanese Case" was tried about that time, I think in 1893, by the Supreme Court of the United States. It rendered a decision that the executive branch of the Government had the right, under the immigration laws, to hear and determine these cases, and to hold these people, and the immigrant had the right of appeal from the decision of the board of inquiry that I spoke of, to the Secretary of the Treasury. That practically did away with the right of courts to interfere, and, as I told you, we are sustained by that decision, and the consequence has been that when these cases have recently been taken before the courts upon writs of habeas corpus the immigrant has been remanded to the custody of the immigration officials, and a like decision was made in Chinese cases.

Q. When your board in New York decides to deport an immigrant, has the immigrant the right to appeal?—A. Yes, sir.

Q. Has the inspector the right of appeal also?—A. Yes, sir; that was a new feature in that law. The idea was that many persons were landed there through sympathy or for reasons of humanity when they should have been deported, so the right of appeal was given the inspector as well as the immigrant

Q. What was the percentage of deportations there under your administration out of the whole number arriving?—A. I do not think it ever reached over 1 per cent, and prior to my administration the proportion was very much less.

Q. Have the general immigration laws as amended up to 1897 and the alien contract-labor law practically suppressed the padrone and alien contract systems?— A. I think they have, in a very great measure. I think, with few exceptions, isolated cases, the importation of contract labor has been suppressed; but there is some padroning still existing in the case of the importation of Armenians, Assyrians, Turks, and Arabs. You can find bodies of Armenians in the wire works about Chicago, and another body about Lynn, Mass., and you will find beggars and others scattered throughout the United States, and I think the duty of the immigration authorities is to eradicate this condition.

I heard of a case the other day. There were about forty of them and they got separated. The authorities got their story separately from each of them, and it gradually leaked out that, although they stated they were going to New York, they were obliged to state that a certain party, naming him, had induced them to come and had furnished them with money, and it developed that they were going to a certain place in the South for the purpose of peddling goods to be furnished by this padrone.

Q. (By Mr. SMYTH.) Is that the padrone system?—A. The features of it are the same that formerly existed with regard to Italian labor.

Q. (By Mr. PHILLIPS.) Is it a fact that crime and pauperism are decreasing among the most enlightened nations of Europe, while it is on the increase in America?—A. Oh, I do not agree with that at all; I think it is really the reverse. I do not think crime and pauperism are increasing in the United States; certainly not in our prosperous times now.

Q. I have seen statistics sustaining that view, but I quote from memory only. The statement was made that both crime and pauperism were on the increase in America.—A. I can not think that is so. I think the statistics must be wrong. Take the foreign population—the Italian, or the Jew—can you name any Jews who are paupers in any almshouse in the United States? Can you name any Italian? These people are able-bodied workmen and when they land here they are able and willing to go to work. We admit only such persons. Such a man is of value to this country the moment he lands. He has not cost us anything. He has lived in the old country. He is ready now to give us the benefit of his labor, and he does it willingly. If the next day he meets with an accident, he has no place under heaven to go to. You would naturally suppose you would find him in an almshouse. When you consult the statistics of those who were born in foreign countries and look for them in the almshouses, you really do not find them; their friends try to take care of them. In the statistics which come from our eleemosynary institutions you will find the so-called foreign inmates are of foreign parentage. They are naturalized citizens and they are entitled to such care, but you will find very few who were born abroad in the almshouses here. By the act of 1892 a head tax of a dollar was levied—50 cents then, now a dollar—on every immigrant coming into the United States, which supports the Immigration Bureau, and it is provided that that money shall be paid into the Treasury for the purpose of paying the cost of the administration of the law and for taking care of such immigrants as fall into distress. The Immigration Bureau has always, for a period of one year, paid the expenses of every immigrant who went into any one of the almshouses of the United States, and under that law I suppose we have paid twenty, thirty, or forty thousand dollars a year for the care of those who were overtaken by sickness or accident. I know of no immigrant who landed in the United States who within one year was a charge upon any charitable institution. We invited all institutions to send us statistics.

Q. (By Mr. FARQUHAR.) Allow me to call your attention to section 11 of the act of March 3, 1891. As I read that law, if the transportation company or the corporation that brought this immigrant into the country can be found, it shall bear the expense. Is that the understanding?—A. Yes. The records kept by the immigration authorities are kept by such a system that at any time you can get the record of any immigrant who landed in the United States. If you could give us the name, the vessel, and the date, we will find a record of his landing, his condition, and where he went to. You will find in my reports that I sent persons back at the expense of the steamship companies, or paid for temporary sickness or disability out of the immigration fund. But I speak of those going to the almshouses who, having been landed, met with an accident or were taken temporarily sick with typhoid or scarlet fever, or anything of that kind. The steamship companies can not be held responsible for them, and their trouble is of such a temporary nature that the United States would not be justified in sending them back. But if a steamship company brings a person here who is, say, half gone with consumption, and within one year we find that man in an almshouse, we write to that company and say, on such and such a day we will send you such and such a person who has become a public charge from such and such a cause, from which he was suffering on his arrival. We have sent many insane back in that way. These are the people you will find mentioned in our reports.

Q. How is the immigrant head money expended?—A. It can not, under the law, be used for any other purpose than as expressly authorized by section 1 of the act of 1882. It is most scrupulously guarded by the Treasury officials. That fund is turned in to the Treasury and you have to draw your warrant showing the purposes for which it is drawn. Section 1 of the act of 1882 provides as follows:

" That there shall be levied, collected, and paid a duty of fifty cents for each and every passenger not a citizen of the United States who shall come by steam or sail vessel from a foreign port to any port within the United States. The said duty shall be paid to the collector of customs of the port to which such passenger shall come, or if there, be no collector at such port, then to the collector of customs nearest thereto, by the master, owner, agent, or consignee of every such vessel within twenty-four hours after the entry thereof into such port. The money thus collected shall be paid into the United States Treasury and shall constitute a fund to be called the immigrant fund, and shall be used, under the direction of the Secretary of the Treasury, to defray the expense of regulating immigration under this act, and for the care of immigrants arriving in the United States, for the relief of such as are in distress, and for the general purposes and expenses of carrying this act into effect. The duty imposed by this section shall be a lien upon the vessels which shall bring such passengers into the United States, and shall be a debt in favor of the United States against the owner or owners of such vessel, and the payment of such duty may be enforced by any legal or equitable remedy: *Provided*, That no greater sum shall be expended for the purposes hereinbefore mentioned, at any port, than shall have been collected at such port."

It is under that act we care for immigrants in charitable institutions for the period of one year after their arrival.

Q. (By Mr. PHILLIPS.) Does that fund accumulate each year or is it exhausted?—A. Oh, I have always had, during my administration, and I think there is now, $150,000, or $200,000, or $250,000 surplus, and not one of the immigrants nor the administration of the law has ever been a charge on the people of the United States.

Q. (By Mr. FARQUHAR.) Has it been used properly as a help to the immigrant?—A. Before I came into the office the immigrant fund contributed very largely to the payment of the construction of the buildings on Ellis Island. Acts of Congress to assist the immigrant fund were passed, one, I think, for $100,000 and another, I think, for $150,000; and it was stated that the $100,000 appropriated was to be repaid from the immigrant fund in four annual payments. During my administration I paid that $100,000, and had an accumulation, in round numbers, of about $250,000 more, and then we were really acting against ourselves, because we were passing laws to restrict immigration, thereby curtailing the funds we were receiving. On the 14th of June of last year the buildings on Ellis Island were burned down, and I do not know whether Congress has appropriated money for reconstructing them or whether this surplus will be used for that purpose.

Q. Did the Government establishment on Ellis Island cost about $750,000 before it was burned?—A. Yes, sir.

Q. (By Mr. KENNEDY.) Was that paid out of the head tax?—A. Nearly all of it.

Q. What will be the cost of the buildings they contemplate erecting now?—A. I think the estimate was about $1,300,000.

Q. Would the head tax have to be increased to pay for these buildings?—A. I think the Government has appropriated that money out of the general Treasury, and not made it a charge on the immigrant fund, but the immigrant fund will be obliged, probably, to put up the surrounding buildings. There is a hospital, the main building, kitchens, restaurants, and other buildings.

Q. (By Mr. PHILLIPS.) Under your administration did many criminals come over?—A. Very few that we knew of. We would have to ask a man if he were a criminal or not.

Q. Are there any means taken to detect criminals?—A. I do not think we sent back more than two or three such characters each year. If a man had committed an act abroad against an immigrant who was at present in America, when he came over that man would be right at the door to see that he should be sent back because he had done certain things abroad.

Q. It is generally stated, and believed, by a large per cent of our people who look into this matter abroad, that criminals are sent to this country as well as paupers.—A. I have not found that the steamship companies do anything of that kind.

Q. Do the municipal governments send them through the agents?—A. There is a great deal to be said about the steamship companies, but I am of the opinion that it is really the municipal governments that send them and pay their passage to the steamship companies. The steamship company is bound to receive and carry them unless they can discover that they are not proper persons to be landed in the United States, and then they will not receive them.

Q. Have the municipal governments abroad connived with the agents for the purpose of shipping here criminals who have served time?—A. I went to the Prisoners' Aid Society in London, and they did not know who I was. I questioned them with regard to what they did with their ticket-of-leave men. They had not gone far when I thought I was not acting fairly, and I told them who I was. The official stated that during the war (we passed an act to encourage immigration in 1864, when we wanted men over here they did send us all their ticket-of-leave men, and he supposed they went into the Army. He said that continued until 1893 and that his jurisdiction was London and a certain territory. He assured me that when the act of 1893 was passed, by which, as he supposed, the emigrant had to swear that he had never been convicted of crime, their society had voted that it would never send any more, and he did not think any from England had gone.

I did find one case in Switzerland, and it was a source of great annoyance to the Swiss minister. There was an habitual drunkard in one of the cantons in Switzerland. In Switzerland every inhabitant has an interest in the property of the canton in which he lives. They wanted to get rid of him, and in order to do so they had paid him his interest in the public rights and with the money purchased him a ticket for America. He came over here and we captured him and his papers. We immediately brought the case to the attention of the Swiss Government, and it apologized and said it should not occur again. That man was not a criminal, but merely a worthless fellow that they wanted to get rid of. I do not know during my administration of any landing of criminals upon us or of any landing of paupers, except aided and assisted Jews.

Q. Can you show the proportion of crime committed in this country by foreigners and Americans?—A. no; I can not.

Q. Are there statistics that define it fully?—A. I have heard of such statistics. I think you will find them in the State reports. As I told you, they are generally persons of foreign parentage.

Q. (By Mr. KENNEDY.) Do you know whether Russian Jews are still coming in this country through the Baron Hirsch fund?—A. Yes; I went over there to make an investigation in regard to that. I have letters from Baron Hirsch. I think you will find one of his letters published in my reports. I went to Hamburg and found one of the directors of the company. It is an incorporated company, limited. I ascertained that the company's capital was, I think, £2,000,000 ($10,000,000). Of that I think Baron Hirsch contributed about $9,999,000 and gave a small interest to five men in whom he had confidence and made them directors. At Hamburg I met one of them. He agreed to have the other four directors meet me in Paris at Baron Hirsch's house, and I went there and found the directors there, but Baron Hirsch was away. He was in Austria shooting. When I came home I received a letter from him. I also got all the notifications and warnings which they gave to the Jews with regard to coming to America.

The letter referred to by Mr. Stump as having been received by him from Baron Hirsch follows:

"[Telegraph address, Abrahirsh, Paris.]

"JEWISH COLONIZATION ASSOCIATION, 2 ELYSEE STREET,
"*Paris, October 15, 1894.*

"The SUPERINTENDENT OF IMMIGRATION, *New York.*

"DEAR SIR: On learning that you came to pay me a visit in Paris at the time of your recent voyage, I sincerely regret to have missed an interview, which would have procured me the honor of making your acquaintance and would have furnished me the occasion of explaining to you personally my ideas on the emigration of the Jews of Russia better than I can do it to-day in writing. It would have been easy for me to reassure you on the question of their emigration to the United States. Far from favoring this emigration, I have busied myself since a few years to turn it toward the Argentine Republic, where, as you know, without doubt, the work of the Jewish Colonization Association has already founded several colonies and is now preparing others. In fact, in consulting the latest statistics, you can not fail to notice that to-day the greater part of the Jews in search of a new fatherland (country) turn their looks toward Argentina, thanks to the efforts of the Jewish Colonization Association. Therefore, I am convinced that in a few years the United States will perceive how mightily our action will have contributed in turning from them the flood of emigration of which they are so apprehensive.

"I should add that the Jewish Colonization Association not only does not contribute in directing the emigration toward the United States, but to my knowledge there does not exist a single society whose aim would be to push our coreligionists to establish themselves in your country by helping them directly or indirectly. Nobody could possibly hinder a certain number of isolated ones from going to North America of their own impulsion and at their own expense and risk. Nevertheless, it is to be presumed that this class of emigration will become more and more scarce when we will have succeeded in creating a stream of colonization toward the countries of South America.

"I would have liked, dear sir, to have given you all these explanations with more details, but as this pleasure has been denied me I hope that the declarations preceding are sufficient to enlighten you as to our intentions and to dissipate the apprehensions which you might otherwise have conceived.

"Accept, dear sir, the expression of my most distinguished feelings.

"M. DE HIRSCH."

Q. (By Mr. FARQUHAR.) Did any of these colonies go into New Jersey?—A. I have heard it said that that New Jersey colony was from Baron Hirsch.

Q. Do you know anything about the condition of the colony now?—A. I do not. I think they came to grief. I have had during my administration the rabbis and others beg that we return these Jews, saying they were unable to take care of so many and that they ought to be returned. They have done so in New York and in other cities. The Jew will take care of one of his race to the utmost of his ability, but they came so thick and fast they could not do any more and wanted us to keep them out.

Q. (By Mr. PHILLIPS.) Did they come largely from Russia?—A. They came from Russia. They came from a place called Libeau. Principally Russian Jews come from there. They came also from the frontiers of Prussian Russia; but, to the credit of the Hamburg and Lloyd people, they have instituted, and I think they have got an enactment of legislation in Germany, a law which prevents any person from entering Germany from Russia. This was directed principally against the Jews, with the view of preventing them from embarking for America, unless at the frontier they showed they were desirable people to come here and would not come within the prohibition of the law. That was done by force of the act of 1893, because when these people arrived, we will say, at Hamburg, or at Bremen, and were rejected, they became paupers upon those cities at once, so the German Government took the precaution to institute an inspection on the borders of their country to prevent these Jews from crossing their frontier, ostensibly to go to the United States. All those things combined tended very greatly to restrict immigration.

Q. (By Mr. FARQUHAR.) Did the action of the Italian Government under Rudini make any difference whatever in the restriction of immigration from Italy?—A. The Italian Government is perfectly willing. both Premiers Crispi and Rudini told me, that their subjects should come to the United States. They think an Italian will never expatriate. They go to America and make money and return. If they do not return one year they return the next. What the Italian makes here he sends home; and I have had pointed out to me little towns and villages in Italy where there are improvements, and they will say, " Those people have been in America." They say they will not encourage emigration from their country to this country, yet they are not inclined to restrain those to whom we have no objection, and will take advantage of what there is for their people here. So many Italians were returned as likely to become public charges, they inquired what we meant by "likely to become a public charge," and wanted to have explained to them the features of the contract labor law. It was rather impolitic for us to write a definite explanation and say what we meant by becoming a public charge, because we can confine or enlarge it to suit almost any class of people we desire to exclude. Mr. Carlisle and our Secretary of State said that I should go over and explain it to the Italian Government verbally, and have no correspondence. I was sent, and I reported the results of my visit when I came back. The report was thought of sufficient importance to be sent immediately to the House and Senate, and you will find it in Senate Document No. 9, reported to the Senate December 3, 1896. I found those people exceedingly anxious—while they would not do anything in violation of our law and would do anything to prevent undesirable people from leaving Italy, still they were rather inclined to hold that those who were eligible should not be prevented from coming across the water.

[Mr. Stump's report and the action taken by the Italian Government is given in Senate Document No. 9, second session Fifty-fourth Congress.]

Q. (By Mr. PHILLIPS.) Would you oblige the commission by giving it a list of documents, reports, and books on the subject of immigration?—A. I will try to do so. There are not many of them.

Q. (By Mr. FARQUHAR.) While we were on that question of the head money and the $100,000 voted for the alien contract-labor law—do you really think that the head money received, and that amount of money from Congress, is sufficient to make that Bureau of the Government in its administration efficient enough to carry out the law?—A. The head money yields a surplus for carrying out the purposes of the act of 1882. As far as the alien contract-labor laws are concerned, I found $100,000 amply sufficient. I never did expend the whole sum in any one year during my administration. I always returned money into the Treasury.

Q. I notice in the conclusion of your report of 1897 that you say it seems proper to suggest the importance of maintaining the immigration service separate and dist'nct from the customs administration. Where is the trouble? Are the immigration servants customs servants also and inspectors?

WASHINGTON, D. C., *January 12, 1899.*

The examination of Mr. Stump was resumed at a meeting of the Industrial Commission convened at 11 a. m., January 12, 1899.

Mr. STUMP. A question was asked me in regard to customs, which would properly be the first one to come up. Under the act of 1892 the collectors of customs of a port were directed to collect the head tax, and the officials under him were placed in charge of the administration of the law regarding immigration. Subsequently immigrant inspectors were appointed by the Secretary of the Treasury. Article 3 of Regulations of Immigration, issued by the Treasury Department, says: "Collectors of customs on the Canadian frontier and at all points where commissioners of immigration are not employed are charged within their respective districts with the execution of the laws pertaining to immigration and all importation of laborers under contract or agreement to perform labor in the United States. They will employ all customs, immigration, and other officers assigned to them for duty in the enforcement of the immigration acts; and all such officers are hereby designated and authorized to act as immigration officers."

Q. (By Mr. FARQUHAR.) Were they to be both custom-house and immigration inspectors?—A. Yes; when the Immigration Bureau was created and immigration officers appointed they were charged solely with the execution of that duty, and the immigration service became efficient. What I allude to in my report is that while the immigration fund is amply sufficient for the compensation of all immigration officers, my experience had been that where customs officers were charged with the duties pertaining to customs and also to immigration that the one or the other would be neglected, and it is policy, I think, to have them entirely separate in order that there should be more efficient duty performed by each. I do not think either should be charged with the other except in places where there is very little customs or very little immigration.

Q. Were the immigration officers charged with looking into infractions of the law of customs as well as smuggling, etc.?—A. Oh, yes; the immigration officers were also directed, wherever they saw any violation of the customs laws of the United States, to make arrests.

Q. It is your opinion that they should be entirely separate?—A. I think so; as far as possible.

Q. Are the functions of the immigration officers sufficient to take all their time, instead of being troubled with the investigation of smuggling, etc., on the borders?—A. Yes; except in isolated cases where there is very little to be done. Where there is little dutiable goods coming and very few immigrants, I would not make objection. I think one officer of the United States Treasury Department should be sufficient to execute both duties at such a place.

Q. Are the duties of a United States inspector of immigration in Canada simply to inspect immigrants who have declared their intention to come to the United States and who have come that way?—A. Yes, sir.

Q. Have they no inspection duties over the general Canadian immigration?—A. None at all.

Q. Is it a fact that on the whole Canadian frontier, certainly as far as Winnipeg, that the trades unions and organized labor have done an immense amount of work through their own officers and their own means in spying out foreigners or Canadians who attempt to come into this country in violation of the law?—A. As to the European immigration through Canada, by an arrangement I made with the steamship companies landing passengers at Quebec, which permitted a United

States officer to go aboard those ships there and make the inspections under the laws of the United States, as is done at the port of Boston or New York, you must recollect that we have no law to prevent Canadians coming and going as they see proper. For instance, take Detroit and Port Huron, and all along the lakes, wherever a foreigner presents himself he is obliged to exhibit a certificate that he has been examined and passed at Quebec, which is provided for under this agreement; but if a Canadian is coming into the United States he is not interrupted, because there is no head tax. It is expressly provided by law that there should be that intercourse between these countries until Congress should enact laws to meet that case. I will show you that act, which may be of interest to you. I find it in section 22 of the act of 1884. There has never been an act to provide for persons coming in by land carriage, neither has there been one providing for persons coming by water, from contiguous territory.

Q. Would the question be on the alien contract-labor law?—A. That is all there is to it. Another matter that has occupied the attention of Congress, both by my recommendations and more especially by the various trades unions, is this: I have been to Detroit, and while on ferryboats between Windsor and Detroit, with the committee, of which Mr. Owen was chairman (see Mr. Owen's report), saw how many carpenters, masons, etc., came daily with dinner buckets from Canada into the United States to work. That is a sore which Congress has not remedied. I think Mr. Corliss had a bill two years ago, as had Mr. Mahany, of Buffalo, on this subject. It has caused much friction between the two Governments and, I think, entered into the work of the joint commission of Canada and the United States in regard to settling immigration and other matters.

Q. When you were Commissioner General were you not the authority in the Treasury Department to decide whether when Canadians, who were members of the International Typographical Union and of a local union, say of Ottawa or Toronto, came to Detroit and had well-defined notions where they were to work in the United States, were under contract for labor or not?—A. It would depend entirely upon whether we could arrest them. We would certainly examine into the matter, and if no contract had been made abroad we could not hold them. If they were induced to come in without any contract, it is that very amendment that I spoke of the other day as being necessary for us to hold such people. We had, at Buffalo especially, an inspector at the end of the bridge and also a Mr. De Barry in Buffalo, and they were very efficient officers, and while I think Mr. De Barry stretched the laws considerably, yet we never interfered with him if he did send a person out. Had some of these cases been brought to our attention by appeal they would have been decided on their merits. But Mr. De Barry sent a good many out when I did not think the law justified his action.

Q. (By Mr. SMYTH.) What is your opinion as to the effects of immigration on the wages of skilled and unskilled labor in this country?—A. I suppose immigration in some branches has had a slight effect. My view in regard to this matter has been that while our country is so great and comparatively sparsely inhabited, when you compare it with European countries, there is a constant demand for labor and it is seeking new fields all the time. In that way immigration has no great effect on the prices which have prevailed heretofore. Skilled labor coming into this country tends naturally to diminish, but owing to our increasing demands does not effect prices to any perceptible degree.

Q. What is the effect on unskilled labor?—A. I think the demand for unskilled labor is so great that it will not have any effect at all. The only trouble is the distribution of immigrants when they come here. When they arrive they get into our Eastern States and go into our cities, and in that way labor here is congested, but gradually they work their way out to where there is a demand for them, and we find that while there is no great demand in the East, there is a great demand in the West, and, like water, labor will seek its own level. If our country were fully settled, of course every addition to its population would have an effect on the working people, but it will not have an effect on them here for years and years to come.

Q. It has been stated, and generally believed, that in certain congested portions of the United States there is a large number of unemployed people seeking employment and unable to find it. Does not this large mass of unskilled labor, brought into this country by immigration, tend to swell the number of unemployed?—A. That is very true of localities. You can go into the mines of Pennsylvania and to a few other portions of the United States and you will find that immigrants are induced to come by letters written by persons who have employment in these various localities, and you will find that when these immigrants come many of them will be unable to find work there. In that way those places have become overcrowded. As I said the other day, a bureau for distributing immigrants would be a vast benefit to the United States.

IMMIGRATION.   17

Q. As you proposed having on Ellis Island?—A. I only mentioned that as one place, but I do not see why smaller bureaus could not be put in other localities, so as to distribute these immigrants.

Q. Can you tell the commission about what proportion the number of skilled immigrants in this country bear to the whole number?—A. I am hardly capable of answering that question. You know I am an agriculturist and lawyer, and my mind has never been directed to that. When I came into public life, I was assigned to this immigration question, and afterwards to the execution of the laws under it. When you go into those questions of labor and industries, I am not a competent witness. But I will tell you what the Bureau has done. It has given the most exact data with regard to each and every immigrant who has come into this country. You will find in the reports the tables which furnish this information, and it will enable you to arrive at your own conclusions. If I considered myself an expert on labor and industries, I would gladly give you my opinions, but they are not worth anything except as mere surmises. In the first tables we give the number of immigrants arriving at the various ports; that is, the total immigration.

Table No. 2 shows the immigrants arriving in the United States, their sex and their nationality, and those debarred and returned during the fiscal year. We next give the age of immigrants and number of illiterates over 14 years of age, by countries of origin, arriving during each fiscal year. We next give a table of the immigrants over 20 years of age, by nationality, bringing $30 and over. In one year they brought over $5,000,000, and probably they brought $10,000,000 that we could not ask about, being over $30 each.

Q. (By Mr. FARQUHAR.) Is that the report of 1896 and 1897?—A. Yes, sir.

Q. (By Mr. PHILLIPS.) I understood from a speech made by Senator Gibson on the immigration question, in the Fifty-fourth Congress, that he estimated that they brought about $800 per capita.—A. I have always estimated that they brought four or five times more than what was actually ascertained from examination.

Q. Is there any data from which you could get those facts?—A. No, sir; only what you see.

Q. Do you think $800 per capita is an overestimate?—A. This statement is made on page 4 of that report:

"The fact disclosed by the table on this subject is that the immigrants during this fiscal year brought with them and exhibited $3,541,241. How much more these immigrants brought can not be stated. From experience it can be safely estimated that the money brought into this country by these immigrants is very much greater than the figures herein given."

Table No. 5 gives the arrivals, by nationalities, during the fiscal year, with relation to those who have not been in the United States before, going to join families, etc. Table 6 shows the increase and decrease each year. Table 7 gives the nativity of alien steerage passengers landed at the ports of the United States in that year. It tells whence they came, nativity, and gives the States to which they went.

Table 8 gives the nativity and occupation of alien steerage passengers landed at the ports of the United States, and in Table 9 you will find the number of actors, artists, clergymen, editors, engravers, lawyers, and everything, and the skilled and unskilled labor. That is exact. The last thing I did was to have a table prepared which gives the destinations and occupations of alien steerage passengers landed at the port of New York, so we can see how many skilled and unskilled laborers went into each State and the occupation of each of them.

Q. (By Mr. A. L. HARRIS.) Do your tables give the percentage of illiteracy among the immigrants that reach this country?—A. Yes, sir; as far as we were able to get it. We had no law authorizing us to examine in regard to that, because it does not matter at the present time whether they can read and write—it is not essential to their admissibility; but, in view of legislation in Congress, we had instructed our registers to ask every one of them whether they could read and write and we took their answers down, and that is the table I presented to you.

Q. (By Mr. KENNEDY.) Mr. Shulteis says that if this commission would probe into the question of immigrants escaping the head tax by coming in from the Canadian border, they could suggest legislation that would result in reimbursing the Government for the entire expense of the commission. What is your opinion in regard to the efficiency of the service in that particular? Could anything be suggested by the commission to remedy the trouble?—A. I will explain how that agreement was entered into. I was directed by the Secretary to go there and see what inspection of immigrants could be inaugurated throughout our border line. That line is nearly 4,000 miles long. I had authority to see all customs officers at the various ports of entry along that line as immigration officials. Before I left here I suggested to the Secretary that if I could make an arrangement with the Canadian government by which at the seaboard, the port of entry of all European immigrants, I could have an investigation, that it would obviate the expense and the necessity of establishing this border line. I visited Ottawa and communicated with the government and the government was inclined to grant it, but the newspapers got hold of it and there was great excitement in Canada in regard to Canadian officials permitting United States officials to exercise their functions within their territory, whereupon the Canadian government retired from the arrangement. I then made an arrangement with the transportation companies themselves; that is, I found four or five trans-Atlantic lines bringing immigrants into Canada and I found only two railroads, the Grand Trunk and the Canadian Pacific, conveying these immigrants west. You will find it on page 17 of the report for the year ending June 30, 1894. The steamship lines were exceedingly anxious to have the business of bringing the immigrants by way of Canada into the United States and to give us every facility for inspection. They were not inclined to pay any head tax.

There was no law for us to compel them to pay a head tax. If they could bring immigrants into Canada, and in that way into the United States, without paying any tax, the steamship lines running into New York might just as well close their business. I told them I would discontinue negotiations unless they paid the head tax, and finally they agreed to it. I fear Mr. Shulteis is not an authority on this subject at least, and that the Commissioners will be without pay if they depend upon getting it from this source. They agreed, as you will see, to allow our inspectors to go aboard their ships and inspect in the same way they do at the ports of the United States. Those destined for the United States were examined by us. When immigrants were not eligible to enter the United States they were not permitted to enter. In order to prevent their entering after we had rejected them, we required our authorities to give each one a certificate, showing to what place he was destined, the description of the person, and that he had been examined. He was required to present that certificate to the customs or immigration officials when he entered the United States, and it entitled him to land. The railroads entered into a compact that they would transport no one destined for the United States without that certificate. If that law is properly administered—and it was during my administration—I do not see how they could get in. Subsequently I ascertained that persons would come, ostensibly for Canada, and they would stay maybe a month or two in Canada, and then come to the United States. Whereupon I instructed our officials to enter into a new contract with the steamship companies providing that they would pay the head tax on all those persons who entered the United States so many months after their arrival, and they paid it. In that way every business safeguard was thrown around it while I was in office, and, I believe, still continues. You will find that agreement in my report; and the supplemental one follows, I suppose, a year or two afterwards.

Q. (By Mr. FARQUHAR.) Who really pays the head tax, the steamship company or the immigrant?—A. It is very much like the question who pays the tariff duty. One says the consumer pays it, and the other says the importer pays it. The steamship companies add it to the passage money. It is not only the immigrant who pays that head tax, but every alien coming into the United States. If he comes for pleasure, or comes a dozen times a year on business, he pays it every time.

Q. (By Mr. SMYTH.) Does he pay it to the steamship company or to the Government?—A. He pays it to the collector of the port. For instance, here is the tourist visiting the United States for pleasure; he is manifested on the steamship company's manifest as Mr. Jones, of England. Being an alien, the collector of the port collects the tax from the steamship company, and it goes into the immigration funds, the same as a head tax from an immigrant.

Q. (By Mr. FARQUHAR.) Do you collect directly from the immigrant or from the steamship company? Do not the steamship companies pay this head tax?—A. Oh, yes; but the bill presented to the steamship company is presented by the collector of the port. In New York we found that that business was better attended to by the immigration authorities, so that the manifest of all passengers was sent to our depot there, and we made up the bill of all tourists and aliens and sent it to the collector of the port and the steamship company also, and the company paid the collector.

Q. (By Mr. PHILLIPS.) Do nations in Europe charge a head tax?—A. No, sir.
Q. No nation?—A. I could not say they do. I never heard of it.
Q. (By Mr. KENNEDY.) Do you know anything about the case of a gentleman, formerly a United States Senator, who contracted to build a State house for the State of Texas, at Austin, imported thirty Canadians into Texas or brought them in under contract to work, was fined $30,000, and the fine never collected?—A. No, sir; I do not.

Q. (By Mr. FARQUHAR.) Could they make a fine of $30,000?—A. Yes, sir; it is $1,000 in each case.

Q. Under the alien contract law?—A. Yes, sir; I think I have had a fine of as much as thirty, forty, or fifty thousand dollars against a concern in Rhode Island.

Q. (By Mr. SMYTH.) Were those amounts paid?—A. The Solicitor of the Treasury, at the suggestion of the United States district attorney, who had found the bills and had the cases docketed, consented to a compromise. The defendant paid three or four thousand dollars and all the expenses of the cases, and they were dropped. I think that was in the Phillips Hosiery Case, up somewhere in Rhode Island. In one of my reports I showed how many cases I prosecuted. I do not know of any cases where there has been a conviction upon trial before any court, and for that reason wherever we had these cases and parties desired to compromise it has generally been done because of the impossibility of getting testimony necessary to convict the employer. The poor immigrant who came in—the innocent party—was sent back, and it was almost impossible to convict an employer.

Q. (By Mr. FARQUHAR.) We spoke of the displacement of American labor by the importation of both skilled and unskilled laborers to this country. It has been stated that in 1860 or 1864, until the alien contract-labor law became thoroughly operative, all the labor employed in the coal mines of this country during, say, twenty-five years was displaced by European labor. Is that a fact?—A. Of course I knew of those things when they were brought to my attention. I believe it to be a fact. We endeavored to return every person going into the mines of Pennsylvania to Europe. That is one of the congested localities I said I wanted to eradicate. I think the case of the Pennsylvania coal fields is always cited by persons opposed to immigration, forgetting its benefits elsewhere.

Q. (By Mr. KENNEDY.) If a person is found in the United States in violation of the immigration laws within a period of one year from his arrival, may he be deported?—A. Yes, sir.

Q. A high officer of the immigration service—not the Commissioner General of Immigration—says he thinks the law might very well be amended by extending that limit to five years. I would like to ask your opinion in regard to that.—A. It might be extended to five years. An alien comes into this country, is examined, and swears positively that he has no contract to work for any particular person. You may feel assured that that man is telling you an untruth. We have traced such men to the mines in Scranton, exactly where we knew they were going, though they swore they were going to some other point. Knowing the provisions of the law that within a year we could arrest them, we have permitted them to go and subsequently arrested them and sent them out of the United States. Whether it is necessary to have that period extended over a year or not is a matter of fancy. I think it is scarcely necessary to increase the period, because if you do not get the man immediately you may as well give up.

But there are other cases. When a criminal comes in and you do not discover it for four or five years you can not send him back. A man comes who has a weak mind, and maybe insanity develops. In that case you want to return him after a year; but in regard to the alien contract-labor law I see no necessity for a change. I will tell you another very important amendment that I have contended for; the right to arrest a party after he has been landed. An immigrant, by false statements, secures his admission into the United States. The law says that the immigration authorities can return the man at any time within a year. There is no person appointed to execute that law and arrest the man. The United States marshals have refused over and over again to do it. It is simply like the acts declaring a thing illegal without attaching a penalty clause to it. You must give the immigration authorities power to sue and right to make an arrest, or you must give it to the marshals of the United States. When I came into office I found that each Secretary of the Treasury had positively declined to issue an order to that effect. I applied to Mr. Carlisle, and we examined into it, and he was the first Secretary that ever issued an order to arrest a contract laborer after he was landed, and the first case I know of was a very hard case. It was a South Carolina case. I arrested a man by the name of Williams, who had made a contract to go into partnership with a man. Williams said they got hold of what little substance he had and then informed upon him; that the company wanted to get rid of him. They had actually robbed him and then informed upon him, and obliged us to deport him. It was making us use the machinery of the Government to gratify private spite and hatred.

Q. Do you believe, for certain purposes, the time limit should be extended?— A. Yes; it might be in certain cases, but I do not think so in the matter of alien contract labor, because all labor unions are anxious to get rid of a man at the time, but if there is delay nothing can be done.

Q. There is quite a general belief throughout the country that the steamship companies exert an influence to prevent the adoption of new legislation on the immigration question. Have you any knowledge of other influences working in that direction?—A. I have not. On the contrary, while I suppose it is perfectly natural, I am not aware of their using any influence one way or the other. In regard to the laws as enacted, I always found that they cordially aided and assisted the service and observed the law as far as they could. I have had friction with them, but it always ended agreeably, and the matter, upon investigation, was adjusted one way or the other and things went on as usual.

The steamship companies have their agents through Europe as they have in America. They have their agents in America selling tickets in almost every city and village. Their greatest business is the selling of prepaid tickets; that is, families here will prepay a ticket for a relative or somebody over there and inclose it in a letter. and that relative or friend comes over. I told you that the steamship companies, in accordance with the act of 1893, did establish rules and regulations in Europe. I will show you the rules established by the American Line, and I know it was done by the Hamburg-American and by the North German Lloyd, but I take this one set of rules:

"The classes not admitted to the United States are such immigrants as are liable to become a burden to the State, paupers. criminals, consumptives. and those suffering with loathsome and contagious diseases: the blind, lame, deaf and dumb, and crippled persons, women with children without any relatives in the country, single females in pregnant condition, and single females with children.

"We beg to advise you that the law will be enforced strictly. In view of this we request you to use the utmost care in accepting emigrants for transportation, and in doubtful cases to consult us, giving all the details and conditions, before you enter into a contract.

"If we approve of the acceptance of a passenger or passengers, you will be in no way held responsible, but if you enter into a contract for transportation of emigrants of whom with a certain degree of attention you could have known beforehand that they would come under that class of emigrants who are refused admittance to America, we will be compelled to charge you 80 marks for every adult for return transportation and also the transportation cost from the port to the home of the passenger."

That was issued by the steamship companies when the act of 1893 went into effect, but, as I told you, whenever an agent located in these villages sold a person who would not be admitted into the United States and he was returned, they were fined the cost of transportation, so it really made it the best inspection.

Q. Did you know the late Dr. Glavis?—A. Yes, sir.

Q. Did Dr. Glavis ever attempt to interfere with you in your administration of the Immigration Bureau?—A. When I went into the office I immediately came into contact with Dr. Glavis, and for probably eight months or a year our relations were not as agreeable as they became subsequently. Subsequently our relations when we got into working condition and he found that there was nothing to be gained became harmonious.

When I came into office the main question was the maintenance of immigrants by steamship companies on Ellis Island. For instance, a wife coming to her husband would be detained four or five days while they were telegraphing, finding out whether she had a husband or not. Sometimes there were contract laborers. They were detained four or five days or more so as to give everybody a hearing. We claimed their expenses should be borne by the steamship companies. At that time the question had not been settled. The contention on the part of the steamship companies was that we should examine these parties, and if we held them over for our purposes that they should not bear the expenses. I contended that they were liable, and I prepared what we called the rules and regulations for the maintenance and support of immigrants while they were detained and rules for maintenance and deportation of alien immigrants were embodied in Circular 177, of November 29, 1893.

[The substance of this circular is embraced in Department Circular 159, of August 16, 1898.]

After they were issued we had no further friction. I found the steamship companies always ready to cheerfully comply with all laws and regulations when they thoroughly understood them and they were conclusively established; but, as a matter of course, while they thought they had the right to contend they contended, and I think the rules and regulations which were drawn at that time have subsequently been submitted to the Attorney-General and been approved by him. You will find that on page 31, report of 1894, and in Treasury Circular No. 1774, the Secretary approved them and they became Treasury regulations. which are equivalent to law, because by the act of 1892 the Secretary of the Treasury is given power to make these regulations. As it is now a law, I apprehend there will be no further difficulty. The only friction grew out of the fact that the Immigration Bureau was then new and did not get into working order until I took charge of it. Mr. Owen preceded me, but there was some difficulty which prevented the Bureau from exercising its just powers.

IMMIGRATION. 21

Q. Have you familiarized yourself with the Lodge bill now pending in the House?—A. I do not know the one now pending. I recall the one that was vetoed by Mr. Cleveland.
Q. You know something about the educational test that was in that bill?—A. Yes, sir.
Q. That is the same test. It provides that the immigrant shall be able to read in some language a few sentences from the Constitution of the United States?—A. Yes, sir.
Q. In view of your testimony of day before yesterday in regard to the very small percentage of illiterate immigrants coming to this country from Germany, England, Sweden, and all those countries of northern Europe, would such a test interfere very much with the volume of immigration coming into this country from those desirable parts of Europe?—A. Very little.
Q. (By Mr. PHILLIPS.) Do you think such a law would be of great benefit in restricting undesirable immigration to this country?—A. It would restrict the undesirable, but I would say that the educated rascal that comes into this country is the most dangerous, and if you want "hewers of wood and drawers of water" you better not turn these immigrants back and let the forgers, scoundrels, and thieves in.
Q. Is the law pretty comprehensive on that question now?—A. Yes. I believe, as is now the case, that able-bodied and healthy immigrants, able and willing to work, who come here for the purpose of settlement, should be admitted into this country; but I think the utmost pains should be taken by immigration authorities to rigidly deport all undesirable immigrants—the class meant in the act of 1891, section 1. I want a strict examination and inspection of immigrants.
Q. Have you any suggestions to make in regard to further legislation on the immigration question?—A. No; I do not think I have, except the amendments I suggested to the act of 1893 and the amendments recommended by the Immigration Investigating Committee. I do not know what other provisions you could make.
Q. Do you think the Lodge-McCall bill would be very effective if enacted into law?—A. That would be effective only in restraining Italians, Poles, and Russians from coming in on account of their want of education.
Q. (By Mr. FARQUHAR.) When the alien contract-labor law came into somewhat effective force toward the end of your administration, was it your opinion that the law had effected very nearly a thorough remedy in respect to the importation of alien labor?—A. Except in isolated cases—individual cases chiefly at the present time. Sometimes you will find that immigrants will meet aboard ship and form plans as to where they are going, and sometimes four or five of them will unite and together go to some particular locality. They will go to the mines of Pennsylvania, the iron works at Chicago, or the wire works, and so on. In that way they are liable to suspicion. When they say they are going to one place, the immigration officials might think they are contract laborers and examine them very rigidly. Sometimes, in fact, they have come over because some friend has written them to come to a certain place, saying they will get work, and they are going there. While the wholesale importation of laborers under contract has been very greatly decreased and almost exterminated, a man abroad will make arrangements so that he won't land in a foreign country without anything to do. He has prudence to secure a place for himself when he does land, and he is a great deal more desirable immigrant than those who leave without any definite purpose or intention. I sent back many a deserving man, and the men who were sent back as alien contract laborers are as distinct as a class from those who are sent back as paupers as day is from night.
The very best immigrants in a great many cases were those who went back as contract laborers, because they had been prudent in making arrangements for their livelihood.
Q. (By Representative OTJEN.) Where you find an immigrant has made arrangements through his friends here do you send him back?—A. We were obliged to do so under the law. I have sent back men who came to a brother. A baker will write for his brother to come over here, saying he has employment for him and will pay him so much wages in his own bakery. I was obliged to send that man back, and for that reason I have suggested another amendment to the law. It is contained in the "Report on Immigration Investigation," page 42 (reading):
"Nothing contained in the immigration or alien labor laws shall prevent near relatives, not more remote than first cousins, from aiding each other to migrate to the United States, either by pecuniary aid or by the promise of maintenance until the immigrant can obtain work, or the promise of or contract for work in the business or trade of such relative, conducted personally by himself and under his own direction and management. The burden of proof in all such cases shall be upon the immigrant or such relative."

That would enable a man to bring a brother to work in his own business.

Q. (By Mr. PHILLIPS.) Have the nations of Europe or any part of them restraining laws similar to ours in regard to immigration?—A. No; but the nations of Europe, particularly Germany, and other nations, are passing laws to prevent as far as possible the emigration of their own people anywhere. The emigration to the United States has been so great and so injurious to Germany and other countries of Europe that they are passing legislation to prevent any persons going there to solicit persons to migrate, and for that reason there has been a great deal of talk about consular inspection and all those bills. I always contended they were an injury, instead of a benefit, to immigration of the United States. Those bills were all defeated.

Q. (By Mr. KENNEDY.) Do Austria and Turkey, as well as Germany, prohibit the Russian Jews from crossing their borders?—A. Russia has passed many laws in regard to the Jews which seem to be exceedingly oppressive and inhuman to us, but when Russia banishes whole races of people in that way there must be some reason for it. The recent laws of Russia in that regard provide that every State is entitled to the military service of its inhabitants. They are also entitled to certain degrees of taxation and so on. The Jews in Russia that I speak of claim they are subjects of Turkey and owe no allegiance to the Russian Government. They do not pay taxes; they will not render military service, and Russia has simply said, Why, you must become our subjects or leave our territory. That, I understand, is the true state of affairs, and a great many of them come to this country.

Q. (By Mr. SMYTH.) Do you think the padrone system among the Italians is obliterated?—A. What you speak of is something that has existed heretofore and for which we want a remedy. The Italians, if they remain long in the country, finally get their eyes open, and those who do not must undergo this oppression by their bankers—the padrones.

Q. (By Mr. A. L. HARRIS.) Is there a disposition on the part of foreign immigrants to colonize in localities; and if so, what is the effect in preserving their own customs?—A. I find when I go to the cities—take New York, for instance—Italians are all in one section. Great colonies of them are about Mulberry street. All the Jews are in certain wards and all the Chinese are in Chinatown, and so on; but when they leave those places, I did not find them in bands, except in charge of padrones in the case of Italians. The Scandinavians, who are really the best immigrants who come to the United States, are farmers They generally come well provided with funds. They are hard-working, industrious people, and from my knowledge of them they go to the West, and after a while they are congregated in communities and they retain their own language. Probably, where large communities of, say, Huns and Poles, go into the mines of Pennsylvania, they speak their own language because they are congregated. I did not find a disposition to colonize except in the cases of Scandinavians. They seemed to go in bodies to certain localities where their friends are and where their language is spoken—that is in the West. I think that is the true reason for the great crops of wheat and products of the United States raised there. I did not find colonies of Italians nor of any other people throughout the United States; but in every town there is an Italian quarter, a Chinese quarter, and so on; but you do not find it in the country.

Q. Do they preserve their language to the extent of having it taught in the public schools; and if so, are they becoming Americanized?—A. I could not say except from what I have heard from people from the Western States where these people are. I have heard that in Montana and through there the people have preserved their own language in the places of worship, and so on. In regard to this educational problem and other matters, I would suggest to you that you look upon immigration as entirely separate and distinct from naturalization and the elective franchise, otherwise you will get into a vast deal of trouble. I apprehend that the greatest opposition—that is, general opposition—to immigration is that ignorant foreigners who reside here for five years are allowed to vote. I do not think that this commission has anything to do with that. The elective franchise is one thing and immigration is another. Some people apprehend that immigration is dangerous because the most of the immigrants that come here are Catholics. You have nothing to do with religion, neither have you anything to do with the elective franchise. My views about elective franchise and giving the right to a foreigner to vote are independent of my views on the pure question of immigration. Immigration as it affects labor is the other ground, and that is a very serious ground, and that is really the subject-matter before your commission, and I am only sorry that I can not enlighten you more upon that subject.

Mr. FARQUHAR. There are just two points so far as the commission is concerned, the economic condition and the social conditions which affect all American civilization and the standard of American workingmen.

IMMIGRATION. 23

Mr. KENNEDY. You may be assured that in the consideration of the immigration question no question as to any man's religion will ever be asked by this commission.

Mr. STUMP. I have no doubt of that. I only alluded to that generally. I stated it as an illustration of my conception of your duty, that you would burden yourselves very much if you allowed the matter of a man's education and his ability to vote intelligently, or, I stated incidentally, his religion to bear upon this subject. That is all I meant to say. I did not mean that you would investigate either one or the other. A great many of my troubles arose, and I find the chief attacks upon permitting immigrants coming to the United States have been because in a few years they get the right to vote, and a great many get that right without being here a few years.

WASHINGTON, D. C., *January 13, 1899.*

TESTIMONY OF MR. HERMAN J. SCHULTEIS,
Ex-Special Commissioner.

The commission met at 11 a. m., Vice-Chairman Phillips presiding.

Mr. PHILLIPS. I will state that Mr. Schulteis is before the commission by invitation. He was one of the five commissioners who visited Europe in 1891 to investigate the subject of emigration to the United States.

Mr. SCHULTEIS. I have not prepared a general statement. If the commission would like to have suggestions which I may be able to make, which are dictated from experience and familiarity with the subject, I would be glad to make a short statement as to what I think the commission could do in the matter of the restriction of undesirable immigration and how it could be of service in relation to pending legislation.

Q. (By Mr. PHILLIPS.) We would be pleased to have you make a statement in your own way, Mr. Schulteis.—A. In the first place, I will speak of the pending illiteracy bill. That bill passed a previous Congress and is now before the House, having passed the Senate. In all probability it will be called up again, although the House refused to consider it the other day. In my judgment, it is the best method of restricting undesirable immigrants that could be devised. It restricts only the undesirable element of European immigration, and does not bar any citizen of Europe who would become a desirable citizen of this country. The questions of illiteracy and undesirability, as former Commissioner Stump told you the other day, go hand in hand, and the statistics of illiteracy particularly show that only emigrants from south European countries would be affected by that legislation if it were enacted into law, and it would reach the lowest element which degrades our citizenship when allowed to land here and at the same time depresses the price of wages. I do not agree with Mr. Stump that the lowest element of European citizenship is desirable on the ground that we have not enough men in this country to do our rough work. I know the contrary is the fact. I know that there are several millions of idle, illiterate workmen in this country who would like to have work. For that reason I do not see why we should import that class of workmen and further increase the ranks of the idle and thus further depreciate wages. It is the lowest class of workmen that depreciate wages. That is an economic truth. Wherever a hod carrier gets good pay a bricklayer will get good pay—much higher in proportion—and vice versa. If the lowest labor is illy paid all the higher labor will suffer correspondingly. For that reason the efforts of labor organizations have been directed against the lowest elements of European immigration. My experience in traveling, particularly through the various countries of Europe, convinces me that the south European immigration is the lowest class that comes to this country, and they are the people among whom the percentage of illiteracy is greatest. In southern Sicily the percentage of illiteracy runs as high as 90 per cent, according to the statistics of Señor Bodia, who is the greatest Italian statistician. He is the Giffen of Italy. He is an authority second to none in Europe. In northern parts of Italy the percentage of illiteracy decreases, and also the number of immigrants that come from that country decreases. In other words, the more desirable Italians do not emigrate in such great numbers as those from southern Italy, who embark from Naples and Palermo.

The Huns, Slavs, and Greeks have an average of 50 per cent illiterate, and they are a very undesirable class. They come over without skilled trades. They are merely rough laborers, such as we have in large numbers in this country, and if there should be a scarcity of that class of labor it could be had from the South, where there are 3,000,000 colored men who can do all the rough labor such as railroad digging and building and work in the mines. Aside from that, a large proportion of these foreigners, who are unable to read and write, and who are already in this country, flood the labor market, settle in the great cities, form colonies, and breed diseases and disorders of all kinds. I believe that the "Lodge bill" would largely restrict this class of immigration. I believe that it would affect 27 per cent of the number that are now admitted. When we can by one act restrict one-fourth of the least desirable of all immigrants, I believe it is a very good law to enact. I am very strongly in favor of it. I recommended it in my report of 1892-93. After a thorough investigation of the question both before I went to Europe, and while in Europe, and after returning, I am convinced that there is only one more effective way to restrict immigration, and that way would restrict all classes. That method is to increase the head tax. But Congress for years has not been disposed to offer any drastic remedy in the form of a head tax to prevent a large influx of labor into this country. Still I think the tendency is toward a head tax that would pay the expenses of the immigration service, which the $1 head tax does not do. In my judgment the head tax should be at least $10, so that only immigrants with a well-determined purpose would come here. At present thousands of them come to this country when they really would prefer to go to South America, which is more of a Latin-speaking country. Their language, manners, and customs are more similar to South American than to our manners and customs, yet it costs $8 more to go there than to the United States, and that $8, which to us seems a small amount, appears very large to them. Where wages are from 14 to 19 cents per day, as in southern Italy, to save $8 requires considerable time.

Q. (By Mr. KENNEDY.) Then the steamship companies make it an object to the immigrants to come to this country instead of going to South America?—A. Yes; the steamship companies and the railroad companies, particularly the land-grant railroad companies, have a direct interest in fostering immigration and getting people to buy their lands, and they make very low rates from New York to their lands for the purpose of getting those who have anything to settle there. The idea that there is a large amount of free public lann to be had in the West, although advertised extensively by the steamship companies abroad, is a myth, and when the immigrants come here they find that out. They find that all the available and good public land in this country is fenced in, and if they want it they have to pay for it, and the lowest price I have heard of is $1.25 per acre. Thousands of disappointed free-land seekers are now filling the slums of the great cities. But the steamship companies still hold out inducements of large areas of land that can be had for nothing. I read advertisements in Europe that immigrants could get 160 acres of land, an additional 160 acres for timber culture, and 160 acres additional for each adult in the family. In fact, there were four offers of 160 acres each that the immigrant supposed he could get gratis when he landed in this country. When they get here they find they can't get the land and that they have to settle down in the large cities, where they are at present. They are in every city, and even in this city the unemployed number 7,000. I made an inquiry some time ago at the Commissioners' office and looked over the list of those seeking employment in the street-sweeping and sewer department. I found there were 7,800, white and black, anxious to work at $1.25 per day. They put on large numbers of them whenever a snowstorm comes, and the other day there were 648 additional men engaged to clean the streets of snow.

When I last examined into the condition of Chicago there were nearly 200,000 idle men looking for jobs. That was some years ago. The fact that immigration slackens in some years is due to the fact that times are hard here and we have labor troubles, which are reported in the papers, and the newspapers are sent abroad. The foreign papers republish these articles, and the people find that conditions are poor here and large numbers of them are deterred from coming. The only opposition I have noticed to the Lodge bill is that which comes from the literary bureau of the steamship companies and from the managers of the Hirsch fund of New York, and their labors here at the Capitol are a matter of public notoriety.

Q. I would like to have you tell us something about the operations of the steamship lobby in Washington to prevent proposed immigration legislation.—A: In my judgment the most dangerous thing that the steamship people have done is to try to get the press to be silent by giving them excursions to New York and by entertaining them on the steamers for two or three days. I remember an excursion of nearly all the newspaper men, some 78 men and their families, that went over the Pennsylvania Railroad—free passes, Pullman cars, everything to eat and drink they wanted; and they were entertained on the steamer *Spree*, of the North German Lloyd, and then brought back to Washington. Of course this cannot be looked upon as a direct bribe, and yet it is in its influence on these newspaper men. They do not like to say anything unkind of these steamship people or against immigration. They also do everything they can to influence the newspapers by editorials they write, a great many of which are published. I have seen editorials in Chicago and St. Louis papers that were duplicates.

Q. In what kind of papers?—A. German papers mostly. They advertise very largely in those papers. They advertise from a column to two columns all the year round. When they send these prepared editorials the editor lets them go in, not because they express the opinion of the editor or of the community where he resides, but because they get from two to five hundred dollars per year for advertising from them, and they hate to refuse an article they are asked to publish; and the result is it is published as though it was the opinion of the public or the editor. They have a great advantage in that, inasmuch as they have to advertise mostly in those foreign papers, for the foreigners are the ones who use tickets to return to their homes. Some of them visit their old homes two or three times. I have known persons to go half a dozen times, if they could afford it, in the course of ten or twelve years.

Q. What do you know about the opposition to proposed immigration legislation on the part of German-American citizens?—A. My experience has been that the German people who understand the question are all in favor of the Lodge illiteracy bill. It is only those who have been told it is a different bill from what it is who oppose it. The literature which is sent out from New York by Dr. Senner, formerly commissioner of immigration at New York, misrepresents the bill, and large numbers of Germans signed petitions against it without knowing what the petitions contained. When they found they were on record as opposing an illiteracy provision, they recalled their statements. The Immigration Restriction League of Boston has published a pamphlet on that subject in which it shows exactly how those petitions were signed and how the signatures were secured throughout the country by Dr. Senner's bureau in New York. He is one of the agents of the Baron Hirsch fund. He is an Austrian, was a countryman of Baron Hirsch, and wrote articles against restriction of immigration from the time he landed until he became commissioner of immigration at the port of New York. He was employed on a Milwaukee paper, and nearly all the antirestriction articles in the New York Staats Zeitung were written by him. For some reason or other he was made commissioner at the port of New York to keep out people he had advocated letting in for years, and after he went out of office he immediately went back into the same service, and tried to do all he could to defeat any restriction legislation. He is the principal agent of the opposition to the Lodge bill.

Q. Was Dr. Glavis the head of the steamship lobby here?—A. He represented the North German Lloyd, and he afterwards took charge of the business of the entire steamship trust, and was very energetic about the Capitol for years trying to prevent any restriction legislation. He had his offices in the Post building for some years. He died not long ago. I do not know who his successor is, but I know that some of his coworkers are still very active and busy, and succeeded recently on the floor of the House in defeating consideration of the Lodge bill. They can afford to engage able counsel because all above deck and first-class passage is clear profit when the steerage is full. They charge on an average of $23.50 for passage, and it costs them $1.70. The rest is clear profit. They walk into the steerage and walk out. They do not have to be wheeled in like freight or carried out. It is the most profitable ballast a foreign steamer can have. Of course, as business men, they are very anxious to procure all such passengers they can both going and coming. Their argument generally is that this class of immigrants is valuable to this country, but it has no weight with them when they try to get them to go back to Europe. They are just as active in trying to get them to return, for the purpose of getting the steerage-passage money, as they were to have them come this way. They have their agents all over this country where these people are most numerous, and sell tickets in blocks, prepaid, to both come and go. I have a copy of some prepaid tickets which were deposited, particularly in the mining regions of Pennsylvania, with agents and even with postmasters, who get a commission on all the tickets they sell. Naturally they want to sell as many of them as they can, both going and coming. The alien steamship companies have a large capital invested. When I examined into the question some years ago, I found they had $118,000,000 invested, and that their percentage of profit was larger than any other colossal investment in existence. There is no large investment of money that pays as well as ocean-passenger traffic. It runs as high as 17 per cent per annum.

Q. How much of that is American capital?—A. A very small quantity of it is American capital. Even the so-called American Line, when I looked into the question, was nine-elevenths foreign and two-elevenths American, as far as their steamers were concerned—foreign built and registered. The capital of this one line, however, is largely American capital, and all the other steamship lines are in the hands of foreigners, and they are largely owned by one clique of bankers, who have their headquarters in London, Frankfort, Vienna, and Paris. They own the English, German, Scandinavian, and Italian lines of ocean steamers.

Q. (By Mr. PHILLIPS.) Is there a name given to this company?—A. They are all under different names.

Q. The same individuals own a large amount of stock?—A. The same individuals own the stock. The capital invested is foreign capital. Even steamers that have American names and registers now were not built here.

Q. (By Mr. KENNEDY.) Mr. Stump, ex-Commissioner-General of Immigration, said yesterday that he thought the time limit in which certain classes of immigrants who had come in in violation of the laws of this country could be deported might well be extended to three, four, or five years, but he made an exception in the case of those who came in in violation of the alien contract-labor law. Have you anything to say as to that matter, any suggestions to make?—A. I believe the time limit could be extended. I think that the pauper who was pauperized abroad should be supported by the community where he was raised and pauperized, and I believe that at any time when he becomes a public charge here, within four or five years, we ought to have the authority to send him to the community that neglected him or that caused his degraded condition. I do not think we are responsible, or that we ought to be held responsible, or ought to be taxed to support the people who are degraded by the conditions that obtain in certain countries abroad. They tax the people to death to keep up large standing armies and navies, and grind them down to the starvation line of wages by keeping them ignorant, and when their burden is so heavy they can not stand it, whenever they become charges, or when they get to the revolting point, they are anxious to get rid of them. Large masses of them have been sent here simply because they have arrived at the danger line. And societies abroad aid and foster the sending of that class of people to this country. I have in my report a list of 160 societies in England alone, called prisoners' aid societies, that make it their business to influence prisoners when their terms are over to come here. The judges often give them short sentences in prison, and the periods of surveillance are made very long and so objectionable and burdensome that they are anxious to get away. They have to report where they have been regularly to the officers of the law, or else they are thrown into prison again under what is called surveillance. These prisoners' aid societies have no difficulty in getting rid of these criminals for life when they offer them the small amount that is required to come here—£3 10s. It would cost as much to sustain them for two months at home as it does to send them here.

Q. (By Mr. PHILLIPS.) The law in this country prohibits the landing of paupers and criminals. Do you think it is not effective?—A. It is very laxly administered. Unfortunately the heads of the bureaus at the port of New York, where nine-tenths of the immigrants land, are old officials, kept in office under all Administrations since Colonel Weber took charge there. I investigated the prisoners' aid societies, and in one of my reports I gave the names of the people sent here, and gave the numbers of the post-office money orders which the societies sent to them after they got here. Then they have a system of sending their superannuated people over here. Under the English governmental system after they work twenty-five years they are pensioned, and the pension is paid them in a lump sum if they will emigrate here; but for fear they will not emigrate it is paid to them after they get here. Criminals are sent here, as well as paupers and the superannuated. They dump their poorhouses here. I have not looked into the matter of late years, and do not know of my own personal knowledge whether the percentage is kept up to the large proportion it was before, but it was done to a very large extent prior to the former commission's visit to Europe.

Q. Have you any statistics or facts that you could leave with the commission bearing on this question?—A. Yes; I would be very glad to leave the names of the secretaries of these societies as they existed at the time I visited them, and their addresses, and give any further data that I have. I looked into the post-office money-order office here and verified the statements I got on the other side, and found the money orders had been cashed on this side by the criminals, and they instanced that as a sharp way in which they got rid of their criminals. One of them, a Colonel Buchanan, showed me a letter he got from a criminal, stating that he had received his post-office money order on this side. I read the letter to Commissioner Powderly, who was with me at the time, and in it the criminal stated he had some difficulty in being identified at the Post-Office Department in getting his order cashed; that he walked out and looked around and copied a sign on the street to put on the order, and went in and got it cashed; and Colonel Buchanan gave that as an instance to show how smart their people were in outwitting us in our regulations here.

Q. (By Mr. KENNEDY.) Your identity was not known to them?—A. No. I introduced myself in my capacity as a member of the Congress of American Charities and Corrections. I was one of the representatives of the District of Columbia in the American Congress of Charities and Corrections at the time, and showed him my commission as such, and pretended I wanted to know how they did things for the purpose of doing the same thing here. Frequently persons are discharged from the courts here on condition that they leave the locality. We have them go to Baltimore and sometimes some of them come here from Baltimore and surrounding places.

Q. (By Mr. PHILLIPS.) Did you find a large number sent here?—A. Yes; one society sent 40,000.

Q. (By Mr. KENNEDY.) In what period?—A. Since it was organized. I can refresh my mind by looking at the report. It must have been a considerable length of time.

Q. (By Mr. PHILLIPS.) And they were principally criminals and paupers?—A. Yes; poor people who had been convicted of some trivial crime and then released.

Q. And some paupers?—A. Yes; they were mostly paupers. The paupers are much more numerous abroad than in this country. The conditions are worse there. We have no idea of poverty in this country as it exists there. In Liverpool I have seen children of 16 years of age who have never had shoes on their feet or hats on their heads; their hair stood up like bristles on a hog's back; they had on one garment, held up with a string from northeast to southwest, and walked the streets. They are called wharf rats in Liverpool. We have no such class of illiterates. They have never seen the inside of a school building, and have never heard of a Supreme Being, or anything else except what they can see. They grow up in utter ignorance and squalor, and they have societies in England which gather them up and send them to this country. Dr. Bernado's Home has sent large numbers of these children here. They find their way into our eleemosynary institutions, and our statistics show that 40 per cent of the inmates of these institutions are foreigners or of foreign descent. There should be no such percentage of foreigners in institutions that we have to support.

Q. Do you know whether statistics show that crime and pauperism in this country are on the increase?—A. They increase very largely, strange to say, in years when immigration is very large. Crime increases in the localities where the immigrants settle. In Allegheny County, Pa., in the year 1891, there were 58 homicides, all of them committed by aliens or naturalized foreigners. I stated in my report: "The alarming proportion of the unemployed proletariat, the increase of insanity, pauperism, and crime is attributable to no other such prolific source as immigration."

If the commission would look after the lax counting of immigrants at the various ports of landing and recommend a cure for the evil, I think the Government would save enough money to pay the entre expenses of the Industrial Commission. The statistics at the port of New York showed 445,290 steerage passengers landed at the Barge Office in New York in 1891. That does not include the number of passengers that were landed at Baltimore, Boston, Barnstable, Brunswick, Galveston, Gloucester, Jacksonville, Key West, Mobile, New Orleans, New Bedford, Norfolk, Newport News, Philadelphia, Providence, Portland, Me., Portland, Oreg., Port Townsend, Pensacola, San Francisco, San Diego, and Wilmington, and those crossing the borders of British Columbia, Canada, and New Mexico; and, in my judgment, if these had been added there would have been 750,000 instead of 445,000 immigrants who came in. The statistics at the British Columbia and Canada borders were dropped in 1885, for some unaccountable reason, and we have no idea how many people have come across the border either of Mexico, British Columbia, or Canada, since then, except in late years, when they were, on my suggestion, resumed. Even now large numbers of them cross the borders and come here, pay no head tax, and are not counted. For years they had a rule, which was allowed by the Treasury Department, by which they counted two children as one person, and that falsified the statistics to a great extent, because there are more children than there are grown people in any community. In foreign families there are 6 or 7 to the family, and in this country they average 5. I made a protest to the Secretary of the Treasury, and that rule was rescinded.

Q. Are there not statistics in the various places you name, such as Baltimore, Norfolk, Port Townsend, etc., of the number that land?—A. There ought to be. The trouble is they take the steamship company's count, and the steamship companies frequently land large numbers of people as employees when they are actually passengers. Those who work their way over, if they only peel potatoes for a meal of victuals, are considered and counted as employees and are landed without being recorded, and that is the last of them. I think the commission should devise some plan by which a check could be had on the steamships' manifests, and that every passenger should be counted as he lands. The office of landing inspector was abolished by the Department, and, in my judgment, it was a very necessary office and ought to be reestablished. There should be a landing inspector at the port of New York to count immigrants as soon as they walk over the gang plank, and the manifest verified by the count of the landing inspector. I have seen steamship manifests sworn to and duly signed abroad which had no names on them at all, showing that they are signed and sworn to with the idea of being filled out later on by the steamship companies. The immigrants never pay the head tax themselves, and the Government loses hundreds of thousands of dollars in the course of years by the inaccurate count of those who actually land.

Q. You spoke of those in Canada who come across the border. Mr. Stump, in his examination before the commission yesterday, stated that under the Cleveland Administration, in which he was Commissioner of Immigration, he had made arrangements with the steamship companies to pay themselves, and give to immigrants who arrived certificates so that they could present them at the border, and he believed that was being carried out faithfully. Have you any knowledge of that?—A. I understood that a vast amount of immigrants evaded the head tax by saying they were going to stay in Canada. Then they take the very next train for the United States. We lose a great deal by not having an efficient system of inspection on the border, and by a lax scrutiny of the steamship manifests.

Q. (By Mr. KENNEDY.) You say they evaded it by saying they were going to stay in Canada?—A. Yes, sir; they stay there one, two, or three days. They first look around to see if they can find employment. The proportion of idle in Canada is as large as it is in the United States. Large numbers of them come over here and get work and large numbers come over and work and go back at night. It has got to be a great evil in places like Detroit. In the morning the "bucket brigade" comes over and takes American workingmen's places and go back in the evening and spend their money over there where they can live cheaper than in the United States. We have endeavored to get legislation on that, to compel them to live on the American side if they work there. I was in Detroit on and off for a year and a half and noticed the large numbers that came over every morning and went back every evening. The fare across the ferry is only 2 cents, and they make 25 to 50 cents more per day on the American side than they can on the other side. The Canadian workingmen have protested against the British immigration policy on the ground that there are so many unemployed in Canada and they do not want the influx of foreign workingmen to take their places. The labor organizations have sent a committee abroad, and whenever they get together and send a committee to Parliament it shows the evil must be galling or they would not take that trouble and expense. The English Government gives nice positions to these envoys and that is generally the end of it.

Q. (By Mr. PHILLIPS.) Have you any suggestion to make in regard to better restricting the undesirable immigrants that come through Canada, and also for collecting the tax that is due this Government according to law?—A. Yes, sir; I should advocate two things: The increase of the head tax and the increase of the immigration inspector's force. I would put an inspector at every place where they cross.

Q. (By Mr. KENNEDY.) The increase of the head tax would pay the expense?—A. Yes, sir; and at the same time increase the revenue, a tax which the foreigner pays, in this instance, beyond cavil.

Q. In your travels abroad did you learn that other nations had restrictive laws in regard to immigration, or is it peculiar to the United States?—A. They have restriction in nearly all European countries, and they are far more strict in some of them than we are. They laugh at our way of administering restrictive laws. I have copies of sworn testimony taken before a Parliamentary committee in England from men at the head of Jewish societies, who say they have no trouble in passing their people here, but they can not pass them in European countries. For instance, the laws are so strict in Turkey and Austria that they will not allow an immigrant to land for a moment for fear he will stay there. They force him to stay on the car and go through. That is the case particularly with Russian Jews.

Q. Is that so with regard to other people besides Jewish people?—A. The law is so worded it affects all classes of people, but it is this class of people against whom it is aimed and enforced. There have been protests in England against Italians coming, on the ground that they take work from the English workingmen, and the London Association for Preventing the Immigration of Destitute Aliens is pressing for legislation on that line.

Q. (Mr. KENNEDY.) That statement is not clear. You say that is the class that emigrates mostly. When Mr. Phillips asked you in regard to restriction laws you said that the Russian Jews were the chief class of immigrants. Is that so?—A. That is only in late years—since the creation of the Baron Hirsh $10,000,000 fund—that influx of Russian Jews, since the Russian Government passed edicts

IMMIGRATION. 29

compelling them to live in the pale of settlement which includes the warmer and more fertile parts of Russia and the whole of Poland, extending from the Baltic to the Black Sea, and into the interior to the border of Courland and to the Sea of Azoff, where they were born and raised; and the Government did that for the protection of the Russian people. The Hirsh Immigration Society expects to bring all the pauper Jews to America.

Q. The Russian Jews are not criminals and do not become charges on the charitable institutions of this country, do they?—A. Their own charitable institutions take care of them. They do that in Russia, too. It costs the wealthy Jews of England, Germany, and France $30,000,000 a year to sustain the pauper Jews in the pale of settlement in Russia. They are anxious to get rid of them and have them come to this country, and they give them a start here, peddling outfits, and they become self-sustaining after that. There are 3,000,000 pauper Jews in Russia, and at $10 per head, which is the lowest estimate, it costs the wealthy Jewish committees $30,000,000 annually to support them.

Q. Are they looked upon as an undesirable class of immigrants in this country? Do the labor organizations take any interest in restricting that class of immigration?—A. They do not enter into the labor unions, except in such trades as are very little worked—tailoring and clothing business, for instance, which they monopolize altogether. They also make hats and caps and do other light work. They will not dig, nor carry a hod, nor farm, nor do any productive labor. They do not interfere much with the labor organizations, except that they increase the class of middlemen in this country very largely, and the middleman is always a drain on the producer.

Q. What was your connection with the immigration service of the country?— A. I was connected with labor organizations some years ago, and was on their legislative committee before the committees of Congress as far back as 1884, and have acted in that capacity for some years. I was appointed at the request of the American Federation of Labor on the European Immigration Commission. Mr. Powderly was appointed to represent the Knights of Labor and I had the indorsement of the American Federation of Labor, which was then, as it is now, under the presidency of Mr. Samuel Gompers.

Q. This Mr. Powderly is not the present Commissioner-General of Immigration?—A. No; he is a brother of the present Commissioner. We investigated the question of immigration in the various countries of Europe, and submitted a report, which first appeared in January of 1892, and Congress has done me the honor to reprint my report in 1893. The other reports were not reprinted. There were reports made by Colonel Weber, and Dr. Kempster, Captain Cross, Mr. Powderly, and myself. We investigated the matter in all except the Scandinavian countries, and we did not go to Spain or Portugal, because there is very little emigration from there. We did not consider it worth while to go there. Scandinavian immigration is very desirable, and there is no more objection to it than there is to the German, French, English, or Irish. They are all welcome when they come up to the requirements of existing law.

Q. That is so of all the countries of north Europe?—A. They are all welcome, and are generally a good class of people and make good citizens.

Q. Have you any other suggestions to make, Mr. Schulteis?—A. I hope that the commission will investigate this subject by looking into the questions that are in their syllabi, and make a report before this Congress adjourns, because, if Congress is to have the benefit of their work and labor, now is the time, when an act is pending. I think the first report ought to be on the subject of immigration, and it would aid Congress materially in coming to a conclusion on this question, which has been before Congress for four years. It was passed by one Congress preceding this and vetoed by President Cleveland, and it was passed over his veto in the House within twenty-four hours after the veto message arrived by a vote of something like 197 to 25; it may have been 175 to 27.

Q. The educational clause of the Lodge bill would not even affect the Russian Jews, would it?—A. They can nearly all read and write the Jewish language. The bill as it was originally drafted would have affected the Russian Jews.

Q. How would it have affected them?—A. The original wording of it was in accordance with a recommendation in my report, "native language," and the words "native language" were struck out. The native language of the Russian Jew is the Russian language. They can not read and write the Russian language, but most of them can read and write the Jewish language. Lots of them are born in other countries and never take the trouble to learn the language of the country where they are born and raised. The prepaid-ticket clause in the existing law, if enforced, would bar them.

Q. Have you German statistics that show the number of Germans that come to this country for a certain year and then our statistics to put by the side of them?— A. Yes; I have here German statistics in one volume, Statistical Yearbook of the

German Empire, from 1871 to 1890, a period of nineteen years, and it will be found on page 14.

Q. Can you pick out a certain year when there was large immigration to this country and show the number that left German ports and then show our own statistics to show a discrepancy?—A. I believe I have that in my report on Italian statistics, immigration from 1869 to 1879. These tables are compiled from information received at the mayors' offices and the registered number of passports delivered and corresponds with the amount paid for them, and therefore these statistics are absolutely correct. They charge $3.50 for a passport, and they get that money from the emigrant, and we only charge $1 head tax. The foreign government makes more from the passport than we get from the head tax. The same is the case in Germany. That is another reason, in my judgment, why the head tax should be increased here. They make their service self-sustaining, and the money they get for the passports pays for every particle of the service and brings a revenue besides. The grand total for six years was 1,174,901, and in our statistics for 1890, published by the Hon. Carroll D. Wright, a smaller number is given for the entire country than appear in the city of New York alone. Italian papers make great sport of the fact that our statistics are so unreliable. I have read a statement in an Italian paper which makes this point that American statistics can not be taken as a basis: "It will be sufficient to quote the fact that the census of 1890 gave only 182,000 Italians living in the United States, while it is certain that the number then approached and now exceeds 500,000." This is taken from Bollettino della Soc. Geog. Italiana, Ser. III, Vol. VIII, Fas. X, p. 325. It is found on page 63 of the Quarterly for March, 1896, of the American Statistical Association, of which Mr. North, one of the members of this commission, is one of the counsellors. That is an authoritative statistical association, the best in the United States.

Q. Goes back for a series of years, does it?—A. Yes, sir.

Q. I would like to have you give us the total of emigrants leaving the ports of the German Empire for, say, a period of ten years, that we may compare that with our immigration reports to see if there is any disparity.—A. I will state that each port has its own separate reports.

Q. Are they not consolidated?—A. Yes; but that consolidation is, in my judgment, not as effective as to get the special reports. Take ports like Bremen and Hamburg and those ports where they go into the nationality of the emigrant. For that reason I prefer them to these. In our statistics we take everybody that comes from Hamburg and mark them down as Germans, although only one-third that emigrate from that port are Germans. All the Jews that come from Russia go on the boat at Hamburg, and the statistics we have in this country on immigrants from Hamburg are unreliable and are not to be depended upon. That is one thing I hope this commission will investigate and see that they are counted properly and according to the place where they were born, and not charged as being of the country from which they ship. English statistics are swelled by the fact that large numbers are sent to Liverpool and from there here and are called English people. They distribute them; particularly the Hirsch Society makes it a business of distributing them. I met immigrants that had been shipped at Hamburg to Liverpool and then from Liverpool here. It sends them down to Genoa. They used to be counted as Italians when they arrived in New York because they arrived from Genoa or any place in Italy or Palermo. That matter has never been presented to committees in Congress or been investigated; and yet my own investigation shows me that in order to get accurate statistics we should have the nativity of the immigrant and count him from that place as it appears on the steamships' manifests, rather than from the port from which he sails.

Q. (By Mr. PHILLIPS.) Have you any given year, taking the foreign statistics, complete or not complete, and ours, to show that there are more shipped from abroad than land here?—A. Yes; the year 1891; I examined into the question.

Q. What discrepancy did you find?—A. In Italian immigration, 50 per cent only were counted at the port of New York.

Q. (By Mr. A. L. HARRIS.) How far is the padrone system in execution in this country?—A. I believe there are about 80 Italian banks in New York City now, and most of them still keep up that system, but not to so large an extent as they did some years ago, because their own people have protested against the slavery that they impose upon Italians. There have been meetings in places like Boston and New York of Italian citizens, protesting against this state of slavery, and protests have been made here at Washington, and they do those things largely under cover now. I have copies of newspapers published in New York City—Italian papers—by these so-called bankers, who are simply immigration agents, and some of their sheets I have here. One is called "Bollettino Della Emigrazione." This was the official organ of the Italian Society of Immigration (Limited). Another is called "Il Fieramosca." Both are published in New York. These bankers

IMMIGRATION.

take care of the immigrants' money and write their letters and answer them. The Italian people are so illiterate that they have, in the streets of Naples, for instance, men as numerous as peanut venders are in this country whose business it is to write letters for them. The bankers take care of their earnings until they get enough money to go home—say, $350 to $400. That is the average capital for an Italian. He never has to work himself when he gets home. He is a boss, and wears velvet knee breeches and silk hat and has his fellow Italians work for him at from 14 to 19 cents per day. He is a shining advertisement for the steamship agents.

Q. To what extent could persons or firms wanting labor be supplied through the padrone system?—A. They can get from 50 to 100 men at a time. I was offered 50 a day by one agent when I was in Italy. I pretended I was looking for contract laborers there.

Q. (By Mr. FARQUHAR.) Do you believe there are any blocks of alien contract laborers brought into this country any more?—A. Not in very large blocks any more, because, as I said. the Italians themselves have protested. Wherever there are blocks, the padrone system prevails, and that has been discountenanced by the Italian Government itself, and they now move in small lots of five or six.

Q. (By Mr. A. L. HARRIS.) You think it is passing away, partly through the execution of the law in this country and also the sentiment against it in Italy?—A. The sentiment against it, in my judgment, has more to do with it than the rigid enforcement of the law, because it has never been a popular law with the immigration officials, and yet it has had its effect. The mere knowledge on the other side that these things were prohibited has shown workingmen that there must be some reason why he is not wanted here, and as soon as he finds that the conditions are not as pictured to him (that this is a land of milk and honey and that gold can be picked up on the streets) they think twice before they emigrate, and in that way it has done a great deal of good. I think the law would have helped very largely and would have been more efficient if it had been enforced, but we had no means of finding who came under contract, except by going among the immigrants when they arrived. There should have been an inspector on these steamers unknown to them.

Q. You have made the immigrant question a considerable study, have you not?—A. Yes; I have studied it since 1884, and have been interested in the subject as a student of political economy and social science.

Q. I wish you would state what effect, if any, the colonization of immigrants in this country has on their customs and the inhabitants of this country and upon themselves?—A. I do not think the effect is very good, but very fortunately the question settles itself in time. The second generation, in spite of their colonization, generally learns how to read and write and speak the English language. It has a bad effect, unquestionably, to colonize them as I saw them colonized in the cities of New York, Chicago, St. Louis, Milwaukee, and Cincinnati. It is not a good plan, but they settle that way for convenience. Blood is thicker than water, and they would rather get together than to scatter, and for that reason the Latins would rather go to South America, if it were made convenient. They have a hospital in New York and treat immigrants when they land here. I have known as high as 600 to be in there at a time. If they were sound, as the ship surgeons swore they were, there would not be quite so many sent to the hospital on their arrival here.

Q. (By Mr. KENNEDY.) Do you think that Congress would, in twenty years, or any period of time, entertain such a proposition as increasing the head tax to $10?—A. Yes; I believe Congress is ready, and I believe the next legislation will be on the head-tax question, and the head tax will be largely increased. The present Commissioner of Immigration, I understand, recommends an increase of the head tax.

Q. Yes; $2.—A. Two dollars. That is only to cover the expense of buildings at Ellis Island. It will not make the service self-sustaining. The steamship people add it to the price of the ticket, and it is effectual as a remedy in proportion to the amount added. Two dollars would not be appreciable.

Q. (By Mr. FARQUHAR.) You mentioned that in Detroit you saw with your own eyes hundreds of Canadians come over there and work and pass back into Canada at night. What year was that?—A. That was in 1876-77.

Q. I thought it could not have been during late years.—A. I was in the governmental service at the port of Detroit for a year and a half at that time, and have visited there several times since.

Q. Are you aware that now there is no such thing in existence—that it is almost impossible to bring a Canadian over there and have him work and return the same day?—A. I understand that the present Congressman from Detroit, Mr. Corliss, endeavored very strenuously during the last two Congresses to get an amendment to the Lodge bill compelling persons who worked on the American side to live there also.

WASHINGTON, D. C., *February 10, 1899.*

TESTIMONY OF HON. T. V. POWDERLY,

Commissioner-General of Immigration.

The commission met at 2 p. m., February 10, 1899. Vice-Chairman Phillips presided and introduced the witness, Hon. T. V. Powderly, Commissioner-General of Immigration. He suggested that Mr. Powderly make a general statement, being guided by the commission's syllabi.

Mr. POWDERLY. I note from your remarks that you very kindly afford me the opportunity to make a statement, but I did not come prepared to do anything of the kind; in fact, I have had no opportunity, since the receipt of your first invitation to come before the commission, to prepare anything; I have been very busy, and I would much prefer that you ask some questions which, of course, will lead up to the making of statements. I note here, " Effects of immigration in the several industries: on employment in skilled trades and unskilled occupations; on wages; on morale." In relation to the effects of immigration on the several industries I am not prepared to make any authentic statement; that is, a statement based upon any facts or data in my possession. No effort has been made, so far as I am aware, to gather information on this particular point except from among workingmen through their organizations, and they note that the effect of immigration on some trades and occupations has been bad, particularly the calling of mining. In the anthracite region the effect has been very bad, and in order to get at a fair idea of it I think it would not be unwise for your commission to visit that region. You will there learn that—I believe in 1869, during a miners' strike which was then in progress—a man who was connected with one of the coal companies made the statement that in order to defeat the men in their demands it would be necessary to bring cheap labor from Europe; and shortly after that miners were noticed coming to the anthracite region in large numbers from Italy, Hungary, Russia, and other far-off lands. I do not think I am making an exaggerated statement when I tell you that at least three men are standing around in the coal regions awaiting each place. I do not think I make that statement too broadly when I make it in that language. The mines are not working full time, and those who are working find that neighbors of theirs are ready and anxious to take their places. You will find also, if you go to the coal regions, streets in towns—I will go further than that—a small town, where you may walk from end to end, and you will hear the American language spoken very rarely. Within the last two years I walked through that place, and I did not meet a man nor a woman who could speak our language. These people came here originally in response to the demands of the employers of miners. Their effect was bad upon business, because they consented to work for the lowest possible wage on which men could subsist; as a consequence the merchants felt it, the entire business community felt it, and it has had a very bad effect, not alone upon the miners but those who depend upon them. It has also been the means of draining our country of a vast amount of money. I am not prepared to give you figures, for I could not do it without consultation with the post-office authorities, but in the year 1896 something like $80,000 went out of two communities in Luzerne County, Pa.; I give you this on hearsay; I am not prepared to make the statement and assure you that it is correct. In Lackawanna County, from the upper end, I have been told by business men that over $100,000 went to Europe from men who are not citizens, who do not speak our language, and who have undersold the American miner in the market.

Q. (By Mr. NORTH.) Do these men intend to remain permanently in this country?—A. Very rarely do such men intend to remain. We have in Lackawanna County a vast number of Italians who came, and who have purchased little homes. They are paying for them and they are bringing up their children as Americans. They intend to remain. They are good people. We have Hungarians and Polanders who do the same, who make very good citizens; but, in the main, the vast majority of those who come stay but a short time, and they will tell you that their desire is to reap the benefit of their labor here and carry a few hundred dollars home with them.

Q. To what nationality does that refer?—A. It does not apply to any particular nationality; the Hungarians, the Italians, and some of the Polanders desire to go home, but, in the main, the majority of those who want to go back, and do go back, are from southern Italy. Those who come from northern Italy like our climate; they like our country, and remain. They make very good citizens.

Q. (By Mr. FARQUHAR.) Do you know, or believe, that the padrone system exists in mining in Pennsylvania?—A. I believe the padrone system has existed for years, and in one form or another it has flourished. I believe it still exists, in that it has never gone out of existence since it was first inaugurated or established.

Q. Then the alien contract-labor law is not apparently sufficient in suppressing this padrone system?—A. No; because they adopt a method that is very hard of detection. For instance, a man comes to this country, bright, active, and intelligent; he learns the American language. He is taken in charge by his employer, who says to him, "You are acquainted in Italy (in Hungary, Belgium, or whatever land he comes from); I want four or five good men (or a dozen, as the case may be), but, under the law, I can not send for them. You can write for them and warn them against making any disclosure on arriving here that would indicate that they are contract laborers or coming here under any agreement." And these men come. Not long ago thirty men came from Syria, and they claimed they were all of one family. There were two facts. One was that they claimed they were of one family, the other that they were going to the one destination. Those were the only suspicious circumstances connected with that case, but I am convinced that they came here under an agreement. We are now investigating the matter.

Q. (By Mr. NORTH.) Have you any remedy under the alien contract-labor law?—A. W ɔ have no remedy unless we prove a contract. We must show that a contract was made abroad. There are rulings and decisions of the courts to that effect, taking the ground that unless a contract, expressed or implied, was made abroad we have no right to send them back.

Q. Have you any suggested amendment to the law?—A. In that respect I would suggest that when the fact that they came in response to an invitation of any kind is proved, even though they did not become a party to a contract on the other side, that that should be sufficient to class them as alien contract laborers.

Q. (By Mr. OTJEN.) Do you think that would be practical?—A. I do.

Q. Would men be privileged to write to their relatives suggesting that they come?—A. That, of course, would be different. There is nothing to prohibit one from giving information to his relatives abroad, sending for them, and paying their passage. I had reference to an invitation from an apparently uninterested party—from one not a relative.

Q. (By Mr. FARQUHAR.) The hiring must have something of a contract in it to come under the law?—A. Yes.

Q. (By Mr. PHILLIPS.) You spoke of those people—foreigners—having "undersold" our people. Do you mean underselling their labor?—A. I mean their labor. They sell their labor much cheaper than our people do; but when I say our people I do not mean native Americans, I mean foreigners who have become naturalized, as well as those who were born here.

Q. (By Mr. FARQUHAR.) What have been the changes in nationality in the mining regions of Pennsylvania, say, for the last forty years? Were the original miners Americans?—A. The original miners in the anthracite regions were Irish, Scotch, English, Welsh, and German, in the order in which I give them.

Q. (By Mr. NORTH.) Naturalized?—A. Yes.

Q. (By Mr. FARQUHAR.) Have they been entirely driven out of mining by the nationalities that succeeded them?—A. I will take you to towns in the anthracite regions and point out to you houses, with four or five rooms, which I have visited, now occupied by anywhere from ten to twenty, twenty-five or thirty people and upward, maybe men, very few women. These houses were formerly occupied by a father, a mother, and three, four, five, or six children. They are now occupied by a number of men, poor fellows, stalwart men some of them, and good men, but in ignorance of their rights, with but little ambition save to work. They are industrious, and they have taken the places of the men of families.

Q. What is the prevailing nationality of the miners in Pennsylvania?—A. I do not think I could tell you. There are a vast number of Italians.

Q. What nationality stands first in numbers?—A. I think the Hungarians and Italians are about equal. There are a number of Welshmen yet.

Q. Was the standard of living of the old miners of Pennsylvania as good as the average standard of that class of labor throughout this country in any other calling?—A. The miner of Pennsylvania aspired to the very best in the land, and he had it as far as his means would go. He had his carpets on his floor, he had his sewing machine for his wife, his children were well dressed, there were pictures on the wall, mirrors, and all the comforts of a modern home, including in many instances organs and pianos.

Q. Under the law of July, 1864, which was virtually repealed in 1868 or 1869, we opened wide the gates of this country to immigration. Is it a fact that nearly all these changes came into the mining regions during that time because of this foreign population?—A. The change began immediately following the war, even during the war.

Q. (By Mr. PHILLIPS.) In naming the various nationalities that were prominent in mining, in their order, you did not name Americans; were there any Americans employed?—A. There were Americans; yes. I thought the question related only to foreigners. Of course there were Americans.

Q. What per cent would there be of Americans now?—A. Very few Americans; that is, since the foreigners came. Americans, as a rule, took to mining very rarely.

Q. (By Mr. FARQUHAR.) Were the succeeding generations of foreigners there—which were mainly Britons—driven out by a lower race?—A. I would hate to say they were a lower race.

Q. I mean less skilled and working for less wages.—A. Put it in this way: Less desirable.

Q. (By Representative OTJEN.) Less educated?—A. Less desirable. The children of some of these people are very bright, very good, and will make good Americans.

Q. (By Mr. FARQUHAR.) Do those of this second generation, or even the original immigrants, naturally take to trade organizations?—A. I think they do. I have known of great numbers of them joining labor organizations.

Q. Can you state the difference in the wage scales of the sixties and the early seventies and the present rate of wage there?—A. No; I could not. There are a number of other elements that enter into the lowering of wages and the lack of activity in the coal trade. Anthracite coal is expensive, and in recent years the gas stove, the gasoline stove, and the oilstove have displaced the anthracite cooking stove in the cities. Great inroads have been made upon the anthracite trade through these agencies.

Q. (By Mr. PHILLIPS.) Have combinations or trusts had anything to do with reducing the number of laborers or the output of coal?—A. No; I can not say that they have. The coal pool, which was intended to limit production for the purpose of keeping up prices, is the only thing in the shape of a trust that the anthracite region has had to complain of—at least that approaches nearest to a trust—but that was a matter of protection, and I do not think the trusts have figured very greatly in the reduction of wages of the men.

Q. Are there many combinations between large firms in the coal regions—have they any big combination regulating the output, to your knowledge?—A. No; I do not know of any, only, of course, what is known as the "coal pool" of New York.

Q. (By Mr. C. J. HARRIS.) Is it not true that instead of this former labor being forced out of employment it has gone up into a higher scale of employment into occupations which require more education? Does not the second generation go out of mining because it goes into those positions?—A. That is true largely, but the miners themselves—those who were actively engaged in mining—were obliged to go away. You read of the shooting of the miners who were on a strike at Hazleton, Pa., a year ago last September. It was known as the "Latimer shooting affair." A number of men were shot that day and they belonged to these nationalities that we have discussed here, and among those who did the shooting were the sons of former miners. I went to Wilkesbarre once during the trial of those who did the shooting, and engaged in conversation with one of the men whose father was at one time a miner in that region. He was among the deputies, or among those who made up the sheriff's posse. I asked him how he could find it in his heart to shoot at those poor fellows without orders, for that, as I understood it, was what they had done at the time, and I put the question to him in that way. His reply recalled an incident in my own experience. Sometime in 1881 I addressed a meeting in the Latimer schoolhouse, or that neighborhood, at the very spot where the shooting took place. There were present in the meeting a number of Irish, German, Welsh, English, and Scotch miners, and one of them made the statement that, "We will have to go away before this influx of cheap labor and leave here, leave our homes." There was a Scotchman who took up the discussion toward the close, and he said: "I am told we must leave here, and go away from these hills and valleys that we have beautified with our labor. I brought my family up here. I came here thirty-five years ago, raised my family, and gave them an education, and now, in the latter end of my life, I am told I must leave my home and go away. I will not do it." But he did do it, and relatives of his were among the men who held rifles that day, so that it did not require the order of the sheriff to impel at least some of them to shoot. I have this from his own lips; so that while I have nothing to say as to the shooting or its legal or moral aspect, that is a fact that must be taken into consideration in discussing it.

Q. (By Mr. PHILLIPS.) Did the "Molly McGuires" create a great disturbance in that region? It might be of interest to the commission to know how that originated.—A. I can not say so much about that, because I never was a "Molly McGuire." I have so often been called a "Molly McGuire" that I look with suspicion upon any charge against another; and they charged the "Molly McGuires" with a number of things that they never did, and that no one else did.

Q. Was there any condition in the coal regions that led up to what was called the "Molly McGuire" movement?—A. Yes; there were conditions there, such as favoritism; I believe the principal offense on the part of those who were punished by the "Molly McGuires" was that they discharged certain miners and hired their friends and relatives in preference, giving them the preference in good chambers, drifts, and headings, and such things as that, known to the miners. They were largely personal matters.

Q. (By Mr. FARQUHAR.) Was it an organized labor quarrel?—A. The "Molly McGuires" was not a labor organization at all. It is charged they were a branch of the Ancient Order of Hibernians, but the Ancient Order of Hibernians had nothing in common with the "Molly McGuires."

Q. In what way do you think the alien contract-labor law is insufficient to exclude the undesirable and at the same time suppress the system of contracting for foreign low-priced labor in this country? Can you suggest any amendment, or can you state how it operates, what your means are for discovering where these contracts are made, how they are made, and whether steamship companies or the foreign boards of relief are concerned in bringing this class of labor to the country.—A. I believe that until very recently some of the poorhouses or charitable institutions in England, Ireland, Scotland, Wales, and Italy were drawn upon for immigrants to come to this country; but the inspection now is so rigid that they seldom attempt to send their cripples, imbeciles, and persons afflicted with disease here. I made a recommendation which the Secretary of the Treasury was kind enough to incorporate in his report. In this recommendation I said [reading]:

"In this connection it is deemed advisable to suggest that a law be passed which will exact a rigid medical examination of every immigrant. Its importance can not be overestimated when we consider that a vast tide of immigration from eastern Europe and the Orient finds its way through England to this country."

The tide soon changed from the Orient. We get a vast number of Asiatics, and they come afflicted with a number of diseases. A prominent physician in New York assured me that great numbers of them were tainted with venereal disease, and he had no doubt that leprosy frequently came through our ports. I delegated an inspector—Robert Watchorn—to go to Europe and watch the methods in sending people here from England, and he reports in this way:

"The inspection to a layman looks like a very rapid affair, the passengers passing the physician at a rate approximately of 2,000 an hour. Only in a few instances were heads uncovered. * * *"

To show you the relevancy of that remark, there is a skin disease known as favus, a disease prevalent among children. It originates in filth, and eventually removes the hair from the head. Once the disease attacks the head it takes months, sometimes years, to eradicate it, and once the hair comes off it never comes back again. A great many good people find fault with sending back a child thus afflicted; they say that the child should not be returned. They say, furthermore, it is inhuman to send such a child back and oblige the father and mother to go with it. I took this view of it—that it would be more humane to send that child back than allow the little creature to run around among the children of our own citizens and spread its disease; that our duty was first to our own children; that we might inflict hardship on a dozen, a hundred, or a thousand, but we would in like proportion save our own children from contact with this disease or those afflicted with it. [Reading:]

"Only in a few instances were heads uncovered, so that it can not be said to have been a very searching inquiry, although it must be remembered that he had seen most of them at the lodging houses the night previous. This physician, it must be borne in mind, is under no obligation to point out that this or that emigrant is likely to be objectionable to the United States immigration authorities. His sole duty, under British laws and regulations, is to protect the health of the emigrants while on board ship."

I have recommended that we station agents of the Immigration Bureau, directly responsible to the head of the Bureau, at foreign ports, to examine those who come as to their health and morals—I mean those who have been convicted of some crime—and to examine them generally to see what class of people we are getting. If that is done we will be able to keep a great many people at home who would otherwise go to the expense and hardship of an ocean journey to our shores; it would be a benefit to the immigrant, and a benefit to our own people.

Q. Do you think you would get the cooperation of the foreign governments to carry out such a plan as that?—A. We have our consuls abroad now to examine them, but they do it so rapidly that they can not do justice to the law. We have at this moment a request from the consul at Naples, asking that an immigration official be stationed there, and who states that he can not in any way do justice to the immigration laws in making the inspection.

Q. (By Mr. KENNEDY.) Do you desire to have that recommendation put in the form of legislation?—A. Yes.

Q. Do you not anticipate opposition from the steamship companies' lobby in getting such legislation as that?—A. No; I do not think the steamship companies would oppose that; I do not see why they should, because when we discover that a person who comes over is afflicted with a disease we send him back at the expense of the steamship company. It would be a saving to them, you know, to have the inspection made on the other side.

Q. (By Mr. NORTH.) How powerful is this steamship company lobby?—A. You are now leading me to unknown depths; I have never waded in.

Q. (By Representative OTJEN.) Under your present laws or regulations, have you inspectors stationed at any of these places?—A. No.

Q. (By Mr. PHILLIPS.) You have spoken of a class of people coming from Asia. What race or nationality are they?—A. A number of Syrians are coming. Japanese are coming in in vast numbers now on our Western coast.

Q. Are they subject to such diseases as you speak about?—A. Many of them are.

Q. (By Mr. NORTH.) What is the physical condition of the Russian Jews who come here?—A. The physical condition of many of them is rather poor.

Q. Are many of those people coming?—A. The tide is increasing; yes.

Q. Are they desirable citizens?—A. Some of them are; but, in the main, I think not.

Q. (By Mr. FARQUHAR.) Are they assisted immigrants, mainly?—A. A great many of them are assisted.

Q. From foreign funds?—A. Yes.

Q. (By Mr. KENNEDY.) Set up in business, after they get here, through the same agency?—A. There is no doubt of that. They come here and engage in peddling and in the vending of fruit, managing push carts, and following like occupations.

Q. (By Mr. NORTH.) How about settlements of Russian Jews—is there one in Tennessee?—A. I do not think that was successful. I have been informed it was not a success, but as to its progress I have no information. There was one organized, I believe, in New Jersey, with the intention of tilling the land, but it proved a failure.

Q. Was that a Baron Hirsch colony?—A. Yes.

Q. (By Mr. KENNEDY.) Have you heard any denials from the Baron Hirsch people of the charge that they are assisting Russian Jews to this country?—A. I have heard none. I make no charge that they are assisting, but it is quite evident that somebody must be doing it; of course, we can not tell.

Q. (By Mr. FARQUHAR.) In article 12 of the Treasury circular of August 16, 1898, we find the following:

"ART. 12. There shall be delivered to the commissioner of immigration at the port of arrival, by the master or commanding officer of the vessel, lists or manifests made at the time and place of embarkation of such immigrants, which shall, in answer to questions at the top of said lists or manifests, state to each of said passengers: (1) Full name; (2) age; (3) sex; (4) whether married or single; (5) calling or occupation; (6) whether able to read or write; (7) nationality; (8) last residence; (9) seaport for landing in the United States; (10) final destination in the United States; (11) whether having a ticket through to such final destination; (12) whether the immigrant has paid his own passage or whether it has been paid by other persons, or by any corporation, society, municipality, or government; (13) whether in possession of money; and, if so, whether upward of $30, and how much if $30 or less; (14) whether going to join a relative; and if so, what relative, and his name and address; (15) whether ever before in the United States; and if so, when and where; (16) whether ever in prison or almshouse, or supported by charity; (17) whether a polygamist; (18) whether under contract, expressed or implied, to perform labor in the United States; (19) the immigrant's condition of health, mentally and physically, and whether deformed or crippled; and if so, from what cause."

The commission would like to know if, in every report, this list or manifest is made out in Europe in good faith and supervised by our consuls; and also whether, when the immigrants reach this side, say, at Ellis Island, there is an adequate inspection to know how thoroughly it is carried out, and whether that regulation itself is sufficient in safeguarding this country against undesirable immigrants?—A. The circular to which you refer grows out of this law, section 1 of the act of March 3, 1893 (reading):

"* * * That, in addition to conforming to all present requirements of law, upon the arrival of any alien immigrants by water at any port within the United

States, it shall be the duty of the master or commanding officer of the steamer or sailing vessel having said immigrants on board to deliver to the proper inspector of immigration at the port lists or manifests made at the time and place of embarkation of such alien immigrants on board such steamer or vessel, which shall, in answer to questions at the top of said lists, state as to each immigrant the full name, age, and sex; whether married or single; the calling or occupation; whether able to read or write; the nationality; the last residence; the seaport for landing in the United States; the final destination, if any, beyond the seaport of landing; whether having a ticket through to such final destination; whether the immigrant has paid his own passage or whether it has been paid by other persons or by any corporation, society, municipality, or government; whether in possession of money; and if so, whether upwards of thirty dollars, and how much if thirty dollars or less; whether going to join a relative; and if so, what relative and his name and address; whether ever before in the United States; and if so, when and where; whether ever in prison or almshouse or supported by charity; whether a polygamist; whether under contract, expressed or implied, to perform labor in the United States; and what is the immigrant's condition of health, mentally and physically, and whether deformed or crippled; and if so, from what cause."

That is done on a manifest of steerage immigrants alone, and you notice in reading the law that it applies to no class of immigrants in particular, that it deals alike with the immigrant who comes in the first or second cabin as well as the immigrant who comes in the steerage. Year before last, shortly after I was appointed, I heard from a friend of mine in England that one of the most notorious and dangerous anarchists in Europe was to take passage for this country. He gave me the name of the vessel and stated the he was coming in the first cabin. He was an immigrant; it was his intention to take up his residence in the United States. I am not prepared to say just how he was forbidden or, rather, how he was prevented from coming here. I would rather not make the statement, but he was checkmated in his designs upon our people.

In October last, noticing for some time that there was no examination made of alien immigrants in first and second cabins, I drew up a circular requiring that it be done. Americans who go abroad dislike very much to be called into an office on the other side just as they are going aboard a vessel and answer all these questions. We would endeavor to make it easy for the steamship company and for the passengers—travelers—by having the inspection done on board the vessel and sworn to on this side, but, of course, that would not be in accordance with law, and we could not do it. I would like very much to see the law amended so as to allow the inspection to be made on board the vessels.

Q. (By Mr. NORTH.) Aliens only?—A. Aliens only. Of course, when it is once established that a man or woman is an American citizen or is coming here merely on business or a visit, we ask no further question. I suppose you saw in the papers recently an account of a prominent Englishman who was asked the question if he was ever in prison or convicted of any offense. He became highly offended. It is absolutely necessary for us to know who comes, but, inasmuch as the rates in the cabins have been reduced, a number of the most dangerous people will come that way. I have no fear of a poor man who comes in the steerage or cabin, honestly intending to live here, with no anarchistic tendencies. He will make a good citizen; but the man who comes here to stir up strife and act the demagogue, rich or poor, I would keep out, no matter who he is or where he comes from, and it is against such people that we make the provision.

Q. Is there no provision that pertains distinctly to anarchists?—A. None whatever.

Q. (By Mr. KENNEDY.) Do you mean that you would have the examination take place after they go aboard and the vessel has sailed?—A. Yes.

Q. And then have them sent back at the expense of the steamship companies if they are found to be undesirable?—A. Yes.

Q. Would the powerful steamship companies contend against that?—A. At present we are making the examination abroad as well as here, and it would be much better for the steamship company, it seems to me, to have the required examination made on the other side. The steerage immigrants are all inspected before they come over.

Q. (By Representative OTJEN.) Who makes that inspection?—A. Our consuls.

Q. (By Mr. FARQUHAR.) It has been stated that the counting of the immigrants that come into this country under these manifests in the collection of the head tax is not rigidly performed. Is the head tax paid under this manifest?—A. Yes.

Q. Is there any way of avoiding the counting, from these manifests, of the number of immigrants and the head tax in the system you have at New York?—A. Yes, there is, by reason of not making the examination of the cabin immigrants. We have, only to-day, a complaint of men coming over in the cabins of certain vessels who were not manifested at all. We have also information that seven or eight men who notified the agent of the vessel on the other side that they were American citizens never were in this country at all. They are not on the manifest of the vessel. Now, what we want is—and 1 believe it is the wish of the Department generally—not to harass or embarrass either the traveling man or woman or the steamship company, and for that reason, to have these questions asked on board ship. We could arrange to have a slip of paper containing the questions and stating the reasons why they were asked handed to each passenger, so that before he went to the purser to make his statement he would know what it meant; but that, of course, we could not carry out, because it would be a violation of the law as it now exists. But if the law can be amended so as to do that it will be the practical way to do it.

Q. What percentage avoid paying the head tax?—A. I do not know.
Q. Is it 2 per cent or 3 per cent?—A. No; perhaps 1.
Q. Nothing like half?—A. Oh, no.
Q. Have you not made a recommendation to enlarge the head tax?—A. I have recommended that it be increased to $2.
Q. What are your reasons?—A. My reasons are that we may have a sufficient force to patrol the entire Canadian and Mexican borders, and establish agents of the Immigration Bureau abroad. At the present time immigrants who feel that they will not be permitted to land at New York, whose ailments are manifest, take passage for Canada; purchase a ticket, we will say, to Montreal. We have a station at Quebec, and in the winter time they land at St. Johns and Halifax. It is removed to St. Johns and Halifax in the winter. We have no right to examine the immigrants landed there if they are manifested to any part of Canada, but if they are manifested to any part of the United States, then our commissioner and his inspectors at Quebec have the right to examine them. They have learned abroad of this method of making examination, and manifest the undesirable ones to some point near the American border. They come there, escaping inspection, and in a few days walk over the line, and we have them. We are constantly sending them back, but under the law we can deport them only to the country whence they came, which is Canada; and they cross the line at some other point.
Q. (By Mr. NORTH.) Would you have the law so amended that you could deport them to their original country?—A. I would. They are not citizens of Canada, and therefore can not claim to be citizens of Canada. Once the fact is established that they are citizens of a foreign country they should be sent back.
Q. (By Mr. A. L. HARRIS.) If they should be sent back, who would bear that expense?—A. The steamship company that brought them here.
Q. Suppose you could not prove it?—A. We would not have much difficulty in doing that.
Q. (By Mr. FARQUHAR.) What is the percentage that surreptitiously crosses the Canadian frontier?—A. I am not in position to answer that question. It is said some place that "All men are liars." They come over the border to us and they lie. They say they have been in this country five, six, or ten years. They go into a poorhouse. They change their names. Every once in a while it develops that a certain man or woman in a public institution was known by another name on landing. I have not the least doubt that the greater part of the infirm people that come to us, aliens that drift into our institutions, come by way of Canada.
Q. (By Mr. NORTH.) Are the statistics of immigration through Canada defective?—A. Yes; very.
Q. (By Mr. FARQUHAR.) How is your inspection there?—A. The inspection is all right, but we have no right to inspect a person who is not coming to this country.
Q. Would you catch them coming this way?—A. Yes.
Q. You desire the increase in the head tax, to put on more inspectors on the Mexican and Canadian frontiers?—A. To police the entire border; it ought to be done.
Q. (By Mr. NORTH.) Is that the only remedy?—A That is not the only remedy; no. Another remedy is to make a thorough medical examination of all who come.
Q. Through Canada?—A. Everywhere. I would examine the men as carefully as our troops were examined when applying for enlistment during the late war. I contend that if it were necessary to select good, sound, healthy men, physically and mentally, to engage in the work of killing and being killed, that it is even more necessary to examine those who come to this country with a view of enlisting in the army of producers and to become the future citizens and fathers and mothers of citizens in this country. If that is done, we will send back every unsound man. If we have the inspection as it ought to be, in Europe and at these foreign ports, we can detect a great many who are coming here as alien contract

laborers, if the law is slightly amended so as to make any evidence of agreement or of an influence used abroad to bring people here, other than through family connections, a sufficient ground to deport. As to the healthy immigrant, I have no objection; I do not think anybody else has. There is another idea I advanced in my recommendations which I will read, and that is (reading):

"There is at present no way of certainly determining where the great bulk of immigrants go to after passing inspection at the ports. While they are manifested to certain points, they may in reality intend going to other places. Under existing laws and conditions they can not be directed to any designated locality or State with any degree of certainty that they will find employment on arriving at their destination. There are bureaus of labor and statistics in 32 States where manufacturing, mining, and commercial life is most active. The enactment of a statute designating each head of a State bureau of labor statistics an agent of the Federal Government, for the purpose of collecting information which would show where trade was brisk and where it languished; where certain classes of labor were in demand and where the labor market was overstocked, and at stated intervals forwarding this information to the Bureau of Immigration, would be of great benefit to arriving immigrants.

"With such information at hand the immigration authorities could intelligently direct the immigrant to a point where he would find employment. It is possible that many would not avail themselves of the opportunity thus presented, but the number who would go direct to places where they would find work, and thus save the money which would otherwise be expended in a fruitless search for employment, would be considerable. Through the post-offices or other governmental agencies accurate information concerning the state of trade and labor could be obtained from all points, and in States where no labor bureaus exist an agent of the Immigration Bureau could be stationed to attend to the compiling and forwarding of the statistics above indicated. It is not necessary to do more than suggest the plan here. The details will be submitted if it is deemed advisable."

Q. Are you aware of any part of the United States where there is an under supply of labor?—A. I am not.

Q. (By Mr. FARQUHAR.) You are aware where there is some congestion of labor?—A. I am.

Q. (By Mr. KENNEDY.) Ex-Commissioner General Stump, when before the commission, expressed approval of the illiterate immigration to this country, having the idea that it had a tendency to elevate the American; that there were not enough of the native Americans to fill the lower grades of labor, and that the foreigners came in and did the work, and that elevated the Americans. I would like to have you express your opinion on that.—A. I do not care to appear as taking issue with anyone who has preceded me; I simply say there are more workingmen in this country than are necessary. The labor market is overstocked.

Q. (Mr. C. J. HARRIS.) Could the mills of New England run without this influx of Canadians?—A. Most assuredly they could.

Q. Where would they get their help from?—A. They could get their help in this country if they pay decent wages. Let them pay living wages and they can get all the help they want.

Q. In New England there seems to be no mill class that could be gotten unless these Canadians came in and took the places. Some three or four years ago the Americans all had large families; their children and women worked in the mills; now there does not seem to be any of that class of people there. What is your opinion about that?—A. I understand they have a curtailed production of children up there; but I think that industry would flourish again if the young men and women could afford to marry and raise families.

Q. (By Mr. PHILLIPS.) Do other nations of Europe have laws similar to our immigration laws?—A. They have educational tests in some European countries and in Australia and New Zealand.

Q. How is it in Europe?—A. I believe there are such laws in England. I will place at your disposal a report made by Inspector Robert Watchhorn. It gives a great deal of information, and I know it will answer a great many of your questions as to foreign immigration.

Q. (By Mr. FARQUHAR.) Was your reason for recommending a head tax of $2 to raise sufficient revenue from that source alone to pay the expenses of inspection and to make the Bureau self-supporting?—A. Yes.

Q. Was it your intention to make it in any way a restrictive measure against immigration?—A. Not by fixing it at $2; that would not be restrictive.

Q. Will you name a figure that would be restrictive?—A. No; I do not know what figure would be restrictive. Here is the difficulty: Many a man who can not raise $5 will be more desirable than the fellow who can raise $100; and sometimes the dangerous man will, on the strength of his sharp practice, get money that would enable him to pay his head tax, while the poor, decent, honest fellow could not.

Q. (By Mr. NORTH.) Could the steamship companies pay a big head tax?—A. Ostensibly the steamship companies pay it.

Q. They really pay it, do they not, now?—A. They pay it, but they collect it from the immigrant.

Q. In every case?—A. Yes; they are not in business for their health; it is part of the fare. There are some steamship companies that feed the immigrants very well on board; they supply them with every necessity, that is, plain food; but there are one or two companies that take the price of their head tax out of their stomachs.

Q. (By Mr. FARQUHAR.) So you think there is no advantage in making the head tax $10, $15, or $20?—A. I do not think it would affect the question much. I did at one time think $5 would be enough to pay all expenses.

Q. Under section 11 of the act of March 3, 1891, it is provided (reading): "That any alien who shall come into the United States in violation of law may be returned, as by law provided, at any time within one year thereafter, at the expense of the person or persons, vessel, transportation company or corporation bringing such alien into the United States, and if that can not be done, then at the expense of the United States; and any alien who becomes a public charge within one year after his arrival in the United States from causes existing prior to his landing therein shall be deemed to have come in violation of law, and shall be returned as aforesaid."

Q. Do you think that one year's time is a sufficient protection against immigrants who come here either with a disease that is not apparent to the inspector, or who through their own vicious habits contract disease, or in any other way become a public charge?—A. Most emphatically, no. I believe that until a man becomes a citizen of the United States, if he commits a crime or in any other way becomes a charge, he should be sent back to his own government.

On the 1st of January of this year I was at home in Scranton, and a former client called upon me and asked me to take up the case of a man in jail; he wanted me to procure a writ of habeas corpus and get the man out. I turned it over to another attorney, but visited the jail, and found that over 20 per cent of the inmates—248, I think, was the population of the jail—were aliens. The percentage of aliens in the population of our county is not so great as that, so that they exceeded their ratio in the jail. Last year, in May, I asked Inspector Layton to make an investigation in Pittsburg, and in one institution he found on a certain day that 1 per cent over one-half of the inmates were aliens. I sent a letter to the heads of several charitable and penal institutions, asking a question as to aliens in their institutions from the 1st of January, 1898, to the 1st of May, 1898, and the answer came back that, according to their books, they had so many foreigners. That led to the statement to them that it was not foreigners I desired to procure information about, but aliens; and I then learned for the first time that our institutions do not keep a record of aliens. If anything happens any of these in a public way, indemnity is demanded by the foreign government of which he is a subject, even if the man has resided here twenty years if he is still a subject of that government. So it would appear that if they have the right to demand indemnity for injuries inflicted we certainly have the right to send them back during the same period; at least I believe we have.

Q. (By Representative OTJEN.) Do you think a law requiring an educational test in the way of reading would be beneficial?—A. I am not so much in favor of the educational test, for the reasons I have given before. The worst people we have to treat are not the people who can not read and write; the curse we have mostly to treat is of those who can read and write in several languages.

Q. (By Mr. KENNEDY.) Would the educational test have kept out immigrants from Italy and Hungary?—A. I doubt it, because the Italians are very bright; and a friend of mine, now in Italy, has informed me by letter that the children over there, and older people, are rapidly learning to read and write, so that by the time this law would be passed we would keep few out. You know the law requires that the immigrant be required to read a passage in his own language.

That idea grew out of the agitation that began some fifteen or sixteen years ago, looking toward the improvement of our naturalization laws. I took the ground then, and do now, that no man should be naturalized who can not read and write the American language. I would not naturalize any man, no matter what language he reads or writes, to American citizenship unless he can read and write our language. The anarchist has a field there that we can not invade, and for that reason I would have the man who is admitted to American citizenship read and write the American language.

IMMIGRATION. 41

Q. (By Mr. NORTH.) Would you have him read and speak English?—A. I would have him able to read and write it.

Q. Is everything that tends to restrict immigration a good thing per se?—A. Everything that tends to restrict undesirable immigration.

Q. Educational test or otherwise?—Yes. I have in my mind an Irishman and a Scotchman; neither one could read nor write. They came to this country poor; they built homes for themselves; they raised their families here; the children of both are occupying high positions to-day, and neither of these men could read nor write. They were desirable acquisitions to our citizenship. They became citizens as soon as they could. I would not want to be accused of harboring race prejudice or bigotry, because I have not anything of it about me, but if the immigration was as it was that day, we could not get a better race than came from the British Isles and Germany.

Q. (By Mr. KENNEDY.) Would you place in the desirable class the Swedes and Norwegians from northern Europe, who go out on the farms in Dakota?—A. They are a very excellent people. I would put no bars against them whatever; in fact, against no industrious man, if we can determine he is such. I would have the supply regulated by the demand for labor. Our institutions are becoming perfect in that respect, and it seems to me it can be done through the agencies we have.

Q. (By Representative OTJEN.) Would you admit no more than we needed?—A. Yes. I made an effort some time ago, through the labor organizations, to notify the people abroad of the exact conditions here, and it had a good effect at that time. I believe it checked a good many immigrants—prevented them from coming.

Q. (By Mr. FARQUHAR.) Do you think the present law is adequate in the matter of alien contract labor, or does it need amendment?—A. The alien contract-labor law is not what it ought to be, not by any means.

Q. Will you state why?—A. The courts have ruled that we must produce evidence showing that a contract has been made abroad. That should be amended so as to include evidence of an agreement made either abroad or here, or the using of undue influence to bring people here other than, as I stated, through family connections.

Q. Do you think a guaranty from the steamship companies against pauperism for five years instead of one would be restrictive enough to separate the desirable from the undesirable?—A. It would go a long way toward safeguarding them this way, that no parties in Europe or elsewhere would ever send an immigrant to this country, providing they knew there was a bonded condition here of $500, to last for five years, with two responsible bondsmen possessing real estate worth double the face of the bond. That would be a safeguard.

Q. If such a law has proven to be a safeguard in Australasia, colonies which are materially conditioned very much like America in respect to their naturalization laws, why would not that be a good law for this country?—A. Yes; I believe such a law should be passed.

Q. (By Mr. KENNEDY.) If a Norwegian owning a farm in Minnesota writes to his brother in Norway that he has work for him on his farm if he will come to America, and the brother accepts and comes, and you learn of that fact, would that be accepted as an agreement made on the other side, and would the brother be sent back to Europe?—A. No; I do not so consider it.

Q. We have been so informed.—A. Under certain conditions, yes; but as the brother owns a farm the question is viewed differently. If I have a brother in Europe and I own a farm and am engaged in farming, I see no reason why I could not inform him of that fact and have him come. The present law can be made to appear odious or ridiculous by applying its operations to cases not contemplated by those who favored its adoption.

Q. (By Mr. PHILLIPS.) Can you give us some information in regard to the effect of immigration on agriculture and manufacturing?—A. No; I can not. As to farming, I do not know how that is affected. I know of no means of gathering any statistics on it; I know of none that have been gathered on it. The farm is not troubled so much with immigration, because a great number of those who come here manifested as farmers do not engage in farming.

Q. (By Representative OTJEN.) Do they mostly congregate in the big cities?—A. An examination of the tables will show that 16,242 farmers and 1,604 miners were landed during the year according to their own statements on the manifests. (Reading):

"It will be noticed that the great bulk of the farmers were destined to California, Connecticut, Illinois, Iowa, Massachusetts, New Jersey, New York, and Pennsylvania, States in which the large cities are located, and it is reasonable to assume that they went direct to the great industrial centers of these States. Advices from the mining towns of Pennsylvania, Ohio, Indiana, and Illinois are to the effect that the number of immigrants that arrived during the year was at least double that given in the foregoing table as miners, while a reference to the table giving destination and occupation will show that but 412 of those designated as miners were manifested to Pennsylvania, Illinois, Indiana, and Ohio."

They may have been farmers at home, that is true, but on arriving here they go right into the mines and the lower occupations. The skilled trades are not so greatly affected as are the unskilled.

Q. (By Mr. PHILLIPS.) Have you any remarks to make in regard to manufacturing?—A. The stonecutting trade and the shoe trade of New England are badly cut up. Take the shoe trade as an illustration: Five years ago, I think, when I was connected with the labor movement officially, I think it took fifty-four parts to make a shoemaker; a tailor was composed of nine. I believe it is increasing. The less a man knows about his rights the better machine he will make. As a consequence, such people are welcomed to New England, where they will manage a part of the machine and work for the lowest possible rate of wages. He who receives small wages can spend but little, and it works its way around and around until it strikes at all. The "sin of cheapness" that Donald McCloud talks about is the sin of this century, and to get people cheap is why they wish to get people over here and in every way they can to stimulate the immigration to this country.

Q. (By Mr. FARQUHAR.) About what is the percentage of skilled and unskilled labor that comes into this country now, and what proportion does the skilled labor bear to the whole immigration?—A. The skilled labor bears a small proportion. Those who come are practically laborers—ordinary laborers and farmers. A great number of tailors come. They go to New York.

Q. (By Mr. KENNEDY.) Are you familiar with the provisions of the Lodge bill now pending in Congress?—A. The one that requires the educational test?

Q. Yes.—A. I have read it, but at this moment am not informed enough in regard to it to tell what its effect would be if it became a law.

Q. (By Representative OTJEN.) Would such a law tend to check immigration from Asiatic countries?—A. The educational test?

Q. Yes.—A. Yes; it will check them.

Q. (By Mr. KENNEDY.) Would it check the Chinese immigration?—A. It would not check the Chinese, the Japanese, nor the Russian Jews. It would check very few Russians.

Q. (By Representative OTJEN.) Can the Russian Jews read?—A. Nearly all read. As I stated, the original idea in that measure was that it should be grafted on to our naturalization laws. Some fifteen or sixteen years ago, when we began that agitation, it was not the intention to apply it to the immigrants on landing. It would be a temporary check, but in a few years they would learn to read a passage; that would be all they would know; it would practically be of no benefit to us at all. You may have read within the last week or two of a family named Becker arriving at New York—a woman and four children. Her husband, who lived in Richmond—her alleged husband—went up to New York to meet her. She came from Russia. In answer to questions put to her by the board of special inquiry, she said her husband was in Russia; that she left him there; saw him the day she left; that he paid her way. She gave her name as Margioli Franck. She had four children, and one of them had favus, that contagious disease, and was sent to the hospital for treatment, or, rather, to know if she had it or not. We ascertained it was favus. She came on the 1st of January, was held by the board of special inquiry, and a man appeared on the 2d of January, calling himself Moritz Becker. He claimed he was her husband. When he was brought into the board room the woman was pointed out to him, and he was asked if that was his wife. He said, "Yes." She was then asked, "Is this your husband?" She said, "No; that is my brother." To the children: "Who is this man?" "He is our uncle." He claims and contends that he was in this country, came under the age of 18, for he goes back to Richmond immediately, and on the 4th of January, last month, takes out his naturalization papers, procuring witnesses to swear he came here under age and was thus entitled to them. He was asked to name his wife. He said her name was Dora; she gave her name as Margioli. He was asked to state the age of the oldest child. He said 15; she said 11; and he gave different names and ages to each one of the children. He said in an affidavit that he made that he went back in 1889 and came to this country in 1893. She had a child 4 years old with her, so that at least two of his children—

Q. (By Mr. KENNEDY.) Were they not his children?—A. It is at least reasonable to assume that there was a stretch of the procreative laws in some way. I do not know how to put it. He certainly could not be the father of the child 11 years old, for he was in this country when the child was born, and he was here two years before the other child was born. He claimed his first wife was dead, and he left his second wife in a pregnant condition when he came.

Q. (By Mr. PHILLIPS.) What did you do in this case?—A. We were obliged to send the child back, and it would not be well to send her back alone, so we sent the mother back with her. We are endeavoring to ascertain the facts in the case. If my suggestion relative to landing certificates had been the law it would be difficult for the man to procure fraudulent naturalization papers.

Q. (By Mr. FARQUHAR.) What is the reason of the mystery in the matter; why should Becker assume the relation of father; to land them?—A. Having no husband, they must procure one.

Q. He was a convenience?—A. Yes; in every steamship that comes over we find a man and woman traveling together as man and wife. Investigation shows that they are not such; that they simply contract the marriage relation on shipboard for the purpose of escaping through the port at New York. I have here a list of cases, some eighty-four in number, of persons applying for relief in New York City, who came in in that way. The board of charities there reports them; and the last time I was at Ellis Island or at the Barge Office, a man came in, owing to a newspaper report that said Mrs. So-and-so—Mrs. Cooper, her name was—was destitute, giving the number and street in New York; that she came to meet her husband, and could not find him. We investigated and found she came over as a Mrs. Drew, I believe. We hunted up Mr. Drew, and he said he kindly consented to officiate as husband on board, and that he was doing it as an accommodation to her husband who could not come over then, but would come later. So you see we have all manner of people to meet, and owing to the fact that they are so extremely accommodating in that way, we have to be very cautious; sometimes we may do an injustice, but I think that is rare.

Q. (By Mr. NORTH.) They must be very anxious to come here.—A. They are anxious to come here.

Q. (By Mr. KENNEDY.) Is there such a thing at Ellis Island as the Italian Immigration Agency?—A. There is an Italian bureau. It was established, I think, in 1894 or 1895. I do not recall the year, but during Secretary Carlisle's administration of the office.

Q. Did you abolish that agency during your administration and then permit its reestablishment?—A. Yes; I did. I had reason to believe, from the reports made to me from inspectors there, that agents of this Italian bureau would go among immigrants before they were inspected, and thus prompt them to evade our laws before our special officers put the questions to them, and in that way were endeavoring to neutralize, or, rather, set aside our laws.

Q. No other country has such an agency at Ellis Island?—A. No; that was one of the reasons why I favored its abolition.

Q. Have you ever suspected that the padrone system was linked in any way with that agency or bureau?—A. I have been told that it was.

Q. Was Baron Fava, the representative of the Italian Government, the one interested in having it reestablished?—A. Yes. There is a man here in the city named Cæsar Celso Moreno, and from him I have heard that that bureau is simply an agency for the padronni, and many of the things he told me, I know, were not borne out by the facts or by the circumstances as they transpired under my own observation at New York; others, I have reason to believe, he is pretty well informed on.

Q. What is the work of that bureau?—A. Its object was to take charge of Italian immigrants after they were landed or passed by the board of special inquiry, and if they were in want of information, give it; and in a general way look after their own countrymen, and see that they were not embarrassed in any way.

Q. (By Mr. FARQUHAR.) Is it a fact that the so-called "Italian banks" are agencies?—A. I believe nearly every one of the Italian banks in New York City is an institution having, for at least one of its objects, the procuring of men for employers. There is one there that I know is a very responsible bank. I do not think it is engaged in any such business.

Q. (By Mr. NORTH.) How many such banks are there?—A. There are a number of them—a great many.

Q. (By Mr. FARQUHAR.) If Germany, Sweden, and other nations ask for the same privileges as the Italians did, would they be granted to them?—A. No.

Q. Why not abolish the Italian bureau?—A. A representative of another government drew up a request for the establishment of such an institution there, and I refused to consider it, having this other matter under advisement at the time.

Q. It is not possible that the Italian Government has a special clause in its treaty rights under which it can claim such a privilege?—A. I believe not. I believe that when our buildings are erected at Ellis Island we can properly take care of every immigrant that comes—see that he is properly housed and attended to without the aid of any other institution. In fact it will be done. The Hebrew Board of Charities never interfere; they never go on the floor of the board room to examine anybody at all; but once the immigrant is passed they afford him every kindness that can be shown to a man or woman. The Irish and the Germans the same, and it seems to me that every nationality should stand upon the same footing as regards the immigrant. Until he is landed by authority or due process of law they have no right to interfere with him.

Q. (By Mr. A. L. HARRIS.) Are there any cities outside of New York that have padrone banks?—A. I believe there are. I believe its ramifications extend pretty generally throughout the country.

Q. Are you acquainted with the hardships imposed on the laborer by the padrone system; to what extent are the laborers imposed upon by the boss padrone?—A. While making an investigation some years ago I discovered that a corporation in Pennsylvania had a foreman who advanced one of these men who had learned to speak English, and through him sent to Europe for workingmen. He advanced the price of their passage, and when they arrived they were obliged to enter into a contract with him to set aside so much per month from their wages to reimburse him for the outlay in sending for them; and then, in addition to that, he demanded a fee for his services in procuring the situations for them, so that they were bled pretty well for a year and a half or two years after they landed. I followed it up and discovered that these men were discharged to make room for a new set of victims later on.

Q. (By Representative OTJEN.) After they had paid their bills?—A. After they had paid for their tickets. You will find in nearly every mining camp a certain man who is preferred by the boss, as they call him, who is a ticket agent, and while he ostensibly advances the money to pay for the tickets, the man back of him who desires the services of these men really advances the money. He does not pay it himself; he does not have it; he could not afford to do so; therefore those who want the men advance the money.

Q. (By Mr. NORTH.) Is he a broker?—A. He is a broker; intermediary; middleman.

Q. (By Mr. A. L. HARRIS.) Who furnishes the habitation or tenement for these people?—A. They usually have a few huts, small houses, or shanties around the mines; but they often rent them from residents of the place. Many of the men who formerly lived close to the mines have moved away now, and their houses are to let for those who work in the mines.

Q. Do the padronni make a profit out of these houses?—A. Of that I am not informed. If they invest their money in them, you may rest assured they do.

Q. Do you know anything about their charges for subsistence, whether there is an advance upon the ordinary price?—A. In a great many instances four or five men occupying a room will club together and buy a sack of flour, when they use it, or meal, more frequently, and in that way, while they may charge an extra rent for the house or room, it is in reality cheaper for them in the end than for our own people.

Q. Their living is of the cheapest kind?—A. The very cheapest. Very often the padronni leave very little money in the place where the work is done, owing to the cheap way in which they live. It was estimated by some statistician that they could live on 15 cents a day—receive a dollar and save 85 cents out of each day's wage.

Q. If the laborer got the 85 cents and went back to Italy, the 15 cents would be all that this country would get out of him?—A. Not only that; I do not say Italy, mark you; I do not speak of any country, but I speak of the people who are up there with us. Some of them are killed in the mines occasionally, and when brought home to their boarding house the boarding boss or the boarding mistress will close the door and say, "No; no admittance to a dead man." You will hear the expression all through the anthracite-coal regions, "Dead man no good." They will not allow them in. Where do they go? The undertaker takes charge of them and they are buried at the expense of the poor board, so that in Scranton and Lackawanna County we are constantly called upon to pay the funeral expenses of men who have sent their last penny to Europe and whose bodies have been turned out of their boarding houses. One visit to that county will establish that fact.

Q. (By Mr. PHILLIPS.) What will they do if they die in the boarding house?—A. If they can get them out before anybody knows it they will set them out on the street.

Q. (By Representative OTJEN.) No sympathy for them?—A. No sympathy at all on the part of their own people. I suppose, of course, in the scope of your investigation you will consider naturalization, and I hope you will lend your influence in behalf of this measure (reading):

"The naturalization laws of the United States have been violated in many instances by unscrupulous persons, who affirmed or swore in open court that they had resided the required time in this country. Conscienceless witnesses were produced to corroborate the statements made by the applicants for naturalization papers. An alien, whose minor child arrived at the port of New York recently, and was debarred because she was afflicted with a dangerous contagious disease, fraudulently obtained naturalization papers for the purpose of claiming his child and preventing her deportation. The alien was indicted, the case tried, the defendant found guilty, and his naturalization papers revoked. A similar case is now being investigated.

"In a number of instances international questions have been precipitated through the arrest of persons abroad who claimed the protection of this Government because they had resided a short time in the United States, and during their stay had taken out 'first papers' declaratory of their intention to become citizens. The genuineness of some of these papers, questioned at the time, has never been established.

"Each arriving immigrant, when admitted to the United States, should be provided with a landing certificate setting forth the name, age, sex, birthplace of the immigrant, government to which allegiance is due, the port from which the vessel sailed, the name of the vessel, the line it belongs to, the port it arrives at, and the date of landing. The immigrant should be instructed, by means of a circular, to retain the certificate for presentation when applying for naturalization papers.

"A record of the facts stated in the said circular as to each immigrant, to be known as an immigrant directory, should be kept for each fiscal year by the Bureau of Immigration. An act of Congress authorizing such a course of procedure and requiring of the alien presenting himself for naturalization to produce such a certificate, or a duplicate from the immigrant directory, would facilitate the work of the courts and go far toward preventing the issuance of fraudulent naturalization papers in the future."

With such a law in force, the procuring of naturalization papers through fraudulent means would be reduced to the minimum, and each alien, on applying to a board of charity or other charitable institution, would be required to present his or her certificate. Immigration authorities are frequently called upon to land immigrants on bond. Good, well-disposed, charitable people will invariably come forward, sometimes with a mistaken idea of duty, I believe, and will become security that the immigrant will not become a public charge. Let me illustrate a case:

A man, whom we will call Joseph Zandol, arrives at one of the ports of this country and has an appearance indicating that he is likely to become a public charge and is refused admittance. His case appeals to the sympathies of such people as I have heretofore mentioned, who present a bond and it is accepted. Mr. Zandol goes to some point in the interior, where he remains, and some months later falls into distress, being unable to work, and is thrown upon the charity of the community; he applies for relief to some poor board or other charitable institution. The law requires that his bondsmen must make good any losses incurred by the institution, but Mr. Zandol, either through collusion with his bondsmen or because of his own dishonesty, selects another name than Zandol, and appears on the record of the institution as John Smith; he will also add to the deception by stating that he arrived at another port than the one he really landed at, from a different country, and on a different vessel than the one he really came over on. Under such circumstances the bond given in his case is worthless. You will see that, with such a certificate as I recommend, this practice will become obsolete, for the instrument will always serve to identify the holder. It will also protect the good, honest, deserving immigrant who may fall into distress, and who will have no hesitation in acknowledging the truth.

Q. (By Mr. PHILLIPS.) Would you advise that an educational qualification be embraced in our naturalization law?—A. I stated that emphatically. I wish to be as emphatic as I know how on that point; that no man should be naturalized until he can speak the American language.

Q. (By Mr. KENNEDY.) Then, a man 50 years of age coming to this country, being illiterate, would probably never become an American citizen?—A. Probably not, but he has every right that the citizen has, except to vote, and I contend that every man should be able to read and write before he is permitted to vote. A man who can not read his ballot does not know what he is doing at the ballot box. If you wish to have your watch repaired, you will not take it to one who does not know how to do it; and how much more delicate is the machinery of our institutions!

Q. (By Mr. NORTH.) Do you think that socialism, or the industrial collectivism as opposed to individualism, is increasing among the American workingmen?—A. I do not think it is; at least, I have no evidence of it.

Q. Is it spreading among the English workingmen?—A. Yes; it seems to be spreading among the Englishmen.

Q. And very strongly among the German masses?—A. Yes; but I do not see any united action at all among our American workingmen. And the American workingmen, no matter what their origin may be, are opposed to anarchy, except in very rare instances. I know of many bright people who would like to proclaim themselves socialists, but do not do so because of the odium attached to the name alone.

Q. Do you think there is any danger of establishing institutions in this country through the organized efforts of socialistic movements?—A. No; I do not.

Q. (By Mr. KENNEDY.) How do you define the socialism that you say you are not opposed to?—A. Well, the socialist who is defined as a man who would improve the existing order of things by reasonable methods—rational, and without violence—is the socialist that we can say amen to.

Q. (By Mr. NORTH.) Is he the collectivist?—A. Yes; the collectivist.

Q. Are you in favor of collectivism?—A. I have no pronounced views on either of them; I do not want to go into them. The anarchist is the man who would improve the existing order by abolishing it.

Q. (By Mr. FARQUHAR.) Is one the destructionist and the other the constructionist?—A. Yes.

Q. Is it a fact that all the American labor unions are founded on the voluntary adherence of the man who goes into them?—A. Exactly; no compulsion.

WASHINGTON, D. C., *April 8, 1899.*

TESTIMONY OF MR. PRESCOTT F. HALL,

Secretary Immigration Restriction League.

The commission met at 10.45 a. m., Vice-Chairman Phillips presiding. Mr. Prescott F. Hall, secretary Immigration Restriction League, testified as follows on the subject of immigration:

Q. (By Mr. FARQUHAR.) Please state your name, residence, and official position.—A. Prescott F. Hall; residence, Brookline, Mass.; place of business, Boston, Mass.; business, attorney at law. I appear here as the secretary of the Immigration Restriction League, which is a national organization, nonpolitical, nonsectarian, with members from all parts of the United States. The actual membership is about 700 persons; that is to say, active members. There are about 5,000 other persons who are not strictly members of the league, but who assist the league in its work and receive the league's documents, and for all practical purposes might be considered members, although they do not pay any annual dues.

Q. Please state the objects of your league, and when it was formed?—A. This league was formed in May, 1894, with the objects, as stated in the constitution, "to advocate and work for the further judicious restriction or stricter regulation of immigration, to issue documents or circulars, solicit facts and information on that subject, hold public meetings, and to arouse public opinion to the necessity of a further exclusion of elements undesirable for citizenship or injurious to our national character. It is not an object of this league to advocate the exclusion of laborers or other immigrants of such character and standards as fit them to become citizens." In other words, the league advocates not a mere reduction of the number of immigrants by any particular plan, but simply the weeding out by some process of the least desirable portion of the immigrants who come to us now ; and it believes that there is need for some such further sifting process.

I will very briefly take up certain features in the history of immigration which have a bearing upon what the league wishes to accomplish. The league was practically instrumental in drafting the bill introduced into the Fifty-fourth Congress by Senator Lodge in the Senate and by Congressman McCall in the House, which afterwards became the so-called Lodge Bill in the Fifty-fourth Congress, and also the bill introduced by Mr. McCall in the Fifty-fifth Congress.

Q. You mean by that the educational test bill?—A. Yes. The league was not the first body to advocate such an idea, but it had a great deal to do with introducing and advocating that measure in those two Congresses. I have prepared here some rather rough diagrams which bring out certain features in the history of immigration, to which I desire to call particular attention :

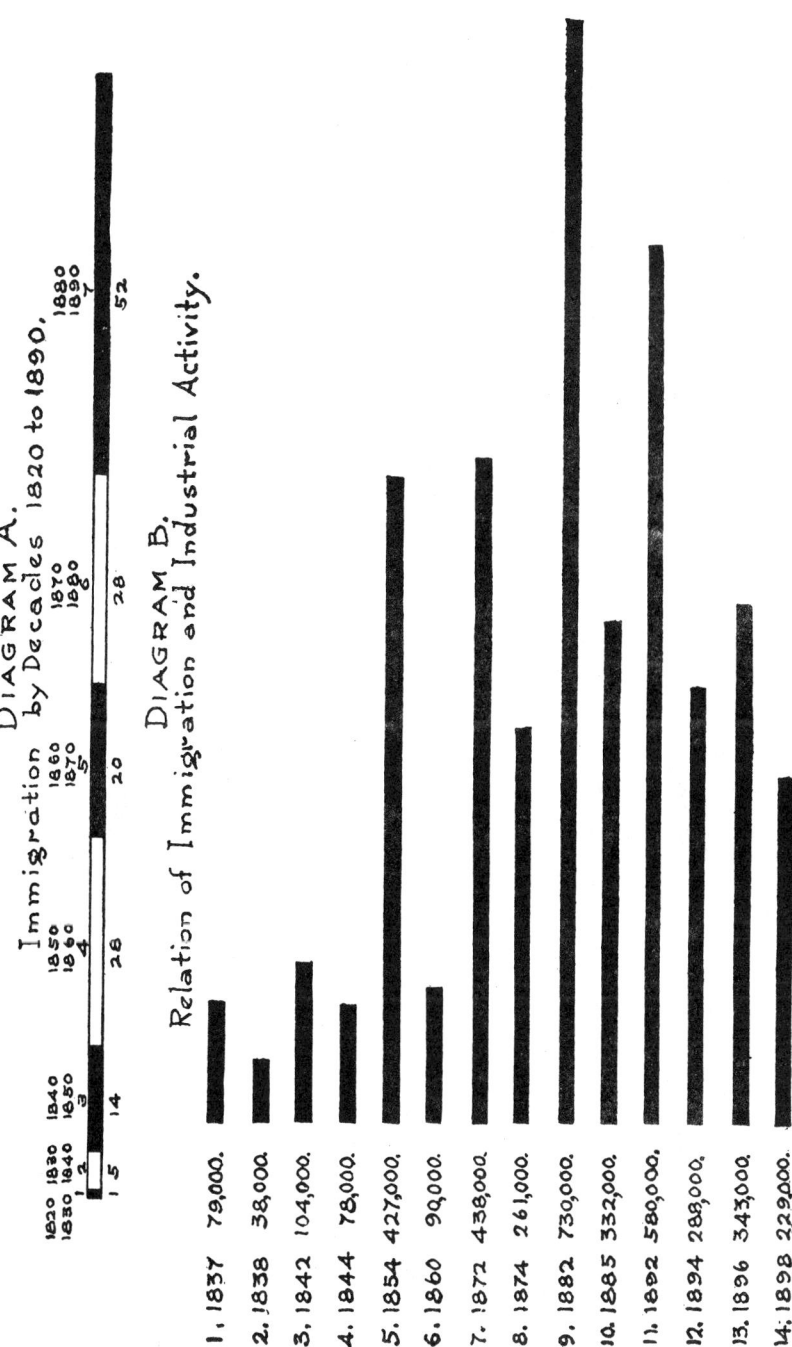

DIAGRAM C.
Immigration from South Eastern and from North Western Europe. 1869 to 1898.

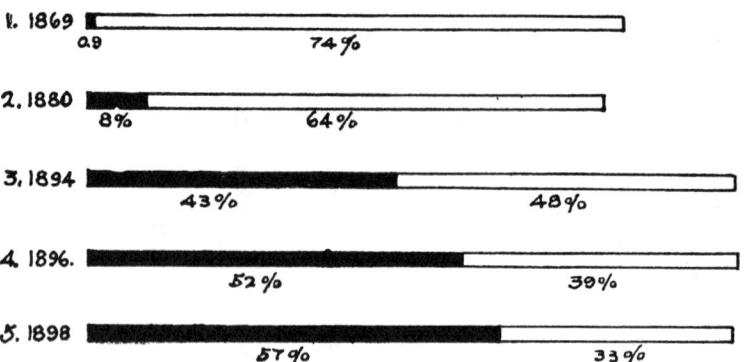

1. 1869 — 0.9 — 74%
2. 1880 — 8% — 64%
3. 1894 — 43% — 48%
4. 1896 — 52% — 39%
5. 1898 — 57% — 33%

DIAGRAM D.

PERCENTAGES OF ILLITERACY AMONG IMMIGRANTS FROM THOSE NATIONS OF EUROPE WHICH SENT UPWARDS OF 2,000 IMMIGRANTS TO THE UNITED STATES DURING THE FISCAL YEAR 1895–96.

Coming from Northwestern Europe.

Average of Group, **4.5%**.

The black part shows the proportion of those over fourteen years of age who could not read and write in any language.

Coming from Eastern and Southern Europe.

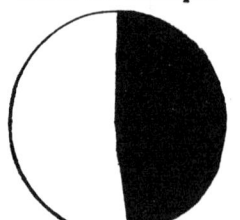

Average of Group, **47.9%**.

DIAGRAM E.
Occupations of Male Immigrants. 1896.

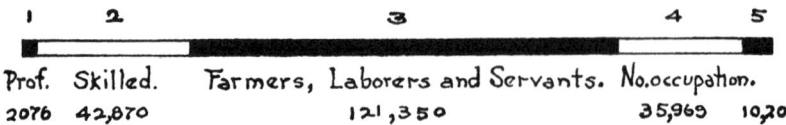

1	2	3	4	5
Prof.	Skilled.	Farmers, Laborers and Servants.	No. occupation.	
2076	42,870	121,350	35,969	10,201

IMMIGRATION.

Q. Before you proceed, please state the basis of the data, whether diagram or statistics.—A. Diagram A (p. 47) was taken from the reports of the Bureau of Statistics, and represents the immigration by decades from 1820 to 1890. From this diagram it appears that 35.1 per cent of the total immigration from 1820 to 1890 came in during the last period—1880 to 1890. The object of that is to call attention to the immense increase in very recent years, which, of course, is well known to everybody. Diagram B (p. 47) is taken from the same reports and shows the immigration for certain different years. This is with the view of showing the close relation between commercial and industrial activity and depression in the United States and foreign immigration. Here, for instance, is 1837, in which the immigration was, in round numbers, 79,000; then the panic came, and in 1838 the immigration dropped to 38,000. In the next year, shown on the diagram, 1842, immigration was 104,000. In 1844 it dropped to 78,000. In 1854 it increased to 427,000; that increase was due largely to the Irish famine of 1846 and the revolution of 1848 in Germany. In 1860, the outbreak of the war, immigration fell again to 90,000. After the close of the war, in 1872, it increased again to 438,000. In 1874, after the panic, it fell again to nearly half, 261,000. From that time it increased until it reached the maximum figure in 1882, 730,000.

Q. Have you any reason for that immense increase?—A. I do not think there was anything very special excepting the general increase of prosperity in this country following the revival from the panic.

Q. Was it due to the great amount of literature sent out from this country about the farming lands in the West, etc.?—A. Undoubtedly that had a great deal to do with it. In 1885 again there was a period of some depression, in which immigration fell to 332,000. It increased in 1892 to 580,000. Then came the cholera year and the panic year, when immigration fell off a great deal.

Q. You mean by "the cholera year" the action of the House of Representatives looking to the prohibition of immigration for one year?—A. Yes; quarantine. In the fiscal year of 1898 immigration stood at about 229,000, represented by the last line on Diagram B (p. 47). The point to which I wish to call attention is that while immigration at the present time is comparatively small, being only a little over a third of what it was at the maximum, there is every reason to expect, in the absence of some other cause coming in, that as soon as industrial conditions are improved here this tide of immigration will increase again, and therefore the fact that it is low at the present time is not conclusive as to the need of further restriction at the present time. I was about to mention the causes for this great increase in numbers. Of course the knowledge of conditions here, spread by immigrants, was very important; and another factor of perhaps equal importance was the reduction in steerage rates from the original rates on sailing vessels to the very low rates which prevailed when there was a rate war. Sometimes the rate was as low as $9 from Liverpool to New York. Also the fact that the United States has been the cheapest place to go to; cheaper than Australia, South Africa, or South America. Another element has been the spreading of advertisements by railroads and steamship lines, especially in southeastern Europe, and also the establishment of the Mediterranean service of the German steamship lines. Another factor which you will all think of is the very large number of steamship agents in all the small towns in Europe, and the fact is well known that their representations have been so extreme that it has been necessary to prohibit the posting of various circulars and notices, limiting the agents in fact to posting the times of sailing of the steamships.

Q. Have you not omitted one very material reason—the Russian laws of 1882 and 1891?—A. You mean in regard to the antisemitic agitation?

Q. Yes.—A. Yes, that undoubtedly accounts for a great many of the Russian Jews coming in at that time. The part played by the people already here in inducing relatives to come, is shown by the large number that came in intending to join their immediate families. The reports for 1896 show that of 263,000 arriving at the port of New York 95,000 were going to join immediate families.

Q. Those were brought here under the prepaid-ticket arrangement?—A. Yes; families in this country sent over tickets to their friends, and various estimates have been made of the amount of money sent over.

The next point to which I wish to call your attention in the history of immigration is a very marked change in the locality from which the immigrants come, owing to some of the causes I have mentioned, particularly the increased facilities to come from certain parts of Europe. These figures (referring to Diagram C, p. 48) are taken from the reports of the Bureau of Statistics and the Superintendent of Immigration. The first line represents the year 1869. The first part of the line represents immigrants from southeastern Europe, under which head are included those from Austria-Hungary, Italy, Russia, and Poland; perhaps eastern Europe would be a better term. The balance of the line represents immigration from northwestern Europe, under which head are included those from Great Britain, France, Germany, and the Scandinavian countries.

Q. Do you include Belgium in that?—A. Not Belgium. The Belgium immigration has not been very large. In 1869 immigration from southeastern Europe was only 0.9 of 1 per cent, while that from northwestern Europe was 74 per cent; in other words three-fourths of the immigration in 1869 was from races closely akin to us—either British or Teutonic races. In 1880 this had changed to this extent, that southeastern Europe furnished 8 per cent and northwestern Europe had fallen to 64 per cent; or about one-tenth in 1880 came from southeastern Europe. In 1896 southeastern Europe had increased to 52 per cent, or more than one-half the total, while northwestern Europe had fallen to 39 per cent, or less than two-fifths. In the last fiscal year the same process has been going on, and we find 57 per cent of the total from southeastern and only about one-third from northwestern Europe. That is very marked, you observe; and that has a close bearing on the question of new laws and on the need of further restriction at the present time.

These charts (referring to Diagram D, p. 48) are taken from the same sources. The upper circles represent the matter of illiteracy in the year 1896 of the two groups previously mentioned—northwestern Europe, and southeastern Europe representing Austria-Hungary, Italy, Poland, and Russia. In that year 4.5 per cent of the immigrants from northwestern Europe were illiterate—that is, unable to read or write; 47 per cent of the other group were illiterate. I might say these figures were taken for the year 1896 rather than any later year, because the last year or two the conditions which have made immigration fall off have been such as to make the basis of comparison more satisfactory when the numbers were somewhat larger, but I think the result would be very much the same. The line under the circles (Diagram E, p. 48) represents for the year 1896 the division of immigrants according to occupation. The little part of the line to the left represents the professional, and the next portion the skilled, forming together one-fifth only of the total immigration. The large class represented by the next portion call themselves farmers, laborers, or servants, and I might say here, what is doubtless very familiar to you, that "farmers" in the immigration reports does not mean farmers in all senses of the word, the landowner who understands the sowing of crops and that sort of thing, but more strictly a farm laborer, a peasant in most cases, who has slight knowledge in the way of practical farming, of crops, expenses, or control.

Q. (By Representative LIVINGSTON.) Do these "farmers" stop in the cities?— A. Mostly in the cities. This, by the way, is only the male immigrants, of course. The next portion of the line represents those with no occupation whatever. They formed in 1896 one-sixth of the total immigration. The next portion of the line represents the balance.

Q. (By Mr. SMYTH.) The chart showing the illiteracy does not apply alone to the males but to the total?—A. That applies to the total.

Q. (By Representative GARDNER.) Can you separate the male from the female in the matter of illiteracy?—A. I think you can under the reports of this year. In some of the older reports I do not think it is given in that way.

Q. Do you know whether there is any correct data whatever on that subject?— A. The females, as a rule, are more illiterate, I think, except in case, possibly, of those from Denmark. I think there is an exception in portions of Denmark, where the girls seem to have a better chance to go to school than the boys do, who have to work. On that, however, I have no special knowledge.

Q. (By Mr. FARQUHAR.) Is the basis of your illiteracy taken on persons over 15 years of age?—A. It is not in that chart. Statistics at that time were not available to show what that was. They have since been made so in response to a request from this league. In the statistics at the present time 14 is taken as the age, probably on account of the fact that the factory laws in a number of the States make 14 the limit of the school age. I have reckoned the illiteracy for the last 6 months—July to December, 1898—from figures furnished me by the Commissioner-General of Immigration, and have calculated the illiteracy for those over 14 years of age, and find it to be 21.8 per cent as against 23 per cent last year, so that the number of children does not make a great deal of difference in that respect.

I will now, if you please, take up certain effects of immigration, as shown at the present time by various other official reports. The Census of 1890, Part II, page 169, shows that of the foreign white element in the United States—that is, those of foreign birth and foreign parentage—representing two-fifths of the total white element, that element of two-fifths furnishes three-fifths of all the white criminals in the United States. In the New York City prison in 1891 three-fourths of all the prisoners were foreign born, and nine-tenths of the balance were of foreign parentage. In Massachusetts the report of the prison commissioners for the year ending September 30, 1894, shows that 85 per cent of the commitments for the year were of persons of foreign parentage, 30 per cent those of foreign birth; and taking the proportion which the foreign born were of the total population, namely, 29 per cent, it appears that 100 persons of foreign birth furnished ten times as many criminals as 100 of native birth and parentage; and contrary to what is commonly supposed, the second generation, namely, those who were the children of immigrants and born in this country, furnished five-sixths as many criminals as the foreign born themselves.

Q. How many years does this comparison cover?—A. One year; the year ending September 30, 1894. These were the commitments during the year, and if we could take the matter of drunkenness alone, apart from other crimes, the foreign element furnishes three times as many commitments as the native element in the State of Massachusetts. I have prepared a table showing the commitments for the same year of persons from various nations, leaving out of account the matter of drunkenness. I would leave it out of account for this reason: a great many people are very good workmen, get paid off on Saturday, get hauled up in the police court on Monday morning, yet the balance of the week are comparatively proficient, and it seemed to me that it was perhaps fair, for this purpose, to leave out the matter of drunkenness on this account—that is, in considering purely criminal tendencies. I have taken the number of commitments for crimes, excluding drunkenness, for that year of persons of various nationalities, proportioned to the population in the State, coming from these different countries. I find the fewest from Germany, 3.6 per thousand; next comes Scandinavia, then Scotland then France, then Ireland, then England, then Russia. England has 7.2 per thousand; Russia has 7.9; then comes Austria, 10.4; Hungary, 15.4; Poland, 16; Italy, 18.2. The average of the native born is only 2.7 per thousand; the average of the foreign born 5.4; exactly twice as many. The idea to which I wish to call your attention is on the order of progression of these countries. Germany, Scandanavia, and the United Kingdom show the lowest; Russia, Austria, Hungary, Poland, and Italy show the most. That progression is exactly parallel to the illiteracy of foreign immigration, practically the same order. That is to say, you have a progression in the matter of illiteracy (with one exception, the Germans being more illiterate than the Scandinavians, but the discrepancy is slight), you have an exactly parallel progression between the number of commitments for crime and the illiteracy of those different races.

Q. Do you intend to show by that the relationship of illiteracy to crime?—A. I do not, because I do not think it is possible to do that exactly; the statistics are not full enough. At my request the prison authorities of Massachusetts attempted to prepare some for the following year, but they are not very conclusive either way. I am informed that in England the economists consider that there is some relation between the two, but in France, on the other hand, they do not consider there is any relation.

Q. Would you not stumble against the economical question that in England in that element there is hardly any crime at all?—A. Undoubtedly. I do not argue that the educational test is any evidence of moral worth. All I am citing this for is to show that any law that would tend to keep out illiterates would tend to keep out the large proportion of those who furnish the most commitments to prisons in the Eastern States. It is very unfortunate that the State statistics are very incomplete. Massachusetts is the only State I am aware of that gives the illiteracy of prisoners at all, and in fact the nationality is not given in most of the States. I think it is given in New York and Pennsylvania, but in most of the other States it is not. Conversely, we find what would be expected, that the proportion of the total number committed to all the prisons who are illiterate varies in very much the same ratio.

Q. (By Mr. PHILLIPS.) Would you think it advisable for this commission to suggest legislation to the various States along the line of nationality and illiteracy of prisoners in reference to statistics?—A. I should think it would be very valuable for future purposes. It would take some little time before the matter collected would be very valuable.

Returning for a moment to the census of 1890, we find, to sum up the matter, without going into details or figures, that the foreign-born population, constituting one-seventh of the total population, furnished about one-third of the total of the insane. In the matter of pauperism we find from the census of 1890, Part II, page 174, that the foreign-born white population, being one-sixth of the total white population, furnished one-half of the paupers supported in public institutions in the United States. In Boston, for the year ending September 30, 1897; of the persons given aid by the Industrial Aid Society, which does most of that work, 56 per cent were foreign born; and 66 per cent of those aided by the Provident Society, the next largest body of that sort, although according to the census of Massachusetts for 1895, Volume I, page 803, only 30 per cent of the population of the State were foreign born. In other words, the foreign-born population, being less than one-third of the total population, furnished more than one-half of the persons relieved by these societies. I mention this to show the large proportion of persons relieved outside of the regular almshouses, supported by the societies, showing that the same results, or even larger, are true, than shown by the census figures. We can sum up this matter by saying that, taking an equal proportion of foreign born and native born, the foreign born furnish once and a half as many criminals, two and one-third times as many insane, and three times as many paupers as the natives. The census of 1890 enumerates those persons, and gives a total of 80,000 criminals, insane, and paupers, being supported at the public expense. The cost of supporting a criminal in Massachusetts in 1893 was $164; in the New York Penitentiary, $110. In Massachusetts in 1893 the cost of maintaining an insane person was $186. If we take $150, roughly, as the average, we have a bill of $12,000,000 a year for the United States for the public institutions alone in supporting these worthless persons who have come in, and this does not include the additional cost of police, law courts, or private charity. The legislative committee of Pennsylvania, in its report to the legislature in 1897, found in the public institutions of that State 20,000 alien paupers, costing the State $1,500,000 a year. To offset this it will occur to you all that immigrants bring in a certain amount of money. I do not mention this as being connected with an immigrant's worth. The organization I represent has refused to consider a large head tax on the ground that it is an un-American test and that it furnishes no key to the immigrant's moral worth or his ability to become a good citizen in the future. It may be that that will be a necessary thing to do. I am only pointing out that the amount of money an immigrant has with him is not necessarily a test of what he is worth. We can all think of poor boys who have come in and risen to be prominent citizens.

Q. (By Representative LIVINGSTON.) Still you do not object to these immigrants paying the expense of our bureau?—A. Not at all. It may be that the head tax is not high enough.

Q. (By Mr. FARQUHAR.) Do you know whether there is any surplus of head tax in the Treasury now?—A. I can not say as to that. There has been for some years.

Q. How much do you think there is, a quarter of a million?—A. I was going to say about $200,000. The average of money brought in has varied from about $11 in 1896 to $19.50 for the last 6 months, but if we examine the money brought by persons of various nationalities we find the same progression as in the matter of illiteracy and crime. France, for example, in 1892, as appears from the report of the Commissioner of Immigration, brought $55 per capita; Germany, $35; England, $26; Sweden, $21; Russia, 22; Austria, 14; Poland, $12; Italy and Hungary, $11. In other words, roughly speaking, the more illiterate races brought in anywhere from one-fifth to one-half less money than the northwestern races.

Q. (By Mr. PHILLIPS.) Does that mean men, women, and children—total?— A. Average total brought by everybody. It is to be said in that connection that a larger portion of immigrants from Ireland, Germany, and Sweden are females than from Italy, Austria, and Hungary; so that that is more favorable in a certain way to the people of southeastern Europe than it otherwise would be. Then, against the amount of money brought in we have to consider the amount sent out. A great deal has been written on that subject, and there has been a good deal of discussion of it, but there is very little that is definitely known. The British board of trade reports show that in 1886 for each immigrant from Great Britain and Ireland to the United States $32 was sent back. That I have taken from Mr. Mayo Smith's book, page 99. The New York Herald in 1892 made an investigation of the matter, and found that $25,000,000 were taken back to Europe every winter, but the chances are that that is very much underestimated, and the exact amount I do not think anybody could tell. A very large amount is sent back to Italy at the present time through Italian bankers.

Q. (By Representative GARDNER.) What is the amount of money that is annually sent from this country back to Italy by Italians?—A. That is a matter on which I am sorry to say I have no very definite information. I have recently seen some estimates obtained by inquiry among Italian bankers, but I would suggest that Mr. McSweeney, of New York, can probably give information on that point.

Q. Is the money sent to the relatives in Italy for their benefit or is it stored in

Italy by Italians in this country who have no intention of remaining longer than is required to accumulate a sum of money sufficient to make them respectable at home?—A. I have no statistics on that subject, but my general information and belief is that the latter is usually the case. I have talked with friends of mine who have traveled in parts of Italy, and who say it is possible to recognize districts and villages where more or less of the people have been to this country and returned, by the improved looks of the dwellings, etc.

Q. Do Italian immigrants from some districts come to accumulate $500 to purchase a home; in other districts $800, and in other districts, say, as high as $1,200?—A. I can not say as to that. Of course a great many Italians come over several times, so that the amount of money they take back or send back on any one trip would not be conclusive of the amount they have sent back to Italy.

Q. Is there a considerable number of Italians who come here with no intention of becoming citizens, whose object is to accumulate what they consider a competency?—A. I personally examined a thousand manifests of Italian immigrants at Ellis Island, and found that quite a large number of those had been in the United States two, three, four, five, and six times before, according to their own statements, aside from any other evidence.

Q. (By Mr. FARQUHAR.) Do you mean the "birds of passage?"—A. Yes.

Q. Have you any figures on the "birds of passage?"—A. In April, 1896, of 3,174 Italians landed at the port of New York, 27.7 per cent had been here before. That is from personal observation. From data furnished me by the Superintendent of Immigration at the port of New York, in the fiscal year of 1895, 25 per cent had been here before.

Q. (By Representative GARDNER.) Including the entire number of Italians or only the male?—A. Entire number, males and females.

Q. You kept nothing to distinguish between the male and the female?—A. No, except at that time there was practically no female immigration among those I examined. I can give you that exactly. The percentage of females among those I examined was 10.8 per cent.

Q. Do you know whether or not they were generally of families, Italians who had been here before?—A. I can not say as to that. There was nothing to show on the manifest. I might say, however, as to that that Dr. Senner told me when he was commissioner at the port of New York that they had been obliged to make a rule that an Italian immigrant should bring over his wife before anybody else; that the custom had become so great of bringing other people over that they had to make a rule. An Italian's wife would come over and land on the dock, perhaps, with some other friend of the previous immigrant; the immigrant would go off with his friend and leave her there standing on the dock, from which I inferred that they are not particularly anxious to bring over their families.

Q. What reason did the Bureau of Immigration have for requiring that they bring the families before anybody else?—A. Simply on the grounds of general propriety and morality, and also thought they would be more likely to be permanent citizens.

Q. Is it true of immigrants in this country that on matters of morality the Italians are almost universally under the influence of the church to an unusual degree, and that the one thing to be said about them is that conjugal fidelity is very great?—A. I believe that to be generally true of the Italians, although I understand in some parts of Pennsylvania, where they are beginning to go into the mining regions—possibly from association with other races—that is not so true as in other places where they are settled by themselves.

Q. (By Mr. FARQUHAR.) Was it not the custom of Italian immigration for, say, 10 or 12 Italians coming from the same section to bring a woman with them, whether a relation or not?—A. That, I have been informed, is true in the case of Hungarians, Slavs, and others in the mining regions of Pennsylvania, and it is sometimes true of Italians.

Q. That accounted for the one-tenth?—A. I can not say.

Q. The woman was a servant?—A. I do not want to say as much as that. I do not mean to say that this 10 per cent of female Italian immigrants came over for any such purpose. I do not know anthing about that. There is nothing to show.

Q. (By Representative LIVINGSTON.) What do the Italian females come over here for?—A. I do not know what the relations of the men and women may have been, but the rule which was established at Ellis Island was made because the Italians bring their friends, neighbors, male friends, while the wife may be left at home without any means of support or means of getting here, and some cases which were investigated I think were the cause for making such a rule.

I may allude once more to the fact in a general way that a very large per cent of immigrants have practically no occupation, or those who are farm laborers or servants. In 1893 this amounted to 81 per cent of the total immigration, and it is about the same each year. It does not vary very much. Most of these Italians that I examined came from southern Italy; 85.8 per cent were laborers, practically unskilled; the few that were skilled were shoemakers, barbers, stonemasons, and sailors. If we take the occupation of the immigrants of various nationalities, the report for 1893 of the Superintendent of Immigration shows that among immigrants from Scotland there was only 1 skilled in 4; from England and Wales, 1 in 5; Belgium, 1 in 7; France, 1 in 9; Germany and Norway, 1 in 10; Italy, 1 in 14; Russia, 1 in 18; Ireland, 1 in 19; Poland, 1 in 27; Austria-Hungary, 1 in 29. In other words, there is the same progression in regard to nationality in the matter of skilled occupation; in regard to crime, in regard to pauperism, in regard to the amount of money brought, in regard to illiteracy. All that is important for these reasons: in times when there is a surplus of labor, these persons having no grade can do only one thing; if a person is a mechanic, in the time of trouble he can turn to unskilled labor; but if he is entirely unskilled he then becomes one of the large number of the unemployed. It is a somewhat curious circumstance that in 1893 in Massachusetts, 180,000 males, or about 30 per cent, were unemployed who had been employed before. You will remember that was a time when a large number of persons were out of employment all over the country. Of these 180,000, 30,000 were unskilled, and the previous year 25,000 unskilled laborers had landed at the port of Boston, giving their destination as the State of Massachusetts. I suppose that is, to a certain extent, a coincidence, but it is a rather curious coincidence; the number of unskilled men unemployed in 1893 was the same as the number of unskilled immigrants that landed the year before, and the officers whose business it was to find employment for persons out of employment in Boston, tell me their work is made very much more difficult by the large number of unskilled persons that come in from time to time; in other words, there does not seem to be now the exact adjustment between the amount of unskilled labor required and the number who come in. (See report of the Massachusetts board to investigate the subject of the unemployed. House Doc. No. 50, March 13, 1895, pp. xxxvii-xxxviii.)

Q. (By Mr. FARQUHAR.) Did all that immigration become residential in Massachusetts?—A. The immigration which came in the year before gave its destination as Massachusetts. It is impossible to say that all those became residents.

Q. It is simply a coincidence?—A. Simply a coincidence. Mr. Charles Stewart Smith, president of the New York Chamber of Commerce, in an article in the North American Review in 1892, quotes the president of the Board of Education of New York City as saying that it costs $30 a year to educate children in the common schools of that city; and Professor Smith has shown that about 40 per cent of the foreign born that come here are above school age and are not likely to receive a school education. I simply mention that as having a bearing upon the probability of immigrants learning English, and learning that knowledge of trade conditions which comes from ability to read the newspapers, as bearing upon the general assimilation.

Q. Their schooling is paid for by the countries they come from. That is not a burden upon the United States.—A. They often have no schooling, and the fact they are above school age bears upon assimilation. Now, another very important matter in regard to distribution of immigrants after they come here: One gentleman asked me whether peasants, those who class themselves as "farmers" in official reports, settle on farms after they come here. The quarterly report, Bureau of Statistics, No. 2, for 1892, shows that of immigrants 44 per cent were found in 124 of the principal cities. When we investigate this matter by nationality we find exactly the same progression which I spoke of in other matters. Of persons born in Norway 20 per cent live in cities; then it goes up. England, 41 per cent; Germany, 48 per cent; Ireland, 55 per cent; Poland, 57 per cent; Italy, 59 per cent. In other words, the Italian in most cases has not the inclination to go West and settle the uncultivated regions, as the Germans, English, and Scandinavians have done. We all know how the Northwest has been built up by these latter races. The Italian usually has not money to go West, and by the time he has, he stays on the seaboard, except some who go into California and go to fruit raising.

Q. Do you not account for that very much on the idea of the old colonization system of the West?—A. I think it is probably that; it is fundamental in the character of the people. I do not think they have the energy and the roving disposition to face hardships.

Q. Do you not think, if you analyze the Scandinavian population, that the State of Minnesota alone has drawn seven-eighths of it, more by being colonized by Scandinavians?—A. Undoubtedly that has a great deal to do with it.

IMMIGRATION. 55

Q. Have not many gone back to the old countries again and brought these people to this country, and entered in with the Scandinavian population, and the British population, and the German rural population, and settled and colonized in great sections; and have brought the whole of their families with them and settled, very much as the New Englander did by taking his family with him? Does not that account for the whole matter of the Italian holding on to the city?—
A. After some of them have got there, but not originally. There are plenty of unsettled regions in the country to-day where the Italians could now go if they had the energy and disposition to do so, but they do not.

Q. You will concede that both the Slav and Italian have not the inducements of other nations?—A. They have not.

Q. (By Mr. PHILLIPS.) Has the climate considerable to do with it, being colder than Italians are used to?—A. The difficulty with that is that the Italians do not go to the South.

Q. (By Representative LIVINGSTON.) What is the reason they do not go to the South?—A. The Hamburg-American line and North German line touch at Baltimore and do not touch at Texas; they have recently established a line to Texas, and in view of the fact I look for more Italian immigration to that point. The fact is that about 78 per cent of the Italians have settled in the Northeastern States, shown by the census of 1890, Part I, page cxxxvi; and it appears that only 4.6 per cent of Poles, 4.8 Hungarians, 10.8 Russians live in the Southern States or the western division, while in the Atlantic States there are 66 per cent of the Russians, Hungarians, and Italians.

Q. (By Representative GARDNER.) In the first place, has the climate anything to do with those people going South?—A. No, not very much.

Q. (By Mr. SMYTH.) Do you think it is more the objection to the negro?—A. I think that may have something to do with it.

Q. (By Representative GARDNER.) To what extent is it influenced by the fact that New York is the chief landing, and the inclination of people to get off at the first point near the destination?—A. I think that has a great deal to do with it, and another fact that they can obtain employment through bankers and the padroni in New York.

Q. If by some requirement the Italian immigrants had already been landed at Galveston, do you suppose a much larger number of them would now be in the South?—A. I think if there was a steamship line touching at that point you would immediately find the Italian bankers making such arrangements there to take care of them.

Q. (By Mr. FARQUHAR.) Is it a fact that the Italians stay in the northeastern States simply because they have a market for their labor there?—A. That is the principal reason.

Q. (By Representative LIVINGSTON.) Do I understand you to say there is a great deal of demand for that kind of labor in the Northeastern States?—A. There has been, yes.

Q. In what lines?—A. Chiefly in unskilled labor, contract work on sewers, railroads, engineering work, etc.

Q. Are you aware of the fact when we do that work in the South we can not get them to labor there?—A. I have no personal information about that. I simply know that they do not go there to settle; what the reason may be I do not know.

Q. They build railroads and sewers down there; the question is, Why do not our men in the North, when the labor is wanted, get this labor?—A. I think my answer would be, there is plenty of unskilled labor right on the spot.

Q. What per cent of Irish go South and what per cent stay in the North?—A. 72 per cent in 1896 of all immigrants were destined for Illinois and Massachusetts, New York, and Pennsylvania, and only 11 per cent were destined for States south of the Potomac River and west of the Mississippi River.

Q. (By Mr. SMYTH.) Do you take out the South Atlantic States?—A. No. The largest percentage from any nationality going in the Southern States, according to the census, is from France. This is from the census of 1890, showing the distribution of the different nationalities, Part 1, p. cxxxvi.

Q. (By Mr. FARQUHAR.) How do you account for the large Italian population in New Orleans?—A. I have not considered that subject especially; I suppose that New Orleans is rather central for the distribution of unskilled labor in the South, and possibly it has something to do with the kinds of crops; some Italians are skilled in growing different sorts of things down there; I can not answer that exactly. The fact that illiterate races settle entirely on the Atlantic seaboard disposes of the argument that further restriction of immigration by means of an illiteracy test would be an injury to the South—the argument always brought up that you are hurting the regions of the country which are not developed;

these facts go to show that such restriction would not cut off any of the people who go there.

At Ellis Island, of about 3,174 Italian immigrants examined by the league only 11 were going to the South and only 3 going to the Southern States. Of 1,000 of various nationalities examined only 1 was going to any Southern State, a German going to Georgia.

Q. (By Mr. C. J. HARRIS.) What reason do they give for not going to the South?—A. Those we talked with had no reason; they did not know anybody there to go to, and knew of no possible opening, and if they did, did not want to say so, on account of the contract-labor law; I think that the principal reason.

I will pass rapidly over the fact that in the Northern and Eastern States the races from southern and eastern Europe not only congregate in the cities, but in certain sections of the cities, and simply refer in that connection to publication No. 16 of the League, pages 5 and 6, taken from the Senate report of 1896, No. 290, Fifty-fourth Congress, or rather prepared by Prof. Davis R. Dewey, of Boston, and given by me to Senator Lodge to put into the report. This simply goes to show the congestion in certain cities and counties. Probably this is on account of factory employment; that is the case with the immigration we have had since 1880.

Q. (By Representative LIVINGSTON.) That 85 per cent which came in here without any occupation, if I understand you, stop chiefly in the large cities; would not the remedy be local? If New York does not want it they could prevent it; if Boston does not want it they could prevent it.—A. The experiment has been tried in New York by the Hebrew Aid Society in colonizing Hebrews. I think $600 per family was expended in carrying some families out of New York City. In 2 years most of them were back again; they will not stay. I think you will find it the same way with the Italians, Armenians, Hungarians, and Slovaks. When I ask where the illiterates do go, I find they go to the cities; they go to the slum portion of the cities very largely.

Q. Where they have inducements to drink, make crime, and become paupers, etc.?—A. To a great degree.

Without going into details on the matter, on page 8 of the league's document No. 16, taken from the Seventh Special Report of the United States Commissioner of Labor, it appears that southern Europe furnishes 3 times as many inhabitants as northwestern Europe to the slums of Baltimore, 19 times as many to the slums of New York, 20 times as many to the slums of Chicago, 71 times as many to the slums of Philadelphia. That, of course, does not mean that all these people from southern Europe are in the slums, but that the slums are supplied in that proportion, and it shows that many of them are to that degree undesirable.

Q. Do you know any difference of character of the Italians, whether on account of the section from which they come, or family, or any other cause, by which they could be separated into people of entirely different classes without respect to the educational test?—A. There is a very clear and sharp distinction between Italians from northern and from southern Italy.

Q. Do you know whether those contractors or employers have any test by which they can separate people as to character at once, and do do it?—A. I do not know that they have any definite test as to personal knowledge of the men but the knowledge they get from other persons whom they have in their employ; they do not always succeed.

Q. Do you know, as a matter of fact, whether they do sort them for certain purposes?—A. I do not; of course, it stands to reason they must send a reasonably good grade of men; they would be liable to damages in some cases if their men were disorderly and produced destruction and damage. Of course, it stands to reason, and we know it to be a fact from the same reports, that illiteracy is very great among the elements of the slums, and it is very much greater among those coming from southeastern Europe than among those from northwestern Europe. In regard to the general population, for instance, the average of illiteracy of northwestern Europe in the slums of these four cities is 25 per cent; of southeastern Europe it is 54 per cent. The average illiteracy of the native American in the same slums is 7 per cent. It also appears from the census of 1890, Part II, p. 683, that 33 per cent of the aliens in the United States do not speak English. In Massachusetts it is 13 per cent.

Q. What is the per cent of all the immigrants?—A. That do not speak English? It is 33 per cent. A certain difference is noticed also in regard to another matter of assimilation besides the matter of language. Of course language is very important on account of the new standard of living and trade conditions which is required by it, but another matter is the question of naturalization. The census of 1890, Part II, pp. 600, 688, shows that the Slav, Latin, and Asiatic elements tend much less to become citizens than the British, Germanic, and Scandinavian.

The average of the Slav, Latin, and Asiatic aliens is about 32 per cent, and the average of the British, Germanic, and Scandinavians is about 9.9 per cent.

Q. (By Representative GARDNER.) What have you to show how long they have been here?—A. Nothing to show.

Q. Has this Slav and Italian immigration been gradually on the increase?—A. It has.

Q. Would their recent arrival here, the want of 5 years' time, account for their not being citizens, or are there other reasons?—A. It would to some extent, but I do not think to the extent of the difference between 9.9 per cent and 32 per cent. By an examination of the records of the courts you will find few applications for naturalization, even among those who have been here for some time. I can not say of the entire number of Italians who have been here a certain number of years how many apply for naturalization papers. I do not know. Some contractors and employers of labor are very desirous that employees should take out the first papers, and in many cases Italians who intend to go back to their country take out the first papers in order to facilitate passing inspection in returning to this country. It seems to me any data on that point would be rather misleading and not conclusive.

Q. Have you any idea how this commission could get at some estimates as to the number of Italian immigrants and Slavs and others who come to remain?—A. The only way that occurs to me would be to have some special agent look into the matter. If I might suggest at this point, it occurs to me that Henry E. Rood, former editor of the New York Mail and Express, went into the mining regions of Pennsylvania and spent a long time there, and is very familiar with the conditions of New York City and other cities on this point. I should suggest that he would be a very important witness. I am not able this morning to give his present address. He is no longer connected with the Mail and Express.

The report of the Immigration Investigating Commission of June, 1896, gives a large number of replies from governors of States and from commissioners of labor, showing what immigrants were desired and preferred. I have tabulated this in the following form: Of 52 replies, 15 expressed a preference for Germans, 12 for English, Scotch, and Irish, 3 for French, 2 each for Swiss and Italians, and 1 each for Dutch, Belgians, "North of Europe," and Americans. Ten States said they did not want any immigrants at all—Massachusetts, Rhode Island, New York, Pennsylvania, Illinois, Iowa, Mississippi, Minnesota, Nebraska, California.

Q. (By Mr. NORTH.) No Southern States?—A. Mississippi. Only 2 replies desired any Italian immigration at all; of these, one did not want unskilled labor and the other wanted only Italian farmers with money and with families. It is also an interesting point, although not an economic one, that on March 16, 1896, the city council, city of Duluth, composed entirely of foreigners, judging by the names, passed unanimous resolutions in favor of further restriction of immigration.

Now, coming down to what is wanted by this league in the way of legislation, we believe it is wiser to go somewhat slowly, to pass some restrictive measure and then wait and see what the effects of it are. The statistics are very indefinite. I believe we should get better results by trying some one plan first, and then perhaps trying something else; on that account the league has advocated the educational-test bill. We do not advocate this test on the ground that every illiterate person is undesirable, for it is of course true that there are many moral and desirable persons who can not read and write; but on the whole the statistics I have cited show conclusively that the illiterate races are those which send us immigrants who are ignorant of any trade or occupation, who bring little money, who drift into our city slums, who form a large proportion of our criminals, insane, and paupers, who do not assimilate with us or adopt our standard of living, who do not become citizens or permanently interested in our government or institutions. Exceptions are made in this bill in the case of aged parents or young children of immigrants coming in or already in this country.

Q. (By Representative GARDNER.) How do you establish that the percentage named by you of criminals, paupers, and insane who are foreigners and who are Americans is correct?—A. The figures which I have given, together with the source which I gave at the time I stated them, and the documents which I offered as exhibits in connection with my testimony, show that the illiterate countries do furnish a very large number of criminals, that they do populate the city slums, that they do furnish a large element who do not assimilate. The Massachusetts prison commissioners' report which I referred to will show the proportion. That is only from one State, for the reason that no other State gives them. I feel that it is not unjust to cite it, because a much better class of immigrants land at Boston than New York. In New York the information on pauperism comes from a source which I have given from the testimony of people engaged in relieving distress, the Seventh Special Report of the United States Commissioner of Labor, and in connection with that the census, shows where these people tend to congregate. There are no figures showing whether the larger portion of the foreign insane are illiterate or not.

Q. You did not make any statement of that, but I want to know from what source you gave the information on which you based your statement on the percentage of insane?—A. Taken from the census.

Q. The best standard of fitness for citizenship upon which your association has been able to hit, according to its judgment, is the educational test?—A. Yes.

Q. Have you never found any connection between the large immigration and the succeeding depression?—A. I have found a connection in the diminution.

Q. I want this expert to say if immigration had anything to do with precipitating panics?—A. I have not considered that as an aspect of it, no.

Q. (By Representative LIVINGSTON.) What have you to say about a recommendation to keep out a certain per cent for a while?—A. You mean in what way; by limiting the number? I think that would involve us in diplomatic trouble.

Q. I do not mean immigration entirely, I mean that class of people you have been talking about, represented by that line in the center [Diagram E, part 3, page 48].—A. You would have to have some other test than simply what the immigrants said themselves, of course, because the minute you announce you are going to keep out the farmers, laborers, and servants, you do not keep out any at all.

Q. How are you going to keep it out if you are going to prohibit it at all?—A. It would be very desirable it seems to me to shut out a large number of that class, but you must have an artificial test to find out. You can not examine to see whether a man is an expert in machinery. It would be impossible for the Government of the United States to go anywhere and prohibit farmers and all these other classes from coming. There must be some artificial test like illiteracy.

Q. Suppose you have an immigrant, you examine him to know whether he is a criminal and all that; you have asked these questions; why not ask one or two more?—A. The immigrants would give false answers.

Q. (By Representative GARDNER.) Suppose the man was an expert stonecutter, he could not get in.—A. Then to that extent there is a hardship. There is hardship about any test on some people.

Q. Do you know whether any considerable percentage of Italian immigrants are deserters from the Italian army?—A. I do not know.

Q. (By Mr. FARQUHAR.) You think that this educational restriction act would remedy a great deal of the trouble that we have in not being able to select the desirable immigrant from the undesirable?—A. I do for this reason: Under the present law the largest number of persons excluded is about 1 per cent. It varies from about half a per cent to 1 per cent; and of those who are excluded the largest number consists of those who are liable to become public charges. That question is not a definite question, capable of definite answer. It depends upon the judgment, in the first instance, of the inspector who asks the question; it depends, in the second instance, on the report of the board of special inquiry. In a great many cases where there are numbers of immigrants coming in, the inspector is hurried; he can not ask questions in enough detail perhaps to get at the whole facts. Even the board of special inquiry, which is a long and cumbrous proceeding, may not be able to do very much better. If an appeal is taken, as it can be done under the law, from the report of the board of special inquiry and that report is not sustained, in a great many cases the practical working of it is that it makes a great deal of trouble for the department and the department does not like it. And the result of that is that there is a tendency to be a little under the line of exclusion and a little less strict rather than a little more strict, so as not to have the decisions overruled by the Secretary of the Treasury. On the other hand, if you have a test which is not elastic, or which is as little elastic as you can get it, as when an inspector asks a man to read and write, you can tell right off in a minute, although that may be hard on some individuals. So that on the whole we can conclude from our personal investigations that that law would shut out a great many undesirable people. You have something definite which the immigrant can not evade, which he knows before he starts from home, so that there is no question of hardship in separating himself from his family; and if he chooses to take the trouble to stay at home a little longer and learn to fit himself for assimilation it is not such a hardship.

Q. (By Representative LIVINGSTON.) What about this recommendation also, that he must not only read and write before leaving his own country, but in addition he must declare his intention to become a citizen of the United States?—A. I have never made up my mind whether it was better to have this class of people vote or not vote.

IMMIGRATION.

Q. If he is required to declare his intention, permitted to do so under the law of the State in which he would settle, would that help to keep out the undesirable class?—A. I do not think it would have any effect at all one way or the other. They do it now if it is for their own advantage.

Q. And generally they lie all along the line?—A. Yes, and that is the advantage of the illiteracy test; they either read or they do not.

Q. (By Mr. FARQUHAR.) Have you had acquaintance in the large cities there with the class of immigrants who settle and acquire homes?—A. Not any very large acquaintance; I have known some.

Q. Do you think that those connected with your association have ever examined into the social and economic conditions surrounding foreigners that live in our big cities, not particularly in Boston or New York, to know what the character of the men is, the families that are being raised, and the readiness of their assimilation to our American customs and ideas?—A. We have done something of that sort, I believe.

Q. It does not need figuring; it would need personal inspection.—A. As I say, this Mr. Rood whom I have mentioned has made such investigations. He is a member of the league, and I think he can give you personal testimony on that point. We have also a number of members who are public officials and who come in contact with people in that way.

Q. Are you aware, if you take the city of Chicago, the city of Buffalo, Pittsburg, and Cincinnati there, that those cities have really been built up by foreigners? They have made the city and pay the bulk of the taxes to-day?—A. Yes.

Q. In Buffalo 20 years ago there was a population of 1,500 or 1,600 Poles, which has increased to a population of 68,000 to-day. Probably two-thirds of these Poles own their own buildings, and many of them support their own schools, belong to the Catholic church or their own churches, own their own homes, and in the purchase of property and the transfer of deeds there is not one-half of those old Poles, possibly, that could sign their names to the deeds themselves. Would your association exclude these men?—A. I will answer that question by asking another; that is, if these Poles did not come over at least as long ago as 10 years?

Q. They have been over here nearly 20 years, but have increased to the present population—I mean the young Polish population that has grown up, families that average from 4 to 8 in the family; they are now American citizens; they have built in all this part of Buffalo there. Where would you apply your educational test?—A. I should have been the last person to apply the educational test 10 or 15 years ago, because the conditions of immigration were different then from what they are now. It cost more money to come here, it was harder to come here, and it was altogether a different class, even of Poles and Italians, that came here 10 or 20 years ago from that coming to-day. Ten or 15 years ago the Italians were from the north of Italy; they were a very energetic and desirable class, very different from the people who are coming now. It may be that some of the Poles that are coming to-day are good people. But now they do not go and build up Buffalo; they go down to the mining regions and live a life that is indescribable in its degradation. I think it ought to be borne in mind that the immigration problem is not the same thing to-day as formerly; there is not the same class of people.

Q. Do you care to make any further statement in respect to the educational bill for the restriction of immigration?—A. There are one or two words I might say, as comparing the educational test with the two or three other principal methods that have been suggested, namely, the head tax and the consular-certificate plan. At first the consular-certificate plan, I think, had the support of a very large number of persons; but the more that plan is examined the less satisfactory I believe it will be found to appear. And I have summed up here in the league's publication No. 14 certain reasons why the consular-certificate plan is not desirable, and, on the other hand, why the educational plan is desirable in those respects. The plan of having the consuls on the other side examine immigrants and certify to their fitness to come over at first sight looks very attractive, because it is supposed that the consuls, being near the points from which the immigrants come, will have better opportunities of information, and if the immigrant is stopped on the other side, it saves, of course, a great deal of trouble to him and it saves the trouble of an inspection here. That would necessitate in the first place a very large increase in our consular force. I do not know what the number of consuls, for example, in Russia is. I believe it is very small, and it would be totally inadequate to the examination of the large numbers of immigrants from that country, and an increase in the number would involve considerable expense. But the principal objection to that bill, as I see it, is that it divides the responsibility between the people in this country and the people in Europe. If you have any inspection on this side at all, the inspector here in a doubtful case is apt to say to himself the man over there knows more about it than I do and therefore I will let the immigrant in. On the other hand, the man in Europe says if there is anything wrong in this man, the man in America will detect it, and therefore I will let the man go. You have that divided responsibility which is always a bad thing, and I believe there would be a lot of doubtful cases where the immigrant would be passed. Then it works a hardship on the immigrant, unless you make the consular certificate conclusive, because then there is always a doubt as to whether he will be allowed to land or not. He makes his voyage with that uncertainty; the immigrant may be turned back after he gets here. In practice at least, unless you increase the number of consuls very much, that work would be done, not by the consul himself, but by some clerk who would usually be a native and would be working on a small salary with considerable temptation to corruption and every inducement to favor his own countrymen as against anybody else. I do not mean to make any specific charges, but it would be apt to work that way. When you have 2,000 immigrants leaving Hamburg in a day, you can see how difficult it would be to get a subordinate official to examine them carefully; and I have myself seen, both at the port of Boston and the port of New York, manifests sworn to in blank; that is, I have found the consul's certificate to the oath of the steamship officer to the truth of the questions asked by him of the immigrants. I have seen the manifests filled in in blank beforehand with nothing else written in afterwards; that is to say, they were apparently made in blank and some of them were filled up by the ship's officer and some of them were not needed to be used and were left blank, therefore showing that such certificate does not amount to anything at all under the present system. And there would be a constant temptation to do something of that sort under any system.

Q. What do you think about the plan they call local certification?—A. I do not know it by that name.

Q. That is, that the certification should come from the officers of the Government itself, the country there, as to the character of the immigrants, and whether they have been convicted of crime, and the age and ability to make a living and everything of that kind?—A. Judging by the way things have worked in the past, I doubt very much if it be wise to transfer the sovereignty of the American Government to any other Government with the expectation of having these duties well done. And then they desire to get rid of their undesirable population while the other part must be retained for the army. There has been considerable complaint in the past with regard to Italy. I do not know whether it is true now.

Q. Do you not think, in the matter of consular inspection and local inspection, that the military laws of Europe have always stood between our being able to get good immigrants?—A. Undoubtedly.

Q. Is it not your experience and knowledge, after investigation, that a great deal of immigration we get is what we might call escaped immigration, that does not come under the military laws nor the local immigration laws of the various countries?—A. Undoubtedly.

Q. That is, as expressed by some, a catch-up?—A. No doubt the emigrant laws of foreign countries have hitherto and probably still to some extent operate to ship undesirable persons over here. A good while ago that was done a great deal, as it was charged, and within two years, I have been told by a gentleman who was visiting in England—this is only what he told me, to be sure, but it illustrates the principle, the way the thing works—that he went into one of the lower courts, and there were 2 men up for some crime like petit larceny or something of that sort.. The father of one of those accused persons came in and stated that it was the first offense, and that he wanted his son to go to America, and produced a prepaid ticket to New York. The other unfortunate accused had no such offer to make. In this one case the party who had the ticket to go to New York was let off, and the other fellow was given 6 months. I do not know that this is often done, but there is one specific case that has come under my observation; and probably without such extreme cases, there are plenty of cases where undesirable persons who can not support themselves are assisted somewhat to emigrate.

Q. Have you any knowledge of the British societies for the help of discharged prisoners or convicts working among certain immigrants?—A. That is denied now, and I have no proof of it. It used to be done, and I believe it was proved in some of the Government reports. I think there is some testimony to that effect. Another objection to the consular-certificate plan is that unless something else is added to it, it does not add anything to the excluded classes—that is to say, it simply gives the consul the same power and authority which is now held by our inspectors. It does not add at all to the class which is to be kept out, and we believe that something in that direction is desirable still. And almost identical with that objection is the objection that it does not furnish any more definite line of exclusion, does not diminish at all the discretion which the present law gives.

Q. Can you suggest any remedy for this, any remedy at all, any new legislation that is needed to enforce the present laws of this country in respect to the inspection on the other side or the manner of certification?—A. I can not do that; no. It seems to me that you must attack it in some other way. I do not believe it could be done in Europe at all. I think that would be a great deal worse than the present system. Undoubtedly, with higher salaried inspectors and more of them the inspection could be increased indefinitely on this side; it could also be made more uniform at the different ports. There is considerable difference, or has been, at the different ports in regard to the strictness and the method of inspection.

Q. You made a statement a minute ago that you found a manifest signed in blank. Would simply the addition of more consular agents or commercial agents help us any if that is anything like the way matters work now?—A. I do not think that would help at all.

Q. (By Mr. KENNEDY.) Do you believe that this legislation which you believe to be desirable would be easy of accomplishment if it were not for the selfish position of the steamship companies and the racial prejudices which they stir up in opposition to it?—A. That undoubtedly had a great deal to do with the inability to pass the bill in the Senate over the President's veto in the Fifty-fourth Congress. The bill which we proposed passed the Fifty-fourth Congress, both the House and the Senate, by very large votes, and it was then vetoed by President Cleveland, and was passed by the House over his veto by a large vote, but failed to pass in the Senate. And I think that that would probably have been passed in the Senate if it had not been for the opposition to which the gentleman alludes, which also has somewhat prevented its consideration by the House in the last Congress. Practically the same bill passed the Senate in the last Congress by a vote of about 2 to 1, but consideration was refused in the House, and I think largely on account of this opposition to which the gentleman alludes, which made the members think they did not care to pass it last spring. Therefore consideration was postponed, and the war intervened, and the mind of Congress was taken up with other matters.

Q. The opposition is very largely reported to have come from the Germans in this country, and I see that you have a document that shows that a very small percentage, a little over 1 per cent of the Germans, are illiterates. Therefore that opposition based upon that ground does not seem to be good coming from that source?—A. I think as far as the Germans are concerned it is purely worked up, as far as I can find out, and in some instances it is based on a misunderstanding of the facts. There is one case I remember where a letter was written to Senator Fairbanks, who was at that time chairman of the Senate Committee on Immigration, in regard to some Germans of Evansville, which stated that they had indorsed a petition sent to them by the steamship people against the bill under a misapprehension, supposing it was intended to cut off a much larger proportion of immigration than it actually would. In the circular sent out by the steamship people they used this language: "If, in particular, the now comparatively feeble stream of German immigration is completely cut off, then they will succeed in oppressing Germans in this country and ruin the German element politically and industrially. To the great satisfaction and delight of the English-American press many a German newspaper, whose competition is a thorn in their flesh, will be forced to the wall. No German church building will then be erected any more or conserved; no German school could exist, and the German language will disappear from the public schools." I think any German who did not know the facts and received a circular of that kind might well be pardoned for protesting against legislation of that sort. The fact that such a circular was issued and protests came in, I think, proves conclusively that a good deal of it was manufactured opposition.

Q. (By Mr. FARQUHAR.) Have you examined very thoroughly all the circulars issued by the main steamship lines to their agents and subagents in Europe?—A. Yes, from time to time.

Q. Through the circulars you have seen, and the instructions, especially to agents and subagents, where they have imposed heavy fines for sending undesirable immigrants to this country, is it not your opinion that the steamship companies have really done as much as it was possible for any carrier to do to keep out undesirable immigration?—A. I think they have to a large degree. On the other hand, I understand that the thing works in this way: They take a doubtful immigrant and charge him double the passage money; that is, the passage over and back in some cases, and then if he succeeds in passing the examination, they keep the fare back, pocket it; and if he is rejected, they carry him back and make a profit on carrying him back. And that was done to such an extent that Baron Fava made a protest against it, and I believe the Italian Government passed some act giving the Italian people a right of action against the steamship companies, to prevent that thing being done.

Q. (By Mr. RATCHFORD.) Has the organization which you represent obtained any facts in relation to the encouragement of immigration either by employers or contractors, or by transportation companies, or by the home Governments?—A. No, we have no definite facts on that subject at first hand. I may say, in passing, that it may be of some use to the commission to have the statement of the contract labor law with all the decisions on the subject and some of the recommendations for changes in it, which is in an article in the Harvard Law Review for last April (1898), and I will put that in as an exhibit. Any system of consular inspection which was thoroughly carried out on the other side would be, as has been suggested, a direct notice to the foreign government as to the desirability of the immigrant, and therefore, as has been suggested, they would make every effort to prevent the emigration of the desirable people who might be available for the army, and the inspection, if it was public, would give them that information if they did not possess it already. On the other hand, if you had a secret inspection, ordinarily the chances are that the foreign government would not submit to it.

Q. (By Mr. FARQUHAR.) Is it not a fact that we must have treaty stipulations in order to carry out any part of this programme you are speaking of?—A. Yes; I think that would be another difficulty.

Q. That is, that the national legislation we may make is not binding on any of these countries unless through treaty stipulations, and we have no right to infringe on the sovereignty of any other country by these laws?—A. It would be practically an extraterritorial court.

Q. (By Representative LIVINGSTON.) The purpose of your association is not to get a better class of immigrants, but fewer of them?—A. I should say that we want to get a better class, without reference to the number particularly.

Q. You do not complain, then, of too many immigrants?—A. We do not complain of too many immigrants of a certain kind, if they are first class.

Q. (By Mr. FARQUHAR.) Are there not only just two reasons for making reductions or restrictions by law in the exclusion of immigrants—the moral reason and the physical reason? Do they not cover the whole ground?—A. There might be political reasons. I mean to say in the sense of unfitness for the body politic. I should say, if we demand a public school education as a basis of citizenship in this country, that illiterate persons from abroad are unfitted for civil life here to that extent according to our ideas of things, and we should, therefore, keep them out, although they may be morally good.

Q. Is it not a fact that the United States can restrict against a whole race on the ground that their civilization is not desirable in this country?—A. They have done so in the case of the Chinese.

Q. Why not others? Have you any reasons? Did your organization ever take up that matter?—A. The only ground, it seems to me, is that it would be practically impossible, on account of the political opposition of foreign countries. We should get into a war right off with other nations if we attempted to put them on the same level with the Chinese. Any nation that would be put on a level with the Chinese would regard it as a national insult.

Q. Is not the right to restrict and prohibit immigration based ultimately on the sovereignty of a nation over its own territory?—A. I suppose it is, politically speaking. I suppose, sociologically speaking, it rests on the doctrine of selection—of artificial selection rather than natural selection.

Q. (By Representative LIVINGSTON.) Have you looked into the rights of the States to regulate immigrants coming within their limits?—A. Not particularly, because we have been occupied in urging Federal legislation; but the different State laws were compiled by Mr. Endicott when he was Assistant Secretary of State. There has been more or less legislation affecting the conditions of employment on public works. (See report of the Department of Labor, 1896.)

Q. You are aware, I suppose, that the State of New York has a right to compel them to read and write the English language?—A. Yes.

Q. The foreigners must present certificates of good character, etc. Have you looked into that?—A. We have that same provision in Massachusetts as far as the reading and writing goes; but the trouble is there are 16 States that admit people to vote who are not citizens of the United States by naturalization. They may be citizens of the State for the purpose of voting, not being citizens of the United States by naturalization. But the trouble is when you try to have State legislation. Once an immigrant is inside you can not follow him, and it is pretty hard to do much with him. We see that in our relations with Canada. It is a great deal easier to stop a man on the seaboard than it is after he gets in. How can we prevent their coming in?

Q. Why can you not make State enactments?—A. Because Congress having acted on the subject of immigration by Federal law, I imagine the Supreme Court would say that that settled it.

IMMIGRATION. 63

Q. That does not prevent your asking it?—A. The State could do something with it, of course.

Q. (By Mr. FARQUHAR.) Has your association ever taken up the matter of issuing a certificate to an immigrant as soon as he lands containing an exact identification of him, where he is from, and everything in relation to him, to which he swears himself, the man to carry that about until the day of his naturalization, and only be naturalized upon producing it?—A. That might apply as to naturalization, but it would not furnish any protection against other difficulties.

Q. Suppose the United States laws were changed to exact a bond from every steamship company in a penal sum of, say, $1,000 or $2,000 on each immigrant brought here by a steamship company, that bond to be good for 5 years until naturalization; why would not that possibly be better than an educational qualification?—A. That law was passed in the State of Massachusetts in 1799, I think, and was in force until 1872, and was repealed as being absolutely unworkable. The trouble is, an immigrant comes in, and he may be a Hungarian or a Pole with a name of five syllables. He finds that he has not a good name to do business under and changes it to John Jones. There is no possible way to identify that man afterwards. You could provide that unless he could produce some certificate, as you suggest, he should be locked up, but the trouble is shown right here. It is provided now, as you know, by law that persons becoming public charges within one year after landing must be sent back to the country from which they come at the expense of the steamship company that brought them in; and right there in our own State of Massachusetts, in the fiscal year 1896, of 372 cases of sick poor for which the State of Massachusetts had to pay, only 133, or 35.7 per cent, could be identified, with all the efforts of the State officers, to such an extent as to be turned over to the United States for deportation. They give false names, they give false dates of the steamer, and when you look up their cases you do not find them there, of course.

Q. Are you aware that such a law as I gave you the main points of is the rule in the whole Australian colonies, and has worked to perfection?—A. I was not aware of that.

Q. It has in every one of them. I merely desired to know if you had looked up the whole of these Australian laws with respect to the bonding of the steamship companies there and the immigrants that come in?—A. I am not at all familiar with the bonding system in Australia. I do know myself that the bonding system in Massachusetts has not worked at all, and that the commissioners of charities there, and Mr. Wrightington, who was for some time the superintendent of immigration at the port of Boston, all agree that the bonding system would not work with the class of people we get there. Possibly they do not get the same kind in Australia.

Q. Are you aware that for hundreds of years it worked in Great Britain?—A. No, I did not know that. I may say, however, that 78 per cent of the foreigners in England are in London, which simplifies the matter; also, they do not have as much of a mixture of races to contend with as we do. The Russian and German Jews are the principal immigrants with whom they have any trouble; most of the other races come through to the United States.

Q. In your criticism of the immigrants in respect to pauperism and crime, have you excepted the Jews out of all of those you characterized as foreigners?—A. No; they are included.

Q. Have you ever had any statistics to show how many Jews are in the poorhouse and how many are in jail?—A. I have seen them; I have not them with me. There are very few in either the jails or poorhouses; but in the case of the poorhouse that is made up for by the fact that there is a very large demand upon the Hebrew societies for private charity, so it does not mean that they do not have to be supported.

Q. Does it not mean that the Jews take care of their own people?—A. Very largely.

Q. I mean entirely; you do not find Jewish beggars?—A. There have been a great many applications for work.

Q. Do they not furnish them means and work as much as they can?—A. To a large extent. It should be stated that Mr. White, I think it is, who is secretary of the Jewish society in London, complained of a certain class of Russian Jews who were incorrigible paupers, of whom nothing could be made, and I have been told that the Hebrew societies in New York are troubled the same way. They are a very bad class to deal with, but they do not come upon the community so far as their own people can prevent it.

Q. Have you anything to say about the system of inspection of immigration, or any suggestion to make as to better inspection?—A. I think the inspection recently has been very good as far as I have observed it; four or five years back it was by no means as good, but I think it has improved very much since the agitation of this question.

Q. (By Mr. KENNEDY.) What have you to say about the exclusive privilege given to the Italian Government to have an agency on Ellis Island?—A. Of course, the purpose of it was to prevent the Italians getting into the clutches of the Padroni without proper instruction as to their rights and privileges, and so on. It was established as a matter of convenience to both sides. I am inclined to think, on the whole, it has worked very well. There have been charges made occasionally, when a man turned up as being the uncle of a great many different immigrants coming over in successive years, for instance, and getting them through, helping them through the inspection, agreeing to be responsible for them. and so on ; and the charge was made that that was done more or less with the collusion of the Italian bureau, but as to that I have no personal information.

Q. (By Mr. PHILLIPS.) With inspection by the consular agencies or establishing a court there to make this investigation, would it not prevent almost all who are subject to military duty coming to this country?—A. It would have that effect.

Q. If I understand correctly, there are in Germany and other nations quite a number of people who are subject to military duty, people who would like to emigrate to this country, and it has been said that this inspection there would prevent largely that class from coming to this country?—A. Of course; they are prevented now so far as the various governments can do it, but inspection would make it harder for them to escape.

Q. They would have to be inspected, and they would have persons there guarding that point, watching for them?—A. Yes. And that would be true of a German who immigrated from a Russian port, or a German who immigrates from an Italian port, because the government can have their agents there for inspection.

Q. (By Mr. KENNEDY.) Was your league making an investigation of Ellis Island just previous to the burning of the building there?—A. I do not think we were immediately previous; we were there in the course of a year, but I do not remember just when.

Q. Were any matters or records in which you were particularly interested destroyed at that time?—A. I think there was a committee appointed to report upon the effect of immigration on manufactures, and I think Mr. McSweeney was the secretary. I guess that was the final report of the Immigration Investigating Commission. The final report was made and some very interesting facts and figures given in that by one or two Boston people. I think Mr. George E. McNeill, perhaps, has appeared before this commission. He furnished a considerable number of figures, and that report was destroyed in the fire, as Mr. McSweeney informed me. I do not know whether that answers your question or not.

Q. (By Representative GARDNER.) The question was asked if it were not possible to exclude immigration by races as the Chinese have been excluded. Is there any other race which could be excluded without running into several nationalities?—A. I should hardly think so.

Q. If the Latin race, for instance, were included, that would hit several nations, say, Spain, Italy, France, and Austria?—A. Yes; I understand so.

Q. You stated a few moments ago that in the relief of the poor among some people that it was impossible to get their identity, that they assumed names and all that sort of thing; to what nationality or race did they belong?—A. I have looked into that matter with considerable care, and it is rather curious, although it may not be essential, that, for instance, in 2 months there were 35 people relieved in the Boston City Hospital about whom too little information could be gained to satisfy the United States authorities. These 35 persons were all Russians, Hungarians, and Italians, and all were illiterate except 2 Italians.

Q. The proportion of Russians and Hungarians and Italians was not stated?—A. No; that we have not got.

Q. As one interested in the question of immigration, and also being a lawyer, is there any race or nationality among the immigrants that you find so disregardful of the value of citizenship that it is found impossible, practically, under our system, to convict any of their number, because where people of that nationality or race are witnesses they will fix the crime on one party before the grand jury and on another party before the petit jury?—A. I can not say as to that. Of course, there is a great difference in the criminality of the different races. Italians get into a row and knife each other; there may be very few involved in it, whereas there may be a large number of Irishmen who go on a spree, drink too much, and get hauled into court for being a little jolly; a large number of commitments in the one case and a few in the other. The two crimes may be very different in intensity.

Q. As a matter of fact, can you convict an Italian, for instance, for slashing anybody anyhow if the only witnesses obtainable are Italians?—A. It is very hard to do it, but I think it is through having to work through interpreters.

Q. (By Representative LIVINGSTON.) Do you consider that class of immigrants that you call farm laborers and common laborers needed in this country at all?— A. From the replies I alluded to from different States, I should say we did not.

Q. Then why not just exclude them entirely?—A. That would be all right if you can devise any method of doing it.

Q. Would not that remedy the trouble to a large extent?—A. I do not believe they are the worst class.

Q. If they were excluded as a class, would not that go a long way toward eliminating the troubles you have mentioned to-day—insanity, criminality, pauperism, and all those things?—A. It would undoubtedly to some extent; I am inclined to think, however, you would shut out some of the best elements.

Q. If you included the percentage of unskilled immigrants, it would be a very large exclusion, would it not?—A. Yes.

Q. On that point, have you any knowledge of what kinds of farm labor an Italian immigrant can do even when he says he is a farmer?—A. I think I mentioned that the farmer, in the immigration reports, practically means farm laborer and practically means manual laborer without any particular skill or capacity for direction or undertaking or managing crops or soils, except in the case of vine growers and fruit raisers and that sort of thing.

Q. The Italian farmer, as he calls himself, is rather expert in vines; he can use a hoe and cut weeds; he can lead a mule, he can not drive him. I live in a country where they abound. I have never seen an Italian who could plow before he had been over 3 years. I have never seen 5 persons competent at any time to take a team and plow, and I simply wanted to know if you knew anything about what they could do after they became farm laborers?—A. I have no personal knowledge, but all that I have heard coincides with what you say precisely.

Q. Does the bulk of the money come with that small per cent which do not come in as common laborers?—A. I understand so; yes.

Q. And the intelligence comes with the remainder and the skilled labor comes with the remainder; now, if you should cut off the 72 per cent, you would only lose in number the common laborers who come in here to compete with the hundreds and thousands we already have that are not half employed?—A. Yes.

Q. Would not that be a quick way to get rid of that trouble and at the same time get just as much money as the way it is?—A. You would find the labor organizations object quite as much, even more, to the skilled people than to the unskilled, because the skilled people compete with the organized industries where the unskilled do not. And that was so much the case that at one time it was more or less the custom at Ellis Island to shut out the skilled mechanic with $100 in his pocket and let in the Italian peasant with 52 cents. This happened some years ago, but it may illustrate the point I am making. A cotton spinner from Manchester—a very bright, active fellow—found he could not do as well as he thought he ought to at home and came over here; and while he was here in detention for examination, he was so clever that he was employed in preparing some tables of statistics. His handwriting was remarkably good. While he was doing that he had occasion to go into New York City once or twice for some of the officers on this matter, and somehow there he learned there was not as good a chance for him as he had thought. He then wanted to do everything he could to be sent back free of expense. I happened to be at Ellis Island at that time, and I said that it was odd he should be excluded because he knew a good deal more than most other immigrants. When the thing was put in that way it did seem, perhaps, a little queer, and they let him through. But that was the policy at one time, on the theory that this country could absorb any amount of unskilled labor, whereas in the skilled occupations there was more competition. I do not mean to say this is true at the present time; it was some time ago. I simply tell this as bearing on the point of unskilled labor.

Q. (By Mr. FARQUHAR.) In view of the treaties we have with foreign countries, do you think we could make any more restrictive laws than we have now against the undesirable and the defective to exclude them?—A. I should say so; yes.

Q. You think that this educational test is one of them?—A. It seems to me so.

Q. And you really think that is substantially the remedy?—A. It seems to me that is the first thing. If that does not work it may be necessary to increase the head tax. Of course, the head tax is paid by the steamship companies and taken out of the steerage rate, so that it would not tax as heavily as it might appear at first sight, for in many cases the tax would be paid by persons in this country.

Q. (By Representative LIVINGSTON.) Suppose we say any man is a pauper that has not $500 good money in his pocket when he lands?—A. That would stop immigration a good deal. The objection to that from my point of view is that the difficulty would be in getting such a measure through Congress.

Q. (By Mr. PHILLIPS.) Have you anything further to say as to the Lodge-McCall bill?—A. The only thing I would like to present is a single word on the other people who agree with me. I do not wish to cite a bushel basketful of authorities, which would not be conclusive, of course, about the desirability of the thing; but I would like to call attention to a few of the different kinds of organizations that do advocate this educational test, people who have looked into the matter and who have had practical dealings with just the kind of immigrants we wish to exclude. There have been quite a number of chambers of commerce, Boston, Cleveland, and various other cities; there have been a very large number of labor organizations, American Federation of Labor, the general convention of Knights of Labor, and a very large number of local and national organizations which appear in the list which I have handed in. And another class which we rely upon very much, the class of organizations which you would suppose would be heartily against this kind of thing, is the associations of the Northwestern States which were organized for the sole purpose of promoting immigration into those States, such as the Montana mining and immigration committee, the South Dakota Immigration Association, the Washington Immigration Association, the Sixth Congressional District of Minnesota Immigration Association. There is the legislature of Nevada, the legislature of Washington, and the legislature of California, the Nebraska Club, the Washington State Society at Seattle, the Montana Bureau of Agricultural Labor and Industry, the Farmers' Congress at Indianapolis. And then another class of people is the factory inspectors in the different States; the factory inspector of Pennsylvania, the chief inspector of the State of New York, and the convention of the factory inspectors that met last year. (See publications of the League Nos. 20 and 23.)

Q. (By Representative LIVINGSTON.) You sent out circulars to all these organizations asking them to join in this request. Is that the way you got that done—like the steamships got the other thing done?—A. Not precisely; we did it with this difference: What we put in were the actual facts and a great many of them, and we left it with them. With many of these bodies we held no communication whatever.

Q. (By Mr. FARQUHAR.) Is it not a fact that mainly these protests are on the Canadian line; that you had them from the local unions all along the Canadian line clear to Washington, a nearly uniform protest against any class of immigration coming in?—A. They are against it, but you will not find them in this list.

Q. Would not all of those organizations have sent in and given their approval of any restrictive legislation?—A. I suppose they would from the fact that Mr. Corliss introduced the amendment which he did. I suppose you mean the labor unions in the towns on the border line, like Detroit.

Q. (By Mr. PHILLIPS.) Will you please tell us the protest that came back from them against the passage of the bill and from what class of people?—A. The point I wish to make in reference to the immigration associations was this: That in the Northwest, which is not as much settled as other parts of the country, there is no demand for immigrants of this character. There is even a protest against immigrants of this character. The trouble along the border line, as I understand it, does not go as far as Washington, Montana, and Idaho—that is, the principal trouble is not out there with the Canadians. The trouble, as I understand it, with the Canadians is at Detroit, Suspension Bridge, and places along the border line of New York as far west as Minnesota.

Q. (By Mr. FARQUHAR.) Let me supplement what you were saying, by the whole border line, lumber line; the fight between the American unions on this side of the line as against all Canadians coming in—that is, where there was lumbering. There are two or three thousand people engaged in it. These are the people who have fought so fiercely against this Canadian immigration.—A. Yes; that would not apply to California; the trades and labor assemblies of Massillon, Ohio; here is Mr. J. H. Brigham, the president of trustees of Ohio State penitentiary; the Glass Bottle Blowers' Association of Philadelphia; the Trades and Labor Assembly of Ohio; the American Agents' Association of Louisville, Ky. In other words, it is true that some of the indorsements are on the border line. I do not mean to deny that those on the line are anxious to have the Canadian immigration restricted.

Q. (By Mr. PHILLIPS.) From what source did the protest come to Congress, if any, against the passage of this bill?—A. Up to the beginning of the session of Congress in the fall of 1898, so far as I know, there were two classes of objections.

One came from theoretical economists, like Mr. Edward Atkinson and Mr. David A. Wells, who said there was more gain from immigrants of any kind from an economic point of view than there was harm that they could do in a social way. There was another class of people who felt that we had no right to shut anybody out, like Mr. William Lloyd Garrison. That opposition was confined to a dozen individuals; at any rate, I did not hear of any more. After that the steamship people, apparently finding the bill was likely to become a law, sent out a large number of circulars, and the protests that came in were apparently very largely in answer to those circulars. There was also a certain amount of protest from certain Roman Catholic societies, who seemed to think this bill was affecting chiefly the Roman Catholic countries—was framed for that purpose. I think in their case they did not understand exactly the object of it, and, as I said before, in some cases where it was explained to them they changed their protest. There were something like 2,300 petitions, I think, in favor of the bill sent to the last Congress; I do not think there were over 50 against it.

STATE OF MASSACHUSETTS, *County of Suffolk:*

I swear that the statements made by me of my own knowledge in the foregoing report of my testimony before the Industrial Commission are true, and that all other statements I believe to be true.

PRESCOTT F. HALL.

Sworn and subscribed before me this 8th day of November, 1899.

FREDERIC S. GOODWIN,
Notary Public.

(Mr. Hall subsequently submitted the following supplementary testimony:)

APPENDIX A.

SUPPLEMENTARY NOTE ON ITALIAN IMMIGRATION.

The very remarkable increase in the last few years is worthy of comment. Whereas in 1869 the entire immigration from Austria-Hungary, Italy, Poland, and Russia was only nine-tenths of 1 per cent of the total immigration, during the fiscal year 1899, 76,489 Italians landed at the port of New York, constituting nearly one-fourth of the total immigration for the year. I speak of the port of New York because nearly all Italian immigration comes to that port.

Under the recent improvement made by the Government in the tabulation of immigrants according to races, the Italians are divided into northern and southern Italians. Northern Italians include the natives of Tuscany, Emilia, Liguria, Venezia, Lombardy, and Piedmont, also the people in other countries whose mother tongue is Italian. Southern Italians include the natives of the remaining parts of Italy, Sicily, and Sardinia. This distinction between the northern and southern Italian has been made in view of the great difference in characteristics and desirability of the people from the two regions.

Of the 76,489 above mentioned, 63,481, or 83 per cent, were southern Italians. Of both southern and northern Italians about 30 per cent were women, which is a much larger proportion than heretofore. Of southern, 2.1 per cent were debarred and returned, as against 0.7 per cent for northern Italians. The average illiteracy of all Italians over 14 years was 48.7 per cent; of southern Italians, 57.4 per cent: of northern Italians, 1.2 per cent. The average amount of money brought was for all Italians, $13; northern Italians, $21; southern Italians, $8.

The very large number of 85 Italians were debarred as having loathsome or dangerous contagious diseases, and it is noticeable that of these only 6 were northern Italians, while 79 were southern Italians.

It thus appears that northern Italians are in many respects very desirable and are on an equal plane of intelligence with the natives of Germany, France, and Scandinavia, while the southern Italians show almost the largest per cent of illiteracy of any nation and are in other respects very undesirable. This simply confirms the evidence of actual inspection and knowledge of the immigrants after they land here.

APPENDIX B.

RECENT CHANGES IN THE NATIONALITY OF IMMIGRANTS.

[Specially prepared for the league from Quarterly Report, Bureau Statistics, No. 2, series 1892-93, and reports of superintendent of immigration.]

Year.	Immigrants from Austria-Hungary, Italy, Poland and Russia.	Immigrants from United Kingdom, France, Germany, and Scandinavia.
1869	3,515	260,083
1880	36,812	292,903
1886	71,734	240,770
1887	124,781	332,748
1890	154,873	262,749
1891	222,020	292,059
1892	259,967	312,502
1893	188,149	212,16C
1894	122,834	137,217
1895	102,850	136,790
1896	178,991	132,374
1897	122,443	86,877
1898	132,964	76,404

Year.	Per cent of immigrants from Austria-Hungary, Italy, Poland, and Russia, to total immigration.	Per cent of immigrants from United Kingdom, France, Germany, and Scandinavia to total immigration
1869	0.9	73.8
1880	8.5	64.5
1890	34.	57.7
1891	39.6	52.1
1892	44.8	53.9
1893	42.7	48.2
1894	42.6	47.9
1895	39.8	52.9
1896	52.	39.0
1897	53.4	37.6
1898	57.9	33.3

INDORSEMENTS OF THE ILLITERACY TEST FOR THE FURTHER RESTRICTION OF IMMIGRATION.

[Over 97 per cent of the press of the country having editorials upon the immigration question are in favor of further restriction, and these papers all but a few are in favor of the educational test.]

Boston Chamber of Commerce, January 22, 1896.
Horseshoers' International Union, Buffalo, May 30, 1896.
Common council and mayor of Duluth, Minn., March 16, 1896, by a unanimous vote.
Chicago Board of Trade, December 15, 1896.
Cleveland Chamber of Commerce, December 15, 1896.
Arkansas house of representatives by a vote of 80 to 2, January, 1897.
Hoisting Engineers' Association, Chicago, Ill., March, 1897, indorsing House bill No. 1.
Council of Trades and Labor Unions, Detroit, February 11, 1897.
John M. Haines, esq., secretary Idaho immigration association.
Sewell Davis, esq., secretary Montana mining and immigration committee, Butte, Mont.
S. W. Narregang, esq., secretary South Dakota immigration association.
D. R. McGinnis, esq., secretary Northwestern Immigration Association.
Sixth Congressional District Immigration Association, Aikin, Minn., March 17-18, 1896.
L. B. Wombwell, esq., commissioner of Agriculture, Florida.

IMMIGRATION.

Mr. Justice Cornell, New York City.
Glass Blowers' Association of United States and Canada.
Commercial travelers of United States, 229 names.
South Dakota Immigration Association.
New York Central Labor Union.
New York Protective Labor Union.
The legislature of the State of California.
Branch No. 1, American Workmen's Protective League, Brooklyn, N. Y.
National Board of Trade, Philadelphia.
Park Street Club, Boston.
Legislature of State of Washington.
The Bostonian Club, Boston, Mass.
Lodge No. 21, Amalgamated Association of Iron, Tin, and Steel Workers, Cambridge, Mass.
Cigarmakers' Union, No. 295, Scranton, Pa.
Knights of Labor Local Assembly, No. 1562.
Knights of Labor District Assembly, No. 66, Washington, D. C.
Legislature of State of Wyoming.
Cigarmakers Local Union, No. 22, Detroit, Mich.
Typographical Union, Port Huron, Mich.
Trades and Labor Council, Port Huron, Mich.
Cigarmakers' Union, Port Huron, Mich.
Journeymen Barbers' Union, Port Huron, Mich.
Longshoremen's Union, Port Huron, Mich.
Edison Union, Port Huron, Mich.
Trades and Labor Assembly, Massilon, Ohio.
The Nebraska Club.
Central Labor Union, Brockton, Mass.
National Brotherhood of Carpenters and Joiners, Cleveland, Sept. 29, 1896.
S. M. Emery, esq., director Montana Agricultural Experiment Station.
Washington State Immigration Society, Seattle, Wash., Jan. 14, 1896.
Hon. Thomas Thorson, secretary of state, Pierre, S. Dak.
Jas. H. Mills, esq., commissioner bureau of agriculture, labor, and industry, Helena, Mont.
J. H. Brigham, esq., president of trustees of Ohio State Penitentiary, Delta, Ohio.
Dr. J. H. Senner, formerly United States commissioner of immigration, port of New York.
Glass Blowers' Association of America.
Glass Bottle Blowers of United States and Canada.
Seattle Chamber of Commerce, Seattle, Wash.
Glass Bottle Blowers of Philadelphia.
General Assembly Knights of Labor, Rochester, N. Y., November 14, 1896.
Farmers' Congress, Indianapolis, Ind., 1896.
Trades and Labor Assembly of Ohio.
Journeymen Tailors' Union of Bloomington, Ill.
United Wood Carvers' Association, New York, December, 1896.
Brass Molders' Union, New York City, December, 1896.
Stair Builders' Union, New York City, December, 1896.
Stone Cutters' Union, New York City, December, 1896.
Typographical Union, New York City, December, 1896.
Bostoniana Club of Boston.
Core Makers' International Union, Newark, N. J., August 25, 1897.
Chandelier Workers' Union, No. 6913, Detroit, Mich., September 3, 1897.
Henry Weil, esq., Sec. Amer. Diamond Verstellers' Union, New York.
Blacksmiths' Helpers' Union, No. 6931, New York City, September 3, 1897.
American Agents' Association, Louisville, Ky., August 30, 1897.
Central Saw Mill Workers' Protective Union, No. 6724, Duluth, Minn., September 4, 1897.
Cooperative Trades and Labor Council, Hamilton, Ohio, September 8, 1897.
Central Labor Union, Washington, D. C.
Carpenters' Union, No. 10, Chicago, Ill.
Bridge and Structural Iron Workers' Union, No. 1, Chicago, Ill.
Daniel O'Leary, esq., chief factory inspector, State of New York.
Henry White, esq., general secretary United Garment Workers of America.
Zinc Workers' Protective Association, No. 6500, Collinsville, Ill., September 11, 1897.
Screw Makers' Union, No. 6585, Elizabeth, N. J., September 27, 1897.
W. T. Levy, esq., United States inspector of immigration, Galveston, Tex.

Hon. Charles Stewart Smith, ex-president New York Chamber of Commerce.
Granite Cutters' National Union.
Local Assembly, No. 2672, Knights of Labor, Washington, D. C., October 11, 1897.
General Assembly Knights of Labor, November, 1897, indorsing Senate bill No. 112.

A very large number of important names of those favoring any measures for restricting immigration, though not in terms advocating the educational test, may be added to the above. A few of these are:

Massachusetts House of Representatives, 1895.
Boston Clothing Cutters and Trimmers' Union, April, 8, 1895.
International Brotherhood of Bookbinders, Local No. 16.
Atlantic Coast Seamen's Union.
National Association of Hatmakers of the United States, New York, January 25, 1895.
Connecticut Branch American Federation of Labor, Hartford, October 14, 1896.
Bricklayers' International Union, Worcester, Mass., January 21, 1897.
Hon. Wm. Ruhrwein, Labor Commissioner of State of Ohio.
Local Assembly 4907, Pittsburg, Pa., June, 1897.
Eighty-five local unions of the Journeymen Tailors' Union of America, 1897.
Farmers' National Congress, St. Paul, Minn., September, 1897.
George Hoffman, esq., Examiner of Department of Charities, Pittsburg, Pa.
Secretary Pearce, of the United Mine Workers.
Brockton Branch of Lasters' Protective Union, Brockton, Mass. (1,100 members).
International Convention of Factory Inspectors, Detroit, September 2, 1897.
Mrs. Lucia T. Ames, Factory Inspector, State of Massachusetts.
Hon. Roger Wolcott, Governor of Massachusetts.
Hon. Robert B. Smith, Governor of Montana.
E. E. Clarke, esq,, Grand Chief of Order of Railway Conductors.
Illinois State Branch American Federation of Labor, Bloomington, Ill., September, 1897.

NEW YORK, N. Y., *July 24, 1899.*

TESTIMONY OF MR. THOMAS FITCHIE,

Commissioner of Immigration at the Port of New York.

At a meeting of the Subcommission on Manufactures and General Business, held in New York City, July 24, 1899, Chairman Smyth presiding, Mr. Thomas Fitchie, sworn as a witness at 2 p. m., testified as follows:

Q. (By Mr. SMYTH.) Where do you live?—A. Brooklyn.
Q. What is your business?—A. Commissioner of Immigration of the port of New York.
Q. Instead of asking you questions we will request that you give us a general statement of the working of the immigration law.—A. We are authorized by law to examine all immigrants that land at the port of New York, as to their eligibility under the law of 189℃. That is the latest law. Under our mode of procedure, our boarding officers go down the bay with the customs officers and meet the vessels. The boarding officers examine the first and second cabin passengers to ascertain if among the aliens therein there are any undesirable or coming in violation of law. If none, all are discharged at the dock. The steerage passengers are brought to the station in barges and examined by the registry clerks, and questioned as to their standing. The usual questions asked are, how much money they have, where they are going to, and where they are from; in fact, all the questions asked on the manifest of the ship that brings them over. If they are undesirable they are made what we term "S. I." and sent before the board of special inquiry for further examination. If there is any doubt in the mind of an inspector or registry clerk of their being of that character of people that are undesirable they are sent before the board and are there examined. One hearing is held without anyone being present, and at the second hearing their friends, if any, call for them, have an opportunity to come before the board and make such statements as they desire, and if satisfactory to the board, and they think that the immigrants ought to be landed, they are landed. Their finding is final unless an appeal is taken to the Department in Washington.

They are also examined by a Marine Hospital surgeon as to their health, who, if they are suffering from contagious or other disease, furnishes a statement to that effect, which is submitted when they come before the board of special inquiry, and they are usually excluded unless appeals are taken to the Department, which are submitted with my opinion to the Commissioner-General, and through him to the Secretary of the Treasury. If on appeal the Secretary of the Treasury reverses the decision of the board of special inquiry, they are admitted; but generally the decisions of the board are sustained by the Department. The men who are appointed on the board are specially designated by the Secretary or the Commissioner-General, from the force of inspectors employed here.

If they are barred, papers are then made out and furnished to the steamship companies, who, at the next sailing of any of their vessels, must take them back to the other side.

Sometimes security is offered for people who are excluded as likely to become public charges, and occasionally bonds are accepted under the provisions of section 7 of the act of 1893.

The officers are instructed to be very careful in carrying out the provisions of the law. The manifests are supposed, in every instance, to be sworn to by the officers of the steamship company, but notwithstanding that, there are a great many people brought here who have contagious diseases, as has been shown on a great many occasions. If the same care were taken on the other side as is taken here, a great many of the cases would never be allowed to embark.

Q. Do you know of any instance of immigrants having contagious diseases returned to the other side and being returned back here?—A. Yes.

Q. Can you give an instance?—A. One of the last was a woman who came here and was certified to by one of our physicians as having trachoma, a dangerous, contagious disease. She was deported and came back on the next sailing of the ship in the second cabin.

Q. She came over first in the steerage?—A. Yes, and she made an affidavit to the effect that a ticket was brought to her, and she was informed that she could return as a cabin passenger, and she came on the return of the same ship, and was detected again, I think, by the same surgeon at quarantine, and was de-deported. She was ticketed in the second cabin. A surgeon goes down with the customs officials and boards these ships at quarantine, and makes an examination as well as he can between the quarantine and the city, and he has detected a great many cases of that kind.

Q. Have you any reason to believe that the steamship company was a party to her returning the second time?—A. That we can not say. We were instructed a short time ago, owing to the looseness of the law as drawn, that a suit will not lie against the steamship company for bringing people of that character over here.

Q. What steamship company was this?—A. The French line.

Q. Do you suggest that the law ought to be more clearly drawn in that respect?—A. Yes. Some 2 or 3 years ago an order was issued by the Secretary that people coming with dangerous, contagious diseases should be placed in the hospital and cared for and cured, if possible, at the expense of the steamship company; but that order was changed afterwards, and people coming with contagious diseases, under the later order, were to be returned to the country they came from. Since that order has been received trachoma and favus have been on the increase. Trachoma particularly, to an enormous extent. I think about 65 cases have came in in 1 week. Of course, they are not all confined to one company.

Q. Can you suggest any changes in the law that you would recommend?—A. Yes; the law is susceptible of a great deal of amendment, or rather change, making a new law that will bear on the whole subject; and it could be made more practical than it is. I understand the reason the Attorney-General held that cases would not lie against the steamship companies was because these people were not landed. The law ought to be changed to "landing or attempting to land." They are not considered as landed until they have passed through the Barge Office, and as they are excluded and returned immediately they are not really landed. That bears not only on contagious diseases but upon contract labor. The whole contract-labor law ought to be revised so as to make severer penalties and penalties that can be levied and collected. My idea is that there ought to be a fine fixed for bringing in dangerous contagious diseases or contract labor sufficiently large to prevent the steamship companies from bringing them. It is utterly impossible for so many cases to develop in the course of a week on the voyage. European points are ten days, and yet our surgeon has repeatedly certified that if there had been any caution used by the surgeons of the ship or examiners, the disease could have been detected as well there as here.

Q. There is no medical certificate required on the other side before sailing?—A. Section 3 of the law of 1893, provides, "That the surgeon of said vessel sailing therewith shall also sign each of said lists or manifests before the departure of said vessel, and make oath or affirmation in like manner before said consul or consular agent, stating his professional experience and qualifications as a physician and surgeon, and that he has made a personal examination of each of the passengers named therein, and that said list or manifest, according to the best of his knowledge and belief, is full, correct, and true in all particulars relative to the mental and physical conditions of said passengers."

Q. (By Mr. FARQUHAR.) Is the examination made on board ship on the other side?—A. As they come on board, I presume. These manifests have to be sworn to by the consul at each station. "If no surgeon sails with any vessel bringing alien immigrants the mental and physical examinations, and the verifications of the lists or manifests may be made by some competent surgeon employed by the owners of the vessels."

Q. (By Mr. SMYTH.) You recommend a more rigid medical examination?—A. Or some other means to prevent the steamship companies inducing so many of their agents to bring here the very class of people we do not want. If a fine were fixed against steamship companies for every violation of the law they would be more careful. Of course we have had complaints from several of them because of our sending so many back. Invariably I have said, if they did not bring that class of people they would not have to take them back. I think we sent back about 10 per cent of one load at one time. I suppose they felt very sorry, but under the law we could not do anything else, and we did not propose to do anything else.

Q. (By Mr. FARQUHAR.) How many departments or divisions have you down there?—A. About 6 or 7. There is the contract labor bureau, Marine-Hospital Service, registry division, board of special inquiry, statistical division, boarding division, matron's division, where we have women that take charge of all the women and make an examination of all cases where it is necessary, and our counsel, who probably would give you a great deal of information in regard to the obstacles that he incurs in the prosecution of any cases that go up. I presume he would give you more suggestions in regard to the changing of the law than I could, because that is part of his business. He is the legal adviser of the board. Mr. Quinlan has charge of the contract labor bureau; Dr. Williams is the Marine-Hospital surgeon; William Weihe is chairman of the board of special inquiry; Mr. Holman is secretary of the board; Mr. Eichler is chief of the statistical division; Mr. Dobler is chief of the boarding division; Mrs. Stucklen is in charge of the matron's division, and Dr. Lorenz Ulio is counsel. That covers every division in our department. Mr. McSweeney is the assistant commissioner and executive officer. He is bristling all over with knowledge of immigration; probably no man in the country is better posted.

Q. Do you have frequent changes in your office?—A. There have been no changes since I have been here.

Q. How long have you been here?—A. Two years the 5th of next month.

Q. When you assumed your duties did you retain the old staff?—A. Every officer above laborer is protected by civil service, and there has been no change. I have recommended the dismissal of 1 or 2 or 3 since I have been there in the interest of the department on account of excesses while on public duty, drunkenness principally; and 1 man for interpreting something falsely.

Q. For good reasons?—A. Yes; very good reasons. There were a few changes, transferring from one place to another, above laborers, and a few laborers. Practically the same force is there as for the last 4 years prior to my time.

Q. Who preceded you in the office?—A. Dr. Joseph H. Senner, and prior to him Hon. John B. Weber.

Q. Have you made any changes for political reasons?—A. No.

Q. In the terms preceding yours, were any changes made there, to your knowledge, prior to the blanket of civil service being thrown over them?—A. There were changes, I believe, under Dr. Senner's administration; but a number of men under Colonel Weber are there now, and I expect they will remain there so long as they discharge their duties properly and keep sober.

Q. Do you regard the civil-service laws as advantageous in the discharge of the duties of your office?—A. No, I do not. In some departments civil service does well, but I do not think there is any civil-service examination that could test a man's qualifications for immigrant inspector. His knowledge of the law might come in, but a man in a business of that kind wants to be honest, and have a good deal of common sense, and a desire to carry out the law. You can not test a man's honesty by a civil-service examination. We have had some difficulty with men who were civil-service men. We have added some engineers and firemen since I have been here, on account of vacancies by death; but no removals. There was one man who was there on test and he turned out to be good for nothing. He came here on trial and did not fill the bill as we thought he ought to and we asked the Commission to send on others in his place, which they did, and we have a very good class of men now. A short time ago a watchman's position was established, but he had to have the qualifications of an oarsman, and we had a good deal of trouble until we finally discovered a man that we thought would fill the bill and asked for his temporary appointment. He was appointed for 30 days and before the 30 days were up, along came a list of men for watchmen, and I sent for them all and asked if they had ever rowed a boat, and they were surprised. I classified them as watchmen so as to give more pay than a laborer, as it is an important position. It is to watch the telephone lines that run from Governors Island to Ellis Island, which was destroyed a short time ago, and we had the cables laid again at a very considerable expense to the Government, and established a watchman in a hut in a certain place to watch and keep vessels from anchoring, to keep them off. It is all at night time. No one on the list knew how to pull a boat. Of course I returned their applications with information as to what we wanted. They found 2 men on the list who had been sailors, and thought that they would fill the bill, and sent them on here, and I put them through the same examination. One of them said that 25 or 30 years ago he could pull a boat, and said he thought it was to watch railroad crossings. After a long while the Department finally consented to have this place made permanent provided each of the men would sign a note declaring he did not want the place. We got a man finally. It takes a good oarsman, and he is on duty all night. He has very little time to occupy the hut, but it is intended to shelter him from the weather. There are a great many cases where practical experience is of more service to the department than civil-serice examinations. In the clerical positions civil-service is a good thing, but in the case of immigration and contract labor inspectors I do not think any examination will ensure that men who may perhaps be able by book learning and linguistic knowledge to pass, will have the requisite common sense and honesty to occupy one of the most important positions under the Government, and have the power to decide whether undesirable immigrants may be allowed to land or not.

Q. Has there been a request on the part of the Commissioner-General of Immigration to take it out of the classified service?—A. Yes. I wrote myself to the President about it, and I have made the request of the Commissioner-General, but no change was made.

Q. You think it would be an advantage to the service to have some of your employees taken out of the classified service?—A. Yes, I think we could improve on it. Then, again, there are some there that are invaluable on account of their long experience and willingness and anxiety to carry out the letter of the law.

Q. (By Mr. CLARKE.) If the classified service did not apply to these employees, how could you protect and keep there in the office those who were valuable?—A. By keeping them there.

Q. Suppose you were a politician and cared more about promoting the interests of the party than you did for the efficient discharge of the duties of the office, would they be kept there?—A. Yes, valuable men would be kept there.

Q. Suppose your successor was more of a politician than you are?—A. I could not tell what my successor would do.

Q. Is not there danger of that?—A. During the administration of General Harrison we had a good force there, and I guess a good many were kept over. It was not under civil service then.

Q. Suppose there was an administration that wanted to promote the party interest and reward some party workers.—A. They all do. My idea of the business is, that where you have good and efficient men in any position retain them; and not only in the United States service, but in all services.

Q. How can you make sure they will be retained unless protected by the civil-service law?—A. The civil-service law protects, in my judgment, men that ought never to be placed under the blanket of the civil service, because they have never taken an examination. I hold the Government is entitled to the service of the best men it can get. There are only two conditions we are interested in, the Government and the immigrant, and so far as I am personally concerned there are men in our department whose services are invaluable and there is not power enough in any organization to get me to recommend their dismissal.

Q. But do you not understand it has been the common experience throughout this country that good men have been displaced to make vacancies for party workers, irrespective of their qualifications for that service?—A. That is true not only in the United States but in the States and cities, and particularly in New York and Brooklyn.

Q. I would like an opinion as to how these men can be protected and kept in the service, whose services are so valuable to the Government?—A. By the appointing power in charge refusing to recommend their dismissal.

Q. But suppose he does not refuse?—A. You can not tell what Mr. Jones 4 or 5 years hence will do.
Q. We can tell what he will have to do if we have the law.—A. Even the law does not protect.
Q. In what respect does it not?—A. Your observation all over the country must have given you an impression that the law has been winked at not only in the United States but in States, cities, and in counties where it exists.
Q. If you know of any specific instance in your department of the public service —— —?—A. (Interrupting.) Not in my department; there have been no changes there. I am speaking in a general way of the law being winked at in States and cities. In one instance it operated very hard against a very excellent man in our department, where they were so anxious to get a position as engineer for a man who was on the eligible list. He was entirely incompetent and had not had the experience of a man whom we had temporarily employed. Last winter we asked for an assistant engineer during the cold season. I recommended a competent man of 15 or 18 years' experience in steam and electrical engineering, and I recommended him because I knew he was a first-class man. I induced him to take this place with the expectation that he would be continued after the term for which he was called. During the first 30 days I received notification that a list of 3 men had been forwarded and to select one for this man's place. I immediately sent for the men and asked them where they were employed and what experience they had had, and took in their general physical appearance. One had never been an engineer but had passed the examination; another run a light dynamo at Long Island, and did not seem to me competent to start an engine; the other run one of the engines on a dock where they hoist coal. I did not want to reject the men because there were places which they could fill all right. I returned them with the information that, in my judgment, none of them could fill the position. The man we had employed temporarily was held up 2 or 3 months without any pay. I called in Washington on the chief of the Appointment Division shortly afterward and explained the situation we were in; that we wanted this man for 4 months, and that I would like to continue him until the end of the term. He wanted to know if the same conditions would not arise next fall. I told him I could not tell that, and after a long time they finally concluded to let this man remain the 4 months, and after the 4 months he was dropped. In that particular case, where the recommendation came from the head of the Department, it ought to be sufficient. Afterwards, when I wanted an extra man, a laborer, I employed the same man because he was a valuable man, and I have him down there now as a laborer or as assistant, to assist the engineer, make repairs, etc., knowing he has the qualifications. This man I never saw until he was appointed, but I had heard from competent engineers as to his caliber.
Q. Do you think the evil is greater by reason of their recommending incompetent men than it would be under the old system of political appointments?—A. That I would not want to say, but I will say that one of the men whom our chief engineer rejected as unfit for a position, headed the very next list that came down. The man that was rejected by the practical man was placed first on the list by the Civil Service Commission in Washington.
Q. I understand your position is that when the appointing power is competent and honest he will make better selections than the Civil Service Commission can make for him?—A. Yes.
Q. When he is not competent and is strongly partisan, is it not better that competent employees should be protected by law?—A. It is, providing they are not strangers to the place. For instance, a man is sent here to New York from Ohio or Pennsylvania or West Virginia. He has passed the civil-service examination. What does he know about our work? I always have been a partisan. I am probably as radical a partisan when national questions come up as any man living, but that would not interfere with my keeping a competent man. As I said, there is not influence enough in any party to make me displace a competent man.
Q. (By Mr. SMYTH.) Would not that feeling cause you to appoint a man from your party?—A. They would be competent men.
Q. But all from one party?—A. Not necessarily.
Q. (By Mr. CLARKE.) You have had considerable experience and observation in politics?—A. I have.
Q. And in the public service?—A. More out than in it.
Q. Is it not your observation and experience that in a great many cases competent men have been removed to make place for mere party workers?—A. That I have noticed in both the State and city, and my experience since I have been in the Federal service is, as a rule, that nearly all in the service have been in the customs and post-office. Men have been there for 25 years. There have not been

very many changes in the national service in New York and Brooklyn until this last order came out. In the Internal Revenue Department there have been some changes, but most of the men placed had been in the service previously.

Q. The changes have been much less frequent than before the civil-service law was enacted?—A. It has been in force a good while, but has not been made applicable to as many positions until two or three years ago. I hold wherever it was made applicable there should have been an examination, because there are in the public service hundreds of men who never passed an examination.

Q. Do you mean to tell the commission that you seriously recommend the repeal of the civil-service law, so far as it applies to the Immigration Bureau?—A. No; I say there are clerical positions which the civil service was intended to cover that ought to be protected; but as to immigration inspectors I do not see why or how an examination can produce one man for a position in the Immigration Bureau better than any other man that the Commisioner-General or the Secretary might select.

Q. Can you suggest some amendment to the law by which there may be a more efficient examination of men for these places requiring expert knowledge?—A. The expert knowledge that the man requires is his honesty; a dishonest man in the Immigration Bureau is a dangerous man.

Q. (By Mr. FARQUHAR.) What do you consider the most pressing reform now necessary in the immigration service, so far as the port of New York is concerned?—A. I believe that the law should be so amended as to more clearly define the powers of the commissioners at the various ports. As it now stands, the commissioner of immigration is the responsible officer—holding the President's commission—and is held accountable for everything that happens at his port. He can, under the present laws, control it in a measure, but the work would be much simplified if it were legally defined. For instance, the evolution of the law of immigration has vested a number of men who were originally appointed as interpreters, and for that purpose only, with powers of admission and, if they are members of the board of special inquiry, exclusion of immigrants applying to be landed. To those who are excluded the avenues of appeal are open, but the other side of the question—the admission of undesirable immigrants—is absolutely under the control of the inspection officer without any right of appeal from his decision. The law says that the inspection officer "shall hold for special inquiry *those who are not clearly and beyond doubt entitled to admission.*" It thus becomes a matter of conscience with the inspection officer. If there is no doubt in his mind, he admits the party regardless of the facts in the case, and the commissioner has no definite right in law to reverse this decision pending further investigation or appeal. So also with the boards of special inquiry chosen from subordinate officers. They are sometimes without very much legal or judicial qualification, but they are placed in the position where they are, for the time being, judges. If their decision should be ever so wrong, it is final after the immigrant is admitted. I believe that, as the commissioner of immigration represents the President and the Secretary of the Treasury directly, and is the responsible party, he should be given the right to veto any act of his subordinate officers, subject to proper report and appeal to the Commissioner-General of Immigration and the Treasury Department. I believe this is absolutely necessary to a proper and wise execution of the laws.

Q. Is section 7 of the act of 1893, in regard to admitting immigrants under bond, taken advantage of frequently?—A. The bonding of immigrants is growing less and less each year, but, in my opinion, the whole question of bonds needs to be carefully revised.

Q. Will you state your opinion of this matter?—A. As I understand the matter, the provision admitting the taking of bonds was inserted as the equity part of the law, and should be continued; but, as a matter of practice, the taking of bonds is not in any measure accomplishing the object intended. I have examined the records and find that a few years ago large numbers of bonds were accepted. I also find, on examination, that it has been decided by one of the law officers of the Government, that, under certain conditions, even members of the excluded classes, such as idiots, diseased persons, etc., can be admitted upon bond, I do not believe that the law contemplated this. Again, as at present executed, the giving of a bond to the Government does not constitute a lien on the property of the parties giving the guaranty, and I am morally certain that there are people who have been bonded not to become a public charge now in public institutions at the public expense. In one case on record in this office a blind girl arrived, going to her parents in New York. The parents were poor but apparently worthy people, and stated that they had sent for their child and intended to support her as a member of their family. Owing to her condition it was decided that the Government should be fortified with a bond before she was landed, which action was taken. About a year after, it was discovered that within a fortnight after her admission she had assumed a false name, and, claiming a man who had been in the United States for more than a year as her parent, secured admission to one of the institutions for the blind in the city of New York. She had then been an inmate for nearly a year and her real identity was discovered only by accident. In this case the bondsmen were sought out and compelled to idemnify the city for the amount of her maintenance while in the institution. This is the usual method of evading the bond—taking the names of persons who have been in the country more than a year, so that when verification is sought here our records will show that the parties are no longer immigrants within the meaning of the law, and the hospitals, asylums, and institution of New York are full of such people, although not all of them have been admitted upon bonds. I would recommend strongly that every bond taken should be made a matter of record and that one of the conditions of the bond should be that a semiannual or annual report be made of the case and the immigrant produced here for inspection. It is due to the department to say that, as I stated before, the accepting of bonds, except in cases involving the separation of families, has become more and more rare.

NEW YORK, N. Y., *July 24, 1899.*

TESTIMONY OF MR. EDWARD F. McSWEENEY,

Assistant Commissioner of Immigration at the Port of New York.

At a meeting of the Subcommission on Manufactures and General Business, held in New York City July 24, 1899, Chairman Smyth presiding, Mr. Edward F. McSweeney appeared at 2.45 p. m., and, being duly sworn, testified upon the subject of immigration as follows:

Q. (By Mr. SMYTH.) What is your residence?—A. New York City.

Q. What position do you hold?—A. Assistant Commissioner of Immigration under Mr. Fitchie.

Q. And executive officer?—A. Yes.

Q. We will ask you to make a general statement of the workings of your office and any suggestions you have as to remedial laws or changes in the existing laws.—A. On last Thursday Mr. Fitchie requested me, as executive officer and assistant, having been in the Immigration Bureau since July 1, 1893, and having a fair knowledge of the subjects, to prepare hurriedly for the commission a statement of the difficulties that we encounter in the practical enforcement of the law, and such remedies as might be suggested in that connection; and to that end I have prepared a few points to submit to you.

Q. (By Mr. FARQUHAR.) At what time did the supervision of immigration at this port pass to the United States Government?—A. Under Secretary Windom, in 1890.

Q. Before that time the State of New York had control of it, did it not?—A. It was under the control of a set of commissioners appointed by the governor, with the presidents of the Irish and German societies acting ex officio. They controlled all matters of immigration at Castle Garden. Secretary Windom, after an investigation of certain complaints made to him, took advantage of that provision of the law which gives the States the right to manage the immigration laws, subject at any time to be abrogated by the Secretary of the Treasury. He decided it should be brought under Federal control, and that was done in 1890. Col. John B. Weber was appointed commissioner and in January, 1892, the Ellis Island station was occupied.

Q. The Commissioner-General of Immigration at that time was Mr. Owen?—A. He was then Superintendent of Immigration. The title was changed to Commissioner-General of Immigration in 1895.

Q. Then the authority of the State of New York over immigration ceased?—A. They had some subsequent dealings with Ward's Island, but all practical matters of examination were passed into the hands of Secretary Windom.

Q. Please give us a general statement of the methods of handling immigration at this port under the present laws, beginning at quarantine here.—A. It must be understood, first, that the law of 1891, which was passed after Colonel Weber came into power, practically represented the new idea of Federal inspection of immigration. However, the law under which we are now working and the law under which the administrative features were outlined, is the act of 1893, which was in many respects an administrative act and changed in many particulars the methods of executing the laws. The law of 1891 did not make many changes, except as to defining the excluded classes and the methods of exclusion. The law of 1893 definitely placed the responsibility on the steamship companies. It changed the methods of manifesting the emigrants to groups of 30. It took from the collectors of customs the authority to exclude immigrants, and vested that power in the hands of a board of special inquiry, which was to be appointed by the Secretary of the Treasury or the then Superintendent of Immigration, now the Commissioner-General, and put it in their power to exclude or admit absolutely, subject only to appeals through the commissioner at each port. It must not be forgotten that this was a great change in the methods which pertained to immigration, because prior to that time the commissioner had this power. With the law of 1893 the number of immigrants excluded became very much greater. It was estimated and stated before a committee of Congress that as a result of that law 50,000 persons were refused the sale of a ticket within the year after the law of 1893 was passed. Before an emigrant can get a ticket to come to the United States he must apply to the nearest agent of the steamship company, and if that agent sells an unfit emigrant a ticket all the expense of his return comes on the steamship company and in some cases on the agent. The emigrant on buying his ticket answers a list of questions which are identical with those on the manifest list—19 questions—how much money he has, where he comes from, where he is going to, and all that sort of thing. When the emigrant finally gets his ticket this list is forwarded to the captain at the port of embarkation, and the names are made up in the lists of 30. Each list of 30 being practically complete, each emigrant is provided with his card for identification. These lists are sworn to by the captain and attested by the consul. After the emigrant reaches quarantine he is examined first under the authority of the State of New York by Dr. Doty; if there is no quarantinable disease he is allowed to pass through, and comes to the immigration station, being removed from the ship on barges, the law expressly stipulating that the immigrant is constructively on the vessel all the time during the pendency of the examination.

Q. Until passed on or landed under the direction of the Government?—A. Yes. The law on immigration has been the result of separate statutes which have been enacted from time to time. The law has not been uniform, and the courts have found it very perplexing when called upon to decide questions.

The first law was rather to regulate immigration than to restrict it. That was in 1882, and it is the one which provided for a head tax, which was specially intended as an immigration fund to defray the expenses of regulating immigration under this act, and for the care and relief of immigrants who fell into distress, and for the general expenses of carrying this act into effect. This law provided for the examination "into the different conditions of passengers arriving at this port" and authorized the exclusion of, first: "Any convict, lunatic, idiot, or any person unable to take care of himself or herself without becoming a public charge." The law then authorized such exclusion by simply enacting that such person "shall not be permitted to land." It does not provide for anything further, except for convicts, concerning whom it says that "all foreign convicts * * * shall be sent back to the nations to which they belong and from whence they came." Courts have found it difficult to enforce this law, as has also the executive office of the Immigration Bureau, as cases have arisen where the convicts belonging to one nation have come from the port of another. This law is not repealed, but another law, that of 1891, has been added to it.

In the interval between 1882 and 1891 Congress restricted immigration as to contract laborers. The statute is known as the contract-labor law of February 26, 1885. The working of this law has not been satisfactory from the point of view intended by Congress. The spirit of the law was that it should be made unlawful to import persons under contract. It provides for a fine of not more than $1,000 to be imposed upon the importer. The courts have strictly construed this law, holding closely to its letter, and consequently not many fines have been imposed in the many cases of flagrant violation of the law, for the simple reason that the contract referred to by the law must be fully proved to be such as, but for the law declaring it unlawful, would entitle the contracting parties to enforce it. The courts have also held that, inasmuch as the act consists in the "importation or migration of any alien into the United States on the contract made previous to the importation," the fine can not be imposed except after the alien has landed, so that such landing would constitute the importation and migration.

Here, again, a difficulty arises in the executive department; if these contract laborers are to be deported and not allowed to land, no importation or migration takes place and the fine can not be imposed.

Again, in order to prove the contract, the testimony of the alien is necessary. If he is deported, the suit must begin at once before his deportation and his testimony taken in the suit; for if not taken then we could not very well trace him abroad in order to get his testimony on interrogatories by commission later on. If, on the contrary, the alien is allowed to land, then it is to be presumed that he goes straight to work for the person importing him, whom he is not likely to betray, and the result is that he is no help to the Government to prove the contract.

So far the power to deport the contract laborer has been supposed to exist, but no line of this law justifies such a power except the title to the act, which is—"To prohibit the importation and immigration of foreigners and aliens under contract or agreement to perform labor in the United States, its Territories, and the District of Columbia." This act was amended February 23, 1887, but even in this amendment no power is given to deport a contract laborer, unless perhaps it is found in sections 6 and 8. By section 6 immigrant inspectors are authorized to examine passengers and if "any person included in the prohibition in this act" shall be found among them, such persons shall not be permitted to land.

Section 8 provided that all persons "included in the prohibition in this act" shall be sent back to the nations to which they belong and whence they came. Who are the persons included in the prohibition? Again the answer is to be found only in the title. Neither the original act nor the amended act says who are the persons included in the act. The prohibition of the act is to enter into a contract with an alien to import him, and a fine is imposed on the importer of such contract laborer or alien. There is no other prohibition in the act. The amendment of 1891 was virtually a recapitulation of previous laws. By it the aliens are "excluded from admission" if found to belong to the following classs, to wit: "All idiots, insane persons, paupers, or persons likely to become a public charge, persons suffering from a loathsome or a dangerous contagious disease, persons who have been convicted of a felony or other infamous crime or misdemeanor involving moral turpitude, polygamists, and also any persons whose ticket or passage is paid for with the money of another, or who is assisted by others to come, unless it is affirmatively and satisfactorily shown in special inquiry that such person does not belong to one of the foregoing excluded classes, or to the class of contract laborers excluded by the act of February 26, 1885." The law is peremptory as to these classes. These questions have arisen: Who is an idiot? Who is an insane person? Is there a middle distinction between the two? Where should the line be drawn? Cases have arisen of a child, a member of a family, coming here, brought by its parents. Such a child, whether an idiot or an insane person, must be "excluded from admission," the law being peremptory. No power is given to the commissioner to take into consideration that the parents are coming here to establish a home with their children, among whom is this unfortunate creature. The parents and the rest of the family are qualified for admission. What is the commissioner's duty, since he can not fathom the dictates of humanity? Is it to allow the parents and the other children to land and to send back the idiot or insane child, or to send the family back?

The same considerations are to be had for such persons as may be found suffering from a loathsome or a dangerous contagious disease, inasmuch as many cases have occurred where children suffering from a loathsome contagious disease had to be sent back while their parents had a right to land. The Treasury Department by circular of October, 1897, made a regulation that in case a minor child is suffering from a loathsome contagious disease and comes here accompanied by its parents "one parent should be returned." This rule was made for humane considerations.

I recall a case where, acting upon such a rule, a child suffering from a loathsome contagious disease was ordered deported, and the mother, although qualified to land, was ordered returned with the child. The mother sued out a writ of habeas corpus, claiming that she was entitled to land, and the judge before whom the habeas corpus came stated that the Government had no power to make such a regulation; that if the parents did not have sufficient humane regard for their afflicted children to go back voluntarily with them, the law was not supposed to be more humane than the parents.

Public opinion does not tend to sustain the present law as applied to individual cases. Strong appeals for relaxation of the present law can be and are made on the ground of sympathy and humanity in every case of insanity, loathsome or chronic contagious disease, idiocy, or the young physically so crippled that they are sure to be always dependent on someone for support. In case of insanity, idiocy, and loathsome and dangerous contagious diseases the law is peremptory, but even in these cases deportation is often effected with difficulty. Where the breaking of family ties is concerned the contention of "likely to become public charges" often fails to hold, and miserable degenerates, crippled children, and the physically unfit to live are released sooner or later to become burdens upon the community. The giving of bonds, even strictly as it is regulated at present, is inefficient.

The next class to be considered is that of persons who have been "convicted of a felony, or other infamous crime or misdemeanor involving moral turpitude." Experience has taught us that other undesirable persons could be included in that class. I recall an instance of a man charged with murder in the first degree, who was a fugitive from justice, and who was confronted at the Barge Office with the witnesses to the murder. The Government of the nation to which he belonged was notified of the case, but did not take any action. Why should not such a person, whose nation does not care to recall him back for punishment, but are glad to be rid of him by his self-imposed exile, be excluded from admission? Yet if he comes with sufficient money, so that it would be against the consciences of the inspectors to declare him to be likely to become a public charge, they can do nothing but admit him. We had another case, of a person charged with fraud, embezzlement, with a felony. His extradition was demanded and the United States Commissioner decided that there were good grounds for believing that the charge made against him was true; but a technical question arose as to whether the felony was committed in the country which asked for his extradition, or in another country which did not ask it, and because of the doubt the Secretary of State withheld the warrant for his extradition. Why should such a man, declared by one of our tribunals likely to become a convict, be admitted?

The next class is that of polygamists. Several cases have occurred of runaway love affairs, say, between a married man and woman. The fact is known and admitted by the parties on examination. They are not polygamists, because they do not profess polygamy, nor have they married each other, because one or both of them is already married. But why is not his case of greater turpitude than that of a man who openly professes polygamy according to his convictions?

Again, we have had cases of women not the wives of persons with whom they came in company. Are they to be admitted, and polygamists not, or should they not be included in this class?

Again, a girl runs away with a man, or, vice versa, a young boy under age runs away with a woman who may have enticed him. A recent case was that of a prostitute coming here with a boy of 18 years. The parents from the other side cabled of the occurrence and asked protection. Of course no protection, as such, ought to be given in such a case; but why should not the Immigration Bureau have power to exclude such persons from admission?

The next class referred to by this law is that of persons who come here assisted with the money of others. The law makes this assistance a cause for exclusion, unless the alien proves affirmatively that he does not belong to one of the excluded classes already enumerated, or does not belong to the class of contract laborers.

A careful revision of the contract-labor law should be made in the light of the experience had since the first law was enacted.

To exclude aliens coming here under contract to perform labor is a matter of easy conception, but it is very difficult to put into execution, as it is difficult to prove contracts made abroad. It can only be proven in three ways: First, by parties present to the contract, and inasmuch as the contract must be made outside of the United States, necessarily, in most cases, the witnesses are outside of the United States and the difficulty is to bring them in to prove the contract; second, by the confession of the alien asking for admission; he knows that by confessing it his punishment is deportation, and the threat of deportation makes it difficult to get out of him the fact that the contract exists; third, by the party importing the alien, who by law is threatened with a fine, so he certainly will not prove the contract.

Experience has shown us that very few convictions have been had. Deportations have been very many. Certainly the number of deportations is out of all proportion to the number of convictions for the fines imposed; but no criticism can be made of such glaring discrepancy. The fact is that those who decide for the deportation of the aliens are executive officers who value the evidence before them differently from the way a judge would, and are not fettered by any restrictions as to the legal import of testimony, and are guided solely by their consciences and impressions which arise during the examination, and in this way reach their conclusions. On the other hand, when the fine is to be imposed, regular pleadings before a judge are brought and the judge has first to decide whether from the allegations in the pleading a contract can be spelled out, and being by law compelled to stand on legal rules obviously weighs these allegations by a legal criterion. Invariably the judges have decided on demurrer to the pleadings without leaving the question to the jury.

The law should not be such that strict proof of a contract should be required. An inducement to come here to perform labor, an allurement of aliens to come and perform labor, should be sufficient to make any importer of such aliens liable for the fine. What amounts to inducements or allurement the jury might find out after due instruction from the judge.

Another class of laborers is also taken into consideration as not desirable under any circumstances. Many aliens come here during the laboring season and go back during the winter to their homes. As a matter of fact, millions of dollars go out of the country to enrich other countries in this way. In other words, millions of dollars are made to circulate outside of the United States, which ought to remain for circulation in this country. How to prevent the landing of such birds of passage may be very difficult, but the board of special inquiry ought to be given discretion to exclude this class of aliens when known to be such, when the circumstances show them to be birds of passage. That they are undesirable there is no question. They do not make good citizens, because they are not even residents. They earn money for the purpose of accumulating it, and spend their savings abroad. They work for less wages, thus impairing the local wage scales. They come here for half the season and then disappear and others replace them, and they necessarily take the place of laborers in the United States.

The alien contract labor laws were passed at the demand of labor organizations, and they should be fully informed of the difficulties attending their enforcement, so that they will not expect impossibilities from the immigration officials. If the courts construe the laws so as to thwart the intention and spirit of the men who urged their passage, I think it wise to show them wherein the law has failed to reach the evils aimed at and assist them to supply the defect by remedial legislation.

The spirit of the present immigration laws, as well as the theory upon which they are most all founded, is sound; the only difficulty being in omitting to clearly and accurately define remedies for the evils existing in undesirable immigration.

The courts are honest and conscientious in their enforcement of the laws, but are fettered by the faulty construction of the statutes. I believe the immigration officials are faithful and fearless in the discharge of their duties. These facts being found to exist, it ought to be easy to supply such remedies as will make the protection sought for almost complete if not entirely so.

Give the commissioners of immigration at the various ports plenary powers to act according to their discretion in all cases where it is found difficult to enact a precise remedy by law, subject to appeal and review by the Department.

Make false swearing a misdemeanor and prescribe a punishment, not too severe (so as to render it difficult to convict), but so elastic as to fit the crime.

While the terms "pauper" and "public charge" are sufficiently broad to reach most all undesirable immigrants, there is yet a class whom it does not reach. There is a class of immoral persons, not convicted as such, but in the eyes of any unbiased person they would be considered unfit for good citizenship. They usually come with a good supply of money in their possession, and the likelihood of their actually falling into distress and becoming a public charge is too remote oftentimes for a verdict of exclusion to sit lightly upon the consciences of the inspectors acting on boards of special inquiry. Criminal persons, not convicted according to the terms of the existing laws, generally come well supplied with money, and there is no way to reach them except under the class of persons likely to become a public charge. Surely the law does not intend to consider a person who has been convicted of a felony or other crime involving moral turpitude as any more undesirable for citizenship in this country than one who, though equally guilty, has escaped from the scene of his crime and comes here a fugitive from justice. I hold that all such cases should be left to the wise discretion of competent persons sitting as a board of special inquiry, subject to the concurrence of the Commissioner of Immigration, and with the usual right of appeal lying to the Department at Washington. These would constitute sufficient safeguards for the protection of the immigrant as well as the country.

I do not believe in the plan of trying to reach every little evil in immigration by a precise enactment, for this would oftentimes so bind the executive officials as to compel them to be unnecessarily severe in all cases, whereas their acts should in each particular case before them be tempered with justice and mercy, as the exigencies of the case require. This difficulty could be effectually obviated in many cases by making the board of special inquiry approach as nearly as possible to a jury, guided by instructions and regulations.

My experience has taught me that where an unbiased body of sworn officials, after a careful examination, believe an immigrant should be rejected, he is generally a bad immigrant and would not make a desirable citizen. On the other hand, I have seen cases where an immigrant would fall within the letter of the law and still in the opinion of the inspectors be a desirable immigrant. For instance, if an alien, through no fault of his own, should not be manifested according to law, the punishment under the present law does not fall upon the steamship company, where it rightfully belongs, but falls upon the immigrant. The fine must be paid, or what occurs? Not a punishment of the steamship company, but the immigrant must be deported as any other excluded person; this, too, in the face of the fact that the immigrant so improperly manifested must first be adjudged qualified to land before the fine can be assessed.

The status of an alien who has acquired a residence here and returns to his native land should be clearly determined in some manner, so that we will know in what light to consider him when he returns to the United States.

Finally, I believe the time has arrived when all the laws touching immigration should be carefully revised and an entirely new law enacted, embodying all that has been found by experience to be beneficial in the old laws and such new enactments as wisdom shall dictate.

Q. (By Mr. FARQUHAR.) How are you advised here at your office of the sailing of criminals from the other side?—A. We are not advised at all, unless occasionally the governments from which they are fleeing advise the State Department, and the State Department sends the Department notice.

Q. In case of escaping criminals from Great Britain, have the Scotland Yard detectives anything to do with the Bureau of Immigration?—A. Very frequently they send word direct to the police department in New York, and they notify us.

Q. What have you to say as to the closeness with which you keep count of the immigrants that come here?—A. It is absolute.

Q. No possibility of a small percentage passing without being accounted for?— A. They do pass occasionally, but we always know it. With all the precautions we take an immigrant sometimes escapes, and we notify the company; and in a majority of cases the immigrants are returned, or it is proven that the escape has been of such a character that no one has been to blame. But as to any wholesale escapes, that would be utterly out of the question. I think there is a chance for the entry people coming in here, over whom we have no jurisdiction. They come as sailors to the United States with sailing ships, and even with transatlantic vessels. There is some leak there, but we have no control over that, although our attorney has been looking the matter up and we have gone into it with the foreign governments. As to the statement that there is an incorrect count of immigrants coming to New York, it is utterly preposterous.

Q. What jurisdiction, if any, have you over the first and second class passengers on these steamers?—A. As to aliens, equal jurisdiction with the steerage passengers.

Q. Does the head money attach to the aliens?—A. Every person who comes in the first or second cabin, not a citizen of the United States, pays a head tax.

Q. Have you ever discovered any discrepancy between the names carried on the manifest and the actual count of the immigrants on board? Do you find more or less at any time?—A. We find less sometimes, and occasionally more.

Q. How do you account for that?—A. There are 30 names on each manifest. These 30 names have been sent in from the general office to the ship, are made up on the ship, and at the last moment before the ship goes out are signed by the master and certified to by the consul, and it is quite possible that of the 600 or 700 or 1,000 people that come over in the ship a man or woman, or a number, may back out at the last moment. The consul always certifies that a certain number are booked. If the consul knows that such a party is not on the ship's manifest, he will say "No. 17 omitted; not on board." Or it is quite possible they might not be on board and he not know it, as they might walk off at the last moment. So the steward or purser would draw a line through that name. But we get so very few in that way that when the line is drawn through, Commissioner Fitchie collects the fine just the same and makes them go through the regular legal process of having the fine remitted through the Department at Washington. On the other hand, parties run on board at the last moment. You will find hundreds of people on board 5 minutes before the ship leaves. If they should come over they might be perfectly proper immigrants, but if we were unable to find them on the manifest they would have to pay a fine of $10 each, and they would have to go back unless the fines were paid. That is according to section 4 of the act of 1893.

Q. Do you receive these manifests at quarantine?—A. They are received by our officer from the purser at quarantine

Q. What process is gone through to verify the manifests?—A. Every immigrant is examined.

Q. How many inspectors have you in the examination?—A. Seven to ten registry clerks in the direct examination of the groups of 30.

Q. Suppose you have 500 immigrants?—A. We have 7 or 8 lines working, each line containing 30. Thirty would be coming through at one time. Mr. Fitchie has examined in his time over 4.000 in a day during the past spring.

Q. So the verification of these manifests, to your mind, is sure almost?—A. I think I can state so positively.

Q. What reliability can be placed on statistics that you annually put forth from this port through the Commissioner of Immigration?—A. Prior to the beginning of the fiscal year 1899 I think very little reliability could be placed on their value.

Q. Wherein lay the faults of the old figures?—A. They did not give what they purported to give.

Q. Did your bureau follow out pretty much the system of the New York commissioners?—A. Constant changes were being made in statistical methods, but the changes were in the way of correcting manifest errors rather than making a complete change in the system.

Q. Where were the manifest errors in bringing these statistics out?—A. I think the failures in the old way were caused by lack of knowledge of the peoples coming to the country. There was no intentional falsifying of statistics. As we have gone on we have come to know more of the peoples, more of whence they come, and what their characteristics are.

Q. In accounting for immigrants by nationalities how accurate are your figures?—A. They are only true in regard to political divisions from which the immigrants come.

Q. Nativity?—A. No. Their race is not true.

Q. Are a good many of the manifests merely from the ports independent of the nationality?—A. I think not. They are manifested from the political divisions from which they come. That would be no criterion as to their race or industrial possibilities here.

Q. So that in the reports furnished by the Government every year the designation or the nationality is no real criterion at all of the immigrant himself?—A. Very little. The present Commissioner-General, Mr. Powderly, has gotten together a new system of statistics which I think will meet any objection which might be urged against our past statistics.

Q. Does the same fault apply to the reports of the occupations of the immigrants?—A. The occupations of the immigrants are absolutely of no value even now.

Q. In what way?—A. The average immigrant from Europe coming here has followed in Europe that occupation given him. He was merely a land workman, not a farmer. Usually they are laborers on farms, and when they come here they are ready to go into anything that offers. They are ready to go into mining or anything that comes their way, and the probabilities are nine-tenths follow a different occupation from that they followed in the old country. Of course, if a man is a carpenter he perhaps remains a carpenter, but if he is an unskilled laborer he becomes that which chance gives him here.

Q. Have you a classification of skilled labor?—A. Yes.

Q. Does it cover nearly all trades?— A. I think our present classification is fairly comprehensive.

Q. So that, taking the old statistics, this commission or anybody that intended to find in general immigration the skilled or unskilled, or the nationalities of European immigrants, would be at an entire loss if they took the official tables as furnished by the Government?—A. I think so.

Q. (By Mr. SMYTH.) Can any reliance be placed on the destination as given by the immigrant and his friend, and as shown by your statistics?—A. Only partially.

Q. Can you give any incidents where you have been misled in that way?—A. Of all the immigrants that land at New York it is estimated that 45 per cent stop temporarily in New York to get their bearings. We confine our statistical divisions to the State. Between the years 1880 and 1890, in round numbers, five and a half to six millions of immigrants were landed at the port of New York. On the basis of 45 per cent coming to New York, there would have been at least, say, 2,000,000 giving their destination as New York. The census of 1890 showed the population of New York had increased during that period less than a million, some 900,000.

Q. In your Government reports you state a great many Russians have been received in this country. Is that true?—A. No, very few have ever come to this country.

IMMIGRATION.

Q. How many did you report last year?—A. I should say that of about 40,000 reported as coming from the political division of Russia last year, as an estimate probably 200 might be Russians.

Q. Are there many variations of that kind, Germany and France, for instance?—A. Not in Germany and France; but there are from the political divisions of Austria-Hungary and Russia. Austria-Hungary now comprises a tremendous factor in our immigration, yet we can hardly say there is such a thing as an Austrian. In our new statistics he would be classed as a German. The immigrants coming from Austria-Hungary are Slovaks, Slavonians, and Croatians, etc.

Q. Are there many Hungarians?—A. If Magyars are meant, very few. Many come from Hungary, but they are not Magyars.

Q. What are they?—A. Poles, Slovaks, Croatians, Dalmatians—all those people that comprise the Hungarian Kingdom.

Q. Do you think that the statistics of the Russian Jews are correct?—A. We have no statistics as to the Russian Jews. They were not classed as to races previous to the last fiscal year.

Q. Instead of the general statement made as to the Huns having displaced the American and Irish miners in Pennsylvania, you would substitute the Slovaks, Lithuanians, Polaks, and Croations?—A. Yes.

Q. Is it a fact in their own homes the Slovaks are nearly all miners?—A. They do some mining there.

Q. The general term Hun, you take it, is not a proper title to give to that class of immigrants?—A. I do not think it would be fair to the Magyar race, who are the real Hungarians.

Q. How do you classify Polish and Russian Jews?—A. That is one of the things in which the falsity of the old system was manifest. When Poland was divided between Austria, Russia, and Germany each part became part of the political entity to which it was given. The Poles not having given up their national characteristics, the Russian Pole is practically as much a Pole now as before the division of Poland; whether he comes from Russia or Austria he is of the same race. The Pole that comes from Germany may be better educated on account of the compulsory laws, but he is a Pole and would be of the same industrial possibilities.

Q. Do not a good many Jews come in from the interior of Turkey?—A. A good many have come from that political division.

Q. In your eastern Asiatic immigration what nation predominates?—A. The Syrian, Armenian, and Greek predominate.

Q. What are their callings or professions?—A. Usually merchants and laborers. The Armenians have gone into Massachusetts particularly, having colonized certain sections. You will also find a good many Greeks in the textile business in Lowell and Lawrence. You will find them also to a certain extent in New Bedford and Fall River, etc. We get a great number of people at our port who are going to Lowell and Lawrence and have acquaintances there. The Armenians have also a large colony in Worcester. The Washburn-Moen Company started a factory in Illinois somewhere, and a great many of that people are out there. The Syrians, on the other hand—if they have gone into producing pursuits, I have not known of it—are mostly peddlers. They have certain distributing agencies all over the country. They are peddlers and go around the country under the control, as I understand it, of certain people interested in notions.

Q. Have you any knowledge that in the case of Armenians and Greeks there is something of the old padrone system?—A. Yes. We are morally sure it exists. When the immigrants of that class come all provided with American gold and having about an equal amount of money, there must be something more than chance accountable for it.

Q. Have you formulated any amendments to the present immigration laws or the alien contract labor law?—A. I had the honor of being a member of the commission appointed by Secretary Carlisle. That commission recommended some 29 changes in the present law covering immigration, which were reported in a printed book. They are all administrative except one or two, and such as the commissioner at the port of New York would find to his benefit every day in the year. I have taken the liberty of putting these down in the form of laws, with the assistance of Dr. Ullo, in a memorandum I will submit later. It points out many defects in the law, which everybody is agreed should be changed.

Q. Practically you have had no amendments to the law since 1893?—A. The only amendments made were those changing the title of the Commissioner-General of Immigration, making the decision of the commissioner at the ports final, and increasing the head tax from 50 cents to a dollar. That was put in the law as a rider on some of the emergency bills in 1894.

Q. Do the circulars from the Treasury, issued as instructions, modify these laws in any way, or are they more in the nature of amplifications of the law?—A. I should say so.

Q. Have you any opinion to give as to doubling the head tax?—A. I should think it would be a very good thing.

Q. What are your reasons?—A. So that at no time the immigration service would be liable to be crippled for funds as it was in 1892. Since the fire at Ellis Island they have taken away from us several hundred thousand dollars, which our fund will have to pay, and if it should happen that immigration should be reduced we would be bankrupt as we were in 1892.

Q. In rebuilding Ellis Island is there not an appropriation by Congress?—A. There is some provision for reimbursement from the immigration fund.

Q. Do you think the guaranty of one year on the part of the steamship companies is sufficient to cover the immigrants who lapse into the undesirable classes?—A. No; I believe that it should be extended to at least 2 years.

Q. Do you think it would meet a good deal of opposition on the part of the steamship companies?—A. I do not think so.

Q. Have you ever heard them express a willingness to make it 2 years?—A. No.

Q. Have you heard any expression of willingness to extend it?—A. No; but I have no idea the responsible steamship companies would oppose such an enactment.

Q. Is it your understanding that the head tax is paid by the steamship companies?—A. Yes.

Q. That is added to the cost of the ticket from the other side?—A. I presume so.

Q. (By Mr. CLARKE.) Where is your office?—A. The Barge Office in New York.

Q. Why is it called the Barge Office?—A. I do not know. When the building was built it was intended to receive all the cabin passengers. It was built some time about 1878 or 1879. The idea was that all the cabin passengers would not land on the docks as they do now, but would be brought to the Barge Office and there landed and their baggage examined.

Q. Where is this building located?—A. At the end of Whitehall street, on Battery Park.

Q. Do the trans-Atlantic liners land there?—A. No. They land from Cortlandt street, to about Twenty-third or Twenty-fifth street, and in Hoboken.

Q. How are the immigrants taken from these steamers to what you call the Barge Office?—A. By barge.

Q. Is that probably why it is called the Barge Office?—A. Perhaps so.

Q. How is that building arranged inside for the inspection of these immigrants?—A. We have had to take the rooms as they were constructed originally, and make the best of them, but we have arranged them as nearly to a reproduction of the arrangement at Ellis Island as we could. We have a large central inclosure for the chief registry clerk; have on each side four aisles capable of holding 30 immigrants passing in review before the registry clerk, sitting at the end of the line. We have in addition to that the balance of that main floor subdivided by iron railings, so the groups of 30 in the aisle, waiting for examination, can be placed in there and arranged according to their groups.

Q. Are these registry clerks skilled in more than one language?—Yes; they have to be.

Q. What languages do they speak?—A. Almost all speak German, Italian, and Yiddish, and we have others who speak the Slavonic languages and dialects; and we have another clerk who speaks the oriental languages. We have had three until lately.

Q. Does the registry clerk converse with every immigrant?—A. Yes.

Q. What does he hand to the registry clerk when he approaches?—A. He hands him generally his inspection card, his doctor's card, a card he receives on the other side, which is supposed to be punched every day by an officer of the ship. It also contains the immigrant's name, the ship on which he came, in some cases his country, his age, his group, and list number.

Q. Does the registry clerk examine them and compare them with the ship's manifest so as to see whether they agree or not?—A. The manifest is before the registry clerk, and that is the basis on which he examines each applicant. He marks any discrepancy, and if there is any doubt at any time that he is the immigrant on the sheet he marks him for special inquiry.

Q. After these immigrants have passed these registry clerks what official do they next come in contact with?—A. That would depend on the class they came in. If they are going to a Western point they are immediately passed down to where the railroad companies have their offices, and are ticketed and sent forth under the protection of the railroad company and auspices of the Government. If they are held for further inquiry, such as a wife coming to her husband and it is desired the husband should come for her, or girls coming to relatives, or for any reason their story needs verification, they are held in the New York detention pen in the building, and the information office afterwards verifies the statements of the applying friends with the statements of the immigrants, and if everything coincides and the subsequent examination verifies that of the registry clerk the immigrant is admitted. If there is any discrepancy he is held for special inquiry. If the clerk does not deem him beyond doubt entitled to land, he goes to the "S. I." detention room where he comes in due course before the board of special inquiry.

Q. Is there any medical inspection in that building?—A. The medical examination is the first that is held.

Q. Held in that building?—A. On the same floor. All those who are considered suspicious by the doctors as the line passes in review before them are placed to one side and taken to the doctors' apartments, where they are especially examined, and if ailing a certificate of rejection is made.

Q. Are there many instances of immigrants being tampered with by any class of persons hanging about the Barge Office?—A. There has always been a class of persons, whose representatives have been hanging outside to get immigrants under their control, but of late years that has been reduced to a minimum. The minute any extortion or wrong doing is known the commissioner immediately prosecutes, and there are a number of people in the States prison for such offenses now.

Q. You think that protection is more efficient under the United States administration than under the State administration?—A. I think it is absolutely and unqualifiedly so. The best testimony to that fact is the unanimous testimony of every missionary organization connected with the institution.

Q. Will you not explain briefly what missionary associations are represented there and what attention they give to the immigrants?—A. There are altogether upward of 15 missionaries there. A number of well-known and responsible societies that immediately come to my mind. The united Hebrew societies, representing all the Hebrew organizations of New York, have a representative at the Barge Office for the special care and protection of Jewish immigrants. This society has an agent and assistant at the Barge Office. The poor of its faith that come in are visited and receive assistance if necessary. Those that are detained are visited by this agent, and if they need money to telegraph, or clothes, or any material assistance it is given them, and in that way this society is helpful in administering the laws, and has worked for the benefit of the immigration laws. And I think the next largest is the society of Our Lady of the Rosary, for the protection of Irish girls. All Irish girls that come to this port can be sure that they will be met at the immigration station, and after they are examined and adjudged fit to land they go to the mission, where they receive a pleasant home, and the moral responsibility for their being placed in safe hands is assumed by that institution.

Q. Is that near the Barge Office?—A. Right across the street. We have the German society and the Irish society. The Irish society was formed as a branch of the Irish immigrant board, and is ready at all times to assist detained Irish of any faith. The Women's Home Mission of the Methodist Episcopal Church have an excellent place at No. 9 State street, where the immigrants of that faith are received and kindly and courteously cared for. These societies that I have mentioned are all supported by outside contributions, and their assistance given to the immigrant without cost. The New York Bible Society, under Mr. Jackson, has been in immigration service for something like 25 years. He gives Bibles and tracts to those who desire them. The Protestant Episcopal Church, under Bishop Potter, has a representative, and a number of others that at the present moment I could not mention. I think I can safely say the societies I have enumerated are great aids to the executive office in the enforcement of the law in many ways besides their legitimate functions.

Q. (By Mr. FARQUHAR.) Is there an Italian society?—A. One called the St. Raphael Society, which has been in existence for a short time under its present management. It came in about 3 or 4 months after Mr. Fitchie came into office. It had formerly been there, but had gone out. Personally I do not know of any hurt it has done; but I do not know of any good it has done either.

Q. These societies exercise more religious functions than anything else?—A. They have no religious functions; it is pure charity.

Q. Do they make provision with money and otherwise for the comfort and assistance of the immigrants?—A. Some of them do.

Q. (By Mr. SMYTH.) They look after lonely women and protect girls?—A. Yes.

Q. (By Mr. CLARKE.) Before the immigrants pass out of the building, and while detained, is there any provision for feeding them?—A. Yes.

Q. At whose cost?—A. At the cost of the steamship companies.

Q. What is the cost?—A. Fifty cents a day. Under the new contract, which went into effect the 1st day of July, 1899, it is 35 cents a day.

Q. What kind of food and in what quantities?—A. As much as they can eat. In the morning coffee, bread, etc. They can eat all they want; we have never received a complaint. They eat 3 times a day; at noon they receive a meal of soup, meat, bread, and potatoes; at night, coffee, bread, and prunes.

Q. (By Mr. SMYTH.) This is furnished by the immigration department?—A. Under their supervision, but not by them; there is a contractor; it is given under competitive bids.

Q. Is it open to inspection?—A. Yes.

Q. What kind of meat, and how is it cooked?—A. All sorts, lamb, beef, boiled beef. I can supply the commission with the menu which Mr. Fitchie has.

Q. Is it in the power of the commissioner to supervise the character of this supply of food?—A. Entirely so.

Q. So that it must be satisfactory to him?—A. Yes.

Q. He makes out the menu?—A. Yes.

Q. (By Mr. FARQUHAR.) Is there any arrangement by the consular agents here of European nations, or their ministers in Washington, in respect to the supervision over their immigrants that come here?—A. There are by two Governments, the Italian and the Austro-Hungarian.

Q. How long has the Italian Government had any supervision?—A. Since June, 1894.

Q. What privileges have they had, and who granted them?—A. The then ambassador to Rome, the Hon. Wayne MacVeigh, forwarded a copy of an Italian paper which went with some elaboration into the wrongs done the Italians in the United States; which said that nowhere in the world were the *colonies* of the Kingdom of Italy so rich and so powerful as they were in America; that the Italians in America were *Italian colonists*, and subject to their Italian Government. The article went on to say that those Italians that went into the United States with the intention of remaining and becoming citizens were loved and respected here. It was not expected that such a feeling could be entertained for those who only came to the United States with the intention of acquiring riches and returning to Italy. It went on to say that the minister of foreign affairs had interested himself in this problem and would immediately bring it to a successful conclusion. Shortly after, Baron Fava visited Dr. Senner at Ellis Island, and negotiations were entered into between Secretary Carlisle and Baron Fava whereby Baron Fava was to have the right to appoint an agent of the Italian Government to be stationed at the immigration office at the port of New York, for the purpose of protecting the Italian immigrants against the evils of the padrone and, if necessary, when he fell into the clutches of the padrone, to rescue him. After a great deal of correspondence, which is on record, it was finally agreed by the Secretary of the Treasury that such an office could be established at the immigration station for the purpose stated, it being distinctly agreed that this establishment was an experimental one. The office was established, with a gentleman named Professor Oldrini in charge. That office went into existence in July or August of 1894. There was considerable space on the floor of Ellis Island at the time, and a space very much removed from our immigration processes, a large room 100 feet removed from the last inspector, was set apart so that the immigrants could go through and get into this floor, and it was supposed that in this office the immigrants would be advised that it was not necessary for them to go to the padrone to secure employment; that they could secure employment themselves; and it was thought that this Italian office would simply break up the padrone, because after it was established no padrone would ever come there. All the immigrants coming into New York were sent to them, and they made their examination, and examined all their passports, etc. Shortly after that there was a colony of Italians, which was a part of the colonization scheme of the late Austin Corbin, started in Sunnyside, Ark., and Professor Oldrini resigned and went to this colony, and a representative of the San Raphael mission resigned and went also. In his stead was appointed Dr. Egisto Rossi. Dr. Rossi had written a book on the agricultural resources of the United States. He is a very learned and accomplished gentleman. Shortly after the establishment of the bureau the contention was made by Professor Oldrini that the Italians who were going to the railroad points were not allowed to go into this bureau, and the matter was referred to Washington, and the authorities decided that as those who were going to the railroad points were presumably going to points which they had themselves selected, and were in no danger of getting into the clutches of the New York padrone, there was no need of their being directed to the bureau, and so they were not given that privilege. The matter has gone on until now we have an Italian bureau, which I do not believe is in accord with the spirit of the immigration service.

Q. Has it been maintained there since its first establishment?—A. Yes.

Q. And Austria also has the same?—A. The Austria-Hungarian Government has quite a different institution. The Austria-Hungarian consul at New York, then Baron Stockinger, and Baron Hengelmüller, the Austrian ambassador at Washington, organized the Austria-Hungarian society here in New York, the object of which is to furnish the protection of home to the Austrians of all classes, Austria having made a subvention of some special amount of money which is given for a protection and home for Austrians of all classes in this country. The subvention from the Government provides that a certain number of days lodging—it runs up to several thousand—is provided each year free, on application, to the needy people who apply. They have in connection with it a free labor bureau, which is paid for out of the subvention. Austria-Hungarians can go to this place and find a home. There is an agent of the Austria-Hungarian office at the Barge Office, and occasionally a representative of the consul comes down and looks around to see if there is anything he can do for his countrymen; but he has no office there and his visits are only semioccasional.

Q. Have you any idea that there could be, through admitting these foreign representatives, opportunities to cover up a great deal of assisted immigration and found a padrone system; do you not think it is dangerous?—A. Yes, absolutely.

Q. Absolutely dangerous?—A. Yes.

Q. Have you any particular statement to make about the workings of it, so far as you have seen it?—A. I desire to preface any statement I might make with reference to the Italian bureau with the statement that I consider Dr. Rossi, who represents the Italian Government at the Barge Office, as a thoroughly honest and careful and conscientious gentleman. He is performing a difficult task in the best way that he can, and whatever I say—and saying this I simply embody the opinions and feelings of my chief—is with no malice toward him, because he has done nothing personally to cause us to lose our great regard for him, but we find that while the Italian Government continues the quasi official supervision over its immigrants there, the United States Government's inspection must be necessarily offset to some degree; that the establishment of such a bureau there in a measure tends to encourage the undesirable Italians to come here, because they feel that they might be protected when coming here. We further believe that the objects for which the Italian bureau was created have not been in any measure achieved; that the padrone system has not been broken up, and that criminals from Italy have not been stopped from coming here.

Q. (By Mr. SMYTH.) Do you still think there is to some extent assisted immigration to this country?—A. I do.

Q. From more than one country?—A. Yes.

Q. Would you say what countries you think that immigration comes from?—A. I think from many countries, but think it generally comes here from England by way of Canada.

Q. Not so much from the continental or Mediterranean sections?—A. No; the Commissioner of Immigration at the port of New York has established the line so that the steamship companies now do not dare to bring them.

Q. Can you suggest any way to check that immigration coming by way of Canada?—A. It is a pretty difficult problem.

Q. (By Mr. FARQUHAR.) Is that the English system of sending out farmers, mechanics, servant girls, and even schoolboys to Canada?—A. That is quite a different system. Coming into Portland and Quebec there is always a number of ships of these boys, picked up and sent to Canada for the purpose of putting them out to farm. I have seen a shipload of these boys myself whose only fault was that they were born poor, and if Canada wishes to encourage it and the boys are willing to grow up with the country, there should be no objection here. I refer to that class of real paupers sent here to get rid of them. It is that kind of people we are getting here as assisted immigrants.

Q. (By Mr. CLARKE.) By whom are they assisted generally?—A. As a member of a special commission I went to England in 1896, and I found out that the wholesale giving of assistance to criminals and paupers and sending them to America was supposed to be, and I believe really has been, broken up. There always has been an effort to move the pauper on, from outside of London into the heart of London, and from London to somewhere else. Finally he gets to Liverpool, and his passage is paid to Quebec, and finally to New York. The United Hebrew Charities of New York, while Mr. Roseneau was manager, had a large number of such cases of their own people that they had to take care of after being shipped from the other side, and it was a matter of almost daily happening for them to send to us persons who had come into the country by way of Canada, and who could not have been landed at any port in the United States. These things are well known by everybody in the office.

Q. Have you any reason to believe that governments, either national or municipal, assist these immigrants through charities?—A. I think that has been broken up. It has not existed to any considerable degree since Colonel Weber's trip to Europe.

Q. (By Mr. FARQUHAR.) Do not the British authorities usually deny that there is any of that assisted immigration now?—A. Officially, I believe that is true; but in Liverpool I was told by officers of the Cunard and White Star lines that it was a common boast, with reference to the inefficiency of our immigration laws of the United States, that they were valueless, and that immigrants who would not try to get in at New York could find their way in by the back door.

(The subcommission adjourned until 10 a. m., July 25, 1899, at which time the examination of Mr. McSweeney was resumed.)

Q. (By Mr. SMYTH.) What is the present status of the padrone; is he still in existence?—A. I think the padrone still exists in this country. They have, as the result of the growth of Italian immigration, changed their character, but if by the padrone we understand that Italians are still controlled after they come here, are sent to work under contractors, that the commissariat is regulated by the man who sends them there, that their wages are controlled by these men, that their wages are sent back to Italy by these same bankers or padrones—if this is what is considered the padrone system, it still exists. The system which was represented to have obtained years ago, whereby these bankers or padrones induced the immigrants to come here, I do not think exists any longer, because there is no need of it. The immigrants now come here of their own accord. When they come to this country, or before they come, they know that if they will go to a certain banker, that that banker is from their particular province, and that they will find employment and all those things through him; and so he does not now need to send them over money. They come and report to him and stay with him. Some few of them break off and become American citizens, but the rest remain under his control or return to Italy when they have satisfied themselves as to the amount of money they have acquired.

Q. We have all through the South colonies of—we call them "dagos" down there, or peddlers—who live together and seem to be under the leadership of one man, and they travel all over the country for 50 miles around. Are they Italians?—A. I think they are Orientals.

Q. A different race, but it seems to be the same system?—A. It is the same system, only on a different basis. We have been unable to get very definite information as to the methods of bringing the Orientals to this country on account of our inability to know their language, to converse with them. As I said, it is very suspicious that large numbers of this class arrive here with a stated amount of American gold, and I think it is established beyond doubt that these people are controlled by a centralized body of notion peddlers, with general headquarters here in New York, and with branches all over the United States, and that these people are representatives of some branch of this padrone traffic.

Q. You think, then, coming back to the Italian padrone, that they still bring in immigrants in violation of law?—A. I do not think they do to any considerable extent.

Q. Do you find the Italian immigrant wants to be released?—A. My personal impression is that the Italian immigrant would prefer to be under the control of the padrone.

Q. He looks to him as a sort of protection?—A. He looks to him for protection. The Italian immigrant, as far as my experience goes, would rather deposit his money with an Italian banker who has no standing outside of his little community than to deposit it in the regular national or State bank.

Q. He knows about one and does not know about the other?—A. I do not know whether it is dislike or distrust.

Q. What other races are held in industrial bondage besides these Italians and Orientals?—A. There has been a species of selling labor going on in New York for a long while, but I believe under Dr. Senner and Commissioner Fitchie that has been broken up—the system of getting girls from the Austrian-Hungarian empire and, not exactly selling them into bondage, but getting them into families and keeping them there for years at just mere nominal wages. I believe that the rigid enforcement of the rules and regulations of the Barge Office have succeeded to a great extent in breaking that up.

Q. Are these girls brought here for immoral purposes?—A. They have not been brought here for immoral purposes, but the gradation to immoral life is very easy, and it has been stated that a large number of these girls are leading that sort of life in New York. This was stated by the police.

Q. Does the Italian bureau or the San Raphael Society give any material assistance to these immigrants?—A. I never knew of them giving any material assistance to immigrants in distress.

Q. Do you think the Italian Government encourages immigration?—A. Commissioner-General Stump went to Europe in 1895, and when he returned he said in his report that one traveling through Italy could tell those provinces from which immigrants were coming to the United States by reason of the thrifty and home-like and well kept appearance of the little houses; that this thrifty condition was due to the money of the emigrant who had emigrated to the United States. Mr. Stump further said that a large amount of the taxes and other burdens were borne by reason of this money coming to them; that in parts of Italy from which emigrants were coming to the United States there was a marked difference in the character of the farms and homesteads.

Q. The money of the immigrant was sent back and used in building up Italy?—A. I was told on last Friday by a gentleman who is engaged in the railroad business here in New York, that on the evening before sailing days almost all the bankers and dealers in Italian money are kept busy until 11, 12, and 1 o'clock at night.

Q. How did the Italian bureau here act during the late war with Spain?—A. I remember a circular that was given to Commissioner Fitchie by Dr. Rossi, in which the cabinet officers or ministers in Italy had sent out a notification that owing to the number of immigrants that were being returned from the United States to Italy as coming in contravention of the local laws of immigration, and because of the great suspension in industry and labor *due to the war with Spain*, the prefects of the kingdom were instructed to discourage emigration to the United States, and were asked to curtail the giving of passports to the greatest possible extent.

Q. When was this warning of Dr. Rossi's sent?—A. I think it was dated on the 21st of April, *four days before war was declared*.

Q. Did he furnish the commissioner with a copy of these circulars of the Italian Government?—A. I think so, in May. It is only a memory.

Q. Did that have any effect in curtailing the emigration from Italy during the summer and fall of 1898?—A. Immigration was rather low during that year.

Q. Especially from Italy?—A. Not particularly. The Italian immigration rather kept up.

Q. After the war was over, did the Italian Government take any steps to encourage emigration to the United States?—A. In October or November of last year Commissioner-General Powderly forwarded a letter, or copies of a letter, received from the embassy at Rome, wherein he reported on the subject of assisted emigration, and stated that in October the Government had reduced the railway fare to the seaboard for all emigrants 50 per cent. I think the name of the official is Lewis M. Iddings, who is connected with the American embassy at Rome.

Q. Does the Italian bureau here have any right to influence the admission of immigrants who have been detained?—A. Absolutely none.

Q. Have they ever tried to exercise such right?—A. Yes.

Q. Can you give some information on that? When, and what was done? Was there any protest made?—A. When we were at Ellis Island, the Italian bureau was removed from all our governmental processes by reason of being in the end of the building away, removed from the inspection floor, and immigrants were directed through the railroad floor, going 75 feet before they got to their control, and any interference with governmental processes would be immediately noticed. When we came to the Barge Office, as they were a part of our institution, and we had to give them room in our cramped quarters, which necessarily brought them right in with us. Their quarters are right adjoining the detention department. While Dr. Rossi has never to my knowledge tried to exercise that right, his assistant did to such an extent that the board of special inquiry had to make a written protest to the Commissioner. Since the suspension of the bureau in April of last year, which was supposed to have gone into effect on the 15th of April, and which was afterwards rescinded, there has been little interference of the Italian bureau with our administrative processes; they have kept their proper function; and whenever Dr. Rossi or his assistant has asked for interference in behalf of a detained immigrant, he has done so as any common citizen would do, and has been treated with all the courtesy that Dr. Rossi's personality and the standing of his Government would warrant. He has been given exactly the same rights and treatment that any citizen would get who was coming in to ask about the case of an immigrant detained for any reason.

Q. (By Mr. CLARKE.) What department of your bureau do you consider the most important?—A. All the departments are equally important, but to my mind the department upon which most depends from the standpoint of the citizen is the registry department; and what applies to that is also true of the contract-labor bureau in its special field. The registry clerk is the first examining officer that comes in contact with the immigrant, and if in his judgment he thinks the immigrant is a qualified person he can allow him to land. So he acts as an absolute judge of the immigrant's eligibility. If he decides the immigrant shall land, there is absolutely no one who can say no unless some other inspector might be there and protest and hold him for special inquiry; so I believe the most important function in our process is that of the registry clerk. The board of special inquiry is also important, but their importance is somewhat qualified when it is realized that they can only act on those persons whom the registry clerk sends to them.

Q. I assume, then, a good deal of care was shown in the selection of these registry clerks, as to their fitness for their positions?—A. Most all of the registry clerks have been connected with the department for years.

Q. They are protected by the civil service?—A. Yes.

Q. What proportion of immigrants are admitted by the registry clerks?—A. From 85 to 87 per cent of all that pass before them.

Q. Of the something like 13 per cent remaining, how many are excluded and deported by the board of special inquiry?—A. The 13 per cent, or in round numbers—say, the 13 to 15 per cent—last year amounted to 25,000 people, who went before the board of special inquiry; and of that number 10 per cent were finally excluded, or less than 2 per cent of the total arrivals.

Q. Are any polygamists admitted?—A. We have not intentionally admitted polygamists, but there has been a constant stream of Mormon converts coming to this country in the second cabin of certain ships for many years—from 30 to 75 Mormon converts, weekly recruited in Sweden and Scotland and other European countries—going to Salt Lake City. They all deny that they are polygamists, and claim to be Mormon converts. About 3 years ago one of the inspectors held up over 50 of them, and the leaders or elders who had been over there converting them stood on their rights as American citizens and defied the efforts to prove they were polygamists, and as there was no way to bar them they had to be admitted. We have received some complaints as to these girls afterwards that they were badly treated, but we have not been able to verify them.

Q. What proportion as to sex?—A. The female sex predominated. I am informed that 90 to 95 per cent are women.

Q. Do these women seem to be accompanied by some man who has charge of a certain number?—A. As I understand it, these Mormon elders at a certain period have to give up their business and go into the field and make converts, go to Europe at their own expense, and bring back their converts with them.

Q. What was the total number of this class that came in last year?—A. I could not tell you. While our new statistics will give you absolutely the religions of all arriving immigrants in the steerage, Mr. Powderly's circular in relation to the cabin inspection has not progressed far enough to enable us to obtain the statistics we want as to first and second class passengers.

Q. From a personal observation of these people by yourself and the registry clerks and the board of special inquiry, is it your opinion that this large preponderance of women suggests that they are polygamists or come to practice polygamy?—A. I could not say. It is rather peculiar that there should be so many females. We have been unable to get any knowledge.

Q. (By Mr. FARQUHAR.) In your examination of these persons in charge of parties of these Mormon people, do they claim that they are members of the Church of Latter-Day Saints and not polygamists?—A. Yes.

Q. Have they ever said that they intended to live under United States laws abolishing polygamy in Utah?—A. They all make the claim with a great deal of force and feeling that they are citizens and, therefore, not amenable to our immigration laws and restrictions. "I am a United States citizen and you have no right over me." They are absolutely within their legal rights.

Q. So their claim as United States citizens safeguards the parties that are under their control or brought over?—A. It does not safeguard the parties, because they are under our control; but the elders are the leaders and controlling element and influence in the party, and the rest say, "I am going out to Utah; I am a convert to Mormonism; I am going to seek employment;" and as they are healthy and have money we have no alternative but to admit them.

Q. Is it not a fact that the females are more susceptible to be proselyted into the Mormon Church than males?—A. I know nothing about that.

Q. Have you any knowledge that in Europe the proportion is three-fourths of females and one-fourth of males, members of the Church of the Latter-Day Saints; that the faith is more captivating to the women than to the men generally?—A. I have seen that stated in the newspapers, but know nothing of it.

Q. (By Mr. CLARKE.) What have you to say as to their giving false destinations in the manifests?—A. I believe there is a great deal of falsifying on the manifests, and my statement before will bear that out, that a large proportion of people who come giving their destination as the city of New York do not remain in New York City. While the majority of these people are honest in their desire to come to New York City, which is the distributing point, there is a considerable amount of falsification done wilfully, and I would suggest that a law which would punish the steamship companies or the immigrants for the wilfull falsification of destination would be very grateful to the immigration authorities and serve a good purpose.

Q. Could you furnish proof so the law could be executed?—A. I think in many cases presumptive evidence would be enough to convict. For instance, if a party of 50 arrives to-day and they say they are going to relatives in New York and they have ample money, say $50, $60, or $70, which would be sure to admit these people after all our registry and contract-labor examinations were gone through with; if these immigrants had $70 apiece that would be one of the most potent reasons for their admission; if they go to New York and on the afternoon of the same day they sail away on the steamship to New Orleans or go on the train to San Francisco, there is no doubt their destination has been falsified; and they have not only succeeded in falsifying as to our statistics, but they have been admitted by reason of having money which is immediately taken away from them, and they land in San Francisco without a cent. If an immigrant comes without a cent going to San Francisco, we demand he shall prove to us his ability to care for himself in San Francisco. We do not recognize his landing in San Francisco without a cent as any different from landing in New York under the same circumstances. It does not only falsify statistics, but allows undesirable immigrants to land who are liable to get into distress at their final destination.

Q. Have you any idea what proportion of immigrants are sent for by their friends already in this country?—A. I think that the steamship companies will be able to answer that accurately. Our information is that of all the immigrants coming to this country 65 per cent come on tickets that have been bought and paid for in this country.

Q. (By Mr. FARQUHAR.) I see by the issue of the morning paper here the claim made by an American Hebrew that your classification does not do the Hebrews justice, and also a claim that the Hebrew is the only religion that is distinctively and particularly brought out in the last annual report. What have you to answer to that?—A. May I see that clipping? (After reading clipping.) This is absolutely founded on a wrong assumption, and the gentleman, whoever he was, that wrote this, does not know what he is talking about. I am glad to have an opportunity to answer this. I have here the report for the fiscal year just ended the 1st of this month, which shows from what quarter of the earth these 27,086 Hebrews came. For instance, we will take Austria-Hungary; as I said before, Austria-Hungary under the old classification would be put down as Bohemian, Galician; under our new classification we will find that there were 1,795 Bohemians, 6,818 Croatians and Slavonians, 367 Dalmatians, 2 French, 3,262 Germans, 9,921 Hebrews, 1,044 Italians from the North, 3 southern Italians, 3 Lithuanians, 4,503 Magyars, 9,740 Poles, 10 Roumanians, 1,344 Rusniaks, 6 Servians, 13,545 Slovaks, 2 Transylvanians, making a total of 52,365 from Austria-Hungary. I simply give you this classification as emphasizing my statement that the former classifications are not at all accurate. I think this will demonstrate it. You will notice further in this that we have differentiated as between the Italians of the North and the South. We have not done this because we wished to make any invidious distinction or throw any aspersions on any race, but simply in order to get at these races industrially as they come to this country. In some cases their mother tongue might give us an idea of the races, but sometimes the tongue would not do that and then we had to ask what their religion was. For instance, there is a great difference between the Arab who is a Mohammedan and the one who is a Christian. It is the Christian Arab which we get in this country. This statement is absolutely false, as a reference to our report of their religions will prove. During the past fiscal year, out of the grand total of 291,814 immigrants arriving at New York, there were 46,196 Protestants, 160,633 Roman Catholics, 12,591 Greek Catholics, 27,145 Israelites, 9 Brahmins, 107 Mohammedans, 144 miscellaneous.

Q. How long since this classification was adopted?—A. Since the 1st of July, 1898. This will absolutely and once for all answer the criticism which has been made by persons who either do not know or wish to misrepresent that these new statistics are intended as a slap at any faith. I wish to repeat, these statistics have been approved by some of the most diligent students of the immigration question in this country, and they are intended simply to classify industrially the people who are coming into this country, so we may know who they are better than we did before, and our asking the religion is simply a means to this end, and as it is asked of all peoples there can be no ground of complaint.

Q. In the old system of statistics, then, the Russian Jew embarking at Hamburg might often be recorded as a German, simply on account of the port of embarkation point?—A. He might if he had lived a few months in Germany, and the shipping agent had said, "Where do you come from?" "I come from Freiburg." He would put him down as a German, and we would classify him as a German.

Q. Suppose 8 or 10 Jews from Poland proper come to Hamburg and place their names on the manifest as Germans, or as citizens of any other nation; are there any means at the port of embarkation of verifying or correcting any such statement that they make?—A. No.

Q. So that the foreign manifest is entirely dependent on either the honesty or caprice of the emigrant?—A. Quite so.

Q. Neither the captain of the ship, the inspecting surgeon, nor the consul have any means at hand to verify the statement as to its truth?—A. If the emigrant makes a false statement?

Q. Yes; in case of their attempt to escape the martial laws of the country, from service in the Russian army, for instance, would it be easy for the emigrants to take a German title or name and pass under the German name?—A. He would find it difficult to get out of Russia unless he got out clandestinely.

Q. But is there an opportunity through this manifest to so register themselves as to even escape from justice?—A. Yes; the only bar to that is the acuteness of our officials. Of course, under our new system of statistics we do not depend on the manifest given us by the steamship companies, but besides the manifests supplied we have an additional manifest which contains the statistical information called for by this new method of statistics.

Q. Do you know whether tickets sold by steamship agents in the various countries of Europe would give an intelligent statement of where the ticket was sold, to whom, and other information that would lead to the identification of the emigrant?—A. It might and it might not, because we have numerous cases where tickets are sold and then transferred. It would in a generality of cases.

Q. Now, is it not a fact that Great Britain is credited with a good deal of immigration that is really continental, simply because they ship from Liverpool?—A. I can furnish to your committee the monthly report of the labor bureau connected with the English board of trade, that will give for any period you might name the immigration to and emigration out of the United Kingdom, and telling whether that immigration was from the Continent or the Orient. Mr. Burnett, who is the chief labor correspondent of the board of trade, has a monthly compilation in the Labor Gazette on this feature, so it is easily obtainable; in fact, I have it for you if you desire it.

Q. Do you think under your new statistical arrangement that your reports will become more intelligible both for Congress, political economists, and the people at large in finding the true nationality of immigration and also the religious divisions?—A. And their industrial possibilities, which is the main thing.

Q. From what source was this matter urged to make this new classification?—A. It was suggested to Commissioner-General Powderly and by him put in effect. He appointed a commission to go into the matter, and, accepting the commission's report, he put it into effect.

Q. What are the predominant races that are coming here now?—A. I have a chart that will show that. This chart is based on the old classification, but I think it will convey the idea better than any words. It is a chart which was originally gotten up by Dr. Safford, of our medical office. Our statistical office can bring that chart up and make the comparison with our last year. It would have to be made on the old basis, but as far as the immigration from the countries is concerned, it would probably be interesting to embody it in the report. (Said chart follows.)

Q. What proportion have you of Canadian immigration?—A. Canadian immigration proper or European immigration by way of Canada?

Q. Both ways, coming into the United States from Canada to labor, and foreign immigrants shipping to Canada and ultimately crossing the border.—A. There are a large number of Canadians proper who come yearly into the United States and work here, and then return. That problem is very much more pressing at Boston than here. In connection with my work on the commission appointed by Secretary Carlisle, it was estimated at that time that from 50,000 to 70,000 Canadians came into the United States every year, working during the busy season, and then returning. They go as far as New Orleans, working and returning again, and the matter has been brought up in the Canadian parliament many times. If you will allow me, I would like to read an extract from a speech in the Canadian parlia ment, delivered by Mr. Charlton, February 10, 1890. It is pertinent to tne conditions now:

"We have to scrutinize the immigration returns to see if we can not arrive at some clew that will enable us to form an opinion as to the loss of immigrants coming into this country from the Old World and leaving this country for the United States. We had in Canada, according to our own census in 1871, 582,668 persons of foreign birth; we had in Canada 10 years later, in 1881, 599,388. The increase in the foreign element in our population in ten years has been barely 15,720 souls. Mark that fact, 15,720 souls was the increase according to the census returns in the foreign-born population from 1871 to 1881, but during that period we had received from the Old World 342,675 immigrants.

"Now, what has become of all these 342,675 received, and only 16,000, in round numbers, more in the country in 1881 than there were in 1871? Where have they gone? They have left us. When we come to make a calculation, and do so properly, we must take the death rate and strike the balance year by year. We should take the number of people in Canada, foreigners, which in 1871 was 582,668; we should add to that the immigration each year; we should take the death rate and see what the loss by death was in each year; we should add to that number the immigration in the following year, and so on, carrying the calculation through for the ten years. There should have been in Canada in 1881, as the result of this calculation, 783,208 persons of foreign birth, and there were in Canada 599,388, showing that with a death rate of 20 to the 1,000 we have lost 184,820 immigrants in the decade from 1871 to 1881, who at the end of that period were living in the United States.

"Now, the immigration from 1881 to 1890 has been 653,510, estimating the immigration for the present year at 34,000. Six hundred and fifty-three thousand was the immigration into this country from 1881 to the 1st of January, 1890. Now, we lost of that number that came between 1871 and 1881, according to the calculation I have made, based upon the census returns and the death rate of 20 to the 1,000 per annum, 53 per cent of that acquisition of our population from immigration, who have left us and gone to the United States and were in that country alive in 1881. And if we take the same proportion of immigrants from 1881 to 1890 as having emigrated to the United States, we have remaining in that country at the commencement of the year 53 per cent of the entire number, or 346,000 souls.

"For the entire period from 1871 to 1889 the total immigration to Canada was 996,185, and to the United States 7,607,039, showing a per capita excess in Canada of 54 per cent; yet in view of these facts we have fallen behind in the race, and our proportion of increase of population is 11 per cent less than that of the United States. This in the face of the fact that the per cent of natural increase in Canada is greater than in the United States, and that the per capita increase by immigration was 46 per cent greater between 1870 and 1880, or 54 per cent for the entire period of 20 years between 1870 and 1890."

I do not believe there has been any objection, especially in Massachusetts, to the Canadian who comes to remain there, but there is a constantly growing feeling against the Canadian immigrants from the provinces who come into the building trade in Boston and all that region around there, coming to work during the busy season, reducing the rate of wages, and returning. The port of Boston receives as many immigrants from Canada as it does across the Atlantic, and without any head tax,

Q. What is your system of inspection at Quebec, or is that more under the control of the general office at Washington?--A. We have nothing to do with it. I only know incidentally of the system of inspection at Boston.

Q. Why does Canada feel sorry to see laborers come here and the United States feel sorry to see them come?--A. I do not think it is beneficial to either country. I think the Canadian Government would rather have these people stay there and work all the time and develop the resources of the country. When they do go back with their savings they harbor them so that they are not of great benefit. On this side they come here and earn money and take most of it back, their living expenses being quite small. Canada loses by not having the benefit of their labor to develop its industries. We do not lose in a real sense because they have been giving value for the money they earn, but we lose in their not spending the money in this country, and more important than all, because they work for less wages than the United States citizens with whom they come in competition, thus lowering the rate of wages.

Q. Is it a fact that many of these workers in New England, the French Canadians, have small holdings in Canada, and in the fall they return there, and come back every spring and summer to work in the United States?--A. That is the complaint; but, particularly in Massachusetts, that thing has been growing less and less each year as far as it refers to the French Canadians. They have been remaining and getting little holdings in the factory towns where they are located.

Q. The French Canadian is generally an industrious man, and makes a good citizen when he once makes his anchorage in the United States?—A. I think so; yes.

Q. What is the effect on the labor market here of these immigrants settling in New York?—A. It has had a great effect on the labor market. Of course, it has driven out of certain trades the former occupants of those trades. For instance, in the clothing trade, in all those trades that are known as the Jewish, the sweating trades, the Russian Jews have driven all other nationalities out. In 1885, practically, the sweating trade began; from 1880 to 1890 we received one-third of all the immigrants that had ever landed in the United States. I know of my own investigation that the Italians have gone into competition with the Jews in the sweating trade and are taking the sweating trade away from them; and Mr. Jacob Riis told me a short time ago that the Greeks had now begun to take it from the Italians. It has moved east across the Bowery to the Italian district, and is now going to the lower West Side to the Oriental quarter.

Q. (By Mr. SMYTH.) Do you consider that the sweating business has increased in New York in the last few years?—A. I do not think so. A peculiar thing about the sweating trade is, as I understand it, that whenever they have gone on a strike for wages they have never lost. There are 75,000 engaged in these industries in New York.

Q. (By Mr. FARQUHAR.) Are these people organized?—A. When necessity compels their organization. I have been told by the managers of these organizations that sometimes, at certain periods, the organizations would dwindle down to 500 to 1,000 paying members, and then in a week there would be 25,000 paying members. They get crowded down to a point where they can not stand it, then all band together.

Q. So that the organization is somewhat of a fast and loose matter, owing to the state of the trade?—A. I think they never lose their allegiance to the organization, though they may lose interest in it when times are good.

Q. Do the Jews generally go in these organizations?—A. I think so. I think the Hebrews in the sweating trade finally wind up in the labor organizations.

Q. What is the physical condition of the Jew compared with the general immigration from Europe?—A. The Russian Jew physically is not of as large stature, but our doctors say he has very much less tubercular disease than the other nationalities. The tubercular disease of the lungs, although they have it of the joints, is very rare comparatively.

Q. Is there a society here that takes care of the Jews?—A. The United Hebrew Society.

Q. Is it a charitable organization?—A. It is a society representing all the Jewish societies and maintained by the wealthy Hebrews of New York.

Q. Is it helpful in caring for the social condition of the Jew?—A. It is exceedingly so. The problem of the sweat shop was old in England before it was known here, and, as a report published in England in 1892 stated, a peculiar thing about the Jew was that those poor immigrants who to-day were receiving assistance in 5 years from now would be contributing to the various charitable organizations. In other words, they do not get pauperized by this assistance.

Q. Could you state where in New York and Brooklyn the centers of the colonization of these various peoples are?—A. Of course the Jews are in that section which I suppose would center at the Essex Market. The Italians have one colony centering on Mulberry street and another on the east side, about One hundred and sixteenth street. Greenwich street is about the center of the district devoted to immigrants from the Orient—the Arabs, Syrians, and those people. The Bohemians are on the east side; they have a strong colony about the Seventies on the east side. The Poles have no colony that I know of. They have a church here and there and are scattered about. Of course, there may be isolated colonies, but those named are the large communities. The Chinese are on Mott street.

Q. Is there a large Jewish colony at Brownsville?—A. Yes; practically all Jews.

Q. Could you give us your views and testimony as to the protection against shipwreck and accident at sea, so far as immigrants are concerned?—A. That does not come as a branch of immigration; it is not under the control of the immigration service, but I think it should be. I do not think there is an adequate provision during the busy season for immigrants at sea. I think if there should be a shipwreck and anybody suffered from inadequate supply of life-preservers, etc., it would be the immigrants. The Commissioner-General at Washington should have some supervision over the matter of protection of life of immigrants at sea.

IMMIGRATION.

Q. Have you heard any complaints made about the air space allowed on shipboard?—A. The immigrants rarely complain about anything.

Q. Was there not an enlargement secured of the amount of air space that immigrants should be allowed on steamships to save overcrowding?—A. I understand so; yes.

Q. You heard the testimony of Mr. Schwab this morning about prepaid passage, etc.? Have you any knowledge of the ticket brokerage with respect to these steamship companies?—A. Yes.

Q. We would like to hear from you on that matter.—A. Mr. Schwab and the other gentlemen said the prepaid ticket business amounted to about 40 to 55 per cent, while I state that 65 per cent would be the prepaid business. My estimate comprehended that which was really prepaid, except that instead of buying a ticket here the friends on this side sent the money over and they purchased the ticket there themselves; that would make up the difference. I would like to recommend a remedy by law against a certain method of selling prepaid tickets. The majority of prepaid tickets, those that are sent from a brother, father, or direct relative, where they come and put down the money, that is a very little danger, and I believe brings a good class of immigrants; but there is a class of peddlers who go around peddling wood and what not, who combine with the peddling business the selling of prepaid tickets. The peddler goes into a family to sell a picture, or whatever article he has, and finds out from that family that there is another member of the family in Europe, and he says, "Now, I want to sell you that ticket." They say, "I haven't any money." He says, "I will arrange that for you. You pay me $1 a week, and when you have paid half of the price of the ticket I will furnish the ticket." So when the half of the $30 is paid a ticket is bought by this peddler, turned over to the purchaser, and sent to the other side, and by the time the ticket gets from this side to the other side and returns enough time has elapsed to enable him to collect the balance of the money. They have become so bold that on one or two occasions these peddlers have come and asked us to assist them in collecting the balance remaining unpaid, the immigrant having refused to pay any more; they come to us and ask us to send the man back.

Q. In that way it has come to your positive knowledge?—A. Yes.

Q. (By Mr. CLARKE.) Do you think most of these tickets which are prepaid on the installment plan are sent to the immigrants who are undesirable?—A. Not necessarily, but the chances are that they are more undesirable than if they had come in the regular way; and I have suggested a law providing that no ticket shall be sold except by the regular authorized agents of the steamship companies. Then we can hold the steamship companies responsible.

Q. (By Mr. FARQUHAR.) Do you think there has been much done in this class of ticket brokerage?—A. I think so; yes.

Q. Do you think it is growing?—A. I fear so, but the reputable companies discourage it. They would work to have such a law passed.

Q. Do you know how much they charge for the tickets?—A. They can charge anything they want, anything they can get. They have to charge more because the man they buy it from is necessarily limited to his legitimate discount or commission.

Q. (By Mr. CLARKE.) In regard to the charges for feeding detained immigrants, will not the per capita amount paid by the steamship companies be an indication of the quality of immigrants brought by each?—A. Absolutely.

Q. Then the amounts vary with the different companies?—A. Yes; greatly.

Q. What are they?—A. They vary from 2 to about 50 cents per capita on the whole number of immigrants carried.

Q. What steamship companies pay the higher prices?—A. The companies bringing the southern Italians, Galatians, and Poles, and those immigrants from the north of Austria-Hungary and the south of Russia.

Q. Will you name these companies?—A. I can only name them in a general way; such a line as the Cunard line, bringing Irish and Swedish immigrants here, will probably pay about 3 or 4 cents for their immigrants' maintenance; the White Star about the same; the lines running direct to Swedish ports less; the North German-Lloyd and the Hamburg line, in their German service, which also bring some of these Gallicians, would run up to 9, 10, 11, or 12 cents; and the Prince line, running to Italy, newly organized, or the Fabre line, would run up to 40 cents.

Q. That shows their greater poverty—the more the companies have to pay?—A. It shows that the inspection processes are longer and more of them detained. I remember one ship of the North-German Lloyd that came in only a few months ago. It brought in here about 700 Russian Mennonites. They are an exceedingly desirable people. Of the 700 who came here, 550 were going to points west of the Missouri and had railroad tickets there. The whole ship had an average, including babes in arms, old people and everything, of $55 per capita. Now, of that ship, probably 3 or 4 were detained temporarily and probably not one was returned. Some ships bringing immigrants from Sicily and other provinces will come in there with, say, 500, of which number perhaps 300 will be held for the various processes of inspection and 200 passed out. Some of the others would be held by the contract-labor bureau, and 150 to 200 would go to the board of special inquiry, and when it came to be finished up 10 per cent would go back. One ship of 300 of these undesirable people will keep our whole force busy 3 days, as long as a ship carrying 1,000 of the kind I first mentioned. If a White Star line ship comes in here loaded down with Irish girls, they pass right through, and Father Henry takes them over to his mission, and when the ship is through we are through. But when the poorer ships come in our work begins, and it goes on for days and days; and sometimes we have had as many as 4 and perhaps 5 boards of special inquiry sitting, trying to decide as to the eligibility of these people.

Q. Is a good deal of the delay caused by a lack of the English language?—A. No. With the exception of the Oriental tongues we are prepared to handle expeditiously all other people.

Q. It is more the character of the immigrants than anything else?—A. Yes.

Q. What have you to say as to the present market for unskilled labor of immigrants?—A. We have no means of officially determining the labor market, but at the present time representatives are coming to us from large employing interests, people who believe that the immigration authorities control and can give out the labor of the immigrants coming in. They are continually applying in person. Yesterday morning 3 such persons came in and said that in points in Iowa, Pennsylvania, and another in Massachusetts they wanted certain numbers of men to do certain unskilled work. I am stating it low when I say since the 1st of July I have heard through the Labor Bureau, which has a quasi connection with us, and from requests of Mr. Fitchie and myself, of places where at least 10,000 such unskilled immigrant laborers could be employed, and they could not find them anywhere.

Q. Who make these applications?—A. Yesterday a gentleman came down representing a railroad, and said he had a union mine, at which there was no strike, and he would like 200 miners to come in there. That was in Illinois. It is a common thing since business revived in the spring.

Q. Do you think it is due largely to the revival of business?—A. I am sure it is. A man came from Pittsburg a short time ago and asked the same thing. Of course, we have no means of knowing the conditions except from what they say. We say to them when they make such requests that we have no power to help them in any way.

Q. (By Mr. FARQUHAR.) In your opinion this indicates the country needs immigration?—A. I should think immigration of the right sort was not hurting it particularly at the present time.

Q. Have you also a notion that if immigration was properly distributed it would not hurt the country?—A. We have gone on record to that effect.

Q. You spoke of the investigations made by a commission; that commission consisted of Dr. Senner, Mr. Stump, and yourself?—A. Yes.

Q. Did that investigation ever result in any legislation? Did the Secretary of the Treasury take any action on it?—A. Nothing further than the simple printing of the report, and I believe its submission to Congress by the then Secretary of the Treasury. Further than that I do not know of any action. I do not know of any legislation. I have here the report of that commission complete, which I submit for your information, and such action as you desire to take; and I desire to say this report is the work of Dr. Senner, Colonel Stump, and myself. I have no direct authorship in it except in conjunction with these gentlemen.

Q. Have you thought of any other modifications since these findings were published?—A. The recommendations I made in the first part of my testimony are in addition to those contained in that report.

Q. What became of the recommendation to set aside for the benefit of the various States an exhibition hall on Ellis Island for the products of the States, showing the desirability of the different localities for immigrants?—A. Nothing.

Q. What is your opinion about the recommendation?—A. As a member of the commission I signed my name to the report; but I am somewhat skeptical, in view of my subsequent investigations, as to whether it would be a mistake or not. I think it would be an experiment, at best.

Q. Do you see anything practical in this scheme?—A. The scheme is plausible in theory, but I think it would be difficult to work out in practice.

IMMIGRATION.

Q. Do you desire now to present those amendments?—A. Yes. It would take a long while to read them, and they will speak for themselves in the printed report.

Q. You might read them, making a running commentary on the matter as you proceed, so that the reader of the testimony will understand the reasons for whatever change or amendment may be suggested to the present laws.—A. The first suggestion was: "That in addition to conforming to all present requirements of law, all transportation companies engaged in transporting aliens to and from the United States shall be required to furnish to the Commissioner of Immigration, at the port of embarkation from the United States, lists or manifests, which shall, in answer to questions at the top of said lists or manifests, state as to each outgoing alien or passenger, the full name, age, sex, nationality, calling or occupation, whether he has ever declared his intention to become a citizen of the United States and whether he intends to ever return to the United States. That in the case of the failure of any transportation company to furnish to the Commissioner of Immigration, at the port from which such outgoing alien passengers embark from the United States, such lists or manifests containing the information above described, the said transportation company shall pay a fine of $10 to the collector of customs of said port, and the vessel of said transportation company shall be refused clearance from any port of the United States while said fine is unpaid."

The second is a suggestion which Colonel Clarke made as to prohibiting the sale of peddlers' tickets, "That the sale of prepaid ocean tickets or ticket orders or the soliciting of orders for tickets or ticket orders is hereby prohibited by any other than the duly authorized agents of the steamship lines, who shall have their authority as such agents posted in their offices, and the steamship lines shall furnish to the Commissioner of Immigration at the nearest port a list of such duly authorized agents; that the sale of any but regular tickets or ticket orders is also prohibited, and any person, company, or corporation who shall be guilty of violation of any of the provisions of this section shall, upon conviction, be fined not less than $100 and not exceeding $1,000, and shall stand committed until the said fine is paid."

Third. "That section 1 of the act approved March 3, 1891, be, and hereby is, amended by adding after the words 'contagious disease,' in the seventh line, the following words: 'Persons imported into the United States for the purposes of prostitution.'"

Fourth. "That section 11 of the act approved March 3, 1891, be, and hereby is, amended so as to read as follows: 'That any alien who shall come into the United States in violation of law may within 2 years thereafter, upon application of the Commissioner of Immigration at the port of arrival of such alien to the Secretary of the Treasury, be arrested upon a warrant from the Secretary of the Treasury and brought before the Commissioner of Immigration at the port of arrival, and given a hearing in accordance with the provisions of section 5 of the act approved March 3, 1891; and if the said alien shall be found to belong to the excluded classes he shall be deported to the country from which he came at the expense of the person or persons, transportation company or corporation bringing such alien into the United States, or if that can not be done, the said alien shall be deported at the expense of the United States. And any alien who becomes a public charge within 1 year after his arrival in the United States from causes existing prior to his landing therein shall be deemed to have come in violation of law, and shall be returned as aforesaid, and all the fines and penalties against the person or persons, transportation company or corporation bringing such alien to the United States shall apply as in other cases.'"

The fifth is to add a little more stringency to the contract-labor laws: "That section 1 of the act approved February 26, 1885, be, and hereby is, amended by adding thereto, after the words 'into the United States, its Territories, or the District of Columbia,' in the seventh line, the words, 'by any undertaking or promise of employment upon arrival in the United States.'"

The sixth is to give the right to immigration officials to administer oaths in taking testimony: "That the Commissioner-General of Immigration, commissioners, and assistant commissioners of immigration, immigrant inspectors, registry clerks and officials sitting as members of boards of special inquiry are hereby empowered to administer oaths and to take testimony orally or by depositions touching all matters and questions growing out of the proper administration of the United States immigration and alien contract-labor laws and their supplements."

Seventh. "That all aliens who may unlawfully come into the United States shall if practicable be immediately sent back on the vessel by which they were brought in, or by a vessel belonging to or controlled by the same line, company, or owners upon the final disposition of their cases. Should, however, there be no such vessel sailing within a reasonable time, then they shall be returned by a vessel belonging to some other line, company, or owners. The cost of their maintenance while on land as well as the expense of return of such aliens shall be borne by the line, company, consignees, or owners of the vessel on which said aliens came, and if any master or officer in charge of said vessel belonging to said line, company, consignees, or owners refuse to receive back on board one of these vessels such alien, and give to the immigration official in charge of such alien a receipt for such alien, together with an undertaking to comply with the terms of this section, or shall neglect to retain them thereon, or shall refuse or neglect to return them to the country whence they came, or to pay the cost of their deportation to the country whence they came by a vessel other than that belonging to the line, company, or owners which brought them, they shall be fined not less than the sum of $300 for each and every offense, and any vessel belonging to said line, company, or owners shall be refused clearance from any port of the United States while said fine is unpaid."

All privilege moneys now received from the restaurant and other things go into the general fund of the Treasury Department, and it is proposed: "That all moneys received from privileges and benefits, all fines and penalties, and all moneys collected from any source whatsoever growing out of the administration and enforcement of the immigration laws shall be paid into the immigration fund, created by the act entitled 'An act to regulate immigration,' approved August 3, 1892."

Dr. Senner, while commissioner, made the discovery that some of the immigrants were counted as many as 10 times, and that in a total of 17,000,000 or 18,000,000 of immigrants there are thousands and thousands that are counted as many as 5 times possibly; so that we ask in this law: "That all transportation companies engaged in transporting aliens to and from the United States shall require every alien who desires to take passage to the United States to fill in a blank form containing all the questions to be answered in the lists or manifests as hereinbefore prescribed by law and the following additional questions: 'Has the intending immigrant been in the United States before? If so, how many times? How much money did he bring each time? How much money did he carry back each time? Does his family accompany him? If not, has he a family in Europe, and how many constitute this family? Does he intend to send for his family later? Is any member of his family likely to be excluded by the immigration laws of the United States? If so, why? Has he any property in Europe? If so, what is its value?' That the said immigrant shall bind himself to the truth of all his statements and take an oath thereto, attested by his signature, if requested to do so by an immigrant inspector, and shall further state that he knows that he will be returned if his answers are found to be false in any substantial particular. That the said forms when filled in shall be delivered to the steamship company, whose duty it shall be to deliver the same to the Commissioner of Immigration at the port of landing. Provided that this statement made by the immigrant shall in nowise relieve the transportation company from any responsibility for bringing undesirable immigrants to the United States. And for each and every violation of any of the provisions of this act the transportation company so violating shall be fined the sum of $100, and any vessel belonging to the said transportation company shall be refused clearance from any port of the United States while said fine remains unpaid."

Tenth. We suggest that the words "if $30 or less" in the original law shall be stricken out, and that we be empowered to ask how much money they have. We can not legally ask how much more than $30 they have. A man says he has more than $30, but we can not ask how much more. We put down $30 and he may have $1,000, and we lose that statistical information. We suggest "that section 1 of the act approved March 3, 1893, be, and hereby is, amended as follows: Add in line 12, after the words 'or Government' the following words 'and if so, by whom;' strike out in the 12th and 13th lines the following words, 'whether upward of $30, and how much if $30 or less,' and substitute the following words, 'how much.'"

Eleventh. "That so much of section 1 of the act approved August 3, 1882, as reads as follows: 'Provided that no greater sum shall be expended for the purposes hereinbefore mentioned at any port than shall have been collected at such port be and hereby is repealed."

Twelfth. "That the lists or manifests of incoming vessels shall contain the exact number of passengers on board, and if after all the names of the passengers have been properly entered thereon there shall remain any unfilled spaces for names, the same shall be crossed out with lines, and after all the lists or manifests are so prepared they shall be verified by the signatures and oaths of the master and surgeon of the said vessel, and thereafter it shall be unlawful for any alteration or erasure or other defacement to be made thereon, and for every violation of this section the person, or persons, company, or corporation owning the said vessel shall be fined the sum of $100, and the said vessel shall not be granted clearance from any port of the United States while said fine is unpaid."

Thirteenth. "That debarred immigrants shall be returned to the country from whence they came; provided, however, that those who come in transit to contiguous territory shall be returned to the country in which they were last resident."

Fourteenth. We have found that when we send back immigrants suffering from diseases, or as likely to become a public charge, or as paupers, or as contract laborers, if the steamship company finds that they have money and can get control of that money, they will take enough to reimburse themselves for their passage back, although the theory of the law is that the steamship company shall be responsible for the passage back; so we have provided that it shall be unlawful to take any return money for their back passage. We suggest: "That it shall be unlawful for any transportation line, person, company or corporation engaged in the transportation of aliens to and from the United States, to collect directly or indirectly from any debarred immigrant the expense of returning him or his belongings, and for each and every violation of this section shall pay a fine of $100, and no vessel of the line committing such violation shall be granted clearance from any port of the United States while said fine remains unpaid."

Fifteenth. "That section 4 of the act approved March 3, 1893, be, and hereby is, amended so as to read as follows: 'That in the case of the failure of said master or commanding officer of any vessel to deliver to the said inspector of immigration lists or manifests, verified as aforesaid, containing the information above required as to all alien immigrants on board, the person, company, or corporation owning the vessel shall pay to the collector of the port of arrival the sum of $10 for each person concerning whom the above information is not contained in any list or manifest as aforesaid, without prejudice to the standing of the immigrant, and any vessel belonging to the said person, company, or corporation shall be refused clearance from any port in the United States while said fine is unpaid. Provided, that the commissioner of immigration at the port of arrival may in his discretion remit said fine if it should appear to him that the error was committed without the knowledge or consent of the steamship company, or was unavoidable and not due to neglect or intent to deceive."

Sixteenth. The next is the most important of all, and provides that false testimony before the board of special inquiry can be punished as perjury. In our practice now there is no hindrance to any immigrant or any witness making any sort of a statement, and doing it with safety and impunity, and we believe that if a law be given us which will make that perjury within reasonable bounds so that we can punish them, it will put the immigration laws on a better footing. We suggest: "That false testimony given under oath before the board of special inquiry in behalf of detained immigrants, made willfully and for the purpose of inducing the admission of a detained immigrant, shall constitute perjury; and if any person or persons shall knowingly or wilfully procure such perjury to be committed every person so offending shall be deemed guilty of subornation or perjury, and shall, on conviction, be fined not exceeding $100, or be imprisoned not exceeding five years, or both, according to the aggravation of the facts. That if any person or persons shall wilfully and knowingly make a false affidavit as to his financial responsibility as a surety upon a bond or undertaking given for the purpose of inducing the admission of an immigrant he shall be deemed guilty of perjury, and shall be, on conviction, punished by a fine not exceeding $1,000, or by imprisonment not exceeding five years, or both, according to the aggravation of the facts."

Seventeenth. As I said before, the registry clerk has the right to admit, and does admit over 85 out of every 100. The commissioner has no right in law to stop that. If the board of special inquiry should decide to allow an immigrant to come in there is no power with the commissioner to say no. It is proposed to give the commissioner that power, subject to review by the Secretary of the Treasury. We suggest: "That the commissioners of immigration be, and hereby are, empowered to temporarily suspend execution of decision of boards of special inquiry, subject to the final decision of the Secretary of the Treasury."

Eighteenth. "That any person or persons found to be guilty of 'coaching' or assisting immigrants to evade or falsely answer inquiries made of them upon inspection shall be deemed guilty of a misdemeanor, and shall be fined $100 and stand committed until the said fine is paid."

Nineteenth. "That in addition to the excluded classes already established by law, boards of special inquiry are hereby empowered to exclude from admission such aliens as appear to them to be suspicious or disreputable characters, suspected convicts, anarchists, or persons unfit to be admitted to the United States, unless the said person or persons shall establish for themselves, or through their friends, a good reputation."

Q. (By Mr. FARQUHAR.) The intention of that is to make the immigrant give the proof?—A. To throw the burden of proof on him. Now we can not send him back unless we can prove he is likely to become a public charge. Under such an amendment we could say to a suspicious or disreputable person: "You must prove your reputation; otherwise you will be debarred."

Twentieth. "That it shall be lawful to take the testimony in a summary manner of an immigrant ordered to be deported, after giving a short but reasonable notice to the party charged with inducing him to migrate in violation of the alien contract laws; and the parties so charged shall have the right to appear in person or by counsel and cross-examine a witness; the testimony thus taken may be used as evidence in any action instituted, or to be instituted, to punish the person so charged, and to have the same effect as if the witness had so testified in open court."

Twenty-first. "That boards of special inquiry, by and with the sanction of the commissioner of immigration at the port of arrival, may in their discretion admit conditionally into the United States such persons as intend to settle here and later on to bring their families here; and within one year thereafter, upon the arrival of their families, it shall be the duty of the board of special inquiry to reopen the case of such immigrant conditionally landed and take into consideration the admission of the whole family in the same manner as if all of them had arrived at the same time, and to admit or deport any or all of them, including the 1 conditionally landed, according to the immigration laws governing excluded classes."

I presume a good many of these things will fail to receive the sanction of Congress, but they will do away with difficulties that we have. A man, as I have said, comes in and says, "I am all right, but my family and six children are on the other side." The immigration authorities should have the right to say, "Are they all right; is there anything the matter with them?" "No; they are all well." "You appear to be responsible and eligible. Are you willing in case we admit you, and your family comes in and is found to be, one an idiot and another consumptive, to go back with them?" That is the point we wish to bring to your consideration.

Q. What are your suggestions in respect to a recodification of the immigration laws?—A. I believe that we are in the same position exactly that the United States was before the Revised Statutes were put into effect, and if we could codify all the laws and add to them only so far as to make the present theory of the law effective, we could go into the courts and do what the general public supposes we can do. The general public supposes the Contract Labor Bureau has absolute power to restrict contract labor and go into the courts to punish the contractors. I believe in such codification of the laws as practical experience has found necessary.

Q. (By Mr. CLARKE.) Do you understand that a person who brings another here under contract to perform labor for him can not be punished in our courts under the present law?—A. We find it exceedingly difficult. Dr. Ullo has found great difficulties in court.

Q. Have you made any investigation with reference to immigration and crime?—A. Somewhat, yes.

Q. Have you reported it to the Commissioner of Immigration?—A. Mr. Fitchie has, yes. I have made that investigation, and have been assisted by Dr. Safford, of our medical division.

Q. Do you know whether that will be embraced in his next annual report?—A. I do not.

Q. If not, can you furnish it to this commission?—A. I should think Mr. Powderly could. It is within his province now.

Q. I would like to ask you whether the census of 1890 investigated, in regard to criminals, those who were children of foreign-born parents?—A. It did. Professor Wines has a special report on that subject.

Q. In your opinion, has that investigation been carried far enough to fairly indicate the relation of criminality to immigration?—A. I think the special question of immigration and crime would merit the fullest investigation, which it has not received.

Q. (By Mr. FARQUHAR.) As you have examined that question, what have you to say with reference to the testimony here this morning that the more intelligent immigrants are most apt to form the criminal classes in this country?—A. Certain classes, yes; but there are special crimes which I think are positively established as the result of the introduction of foreign peoples into our country; certain classes of crimes which are now becoming prevalent.

Q. Do you think immigrants from the more intelligent nations of the Old World are more apt to commit crimes than those from the south of Europe?—A. I think they commit different classes of crimes. There is always the fear, in making that comparison of immigrants of confusing with the good immigrants those who are forced out of their own country because of their criminal habits, and they come in force here and increase the average, and we must, in making any fair comparison, take that into account. But the matter is one that it seems to me is vitally important in this connection, that the moral dangers from immigration are equally, if not much more pressing than the economic dangers.

(At this point the examination of Mr. McSweeney was suspended, and was resumed at 10 a. m., July 26, 1899.)

Q. (By Mr. SMYTH.) Are all the questions on the ships' manifests uniformly answered in full, so far as you know?—A. They are answered in full, but the last 4 questions are answered generally—all in the same tenor. The immigrant's health is generally reported good, and there seems to be very little attention paid to it. The last 4 or 5 questions are always answered pro forma.

Q. Are these manifests common to all the shipping lines?—A. Yes.

Q. Mediterranean, continental, and British?—A. Yes. In this connection I suggest that the character of the paper and the character of the writing material now used will make these manifests absolutely valueless in less than 10 years; and these are among the most important records the country has. I think some legal requirement ought to be made as to the quality of the paper and ink. In many of our ships the paper falls to pieces before it is handled by our officers, and the ink is of all sorts. There should be some legal requirement to protect these very valuable statistics.

Q. How many interpreters have you at the Barge Office?—A. About 20 all together; men who are conversant with all sorts of languages.

Q. How many languages are spoken?—A. We speak every language that comes in with the exception of 1 or 2 of the Slavish dialects. We have not a good interpreter in Lithuanian, for instance, but we can always get one, because in the railroad department or in some of the other departments there are always men who can fill these breaches.

Q. How about the Arabian?—A. We had up to a month ago 3 Oriental interpreters, but 1 was discharged about 2 weeks ago, and I understand the discharge of another is pending, so it leaves us 1. We have 1 Oriental at present.

Q. You think you have ample provision; immigrants can communicate their ideas to a competent party who can communicate with you?—A. As to the races which come in, the German, Yiddish, and Italian languages are spoken in the bureau, and we all have a smattering of all of them, so we are pretty well provided; but there are expert interpreters in almost every language with which we have to deal.

NEW YORK, N. Y., *July 25, 1899.*

TESTIMONY OF MR. GUSTAV H. SCHWAB,

Agent, North German Lloyd Steamship Company, New York City.

At a meeting of the Subcommission on Manufactures and General Business, held in New York City, July 25, 1899, Chairman Smyth presiding, Gustav H. Schwab appeared at 11.15 a. m., and, being duly sworn, testified concerning immigration as follows:

Q. (By Mr. SMYTH.) What is your place of residence?—A. 31 West Forty-seventh street, New York City; place of business, 5 Broadway.

Q. What is your business?—A. Member of the firm of Oelrichs & Co., agents of the North German Lloyd Steamship Company.

Q. How long have you been in that business?—A. Twenty-three years.

Q. If you can give us any information or have any statements you would care to make with reference to the immigration law and its rulings we would be glad to hear from you, and after that we will ask you questions.—A. I would like to preface what I have to say by saying the representatives of the foreign steamship lines are nearly all citizens of the United States and reputable merchants, and whatever opinions they have they believe they represent as citizens. What I shall have to say will be from the standpoint of an American citizen. We do not wish to disassociate these two. The foreign steamship lines on the other side are managed by directors who are the foremost business men of their respective cities, and also desire to comply with the laws of this country and forward the interests of this country, because they take a high view of things and do not wish to send their steamers here for the purpose of throwing upon this country a mass of immigrants that can not be assimilated and should not properly come. We believe, the steamship companies, that the immigration laws as they exist at present are certainly carried out most efficiently at this port and at the other ports equally well. As to the laws themselves, while I suppose they could be amended and improved in some particulars, I believe they represent the right principle, and that is this: As far as the steamship lines are concerned, they are held responsible for the passenger. For instance, if a passenger on landing here is found in any way not to conform to the requirements of the law, that passenger is returned by the same steamship line. If the line has made a mistake, it is ready to take him back. Through their agents on the other side they exercise a careful scrutiny of every passenger who comes to them for passage. They have instructed their agents and given them a full statement of the laws as they exist in this country and the various objections that are made to immigrants, and they require these laws to be complied with. They give to the Secretary of the Treasury, as required by law, a statement showing that their agents are informed. It is given every 6 months, I believe. That I hold to be the right principle; to hold the steamship companies responsible for the people they bring, and oblige them to investigate the passengers, and if they make a mistake to send them back. I believe that such an investigation is far more valuable than any consular inspection such as has been proposed. I hold that to be absolutely impracticable, and I believe the investigation through the steamship lines is more thorough. We have only a few consuls in the countries the immigrants come from. I believe in Hungary we have only one consul, a country from which as high as 30,000 immigrants have come in one year. Manifestly it is impossible for that consul to investigate the antecedents of the immigrant properly. The agent of the steamship company, who is resident in the country, is the man to hold. The steamship companies not only have their instructions to their agents to carefully examine any passenger in the light of the law, but they also hold the agents responsible; at least our company does. If the passenger is returned, it is at the expense of the agent who booked him. Now, where a man's pocket is affected you can probably have more control over him than in any other way. I believe that this control, through the steamship companies, of their agents in booking passengers is the most reliable one. It is more satisfactory, it seems to me, to the immigration authorities than any other investigation on the other side could possibly be. Aside from this fact, it is problematical whether the investigation of passengers on the other side would be permitted by the foreign government, if carried out by the United States Government, whereas now the investigation is carried out by private persons.

In suggesting any changes in the present law, I would like to state that I hardly have had an opportunity to carefully consider the present law as to the features in which it might be improved. It has always seemed to me that the contract-labor law could be improved in this particular, that it now does not hold the employer in this country who sends for the contract laborer, but it visits the whole wrath of the law on the unfortunate laborer who comes here absolutely ignorant of the United States law, and does not hold the employer himself, who is the man to be held by right. I suggest that an improvement ought to be made in that way.

Then, I have learned of some suggestions as to the extension of the time during which a man should be here, from 1 to 2 years or even longer; also an increase in the head money. I would say, as far as that is concerned—I do not attempt to speak for all the steamship companies—that in whatever is deemed wise and reasonable and proper for the protection of this country, I think you will find the steamship lines will acquiesce. Of course, I believe it would be a mistake to raise the head money to an inordinately high figure, say $5 to $10; it would be prohibitory. In other words, you prohibit all immigration except of those who can afford to pay the $5 or $10. As I take it the principle to be followed in the matter of immigration is the question of whether a man is capable and willing to work, is honest, and will make a good citizen. Now, whether he is going to bring in here $30, $50, or $100 is of minor importance compared to whether he will develop into a good citizen for the country; that is entirely left out of sight if the plan of a high head tax is introduced or a high money qualification.

As to the question of illiteracy—educational test: That strikes one quite favorably on first contemplation, but there, also, you must remember that you not only prohibit the admission of a large number of people who are absolutely necessary in this country for the development of the natural resources of the country, but you commit an injustice by adopting such a measure as that. I do not know that you have had an opportunity of investigating the prison returns in the various cities, but it is certainly a most startling fact that those countries whose immigrants into this country are most literate show the largest percentage of prison commitments and jail commitments for vagrancy, drunkenness, etc. I refer to such States as New York, Pennsylvania, New Jersey, and Illinois, where you have a large number of immigrants coming from countries such as Italy, Austria, Hungary, Russia—those which are said to send us the worst immigrants. I would earnestly commend a study of these statistics. You will find them most startling. It is shown that illiteracy has nothing to do, as far as these statistics would seem to show, with crime.

There is another thing that has been quite surprising to me, and that is the statements that were made by a number of gentlemen—I believe one gave testimony before you in Washington—with reference to the reduction in wages. Now, if you will investigate the matter, I believe you will find that within the last 25 years, during which a large immigration has come into this country, wages have actually risen. There is not a single occupation in which wages have not risen in the last 25 years, and that, taken together with the enormous decrease in the cost of living in the last 25 years, which was obtained by the large immigration enabling us to produce things and create more cheaply, seems to me to show that labor has rather gained than suffered by the large immigration to this country.

I believe that the present laws are ample to protect this country. Whatever further improvements are deemed wise and seem to be agreed upon by all—the general consensus of opinion—the steamship lines will cheerfully acquiesce in anything that promotes the welfare of the country. They believe the immigrant that comes into this country now is absolutely needed. Construction work on highways, sewers, etc., is done by the Irish, Hungarians, and Italians as the Americans advance in intelligence and better their condition. We could not get them to work on these more or less brutal tasks, which are attended to by these lower classes that come in. I do not think it would be best to go back to the old conditions. It is merely a question of modern improvement.

Q. We have had testimony in Washington that the steamship lines issued circulars to their agents with reference to inducing immigrants to come to this country. Have you some circulars that your company has issued in the past you could give us?—A. I could only say in regard to that, that no steamship line that I am familiar with would be guilty of doing such a thing, nor would any country from which these lines come, and in which they are domiciled, permit such a thing to be done. The countries of Germany, Italy, Austria, France, and, I believe, also of England and Scandinavia, all have very stringent laws prohibiting the inciting to emigration from those countries, for the reason that these countries are all dependent on the young emigrants for their armies. That also is sufficient inducement for them to exercise a more stringent inspection of emigrants leaving their countries. They go so far as to permit only certain licensed agents to exercise the trade of emigration agent, and these licenses are paid for with a very high fee and subject to revocation at any time. We have had any number of agents in former years who have tried to send out circulars to people they thought would emigrate, and who have had their licenses revoked without any mercy. It is absolutely impossible, in my opinion, for the steamship companies and agents to incite to emigration on the other side. It can not be done; not even to invite.

Q. The statement that agents have in foreign countries employed subagents to induce emigration is a mistake?—A. Entirely wrong. Of course, they have subagents to sell tickets in various cities, but they are all subject to the laws of the country, which are carried out very stringently.

Q. Is the carrying of immigrants a very lucrative part of your business?—A. It was in former years. I consider that the cabin business has assumed greater proportions and more importance with a number of the lines. The cabin business has increased in much greater proportion than the steerage business. We calculate the increase in cabin about 10 per cent a year on the average.

Q. How does the steerage rate compare with the rate of, say, 10 years ago?—A. The steerage rate at present is very much higher than it was 10 years ago. That is due to an agreement of the lines among themselves.

Q. Which is being carried out in good faith?—A. Yes.

Q. What percentage of increase since 1880?—A. I do not remember what the rate was.

Q. Can you give it in figures?—A. I should say the rate is now probably fully 50 per cent higher than in 1880. That is a rough guess.

Q. What is the rate to-day?—A. We have two classes of steamers. One is the

the so-called express steamer, and the rate is $38.50 in steerage from Europe. The rate of the slower steamers is $36.50 to New York from Bremen. That is about 50 per cent higher than in 1880 at a rough guess.

Q. Have you had many of your immigrants rejected at the port of New York and returned on account of having contagions or loathsome diseases?—A. There has been a certain number rejected. I do not think we have had a large number rejected.

Q. Do you know of any case in which such rejected immigrant has been returned on a subsequent or the same ship of the company?—A. I know of no case on our line.

Q. Your board of directors on the other side has never considered that such a passenger should be admitted and sent him back?—A. They would never think of such a thing. Speaking of the circulars sent out by the lines on the other side, I would like to hand you here a circular to agents issued in this country, on which you will find instructions to agents giving the classes that are prohibited and not to be booked. You are probably not familiar with the fact that so-called prepaid tickets are a feature in the business of the steamship companies of great importance. By prepaid tickets is understood a ticket bought in this country for passage from the other side; that is, a ticket that takes the place of money, as it were. It is a ticket bought in this country by a man who has come over here, worked here, and accumulated a fund, and to bring his folks from the other side, sends them a ticket for the passage. This is a very large business, and it is to that business that must be ascribed either the increase or decrease in immigration. Of the whole immigration into this country about 60 per cent is due either directly to prepaid business or such business as is brought in with the prepaid passenger.

Q. That is, assisted immigration?—A. That is assisted immigration of the right kind. The prepaid ticket is sent to John Smith in some village of Germany, and the whole village knows he has a ticket from his brother to come over; that he is working on a farm, not subject to military duty, paying very little taxes, and generally thinks he is in a pretty good country and would like his brother to come. His brother tells all his friends and neighbors, and he brings with him 2, 3, or 4 men coming over to this country they have heard of. So this prepaid business is of immense importance, and that is the barometer, as it were, of business. For instance, if we have had bad times in this country, prepaid business falls off; where 100 are usually sold in a day only 25 or 30 will be sold. If the immigrant is poor the immigration falls off. Immigration is induced by the condition of things in this country, the condition of the labor market, agriculture, and business generally; upon that depends immigration absolutely and entirely. Nothing else in the last 10 or 15 years has induced immigration from the other side.

Q. In such periods of depression as you speak of, there is really a return of immigrants to the other country?—A. Yes; that is a fact. The list of persons who return from this side increases. Our steerage list shows very much larger numbers in times of depression than in times when everything is prosperous and business doing well.

Q. Have you any way of telling whether immigrants come over for a brief season and then return—birds of passage?—A. Hardly to the north. I do not know but that may apply—to some extent to the Italian.

Q. (By Mr. CLARKE.) I suppose you are aware that formerly large landowners in this country, whether individual or corporate, exerted themselves in Europe to induce immigration?—A. Yes.

Q. Is that practice kept up now?—A. As far as I am informed that has entirely disappeared. In former years the railroads did a very large work in that direction, especially the land-grant railroads, and corporations also; but I have not heard of anything of that kind being done in the last 10 or 15 years.

Q. The class of people in this country who send over there for their friends is generally in favor of immigration, and would be opposed to restricting immigration?—A. I suppose so; undoubtedly.

Q. So that if Congress should undertake to prohibit immigration entirely for a period of time it would probably incur the opposition of this class of people?—A. Oh, yes; undoubtedly; and cause a great deal of hardship also.

Q. And therefore your agents abroad, while being careful to have our laws complied with, notwithstanding work chiefly in the interests of the steamship company—I mean to say you go as near the limits of the law as you safely can so as to bring an immigrant?—A. I think I will have to correct that. The companies on the other side, I believe, judging from our experience, are apt to err. They wish always to leave a safe margin. We have frequently had cables inquiring whether it would be wise to take a certain family that has applied, and has, we will say, a child or a person that might possibly come under the prohibitory classes. As Mr. McSweeney will confirm, we frequently apply to him as to whether we can safely carry such persons, and our company usually decides not to bring them.

Q. Your interest, you think, is in favor of rather excessive caution than the other way?—A. I think so. That is the way the system works.

Q. How would it do to have some United States Government immigration agents to make a careful inquiry in cooperation with your steamship agents?—A. I think that would involve such an enormous expense that it would practically not be feasible. You would have to have practically an agent of the United States, an immigration agent, by the side of everyone of our agents.

Q. The steamship companies would not object to it, I suppose?—A. I think they would probably welcome it, for they would have someone on whom the responsibility could be placed and have the matter settled there; but I doubt very much if that would be feasible.

Q. In reference to head money, that is exacted from only the first and second class passengers?—A. No; from all alien passengers, whether they come in steerage or cabin. Of course, we are obliged to depend on the statements of cabin passengers as to whether they are aliens or United States citizens.

Q. Do you not think it would be an advantage to increase that, even for the sake of revenue?—A. I do not like to express an opinion on that. I do not know if it would be necessary. Probably the immigration officials are more capable of expressing an opinion as to whether it is needed. If it is absolutely necessary, the steamship lines would acquiesce in anything reasonable.

Q. Is this head money paid by the steamship company?—A. Yes.

Q. And added to the fare of the passenger?—A. It is in a certain way. It is not added directly. The steamship companies of course fix their rates, including all expenses they have to pay. I presume the rate of fare would be increased by that much if the head money was increased, so it would ultimately fall on the passenger. It is one of the items of cost.

Q. Do you not think a moderate increase of that head tax would tend to improve the quality of the immigrants?—A. No; I do not think so.

Q. If there is any assisted immigration, I suppose it would not help that, as the people would put up more money if necessary?—A. I have not heard of any assisted immigration for a number of years.

Q. (By Mr. SMYTH.) Except in the way of prepaid tickets?—A. That we do not call assisted immigration; that is regularly prepaid business.

Q. It is assisted?—A. It is a ticket presented to a relative on the other side, yes. I have recently observed a statement of the enormous revenues to the steamship lines from the passenger business, and also as to the cost of transporting business. This morning I ran over the reports of the North German Lloyd for the last 20 years, and I find the average dividend paid in the last 20 years was 5 per cent, and the shares are now quoted at 119 and 120. That does not show that it is such an enormously lucrative business.

Q. Of course there is a great depreciation in the steamers?—A. Yes; certainly.

Q. (By Mr. FARQUHAR.) Are you practically acquainted with the manner of inspection on the other side, medical inspection?—A. I am to a certain extent.

Q. Have you been present while the inspection was made?—A. I know that our company has a doctor, who is detailed and paid for the purpose of examining all emigrants before they embark, and if there are any cases coming from suspected districts, such as the south of Russia, where there is a great deal of smallpox, they are kept in control stations. Our company has at present 7 control stations which have been established and maintained with its own means, together with those of the Hamburg-American, and, I believe, the Red Star Line. They are located near the frontier between Prussia and Russia. They are established for the purpose of passing through them all emigrants intended for this country, coming from south Russia. I will read this: (Reading.)

"The North German Lloyd Steamship Company now offer to immigrants from Russia the use of its control stations established on the Russo-German frontier at Bajohrem, Eydtkuhnen, Prostken, Illowo, Ottlotschin, Tilsit, and Insterburg."

The other steamship companies contribute to their maintenance, though they are practically owned by the North German Lloyd. (Continuing to read.)

"These control stations, built and owned by the North German Lloyd, are completely equipped for the comfort and convenience of its passengers. Each of them is under the supervision of a competent manager, and is provided with the necessary sleeping and living rooms, with bathrooms, steam-heating arrangements, and restaurants. A practicing physician and a force of male and female attendants are attached to each of them, and they are under the continual control of the Imperial German Government and have received official approval.

"In these control stations emigrants from Russia, intending to take passage in the steamers of the North German Lloyd Company are examined as to their compliance with the requirements of the United States immigration laws, bathed, and their baggage disinfected for the sum of 2 marks (50 cents) each person, after which they receive a certificate that entitles them to continue their journey to the port of departure."

These stations are in some cases 24 hours by rail east of Bremen, and they have to continue their journey 24 hours to reach the port of departure. I believe the Rotterdam line is interested in these control stations, besides the 3 I have mentioned.

It is well known that most of these contagious diseases come from the south of Russia, and countries where cleanliness is not very great.

Q. You have also local inspection at the port of embarkation?—A. There is a local medical inspection at the port of departure.

Q. On board ship?—A. No; on land. The port of Bremen is an inland port, situated 30 miles up the river Weser, and the river Weser is not navigable by the large steamers. Therefore, all emigrants, before they embark in Bremerhaven, are sent by train from Bremen to Bremerhaven and there put on board steamer. Before they leave Bremen, in the railway station there is a special station arranged for these emigrants, where they are ticketed, have their baggage attended to, and are examined by the physicians. I think there are 2, at least 1, paid by our line for the purpose of examining and disinfecting passengers. If there are any persons who are at all suspicious, they are quarantined in Bremen and kept there until developments show whether they prove to be harmless.

Q. Is there any medical inspection made on board the steamers before starting?—A. On our large steamers we have 2 doctors; on the small steamers 1. The medical inspection is carried out at least once a day.

Q. To comply with the United States regulations?—A. No; with our company's own regulations.

Q. In compliance with the law?—A. I do not recollect that the United States regulations call for any.

Q. Suppose you have 1,000 steerage passengers, how long does it take the medical inspector to pass on that 1,000 aboard ship at the gang plank?—A. If the weather is fine they are brought on deck and passed in that way, but very often, and probably generally in the fall and winter, that inspection has to be done below deck, and the doctor goes down and examines every passenger and sometimes in his bunk.

Q. Complaint has been made as to the insufficiency of that medical inspection on board ship on the part of the steamship's doctors. First of all, that it is hurriedly done; that there is not sufficient time given for anything like the proper inspection; and secondly, that the medical inspectors are not experienced surgeons and physicians, but mostly young graduates of medical colleges?—A. In relation to that I would say the inspection can take place through the whole day. The doctor has 24 hours, and at least 12 hours of daylight in which to make the inspection. To my knowledge the inspection has taken at least 2 or 3 hours, and it can, if desired, be made more minute. In most of our large steamers we have 2 doctors.

Q. (By Mr. SMYTH.) Does he inspect every immigrant, or only those who are sick?—A. They all pass.

Q. Every day?—A. Yes; it is his duty and prescribed by the company. Of course, you will understand in very stormy weather it is almost impossible at times to carry out an inspection of that kind. With reference to the character of the physician or surgeon, I will say it is true there are some physicians who are young, but the greater number of surgeons on board the transatlantic liners are men who have been in the service for a number of years. I recollect on the largest steamer on our line a doctor who has been in our service at least 15 if not 20 years as ship surgeon, and I remember one man who was in our service 30 years as surgeon. Of course, it is not possible to secure the services of physicians of a great deal of experience; a man who has a large practice on shore would never think of taking a position as ship surgeon. They are required to be physicians of experience, and those on our line must have passed the German medical examination, and that is a very rigid examination. We have applications daily from doctors in this country for positions as surgeons, but I am obliged to inform them that they can not be passed unless they have seen experience and have passed the German examination.

Q. (By Mr. FARQUHAR.) Is the examination of passengers on board ship in the character of the sick call of the army?—A. No; I do not think it can be compared with that, because it is to the interest of every steamship company and every captain to have his ship examined every day carefully to ascertain if there are contagious diseases on board. If we arrive here and have a case of smallpox on board, not detected by the physician as soon as it broke out, that ship is held in quarantine. The passengers are taken to Hoffman Island, and kept there at our expense at a cost of many thousands per day if the number is large. That is the interest that appeals to the steamship company's pocket, and they do not wish to incur anything of that kind. The strict injunction is given to examine every passenger every day to see if there are any possible signs of smallpox, cholera, or any contagious disease. Do not misunderstand me. We will only be too glad to introduce any improvements that can be introduced.

Q. Do you not think it would be an advantage to all the steamship companies and a great help here to the inspection service on this side of the Atlantic to make your examination at your ports of embarkation more rigid than they are at present?—A. I do, personally, yes; and I can give you the assurance that whatever I can do on my part will be exerted to comply with your wishes.

Q. (By Mr. CLARKE.) Who sell these prepaid tickets on this side?—A. The steamship companies and their agents.

Q. Are they in the hands of the railroad companies?—A. No. In some cases railroad companies are at the same time steamship companies; but in my experience in comparatively few cases.

Q. Are they sold by the railroad and steamship ticket brokers also?—A. Yes, in some few cases; generally by steamship agents who at the same time sell bills of exchange and money orders and do a general money business, but I think in very few cases by railroad agents. That applies to our own lines; possibly the other lines may have some other experience.

Q. You have no instructions to your agents as to the solicitation of this class of trade?—A. Nothing further than is contained in the circulars we have issued to them. That is hardly a business that could be solicited. For instance, an agent is in a small village in Wisconsin, and a farmer drives in from the country and buys a ticket. Among the farmers around there a man could not do a large soliciting business, it would not pay.

Q. The commission on the sale of these tickets is not very large?—A. I think it is $2 now.

Q. (By Mr. FARQUHAR.) Will you state the aims of this North Atlantic conference?—A. There are 3 conferences, North Atlantic, Mediterranean and Continental. They are solely for the purposes of trade and discussion of matters of general interest concerning all the lines.

Q. Do they discuss rates?—A. That is fixed by the various lines on the other side.

Q. (By Mr. CLARKE.) It is not in the nature of a trust?—A. No; it is not a trust.

Q. In the testimony given before us in Washington a statement was made that the steamship lines employed a very powerful and extensive lobby in Washington?—A. That is an absolute and unmitigated untruth; there is absolutely nothing in that. The steamship lines have maintained no lobby of any kind in Washington. The late Dr. Glavis was in Washington as a representative of the steamship lines, but he was never engaged as a lobbyist, and since his death the steamship lines are not represented in Washington, except by agents for the transaction of passenger business.

Q. (By Mr. FARQUHAR.) The general assertion was made some time ago in respect to a pool formed by all of the steamship companies between the United States and Europe. Was or is there such a pool or pooling arrangement with respect to steerage rates, or in your conference was such an arrangement considered?—A. Not in this country. There is an agreement on the other side with reference to rates and the general conduct of business.

Q. Has there been a division of European territory made to suit or accommodate the lines and ports the steamships enter?—A. You refer to the Continental conference. I have never heard of any; I do not think there is any. The ports are all open, except that the Continental conference does not book passengers in Italy, but leaves that to the Mediterranean conference.

Q. Is the French line in that conference?—A. It is not exactly a member. It accommodates itself and generally agrees to what is adopted.

Q. Whatever arrangements are made with respect to rates are made on the other side?—A. Yes.

Q. And the arrangements are merely business arrangements, not in the character of a trust or pool or syndicate or anything of that kind?—A. Oh, no.

Q. No control put into any board of officers?—A. The lines retain their individual control and management absolutely.

Q. So it is simply give and take, free trade, as is often done between parties in the same business?—A. They do control the rates. They agree on certain rates.

Q. Could you give us a reason why steerage rates have risen within the last 15 or 20 years, or have been increased 35 to 50 per cent?—A. It is probably due to the fact that wars have been avoided among the steamship lines, and there has been this agreement on the other side with respect to rates.

Q. On the other side they found that the competition was destructive of profits and expensive to carry through?—A. Yes.

Q. So it was for the restriction of competition, the competition in the matter of agencies, and at the same time to get a proper return in the steerage rate for the lessened immigration that occurred?—A. There is no combination of agents. Each line retains its own agents and all its outfit. It is simply an agreement with reference to rates, introduced to avoid competition, the same as railroads have had to enter into agreements with reference to rates. Otherwise they would cut each others' throats.

Q. With respect to section 11 of the act of March 3, 1891, which requires the guaranty on the part of the transportation companies to care for the immigrant for the space of 12 months, and provides that the immigrant may be deported by the same line, have you anything to say why that length of time should not be extended more than 12 months?—A. No; I have no opinion to express. The immigration officials, I think, would be more competent to express an opinion. I do not know how many we have taken back that have been here more than 6 months. However, if it is decided that it is wise to extend it to 2 years—

Q. (By Mr. SMYTH.) (Interrupting.) You would not consider it a hardship?—A. We would consider it a hardship, but would agree to it.

Q. Would it lead to a rise in steerage rates?—A. I doubt that.

Q. (By Mr. FARQUHAR.) Do you know what the system is in the Australian colonies—the length of time of guaranty?—A. No; I am not familiar with that.

Q. Suppose it was for 5 years, and that a bond should be entered into in the sum of $2,500?—A. I think that would be a very long period of time—5 years. A great deal can happen in that time. Surely 2 years might be sufficient.

Q. Are there not a great many immigrants who neglect or refuse to become American citizens?—A. Really I am not familiar with that; I would not express an opinion on that.

Q. Provided that such a thing does occur, do you not think that it would be a matter of injustice to the United States to be compelled to take care of men and women who are in fact the subjects of a foreign nation and not American citizens?—A. I do not know that I am competent to express an opinion on that. As long as they are benefiting the country by their labor, it seems to me they have a certain amount of right to apply for the protection a government can give even if they are not citizens. That is my private opinion. I think if I had the control I should raise the time necessary to naturalization in this country. That seems to me to be of more importance than the restriction of immigration.

Q. If you raise the time of naturalization you debar these men from becoming citizens?—A. I should not permit it unless they knew the language and could read and could understand the Constitution of the United States. But I draw an absolute distinction between admitting these people to the country and admitting them to the franchise. A very great distinction should be drawn between the two.

Q. Do you not think it is quite a disadvantage to have foreign immigrants entering and maintaining their allegiance to the foreign country, and after being here 4, 5, 6 or 7 years, leaving to go back home and remain there?—A. I should say not, if they produce and contribute toward the welfare and advance of the country, which they undoubtedly do. I declare I should just as soon have them come in as to have cattle come in or brute labor force that we need in this country for the development of the country.

Q. They are largely in the lower grades of labor?—A. Yes. I should not admit them to citizenship unless they understood the English language. I do not believe we could have built the Pacific railroads if it had not been for the Chinese labor. If we had prohibited that labor, we would not have had any transcontinental railroads whatever. The Americans would not have built them.

Q. But on the question of guaranty you are free to say the steamship companies would cooperate even to the extension of another year?—A. I am speaking personally. I am not competent to bind the steamship lines. If it is considered wise and necessary to raise the time by the immigration officials, we should certainly not raise any objections.

Q. How about doubling the head money, temporarily at least, to meet the expense of rebuilding the depot, etc.?—A. We would rather not see the head tax advanced, but if it appears impossible to carry on the work of the immigration bureau here and at other ports without advancing the head tax, of course we would be obliged to submit.

Q. You think it fair that all expense attending immigration should be borne by the immigrant or the transportation company?—A. That is a question. As it is, we are accustomed to it; the fact is there, and I do not wish to raise the question.

Q. (By Mr. CLARKE.) Since the steerage rates of the different lines have been fixed by conference on the other side at what you call a reasonable figure, what restrained the conference from fixing them at a higher figure?—A. Well, no doubt the fact that if the prices advance too high it simply acts in a prohibitive way, or induces competition, one of the two. In the same way, for instance, that the rates are fixed for first and second cabin travel. Certain rates are fixed beyond which it is not considered judicious to go.

Q. This conference constituted a sort of temporary monopoly, but the monopoly was restrained by prudential considerations from abusing its power?—A. Yes; it would undoubtedly have called in competition if rates had been advanced too high.

LETTER AND INCLOSURES APPENDED TO MR. SCHWAB'S TESTIMONY.

NORTH GERMAN LLOYD STEAMSHIP COMPANY,
OELRICHS & CO., AGENTS,
New York, September 8, 1899.

WILLIAM E. SACKETT, Esq.,
Secretary Industrial Commission, Washington, D. C.

DEAR SIR: Pursuant to the request of the chairman of the subcommission of the Industrial Commission that heard testimony in this city some weeks ago on the subject of immigration, I take pleasure in sending you under separate cover a large number of circulars and letters of instruction addressed to agents and passengers and containing instructions with regard to the booking of emigrant passengers to this country.

These documents are in use by our company for their northern lines from Bremen to New York, Baltimore and Galveston, and for their Mediterranean service from Genoa and Naples to New York.

The documents that I send you are the following:

1. Circular to agents and passengers, containing on the reverse a reference to the United States immigration laws as to passengers who are not permitted to land in this country in use for the service from Genoa.
2. Circular of the same nature in use for the service from Naples.
3. Circular containing instructions with regard to the interdiction of cases of conjunctivitis, trachoma, etc., in use for the service from Naples.

The following letters of instruction, circulars, and tickets are in use for our company's service from Boston to New York, Baltimore, and Galveston.

4. Circular to agents containing the questions to be addressed to alien passengers.
5. Instructions addressed to agents with regard to the manifesting of cabin passengers.
6. Question blanks to be answered by cabin passengers.
7. Circular to agents with regard to exposing the United States laws with reference to immigration in such position that all persons can read them.
8. Circular to agents with regard to favus.
9. Circular to agents with regard to trachoma and conjunctivitis.
10. Circular to agents with regard to bringing to the attention of passengers the provisions of the United States laws on immigration.
11. Printed letters addressed to steerage passengers containing full reference to the excluded classes under the United States immigration laws.
12. Circular intended for passengers also containing reference to the excluded classes under the United States immigration laws.
13. Samples of tickets issued by the North German Lloyd containing on the face of the tickets in large type a reference to the classes excluded under the United States immigration laws.
14. Circulars to agents and passengers with regard to the examination of passengers before embarking on the steamers of the North German Lloyd for the United States.
15. Circular addressed by the agent of the North German Lloyd in Berlin, who has charge of the seven North German Lloyd control stations at which all immigrants from Russia and Austria are held for examination before being sent on to Bremen for embarkation. In this circular reference is again made to the classes excluded under the United States immigration laws.

16. Copies of the translation of the immigration laws of the United States into the various languages in use by the passengers of the North German Lloyd, namely, German, Polish, Hungarian, Bohemian, Slavonian, Italian, Dutch.

These documents are all of the latest editions, as you will observe. We have attached to those that do not explain themselves the translation of the particular passages referring to the United States immigration laws.

I have requested our friends in Italy to send me copies of the Italian emigration laws and expect to be able to send you a copy of these laws in a few weeks. The steerage passengers before embarkation in Genoa and Naples, but especially at Naples, where the largest number of Italian emigrants embark, are subject to an examination by a physician representing the Royal Italian Emigration Commission, by another physician engaged by our company, and whose specialty is the examination for favus and trachoma, by the United States medical inspector who is appointed for the examination of steerage passengers embarking at Naples, and by the steamship surgeon.

Trusting that the documents and the information given may be of some service to the commission, I am, my dear sir,

Yours, very truly, GUSTAV H. SCHWAB.

---

1. *Extract from circular to agents and third-class passengers, service from Genoa. Dated July 1, 1899.*

The law of February 26, 1891, prohibits the entrance into the United States of America—

1. Blind persons, lame persons, humpbacks, deaf-mutes, mutilated or deformed persons.
2. Women with infants who can not prove that they have been called there by relatives.
3. Unmarried woman, pregnant or with offspring.
4. Those afflicted with nauseous or contagious diseases.
5. Persons condemned for infamous acts or transgressions which imply moral turpitude, polygamists, persons under contract to labor, be the contract in writing, verbal, or self-understood.

N. B.—In case a passenger in a condition above enumerated would elude the authorities and embark, and upon his arrival at destination be debarred from landing, the agent or subagent who booked the passenger will be held for the return fare of £.155 in gold in addition to the loss of the passage money.

2. *Extract from circular to agents and third-class passengers, service from Naples. Dated August 1, 1899.*

The Government of the United States prohibits the landing at New York of idiots, insane persons, blind persons, cripples, deaf-mutes, persons afflicted with contagious diseases, persons condemned for infamous acts, polygamists, contract laborers, and persons unable to support themselves.

3. *Circular to agents, service from Naples, concerning contagious diseases. Dated October, 1898.*

To Subagents:

To our regret we observe that recently several emigrants bound for New York, in the act of embarking, have been prohibited to travel by the sanitary commission on account of contagious diseases with which they were afflicted.

This creates considerable loss to the passengers, who are then compelled to return at their own expense, or, the means to do so failing them, the expense falls upon us.

To eliminate such serious inconveniences we earnestly request your attention that before sending passengers here you will assure yourself of the perfect state of their physical condition, and, above all, that they are not afflicted with contagious diseases, such as **favus and diseases of the eye, conjunctivitis, trachoma**, etc.

We therefore request you strictly to observe our instructions and not to forward passengers afflicted with such diseases; otherwise, to our regret, we will hold you responsible for the consequences. In doubtful cases it is necessary that the passenger be provided with a certificate from the health board affirming that his disease is not contagious.

IMMIGRATION. 111

Also take note that all persons over 60 years of age must be furnished with an affidavit upon their arrival at New York, by which the relatives residing there guarantee to provide for and maintain the passengers at their own expense.
Respectfully,

THE EMIGRANT AGENT.

4. *Circular to agents, Bremen service, containing question blanks. Dated June, 1898.*

To our Agents:

The regulations of the new German emigration law and those for filling out the new receipts approved by the imperial chancellor to be used from now on do not imply a discontinuance of the American requirements as to the use of the question blanks.

With every steerage receipt a question blank must be filled out and attached to such question blank, in order that we may take the question blank so filled out from the passenger here for the preparation of the American lists.

5. *Question blank.*

Name in full
Age { years / months
Sex
Married or single
Calling or occupation
Able to { read / write
Nationality
Last residence
Seaport for landing in the United States
Final destination in the United States (State, city, or town)
Whether having a ticket to such final destination
By whom was passage paid
Whether in possession of money; if so, whether more than $30, and how much if $30 or less
Whether ever before in the United States; and, if so, when and where
Whether going to join a relative; and, if so, what relative, their name and address
Ever in prison or almshouse or supported by charity; if yes, state which
Whether a polygamist
Whether under contract, express or implied, to labor in the United States
Condition of health, mental and physical
Deformed or crippled, nature and cause

6. *Instructions to agents, Bremen service, as to manifestation of cabin passengers. Dated January, 1899.*

The United States Government in Washington has ordered that, in accordance with the law of March 3, 1893, all cabin passengers (I and II cabin) must answer the prescribed twenty questions, in the same way as steerage passengers. These answers are to be obtained by the agents when making out the passage orders, and to be entered on the forms intended for that purpose. This form and the passage order must be delivered by the passengers to us in Bremen.

The following cabin passengers need not be manifested:
1. Citizens of the United States.
2. Tourists (those who return to Europe after a short sojourn).
3. Transit passengers (those traveling through to Canada, Mexico, and Central America).

All such exceptions must be plainly noted on the passage orders as "U. S. citizen," "Tourist," or "Transit passenger."

Holders of American return tickets not American citizens (those who only have the so-called "first citizen's paper" are not citizens) must also answer the twenty questions.

Forms for the manifestation of cabin passengers are supplied upon demand.

7. *Circular to agents, Bremen service, as to displaying United States laws.* Dated June 30, 1899.

Referring to our circular of April 28, 1893, with which we sent you copies of the immigration act of the United States, and particularly to the section stating that "all agents must display a copy of this law, printed in large, legible type, in the language of their country, in their office, and must draw the attention of all intending passengers to this law before their departing," we request you to observe these laws strictly according to their provisions. Where necessary the above law must be translated into the local language.

Should the copies in your possession require replacing, kindly advise us and we will supply you with additional ones.

8. *Circular to agents, Bremen service, as to favus, etc.* Dated August 5, 1899.

We desire to call your attention to a recent decision of the Treasury Department of the United States of North America, according to which any steamer bringing passengers afflicted with contagious or loathsome diseases, such as favus, etc., will be prosecuted, and we urge you not to permit any passenger to embark who does not in every way satisfy the requirements of the United States Government in the above respect.

We request you to be guided by this circular and most carefully to see that no passenger is accepted who comes under the above heading, as we shall hold you responsible for any consequences that may arise.

9. *Circular to agents, Bremen service, regarding trachoma and conjunctivitis.* Dated May 16, 1899.

As it has recently repeatedly happened that the American immigration officers have returned steerage passengers on account of trachoma, whose cases have here been diagnosed as conjunctivitis, I would request you, at the desire of the North German Lloyd, to take particular pains that a thoroughly careful examination of all passengers be made. Persons afflicted with trachoma or any other dangerous disease of the eyes must under all circumstances be refused transportation, whereas in the case of slight diseases of the eyes which may be cured before the departure of the passenger from here, such passengers as are able to bear the expense of curing their maladies, which amounts to 20 marks, may be accepted for transportation. The North German Lloyd holds you responsible for the strict enforcement of this order.

Kindly acknowledge receipt of this circular.

12. *Notice appended to printed letter sent to applicants for steerage passage, Bremen service. (Form printed 1898.) Same also inserted in advertising circular.* Dated July, 1899.

TAKE NOTICE: According to the immigration act of the United States only those immigrants are permitted to land who are able to support themselves. Feeble-minded persons, idiots, cripples, lame persons, blind persons, deaf mutes, persons afflicted with contagious or incurable diseases, unmarried females when pregnant, unmarried females without means with their children, and criminals and convicts are not permitted to land. The American immigration authorities as a general rule demand health, sturdiness, ability and desirability to work, and respectable attire before giving permission to land to immigrants.

Attention is especially drawn to the fact that all persons who have, before embarkation, entered into a definite labor contract, or have otherwise tacitly obligated themselves to labor in the United States, will be unconditionally returned.

While the permission to land in America is not dependent upon the possession of any certain amount of money, the passengers are nevertheless advised to provide themselves with such funds aside from passage money. The immigration commissioners demand that cash money be produced by the immigrants.

13. Samples of tickets from Berlin to Baltimore and New York, containing on their face identically the above notice, and on the reverse side the question blank above quoted.

IMMIGRATION. **113**

14. *Circular to agents and passengers, Bremen service, as to excluded persons. Dated January 1, 1899.*

A law of the United States of America prohibits the immigration of the following persons:
1. Persons without means.
2. Persons afflicted with incurable disease.
3. Persons afflicted with contagious or loathsome diseases.
4. Cripples.
5. Aged, feeble persons.
6. Prostitutes.
7. Criminals.

All immigrants are most carefully examined on landing in the United States. All immigrants to whom the above applies, as also those who within a space of even two years after their landing may be found objectionable, are returned to their homes. It is, therefore, in the interest of the immigrants that they undergo a medical examination before embarking.

This medical examination takes place every evening, excepting Sundays, at the railway station of the North German Lloyd. Women, girls, and children are to appear at this station at 5.30 p. m., and men at 6.30 p. m., on the day of their arrival in Bremen. Every immigrant who has been examined medically is furnished with a certificate and no emigrant will be permitted to board the steamer without this certificate. Emigrants arriving in Bremen late on the evening preceding the day of departure of the steamer on which they are to be forwarded must appear one and one-half hours before the departure of the special train at the depot to receive their certificate. Emigrants who become ill on their way to Bremen, or after their arrival in Bremen, must await their cure before they can be forwarded to America.

15. *Circular to agents of the seven North German Lloyd central stations as to medical examinations there. Dated April 23, 1897.*

In a like manner as the German Government to protect the sanitary condition of Germany has given orders permitting only such foreign emigrants to pass through Germany as are perfectly healthy, have the steamship companies the greatest interest in preventing the embarkation of passengers who may be afflicted with contagious diseases. In view of the many hundred passengers who daily come in contact with each other on board the vessel it is necessary that even greater care be exercised for the ocean voyage than for the journey on land. The American Government conforms to these provisions of the German Government and of the steamship companies, but besides it considers whether the means of the immigrant to gain a livelihood are in any way impaired by physical infirmities. The examination of immigrants when landing in the United States is therefore a very thorough one. Aside from those who have become ill during the voyage every passenger who, on account of pimples, boils, or other skin eruptions, makes an unfavorable impression upon the immigration authorities is objected to and sent to a hospital for detention. Especially persons who are found to be afflicted with hair diseases, for example, existing or healed favus, regularly meet this fate, and are then later on generally returned to Europe as suffering with a loathsome disease.

The following persons are regarded as unsuitable for transportation:
1. Cripples.
2. Lame persons.
3. Blind persons.
4. Idiots.
5. Aged feeble persons.
6. Persons unable to support themselves.
7. Unmarried pregnant females.
8. Persons afflicted with contagious or loathsome diseases.
9. Persons afflicted with diseases of the head, hair, or eyes, whether such disease be curable or not.

Persons enumerated under the headings 1 to 7 may, however, embark if they can produce a certificate signed by the American immigration authorities, permitting their landing in America.

As for the remainder, however, the American immigration authorities exercise their own judgment as to whether the immigrant is to be regarded as admissible to the United States, and permit no one to land who, in their opinion, is afflicted with a loathsome disease or unable to support himself.

It is therefore the duty of our doctors, agents, and employees to see that such passengers as are not permitted to land in the United States are not accepted for transportation, especially at the control stations established by the German steamship companies for this purpose on the frontier between Germany and Russia and at Ruhleben.

The doctors at the control stations are therefore instructed not to give a certificate to anyone who according to the above list is not permitted to land in the United States, and the agents of the companies are requested not to sell tickets to such persons at all. In doubtful cases inquire of the respective steamship company, but under no circumstances must the passenger in question be permitted to depart before an answer is received from the steamship company. The principle is rather to refuse one passenger too many than forward a doubtful one.

16. *The tranlations of the American immigration laws of 1891 and 1893 into German, Polish, Hungarian, Bohemian, Slavonian, Italian, and Dutch give their provisions in full.*

17. *Summary of Italian emigration law of December 30, 1888.*

ARTICLE 1. Emigration is free aside from the obligations imposed upon citizens by the laws. Those subject to military service, whether in the permanent army or in the militia, can not emigrate unless they have obtained a permit from the minister of war.

ART. 2. No one can solicit emigrants or sell tickets without having received a certificate as agent from the ministry or a license as subagent from the prefect.

ART. 4. The grant of the certificate as agent is obtained upon a deposit or a guaranty of 3,000 to 5,000 lire.

ART. 5. The certificate is withdrawn whenever an agent has knowingly procured the departure or the emigration of criminals or of those who have escaped from prison or from penal colonies, or of minors destined to occupation included in the terms of the law of December 21, 1873.

ART. 6–69. Subagents are similarly responsible for violations of the law and agents are responsible for the acts of their subagents.

Article 12 of the ministerial regulations for the execution of the above law provides that the agent is prohibited from procuring the departure or the emigration of persons who are not permitted immigration into the States to which they are destined. It provides that the agent is bound to conform to the prescriptions which the minister may give for the protection of our emigrants in accordance with the provisions adopted by the Government of the States to which the emigrants are directed.

NEW YORK, N. Y., *July 25, 1899.*

TESTIMONY OF MR. JACOB TER KUILE,

Passenger Agent of Fabre Steamship Line, New York City.

At a meeting of the Subcommission on Manufactures and General Business held in New York, July 25, 1899, Chairman Smyth presiding, Jacob Ter Kuile appeared at 12 o'clock, and, being duly sworn, testified on the subject of immigration, as follows:

Q. (By Mr. SMYTH.) What is your residence?—A. I reside in Mont Vale, N. J.

Q. Your business?—A. Steamship passenger agent of the Fabre Line.

Q. If you have any suggestions or statements to make in the matter of immigration, we would be glad to hear from you, and then we will ask you some questions.—A. I think Mr. Schwab has made such a full statement, that as to general suggestions I can not add any.

Q. (By Mr. FARQUHAR.) Between what ports is your line?—A. Between Naples and New York.

Q. Have you copies of any circulars that you place in the hands of your foreign agents?—A. I have not.

Q. There are such circulars?—A. Yes, I will be glad to procure them and send to you.

Q. Do you know of any case on your line where an immigrant has been rejected at this or any port, for any cause, and then subsequently returned by your line?—A. No.

IMMIGRATION.

Q. How often do your steamers run?—A. We have a steamer about every fortnight.

Q. How many immigrants did you bring in last year?—A. The exact number was 12,110.

Q. Do you remember how many were rejected at this port?—A. I do not.

Q. (By Mr. CLARKE.) Are all of your immigrants aliens?—A. Nearly all of them.

Q. Are the agents whom you employ at Naples aliens?—A. Yes.

Q. Do you have any agents in other cities or towns of Italy?—A. Yes.

Q. What is the fare of the immigrant from Naples to New York?—A. Twenty-eight dollars.

Q. What was it in 1880?—A. We only commenced running in 1881. I think it was about $25 then.

Q. Have you any knowledge as to the percentage of prepaid tickets from this side?—A. We ticketed 6,700 last year.

Q. Nearly one-half of all you had?—A. Not quite that. I should think, on an average, from one-third to two-fifths.

Q. Is there considerable return of these immigrants on your line?—A. Quite a number are going back, but it seems to me it is diminishing from year to year. They used to flock back almost to the extent of one-half every fall, but I doubt if the proportion now exceeds one-quarter, if it is that.

Q. How do you account for that?—A. I presume they are getting more used to the country, and prefer to settle here. Eighteen years ago they came here perfect strangers, but now they know somewhat of the country through friends and relatives.

Q. (By Mr. FARQUHAR.) Of those returning to Italy, do they usually permanently settle in Italy, or are they what we generally call birds of passage?—A. I think they are apt to go back and come again, perhaps to settle. They are mostly young men who have tried to make some money and then go back to see the old folks; and then we very often see them come back in a subsequent year.

Q. Have you noticed any improvement in the class of immigrants from Italy during the last 5 or 6 years?—A. It has decidedly improved.

Q. Is the immigration drawn from about the same sections of Italy as it was 10 years ago?—A. Yes; it is drawn mostly from the agricultural districts. There are none coming, so to speak, from Naples and the large cities.

Q. Do you know anything of a medical inspection of your immigrants at Naples?—A. There is a very rigid one.

Q. Please state to the commission what length of time it takes, and the means employed, to make the inspection.—A. I do not think I could give you the details. I only know in a general way that it is a very rigid examination.

Q. Are you aware that a few years ago the American commission in Europe reported that it was the most inefficient examination held in Europe?—A. I think it was improved in consequence of that report. I believe the American consul exercises a general supervision.

Q. Does the Italian Government aid the companies in making rules and regulations in respect to inspection?—A. It does. In the first place, it does in the rejection of immigrants that might be rejected in this country.

Q. How do the people of Italy generally know of the immigration laws of the United States?—A. I have a proclamation here from the Italian Government, dated in November, 1886. It says finally: "Hence arises the obligation on the part of the prefects to refuse passports to the United States of those who are included in the prohibited classes, under the amendments of the immigration law." It further states: "I beg the proper officers to make known to the public, either through print or through the syndaci (mayors or authorities), the foregoing rules, and to acknowledge in the meantime the receipt of these presents."

Q. (By Mr. SMYTH.) Has your line any connection whatever with the Italian bureau here in New York?—A. We are somewhat subject to their authority.

Q. That is, by authority of the Italian Government?—A. By authority of the Italian Government.

Q. Do you think immigrants are still brought from Italy in defiance of the law?—A. There are some, but the number is reducing constantly.

Q. Do you know anything about the existence of the padrone here in New York?—A. It used to exist, but it does not now, to my knowledge.

Q. You do not think it exists at all now?—A. I doubt it.

Q. Does the Italian immigrant want to be released from the padrone, or does he prefer that system of service?—A. Years ago he preferred it. He was unfamiliar with the language, was not educated, and the padrone was, as it were, the most educated among them, and protected them. Nowadays he does not need so much the assistance of the padrone.

Q. You think the system was rather a help to the immigrant in former days?—
A. At that time; yes.
Q. Did it become a great evil?—A. It did, years ago.
Q. You think now its evil effects have been entirely wiped out?—A. To my knowledge, entirely; but that, of course, I will not vouch for.
Q. Does not the Italian immigrant, as a rule, deposit his savings with rather irresponsible bankers of his own race?—A. Some are responsible and some are not. There is now one Italian savings bank in New York established under the laws of the State of New York.
Q. Does the San Raphael Society do much to help the ignorant Italian immigrant on his arrival in New York?—A. It does a great deal.
Q. Does that society render material assistance if necessary?—A. I believe it does.
Q. And take care of his money and deposits?—A. I do not believe that; not to my knowledge.
Q. In what form does it render material assistance to these immigrants?—A. It will assist them in finding their relations, and gives them a good deal of help in the Barge Office.
Q. Does it give them charity?—A. Not to my knowledge.
Q. You say with reference to the padrone that, as far as you know, it has been entirely done away with. Do you think you have a full knowledge on that subject?—A. I have not; only from what I hear.
Q. Is that the opinion here, you think, of this Italian bureau—of Dr. Rossi, for instance?—A. I could not say. I have not spoken to him on the subject. I do not meet him myself. It is my landing clerk that meets him.
Q. Has the Italian bureau any right to influence the admission of immigrants detained, when the officers here object to their being received either on account of contagious or loathsome diseases or on account of being criminals?—A. If they are objectionable, they certainly should not use influence; but if they are not, I should judge that their influence is not objectionable.
Q. Will you tell us exactly what is meant by the padrone system?—A. It originated from the sense of helplessness on the part of the majority of the Italian immigrants. They looked to the padrone for protection, especially in receiving the wages that were due them, and in procuring them quarters. They had to go out in the fields and work on the railways, and the padrone would see to it that they were fairly well settled.
Q. Of course, he secured them employment?—A. He would do that.
Q. He would take contracts and they would go to him and work?—A. Exactly.
Q. I suppose one of the evils came from his deducting large portions of their pay?—A. It was simply the abuse of the system that brought the evil; robbing the poor immigrant.
Q. Was that system in effect here in New York City as well as in the country?—
A. I believe mostly in the country.
Q. In town, with reference to municipal work?—A. I am not familiar with that. If you will allow me, I will lay before you the law of the Italian Government, which makes the subagent in Italy responsible for his agency and his transactions with the passengers. In the first place, they have to give security to the amount of from 3,000 to 5,000 lire; then it states the penalties, and makes further regulations. Article 12 of said regulations reads: "It is, further, forbidden to procure the departure or embarkation of persons whose immigration is not permitted to the countries to which they are directed."
Q. Does the Italian Government encourage emigration to this country?—A. I think the Italian Government is like most governments in Europe—they discourage emigration. They need the intended emigrants for their armies.
Q. (By Mr. FARQUHAR.) That is one of the greatest industries of Europe, keeping up armies?—A. It would seem so.
C. (By Mr. SMYTH.) How did this Italian bureau act during the recent war between Spain and the United States; did it discourage emigration?—A. I think it did; took steps in the very beginning of the war, pointing out the danger, in the first place.
Q. Was it in the shape of a warning sent by that bureau to the Italian people?—
A. I would not be sure whether it was the Italian Government. I think the Government advised the people not to go for the time being. Whether they kept it up during the whole war I do not remember.
Q. Since the war, has the Italian Government taken steps to encourage emigration or prevent it?—A. It certainly tries to prevent emigration, and regulates it in a very stringent way.

IMMIGRATION. 117

New York, N. Y., *July 25, 1899.*

TESTIMONY OF MR. ROBERT FLOYD,

Chief Clerk of the Cunard Steamship Line, New York City.

At a meeting of the Subcommission on Manufactures and General Business, held in New York City, July 25, 1899, Chairman Smyth presiding, Robert Floyd appeared at 12.15 p. m., and, being duly sworn, testified concerning immigration, as follows:

Q. (By Mr. SMYTH.) What is your address?—A. 7 Fifth avenue, New York City.

Q. What is your business?—A. Chief clerk Cunard Line, New York.

Q. How long have you been connected with the Cunard Line?—A. Eleven years.

Q. We would be glad to have any statement from you in reference to the working of the immigration law, and any suggestions which you have to make.—A. Mr. Schwab has spoken so fully on the subject, and his views agree so well with those of the company I represent, that I think there is nothing for me to do except to answer such questions as you may put. I fully agree with all he said on the general subjects.

Q. The Cunard Line, I believe, runs to England?—A. Yes.

Q. Therefore you have not very much of the continental steerage business?—A. Our steerage passengers are mostly Irish and Scandinavians.

Q. What is your rate of steerage passage?—A. $25 to some and $27.50 to others.

Q. How does that compare with the rate in 1880?—A. It is higher.

Q. How much?—A. I can not answer.

Q. Do you think it is as much as 50 per cent?—A. I think fully. If I remember rightly, I think in 1880, in consequence of competition, rates ruled unusually low.

Q. Has the increase of rate tended to discourage immigration?—A. I think not. I can not speak correctly of the days when this heavy competition was on. No doubt at that time the extremely low rate induced them to come when they would not have otherwise.

Q. But the higher rates now you do not think tend to retard immigration?—A. I think the rates at present are reasonable ones and immigrants so consider them.

Q. Do you know of any case where the immigrant on your line has been rejected and returned by the immigrant officers in the port of New York, and subsequently brought back on your line to the United States?—A. I know of no case, and I am sure our company would prevent any immigrant who had been deported coming back by our line if the matter came under their observation. They would not run the risk of having to repeat the same experience with the same individual.

Q. Have you a copy of your instructions issued to your agents?—A. I have not.

Q. You have issued such circulars?—A. Our circulars on the other side are merely circulars giving information as to rates of passage and sailing dates, so far as I am informed.

Q. Can you procure for the use of the commission copies of these circulars and have them sent to us at Washington?—A. I will send you anything our steerage department issues regarding the business.

Q. (By Mr. CLARKE.) Have you any system of detention and inspection in the interior of the country from which your passengers come?—A. No, except in Scandinavia. All our British and Irish passengers come but a short distance. They are all examined prior to embarking at the port of embarkation.

Q. Is there any examination except the medical examination?—A. The intended passengers are all questioned on the subjects referred to in the list, under these several headings [referring to manifest].

Q. Is there any other evidence sought except their own in regard to these subjects?—A. Not to my knowledge.

Q. Would there be in case you had suspicions that the man was really prohibited by law from coming?—A. There certainly would.

Q. Do you ever extend these inquiries back to the homes and ask people there what they know about these immigrants?—A. I think the booking agent, before booking the passenger, is very careful to inquire of them particularly on all these points, for the reason that if he books a passenger who upon landing here is found to come within the prohibited classes and is returned, he is disciplined at once; so that the inquiry starts with the agent who books the passenger. We hold them to a strict account for every passenger returned in consequence of booking them illegally according to the United States law.

Q. How long have you been connected with the Cunard Line?—A. Eleven years. I have been in the steamship business 31 years.
Q. Have you noticed any improvement in the character of the immigrants since the enactment of our present immigration laws?—A. They never come under my observation.
Q. What officer could tell most about that?—A. Probably the heads of our steerage department. I seldom ever have occasion to see the passengers when they arrive here.
Q. (By Mr. FARQUHAR.) Does your line take part in the consultations of the North Atlantic conference?—A. Yes.
Q. Have you ever attended any of their meetings as a member yourself?—A. Occasionally.
Q. What is the character of the consultation usually had by them?—A. Generally the general methods of conducting business, regulations adopting agencies, and sometimes discussion as to rates of fare.
Q. Purely a voluntary business arrangement?—A. Yes.
Q. (By Mr. SMYTH.) Has it anything to do with the passage of the steamers—the course they take?—A. No; that is regulated by the principals at home, on the other side.
Q. Simply the commercial side of it?—A. Simply the commercial side of it.
Q. Have you any suggestions to give this commission as to remedial legislation with respect to immigration?—A. I have no suggestions to make. I think the present law seems to be adequate.

NEW YORK, N. Y., *July 25, 1899.*

TESTIMONY OF MR. ARTHUR LEDERER,

Passenger Manager of the American and Red Star Steamship Lines, New York City.

At a meeting of the Subcommission on Manufactures and General Business, held in New York City, July 25, 1899, Chairman Smyth presiding, Mr. Arthur Lederer appeared at 12.30 p m., and, being duly sworn, testified concerning immigration, as follows:
Q. (By Mr. SMYTH.) What is your residence?—A. 211 East Sixty-first street.
Q. What is your business address?—A. 73 Broadway.
Q. What is your occupation?—A. Passenger manager of the American and Red Star Lines.
Q. How long have you been in that position?—A. The last 11 years.
Q. How long have you been in the steamship business?—A. Twenty-six years.
Q. You have heard the testimony of Messrs. Floyd and Schwab. Have you any statement you would like to make in addition to their testimony?—A. I do not think I could very well improve on the same; but I have a few documents with me which, perhaps, will be useful to your committee.
Q. We will be glad to have any circulars that you give to your agents in other countries with reference to immigration.—A. Mr. Schwab has presented me as representing the American Line. Unfortunately, I have only in the last moment before being invited to come before you been able to pick out from my documents a copy of a circular issued for the use of agents of the Red Star Line on the European Continent, dated April 20, 1893, and giving the law of March 3, 1891, verbatim, and on the third page an extract of the law. It also gives instructions to subagents, and incloses, with the instructions in that circular for German-speaking agents, a translation of the immigration law of the United States into German, also of the law of March 3, 1891, as well as the supplemental laws or amendments of March 3, 1893, with instructions to exhibit it in prominent locations in their offices. There are also translations in other languages for the use of agents in other countries.
Q. What ports does your line ply between?—A. Antwerp and New York, and Antwerp and Philadelphia. I will be very glad to supply you with translations in other languages. The one I here hand you is in German.
Q. How many immigrants did you bring in last year?—A. Probably 25,000; it generally runs between 25,000 and 30,000.
Q. Have you any idea how many of these were on prepaid tickets?—A. I am inclined to think the sales of prepaid tickets with our lines run about 40 per cent, maybe 45. It depends entirely on the condition of this country. When we have prosperous times the prepaid sales are greater.

Q. Do you recollect any instance of any immigrant on your line being rejected at the Philadelphia or New York port by the Immigration Bureau and returned to the other side, and then subsequently returned in one of your steamers?—A. I do not know of such a case and do not think that such a thing is quite possible, because the penalty would be at our expense, and I think taking an immigrant back once is sufficient.

Q. What is the steerage passage between Antwerp and New York or Philadelphia?—A. $29.50 for either port.

Q. How does that compare with 1880?—A. I am not prepared to say accurately, but I would guess about 50 per cent higher than it was.

Q. How has that increase in passage money affected the immigration? Has it caused much decline?—A. Not a particle. I am under the impression that the rise and decline of immigration depends entirely on the conditions prevailing in this country. If the farmer has made money to send for his family, the number is increased; if he gets little for his crop or for his work, he waits another year or two; and that probably explains the ups and downs in immigration. I would like to leave with you, also, another document which goes with those I have mentioned. It is the inquiry sheet which is submitted by each of the agents to passengers applying for passage in Europe, and which is sworn to by the immigrant. The documents which are the basis for the sheet of 30, manifest of 30, is also printed in the different languages, so that the booking agents in Europe, as well as the immigrants, may be in a position to properly explain it and read it.

Q. Do you agree with all you heard Mr. Schwab say and the suggestions he made?—A. I do.

Q. Your line works in harmony with the United States laws?—A. We have particularly impressed on the representatives on the other side that they must comply with the rules and regulations.

Q. Have you any suggestions to make as to changes?—A. I think they are entirely adequate. This circular also says, Immigrants must be at the port of embarkation 48 hours, or 2 days, prior to departure. This is for the purpose of medical and other inspection. It also says that the law of March 3, 1891, prohibits any agents directly or indirectly issuing any printed matter or verbally encouraging or inviting immigration, and that only the ordinary business means, such as circulars, published announcements, and statements as to the sailing of vessels, prices of passage, and advantages of ships can be explained. In any case where there is any question as to the admission of the immigrant, it is absolutely necessary that the company must have all of the particulars of the case, for which one of the inquiry sheets is to be used. We do not cater to that class of business which we are likely to have to return. I also wish to leave with you 2 circulars issued in this country to subagents, with instructions which, among other things, repeat the extract of the immigration law, showing just exactly what classes are prevented from landing in this country, so they may have no excuse for making a mistake in that regard.

Q. (By Mr. FARQUHAR.) These are all of recent date?—A. One was issued only 2 days ago, and the other issued March 30, 1899; one by the American Line and the other by the Red Star Line.

Q. The statement has been made before us that the immigration business of the steamships was exceedingly remunerative, and they were making large profits. Would you mind telling what dividends your lines have paid within the last few years?—A. I am not familiar with the financial parts of our companies, but so far as I have been advised they have never paid a dividend. They have coupons on the bonds, but no dividends on the stocks.

Q. (By Mr. CLARKE.) Does your company have any agents who keep up an acquaintance with immigrants after they have settled in this country, to any extent?—A. We have agents in this country—storekeepers, merchants, and banks—who sell these prepaid tickets. They are the only kind of agents that we maintain.

Q. Do these agents solicit the fellow-countrymen of possible immigrants to invite them to come over?—A. No; I do not think that has ever been tried, or if tried would be successful. You can not encourage a man to lay down his money to bring somebody over. When he has the money and has use for his brother or family, he finds the man who will sell him a ticket. If he does not write to the company's office in New York or Chicago, he will apply to the postmaster, or the cashier of the bank, and they will secure him the steamship ticket. If he is not the agent, he applies to the steamship company and they furnish him the ticket.

Q. You mean to have us understand your company does not solicit immigration either in the countries from which immigrants come or through their friends in this country?—A. Exactly. It is even prohibited on the other side.

NEW YORK, N. Y., *July 25, 1899.*

TESTIMONY OF MR. JOHN J. QUINLAN,

Supervising Inspector of the Contract Labor Bureau, Port of New York.

At a meeting of the Subcommission on Manufactures and General Business held in New York City, July 25, 1899, Chairman Smyth presiding, Mr. John J. Quinlan appeared at 2 p. m., and, being duly sworn, testified on the subject of immigration as follows:

Q. (By Mr. SMYTH.) What is your name?—A. John J. Quinlan.
Q. Occupation?—A. Supervising inspector of the contract labor bureau, port of New York, for a little over 6 years.
Q. Is there more than one inspector in the bureau?—A. Yes; in the contract labor bureau of the Barge Office there are about 30 employees all told. Of these about 15 are full-fledged inspectors and receive $5 a day, and 6 I think are assistant inspectors, and the remainder are interpreters.
Q. Are you chief of the bureau?—A. Yes.
Q. Will you please explain the operations of your bureau, and also the law, so far as you know it, that governs your inspection?—A. I may state, briefly, that the Contract Labor Bureau is divided into 3 sections: The section which may be called, for the sake of convenience, the quarantine division, consists of 2 inspectors, who board and carefully examine the passengers of ships coming from South America and all other vessels other than regular liners; the boarding division consists of 3 inspectors usually, who are interchangeable, and 6 assistant inspectors, who go down the bay in one of the revenue cutters, board the incoming steamers at quarantine, and make an examination of the cabin passengers between quarantine and the dock. The purpose of this examination is to ferret out any suspicious case of infringement of the contract labor law or violation of the immigration laws in general. The third and most important division is the Contract Labor Bureau proper of the Barge Office, of which I am the chief or supervising inspector. Our main business is to detect violations of the contract labor law wherever such exist, and work them up in shape for presentation to the Board of Special Inquiry and, when warrantable, for prosecution and recovery of the fine as prescribed by section 3 of the act of 1885. The method is to have the inspectors of my bureau stand beside the registry clerks and interpreters at the end of each inspection aisle on the "main floor" of the Barge Office station, and if, as the immigrants pass through during the formal inspection process, any case attracts attention, the suspect is taken to one side, where an examination is made, with the assistance of a suitable interpreter. Such action is taken in pursuance of the provisions of section 5 of the act approved March 3, 1893, which requires that " it shall be the duty of every inspector of arriving alien immigrants to detain for a special inquiry * * * every person who may not appear to him to be clearly and beyond doubt entitled to admission," etc. If, in the opinion of the inspection officer, the suspected immigrant is coming here in violation of law, he is handed a card and taken into the detention compartment, and after the immigrants pass through he is then taken into the examination room and there put through a thorough examination touching his right to land, suitable notes of his testimony being taken for future reference.

For the information of the commission it may be stated that the original act governing the exclusion of aliens brought to this country under contract to work here was approved February 26, 1885, and amended in the act approved February 23, 1887. Further acts, approved March 3, 1891, and March 3, 1893, respectively, relate also to the importation of alien contract labor.

Q. Have you any means of obtaining information in this investigation independent of your own observation?—A. Yes. Sometimes we are notified that such and such a man is coming here for the purpose of taking somebody else's position. In that case usually the Commissioner, or myself, issues a notice requesting that a thorough examination be made, and if that man is found, to bring him to the Barge Office for the purpose of further inquiry as to his eligibility.

Q. Do you receive any information so as to identify these contract laborers through organized labor associations of this country?—A. Strange to say, we receive very little assistance from organized labor. I might, however, give a case where they were of great service during the last 10 days: Six stevedores left St. Johns, New Brunswick, last Saturday, arrived in Boston the following day, and came through by the Fall River Line to New York, arriving here on Monday morning, and reported to the contractor. They were taken down to what is called Black Tom, a place in Jersey City, and went to work—I think it was on Monday afternoon. The same day they went to work a gentleman identified with organized labor called and showed me a letter that he had, and the letter simply said these people were going to a "boss" stevedore of a certain name in Long Island, but did not give his address. I sent one of my inspectors for the Brooklyn city directory, and there we found this man as a stevedore. We also learned that this man had an office on West street, and we found later all these 6 men loading ships for 40 cents an hour. We took their affidavits in the usual way, and also an affidavit from the alleged contractor, in which he partly corroborated the 6 stevedores, and they made themselves out contract laborers. The inspectors brought that news back on Tuesday afternoon, and that night, through the Commissioner of Immigration, we asked for warrants for the arrest of these men. The warrants came from the Secretary of the Treasury on Thursday, we arrested the men, and on Saturday they were sent to Boston, and yesterday they were deported from Boston on the same steamer on which they came back to St. Johns. In connection with that case I might state that, feeling that it was a good cause to prosecute for the penalty, I sent for Dr. Ullo, the Government counsel, and after reading over the affidavits of the immigrants and the alleged contractor he told me, "Quinlan, that is the same old case. The immigrants have convinced you, they have convinced me, they would convince a jury, that they came here in violation of the contract labor law, but unfortunately we can not convince the judge, because the inducement to come here was a letter to one of these men with a request to bring as many as he could, and it was only an offer. Therefore, I do not think we can sue advisedly for the penalty." I then said, "Dr. Ullo, I would like to have you talk to the immigrants (then in the Barge Office), and if you can strengthen the case in any way, get any additional evidence, I would like to have you do it so we can bring an action for the penalty." He said, "If I come to the office I think I will only make the case worse." He did come, however, and when he appeared again he said, "It is just as I told you. The case is in no better, and, if anything, is in worse, shape than when I went there." That is the characteristic of pretty nearly every case we have where we attempt to recover the penalty. We have tried all sorts of things. I remember now two cigarmakers coming from Havana prior to the war. They had a written contract—that is, a letter from this country—stating, "If you come over here you can go to work in my factory on Murray street at $20 per week." After a conference with the attorney—I think Mr. Corcoran was then the attorney—he said, "Mr. Quinlan, that looks like a clear case of a violation of the contract labor law, and I think we can recover the penalty; but to strengthen the case I would advise you to let the immigrants go to work; let them leave here, follow them, after they are at work ask for warrants for their arrest, and then I think that will strengthen the case." We did that; we found them at work and took them out on warrants of the Secretary of the Treasury, brought them to Ellis Island, took them before the United States officials—district attorney, I think—where their depositions were taken, and all agreed that was a case where we would recover the penalty; but Judge Benedict charged the jury that as the contract was not made in foreign lands it was no case for the jury. I simply state these cases that are fresh in my mind; there are hundreds of such cases which might be cited.

Q. What do you regard as the main defects in the law?—A. That is the main defect. It must be proven that the contract was made in the foreign country; the judges require the contract must be made there. Of course if we could convict the importer on the promise or the inducement held out to the immigrant it would not be very long until we would be able to stop the importation of foreign labor.

There is one thing that has always seemed to me a great obstacle in the way of convicting the alleged contractor; that is, that the law makes it imperative that the district attorney should bring the action. I think if the law were amended so that any attorney, who was admitted to practice in the United States courts, could bring the action, or bring the evidence before the district attorney, and if he refused to prosecute on that evidence, then be permitted to do it himself, and in the event of his recovering the penalty, be allowed, say, one-half of it, and the witnesses assisting him the other half, it would go a great ways toward breaking up the importation of contract labor. Of course, there is always an objection to that; it has been said by people that that would amount to blackmail, but it seems to me it would make every labor organization, and every man identified with organized labor, more or less of a labor inspector.

Q. Does your law cover the persuasion as well as the inducement?—A. No. It seems to me the law itself is strict enough provided we could convict the importer on the inducement or the request, whatever it might be. If we could do that we could make the connection readily enough. The only case that I have in mind now, that came up before the judge and the jury, was the case involving John Wanamaker. I think it was the head of his dress-goods department, who advertised in a London paper that he could give employment to dress-goods salesmen at £3 per week. A man who had been an employee of a store there in London replied, and was engaged to come to Philadelphia, and his passage was prepaid. He arrived here on Saturday or Sunday, and the following Monday he went to work in Wanamaker's, replacing a man who had been dismissed on Saturday night. That case was tried, and, as I say, the judge allowed the case to go to the jury. Mr. Wanamaker was convicted, fined $1,000 and cost, and paid into the Treasury of the United States about $1,180. There have been many convictions, but that was probably the best case, or rather the best conviction, we have had under the law. Most of our cases have been compromised. They come to a point where the district attorney is undecided, and the other side offers to compromise, and it is usually accepted with the consent, of course, of the Solicitor of the Treasury.

Q. Have you any suggestions as to the amendment of the law?—A. Only in that respect. I struck off hurriedly this morning an idea of mine (reading): "The alien contract-labor law should be amended so that there will be no possible loopholes of escape, as at present, either for the alien or for the person contracting with him or inducing him to come to this country. I would suggest an amendment, in the first place, to the effect that any alien coming to this country under any inducement, request, or suggestion that work or labor can or may be secured here, although there be no contract or agreement of any kind, shall be excluded, and that all persons offering or holding out any such inducement, request, or suggestion, even though there be no proof of any contract or agreement, shall be subject to the penalties already provided for contractors; also, that the same penalties be visited upon contractors and offerers of inducements, requests, or suggestions, whether the contracts, inducements, requests, or suggestions be made in this country or elsewhere." The last suggestion is made in view of my understanding that the courts have held that to secure a conviction under the present law it must be proven that the contract was made in the foreign country.

And I struck off another little idea here (reading): "Another suggestion to facilitate prosecutions, which are commonly subject to long delays: At present only a United States district attorney can, as I understand it, prosecute contractors for violations of the law. I would suggest that the law be so amended that any attorney admitted in the United States courts, who states that he has evidence, may go before the United States district attorney and lay his case before him, and if the district attorney does not see fit to take up the case, any such attorney may himself prosecute the alleged offenders, and, upon conviction, be awarded by the court one-half of the penalty, and that the court have power to award to informing witness or witnesses the other half of the penalty so secured."

There is one other thing that occurs to me now. I remember the day that Senator Hill's senatorial committee on immigration came to Ellis Island. I told Senator Hill that I had examined a group of 30 Italians that day; 15 of them had been in the United States before, each one carrying back all the way from $200 to $1,000. The 15, on returning, had an average of about $15 apiece. When I asked them what they did with the money they carried over, I think about two-thirds told me they had bought a little place in Italy, a little house and a plot of ground; that they had paid a certain sum; that there was a mortgage on it; that they were returning to this country for the purpose of making enough money to pay that mortgage off, and as soon as they had accumulated sufficient they would return and spend the balance of their days in Italy. At that time this struck me as one thing that was very wrong, and there ought to be some way of righting it. I have never changed my mind on that, after 6 years. I have personally investigated at least 1,000 such cases. I have found that they consume nothing but what they eat. They bring with them all that they will require in the way of clothes, and everything else sufficient to do them while they are here, and while they are in this country they will not purchase a thing probably except what they eat, drink, and smoke. I have heard it said that these so-called birds of passage take out of this country about $20,000,000 every year. I do not know what that statement is founded on, but it has been observed that through the fall of the year we will find the North German Lloyd ships and other lines going back with every available inch of space taken in the steerage by these people returning to Italy. I speak of the Italians because they probably practice that more than any other nationality. Of the others, there is one class that comes here in the spring from the north of Ireland, Scotland, and England. They are carpenters, stonecutters, bricklayers, and skilled mechanics, who thoroughly understand the immigration laws. They come here in March or April, remain until November, and then go back carrying with them the proceeds of their labor. They also bring with them all they require in the way of clothes while here. Now, I do think it would be one of the very best amendments to the law that could be passed if there were some way of stopping the migration of these people. We have found no way on Ellis Island or at the Barge Office to stop them, except where we find them with very little money, and then we adjudge them public charges and deport them under the law. Where we find the birds of passage with as little as $15, no matter what their condition is, we endeavor to return them to the other side.

Q. How do you identify these birds of passage?—A. Simply by examining them. We ask them their object in coming here. They tell us they were here before; that they are carpenters, for instance, and worked for so and so, on such a street, in such a city, and that they are going back to that city; and if you ask them such questions as "Are you going to work for your former employer?" they answer, "I do not know." "Had any letters from him?" "No." "How often have you been in this country?" "Two, 3, or 4 times." "How long did you stay?" "Five months or 7 months." They come in the steerage and go back, finding it is cheaper to live with their families during the winter months than to remain here.

Q. Of course, in many of these cases these skilled workmen are holding international union cards?—A. Not as a rule, but some of them do.

Q. In a case of that kind you could not prove a contract?—A. I speak of those who are not members of organized labor.

Q. Take the Amalgamated Carpenters' Union.—A. We do not have trouble with those people.

Q. What is your best judgment as to what would be the best amendment of the law?—A. In the original law, after the words "District of Columbia," on the seventh line, I would suggest the insertion of the words " under any inducement, request, or suggestion that work or labor can or may be secured in this country, or under any contract or agreement," etc. It seems to me—I am not a lawyer—that with such an amendment we could successfully prosecute the contractor.

I am also convinced that I could do very much better work if we had a larger force of men. I think that the contract-labor law is so important to organized labor and the men of this country that we ought to have a larger appropriation than $100,000 from Congress. I think we ought to have at least 10 more inspectors and interpreters than we have now at the Barge Office. If we can not get a larger appropriation from Congress, I would be in favor of increasing the head tax from $1 to say $2, and using that for the purpose of increasing our force as well as for other immigration matters.

Q. Has your commissioner here made any recommendations to the Secretary of the Treasury with respect to an increase of force?—A. I can not say. I have written him several urgent letters, and I have tried to point out to him how important it was that our force should be increased. Some 2 years ago they dropped from the force at one time some 5 or 6 inspectors. Since that time, by resignation and death, we have lost 4 or 5 more, and they have not been replaced. During the 6 years that I have been chief of the contract labor bureau we have deported from this port about 4,000 contract laborers, with very few convictions of the alleged contractor.

Q. All the punishment has been on the immigrant?—A. Yes.

Q. Do you know anything about the case of contract laborers who went to Rathbun, Iowa?—A. Yes. About 1 month ago, or just prior to 1 month ago, we received from the Commissioner-General a request to thoroughly investigate all Croatians coming through our station. Some few days after that a group of 15 were discovered, and after a thorough examination we ascertained, according to their story, that they were farmers principally; that they were going to Rathbun, Iowa; and they had prepaid tickets there; they had no friends there, and had not any relatives, and could not give a satisfactory excuse for their going there. I inquired about Rathbun and found that in the past some French and Italian miners had passed through and gone to Rathbun, but these were the first Croatians that we knew of. I reported the matter to the Commissioner and requested that he forward my findings to the Department in Washington, and that it be looked into, and I believe an inspector from Chicago was detailed on the case, and found that these people had gone to work the following day after their arrival in Rathbun in a coal mine about half a mile from the village. He reported his findings to Mr. Powderly, and warrants were issued, and the immigrants are now on Ellis Island, and will be deported this week.

Q. Can you give the names of the owners of the mine at Rathbun?—A. No; but I can get them for you.

Q. We would like to have them. Has any action been taken by the Department at Washington with respect to the prosecution of the mine owners?—A. I have not heard of any, but I do not think they have connected the owners. You know that thing is done, not through the owners of the mine, but relatives and friends of these men. The foreman of the mine will say, "How do you like your job here?" "Pretty well." "Have you not a brother or cousin or some friends in your home that you would like to bring out?" "Yes." "If they come here we think we can put them to work." It seems to me we would have great difficulty in convicting the mine owners under the present law.

Q. Do you know of any strike at the mines in Rathbun?—A. No.

Q. The only reason of the owner or superintendent in sending for these people was to get cheap labor?—A. That was the idea, I suppose. In every case I have investigated I found that to have been the object; to replace the American or more intelligent workman by a man who is usually willing to work for less money.

Q. (By Mr. CLARKE.) You say you regard the alien contract-labor law as of great importance to organized labor; is it not of equal importance to unorganized labor?—A. Yes; to every man who works for a living.

Q. In regard to the recommendation to amend the law so as to attach a penalty to an inducement to come to this country, can you think how that could be framed so that it would not prevent a brother who lives here from writing to his brother abroad what a fine country this is for a workingman?—A. I want to say this, a brother coming to a brother is never interfered with at the Barge Office, if he is going to work for his brother. We have had cases where one brother found employment for another, and we convicted him as coming in violation of law and returned him. But where a brother is coming to work for a brother—there is no case that I know of where such a man has been deported as coming in violation of the law.

Q. Suppose the relationship is a little more remote?—A. Then I think we would enforce the law against him.

Q. Then as a matter of fact it would be unsafe for anybody in this country to write to a friend abroad, unless he is a brother, what a fine country this is for a workingman or woman?—A. If he wrote him to come to a farm in the West, if a farm laborer, he would not be interferred with; but if a tailor, shoemaker, or in any skilled trade, and he wrote to his first cousin that this is a fine country, and "if you come over here I can get you a job," not even saying "I can give you one," I think such a man ought to be sent back.

Q. Suppose the farm laborers in the West were organized and objected to the bringing over of men under any inducement whatever to compete with them, you would then enforce it in regard to farm labor?—A. I think the conditions of the country might control me. I would cross that bridge when I came to it. So far we have held no farm laborers. There is such a thing as making this law ridiculous; I do not propose to do that if I can help it. What I want to do is to protect the laboring man in established industries against the foreigner who is willing to come here and work for less money; but I believe we want more farmers and farm hands, and we have not interfered with that class.

Q. Is it ever possible that we need more help in some lines than is now here?—A. Mr. McSweeney spoke of a condition that to him was peculiar—of the great demand for unskilled labor during the last month. That has been my observation during the last 4 or 5 months. I was talking to a gentleman yesterday, and he told me that he wanted men to work on a railroad and in a mine; that he would rent a little house at $5 a month (that was in Illinois), where they would have a good well and all that kind of thing, and that they could make $1.50 to $1.75 a day. I asked him why he did not get his help in Chicago, and he told me he had tried and could not get a man unoccupied or out of work in Chicago who was able or willing to work in the mines or on the railroad. He is one of many who have applied to me for assistance, to find out how they could procure unskilled labor, principally to work in the mines. The coke mines through Pennsylvania want men very much. I assume that the great boom in the iron industry is responsible for this demand.

Q. You do not think, then, it is the desire of these men to displace other men, but that they need them on account of extending their business?—A. These particular men I speak of want them to extend their business—these few men I have met with in the last 3 or 4 months—but that is a new condition. Prior to that, for 3 or 4 years, I did not have one request. We sent back probably 2,000 or 3,000 people who were coming here for no other purpose than to take the places of our own people and work for less money. In pretty nearly every case we investigated we found this was the case.

Q. What proportion do the deportations bear to the total number of immigrants on account of their being contract laborers?—A. In the fiscal year ending June 30 291,000 immigrants landed at this port, of which 3,500 were deported for all causes—18 insane persons, 2,381 paupers or likely to become paupers, 328 loathsome or dangerous contagious diseases, 3 convicts, and 635 contract as laborers.

Q. Do you think you would have been able to deport a good many more alien contract laborers if you had had a larger inspecting force?—A. Yes.

Q. You think that a good many alien contract laborers have gotten in in spite of your vigilance?—A. Yes. These groups of 5, 7, 11, and 15 could have been followed up if we had had more inspectors, but we have not the force to do that now.

Q. What reason have you for thinking these men that escaped were alien contract laborers?—A. They are just like the case of the Croatians going to Rathbun, Iowa; they looked suspicious, and in the bustle, owing to the shortness of inspectors, we think that many of them have slipped through that we might have prevented had we had a larger force.

Q. In what respect do they look suspicious?—A. The fact that they are going to, say, some place in Pennsylvania, a group of seven, each man having, say, $12 or $15. One man was here for some time before. This is his second trip. He is in charge of the others, and they are going out there, but they can not tell you the reason why, and hence the case looks suspicious.

Q. Now if you had a larger force how would you follow up these men?—A. By sending a man after them. We might send a man with them.

Q. Every case that looks suspicious you investigate here as fully as you can?—A. Yes; in New York or close by we give it a more thorough investigation, and where it looks very suspicious I report it to the Commissioner and he in turn to the Commissioner-General, who investigates it from Washington, as in the Rathbun case.

Q. Have you considered the difficulty of getting these very stringent provisions enacted by Congress?—A. Yes, I realize how difficult that is. I have conferred with several United States district attorneys, and they always tell me the difficulty of making a conviction. I may be pardoned for suggesting to the commission that it might be well to call these gentlemen, and also our counsel, Dr. Ullo, as they can tell you more fully just the reason the judges give for not permitting these cases to go to the jury, or, when they do, charging the jury in such a way that we do not secure convictions. Mr. McFarland, who was formerly district attorney here, is very familiar with all these cases, and he has expressed to me personally what he called the contempt the United States judges had for the contract labor law.

Q. How does the size of the force of inspectors in your department compare with that in the other departments of the inspection bureau here?—A. As I say, we have lost altogether about 10 men through dismissals, resignation, and death. I think there are other branches short, but not nearly so short as the contract-labor force. We came from Ellis Island 2 years ago with 10 men more than we have now.

Q. Do you know why they have not been replaced?—A. No; I could not say. I have recommended to Mr. Fitchie at different times that the contract-labor bureau ought to have more inspectors and interpreters, and I assume that he has said as much to Mr. Powderly, although I do not know.

Q. You do not know the number of inspectors in the other departments, do you?—A. The inspectors are the registry clerks; I consider them very efficient.

Q. They assist you, do they not?—A. Yes; at times we work together and assist one another. At times you will find some of our contract-labor inspectors or interpreters registering or helping out the other bureau.

Q. Do not the other bureaus have any inspectors except the registry clerks?—A. Not that I know of. They had the boarding officers, but they are in the contract-labor bureau. Mr. McSweeney speaks of some people who were transferred to the contract-labor bureau. They are known as assistant inspectors.

Q. They are not in addition, then, to the force you have named, the 28 or 30?—A. No; they are included in that.

Q. How many of these registry clerks are there who assist you?—A. They do not assist us unless we call upon them to act as interpreters or something of that kind. The so-called contract-labor inspector stands at the end of the line during the process of inspection. He listens to both what the immigrant says to the registry clerk, who is an inspector, but not in the contract-labor bureau, and after he passes this man, if the contract-labor inspector is suspicious of anything, my inspector takes him to one side, as I said, and interviews him at length.

Q. Does the registry clerk ask questions that bear on the contract-labor subject?—A. Not as a rule; sometimes they do and call our attention to it; it is where the man volunteers, or they discover something suspicious, and they simply invite our attention to the fact.

Q. They have this subject in mind as they have other disqualifications of the immigrant?—A. Yes. I have always found them very willing and very able to assist us in any way.

Q. (By Mr. FARQUHAR.) Do you ever come in contact with the so-called Italian bureau in your business?—A. No; very seldom.

Q. You have had very little to do with that?—A. Very little. They deal more with the other branch of the service.

NEW YORK, N. Y., *July 25, 1899.*

TESTIMONY OF DR. LOUIS L. WILLIAMS,

Surgeon, Marine-Hospital Service, detailed to inspect immigrants at the port of New York.

At a meeting of the Subcommission on Manufactures and General Business, held in New York City July 25, 1899, Mr. Farquhar presiding, Dr. Louis L. Williams appeared at 4 p. m., and, being duly sworn, testified concerning immigration, as follows:

Q. (By Mr. FARQUHAR.) What is your residence?—A. No. 35 Madison avenue, New Brighton, Staten Island.

Q. What is your official position?—A. Surgeon, Marine-Hospital Service, at present detailed to inspect immigrants at this station.

Q. I wish you would explain to the commission your official connection with the immigration service at the port of New York, and also your general duties with respect to immigrants.—A. According to the immigration law of 1893, the medical inspection must, when practicable, be made by a medical officer of the Marine-Hospital Service, and one is detailed from time to time for that purpose; and in addition to that work it has been found convenient by the commissioner to have the medical inspector take charge of the immigrants detained in the hospital and have supervision of the hospital work, which is under the control of the commissioner directly.

Q. Do you have to report to the commissioner here, or to Washington?—A. To the commissioner, and incidentally to make certain reports to the Marine-Hospital Bureau in the way of information or anything directly connected with my duties here.

Q. What other medical inspection is there here of incoming ships?—A. The inspection at quarantine.

Q. Is that under Dr. Doty?—A. Yes. Some of our inspectors board all ships at quarantine for the purpose of examining the first and second class passengers. The steerage are examined in the Barge Office. The medical inspection is the first inspection made.

Q. How many are engaged in this medical examination at the Barge Office?—A. In the Barge Office, besides myself, there are 1 acting assistant surgeon and the chemist, who acts as bookkeeper and, in a certain sense, as executive officer and assists in the inspection. That is the force, with the exception of the clerk and 1 attendant. The three assistant surgeons who inspect the cabin passengers also assist in the steerage inspection when practicable.

Q. So that practically the whole medical inspection here at the port of New York is in your hands?—A. Practically.

Q. Do you find your force sufficient to perform all your duties?—A. Just sufficient. At the present time it keeps the force all employed. It would not be sufficient had I not found here a very competent set of assistants. I found the office exceedingly well organized.

Q. You would say that your means of inspection and the time of your inspection are sufficient?—A. Quite sufficient.

Q. Do you know anything at all about the inspection on the other side?—A. A little only as regards the inspection at Liverpool. I inspected the immigrants there under a special detail in 1893, the cholera year, so I became somewhat familiar with their methods at that port.

Q. What is your opinion as to its thoroughness?—A. It is fairly good, in a way. The inspection by the ship's surgeon I know very little about. I know they made an inspection, sometimes on shore, and sometimes necessarily on board, for the reason that many of their passengers would come from Hull; passengers coming from Rotterdam or Hamburg or Bremen would be railroaded across from Hull and sometimes arrived only in time to be put aboard. In that case I do not see how the ship's surgeon could make an inspection before they went aboard, though he might have inspected them en route. In addition to that the British board of trade has 2 medical inspectors who examine all the steerage and second-cabin passengers. That examination is made on board and, I believe, is fairly good. I knew the inspectors at that time personally, and I believed them to be competent, though the inspection, so far as they were concerned, did not practically concern the work of the immigration office here, because the idea was merely to exclude passengers who were likely to become ill on the voyage or persons afflicted with a contagious disease.

Q. Some contagious diseases, of course, develop on the voyage?—A. That cannot be avoided, of course.

Q. What is your experience as to the efficiency of the inspection on the other side; take it from any port?—A. You mean from the standpoint of the office here? I do not think it is very efficient. It can not be, else we would not have discovered so many cases on this side. I believe, however—in fact I know—that we get less, for instance, from Liverpool than from any other port. The majority of the cases we get from some of the French and Italian ships, and some of the Hamburg liners bringing Italians and Syrians.

Q. Have you discovered here many diseases common to the Asiatic countries?—A. There is one disease especially common. We have among the Syrians a very large proportion affected with trachoma, granular lids, a disease of the eye.

Q. What do you regard as the greater deterrent, the detention of the immigrant here at the expense of the steamship company or the dread of deportation?—A. I believe the detention here would be the greater, for the reason mentioned by Mr. Schwab, that it would be an appeal to the pocket of the steamship company. The diseases in question, as far as trachoma or favus are concerned, are so obstinate, and the period of treatment so long, that it would involve them in very great expense to pay for the treatment on this side, and I believe they would be extremely careful in bringing them over if that was to be the outcome. As it is now, if they do not make money they at least may not lose if the case is deported.

Q. How many have you had to deport since you have been the official here?—A. I have brought some data as to that [reading]:

Number of hospital cases for past year	1,862
Number of landed cases applying for relief for past year	235
Number of arriving immigrants certified to during past year	1,244
Number of cases certified loathsome or dangerous contagious diseases:	
Favus	48
Trachoma	312
Number of contagious cases deported:	
Trachoma	298
Favus	36
Number of cases contagious diseases certified to during month of June, 1899:	
Trachoma	123
Favus	3
Number of contagious cases deported:	
Trachoma	116
Favus	1
Total number of immigrants rejected during month of June	261

That would give the idea of the proportion, trachoma being the largest factor in the cases rejected medically.

Q. In case of deportation, to what port are they sent usually?—A. They are returned on the ship that brings them.

Q. Where is the usual shipping point?—A. Ordinarily Havre. They collect for the most part at Marseilles, and take ship at Havre. Some occasionally come on other lines. Some come on the Holland line; but the other is the most common route.

Q. (By Mr. CLARKE.) Do you think the inspection on the other side is less rigid in case of these French and Italian lines than the other lines?—A. I would not be prepared to say that. The possibility is that they have the opportunity to bring more of these people for the reason I have mentioned. I could not of my own knowledge say it was less efficient.

Q. Do you think it would be advisable for the United States to employ medical examiners at the ports of departure of these immigrants?—A. It might possibly be of advantage, but it would appear to me that it might be reached otherwise, by making it undesirable for the companies to bring them, and at less expense to the Government.

Q. How do you think the law can be improved so as to make it more difficult or more undesirable for them to bring them?—A. Only in the manner I have indicated—to leave it to the discretion of the commissioner whether such a case should be immediately deported or kept in hospital. Apart from the deterring effect there comes in the question of humanity. It is a rather difficult thing for the commissioner to deport a case of that sort, leaving portions of the family in this country. If it was kept in hospital that difficulty would not obtain to the same extent. There could be no reasonable objection to the case remaining in the hospital under treatment if it was to be a source of trouble to the community. In other words, it would be treated as any other case would be treated.

Q. Has any complaint come from any part of the country that your medical examination here is not strict enough and that dangerous diseases escape your vigilance?—A. The only thing that I have seen was a statement to the effect that certain cases of leprosy came from Finland. What truth there is in that I can not say. Certainly the inspection is reasonably rigid here, and I believe few, if any, such cases have occurred. I have seen none during the period I have been on duty here; while it is possible for incipient cases of leprosy to pass the line, certainly not an aggravated case. There are some cases of leprosy that would exist in the community for many months undiscovered even by those in close contact; that is quite possible.

Q. How much time do you and your assistants give to the medical examination of any immigrant?—A. That depends very much on the immigrant. There are some shiploads that are so obviously in good condition that a very casual inspection is all that is necessary, and they are passed with reasonable rapidity; others require more careful looking after. I refer particularly to the Syrians. Such a large proportion of them have trachoma that it is customary to stop all and examine their lids. That, of course, takes a good deal of time. The Scandinavian immigrant is usually in good condition. There are so few physically defective that they are passed quite rapidly. Of course a more careful examination is subsequently made of the suspects, all the time being given to it that is necessary.

Q. Is it your policy to exclude every person afflicted with a contagious and loathsome disease of any character?—A. That is the ruling. At least, that is the law on the subject; and the Department has ruled, for instance, that trachoma and favus shall be excluded as contagious diseases. Practically these are the diseases that there can be any question about, for the reason that the more severe diseases, such as smallpox are stopped at quarantine. The mild diseases, like scarlet fever and measles, would be allowed to pass quarantine, but would be taken up here and put into the isolation hospital. They are cases which develop en route, and it would not do to return them.

Q. Do you know of any instance of a person deported for having a loathsome and dangerous contagious disease returning again to this country?—A. Several instances.

Q. (By Mr. FARQUHAR.) Can you relate any of the instances?—A. I have put down 4 instances from the records of the office: The first is the case of Maria Laham, 29, Syria, arrived April 11, 1899, per steamship *Alesia* (Fabre Line); deported for trachoma. Returned to the United States July 5, 1899, per steamship *Spaarndam* (Holland Line), under name of Martha Jousef Simon, and again deported for trachoma. In this case I understand the party admitted the fact of her identity. Second: Maria Hatzopoulos, 22, Greek, arrived June 4, 1899, per steamship *La Champagne* (steerage); deported for trachoma by same ship June 10, and returned to the United States in cabin of same ship July 2. She was again deported. Third: Mrs. Moses and 2 children arrived November 5, 1897, per steamship *Oledam*, and deported on account of favus (children). Returned to the United States January 22, 1898, per steamship *Amsterdam* (steerage); held in hospital 4½ months, and finally landed. They were held thus by order of the Department until regarded as cured. Fourth: Jacobus Van Hoorn, 7, Holland (accompanied by mother); case of favus; arrived May 8, 1898, and deported; returned to the United States June 9, 1898; held in hospital for 4 months and 10 days, and finally landed.

In addition to these I can recall a case that occurred recently—a case of trachoma coming on one of the Liverpool ships, and deported on account of this disease, and a short time after that coming into the port of Philadelphia. The inspecting officer wrote to know if he had not been here. He was evidently suspected from some circumstance, and I presume he was deported from that port. These are simply instances; there are others.

Q. (By Mr. CLARKE.) Suppose you give the English of favus?—A. The ordinary name is scaldhead; that is the common term.

Q. Are the agents of the steamship companies informed of all these cases of deportation as soon as they occur?—A. They are informed before deportation.

Q. All the cases?—A. Yes; they are invariably informed.

Q. So that by that notice they are put on their guard against bringing back these persons?—A. Precisely.

Q. How many appeals are made against deportation?—A. That is a question which comes before the commissioner, usually. I would only hear of it incidentally. In the medical division we only deal with the question of fact, properly.

Q. (By Mr. FARQUHAR.) On the basis of your report the commissioner makes his decision?—A. The cases rejected medically are certified, and that certificate passes through the hands of the registry division to the board of special inquiry. If the case calling for special inquiry has been certified to be a case of trachoma or favus or any disease which has been determined to be a loathsome and dangerous disease it is equivalent to a decision of deportation. As I understand it, the board of special inquiry has no further jurisdiction except to formally give an order for deportation. In the case of those certified for physical defect simply, it is optional with the board whether it shall admit the immigrant or not.

Q. (By Mr. CLARKE.) Have you any means of knowing whether the ships' surgeons discover these loathsome diseases in any case on the passage over?—A. I have no means of knowing. Officially they do not know of any such thing on board. I believe in one or two cases they have discovered trachoma or favus, but it is rare.

Q. What is their practice with reference to cases of dangerous diseases when they do discover them?—A. Each ship is required by law to have a hospital, which is usually a very small compartment, in which these cases are placed—cases like scarlet fever or smallpox. There is no isolation of trachoma or favus; they do not recognize them as a rule.

Q. Do you not think the law should be amended so as to require the isolation of such cases?—A. It would be of advantage if they ever admitted the fact that such a thing was on board the ship, but practically, with rare exceptions, they deny the existence or claim they have not recognized any disease aboard. Therefore the question of isolation would not come up at all.

Q. Have you any means of knowing whether their medical examiners on the other side have rejected any cases of trachoma or favus?—A. I have been told by some of the agents of the lines and some of the ships' surgeons that a number of cases have been eliminated, and I believe, to a certain extent, that is the case. I have recently received a private letter from one of my colleagues, formerly associated with me in the medical division of the Barge Office who has recently been ordered to Naples to carry out the quarantine law of 1893—that is, inspection of passengers from that port to prevent the introduction of contagious diseases—and incidentally he has advised against bringing certain cases likely to be barred under the immigration law, and he informs me the steamship companies have very readily taken his advice, and he believes they have eliminated some cases of trachoma. There are certain diseases of the eyes which attract much more attention than a very bad case of trachoma would. Many cases of this disease, to the casual observer, would present nothing until the lids were everted.

Q. By whom is the medical examiner here appointed?—A. He is examined by a board of medical officers of the Marine-Hospital Service, and is then commissioned by the President.

Q. On whose recommendation?—A. The recommendation of the Secretary of the Treasury, after the examination required by law.

Q. To whom do you make your reports of inspections?—A. The report of the year's work is made to the commissioner.

Q. You do not make any reports direct to Washington?—A. None at all, except incidentally and by request of the Marine-Hospital bureau, so as to give that bureau certain information in regard to the number of cases, rejected cases, etc.; matters of purely medical information.

Q. Are all immigrants thoroughly bathed and their clothing disinfected before they are allowed to come on board at the foreign ports?—A. Officially there is nothing of the sort done except in those cases where it has been required by the quarantine law of 1893, which law empowers the President to detail any medical officer of the Government to proceed to any foreign port for duty in the office of the consul, for the purpose of making inspections of all passengers and of giving bills of health, the hold upon the ship company being the bill of health.

Q. Do you not think it would be a good plan if the law required such bathing and disinfection?—A. It unquestionably would be a good hygienic measure in any case. They are certainly anything but clean, the majority of them.

Q. (By Mr. FARQUHAR.) Would it not be inexpensive as a preventive?—A. Some of the lines carry it out. I am told they had it in Rotterdam, or used to. I should think it would be a very good thing.

Q. (By Mr. CLARKE.) It might tend also to awaken a wholesome respect in the mind of the immigrant for the country to which he is coming?—A. It would be a good plan, but it might present some practical difficulties, and it might be opposed by the steamship companies on the score of expense—not so much the soap and water, but they would be compelled to detain the immigrant on the other side for a certain length of time to carry that out. I meet with that opposition in carrying out all quarantine laws. While on duty at Liverpool, whenever I came across an immigrant whose place of departure was an infected port of Europe, I kept him over a trip and required him to be washed and his baggage steamed. They were very reluctant to do that. That would be the only practical difficulty.

Q. Do you know of any institution, charitable or penal, in our country to which persons are admitted without being required to be bathed thoroughly and their clothing disinfected?—A. As far as the disinfection is concerned, I do not think that is uniformly carried out except in cases of persons suspected of having a contagious disease, but certainly they are in the better class of institutions required to be bathed.

Q. There is as much reason why they should be required to go through that process in going on shipboard?—A. There is more reason, because they are necessarily crowded on shipboard. It would be practically impossible to give a passenger all the air space that he should have in a hospital or even in his house. Theoretically, he should have a very large air space, but practically on shipboard he can not get it. The conditions are such that he could not get more than a certain amount of space, and he is therefore crowded, particularly in bad weather, and certain contagious diseases are more likely to show themselves under the filthy conditions that exist in the average steerage.

Q. (By Mr. FARQUHAR.) Have there been any formal complaints made as to the inadequency of the air space?—A. No; and in the ships I am mostly familiar with the air space, I believe, is practically sufficient; that is to say, not sufficient to live in indefinitely, but sufficient for ordinary sustenance for a passenger to cross the Atlantic. There were a few of the old ships which had inadequate conditions, but in all of the newer ones which I have seen—the English lines—the conditions are very fair indeed.

Q. Is the sanitary condition of the ships that arrive here good?—A. Fairly good. It is scarcely just to judge the ship by the condition you see the steerage in on arrival, because they carry some very filthy people, who make a great litter in the steerage. We see the same thing here in our detention pens and the detention boat on Ellis Island. Immigrants have to be followed very closely in order to secure cleanliness, and it is therefore very hard to judge by conditions seen on arrival.

Q. You would not think it was dangerously dirty?—A. Most dirt is not dangerous, but it is repulsive. You may have a very bad state of affairs with a practically clean steerage if infected people are put in it.

Q. Have you anything to suggest in the way of amendment to your inspection or the breadth of your jurisdiction, or as to a separate staff, entirely outside of the Marine Service, to be brought into the immigration bureau?—A. No; I can not say that I have any suggestions to make, for the reasons mentioned. I found the medical inspection service in an exceedingly good condition. I have been in charge for barely more than 3 months. I think it would be very unwise to make any slipshod amendment that had not been very carefully thought over. At present I see no necessity for it.

Q. Who preceded you?—A. Dr. Joseph H. White.

Q. Is he still in the Marine Service?—A. He is on duty in Washington at present in the Marine-Hospital Bureau.

NEW YORK, N. Y., *July 25, 1899.*

TESTIMONY OF DR. M. VICTOR SAFFORD,

Surgeon, United States Immigration Service, Port of New York.

At a meeting of the Subcommission on Manufactures and General Business, held in New York City July 25, 1899, Mr. Farquhar presiding, Dr. M. Victor Safford appeared at 4.30 p. m., and, being duly sworn, testified concerning immigration as follows:

Q. (By Mr. FARQUHAR.) What is your address and official position in the bureau?—A. Address, 121 West Eleventh street; surgeon, United States Immigration Service.

Q. How long have you held your present position?—A. Since October, 1895.

Q. What are your special duties?—A. To pass upon the landing of immigrants, in connection with a Marine Hospital officer and other assistants. We pick the suspicious ones out and after the remaining passengers have passed the line, these are examined as thoroughly as necessary. Those in need of hospital treatment are sent to the hospital; those who have diseases which are prohibited by law, such as loathsome and dangerous contagious diseases, are certified to by the surgeon in charge. Those who have physical defects like partial paralysis, incipient blindness, consumption, and heart disease, are also certified to and are sent before the board of special inquiry for a decision as to whether or not they are likely to become public charges. We also relieve usually those who have already been landed and come back to the immigration bureau for relief, either of their own volition or by direction of the department of charities of the State. These cases already landed usually come to us first and our reports accompany them to the commissioner. We state, for instance, whether the man is likely to be permanently incapacitated, and if so our certificate is really final in disposing of the case. The commissioner requests his deportation on the medical certificate alone, and in other cases, where there is only temporary trouble, the immigrant may be sent to the hospital; or where his condition does not warrant medical treatment it is so stated, and he is sent with that statement to the commissioner to be dealt with as is deemed advisable.

Q. In case an immigrant comes here, and you make no special record of him; he is landed, and a few months afterwards a disease develops which had been contracted previous to his landing here, so that you have no record in your first inspection. Do you take the voluntary affidavit of this man if he wants to go back to Europe or elsewhere?—A. Perhaps, to a certain extent, we do depend upon his statement, but that is rarely wholly necessary, because usually a diseased condition will speak for itself. We can form something of an idea whether the disease existed and escaped detection at the time he landed or not.

Q. In your records are you quite careful in giving the indications of diseases, even if the board of inquiry would ultimately pass him? Do you make a report sufficiently explicit so as to trace the man within 12 months?—A. Without question; and not only that, but we also keep a record of minor defects in cases which we do not send before the board of special inquiry at all, but which we detain, examine, and send before the registry clerk. These defects being recorded on the ship's card, the registry clerk takes them into consideration as a factor; for instance, a man a little below the standard in physique, or the loss of an eye, or the loss of a finger, or a man who is rather deficient in stature, in which case there is some doubt about his securing employment—these cases are not made special inquiry cases by us. For the month of May we rejected 178 cases; that is, those cases were either of the prohibited classes or else were of sufficient importance that we thought their conditions warranted deportation; but in addition to that there are 1,224 minor-defect cases, where we made comment on the card for the information of the registry clerks, out of a total of 44,754 examined during the month of May.

Q. Can you explain how you are able to trace these cases that you report and pass on, once they are landed?—A. Those cases which apply for assistance or come to the attention of the bureau are sent to the statistical office to obtain a verification of landing; in other words, a statement showing name of ship, date of arrival. etc., and then they usually come to our office. We have in our records a copy of every certificate made during the year—in fact, since the bureau has been established; at least ever since the fire. We also have a record of every minor defect which we have recorded, and having the name of the ship the man came on, we can easily see whether we have made at the time he landed any comment as to his physical condition.

Q. What do you know of any rejected persons being brought back here?—A. I remember those cases of which Dr. Williams has spoken. This spring an Italian came to the Barge Office to get some members of his family out who had arrived that day on the ship, and he was identified as an Italian who had been deported several months previously for trachoma. His own statement was that he came back to this country on the same ship, as a cabin passenger, directly the ship got on the other side. That occurred before the medical inspection of cabin passengers was made. Such inspection has only been in existence since the 1st of November, 1898. I remember one instance, though it was not a medical case, where a number of Ruthenians came here on a ship from an Italian port and were deported, and subsequently came by a ship of another line from Italy and were deported a second time. I think there are other instances, of which we have no official record, but I do not at this moment recall any more.

Q. What had you to do with the change to the new statistical classification of nationalities, vocations, etc.?—A. I served with Mr. McSweeney, and Mr. Campbell, of Washington, and Mr. Rogers, of Philadelphia, the committee which had the revision of statistics in charge. I was secretary of that committee.

Q. To whom was that report made?—A. To the Commissioner-General. Its recommendations were adopted immediately.

Q. How long has the new plan been in operation?—A. Since the 1st of July, 1898. That plan could be best stated as, substituting for the territorial classification of the people who come here the language or race classification. In other words, people that speak the same language and that have the same religious ties and that are bound to ally themselves together in this country and, whether they want to or not, be forced into the same occupations, were classified together. That was the main change. The old political division is still retained. For instance, we can tell now how many come from the political divisions of Austria-Hungary, and from Russia, and the statistics of their occupations and destinations.

Q. What have you to say as to the accuracy of the old statistical methods of this office?—A. In regard to the number of people coming from political divisions it was, I think, accurate within very close limits, but where, for instance, in the case of Austria-Hungary, the country was divided up into territorial subdivisions, each of these subdivisions did not, in fact, in every instance, get the number of immigrants that should be credited to it. But it should be understood that we have now more information on which to base our statistics than previous to July, 1898. This new system included the obtaining of new information not available prior to July 1, 1898.

Q. Do you know of any way you can take the old statistics and conform them to the new methods so as to make them more intelligent and more correct?—A. That would be very difficult, and could not be done with any degree of accuracy. Of course the man's name, to one familiar with the country, will give a clew to the race to which he belongs. For instance, in 9 cases out of 10 you could separate in that way the Jews from Poland from the Poles themselves. In some such way as that it might be partially done, but I do not think the result would be of much value.

Q. You know there are 1 or 2 treatises on immigration, written in this country, which, together with the conclusions of political economists, are based on the figures furnished to the old New York Board. What have you to say as to the correctness of any of those conclusions?—A. I do not think those conclusions are impaired. I think, in the past, the number of people from Russia, as a political division, was correct within close limits, and in the same way from Austria-Hungary. It was only as regards the subdivisions that there might be a question, and I do not think that the element of subdivisions enters to any extent into economic deductions from these old figures.

Q. (By Mr. CLARKE.) Are there some loathsome and contagious diseases that are so obscure that they are not readily detected on a cursory examination of the person?—A. Yes, that may be so. Perhaps in that connection I might explain, in detail, our form of inspection. The first inspector stops the immigrant, looks at his hands, head, and eyes carefully. Skin diseases will usually show themselves in one of these 3 localities. For instance, in leprosy the first indication would be in the appearance of the hands. Then he is passed along probably 30 feet and brought to a second and perhaps a third inspector. The second inspector disregards, as a rule, the head and hands, but looks for anything else which attracts his attention, and checks the first inspector on the eyes. Then, if there be a third inspector there, he tries to check the other two, and in that way it is really more than a cursory examination, because the men who are working on each are men who have had the opportunity and training to make them experts, and they pick out things which would pass a man with any ordinary training of that sort. Anything which attracts suspicion in any way is turned to one side and later gone over as carefully as may be necessary.

Q. Do you sometimes require an immigrant to remove his clothing?—A. Certainly, or send him to the hospital for observation; that is frequently done.

Q. Have you any knowledge of contagious diseases developing which pass you?—A. I do not recollect any instance at present, but I think that is possible.

Q. Do you think there would be enough such cases that the danger would be very great?—A. No; I do not think so. They have not been brought to our attention, or I would certainly recollect such cases. I do not recollect any.

Q. You agree with Dr. Williams as to the desirability of bathing and disinfecting at the port of departure?—A. Yes; though I presume that is of greater value as a quarantine measure than for the purpose of immigration strictly.

Q. (By Mr. FARQUHAR.) Is there any matter you can suggest that has been omitted in the examination; anything to which you desire to call the attention of the commission?—A. There was one thing in regard to favus; the commission asked the common name for that, and Dr. Williams responded "scaldhead;" that should not be confused with eczema, sometimes also known as scaldhead. It is a parasitic disease of the scalp, and was practically unknown in this country until the Russian Jews and Italians began to come here. Then, in regard to trachoma, our attitude in ruling that as a dangerous, contagious disease is due to the order from the Department placing it in this category, which order was issued at the instigation of a convention of oculists in this country, who said the disease would probably die out in this country if it were not for fresh accretions from Europe.

IMMIGRATION.

NEW YORK, N. Y., *July 25, 1899.*

TESTIMONY OF MR. CHARLES G. EICHLER,

Chief of Statistical and Record Division, Bureau of Immigration, New York City.

At a meeting of the Subcommission on Manufactures and General Business, held in New York City July 25, 1899, Mr. Farquhar presiding, Mr. Charles G. Eichler appeared at 5 p. m., and, being duly sworn, testified concerning immigration, as follows:

Q. (By M. FARQUHAR.) What is your name?—A. Charles G. Eichler.
Q. What is your position?—A. Chief of statistical and record division, Immigration Bureau, port of New York.
Q. Where do you live?—A. 249 West One hundred and twenty-sixth street; office at 45 Pearl street, New York.
Q. How long have you held that position?—A. Since April 19, 1890, under the United States Government, and 10 years previous under the State government.
Q. What are the duties of your office?—A. I make up statistics for the Commissioner of Immigration, who transmits them to the Commissioner-General.
Q. Did you have in charge all the statistics at the time the fire happened at Ellis Island?—A. Yes.
Q. Did you lose everything at that time?—A. Very nearly everything. We had old records there from the old State board of immigration for the past 50 years, since 1847, and I guess they were very nearly all destroyed.
Q. Have you ever examined to find if duplicates of any of these records were in Albany?—A. There are no duplicates. The only duplicates are in the United States customs-house at this port.
Q. Were there any copies furnished to the municipality of the city of New York?—A. No.
Q. Do you regard these documents of great value?—A. I do.
Q. What have you to say as to the real value of the statistics other than simply numbering the people that come in?—A. At the present time they are very good.
Q. What was it 2 years ago?—A. Not so good.
Q. Did the Government keep the old State form when the United States came in to take jurisdiction?—A. No;. an act of the legislature turned it over from the State to the United States.
Q. As to manner of collecting statistics, when the United States Government took charge was the same system carried out as was carried out by the old State board?—A. Yes; same form. We started first to register the passengers the same as the old State board.
Q. As for the number of immigrants that have arrived, there is sufficient data in the papers of that time and other reports to have a comparative view of the old immigration, the present immigration, and the changes that have occurred in the immigrants, nationalities, and all?—A. Yes.
Q. Did your old statistics of the State board go beyond 1846 and 1847? A. May 10, 1847.
Q. Do you know what dependence can be placed on statistics from 1824 to 1847?—A. I could not tell.
Q. Do you know how it is the political economists usually adopt 1824 as a basis of their comparisons with respect to American immigration?—A. I do not.
Q. You have no knowledge of handling any figures prior to 1847 on the old board?—A. No.
Q. Is there now in the possession of the United States statistics from 1847 to the present time that this commission can reach?—A. You might get it through the Bureau of Statistics, Washington, Treasury Department.
Q. Records made through collectors of the ports?—A. Customs districts.
Q. Can you suggest any amendments in reference to the statistical matter?—A. No; I think they are very good now. As Mr. McSweeney said, after a while we will get into the cabin business, and that will make it final.
Q. Have you in your possession here any body of comparative statistics that would be of value to this commission in making its report to Congress?—A. We could make up some illuminated tables or something like that.
Q. Have not bodies advocating restriction of immigration obtained considerable statistics from you?—A. Yes, several, through the Commissioner of Immigration.
Q. We take it from your testimony the new arrangement is of great advantage over the old one?—A. Yes; and we will still do better when we get the cabin business in shape. The Commissioner and I are working at it now.

NEW YORK, N. Y., *July 25, 1899.*

TESTIMONY OF MR. EDWARD B. HOLMAN,

Inspector and Secretary of the Board of Special Inquiry, Immigration Bureau, New York City.

At a meeting of the Subcommission on Manufactures and General Business, held in New York City, July 25, 1899, Mr. Farquhar presiding, Mr. Edward B. Holman appeared at 5.30 p. m., and, being duly sworn, testified concerning immigration as follows:

Q. (By Mr. FARQUHAR.) What position do you occupy in the Bureau of Immigration?—A. Immigration inspector assigned to duty as secretary and member of the board of special inquiry.

Q. What are the duties of that board?—A. That is a board of special inquiry created by act of Congress, consisting of 4 officers sitting as inspectors, who hear such cases as are sent before them for special inquiry and determine whether they shall be admitted or deported. They are designated in writing by the Secretary of the Treasury or the Superintendent of Immigration, who is now the Commissioner-General of Immigration. We hear such cases as the registry department send down to us, known as special-inquiry cases. Those consist of cases that come directly from the registry department; sometimes from the medical department, although all medical department cases come through the registry department and then to the board of special inquiry. We swear these immigrants and take their statements, and after we have heard all the testimony that we think is material to the question of their landing here we vote on whether we will land them or not. It takes the affirmative vote of 3 members to land an immigrant. Any member dissenting can appeal to the Secretary of the Treasury and hold such immigrant until such appeal is determined; and, on the other hand, the immigrant has the right to appeal to the Secretary of the Treasury, which acts as a stay on his deportation until that is determined. We have interpreters for the different languages, and some of us know their language enough to speak with the immigrants. I act as the secretary, and take down all the evidence in shorthand and keep a record of it. I have with me Mr. Smith, who is also secretary—2 secretaries to the board of special inquiry—and we do the same character of work.

Q. How speedily can you dispose of the cases submitted to you?—A. We handle them very fast. Sometimes I am afraid the business is so large that perhaps we do not have sufficient time to give to each case. Of course, sometimes one case will demand more attention than another. Take, for instance, where we have a number of immigrants who have not means to reach their destination. We can not turn them out. They do not present any sufficient reason for being deported, except they are in a helpless condition for the time being, and we can not dispose of them very rapidly. We have nothing to do but wait, and see whether their friends and relations will show up later on. We can dispose of some cases in a couple of minutes, and then again we may strike a case of contract labor or something suspicious, and we will have to question them very closely. We try to be very thorough in our examination. We handle on an average during the busy season 100 cases a day.

Q. Out of how many immigrants arriving?—A. That would be hard to say. Some days we might have 5 or 6 ships all land at once, and we would be flooded with special-inquiry cases; have 400 or 500 cases held for special inquiry. We would try to dispose of them as fast as good service would warrant, and we would have more than 1 board running, Sometimes 3 and 4 boards run at one time, and each board would treat about 100 cases a day. That is a good day's work, indeed. To treat 100 cases, and treat them properly, does not leave much time for each immigrant

Q. How do you constitute more than 1 board?—A. The commissioner calls in whatever the emergency requires. If it is necessary to have 2 boards, we have 2, and if that does not seem equal to the cases we have more. Usually 1 board is sufficient for the ordinary transaction of the business, but during the very busy times, when they are coming in in great numbers, it is impossible to dispose of them promptly with 1 board.

Q. How frequently are your decisions overruled in Washington?—A. I do not think they are overruled very often. I should say a very small percentage of the board decisions are overruled. The Commissioner of Immigration usually sends his opinion along with the record and testimony of the special board of inquiry, and there is not often much difference of opinion between us in regard to the admissibility of the immigrant.

Q. Have you anything to do particularly with this Italian bureau?—A. I do not know of any reason why we should have any relationship with them beyond what we might with private citizens. I do not recognize any right—the board has never recognized their right to take any part in our proceedings. They are there, of course, and have been there for a number of years, and it is generally understood that they have been interested in the relief of their countrymen.

Q. Do you find it in any way an interference with the proper execution of your duties?—A. At the present time it does not interfere in any way that I know of with the duties of the board of special inquiry, but at one time it did, and so seriously that I felt it my duty to communicate with the Commissioner of Immigration in regard to it, and told him such facts as had come to my knowledge in regard to the Italian bureau However, I have never known of any obnoxious actions on the part of Dr. Rossi himself. He is the head of the bureau.

Q. Did you ever see any necessity for any nation having a bureau of that kind so immediate to United States officials?—A. No.

Q. Do you know of any practical use for it now?—A. I do not.

Q. Is there any reason you know of why they should be in such immediate contact with the immigrant as a benefit to the immigrant or their own Government?—A. I do not know of any possible benefit.

Q. Have you ever had a talk with Dr. Rossi to learn the reasons why they seek closer contact with the immigrant than other nations?—A. The only conversation I had in which Dr. Rossi took part was a little consultation that took place after the communication I wrote to the Commissioner. Dr. Rossi was called down to the commissioner's office and quite a conversation was had, and the Doctor disclaimed any knowledge of the practices that I had spoken of in the communication, and was told by the commissioner of immigration that the bureau should not interfere with immigrants until after they were landed. That was about the only conversation I have had in reference to the matter.

Q. (By Mr. CLARKE.) To what class of detention cases does the board of special inquiry give the most time?—A. It usually takes more time to try a contract-labor case than a public charge case, for this reason: When a contract-labor case is discovered by the inspector he makes an examination, and if convinced that he is here in violation of the alien contract labor law he reduces that examination to an affidavit which he has read over to the immigrant and duly signed. Then he appears before us with the immigrant and submits this affidavit and the immigrant to the board of special inquiry for further examination. We have the affidavit read over to him by the interpreter, and if he verifies it and says it is true, that he comes here in violation of the alien contract labor law, and in pursuance to an agreement to perform service, he is excluded. So far, that is nothing but an ex parte hearing. In a few days the man that he says he has the work with appears and we must hear him. So you may say we are sure of 2 hearings on that contract-labor case, and they usually have means to employ lawyers and create activity generally in their behalf. I should say they take up more time as individual cases than others, but there are not so many of them as public charge cases.

Q. Does your board afford the fullest possible opportunities to the contract-labor inspectors to present their cases to you? A. Yes, they usually have the call on the situation. For instance, we will have a room full of people, and if the contract-labor inspector comes in with a case we usually give it prompt attention, because in that sort of case it will not do to wait very long, for you have to depend for the making of that case on the confession of the immigrant. If that immigrant finds out he is going to be deported, he may change his mind and say he is not under contract, so we give it prompt attention. We do not try to hurry the matter, in fact, we warn him usually that it is not necessary for him to say that he has work in this country in order to land, but must simply tell the plain truth. Some of them, perhaps, might have the idea that if they did not have work here we would send them back as a public charge, and unwillingly trap themselves, but in order to prevent that we warn them, and tell them we want them to tell the truth.

Q. While you aim to be fair to the immigrant you cooperate, so far as you can, with the inspectors who bring the case before you?—A. I would not use the word cooperate, because it would seem to my mind to convey the impression we were paying attention more particularly to one part of the special inquiry cases than another. We try to examine every case that comes before us with absolute fairness and thoroughness, and in doing that we give the contract-labor bureau every service we can.

Q. There is never any antagonism between you and them?—A. Oh, no.

Q. (By Mr. FARQUHAR.) Does anything suggest itself to your mind that would be valuable to the commission, any suggestions?—A. I would like to say that

I have been associated with Mr. McSweeney for many years and am familiar with his views, and the recommendations he has made I thoroughly agree with. I believe in preserving the spirit of the laws as they now exist. I believe we should preserve them, and try to amend such defects as may be found to exist in them without taking chances with experimental things. We have got established by law now pretty near all of the people that I can think of that ought to be excluded from this country—contract laborers, idiots, public charges, paupers, and all those enumerated in the act of 1891. That seems to me to cover the ground, and the only difficulty that remains is to render more effective the means of detecting them and sending them back. I am very much in favor of anything that will tend to reach these excluded classes more effectively, if it is possible to do so; but, on the other hand, I do not believe that it is a wise policy to try to reach every little evil that may exist by some precise act of legislation. I would prefer to see the commissioner of immigration and the board of special inquiry given such power of discretion as would enable them to do justice in every case that arose. It is hard to depend on a specific enactment for a remedy in every matter. Unless there was some discretion it would sometimes be hardship. I have seen some very heartrending things we have had to do in the line of duty, and sometimes have been brought face to face with the unnecessary hardships that will exist when you depend on the letter of the law.

Q. (By Mr. CLARKE.) Do you think an educational test would be of any value for protecting American labor?—A. I doubt it very seriously.

Q. Do you think, from your observation of immigrants, that it would improve the quality of the immigrant and help us to a better class of citizens, industrially and morally?—A. I am in favor of anything that will increase education among the immigrants or anybody else we have to make citizens out of, but I do not believe it is an absolute sure test of the persons that come here. I have seen some persons come here that were well educated that I would rather keep out than persons, young, able-bodied, and not so well educated. It is not a safe test at all. An educational test might sometimes hit some sections right that furnish undesirable classes of citizens; otherwise I do not like the principle of it, and I do not think it is an absolute safe test of the desirability of the immigrant.

Q. You state it would apply to certain classes who are undesirable for other reasons, as I understood you. Now, is not that about the only test that can be applied beyond our present laws toward the exclusion of undesirable immigrants?— A. That might be, and still it does not come up to my idea of how these questions ought to be met. If an undesirable person happens to come within the prohibition established by this educational test, would you be barring him on account of the real ground of his undesirability? Q. It would be incidental?—A. I would rather stand up and give the reason why we did not want him.

Q. Is it not true that a larger proportion of the immigrants from the British Islands and the north of Europe would pass the educational test than those from the south of Europe and the east?—A. Yes.

Q. You think the educational test would be of some value toward the exclusion of classes that are thought to be less desirable than other classes?—A. Yes; there are some undesirable sections that would be prohibited by the educational test.

Q. (By Mr. FARQUHAR.) In this educational test, do you take the view of the immigrant as an ultimate citizen of the United States or simply as a worker and developer of material resources?—A. I look on that in this way: As I look at the immigration question generally, it is from the standpoint of the immigration official dealing with his eligibility to land when he reaches here, and I think the question of his citizenship is a separate and distinct one. If I thought that man coming here and applying for admission in an ignorant condition was going to remain in that ignorant condition, I would not want him to land here. We can deal with his citizenship after he has shown his character and physical ability and willingness to work. When admitted he is supposed to go on and become an intelligent and useful citizen. He is supposed to take up from that time the study of the problem of good citizenship and learn it by residence here and complying with our laws, and then when the time comes to naturalize him that can be determined by the proper functions. I think it would be a very difficult matter to say that every person who comes here uneducated would not make a good citizen; on the other hand, I would not like to say that every man who comes here educated would make a good citizen. If the man impresses the inspector that he is fit to land he is not apt to become a bad citizen. I would not naturalize anybody that could not read and write. I believe in preserving our naturalization on as high a plane as possible.

Q. (By Mr. CLARKE.) Would it be safe to leave the application of the educational test to the discretion of this board of special inquiry?—A. Yes. I think the board of special inquiry ought to have sufficient discretion to be able to take all these things into consideration. If a man can not read and write that is a factor. He certainly will not be as well equipped to go out and make a living as if he were educated, and that is unwittingly taken account of, in our general opinion, as to whether he is equipped to land. But not being educated, and having the ability in other ways, ought not to constitute sufficient reason for sending him back if he is otherwise desirable. It is merely a factor that should be taken into consideration, but it ought not to be the decisive point.

Q. You mean it ought not to be a reason for exclusion?—A. I do; not the sole reason.

Q. You think it is going too far?—A. Yes.

Q. And when you establish an educational test you place up the bars at once, and that ends it; the question of desirability does not enter into it at all?—A. Yes. You see, we have the excluded classes established by law—idiots, public charges, and all that. When this man is examined we ought to ask him, and nearly always do, if he can read and write. That has to be taken into consideration in making up our verdict, but it ought not to be decisive. Take a young man 18 or 19 years of age; he has not been blest with the opportunities of getting an education, but otherwise may be bright. He comes here as a laborer, coming into a field where his labor can be employed; in every respect is admissible except he may not be able to read and write. Surely he can overcome that difficulty, and if he has the elements of a good citizen he will overcome it.

Q. If the law provided the educational test to be applied in the discretion of the board of special inquiry, how many—what proportion—of the immigrants who are now admitted would properly be rejected by the board?—A. Among the Italians it would be quite large, and I should say, taking it as a whole, it would make quite a difference. We have figures which show the relative percentage of illiteracy in the different countries and figures to show the excluded classes from the different countries. I am not prepared to say what the figures would be. It would make a large difference in some sections where I do not believe we want to restrict immigration at all. Suppose it should send back the virtuous and industrious Irish girls that come here; on what grounds of humanity and broad lines of thought could we justify that to the world—excluding persons who come here speaking our own language and who perhaps, by no fault of their own, had been unable to enjoy the opportunities of learning to read and write?

Q. If this were left to the discretion of your board, would there be any danger of some races being unfairly discriminated against?—A. No. My idea about the board is that it ought to be made to approach as nearly as possible to a jury. It ought to be built somewhat on that plan, so that when they look a man over and give him a careful and conscientious investigation and then believe he ought to go back, he ought to go back. The chances are that such a man would not make a good citizen. Sometimes we find after an examination of an alien that he is not desirable, and yet he does not come within the excluded classes, and we can not force him into one of these excluded classes, and have to vote to admit him. If the law is changed at all so as to reach any more people, I believe in making it elastic along these lines, so as to give discretionary power. If the board of special inquiry had the power to send a person back solely because he could not read and write, it might be sometimes that a person might come here that we could use that to advantage against. Anything that will tend to make the man who makes the contract for labor suffer a little more would also be a good thing. The alien is not going to make a contract unless he has somebody to give the inducement.

Q. Have you thought of any new way to reach him?—A. I must confess it is an extremely difficult matter, and I am not prepared to give any solution of it.

NEW YORK, N. Y., *July 26, 1899.*

TESTIMONY OF DR. LORENZO ULLO,

Legal counsel, Immigration Bureau, Port of New York.

At a meeting of the Subcommission on Manufactures and General Business, held in New York July 26, 1899, Chairman Smyth presiding, Dr. Lorenzo Ullo appeared at 10 a. m., and, being duly sworn, testified concerning immigration as follows:

Q. (By Mr. SMYTH.) State your name.—A. Lorenzo Ullo.

Q. Residence?—A. City of New York, Borough of Brooklyn.

Q. Are you connected with the Immigration Bureau; and, if so, in what capacity?—A. Practically, I am the legal adviser of the Immigration Bureau.

Q. How long have you held that position?—A. Since 1893.

Q. Will you state to the commission the workings of your department, and any suggestions you have to make with reference to changes in the present laws? We will then ask you some questions.—A. The law, as it has been enacted from time to time, has been trying to cover special cases, which method has resulted in some instances in very awkward and contradictory statements and enactments. The original law was passed in about 1875. I speak from memory. It particularly excluded children coming under what was known as the padrone system. In 1875 there prevailed a great deal of what was known then as the padrone system, which is now practically extinct. The law also prohibited the importation of persons for the purposes of prostitution. Then came in 1882 a law which was properly a law trying to regulate immigration, which was the outcome of several State laws which were considered unconstitutional. The State of New York had legislated and imposed a head tax on the different steamship companies, to be paid on the arrival of each passenger. Those laws were declared unconstitutional by the Supreme Court of the United States, and this brought about the law in 1882 to regulate immigration imposing a tax on each passenger brought into this country, and that tax was to be kept as a separate fund, called the immigration fund, for the purpose of protecting and caring for the immigrants. In it, if I am not mistaken, there is a list of persons who are undesirable, such as paupers, idiots, criminals, and convicts, excepting those for political offenses. Then came the first difficulty; the law speaks of the passengers who are undesirable and who shall not be permitted to land, and of convicts it says they must be sent to the nation to which they belong and from whence they came. This expression has also been used in some subsequent legislation. The port whence the immigrant came may not be a port of the nation to which he belongs; to which are we to send him? A great many come from the eastern parts of Europe, inland parts of Germany, and inland parts of Austria-Hungary and Italy, thus causing confusion, and take passage at Bremen. If they are sent back to that port they are turned out there helpless, where they have no claim for protection.

Q. (By Mr. FARQUHAR.) Do you think it would be an advantage to have the law so that the immigrant would be returned to the nation to which he belongs, independent of the port from which he departs?—A. I do not think we could have any jurisdiction or even actual power to enforce our order if we did so. How could we enforce it? Suppose we decided he should go to the nation to which he belongs; how can we force the captain or the owners of the vessel at Bremen to send that passenger from Bremen to Russia?

Q. You think it would be better to send to the port of embarkation, and by the line on which he came?—A. I think we should stop at "Not permitted to land." Let the vessels do what they think best. It would then be a question between them and the immigrants.

Q. The law considers it now as a private contract between the carrier and the immigrant, and the question of the regulation occurs as soon as the ship comes within the marine league.—A. But if we order them deported, when the ship gets beyond the three miles we have no jurisdiction and can not enforce the order; therefore the best way is to say these undesirable people shall not be permitted to land. The vessel will take them on board and find its own way to execute its contract, or give damages for the nonexecution of the contract, with which we have nothing to do. There is another point. Sometimes a steamer brings immigrants from Europe here on its way to Cuba or the West Indies. We are bound, under the law, to send the immigrants back to the port whence they came; but the steamer is going south. What shall we do? I say the best way to keep within our powers is not to permit them to land, and let the vessel and the immigrants fix their respective rights between themselves. If an immigrant has a case of damages, let him have it before the proper tribunal. We say, "We bar you from landing that person," and that is as far as our jurisdiction can go. I could not devise a way of enforcing an order of the Commissioner-General to send a person from Bremen to an inland city.

Q. Then, after the inspection is made here and the parties have been found undesirable, there is an arrangement between the Treasury Department of the United States and the steamship companies to deport such undesirable immigrants?—A. As it is now, we order them deported to the ports from which they come. That order is served on the steamship companies.

Q. None of the representatives of that man's country in the United States interfere in any capacity with this deportation, so that it is simply an arrangement, and nothing more, between the steamship companies and the Treasury Department at Washington?—A. Yes; it is a result of the law as it stands, executed as best we can. It is not purely an arrangement; we order it; we claim it to be a right of the Commissioner to order the steamship companies to deport them. Under the law the examination of every passenger is supposed to take place on board; but, for the convenience of the Government and its officials, the law allows the immigrants to be temporarily removed, but provides that "such a removal shall not be construed a landing." As soon as a person is considered undesirable and is to be deported, we order him sent back, as if he had always been on board the steamer; order him to be taken back out of our jurisdiction. If it happens that the port whence he came is the port of his nationality, so much the better for the man. If it does not happen to be so, we can not execute that part of the law.

Q. In case of detention of this immigrant, pending his examination here, or an appeal to Washington, the cost of his care and maintenance is charged to the steamship company?—A. I understand it to be so.

Q. Have the steamship companies at any time made any complaint as to the execution of the law, with respect to the care, maintenance, and detention of immigrants?—A. I understand they have made a great many, but I do not know that they have ever objected to the order of deportation.

Q. Do they object to the kind of inspection that you have here over immigrants?—A. I do not think there has been any complaint on that line. I can say as much since 1893, since which time I have been there, and I have had experience even beyond 1893. Before I was connected with the office in my present position I was connected with benevolent societies, and my experience runs from the time when it was under State laws, and I must say there has been a most decided improvement in the workings of the department. It is now organized. It has its regular organization. There was a time when it was merely chaotic. Under the present law there are two kinds of examinations, which now put the inspection in very good order; there is a preliminary examination on board or at the Barge Office; there is then a second examination, which is an examination by special inquiry. When the officers who make preliminary examinations, called the boarding officers, have, in the words of the law, reasonable doubt that the person is not a person entitled to be landed, their powers are limited to sending him before the board of special inquiry. It is the board of special inquiry that finally excludes a person under the law. The steamship companies do not complain much as to the judgment passed upon the immigrants; they do complain mostly of the fact that these immigrants take appeals to the Secretary of the Treasury in Washington and prolong their appeal, which prolongs their detention and increases the expense. I understand, and it must be known generally, that these steamship companies take some precaution in cases of persons which they consider of doubtful admission. They compel such persons to make a good deposit before accepting them for transportation to this country. So the company is guaranteed against the expenses of their stay here and deportation. So far as the steamship lines are concerned, there is not much complaint as to the law as executed now. I think there were complaints in the first year of its execution. Of course, it was a new law.

Q. Cases of infraction of the alien contract-labor law—have you had many of these cases in the courts?—A. I have had charge of nearly all those cases on the Atlantic side, preparing them for the courts. Under the law the district attorney is designated to sue, but frequently I have had the preparation of testimony, and have even drawn the pleadings in some cases. There has been the greatest difficulty. It has reached a point under the decisions where, I will say, not one case in a thousand can be brought to a satisfactory result or conviction. In fact, in my experience of 5 years, I think only one case has been successful.

Q. Are you speaking of the contract-labor law?—A. The contract-labor law alone. In the others we are mostly successful. The original contract-labor law was passed in 1885. It was amended or rather extended in 1887. It was in some way made, without amending or abrogating these two acts, a part of the act of 1891. Then, in 1893, the law has not been revised, but patched on. Under this law any legal mind can not but find the difficulties which have been encountered. The law of 1885 declares in so many words in the third line: "It shall be unlawful for any person, company, partnership, or corporation, in any manner whatsoever, to prepay the transportation, or in any way assist or encourage the importation or migration of any alien or aliens, any foreigner or foreigners, into the United States, its Territories, or the District of Columbia, under contract or agreement, parol or special, express or implied, made previous to the importation or migration of such alien or aliens, foreigner or foreigners, to perform labor or service of any kind in the United States, its Territories, or the District of Columbia."

The law says it shall be unlawful to import into the United States a man under contract made previous to his importation. That contract must be made *previous* to his importation. It must be a contract solemnly entered into. The words "express or implied" refer only to the mode of proof, by direct or circumstantial evidence; but it must be a contract as solemn as any other contract. How can that be proved? The courts have held, and, I think, held justly as far as that law is concerned, that it must be such a contract as could have been enforced if not performed by either of the parties. It is very rare that anybody makes such a contract, and it is rare, too, that the Government can find the proofs of such a contract; there is the great difficulty.

Q. How do you propose to remedy that? What amendment would you make?—A. It is very hard to propose an amendment, but I think inducements to bring a person, inducing him to come for the purpose of giving him labor, would reach much further. If you make a law that would condemn inducements to aliens to come and perform labor here, then, under our system of jury, we will have 12 men who will find out whether it really amounts to the inducement intended by law, or mere frivolous or casual praising of the country; but if it must be a contract, how can we on this side find proofs of the contract made on the other side? It is practically an impossibility.

Q. You say you have had only one conviction under the law?—A. I can recollect only one, and that case went to the jury. On account of this any lawyer can see it is very hard to prove a contract.

We have had another difficulty; importation is an essential element of the prohibition; if we deport a man who is imported, the courts have released the importer from the fine on the ground that the man has not been imported. If we find he is a contract laborer he is sent back and therefore there has been no importation. That has also been found in one of the cases.

Then we come also to this trouble: There are some cases where contracts can be proved, but where the defense is that the alien was brought to perform work in a new industry, which case is excepted under the law; so there again we have a good deal of work.

In the Keck diamond case they imported all the diamond cutters. It took over a week's trial to find out whether it was a new industry in this country to cut diamonds. The Government proved that cutting of diamonds was done in this country since 1830, but whether it was a new *established* industry was a question. They claimed that we may have had special cases of diamond cutting here and there in the States, but the judge charged the jury in that case that under the testimony it must be not a special case of diamond cutting but whether it has been an established industry or not.

Again we find the law defective in this: In section 5—"Nor shall this act be so construed as to prevent any person, or persons, partnership, or corporation from engaging, under contract or agreement, skilled workmen in foreign countries to perform labor in the United States in or upon any new industry *not at present established* in the United States: *Provided*, That skilled labor for that purpose can not be otherwise obtained; nor shall the provisions of this act apply to professional actors, artists, lecturers, or singers, nor to persons employed strictly as personal or domestic servants." "New industry not at present established,"—what does "not at present established" mean? Not established in 1885? Then if established in 1886—and we are in 1899—and has since become established, are they still permitted and privileged to bring laborers under contract because their industry was not established in 1885? Under the law as it stands, we have to meet this point.

Then there is another thing which has worried the department a great deal, and that is that in no place in that law is it stated that we have the power to deport the contract laborers, except in the title. The title speaks of an act to prohibit the importation and immigration of foreigners. Not a word in the 5 sections provides for the deportation or the power to deport. It is in the law of 1891 implied, and we gather our power from the implication in that law, where the classes of undesirable aliens are enumerated. This says the following classes shall be excluded: "Idiots, insane persons, paupers, or persons likely to become a public charge," etc. Then it says "also any person whose ticket or passage is paid for with the money of another or who is assisted by others to come, unless it is affirmatively and satisfactorily shown on special inquiry that such person does not belong to one of the foregoing excluded classes, or to the class of contract laborers excluded by the act of February twenty-sixth, eighteen hundred and eighty-five." In the law, as amended in 1887, we find this expression—section 6, that if after examination, etc., "there shall be found among such passengers any persons included under the prohibition in this act * * * such persons shall not be permitted to land." The act does not include any but the person who made the contract, who is fined, still we must gather our authority from these words. Again section 8 says: "All persons included in the prohibition in this act, upon arrival, shall be sent back to the nations to which they belong and from whence they came." That clearly means that the contract laborers must be sent back, because the other party is supposed to be within the United States. So we have to gather our authority to deport merely from the spirit of the law and not from the letter of it.

Q. Do you find any sections in these laws conflicting since the adoption of the ater amendments to the previous law?—A. There are cases of patching, at least adding one without amending the other. They are all laws. They are the law of 1875 and the law of 1882, 1887, 1891, and 1893.

Q. Do you find amendments there where the amended section has not been repealed at all? Do you find two bodies of law bearing on one feature?—A. Yes; and the law of 1882 is not amended at all, and when the classes of undesirable persons are mentioned in the law of 1891, which law is somewhat expansive of the classes mentioned in the law of 1882, the law does not expressly abolish the law of 1882.

Q. What remedial legislation would you propose in this matter?—A. A general revision. It has been working since 1890 under the United States control. Since then we have had a great deal of experience, and the thing has in some way crystallized. There is enough experience to make a recodification of the law, without even adding to what is known to be the spirit of the law.

Q. Have you formulated at any time a recodification of these laws?—A. I did during Dr. Senner's time, I think about 4 years ago.

Q. Was that matter presented to the Treasury in Washington, or did it go beyond Dr. Senner?—A. I can not tell. I know Dr. Senner had gone to Washington and I sent it to him there, but how far it reached I can not tell. It was only suggestions for recodification, and that is merely more or less what I am mentioning here.

There is one other point with which we have found great difficulty; in fact, a case involving it is still pending and may go to the United States Supreme Court. The law uses the word "aliens" and sometimes uses the words "alien immigrants." This has produced some difference of opinion among the judges. The judges in this circuit, Judge Lacombe, especially, have decided that the law only is applicable to alien immigrants and not to aliens generally. After the first decision we found that all were taught to say they came here to see the country or to see their father or sister or brother, and were not coming as immigrants but as tourists. We tried to avoid that the best we could afterwards. A great many so-called birds of passage come here for the summer and go back in the winter. The judges held that they are immigrants the first time they land, and after the first landing they are no longer immigrants and are beyond the jurisdiction of the Bureau of Immigration. This went on until 1894, when in the appropriation for the enforcement of the Chinese exclusion act, after allowing an appropriation, the statute went on to say that the examination of all aliens shall be final unless an appeal be taken to the Secretary of the Treasury, and his decision will be final. The Supreme Court of the United States in the case of a Chinese decided that that law, although found in an appropriation statute, makes it final and takes away the jurisdiction from the courts in all examinations of immigrants, "at least for Chinese immigration." The inferior courts, Judge Lacombe and Judge Brown, since then have followed the decision in the cases of aliens, whether Chinese or not Chinese; but there is at this moment pending an appeal from a habeas corpus where an Italian contends that that law does not apply to all aliens, but is restricted to Chinese alone. The question may come up before the United States Supreme Court in October or November, when that appeal may be reached. We have now reached a point with the inferior courts where this is no longer a difficulty, because they have recognized that all aliens are within the jurisdiction of the Immigration Bureau.

Q. Under the statute, in your prosecutions do you not find considerable difficulty in the definition of "criminals?"—A. Yes, a great deal. We have "convicts." Who is a convict? In the law of 1882 the word convict was generic, was not qualified at all. In the law of 1891 it is qualified by the words "has been convicted of a felony or other infamous crime or misdemeanor involving moral turpitude." We have also had this experience: a man comes charged with murder, and is confronted with the person who charges him and who was a witness to the murder. We try to hold the man for further instructions, and notify the Government to which he belongs, and ask whether they desire to take any action. They do not. What can we do? We have no power to deport him, if he is otherwise qualified to come in. Under this law we have no other alternative than to allow him to come in. We had a case of a man charged with felony. His Government asked for his extradition. We turned him over to the judicial authorities and retained our rights of jurisdiction to examine him further. We turned him over to the authorities to find out whether under our treaties with the Government to which he belonged our judges would declare that there was sufficient evidence to justify his extradition. The magistrate before whom the case came decided that there was sufficient evidence for extradition, and the Secretary of State thought there was also, but there arose a technical question whether the felony was committed within the jurisdiction and territory of the Government asking for his extradition, or within the territory of another nation, to which the man belonged, and on account of that technical question the Secretary of State thought proper not to grant the extradition. Now, we had this man adjudged by our own tribunals likely to be a convict. He came back to us for his examination as if nothing had happened. He came before the board of special inquiry, and he appeared by himself and by counsel in his behalf. He was sent back because he said he had no money; he was sent back only because he was likely to become a public charge. We have cases of persons running away with the wife of another; for example, a wife becomes unfaithful and finds another man to bring her over. Her husband remonstrates, "that is my wife coming with another man." The case does not come under the provision against "Importing for purposes of prostitution," nor under polygamy, but here is a vicious life and we have no power to send her back if she has money enough to bring her in.

Q. Have you ever deported a Mormon?—A. I can not tell you. I never have been called to give an opinion for a Mormon.

Q. (By Mr. CLARKE.) Are you a member of the legal profession?—A. I am.

Q. Doctor of laws?—A. Doctor of laws.

Q. Admitted to practice in the New York courts and in the Federal courts?—A. Yes.

Q. There is no question I suppose but that our Government has jurisdiction over these steamship companies?—A. None whatever.

Q. What then is to hinder the enforcement of a law, if Congress should enact one, requiring the steamship companies to send back to the country of their origin, such immigrants as are rejected, even though that might involve some land transportation after reaching the foreign port?—A. None whatever, so far as jurisdiction is concerned. The difficulty is in the practical way of enforcing it. Suppose a vessel hails from Bremen, what can we do? The thing I advise is to stop the clearance of such steamer when it comes into port again. I do not deny the power to obtain jurisdiction, but the difficulty is in its enforcement.

Q. Do you not understand Germany has such a law?—A. But will Germany help us to enforce it?

Q. Do you not think, as a matter of practice, with this complete jurisdiction over the steamship companies, you could secure such a complete deportation in most cases?—A. With proper treaties to enforce our orders through the countries through which the parties have to travel. Virtually the person deported would be restrained of his liberty in being sent through a country which is not ours.

Q. In case an immigrant is ordered to be deported before being permitted to land, what occasion is there to prosecute anybody?—A. There is no occasion, unless the importation of that person was willful. If the company willfully brings a person who has to be deported, I think there ought to be some way in which that company should be punished. For example, a company brings an idiot or a lunatic here, and compels us to keep machinery sufficient to deport that man, is not that a willful act, and why should not the company be punished for it when it is willful?

Q. Would there practically be many such cases as that?—A. We have had such cases, and have found where the company knew it, and took deposits from the passenger in order to protect themselves in case he was not admitted.

We have had cases where the immigrant comes back again by the next steamer, and he says that the officers on board and the agents on the other side told him he could come back by the next steamer; and they put him in the first or second cabin in order to have him pass through. That is a willful act again. On his way back he is told if he pays his own passage they will pass him through. The company ought to be made responsible for that. As the law stands it is very hard, because it makes it a misdemeanor only for the person who does it, but whether it was the act of captain, officer, or of the agent on the other side—you can not prove it. You could make the vessel responsible for such an act.

Q. Is there any reason why the contract-labor law should be executed differently from the laws excluding other prohibited classes?—A. I can not see any reason; it is one of the prohibited classes and there ought not to be any special legislation for it. It is made by law as much an undesirable class as the idiot or pauper.

Q. Do you see any reason why, in case of neglect or refusal of the district attorney to prosecute, a private party might not prosecute and take a moiety of the penalty as an inducement?—A. I am fully in favor of allowing a private party to sue, and that the fine should go to the contract laborer. The contract laborer is frequently an innocent man. He is not presumed to know the law of this country. He is a foreigner. A man comes to him or he is written to, "If you come to the United States I will give you $15 or $20 a week." He knows nothing of our laws and no law presumes that he ought to know our law. He auctions, perhaps, his property, whatever he has, his furniture, perhaps, and breaks up his home; he has a wife and children; and he comes here, taking it from a practical sense, thinking he has done a prudent act by securing a way of livelihood for his family on this side. He is sent back and he has to build up a home again on the other side. He gets nothing for it, and there is $1,000 penalty for that here. Should he not have the most part of that for damages from the man who lures him? Our law presumes that the man who is here, the American who contracts with him, does know the law; and he does all this damage to this man. Why should not the penalty go to this man? It would work much better for us, and the spirit of our law would be much more satisfied. If we leave it to private action the employers who violate the law will be very much more careful.

Q. Would you extend that power of private prosecution to other cases that are prohibited under the law, or would you confine it to contract-labor cases?—A. I would even give the passengers the right of prosecution against the steamers when the steamers have induced them to come over. We have had cases, for example, of a family—father and mother coming with one child, an idiot; that idiot can not come in; the company knew it. In that way you could force the companies to be more careful. The companies are more afraid of a private action than they are of a Government action, and the spirit of the law is much more satisfied if you leave it to private action.

Q. You say you would have the law amended so as to prohibit the inducements to the people to come, which would extend it beyond a contract?—A. Something which is not strictly a contract.

Q. Do you not anticipate there would be a good many difficulties in the enforcement of that law, in getting proof and a legal determination as to what was an inducement?—A. But the difficulty would be more on the side of the importer to get out of the broad significance of the word "inducements," and an intelligent jury can decide what is an inducement after instruction from the court.

Q. Do you not think there would be a great difficulty in getting Congress to enact such a law?—A. That is a practical question.

Q. As a matter of fact, is it not common for the people residing in this country to write to their friends abroad that they have secured an opportunity for them here and thus induce them to come?—A. Yes; but that would not be an inducement perhaps—merely saying that. The matter must be defined; there must be a definition given.

Q. Suppose you were running a coal mine and hiring men, in Pennsylvania, and wanted some help; you had a good many from abroad and persuaded them to write to their friends on the other side to come over, and tell them they can have employment?—A. That would not be an inducement. I think the line of demarcation would be this: When a man comes here relying upon his own efforts and resources to find employment he ought to be admitted.

Q. Is it not a common practice within our own country for young men, going from the country to the city, to make sure of employment in the city before leaving home, through their friends?—A. No question about it.

Q. The same rule would apply to people coming from abroad, would it not?—A. I am talking from a legal point of view, irrespective as to whether the restriction of foreign contract labor is advisable. If it is advisable to restrict contract labor, the law as it stands does not restrict it.

Q. Do you think it would be advisable to enact a prohibition of the efforts of friends to help their friends get positions?—A. No; the law makes a special distinction for that, where it says that nothing in this act shall be construed to prevent an individual in the United States from sending for a relative or friend who is not of the excluded classes to emigrate for the purpose of settlement here. And then again in the law of 1891, this exception has been kept up by saying they can be assisted by brothers and friends, and the burden of proof is on them to prove that they are not paupers or of the excluded classes or contract laborers.

Q. Do you think you could sufficiently define "inducement" so that you could make it effective to prevent the importation of persons who are really contract laborers in disguise?—A. In the criminal law we have the inducement or inciting to crime as itself a crime. We can go as far as the criminal law goes in defining the inciting or inducing, and therefore we have some rules of law to reach the point.

Q. Can the testimony of immigrants now be taken *de bene esse* before being deported by the board of special inquiry?—A. Yes; but in our practice, what does that amount to? Before they are deported their testimony can be taken *de bene esse*, but as a matter of practical results how does cold type and cold reading of testimony compare with viva voce testimony given by the defendant? When the lawyer takes that testimony *de bene esse* he does not know the defense of the other side; he has not formed a theory of the defense in his mind; the examination is merely an examination of the principal elements in the case, perfunctory, and no lawyer can be ready to go to trial with what can be said just at the beginning without the pleadings. You can take testimony *de bene esse* as soon as you get in your complaint, but you have no defense. You might ask the defendant as to his defense, but what he says is not sworn to and you have to take what he says as to his defense.

Q. Is there anything to prevent the deportation of persons after they have landed, when it is found they were not entitled to be admitted?—A. We have 1 year's time to take it up, but if he goes to work, how much of his testimony can we rely on when he is at work for the person who is the defendant in the contract-labor case?

Q. Is there any inconsistency in the law with reference to arrests, and why should it be confined to contract-labor cases as it is now?—A. It is not an inconsistency. The law originally gave power to the Secretary of the Treasury to deport any person found in the United States within a year after his landing, who has been a contract laborer—only for contract labor; but later on, by the act of 1891, the provision is: "That any alien who shall come into the United States in violation of law may be returned as by law provided, at any time within 1 year thereafter, at the expense of the person or persons, vessel, transportation company, or corporation bringing such alien into the United States, and if that can not be done, then at the expense of the United States." This rule governs all persons coming in in violation of the law. And there is this: "And any alien who becomes a public charge within one year after his arrival in the United States from causes existing prior to his landing therein shall be deemed to have come in violation of law and shall be returned as aforesaid." So the burden of the proof is on the Government, in cases of public charges, to prove that the conditions existed prior to the alien's importation. The mere fact of his having become a public charge is not sufficient to deport him.

Q. The law should be so amended to make the mere fact of his becoming a public charge sufficient to cause the deportation?—A. Precisely.

Q. Would you make that same provision apply to contract labor?—A. Yes In practice we find out the contract between the alien and the importer 2 or 3 years after, because after the alien has worked there for a year or two he finds himself abused or discharged. Many times they use it as a pretext to go back. Then they come and expose the fact 2 or 3 years after, instead of at the time of the importation.

There is another difficulty with respect to persons who come here under contract to do work excluded under this act. We have had cases where a house has its branch in this country for general business. They have here a general manager under a salary. After assisting here for so many years he is sent back, and another is promoted, and he comes here as a manager from England, Germany, etc. Should he be excluded or included under the spirit of the law? We have had many such cases. The Singer Sewing Machine Company abolished their London branch, and their clerks were brought over here to take charge of the foreign department here instead of there. Could these come in or not? The law there is very vague.

Q. You think it would be easy to provide for such case?—A. The board may remember that our Trinity Church here in front of Wall street brought in a minister. The circuit court decided that as he was a minister of the gospel who came under a contract to perform labor he was excluded. The Supreme Court of the United States decided that was not the spirit of the law, and established a principle which had not been established in this country before; that is to say, that courts have power to inquire into the discussion of the legislature to find out the spirit of the law, and they did inquire into the discussion and quoted from the discussions of the Senate, and I think also from the House, in order to arrive at the conclusion that a minister of the gospel was not intended to be excluded even if he came here to labor at a salary. After that decision there was an amendment. The law of 1885 was merely, "provided that skilled labor for that purpose can not be otherwise obtained, nor shall the provisions of this act apply to professional actors, artists, lecturers, or singers, nor to persons employed strictly as personal or domestic servants;" and under these words a minister of the gospel was not

IMMIGRATION.   145

included. Now, the law of 1891 added, " nor to ministers of any religious denomination, nor persons belonging to any recognized profession, nor professors for colleges and seminaries." The exception proves the rule again; therefore, a manager of a great business is not included in the exception, nor clerks of a higher order.

Q. Nor newspaper men?—A. Nor newspaper men. They can not come in. The courts may hold the words "recognized profession" have a very restricted sense. Under the old style they only included "divinity, law, and medicine," but we have a decision of the Supreme Court that a chemist is of the recognized professions, and they allowed a chemist to come in. This law was amended prior to the decision of the Supreme Court in the Trinity case, but no reference is made to that amendment in the decision.

Q. (By Mr. FARQUHAR.) About these propositions that you made through Dr. Senner—do you know if there are any copies in existence?—A. I have made drafts. There were amendments proposed, and there was a conference held; my recollection is that there was a report subsequent to that. It was a work that was done for an investigating commission which was then composed of Mr. Stump, Dr. Senner, and Mr. McSweeney, and whatever was given in those suggestions may be found in their reports.

Q. You spoke of an amendment to the law with respect to the inducement. Do you not think the province of the law itself has been to suppress this cheap labor from coming into the country?—A. That is the spirit of the law.

Q. Is it not the law desired by the people of the United States?—A. It seems to me so.

Q. Is it not the intention to keep the hirer of labor from acquiring in a foreign market that which he can acquire here?—A. That is the intention.

Q. I am speaking generally of this cheap labor that comes in—working in mines, railroad building, etc.—A. No question about that.

NEW YORK, N. Y., *July 26, 1899.*

TESTIMONY OF MRS. REGINA STUCKLEN,
Matron, Immigration Bureau, Port of New York.

At a meeting of the Subcommission on Manufactures and General Business, held at New York July 26, 1899, Chairman Smyth presiding, Mrs. Regina Stucklen appeared at 11 a. m., and, being duly sworn, testified concerning immigration as follows:

Q. (By Mr. SMYTH.) What is your name?—A. Regina Stucklen.
Q. Where do you live?—A. Brooklyn.
Q. You are connected with the bureau of immigration?—A. I have held the position of matron under the Government since 1890, and before that under the State continuously from 1885.

Q. Will you explain to the commission the work of your department?—A. When the immigrants come in from the steamer, the first work of the matron is to stand on the line of inspection, the same as the doctors, and inspect all females as they come through as to whether or not they are in a delicate condition, simply from their appearance. The matrons have not studied medicine; it is only experience that teaches them the way of detecting a woman in that state. Sometimes it is very difficult and sometimes it is quite easy. These women are placed to one side for later examination after all the passengers are in. If it is found by the second examination that they have husbands with them, or are going to their husbands, and have a legal right to be in that condition, and otherwise are eligible to land, have money, transportation, and we see they can get along in this country all right, we allow them to pass through the same as the registry clerk would. In that capacity the matron takes the place of the inspector. That is one of my titles—inspectress of immigration.

Q. How many assistants have you?—A. I have one in that work, and one who simply cares for the women and children when they are detained.

Q. Is that a sufficient number?—A. If we had more we could do the work better than we do now. The matron's department is not the easiest worked department there now. If the gentlemen will come down and see the work we do in one day, you will see for yourselves that the matron's work is very heavy. If we find in

607A——10

that second examination that the woman we have detained is an unmarried person and she is going to her intended husband, we try to get this intended husband to the Barge Office and try to make him see it is his place to marry this girl. Quite often we succeed. We have an average of 1 marriage a day during the year, perhaps a little more.

Q. Under these circumstances?—A. Largely under these circumstances. Sometimes they have been living together, and while there is no pregnancy, yet they should be married; probably have children, or have been cohabiting, and ought to be married. Then, sometimes we find the girl's intended husband is on the other side, and in such case she is generally returned. She is sent by the matron's department to the board of special inquiry with the information the matron has. She there again states the same thing. She may change her story, but most likely she will tell the same story and be returned to Europe. We try to induce such that come together to marry; we can not make them marry; we have no right to do that. In some cases the relatives of the girl appeal to the Government and have the girl landed. During the last fiscal year we have detained in all 1,441 pregnant cases, which will speak itself for the work done in the matron's department. Of these there were 52 deported, all single girls. Thirty-three were married out of that 1,441. The rest of the marriages were between such as had been cohabiting. Twenty-four of these 1,441 were admitted to the relatives, either on bond or by appeal to the Government. Bonds are not very often accepted in any case. The Government does not try to have these people landed, but tries to prevent it if possible. The rest were all legally in that condition, and were allowed to land. We have had probably 50 cases during the year of women who had been unfaithful to their husbands, and come to their husbands in that condition, and with the exception of 3, who returned, the husbands all forgave them and took them, and we believe are providing for them the same as if nothing had happened. Then a number of women and children are detained by the registry clerks awaiting the arrival of relatives; also, young girls are placed in the detention department, and are under the care of the matron until called for or returned. We give them all the comforts we can under the circumstances.

Q. Do any of the detained immigrants ever die at the Barge Office?—A. If any are sick we place them immediately in the hospital. That is out of the hands of the matron. They have medical nurses there. The medical department makes an inspection twice a day of the detained passengers, and if there are any signs of sickness at any time the matron calls the attention of the medical department to it.

Q. Children traveling alone come under the care of the matron?—A. Sometimes we have them as young as 2 and 3 years old sent here by the relatives on the other side to the relatives in this country. Sometimes they are orphans, and sometimes their parents came before them. These children generally have their transportation all the way through, or the agent has it for them. They generally have a ticket on them with the name and address or destination of the child, and we give it into the hands of the railroad official, and he will see that the child is placed in the car properly in the charge of the conductor. We telegraph to the relatives at what time and on what train the child will leave this port and when it is due there. Where it is going to the vicinity of New York, where it can be called for, we keep it in our care until they call for it.

Q. (By Mr. CLARKE.) Do you think of any respect in which the law can be amended to promote the efficiency of the work in your department?—A. Yes; I think the law ought to include the immoral women that come to this country. There is nothing in the law as it stands under which we can send a girl back if she comes for that purpose. We can only bar her as an undesirable immigrant or likely to become a public charge.

Q. Could you get proof to establish such cases?—A. I think I could by looking over the minutes of the board of special inquiry.

Q. Do they find out whether a person is of that character or not?—A. In cases where the matron learned that girls came over here for anything else than a good purpose and sent them before the board they have found out that they have been immoral women on the other side and came here for that purpose. There have been some deportations on that line. In fact, I remember one case before the board where a girl came with a man. They came as man and wife. The examination showed they were not man and wife, but had only been cohabiting. The couple were returned to Europe, and 2 months afterwards they came back in the cabin. They were found out by one of the agents of the immigration service when the house that the girl was in was raided. The girl was arrested and held as a witness against the man who had imported her. The court held the man under bail and he skipped his bail. What became of the girl I do not know. That is out of my line. We have a girl there now with her young man. They came over in the cabin and were sent to the Barge Office because they did not have a cent of money. We found on the examination that she had been living with this man for a year and intends to do so in this country if landed. She had no thought of marriage at all until she found she was detained. She at present is quite willing to be married, but they are both excluded as likely to become public charges, as they have no friends and no money. She is one of the lower class of actresses, singing and playing on the violin in concert halls, and the man is a designer for millinery. His mother, he says, is the first lady in Worth's establishment in Paris, and sent him over to America to get rid of this girl. She gave him a little more money than he needed for his passage, and he quietly took the girl along. His mother does not know he brought the girl along. If they had had money they would have passed as cabin passengers and landed on the streets of New York, and the end of that girl would be the same as on the other side, and we would have one more unfortunate in this city.

Q. Does the board recognize the common-law marriage where it is claimed by the parties?—A. They have in one case, but in all the other cases they try to convince the parties that they ought to get married. They are held until the matron can have a talk with them and call in a missionary, perhaps, to help her out, and succeed finally in having them marry legally.

NEW YORK, N. Y., *July 26, 1899.*

TESTIMONY OF MR. ROMAN DOBLER,

Inspector, Immigration Bureau, Port of New York.

At a meeting of the subcommission on Manufactures and General Business, held in New York City, July 26, 1899, Chairman Smyth presiding, Mr. Roman Dobler appeared at 12 m., and being duly sworn, testified concerning immigration as follows:

Q. (By Mr. SMYTH.) What is your residence?—A. New York.
Q. What is your official position?—A. Immigrant inspector.
Q. How long have you held that position?—A. Six years. I was stationed for 3 years as border inspector at Cleveland, Ohio, and have been stationed at the Barge Office and Ellis Island for the last 3 years.
Q. The commission would be pleased to hear from you any suggestions you have to make with reference to the working of the law as it comes under your inspection.—A. I think for the information of the gentlemen I had better give a full detail of my duties and that probably will bring out such questions as you may desire to ask. I have charge of the boarding inspectors, who board the incoming passenger steamers. I have 3 contract-labor inspectors under my charge and 6 assistant inspectors. Our duties are to go on board of ships and get the manifest or passenger list from the pursers, and then go into the first and second cabins, and there make such an examination as will determine the eligibility of the passengers to land under the immigration laws. The authorities have seen fit to designate four classes in the cabin, American citizens, tourists, transient passengers, and alien immigrants, those who express a desire to come here and remain in the United States. We examine these passengers as to whether they are likely to become a public charge and whether they are physically disabled in any way, and whether they have any engagements to perform labor in the United States. There are a great many unprotected females coming in the cabin who are going to relatives, and when they land here they have no way of getting to their destination, and by direction of the immigration authorities we generally bring them to the Barge Office. There are a large number of that class traveling in the second cabin. There are a great number who, in my opinion, would likely become public charges, who belong to some of the clerical professions in Europe—clerks, bookkeepers, and that class. They come here with very little money, $30 or $40, and my experience leads me to believe that they are among the first to become public charges after landing. After we have made an examination of the cabin passengers and passed them or held them, as the case may be, we bring the steerage passengers to the Barge Office for an examination there. On shipboard we act as registry clerks and inspectors and pass on the right of the passengers to land at the dock. That admits them into the United States. Of course, if we find any cases that might be coming under contract we bring them to the Barge Office for special examination, and make out an examination affidavit from their statements or any other

circumstances we may have cognizance of and present it to the board. If not on that duty, we do duty at the Barge Office the same as other inspectors. We often go on the line and pass on steerage passengers, or we write up affidavits for alleged violations of the alien contract-labor law or any other duties which may devolve on us. I have a list here of the different steamers of the different lines arriving within the last 30 days, showing the comparative number of cabin and steerage passengers coming here (reading):

Steamship line.	Steamship.	First cabin.	Second cabin.	Steerage.
Hamberg American Line..	Fürst Bismarck	172	192	270
	Palatia		117	300
Cunard	Lucania	263	182	447
American	Friesland	12	59	479
	St. Paul	305	129	300
North German Lloyd	Prinz Reg. Luispold	61	92	732
	Kaiser Wilhelm der Grosse	315	158	658
Anchor	Furnessia	·34	104	112
French	La Bretagne	31	61	297
	La Gascogne	32	91	251
Holland	Statendam	71	65	487
White Star	Majestic	215	169	344
Danish	Thingvalla	3	14	82

I have here also a similar list of 6 of the Mediterranean ships that come here, belonging to the different lines, which bring the Italian immigrants:

Steamship company.	Steamship.	First cabin.	Second cabin.	Steerage.
North German Lloyd	Ems	20	22	933
Anchor	Bolivia			300
Prince	Tartar Prince	11		1,077
Italian Navigation Company	Sempione			687
Fabre	Chateau Yquem	3		286
Portuguese Navigation Company	Peninsular	21		190

Q. Compared with the other 12 months of the year, do you regard July as a rather slack month on immigration?—A. Yes, it is one of the lightest summer months we have.

Q. What is the capacity under law of the Fürst Bismarck in bringing steerage?—A. I have no figures to show that, but I presume they would have room for 1,200 or 1,500 steerage.

Q. Do you board at quarantine?—A. Yes.

Q. How thorough is your inspection from quarantine until these immigrants are turned over here to the commissioner of immigration?—A. I would state here that with the force we have we make as thorough inspection as we can, but in my opinion the inspection is not thorough enough. We have not sufficient force at the Barge Office. To give you an understanding of the force required for a thorough examination, I will say that the registry clerk is confronted by 30 immigrants; he has a group list of 30; they have a card giving their name and their number and letter on the manifest, which they present to the registry clerk, and that designates to him the exact location of the immigrant on the list. He then scans the list and sees what questions have been answered, and verifies that list from the statement of the immigrant. In the cabin we have generally 2 men, and in rare cases 3, because we can not spare more. We are confronted usually by 100 or 150 in the second cabin. There is no order or system, because they are not in line. They can not be grouped, and we have to take them as they come to us. We take the statements and hold or pass them, as the case may be. The inspection is not as thorough as it would be at the Barge Office, but it could be made so by sending a sufficient force.

Q. How many are with you on one steamer at the quarantine?—A. Usually 2; in rare cases, as when the *Kaiser Wilhelm der Grosse* comes in, we send 3.

Q. It depends on the number of steerage passengers as to the number of inspectors you send?—A. We do not examine the steerage passengers on the ship; simply see that they are all brought to the Barge Office.

Q. Is it possible for any of them to escape before coming to the Barge Office?—A. It is possible, but rarely happens. The steamship companies are very diligent and careful, because they are responsible for every immigrant on the manifest.

Q. It is not possible for half the immigrants to pass without examination—the steerage or the second cabin?—A. The steerage passengers are all examined; they can not escape the examination.

Q. (By Mr. FARQUHAR.) How do you verify the count of the manifest?—A. We lay the manifest down before us and as the first passenger comes along and is examined, we check his name off. When we get through we compare our lists and we see whether we have checked off all the passengers on the list.

Q. Do you see or come in contact with each cabin passenger as the name is read?—A. We attempt to do that, but sometimes from the lack of forces we have no means of holding these passengers, especially the first-cabin passengers, and it is not the practice of the board to hamper or distress the passengers or detain them.

Q. You make no inspection, really, of the steerage passengers?—A. No.

Q. Your attention is called more especially to the first and second cabin?—A. We only have usually from an hour to an hour and a half, and sometimes we find when we get to the dock we have not had time to examine all the passengers, and in that case we usually issue an order to the captain and order them detained on shipboard until they are all examined, which detains them that long.

Q. Your inspection, then, covers the first and second cabin?—A. Yes.

Q. It is in connection with the cabins that you take the place of the various boards found at the Barge Office, and you have the same latitude with respect to contract labor, diseases, and everything of that kind?—A. Yes. A doctor of the Marine-Hospital Service goes on board and passes the cabin passengers medically.

Q. Your inspection takes in nearly all the phases of the inspection of the Barge Office proper, as far as the first and second cabin passengers are concerned?—A. Yes.

Q. Have you found contract-labor people in the first or second cabin?—A. In recent years a great many who desire to escape the rigid examination at the Barge Office that they would now have to undergo if they came in the steerage, pay the difference and come in cabin, expecting to escape that examination. In my opinion a great many contract laborers come through the cabin. Of course we find some, and some we do not find. We can only take their statements and have to land them, having no other evidence. A great many of the Mediterranean ships bring in cabin people who are practically destitute, but will spend the difference in the price between steerage and cabin to come that way, expecting to be landed. We bring them to the Barge Office and hold them up. We have brought a number that way and they have been sent back.

Q. When you board at quarantine are there any but the medical officers and yourselves?—A. The customs officers and the medical staff.

Q. Is it permissible for any officers of foreign countries to appear at quarantine and board the vessel and go to the dock—I mean anyone not the consul-general or the minister of foreign nations?—A. Yes; they get a permit.

Q. For what purpose?—A. I could not say for what purpose. A number of persons come on the revenue cutter and board the ships at quarantine by permission of the collector of customs. He issues a permit for that purpose. Sometimes members of the embassies at Washington have permits issued by the Secretary of the Treasury to board ships at quarantine.

Q. They have free access to all passengers on board the ship?—A. Yes; after they get on shipboard.

Q. What is the time between quarantine and dock?—A. Generally we calculate about an hour and a half from quarantine until the ship is docked. It depends on the speed of the vessel.

Q. Can any of these parties accompany the vessel to the Barge Office?—A. With the steerage passengers; no.

Q. They then leave with the first and second class?—A. They land with the cabin passengers. No one is allowed to mingle with the steerage passengers. Sometimes, as a matter of humanity, if a father or husband wants to see his child or wife, we accompany him to the person, but it is always in our presence.

Q. There is no possible tampering with the steerage passengers between quarantine and the Barge Office?—A. No; there are cases where railroad agents and others attempt to communicate with the steerage passengers, but it is always detected and prohibited. Another duty we have is to discharge the American citizens who may be coming in steerage. As soon as they present evidence that they are American citizens they are immediately discharged.

Q. But after they reach the Barge Office they are subject to the inspection and the care and surveillance of the barge officers proper?—A. Yes.

Q. Are there any societies or bureaus of the foreign governments that have privileges there at the Barge Office in respect to communicating with immigrants?—A. Yes; I understand the Italian society is located at the Barge Office, and I suppose they communicate more or less with the passengers, as they are right there in the building. I myself, as an officer, do not approve of any communication whatever with the passenger until he has been examined and passed by the Government inspectors. I do not think they should be communicated with at all.

Q. In the case of detention, until your boards pass on the case of a passenger or immigrant, are outsiders allowed to communicate quite freely with them, in calling on and caring for them, and furnishing them with money, or anything of that kind?—A. I believe not. I suppose the steamship agent or a near relative, in the presence of the inspector, has a right to communicate with the passenger and give him means or whatever information is necessary, not detrimental to his examination.

Q. These communications between the immigrants and the outsider are always in the presence of an officer of the Barge Office?—A. Yes; so far as I know.

Q. They would not have the permission unless through the commissioner of immigration?—A. He gives them permission; or, if it is a contract-labor case, Mr. Quinlan gives the permission and sends an inspector with the person.

Q. (By Mr. CLARKE.) To what class of cases do you give the most attention on shipboard?—A. Well, we aim to examine the passengers in the first place as to their occupations, to ascertain whether they are coming here under contract. Then we examine them as to their intentions in coming here, their business and their means, and whether they have an address or any place to go to where they will be taken care of; and if we find a man has no trade or occupation, or is not a laborer, and has very little means, we bring him to the Barge Office and let the board of special inquiry pass on his case. If it is a case of an old person, a female going to her son or some relative, we try to verify their statements by communicating with the relatives. If it is a young girl traveling in cabin unprotected—frequently there are persons traveling in the cabin who make the acquaintance of female passengers—we consider it would not be safe to allow them to go through without examination and without anyone to take an interest in them, and the authorities at the Barge Office see them through to their destination.

Q. If, for instance, you have a reasonable suspicion that the immigrant comes in violation of the alien-contract-labor law, you send that immigrant to the Barge Office?—A. Yes. When I am examining the passengers, to facilitate the examination, I usually place him to one side and reexamine him when I get through with the passengers, and question him closely, and state to him that it is not necessary for him to have employment. I think a great many of the passengers are coached and instructed. They have been told to say certain things in order to be landed. I have had cases in which men state positively that they are going to some employment on an agreement made at a certain stated price, and afterwards they admitted they were told to say that in order to be landed. So I always caution them that it is not necessary to have employment in order to be landed, but if he insists on his statement being true, I bring him to the Barge Office and before the board.

Q. (By Mr. FARQUHAR.) Have you matrons as inspectors of women on shipboard?—A. No; at the Barge Office we have two.

NEW YORK, N. Y., *July 26, 1899.*

TESTIMONY OF MR. WILLIAM WEIHE,

Inspector, Immigration Bureau, port of New York.

At a meeting of the Subcommission on Manufactures and General Business, held in New York July 26, 1899, Chairman Smyth presiding, Mr. William Weihe appeared at 12.45 p. m., and, being duly sworn, testified on the subject of immigration as follows:

Q. (By Mr. SMYTH.) What is your name?—A. William Weihe.
Q. Is your residence here?—A. New York City.
Q. In what capacity are you connected with the Bureau of Immigration?—A. Immigrant inspector.
Q. How long have you held that position?—A. Over 3 years.
Q. Does that cover your full service?—A. Yes.
Q. Will you explain to the commission the working of the department with which you are connected?—A. I have been most of the time on the board of special inquiry, where the immigrants are examined after they leave the registering department, and where there is a doubt we get them there. Sometimes I suppose we get from 75 to 100 or 125 a day, according to the number of immigrants that arrive.

We get the card that is signed by the inspector on the line, and it states simply what the cause of the detention is, and on the line of that we examine the immigrant. If there are families we take the names of the father, mother, and children, ask them their destination, who pays their passage, and where they obtained their money. If they prove to have relatives here, or have means on which the board believes they are able to get along, they are admitted. If it is thought by the members of the board that they should be held until it is learned whether the parties to whom they are going are able to take care of them, they are so held. Cases come there in which we find out many things not discovered on the line when being registered, and in case we think they ought to be further investigated we hold them on what is called the deferred system. They have to produce evidence, or get their friends to write or come, in order to show that what they have previously stated is correct and that their friends are willing to take care of them. We examine them as to whether they have ever been guilty of crime, and also as to whether they are coming in under contract, notwithstanding that such has previously been gone into by the contract-labor bureau. Sometimes the immigrants deny it. Often it appears from their statements that there are conditions which constitute violations of the alien-contract-labor law. We have held cases for 2 or 3 days before they would develop, and finally they would give us the full information, where they were going and how they happen to be going there. If we can not make a case directly we refer it to the bureau of contract labor, or commissioner, to make a further investigation, after they have left for the place they intend to go to, and thus get direct information.

Q. (By Mr. FARQUHAR.) What is the longest period of detention that you know of?—A. Sometimes 3 weeks, sometimes 4 weeks. I know of a case where they were held for 4 weeks. Some 5 Italians came in last summer; the board had doubts, and all were held 4 weeks.

Q. (By Mr. CLARKE.) Under what circumstances?—A. Believing they had come under contract with some parties in Pennsylvania, but had not a good direction.

Q. (By Mr. FARQUHAR.) The address was not clear?—A. They would not give it as clear as we thought they should. We finally learned that they wanted to go to Wampum, Pa. Each claimed to have a cousin, but neither of the cousins knew they were coming. Their cousins only had been there some 6 months or a year, as they claimed.

Q. (By Mr. SMYTH.) They all told the same story?—A. Each had a separate cousin, but all told the same story. We finally found a letter for each of the immigrants written by one man. He had signed different names, but the handwriting was the same. After being held that long they received from friends, I think, in the neighborhood of $50 or $60, and of course we could not hold them any longer. We could not directly prove a contract and they were not a public charge. They had addresses to a certain destination—Newport. At first we thought it was Newport, Ky., but being from the western part of Pennsylvania, I found it was near Wampum, Pa., a little town opposite, where the Pennsylvania road makes connection with the Pittsburg and Erie.

Q. (By Mr. FARQUHAR.) Were they going to the coal mines?—A. They did not state, just going to these cousins. I went out there a month afterwards, and made some inquiries near there, and found they had gone to work in the limestone quarries.

Q. Do you not find a great deal of difficulty in preventing infractions of this alien-contract-labor law by these immigants and the parties who were instrumental in bringing them in?—A. Oh, yes; it is very difficult to get direct information.

Q. Do you discover more of these infractions of law through the confessions of the immigrants under detention than in any other way?—A. That is the only means we have to get it.

Q. And in every case they acknowledge it, it is deportation?—A. Not always.

Q. Do you take an equity view of the thing?—A. Yes. Supposing a man comes and claims he has work; he is held. We generally take his affidavit, and then the immigrant or the steamship agent writes to the contractor that such and such an immigrant is held for certain purposes, and then they come or send an affidavit. In most cases they deny it. We have had parties come and acknowledge that they had made arrangements—had spoken to a boss and secured work; but that is not often the case. Very often we believe that they avoid the questions, even though they have made the arrangement; that they have secured work for the immigrant, but make an affidavit that they invited them to come and sent passage money merely as friends. The board generally considers that for what it may be worth.

Q. Has the execution of the contract-labor law on the part of the Government broken up this gang system, importing laborers in groups of 5, 10, 15, 50, or 100?—A. They come in that way yet in a number of cases.

Q. From what countries?—A. Generally from Italy, Austria-Hungary, Poland, and Russia. I will cite a few late cases. There are 15 now at the Barge Office that came through here on the 17th of June, 1899; they are Dalmatians or Croatians. They arrived here and passed through. There were 19 or 20 They could not give directly any information as to where they were going to work, but were going to Rathbun, Iowa. We let them go and notified the Department at Washington, which instructed the inspector at Chicago, who traced them as far as Rathbun, Iowa. He went there and found they were working in the coal mines of the Star Coal Company at that place.

Q. Do you know who are the owners of the mine?—A. No. This inspector reported to the authorities at Washington, and on the strength of that the Secretary of the Treasury issued a warrant for the arrest of these 19 men. The inspectors went there from New York and Baltimore and found them at the mines working, arrested them, and brought them here to New York.

Q. Was there any appeal taken to the Secretary of the Treasury?—A. There was a stay taken after they got here; I could not say through whom. They are still here. They got back a week ago.

Q. Who pays the maintenance of these 19 Croatians at the present time?—A. I think the steamship company. That is the way the warrant reads; they were to be deported at the expense of the vessel on which they arrived.

Q. And the judgment of your board was that it was contract labor?—A. They did not appear before the board; they would not say they had a contract. I was there at Rathbun myself as one of the inspectors. We were informed that the next day after they arrived at Rathbun they were given caps and lamps and put to work with other miners in the mines. I understood that some of their relatives or friends there had secured this work for them, and on the strength of that they had come here and started to work, but they all claimed they had no work when they arrived at the Barge Office.

Q. Your board did not pass on the case?—A. No; it was done by the Commissioner-General. After they landed the Secretary of the Treasury issued the warrant, and on the strength of that they were arrested and will be deported.

Q. That was done through the action of the Commissioner-General in Washington?—A. Yes.

Q. Do you know of any of that contract labor going into Pennsylvania, in the coke or mining regions?—A. Yes. I think the Polacks, Slovaks, Hungarians, and Russian Poles—over 50 per cent of that labor goes into Pennsylvania; not only in the coal mines, but in other industrial lines, such as iron and steel mills and blast furnaces.

Q. Have you a knowledge of many cases where you discovered contract labor going into the mining regions there last year?—A. While we have not discovered it, we have every reason to believe that it is done. It is very hard to prove it. I take it that they are coached on the other side, and on the way over, to avoid the law. Very often they arrived one day and started to work the next. I could cite another instance which happened over a year ago, where a half dozen or more arrived and were going to Steelton, Pa. One party who came with them had been in this country before, and it was supposed he had brought them over. An investigation was made and that man was found at work, but we could not prove a contract. The manager or some one in authority employs one of their countrymen as foreman of the gang, and in that way they are put to work. They understand the language and are apt to work at jobs around the plant. In the last 10 or 15 years machinery has done away with a great deal of skilled labor, and I have heard of cases where skilled labor was willing to work, but foreigners had the preference because the work was not as skillful.

Q. Can you give the names of the firms?—A. I do not want to be personal.

Q. You know that of your own knowledge?—A. Yes.

Q. I do not think it would do any harm to mention any of these cases.—A. The reason I say that is because of my former connection with the organizations and the manufacturers. I will state one particular case; the La Lanc Gros Jean Company at Harrisburg, through its manager, wrote on for a roll turner and an annealer, promising the roll turner $30 per week and the annealer $25. We had the letters written by the manager on the letterhead of the company. The whole thing was investigated. These men came here and worked. We could not prove directly that the president of the company had authorized the manager to hire these people, and, it being under the criminal law, we were told we could not prosecute the company on account of the acts of the manager, who was a hired man; and we had to let the case drop. Everything was proven—that the money was sent, and even that the passage money was retained out of their salaries; but we could not prove that the president of the company authorized it. This happened, I think, in 1897.

Q. Were they Welsh immigrants?—A. Yes, these two came from Wales.

Q. They are now in this country, so far as you know?—A. No, these two men left again. The organization held them here for a while, but it took too long to get the case before the courts, and they went back. They were willing to go on the stand, but under the present law the district attorney said they could not be prosecuted for some time, and the case had to go by default, as it were.

Q. (By Mr. CLARKE.) Were you formerly president of the Amalgamated Association of Iron and Steel Workers?—A. Yes.

Q. Is your time as inspector and member of the board of special inquiry principally devoted to these contract-labor cases?—A. No, it is general. As a member of the board of inquiry, we take up all cases.

Q. But you are all the while on the watch for such cases as that?—A. I more particularly interest myself in that part.

Q. Can you think how the law can be made more effectual in preventing the importation of such people?—A. By placing more restrictions on the steamship company, I think, and having an inspection on the other side the same as in this country.

Q. You would have the United States employ agents on the other side?—A. I would make that general. I am speaking generally, not alone on the contract-labor part. For instance, a man is coming with his family, he may have 3, 4, or 5 children. He arrives here with little money; his whole aim has been throughout his life to bring his children to this country; he has practically nothing to start out with. It is very hard to decide to send a family of that kind back after spending all their money on the voyage. I think if a case of that kind was investigated on the other side, and it was shown they did not have means, they would be held back.

Q. You do not think the steamship companies could be depended on to exclude that kind of people?—A. I think if they can only get the passage money they will take them.

Q. Take the case of these men retained here, the Rathbun people; on what evidence are these men detained for deportation?—A. On the examination of the inspector at Chicago, made at Rathbun through parties who informed him when they had arrived there, and were immediately put to work.

Q. He has given that evidence under oath?—A. He has at Washington, I suppose.

Q. So far as you know that is the only evidence against these men?—A. Yes.

Q. They are under accusation of violating a penal statute, I suppose?—A. Yes.

Q. And are held here without opportunity for defense on the affidavit of one man; is that the situation?—A. I can not say whether on the affidavit of one man or not. All I know is the warrant was issued to arrest them.

Q. Do you know whether they displaced American labor there or whether the works were so full that the employers found room for them in addition to all the labor they employed before?—A. I could not say they displaced American labor; but I was informed that other mines in that locality were only working half time, and this one was working steady.

Q. Do you know the reason of that?—A. No. I will say this: The majority of the men employed in that mine were Croatians.

Q. If there is an abundance of work in this country for all the people now here who desire work, and the development of industries requires labor, you have no objection to that labor coming, if it comes without previous contract?—A. If they come voluntarily, and take their chances the same as any other person who arrives here, like they did formerly.

Q. You understand that to be the attitude of labor organizations generally toward immigration.—A. If they come in the proper way they have no objections.

Q. (By Mr. FARQUHAR.) You have foreign societies and bureaus here that somewhat come in contact with the Barge Office and its administration. Do you think that it is good judgment to allow any societies to have direct communication with immigrants until they are landed legally?—A. No, I do not think it is proper for any foreign Government to have an office there, or at any landing port, to look after immigrants.

Q. You think that if they desire to take care of them, or direct them to their destination, or give any help through local societies, it would be proper after the United States had passed on the immigrant, rather than having, in any way, contact with these immigrants while in the hands of the United States?—A. If a man with a family arrives, or a man and wife only, and they are healthy and can land,

I would not object to the society taking charge of them and putting them in the industrial centers or agricultural sections.

Q. That it should not be a matter of foreign interference; that is what I mean.—A. I would be opposed to having societies of that kind.

Q. Do you know whether there is anything of that sort here at Ellis Island or the Barge Office?—A. There are a number of such societies that make inquiries.

Q. Has any society any special privilege?—A. The Italian Government has.

Q. Do you know who is at the head of it?—A. Dr. Rossi.

Q. (By Mr. SMYTH.) You think if the law were amended so that the contractor in this country should pay a fine instead of the immigrant himself, it would be better?—A. I understand the intent of the law was to prosecute the contractor who brought them. It was not understood at the time that the immigrant should be deported in the way they are doing it. The organization with which I was connected helped to draw up that law. That was the intention at the time, but such has not been done. It is impossible to convict such people. There are ways to avoid the law. There are always one or more foreigners in a community somewhat more intelligent than their native countrymen, and through them the immigrants are induced to come, at the suggestion of others, and thereby the parties that ought to be punished escape; and yet the immigrants come here and take the places of our workmen in the face of the present law, under which it takes so long to reach the courts for trial, even when a contract is made.

NEW YORK, N. Y., *July 26, 1899.*

TESTIMONY OF DR. EGISTO ROSSI,

Chief of Italian Bureau, Port of New York.

At a meeting of the Subcommission on Manufactures and General Business, held in New York City July 26, 1899, Chairman Smyth presiding, Dr. Egisto Rossi appeared at 1.30 p. m., and, being first duly sworn, testified concerning immigration as follows:

Q. (By Mr. SMYTH.) What is your name?—A. Egisto Rossi.

Q. Your residence?—A. Mount Vernon; 159 North Fulton avenue; near New York.

Q. What is your business?—A. Chief of Italian bureau.

Q. You hold an official position in that bureau?—A. Yes.

Q. By whose appointment?—A. By the Italian Government.

Q. An official bureau established here by the Government of which you are a representative?—A. Yes.

Q. How long?—A. Since September, 1895.

Q. Was the bureau in existence prior to 1895?—A. It had been in existence only one year.

Q. Does your Government encourage emigration to this country?—A. Not at all.

Q. What was the object of your Government in establishing the bureau?—A. The principal object was to keep the people well informed of the existence of the padrone system and its evils, and to warn them against the same.

Q. To keep your people in Italy informed?—A. Yes. And on their arrival here to have a bureau so well posted as to be able to give them all necessary information; so one of our first duties is, as soon as they are discharged and come into the bureau, to ask where they come from, where they are going to, if they have a relative or friend to care for them, what they intend to do in this country, and to try and help them as far as we can.

Q. What special privileges does your bureau enjoy at the Barge Office?—A. No privilege at all. We have only the right to mingle with the immigrants as soon as they are discharged from the board of special inquiry or from the examination of the registry clerks. As soon as the people are discharged, they come into my bureau, and they are questioned, as already stated, and put on their guard about the dangers to which they are exposed by going to live in New York.

Q. Only Italian immigrants come to your bureau?—A. Only Italians.

Q. You have no access to these immigrants before they pass the special inquiry?—A. No access whatever; and I must also call your attention to this point especially. It would not be easy for the men of the Italian bureau to have access to the Italian immigrants when they are under the control of the Federal authorities. Probably you know that from the moment the immigrants arrive on the steamer and leave the steamer and go on the barge which has been sent by the Federal Government to take them to the Barge Office for proper examination there is such a close watch by the Federal employees that I think I could assure you that it is absolutely impossible that anybody could come in contact with the immigrants, not only a clerk of the Italian bureau, but anybody else. They are closely watched from the moment they arrive at the dock to the landing point. They pass also through a kind of escort of Federal employees, who watch every movement of the immigrants. If, by chance, somebody should try to approach the immigrant it would be immediately detected and he would be invited to appear before the commissioner. Then I do not know how anyone may say that the Italian bureau tried to interfere with the Italian immigrants, or to instruct them before they come into contact with the proper authorities. I should like to have these charges substantiated by proofs, facts, data, names of the immigrants, and also of the clerks who had approached these people.

Q. (By Mr. FARQUHAR.) Have you at any time since the foundation of your bureau, before the immigrant was officially and legally landed in this country, while in and under the jurisdiction of the Barge Office here—have you or any of your agents employed, in any way, prohibited means to reach any immigrants from Italy?—A. None.

Q. You positively swear you never did?—A. Positively. There is, as you know, a detention pen where immigrants are temporarily detained. The reasons are very simple—because they have stated they are going to their relatives, as for instance a wife is going to join her husband, or a son a father, or vice versa. They are not liable to be under the jurisdiction of the board of special inquiry. They are detained simply because the relative to whom they are directed has not come. My clerks have sometimes approached them in order to ask the address of their relatives, as is constantly done also by the representatives of all steamship companies, benevolent societies, missionary ladies, etc. And when the relatives are found out we telegraph them to come down, or the son or husband is sent for if in the city. Often times I have allowed myself to do this kind of work, which has not been in violation of the law, or considered bad practice, since my attention has never been called to it by the commissioner, otherwise I would have discontinued it at once. But I have never allowed myself or my clerk to approach any immigrant who has not been regularly examined, never.

Q. Can you tell us something about the condition of the padrone system when your bureau was first established?—A. When the bureau was first established the conditions of the padrone were very bad, and especially to the department of our immigration. The padrone system has two parties, one here, the other in our country; the padrone here is in correspondence with the agent of the immigration on the other side of the ocean. So one of the practices used by this padrone was to write to the agents in Italy that every immigrant coming to this country should arrive with a letter of introduction to some banker or some boss or contractor. So a great many of these immigrants on arriving had some letter of introduction of this kind. Now, I think it is a fact that this was a great deal of trouble and constituted one of the greatest inconveniences for our immigrants. Now much of that has been stopped through the assistance of the Italian bureau. You must know that every immigrant coming to my bureau, who is directed to some hotel keeper or contractor or banker, has to say to the bureau what reason he has for going there, especially when he is destined to points distant from New York. One of the special duties of the bureau is to inquire, " Where are you going?" " I am going to Pittsburg, but I have to go first to New York." "I have a letter and I have to go to a banker to get it cashed." " You have no need to go; your banker has to come here." And so, in many of the cases, the Italians directed to distant points from New York are prevented from coming into the hands of the middleman and speculator, and we aid them to start at once for their destinations; and so, in many cases, we advise the family, the uncle, or the father or the son, to meet such and such a train : " Your relative will arrive on such a train, so please take proper care of him." In this way, I think, we have done much to reduce the evils of the padrone system. It is too great a problem to be solved entirely by a bureau like ours, of a little force ; but certainly we have done a great deal toward preventing our immigrants from coming into contact with the padrone.

Q. They were sending to Italy for immigrants to come to this country so that they might control their labor?—A. Yes. But now every Italian who has come here in violation of any law, and is deported by order of the Federal authorities, has to receive from the Italian bureau a printed card, in which is clearly stated the reason why he is deported. Now, you must know there is an article in our emigration law which says every man who has been deported from the United States by order of Federal authority, on receiving the card of the Italian bureau, is entitled to prosecute the agent who has sold him his ticket. This thing, which seems very small, has done a great deal to remove the abuses of the padrone system in Italy, because now the agents of emigration, before listing an emigrant, knowing that the emigrant, if he is sent back, has a right to prosecute them, are very careful. They are also very careful since the Government, on our complaint, has condemned or imprisoned some of these agents.

Q. What is the condition of the padrone now here in New York?—A. As I have already implied, the system is much weakened for the reasons just given, also the recent failures of some of the smaller Italian banks, which were great gainers under the boss system, would be an additional proof of what I have said. The problem is still too huge a one to solve in so short a time, since the existence of the bureau, but it has been modified a good deal.

Q. Is the Italian labor in this country now controlled by padrones?—A. To some extent.

Q. Directly or indirectly?—A. Both directly and indirectly. Now, however, every case of padrone abuse which is brought to the attention of the Italian bureau is put under the attention of our Italian consul.

Q. The immigrant in this country, if still the slave of the padrone, has some claim on your bureau?—A. Certainly. I can always send a complaint, no matter how long he has been here.

Q. He can look to you for help?—A. Yes, and in many cases we have succeeded in having the wrong redressed.

Q. How many cases have you had in the past year?—A. Twenty-five or thirty; maybe more.

Q. Do they still send to Italy for immigrants?—A. They still do, but in smaller proportion.

Q. Is it not a fact that the labor of these newly arrived Italian immigrants is still controlled by padrones?—A. To some extent.

Q. Does the average Italian immigrant, coming to this country, have anything to do with securing his own employment? Does he not have to go to the padrone?—A. Some come with this idea, certainly, of needing the help of the padrone to find work.

Q. After a man goes to the padrone and gets work, does not this padrone still control his wages?—A. Yes, somewhat; but if he has come in contact with our bureau it will give him such information as to prevent many going to the padrone.

Q. Where does the average Italian immigrant deposit his money?—A. Formerly he used to deposit it with Italian bankers, but now, on account of many failures, there has been so much discredit cast upon the Italian bankers that many of our immigrants prefer to keep their savings in their houses and in their pockets. Still we have among our bankers some who are very honest and straightforward, who do their business with the same honesty and punctuality as the American banker of the first class, and these are well known also to the commissioner. We have some above reproach.

Q. How much money do you suppose is sent back to Italy by Italian immigrants?—A. I do not think we could give the data, because the money is sent sometimes through the post-office, sometimes through the bankers by draft, sometimes it is sent in a registered letter, the cash itself; so I can not dare to give any amount.

Q. It amounts to millions, does it not?—A. I could not say.

Q. Do you regard all Italian immigrants in the United States as colonists of Italy, as still being under the protection of the Italian Government?—A. If they have naturalization papers I do not consider them as subjects of the Italian Kingdom.

Q. But the general run of the Italian immigrants you consider as colonists?—A. We consider them as colonists unless they have taken naturalization papers and, if subject to military service, have written to the foreign department in Italy informing the Government that they have taken naturalization papers, and, therefore, are willing to renounce their allegiance to King Humbert; then, in that case, he is not considered a colonist.

Q. Unless the immigrant does so write to your Government, the Italian Government does still consider him as a colonist?—A. Yes, if subject to military service.

Q. How many reports has your bureau made to the Bureau of Immigration in this country as to the padrone system in this country?—A. Of the cases that come under our knowledge we have taken notes in our books, and call it to the attention of the Italian consul, being cases which were outside of the jurisdiction of the commissioner. However, I have called to the attention of the commissioner many cases of Italian hotel keepers who have tried to get hold of the Italian immigrants in order to speculate upon them; because, you see, many keepers of our lodging houses here are a set of speculators on our own people by engaging them for some kind of work in which the padrone system is exercised.

Q. Why does not the Italian Government itself, by its authority over these immigrants, place them in the hands of their consular agent here? Can you explain that?—A. And the bureau do the work outside of the Barge Office?

Q. We do not see why you have any right to do any business in the Barge Office.—A. I have considered the matter myself and I would be very glad in some way to be outside, but how can you give me the means of approaching these people before they come in contact with the great many people waiting for them outside the Barge Office?

Q. Simply as I have proposed to you, that your Government, which seeks so much the welfare of the Italian immigrant, should make arrangements at home that the Italian immigrant would know where to go and would escape these agencies. It is apparently the fault of the Government at home, is it not?—A. I do not think so; I want to call your attention to one fact. Whenever an Italian steamer arrives there are hundreds of people outside of the Barge Office waiting for them. When the immigrants are discharged from the registry clerk or the board of special inquiry, and when they have left the Barge Office, these people waiting for them are anxious to get possession of them. I could not get hold of the immigrant at all. I have thought a great deal of this. We have no desire to be in the Barge Office, no other purpose except to protect the immigrants in the way I have told you. It is immaterial to me whether I am inside or outside. Our work could be done by the consul, but how could the consul get hold of our people after they are carried off by their friends and relatives? How could the consul prevent their falling a prey to the padrone? You say provided I can do the same work; but this does not seem to me possible outside of the Barge Office.

Q. If the Italian consul and his officers could not do that, how can you with one or two clerks do it?—A. I can——

Q. (Interrupting.) The futility of your bureau then is manifest by your testimony, is it not?—A. No, I say I can do that because the emigrants are obliged to come in my bureau directly; there is no egress between the immigrant and the railway. The immigrant, as soon as he is discharged, is sent through my bureau. There is no need of force, because he has not left the Barge Office.

Q. (By Mr. SMYTH.) Is it not true that your one official will pass through the same number that it has taken perhaps a half dozen men in the immigration bureau to attend to?—A. Yes, but the questions are not so many as in the first examination; after giving the usual information, if there are not suspicious cases, we allow them to go; if they come to friends or relatives, we call the friend or relative inside to get the immigrant into their hands and say, "This immigrant is intrusted to you and you will have to take care of him." In case this man should complain, he will call it again to the attention of the bureau.

Q. How can your one man attend to this work that it takes a half dozen men to attend to in the other room?—A. I am not alone. I have three clerks, who have their special business, and as soon as the people enter my bureau we take their names, ask where they are going to, and what kind of relatives they have.

Q. Do you think it possible for your small force to attend to that work?—A. Yes. Most of the cases are so simple that they do not require much further examination, but there are some who look suspicious; so we hold them for more extended investigation.

Q. Do you think the work is done very thoroughly by your bureau?—A. As much as we can. If we could have more help the work would be more successful.

Q. What caused the establishment of this Italian bureau in New York?—A. I have already said it was organized especially in order to break up the padrone system.

Q. What privileges do you have from the United States Government?—A. None except to occupy a room in the Barge Office to receive the immigrants as soon as they are discharged.

Q. Your immigrants are sent to you instead of being sent outside?—A. Yes.

Q. No other nation has it?—A. No other nation has it, but no other nation has an immigration of our kind. I mean, for instance, the German and Irish, who, when they arrive here, are at home. The English and the Irish speak English. On the contrary, our immigrants arrive here devoid of even elementary knowledge of the customs and language.

Q. Is there not another reason—that you have the padrone system—that does not exist as to other nations? Is that one reason?—A. The padrone system has its principal origin here. Our immigrants, being strange to the language of the country, ignorant of the conditions of this country, are in some way naturally attracted by those who have some experience, and these offer themselves to help them. The padrone system has originated in this way. It is the capturing of the ignorant by those who have been here some years, who know the language and know the customs of these people who have just arrived and do not know anything. So by keeping them informed we prevent somewhat the contact of those newly arrived with the old residents.

Q. Did your Government agree to give penal certificates to all emigrants going to the United States?—A. That was agreed to.

Q. Why have not they done so?—A. In cases where the emigrant has never had to do with the police they do not give any certificate.

Q. Is it not true that less than 10 per cent come in with these certificates?—A. That may be explained by the fact already stated, viz: that having looked over the books of the police and finding that this man never has been convicted of crime, no certificate is given; but in any case where the immigrant has been imprisoned they give a penal certificate in which is given the reason and how long he has been imprisoned.

Q. Do you know of any criminals bearing passports, but no certificates, that have come to this country?—A. There was a case.

Q. Has not there been more than one?—A. To my knowledge only one. That was the case of a man who was convicted in Genoa, and he was condemned to twenty years of imprisonment; but this man received his passport by mistake. He was ticketed by the official in Genoa. It was brought to my attention, and as soon as I knew it I wrote to Italy asking why this convict was given a passport to this country. This man had a wife and children in the United States who were American citizens, and the officer thought that in spite of his having been a convict the American law could not bar him from his family, so he would have to be admitted anyhow, and in his ignorance he gave him a passport. I know of many other criminals who have come to this country, but from other foreign ports—Antwerp, Hamburg, Marseilles, Havre—and, as you know, the Italian Government can have no control of that.

Q. Your system of registration is considered very perfect?—A. Yes; the same as in France.

Q. Is it true, as stated in the New York papers, that your Government will not seek to extradite criminals after they have secured entrance into the United States?—A. I know nothing about it.

Q. Is it true that you issued a circular letter last spring advising your Government that owing to the war with Spain labor and industry had ceased in this country, and directed the cessation of Italian immigration?—A. I am certain that the person who gave you this information did not understand my Italian circular, because my circular was general and occasioned by these facts; it was about a year ago in April—

Q. Was it the 21st of April?—A. I do not remember exactly. It was during the Spring of last year when we had had many Italian immigrants who arrived here without proper address of relatives and without sufficient money to be landed as the American law requires; so I invited the Government to urge that the mayors and prefects should pay attention to this fact; that unless the emigrant had the conditions required to be admitted to this country, not to give any passport, and extend his instructions to the agent of emigration; and I added, so much more is it to be recommended to the prefects not to send to this country people in no condition to land, since the country is engaged in the war with Spain, and of course, as a natural result of the war, many enterprises will be reducing their work and will have less demand for labor.

Q. Did not your letter rather anticipate the war? Was not that in April, before war was declared?—A. I can not remember exactly.

Q. When the war was over did Italy again seek to increase emigration to this country?—A. Emigration to this country naturally increased afterwards.

Q. Is an effort being made on the part of your Government to induce emigration?—A. No, as I have already stated.

Q. (By Mr. FARQUHAR.) Have you a copy of that circular?—A. I think I have.

Q. Would you present it to this commission?—A. Certainly.

Q. How long have you lived in the United States?—A. Consecutively, I might say four years.

Q. How long have you been in this country?—A. In 1882, 1883, 1886, and from 1895 to 1899.

Q. Have you any knowledge practically of the New York padrone system and the so-called Italian banking system here? Have you ever been engaged in it?

IMMIGRATION.

Have you had friends in it? Have you examined as to its workings?—A. No, I have been engaged in no business whatever except this of the bureau.

Q. Are we to understand you take common report very much for the matters you have given here in evidence; that you have not come practically in contact with them yourself?—A. Only, as I say, in redressing a wrong.

Q. Have you had any dealings with these Italian banks?—A. Except to make them bring money to the immigrants when I have drafts to cash in a padrone bank.

Q. Do you know that the Italian labor in Greater New York is entirely controlled by the padrones?—A. There are still some contractors who try to get hold of the immigrants as soon as they arrive, but the proportion is a good deal less than it was before. I could not state exactly how many are still victimized by the padrone system.

Q. Because there is not so much demand for them; not so much necessity for the padrones or banks?—A. And above all because they are frightened at the idea of our bureau punishing the agents who in any way try to abuse the immigrants; giving the immigrants to the padrone. We are also in communication with the agents in Italy. When we know that one has been abused by a padrone, we make inquiries, and if it is a padrone in connection with the agent in Italy, then if the agent is found to be in communication with the padrone his license is withdrawn.

Q. In constructing our sewers here, in making our roadways, in private and municipal improvements that are going on, do you or not know that the Italian help on these works is practically padrone—controlled labor? This, practically, not theoretically, of your own knowledge, and with all the experience you have had in this bureau; do you know that practically nearly all your Italian labor is in slavery?—A. It is in slavery to a certain extent, but it is not as it was before.

Q. Because there is not so much employment for it; is that one reason?—A. You must allow me to believe also it is due to the amount of information they receive as they come through my bureau, and the penalty inflicted upon the agents in Italy who have had to do with the padrone in the United States.

Q. It was officially stated that in the late enlargement of the Erie Canal there were employed 10,500 Italians, and a little over 2,000 Americans and people of all other nations. These Italians worked for less than the American wage; they were operated in shifts, provided for by padrones, boarded in shanties, controlled by their bosses, and their whole money and financial matters conducted by these bosses.—A. That may be.

Q. When you take such an American improvement as that, where $9,000,000 of the money of the State of New York was expended, unless there is a perfect system of padronism how is it possible that these contractors could be furnished with 10,500 of these people for over two years in doing that work?—A. I wish, before giving my answer, I could know the details of those facts. I do not deny the possibility that there may be in the United States still, as I told you, many cases of the padrone system existing, but while you give Italian examples I could give many examples of American contractors who, in despair of finding Italian padrones, because, as I say, they are frightened by the presence of this bureau, have employed for the same purpose American foremen exercising the same prerogatives as Italian padrones. As I told you, the padrone system is not possible to destroy with the means the bureau has at its disposal now, but you must not forget that in founding this bureau the Italian and American Governments had two objects in view; first, to try to remove the contact of the Italian immigrant with the padrone through the information given him by the bureau, and the second object was to find employment directly for our people and to scatter them through the States, especially in the agricultural districts. That part of the programme has not yet been carried out, for the reason that when the bureau was started circulars were sent to all the agricultural State boards asking them to give information as to the lands to be colonized and as to the conditions they were ready to make with the Italians, and so on. When we received good offers asking us to send there 200 or 300 people, I thought it was necessary to send a man on the spot to examine the conditions. After consulting with my Government I replied and said: "With the means at my disposition I can not do the task; there is too much responsibility. On the simple information you have given me I can not send people to you unless I know what conditions you make." Therefore, the Government recognized the necessity of establishing an Italian labor bureau, in order that the Italian immigration could find employment in agricultural districts, because most of our immigrants come from rural districts and their only natural occupation would be in the Western States, and the Government has acknowledged that in order to carry out the second part of our programme it would have to organize an Italian labor bureau; and as this would require a good deal of expenditure there are in view measures to modify the present law of immigration. After many complaints made by our bureau in Italy, we have been able to show to the Government that there are many deficiencies in the present law, so the Government has just now presented to Parliament a bill, which I hope will be approved, and which has some new provisions which will be of greater benefit to our immigration in breaking up the padrone system.

Q. (By Mr. CLARKE.) I would like to ask if your Government receives any benefit from these immigrants in any way?—A. No, at least no direct benefit.

Q. Do they send home large sums of money to their friends, which is used for the purchase and improvement of real estate?—A. Yes, it may be.

Q. And the payment of taxes?—A. It may be—taxes on their houses.

Q. You think that probable?—A. I am certain of that.

Q. For that reason the Government indirectly receives a great benefit from the emigration of these people and their profitable employment here?—A. No profit besides the payment of the regular tax in Italy. Everybody who is the owner of a house has to pay taxes, whether in Italy or abroad.

Q. The Government is in that way indirectly benefited by the presence of these people here more than it would be by their presence at home?—A. I do not see any special benefit from that any more than in any other nation.

Q. In spite of the safeguards that you speak of, and your preparation to send your men who are said to be farmers, and never were farmers. to the far West, is it not a fact that your people have congested in the large cities here and are subject to the padrone system or employed in gangs?—A. Although the congestion of Italians here is still existent, that is due also to the fact that immigration has substantially increased in the last three years. It is not due to the mere fact that they want to stay in New York, but there is a great increase over previous years. This year we will have about 78,000, against 59,000 last year, and when the bureau was founded we had only 30,000.

Q. Could you tell us what good your bureau has accomplished?—A. As I have already said, we do a great deal of good to the immigrants as soon as they are discharged, in the way of informing them, and asking them for information as to where they are going, and taking the addresses of relatives and friends, and, if possible, correspond with the relatives, and if the relatives are in New York we send for them and try to give the immigrant into their hands. Or, for instance, if the immigrant has no ticket to go to his destination we telegraph to relatives to send money for the journey, so the immigrant is sent direct. If there are women or children along, we take special care of them. If children go to points near to New York, we try to accompany them by a clerk of the bureau. If they are going to New York and have no friends there, we advise them to go to proper places where they can not be robbed. If they have relatives there we call them and talk with them, and give them special directions where to go in order to escape the speculation of the owners of the lodging houses and other speculators. Where, for instance, an immigrant complains of having been robbed, we make special inquiry. If they have lost baggage or if the baggage has gone astray we make a special effort to find it. Many of these immigrants do not know anything about salaries, what is paid, and we give all kinds of information, and advise them not to receive less than a certain salary, because it is the common salary that is paid.

I must call your attention also to the so-called "birds of passage." You seem to reproach the Italians who come here in the spring and go back in the winter. Now, you must consider that most of these men who come here in the spring and go back in the winter or fall are glad to be here while they find work to do, but as soon as winter comes many of these constructions are suspended, and, therefore, they have to return to Italy. You consider these "birds of passage" as being to blame, and they are held by the board of special inquiry, because they have simply stated before the registry clerk that they have been here two or three times. I do not find anything to blame them with, because if they could find work during the whole year they would be glad to remain. I could give you statistics of men who come back here in the spring and bring their families, showing that our immigration is becoming more and more permanent and losing the character of "birds of passage."

I have just received the following communication from an American gentleman here present, which says: "Tell them that many Americans, including John Jacob Astor, take annually to Europe and spend millions of dollars which they have taken from American people in rents, so why object to a few poor Italians taking back a few hard-earned dollars to Italy?" I submit the same to your consideration.

IMMIGRATION.   161

STATEMENT OF MR. W. H. ALLEN,

On Restriction of Immigration.

348 REID AVENUE, BROOKLYN, N. Y., *October 20, 1899.*

WILLIAM E. SACKETT,
Secretary Industrial Commission, Washington, D. C.

DEAR SIR: I subjoin a brief statement of the argument I made before the commission in favor of immigration restriction, together with authorities for every statement made.

The main points I advance in support of this policy are:

First. That a large proportion of the immigrants of later years only come here to hoard up money.

Second. There are nearly 500,000 of this class of aliens in the country (including Asiatics), and the amount of their hoardings reaches the enormous sum of $118,000,000 yearly.

Third. This steady absorption of gold is a serious menace to our financial stability.

I represent the Advance Labor Club of Brooklyn, N. Y., an organization that has always taken an active interest in the subject of immigration. About 10 years ago we adopted resolutions in favor of immigration restriction, and a committee, consisting of James McKay, T. J. Meany, and myself, were appointed to agitate the question in other labor bodies. This committee visited about 150 labor unions, of which number all but 5 or 6 approved of our resolutions. In 1896 we had resolutions in favor of the Lodge-Corliss bill indorsed by the 2 Central Labor unions and the 5 district assemblies of the Knights of Labor of New York and vicinity. We also had them approved by the United Brotherhood of Carpenters at their national convention, and the General Assembly of the Knights of Labor in the fall of 1896.

In view of the efforts that have been made to prove that this agitation is a nativist movement I desire to say that such is not fact. It is an economic, not a Know-Nothing movement.

We advocate restriction because a large portion of the immigrants of later years do not intend to become citizens. They are only here to hoard a small fortune, and as soon as that object is effected they return home.

The last Congress saw fit to reject the Corliss amendment, which provided for the exclusion of these migratory immigrants, and in so doing I think it acted unwisely, for while my organization heartily supported the Lodge bill. we yet believe that the immigrant who does not intend to stay here is worse than the uneducated immigrant. He is worse because the loss of the money he absorbs is a serious menace to our financial stability. This is a phase of the immigration question that has been entirely overlooked; but when the American people properly understand it, when they realize how much these aliens absorb, and the financial and economic effect of such absorptions, they will demand the enactment of more drastic legislation than any that has yet been proposed.

At one time it was supposed the Chinese were the only class of aliens who came here just to hoard up money; but about 1863 it transpired that the Canadians were nearly as bad; and still later, owing to reduced passage rates, it was seen that large numbers of the same class were coming from Europe. In the last 12 or 15 years the proportion of migratory immigrants has been steadily increasing, so that at the present time there is good reason to believe they constitute three-fourths of the whole number.

According to the reports of our Immigration Bureau the number of aliens landing here during the decade ending June 30, 1891, was 5,246,613; but these reports are incomplete, as they do not include the immigrants arriving here from Canada and Mexico since 1885. In his report for 1893 our Chief of the Bureau of Statistics cites Canadian official reports to show that 418,000 immigrants arrived at Canadian ports from European countries en route for the United States, between the years 1885 and 1890. In addition to these, there are the native Canadians who come and go every year. In 1891 Congressman Chipman, of Michigan, put their number at 250,000, while the Immigration Investigating Commission of 1895 estimates the number at 100,000, "not including those who come daily into Buffalo and Detroit and other border towns and cities, or the seamen on the Great Lakes," so that it is safe to put the whole number of immigrants coming from Canada, or through there from Europe, between 1885 and 1890, at 950,000. Add to these the number reported by the Immigration Bureau and it makes a total of 6,196,613

607A——11

aliens that landed here between 1880 and 1890. And yet, according to the census reports, there were only 2,569,604 more foreign-born persons here in 1890 than in 1880.

If all these immigrants remained here the usual allowance for deaths in 10 years would be 20 per cent; but as most of them only remain here from 1 to 3 years, 10 per cent is a fair allowance. Now then, if we deduct this 10 per cent (619,661), it appears that 3,007,348 of these aliens must have returned home in those 10 years; that is, an average of 300,734 yearly.

Along with this number must be added the immigrants from China, Japan, and Mexico. The census of 1890 makes no mention of Chinese immigrants; it assumes that after the restriction act was passed none came in except those who were here before, while the testimony of United States officials before the Stump committee in 1891, and numerous newspaper reports, show that they have been stealing their way in ever since the act went into force. According to the report of the House Committee on Immigration (1892) the Chinese were being smuggled in at the rate of 20,000 a year. The census of 1890 puts the Chinese population at 107,475, but Wong Chin Foo, secretary of the Chinese Equal Rights League, in his petition against the Geary law, claimed that there were 150,000 Chinese in that organization in this country; and he ought to know better than the census officials, because the Chinese are stowed away in their dwellings in such manner that no correct count can be made of their numbers. As to the number of Japanese and Mexican immigrants here, from the testimony of witnesses before the Stump committee in 1891 it appears that there must be not less than 25 000 of both nationalities in the United States. This would make the whole number of these migratory immigrants here about the year 1891 about 475,000.

Now, as to the amount of money taken away by these aliens: In 1892 the New York Herald investigated this matter, and, from the testimony of padrones, labor contractors, and steamship agents, it reached the conclusion that the average amount taken by the Italians was $250 each, while the English and Scotch immigrants took on an average $300 each. These estimates may be fair for the unskilled laborers who stay here only 3 years; but it is too low for the skilled laborers who earn from $3 to $4 a day, and who can save from $350 to $550 in one season, working 8 months in the year. It is also too low for the Chinese and others who stay here from 3 to 10 years, and who take away an average of $400 each. Besides these, there are a number of these aliens who are in business for themselves; they own fruit stands, boarding houses, rum shops, laundries, barber shops, and they act as padrones, bankers, labor contractors, and steamship agents, and their hoardings run up into the thousands.

However, even if we take the lowest estimate as a basis, and assume that these aliens take on an average only $250 each, the total amount absorbed by the whole number reaches the enormous sum of $118,000,000 yearly. This does not include the passage rates both ways that is paid out of the wages earned here, and if added up would more than offset all the money that is brought by those who come here to stay.

In reply to those who may think I have exaggerated the amount taken by these aliens, I beg to refer to F. L. Dingley on "European immigration" (p. 249), Special Consular Reports, 1890, wherein he estimates that in the 2 previous years alien laborers and American tourists took from us upward of $500,000,000. As the latter item—tourists' expenses—is usually estimated at $100,000,000 yearly, it leaves $150,000,000 as the amount that alien laborers take away each year, which is $32,000,000 a year more than my estimate.

Now, in order to realize the true significance of the facts here set forth it is necessary to remember that the export movement of gold, which began in 1889 and continued up to 1893, when it precipitated the worst panic we had had in 50 years, averaged only $54,000,000 for each of those years. That is less than the amount which the immigrants from Europe alone had been absorbing about that time, and less than half of what the whole number took away. Hence I was convinced that the gold which we had exported in these 4 years largely represented the hoardings of these aliens.

Our financial leaders, however, had another theory of the cause of the gold exports. Their theory was that the exports of gold were to pay for stocks that had been returned by foreign investors who had become alarmed about our silver policy. Hence it was claimed that if the Sherman law was repealed the confidence of foreign investors would be restored and they would cease to return their stocks; then the export of gold would cease, and prosperity would return.

This theory became popular enough to force the repeal of the Sherman law; but as the export of gold continued, and as prosperity did not return after that law had been wiped off the statute books, it became evident that this theory was false, and that our financial leaders were on the wrong scent.

Now, the reasons which convinced me that the absorptions of these aliens had more to do with the outflow of gold than the Sherman law were as follows: In the first place, this outflow began in 1889, a year before the Sherman law was enacted. In the second place, while it was claimed that foreigners were losing faith in our stocks, it was an undeniable fact that they were making investments right along. At the time of the panic, when the prices of all stocks were lowest, foreign capitalists were the heaviest purchasers. In the 12 months preceding this panic the financial reports certainly show that foreigners bought more of our stocks, bonds, industrial plants, and mining properties than they sold. In the third place, if it were true that this gold was being sent abroad in payment for returned stocks, then the most of it certainly ought to have gone to those countries where the largest portion of our stocks are held. But such was not the fact. England, as is well known, holds more of our stocks than any other country, but she did not get the most of this gold that was exported between 1889 and 1893. Most of the gold we shipped abroad in these 4 years went to the south of Europe. According to the Mint report of 1892, out of $55,000,000 exported at New York from July 1, 1891, to September 21, 1892, only $6,000,000 went to England; the rest was shipped to France and Germany, from whence, according to the same report, a large portion was reshipped to Austria.

Now, according to a statement of ex-Minister Fred. D. Grant as published in the New York Morning Advertiser of July 9, 1893, Austria did not hold any of our stocks at that time. Consequently the Sherman law could not be held responsible for the shipment of gold to that country. Besides, it is well known that our gold continued to go to Austria after this law had been repealed. In regard to this later movement, it was claimed at the time that the Rothschilds, who were floating the Austrian loan, were borrowing the gold from us. But this could not have been true, because those astute bankers would not be very likely to try to borrow gold in the United States, where its growing scarcity and dearness had produced a disastrous panic, when it was plentiful and cheap in England. In a letter to the New York World, under date of June 25, 1893, Julian Ralph calls attention to the abundance and cheapness of money in England at that time. He says: "So phenomenally cheap is money in London to-day that it is possible to borrow practically an unlimited amount at the rate of 25 cents a day for every $50,000. There is now on deposit in the Bank of England alone more than $250,000,000 more money than was lying there 9 months ago." In view of these facts it is preposterous to assume that Europe was borrowing any gold from us at that time.

Hence, the only reasonable assumption is that, inasmuch as we did not owe Austria any great amount for imports of merchandise or tourists' expenses, this gold represented the hoardings of the thousands of Austrian laborers that are scattered all over this country. Some idea of the extent of their hoardings may be gathered from the evidence submitted to the Joint Committee on Immigration in 1890 (p. 580), which shows that as much as $75,000 a month was being sent from the town of Mount Carmel, Pa., by the Huns in that vicinity. In this connection it is to be noted that it is only since her people began to come here in such large numbers that Austria has been taking our gold.

Of course, the Austrian immigrants were not the only factors in this movement of gold. In later years the Italians have begun to take vast sums of our money. One Italian banker testified before the Senate committee in 1893 that his firm alone sent away $2,000,000 the year before, and that there were about 80 other such firms in New York City, some of which sent away even larger amounts.

Until 1889 the extent of the hoardings of these aliens was not noticeable because our excess of exports and sales of stocks was sufficient to offset them; but about that time there was such an enormous increase in this class of aliens, principally from the south of Europe, that our excess of exports was not large enough to offset their hoardings, and hence we had to ship gold to make up the difference. And it was about this same time that a change took place in the personnel of the gold exporting trade. About 1889, and afterwards, the French and German houses, not previously active in the trade, began to take most of our gold. (U. S. Mint Rep., 1892.)

Now, as before stated, the outflow of specie from 1889 to 1893, when the panic occurred, averaged only $54,000,000 a year; and as that is actually less than the amounts which the aliens from Europe alone were absorbing, it seems very evident that if it had not been for such absorptions the panic could not have happened, as our excess of exports would have been more than sufficient to offset our annual foreign debts.

That is my explanation of the panic of 1893; and I have a right to say here that in a letter to the Brooklyn Eagle, dated June 1, 1893, before the Sherman law was repealed, I predicted that such repeal would not stop the outflow of gold. As this prediction turned out to be true, I have certainly a much better right to assume that my explanation is correct than those who contended that the Sherman law was the cause of the panic.

Now, that panic of 1893 was the worst one that we had had in 50 years. It caused the failure of 50,000 business firms, with liabilities of over $800,000,000, a shrinkage in values of many millions more, and a loss of over $300,000,000 in wages, besides inflicting untold hardships and poverty upon thousands of our people. And if, as I contend, the hoarding of gold by these aliens hastened this event, then that is sufficient reason for excluding them. For, if their absorptions could inflict such injury upon us in 1893, it is very likely to have the same effect upon our prosperity again.

It may seem rash to hazard such a prediction now, when our financial leaders are making such boasts about our solid business prosperity; but I contend that the facts of current history prove that we are not as safe as these leaders seem to think. I contend that our present financial condition is such that we can not afford to lose the gold which these aliens are taking away, and that even now their absorptions are threatening the prosperity of the country.

Last year the balance of trade in our favor was $530,000,000, while our net imports of specie (gold and silver) were only about $25,000,000. The Wall street explanation of the reason why we got so little cash for all this excess of exports is that about $250,000,000 of it went to pay for returned stocks, and the balance was used to pay interest on foreign investments, tourists' expenses, and ocean freights. (New York Evening Sun, June 17, 1899.) This explanation, however, does not fit in with the facts. The financial reports of the New York Sun and the Press certainly prove that from July 1 to December 31, 1898, foreigners bought more of our stocks than sold. Besides, there were outside purchases of stocks by foreigners that are not included in the regular market reports. Thus, about October 13 a large block of Pittsburg and Western bonds were sold in Europe; the next month, November 18, the Speyer Brothers sold in London $10,000,000 worth of Southern Pacific bonds. If there were any sales to offset these purchases by foreigners, they are not recorded in the reports.

In regard to the latter half of the last fiscal year, up to June 24, R. G. Dun's report of that date says that "according to the best obtainable evidence the sales of stocks by foreigners since the 1st of January did not exceed the purchases by over $12,250,000."

Now, I think that where the experts are wrong in this matter is in underestimating the amount of our annual foreign debts. I think they underestimate the amount due as interest on foreign investments. But the biggest mistake they make is in wholly ignoring the fact that we have this vast army of migratory immigrants sending their hoards to the old country. And yet the evidence that there is such an army is as plain and unmistakable as is the evidence that we have an army of Americans who go to Europe every year. That evidence consists of the census reports on immigration and population, as well as the testimony of numerous witnesses before our various Congressional committees. And there is certainly better evidence that these aliens absorb a big part of this trade balance than there is that it went to pay for returned stocks. For instance, one part of this trade balance is the result of our commerce with Canada. Last year it amounted to $52,000,000, for which we received only $13,500,000 in cash. Now, we certainly do not owe that country any big amounts for tourists' expenses or ocean freights; and as her people have none of our securities to dump on our market the only rational explanation is that the most of this balance has gone to offset the hoardings of the army of Canadian laborers that are scattered all over the United States.

In the same way it is evident a good portion of the remainder of our trade balance has gone to offset the hoards of other aliens from Europe and Asia. For the first few years after the panic the number of immigrants declined, and the amount of money sent away was not so large as in former years; but at the present time there is good reason to believe that as much money is sent away by alien laborers as ever before.

The number of Chinese and Japanese is certainly larger than it was in 1893. We see proof of this in the streets of our towns and cities, in the steady expansion of the Chinese quarters of New York, and also in the frequent reports of their being smuggled in at various parts of the country. Here are a few of these reports which give some clew to violations of the restriction act that have been going on for the last fifteen years.

IMMIGRATION. 165

HERALD BUREAU,
CORNER FIFTEENTH AND G STREETS NW.,
Washington, D. C., November 28, 1896.

Chinese Inspector Scharf, stationed in New York, has submitted an elaborate report to the Secretary of the Treasury on the smuggling of Chinese into the United States. He makes several specific charges against United States officials at the ports of New York and Malone, N. Y.

Those at the latter port, he charges, are in collusion with officials of the Canadian Pacific Railroad, and says that through such collusion great numbers of Chinese not entitled to enter the United States are yearly admitted into its territory.

The great extent of the northern border of the United States has during the past few years afforded Chinese many opportunities to surreptitiously enter the United States. It is almost impossible to maintain an effective guard along its great length, and the vigilance exercised at most of the ports on the Atlantic and Pacific has compelled those Chinese who desired to smuggle themselves into this country to resort to the northern border. Most of these Chinese come by way of Halifax.

CHARGES ACTUAL COLLUSION.

Mr. Scharf now charges that in Malone, which is in the custom district of Plattsburg, the officials of the Canadian Pacific Railroad, who encourage Chinese travel on their road, assist, by advice, and in many cases by actual collusion with United States officials at that port, in getting the Chinese into the United States.

His charges against the New York officials are directed more against the practice of examination, which, he holds, affords loopholes for illegal entry of Chinese, than against the officials themselves.

Copies of Inspector Scharf's report, which has not been made public, have been sent to the collectors of customs in New York and Plattsburg, N. Y., with instructions from Acting Secretary Hamlin to investigate the charges and criticisms made by him and report back to the Treasury Department the facts found.

MAY BE REFERRED TO ENGLAND.

In case it is found that Mr. Scharf's charges, that officials of the Canadian Pacific Railroad are conniving with United States customs officials, are true, the matter will be brought to the attention of the British Government. The Treasury Department will attend to the cases of their own officials in Malone should Inspector Scharf's allegations prove well founded.

It is announced this afternoon that W. B. Howell, special employee of the Treasury; J. J. Crowley, chief of the special agents, and John M. Comstock, chief of the customs division, will be in New York Monday to meet the customs officers on duty at the lake ports and along the Vermont and New York boundary line. The purpose of the conference is to arrange for a better uniformity in carrying out the Treasury regulations and customs laws.

CHINESE EVADE LAWS—COMING HERE IN GREAT NUMBERS—SMUGGLED INTO THE COUNTRY IN THE GUISE OF MERCHANTS OR UNDER BONDS.

Despite the stringent laws on the subject, there is no doubt but that Chinese laborers in great numbers are being brought into this country, and many of them land right here in New York, and here they stay. The principal point from which they reach here is Havana, and so long as the rules laid down by the Treasury Department are in force the local officers have no remedy. The way the game is worked on Uncle Sam is very simple, but at the same time very effective. At Havana the Chinese laborers can easily become merchants by the payment of $25, that sum securing them a nominal interest in some mercantile house, and for a few dollars more there is no difficulty in securing affidavits to the effect that they are bona fide merchants. Of course, when these are presented to Consul-General Williams he promptly vises, and the holders are entitled to admission to this country. With these the local inspection officers have nothing to do; it is the laborers who give all the trouble. These men come here on the way to Montreal, and are permitted to land under a bond of $200. This bond once given, they are allowed to roam about the city at will for twenty days, and it is during this time they perfect arrangements for staying in this country.

They find some bona fide merchant who either wants to return to China or is willing to make the journey to Montreal, for a consideration, so that when the twenty days are up the Canadian Pacific Road transports the number of Chinamen they have given bond for, but not the same Chinamen. The deputy collector at Malone, N. Y., certifies that the proper number has passed over the border, the bonds are canceled, and the whole transaction, so far as that particular batch of Celestials is concerned, is at an end. The law has apparently been enforced, but in reality it has been evaded in the most barefaced manner.

As for European immigration there are sure signs that it is rapidly reaching the higher rate of former years. The increase the last 6 months has been larger than for many years back. A significant feature of last year's immigration is the evidence of an increase in the proportion of migratory immigrants. Of the 311,707 aliens who came last year, Italy sent more than any other country, 78,000; and according to ex-Commissioner Senner, 80 per cent of them are birds of passage. Among these migratory immigrants there is always a greater proportion of males, and last year's immigration figures show this proportion to be greater than in former years.

In view of these facts, and considering that labor of all kinds commands higher wages than it has for many years back, I am convinced that these aliens are draining the country of as much money now as they ever did before. And every dollar they send away goes to offset what is owing to us abroad for excess of exports.

That, I contend, is the true reason why we got so little cash for our enormous trade balance last year. The greater part of what was left after paying interest dues, tourists' expenses, and ocean freights, has gone to offset the drafts and money orders of these aliens.

And hence it follows that the money famine, which at this moment hangs like a dark cloud over the country, threatening ruin and disaster to our people, owes its origin to the same cause as that which precipitated the financial crash of six years ago. Even if the existing money stringency should disappear for a time, the indications are that it is almost certain to appear again in the near future and produce serious results.

The fact that we got so little cash for last year's trade balance proves that our annual for debt amounts to about $500,000,000. Next year one item of this debt (tourists' expenses) will be doubled, perhaps trebled, on account of the Paris Exposition. Suppose now that while this debt is growing bigger there should come such a change in crop conditions, here and abroad, as to cause a decline in our exports. Such changes have happened before. Thus in 1892 our excess of exports amounted to $202,000,000, and the very next year it was the other way. There was an unfavorable balance of $18,000,000. Now, even if the decline in our excess of exports should only be to what it was two years ago (1897), when it stood at $359,000,000, the result would be that in order to settle these foreign debts we might have to pay out every dollar of gold there is in the National Treasury. And with the experience of 1893 before us we can well imagine what would be the consequences of such a drain.

Under these circumstances I hold that there are good and sufficient grounds for the absolute restriction of immigration. It is not right that the welfare of 80,000,000 people should be put in jeopardy for the benefit of a class of alien vampires who have no other object in coming here but to rob the country of that which is the life blood of its trade and industry.

Respectfully submitted,

W. H. ALLEN.

WASHINGTON, D. C., *October 12, 1899.*

TESTIMONY OF JOSEPH H. SENNER,

Formerly Commissioner of Immigration at the Port of New York.

The commission met at 10.30 a. m. Vice-Chairman Phillips presided and introduced Dr. Joseph H. Senner, who, being first duly sworn, testified concerning immigration as follows:

Q. You will please give your name and address.—A. Joseph H. Senner, 16 Nassau street, New York City.

Q. How long were you commissioner of immigration at the port of New York?—A. From March 29, 1893, to August 5, 1897.

Q. I believe that you have some statement that you wish to make to the commission.—A. I preferred to put at least the general scope of my remarks on paper, in order to give the commission an opportunity to ask me about any specific point,

IMMIGRATION. 167

either in connection with same or independently of that, in reference to the immigration question. If I am permitted to read——
Mr. FARQUHAR (interrupting): Go right ahead and read.
The WITNESS: Newspapers have a great deal to say at present about the recent large increase in immigration. There is again, as often before, much ado about nothing. The report of the Immigration Bureau for the fiscal year ending June 30, 1899, shows a total of only 311,707, which is more than 10 per cent smaller than the immigration in 1896 and a great deal less than in any year from 1880 to 1893. While it is true that there is some increase over the preceding two years, the total immigration of last year was nevertheless abnormally low, considering the almost unprecedented prosperity the country enjoyed after a successful war, and the rapidity with which reports of such prosperity spread all over the world in modern times. Industrial and commercial activity and financial prosperity of such dimensions ought to have brought to the United States, according to all theories of immigration, at least twice as many immigrants as actually landed. According to the same theories, the largest number of immigrants ought to have come from the most densely populated European countries; in fact, just these countries, like, for instance, Germany, show a decided tendency of decrease in their immigration, while some of the most numerous types of immigrants come from countries which could easily support twice as large a population as they possess. Immigration depends upon a variety of causes, partly local, partly individual, partly national, partly economical, but in all these directions so diversified that it is hardly possible to establish rules about it. To regulate immigration by statute is almost as impossible a task as to control prosperity or a financial crisis by legislation. Some of the most potent factors of immigration, which is naturally based on emigration from other countries, are entirely beyond our own control. All we can do is to discourage the immigration of undesirable persons, and even then opinions may greatly differ as to the desirability or undesirability of certain classes of immigrants. Besides, persons who may be very undesirable in a certain location are most desirable in another section of this vast country. This was clearly shown by the replies from governors or heads of bureaus of the different States, to whom the Immigration Investigating Commission in 1895 issued official inquiries on that subject. I beg to quote from the report of this commission, of which I was a member:
"The immigration question is preeminently a national one. This nation consists neither of a few large cities, which, as in all countries, furnish only limited employment to a dense population, nor of the few States whose farms are deserted and whose manufacturing cities are overcrowded with idlers. Immigration concerns the West not less than the East, and South as well as the North, and the only line of policy which can be consistently recommended is one which will benefit the whole country most and harm each part of it least. Certain classes in the community have demanded the complete abolition of immigration because of abuses of the naturalization laws in conferring the right of franchise upon newly arrived immigrants; of religious or race antagonisms; or because of the discouragement induced by the recent financial depression. But it is a remarkable fact that, notwithstanding the financial crisis, and the widespread agitation against immigration, a large number of the governors of States have emphasized a desire for immigrants."
A great deal has been said recently about the noticeable change in the nationalities which predominate among immigrants. It stands established as a fact that in recent years immigration from the United Kingdom, Germany and Scandinavian countries is smaller in numbers than that from Austria-Hungary, Italy, and Russia (including the Poles, which have no empire of their own). I do not dispute this fact, though I do not hesitate to declare the statistics cited in connection with it as inaccurate and partly misleading. As to the causes of the remarkable change, I decidedly differ from the members of the Immigration Restriction League, who apparently hold the steamship companies almost entirely responsible for it. I believe I am justified in the statement that the remarkable increase in immigration from southern Italy during the last years was to a large extent, if not entirely, due to nothing else but the agitation of the American restrictionists, and especially for the so-called Lodge bill. It is not at all surprising that tens of thousands of Italians from the South, if illiterate, hastened to the United States before they were barred out by a new law. Only three years ago a new steamship line was actually started in business exclusively on this theory. As a matter of fact, immigration from southern Italy during the last years of financial depression and business inactivity, but of liveliest agitation of the Boston restrictionists, was larger than in the present year of prosperity and enormous business activity.

On the other hand, immigration from Germany decreased to only about 10 per cent of what it used to be ten or fifteen years ago. The extraordinary development of the German Empire in the last decade furnishes but a partial explanation of this very startling phenomenon, because some of the largest immigration from Germany fell just in this period of German imperial rise, while the largest decrease only occurred during the last few years. Besides, Ireland, which is certainly all but equally prosperous, shows during these same last few years an enormous decrease in immigration to the United States. The same is true of the Scandinavian countries, Sweden, Norway, and Denmark. Why, then, it may be asked, have the United States lost so much of their attractive powers for the thrifty and enterprising people of these European countries? Nobody can justly claim that the richest country of the world in natural products, with its, on the whole, still scant population, does not any more offer sufficient opportunities. Nobody can justly claim that this country is thoroughly settled, and much less, that our demands for domestic help, with high wages and abundant opportunities for marriage, is in any way filled. Every housewife will certify to this fact. Why, then, was the influx so materially and almost instantly stopped?

There is but one reasonable reply to these questions, and that is that the unequaled vexations to which any steerage passenger was subjected since 1893 have done their full work. The restrictive force of the law of 1893, which I personally had the privilege to inaugurate practically, has as yet not been sufficiently recognized. The very large decrease in immigration since 1893 was heretofore almost exclusively attributed to our financial depression. That the entire removal of this depression and the return of extraordinary business activity for more than a year, combined with an unusually successful war, ordinarily a great attraction by itself, had comparatively so little effect on our immigration may perhaps open the people's eyes. The law now in force works immensely as a restrictive measure, not so much by actual prevention of the landing of undesirable persons as by the deterring of them, and also of many desirable, from taking passage. This is done in two ways: First, directly, by imposing upon the steamship companies heavy financial responsibilities not only for maintenance and return of all undesirable passengers detected at the landing, but also for maintenance and return of all landed immigrants who become public charges within 1 year after landing, from causes existing prior to landing. The steamship companies, on the other hand, hold their agents strictly responsible, and no agent sells a ticket to any possible deportee without proper deposits or guaranties. Besides, the agent, especially in Italy, has, since the enforcement of said law, been held responsible to any deported person for the passage money and other damages. Tens of thousands of would-be immigrants were refused tickets annually by the agents, and a still larger number was deterred by the annoyances of the minute inquiries made by agents in self-protection. This was and is a wholesome and beneficial restriction, because its effects naturally extend principally to the less desirable.

Quite different, however, is the second more indirect and harmful effect of restriction caused by the law of 1893, and I can speak of it so much more freely as it is universally recognized that during the four years and four months of my term as commissioner of immigration at the principal American port I faithfully enforced the law. Even the most eligible, desirable immigrant coming, as they usually do, in steerage does not succeed as a rule in landing in less than 24 hours later than his more fortunate fellow-passenger in the cabin, and not without a long series of vexatious, annoying, oftentimes distinctly hard tribulations, as they are almost unavoidable in the present procedure, requiring frequent removals and repeated examinations. And if the admission of any immigrant be in any way questionable, it has become quite usual that one or more weeks pass before the immigrant, whether male or female, adult or child, is landed. This frequently extended period of detention, during which the immigrant is practically treated as a prisoner, and by no means as well as an inmate of a modern and humanitarian prison, brings forth so many and manifold hardships to the immigrant that people belonging to nations of higher civilization keenly resent it. I have called these vexations unequaled, and, as a matter of fact, they have no equal in any civilized country in the world. The statement of Mr. Schulteis that "They have restrictions in nearly all European countries, and they are far more strict in some of them than we are" (page 28 of his testimony), is entirely without foundation.

Incidentally I may remark right here that one of the principal objections against the Lodge bill rests in the necessary enormous increase in these vexations, and in its natural influence on immigrants from nations of a higher civilization. It has been repeatedly stated, with some pretense of surprise, that Americans of German or Bohemian or Scandinavian descent are unanimously opposed to the Lodge bill, although they are with hardly any exception fully able to pass its examination. As a matter of fact, however, it does not help very much any single immigrant, whether he or she is able to read and write, if his or her group of 30 is admitted to examination in order, perhaps a day later, or if in his group he or she stands at the end of the line and has patiently waited until those preceding have passed the curious examination of reading, and, as originally intended also, of writing the translation of the American Constitution—a performance, by the way, which in many cases can be nothing but a farce, because the immigrant inspector, in nine cases out of ten, does not understand the language at all in which the document is read or written, and therefore has no possibility of proper and fair judgment. Based on my extended practical experience in charge of the paramount immigration station, I state that with the present number of inspection aisles and of available registry clerks an introduction of the Lodge bill would much more than double the time for examination and thereby double the hardships of steerage passengers. Its practical effect would, therefore, in my opinion, come dangerously near to an annihilation of immigration from nations of higher grade.

In order to dispose right here of the Lodge bill, I wish to state that our opposition to the same is principally based on our conviction that the proper time for such an educational test is at the time of naturalization and not upon admission to the country. We further regard its application to women not only generally unjust, but practically, also, as a severe aggravation to our much vexed servant-girl question. We believe that its introduction for immigrants stands in a rather curious contrast with the present policy of expansion and its consequence as to wholesale reception of illiterate, if not savage, co-citizens. And finally, as a protective measure for American workingmen, the Lodge bill would be simply a farce, because the skilled laborer, whose competition organized labor wishes to restrict, could at any time pass any such examination.

I believe I have sufficiently shown that the immigration laws now in force have a decided restrictive effect. I am far from stating that the present laws are perfect. As member of the Immigration Investigating Committee I joined in the recommendation of not less than 29 amendments, some of which could be easily carried out in an administrative way, and a good many of which I personally only agreed to as a compromise with the two other members of the commission. But while it is a fact hardly disputed by any student of the laws, and much less by any person connected with their practical handling, that the wording of the laws often is ambiguous and defective, I hesitate to recommend a new codification, because I apprehend only new complications and difficulties and reopening of all questions pertaining to immigration. I believe that in due time all existing disputes can easily be worked out by decisions of the courts and by improved regulations of the department. It appears to me that the present laws could be enforced more efficiently, and that all difficulties with future immigration could be solved with the existing laws, provided ways and means could be found for a better distribution of the immigrants. I stated intentionally that the difficulties with future immigration could be solved in this way. There are unquestionably many difficult problems to solve as consequences of the large immigration of former years and of its partly unwholesome distribution; but these problems do not fall within the province of the immigration laws and their handling, as there are no more immigrants to deal with, but residents of the States, and to a large extent often citizens. American civilization, assisted by restriction of naturalization, will readily dispose of the problems from old immigration.

As to my remark that the immigration laws could be enforced more efficiently than they are, I do not wish to reflect on the honesty and conscientiousness of the officers. Their shortcoming, however, is unquestionable, an unavoidable consequence of the prevailing system in their selection, qualification, and compensation. If there is any public service in the United States which requires peculiar qualifications in knowledge additional to the standard qualifications of any public officer, such as honesty, faithfulness, and energy, it is certainly the immigration service. The officer has not to deal with goods, but with living and speaking subjects. He has no established standard of appraisement which may be passed upon in wholesale, but he has to judge of every single individual according to his merits. And these individuals who appear before the examining officer speak not the American language and are not brought up in the American way. They are entitled, however, to all consideration due to human beings, and as to their eligibility as American residents to a fair and just judgment of their natural qualifications.

An officer who has no knowledge of foreign countries, their peculiarities and language, will be seriously hampered in passing a fair judgment on the immigrant unless he has another officer on hand who can act as an intelligent interpreter, and who, therefore, practically does what the American officer is supposed and paid to do. The prevailing system of appointing the largest number of

American officials without any requirement as to knowledge of foreign languages or countries, and to supply them with a few poorly paid and, therefore, naturally neither select nor competent interpreters—this system, as a matter of course, cripples the efficiency of the service. My former assistant in New York, Commissioner McSweeney, evidently came to the same conclusion as to the necessity of a knowledge of foreign languages for an efficient service, as he has taken considerable pains to study Italian; and he will surely bear me out in the statement that he was materially helped in his administration of the office by the ability not not only to control the interpreter, but, if necessary, to dispense with him entirely. I heard it repeatedly stated, even by gentlemen of high public standing, that the immigration service should be exclusively handled by native Americans, who are alleged to possess, exclusively, sufficient determination to carry out the law. The implied insinuation against foreign-born Americans may well be overlooked, but it can be emphatically stated that an immigrant inspector, or a member of the board of special inquiry, or a contract-labor inspector, who has entirely to rely on the usually poor interpreter, rarely receives correct information, and therefore, as a rule, is unable to do justice to the country and to the immigrant.

Some years ago, shortly after I assumed charge of Ellis Island, I suggested to Mr. Samuel Gompers, the president of the American Federation of Labor (by the way, also foreign born), the advisability of sending immigrant inspectors abroad to return among the immigrants and to detect by personal observations all attempts of circumvention. Mr. Gompers embodied this suggestion in a widely reprinted letter to the then chairman of the Senate Immigration Committee. Nothing, however, was done in this direction, for the very simple reason that we had no available inspectors conversant with these foreign languages who could have mingled with immigrants and gained their confidence without being detected at once in their true position.

I do not hesitate for these reasons to go on record as decidedly differing with my successor in office, who stated before your subcommission that honesty and determination to carry out the law are the principal, if not the only, requirements for an immigrant inspector, and therefore declared himself opposed to civil-service regulations in this department. I, on the other hand, can not see any reason whatever why honesty and determination to carry out the law should not be combined with the ability to understand and to properly handle the various nationalities asking for admission to a free country. The immigration service suffers in its efficiency more than any other under the burden of political drones who are officially called to the sifting of persons whose language they understand as little as their character.

A person who is still struggling with the national language, and can not as yet express himself to the full understanding of others, is naturally at a disadvantage, not only in his fight for daily bread, but also and especially as to the recognition of his merits. It is therefore but natural that the foreigner is met with prejudice, which, as a rule, grows stronger and stronger, especially if commercial depression impairs the livelihood of the natives, and strengthens the belief that any increase in the supply of the labor market only increases the struggle for a living. In such cases men are apt to lose sight of the fact that but for immigration the United States could never have built up its unparalleled home market, and that every immigrant very soon turns up as a consumer. Any American only needs to watch the reception of immigrants by their relatives or friends at the immigration station to convince himself at once of the immense difference in the appearance and outfit between the newcomer and his waiting friends, most of whom only preceded him a short while, but all of whom are stylishly dressed in American goods. This important point is generally overlooked, and not the least by workingmen who earn wages in the production of these very goods.

Now, as to the character of such nationalities which recently furnished the largest part of immigration, I have to mention first of all the Italians. That they are an orderly and law-fearing class is hardly ever denied. Isolated cases of too free use of the knife are much too rare exceptions to annul the rule. No doubt they are frugal, and their standard of life is in the first years a good deal lower than that of the average American. But this, too, is only temporary, and American civilization exerts its overwhelming power in due time. True enough, a good many Italians maintain for some years the habit of returning to Italy for a time, and either take along or send their savings home. Close observation, however, convinced me that this also is rapidly decreasing, and that at the second or third return to America their families come along for permanent settlement, which of course makes an end to all sendings of money abroad. This change of condition is plainly shown by the statistics of Italian immigration of the last years as compared with former times. In 1883 arrived 28,217 males and 3,567 females; in 1890 arrived 40,717 males and 11,082 females; in 1898 arrived 40,248 males and 18,365 females from Italy. The number of Italians under 15 years in the same years was

2,528 in 1883, 8,759 in 1890, and 11,935 in 1898. Immigrants from Italy are Americanized fast enough, as stated by me in the North American Review of June, 1896, and meanwhile they are certainly very much more welcome than the Chinese, whose places they have taken in building railroads and waterworks, and doing other labor which the native American and the immigrants from the English-speaking countries have long ceased to undertake.

Another very much misjudged nationality are the Poles, whom not a few of our restrictionists are pleased to call Huns; of course, with very little regard to ethnology and similar minor matters. I happened to get a copy of a letter addressed in March, 1893, by the collector of customs in Buffalo, Mr. William J. Morgan, to a gentleman very much interested in the question. Buffalo is known as a Polish-American center. Permit me to read verbatim part of the interesting letter dated March 6, 1893:

"The Polish colony in Buffalo is quite large. The total number is 55,000, who own about 3,000 lots, valued at $6,181,100, and also 5 large churches and 4 schoolhouses, valued at $450,000, in addition making the total Polish real estate investment in this city $6,631,000. No class of foreigners reaching here display as much anxiety to secure a little home at once as do the Poles. Whole streets are owned by them and several election districts are nearly exclusively peopled by them. They are well organized for the promotion and protection of Polish interests, there being at least one society for this purpose in nearly every Polish election district.

"As a people they pay their taxes more promptly than any other nationality, not excepting the Americans. They take great interest in informing themselves as to American institutions, particularly as to American politics, and for foreigners they are remarkably well informed as to our election laws. It is a well-known fact that when the political organizations established schools in the various localities for the enlightenment of voters as to the practical workings of the new ballot law, the Poles were found to be the best informed as to the subject of any nationality, not excepting the Americans. They had been making the new law a special subject of study in the societies already mentioned and were very well posted. As regards the matter of general education, I think they surpass many people now flocking to our shore. They are industrious and frugal and fill an important place among the army of unskilled labor. Socially, morally, and as regards drink they are as good as the generality of mankind."

Immigration of Russian Jews was at one time alarmingly strong during the years of suppression and expulsion by the Russian Government. It attracted the attention of Americans principally because it appeared to be, and probably was, assisted. It invaded and actually revolutionized many lines of trade and, besides, aroused quite strong race prejudices. We have, however, for some time passed the tail end of this specific immigration, because the effects of the famous Russian edicts had to stop at the end of the few years which the Russian Government fixed for their enforcement. Merely from old habit our statesmen continue to worry about the Baron Hirsch fund, and about its alleged but never proven systematic assistance of immigration. As a matter of fact, this Baron Hirsch fund was for years only applied to some more or less ill-fated agricultural experiments, and principally to educational purposes, the tendency of which is strongly Americanizing. Whenever we succeeded in tracing an influence of the fund or of the Alliance Israelite on immigration, it was exclusively in the direction of helping a wife or children of an American resident to join the husband and father. If there are evils in this immigration of Russian Jews, they belong to the category of old evils which are beyond the sphere of immigration laws.

We heard quite frequently, and especially from the advocates of further restriction by educational or other tests, that the change in the character of immigration which took place in the last 10 or more years greatly added to the increase of crime. It is alleged that the formerly prevailing immigration from the United Kingdom, Germany, or from Scandinavian countries brought more law-abiding persons than the more illiterate recently stronger immigration from Italy, Russia, or Austria. In fact, the alleged close connection between illiteracy and crime always appears as one of the most powerful arguments for the Lodge bill. A careful examination of the official records about the nationality of inmates of State prisons shows, however, quite different results.

I beg to submit in Appendix A reliable abstracts from official records, prepared by a student of the question and revised by myself. Special attention is suggested to the statistics from Massachusetts, the center of agitation for restriction, and from New York, where the greatest congestion of the so-called undesirable immigration takes place. A summary of the commitments to the enumerated institutions in 11 States and of their proportion to the total immigration into this country from 1886 to 1897, from the United Kingdom, Germany, Italy, Austria,

Russia, Sweden, and Norway, also including that from so-called Poland, furnishes a quite interesting result:

	Total commitments.	Immigration 1886-1897.	Percentage.
England	3,199	530,872	0.60
Ireland	15,819	605,968	2.61
Scotland	1,027	124,494	.82
Germany	1,214	945,008	.13
Italy	733	613,531	.12
Austria	253	642,642	.04
Russia	445	537,201	.08
Sweden and Norway	745	518,602	.12

In this table the figures from Poland, which was recognized as an independent country only by the American statisticians, but unfortunately had ceased to exist long before these statisticians were born, were evenly distributed between Russia and Austria, thereby following quite closely the proportion on the actual partition. It appears from this table that Italy, Austria, and Russia furnished a much smaller proportion of commitments than their more literate fellow States from the north of Europe. The plea of danger to our national morals, of contamination by the larger influx of illiterates, hardly stands the illumination of facts. I wish to state, however, that the statistics are only submitted for what they are worth, as I am in general not an admirer of and much less a believer in statistics, unless they are prepared with far more accuracy than has been and largely still is the case for immigration matters.

The large and complex subject of the influence of immigration on wages can not be treated in the ordinary way of jumping to conclusions from a few facts within the much-limited eyesight of a casual observer. Wages depend upon the iron law of demand and supply, only limited by the minimum standard of life on one side and by the maximum power of organization on the other. Furthermore, the standard of life stands in close connection with the much-varying purchasing power of money, and organized labor is met by combinations of capital, which at times are forceful, at other times windy. It is therefore enormously difficult to draw any reliable conclusion from mere statements of the amount of wages, without taking into close consideration the influences prevailing at the specific time.

The late Henry George, who built up his brilliant syllogisms on the abnormal conditions of a pioneer State of gold miners, furnished a warning example of the danger in treating this perplexing subject, even for the most brilliant and loftiest minds. In this place I desire but to contradict emphatically the widespread opinion that wages have fallen with the setting in of great tides of immigration. As far back as 1891 an exhaustive report of a Senate committee charged with the duty of ascertaining the cause of prices and wages of labor stated that wages have been highest during the years of heaviest immigration, which were naturally coinciding with the periods of prosperity, and further that they have steadily increased during the last three decades. The Immigration Investigating Commission before mentioned stated on this subject, page 10: "It would be manifestly unfair, however, to jump to the conclusion that immigration has increased wages, though for that position something may be said. Trade unions have unquestionably been a potent influence in increasing wages, and immigrants have made, broadly speaking, first-class trades-unionists."

In Appendix B I beg to submit a few tables, based on official bulletins and reports. Table I proves that in no single instance average wages were lower in the twelve largest cities in the year 1896 than in 1870; that, on the contrary, an increase in wages took place in spite of the large immigration that poured in since 1870, in many trades such advance even assuming quite respectable proportions. Table II compares the average retail prices of 1872 with those of 1897; Table III compares the purchasing power of money in the same years in Massachusetts, and, finally, Table IV shows the course of wages in each year from 1870 to 1897, with percentages of increase and amount of immigration in the corresponding years.

These tables, as far as statistics are at all able to prove, show that, with but two exceptions, larger quantities of all commodities enumerated could be purchased in 1897 than in 1872, or, in other words, that the purchasing power of wages was larger. It will be noticed that flour, sugar, dry goods, and coal show especially large percentages of increase. The laboring classes ought to consider whether or not without immigration such a development would have been possible, and principally whether or not the commodities enumerated could ever have been produced so cheaply. Table IV deserves the greatest attention by the laboring classes, as it clearly shows that the highest increase in wages as compared with 1870 took place in the years when immigration into the United States was the greatest.

I expressed before my skepticism as to immigration statistics, and desire to emphasize it on the strength of close observation during several years. Apparently we have very complete records, at least since 1856, about the number, nationalities, ages, destination, and money of immigrants. The most superficial comparison of census figures and immigration statistics, however, shows at once that either of the two must be entirely wrong, even as to the simplest of all accounts, the number of immigrants. Some of these very large discrepancies may be explained by the neglect, prior to 1893, of determining whether an immigrant had been in the United States before, and therefore had not been counted twice or even more times.

The immigration station in New York, which was under my personal charge, had beyond doubt the best organized statistical bureau as to immigrants. Nevertheless, in carefully looking up old records, I found that the largest part of statistical figures was based on guesswork without actual counting of numbers, and as to nationalities, ages, or destination often without records of any examination as to these points. It can not be different as long as appointments to office are principally dictated by the desire to give to a friend an opportunity of drawing a salary from Uncle Sam. As to destination and money the statistics are simply absurd. About one-half, if not all, of the immigrants are recorded with destination as New York. No immigrant will ever tell the truth about his available money, and the law of 1893, which only obliges him to disclose his treasure if he has less than $30, made any kind of exactness about the amount brought into the United States by immigrants plainly impossible. I know personally of more than one case where immigrants held as paupers on account of their own statements and appearance, under the pressure of impending deportation disclosed thousands, and I remember one case in which we were all startled by a Russian immigrant showing, finally, not less than $40,000 in good drafts and money. As to nationalities, our statistics are equally unreliable, and not the least on account of the ignorance of inspectors as to the manifold nationalities of polyglot Europe, or on account of the frequent not always well-advised changes in the make-up of the tables. I lay stress on these findings as important, because of the general overestimation of so-called official statistics.

Permit me finally, before concluding this testimony with a few general remarks, to turn to the different attacks made upon me on account of my determined position on the immigration question. Your own pamphlet on immigration contains, on page 25, the statement of Mr. Shulteis that I am one of the agents of the Baron Hirsch fund and a countryman of Baron Hirsch, and that after I went out of office I immediately went back into the same service. These statements are as equally malicious as untrue. It is a matter of record that I had at no time any connection whatsoever, in business or otherwise, with the Baron Hirsch fund, and as an Austrian I could never have been a countryman of the Bavarian Baron Hirsch. Only a few weeks ago the New York Press designated me as an agent of the German colonial party, indeed a very high compliment for an Austrian who never had any bonds of allegiance to the Kaiser. If anything, these two statements prove clearly the lack of knowledge of European geography and ethnology, which I mentioned as an obstacle to a proper enforcement of immigration laws. Other insinuations, including those from a United States Senator on the floor of the Senate, are of the same character. I may take it as a personal compliment if such personal attacks are believed necessary to weaken the force of my arguments.

In conclusion, I beg to state that in my conviction the danger from immigration to the welfare of our country is actually decreasing from year to year. It is obviously clear that a nation of 70,000,000 inhabitants assimilates very much easier 300,000 or 400,000 foreigners than a nation of 40,000,000 could ever assimilate 700,000 to 800,000 a year. Besides, while the United States are continually progressing and strengthening as a nation, Europe does by no means stand still. From year to year education, civilization, and wealth, and with this the general standard of life, advance also in Europe. If the Lodge bill, as I believe, can not be passed within the next few years, it will become obsolete from lack of illiterates in Europe. I freely admit that the immense immigration of former years, prior to the new law of 1893, created quite a number of difficult problems for the United States, especially on the political field, but no new law on immigration would or could assist in solving the problems of old immigration. As stated before, American civilization will work them out successfully. We may help it by strictness in the admission of foreigners to the privilege of voting, but it is absurd to protect the ballot box at the ports of entry and to exclude sturdy and useful immigrants who desire to be admitted to the blessings of this free country of ours and are ready to assume the duties of American citizenship in the course of time. We may further assist the forceful work of an American civilization on the millions of former immigrants by a systematic influence on their better distribution over the country; and in this respect the suggestion of the present commissioner-general, in designating by statutes the heads of State bureaus of labor statistics as agents of the Federal Government for collecting information about the condition of trade and labor, may be more fruitful than if applied to newcomers.

As to immigrants proper, I suggested to the Immigration Investigating Committee, and it was embodied in their report, that an immigrant clearing house, with permanent exhibition, should be erected by private enterprise under Government control for the purpose of influencing a better distribution. This country is not yet ripe, and will not be in the lifetime of any of us, for shutting our doors tightly to the brawny laborer who is willing and able to at least improve our much neglected roads and to perform other menial work which the Americans, for one reason or another, are loath to perform. What we need, besides improvement of our naturalization laws, are ways and means for a more appropriate distribution of the immigrants, so that the newcomers may be directed to the localities where they are peculiarly needed and into the work for which they are fitted; in other words, where they could do the most good to the country as well as to themselves. As to restrictions, however, the law of 1893, if properly enforced, is amply restrictive, and as a matter of fact we have now rather more restriction than is beneficial to the country.

Appendix A.

STATISTICS ABOUT IMMIGRATION AND CRIME.

According to the State reports from Massachusetts for the year ending September 30, 1897, of 826 inmates of the State prison in that year 84 were natives of Great Britain (27 of England and 57 of Ireland), whereas only 35 were born in Italy, 8 in Russia, 2 in Poland (so called), and 2 in Austria. Taking the official returns of the jails and houses of correction in the State of Massachusetts for the year ending September 30, 1897, of 28,755 inmates of these institutions 10,006 were natives of Great Britain (1,615 from England, 510 from Scotland, 7,881 from Ireland), and 491 were natives of Sweden and Norway, as against 252 Italians, 78 Poles, and 94 Russians, 30 from Austria, 10 Armenians, 2 Syrians, 16 Hungarians. The commitments for drunkenness to all penal institutions in the State of Massachusetts for the year ending September 30, 1897, furnish considerable food for reflection. Of 21,443 commitments for drunkenness, 8,360 were natives of Great Britain (6,777 from Ireland, 1,170 from England, 413 from Scotland), 299 from Sweden and Norway, 440 from Germany, 59 from Italy, 71 from Finland, 41 from Poland (so called), 25 from Russia. The three State prisons of the State of *New York* for the year ending September 30, 1896, had 3,120 inmates, 339 of which were natives of Great Britain (105 of England, 37 of Scotland, 197 of Ireland), 192 were German, 156 Italians, 60 Austrians, 47 Russians, 36 Poles. The Matteawan State Hospital for the Criminal Insane during the year ending September 30, 1896, contained 21 natives of Great Britain (6 England, 15 Ireland), 15 Germans, 8 Italians, 2 Austrians, 1 Russian, and 1 Pole.

An investigation of the nationality of the persons committed to the State prisons in *Illinois* (containing the second largest city and a very great proportion of immigrants) during the year ending September 30, 1896, shows, of a total of 2,218, 126 natives of Great Britain (35 England, 88 Ireland, 3 Scotland), 130 natives of Germany, 24 Italians, 19 Russians, 19 Austrians, and 22 Swedes and Norwegians. The Illinois State reformatory during the year ending September 30, 1896, contained 694 inmates, of whom 8 were natives of Great Britain (4 Ireland, 4 England), 30 of Germany, 8 of Sweden and Norway, 10 of Italy, 1 of Austria, 2 of Russia, and 7 of Poland (so called); Southern Illinois penitentiary at Chester, out of 869 there were 37 from Ireland, 15 from Germany, 2 from Italy, no Hungarians, and no Poles.

Pennsylvania, another one of the States which receives a large percentage of foreign immigration from Austria and Italy, has but incomplete prison statistics; but an examination of the official reports shows that of 947 inmates of penitentiaries in 1896, 47 were natives of Great Britain (25 from Ireland, 22 from England), and 42 natives of Germany. The other foreign-born inmates are bunched together, and the reports show 61 natives of all other foreign countries as against 89 natives of Great Britain and Germany. The commitments to county jails and workhouses in Pennsylvania show 558 natives of Great Britain and Germany as against 485 natives of all other foreign countries not specified. The statistics of outdoor relief in Pennsylvania show 1,090 natives of Germany, 3,134 natives of Great Britain (2,101 Ireland, 930 England, 103 Scotland), as against 835 natives of all other foreign countries not specified.

The official reports of the *New Jersey* State prison show of 1,131 inmates, during the year 1897, 80 were natives of Great Britain (44 of England, 9 Scotland, 27 Ireland), 61 natives of Germany, 45 Italians, 7 Austrians, 10 Russians, and 2 Poles. The Essex County penitentiary in 1897 contained 839 inmates, of whom 135 were natives of Great Britain (35 England, 6 Scotland, 94 Ireland), 79 were Germans, 35 Italians, 9 Russians, 10 Austrians, and 4 Poles. The Hudson County penitentiary showed 815 inmates in 1897, of whom 153 were natives of Great Britain (23 of England, 11 Scotland, 119 Ireland), 101 Germans, 40 Italians, 11 Russians, 9 Austrians, and 8 Poles.

The State of *Connecticut* (like the former one of those States in which the proportion of Italian and Slavonic immigration is comparatively large) shows in its prison reports for 1897 of a total number of 444 confined in the Connecticut State prison, 40 were natives of Great Britain (10 of England, 30 of Ireland), 18 Germans, 32 Italians, 4 Poles, 8 Russians, and 2 Austrians. The total commitments to the Connecticut School for Boys at Meriden, Conn., during the year 1896–97 were 166. Of this number 42 were Irish, 15 Germans, 5 Italians, 8 Russians, and 2 Austrians. The Connecticut Industrial School for Girls at Middletown, Conn., showed the number of inmates committed in 1896 to be 1,257, of which 277 were Irish, 55 Germans, 8 Italians, 1 Hungarian, and 1 Russian-Pole.

Taking the State of *Ohio*, we find on examination of the official reports that the total number confined in the Ohio penitentiary in 1897 was 2,435. Of this number 49 were natives of Great Britain (23 of England, 7 of Scotland, 19 of Ireland), 68 of Germany, 7 of Italy, 14 of Austria, 8 of Russia, and 1 of Poland (so called). Of a total of 350 commitments to the Ohio State reformatory in the same year 13 were natives of Great Britain (7 of England, 1 of Scotland, 5 of Ireland), 3 of Germany, 1 of Austria, 1 of Russia, and 2 of Poland (so called).

The State of *Indiana* shows the following comparative nationalities among its prisoners: The Indiana State prison (north) in 1896 contained 842 inmates, of whom 10 were from Great Britain (4 from England, 6 from Ireland), 26 from Germany, 2 from Hungary, and 2 from Italy. The Indiana State prison (south) contained 817 inmates in 1896, of whom 5 were natives of Great Britain (4 from England and 1 from Ireland), 11 natives of Germany, and 2 of Italy.

The State of *Missouri* shows the following figures: The State penitentiary in 1896 contained 1,923 persons, of whom 44 were natives of Great Britain (20 from England, 2 from Scotland, 22 from Ireland), 54 natives of Germany, 4 of Austria, 3 of Russia, and 3 of Italy.

The *Wisconsin* State prison in 1896 contained 318 inmates, of whom 17 were natives of Great Britain (6 of England, 2 of Scotland, and 9 of Ireland), 28 natives of Germany, 1 of Austria, 15 of Sweden and Norway, 1 of Italy, 2 of Russia, and 1 of Poland (so called).

The State penitentiary of *Minnesota* in 1895 contained 410 inmates, of whom 27 were born in Great Britain (12 in England, 15 in Ireland), 35 in Germany, and 7 in Russia.

The State of *Michigan* does not appear to publish any prison statistics. The only report that is accessible is that of the Detroit house of correction, which contained 2,143 inmates in 1897. Of this number 201 were natives of Great Britain (63 of England, 27 of Scotland, 111 of Ireland), 192 were natives of Germany, 6 of Italy, 4 of Austria, 28 of Poland (so called), and 2 of Russia.

APPENDIX B.

STATISTICS ABOUT IMMIGRATION AND WAGES.

The bulletin of the Department of Labor in Washington, No. 18, September, 1898, in its first article, entitled "Wages in the United States and Europe, 1870 to 1898," quotes the average daily wages in 12 of the largest cities in the United States in the years 1870 to 1898. For purposes of comparison we take the average wages in each occupation in the years 1870 and 1898 in these 12 cities.

TABLE I.

Occupations.	1870.	1898.	Occupations.	1870.	1898.
Blacksmiths	$2.43	$2.43½	Iron molders' helpers	$1.53	$1.58¼
Blacksmiths' helpers	1.40¼	1.52¼	Joiners	2.25¾	2.47
Boiler makers	2.35¾	2.56½	Laborers, street	1.46¼	1 65½
Boiler-makers' helpers	1.41	1.53¼	Laborers, other	1.39¾	1 45
Bricklayers	3.15¼	3.51¾	Machinists	2.30¼	2 41
Cabinetmakers	2.14	2.29¾	Machinists' helpers	1.34	1 35½
Carpenters	2.36¾	2.52¾	Masons, stone	2.80¼	3.20¼
Compositors	2.52¼	2.81½	Painters, house	2.22½	2.60
Conductors, railroad	3.43	4.03¼	Patternmakers, iron works	2.70	2.90
Engineers, railroad	3.22¾	4.42¾	Plumbers	2.74½	3.15½
Firemen, railroad	1.75	2.26	Stonecutters	3.07	3.23
Hodcarriers	1.75¼	2.00½	Teamsters	1.58¾	1.88½
Iron molders	2.60½	2.60½			

In order correctly to estimate the actual advance that wages have made in this country since 1870 the prices of ommodities and the purchasing power of money must be taken into account. For this purpose the Twenty-eighth Annual Report of the Massachusetts Bureau of Statistics of Labor, published in March, 1898, may be consulted. This report contains a table showing the average retail price of commodities during certain years between 1860 and 1897 in Massachusetts. We select the year 1872, and compare the average retail prices, expressed in the gold standard, for that year with the year 1897.

TABLE II.—*Average retail prices for the years 1872 and 1897.*

Article.		1872.	1897.	Increase (+) and decrease (−) in 1897, as compared with 1872.
Flour:				*Per cent.*
Wheat, superfine	barrel	$10.75	$6.62½	−38.37
Wheat, family	do	12.75	5.80	−54.51
Rye	pound	.03¼	.03⅙	− 2.56
Cornmeal	do	.01¾	.03	+71.43
Codfish, dry	do	.08¼	.07 3/10	−12.12
Rice	do	.11¼	.07 6/7	−30.16
Beans	quart	.09½	.07	−26.32
Tea, oolong	pound	.69	.46⅖	−32.75
Coffee, Rio:				
Green	do	.34¼	.31⅕	− 8.91
Roasted	do	.42½	.28	−34.12
Sugar:				
Good brown	do	.10¼	.04 7/9	−53.66
Coffee	do	.10½	.04⅔	−55.56
Granulated	do	.12	.05¾	−52.08
Molasses:				
New Orleans	gallon	.70	.50	−28.57
Porto Rico	do	.76¼	.49½	−35 08
Sirup	do	.75	.52 6/7	−29.52
Soap, common	pound	.08	.04¼	−46.88
Starch	do	.12¼	.07⅕	−41.22
Beef:				
Roasting	do	.19	.14⅔	-22.81
Soup	do	.07½	.05⅗	−25.33
Rump steak	do	.29½	.25⅔	−12.99
Corned	do	.10½	.09 3/7	−10.20
Veal:				
Fore quarter	do	.10½	.08	−23.81
Hind quarter	do	.17	.12 7/9	−24.84
Cutlets	do	.28¼	.21¾	−23.01
Mutton:				
Fore quarter	do	.10¼	.07⅐	−30.63
Chops	do	.15¼	.20	+31.15
Leg	do	.19	.11¾	−38.16
Pork:				
Fresh	do	.12½	.10	−20.00
Salted	do	.11	.09 2/9	−16.18
Hams, smoked	do	,13½	.13⅓	− 1.28
Shoulders, corned	do	.10¼	.09	−12.20
Sausages	do	.12½	.10⅚	−13.36
Lard	do	.14¾	.08	−45.76
Butter	do	.39¼	.24⅓	−38.00

TABLE II.—*Average retail prices for the years 1872 and 1897*—Continued.

Article.	1872.	1897.	Increase (+) and decrease (−) in 1897, as compared with 1872.
			Per cent.
Cheese .... pound..	.17½	.14	−20.00
Potatoes .... bushel..	1.02	1.01⅓	− .65
Milk .... quart..	.08	.05⅔	−29.17
Eggs .... dozen..	.30	.23½	−21.67
Coal .... ton..	9.25	6.00	−35.14
Wood, hard .... cord..	10.12½	8.41⅛	−16.92
Wood, pine .... do....	7.00	6.97	− .43
Shirting:			
4-4 brown .... yard..	.13	.08½	−34.62
4-4 bleached .... do....	.16	.08½	−46.88
Sheeting:			
9-8 brown .... do....	.14	.08½	−39.29
9-8 bleached .... do....	.19½	.09¾	−50.00
Cotton flannel .... do....	.27½	.10	−63.64
Ticking .... do....	.24	.11	−54.17
Prints .... do....	.11¾	.05⅓	−54.61
Men's heavy boots .... pair..	3.94	2.05½	−47.84
Rents:			
4-room tenements .... month..	14.75	8.63 5/7	−41.44
6-room tenements .... do....	16.00	11.61	−27.44
Board:			
Men .... week..	5.62	4.62	−17.79
Women .... do....	3.75	3.66	− 2.40

The full significance of these price comparisons will be more apparent if the following table is studied, showing the quantity of each article purchasable for $1 in the years 1872 and 1897 in Massachusetts:

TABLE III.—*Purchasing power of money for the years 1872 and 1897.*

Article.	What $1 would buy in—		Increase (+) and decrease (−) in 1897, as compared with 1872.
	1872.	1897.	
			Per cent.
Flour:			
Wheat, superfine .... pounds..	18.18	30.30	+ 66.67
Wheat, family .... do....	15.38	34.48	+124.19
Rye .... do....	31.25	32.26	+ 2.23
Cornmeal .... do....	55.55	34.48	− 37.93
Codfish, dry .... do....	12.20	13.89	+ 13.85
Rice .... do....	8.93	12.82	+ 43.56
Beans .... quarts..	10.52	14.29	+ 35.84
Tea, oolong .... pounds..	1.45	2.16	+ 48.97
Coffee:			
Rio, green .... do....	2.92	3.21	+ 9.93
Rio, roasted .... do....	2.35	3.57	+ 51.19
Sugar:			
Good brown .... do....	9.80	21.28	+117.14
Coffee .... do....	9.52	21.74	+128.36
Granulated .... do....	8.33	17.86	+114.41
Molasses:			
New Orleans .... gallons..	1.43	2.00	+ 39.86
Porto Rico .... do....	1.31	2.02	+ 54.20
Sirup .... do....	1.33	1.89	+ 42.11
Soap, Common .... pounds..	12.50	23.81	+ 90.48
Starch .... do....	8.19	14.08	+ 71.92
Beef:			
Roasting .... do....	5.26	6.85	+ 30.23
Soup .... do....	13.33	17.86	+ 33.98
Rump steak .... do....	3.39	3.89	+ 14.75
Corned .... do....	9.52	10.64	+ 11.76
Veal:			
Fore quarter .... do....	9.52	12.66	+ 32.98
Hind quarter .... do....	5.85	7.87	+ 34.53
Cutlets .... do....	3.54	4.61	+ 30.23
Mutton			
Fore quarter .... do....	9.80	14.08	+ 43.67
Leg .... do....	5.26	8.55	+ 62.55
Chops .... do....	6.61	5.05	− 22.43

TABLE III.—*Purchasing power of money for the years 1872 and 1897*—Continued.

Article.	What $1 would buy in— 1872.	What $1 would buy in— 1897.	Increase (+) and decrease (−) in 1897, as compared with 1872.
			Per cent.
Pork:			
Fresh .... pounds..	8.00	10.00	+ 25.00
Salted .... do....	9.09	10.27	+ 19.58
Hams, smoked .... do....	7.41	7.52	+1.48
Shoulders, corned .... do....	9.80	11.24	+ 14.69
Sausages .... do....	8.00	9.26	+ 15.75
Lard .... do....	7.87	12.66	+ 60.86
Butter .... do....	2.55	4.13	+ 61.96
Cheese .... do....	5.71	7.19	+ 25.92
Potatoes .... bushels..	.97	.99	+ 2.06
Milk .... quarts..	12.50	17.86	+ 42.88
Eggs .... dozens..	3.33	4.27	+ 28.23
Coal .... pounds..	217.39	333.33	+ 53.33
Wood:			
Hard .... cubic feet..	.79	.95	+ 20.25
Pine .... do....	1.14	1.15	.88
Shirting:			
4-4 brown .... yards..	7.69	11.76	+ 52.93
4-4 bleached .... do....	6.25	11.76	+ 88.16
Sheeting:			
9-8 brown .... do....	7.14	11.76	+ 64.71
9-8 bleached .... do....	5.13	10.31	+100.97
Cotton flannel .... do....	3.63	10.00	+175.48
Ticking .... do....	4.17	9.09	+117.99
Prints .... do....	8.55	18.87	+120.70
Rents:			
4-room tenements .... days..	2.03	3.53	+ 73.89
6-room tenements .... do....	1.87	2.62	+ 40.11
Board:			
Men .... do....	1.24	1.52	+ 22.58
Women .... do....	1.87	1.92	+ 2.67

Following is a summary of the average wages in the industries enumerated above, by years, showing the course of wages in each year, taken from the Bulletin of the Department of Labor for September, 1898.

TABLE IV.

Year.	Average wages.	Increase as compared with 1870.	Immigration into the United States.
		Per cent.	
1870	$2.20½	....	387,203
1871	2.39¼	8.5	321,350
1872	2.45	11.1	404,806
1873	2.35½	6.8	459,803
1874	2.30¼	4.4	313,339
1875	2.24¼	1.7	227,498
1876	2.18	1.1	169,986
1877	2.24½	1.8	141,857
1878	2.30¾	4.6	138,469
1879	2.32	5.2	177,826
1880	2.34	6.1	457,257
1881	2.40¾	9.2	669,431
1882	2.44¾	11	788,992
1883	2.47	12	603,322
1884	2.49	12.9	518,592
1885	2.47¼	12.1	395,346
1886	2.47¼	12.1	334,203
1887	2.49¼	13	490,109
1888	2.50¾	13.7	546,889
1889	2.51½	14.1	444,427
1890	2.52¾	14.6	455,302
1891	2.54½	15.4	560,319
1892	2.56	16.1	623,084
1893	2.54¼	15.3	502,917
1894	2.49¼	13	314,467
1895	2.47¼	12.1	279,948
1896	2.45¾	11.5	343,267
1897	2.44½	10.9	230,823

Q. (By Mr. FARQUHAR.) In your statement just read to the commission, you have, in several places and in several particulars, somewhat severely criticised the inaccuracy of immigration statistics. Now, could you state to the commission particularly some of the faults that you have discovered as to the executive office at Ellis Island, and could you suggest any remedy outside of the registry system that we have there now?—A. I assumed charge of Ellis Island on the 1st of April, 1893, just during the time when, in view of the new law about to take effect, there was an immense immigration brought into our country. We had a record of not less than 72,000 in 1 single month, in April and May, 1893. I had an opportunity during this time of acting under the old law and I had an opportunity to watch the system as it had been enforced before. I made a study of it for the purpose of deciding about the changes which I regarded as necessary, and I found, especially in looking up the old records which were all kept on Ellis Island, that while the few registry clerks in the office were supposed under the old law to take a statement from the immigrants about their nationality, destination, and ages, that, as a matter of fact, whole pages did not contain any reply to any of these points. They were nothing more than an index of names of people arriving at the port. It was, as a matter of fact, physically impossible for these people—the port officers—to do more. There were but a few of them, who had to register sometimes 4,000 or 5,000 in a day. Now, under no circumstances could it be expected from them that they could examine the immigrants as to all these specific points, and put them down, and then expect that when through with the day's work they would make up the statistics. I saw immediately the importance of condensation of such a system. I asked the officials, "How do you get these figures which we now have in our reports?" They freely admitted that, in most cases, it was merely guesswork on their part; even the count could not be accurate and complete. Now, this was especially the case under the old Castle Garden administration. As long as the State authorities and, you may practically say, the municipal machine had control of immigration, where immigration was especially large and where the employees were few—at least, where the employees who worked were few, while more may have drawn salaries—it is a matter of impossibility to rely in any way on these old statistics; and I speak from my personal observation and examination of the officers who had it in charge.

Q. What do you say as to the statistics taken since 1893?—A. They are vastly improved.

Q. Would you suggest any improvement to the present way of taking statistics?—A. I would suggest one remedy, which I believe would facilitate proper examination as well as statistics. The immigrant is supposed to answer a number of questions submitted to him by the ticket agent. I can not see any reason why these replies should not be taken in writing, together with the interrogatories. As a matter of fact, when the law of 1893 was introduced, the steamship companies originally started out that way and submitted to me these answers to interrogatories, and I found them immensely beneficial for everything. These interrogatories should be signed by the immigrant himself, and if he can not sign his name it would at least establish the fact finally as to his illiteracy from the very start. Such interrogatories should be turned over to the statistical bureau. They certainly could collect reliable total figures. That would change the whole system at once.

Q. Would not that in a great measure relieve the inspectors and also your special-inquiry bureaus there?—A. It would.

Q. Would it not simplify the matter?—A. Very much in that way. The inspector would then have before him in a much better way the answers to the different questions which the immigrants have to reply to.

Q. You say the law of 1893, to your mind, is sufficiently restrictive without any additional legislation?—A. That is my conviction, and I believe that the immigration since last year proves it better than anything else. Up to last year we did not know how much of the decided, conspicuous falling off of immigration was due to the prevailing financial depression, and how much to the restrictions of the law. We hesitated about expressing an opinion about it, and the annual report of the superintendent was rather hesitating in that direction. But the experience of the last year, a year of undoubted, almost unequaled, prosperity, proves that there is but one explanation of the decided decrease in immigration, and that is the restrictive power of the law, and it is natural. If you, especially the gentlemen of the subcommission, who have seen it themselves working on Ellis Island—if you bear in mind how much trouble an immigrant now has before he gets his ticket at the port, and how much trouble he is subjected to after he lands at New York, you will realize that it is but natural this should have a restrictive effect on immigration.

Q. But is it not also a fact that the steamship companies themselves, in the series of questions that they furnish their agents in Europe, furnish a shadow of what the immigrant is to meet here, and the immigrant knows how difficult immigration is made?—A. Exactly. The first examination by the ticket agent, who is held personally, officially, responsible for every deported immigrant, is the most efficient of all.

Q. Would you suggest any amendment to the 1893 act?—A. I have expressed my opinion that I am rather reluctant about suggesting any new legislation on this question, because I know too well that the whole question would again be reopened, and there is evidently a confusion prevailing on this whole question, and a very important one. As I stated, there were a number of evils, unquestionably from the form of the law, in unrestricted immigration, and I fully understand that our people, and especially the laboring classes, and mostly in times of financial depression and enforced idleness—that they in such times are sore on immigration, also for the future; though it is a matter of fact that no matter how much we would restrict immigration at present, even if we shut our doors entirely to new immigrants, this would not do a particle of good in the solving of our own problems of congestion of labor at certain points, of massing of people of the same nationalities, of the same language, in certain points, and of their influence on politics.

Q. Would it not only take a very few minutes to make the physical examination of a group of 30?—A. Certainly, the physical examination takes place before they come off.

Q. Now, then, do not the delays you speak of, of one day or two days and sometimes a week, result more from detentions on account of alien contract labor law than from any other difference that may be in the minds of the inspectors or the board of inquiry; is not that the cause that usually detains the immigrant?—A. First of all, they are detained very much longer than cabin passengers in being landed. The first immigrant leaves the ship after the last cabin passenger has left. Then his examination of baggage commences. Then he is taken over the tedious trip to the Barge Office; after being grouped in these groups of 30 they are taken down to the Barge Office, and there commences the unloading. They then pass in single file, and if there are 800 of them you can imagine how long it takes. Then again, if grouped in groups of 30 they have to pass the physical examination first. If there are only 800 passengers, for instance, to take this as an example; that will furnish 27 groups, in round figures. There are only 4 or 5 registry aisles, through which but 1 group can go at a time; say 4 groups can only be dispatched at the same time; if there are 27 it takes about 7 turns for all of them to pass. Meanwhile it is getting dark; the officials are expected to work overtime when necessary, but not too long. They adjourn until the next morning. The very best man may be in the last group. The last 10 groups are not handled until the next day, and they have to wait until the next day. These are hardships.

Q. How would the lessening of the group or the multiplication of aisles assist this inspection?—A. Very much, certainly.

Q. Well, how are the quarters there at the Barge Office now?—A. We could not do very much under any circumstances. We made the most of the Barge Office as it was.

Q. Then could your suggestion be practiced at Ellis Island, when you go there? What improvements would you make of inspection?—A. There must be at least ten aisles working at the same time, and they must all be filled by inspectors who understand the language; otherwise it takes twice the time. He gets the reply through the interpreter as it is now. What enormous difficulty is to be met with under such circumstances you can well understand——if you consider that in this group of 30 there are sometimes five or six nationalities represented, and that nevertheless the same inspector is supposed to examine these people individually as to their eligibility to land. We had many times to hunt around for interpreters to understand at all what the immigrant desired and to put any questions to him. Of course, meanwhile, we did not delay the whole work.

Q. What is the ordinary salary paid the interpreter?—A. A thousand dollars. Cities pay $2,000 to every court interpreter—$2,000. The Government interpreters have $1,000, which is not very high, and you can not expect good work from them; it is simply impossible.

Q. Has there not been at the port of New York a great improvement in the last 10 years, last 6 or 8 years, in the number and ability of interpreters?—A. No.

Q. While you were commissioner there, did you have a sufficiency of interpreters to make at least a partially intelligible examination?—A. No, I did not; and a great many nationalities I could not handle at all by Government employees—for instance, the Portuguese. I should have had a particular interpreter in the Portu-

IMMIGRATION. 181

guese language. We could not do it. All we could do was to take an employee of the ship to act as an interpreter for us. Now, that is not a proper way.

Q. Well, did you have any trouble with Asiatics in respect to language?—A. We had one or two interpreters, one especially excellent interpreter, but the difficulty again was that we had to rely entirely on him and on his statements, and sometimes there was quite a good reason to doubt some of his statements; but we had to rely on them, we were entirely helpless.

Q. They were liable to be in favor of their own countrymen in the matter?—A. Certainly.

Q. (By Senator MALLORY.) Those positions are not under civil service?—A. They are now. They are under civil service by the last order of 1896.

Q. Is it feasible to cultivate a corps of interpreters?—A. Certainly. Why have the courts proper interpreters? Because they are paid accordingly.

Q. Well, the courts very often have to call in certain interpreters to suit the language spoken. I assume that you have at your office at Ellis Island almost every language spoken on the face of the earth, in the course of a year, and I should think it is necessary to have a large corps of interpreters, or at least a corps of men who speak a very great variety of languages?—A. It could be done in this way. For the most prominent languages, permanent employees should be employed, while in extraordinary cases of languages which are rare—like, for instance, Asiatic——

Q. (By Mr. FARQUHAR.) (Interrupting.) Armenian, Turkish, and Greek?—A. Yes; a good many of those—it might be arranged that persons should work only by the day who are selected as having passed the civil-service examination, and only to be employed for that specific day. It would be no extraordinary hardship, especially on this class of immigrants, to be detained for one day and wait until an interpreter was available; but it would be for the more common languages—Slavonian, German, French, and Portuguese, if permanent interpreters should not be employed. Spanish is one of the rare languages, but of Portuguese there is a permanent immigration. We also never had interpreters for the different Slavonic dialects, which are so different that the same interpreters ought not to be employed for all.

Q. (By Senator MALLORY.) That is done now under the civil-service system, is it not?—A. That is not done as yet. A good deal of the money is spent differently, and not for the proper kind of employees, in my opinion.

Q. You think it is essential, then, so far as the statistical part of the duties of that bureau is concerned, that you should have court interpreters?—A. Not only for the statistical portion, but for the direct enforcement of the law, in order to understand whether a certain person is really desirable or not; to examine him properly; and the board of special inquiry most of all and first of all ought to have competent interpreters.

Q. (By Mr. FARQUHAR.) Interpreters as advisors?—A. Advisors or as members.

Q. In fact they ought to be members?—A. Certainly.

Q. (By Mr. CLARKE.) Why did you speak specially of the Boston immigration restriction efforts?—A. I had only to do with the Boston Immigration Restriction League during the time of my term of office, and later on.

Q. Is there any other restriction league in the country?—A. Not that I know of. That is the only restriction league.

Q. Is there no opposition to wholesale immigration anywhere in the country except in Massachusetts?—A. Oh, certainly there is; no doubt. I only mentioned those who have been most pronounced and best organized.

Q. You admit, then, that the Boston restrictionists represent in a sense large numbers of people throughout the country who entertain the same views?—A. Numbers and perhaps not. I am not quite sure about that. Congress receives quite a number of petitions from other parts just as well as from our part, I have learned from my opponents. I organized the Immigration Protective League, as I suppose is known to the commission, and we did exactly what the immigration restrictionists did; that is, sent out petitions for signature, which were submitted to Congress, when we learned the opposition was in favor of the Lodge bill. If the sentiment on one side is really representing a large number of people, it is exactly the same on the other. It would be hard to count one or the other, or even to measure them up against each other.

Q. Then your latest statement means that it is not a local question or local prejudice?—A. Oh, certainly not, and I have emphasized it before. I wish to state again that a time of commercial and financial depression, such as we had a few years ago, is liable to come again in a very pronounced and very determined way. At present there are hardly any idle hands. Our factories work many of them with 1 or 2 years' advance orders. They employ a good many people, perhaps instigated by the demand of labor, and new arrivals may come and may be employed. Overproduction will naturally set in, and some establishments which at the present time work over time, day and night, and hardly are able to fill their orders, will again shut down for a while, and a good many of the old and of the new men will again be idle, as they have been in the last five years. It would be but natural that in another turn of the same kind the first sentiment of the Americans would go against the foreigners, who have furnished, as they believe, the abundance, the surplus of supply against the demand.

A. Now, if, unfortunately, we should have a period of depression so that labor seeks work, rather work seeks labor, and there should be a large tide of immigration, would not one effect of that be to displace considerable American labor?—A. If we had another time of depression then it would be only natural that no tide of immigration would set in at that time. Depression and large immigration practically exclude each other.

Q. There has been considerable immigration even in depressed times, has there not?—A. Very little, as compared with former years; and especially very little, if immigration is sifted down to its actual character. If there are, for instance, 300,000 arriving at the port of New York, and we find in examining them, that about 50,000 had been here before, had gone abroad and returned, and that of the other 250,000, 100,000—that is the ordinary percentage—are members of the immediate families of former immigrants, then the actual immigration remaining, to be counted as immigration on the labor market, is reduced to only 150,000 a year. And then, if taken into consideration the number of such persons who leave this country even for good, the labor market will appear to suffer very little from immigration at such times.

Q. You have referred to the comparative decline in immigration recently. Do you think that is due more to the effective administration of our law, or to the law itself, than it is to the fact that there has been a revival of prosperity in Europe as well as in America, so that these people have less inducement to come here than they had before?—A. I state distinctly that the causes are many. There is no doubt that the increase of prosperity in Europe serves to offset ours to a certain degree; but aside from that our prosperity had no large attraction on the European surplus of population. It proves, in my opinion, the restrictive efficiency of the present law.

Q. At the present time is there any advertising in Europe by land-grant railroads, and by other associations in this country, to induce immigration?—A. This has been overestimated in many ways. There is advertising perpetually done. It is done in every way. It is done with our products as well as by our land-advertising companies. There is no doubt the people have been educated to take our advertisements with a large grain of allowance. They look rather more skeptically on these matters than they did 15 to 20 years ago. When first this advertising started, it had a kind of vivid and startling effect. Europe has been educated to advertising just as well as America has. The effect of American advertising in Europe is very slight at present, very small.

Q. (By Senator MALLORY:) Are there any States that have advertising agencies or bureaus in Europe now?—A. There are, certainly; Michigan, Wisconsin, and a few others. They maintain permanent colonization bureaus in Europe.

Q. Kept for furnishing information?—A. Kept for furnishing information of all kinds. Texas has certainly one, I am sure. Mr. Johnson is the general representative. I know of that personally.

Q. Do you know anything about the efficiency of those bureaus—their success in inducing immigration?—A. They certainly have some success or else they would not be maintained and continued, but their success is very small. Colonization in the States, in the United States, has been very limited. The most successful colonization to my knowledge has been carried out by the Italians in Arkansas, the Sunny Side colony. Another quite successful organization is on the way in Georgia. Now, I shall never believe, no matter how often I hear it, that the American land is given away and being settled. It may be possessed, it may be owned, but is certainly not cultivated as yet, and there is ample room, in my thorough conviction, for a great deal of new settlement; and certainly our roads of the West and South, our railroads, would have prospered, at least four or five years ago, at the time of the depression, if we had had anything of immigration. In fact, beyond doubt, in addition to the poor crops, it was the decrease in immigration which drove a good many of those roads, like the Pacific roads, especially the Northern Pacific, into the receivers' hands.

Q. (By Mr. CLARKE.) Have you ever studied the history of immigration from New England to Ohio and other parts of the West?—A. Yes.

Q. Which began only a year ago or more?—A. Yes.

Q. Is it your understanding that the people left Massachusetts, Connecticut, and Rhode Island at that time because they believed in the overpopulation of those States?—A. No.

Q. To seek new and larger fields?—A. Not the overpopulation of their own States, but their enterprise for seeking larger fields.

Q. Does that motive actuate the immigration from Europe largely?—A. Great many; largely, largely. Those people who come for settlement in this country have a desire and feel the ability in themselves to expand, to look out for larger and better fields for their activity than they can find at home. We get some of the very best settlers from Russia, and there is room enough there, as you well know. There are large tracts almost equal to our own, but nevertheless they come here and bring their good money here, and are most excellent settlers, because they feel the possibilities are greater in the United States in the free air and the civilization of America.

Q. Are republican principles one of the inducements to this immigration?—A. Not very much. It is among Russian Mennonites to a large extent; they are sick and tired of Czarism.

Q. As a rule, then, if I understand you, it is not so much the difference in the form of government and a desire to participate in the government that induces these people to come here, as it is their belief that here is a better opportunity for prosperity?—A. Directly an opportunity for prosperity, and more particularly for liberty.

Q. Have you watched them pretty carefully after they have landed, and seen what their condition has been generally where they have gone?—A. We can not follow them; that is a matter of impossibility. The only thing we could watch— we had attempted to watch—was in our immediate neighborhood in the lower part of New York, the settlement of those unfortunate Russian Jew refugees.

Q. Your reference to the Polish quarter in Buffalo led me to think that you had followed them to some extent.—A. My reference to the Polish quarters is based on the statement of the gentleman whom I quoted.

Q. That statement shows that they were studying our institutions and learning our method of voting, etc. Do you understand that they become active participants in our politics wherever they go?—A. I do understand so, and I had some experience of it myself in the West during the two years that I lived there in Milwaukee, where there is also a Polish settlement.

Q. Do you think that their colonization is an evil?—A. To a certain extent, but a necessary and unavoidable one. Those people are naturally first drawn to such surroundings as are more congenial to them, and where they can make themselves understood. By and by they flock off from there; they do not stick together very long, the second generation especially; they flock off; they are not to be held.

Q. You think, then, it is only a temporary evil?—A. It is always only temporary and unavoidable.

Q. Is there an equal tendency among the different classes of immigrants—that is, those from different countries—to become Americanized?—A. My personal experience in many directions has convinced me that the desire to be Americanized is intense among the foreign-born population, and absolutely boundless in their church. Many an old immigrant I have found to be rather sore on the Americanizing power of this country. He would like to preserve, for instance, his old German language in his house. He can not do it. His children will all speak English, not only among themselves but also to him and to the mother. Our German newspapers feel it very strongly, that the second generation is drifting away from them rapidly; and the same is true of Italians, of Frenchmen, of Scandinavians.

Q. You have expressed the opinion that the proper place to make an application of an educational test is at the naturalization office?—A. I am distinctly, decidedly in favor of that, and by any even more difficult test than that proposed in the Lodge bill.

Q. Are you familiar with the registration and voting laws of the several States?— A. I know we have States where a residence of about 6 months is sufficient to enable you to cast your vote. I myself cast a vote for president after having been 4 years in this country.

Q. Are you aware that there are 15 States in the United States in which aliens are allowed to vote after declaring their intention to become citizens, and in many of those States on 1 year's residence?—A. Only 6 months' residence—oh, yes, I am fully aware of that; and I am also aware of the necessity, fully conscious of the necessity, of reform in this direction.

Q. What would you say to the idea that qualifications for voting should be regulated by a national law, the same as naturalization is?—A. If it is a constitutional possibility?

Q. Yes; certainly.—A. I believe that is the weak point in it. I would be certainly in favor of it; most decidedly.

Q. You think, in view of the cosmopolitan character of our population, that such a change as that would be beneficial?—A. I do not wish a cosmopolitan character of our population to be continued. I wish the character of our population to be American, distinctly American; but I do not object to people becoming Americans.

Q. (By Mr. KENNEDY.) You submitted a statement which seemed to show that this immigration was not detrimental to organized labor. I want to ask you if you know that the representatives of organized labor who came before this commission have almost without exception been in favor of further restriction of immigration?—A. I am fully aware of that, and I had plenty of opportunities during my official term to confer with members and leaders of organized labor on that subject. I find that they are sadly misinformed on that subject. I have tried my very best to make them understand that all the evils they complain of date back in their origin to a time prior to 1893. I tried my very best to make them understand that any new immigration laws would not be able to change, for instance, the condition in Pennsylvania, in the mining districts. If you read the testimony of Commissioner-General Powderly before you, you will find that the conditions of the mining district of Pennsylvania originated from the large immigration in 1881. You can not change that now by any new law. The Americans have been driven from the mining occupation there, but you can not remedy that condition now by any change in the law; that is a settled fact. The same is true of the clothing interests, of the interests in the shoe manufacturing. You can not change it now. This has been changed, and we have to accept these facts as they are at present. I believe that this commission should find out what is to be done in the future, if possible to find out remedies against the existing economic evils. In the same way, I have endeavored my very best to convince labor leaders of the fact that there is a positive restriction at the present time in force, and that any change in the law would not benefit them, especially such a change as the Lodge bill intends. The immigrants they are mostly afraid of would not be excluded by an illiteracy law.

The statement was also made here that any decrease in the wages of unskilled labor brings about in the course of time a natural decrease in the wages of skilled labor. This is a statement which sounds very well, but is not true. We have not to take our experience from exceptional conditions of any kind, as, for instance, Henry George, to whom I alluded, took the experience of California, where there was a scarcity of supply of labor, and therefore immensely high wages. Mr. Henry George complained that in the course of time the more labor that came there—I mean the more immigrants that arrived there—the wages would naturally decrease; but, on the other hand, the purchasing power of these same wages increased, even of the lower wages. Now I wish to remind you of what I said about wages for skilled labor, and refer you to the table which I submitted here, taken from the Bulletin of the Department of Labor at Washington, No. 18, September, 1898.

The table shows that in some special trades a decrease in wages took place, and that influenced the leaders; but as a matter of fact wages not only have increased in the average since 1870, but, as is proven by the other tables, the purchasing power of the same wages has increased.

Q. You are aware, I presume, that very many of the labor leaders of this country are of foreign birth, or the sons of foreigners, and if organized labor is sadly misinformed, as you state, it is largely due to their representatives who are of foreign birth. You know, I presume, that Mr. Gompers, president of the American Federation of Labor, is for further restriction?—A. I know very well. I mentioned him in my statement.

Q. It is remarkable that those who are of foreign birth, or the sons of foreigners, who have been before this commission—and I think perhaps a few of them are such—are emphatically in favor of restriction.—A. I fully understand this, and for that reason I took the pains to work out these facts, especially in reference to immigration.

Q. (By Mr. A. L. HARRIS.) Is this country sufficiently protected by this law, even when ordinarily executed, to save it from the expense of taking care of pauper immigrants?—A. I believe so, as a whole; by all means. We took considerable pains during the term of my office to ascertain whether any foreigners were public charges. There have been a good many, but all from former immigration. A person may change his name in the institution, and therefore it would not be found out whether or not he was a recent immigrant; but this happens only in isolated cases, and has no bearing on the answer in general, which I can give in a most decided way, that I believe our country to be sufficiently protected by the present laws, even as they are enforced.

Q. Those exceptions you speak of are liable to occur?—A. Oh, certainly; everywhere. There is no doubt that undesirable immigrants land, just as there is no doubt that a great deal of merchandise is smuggled; but at the same time we maintain a customs service to prevent a wholesale smuggling, and we maintain an immigration service for preventing this same effect in the question of wholesale undesirable immigration, and successfully.

Q. (By Mr. PHILLIPS.) Do you believe we are sufficiently protected in regard to the criminal class that comes to this country, as well as to the pauper class?—A. No doubt; positively. Of course we can not prevent exceptions. There may be fugitives of law that we are not aware of. There is no doubt of it. But as a rule the present laws and regulations are strong enough. I beg to refer especially to the former notions about the deportation of that undesirable immigration— ticket-of-leave men who are brought to this country. This has been a practice in the past, but the laws of 1893 cut it short absolutely, simply by shifting the financial responsibility and moral responsibility on the steamship companies.

Q. (By Senator MALLORY.) I understand you to say that the conditions existing in the coal regions of Pennsylvania and some other special districts are the results of legislation many years ago, or rather lack of legislation anterior to 1893, and that they can not be reached, those evils, by any legislation now; that we have got to simply take these things as they stand. I do not know myself what those conditions are exactly, but I understand that the character of the immigrant, the character of the labor that is employed there, is of a lower order than that usually brought into this country. Now, is it not a fact that most immigrants, you may say as a general rule all immigrants, coming to this country are followed by their next generation, who are assimilated very readily into the American people? I believe you stated about that.—A. Yes.

Q. Why is it these people who came here anterior to 1893 and went to certain districts of Pennsylvania, the coal regions, and those Jews in New York—why is it they are an exception to the general rule, which seems to be almost universal, that after the first generation they almost become unrecognizable as foreign-born people?—A. I beg to state that as far as the Jews in New York are concerned, or in any large city, they are no exception; they are rapidly assimilating and rapidly Americanizing; more rapidly, perhaps, than the majority of all other immigrants. As far as the Hungarian colonies in Pennsylvania are concerned, I beg to risk the statement that they could be Americanized very much quicker if they were not treated as a kind of an outcast; if they were not left alone, and if people would not look down on them, and practically despise them; if they were taken in hand the same as the large cities like New York take them in hand, because there people can not help but come in contact with them. Then these Pennsylvania settlers would also assimilate just as quickly as their own brothers and sisters in any other section. They are left alone too much, in my opinion, and they are left to live among themselves, exclusively among themselves, a good many of them; and especially their children would like very much to go out and mingle among the Americans, but they have no opportunity.

Q. Well, is that due to their segregating themselves from the rest of the community, or is it largely due to the dislike or distaste for them and for their association?—A. That is what I believe—the latter part.

Q. Is not that exceptional?—A. It is exceptional.

Q. And is not that about the only instance—these Pennsylvania Hun miners—of immigrants who come to this country and stay here and raise their families here, but do not assimilate with the American people? Are they not about the only exception?—A. They are about the only exception, and the Syrians, some portion of the Syrians. But even those in Pennsylvania, whom you call Hun miners, will not resist the Americans very long. It is simply impossible; it is too strong an assimilating factor.

Q. (By Mr. CLARKE.) You explained the desirability of some method being entered upon to cause a better distribution of the Americans in different parts of the country. I think the suggestion very wide, and I would like to have you elaborate the point a little and suggest, if you have convictions on the subject, what method would be most effectual to that end?—A. I suggested to the Immigration Investigating Commission a plan which the two other gentlemen, Mr. Stump and Mr. McSweeney indorsed, and that is to erect on Ellis Island, in close connection with the landing place, a large permanent exhibition hall, where different States may have their permanent bureaus, their permanent representatives; where different railroads may have their permanent exhibitions. I had even drafted the plans for such a building, into which only landed immigrants should be admitted before being sent to New York or to their railroad depot. If they had an opportunity there, guided by intelligent Americans able to talk to them and make themselves understood, to learn about the condition of labor in the different sections of the United States; to know whether their own trade, for instance, is overstocked in one direction, and looked after in another; if they could find out exactly by maps and an exhibition of local products what they could look for in any section of the United States, and under what plans they could acquire land there, and so on; and if all people admitted to this institution, which would be under Government control, had to pass a rigid examination by a Government official as to their honesty and reliability, so that only responsible persons would be introduced into such an exhibition hall to give information at all; if the knowledge of all this could be spread abroad officially through the countries, imparted to all steamship agents abroad, then I believe the immigrant could easily be taught to look out for his own betterment, for the proper place to go to, and for the proper occupation to look for. As it is at present, I found, by personal observation, that unless a person goes directly to his family he does not know, in one case out of a hundred, what he is going to do in the United States when arriving. He is a carpenter, he is a plumber, he is a common laborer, he is a bookkeeper, but he has no idea what he will do in the United States. It is actually pitiable how little they know when they arrive. If such persons could receive reliable information, and especially if landed would-be settlers could know from the very start that when coming to, say, New York, or to Boston, where a branch of this institution may be established, or to the port of Philadelphia or Baltimore, that they could then and there find proper and reliable information about their future, they would fall back on it, and they could be properly guided. The State bureaus of labor would have to furnish their information to the central office at Washington at the same time; I mean the Bureau of Immigration in Washington would have to supply all information. And I believe that if properly worked such an institution would very soon become actually what it proposes to be, a land and labor clearing house.

Q. (By Mr. KENNEDY.) Can the State of Pennsylvania furnish public-school facilities for the Hun population to which you referred a short while back?—A. I do not think they are sufficient.

Q. You do not think they are sufficient?—A. And I am afraid that there are too many truants: I mean too many who do not make use of it.

Q. Do the Huns keep their children out of these schools?—A. They do not do it unless they have opportunity to do it; unless they are permitted to do it.

Q. Then you think the only way to get the truants in these schools would be by compulsory education?—A. By compulsory education.

Q. Then it seems that the Huns are resisting this Americanizing influence you speak about?—A. Pardon me; the word "Huns" I should like to have eliminated from this whole discussion, because they are neither Huns nor anything near them at all, neither by race nor in any other way. They are mostly of a Slavonic race, a race similar to that of the Poles, but somewhat inferior. They did not have the advantages which the Poles had, of an empire of their own, of some splendor and achievements through several centuries, which made the Poles after all a partly civilized nation; but they are akin to the Poles, only a little more neglected in the country of my birth, in Austria, which, as you know, suffered immensely up to about 1860 under misrule and mismanagement in every direction. These Polacks or Croats, neither of the two, are by no means Huns, even in the sense of their brutality; not at all. They are very tractable, peaceful people if let alone and not maltreated. There is a great deal of prejudice against them, which is usually brought about by wrong information from the start. They do not resist our civilization; they have no opportunity; they do not know it. Most of them were imported as far back as about 1881, from 1881 to 1885, and I really believe that most all of them were imported under contract at that time, and, in fact, their importation induced, more than anything else, the establishment of the law of 1885, the first contract-labor law. They do not resist American civilization; they do not understand it yet.

Q. I take it that you would concede that the most Americanizing of all influences is the public school?—A. No doubt.

Q. Upon population like that?—A. Yes.

Q. And you think that if there were public schools there and they did not use them, it was because they were not compelled to use them?—A. They were not compelled. They are used to being compelled in their own old home, in Austria. There are laws there for compulsory education which have been in force for more than fifty years, but at the same time they are not enforced there. People evade the law, and they are used to it. Now, here, if they could be forced to attend the public schools, the process of assimilation would be very much accelerated.

If I may be permitted, I wish to call the commission's attention to a matter in close connection with the immigration statistics, which is, in my opinion, immensely misleading—the frequent changes in the classification of immigrants made by the United States officials. For instance, an important change took place last year, as I believe your subcommission found out. A commission was appointed which decided, approved by the secretary and by the Commissioner-General, to classify immigrants from now on according to races. Formerly they used to be classified, at least professedly, by nationalities. This was never done correctly, but at least a certain basis for calculation was given which, if not accurate to the figures, was at least accurate in its general proportions. Now. last year a change was effected by establishing races. The consequence is that we find statements, as I have them here before me, of only one Swiss arrival. That is from the New York Times of July 24. which says, speaking of the last official statistics, "Only one Swiss was reported as arriving last year. There used to be about eight thousand every year"; which is easily explained. Formerly they spoke of the Swiss as a nationality, coming from Switzerland. Now, they start to establish a race basis. There is no Swiss race. Only one person was fool enough to state his race as Swiss, and only one inspector was fool enough to put him down as such. There did not arrive less people from Switzerland than before, not very many; but simply a change in the classification was carried out, which has to be understood also by the commission in order to enable it to make proper comparisons. I find "there were less than 1,000 Hungarians, which is a tremendous falling off from the average of 30,000 a year, which formerly arrived." Hungarians are no race. There is a race, Magyars. Hungary is an empire, part of the Austrian-Hungarian Empire. Under the new classification we shall find probably 15,000 Slavs and 20,000 Croats, all coming from the Empire of Hungary. That means that immigration has not decreased, but we have changed our point of view; and if now somebody is ignorant of this change and makes comparisons, as this editor of a respectable paper has done, he is not only entirely misled, but he is apt to mislead all his readers. I believe that while a certain improvement is effected by an investigation into the race quality of an immigrant it ought to have been combined with a continuation of the old statistics; the old statistics ought not to have been abandoned; new statistics ought to have been introduced only for supplementary scientific work. As to the practical value of the new statistics, they are only misleading, especially misleading in the way they are made up. They contain quite a number of ethnological errors.

Q. Have you any present official connection with the immigration of our country?—A. Not at all. I was a member of the Immigration Investigating Commission, but this commission, I do not know for what reason, simply expired with my leaving my office. We have never been officially removed or discharged.

Q. Are you an officer of an organization which exists for the purpose of combating the work of the Immigration Restriction League of Boston?—A. Yes.

Q. What is your office?—A. I am secretary of the Immigration Protective League. Of course that is an unsalaried position. I am publisher of a trade paper, and of books. That is my business.

Q. (By Mr. PHILLIPS.) What is the chief object of this league to which you belong?—A. The object is (reading from constitution of league) "To oppose any further restriction on immigration to the United States, and to protect and advance the interests of persons immigrating to this country."

Q. (By Mr. FARQUHAR.) Have you a copy of the circular there?—A. Yes; I submit the constitution, and will leave it with the commission.

WASHINGTON, D. C., *January 11, 1900.*

TESTIMONY OF MR. JULES ROSENDALE,

Special agent of the department of agriculture of the State of Pennsylvania.

The commission met at 10.55 a. m., Vice-Chairman Gardner presiding. At that time Mr. Jules Rosendale, of Philadelphia, Pa., special agent of the department of agriculture of the State of Pennsylvania, was introduced as a witness and, being duly affirmed, testified as follows, the Topical Plan of Inquiry on Immigration being followed:

Q. (By Mr. FARQUHAR.) Please give your name, address, and business.—A. Jules Rosendale; 1413 Jefferson street, Philadelphia, Pa.; occupation, agent for the dairy and food commissioner of the State of Pennsylvania.

Q. How long have you been a resident of the United States?—A. Forty-four years, some time during this year.

Q. What opportunities of observation have you had to enable you to give testimony before this commission on immigration matters?—A. In 1894, during the dull times and the panic, by assisting the factory inspectors, not officially, I admit, but simply for courtesy, in regard to the sweatshops and the overcrowded condition in the tenement houses, sweatshops, among the Polish Jews and Italians and Hungarians in the city of Philadelphia, in one word, the foreign element. That was my first observation—in 1894. The next opportunity I had of studying the condition of the foreign element or the working classes was in 1897, when the Pennsylvania legislature appointed two committees to inquire into the condition of the bituminous and the anthracite coal miners. I was then acquainted with Senator Saylor and went with him to the anthracite region to study the condition of the miners at that time. The first opportunity related only to the clothing trade and tailors; the second to the miners only. The third opportunity was after I was appointed one of the agents of the dairy and food commissioner. Professor Hamilton and Mr. Welch, the dairy and food commissioner, both requested me to take up the slum districts in Philadelphia, because they said they could not get any satisfactory report, and that a majority of those who were inspectors could not talk their language; so I told them I would oblige them. I can assure you that it was not a very pleasant job, but I got a great deal of information because I had their jargon, their language. I had no difficulty whatever to get along with the Russian Jews, but sometimes when I could not get along with the others I tried to get an interpreter. I had a little bit more difficulty with probably the Italian, because, speaking the French language fluently, he could not understand some. I found that they had a certain jargon like the Jews' jargon that I could not get along with. I took two students from the University of Pennsylvania, both interested in social science, and we found out a great deal, because they could get along and assist me in my work. Those were about the opportunities that I had in observing the conditions, first, of the miners, and next of the foreign element, including nearly every occupation in the slum districts in Philadelphia.

Q. You may state your observations in respect to the labor in the anthracite coal fields first, and state it in your own way.—A. I think I omitted to bring you the Pennsylvania legislature's report of the conditions in the bituminous region. None was issued as to the anthracite region; that is, one was made by the legislature, but not printed. It was late in the session, Mr. Saylor told me, and I think on account of the appropriation and one thing and another it was not printed. But I had the report of the bituminous. Shortly after I came back from the war of 1861, after 1865, in 1867, 1868, and 1869, I think I was up in the mining region, and found there that most of the miners were Welsh, Irish, Americans, Germans, and Scandinavians. I was then employed there as a mining engineer for 15 or 18 years, but finding mining engineering was not to my taste I left. But I had an opportunity in the beginning of 1870 to study the conditions there, so I was able to compare them with those of 1897, when I was up there with Senator Saylor. I found most of the miners there foreigners; the original report is, 60 per cent foreigners. I think I would make it even higher. Of course, I did not take any statistics. They took statistics and made it 60 per cent foreigners; and Hungarians and Italians I found in the majority. They generally use the word for Hungarians, Huns, and the Italians, Hides; those are the nicknames they gave them. I found out there were fights and quarrels between them very frequently; living in dilapidated shanties and frame houses, huddling together just like cattle. I found in one house, in one shanty, 20 Hungarians, and they hired one woman to do the cooking for them. I made no inquiry in anything else, but that was the actual state of affairs that I found.

Q. Can you mention the county or city where this occurred?—A. That was near Shickshinny, near Wilkesbarre, in the anthracite coal region. I even found children, boys and girls, occupying the same room with the parents. The average earnings that I found—I am speaking now of 1897, and I am confirmed in my view; the report of the legislature I have not copied because I went into that same county—the amount was from $4 to $5 a week per adult; $1.50 and sometimes $2.50 for boys and girls. They have to purchase at company stores at prices from 20 to 25 per cent higher than in Shickshinny. I tried to find out the religious and ethical mode of living of the people who were there in Shickshinny; and in the neighborhood I found 5 Roman Catholic churches presided over by either Italian or Polish priests; 1 Greek Catholic church; 2 Polish Jewish synagogues; 1 Methodist meetinghouse, and another meetinghouse divided in time between the Presbyterians and the Episcopalians. I had an interview with 50 of them on the subject of citizenship; 2 had applied for citizenship and 4 were naturalized. The Polish Jews I found there were originally not so many of them miners; they were mostly traders and peddlers. I think the first Italians which were brought over to this country were brought over by the wife of a coal man in Wilkesbarre. She was traveling in Italy.

Q. At what year?—A. I think, as far as I can trace it back, in 1884; I would not say positively. She took pity on the condition of the poor workingmen and sent them over here at her own expense. No doubt her intentions were very good, but it created a very bad state of affairs in the mining region, because they were followed afterwards by the Hungarians and by the Italians.

Q. Do you regard the bringing of these Italians at that time by this lady as a pure act of philanthropy, or was there some business arrangement in her relations with the miners?—A. No; I am not one of the radicals who think that that woman did that to get cheaper labor. I think it was a pure act of philanthropy on her part. As far as I could find out, she is a very estimable woman, and bears a very good reputation, and I do not think for one moment that she had any intention to bring those miners over to compete with American labor, to lower wages. I found out at that time—I can not say about the present condition—but at that time, in 1897, if mines were worked to their full capacity they could not give employment to all the miners for more than 6 months, which clearly proved to me that the supply of labor in the mining region is double the demand. I had another opportunity of studying their condition, or rather to find out something that brought out—that a large number of them were brought here, enticed, not like by that lady, whom I referred to, but by circulars that were thrown in their houses, and so on, and I could not get to the bottom of it, but I think that the steamboat agents who have their agents in those little villages wherever they are, have men who have enticed them to come over here as miners. I found probably out of 80 or 90—well, I would ask one, for instance, "What made you come over to this country? You are suffering now, and you tell me you can not make a living, and you would be glad if you could go back." "Well," he says, " we were enticed by circulars thrown into our huts and into our villages by steamboat agents." That is what I found out those circulars contained. I had several of them, and I lent them to some friend of mine and he never returned them to me. Those circulars stated that a miner could earn from $2.50 to $3.50 per day in the coal regions, which is virtually for those people out there a fabulous sum. I found out—I am speaking of 1897, when there was stagnation in the coal trade and the people were suffering; I am not speaking of the present time—they were actually so dissatisfied and so disgusted with their condition that they would be glad to return to their own countries. That is about, in brief, what I found out among the miners in the anthracite region of the State of Pennsylvania. Here is another statistic I have. Out of 50 whom I interviewed 8 could read and write English, 20 their own language, while 22 were illiterate. I also found that very few of their children attended the public schools. They were working mostly as helpers, pickers, etc., in the mines. I found virtually a great many women as helpers, doing work in the coal mines; and they left their infant children, sometimes 2 months, sometimes 12 months old—I could not always judge—under the shade of a tree while they were working in the mines. I have here a comparison which I made with the conditions when I was there and studied them before, in 1884. In 1884 I found another, an entirely different class of people; I found towns, and contentment among that same class of people. I found them inhabiting clean dwellings; probably a little fighting and a little rioting once in a while, but, as a rule, contented; and it impressed me as very deplorable that in from 10 to 12 years in our State we had come to the state of affairs existing in the coalmining region, and no doubt, by that means, to a lower standard of morality in this country, owing to that class of people.

Q. What became of these foreigners, the Irish and Welsh and others, that had been in these mines before the Italians and Hungarians came in?—A. I tried to learn that, and in Pottsville and other places old acquaintances that I knew before the war in different regions told me that a large number of those Welsh and Irish miners could not stand it, and had emigrated; a great many of them went to the West and tried to find employment in other mines where the influx of the foreign element was not so strong at that time. When I was up there the strongest elements were the Hungarians and the Italians. Being so close to the landing place at Philadelphia and New York or Boston, all came to the anthracite or to the bituminous regions, and the majority of the miners who had been there, the Irish and the Welsh and a great many Scandinavians, had emigrated farther west and looked for employment in some place where their conditions were slightly better. That was the answer I got. Of course, I could only go by hearsay, what they told me.

Q. Was the displacement of these other miners caused by the lowering of wages, or what?—A. By the lowering of wages and the conditions under which those people can exist, and under which no American or any respectable foreigner can exist. I am speaking of the American and foreign workers together who try to live under favorable conditions. I tried to find out the cost, but I do not like to give the figures, because they were very unsatisfactory to me. I tried to find that out with respect to these Hungarians, who live 20 in one shanty and hire one woman to do the cooking and all; and they can exist for one-half the wages which the others can. I find the same conditions in Philadelphia.

Q. Did you ever have the opportunity to examine into the prices of coal, to learn whether there were economic causes why the wages of workingmen should be driven down to this Hun and Italian standard?—A. Yes. I do not think the changes of the prices of coal have been commensurate with the lowering of the prices of their wages in the anthracite. I am not speaking of the bituminous. There are different conditions in the bituminous and individual mines, etc. The lowering of the wages and the shutting down of the mines—it is not so much in the anthracite a question of lowering the wages, but of restricted production, making a man only work 6 months or 3 months or whatever it is in the anthracite, which, of course, is equal to a reduction of wages. That is, it reduces the earning capacity of the miner if he only has 6 months' work or 3 months' work—often not even at such a rate—instead of a whole year's work.

Q. So you would argue it in this way, that it was the restricted output and overplus of labor?—A. Overplus of labor to do the work, and the actual consequence of restricting the labor and lowering the wages.

Q. Is it general that anthracite mines are owned by large corporations or operators or railroad companies, or by individuals?—A. I think there are a few individuals who own mines; but it is difficult for me to state a rule connected with corporations. For instance, there is a firm, Arrio, Pardee & Co., and several other firms in the anthracite regions, but it is difficult—I had no opportunity to find out whether they are not connected after all with the Pennsylvania Company; how they are interested. Working as I did, I had no chance to find out; but as a rule I found out that the controlling interest of the anthracite was in the Pennsylvania, the Philadelphia and Reading, the Lehigh Valley, the Delaware, Lackawanna and Western, and, well, it amounts to about 6 or 7 companies who hold the controlling output, who control the output of the mines, and then again the distribution of the mines at the same time. My observation, when I was there in 1880, was that the great difficulty at that time which the individual owners of the mines in the anthracite were having was the discrimination by the railroad companies in not giving them cars in order to bring their coal to the market. I am not speaking of 1894. In 1894 I heard very little complaint of that; but it seems to me there are no more individual operators. I think that is the reason I did not hear any more complaints.

Q. (By Mr. RATCHFORD.) Has your investigation or observation in the anthracite region brought out any connection between the mining companies and the railroad companies?—A. It is a very difficult question to answer. I think there is. There certainly must be in the Reading, because there is the Reading Coal and Iron Company and the Reading Railroad.

Q. Can you describe it?—A. I am not enough of a lawyer to give you the technical points, where the difference comes in; I could not, but I know one thing, that it is well known that the Philadelphia and Reading Coal and Iron Company are miners of coal, and that the Philadelphia and Reading Railroad Company are, of course, carriers of coal. They have been operating under the old charter issued previous to the constitution of the State of Pennsylvania in 1870, adopted in 1872 or 1873, which provides that no railroad company and no mining company can combine together. The Reading Railroad said that they were not liable to that, because their charter antedated that new constitution; neither was the Pennsylvania Company. I can not say when the Reading Railroad Company was chartered, as to-day it is reorganized and running under a different management, whatever it is, nor whether they have changed them or disconnected the two companies. I never made any inquiry, of course.

Q. We have testimony before this commission to the effect that the coal producers in the anthracite region have nothing to say as to the selling price on the seaboard; that there is an arrangement between the producers and the carriers which gives to one 40 per cent of the selling price and to the other 60 per cent. What do you know about that?—A. I could not tell, because that is not in my line; I did not investigate it. As I told you, all the investigation I have made for years has been on the simple condition of the workingman, on the economic grounds, and, in fact, I would not have the time to go into those details fully and give you a satisfactory explanation of that question.

Q. (By Mr. FARQUHAR.) What observations did you make there in respect to the attendance of the children of these foreign miners at school?—A. In 1897 not 1 out of 50 went to school. I make that sweeping assertion. The boys are helpers and pickers, and the girls were there to do the housework.

Q. Is there no law to compel attendance?—A. We have a compulsory law now in the State of Pennsylvania, but it is a dead letter in the mining regions, so far as I know. I see that they are trying to enforce it in the city of Philadelphia, but I do not hesitate to say that it is a dead letter in the slum districts. I saw the other day where a few people were arrested, but it is virtually a dead letter in the slum districts. I have my notes in regard to the condition of the children in the slum districts in Philadelphia. I found that they are not attending public schools.

Q. How many years have these Huns been in these mining districts?—A. Twenty years. Twenty years ago you could not find an Italian or a Hungarian. Those nationalities were scarce in the coal region. The present condition commenced, probably, with the large influx since 1885, 1886, 1887, and 1888. There might have been a few scattered. I doubt whether, up to 1880 or 1882, 2 per cent of the miners there were adult Italians, Hungarians, or Polish Jews; possibly up to 1884 or 1885.

Q. You can not say, on account of the recent immigration there, what the characteristics are of this coming generation?—A. Well, yes, I would say that the characteristics of the rising generation, brought up under that influence, if we keep on holding that undesirable thing, will be detrimental. I answered that the other day, if you will allow me to make that allusion, to a professor of economics. He asked me whether it was not true that our cry for this restriction of immigration came only from organized labor, and that the labor unions wanted to create a trust and make labor scarce. I replied: "I am not connected with any labor association, though I admit I am very friendly to them; but I am arguing the question from the purely moral ground, and I would like you to answer this: Supposing this city has a reservoir capable of holding 10,000,000 gallons of water, and at the same time there is only one stream where they can take a pure supply from, and they can not, with all their pumping facilities, get more than 5,000,000 gallons of pure water into that basin. According to your doctrine (you say this country is big enough and large enough to employ three times what there is here and there will be room for more), the city should go to a polluted stream and pump 5,000,000 gallons of polluted water into the pure. And that is just what we are doing."

Q. (By Mr. RATCHFORD.) You stated that a legislative committee of the State of Pennsylvania made an investigation of the mining conditions?—A. Yes; in 1897.

Q. Both in the anthracite and in the bituminous?—A. Yes; and it is even stronger than what I give you here to-day. The one as to the bituminous you can get; it is printed. I neglected to bring it.

Q. Can you state what the findings of this committee were and their recommendations?—A. The findings of the legislative committee in the anthracite and bituminous coal regions did not touch any subject that I touched. They simply described the miserable condition of the miners. Senator Saylor, of course, advocated in his report, and he was fully sustained by the majority, the proposition that it would be advisable for the legislature of the State of Pennsylvania (in view of the fact that the State of Pennsylvania could not pass any bill restricting immigration), under the existing conditions in the bituminous region, to pass a law prohibiting the importation of pauper labor into the State. I do not think there was anything done, but you will find that recommendation in the report.

Q. As the conditions in the anthracite region differ materially from those found in the bituminous region, I believe the commission would prefer that you treat the cases separately.—A. Oh, I can only speak of the anthracite. My observations were not in the bituminous. I am only speaking from hearsay.

Q. You know of the recommendations made, do you?—A. Made by the Pennsylvania legislature, from reading their report, but I could not speak on the condition of the bituminous men from my own observation, because I was not there.

Q. Can you enumerate the recommendations?—A. I am very sorry that I neglected to bring them. They are so numerous that to a certain extent I am not very familiar with them. For instance, the weighing of coal, the sliding scale, and all that, going into the details; and they passed some laws in 1897, on the strength of that, which were recommended by the committee.

Q. What laws have they passed?—A. The inspection law; and now what do you call that, for instance, loading the car above the——

Q. Limiting the weight of cars?—A. Yes; they passed several laws about that.

Q. They passed an antiscreen law?—A. Yes; and they passed another law at the recommendation of the Pennsylvania legislature, which was vetoed by Governor Hastings, taxing the so-called company stores 10 per cent on scrip, and so on, on the books.

Q. What is the effect of those laws? How many of them are in operation?—A. I could not tell you. I have not been there lately and can not give you a satisfactory answer as to how many there are in operation.

Q. Do you know if there are any in operation?—A. Yes. I know several of the labor leaders, and I met Mr. Fay, from Schuylkill, several times in Harrisburg, and he told me it is a little better, but it is not what it should be.

Q. Would you be kind enough to submit to this commission as a part of your testimony, if you wish, the findings of that legislative committee and its recommendations?—A. I can mail it. I have a copy—it is in my desk in Philadelphia—of the bituminous; they were printed. I can not give you a copy of the anthracite. The anthracite report, as I have explained here before, was only submitted by the committee. It never was printed, and that does not exist. The anthracite had more recommendations than the bituminous, and the anthracite virtually had that recommendation—or upon the strength of the recommendations the bill was passed to tax those company stores 10 per cent. I could bring before the commission something of the record which might be of some interest to you, such as the slips which those companies issue. I have a large number of them; I gathered them up there.

Q. Have you found that the existence of the company store is a detriment to the miners?—A. In 1897, when I was up there, there was nothing else there but company stores, and the only way was for miners to get things from the Polish Jews, who carried their packs and supplied them to the women in the house. I found the small grocery store and the small dry goods store that used to exist 20 or 30 years ago completely broken up. I found worse conditions there; I found, judging from what experience I have, that the prices were higher. One man showed me a slip which had a circle and a red cross in it; he only purchased during that month $2.75, and he said, "You know what that red cross means?" I said, "No." He said, "That if I do not deal more with the company store I can get no work." And several of these I have got.

Q. (By Mr. FARQUHAR.) Have you a scale of prices of the company stores, that you could compare with ordinary prices?—A. I can get it for the commission from Mr. George Chance, president of the United Labor League of Philadelphia, who made that a special study when he was up there. He has got it calculated. He found it from 20 to 25 per cent higher. Of course, when I was up there I did look into the condition and found it bad, but I did not give that sharp detail attention to it that Mr. Chance did.

Q. (By Mr. RATCHFORD.) You found that the men are obliged to deal there?—A. Yes; I make that statement from my best knowledge, and I can confirm it, and I can bring those slips containing the circle and the red cross, which that man told me is warning or a notice that you must purchase more of the company store. I am now speaking of 1897, but I am told the same condition exists to-day.

Q. What company was it that sent out such letters?—A. Some of the slips I had were from Arrio, Pardee & Co., and the Pennsylvania Supply Company, I think. I got some slips from Arrio, Pardee & Co., and the Pennsylvania Supply Company; the others I do not remember.

Q. (By Mr. FARQUHAR.) Now, suppose you take up the sweat-shop investigations that you made and give us your observations?—A. That happened in 1894, and I stuck to it for 2 days with Mr. John Keefe and by the advice of Mr. Watchhorn—he was factory inspector—and I did it because they always got me to do those things, because I could help on account of my knowledge of the dialects, etc.; but after 2 days, by the advice of my wife, I gave it up. I found the conditions too hard; I found such filth, such dirt, such vice, immorality, so much suffering, starvation, actually—I would rather speak about the conditions of the working class and the foreign element in Philadelphia in the slum districts for the last 8 months, because I have given that very close investigation.

Q. Well, proceed in your own way; tell us all you know.—A. I have numbers; I never mention any names. No. 14: House occupied; two-story frame; formerly a dwelling house; now, front room used as a grocery store; back room rented as a working room to make shirt waists; occupied by 6 working girls; second story contains 4 bedrooms, occupied by 3 different families; 22 people in all living in the house; all Russian Jews; only 2 adults could speak English, and that was very poorly; the rest speak the Jews' jargon only; 8 children, who did not attend public school, but they are sent to the Hebrew school to learn to read Hebrew, but not to translate it, simply so they can say their prayers, and that is about all. Children are engaged in selling matches and newspapers. Rent of the house, $30;

received $25 from subtenants; everything in a filthy and dirty condition and no sanitary regulation.

Case No. 20: Grocery store; looked in a fair sanitary condition; occupied by a woman about 30 years old; speaks only the Jewish jargon; married and has 3 children; her husband left her and she really does not know where he is to-day; left her several years ago; she is married again. On questioning her about it, I said, "How did you get a divorce from your first husband?" and she said, "The easiest way I could get it;" that is, a divorce from the rabbi, not legal in any court; simply goes to the rabbi and states the case to him, that her husband has left her for some years, and he gives her a paper written in Hebrew hieroglyphics, and simply divorces her, and the same rabbi marries her to another man. That is the condition I found there.

Now, here I have a very interesting case. I must give you some Jewish words in order to explain to you the man's occupation. It is a very interesting case to me; I devoted a great deal of time to it. In making the explanation you must remember one thing—that in all those districts you can not find a single English sign; all Jewish.

Q. What is the number of this case?—A. No. 24. He makes a specialty of what he calls koscher food. That means something which is allowed according to the dietary laws of the orthodox Jews—something which has not been mixed with anything impure, or anything of the kind. I found the sign in his window, which took a long time for me to understand—only three Hebrew words. The first Hebrew word was "Schocker," killer of animals. Of course, some of the gentlemen here know that the orthodox Jew is not allowed to eat the meat of any animal unless it has been killed according to the Jewish rite; that is, the cutting of the throat and leaving out all the blood. This is ridiculed by some. Through that same man I got a great deal of valuable information. According to the law the blood is injurious. That was his first occupation. His next occupation was called "Mohul;" that is, he is licensed by the chief rabbi to perform the rite of circumcision. The third license—you do not need to have the Hebrew word there—was to perform the marriage ceremony; that is, authority given to him by the Jewish rabbi to perform marriages; and a divorce is considered legal from him, from the Jewish standpoint; that is, as far as the Talmudic law is concerned. He is a very thorough student of that law. I was perfectly surprised at his knowledge. When I explained to him how it was, he was bitterly opposed; he said it never ought to be taken away from the rabbi—the right to perform marriages.

Q. Or grant divorces?—A. Or grant divorces. That never ought to be given away. I need not go into that. I was very much interested in the Jewish side, but it is not interesting to the commission here. The only thing, probably, may be how these men try to have those poor ignorant people keep up their superstitious habits, and do it for no other purpose, as I can see it, but to keep control over them. Now, while I was there, some boy came in and he asked for a certain Hebrew document. Of course, I was raised by the École Polytechnique, under the direction of Prof. Samuel Monk, probably one of the ablest scholars in Talmudic languages, and he taught me all those things, not from the same standpoint of superstition, but to get an insight—knowledge; and I was perfectly amazed. I said, "Do you give that document?" His mother was confined in childbed, and he came to that store to get those papers and pin them around the room to keep the evil spirits out. And that is encouraged by these people, to my mind, simply to keep that superstitious habit up and keep them in ignorance. Prof. Samuel Monk was professor of Semitic and Talmudic languages at the École de la Science, Académie de la Science.

Case No. 30: Grocery and fruit store on the first floor; basement used for the storage of bananas and other fruit; in the month of July; family consists of 9, the oldest a girl of 15 years; they are Italians; none of the children attend school; the boys are bootblacking, and the girl, 15 years old, worked in a candy store. Out of the whole I could only find the girl of 15 and 2 boys who could read and write English; the husband and wife were illiterate.

Case No. 34: Three-story building; grocery and fruit store; rent out rooms to families. The dwelling is a 10-room house, occupied by 18 people, all illiterate.

Case No. 50: Grocery store, occupied by a single man; had arrived in this country and was supported by a Jewish charitable association for some time; after about 4 months he got desperate and tried to get work, and was enticed by the crimps and shipped as a sailor (another nuisance and another very bad thing in our city of Philadelphia). They made him drunk and landed him on board of a vessel. That is his story, and I know it is true. He worked for 4 months on the vessel, and his wages, when he landed back in Philadelphia, was $3.75. I guess those are about the extracts I made of those cases.

Q. Now, has the State of Pennsylvania taken any legislative action in respect to the slums of Philadelphia that you have just described?—A. The board of health does interfere, but can not enforce its regulations; clean them out one day and they come back the next day. The Pennsylvania legislature passed a factory-inspection bill, and the inspectors are doing their duties. They are trying to do all they possibly can, but they clean them out in one place and they appear in another. And one thing is that no factory inspector can find out—for instance, the first case which I reported is impossible for the factory inspector; it is only by accident that I stumbled on it; that is, where they have a small grocery store and a small room back, and they have 10 or 12 girls working there, and they are not registered. They have passed a law that they must be registered and take out a license and give every girl so much space, so much room, so many feet. Well, while this is enforced in large factories it is not enforced in the slums, because I came across any number of places in the months of July and August where 10 or 12 girls were huddled together like sheep in a little shop; and the factory inspector does not know enough about it and could not touch them.

Q. What personal knowledge have you of sweat shops in Philadelphia?—A. My personal knowledge of the sweat shops in Philadelphia was acquired when I was there in 1894, and since that time I have made very little observation—in fact, I would only give hearsay evidence. I have not paid much attention to it, but I think they are existing to a very large extent yet, and will exist as long as we have two persons applying for one job.

Q. What would be your opinion of the moral standing of the Jews in Philadelphia compared with other foreigners in like conditions?—A. I think, judging from the influx of the lower class of people into the slums, especially Russian Poles and Jews, that in certain things they are lower than other foreigners, except perhaps the Italians. There is one thing I will say in their favor—I find very little drunkenness among them, but, on the other hand, regarding pure sanitary conditions they are far below the others.

Q. Do you mean viciousness in person or viciousness in mind?—A. Not so much in mind as in person; for instance, their uncleanness; they are filthy, dirty. They seem to prefer to live in dirt. That is about the only explanation I know of.

Q. Do you believe that taking an equal proportion of that class of Jews to the Italians or other foreigners in like condition, that you find them more in the police court or in the jurisdiction of the police authorities than the others?—A. Yes.

Q. You find more of the Jews than you do of the Italians?—A. No; more of the Italians than of the Jews; but more of the Jews to-day than there used to be; an alarming increase over what it was 40 years ago. Forty years ago the average of criminals among the Jews in this country was the lowest; there were very few; but to-day it is largely on the increase. Of course, there are more Jews, but I mean according to the increase of the population.

Q. What class of crimes is the Jew increasing in?—A. The increase of crime is, in the first place, for instance, in buying goods under false pretenses, swindling; that is one thing. I would say, for instance, that there is a great deal more among the Polish Jews, in setting their stores on fire; more than among the other Jews. Of course, I am only speaking of what I hear. That is greatly on the increase—not observing the laws of the land; that is the principal thing. They do not keep Sunday; they keep all their places open on Sunday. They try to enforce it in Philadelphia. I am not speaking of strict enforcement of the Sunday law; but they will keep their places open on Sunday, and they even work on Sunday.

Q. Do they keep their places open on Saturday?—A. Yes. Even the rabbi says, "We are in a condition in this country where we have to keep open."

Q. Do these Jews usually come onto the list of the poor board for support, or do the Jewish societies usually keep them?—A. The Polish Jews?

Q. I do not care which.—A. The United Hebrew Relief Association tells me that nine-tenths of their charity goes to the Polish Jews. I find another thing, that philanthropic movements, such as, for instance, the Baron Hirsch fund, have frequently been a detriment to the people—that class of people I take an interest in, the workingmen in this country; I mean the workingmen at large. Now, in these colonies over there in Woodbine, started by Baron Hirsch, they simply try to make farmers of them, but they all end in factories in competition with American workmen. I think that the agricultural occupation in Woodbine, and all these persons who were brought over by Baron Hirsch, I think they have all been a complete failure. They have been a failure in the Argentine Republic, and they are a failure in this country.

Q. (By Representative GARDNER.) Do you know of a single instance of the Jews prosecuting agriculture for a living?—A. Very few; very, very few. I am not making a charge. I was born of orthodox parents. It is not his fault, but of his Christian brother. It is the fault of his Christian brother in Europe, who prevented him from being anything else, but compelled him to have a certain occupation. But the reason I am one of those who speak so strong against that class of Jews—Polish, or any other class of Jews in this country who still carry on the occupation of barter and trade—is because it is the duty of the Jew in this country, having equal opportunities and privileges, and being the first country that gave it to him, to show that he will try to become as good a citizen as his neighbor.

Q. Are the Jews within your observation, whether within the mining regions or the city, an exceptionally healthy race of people, or otherwise?—A. Healthy; only in the slum district I find there is a great deal of consumption, owing to the overcrowded condition. I find delicate children, and delicate girls—a good deal of consumption in the slums, but I attribute that to the overcrowded and unsanitary conditions they live in.

Q. An impression seems to prevail that the Jews are an exceptionally healthy race of people in this country. I want to ask how that is harmonized with the sanitary condition you described?—A. I do not think the average age of the Jews is any greater than that of his Christian fellow, if he lives in worse sanitary conditions. I believe that the condition they live in is below the average.

Q. What percentage of the Jews follow any productive occupation.—A. You mean down in the slums?

Q. I am distinguishing now the productive occupations from nonproductive occupations—the difference between making, and living off what somebody else makes.—A. You mean as regards manufacturing or distributive selling, trading?

Q. Yes.—A. I could not very well give that, but I think, as a class, a large number of Jews in Philadelphia are engaged in production. I think we have a full ratio of manufacturers in Philadelphia among the Jewish people. I am speaking now of the Jews, and including myself—those who were born of Jewish parents.

Q. (By Mr. RATCHFORD.) Would the conditions in Philadelphia in that respect hold good generally?—A. All through the United States?

Q. Yes; as far as you know.—A. I think there is the same condition in New York and all over. I think the Jews, as a class in this country, having equal opportunities, which they do not have in Germany and other places, are trying to work on a different line, and no longer pursue the same occupation. I think in the professions they are fully represented—those that take up the study of law and medicine, and even in the mechanical arts. I find that in the University of Pennsylvania, the mechanical department, the ratio of Jews is on the increase, I think, more than the population is.

Q. (By Mr. FARQUHAR.) Do you find a more peaceable race than the Jews in this country, whether native or foreign—and law observing? I want to know if in your observation you find them in the lower saloons, in streets fights, in mobs, in riots?—A. No.

Q. In brothels or what else?—A. No, no. I find that even in the lowest strata of the Polish Jews, they are not given so much to drunkenness as the others. They are more temperate, more of a temperate people.

Q. Do you find in the slums of Philadelphia, which you investigated there, that many of these people are a charge on the poor rates of the city of Philadelphia?—A. No; not so much on the poor rates but on the Jewish United Hebrew Charitable Association; mostly on that. The Italians are coming very largely to be supported by the poorhouses—inmates of the almshouses.

Q. Can you give the reasons why these foreigners herd together in the cities when the opportunities for labor are so good outside of the cities?—A. Yes; I made a special inquiry. I said, "Why is it that you people prefer to live this way? Why is it you people huddle together in this court or alley? What rent do you pay?" They said so much. "You can get an elegant house in the country; why don't you move out?" For instance, they will say, "We are amongst our people here; everybody understands me and I understand everybody. If I move out to the country, I can not talk and nobody understands me. Then, everywhere I go, they say, 'Sheeny! Sheeny! Polish Jew!' they halloo after me. Then, here we have our theaters, and we can go in the evening, only a few squares, and in the country we could not have them." They seem to prefer to live that way. You can pretty nearly draw a line, and make wards out of it—from Broad street, beginning at Shippen and Fitzwater, you find nothing along there but Polish Jews. I am speaking of Polish Jews, Russian Jews—no matter where they come from—Armenian, all that same class, speaking that jargon. When you come to Carpenter, to Fitzwater, between Eighth and Thirteenth, you find nothing but Italians. We call it "Little Italy," and the other we call the slum.

I think these Italians huddle together for the same reason, because they find more congeniality amongst themselves; but apart from that, I think a great deal may be attributed to the following: Now, for instance, there are a few Irish people living in that neighborhood, keeping grocery stores, and a few Americans; and I go in and talk with them, and they say, "We will have to get out of here; we can not stand the smell." It makes a clash between these two. These people in former times made a good living, and now they are driven out by these people who live on half what they ought to eat; and they are driving them out, and there is a certain clash between them, and that is, I think, the chief cause why they gather in these sections. I frequently hear of fights between these Irish boys and the Polish Jew boys. "Look at the Sheeny!" And they would turn around and call the Irish boys other names. They do not mix together. The Italians and the Polish Jews keep separate, keep in their own districts. One gentleman told me, and he has made it quite a study, "I have come to the conclusion that these people prefer to live in the slums because if they have clean neighbors they see the dirt, and if they have dirty neighbors they do not take any notice of it."

Q. Still you have not got to the bottom of the "why" of this colonization and this huddling together in poverty. Do you have any other reasons than those you have stated?—A. No; I have no other reasons; but it seems to me that they try to form a social club amongst themselves; that they find it more congenial to live in that atmosphere and in those surroundings and conditions.

Q. As to the rising generation of these foreigners, Jews, Italians, Huns, and all that, what is your observation? Do they intend to live in these same surroundings that their parents did?—A. Yes, the majority of them.

Q. You have no information of them learning mercantile trades?—A. There are some few bootblacks, newsboys, and similar occupations.

Q. But they can not stay bootblacks always; you will come on to an age limit when you speak of that kind of work.—A. I think the bootblack will, afterwards, when he gets stronger and older, land in a position of unskilled labor—a porter, a street sweeper, or something of that kind.

Q. (By Mr. KENNEDY.) Is there not a character of slavery which has an influence in keeping these people together in that way?—A. Do you mean the padrone system?

Q. Yes.—A. I have not been able to trace any of the padrone system as it has been described. But that exists among the Italians mostly, and I have not been able to trace these things among the Italians as I have been among the Polish Jews, because there I can understand their jargon and I can get along with them; but there is no padrone system among the Polish Jews, except only as to the sub-contractors in the sweat shops.

Q. Do you believe that there are any influences controlling their labor, interested in controlling their labor and keeping it cheap, thus keeping them in the community?—A. Well, no. I think that is the natural outcome of their condition and the constant large influx of new immigrants who, as I say, have to take the same occupation, and that will certainly keep the wages down. Now, in the clothing manufacture, cap manufacture, and all that, the revival of trade which we have now had for a year gives these people a little better wages, but the question is, How long will it last? I find now they are mostly employed, and there is not that misery and starvation that existed in 1894 and 1895, and up to 1897; but if the ratio increases and keeps constantly flocking in, of course the result will be exactly the same as in 1894—a surplus supply of labor; and it is getting worse and worse.

Q. (By Mr. FARQUHAR.) Can you suggest any remedy for the congestion of these foreigners in the cities?—A. Yes. In the first place, Senator Lodge's bill—an educational test.

Q. How would Lodge's bill, with its educational test, affect these colonies in the cities? Have you any remedy to propose to break up these colonies of foreigners in the cities, so that they can establish productive enterprises and become American citizens?—A. You can bring them out of the slums to somewhere else. The only remedy I have to suggest is what the city of Berlin has done. It has a different sort of board of health than we have in the city of Philadelphia. The city of Berlin goes down in the slums and finds conditions as I have found them, dangerous to the community. They give notice to the landlord or owner of the building that that building has to be put in sanitary condition, and kept so. If it is not done, and kept clean, the city takes these people and puts them in quarantine outside of the city, in the suburbs, and there, under police surveillance, they are forced to keep clean, to take their baths and keep their houses clean. They are forced to stay in the suburbs so long they become used to that kind of living, and then when they come back to the city they are kept under watch. We want to adopt desperate means to clean out the slums in Philadelphia. The city of Berlin has cleaned out its slums, and the city of Edinburgh is doing the same thing, but the ordinary sanitary laws, such as we have in Philadelphia, will not do it.

Q. You spoke of the Lodge bill?—A. It will be desirable in so far as it keeps that undesirable element out.

Q. (By Mr. KENNEDY.) Will it keep any of these Jews out?—A. Two-thirds of them.

Q. Can they not read some language?—A. I would not recognize the Hebrew jargon as a language.

Q. It is a printed language, is it not?—A. Yes. A large per cent of them can read that, but they can read only so far that they go to school and learn to read their prayers—read Hebrew. He can read Hebrew, but he does not know it. I can take any gentleman here and teach him to read the Hebrew language in an hour, but of course he would not know what he reads. It would keep a large percentage out, and mostly women.

Q. (By Mr. FARQUHAR.) What other nations would it keep out?—A. The Italians, as a class, and the Hungarians, because they can not read their own language.

Q. What would be the physical characteristics of the people it would keep out—their producing qualities as laborers and developers of industry?—A. Of course I can not say whether they are producing as much as the others, but they become competitors and have to sell their labor at almost anything they can get for it.

Q. So you think that the educational test would be a measure to retard immigration?—A. To restrict immigration.

Q. Without sampling out the good and bad?—A. I hold, and I find by my experience, that the man who is so ignorant can be influenced and brought under the control of these Jewish rabbis and priests far more than the man that can read and has a mind of his own. I only would judge it by that. I do not mean to say that they are less inclined to commit crimes or anything of that kind.

Q. Do you think this legislation would give us a better class of immigrants?—A. It would give us, at any rate, a better class of immigrants than absolutely no restriction.

Q. Would that same test exclude a good many honest, hard-working immigrants?—A. Yes, I admit it.

Q. (By Mr. KENNEDY.) Do you know anything about organized labor?—A. I had some experience when I was connected with Local Assembly 6401, Knights of Labor.

Q. Do you know what is the sentiment of the organized working people?—A. Unanimously in favor—all those I have spoken to are unanimously in favor of restricting immigration. The only class that I can find against it is the newspapers and the steamboat agents.

Q. A great many of the leaders of organized labor are foreigners or sons of foreigners, so far as you know?—A. Mr. Gompers, of course, is a foreigner. George Chance, of course, was born in England. I do not know whether they can be called foreigners any more—they are 50 and 60 years in this country.

Q. The question I desire to ask is whether the leaders of organized labor, native born or foreign born, are in favor of restricting immigration?—A. Yes; all those I have come in contact with are in favor of restricting immigration, and say something should and must be done.

Q. (By Mr. FARQUHAR.) What are the reasons for it? Is the labor market overcrowded?—A. Overcrowded. The reason given is that, with all the prosperity we have to-day, there is a surplus, an oversupply of labor. The reason I give you, and there are a great many who agree with me, is that while we have a protective tariff—and I am in favor of protection to the manufacturer—the manufacturer can scour the markets of Europe where he can get the cheapest labor and import it free of duty. I think if protection is given to the manufacturer, protection should be given to the workingman, and the only protection he needs is not too much competition in the labor market.

Q. (By Mr. RATCHFORD.) You spoke of the leaders of labor organizations being unanimously in favor of restricting immigration.—A. Yes.

Q. Have the great labor organizations of the country expressed themselves?—A. So far as I know, the leaders have. I do not know whether they have passed resolutions at their business conventions. I have not looked over the proceedings of the American Federation of Labor, and I do not know.

Q. Can you state to what extent they are in favor of such restriction?—A. In favor of such restrictions that the Hungarians, the Italians, and these others will not come over.

Q. That is the thing they want to meet, but what are the remedies that they apply? To what extent are they in favor of restriction?—A. Of course, as I say, Senator Lodge's bill goes to the educational test. I am very much in favor of another bill, which was introduced by Congressman Stone, suggesting the following remedy: "Section 4. That it shall hereafter be unlawful for any male alien, who has not in good faith made his declaration before the proper court of his intention to become a citizen of the United States, to be employed on any public works of the United States or to come regularly or habitually into the United States by land or water for the purpose of engaging in any mechanical trade or manual labor, for wages or salary, returning from time to time to a foreign country." This bill was mostly aimed, I think, against the Canadian immigration.

Q. (By Mr. FARQUHAR.) That bill went through Congress?—A. It went through Congress once and was vetoed by President Cleveland.

Q. (By Mr. RATCHFORD.) You state that so far as you know the labor organizations of the country have expressed themselves in favor of restriction of immigration. Is it not a fact that some of the labor organizations of the country admit to membership in their unions and to places in their factories and workshops immigrants who come to this country with the union card?—A. Yes; but that class of people would not be kept out, I think, under restriction.

Q. (By Representative GARDNER.) Do you mean to intimate that there is an educational test anywhere in Europe for membership to the labor unions, and that it is impossible for a member of a labor union, entitled to the international card, to not be able to pass an educational test?—A. Yes. I make this sweeping assertion: That in Germany there is not a member of a labor union who is not only able to read and write his language, but has actually got a good education.

Q. Yes, in Germany; but any country in Europe?—A. Italy has no labor unions. You will find no labor unions in Russia, Poland, Austria, or any country where that class of people come from. They are not tolerated.

Q. Take it in London?—A. Even in London, in that class of immigrants who come over here from London, if a man is a member of a union, that class of people become more intelligent, more educated, more enlightened. That is my experience.

Q. You say a man that has been a member of a labor union for several years will be able to read and write, because that is a kind of a school. I admit that to be true, but still might there not be many members coming here with cards that would not be members for a number of years, but comparatively new; and suppose an immigrant should appear and be submitted to the educational test, and should fail to pass, and should then produce his union card, what would you do with him?—A. I do not think that case would arise; but of course if it should, under the strict interpretation of the law, the law of the United States could not recognize the trade-union card, and he would have to be excluded. But I do not think this case would come up.

Q. (By Mr. KENNEDY.) If the immigration laws were amended to meet the desires of the workingmen of this country, and there should follow an educational test in the immigration laws, would the workingmen raise any question that because a man who was illiterate came with a union card he should therefore be admitted to American citizenship?—A. You mean whether the labor unions would protest if the man were to be excluded?

Q. Yes.—A. I do not think they would.

Q. (By Mr. RATCHFORD.) You say you are not a member of a labor union now?—A. I am not a member of a labor union.

Q. (By Mr. FARQUHAR.) You spoke of this class of labor being brought in, up to the present time, in large bodies. Do you think the alien contract labor law is imperfect?—A. Yes.

Q. Can you suggest anything better?—A. The alien contract labor law should be so that the American manufacturers should have the right in all new arts and in all new industries to go to Europe and bring men over to teach American workmen that new industry.

Q. (By Representative GARDNER.) Following that very point that you have now brought out, that the manufacturer, in your judgment, should be permitted to go anywhere to get men of special skill: Suppose that we had had a rigid immigration law for the last 50 years, would or would not, in your judgment, the people of this country, up to this time, have been able to establish successfully the potteries of the country, the tin-plate industry, and many others, the hardware and cutlery business, and so on? Put the question in a different form: Do we not owe the establishment of our potteries, cutlery business, and a long list of industries that are now employing many thousands of skilled workmen in this country to our ability to first draw from foreign countries for the skill to make these goods?—A. We would have never come to the present condition unless it was through the foreign element. That is what has made the American manufacturer and the American inventor so successful. For instance, in Germany there is only one class of people working in the same class; in England the same way, in France the same way. The great advantage of the American manufacturer is in drawing his people from those who have seen the different methods and ways of another country, and taking what is the best of all and combining it. That is what has made the American manufacturer so successful.

Q. Do you know of any man who would now agree to a law that would have excluded him when he came?—A. Yes; I think a great many of these Polish Jews and Hungarians are sorry they came here, and would be only too glad if they could go back.

Q. The question now is, while each man, in a general way, expresses himself for restrictive laws, would that same man, when you come down to particularize with him, agree to a law that would have excluded him or any of his family?—A. I do not know. I have never had much experience. I do not know that I could answer that question. For instance, you know, of course, if a man was illiterate he would say he opposes the educational test, because he could not read; but the question is, Would he not want it enforced to-day after he is here? That I do not know.

Q. (By Mr. KENNEDY.) Do you believe the position of the workingmen of this country, and especially those that are foreigners, is very much the same as that of a manufacturer who wants the protective tariff; that it is self-interest and self-preservation that impels them to be in favor of further restriction of immigration?—A. I do not blame them. Self-interest always come first. Self-protection, I believe, is the first law, and they would be foolish if it were not so. I perfectly agree with you there.

Q. Do you admit that certain industries have been built up that could not have been built up without the aid of foreign workmen?—A. Most surely.

Q. Now, these foreign workmen and the American workmen engaged in these industries want to preserve their own status and high order of living in this country; is that not the object?—A. Certainly it is, to a certain extent—to better their condition and not be compelled to live in the slums like those who are coming over here.

Q. You do not think it is a good argument against further restriction of immigration to admit that these industries were built up by foreign workmen?—A. Yes; I say they were built up by the combinations of foreign workmen; but the difficulty lies here, and you forget one thing—that that was an intelligent class. The restriction of immigration which we are after now is to keep out the lowest strata. I do not think there is anyone who wants the working classes of Europe kept out, but the difficulty is to keep the undesirable element out.

Q. (By Representative GARDNER.) The questions asked have already drawn a distinction between protection to labor and the idea of good citizenship. A man may be kept out because he will come in competition with some other workmen, or he may be kept out because we do not think he would make a good citizen. They are two things. Do you think that the educational test, reading, writing, etc., has anything to do with a man's ability to run a jigger machine in a pottery, for instance, or doing any other thing that requires quickness of eye and hand?—A. I do not think that the educational test is anything to gauge the ability of a workman by, but the majority of workmen coming from countries like Germany—all good workmen—are educated, and those not educated are not good workmen to-day any more. They are only that class of people who are fit to sweep the streets and do that kind of work. They are not, in other words, skilled mechanics.

Q. You speak more particularly of Germans?—A. Not alone of Germans. The immigration from Germany and France is down to zero. There is no more immigration, practically. The statistics show the immigration from Germany is down to 12,000. I think that is what it is. That is the whole sum and substance from Germany—the whole immigration we are getting to-day. At the time I was connected with the Knights of Labor, Local Assembly 6401, it was a mixed assembly, and my experience at that time was that there was not a single man who could not read and write; in fact, hardly any one of us who could not be elected an officer of the association. I found very few who could not read and write.

Q. The better class of workingmen is naturally a different thing from the class of better workmen. A man may belong to a very bad class of workingmen, speaking in a general sense, and yet be a very skilled performer at his machine, or whatever it is?—A. Yes. There is, if you sift that matter—I still hold that view, and I think I am supported in my observation, that if we should take statistics to-morrow among the better class of workmen we would find that they are capable of reading and writing and have an education.

Q. (By Mr. KENNEDY.) Is the sentiment, which we read about in the newspapers, in opposition to further restriction of immigration a general, spontaneous expression, or a worked-up sentiment?—A. No; I do not think it is worked-up sentiment. I think it is genuine. Of course I can only speak from my limited experience.

Q. (By Mr. CLARKE.) Do you know any manufacturers who have imported low-priced, low-conditioned, contract labor?—A. No; not especially of late; but I hear a great deal of inquiry about it; it is done in a certain way. For instance, those men in the coal regions have told me that agencies in small town distribute circulars, giving a glowing description of the conditions of the American workingmen.

Q. You do not know that the manufacturers have done anything of that kind, do you?—A. No. I do not think I have heard of a single manufacturer that has done anything of that kind.

Q. You do not know of any manufacturer who does not prefer the high class of intelligent labor to the low class of ignorant labor?—A. The majority of them do. The majority of them do think they are better, and there is a reason: You find that those Italians and Polish Jews have so few occupations to follow in this country that they are only left with the sweat shops or with the coal mines.

Q. You do not know of any manufacturer who seeks protection for himself and is not willing to grant equal protection to the working people, do you?—A. Well, that is impossible to answer. No; I do not think a good many of them are willing to give equal opportunities to the workingmen; they want it all themselves.

Q. How do you know that?—A. It is easy to tell by the way they treat their workingmen, by the sharp practices they apply on workingmen, which come to my knowledge. For instance, in some of our machine shops, the contract system and the docking system; but at the same time there are plenty of manufacturers who treat their workingmen as good as any man can treat them, and do not want to cut down wages if they can possibly help it.

Q. I did not ask you about the way they manage with their help, but I asked about the application of the principle of protection.—A. Well, I think the average manufacturers in this country are trying to get all the protection they can, and make as much money as they can out of the workingmen as a class.

Q. Is not everybody else trying to do so?—A. Yes; and consequently I say the trades unions' duty is to see that they get a fair share of the profit.

Q. (By Mr. A. L. HARRIS.) When did this class of immigrants that you speak of come to this country?—A. As I said before, they began to arrive here in small numbers in 1884, and in alarming numbers up in 1888, 1890, 1892, and 1894. It decreased slightly in 1894, owing to the depressed conditions—what we called the panic; but rapidly increasing again at the present time.

Q. Has the present legislation and its execution, upon that question, had any effect upon increase or decrease?—A. Well, it has not kept them out; they were admitted as before, with the exception of a few formal questions asked—whether they had $30, and whether somebody would vouch for them. They were indiscriminately, to a certain extent, admitted.

Q. Was there no effort to execute the law we have upon the statute book, at the ports of entry?—A. I know; but the difficulty lies in the crowded condition. I do not think, under the present inspection, that it is possible to take care of the immigrants rapidly enough. I think there is where the trouble lies. I do not think it possible for a thousand immigrants to go through, especially when they have 4 inspectors.

Q. Is the same encouragement, distributing circulars in the old country, continued as in former years?—A. I can not tell that, because I have not heard of it; but the same thing springs up again and is established as before. That is a system I did not mention. They do not need to have the circulars distributed in the old country. The steamship agents in Philadelphia, on Second street, Third street, or Fourth street, go around to families and ask: "Have you a brother, sister, or father? Have you not some relative? Why don't you bring them over?" They sell tickets on the installment plan to those people. For instance, for $20 they pay 50 cents a week. They are like life insurance agents. These people are hunted up and tickets are sold to them to bring these people out. That exists; that I have found out.

Q. You say many of these people are dissatisfied with their condition here. Do they encourage their kinsmen to come over and place themselves in the same conditions they are in?—A. I spoke of some who are dissatisfied; some are not dissatisfied, because under the low conditions and the way they live they are doing better here than they were doing in their own country. Even in my paper I remarked, for instance, that 1 house rented for $30, and by taking 25 subtenants, living 20 to 30 in 1 house, and all that—under these conditions they will accumulate more money than out of what they had in Russia.

Q. (By Mr. CLARKE.) Do you not think that if the Berlin plan were put in force rigidly in our cities, sanitation was required, and the highest style of living enforced, it would have the effect after a little while to restrict immigration of those poorer classes?—A. Decidedly so. It would have a good effect on it, decidedly, because it would break up that system, as I describe, of 20 people living in 1 house. It would not be tolerated; consequently they would be compelled to have a higher standard of living.

Q. (By Mr. A. L. HARRIS.) You spoke about the large charity fund going to a certain class of immigrants. Do they find their way in the almshouses in this country?—A. No, the Jewish class, as a class, do not find their way in the almshouses. As a rule the Jews of Philadelphia—I do not speak from experience; I do not belong to a synagogue, or anything of the kind—try to keep their own poor as long as they can. The United Hebrew Charity Association, as they call it in Philadelphia, I think distributes annually a large amount to keep these people out of the poor house. Then they have their own organization. For their benefit they are kept out of the poor house, but they are kept in a condition which makes it dangerous to the surroundings. What I mean is that their unsanitary condition, their low method of living, poisons the atmosphere.

Q. Can not the sanitary condition of the locality be controlled by local legislation?—A. No, it can not. If we would once get a city council in our cities out of political control, as in the city of Berlin, a different class of men—it can not be done under our present conditions.

Q. Do you think that the politics of this country weakens the power of a city to protect itself?—A. Great influence over it, but the sanitary conditions——

Q. (By Representative GARDNER, interrupting.) You say the city can not protect itself because of politics?—A. I do not say it can not. There is no such thing as "can't."

Q. Do you mean that the presence of these people, of their voting power, or political power, makes it impossible for a council to correct the evils and still hold office?—A. No; I do not mean that by any means. I mean that to clean them out, the sum of money that would be required, and all that, would be too big for the city of Philadelphia, even if they tried to do it.

Q. Then, the difficulty is financial and not political?—A. The difficulty is a financial one and not a political one. I do not think politics has anything to do with it, because I do not think they have any political influence.

Q. (By Mr. CLARKE.) Do you see any objection to the State taking hold of that work?—A. I would be in favor of anyone who would take hold of that work; but the point is here: Just as soon as you clean out that district another ship comes here with 2,000 or 3,000 or 20,000 for New York, Philadelphia, or Boston, their landing places, and you will have to do the work over again. It is an endless chain as long as you bring them over.

Q. But you say they will not come in in such numbers when they are obliged to live decently?—A. They would get around that and live in the other way, and of course the expense to the State would be enormous.

Q. (By Representative GARDNER.) If a part of a shipload of immigrants came into the Italian district of Philadelphia next week and found all quarters in a sanitary condition and found their countrymen living as they had never seen them live before, and were told that they had to live that way under the law or else the penalty, whatever the existing code prescribed, would be visited upon them—it might be, perhaps, to the extent of deportation to their own country—do you suppose they would proceed to comply with the law as they learned it from their countrymen and saw it had been enforced upon them?—A. No; I do not. They live in the same condition as they did on the other side. For instance, you go in the slum districts, and you need not go out of their districts to see that they still stick to their old habits.

Q. Have you observed that the administration of the office of Commissioner of Immigration of late, by Mr. Powderly, has had the effect of returning to the countries from which they came applicants for admission into this country who heretofore would have been admitted, and that that in turn has had a material influence on the starting of others from those countries?—A. Yes. I think the rigid enforcement by Mr. Powderly of the immigration laws as they exist will have a beneficial effect in Europe, but the trouble is that they are not strict enough yet.

Q. But they have had a double effect, by returning people?—A. Those returned, and also those who voluntarily go back to Europe, will spread the news; that I admit.

(Testimony closed.)

WASHINGTON, D. C., *December 5, 1900.*

TESTIMONY OF MR. GOODWIN BROWN,

Counsel for the New York State Commission in Lunacy.

The commission met at 10.15 a. m., Vice-Chairman Phillips presiding. At that time Mr. Goodwin Brown, of New York City, counsel of the New York State Commission in Lunacy, was introduced as a witness, and, being duly sworn, testified as follows:

Q. (By Mr. CLARKE.) Will you please give your post-office address?—A. 192 Broadway, New York City.

Q. How long has the New York State Commission in Lunacy been established?—A. Since 1889.

Q. What is its particular duty?—A. If you will permit me, I might make a little statement in regard to it. The system is so extensive that I hardly know where to begin, but I might make a few preliminary observations. New York State is peculiar in this, I think, that it is the only State, so far as I am aware, that has established solely and exclusively what is known as State care of the insane. In other words, the State of New York, since 1893, or practically since 1890, pays absolutely for the support of all the dependent insane within its borders. One great difficulty in regard to the treatment of this subject of caring for the insane—as of all the dependent classes, I conceive, in the past in the various States—is the conflict between the State and the various municipalities. Prior to 1836 in the State of New York, or I might say prior to 1843, for the first act was passed in 1836, the care of the insane was purely a local affair—that is, they were cared for by towns, by cities, by municipalities, counties, etc. In 1843 the first lunatic asylum was established in the State, at Utica, to care for a limited number of insane; and from that time up to 1890 a large number of institutions have been established, the State paying a portion of the expense and the counties a portion, sometimes the cities. But the abuses became so great in the care of the insane by the local authorities, principally by reason of the fact that the local authorities were unwilling to appropriate the necessary money, that an act was passed in 1890 providing for the care of all the insane by the State. Certain counties were exempted, notably New York, Kings, and Monroe, and the act provided that those counties might turn over their insane to the State on certain terms. The last of those counties turned over its insane in 1896, so that from 1896 down, under the provisions of the act of 1890, as I said before, New York pays absolutely all the expenses whatsoever. It has ceased to be a local affair in any sense, with this possible exception, that the local authorities are obliged to provide the clothing and pay the expenses of the commitment; after that has been done the State from that time on assumes all expenses.

Q. You believe that is the only State in the Union which does that?—A. Well, I will not say that absolutely. I think there are one or two States in the West— the newer States—that started out at once with a system of State care. I never have looked into it particularly, but I think that is the case, possibly. There are some States which divide the expenditures—that is, where they have, you might say, State control with a portion of the expense paid by the counties or the municipalities, but in New York the municipalities, towns, cities, and counties were relieved of all taxes whatsoever. The burden absolutely was shifted to the State. To-day there is a great confusion in the State of New York in the minds of many people who do not understand it, and who think that the expenses of the State government have enormously increased. They have increased theoretically, you might say, by about $5,000,000, for the cost of caring for the insane in the State of New York to-day is about $5,000,000 a year. On the other hand, of course, the municipalities have been relieved entirely from that tax.

In 1889, about coincident with the passage of this State-care act, the State provided for the establishment of a State Commission in Lunacy—that is, the interests had become so vast and so complicated that it was felt that it was necessary to have a separate board having jurisdiction and control over the matter. Therefore the State legislature created what is now known as the State Commission in Lunacy, consisting of 3 paid members, which has sole and exclusive jurisdiction over the insane, and this was followed in 1894, in the last constitutional convention, by making the commission a constitutional body and devolving on this commission the sole and exclusive care of the insane, and excluding from its jurisdiction the care of idiots and epileptics, a jurisdiction which up to that time— up to the 1st of January, 1895—they had. So that the State of New York is unique in this, that the care of the insane is not complicated, if you please, with any other question whatever. The commission at that time resented somewhat the removal of its jurisdiction over idiots and epileptics, on the ground that they were so interlocked, if you please, that it might lead to some serious question, but on the whole I think it has been a satisfactory thing. The minute that that happened, the whole organization became centralized, and the legislature, from the time of the creation of the commission, began constantly to extend its powers, and, beginning with 1893, it gave it control over expenditures for fixed charges, what we call ordinary board or maintenance; that was extended in 1895 to cover expenditures for buildings, and, by subsequent acts, all expenditures whatsoever.

Now, following as a necessary consequence of all that, a very elaborate system in that State has grown up, which has enabled the State to go into all sorts of questions in a careful and scientific way which it was impossible that the State could go into prior to that time on account of the conflicting jurisdictions. I recall very well when I was appointed in 1889 that we had to deal in some instances with towns, in some instances with counties, sometimes with cities, and there was a constant conflict. We had great difficulty in procuring information, getting statistics, etc. It was almost impossible for a time there to know what the cost of caring for the insane was. So that we felt, in order to bring about any systematic effort, that we should have absolute control. And about that time the State conferred the authority of removal of insane from its borders that belonged to other States and countries. Up to that time that duty had devolved on the State board of charities. After this organization had been perfected and after the financial side of it had been settled, then the commission began to turn its attention to various other questions. Of course, the first thing to do was to establish a uniform system of accounts, a uniform system of commitment, a uniform system of dietary, of wages, of officers' salaries, etc.; all of that has been worked out. Then came other questions. Up to that time the State was in the habit of receiving everything that came and asking no questions; and, in fact, practically to-day that is what the State is obliged to do, although it is empowered to return lunatics before or after commitment, in its discretion. Now, the most startling thing that we found when we came to look at this question was the disproportion between the number of insane of foreign parentage as compared with the inhabitants of the State; that certainly was the most startling thing. And I might say here something about the increase in the number of the insane. There has been a great deal of public talk, you might say, a great many observations in regard to the increase of the insane. It is a very questionable whether the insane actually are increasing. I do not think at this time it can be known that it is true. For instance, apparently they increase much faster than population. We attribute that very largely to the fact that more of the insane are being given public care and treatment than formerly. The management of the institutions of the State of New York to-day is so satisfactory that relatives and friends are no longer unwilling, as they were formerly, to commit insane persons to the public institutions. So that I can conceive that the increase can largely be accounted for in that way; that is, so far as the native population is concerned, laying aside, of course, this question of insane being brought in here from other countries. I can recall very well when I was a young man and lived in the country that it was not an uncommon thing at all to have pointed out to me by my father a certain house in the locality where an insane person was kept. I think that, practically, has passed away. The insane up to 1890 were increasing in the State at the rate, perhaps, of about 1,000 a year—that is, there was a net increase. In the last few years the number has dropped down, and I think the last year it was between 600 and 700, and I think that has been the average for the last 4 or 5 years—that is, the absolute net increase. I always believed personally that the time would come when the increase in the insane would just about keep pace with the population, and, in fact, that as medical science advanced the number would tend to diminish, as, in other words, insanity now is regarded as a disease to be cured. Of course, it is a disease which is likely to grow. Then, further, a good many of these people are committed over and over again, discharged as cured, and perhaps in a few months they come back. And I might say here that the State of New York has unlimited means, of course, at its disposal, and that no reasonable expenditure has been spared to discover the causes of insanity, to employ the most skillful physicians, to give these people proper food, clothing, nurses, and attendants; and violence in an institution has almost practically ceased. That is, there is not 1 violent case now where there used to be 10.

Q. (By Mr. CLARKE.) What do you mean by violence—on the part of the attendants or on the part of the insane?—A. On the part of the insane. I remember in 1890 that I walked through one of those wards, and it was so terrible that I came back outside. Now, that has all practically disappeared simply for the reason that the State employs a vast number of people to take care of them; and perhaps a few figures here will not be out of place. The State to-day employs in round numbers 1 employee to every 5 insane persons, to care for them, and there is—I am only giving round numbers here—perhaps 1 physician to every 170. The number of insane during the past year, as I see by the last report of the lunacy commissio ', is something over 23,000; about 1,000 of those are in the private institutions, so that there is a permanent number at the present time of about 22,000 dependent cases, and they are increasing at the rate of about 700 a year.

Q. Does that increase include recommitments?—A. No, that is the net increase; for instance, there are 700 more at the end of any one year than there were the previous year—actual persons. So you see this is becoming an immense thing. In 10 years more at that same rate of increase there will be 6,000 more. To-day, say, we have 22,000 in all—in 10 years more there will be 29,000. It does not require very many figures to show where this is likely to lead.

Of course, personally I do not have the same feeling of apprehension about it perhaps that a person might who had no experience. These people must be cared for somewhere, either in homes or in public institutions. My own judgment has been, and that has been the judgment of the commission, that it is better to care for these people in public institutions than to have them cared for at home or wandering about the country, because they are constantly committing acts, if not of violence, of depredation; and often when they are cared for at home, they break up families, they destroy earning capacity, they cause untold suffering and misery; so that it has been the policy of the State to take in every person that is properly committed. And I might say right here that the safeguards in regard to the reception of persons other than insane are very carefully drawn. The superintendent of a State hospital in New York can override a judge's order. That is, a judge may sign an order for the commitment of a lunatic; and if that lunatic is brought to the hospital for reception and the superintendent believes that the person is not insane, he can refuse to receive him. Of course the State is very anxious to return these people, to discharge them and get rid of them. Vast numbers of writs of habeas corpus are taken out. The position of the State is that it simply throws the responsibility on the courts. It makes no objections before a court to the discharge of any person, except to insist that the court shall have before it ample information. Then if the court decides to take the responsibility, the State makes no objection.

Now, another point—in regard to the extent to which private individuals pay for the support of the insane: The ratio is about 1 to 16; in other words, the fixed charges for caring for the insane in the State of New York are about, in round numbers, $4,000,000 a year, and the friends and relatives contribute about $250,000; I think that is about one-sixteenth. In the State of Ohio, if I am correctly informed, no charge is made by the State whatsoever, and any person can be committed as a State charge—that is, so far as the h ·spitals for the insane are concerned. Vast numbers in Ohio are cared for in the county houses, as I understand it.

Now, with that as a preliminary statement, the thing which I conceive this commission is more particularly interested in is the effect of foreign immigration. There are some things about that that are certainly very puzzling. By the census of 1890—and I think the last census shows the same thing practically—the foreign population of the State of New York constitutes 25 per cent of the whole. The foreign population in the hospitals for the insane in New York is 50 per cent and a fraction over. Exactly how that is to be accounted for, you gentlemen perhaps can determine.

Q. (By Mr. KENNEDY.) You mean foreign born?—A. I mean foreign born—exactly 50 per cent, while there is only 25 per cent in the State. Now, the conclusion is inevitable in my mind that in the admission of immigrants here the defective classes have not been kept out. I will not undertake to say that it has been a systematic effort on the part of foreign countries, or a deliberate effort, to send out of those countries defective persons for the sake of their care and support in this country; but I do say this, that it has been done, that an undue proportion of those persons have been sent out and have been received here. Of course the State of New York suffers more by this than any other State.

Q. (By Mr. CLARKE.) Have you any information as to whether there has been an increase or a decrease in the immigration of these insane people, or mentally defective people, in recent years?—A. I do not think so. I am sorry that I have not here the last report of the commission in lunacy, but there they present a table showing the fluctuations. In 10 years it has varied from, say, about 40 per cent up to 50; some years it has risen to 50, and last year it had risen to 50 per cent—the year ending September 30, 1899, what we call the last fiscal year.

Q. Do the statistics show what countries they come from mostly?—A. Yes; that of course is a thing that could be figured out; but I could not give it to you offhand here except to say that, of course, the greatest number come from Ireland.

Q. (By Mr. FARQUHAR.) Can you furnish this table with your testimony now?—A. No; I can not.

Q. Well, you can send it to us with your revised testimony?—A. Oh, yes; I can send the figures in regard to that, showing exactly the countries where they come from. It is well known that that is not only true in regard to the insane but it is true in regard to the prisons; it is true in regard to all public institutions. I have noted that repeatedly in the State of New York. And I might say in this connection that prior to being a State commissioner in lunacy, which office I occupied for 10 years, I was for nearly 7 years in the governor's office in New York and had charge of the criminal business; that is, the extradition of fugitives and looking after criminals generally.

Q. (By Mr. KENNEDY.) May I ask you if you have any information as to whether that large percentage from Ireland is assisted from the other side or more largely from this side by relatives and friends?—A. I could not answer that. Of course I think we all appreciate this fact, that owing to the unfortunate conditions which prevail in Ireland, there are more of these people there; but this happens right along, that when people come over from Ireland or from any other of those countries and become a little bit prosperous, they immediately try to bring their friends over here. They are exceedingly clannish—I have observed that—much more so than our own native population. They seem to care much more for their own people, and they will save money and put forth efforts, and make sacrifices which, I feel free to say, would not be made by the native-born people. It is astonishing how they get those people over here. I can conceive in some instances perhaps—in fact I feel pretty confident that in England that was the case, certainly for a number of years—deliberate efforts were made, fare was furnished, transportation was given for those people to come. The fact remains that that is the condition of things.

In regard to the cost of caring for those people, to show what an enormous thing this burden is, and how, I believe, it is worthy of the most serious consideration that this honorable commission can give it, we have, for instance, a net increase in the State of New York of 700 per year. Half of that is foreign-born population, just one-half of it—in other words, 350 a year. It is known, so far as anything can be known, that the average duration of life of the insane—that is, in an institution—we will not say anything about how long they have lived outside or how long they live after they get out—but the average length of time which they live after they get in is supposed to be about 12 years; and we will call it 10 years for convenience. Last year the fixed charges of caring for the insane were the lowest in the history of the State.

I might say here, as perhaps being germane to some of the questions that come before you on the value of cooperation, that in 1893, when the State consolidated all its hospitals for the insane under one charter, and had them operated from one central office, the average cost of caring for the insane was $222 per year. The first year that the commission had charge of the finances the cost went down to $187; and it has been dropping ever since, so that last year the average cost of caring for the insane in New York dropped down to the unprecedented low figure of $165. As compared with 1893, say—that is, in round numbers—a saving of nearly $60. That would mean a saving to the State, on a basis, say, of 20,000 insane, of $1,400,000 a year. That has been brought about by cooperation. I am not here in behalf of trusts, but I just simply desire to say a word showing what can be accomplished by intelligent, well-directed, centralized effort—what has been accomplished in one direction in the State of New York.

Q. (By Mr. CLARKE.) And at the same time you claim they have been very much better cared for than before?—A. I can say this, that it is said by competent judges that the system of caring for the insane in New York is the finest in the world. I venture to say that you gentlemen could not be any better entertained than to visit one of the hospitals for the insane in the State of New York and see how these people are cared for. They are comfortably clothed, they are well fed, they are kept warm, they are supplied with trained nurses; there is not a hospital that has not a training school; they are given the best medical attendance that can be had; the recovery rate is rising constantly; and all that has been brought about with a constantly diminishing rate of expenditure. Why? Simply by cooperation. The State has now in round numbers a dozen State hospitals. In the old days when it had six, or seven, or eight, each of these institutions was governed by a board of trustees and each was going independent of all the others. They never compared notes; they never visited each other's institutions; their own methods prevailed. Every 2 months, in the State of New York, each superintendent of a hospital meets in Albany in consultation with the commission, and all of these questions of finance, of medicine, and of internal management are discussed. The purchase of supplies on joint account has been extensively introduced, so that, as I say, while the standard of care has enormously improved, the rate of expenditure has enormously decreased. But even taking it on the basis of $165 a year, if these people live 10 years—and that certainly is the lowest estimate; my own judgment is that it is more than 12 years, but for practical purposes we will say it is 10 years—there is $1,700, saying nothing about the rate of interest. The credit of the State of New York is very high, as the credit of all the States is to-day. The State of New York can borrow money for about 3 per cent. If you add the interest charge, it will bring the cost to the State up to about $2,000 during that period.

Then you must consider the cost of erecting all these vast buildings. In the old days, Major Farquhar, I used to live in Buffalo myself, and we both recall the Buffalo Hospital for the Insane. That institution when it was put up, in the days when it was desired to do something for the district, cost nearly $4,000 per capita for every lunatic in there. Of course it was a magnificent structure. Its towers I will not say are quite as high as the Washington Monument, but it is a magnificent structure. And that sort of thing went on for years, so that the State of New York has to-day invested in public buildings for the insane in round numbers $20,000,000.

Coincident with the passage of the State care act, the legislature, as the result of frequent investigations, numerous scandals, charges, and bickerings, etc., became satisfied that the ratio of expenditure was too great and they limited the lunacy commission in buildings to $550 per capita, and that is the rate to-day, which includes furniture, fixtures, and everything that goes to make up the institution. Now, how long those buildings will last is a question. I was looking over, several years ago, a statement by the National Fire Underwriters and, as I recall it, they determined that the life of a brick store building was about 20 years. If you put up a brick store building and did not make a dollar's worth of repairs on it, in 20 years the building would fall down, would be destroyed. In other words, you have practically got to expend what the building would cost in an ordinary structure. Now, I use this illustration of the brick store building because I think it more nearly corresponds to the class of buildings they put up for the insane, all ordinary structures. If we assume that in 20 years the buildings would have to be duplicated, and if we assume the life of a lunatic is 10 years, why it costs for buildings for each lunatic $275.

Q. (By Mr. PHILLIPS.) Do you think that is a fair estimate of the brick building? Are not a great many of those torn down in order to erect larger ones, which would not be the case with an insane institution? A very large per cent of the buildings that are 20 years old are supplanted by larger and better buildings.—A. If I recall it correctly—I gave a good deal of study to it at that time—that estimate was confined to the ordinary building which simply was allowed to live out its course. That is, if they were going to pay a loss they would figure as to what it would be worth on that basis of depreciation. That is my general recollection. At any rate, of course, the cost of caring for buildings for the insane obviously must be much greater. A certain number of them are destructive. I said awhile ago that the number of destructive insane persons has diminished, and that is true. In the old days they would tear a building practically to pieces in a few years. Of course, as they employ more people, that is diminished to a very large extent, but even to-day they are a destructive class of people. And if we assume that $275 would represent the cost of a building for each person, you have to add that to your $2,000; you have to add interest to that; then on top of that you have to take the appropriation for expenses of the central administration to add to this amount. The maintenance of the State Lunacy Commission at Albany with its great force of employees, with its machinery for sending these people out of the State into other countries, etc., all that aggregates a large amount of money; you have to add that to it. Then, as I say, the interest charge on these buildings and the interest charge on all these other things has to be added; so that I should say that $3,000 per lunatic would be a very conservative estimate.

We figured out, so far as the State is concerned, a few years ago, in the case of native-born insane, the loss to the State by reason of the insanity of persons during the 12-year period. Horace Mann, away back 40 years ago, figured out that the average earnings of each inhabitant of the State amounted to at least $150 a year. That is probably much higher to-day. I have not gone into the subject, but even taking his figures, in 10 years the earnings lost by reason of one lunatic would be $1,500. We figured it out at that time that if we took earnings into consideration, interest, buildings, and all those things, it would amount to about $6,000; but for the sake of being conservative on that question, we might cut that rate in two and say $3,000. We have 350 a year of foreign-born people admitted into these institutions. They live 10 years at the rate of $3,000 a piece, and you can multiply that $3,000 by 350 and see what you get—in round numbers you get $1,000,000.

Q. (By Mr. KENNEDY.) For the State of New York alone?—A. For the State of New York alone. Now, mind you, that is going right along indefinitely; and unless the United States Congress, through the medium of such a commission as yours, can provide some remedy for this evil it will require more figures than we could put on this table here to see where this will end.

Q. (By Mr. CLARKE.) Have you studied our immigration and the practice at the barge office in New York with reference to a diminution of this evil?—A. Only in a general way. I was going to speak of that a little bit later. I have never visited the barge office, but, of course, we know something about it. We are to-day, of course, caring for over 5,000 people in excess, according to our figures, of what is the normal percentage in the State of New York. In other words, we have got over 50 per cent—11,000, of these people who are foreign born, whereas, according to the foreign-born population in the State, we should have only 5,000 or between 5,000 and 6,000. It already runs into millions and millions, and it will run into millions and millions more; it is a vast thing. I am not prepared here to-day, for instance, to give the figures in regard to the idiots and epileptics; but I might say in this connection, although I am not charged especially to do so, that the State of New York has assumed practically the care of all the epileptics in the State; it has assumed practically the care of all the idiots; and then when you come to take into consideration the prisons of the State, when you come to take into consideration the vast number of reformatories, its houses of refuge, its various charitable institutions, why, the figures simply reach an appalling size. As I say, I am simply interested in this question of the insane.

Now, we get down to the practical question why the lunacy commission was charged with the duty of deporting persons who belonged to foreign countries. The insane are a very difficult class to deport. For instance, you take the average paupers, and they are shifted about from one city to another by the purchase of a railroad ticket; they are generally ready to move on if anybody will give them a ticket. But you can not do that with a lunatic; as a class they are difficult; and it is especially difficult to send them back to Europe. I think, in round numbers, they send out of the State to other States and foreign countries about 168 a year; a large number of them—I think about 100—are sent to foreign countries, sent back, and the others are distributed to other States.

Q. By Mr. PHILLIPS.) How are they cared for in being sent back; what provisions do you have for them?—A. I am very glad you suggested that. The policy of the State commission in lunacy—we do not claim to be any more moral than other people, but as a matter of sound public policy when the State of New York assumed the entire care of the insane and when all this was placed under charge of this commission, a commission which could be held directly responsible, three men, by the legislature and by the public, it was felt that it would hardly do to tolerate certain practices which had theretofore existed by the local authorities. Now, I will not go into the cases and mention the States, but I know of instances after instances—I can recall one State in particular that makes it a regular practice to send an agent around to its hospitals for the insane like this: They come across a patient and say: Where did you live before you came here? I lived in New York. Got any friends there? Yes; oh, yes. Like to go back there? Very glad to. Well, I will see if I can fix it. They literally gather up those patients, take them to a railroad station, buy them a ticket, give the train men half a dollar or a dollar and say, If you will kindly look after this patient until he gets to the Grand Central Depot you will confer a favor. Now, what happens? They are dumped out at the Grand Central Depot and go out on Forty-second street, and the police see them wandering around, and they are taken to the police station and examined and found to be insane, and taken to the receiving pavilion, kept under detention for a week and committed to the State hospital. Then the State of New York has to begin to get those persons back; and, of course, the question of domicile is a difficult one to determine, especially in cases of that kind. So that they are constantly pouring into the State of New York, and ultimately they drift and gravitate from the State of New York to other States for various reasons. Of course the State has always been willing, and I would not undertake to state that we had been entirely free from guile; but we never have taken a poor, helpless lunatic and put him on a train and paid anybody for doing it. If we have sent anybody out of the State, we have always sent a trained attendant and made arrangements beforehand with friends and relatives to take care of him.

Q. (By Mr. CLARKE.) Do you send any out of the State unless you have reason to believe that their proper domicile is in the State to which they are sent?—A. No; and the most careful investigation will not show one instance since the State commission in lunacy has been organized. We have considered it a matter of sound policy not to do that, because we would have difficulty the minute we did it. We have had difficulty. For instance, here is a patient whose husband has gone to some other State and is employed there, and perhaps we have sent an agent to go and see him, and if he has expressed any desire to have her back, or found any friends, why we send her back. Now, that is an easy matter, comparatively speaking, to get people back between the States, although we are trying to get certain legislation in Congress to cover that question; but, as I conceive it, that does not interest you. The trouble in regard to sending insane to foreign countries is a serious one. Now, the immigration laws provide substantially—and I will not burden you with going into details at this moment—that if it can be shown that an immigrant becomes insane within 1 year from the time of his arrival, from causes which arose prior to his departure for this country, he can be shipped back at the expense of the steamship company. That is one provision of the statute. You can see how exceedingly difficult that is to establish. It is hard work to say who drew that law or at whose instance it was drawn. We find that the superintendents of the State hospitals in New York—they are all conscientious men, and if they were not conscientious, good men no man with any professional reputation would be willing to make out a certificate that any lunatic became insane from causes which arose prior to his departure for this country. They simply can not get at it. Of course, an alienist studying the history of one of these cases might very well come to the conclusion that the causes arose more than a year before he came here, but not by the most remote possible stretch of the imagination could he certify to it satisfactorily. In some cases they refuse outright to do it; in others they do it very grudgingly; but unless that certificate is made the steamship-companies refuse actually to take them.

The United States statutes provide, among other things, as I recall them, that if a person becomes dependent within 1 year he may be sent back at the expense of the Immigration Bureau. Now, the State has gone a little further than this; we have sent people back as far as Japan—that is a rare instance—I do not recall but 1 case; we did send a Japanese back who came over here to study for the ministry, became insane, and was in our hospitals for 2 or 3 years; and through correspondence we found that his friends were willing to receive him, and we paid the expense and sent a trained nurse with him to Vancouver; and it cost the State $500. But we regard it as cheap to do that and the State was willing; and the State could afford to-day to pay out $500 for every lunatic to get rid of them.

Q. In sending them abroad do you compel them to leave the State or just make amicable arrangements?—A. Oh, we have to make amicable arrangements. There is no way by which we can compel any lunatic. They are usually willing to go, they are usually glad to go, but then comes the difficulty of arranging the matter with the steamship company, and that is what I want to speak of here—those cases, of course, where they are obliged to return. That is a very difficult thing to establish, a difficult thing to get that certificate, and difficult in every way. And even when we are willing and the person is accompanied by a trained attendant—for instance, there is one woman in the employ of the State who speaks several languages who is constantly traveling back and forth between this country and Europe taking these people home. The State would be willing in every case to furnish a trained attendant to take the person back, but while the State is willing to do its share, if the steamship company knows it, it will not receive a lunatic on board, no matter how harmless or how quiet or how well attended; so that the State or the agents of the State have to resort to various petty, minor artifices to get rid of these people.

Q. (By Mr. KENNEDY.) Is that because of regulations in the ports on the other side?—A. No; I think not. The steamship companies simply object to having a lunatic on board; they are afraid of them; they do not know exactly what will happen. Of course, as a matter of fact, any person who is accustomed to handling lunatics is no more afraid of them than they are afraid of a sane person. They are very tractable in the hands of a trained person, and the State always pays second cabin and sends over a very competent person, and sometimes by various arrangements they succeed in getting them on board; sometimes they are refused absolutely.

Q. (By Mr. PHILLIPS.) They are compelled to take them back if they have not been here over a year?—A. Yes; they are compelled to take them back, as I have pointed out.

IMMIGRATION.   209

Q. Then who provides for them?—A. The steamship company.
Q. They provide the nurse?—A. No; I do not know what they do; we simply deliver them. That is a thing which I think might very well interest this commission, because I imagine the suffering and hardships of those people must be very great when they are transferred back under those circumstances. Of course, all the State does is simply to take them down to the Barge Office; it is arranged by the immigration authorities. The number of those cases is very small, because it is a very difficult thing to establish that a person became insane from causes which arose prior to departure for this country. Now, it does seem to me that some provision should be made whereby if the State desires to return lunatics or other dependent persons to a foreign country the steamship company should be obliged to take them, if they are properly accompanied. I do not think any State would object to that.

Then, again, this question of a year. Now, that is altogether too short a time. You take the history of those people. They come over here, even the very poorest of them, perhaps with a little money. They may have the promise of employment, and it may be pretty nearly a year, and often is, before this malady begins to develop. After money is gone and employment ceases and loss of friends, etc., despondency ensues, a case of melancholia results, and the consequence is that a year elapses before the disease becomes apparent. We believe that that time should be extended.

Q. (By Mr. FARQUHAR.) How much extension?—A. I should think it should be extended to 2 years; I think that would be a reasonable time.

Q. Why should you not make your extension to cover citizenship? These people are not citizens of the United States.—A. Not at all.

Q. You mentioned it simply as an arbitrary term?—A. That is all. We should prefer to have that time very much extended. I mention 2 years as the shortest time. Of course you would have to adopt some arbitrary period, I conceive. I mention 2 years as the shortest time.

Q. (By Mr. LITCHMAN.) Would you not also in that connection adopt a regulation that in case they became insane they should be deported anyhow, without reference to this examination that you speak of to show that the primary cause existed at the time of the immigration from the foreign country?—A. I do not think that would be an unreasonable thing at all. I think that question you ask is a very pertinent one, and I say it for this reason: A very elaborate system of records is kept. For instance, when a hospital is notified that a person is ready to be received, a trained nurse goes to get this person. They are not only trained in that particular, as to the care of the insane, but they are trained in regard to the question of issuing the certificates; and they take long blanks and they question the relatives and friends, because the history is a very important thing in relation to the care of a case. We find in almost every instance where the history can be known that heredity plays a very important part. It is wonderful. On the records of the wards of the State of New York I have seen grandparents and grandchildren. I have seen as many as 2 sisters at a time. It is not an uncommon thing to see 2 brothers and sometimes 3 sisters. I do not mean to say that that is very common, but it occurs, and it only points out that heredity plays a very important part in this matter.

Q. Is that heredity manifest more in the female than in the male?—A. I do not think there is any difference. Experience shows in New York, and I imagine almost everywhere, that the sexes are almost equally divided. There is a slight excess as to women, but I attribute that entirely to the fact that women are more tractable. When the question comes up about their commitment, if they go, they do not make any resistance as a rule.

Q. Have you investigated the question as to the age at which insanity manifests itself?—A. Why, as I recollect it, it manifests itself more particularly between 30 and 45.

Q. That applies to both sexes?—A. Applies to both sexes. I desire to say that I am not a physician. I am simply a lawyer, representing the legal end of this commission; but, of course, I acquire some information, some knowledge, which a physician perhaps could only be expected to know. But that is generally the case. In other words, you find very few young people, you find scarcely ever a child in these institutions.

Q. Do you find any special cause for the insanity manifested?—A. That would be difficult.

Q. That would be a physician's answer?—A. That would be a physician's answer. Of course, in round numbers, in generalizing you might say that heredity is the most important cause, if you are pleased to call it a cause. Then comes in the question of intemperance and excesses of various kinds. Take a person who has a heredity of insanity, of a grandparent or a parent, there is insanity in the family. That does not mean that that person would inevitably become insane; but it does mean that there is a predisposing cause, and if that person goes through life in a temperate way and in a fairly prosperous way, and is not given to drugs and narcotics, the chances are that that person will not become insane. But if any of these things happen, loss of employment, or loss of influence or misfortune, he very often will. Now, we know that most of these immigrants that come over here—I think it is safe to say that most of them are from the very poorest class. They have lived on a low diet, the poorest diet, and they have suffered great hardships, and they are very much more prone to become insane than any other class. I think that explains that.

Q. (By Mr. FARQUHAR.) Do you omit in that the continuous marriage of kin?—A. No; I think it would include that, because I think that is very well recognized. But there are numberless causes which enter into this thing.

Q. (By Mr. LITCHMAN.) Of course this question may not be properly put to you as a lawyer, but more properly to a physician, but how near in consanguinity may marriage safely take place?—A. Well, I should draw the line at cousins.

Q. Not nearer than that?—A. Not nearer than that.

Q. First cousins or second cousins? Would you have the marriage of own cousins?—A. Well, I think it has been generally thought even in that case that the results are very bad and that there ought to be a wider margin. That is my general recollection and impression—that you ought to have more margin.

Mr. FARQUHAR. If you will go back, Mr. Brown, to the question of sending these people back under the immigration laws, I think it would help your testimony somewhat to quote into it sections 1 and 11 of the immigration law of 1891. It would make your testimony more complete. Just look over it a minute—the excepted classes and the deportation clause.

The WITNESS. I did not intend, I might say here, to go into this subject so generally. I will read section 11 of the law of 1891, approved March 3, 1891. [Reading.]

"Section 11. That any alien who shall come into the United States in violation of law may be returned, as by law provided, at any time within 1 year thereafter, at the expense of the person or persons, vessel, transportation company, or corporation bringing such alien into the United States; and if that can not be done, then at the expense of the United States; and any alien who becomes a public charge within 1 year after his arrival in the United States from causes existing prior to his landing therein shall be deemed to have come in violation of law and shall be returned as aforesaid."

Now, as I say, I would amend that section by extending the time. I should say that the limit of time should be 2 years. I should also strike out "from causes existing prior to his landing therein," because that is a thing which possibly can not be found out practically. It could only be known by a very elaborate investigation.

Q. (By Mr. FARQUHAR.) Now, to the inhibited classes named in the first section would you add any others so as to make it more of a drag net?—A. The first section of this act says [reading]: "That the following classes of aliens shall be excluded from admission into the United States, in accordance with the existing acts regulating immigration, other than those concerning Chinese laborers: All idiots, insane persons, paupers, or persons likely to become a public charge," etc. It seems to me that is a pretty broad section. Of course, to be more exact, they might put in the word "epileptic," for instance. I would amend that section by providing that if it could be shown or there was reason to believe—and of course the United States would have to determine that question, I take it,—that the person was or had been an idiot—of course, once an idiot always an idiot. That might be said also in regard to epilepsy. It is practically an incurable disease. It could be said in regard to an insane person. I would absolutely exclude them if it could be shown that the person was an idiot or was an epileptic or had been insane for—well, we will say 10 years—because it is known—I have known of instances and you perhaps have known of instances—where a man has been insane for a while and recovered, and the disease has never recurred. I think it would be a hardship, if a person had had no insanity for 10 years, to exclude him, but I certainly would put a time limit on it. A person who has been insane once will be almost certain to be insane again unless the conditions are exceedingly favorable. Therefore I would exclude those persons absolutely; that is, if it is the policy of this Government—and I presume it is—to exclude defective and undesirable persons. I would say they were a very undesirable addition, and I would exclude them without reference to whether they had property or not.

Q. You would include epileptics in the excluded class?—A. I certainly should.

Q. Would you use the expression "weak-minded" to cover other classes?—A. That is a very troublesome question, For instance, we had an immense amount of difficulty under the constitution of New York. The lunacy commission's jurisdiction was cut off from idiots. Now, legally, an idiot is a person without a mind. An idiot may be born as such—that is, without a mind—or it may be a case of arrested development. For instance, a child may live for 6 months or a year and it may have scarlet fever or some other disease and practically the mind be destroyed. Now, there is much dispute between alienists as to whether that person is an idiot, and the State has had considerable difficulty in framing a suitable definition. But I would include imbeciles. There is a distinction between an idiot and an imbecile. That is a word that may be used with perfect safety. An imbecile may be known. If you go to the idiot asylum at Syracuse or the institution at Newark for feeble-minded women, you can see the distinction between idiots and imbeciles and persons of weak minds. I think that such legislation as that could be safely, and should be, provided.

Q. How full are your statistics in New York as to those aliens that have come under that law concerning lunacy?—A. You mean as to what country they come from?

Q. Yes; are they very full and go back for several years?—A. Yes. We could furnish them back to 1890.

Q. Can you furnish also the statistics of deportation?—A. Oh, yes. Of course, in some instances it is very difficult to find out the private history of these people, but every effort is made, and I think that could be furnished.

Q. (By Mr. PHILLIPS.) Have you ever gone into the question of insanity among the uncivilized—for instance, the North American Indians—and whether older nations are not more liable to have their subjects become insane than newer ones?—A. No; not especially. We have some Indians.

Q. You have some insane Indians?—A. Yes; but there are very few Indians in the State of New York, and it would be very hard to generalize, the number of Indians we have is so small; but in regard to the old countries—I suppose you are referring to China and Japan—it would be practically impossible to get any information that would be of any real value in regard to the matter. It is astonishing how much of inaccuracy there is in regard to statistics. Now, I undertook to go into one of our neighboring States—one of the most highly civilized—to find out about the cost of maintaining the insane, and I found it necessary for me to make a special study of their institutions to find out anything about it. The methods were so entirely different.

Q. Have you studied in regard to the proportion of insane to the population in England, Ireland, France, and Germany, as compared with those in the United States?—A. Our figures would show that. Of course, in New York and in other of the Eastern States the whole thing is vitiated by the fact of this stream of immigration; and there is another thing: We put down a person as native. Here is an Italian family that comes into this country and a child is born a few days after arrival; that child has to be put down as a native, and yet, practically it is foreign born to all intents and purposes.

Q. (By Mr. FARQUHAR.) Have you found in your investigations that any organizations or municipalities or smaller subdivisions of states in Europe do deport their insane to this country?—A. It is only on information and belief. We never have gone to the extent of going over there and thoroughly investigating it.

Q. Do you recollect the report made by a special commission in 1891 that went all over Europe and reported that in Switzerland and England, and especially Ireland, they deported many of their insane and imbeciles to this country?—A. I recall that.

Q. Do your later investigations show there is anything of that now at all?—A. We do not know, except there are certain earmarks which indicate that thing is being done. We do not know it to a certainty.

Now, as to the remedy, outside of this matter of legislation: I might say the lunacy commission had a bill introduced in both Houses of Congress a year or two ago on this very subject. We should like to get that legislation if we could, and we would like to get the support of this commission in regard to it.

Q. What was your proposed law to cover?—A. Substantially the lines we have discussed.

Q. Was it an amendment to the immigration law or a separate law itself?—A. It was an amendment. It was prepared and introduced in the Senate of the United States by Senator Fairbanks on May 2, 1898; it was an amendment to the act of 1891.

Q. What is the form of the amendment?—A. Shall I read it?

Q. Yes; if you please.—A. (Reading:)

"Be it enacted by the Senate and House of Representatives of the United States of America in Congress assembled, That section 1 of the act of March 3, 1891, in amendment of the immigration and contract-labor acts, be, and hereby is, amended by adding to the classes of aliens thereby excluded from admission to the United States the following:

"All persons who have been confined in an asylum for the insane, or have been insane before landing in the United States, or who shall within 2 years after arrival in the United States become insane, unless it shall affirmatively appear on special inquiry that such insanity is due to causes arising after such arrival."

Of course that covers substantially what we have been talking about. [Reading:]

"Section 2. That section 1 of the act of March 3, 1893, to facilitate the enforcement of the immigration and contract-labor acts of the United States be, and hereby is, amended by adding to the statements which are now required in the lists or manifests in answer to questions at the top of said lists statements as to each immigrant, 'Whether ever insane or confined in an asylum for the insane.'"

Q. Adding just one question?—A. Just one question. [Reading:]

"And section 2 of said act is hereby amended by adding after the words 'insane persons' in said section the words 'or been insane or confined in an asylum for the insane.'"

That covers substantially the same ground. Section 3 of this proposed bill provides that [reading]:

"SEC. 3. That every alien immigrant landing in the United States furnish to the inspector of immigration a certificate of a surgeon of the immigrant's last place of residence, showing whether such immigrant has ever been insane or confined in an asylum for the insane, or whether either of the parents of such immigrant was ever so confined, accompanied by a certificate of a consul or consular agent of the United States, in the same State, province, or country, that such surgeon is a qualified and practicing surgeon thereof.

"If such certificate is not furnished, the inspector of immigration shall, with the medical examiner or examiners, make careful inquiry as to the matters required to be shown by such certificate, and if it shall appear that a parent of an immigrant who is permitted to land has ever been insane or confined in an asylum for the insane, the fact shall be reported by the inspector of immigration to the superintendent of immigration.

"SEC. 4. That any alien or foreign-born insane person in the United States, whose return to a foreign country from which he migrated is not now provided for by the immigrations acts, but whose return may be voluntarily had upon the request of the family or relatives of such insane person or other persons in interest, shall, upon the demand of the superintendent of immigration or of a State board or officer having charge of the insane in any State, the furnishing of the necessary attendant or attendants and the payment of the regular fare of the persons carried, be transported to the country from which such insane person migrated to the United States by any steamship or transportation company, or owners of vessels doing business between any port of the United States and any foreign port in the line of travel to such foreign country. And any company or owners violating the provisions of this section shall pay a fine not exceeding $500, to be recovered in the proper United States court, and said fine shall also be a lien upon any vessel of said company or owners found within the United States.

"Section 5. That this act shall take effect three months after its passage."

This bill I recall now, upon reading it. I have been out of office nearly 2 years, but when this bill was prepared it was very familiar with it. I certainly think that would be a very wise provision, and I do not see how any great hardship could be worked out. If it could be shown that any person contemplating migration to this country had been insane, it does not seem unreasonable to say that that person should not be admitted here. I think the United States could go a great deal further. I never was down to the Barge Office, and do not know what the system of inspection is, but I do say this: If the exclusion of these people could be predicated upon the determination of the fact, even to be ascertained on this side, that the person was of the defective class—an idiot, insane person, or epileptic—it would be worth to the State of New York alone any sum of money. The State could afford—to say nothing of the United States—to keep at every port one or two trained alienists to examine these people as they come. Now, the manifestations of degeneracy, if you please, are so striking in most instances, that any expert would know it instantly.

Q. (By Mr. CLARKE.) Is it your opinion that a person who has been insane could be detected ordinarily by one or two physicians when that person might pass in line before them?—A. No; I think in many instances that they might escape observation, but I think in a large number of instances it would be perfectly apparent; that the manifestations of physical degeneracy would be so apparent that it would result in their being set aside and detained for a further inquiry. That is what it would result in.

Now, it is very curious. These alienists, trained men with experience, can detect certain manifestations of the eyes and the ears—you might say of the face. I have watched these physicians in a hospital; they would have the person cross his legs and then strike a sharp blow with the hand below the knee. What that sign is I can not recall, but I have seen it done repeatedly, and it is certain to show a certain—you might say a nervous lesion—if I use the expression correctly. Now, I believe that might be done, and I do not believe with the large number that is admitted here it would be any great hardship. It is certainly the case that these people are coming here in vast numbers, and I certainly think that legislation should be obtained somewhat on the line of this bill.

Q. (By Mr. FARQUHAR.) It is also a very expensive class of immigration?—A. Very; the most so. For instance, the inmates of our workhouses and reformatories, and the epileptics and insane are capable of largely supporting themselves. The insane are at work some, but their working is only an incident to their cure and treatment. They are only given that amount of work which will benefit them. You can see the enormous number of employees. I stated it is 1 to 5; my recollection is it is greater than that—between 4 and 5—approximately 1 to 5.

Q. (By Mr. KENNEDY.) I would like to ask one question about something you said in regard to the people of a certain country. You said, I believe, that 25 per cent of the population of New York was foreign born, and 50 per cent of the insane were foreign born, and that about 40 per cent of that 50 per cent were Irish.—A. That is the general impression that I have.

Q. General impression? You think there can be no question about that?—A. I do not think there is much.

Q. Is it not a fact that the Irish are generally a pretty hardy and healthy race, and you do not look for insane people among them?—A. The trouble about that is this: I apprehend that the thrifty Irish largely do not come over here—that is, they have not in the early days and to this time. They naturally come over here to better their condition, and they come over here as a result of severe poverty. In other words, we might apply the same thing here. If emigration were to take place from this country, only those would go whose condition had become desperate by reason of great hardship, poverty, etc. I believe it to be the case that these people live largely on a low diet. I believe it to be the case that the Irish are peculiarly prone in this country to tuberculosis—peculiarly prone to it. I think, without stating it as a fact, that statistics will show that that race is taken off more rapidly by tuberculosis than any other class. As to tuberculosis, I might mention here what Dr. Trudeau told me in the Adirondacks. I had quite a long talk with him, and he said that the germs of tuberculosis existed everywhere. He said, "You are just as liable to get it in Albany as here. Everybody breathes the germs, but if a person is in excellent physical condition, the germs pass right through and do no harm, but if persons are in a low physical condition—if their diet has been poor and they are run down, disease readily attacks them." And I certainly think that is so in regard to the Irish. Their climate is a severe one, as I understand it; it is moist.

Q. You would not find many predisposed to insanity among the police force of New York City?—A. They are a picked class.

Q. Picked from the Irish class, too?—A. Generally from that race, but the hardy ones are picked out.

Q. (By Mr. CLARKE.) Have you studied the subject of intemperance among immigrants as a cause of insanity?—A. No; except that we know in a general way that intemperance plays an enormous part in this thing. I think it is generally true. For instance, take the English, I think intemperance is much greater over there than it is here. That is my impression. I think that is so among the Irish; but I would not speak with any authority on that subject.

Q. (By Mr. PHILLIPS.) You say the larger per cent of the foreign-born insane are from Ireland. If we now had statistics of the number of insane in Ireland and England in proportion to the number of inhabitants, and from some of these other countries, we might find that their per cent may be much larger; and that therefore we are not getting so many shipped in on us as there would seem. Is there any way to do that?—A. I see what your point is. In New York, Pennsylvania, Ohio, Massachusetts—in fact, all the Eastern States—the ratio of insane persons to the whole population is pretty nearly constant. The last time I looked at it it was about 1 to 300. As you go farther west you will find it grows less and less until you get out in the far Western States, where the proportion runs to as high as 1 in 1,500.

Q. The conditions surrounding the American people are different?—A. Of course it is different. The tendency is with these people to go into the Eastern States when they come into the ports of Boston, New York, or Philadelphia. The number has been so great that there is in the Eastern States 1 lunatic to every 300 of population. I do not know what this last census will show, but that was the condition when I looked at it last. When they migrate and go West it is only the hardy ones that go. The same rule does not seem to apply here as applies when they come from the foreign countries over here. Only the hardy ones go to the Western States; they leave the feeble and defective ones behind them here. So you get a proportion out there so small that you might practically say there are no lunatics at all out there. I still think—no matter what the statistics might show in Great Britain, Ireland, Germany, and France—I still think vast numbers of these people could be kept out.

Q. Do you not think there is a greater per cent of these in the old nations, where they are thickly populated, compared with America?—A. I should think so. I do not know how many of you have ever undertaken to look through lunacy reports, or the reports of Great Britain, that we concede to be about the most highly civilized country across the water; and yet I should say, to the most expert man it would be impossible to take their reports and figure out anything satisfactory. That is because they have no centralized administration. Take it in London—it is one of the most confused things. There is the county council, the borough of this and the borough of that, and they do not seem to have any responsible head there anywhere. So it is almost impossible. And then they allow far greater numbers of their affected people to roam at large. In the State of New York it could not ever be known with any certainty how many lunatics there were. We know of instances, all of us, where there are people who should be committed, but out of sentiment and considerations of humanity, mistakenly socalled, no steps are taken to lock them up. I think that condition prevailed much more generally in the old days. I meant to have brought that out more fully. It was true in the State of New York just as long as the insane were a municipal, or county, or town charge, and had to pay the State a certain rate per week, they were unwilling or reluctant to commit the people. They said, "Let this crazy Mary wander around. We will have to pay $4 a week for her board, and we can care for her in the poorhouse better and more cheaply." That ceased to operate the minute that the State took hold of it. They saw that they were relieved of local taxation, and said, "We might as well get this person out of the poorhouse." So the State now has them all. But the benefit has been such that the people recover quicker now, get cured quicker. And, in spite of the fact of all these people being brought in, the number appears to be diminishing.

Q. (By Mr. FARQUHAR.) The whole expense in New York comes out of the general fund?—A. Out of the general fund. The $250,000 which is now received goes into the treasury, but it is a general State tax. I want to emphasize the fact that the State of New York has ceased to treat the question as a matter of charity, but simply as a matter of the highest financial consideration.

Q. (By Mr. PHILLIPS.) Do you admit persons to the insane asylum whose people are able to support them?—A. They have to be admitted.

Q. Do you not charge it up to them?—A. The State has 7 or 8 agents, whose duty it is to investigate all of these cases. For instance, in the city of New York an agent stands there at the receiving pavilion, where the persons are brought for preliminary examinations, and if it is found there is anybody liable for their support, they are charged with it. But to show the poverty-stricken condition of these people it is only necessary to point out that the State receives less than $300,000.

Q. Out of the $5,000,000?—A. Out of the $5,000,000. Of course, this may be said, that the policy of the State of New York to-day is not to pauperize the family. For instance, here is a mechanic whose wife becomes insane. He may be earning $2.50 per day. He has 3 or 4 children to care for and has to hire a housekeeper. To make that man contribute the average cost of support, $3.50 a week, would cut into his wages so as to impoverish the family. So the State says, "We will remit this charge." We had the criminal procedure amended a couple of years ago extending the liability to brothers and sisters and husband and wife.

Q. It stops with the immediate family?—A. No; it takes in everybody in the order of their relationship; brothers and sisters would come first. The liability of parents always continues. The liability of the husband always continues. The liability of the wife always continues, and the other relatives in point of order.

Q. Down to cousins?—A. As a practical question I do not think they ever pay.

Q. They have compelled brothers and sisters?—A. Yes; but if the State chose to exercise its power it could bring these people under court under our amended criminal procedure and have a judicial order made establishing their liability. But in spite of all that to-day they only get about 1 in 16.

When you come to get the statistics of Germany or England—I will not speak of France, because their government is much more centralized—I think they would only show approximately the number of insane in proportion to the population. Under our census, of course, that would be a matter of opinion—the number of insane persons outside of institutions. The census taker would have to form his own judgment as to whether a person was insane. He would have to guess at it. Naturally relatives are very reluctant to make any admission. They have an idea it casts a stigma and interferes, perhaps, with the marriage of sons and daughters. They are very reluctant to admit anything of the kind.

Here is a thing that happens, and it seems to me there ought to be some remedy: We will say here is an immigrant that starts here from way back in some interior port—away from the coast. The steamship company, when it returns him, simply deposits this person right at the point of departure and leaves him. Now, I conceive that there ought to be some provision made for these persons being sent back to the place they came from. It has led to an immense amount of difficulty and hardship.

Q. (By Mr. CLARKE.) Would not that be a matter for foreign determination, or to be provided for by treaty provision?—A. Perhaps. I leave it with you, gentlemen, if they undertake to return them, whether they should not send them back to the point of original starting. Of course, as a matter of fact, I think they purchase tickets right through.

Q. I would like to inquire if your insane in New York are employed in any productive industry?—A. Yes. If you are interested, I could say a word about that. Of course, labor on the part of the insane in New York is only an incident. It is simply with reference to their cure. In other words, no lunatic is permitted to labor except practically on the certificate of the physician. The State seeks to make no profit out of them. It simply employs them for their own benefit. But, as a matter of fact, in the last few years all the shoes used in these institutions and all the clothing is made by them; all the hats and caps—I won't say all, but practically all. Then the State has gone into the business of making its own soap; has a finely equipped factory at Rochester, where all the soap is made. They simply employ one soap maker, and the patients assist him. They make all the soaps used, even the shaving soap. At Utica all the coffee is taken there and ground and distributed, and all the spices.

Q. You mean all the supplies for the various insane hospitals or for other State institutions?—A. Confined absolutely to the hospitals for the insane. Of course the other institutions have sought to get the privilege of buying their own coffee. We used to pay 25 cents a pound, the average wholesaler's price, for coffee up to about 3 years ago. Now this coffee is bought directly by the broker from the importers, taken to Utica and roasted, cleaned, ground, and distributed, and it is simply a matter of bookkeeping. The actual cost is taken into consideration and it is distributed according to that cost, and to-day it is billed to them at 11 cents. It is so fine that the officers drink it on their tables. I venture to say if you would drink a cup of that coffee you would say you never had better coffee in your life.

Q. Are any goods produced for the general market?—A. No; not a dollar.

Q. That is prohibited by law, is it not?—A. I do not know that it is prohibited as far as the hospitals are concerned, but in the penal institutions it is. They carry out that rule to such an extent that a warden is not allowed to be shaved by a convict. But, so far as the hospitals for the insane are concerned, they manufacture their own supplies, and they are distributed from one point to another.

Q. I suppose there are farms connected with some of the hospitals?—A. Yes. Every institution in the State of New York has a farm; and that is a very interesting thing, that question of the running of these farms. We found, when we came to go into the matter from a financial standpoint, that in some instances it would be better to abandon the farms altogether and buy everything than to undertake to operate them. We found that on their balance sheet they showed a profit. Of course they would give themselves credit for the milk and for the hay, and give themselves credit for the corn that the hogs ate and also for the pork; but when we came to analyze their accounts and charge it on a proper basis we found that about half of them paid the State and the State more than got its money back, and that the remainder of them were bankrupt. So that led to a reorganization. None were absolutely abandoned, because it is an advantage to keep a certain number employed. Generally speaking, we found that the old methods of agriculture were not the best. The State in some instances has farms amounting to 1,000 acres. Willard and Binghamton each has a farm of about 1,000 acres. We found that the raising of the ordinary farm products, such as are commonly raised in the East, were financially a failure. So we instructed the people to turn the farms so far as possible into market gardens, and we began to raise immense quantities of asparagus and fine fruits and raspberries, gooseberries, and all sorts of fruits of that kind. In some cases they have 3 or 4 acres in strawberry beds. At one time when I was at Utica the patients were gathering 1,000 quarts of strawberries a day. Those were things the State could not afford to buy. We used to give these people a certain amount of fruit, but we could not, of course, begin to do anything like what we ought to do; and when we turned these farms into fruit gardens and market gardens they began to pay. The State could not compete in raising corn and barley and oats and rye with the West. The things were laid down in our market at a cost much less than the labor; but the moment we began to raise small stuff it began to pay.

Q. You raise these garden products for the general market?—A. No; simply for the insane. We used to purchase it.

Q. Do not sell anything?—A. Do not sell anything. But of course it was much more valuable. You take an acre of asparagus and compare it with an acre of corn as to value, and you will see what a difference it will make. Of course that would diminish the amount of meat we would have to give them. Of course they raised vast numbers of hogs. That is something we gave a great deal of attention to. In the old days the hogs used to die off and the herds were destroyed every year or two. Right here I should say that we employed Professor Atwater, of the Wesleyan University at Middletown, Conn. He has been employed for 2 or 3 years in working out a dietary for the insane, finding out by experiments and observations the class of food used, and seeing what foods could be substituted for the present food and what waste could be prevented. In his preliminary report he showed to us beyond the cavil of a doubt that at least 25 per cent could be saved on the food supplies alone. Now, the State of New York is doing all these things, and yet in spite of all this and an enormous reduction in expenditure the number is piling up at a fearful rate.

Q. (By Mr. KENNEDY.) Do the hospitals of the State of New York use any of the products of the inmates of the penal institutions of the State?—A. Yes; I should have spoken of that.

Q. I want to ask in that connection if that has had any effect on the marked reduction in the cost of maintaining the convicts you spoke of?—A. I should say not. I want to say a word about that. When the constitution prohibited convict labor the legislature, in carrying out the provisions of the constitution, among other things, provided that the convicts should be employed solely in the manufacture of articles for the use of State institutions and for the use of the political divisions of the State. On that basis the penal institutions have been making furniture and clothing and all sorts of things, and to a certain extent they have the convicts employed, but only partially so. The amount of stuff they can turn out is so great, compared with the consumption of the State, that they can keep these people employed only a part of the time.

Q. Through labor-saving machinery?—A. Yes. The act provided that the hospitals should pay the State a price which should be as near as possible the market price. The State has found it can go out in the market and buy a better iron bed, for instance, than the State can make, and for a lower price. You can go down to Wanamaker's store and buy a better iron bedstead than the State can make, and at a less price, and buy at retail. Of course there has been a great deal of dissatisfaction in regard to that.

Q. Does it cost the State a good deal less now?—A. No. There are two forces at work. The prison system wants to be as nearly self-sustaining as possible, and they claim that they only charge for the goods they turn out what the goods could be obtained for on the outside; but that is a question. I notice they charge the State more generally than the same article can be bought for outside, but they are supposed to pay the same.

Q. (By Mr. FARQUHAR.) Does not the State get the whole of the convict's labor that is in the iron bedstead, or pair of shoes, or school bench, or desk? If you had to pay an outside mechanic for doing that and you do not pay your convict for doing it, is it not a saving for the State?—A. Not very much. The difficulty is with convict labor and the way it is applied. It is applied under such peculiar conditions. The overseers or assistant labor is such a heavy element in the cost that large numbers of them are practically without free labor. I do not know that you could say their labor was worth one-fifth what the labor is outside. It is worth very little.

Q. (By Mr. LITCHMAN.) Do you know that of your own investigation?—A. I know it from an investigation I made at the time. We looked into it pretty carefully. When I was a member of the lunacy commission our object was to keep down the cost of running the hospitals; and they would often charge us for bureaus, bedsteads, and various articles prices which we believed to be in excess of the market prices. They took the ground: Here is all this labor that goes in. We call our labor worth so much a day, and it takes us so many days' labor to produce these articles. My answer was: I do not care what it costs you. You can not charge us for those beds more than the beds can be purchased for in the open market. That is your loss. The price charged in the regular market is so much.

Q. The price charged in the regular market is the compensation to the State for the labor of its convicts, is it not?—A. That is all.

Q. Now, if it is charged to your department, it becomes a part of the expense of managing the insane, does it not?—A. Yes; it would.

Q. Then in the last analysis there is a saving to the State, is there not?—A. Possibly there would be.

Q. It is simply a matter of bookkeeping?—A. Possibly it is a matter of bookkeeping, of course, affecting the labor question. Years ago I used to know considerable about it. The difficulty is that all these people come in there untrained and with no trades. There is not one man in a hundred that has a trade, and they only work comparatively few hours a day, and there are certain rules and regulations in there, and they have to have a great many trained employees over them. They tried to have convicts trained, but that did not work.

Q Is it not true that the convict in the prison learns as much of a trade as the workman outside of the prison?—A. Under the present management I should say that he learned a good deal more than he used to. That was one of the evils of the old contract system that I was opposed to when I had something to do with the prisons. For instance, they used to have great stove contracts at Sing Sing. They used to do more than one particular thing, but when they got into the prison they never did anything else; a fellow would stay in prison for 5 years or 10 years, and he would be an expert driller or an expert polisher, but he would not learn a trade. Of course, when they started in with this new scheme they said, Here, we will teach these people trades as distinct from making them mere laborers. Now, that would be an excellent idea; and my own judgment is, of course, that we are branching out into other things, and that it would pay every State in this Union to teach these people in these prisons trades.

Q. Even if it did cost a little more?—A. Even if it costs a little more.

Q. (By Mr. FARQUHAR.) Is not there a proposed amendment now coming before your present legislature to make it hand work, the same as Pennsylvania?—A. I presume likely. Of course the labor people look at it as competition, and they are looking after it. An iron bedstead from the prison standpoint would cost 10 times more if they undertook to do it by hand.

Now, the best-managed penal institution in the world, so far as I know, is the reformatory at Elmira. The very last thing I knew anything about it they had in round numbers 40 different trades, and a fellow actually was taught bricklaying. They had fellows learning the trade of stone masons, blacksmithing, and barbering, and when a man went out into business he had a trade. Run on that basis, the State ultimately will get a return, because when they go out they have some occupation to turn to and be useful; and having an occupation, in my judgment, would diminish crime in this country more than anything else.

Q. Have you noticed statistics of the State of New York in the last two years since this bill came into operation? What is the difference between commitments now in penitentiaries and reformatories and before this went into operation?—A. The diminution of crime in the State of New York has been enormous in the last 3 or 4 years.

Q. (By Mr. CLARKE.) That might be owing to the general prosperity, might it not?—A. Well, good times have undoubtedly affected it some, and of course better police supervision and better education; the people know more than they used to. There are some county jails in the State of New York that practically haven't got an inmate.

Q. (By Mr. FARQUHAR.) Is it not a fact, since the enactment of that law in the State of New York, that there is not any inducement for a justice of the peace, or a judge of a municipal court, or whatever court may have jurisdiction of that small class of crimes, to convict and send anyone to the penitentiaries or to the reformatories?—A. I think so.

Q. It does not pay now to send any?—A. No.

Q. Constantly diminishes?—A. Diminishes. But if I had my say about it, if I was superintendent of prisons of the State of New York to-morrow, I would turn every one of these prisons into institutions for teaching these people trades; I would wipe out every possible source—I think it has been wiped out legally—every source of profit. I would abolish, for instance, the fee system among petty officers; I would abolish the mileage system; I would remove all temptation. I believe it is the cause, not only in New York, but in the States generally, of numbers of instances where these people, for instance, are sent to various penal institutions for what there is in it.

Q. (By Mr. KENNEDY.) We have testimony here to that effect.—A. That is my judgment, and I was connected with prisons indirectly for several years, and in fact I take great interest in prison associations in New York to-day. My views, however, have entirely changed in regard to that from what they were 10 or 12 years ago. I was in favor of the contract system, and at the time they tried to abolish it I was very much opposed to its abolition, but I believe it was a mistake.

Q. (By Mr. FARQUHAR.) The only argument in its favor was revenue?—A. That is all.

Q. And it admitted of division of revenue among politicians?—A. No doubt about that at all.

I was just going to say in conclusion—I won't say that humanity and charity, that side of human nature, should be eliminated, but I do think that the sooner that our Government and our States come to recognize this whole question as one of sound financial policy, the sooner they will eliminate the difficulties with which they are surrounded; just as in the State of New York in regard to its care of the insane, which was regarded as a charity, and the question was to do or not to do, and we had a constantly increasing burden. The minute the State came to look at it as a business proposition, and endeavored to see what was best to be done, it began to succeed.

Q. (By Mr. LITCHMAN.) Do you think the State management of the insane has eliminated to any degree the brutal treatment of inmates of institutions?—A. Practically it is impossible. I do not believe I have seen in a paper in the State of New York—I can not recall a single instance where a matter of that kind has been mentioned. It used to be a common thing, and the reason why it has been discontinued is that the State employs more people; their tenure is secure. In the State of New York both parties by common consent leave the hospital for the insane outside of the domain of politics. There is not a political party in the State that pretends to interfere with the appointments of attendants or nurses. The whole thing is under the civil-service regulations, but outside of that there is no sentiment in favor of it.

Q. What State inspection is there?—A. None whatever. The lunacy commission is held simply and solely responsible, and they are subject to removal by the governor on charges.

Q. Do you know how often inspections are made by that commission?—A. They are required to visit each institution at least twice a year. As a matter of fact, they are visited more often; every inmate has an opportunity of being heard, etc.

Q. (By Mr. CLARKE.) Coming back to this question of the financial aspect in the management of the insane, have you any statistics showing the diminution of the cost?—A. Yes; we can give you the statistics as to the cost of caring for the insane in the State hospitals. When you come to the State of New York, for instance, in the counties of New York and Kings, which include Greater New York, nobody on earth knows what it formerly cost to care for their insane, because their figures were constantly juggled. The cost of caring for the insane in the poorhouses were inextricably mixed. For instance, the care of the insane and the care of the paupers were together; but when we came to aggregate the whole thing we found that the cost became diminished; it became diminished so far as the State institutions were concerned. It went down from $222 to $165 last year.

Q. Is it not possible to get statistics from some of the cities, or counties, or towns, which will show that this State assumption of the cost of maintaining the insane has been economical to them in the respect that it has diminished their local charges?—A. That brings up the great question of taxation. It is a curious thing. Now, for instance, we can only approximate what it cost the city of New York and the county of Kings to care for their insane. We know what the figures were, but we know that the figures are very much less; that is, they juggled with them. Some years they included the buildings, and in other years they struck them out. In other words, the city government of New York would make a favorable showing. They would juggle with those figures and we never could arrive at a satisfactory conclusion. Neither could we in the counties. Now, for instance, in some counties, in round numbers, it cost $2 a week to care for their insane. We found when we went to investigate it that it cost a great deal more to care for the insane than for the paupers, but to show what that difference was they kept no separate books; it was impossible to get at it.

Q. (By Mr. LITCHMAN.) Do you have under your control the epileptic colonies?—A. No; that is under the control of the State board of charities. That is a new experiment on the part of the State. They are gathering up those people very rapidly, but there is a class that is perfectly hopeless, and the only thing you can do for them is to care for them properly. That is a disease that is practically incurable, as I understand it.

Q. You made a statement that the convict was worth about one-fifth as much as outside labor. That you do not know from any investigation of your own?—A. Not at all. That is a mere guess.

Q. I asked that because of an investigation by the legislature of Massachusetts showing under the conditions then prevailing that the convict in the prison was worth about two-thirds as much as outside labor.—A. I should doubt that exceedingly.

Q. It was proved before that commission, of which I was a member.—A. Of course it would depend on what work they do; they might be employed in certain lines of work where they would be worth that much.

Q. But on the long-term men they were worth exactly as much, hour for hour, but of course their pay was very much less?—A. Here is a long-term man, for instance; he becomes expert in a certain trade. Now, you can say he produces as much under good conditions as the man outside, but then you have got to take into consideration what it costs to maintain that man—what it costs to operate that prison.

Q. That is not the point. The point I asked you was as to his comparative productive power compared with the outside mechanic.—A. For instance, here is a fellow who gets in for what we call a 2-year term—that means 1 year and 8 months; here is a fellow that gets in for 5 years—that means 3 years and 7 months; here is a man that gets in for 10 years—that means 6 years and 6 months. Now, there are lots of those convicts who do not really get into the harness before their term is out. Take the average hours of labor of those people, and the average production, and that is the only way you can get at it. When a man becomes expert in one thing he is suddenly removed, sent out, and a new man takes his place. Take the average hours with the average number of men right through and undertake to compare their productive labor with the things they ordinarily work at, I do not believe that my one-fifth would be so much out of the way.

Q. Our prisons were conducted in Massachusetts at that time under the contract system, under which the labor was contracted out to private employers, who used exactly the same machinery in the prison as outside the prison, and the testimony before that commission was to the effect that the convict was worth about two-thirds as much as the outside man.—A. Well, I should doubt it.

Q. We got it from the manufacturers themselves, who were in a position to know.

(Testimony closed.)

NEW YORK, *May 21, 1901.*

TESTIMONY OF MR. THEODOR RITTER,

Manager of the Austro-Hungarian Home, of New York.

The special subcommission being in session at the Fifth Avenue Hotel, New York, Mr. Clarke presiding, Mr. Theodor Ritter was introduced as a witness at 12.14 p. m., and, being first duly sworn, testified as follows:

Q. (By Mr. CLARKE.) Please give your name and post-office address.—A. Theodor Ritter; 14 Greenwich street, New York.

Q. What is your occupation or official position?—A. I am the manager of the Austro-Hungarian Home and Free Employment Bureau.

Q. Will you please describe that home, how it was instituted, and by whom it is supported?—A. This home was founded for the purpose of giving aid to the immigrants coming from Austria-Hungary, and it originated in the fact that many of these men and women were put in places on the East Side of New York, in the lower part of the city, where they had no good places to stay and no help in their troubles. Therefore this house was founded. The Austro-Hungarian Government sends over to this country every year a certain sum for the support of the house, and the money to pay the rest of the cost is raised by the Austrian Society of New York and the Hungarian Relief Society. All we have to do in said house is to take in charge the people coming from the other side—from Austria-Hungary—and bring them to the home and find out what they want to do. Most of them want to get work in this country, while many come on invitation of their relatives. Of course, when they have the address of relatives where they want to go, our task is fulfilled as soon as they go there. The others we put into positions as laborers or mechanics or office workers or servant girls, and that is the part of our work, I suppose, that interests this commission.

In securing employment we have to make discriminations between men and women. The laborers, of course, we try to put into work in factories or on farms, and a great part of them with hotels and similar places, according to the ability of the men. Certainly the hardest thing is the language, because nobody coming from the other side speaks the language of this country; therefore it is absolutely necessary to put even intelligent men to work as laborers, the only positions we may be able to secure for some of these men being such as porters in hotels or restaurants or that kind of position.

As to laborers, farmers, and factory hands, we try to come into contact with factories, and in the last few weeks we sent out circulars. Of course, all that goes very slow. It is not possible to do it all at once. We tried every way, and finally we came to these circulars which we sent to the factories known to us and asked them to answer certain questions—what kind of laborers they want, whether mechanics or whatsoever, and how they pay their wages; whether there are houses there, and so on. We have got quite a number of answers to that circular, and it seems it will be quite possible to dispose of these laborers coming from the other side in some of these factories. We will try our best to get families who will settle down in these places where there are big factories, such as sugar factories, etc.

Q. (By Mr. KENNEDY.) You say, "We will try our best to get families to come over." It is your object to induce families to come?—A. No. I did not mean that I will induce families to come over, but I will try my best to get the families coming over to settle down in places like these sugar factories, for example. That is the meaning of the circulars, and I thought I could put that in because I thought in many places outside of the cities there are factories that need laborers, and the only way I could give them steady laborers is to make the families settle down there, and then they would do good work. Most of the single men settle down near New York or in some of those other cities not very far from New York. Those cities are as stuffed with laborers as can be; whereas farther away from New York there are many places where they could use laborers, but have none. Many times I hesitate to send them to these places, because I do not know them, and there are many cases where men are lured to these places on the promise of good work and good earnings, and when they get there it turns out that the agents of those places would promise anything without having authority from the factories. That is the reason why we are very careful not to send them out until I can find through other people which factories are reliable in doing what they promise.

Q. (By Mr. FARQUHAR.) How far West does your work extend?—A. The farthest which I have in mind now is Michigan and Nebraska, with which States we have correspondence. We have many correspondents in Ohio and Pennsylvania.

Q. Have you any in Kansas?—A. Not yet.

Q. Any in Indian Territory?—A. None.

Q. Any from coal miners in the West?—A. Oh, yes; I have had from coal miners in Virginia and West Virginia—the Pocahontas fields. I do not now remember all the places. A very important factor in these factories is the employment of able foremen. Some of them make it nearly impossible for green men to go to work. In many of these places everything is in the hands of the factory. The justice of the peace, the policemen, and everything belongs to the factory, and the laborer who is unable to speak the language of the country is not able to make himself understood, but is at a great disadvantage, just as much on account of the labor as on account of the payment and anything that he wishes, and that is the reason I never send any men to the coal mines any more.

Q. Do you or others in this city keep a registry of immigrants from Austria-Hungary?—A. Oh, yes.

Q. Is it taken from the ship's manifest or records?—A. No. I have a few of these records here, and if they interest you I will submit them for your inspection. Every person who comes to our house is asked his name, the place he comes from, the language he speaks, how much money he brings to this country, the ship by which he arrived, the destination to which he desires to go, his occupation, and in the case of girls, the address of relatives. Then, when sent out of the house the first time, it may be to a position as laborer, servant girl, or whatever it may be—the facts are all entered on the sheet, and we keep a record of all persons so that we can trace them.

Q. How are they directed from Ellis Island to your headquarters, and where is your headquarters?—A. Our agent has a permit to go to Ellis Island and take out our countrymen. In some cases he has to bring them before the board, and it is investigated as to whether they will be delivered into our care. If they are discharged in our care, he brings them to the house, and from that moment I take care of them and try to put them into a position, or send them to their relatives, or do whatever it is necessary to do.

Q. What proportion of the Austro-Hungarian immigration do you handle through your office?—A. I think about half. I am not prepared to answer that question exactly.

Q. What is the character of the employment of the Austro-Hungarian immigrants to this country?—A. The men generally are laborers—farmers or laborers. Some are mechanics, blacksmiths, and machinists.

Q. Are there many miners?—A. Very few.

Q. (By Mr. TOMPKINS.) Have many of the people gone to the Southern States?—No. We handle very few.

Q. Farmers or cotton mill operators?—A. Very few of them; very few.

Q. (By Mr. CLARKE.) Have you any complaint to make of any of the methods of the steamship companies?—A. No; I have no complaint to make about steamship companies.

Q. Are there any agents employed in Austria-Hungary by any corporations in this country to induce persons to come here?—A. That is a question which I will answer with yes and no. I know there are such agents, but I know that none of the people are engaged by any person who has a good interest in them. They are only engaged by persons who want to do business with them. For example, nearly all these Hungarians or Slovaks get their tickets from these agents who induce them to come over, but that is all private and officially unknown.

Q. Do you know who these agents represent in this country?—A. No; I do not. I guess they represent their own interests. I do not think they are engaged by anybody. I think they sell the tickets and work in their own interests, and I do not think they are engaged by anybody in this country.

Q. You think they receive a commission on the sales of tickets?—A. Certainly. That is their business.

Q. And therefore they are in a sense in the employment of the steamship companies?—A. I can not answer that question. I never looked into that side of the subject.

Q. Is it desired by the Austro-Hungarian Government that there shall be emigration to this country?—A. No; it is not.

Q. Do they prefer to keep their people at home?—A. Yes.

Q. But since they will come, they deem it necessary to take some measures to help them when here?—A. Yes.

Q. Are you paid by the Government?—A. No; I am paid by the two combined societies here.

Q. And your Government contributes to those societies?—A. Yes.

Q. (By Mr. KENNEDY.) I should like to ask whether the Government or provinces or municipalities have assisted undesirable people to come to this country; such as, for instance, criminals, paupers, or diseased people?—A. No; on the contrary, it is very difficult to come over to this country from our old country. They do not encourage it at all; on the contrary.

Q. Do you find any such people—criminals, paupers, or cripples—coming from your country?—A. I do not think it is possible for them to land, because if they are criminals they are caught at the ship before they can land; and if they are paupers or unable to work for their living they are not allowed to land on Ellis Island. Then, we are held responsible in case a pauper or cripple should be taken out by mistake. We would, of course, not be allowed to take out anyone who would become a public charge. To prevent such is what the house is for. There may be a man well able to work, but without any means; we take care of him and get work for him and start him out, and then all is right. We have many cases like that where all the men got work.

Q. (By Mr. LITCHMAN.) Do you in those cases give bond to the Ellis Island authorities that the immigrant shall not become a public charge?—A. We do not give bond in writing or in cash, but we give bond in so far that the authorities hold us responsible, and in case there should be a pauper delivered to us—there have been none so far as I know since we have had the right to go to Ellis Island—but if there should be a case like that, we would be held responsible. That is the purpose of these societies—to take care of our people and see that they get work and do not become public charges.

Q. The law provides that a person may not land where there is any fear that he may become a public charge unless a bond be given in a certain sum. I did not know whether you had given such bond at any time. You say you have not, however?—A. I could not tell you anything about that. I know we have not given any bond from the management of the house, but it may be there is an arrangement between the consulate and the Government, because the consulate has the supervision of the house.

Q. When you put out the help, either men or women, are the wages paid to the help or to your society?—A. The wages are paid to the help unless there be some misunderstanding. I hold the parties responsible to pay in our office, if their hired help complains.

Q. If any of the help put out by you has a dispute with the person who employs him, do you assist the help, as far as you are able, in securing justice?—A. Yes.

Q. What is your method?—A. If there is any trouble like that I write a letter first to this party, and a very polite letter, too. Then, if I do not get a suitable answer, I write a letter, "If you do not pay the wages in 24 hours I will sue you." Then I turn the matter over to our lawyers.

Q. Have you found that your system of distributing the immigrants in different parts of the country has on the whole worked well for your people?—A. Yes.

Q. And they seem to have confidence in your establishment and report the fact to their friends in the old country who are coming over here?—A. Yes. Of course, at first it was quite different, because these people did not understand what we were and how we worked, and there were many cases where they tried to get as far away from the house as possible. After some time (it is now the third year the house has existed) they came to a right understanding of our ways, and we have many cases where people who have gone away from the house have come back and asked us to forgive their mistrusting and help them. So it shows the society is a good one and is the right thing for the interest of these people.

Q. How far are you able to protect the women from falling into habits of vice?—A. Well, that depends. If these women are discharged to our house and we put them into positions, we have the right to look after them for a full year, because they are supposed to be landed conditionally, and this condition prevails for a year's time. During the year I have the right to take a woman away from any position or put her in any position I want; but after this time it is impossible. The percentage going astray now is practically nothing in comparison with what it was formerly. One reason why this house was founded is the fact that these women were getting into bad habits and even sometimes into disorderly houses.

Q. You spoke of conditions. Do you refer to the condition that the immigrant shall not become a public charge within a year?—A. Yes; that keeps us responsible.

Q. You have to keep track of the immigrant in order to protect yourselves?—A. Yes.

Q. (By Mr. FARQUHAR.) What experience have you had with these so-called intelligence offices here that propose to provide employment for immigrants?—A. That is a very hard question to answer in a few words, because it is with intelligence offices just as it is with people. Some may be very good and some not. But there are many employment offices that do not act in the interest of the people who go to them. Of course, you could not expect much different, because these people are there to do business, and certainly our idea is quite different from the employment offices' idea. We want to raise these people intelligently as well as morally, but they are there to do business; and that is quite a different thing. There are many houses on the east side of New York City, in the lower part, where the Slovaks or Hungarians live, and without having a regular intelligence office and even without having a boarding house, they keep their "friends" with them. These people are "friends" that come from the same part of the country, and they keep them there for a few days and then put them into a position with some family and give them all the good advice they can: "You must not work too hard;" "you must go out every day;" "you must not work on Sunday," and "you must get so much wages every month." This is the first influence upon these people. You know these immigrants have to be considered from quite a different standpoint than an American. They must be treated in a different way. You could not talk to a Slovak the same way you could to an American girl; and that is the reason why these boarding houses on the east side should be checked.

Q. You say that the Austro-Hungarian Government does not desire to have these people emigrate to this country. Feeling that way, I would like to ask you how your people would view further restrictive legislation on the immigration question by this country?—A. You mean to prevent them from landing in this country?

Q. Yes. That question has been discussed by many people; not to prevent them altogether, but to further restrict the volume of immigration from your country.—A. Yes; but I do not see in what way it should be done. Do you mean the laws enforced more strictly than now to prevent paupers and such people from landing?

Q. For instance, would your people object to an educational test—that is, reading, for instance, a selection from the Constitution of the United States or any other instrument in their own language?—A. I do not see how they could object. If the law is here it is not their place to object, but to obey.

Q. I mean what would be the sentiment of your people in this country in regard to such legislation as that? Would they feel it was directed against them as a people or a race?—A. I guess they would feel like it was a restriction upon their landing, and so it would be.
Q. Are you a German or a Hungarian?—A. I am a German; from Vienna.
Q. How long have you been in this country?—A. Ten years.
Q. You have perhaps been aware of efforts to pass immigration bills with educational tests in them?—A. Yes.
Q. You are also aware of the opposition in German societies, for instance, against this measure?—A. Yes.
Q. I would like to ask you if you are aware whether that opposition is a spontaneous opposition on the part of the German people, or whether it is a prompted opposition on the part of certain individuals in the interests of the steamship companies?—A. I think that it may have been more an opposition by some individual interests than for any other reasons, because you know these Hungarian Slovaks are the very best laborers—no doubt about it. They are good laborers, but there are many educated among them, and there are many that are not able to read and write, although, of course, not so many of them as there used to be.
Testimony closed.

TESTIMONY OF MR. JOHN J. BEALIN,

Superintendent Free Employment Bureau, New York.

The subcommission met pursuant to recess at 2.11 p. m., Mr. Clarke presiding. At that time Mr. John J. Bealin was introduced as a witness, and, being first duly sworn, testified as follows:

Q. (By Mr. CLARKE.) Please give your name and post-office address and official position.—A. John J. Bealin; 107 East Thirty-first street, New York City. I am an employee of the department of labor of the State of New York, officially designated as the superintendent of the free employment bureau. My duties are to superintend the bureau, to see that the law is carried out, to keep such books and records as the commissioner may direct, to collect statistics, and to work generally under his instructions.

Q. What class of people do you look after?—A. The law directs us to register all applicants for labor—that is, to register every one that will come to us seeking employment, and to keep a register of all people who wish to employ them. In carrying out the work of the bureau we have a form which is filled by all applicants who desire to place their labor on the market through the bureau. This blank, when filled out, will give the name of the applicants, their address, their occupation, their nativity, the name of the last employer, the character of their employment, the duration of their employment, the cause for being unemployed, and whether they would be willing to go to the country if employment was found there for them. When this blank is filled out a reference blank is sent to the last employer, asking for a verification of the statement made by the party seeking employment. This inquiry asks as to the character and ability of the party, the duration of employment, somewhat as to their temper, asking whether they were willing and obliging. We have found some few people who give us fictitious addresses as to the last employer, and we have found very few people whose last employer did not speak of them as being competent, sober, honest, willing, and obliging.

The bureau has now been in operation since July 20, 1896. We have worked under and we have lived up to the law. We have met with the commendation of such people, for instance, as Bishop Potter, the Society of St. Vincent de Paul, the Charity Organization Society, and other kindred bodies.

We will average a little over 5,000 applicants for labor in the course of a year—say 5,500. Year before last we found employment for 45.4 per cent of the applicants; last year for 51.7 per cent.

Some things we have learned that I wish to state. For instance, the average woman who earns her living as a domestic is commercially dead after she is 45 years of age. There is no place for her if she has not saved sufficient money to keep herself, unless she goes to the almshouse. There is no place for a man that is 50 years of age if he is a common laborer, if he shows his age. There is no place for him unless he has saved sufficient from his former earnings or is kept by his children if he is married and has such. Except in rare instances he has to face toward the workhouse.

The labor market in New York is very singularly situated. Skilled labor is highly organized here, and the organized workers, all of them, in some form or other, maintain employment agencies of their own. Some of them, for instance the painters and stationary engineers, have places where men go when they are out of employment—places where they are taken care of. All the men in organized labor who are unemployed report to their organization if they are out of employment, and it is the business of the much condemned so-called walking delegate to find employment for these people.

I would say that the free employment agency was called into existence at the solicitation of the Working Woman's Association of New York City, which at that time had as its president Miss Alice Woodbridge. It was called into existence to benefit working women, and its mission has been principally along that line. As I have stated, organized labor takes care of its members through its employment agencies. The average everyday laborer, if he does not belong to the ranks of so-called organized labor, and he wants to find employment in the city of New York digging a sewer, if you will, on that subway that they are building that is mortgaged to the dominant political party of this city, has got to go to his district leader and he has to be verified by his election district leader; and then when they know he is of the faithful he will get work for a certain period of time, only to be displaced later on because of the swarms of people going to the headquarters of the organization looking for employment.

In the fall of 1896 the commissioner of labor, who was at that time Mr. John T. McDonough, our present secretary of state, at the solicitation of the Working Woman's Association, held an investigation as to the methods of employment agencies in this city. I would respectfully ask permission to file later on the testimony taken there under oath. A summary of it is of this character: That women were treated very coarsely and brutally in some of the employment agencies; that, contrary to law, the fees paid by them were kept and not returned when work was not found for them. Since then it has been constantly reported to our office that the same condition of things prevails, and I say that to the best of my knowledge and judgment and belief in very many instances the law is not lived up to by many employment agencies in this city. No later than last week a woman called my attention to an evasion of the act. I asked her why she did not go and get her money. She said: "It is too much trouble. I would have to do this, that, and the other." No later than last week people who had put advertisements in the World were answered by requests to call at a certain institution; and finding out the character of the institution they reported the matter to the office—Broadway, Sixth avenue, and Thirty-sixth street. The people at the World office called my attention to that. Now, I may be asked, why the commissioner of the bureau of labor statistics, when he held this investigation, did not report the matter to the mayor. He reported it just where the law instructed him to report it—to the legislature of the State of New York. Reports that come to me of the management of some of the employment agencies I bring to the attention of the commissioner. It is my duty. I am not the prosecuting officer of this county.

We have investigated this employment agency business not only in New York but in other cities of the State. I was sent by the commissioner to the city of Buffalo some 2 years ago. I sat on the bench with Judge King, and I asked him his opinion as to the condition of things in that town. He said it was infamous. He said: "Just wait a while and we will see." That morning there were 3 cases. The judge looked at the man that was running the agency. He was a young man. His parents were known to the judge, and Judge King said: "It makes an honest man's eyes sore to look at you." And so it would. This condition of things brought on a terrible strike in the city of Buffalo a little over a year ago. It was known as the freight handlers' strike. Thousands of men were out on strike, simply because in order to get employment they had to go to a certain employment agency that was kept by a liquor dealer. He was master of the situation, and they had to drink a certain amount of beer. For the man that drank the most beer and spent the most money at the bar, he got employment as a grain shoveler. That thing went on for a long time until it was finally settled by Bishop Quigley. Since then the men are free to find employment through any channel they like. They do not have to go to the employment agency; they can go direct to find employment.

In the city of Rochester the same condition of things prevails. Testimony of that character was filed in the records of the department of labor, including a letter from the assistant chief of police.

And so we find all over the State the same condition, and in order to remedy that wrong there was drafted an act placing all the employment agencies in the State under State control. This act was drawn in obedience to the recommendation to the State legislature of Governor Roosevelt. State control was asked because it was not a local complaint. It was all over the State, and it was considered wise to have a State law enforced by a State department, where the discipline would be uniform.

This bill, a copy of which I hold in my hand, was drafted and presented in the senate by Senator John Ford and by Mr. Kelsey in the assembly. After a conference

IMMIGRATION. 225

it was sent back to New York City, with the instruction that the people interested here should have a hearing—that is, that the employment agencies should be heard. There was a conference held at the office of the bureau of labor statistics, at which conference were three representatives of the employment agencies. There was a representative of the Society of St. Vincent de Paul; the University Settlements had a representative. As the result of the conference this bill was submitted to the legislature. It was passed by the assembly, twice amended in the senate, and at the end of the session it remained in charge of the senate committee on cities, not being reported to the body for final action. I will read this bill with your permission and explain it in order that there may be no misunderstanding of the terms.

(Witness read as follows:)

AN ACT to regulate the keeping of employment agencies in cities of the first and second class where fees are charged for procuring employment or situations.

The people of the State of New York, represented in senate and assembly, do enact as follows:

SECTION 1. The term person when used in this act means and includes persons, company, society, association, or corporation; and the term employment agency means and includes the business of keeping an intelligence office, employment bureau, or other agency for procuring work or employment for persons seeking employment, or the acting as agent for procuring such work or employment where a fee or other valuable thing is exacted, charged, or received for registration or for procuring or assisting to procure employment, work, or a situation of any kind, or for procuring or providing help for any person, excepting procuring employment as school teachers exclusively.

SEC. 2. No person shall open, keep, or carry on any such employment agency in the cities of the first and second class, unless every such person shall procure a license therefor from the State comptroller, authorizing the licensee to open, keep, or carry on such agency at a designated place, which license shall be issued by the comptroller upon the payment to him of a fee of fifty dollars for the first year and twenty-five dollars for each succeeding year for each and every such employment agency in cities of the first class, and a fee of twenty-five dollars for the first year and twelve and one-half dollars for each succeeding year for each and every such agency in cities of the second class. Every license shall contain a designation of the city, street, and number of the house in which the person licensed shall carry on the said employment agency, and the number and date of such license. No saloon keeper shall conduct an employment agency, or act as agent for procuring work or employment in any building where liquor is sold or offered for sale.

SEC. 3. The State comptroller shall require such person to file with his application for a license a bond in due form to the people of the State of New York in the penal sum of two thousand dollars in cities of the first class, and one thousand dollars in cities of the second class, with one or more sureties to be approved by the comptroller and conditioned that the obligor will not violate any of the duties, terms, conditions, provisions, or requirements of this act. The comptroller is authorized to cause an action, or actions, to be brought on said bond in the name of the people of the State of New York for any violation of any of its conditions; and he may also revoke any license whenever, in his judgment, the person licensed shall violate any of the provisions of this act.

SEC. 4. It shall be the duty of every person so licensed to keep a register in which shall be entered, in the English language, the name and address of every applicant for employment, and the name and address of his or her last employer, and the name and address of the person or persons who shall employ such applicant. Such licensed person shall also enter in a register the name and address of every person who shall make application for help or servants, and the name and nature of the employment for which such help shall be wanted. Such registers shall at all reasonable hours be open to the inspection and examination of the commissioner of labor or his agents.

SEC. 5. It shall be the duty of every such licensed person to give to each and every applicant for employment or work, from whom a fee or other valuable thing shall be received for procuring such employment, a receipt in which shall be stated the name of the applicant, the amount of the fee or other valuable thing, the date, the name or nature of the employment or situation to be procured, and on a separate receipt the name and address of the person or persons to whom the applicant shall be referred or sent for employment or work. In case the said applicant, shall not obtain or accept a situation or employment through or by the procurement or agency of such licensed person within one month after registration as aforesaid, then said licensed person shall forthwith repay and return to such applicant, upon demand being made therefor, the full amount of the fee or other valuable thing paid or delivered by said applicant to said licensed person. Every receipt aforesaid shall have printed on the back thereof, in the English language, a copy of this section, and every such licensed person shall cause a plain and legible printed copy of this act to be posted in a conspicuous place in such agency or place of business. No such licensed person shall print, paint, publish, or display on any sign, window, or in any publication, the name or a similar name to that of the State of New York free employment bureau.

Sec. 6. It shall be the duty of every licensed person to investigate at least two of the references of every applicant registered for employment. No such licensed person shall knowingly send or cause to be sent any female help or servants to any place of bad repute, house of ill fame, or assignation house, or to any house or place of amusement kept for immoral purposes. No such licensed person shall publish or cause to be published any false or fraudulent notice or advertisement, or give any false information, or make any false promise concerning or relating to work or employment to anyone who shall register for employment; and no such licensed person shall make any false entries in such register, or violate any of the provisions of this act.

Sec. 7. It shall be the duty of the commissioner of labor to look after the enforcement of this act. If he shall have reason to believe that any of its provisions are disregarded or violated, he shall report to the district attorney of the county wherein such alleged violations shall take place, the facts relating to the violating thereof, whereupon it shall be the duty of such district attorney to begin and carry on a proper criminal prosecution for such violation. Any person convicted of a violation of this act or any part thereof shall be guilty of a misdemeanor. One-half of the fines imposed and of penalties recovered under this act shall be paid to the commissioner of labor, who shall use and expend the same in payment of the expenses of investigating violations of this act, and in securing information regarding the same.

Sec. 8. All acts or parts of acts heretofore passed relating to employment agencies in cities of the first or second class and all acts or parts of acts inconsistent with this act are hereby repealed, except the provisions of chapter four hundred and fifteen of the laws of eighteen hundred and ninety-seven, known as the labor law.

Sec. 9. This act shall take effect July first, in the year nineteen hundred and one.

Section 4 would prevent fraud. This section would prevent bringing people to employment agencies to get their fee for registering when there was no possible chance of getting them employment. It is only by putting out decoys, by making false statements, that this thing can be carried on to the limit it has been carried on in the city of New York; but in this bill they are prohibited from putting out a sign or an advertisement that they have employment when they have not. By it they are required to keep a register—a tabulated list—of everyone who sought employment or sought to employ people; the character of the work that they could give. Then it would be easy, when the commissioners' authorized agents would go in, to see whether there was deception or not. Objection is raised to this fourth section, saying that it violates the privacy of a man's business; that it invades his private books, papers, etc. I would call attention to the fact that the United States Government insists upon every wholesaler and rectifier of liquor keeping a special book. Now we will take, for instance, a wholesaler or rectifier. He has withdrawn from the bonded warehouse the goods placed there on bond, and before he can withdraw any of the spirits from bond he has to pay into the United States Treasury, through the collector of internal revenue in that district, every cent that is due the Government against those spirits. Naturally one would think that now the spirits is his property. The law says when those goods have come on his premises they must be designated by the peculiar stamp—a warehouse stamp—stating the serial letter and number, the number of wine and proof gallons that are in the package, by the revenue stamp—the tax-paid stamp—which declares the number of wine and proof gallons that are in the package when withdrawn from bond, and which satisfies everyone, so far as can be seen, that there is nothing due the Government. But still the Government says that it has a right, and it exercises that right, and makes that man keep the register and show that package of whisky, or spirits, as it is denominated, from the point of its production to the point of its consumption; and likewise, when a man buys tobacco, the name of the manufacturer of cigars and cigarettes has to be entered into the form. He has to tell who he buys it from, how much he uses during the month, what it is used for, in what way the cigars were packed—for instance, 25 in a box or a box of 50; the number of samples used, the number of samples on hand. And such records are open at all times for inspection by the revenue officers, and the revenue officer has promised, under oath, to inspect every such place at least once a month. That is, in my judgment and the judgment of men—many men—sufficient warrant for section 4.

The next section states just how the business shall be conducted; that when a man or a woman comes in and makes application for work, and as soon as he or she is registered he has to get a card. Applicants have to get a receipt acknowledging they have been there; that the money has been paid, and what paid for, and at the end of the month, on demand—not otherwise—if there is not work procured, that fee is returned. If there is work procured, the fee belongs to the parties operating the employment agency. In addition to that, they get the usual percentage that they demand, the matter of sometimes 10 per cent, for instance, on the first month's salary. If this could have passed and become a law the commissioner would have been instructed to look for the enforcement of the act, to see that it was carried out in all its details. It did not pass. Why I do not know.

Q. (By Mr. FARQUHAR.) In the absence of a law what jurisdiction has the State bureau now?—A. None whatsoever.

Q. Is there exercise of police power over these employment agencies?—A. The mayor's marshal has some authority. There is a law governing employment agencies in the city of Buffalo at present. There is one covering Brooklyn and one in New York. The mayor's marshal issues the license, but the mayor's marshal has not power to go in and see that they keep this register. The mayor's marshal has not power to see that the register corresponds with the advertisements; but if this act became a law, then the commissioner would have the power to appoint officials who would go in there and see that that law is lived up to.

Q. Was this law submitted to the attorney-general of the State as to its constitutionality?—A. It was not.

Q. You have no means of knowing what the objections of the committee were as to its final passage?—A. Want of time, more than anything else. It was late in the session; but the constitutionality of the bill is vouched for by the present secretary of state, by John Ford, especially the portion of it prohibiting the putting out of signs and decoys when there was not employment. That is taken from the Illinois law; it is taken from various laws enacted in various States, and it was agreed upon. It met the emergency—came up to the necessities of the hour.

Q. Have you anything to say about the efficiency of the carrying out of the present law in the city of New York, your local laws?—A. The trouble is simply this, that the people who are victimized, and I am satisfied that there are thousands and thousands of them in the city of New York, get sick and tired of it. As they have said to me, "What's the use?" Last year or the year before there was quite a sensation here. A newspaper in the city had one of the proprietors of one of the agencies on Sixth avenue arrested and brought into court, and there were two, three, or four more arrests. The licenses were revoked in one case, and another one left the city. The other people, operating an agency on Sixth avenue, are there still; they are doing just now what was charged in court, and what was proven in Judge Mayo's court. When that trial was going on I went in and sat down there a little amongst the people, and that court was literally packed with people victimized by employment agencies right here in New York City.

But the worst has yet to come. There is some supervision over the employment agency; it has to buy the licenses. The mayor's marshal can reach them, but there are institutions, such as we have spoken of this morning, that are doing business without any licenses whatsoever. I know this, because it is part of my business to read the morning papers carefully, the advertising columns. In them you will see, day after day, sometimes with an intermission of one day, but as a rule day after day, announcements that certain people can be found at a certain address, a girl, a housekeeper; for instance, a young girl just landed; and then it will be a Swedish housworker, or a waitress, or a chambermaid. They are getting employment through employment agencies that are not registered, that have not taken out a license. I am morally certain of that, and, talking over this phase of the question with the mother superior of the Sisters of Mercy, who has charge of the Working Girls' Home, she said to me what I had already concluded in my own mind, that the institutions of this kind were the worst, morally speaking. You get a girl; she would go to one of those places; it is a friend's house. She knew that when she got out of work she could come back there again, and after a month, perhaps, she would return there with her month's wages to have a good time, and she would get into the drink habit. That is the truth. This is the experience, not only my experience but the experience of this Sister of Mercy in control of the Regina Angelorum. That is a form of finding employment that should be wiped out. A remedy could be provided if there were men whose special duty it was to run down such places under the commissioner, and they could do that, if that law were passed, without any more expense to the State. I say that the department should have agents all over the State and could enforce that law without one cent extra expense; and to give you an idea just how they do some things, I will read from our report a statement of the case.

Mr. LITCHMAN. And the number of the report and the page.

The WITNESS. June report, 1900, page 104. This is a clipping taken from the Times of Friday, April 13, 1900. [Reading:]

"As Recorder Goff was about to sentence Amelia Monach, a pretty Hungarian girl, living at 105 Lewis street, who had pleaded guilty in general sessions to having stolen merchandise worth $800 from her employer, David Rosenbach, of 452 East Eighty-fourth street, Mrs. Foster, the 'Tombs angel,' came forward and asked the recorder to be lenient.

"'The girl has told me that she is thoroughly repentant for what she has done,' said Mrs. Foster; 'besides, she has told me that it is her first offense.'

"This speech seemed greatly to excite a man in the court room. 'It isn't her first offense,' he said, hastening up toward the bar. 'She worked for me as a servant and cleared my flat out entirely, taking away $275 worth of goods. My name is Abraham Spitzker, of 330 East Seventy-ninth street, and I will identify her and swear to her guilt on the witness stand.'

"Two other men in the court room also came forward and said that they had employed the girl as a servant, and that she had stolen money from them.

"Recorder Goff listened to what the men had to say, and sentenced the girl to 2 years and 6 months in the penitentiary.

"'This is a splendid commentary on methods adopted by employment agencies,' he said. 'This girl is a specialist in the business of robbing her mistresses and helps to support her parents in Hungary in that way. She says that she secured all her positions through the assistance of employment agencies. Some of them make a practice of sending thieves into the homes of respectable citizens, giving them recommendations and first-class certificates of character.'

"Five pawnbrokers were then called to the bar, forced to acknowledge numerous pawn tickets found in the girl's possession as their own, and ordered to return the goods. One wept bitterly at his loss.

"In order to make sure of this most remarkable news item, Recorder Goff was interviewed by a representative of this bureau. On stating the purpose of the visit to the recorder, he said that this fact was brought out by the evidence in the court at the trial of Amelia Monach; that she gained admittance into two families in three weeks on certificates of character given her by East Side employment agencies; that she had committed robberies in each of the places where employed, and that the agencies in question were, to say the least, criminally negligent in not investigating the references before introducing the girl into families."

This is a brief outline of conditions that exist in New York to-day. I charge no one with being the cause of it. I believe myself that this condition can not be changed unless we have a change in the law on the lines laid down in this act.

Q. (By Mr. LITCHMAN.) This you refer to as a suggestion for a law that will reach these evils you complain of?—A. That is just it. Now, I want to say in addition that there are many respectable employment agencies in New York City, many of them that recognize wrongs that exist; very many of them that would wish to have the wrongs righted, and that these people were with the bureau a year ago and asked that the bill proposed become a law.

Q. What objections were given by the Legislature at that time?—A. Simply want of time. The bill was amended twice or three times; sent back first to New York to have a conference with the people who were interested, and then it was amended twice or three times, and was not reported from the committee; consequently it died there. Some say that the breweries had a little something to do with it. I do not know positively, do not know officially, do not know that it is so.

Q. Was the matter brought to the attention of the governor to enlist his cooperation in the passage of the bill at all?—A. The governor did all he could. He recommended the legislature to move; he asked the committee to report it; but things were in a bad shape last year. You see the Republican party did not have that majority in the senate that it always depends upon to do what it wants to do.

Q. You have not tried this year to get the legislature to act?—A. The bill was introduced, but rather late. There was another bill that went through which was vetoed by the mayor April 14, and vetoed by the governor on May 4. It was not a bill that we were at all interested in; we did not think it covered the ground, and consequently did not bother our heads about it. That bill of last year was introduced by the United Charities, by the Hebrew Charities, by the Society of Ethical Culture, by the Social Reform Club, by the Society St. Vincent de Paul, by the Church Association (Protestant Episcopal, to improve the condition of labor), by the Church Temperance Society (Protestant Episcopal), and the Catholic Total Abstinence Society of America.

Q. You understand, of course, that legislation of this kind necessarily must be by the States?—A. Yes.

Q. I presume your experience has taught you that legislation is not always given for the asking, but that it is gained after long and patient trouble?—A. Yes; and continued fighting.

Q. I suggest to you that you be on hand early next year—that you get there the early part of the session.—A. We will try to do that. The Republican party in its platform last year indorsed the position of State control, and we will try again.

Q. A part of the duty of the commission is to receive recommendations for laws, not only national but State, and the suggestions you make are right in the line of our work, but of course the initiative of this legislation, you understand, must be taken in the State itself.—A. Most assuredly.

Q. (By Mr. FARQUHAR.) Have you any statement to make of the operations of your State bureau in the enlargement of its work or of its opportunities?—A. I believe that there should be in this State, and under the control of the State, knowledge at all times as to where there is a vacancy of any considerable extent in the labor market, and that that information should be sent to various centers of population. In Australia, where they do things in a more advanced shape than in any part of the world, the department of labor looks after matters in that way, and it does more than that, it helps people to go to where they can find labor, and anything the State can do to help a person to keep the home over there is done within certain limits. I do not believe in paternalism, but anything the State can legitimately do should be done. Take, for instance, a poor old woman who came to me. She was a decent woman and had raised a family. They all died, one after another. She was left at 50 years of age to commence life again. She turned to our place; we got her employment. Now, the State would either support her as a pauper or give her a chance to support herself. The State did give her a chance to support herself, and she is doing it now.

Q. Suppose that the State had agencies of the character of yours—State agencies and branches—would there be any means of cooperation between States to relieve the existing idleness of immigrants, or even Americans out of employment?—A. Any exchange of weekly reports would settle that. There are many such institutions throughout the country. Through the labor organizations—the large bodies—they take care of that for themselves. You take the printers; they know where there is work and where there is not, and they are told it officially through journals. They have not to go and pay a tax for the privilege of getting work. The idea of a civilized people in this age of ours being taxed to get the privilege to work, when it is a natural necessity and a natural right!

Q. You are mainly speaking in your criticisms of unskilled labor?—A. Yes.

Q. Not the organized labor?—A. Organized labor takes care of itself. It is a blessed thing that it does. Every labor organization that is in this State, in this union, is a blessing for the State and a blessing for the union. The one thing they do, in the darkest hour, when things are blackest, is to keep up a record of the labor wage, and when times get better men will be reemployed at the wage rate that was kept up by the labor organizations.

Q. (By Mr. LITCHMAN.) And in this advantage the unorganized labor receives the advantage equally, does it not?—A. Most assuredly, and the men who are working at trades who are not in the organization receive an advantage. The gentleman on the stand this morning—his men received the advantage of those who are willing to stand out, risk something to keep up the wage to a living scale. The mission of the American trades unions is to have a home on the American plan; to live as Americans.

Q. (By Mr. FARQUHAR.) What do you say to the proposition that it is the positive duty of the State to protect a subject if possible; to bring into productive industries that class that stand nearer pauperism?—A. Yes.

Q. Is it not a positive benefit? Is it not the policy of many States to care for these productive agencies through the unskilled in finding work for them and to enable laborers to support themselves instead of being supported out of the general tax?—A. Yes, and it is a benefit to leave a man a free man to work—not to go to work and to mortgage his vote before he gets his work. There is no such freedom here for the unorganized workers in New York. They are the chattels of the dominant party.

Q. (By Mr. CLARKE.) How is it with organized workers?—A. They are able to take care of themselves.

Q. They are not subject to the political influences of those in charge of your contracts?—A. No; and men that are now were not some time ago. For instance, the car drivers of the city of New York. I remember that the organization of car drivers forced the labor law into existence. They had a great deal of trouble about it; but after a while the State came to the rescue, and now the law is on the books that they shall work only 10 hours a day. And they would not have gotten through only for men, now in their graves, who worked themselves out trying to get them to organize.

Q. (By Mr. KENNEDY.) How long did the men work?—A. From early morning to late at night. They were forced to do it. There was no law to protect them; but they did pass a law themselves through their organization, and afterwards the State took up that law. The State refused to assist them. It was not until after years of agitation that the law was placed on the statute books

Q. Why did you favor State control of this matter rather than local home rule control of it?—A. For the very simple reason that you have to have a uniform discipline. It is all over the State from one end to the other. You have to have one man responsible for the enforcement of the law. And it will work to the advantage of the public just as much as to the State now to license men who work for a living, which will do away with the sweatshops, or control them.

Q. Could not the mayor of the city of New York, or some other high official of this city, be made responsible for the execution of such a law?—A. If they have those registers, and if they have men that will examine them I would not have very serious objection to making the law local, but still my judgment is, by preference, for a State law. It has worked well in Illinois.

Q. You speak about the good work of organized labor and the great affairs in which they have accomplished for good; why can't you get organized labor interested in the movement of this kind and hope for good results?—A. They have indorsed that bill, the copy of which is in the hands of the commission. The organized labor of this State, the State Workingman's Assembly, had already indorsed it when it was presented to the legislature, and it was indorsed by the local bodies as well. It was first asked for by labor organizations. The first organization that asked for that was the German waiters.

Q. I would like to ask if you can name any other States that have agencies under the State control or local control?—A. There is one State in which the question is under the control of the State—Illinois.

Q. Do you know of any other States?—A. I have no knowledge.

(Testimony closed.)

TESTIMONY OF MR. GEORGE W. BROWN, JR.,

Deputy chief, bureau of licenses, mayor's office, city hall, New York.

The special subcommission met in the rooms of the Fifth Avenue Hotel at 10.37 a. m., Mr. Clarke presiding. At 3.10 p. m. Mr. George W. Brown, jr., deputy chief, bureau of licenses, New York, appeared as a witness, and, being duly sworn, testified as follows:

Q. (By Mr. CLARKE.) What is your name?—A. George W. Brown, jr., bureau of licenses, mayor's office, city hall. I am deputy chief of the bureau.

Q. What are the duties that you have to perform, in a general way?—A. The bureau of licenses issues licenses under the municipal ordinances and also under the State laws, more especially to intelligence offices and pawn brokers. The chief of the bureau of licenses under the municipal ordinances is not only charged with the administrative powers of issuing licenses, but also with seeing that the provisions of the ordinances are enforced, and in that way he hears complaints against licensees for violations of the provisions and regulations of the ordinances.

Q. Then you are familiar with the condition of the employment agencies in this city and of the regulations concerning them and of abuses which creep in, perhaps?—A. So far as they come before the bureau of licenses and so far as concerns that bureau.

Q. Can you tell how many private management agencies there are in the city?—A. I have here 2 memoranda, 1 showing the number of licenses issued by our bureau during the year 1900, and 1 showing the licenses that were issued in the old city of New York for the past 10 years; that is, the former city of New York. During the year 1900 there were issued in the principle office of the bureau of licenses located in the borough of Manhattan, and covering the territory of the former city of New York, now the boroughs of Manhattan and the Bronx, 72 licenses, and 276 renewals. In the borough of Brooklyn, a branch of our office, covering the territory of the former city of Brooklyn, we issued 18 new licenses and 52 renewals. In the borough of Queens, occupying chiefly the territory of the former Long Island City and adjacent towns and villages now included in the borough of Queens as a part of Greater New York, there were issued 3 new licenses and 2 renewals. In the borough of Richmond, which was formerly the county of Richmond and Staten Island, there were issued 5 renewal licenses. That makes a total during the year 1900 of 91 new licenses and 335 renewals, showing a total of 426 intelligence offices licensed by our bureau. If it is at all of interest I can give you the statistics of the past 10 years in the former city of New York, now the boroughs of Manhattan and the Bronx, which is the most important part, perhaps, of the Greater New York, if you care to have them.

Q. Unless you see some value in them connected with further testimony which you are to give it does not occur to me that they would be of much interest to us, except you may state in a general way whether there has been a growth in the number.—A. There has been a gradual growth, and fairly uniform. Starting in 1890 there were 39 new licenses and in 1900 the number had gotten up to 70 new licenses; there were 152 renewed in 1890 and 276 renewed in 1900. The greatest number of new licenses issued during that period was in 1895, when there were 106 new licenses issued. Generally speaking, I think it fair to say that there has been a gradual and uniform growth, and that the institutions once licensed renew their licenses and stay in business, and are fairly permanent institutions.

Q. Are most of those agencies conducted by firms or by single individuals?—A. There are no statistics that I know of that are available on that point, for the reason that it used to be the practice of the bureau of licenses to issue a license to some individual for the purpose of holding that individual responsible for the conduct of that office, the license being in that individual's name; whereas perhaps as a matter of fact there were others associated with him in the conduct of his business, but he was the one held responsible for it. In some instances licenses have been issued to church organizations, or charitable organizations in the name of the organization. I do not think there are any trustworthy statistics showing whether these agencies are conducted by individuals or firms.

Q. Have you any information as to whether they are generally conducted by the persons holding the licenses?—A. Yes; they are generally conducted by the person to whom the license is issued, but I do not wish it to be understood that one man does all the work of any particular office. He has clerks and agents and various persons for whom he is responsible.

Q. Are the licensees mostly men, or are there some women?—A. Oh, both; both men and women.

Q. There is a license fee, is there not?—A. Yes; there is a State law that regulates the issue of the licenses. The law provides for a fee of $25 for taking out new licenses, and a renewal fee of one-half of that amount when the license is renewed for each time that it is renewed.

Q. Into what treasury does that fee go?—A. In the city it goes into what we term the city treasury, as distinct from the sinking fund or any special funds. It goes into the general treasury account.

Q. Does your bureau have the exclusive supervision of the conduct of those agencies?—A. So far as they violate the municipal regulations, yes. They might violate some other law. Of course then they might be amenable to our bureau and at the same time amenable to some criminal law. We have the authority under the municipal regulations of hearing complaints against any licensees, and, as a matter of fact, we have frequent complaints of both employers and employees against intelligence offices.

Q. Do these agencies and people whom they serve have some relation to racial lines?—A. Oh, yes. Some agencies restrict themselves to the furnishing of female help; some agencies restrict themselves to the furnishing of male help; some agencies do both; some agencies restrict themselves to nationalities; and some agencies restrict themselves to certain kinds of service—for instance, cooks, or waiters, or barbers. I think that this is simply a matter of custom, perhaps, or accident. I do not think that there are any agencies that are so exclusive that they would help only those of a certain race.

Q. (By Mr. CLARKE.) Is it the common practice of these agencies to exact a fee in advance from a person who applies for employment?—A. There is no uniform custom that I am certain of among the agencies in regard to the fees. Some agencies have one regulation and some another. Some charge a fee for registration, which entitles the person that pays it to the facilities of the office. Others collect a fee in advance, which includes all the charges for the service rendered. Others have no fee for registration, and get their fees sometimes before and sometimes after the services are performed. The law regulating the services performed by the bureau toward the employer and the employee, generally speaking, provides two conditions. One is that a servant shall remain at least a month with the employer for a given fee paid; that is to say, an employment office is under obligation to furnish a servant to an employer who shall stay at least 1 month for 1 fee. There is an obligation also on the part of the offices to the employees in refunding to them the full amount of the fee paid where no services have been actually rendered and no situation secured. In other words, they must return the fee paid if they do not do the work—the whole fee. There is in addition to that a further responsibility of the expenses incurred where an employee is sent to a place of employment where there is no employment and the intelligence office had good reason to believe or did actually know that there was no employment there. In other words, the false pretense will necessitate a return of the fee paid.

Q. Does your office employ inspectors to constantly inquire into the conduct of the business of these bureaus?—A. The bureau of licenses has attached to it, as a part of the police department, a squad which is called the "ordinance squad," and who are charged with seeing that the municipal ordinances are enforced. There are usually 1 or 2 men who are specially charged with seeing that the exactions of the licenses issued to intelligence offices are complied with, and that there is no one doing business in the city of New York without a license who requires a license.

Q. Are complaints numerous?—A. Well, some days we have quite a number and other days none at all. Of the number of persons licensed—and I speak from an experience of some 18 years or more in the bureau—I know intelligence offices in this city that have been licensed uninterruptedly during that entire period of time, and against whom no complaint has ever been made to our office. I know of others who have been "down" much more frequently in that time.

Q. (By Mr. KENNEDY.) What do you mean by "down?"—A. Have been down to our office on a complaint. There are, as I have stated, 426 licensed employment agencies in the city of New York, and I think out of that number the complaints are confined perhaps to 10 or a dozen, maybe 15. I think a very large majority of those actually licensed we never hear any complaint against.

Q. (By Mr. LITCHMAN.) Will you designate briefly the nature of the complaints?—A. They are generally made by the employees, that they have paid a fee and that no situation has been secured for them by the agencies; or by employers, that they have paid a fee and the servants have not remained the 30 days required by law. They all fall into one of those two classes.

Q. What has been your method in dealing with these different complaints?—A. When a complainant appears we issue a notification to the licensee to appear at a certain time, and we invite also the complainant to appear at the same time, and we hear the dispute between them, and adjust it according to the law and our understanding of what is right.

Q. Now, in these adjustments that you have made what penalty have you inflicted in any case; or, rather, what has been your usual penalty?—A. In the case of employees who have paid a fee and no situation has been secured, the return of the fee to the person who paid it. In the case of an employer who has not been served for a month, a mandate to the intelligence office to supply the servant for the required period of law or return of the fee that has been paid.

Q. Have you ever gone to the extent of revoking licenses in any case?—A. Yes.

Q. And for what cause?—A. Where we had reason to believe that the office was not fairly conducted.

Q. What have you to say as to the possibility of moral abuses through some of these employment agencies?—A. I do not know. I never have seen any proof that such things exist.

Q. Have you any knowledge of complaint being made that such things exist?—A. We have had statements occasionally in our office that sometimes persons had been sent to places of ill repute. We never could find out that it was so.

Q. You would of course consider that a sufficient cause for immediate revocation?—A. If it could be proved, certainly.

Q. A suggestion made on the administration of the law by the previous witness was that there should be some system of registration by which a trace could be kept of the employment agencies, compelling them to register the application and giving a sort of history of each case. Have you anything to say in favor of that?—A. I think the agencies generally do that. I know that there are offices in this city which have set rules. They invariably investigate the references in advance, and they very frequently say to the employers, "I have not" or "I have investigated this person," and "I do" or "I do not know all about him or her."

Q. Are these records open to your inspection or the inspection of your department?—A. Yes.

Q. As a matter of favor or a matter of law?—A. Well, we take it as a matter of right.

Q. Have you really any right?—A. We have no right, except in this way. In the first place, such records are not required to be kept.

Q. Then you have no legal right, of course?—A. But as a matter of fact we say to a person who has a license, "You must conduct your business right or go out of business," and we say, "You must keep a record," and that requires them to give a receipt to the employee of the money paid by them, and we require that books shall be kept. There is no broad formality laid down. It is the practice with a great many of them to have an application blank, and these have certain spaces upon them that are filled in, and then they are pasted into a scrapbook, regularly.

Q. You see no objection to having this register and supervision required by law?—A. Not at all. I am here to-day to give the benefit of what experience I have to the commission, but I am not an advocate of any distinct procedure.

Q. We understand that. A part of our duty is, you understand, to give recommendations for remedial legislation both State and national. I am asking these questions along that line to ascertain if you have anything to suggest.—A. My experience, as I say, extends over quite a number of years, and under 7 different mayors, some of those of different political complexions and aspirations, and I think I know something of the situation in this town.

Q. Have you any suggestion for remedial legislation?—A. I think the gentleman on the stand here this morning, Mr. Redfield,[1] has the right idea. You can not make the people good or honest, nor well behaved, nor efficient, by law. You can watch those that have a tendency to do things they ought not to do. As I say, we

---

[1] See testimony of William C. Redfield, volume on manufactures.

IMMIGRATION.

have upon our books intelligence offices that have been licensed, and many of them for 18, 19, and 20 years right straight along; that have done business, not very philanthropic business, but on the same sort of basis as Mr. Redfield, and we have never had a complaint against those offices. We see their representatives only once a year, when they come down to renew their licenses. There are a few offices in the city, and very few, which do business and take long chances. For instance, you can see exactly how it is. Suppose I am an intelligence-office keeper and a man comes to me that wants work awful bad, and he has got a $5 bill, and that is all he has, and I know a job he can get, and I say to him, "If you will give me that $5 bill, I will give you the job," and he does it, although morally speaking the place he gets is not worth it. There might be another intelligence-office keeper under the same circumstances who has sympathy for the man and would say, "Here, I will not take your last $5; you give me 50 cents and I will find you a job." We do find occasionally people that get into the business, notwithstanding our best efforts to see what their past record has been, who will take any sort of fee and promise anything for it. Once in a while they perform those promises, but usually they get as many fees as they can and then go out of business.

Q. Do these offices specialize in procuring work for female help or for male or for both?—A. There are a few that supply only female help and a few only male help, but most of them supply both.

There is perhaps one suggestion: Mr. Bealin referred to the law that had been vetoed by the mayor and vetoed by the governor which proposed an amendment to the present law. The present law has been on the statute books for some time, and prescribes, as I read it, that the fee may be divided into two parts or may cover all the service rendered. The intelligence office is usually kept in some place where rent has to be paid and where clerical help must be employed. It is a sort of exchange between the employer and employee. Some of them charge a fee, which they call a fee for registration, which entitles the person who pays that fee to the privileges of that office for a certain period, and he takes the chances of meeting there somebody that wants to employ him. That is what they call a fee for registration.

Q. That also applies to those who desire to employ help?—A. Some intelligence offices charge the employer and the employee both a fee; others charge only the employee. Then, if the position is secured, there is an additional fee, which is generally a fixed charge, but sometimes a percentage on the pay.

There are others that charge a fee which shall include both the privileges of the place and the service secured. I think an intelligence-office keeper has a right to divide the fee up into those two parts if he sees fit. The part paid for registration, if it be reasonable, is not subject to be being returned if it is understood for what it is paid; but if, in addition, anything has been paid for a situation which has not been secured, it must be returned. If the intelligence-office keeper receives a fee which is not specifically applied on either of these divisions, but is for a position to be secured, and he does not secure the position, although the applicant may have had the privileges of the office for an indefinite length of time, he must return the whole amount.

Q. Is there any legal limit on the fee that may be charged?—A. No.

Q. You spoke of the fee being sometimes a fixed sum and sometimes a percentage on the prospective salary. In the latter case how is it collected?—A. We have nothing to do with that. The intelligence-office people take their chances.

Q. Have any complaints come to your knowledge of abuses because of that contingent fee and the manner of its collection?—A. No complaints, because we have nothing to do with the matter. But I have information that a great many intelligence offices do not get all their fees because of the dishonesty of the people, who promise to pay and get beyond their reach.

Q. Do you know whether any arrangement is entered into by the party employing that they will deduct the fee from the salary and pay it to the intelligence office?—A. We know nothing of that. I dare say there are instances of that sort. It certainly would not be contrary to the law. There is no law on the subject. It is purely a matter of agreement.

Q. That case would be very likely to happen, or more likely to happen, where the employer sought the help than where the help sought the employment?—A. Under the present law there is a very large discretion in the licensing power, and that is used as judiciously and with as good judgment as we can.

Q. Is it not practically a fact that the only penalty for a breach of the law is your power to revoke the license?—A. After an agency is licensed, yes; but not before it is licensed; of course the criminal law would apply.

Q. They are prohibited from doing business unless they are licensed?—A. That is it. There is one other suggestion, and that is that there seems to be no definition as to what an intelligence office is. It is a pretty open question as to what offices must have a license. Where they supply help of a domestic character there seems to be no doubt; but where they supply help which is more or less skilled, then it is an open question. For instance, there are theatrical agencies in this city, and teachers' agencies, and agencies of that sort—a great many typewriter agencies nowadays.

Q. They all come under the official designation of intelligence offices?—A. There is no official designation. There is a designation in the law which does not define, and so far as I am aware it has never been entirely determined what constitutes an intelligence office, and it is very hard to draw the line. If you start with domestic servants and end up perhaps with some agency that supplies professors to colleges, and take in all the intermediate steps, how far are you going to make that law apply?

Q. You have not thought the matter out far enough to make a suggestion as to practical legislation along that line?—A. My opinion is that the less legislation we have and the better enforcement of the law as it exists, the better off we are.

Q. But is it not true that the designation that you speak of must be a matter of legislation?—A. The difficulty is that the law in regard to intelligence offices was passed originally in 1888. Times have changed very much since then. It simply says, "No persons shall engage in the business of keeping an intelligence office, employment bureau, or other agency," except under specified conditions. There is where the trouble comes in—with the expression "other agency." That is broad enough to include any brokers' office, almost. I do not see how you are going to define an intelligence office.

Q. (By Mr. KENNEDY.) I would like to ask if you would favor the fixing of the fee, say at $1 for men and 75 cents for women, as I understand is the case in Massachusetts?—A. I am inclined to think that perhaps is the best way of legislating on the subject, and that practically it is the only way. Pawnbrokers, for instance, are regulated in their charges, and I see no reason why intelligence-offices should not be regulated in their charges. I believe that they have the right to charge justly a fee for registration, which shall include the facilities of a place of meeting between help and employers; and whether we can go further and say that the additional charge for the service rendered shall include a certain percentage of the first month's pay, or of the year's salary, is an open question.

Q. What action would be taken by your bureau in the event a judge of the city of New York should declare certain intelligence-offices, which you have licensed, to be fraudulent? Has that ever happened in New York?—A. We have had this happen once or twice. Under the law a fee that has been paid upon the promise of a position must be returned if the promise is not fulfilled. I have known of instances where a number of applicants have paid fees to a person and that person has disappeared. He simply collected his fees and got out of town, and consequently there was no chance to have the fees returned.

There is one other thing, and that is the question of a bond for the faithful performance of duties under the ordinances. There are a great many of the intelligence offices in the city, I think, that are kept by married women, who use it as a means of increasing the family income, and very often it is kept in their own houses, especially among the poorer classes on the East Side. It would come pretty hard on them to furnish a bond, and almost invariably they do maintain a perfectly respectable office and there is no objection to it. I think the fact that there are so very few of these offices that are complained against shows that the law that we now have is a pretty good one, and as a rule the people in the business are very reputable people.

Q. I have been informed to-day that this sort of practice prevails in regard to this system; that is, that when complaints are made to your office against these Intelligence Offices which you have licensed, the politicians of the political parties are rushed to the front to intercede for them and get them off, so to speak. Does that practice prevail at all?—A. Not that I am aware of. If any such application was made, I am very sure it would be of no effect. The appointees and the officials are all under an official oath to do their duty, and I think they would do it.

Q. (By Mr. FARQUHAR.) Have you any license or any regulation of the so-called padrone system of employment?—A. No.

Q. Are these licensed places chiefly for domestic help?—A. Yes.

Q. Are there many mechanics who make application to them and get work?—A. We have no means of knowing that. Most of the offices have on their books records of situations in the country as workmen in the summer season and as waiters or waitresses at different hotels, or various work done about summer hotels. As Mr. Bealin stated, any person that belonged to organized labor would probably go to his union for the line of business in which he was educated.

Q. Do you think that under the present law the rights of applicants are properly safeguarded against extortion and misrepresentation?—A. I am inclined to believe the operation of the present law in regard to intelligence offices is perhaps as satisfactory as can be formulated. A person likes to keep the fee, and he knows he must return it if he does not earn it; and the presumption is that he will try to earn it.

Q. The keeper of an intelligence office is in the line of a broker furnishing employment, subject to regulation under the State. Now, with reference to the unfortunates that are out of employment, is it not the duty of the State and of the municipality, if necessary, to so frame laws and put safeguards over the rights of these people and over whatever little money they may provide to get a situation that they may labor and keep themselves from being public charges?—A. That is a question for a statesman.

Q. You have had 18 years' experience and have handled the business every day, and you are in a city which is congested with foreign immigration and with people wanting and seeking situations?—A. There is this difficulty about it. Take an intelligence-office keeper; a man or woman goes to that keeper and says: "I want a place." Now, as a matter of fact, that applicant may be such that you might hunt the city over and yet find nobody that would have him or her. How are you going to get that man or woman a place?

Q. I am speaking of the worthy.—A. That is a very different thing. My experience and observation are that the worthy are pretty apt to get there if they work hard enough.

Q. How is it, when the city of New York has such a large fund for providing for the unemployed, that you have so many almshouses and institutions covering Blackwells Island and everywhere else?—A. I think that is because, as Mr. Carnegie says, everybody wants to come to New York, and the large proportion of them have no business here. Competition is too fierce. The struggle for existence is too much, and they simply become a part of the submerged tenth, and you will never be able to float them.

Q. Does not that circumstance emphasize the fact that you must have municipal or State control as a safeguard to the public?—A. I am not an advocate of a paternal government. I think the less government we have the better we are off. My impression is that if there were rules here that would make it absolutely sure that whoever came to the city of New York would get a job we would have the whole population of the United States here inside of 24 hours.

Q. If you were to establish that kind of agencies all over the State, could you not find employment for all applicants, and thus equalize matters and relieve New York and other large cities?—A. That is a theoretical demonstration, but it can not be carried out in the nature of human affairs. There are men and women who would rather live on a crust of bread in the city of New York than have a full meal served at Delmonico's in Hoboken or some other place, and you can not help it.

Q. Is it not a fact that worthy people often become stranded, on account of sickness or otherwise, and that the safety of the public, in the moral view as well as in the political view, lies in providing, through the State or municipality, in some way, employment for those who are willing to work and who are not vicious?—A. It is within my knowledge that in a great many instances servant girls and applicants for various sorts of work have gone to intelligence-offices and been provided with places without paying one single cent. Often the intelligence-office keeper has to rely on the honesty of the individual to pay the money when he or she gets it. I do not know of any place where a man who has the push and ability and determination to get along can do any better than right here.

Q. To come back to the original proposition. Have you, out of your own experience, any suggestions to make amendatory of the present law or to make it more efficient and better in its operation?—A. I have no suggestions that I have any reason to believe would make it any better than it is to-day. I have a number of theories. The only suggestion that possibly might be an improvement would be the division of the fee paid so that a part of it might be applied to what might be termed a registration fee, which should be regulated and made small, and the other part of it made in proportion to the service rendered and paid when the services are rendered; and if those services are not rendered, and it has been paid in advance, it should be returned. I think that would be fair to everybody concerned. I see no reason why intelligence-office keepers should provide a place of meeting and go to the expense of keeping a register of all people that want help and of all help that want places, and employ the necessary clerical help, and pay for a thousand and one things necessary to do it, without remuneration. I think they are entitled to a fee which shall be paid to them when they place the facilities of their place at the disposal of the applicant. Then, if they render more service they are entitled to more pay. And if they get a good place I think they are entitled to more pay than if they get a poor place. A place that will pay $1,000 a year is worth more than one that pays $10 a month. Now, whether any rate can be established that will gauge that fee is a question. The only way that you could get at that would be on a percentage basis, probably. But a percentage on what? The first month's pay or the first year's pay? Manifestly, if you make it a percentage of his first year's pay it can not be collected until the man has been there a year, and what guaranty has the intelligence-office keeper that he will be able to trace his man after a year? How is he going to make that man pay it? You do not have him under your jurisdiction. You license the intelligence-office keeper, and he is the man you can put your finger on. He is the man you can make do what you think is right; but you can not make the employer or the employee do what is right. Many times we have complaints of a servant who has been sent to a situation and who has not paid anything, and yet there are thousands of people who would be glad to take the place and pay for it. Sometimes domestics want a great deal; on the other hand, the employer sometimes wants a great deal and pays very small wages. That is a matter that, to my mind, must be regulated by the law of supply and demand and the various incidents and circumstances of life.

Q. (By Mr. KENNEDY.) What can you say as to the comparative efficiency of State employment bureaus and of these local ones?—A. I have seen nothing at all of the operation of the State employment bureaus. I am not in a position to know anything about them, but I think I do know something about our bureau of licenses.

Q. You do not know whether they are more efficient in the matter of securing employment for persons seeking it than the local agencies?—A. It is the old question of any organization that has more far-reaching influence which can in all probability better serve its purpose, yet at the same time they may go so far and reach out so far that their lines are so stretched out that they are absolutely weak and break down of their own weight and do not accomplish any good. I think the matter of intelligence offices is one of which it may be said that the more thoroughly they are organized and the more restricted or local they are in their operations the better they will serve their constituents. They must of necessity be more thoroughly informed. It would be pretty difficult for a man out in Illinois, where they have some such law as that, to be as thoroughly informed of the conditions here in New York as those who are living here every day and keep up with the changes that are continually occurring. Take, for instance, any question like strikes. When employers want laboring men they do not get them through intelligence offices, but they learn it through the newspapers that certain men are out and they go there, but that information is not disseminated through any organization except the press.

Q. I referred to such State employment bureaus as you have in New York.—A. I know nothing about the State bureau here. I never have, to my knowledge, seen anyone that had any complaint to make about it or had anything to say in praise of it. In other words, so far as I am concerned, I have myself never heard of it except as a matter of hearsay.

Q. Your opinion, then, is that it is inoperative and ineffective?—A. No; I do not mean to say anything of that kind. There are likely many concerns in New York that are very active that I have never heard of.

Testimony closed.

TESTIMONY OF MR. THOMAS W. HOTCHKISS,

Counsel, Protective Association of Employment Agencies, New York.

The special subcommission being in session, Mr. Clarke presiding, Mr. Thomas W. Hotchkiss was introduced as a witness at 4.03 p. m., and, being first duly sworn, testified as follows:

Q. (By Mr. CLARKE.) Please give your name and address and occupation or official position.—A. Thomas W. Hotchkiss, in care of St. Bartholomew's Employment Bureau, 211 East Forty-second street, New York City. I am the superintendent of the mercantile, professional, and labor departments of that bureau. I am also the counsel for the Protective Association of Employment Agencies of this State, an organization which was formed in the winter of 1899–1900 to oppose the Ford-Kelsey bill, which Mr. Bealin offered. Since the matter of legislation seems to be the central matter of inquiry by the commission, I would select that as my topic, if I am permitted to do so.

Q. Proceed in your way to develop the points that you wish to bring out.—A. I wish to make the preliminary statement that St. Bartholomew's bureau makes no charge at all until employment is obtained. It may collect its fees before the position is obtained, but it refunds those fees if the employment is not obtained. In other words, we are operating strictly within the law of this State. St. Bartholomew's Bureau is not a member of the Protective Association of Employment Agencies; and upon this question of legislation I would speak as a representative of that association and not as a representative of St. Bartholomew's Bureau.

I refer directly to the matter of legislation because I do not want to take up too much time, although I might speak at considerable length on the general question of the unemployed.

The Protective Association of Employment Agencies opposed the Ford-Kelsey bill for several reasons. All legislation affecting employment agencies is intended to regulate their operation and to prevent frauds being perpetrated against employers and employees. That would be the starting point of all legislation. The Protective Association of Employment Agencies concedes that these frauds may be perpetrated, but to my knowledge none of its members have ever been guilty of any of those frauds. I have to take the evidence from hearsay as to these existing frauds. I derive it from the statements of Mr. Bealin, whom I have heard on former occasions, and from the bureau of licenses. I cite also the paper of Prof. E. L. Bogart, of Indiana University, printed in the Quarterly Journal of Economics for May, 1900, in which he makes a very clear statement of specimen frauds. The Encyclopedia of of Social Reform, in an article under the title of "Unemployment," wrtten by Mr. Bliss, also gives samples of fraud. These are the sources of my information as to existing frauds. I have Mr. Bogart's paper before me, and I read his mention of such frauds. (Reading:)

"The least of the abuses which are perpetrated is the universal practice of accepting a fee whether there is a prospect of finding a position or not, and of refusing to refund it when a position is not secured. No pay agency will ever admit that the labor market is overstocked. Worse than this is the practice of advertising for laborers to undertake work in distant cities, and of sending them to fill purely fictitious openings after accepting their fees. In the case of some of the more dishonest agencies there is an agreement between a foreman and an agency, according to which men sent by the agency are employed, but only for a few days, and then discharged to make way for others. The fees are divided between the agent and the foreman. An additional refinement, which is reported from New York, consists in an illicit connection of employment agencies with alleged employers, who refer an applicant to a guaranty agency which is also in the league, and which exacts another fee for looking up the reference. It is a not uncommon plan to have the employment agency located in the rear of a dramshop, which the men, who are purposely kept waiting in the hope of securing a position, will unfailingly patronize."

Now, the Protective Association of Employment Agencies wants to see the business of employment agencies in New York State conducted according to law. We consider it a matter of protection to ourselves. An agency which is licensed and which is put under bonds, which is inspected by proper officers of the municipality, which is liable to fines or penalties or punishment for misdemeanors, is protected against the unwarranted statement that frauds are perpetrated. There has been a good deal of talk concerning frauds practiced by employment agencies, without specific proof of frauds. It is much easier to make the allegation of frauds than to prove it. I make that statement not only because the evidence may be difficult to get, but because the circumstances of the case are such that the allegations come easy, especially to a person who is out of employment. The person who is out of employment is a very discontented person, and he looks at life with distorted vision. He thinks he is an object of fraud, and in many cases will make himself believe that he is a victim of fraud. If fraud is perpetrated, the fraud must be proved; but in many cases the allegation has been made when the proof was not forthcoming. Instead of indulging in an indiscriminate denunciation of employment agencies, the most direct, radical, and effectual remedy for wrongs that really exist is to bring the wrongdoers to justice. The courts are open, and the mayor's marshal stands ready to see that substantial justice is done to any person wronged by any employment agent in this city.

The employment agency which is self-supporting, that is, which charges fees for its services, and which is not a free bureau of the State or a charitable organization, has got to guard its earnings very carefully. It has already been explained as to how fees are charged and something of the amount charged.

The Ford-Kelsey bill, inspired by a zeal to reform, went far beyond the steps necessary to make that reform equitable. It overlooked the rights of the employment agents.

The objection of the Protective Association of Employment Agencies to Mr. Bealin's bill was, first, in regard to its first section. The Ford-Kelsey bill made an exception of agencies operated for teachers and members of the theatrical profession. Now, it seems to us that employment agencies of that character are operated for the same purpose and in practically the same way and may be guilty of the same frauds which may be practiced in any other agency. I make that statement as applying not only to domestic employment agencies, hotel agencies, and agencies for laborers or workers at mechanical trades, but also as applying to professional and mercantile agencies and so on, covering the whole field and making no exceptions whatever. It is stated that the object of this legislation is to check frauds. I never heard any other reason given, and frauds may be practiced in any of those agencies. So that making an exception of agencies operated for school teachers and theatrical people seems to me to be unfair to the other agencies—a sort of legislative favoritism.

Secondly, the Ford-Kelsey bill, when first presented, charged an annual license fee, so called, of $200. That is the amount in the Illinois law, and there is no other State which requires so high a license fee. The States of Colorado, Minnesota, and Washington have an annual license fee of $100. The only other State requiring any annual license fee is Pennsylvania, where the amount is $50. Now, $200 a year is not a license fee, but a tax, and is so large that it would wipe out of existence many employment agencies.

The Protective Association of Employment Agencies maintains that employment agencies are necessary to the public good and for the benefit of both employers and employees, and the orderly and convenient marketing of labor. Therefore, any law which is prohibitive and prevents agencies doing such a business, by charging too high a license fee or a fee that becomes a tax, is unfair to those agencies and detrimental to the public good.

In that connection I want to call the commission's attention to a decision in the State of North Carolina taking that position. The case was decided by the supreme court in 1893. It is the State v. Moore (113 N. C., 697). This is a case upon the constitutionality of chapter 75 of the acts of 1891. That chapter of that act is by this decision held to be unconstitutional, because the occupation defined in this chapter (that of an emigrant agent) does not belong to that class of trades or occupations which are so inherently harmful or dangerous to the public that they may either directly or indirectly be restricted or prohibited.

I maintain that what is true of emigrant agents is also true of employment agencies for the same reason, and that any tax which is too large (although that tax may be imposed, as was attempted in this statute, under the police power of the State) is unconstitutional. I am not a constitutional lawyer, but I offer this as evidence of what was found in the State of North Carolina.

As to the amount of annual fee which seems to me to be fair for these employment agencies, I should say that $100 for the first year and $50 annually thereafter would be a fair maximum charge or license fee for the purpose of properly administering such a law, including all the expenses connected with the inspection of the offices, for I am in favor of the inspection theory. In connection with the Ford-Kelsey bill, the Protective Association was willing to concede that amount, but opposed the $200 license fee as proposed by the original bill.

Under the third section of the Ford-Kelsey bill, which is the section referring to the bonding of the offices, the Protective Association is in favor of such bonding to the amount of $2,000. We do not say that such a bond must be obtained from any certain surety company, but a bond with responsible sureties; and it is my individual opinion that such a bond should run, not to the municipality, but to the party aggrieved. If the law is administered by the municipality, a suit on such a bond would be brought by the municipality against the licensee who is accused by a citizen of having fraudulently taken money. Now, in a suit on a bond, as I understand it, if it go to the question of the payment by the sureties, such payment should be reached by the terms of the statute, so that the aggrieved party, if he has been defrauded, may be reimbursed. It should not stop at the municipality. The bond should not be paid simply to the municipality, but to the aggrieved party. For that reason we favor such an amendment to the Ford-Kelsey bill.

We are heartily in favor of the regulation which requires that books shall be kept and certain information be entered in those books which is required by the fourth section. That is to enable the proper officers to make such inspection and also to aid the police in tracing thieves who may have registered at the employment offices. But we do not agree with Mr. Bealin that the books should be kept as outlined in the Ford-Kelsey bill. Such a system is practically impossible in an office where cashbooks and receipt books are necessary, as well as the registers of employers and employees. That section should be revised. The inspection of employment agencies should be made, in my opinion, by the inspection officer, only on the sworn complaint of an applicant for employment or an employer. This would avoid an unnecessary disclosure of confidential communications on file in these offices concerning the condition, character, and ability of persons out of employment, and private information as to the needs of employers It would also avoid the possibility of lists of unemployed workers being made for partisan election purposes

Under the fifth section the association is concerned with the character of the contract entered into between the applicant for employment and the employment agent. We oppose the Ford-Kelsey bill as unconstitutional in its fifth section, and I have here the opinion of Mr. Carl L. Schurz, jr., attorney and counsel of the Legal Aid Society, that this section 5 is unconstitutional because it takes away the property of the employment agent without due process of law. Applicants for employment who fancy that they have been defrauded by employment agents should know that (as stated in its report for 1900), "It is the object of the Legal Aid Society to assist the poor and helpless whenever they appear to have been wronged."

(Witness submitted opinion, which is as follows:)

THOMAS W. HOTCHKISS, Esq.:

DEAR SIR: I beg to submit that the bill submitted by you to me is, in my opinion, unconstitutional as to so much of section 5 thereof as I quote: "In case the said applicant shall not obtain or *accept* a situation or employment through or by the procurement or agency of such licensed person within one month after registration as aforesaid, then said licensed person shall forthwith repay and return to such applicant the full amount of the fee or other valuable thing paid or delivered by said applicant to said licensed person." That it is unconstitutional for the reason that it deprives a citizen of his property without due process of law.

At the time of the payment of the deposit by the person seeking a situation it is within the contemplation of the parties that the licensed person expend his time and his money in seeking a situation for the applicant. To require the licensed person to return the full deposit to the applicant is to take from the licensed person his time and his money without reimbursement for the same. This is taking his property without due process of law. The law of the land in any form has no more right to require a licensed employment agent to do work for nothing, or to expend money without return, than it would have to require a baker to buy materials, bake bread, and then give away the baked loaves without payment.

The only question remaining is whether the contract to find a position for the applicant can be carried out without the expenditure of time and money. Clearly not; for even to be entitled to make such a contract the agent must have his license, for which he pays; must give his time, and must have a place in which to do business. There is no question but what to require him to return the full deposit paid takes from the agent this property.

Labor is property.
In re Jacobs (33 Hun., 379).
Slaughterhouse Cases (16 Wall., 127).

The police power is not without limitations, and in its exercise the legislature must respect the great fundamental rights guaranteed by the constitution.

In re Jacobs (98 N. Y., 110).
Quoting Slaughterhouse Cases (16 Wall., 36–87).
Coe v. Schultz (47 Barb., 64).

The right of the legislature to regulate certain things in regard to businesses affected by a public interest is recognized. Admitting for the purpose of argument that this is a case of that kind, we can not lose sight of the fact that so much of this act as we object to does not regulate the price to be paid or the manner of conducting the business, but deliberately orders that all the requisite work for the carrying out of the contract in question shall be done and shall not be paid for in any way. Especially is the phrase "or accept," at line 20 of paragraph 5, objectionable. By this it is left at the option of the applicant to take from the employment agent the entire fruit of his labors, however faithfully and successfully performed and carried out.

It is, however, even questionable whether this business is one which is "affected with public interest." All the cases in the United States which have sustained such regulations relate to commercial carriers, ferrymen, hackmen, etc., i. e., those whose business was affected by a public interest. On this basis the leading case of Munn v. Illinois (94 Ill., 113) upheld the control of rates of the use of grain elevators in Chicago and in New York. A similar provision was sustained in People v. Bobb (117 N. Y., 1); but even in this last-named case there are strong dissenting opinions by Gray, J., and Peckham, J. In his dissenting opinion Gray, J., says:

"The learned judge writing the opinion concedes that the uses to which a man may devote his property, the price which he may charge for such use, how much he shall demand or receive for his labor, and the methods of conducting his business are, as a general rule, not the subjects of legislative regulations. He well says that 'these are a part of our liberty, of which, under the constitutional guaranty, we can not be deprived.' He believes, however, that he finds in this particular business of elevating grain 'special conditions and circumstances' which justify legislative control. In my view, the concession which the learned judge is obliged to make with respect to our constitutional liberties impairs the force and effect of his opinion, unless he is able to show that the business in question is affected with a public use or interest, within the strict and proper meaning of the term. This I do not see that he accomplishes."

Peckham, J., in his dissenting opinion, states:

"As is said, there can be no legal objection to the power to direct the weight of a loaf of bread, for that is a mere police regulation, interfering with no man's real liberty, and it is the same as if the length of a yard were declared by law, or the weight of a ton. But I deny the right of any legislature in this country to limit the price for which an individual baker shall sell his bread per loaf, or the price per ton for which a coal dealer shall sell his coal, or the price which a tailor shall charge for his coat, or the shoemaker for his shoes."

Section 5 of this act is a taking of property without due process of law.

C. L. SCHURZ.

I agree with Mr. Brown in his testimony that an employment agency is entitled to a reimbursement for services rendered, even though no employment results from his efforts, and a law which does not recognize that right is, according to the opinion of Mr. Schurz and according to the minds of employment agents, unfair and unconstitutional. Labor is property. If the agent performs service, he does not wish to perform that service and not be compensated for such performance.

What is the operation of the employment office? If it be considered only as a registry of names and a place where the agent's sign hangs out before the public, it seems to me that the applicants for employment may reasonably be expected to pay their registration fees for the maintenance of such registry. But an employment agency is not a mere registry of names; it is an active agency. You must take into consideration not only the equipment of the office and its wear and tear, but the expense connected with advertising, stationery, postage, and also the intelligent conduct by the agent in seeking employment for the applicant. Those are actual services rendered for every applicant for employment, and any statute intended to regulate the conduct of employment agencies should recognize the right of the agent to be compensated for services thus rendered

I wish to refer to the ordinances of the city of Buffalo, which has a schedule of such rates as the agent may charge and keep, whether employment results or not; also to the ordinances of the city of Boston, and to the law of the State of Maine, which permits a fee of not over $1, which may be retained by the office if no position has been secured. So the Protective Association of Employment Agencies would favor a definite scale of fees, arranged according to the character of the different kinds of offices, which the agent may keep although no employment may result from his effort, and a certain percentage in case employment is obtained by the applicant for employment, just as outlined by Mr. Brown in his testimony.

Q. You mean to say that there ought to be a scale from, say, $3.50 to $4 a week, up to $50 a week, and that the man that simply brings together an employer and employee is entitled to any of the usufruct after the first fee? What right has the man that simply brought together the two parties to any part in the amount that is earned? What right has he who simply is an errand boy, and has no money in it at all; who pays probably a few dollars of rental, who may have a few blanks, and use a few postage stamps and some shoe leather? Do you advocate that he has the right, after the contract is made, to get a percentage out of the earnings of that man simply because of getting the position for him?—A. I can answer that best by referring to my own experience in St. Bartholomew's Employment Bureau, and that evidence is contained in the Parish Year Book for 1900. The expenses of the conduct of that office for the year ending October 31, 1900, were $5,759.93. The number of persons placed in employment by that office that year was 2,592. In other words, the per capita expense of placing those applicants in positions was $2.22, and that office is operated as economically as an office could possibly be. The average per capita expense in the last five years has been $2.15. Money received in fees and not applied to defray current expenses for the operation of the bureau, has been used for the benefit of applicants for employment through advertising, or turned over as a surplus to the parish treasurer to offset the advantages the bureau receives in the use of rooms, electric lights, and telephone service.

Q. And you charge a fee?—A. You are speaking of free offices; but where are they going to derive a revenue? An employment office is just like a doctor. Many of the cities have their free dispensaries, but the doctor is entitled to his compensation even if he does not cure the patient; the lawyer is entitled to his compensation if he does not win his case. The free employment offices are all right, and the charitable office operated by public contributions is all right; but those that are self-supporting have to look out for their finances. These offices, whether operated under church auspices or as private enterprises, should, as I have stated, be regulated by law, but the law should not be prohibitory.

Q. (By Senator KYLE.) May I ask what are the number of applications you had during the past year?—A. In the year 1899 to 1900 the number of applications from employers in all departments was 3,713; the number of applications from workers in all departments was 5,169.

Q. So you place more than 50 per cent?—A. We have placed exactly 50 per cent. In that connection I want to call your attention to the fact that St. Bartholomew's Employment Bureau, perhaps unlike most employment bureaus, covers the whole field of industry, and operates in four distinct departments—the domestic department, the professional department, the mercantile department, and the department of labor and mechanical trades—and we have kept statistics separate in those four departments. We placed last year 72 per cent of the applicants in the domestic department, 20 per cent in the mercantile, 11 per cent in the professional, and 36 per cent in the labor department.

Q. How do you regulate your fees of parties seeking employment? In the two cases of a girl that wishes employment in a store at $4, $5, $6, or $7 a week, and another party who wishes a position, probably a position in a store, at $75 a month, how do you regulate the fee in that regard; do you charge the same for each?—A. Yes; on a percentage basis.

Q. Percentage of what?—A. Of the first month's salary.

Q. So that a girl getting a place at $5 per week has to pay what?—A. Fifteen per cent of the first month's salary, as a sales girl, for example. We charge 10 per cent of the first month's wages when we place an applicant in the domestic or labor department. In the mercantile and professional departments we charge 15 per cent of the first month's salary. That is the customary charge in New York City, and I want to explain that. In the last 4 months St. Bartholomew's Bureau has been operating without charging any registration fee, and for the first time in its history is operating at a loss. In other words, when the fee charged for the use of the office, to reimburse the office outlays, the actual expenses, is cut off, the office operates at a loss.

Q. Then the fee for registration is required whether you secure a position or not?—A. We have no fee for registration at present. We charge now only in case employment is obtained. This method is all right for St. Bartholomew's Bureau, which is backed by a substantial church corporation. The private, self-supporting agency, which must derive its income from its fees and cover expenses or go out of business, must demand of most of its applicants for employment the payment of the fee in advance as a guarantee of the applicant's good faith, and to reimburse the agent for actual outlays which must be made for the applicant's benefit whether employment results or not.

Q. What fee was formerly charged?—A. Twenty-five cents for the domestic department and 50 cents for the other three.

Q. You say you have 3 or 4 departments. What are they?—A. Domestic, mercantile, professional, and labor.

Q. The first is 10 per cent?—A. Ten per cent in the domestic and labor departments.

Q. Then in the two higher, or the two or three higher, what is your percentage?—A. Fifteen per cent of the first month's salary in the mercantile and professional departments.

Q. That is higher?—A. That is higher. That is a very fair charge, made only to cover expenses.

Q. (By Mr. KENNEDY.) What do you mean by "professional?"—A. Well, that is realy semiprofessional, for our applicants in that class are mostly matrons for institutions, housekeepers, nurses, trained and untrained attendants, and that class of workers. We do not pretend to compete with the teachers' agents in placing teachers; we do not pretend to compete with other agents who deal with a particular kind of employment, and it is an interesting thing to know that the agencies are more and more specializing.

Q. You do not get employment for printers, do you?—A. We have few applications from organized trade workers. They, as has been stated by Mr. Bealin, can take care of themselves. In that connection I will refer again to Mr. Bogart's paper. The title of his paper is "Public employment offices in the United States and Germany," and he concludes, so far as the offices in the United States are concerned:

"'And thus, as to the general outlook for the free offices, the following paragraph from the exhaustive report of the English department of labor on 'Agencies and methods for dealing with the unemployed' will apply equally to the United States:

"'With the best of conditions, labor bureaus can hardly be expected to become the sole or principal means of bringing together employers and unemployed. The bulk of the work of hiring labor and seeking employment will, in most trades, continue to be done directly between workmen and employers, as in the case where, as in France, the system of bureaus has been carried much further than in the United Kingdom. Nor as regards the organized trades can labor bureaus, as a rule, compare in utility, so far as workmen are concerned, with the work of a well-managed trade society. The chief field of usefulness of labor bureaus is likely, therefore, to be found for some time to come in the less highly organized trades.'"

Q. (By Mr. LITCHMAN.) In the less skilled trades?—A. By no means. Many of the most skilled trades are unorganized. As has been stated by Mr. Brown, you must remember that agencies are springing up for professional workers, for all kinds of workers, and those are mostly, as stated in this quotation, unorganized.

Q. (By Mr. KENNEDY.) I should like to ask your opinion of that fee which is permitted by law in the State of Massachusetts, to which reference was made a while ago, $1 in the case of males and 75 cents in the case of females. Do you think this would be a proper fee to be permitted by law in the State of New York?—A. You mean, to be retained by the agent whether employment results or not?

Q. Yes.—A. I think that is a very fair rate for domestic or hotel agencies, and all agencies which place workers at labor and mechanical trades. I do not think it is adequate for the teachers' agencies. I am not so familiar with any of the others. But, you must understand that if the agent succeeds in placing the applicant, a larger fee than $1 or 75 cents is required. The amount you name would only cover incidental expenses. It would not compensate the agent for his services.

By Mr. COMMONS. I think that in Massachusetts that fee is required to be refunded in case there is no employment found. That is the law in Massachusetts.

WITNESS. Yes. I verified the tabulated digest which Mr. Bogart has printed in his paper. There are two matters in which he is incorrect, and I may say that only two State laws require that the agent shall receive no fee unless a position is obtained.

Q. (By Mr. KENNEDY.) I stated that the fee was not returnable. You say you verified that?—A. The State of Massachusetts is one of those States where the agent is not permitted to receive and retain a fee unless a position is obtained. The State of Maine recognizes the right of the agent to make a charge for his services and be reimbursed for his outlay. The law there was revised in 1899 permitting the agent to receive and retain $1, although no employment results from his efforts. The ordinance of the city of Buffalo is the same or similar

Q. You would not consider that an adequate compensation in the State of New York if the fee were to be returned in case of failure to procure employment?—A. As I say, a scale should be arranged which would accomodate itself to the different agencies. It seems to me the more professional agencies should have a larger compensation on account of the special learning; and then there are certain agencies which do business with out-of-town employers almost altogether, as in case of most teachers' agencies, requiring a larger amount of correspondence.

I do not know whether the opposition of the Protective Association of Employment Agencies had to do materially in preventing the passage of the Ford-Kelsey bill or not, but I will take the same stand as heretofore if that bill is introduced again. Our great principle is the principle of home rule, the principle which we wish to emphasize most emphatically. There are State enactments in 13 States, regulating private employment agencies. In one there is no supervision, State or municipal; in Illinois there is State supervision; in the other 11 States the agencies operate under license of the municipality, town council or common council, or by permission of the mayor. Our objection to State supervision lies in the fact that the State bureau of labor statistics has a free bureau in the city of New York, which is conducting a business in opposition to ours. The placing of the business of inspection in the hands of that free office, to examine the books of our offices which are doing business in competition with them, is manifestly unfair, it seems to me; and, moreover, the proposition of the commissioner at the time the Ford-Kelsey bill was introduced was that employment offices should be reduced in number by a large license fee, in order to keep them more easily under inspection, and then to use the revenues derived from the balance of the agencies for the establishment of free bureaus throughout the State of New York. In other words, the offices in New York City were required to pay taxes for the establishment of free offices in New York and up the State.

Q. (By Mr. FARQUHAR.) Do you speak of competition for St. Bartholomew's in this intelligence agency? Do you mean in this modern age that it is run for business profit?—A. I simply stated our aim, which is to cover our expenses, and the purpose is to have an office which will deal with perfect fairness with all concerned.

Q. What are the competitive features of the State bureau as to your work?—A. I may say that it is antagonistic to the private offices. That antagonism is shown in their printed reports, and I think that while there are frauds and abuses, as I said in the beginning, it is easy to check them. The objections to the private "pay" agencies may outrun reason, may outrun justice, may outrun equity, and the officers of the State Labor Department must guard themselves against that.

Q. Do you think that the Ford-Kelsey bill, if enacted into law, would have been an advance or of benefit in the regulation of the employment agencies over and above the present laws you have in the State?—A. I would much prefer the existing law in the city of New York to the Ford-Kelsey bill.

Q. What percentage of the agencies in your own city are semicharitable or philanthropic?—A. Some of the philanthropic agencies in the city of New York are the Young Woman's Christian Association agency, the agency of the Salvation Army, and the Alliance Bureau, which is affiliated with about 20 charities. And I want to say that every semiphilanthropic employment agency in the city of New York indorsed the Price-Fuller bill, which the Protective Association of Employment Agencies advanced at the last legislature, which was passed by the legislature, vetoed by the mayor, repassed over the mayor's veto, and then vetoed by the governor.

Q. (By Mr. KENNEDY.) Why did the mayor veto it?—A. I am sorry I have not a copy of his veto here. I think Mr. Brown might more easily answer that if the question was referred to him.

Q. (By Mr. FARQUHAR.) Was it the present administration at Albany—the present governor—that vetoed it?—A. Yes.

Q. (By Mr. KENNEDY.) Do you know why the governor vetoed it?—A. I have no means of knowing; I can only guess. I think it was merely because the mayor had vetoed it. I think that our bill, the Price-Fuller bill, could have been improved upon had the Protective Association of Employment Agencies, who had the drawing of that bill in charge, consulted with the mayor's marshal, Mr. Roche, chief of the bureau of licenses, and the deputy chief, Mr. Brown. We might have agreed upon a bill which would have passed and would have been signed by the mayor. It is my desire to draw another bill, either as an amendment to the existing law or an entirely new law, for the next session of the legislature, so that all interested can agree upon its terms and to avoid in the future having this question reopened.

Q. (By Mr. FARQUHAR.) Has the establishment of the State bureau or this intelligence office by the State been of any advantage in the regulation of intelligence offices of this city?—A. I have no knowledge that it has ever had any advantage. I am not posted as to that

Q. Has there any advantage come from the bureau in this city in respect to the management and mismanagement of intelligence offices through that department of the State government?—A. They attempted legislation in the Ford-Kelsey bill, and legislation failed. At that time there was a crusade against employment offices, conducted by the New York Journal, which resulted in closing, I believe, only one or two employment offices in the city.

Q. (By Mr. LITCHMAN.) What difference is there between the fees charged by the association you represent and the ordinary fees charged by employment agencies? I am not speaking now of the semicharitable, but I am speaking of the ordinary agencies that come into the work as a matter of business.—A. The Protective Association of Employment Agencies has no uniform charge for all its members. The charge is left to the discretion of the separate agencies, and the charges are quite different among those agencies, as has already been stated by Mr. Brown.

Q. Are your fees less than the average of other societies in the same business? I am speaking now of the St. Bartholomew Society that you belong to?—A. There are some agencies that are not under philanthropic auspices. Charitable societies, church societies; they have the same basis of fees that we have. That is, they make a charge on the same principles that we do, but I think their charges are less in amount. One reason we make a charge is to avoid the charity basis. The other is to give support to the Employment Bureau.

Q. Do the bulk of them have higher fees?—A. Am not informed as to that. I do not think so. I think, as far as I am informed, that there is a good deal of freedom of contract on that point.

Q. You have testified, as I understand, that the fees now charged by you are not remunerative—that you are conducting part, at least, of your business at a loss. Are you recouping on the other part of your business for the loss in the free work you are doing?—A. What other part, sir?

Q. Well, is there any part of the business you are doing at a loss?—A. I am speaking of St. Bartholomew Employment Bureau as a whole; for January, February, and March there was a deficit. Whether there will be a deficit at the end of the fiscal year or not I am not prepared to say.

Q. But under the conditions you have reason to anticipate the same?—A. I have reason to fear there will be a loss.

Q. How is that loss recouped?—A. I do not see how it can be, except through the treasury of the parish.

Q. That is, if it can not come out of the business.—A. If it can not come out of the business.

Q. Are you practically running a free establishment to that degree?—A. Philanthropic to that degree.

Q. Then it is only a question of degree between you and the State establishment, is it not? I understand you that the State establishment is free entirely.—A. Entirely free.

Q. And yours is practically so?—A. We do not aim to be. I think we can arrange that by cutting down expenses so that we will come out even at the end of the year. We are going to try to do so. That is what we aim to do. We want to do it.

Q. You are not running the institution as a money-making concern?—A. By no means. We want it to pay its own way, and we are going to make it do so if we possibly can. It ought to, if possible.

Q. (By Mr. CLARKE.) Do you think it is any part of the business of the State to furnish or find employment for people?—A. I have no reason to oppose the State free employment bureau in any of its purposes or operations if its purpose is to place needy employees in position. There are many applicants for employment who do not go to that office because it makes no charge for positions, as they think they would be receiving charity. Mr. Bealin contends that it is not a charity, that it is supported by the taxpayers of the State, but the applicants for employment do not all see it that way. They prefer the private pay offices, just as a man seeking medical attendance prefers his private physician rather than the free dispensary. Applicants for employment are not taxpayers. The benefits derived by these applicants from the State free bureau are paid for not by themselves, but by some one else. In this sense they may be right in maintaining that the free bureau, as to them, is a charity. The taxpayers derive a benefit from the free State bureau in only one way—it is a convenience to some of them as employers. It can not be said that employers are saved by that bureau from the annoyance of having their premises invaded by applicants for employment, because 9 out of 10 of the applicants for employment in that bureau are women for domestic service, a class of applicants who never solicit work by going to the homes of employers uninvited. Then, too, so far as employers are concerned, many of the taxpayers who, as Mr. Bealin claims, are the persons who pay for the maintenance of the free State bureau, are not employers of help of any kind, and of those taxpayers who are employers few patronize that bureau as compared with the number of employers who patronize the 426 private pay employment agencies in Greater New York. I do not mention this as an objection to the free bureau. I mention it only for the sake of distinction between the private pay agency and the free public agency. The same distinction exists, possibly, as regards taxpayers that exists between private and public schools. Each has its field and proper place and should not attempt to impair the usefulness of the other, but rather set an example of excellence which the other may emulate. Many employers do not patronize the free bureau because they assume that the free bureau attracts the unthrifty or the otherwise undesirable applicants. My observation has been, after considerable experience in studying applicants for employment, that lack of money is not, prima facie, an evidence of lack of character or ability, although the possession of money may be good evidence of the possession of both. It is a fact, however, that the free bureau, while aiding the deserving poor who are in need of work, does not obtain the registration of self-reliant persons who do not choose to be dependent upon State aid. I do not mean the poor and proud only, but the fairly well-to-do and independent, who, when out of work, prefer to do business on a business basis. An employment agent who is paid by employers or employees for his services is under not only a moral obligation, but is bound by a legal obligation, having in it a monetary consideration, to perform the services and do them well. The pay office has this advantage over the free office. It has the activity of enterprise. It wins clients and patrons by deeds of kindness, also, which are impossible in the free office, however charitably inclined. Besides giving counsel and encouragement to assist the struggling applicants to seek employment, they lend money without interest to applicants who are well known to them, they advance car fares, place many applicants in positions, and trust them for payment or make no charge whatever, or act as bankers for the saving of wages which servants going to distant places for a season's work do not wish to take with them, but which they may wish to draw upon during their absence or receive in full on their return to town. There is charity in abundance given in the private pay employment agencies as occasion requires. So far as the State is concerned, I do not think it is a necessary part of its business to furnish or find employment for people in the city of New York in normal, prosperous times like these, nor do I think the State ought to create avenues for bestowing charity if the occasion does not require it. The private employment agencies in the city of New York relieve applicants for employment from having to ask charity, while dealing charitably with all; and being self-supporting they relieve the general public of the burden of supporting them. They are maintained only by those persons who pay for services rendered them under the contract of agency. As to the success of the free State employment bureau in this State and other States, I respectfully refer your attention to the excellent compilation of facts and opinions contained in Mr. Bogart's paper, already mentioned.

Since giving my testimony to the commission and before presentation of the proof of it to me for revision, I have made a thorough inquiry into the condition of employment agencies in the city of Buffalo. The information I obtained modifies Mr. Bealin's testimony materially in one very important particular. Judge King has not been on the bench there as police justice for about 3 years. The ordinance now regulating employment agencies there went into effect in June, 1898. This was before the Ford-Kelsey bill was presented in Albany. It is the testimony of the present justice (Murphy), the license clerk in the mayor's office, and 9 employment agents whom I interviewed, the best in the city, including the Women's Christian Association, that the ordinance has worked very well indeed, having reduced the number of agencies to 23 through its annual license fee of only $24, and easily and effectually removed the fraudulent practices described by Mr. Bealin, which were prevalent there in Judge King's day, before the ordinance went into effect. That ordinance is a municipal ordinance, and it recognizes the right of the agent to be compensated for services and reimbursed for outlays although no employment results from his efforts. Some of its provisions could be improved upon, I think, but as it is it has worked so well that no criticism can be made to-day about the condition of the employment agencies in Buffalo.

Testimony closed.

WASHINGTON, D. C., *March 9, 1901.*

TESTIMONY OF MR. SIMON WOLF,

Attorney at law, Washington, D. C.

The commission met at 10.40 a. m., Mr. Phillips presiding. At that time Hon. Simon Wolf, Washington, D. C., an attorney at law, was introduced as a witness and, being duly sworn, testified as follows:

Q. (By Mr. LITCHMAN.) Will you kindly give your name, post-office address, and occupation?—A. Simon Wolf; 926 F street, Washington, D. C; attorney at law.

Q. You have been the representative of the United States Government abroad at one time?—A. I have. I was consul-general and agent diplomatique to Egypt.

Q. You have been for a great many years connected with the fraternal and benevolent societies of the Hebrew people?—A. Yes.

Q. You are familiar in a general way with the measures taken by those people for the reception and dissemination of the immigration that comes into this country?—A. I am.

Q. You have been connected with the organization of B'nai B'rith, have you not?—A. Yes.

Q. You are at the present time vice-president of that organization?—A. I was up to last May.

Q. Is that an organization having in a general way charge of these matters?—A. No; I will explain.

Q. Then go on in your own way.—A. In the first place, the Jews of the United States have never, either in their collective or individual capacity, had any organization looking to or aiming at Jewish immigration in any way or manner. The exodus caused by persecution in Russia in 1882 was the first cause which stirred the people of our faith, citizens of the United States, to care for, to distribute, and assimilate those of the sufferers who had found their way to this country. At that time leading representatives of the Jews of the United States met in the city of New York, and, fearing that the large number of people that would be dumped on the United States would become not only a menace for the moment but a great burden upon their coreligionists, they appointed representative men to go to Europe and confer with leading Jews of London, Berlin, Frankfort, Vienna, Paris, and other centers, and to prevent this wholesale immigration and divert as much as possible the large stream of unfortunate refugees. Notices were published in the Jewish press of the disturbed districts warning the people against precipitate flight from their homes, and especially against indiscriminate emigration to America. A great deal was accomplished at that time, and but a fraction of the immense number of expatriated Jews of Russia came here. Of those who came, many were impoverished, and to the end that these should not become a burden to the country or to local communities the generous-hearted citizens of the United States of Jewish faith took them in hand. Thus, for instance, we received some 10 or 15 families in Washington, for whom we cared. They were men that were engaged in various industries. One was a shoemaker, another a carpenter, another had been a dairyman. For one man we purchased cows, and he sold the milk; for another we purchased a horse, and he did work on the roads; to another man we furnished tools for his carpenter's trade, and for another man tools for his work as a shoemaker. These people have maintained themselves, and are now in this city, as others like them are in nearly every center of our country, and are industrious, law-abiding, prosperous citizens.

The exodus continued for a year or two and then diminished for 7 or 8 years, until 1891, when all at once the same conditions, only aggravated, broke out again in Russia. It was at that time that Baron Maurice de Hirsch, the well-known Jewish philanthropist, whose acts of benevolence have become known throughout the world, offered the Czar some $10,000,000 for the purpose of establishing secular primary schools for the Russian Jews, whose children were practically debarred from the public schools. Historically, it is stated that the Czar was willing and anxious to comply, but the ruling party of the nobility in Russia prevented it, and persecutions, more terrible than ever, were renewed. The neighboring states of Austria and Germany attempted to stem the tide of the fleeing refugees, and these poor people were hounded from pillar to post, until their condition became most deplorable. Nothing in the history of mankind has been more heartrending than the condition of these unfortunate Jews. Despite the efforts to avoid it, a considerable number of the refugees came to the United States, and a large proportion of the immigrants settled in New York City. The American Jews at once addressed themselves to the task of Americanizing the newcomers. Special attention was given to the danger of pauperizing these people by unscientific charity, and therefore the greatest efforts were directed to educational methods. To advance these and the moral, mental, and physical conditions of the poorer Jews, a considerable fund was provided by Baron de Hirsch, and the same was augmented later by his widow, the baroness. What is known as the Baron de Hirsch Fund is managed by a board of trustees, of which Judge Meyer S. Isaacs is the president, and of which Hon. Oscar S. Straus, lately our minister to Turkey, Mr. Jacob H. Schiff, Mr. Seligman, and Mr. Hoffman, of New York, and Mr. W. B. Hackenburg and Judge Meyer Sulzberger, of Philadelphia, are members. The trustees have built industrial schools at various centers, and have in general achieved splendid results. The Jews of New York established the great Educational Alliance on East Broadway, the attendance upon which averages in excess of 5,000 persons per day. The Baroness de Hirsch made a loan of $100,000 to the building fund of this institution, and thereafter, being so much impressed by its usefulness, made a gift of the mortgage to the alliance. This institution has taken an active part in the vice crusade that is now being waged in New York City. Mr. Isadore Straus is president. There also exists the Hebrew Technical Institute, which educates Jewish boys for mechanical and scientific pursuits. Mr. Steinem, of New York City, recently gave $100,000 to establish the metal-working department. The institution has been achieving wonderful success, and is one of the great factors in eliminating mendicancy and pauperism.

Q. Is that the one with which Mr. Blaustein is connected?—A. Yes. That has been thoroughly established and is doing a vast amount of good. No doubt you are aware of the educational methods pursued in all these institutions. The Constitution of the United States and the Declaration of Independence are made a part of the educational system, and on every desk of the children there is a tiny United States flag. The duties of patriotism are inculcated in the fullest degree. The De Hirsch trust has also founded, or rather has stimulated and encouraged what had previously been founded under the first exodus of Russian refugees, the well-known "Vineland Colony," and other colonies in New Jersey, and various settlements in Connecticut. Those in New Jersey, however, have proven most effective and prosperous. They are doing admirable work there. In these different settlements are farmers, tilling the soil as their ancestors did thousands of years ago. They are a sober and law-abiding people. They have no drinking shops and no police. None are necessary. They take care of themselves and various industries have been built up there in Vineland and other parts of New Jersey.

Q. (By Mr. PHILLIPS.) What is the population, please, of Vineland?—A. The figures are given in an article relating to the colonies, which I will submit:

"THE NEW JERSEY COLONIES.

"From the independent New Jersey colonies at Alliance, Norma, Carmel, and Rosenhayn, we are in receipt of detailed reports by Mr. J. C. Reis, one of the most earnest-minded and resolute of the later settlers at Norma. From these it appears that the settlement at Alliance and around its railway station, Norma, contains 512 inhabitants, composing 96 families. Of these, 33 families are devoted exclusively to farming; 12 to farming and tailoring combined; 36 to farming and other workshop occupations; 15 to tailoring exclusively. They own over 1,500 acres of land, of which 530 are in fruit cultivation, 577 are devoted to truck raising, and the remainder is uncultivated. There are 87 dwelling houses and 141 additional buildings. The total valuation is $112,000, of which $44,000 is unpaid. The value of last year's product was $17,808, of which $10,712 worth was sold and the remainder consumed. They own 55 horses, 79 cows, and 4,700 chickens.

"Carmel contains 89 Jewish families, comprising 471 individuals. The exclusively farming families number 19, farming and tailoring 14, farming and trades other than tailoring 23, and tailoring exclusively 33. They own 1,029 acres of land—113 under fruit, 504 under truck, and 456 uncultivated. There are 46 dwelling houses occupied, besides a number that are vacant, and 86 occupied outbuildings. Their holdings are valued at $84,574, on which there remains an indebtedness of $26,273. The yearly product is valued at $12,585, of which $8,200 was sold and the remainder consumed. They have 36 horses, 114 cows, and 3,300 chickens.

"The figures for Rosenhayn were obtained by Prof. A. L. Sabsovich, the well-known superintendent of Woodbine Colony. At this place there are 47 settlers, holding a total of 1,388 acres, of which 948 are under cultivation. These colonists have 7,215 fruit trees, 28,770 grape vines, 128 horses and cows, and 6,000 chickens. The valuation is $85,520, on which there is an indebtedness of $26,986.

"From these accounts it is manifest that these colonies have quite passed the problematic stage, although some of the colonists are still insecure in their holdings. All would be greatly helped and the general cause be greatly furthered if some of the efforts now being given to less promising fields of philanthropy were devoted to the educational and material upbuilding of these settlements. The establishment of a properly equipped wine press and of a canning factory, under competent business direction, would be a great desideratum to the end in view."

Q. (By Mr. LITCHMAN.) You speak of Vineland. That is a village adjoining Vineland? It is not Vineland proper?—A. No; but it is usually so designated. Vineland was the post-office originally. Now there are 4 post-offices in the colonies.

Q. There is another settlement farther down in Jersey, Woodbine, is there not?—A. Yes.

Now, in all these movements and in all these endeavors there has never been on the part of the Jews of the United States any organization that stimulated, encouraged, desired, or wished this wholesale influx of their coreligionists, and for the very natural reason that, as the traditions and customs and habits of the Jews from time immemorial have been to help their own, the larger the number of unfortunates that would come here, the larger the burden that would fall upon the shoulders of our older Jewish communities. And while our hearts were surcharged, as every human being's should be, with pity and sympathy, we naturally preferred that they should remain in the countries in which they had been born, provided they could there enjoy at least the immunities, if not the privileges, of their fellow-countrymen. But this has legally been made impossible in Russia and in Roumania. By studying the tables of immigration, as furnished by General Powderly, you will find that the streams of immigration or rather of refugees, came mainly from the Slavic States, and, within the last few years, from Austria and its Slavic provinces. From the countries where the Jew is treated with equality and is recognized as a citizen, there has been scarcely any immigration at all. The people are reasonably happy in their respective countries, and they accordingly do not leave their native lands, even for the greater opportunities they would naturally enjoy here. In 1870, when the political ferment in the Balkan States, which afterwards resulted in the Russo-Turkish war, was beginning to be of international importance, our Government, for the first time, felt called upon to have a diplomatic agent in Roumania, and for that purpose President Grant accredited Mr. Benjamin F. Peixotto to the Roumanian Government. Mr. Peixotto had been for five years the head of the order of B'nai B'rith, and, with the consent of our State Department, he took steps looking to the political amelioration of the Roumanian Jews, with a view to preventing their enforced immigration from their homes. He founded the Society of Zion, on the exact model of the order B'nai B'rith, and organized it especially as an educational agency, open and subject to governmental supervision. This society, through Mr. Peixotto, brought about the recognition of the Jews in the Treaty of Berlin in 1878. By the provisions of this treaty, through the efforts especially of Lord Beaconsfield and Prince Bismarck, the political rights of the Jews in Roumania were guaranteed, and for a number of years the Jews of Roumania did enjoy a higher degree of tolerance and protection. But, within the last two years, as a result of the Dreyfus agitation, anti Somitism has broken out afresh in Roumania, and over 20,000 men and women of that country have recently been compelled to leave their country, harassed, antagonized, persecuted, maligned, with every privilege of humanity denied them, through the malignant conduct of the ministry of that period. The present ministry is more liberal, but how long it will last remains to be seen. A fraction of the refugees from Roumania came to this country; but the larger number of them required no assistance, inasmuch as they possessed some means with which to establish themselves in the United States. Believing it to be inexpedient that the most helpless ones should settle in large cities, the order of B'nai B'rith addressed itself to the task of securing employment for these in different parts of the country, and so distributing them that they might the more readily become Americanized. The plans of the order have been carried out and about 2,000 Roumanians have been distributed to over 200 different places in the United States. Prior to this, however, correspondence by cable as well as by post had been carried on with the various communities of Europe by Leo N. Levi, president of the order, urging them to prevent all but those fully competent to maintain themselves from coming to these shores. The stream of immigration has been, accordingly, largely diverted. Some of these people were attracted by the Zionist movement to Palestine and went there; others went to Anatolia and to Cyprus, and some went to Argentina. Every effort was made by the Jews of the United States, and especially by the order of B'nai B'rith, to prevent wholesale immigration to this country, and we accomplished our purpose. The number of immigrants and refugees that have come here has been comparatively small, and they have been of a very high order of manhood and womanhood—people of a very superior character, artisans and mechanics. One ship came over with 119 persons, every one able to care for himself or herself and to go forward at once to the various centers in the interior of the country to make a living without becoming a burden.

You will find from the report of Robert Watchhorn, special agent of the Bureau of Immigration of the Treasury Department, that he found the condition in Roumania exactly as I have described it, and he praises in no unstinted words the character, ability, intelligence, and moral worth of these people.

The order of B'nai B'rith is nearly 60 years old. It was founded by a number of earnest-minded men (German immigrants, mostly), who had come here under normal conditions, as other immigrants came in those times. It has had for its main object the Americanization of its members, and in this direction has accomplished a vast amount of educational work. The president of the organization during the 35 years ending May, 1900, was Mr. Julius Bien, of New York, well known as a leading cartographer and as a map maker for many departments of our Government. Under his direction the order spread throughout America, and has been successfully established in Europe. There are lodges of the organization in Austria, in Germany, in Roumania, in the Holy Land, and efforts are now being made to start one in France.

Thus you will see the scope and wide range of usefulness of this order of B'nai B'rith as an agency of commercial and national progress. Its function is primarily one of education, and it strives to elevate the moral and intellectual standard of its members and to fit them to become worthy citizens of the United States.

Q. Right there would it not be well to say something concerning the membership and resources of the organization in this country and so on?—A. The membership of this organization is at present about 20,000. It has 7 districts in the United States and 3 in Europe. The fifth district, for instance, in which Washington is included, combines the District of Columbia, Virginia, Maryland, North and South Carolina, and Georgia.

I would state that it is not only in the direction of education that this organization and kindred organizations have worked, but also in the founding of hospitals, of homes for the aged, of orphan asylums for unfortunate children, of free libraries, and of industrial schools. In the city of Cleveland there exists, I suppose, the model orphan asylum of the world. It has been so regarded. In the city of Atlanta there is an orphan home, which was established by the order and of which I have been the president since its foundation 25 years ago. In Yonkers the order has a home for the aged. In New Orleans there is an orphan asylum of the highest efficiency, managed and supported in part by the order. At Denver it supports a national hospital for consumptives which is open to the world without reference to creed or nationality. In Philadelphia there is a hospital, originally initiated by the order and open to all people irrespective of faith, and a manual-training school directly controlled by it. In New Orleans there is a hospital and a home founded by Judah Touro, but now largely maintained and endowed by this order. In New York there is what is known as the Maimonides Library, and the number of books taken from that library, in comparison, is far in excess of the number taken from the public libraries of New York.

But the work of the B'nai B'rith is only part of what has been done to further the effective assimilation of the Russian Jewish refugees in our American Commonwealth. In every large city, and in many of the minor towns of the country, societies have been organized and have worked earnestly to that end. In New York there is a vast network of affiliated organizations which are ramifications from the central body of the United Hebrew Charities, and which all deal, almost exclusively, with this element of the population. Besides the aid given for the relief of actual physical necessities, including hospitals, orphan asylums, churches, and other like institutions, there is centered in the Educational Alliance a system of day schools, night schools, and manual-training schools, which afford instruction to thousands of pupils of all ages and of both sexes. A similar situation is presented in Philadelphia, where the Foster Home, the Hebrew Convocation Society, with its day, night, and industrial schools, the Maternity Hospital and the United Hebrew Charities, as well as the National Farm School at Doylestown, all deal with practically no other class than the Russian Jews. A similar condition prevails in Baltimore, in Boston, in Pittsburg, Cincinnati, Chicago, St. Louis, San Francisco, Portland, Oregon, and, in fact, as already stated, in all the larger communities throughout the land. In Chicago, notably, a very widely varified system of charity has been established, which includes, especially, a manual-training school of the first rank. There is also the great hospital founded by the heirs of Michael Reese and open to comers of every faith.

You will understand, gentlemen, that the revolution of 1848 brought the first notable number of Jews to this country. They were principally Germans, who have since become some of the foremost citizens of our country, active in war as well as peace. Many of these immigrants still live and they and their descendants feel a keen interest in their coreligionists who are oppressed and persecuted, aside from the keen interest they take in the cause of humanity generally.

I have been for the last 25 years the president of the committee on civil and religious rights of the Union of American Hebrew Congregations of the United States. This organization maintains a college in Cincinnati, which was founded by the late Dr. I. M. Wise, and which is well known and recognized as a great educational institution. And throughout these 25 years I have had more or less intimate connection and frequent contact with the various branches of our Government, especially the Immigration Bureau and the State Department, through my work in caring for and protecting the rights of the Jews, individually and collectively, at home and abroad, so far as it came within the power of an American citizen so to do without infringing the constitutional laws of our country.

As I said, so far from there having been any systematic effort to stimulate immigration, all our strivings have been to regulate, and, if possible, to reduce it. Whatever has been done has been in the nature of humanitarianism, of protection, of education, of assimilation; and we are thoroughly in sympathy with every effort of this Government to prevent improper immigration, or such as may prove inimical to this country.

We are in full accord with the laws that have been passed to prevent the immigration of criminals or paupers, or diseased persons, or any persons that are unfit to enjoy the franchise of our Government; but we do know one fact, and it can not be too strongly emphasized, and that is that the vast majority of the immigrants of all nationalities who have in the last 50 or 60 years come to this country, and who are now the bone and sinew of American citizenship, came in practically the same condition of financial poverty as that in which the majority of the immigrants come now, a poverty which is often made the pretext for projects of exclusion.

I remember that when I came with my grandparents in 1848 we had scarcely $5 to our name. A relative who had come 5 or 6 years before met us and cared for us. I do not wish for a moment to insinuate that the country has specially profited by my being permitted to land, but I am sure it has not lost anything; and so it has been with nearly all of the immigrants who have come here, and many of whom have made this country greater and more happy.

There is no fund available in this country, either out of the funds of the Order of B'nai B'rith or out of the Baron De Hirsch Trust Fund, for paying the transportation hither of any of these refugees or unfortunate immigrants.

Q. How are the funds provided for this charitable work, and this work of distribution to which you have referred?—A. The transportation to the different points in the interior of the country is paid out of the charity funds of the various larger communities. At the seaboard cities, the Baron De Hirsch Trust Fund contributes to relieve these centers and to send these people to the various places to which they have been allotted.

Q. How are these various asylums maintained, to which you have referred?—A. They are maintained solely by the voluntary contributions of the members of the order and of the Jews generally in the respective districts.

In addition, I may take occasion to state that in Denver there was founded last year a hospital for Jewish consumptives, which is maintained largely by the Order of B'nai B'rith, each member of the order in the United States contributing 25 cents annually toward the maintenance. Jews from all over the country become annual subscribers. One of the lady agents of this institution was here the other day, and I went around with her, and in a short time we succeeded in raising $500 in annual contributions for that very worthy charity, which takes in no pay patients whatever, but only those who are unfortunate and unable to care for themselves.

Q. (By Mr. PHILLIPS.) Is there any objection to the existence of that institution in Colorado?—A. Objection?

Q. Yes; among the citizens in the community?—A. None at all. In Denver there are 6 or 7 hospitals caring for consumptives who pay, and this institution is only another of similar character. You see, Jewish consumptives were flocking to Denver on account of the climate, and they became a great tax and burden upon that small Jewish community; and hence their coreligionists throughout the country and the order of B'nai B'rith took the matter up and assisted. A number of philanthropists in different parts of the country gave a thousand to five thousand dollars each. One gentleman gave ten thousand and Mr. Grabfelder, of Louisville, the president of the hospital, gave $20,000.

Q. (By Mr. LITCHMAN.) These institutions are also sustained by bequests by benevolent Jewish people?—A. Yes. For instance, I received for the home in Atlanta, from the Baroness de Hirsch $7,500; and she showed her liberality and her world-wide recognition of all faiths in that, when I wrote to her, she sent me a check for $5,000 for Garfield Hospital of this city. Furthermore, quite a number of members of the order, and other Jews, have insured their lives for the benefit of the homes for the aged and of the orphan asylums. The other day I received checks from the relatives of three persons who had died and who had insured their lives for the benefit of the orphan home in Atlanta, each of them for $1,000. Bequests are made frequently. I was called up day before yesterday by a gentleman from Richmond who wanted to know the exact title of the Hebrew Orphan Home in Atlanta, as a client of his wanted to leave something by will. And what is true of the home in Atlanta is unquestionably equally true of almost every one of these institutions. They do not receive a dollar from any public or State treasury. Of course there are quite a large number of Christian friends living in the communities where these institutions exist who recognize the worth and value of these institutions and who undoubtedly contribute annually and possibly leave something in their wills. But they are not very numerous, as we do not make propaganda in that direction. We have a pride in caring for our own, apart from doing our share as citizens in every other direction.

Q. Does your work contemplate and carry out, in some localities, manual training for the younger portion of your people?—A. It does in Cleveland, in Philadelphia, and in Atlanta. In the Atlanta asylum we not only care for the orphans while they are with us, but we try and secure for them employment afterwards. We educate the girls to be housemaids and cooks—the great social problem in the future of our country; and the boys become mechanics, artisans, and stenographers and typewriters. We have had two weddings in our orphan home in the last three years. After the girls have gone away they consider themselves still under our guardianship, and the weddings were held at the home. All the children were present and had a glorious time.

Q. Is not this the case also at Woodbine, in New Jersey?—A. Absolutely; and in Philadelphia, as I have already remarked, there is an industrial school under the order of the B'nai B'rith; and we have industrial schools under the order of B'nai B'rith in Jaffa and in Jerusalem. Indeed, when I was consul-general to Egypt I aided in the starting of a lodge of the order at Cairo, Egypt, which has done a large amount of good; and all the good done in this direction naturally, like a wave current, reacts to aid us here.

Q. (By Mr. PHILLIPS.) At some point in your statement will you come to the number of the Israelites or Jewish people in the world? Have you an idea of about the number?—A. Yes; there are at present between nine and ten millions.

Q. How are they distributed?—A. There are between five and six millions in Russia.

Q. Indeed?—A. Yes; and the others are scattered all over the world.

Q. Could you give the reason why so many drifted into Russia?—A. Yes; briefly. They moved eastward from the Rhineland under the stress of persecutions during the Middle Ages, and were welcomed by the Kings of Bohemia and Poland. They grew in numbers there and lived at peace until Bohemia was conquered by the Hapsburgs of Austria, and Poland, later, became a prey to the Muscovites. Since then, especially in Poland and Lithuania, the Jews have suffered, in common with the Roman Catholics and Baptists, from the political and religious enmity of the Russians. A considerable number found their way to central Europe after their expulsion from Spain.

Q. About the time Columbus discovered this country? In that persecution?—A. Yes.

Q. At the time of the establishment of the Inquisition?—A. Yes. In 1876 Mr. Hackenburg, of Philadelphia, and myself tabulated a census of the Jews of the United States, and at that time—in 1876—there were only, as far as we could find, 150,000 Jews in the United States. But owing to these persecutions in other lands that number has of course very largely increased. I suppose there are at present in the United States between 800,000 and 900,000 Jews. Yet, as I have shown in a book published by me, entitled The American Jew as Soldier, Patriot, and Citizen, there were a larger number of Jews in the Northern and Southern Armies, in proportion to their numbers, than of men of any other faith in the United States.

Q. (By Mr. LITCHMAN.) Is there any means by which the Jewish population of the United States is shown in the census of 1900?—A. I think not, except so far as the congregations would show. There has been a question and a contention, of which you are no doubt aware, as to scheduling or tabulating the immigrant Jews as Jews. I protested against this classification to Mr. Powderly, and we had a conference in the city of New York, at which he and some of his agents were present. People come in as Austrians, Italians, Germans, Greeks, and not as Catholics or Protestants. The religious proclivities of the individual is no concern of the United States. And I believe the Attorney-General, in answer to the question propounded by the Superintendent of the present census, sustained that view. That is a matter, however, which you can easily ascertain.

Q. How, then, can you form an estimate that there are but 800,000 Jews in the United States?—A. I say we ourselves have estimated that number. The number of synagogues is given, with their location and their membership, just as are other places of worship.

Q. (By Mr. PHILLIPS.) About what per cent of the Jewish people belong to the church—attend synagogue worship?—A. Among those who adhere strictly to the ancient Jewish ritual and liturgy nearly all are members of the synagogue; of the reform Jews there is quite a contingent who are not members of any congregation, yet who contribute to every Jewish charity and every Jewish educational enterprise. Of course I do not suppose you want to go into the difference between the orthodox and the reform element?

Q. You spoke of the general thrift of the Jewish people. How is it in New York, in the Jewish settlements there? Are not a great many of them, or quite a large per cent, engaged in the sweat shop work in that quarter of the city?—A. There have been and undoubtedly still are many undesirable conditions in that respect, but much has been done to ameliorate these conditions and to prevent their growth. The so-called sweat-shop system is not at the present time so serious a condition as it was a few years ago, owing to the fact that the people in New York have taken hold of it energetically and systematically and intelligently.

Q. Well, in that portion of the city about where Five Points used to be, how do the Jewish people compare with the Italians and others that are immigrants to this country in sweat-shop work?—A. There is, strictly speaking, no such comparison to be made, because the Jews of that section are of a far higher grade of manhood and intelligence. As the New York Sun stated in an editorial a few years ago, when there was a great deal of trouble among the laboring men, the Jewish laborers, when Friday evening comes and the Sabbath commences, withdraw from all the deliberations and from the vicinity of their shops to their places of worship, and are always law-abiding and orderly, showing a high grade of moral and religious instinct, which the others never do.

Q. You think there are not as many of them engaged in the sweating industry as of other elements?—A. The sweat shops, or, more accurately, the small shops, are those of the tailoring industry, and the operators are nearly all Russian Jews. But the Educational Alliance and the industrial schools, of which I have spoken, are all in that locality, and thus, as you can easily imagine, a very beneficial influence is exercised in that quarter.

Q. The impression is prevalent, however, that a large per cent of the immigrants and of the Jewish people have been engaged in the sweat shop service and work. That impression seems to prevail.—A. I am aware of it. But it is not accurate. The subject has been taken hold of and investigated by intelligent and impartial American citizens not of the Jewish faith, and much of the popular impression regarding the matter was found to be exaggerated.

Q. Have the Jewish people been as competitive among themselves as the Aryan race?—A. There is far more mutual help and charity among these Russian-Jewish working people than among immigrants of other faiths, but there is also a keener and more searching competition. The Jew is innately individualistic, optimistic, and ambitious. He accepts charity only as a last resource, and would rather work for half a loaf than take a whole one in charity. The poor immigrant may accept a low wage as better than none, but he is sharp to further his own interests, and uses the low wage only as a stepping stone to a higher one. As a result, the strife between the wage taker and the wage giver and between the members of each class comparatively is sharper and keener than among the other newcomers. In general I may say that the economic question involved in the presence in this country of the Russian Jews is one that would quickly solve itself and vanish from our consideration if but the condition out of which it has grown were normalized. So long as these people are forced out from their homes, as they have been, we here, in this land of freedom and of hope, must permit them to find here an asylum, as all of us here have found one in the past. But we may reasonably suggest to our Government, and this commission is in a position to make the suggestion, that it might use its influence with the Government of the Czar to do justice to his Jewish subjects, and not to enforce on the American people the alternative of taking the burden of alleviating the miseries of Russian oppression or shutting our gates against its victims.

The late President Harrison stated, in the following forcible language, in his third message to Congress, the feeling of each and every citizen of the United States:

"This Government has found occasion to express in a friendly spirit, but with much earnestness, to the Government of the Czar its serious concern because of the harsh measures now being enforced against the Hebrews in Russia. By the revival of anti-Semitic laws, long in abeyance, great numbers of those unfortunate people have been constrained to abandon their homes and leave the Empire by reason of the impossibility of finding subsistence within the pale to which it is sought to confine them. The immigration of these people to the United States—many of the other countries being closed to them—is largely increasing, and is likely to assume proportions which may make it difficult to find homes and employment for them here and to seriously affect the labor market. It is estimated that over 1,000,000 will be forced from Russia within a few years. The Hebrew is never a beggar; he has always kept the laws, often under severe and oppressive civil restrictions. It is also true that no race, sect, or class has more fully cared for its own than the Hebrew race. But the sudden transfer of such a multitude, under conditions that tend to strip them of their small accumulations and to depress their energies and courage, is neither good for them nor for us.

"The banishment, whether by direct decree or by not less certain indirect methods, of so large a number of men and women is not a local question. A decree to leave one country is, in the nature of things, an order to enter another, some other. This consideration, as well as the suggestions of humanity, furnish ample ground for the remonstrances which we have presented to Russia, while our historic friendship for that Government can not fail to give the assurance that our representations are those of a sincere wellwisher."

Mr. Louis E. Levy, of Philadelphia, has written a very able and exhaustive report which contains a great deal of very substantial information in regard to statistics and to what has been accomplished by the various organizations in this country, which I submit. Mr. Levy is one of the most recognized authorities on the subject.

JEWISH IMMIGRANTS.[1]

[By Louis Edward Levy.]

LOCAL STATISTICS.

In submitting to the association this report for the year ending November, 1, 1900, I have to note my regret that my prolonged absence from my accustomed post, in connection with the exposition in Paris, has belated its presentation. Our secretary, Mr. Hoffman, and our treasurer, Mr. Fels, were also in Europe during a part of this time, but the association's work, I need scarcely add, suffered no interruption throughout this period, having been continued as usual by our agent, Mr. Ehrlich, under the supervision of our honored vice-president, Mr. Abraham Kaufman. That those who had charge of the association's interests during the summer and fall of the past year found their offices no sinecure will be apparent from even a brief review of the data at hand. The number of Jewish immigrants at this port during the year ending November 1, 1900, was 3,870, more than double that of the preceding year, which was 1,649; and of this year's arrivals more than two-thirds—namely, 2,708—reached here during the last 6 months of the term. The summer is naturally the season when immigration is always the heaviest, but the disproportion has this year been greater than usual. The cause of this has been the sudden disturbance of the Jewish populations of Roumania and southern Russia, and the continued disorganization in Galicia, a condition to which I will have further occasion to allude.

The general immigration to this port during the past year numbered 20,081, as against 14,079 for the preceding period, an increase of some 42 per cent. Thus, while the Jewish immigration at Philadelphia in 1899 was 11.7 per cent of the total, the proportion in 1900 was 19.2. In 1898 it was 18.5, and in 1897, 14.5; but in 1894 it was 20 per cent, and in 1893, 25 per cent. These fluctuations result in the main from exigencies of the trans-Atlantic steamship service, the strike of dock laborers at the North Sea ports last summer affording a notable example.

GENERAL STATISTICS.

The improvement in the condition of industry and commerce in our country during the past year or two, together with a tendency to a reverse condition in Europe, has resulted in greatly augmenting the general immigration movement to our shores.

In 1899 the total immigration to the United States was figured by Commissioner-General Powderly (for the fiscal year) at 337,000; for 1900 his total, counting immigrants by both steerage and cabin, foots up to some 515,000, an increase during the latter year of some 53 per cent.

From figures at hand regarding our larger landing places, together with close estimates of the remainder, it appears that the total Jewish immigration to the United States during the year ending November 1 ultimo was about 63,000. During the preceding 12 months the number was about 37,000, showing an increase during the present year of some 67 per cent. Our figures are for a period 4 months later than the Government data, and as these 4 months are those of heaviest immigration, the discrepancy between the two ratios is probably very much less. Making some calculated allowances for this difference, it appears that while the percentage of the Jewish contingent in the total immigration was 11.9 in 1899, it was 12.2 in 1900, exactly the same as in 1898.

SOURCES OF THE IMMIGRATION.

Of our local arrivals more than 99 per cent were registered as coming from the Slavic countries of Central Europe, and of the remaining 1 per cent a number probably were natives of that region. With regard to this aspect of the movement Commissioner-General Powderly's official tables afford an instructive study. From these compilations it appears that of the total immigration from the Russian Empire, numbering 90,787, only 1,165 were Muscovite Russians, the remainder consisting of 12,515 Finns, 5,349 Germans (probably Stundist Baptists), 32,797 Poles and Lithuanians, 1,859 Scandinavians, and 37,011 Jews, the latter belonging to all the various nationalities of the Empire.

Of the immigration from Austria-Hungary, which reached the enormous total of 114,847, the highest figures in the list, there were 22,802 Poles (Galicians), 29,183 Slovaks (Moravians), 13,776 Magyars (Hungarians), 2,832 Ruthenians (Stundists), 17,163 Croatians and Slavonians, 3,056 Bohemians, 6,901 Germans (Austrians), and besides some small numbers of Italians and Dalmatians there were 16,920 Jews.

The majority of these latter, as we know from the current history of the dual monarchy, and as is further indicated by our own records, are of Galician, Bohemian, and Austrian nationality, natives of the lands where the miasma of clericalism has sickened the body social.

---

[1] President's report, presented at the sixteenth annual meeting of the association, February 7, 1901.

The most marked illustration of the effect of this pestilence is afforded by Roumania. Of the 6,459 immigrants from that country 214 only were classed as Roumanians, 58 were Germans, 2 were Poles, 1 was a Bohemian, and 1 a Slovak. All the rest—namely, 6,183—were Jews, Roumanians by nationality, natives of the soil, and not only native, but doubtless in a large majority of cases descendants of those who had been natives of the country for centuries before Roumania had being as a State. Of these refugees from Slavic civilization 672 (nearly 11 per cent) landed in this city.

On the other hand, in the vast concourse of Italians who thronged hitherward during the closing year of the nineteenth century, numbering over 100,000 souls, there were two Jews, but whether Italian Jews or possibly Tunisian, Egyptian, or Palestinian Jews, the record sayeth not. There are many Jews in Italy, some in Parliament, some in the army, some in all the walks of civilized life, but there is no legalized anti-Semitism there, and so the Italian Jews stick to their native soil because they can.

A similar object lesson is afforded by France, which among its meager contingent of 1,739 emigrants included 17 Jews, none of them, in all probability, natives of French soil. Germany sent us last year 18,507 emigrants; of these 16,484 were Germans, 1,663 were Silesian Poles, and 337 were Jews; but the latter, if classified by their nationality, would probably have brought the number of Silesians up to 2,000. Belgium, with a considerable Jewish population represented in its Parliament, sent out 968 Flemings and 218 French, and in addition to these 4 Jews, of what nativity is not stated. Holland, among 735 immigrants to our country, included 2 Jews, possibly Dutch. From the United Kingdom, among a total of 48,237, there were 133 Jews, probably not all of British birth. From the Turkish Empire, among 4,247 immigrants, 114 were Jews, but among the 31,151 arrivals from Denmark, Sweden, and Norway, although these countries contain a considerable number of Jewish inhabitants, there was not a single Jewish immigrant. On the contrary the Jewish population of the north countries is noted as increasing through settlers from outside, probably from the disturbed Slavic districts.

CONDITIONS ABROAD.

For many years past, indeed since the first great revival of mediævalism in Russia in 1882 drove such large numbers of the refugees to our shores as to necessitate the organization of this society, we have anxiously scanned the eastern political horizon in the hope of discerning the promise of a better day. But as yet the only certainty we have is that history will repeat itself, and that this storm will pass as others have passed in the centuries on which we look back. For the present the outlook for the immediate future is far from being clear, and the retrospect of the immediate past is very saddening.

IN ROUMANIA

In Roumania especially the past year has been perhaps the darkest of any recorded in any modern Jewish history. Roumania is a little kingdom, containing a population of some 5,000,000, including 260,000 Jews. It was established as a separate State in 1878, under the treaty of Berlin, in which were included special guaranties of civil and religious rights for its Jewish people. But the Roumanians are Slavs—Latinized in language and religious cult—but Slavs in affiliation and sympathy. So, when the reactionary movement in Russia, following the war of 1878 and the treaty of Berlin, took form in the repression of all nonconforming sects, and especially in outrages on the Jews, the Roumanian Government followed suit and the treaty of Berlin was practically, though not formally, repudiated. The provisions of equality of rights for the Jews were deliberately and persistently evaded, the Jewish inhabitants were placed by gradual encroachments in the legal status of foreigners, and naturalization laws were so framed as to make the acquisition of citizenship by Jews practically impossible. Jewish children were excluded from the public schools, the private schools established by the Jewish people were harried and taxed into insignificance, and the existence of the Jewish community made impossible, except on the single condition of pay, pay, pay. Every recrudescence of anti-Semitism arising from time to time in Russia, in Germany, in Austria, and especially the Dreyfus agitation in France, gave the cue for further outrages, until finally, in the early winter and spring of 1900, under the constant goading of the money-hungry Government and its horde of yet more hungry officials, the Roumanian Jews were brought into a state of panic, and an emigration movement en masse began.

THE ROUMANIAN EXODUS.

Within a short time—in May, June, and July of the past year—more than 20,000 Roumanian Jews took up the wanderer's staff and streamed out in all directions. Some turned south to find refuge with their former suzerain, the Turk, and found a welcome reception, but only a more or less precarious foothold in Anatolia; some reached as far south as Cyprus, only to find their poverty an insuperable obstacle to their existence there, and the rest turned westward, lured by the hope of that liberty to live and to work which the flags of England and America symbolize for the oppressed of Europe. The spectacle of suffering, of hunger, misery, and death that was enacted by this unorganized and impoverished throng on the highways and byways of the Roumanian land; the waiting of this hapless multitude at the frontiers; the despair of those who found their way barred and compelled to halt and return, all these tragedies and their minor episodes have gone to swell the history of that greater tragedy of which they form a part.

The suddenness and magnitude of the movement overwhelmed the Jewish organizations of Europe and practically overtaxed their machinery of charity. The Israelitische Allianz of Vienna, the Alliance Universelle of Paris, the Board of Guardians at London, strove to meet the terrible exigency, and the Jewish communities of those cities and of Budapest, Berlin, Frankfort, Hamburg, and Rotterdam taxed themselves heavily to help. By August the movement had been tempered down and brought under control.

Meanwhile the world was busy contemplating the triumphs of civilization in the Exposition at Paris and the triumphs of the Gospel of peace and good will in China and other outlying quarters of the globe, and the passing efflorescence of Roumanian treachery went unrebuked and unnoticed by the powers whom Roumania had deceived.

THE ROUMANIAN PROSPECT.

But the nature of things, "la force de choses," is stronger than treaties, or the powers that sign them, and the commercial crisis which inevitably followed the industrial disorganization resulting from the governmental policy, brought about a revulsion which overturned the anti-Semitic cabinet. A new ministry was installed in September and saner counsels have followed, but what these will accomplish or how long they will last remains to be seen. So far a majority of Roumanians have found out that oppression of their Jewish fellow-countrymen is not only a craven crime, but a costly blunder as well, and it is impossible that its people will not, sooner or later, have the sense to see and understand the significance of what our government agent, sent out to investigate the matter, saw and reported. Inspector Robert Watchorn, in his report to the United States Immigration Bureau, makes the following statement:

"The Roumanian Jews who will emigrate from Roumania in the near future, and those who are now actually en route to American ports, are not only self-supporting, but by signal abilities, despite the unfavorable condition under which they have lived, had acquired a competence, and on reaching our shores will be amply prepared to take care of themselves. Having seen many of the families, I am quite certain that they will be a desirable accession to our population."

It is the misery of these people, whom their surroundings have made miserable, that taxes our charitable efforts here, and hence it is that we are directly interested in their home conditions.

THE STATUS IN RUSSIA.

Of the status of the Jewish population of Russia scarcely better can be said than that their situation has not become worse during the past year. There are, indeed, some flittering signs of improvement, notably a distinct tendency on the part of the higher authorities of the Empire toward a more liberal construction and less harsh enforcement of the laws bearing on the Jews. The manifestly settled policy of the governing senate to establish a uniform administration of these laws instead of leaving them, as heretofore, to the caprice and self-interest of irresponsible officials, is an important factor of permanent improvement, and the growing sentiment among the small but influential class of manufacturers and merchants in favor of a wider and fuller liberty for the Jews is also making itself felt. Against these favorable symptoms are to be noted the famine which last year afflicted the Jewish farmers in the Bessarabian provinces of southern Russia, and the outbreak of mob violence in the Jewish quarter of Odessa. The former was combated by the charity of the Russian Jews themselves, and the latter lost its merely Jewish significance through having developed into a plunder riot which devastated the finest business quarter of the town and destroyed the property of prominent Russian, French, Italian, and other Christian families of the city. The military was called out, about 1,500 rioters were arrested, some of them imprisoned, and many of them flogged. These measures will at least tend to confine further plunder riots to the Jewish quarter, and perhaps result eventually in their entire suppression.

CONDITIONS IN AUSTRIA.

In Austria, more particularly in Galicia, Bohemia, and in Vienna, the agitation appears to be subsiding, though by no means at an end as yet. The outcome of the Dreyfus case, the object lesson of Roumania, and the inevitable revulsion of the populace, has checked the spread of the anti-Semitic fever in Austria, as was made apparent by the losses of that party at the recent elections. Much remains to be gained for the cause of reason in those unfortunate sections of Europe, and much is yet to be feared from the disturbances which threaten when the present already aged Emperor of Austria passes away; but, on the other hand, much is to be hoped for from the certain, however slow and halting, process of general enlightenment.

THE ZIONIST MOVEMENT.

Meanwhile the broad gleam of hope afforded by the Zionist movement, though seeming but scarcely to have become brighter, has at least not lessened during the past year. In the ghettos of Eastern Europe, in the great ghetto of the Russian "Pale," especially, and in many a dark spot in other lands of the Dispersion, this hope is affording weary sufferers a larger reason for existence, without which the problem would seem useless of solution. For us who live in the radiance of modern enlightenment, under the ægis of religious liberty and political freedom, the value of this Zionistic hope is not easily appreciated, and the import of its realization scarcely understood. But for the Jews who yet live in the shadow of the Middle Ages, out in Russia, Roumania, Austria, the way east to Palestine is the nearest to redemption, and its goal is nearest to their hearts. They are waiting for the Sultan to lift the bars, but the Sultan is not ready. But they have waited and prayed through centuries of history, and history is not yet at an end.

COLONIZATION IN PALESTINE AND ARGENTINA.

The existing colonies in Palestine were last year transferred by their founder, Baron Edmond de Rothschild, to the control of the De Hirsch foundation, the Jewish Colonization Association. Under the stimulus of the new régime, and with the continued support of the founder, these colonies give promise of expanding their growth and becoming finally independent. A similar note of progress comes from the De Hirsch colonies in Argentina, where conditions have so far improved as to open the way for the addition of a limited number of immigrants to their population.

THE NEW JERSEY COLONIES.

The status of the older colonies established near us in New Jersey remains much the same as a year ago. A number of new settlers were directed by us to Alliance, Rosenhayn, and Carmel during the past year, and a few are reported to have removed from there. The statement of the property holdings of the colonists, as noted last year, might be somewhat extended now, but in general the progress of these settlements is very slow. The colony of Woodbine, established under the De Hirsch trust fund, is being steadily advanced by the trustees, and will clearly develop into a thriving agricultural and industrial center. The agricultural school established at Woodbine was recently installed in a new and commodious building, fitted with a full equipment of appliances for scientific research, and surrounded with all the requisites of thorough agricultural experimentation. Altogether this settlement, under the competent lead of Professor Sabsovitch, is making marked headway. As much would certainly be true of the older colonies if some similar measure of support, educational especially, were afforded them.

A movement in aid of these colonies, by way of giving the farmers special facilities and cost rates in the obtainment of manures, was inaugurated during the early season of last year by Messrs. Joseph Fels, Maurice Fels, and Samuel S. Fels, the latter the worthy treasurer of our association. Reports from Mr. I. C. Fels, one of the colonists at Alliance and teacher at the Woodbine school, give details of the encouraging results which this effort has afforded, and pointing anew to the desideratum of a canning factory at the colonies.

IMMIGRATION.

DISTRIBUTION OF THE IMMIGRANTS.

Besides the few immigrants whom we found occasion to forward to these colonies, a great number of the others landing here came in for a like exercise of our offices. Our functions were in fact so entirely similar to those which I have reported from year to year that I leave the details to be gleaned from the report of our agent. I will only remark that, of the 3,870 arrivals at our port, 2,420 settled in this city, the other 1,450 scattering to nearly 100 other destinations in various parts of the country. Among those who were distributed were 295 individuals who had no definite destination, but who were forwarded by us to friends and relatives whom we located in 62 different places in the Union, where their people were glad to receive them. These immigrants, without some proper direction, would have been stranded in this city, and eventually have found a settlement only after much suffering on their part and costly charity on the part of the community.

OUR FINANCES.

From our treasurer's report it appears that our expenditures during the last fiscal year were $653.78, and our income for the same period was $583.19, leaving a deficit of $70.59. The generous annual donation of $100 by Miss Emily Phillips, an anonymous donation of $30, the contribution of $125 by the Charity Ball Association, and the amount of $270.40 from memberships make up the main items of our income, the balance of $57.79 accruing from investments. The expenditures in our work have been restricted to the closest possible limits, closer indeed than many of its exigencies would dictate and its broader requirements demand. There is need of a fuller support of the association's work by the community, and this I believe to be obtainable through efforts to increase our membership.

(Testimony closed.)

PART II.

GENERAL STATISTICS OF IMMIGRATION AND FOREIGN-BORN POPULATION.

A REPORT PREPARED UNDER THE DIRECTION OF THE
INDUSTRIAL COMMISSION

BY

E. DANA DURAND, Ph. D.

GENERAL STATISTICS OF IMMIGRATION AND FOREIGN-BORN POPULATION.

CHAPTER I.
THE FOREIGN-BORN IN RELATION TO TOTAL POPULATION.

Percentage of foreign-born, 1890.—In the following table is shown the percentage of the foreign-born to the total population for the United States as a whole, for each of the main census divisions, and for the separate States. It will be seen that a trifle over one-seventh of the entire population of the country (14.77 per cent) was born on foreign soil. This foreign-born element is confined almost entirely to the Northern and Western States, the Southern States having less than 3 per cent of their population foreign-born. The mining States of the West show the largest proportion, over one-fourth for the division as a whole, the number being swollen by the Chinese and Japanese laborers who have come to that section. The next division in rank as to the proportion of foreign-born is the North Atlantic, the original core of the nation, where the percentage is 23.34. In the North Central Division 18.16 per cent are foreign-born. Several of the farming States of the North Central Division show a very large proportion, North Dakota having no less than 44.58 per cent of foreign-born. For the most part, however, the foreign-born are found in largest proportions in the States containing a high percentage of urban and manufacturing population, Massachusetts, Rhode Island, Connecticut, New Jersey, New York, Illinois, Michigan, and California all showing more than one-fifth of their population of foreign birth. The tendency of immigrants toward concentration in cities, and the causes thereof, will be discussed later.[1]

Percentage of foreign-born by States, 1890.

[Census of 1890, Population, Part I, p. lxxxii.]

The United States	14.77
North Atlantic Division	**23.34**
Maine	11.94
New Hampshire	19.21
Vermont	13.26
Massachusetts	29.35
Rhode Island	30.77
Connecticut	24.60
New York	26.19
New Jersey	22.77
Pennsylvania	16.08
South Atlantic Division	**2.35**
Delaware	7.81
Maryland	9.05
District of Columbia	8.15
Virginia	1.11
West Virginia	2.48
North Carolina	.23
South Carolina	.54
Georgia	.66
Florida	5.86
North Central Division	**18.16**
Ohio	12.51
Indiana	6.67
Illinois	22.01
Michigan	25.97
Wisconsin	30.78
Minnesota	35.90
Iowa	16.95
Missouri	8.77
North Dakota	44.58
South Dakota	27.69
Nebraska	19.13
Kansas	10.30
South Central Division	**2.93**
Kentucky	3.19
Tennessee	1.13
Alabama	.98
Mississippi	.62
Louisiana	4.45
Texas	6.84
Oklahoma	4.43
Arkansas	1.26
Western Division	**25.46**
Montana	32.61
Wyoming	24.57
Colorado	20.38
New Mexico	7.33
Arizona	31.52
Utah	25.52
Nevada	32.14
Idaho	20.69
Washington	25.76
Oregon	18.27
California	30.32

[1] p. 278.

Relative percentages of foreign-born, 1850–1890.—By comparing the percentages in the following table for the different census years we see that the most rapid increase in the proportion of foreign-born for the nation as a whole was from 1850 to 1870, when it rose from 9.68 to 14.44 per cent. There was a check in the influx of immigrants during the decade from 1870 to 1880, although part of the relative decrease in the foregn-born shown in that decade is believed to have been due to an understatement of the total population, especially the negro population, in the Southern States, by the census of 1870. The Northern States themselves, however, show a relative decrease of foreign-born during this decade. During the period from 1880 to 1890 there was again a considerable increase in the proportion of foreign-born, from 13.32 to 14.77 per cent for the country as a whole, the increase being wholly confined to the North Atlantic and North Central divisions.

Roughly speaking, the relative condition of the various divisions and States as regards the native and foreign born elements has varied comparatively little at the different census periods. The increase in the foreign-born has gone chiefly to the States already having the largest proportion. However, in Wisconsin, Minnesota, Nebraska, Kansas, and nearly all of the Southern and Western States there has been a decrease or very slight increase in the percentage of foreign-born since 1850. The most marked increase has been in the New England States and Illinois. The States which have shown the most striking increase in the proportion of the foreign-born in the decade between 1880 and 1890 are the New England States, New Jersey, New York, Pennsylvania, and Illinois, which constitute the great manufacturing and urban States. In each of these States the percentage of foreign-born increased by from 2 to 4 during the decade.

Percentage of foreign-born of total population, 1850 to 1890.

[Census of 1890, Population, Part I, p. lxxxiii.]

	1890.	1880.	1870.	1860.	1850.
The United States	14.77	13.32	14.44	13.16	9.68
North Atlantic Division	23.34	19.40	20.49	19.10	15.37
Maine	11.94	9.07	7.80	5.96	5.46
New Hampshire	19.21	13.34	9.30	6.42	4.49
Vermont	13.26	12.33	14.27	10.39	10.73
Massachusetts	29.35	24.87	24.24	21.13	16.49
Rhode Island	30.77	26.76	25.49	21.41	16.20
Connecticut	24.60	20.88	21.14	17.54	10.39
New York	26.19	23.83	25.97	25.80	21.18
New Jersey	22.77	19.60	20.85	18.27	12.25
Pennsylvania	16.08	13.73	15.48	14.81	13.12
South Atlantic Division	2.35	2.29	2.85	3.03	2.24
Delaware	7.81	6.46	7.31	8.17	5.74
Maryland	9.05	8.86	10.68	11.28	8.78
District of Columbia	8.15	9.64	12.34	16.63	9.51
Virginia	1.11	.97	1.12	2.20	1.62
West Virginia	2.48	2.95	3.87		
North Carolina	.23	.27	.28	.33	.30
South Carolina	.54	.77	1.14	1.42	1.30
Georgia	.66	.69	.94	1.10	.72
Florida	5.86	3.68	2.65	2.36	3.17
North Central Division	18.16	16.80	17.97	16.97	12.04
Ohio	12.51	12.35	13.98	14.03	11.62
Indiana	6.67	7.29	8.42	8.76	5.62
Illinois	22.01	18.96	20.23	18.96	13.14
Michigan	25.97	23.73	22.63	19.90	13.76
Wisconsin	30.78	30.82	34.56	35.69	36.18
Minnesota	35.90	34.28	36.55	34.14	32.53
Iowa	16.95	16.11	17.14	15.72	10.91
Missouri	8.77	9.76	12.91	13.58	11.23
North Dakota	44.58}	38.32	33.95	36.68	
South Dakota	27.69}				
Nebraska	19.13	21.53	25.00	22.02	
Kansas	10.36	11.05	13.28	11.84	
South Central Division	2.93	3.08	3.62	3.99	3.18
Kentucky	3.19	3.61	4.80	5.17	3.20
Tennessee	1.13	1.08	1.53	1.91	56
Alabama	.98	.77	1.00	1.28	.97
Mississippi	.62	.81	1.35	1.08	.79

NATIVITY OF FOREIGNERS.

Percentage of foreign-born of total population, 1850 to 1890—Continued.

[Census of 1890, Population, Part I, p. lxxxiii.]

	1890.	1880.	1870.	1860.	1850.
South Central Division—Continued.					
Louisiana	4.45	5.76	8.51	11.44	13.18
Texas	6.84	7.20	7.62	7.19	8.32
Oklahoma	4.43				
Arkansas	1.26	1.29	1.04	.83	.70
Western Division	25.46	28.29	31.64	28.92	15.11
Montana	32.61	29.42	38.74		
Wyoming	24.57	28.14	38.53		
Colorado	20.38	20.48	16.55	7.78	
New Mexico	7.33	6.73	6.12	7.19	3.49
Arizona	31.52	39.69	60.15		
Utah	25.52	30.56	35.38	31.67	17.96
Nevada	32.14	41.40	44.25	30.10	
Idaho	20.69	30.59	52.57		
Washington	25.76	21.04	20.97	27.12	
Oregon	18.27	17.45	12.76	9.76	7.69
California	30.32	33.87	37.45	38.56	23.55

CHAPTER II.

FOREIGN-BORN POPULATION ACCORDING TO COUNTRY OF BIRTH, 1890.

The following table shows the number of natives of the leading countries of the world found in the United States at the census of 1890, together with the number for each leading race group. The percentage which the number of each nationality and race bears to the total number of foreign born is also indicated. It will be seen that of 9,249,547 persons of foreign birth the United Kingdom and the Germanic nations contributed practically the same number, a trifle over one-third of the total in each case. The Scandinavian nations and the North and South Americans (chiefly Canadians) contributed somewhat over one-tenth each; the Slav nations 5.52 per cent; the Latin nations 3.46 per cent, and the Asiatic nations 1.23 per cent. The Irish constituted nearly two-thirds of the immigrants from Great Britain and the Germans nine-tenths of those of Germanic race. Italy furnished about 2 per cent, the larger part of whom had come to us during the decade of 1880 to 1890. The French have never been conspicuous as an emigrating nation

Foreign-born population according to country of birth, 1890.

[Census of 1890, Population, Part I, p. cxxxv.]

Country of birth.	Number.	Per cent.	Country of birth.	Number.	Per cent.
Total foreign born	9,249,547	100	Germanic nations	3,119,583	33.73
North and South Americans	1,088,245	11.76	Germany	2,784,894	30.11
			Austria	123,271	1.33
			Holland	81,828	.88
Canada and Newfoundland	980,938	10.61	Belgium	22,639	.25
Mexico	77,853	.84	Luxemburg	2,882	.03
Central America	1,192	.01	Switzerland	104,069	1.13
South America	5,006	.05	Scandinavian nations	933,249	10.09
Cuba and West Indies	23,256	.25			
			Norway	322,665	3.49
Great Britain and Ireland	3,122,911	33.76	Sweden	478,041	5.17
			Denmark	132,543	1.43
England	908,141	9.82	Slav nations	510,625	5.52
Scotland	242,231	2.62			
Wales	100,079	1.08	Russia	182,644	1.97
Great Britain, not specified	951	.01	Hungary	62,435	.68
			Bohemia	118,106	1.28
Ireland	1,871,509	20.23	Poland	147,440	1.59

Foreign-born population according to country of birth, 1890—Continued.

[Census of 1890, Population, Part I, p. cxxxv.]

Country of birth.	Number.	Per cent.	Country of birth.	Number.	Per cent.
Latin nations	319,822	3.46	All others	41,729	0.45
France	113,174	1.22	Africa	2,207	.02
Italy	182,580	1.98	Atlantic Islands	9,739	.11
Spain	6,185	.07	Australia	5,984	.06
Portugal	15,996	.17	Europe, not specified	12,579	.14
Greece	1,887	.02	Pacific Islands	2,065	.02
			Sandwich Islands	1,304	.01
Asiatic nations	113,383	1.23	Turkey	1,839	.02
			Born at sea	5,533	.06
Asia, not specified	2,260	.03	Other countries	479	.01
China	106,688	1.15			
Japan	2,292	.03			
India	2,143	02			

Foreign-born population according to country of birth, 1850–1890.—The following table shows the total number of persons of foreign birth for each leading nationality at the last five censuses, together with the proportion which each bore at the time of the census to the total foreign born. We can thus trace the changes in the relative importance of the different nationalities in our population. The Census of 1890 makes the following comment on this subject:

"In 1850 the leading foreign nationality was the Irish, which comprised nearly 43 per cent of the whole foreign-born element, while the natives of the United Kingdom jointly constituted nearly three-fifths of all the foreign born. Next to the Irish were the natives of Germany, who constituted one-fourth of the entire foreign-born population.

"In 1860 the Irish, as well as the natives of the United Kingdom, had relatively diminished, the Irish constituting less than 39 per cent, and natives of the United Kingdom as a whole constituting but little more than one-half of the foreign-born population, while the Germans had increased nearly one-third.

"In 1870 the proportion of Irish and of natives of the United Kingdom had still further diminished; the proportion of Germans had remained practically at a standstill, while that of natives of Canada and Newfoundland had slightly increased.

"In 1880 the proportional diminution of the Irish had continued; the Germans showed a slightly diminished proportion, while the proportion of natives of Canada and Newfoundland had still further increased.

"In 1890 the proportional reduction of Irish had continued; the natives of the entire United Kingdom constituted barely one-third of the whole foreign-born element; the Germans had slightly increased; the natives of Canada and Newfoundland had held their own; the Scandinavians had largely increased, while several other elements, especially the Russians, Hungarians, Bohemians, Poles, and Italians, which previously constituted very small proportions, became noticeable."

"The Irish have in 40 years diminished from 42.85 to 20.23 per cent. They have become relatively less than half as important in 1890 as in 1850. The Germans have increased from 26.01 to 30.11 per cent, but this increase has not been continuous, since this nationality constituted a larger percentage of the foreign-born population in 1860 and 1870 than in 1890. The natives of England and Wales, who in 1850 constituted 13.75 per cent, have diminished continuously until in 1890 they constituted 10.91 per cent. The natives of Canada and Newfoundland have in the 40 years increased from 6.58 to 10.61 per cent, the maximum being reached in 1880, when the proportion was slightly greater than in 1890. The Scandinavians, starting in 1850 with the insignificant proportion of 0.81 per cent, have increased until in 1890 they constituted 10.09 per cent of the total foreign-born element, this increase having been the most rapid in recent years."

The Slav countries, Italy, and China were scarcely represented in our population in 1850, and, with the exception of Bohemia and China, their chief growth has been since 1880. Combining the Bohemians, Hungarians, Poles, Russians, and Italians we find that they bore the following proportions to the total foreign-born at each census:

1850	0.22	1880	3.38
1860	.51	1890	7.49
1870	1.44		

These nations have been sending still greater numbers of immigrants to this country since 1890, and the census of 1900 may easily show more than one-tenth of the total foreign-born belonging to them.

NATIVITY OF FOREIGNERS.

Foreign-born population according to countries of birth, 1850 to 1890.

[Census of 1890, Population, Part I, p. cxl.]

Countries of birth.	1890.		1880.		1870.		1860.		1850.	
	Number.	Per cent.	Number.	Per cent.	Number.	Per cent.	Number.	Per cent.	Number.	Per cent.
Total	9,249,547	100.00	6,679,943	100.00	5,567,229	100.00	4,138,697	100.00	2,244,602	100.00
Canada and Newfoundland	980,938	10.61	717,157	10.74	493,464	8.86	249,970	6.04	147,711	6.58
Mexico	77,853	.84	68,399	1.02	42,435	.76	27,466	.66	13,317	.59
England	909,092	9.83	664,160	9.94	555,046	9.97	433,494	10.47	278,675	12.42
Scotland	242,231	2.62	170,136	2.55	140,835	2.53	108,518	2.62	70,550	3.14
Wales	100,079	1.08	83,302	1.25	74,533	1.34	45,763	1.11	29,868	1.33
Ireland	1,871,509	20.23	1,854,571	27.76	1,855,827	33.34	1,611,304	38.93	961,719	42.85
Germany	2,784,894	30.11	1,966,742	29.44	1,690,533	30.37	1,276,075	30.83	583,774	26.01
Austria	123,271	1.33	38,663	.58	30,508	.55	25,061	.61	946	.04
Holland	81,828	.88	58,090	.87	46,802	.84	28,281	.68	9,848	.44
Switzerland	104,069	1.13	88,621	1.33	75,153	1.35	53,327	1.29	13,358	.60
Norway	322,665	3.49	181,729	2.72	114,246	2.05	43,995	1.06	12,678	.57
Sweden	478,041	5.17	194,337	2.91	97,332	1.75	18,625	.45	3,559	.16
Denmark	132,543	1.43	64,196	.96	30,107	.54	9,962	.24	1,838	.08
Russia	182,644	1.97	35,722	.54	4,644	.08	3,160	.08	1,414	.06
Hungary	62,435	.68	11,526	.17	3,737	.07				
Bohemia	118,106	1.28	85,361	1.28	40,289	.72				
Poland	147,440	1.59	48,557	.73	14,436	.26	7,298	.18		
France	113,174	1.22	106,971	1.60	116,402	2.09	109,802	2.66	54,069	2.41
Italy	182,580	1.98	44,230	.66	17,157	.31	10,518	.25	3,645	.16
China	106,688	1.15	104,468	1.56	63,042	1.13	35,565	.86	758	.03
Other countries	127,467	1.38	93,005	1.39	60,701	1.09	40,445	.98	56,875	2.53

Distribution of leading nationalities by divisions and States.—The Germans, who are in the nation as a whole 1½ times more numerous than the next largest nationality, the Irish, are the most numerous of the foreign-born nationalities in 26 of the States, including New York, New Jersey and Maryland, and nearly all of the North Central and the Southern States. The Irish are the predominant foreign-born nationality in 7 States: Massachusetts, Rhode Island, Connecticut, Pennsylvania, Delaware, Virginia, and Nevada. The Canadians outnumber other nationalities in the border States of Maine, New Hampshire, Vermont, Michigan, Montana, and Washington. The English are most numerous among the foreign-born in Idaho, Colorado, and Utah, mining States; the Scandinavians in the two Dakotas, farming States; the Mexicans in Arizona and New Mexico, and the Chinese in California.[1]

---

[1] Census of 1890, Population, Vol. I, Table 32, p. 608.

Distribution of nationalities by States, 1890.

[Compiled from tables in Census of 1890, Population, Part I, pp. cxliii-cl.]

States and Territories.	British Americans. Per cent of total population.	Per cent of foreign population.	Irish. Per cent of total population.	Per cent of foreign population.	British. Per cent of total population.	Per cent of foreign population.	Teutons. Per cent of total population.	Per cent of foreign population.	Scandinavians. Per cent of total population.	Per cent of foreign population.	Slavs. Per cent of total population.	Per cent of foreign population.	Greco-Latins. Per cent of total population.	Pr. cent of foreign population.	Asiatics. Pr. cent of total population.	Pr. cent of foreign population.
The United States...	1.57	10.61	2.99	20.23	2.00	13.53	4.98	33.73	1.49	10.09	0.82	5.52	0.51	3.46	0.18	1.23
North Atlantic Division..	2.82	12.61	7.13	31.92	3.55	15.88	5.29	25.92	.68	3.06	1.19	5.33	.96	4.30	.05	.23
Maine	7.88	65.95	1.73	14.49	1.48	12.39	.19	1.56	.41	3.43	.07	.62	.12	1.04	.02	.14
New Hampshire.	12.30	64.03	3.95	20.58	1.79	9.33	.48	2.50	.41	2.11	.06	.33	.15	.78	.03	.16
Vermont	7.52	56.71	2.95	22.25	1.87	14.08	.31	2.35	.29	2.19	.08	.58	.20	1.51	.01	.11
Massachusetts	9.27	31.59	11.61	39.55	4.46	15.21	1.39	4.74	1.01	3.45	.52	.77	.66	2.25	.08	.26
Rhode Island	8.08	26.28	11.26	36.61	7.55	24.54	1.07	3.48	1.11	3.60	.26	.84	1.10	3.57	.05	.16
Connecticut	2.84	11.56	10.44	42.42	3.64	14.81	4.11	16.69	1.61	6.55	.78	3.39	1.02	4.15	.05	.22
New York	1.55	5.93	8.06	30.77	3.13	11.96	9.22	35.20	.72	2.75	1.77	6.74	1.45	5.53	.07	.26
New Jersey	.33	1.43	6.99	30.12	4.02	17.64	8.55	37.56	.59	2.59	.88	3.85	1.24	5.44	.06	.26
Pennsylvania	.23	1.44	4.64	28.83	3.72	23.12	4.97	30.92	.45	2.79	1.32	8.21	.65	4.03	.03	.19
South Atlantic Division	.06	2.59	.54	23.02	.34	14.60	.97	41.24	.03	1.48	.13	5.39	.09	4.00	.01	.45
Delaware	.18	2.35	3.63	46.51	1.43	18.33	1.54	19.66	.18	2.29	.39	4.95	.38	4.92	.02	.29
Maryland	.10	1.08	1.80	19.87	.83	9.20	5.21	57.60	.06	.64	.75	8.29	.20	2.26	.02	.25
District of Columbia	.28	3.49	3.14	38.49	1.21	14.79	2.68	32.90	.12	1.44	.16	1.92	.39	4.85	.06	.72
Virginia	.05	4.25	.28	24.92	.28	25.52	.29	25.91	.03	2.31	.06	5.42	.10	8.99	.01	.90
West Virginia	.05	1.98	.63	25.41	.53	21.25	1.07	43.32	.02	.65	.06	2.31	.11	4.51	.00	.14
North Carolina	.02	9.59	.03	12.18	.08	34.14	.07	31.98	.01	2.43	.01	2.94	.01	2.62	.00	.73
South Carolina	.01	2.54	.14	26.56	.08	14.31	.23	42.14	.01	1.90	.02	4.23	.03	4.99	.00	.54
Georgia	.03	5.02	.18	27.80	.83	19.05	.22	33.11	.02	2.80	.02	3.44	.03	4.89	.01	.87
Florida	.29	5.02	.27	4.60	.87	14.79	.54	9.27	.21	3.55	.05	.79	.29	4.98	.04	.73
North Central Division	1.80	9.89	1.94	10.68	1.92	10.55	7.79	42.91	3.17	17.47	1.20	6.58	.28	1.53	.02	.10
Ohio	.45	3.60	1.91	15.27	2.02	16.16	6.92	55.36	.11	.92	.73	5.87	.31	2.45	.01	.09
Indiana	.23	3.39	.95	14.24	.69	10.28	4.14	62.13	.25	3.77	.20	3.02	.17	2.62	.01	.11
Illinois	1.03	4.69	3.25	14.73	2.49	11.29	9.57	43.48	3.37	15.30	1.75	7.96	.45	2.05	.03	.13
Michigan	8.66	33.36	1.87	7.18	3.26	12.54	8.28	31.88	1.98	7.63	1.46	5.61	.40	1.54	.02	.06
Wisconsin	1.97	6.39	1.97	6.41	1.98	6.44	16.78	54.51	5.91	19.21	1.92	6.25	.18	.61	.01	.04
Minnesota	3.35	9.32	2.15	5.99	1.65	4.61	9.93	27.65	16.53	46.05	1.97	5.49	.?	.59	.01	.05
Iowa	.91	5.39	1.95	11.53	1.96	11.58	7.46	43.99	3.81	22.49	.65	3.82	.15	.90	.02	.05
Missouri	.32	3.63	1.53	17.44	.94	10.70	5.09	58.09	.28	3.18	.29	3.36	.25	2.88	.02	.24

NATIVITY OF FOREIGNERS.

North Dakota	12.61	28.29	1.62	3.64	2.86	6.40	5.39	12.09	18.73	42	3.10	6.94	.13	.29	.02	.05
South Dakota	2.89	10.43	1.45	5.24	2.25	8.11	6.44	23.25	9.54	34.45	4.71	17	.19	7	.07	.25
Nebraska	1.14	5.98	1.51	7.88	1.84	9.62	7.63	39.87	4.38	22.88	2.36	12.36	.19	1	.03	.15
Kansas	.83	8.03	1.11	10.73	1.83	17.67	3.81	36.76	1.54	14.89	.98	9.43	.20	1.97	.01	.14
South Central Division	.07	2.53	.39	13.42	.30	10.29	1.21	41.14	.07	2.46	.09	3.02	.26	8.86	.02	.53
Kentucky	.06	1.98	.75	23.46	.30	9.35	1.89	59.07	.02	.67	.04	1.16	.10	3.23	.00	.12
Tennessee	.06	5.09	.28	25.04	.24	20.87	.38	33.17	.03	2.32	.05	4.57	.07	6.53	.00	.41
Alabama	.04	4.20	.17	17.62	.31	32.04	.29	29.60	.03	2.79	.03	3.40	.07	6.96	.01	.84
Mississippi	.03	4.34	.14	23.45	.09	13.97	.20	32.43	.03	5.65	.02	3.03	.07	11.93	.01	1.55
Louisiana	.07	1.53	.83	18.57	.27	8.07	1.44	32.30	.06	1.40	.05	1.06	1.54	34.67	.03	.76
Texas	.13	1.87	.37	5.36	.53	7.80	2.67	39.01	.21	3.12	.27	3.93	.24	3.48	.04	.54
Oklahoma	.68	15.83	.53	12.01	.69	15.58	1.39	31.39	.34	7.70	.55	12.48	.16	3.5	.04	.99
Arkansas	.08	6.64	.18	14.17	.19	14.93	.63	50.03	.05	3.63	.04	3.48	.06	4.4	.01	.60
Western Division	2.49	9.79	3.48	13.68	4.69	18.43	5.	19.64	3.10	12.17	.49	1.93	1.78	6.98	3.23	12.68
Montana	6.84	20.98	5.03	15.43	6.65	20.39	5.44	16.67	4.85	14.88	.72	2.22	.95	2.91	1.96	6.01
Wyoming	2.16	8.81	3.13	12.74	8.34	33.94	3.97	16.17	3.92	15.97	1.42	5.77	.66	2.7	.81	3.29
Colorado	2.22	10.88	3	14.71	5.05	24.80	4.72	23.14	2.96	14.53	.52	2.56	1.29	6.33	.37	1.81
New Mexico	.44	6.05	.63	8.58	1.18	16.13	1.17	15.90	.16	2.18	.07	1.01	.44	6.01	.25	3.44
Arizona	1.23	3.89	1.96	6.23	2.55	8.09	2.47	7.88	.68	2.17	.13	.42	.92	2.93	2.02	6.41
Utah	.59	2.30	.93	3.85	12.87	50.44	1.84	7.22	8.11	31.78	.16	.64	.29	1.12	.40	1.58
Nevada	3.63	11.30	5.73	17.99	5.95	18.50	4.68	14.57	1.56	4.86	.21	.65	3.62	11.26	6.13	19.07
Idaho	2.12	10.26	2.27	10.98	5.39	26.07	3.15	15.25	4.15	20.08	.18	.85	.86	4.18	2.40	11.58
Washington	4.98	19.35	2.23	8.67	4.31	16.72	5.26	20.43	6.13	23.79	.76	2.97	.76	2.95	1.06	4.10
Oregon	2.06	11.27	1.56	8.53	2.64	14.47	5.01	27.45	2.34	12.79	.90	4.94	.53	2.88	3.04	16.65
California	2.15	7.11	5.25	17.24	3.86	12.74	6.32	20.84	1.85	6.11	.39	1.27	3.17	10.46	6.01	19.83

The British Americans in 1890 were found mainly in the New England States (except Connecticut), where they constitute from 7 to 12 per cent of the total population, and from one-fourth to two-thirds of the entire foreign-born population. A large proportion of them are also found in North Dakota and Michigan, while several other border States show a larger percentage of British Americans than is found in the country as a whole. It is well known that the French Canadians are competing sharply in the manufacturing industries of New England, while in the more western States they enter agricultural and lumbering.

The Irish, who, as we shall soon see, are specially inclined to urban life, are relatively most numerous in the North Atlantic division, where they constitute 7.13 per cent of the entire population as compared with 2.99 per cent for the nation as a whole. The proportion is greatest in the States of Massachusetts, Rhode Island, Connecticut, New York, and New Jersey, in the order named. In the North Central division they represent only 1.94 per cent of the total population, the proportion being quite uniform in each State, except in Illinois, where it is much higher. The States of the Far West show also a considerable proportion of Irish.

The English, Scotch, and Welsh are likewise found in larger proportions in the North Atlantic than in any other division except the Western, where they enter largely into mining. Constituting 2 per cent of the entire population and 13.53 per cent of the foreign population of the whole country, they show the corresponding percentages for the North Atlantic division 3.55 and 15.88 per cent. The largest proportion in each case is found in Rhode Island and Massachusetts. The proportion of British to the total foreign-born is more uniform throughout the 5 grand divisions than that of any other race. The proportion of British to the foreign-born in Pennsylvania and in several of the States of the South Atlantic division in Ohio, Tennessee, and Alabama is considerably above the average for the entire country.

The Teutons, mainly Germans, constituted about one-twentieth of the entire population and one-third of the foreign population of the United States in 1890. Their proportion in each case is considerably higher than these figures in the North Central division, while the proportion to the entire population is also somewhat greater in the North Atlantic than in the country as a whole. In Wisconsin the Teutons are more than one-sixth; in Minnesota, Illinois, and New York nearly one-tenth of the entire population. They show less inclination to the New England States than to any other. In Missouri, Indiana, Maryland, Ohio, and Wisconsin, the Teutons are more than one-half of the total foreign-born, while in Iowa, Illinois, Nebraska, New Jersey, Kansas, and New York they exceed one-third of the foreign-born. The Germans, as we shall see, enter more largely into agriculture than any of the other race groups except the Scandinavians.

The Scandinavians appeared in 1890 in a considerable body in Rhode Island, Massachusetts, and Connecticut, but they bore a much larger proportion to the total and to the foreign-born population in the farming States of the Northwest. In Minnesota they constituted about one-sixth of the entire population and one-half of the foreign-born. In North Dakota the proportions are much greater, while in South Dakota the Scandinavians are nearly one-tenth of the total population and more than one-third of the foreign-born.

The Slavs, in 1890, were found mainly in the North Atlantic division, especially in New York and Pennsylvania, where they constituted between 1 and 2 per cent of the entire population; and to a secondary extent in the North Central division. The largest proportion to total population and to foreign population is found in the farming States, South Dakota, North Dakota, and Nebraska.

The Greco-Latins, including especially the French and Italians, are found principally in the North Atlantic and Western divisions. The largest proportions are found in New York, where they constitute 1.45 per cent of the total population and 5.53 per cent of the foreign-born population; in California and Nevada where the proportions respectively are about double those in New York; in Rhode Island, New Jersey, Connecticut, Louisiana, Colorado, and Massachusetts.

The Asiatics, mainly Chinese, are found principally in the Western division, where they constitute 3.23 per cent of the total population and 12.68 per cent of the foreign-born. The proportions in Nevada and California are considerably higher than these. In other parts of the country their number is insignificant.

CHAPTER III.
STATISTICS OF IMMIGRATION.

Total immigration, 1820-1899.[1]—A different way of looking at the problem of the foreign-born is by considering the current of immigration into the country rather than the number of foreign-born already there at any particular time. We shall naturally reach somewhat similar conclusions by this system to those obtained by the preceding one, although the two methods do not give strictly parallel results. Thus the amount of immigration of a given nationality during any decade may be relatively small, and yet the proportion of the persons of that nationality in the country at the end of the decade may be large, owing to preceding immigration. In order to obtain a satisfactory view of recent and present tendencies, the current of immigration gives the more instructive results. Another reason why the results obtained by the consideration of immigration differ somewhat from those obtained by considering the population at a stationary point is that there is a certain return current of persons of foreign birth from this country of which no statistical record is kept. The Italians especially are apt to come to this country as "birds of passage," so that it will be quite possible that the census of 1900 will show fewer Italians in the country than were reported to have come here during the preceding decade, a phenomenon which was also observable at the census of 1890.

The following table shows the total number of immigrants, by decades, 1821 to 1899. It is to be observed, however, that previous to 1856 no distinction was made between those who came here to settle and mere travelers. Moreover, since 1885 the immigrants from the British North American provinces and from Mexico have not been included, while only since 1894 have the numbers of European immigrants arriving in Canada but destined for the United States been included:

Number of immigrants by decades.

1821 to 1830	143,439	1871 to 1880	2,812,191
1831 to 1840	599,125	1881 to 1890	5,246,613
1841 to 1850	1,713,251	1891 to 1900	3,687,564
1851 to 1860	2,598,214		
1861 to 1870	2,314,824	Total	19,115,211

Immigration first becomes of marked importance during the decade from 1830 to 1840. During the next 20 years the influx of the foreign-born was greater relatively to the amount of native population than at any other period. Three principal causes of this increase were the hard times in Germany, the great famine in Ireland, and the discovery of gold in California. Financial depressions have always a marked influence in decreasing immigration. That of 1857 was followed closely by the civil war, and the number of foreign-born coming to this country was greatly decreased. The era of prosperity succeeding the war, coupled with the marked improvements in methods of transportation, rapidly swelled the tide so that the total immigration for 1861 to 1870 was but little less than that for the preceding decade. The severe depression which succeeded the crisis of 1873 once more greatly reduced immigration so that the entire influx for the decade was not greatly above that for 1851 to 1860. The next decade was one of prosperity in this country. The opening up of the great farming regions of the West was still actively going on, while manufacturing industry was being developed with great rapidity. We find the total immigration for this decade accordingly more than equal to that for the 20 years preceding. The year 1882 marked the climax of the movement, 788,992 immigrants coming to our shores. The movement continued with little abatement till the crisis of 1893. During the years of depression which have followed, immigration has fallen off to about half the average of the years preceding. The tendency toward returning prosperity was apparently already shown, however, in the year ending June 30, 1899, when 311,715 immigrants arrived as compared with the minimum of 217,786 for the preceding year. The almost complete occupation of the farming lands of good quality in the West, however, is likely to reduce the attractiveness of this country as a place of settlement to many foreigners.

·The movements which have been described in the preceding paragraphs may be more accurately traced by the figures of the following table, which show the immigration for each year. The fluctuations may be traced more easily by means of the diagram:

---

[1] Based on Report of Immigration Investigating Commission, 1895, pp. 8, 9.

268   THE INDUSTRIAL COMMISSION:—IMMIGRATION.

Number of alien passengers arrived in the United States, 1820 to 1855, and number of immigrants arrived, 1856 to 1900.

Year	Number	Year	Number
1820	8,385	1861	89,724
1821	9,127	1862	89,007
1822	6,911	1863	174,524
1823	6,354	1864	193,195
1824	7,912	1865	247,453
1825	10,199	1866	314,917
1826	10,837	1867	310,965
1827	18,875	1868 (6 months)	138,840
1828	27,382	1869	352,768
1829	22,520	1870	387,203
1830	23,322	1871	321,350
1831	22,633	1872	404,806
1832 (15 months)	60,482	1873	459,803
1833	58,640	1874	313,339
1834	65,365	1875	227,498
1835	45,374	1876	169,986
1836	76,242	1877	141,857
1837	79,340	1878	138,469
1838	38,914	1879	177,826
1839	68,069	1880	457,257
1840	84,066	1881	669,431
1841	80,289	1882	788,992
1842	104,565	1883	603,322
1843 (9 months)	52,496	1884	518,592
1844	78,615	1885	395,346
1845	114,371	1886	334,203
1846	154,416	1887	490,109
1847	234,968	1888	546,889
1848	226,527	1889	444,427
1849	297,024	1890	455,302
1850 (15 months)	369,980	1891	560,319
1851	379,466	1892	579,663
1852	371,603	1893	439,730
1853	368,645	1894	285,631
1854	427,833	1895	258,536
1855	200,827	1896	343,267
1856	195,587	1897	230,832
1857	246,945	1898	229,299
1858	119,501	1899	311,715
1859	118,616	1900	448,572
1860	150,237	1901	487,918

Immigration by nationalities.—1820-1899.[1]—Since the total amount of immigration into this country has considerably fallen off during the past decade, greater attention is now being given by the public thought to the character of the immigrants. A comparison of the statistics of the immigration of persons of different nationalities shows that there have been marked changes in this regard in the more recent decades and especially during the past 10 or 15 years. The following table and accompanying diagrams show the number of immigrants of each leading nationality by decades:

Nationality of immigrants by decades.

	1821 to 1830.	1831 to 1840.	1841 to 1850.	1851 to 1860.	1861 to 1870.	1871 to 1880.	1881 to 1890.	1891 to 1900.
Total	143,439	599,125	1,713,251	2,598,214	2,314,824	2,812,191	5,246,613	3,687,564
United Kingdom	75,803	283,191	1,047,763	1,338,093	1,042,674	984,914	1,462,839	661,742
England and Wales	22,167	73,143	263,332	385,643	568,128	460,479	657,488	228,596
Scotland	2,912	2,667	3,712	38,331	38,768	87,564	149,869	44,181
Ireland	50,724	207,381	780,719	914,119	435,778	436,871	655,482	388,965
Germany	6,761	152,454	434,626	951,667	787,468	718,182	1,452,970	505,152
British North American Provinces	2,277	13,624	41,723	59,309	153,871	383,269	a 392,802	
Norway and Sweden	91	1,201	13,903	20,931	109,298	211,245	568,362	321,281
Austria-Hungary					7,800	72,969	353,719	592,707
Italy	408	2,253	1,870	9,231	11,728	55,759	307,309	651,893
France	8,497	45,575	77,262	76,358	35,984	72,206	50,464	30,770
Russia and Poland	91	646	656	1,621	4,536	52,254	265,088	602,010
China	2	8	35	41,397	64,301	123,201	61,711	17,527
Switzerland	3,226	4,821	4,644	25,011	23,286	28,293	81,988	31,179
Denmark	169	1,063	539	3,749	17,094	31,771	88,132	50,231
Netherlands	1,078	1,412	8,251	10,789	9,102	16,541	53,701	26,758
Other countries	45,036	92,877	81,979	60,058	47,682	61,587	107,528	196,314

a 1881 to 1885; no figures since.

[1] Based on Census of 1890: Population, vol. i, pp. lxxx, lxxxi, supplemented by later figures from the Reports of the Commissioner-General of Immigration, and corrected by Immigration and Passenger Movement, 1894, p. 72.

STATISTICS OF IMMIGRATION. 269

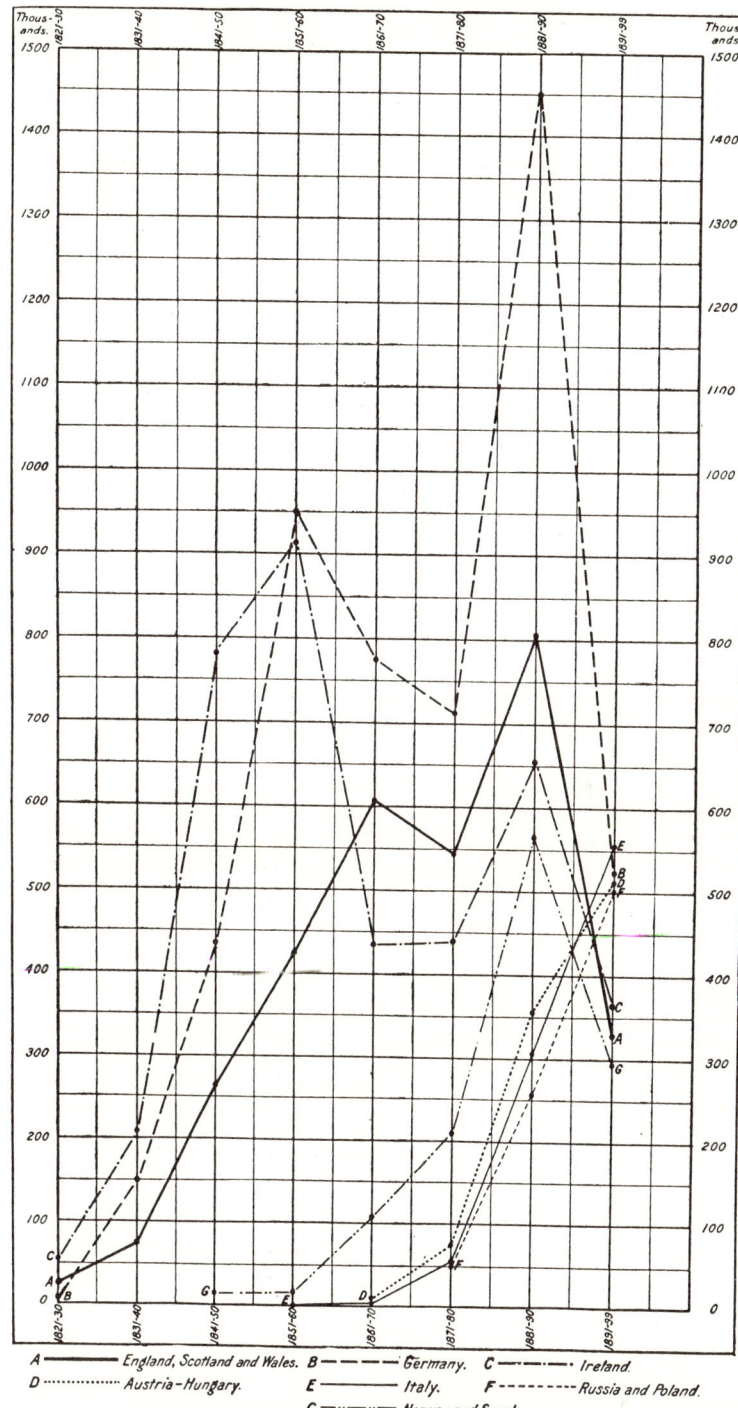

A ——————— England, Scotland and Wales.　B — — — — Germany.　C — · — · — Ireland.
D ················· Austria-Hungary.　　E ——————— Italy.　F - - - - - - Russia and Poland.
G — ·· — ·· — Norway and Sweden.

Immigration of Leading Nationalities by Decades, 1821-1899.

270   THE INDUSTRIAL COMMISSION:—IMMIGRATION.

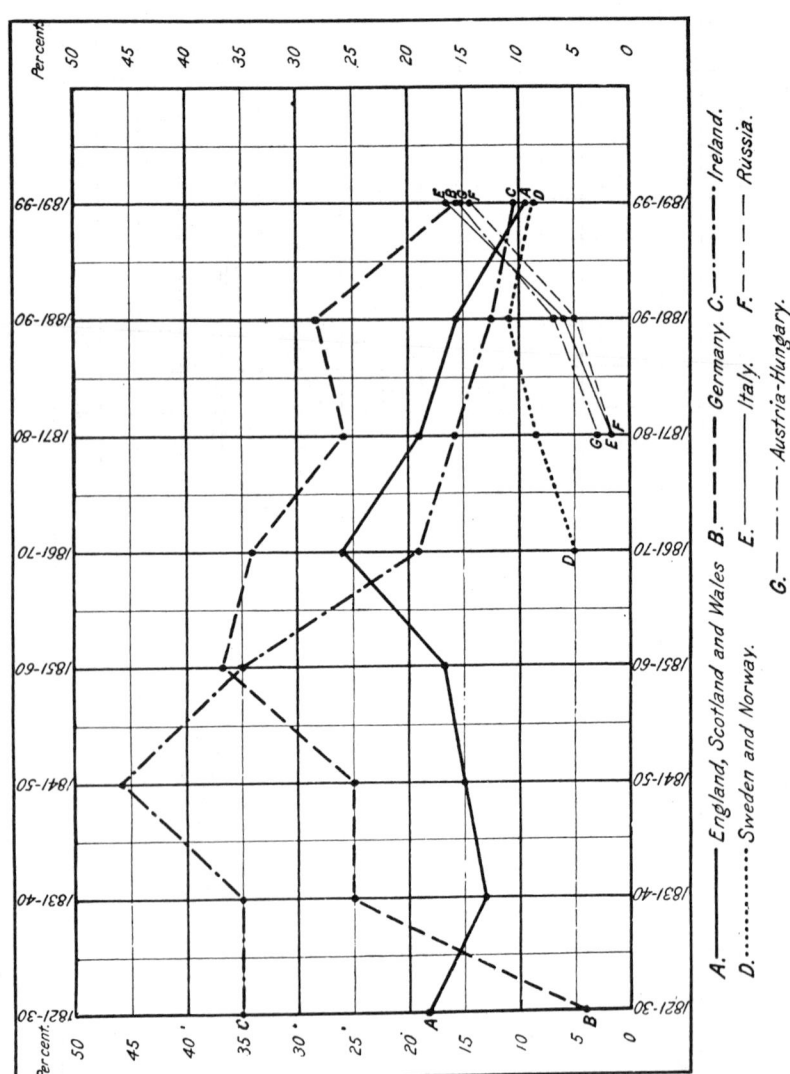

Nationality of Immigrants. Percentage of Total for each Decade, 1821–1899.

STATISTICS OF IMMIGRATION. 271

The Irish were the first to appear in large proportion among our immigrants. They came most rapidly during the decades from 1841 to 1860, since which time they have fallen off greatly in absolute numbers and in the proportion which they bear to the total immigrants. The course of German immigration has been more regular, but shows a falling off in the decades 1861-1870 and especially 1891-1899, as compared with those immediately preceding. The English and Scotch have been even more regular, gradually increasing in absolute numbers each decade except the last. Immigration of other nationalities was not important enough to be noteworthy until 1860. The Scandinavians then began to come, and since 1880 they have come to constitute about one-tenth of our immigration. The Russians and Poles, the Hungarians and Italians began to appear in moderate numbers during the decade from 1871 to 1880, increased with enormous rapidity during the following 10 years, and for the decade 1891-1900 constitute 50 per cent of our total immigration.

To present these changes somewhat more specifically it may be noted that from 1830 to 1840 the proportion of Irish among the total immigrants was about 35 per cent, that of other British about 12½ per cent, while the Germans constituted 25 per cent. The French immigration at this time was also considerable, amounting to 8 per cent.

From 1840 to 1850 the proportion of Irish increased to 46 per cent, of other British to 15½ per cent, that of Germans remaining unchanged. During the next decade the Irish, although increasing in absolute numbers, were only 35 per cent of the total immigrants, the English and Scotch had still further increased to 16 per cent while the Germans were a little less than 37 per cent. In the decade from 1860 to 1870 the importance of the Irish still further diminished, their percentage being only 19, while that of the other natives of Great Britain had risen to 26, and that of Germans had fallen slightly, to 34 per cent. Norway and Sweden now furnish 5 per cent and the Canadians 7 per cent. The following decade shows the Irish only 16 per cent of the total immigrants, the other British somewhat reduced, to 19 per cent, the Germans likewise fallen off to 26 per cent, while the British Americans and the Scandinavians had shown a marked increase, the former furnishing 14 per cent and the latter 8 per cent. From 1880 to 1890, when the tide of immigration was at its height, the Irish constituted only one-eighth and the other British only one-seventh of the total immigration. The Germans doubled in absolute number as compared with the preceding decade, and increased slightly, to 28 per cent, in their proportion to the entire inflow. Norwegians and Swedes rose to 11 per cent. Russians and Poles now amount to 5 per cent, Hungarians to 7 per cent, and Italians to 6 per cent, each of these nationalities having at least quadrupled its absolute numbers and doubled its proportion of the total immigration as compared with the preceding 10 years. The immigration from Canada, had statistics been continued, would apparently have fully held its own.

Detailed immigration by nationalities, 1875-1899.[1]—So marked have been the changes in the proportions of the different nationalities among our immigrants during the past 25 years, that it will perhaps be profitable to present more detailed statistics. The following table shows the absolute number of immigrants of each leading nationality by five quinquennial periods, together with the proportion which each bore to the total immigration for the same periods, these proportions being indicated graphically in the diagram:

Immigration by leading nationalities, 1875-1899.

	1875-1879.		1880-1884.		1885-1889.		1890-1894.		1895-1899.	
	Number.	Per cent.	Number.	Per cent.	Number.	Per cent.	Number.	Per cent.	Number.	Per cent.
All countries	855,636	100	3,037,594	100	2,210,974	100	2,320,645	100	1,373,649	100
England, Scotland, and Wales	152,880	17.9	400,192	13.2	410,704	18.6	236,259	10.2	92,832	6.8
Ireland	108,046	12.6	365,107	12	308,854	14	233,922	10.1	172,460	12.6
Germany	172,919	20.2	920,215	30.3	524,966	23.7	457,894	19.7	121,178	8.8
Sweden and Norway	60,516	7.3	330,455	10.9	255,986	11.6	225,242	9.7	108,816	7.9
Total above countries	494,361	58	2,015,969	66.4	1,500,510	67.9	1,153,317	49.7	495,286	36.1
Austria	27,386	3.2	92,392	3	112,413	5.1	176,492	7.6	130,414	9.5
Hungary	3,057	.4	46,156	1.5	63,826	2.9	123,744	5.3	103,408	7.5
Italy	19,976	2.3	108,216	3.6	159,444	7.2	304,811	13.1	298,950	21.8
Russia and Poland	30,350	3.5	68,591	2.3	157,027	7	343,544	14.8	214,350	15.6
Total above countries	80,769	9.4	315,355	10.4	492,710	22.2	948,591	40.8	747,122	54.4

[1] Tables compiled from Reports of Commissioner-General of Immigration, 1892-1899. Immigration and Passenger Movement, 1894, pp. 73, 74.

From this table it appears that the natives of England, Scotland, and Wales reached their highest absolute numbers among our immigrants in 1880–1884 and 1885–1889, with over 400,000 for each period. In the latter period they constituted no less than 18.6 per cent of the total immigration. The number of these nationalities fell off considerably during the next 5 years, while during the years 1895–1899 about one-fifth as many came to us as from 1885 to 1889. The proportion in the latter period was little over one-third as great as in the former, 6.8 per cent. The year 1899 shows by far the smallest proportion ever known, 4.4 per cent.

The proportion of the Irish among the total immigrants has varied much less but, it also reached its maximum in 1885–1889, 14 per cent, the absolute number occurring in the preceding 5 years being, however, greater—365,107. For the years 1895–1889 the percentage has been 12.6, and the absolute number of Irish immigrants less than one-half the number from 1880 to 1884.

The number of Germans coming to our shores reached the enormous total of 920,215 for the period 1880–1884, when it constituted no less than 30 per cent of the entire number of immigrants. The total number of Germans arriving during the next ten years was only about 60,000 more than during the 5 years preceding. The proportion of Germans had fallen off to one-fifth during 1890–1894. The most striking change, however, was during the 5 years last past, when only 121,178 natives of Germany landed in this country, constituting but 8.8 per cent of the total immigration.

The proportion of Scandinavians reached its highest point from 1885 to 1889, 11.6 per cent. The decrease since that time, however, has been less rapid than for Germany, and the proportion for the past 5 years is still 7.9 per cent, although the total number of Scandinavians arriving during that period was barely one-third of the number arriving from 1880 to 1884.

The losses which have been thus shown in the immigration from the countries of western and northern Europe have been made up by an increased influx from southern and eastern countries.

Italy shows the most striking increase of all. While only 19,976 Italians came to this country from 1875 to 1879, the arrivals from 1890 to 1894 were no less than 307,077, while those for the succeeding 5 years were scarcely less, despite the great falling off in the total immigration. The proportion of the Italians to the total immigrants has increased by geometric rather than by arithmetic progression. It rose from 2.3 per cent in 1875–1879 to 13.1 per cent, in 1890–1894, while the proportion for the past 5 years has reached 21.8 per cent more than one-fifth of the total. For the year 1899, in fact, almost one-fourth of all our immigrants were Italians.

The increase in the absolute numbers and the proportions of the Russians and Poles was up to 1895 even more striking than that of the Italians, the number for 1890–1894 being 343,544, or 11 times greater than for 1875–1879. In the two years after 1896, however, there was a very considerable falling off in their absolute number, the proportion to the total immigration for 1895–1899, however, increasing somewhat as compared with the preceding 5 years, and amounting to 15.6 per cent.

The number and proportion of the Hungarians coming to this country, while less than half as great as that of the Russians and Poles, has increased during the period since 1875 with about the same proportionate rapidity. While barely one hundredth of the total number of immigrants from 1875 to 1884 were Hungarians, the proportion from 1895 to 1899 was 7.5 per cent. The immigrants from Austria are, on the whole, of a higher class than those from Hungary, but there has been a tendency in recent years for relatively fewer of the inhabitants of that country of German birth to immigrate, while a larger proportion of those belonging to the Slavic races have been coming to this country. The proportion of Austrians to the total immigration has increased from about 3 per cent for 1875–1884 to more than 9 per cent during the past 5 years.

It is customary to consider the immigrants from the more western and northern countries of Europe as higher in character than those from the south and east of the continent. Taking only the leading nationalities, as indicated in the table, a broad view of the recent change in the character of our immigration may be obtained by comparing the proportion which the number of immigrants from Great Britain, Germany, Sweden, and Norway has borne to the total immigration for each 5-year period with the proportion borne to the total by the immigration from Austria-Hungary, Russia and Poland, and Italy. The figures thus obtained are shown in the above table and in the accompanying diagram. It will be seen that the immigration from the northern countries reached its maximum during the decade from 1880 to 1889, when it represented a little more than two-thirds of the total influx. For the past 5 years, on the other hand, the absolute number of immigrants from these countries has been barely one-third the number for the 5 years from 1885 to 1889, while the proportion to the total immigration has fallen to 36.9 per cent. The immigration from the southern countries of Europe began to increase greatly during the period from 1880 to 1884 but reached its maximum in absolute numbers from 1890 to 1894, when the immigration was more than 10 times greater than from 1875

STATISTICS OF IMMIGRATION.

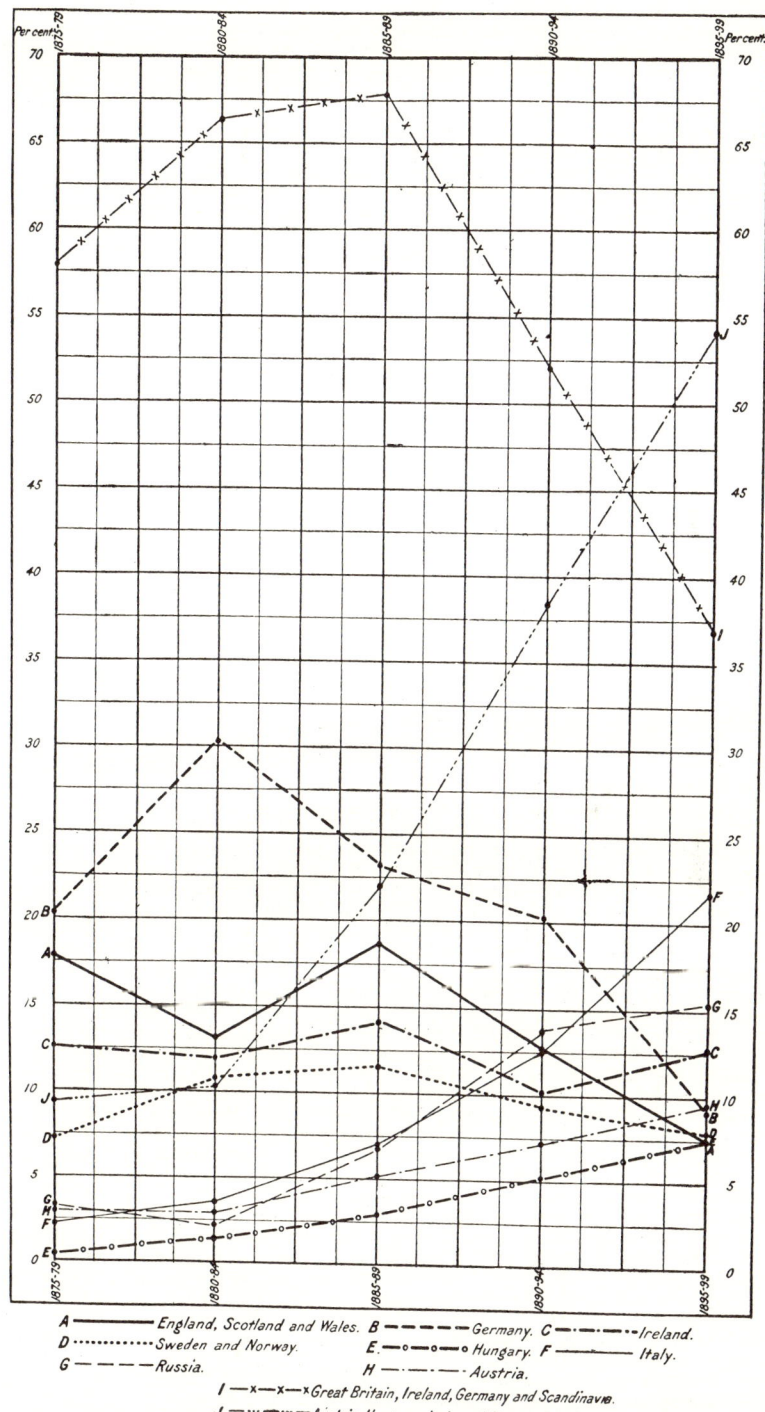

A ——————— England, Scotland and Wales. B ————— Germany. C ———·——— Ireland.
D ·············· Sweden and Norway. E —o—o—o Hungary. F ——— Italy.
G ———— Russia. H ———·——— Austria.
I —x—x—x Great Britain, Ireland, Germany and Scandinavia.
J ———··——— Austria-Hungary, Italy and Russia.

Nationality of Immigrants. Percentage of Total for each 5-Year Period, 1875–1899.

to 1879, the proportion to the total number of immigrants having risen from 9.4 per cent to 38.6 per cent. The proportion borne by the immigration from these countries to the total for the period from 1895 to 1899 is still greater, amounting to no less than 54.1 per cent.

Yearly immigration, by nationalities, 1890-1899.—The following table shows the number of immigrants of each leading nationality for each year from 1890 to 1899. It confirms the general results of the preceding table for the period from 1875 to 1899, although the marked fluctuations in the total immigration during the past 10 years make comparisons of the proportions of the different nationalities difficult. It will be seen that the immigrants from Great Britain, Germany, and Sweden and Norway have steadily decreased in absolute numbers from year to year, as well as in their proportion to the total number of immigrants. The immigrants from Italy, on the other hand, have nearly held their own in absolute numbers, despite the falling off of the total immigration, while for the year 1899 the number is the largest ever recorded. The immigration from Hungary and from Russia and Poland has decreased somewhat along with the general decrease, but the falling off has not been so great as in the case of the nations first mentioned.

Number of immigrants by leading nationalities, 1890-1899.

Year.	Total.	England, Scotland, Wales.	Ireland.	Germany.	Austria, including Bohemia, etc.	Sweden, Norway.	Hungary.	Italy.	Russia.
1890	455,302	69,730	53,024	92,427	34,137	41,002	22,062	52,003	46,671
1891	560,319	66,605	55,706	113,554	42,676	49,448	28,366	76,055	74,923
1892	579,663	42,215	51,383	119,168	41,213	56,170	35,724	61,631	122,047
1893	439,730	35,189	43,578	78,756	34,528	51,225	22,892	72,145	58,684
1894	285,631	22,520	30,231	53,989	23,938	27,397	14,700	42,977	41,219
	2,320,645	236,259	233,922	457,894	176,492	225,242	123,744	304,811	343,544
1895	258,536	28,833	46,304	32,173	18,195	22,942	15,206	35,427	36,697
1896	343,267	24,556	40,262	31,885	34,205	30,032	30,898	68,060	52,136
1897	230,832	12,727	28,421	22,533	18,006	19,004	15,025	59,431	29,981
1898	229,299	12,893	25,128	17,111	23,138	17,336	16,659	58,613	34,554
1899	311,715	13,823	32,345	17,476	36,870	19,502	25,620	77,419	60,982
	1,373,649	92,832	172,460	121,178	130,414	108,816	103,408	298,950	214,350

The race elements that have entered into the immigration problem, decade after decade, are shown in the table and chart, on pp. 275, 276, giving the percentage afforded by immigrants of certain nationalities to the total immigration of successive decades. It will be noticed that down to 1870 immigration was mainly British, Irish, and German, and that from 1870 on there was a progressively rapid decrease in the percentage of British, Irish, and German immigration and a proportionate increase in immigration from Italy, Austria, Hungary, Russia, and Poland. Immigration from all these countries put together did not amount to 1 per cent of the total immigration until the decade 1861-1870, when precisely that proportion was reached. In the next decade each of the three countries furnished notable percentages of the immigration, and in the decade just passed (1891-1900) had increased so much as to outweigh the British, Irish, Germans, and Scandinavians combined.

The progressively rapid rate of change is seen more plainly by comparing the proportions for the last years of the decade with each other and with the decade as a whole (see chart). In 1898-99 immigrants from Great Britain, Ireland, Germany, and Scandinavian countries made up only a little over 27 per cent of the total immigration, while immigrants from Italy, Austria, Hungary, Russia, and Finland (not Poland as in the proportion for the decade) made up about 65 per cent of the total. The following year the first group of peoples was reduced to 22 per cent of the total; the second group rose to 68 per cent.

Part of this change is due to a difference in grouping the nationalities between the single years as given and the decades. Immigrants from Finland have been added to the Russian group in the statement for the two separate years, making that group by so much the larger. Poland has been omitted as a separate heading in the 2 years named, but this omission makes a difference in the relative proportions of Austrian and Russian immigrants only—not in the relative proportions of the two great groups—as the immigrants formerly classed as Poles are now simply distributed between Austria and Russia.

These analyses are based upon the census classification of foreigners by country of birth, irrespective of race. A more satisfactory method, however, is to use a race classification, as is now done by the immigration department. The reasons why this is more satisfactory are obvious. Under the old system groups with most unlike

STATISTICS OF IMMIGRATION. 275

social traditions, characteristics, and possibilities are united indistinguishably in one group, while the elements of what should be one social group, as far as their characteristics and possibilities are concerned, are scattered about among several other groups. For example, under "Russia" of the census classification were gathered Germans, Hebrews, and Slavonic peoples of various kinds; under "Austria-Hungary" were collected Germans, many distinct Slavonic peoples, Hebrews, the true Hungarians or Magyars, and many Italians; while, on the other hand, no one group designation covered all Germans coming here, all Italians, or all Hebrews.

Analyzing the arrivals for the year 1899-1900 by races, then, and adding the Finns to the Scandinavians, where, for our purpose, they belong, it is seen (compare chart) that British, Irish, Germans, and Scandinavians made up about 28 per cent of the total immigration for the year, a slightly larger proportion than is shown by the corresponding general group taken by nationalities, while Italians, Hebrews, and Slavs of various kinds (Croatians, Slovaks, Poles, Bohemians, etc.) made up about 61 per cent, a somewhat smaller proportion than that shown by the nationality group for the year.

PER CENT NATIONALITIES IN TOTAL IMMIGRATION TO UNITED STATES.

[To accompany chart.]

Period.	I. England, Scotland, and Wales.	II. Ireland.	III. Germany.	IV. Scandinavian countries.	V. All others.	VI. Italy.	VII. Austria-Hungary.	VIII. Russia and Poland.	Total.
Decades.	Per ct.	Per ct.	Per ct.	Per ct.	Per ct.	Per ct.	Per ct.	Per ct.	Per ct.
1821–30	17	35	4.8	0.2	42.6	0.3		0.06	100
1831–40	12.5	35	25	.5	26.5	.4		.1	100
1841–50	15.5	46	25	.8	12.6	.1		.04	100
1851–60	16	35	37	.9	10.7	.3		.06	100
1861–70	26	19	34	5	15	.5	0.3	.2	100
1871–80	19	16	26	8	24.5	2	2.5	2	100
1881–90	14.5	12.5	28	11	16	6	7	5	100
1891–1900	7.4	15	13.7	10.1	3.8	17.7	16	16.3	100
Years.									
1898–99	4.1	10.4	5.6	7.1	8.3	25	20	19.5	100
1899–1900	2.8	8	4.1	7	10	22.3	25.6	20.2	100

PER CENT OF DIFFERENT RACES.

Period.	English, Scotch, and Welsh.	Irish.	German.	Scandinavian (including Finns).	All others.	Italians.	Hebrews.	Slavonic races.	Total.
1899–1900	3	8	6.6	10.2	11.1	22.6	13.5	25	100

276   THE INDUSTRIAL COMMISSION:—IMMIGRATION.

STATISTICS OF IMMIGRATION.

Effects of immigration on the increase of population.—It is, of course, impossible to measure the effect of immigration upon the population of the country, but at any rate it is a hasty assumption which holds that immigration during the nineteenth century has increased the total population. The late Francis A. Walker, superintendent of the censuses of 1870 and 1880, maintained that had there been no immigration whatever into this country during the past 90 years, "the native element would long have filled the place the foreigners have usurped." (See article in Forum, 1891, pp. 634–743; reprinted in Discussions in Economics and Statistics, Vol. II, pp. 417–426.)

Population and immigration.

	Population.	Watson's estimate.	Watson's error.	Foreign immigration for decade.
1790	3,929,214			
1800	5,308,483			50,000
1810	7,239,881			70,000
1820	9,633,822	9,625,734	—8,088	114,000
1830	12,866,020	12,833,645	—32,375	143,439
1840	17,069,453	17,116,526	+47,073	599,125
1850	23,191,876	23,185,368	—6,508	1,713,251
1860	31,443,321	31,753,824	+310,503	2,598,214
1870	38,558,371	42,328,432	+3,770,061	2,314,824
1880	50,155,783	56,450,241	+6,294,458	2,812,191
1890	62,622,250	77,266,989	+14,644,739	5,246,613
1900	75,559,258	100,235,985	+24,676,727	3,687,564

President Walker's argument gains statistical plausibility from the estimates, which he quotes, made by Elkanah Watson in 1815, of the future population of the United States, on the basis of the first 3 censuses. Taking Watson's predictions and comparing them with the actual census returns (see table above), Walker found that in the censuses of 1820 and 1830, when immigration was so slight as to be negligible, the predictions were within four one-thousandths of the actual population; and again, in 1840 and 1850, with immigration amounting to 599,125 in one decade, and 1,713,251 in the second decade, Watson's predictions were again as close as before. Speaking of these predictions, Walker says:

"Here we see that, in spite of the arrival of 599,000 foreigners during the period 1830–1840, 4 times as many as had arrived during any preceding decade, the figures of the census coincided closely with the estimate of Watson, based on the growth of population in the preimmigration era, falling short of it only by 47,073 in 17,000,000; while in 1850 the actual population, in spite of the arrival of 1,713,000 more immigrants, exceeded Watson's estimate by only 6,508 in a total of 23,000,000. Surely, if this correspondence between the increase of the foreign element and the relative decline of the native element is a mere coincidence, it is one of the most astonishing in human history."

It might be added to what President Walker says, that even in 1860, 45 years after Watson's predictions, and following an immigration of 2,598,214 during the preceding decade, Watson's figures were within 1 per cent of the actual figures.

The explanation given by Walker for the check on the native increase following the increased immigration of foreigners is based partly on sentimental and partly on economic reasons. "The American shrank from the industrial competition thus thrust upon him. He was unwilling to engage in the lowest kind of day labor with these new elements of population; he was even more unwilling to bring sons and daughters into the world to enter into that competition."

After the civil war new causes entered, especially city life and more luxurious methods of living, and Watson's predictions fall wide of the actual population, mounting as high as 33⅓ per cent in 1900. "Yet," says Walker, "still the great fact protrudes through all the subsequent history of our population, that the more rapidly foreigners came into the United States the smaller was the rate of increase, not merely among the native population separately, but throughout the population of the country as a whole, including the foreigners. * * * If the foregoing views are true, or contain any considerable degree of truth, foreign immigration into this country has, from the time it first assumed large proportions, amounted not to a reenforcement of our population, but to a replacement of native by foreign stock." (P. 425.)

CHAPTER IV.
TENDENCY OF FOREIGN-BORN TOWARD CITIES.

Although principal stress is laid in most discussions of immigration upon its economic effects, its social and political effects upon this country also call for very considerable attention. Light upon certain of these effects can be obtained from the statistics of the United States census and of the Bureau of Immigration.

It is a familiar fact that a large proportion of those who come to our shores remain in the great cities. The crowding together, often in colonies composed almost exclusively of persons of a single nationality, of large numbers of poor and ignorant immigrants, is considered a serious economic, social, and political menace to our municipalities.

As will be seen by the following table,[1] the United States census of 1890 shows that whereas the foreign-born constitute only 14.4 per cent of the total population of our country, they constitute more than twice as large a proportion, 29.18 per cent, of the population of the principal cities of the country, to wit, those over 25,000 in population. If we consider the rural population alone, excluding the cities, we shall find that only a little over one-tenth of the total number of inhabitants are of foreign birth. The table shows by grand divisions and States the percentages borne by persons of foreign birth to the total population in the principal cities and in the remainder of the country. The individual States of the South Atlantic and the South Central divisions are omitted on account of the small proportion of foreign-born and the small number of great cities, as are also most of the States of the Western division.

Proportion of foreign-born in the principal cities and in the remainder of the country compared with the total population—1890.

States and Territories.	Number of principal cities.	Per cent of foreign-born of total population—		States and Territories.	Number of principal cities.	Per cent of foreign-born of total population—	
		In principal cities.	In remainder of country.			In principal cities.	In remainder of country.
The United States	124	29.18	10.63	North Central division—Continued.			
North Atlantic division	56	32.38	15.37	Michigan	4	37.52	23.73
				Wisconsin	2	38.31	29.59
Maine	1	21.48	11.39	Minnesota	3	39.26	34.75
New Hampshire	1	45.53	15.72	Iowa	4	22.82	16.47
Vermont			13.26	Missouri	3	22.43	4.51
Massachusetts	16	35.10	23.22	North Dakota			44.58
Rhode Island	2	31.12	30.47	South Dakota			27.69
Connecticut	4	28.87	22.91	Nebraska	2	21.22	18.65
New York	13	36.23	15.07	Kansas	2	13.24	10.21
New Jersey	7	30.69	16.81				
Pennsylvania	12	24.70	11.76	South Central division	13	12.46	2.16
South Atlantic division	10	10.93	1.17	Western division	9	34.78	22.66
North Central division	36	30.74	15.20	Colorado	1	23.86	19.16
				Washington	2	32.93	23.67
Ohio	9	26.13	8.03	Oregon	1	37.35	14.96
Indiana	4	14.43	5.80	California	4	38.11	26.10
Illinois	3	39.67	14.22				

The following table shows, for all cities having more than 100,000 population, the percentage of foreign-born to the total population, together with the proportions of the leading nationalities, as shown by the percentages borne by the number belonging to each nationality to the total number of foreign-born in the city.[2]

---
[1] Census of 1890, Population, Vol. I, p. xc.
[2] Ibid., p. cli.

Foreign-born in great cities, 1890.

City.	Per cent of total population foreign-born.	Per cent of total foreign-born in—						
		Canada.	England.	Ireland.	Germany.	Russia.	Hungary.	Italy.
United States	14.40	10.61	9.83	20.23	30.11	1.97	0.68	1.98
New York	42.23	1.31	5.64	29.76	32.93	7.62	1.91	6.24
Chicago	40.98	5.39	6.29	15.54	35.73	1.71	.40	1.26
Philadelphia	25.74	.96	14.45	41.17	27.82	2.92	.50	2.52
Brooklyn	32.46	2.25	10.16	32.38	36.22	1.30	.25	3.65
St. Louis	25.43	1.75	5.68	21.13	57.45	1.34	.22	1.13
Boston	35.27	24.21	8.52	45.17	6.55	2.72	.12	2.98
Baltimore	15.88	.75	4.49	19.40	59.00	5.88	.24	1.19
San Francisco	42.41	3.45	7.78	24.22	20.84	.84	.13	4.11
Cincinnati	24.05	1.32	4.13	17.26	69.20	1.37	.17	1.03
Cleveland	37.15	5.31	11.28	13.92	41.09	1.53	3.31	.65
Buffalo	35.00	11.86	7.99	13.03	47.67	.68	.09	2.05
New Orleans	14.20	1.01	4.65	23.05	32.99	.43	.07	10.54
Pittsburg	30.71	.86	13.85	28.80	34.61	3.11	1.08	2.59
Washington	8.15	3.49	11.34	38.49	30.78	1.30	.22	2.49
Detroit	39.69	23.00	8.77	9.11	43.42	.82	.14	.41
Milwaukee	38.92	1.57	3.03	4.32	68.83	·69	.25	.17
Newark	30.56	.94	10.12	23.82	47.72	2.33	.77	5.26
Minneapolis	36.76	12.83	4.11	6.20	12.75	1.64	.44	.23
Jersey City	32.73	1.73	10.20	41.53	30.15	1.08	.15	2.80
Louisville	14.59	1.66	4.20	22.39	59.95	1.16	.05	1.12
Omaha	24.95	5.57	6.94	11.61	23.63	1.75	.39	1.53
Rochester	29.71	14.63	12.58	16.30	43.57	2.73	.10	1.30
St. Paul	39.94	9.08	4.82	11.36	30.56	1.23	.77	.60
Kansas City	15.72	7.59	11.53	22.18	29.29	2.60	.08	2.93
Providence	30.55	11.12	20.18	47.17	4.03	1.53	.03	3.76
Denver	23.86	10.49	13.11	16.56	21.10	1.87	.42	2.39
Indianapolis	13.74	3.26	6.78	24.48	54.48	.97	.39	.77
Allegheny	24.82	1.23	8.67	21.19	50.83	.25	1.19	.52

It will be seen that the two cities possessing the largest proportion of foreign-born population are New York and San Francisco, each having no less than 42 per cent, or nearly three times as large a proportion as that for the United States as a whole. Chicago has almost as large a proportion, while St. Paul, Detroit, Milwaukee, Cleveland, Minneapolis, and Buffalo follow in the order named, each having more than one-third of its population of foreign birth. Eighteen out of the 28 great cities have more than one-fourth of their population of foreign birth, while the only cities having a less proportion of foreign-born than the average for the United States as a whole are New Orleans, Indianapolis, and Washington.

Great differences exist as to the relative tendency of the different nationalities toward city life. The following table shows the percentage of the total number of the various nationalities in the country who are residents in cities:[1]

Percentage of total foreign-born in principal cities.

Total foreign-born	44.13	Norway	20.78
Canada and Newfoundland	31.36	Sweden	31.81
Mexico	7.97	Denmark	23.24
England	46.70	Russia	57.90
Scotland	41.25	Hungary	44.78
Wales	25.80	Bohemia	48.32
Ireland	55.97	Poland	57.11
Germany	47.71	France	45.69
Austria	48.33	Italy	58.79
Holland	33.54	China	40.19
Switzerland	31.15	Other countries	39.22

This table shows the marked aptitude for urban life of the Russians, Italians, and Irish, each of which nationalities has more than one-half of its numbers in this country dwelling in large cities. Owing to the much greater absolute number of the Irish, as well as of the Germans, we find from the table on page 3 that these two nationalities constitute more than one-half of the total foreign-born population in the cities of the country as a whole, the Irish furnishing 20 per cent and the Germans 30 per cent.

---

[1] Census of 1890, Population II, p. cl.

The table on page 3 also indicates that the Germans are the predominant foreign nationality in most of the cities individually, as well as in the urban population as a whole. They constitute more than two-thirds of the total foreign population in Milwaukee (68.8 per cent), Cincinnati (69.2), Louisville, Baltimore, St. Louis (57.4), Brooklyn (36.2), Chicago (35.7), and numerous other cities.

The Irish are either the most numerous or the next most numerous foreign nationality in nearly every city. In the following cities they exceed the Germans: Providence (47.2 per cent), Boston (45.2), Jersey City (41.5), Philadelphia (41.2), Washington (38.5). The Irish constitute 32.4 per cent of the foreign-born population in Brooklyn, 29.7 in New York, but only 15.5 per cent in Chicago.

CHAPTER V.

ILLITERACY AMONG FOREIGN-BORN.

It is a well-known fact that the immigrants who come to this country are frequently from the less educated classes of the countries from which they come, while the general standard of intelligence and education in several of those countries is much lower than in the United States. The only statistical method which has been employed for ascertaining the relative intelligence of the native and foreign born is by the test of ability to read and write, which is applied both at the taking of the census and at the entrance of immigrants into this country. It is scarcely fair to compare the illiteracy of our total native population, including the exceedingly illiterate negroes in the South, with that of the foreign born, who are mostly whites. The following table, which compares the percentages of illiteracy among the native whites, ten years of age and over, in the various grand divisions and States, with the percentages among the foreign whites, gives a fairer view.[1] Owing to the small proportion of the foreign born in the South Atlantic and South Central divisions, the figures for separate States are omitted.

Comparative percentages of illiteracy of population 10 years of age and over, classified by general nativity—1890. (a)

	Per cent of total native whites illiterate.	Per cent of total foreign whites illiterate.	Native whites of native parentage.	Native whites of foreign parentage.
United States	6.23	13.06	7.45	2.24
North Atlantic Division	2.31	15.59	2.42	2.07
Maine	2.45	24.09	1.78	8.22
New Hampshire	1.48	26.32	1.07	4.43
Vermont	3.15	25.84	1.85	8.50
Massachusetts	.82	16.23	.53	1.38
Rhode Island	2.33	22.14	1.46	3.94
Connecticut	1.02	14.88	.87	1.35
New York	1.77	13.11	1.88	1.59
New Jersey	2.71	13.26	3.22	1.62
Pennsylvania	3.50	17.81	3.81	2.50
South Atlantic Division	14.62	12.24	15.40	2.99
North Central Division	3.45	10.58	4.08	1.90
Ohio	3.53	11.13	4.05	2.00
Indiana	5.26	10.97	5.70	2.90
Illinois	3.14	9.36	4.07	1.25
Michigan	2.49	12.41	2.35	2.74
Wisconsin	2.07	13.45	1.80	2.25
Minnesota	1.40	11.10	1.12	1.61
Iowa	1.85	9.28	2.11	1.25
Missouri	6.84	9.08	7.93	2.32
North Dakota	1.76	8.68	1.11	2.40
South Dakota	1.22	9.00	1.05	1.47
Nebraska	1.30	7.30	1.35	1.16
Kansas	1.96	8.78	2.05	1.57
South Central Division	14.98	20.20	15.59	7.03

a Native white and foreign white, Census 1890, Population, II, p. xxxv; native white of native parentage, p. xxxix; native white of foreign parentage, p. xl.

[1] Census of 1890, Population, II, xxxv.

ILLITERACY OF THE FOREIGN-BORN.

Comparative percentages of illiteracy of population 10 years of age and over, etc.—Cont'd.

	Per cent of total native whites illiterate.	Per cent of total foreign whites illiterate.	Native whites of native parentage.	Native whites of foreign parentage.
Western Division	4.49	10.36	5.55	1.98
Montana	1.59	8.20	1.61	1.56
Wyoming	1.31	7.06	1.19	1.62
Colorado	3.83	7.80	4.57	1.18
New Mexico	42.79	30.54	45.03	19.37
Arizona	7.87	42.22	5.20	13.84
Utah	2.34	10.27	2.68	2.05
Nevada	.85	10.00	1.03	.60
Idaho	1.91	8.29	1.98	1.75
Washington	1.33	6.99	1.33	1.35
Oregon	1.77	7.87	1.84	1.46
California	1.65	10.48	1.79	1.41

From these figures it will be seen that, for the United States as a whole, 6.2 per cent of the native whites are illiterate, while more than twice that proportion, 13 per cent, of the foreign-born whites are unable to read and write. The disparity between the natives and the foreign born is especially marked in the North Atlantic Division. The proportion of native whites in that division who are illiterate is only 2.3 per cent, while 15.6 per cent of the foreign born are illiterate. Among the foreign born in the New England States especially the illiteracy is great. In the two southern divisions of the country the proportion of illiteracy, even among the native whites, is very high, and in the case of the South Atlantic States fully exceeds the proportion among the foreign whites, although the latter figure has comparatively little significance, owing to the small total number of the foreign born in those States. In the North Central Division the illiterates among the native whites are 3.4 per cent; among the foreign whites, 10.6. In the States of that division where large cities are less important, the percentage of illiteracy among the foreign born is much less, showing that the agricultural population of foreign birth which settles in those States is of a comparatively high degree of intelligence.

Owing to the large proportion of the immigrants who settle in our great cities the question of the ignorance of the foreign born in them is especially significant. The following table shows the percentages of illiterate population, 10 years of age and over, in each of our leading cities, classified by general nativity:[1]

Percentage of illiterate population 10 years and over, classified by general nativity, for cities having 100,000 inhabitants or more—1890.

Cities.	Native whites.		Foreign whites.
	Native parentage.	Foreign parentage.	
New York	0.52	0.66	14.06
Chicago	.38	.45	8.31
Philadelphia	1.16	1.24	11.29
Brooklyn	.28	.60	6.96
St. Louis	1.70	1.15	9.07
Boston	.23	.50	12.77
Baltimore	2.38	2.02	12.40
San Francisco	.35	.32	6.56
Cincinnati	1.32	.77	8.06
Cleveland	.98	1.06	12.66
Buffalo	.48	.83	11.37
New Orleans	2.90	2.24	15.61
Pittsburg	.92	1.52	14.22
Washington	1.86	.89	9.26
Detroit	.88	1.17	12.06
Milwaukee	.52	.67	9.91
Newark	.57	1.13	10.13
Minneapolis	.31	.59	4.65
Jersey City	.50	.96	12.86
Louisville	2.63	1.58	9.46
Omaha	.58	.41	6.16
Rochester	.31	.65	8.87
St. Paul	.65	.86	8.11
Kansas City	1.19	.97	9.21
Providence	.55	2.29	18
Denver	.36	.38	5.50
Indianapolis	2.16	1.35	11.83
Allegheny	.59	1.04	8.95
Wheeling	3.17	1.85	9.72

[1] Census, Population, II, p. lviii.

It will be noticed that among the native whites, both of native and foreign parentage, the percentage of illiteracy in our cities is, on the whole, less than the percentage in the States in which they are situated. The efficiency of the common school system is especially indicated by the fact that the illiteracy is scarcely greater among native whites of foreign parentage than among those having native parents. The illiteracy among the foreign-born city dwellers, on the other hand, is very much greater than that among the natives. Thus in New York City the percentage of illiteracy among the native whites of native parentage is only 0.52; among the native whites of foreign parentage, 0.66, while among the foreign whites it is 14.06.

The statistics secured by the Bureau of Immigration regarding the ability of those who enter the country to read and write confirm the evidence of the above tables. In fact the percentage of illiteracy shown is even higher than that of the foreign-born resident population, indicating apparently that a certain proportion of immigrants learn to read and write after landing. The proportion of illiteracy among immigrants of 14 years of age and over during the 6 years from 1895 to 1900 averages above 20 per cent. It varied considerably from year to year, the specific figures being as follows: 1895, 20.37; 1896, 28.63; 1897. 23.1; 1898, 23.2; 1899, 22.9; 1900, 24.2.

The relative degree of illiteracy differs greatly among immigrants of different nationalities. The following table shows the percentage of illiteracy among the immigrants according to nationalities and according to races for 1899 and 1900.

Total number of immigrants in 1900 and percentage of illiteracy among immigrants 14 years of age and over for the years 1899–1900, by races.

[Compiled from annual report of Commissioner General of Immigration, 1899, p. 6; 1900, p. 6. The table is arranged according to the precedence of illiteracy in 1900.]

Races.	1900.		1899.
	Per cent of illiterates 14 years of age and over.	Total number arriving.	Per cent of illiterates 14 years of age and over.
Turkish	78.7	184	11.5
Portuguese	60	4,241	65.6
Syrian	56.4	2,920	56.5
Italian (southern)	54.5	84,346	57.3
Filipinos	50	9	
Ruthenian (Russniak)	49	2,832	42.6
Pacific islanders	41	112	
Mexican	38.3	261	5.1
Croatian and Slovenian	37.4	17,184	24.9
Bulgarian, Servian, and Montenegrin	35.9	204	13.4
Dalmatian, Bosnian, and Herzegovinian	32.9	675	28.8
Lithuanian	32.1	10,311	32.5
Polish	31.6	46,938	31.3
Russian	28.8	1,200	13.5
Slovak	28	29,243	27.7
Roumanian	25.1	398	17.9
Armenian	24.4	982	18.9
African (black)	23.9	714	30.4
Spanish-American	22.8	97	
Hebrew	22.8	60,764	23
Korean	22.5	71	
Greek	17.5	3,773	23.8
Magyar	16.9	13,777	10
Italian (northern)	11.8	17,316	11.4
Dutch and Flemish	9.9	2,702	9.3
Japanese	8.9	12,628	4.8
Not specified	7.9	73	
Cuban	6.9	2,678	2.5
German	5.8	29,682	3.2
West Indian	5.4	78	26.3
Spanish	5	1,111	6.1
French	4.1	2,095	3.5
Welsh	3.7	762	4.6
Irish	3.2	35,607	4
Bohemian and Moravian	3	3,060	3.4
Finnish	2.7	12,612	1.2
Scotch	2.1	1,757	1.5
English	2.0	10,897	1.7
Hawaiian	1.9	67	.8
Chinese	1.4	1,250	.1
Scandinavian (Norwegians, Danes, and Swedes)	.8	32,952	.6
South Americans			2.6
Total	24.2	448,572	22.9

ILLITERACY OF THE FOREIGN-BORN.

Illiteracy of immigrants 14 years of age and over by nationality, 1896.

Nationality.	1896. Total arrivals.	1896. Percentage of illiteracy.	Nationality.	1896. Total arrivals.	1896. Percentage of illiteracy.
Austria-Hungary:			Wales	1,581	12.54
Bohemia and Moravia	2,709	11.45	Europeans not specified	9	
Galicia and Bukowina	12,696	60.37	Mexico	150	40
Other Austria	18,800	36.38	British Honduras	5	
Hungary	30,898	46.51	Costa Rica	3	
Belgium	1,261	14.46	Guatemala	1	
Denmark	3,167	.95	Honduras	2	
France (including Corsica)	2,463	4.88	Salvador	5	50
Germany	31,885	2.96	Quebec and Ontario	191	5.95
Greece	2,175	26.21	Nova Scotia	23	
Italy	68,060	54.59	New Brunswick	9	
Netherlands	1,583	4.16	British Columbia	22	
Norway	8,855	1.18	Newfoundland and Labrador	28	
Portugal	2,766	77.69	Cuba	6,077	21.49
Roumania	785	21.03	Other West Indies	751	33.18
Russia (proper)	45,137	41.14	South America	35	6.90
Finland	6,308	11.82	Turkey in Asia	4,139	46.66
Poland	691	47.78	China	1,441	17.85
Spain	351	15.81	Japan	1,110	10.73
Sweden	21,177	1.16	Asia (not specified)	74	7.04
Switzerland	2,304	.79	Australia	87	6.56
Turkey in Europe	169	31.43	Africa	21	11.76
England	19,492	5.44			
Ireland	40,262	7.			
Scotland	3,483	5.70	Total	343,267	28.63

From these figures it appears that the immigrants from the northern countries, Great Britain, Sweden, and Germany, show a very low percentage of illiteracy. The illiteracy among the immigrants from Germany and Sweden is no greater than among the native-born Americans in our most highly educated States. The Irish are somewhat more illiterate than the natives of the rest of Great Britain, but even here the percentage is not high. The immigrants from the southern and eastern countries of Europe, on the other hand, show an excessive proportion of illiteracy, and it is those classes that are now coming to our shores in the largest numbers. More than one-half of those from Turkey, Italy, and the Portuguese Islands are unable to read and write, about two-fifths of the Ruthenians from Russia, about one-third of the Croatians, Poles, and Lithuanians from Austria-Hungary and Russia, and more than one-fifth of the Slovaks from Hungary, and the Hebrews.

The foregoing distinction is brought out still more clearly by the following tables, in which the illiteracy of the different races is shown by three groups, namely, those coming from western Europe, those coming from eastern Europe, and other races, mainly Asiatic. The line adopted as dividing eastern from western Europe is as follows: Beginning at the boundary between Finland and Russia the line leaves Finland and Germany on the coast, then follows the boundary between Bohemia, Austria, and Corinthia on the west and Galicia, Hungary, and Croatia on the east. The line then follows the division between northern and southern Italy. Spain and Portugal are also included in the eastern division because of their high illiteracy.

The tables show that in 1899 the per cent of illiteracy from western Europe was 2.8 and in 1900 4 per cent, whereas from eastern Europe the per cent of illiteracy in 1899 was 38.4 and in 1900 36.6.

Percentage of illiteracy among immigrants 14 years of age and over for the years 1899–1900, arranged in groups of eastern and western European races and others.

	1899.	1900.		1899.	1900.
Western Europe:			Eastern Europe—continued.		
Scandinavian	0.6	0.8	Russian	13.5	28.8
English	1.7	2	Polish	31.3	31.6
Scotch	1.5	2.1	Lithuanian	32.5	32.1
Finnish	1.2	2.7	Croatian and Slovenian	24.9	37.4
Bohemian and Moravian	3.4	3	Ruthenian	42.6	49.3
Irish	4	3.2	Italian (southern)	57.3	54.5
French	3.5	4.1	Portuguese	65.6	60.2
German	3.2	5.8			
Dutch and Flemish	9.3	9.9	Average	38.4	36.6
Italian (northern)	11.4	11.8			
			Other races:		
Average	2.8	4	Chinese	.1	1.4
			Cuban	2.5	6.9
Eastern Europe:			Japanese	4.8	8.9
Magyar	10	16.9	Syrian	56.5	56.4
Greek	23.8	17.5			
Hebrew	23	22.8	Average	20.4	14.1
Slovaks	27.7	28			

Illiteracy and financial condition of immigrants.—There is a close connection between the amount of money brought by immigrants and their illiteracy. In the following table the per cent of illiterates 14 years of age and over is given for the more important races for the year 1900, and also the amount of money per capita. The per cent of illiteracy for all immigrants is 24.2, and the money per capita $14.84. Comparing these averages with the figures of the individual races, it will be seen that in only one case was more money per capita shown than the average by a race with a per cent of illiteracy above the average. This was the Russian. The smallest amount of money was brought by the Lithuanians, whose illiteracy was 32.1 per cent. The southern Italian, with a very high per cent of illiteracy, showed a small amount per capita. On the other hand, the highest amount of money per capita was $41.51, brought in by the Scotch, with an illiteracy of only 2.1 per cent. Of those races then having an illiteracy below the average, only the Hebrew, Magyar, Irish, Finnish, and Chinese showed less money per capita than the average for all. In general, then, the amount of money brought seems to vary inversely with the illiteracy of the immigrants, so that those with the greatest illiteracy have the least money, and the largest amount of money is found among the least illiterate.

Illiteracy and money shown by immigrants per capita for certain races.

| Races. | 1900. | | Races. | 1900. | |
	Per cent of illiterates 14 years of age and over.	Amount of money shown per capita.		Per cent of illiterates 14 years of age and over.	Amount of money shown per capita.
Portuguese	60.2	$10.47	Japanese	8.9	$39.59
Syrian	56.4	14.31	Cuban	6.9	19.34
Italian (southern)	54.5	8.84	German	5.8	28.53
Ruthenian (Russniak)	49.3	0.51	French	4.1	37.80
Croatian and Slavonian	37.4	12.51	Irish	3.2	14.50
Lithuanian	32.1	7.96	Bohemian and Moravian	3.0	23.12
Polish	31.6	9.94	Finnish	2.7	13.06
Russian	28.8	14.94	Scotch	2.1	41.51
Slovak	28.0	11.69	English	2.0	38.90
Hebrew	22.8	8.67	Chinese	1.4	13.98
Greek	17.5	28.78	Scandinavian	.8	16.65
Magyar	16.9	10.39			
Italian (northern)	11.8	22.49	Total for all races	24.2	14.84
Dutch and Flemish	9.9	21.00			

CHAPTER VI.
PAUPERISM AND CRIMINALITY AMONG THE FOREIGN-BORN.

It is often charged that the large influx of foreigners of low class has been especially injurious in its effects on account of the relatively large proportion of pauperism and criminality among these classes. The recent immigration laws of the United States have sought to debar, so far as possible, the entrance of those who are likely to become dependents and criminals. The working of these laws, the number and character of those debarred, etc., will be discussed in another place. It is doubtless true that they have had some beneficial effect, which will perhaps show itself in the statistics of the census of 1900, although the relatively lower standard of immigration as a whole since 1890 may offset any effect of closer inspection or debarment.

The following table from the census of 1890 shows the relative proportion of the different elements of the population who were found among the dependent, defective, and delinquent classes. The figures show the proportions to 1,000,000 of the population. Thus the number of prisoners of foreign birth among 1,000,000 of the total number of foreign born is ascertained and compared with the similar proportions of the other elements of the population:

Proportion of inmates of penal and charitable institutions to 1,000,000 of total population.

[Census, 1890, Crime, Pauperism, and Benevolence, I, 10.]

Classes.	White.				Colored, total.
	Aggregate.	Total.	Native born.	Foreign born.	
Total	4,505	4,431	3,708	8,065	5,040
Prisoners	1,315	1,042	898	1,768	3,275
Juvenile offenders	237	235	250	159	254
Paupers in almshouses	1,166	1,211	829	3,131	847
Inmates of benevolent institutions	1,787	1,943	1,731	3,007	664

On the basis of these, and of other similar figures, the compiler of the volume on Crime, Pauperism, and Benevolence of the United States Census of 1890 makes the following comments:[1]

"The total white population of the United States (54,983,890) is divisible into two parts—native white, 45,862,023; foreign white, 9,121,867.

"The white inmates of penal and charitable institutions whose nativity is known (235,782) are also divisible into two groups—native white, 164,475; foreign white, 71,307.

"Of the total white population therefore 16.59 per cent is foreign born, of the corresponding institution population 30.24 per cent.

"Of the total native white population (45,862,023) the number with native parents is 34,358,348; with foreign parents, 11,503,675. By adding the latter to the foreign population we find the total number with foreign parents to be 20,625,542. The percentage of those with native parents is 62.49; of those with foreign parents, 37.51.

"We have seen, however, that the nativity of 396,416 parents of inmates of institutions is known, and that the percentage of native parents is 38.60, but of foreign parents, 61.40.

"In other words, if attention is confined to the nativity of the inmates of institutions 16.59 per cent of the entire population furnishes 30.24 per cent of the institution population. But if attention is directed to the nativity of the parents (a) of inmates 37.51 per cent of the entire population furnishes 61.40 per cent of the entire institution population."

The conclusions thus reached, however, require very material qualification before they can be accepted. So far as the statistics concerning the prisoners are concerned the figures in the above table have almost no significance whatever, because they fail to consider the great differences as to the relative number of males and the relative numbers belonging to the various age periods among the foreign born as compared with the native born. This point will be developed in detail further on. The proportion of males and the age distribution, however, should have much less influence on the number of persons who become paupers or who are inmates of

---
[1] Census, Population, II, p. 38.

benevolent institutions. At any rate, it is impossible to trace any close causal connections or to demonstrate them statistically. The proportion of paupers in almshouses is seen to be nearly 4 times greater for the foreign-born whites than for the native whites, while the proportion of the former in other charitable institutions is more than 75 per cent greater than in the case of the natives.

It will be interesting to know what nationalities among our foreign-born population furnish the largest contributions to our criminal and dependent classes. The following table, condensed from the census of 1890, shows the proportion of the different classes of defectives, dependents, and delinquents to the total population of each nationality in this country. The ratios are reduced to the basis of 1,000,000 of the total population:

Ratio of criminals and dependents of each nationality to 1,000,000 of total population of that nationality, 1890.

[Census, Crime, Pauperism, and Benevolence, I, 35.]

Birthplace.	Total.	Prisoners.	Juvenile offenders.	Paupers in almshouses.	Benevolent institutions.
Total	7,818	1,747	154	3,031	2,886
Canada and Newfoundland	4,037	1,626	218	949	1,244
England	7,160	2,114	211	2,163	2,672
Ireland	16,624	2,971	146	7,550	5,957
Austria	4,805	1,404	16	779	2,606
Belgium	4,685	1,149	133	1,370	2,033
Bohemia	2,447	305	102	1,439	601
Denmark	2,997	853	38	868	1,238
France	10,864	2,468	248	3,636	4,512
Germany	5,662	1,065	113	2,436	2,048
Hungary	6,794	2,083	112	785	3,814
Italy	9,877	3,115	784	817	5,161
Norway	2,852	645	74	1,144	989
Poland	4,580	1,011	285	1,486	1,798
Portugal	3,897	575	192	1,425	1,405
Russia	5,202	1,144	110	586	3,362
Sweden	3,468	728	38	1,351	1,351
Switzerland	7,255	1,480	144	2,969	2,662

Taking the inmates of all penal and charitable institutions, we find that the highest ratio is shown by the Irish, whose proportion is more than double the average for the foreign born, amounting to no less than 16,624 to the million. The French, Italians, Swiss, and English furnish the next largest contributions to these undesirable classes. The relatively low proportion of dependents and delinquents among the Russians, Poles, and Bohemians is noteworthy. The immigrants from Sweden, Norway, and Denmark appear to be especially desirable from this standpoint.

Although, as we see, the comparison between the number of prisoners of foreign birth and those of native birth is entirely misleading, we can yet gain some information by comparing the different nationalities of foreigners among themselves, since differences in the proportions of sexes and in the age groupings are not so marked between the different nationalities as they are between the foreign born as a whole and the native born. Nevertheless the comparison even between nationalities is much less satisfactory as regards criminals than as regards paupers and inmates of benevolent institutions. The Italians appear to furnish the largest proportion of criminals, a fact which is doubtless connected with the exceedingly high proportion of males of ages capable of committing crime. The Irish come next, and the French follow the Irish. The Russians, Poles, and Germans stand almost on a par with one another, having a comparatively low proportion of criminals, while, as before, the most northern countries appear to furnish the most desirable immigrants, judging from this standpoint alone.

The proportion of the different nationalities among the paupers in our almshouses varies very greatly. The Irish show far and away the largest proportion, no less than 7,550 per million inhabitants, as compared with 3,031 for the average of all the foreign born. The French come next, while the proportion of paupers among the Germans is somewhat unexpectedly high. The remarkably low degree of pauperism among the Italians is possibly due to the fact that such a large percentage of them are capable of active labor, coming to this country especially for that purpose.

The Italians, on the other hand, show a very large proportion of inmates of other benevolent institutions—insane asylums, hospitals, etc.—falling first after the Irish in the proportion of such classes. The Russians, also, who are to a very slight degree represented in our almshouses, are in comparatively high proportions in the various benevolent institutions. It should be noted that the benevolent institutions referred to include those supported by private charity, whereas almshouses are mostly public institutions. Several of the nationalities among our foreign-born inhabitants, notably the Jews, maintain institutions for persons of their own birth, which explains the marked discrepancy between the figures in the last two columns.

As already intimated, the gross statistics as to the proportion of foreign-born criminals to the total number of foreign born in this country are entirely misleading. The proportion of males in the United States, as we have already seen (p. —), is very much higher among persons of foreign birth than among those of native birth. We have also seen that the proportion of our inhabitants born abroad who are between the ages of 20 and 45 is 51 per cent, as compared with 34 per cent for persons of native birth. The proportion of males among the foreign born from 20 to 45 years of age is considerably higher, even than the proportion of males among the foreign born as a whole. It is a familiar fact that the amount of criminality among males is from 3 to 5 times greater than among females. Moreover, persons under the age of 20 years seldom commit crime, so that the immense numbers of persons below that age of native birth contribute very little to the number of prisoners in the country.

A somewhat fairer view of the actual tendencies toward criminality on the part of the foreign-born as compared with the native-born is obtained from the following table, which gives the proportions of prisoners to 1,000,000 of the total population by age groups. This table, however, fails to make the exceedingly important distinction between the males and the females.

Proportion of prisoners to 1,000,000 of total population, for each element of population by age groups, 1890.

[Census, 1890: Crime, Pauperism, and Benevolence, I, 166.]

	Under 15 years.	15 to 19 years.	20 to 24 years.	25 to 29 years.	30 to 34 years.	35 to 45 years.	45 to 54 years.	55 to 64 years.	65 years and over.
Total	31	1,370	3,180	3,127	2,419	1,964	1,356	867	403
White	12	891	2,285	2,430	2,019	1,708	1,222	785	354
Native	12	860	2,255	2,401	1,903	1,514	950	552	230
Foreign	36	1,199	2,434	2,528	2,416	2,222	1,774	1,216	632
Colored	148	4,451	9,695	8,701	6,243	4,123	2,534	1,713	906

It will be seen that this table makes a much more favorable showing for the foreign-born than the first above presented. According to the previous table there were 1,768 foreign-born prisoners per million of the foreign-born population, as compared with 898 among native-born whites. If in the above table we compare the ages from 20 to 45, in which much the largest proportion of crimes are committed, we shall see that the number of foreign-born prisoners in proportion to 1,000,000 of the total population is not more than 15 per cent greater than the number of the native born, the disparity being greater during the last two age periods than during the first two.

An article in one of our sociological journals[1] recently attempted to show that the proportion of criminality among the foreign-born whites was considerably less even than among the native whites of native parents, if both be properly estimated. The calculation was made on the basis of the number of male prisoners and number of males of voting age. Investigation shows, however, that this writer used erroneous methods of ascertaining the actual number of native prisoners of native parentage and of foreign parentage, respectively. There are a considerable number of prisoners whose parentage is unknown, and also a large number only one of whose parents is of foreign birth. All of these prisoners were included by the writer as being native whites of native parentage. The practice of the census authorities, on the other hand, in stating the total population, is to include all having one foreign parent under the natives of foreign parentage, and the writer referred to took this grouping as his basis for reckoning the population, while using the other in reckoning the number of prisoners. In the following table prisoners of unknown birth have been apportioned between the respective classes in proportion to the number of known birth, while the correct definition, according to the census authorities, of natives of foreign parentage has

---

[1] H. H. Hart, Am. Jour. of Sociology.

been applied. The table therefore shows the number of male prisoners of native birth, distinguishing those having native parents from those having foreign parents and of foreign birth, per million of the total male population of voting age belonging to these respective classes.

Number of male prisoners per million of voting population, 1890.

[Compiled from Census, 1890: Population, I, 751; Crime, Pauperism, and Benevolence, II, 4.]

	Native white.		Total native white.	Foreign white.
	Native parents.	Foreign parents.		
United States	2,517	7,435	3,482	3,269
North Atlantic Division	2,839	10,636	4,756	4,373
South Atlantic Division	1,553	4,343	1,722	2,449
North Central Division	2,414	4,523	2,940	1,913
South Central Division	2,827	6,453	2,693	5,086
Western Division	4,388	10,443	5,910	4,658
Massachusetts	3,090	18,839	6,999	5,903
New York	3,779	10,258	5,964	4,024
Pennsylvania	2,485	5,210	3,619	3,777
Illinois	2,649	5,918	3,535	2,322
California	6,362	12,935	8,181	5,632

From this table it will be seen that, taking the United States as a whole, the whites of foreign birth are a trifle less criminal than the total number of whites of native birth. But there is a wide difference in criminality between native whites having native parents and those having foreign parents. The number of native male whites of native parentage in our prisons is 2,517 per million of the voting population, as compared with 3,269 for the foreign born, and 7,435 for the native born of foreign parentage. The excessively large proportion of prisoners among the latter class, it should be noted, constitutes just as strong an argument as to the injurious effects of immigration as would a high proportion among the foreign-born themselves. It seems to show that the second generation of the foreign element, having become more accustomed to the ways in this country and more familiar, so to speak, with crime, and less under the control of their parents whom they learn to look upon as ignorant and out of date, present an excessively high proportion of criminality.

The general statistics for the country as a whole are borne out, with some exceptions, by the figures for the separate great divisions and for certain leading States, which are included in the table. In every grand division except the North Central the foreign whites show a somewhat larger proportion of prisoners than the native whites of native parents. The relative proportions in the North Atlantic Division, where the foreign-born population is exceedingly large, are especially noteworthy, the foreign-born showing a proportion of 4,373 to the million, the native born, 2,839. In almost every case, on the other hand, the criminality among the foreign-born is somewhat less than that among the total native white population, while in every case the criminality of the native whites of foreign parentage is very much higher than that of the other classes. Notice especially the high proportion of prisoners among this class in Massachusetts and New York. The figures for the South Atlantic and South Central divisions are of comparatively little significance, owing to the small foreign-born population of those States.

If we inquire somewhat more closely into the offenses committed we shall discover interesting differences between prisoners of native and those of foreign parentage. The following table shows the birthplaces of the 114,620 parents of the 57,310 white prisoners by specified crimes. It appears that in two groups, namely, homicide and forgery, the prisoners of native parentage predominate, but that in case of public intoxication foreign parentage has more than three times the influence, and in disorderly conduct slightly less than three times the influence. In the other groups, namely, assault, burglary, larceny, and grand larceny, there is a slight predominance of foreign parentage. When it is considered that the proportion of white male population of foreign parentage between the ages of 18 and 44 was 38.02 per cent of the total white male population (Census, Population, p. clxxvii), it becomes apparent that the influence of immigration, taking into account both the immigrant and his native-born children, accounts for a much larger proportion of prisoners than does the native stock, and that this disproportion in the case of misdemeanor, such as intoxication and disorderly conduct, amounts to two-fifths of the population producing more than three-fourths of the punished offenses.

CRIME AND PAUPERISM. 289

Birthplaces of 114,620 parents of 57,310 white prisoners, by specified crimes.

[Census: Crime, Pauperism, etc., Part II, p. 280, ff.]

	Aggregate.	United States.	Foreign.	America.	England.	Scotland.	Ireland.	Germany.	Italy.
All offenses	114,620	45,732	60,153	6,036	5,997	1,996	29,184	9,987	1,209
Public intoxication	10,666	2,102	7,858	646	731	266	5,330	514	10
Disorderly conduct	6,450	1,493	4,645	207	351	149	2,916	589	40
Homicide	8,850	4,614	3,604	459	318	93	1,255	765	214
Assaults, all sorts	9,774	3,625	5,556	485	500	140	2,543	910	374
Burglary	13,756	5,674	7,345	731	766	239	3,518	1,418	58
Larceny	10,024	4,411	5,036	602	546	146	2,282	924	35
Grand larceny	9,490	4,368	4,477	483	536	180	1,695	930	69
Forgery	3,016	1,804	1,053	106	172	55	203	348	9

The following table, compiled from the reports of the prison commissioners of Massachusetts and the census for 1895 of that State, shows also the significance of intoxication as a prominent cause of offenses amongst the foreign-born. It appears from the table that prisoners committed to all institutions in proportion to a thousand population of the same nativity indicates that those born in Massachusetts numbered 7.3 per thousand, but that, omitting those committed for intoxication, the number is 2.6 per thousand. Below this proportion stands immigrants from Portugal, Austria, Germany, Russia, and Finland. The leading nationality above this average is that of the Irish, whose commitments per thousand were 27.1, but omitting intoxication was 6. Next in order of commitments are Welsh, English, Scotch, and Norwegians, all of which show a large predominance of intoxication. The Italians are a marked exception, the commitments numbering 12.9 for all causes, and 10 for causes except intoxication.

Prisoners committed to all penal institutions of Massachusetts, except the State farm, during year ended September 30, 1895.

[From Prison Commissioners' Report, 1895, and Census, 1895, Vol. II, pp. 699-707.]

	Commitments per 1,000 population of same nativity.	Commitments per 1,000, less intoxication.		Commitments per 1,000 population of same nativity.	Commitments per 1,000, less intoxication.
Portugal	0.6	0.3	France	11.8	3.5
Austria	2.1	.5	Italy	12.9	10.0
Germany	5.4	2.7	Hungary	14.5	9.3
Russia and Finland	5.9	3.3	Norway	10.6	4.4
Massachusetts	7.3	2.6	Scotland	17.0	4.3
Sweden	8.3	2.9	England	17.7	5.4
Denmark	9.0	3.4	Wales	24.9	7.5
Canada and provinces	9.1	3.4	Ireland	27.1	6.0
Poland	9.5	6.2			

Deportations by the Bureau of Immigration.—In addition to the foregoing tables showing the relation of immigration to the problems of crime and pauperism, the following table is of interest as showing the operations of the Bureau of Immigration under the laws restricting immigration. This table gives for the year 1900 the deportation by races, arranged in the order of the percentage of total arrivals that were debarred. It will be noted that the high percentages of Pacific Islanders, Japanese, and Bulgarians is owing to the number of contract laborers deported, but that in other cases those debarred as likely to become public charges are the leading factors in the statistics. From Scotland this was almost the sole cause for deportation, while from Italy it was by far the leading cause. The same is true of the Hebrews, the Syrians, the Finns, Scandinavians, and Irish.

607A—19

Deportations by races, 1900.[1]

Races.	Percentage debarred.	Arrivals.	Total debarred.	Public charge.	Loathsome and dangerous diseases.	Contract laborers.
Pacific Islander	58.92	112	66		2	64
Bulgarian, Servian, and Montenegrian	6.37	204	13	7		6
Japanese	3.45	12,628	437	137	39	261
Roumanian	2.51	398	10			10
Armenian	2.34	982	22	10	11	1
Spanish	2.33	1,111	26	21		5
Scotch	2.21	1,757	39	38	1	
Greek	2.01	3,773	76	63	9	4
Italian (southern)	1.44	84,346	1,215	1,015	32	168
English	1.35	10,897	148	133	2	13
Croatian and Slavenian	1.18	17,184	204	131	2	71
French	1.09	2,095	23	20	1	2
Hebrew	.95	60,764	578	446	114	18
Italian (northern)	.93	17,316	161	99	8	54
Welsh	.78	762	6	5		1
German	.72	29,682	216	167	16	33
Lithuanian	.70	10,311	73	41	19	13
Portuguese	.66	4,241	28	26	2	
Slovak	.64	29,243	190	131	9	50
Nagyar	.56	13,777	78	69	2	7
Polish	.53	46,938	252	173	33	46
Dalmatian, Bosnian, and Herzogovenian	.44	675	3	3		
Ruthenian (Russniak)	.42	2,832	12	8		4
Syrian	.41	2,920	120	71	48	1
Dutch and Flemish	.37	2,702	10	9		1
Bohemian and Moravian	.26	3,060	8	5	2	1
Finnish	.26	12,612	33	13	20	
Russian	.25	1,200	3	3		
Irish	.23	35,607	83	69	12	2
Scandinavian	.19	32,952	36	27	8	1
Total	.94	448,572	4,233	3,007	393	833

[1] Compiled from Report of United States Commissioner-General of Immigration, 1900.

Religious faith of immigrants.—Questions concerning their religious faith were addressed to immigrants by the immigration authorities during a limited period in 1899 and 1900, and have since been discontinued. The following table, compiled for the only year for which complete records were obtained, shows the number of adherents to each faith by nationalities, and the percentage of each religion in the aggregate. It appears that in that year 52.14 per cent of the immigrants were Roman Catholics, and 4.03 per cent were Greek Catholics; of Hebrew 10.39 per cent of the immigrants, of Protestants 18.54 per cent, and the miscellaneous religions were 13.91 per cent. The Roman Catholics came mainly from Austria-Hungary, Italy, and Ireland; the Protestants from Germany, Norway, Sweden, and England; the Israelites from Austria-Hungary and the Russian Empire.

CRIME AND PAUPERISM.

Total number of passengers arriving in 1899 distributed by countries and religious faith and percentage of each religious faith.

Countries.	Total.	Protestants.	Roman Catholics.	Greek Catholics.	Israelites.	Brahmins and Buddhists.	Mohammedans.	Miscellaneous.
Austria-Hungary	64,835	5,009	39,694	7,699	11,082			1,351
Belgium	1,728	94	967	2	4			661
Denmark	3,253	2,629	44		2			578
France, including Corsica	4,902	165	1,736	3	12		2	2,984
German Empire	25,904	10,258	6,758	18	401			8,469
Greece	2,450	14	14	2,350				72
Italy, including Sicily and Sardinia	79,664	50	78,306	26	1			1,281
Netherlands	1,994	839	190		8			957
Norway	7,113	6,674	2					437
Portugal, including Cape de Verde and Azore Islands	2,269	2	2,056					211
Roumania	1,655	160	60	31	1,350			54
Russian Empire and Finland	62,537	13,295	22,462	1,470	24,351		1	958
Servia, Bulgaria, and Montenegro	59		4	47	1			7
Spain, including Canary and Balearic Islands	1,428	15	704					709
Sweden	13,541	12,708	9					824
Switzerland	2,294	710	608	7	6			963
Turkey in Europe	137	5	5	33	27		13	54
United Kingdom	65,390	12,611	31,216	4	197		1	21,361
Not specified	8				5			3
Total Europe	341,161	65,238	184,835	11,695	37,442		17	41,934
Total Asia	9,726	452	1,390	2,833	48	3,373	77	1,553
Africa	109	13	9		5		16	66
All other countries	10,440	1,274	2,178	11	28	228		6,721
Grand total	361,436	66,977	188,412	14,539	37,523	3,601	110	50,274
Percentage in each religion	100	18.54	52.14	4.03	10.39	.99		13.91

PART III.

IMMIGRATION AND ITS ECONOMIC EFFECTS.

A REPORT PREPARED UNDER THE DIRECTION OF THE
INDUSTRIAL COMMISSION.

BY

JOHN R. COMMONS, A. M.

IMMIGRATION AND ITS ECONOMIC EFFECTS.

CHAPTER I.

OCCUPATIONS OF IMMIGRANTS.

The chief question which is usually raised regarding the advantages and disadvantages of immigration into this country has to do with its effect upon industry, and especially upon native labor. It is claimed by many, especially among the working classes themselves, that the large immigration of laborers, accustomed to a lower wage and an inferior standard of living, tends to drive out American-born labor from various occupations, or at any rate to force down the general level of wages. It is claimed on the other hand by many persons that, so far as American labor is displaced by the lower grade of foreign labor, it finds occupations in higher forms of industry. The result thus is, according to this argument, that the severest and most unpleasant work is done for us by immigrants while the level of American labor is continually raised.

Some light upon the degree to which the foreign-born enter into productive labor and into the respective classes of occupations can be gained from the statistics furnished by the United States Census and by the Commissioner of Immigration.

Predominance of males among immigrants.—It is noteworthy that a much larger proportion of immigrants are adapted for gainful labor than is the case among the native-born. In the first place, the proportion of males among the total number of immigrants is much higher than the normal proportion in a fixed population. In an ordinary population the number of females is approximately the same as the number of males, although in the United States, as a whole, the proportion of males in 1890 was slightly more than half of the total, 51.21 per cent.[1] The proportion of males among the native-born in that year was 50.6 per cent, while among the foreign-born it was considerably larger, 54.9 per cent. The following table shows the proportion of males among the immigrants to this country from 1881 to 1889:

Percentage of males among immigrants of each nationality, 1881-1889.

[Report of Superintendent of Immigration, 1892, p. 14.]

	Per cent.		Per cent.
All nationalities (1881-1890)	61.0	Italy	79.4
		Russia, including Poland	65.8
Germany	57.6	Austria	62.9
Ireland	51.0	Hungary	73.8
England	61.3	Scotland	61.6
Sweden and Norway	61.0		

It will be seen that 61 per cent of the total number arriving during that period were males. Comparing the different nationalities, we find that the Irish and Germans show the largest percentage of females among the total immigrants. This is in the case of Ireland probably due to the large number of Irish women who come to this country as servants, while in the case of Germany a large proportion of the immigration is by families. The natives of the more southern and eastern countries of Europe, on the other hand, are much less given to bringing their families with them, and the proportion of males ranges from 65.8 for Russia and Poland to 79.4 for Italy.

Age distribution of immigrants.—From the fact just noted that a considerable proportion of immigrants do not bring families to this country, we should expect to find the relative number of children among immigrants and among our foreign-born population much less than among the native-born population. This fact is shown conclusively by the following table from the census of 1890:[1]

---

[1] Census of 1890, Population, Vol. II, p. xix; Census of 1890, Population, Vol. I, pp. lxxii, 486.

Relative age distribution of native and foreign born, 1890.

Age periods.	Native white.	Foreign white.
	Per cent.	Per cent.
All ages	100.00	100.00
Under 10 years	27.73	3.67
10 to 19 years	23.44	10.06
20 to 29 years	17.67	21.81
30 to 44 years	16.95	29.30
45 to 54 years	6.63	16.41
55 to 64 years	4.04	11.00
65 years and over	3.33	7.48
Age unknown	0.21	0.27

From this it appears that while more than one-half of the total native white population belong to the periods of childhood and youth, less than 20 years of age, only 13.73 per cent of the foreign whites are under 20. The years of life from 20 to 45 may be considered as the most productive. The proportion of the native-born population falling within these years is only 34 per cent, while the proportion of the foreign-born population is 51 per cent.

The same facts appear from the statistics of the ages of immigrants. The following table shows the percentage of immigrants under 15, between 15 and 40, and over 40, during the years 1873-1890:[1]

Percentage of immigrants under 15 years of age, between 15 and 40, and over 40, from 1873 to 1890.

	Under 15 years.	15 to 40 years.	Over 40 years.
Total	20.9	68.0	11.1
England and Wales	22.8	65.0	12.2
Scotland	23.0	64.6	12.4
Ireland	14.6	77.4	8.0
Hungary	15.4	74.2	10.4
Austria	23.9	64.2	11.9
Germany	25.8	62.5	11.7
Italy	15.6	69.0	15.4
Norway	20.7	67.9	11.4
Russia and Poland	26.2	63.8	10.0
Sweden	17.5	73.6	8.9
British America	19.4	67.9	12.7
China	7.4	88.9	3.7

It will be seen that the proportion of all immigrants under 15 years of age is slightly over one-fifth, whereas among the native whites the proportion was almost exactly two-fifths in 1890.[2] The immigrants belonging to the more productive years, from 15 to 40, constitute no less than 68 per cent of the total number. This table shows also that the nations from which the largest proportion of immigrants fall within the ages of 15 to 40—indicating that immigration by families is relatively less than the immigration of the unmarried—are Ireland, Hungary, Italy, Sweden, and China.

The relative proportion of immigrants belonging to ages from 15 to 40 is still greater during the 5 years from 1895 to 1899 than during the period covered by the above table. The proportion under 15 during these last 5 years is 15.9 per cent; from 15 to 40, 74.1 per cent; and over 40, 10 per cent.

Relative proportions of native and foreign born engaged in gainful occupations.—Chiefly because of the predominance of males and of persons in the more productive years of life among the foreign-born, we find that a much larger proportion of the total number of foreign-born in this country is engaged in gainful occupations than among the native-born. This means, of course, that the foreign-born compete to a greater degree with native labor than their mere aggregate numbers, compared with the number of native-born, would indicate. The following table shows the proportions which the different elements of the population bore to the total population according to the census of 1890, together with the proportion belonging to each class engaged in occupations, as compared with the total number of persons occupied.[3]

---

[1] Report of Superintendent of Immigration, 1892, p. 15.
[2] Census, Population, II, xvi.
[3] Census, Population, II, cxvii.

OCCUPATIONS OF IMMIGRANTS.

Percentages of each group of occupations, by nativity and color.

Nativity and color.	Proportion of total population.	All occupations.	Agriculture, fisheries, and mining.	Professional service.	Domestic and personal service.	Trade and transportation.	Manufacturing and mechanical industries.
Native white, native parents.	55.30	47.92	56.83	67.86	30.78	51.79	40.60
Native white, foreign parents	18.37	15.58	8.81	16.34	14.15	22.09	24.40
Foreign white	14.40	22.45	14.49	12.08	31.53	21.42	31.37
Total colored	11.93	14.05	19.87	3.72	23.54	4.70	3.63

From this table it appears that whereas the foreign-born whites constituted only 14.40 per cent of the total population in 1890, those foreign-born whites who were engaged in gainful occupations constituted no less than 22.45 per cent of the total number in such occupations. The competition of the foreign-born is most conspicuous in the groups of industry classed as "domestic and personal service" and "manufacturing and mechanical industries." In each case the number of foreign-born whites occupied is more than 31 per cent of the total number engaged in these occupations. The foreigners are less inclined to enter agriculture, and usually are less competent for professional service, which explains the fact that the proportion of the foreign-born occupied in these groups of industries, as compared with the total number engaged in them, is not greater than their proportion to the total population.

While, as has been said, the greater proportion of the foreign-born engaged in gainful occupations is primarily due to the predominance of males and of persons belonging to the productive age groups, it will be seen from the following table that within each age group—including those groups where the largest proportion of all classes is engaged in gainful occupation—the foreign-born show a larger proportion of persons so occupied, both among the males and among the females, than do the native-born, whether of native or foreign parentage. The difference between the proportions occupied is naturally least during the ages from 25 to 54, but even here the foreign-born show approximately 1 per cent more employed than the native-born among the males, while the disparity in the case of the females is, as might be expected, considerably greater.

Percentage of total population of each element above 10 years of age engaged in gainful occupations, by age groups.

[Census, Population, II, p. cxxii.]

Sex and age periods.	Native white—		Foreign white.	Colored.
	Native parentage.	Foreign parentage.		
Males	73.91	70.28	90.54	79.94
10 to 14	7.41	7.54	15.64	29.65
15 to 19	49.41	63.79	81.70	73.49
20 to 24	89.92	92.56	96.56	94.14
25 to 34	97.06	97.19	98.35	97.15
35 to 44	97.64	97.71	98.32	97.96
45 to 54	96.21	95.45	97.03	98.23
Females	10.90	20.78	19.35	36.02
10 to 14	2.52	3.70	9.81	20.42
15 to 19	15.80	33.68	58.78	43.45
20 to 24	19.94	36.58	45.45	47.05
25 to 34	11.45	19.18	19.79	37.16
35 to 44	9.16	12.07	12.02	36.77
45 to 54	9.84	10.89	10.51	37.59

Occupations chiefly entered by foreign-born.—We have already commented upon the fact that the foreign-born show a special inclination to enter the industries belonging to the groups of domestic and personal service and manufacturing and mechanical industries. While a considerable proportion of the immigrants on their arrival declare that their occupation is that of farming, comparatively few of these, at least in the case of the more southern and eastern nationalities of Europe, actually enter into agriculture in this country. They drift into unskilled forms of labor, the

298   THE INDUSTRIAL COMMISSION:—IMMIGRATION.

males going largely into mining, into common day labor, and into work of a less skilled character in our factories. A record is kept by the Commissioner of Immigration of the occupations to which the immigrants declare that they belong, but this, of course, gives comparatively little light as to the occupations which they actually enter. These occupations are grouped as professional, skilled, and unskilled, but it naturally does not follow even that those who declare themselves as belonging to one of the skilled occupations actually enter upon skilled labor in this country. A large proportion are returned as being without occupation, but these are chiefly children and women. The following table shows the number and the percentage belonging to each of these groups among the immigrants arriving in this country from 1881 to 1890:[1]

Classes of occupations of immigrants arriving in this country, 1881 to 1890, inclusive.

	Males.	Females.	Total.	Per cent of males.
Professional	25,257	1,749	27,006	0.8
Skilled	514,552	25,859	540,411	16.1
Unskilled	1,833,325	245,810	2,079,135	57.1
Not stated	73,327	42,830	116,157	2.2
Without occupation	759,450	1,724,454	2,483,904	23.7
Total	3,205,911	2,040,702	5,246,613	100

It will be seen that only 16 per cent of the males declared themselves as belonging to skilled occupations, while 57 per cent are rated unskilled, and 23 per cent as without occupation.

The following table, compiled from the United States Census of 1890, shows the absolute number of foreign-born males engaged in the leading occupations entered by them, together with the percentage which they bear to the total number of workers engaged in that occupation.[2] These figures should be considered with the fact in mind that the total number of foreign-born males in this country at that time was equal to 15.8 per cent of the total male population.

Foreign-born males in principal occupations.

	Number.	Per cent of total workers.
Agriculture and mining:		
Agricultural laborers	243,947	9.54
Farmers, planters, and overseers	743,161	14.70
Gardeners, florists, nurserymen, and vine growers	31,232	44.50
Lumbermen, raftsmen, and wood choppers	28,677	28.82
Stock raisers, herders, and drovers	16,110	23.00
Fishermen and oystermen	12,619	21.07
Miners and quarrymen	188,436	48.71
Professional service:		
Clergymen	18,238	20.95
Lawyers	6,008	6.72
Officials (Government), etc	11,985	15.42
Physicians and surgeons	10,402	10.37
Professors and teachers	8,834	8.72
Domestic and personal service:		
Barbers and hairdressers	21,821	26.56
Bartenders	19,888	35.73
Engineers and firemen (not locomotive)	38,440	27.51
Hotel and boarding and lodging house keepers	15,024	29.72
Laborers (not specified)	664,614	35.76
Restaurant and saloon keepers	42,695	49.66
Servants	55,611	23.35
Watchmen, policemen, and detectives	26,181	35.22
Trade and transportation:		
Agents and collectors	23,723	17.51
Bankers, brokers, and officials of banks, etc	11,999	17.34
Boatmen, canal men, pilots, and sailors	21,916	28.53
Bookkeepers and accountants	21,188	16.10
Clerks, copyists, stenographers, and typewriters	72,893	14.43
Commercial travelers	8,398	14.46
Draymen, hackmen, teamsters, etc	87,541	23.77
Hostlers and livery-stable keepers	18,623	23.07

[1] Report of Superintendent of Immigration, 1892, p. 15.
[2] Census, Population, II, cxviii; I, 486.

OCCUPATIONS OF IMMIGRANTS.

Foreign-born males in principal occupations—Continued.

	Number.	Per cent of total workers.
Trade and transportation—Continued.		
Hucksters and peddlers	30,190	53.13
Merchants and dealers	176,200	26.46
Messengers, packers, porters, etc	17,281	19.02
Salesmen	34,039	16.53
Steam railroad employees (d)	112,132	24.33
Telegraph and telephone operators	3,072	7.02
Manufactures and mechanical industries:		
Apprentices	10,284	13.81
Bakers	34,466	59.52
Blacksmiths and wheelwrights	67,319	30.86
Boot and shoe makers and repairers	72,075	40.07
Brick and tile-makers and terra-cotta workers	22,475	37.42
Builders and contractors	14,054	30.57
Butchers	38,748	36.59
Cabinetmakers and upholsterers	27,614	46.17
Carpenters and joiners	158,792	25.98
Coopers	15,766	33.23
Cotton, woolen, and other textile mill operatives	98,496	46.05
Harness, saddle, trunk, valise, leather case, and pocketbook makers	13,412	27.88
Iron, steel, and other metal workers	129,670	36.05
Leather curriers, dressers, finishers, and tanners	18,592	47.62
Machinists	56,160	31.74
Manufacturers and officials of manufacturing companies	26,217	25.89
Marble and stone cutters	28,238	46.28
Masons (brick and stone)	60,444	38.04
Millers (flour and grist)	9,476	17.97
Painters, glaziers, and varnishers	55,310	25.30
Plasterers	10,279	26.36
Plumbers and gas and steam fitters	12,556	22.20
Printers and compositors	17,684	16.86
Saw and planing mill employees	41,359	29.89
Tailors	86,471	71.12
Tobacco and cigar operatives	27,972	33.45
Wood workers (not otherwise specified)	21,577	33.93

It will be seen that a large number of our immigrants have entered our mines and quarries, the percentage of the foreign-born in those occupations being no less than 48.71 per cent. A large percentage of the total number engaged in the leading forms of domestic and personal service are also foreign-born, the proportion of restaurant and saloon keepers being very nearly one-half. The largest absolute number of the foreign-born engaged in any one occupation (with the exception of agriculture) are those classed as "laborers, not specified." The proportion of the foreign-born is slightly over one-fourth of the total number of such laborers.

A large number and proportion of the foreign-born are also engaged as boatmen and sailors, as hucksters and peddlers, and as merchants and dealers. Nearly one-fourth of the total number of railroad employees also are of foreign birth. It should be noted that this class, as given in the census, does not include mere track laborers.

In many of the mining and mechanical industries the foreign-born constitute from one-fourth to one-half of the total number of employees. Their competition is most conspicuous apparently in the following occupations: Tailors, bakers, boot and shoe makers and repairers, brick and tile makers, butchers, cabinetmakers and upholsters, textile mill operatives (46.05 per cent), leather dressers and tanners, marble and stone cutters, masons, and tailors.

The following table shows similarly the percentage of foreign-born females engaged in the principal occupations entered by them to the total number of females in those occupations. The proportion of foreign-born females to the total number of females in the country in 1890 was 13.7 per cent.[1]

---

[1] Census, Population, II, cxix, I; 486.

300   THE INDUSTRIAL COMMISSION:—IMMIGRATION.

Foreign-born females in principal occupations.

	Number.	Per cent of total workers.
Agricultural laborers	2,917	0.65
Farmers, planters, and overseers	29,106	12.85
Professors and teachers	13,804	5.61
Musicians and teachers of music	2,576	7.46
Boarding and lodging house keepers	9,736	29.97
Housekeepers and stewardesses	19,775	22.97
Laborers (not specified)	4,746	8.66
Laundresses	31,983	14.76
Nurses and midwives	13,164	31.80
Servants	374,253	30.76
Bookkeepers, clerks, stenographers, and typewriters	10,050	8.87
Saleswomen	6,944	11.88
Boot and shoe makers and repairers	4,537	13.47
Cotton, wool, and other textile mill operatives	80,923	36.18
Dressmakers	49,728	17.25
Milliners	7,199	11.98
Seamstresses, etc	26,030	15.49
Tailoresses	20,357	31.90
Tobacco and cigar factory operatives	7,124	25.45

Another way of looking at the same facts shown by the above tables is to take the proportion of persons belonging to each class of the population who are engaged in each leading industry as compared with the total number in that class who are engaged in productive labor. These proportions for males only are shown in the following table, the total number of each class employed in all industries being taken as 100:

Percentage of total number of males employed of each element of population in principal indusies entered by them, 1890.[1]

Native white, native parents	100.00	Foreign white	100.00
Farmers and planters	35.03	Farmers and planters	17.16
Agricultural laborers	13.76	Laborers not specified	15.35
Laborers not specified	6.59	Agricultural laborers	5.63
Merchants and dealers	3.86	Miners and quarrymen	4.35
Carpenters and joiners	3.68	Merchants and dealers	4.01
Clerks, stenographers, etc	2.94	Carpenters and joiners	3.67
Steam-railroad employees	2.32	Iron and other metal workers	2.99
Draymen, teamsters, etc	1.63	Steam-railroad employees	2.59
Iron and other metal workers	1.26	Cotton and textile workers	2.27
Salesmen	1.23	Clerks, stenographers, etc	2.17
Native white, foreign parents	100.00	Colored	100.00
Farmers and planters	15.52	Agricultural laborers	33.45
Agricultural laborers	9.46	Farmers and planters	24.66
Laborers not specified	8.51	Laborers not specified	15.02
Clerks, stenographers, etc	5.34	Servants	5.34
Merchants and dealers	4.05	Steam-railroad employees	2.28
Iron and other metal workers	3.73	Draymen, teamsters, etc	1.99
Draymen, teamsters, etc	2.97	Miners and quarrymen	1.19
Steam-railroad employees	2.80	Carpenters and joiners	1.01
Miners and quarrymen	2.23	Launderers	.98
Carpenters and joiners	2.87	Planing-mill employees, etc	.80

While in each group of the population the largest proportion of the total number occupied is engaged in farming or in agricultural labor, the relative proportions in the cases of the different groups differ very greatly. While 48.79 per cent of all native whites of native parents are engaged in agriculture, only 22.79 per cent of foreign whites are so engaged. The second generation of the foreign classes shows only a slightly greater inclination toward agricultural life than the first generation, the percentage of native whites of foreign parents on the farms being only 25 per cent.

The extent to which the foreign-born and their immediate descendants perform the unskilled labor of the country is shown by the fact that 15.35 per cent of the total number of foreign-born engaged in all occupations are classed as common laborers, and 8.51 per cent of the native-born of foreign parents, while only 6.59 per cent of the native whites of native parents engaged in productive labor belong to this class. Similarly 4.35 per cent of foreign whites are occupied in mines and quarries,

---

[1] Census, Population, II, cxx.

OCCUPATIONS OF IMMIGRANTS.

while the proportion of native whites of native parents so occupied is barely 1 per cent. The proportion of foreign whites working in cotton and textile mills is more than twice as great as the proportion of native whites. Other interesting comparisons may be made by studying the above table.

Marked differences in the degree of skill and in the relative inclination of adaptability for different industries manifest themselves among the different nationalities of the foreign-born. These differences are brought out in the following table, which is prepared in the same manner as the one just preceding, so as to show the proportion of those out of the total number of each nationality engaged in gainful occupations who enter into each of the leading industries.[1] The figures for each nationality may be profitably compared with those already given for the native whites of native parents and the foreign whites.

Percentage of total number of males employed of each nationality, in principal industries entered by them, 1890.

Germany	100.00
Farmers and planters	21.14
Laborers not specified	11.58
Agricultural laborers	5.90
Merchants and dealers	5.48
Carpenters and joiners	3.78
Tailors	2.72
Iron and other metal workers	2.67
Shoemakers and repairers	2.09
Draymen and teamsters, etc	1.87
Butchers	1.82
England and Wales	100.00
Farmers and planters	14.82
Miners and quarrymen	8.18
Laborers not specified	7.47
Iron and other metal workers	4.78
Cotton and textile workers	4.76
Agricultural laborers	3.71
Merchants and dealers	3.65
Carpenters and joiners	3.49
Machinists	2.67
Clerks, stenographers, etc	2.46
Canada (English)	100.00
Farmers and planters	18.39
Laborers not specified	10.03
Carpenters and joiners	7.61
Agricultural laborers	6.42
Merchants and dealers	3.39
Lumbermen, wood choppers, etc	3.01
Draymen, teamsters, etc	2.99
Steam-railroad employees	2.74
Clerks, stenographers, etc	2.63
Blacksmiths and wheelwrights	2.36
Sweden and Norway	100.00
Farmers and planters	27.12
Laborers not specified	14.95
Agricultural laborers	11.14
Carpenters and joiners	5.36
Miners and quarrymen	3.66
Steam-railroad employees	2.72
Saw and planing mill employees	2.42
Iron and other metal workers	2.03
Tailors	1.78
Merchants and dealers	1.77
Ireland	100.00
Laborers not specified	25.16
Farmers and planters	11.60
Steam-railroad employees	4.53
Iron and other metal workers	4.04
Draymen, teamsters, etc	3.57
Miners and quarrymen	3.47
Merchants and dealers	3.31
Agricultural laborers	3.11
Cotton and textile workers	2.29
Carpenters and joiners	2.01
Scotland	100.00
Farmers and planters	13.64
Miners and quarrymen	9.98
Laborers not specified	6.61
Carpenters and joiners	5.17
Iron and other metal workers	3.98
Cotton and textile workers	3.75
Machinists	3.48
Merchants and dealers	3.47
Marble and stone cutters	3.18
Agricultural laborers	3.14
Canada (French)	100.00
Cotton and textile workers	18.64
Laborers not specified	16.43
Farmers and planters	8.80
Carpenters and joiners	6.34
Agricultural laborers	4.01
Boot and shoe makers	3.39
Brick and tile makers	3.28
Lumbermen and wood choppers	2.98
Saw and planing mill employees	2.88
Draymen, teamsters, etc	2.62
Denmark	100.00
Farmers and planters	27.41
Agricultural laborers	13.37
Laborers not specified	13.30
Carpenters and joiners	4.48
Steam-railroad employees	2.56
Merchants and dealers	2.45
Blacksmiths and wheelwrights	2.04
Draymen, teamsters, etc	1.92
Painters, glaziers, etc	1.51
Servants	1.47
France	100.00
Farmers and planters	16.87
Laborers not specified	8.89
Merchants and dealers	6.13
Miners and quarrymen	4.65
Agricultural laborers	4.65
Servants	4.51
Carpenters and joiners	2.79
Iron and other metal workers	2.25
Cotton and textile workers	1.74
Butchers	1.73
Russia	100.00
Tailors	13.98
Farmers and planters	11.03
Laborers not specified	10.96
Hucksters and peddlers	9.52
Miners and quarrymen	8.55
Merchants and dealers	7.73
Agricultural laborers	4.16
Lumbermen and woodchoppers	2.00
Iron and other metal workers	1.72
Boot and shoe makers	1.70

[1] Census, Population, II, cl–cliii.

Percentage of total number of males employed of each nationality, in principal industries entered by them, 1890—Continued.

Bohemia	100.00	Hungary	100.00
Farmers and planters	28.16	Laborers not specified	32.44
Laborers not specified	15.90	Miners and quarrymen	19.97
Agricultural laborers	6.45	Iron and other metal workers	6.73
Tailors	6.42	Tailors	5.01
Tobacco and cigar operatives	3.83	Merchants and dealers	3.77
Carpenters and joiners	2.88	Steam-railroad employees	3.55
Saw and planing mill employees	2.55	Farmers and planters	2.12
Merchants and dealers	2.48	Hucksters and peddlers	1.87
Iron and other metal workers	2.46	Agricultural laborers	1.80
Miners and quarrymen	1.77	Coke and lime burners, etc	1.68
Italy	**100.00**	**Other countries**	**100.00**
Laborers not specified	34.15	Laborers not specified	20.38
Steam-railroad employees	10.56	Farmers and planters	10.78
Miners and quarrymen	8.51	Agricultural laborers	7.95
Merchants and dealers	6.33	Miners and quarrymen	6.85
Agricultural laborers	3.92	Servants	5.04
Hucksters and peddlers	2.96	Launderers	4.69
Barbers and hairdressers	2.91	Merchants and dealers	3.87
Boot and shoe makers	2.80	Tailors	2.73
Tailors	1.99	Tobacco and cigar operatives	2.19
Farmers and planters	1.89	Steam-railroad employees	2.19

While in no case does the proportion of immigrants who are occupied on the farms equal the proportion of native whites of native parentage so occupied, it will be seen from this table that the following nationalities, in the order specified, are more inclined toward agricultural life than the average of the foreign whites: Denmark (40.78 per cent), Sweden and Norway (38.26 per cent), Germany (27.04 per cent), and Bohemia. The immigrants from Great Britain show comparatively little inclination toward the farms, the Irish especially having but 14.17 per cent of their total number in gainful occupations thus engaged. The lowest proportions of farmers are found among the Russians, Italians (5.81 per cent), and Hungarians (3.92 per cent).

The nationalities showing the largest proportion of unskilled labor are, respectively, Italy (34.15 per cent), Hungary (32.44 per cent), Ireland (25.16 per cent), and French-Canada (16.43 per cent). The lowest percentages of unskilled laborers are found among the foreign born from England and Wales, Scotland, and Germany.

Immigrants from Hungary, Russia and Poland, and Italy are especially engaged in mining and quarrying, nearly one-fifth of the Hungarians being so occupied.

The most conspicuous fact indicated in the above table, aside from those already brought out, is the large proportion of Russians and Poles engaged as tailors and as hucksters and peddlers. It must be remembered that most of the immigrants from those countries are Hebrews, and largely settle in the sweat-shop districts of our great cities.

The following table, compiled from the report of the Commissioner-General of Immigration for the year 1900, shows, by races instead of countries, the proportion of males among immigration. The table is arranged in the order of precedence. It will be seen that the largest proportion of males is among the Chinese, Japanese, and Greeks, amounting to more than 99 per cent in the case of the Chinese and nearly 97 per cent in the case of the Greeks. The Croatians, who are immigrating in large numbers at the present time, show nearly 87 per cent males, indicating the recent beginning of that immigration. The same is true of the Slovaks, numbering 72.6 per cent male. This table brings out clearly the difference between the Russians and the Hebrews as contrasted with the preceding table based on countries of origin. In this table the Russians show 72 per cent males, whereas the Hebrews show 59.88 per cent. The Hebrew immigration is a permanent one, and the families are brought to this country as rapidly as they are able to pay the expenses. The Irish immigration shows a considerable smaller proportion of males than the preceding table, namely, 46.82 per cent, indicating the increasing immigration of Irish girls as servants.

OCCUPATIONS OF IMMIGRANTS. 303

Per cent of males among immigrants, distributed by races, 1900.

[Compiled from original figures in Annual Report of Superintendent of Immigration, 1895-1899.]

All races	67.80	Cuban	65.83
Chinese	99.27	Dutch and Flemish	65.32
Japanese	97.08	Finnish	63.43
Greek	96.87	French	62.57
Croatian	86.90	Syrian	62.09
Italian (northern)	78.19	English	61.57
Ruthenian	75.70	Scotch	60.60
Italian (southern)	75.50	Hebrew	59.78
Lithuanian	74.51	Scandinavian	59.26
Magyar	74.08	German	58.23
Slovak	72.61	Portuguese	56.26
Russian	72.16	Bohemian	51.04
Polish	68.49	Irish	46.82

Unfortunately no statistics are available to show how many of the unmarried men coming to this country as laborers are "birds of passage," who return at the end of each season or after a short period of years to their native land. It is quite generally believed, however, that this practice is very common, especially among the Italians.

The following table, compiled from the report of the Commissioner-General of Immigration for the year 1900, shows, by races and numbers, the proportion between skilled and unskilled laborers. Unfortunately the proportions are not conclusive, since the reports include women in the class indicated as having "no occupation." At the same time the table is fairly indicative of the relative position of different races in this respect. It will be seen that the race which shows the largest proportion of skilled laborers is that of the Cubans, namely, 40.93 per cent. This is owing to the large immigration of cigar makers. The next are the Hebrews, 34.6 per cent, largely tailors. Following this are the immigrants from England, with 28.9 per cent skilled laborers, and the Scotch, 31.7 per cent. Next are the French, with 24.8 per cent skilled. On the other hand, the races having the largest proportion of unskilled and miscellaneous laborers are the Chinese, Japanese, Croatians, Russians, Greeks, Italians, Lithuanian, Magyar, Polish, Portuguese, Ruthenian, Scandinavian, and Slovaks.

Occupations of immigrants, divided by races, 1900.

Races.	Total.	Skilled.	Unskilled.	Miscellaneous.	No occupation.
Bohemian	3,060	540	783	140	1,597
Chinese	1,250	3	618	600	29
Croatian	17,184	993	13,243	377	2,571
Cuban	2,678	1,097	30	218	1,333
Dutch	2,702	340	965	77	1,320
English	10,897	3,151	1,824	1,516	4,406
Finnish	12,612	238	9,094	231	3,049
French	2,095	521	718	141	715
German	29,682	4,660	9,075	1,270	14,677
Greek	3,773	595	2,287	205	686
Hebrew	60,764	21,047	6,872	2,865	29,980
Irish	35,607	1,943	28,557	818	4,289
Italian—					
Northern	17,316	3,359	9,899	359	3,699
Southern	84,346	10,432	50,118	986	22,810
Japanese	12,628	1,793	6,055	4,073	707
Lithuanian	10,311	310	7,296	49	2,656
Magyar	13,777	690	9,068	114	3,905
Polish	46,938	1,865	28,317	280	16,476
Portuguese	4,241	288	3,139	39	825
Russian	1,200	147	424	115	514
Ruthenian	2,832	33	1,732	20	1,047
Scandinavian	32,952	3,658	23,098	951	5,245
Scotch	1,752	565	342	163	682
Slovak	29,243	987	19,529	132	8,595
Syrian	2,920	478	933	165	1,344

Per cent of immigrants in specified classes of occupations, divided by races, 1900.

Races.	Total.	Skilled.	Unskilled.	Miscellaneous.	No occupation.
Bohemian	100.00	17.64	25.25	4.60	52.51
Chinese	100.00	.24	49.44	48.00	2.32
Croatian	100.00	5.77	76.99	2.30	14.94
Cuban	100.00	40.93	.83	8.13	50.11
Dutch	100.00	12.59	35.47	2.79	48.88
English	100.00	28.90	16.73	13.95	40.42
Finnish	100.00	2.22	71.38	2.21	24.19
French	100.00	24.80	34.19	6.97	34.04
German	100.00	15.70	30.57	4.28	49.45
Greek	100.00	15.78	60.61	5.42	18.19
Hebrew	100.00	34.60	11.30	4.80	49.30
Irish	100.00	5.45	80.21	2.33	12.01
Italian:					
Northern	100.00	19.41	57.21	2.00	21.38
Southern	100.00	12.36	59.41	1.19	27.04
Japanese	100.00	14.19	47.94	32.24	5.63
Lithuanian	100.00	3.00	70.83	.38	25.79
Magyar	100.00	5.00	65.80	.87	28.33
Polish	100.00	3.97	60.32	.61	35.10
Portuguese	100.00	5.61	74.03	.91	19.45
Russian	100.00	12.25	35.33	9.76	42.66
Ruthenian	100.00	1.16	61.19	.66	36.99
Scandinavian	100.00	11.10	70.09	2.88	15.93
Scotch	100.00	31.71	19.51	9.81	38.97
Slovak	100.00	3.37	66.78	.46	29.39
Syrian	100.00	16.48	32.17	5.01	46.34

CHAPTER II.

RELATION OF IMMIGRATION TO OTHER CAUSES AFFECTING WAGES AND EMPLOYMENT.

In addition to the general data regarding the distribution of immigrants among the several occupations, given in the preceding chapter, a more detailed examination is made in the following pages of certain occupations in which immigration has played an important part. These are especially the clothing manufacture and coal mining, and, to a lesser extent, cigar making and common unskilled labor. Preliminary to this detailed examination, the following introductory observations are thought to be in place:

The effect of immigration on wages and unemployment can not be considered apart from other causes which tend either to depress or to elevate wages, or to increase or diminish the amount of employment. Among the principal of these other causes are the cycles of business prosperity and depression, the introduction of machinery and subdivision of labor, the competition of women and children, country competition, and labor organization. The problem of separating out immigration from these other causes is one of extreme difficulty. It will be found that immigration exerts its greatest influence in those occupations where without immigration other causes tend already to depress wages. If machinery and minute subdivision of labor opens a place for the unskilled immigrant, they also open a place for women and children. And in other cases, where the immigrant might be supposed to have cut wages, it is found that in country competition native Americans are doing the same class of work at even lower prices than those received by the immigrant.

The competition with American labor created by immigration may affect wages in two ways, first, by an oversupply of labor, and, second, by the displacement of higher standards by lower standards of living. These two causes may be separated in our consideration and each judged upon its own merits. Suppose, in the first place, that all of the incoming immigrants for the past fifty years held the same standards of living as those Americans with whom they competed for jobs, would such immigration have overstocked the labor market and brought about depression in wages, or an increased amount of unemployment? This question may be stated in another way: Suppose, instead of immigration during the past fifty years, the same growth of population would have occurred through the natural increase of American stock already in the country, as maintained by President Walker in the article quoted on page 277, would such natural increase have caused a fall in wages and lack of employment?

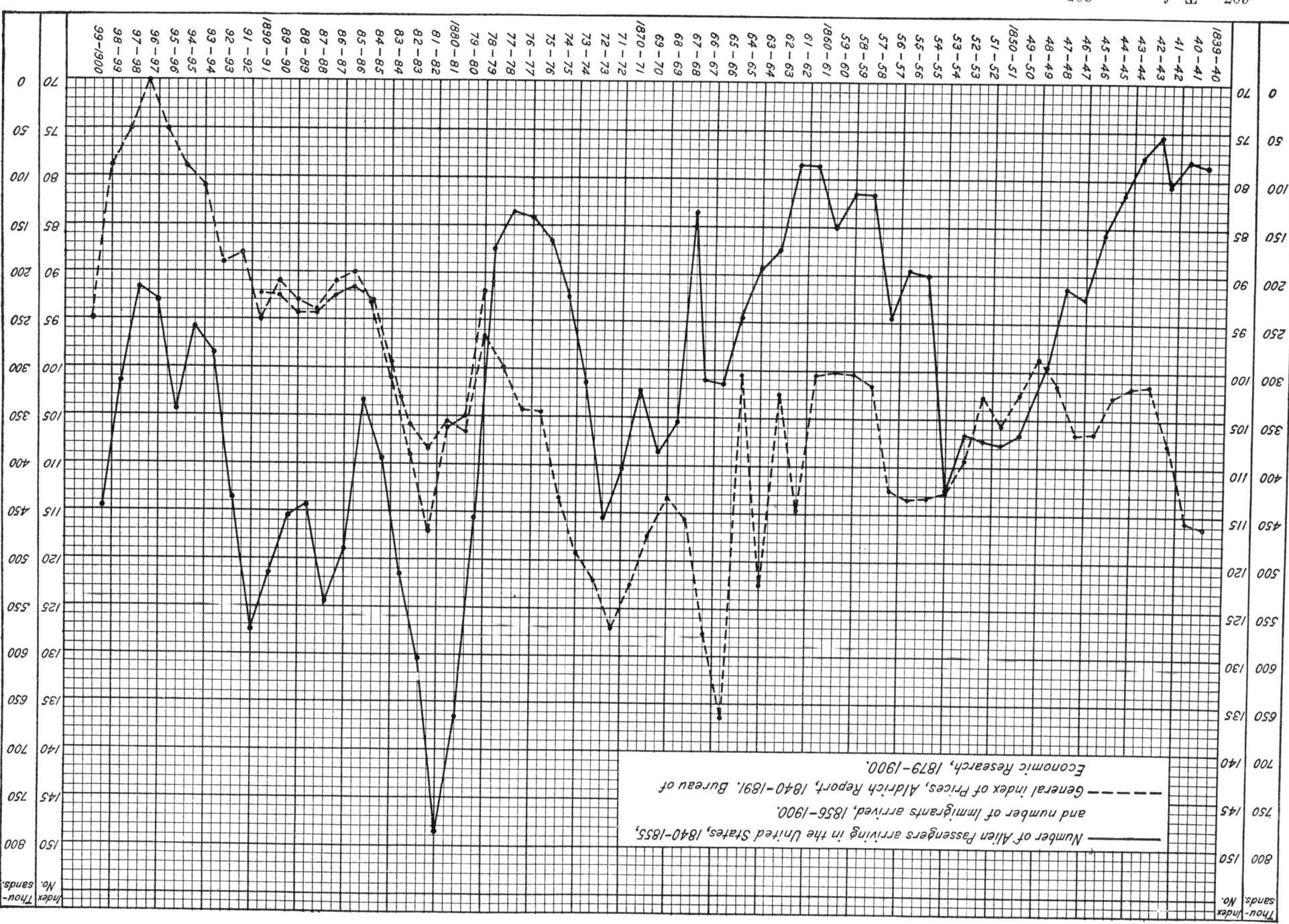
607A—To face page 305.

FACTORS CONTROLLING WAGES AND EMPLOYMENT. 305

To be sure, immigration, as has been shown in the preceding chapter, on account of the large proportion of adults and males, contributes to the working population more than would the natural increase of population, and, moreover, the immigrants crowd into the occupations unequally, and are not evenly distributed through all, as is the natural increase. Neglecting, for the present, these differences, and assuming that the new population comes with the same standard of living as the existing population, and is distributed evenly, it follows that the opportunities for the new hands depend upon the expansion of industry and the resources of the country. If the resources of the country are not yet diminishing, then the new hands which go into agriculture, mining, manufactures, transportation, etc., continue to produce wealth in the same proportion as formerly, and continue to get their wages by exchanging their products among themselves the same as before. Now, American industry has been expanding even more rapidly than population. New lands have been opened up either by clearing or by irrigation, and the expansion of agriculture creates a demand for increased manufactures. There has been, also, a more intensive utilization of old lands through more scientific farming. Again, in manufactures, mining, and transportation there has been a rapid advance in machinery and a better organization and division of labor, whereby the resources of the country are made more productive. This advance in machinery and division of labor often appears in itself to be a means of displacing labor and so of depressing wages, and such would be the case if industry as a whole were not continually expanding. The effect of machinery in displacing labor is similar to the effect of immigration in displacing labor. In both cases a third factor is essential, namely, business conditions. Business prosperity is but another name for expansion of trade, the opening up of new resources, the investment of new capital. Provided this expansion occurs there is no overcrowding of the labor market. The new resources and new investments demand new labor; and, if the expansion is strong enough, the new labor as well as the existing labor may secure advances in wages. But if business prosperity gives way to business depression then not only is the new labor a surplus but the existing army of laborers lacks employment. In time of depression not only machinery, but also immigration, and even the natural increase of population, add their influence in a cumulative fashion to overcrowd the labor market and displace labor.

I. CYCLES OF PROSPERITY AND DEPRESSION.

These observations are pertinent when we come to consider the alternations of prosperity and depression. Whatever the causes, the cycles of business activity and stagnation seem to be world-wide. These cycles are measured commercially in the rising and falling of the prices of commodities and in the volumes of sales. The so-called series of "index numbers" of prices present in concise form the movement of the general level of prices over a period of years. The accompanying chart is based on the index numbers of the Aldrich Report, compiled by the United States Department of Labor for the years 1840 to 1891, supplemented by the index numbers of the Bureau of Economic Research for the years 1879 to 1900. Taking the prices of a given year or set of years (Aldrich, 1860; Bureau, 1879-89), as a basis, the prices of the same commodities, including the leading staples at wholesale, are computed in percentages of the basis. These percentages, or "index numbers," will show, therefore, the rise and fall of prices, each general rise being usually coincident with increasing volume of sales, and indicating business activity and prosperity, and each general fall being coincident with decreasing volume of sales and business depression. In the diagram the annual volume of immigration is also presented, in order that it may be compared with the business prosperity and depression of the country.

In examining the diagram it will be seen that there is a striking coincidence, since the year 1868, between business conditions and the volume of immigration. From 1869 to 1872 there is an increase in prices of 13 per cent, and an increase in immigration which had begun to increase in 1869 from 352,768 and continued until 1873, when it reached 459,803, an increase of 30.3 per cent. The depression from 1872 to 1879, shown in a fall of 24 per cent in prices, was accompanied with a decline in immigration to 138,469 in 1878, a decrease of 69.8 per cent. The business recovery to 1882 shows an enormous increase in immigration, reaching the highest figure of the century, 788,992. The decline in prices to 1886 was accompanied with a decline in immigration, and the industrial recovery to 1892 by an increase in immigration. The decline in immigration after 1892 came at the same time as the new administrative law of 1893, which improved the efficiency of the restrictions on immigration, and, were it not for the regular cycle of immigration accompanying the cycle of prosperity and depression, the influence of that law might be cited as a cause for the decline. Lastly, the recovery in business since 1897 is reflected in the rise of mmigration in 1899 to 1900.

Taking these considerations into account it may well be said that immigration since the civil war is a reflection of industrial conditions. Going back to years prior to the civil war we find that political causes were added to industrial causes. The increase in immigration from 1843 to 1847 accompanied an increase in business activity, but the panic of 1847 did not cause a decline in immigration, because at that time the political revolutions on the Continent and the famine in Ireland occurred at the very time when the depression was at its depth. Again, 2 years before the rise in prosperity had received its check in 1857, the decline in immigration had begun, and very low points were reached during the civil war. Following this period, however, as already shown, immigration follows closely the state of industrial activity.

It must not, however, be assumed that in recent years immigration is strictly economic. While there has been an increase along with returning prosperity in the United States, this increase has not come in a marked degree from prosperous countries with advanced constitutional Governments nor from the dominant races of other countries. From Russia in 1900 there were only 1,165 "Russians," but there were 37,011 Hebrews, 12,515 Finns, 10,297 Lithuanians, 22,500 Poles, 5,349 Germans. From Austro-Hungary there were 13,776 of the dominant Magyars out of a total Magyar population of 19,000,000, but there were 17,163 Croatians and Slovenians from a population of 2,200,000, 22,802 Poles from a population of 3,700,000, 29,183 Slovaks from a population of perhaps 3,000,000.

Even of Italy the large immigration comes mainly from southern provinces, which, on account of their lack of political suffrage, have been discriminated against in taxes and landlord exactions. While, of course, economic considerations are always present in immigration, the foregoing considerations suggest that it is the unequal distribution of this economic pressure through political and racial oppression that drives subject races to our shores.

Average daily wages in gold, 1870–1898.

[Compiled from Bulletin Department of Labor, September, 1898, pp. 668–682.]

Year.	Average daily wages in gold of all occupations.	Blacksmiths.	Blacksmiths' helpers.	Boiler makers.	Boiler makers' helpers.	Bricklayers.	Cabinetmakers.
1870....	$2.20½	$2.43	$1.40¼	$2.35¾	$1.41	$3.15¼	$2.14
1871....	2.39¼	2.65½	1.51¼	2.53	1.52¼	3.61	2.23¼
1872....	2.45	2.70	1.55	2.58	1.57	3.67	2.32½
1873....	2.35½	2.60¾	1.51¼	2.53¾	1.51½	3.35	2.20¾
1874....	2.30¼	2.59	1.50¼	2.53¾	1.52¾	3.14½	2.23¾
1875....	2.24¼	2.47	1.45¾	2.47	1.53¼	3.11	2.16¼
1876....	2.18	2.43¾	1.41¼	2.41	1.46½	3.00	2.11½
1877....	2.24½	2.51¼	1.48	2.51¾	1.52½	3.07½	2.20½
1878....	2.30¾	2.59¼	1.52¼	2.59	1.59	3.15	2.25½
1879....	2.32	2.59¼	1.53	2.62	1.61¼	3.14½	2.28½
1880....	2.34	2.59¾	1.51¼	2.59¾	1.56¼	3.18½	2.28¾
1881....	2.40¾	2.64¼	1.54¼	2.56	1.58	3.46¾	2.38¾
1882....	2.44¾	2.64½	1.54¼	2.66	1.61¾	3.72	2.38¾
1883....	2.47	2.64½	1.56½	2.67¾	1.60½	3.89	2.36¼
1884....	2.49	2.66¼	1.56¾	2.69	1.60	3.95	2.37
1885....	2.47¼	2.62	1.53	2.61¾	1.58¾	3.99½	2.38½
1886....	2.47¼	2.64¾	1.54¾	2.60¼	1.58¾	3.93	2.38
1887....	2.49¼	2.66½	1.56¾	2.61¾	1.56¾	4.01½	2.35
1888....	2.50¾	2.65	1.58¼	2.66¼	1.59¼	4.03	2.39½
1889....	2.51½	2.64½	1.59	2.65¾	1.59½	4.13	2.41
1890....	2.52¾	2.63¼	1.58	2.64½	1.57½	4.13	2.44¼
1891....	2.54¼	2.58	1.54¼	2.62	1.57¼	4.28½	2.43
1892....	2.56	2.59½	1.54¾	2.59½	1.55¾	4.23½	2.47¼
1893....	2.54¼	2.59¼	1.55¾	2.58	1.53¼	4.12¾	2.39¼
1894....	2.49¼	2.49½	1.50	2.56½	1.53¾	4.12¼	2.33¾
1895....	2.47¼	2.47	1.49¼	2.54¾	1.52¾	4.02½	2.31½
1896....	2.45¾	2.44½	1.50¾	2.55½	1.53¼	3.82¾	2.35¾
1897....	2.44½	2.41	1.50¼	2.54	1.54	3.73½	2.32½
1898....	2.43¼	2.43½	1.52¼	2.56½	1.53¼	3.51¾	2.29¾

Year.	Carpenters.	Compositors.	Conductors, railroad.	Engineers, railroad.	Firemen, railroad.	Hod carriers.
1870....	$2.36¾	$2.52¼	$3.43	$3.22¾	$1.75	$1.75¼
1871....	2.57¾	2.75½	3.57½	3.48	1.82¼	1.91
1872....	2.60	2.77½	3.61¼	3.63¾	1.88¼	1.93
1873....	2.47½	2.72	3.52½	3.64	1.81¼	1.84½
1874....	2.45	2.74	3.49	3.53¾	1.79	1.67½
1875....	2.37½	2.71¾	3.36¼	3.49¼	1.75½	1.63½
1876....	2.30¾	2.64¾	3.28¾	3.52¾	1.76¼	1.58¼
1877....	2.31½	2.74	3.51	3.76	1.87¾	1.63
1878....	2.28	2.74½	3.62¾	3.82½	1.94	1.77¼
1879....	2.34¾	2.76½	3.66½	3.86	1.96¾	1.79½
1880....	2.37¼	2.77½	3.65¾	3.91½	1.95¼	1.82¾
1881....	2.49½	2.78¼	3.65½	3.93¾	1.94¾	1.91½
1882....	2.55	2.81	3.65¼	3.90¼	1.96½	1.99½
1883....	2.58½	2.80½	3.68	3.88¾	1.94¼	2.08
1884....	2.60¼	2.82½	3.68¼	3.90¼	1.94	2.11¼
1885....	2.57¼	2.82¾	3.72¼	3.94¾	1.96	2.15
1886....	2.55½	2.80¾	3.72¼	3.93¾	1.95¾	2.11¾
1887....	2.52¾	2.81½	3.74¼	3.93½	1.95¾	2.15¾
1888....	2.56	2.80¾	3.74	4.00	1.96	2.20½
1889....	2.54	2.80	3.73	4.02	2.01½	2.20¼
1890....	2.59¼	2.79¾	3.76	4.03	2.03¾	2.21¼
1891....	2.64¾	2.76½	3.98¾	4.11½	2.11¼	2.17½
1892....	2.65	2.78¼	3.95½	4.00	2.40½	2.19¼
1893....	2.67	2.77¾	4.11½	4.63	2.27¾	2.18¾
1894....	2.62½	2.79½	3.91½	4.35¾	2.27¼	2.15¾
1895....	2.55¾	2.81	4.05¾	4.44	2.29¾	2.06¼
1896....	2.52	2.82½	4.08½	4.56¼	2.33	2.00
1897....	2.56¾	2.80	4.09¾	4.48¼	2.29¾	2.03
1898....	2.52¾	2.81½	4.03¼	4 42¾	2.26	2.00½

Year.	Iron molders.	Iron molders' helpers.	Joiners.	Laborers, street.	Laborers, others.	Machinists.	Machinists' helpers.
1870....	$2.60½	$1.53	$2.25¾	$1.46¼	$1.39¾	$2.30¼	$1.34
1871....	2.74½	1.65½	2.44¾	1.62¾	1.49¼	2.46½	1.43¾
1872....	2.79½	1.65¾	2.49¼	1.63	1.58½	2.48	1.47
1873....	2.70¾	1.61	2.44½	1.58¼	1.50½	2.41¼	1.40½
1874....	2.61¼	1.57¼	2.38¼	1.58½	1.46¼	2.41¼	1.41¼
1875....	2.50¼	1.51¼	2.28¾	1.51½	1.45¼	2.32½	1.37½
1876....	2.36½	1.45	2.17½	1.45½	1.43¼	2.22	1.31½
1877....	2.44½	1.51¼	2.17¼	1.48¼	1.40¾	2.32¾	1.34¾
1878....	2.52½	1.60	2.19½	1.46¾	1.44¼	2.40¼	1.42
1879....	2.48½	1.58¾	2.27¼	1.50	1.45	2.39¼	1.41½
1880....	2.56¾	1.61¼	2.36¾	1.50	1.48½	2.44¼	1.43½
1881....	2.61¾	1.61¼	2.55½	1.51½	1.51¾	2.47¼	1.44
1882....	2.61½	1.61	2.64	1.50	1.55½	2.49¾	1.47½
1883....	2.67¾	1.61¾	2.62¼	1.55½	1.56½	2.49	1.43
1884....	2.66¼	1.59½	2.66¾	1.55½	1.55¾	2.52¾	1.45¼
1885....	2.59¾	1.56	2.61¼	1.54¾	1.54¾	2.48¾	1.43¾
1886....	2.58¾	1.55	2.54½	1.57	1.54½	2.48½	1.42¾
1887....	2.66	1.58	2.56¾	1.59¾	1.57¼	2.51¾	1.46¼
1888....	2.65¼	1.58¾	2.58	1.60¼	1.56½	2.51¾	1.46¾
1889....	2.63¾	1.59½	2.64¾	1.59¼	1.57¼	2.52¾	1.46¾
1890....	2.68½	1.60	2.63¼	1.59¼	1.55	2.51¼	1.43¾
1891....	2.73¾	1.62	2.62¾	1.59¼	1.54¼	2.50¾	1.43
1892....	2.70¼	1.63	2.57¾	1.59	1.51	2.52	1.44½
1893....	2.67	1.62¼	2.54¼	1.61½	1.54½	2.48½	1.39¼
1894....	2.59¾	1.56½	2.57½	1.62	1.49	2.40	1.39¼
1895....	2.58	1.56	2.50½	1.62	1.48	2.38	1.37
1896....	2.55¾	1.57¾	2.44¼	1.62	1.48¾	2.40½	1.33½
1897....	2.59¼	1.57½	2.44½	1.61¾	1.46	2.42	1.34½
1898....	2.60½	1.58¼	2.47	1.65½	1.45¼	2.41	1.35½

Year.	Masons, stone	Painters, house.	Pattern makers, iron works.	Plumbers.	Hone cutters.	Teamsters.
1870....	$2.80¼	$2.22½	$2.70	$2.74½	$3.07	$1.58¾
1871....	3.26	2.40¼	2.92¾	2.96¼	3.32¼	1.73¾
1872....	3.39¼	2.52¼	2.98¼	2.87¾	3.64¾	1.78¼
1873....	3.21	2.35½	2.94	2.80	3.37¼	1.72½
1874....	2.90½	2.23¼	2.94	2.83	3.19	1.74
1875....	2.81½	2.23¼	2.85½	2.84¼	2.99¼	1.71
1876....	2.94	2.16	2.68	2.79	2.75½	1.71¼
1877....	2.94½	2.25¾	2.76½	2.91¼	2.66¾	1.79
1878....	2.97½	2.34½	2.91½	2.92¾	2.76¾	1.86¼
1879....	3.06¾	2.31¼	2.85¾	2.97	2.74	1.87½
1880....	3.11¼	2.41½	2.82	2.93½	2.83	1.88¾
1881....	3.44¼	2.47¼	2.86¾	2.97	3.06½	1.88¼
1882....	3.52	2.51	2.88¾	2.99½	3.16	1.89¼
1883....	3.50¼	2.61¾	2.88¾	3.01½	3.19¾	1.90¾
1884....	3.62½	2.66	2.93	3.03¾	3.21½	1.89¼
1885....	3.60¼	2.64	2.84½	3.05	3.14	1.88¾
1886....	3.55¼	2.63¼	2.88	3.09¾	3.23	1.92½
1887....	3.57¼	2.63¼	2.93¼	3.13	3.27¼	1.94
1888....	3.55	2.64	2.95½	3.13¼	3.36	1.95
1889....	3.51¾	2.61¼	2.93½	3.15¼	3.38¾	1.94¼
1890....	3.71	2.59½	2.98	3.13½	3.45¼	1.94¾
1891....	3.73½	2.61¼	3.05	3.18	3.50¼	1.94¾
1892....	3.60½	2.68¾	3.01½	3.20¼	3.49¾	1.95
1893....	3.61¾	2.69	2.96¼	3.21½	3.45½	1.90½
1894....	3.45	2.67½	2.89¼	3.19¾	3.34¼	1.90¼
1895....	3.37	2.60¼	2.90½	3.17¼	3.36½	1.90
1896....	3.36½	2.58¾	2.82¾	3.17¼	3.33¾	1.88¾
1897....	3.29¼	2.57¼	2.82¼	3.14¾	3.30½	1.87¾
1898....	3.20¼	2.60	2.90	3.15½	3.23	1.88½

At the same time, it is quite plain that in times of business expansion, when capital is seeking investment and the resources of the country are being eagerly developed, these immigrants enter in increasing numbers to take a share of the increasing wages and employment, but in times of business depression their numbers decline.

That immigration, however, is not a leading cause affecting wages of American labor may be inferred from a study of the movement of wages during the past 30 years. The accompanying table and chart give a comparison of the movement of prices of commodities and the movement of wages for the years 1870 to 1900. The line of prices is the same as that contained in the chart opposite page 305.

The wages are derived from Bulletin of the United States Departmemt of Labor for September, 1898, and July and September, 1900. The Bulletin of September, 1898, presents 255 wage quotations for 12 leading cities of the United States (Baltimore, Boston, Chicago, Cincinnati, New Orleans, New York, Philadelphia, Pittsburg, Richmond, Va., St. Louis, St. Paul, San Francisco), including skilled and unskilled labor in 25 occupations.

The later Bulletin presents 192 occupations in 26 industries and 148 establishments. In the accompanying table and diagram these series of wages, for the sake of comparison, have each been converted into "index numbers," using the average wages of the year 1891 as a basis equivalent to 100. It will be seen that the wage movements indicated by the two sets of index numbers for 1891 to 1898, while not parallel, are nevertheless indicative of similar conditions operating in both cases.

Average wages and index number of wages, 1870–1900.

Years.	Average wages, 25 occupations.[1]	Index number average wages for 1891 being 100.	Index number of 192 occupations, average wages for 1891 being 100.[2]	Years.	Average wages, 25 occupations.[1]	Index number average wages for 1891 being 100.	Index number of 192 occupations, average wages for 1891 being 100.[2]
1870	$2.20½	86.64		1886	$2.47¼	97.15	
1871	2.39¼	94.00		1887	2.49¼	97.93	
1872	2.45	96.26		1888	2.50¾	98.52	
1873	2.35½	92.13		1889	2.51¾	98.82	
1874	2.30¼	90.46		1890	2.52¾	99.31	
1875	2.24¼	88.11		1891	2.54½	100.00	100.00
1876	2.18	85.65		1892	2.56	100.59	100.30
1877	2.24½	88.21		1893	2.54½	99.94	99.32
1878	2.30¾	90.66		1894	2.49¼	97.98	98.06
1879	2.32	91.12		1895	2.47¼	97.19	97.88
1880	2.34	91.94		1896	2.45¾	96.60	97.93
1881	2.40¾	94.59		1897	2.44½	96.11	98.96
1882	2.44¾	96.16		1898	2.43¼	95.62	98.79
1883	2.47	97.05		1899			101.54
1884	2.49	97.83		1900			103.43
1885	2.47¼	97.15					

[1] Bulletin of the Department of Labor, September, 1898, p. 668.
[2] Bulletin of the Department of Labor, September, 1900, p. 914.

Comparing the level of wages with the level of prices (the latter indicating the expansion and depression of business) it can be seen that from 1870 to 1872 both show a rise. From 1872 to 1876 wages decline from 96.26 to 85.65, and then show a steady recovery until 1884. But prices decline rapidly until 1879, and then more even more rapidly until 1882. The depression in prices of 1884-85 shows a slight depression in wages, but there is a steady recovery until 1892, after which both prices and wages fall until 1897-98. In the two years of 1899 and 1900 both prices and wages show a marked increase.

In making a comparison like the foregoing, with the view of showing the part played by business expansion and depression upon wages, it must be noted that two important factors are omitted, namely, the volume of trade and the amount of unemployment. This defect is owing solely to the absence of statistical compilations bearing upon these factors. The movement of average wages, as shown by the diagram, does not respond promptly to the movement of prices simply because the wages quoted are the rates of daily wages and not yearly earnings. They do not take into account the quantity of employment during the year. If this factor were introduced, and if the rate of wages were qualified by a coefficient of the amount of employment, it would doubtless be found that the parallel between the movement of prices and the movement of yearly earnings is very close. Evidence of this can be

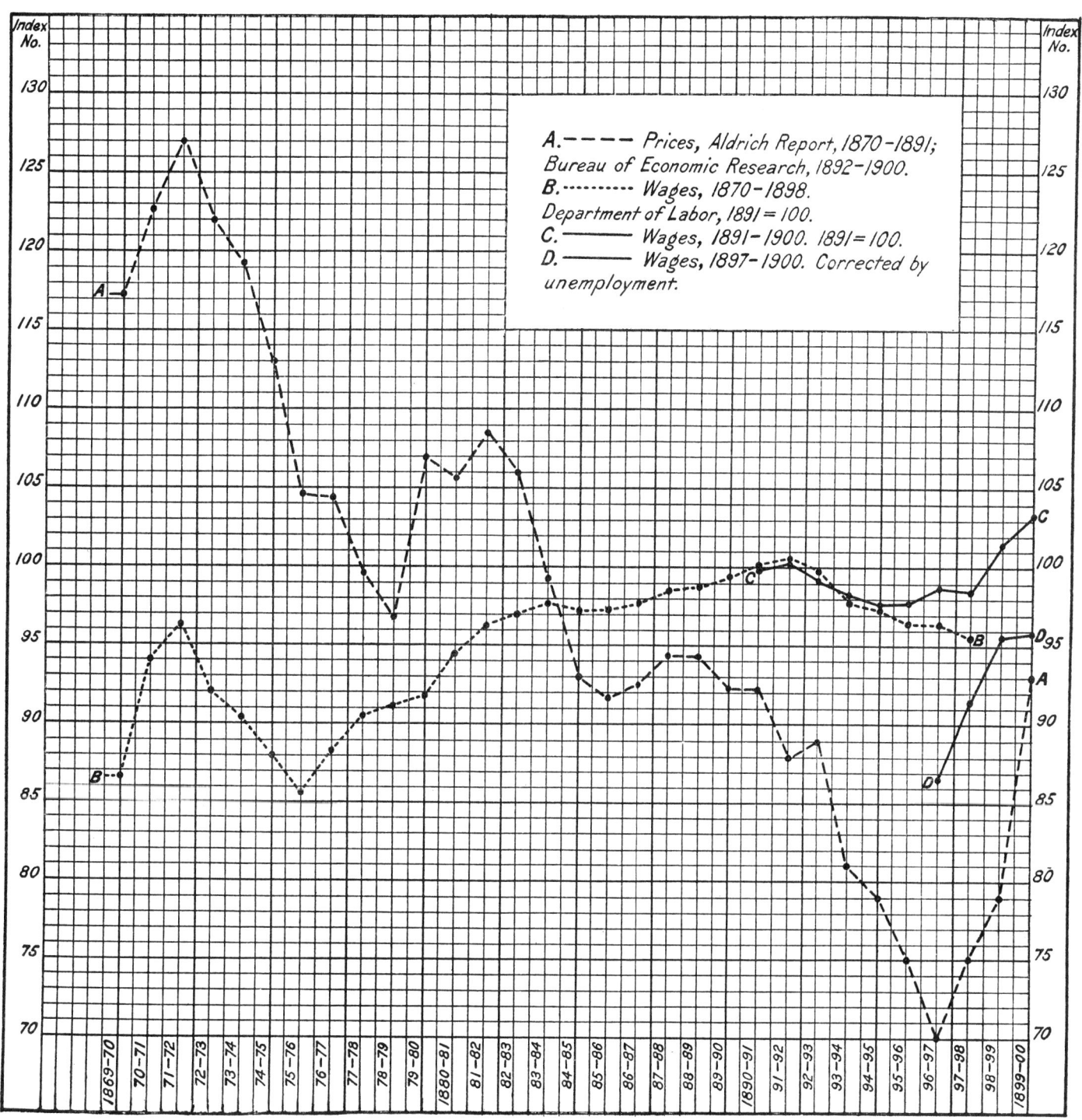

607A—To face page 308.

found in the following table, wherein the index numbers of wages, as given in the Bulletin of 1900, have been corrected by an index of the amount of yearly employment:

Year.	Index numbers of rate of wages, Bulletin of Department of Labor.	Per cent of employment of organized labor in the State of New York.	Index numbers of yearly earnings.
1897	98.96	87.8	86.88
1898	98.79	92.3	91.18
1899	101.54	94.1	95.63
1900	103.43	92.7	95.89
Increase per cent, 1897-1900	4.51		10.37

The index of employment is derived from a percentage of the number of unemployed members of the labor unions reporting to the New York Bureau of Labor Statistics, compared with the entire membership of such unions. For example, in 1897 the number of members unemployed through the year was 12.2 per cent of the total membership, or, conversely, the number of members employed through the year was 87.8 per cent of the total membership. In 1900 the number employed was 92.7 per cent. Using these percentages of employment as a coefficient of the index numbers of the rates of wages, in order to get an approximate index of yearly earnings instead of daily rates of wages, it will be seen that the index number of yearly earnings for 1897 is 86.88 and for 1900 is 95.89. In other words, the yearly earnings in 1900 were 10.37 per cent higher than in 1897, although the daily rate was only 4.51 per cent higher. Comparing the movement of this index of yearly earnings with index of daily rate of wages it will be seen that it lies much closer to a parallel with the movement of prices. (See chart, line D.) Were it possible to compile a series of percentages of unemployment for the years preceding 1897, doubtless the coincidence year by year would be found quite close between yearly earnings and business prosperity and depression. This being so, the conclusion is strongly reenforced that, since immigration follows business conditions in obedience to the opportunities for employment, it is a secondary cause in affecting wages and is indeed in importance far below the primary cause. With expanding business there is increasing room for both immigrants and natives. It is possible, of course, that the presence of immigrants in large numbers may prevent wages from reaching as high a level in time of prosperity as they otherwise would reach, but this can not, in the nature of the case, be demonstrated. On the other hand, in times of depression the lessened numbers of immigrants are entering an overstocked market and are thereby adding to the critical unemployment and depression of wages.

It must be remembered that the foregoing conclusions depend for their accuracy upon the two assumptions that the immigrant brings the same standard of living as that maintained by American labor, and that immigrants are proportionately distributed among the various occupations. That these assumptions are not valid need not be stated, and it is necessary now to inquire what modification shall be made in the conclusions after correcting these invalid assumptions.

II. STANDARD OF LIVING.

The following table shows in a comparative way the wages of unskilled laborers in Europe and in American cities and farming communities.

In this table the rates of wages quoted are to be considered as only indicative of the relative wages in the different States and localities, since it has not been possible to compile an exhaustive report covering accurately so wide and uncertain a field of research. The different sources drawn upon are the Bulletin of the Department of Labor (September, 1898); reports of the United States Department of Agriculture; the Royal Commission on Labor, 1894; King & Okey's "Italy To-day," 1900; personal correspondence with American farmers, and personal interviews with immigrants from the several countries of Europe.

The significant comparison in this table is that between the wages of agricultural labor in Europe and the wages of common labor in American cities, for it must be remembered that immigration is a part of the modern movement from the country to the city. From this point of view it will be seen that in those countries of eastern and southern Europe from which immigration has largely increased in recent years the wages of agricultural labor are about one-fifth of the wages of unskilled labor in American cities.

Average daily wages for unskilled labor in United States and in Europe.

Locality.	Agricultural labor, outside harvest.	Laborers in cities.	Hod carriers.	Blacksmiths' helpers.	Boiler makers' helpers.	Iron molders' helpers.	Machinists' helpers.	Miners.
United States:								
New England	$1.40							
Boston		$1.37½	$1.96⅔	$1.84	$1.46¾	$1.61¼	$1.70	
Middle States	1.22							
New York		1.63¼	2.40	1.80	1.40		1.10	
Philadelphia		1.50	2.00	1.28	1.73¾	1.28½	1.34½	
Southern States	.75							
Baltimore		1.25	1.89	1.35¾	1.36½	1.36	1.37½	
North Central	1.32							
Chicago		1.50	2.00	1.71	1.67½	1.83	1.64	
Cincinnati		1.42½	2.00	1.37½	1.18¾	1.47½	1.19¾	
St. Louis		1.50	2.70	1.53	1,43½	1.50	.64½	
St. Paul		1.50	1.75	1.50	1.75	1.72½	1.73¾	
Western	1.50							
San Francisco		1.59	3.00	1.92¾	1.94¼		1.84	
Europe:								
Great Britain, England	.53							
London					1.46			
Manchester				.93¼	1.29¾			
Glasgow				.85¼				
France	.51							$0.74
Paris		.96⅓	1.06¼	.99½	.96½	.93¾	.98¼	
Germany	.36							.42
Italy	.16 to .28	.29 to .48						.46
Russia	.30		.20					
Austria	.35							
Bohemia	.36							
Hungary	.30							.80
Croatia	.30							.75
Uhrosko (Slovaks)	.30							.50
Portugal:								
Azore Islands	.45							
Cape Verde Islands	.25							
Syria		.30						

While wages are lower in Europe and Asia, it is also true that the cost of living is lower. It is generally claimed by immigrants that 30 to 40 cents on the Continent of Europe will go as far as $1 in the United States. Comparing Italy, for example, it is held by immigrants that wages in the United States are five times as high and cost of living is three times as high as in their foreign home. This would indicate that the Italian can live on wages three-fifths as high as the wages of American labor with which he competes. But this comparison is inadequate, because it omits an element which is difficult of measurement, namely, the necessary change in the standard of living in order to work in America. It must not be assumed that in all cases low standards of living are an economic advantage in competition with high standards. The Italian who lives largely on vegetables in Italy can not do the work of American laborers unless he has meat and bread. It is everywhere found in all American occupations that the immigrant can not keep pace with American mechanics and laborers. For the first year or more the pattern of speed set for him exhausts his strength. It is not merely that he is ignorant of American methods and devices; he is also unequal to the American intensity of exertion. He must necessarily, therefore, begin at a low rate of pay or not work at all. This is one reason why, in occupations controlled by strong labor organizations, there is entire reciprocity between the American and European unions. The Europeans bringing their "cards" are admitted to the full privileges of American members, provided they do not work for less than the scale of wages. But at that scale and with their lower energy they are at first unprofitable to the employer. On the other hand, in the unorganized trades where there is no scale of wages, and where the employer makes an individual bargain with each workman, a place can be found for immigrants at very low pay. The employer is not usually willing to resort to such labor, preferring to pay higher wages to skilled workmen, but he finds their presence useful in order temporarily to take the places of skilled workmen who go out on a strike, or to hold as a club to threaten those who demand higher pay.

This hot exertion of American mechanics and laborers is directly traceable to the mobility of American labor, including under that term immigration. Men who have left their homes and gone among strangers are thrown upon their individual merits, and are spurred to activity greater than they ever felt before. Their traditions and habits of life are broken. They leave the customary track and break across into new paths. Moreover, with mixed nationalities and languages, labor organization and labor traditions are weakened, and it becomes less feasible to restrict arbitrarily the amount of work a man shall be permitted to do. Where employers concentrate on that point they are able to make a stronger fight in favor of removing all restrictions, both to the introduction of machinery and to the speeding of the workmen, than the employers of other countries with homogeneous labor are able to do. It is in the mixed nationalities and the mobility of labor that the resisting power of labor is weakened. This shows itself not only in the more vigorous exertion which the employer can exact but also in the repeated reductions of wages.

Here we touch a striking feature of American labor conditions. Where divergent nationalities have been introduced and the former high-standard labor has been displaced, labor organization is usually effectively stopped. Race antagonisms are usually combined with religious antagonisms, and even politics is introduced to buy up the leaders. Cutthroat competition of the severest kind now depresses wages year after year, and even the return of prosperity affords little or no relief. Finally, the point of desperation is reached. The increased exertion and exactions require at least a minimum wage in order to provide the necessary food. Even though wages be not reduced, yet the amount of exertion may have been steadily increased until the former wages no longer furnish even the vital energy required. The standard of living now becomes a question of merely sustaining the needed physical endurance. At such a point the incomers are ready to drop all questions of race, religion, and politics. Their animal necessities compel them to organize on the strictly economic basis of getting enough food, shelter, and rest to continue work. This was the point reached by the bituminous coal miners in 1897 and the anthracite coal miners in 1900, and the remarkable organization in that occupation at the present time is a result of the direst poverty to which a large class of labor in this country has probably ever been reduced. In the clothing trade, indeed, a similar condition has been reached, but, in addition to the opposition of a class of highly skilled workmen not found in mining, the continuous influx of immigrants has not yet afforded a breathing spell for organization.

Another reason why in the clothing trade the depression in wages has not brought determined and general resistance is because, in that trade, the labor of wife and children can be drafted to aid that of the husband and father. As will be seen below, the race or class of labor which learns to depend on the labor of wife and children clings to the cities and factory towns where these can be employed. The race where the standard of living of the family is not supported by the husband alone has an advantage over other races which are averse to employing their women and children. It is in this way especially, and not because his standard itself is low after a few years' residence, that the Italian is a formidable competitor of the Jew in clothing, and of all nationalities in common labor.

III. UNEQUAL DISTRIBUTION OF IMMIGRANTS.

There is still another correction to be introduced in our assumption of the probable effects of immigration compared with a natural increase in population of the same extent, namely, the unequal distribution of immigrants in the several occupations and localities. This unequal distribution has already been pointed out (p. 298). From the eastern ports and the Canadian border much louder complaint is heard than from the interior. From unskilled and unorganized occupations in cities the complaint is more urgent than from those which have been able to protect themselves. Certain unions, such as glass blowers, charge an initiation fee higher for aliens than for citizens. Others, like the eccentric firemen in New York, have secured a State license law restricting the license to citizens. This, of course, keeps the immigrant from obtaining work until he has been a resident at least five years. On public work legislation has frequently restricted employment to citizens. But where these attempts to lessen the pressure of immigration are not applicable, the immigrant operates with concentrated effect. This is especially true in ordinary, common labor, coal mining, clothing and textile manufactures. Here there is overcrowding, displacement of American or of earlier immigrant labor, without directly depressing wages in other employments. A part of the displaced classes seek other occupations where a higher standard can be maintained. Many coal miners sought the western and northern metal mines; others turned to farming. In case migration is not available, the displaced workman may be able to rise on top of the immigrant and become his foreman, his boss, or the proprietor of his working place. On the other hand, the inferior individuals of the displaced classes, refusing to compete alongside the immigrant, and incapable or unwilling to rise and better their condition, fall into the class of hoodlums, tramps, and paupers. There is a hardship in the transition, and there is a restriction on the growth of population of the displaced classes, both of those who rise and those who fall. Those who rise restrict their numbers by late marriages and small families, in order to lessen the pressure of competition, and those who fall reduce their numbers by vice and pauperism. In either case the intensity and extent of the result depends upon the general industrial prosperity or depression.

The fate of the immigrants themselves who have displaced the earlier workers is a matter of organization next to be considered.

IV. LABOR ORGANIZATION.

As already noted, the leading influence which at the present time resists or overcomes the depressing effect on wages of immigrant competition is labor organization. While the fate of those who are displaced by increasing numbers of immigrants turns, as already stated, upon the industrial conditions of the country and the demand for employment, a leading object of labor organization is to sustain its members in times of industrial depression and to protect them from this very displacement and to maintain the rates of wages and standards of living to which they have been accustomed. Owing to the unequal pressure of immigration, certain occupations, as above mentioned, have been brought to such a low state that the American workman finds himself miserable if he can not escape from them. Such occupations fail to respond even to a period of prosperity, since this very prosperity brings an increase of immigration which falls mainly into their overcrowded confines. Now, labor organization in America, as regards immigration, has two aspects. It is, first, apart from legislation, the only bulwark which the Americanized workmen are able to erect against the flood of immigration, and, second, in case this bulwark is broken down and the occupation has been filled by immigrants, organization is the only means by which the immigrants themselves can rise to the standards of those whom they displace. The first aspect is seen in those strong trade bodies based upon skill and not seriously affected by machinery, which, like the glass blowers, printers, molders, building workmen, and several others, have forced the immigrant to take himself to other lines of less resistance. The second aspect is seen in those occupations with less skill or more machinery, like those of the coal miners, textile workers, clothing workers, or common laborers, which have already in years passed been largely given over to the immigrant. In either of these aspects the menace of immigration is present more or less in three ways.

First, as workmen imported from abroad under contract or by solicitation to take the place of organized labor at times of strike or lockout. At such times the position of the organization is critical, since the result of the dispute determines for months and years to come the wages and standards of the occupation. The employer of course, appreciates the crisis and goes to the furthest limit in his effort to break the organization. If he can bring workmen from abroad, ignorant of the issues and the nature of organization, he has a decisive advantage. For this reason labor organizations at an early day directed their first attention to prohibiting importation of laborers under contract. This led to the alien contract labor laws in 1885 and amendments in the following years. This law and its workings are fully described in the following pages, but it is important to notice at this place that if labor organization is to be considered a desirable means of protection for American labor then the alien contract labor law and its effective enforcement are a first essential. By weakening or breaking down this law, labor organizations in the United States can be crippled and in many cases destroyed.

2. The second menace of immigration to the labor organization is in the steady immigration of poor but hardworking people who are unfamiliar with the traditions and customs of organization, unaccustomed to the rules and the control which it imposes, incapable of learning the same through their ignorance of the language, and, moreover, forced by their poverty to work for low wages, and, by their lack of friends, to work with docility and desperate energy for him who first gives them a job. This phase of immigration is undoubtedly by far the principal characteristic at the present time, and so predominant is it that there is much less inducement for employers to contract with laborers abroad than there was when immigration was an unknown risk. The constant influx of this class of immigrants into a trade nullifies, as in the clothing trade, the educational work of organization almost as rapidly as it is conducted. About 2 or 3 years after landing are enough to bring the immigrant to a realizing sense of the need of organization and to train him up to a certain ability in promoting it, but by that time a further crowd of inexperienced immigrants, who can not be reached by the organization, has gained a decisive influence in the trade. This accounts partly for the remarkable fact in the clothing trade in New York that the unions have won nearly every strike that they have conducted, but have been unable to hold the contractors to their agreements, because the latter were able so easily to introduce green laborers. This accounts also for the fact in the mine workers' organization that the State of Illinois is far better organized than the State of Pennsylvania. The latter State has the reputation throughout the

labor element of the entire Union as a State of cheap labor, and in no State are the problems of organization more trying. Immigrant labor from all nationalities of Europe, which 30 years ago was largely imported from abroad into that State and was used to break down strikes and unionism, has in later years come in large numbers by the mere attraction of those already here. To bring this constant influx of new labor into the unions is practically impossible. The fresh immigrant, who has for the most part been a farm hand, must first have a few years' practical experience of the results upon himself of his unrestricted competition, must have time to understand the conditions of the occupation and the objects of unionism, and must have opportunity to know the leaders whom he can trust. This brings us to the third aspect in which immigration menaces the organization of labor.

3. There is no country in which the problem of labor organization is more complicated by a multitude of disintegrating causes than in the United States, and these causes are based directly on immigration. In the same occupation, working side by side or in the same competitive field, are often found Irishmen, Negroes, Englishmen, Germans, Poles, Slovaks, Magyars, Lithuanians, Italians, Croatians, and in others French Canadians, Armenians, Syrians, and so on. These have largely come from despotic countries, where organization was put down by the military power and where violence is the accepted remedy for oppression. They bring with them differences in language, so that in their business meetings the motions and speeches must be translated by several interpreters. Their race differences are accompanied by the religious differences of Roman Catholic, Greek Catholic, Protestant, and Hebrew. Often within their own races and religions are factional differences, sometimes more bitter than race differences, as between the north and south Italians, or between Russian and Austrian Poles. With all of these differences it is an easy matter for employers and foremen to play race, religion, and faction one against the other. As a practical fact, shown hereafter in many cases nothing short of the verge of starvation is adequate to eliminate these conflicts and to bring these diverse races, religions, languages, and factions down to the simple economic basis of labor organization. Even this is not enough where the women and children of immigrant races can be introduced to take the places of men. In such cases the men necessarily seek work elsewhere, but, apart from women and children, poverty may be relied upon, sooner or later, to bring the nationalities together.

This problem of mixed nationalities results in at least one novelty in the method of organization of American labor unions compared with those of other countries, namely, branch organizations based on race. The difficulties of language preclude a mixed meeting of all races. The members of each naturally cling together and follow their own race leader, and are jealous of the leadership of others. These leaders, however, once elected by their own race constituencies, are able to come together in a council or governing body for all the branches. The result is that each local is based on representative government rather than the primary assembly which usually characterizes the local bodies of labor unions. This feature of organization is noted in the following pages in the case of the longshoremen, hod carriers, and coal miners. It tends to disappear in proportion as the races assimilate or the needs of the industry dictate.

The foregoing considerations regarding labor organizations lead to the conclusion that, while the general effects of immigration on labor conditions turn upon the rise and fall of industrial prosperity, yet without organization the majority of laborers are not able to share in the rise nor to resist the fall, and at the same time, where the organization already exists, their ability to maintain it, based on their power to strike, is menaced, and in some cases is overcome by the inroads of immigrants. On the other hand, where there is no organization, their struggles to organize are fruitless or long postponed if they are being continually menaced by green immigrants or are themselves made up of mixed races, religions, and languages.

V. MACHINERY AND DIVISION OF LABOR.

The remarkable development of machinery and division of labor in the United States has been coincident with the enormous immigration of foreign laborers. There is a close relationship between the two movements. In the first place, from the earliest beginnings of modern industry both skilled and unskilled laborers in England and America have implicitly argued that these mechanical innovations, which before their very eyes both substituted unskilled for skilled labor and displaced both kinds of labor, were hostile to their interests. Where, as in England, it has been possible for labor to organize, or where, as in England and Germany, without effective organization, there have been long accepted traditions and customary lethargic methods of doing work, the introduction of machinery and division of labor have been seriously checked. But in America, in the past 20 years, with its mixed races, there has been neither organization nor tradition, or, rather, obstacles imposed by tradition and organization have been easily broken down. The same is true in England itself in those few trades where the immigrant has entered, as in the clothing trade. It was the Russian Jew who, in that country, introduced the sewing machine and the minute subdivision of labor in the face of the English journeyman tailor, who despised these innovations as destructive to his trade skill. In America this process has been nearly universal in all trades, and the high degree of machine industry in this country, with its low cost of production and large growing exports, may almost be said to be a direct effect of immigration. The industrial menace to Europe from American manufactures is very largely the work of the European immigrant himself removed to America. Not that the immigrant has been prominent as an inventor and organizer of machine production, but that he has removed all obstacles to its free and rapid introduction, and so has stimulated invention and business organization. The minute subdivision of labor in the sewing trade, described in the following pages, has indeed been devised in order to put the hordes of unskilled immigrants easily to work, and they have created for themselves practically a new industry, that of ready-made clothing for the country at large, alongside that of the journeyman tailor, who continues his traditional methods of work for the more expensive custom garments. In other trades, likewise, the objections of the old-time trade unions to the introduction of machinery or to its rapid speeding have been nullified by competing establishments springing up and entering the race with him on the basis of machinery and immigrant labor. Ultimately he, too, has been compelled to accept the innovations or lose his job. The last few years have seen a number of unions, like the glass blowers and the iron and steel workers, formally remove through their national conventions several, if not all, their restrictions on machinery, business management, and speeding of work.

In the second place, the fact that machinery and division of labor opens a place for unskilled immigrants, makes it possible not only to get the advantages of machinery, but also to get the advantages of cheap labor. If machinery were to be considered as strictly an economic force, then the labor employed to operate the machinery should receive the same wages as the skilled labor which it displaces. The economy would show itself in the greatly increased output. This has been the actual outcome in the case of the printers who, owing to their strong organization and their natural protection against immigration in the fact of the English language, receive even better wages on the typesetting machine than they formerly received in setting type by hand, and, at the same time, the cost of the work has been greatly reduced. But if, on the other hand, the new machinery is used to displace well-paid labor by ill-paid labor, it is a means of increasing permanently the proportion of low standard population in our midst. This result in past years has, in many cases, accompanied immigration. It is shown in the cotton textile industry, where, with the chronic revolution in machinery, there has been found a place for continuous succession of lower and lower standards of living, following in order the native American, the Irish, the French Canadian, the Armenian, and the Syrian. As already stated, the fate of the higher displaced classes and their ability to make the transition to other industries depends upon the expansion of industry and the restriction on the growth of their numbers. While, therefore, immigration has furnished a field for the rapid expansion of machinery, it has permitted that machinery to be used as a refuge for the low-standard population. Whether this population in course of time is itself able to rise in the scale is a problem of organization already touched upon and to be further dealt with in the description of particular occupations in the following pages. Hitherto organization has been able to do but little for those industries where automatic machinery and division of labor have displaced skilled labor by unskilled labor. This is partly owing to another factor—the introduction of women and children.

VI. COMPETITION OF WOMEN AND CHILDREN.

While it might appear at first sight that machinery would seem to offer a place for women and children, yet their competition with men is strictly limited. In the case of children legislation has in later years definitely limited the number. As regards women, comparatively a small number who are found in factories are married. They usually begin work at 14 years of age and continue 5 or 10 years. They do not work long enough to acquire skill and speed. One manufacturer states that usually the best workers are those that marry earliest. Another witness before the Industrial Commission affirms that women are not suitable in factories on account of carelessness, ill temper, and unreliability. (Reports Industrial Commission, vol. 7, p. 61.) But more important than this is the fact that machinery, while it offers opportunity for unskilled labor, at the same time requires great endurance on account of the high speed with which American factories are operated. It is for this reason that employers do not find women help profitable unless at much lower wages than men receive; and it is found in those establishments where unions have been able to maintain the same scale of wages for women as for men working by the week, or in those

FACTORS CONTROLLING WAGES AND EMPLOYMENT. 315

establishments where piecework is fixed at the same price for both men and women, that the number of women employed is very small. The census figures show the following proportion of males and females above 16 years of age and of children below 16 years of age employed in manufacturing establishments:

Per cent of men, women, and children in manufacturing establishments.[1]

Year.	Males.	Females.	Children.
1850	76.39	23.61	
1860	79.34	20.66	
1870	78.66	15.76	5.58
1880	74.48	18.97	6.55
1890	80.40	16.92	2.68

[1] Census 1890, Manufacturing Industries, Part I, p. 14.

From these percentages it will be seen that from 1880 to 1890 the per cent of females decreased from 18.97 to 16.92. If we take individual occupations employing the largest proportion of females in 1880, we have the following table:

Per cent of women in industries employing the largest proportion of women.[1]

Industry.	1880.	1890.
Boots and shoes, factory product	22.60	29.01
Boxes, fancy and paper	70.63	64.81
Clothing, men's	50.37	39.94
Clothing, women's, factory product	88.33	62.64
Cotton goods	49.14	48.15
Hosiery and knit goods	61.30	66.86
Shirts	86.37	78.57
Silk and silk goods	52.32	57.06
Tobacco, chewing and smoking, and snuff	32.90	33.87
Woolen goods	33.95	38.11
Worsted goods	50.38	46.13

[1] Census 1890, Manufacturing Industries, Part I, p. 17.

It will be noticed in the foregoing table that the largest decrease relatively in the proportion of females is in men's clothing and women's factory-made clothing. This, as will be shown later, is attributable largely to immigration and to the high speed attained in the manufacture of this product.

It will be found that in those occupations where women find employment the wages of men are correspondingly low. This does not always appear as such from the census figures, from the fact that men are usually advanced to the more skilled and better-paid occupations in the establishment, while the women monopolize the others. It appears from the census of 1890 that the average wages of men by the week were $498 and the average wages of women were $276. In other words, the wages of women were 45 per cent less than the wages of men. These low wages are attributed not only to the causes cited above, but also to the exceptional difficulty in the way of organizing women in an effective trade union. It follows that in those particular occupations where women compete with men only the class of men who are willing to work for low wages will be employed, and these are largely immigrants, who by their greater endurance than women are able to earn more wages in a given time, though at a less cost per piece to the employer. Where men work at the same occupation as women it is usually found that the women are their own wives and daughters; and this is a secondary and highly important phase of immigration, namely, that the women and children who enter factories are the wives and daughters of recent immigrants. Nationalities differ in this respect. Among all of them the girls go to work; but while the wives of Italians are found in the shops, the wives of Jews stay at home. The daughters of the native Americans and of the earlier immigrants when they enter productive occupations are usually able to find employment as clerks, school-teachers, and in similar occupations. In conclusion it may be stated that while machinery in itself affords a place for women and children, it also places the limit upon the number that can be practicably employed unless at low wages. Since women's wages are 25 to 50 per cent below those of men, the difference is so great that the men who continue to compete with women must accept wages at a substantial reduction; and, finally, the women and children who actually work in factories are mainly the wives and daughters of immigrants, and it is against them that the immigrants themselves compete.

316   THE INDUSTRIAL COMMISSION:—IMMIGRATION.

VII. COUNTRY COMPETITION.

Another factor which in many occupations obscures the effect of immigration, by cooperating with it to reduce wages, is country competition. The complaint of labor representatives against immigration usually proceeds from the cities, where the immigrants congregate and where they can be actually seen taking the jobs of the complainers. At the same time, upon careful inquiry, it is often found that the pressure to reduce wages or to cause unemployment proceed from the cheaper labor of country districts employed in the same line of production. Wages are necessarily higher in cities than in the country for the corresponding standard of living. In the city there are such additional demands as car fare, the food costs more and must be paid for in cash, because the laborer does not have his patch of ground from which, by the help of wife and children and by his own extra work mornings and evenings and idle days, he can secure a large share of his necessary food supplies. With these incidental advantages the wages of country labor per day to the men are usually very much lower than the wages of corresponding city labor. Whether the city or the country is the more economical place from the manufacturer's standpoint in locating his enterprise turns on many considerations, an important one being the cost of labor. Highly skilled or excellent work can not be done in the country, because the labor market is not there. The cheaper goods can, however, be sent to the country for manufacture while the better grades are made in the city. This is markedly the case in the manufacture of cigars and clothing, which are affected more seriously by immigration. Even in coal mining there is an analogous situation in those new and richer mines of southern Illinois and West Virginia just entering the older competitive fields, where the greater thickness of the seams, their proximity to the surface, and the purity and quality of the coal render it possible for American-born farmers and laborers through competition to cut down the wages of miners in the older fields. At the present time, since foreign-born miners in these older fields have been able to build up an organization and to gain a notable increase in wages, more serious to them immigration is the competition of these richer mines with unorganized native labor. And the stronger the organization and the higher it forces wages, the larger the share of the output which is diverted to these competitors.

The encouragement of country competition in its various forms would, indeed, be one of the methods for lessening the pressure of immigration in the cities in case the country should draw off the immigrant, but such is not usually the case, since it is native labor or earlier immigrant labor that is mainly attracted to these fields. For this reason country competition of native labor is one of the causes which must be taken into account in any attempt to measure the effect of immigration on wages and employment.

CHAPTER III.

FOREIGN-BORN LABOR IN THE CLOTHING TRADE.

I. NUMBER OF FOREIGN-BORN EMPLOYED IN THE TRADE.

The clothing trade leads all others in the United States as an occupation controlled by immigrants. The census of 1880 showed that, of 133,756 tailors[1] of both sexes, the foreign-born were 71,591, or 61 per cent.

In 1890 the foreign-born male tailors, numbering 86,471, were 71 per cent of the total number in the trade. This was 11.5 per cent higher than the occupation next in order, namely the bakers, in which the proportion of foreigners was 59.5 per cent. Below that came hucksters and peddlers with 53 per cent foreigners; miners with 48.7 per cent foreigners, and so on. Even unskilled laborers (i. e., "laborers not specified"), numbering 664,614, show only 25.76 per cent foreign-born.

The foreign-born females reported in 1890 as tailoresses were 31.9 per cent of the 63,809 tailoresses in the country, and there is but one occupation in which the proportion is exceeded, that of textile mill operatives, where the proportion is 36.18 per cent.

The following table shows, in comparative form, the extent of this immigrant influence by nationalities. It will be seen that the predominating nationality in 1880 and 1890 was German, although in the latter year the appearance of the Russian

---

[1] I. e., "Custom tailors," not factory operatives. The latter are considered on pp. 5 ff.

Jew reduces relatively the numbers of Germans, as well as other nationalities. Unquestionably the census of 1900 will give an added weight to the Jews:

TABLE 1.—*Tailors by sex and nationality.*

	1890.[1]		1880.[2]	
	Male.	Female.	Male.	Female.
Total number	121,591	63,809	81,658	52,098
Total per cent	100.00	100.00	100.00	100.00
Native born	26.17	67.39	30.34	71.77
Germany	29.89	10.23	38.58	11.85
Great Britain	8.72	5.46	13.72	7.88
Norway and Sweden	5.95	1.89	3.87	1.71
Italy	1.88	1.48		
Russia	10.33	3.44		
Hungary	1.55	.53		
Bohemia	2.75	1.90		
All other countries	12.76	7.68	13.49	6.79

[1] Census 1890, Population, Part II, Table 109; Census 1890, Population, Part II, CXVIII.
[2] Census 1880, Population, pp. 754, 759.

The following table shows the immigration of tailors, by years, from 1875 to 1900:

TABLE 2.—*Immigration of tailors, 1875–1890.*[1]

Years.	Total number tailors.	Years.	Total number tailors.	Years.	Total number tailors.	Years.	Total number tailors.
1875	1,463	1882	3,748	1889	3,809	1895	3,869
1876	969	1883	3,235	1890	3,879	1896	4,021
1877	668	1884	3,317	1891	5,864	1897	3,454
1878	815	1885	2,228	1892	9,274	1898	3,826
1879	1,062	1886	2,682	1893	5,914	1899	5,833
1880	2,134	1887	3,769	1894	7,539	1900	9,899
1881	3,106	1888	3,469				

[1] Reports Commissioner-General of Immigration.

The leading nationalities contributing immigrants to this occupation prior to 1890 were the Germans and Scandinavians. The German immigration reached its highest point (1,935) in 1882, and has since then declined, until in 1899 it was 224, and in 1900 270. The Scandinavian immigration has declined from 238 in 1880, 240 in 1887, and 238 in 1888, to 133 in 1900.

Since 1890 the Italians and Hebrews have taken the leading part. The Italian immigration has steadily increased from 16 in 1877 to 1,502 in 1900, and the Hebrew immigration from 59 in 1877 (Russia and Poland) o 7,031 in 1900.

The following table shows the distribution by races for the years 1899 to 1900:

TABLE 3.—*Distribution of tailors by races.*[1]

	1900.	1899.
Hebrew	7,031	3,664
Italian:		
South	1,312	1,061
North	180	119
German	270	224
Polish	260	163
Scandinavian	133	122
Other races	703	480
Total	9,899	5,833

[1] Commissioner-General of Immigration, 1899–1900.

The direct effect of immigration on the tailoring trade is found in the number of immigrants who have learned the trade in their native country, while the indirect effect is in the number who have learned the trade after migration. The direct effect can be judged from the preceding table, which shows the number of tailors coming to this country by years since 1875. It will be seen from this table that in 1880, when the Census returns showed 133,756 tailors in the country there were 2,134 immigrant tailors, and in 1890, when the Census showed 185,400 tailors, there were 3,879 immigrant tailors. In 1880 the immigrants were 1.6 per cent of the residents, and in 1890 they were 2.1 per cent.

The indirect effect of immigration is even greater than the direct effect. Formerly, before the division of labor had advanced to its present minuteness, it required 4 to 5 years to learn the trade, but at the present time in the ready-made work less than 1 man in 4 is a tailor. In the ordinary task shop the baster is the skilled mechanic, while those who learn the other divisions of the trade, such as operating, pressing, sewing on buttons, felling, and so on, are able to earn wages in 2 or 3 months, although a longer time is required to develop speed and endurance. Consequently, these unskilled divisions are open not only to the influx of the unskilled labor of all kinds, but also to the skilled labor which is unable in a strange land and a foreign language to find its own special field. The more recent factory system, with a division of labor much more minute than even that of the task system, to be described below, opens the way for still greater indirect effects of immigration.

The influence of immigration on the ready-made clothing trade can not be measured by a single comparison of the number of immigrants with the number of resident tailors, as could be done in other trades, for the peculiar reason that the business has largely concentrated in New York City, where it meets the first impact of the flood of immigration. This movement is believed to have proceeded with great force during the past 10 years, largely as a result of the cheap immigrant labor which has concentrated in that city. In the absence of census figures it is impossible to show this movement statistically, but estimates made from the incomplete reports of factory inspectors indicate the following numbers employed in the leading centers of New York, Chicago, Philadelphia, and Boston. These estimates give color to the generally accepted statement in the trade that one-half of the ready-made clothing in the United States is manufactured in the city of New York.

TABLE 4.—*Estimate of employees in clothing trades.*

Greater New York	103,000
Chicago	48,000
Philadelphia	20,000
Boston	7,000

2. Foreign born in New York clothing trade.—If it be true that one-half the ready-made clothing is made in New York, comparison should be made with the census returns of 1890, which show in that year 27.4 per cent of the men's factory product and 62.9 per cent of the women's factory product made in New York. In that year also 26.4 per cent of the factory operatives on both men's and women's clothing lived in New York. The tables from which these percentages are computed is given herewith.[1]

TABLE 5.—*Clothing industry.* (a)

Cities.	Men's factory product.		Women's factory product.	
	Average number of employees.	Value of product, including receipts from custom work and repairing.	Average number of employees.	Value of product, including receipts from custom work and repairing.
Total for United States	156,341	$251,019,609	42,008	$68,164,019
New York	37,438	68,796,405	24,791	42,779,286
Chicago	15,616	32,517,226	2,673	6,422,431
Cincinnati	14,532	17,951,525	1,648	2,285,598
Baltimore	13,094	15,032,924	605	870,681
Philadelphia	6,666	24,490,218	2,456	3,335,746
Boston	6,478	19,640,779	1,073	1,506,212
St. Louis	5,033	6,554,982	499	541,894
Rochester	3,123	9,133,562	331	405,400

a Census 1890: Manufacturing industries, Pt. II, statistics of cities, pp. 654–655.

[1] It should be noted that in the census returns the employees upon "Factory Product" are not classified as tailors in the occupation tables. That is to say, the 133,756 tailors considered in preceding pages are custom tailors, who make the entire garment, whereas the employees in Table 5 are those who make the garment by division of labor. The census does not give the nationalities of these factory operatives.

IMMIGRATION AND THE CLOTHING TRADE. 319

The decisive influence of New York in the clothing trade is well known. Organizations of employees in other cities are met with the threat, "We will get our work made in New York." It is only as the conditions in New York are improved that the trade can be improved elsewhere.

The part played by immigration in New York is indicated by the fact that whereas in the country at large the foreign-born tailors (not factory operatives) in 1890 were 71 per cent of the tailors, in New York they were 91.5 per cent. The following table shows the percentages for the 4 leading cities of New York State, and also for the rest of the State outside these cities:

TABLE 6.—*Per cent of males 10 years of age and over employed as tailors (not factory operatives) in New York, 1890.*[1]

	Foreign white.	Native white, foreign parents.	Others.
New York City	91.5	7.2	1.3
Brooklyn	73.8	22.9	3.3
Buffalo	72.5	24.8	2.7
Rochester	57.3	38.5	4.2
State, exclusive of above cities	54.2	18.9	26.9

[1] Eleventh Census, Population, Pt. II, table 118.

The desirability of an occupation may be roughly judged from the rate at which the children of the workmen follow the footsteps of their parents. The following table compares on this point "all occupations" with the occupation of tailoring (not including factory operatives). It appears that in all occupations the foreign-born males number 26.12 per cent and their children number 18.13 per cent, yet among tailors, whereas the foreign born are 73.1 per cent, their children are only 14.9 per cent. In other words, while foreigners crowd into tailoring to the extent of three times their proportion in all occupations, their sons enter that trade even one-fourth less than their proportion in all occupations. On the other hand, the daughters of tailors are more likely to follow their parents' calling, since their freedom of choice is not so great as that of their brothers, and tailoring is more suitable for female help. It may, indeed, be held, from a study of this table and a knowledge of the clothing trade in the city of New York, that this trade is peculiarly the refuge of the immigrant and the school of his Americanization:

TABLE 7.—*Distribution of immigrants and native born and children of immigrants in "all occupations" and tailoring (colored and Chinese omitted).*[1]

	Males.		Females.	
	All occupations.	Tailors.	All occupations.	Tailors.
Total	100.00	100.00	100.00	100.00
Foreign white	26.12	73.10	26.04	32.13
Native white, foreign parentage	18.13	14.90	16.50	43.16
Native white, native parentage	55.75	12.00	57.46	24.71

[1] Census, 1890.

With the foregoing general summary of the statistical features of immigration in the clothing trade we shall proceed to a detailed account of the industry itself as affected by the movements of nationalities in the leading centers, New York and Chicago.

This portion of the report has been prepared with the assistance of Mr. A. Bisno, a practical tailor.

II. THE "SWEATING SYSTEM."

The term "sweating" or "sweating system"[1] originally denoted a system of subcontract, wherein the work is let out to contractors to be done in small shops or homes. "In practice," says the report of the Illinois Bureau of Labor Statistics

[1] See Dictionary of Political Economy, art. "Sweating."

(1892, p. 358), "sweating consists of the farming out by competing manufacturers to competing contractors of the material for garments, which in turn is distributed among competing men and women to be made up."

The system to be contrasted with the sweating system is the "factory system," wherein the manufacturer [1] employs his own workmen, under the management of his own foreman or superintendent, in his own building, with steam, electric, or water-power. In the sweating system the foreman becomes a contractor, with his own small shop and foot-power machine. In the factory system the workmen are congregated where they can be seen by the factory inspectors, and where they can organize or develop a common understanding. In the sweating system they are isolated and unknown.

The sweating system has undergone significant changes during the past 50 years. The early part of the last century, when the term seems to have originated in England, it applied to ready-made new clothing in the form of army clothing given out to contractors. At that time each tailor usually made the entire coat at home. The manufacturer of ready-made clothing and army clothing would give his work to a contractor who was a responsible party, usually not a tailor himself. This contractor would then give the work to some man who kept a tailors' boarding house or a saloon where the tailors were accustomed to come together. This boarding-house keeper or saloon keeper was a subcontractor, though not a tailor. He in turn would give this work out to the individual tailors whom he personally knew and who were responsible for the work. The money received by these subcontractors for their part was called "sweat money," implying that their profit was the difference between the price they received from the manufacturer or contractor and the price paid to the tailor for making the garment, and that they invested no labor in the transaction.

There was an agitation against this system in the early fifties because of the low condition of the tailors. They worked for very low wages and many of them were unemployed much of the time. The work used to be made in between seasons for one-third and one-fourth of the regular price.

In the sixties the influx of the Russian Jews in the ready-made clothing trade, who replaced the native and Irish tailors, began to be felt. Here the incursion of the foreigner seems to have been irresistible. His success was due, not alone to the lower wages he was willing to take, for he was competing with the outcasts of the English tailoring trade, the unskilled English woman and the wretched and often imported Irishman, whose wages were as low as the contractor was willing to pay. But the success of the immigrant was due to his willingness to change the mode of production by using the sewing machine and division of labor against which the native tailor showed a decided aversion. Here the influx of the foreign Jew has wrought a complete change in the contract system. The old contractor was a mere middleman and had no need for any knowledge of the tailoring trade, and was mostly a lodging-house keeper, who secured the work by giving a cash deposit for the goods he took from the manufacturer and distributed among the wretched tailors in the lodging house and the helpless women in his vicinity who completed the whole garment. He was replaced by the Jewish contractor, who made his work in a shop. This Jewish contractor was not a mere middleman; he was necessarily a tailor and an organizer of labor, for his work was done by a system of division of labor calling for various grades and forms of skill, viz, the baster, machinist, and presser, with various subdivisions, such as fitter, busheler, finisher, buttonhole maker, feller, basting puller, etc.

The position of the contractor or sweater now in the business in American cities is peculiarly that of an organizer and employer of immigrants. The man best fitted to be a contractor is the man who is well acquainted with his neighbors, who is able to speak the language of several classes of immigrants, who can easily persuade his neighbors or their wives and children to work for him, and in this way can obtain the cheapest help. The contractor can increase the number of people employed in the trade at very short notice. During the busy season, when the work doubles, the number of people employed increases in the same proportion. All of the contractors

---

[1] The term "manufacturer" in the clothing trade has a peculiar significance. It means the wholesale merchant or warehouseman. The exact designation would be "merchant manufacturer." Such a manufacturer usually has an "inside shop" and several "outside shops." The inside shop is usually on the manufacturer's own premises, and includes the cutters who cut the cloth for the contractors, the examiners who inspect the garments on their return, and the "bushelmen" who repair and reshape the garments if necessary.

The "outside shops" are the shops of contractors who take the goods out from the manufacturer for stitching and finishing. If the manufacturer does his own work directly under a superintendent or foreman, instead of indirectly through a contractor, this shop also is known as an "inside shop." Workmen employed by a contractor often speak of themselves as employed by the manufacturer who furnishes the work to the contractor. Since the manufacturer sets the contract price, it might almost be said that the contractor is really the manufacturer's foreman, who takes the responsibility of finding help, doing the work, and making such wages of management as he can at the price set by the manufacturer.

are agents and go around among the people. Housewives, who formerly worked at the trade and abandoned it after marriage, are called into service for an increased price of a dollar or two a week. Men who have engaged in other occupations, such as small business, peddling, etc., and are out of the business most of the year, are marshaled into service by the contractor, who knows all of them, and can easily look them up and put them in as competitors, by offering them a dollar or two a week more than they are getting elsewhere. It is the contractor who has introduced the Italian home finishers in the trade; he has looked them up and taught them the work, and is getting it made for less than half the wages that he formerly paid for the same work.

The contractor never has at one time a large amount of work. Through him the industry is scattered over a wide area, among all kinds of people, and he thrives as long as they do not know one another. The contractor is an important factor in the clannishness of the immigrant nationalities. It is to him due in part that we have in large cities the Jewish districts, Polish districts, Swedish districts, etc., with very little assimilation. The contractors establish their shops in the heart of the district where the people live, and since they can practically earn their living at home, they have no opportunity of mingling with others or of learning from the civilization of other people.

The following is a typical case: A Polish Jew in Chicago, at a time when very few of the Poles were tailors, opened a shop in a Polish neighborhood. He lost money during the time he was teaching the people the trade, but finally was a gainer. Before he opened the shop he studied the neighborhood; he found the very poorest quarters where most of the immigrant Poles lived. He took no one to work except the newly arrived Polish women and girls. The more helpless and dependent they were, the more sure they were of getting work from him. In speaking about his plans he said: "It will take these girls years to learn English and to learn how to go about and find work. In that way I will be able to get their labor very cheap." His theory turned out to be practical. He has since built several tenement houses.

he contractor in the clothing trade is largely responsible for the primitive mode of Troduction; for the foot-power sewing machine; for the shops in the alleys, in thepattics, on top floors, above stables, and, in some cases, in the homes of the people. These small shops are able, on account of low rent and meager wages, to compete successfully, although with foot power, against the large shops and factories with steam or electric power. Usually it is not necessary to have more than $50 to start a shop with foot-power machines. As there is no investment in goods, the contractor runs no risk. Little managing ability is required, because the number of employees is small.

The unlimited hours of work, often 7 days in the week, is a feature of the contracting system. The contractor himself works unlimited hours. His shop is open most of the time. He deals with people who have no knowledge of regular hours. He keeps them in the dark with regard to the prevailing number of hours that other people work.

The contractor is an irresponsible go-between for the manufacturer, who is the original employer. He has no connection with the business interests of the manufacturer nor is his interest that of his help. His sphere is merely that of a middleman; he is practically useless in a large factory. He holds his own mainly because of his ability to get cheap labor, and is in reality merely the agent of the manufacturer for that purpose. In this he in the main succeeds, because he lives among the poorest class of people, knows them personally, and knows their circumstances and can drive the hardest kind of a bargain. A very large number of the people who work in the sewing trade for contractors usually hope to become contractors themselves. When they succeed in this they reduce the prices, since the contractor when he first takes work out takes it for less money than other contractors.

Usually when work comes in to the contractor from the manufacturer and is offered to his employees for a smaller price than has been previously paid, the help will remonstrate and ask to be paid the full price. Then the contractor tells them, "I have nothing to do with the price. The price is made for me by the manufacturer. I have very little to say about the price." That is, he cuts himself completely loose from any responsibility to his employees as to how much they are to get for their labor, throwing the responsibility on the manufacturer who originally gave him the work. The help do not know the manufacturer. They can not register their complaint with the man who made the price for their labor. The man who did not make the price for their labor—the contractor—claims that it is of no use to complain to him. So that no matter how much the price for labor goes down, there is no one responsible for it.

In case the help form an organization and send a committee to the manufacturer, the manufacturer will invariably say, "I do not employ you, and I have nothing to do with you;" and when they go back to the contractor and file their complaint, he will invariably say, "I am not making the price for your labor. I am simply paying you as much as I can out of what I get from the manufacturer." This is also true with regard to any agreements of a labor organization that may be made. If an agreement is made with a contractor, it is usually worthless, because he has no property invested that can be levied upon. If the agreement is made with the manufacturer, it does not hold, because he is not violating it. In this irresponsible state of the business it is extremely difficult to devise any way in which organizations can make agreements and enforce them.[1]

There is always a cut-throat competition among contractors. A contractor feels more dependent than any of his employees. He is always speculating on the idea of making a fortune by getting more work from the manufacturer than his neighbor and by making the work cheaper. Usually when he applies for work in the inside shop, he comes in, hat in hand, very much like a beggar. He seems to feel the utter uselessness of his calling in the business. Oftentimes the contractor is forced to send work back, because he can not make it under the conditions on which he took it, yet he does not dare to refuse the offer for fear the manufacturer will not give him more of his work. So he tries to figure it down by every device, and yet, perhaps, in the end is forced to send it back.

The contractor is always speculating on what is coming next in the busy season, and sometimes in the busy season he can, as a matter of fact, save some money; but this is only for a short time. The most of the year, probably for about 9 months, he is in this cut-throat competition. This is, indeed, the worst factor in the trade.

It must not be inferred from what precedes that the contractor is the cause of the sweating system, or that the sweating system is identical with the contract system. Both the contractor and the sweating system are the product of a disorganized and crowded labor market. This distinction is not apprehended even by the tailors' unions, who direct their energies mainly to the abolition of the contractor instead of the abolition of the conditions which produce the contractor. The factory system itself is not always clearly marked off from the contracting system. A factory foreman may send work out at night to be done by his own employees at their homes. A factory may use partly mechanical power and partly foot power. A manufacturer may employ subcontracting within the factory. On the other hand, the small manufacturer may practice the same oppression and impose the same insanitary conditions upon his employees as would be done by a contractor. In the manufacture of cigars the "sweater" is not a contractor, but is a manufacturer who buys his material on the market and sells his product to jobbers or regular purchasers. In the manufacture of clothing the "sweater" is a contractor who agrees to take out material owned by the merchant and to return it to him as a finished garment. The only difference is that in the cigar business the raw material is owned by the one who directly employs the labor, while in the clothing business the raw material is the property of the merchant. In both cases the labor is equally "sweated."

The futility of directing the energies of reform solely against the contractor may be seen in New York in one branch of the clothing trade, that of ladies' ready-made garments, including cloaks and so-called "tailor-made suits." Already in this line of manufacture fully 75 per cent of the product has passed out of the hands of contractors into those of "manufacturers." Ten years ago probably 90 per cent of women's clothing was made by people who worked for contractors, while now only about 25 per cent of the trade are working for contractors. But so far as the people employed in the business are concerned, there has not been any material change for the better, since these small manufacturers retain all the abuses of long hours, small pay, and insanitary shops. The way in which this new class of manufacturers has arisen in the clothing trade and has driven out of business the large manufacturer on Broadway who sent his work out to contractors is one of the remarkable developments of this remarkable trade. These former large manufacturers who have abandoned the ready-made business have gone into the retail or custom trade, and have set up model "inside" factories on Broadway, where they cater to the more well-to-do purchasers. Small manufacturers on Division and other streets, who have absorbed the former wholesale trade, have followed a method somewhat as follows:

A contractor who had been able to save $500 or $600 makes up in a small shop a number of samples and designs. He then communicates with the buyers of wholesale dry goods, or clothing houses, or cloak jobbers, or country merchants, or "mail-order" houses, stating that he had opened a shop and is able to sell new and first-class designs in the several patterns of cloaks and suits at a much lower price than the cloak manufacturers were doing. He does not send out traveling salesmen, but waits for buyers to call and see his samples and leave their orders. Having received an order, he takes it to some convenient bank, which usually extends him credit with a woolen house somewhat approximating the amount of the order, furnishing

---

[1] See testimony of I. A. Hourwich. in Vol. VII, Manufacturers and General Business, p. 150.

also a certain amount of cash to pay his help. The bank takes the order from him as guaranty, and also collects the bill after the goods are made and delivered. In this way a man with very little money is able to blossom out from a contractor into a manufacturer and to do business to the amount of the orders he is able to get.

The saving by this small man as against the large cloak manufacturer, it is claimed, is in the following ways: He does not have to pay a high-priced designer, since he designs his own patterns; he does not have to pay a superintendent, since he manages his own business; nor does he pay high rents, since he is usually located in a poor quarter of the city. He can get labor as cheap as any contractor because he runs his shop in the same method when he becomes a manufacturer as he ran it when he was a contractor; that is, his shop is open day and night, and people can work as long hours as they want to. He is always on the lookout for cheap help and he is careful in regard to saving the goods and pieces, which can not be saved in the same manner in the large factory. So he can give the buyers of these wholesale and jobbing houses and also the retail and department stores the benefit that was formerly derived by the large wholesale cloak manufacturer, selling goods in some instances for 30 and 40 per cent less than the large wholesale manufacturer can possibly do. In reality he is little more than he used to be—a contractor, with the difference that he now does his own cutting and his own marketing; and the profits on his labor and on the capital invested in the business are shared with the banker.

It is possible that the racial characteristics of the Jew have entered as a factor in bringing about the above-mentioned results. The Jew likes to be "his own boss," even if it is merely in name; from the operator and tailor he becomes a contractor, and from the contractor he becomes a small merchant manufacturer, working for jobbers and wholesalers until in time he becomes a jobber and wholesaler himself. While this is true of other nationalities to some extent, it is very largely true of the Jews, who, when they manage to acquire $300 or $400, will go into business and hold their own against the large manufacturers, and probably also the fact that the Jews do not like to work on Saturday has something to do with the system. These shops are usually open on Sunday and the religious Jews have the opportunity of keeping their Saturday as a day of rest, while in the large factories business is done on Saturday and on Sunday the shop is closed. In a number of instances the Jews prefer to work for smaller wages per piece with the opportunity of working Sunday instead of Saturday.

Probably the nature of the business also has something to do with this displacement of the large manufacturer by the small one. Nobody can now manufacture women's clothing very far ahead of time. Styles change every 3 months and even in shorter time, so that one can not safely produce a large stock of women's suits 6 months ahead. The manufacturers figure on selling all their goods within 3 months, and the most successful way for the large wholesale houses to buy, therefore, is in small lots, consulting the latest fashion. This could not very well be done economically in a large factory, with large investments.

The wages which these small manufacturers pay their employees vary very greatly In some places they pay as good and even better wages for first-class work than the large manufacturers, but in the majority of cases the wages per cloak are smaller. But then the people say that since a man can work in one of these small shops a longer number of hours than he can in the large cloak factory on Broadway, a man can earn more money at a smaller rate.

There is one respect in which these small manufacturers are a greater disadvantage to the employees as a class than were the contractors whom they displaced. The opportunity for labor organization is diminished. Formerly, when several contractors worked for one large manufacturer, it was possible for the cloak makers in the employment of this manufacturer to make a common cause. The unions were indeed largely based upon a system of shop organizations. The cloak makers who worked for one large firm and for the several cloak contractors employed by that firm would meet together in one association. Although working for different contractors they would join forces and make their appeal direct to the manufacturer. But as the large manufacturer disappeared from the business and the small contractors opened shops for themselves and became small manufacturers, there arose a competition in each small shop on the part of the help against all outsiders, with no common interest to join them together. There is an immense competition among these small manufacturers' shops. The manufacturer will usually say to his people: "You know there isn't work enough for all of us all the time. Now, in order that I may be able to employ you for a longer period during the year than my neighbor employs his people, I will have to underbid him in the price of my goods. I will have to sell clothing, say, to such and such a firm. who are buying both from him and me, for less money than he does so that I can get all of the trade." There are many cases where the help will agree to produce a garment for a lower price than they have been receiving, figuring on the proposition that they will have work for a longer period through the year than they have had before, and so the wages are reduced as the years go on. In these small factories the employment is very irregular and the men work in one year for several different firms, so that it is difficult to establish union conditions.

The conclusion to be drawn from the foregoing considerations is that the sweating system is not identical with the system of contracting, although the latter has the peculiar evil of introducing an irresponsible party to whom the real employer shifts his responsibility. In view of the overlapping of conditions, the attempt to give exact meaning to the term "sweating system" as a method of business was abandoned by the committee of the House of Lords appointed in 1888 to investigate the subject, but the evils known by the name were said to be:[1]

"1. A rate of wages inadequate to the necessities of the workman or disproportionate to the work done.

"2. Excessive hours of labor.

"3. The insanitary state of the houses in which work is carried on."

While the sweating system is not identical with a contracting system, yet, as already stated, in the clothing trade the wide development of the contract system with "outside" shops is a phase of immigration. Consequently the description of nationalities, organization of labor, and modes of production in the following pages must always be interpreted, both as growing out of the contract system and as furnishing the field in which the contractor develops.

III. POSITION OF VARIOUS NATIONALITIES IN THE CLOTHING TRADE.

New York.—Ready-made clothing for men was manufactured in New York as early as 1840. It was partially made in the shops of the manufacturer and partially at the homes of the tailors, each tailor making the whole garment. Most of it was made between seasons by the journeymen tailors, who worked for the merchant tailors. It is said that about 1840 the price for a ready-made coat was about one-half the price of a coat made by the merchant tailor. A coat for which one paid $5 to $6 to the merchant tailor would be taken home by these tailors in the dull season and made for from $2.50 to $3. The majority of tailors then were English, Scotch, and American. About the year 1850 the Irish came largely into the trade and along with them some Germans. It was customary for the Irish tailor to work in the back shop of the merchant tailor and for the German tailor to take his coats, pants, and vests home and do the work there, usually assisted by his wife and children. The first attempt to introduce a division of labor in the manufacture of ready-made clothing was probably made by the Germans who developed in their homes such separate divisions as machine sewing, basting, etc., though the division was not definite.

All told, the manufacture of ready-made clothing was not extensive. It was not until after the war, in 1866-1870, when the tailors and journeymen tailors formed a union and raised the price for their labor that the manufacture of ready-made clothing began to be developed on a larger scale. Previous to that the bulk of such clothing was of very poor quality, made from cheap goods for sailors, for cattle rangers, for the people on the cotton plantations of the South, for miners, etc. But very little men's fine wear was made until after the war. Beginning with 1865 this class of business began to develop and increase. It was carried on at this time mostly by the German tailors in their homes.

About the year 1873 Hungarian, German, and Austrian Jews began to migrate to this country, a number of whom were tailors, and they entered this business. They introduced the man working as a sewing-machine operator. It was said at that time that the Germans preferred these Jewish men as help because they were able to produce a quicker and better garment, but before long the Jews themselves came into the business as contractors.

Beginning with 1882 the immigration of Russian and Polish Jews to this country increased very greatly and many of them entered the sewing trade, so that the competition for work began to be fierce. The price for labor fell and coats which were made in 1876-1880 for $1.50 to $2 were reduced to $1.25 and $1.50. As early as 1890 the Jews had gained control of the clothing trade in New York, the German shops being only remnants. Beginning with 1890 the Italians entered the trade in large numbers, especially in those branches which after the development of the shop and factory system continued to be carried on at home.

The prevailing nationalities in Boston and Philadelphia have been similar to those in New York.

---

[1] Parliamentary Papers, Reports from Committees, 1890, Vol. XVII, 169; Fifth Report of the Select Committee of the House of Lords, p. xlii.

Chicago.—The clothing industry in Chicago, although less extensive than that in New York, has a peculiar interest from the standpoint of immigration, on account of the more even balance between the nationalities there employed. Whereas in New York the Jews largely predominate, yet in Chicago they number only about 25 per cent of the trade. The following is believed to have been the distribution of the nationalities in 1886:

TABLE 8.—*Distribution of clothing workers by nationality, Chicago, 1886.*

	Per cent.
Swedes	30
Bohemians	30
Jews	25
Germans	10
Others	5
Total	100

Prior to 1870 the trade was mainly custom work, the tailors being German and Irish. The Germans took up the ready-made work in their homes prior to 1880. It was in 1880 to 1884 that the Bohemians, Jews, and Scandinavians took up the manufacture of ready-made garments, and from that time is dated the expansion of that trade. The Poles did not enter the trade until 1889, but have already increased to probably 15 per cent of the total number, and have driven Bohemians and Jews out of the ready-made branches. These displaced nationalities have created places for themselves by developing the "special order" trade (see page 331), or by opening small custom shops. Following is the probable distribution of nationalities in Chicago at present:

TABLE 9.—*Distribution of clothing workers by nationality, Chicago, 1900.*

	Per cent.
Swedes	25
Bohemians	25
Jews	25
Germans	5
Poles	15
Others	5
Total	100

The Jew occupies a unique position in the clothing trade. His physical strength does not fit him for manual labor. His instincts lead him to speculation and trade. His individualism unsuits him for the life of a wage-earner, and especially for the discipline of a labor organization. For these reasons, when the Jew first lands in this country he enters such light occupations as sewing, cigar making, shoemaking, etc. Only about 11 per cent of the Jewish immigrants were tailors in Europe. The reason why so many of them take up that occupation in America is because the work is light. They begin as helpers and advance to full-fledged mechanics. After they have worked for some time and have learned the trade they open contractors' shops for themselves. They can begin with a capital of $50. From that they go into the wholesale manufacture of clothing. A similar development occurs in the cigar manufacture. Jews do not enter largely those industries where machinery plays an important part, but if they do enter they strive to set up as small manufacturers or contractors. Probably the only place in the United States where shoes are made outside factories by the old sweating system is among Jewish contractors in New York.

Jewish women are employed to a much less extent than the women of other nationalities, and their children are kept in school until 15 or 16 years of age. It is quite unusual for Jewish tailors to teach their children their own trade. The young generation seek other callings.

The Italian tailor in his own country receives only about one-half the wages received by the Russian, Polish, Hungarian, and Roumanian Jews in their own countries, and about one-quarter of the wages paid for similar grades of work in Western Europe. Consequently, in the United States, with his standard of living, he can successfully compete with the newly arrived Russian Jew and 4 to 1 against the newly arrived German or Englishman. The Russian Jew who is not a tailor, but learned his work in this country and works in the shop as operator or presser, is usually from the stock of small business men in the old country, who have a fairly good standard of living, and is regarded among the clothing workers as of the better class. He will insist on better living and higher wages for his particular kind of work than the tailor. This accounts for a curious paradox in the task system in New York, where the operator, who usually comes from the commercial classes in Russia, will command $3 instead of $2.66, which is paid to the skilled tailor for the basting. This also holds true in other branches, such as cloak making and pants and vest making, the operator usually gets more money than the tailor, due to the fact that this line of employment has been taken up by a class of people who did not work in the clothing trade in the old country and whose standard of living was not as low as that of the tailor.

But when we come to the Italian we find that he will work at operating, or pressing, or any branch of the trade which he learns in this country, at exceedingly low wages. He has usually been a farmer or farm hand, and the standard of living of the Italian farmer is even below that of the tailor. While as yet the Italians have not come into the trade in very large numbers, since they have sought mainly the common outdoor employments, yet those who have taken up this branch of work usually accept much less wages than skilled tailors. Considering the large immigration of Italians it seems that the future clothing workers in this country are not likely to be the Jews, but the Italians.

One point at which the Italians have an advantage is the employment of their wives and sisters. The Italian and his wife will come to the shop together. If he is a pants operator she is usually his helper, or if he is a cloakmaker she is his handsewer and finisher, and so both labor together to cover the expenses of the family. In the case of the Jews, the Jewish woman after she is married will not go to work in the shop. There are numbers of cases where the Italian and his wife together work for the same price which the Jew receives for his labor alone, and in this way the Italian is able to crowd the Jew out of the trade.

The Italian, like the Jew, has a very elastic character. He can easily change habits and modes of work and adapt himself to different conditions; he is energetic and thrifty and will work hard, with little regard to the number of hours. It is quite usual for an Italian cloakmaker, like the Jew, after he has worked 10 hours in the shop with his wife to take a bundle of work home at night. But, unlike the Jew, he not only does the work at home himself but he is assisted by the women in his family, and often leaves a part of the work for them to do during the day.

If the Italian and the Pole are compared, it will be found that it is the Polish women who enter the sewing trade, whereas the former Polish farmer clings to common work requiring hard labor. The Italian is able, on account of his national characteristics, artistic ability, etc., to control such work as the manufacture of clothing, silk weaving, hat making, and other trades where taste and a fine sense of touch are essential for a successful performance of the work. The Polish farmer can successfully compete in factory work, where hard, automatic labor is necessary; but the Italian dislikes mechanical work and is better adapted to diversified pursuits where manipulation is required.

The mode of production among the Germans and Bohemians is about the same; the women and girls operators, edge basters, and finishers, with men as first basters and trimmers. The Bohemians employ their children in the shops probably more than the Germans. The Bohemians are a fairly well educated people, and have a number of unions among their working population. When the price for labor is reduced they usually start a movement in resistance.

The Poles work in the same way as Germans and Bohemians. Owing to the opposition of their priests they have never made any attempt to join a labor organization. During the strike in Chicago in 1896 it was the Polish shops that continued at work and defeated the strike. The Poles are a submissive people while working, and it is in their shops that the hardest driving is done. They have greater endurance and will work for a lower rate of wages than any other nationality. The contractors are mainly Jews. Their children begin to work early. In a shop of sixteen persons there will usually be four to six children under 16 years of age.

Notwithstanding the competing power of Polish women they can probably be outclassed by Italian women. While a great many Polish women have entered the trade they have not yet developed great speed nor been able to work in factories producing the best grades of work, while Italian women are almost perfect imitators. The Italian woman can develop speed and can work with skill. Like the Poles, they also are obedient to orders.

The best people in the clothing trade in Chicago are the Scandinavians, including Swedes, Norwegians, and Danes. They are engaged in the manufacture of pants and vests, under contractors of their own nationality. They do not work more than 10 hours a day as a rule, usually in large shops with steam power. They uphold the price for their labor more than the Bohemians or Poles, and have developed the best labor organizations in the trade. Their standard of living is high, and many of them are fairly well educated. The Swedes do not put their children to work, but send them to school.

The women of the above-mentioned nationalities—Germans, Bohemians, Poles, and Swedes—are principally employed in the shops. In many cases they work even after marriage. The mother or grandmother stays at home keeping house and taking care of the children while the younger women of the family are in the shop. There are about 5 women to 1 man in the Swedish shops on pants and vests, and about 2 women to 1 man in the Polish and Bohemian coat shops. In the Jewish shops there are about equal numbers of men and women, although the women are mainly of other nationalities.

The standard of living of all nationalities has been gradually raised after their immigration to this country. Probably the Jewish immigrant changes his standard of living soonest. When the Jew wants to make more money he will leave his former occupation as operator or baster, etc., and will become a contractor or storekeeper. So that, instead of trying to raise the standard of living in the trade, he will try to leave the trade and throw his lot in with people whose standard of living is somewhat higher. In this way his commercial instinct militates continually against making active efforts to better the condition of his trade.

The Poles and Italians adhere to a lower standard of living for a longer time. During the last few years immigration from those countries has been continuous, yet there is not much evidence of a material rise in the standard of living among the clothing workers. While it may be that the clothing workers are earning more money, and are living under somewhat better conditions than they did in the old country, yet here in this country their lot in life has not improved. The low standard of living on the part of those immigrants who are continuously coming into the trade is always a successful check on the efforts that the people may make to better their condition. So they have no choice except either to stay in the trade and submit to the conditions of the newly arrived immigrant or to leave the trade and go into some business. The Jews have been successful in doing the latter. As regards the condition of the clothing workers, it is about the same as it would be if all these Poles, Jews, and Italians had begun to engage in the trade yesterday. Those who have had a better standard of living, such as the Germans and Irish, have been crowded out of the trade and have been replaced by the Italians, Jews, and Poles.

IV. LABOR ORGANIZATIONS IN THE CLOTHING TRADE.

1. Generally.—The movement of wages in the clothing trade is directly affected by the fate of labor organizations. With the continual influx of immigrants unaccustomed to unionism, with the employment of women and children, and with the prevalence of home work, the problem of organization is indeed serious. In New York, for the past 20 years, the Jews have controlled the trade, so that it has not been conflicts of nationalities within the union that have occasioned difficulty. The problem has been the nature of the Jew himself. The Jew's conception of a labor organization is that of a tradesman rather than that of a workman. In the clothing manufacture, whenever any real abuse arises among the Jewish workmen, they all come together and form a giant union and at once engage in a strike. They bring in 95 per cent of the trade. They are energetic and determined. They demand the entire and complete elimination of the abuse. The demand is almost always unanimous, and is made with enthusiasm and bitterness. They stay out a long time, even under the greatest of suffering. During a strike large numbers of them are to be found with almost nothing to live upon and their families suffering, still insisting, on the streets and in their halls, that their great cause must be won.

But when once the strike is settled, either in favor of or against the cause, they are contented, and that usually ends the union, since they do not see any practical use for a union when there is no cause to fight for. Consequently the membership of a Jewish union is wholly uncertain. The secretary's books will show 60,000 members in one month and not 5,000 within 3 months later. If perchance a local branch has a steady thousand members from year to year, and if they are indeed paying members, it is likely that they are not the same members as in the year before. A German union, on the contrary, will have the same members year after year, well or ill, with little change. The Jew joins the union when it offers a bargain and drops it when he gets, or fails to get, the bargain.

The Jew is also exceedingly abstract and metaphysical, and greatly interested in general principles. His union is always, therefore, except in time of a strike, a forum for the discussion of socialism and the philosophy of the labor movement. The Socialist element acquires control when the workingmen stay away from the union, and they urge an organization devoted mainly to education on the principles of the solidarity of all labor, without much attention to trade differences. The Jewish labor press, pamphlets, and speakers, nearly all recruited from the Socialists, have continually engaged in these discussions, neglecting the formation and strengthening of their unions.

These statements are substantiated again and again in the history of the trade in New York. It is a saying on the East Side that there is always a strike going on somewhere. Following is a brief survey of the more important events of the past 25 years:

2. **Coat makers.**—The first union of tailors employed in the ready-made clothing trade in New York was organized in 1877. At that time the home shop was the prevailing mode of production. The union was a sort of educational society with the purpose of educating its members to establish separate shops. It existed only a few months, because no practical work could be done. In 1879–80 a union was organized, led a strike, lost, and went to pieces. In 1882 there was a strike against the increased number of coats to the task. At that time the contractors first organized against their people. The strike was lost and the union broken up. Two years later, in 1884, the tailors organized again under the leadership of the Knights of Labor, and the contractors also organized. At this time the number of coats to be made in the task had been increased. The contractors refused to employ union men. The fight was on the right to organize in both cases. The strike lasted several weeks and resulted in a complete victory for the men. A large number of contractors even paid a fine of $25 to $50 for having done violence to the interest and spirit of the tailors and gone into an association of their own.

About a year later the contractors again organized and locked out the men. After 4 weeks a compromise was made and the number of coats in a task was somewhat reduced, but the union was not recognized and neither body gained a complete victory. Later, in 1885, another strike occurred against nonunion buttonhole workers. During the years when the tailors were under the leadership of the Knights of Labor there was dissatisfaction with the methods of settling disputes. They claimed that the executive board of the Knights, composed of bricklayers, teamsters, and other trades, had no knowledge of tailoring, and in 1886–87 the union went out of existence. In 1888 an independent union was organized, called the Tailors' Progressive Union. This union was governed entirely by the tailors, and did not belong to any national or superior body.

In 1891–1894 there was a vigorous agitation among the tailors against the task system. The number of coats per task was being increased continually. Competition was very severe. In 1894 a strike was instituted and won. Contractors were forced to file a pledge with the union that they would employ their people by the week with no reference to the number of coats they made per day, and also that they would not compel them to work longer than 10 hours a day. A certain scale of wages was insisted on, namely, $16 per week for the operator, $14 per week for the baster.

During the season of 1895 the contractors came together, formed an association, and locked their men out. The men held out for a long time, but were finally defeated, and the task system was again introduced, with longer hours of labor and lower wages.

In 1897 the union was again reorganized, but it has not up to the present time been strong enough to effectively control the trade.

3. **Pantsmakers.**—Among the pantsmakers the union has had more effect than among the coatmakers. They, too, have had the same history of organizing, striking, leaving the organization, and again reorganizing, time after time during the past 15 years. During the last 3 or 4 years they have interested themselves mainly toward securing a regular number of hours for their members. While they do not control all of the trade, they do control a large number of shops and have made a very hard fight against long hours in the contractor's shop. Out of the 3,000 pantsmakers in New York and Brooklyn about 1,100 are organized, controlling most of the large shops. Unlike the coat trade, within the past 12 years there has been almost no change in the price paid for the best operator. He now gets 9 to 12 cents for operating an ordinary pair of pants, just as he did 10 or 12 years ago.

This is not so in the other branches of the trade. On coats, vests, cloaks, shirts, caps, and most of the other occupations in the sewing trade the price has fallen. The contract price for pants has fallen so that it is now extremely difficult for a contractor to make a profit. The contractors' shops for pants have become somewhat larger, since it is not possible to run a small shop on the small margin which the contractor makes. If in the future the pantsmakers are able to hold their price as they have done for the last 5 years, it is probable that it will not be long before the contractor is entirely driven out of that business. Already, in the last few years, manufacturers are going into the pants business on a small scale, and former contractors are becoming pants manufacturers.

4. **Ladies' cloaks and suits.**—Women's ready-made clothing existed only to a very limited extent prior to 1880. About this time, when the Russian Jews began to migrate, an industry was established known as the ladies' cloak and suit business. The development of this business was similar to that of the men's ready-made clothing. At first cheap help was employed to work on cheap materials, but before long skill and taste were developed in the business, and very expensive plush and cloth garments were made for women's wear and distributed broadcast among the stores of the country. New York City was the center for the development of that

class of manufacture, and it is probable that at the present time over 75 per cent of the cloak business of the country is located in that city, where there are about 15,000 people in the trade.

During the busy season the average operator earns $15 to $20 per week; the baster, $9 to $15; the presser, $12 to $15. But the seasons are very short in this trade, usually 5 or 6 months. For this reason the prices fluctuate enormously. An expert operator can sometimes earn $40 per week for 3 or 4 weeks in the busy season at piece work, and such wages are sometimes cited as indicating a prosperous condition of the trade. But they indicate only a disorganized state of business, with occasional famine prices. The same expert operator on the same class of work in the dull season could earn only $10 if he worked the same number of hours. The highly speculative character of this work makes it peculiarly a field for the Jewish workman. With the high prices of the busy season he is spurred to exert himself to the utmost, day and night. At the same time Italians have recently entered the trade and have become a more serious factor than in other branches. The Jewish cloak and suit makers in New York now number about 12,000 and the Italian 3,000.

In this field the immigrant has created an industry which did not exist prior to his coming. These ready-made suits for women have indeed cut into the business of the dressmaker and home worker, but they are sold in the stores for less money than a woman would pay were she to buy the cloth and have it made up.

The manufacture of ladies' cloaks and suits is the branch of clothing which in New York, as already stated, has passed out of the hands of contractors working for large manufacturers and into the hands of small manufacturers working in their own inside shops. The reasons for this change have been considered on page —.

The cloakmakers were first organized in 1884. The history of their organization is somewhat similar to the history of the other organizations in the Jewish trade, but the features are intensified. It is customary for them to come together in large numbers after samples are made for a coming season and before the prices have been made. They form a strong organization, send a committee to the manufacturer, make terms for the price of labor for the season, and then neglect the organization until the next season. The initiation fee in the union has usually been small, from 25 cents to $1.

The first large strike was in 1890, when they were out for 8 weeks and endured great suffering, but they finally won the strike. The price for labor was raised to such an extent that the cloakmakers were able to earn as much as $25 to $30 per week, making at that time a sort of standard for the price of labor, which has had a strong influence in all succeeding years. When in the busy season they are able to earn what they did in 1890 they are satisfied. If not, they strengthen their union and institute a strike.

The following are the local branches of the cloakmakers' union: Operators' Local, No. 1, with about 2,000 members out of 4,000 in the trade; Tailors' Local, No. 2, with about 1,000 members out of 4,000; Pressers' Local, No. 3, with about 500 members out of 2,000; Ladies' Branch, composed of the women tailors in the trade; No. 6, with about 300 members out of 2,000 all told; Italian Branch, with about 300 members out of 3,000; Skirtmakers' Local, with about 100 members out of 2,000.

There are more Italians in the cloak business as tailors than in any other branch of the clothing trade. They usually conduct themselves about the same as the Jews. They join the unions in large numbers when the Jews join and stay out of the union when the Jews stay out. They have not as yet successfully entered the trade as a people. They work somewhat cheaper than the Jews do, but they are not so much alive to the different changes in the trade, and do not take up so easily the different modes of production and the different styles. For this reason they have not the same opportunities in the trade as the Jews. But their number is slowly increasing, and it is probable that before long they will be the most formidable factor in the trade. As it is they form about 20 per cent of the people engaged in the cloak business.

In Chicago cloaks were originally made in large shops, by women and girls, working by piece work. When the immigration of Russian Jews began in 1881 the contract system was first established in the home shops, where they were able to do the work cheaper than in the large shops.

The price for labor fell so seriously that the Jews organized their first union in 1886 under the Knights of Labor. Following that, a strike occurred at the beginning of each season, when prices would be made at about double the figures of the preceding dull season. In 1890 a strong organization was effected which lasted until 1894. By several large strikes the union was able to regulate the wages of the workmen without so many small strikes as were necessary in the preceding years. Earnings at that time were $16 to $20 in the busy season and $8 to $10 in the slack season. The union also gained a ten-hour day in place of the preceding unlimited hours. During the depression of 1893, 1894, and 1895 the union was almost broken up. The price for labor went down to nearly one-half. The union was again strengthened in 1896 and lasted until 1898, when it was again broken up by a hard-contested fight against large cloak manufacturers. In 1901 it was again reorganized.

In 1889 the cloak manufacturers began to replace men's outside shops by women's outside shops in districts populated by immigrant Poles and Bohemians. These girl's shops have never been organized, and they have practically displaced the Jewish men on all the cheaper work, their contract prices being about two-thirds of the prices paid to the men. A large number of the men who were driven out of the trade by the girls have gone into the ladies' tailoring business, opening small shops and making ladies' garments to order. Those who continue to work at the better grades of ready-made work are able to earn about the same wages as in 1890.

The ten-hour day which they gained at that time is still customary with a large number of men, though not under the control of a union.

5. Knee-pants makers.—The nationalities engaged in the manufacture of knee pants in New York number about 1,300 Jews and 200 Italians in shops and 1,000 Italian home finishers. About 800 are working with foot power and 700 with steam power. The steam-power shops are "inside shops," and the foot-power shops are run by contractors. In the steam shops 80 per cent of the employees are men. The first steam shop was started in 1895, in Brooklyn, with an intense division of employment and the employment of men, which continues even at present. This manufacturer moved to New York in 1897 to gain Italians.

In 1890 the shops were in the homes of the Jews. Contractors employed from 5 to 7 persons. Each person had to furnish his own machine and bring it to the home of the contractor. The trade was driven from the tenements by the legislation against tenement-house manufacture, and the contractors then rented little shops.

In 1893, when the manufacture was still in tenements, there was a strike to compel the contractor to buy his own machines. The strike was lost. The union was reorganized and struck again for the same reason in 1894, and won. Since then the manufacturer and contractor supply the machines.

In 1897 there was a strike against the manufacturers direct, on the demand that they should hold themselves responsible for the prices. Two-thirds of the manufacturers signed the agreement. Of these only three lived up to it. The agreements were not sustained in court, on the ground that they were given by the manufacturers under duress.[1] In 1899 there was anothe strike, and this time promissory notes were demanded. This strike was successful. The demand for this security by notes was not continuously nor extensively practiced, because the other trades being unorganized, the members of this union were replaced.

At the present time the union is comparatively strong. It controls one large shop and 25 to 30 small ones. It numbers about 500 members, although the membership is continually changing. Every general strike at the beginning of a season has been won, but prices have always gone down within 3 weeks. In the last 3 or 4 years Italian women have taken the places of strikers. They begin work at $1.75 per week.

The earnings of the men are now about the same as in 1890, namely, $12 per week in the busy season of about 6 months, and $8 in the slack season. But the workmen have a 10-hour day instead of 14 hours, and their efficiency through division of labor and increased speed has so increased that they produce as much work per day as formerly.

In Chicago, in the early years of the knee-pants industry, the prices offered were $2 to $2.50 per dozen, and the people employed made fairly good wages. But as the business developed and a large number of immigrants entered, principally Russian Jews, the price began to fall, so that at the present time the knee pants are taken out by the contractor at from 80 cents to $1.20 a dozen. Machine operators formerly earned about $12 per week. Now they only earn $8 to $10, while their efficiency has almost doubled.

In 1890 a union of knee-pants makers was formed in Chicago and it has been in existence since that time, although very weak. When there is plenty of work, the people are generally alive to the fact and strike for higher wages. When work is not plenty, they feel helpless and wages run down, so that men work for $4 and $5 during the slack season. On knee pants in Chicago the people work more hours per day than in any other branch of the trade, in most of the shops the men going to work at 5 o'clock in the morning and working until 9 or 10 in the evening. This is the case not only in the busy season, but even during the slack season.

The people are continually changing in this trade. After a few years, many of them, exhausted and with health destroyed by foot-power machines, are supported by charity. A large number live partly on charity even while they are working at the business. The trade is more seriously affected by home work for pin money than other branches. When the knee-pants makers strengthen their union and inaugurate a strike, they usually find that they strike the work away from them-

---

[1] See also testimony of I. A. Hourwich, Manf. and General Business, p. 150, vol. vii.

selves. In the last few years Polish girls' shops are replacing the men's shops, although the Jewish men still make the larger number of knee pants because they work harder. The contractors themselves have not succeeded in the business. Only a few of them have been able to build their own homes or shops.

6. **Children's clothing.**—The manufacture of children's coats in New York is carried on mostly in large shops, where there is an intense division of labor. The majority of the employees are men. Foot power prevails. The great majority of the people in the trade are Russian Jews. Probably 10 per cent are Poles and 5 per cent Lithuanians. The shops work by the week, 11 hours a day, and in many cases still longer hours. Where the division of labor is not very intense, they work by the piece, and work an unlimited number of hours. The price for labor is almost as low as the prices paid in the knee-pants business, the operators and pressers earning from $6 to $12 a week, the majority getting $7, $8, and $9, working eleven hours a day.

The trade is being extended very much year after year and more and more people are being engaged in it, but the condition of the workers has become worse within the last few years. At one time they formed a union, but were sold out by their leaders and the union was broken up. Efforts are now being made to reorganize. There have been many strikes and the men have won, but they have not gained any lasting benefit.

In Chicago the manufacture of ready-made clothing for children was introduced about the year 1888 in colonies of Poles, Jews, and Bohemians. As years went on, the Polish girls succeeded in getting almost a monopoly of the business. A machine girl would earn $4 to $7 a week; probably the majority earn between $4 and $5. Steam power has recently been introduced in a number of these girls' shops. The hours are usually 10. The work is done in section work, so that but little skill is required and each girl learns only a small part of the work. There is a good deal of "driving" done in these shops. Although most of the girls work by the week, it is the custom of the contractors to hurry them all the time. This is done in the larger shops by an ingenious system of "work records" by which the number of pieces completed by each girl is recorded at the end of each hour during the day. Since the girls begin work at $1.50 a week, and there is no scale of wages for the shop, but individual bargains are made with each employee on the basis of the amount of work done, it can be seen that this continual comparison of records is even superior to piecework in its capacity of urging the girls to their utmost exertion. The system requires constant oversight and prodding, such as would be resented by other nationalities. In this way the contract price on children's coats is about one-half the price of 10 years ago, but the hands do not earn much less per week, since they work much faster. A detailed account of one of these Polish shops is given in establishment No. 6, on page 358.

No effort has ever been made to organize any of the employees in the children's coat shops in Chicago.

7. **Special-order trade in Chicago.**—Within the past 10 years there has grown up in Chicago a branch of the clothing industry known as the "special order" or "country order" trade, in which suits are made to measure for very little more than they cost when bought ready made. They are made up on the same system as ready-made clothing; that is, by the division of labor, such as machine hand, baster, finisher, presser, buttonhole maker, hand sewer, etc. Each garment is cut separately and not in lots, as is the case with ready-made clothing.

Originally this business helped to intensify the sweating system and home production. Tailors would take home with them 2 or 3 coats, pants, or vests and make them up. The trade has now developed so that the shops are growing larger and larger. There are certain manufacturers who do that kind of work in their inside shops, and there is a tendency for the inside shop to replace the contractor; but the bulk of the coats as yet are made by Jews in the outside small shops.

In these shops there is no organization. The hours of labor are long during the busy season. Following are customary earnings:

TABLE 10.—*Earnings, special-order trade, Chicago, unorganized shop.*

	Per week.
Men operators in Jewish shops, week workers: first hand	$13 to $15
second hand	9 to 11
Piece workers, operating on $1.25 coat, 22 to 23 cents; on $2 coat, 30 to 35 cents; usual weekly earnings	16 to 20
(During the slack season the income is less.)	
Basters, week work:	
First hand	11 to 13
Second hand (usually girls)	7 to 9
Hand buttonhole makers (usually girls)	10
Hand finishers (felling, buttons, etc.)	4 to 7
Pressers	9 to 12
Hand pressers	5 to 7

In the large inside coat shops the price for labor is about $1 to $2 per week less than in the contractors' shops, but the work is steadier, the hours are shorter, and not quite as much is required. The supervision is less rigid.

Pants and vests in the special-order trade in Chicago are made by Swedes. Girls do most of the work, only the trimmers and pressers being men. The Swedes drifted to this branch of work when they were crowded out of the ready-made work by Poles, and by their capable labor organization they have here developed the most favorable conditions to be found anywhere under the contract system. They are practically the only tailors in the country who have successfully organized the outside home finishers, including Swedes, Germans, and Italians. The Italian finishers have come into the trade only within the last 7 or 8 years, and an Italian settlement was established a few years ago in the very heart of the Swedish district, where the Swedish pants and vest makers have kept their shops. Out of 1,400 outside finishers there are about 1,000 Italians and 400 Swedes and Germans. Formerly all the finishers were Swedes and Germans. The significance of organizing the Italian finishers is seen in the price which they receive for their work, namely, 14 cents, whereas the same work is done by unorganized Italians for 9 cents in Chicago and 5 cents in New York.

The union of the special-order pants and vest makers is known as the Custom Clothing Makers' Union of America, and controls about 75 per cent of that class of the trade, having about 3,500 people organized, under the following branches: Pressers' local, composed entirely of men; fitters, trimmers, bushelers, and brushers-off, mostly men; machine operators, girls; basters, girls; finishers, two branches, one Italian, the other Swedish and German.

The following are the wages earned in the union shops:

TABLE 11.—*Wages, special-order pants, Chicago, union shop.*

	Per week.
Machine operators (girls)	$10 to $15
Pressers	12 to 15
Trimmers	12 to 14
Finishers	5 to 9

The Swedish pants makers work 7 months in the year. Their earnings are about one-third more than the pants makers in the ready-made clothing trade, and one-third more than they themselves were earning before the organization of their union.

8. Central and national organizations of tailors.—The organizations in different branches of the clothing trade in New York mentioned in the preceding pages were organized separately at different times. In 1892 the locals in the manufacture of ready-made clothing formed a central body for Greater New York, known as District Council No. 7. This council meets weekly as an executive committee for the trade. The following locals are represented:

No. 2, United Brotherhood of Tailors, composed of the coat tailors in New York.
No. 10, composed of children's jacket and coat makers.
No. 15, a mixed organization in Brooklyn.
No. 16, vest makers of New York.
No. 17, vest makers of New York.
No. 25, German tailors of Brooklyn.
No. 24, mixed organization of Newark.
No. 55, coat tailors of Brooklyn.
No. 6, pants makers of New York.
No. 9, pants makers of Brooklyn.

The clothing cutters are not included.

In July of 1901 the clothing trades council of District No. 7 of New York inaugurated the first general strike of all the clothing workers that has occurred. This strike was inaugurated with a view of enforcing the policy indicated in the above series of resolutions. Hitherto each local had conducted its own strike and made its own agreements, but in this case the federation of these locals in the form of the district council has taken the matter in charge. Another new feature of this strike is the demands made directly upon the manufacturers. Hitherto contracts were made with the contractors; but in this case the district council passed over the heads of the contractors and made the demands directly upon the manufacturers. In these demands the manufacturers are asked to guarantee that the wages owing to employees shall be paid by contractors, thus making the manufacturers responsible for his contractor. Following are copies of the two agreements usually signed:

AGREEMENT WITH MANUFACTURER No. 1.

Whereas the United Garment Workers of America, a duly organized and incorporated association of the State of New York, on this —— day of ——, 1901, promises and undertakes to furnish skillful hands of both sexes to —— for the period of 1 year successively, whenever same are at their disposal and as may be called for by the said ——.

LABOR ORGANIZATIONS. 333

Now, therefore, know all men by these presents, that ―――― of the city of New York, borough of Manhattan, am hereby held and firmly bound unto the United Garment Workers of America, and the conditions of this obligation are as follows:
That if the above United Garment Workers of America furnish the said ski.lful hands or employees to the said ――――, I obligate myself in consideration thereof to guarantee to the said United Garment Workers of America that any employees by them furnished as above shall be employed in none but sanitary shops as provided by the State factory law; and I further guarantee that whatever earnings or wages, weekly or otherwise, that may at any time hereafter and during the period of 1 year from date be lawfully due to the employees furnished as aforesaid for a period not exceeding 1 week at a time, shall be promptly and fully paid by the said ――――, then this obligation to remain in full force and effect, otherwise it is to be void.
Signed in the presence of ――――.

AGREEMENT WITH MANUFACTURER, NO. 2.

The following agreement is hereby entered into between the firm of ―――― and District Council No. 1, United Garment Makers of America:
First, all contractors doing work for said firm shall employ only members in good standing of the United Garment Makers of America, and the following conditions shall be observed in all shops conducted by said contractors:
A. The working time shall be limited to 59 hours per week.
B. Wages of employees to be paid on the last working day of each week.
C. The union rate of wages shall be paid in said shops.
Second, the firm agrees to withhold work from any of the said contractors not observing the above-mentioned conditions.
Third, the firm agrees also to be responsible for all wages that may be due the employees of said contractor at the end of each week on such work as performed on garments of the above firm, limited to 1 week's wages, and on further condition that the undersigned is to notify of any default of the contractor by 12 o'clock noon on the following day.
This agreement entered into ―――― day of ――――, 1901, to terminate 1 year from date.

(Signed.)

Under the foregoing agreements it will be seen that the manufacturers guarantee that the contractors shall pay the union rate of wages, but this is done without any direct agreement as to what those wages shall be. The question of wages is dealt with in another agreement made with the contractors. This agreement specifies wages, hours, and conditions of work, and the contractor is required to give a bond to the amount of $10 for each machine operative. Following is a copy of the contract made with the tailors:

AGREEMENT WITH CONTRACTOR.

Articles of agreement made and entered into this ―――― day of ――――, 1901, by and between ――――, party of the first part, and ――――, parties of the second part, by their attorneys in fact, to wit: United Brotherhood of Tailors, District Council No. 1, of the United Garment Workers of America, all of the city, county, and State of New York, witnesseth:
1. The part― of the first part hereby covenant― and agree― to employ the parties of the second part as operators, basters, finishers, pressers, fitters, bushlers, and buttonhole makers, each in his own capacity, in the tailoring shop of the part― of the first part, at No. ―――― street, New York City, borough of ――――, for the period of 1 year from date thereof.
2. In consideration of the premises, the parties of the second part hereby faithfully, skillfully, and diligently to perform the work of operating, basting, finishing, pressing, fitting, busheling, and buttonhole making, each in his own capacity for the part― of the first part, and further agree to accept wages hereinafter mentioned as the minimum scale, and are to work 59 hours each week, as hereinafter specified.
3. It is also mutually agreed by and between the parties hereto, that the parties of the second part are to remain in the employ of the part― of the first part as long as they will remain members in good standing in the union above named, and that should the part― of the first part need other hands ―――― shall employ only members in good standing in said union on the same conditions.
4. The part― of the first part hereby agree― to abide by the rules of said union as known in the trade, and to permit said union's representatives to enter ―――― shop or shops for the purpose of enforcing said rules.
5. It is also mutually agreed by and between the parties hereto that the system of work shall be that known as week work only; that wages are to be paid weekly on the last day of each week s work, and not later than 5 p. m. of said day, and that the above-mentioned 59 hours of labor are to run as follows: First 5 days of the week, 10 hours per day, to wit, from 7 a. m. to 12 noon and from 1 p. m. to 6 p. m.; the last day 9 hours, from 7 a. m. to 12 noon and from 1 p. m. to 5 p. m., and under no circumstances shall the part― of the first part cause the parties of the second part to work any overtime. Work to be begun Sunday or Monday, according to the religious faith of the employees.
6. The part― of the first part hereby further agrees not to employ any more than 1 helper to every 2 operators, and not more than 1 helper to every 2 basters, and not to employ any apprentices.
7. The following is the minimum scale of wages to be paid by the part― of the first part to each of the parties of the second part in consideration of the premises:
Operators, $16 per week and upward; basters, $15 per week and upward; finishers, $12 per week and upward; pressers, $13 per week and upward; fitters, $12 per week and upward; bushlers, $11 per week and upward.
8. It is also mutually agreed by and between the parties hereto, that the part― of the first part shall give to the parties of the second part a promissory note for ―――― dollars as security for the pay ment of wages and for the faithful performance of the covenant of this contract.
9. It is also mutually agreed by and between the parties hereto that the parties of the second part may quit work during the so-called sympathy strike, provided that no new demand be made by them.
10. This contract shall be binding upon all the parties hereto and their legal representatives during the period of 1 year from date hereof.
In witness whereof the parties hereto have set their hands and seal the day and year first above written.
In presence of―
―――― ――――,
United Brotherhood of Tailors, District Council No. 1, of U. G. W. of A.

Similar contracts were made with the other locals of the district council.

A significant development of the foregoing demands upon manufacturers is the organization of the contractors to the number of some 2,500 and their counter-demands. The contractors' association being placed between the manufacturers' association and the tailors' unions, presents a most interesting problem in this curiously disorganized trade. The contractors are really in the position of a trade union of foremen paid by the piece, since the agreement of the manufacturers with the workmen regarding the scales of wages gives them in effect such a status. Being paid by the piece by the manufacturer, and the wages being fixed over their heads by agreement between the manufacturers and the union, it is all-important to them that the manufacturers should also agree upon the contract prices for which they shall be compelled to take out work. Such is the demand of their organization through the union which they effected. Since the contractors' side is not usually presented to the public, and since this version of the situation is necessary to an understanding of the whole, the following copy of the contractors' official statement is reproduced in full:

THE CONTRACTORS' VERSION—AN OPEN LETTER.

Since the last few years the clothing trade has been agitated by numerous strikes, the causes of which were not understandable to the general public. Every year the workers went out on strike, and apparently won all they demanded, yet a few months later would witness again the same outcry in the press—"Long hours and small wages."

This ignorance of the true state of affairs arises partly from the natural sympathy of the press and the public for the downtrodden "laborer," partly from the false and highly exaggerated statements of labor "leaders," partly because the contractors, in the public eye notorious sweaters, were denied the privilege of the press columns, and feared to denounce the wholesale manufacturer as the fountain head of all the evil conditions extant.

Did the manufacturer accede to the demands of the laborer, when forced by the fact that his customers were waiting the shipment of their orders, so that the contractors could satisfy their just and righteous demands, no sooner was the busy season over than the manufacturer again reduced the contract price so that of necessity the contractors were compelled to cut down the wages of their employees.

For these reasons, the contractor is to-day loath to reopen his shop until the manufacturer shall have guaranteed to both workman and contractor to keep the terms of his agreement.

The statement of various labor agitators to the effect that the manufacturer will open inside shops and thus abolish the contract system, does not frighten the contractor. He well knows that the manufacturer is not in business from philanthropic motives. He knows that as long as he can make the work cheaper than the manufacturer himself, as is evident by the very fact of his existence, his position is not in danger. It is true that some manufacturers have a small part—the higher grades—of their work made up on their own premises, but this is only to throw sand in the public eye.

What the manufacturer loses here, and he undoubtedly loses, he more than recompenses himself for by grinding down the prices of the cheaper lines, which he gives out to the contractors. Since, then, the contractor is now between two fires, he wishes to show the public the true state of affairs and asks the manufacturer, who has his work made partly inside and poses as a philanthropist and friend of the workingmen, not to give any more work to outside contractors.

The contractor wishes to show the workmen that he does not fare any better than they, so that they include in their demands of the manufacturer not only a 59-hour week and a guarantee for their wages, but also such an advance in the contract price which will enable him to meet their demands, and then the contractor pledges himself to turn over this entire advance to the workingmen's wage.

GAP KAIMES,
Secretary Clothing Contractors' Association.

Custom tailors.—The first organization of custom tailors in New York was formed in 1862 with 2,000 members. It has never been as prosperous as it was during the first years. At that time it succeeded in doubling the wages. The members were Irish and German, and these have predominated until the present time. The Swedes have been coming in for 20 years, but in 1894 they left in a body and formed a separate union of 600 members. Italians joined in 1891-92 during a strike, but left of their own accord when the strike was settled. The Italians work almost solely on ladies' tailoring. During the history of the union prices have been raised several times, and the price of $14 for a sack coat in 1894 was much higher than in the early years. Neither the best tailors on Fifth avenue are in the union, nor the Jewish custom tailors on the east side. The Jews are never first-class custom tailors. Their field of activity is ready-made clothing.

Clothing cutters.—Among the clothing cutters in New York almost one-half are Jews, one-quarter Irish, one-quarter German. The unions include, perhaps, 1,700 members out of a total of 3,000. Wages in union shops and the best nonunion shops are $18 per week, running as high as $24. On East Broadway they are as low as $6 to $10 per week.

Organization of Jewish trades.—A central organization of all Jewish trades, known as the "United Hebrew Trades," was organized in 1888. Here the great questions of trades unionism and socialism were discussed and the ideas disseminated amongst the p ople. The labor movement among the Jews has been reflected in this council more than in any other single place, and it is there that new movements were usually inaugurated. The following list of organizations which now belong to the United Hebrew Trades shows the marked predominance of the clothing trades:

United Brotherhood of Cloak Makers, representing the 7 locals.
United Brotherhood of Tailors, representing the Coat Makers' organization, probably having 1,000 members.

Wrapper Makers' Union, who make ladies' cotton wear, having some 800 members, three-fourths of whom are women out of an entire number in the trade of about 2,000.
Vest Makers' Union No. 2, with about 200 members, and No. 1, with about 300 members.
American Protective Musical Union, 50 members.
Bottlers and Drivers' Union, 40 members out of 150.
Bill Posters and Ushers' Union, 32 members.
Bakers' Union No. 86, of New York, 550 members out of 800.
Bakers' Union No. 156, of Brooklyn, 83 members out of 83.
Clothing Cleaners' Union, 50 members out of 150.
Chorist Union of New York, 42 members.
Hebrew American Typographical Union No. 83, 65 members out of 200.
Hebrew Actors' Protective Union, 48 members.
Knee-pants Makers' Union, 400 members out of 2,000.
Paper Cigarette Makers' Union, 350 members out of 500.
Progressive Rolled Cigarette Makers' Union, 700 out of 3,000.
Pants Makers' Union, 600 members out of 3, 000.
Sailor Jacket Makers' Union, 300 members out of 600.
Shoe Fitters' Union, 125 members out of 300.
Suspender Makers' Union, 200 members out of 300.
Skirt Makers' Union.
Salesmen's Protective Union, 18 members.
Silk Waist Makers' Union, 650 members out of 2,000.
Theatrical Costumers' Union, 650 members.
Vest Makers' Hungarian Branch.

It was not until 1891 that the first attempt on the part of the tailors of the United States was made to organize a national body together with the clothing cutters. On April 12, 1891, representatives of some 18 or 20 unions, who represented the tailors of Boston, New York, Brooklyn, and Philadelphia, in all 47 delegates, met at Clarendon Hall, New York, and formed a national body, called the United Garment Workers of America, and decided to join the American Federation of Labor.

Union label movement—Attack on contract system.—At the present time the point of attack on the part of the labor organizations in the clothing trade is the contract system. It is claimed that all efforts toward bettering the condition of the tailor fail, mainly, because their so-called employers are middlemen, and not responsible. That they take advantage of the lack of work during dull times to destroy effectively their agreements with the unions. The national executive board of the United Garment Workers of America has resolved to use the label for the purpose of eliminating the contractor. On April 11, 1901, the following resolution was adopted:

It being agreed that the contract system made it extremely difficult to enforce the laws and control conditions, and as the members were preparing for a movement having for its object the abolition of the contract system, it was agreed as follows:

First, the label be granted to no more firms unless they agreed to do their own tailoring directly in their own shops.

Second, to grant the present firms using the label six months' time in which to comply with the above condition.

Third, labels not to be given to shops employing less than ten persons.

Fourth, no labels to be given to any shop until first inspected and reported upon favorably by the label secretary.

Voted to announce publicly the policy of the national union in regard to the contract system and to institute the same movement as soon as practicable in all other clothing cities.

The foregoing resolution was followed by a demand upon the manufacturers by the Clothing Trades Council of New York for the abolition of the contractor. Following is the resolution:

Whereas it has now become impossible for the average workman in the tailoring trade to earn sufficient to keep body and soul together, the strikes in the past having accomplished but little for the tailor because the competition among sweater contractors made it impossible for them to live to their solemn promises to the unions;

Whereas the tailor works in the shop wholly unsanitary; shops that were not whitewashed for years, shops where windows, floors, and toilets are never cleaned; shops that are transformed during the night into lodging houses—the clothing being turned into quilts, pillows, and beddings, breeding vermin; shops that are a menace and danger to the workman as well as to the consumer of the clothing there made;

Whereas in hundreds of cases the tailor suffers the loss of his toil, the sweater absconding with the hard-earned wages, and the tailor getting paid waits two or three weeks for his bare, miserable pittance, with the result that he works and starves;

Whereas contractors have ceased to be contractors, and have become mere tools of oppression, exploiting the hands;

Wherefore in consideration of the great evils aforementioned, be it

Resolved, That we, the representatives, delegates of all the tailor unions representing the local unions of New York, Brooklyn, Newark, and Brownsville, when the opportune time arrives, refuse to submit to the sweater, and we now notify all manufacturers in the clothing trade to establish shops under their own control and under their own supervision.

V. WAGE STATISTICS IN THE CLOTHING TRADE.

The main obstacle in the way of measuring the effect of immigration on wages over a period of years is the uncertainty of the wage statistics. The clothing industry is conducted in small shops where the employer carries his accounts in his head, and leaves the business as soon as he can or must, either by advancing to the position of a manufacturer or returning to the position of an employee. It is practically impossible to find a contractor who has a set of books covering five or ten years, to say nothing of the past twenty years, during which immigration has been playing its part. In lieu of the contractors' books, the New York bureau of labor statistics, since the year 1889, has undertaken to secure information from the officials of labor organizations. The conjectural character of these statistics can be judged from the following example:

TABLE 12.—*Daily rates of wages as stated by labor organizations in the clothing industry from 1891 to 1895.*

[New York Bureau of Labor Statistics, 1896, pp. 738 ff. Selected occupations.]

Organizations.	1891.		1892.		1893.		1894		1895.	
	Highest.	Lowest.	Highest.	Lowest.	Highest.	Lowest.	Highest.	Lowest.	Highest.	Lowest.
Basters	$2.16⅔	$1.66⅔	$2.16⅔	$1.66⅔	$2.16⅔	$1.66⅔	$2.33⅓	$1.83⅓	$2.33⅓	$1.83⅓
Bushelers	1.33⅓	1.00	1.33⅓	1.00	1.33⅓	1.00	1.50	1.16⅔	1.50	1.16⅔
Cutters	3.33⅓	....	3.33⅓	....	3.33⅓	....	3.33⅓	....	3.33⅓	....
Coat makers	2.33⅓	2.00	2.33⅓	2.00	2.33⅓	2.00	2.50	2.00	2.50	2.00
Operators	1.33⅓	1.16⅔	1.33⅓	1.16⅔	1.33⅓	1.16⅔	1.33⅓	1.16⅔	1.33⅓	1.16⅔
Pressers	2.16⅔	1.33⅓	2.16⅔	1.33⅓	2.16⅔	1.33⅓	.83⅓	.50	2.50	1.66⅔
Tailors	3.33⅓	2.00	3.33⅓	2.00	3.33⅓	2.00	3.33⅓	2.00	3.33⅓	2.00
Vest makers	1.33⅓	1.16⅔	1.33⅓	1.16⅔	1.33⅓	1.16⅔	1.25	1.08⅓	2.00	1.83⅓

The well-recognized fallacy of comparative average wages is especially apparent in the clothing trade. The following averages are taken from the reports of the New York Bureau of Labor Statistics:

TABLE 13.—*Average annual wages paid in the clothing trade, New York.*

[New York Bureau of Labor Statistics, 1896, pp. 78, 79.]

Year.	Number reporting.	Yearly average wages.
1891	22,622	$384.26
1892	23,687	384.85
1893	26,100	392.67
1894	25,414	357.92
1895	30,979	361.77

The following table shows that the wages of operatives in clothing manufacture range from $1 per week to $60 per week. It shows also that even within a single occupation the range is as great as $1 to $15 (coat makers) and $3 to $50 ("tailors"). Plainly an average derived from such a wide range can have but little meaning.

TABLE 14.—*Rates of wages per week for all males.*

[New York Bureau of Labor Statistics, 1889, pp. 482 ff.]

	Per week.
Buttonhole makers	$4 to $18
Coat makers	1 to 15
Cutters	12 to 35
Finishers	6 to 7
Pressers	6 to 11
Tailors	3 to 50
Vest makers	3 to 12
MERCHANT TAILORS.	
Basters	7 to 13
Bushelmen	8 to 19
Cutters	16 to 60

While average wages for the trade can not be relied upon, it is even questionable whether the reported wages of a single occupation over a period of 10 or 20 years can be relied upon. In the course of 20 years so many changes have occurred in the trade in the way of subdividing the work that a given occupation does not designate the same degree of skill as formerly. It is for this reason that the existing wide range of wages within even the same occupation is found. Consequently a comparison between the wages of a given class of workmen at different periods, compiled from different sources, must be taken with the caution that perhaps the compilers have not agreed upon the identical kind of work throughout the time covered. Prbobably the most satisfactory effort of this kind is found in the following table from the report of the Massachusetts bureau of labor statistics (1897, p. 5). This shows the average weekly earnings for specified occupations for the years 1860, 1872, 1878, 1881, and 1897. Prior to 1880 the Jew and Italian had not influenced the trade materially, and, moreover, the trade had not developed largely its ready-made side. Comparing, therefore, the wages of 1881 with 1897 it appears that the wages of cutters and women custom workers on pantaloons and vests have risen, whereas the wages of overseers, cutters, trimmers, pressers, basters, home finishers, shop finishers, and custom finishers have fallen. The marked fall in the case of home finishers is the well-known result of Italian immigration. These comparative wages should be compared with the subjoined average wages, for the same years, of the 23 occupations compiled by the United States Department of Labor, which show a rise of 1.2 per cent during the same period—1881 to 1897.

TABLE 15.—*Average weekly wages, ready-made clothing, standard gold.*

[Massachusetts, Report on Statistics of Labor, 1897, p. 5.]

	1860.	1872.	1878.	1881.	1897.
Overseers	$19.45	$24.45	$24.82	$28.33	$18.35
Cutters	13.92	19.85	16.00	19.81	20.35
Trimmers	11.06	11.26	14.31	13.69	8.20
Pressers	9.17	16.05	10.28	14.70	13.44
Basters (women)	6.32	7.77	6.46	8.00	5.92
Machine operators (women)	5.53	10.81	5.92	9.47	6.42
Finishers at home (women)	4.00		3.46	5.42	1.79
Finishers in shop (women)	4.56	4.74	4.58	4.95	3.75
Finishers, custom (women)	6.00		8.00	8.71	6.00
Pantaloon and vest makers, custom work (women)	5.58		6.90	8.54	10.29
Average daily wages, 23 occupations [1]		2.45	2.31	2.41	2.44

[1] United States Department of Labor Bulletin, 1898, p. 668.

The following table shows for the fourth quarter of 1898 the wages received per day worked and the number of employees receiving the specified wages:

TABLE 16.—*Wages and number receiving specified wages in different occupations of the tailoring trade for the fourth quarter, 1898, New York City.*

[Computed from New York Bureau of Labor Statistics, 1899, pp. 318-319.]

Daily wages.	Number.	Daily wages.	Number.
Cloak makers:		Jacket makers—Continued.	
$1.25	300	$2.00	382
1.33	200	2.50	68
1.50	500	Pants and knee-pants makers:	
1.60	490	$1.25	600
2.00	700	1.75	800
Cutters:		Pressers:	
$1.50	6	$1.00	200
1.65	10	1.50	100
1.80	8	1.60	40
2.00	26	2.00	140
2.40	4	Tailors:	
2.50	3	$0.80	14
2.50	6	1.50	28
2.60	6	1.60	20
3.00	451	1.90	150
3.30	578	2.00	300
3.40	11	3.30	90
3.70	6	Vest makers:	
4.00	153	$0.60	10
4.15	2	.80	10
Coat makers:		1.00	30
$1.50	45	1.20	20
2.00	600	1.60	30
Jacket makers:		2.00	30
$1.25	25	2.25	30
1.50	145		

Of even more importance than the movement in the rate of wages in the clothing trade are changes in the hours of labor and the exertion of the laborers. On this point statistical records are lacking, but it is a significant fact, as already stated, that in the "task" system as practiced in New York, whereas 15 years ago the task was 8 or 10 coats for 1 day's work, the task is now 20 to 22 coats of the same quality. Formerly the operator, baster, and finisher could complete their task in 8 or 10 hours of leisurely work; now it require 14 hours of intense application. On the basis of 12 hours' work it is generally found that the team can turn out only

5 tasks—i. e., 5 day's work in the week. The so-called "driving" is the characteristic of every sweat shop. Accepting the foregoing basis of 10 coats in the task compared with the present basis of 20 coats, and no changes in the method of production, the workmen do twice as much work for the same money, and since they work 2 to 3 hours longer, it follows that the exertion of the workman for the same amount of money has increased 20 to 40 per cent.

It is possible, however, that the overexertion can be traced as much to antiquated methods as to overcrowding the labor market. This point will be carefully examined in later pages of this report, wherein the task system is compared with the newly introduced "factory system." It is there shown that this factory system produces in 10 hours, at slightly higher wages, the same product that the task system produces in 12 hours. But, on the other hand, in the factory system, owing to the minute subdivision of labor, the intense exertion of the workmen is even greater than in the task system. On the whole, if we measure wages by the amount of his life energy which the workman gives up, it seems clear that in the past 15 years there has been a decided fall in the amount of return received for his labor.

Beginning with the year 1897, the New York bureau of labor statistics has compiled quarterly reports from the officials of labor organizations in the clothing trade, and by a system of subdivision of occupations and careful instructions to the officials has been able to present the most nearly accurate body of wage statistics that can now be found in the clothing trade. The following tables have been compiled from the reports of this bureau. They show for the 20,000 organized employees the number of days worked each quarter and each year, the average earnings per quarter and per year, the average earnings per day worked, and the average earnings per working day of the year. It should be noted that organized labor, which alone is represented in these reports, includes those employed in the better shops, with the shorter hours, higher pay, and more regular employment. Consequently the 20,000 employees covered by the tables indicate an average of the better conditions of the trade, while the remaining 80,000 or more are on a distinctly lower level.

It will be seen, taking the trade as a whole, that the average number of days worked each year ranges from 217 to 255 for men and from 228 to 272 for women. Allowing 310 days as the working period of the year, this represents employment of 70 to 90 per cent of full time.

The average earnings per year range from $415.30 to $580.78 for men and from $245.28 to $312.98 for women. The average earnings for each day worked range from $2.04 to $2.27 for men and $1.07 to $1.26 for women, and the average earnings per working day on the basis of 310 days per year, representing the amount of money available for daily living expenses, ranges from $1.34 to $1.87 for men and from 79 cents to $1 for women.

The best-paid workmen are the cutters—earning from $3.14 to $3.29 for the days worked, equivalent to $2.64 to $2.72 for each working day. These include 5 to 10 per cent of the total number reported. Coat operators earned in 1897 $1.78 per day, equivalent to 89 cents for each working day. Other occupations can be followed by consulting the table.

TABLE 17.—*The clothing trade in New York City.*

[Compiled from reports of the New York Bureau of Labor Statistics.]

Quarter.	Number of members employed.		Average number of days each member was employed.		Average earnings of each member.							
			Per quarter.	Per year.	Per quarter.		Per year.		Per day worked.		Per working day.	
	Male.	Female.	Male.	Female.	Male.	Female.	Male.	Female.	Male.	Female.	Male.	Female.
1897—First	9,998	1,213	55	60	$119.45	$70.46						
Second	14,462	1,349	44	50	81.55	57.09						
Third	23,871	2,563	64	68	146.46	86.84	$482.93	$289.42	$2.22	$1.26	$1.55	$0.93
Fourth	23,495	3,520	54	50	135.47	75.03						
1898—First	23,074	3,145	57	58	121.14	64.46						
Second	17,394	3,565	37	45	85.36	47.95						
Third	16,513	3,284	59	64	105.06	66.69	415.30	245.28	2.04	1.07	1.34	0.79
Fourth	8,650	2,059	50	62	103.74	66.18						
1899—First	14,670	3,540	58	65	138.17	74.62						
Second	16,697	3,916	68	72	158.35	78.84						
Third	19,453	4,029	68	70	149.38	83.54	580.78	312.98	2.27	1.15	1.87	1.00
Fourth	23,121	3,899	61	65	134.88	75.98						
1900—First	19,691	4,258	63	61	140.09	72.08						
Second												
Third	13,623	3,568	59	59	111.93	63.50						

WAGE STATISTICS IN CLOTHING TRADE. 339

TABLE 18.—*Cutters (males).*

Quarters.	Number of members employed.	Average number of days each member was employed.		Average earnings of each member.			
		Per quarter.	Per year.	Per quarter.	Per year.	Per day worked.	Per working day.
1897—First	2,770	60	} 261	$193.98	} $820.75	$3.14	$2.64
Second	1,405	64		187.73			
Third	1,498	71		227.45			
Fourth	1,658	66		211.59			
1898—First	1,663	73	} 266	232.08	} 845.33	3.17	2.72
Second	1,658	70		225.92			
Third	1,625	62		195.68			
Fourth	1,616	61		191.65			
1899—First	1,219	63	} ¹198	200.30	} ¹651.40	3.29	
Second	1,281	64		207.92			
Third	1,327	71		243.18			

¹ For three quarters.

TABLE 19.—*Coat operators (males).*

Quarters.	Number of members employed.	Average number of days each member was employed.		Average earnings of each member.			
		Per quarter.	Per year.	Per quarter.	Per year.	Per day worked.	Per working day.
1897—First	300	45	} 155	$67.50	} $277.49	$1.78	$0.89
Second	1,500	25		43.75			
Third	1,675	29		49.91			
Fourth	1,350	56		116.33			
1898—First	1,150	51		97.24			
Second	200	36		60.00			

TABLE 20.—*Basters (males).*

Quarters.	Number of members employed.	Average number of days each member was employed.		Average earnings of each member.			
		Per quarter.	Per year.	Per quarter.	Per year.	Per day worked.	Per working day.
1897—First	200	45	} 197	$93.75	} $414.24	$2.10	$1.33
Second	1,500	25		50.00			
Third	1,300	72		158.59			
Fourth	1,000	55		111.90			
1898—First	800	49		92.29		1.88	

TABLE 21.—*Coat makers.*

Quarters.	Number of members employed.		Average number of days each member was employed.		Average earnings of each member.						
			Per quarter.		Per year.	Per quarter.		Per year.		Per day worked.	Per working day.
	Male.	Female.	Male.	Female.	Male.	Female.	Male.	Female.	Male.	Female.	Male.	Female.
1897—First	520	20	39	26	} 224	} 173	$47.83	$25.00	} $349.23	} $207.16	$1.56 $1.19	$1.12 $0.67
Second	1,265	72	50	41			79.82	33.83				
Third	1,626	15	70	60			123.09	90.00				
Fourth	1,455	45	65	46			98.49	58.33				
1898—First	725		59		} 223	} 127	84.96		} 344.80	} 164.58	1.54 1.29	1.04 .53
Second	915		34				56.60					
Third	833	65	76	85			101.11	127.47				
Fourth	687	194	54	42			102.13	37.11				
1899—First	377	141	34	40	} ¹167	} ¹192	50.43	43.50	} ¹325.10	} ¹163.66	1.94 .85	
Second	1,464	221	60	76			106.00	55.72				
Third	2,120	292	73	76			168.67	64.44				

¹ For three quarters.

THE INDUSTRIAL COMMISSSON:—IMMIGRATION.

TABLE 22.—*Pressers (males).*

Quarters.	Number of members employed.	Average number of days each member was employed.		Average earnings of each member.			
		Per quarter.	Per year.	Per quarter.	Per year.	Per day worked.	Per working day.
1897—First	410	43	} 202	$64.90	} $375.50	$1.85	$1.21
Second	1,160	27		42.17			
Third	1,535	73		155.72			
Fourth	1,202	59		112.71			
1898—First	1,175	58	} 198	92.87	} 317.36	1.60	1.02
Second	685	39		59.20			
Third	200	51		91.96			
Fourth	480	50		73.33			
1899—First	80	75	} [1]204	118.75	} [1]331.55	1.62	
Second	100	60		74.80			
Third	700	69		138.00			

[1] For three quarters.

TABLE 23.—*Finishers (edge basters).*

Quarters.	Number of members employed.		Average number of days each member was employed.		Average earnings of each member.							
			Per quarter.		Per year.		Per quarter.		Per year.		Per day worked.	Per working day.
	Male.	Female.	Male.	Female.	Male.	Female.	Male.	Female.	Male.	Female.	Male.	Female.
1897—First	300		45		} 198	} 25	$135.00		} $407.96	} $37.50	} $2.08 $1.50	} $1.31 $0.12
Second	1,650	50	25	25			37.50	$37.50				
Third	1,450		72				125.64					
Fourth	1,100		56				109.82					
1898—First	985	50	50	47	} [1]162	} [1]97	77.59	73.24	} [1]265.83	} [1]123.24	1.64	1.27
Second	100	20	53	50			83.42	50.00				
Third	65		59				104.82					

[1] For three quarters.

TABLE 24.—*Vest makers.*

Quarters.	Number of members employed.		Average number of days each member was employed.		Average earnings of each member.							
			Per quarter.		Per year.		Per quarter.		Per year.		Per day worked.	Per working day.
	Male.	Female.	Male.	Female.	Male.	Female.	Male.	Female.	Male.	Female.	Male.	Female.
1897—First	250	50	52	52	} 210	} 213	$96.33	$74.13	} $375.85	} $143.79	$1.78 $1.15	$1.20 $0.78
Second	100	100	78	78			120.38	73.10				
Third	244	200	41	43			70.69	46.48				
Fourth	595	379	39	40			87.45	50.08				
1898—First	580	390	38	38	} 137	} 133	80.82	53.63	} 260.45	} 154.49	1.90 1.16	.84 .50
Second	385	240	29	28			53.97	35.67				
Third	185	140	31	28			54.09	28.63				
Fourth	110	50	39	39			71.57	35.56				
1893—First	35	15	66	66	} [1]183	} [1]183	121.00	60.50	} [1]412.00	} [1]106.00	1.25 1.12	1.32 .66
Second	34	34	48	48			84.00	42.00				
Third	100	50	69	69			207.00	103.50				

[1] For three quarters.

WAGE STATISTICS IN CLOTHING TRADE. 341

TABLE 25.—Jacket makers.

Quarters.	Number of members employed.		Average number of days each member was employed.				Average earnings of each member.							
			Per quarter.		Per year.		Per quarter.		Per year.		Per day worked.		Per working day.	
	Male.	male.	Male.	Female.	Male.	Female.	Male.	Female.	Male.	Female.	Male.	Female.	Male.	Female.
1897—First	1,789	125	51	58			$82.05	$95.58						
Second	2,259	274	36	34	204	144	62.87	38.53	$339.39	$176.39	$1.66	$1.22	$1.09	$0.57
Third	2,358		51				87.05							
Fourth	2,930	605	66	52			107.42	42.28						
1898—First	2,375	300	62	56			77.58	37.13						
Second	715	225	39	50	201	214	70.53	42.06	361.01	283.19	1.79	1.32	1.16	.91
Third	895	50	62	72			139.66	132.00						
Fourth	595	25	38	36			73.24	72.00						
1899—First	175	75	63	62			131.16	126.00						
Second	25		60				75.00							

TABLE 26.—Pants makers.

Quarters.	Number of members employed.		Average number of days each member was employed.				Average earnings of each member.							
			Per quarter.		Per year.		Per quarter.		Per year.		Per day worked.		Per working day.	
	Male.	Female.	Male.	Female.	Male.	Female.	Male.	Female.	Male.	Female.	Male.	Female.	Male.	Female.
1898—Fourth	1,214	236	51	47	243	248	$75.71	$79.03	$366.05	$324.64	$1.50	$1.30	$1.18	$1.04
1899—First	1,060	75	61	69			93.46	81.53						
Second	2,516	234	58	63			76.03	79.21						
Third	3,239	236	73	69			120.85	84.87						

TABLE 27.—Pants and vest makers.

Quarters.	Number of members employed.		Average number of days each member was employed.				Average earnings of each member.							
			Per quarter.		Per year.		Per quarter.		Per year.		Per day worked.		Per working day.	
	Male.	Female.	Male.	Female.	Male.	Female.	Male.	Female.	Male.	Female.	Male.	Female.	Male.	Female.
1898—Fourth	6	217	68	74	283	310	$93.61	45.34	$445.34	$210.27	$1.57	$0.68	$1.43	$0.68
1899—First	5	268	77	83			117.00	47.48						
Second	13	440	60	75			97.45	56.89						
Third	50	400	78	78			137.28	60.56						

342   THE INDUSTRIAL COMMISSION:—IMMIGRATION.

TABLE 28.—*Pants and knee-pants makers.*

Quarters.	Number of members employed.		Average number of days each member was employed.				Average earnings of each member.							
			Per quarter.		Per year.		Per quarter.		Per year.		Per day worked.		Per working day.	
	Male.	Female.	Male.	Female.	Male.	Female.	Male.	Female.	Male.	Female.	Male.	Female.	Male.	Female.
1897—First	1,078		58				$85.67							
Second	1,095		56				75.37							
Third	2,672		72		246	62	111.93		$363.75	$92.25	$1.47	$1.48	$1.17	$0.29
Fourth	2,710	100	60	62			90.78	$92.25						
1898—First	2,400		75				125.78							
Second	1,580	20	45	60	¹176	¹120	70.42	90.00	¹283.18	¹105.00	1.60	1.62		
Third	2,300	150	56	60			86.98	105.00						

¹ For three quarters.

TABLE 29.—*Cloak makers.*

Quarter.	Number of members employed.		Average number of days each member was employed.				Average earnings of each member.							
			Per quarter.		Per year.		Per quarter.		Per year.		Per day worked.		Per working day.	
	Male.	Female.	Male.	Female.	Male.	Female.	Male.	Female.	Male.	Female.	Male.	Female.	Male.	Female.
1897—First	950		68				$118.23							
Second	1,276		78				107.10							
Third	7,000	1,000	68	68	248	99	188.92	109.68	$585.57	$209.68	$2.40	$2.11	$1.89	$0.67
Fourth	6,800	1,200	34	31			171.32	100.00						
1898—First	7,815	800	52	52			140.34	62.40						
Second	7,651	1,400	34	29			83.62	38.90						
Third	8,359	1,200	60	60	181	190	95.34	50.00	377.74	200.05	2.08	1.05	1.21	.64
Fourth	1,900	200	35	39			58.44	48.75						
1899—First	9,170	1,844	60	60			151.20	75.00						
Second	9,217	1,853	72	71	¹197	¹197	183.54	88.16	¹482.52	¹262.32	2.44	1.32		
Third	8,000	1,800	65	66			147.79	99.16						

¹ For three quarters.

TABLE 30.—*Custom tailors.*

Quarter.	Number of members employed.		Average number of days each member was employed.				Average earnings of each member.							
			Per quarter.		Per year.		Per quarter.		Per year.		Per day worked.		Per working day.	
	Male.	Female.	Male.	Female.	Male.	Female.	Male.	Female.	Male.	Female.	Male.	Female.	Male.	Female.
1897—First	841	25	46	41			$100.30	$47.64						
Second	971	32	63	76			142.26	90.89						
Third	1,672	31	48	34	225	212	95.59	39.40	$497.14	$271.93	$2.20	$1.28	$1.60	$0.87
Fourth	1,957	15	68	61			158.99	94.00						
1898—First	1,532	41	51	64			123.33	55.49						
Second	1,592	370	56	55			130.10	54.18						
Third	1,041	406	37	65	202	251	68.36	56.10	442.77	210.38	2.19	.83	1.42	.68
Fourth	1,409	263	58	67			120.98	44.61						
1899—First	1,995	165	42	76			76.55	75.00						
Second	1,682	250	73	78	¹182	¹228	156.66	72.32	¹369.18	¹203.00	2.02	.89		
Third	3,411	253	67	74			135.97	55.45						

¹ For three quarters.

VI.—MODES OF PRODUCTION AND RELATION TO NATIONALITIES.

The foregoing compilations of statistics are designed to present, as far as they go, the general or average conditions of labor in the clothing trade at different times. We have already mentioned the defects of method and inadequacy of data. There remains another method of study, that of individual typical shops. In the course of the past 25 years the changes in mode of production are as important as the changes in nationalities, and new modes have usually accompanied new nationalities. At the same time there can be found in existence side by side types of all the different shops and the different nationalities that have engaged in the business. Old methods and new methods are competing together, and also the remnants of earlier nationalities, with the vanguard of later nationalities. By studying these nationalities comparatively we can get, as it were, a contemporary epitome of the history of the trade. We can then draw our inferences upon the relative competing power of the several factors involved, especially those of immigration, women and children, and modes of production. In other words, as we find that one nationality or one mode of production has greater competing power than another nationality or mode of production, we can endeavor by a minute comparative study of the shops in question to separate the one cause from the other. After a careful study of some 150 shops in New York, Chicago, and Philadelphia, 12 have been selected as representative. These are described in detail in the following pages, and the accompanying comparative table (Table 31, page 344) has been drawn up showing the results reached in the later study of individual shops. This table should be referred to in following the discussion.

Only coat shops have been selected for detailed study, since this gives a uniform basis. The manufacture of trousers, vests, cloaks, etc., show similar comparisons, which have already been more briefly referred to.

344 THE INDUSTRIAL COMMISSION:—IMMIGRATION.

TABLE 31.—*Comparative showing of typical coat shops of different nationalities and modes of production.*

	A.	1.	2.	3.	4.	5.	6.	7.	8.	9.	10.	11.	12.
Character of shop..	Journeyman tailor.	Task system.	Factory...	Factory .	Factory .	Factory..	Small shop	Successor to family shop.	Successor to family shop.	Custom work, factory system.	Custom work, shop system.	Inside shop.	Factory.
Location............		New York.	New York.	Brooklyn	Chicago .	Brooklyn	Chicago .	Chicago ..	Chicago ..	Chicago .	Chicago .	New York.	Egg Harbor, N. J.
Character of work.	Coat....	Coat.... 300	Coat.... 1,650	Coat.... 600	Coat.... 400	Coat.... 3,000	Boys' coat 350	Coat.... 120	Coat.... 75	Coat.... 300	Coat.... 150	Coat...... 600	Coat. 500
Output per week..	Foot... 3	Foot.....	Steam ..	Steam ..	Gas.....	Steam ..	Gas.....	Foot.....	Gas.....	Gas.....	Foot.....	Steam "Inside	Steam.
Power.............		Jew	Jew	Lithuanian.	Jew.....	Jew	Pole.....	Bohemian.	German .	Jew	Jew	shop,"	German.
Nationality of contractor.													
Nationality of employees.	Jew	Jew	Jew, Italian.	Lithuanian.	Polish women & girls.	Poles, Jews, Italians	Polish women.	Bohemian.	German .	Jews, Polish women.	Jews, Bohemians, et al.	Jews, Italians.	German-Americans.
Number of employees.		19	104	57	32	50	17	13	16	35	19	124	34
Hours per week ..		72	60	66	60	66	60	60	60	60	60	59	60
Contract price per coat.	$6	75 cents..	75 cents..	75 cents..	75 cents..	19 cents..	30 cents..	$1.00	$1.75	$1.35	$2.00	$1.50	45 to 52½ cts.
Labor price per coat.	$6	59.3 cents.	55.7 cents.	67.5 cents	58.4 cents	16.1 cents	26 cents...	93.8 cents.	1.47	1.06¼	1.43		
Cost of operating per coat.		15 cents...	19 cents...	18.7 cents	23.7 cents	9.6 cents	10.3 cents	23.2 cents	39.4 cents	30.4 cents	30.7 cents	31.8 cents	39.8 cents. 13.8 cents.
Cost of basting per coat.		23.3 cents	13.7 cents	25.5 cents	13.9 cents	0.5 cent .	5.7 cents	47.4 cents	56 cents..	34.8 cents	39.4 cents	46.3 cents	14.2 cents.
Cost of pressing per coat.		8 cents....	8 cents....	9.3 cents	8 cents...	3.2 cents	3.1 cents	9.1 cents	27.3 cents	18 cents..	24 cents..	22.8 cents	3.4 cents.
Average wages per hour.	25 cents..	15.1 cents	14.7 cents	12.7 cents	12.2 cents	14.7 cents	8.9 cents	14.4 cents	11.5 cents	15.2 cents	19.7 cents	11.8 cents	9.7 cents.
Operators' wages per hour.		20.9 cents	20.1 cents	18.7 cents	13.2 cents	17.6 cents	7.5 cents	15.5 cents	9.7 cents	15.2 cents	25.6 cents	19.1 cents	8.8 cents.
Basters' wages per hour.		18.4 cents	5.1 cents	13.6 cents	12.2 cents	10.6 cents	9.1 cents	15.8 cents	14 cents..	17.4 cents	16.1 cents	10.3 cents	13.2 cents.
Pressers' wages per hour.		16.6 cents	22 cents...	16.9 cents	17.7 cent	14.4 cents	11.5 cents	18.3 cents	16.6 cents	22.5 cents	30 cents..	23.3 cents	14.2 cents.
Edge basters' wages per hour.		13.8 cents		9.2 cents									
Time per coat	24 hours..	3 hours 55 minutes.	3 hours 41 minutes.	5 hours 16 minutes.	4 hours 48 minutes.	1 hour 6 minutes.	2 hours 27 minutes.	6 hours 30 minutes.	12 hrs. 48 minutes.	7 hours ..	1 hour 36 minutes.	12 hours 11 minutes.	4 hours 5 minutes.
Operators' time per coat.		43 minutes	57 minutes	1 hour ...	1 hour 40 minutes.	33 minutes.	1 hour 24 minutes.	1 hour 30 minutes.	4 hours 41 minutes.	2 hours ..	1 hour 12 minutes.	1 hour 37 minutes.	1 hour 22 minutes.
Basters' time per coat.		43 minutes	54 minutes	1 hour 6 minutes.	1 hour 3 minutes.	2.6 minutes.	20.6 minutes.	3 hours...	4 hours ..	2 hours ..	2 hours 47 minutes.	4 hours 25 minutes.	1 hour 5 minutes.
Pressers' time per coat.		28.8 minutes.	21 minutes	33 minutes.	27 minutes.	13 minutes.	30 minutes	30 minutes	1 hour 36 minutes.	48 minutes.	48 minutes.	59 minutes	14 minutes.
Edge basters' time per coat.		43 minutes		1 hour 6 minutes.									

It will be seen that the shops selected cover four modes of production: First, the journeyman tailor who makes the complete garment (No. A); second, the successor to the home shop (Nos. 7 and 8); third, the small shop (Nos. 1, 6, 7, 8, 9, 10, and 12); fourth, the large shop or factory (No. 2 and 11).

The shops also cover the two methods of employment, namely, the contract system (Nos. 1 to 10) and the direct employment by the manufacturer or "inside shop" (No. 11). There is also one shop, No. 12, which is a "country shop," all of the others being located in large cities.

The predominating nationalities represented among the employees are six: Jew (Nos. 1 and 2), Lithuanian (No. 3), Polish (Nos. 4, 5, and 6), Bohemian (No. 7), German (No. 8), Italian (No. 11). These are shops which may rightly be described as belonging to the nationalities named, although in all cases certain parts of the work are done by a few persons of a different nationality. But there are two shops (Nos. 9 and 10) where the nationalities are distinctly mixed, including Jews, Germans, Poles, Bohemians, etc.

Lastly, these shops are selected so as to exhibit men's shops (Nos. 1, 2, 3, 5) and women's shops (Nos. 4, 6, 7, 8). Here again only the predominating character is indicated, since certain parts, especially pressing, trimming, and busheling are always done by men, even in women's shops. By predominating character is meant the character of the employees upon the machine operating and the basting. There are also 3 shops which are mixed as to sexes (Nos. 9, 10, 11).

The comparative study of these shops is designed to show, as already intimated, the competing power of nationality, sex, and mode of production. In each case is given the contract price of the coat, which serves to identify the quality of work; the labor cost of the same and the time required to make the coat; the wages per hour for the entire shop and for each of the three leading divisions of labor, operating, basting, and pressing. Each schedule is also accompanied by a commentary, in which the several factories are analyzed and the different shops compared.

VII. THE TASK SYSTEM.

Accompanying the immigration of Jews, from 1876 to 1882, the remarkable "task system" was introduced in New York. This system produces at the present time perhaps one-half the coats made in that city. The task system is peculiar to the city of New York, where it originated and continues. It exists neither in other cities of the United States nor in other countries. It is peculiar, also, to the Jewish shops.

The task system was the first real division of labor in coat shops. It has a double characteristic. It is a "team," or "set" of workmen, and the wages are paid by the piece. The number of workmen in the set is 3: The machine operator, the baster, and the under baster or finisher. The pressing is usually done by a fourth man, who is not a member of the team. With such nicety has this system been adjusted, through the pressure of competition, that at the present time it is found that 1 presser can press more coats than 1 team can complete in a day; and, on the other hand, 2 teams can furnish more work than 1 presser can complete; consequently the standard shop in which four-fifths of the task work is done is that of the "3-machine" shop, i. e., the shop of 3 teams of operator, baster, and finisher, to 2 pressers. Sewing on buttons and tacking pockets is done by a girl working by the week. In many cases, originally, where the shop was small, the contractor himself was one of the team, but at the present time, with 3 teams, he is the fitter or bushelman. Each team, therefore, as will be seen from the schedule of Establishment No. 1, below, is composed of the following: 1 operator, 1 baster, 1 edge baster or finisher. To every 3 teams, 2 pressers. Two girls for sewing on buttons, tacking pockets, etc. One or 2 girls for felling armholes and bottoms, etc.

When the task system originated with the Jewish immigrants, about the year 1877, it took the place of the journeyman tailor in the ready-made work. The coat for which the tailor received $5 or $6 as custom work, and for which he received $2.50 to $3 in the dull season as ready-made work, was made in these Jewish task shops for $1.50 to $2. At this price the Jews earned as much and even more money than the merchant tailor. The latter made very little use of the sewing machine. Most of the work on the coat was done by hand. When the division of labor was introduced in the Jewish shops each particular division became a trade in itself. The machine operator did not know how to do pressing or basting, the presser could not do the work of the others, and so on. The sewing-machine operator now became an important factor in the trade. He was able to do many parts of the work by machine that were formerly done by hand, and as a result the coat was made much quicker. Then again, the men who were engaged only in basting were able to do their work much quicker and probably better. The same was true of the presser and finishers.

In addition to the division of labor, the characteristic of the task system as distinguished from a piece system consists in the fiction that the workmen are earning a standard amount of wages per week. The scale originally fixed upon, and adhered to at the present time, was $18 for the operator, $16 for the baster, and $7 to $9 for the girl edge baster or finisher, or $11 to $12 for the man edge baster who has latterly taken the girl's place. Starting out upon this basis, it was found, 20 years ago, that a team could complete 8 or 9 cheviot coats per day, with plain seams and with welts on the outside. At this rate the price per coat for the team was about 80 cents. The present price is only 28 to 35 cents.

The process by which the price of labor was reduced, following the great influx of Hebrews in 1882, was somewhat as follows: The contractor, who was, perhaps, himself a member of the team on a kind of cooperative basis with the others, would go to the manufacturer and ask for work. Finding that there was but little work to be had, he would offer to take the coats cheaper than the price theretofore paid. When he came home, he would tell his men that there was not much work and he was obliged to take it cheaper, and, since he did not want to reduce their wages and pay them less per day, all they would have to do would be to make another coat in the task. That is, if they were accustomed to make 9 coats in the task, they would be required to make 10, then 11, and so on. The wages were always reduced on the theory that they were not reduced at all, but the amount of labor increased. In this way intense speed was developed. The men who had been accustomed to making 9 coats in a task would make 10, and so on up to 15, 18, and even 20, as is the customary task at the present time. The hours began to be increased, in order to make the task in a day. Within the last 3 years it is said by the men that it is only in very rare cases that a set can make a task in a day; that it is usual for these sets of 3, even when working 12 or 13 hours per day, to make only 4½ or 5 tasks in a week. In previous years, they claim, men were able to make 7 and 8 tasks or days' work per week.

This increased number of coats per task probably explains why, in the evolution of the trade, women could not hold their own as edge basters and finishers. About 1,500 to 2,500 girls have been driven out and men have taken their places at wages 50 per cent higher. This is because both the hours and the speed were increased continuously so that women were physically unable to perform the task.

The task system, it is said, has two advantages: The men work substantially by piecework and have a personal inducement to perform their work as quickly as they can, and, since they are in a team, each has to keep up with the others, so that a higher speed by anyone induces higher speed by the other two. So nicely are the members of these teams adjusted to each other that frequently a baster or an operator is out of work because, for the time being. he can not find the other two members whose speed is exactly fitted to his. By this queer cooperative production in the form of team work, combined with the personal interest of piecework, the Hebrew tailors in New York have devised what is, perhaps, the most ingenious and effective engine of overexertion known to modern industry.

One reason why piecework and high speed have become the framework of the contractors' shops is probably because the Jewish people are peculiarly eager to earn a big day's wages, no matter at what sacrifice. The Jewish workman is willing to work very hard for this, and does not want to have it said that there is a limit to his earning capacity. It is the desire of the Jew to have his employment so arranged that he can speculate and bargain upon his earning capacity, and can make use of the seasons. Piecework gives him that opportunity. In a rush season he will demand a decrease in the number of coats to the task, making more tasks per week and consequently earning higher wages. If the work is slack and the number of coats in the task is increased, he will speculate upon his ability to work harder and still earn high wages. Usually he is anxious to accumulate money and open up a contractor's shop for himself, or go into some kind of business. It is not for love of hard work nor because of lack of other enjoyment that the Jew is willing to work so hard, but for the sake of getting rid of work. At the same time it is true regarding green immigrants of all races that the conditions of a strange land stimulate them to the hottest exertion of which they are capable. The Jewish immigrant is peculiar only in that he is not by nature a wage-earner, and he keeps before himself continually the goal of emancipation from hard work.

This characteristic of the Jew shows itself in his irritation under the discipline of the factory. He is willing to work long hours, but does not like to have anyone dictate the time when he shall begin work or stop work. He does not like to be driven nor have his attention called to the fact that he has not made much work. He wants to have freedom. This he usually has in the contractor's shop. He is very nearly "his own boss;" he can smoke, talk, run around, stay at work an hour longer, come in an hour earlier, or come later. The conditions of sweatshop employment which favor this are piecework, with an almost complete absence of factory regulations and factory management. The contractor's shop is a sort of ideal worked out by this individualistic people, which holds out a fair hope to everybody of some day becoming his own boss, and, to a certain extent, of being his own boss while still at work in the shop. It is mostly from the employees of the contractors' shops that the contractors themselves are recruited, and it is from both the employees and from the contractors that the better class of help in the clothing trade, such as designers, is recruited. It is also from these same people that the small clothing manufacturer starts out, building his trade up until he becomes a large clothing manufacturer.

Following is the schedule, in detail, of a typical shop of the task system. In explanation of this schedule it is necessary to describe the usual method of figuring the contractor's interest in the amount of work done. It is as follows:

Out of not less than $15 worth of work, which the contractor takes out from the manufacturer, he pays $3 to the operator; $2.66 to the baster; $2 to the finisher or edge baster. In addition to this he has to pay for sewing on buttons, felling armholes and bottoms, tacking pockets, trimming the coat and pressing, expressage, rent, oil, and repair for machines, etc.

The pressing is usually done by the piece, at the rate of 8 cents per piece for a 75-cent coat; the presser would get $1.60 to $1.80 out of the $15.

The women who fell the sleeves, at home, usually would get 80 cents to $1.

The busheling, trimming, and fitting is usually done by a man, who gets from $12 to $15 per week, working at the rate of 4 to 6 cents for a 75-cent coat, or 80 cents on the $15 worth of work.

The girls who sew buttons on, in the shop, usually get from $4 to $7 a week.

TABLE 32.—*Cost and profit of contractor, on task system.*

[Per task of $15 worth of work.]

Operator	$3.00
Baster	2.66
Edge baster	2.00
Presser	1.60
Sewing on buttons and tacking	.60
Felling	.80
Fitting and busheling	1.00
Buttonholes	.48
Expressage	.30
Total	12.44

Leaving a profit of $2.56 on each task. With three sets the balance would be $7.68 per day, and for 4½ days' work per week, $34.56. Out of this the contractor must pay about $6 rent per week, and $3 for oil and repairs, leaving a net profit for the week of 4½ days of $25.56.

ESTABLISHMENT NO. 1.

[Task system: New York; coat shop; foot power; contractor, Jew; employees, Jews; 19 employees, in 3 sets; 300 coats per week; 72 hours per week; system introduced about 1877.]

	Cents.
Contract price	75
Labor cost	59.3
Average wages per hour	15.1

	Hour.	Week.	Two-thirds year.	Average per week per year.
	Cents.			
Operator's wages	20.9	$15.00	$520.00	$10.00
Baster's wages	18.4	13.00	450.00	8.66
Edge baster's wages	13.8	10.00	346.00	6.66
Presser's wages	16.6	12.00	416.00	8.00

	h.	m.
Time per coat	3	55
Operator's time per coat		43
Baster's time per coat		43
Edge baster's time per coat		43
Presser's time per coat		28

Individual occupations in establishment No. 1.

Number.	Occupation.	Nationality.	Sex.	Week or piece.	Cost per coat.	Earnings per week.	Total earnings per week for the occupation.
					Cents.		
3	Operator	Jew	Male	Piece	15	$15.00	$45.00
3	Baster	....do	....do	....do	13.3	13.30	39.90
3	Edge baster or finisher	....do	....do	....do	10	10.00	30.00
2	Presser	....do	....do	....do	8	12.00	24.00
1	Trimmer and busheler (contractor).	....do	....do	....do	6		18.00
1	Buttons and tacking	....do	Female	....do	3	9.00	9.00
¹6	Outside finishing (felling).	Italian	....do	....do	4	2.00	12.00
19						59.3	177.90

¹ Estimated equivalent to 3.3 inside finishers at 10 hours per week.

While the task system displaced the journeyman tailor in the manufacture of ready-made coats, it has itself in the past 5 years met a competitor in the factory or large shop, described below as establishment No. 2. In this contest the task system appears to be antiquated and uneconomical. During the 25 years of its existence in New York it shows no material change. The division of labor is but slightly different from what it was originally. We now have the operator, baster, and edge baster or finisher, with a helper or two in each branch of work, just the same as formerly, except that the edge baster or finisher is now a man, while originally this work was done by women. But the task itself, instead of being 8 or 10 coats, is now 20 to 24 coats. The workmen make up in overexertion what they lack in shop organization and division of labor. The team system lacks elasticity and the power of expansion. The division of labor can go no further than to pass the coat through the hands of not to exceed 9 or 10 persons. If the shop grows in size the growth is not organic—it is segmentary. It can not add a man here and a girl there, but must add an entire team—in fact, it must add 3 teams in order economically to adjust the work of the 2 pressers.

There has, indeed, been a cumbersome attempt during the past 10 years to introduce a further division of labor in the task system. It consists in a curious reduplication of the team. The operator in the original team becomes the first operator, who does the parts requiring more careful work. He takes with him another man, called "two-thirds of an operator," who does operator's work requiring less skill, and who is paid two-third wages, and still a third man, called "one-third of an operator," who does the least skillful work and gets one-third pay. The same threefold division is made for the baster and edge baster, so that there is also a "whole baster," a "two-thirds baster," and a "one-third baster." A shop of this kind is called, not a three-team shop, but a "two-team" shop, since it requires a whole man plus a two-thirds man plus a one-third man to make two "whole men." This awkward subdivision is not making headway, but the entire task system is yielding to the more elastic and organic factory system.

VIII. THE FACTORY SYSTEM.

Quite recently what may be described as a factory system has been introduced in a few establishments in New York. This is known in the trade as the "Boston system" in order to distinguish it from the task system which is peculiar to New York. It is not really a "Boston system," since it is found also in Philadelphia, Chicago, and elsewhere, but it has been slow to gain a foothold in New York because the task system has met it by its unique capacity for overexertion. Now that it has been introduced on the basis of New York's wages and standards of exertion those contractors who have adopted it are confident of its future. The "factory" employs 50 to 200 persons, where the task system employs 10 to 20. It has a minute division of labor and an elasticity of expansion far beyond that of the task system. The following schedule of Establishment No. 2 represents this system. This is a shop employing 104 people and making 1,650 coats per week, at 75 cents each.

THE FACTORY SYSTEM. 349

ESTABLISHMENT NO. 2.

[Factory system: New York; coat shop; steam power; contractor, Jew; employees, Jews and Italians; 104 employees in one system; 1,650 coats per week; 60 hours per week; system introduced about 1897.]

	Cents.
Contract price	75
Labor cost	55.7
Average wages per hour	14.7

	Hour.	Week.	Two-thirds year.	Average per week per year.
	Cents.			
Operator's wages	20.1	$12.00	$416.00	$8.00
Baster's wages	15.1	9.06	308.04	5.92
Presser's wages	22	13.20	457.60	8.80

	h.	m
Time per coat	3	41
Operator's time per coat		57
Baster's time per coat		54
Presser's time per coat		21

Individual occupations in establishment No. 2.

Number.	Occupation.	Nationality.	Sex.	Week or piece.	Earnings.	Total earnings for the occupation.
1	Pocket maker	Jew	Male	Week	$17.00	$17.00
1	....do	....do	....do	....do	15.00	15.00
1	....do	....do	....do	....do	14.00	14.00
3	....do	....do	....do	Piece	.06	48.00
1	Sewing in sleeves	....do	....do	Week	16.00	16.00
1	Sewing around	....do	....do	....do	17.00	17.00
1	....do	....do	....do	....do	15.00	15.00
1	Seamer	....do	....do	....do	12.00	12.00
1	Stitching coat	....do	....do	....do	12.00	12.00
1	....do	....do	....do	....do	10.00	10.00
1	Stitching bottoms on lining	....do	....do	....do	7.00	7.00
1	Sewing around pockets	....do	....do	....do	6.00	6.00
1	Stitching under collars	Italian	....do	....do	6.00	6.00
1	Lining maker	Jew	....do	....do	14.00	14.00
2	....do	....do	....do	....do	10.00	20.00
2	....do	....do	....do	....do	9.00	18.00
1	....do	....do	....do	....do	8.00	8.00
1	....do	....do	....do	....do	6.50	6.50
1	Stitching canvas	....do	....do	....do	3.00	3.00
2	General hand	....do	....do	....do	17.00	34.00
1	Piping facing	....do	....do	....do	15.00	15.00
26						313.50
	Basting and edge basting.					
1	Head baster	Jew	Male	Week	14.00	14.00
2	....do	....do	....do	....do	13.00	26.00
2	....do	....do	....do	....do	12.00	12.00
1	....do	....do	....do	....do	11.00	11.00
4	Edge baster	....do	....do	....do	10.00	40.00
1	Canvas baster	....do	....do	....do	10.00	10.00
1	....do	....do	....do	....do	6.00	6.00
2	....do	....do	Female	....do	8.00	16.00
1	Shoulder baster	....do	....do	....do	7.50	7.50
1	....do	....do	Male	....do	7.00	7.00
1	Pairing sleeves	....do	....do	....do	12.00	12.00
2	Padding lapels	Italian	Female	....do	4.50	9.00
1	Under presser	Jew	Male	....do	9.00	9.00
3	....do	....do	....do	....do	8.00	24.00
1	....do	....do	....do	....do	7.00	7.00
25						226.00
10	Presser	Jew	Male	Piece	.08	132.00

Industrial occupations in establishment No. 2—Continued.

Number.	Occupation.	Nationality.	Sex.	Week or piece.	Earnings.	Total earnings for the occupation.
	Busheling and trimming.					
1	Foreman	Jew	Male	Week	$17.00	$17.00
1	Shorter	do	do	do	15.00	15.00
1	Lining cutter	do	do	do	11.00	11.00
2	Trimming small lots	do	do	do	12.00	24.00
2	Busheler	do	do	do	12.00	24.00
1	do	do	do	do	7.00	7.00
9						113.00
	Sewing buttons and tacking.					
8	Buttons and tacking	Jew	Female	Week	6.00	48.00
1	do	German	do	do	7.00	7.00
1	do	Italian	do	do	5.00	5.00
3	Pulling bastings	do	Boy	do	3.00	3.00
13						69.00
	Felling ("outside" finishing).					
18	Felling	Italian	Female	Piece	.04	56.56
3	do	Jew	do	do	.04	9.44
21						66.00
104						919.00

This particular shop, chosen as establishment No. 2, has been selected because it is known in the trade throughout the country as able to produce the cheapest coat of this kind. It is claimed by competing contractors in New York and other cities that contractor No. 2 enjoys his superiority because he employs immigrant labor and gets it very cheaply; but it can safely be said, after a careful examination of the trade in general, that the better grades of labor on this grade of work are paid more per hour in this shop than any other place in the country. Also, the employees are working 10 hours a day instead of 12, 13, and 14 hours, as is done in competing shops. As regards the employing of immigrant labor, contractor No. 2 employs labor that has probably been in this country longer and has had better training than the majority of the trade outside. The advantage which this establishment has over other shops is in the mode of production. With its minute division of labor, skilled labor is employed where skill is required, and unskilled labor where less skill is required.

The labor cost on a coat, on the basis of 10 hours' work a day, in establishment No. 2, is 55.7 cents. The labor cost on a coat in establishment No. 1, where the division of labor is not so minute, is 59.3 cents, giving No. 2 an advantage of nearly 4 cents.

The time required to make the coat in establishment No. 2 is 3 hours 41 minutes, as compared with 3 hours 55 minutes, in the case of No. 1, giving No. 2 an advantage of 14 minutes per coat.

If the wages are compared in their several divisions it will be found that the average earnings of operators in establishment No. 2 are 20.1 cents per hour, working 10 hours per day, or $12 per week; while in establishment No. 1 the operator earns 20.9 cents per hour, working 12 hours, or $15 per week.

But establishment No. 2 has 26 operators of widely different skill, whereas the operators in No. 1 are of equal skill. We should compare the operators in No. 2 who are of the highest skill with those in No. 1 whose skill is the same. In doing this we find that out of the 26 operators in No. 2 there are 7 men who earn $15 to $17 a week, working 10 hours a day, while in establishment No. 1 the operators of the same skill are working for $15, 12 hours per day. There are also in No. 2 two men at $14 a week, working 10 hours per day, making their wages per hour higher than the men who work 12 hours a day for $15 a week in No. 1. Even the 2 men on the schedule who earn $12 a week each are earning about the same wages per hour as the best in establishment No. 1.

The same thing holds true with regard to the baster. The baster in establishment No. 1 gets on an average 18.4 cents per hour, working 12 hours a day, amounting to about $13 per week, while the baster in establishment No. 2 gets 15.1 cents per hour. But in the case of No. 2 the baster includes the edge baster also on the basis

THE FACTORY SYSTEM. 351

of 15.1 cents, while in No. 1 the edge baster gets only 13.8 cents per hour; so that if in establishment No. 1 the baster and the edge baster were combined and an average drawn as in No. 2, it would be found that the basters get about the same amount in both cases. When the wages for the baster are computed it will be found that in No. 2 there is one man who gets $14 a week, working 10 hours, while the skilled baster in establishment No. 1 gets only $13 a week, working 12 hours a day.

With regard to the edge baster or finisher we find that in the case of No. 1 the skilled finisher works 12 hours a day in order to earn $10 a week. In establishment No. 2 there are 2 skilled finishers who get $10 and $12, working only 10 hours a day, and others at $9, $8, and $7, while there are 2 at $8 a week who earn per hour about the same and even a trifle more than the skilled basters in establishment No. 1.

But the output of the basters is about 60 per cent greater. The basters in establishment No. 2 baste a coat in 54 minutes as against 86 minutes in No. 1. Consequently, while establishment No. 2 pays even better wages for skilled labor than does establishment No. 1, and requires the employees to work only 10 hours per day, as compared with 12 hours in the latter case, they are able to produce a coat cheaper than establishment No. 1. On both the question of wages for skilled help and the question of time consumed per coat No. 2 has the advantage.

In view of the counter argument which would naturally suggest itself that, granting establishment No. 2, with its factory system, pays higher wages to a few extra-skilled employees, yet this is likely to be counterbalanced by the larger proportion of cheap help, the following comparison is offered: Taking an average wage of $9 per week as the dividing line between cheap help and skilled help, and calling those who receive $9 and less per week the cheap help and those receiving over $9 the skilled help, it will be seen from the schedule that establishment No. 1 has 9 employees, or 47 per cent of the whole number, receiving more than $9, and 10 employees, or 53 per cent of the whole number, receiving $9 or less; and establishment No. 2 has 48 employees, or 46 per cent of the whole number, receiving over $9 per week, and 56 employees, or 54 per cent of the whole number, receiving $9 or less per week. In other words, in establishment No. 1 53 per cent of the employees are cheap help, and in establishment No. 2 54 per cent of the employees are cheap help. The proportions between skilled and cheap help in each establishment are practically identical.

The reasons for the cheaper cost of production and the better conditions in establishment No. 2 are to be found in the greater skill and speed acquired where the labor is minutely divided. A man who makes only pockets can make more pockets and better pockets than the man who makes a whole coat, and moreover he can do this without the basting required by the latter, thus reducing the time and cost of the operation. As a consequence the pocket makers in the large shops earn about $16 per week working 10 hours a day, while the first-class skilled operator in the small shop will have to work 12 hours per day in order to make $15 per week. The same thing is true with regard to the man who sews around coats or stitches coats. More efficiency and skill are acquired by doing one thing, and higher wages are earned, even though working a less number of hours per week.

It is generally claimed in the trade by people who are running large shops like No. 2 that the only advantage which the small contractor has over them is in running his shop for unlimited hours. It will be seen from the schedule that this idea is verified in figures. Establishment No. 2 pays as good and even better wages than No. 1, and produces a coat in less time and at less cost per coat with 10 hours work, than No. 1 with 12 hours a day. If the labor of all shops were limited to 10, either through the strength of a labor union or through legislation, the following would probably be the result: Shop No. 1 would be compelled to increase the wages of its employees 20 per cent in order to enable them to earn the same wages in 10 hours that they now earn in 12 hours. This, on the assumption that the intensity of exertion would not be increased, would increase the cost of the operating and basting 20 per cent. This assumption is not wholly valid, because, with increased energy, owing to shorter hours, the increased cost would not be quite as great. The present cost of operating and basting is 46.3 per cent per coat, and an increase of 20 per cent would be 9.3 cents. Even now shop No. 2 has an advantage of 5 cents on a coat, and an increase of 9.3 cents would bring the advantage up to 14.9 cents per coat. With such a difference, or even with less difference in the cost of production, the task system would disappear before the factory system.

A probable reason which may be mentioned why shops of this kind have not come into the trade more largely is that the Jews do not submit graciously to this form of production. Establishment No. 2 must enforce discipline; everybody must be on time. There is not as much freedom as in the small contractor's shop. Many Jewish operators, basters, and edge basters would prefer to work 12 hours a day in a shop where they could have freedom than 10 hours in a shop where discipline is an essential part of the mode of production.

Another reason why establishment No. 2 has not developed further is because of the amount of money required to establish it. The contractor who can save $2,000 usually invests it in the manufacture of clothing himself. He claims that there is not much money for the contractor who is working for a clothing manufacturer, but there is money in manufacturing for oneself, even on a small scale, utilizing the labor of the small contractor. Consequently, contractors, instead of investing their money in larger contractor's shops, have made a practice of beginning to manufacture clothing themselves on a small scale. There has, indeed, been a number of large manufacturers who have established just such shops as establishment No. 2, known as "inside shops" to distinguish them from the contractors' shops. But it seems that a manufacturer can not produce a 75-cent coat in the large factory quite as cheaply as the contractor can produce such a coat in the large factory. A hired superintendent is not usually able to obtain as cheap results as those obtained by a skillful contractor. But in these large inside shops a better grade of coat, costing $1.50 to $3, is made to great advantage, while the 75-cent coat (and the great majority of coats are from 62½ cents to $1) is made in shops of the class of establishment No. 1. Probably 50 per cent of the 75-cent coats are made in shops of this class and the rest is distributed through other shops, leaving probably not more than 5 per cent of the 75-cent coats in establishments like No. 2.

ESTABLISHMENT NO. 3.

[Percentage system: New York; coat shop; steam power; contractor, Lithuanian; employees, Lithuanians. 57 employees in 10 teams; 600 coats per week; operators and button sewers, 10 hours; others, 11 hours.]

	Cents.
Contractor's price	75
Labor cost	67.5
Average wages per hour	12.7

	Hour.	Week.	Two-thirds year.	Average per week per year.
	Cents.			
Operator's wages	18.7	$11.22	$388.92	$7.46
Baster's wages	13.6	9.00	312.00	6.00
Edge baster's wages	9.16	6.05	208.00	4.00
Presser's wages	16.9	11.20	388.23	7.46

	Cents.
Cost of operating per coat	18.7
Cost of basting per coat	25.5
Cost of pressing per coat	9.3

	h.	m.
Time per coat	5	16
Operator's time per coat	1	0
Baster's time per coat	1	6
Edge baster's time per coat	1	6
Presser's time per coat	0	33

Individual occupations in establishment No. 3.

Number.	Occupation.	Nationality.	Sex.	Week or piece.	Cost per coat.	Earnings per week.	Total earnings per week for the occupation.
					Cents.		
10	Operator	Lithuanian	Male	Piece	18.7	$11.22	$112.20
10	Baster	....do	....do	....do	15.0	9.00	90.00
10	Edge baster	....do	....do	....do	10.5	6.05	60.50
1	Presser	....do	....do	Week		14.00	14.00
1	....do	....do	....do	....do	9.3	12.00	12.00
3	....do	....do	....do	....do		10.00	30.00
2	Foreman and contractor.	....do	....do	....do	5.0	15.00	30.00
5	Buttons and tacking	....do	Female	....do	5.0	6.00	30.00
15	Outside finishers [1]	Italian	....do	Piece	4.0		24.00
57					67.5		402.70

[1] Estimated equivalent to 8 inside finishers at 10 hours per day.

FACTORIES AND SWEATSHOPS. 353

Establishment No. 3 is a Lithuanian shop in Brooklyn. The people employed in this class of shops number several hundred. The mode of production is quite similar to that in the Jewish task-system shop. Indeed, the Lithuanians probably learned their peculiar division of labor from the Jews. They came from the same localities in Russia, and a number of them speak the jargon of the Jews. Like the shop described in schedule No. 1, which makes almost the same class of work, the Lithuanians have an operator, a baster, and an edge baster or finisher, in teams. They work with steam power, in shops of 10 machines and more. The earnings are divided in about the same way as in the Jewish shops, except that the contractor gets a smaller share. Out of $15 worth of work the operator gets 25 per cent, or $3.75; the baster gets 34 per cent and pays, in turn, the edge baster or finisher 40 per cent, so that out of the $15 worth of work the baster gets $3.06 and the edge baster gets $2.04. Together the operator, baster, and finisher get $8.85 out of the $15 worth of work, instead of the $7.66 received by the team in the Jewish shop. Therefore the labor cost on a 75-cent coat is 67.5 cents instead of 59.3 cents, leaving the contractor a balance of 8 cents, instead of about 15 cents in the case of the Jewish shop.

Probably the reason why these Lithuanian contractors can manage on 8 cents instead of 15 cents is because their shops are usually larger, having 10 or more machines instead of 3.

Notwithstanding the smaller share of the contractor and a piece price per coat 14 per cent higher than that of the Jewish team in the task shop of establishment No. 1, yet the Lithuanian earnings are smaller than those of the Jews. This is partly because the Jews work longer hours and partly because they are quicker and more intense in their work. The Lithuanians are mainly large and robust men, but are not so well adapted to the rapid and artistic kind of work required in the sewing trade.

The Jewish operator is able to make a coat in 43 minutes, while the Lithuanian operator requires an hour to make the same coat, so that while the price for labor paid to the Lithuanian is higher, yet, since he works so much slower, his earnings are less. In the Jewish shop the operator earns $15 per week, working 12 hours per day, as against the Lihuanian operator $11.22 for 10 hours' work.

The same facts are true with regard to the baster and edge baster (or finisher). In the Lithuanian shop it will be seen that the baster receives 13.6 cents per hour, while the baster in the Jewish shop earns 18.4 cents per hour. The Lithuanian edge baster earns 9.2 cents per hour; the Jewish edge baster earns 13.8 cents per hour. The earnings of the presser are about the same in both shops, although the Jewish presser, who works by the piece, gets a somewhat smaller percentage than the Lithuanian, who works by the week. Pressing requires a good deal of hard physical labor and less skill than operating or finishing, and although the Lithuanians, who are stronger than the Jews, get a higher price per piece, yet they earn about the same wages per week.

Comparing the wages on the basis of 8 months worked during the year, it will be seen that when the Lithuanian machine operator earns $11.20 a week while working 10 hours a day, or $387.96 a year, his average weekly wages for the year are $7.46. The Jewish operator in establishment No. 1, on the other hand, while working 12 hours a day, earns $15 a week. On the basis of 8 months worked during the year he earns an average of $10 per week or $520 per year. But making a comparison between the two nationalities on the basis of a 10-hour day, it is seen that the Jewish operator under the task system working 10 hours per day earns $12 per week, in contrast to the Lithuanian who earns $11.20. This shows a difference in the earning capacity of the two nationalities of 7.25 per cent in favor of the Jewish operator. When, however, the element of time is introduced, the difference is more pronounced. The Jew, working 12 hours instead of 10, or an increase of 20 per cent in time over the Lithuanian, earns $520, or $10 a week, in contrast to $387.96, or $7.46 a week, which is an increase of 34.03 per cent. In other words, the two nationalities, working the same number of hours on virtually the same kind of work, show a difference in earning capacity of 7.25 per cent in favor of the Jewish workman. But the Jew, by working 20 per cent longer, is able to earn 34.03 per cent more than the Lithuanian.

The same difference between the nationalities is brought out in an examination of the basters. The Jewish baster in establishment No. 1 earns $13 per week when working 12 hours a day, or $10 a week for a 10-hour day. The Lithuanian baster in establishment No. 3 earns $9 per week on the basis of 10 hours. In the same class of work and for the same time there is thus a difference of 11 per cent in the wages earned, in favor of the Jew.

Introducing the element of time, the difference is more marked. By working 12 hours per day instead of 10, or an increase cf 20 per cent, the Jew earns $13 per week or $450 per year for 8 months, and $8.66 per week for the year, which is a net increase of 44.33 per cent over the earnings of the Lithuanian.

354   THE INDUSTRIAL COMMISSION:—IMMIGRATION.

The difference is further brought out in comparing the finishers or edge basters. In the Jewish shop the earnings per week for a 12-hour day are $10, or for 8 months $346.32, and an average of $6.66 for the year; while for a 10-hour day they are $8 per week. The difference in earnings between these nationalities, taking the 10-hour day, is, then. 32.36 per cent in favor of the Jew; while taking the Jew on the basis of the 12-hour day, in comparison with the 10-hour day of the Lithuanian, the difference in earnings is 65.70 per cent in favor of the Jew. The presser, getting $11.20 a week, or $388 per year, will average during the year $7.46 per week.

It will be seen that this Lithuanian labor, while receiving per coat 14 per cent higher piece price, is able to earn less wages per week, showing that cheap labor is not really cheap in all cases. This Lithuanian team system, while it suffers in comparison with the Jewish team system, suffers still more in comparison with the factory system. It represents but a remnant of the clothing manufacture and must necessarily disappear before the greater economy of a more minute subdivision of labor. It must be added that the majority of these men receiving $4 to $7.46 per week for the year are married men, living in a large city, with families to support.

ESTABLISHMENT No. 4.

[Factory system: Chicago; coat shop; steam power; contractor, Jew; employees, Polish women and girls; 32 employees in one system; 400 coats per week; 60 hours per week; system introduced about 1892.]

	Cents.
Contractor's price	75
Labor cost	58.4
Average wages per hour	12.2

	Hour.	Week.	Two-thirds year.	Average per week per year.
	Cents.			
Operator's wages	13.2	$7.92	$274.56	$5.28
Baster's wages	13.2	7.92	274.56	5.28
Presser's wages	17.7	10.62	368.16	7.08

	Cents.
Cost of operating	23.7
Cost of basting	13.9
Cost of pressing	8

	h.	m.
Time per coat	4	48
Operator's time per coat	1	48
Baster's time per coat	1	3
Presser's time per coat		27

Individual occupations in establishment No. 4.

Number.	Occupation.	Nationality.	Sex.	Week or piece.	Earnings.	Total earnings for the occupation.
	Operators.					
1	Sewing in sleeves	Pole	Female	Week	$9.50	$9.50
1	....do	....do	....do	....do	9.00	9.00
1	Sewing round	....do	....do	....do	8.00	8.00
3	Sewing pockets	....do	....do	....do	8.50	25.50
1	....do	German	....do	....do	8.50	8.50
2	Sewing linings	Pole	....do	....do	6.00	12.00
1	....do	....do	....do	....do	6.50	6.50
1	....do	....do	....do	....do	5.00	5.00
1	Stitching coat	....do	Male	....do	11.00	11.00
12						95.00
1	Head baster	....do	Female	....do	10.00	10.00
1	....do	....do	....do	....do	9.00	9.00
1	Edge baster	....do	....do	....do	7.00	7.00
3	....do	....do	....do	....do	6.50	19.50
1	Under presser	....do	Male	....do	10.00	10.00
7						55.50
3	Pressers	....do	....do	Piece	.08	32.00

FACTORIES AND SWEATSHOPS. 355

Individual occupations in establishment No. 4—Continued.

Number.	Occupation.	Nationality.	Sex.	Week or piece.	Earnings.	Total earnings for the occupation.
	Trimming and busheling.					
1	Trimming	Pole	Male	Week	$12.00	$12.00
1	Busheling	Jew	do	do	9.00	9.00
2						21.00
	Buttons and tacking	Pole	Female	do	2.50	10.00
3	Felling (outside finishing)	do	do	do	5.00	15.00
1	do	Jew	do	Piece	.05	5.00
4						20.00
32						233.50

Establishment No. 4 is the shop of a Jewish contractor, employing in the main Polish female help. It is this class of shops that are the most formidable competitors in the trade in Chicago. Contractors who have entered this business, employing this class of help, have been quite prosperous.

If schedule No. 4 is compared with schedule No. 1 it will be seen that the labor on a coat is 58.4 cents as against 59.3 cents in the task shop, and it has an advantage of less than 1 cent per coat. Probably even this advantage is offset by the difference in the quality of the coat. The Jewish operators and basters are better trained and the coats made in the Jewish shops are on the whole more artistic and have a better appearance.

Comparing the different divisions as to the price of labor it will be seen that the advantage is rather on the side of establishment No. 1, with Jewish help. The cost of operating in the case of No. 4 is 23.7 cents, while in the case of No. 1 it is only 15 cents per coat.

The time required for operating in establishment No. 4 is 1 hour 40 minutes, but the time required for operating in establishment No. 1 is only 43 minutes. The principal saving in No. 4 is in the basting, and as it is the basting that indicates quality, this saving is somewhat effected at the expense of quality. The cost of basting in the case of No. 1 is 23.3 cents, while in the case of No. 4 it is 13.9 cents.

When the wages and income of No. 4 and No. 1 are compared, it will be seen that the advantage is in favor of the Jewish shop. In No. 1 the operator will earn per hour nearly 21 cents, while in No. 4 she will earn only about 13 cents.

The baster in No. 1 will earn per hour 18 cents, while in No. 4 the baster will earn only about 13 cents. The Jewish task shop has the advantage both in wages and in cost per coat, considering the quality, compared with the factory system employing girls, even though the latter are good, steady help working for small wages.

But when establishment No. 4 is compared with establishment No. 2, the advantage is on the side of No. 2, namely, the Jewish shop employing men under the factory system. The difference is about as follows:

Comparison of establishments Nos. 4 and 2.

Establishment.	Labor cost per coat.	All employees.		Operator.		Baster and edge baster.	
		Average wages.	Time per coat.	Average wages.	Average time consumed.	Average wages.	Time consumed.
	Cents.	*Cents.*	*h. m.*	*Cents.*	*h. m.*	*Cents.*	*h. m.*
No. 4	58.4	12.2	4 48	13.2	1 40	13.1	1 03
No. 2	55	14.7	3 41	20.1	57	15.1	54

Establishment No. 2, therefore, has the advantage at every point, showing that while the labor of women is cheaper per hour and per week than that of men, the labor cost on a garment is less in the shop employing men, even when paid almost double the wages paid the women. This will be further shown in a number of cases as the schedules are followed up. The reason why the contractors employing Polish women have been able to crowd out the shops employing Jewish men in Chicago is probably because these contractors first introduced the factory system rather than because they employed Polish women. It was the factory system and not the Polish women that threw the Jewish shops out of business, and when the factory system is introduced in a Jewish shop the Jewish operator and baster, even at much higher wages, evidently can hold their own in competition and can produce a coat just as cheaply as can be done with female labor.

The characteristics of the Jews already mentioned will partially explain why they permitted themselves to be driven out of business rather than establish the factory system. They prefer work in the small shop so as to avoid the discipline which naturally accompanies the large factory. There is a change now taking place in Chicago in the large shops where Jews are employed, and the division of labor is being introduced in the better grades of work.

Probably another reason why the Jews and Bohemians have been driven out and replaced by Poles is because both the Jews and Bohemians were given to forming unions and going on strikes and insisting on their price for labor. The Poles have worked while the others were on strike, so that clothing manufacturers encouraged very strongly the Polish shops, even while they were learning the trade, so as to successfully defeat the tailors' unions.

ESTABLISHMENT No. 5.

[Factory system: Brooklyn; coat shop; steam power; contractor, Jew; employees, Poles, Jews, Italians; 50 employees in one system; 3,000 coats per week; 66 hours per week; system established about 1897.]

	Cents
Contract price (lined coat)	19
Labor cost	16.1
Average wages per hour	14.7

	Hour.	Week.	Two-thirds year.	Average per week per year.
	Cents.			
Operator's wages	17.6	$11.62	$402.48	$7.74
Baster's wages	10.6	6.99	242.32	4.66
Presser's wages	14.4	9.50	328.64	6.32

	Cents.
Cost of operating	9.6
Cost of basting	.5
Cost of pressing	3.2
Cost of trimming and busheling	1.1

	h.	m.
Time per coat	1	6
Operator's time per coat		33
Baster's time per coat	2.	6
Presser's time per coat		13

Individual occupations in establishment No. 5.

Number.	Occupation.	Nationality.	Sex.	Week or piece.	Earnings.	Total earnings for the occupation.
1	Sleeve maker	Jew	Male	Week	$7.50	$7.50
1	....do	....do	....do	....do	8.00	8.00
3	Pocket maker	....do	....do	....do	12.00	36.00
7	....do	Pole	....do	....do	12.00	84.00
1	Lining maker	Jew	....do	....do	11.00	11.00
4	....do	Pole	....do	....do	11.00	44.00
5	....do	....do	....do	....do	10.00	50.00
1	Sewing around	....do	....do	....do	17.00	17.00
1	Stitching	Jew	....do	....do	16.00	16.00
1	Sewing in sleeves	Pole	....do	....do	16.00	16.00
25						289.50

Individual occupations in establishment No. 5—Continued.

Number.	Occupation.	Nationality.	Sex.	Week or piece.	Earnings.	Total earnings for the occupation.
1	Under presser	Pole	Male	Week	$7.00	$7.00
1	....do	Italian	....do	....do	7.00	7.00
1	Off presser	Pole	....do	....do	5.00	5.00
3	....do	....do	....do	....do	10.00	30.00
2	....do	Jew	....do	....do	11.00	22.00
2	....do	....do	....do	....do	12.00	24.00
10						95.00
2	Baster	Italian	Male	Week	7.00	14.00
1	Trimmer	Pole	....do	....do	18.00	18.00
1	Busheler	....do	....do	....do	16.00	16.00
2						34.00
1	Felling armholes	Pole	Female	Week	5.00	30.00
2	Sewing buttons	....do	....do	....do	5.00	10.00
1	....do	Jew	....do	....do	4.00	4.00
1	Turning over coat	....do	Male	....do	3.00	3.00
1	....do	....do	....do	....do	5.00	5.00
11						52.00
48						484.50

Establishment No. 5 produces what is probably the cheapest lined coat in the United States, namely, a coat trimmed, stitched, pressed, felled, buttonholes made, and buttons sewed on and ready for the customer, for 19 cents. The cost of production on this class of goods has fallen more than in any other branch of clothing manufacture, the present contract price being 19 cents compared with a price of 40 to 45 cents 10 years ago.

The striking characteristics of this shop are its minute division of labor and the amazing speed of the workmen. Each man does one particular kind of work, in which he develops great skill and high speed. It is possible for the operator to do fairly good work without the help of the baster. Consequently the cost of basting each coat is only one-half cent, compared with 23.3 cents in the task shop No. 1, and 13.7 cents in the factory shop No. 2. The baster's time is only 2.6 minutes, compared with 43 minutes in No. 1 and 54 minutes in No. 2. Of course, this elimination of the baster depreciates the quality of the coat, but it is compensated to a remarkable extent by the increased skill of the operator.

The entire time required for a coat is only 1 hour 6 minutes, compared with 3 hours 55 minutes in No. 1 and 3 hours 41 minutes in No. 2. The total labor cost is 16.1 cents, compared with 59.3 cents in No. 1 and 55.7 cents in No. 2.

Immigrant and green labor can only come into this shop partially, since it requires trained men to keep up the speed that has been developed. More actual work per hour by the individual is incorporated in a coat in this shop than in any other class of shop. Polish men operators have here developed equal, if not greater, speed than Jews are able to develop under similar conditions.

The Poles before immigrating to this country were farmers. They came from more robust stock than the Jews and their endurance is greater. When once they become a part of this machinery they develop enormous speed.

If we examine the wages we shall find that the average earnings per hour are but little less than the earnings in those shops which produce a better class of goods. The earnings per hour are 14.7 cents, compared with 15.1 cents in No. 1 and 14.7 cents in No. 2, which make 75-cent coats, and 11.8 cents in No. 11, which makes a $1.43 coat. These comparisons, however, are not quite parallel, since on the 19-cent coat there is more operating proportionate to the total cost than on the more expensive coats. If operators alone are compared it will be seen that these Polish operators receive 17.6 cents per hour, whereas the Jews in No. 1 receive 20.9 cents, and in No. 2, 20.1 cents. By the week the operators receive $7.50 to $17, the majority getting $10 to $12. The cheap cost of production does not result mainly from low wages compared with other shops but from a minute division of labor, steam power, and great skill and speed.

ESTABLISHMENT NO. 6.

[Factory system: Chicago; boys' coat shop; gas power; contractor, Pole; employees, Polish women and girls; 17 employees; 350 coats per week; 60 hours per week.]

	Cents.
Contract price (lined coat)	30
Labor cost	26
Average wages per hour	8.9

	Hour.	Week.	Two-thirds year.	Average per week per year.
	Cents.			
Operator's wages	7.5	$4.50	$156.00	$3.00
Baster's wages	9.1	5.46	189.28	3.64
Presser's wages	11.5	6.90	239.20	4.66

	Cents.
Cost of operating	10.3
Cost of basting	3.1
Cost of pressing	5.7

	h.	m.
Time per coat	2	27
Operator's time per coat	1	24
Baster's time per coat		20.6
Presser's time per coat		30

Individual occupations, establishment No. 6.

Number.	Occupation.	Nationality.	Sex.	Week or piece.	Earnings.	Total earnings for the occupation.
1	Sewing sleeves	Pole	Female	Week	$8.00	$8.00
1	Pocket maker	....do	....do	....do	6.00	6.00
1	....do	....do	....do	....do	5.00	5.00
2	Lining maker	....do	....do	....do	3.00	6.00
1	Sleeve maker	....do	....do	....do	3.00	3.00
1	Canvas maker	....do	....do	....do	2.00	2.00
1	Stitching coats	....do	....do	....do	6.00	6.00
8						36.00
1	Seam presser	....do	Male	....do	6.50	6.50
2	Off presser	....do	....do	Piece	.04	14.00
3						20.50
1	Baster	....do	Female	Week	6.00	6.00
1	....do	....do	....do	....do	5.00	5.00
2						11.00
1	Trimmer	....do	....do	....do	12.00	12.00
1	Felling armholes	....do	....do	....do	4.00	4.00
1	....do	....do	....do	....do	2.00	2.00
1	Sewing buttons	....do	....do	....do	4.00	4.00
1	Boy	....do	Male	....do	1.50	1.50
4						11.50
18						91.00

Establishment No. 6 employs female Polish help doing the main sewing and basting and produces the cheapest coat of that class of work that is made in Chicago. If we compare this establishment with No. 5, a shop doing similar work and employing the same nationality, but employing men instead of women, we shall see that the men have the advantage in cheapness of production. In establishment No. 6 the cost of operating is 10.3 cents while in No. 5 it is 9.6 cents. But there is even a greater advantage than can be seen from these figures, since No. 6, employing women, can not make the coat without basting, and the basting for the 350 coats costs about $11. It costs No. 5, employing men, almost nothing for basting, as all the work is done by machine. Yet the average wages of the men operators (17.6 cents per hour) are more than double the wages paid the women in establishment No. 6 (7.5 cents per hour).

The time consumed in operating a coat in establishment No. 5 is only 33 minutes, while with the women operators in No. 6 it is 1 hour 24 minutes—more than twice as much. If the time which is required for basting on this same grade of coats is taken into consideration the difference would be much larger. Consequently, while the girls work for less than half the wages the men receive, their cost of production is about one-third greater.

The average wages for the whole shop in the case of No. 5 are 14.7 cents per hour, while in the case of No. 6 they are 8.9 cents per hour. But the cost of producing the coat is 16.1 cents in No. 5 as against 26 cents in No. 6, showing that where men and women are of the same nationality, working the same number of hours, in each instance with machines propelled with power, the men are able to produce coats for nearly 40 per cent less than the women.

If establishment No. 6 is compared with establishment No. 4, both employing women, Polish shop No. 4 producing a 75-cent coat and Polish shop No. 6 producing a 30-cent coat, it will be seen that in No. 4 the wages are on an average 12.2 cents, while in No. 6 they are 8.9 cents, a difference of more than 3 cents per hour in favor of No. 4. This is probably due in the main to the fact that the help in No. 4 are more skillful and are working on a better grade of work.

It will also be seen that while there is a difference of 3 cents per hour between No. 6 and No. 4, due principally to the differences in skill, yet when two shops employing men are compared, namely, the shops making the 19-cent coat and the 75-cent coat, the average wages for the employees on the cheap coat and on the good coat are about the same, namely, 14.7 cents. This shows that men, by developing greater speed, can earn very nearly as much wages on cheaper grades of coats as they can on better grades of work, where it is not possible to develop such intense speed.

It is thus seen that in cheap coat making the enduring ability of the men is an important factor, and makes them able to compete successfully with female labor at cheaper rates. It is also true that the men stay at the trade longer and develop a capacity to work automatically, while women usually leave the trade after working 5 or 6 years.

Establishment No. 7.

[Successor to family shop: Chicago, coat shop; foot power; contractor, Bohemian; employees, Bohemian; 13 employees in one system; 120 coats per week; 60 hours per week.]

Contract price... $1.00
Labor cost.. .938
Average wages per hour... .144

	Hour.	Week.	Two-thirds year.	Average per week per year.
	Cents.			
Operator's wages	15.5	$9.30	$322.40	$6.20
Baster's wages	15.8	9.48	328.64	6.32
Presser's wages	18.3	10.98	380.64	7.32

	Cents.
Cost of operating per coat	23.2
Cost of basting per coat	47.4
Cost of pressing per coat	9.1

	h. m.
Time per coat	6 30
Operator's time per coat	1 30
Baster's time per coat	3 0
Presser's time per coat	30

Individual occupations, establishment No. 7.

Number.	Occupation.	Nationality.	Sex.	Week or piece.	Earnings.	Total earnings for the occupation.
1	Sewing sleeves	Bohemian	Female	Week	$12.00	$12.00
1	Making sleeves	do	do	do	10.00	10.00
1	Stitching canvas	do	do	do	6.00	6.00
3						28.00

Individual occupations, establishment No. 7—Continued.

Number.	Occupation.	Nationality.	Sex.	Week or piece.	Earnings.	Total earnings for the occupation.
1	Head baster	Bohemian	Male	Week	$16.00	$16.00
1	Second baster	do	do	do	12.00	12.00
2	Edge baster	do	Female	do	8.00	16.00
1	do	do	do	do	7.00	7.00
1	do	do	do	do	6.00	6.00
6						57.00
1	Presser	do	Male	do	11.00	11.00
2	Buttons, tacking, felling	do	Female	do	6.00	12.00
1	do	do	do	do	4.50	4.50
3						16.50
13						112.50

Establishment No. 7 represents a shop where Bohemian girls are employed as edge basters and machine operators and men as first basters and pressers. There is quite a large colony of these shops in Chicago, employing probably 5,000 people, making the better class of ready-made coats at 87½ cents to $1.25 for sack coats, and $1.25 to $2 for overcoats. The majority of them are small shops, with two or three machines, and not a very minute division of labor. From 12 to 20 people are employed, as a rule. It seems that these shops are not able to hold their own in the trade; they are successfully replaced by the shops employing Polish help, and also by the large shops employing the factory system.

It will be seen from the schedule that the time for a $1 coat is 6 hours and 30 minutes, as against 4 hours and 48 minutes for the 75-cent coat in schedule No. 4; showing that it takes the Bohemians a longer time relative to the rate of wages than it takes this factory shop. They are also insisting upon somewhat higher wages individually than the Poles. The Bohemian operators insist on getting 15.5 cents per hour, whereas the average wages of the Polish operators is 13.2 cents, and their ability to produce is greater than that of their Bohemian competitors. Gradually, therefore, the Bohemian girl is being crowded out by the Polish girl.

The same is true in the case of the baster. The baster in the Polish shop gets 13.2 cents per hour; in the Bohemian, 15.8 cents per hour.

With regard to the time required on a 75-cent coat, the Polish baster requires 1 hour and 3 minutes, while on the $1 coat the Bohemian requires 3 hours; showing that the ability to produce is much less in the shop where an intense division of labor is not employed than it is under the factory system with Polish help.

There is a tendency on the part of these Bohemians to go into the "special-order" trade, which has been quite largely introduced in Chicago, and so to put their ability into a calling where skill is required, and where, in the nature of things, the labor can not be so intensely divided as can be done in the manufacture of ready-made clothing. But even in the special-order trade the large shop, as will be seen in establishments 9 and 10, is successfully driving out the small shop.

ESTABLISHMENT NO. 8.

[Successor to family shop: Chicago; coat shop; gas power; contractor, German; employees German; 16 employees in one system; 75 coats per week; 60 hours per week.]

Contract price $1.75
Labor cost 1.47
Average wages per hour .... .115

	Hour.	Week.	Two-thirds year.	Average per week per year.
	Cents.			
Operator's wages	9.7	$5.82	$201.76	$3.88
Baster's wages	14	8.40	291.20	5.60
Presser's wages	16.6	9.96	345.28	6.64

FACTORIES AND SWEATSHOPS. 361

	Cents.
Cost of operating per coat	39.4
Cost of basting per coat	56
Cost of pressing per coat	27.3

	h.	m.
Time per coat	12	48
Operator's time per coat	4	41
Baster's time per coat	4	00
Presser's time per coat	1	36

Individual occupations, establishment No. 8.

Number.	Occupation.	Nationality.	Sex.	Week or piece.	Earnings.	Total earnings for the occupation.
1	Sewing sleeves	German	Female	Week	$9.00	$9.00
1	Stitching coats	do	do	do	8.00	8.00
1	Pocket maker	do	do	do	6.50	6.50
1	Inside pocket and lining	do	do	do	5.50	5.50
1	Stitching canvas, etc	do	do	do	3.50	3.50
1	....do	do	do	do	2.50	2.50
6						35.00
1	Head baster	do	Male	do	11.00	11.00
1	Second baster	Pole	do	do	10.00	10.00
1	Edge baster	German	Female	do	6.50	6.50
2	Sleeve baster, etc	do	do	do	7.50	15.00
1	Seam presser	do	Male	do	9.00	9.00
1	Presser	do	do	do	11.00	11.00
7						62.50
1	Trimming, etc., by contractor	do	do	Piece	.06	4.50
1	Buttons and tacking	do	Female	Week	6.00	6.00
1	Felling	do	do	do	2.50	2.50
2						8.50
16						110.50

What has been said with regard to the Bohemian shop holds good even in a better grade of work. Establishment No. 8 is a German shop, run by gas power, but is a small shop in the rear of a tenement house. The power has probably been introduced because the German girls are not willing to run sewing machines by foot power, as the Bohemian girls and Jewish men do. But the production is on a small scale, and the labor is not very much divided. It is said in the trade that these shops are being crowded out by the larger Polish shops, where the girls are more willing to "drive" their work.

It will be seen that it takes No. 8 12 hours and 48 minutes to make a $1.75 coat. Comparing the unit of time with the price of the product, it is seen that more time is required to every unit of price than in establishment No. 4, employing Polish girls. For example, it takes an operator 4 hours and 1 minute to operate a coat, and the baster 4 hours to baste a coat. But in establishment No. 4 it takes the operator only 1 hour and 40 minutes to operate a 75-cent coat, and the baster 1 hour and 3 minutes to baste a 75-cent coat. It will be seen, by taking into account the difference in quality, that the advantage is on the side of establishment No. 4.

The average earnings are on the side of No. 4. The operator in No. 4 earns on an average 13.2 cents an hour, while in No. 8 she only earns 9.7 cents per hour. On the other hand, the basters in No. 8 include 3 men, since the work requires higher skill than can be obtained by the employment of girls, and their wages are 14 cents per hour, compared with 13.2 cents in No. 4.

With regard, therefore, both to the amount of wages and the amount of time, the German small shop is at a disadvantage compared with the Jewish and Polish shops under the factory system.

362 THE INDUSTRIAL COMMISSION:—IMMIGRATION.

ESTABLISHMENT NO. 9.

[Custom work on factory system: Chicago; coat shop; gas power; contractor, Jew; employees, Jews, German, and Polish women; 35 employees in one system; 300 coats per week; 60 hours per week.]

Contract price $1.35
Labor cost 1.065
Average wages per hour .... .152

	Hour.	Week.	Two-thirds year.	Average per week per year.
	Cents.			
Operator's wages	15.2	$9.12	$316.16	$6.08
Baster's wages	17.4	10.44	361.92	6.96
Presser's wages	22.5	13.50	468.00	9.00

Cents.
Cost of operating per coat 30.4
Cost of basting per coat 34.8
Cost of pressing per coat 18

h. m.
Time per coat 7 0
Operator's time per coat 2 0
Baster's time per coat 2 0
Presser's time per coat   48

Individual occupations, establishment No. 9.

Number.	Occupation.	Nationality.	Sex.	Week or piece.	Earnings.	Total earnings for the occupation.
1	Sewing in sleeves	Jew	Male	Week ...	$16.00	$16.00
1	Making pockets	....do	....do	....do ...	13.00	13.00
1	....do	....do	....do	....do ...	12.00	12.00
1	Making linings	....do	....do	....do ...	8.00	8.00
1	....do	German ...	Female ...	....do ...	9.00	9.00
1	....do	....do	....do	....do ...	8.50	8.50
1	Making sleeves	Polish	....do	....do ...	5.00	5.00
1	Stitching under collar	....do	....do	....do ...	4.50	4.50
1	Stitching coat	German ...	....do	....do ...	11.00	11.00
1	General	....do	Male	....do ...	14.00	14.00
10						101.00
1	Head baster	Jew	....do	....do ...	18.00	18.00
1	....do	....do	....do	....do ...	15.00	15.00
1	....do	....do	....do	....do ...	14.00	14.00
1	Second baster	German ...	....do	....do ...	9.00	9.00
1	....do	Polish	....do	....do ...	9.00	9.00
1	....do	....do	....do	....do ...	8.50	8.50
1	Edge baster	Jew	Female ...	....do ...	7.00	7.00
3	....do	Polish	....do	....do ...	8.00	24.00
1	Padding lapels	German ...	....do	....do ...	3.00	3.00
1	....do	....do	....do	....do ...	2.00	2.00
1	Pulling bastings, etc	....do	....do	....do ...	3.00	3.00
2	....do	....do	....do	....do ...	2.00	4.00
1	Under presser	....do	Male	....do ...	8.00	8.00
1	....do	Hollander .	....do	....do ...	11.00	11.00
17						135.50
4	Presser	Jew	....do	Piece ...	.18	54.00
1	Trimming and busheling	....do	....do	Week ...	16.00	16.00
5						70.00
1	Felling armholes	....do	Female ...	....do ...	6.00	6.00
1	....do	German ...	....do	....do ...	3.00	3.00
1	....do	....do	....do	....do ...	4.00	4.00
3						13.00
35						319.50

Establishment No. 9 is run on the factory system, producing "special-order" coats at $1.35 per coat. This shop, compared with No. 8, clearly expresses the difference between the shop and factory. The time required on a $1.35 coat is 7 hours,

FACTORIES AND SWEATSHOPS. 363

whereas No. 8 requires 12 hours 48 minutes on a $1.75 coat. The advantage in time is 40 per cent. The operator in No. 9 requires 2 hours; in No. 8, 4 hours. The wages of operator in No. 9 are 15 cents per hour, while the operator in No. 8 gets 9.7 cents per hour. This is probably due to two causes: One is that part of the operators in No. 9 are Jewish men, while the operators in No. 8 are German girls; the second cause lies in the difference of production—the factory system as against small production. While the operators in No. 9 earn more money, they work 40 per cent cheaper per coat than those in No. 8.

The same holds true in the case of the basters. The baster gets 17.4 cents per hour in No. 9 and 14 cents per hour in No. 8; but he bastes the coat in 2 hours in No. 9, while in No. 8 it requires 4 hours.

The ability of establishment No. 9 to produce cheaply arises partly from the mixed nationalities of the employees, including Poles, Jews, and Germans, with little resisting power in respect to "driving." The several nationalities working together find it harder to organize themselves or to come to an understanding than in shops where one nationality is employed. This brings about a wide diversity of wages. Some of the basters earn as high as $18, $15, and $14, and the operators $16, $14, and $12. The contractor is able in the high grades of work, where great skill is required, to pay good wages, and to pay low wages for the low grades of work, where he employs German and Polish girls.

ESTABLISHMENT NO. 10.

[Custom work, shop system: Chicago, coat shop; foot power; contractor, Jew; employees Jews, Bohemians, et al.: 19 employees in one system; 150 coats per week; 60 hours per week.]

Contract price $2.00
Labor cost 1.49
Average wages per hour .... .197

	Hour.	Week.	Two-thirds year.	Average per week per year.
	Cents.			
Operator's wages	25.6	$15.36	$532.48	$10.24
Baster's wages	16.1	9.66	334.88	6.44
Presser's wages	30	18.00	624.00	12.00

	Cents.
Cost of operating per coat	30.7
Cost of basting per coat	39.4
Cost of pressing per coat	24

	h.	m.
Time per coat	7	36
Operator's time per coat	1	12
Baster's time per coat	2	47
Presser's time per coat		48

Individual occupations, establishment No. 10.

Number.	Occupation.	Nationality.	Sex.	Week or piece.	Earnings.	Total earnings per week for the occupation.
3	Operator	Jew	Male	Piece	$0.30	$5.00
1	Baster	do	do	Week	18.00	18.00
1	do	do	do	do	13.00	13.00
2	Edge baster	Bohemian	Female	do	10.00	20.00
2	Presser	do	do	do	9.00	18.00
1	do	Pole	do	do	9.00	9.00
1	Under presser	German	do	do	12.00	12.00
1	Padding	Bohemian	do	do	4.00	4.00
1	do	do	do	do	2.25	2.25
1	Sewing buttons	do	do	do	6.00	6.00
1	do	Portuguese	do	do	6.00	6.00
1	Felling	German	do	do	5.00	5.00
16						158.25
2	Presser	Jew	Male	do	18.00	36.00
1	Trimmer	German	do	Piece	.12	30.00
19						224.25

364   THE INDUSTRIAL COMMISSION:—IMMIGRATION.

Establishment No. 10 is a "special order" coat shop in Chicago, producing a $2 coat, with 19 employees making 150 coats per week, working at the rate of 60 hours per week with foot-power machines.

The labor cost per coat is $1.49 as against a labor cost of $1.06 on the $1.35 coat in the factory (No. 9), and as against a labor cost of $1.47 in establishment No. 8, which is run by German girls, on a $1.75 coat.

No. 10 has an advantage over the small shop of the Bohemians and Germans in producing a $2 coat in 7 hours and 36 minutes, as against 12 hours and 48 minutes in the German shop on a $1.75 coat, and 6 hours and 30 minutes in the Bohemian shop on a $1 coat.

It will be seen that Establishment No. 10, making coats with Jewish men as operators and basters, is producing a coat cheaper than establishment No. 8 with German girls, or No. 7 with Bohemian girls, but that it costs more than it costs No. 9, with both Jews and Germans and men and women, running on a factory system.

ESTABLISHMENT No. 11.

[Inside shop: New York, coat shop; steam power; superintendent, Jew; employees, Jews and Italians; 124 employees in one system; 600 coats per week. 59 hours per week.]

Price of coat, if done by contract, about.. $1.50
Labor cost per coat 1.43
Average wages per hour.. .118

	Hour.	Week.	Two-thirds year.	Average per week per year.
	Cents.			
Operator's wages...	19.1	$11.26	$390.00	$7.50
Baster's wages...	10.3	6.07	210.08	4.04
Presser's wages...	23.2	13.68	474.24	9.12

Cents.
Cost of operating per coat 31.8
Cost of basting per coat 46.3
Cost of pressing per coat 22.8

                                                                                                              h. m.
Time per coat... 12 11
Operator's time per coat 1 37
Baster's time per coat 4 25
Presser's time per coat   59

Individual occupations, establishment No. 11.

Number.	Occupation.	Nationality.	Sex.	Week or piece.	Earnings.	Total earnings per week for the occupation.
1	Steamer	Jew	Male......	Week...	$17.00	$17.00
1	Sewing in sleeves.........	....do	....do	....do ...	16.00	16.00
1	......do	....do	....do	....do ...	13.00	13.00
1	Sewing round and sewing in collar.	....do	....do	....do ...	16.00	16.00
2	Sleeve maker	....do	....do	....do ...	8.00	16.00
2	Lining maker................	....do	....do	....do ...	12.00	24.00
1	......do	....do	....do	....do ...	11.00	11.00
1	......do	....do	....do	....do ...	4.00	4.00
1	Stitching coat	....do	....do	....do ...	12.00	12.00
1	Stitching canvas...........	Italian......	....do	....do ...	5.00	5.00
1	Sewing sleeve linings....	....do	Female ...	....do ...	3.50	3.50
4	Pocket makers	Jew	Male......	{Piece... 8 cents..}	12.00	48.80
1	General operator	....do	....do	Week...	11.00	11.00
18						196.50
1	Lining baster................	Italian......	....do	....do ...	9.00	9.00
1	......do	Jew	....do	....do ...	11.00	11.00
1	......do	....do	....do	....do ...	10.00	10.00
1	......do	....do	....do	....do ...	9.00	9.00
1	Basting round	....do	....do	....do ...	12.00	12.00
1	......do	....do	....do	....do ...	13.00	13.00
1	Edge baster	Italian......	Female ...	....do ...	6.00	6.00
1	......do	....do	....do	....do ...	4.75	4.75

FACTORIES AND SWEATSHOPS.

Individual occupations, establishment No. 11—Continued.

Number.	Occupation.	Nationality.	Sex.	Week or piece.	Earnings.	Total earnings per week for the occupation.
2	Edge baster	Italian	Female	Week	$4.50	$9.00
1	....do	....do	....do	....do	3.25	3.25
1	....do	Jew	Male	....do	8.00	8.00
1	....do	....do	....do	....do	5.12	5.12
1	....do	Bohemian	....do	....do	2.75	2.75
1	Canvas baster	Jew	....do	....do	7.00	7.00
1	....do	....do	....do	....do	5.00	5.00
1	General baster and overseer	....do	....do	....do	11.00	11.00
2	Basting in sleeves, tacking lining and canvas in armholes.	Italian	Female	....do	3.25	6.50
1	....do	....do	....do	....do	1.50	1.50
1	....do	....do	....do	....do	2.00	2.00
1	....do	....do	....do	....do	5.50	5.50
1	....do	....do	....do	....do	3.75	3.75
1	....do	....do	....do	....do	3.00	3.00
3	Basting collars and shoulders	Jew	Male	....do	10.00	10.00
1	....do	....do	....do	....do	9.00	9.00
1	....do	....do	....do	....do	7.00	7.00
1	Baster	Italian	....do	....do	7.50	7.50
1	....do	....do	....do	....do	7.00	7.00
3	Padding lapels	....do	Female	....do	1.50	4.50
1	....do	....do	....do	....do	1.75	1.75
1	....do	....do	....do	....do	2.75	2.75
1	....do	....do	....do	....do	3.25	3.25
1	....do	....do	....do	....do	4.00	4.00
1	....do	....do	....do	....do	3.50	3.50
1	Under presser	Jew	Male	....do	12.00	12.00
1	....do	German	....do	....do	8.00	8.00
1	....do	Italian	....do	....do	7.50	7.50
1	....do	....do	....do	....do	5.50	5.50
1	Edge presser	Jew	....do	....do	8.00	8.00
1	....do	German	....do	....do	6.00	6.00
45						275.37
7	Buttonhole maker	Jew	Female	Piece	.02½	60.00
2	....do	Italian	....do	....do	.02½	
1	Fitter	Jew	Male	Week	15.00	15.00
1	Busheler	....do	....do	....do	15.00	15.00
1	....do	....do	Female	....do	8.00	8.00
5	....do	Italian	....do	....do	4.00	20.00
15	Felling armholes and bottoms	Italian (inside)	....do	Piece	.08	48.00
9	....do	Italian (outside)	....do	....do	.08	
1	Button sewer	Jew	....do	Week	7.00	7.00
1	....do	German	....do	....do	5.00	5.00
1	....do	Italian	....do	....do	4.50	4.50
1	Buttonhole maker	Jew	....do	....do	4.00	4.00
1	Sewing ticket	....do	....do	....do	6.00	6.00
2	Pulling bastings	....do	....do	Piece	.01 / .01½	6.00
1	Superintendent	....do	Male	Week	30.00	30.00
1	Foreman	....do	....do	....do	18.00	18.00
1	Office bookkeeper	....do	....do	....do	8.00	8.00
51						254.50
2	First-off presser	....do	....do	....do	13.00	26.00
1	....do	....do	....do	....do	14.00	14.00
2	....do	....do	....do	....do	11.00	22.00
2	Second-off presser	....do	....do	Piece	.12½	75.00
1	....do	German	....do	....do	.12½	
2	....do	Italian	....do	....do	.12½	
10						137.00
124						863.37

Establishment No. 11 is a large "inside" factory in New York employing 124 people, making 600 men's fine coats per week. If the coat were given out to a contractor it would probably cost $1.50, but in the manufacturer's own shop it costs $1.43. Ready-made fine coats of this class can be made much more successfully in the large inside shop, with a minute division of labor, than can cheaper grades of coats. The same manufacturer who operates this inside shop for his fine work sends out his cheaper coats to contractors.

It requires in this factory about 124 people to make a coat. The economies are mainly the following: The division of labor makes each person in the several occupations able to produce more work than would be possible if the labor was not so intensely divided. It also makes it possible to introduce a large number of unskilled workers, at low wages, for parts of the work where skill is not required.

The coat is made in 12 hours 11 minutes, as against 3 hours 41 minutes in Establishment No. 2, and 3 hours 55 minutes in No. 1 for a coat at half the price.

The operators in this factory are mostly Jewish men. They receive fairly good wages, as will be seen from the schedule, one man getting $17 per week; two, $16; one, $13; three, $12, and two, $11, working 10 hours a day. There is only one getting $8, and an Italian man and woman getting, respectively, $5 and $3.50.

The average wages for all operators per hour are 9.1 cents, which is about the same as in establishment No. 2 and establishment No. 1, where Jewish help is employed. Since the time of the operator is 1 hour and 3 minutes, as against 57 minutes in No. 2 and 43 minutes in No. 1, and, taking into consideration that the other two shops are making a 75-cent coat, it is seen that establishment No. 11 can operate a coat in a shorter time and pay about the same wages.

But the main economy in this class of shops is with the baster and edge baster. Here a large number of Italian men and women are introduced, working at low wages. Out of the 45 basters, edge basters, and seam pressers there is only one at $13 a week. There are two at $12; two at $11; two at $10; two at $9; and thirty-six at $8, $7.50, and down as low as $1.50. A large number of Italian girls, as will be seen, are working for $1.50, $2, $2.50, and $3 per week.

The average wages for the baster have fallen far below the wages received by the baster in establishments No. 1 and No. 2. While the baster in No. 1 gets on an average 16 cents an hour, and in No. 2, 13.6 cents per hour, yet in No. 11 the earnings are only 10.3 cents. The time for basting in No. 11 is 4 hours and 24 minutes, as against 1 hour and 26 minutes in No. 1 and 1 hour in No. 2; showing that the basting in No. 11, while it is produced by very cheap help, costs much more per dollar's worth of work than in either No. 1 or No. 2.

The presser in No. 11 gets better wages than in the other two shops, probably because skilled mechanics are required, and the off-pressing can not in the nature of things be very much divided, so that it takes a first-class presser to do the work.

It is this class of shops, making first-class coats, with very cheap help, that is extending the ready-made clothing business among people who formerly wore only custom-made clothing. It is displacing the custom tailor by producing a coat as well, or almost as well, as he does for less than one-fifth of the price required by him.

The example of this shop should be well considered by those who expect that the abolition of the contractor and the substitution of large inside shops will improve the condition of the employees. This particular shop is a model in its external and sanitary aspects; the hours are shorter than elsewhere, and the best-paid employees receive as high wages as elsewhere; but by its subdivision of labor a place is found for women instead of men, and for the very cheapest class of help.

ESTABLISHMENT NO. 12.

Establishment No. 12 is a coat shop at Egg Harbor, N. J., employing girls as machine operators and a few girls as edge basters, making 500 coats per week, working 60 hours per week; contract price per coat, 45 to 52½ cents.

Establishment No. 12 can be favorably compared with establishment No. 8, a German shop in Chicago making a $1.75 garment. It will be seen that the average wages per hour in establishment No. 8 are 11.5 cents, while in No. 12 they are 9.7 cents, showing that in small country towns labor can be procured at somewhat less per hour than in the large cities, employing the same nationality.

If establishment No. 12 is compared with establishment No. 4, which is a Polish shop in Chicago employing girls, it will be seen that the average wages in No. 4 are 12.2 cents, as against 9.7 cents in No. 12, emphasizing the point that female labor is usually cheaper in small towns than in large cities, probably due to the different standard of living and the lower cost of living.

The average wages for the operator in No. 4 are 13.2 cents; the average wages per hour for the operator in No. 12 are only 8.8 cents.

The cost of basting, per coat, is about the same in both cases, being 13.2 cents in No. 12 and 13.9 cents in No. 4.

FACTORIES AND SWEATSHOPS. 367

ESTABLISHMENT No. 12.

[Coat shop, Egg Harbor, N. J.: Contractor, German; employees, German-Americans; 34 employees; 500 coats per week; 60 hours per week; steam power.]

	Cents.
Contract price	45 to 52½
Labor cost	39.8
Average wages per hour	9.7

	Hour.	Week.	Two-thirds year.	Average per week per year.
	Cents.			
Operator's wages	8.8	$5.30	$183.56	$3.53
Baster's wages	13.2	7.92	274.56	5.28
Presser's wages	14.2	8.50	295.36	5.68

	Cents.
Cost of operating per coat	13.8
Cost of basting per coat	14.25
Cost of pressing per coat	3.4

	h. m.
Time per coat	4　5
Operator's time per coat	1　22
Baster's time per coat	1　5
Presser's time per coat	14

Individual occupations, establishment No. 12.

Number.	Occupation.	Nationality.	Sex.	Time or piece.	Earnings.	Total earnings per week for the occupation.
2	Sewing in sleeves and stitching sleeves.	German-American	Female	Week	$8.50	$17.00
3	Pocket maker	do	do	do	6.50	19.50
2	Lining maker	do	do	do	5.75	11.50
2	do	do	do	do	4.25	8.50
2	General workers	do	do	do	2.00	4.00
2	do	do	Male	do	4.25	8.50
13						69.00
1	Presser	do	do	do	9.00	9.00
1	do	do	do	do	8.00	8.00
2						17.00
1	Baster	do	do	do	9.75	9.75
2	do	do	do	do	9.00	18.00
2	do	do	do	do	8.50	17.00
1	do	do	do	do	8.00	8.00
1	Coat-collar baster	do	Female	do	4.00	4.00
1	Under presser	do	Male	do	6.50	6.50
1	Seam presser	do	do	do	8.00	8.00
9						71.25
1	Busheler	do	do	do	6.00	6.00
1	Foreman	do	do	do	12.00	12.00
1	Finisher	do	do	do	3.75	3.75
3						21.75
7	Felling hands	do	Female	Piece	.04	20.00
34						199.00

IX. CONCLUSIONS AS TO CLOTHING TRADES.

The following conclusions relative to wages and prices, based on the foregoing discussion, are made in comparison of the period of 1878-1882, when the immigration of Russian Jews began, and the year 1900-1901.

The clothing trade has been affected more than any other trade by successive waves of immigrants, especially Irish, Germans, Scandinavians, Jews, Italians, Poles, Bohemians, and Lithuanians.

Wages have always been extremely unstable; in the dull season being much lower per day and per piece than in the busy season. This is not the case in other countries where tradition is stronger, nor in other trades where labor unions have better control. In ladies' cloaks and suits, work is less steady than in men's and children's clothing, and the prices are higher in the busy seasons and lower in the dull seasons.

The organization and evolution of the trade have passed through four stages: (1) the journeyman tailor; (2) the home shop; (3) the task shop or small contractor's shop; (4) the factory.

This increasing subdivision has reduced the cost of making a coat about as follows: Task system, 50 per cent below journeyman tailor's price in dull season; factory system, 40 per cent below task system; total, 70 per cent below journeyman tailor's dull-season price or 85 per cent below busy-season price—i. e., from $5 to 75 cents.

The increasing subdivision of labor has substituted simple operations for complex operations and has increased the speed and exertion of the workman.

While wages by the hour, day, or week on factory products have decreased in most cases and remained constant in a few cases, yet the increased overexertion and overtime are more exhausting to the employee than they were 20 years ago.

Custom or journeyman tailors earn higher wages than formerly, not mainly through organization, but partly because of the high skill required, partly because of the new demand for ladies' fine tailoring, and partly because of the growth in wealth of the wealthier classes whom they serve.

The wages per week of male operators and basters on coats in task shops in New York have fallen one-sixth, their hours increased one-fifth, their weekly output has increased two-thirds, the piece price of their product has decreased one-half without any change in machinery or subdivision of labor.

These low wages, long hours, and overexertion in the task shops are partly the result of an antiquated system of production in competition with factory methods, and partly the result of an overcrowded labor market and lack of organization.

The wages of women hand sewers on coats, except finishers and edge basters, have remained constant.

The wages of women edge basters on coats have declined one-fifth, and they have been replaced by male immigrants at wages per week about 50 per cent higher than those which the women formerly received, but per piece the same, owing to the greater speed and endurance of men.

The earnings of women finishers on pants in New York declined one-third when the Germans began tenement-house work 10 years ago, and again declined one-third when the Italians drove out the Germans. In Boston the legislation restricting tenement-house work prevented the latter decline.[1]

Pressers' wages per week have fallen 10 per cent, but per piece 40 per cent, and their hours have increased 20 per cent.

Cutters' wages have been constant, or have slightly advanced, and the hours have been reduced in the better shops, through the aid of the organization. In the small shops, where there is no organization, wages have been reduced. For these wages the cutter has heavier work and has increased his output 50 per cent by shears, 150 per cent by machine, and 200 per cent by knife.

The wages of pants operators in New York have not declined nor the hours increased, owing to the superior organizaton of the union.

Wages in coat shops on the factory system with minute division of labor, are higher per hour, the day's labor is shorter, the skill in each particular operation is greater, and the cost of the coat is less than in the task or small shop system. Moreover, men are not replaced by women.

The competition of the immigrant is not felt until the second or third year after his arrival, even in the simple operations, because he requires that much time to increase his skill and speed to the point where he can earn $10 to $15 per week. At these rates of wages his labor is cheaper than that of the "green" immigrant who can earn $5 per week 3 months after landing.

The condition of the immigrants is better than it was in their native countries, but their standards of living are much lower than the standards of those longer in the country with whom they compete for employment.

---

[1] See following chapter on Tenement House Work, p. 369.

The sons of tailors do not generally enter the clothing trade on account of its uncertainty, low pay, long hours, and unwholesome conditions, but the women and girls who enter the shops are mainly American-born children of immigrants.

Men's labor in shops, owing to greater skill, speed, and endurance, is worth about 50 per cent more per hour than woman's work in shops, and women and girls working for $5 to $9 per week tend to displace men above $8 to $14 per week on corresponding work, but men working at these or lower wages have displaced women. The competition of women has forced men to increase their exertion without increasing their wages. Women are especially available in preventing men from raising their wages through strikes.

Labor organization has been especially difficult on account of immigration, mixed nationalities, female or child labor, country competition, tenement-house work, and the introduction of the division of labor. After male immigrants have been here 2 or 3 years they are willing to organize, but are prevented from bettering their condition by the new arrivals whose necessities compel them to accept low pay. The only enduring organization has been that of the cutters, who are but slightly affected directly by immigration. The most successful organization of factory tailors is that of the Swedish pants and vest makers of the "special order" trade in Chicago. This organization has raised wages at the time when other wages were falling. The "special order" trade furnishes a peculiar leverage for a labor organization, since it requires trained mechanics, and the work can not be postponed in case of a strike.

Different nationalities have introduced different modes of production: The Jews, the task system based on speed, endurance, and team work; the Germans and Bohemians, the female finisher and foot-machine operator; the Scandinavians, the large steampower shop, with minute subdivision of labor, for pants and vests. The factory system in coats has originated with Germans, Scandinavians, and Jews. Immigrants have created for themselves new lines of ready-made products and have displaced the custom tailor, the dressmaker, and the housewife. This is true of all kinds of clothing, whether for men, women, or children. As a result, all classes of people are better dressed, in the latest styles, and they spend much more money every year for clothing.

Tailors who have been displaced by green immigrants of the same or other nationalities have found better positions as contractors, manufacturers, or small tradesmen, or have created a new line of product of a better grade. This displacement has been accompanied by hardship and temporary unemployment similar to that accompanying the introduction of machinery in other callings.

Legislation further restricting immigration would assist tailors now in the trade to organize and secure shorter hours and higher pay.

X. TENEMENT-HOUSE WORK AND LEGISLATION REGARDING IT

1. CONDITION OF HOME WORKERS.

The so-called "sweat-shop" legislation of the several American States, in so far as it adds to factory legislation in general, is simply legislation directed against tenement-house work.

The broad fact first apparent in this legislation is that American States in restricting tenement-house work have been legislating upon the subject of immigration in its most urgent and threatening aspect. Practically all of the work in tenements covered by the laws about to be considered is carried on by foreign-born men and women, and, more than that, by the latest arrivals and the lowest conditioned of the foreign born. The legislation on this subject is more radical and even despotic than any that can be found on the same subject in other countries, and its extremest forms are found in the three States of New York, Massachusetts, and Pennsylvania, whose great ports of entry receive the first impact of immigration. Moreover, this legislation has been forced upon these States, as a matter of fact, by practically two of the races that have been recently crowding into the cities, namely, the Hebrew and the Italian. It is the Italian woman, working in her close tenement, whose cheap labor has almost driven out all other nationalities from that class of work which is still mainly done in the home, namely, the hand sewing on coats and trousers. Of the 20,000 licenses granted by the New York factory inspector for "home finishing" in New York City, it is estimated that 95 per cent are held by Italians. In Boston, where the law has been rigidly enforced against unsanitary conditions, about 50 per cent of the 1,300 licenses are held by Portuguese and 12 per cent by Italians.

"Home finishing," it should be observed, is perhaps four-fifths of the work now done in tenement houses. It is that remnant of the former home shop where the entire garment was made at home. In New York, coats and trousers are "finished" at home; in other cities, only trousers. In addition to home finishing, the only other classes of work affected by tenement-house laws are those of journeyman tailor and the woman who works for "pin money."

The Italian home finisher is usually compelled to take work home, because her husband is not making enough money to support the family. These men work mostly as street laborers, hucksters, and peddlers of fruit, fish, and other merchandise on the streets. When working as street laborers they are employed so few months in the year, and as peddlers their income is so small that they must get aid from their wives at home. The price paid for labor to a home finisher is about one-half that formerly paid to a woman regularly employed in the shop. A pair of pants is lined, bottoms basted or felled, and the buttons sewed on for from 5 to 7 cents at home, while formerly, before the Italians came in, it was 10 and 14 cents in factories and 7 to 10 cents in the homes of German finishers, so that the Italian finisher works for about two-thirds of the price which other nationalities formerly received for the same work. This is not true, however, in Boston, where the strict enforcement of the laws restricting tenement-house work has lessened that form of competition, and where, on this account, the prices continue at 7 to 10 cents.

The Italian family not only makes its living by the aid of home work by the wife and children, but by this process it is made possible for the Italian laborer to bid on much cheaper terms for labor in other employments than it would be possible for him to do if his wife and children were not engaged in the business of sewing at home. Consequently, this practice not only has a damaging effect on the shop worker in the sewing trade, but it also affects the people engaged in the same callings as the Italian laborers. It is possible for the Italian to work on railroads and on streets and buildings for a lower price than he would be able to do if he did not receive this aid from his mother, his sister, his wife, and his children at home.

The following are cases taken at random from notes on the homes of the Italian finishers:

Anabella, 235 Mulberry street, rear tenement, second floor front; pants, 5 cents apiece; woman, her mother, 2 children, husband; she does not know what he does or what he makes. Two women can together earn $3 a week. Old woman looks 80, is 52; been in the country only 5 months; husband worked with shovel in old country; she didn't sew in old country—took care of house; conditions here about same as those in old country; 2 rooms, rent $8.50; 2 windows in outer room; 1 child of 5, 1 of 6 months; licensed place.

Donia Falzia, 235 Mulberry street, third floor, rear tenement; pants, 5 cents; finishing; good grade of work (pants probably sell at $3.25 retail); says it takes an hour; husband works at shovel—$1.25 to $1.50; rent, $7.50, 2 rooms; no children. Came here from Boston to see his family; worked on pants in Boston, but in shops, not in houses; must pay there $15 or $16 for a shop, which must be nice, while here you can work in ordinary rooms; married 2 years (in Boston); been in this country 3 years; was working in shop before she was married; 7, 8, and 10 cents per pair when working in shop in Boston—$4, $5, and $6 per week; earns now $3 a week—sometimes.

Antonia Scarifino, 235 Mulberry street, third floor; 5 cents per pair pants; bastes bottoms, puts lining on; 1 hour to make; 2 years at this business; 4 in this country; married, with 1 baby; sister works with her; can both together make $4 a week; husband peddles fish and makes only $1 to $2 a week; in summer he can make $4 to $5; got married over here; husband been here 5 years; was married 2 years ago; did nothing before making pants; 2 rooms, $8.50 rent; kitchen probably 10 by 12 feet; bedroom, 8 by 10 feet; she gets all the work she wants.

Lafiel Agalo, 235 Mulberry street; 5 cents coat; felling front part of sleeves, felling armholes, bottom, and pulling bastings on 62½ and 75 cent coat; makes 2 or 3 a day; had this coat 3 days; 6 cents on coat when working in shop; husband a baker—$4 to $5 a week; didn't work when husband got more; can make 50 cents a day; does make only $1 to $1.50 a week, for works little; 2 children—little baby; learned in neighbor's house; learned only coat; 2 years in this country; 4 months only in shop; made then 55 or 50 cents a day; husband earned 20 cents a day in Italy; pays $9 a month rent, 2 rooms; 2 windows in 1 room.

Legislation affecting the Italian home worker must of course be general, and must affect other nationalities and other classes of work manufactured under similar conditions. Among the other classes of work thus affected is that of the custom tailor or the journeyman tailor. This is the skilled mechanic who makes the entire coat. He makes one to three of these coats a week, and his home is not seriously encumbered with quantities of material, whereas ready-made clothing is handled in large quantities and is scattered everywhere through kitchen and bedroom, on floor, tables, and beds. Fifteen or twenty years ago most of the ready-made clothing was also made in the homes of the people. The ordinary shop was in the home, where most of the members of the family were engaged, the man, his wife, and such grown-up children and other people as could be marshaled into service. The contractor's shop and what is called the "sweating system" have developed out of this. With the introduction of labor and sanitary legislation as applied to the sewing trade, the largest part of clothing manufacture has gone into shops of contractors, but there still remains a small number of families who are working on clothing in the old mode of production. Coats, pants, vests, and ladies' garments are made in the home, with the help of the wife and children and sometimes of others, and by means of this labor and with the opportunity of working unlimited hours they are able to hold their own in open competition with the shop. Home work is usually practiced by people who prefer isolation and do not like to go into a shop to work, and are not able to establish large shops of their own. It is because of a sort of conservatism with regard to new modes of production that these people still hold their own in these home shops.

The urgent complaint made by tailors of all classes against home work is based on the obstacles which it places in the way of organization and joint protection of their wages and hours of employment. The agitation conducted by the journeymen tailors' organizations of this country is directed more vigorously against their members doing work in their own homes than it is in regard to holding up the regular price for their labor. It is claimed that it is harder to organize the home workers than it is to organize those who work in back shops or in regular shops, because they are scattered through the city and the organization has no means of getting control over them or finding them if they are wanted. They have no opportunity of coming together in an organization with other people employed in the trade. Usually the contractor from whom they take work speaks their language, and in their homes they usually hear nothing but their own language, so that they have no opportunity of acquiring a language common to others in the same industry so as to make it possible for them to be interested in a common cause. Being slow to learn English, they are slow to become Americanized.

Subcontracting is the rule in this business. Manufacturers do not want to be bothered with giving out small lots of work such as would be required by a man who worked only with his family. Consequently, such a family is forced to take work not from the manufacturer direct, but from some contractor in the neighborhood. When the home worker complains, he is told by the contractor, "I am not making the price; the price has been made by the manufacturer for me," and as the manufacturer is never seen, they know nothing about him and so can not influence him. In this way home work reduces the resisting power among the tailors when the price for labor is reduced. As they have no opportunity of becoming acquainted with one another they can not give expression to a common grievance.

The difficulties of organization are especially noticeable in the case of the Italian home finishers. They receive such a small income from their earnings that they are not able to pay dues to carry on the expense of an organization. They work so continuously, and are so busy caring for their families at home, that they can not spare the time to go to meetings or participate in an organization. They seem to be like chattels of their husbands and the other male members of the family, and would be looked upon as a sort of rebels if they participated in any form of protest against their condition. The same is true in their dealings with the contractor. Any effort to resist the oppression of the contractor would be met by him with the threat that he would employ other help and have his work done inside or by other Italians.

An apparent exception to this rule is that of the finishers for certain shops which have been organized by other nationalities. The Swedish women in the "special order" trade of Chicago have required the contractor to pay 14 cents per pair of pants to the Italian finishers at home, and have organized about 600 of them for this purpose. The Swedes have been able to do this because they have a strong union, practically monopolizing their line of work, and because they wish to protect also the 300 Swedish and German home finishers on the same work. So exceptional, however, is this case of apparent organization of home workers that it is looked upon by the people in the trade with great curiosity.

Another class of workers who are beyond the field of organization are the women who work for pin money. These are usually married women or widows of American birth. They may formerly have been engaged in some occupation in the sewing trade, and in case of emergency they strive to help themselves upon the death of the breadwinner or during times when they are not fully supported by their husbands, or when they wish additional money while their husbands are being employed. Such a woman will usually take clothing home, doing the felling or making the buttonholes by hand, and working for less money than the people employed regularly at the trade. Since she is not compelled to wholly support herself by her labor she can get the little that she needs even if she works for half the price that the woman must demand who is dependent upon similar work for subsistence. This line of employment is also practiced extensively in making shirtwaists, wrappers, underwear, children's knee pants, and in some cases on ready-made and even custom-made vests; in almost every case decreasing the price for labor. A dozen women's wrappers will be taken out by the woman who needs some additional money for 45 to 75 cents, when the girl working in a shop, in order to make a living, will have to ask 75 cents to $1.10 for the same thing. The girl in the shop must earn at least $4.50 to $6 a week in order to make a living, while the woman working for pin money will be content to earn $2.50. This reduces the price for labor below the point of subsistence for the girl in the factory.

It is very difficult, almost impossible, to organize in a union the people who do not stay at the trade regularly and only work for the sake of earning pin money. Their intention is not to make a living at the business, and the pay is so low that they abandon it as soon as possible. It is impossible to get them into a labor organization. They cut the price for labor and there is no redress from the grievance. It is probably true that, out of regard for this class of women, American legislation has not taken the advanced step of prohibiting outright tenement-house work and instead of prohibitive laws has adopted the device of licensing such work. This will appear from the description of such legislation in the following pages, where it is shown that the factory inspector is given discretion in granting and revoking licenses. If the inspector is charged with laxity in enforcing the law, he appeals to the cases of individual hardship which it would bring upon women forced by emergency to work at home. The factory inspector of New York, who has not taken the advanced ground of inspectors in other States in enforcing the stringent law of that State, gives an illustration in his report for 1899 (p. 52) of the hardship of strict enforcement compared with the leniency of nonenforcement. He cites the following parallel incidents:

Where the law was not enforced.

The New York Evening World of January 18, 1900, reported the proceedings of the New York Diet Kitchen Association.

At this meeting Dr. Annie S. Daniels, a physician of New York City, reported on her visits to tenement houses where manufacturing is done. Her report is interesting and unquestionably true. During her narrative she spoke of one case which is particularly interesting and which we grant is an illustration of a condition where the law was *not* enforced. She is quoted as saying:

"You might not believe it, but I recently ran across a case where a woman could not spare the labor of a child only 3 years old. Some children at that time are actually useful in fixing trimmings on women's dresses."

It is said that the word picture of the little one at work caused the shedding of tears. And no wonder, for Dr. Daniels was speaking to a sympathetic audience.

A child of such tender years at work in a tenement sweatshop would appeal to the hardest heart and arouse the sympathy of the most callous soul.

Where the law was enforced.

Application No. 3687, asking for a license, was received at our suboffice in New York. The premises from which application came were carefully inspected and a license was refused the applicant, for sanitary reasons. The applicant was a woman, presumably a widow, who had three small children dependent upon her for support.

On January 10, 1900, our inspector who was detailed to inspect and investigate the condition of the premises for which license had been refused reported as follows on the case in point:

NEW YORK, *January 10, 1900.*

[Application No. 3687.]

This person was refused a license on November 22, 1899. The contractor refused to give her more work to do in her apartments in violation of the law. Therefore, she has been obliged to go to the shop to work, to support herself and little ones. I found on my visit to her room three small children, the oldest apparently not over 5 years of age, alone in a cold room, no fire whatever, and the place almost entirely bare of furniture.

I learned from the housekeeper of the premises that this mother goes to work at 7 o'clock in the morning; she returns at noon to give the children some dinner, then goes back to work, not returning until 6 o'clock in the evening. These little children are alone all day with absolutely no one to look after them or keep a fire to warm them.

JOHN H. STORY,
Deputy Inspector.

From a purely humanitarian standpoint, which narration presents the most pitiful picture? On the one hand we have the 3-year-old child helping its mother in the home—never out of her sight—always where the mother could attend to its wants and allay its fears and suffering. While, on the other hand, we see the mother compelled to desert her three little ones of very tender years, going out to the shop to work, because the law prohibits her bringing the work into her home. As a result thereof these unfortunate little ones are thus deprived of the scant care a hard-working mother could bestow upon them, they are left alone in a tenement, shut up in a fireless room with no one to attend to their wants. Is not this a sadder picture than that presented by Dr. Daniels? We do not attempt to mitigate the frightful conditions existing in places that our inspectors have not up to this time reached, but we do say that the strict and unrelenting enforcement of our present law will cause untold misery and suffering.

While individual cases of hardship can often be cited, it is claimed that the price paid for the labor of these women home workers is so low that a widow or other woman in need is not able to make a living wholly by that labor. It is often the case that widows who work at home at this kind of employment are being partially supported by charity. The charity thus received makes it possible for them to work for less wages than they would receive if they had to work in a factory and wholly support themselves.

Since the standard of living of the working classes is generally recognized as equally important with their organization in maintaining a high rate of wages, the question of the influence of home work upon their standard is of vital interest. It is claimed by tailors that home work reduces the standard of living. They do not care for a fine home with good living rooms when the home is almost all of the time used as a shop, with pieces of cloth and rags lying about and with pressing irons and sewing machines crowding upon the space. In the Italian home with its twenty or more pairs of pants or as many coats and jackets scattered through the kitchen and living rooms, and the wife busy plying her needle, it necessarily results that the surroundings are uncared for and filthy and the children neglected and dirty. Furthermore, the husband or other support becomes less energetic in the effort to provide for those dependent upon him, and he feels at liberty to spend in drink or other luxuries the money which he would otherwise have been compelled to expend for his family.

It is claimed also that the man who works at home has irregular hours and usually works all the time he can spare, day and night; he employs his wife and children as helpers, and is usually able at a pinch to get cheap help by employing his neighbors' boys, girls, and wives. Thus in open competition he is able to underbid the man who works in the back shop or the regular factory. As a consequence the price for labor is not stable and there is a constant cutthroat competition between the people in the trade for the purpose of getting work, since the long hours worked per day make it impossible for work to last throughout the year.

The effect on the intelligence and personal initiative of the tailors is also depressing. The man who can rely upon the earnings of his wife and children loses the spirit of enterprise. Improvements in the mode of production are absolutely out of the question. Home shops are usually not able to use improved machinery, nor are they able to subdivide labor so that each laborer is utilized in the most efficient manner. Consequently by the old mode of production the laborers must work longer hours and utilize the labor of women and children in order to hold their own in competition with the better shops.

For these reasons it is quite generally argued by tailors that if the manufacture of clothing in tenement houses could be prohibited they would be benefited. They would earn a better living in factories, with regular hours of work, with a better protective organization, and without the depression of their homes and the oppression of their wives and children.

2. PROTECTION OF THE PURCHASER.

The most effective agitation and legislation against tenement-house work has been undertaken, not on behalf of the workers, but on behalf of the public which purchases clothing. The contagious and infectious diseases which are presumably carried by clothing from tenements to the consumers are phthisis, diphtheria, smallpox, chicken pox, scarlet fever, and measles. It is not known that any definite case has ever been reported where contagion was actually proven, owing to the large number of hands through which the goods pass before they reach the consumer. At the same time, the danger of contagion is apparent. The report of the New York tenement house commission for 1900 says (p. 70):

Tenement-house labor is generally carried on in the dwelling room of the family, where old and young are crowded in with the workers. The danger of contagion, when any member of the family is ill, therefore, is very great. A member of the commission has seen garments piled on the floor in the midst of dirt and rubbish, garments stacked on the bed, and some of them used as pillows for sick children; and in one instance garments were found stored in the same room with a sick man apparently in an advanced stage of tuberculosis. Such conditions the commission regards as a serious menace to public health. It believes that manufacturing can not be continued in the tenement houses with safety to the general public except at great expense in the way of investigation and supervision, in view of the immense amount of labor at present carried on in tenement houses.

"The risk run by the purchaser of a costly cloak," says the report of the Illinois factory inspector (1895, p. 55), "or a custom-made suit is precisely the risk run by the workingman buying a cheap, ready-made suit and by the poor woman who gets from a bargain counter knee pants for her boy. In the cloak trade, the clothing trade, the merchant tailors' custom trade, although the manufacturer or merchant tailor may have shops in good sanitary condition, nothing of his manufacture can be guaranteed noninfectious so long as the greater part or any part of his work is done on tenement-house premises."

Complaints similar to the foregoing have resulted in legislation regulating tenement-house work in the States of Massachusetts (1894, 508, 44), New York (G. L. 32, 100), Pennsylvania (1897, 37; 1899, 64), New Jersey (1893, 216), Illinois (1893, p. 99), Missouri (1899, p. 273), Michigan (1896, p. 233), and Ohio (1899, p. 213). (See Report of Industrial Commission on Labor Legislation, Vol. V, p. 116.) Following is a description in detail of the main features of this legislation.

3. LEGISLATION GOVERNING TENEMENT-HOUSE WORK.

A. Persons permitted to work in tenement house or dwelling.—In no State does the legislature take the radical step of prohibiting outright tenement or home work. If such step has ever been taken it has been declared unconstitutional by the courts, as was done in New York with the statute of 1884, c. 272, prohibiting the manufacture of cigars in tenement houses on any floor partly occupied for residence purposes. (In re Jacobs, 98 N. Y., 98.) The unconstitutionality of this statute was maintained by the court on the ground that it did not clearly appear on the face of the law that its primary object was to secure the public health.

The existing statutes, following the clue suggested in New York decisions, go only so far as to restrict the number of persons who shall be employed in a room or tenement. In Massachusetts, Ohio, Indiana, New Jersey, and Illinois this restriction excludes everyone except "the immediate members of the family living therein."

In Missouri the number is restricted to "three persons not immediate members of the family living therein." In Pennsylvania, New York, and Michigan there is no definite restriction to the members of the family nor any specified number of outsiders, but the factory inspector uses his discretion at this point. In Pennsylvania, where the law does not prohibit the employment of outsiders in the family, the inspector reaches that result by specifying in the license only the names of immediate members of the family who are permitted to work in the room or apartment. While the statute does not, on its face, grant this authority to the inspector, his action has not been tested in the courts. At the same time the statute restricts the number to be employed so that "not less than 250 cubic feet of air space shall be allowed for each and every person."

In New York the minimum air space is also 250 cubic feet in the daytime and 400 cubic feet at night, and there is no specified limit on the family relationship of persons who may be employed in a room or tenement. The factory inspector in his discretion has adopted the rule that in the ready-made trade no outsider shall be permitted to work with the family, but in the custom trade the tailor may bring in one or two outsiders. This distinction is based on the difference between the low-paid Italians who do the work of finishing ready-made garments and the relatively high-grade mechanics who make the custom work. The latter have larger and better premises, but even in this case the character of the premises may be such as to forbid a permit to outsiders.

Certain statutes provide that nothing in the law shall be so construed as to prevent the employment of a tailor (Massachusetts and New York) or seamstress (Massachusetts, New York, Pennsylvania, and Michigan), by any person or family for manufacturing articles for such person's or family use.

B. The tenement described.—The places to which the law governing tenement manufacture applies are usually described as a "room or rooms, apartment or apartments in any tenement or dwelling house" (New York, Massachusetts, New Jersey, Pennsylvania, Indiana, Missouri, and Michigan) to which Illinois adds "used for eating or sleeping purposes." It is especially provided in Massachusetts that "a room or apartment in any tenement or dwelling house which is not used for living or sleeping purposes and which is not connected with any room or apartment used for living or sleeping purposes, and which has a separate and distinct entrance from the outside, shall not be subject to the provisions of this act." In Ohio it applies to every "dwelling or building, or any room or apartment of itself, in or connected with any tenement or dwelling or other building." And New York, New Jersey, and Indiana add also any "building in the rear of any tenement or dwelling house."

C. Articles included in legislation on "tenement" or "home" manufacture.—Legislation upon this subject applies in the first instance to wearing apparel and secondarily to cigars and cigarettes. The laws are not uniform, certain States (Massachusetts and Ohio) covering all wearing apparel whatsoever, and others (New York, Pennsylvania, New Jersey, Illinois, Missouri, Indiana, and Michigan) covering only specified articles.

In Massachusetts (1894, amended 1898) the law covers "the making, altering, repairing, or finishing any coats, vests, trousers, or wearing apparel of any description whatsoever."

The Ohio law (1896) includes "any process of making any kind of wearing apparel for male or female wear, use, or ornament, or for the manufacture of cigars, cigarettes, or tobacco goods in any form, when such wearing apparel or other goods are to be exposed for sale or to be sold by manufacturer, wholesaler, or jobber, to the trade or by retail."

The New York law (1899) includes the "manufacturing, altering, repairing, or finishing coats, vests, knee pants, trousers, overalls, cloaks, hats, caps, suspenders, jerseys, blouses, dresses, waists, waistbands, underwear, neckwear, furs, fur trimmings, fur garments, skirts, shirts, purses, feathers, artificial flowers, cigarettes, cigars, or umbrellas."

By a special clause the New York act excludes "collars, cuffs, shirts, or shirt waists made of cotton or linen fabrics that are subject to the laundrying process before being offered for sale." This exclusion of so-called "white goods" does not occur in the laws of other States. It is apparently an effort to carry out consistently the theory that the law is designed to protect the purchaser, leaving the worker free to do as he pleases where the public health is not jeopardized.

The Pennsylvania law is identical with that of New York except that it uses simply the word "manufacture" and does not include hats and caps, and no exception is made of "white goods." It includes the "manufacture of coats, vests, trousers, knee pants, overalls, skirts, dresses, cloaks, hats, caps, suspenders, jerseys, blouses, waists, waistbands, underwear, neckwear, furs, fur trimmings, fur garments, shirts, hosiery, purses, feathers, artificial flowers, cigarettes, or cigars."

The Illinois law (1893) includes "the manufacture, in whole or in part, of coats, vests, trousers, knee pants, overalls, cloaks, shirts, ladies' waists, purses, feathers, artificial flowers, or cigars."

The New Jersey law (1893) includes "the manufacture of coats, vests, trousers, knee pants, overalls, cloaks, furs, fur trimmings, fur garments, shirts, purses, feathers, artificial flowers, or cigars."

The Missouri law (1899) includes "the manufacture of any wearing apparel, purses, feathers, artificial flowers, or other goods for male or female wear."

The Indiana law (1899) includes the "manufacture of coats, vests, trousers, knee pants, overalls, cloaks, furs, fur trimmings, fur garments, skirts, purses, feathers, artificial flowers, or cigars."

D. **Register of tenements and sweat shops.**—An essential feature in the supervision of sweat-shops and home workers by the factory inspector is the register or list of such places. In the enforcement of the ordinary factory law it is sufficient for the inspector himself to compile such a list from the visits of his deputies or from a city directory. But in the case of small contractors and home workers the number is so large and fluctuating, and individual workers are so completely hidden in the homes, that a house-to-house canvass by the inspectors can not be relied upon. Consequently the statutes of several States place the responsibility of locating these outside workers and shops upon the manufacturer or contractor who furnishes them work. Of course every manufacturer keeps a list of all his outside contractors and finishers for his own use, and it is a simple matter to require him to produce such list for inspection by the factory inspector (New York, Pennsylvania, Missouri, Illinois, and Michigan) or to furnish a copy of the same on demand (New York, Pennsylvania, Missouri, and Michigan). In Massachussets, where the statute does not require the manufacturer to furnish the list, the inspector secures it through voluntary arrangement. The manufacturer furnishes a list of his contractors (and home finishers) and the contractors in turn furnish lists of their home workers. When a manufacturer with an "inside shop" gives out work to his own employees to be taken home at night these also must be included in his list.

The compilation and checking of these lists in the office of the inspector requires considerable clerical help, especially in the city of New York, where the list runs as high as 20,000 names. Usually the names are arranged in card catalogue, by streets, and the constant changing of residence, the overlapping of names on the lists of different manufacturers, and the problematical spelling, require a highly perfected and adjustable system of registration.

E. **Publicity of register.**—The most effective check upon the manufacturer is publicity. So apprehensive is he at this point that a contractor who has once been fined in court is thenceforth unable to get work from him. Therefore, if the manufacturers' lists of contractors are treated as public records, open to the inspection of private citizens, then such agencies as trade unions, consumers' leagues, and charitable societies are able directly to reach the manufacturer, and through publicity to enforce his responsibility. It is undoubtedly a defect in the administration of the law hitherto in New York that these lists are not open to the public, like other records.

F. **License.**—In the enforcement of the ordinary factory and workshop laws the factory inspector is required to come into court and prove his allegations in order to enforce a penalty for the violation of the law. The alleged violator enjoys the benefit of the doubt, and the inspector and prosecuting attorney are held to the strict interpretation of the statute. The delay, uncertainty, and formality of such proceedings render the law often nugatory and always problematical. If, however, the inspector were permitted, upon his own belief, not merely to prosecute the violator, but also himself to impose the penalty without recourse to the courts, the execution of the law would be summary and decisive. This is the intended effect of the "license" or "permit" clause in the recent legislation of Massachusetts, New York, Pennsylvania, New Jersey, Indiana, and Michigan. This license is not merely a means of maintaining a register of the places where clothing is made, but it is a substantial condition, dependent largely upon the discretion and good judgment of the factory inspector, without which the worker or contractor is prohibited from getting employment. The refusal or revocation of a license by the inspector is a more severe penalty than the imposition of a fine by the court. The latter takes away a portion of the man's earnings, but the former shuts him off entirely from his ordinary means of getting earnings. The license is the most powerful weapon in the hands of the factory inspector. It practically removes the workers in question from the ordinary protection of the courts and places them under the direct control of an administrative officer. To the courts there remains not the enforcement of the substantial features of the law, but only the enforcement of the administrative feature, which prohibits a contractor or home worker from working without a license. The inspector revokes the license on his own discretion, and only calls in the courts to punish the one who works without a license. Of course there remains always the judicial remedy by mandamus or injunction, but in the case of the poverty-stricken workers of the tenement houses this is not a substantial remedy.

Massachusetts was the first State to introduce the license feature as a part of its factory legislation. The law of 1891, amended in 1898, prohibited tenement-house work unless a member of the family "shall first procure a license, approved by the chief of the district police," in whose hands is the enforcement of the general factory laws. It was the successful operation of this statute which led five other States to copy the provision. In Massachusetts, New York, Pennsylvania, New Jersey, Indiana, and Michigan the tenement worker is required to make application to the factory inspector for a license, and "no person, firm, or corporati n shall hire, employ, or contract with any member of a family not holding a license therefor," to manufacture the designated article in a tenement or dwelling. In Pennsylvania the license is required also for "any building or parts of building," and in New York and Indiana for any "building in the rear of any tenement or dwelling house." The latter provision was designed principally as a means of registration, in order to bring the rear factories under the observation of the factory inspector for the purpose of the ordinary factory legislation; but since the license can be revoked for these rear clothing factories in New York and Indiana, and for all clothing factories in Pennsylvania, these establishments, as well as the tenements, are brought under the direct control of the inspector. The advantage of this control was referred to by one of the Massachusetts inspectors, who says (Rep. 1900, p. 231):

> The regular workshops inspected were found, with few exceptions, in fairly good order, their great fault being the dirty state of their water-closets. If the owners of these establishments were compelled to obtain a permit from this department similar to the home-workers' license, strict cleanliness and healthier conditions could be easily obtained.

Before the license is granted the factory inspector is required to make an inspection of the room, apartment, or building sought to be licensed, and to ascertain (1) whether it is in a clean and proper sanitary condition; (2) whether there is the legal limit of air space for each person employed (New York, Pennsylvania); (3) whether it is adequately lighted by electricity or other suitable light (New York).

After the license is granted the place must be kept in the proper condition designated by the inspector, and is subject to his inspection at all times for the purpose of "ascertaining whether the garments or articles manufactured are clean and free from vermin and other matter of an infectious or contagious nature." (N. Y., sec. 100; Mass., sec. 44.)

If, upon inspection, the conditions are found not satisfactory, the license may be revoked.

The discretionary power of the inspector in granting and revoking licenses is evident from the terms employed in the several statutes. In New York he shall grant the license if he ascertain that the premises are in "a clean and proper sanitary condition," and it may be revoked if he find that "the health of the community or of the employees require it, or if it appears that the rooms or apartments to which such license relates are not in a healthy and proper sanitary condition." (N. Y., sec. 100.)

In Massachusetts the inspector determines only that the premises are "kept in a cleanly condition." (Sec. 44.) In Pennsylvania and New Jersey the "permit may be revoked at any time the health of the community or those so employed may require it." (Pa., 1897, sec. 1; N. J., 1893, sec. 1.)

The foregoing terms indicate that the criterion of cleanliness and sanitary condition must necessarily be left to the judgment of the inspector. And since inspectors differ materially in their judgment, the efficacy of the law depends largely upon the individual opinion and strength of character of these administrative officers. Indeed, under the terms of the statutes it is conceivable that tenement-house work could be almost wholly abolished, provided inspectors were selected whose standards were high enough. Such would seem to be almost the necessary result where, as in Massachusetts and New York, the instructions printed on the back of the license state that one condition "which must be observed in order to obtain and retain a license" are "absolute cleanliness of apartment and immediate premises, halls, stairs, yards, and closets." Were absolute cleanliness enforced, very few licenses could remain long outstanding.

The Illinois legislation does not require a license for home work, but by ordinance the board of health of Chicago issues such a license. This, however, contributes to the administration of the law by the factory inspector only in cases of infectious and contagious disease.

It should be added that in all States where manufacturers with "inside shops" give out work to their own employees to be taken home for work at night and on Sundays, these also are required to have a license.

G. "Tenement-made" tag.—The legislation of Massachusetts (1891) and New York (1899) has gone further than that of other States in strengthening the licensing prerogative of the inspector. In Massachusetts whoever sells or offers for sale wearing apparel made in unlicensed tenements is required to affix to each garment so made a conspicuous tag or label with the words "Tenement made" legibly printed, and the name of the State and town or city where the garment was made. In New York the law is more effective, since the inspector himself affixes the label whenever he finds goods manufactured without a license. No person except the factory inspector is permitted to remove or deface the label, the penalty being the same as for other violations of the labor law. This label, of course, as long as it remains affixed, renders the goods unsalable. In practice, the procedure in New York is somewhat as follows: In case a license has been refused upon application of a home worker the deputy inspector returns to the place of residence of the applicant within the period of two weeks to see whether the worker has followed the instructions given in the letter of refusal. If the designated improvements have been made he reports favorably and a license is sent to the applicant. But if he finds that no improvement has been made the case is closed, and no further inspection is made on the basis of the application. If the applicant desires a license he must renew his application.

If, upon inspection of premises for which a license has been refused, the inspector finds work is being conducted, he is required to affix the label "Tenement made." The inspector then secures the name of the contractor or manufacturer for whom goods are being made and instructs the workmen to notify the contractor to go to the factory inspector's office and make application for the release of the tag. The inspector also sends notice to the office that goods in the hands of the designated worker and belonging to the said contractor have been tagged.

The contractor goes to the office of the factory inspector usually with the worker, and in applying for the release of the tag, signs a form stating that the goods were being manufactured for him in unlicensed rooms. This signature becomes evidence in court on the complaint of the inspector.

If this is the first offense of the contractor he is simply warned, and is told to take the goods to his office and the deputy will be sent there to remove the tag. If it is a second offense prosecution is decided upon, and the matter is turned over to the district attorney, the deputy of the factory inspector being the complainant and witness.

The efficiency of the "tenement-made" tag is sometimes questioned, on the ground that it can easily be removed by the worker without discovery and punishment. But a consideration of the circumstances will conclusively answer this question. The tag is placed upon the goods by the deputy inspector, who immediately notifies the central office. The unlicensed worker must then go to the office in order to make application to have the tag removed. If he does not go, then it is the duty of the inspector to make another visit to his premises in order to discover the reasons for his nonappearance. If the inspector follows up the case, plainly the only conditions under which the worker could afford to remove the tag would be either by resolving to discontinue work or by moving to other quarters. And, since it is the practice of the department to prosecute not the worker, but the contractor, there is good reason why the worker shall respect the tag and bring his contractor before the inspector. He has a chance of finding another contractor if he secures a license, but he has no such chance as long as he stays in the same tenement without a license.

It will be readily understood from what precedes that the "tenement tag" is a powerful weapon in the hands of the factory inspector for prohibiting work in unlicensed places, and thereby enforcing the inspector's control over this class of manufacture. At the same time, it involves a considerable amount of formality and some uncertainty. In Pennsylvania, on the other hand, where the tag is not in vogue, this formality and uncertainty are avoided by the radical device of authorizing the inspector or his deputies to condemn and destroy all goods found in "unhealthy or unsanitary" places. Such destruction in other States is confined to "contagious and infectious" diseases, and is permitted only to the local boards of health.

The "tag" and the manufacturer.—While the manufacturer is not legally responsible and penally liable for violations of the law by home workers, he can be reached indirectly through restrictions on the sale of his goods (Massachusetts, New York, Ohio, and Missouri), or by the confiscation and destruction of his goods (Pennsylvania).

In Massachusetts (sec. 47) and Missouri (sec. 10) the merchant or dealer whose goods have been made in unlicensed or contagious places is required to label such goods with the "Tenement-made" tag, and in New York (sec. 102), where the inspector affixes the tag, and in Ohio the goods are prohibited from being sold or offered for sale.

The tag, as long as it remains affixed, is an effective prohibition on the sale of goods, and it would seem that on this account the Ohio law, which does not provide a tag, is defective. But the inspectors in Massachusetts and New York do not interpret their law as intended to reach the manufacturer in this way. They consider the purpose of the tag accomplished when the home worker or the contractor is punished if it be an unlicensed place, or when the goods have been disinfected if it be a case of contagion. Consequently, when this result is accomplished they remove the tag and permit the goods to go to the manufacturer and the market. In this way the tag fails to affect the sales of the manufacturer and imposes no restraint upon him.

H. New Zealand legislation.—In this connection the "factory act" of New Zealand, adopted in 1894, is interesting as a piece of legislation which has almost abolished home manufacture from the market. According to that statute, every building or place where two or more persons are employed, directly or indirectly, in manufacturing any article for trade or sale is defined as a factory or workshop, and is thereby brought under the stringent provisions governing factories. Like other factories, it is unlawful for work to be carried on without a license, and in granting or revoking a license the inspector enforces the laws regarding sanitation, prohibiting meals from being taken in the workroom, prohibiting the employment of children (except in special cases), prohibiting the employment of boys under 16 and women and girls for more than 48 hours per week, prohibiting overtime, and providing for holidays and Saturday half holidays. Manufacturers are permitted to give out work without restriction to these licensed places, but every "occupier of a factory, every merchant, wholesale dealer, shopkeeper, agent, or distributer," who gives out work to an unlicensed place—i. e., to a single home worker—is required to affix to such article a manufacturer's label, as follows:

Made by..........................

In No..........................street,

IN A

PRIVATE DWELLING OR UNLICENSED WORKSHOP.

AFFIXED UNDER FACTORY ACT.

Any person unlawfully removing or defacing this label will be prosecuted.

This label, by rendering goods unsalable, has stopped the manufacture of goods in unlicensed places, but the significance of the New Zealand law lies in the fact that all of the licensed places are raised to the same level as the regular factories, not merely in sanitation, as in the United States, but also in the hours of labor and the nonemployment of children.

I. Contagious and infectious diseases.—Since the main object of the existing statutes touching tenement manufacture is the protection of the purchasing public, the sections relating to contagious and infectious diseases have the leading place. In dealing with this phase of the clothing manufacture the factory inspector requires the cooperation of the local boards of health. There are two ways in which contagious or infectious diseases are discovered where clothing is being manufactured: First, by the board of health; second, by the factory inspector.

Local physicians are, of course, required by law to notify the board of health promptly of all such cases under their care. Boards of health in the several States, cooperating through courtesy, though not so required by law, with the factory inspector, send in daily reports to that official containing a complete list of all contagious disease. Where the inspector maintains a street list of home workers, as is done in Boston, New York, Philadelphia, and Chicago, it is an easy matter to refer at once to such list and to locate the presence of the contagious disease in the tenement where clothing is being manufactured. It is the duty of the inspector to go at once to the infected premises and to revoke the license, if necessary. This, of course, stops the lawful manufacture of clothing in those premises for the time being. In New York the inspector affixes the "Tenement-made" tag to such goods as he finds and turns them over to the board of health, who may disinfect the goods and remove the label, or condemn and destroy them.

In other States the board of health is given power to take such action as the public health may require. In Pennsylvania, as already stated, the factory inspector and his deputies have the unusual power to destroy goods both in places of contagion and infection, and also in other places which are merely "unhealthy or unsanitary."

Boards of health also notify the inspector each day of all places which have been disinfected, upon which the deputy returns the license to such as have been deprived of it during the continuance of the contagion.

The question as to whether it is possible to thoroughly disinfect woolen and cotton goods in cases where they have been contaminated by such diseases as phthisis, diphtheria, smallpox, chicken pox, scarlet fever, and measles, is answered differently by different medical authorities. The Pennsylvania law is based upon the theory that such disinfection is at least uncertain, if not impossible. Undoubtedly, were it known to the purchasing public that a certain lot of goods had been exposed to contagion, they would decline to purchase such goods, even though officially assured that they had been "thoroughly disinfected." From the point of view of the consumer, whatever difference of opinion may exist among medical experts, the Pennsylvania law authorizing the destruction of contaminated goods by the board of health or factory inspector is the safest and most satisfactory.

J. Prosecution and penalties.—The penalties prescribed for violation of any of the requirements in the law range from $3 for the first offense in Illinois to $20 in New York, and $50 in Pennsylvania and Massachusetts. The maximum penalties for later offenses are $100 in Illinois, $200 in New York, and $250 in Pennsylvania. In New York and Pennsylvania there may be added imprisonment for not more than 30 days.

The question as to whether these penalties apply equally to home workers, contractors, and manufacturers is an important and interesting one. Plainly the enforcement of the penalties for violation upon the home workers imposes a burden out of proportion with the same penalty enforced upon a contractor, and far more than the same penalty if imposed upon the manufacturer. Also the difficulties of prosecution in the case of the thousands of home workers are far greater than in the case of the hundreds of contractors or the tens of manufacturers. Furthermore, the moral effect upon others is small when a home worker is prosecuted, compared with the effect of a prosecution of the contractor, and insignificant compared with the prosecution of a manufacturer. The home worker is unknown and without influence, and moreover is dependent upon the contractor. On the other hand, if the contractor is held responsible for violation of law on the part of his home workers, he can control every one of them, whether they be ten or five hundred. The simple refusal to give them work is the heaviest of penalties. Consequently, the several statutes forbid contractors from giving out work to families not holding licenses (Massachusetts, New York, Pennsylvania, New Jersey, Indiana), or when notified by the inspecor that such family has not complied with the law (Ohio). In New York the inspector has prosecuted not more than a half dozen home workers and has secured only one or two convictions, but he has prosecuted nearly 150 contractors and secured nearly 100 convictions.

While the penalty imposed upon the contractor is more effective than that imposed upon the home worker, it is the manufacturer who holds the strategic position in the enforcement of the law. If he employs 50 contractors and each contractor 50 home workers, plainly he gives employment to 2,500 home workers. The contractors are dependent upon him just as the home workers are dependent upon the contractor. The manufacturer's position before the community is a responsible one. The sale of his goods depends upon the reputation of his house.

The existing laws do not make the manufacturer penally responsible for violation of law by home workers when employed by his contractor. Of course, if he employs them directly, or if he sends out work at night by his own employees, he is responsible for this home work. But generally, and this is the essence of the sweating system, he gives his work to contractors, and these in turn give it out to the home finishers. Consequently, if the manufacturer were brought into court under the existing statutes for work being done in unlicensed homes, he could claim that it was not he, but his contractor, who gave out the work to the home finisher, and who is responsible for the same. The contract system possesses as one of its advantages, not merely the cheaper cost of manufacture, but also the shifting of legal responsibility from the manufacturer to the middleman.

K. The landlord.—Tenement house workers are usually a floating population with very little property, and their places of residence are rapidly changing. In addition to this, when they are congregated in large numbers, of foreign extraction and illiterate, the mere uncertainty as to the spelling of their names makes the problem of the factory inspector a perplexing one. To reach them all individually and continuously is impossible. They must be reached either through their employer or through their landlord. While the legislation of several States brings in the employer, i e., the contractor or sweater, New York is the only State which makes the landlord responsible. In addition to the ordinary requirements governing the sanitation and safety of dwelling houses, the New York law (sec. 105) prohibits the "owner, lessee, or agent of a tenement or dwelling house, or of a building in the rear of a tenement or dwelling house" from permitting the use of his premises for the manufacture of clothing without a license and contrary to law. The factory inspector is required to serve notice of such violation upon the owner, lessee, or agent, and the latter is given 30 days in which to cause the unlawful manufacture to discontinue, or 15 days thereafter in which to bring proceedings for dispossession, the unlawful manufacture being constituted a sufficient cause for dispossession. Failure in this subjects him to penalties as though he himself were engaged in the unlawful manufacture.

To what extent the provisions holding the landlord responsible can be made of practical value has not yet been determined, since the New York inspector has not relied upon it in the enforcement of the law.

L. Summary.—It may be briefly stated in regard to the effectiveness of the foregoing laws on tenement-house work that—

1. They have cooperated with the economic development of the industry in driving shopwork from tenements. Practically in Massachusetts, New York, and Pennsylvania there are at the present time very few, if any, of the home shops which occasioned complaint 10 years ago. The only remaining home work of significance is that of home finishers, custom tailors, women who work for pin money, and employees who take work home at night from the shop. Home finishing is that subsidiary part of hand work on coats and pants which has not yet been transferred to the regular workshop. It is now the bulk of home work. In Boston, where the law has been strictly enforced, there is very little home finishing, this work being largely transferred to shops, and the wages are 40 to 50 per cent higher than in New York for the same work.

2. With a strict enforcement of the law the system of licensing is superior to the proposed abolition of home work, since the inspector is then able to grant the privilege of home work in cases of emergency where peculiar hardship would otherwise result, while at the same time he reduces the amount of home work to the point where its competition does not seriously affect the condition and wages of labor. This strict enforcement of the law, however, since it depends upon the discretion of the inspector, is very difficult to secure.

3. The statutes, in placing discretionary power in the matter of granting and revoking licenses in the hands of the factory inspectors, intrusts them with the most powerful of weapons, namely, the right to grant or withhold the privilege of earning a living. The great powers of this office, resting, as they do, in the hands of subordinates, render the right selection of appointees extremely important, since its opportunities for corruption and political favoritism are unusually tempting. The success of the law in Massachusetts is doubtless owing more to the civil-service regulation and permanent tenure of the inspectors than to the stringent character of the law.

4. The evident success of the leading States in reducing the evils of tenement-house work through legislation, and the apparent willingness of other States where a less amount of clothing is made to copy their legislation, make Federal legislation unnecessary and inadvisable. The existing defects are not in the laws, but in the administration of the laws.

5. The depressing effects of immigration on wages are materially counteracted by the restriction or prohibition of tenement-house work, and this, together with the jeopardy to the purchasing public through contagious and infectious diseases, render the strict enforcement of the laws restricting tenement-house work of vital importance, both to clothing workers and to the public.

4. PROPOSED ABOLITION OF TENEMENT-HOUSE MANUFACTURE.

The excessive evils of tenement-house manufacture, and the difficulties of regulation, have caused a demand in various quarters for its abolition by legislation. This demand is based on the alleged impossibility of adequate inspection, and the resulting danger to the purchaser of clothing. Says the Illinois inspector (1895, p. 52):

It is clear that even the 1,715 contractors' shops now known to us can not be inspected often enough to render it safe for the public to purchase goods made up in them while they are kept on premises where poverty continually breeds disease, and though any one given shop may be wholesome enough, yet no goods can be guaranteed noninfectious which have passed through it to the rooms of the poverty-stricken home finisher. * * * From this danger nothing short of prohibition can protect the purchaser. * * * The dangers of the shop are much increased by the circumstance that garment making is a season trade, that the season is uncertain, and it is short and very intense. New people open shops who were never contractors before, and knew nothing of the requirements of the law. During the season no staff of inspectors could cover all the shops often enough to prevent violations of the law or give assurance that no infectious disease is in the shops where garments are being made. * * * The city ordinance requires the physician who is attendant upon any case of infectious or contagious disease to report the same to the board of health, but physicians can not report what they do not know, and in many cases among the very poor a physician is called in only when death is imminent to save the annoyance of a coroner's inquest. Meanwhile infected clothing may have been finished and sent out for weeks before the danger is known by anyone.

THE ABOLITION OF TENEMENT HOME WORK.

The following is from the report of the Illinois factory inspector for 1896 (p. 43):

The eagerness of parents to conceal the presence of disease has led them to hide, in all conceivable ways, children sick with infectious maladies, locking the patient in the pantry, covering it with a pile of garments in process of manufacture, and to tear down quarantine cards or to post them on rear doors. Practices of this kind, which caused public protest in the smallpox epidemic of 1894, went on without any outcry during the long struggle with diphtheria in 1896. They baffle at all times, and with varying degrees of success, the efforts of all officials, State and local, who try to protect the public health by enforcing the regulations of tenement-house shops.

No goods can be guaranteed noninfectious which have passed through the tenement-house shop and a home finisher's living room, and so long as the wholesale manufacturer has any goods made up on tenement-house premises none of the goods can be guaranteed free from danger of infection, since neither the retailer nor the purchasers can know which among them are tenement made.

Charges like the foregoing found expression in a demand for Federal legislation governing the subject, the best known of which was the so-called "Sulzer bill," introduced in the Fifty-fourth Congress. (Fifty-fourth Congress, first session, H. R. 3346.) This bill, while in form it provided simply for a license system, would in effect have amounted to prohibition, since the amount of the license was placed high above profitable expenditure. The bill provided that every person engaged in the manufacture of clothing and cigars who shall give out material for manufacture "in rooms or buildings occupied for eating, sleeping, or domestic purposes," shall pay a "tax of $300 annually for each person with whom a contract or agreement to wholly or partially manufacture or make up such articles shall be made." The tax was to be collected by the officers of the United States internal revenue.

One objection to this act, supposing it not to be prohibitive, would be the apparent guaranty which a Federal license would give against State interference. It is probable that Federal legislation on this subject would come under the head of a regulation of interstate commerce, and as such, a Federal law might provide for identification of tenement-made goods by means of a label, such as is described above under the legislation of Massachusetts and New York.

The New York tenement house commission in presenting its preliminary report in 1901, made recommendations going far toward the abolition of tenement-house work (p. 70–71):

The law requiring the licensing of work carried on in tenement houses has undoubtedly led to certain improvements, but the very attempt to enforce the law has furnished additional proof of the undesirability of the conditions. Where workers apply for a license they may be investigated, but if a license is refused it is not always possible to be sure that work will be discontinued, and if the license is not applied for it will only be by chance that the tenement-house workshop will be discovered. * * *

The commission does not feel warranted in recommending the absolute abolition of tenement-house labor. It recommends the amendment of chapter 191 of the laws of 1899 by the insertion of a proviso that no license shall be issued for any room in a tenement house containing less than 1,250 cubic feet of air, or used for the purpose of cooking, eating, or sleeping, or for children, or otherwise than as a workshop. This recommendation regarding the size of the room in which labor should be allowed is based upon the knowledge of the fact that by all the members of the family of any room connected with a living apartment. It is also based upon the universally accepted fact that the average tenement-house family consists of five members, though undoubtedly in frequent instances the boarders taken by such families make the average size higher. Among the Italian garment workers it has been frequently found that two, and even three families, making a total of from 10 to 15 individuals, occupy a single apartment. But taking the conservative estimate and applying the provision of the law that a workshop must have at least 250 cubic feet of space for each worker, your commission believes that 1,250 feet (12 by 12 by 9) should be required as the minimum size of any workroom in a tenement house, because experience has shown that an average of not less than five persons will use the room for a greater or less part of the day.

While the tenement-house commission only recommends a minimum cubic capacity for living rooms in which clothing manufacture is conducted, yet to one who is familiar with the dimensions of the rooms in which at the present time the Italian home finishers are at work, it will be evident that the minimum, 1,250 cubic feet, is so high that but few families could qualify for the license.

The Illinois inspector in his report for 1899 takes a less radical position regarding the abolition of tenement-house work than in earlier reports. He says in advocating for Illinois the enactment of a law similar to that in Massachusetts, New York, and Pennsylvania (p. 15):

This law has had a thorough trial in New York, Pennsylvania, and Massachusetts, and there is no doubt of its successful operation. Not only will it to a certain extent protect the public and employees from the danger of tenement-house manufacture, but it will check the growth of the sweatshop system and aid in the development lately noticeable toward the more wholesome conditions of the factory. In 1894 this department reported that the garment factory was disappearing before the tenement-house shop. In the last two years the number of establishments in the garment trades employing more than 50 people has increased from 70 to 89. This, with other data at hand, leads to the conclusion that the tendency is now in the other direction.

The proposed law in eliminating the most unsanitary shop will also eliminate the most tenacious rivals of the factories. As the economies practised by such places at the expense of the employees and the public are no longer tolerated, they will not be able to compete with the steam-power and progressive management of the modern factory. In this future extension of the factory lies the best hope of doing away with the abuses that are inherent in the sweating system, and will never entirely disappear as long as the system itself survives.

5. PUBLIC CONTRACTS.

While neither the Federal Government nor any State government has undertaken to abolish tenement-house work where the work is sold to private purchasers, yet where the Federal Government itself is a purchaser of clothing it has recently instituted measures for the protection of its public servants. The departments of Federal Government for which clothing and uniforms are manufactured are those of the Army and Navy. The letter carriers purchase their own uniforms according to the Government specifications. In certain cases, as at Philadelphia, the association of letter carriers inserts a clause in the contracts prohibiting tenement-house work. Practically all of the clothing for the Navy is manufactured at the Naval Clothing Factory, navy-yard, Brooklyn.

Army uniforms were formerly purchased from contractors without specifications as to conditions of manufacture, but beginning in 1900, owing to revelations made regarding the contagion of measles and similar diseases in the Army camps during the Spanish-American war, the quartermaster at Philadelphia, under whom the heavy clothing is manufactured, has inserted in his "Information to bidders for the manufacture of military garments," the specification that "all work, including operating, finishing, buttonholing, pressing, etc., must be done in a regularly organized factory, conforming in every detail to the factory laws of the State of Pennsylvania; no sweatshop work will be allowed under any circumstances."
The following article is inserted in the contracts:

ARTICLE III. It is expressly agreed that no part of the work incident to the manufacture of said clothing shall be sublet or made in any place not covered by the factory laws of the State of Pennsylvania and evidenced by the certificate of an authorized factory inspector, and that failure to comply with the conditions of this clause shall be deemed a valid cause for canceling this contract, and withdrawing all work that may be in course of manufacture.

* * * * * * *

That in case of failure of the said party of the second part to comply with the stipulation of this contract according to the true intent and meaning thereof, then the party of the first part shall have the power to have the work done by others of his own selection and charge any additional expense incurred against the party of the second part.

It is stated by the assistant quartermaster-general at Philadelphia that the insertion of these clauses in the contract "has had no noticeable effect on the contract price of making."

The khaki clothing for soldiers in the Tropics is manufactured under the supervision of the quartermaster's department at New York. These contracts include a clause to the effect that all such clothing "must be made by the contractors in their own factories under the most perfect sanitary conditions."

Clothing for the National Guard of the several States is usually purchased from the War Department, and is therefore protected by the specifications of that Department. When the clothing is purchased from other sources there are usually no specifications regarding labor or conditions of manufacture, except in Massachusetts and California. A Massachusetts law provides that clothing shall be made in the city of Boston and not in a sweatshop, and an inspecting officer is detailed at all times to enter factories each day to see where they are made and the manner of making.

For the National Guard of California the only clause affecting labor or its location is a clause prohibiting the employment of either "convict or Chinese labor in or about the manufacture of the material used or in the performance of the labor in carrying out the contract."

All the clothing for the National Guard of Pennsylvania is made in the manufacturing department of the State arsenal.

In New York all contracts for the manufacture of clothing for the militia include a clause which prescribes that all the laws and regulations of the State of New York relative to the employment of labor, the hours or work, places wherein work shall be carried on, shall be strictly observed. A clause of this kind, of course, does not require contractors to go any further than the law requires private manufacturers to go in eliminating subcontracting and tenement-house work.

Canada.—The movement in the government of Canada to suppress "sweating" in carrying out government contracts had its beginning in the post-office department and has extended to the contract work of all branches of the administration.

The first antisweating regulations in Canada were made in connection with contracts for the supply of mail bags and satchels for the post-office department. The militia department was the next to introduce regulations into its contracts. These regulations have been inserted in all contracts awarded since 1898 for the manufacture of militia clothing. The contracts of the several departments have similar "regulations framed with a view to securing the payment to the workmen of fair wages and the performance of the work under proper sanitary conditions."
The following section is inserted in the contracts:

With a view to suppressing the sweating system and securing payment to the workmen of fair wages and the performance of the work under sanitary conditions, this contract shall be subject to the following regulations, and strict compliance with the true spirit and intent of the various provisions herein contained is required:

SECTION 1. All articles included in this contract shall be made up in the contractor's own factory, and no portion of the work of making up such articles shall be done at the houses of the work people. The contract shall not, nor shall any portion thereof, be transferred without the written permission of the minister of militia and defense; and subletting of the contract or any of the work to be performed under the contract, other than that which may be customary in the trades concerned, is hereby prohibited.

SEC. 2. If the contractor violates the condition herein mentioned against subletting he shall not be entitled to receive any payment under the contract for work done by the subcontractor; and the minister of militia and defense may refuse to accept any work performed by a subcontractor in violation of the prohibition herein contained against subletting.

Great Britain.—On February 13, 1891, the following resolution was passed by the House of Commons:

Resolved, That in the opinion of this House it is the duty of the Government in all Government contracts to make provision against the evils recently disclosed before the sweating committee; to insert such conditions as may prevent the abuse arising from subletting; and to make every effort to secure the payment of such wages as are generally accepted as current in each trade for competent workmen.

February, 1892, returns of the forms issued by the war office, admiralty, board of works, and other departments of the Government were called for.

The following extracts from the conditions of contracts made by the board of trade (Parliamentary Papers, 1892, LXIV, 189) are representative of the conditions made by the several departments:

SEC. 5. The contractor undertakes that all garments included in this contract shall be made up in his own factory, and that no work shall be done at the homes of the work people. Any infringement of this condition, if proved to the satisfaction of the president of the board of trade, shall render the contractor liable to a penalty not exceeding £100 for each offense.

SEC. 6. No portion of this contract shall be transferred without the written permission of the president of the board of trade. Subletting, other than that which may be customary in the trades concerned, is prohibited.

In 1896 a special committee was appointed "to consider the working of the fair-wages resolution of the 13th February, 1891, and the administration of the various Government departments."

In considering the question of "subcontracting," the committee came to two propositions:

(a) Subletting or subcontracting may be perfectly legitimate where the particular form of contract in question is customary to the trade or where the contractor in question, in the ordinary course of his business, sublets or subcontracts that particular portion of the work.

(b) But subcontracting or subletting does not appear to the committee to be permissible where it is not customary to the trade; nor should the contractor who, in the ordinary course of his business, could not or would not himself carry out certain work be allowed to sublet it to others. Where a subcontract is allowed, the principal contractor should, as regards the carrying out of the fair-wages resolution, be held responsible for his agent. (Parliamentary Papers, 1897, X, 334, VI.)

The London county council.—"The council's standing orders provide that in all clothing contracts a minimum scale of wages for workers and work of every description shall be fixed by the council, and that contractors shall be called upon to sign an agreement to pay according to the scale. These standing orders were passed by the council as the result of an exhaustive inquiry into the conditions of the clothing trade with the object of securing the payment of a fair rate of wages. * * * Special clauses were inserted in the contract providing that the contract or any part, share, or interest in it should not be transferred, assigned, or sublet by the contractor, directly or indirectly, without the written consent of the council; that the contractors would directly employ and pay all work people employed in connection with the contract wages or remuneration at a rate or scale not less than the rate or scale fixed by the council, and would observe and cause to be observed by such work people hours of labor not greater than the hours of labor also stated in such schedule; further, that the contractors would carry out the work in their own factories.

"The contract also required the contractors to observe the following stipulations at all times during its continuance:

"(a) The rate of wages for every class of work done in any workroom shall be posted up in some conspicuous place in that room.

"(b) Any person authorized by the council shall have at all reasonable times free access to every part of the factory.

"(c) Any person authorized as above may see any worker apart.

"(d) The wages book shall at all times be open to inspection by any person thereto authorized by the council.

"In the case of the clause prohibiting 'home work,' one of the most fruitful sources of sweating which the council had strenuously set its face against, a penalty of £100 had been fixed."

In other clauses dealing with wages and the regulation of the factory a penalty of £25 was fixed for each breach. (London county council, annual report for year ending March 31, 1898; report of the stores committee, pp. 135–136.)

6. LABELS.

The wish of the purchaser to know the conditions under which his garments are manufactured is the basis of the organization known as the Consumers' League, organized May 1, 1899. (See testimony by Mr. J. G. Brooks, Manufactures and General Business, Vol. XIV, p. 137.) The officers of this association enter into contracts with manufacturers binding them to obey the State factory laws in all their provisions, to have all their goods made wholly on their premises, to employ no children under 16 years of age, and to use no overtime work. Manufacturers signing this agreement are furnished with the official label of the league, to be attached to the garments which they place upon the market.

It will be seen that the conditions imposed by the Consumers' League are superior to those of the factory acts in raising the age limit to 16 when it is usually 14 and in prohibiting overtime work. The label has now been granted to 25 manufacturers controlling 26 factories situated in 9 States. Their organized customers are in 30 leagues in the 11 States of Massachusetts, New York, Pennsylvania, Ohio, Kentucky, Virginia, Illinois, Michigan, Wisconsin, and Minnesota, and in the Federation of Women's Clubs in those States and also in the States of Maryland, Tennessee, and Rhode Island. The Consumers' League has also enlisted the cooperation of the Women's Christian Temperance Union, the National Council of Jewish Women, the King's Daughters, and other organizations of women, whose members are recommended to give the preference, in their shopping, to garments bearing the label of the league.

It is noticeable that of the 25 manufacturers who are granted the label, 16 are in the State of Massachusetts and 9 in the rest of the country. This is due to the excellent factory legislation of Massachusetts and the thorough manner in which it is enforced. The standard in that State is so high that the manufacturers need make but few changes in their previous arrangements in order to receive the award of the use of the label.

It is stated by the secretary of the league (May 3, 1900) that no manufacturer in New Jersey or the city of New York appears upon the list, because the methods of enforcement of the factory laws therein have been such that the league has not been able to base upon them any guaranty that all the provisions of the factory law are obeyed in any given factory, or that all its goods are made on its own premises. It is hoped, however, that within the next two years efficient methods may be adopted by the departments of factory inspectors in both these States, and after this is done a large addition of manufacturers in New York City and New Jersey can be added to the list of label-using employers.

Slightly different from the label of the Consumers' League is that of the Garment Makers' Union. This label is granted only to those manufacturers who employ union help or send their work out to contractors with union shops. Heretofore, owing to the weakness of the union, many of these shops have not been superior either in wages, hours, or sanitary conditions to the majority of shops without the label. It was considered by the union officers that if by means of the label a large number of shops could be unionized, they could afterwards secure the better conditions. The label, therefore, has not stood for the absence of sweat-shop conditions, but has stood only for a willingness to lead in the improvements of conditions. This policy has been found unsatisfactory and unfair to the better manufacturers who adopted the label, and it therefore has recently been abandoned. By a resolution adopted May, 1901, by the executive board of the United Garment Workers of America, based upon instructions from their national convention, the label is hereafter to be furnished only to those manufacturers who maintain exclusively their own shops. The union label, like the Consumers' label, henceforth is intended to be a guaranty that the labeled goods are not manufactured by a contractor nor finished in a tenement.

CHAPTER IV.
EFFECT OF FOREIGN BORN ON CIGAR-MAKING TRADE.

The direct effect of immigration on the earnings of cigar makers is slight. In 1900 the number of alien tobacco workers of all kinds who entered the ports was 377. The census of 1890 showed 111,625 tobacco and cigar factory operatives in the country, and it is estimated that in 1900 there were 88,000 cigar makers. (See Industrial Commission, Capital and Labor, vol. —, p. 720.) It is to the indirect effect of immigration that attention must be directed, i. e., the effect of the competition of those who learn the trade after arriving in this country.

Of the 94,176 white cigar and tobacco operatives in the United States in 1890, 35,096, or 37.3 per cent, were foreign born. The following table shows the distribution by nativity, parentage, and sex:

Tobacco and cigar factory operatives.

[Census 1890, Population, Part II, Table 82.]

	Number.	Per cent.
Total white	94,176	100.00
Native white, native parents:		
Male	22,468	23.85
Female	7,582	8.05
Native white, foreign parents:		
Male	20,278	21.52
Female	8,752	9.29
Foreign born:		
Male	27,972	29.72
Female	7,124	7.57

It will be seen that the foreign born of both sexes number 37.29 per cent of the total number of white operatives, and that the foreign born and the children of foreigners number 68.10 per cent of the total number of operatives.

Since the census does not separate cigar makers from other tobacco workers, it is impossible to present data from that source for that branch of the industry. In lieu thereof the following estimates are made of nationalities in the leading centers of cigar manufacture. It may be stated that in New York City probably 25 per cent of the cigars manufactured in the United States are supposed to be produced.

Nationality of cigar makers in leading centers.

	Total.	Germans.	Bohemians.	Jews.	Americans.	Others.
New York	15,000	5,000	4,500	3,000		2,500
Chicago	5,000			2,000		3,000
Philadelphia	4,000	900		1,200	1,900	
Boston	1,600	160		600	680	160

The most serious effect on wages as a result of immigration followed the incoming of the Bohemians in 1879–80. The Bohemians have now established themselves in the trade in New York, and have made efforts to improve their wages. Following the Bohemians the next important wave of immigration was that of the Russian Jews, who have entered the trade during the past 10 or 12 years. It is the immigration of the latter race which at the present time occasions complaint.

Beside immigration, other factors which depress the wages of cigar makers are machinery and division of labor, country competition, and women and girls. Opposed to these are the efforts of labor organization.

The part played by division of labor in the trade may be inferred from the following description: "Booking" consists in straightening out and dampening the leaves. "Stripping" is drawing out the large midrib of the leaf. "Bunch breaking" is the selecting and shaping of the "filler" tobacco. This is usually done by hand on the 10-cent cigars and by a mold on the 5-cent cigars. The hand work without the mold produces the better cigars, since the arranging and shaping of the filler is then adjusted through the delicate touch of the skilled workman. "Rolling" consists in cutting the wrapper and then rolling it around the filler. This is done by hand or by the aid of a "suction table," the latter being a metal plate with perforations for air suction, so as to hold the leaf in place. The plate also cuts the leaf to the exact shape desired for the wrapper. Either with or without the suction table the cigar must be rolled by hand, but the table permits less skilled workmen and girls to take the places of the skilled mechanic. The Cigar Makers' International Union prohibits the use of the suction table by its members, and about one-half of its members are employed on hand work and one-half on mold work. "Team work," i. e., the division of labor where one employee "breaks bunches" for two "rollers," is also contrary to the rules of the union, but this rule is not enforced except in localities, like Boston, where the union is strong.

In order more accurately to compare the part played by immigration, country competition, and labor organization, the following table is compiled, showing the different prices at which a selected standard 5-cent cigar is made at the present time.

Prices for making "clear seed" mold cigars, "shape," 4½ inches, per 1,000.

Locality.	Union scale.	Nonunion large shops.	Jewish sweat- shops.	Nonunion with suction table.	Country competition without suction table.
New York	$8.50	$6.00	$4.00	$5.00	
Chicago	9.50	$5.00 to 5.50	4.00		
Milwaukee	7.50	5.50 to 6.50			
Philadelphia	7.50	7.00		4.50	
Boston	8.00				
Berks, Bucks, and Montgomery counties, Pa.					$5.00 to $5.50
Kingston, N. Y.					4.00 to 5.00

The above prices include both bunch breaking and rolling. Where team work prevails—for example, on a $4.50 cigar—the roller is paid $2.50 per 1,000, and the bunch breaker is usually paid by the week on an estimate of $2 per 1,000.

The significant fact to be noted from the foregoing table is the wide range of prices paid for identical work. Even the scales prescribed by the cigar makers' union range from $7.50 per 1,000 in Philadelphia to $9.50 in Chicago. Outside the union the prices range from $4 to $7. The nonunion shops which pay $5 to $7 for hand work, or $4.50 to $5 with suction table, are usually large establishments, employing in Philadelphia as high as 900 and in New York as high as 2,000 work people. In these shops the employees are largely immigrants, but mainly women and girls, the American-born daughters of immigrants. The "suction table," it will be noticed, effects a very large saving for the manufacturer in the price per thousand cigars, as follows: In New York, $1 below the nonunion shops and $3.50 below the union scale; in Philadelphia, $2.50 below nonunion shops and $3 below the union scale, but only 50 cents to $1 below the adjoining country product in Berks, Bucks, and Montgomery counties. The suction table is not used in Boston on account of the exceptional strength of the union, which includes more than 99 per cent of the cigar makers; nor in Chicago, where immigrant and sweat-shop labor is abundant at low prices; nor in the country shops where labor is cheap. It is not extensively used in New York on account of the strength of the union and because the large manufacturers do not make their 5-cent cigars in New York. The latter are made in their country shops.

The sweatshop labor in New York and Chicago, which produces the cheapest work on this grade of cigars outside country districts, is Jewish. In Chicago this labor is employed not by contractors, but by small manufacturers, in cellars, alleys, and over stables under the most disagreeable surroundings of filth and overcrowding. These small manufacturers obtain their capital partly from the $5 to $15 which they charge the beginner for learning the trade. They also get his labor for three months free. They buy their tobacco and boxes and sell their cigars to jobbers. In New York these shops are strictly sweaters' shops, managed by contractors who take out tobacco belonging to manufacturers and return the finished product at a contract price for the labor. These shops, however, are very few in number, including less than 500 people, although prior to 1885 they predominated. The tenement-house legislation and the strong agitation of the labor organization have practically abolished this form of work. But in Chicago the small manufacturer or sweater controls a large proportion of the trade, including, perhaps, 1,000 employees.

The position of the labor organization in the manufacture of cigars is unique. The International Cigar Makers' Union, with 35,000 members—about 40 per cent of the workmen in the trade—is noted for its high dues, its strong defense funds, and the determined strikes which it has conducted. Through its efforts there has been a continuous increase in the wages paid to its members, so that it is estimated that on a class of work where sweatshop and nonunion labor can earn $6 to $9 per week the union labor earns $12 to $18. In only one city in the country—Denver, Colo.—was there a decline in union prices during the depression of 1893-1897.

But the strength of the union has had a peculiar effect. While its membership has increased and its scale has risen it has lost control of the large factories, and the manufacturers have moved their establishments into country districts. This holds true only of the cigars which sell at 5 cents or less retail. On the 10-cent and higher-priced cigars the union labor retains its hold, but on this high-grade work the non-union workmen get the same prices as the union workmen.

The proportion of large factories controlled by the union may be judged from the following facts concerning shops in Boston, Chicago, Philadelphia, and New York:

In Boston, where the union controls nearly every shop in the city, the 10 largest shops employing more than 20 workmen each have 973 employees, being an average of 97.3 employees per shop, whereas 154 shops, each employing less than 20 men, have 500 employees, being an average of 3.3 employees each. The union rules provide that an employer may have the use of the label if he has been a member of the union 1 year or if he employs at least one workman. Consequently, since the employer counts as 1 workman, it is perhaps true that the 154 small shops in Boston with 3.3 employees each include less than 3 wage-earners each, and that a large proportion of the shops are simply a small manufacturer with an apprentice or a member of his family at work.

In Chicago the union controls 800 small shops, with 1,700 work people, or an average of 2.1 workmen each, including 200 small employers. In that city the large shops employing 20 or more people are, as a rule, nonunion shops. In Philadelphia the largest union shop has 14 employees. In New York the factories of 400 to 2,000 employees are nonunion.

The inference derived from these facts is that the high union scale is partly fictitious, because it represents in many cases merely constructive wages paid by the small cigar manufacturer to himself or to a member of his family, and not actual money wages paid to a wage-earner. The feature of the union by which this situation is maintained is the cigar makers' label. The label secures for those to whom it is granted an exclusive market of a certain class of customers, and is a substitute for the billboard advertising of the large manufacturers. There is a strong competition among label users for the market created by this kind of advertising, and the prices at which the 5-cent cigars are sold to retailers is $2 to $5 per 1,000 less than the price which the large manufacturers receive for their highly advertised cigars.

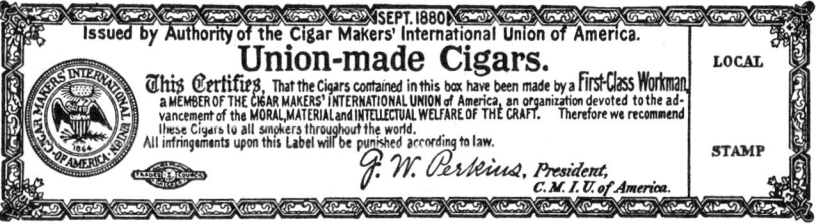

The significance of the position of the Cigar Makers' Union in this connection is that immigrants do not join the union, but are confined to nonunion shops, and even after learning the trade they continue to work on nonunion scales of wages.

More serious than immigration for the city cigar maker is the spread of country factories. In internal-revenue district No. 1, which includes, besides the city of Philadelphia, the counties of Berks, Bucks, and Montgomery, more than one-half the cigars are now made in the country shops. A Philadelphia manufacturer, without changing the number of his district, can plant his annexes in the country, where, in place of $7.50 for union labor and $7 for nonunion labor, he can have the same cigar made for $5 or $5.50. At this price the suction table is not profitable. These country establishments have usually several advantages. Small communities offer favorable inducements for the location of a large factory in their midst. They often donate the ground in fee to the manufacturer; frequently they provide a subscription toward the building, and they grant an exemption from taxes for a term of years. Lastly, the cost of living is lower in these country places, and the working population has not been instructed in the methods and aims of unions. Much of the work, however, is crude, and the 10-cent cigars can not be made on a large scale.

But the cheaper grades are increasing. In the counties of York and Lancaster, Pa., where large quantities of tobacco are raised, there have grown up many good-sized shops, and the tobacco growers themselves with their families occupy winter months and rainy days in making cigars. Prices there are as low as $1.50 per 1,000; but this is on cheaper cigars, without "shape," which sell 2 for 5 cents or 3 for 5 cents.

Large cigar manufacturers in the city of New York who have had labor troubles have within recent years turned especially to the towns of Pennsylvania, where they can find cheap labor, and in several cases have established what may be termed schools for the education of local labor in cigar making. Such establishments are located at Lancaster, York, Ephrata, Manheim, Danville, and Hamburg, Pa.; also in New York at Kingston and Newburg, and in New Jersey at New Brunswick and Elizabeth. These country factories employ from 25 to 1,000 people.

It is important to note, in connection with complaints made on account of the congestion of immigrants in the large seaport cities, that the country employment in the cigar trade is actually drawing immigrants from the cities. Philadelphia manufacturers and contractors to a considerable extent send employees from their city establishments to their country establishments, and frequently green immigrants, instead of stopping in the city, go directly to these country places in order to take up the manufacture of cigars.

Besides the country establishments the most serious encroachment upon the earnings of the skilled cigar maker is in the competition of women and girls. Through the increased division of labor and the introduction of the suction table girls can learn the trade so that a good hand at $2.50 per 1,000 for rolling can earn $7.50 per week. In this occupation, unlike clothing, endurance is not required, and therefore the work of women is a more serious competitor than it is in the manufacture of clothing. The large establishments in New York and Philadelphia which have in recent years extended the sale of advertised cigars employ almost exclusively girls and women, usually American born of immigrant parentage. In New York the recent strike in the largest factories resulted in the displacement of large numbers of men by girls. It is the opinion of the majority of cigar makers representing the local unions in New York that this competition of American-born women and girls is much more dangerous to them than immigration.

In the light of the foregoing facts regarding country competition and woman labor, immigration may be decided as third in importance in the depression of wages of cigar makers. It is doubtless true that the green immigrant, who is of course unable to become an apprentice in a union shop, turns to a "scab" shop of his own nationality. Here he can learn the rudiments of the trade, and can in time become a skilled workman. When he reaches that stage he is ready to join the union if work can be found in that direction. This the Jew has done in large numbers in Philadelphia, New York, and Boston. But in Chicago, with its extremely high union scale and a relative oversupply of union labor, he continues in the small shop of the Jewish manufacturer or enters a large nonunion factory, where at a rate of $5 per 1,000 he can earn $7 to $12 per week. This class of competition has reduced the price on the 5-cent and cheaper cigars within 30 years to the extent of $1 or $2 per 1,000, but on the higher-grade cigars prices remain steady. In the cheapest shop in Chicago, on a 5-cent cigar employing immigrant Jews, the "roller" is paid $2.50 per 1,000, and earns 80 cents to $1.75 per day; the "bunch breaker" is paid $1.50 per 1,000, and earns $1.36 to $1.44 per day. Following is a schedule of this shop, showing for each employee the price per piece, the amount of work done, and the daily and weekly earnings. The highest earnings are $10.50 per week. On the basis of the usual 9 months' work this is an average of $9.86 per week.

Jewish sweatshop, Chicago.

Occupation.	Employees.	Nationality.	Sex.	Cigars per day.	Price per thousand.	Daily earnings.	Weekly earnings.	Yearly earnings (9 mos.).	Average earnings per week.
Roller	3	Jew	Male	500	$2.50	$1.25	$7.50	$292.50	$5.62
Do	2	...do	...do	700	2.50	1.75	10.50	409.24	7.87
Do	1	...do	...do	400	2.00	.80	4.80	187.20	3.60
Do	1	...do	...do	350	2.50	.87½	5.25	204.36	3.93
Apprentice roller	1	...do	...do	250			1.50	53.04	1.02
Do	1	...do	...do	500			6.00	234.00	4.50
Bunch breaker	1	...do	...do	1,000	1.50	1.50	9.00	351.00	6.75
Do	1	...do	...do	1,000	1.75	1.75	10.50	409.24	7.87
Do	1	...do	...do	800	1.75	1.36	8.16	318.24	6.12
Do	1	...do	...do	900	1.60	1.44	8.64	336.96	6.48
Bunch breaker's apprentice	1	...do	...do	250			1.50	53.04	1.02
Do	1	...do	...do	300			4.00	156.00	3.00
Stripper	2	...do	Female				3.00	117.00	2.25
Do	1	...do	...do				2.50	97.50	1.87
Do		...do	...do				4.00	175.24	3.37
Packer	1	...do	Male	3,500			9.00	351.00	6.75

IMMIGRATION AND THE COAL MINERS. 389

Following is a detailed statement of the cost of manufacture of a cigar which is made by a Jewish manufacturer in Chicago, employing 22 men and women of different nationalities, in a shop known as a "hobo" shop, over a stable, whose dimensions are 20 by 15 by 9 feet. This manufacturer sells his cigars to jobbers at $14 per 1,000, the lowest union price for the same being $23 and the price to the retailer being $33.

Jewish sweatshop, Chicago—Bill of expense per 1,000 cigars.

Internal-revenue stamps	$3.60
Filler (10 cents per pound)	1.50
Binder (10 cents per pound)	.50
Wrapper (30 cents per pound)	1.50
Stripping	.50
Bunching	1.50
Rolling	2.50
Boxes	1.00
Packing	.50
Total	13.10

In a few shops in Chicago the Jewish cigar makers have formed a small organization independent of the international body, and have raised the scale of their pay from the prevailing $5 or $6 per 1,000 to $7 per 1,000. The prospects of this organization, however, are not promising.

CHAPTER V.
THE FOREIGN BORN IN THE COAL MINES.
I. DISTRIBUTION OF FOREIGN BORN AND OF NATIONALITIES.

The coal mining industry of the United States has from the earliest times been a field peculiarly affected by the influx of fresh immigrants. Not only have men entered that occupation who had already become skilled miners in their European homes, but in recent years many unskilled laborers from European farms find in the American coal mines their introduction to American industry. In the year 1900 there were admitted to the ports of the United States out of a total immigration of 448,572 persons, only 2,822 miners. On the other hand, of the 163.508 "laborers" who entered the ports, after deducting the 42,101 who remained in New York, there were 47,317 who gave their destination as Pennsylvania; and of the 31,949 "farm laborers," 6,563 were destined to New York and 6,773 to Pennsylvania. It is, of course, not known what proportion of these laborers and farm laborers went into the mines of Pennsylvania, but that large numbers found work about the mines is certain.

The following table shows the destination of immigrants in 1900 who described themselves as "laborers," "farm laborers," and "miners:"

TABLE 1.—*Destination of laborers and farm laborers in 1900.*

	Laborers.	Farm laborers.	Miners.
New York	42,101	6,563	431
Pennsylvania	47,317	6,773	736
Illinois	10,320	2,150	177
West Virginia	749	128	18
Ohio	6,088	1,085	76
Alabama	74	14	15
Maryland	990	67	9
Indiana	668	221	21
Iowa	835	436	22
Kentucky	65	25	1
Colorado	1,143	220	191
Kansas	234	113	37
Other States	52,924	14,154	1,088
Total	163,508	31,949	2,822

THE INDUSTRIAL COMMISSION:—IMMIGRATION.

The following tables show for the years 1875 to 1900 the total immigration of miners and the leading countries and races from which they originate. The falling off in the numbers of English, Scotch, and Irish miners will be noted. English immigration reached its highest number, 2,598, in 1888, and has fallen in 1900 to 645. Scottish miners declined from 1,365 in 1888 to 58 in 1900; Irish from 510 in 1883 to 96 in 1898. On the other hand, Italian miners have increased from 14 in 1877 to 1,260 in 1900, and the Austro-Hungarian contributions from 23 in 1878 to 518 in 1887 and 293 in 1900. The latter figures for Italy and Austro-Hungary by no means fully indicate the existing predominance of these countries, since, as already stated, it is the laborers and farm laborers who contribute mainly to the mining population.

TABLE 2.—*Immigrants giving their occupation as miners, by nationalities, 1875–1898.*

Year.	Austro-Hungary.	Germany.	England.	Scotland.	Ireland.	Italy.	Russia and Poland.	Total.
1875	36	163	1,956	344	267	79	255	4,055
1876	38	91	1,005	113	107	27	162	2,237
1877	24	73	667	64	100	14	198	1,670
1878	23	51	651	73	96	32	50	1,578
1879	30	76	1,169	465	114	34	66	2,588
1880	41	320	2,446	620	348	40	253	6,086
1881	48	655	1,626	1,032	236	132	20	5,204
1882	103	1,090	2,290	1,312	398	354	44	6,485
1883	228	755	1,628	541	510	448	16	4,743
1884	104	398	1,704	339	436	200	16	3,794
1885	70	163	1,361	277	264	181	6	2,940
1886	407	163	1,493	346	173	343	30	3,481
1887	595	518	2,346	793	258	426	127	5,945
1888	150	270	2,598	1,365	251	347	99	6,264
1889	109	254	2,478	752	270	767	94	5,505
1890	738	327	1,194	194	153	374	123	3,745
1891								6,966
1892								6,027
1893								3,160
1894								2,220
1895								2,698
1896								1,743
1897	136	61	516	58	74	573	12	1,743
1898	47	50	415	71	96	517	9	1,604

TABLE 3.—*Immigrants giving their occupation as miners, by races, 1899–1900.*

	1899.	1900.
Croatian and Slovenian	56	99
English	471	645
German	98	195
Italian (north)	763	1,107
Italian (south)	100	153
Lithuanian	37	67
Polish	29	49
Scandinavian (Norwegian, Danes, and Swedes)	28	43
Scotch	63	58
Slovak	59	53
Welsh	109	88
Other races	213	265
	2,026	2,822

The attraction of coal mining to the immigrant is also apparent from the census statistics. In Pennsylvania in 1880 there were 69,415 miners, of whom 35,015, or 50 per cent, were American born. In 1890 the number of miners had increased to 116,756, an increase of 47,341; but the foreign-born miners had increased from 34,400 to 67,790 and constituted 58.1 per cent of the total. In Ohio in 1880 only 41 per cent of the 5,575 miners were native born. In Illinois in 1880 the foreign-born miners were 58 per cent of the total number, and in 1890 they were 57.4 per cent of the total. The increase of 9,197 miners during the 10 years contained an increase of 5,087 foreign born.

TABLE 4.—*General nativity of miners.*[1]

	Total number.	Native white.			Foreign white.	Colored.
		Total.	Native parents.	Foreign parents.		
Pennsylvania:						
1880	69,415	35,015			34,400	
1890	116,756	48,117	23,062	25,055	67,790	849
Ohio:						
1880	5,575	41			5,534	
1890	24,435	16,087	11,597	4,490	7,770	578
Indiana:						
1880	3,684	2,093			1,583	
1890	6,477	4,121	3,124	997	2,184	172
Illinois:						
1880	12,998	5,460			7,633	
1890	22,195	8,919	4,744	4,175	12,720	556
West Virginia:						
1880	3,701	2,777			924	
1890	9,605	6,314	5,523	791	1,375	2,016

[1] Tenth Census, Population Table XXXIV; Eleventh Census, Population, Part II, table 116.

TABLE 5.—*Percentage of miners in each general nativity class.*

	Total.	Native white.			Foreign white.	Colored.
		Total.	Native parents.	Foreign parents.		
Pennsylvania:						
1880	100	50.4			49.6	
1890	100	41.2	19.7	20.1	58.1	0.7
Ohio:						
1880	100	.8			99.2	
1890	100	65.9	47.6	18.3	31.8	2.?
Indiana:						
1880	100	56.8			43.2	
1890	100	63.6	48.2	15.4	33.7	2.
Illinois:						
1880	100	42			58	
1890	100	40.1	21.3	18.8	57.4	2.5
West Virginia:						
1880	100	75			25	
1890	100	65.7	57.5	8.2	13.4	20.9

The change in the character of the immigration into the mining regions, especially the region of Pennsylvania and Illinois, which occurred between 1880 and 1890, is shown by Table 6. It appears that while the number of Irish stood at about 11,000 for the 2 years, and the Germans increased 2,409, or 61.3 per cent, and the miners from Great Britain increased 9,994, or 63.3 per cent, yet the miners from "Other countries" (mainly Slavs and Italians) increased from 2,037 to 21,878, or 974 per cent. In Illinois, during these 10 years, the Irish remained stationary; the Germans increase 159.7 per cent; the British increased 9.2 per cent, but the "Other countries" increased from 604 to 3,218, or 432.7 per cent.

TABLE 6.—*Nationality of foreign-born miners.*[1]

	Total foreign.	Ireland.	Germany.	Great Britain.	British America.	Norway and Sweden.	Other countries.
Pennsylvania:							
1880	34,400	11,224	3,926	15,789	289	1,135	2,037
1890	67,790	11,606	6,335	25,783	277	1,934	21,878
Ohio:							
1880	5,534	45	2	5,047	68	16	356
1890	7,770	806	1,510	4,642	60	46	708
Indiana:							
1880	1,583	239	206	993	16	37	100
1890	2,184	184	353	1,312	21	21	294
Illinois:							
1880	7,633	1,202	1,069	4,428	99	236	604
1890	12,720	1,136	2,777	4,837	85	667	3,218
West Virginia:							
1880	924	274	159	447	17	2	25
1890	1,375	251	161	740	11	2	211

[1] Tenth Census, Population Table XXXIV; Eleventh Census, Population, Part II, Table 116.

The Bureau of Mines of Pennsylvania in 1897 (p. xiv) attempted to find the number of native-born workmen employed in the mines of the State. Inquiries were made of several mine superintendents as to the number of men employed, the number of native born, the number of naturalized citizens, and the number of aliens. The following table gives the results:

TABLE 7.—*Foreign-born and native miners in Pennsylvania.*

	150 anthracite mines.		400 bituminous mines.	
	Number.	Per cent.	Number.	Per cent.
Employees	59,823	100	59,903	100
Native born	23,402	39.1	23,675	39.5
Naturalized citizens	13,561	22.7	14,691	24.6
Aliens	22,860	38.2	21,537	35.9
		60.9		60.5

Mr. G. O. Virtue, in his report to the United States Department of Labor (Bulletin, Vol. II, pp. 749-750) on the anthracite mine laborers, says:

As has been said before, the early miners in the anthracite region were, for the most part, English Welsh, Scotch, Irish, and German, and the growth of the mining population down to the early seventies was mainly through additions from the same stock, either by natural increase or by immigration. It was these people who, putting aside race and religious antipathies, acted together in the movement for the 10 years following the war in the Workingmen's Benevolent Association. But about the time of the collapse of that society in 1875 immigration from another source began. It is at this time we first hear of the Poles, Hungarians, and Italians coming into the mining region. How far their introduction was due to the action of the operators under a system of contracting for their labor before their importation is not clear. It is quite certain, however, that this method of securing laborers was common at the time and had been for many years. * * *

There is no doubt that the anthracite operators made use of this method of securing workmen. But at this time, and for 10 years afterwards, laborers brought in were from the United Kingdom or the northern continental countries, and, while from their presence in large numbers they may have contributed to the defeatof the strikers in 1875, they did not constitute a new feature in the mining population. During the late seventies began that immigration to the United States from southern and eastern Europe which has done more than anything else to change public opinion on the subject of immigration, and which led, only 20 years after the act to encourage the importation of laborers, to a complete reversal of the policy of that act. Indeed, it is difficult to see how a government which was using its power of taxation for the avowed purpose of maintaining a high standard of wages should so long have allowed employers to use so direct a means of defeating the efforts of laborers in their own behalf. But before the passage of the alien contract-labor law of 1885, a strong current of Poles, Huns, Italians, and Russians had already set toward the United States, a large part of them finding their way to the coal mines; and however well the law may have been administered, the current has continued to the present time even stronger than ever before.

The presence of this class of laborers no doubt contributed to the defeat of the strike of 1887-88. It is said that the operators had been making preparations for the conflict they saw approaching by inducing these men, either before or after reaching the country, to come to the mines. However that may be, there were, it is estimated, at the time of the strike, about 5,000 Poles, Huns, and Italians in the Lehigh district, and double that number in the Wyoming district.[1] The United States' census of 1890 shows the total number of these nationalities in the 5 anthracite counties to be 28,216. . This is 10,307 less than the foreign-born Irish in the same counties, 5,627 less than the foreign-born Germans and Austrians combined, while of English there were 22,729 and of Welsh 23,404. There is no means of knowing the number of the various nationalities employed at the mines, but it is certain that a far greater proportion of the Polish, Hungarian, and Italian population are so employed than of the other nationalities named. A fairly accurate indication of the number and growth of this class for the last half dozen years may be had from the following figures, furnished by the Philadelphia and Reading Coal and Iron Company, showing the nationality and parentage, but not the place of birth, of the employees at their mines in 1890, 1895, and 1896:

TABLE 8.—*Nativity of miners employed by Philadelphia and Reading Coal and Iron Company.*

Nationality and parentage.	1890.		1895.		1896.	
	Number.	Per cent.	Number.	Per cent.	Number.	Per cent.
American	4,719	19.1	5,765	20.6	5,838	20.6
English	2,088	8.4	1,960	7	1,799	6.3
Irish	6,887	27.8	6,450	23	6,025	21.3
German	3,709	15	3,471	12.4	3,207	11.3
Scotch	210	.9	223	.8	168	.6
Welsh	1,282	5.2	1,112	4	1,037	3.7
Polish	4,287	17.3	5,955	21.3	6,895	24.3
Hungarian	1,466	5.9	2,800	10	3,180	11.2
Italian	86	.4	245	.9	211	.7
Total	24,734	100	27,981	100	28,360	100

[1] Labor Troubles in the Anthracite Region of Pennsylvania, 1887-88. House Report, Fiftieth Congress, second session, No. 4147, p. 49.

IMMIGRATION AND THE COAL MINERS. 393

The following table shows, for the State of Illinois, the birthplace of the 36,991 coal miners in that State in 1899. It appears that American-born miners are 43 per cent of the entire number, and that the foreign-born miners in the order of precedence are German, English, Italian, Polish, Irish, Scotch, Austrian, Bohemian, Hungarian, etc. In the first district, being the northern district of the State, the American born are only 10.6 per cent of the total number, and the Italian outnumber all other nationalities. These are followed by English, Hungarians, Poles, Scotch, Irish, Germans, and Bohemians in the order named.

TABLE 9.—*Nationality of employees.*[1]

	American.	English.	Scotch.	Irish.	Welsh.	German.	French.	Italian.
First district	842	1,218	621	606	244	476	109	1,283
Second district	1,874	640	279	327	91	535	61	879
Third district	1,254	264	54	53	47	35	2	5
Fourth district	1,783	301	128	300	57	477	80	140
Fifth district	3,370	364	174	537	107	1,095	51	179
Sixth district	2,456	373	96	163	70	1,331	51	195
Seventh district	4,001	234	60	100	29	189	19	335
The State	15,580	3,394	1,412	2,086	645	4,138	373	3,016

	Austrian and Bohemian.	Hungarian.	Poles.	Belgians.	Russian.	Danes, Swedes, and Norwegians.	Unknown.	Total.	Per cent of Americans.
First district	435	664	636	112	88	36	128	7,498	10.6
Second district	135	9	807	173	92	341	388	6,631	28.3
Third district	21					40	24	1,799	70
Fourth district	50	73	383	182	184	202	315	4,655	38.3
Fifth district	250	6	202	5	55		6	6,401	52.6
Sixth district	82	21	82	15	73			5,008	49
Seventh district	2	1	23		6			4,999	80
The State	975	774	2,133	487	498	619	861	36,991	

[1] Illinois Coal Report, 1899, pp. lxii–lxiv

Speaking of the changes in nationalities of the miners in Illinois, a writer in Mineral Industry (1895, Vol. IV, p. 192), says:

The character of the men employed in Illinois coal mines has changed. Formerly English, Scotch, Welsh, and Irish. At present there are some Germans, majority are Slavonians, Russians, Italians. This change has resulted partly from prejudices among old hand miners. When on account of competition and frequent labor troubles a cheap and reliable system became necessary and machines were introduced, there was a great deal of bitterness and the result was that nearly all the old miners left the business, either finding other occupations or leaving the State and a new race was introduced. Many operators think it doubtful whether machine mining would have been practicable without this introduction of foreign labor. The fact is, that under the present system coal mining in Illinois has either ceased or is fast ceasing to be a skilled occupation.

II. EFFECTS ON EMPLOYMENT.

At first sight the most important factor affecting changes in wages is the business activity touching the demand for coal. Not only do reductions in price of coal usually accompany business depression, but at such times the effects of machinery and surplus labor show themselves without restriction. There are two phases of this oversupply of labor—first, the chronic oversupply; second, the periodic oversupply. The following table shows for both anthracite and bituminous coal the annual product, the average price, and the number of days during the year that the mines are active:

TABLE 10.—*Product, price, and number of days active of anthracite and bituminous coal production in the United States.*[1]

Year.	Product.		Price (short).		Days active.	
	Anthracite.	Bituminous.	Anthracite.	Bituminous.	Anthracite.	Bituminous.
	Short tons.	*Short tons.*				
1886	39,035,446	74,644,581	$1.95	$1.06		
1887	42,088,197	85,562,014	2.01	1.12		
1888	46,619,564	102,039,843	1.95	1.00		
1889	45,544,970	95,684,643	1.44	1.00		
1890	46,468,641	111,302,322	1.43	.99	200	226
1891	50,665,431	117,901,237	1.46	.99	203	223
1892	52,472,504	126,856,567	1.57	.99	198	219
1893	53,967,543	128,385,231	1.59	.96	197	204
1894	51,921,121	118,820,405	1.52	.91	190	171
1895	57,999,337	135,118,193	1.41	.86	196	194
1896	54,346,081	137,640,276	1.50	.83	174	192
1897	52,611,680	147,609,985	1.51	.81	150	196
1898	53,382,644	166,592,023	1.41	.80	152	211
1899	60,418,005	193,321,987	1.46	.87	173	234

[1] The Production of Coal in 1899, E. W. Parker, pp. 23, 24, 42, 43.

It can readily be seen from this table to what extreme fluctuations the coal industry is subjected. The average number of days per year during which the mines are operating varies from 171 to 234 in the bituminous fields and 150 to 203 in the anthracite field. That is to say, taking 306 days in the year working time in the bituminous mining, the average employment ranges from 57 per cent to 78 per cent of full time, and in anthracite mining from 50 per cent to 67 cent of full time. Or, to state it differently, in the dullest year the amount of employment in bituminous mines is 73 per cent of the amount in the most prosperous year, and yet in the most prosperous year it is only 78 per cent of full time. And in the anthracite mines in the dullest year the amount of employment is 75 per cent of the amount in the most prosperous year, and yet in the most prosperous year it is only 67 per cent of full time.

TABLE 11.—*Comparison of the average number of days worked in the anthracite and bituminous coal fields of Pennsylvania.*[1]

	Anthracite.					Bituminous.				
	1892.	1896.	1897.	1898.	1899.	1892.	1896.	1897.	1898.	1899.
Average number of days worked	206.6	172.9	148.8	148.4	180	208.6	187.7	188.6	208.5	246
Per cent of possible time worked	67.5	56.5	48.6	48.5	58.8	68.1	61.3	61.6	68.1	80.4

[1] Compiled from Reports of Pennsylvania Bureau of Industrial Statistics and Reports of Bureau of Mines.

The foregoing table shows the average number of days worked in the two coal fields of Pennsylvania and the per cent of possible time thus worked. It is seen that the average for the bituminous field is considerably higher than that of the anthracite. In 1892 the time worked and the percentage of possible time in the two regions were almost alike. In 1896 and 1897 the time in both had decreased, but in 1898 the time in the bituminous region was increased, while that of the anthracite had continued to decrease. In 1899 there was a large increase in both fields, especially in the bituminous mines.

The point of interest at this place is the percentage of possible time that both regions show in prosperous and adverse years. In 1892, a year of uniform and marked prosperity, the percentage of possible time worked was 68 and 67. This may be taken as indicative of the time that can be worked under the most favorable conditions. On the other hand, in years of depression a decline to 48 and 61 per cent is shown. It is evident, then, that the time worked in the Pennsylvania coal mines varies from one-half to two-thirds of the possible working time.

IMMIGRATION AND THE COAL MINERS. 395

TABLE 12.—*Days worked in the mines of the States named from 1890 to 1899.*[1]

Year.	Bituminous regions.						Anthracite, Pennsylvania.
	Illinois.	Indiana.	Ohio.	Pennsylvania.	West Virginia.	Total United States.	
1890	204	220	201	232	227	226	200
1891	215½	190	206	223	237	223	203
1892	219½	224	212	223	228	219	198
1893	229	201	188	190	219	204	197
1894	183	149	136	165	186	171	190
1895	182	189	176	206	195	194	196
1896	184	163	161	206	201	192	174
1897	185	176	148	205	205	196	150
1898	175	199	169	229	218	211	152
1899	228	218	200	245	242	234	173

[1] Parker, 1899, pp. 39-41.

The foregoing table, showing the days worked in the mines of the 5 principal coal States for 10 years, was compiled from the Production of Coal in 1899 (E. W. Parker). The highest number for any 1 of the 5 States in any 1 of the 10 years was Pennsylvania, bituminous, for 1899. This was 245 days, or 80 per cent of full time. At the other extreme, Ohio, in 1894, had an average of only 136 days for the year, or 44.4 per cent of full time. It is thus seen that even in an exceptionally prosperous year, and under other favorable conditions, like those in Pennsylvania bituminous and West Virginia mining in 1899, the maximum time is only 80 per cent of the possible working time.

TABLE 13.—*Average number of days worked.*

Industries.	1892.	1893.	1894.	1895.	1896.	1897.	1898.[1]
Total of 47 for the State	294	268	276	288	276	287	298
Anthracite coal	206.6				172.9	148.8	148.4
Bituminous coal	208.6				187.7	188.6	208.5
Steel	281	270	272	279	219	271	282
Iron foundries	301	279	282	299	289	298	300
Rubber boots and shoes	250	230	248	271	244	222	244
Woolen yarns	299	245	277	293	269	296	274
Hosiery	296	261	273	288	288	288	279
Carpets	280	218	259	277	289	291	286
Woolen goods	299	245	278	298	274	290	289
Cotton goods	303	249	246	285	258	293	298
Window glass	253	195	261	241	229	268	271

[1] Compiled from Reports of Pennsylvania Bureau of Industrial Statistics.

The foregoing table shows the average number of days worked in each of 9 different industries selected from the 47 reported in the industrial statistics of Pennsylvania, the average for the total 47 industries, and also the average number of days worked in both the anthracite and bituminous field. The table is intended to show the small average time worked in the coal mines compared with that of manufacturing industries.

To simplify the comparison the following table has been made from the totals given by the Pennsylvania Bureau of Industrial Statistics, showing the percentage of possible time employed in the two mining regions of Pennsylvania and in the 47 industries investigated by the bureau.

TABLE 14.

	1892.	1896.	1897.	1898.
Industries (47)	96	90.1	93.7	97.3
Anthracite coal	67.5	56.5	48.6	48.5
Bituminous coal	68.1	61.3	61.6	68.1

It is readily seen that the percentage of time employed in the bituminous field varied very little, and remained steady at from 60 to 70 per cent of possible time. The time in all the industries was from 90 to 97 per cent, so that, in fact, the miners in the bituminous field were working only about two-thirds of the time that the men in manufacture were working. On the other hand, the anthracite miner was much worse off, and worked only from 50 to 65 per cent as much time as men in manufacture, or 48 to 67 per cent of possible time.

On the average, then, the workers in iron, steel, cotton and woolen products, and in general manufactures have the opportunity to work from 35 to 50 per cent more of the total time per year than the coal miner in the anthracite field and from 30 to 40 per cent more than the bituminous miner.

This irregularity of employment naturally causes instability of application on the part of the miners. To a large extent they are a floating population. They pass from one mine to another. This makes it difficult to gain accurate information regarding the condition of the individual miners and their families. This is shown in the report of an investigation made by the Illinois bureau of labor statistics in 1890, wherein, among other data, is produced the following table with comments (p. XXVI):

TABLE 15.—*Seasonal irregularity of employment.*

	Whole number of men on pay roll of a mine in Sangamon County during the month.	Number of men required to produce same tonnage if at work full running time.
May	97	85
June	94	84
July	94	87
August	101	88
September	100	80
October	102	89
November	116	95
December	119	98
January	107	99
February	107	96
March	97	89
April	85	80
The year	210	90
Monthly average	102	90

"The figures in this column represent one of the chief difficulties presented in statistics of this kind. The smallest number of men employed in this mine in any given month was 85, in April; the largest number 119, in December. Between these extremes there is more or less fluctuation from month to month, and the average for all months is 102. It does not follow, however, that the greatest number employed in any one month is in fact the whole number of men who found employment during the year. On the contrary, there were 210 different men at work in this place during the year and only 45 of them worked continually throughout the year. * * *

"Of the 97 miners who were paid for labor in May, some never appeared on any subsequent pay roll, others continued to appear several months and then were found no more, while others still disappeared for several months and then began to work again. In like manner names were found on every pay roll which had not appeared on any previous one, and what was true in this case was found to be the characteristic of all coal mines. * * *

"In Establishment I, 320 miners received pay in July, and 466 in February, while for all other months the number fluctuates between these two extremes. The average number for the twelve months was 382 for each; that is to say, this number of men, if continually at work, could have performed all the labor which was required during the year at this mine. In fact, 84 more men worked in the busiest month and 62 less men in the midsummer months, but the greatest number of men employed in any month was far less than the whole number of persons who were given employment during the year. In fact, the names of 685 different men were found on the pay rolls of this company during the year, and, although an average of 382 were at work each month, only 160 of them worked every month in the year. It thus appears that 56 per cent of the whole number of men who worked in this mine, first and last, during the year was sufficient to perform all the labor done, and that only 23 per cent of the whole were constant workers throughout the year.

"The results summarized show that while the labor of 3,111 men, or the total of the various averages, was sufficient to mine and deliver the annual output of these mines, there were, in fact, 5,356 individuals who shared that labor for a greater or less period. Only 869 men out of 5,356 actually maintained their places on the pay roll throughout this particular year, and the inference is justifiable, inasmuch as this was a fairly representative year, that a corresponding degree of fluctuations would be found in any given period of twelve months in any corresponding number of mines equally distributed throughout the State."

The excessive uncertainty of employment above described is more apparent than real, because miners are changing from one colliery to another, and would therefore appear to work only a short time, whereas, if all the mines in the State were examined, these individuals would be found at work for a longer period, although with different employers. At the same time, taking the industry as a whole, the oversupply both of equipment and labor is readily demonstrated. This appears in the Illinois Coal Reports of 1898 (p. 48) and 1899 (p. XXXIX), where it is stated that the possible output of the existing collieries of Illinois, if operated continuously with the present equipment, would produce, in 1894, 41,082,925 tons. The actual output in 1898 was 18,599,299 tons. Consequently the per cent of possible increase were the plants to operate continuously would have been 120.88 per cent. In 1899, assuming the same possible output, the increase would have been 75 per cent had the mines operated continuously, since the actual output had increased to 23,434,445 tons. These estimates are not based "on what might be produced if the hauling, hoisting, and handling facilities should be increased to their limit. The majority of first-class plants, which are the real producers of commercial coal, are capable of indefinite expansion to meet any reasonable demands which may arise in excess of their present capacity. Yet variation is found in the reports of individual mines. Some have a capacity for increase five and even seven fold; others none whatever, owing to the fact that the mineral is nearly or quite exhausted."

TABLE 16.—*Average number of employees, days active, and yearly product of coal fields of Pennsylvania.*[1]

Year.	Anthracite.			Bituminous.		
	Average number of days active.	Average number employed.	Short tons product.	Average number of days active.	Average number employed.	Short tons product.
1890	200	126,000	46,468,641	232	61,333	42,302,173
1891	203	126,350	50,665,431	223	63,661	42,788,490
1892	198	129,050	52,472,504	223	66,655	46,694,576
1893	197	132,944	53,967,543	190	71,931	44,070,724
1894	190	131,603	51,921,121	165	75,010	39,912,463
1895	196	142,917	57,999,337	206	71,130	50,217,228
1896	174	148,991	54,346,081	206	72,625	49,557,453
1897	150	149,884	52,611,680	205	77,272	54,417,974
1898	152	145,504	53,382,644	229	79,611	65,165,133
1899	173	139,00c	60,418,005	245	82,812	74,150,175

[1] Parker, 1899, pp. 39-41.

In the above table comparing the number of employees, the days worked, and the product in short tons for the two fields of Pennsylvania, it is evident that an increase in the number of employees in the anthracite region meant not so much an increase in the amount of the resulting product as a decrease in the number of days worked per man. There was a steady increase in the mined product from 46,000,000 tons in 1890 to 60,000,000 tons in 1899. This was an increase of 30 per cent in product, the employees increased in number 11 per cent, and the average number of days active decreased 13.5 per cent. If, however, the year 1898 is compared with the year 1890, the increase in the product will be found to be 15 per cent and the increase in employees about 15.4 per cent, while the decrease in the number of days active, from 200 in 1890 to 152 in 1898, is represented by 24 per cent.

This difference between the product, number of employees, and days worked is brought out in comparing 1895 and 1896. An increase in employees, while tending to decrease the average days worked, in this case went with a decrease in the product mined.

The report of inspectors of coal mines, Pennsylvania (p. XI), 1896, says of the anthracite region: "There has been an increase in the number of employees every year since 1892. This does not mean, however, that there has been an increase in the number of days of employment each year, especially with reference to the increase between 1895 and 1896, as the reductions in the number of tons of coal mined is pretty strong evidence that while there has been an increase in the number of employees, there has been a decrease in the number of days employed."

The report further says (p. XII): "A somewhat different condition is found in the bituminous region with reference to the proportion of the number of employees to the number of tons of coal mined in each of the years named, for while there was a reduction in the number of tons of coal mined in the anthracite region, there appears to have been an increase in the number of employees. In the bituminous region there has been a decrease in number of tons of coal mined and a proportionate decrease in the number of employees, applying this comparison to the data returned for the years 1895 and 1896."

In the bituminous region it may be well to notice that the increase in the product from 1890 to 1899 was nearly 32,000,000 tons, or 75.2 per cent; the increase in the number employed was 21,000 persons, or 35 per cent, while the average number of days employed instead of having decreased 13.5 per cent, as in the anthracite field, actually increased 5.6 per cent over the average of 1890.

Comparing these percentages with those of the anthracite region, it is seen that the bituminous product increased by a percentage two and one-half times as large as the percentage of increase in the anthracite field; the percentage of employees was more than three times as large, and the average number of days worked was a gain of almost 6 per cent instead of a loss of almost 14 per cent.

There is a distinction in the character of bituminous and anthracite coal relative to the stability of operation. Bituminous coal can not economically be stored, as it disintegrates with exposure. Consequently the mining of that coal is a seasonable industry, like the clothing trade. In the busy season all of the miners are employed, and the output for the time is as great as the output of the mines. It can not, therefore, be said that there is a surplus of labor in busy seasons any more than it can be said that there is a surplus of carpenters and bricklayers because they can not find work in winter. But in anthracite mining it is different. Anthracite coal can, without much injury, be mined and stored during a dull season and the stock can be worked off during a busy season. The surplus of labor, therefore, is not merely seasonal, but is maintained more for the convenience of the operators than for the necessities of the trade.

Concerning the significance of the oversupply of labor in the anthracite mines, Mr. G. O. Virtue says (Bulletin of Department of Labor, Vol. II, p. 753):

> The question of earnings is as much one of time as of rate. The daily earnings, though not high, are not unusually low for the grade of labor employed. The great evil is in the irregularity of employment. There are more than enough laborers in the region to man the collieries at their full capacity. But, as is well known, they are and for years have been kept idle a part of the time to prevent overproduction. The Reading collieries were operated an average of 219.2 days for the six years 1885 to 1890, and for the six years 1890 to 1895 an average of 187.1 days. Of the 354 collieries whose time was reported by the inspectors of mines in 1894 only 20 per cent ran 200 days and over; more than 30 per cent ran but half time and less. It is easy to believe that the estimate of 67,000,000 tons as the capacity of the mines is not too high; while in 1896 only 43,200,000 tons were produced.
> A restriction of production is necessary if profits are to be earned upon the investments made; but as now effected it is wasteful in the extreme. Each company is compelled to maintain itself on a war footing, and aggravates the difficulties by increasing its capacity each year beyond the growth of the market. A restriction which would bring about the closing of the poorest mines and keep only the best running at their full capacity would have the advantage of a lower cost of production, and would also correct, though not remove, the evil of the irregularity of employment. Owing to the periodicity of the demand for coal, it will always be present in some degree. This mode of restriction would undoubtedly mean the departure of many who are now held at the mines by the vain hope of more work next month. But such a mode of restriction can not be expected so long as the ownership of the mines remains, as now, divided among the eleven carrying companies which serve the field, each vitally interested in the question as to whose collieries shall be closed.

III. MACHINE MINING.

The most important change which has taken place in the mining of bituminous coal in the past 15 years has been the introduction of machinery. Illinois took the lead in this development, and as early as 1888 there were 272 machines in the State, mining 20 per cent of the whole output by the labor of 10 per cent of the men. (Illinois Bureau of Labor Statistics, 1888, p. 338.) The following table exhibits for the leading bituminous States the introduction of machinery:

TABLE 17.—*Percentage of total product mined by machines.*[1]

Year.	Pennsylvania.	Ohio.	Indiana.	Illinois.	West Virginia.	Total for United States.
1891	1.01	12.85	7.16	19.33	2.23	6.66
1896	12.29	26.16	24.69	19.57	3.35	14.17
1897	16.35	31.51	24.65	19.66	4.73	16.19
1898	25.34	35.76	28.74	18.36	7.93	20.39
1899	29.67	41.35	28.52	24.90	9.27	23.00

[1] Parker, 1899, p. 63.

IMMIGRATION AND THE COAL MINERS.   399

The effect of machinery is seen, first, in the reduction of prices and, second, in its effect on wages. The reduction in prices may be inferred from the marked economy of the machine method. The Report of the Illinois Bureau of Labor Statistics for 1888 contains examples of the economy of machine production, among which is the following (p. 391):

A company at Peoria got the machine-mined coal shot down, loaded to the rooms, and timbered for 32½ cents per ton, making the machine-mined coal cost the company 50½ cents per ton; or, considering the engineer's wages, wear an tear in machines, and interest on capital, etc., it cost nearly 55 cents per ton. Compared with hand mining prices in the past year in the same locality (which were 75 cents in summer and 80 cents in winter) there is a material difference.

The effect of these economies may be seen in the prices of bituminous coal on the markets. The following table shows for the leading States and for the United States that there has been a steady decline in prices from 1886 to 1898, with a recovery of 7 cents per ton in 1899:

TABLE 18.—*Average prices for bituminous coal at the mines, 1886–1899.*[1]

Year.	Pennsylvania.	Ohio.	Indiana.	Illinois.	West Virginia.	Total for United States.
1886	$0.80	$0.95	$1.15	$1.11	$0.94	$1.06
1887	.90	.88	1.34	1.09	.95	1.12
1888	.95	.93	1.40	1.12	1.10	1.00
1889	.77	.93	1.02	.97	.82	1.00
1890	.84	.94	.99	.93	.84	.99
1891	.87	.94	1.03	.91	.80	.99
1892	.84	.94	1.08	.91	.80	.99
1893	.80	.92	1.07	.89	.77	.96
1894	.74	.83	.96	.89	.75	.91
1895	.72	.79	.91	.80	.68	.86
1896	.71	.79	.84	.80	.63	.83
1897	.69	.78	.84	.72	.63	.81
1898	.67	.83	.81	.78	.61	.80
1899	.76	.87	.88	.85	.63	.87

[1] Parker, 1899, p. 42.

The Report of the Illinois Bureau of Labor Statistics for 1888 (p. 338) explains the changes effected not only in the cost of production, but also in the wages of machine miners (p. 339): "A mining machine not only reverses the methods of work, but it equally changes the system of wages. The coal miner proper takes his own tools into the pit and undertakes to deliver from the wall of mineral before him certain tons of coal ready every morning for a certain sum per ton. He mines and drills and blasts and loads his own coal, timbers his own roof, takes care of his own tools, and is responsible mainly to himself for his personal safety and the amount of his output.

"In the machine mine it takes 7 or 8 men to perform these various functions, and in the mine, as in the mill, the machine is the master and the men are its servitors; the operator and the mechanism simply directs it energies when the motive power is given to it and the coal is undercut or mined. A blaster follows with tools and explosives, loosening the mass; the loaders reduce it and shovel it into pit cars; the timbermen follow and prop the roof, which no longer has the mineral to rest upon. Laborers assist in every process, and a machinist is retained for repairs. Each one does his own certain portion of the work and no more, and doubtless does it better, as well as faster, by reason of his greater skill thus acquired. Herein lies the chief value of the machine to the mine owner. It relieves him for the most part of skilled labor and of all the restraints which that implies. It opens to him the whole labor market from which to recruit his force; it enables him to concentrate the work of the mine at given points, and it admits of the graduation of wages to specific work and payment of wages by the day.

"The results of this introduction of machinery," continues the Illinois report (p. 339), "consist not only in the greater execution of the machine, but in the subdivision of labor which it involves, and the greater per capita efficiency of the force thus secured. The gain is consequently to the employer rather than to the men. The mining machine is in fact the natural enemy of the coal miner; it destroys the value of his skill and experience, obliterates his trade, and reduces him to the rank of a common laborer or machine driver if he remains where it is."

The foregoing complaints of the Illinois bureau of labor statistics in 1888 find apparent verification in certain statistical tables published in the report of the same office for 1890. These are in the form of returns from typical hand and machine mines in different parts of the State. Seeing that the mines operate under a wide variety of circumstances, it is difficult to make average comparisons, but the following selections may be made of mines in neighboring localities and similar circumstances.

TABLE 19.

Establishment X, Macoupin County, hand mining.

[Conditions: Depth of shaft, 420 feet; thickness of coal, 8 feet; working places, dry; system of working, pillar-and-room; mining done by hand; price of mining, 50 cents a ton for screened coal; seam level and uniform.]

Occupation.	Number of men.	Per cent of total number.	Average daily earnings.
Miners	205	58.75	$1.83
Laborers	74	21.20	1.63
All others	70	22.05	1.75
Total and average	349	100.00	1.81

[1] Illinois Bureau of Labor Statistics, 1890, pp. 184, 193.

Establishment XI, Madison County, machine mining.[1]

[Conditions: Depth of shaft, 168 feet; thickness of coal, 7 feet; working places, dry; system of working, pillar-and-room; mining done with machines; operatives paid from $1.25 to $2.50 a day; seam level and uniform.]

Occupation.	Number of men.	Per cent of total number.	Average daily earnings.
Cutters	8	3.74	$2.25
Blasters	9	4.20	2.22
Timbermen	10	4.67	1.99
		12.61	
Helpers	31	14.48	1.63
Loaders	109	50.92	1.77
		65.40	
All others	47	21.99	1.63
Total and average	214	100.00	1.77

[1] Illinois Bureau of Labor Statistics, 1890, pp. 195, 201.

An examination of the foregoing table shows that the average wages of all employees in the hand mine are $1.81 per day, and of all employees in the machine mine are $1.77. It also shows that the wages of loaders, laborers, helpers, and all others are about equal in both mines, viz, $1.63 to $1.75 in the hand mine and $1.63 to $1.77 in the machine mine. On the other hand, it shows that the miners or skilled laborers who received $1.83 per day in the hand mine are displaced by cutters and blasters who receive $2.22 to $2.25 per day, an increase of about 22 per cent in wages. But the cutters and blasters who take the places of the miners are only 8 per cent of the total number employed in the machine mine, whereas the displaced miners were 60 per cent of the total number employed in the hand mine.

Similar results follow in comparing hand and machine mines in Lasalle County under similar conditions.

TABLE 20.

Establishment IV, Lasalle County, hand mining.[1]

[Conditions: Depth of shaft, 110 feet; thickness of coal, 5½ feet; workings, wet; system of working, pillar and room; mining done by hand; price of mining, 80 cents a ton for screened coal.]

Occupation.	Number of men.	Per cent of total number.	Average daily earnings.
Miners	453	71.2	$3.21
Laborers	31	4.8	1.74
All others	152	24	1.90
Total	636	100	3.00

[1] Illinois Bureau of Labor Statistics, 1890, pp. 84, 99.

IMMIGRATION AND THE COAL MINERS. 401

Establishment VI, Lasalle County, hand mining.[1]

[Conditions: Depth of shaft, 74 feet; thickness of coal, 5½ feet; working places, wet; system of working, pillar and room; mining done by hand; price of mining, 80 cents a ton for screened coal.]

Occupation.	Number of men.	Per cent of total number.	Average daily earnings.
Miners	589	70.14	$2.72
Laborers	61	7.13	1.75
All others	191	22.73	1.72
Total	841	100	2.37

[1] Illinois Bureau of Labor Statistics, 1890, pp. 114, 132.

Establishment V, Lasalle County, machine mining.[1]

[Conditions: Depth of shaft, 85 feet; thickness of coal, 5½ feet; working places, wet; system of working, pillar and room; mining done chiefly with machines; operatives paid from $1.75 to $2.50 a day; hand miners employed at entry and other work during October, November, and December; price of hand mining, 80 cents a ton, with extras for driving entries.]

Occupation.	Number of men.	Per cent of total number.	Average daily earnings.
Machine foremen	4	0.76	$2.36
Cutters	26	4.98	²2.41
Blasters	55	.95	²2.30
Timbermen	18	3.44	²2.12
		9.37	
Helpers	38	7.28	1.75
Loaders	174	33.33	1.73
		40.61	
Entrymen	44	8.42	2.01
Hand miners	108	20.69	2.53
All others	105	20.15	1.78
Total	522	100	1.97

[1] Illinois Bureau of Labor Statistics, 1890, pp. 101, 113.   ² $2.28 average daily earnings.

In examining the above tables it is seen that the average earnings per day in the hand mines are $2.37 and $3, but in the machine mines are only $1.97. In establishment No. IV (hand mining) the miners were 71.2 per cent of the men, with wages at $3.21 per day, and in No VI (hand mining) they were 70.14 per cent, with an average wage of $2.72 per day. On the other hand, in establishment No. V (machine mining) the cutters, blasters, and timbermen were 9.37 per cent of the employees and received an average of $2.28 per day. In other words, the hand miners in Establishment IV received 40.3 per cent more than the average wage of cutters, blasters, and timbermen, and 35 per cent more than the cutters alone in the machine mine. Establishment No. VI also shows wages 19.3 per cent higher for the hand miners than for the cutters and blasters in the fifth, or a higher wage by 12.8 per cent than that for the cutters alone. Even the hand miners in the same mine where machinery was used showed an average wage of $2 53 per day as against $2.41 for the cutters, or a wage of 5 per cent higher in favor of the hand method.

A different showing from the foregoing establishments in Illinois is made in the comparison of 2 establishments under hand and machine method by the United States Commissioner of Labor (Report on Hand and Machine Labor, 1899, p. 1579). The following table is computed from the data given in that report. It appears that in establishment No. 654 under hand methods the average wages were 18.4 cents per hour, while in the same establishment 2 years later under machine methods the average wages were 22.1 cents per hour, an increase of 20 per cent. In this case the loaders received an increase of 2 cents per hour and the driver 5 cents per hour, while the operator and helper who took the places of the miners received, respectively, 55 and 25 cents per hour in place of the 18 cents received by the displaced miners.

In establishment No. 655 the average wages increased from 22.1 to 22.5 cents per hour on the substitution of machine methods. In this case the operatives received 25.7 cents in place of 22.8 cents received by the displaced hand miners, and the wages of other classes of workers were not increased.

402   THE INDUSTRIAL COMMISSION:—IMMIGRATION.

TABLE 21.—*Mining coal by hand and machine methods.*

[Computed from tables in Report on Hand and Machine Labor, pp. 1579–1581, United States Department of Labor, 1898.]

Office number of establishment.	Method of work.	Year.	Number of employees.	Hours.	Time.	Labor cost.	Average wages per hour.
					Hr. M.		Cents.
654	Hand	1895	93	10	387 30	$71.21	18.4
654	Machine	1897	60	10	191 0	42.30	22.1
655	Hand	1891	42	10	342 55	77.60	22.1
655	Machine	1897	32	10	168 36	42.40	22.5

NUMBER EMPLOYED AND EARNINGS PER HOUR.

Occupation.	654.				655.			
	Hand (1895).		Machine (1897).		Hand (1891).		Machine (1897).	
	Number.	Earnings per hour.	Number.	Earnings per hour.	Number.	Earnings per hour.	Number.	Earnings per hour.
		Cents.		Cents.		Cents.		Cents.
Miners	80	18			23	22.8		
Machine operator			1	55				
Machine operator (helper)			1	25			2	25.7
Miners (loaders, etc.)	80	18	12	20	23	22.8	9	22.8
Drivers	4	15	20	20	6	20	6	20
Dilly rider	1	20	1	20	1	20	1	20
Tippleman	2	20	10	20	3	20	3	20
Weighman	1	20	1	20	1	19	1	20
Trimmer	1	20	3	20	2	20	2	20
Repair man	1	15	3	20	1	20	1	20
Bit grinder							1	20
Blacksmiths	1	25	1	25	1	25	1	25
Do			2	20				
Machinist							1	27.5
Electrician			2	27.5				
Fire boss	1	40	1	40	1	25	1	25
Mine boss					1	35	1	35
Engineer	1	30	1	30	1	27.5	1	27.5
Fireman			1	20	1	20	1	20

It will be seen that in these two establishments reported by the Commissioner of Labor, notwithstanding the higher average wages, the cost of mining was reduced from 71.2 cents per ton to 42.3 cents in No. 654 and from 77.6 to 42.4 cents in No. 655. Allowing 5 cents per ton for interest, depreciation, etc., on the machinery, the reduction in cost was 24 cents, or 33.7 per cent, in No. 654 and 30.2 cents, or 38.9 per cent, in No. 655. The number of men required to operate the mine was reduced from 93 to 60 in No. 654 and from 42 to 32 in No. 655.

Comparing now the somewhat contradictory results derived from the reports of the Illinois bureau and from the Department of Labor, it is evident that local circumstances play a large part in the effect on wages where machinery is introduced. The following inferences may be drawn:

1. Notwithstanding the large reduction in the number of workers required for a given output, it is to be expected that, in time of prosperity, when the output is largely increased, the surplus labor will be absorbed; and, on the other hand, in a period of depression the number will be reduced. This inference is borne out by the following table, showing the number of employees in bituminous mines for the leading States and for the United States for the years 1890 to 1899: *See Parker 1899*

IMMIGRATION AND THE COAL MINERS.

TABLE 22.—*Average number employed in bituminous mines.*[1]

Year.	Pennsylvania.	Ohio.	Indiana.	Illinois.	West Virginia.	Total for United States.
1890	61,333	20,576	5,489	28,574	12,236	192,204
1891	63,661	22,182	5,879	32,951	14,227	205,803
1892	66,655	22,576	6,436	34,585	14,867	212,893
1893	71,931	23,931	7,644	35,390	16,524	230,365
1894	75,010	27,105	8,603	38,477	17,824	244,603
1895	71,130	24,644	8,530	58,630	19,159	239,962
1896	72,625	25,500	8,806	39,560	19,078	244,176
1897	77,272	26,410	8,886	33,788	20,504	248,144
1898	79,611	26,986	8,971	35,026	21,607	255,717
1899	82,812	26,038	9,712	36,756	23,625	271,027

[1] Parker, 1899.

It appears that in the country at large the number employed showed an annual increase except for the year 1895, and since 1895 the number increased to the extent of 31,065 men, or about 13 per cent. From Table 23 it is seen that the product also showed an annual increase except in the years 1890 and 1895, and since 1895 it has shown an increase of 74,501,582 tons, or 62 per cent. In the State of Illinois, however, the number employed in 1899 was 2,804 less than in 1896, notwithstanding an increase in the product of 4,652,293 tons, or 23.5 per cent. On the whole, it is evident that increasing prosperity overcomes the displacing effect of machinery, but business depression displaces labor whether machinery is introduced or not.

TABLE 23.—*Bituminous-coal product (short tons).*[1]

Year.	Pennsylvania.	Ohio.	Indiana.	Illinois.	West Virginia.	Total for United States.
1872		5,315,294				
1873	13,098,829	4,550,028			672,000	
1874	12,320,000	3,267,585			1,120,000	
1875	11,760,000	4,864,259			1,120,000	
1876	12,880,000	3,500,000			896,000	
1877	14,000,000	5,250,000			1,120,000	
1878	15,120,000	5,500,000			1,120,000	
1879	16,240,000	6,000,000			1,400,000	
1880	21,280,000	7,000,000			1,568,000	42,831,758
1881	22,400,000	8,225,000			1,680,000	53,961,012
1882	24,640,000	9,450,000			2,240,000	68,164,533
1883	26,880,000	8,229,429			2,335,833	76,755,280
1884	28,000,000	7,640,062			3,360,000	82,578,204
1885	26,000,000	7,816,179			3,369,062	72,621,548
1886	27,094,501	8,435,211	3,000,000	11,175,241	4,005,796	74,644,581
1887	31,516,856	10,300,708	3,217,711	12,423,066	4,881,620	88,562,014
1888	33,796,727	10,910,951	3,140,079	14,328,181	5,498,800	102,039,843
1889	36,174,089	8,976,787	2,845,057	14,017,298	6,231,880	95,684,643
1890	42,302,173	11,494,506	3,305,737	15,274,727	7,394,654	111,302,322
1891	42,788,490	12,868,683	2,973,474	15,660,698	9,220,665	117,901,237
1892	46,694,576	13,562,927	3,345,174	17,862,276	9,838,755	126,856,567
1893	44,070,724	13,253,646	3,791,851	19,949,564	10,708,578	128,385,231
1894	39,912,463	11,909,856	3,423,921	17,113,576	11,627,757	118,820,405
1895	50,217,228	13,355,806	3,995,892	17,735,864	11,387,361	135,118,193
1896	49,557,453	12,875,202	3,905,779	19,786,626	12,876,296	137,640,276
1897	54,417,974	12,196,942	4,151,169	20,072,758	14,248,159	147,609,985
1898	65,165,133	14,516,867	4,920,743	18,599,299	16,700,999	166,592,023
1899	74,150,175	16,500,270	6,006,523	24,439,019	19,252,995	193,321,987

[1] Parker, 1899.

2. The large economy in machine methods makes it possible to pay much higher wages with increased profit to capital and without reducing the price of the product.

3. The most important local circumstance which determines whether the mine worker shall gain an increase in wages with the introduction of machinery is the state of his labor organization. This is shown in the following table, which gives the results for Illinois of the strike of 1897, at which time the coal miners, for the first time, perfected an organization of remarkable strength.

Table 24, reproduced from the Illinois Coal Report for 1898, shows, by districts and by hand and machine mines, the number of men included in the strike of 1897, the average duration of the strike, the price for mining before and after the strike, and the average gain. It will be seen that the average gain in machine mines was 36.3 per cent, whereas the average for all mines (including machine mines) was 26.4 per cent.

TABLE 24.—*Results of the strike of 1897.*[1]

Field.	Prices per gross ton.		Average gain per cent.
	Before strike.	After strike.	
	Cents.	*Cents.*	
Northern	51.5	59.2	{ 13.97
			19.68
Rock Island	45.3	46.6	2.96
Peoria	40	44.38	10.97
Danville	30	36.43	21.46
Springfield	31.9	37	19.18
Pana, Mount Olive, and Virden	25.9	32.14	24.12
Belleville	25	38.68	54.75
Duquoin	25.5	38.4	50.61
Big Muddy	27.2	37.15	36.6
Machine mines	21.95	29.41	36.3
Average (the State)	31.53	39.93	26.42

[1] Illinois Coal Report, 1897, Appendix (compiled).

The foregoing table shows the gain in prices immediately before and after the strike of 1897. The following table shows that for the year 1899, following the increase in prices secured at the beginning of that year, the average price for hand mining had been increased 49.38 per cent, and the average price for machine mining had been increased 42.77 per cent.

TABLE 25.—*Average prices, machine mining and hand mining, 1897 and 1899 (Illinois).*[1]

	1897.	1899.	Increase per cent.
	Cents.	*Cents.*	
Machine mining	21.95	31.34	42.77
Hand mining	31.53	47.1	49.38

[1] Illinois Coal Report, 1897, p. 182; 1899, p. XLV.

The Report for 1900 shows a still further increase in the prices of hand mining to 49.3 cents, an increase of 56.6 per cent since 1897, and in the prices of machine mining to 35.78 cents, an increase of 62.7 per cent since 1897.
The effect of labor organization on the prices and earnings of machine miners is shown in even more striking form by the following table. This gives the scale of prices for hand mining and machine mining as agreed upon in the interstate conferences of 1900 and 1901 for the basing districts of Pennsylvania, Indiana, Ohio, and Illinois. It will be seen that in Illinois, where the union is especially strong, the machine price for the basing drict, Danville, which is fixed by the interstate conferences, is 10 cents below the hand price, but for the other districts of the State, where the prices are fixed by the State organization, the differential is only 7 cents. On the other hand, for the States of Ohio and Pennsylvania, where, the unions have developed less strength, the differential is 19.2 cents. These discriminations in the differentials against Illinois account for the fact, which appears in Table 17, that the adoption of mining machinery in Illinois has not progressed as rapidly as in Ohio and Pennsylvania.

TABLE 26.—*Comparative prices for pick and machine mining (per ton), 1900-1901.*

	Illinois.		Indiana, bituminous.	Ohio, Hocking Valley.	Pennsylvania.
	Danville district.	Outside Danville.			
	Cents.	*Cents.*	*Cents.*	*Cents.*	*Cents.*
Pick	49	49	49	57	57
Machine	39	42	36.5	37.8	37.8
Differential	10	7	12.5	19.2	19.2

The conclusion to be drawn from these considerations is that the miner is able to gain from the introduction of machinery, provided he is able to organize, but without organization he does not gain.

IV. LABOR ORGANIZATIONS IN COAL MINING.

Considering that in the foregoing discussion of machinery we are brought to the conclusion that the decisive factor in elevating the wages of mine workers is the circumstances of their organization, our inquiry into the effect both of immigration and machinery upon wages must concern itself largely with their effect upon organization. It will here be seen that we reach the crucial problem of immigration.

In the matter of organization, the mine workers have passed through extraordinary vicissitudes. The early miners were English, Welsh, Scotch, and Irish, and the first union was organized among them in the anthracite region by an Englishman, Bates, in 1849.[1] This was broken the same year. During the civil war the prosperity of the miners was so great that little need of organization was felt. It was not until 1868 that the first comprehensive organization was effected—that of the Workingmen's Benevolent Association. This spread through both the anthracite and bituminous fields. This was not recognized as a national union until 1873, when a convention was held at Youngstown, Ohio. In the strikes which followed from 1873 to 1875 against reduction of wages, following the reduction of prices, the union was defeated, and in 1875 was destroyed. In the anthracite region it had become confused with the Molly Maguires, although the two were separate. It was about this time, beginning in 1870, that the large importations of labor from southern Europe were inaugurated, under the impulse of what is believed by the miners to have been a new policy of the operators to maintain a supply of labor always on hand equal to three men for every job. But however this may be, the failure of the strike of 1875 was not owing to the presence of these immigrants. The miners were defeated outright as the result of a strike against a falling market. They accepted substantial reductions in wages, but even more important than normal wages were the loss of their organization and the consequent transference to the operators of all control over the measurement of coal and the employment of newcomers.

There was no organization of miners which could rightly be termed national in scope from 1875 until 1897 in the bituminous field and 1900 in the anthracite field. There were local organizations in Ohio, Indiana, Illinois, and Pennsylvania in the bituminous fields, and the Knights of Labor had a considerable membership in its mixed assemblies. In 1885 these locals of the mine workers secured the right from the Knights of Labor, after it had previously been refused, to form a national trades assembly of their own craft, thus separating them out from the mixed assemblies where their interests were subject to the influence of other crafts. It was this assembly of the Knights of Labor which, in 1887, made demands for increase of wages in the anthracite region and was utterly defeated and destroyed. The defeat at this time is ascribed with unanimity to the presence of the cheap labor of southern Europe, which could not be controlled and organized according to the methods then pursued. The operators were able to play one section against another section and one nationality against another nationality.

In 1885, as a result of the refusal of the Knights of Labor to grant a national trades assembly to the miners, a separate convention of representatives of local and State unions was called and met at Indianapolis, where was formed the Federation of Miners and Mine Laborers. This had no connection with the Knights of Labor, but it forced the Knights shortly thereafter to recognize the National Trades Assembly, as stated above, exclusively comprised of miners. These two national bodies competed for jurisdiction, but after various negotiations they effected a consolidation in 1890 at Columbus, Ohio, under the title of United Mine Workers, wherein it was agreed that the two bodies should retain separate organizations, but should elect identical officers. This arrangement ultimately fell to pieces in 1895, since when the present order of the United Mine Workers has had no connection with the Knights of Labor, and retains its place as a branch of the American Federation of Labor.

The United Mine Workers had a precarious existence for several years. In 1890 they were strongly organized in the coke region, but when in that year the national body refused to indorse a local strike and the men went out on their own account, they were completely defeated; 11 Slavs were killed in the "Morewood massacre," and no organization has arisen to take the place of the one destroyed.

The first national strike of the United Mine Workers was called in 1894. This was not intended to be a strike but only a cessation of work to enable the overstocked markets to become depleted. But the original purpose was lost sight of, and it became a practical strike, lasting some 3 months. A compromise was effected

---

[1] Bulletin, Vol. II, p. 732.

with a portion of the operatives in Ohio, Indiana, and Pennsylvania, but there was utter defeat in Illinois. The result was a falling off in membership, which reached in 1897 the low point of 10,000 members.

At this time the depression had carried wages so low that the miners were desperate, and it was this desperation upon which has been based the apparently powerful organization of the present time. A general strike was ordered for July 4, 1897, to restore the wages of 1893. This continued 2 to 3 months, and although the union began this strike with only 10,000 members and no treasury, it ended with practically all the miners of the States affected and a favorable treasury. The strike resulted in the advances demanded. In Illinois, where the miners had been treated more arbitrarily and oppressively than in other States, they stood out a month longer than in other States and secured demands considerably beyond those gained elsewhere. They gained not only an increase in wages, but also the universal payment by run of the mine, the "check-off system," whereby the operators actually collect the union dues and pay them over to the treasurer of the union, and other substantial advantages.

In this same year, 1897, the miners of the anthracite region were not successful, one of the incidents of the strike in that section being the famous "Hazelton massacre," where a large body of Austro-Hungarians was fired upon by the militia. But in the summer of 1900 the anthracite miners were called out by the union, although they were not all organized. They, however, responded, joined the union, and although the union was not recognized by the operators, as had been the case in the bituminous field, yet the desired advance of 10 per cent, and the reduction in the price of powder, was granted.

The remarkable and interesting feature of the United Mine Workers is the annual conference with the Bituminous Mine Operators, for the purpose of establishing a scale of wages and conditions of work in the several districts of the competitive field. The first interstate conference of this kind was held in Chicago in January, 1898, following the successful strike of the preceding year. The second conference was held in Pittsburg in 1899, the third in Indianapolis in 1900, and the fourth in Columbus in February, 1901. It is not necessary at this point to describe in detail the nature of these annual conferences, except in so far as they are concerned with the problem of organization and discipline of the diversified races and nationalities in the mining industry. The conferences are supposed to include all of the mine operators and the representatives of all the mine workers in the competitive field. At the present time the States included are Pennsylvania, Ohio, Indiana, and Illinois. The State of West Virginia, which is also in competition with the above four States is not included, because the mine workers have not yet succeeded in organizing the miners.

At these conferences the mine operators appear as an associated body of some 200 firms and corporations, and the 150,000 mine workers appear through their 600 representatives elected from the local unions. This is doubtless the largest industrial parliament in the world in point of numbers. Indeed, the numbers are too large for deliberation, and the real work of agreeing on a scale is done in a small committee of the leading officers and representatives of the two bodies. In the annual conferences held in other trades—such as those of the iron molders, etc.— only the executive officers take part. But in the case of the mine workers it is necessary not only to make an agreement with the employers, but it is even more important to educate the rank and file in a spirit of acquiescence to that agreement. This can be successfully done only by a widely representative body. Each local union throughout a widespread territory sends its chosen spokesman with its particular grievance and demands. This spokesman after listening to the debates for several days is impressed with the conflicting demands and the need of compromise, if any agreement whatever is to be made. When the agreement finally is made by the small committee, he is prepared not only to ratify it, but to return to his local union with a complete account of the negotiations, the difficulties and obstacles, and the necessity of their yielding a part of their demands and their accepting and abiding by what could be obtained for them. In this way each delegate becomes an educational force in his locality on the principles of trade unionism and the obligations of the contracts into which they have entered. Although the expense is very great, yet it is a necessary expense in the present stage of the industrial education of the most refractory constituency that a labor organization was ever called upon to handle.

Additional details in the problem of organization of the mine workers are interesting. In the earlier form of local organization it was usual to organize each nationality separately, in its own branch, in order that it might conduct its business in its own language, and then meet the other branches through a chosen representative. Two objections to this form of organization were raised. First, the non-English miners themselves objected, because they lost incentive to learn the English language as long as it was possible to carry on their business in their native language.

Second, the organization by nationalities brought together workmen from different mines whose legislative problems were different, and this resulted in useless complication. For these two reasons, at the present time the local unions are organized as English-speaking unions for each mine or district. The non-English members are always represented in the executive board. Usually the president is English, Irish, or Welsh, and the other officers are Italian, Polish, Slovak, Lithuanian, etc., as the case may be. The business must be translated for the benefit of the several nationalities, and it often happens that three or four translations are required at a single meeting, so various are the languages spoken.

It is an interesting fact to notice that the majority of the delegates to the State and interstate conferences, as well as the leading officers of the miner's unions, are Irish or Irish-Americans. Naturally the delegates would be English-speaking persons, but the predominence of Irishmen is far beyond their proportion among the miners. It is evident that the Irishman possesses peculiar gifts in bringing together and organizing conflicting nationalities, races, and religions. In the miners' union his leadership is based on his amiability, his shrewdness in negotiation with the employers, and his firmness in enforcing the agreements upon his own membership.

Competition of native Americans.—Considering the fact, which is abundantly demonstrated, that the only force competent to check the fall of wages or to force a rise of wages in the mining industry is a thorough organization of the miners, it is necessary to inquire whether the presence of antagonistic nationalities has stood in the way of organization. It is unquestionably true that this is the case. Were it not for the difficulties of language, the antipathy of race, and the jealousies of religion, the problem of labor organization would have been much easier, and organization would not have delayed so long. But, at the same time, it can not be said that these race problems are confined to foreign races. The jeopardy and defeat of the unions has been owing as often to the competition of unorganized Americans of native stock, in new fields, as in the competition of the foreign born. This is fully demonstrated by the experience of the miners prior to 1897, when they were defeated by the competition of southern Illinois, and, since 1897, when they are jeopardized by the competition of West Virginia. Beginning with 1886, as already stated, the local organization of miners known as the Federation of Miners and Mine Laborers acquired such strength that it was able to summon the operators of Pennsylvania, Ohio, and Illinois to annual conferences for the purpose of agreements regarding the scale of wages in these competitive States. These conferences continued until 1893, when they finally went to pieces, not to be resumed until 1898 on a larger scale by the larger union. During the entire period of these interstate conferences, from 1886 to 1893, it had been impossible for the unions to organize southern Illinois. The miners in that section were predominatingly Americans. They were farm laborers who had turned to the mines as a source of ready cash. The following table reproduced from Table 9, p. 393, shows the prevailing nationalities of the several districts, the sixth and seventh districts being in the southern part of the State:

TABLE 27.—*Percentage of foreign born and native born miners in Illinois, 1899.*[1]

Divisions.	Total number employed.	Per cent Americans.	Per cent foreign born.	Total.
First	7,498	11	89	100
Second	6,631	28	72	100
Third	1,799	69	31	100
Fourth	4,655	38	62	100
Fifth	6,401	52	48	100
Sixth	5,008	49	51	100
Seventh	4,999	80	20	100

[1] Illinois Coal Report, 1899, p. LXXII.

The American-born miners were found in the southern districts, where their rates per ton for mining coal were 28 to 38 cents, as compared with 62 to 70 cents in the northern fields. The nature of the mining differed, however, so that, on account of the thickness of the veins, the southern miner averaged from $4\frac{1}{2}$ to $5\frac{1}{2}$ tons per day, while the northern miner's average product was but 2.6 to 2.7 tons. But, notwithstanding the greater productivity, the price per ton had been reduced so low that the earnings in the southern division were actually lower than those in the northern districts, averaging from $1.53 to $1.72 per day, while in the north the rate was $1.68 to $1.90 per day. (See Table 28.) Since the strike the earnings have increased throughout the State, but the increase has not been marked in the northern mines.

A comparative view of these gains is shown in Table 24 and in the following tables derived from the Illinois Coal Reports. The rate per cent of gain indicates a low price before the strike rather than a high price after. It is to be noted that the high gains are in the southern districts, where the miners are of American stock, and where they had never hitherto been brought into an effective organization, and the low gains are in the northern districts, where the foreign-born miners of Polish, Lithuanian, and Italian stock predominated. The explanation of these divergences will be given below.

TABLE 28.—*Earnings of Illinois coal miners before and after organization.*[1]

Districts.	Average number tons mined per man per day, 1896.	Average amount earned each day.		Increase, per cent.	Average yearly wages.		Increase, per cent.
		1896.	1899.		1896.	1899.	
First	2.70	$1.90	$2.01	5.8	$299.39	$378.00	
Second	2.69	1.68	1.96	16.6	232.33	415.31	
Third	3.04	1.78	1.90	6.8	280.34	288.96	
Fourth	4.22	1.53	2.31	37.8	324.22	465.06	
Fifth	5.69	1.97	2.15	9.2	383.91	416.49	
Sixth	4.44	1.72	2.30	33.7	329.65	436.37	
Seventh	5.53	1.58	2.40	51.3	235.01	388.98	
Averages	3.53	1.77	2.20	24.3	318.65	406.98	27.7

[1] Illinois Coal Report, 1896, p. 21; 1899, p. L.

Going a step further and comparing the prices on hand mining for 1897 with the scale of prices agreed upon by conference of miners and operators in 1900 and 1901, we have the following increase:

TABLE 29.—*Results of the strikes of 1897.*

Cities.	Before strike, 1897.	Scale for 1900.	Increase, per cent.
	Cents.	Cents.	
Wilmington	67.5	81	20
Peoria	40	56	40
Danville	30	49	63
Springfield	31.9	49.7	55.6
Pana	25.9	49	89
Belleville	25	49	98
Duquoin	25.5	45	96

In will be seen, in examining the two preceding tables, that whereas before the strike of 1897 the average daily earnings in the southern districts were less than in the northern districts, yet since the strike the earnings in the southern districts are 35 to 40 cents per day above those in the northern districts; and that the increase in prices in such southern districts as Pana, Belleville, and Duquoin for 1900 have been 89 to 98 per cent above the prices of 1896, but the increases in northern districts are 20 to 40 per cent.

"The greatest average gain over former prices was secured in the southern part of the State, where prices had been less; the least, in the region of Rock Island, where there had been less complaint of prices. This average for the Rock Island field is the average for all the men involved, including those who received no advance. Those who really obtained a gain received about 5 per cent over former prices. The men in the Springfield, Danville, and Streator fields fared about equally well in an advance of substantially 20 per cent. The Belleville and Duquoin miners are credited with an advance in round numbers of 50 per cent, and the Pana, Mount Olive, and Virden men with a gain of 25 per cent. In a more general way it may be said that the advance in the Peoria field was 10 per cent, and in the Braidwood-La Salle field 15 per cent. For the State at large, reducing all percentages to one, the gain was 26.42 per cent." (Illinois Coal Report, 1897, p. 184.)

When it is noted that, at the time when 25 cents was being paid in the Belleville district, the price in the Wilmington field was as high as 67½ cents, it will be seen to what disadvantages the other fields were subjected. According to the agreement in price for 1900 the price in the Belleville district is 49 cents—nearly 100 per cent above the price for 1897—whereas the highest price in the State is 81 cents, for the

Wilmington district, an increase of 21 per cent. In other words, whereas in 1897 the price paid in the Wilmington district was 2.7 times greater than that in Belleville, yet in 1900 the price in Wilmington is only 1.6 times greater. This shows the peculiar equalizing principle which the miners' union has introduced.

This principle is not that of equalizing earnings, as is often asserted, but that of equalizing competitive conditions. That earnings have not been equalized is shown by the foregoing table (see Table 28), giving by districts the average earnings per day and the average earnings per year. In the southern districts, where daily earnings were increased 33.7 and 51.3 per cent, they were in 1899 $2.30 and $2.40 per day, compared with $2.01 and $1.96 per day in the northern districts, where the increases were only 5.8 and 16.6 per cent. In other words, in order to protect the miners in the northern, thin-veined district, and permit their coal to come into the market at living wages, the union has forced the miners in the southern, thick-veined districts to increase their earnings from the lowest in the State to the highest in the State. This is one of the necessities of the system of differentials in arranging scales of prices for different sections of the same competitive field, and it was exactly the evil of the former unorganized condition that the American miners in the southern field had reduced their compensation so low, notwithstanding the greater productivity of the mines, that they were earning less than the meager wages of the foreign-born miners in the northern fields. It was the strategic position held by the cheap labor of the southern district that compelled the union to control that labor in the interest of living wages for their fellow-miners in other parts of the State. The present high wages of the southern field are not, therefore, owing to a higher standard of living or superior capacity for organization of Americans as compared with foreigners, but are owing to the initiative and interference of foreigners, who, in self-protection, forced the Americans to a higher position than the one they were willing to accept.

West Virginia.—Just as southern Illinois prior to 1897, with its native American stock and its thick vein of coal, defeated the efforts of the miners' union to raise wages and maintain a high standard of living, so West Virginia at the present time threatens to play a similar part in the larger movement of the reorganized union. By consulting Table 5 it will be seen that in West Virginia in 1890 the foreign-born miners were only 13.4 per cent of the total number, compared with 58.1 per cent in Pennsylvania. 57.4 per cent in Illinois, 31.8 per cent in Ohio, and 33.7 per cent in Indiana. The native whites of native parents were 57.5 per cent of the total number, compared with 19.7, 47.6, 48.2, and 21.3 per cent in other States. On the other hand, colored miners in West Virginia number 20.9 per cent of the total number, compared with 0.7, 2.3, 2.7, and 2.5 per cent in other States.

Since there is no uniform scale of wages and prices in West Virginia as in the other States governed by the interstate agreement, it is impossible to give a comparative showing which will represent the entire State. In West Virginia payment is usually made by the "box," which was originally supposed to contain 2 to 3 tons, but owing to the absence of a checkweighman, it is believed that these boxes have been gradually increased in size until they hold a larger weight. On the basis of 45 cents per box of 2 to 3 tons, which is the price in certain mines, the cost per ton of 2,240 pounds is 15 to 22.5 cents. This should be compared with the price of 43 cents per ton in the thick vein of the Pittsburg district and 42 cents, the lowest price in the thick veins of Illinois. The following table shows in a comparative way for the year 1900 the prices for mining and the wages of inside day laborers in this particular section of West Virginia and in the four States of the interstate conference. It will be seen that prices and wages in West Virginia are 30 to 70 per cent below those under similar conditions in the other States:

TABLE 30.—*Prices for mining coal and wages of mine workers, 1900.*

	West Virginia.	Pennsylvania.	Ohio.	Indiana.	Illinois.	
					Danville.	Williams County.
Tracklayer	$1.25-$1.35	$2.28	$2.28	$2.28	$2.28	$2.28
Driver	1.00- 1.50	2.10	2.10	2.10	2.10	2.10
Other inside labor	1.00- 1.10	2.10	2.10	2.10	2.10	2.10
Pick mining per ton (run of mine)	.15- .22½	1.52 / 2.43	.57½	.49	.49	.42

[1] Thin vein. [2] Thick vein.

The significance of the West Virginia product is shown partly by the annual increase in that State compared with the increase in competitive States. (See Table 23.) This increase is especially marked since the organization of the miners' union in the other States in 1897. It will be seen by the table that the product steadily increased from 10,708,578 tons in 1893 to 19,252,995 tons in 1899, nearly 100 per cent. Whereas the product of Illinois, which was 19,949,564 tons in 1893, after falling off in 1894 and 1895, increased to 24,439,019 tons in 1899, an increase of 22 per cent. Pennsylvania increased 68 per cent in the same period.

Referring to the increased output of West Virginia compared with other States where the miners' union gained control in 1897, the commissioner of labor of West Virginia says in report for 1897-98 (p. 63):

Of 18,000 men employed in the coal mines of West Virginia, but 206 in the Pan-Handle district report organization in the United Mine Workers of America at the beginning of the strike and subject to the strike call of the executive officers. Beyond suspension of the mines in the Pan-Handle, where the organized operatives were employed, the mining industry of the State was not affected early in the struggle, except to appreciate the stimulus of an increased demand caused by the scarcity of coal in the market. The operators in many parts of the State increased the wages of their men, and paid a bonus, sharing with them the profit of an increased business activity and advanced price of their product. In 1894 the West Virginia operators secured in this way new trade and market, which the excellence of West Virginia coal enabled them to hold after the termination of the strike, and secured to them and their employees great permanent benefit.

The number of persons employed in West Virginia has also steadily increased, whereas the number has actually declined in Illinois since 1896, in Ohio since 1898, and has increased at a much less ratio in Pennsylvania and Indiana. (See Table 22.)

Even more significant are the prices at which the coal was sold. (See Table 18.) Whereas the average prices for coal for the United States rose from 80 cents in 1898 to 87 cents in 1899, and the prices in the competitive States rose 4 cents per ton in Ohio to 9 cents in Pennsylvania, the price in West Virginia rose from 61 to 63 cents, showing the ability of that State to retain cheap labor while other States were required to pay higher wages.

The number of days of operation of the mines conveys a similar lesson. (See Table 12.) The number of days of activity in West Virginia (242) in 1899 exceeded that in other States, except Pennsylvania (200, 218, 228, 245), showing relatively steady employment on account of steady sales for coal.

The low level of wages in West Virginia may be inferred from the low rate of introduction of machinery. The table (see Table 17), giving the proportion of the bituminous coal mined by machinery in the States named, and in the United States, shows that the proportion in West Virginia (9.27 per cent) is less than one-third of that in Pennsylvania (29.67 per cent) and Indiana (28.52 per cent) and less than one-fourth of that in Ohio (41.35 per cent).

The foregoing data and considerations relative to West Virginia are fully appreciated by the operators and miners in the competitive States, as may be seen by consulting the stenographic reports of their interstate conferences. The agreements and scales of wages established in these conferences are becoming more seriously jeopardized every year on account of the competition of the unorganized field of West Virginia. The significance of these considerations for our present purpose is twofold; the miners of West Virginia are mainly native Americans, who have only recently turned from home industry to mining, and the coal veins are thick and the coal is abundant and easily mined. These are the conditions, rather than foreign immigration, which at the present time operate as obstacles to the improvement of miners' wages in the bituminous fields.

Restrictions on the number of miners.—An important restriction introduced by the Miners' Union of Illinois, and one which marks that section of the union as distinctly stronger than any other section, is the initiation fee and apprenticeship period. This is designed especially to keep farmers out of the mines, but it plainly operates with the same effect upon immigrants. A "practical miner" is one who satisfies the officers of the local union that he is practical, and the officers are very strict in their interpretation of the term. Such a miner is admitted to the union and permitted to go to the helper of the coal and have charge of a room, on payment of an initiation fee of $10. An "unpractical miner" must pay $10 to join the union, and then he is allowed to work only as a "top man" for a year. At the end of a year he can go below and work as a "mine laborer," in company with a practical miner, assisting in the loading, etc. At this step he pays an additional fee of $10. Here he must work two years before he can have charge of a room to himself; and at this final stage, when he finishes his 3 years of apprenticeship, he pays an additional fee of $10. This total initiation fee of $30 indicates, as well as any other symptom, the strength of the Illinois union, compared with that of other States, where the aggregate fee is $5 or $10.

It is true that when the "unpractical miner" goes into a room with a practical miner he gets equal pay with the miner, since the union has prohibited the former practice of subcontracting. But it will be seen that as a competitor with the other miners in the State he is compelled to serve a 3 years' apprenticeship. The union has a warrant in enforcing this rule, growing out of an act of the legislature entitled "An act concerning qualification of miners," approved June 7, 1897. This provides that "every person desiring to work by himself in rooms of coal mines in this

State shall first produce satisfactory evidence to the mine manager of the mine in which he is employed or desirous to be employed, that he has worked at least 2 years with or as a practical miner. Until said applicant has so satisfied the mine manager of the mine in which he seeks such employment of his competency he shall not be allowed to mine coal unless accompanied by some competent coal miner until he becomes duly qualified." Any violation of the act works a forfeiture of the certificate of the manager of the mine where such party is employed.

It is not only in the strict enforcement of the law, but also in the preliminary requirement of 1 year's work as a "top man" that the Miners' Union of Illinois protects itself from immigrants as well as farmers.

Contrast now the operations of a somewhat similar law, applicable to the anthracite coal mines in Pennsylvania, where the union is weak. An act approved July 15, 1897, to protect the lives and limbs of miners, etc., in the anthracite coal mines of Pennsylvania, provides for the establishment in each of the 8 inspection districts of the anthracite coal regions of a board to be styled the miners' examining board. This board consists of 9 miners to be appointed from the most skillful miners actually engaged in the business, who have had 5 years' practical experience in the same. Each examining board registers the names of all persons duly qualified to be employed as a miner. A fee of $1 is paid to the board, and a fee of 25 cents is charged where the person has been examined by another board. The amount derived from this source is held by the board and applied to the expenses and salaries. The board is required to grant "such persons as may be qualified, certificates of competency or qualification, which shall entitle the holder thereof to be employed as and to do the work of miners, as may be expressed in said certificate, and such certificate shall be good and sufficient evidence of registration and competency under this act. * * * All persons applying for a certificate of competency, or to entitle them to be employed as miners, must produce satisfactory evidence of having had not less than 2 years' experience as a miner or as a mine laborer in the mines of this Commonwealth, and in no case shall an applicant be deemed competent unless he appear in person before the said board and answer intelligently and correctly at least 12 questions in the English language pertaining to the requirements of a practical miner and be perfectly identified, under oath, as a mine laborer by at least 1 practical miner holding miner's certificates."

It is plain that if the Mine Workers' Union of the anthracite section took it upon itself to enforce this law in spirit and in letter, it could not only enforce a period of apprenticeship upon every "unpractical miner" equal to two years, but could absolutely shut out immigrants who have not learned to speak the English language. But the law, contrary to the experience in Illinois, increases the competition of fresh immigrants, since in practice the examining boards make no examination whatever of the applicants. The payment of the fee and the granting of the certificate are a mere formality and very few applicants are refused. The consequence is that the mine manager who employs a certificated miner is relieved of all responsibility for any accident which the miner may have brought upon himself or others. He therefore employs such miners as he sees fit, usually sending them into the more difficult and dangerous places where experienced miners are reluctant to go. Instead of imposing a period of apprenticeship like that in Illinois, the Pennsylvania law, through the weakness or negligence of the miners' union, actually intensifies the competition from the unemployed who may congregate around the mines.

V. WAGE STATISTICS.

The problem of comparing the movement of wages in the mining industry over a period of years is peculiarly difficult, as will appear from the following considerations:

The companies report the average number of employees and the total wages paid, but not the wages paid to individual employees. Prior to the organization of the union in 1897 in the bituminous region, and 1900 in the anthracite region, the system of subcontracting prevailed, and the only person appearing on the company's book was the contracting miner, who usually had 1 helper, and in the anthracite region sometimes as high as 6 helpers, whose names did not appear on the books. Also, prior to organization, there was no rule preventing a miner from digging out coal on days when the mine was not hoisting, but the companies report the number of days worked as equivalent to the number of days when hoisting. In this way the average daily earnings per man appeared larger than they really were.

Again, before the period of organization the miners were not permitted to station their own "checkweighman," in order to verify the measurements, and it is well known that, in course of time, the "boxes," "cars," and "tons" gradually increased in size, so that in the anthracite region ultimately a ton was rated at 3,360 pounds. In this way the real price per ton was continually falling, though not apparently so.

Lastly, the charges for powder and the introduction or discontinuance of company stores introduce variable factors which do not always appear in the earnings. For these reasons no statistical authority has undertaken to compile a series of miners wages over a period of years, and the averages compiled by different authorities at intervals are not to be relied upon. The nearest approach to a continuous view of miners' wages is that of Mr. Joseph D. Weeks, in the Aldrich report, who gives the comparative wages of day men in an anthracite mine for the years 1840 to 1891. This reported is submitted herewith.

ANTHRACITE COAL.

Rates of wages paid miners on company work at anthracite coal mines in Luzerne County, Pa.[1]

Date.	Rate of wages per week.	Date.	Rate of wages per week.	Date.	Rate of wages per week.	Date.	Rate of wages per week.
1840	$7.20	Oct., 1857	$5.40	Dec., 1869	$17.34	June, 1876	$11.28
1841	6.00	Jan., 1858	4.50	Jan., 1870	15.97	July, 1876	11.34
1842	6.00	June, 1858	5.00	Feb., 1870	14.80	Aug., 1876	11.49
Jan., 1843	5.00	July, 1858	5.40	Mar., 1870	14.85	Oct., 1876	11.43
May, 1843	5.25	Aug., 1858	4.50	Apr., 1870	15.06	Dec., 1876	11.18
July, 1843	5.50	Jan., 1859	6.00	Aug., 1870	15.52	Mar., 1877	10.08
Aug., 1843	6.00	Apr., 1859	6.60	Oct., 1870	15.06	May, 1877	9.64
Jan., 1844	4.50	May, 1859	6.96	Nov., 1870	14.60	June, 1877	9.40
Feb., 1844	5.00	Sept., 1859	6.48	Jan., 1871	15.67	Aug., 1877	9.85
May, 1844	6.00	Nov., 1859	6.00	Feb., 1871	14.60	Sept., 1877	10.36
Jan., 1845	5.25	Mar., 1860	6.96	June, 1871	14.63	Nov., 1877	9.40
May, 1845	6.00	Dec., 1860	6.00	July, 1871	14.04	Jan., 1878	9.51
June, 1845	6.96	May, 1861	6.96	Aug., 1871	14.58	Feb., 1878	10.08
Jan., 1846	6.00	Aug., 1861	6.00	Sept., 1871	14.76	Apr., 1878	10.36
May, 1846	6.96	May, 1862	6.48	Oct., 1871	14.78	July, 1878	10.53
Jan., 1847	6.00	July, 1862	6.96	Nov., 1871	14.68	Aug., 1878	11.78
Mar., 1847	6.96	Nov., 1862	7.98	Dec., 1871	13.54	Dec., 1878	10.08
Jan., 1848	6.00	July, 1863	9.96	Jan., 1872	14.10	Jan., 1879	9.51
Apr., 1848	6.96	Sept., 1863	12.00	Feb., 1872	13.23	Feb., 1879	9.34
Jan., 1849	6.00	May, 1864	13.50	Apr., 1872	13.49	July, 1879	9.51
Feb., 1849	6.48	July, 1864	15.48	Oct., 1872	13.84	Nov., 1879	10.39
Mar., 1849	6.00	May, 1865	13.50	Nov., 1872	14.10	Mar., 1880	11.15
May, 1849	6.96	July, 1865	10.50	Feb., 1873	14.17	Mar., 1880	11.47
Dec., 1849	6.00	Sept., 1865	12.00	May, 1873	14.80	Apr., 1880	11.72
May, 1850	6.96	Oct., 1865	13.50	June, 1873	14.97	Sept., 1880	11.97
Nov., 1850	6.00	Jan., 1866	10.98	July, 1873	15.15	Jan., 1881	12.41
Apr., 1851	6.96	Feb., 1866	11.76	Aug., 1873	15.33	Jan., 1882	11.97
Jan., 1852	6.00	Apr., 1866	10.74	Sept., 1873	15.50	Jan., 1883	11.24
Apr., 1852	6.96	June, 1866	12.00	Oct., 1873	15.67	1884	11.24
Jan., 1853	6.00	Aug., 1866	13.50	Mar., 1874	14.85	Jan., 1885	11.34
May, 1853	6.00	Dec., 1866	10.74	Apr., 1874	14.94	Jan., 1886	11.78
Aug., 1853	6.48	1867	10.74	May, 1874	15.10	June, 1886	11.34
Dec., 1853	6.00	Jan., 1868	11.75	June, 1874	15.29	Oct., 1886	11.59
Jan., 1854	6.96	May, 1868	13.15	July, 1874	15.55	Nov., 1887	12.10
May, 1854	8.46	June, 1868	14.00	Aug., 1874	14.79	Mar., 1888	11.59
July, 1854	7.50	Aug., 1868	15.00	Sept., 1874	15.31	Aug., 1888	11.72
Sept., 1854	7.98	Sept., 1868	16.50	Oct., 1874	14.65	Sept., 1888	11.84
Feb., 1855	7.50	Oct., 1868	17.50	Nov., 1874	14.89	Nov., 1888	11.72
Apr., 1855	6.96	Nov., 1868	18.50	July, 1875	11.52	Dec., 1888	11.59
Oct., 1855	7.50	Dec., 1868	17.50	Aug., 1875	11.89	Mar., 1889	11.47
Dec., 1855	6.00	Jan., 1869	15.35	Sept., 1875	11.94	1890	11.47
May, 1856	7.50	Feb., 1869	15.00	Oct., 1875	11.97	1891	11.47
Dec., 1856	6.00	July, 1869	20.65	Feb., 1876	11.45	1892	11.47
June, 1857	6.96	Aug., 1869	20.64	Mar., 1876	11.17		
Sept., 1857	6.00	Nov., 1869	20.08	May, 1876	11.22		

[1] Aldrich report, part 4, 1893, Table XIII, p. 1561.

BITUMINOUS COAL.

Wages paid in mining bituminous coal in first and second pools of the Monongahela River, near Pittsburg.

The rates given from 1840 to 1857, inclusive, are the rates paid per 100 bushels. It is assumed that the average product of the miner per day, when work is steady, is 100 bushels, which would make the rate given as the price per 100 bushels the daily rate of earnings.[1]

Date.	Ra e of pay (per bushel).[2]	Date.	Rate of pay (per bushel).	Date.	Rate of pay (per bushel).	Date.	Rate of pay (per bushel).
1840	$1.25	1859	$0.02	1872	$0.04	1882	$0.04
1841	1.25	1860	.02	1873	.04	1883	.03½
1842	1.25	1861	.01	1874	.04	1884	.03½
1843	1.25	1861	.01½	1874	.03½	1884	.03¼
1844	1.25	1861	.01¾	1875	.03	1884	.03
1845	1.50	1862	.01¾	1875	.02½	1884	.02½
1846	1.50	1862	.02	1876	.02½	1885	.02½
1847	1.75	1863	.03	1876	.03	1885	.03
1848	1.75	1863	.04	1876	.02	1885	.02½
1849	1.75	1864	.05	1877	.03	1886	.02½
1850	1.75	1865	.05	1878	.03	1887	.02½
1851	1.75	1866	.04	1878	.02½	1888	.03
1852	2.00	1867	.04	1878	.02	1888	.03¼
1853	2.00	1868	.04	1879	.03	1889	.03
1854	2.00	1868	.03½	1879	.02½	1889	.02½
1855	2.00	1869	.03½	1879	.03	1890	.03
1856	2.00	1869	.04	1880	.03	1891	.03½
1857	2.00	1870	.04	1880	.03½	1892	.03½
1858	.02	1871	.04	1881	.03½		

[1] Aldrich report, part 4, 1893, Table XIII, p. 1565.
[2] Rate of pay from 1840 to 1857 is per 100 bushels.

Besides the foregoing report of Mr. Weeks, the principal source of information on miners' wages is the reports of the Illinois bureau of labor statistics, continued latterly as the Illinois coal reports. Following is a summary of investigations made by that office in the years 1881, 1882, 1884, 1890, 1896, and 1899. As will be seen, the several investigations are not upon a uniform basis.

The first investigation made by the Illinois bureau of labor statistics was in 1881. This included 95 families of miners, with 109 persons earning wages, the aggregate earnings for 1 year being $84,563. Average earnings per family were $363.82. No statement is made of the location of families or their distribution throughout the State.

"The question of wages," says the report (p. 225), "is one of the most mooted which has come before us. During the fall and winter season a good workman can earn, in the majority of mines in the State, from $50 to $90 per month. The average earnings, however, hardly exceed $400 the year round, and taken one year with another will not average that amount for the past 10 years."

In 1882 the Illinois bureau continued its investigation. It reported that the price of mining has advanced about 11 per cent during the year (p. 36). The coal companies own the houses and land occupied by the miners and the stores at which they trade. The status of the miners in this case is low. This condition is passing away. The following table is published on page 319:

TABLE 31.—*Braidwood.*

Number in family.	Earnings of head of family.	Earnings of other members.	Total incomes.
10	$450	$480	$930
2	410		410
5	480		480
3	406		406

"Considering the dangers besetting them and the severity of their labor, it is greatly to be regretted that the income is not sufficient to provide them a greater proportion of the comforts of life. Besides the ordinary dangers that surround them, they are especially liable to loss of time on account of the fluctuating demand for the product of the mines" (p. 320).

The report states: "Perhaps no one body of laborers, taken as a whole, have made as little progress from their condition as mere wage workers as the miners of this State, and it is a question which concerns the whole State, as well as the employers of these men and the people who live in their immediate communities, whether this condition may not be much improved in the near future.

"The majority of our mining population is of foreign birth or parentage, and as a rule the sons of miners follow the employment of their fathers."

The next investigation made by the Illinois bureau was in 1884, wherein 290 families of coal miners were reported upon as part of an investigation of 2,129 families in various occupations. This report was made at a time when the Slavic and Italian elements in the mining population were as yet insignificant. The following table shows the distribution of the 2,129 families by nationality and by occupation. In the coal mines the English played the leading part in the investigation, numbering 76, the American born followed with 63, the Irish with 47, the Scotch with 38, and the Germans with 28. Only 5 Italian miners were investigated and no Poles.

TABLE 32.—*Nationalities and their representation in classified occupations in Illinois, 1884.*[1]

Nationalities.	Whole number.	Building trades.	Shop trades.	Metal workers.	Coalmine employees.	Railroad employees.	Outdoor occupations.	Indoor occupations.	Foremen.	Total.
Americans	978	173	202	130	63	74	178	148	10	978
English	152	21	15	20	76	4	14	2		152
Scotch	65	7	7	7	38	1	4	1		65
Irish	348	24	45	43	47	38	144	4	3	348
Welsh	25	1	5	4	12	3				25
Germans	349	33	132	33	28	18	78	26	1	349
Scandinavians	107	10	25	6	13	5	43	5		107
Danes	13		2	22	4	2	5			13
Italians	11				5		6			11
Poles	4	1	3							4
French	21	3	3	1	1	3	8	1	1	21
Swiss	5		2		1		1	1		5
Canadians	22	4	8		2			8		22
Colored	23		2			1	19			23
Bohemians	5		5							5
Portuguese	1		1							1
Total	2,129	278	457	244	290	149	500	196	15	2,129

[1] Ill. Bur. Lab. Stat., 1884, p. 160.

In this investigation the striking result is the low earnings of coal-mine employees compared with those of other occupations. The average earnings of all employees, including one foreman at $1,000, was $399.73. But coal-mine employees earned the lowest of all classes, only $370.33. Coal miners proper, numbering 232, earned $385.43 per year.

Next to coal miners were the "shop trades," earning $373.99; while the "building trades" earned $414.15, and railroad employees $550.

That the wives of coal miners do not find occupation as wage earners to the extent reached in other occupations appears also from the table.

TABLE 33.—*Family earnings by occupation—Illinois, 1884.*[1]

General classes.	Whole number of families.	Number of occupations.	Number of wives at work.	Earnings of—				Cost of living.
				Husbands.	Wives.	Children.	Whole family.	
Building trades	287	8	16	$414.15	$75.95	$64.50	$554.60	$509.89
Shop trades	458	11	19	373.99	158.83	11.97	541.19	497.84
Metal workers	243	5	12	557.23	243.50		800.72	752.30
Railroad employees	149	4	5	550.00	144.00	10.00	704.00	579.12
Coal-mine employees	290	1	6	370.33	104.66		483.33	494.66
Outdoor occupations	500	5	49	478.35	145.28	25.32	650.96	618.29
Indoor occupations	196	2	3	690.00	155.00		845.00	583.25
Foremen	15	1	1	1,000.00	250.00		1,250.00	734.00
Total	2,129	37	111	399.73	147.93	24.96	572.62	511.28

[1] Illinois Bureau Labor Statistics 1884, p. 283.

The same investigation showed that 15 per cent of the blacksmiths do not make a living, and that the same is true of 11 per cent of the bricklayers, 25 per cent of the carpenters, 25 per cent of the cigar makers, 30 per cent of the railroad employees, 37 per cent of the laborers, 25 per cent of the shoemakers, 30 per cent of the teamsters, and 30 per cent of the coal miners. In this respect, however, the coal miners were superior to unskilled workers in general, of whom 35 per cent did not pay expenses.

TABLE 34.—*Earnings by classes of employment—Illinois, 1884.*[1]

Classes.	Whole number.	Pay expenses.		Do not pay expenses.	
		Number.	Per cent.	Number.	Per cent.
Skilled workers	1,175	950	80	225	20
Railroad employees	149	122	81	27	19
Coal-mine employees	290	216	74	74	26
Unskilled workers	500	326	65	174	35

[1] Illinois Bureau Labor Statistics, 1884, p. 258.

Those who show average earnings of more than $300 and less than $400 are representative of 191 individuals, among whom are day laborers, coal miners, railroad section men, hod carriers and others (p. 263).
The Coal Report for 1890 gives record of 5,356 coal miners in 11 different mines, where the average earnings for the year were $384.14, or $2.23 per day, working 11 months in the year.
In 1896, in the Annual Report on Coal Statistics, the Illinois bureau made an attempt to arrive at definite knowledge of the actual earnings of the miners. The method adopted was such that the apparent daily earnings of the miners were greater than their real daily earnings. This is because the number of days of actual employment for each man is based upon the reported number of running days of the mine. But many days, when the work is nominally suspended, the miners are setting props and getting in readiness for the resumption of work. These days are not accounted for. This discrepancy, however, affects only the daily average earnings, and not the yearly averages of $318.65 and $313.59.
The investigation included wages paid by the ton and wages paid by the day.

TABLE 35.—*Earnings of miners, 1896 (Illinois).*

	Paid for by the ton.	Paid for by the day.
Number of men	16,625	2,884
Number of mines	205	191
Average days employed per man	179	177
Average price per ton	$0.53	
Average amounts earned each day while working	1.77	$1.76
Average yearly income	318.65	313.59
Average daily income	.873	.859

In 1899, for the first time in the Reports of the Illinois Bureau of Coal Statistics (p. XLVI), the operators of mines were asked to furnish the total amount of wages paid all classes of employees excepting office help. The totals are condensed in the following summary:

TABLE 36.—*Earnings of Illinois coal-mine employees, 1899.*[1]

District.	Miners.	Day men.	Boys.	Total.	Average number of days worked.	Total wages paid all classes of employees.	Average wages per day, all employees.	Average wages per year, all employees.
First	5,688	1,385	425	7,498	188	$2,835,177	$2.01	$387.00
Second	4,445	1,400	199	6,044	212	2,508,459	1.96	415.31
Third	1,415	335	49	1,799	152	519,883	1.90	288.96
Fourth	2,960	1,415	134	4,509	201	2,096,671	2.31	465.06
Fifth	4,421	1,812	168	6,401	194	2,665,968	2.15	416.49
Sixth	3,579	1,258	165	5,002	196	2,182,747	2.30	436.37
Seventh	3,330	1,491	137	4,958	162	1,927,274	2.40	388.98
Total	25,838	9,096	1,277	36,211	186	14,616,555	2.20	406.98

[1] Illinois Coal Report, 1899, p. L.

The foregoing table, it should be noted, is based on the total number of all classes of employees in the mines, including miners, daymen, and boys. Deducting the 1,277 boys, whose daily wages are estimated at 75 cents each, and 9,096 day men, whose average wages are estimated at $1.90 each, it follows that the average earnings of miners were $434.39 per year or $2.55 per day.

Contrasting these different investigations it is apparent that the bases are not uniform. In 1881 the report is based on families and in the other years on miners or mine employees. In 1882 only four miners are reported and their high wages may not have been typical. In 1884 the earnings of 232 miners reported give a wider basis for comparison. There is no doubt that wages declined during the years 1881 to 1886, the decline amounting to 33 per cent, according to a report of the Illinois bureau for 1886 (p. 356). In 1890 the earnings were about the same as in 1884, but they declined to $318.65 in 1896, a drop of 17.2 per cent in six years. In 1899 they had recovered and reached the highest point in twenty years, $434.39 (excluding the inadequate report for 1882). The following is a comparative table of the foregoing results:

TABLE 37.—*Comparative earnings of miners and miners' families, Illinois.*[1]

Year.	Number.	Designation.	Average yearly earnings.
1881	95	Families..	$363.82
1882	4	Miners ...	436.00
1884	232	....do	385.43
1890	5,356	....do	384.14
1896	16,625	....do	{[2]318.65 / [3]313.59}
1899	25,838	....do	434.39

[1] Compiled from Reports of Illinois Bureau of Labor Statistics and Coal Reports.
[2] By ton.
[3] By day.

In general it may be stated that there was a sharp decline in the earnings of bituminous coal miners in Illinois prior to the year 1884; that earnings in 1890 were about the same as in 1884; that they declined 17 per cent from 1890 to 1896, and that they increased 36 per cent from 1896 to 1899, to a point probably higher than at any time within the past 20 years. A similar movement of earnings has probably occurred in the 3 other States of the competitive field, namely, Indiana, Ohio, and Pennsylvania, covered by the Mine Workers' Union, but the recent rise has not occurred in West Virginia, where the union has not gained a foothold. The decline of wages in 1882 to 1884 followed an enormous immigration of laborers from Europe, but it was also accompanied by a general depression of business, which reduced the coal product from 82,578,204 tons in 1884 to 72,621,548 tons in 1885. (See Table 23.) On the other hand, the daily rates of wages in the 25 selected occupations reported by the Commissioner of Labor (not including miners) (see p. 307 and chart) actually rose 1.73 per cent during these years, but the yearly earnings doubtless declined.

The decline in coal miners' wages following 1892 resulted from the depression of business coupled with a disorganized labor market, as shown by the fact that in the 25 occupations reported by the Commissioner of Labor (see p. 307 and chart) the decline in wages from 1892 to 1896 was 4 per cent, whereas in the coal trade the decline from 1890 to 1896 was 17 per cent.

The recovery of wages from 1896 to 1899 was owing to returning business activity and increased demand for coal, combined with labor organization. This increase was 36 per cent, whereas the average increase in daily rates of wages in 192 occupations reported by the Commissioner of Labor for the same period was only 3.7 per cent. (See p. 308.)

VI. ACCIDENTS IN RELATION TO THE FOREIGN BORN.

That mining is a dangerous occupation is admitted by everyone, but as to the causes and prevention of accidents opinion is divided. The dangerous character of mining is shown by an examination of the accidents in relation, first, to the number of employees and, secondly, to the number of tons mined. The following table shows the number of fatal accidents per thousand employees and the number of tons mined for each fatal accident. This is given for both the anthracite and bituminous mines of Pennsylvania.

IMMIGRATION AND THE COAL MINERS. 417

TABLE 38.—*Fatal accidents per 1,000 employees and number of tons mined for each fatal accident.*[1]

Year.	Anthracite mines.		Bituminous mines.	
	Number tons per fatal accident.	Number accidents (fatal and nonfatal) per 1,000 employees.	Number tons per fatal accident.	Number accidents per 1,000 employees.
1870	59,970	5.921		
1871	66,038	5.601		
1872	83,734	3.709		
1873	83,711	4.647		
1874	77,034	4.325		
1875	87,795	3.401		
1876	86,013	3.235		
1877	113,803	2.902		
1878	99,794	2.923	438,656	[2]1.687
1879	105,708	3.805	237,987	[2]2.278
1880	182,987	2.753	357,967	[2]1.456
1881	110,659	3.591	357,339	[2]1.392
1882	105,349	3.520	273,014	[2]2.098
1883	104,336	3.533	294,597	[2]1.541
1884	98,076	3.284	195,743	2.625
1885	94,160	3.541	333,763	1.630
1886	122,095	2.707	353,175	1.562
1887	117,522	2.965	329,146	1.783
1888	114,391	2.103	380,138	1.445
1889	101,604	3.226	329,766	1.888
1890	106,033	3.463	279,045	2.183
1891	103,796	3.463	177,252	3.183
1892	115,500	3.051	347,560	1.688
1893	106,021	3.224	331,469	1.640
1894	103,659	3.144	324,194	1.441
1895	121,340	2.939	334,278	1.825
1896	95,766	2.354	280,858	2.136
1897	110,725	2.836	366,941	1.723
1898	114,708	2.886	323,483	2.255
1899	117,210	3.286	282,421	2.821

[1] Accidents: Penna. Bureau of Mines, 1899, pp. IX-X, XIV.
[2] The returns not complete.

It is seen from the table that the number of accidents per thousand employees shows a general decrease in the anthracite mines. But it must be borne in mind that the great majority of these accidents happen inside and that the rate based on the total number of employees does not take into account the large number employed outside. Now, this number working outside has increased out of proportion to the number of inside men, so that the rate for 1898 is not absolutely to be compared with the rate of 1870. This difference is not so marked in the bituminous mines because the proportion of inside and outside men has remained more nearly regular than in the anthracite mines.

Comparing the number of tons mined to each fatal accident it is seen that in the bituminous mines there has been a slight tendency for the number of tons per accident to decrease from 1879 to 1898, which would show that mining in the bituminous mines is becoming more dangerous. On the other hand, the tons mined per each fatal accident in the anthracite mines increased over the number in 1870-1876, since which time the rate has remained steady with the exception of 4 years. This would seem to show that there has been an improvement and a slight decrease in the dangerous character of anthracite mining considering the number of tons mined per fatal accident.

But in general it will be seen from the above table that there has been only a slight change in the number of accidents in these mines even in the face of the rules and regulations enforced by State inspectors. The reason for this rate and its continuance may be found in the character of the mines. The difference in the number of accidents in the anthracite and in the bituminous mines is, to quote from the Pennsylvania Report of the Bureau of Mines, 1897 (p. IX), "in part accounted for by the thickness of the seams, their frequent heavy pitch, the depth of the mines, and their gaseous condition." The older the mines, on the other hand, the more dangerous they are and the continuance of a high rate of accidents may show the increasing difficulty of extracting coal.

A more frequent explanation is to attribute the accidents not only to the natural conditions but to the presence of foreigners. The mixture of several nationalities who do not speak the same language, and understand one another with great difficulty, is a disturbing condition and complicates things in the face of danger where quick thought and promptness of execution are often able to prevent accidents.

Language and mode of thought are not the only danger in the employment of foreigners. Their ignorance, combined often with recklessness, leads them into dangerous places without consciousness of the danger. In connection with their ignorance the foreigners are often driven into the most dangerous places, or they may willingly take the greatest risks in order to show their willingness to work. Aside from this their desire to make good earnings, while they at the same time work cheaply, leads them to neglect many of the ordinary precautions because the time spent on that is to them wasted. It is thus that through ignorance they may enter a dangerous place with a naked lamp, or willfully fail to put up props at the proper time.

The increase in the number of accidents in the bituminous mines followed the increase in the number of foreigners who entered the mines. But the difficulty in attempting to study the effect of immigration on the number of accidents is found in the fact that the Pennsylvania Bureau of Mines does not give the nationality of the miners. But this much can be said, that the number of accidents has not, over a period of years, shown any marked change. So far as there has been a change it has tended more toward an increase. This condition may be the result of increasing difficulties or to the increased number of foreign born. More probably both elements combined would largely explain the condition, though it might reasonably be expected that State regulations and frequent inspections would have some effect in reducing the number of accidents.

In this connection it is of interest to make a comparison between the number of accidents occurring among the miners and the accidents to employees of railways. The report of the inspector of coal mines of Pennsylvania for 1895 makes such a comparison.

In the anthracite mines in 1895 1 miner was killed to 342 employed; in the bituminous region, 1 to 544. Among railway employees of the United States in 1895 there was 1 killed to 432. This is more dangerous than in bituminous mines and less dangerous than in anthracite mines. The nonfatal accidents were greater on the railroads than in the mines.

In considering the nationalities of the injured it is not possible to reduce the accidents to rates on the basis of the nationalities employed. The Pennsylvania reports do not state the nationalities of the miners, but they do give the nationalities of those injured. It is then possible to classify the accidents as fatal and nonfatal and give them for the different nationalities. The following table shows the number of accidents for each nationality in the anthracite and in the bituminous mines in Pennsylvania for 1898, and also shows the per cent of accidents to American born and to total foreign born.

TABLE 39.—*Nationality of miners injured in Pennsylvania in 1898.*[1]

Nationality.	Anthracite.				Bituminous.			
	Fatal.	Non-fatal.	Total.	Per cent.	Fatal.	Non-fatal.	Total.	Per cent.
Americans	73	245	318	20.8	51	109	160	26.8
Austrians	27	9	36		12	15	27	
English	21	75	96		25	30	55	
Germans	22	53	75			6	6	
Hungarians	36	64	100		9	28	37	
Irish	58	147	205		11	30	41	
Italians	7	38	45		9	15	24	
Polish	114	267	381	79.2	16	24	40	73.2
Russians	12	20	32		17	35	52	
Scotch	6	4	10		2	6	8	
Swedes	1	4	5		7	19	26	
Slavs	7	27	34		10	16	26	
Welsh	47	138	185		28	51	79	
Greeks		2	2		2	13	15	
Total	431	1,093	1,524	100	199	397	596	100

[1] Pennsylvania Report Bureau of Mines, 1898, pp. LXXX, LXXXII.

The above comparison is inadequate because the percentage of each nationality among the miners is not taken into account. In the Bulletin of the Department of Labor (Vol. II, p. 751), Mr. G..O. Virtue has given the percentage of different nationalities employed in the Pennsylvania and Reading mines in 1896. These mines

IMMIGRATION AND THE COAL MINERS. 419

make up the greater part of the sixth anthracite district of Pennsylvania. Dr. Virtue estimates them at 70 per cent of the district. It is then possible to draw a comparison between the accidents of each nationality in the whole district and the corresponding number of miners in the principal mines of the district. The following table is intended to show the number and percentage of accidents in each nationality for the sixth district, anthracite, in Pennsylvania, and the number and per cent of the same nationalities in the mines of the Philadelphia and Reading Coal and Iron Company:

TABLE 40.—*Sixth district anthracite.*[1]

Nationalities.	Accidents.				Per cent of these nationalities employed in Philadelphia and Reading mines.	Number.
	Fatal.	Non-fatal.	Total.	Per cent.		
Americans	2	4	6	3.6	20.6	5,838
English	4	4	8	4.8	6.3	1,799
Irish	14	16	30	18.1	21.3	6,025
Welsh	6	7	13	7.8	3.7	3,207
Scotch	1		1	.6	.6	168
Germans	5	2	7	4.2	11.3	1,037
Polish	23	46	69	41.6	24.3	6,895
Hungarians	10	20	30	18.1	11.2	3,180
Italians	2		2	1.2	.7	211
	67	99	166	100	100	28,360

[1] Bureau of Mines, Penna., 1896, p. 191; Bulletin Dept. of Labor, Vol. II, p. 751.

From the above it will be seen that the American, English, German, and Irish mine employees have considerably smaller percentages of accidents than their numbers bear to the total number of employees. The Scotch have accidents in proportion to their number. It is thus evident that the American-born, English, Irish, and Germans must exercise more care and have greater experience in dealing with dangerous conditions than the more recent immigrants who are represented by the Poles, Hungarians, and Italians. In the case of these latter people and the Welsh the proportion is very much higher than their proportionate numbers, which shows that these people either do the most dangerous work, are inexperienced and ignorant, or careless and reckless. This is especially the case with the Hungarians and Poles, whose willingness to take chances and disregard even of the ordinary dangers are well known. But the case of the Italian is somewhat different. Very few work on the inside of the mines because they are timid and seem anxious to avoid danger, but the number of accidents happening to them is almost twice their proportionate number.

Upon the causes of accidents and the possibility of reducing them to a minimum the remarks of the mine inspectors are of importance. As to the accidents resulting from inexperience, the inspector of the sixth bituminous district of Pennsylvania said:

Of the 13 accidents that resulted from falls of coal and rock, only 4 were really unavoidable, the others having been caused either by carelessness of the unfortunates or incompetency. I found the latter cause to be in the majority, the inexperience of many of them in mining being so limited that they were not aware of the dangerous conditions when they existed and therefore did not protect themselves.

The carelessness of miners and their willfulness in failing to take the most ordinary precautions is brought out in the Report of the Bureau of Mines of Pennsylvania, 1897 (p. IX):

With all the object lessons presented of men maimed and killed, there is evidence where men deliberately, and against all laws and common sense, enter a mine with a naked light when they have been repeatedly told not to do so, and even going so far as to secrete matches or manufacture a key to open their safety lamps in order to get a light for their pipes. They fail to put up props at the proper time, neglect sprags to protect the coal from falling on them, use an iron bar to ram a cartridge back in a hole, and do many other things that they know themselves they should not do, all of which are prohibited by law. These are conditions that are undoubtedly difficult to combat. No occasional inspections or regulations on paper can take the place of intelligent supervision of the mines.
It appears from the reports sent to this office that 609 fatal and 1,623 nonfatal accidents occurred in and about the coal mines of the State during the year 1898. Two hundred and fifty, or 41 per cent, of the fatal accidents were attributable to carelessness or violations of the mine laws by the victims themselves. Of the 1,623 non fatal accidents, 700, or 43 per cent, were attributed to carelessness or violation the mine laws by the injured."

It is probable that the number of accidents depends somewhat upon the enforcement of the mining law. The chief mine inspector of Pennsylvania touched upon this in the report of 1897 (p. 9):

> There is no question but if the mine rules, general and special, were more vigorously enforced, the number of accidents would be very materially reduced. Some people attribute the cause of so many accidents to the large foreign element employed in and about the mines. I have my doubts as to that being the cause. My experience and observations have been that this class are as careful of danger, if not more so, than many of the experienced miners.

CHAPTER VI.

MISCELLANEOUS TRADES.

In addition to the extended investigation reported in the foregoing pages concerning the effect of immigration on the clothing workers, cigar makers, and coal miners, the following pages contain the results of less complete inquiries made in other trades where immigration does not at present play so important a part, or where its influence is not so great as in former years. This is followed by a summary of an investigation covering practically all the trades in the State of New York, made in 1898 by the bureau of statistics of labor of that State.

Textile trades.—In the textile trades the most striking feature is the great improvement in machinery and the large number of new inventions and labor-saving devices continually introduced. A brief reference to the silk textiles will be found on page 445. The improvements in both silk and cotton manufacture have been among the most remarkable in recent industrial history. When in England steam power was introduced into cotton manufacture in 1842, a weaver would run two looms, work about 13 hours a day, and earn about $1.75 per week. In Fall River in 1848–1850 a skilled weaver would run 3 looms and earn $4 per week. The rate was 25 cents a cut of 36 yards. The length of the cut was gradually increased until in 1870 it was 45 yards and the price per cut was 30 cents. In 1850–1855, 4 looms of 130 picks a minute were tended, then 6 looms in 1860, and in 1872 8 looms of 180 picks. At the present time the loom has from 120 to 225 picks per minute on ordinary prints.

As to production, a weaver can now produce, working 58 hours a week, more work than he formerly could while working 13 hours a day. In 1872 a weaver was able to earn $12 to $13 a week, but it is claimed that at present very few weavers are able to earn that amount—the average is from $8 to $10 per week—and their work is now much harder. The foreman of a weaving shop in Fall River, Mass., says:

> Wages have decreased rather than increased. Not only have they decreased in proportion to the amount of work done, but they have decreased absolutely. A man used actually to earn somewhat more money while producing somewhat less work than he can earn to-day doing double the work.

The Bulletin of the Department of Labor, July, 1900 (p. 783), gives the average daily wages for weavers. In Fall River the average daily wages in 1893 were $1.30¼, and in 1900 $1.37, an increase of 5 per cent.

In considering machinery it is said that skilled help is constantly being replaced by the introduction of new machines. Much less skilled help is now required in the card room and in the spinners' and weavers' rooms. A new machine or a more perfect part of a machine is being introduced almost every day, thus simplifying the mode of production, making it safer and more regular, so that a better thread and a better cloth can be produced at much less cost. For example, improved "ring" spindles are now replacing "mule" spindles. As to the effect on labor as a result of this machine, the testimony of a foreman is important:

> In a few months we will throw out all our mule spindles and put in ring spindles. We can manufacture twice as much thread on the ring as on the mule in the same space, and while it is said that the thread is not as good on the ring as it is on the mule—that is, it is a little harder and does not take on print so easily, yet that has not been my experience. The modern ring spindle can produce almost as good thread with the ring as with the mule, the mule taking up twice the amount of space. Another saving on the ring spindle is in the cost of labor. The mule spinner is a mechanic. He works very hard in order to make a living, and it takes him some time to learn the trade. He earns from $12 to $14 a week and probably can not do much more work than a woman could do on the ring spindle. Now, the woman who tends the ring spinning machine only earns from $6 to $8 a week, so there is that saving on her wages. She does not have to work half as hard as the man, and she can learn the business in a week or two.

As a result of such improvements in machinery the producing capacity of the employee has been greatly increased, and the trade has expanded as a result of the increased productivity of labor. Upon this point a foreman said:

> Weavers have more than doubled their capacity and output in the last 30 years that I have been in business, without regard to the Northrop loom. With the Northrop loom they are able to produce five times as much as they were able to produce 40 years ago. This is mainly due to improvements which have been made in the looms. Not only the loom, but the spindles, both mule and ring, have

TEXTILE TRADES. 421

been so perfected that the warp and the filler do not break as often now as they did with the old-fashioned machinery. Also they do not require half as much fixing as they formerly did, while at the same time the weaver works harder now than he used to work and is producing a great deal more. It is also true that it would not have been possible for him to have worked so hard years ago with the machines and the thread in the imperfect state in which they then were. We are now using better machines and better cotton, and the weaver is able to do several times more work than he could do years ago.

The operatives in these textile mills in Fall River and New Bedford are largely English and Irish, with a large number of French-Canadians. With these nationalities there are also Portuguese from the Azores and the Cape Verde Islands.

There are in Fall River about 5,000 people who are eligible to membership in the Card Picker and Ring Spinning Association. Probably 75 per cent of them are women and 25 per cent men. With regard to nationality there are about 30 per cent Irish, 25 per cent English and Scotch, 30 per cent French, 10 per cent Portuguese, and 5 per cent others. In the union about 75 per cent are English, Irish, and Scotch; 20 per cent French; 5 per cent Portuguese, Poles, and others. It is stated by one of the foremen that immigration has come in as "quite a factor" in the industry. He said: "We can get almost all kinds of help; all we want."

It is said that as a rule the French do not join the unions. The attitude and the condition of the French-Canadians has been expressed as follows by an old weaver who worked both in England and in America since 1850, and is now a justice of the peace in Fall River:

The French Canadians came to New England first in 1866. They used to come by carloads. Conditions then were fairly good, but after that the price for labor began to fall. For a time the manufacturers seemed to prefer them to the English and Irish. It is very easy to enter into the textile business. No skill is required in some work in the card room, and in 3 or 4 weeks a person can learn to run 4 looms and begin to earn some money. It used to be impossible to organize the French at all. But now this has changed somewhat and there are some French in the unions. Their standard of living has also improved. They used to come intending to go back to their farms or to earn enough to help for a farm, and this is often the case now. When the price for labor in New England rises they come in large numbers and when the price falls large numbers of them go back, but more of them stay than formerly. When they first come they are willing to work for almost any wages, and their standard of living is low. But in a few years they improve and want to live comfortably and dress as well as the English, and Irish, and Americans. There are quite a number of them who have accumulated property and are well-to-do, and some of them are foremen or shop bosses. The French are a very saving people and are anxious to own their own homes.

The factory inspector of Fall River also says in regard to the French-Canadians:

My impression is that the standard of living of the French-Canadian is much below that of the English, Irish, Scotch, and Americans in the cotton mills. Those that come here were formerly farmers, and usually come with the intention of going back, and they live as best they can while they are here. Farmers in Canada send their families to Fall River and other New England towns to earn some money and then return. They have to live in our towns 5 or 6 years before they become Americanized and raise their standard of living. They come here now in quite large numbers whenever there is a busy time. When work is slack they go back.

The Portuguese are found in largest numbers in New Bedford, where there are about 8,000. These people come from the Azore Islands, and are here employed in fisheries and fruit raising, and also in the mills. There are also about 2,000 from the Cape Verde Islands.

These Portuguese are employed both in Fall River and New Bedford, but the larger number are in New Bedford. The factory inspector reports that they usually work on unskilled parts of the work in the mills at low wages, and that they both dress and live poorly.

In Fall River in the Card Picker and Ring Spinning Association about 5 per cent of the members are Portuguese and Poles. The secretary says that when the Portuguese join the union they stay in it, and the same is true of the Irish and English, but not so true of the French.

Proportionate to their numbers we have much less of them in the union than of other nationalities. There are few Poles in proportion to their numbers. It is very hard to get them into a union when they are green, but after they have been in the country a while they make good members. The same is true of the Portuguese.

In comparing the French and the Portuguese the secretary of the local Card Picker-Room Operatives in New Bedford says:

The French are not good members, except in some trades, such as the mule spinners, where they have been in the country for a long time and have become Americanized. We are not bothered very much by the Portuguese. Those who do join the union stay in it and are good members. I know of cases where men have gone to sea and when they returned after 5 or 6 months they paid all of their dues before going back to the factory. This is not true of other nationalities. While there are a great many Portuguese in this city, there are not many of them in the mills. They only go into the mills during the winter. In the summer they fish. This is true of many of the French-Canadians. They work in the mills in the winter and in the summer return to their farms in Canada. My impression is that the blacks of the Cape Verde Islands are not as industrious as the whites of the Azores.

Wages in cotton mill at Fall River.

Unloading cotton (male)	per hour	$0.20
Yard men:		
Foremen	per day	1.50
Others	do	1.25
Cotton throwers (male)	do	$0.95 to 1.10
Ropers (male)	per week	7.50
Carders (male)	do	7.50
Grinders (male)	do	10.50
Slubbing (female and male)	do	9.00
Ropers (coarse spinning) (female)	do	8.00
Fine speeders (female)	do	8.00
Dauphers (female)	do	9.00
Sweepers (female)	do	8.00
Fixers	do	10.50 to 11.00
Overseers	do	18.00
Loom fixers	do	11.75 to 12.00
Spinners (boys and females)	do	8.00
Mule spinners	do	14.00
Back boys and dauphers	do	5.00
Winders and spoolers (female)	do	4.00 to 7.00
Warpers (female)	do	8.00 to 9.00
Slashers (male)	do	10.00 to 11.00
Size makers (male)	do	7.50
Drawers in (female)	do	5.40 to 8.00
Weavers (male)	do	8.00 to 8.50
Truckmen (male)	do	6.60
Oilers, scrubbers, and handy men (male)	do	5.00 to 6.00

Shoe trade.—There are probably 250,000 employees in the trade in the United States, 100,000 being in Massachusetts. In April, 1895, the present union was organized, and has now about 20,000 members in the United States, 6,125 being in Massachusetts. This shows that less than 8 per cent are organized. As to immigration, it can be said that the effect at the present time is small, owing to the slight influx of foreigners in the trade in recent years. Probably 85 per cent of the workers are native-born. The reduction of wages that has occurred in this trade has been owing to the introduction of machinery and the lack of organization. This lack of organization in turn is largely owing to the mixed nationalities which have entered the trade in past years. Recently the Armenians and Italians have been introduced in limited numbers, and have been used in breaking strikes. In this respect there has been serious disadvantage from immigration. (See volume VII, Reports of Industrial Commission, p. 369.)

Since there has been no organization to control the introduction of machinery and maintain wages, the policy of the union at the present time, based on the union label, consists simply in effecting arbitration agreements whereby it is hoped that steady employment may be secured.

In New York City the number in the shoe trade is about 40,000 men and 1,000 women, but there is no branch of the National Boot and Shoe Workers' Union in New York or Brooklyn. Twelve or 15 years ago there was an organization of the Knights of Labor in the shoe trade, which was changed about 8 years ago into a Socialist Trade Alliance when the Socialists controlled a part of District Assembly 49. The shoemakers' organization has since split; about 150 belong to the Socialist Trades Alliance and about 700 to an independent organization, called the Independent Shoe Workers' Union. About 550 of this number are men, and the remainder women. About 150 of the Jewish shoe fitters are organized, and of these the majority work in contractors' shops. In New York the Jews take out "fitting" from the contractor. The number of these Jews is about 300. This is probably the only remnant of the sweating system in the shoe manufacture now existing in the United States, unless possibly the Chinese shops in San Francisco are of this character. This work is usually done in "inside" factories by girls, but these Jews in New York under this form of sweating do even a better class of work and at less cost than that done by the girls in the inside shops.

In comparing conditions in the United States with those in Russia a Jewish shoe fitter says:

A shop of 10 people in the old country where I worked would turn out about 400 pairs of uppers in a week. Here in America the same number of people, with better machinery and a more minute subdivision of labor, will turn out 1,500 a week. I used to earn 10 rubles ($4) a week. I now get $14. I think, on an average, that the shoe fitters in New York get about $2 per week more than they used to get rubles in the old country.

In the higher grades of work in New York most of the people are German, English, and Irish-American. In the cheaper grades of work Jews, Italians, and Poles come in very largely. In fitting, however, which is usually girls' work, the girls have come in and make first-class hands.

There is another form of manufacture whereby cheaper grades are made in country towns. Here girls are employed, and this practice cuts into the shoe trade by introducing cheap American labor and making organization among the employees on a national scale almost impossible.

Low wages in the trade, then, are not attributed by the leaders of the national union to immigration, but to the introduction and improvement of machinery, to the lack of organization, and the large number of women and girls employed in the factories of the small country towns.

In Chicago Swedes, Norwegians, Germans, Irish, and English are largely employed in the trade. Here it is held that the chief factors reducing the condition of the trade are immigration, machinery, and the employment of women and boys. The Armenians and Italians, whether members of the union or not, are looked upon as a bad factor in the trade, because it is claimed that they are not to be relied upon.

The influence of machinery comes from the large number of new inventions, introducing minute subdivision of labor, disturbing old forms of the trade, and producing new kinds of skill. It follows, then, that old forms of organization are giving place to new ones as a result of new machinery, so that, in fact, new trades are being produced. All these changes and disturbances require readjustment in the character of the occupations, in the employment of different kinds of labor, and in the prices paid. These conditions, combined with mixed nationalities, seriously interfere with organization.

Wood workers.—This occupation is divided into three groups, that of building material, cabinet, and furniture. The first two are well organized. The third is not organized, because mainly in small centers and controlled by immigrants. The president of the International Union states that there has been no complaint from locals on the score of immigration for the past 10 years. The immigration from Canada is not serious, since wages are equal to those in the United States. There are 15 local unions in the Provinces.

Regarding the different divisions of the trade, 50 per cent of the cabinetmakers in the United States are Germans. They are considered the best men in the trade. Twenty-five per cent are foreigners of all other nationalities and 25 per cent are native-born. The machinists and wood workers are mostly foreigners. The finishers are 45 per cent foreigners. The large furniture cities of the country are Chicago, Grand Rapids, Jamestown, and Rockford, Ill. The Swedes colonized in Rockford a few years ago and contributed to the reduction of wages which took place. The same is true of the Hollanders in Grand Rapids. The Germans in the Northwest work for very low wages, especially in Oshkosh, where within the past 3 years men were getting as low as 50 cents per day and women were doing carpenter work at the bench. Boys and girls were doing glazing and operating light machines. It is comparatively easy to organize the Germans, more difficult to organize the Swedes, but they make splendid unionists. The Bohemians are considered good "stickers." A large part of the wood workers of Chicago are Bohemians, Swedes, Germans, and Poles. The industry has a fairly good organization in factories connected with the building trades, where they have been supported by the latter in their refusal to construct buildings with nonunion material. Since the building trades' strike of 1900, however, their hours of labor have been increased from 8 to 9, owing to the loss of this support. They control 60 per cent of the sash and door employees, 95 per cent of the office, store, and saloon fixtures, only one desk factory, and do not control the regular furniture factories, manufacturing chairs, tables, beds, and folding beds, nor any of the school furniture "trust" shops. Of the 20,276 people in the trade in Chicago the following are organized, perhaps 4,000 in all. The table shows that in the case of Germans and Bohemians organization has been based on line o nationality.

Union number.	Year organized.	Membership.	Nationality.	Occupation.
1	1876–1890	400	German	Cabinetmakers.
4	1890	300	Bohemian	Machine hands, finishers and carvers.
7	1890	650	English speaking	Mixed employment.
17	1890	750	....do	Do.
30	1892	250	Bohemian	Do.
67	[1]1896	400	English speaking (mostly Germans).	Do.
75	[1]1895	50	English speaking	Mixed employments (South Chicago).
78	1894	300	Bohemian	Mixed employments.
85	1897	300	English speaking	Mixed employments (Oakpark).

[1] Reorganized.

The effect of machinery with the opportunities it offers for introducing the work of unskilled immigrants, women, and boys is quite marked in this trade. In the furniture factories which are not organized, out of 75 men perhaps only 5 are skilled mechanics. The rest are only feeders. A large number of children are employed and common labor is done almost wholly by immigrants.

In the box-making trade Bohemians, Germans, and Poles predominate. In the union shops 90 per cent of the labor is skilled and in nonunion shops 90 per cent is unskilled, indicating the success of the union in organizing the skilled mechanics and the difficulty in organizing the machine shops with their large proportion of immigrants, women, and boys. The following table shows the wages in union and nonunion shops in the box-making trade:

Relative wages in box-making shops, Chicago.

	Union wages.	Nonunion wages.
	Per dozen.	Per dozen.
Rip sawyer	$2.50	$1.75
Hand nailer	2.50	1.25 to 1.50
Machine nailer	2.50	1.00
Bottom nailer	2.00	[1] 3.00
Crosscut sawyer	2.00	[2] 1.00 to 1.25

[1] Per week.   [2] Per dozen.

In the piano and organ manufacture, 4,500 persons are employed in Chicago, of which number about 2,200 are organized. The nationalities and numbers in the unions are as follows:

Germans 800
Irish, English, and Scotch 500
Americans 500
Swedes 200
Poles and Bohemians 200

Nationalities outside of the union are mostly Swedes and Poles. The effect of immigration is found most in the nonunion shops. There has been but little effect in union shops. But there is great difficulty in bringing nonunion shops into the organization. Wages some 20 years ago ranged from $25 to $40 per week, but now the rate is $10 to $18 for mechanics, and $6 to $9 for common labor. Causes for this lowering of wages are immigration, machinery, and employment of women and children. The children are mostly of Polish descent, and the women are of different nationalities. A number of the factories are located in the near-by towns, where Italian immigrants are employed in competition with the labor of the cities. But there seems to be little difference in the cost of living compared with that of the city.

Iron, steel, and machinery trades.—A number of highly skilled trades which have to do with the manufacture and operation of machinery are not much affected by immigration and still less by women and children. In these trades the immigrants who come in are usually German, English, or Scandinavians and have followed the same occupation in their native lands, where they have been faithful members of labor organizations. These occupations are included under the iron and steel industry or are closely allied with it.

The immigrant engineers, iron and steel workers, blacksmiths, machinists, and molders are mostly from Great Britain or Germany. In these countries they have learned their trades and have been members of labor organizations, and when they come here they bring their ideas of organization with them, and their cards of membership, and do not enter into strong competition with those already here. They enter the unions, especially the English and Swedes.

The blacksmiths are not much affected by immigration because of the degree of skill required and the long term of apprenticeship necessary before becoming a skilled mechanic.

The men in this occupation are largely Irish and German, and the newer immigrants who may wish to enter the trade must serve a long period of apprenticeship, by which time they have become Americanized.

Besides the distinctly high character of intelligence and skill among the employees in these occupations and the foreigners who come in, there have been restrictions both by statute and in some cases by union rules requiring citizenship of members and of applicants for license. Labor-union members reported to the New York bureau of labor statistics (1898, p. 1070) as follows:

National Association of Stationary Engineers No. 44: "We do not admit anybody unless he is a citizen of the United States." German-American Engineering Association No. 29: "The trade has not been affected by immigrants since the passage of the law of 1897 requiring an engineer to be a citizen before granting him a license."

GLASS WORKERS. 425

Machinists.—The officers of the machinists' organization explain that owing to the difference in methods, machinery, and speed of work in the United States, there is but little danger in the competition of foreign immigrants. Although the wages in the trade are much higher than in Great Britain or Europe, yet the quantity of production is still greater, so that the pay of workmen in proportion to output is less than in Europe. There is a complete assimilation between the machinists who come from the British Isles and from Sweden with the American organization, since such immigrants have had the experience of the strong organizations of those countries. From other countries the only threatening immigration is that of the all-around handy man who can be rapidly trained to American methods. But in recent years there has been no effect whatever on the results of strikes which can be ascribed to immigration, although it is believed that employers have indirectly made efforts to secure immigrants. Especially in the last few years have the wages and employment in Europe been so high in this trade that there has been but little immigration.

Amalgamated Association of Iron and Tin Workers.—This organization ascribes its defeat at Homestead to the importation of aliens, and since that disastrous defeat wages in the steel mills have been materially reduced. This includes the production of rails, slabs, sheet tin, steel billets, and structual-iron material. It is the only branch of the trade where the scale of wages has not recovered since the return of industrial prosperity. In other cases the union has been able to protect members. An essential factor in the inroads of immigrants was the introduction of machinery which displaced the need of highly skilled work. Unskilled foreign laborers who have been thus introduced are Polanders, Hungarians, and Slavs, and a few Italians. The skilled labor is as yet done by natives, but the common labor is done by immigrants. Very few of this lower order of immigrants ever learn the skilled work, but in the second generation they aspire to the skilled jobs. (See Schaffer, Reports Industrial Commission, vol. 7, p. 393.) There is no difficulty whatever with the English, Irish, French, or German workmen in the matter of organization, but in the last 2 years there has been immigration of 40 or 50 Belgians who, it is believed by the leaders of the union, were brought in under contract. Three of these were deported by the authorities at Ellis Island, but satisfactory evidence could not be secured against the others.

The effect of immigration in the last 7 or 8 years has not consisted in breaking strikes, but in the gradual introduction of foreigners through machinery, as above stated. There is, however, another feature of the trade which has been materially affected, namely, the speed of work. It is stated by the president of the association that foreigners, especially those who hope to return to their own country, have no consideration for themselves or their fellow-workmen, but press their output to the extent of their ability. This is shown by the increase in the output of 30-gauge standard sheet, where, prior to 1895, the output for 8 hours, as agreed upon with the manufacturers, ranged from 2,600 to 2,900 pounds. In 1895 it was increased to 5,250 and then to 5,750 pounds by agreement. Individual foreigners, contrary to this agreement, made as high as 7,500 pounds in 8 hours, about double what they made in 1893 and 1894. When expostulated with they did not hesitate to say, "It don't matter. We are going to make our pile while we are here and then we'll go back to the old country again." (Reports Industrial Commission, vol. 7, p. 393.) In this respect it should be noticed that the speed of the American manufacturer is not so great as to keep out foreigners. In the tin mills the competition has accompanied transference of the trade from Wales to this country, and it has consisted of Welshmen, but these men are highly skilled and their organization is the strongest in the association.

Glass workers—Flint-glass workers.—The union in this trade includes about 85 per cent of the workers, and numbers 10,000 members. Being a highly skilled trade, it is not troubled by the immigration of unskilled laborers. Those who come to this country are mainly from Norway, Sweden, and Alsace-Lorraine, where they have learned their trade. There are two considerations which restrict the entrance of immigrants. First, the initiation fee imposed by the union. This fee was formerly $100 for foreigners, and $3 for Americans. The fee has been reduced to $50 for foreigners, the American fee remaining at $3. There is an opinion in the union that this extreme discrimination against foreigners is not advantageous, as it compels them to enter nonunion shops instead of joining the union. This is known to have been the fact in at least one large nonunion establishment manned mainly by foreigners. The second obstacle to the entrance of immigrants is found in the high speed of the American workmen. On this point, however, there is not uniformity. The union covers a large number of highly specialized occupations, and formerly made as many as 14 different agreements with as many associations of employers for the several specialized departments. In the majority of these departments the quantity of output per day for each workman is strictly limited by agreement, but in six departments the "unlimited" system has been introduced at different times. The unlimited system is specially noteworthy in the prescription department, which numbers about 2,100 members, none of whom are foreigners. The skill in this department is of a very high degree, and the speed is so great that immigrants can not attain it. The workmen earn from $6 to $8 per day, paid by the piece, working in teams of 3 members to the team, 2 men blowing and 1 finishing, and the team turns out 55 gross of one-half ounce bottles per day. There is but one nonunion establishment in this country in this department of work.

In another department, namely, the paste-mold department, the competition of foreigners has forced the union to abandon the limited for the unlimited system. This, however, applies only to the thin-ware branch of the work. From 1884 to 1890 immigrants entered this line of work, especially at Cumberland, Md., where they worked by the piece at about 35 per cent less than the union scale. The union shops could not compete and finally, in 1892, the union changed to the unlimited system. The increased production of the system amounted to 100 per cent, and the earnings to about 15 per cent, so that the workmen received about $4 per day, compared with $3.50 under the limited system. When, in 1899, the National Glass Company was organized, including both the union and nonunion factories, the union refused to sign the scale until the entire system was unionized. This resulted in raising the wages of nonunion places about 35 per cent, so that men who had been receiving from $17 to $19 per week were raised to from $30 to $32. Owing to the fact that many of these factories have foreign foremen, it is found that immigrants are still favored in the paste-mold department, where it is easier for them to enter than in other departments.

The introduction of machinery in certain cases has caused both the reduction of wages and an enormous increase in output, especially in the department of machine-made fruit jars. Formerly 3 men made 275 quart jars per day by hand, and now 2 men make 3,400 by machine. The 3 men working by hand were blowers, making $7.50 per day, whereas the 2 men working by machine are a presser at $5 per day, and a gatherer at $2.75 per day.

In this case it is not alleged that immigration effected a reduction in the pay. In the pressed ware department, since 1897, there has existed the unlimited system, and whereas on common tumblers and jellies formerly 800 or 900 per day was the output at $4, the present output is 1,200 on a sliding scale at 15 cents minimum, the wages remaining about the same.

Glass-bottle blowers.—The organization of the glass-bottle blowers includes about 4,500 men and has almost complete control of the trade. Of this number about 600 are foreign born. These were employed mainly in the nonunion factories in New Jersey, which the union succeeded in capturing in the protracted struggle of 1899–1900. The union has a clause in the by-laws of the national organization providing that no foreign blower be admitted into the association during the blast of 1900–1901, but the president and the executive board have power to authorize any branch to admit such workmen if it was thought necessary. The constitution provides that any member who encourages or assists any foreign glass blower to come to this country shall be fined $100 and be suspended for one year. (See Report of Industrial Commission, vol. 17, p. 173.)

Formerly the initiation fee for foreigners was $100, but owing to the stimulus to "scabbing" on account of this discrimination, it has been equalized with the American fee.

The building trades.—In the large cities very few of the workers in the building trades are of the old American stock, but almost entirely they are older immigrants, such as Germans and Irish. These trades are for the most part well organized and, with the exception of carpenters, are not at the present time materially affected by immigration. The bricklayers and masons even claimed that they are benefited. The representatives of that union in New York reported to the bureau of labor statistics, 1898 (p. 1041), as follows: "Immigration benefits our trade. Increased immigration necessitates the erection of more dwelling houses, which means work and prosperity for all the building trades."

Wages at the present time are good throughout the large cities, where it must be borne in mind the men employed in the building trades have themselves been immigrants. In the smaller cities, where the wages are much less than in the larger cities, it is the older American labor which controls the field. In these large cities not only have the wages been increased, but the hours have been reduced from 12 to 10 and again from 10 to 8. In the Bulletin of the Department of Labor, September, 1898, the investigation of wages shows that from 1870 to 1898 the average wages for bricklayers were raised from $3.15¼ per day to $3.51¾; carpenters, $2.36¾ to $2.52¾; hod carriers, $1.75¼ to $2.005; masons, $2.80¼ to $3.20¼; painters, $2.22½ to $2.60; plumbers, $2.74¼ to $3.15½. (See table, p. 000.) This increase will appear the more important when it is remembered that the number of hours has been decreased and that the rates since 1898, when that report was made, have risen still further. Wages in Chicago for carpenters were raised in 1897 from 37½ cents per hour to 42½ cents.

The effect of immigration on the different building trades varies considerably, carpenters suffering more than others. They are met mainly by the immigration of Canadian carpenters, who affect wages at Boston, Buffalo, Detroit, and the smaller Canadian-border towns. This immigration is described in the chapter on Canadian immigration. (See p. 000.) It should be noted, however, that immigration from Canada to these cities is of the same nature as immigration from country districts in our own country to the cities. This is brought out by the situation in Chicago, where it is noted that the principal danger to the carpenters is from suburban and country towns, which send carpenters to the city in the winter. Very few Canadians come to Chicago. It is stated that not over 50 to 75 carpenters are aliens. The work in the cities is so different from that in a country district and in foreign countries that an outsider can not successfully compete except after learning practically a new trade. Furthermore, carpenters in England, whence the large numbers have hitherto come, are at the present time receiving good wages and are not migrating.

In Chicago the building trades unions are organized largely by nationalities. The reasons seem to be that there is difficulty in getting new immigrants into the union, especially when the union is mixed or is controlled by a leading nationality. It has been found by experience that unions which were exceedingly heterogeneous failed to hold together when really tested. In the matter of getting the newcomers into the union, the case is well illustrated by the Swedish carpenters who, when they first came, could not be induced to enter a union whose membership was larger than that of their own nationality. Since they have been organized in a union of their own, they have been very strong unionists. The following is a list of the organization of the carpenters unions in Chicago by nationalities:

Unions of carpenters in Chicago.

Number of union.	Year of organization.	Membership.	Nationality.
1	1881	900	Mixed.
10	1881	1,100	Do.
13	1874–1878	250	Do.
21	1881	100	French.
54	1886	125	Bohemian.
58	1891	500	Mixed.
62	1881	550	Mostly Swedes.
70	1881	50	French.
80	1888	150	Mostly Canadians.
181	1881	600	Scandinavians.
199	1881	225	Mixed.
242	1881	80	German.
416	1888	250	Mixed.
419	1888	200	German.
434	1889	50	French.
504	1900	100	Jews.
521	1881	125	Mixed, Germans.

Hod carriers of Chicago have a similar practice. Their union was first organized in 1886 as a mixed assembly of all nationalities. It broke down on this account. The different nationalities then organized separate independent unions, and in 1896 these effected a federation in the hod carriers' council, a delegate body of 4 locals, as follows: No. 1, German speaking, including a small number of colored men; No. 2, Bohemian; No. 3, Polish; No. 4, English speaking, including Italians, Swedes, and about 250 or 300 colored. The colored members are treated the same as others. These are not strictly locals; they are rather branches, since membership is not localized. The leading locals have business agents and the recruits join the local of the business agent regardless of his nationality. Prior to 1896 and the organization of the hod carriers' council, foreign labor coming in in large numbers depressed wages, but since then the wages has been raised.

Granite cutters.—The granite cutters are strongly organized, as a rule, but have made complaint in New York City of the violation of the State law regarding the prevailing rates of wages by the padroni in the case of Italians. The scale is $4, but it is claimed that these Italians are required to pay the padroni a dollar a day commission, which goes to the contractor. (See p. 435.) The granite cutters in the cities especially complain of work done at the quarries, where mainly immigrant labor is employed and the wages are very low. These quarry laborers are not organized. This is especially true of granite quarries in New England. As far as city employment is concerned, the effect is not serious.

Stonecutters.—The stonecutters have complained in times past of the so-called "harvesters," who come from abroad, work during the busy season, and then return home. The union, however, has been able to stop this practice by requiring an initiation fee of $50 for foreign stonecutters, the fee for American being $10. (See Reports of Industrial Commission, Vol. VII, p. 745.)

Bricklayers.—This is perhaps the strongest organization in the building trades, and it has been successful in protecting itself against immigrants. The New York local has a clause in its constitution making it compulsory for persons desiring to become members to be citizens of the United States. This is directed against the so-called "birds of passage" who come from Great Britain in the spring and return in the fall. One device adopted a few years ago to check this class of competition was a provision that the monthly dues in the union should no longer be paid in advance but must be paid each month, the penalty being that the lapse requires a new initiation fee. Considering that a member must attend the monthly meeting of the union in order to pay dues, it will be seen that this provision compels permanent residence in the locality in order to retain membership and find work.

Plumbers.—This organization receives competition from immigrants only from those who come from England and Scotland, but such immigrants have strong unions in their own country and readily abide by the union rules when they migrate.

Longshoremen.—The organization of longshoremen presents one of the most striking instances of the way in which organization overcomes the disadvantages of race competition. Formerly, under the old stevedore system, which was a system of subcontracting or sweating, the men received very low pay at very irregular work. Since 1897, when the national union was organized, their yearly wages have doubled and they have become their own contractors. (See Vol. IX, p. 309.) In a majority of the ports along the Great Lakes, where the union has its strength, the organization is mixed, but at Ashtabula the men are organized by races, namely, Swedes, Italians, Finns, Slavonians, and Portuguese. Each of these races has its own branch or local, and there is a central council composed of the delegates of each which conducts business in English and has jurisdiction over the several locals. At Newport News, since 1899, a similar arrangement has been made between the white and colored races.

In loading and unloading vessels these different races work in cooperative gangs of their own kindred. The contracts with the dock managers are made by the national union at a fixed price per ton for each port. The several gangs take turns on the vessels as they come in, so that the work is distributed equally in the course of the season. Each gang elects its own foreman, whose pay is the same as that of the other members, and the lump sum received for unloading or loading vessels is paid to these foremen and by him equally divided among the members of the gang. It is by this arrangement, based on the national conference with the dock managers, that these diverse nationalities have been able to come together and secure a most important increase in their earnings.

Bakers.—In the large bakeries mechanics are not required because of the introduction of machinery. In these bakeries women and children tend the machinery. With a mixer, a man or boy can do the work of 6 men. With a dough-brake machine, a man can do the work of from 6 to 7 men. With a bread molder, 1 man can do the work of 8 to 10 men. Besides these improvements there are machines for making cakes and crackers, and improved ovens, so that a man's labor to-day produces very much more than it did 20 years ago.

The so-called "trust bakeries," such as the American Biscuit Company and the National Biscuit Company, are not organized, and the union officers say that whenever they had a strike they were replaced by unskilled and immigrant labor and lost the strike.

Investigation made by the New York bureau of labor statistics.—The fact that the city and State of New York are affected directly by European immigration more than other States gives especial interest to the investigation made in 1898 by the bureau of labor statistics upon the effects of immigration upon wages and employment. Following is the summary of the inquiry made by the statistician.[1] Since this investigation was made at a time (1898) when industrial depression had been severe for 3 or 4 years, it naturally shows the serious effects of immigration at their worst.

In view of recurring complaints from labor organizations as to the adverse effects of immigration on the trades in this State, this bureau determined early in the current year to ascertain the facts from those directly affected—the working people themselves, through their unions or accredited representatives; so toward the close of the first quarter there was sent to every labor organization in the State a schedule containing these questions: (1) "Has your trade been affected by immigration during the past 6 years?" (2) "If so, how many of your members have been displaced by immigrants?" (3) "Have wages in your trade been reduced by reason of competition of immigrants?" Responses immediately came from 1,039 organizations, having a membership of 175,959. Negative answers to the queries were received from 774 unions (74.5 per cent of the whole number that returned replies),

---

[1] Bureau of Labor Statistics of New York, 1898, pp. 1036–1040.

THE BUILDING TRADES. 429

with 105,889 members (60.2 per cent of the total); while 265 organizations (25.5 per cent), returning a membership of 70,070 (39.8 per cent), report that they were directly and detrimentally affected by immigrant labor. This competition was felt by the workers in 85 trades, or 45 per cent of the 189 covered by the research, and its influence was observed to some extent in every general industry except that of glassworking. The building, clothing, coach-driving and livery, food-producing, hat, cap, and fur, iron and steel, leather, marine, stone, tobacco, and wood-working industries suffered the most; but the effect was hardly perceptible in the printing and steam-railroad industries.

The returns show that the unions located in towns at or near the seaboard and those bordering on or easy of access from the Canadian boundary experienced a more adverse effect than did those farther in the interior of the State. In all the boroughs of New York City 181 organizations, comprising 68.3 per cent of the 265 imparting affirmative replies, report that immigration affected the employments of their members. Nineteen Buffalo unions answer in the same strain; so do 9 in Syracuse, 6 each in Rochester and Yonkers, 5 in Watertown, 4 each in Albany, Kingston, Lockport, and Troy, 3 each in Newburg and Poughkeepsie, 2 in Utica, 1 each in Auburn, Cohoes, Ithaca, Jamestown, Mount Vernon, Niagara Falls, and Rome, 2 in the village of New Rochelle, and 1 each in Glens Falls, Hulburton, Mamaroneck, Port Chester, Sidney, and Tarrytown.

It is reported by 154 unions that in 6 years 17,322 members were displaced by immigrants; and 97 organizations, having a membership of 22,318, declare that the term of employment of these members was materially lessened, with a resultant decrease in wage earnings, by the surplusage of labor brought about by newly arrived aliens overcrowding the trades. A few unions, although reporting that their members had been affected, fail to show to what extent.

Of the 265 organizations affected by immigration, 120, with 34,304 members, state that wage rates were reduced as a result of the unequal competition of these newcomers, while 137, having a membership of 34,482, report that immigration has not caused reductions in union rates of wages. Eight unions, membership 1,284, do not make answer to the question.

In the building industry 113 organizations, membership 27,862, engaged in 17 out of 26 trades, report an injurious effect. Seventy-four unions say that 9,815 members were displaced by immigrants; 34 organizations, membership 6,832, record an abridgment of employment, with a consequent reduction of earnings, and 33 unions, 4,760 members, show decreases in wage rates owing to immigrant competition. The workers most affected were bricklayers, building laborers, carpenters, painters, and stone masons.

In the tobacco industry 7 unions of cigar makers, numbering 1,504 members, report a detrimental effect; 3 note the displacement of 112 members; 4 organizations, membership 1,185, state that overplus immigration has caused lack of employment and reduction of earnings, and 4 others, with 1,372 members, report reduced wage rates. One union composed of 30 cigar packers states that 2 members were displaced, and that the others had their employment and earnings lessened.

Thirteen of the 18 clothing trades were affected; 31 unions, with 18,631 members, reporting the extent. Twenty-two state that 3,569 members were displaced; 8, with a membership of 5,061, found less opportunity for employment and suffered a decrease in wage earnings, while 25, having 17,020 members, report reductions in rates of pay.

Three unions of coach drivers and livery-stable men report the displacement of 238 members.

Bakers predominate in the food-producing trades that were affected. Nine bakers' unions, with a membership of 571, report the effect. Four organizations state that 48 members were displaced. Eight unions, 393 members, say that on account of immigration the number of days of employment was lessened and wage earnings fell off. Three unions, having a membership of 140, report wage-rate reductions. A union of butchers states that 24 members were displaced.

In the furniture industry an upholsterers' organization, with a membership of 238, makes return that immigration has decreased the number of days of employment, wage rates, and earnings.

Seven organizations, with 1,359 members, in the hat, cap, and fur industry were affected. Four of these unions state that 173 members were displaced; 100 members in another organization had their employment lessened, and 3 unions, with a membership of 966, report reductions in rates of wages.

Of the 5 organizations, membership 782, of hotel, park, and restaurant employees affected, 1 states that 30 members were displaced; 4 report that 632 members could not obtain steady employment, while 4, with a membership of 717, declare that wage rates were reduced.

Immigrant labor affected all but 3 of the 16 trades in the iron and steel industry, according to the returns from 35 unions, having 4,612 members. Sixteen organizations state that 347 members lost their places owing to immigration; 9 unions, membership 871, report a curtailment of employment and loss in earnings, while 20 organizations, with 2,373 members, say that rates of pay were reduced. The workers most affected were blacksmiths and their helpers, stationary engineers, iron molders, and machinists.

Among the leather workers 7 organizations, membership 1,367, felt the effect of immigration. Five of these unions report that 173 members were displaced, while 1 states that the employment of its 275 members was curtailed, with a consequent decrease in earnings, and 4 others, with 637 members, show reductions in wage rates.

The only workers affected in the malt-liquor industry were 28 maltsters in 1 organization. They were displaced by immigrants.

Four organizations in the marine trades state that, owing to immigrants overcrowding the several occupations, their 1,502 members had their working time and wage earnings reduced, and 1 union reports the displacement of 90 members.

In the metal-working industry 2 organizations, with 210 members, report less employment and reductions in earnings as well as rates by reason of immigration.

Six unions composed of 551 musicians were affected by immigration. One states that 25 members were displaced; 5, with a membership of 382, report that opportunities for employment were lessened, and 4, having 472 members, declare that wage rates were reduced.

The effect was slight in the printing industry. One union of book-cover stampers and gold layers reports that 3 members were displaced. An organization of 120 lithographic artists and engravers states that the employment of members was lessened and that wage rates were reduced. A union of 43 compositors replies that there was a reduction in working time and earnings.

One organization, containing 135 locomotive engineers, states that employment was lessened and wage earnings reduced. Two unions of locomotive firemen, with 86 members, report reductions in wage rates, and 1 lodge in the same calling says 20 of its members were displaced by immigrants.

A district assembly of 4,335 street surface railroad employees replies that immigrant competition caused a decrease in wage rates. The same organization reports the displacement of 1,450 members.

Three of the 11 trades in the stonecutting industry were affected, 7 unions, with 784 members, stating to what extent. Three report the displacement of 106 members, and the other 4, membership 565, show that the opportunities for employment were diminished, resulting in decreased earnings. Three organizations, 219 members, report reduced wage rates by reason of immigrant competition.

Four assemblies of 302 pavers and rammer men were affected by immigration, 1 having had 3 members displaced, and the 233 members in the other 3 unions had their employment lessened.

In the textile trades 1 union was affected. It is composed of 22 lace workers, whose wage rates were reduced. This organization also reports the displacement of 20 members.

A union of 2,700 actors states that at times these members were deprived of employment owing to the immigration of people in that profession. The same organization reports that 300 of its members were displaced.

In the woodworking industry 3 unions of coopers report that 515 members were displaced by immigrants. Two organizations, with 400 members, state that the chances of employment were decreased and wage earnings were reduced. Two unions, 189 members, show reductions in rates of wages. A union of 150 kindling-wood workers reports a reduction in wage rates and the displacement of 20 members.

Among the miscellaneous trades are 4 unions of 341 barbers, who report an adverse effect from immigration. Two of these organizations state that 85 men were displaced, and in another 159 members were compelled to work on short time. Two unions, membership 196, say that wage rates were reduced. A union of clerks and salesmen reports the displacement of 100 members, and the same organization also declares that its members had to submit to a reduction in rates of wages. One union of 54 workers in mixed trades suffered a decrease in wage rates, and 26 members were displaced.

CHAPTER VII.

THE PADRONE SYSTEM AND COMMON LABOR.

I. HISTORY OF PADRONE SYSTEM.

In the period of industrial recovery following the civil war there was a pressing demand for labor. Special legislation was even invoked to aid in supplying this demand. Thus the act of 1864, for the encouragement of immigration, gave manufacturers and contractors the right to import foreign laborers under contract. Speculation in cheap labor ensued; agents were sent to foreign countries in search for workmen. The unenlightened peasants of Italy were the easiest victims of this speculation. Their coming, in fact, was not of their own accord, as was the case with the people of northern Europe, but they came usually under contract.

This difference between the Italian immigrant and the northern people, and the reason for their having been so easily exploited, is brought out by their illiteracy and ignorance of the English language.

The great bulk of Italian immigration has come from southern Italy, the provinces, Abruzzi, Auelbino, Basilicata, Sicily, Calabria, and Naples. Almost the whole number from these provinces are of the peasant class, accustomed to hard work and meager fare. Their illiteracy is very high. In 1899 the illiteracy for all races of immigrants was 22.9 per cent, while for the immigrants from southern Italy it was 57.3 per cent and for northern Italy the illiteracy was only 11.4 per cent, showing clearly the contrast between this ignorant peasant class of unskilled laborers and the skilled workmen from the manufacturing centers of northern Italy. In 1900 the percentage of illiteracy for these immigrants was 54.5 in contrast to 24.2 for all races and 11.8 for the northern Italians.

This illiteracy is brought out by the investigation of the United States Department of Labor of the Italians in Chicago (9th Special Report, p. 383). Out of 4,553 persons 10 years of age and over, 2,752, or 60.44 per cent, were found to be illiterates. Among 2,812 males 51.96 per cent were illiterate, and of 1,741 females 1,291, or 74.15 per cent were illiterate. As to the literacy itself of the 39.56 per cent who were literate, only 18.21 per cent could read and write English and Italian, while 54.80 per cent could read and write Italian only. More than this, the literate males who could read and write Italian only were 60.55 per cent of the literates, which shows how very unfavorably the Italians are situated when they enter industrial activities under American conditions.

The same investigation showed that of the number of persons of foreign birth and 10 years of age and over, 58.62 per cent were able to speak English and 47.38 per cent were not able to speak English. The following table is taken from the above report (p. 33), and shows the percentage of foreign born 10 years of age and over able and not able to speak English, by the number of years in the United States:

THE PADRONE SYSTEM.

Italians of Chicago able and not able to speak English.

Years in the United States.	Able to speak English.	Not able to speak English.
	Per cent.	Per cent.
Total native born	99.33	0.67
Foreign born:		
Under 1 year	1.80	98.20
1 year	19.48	80.52
2 years	28.95	71.05
3 years	39.55	60.45
4 years	44.07	55.93
5 years	52.51	47.49
6 years	56.25	43.75
7 years	69.02	30.98
8 years	65.40	34.60
9 years	64.91	35.09
10 years and over	73.14	26.86
Not reported	78.26	21.74
Total foreign born	58.62	41.38
Aggregate	61.30	38.70

Literates and illiterates, by sex.

[All persons 10 years of age and over.]

	Males.	Females.	Total.
	Per cent.	Per cent.	Per cent.
Read and write English only	19.32	50	26.99
Read and write Italian only	60.55	37.56	54.80
Read and write English and Italian	20.13	12.44	18.21
Total literates	48.04	25.85	39.56
Total illiterates	51.96	74.15	60.44
	100	100	100

Some form of contract was then necessary to induce these people to leave their country, for by temperament they were not the self-reliant people of the north who came of their own volition. The dread of change, the fear of coming to a strange and unknown land, had to be counteracted by material inducements. It was thus that they came not in search of work, but under contract for several years, and thus were assured in advance of permanent work at what seemed to them high wages.

At this earliest stage in the Italian immigration the padrone was the agent of the contractor or manufacturer. Laborers were demanded, and he acted simply as the agent in supplying specific demands. The manufacturer or contractor was of another nationality, but in looking for cheap labor he had recourse to an Italian already in this country. This Italian, undertaking to supply the number of laborers called for, went or sent to Italy for the number, who entered upon a contract binding themselves to service for from 1 to 3 years, and in rare instances even for 7 years. At the same time he furnished transportation and took care of them upon landing here until they were sent to the work for which they were contracted. It was thus that the padrone was merely a middleman, the man who stood between the contractor and the men. He was looked upon by the men as their representative, not as their employer, and upon him they depended.

Under this early system there were numerous ways in which the padrone could make money. In the first place, he had a commission from the men as well as from the contractor for furnishing the men, and commission on their passage. Upon getting them here he had a profit from boarding them until they went to work. This was deducted from their prospective earnings. After that the padrone usually furnished food and shelter for them while at work. This privilege was usually given free by the contractor who furnished shelter and for which the padrone charged rent. Then there was also the commission from sending money back to Italy, and finally the commission on the return passage after the contract had been completed.

But the padrone par excellence was not an agent and did not act for the contractor. He acted primarily upon his own initiative and for himself. Instead of waiting for a call for men, he would upon his own responsibility engage Italians to come, and contract for their labor for a certain number of years. After having brought them here he would farm them out to anyone who wanted them. He boarded them, received their wages, and paid them what he saw fit. Sometimes a laborer would receive $40 a year and as often only $40 for 2 years. Under this system the padrone occasionally would buy outright a minor from his or her parents. Men, women, and children were thus brought into the country, the boys to become bootblacks, newsboys, or strolling musicians. In this stage the padrone system most closely resembled the system as it existed in Italy, which meant in general the employment of children, or minors, in the "roving professions," such as strolling musicians, performers on the harp or hand organ, and street acrobats. These persons were under the direction of a master or padrone more or less inhuman, to whom belonged all the earnings of these persons. This system flourished most widely during the decade 1870–1880, and under its influence Italian immigration was stimulated to such an extent that the flow soon equaled the demand. The sphere of the padrone then changed. His work of inducing immigration was no longer necessary; immigrants came without having previously made contracts, and governmental action was aimed at preventing the importation of contract labor. Under these two influences—the great increase in immigration and governmental opposition—the character of the padrone has changed.

As a result of this demand for laborers and the activities of the padroni, the Italian immigrants have been largely males, and until recent years have not come by families, as have the other nationalities, notably the German and Scandinavian people. In the following table the total number of immigrants and the percentage of male and female are given for 20 years for the leading nationalities:

Total number of immigrants, and percentage of each sex, from leading European countries, 1868–1888.

Nationality.	Total.	Male.	Female.
		Per cent.	Per cent.
Germany	2,080,149	57.3	42.7
Ireland	1,083,191	49.4	50.6
England	980,255	60	40
Norway and Sweden	924,005	60.1	39.9
Italy	803,510	76.7	23.3
Russia and Poland	695,507	62.9	37.1
Austria	482,694	63	37
Hungary	313,964	70.1	29.9
Scotland	224,271	60.8	39.2
Total	7,587,546	60.6	39.4

Of the above nationalities the German, Irish, English, Scotch, Scandinavian, Austrian, and Russian showed percentage of males either below or not much above the average for all. This would indicate that these people came mostly in family groups, with the intention of permanent settlement. But the Hungarian and Italian immigrants showed very high percentage of males, which would indicate that the immigration was not of family groups, but of individuals.

II. PRESENT CONDITIONS.

Under these changed conditions it is probable that the padrone has very little to do with bringing Italians into the country, since it is no longer necessary to have a contract to bring them in, and because it is even unsafe according to Federal statutes. The padrone is now nothing more than an employment agent, and exists only because of the immigrants and their illiteracy and ignorance of American institutions. He procures his subjects at the port, upon their landing, by promising them steady work at high wages. If the immigrant does not get under the control of the padrone by this means, the immigrant need only go to the colony of his race in any of the large cities, where he will readily be picked up by one of the padroni and promised employment. By this means the newcomers are attached to the padrone, who is able to fulfill his promises, because he "stands in" with the contractors, he knows officials and bosses of the railroads, and he is thus in a way to furnish employment for his fellow-countrymen who can not speak English and have no other way of finding employment. It may then be said that the padrone system no longer exists, and that the successor to the padrone is an employment agency, which collects the labor only after it has already arrived in this country, and makes its profit through commissions and keeping boarders.

As Dr. Egisto Rossi, of the Italian Immigration Bureau, has summed up the situation, "The padrone system, or bossism, can be defined as the forced tribute which the newly arrived pays to those who are already acquainted with the ways and language of the country."

Though the character of the padrone is now that of an employment agent, it is undoubtedly true that no Italian has an employment agency license. But it is also true that in nine years there has never been a prosecution of an Italian for carrying on an employment agency without a license. His mode of operation is to go to the regular licensed agencies or to the contractors and furnish the men desired. The padrone also has no office of his own.

But the padrone does not employ the men alone and upon his own responsibility. He works together with the Italian banker, who is a somewhat more responsible party than the padrone; at least the men have more faith in him, because it is through him that they send money back to Italy, and with whom they keep their small savings. It is through the banker that the call is made for the number of men who are wanted, and it is in his office where the arrangements with the men are made. He may advance the money for transportation, and even the commission if the men do not have the money. The padrone takes charge of the men in the capacity of a boss, takes them to the place of work, runs the boarding house or shanty store at the place of work, and acts as interpreter for the contractor.

The padroni may be divided into several classes. The first class is the small boss who furnishes many odd jobs for individuals. The next class is the boss who regularly supplies contractors and others with laborers in large numbers. This is the largest class and really stands for the padrone as he at present exists. Finally, there are bosses who at the same time are independent contractors. But this is the exception, for the padrone, it may be said, is never a foreman and just as rarely an independent contractor. His work is to act as an interpreter for the foreman and run the boarding house or shanty store.

For furnishing employment he receives a commission from the laborer. This commission depends upon the (1) length of the period of employment, (2) the wages to be received, and (3) whether they board themselves. If they board themselves, the commission is higher and varies from $1 to $10 a head. For a job of 5 or 6 months the commission may even rise to $10. In some cases the wages are paid to the padrone, but this is only when the contractor is dishonest and receives a share from the padrone. But if the contractor is honest, he knows that the people are generally cheated, and so he pays the men direct, deducting, however, the board and other charges as shown by the padrone.

Under this system the padrone is in combination with the Italian banker, who furnishes the money to pay for transportation, for the erection of shanties when they are not provided by the contractor, and to buy provisions. All this money is then deducted from the earnings of the men. The profits derived from the venture are finally shared by the padrone with the banker, who, however, finds his chief source of gain in holding the savings of the laborers, sending their money to Italy, and changing the money from American to Italian, in which process great shrinkage usually takes place.

The padrone has a further hold upon these people as a result of irregular employment. During the winter there is almost no employment at all. This means that during the greater part of 5 months these people are without work. When work is plentiful, the laborer who boards with his boss is said to be fortunate if he can save more than one-half of his earnings. Some of these earnings are sent to Italy or frequently squandered, so that the laborer often finds himself in winter without resources of his own. In such cases he finds it convenient to go the boarding house of the boss or banker, where he remains until spring, when it is understood that he shall enter the employ of the boss. In New York there are large tenements owned by Italian bankers which serve as winter quarters for these laborers. Here the men are crowded together, a dozen or more in one room, under the worst sanitary conditions. It is frequently said that the padrone encourages the men in extravagance in order to have a firmer hold on their future earnings. The employment is even made irregular by the padrone, who furnishes employment for several weeks at a time and then keeps them idle, claiming that the work is not regular.

In the Ninth Special Report of the Commissioner of Labor, on the condition of Italians in Chicago, it was found that 21.67 per cent of persons of whom the question was asked answered that they worked for a padrone. Of this number 5.96 per cent reported that they paid no commission to the padrone for securing the job, while 94.04 per cent reported that they paid a commission. It was found that an average of $4.84 per individual, of the number reporting, was paid for the last job at which they worked, and the average time worked on this job was 11 weeks and 4 days per individual. The average amount paid per week to padrones for employment was thus 42 cents.

The Immigration Investigation Commission of 1895 found that from 500 to 600 laborers employed on sewers and waterworks padroni had deducted from their wages 10 cents and 15 cents each day for procuring employment.[1]

---

[1] Report Immigration Investigation Commission, 1895, p. 26.

The padrone provides transportation for the men. But in the rates he overcharges the men, charging for first-class transportation or regular ticket rates, and securing greatly reduced rates because of the large number. If the work is some distance from the city, the padrone often boards the men, and usually buys the privilege from the contractor at a fixed rate per head per month. In some cases the privilege is given by the contractor free, because the padrone saves him trouble in employing men, and is convenient to have around in managing the men. But usually the contractor sells the privilege of furnishing the laborers with board and lodging and wearing apparel, the cost of which is generally deducted from their wages. In consideration of the many advantages which the padroni have in this transaction, they generally have to pay pretty high prices for the privilege, which naturally comes out of the pockets of the immigrants. If the men board themselves, their food must be bought at the shanty store, which is operated by the padrone. Notices are posted to this effect, and fines are imposed for disobedience. Even dismissal is often the penalty. Occasionally a fixed daily amount of purchases is required by the padrone, but usually the men are allowed to spend at their pleasure, but only at the padrone store. For example, in 1894 Italian laborers were shipped from New York to Brunswick, Ga., for work on a sewerage contract. Each man paid the padrone $1 for finding the employment. The passage money, $7 per head, was paid by the banker with the understanding that this was to be deducted from their wages. The agent of the banker paid $25 a month rent for 10 huts, but charged each laborer $1 a month, which for 215 men was $215 a month. All supplies had to be bought at the shanty store, the penalty for disobedience being a fine of $5.[1]

The quality of the food is as a rule very low even for Italians, and the prices are extortionate. The investigation of the United States Department of Labor (Ninth Annual Report) of the Italians in Chicago showed, among other things, that "the prices charged by padroni are frequently double those charged in Chicago markets for similar articles of food of the same quality" (p. 50). The average increase over Chicago prices was as follows:

		Per cent.
Bread		82.19
Macaroni	pound	61.11
Macaroni	box	50.33
Cheese		46.02
Tomatoes		65.38
Sausages		72.40
Bacon		69.91
Lard		77.04
Sugar		44.58
Coffee		74.70
Tea		80.00
Beans		61.70
For all articles of food combined		59.55

In the Bulletin Department of Labor (March, 1897, p. 118) it is said: "The provisions are furnished in a raw state, and cooked, if at all, by the men themselves. The food furnished by the boss is usually of an inferior quality and often unfit for consumption." The following table is then given showing the prices of articles sold at a shanty store "not far from the city of New York" and the average market prices in New York:

Prices of commodities at shanty stores and at New York market compared.

Article.	Unit.	Shanty price.	Market price.
Macaroni	Pound	$0.10	$0.03
Bread	Loaf	.10	.04
Lard	Pound	.20	.05
Cheese	do	.25	.08
Vegetables (sold by weight)	do	.10	.00½
Codfish	do	.10	.05
Olive oil	Gallon	2.00	1.00
Meat (when sold)	Pound	.15	.05
Tobacco	do	.50	.25
Beer	Bottle	.15	.04
Wine	Gallon	.80	[2].30

---

[1] Report Immigration Investigation Commission, 1895, p. 29.
[2] Approximate.

It is seen from the above table that the prices paid at the shanty store of the padrone are from 2 to 3½ times those of the market prices, while in the case of vegetables the shanty price was 30 times the New York market price.

Besides the profit from supplying food to the men, the padrone charges from $1 to $3 a head for the shanties in which the men sleep. These shanties are often furnished without charge by the contractor, but the padrone nevertheless charges the men a rent to pay for his boarding privilege. Sometimes he even charges regular fees for medical service, though a regular physician is called in only in very serious cases.

As to the wages, it is seldom in Eastern States that only $1.25 per day is paid, though in 1894, 1895, and 1897 wages were $1, with very little work to be had even at that price. At present they vary from $1.35 to $1.75 per day. In the investigation of the Department of Labor (Ninth Annual Report, Italians in Chicago) it was shown that the average weekly earnings for Italian males were $6.41, and the average hours of work per week were 59.4. The highest average weekly wage was $8.25¼ in manufactures and mechanical industries, and the next highest was $7.64½ in agriculture, fisheries, and mining. But this throws no direct light upon the wages or earnings received under the padrone. Under the earlier padrone system the padrone would import laborers under contract for 75 cents per day for two years' work. But the padrone could get $1.25 per day from railroads and contractors, and this difference would go to him. At present he is only an employment agent, and the wages are usually paid direct to the men, though only after the deductions have been made in favor of the padrone.

In the investigation of the New York Bureau of Labor Statistics into the alien labor employed on State contract work on the Erie Canal (Report 1898, p. 1153) it is stated that there were 15,000 common laborers employed, of whom 1,000 were American citizens, 13,500 were Italian aliens, 350 Poles, and 150 Hungarians. The highest wages paid these laborers was $1.75, and the lowest $1.20 per day. Of this number 600, or 4 per cent, received $1.20; 4,420, or 30 per cent, received $1.25, and 9,794, or 65 per cent, received $1.50, which shows that the rate for this labor, of which Italian aliens made up 90 per cent, was from $1.20 to $1.50 per day.

As to the amount of employment the investigation of the Commissioner of United States Department of Labor (Ninth Special Report, Italians in Chicago) shows that out of 2,663 persons employed in remunerative occupations 1,517, or 56.97 per cent, were unemployed some part of the year. The average time unemployed for these 1,517 persons was 7.1 months; for the 109 females in the number it was 6.4 months, and for the 1,408 males 7.2 months.

The nominally small earnings of these people thus become really very small when it is kept in mind that they are unemployed on an average from 5 to 7 months during the year, and must live during this time on the small savings which they may perhaps have been able to put aside from their earnings.

As to the kind of labor, it may be said that the padrone undertakes to furnish only unskilled labor in the large cities, though the Immigration Investigation Commission of 1895 reported (p. 27 of the report) "that padroni in New York not only guarantee to supply unskilled labor for sewer, railroad, and waterworks construction, but also skilled labor for building trades, and will, furthermore, arrange for their transportation to a remote point if a small percentage of the passage money is advanced or guaranteed."

But in the country and small towns the padroni stand ready to furnish skilled workmen, masons, carpenters, stone cutters, and machinists. Occasionally Italians are employed through padroni in the endeavor to break a strike. For example, in the lockout in 1892–93 of the granite cutters Mr. Duncan testified before the commission that Italians were employed to take the places of the union men. But he said that they were inefficient and had to drift out of the work because of the minimum wage rate established by the union and the desire of the employer to have only the most profitable men. The general secretary-treasurer of the Granite Cutters' National Union describes a padrone system in New York City which was prepared to supply men to employers in the granite-cutting trade. The union has an 8-hour day with $4 in New York. The padrone gathers the Italians, who comply with the State law by declaring their intentions for citizenship. These men pay the padrone $12 commission, $6 remaining on deposit as a guaranty that at the end of the week the man supplied with work shall return $6 to the padrone; if not, his employment ceases. These $6 per man per week are paid by the padrone to the contractor, who has thus employed men at $3 under a $4 law in New York, which provides that mechanics employed in the State upon municipal, county, or State work shall be paid the prevailing rate of wages and work the prevailing hours. This is one of the very rare instances where skilled labor is furnished in New York by the padrone system, and it can not be taken as representative of the system.

The Italian immigrant, however, does not always limit himself to becoming a common laborer on railroad work and other excavations, but often becomes an artisan. In so far as he becomes an artisan he comes in conflict with American workmen, but the conflict is less sharp than formerly, because the American unions are organizing Italian labor. The Italians themselves are coming to understand the importance of organized labor. This is noticeable especially among the Italian hod carriers, masons, and stone cutters, and where this feeling and sense of organization has developed there is no opportunity for the padrone system.

III. PADRONE SYSTEM ON PUBLIC WORKS.

Formerly the padrone furnished men to contractors in city departments, waterworks, and street-cleaning departments. To see to what extent this is now practiced letters were sent to the mayors of different cities. The questions asked were as to employment on public works, whether aliens or citizens were employed, the nativity of aliens and parentage of citizens, whether employed through agencies or padrone, and whether the work was performed by the city directly or by contracts. The next question dealt with regulations, whether there were any clauses in contracts or ordinances stipulating the wages, hours, and citizenship of employees on public works, and whether such regulations were the result of legislative or municipal enactments. Finally, what were the prevailing wage and hours for common laborers under contractors on public work, on private work, and under direct municipal employment. The following tables show the answers received:

PUBLIC EMPLOYMENT. 437

Employment of aliens upon public works in cities.

Cities.	Employment.		Regulations.			Wages and hours of common laborers.					
						Under contractor on—				Under municipality direct.	
	Aliens or citizens.	Nationality of aliens and parentage of citizens.	Agency	Direct or contract.	Stipulating wages, hours, and citizenship.	Municipal or legislative.	Public work.		Private work.		
							Wages per day.	Hours.	Wages per day.	Hours.	Wages per day.	Hours.
Albany	Citizens	Americans, Irish, Italians, Bohemians.	No	Direct	Yes	Legislative					$1.50	8
Baltimore	....do		No	Both	Yes	Municipal	$1.66⅔	8	[1]$0.13 to $0.15		1.66⅔	8
Binghamton	....do	Irish and Italians	No	....do	Yes	Legislative	1.50	8			1.50	8
Bridgeport, Conn.	....do	Some Italians	No	....do	Yes	Municipal	1.50	9	1.15 to 1.50	[1]10	1.50	9
Buffalo	Both	Italians and Poles	No	....do	Yes	Both	1.50	8			1.00	
Cambridge, Mass.				....do	None		Lowest possible.					
Cincinnati	Citizens	Irish, Germans, negroes.		Direct	Yes	Municipal					1.75	8
Davenport	No requirements as to citizenship; most are citizens.	Germans, Irish, and Americans.	No	Both	Yes; stipulating wages and board.	....do	1.50	8			1.50	8
Dayton, Ohio	Both	Germans, 50 per cent; Irish, 30; Negroes, 20.	No	....do	No stipulations	Legislative	1.50		1.50			
Newton, Mass	Citizens	Italians	No	....do	No city form of contract; citizenship required by State law; heads of departments to fix rates.							
New Orleans	Residents for six months at least.				None							
Newport, R. I.	Citizens	Irish, Americans	No		Citizenship	Municipal	2.00	8	2.00	8	2.00	8
Peoria, Ill	Peoria labor employed first.				None						1.50	8
Philadelphia	Citizens		No	Both	Citizenship	Municipal and legislative.						

[1] Per hour.

438   THE INDUSTRIAL COMMISSION:—IMMIGRATION.

Employment of aliens upon public works in cities—Continued.

Cities.	Employment.			Regulations.		Wages and hours of common laborers.					
	Aliens or citizens.	Nationality of aliens and parentage of citizens.	Agency	Direct or contract.	Stipulating wages, hours, and citizenship.	Municipal or legislative.	Under contractor on—				Under municipality direct.	
							Public work.		Private work.			
							Wages per day.	Hours.	Wages per day.	Hours.	Wages per day.	Hours.
Pittsburg	Citizens	Italians	No	Both	Citizenship	Municipal	1.50	9	1.50		1.50	9
Portland, Oreg			Yes*		None							
Poughkeepsie			No		...do							10
Providence	Residents	Irish, Italians, and Portuguese.		Both	No conditions or contracts.	Municipal					1.50	
Quincy, Ill	Citizens		No	...do	No		1.15 to 1.50				1.50	8
Rochester	...do		No	...do	Yes	Both	1.50	8	1.50	8	1.50	9
San Francisco					City charter fixes wages and hours.	Legislative. Nationality is not mentioned.					1.00	
Dubuque, Iowa	Usually local residents.	Germans and Irish	No	Both	No stipulations		1.50	10	1.50	10	1.35	8
Duluth	...do		No	Both	...do		Not much less than city.				1.60	
Elmira	Citizens	Irish and Americans.	No	Both	Stipulations as to citizenship.	Municipal	1.50	8	1.25 to 1.35		1.50	8
Erie	Citizens by the city; foreigners by contractors.	Italian and Russians.		...do	Wages of city employees by fixed council.	...do	1.25 to 1.50	10			1.75	10
Fall River	Citizens	Irish, French, Jews, Portuguese.	No	Direct	Yes	...do			1.00 to 1.50		2.00	8
Haverhill	Taxpayers and residents.		No									
Hoboken	Citizens	Irish and Italians by contract.	No	Both	Stipulating hours and citizenship.	Municipal and legislative.		8			2.00	8
Holyoke	Few aliens; mostly foreigners.	French and Irish.	No	...do	Wages by board of public works; hours by legislature for city laborers.	...do	Not specified in contract.		1.25 1.50		2.00	8
Lawrence, Mass	Residents	Irish and English.	No	Nearly all direct.	No specifications in contracts.		1.25 to 1.50				2.00	

PUBLIC EMPLOYMENT.

City	Citizens	Nationalities			Specifications		Wages			Wages	Hours
Memphis, Tenn.	Citizens	Irish and colored.	No.	Both.	No specifications in contracts; wages for city employees fixed.	Municipal.				1.50	
Nashville, Tenn.	...do...	Irish and negroes.	No.	...do...	None.						
Newark, N.J.	...do...	Italians.	No.	...do...	...do...		1.25 to 1.75		1.00	1.25	8
Schenectady...	Few aliens.	Italians and Poles.		Both.	Yes; hours, wages, and citizenship not stipulated.	Both.	1.30 to 1.50			1.50	
Somerville, Mass.	Citizens and few aliens.	Italians and Irish.			Yes; stipulated in favor of citizenship; no clause as to wages and hours.	Municipal.	{ 1.25 to 1.50 { 1.50 to 1.75			2.00	
Springfield, Mass.	Citizens usually.	Americans, Irish, and Italians.	No.	Both.	None.		1.50		1.50	1.75, 1.50 to 1.60.	8
St. Louis...			No.	Contracts.	Yes; hours, wages, and citizenship not stipulated.	Both.			10	1.50 to 2.00	8
Syracuse...	Citizens by the city; aliens by the contractors.	Italians and Poles.	No.	Both.							
Taunton, Mass.	Residents of city preferred.	Portuguese and Irish.	No.	...do...	Yes; wages and hours not specified.	Municipal.	1.25 to 1.50	8		1.75	8
Toledo, Ohio...	...do...	Poles and Germans.	No.	...do...	Preference to residents; wages and hours not stipulated.	...do...	1.50	8		1.50	
Trenton, N.J.											
Utica, N.Y...	Citizens; aliens by contractors.	Italians.	No.	Both.	None.	Municipal.	1.50	8		1.75	8
Williamsport, Pa.	Citizens.				Preference for citizens; aliens not excluded.						
Worcester, Mass.	...do...		No.	Direct.	Citizens who apply are registered; veterans of the civil war have preference.	Municipal.	1.50	8		1.75	8
Yonkers, N.Y.	...do...	Italians, Irish,[1] Hungarians, and a few negroes.		Both.	Clauses from State law.	Both.	{ 1.50 { 1.85			2.00	8

[1] Italians.

It will be seen from the above that there is no marked influence on municipal employment by the padrone system. In the Eastern cities regulations are the rule both by councils and by State legislatures. Even in the cases where Italians were employed, answers were received stating that no laborers were employed through padroni, but usually by the city direct and even directly by the contractors, because in every case it was stated that the supply was greater than the demand. The only city from which an answer was returned showing that agencies are common was Portland, Oreg. Upon this point the letter said: "There are a number of agencies in this city. They are licensed by the municipality and are required to give a receipt to each person from whom they receive money as a fee. The receipt shows the amount of the fee paid, where employment is to be secured, and the wages to be paid. All the employment agencies have been kept under strict police supervision, and as a result there is little or no complaint against them." But these are not in any way connected with the padrone, who is found only in a few of the largest cities, principally in the East.

The stipulations as to citizenship are expressed at considerable length by an ordinance of the city of Philadelphia in connection with an act of the State legislature. The following is received from the Philadelphia director of public works:

In reply would state we have in all our specifications a clause stating "any contract awarded under these specifications will be subject to the provisions of an act approved June 25, 1895, entitled 'An act providing that none but citizens of the United States shall be employed in any capacity in the erection, enlargement, or improvement of any public building or public work within this Commonwealth.'"

This matter is also governed by ordinance of councils.

AN ORDINANCE providing for the employment only of American citizens by contractors doing work for the city of Philadelphia.

SECTION 1. The select and common councils of the city of Philadelphia do ordain, that in all contracts hereafter let by the city of Philadelphia or any department thereof for the construction of public buildings, waterworks, sewers, or work of any kind involving the employment of labor, there shall be a stipulation or covenant embraced in the contract that the contractor or contractors shall not employ any laborer, artisan, or mechanic upon the work undertaken or contracted for by him or them who is not a citizen of the United States: *Provided*, That the provisions of this section shall not apply to public work where the cost thereof is paid in whole or in part from assessments of benefits.

SEC. 2. That for every person who has not qualified as provided in section 1, who may be found in the employment of such contractor or contractors on such city work, he or they shall, in said stipulation or covenant, agree to forfeit five (5) dollars per day for every day that such person shall have been employed as aforesaid, and shall, in said covenant, authorize and empower the head of any department where such person or persons are employed to deduct from any sum or sums of money due said contractor under such contract the said sum of five (5) dollars per day for each person not a citizen of the United States, but employed as aforesaid, as liquidated damages for the failure of said contractor or contractors to observe and perform in this respect the conditions or terms of his or their contract.

SEC. 3. That it shall be the duty of the departments to acertain and require satisfactory proof of the citizenship of the laborers, artisans, or mechanics employed upon such work, and to keep a record of the number of days or fraction thereof upon which any person not a citizen as aforesaid shall have been employed.

SEC. 4. That it shall be the duty of the city solicitor to insert in all contracts as aforesaid, and in all specifications of work to be done under such contracts, the stipulations and conditions provided for in this ordinance.

SEC. 5. That any ordinance or part of ordinance conflicting with the provisions of this ordinance be, and the same is, hereby repealed.

Approved this sixteenth day of December, A. D. 1896.

In New York State, by act of the legislature, certain clauses were required to be inserted in all contracts for public work. A copy of these stipulations contained in all city contracts for public works in Yonkers, until the recent decision of the court of appeals with regard to the prevailing rate of wages, is here given. The following is from Yonkers, N. Y.:

The contractor for work under this contract, and each and every subcontractor or person employed by such contractor to furnish any part of the materials required under this contract, will be required to observe all the laws of the State of New York in relation to the employment of citizen labor [the wages to be paid to each class of labor employed], and the hours constituting a day's work; and he shall also furnish to the mayor and city clerk, whenever required, affidavits made by him and by each and every subcontractor that all the requirements of said laws have been complied with.

The contractor for work under this contract [agrees to comply with the provisions of chapter 567 of the laws of 1899, and] agrees that no laborer, workman, or mechanic who is not a citizen of the United States shall be employed by him or by any subcontractor in the performance of any work to be done under this contract, and further agrees that no laborer, workman, or mechanic in his employ or in the employ of any other person doing the work herein contracted for shall be permitted or required to do more than eight hours' work in any one calendar day, except in cases of extraordinary emergency, caused by fire, flood, or danger to life or property; [and he further stipulates that each laborer, workman, or mechanic employed by him or his subcontractor or any other person on or about the work herein contracted for shall receive for each legal day's work a sum not less than the prevailing rate of wages for a day's work in the same trade or occupation in the city of Yonkers. And this contract shall be void and of no effect if the contractor or his subcontractor or any other person on or about the work herein contracted for shall employ on any work herein contracted for any person who is not a citizen of the United States; and this contract shall be void and of no effect unless the contractor and his subcontractors shall comply with the provisions of section 3 of chapter 415 of the laws of 1897, as amended by chapter 567 of the laws of 1899].

These clauses were required by acts of legislature to be inserted in all contracts for public work. Since the decision of the court of appeals in the spring of 1901 declaring the provision of the law relating to the prevailing rate of wages to be unconstitutional, the parts of the above included within brackets have been eliminated from the contracts.

IV.—EMPLOYMENT OF ALIENS ON RAILROADS.

A further inquiry was made into the employment of aliens as common laborers on railroads and the larger public improvements in different States. The object in view was to find what wages were paid; whether or not the labor was secured through padroni or employment agencies; if so secured, what deductions were made by such agencies from the wages paid; finally, as to the extent to which immigrants have displaced Americans as common laborers on railroads. To this end letters were sent to State bureaus of statistics and labor. The results are shown in the following table:

Aliens employed on railroads and public improvements in different States.

States.	Wages paid per day.	Hours.	Secured through padroni or employment agencies.	Displacement of American labor.	Nationalities.
Maine	$1.25		Yes; from New York and Boston.	American by Irish; then French Canadian; now Italian.	Italian; work for 25 per cent less than others. French Canadian; Irish.
New Hampshire					Italian and French Canadian.
Connecticut	1.00 to 1.50	10	Yes; especially in Bridgeport. Padroni deduct 25 cents per day.	Entirely	Mostly Italian.
North Carolina				No influence from immigration.	Railroads built largely by convict labor. Cheap labor is negro.
Tennessee	1.50		No		Only a few Italians in the mines.
Kansas			No	11 per cent laborers are foreigners.	
Montana	¹2.00		Italians and Austrians are shipped into the State through agencies.	75 to 80 per cent foreign labor in smelters.	Italian, Austrian; Cornish and Irish miners; Japanese on railroads.
North Dakota	1.40	10	Yes; shipped from Chicago and the East.	Displace Americans by working cheaper.	Italian, Russian, Hungarian, Norwegian.

¹ In smelters.

In the above it is shown that the employment of foreign immigrants through agencies and padroni is extensively practiced in the North, both East and West. But the wages are not found to be unusually low. Very little, however, is brought out concerning deductions or commissions for the padroni. In Bridgeport, Conn., it is said that the padroni had been in operation to a great extent, and that as much as 25 cents a day for each laborer is deducted. Nearly all street railways in Connecticut are built by contract, and the contractors procure the laborers through padroni. "This evil has grown to such magnitude in the State that the general assembly * * * has before it 2 measures intended to eliminate the possibility of a continuance of the practice." In this railway construction the American labor has been entirely displaced by alien or foreign labor.

In Maine the American labor in construction of large works was displaced by the Irish, then by the French Canadian, and now the Italians brought from New York and Boston have displaced all others and work for $1.25 per day, which is 25 cents less than the wages paid to other nationalities. In the ordinary repair of railroads no Italians are employed, and in the construction of short lines, where small gangs of men are employed, the work is usually done by French Canadians, with some Irish and Americans. "It certainly would be a difficult thing at the present time to build a railroad of any considerable length without Italian labor."

In New Hampshire the labor employed in constructing railroads and section men used in grading is largely foreign. Italians are employed principally in constructing railroads. The Italians and French work at a less rate than the Americans. "I do not think that foreign labor has displaced American labor to any extent, for the reason that there seems to be plenty of work for all who wish to labor."

In the Southern States the percentage of foreigners is so small that there is no influence from them on common labor for which the negro is employed.

In the case of the common laborers on the Pacific coast it will be found that they are mostly Chinese and Japanese. In Montana the Japanese are employed on the railroads, while at the smelters the Austrians and Italians are employed. The mining is in the hands of the Cornish and Irish, with a few Italians and Austrians. The extent to which this common labor at the smelters is performed by foreigners American labor is displaced. All this common foreign labor is "shipped into Montana through employment agencies and such mediums acting in concert with the corporations and at their instance."

In North Dakota it is held that the railroads could not get American laborers at $1.40, so the foreign labor is shipped in from Chicago and displaces Americans by working for less money.

V. SYRIANS.[1]

The immigration of Syrians into the United States commenced to attain significant proportions some 10 years ago, and has grown steadily until at the present time there are probably 25,000 of these people in the United States, of whom 6,000 claim a residence within the Greater New York. Boston possesses a colony 1,200 strong, and smaller settlements exist in all large cities and in many towns. Such colonies are for the most part aggregations of traders. Only in a few mill towns does the Syrian rank as a proletarian. The cities of Lawrence and Worcester, Mass., are unique (Scranton, Pa., and Paterson, N. J., in lesser degree) among American cities as each possessing a considerable population of industrial Syrians. There appears to be a growing tendency to enroll Syrian workers among the working forces in the textile industries, particularly in silk and cotton mills. The creation of a Syrian-American proletariat, however, is slow, although now apparently an assured fact. The strong trading instinct characteristic of the race militates against the acceptance of factory life as a finality. It is as a small trader (shopkeeper) or itinerant trader that the Syrian is better known. "Business" is his lodestar, and in pursuit of it he penetrates if necessary the most remote parts of the Union. No nook escapes him, and neither Canada, Latin America, the West Indies, or the Philippines is foreign to his enterprise. New York, however, always remains his base of supplies, and it is to New York that he plans to return after trying his fortune elsewhere, for in no other American city does the colony of his people attain such numbers and importance. Notwithstanding the superficial scope of his enterprise, an unstable, too versatile, and constitutionally indolent temperament tends to restrict his energies to the nomadic and parasitic pursuits rather than those truly useful to the community.

It is asserted by representative Syrians that within the past 30 years four-fifths of the young men of Mount Lebanon have been impelled to seek in foreign lands the opportunities denied to them at home, and within the same period an aggregate of 1,000,000 Syrians have migrated. Syrians of all factions are practically unanimous in ascribing to the rapacity and misrule of the Porte this wholesale expatriation. While of late years America has become more directly the "land of promise" to these emigrants, Great Britain, and her Asiatic dependencies, the South American republics and Egypt, together with the Mediterranean countries, have absorbed large numbers of the exiles.

So far as the United States is concerned it is primarily to American missionary effort and advice that we owe the diversion to these shores of so large a portion of this stream of dissatisfied Turkish subjects. The influence of the Protestant missions in this direction can hardly be overestimated, and has been the means of introducing thousands of Syrians to increased opportunities. Broadly speaking, the well-intentioned efforts of the missionaries have been abused by their protégés.

Nine-tenths of all Syrians are Catholics, belonging to the Greek or Maronite branches of the Roman Church and to the Metawile and other Catholic sects. The majority of those coming to America are Orthodox Greek Catholics, the Maronites being next in number.

But very few Druse and Mohammedan-Syrian families come to this country. A relatively large proportion of the Greeks and Maronites have coquetted with Protestantism in one way or another; usually perhaps through missionary offers to secure an education, and particularly a knowledge of English, for their children. It is these alleged proselytes who have contributed largely to bring into relief the

---

[1] Information furnished by Mr. James Forbes, district agent of Charity Organization Society, New York.

THE SYRIANS.   443

intrinsically servile character of the Syrian, his ingratitude and mendacity, his prostitution of all ideals to the huckster level. No sooner are they landed than they seek the commitment to institutions of such of their children as have not attained working age, usually importuning returned missionaries and their friends until they succeed. They then, as a rule, affiliate themselves with some Protestant church or mission, abandoning such connections when no longer deemed necessary or profitable. Cases are not infrequent in which a bright young protégé has been educated at a theological seminary here for the express purpose of returning to preach the gospel and when graduated has coolly repudiated his contract upon the plea that he could do better here in trade.

The versatile genius of the Syrian, as evidenced alike in his cosmopolitan scope of trading enterprise and his readiness to use religion as an expedient, is reflected in the principal concession he is willing to make to occidental competitive methods. As has been said, the Syrian, due perhaps to climatic influences, possesses an ingrained indolence better suited to oriental bazaar methods than to American business life, and though entering into direct competition with Americans and men of other races in America only in a small degree, he finds it necessary to make a concession, the more significant when we consider woman's position in the East. This consists in sending his wife and daughters, or the wives and daughters of his countrymen, out to peddle from door to door the silks, rugs, bijouterie, and antiques in which he traffics.

A few Syrians are honest enough to express themselves as ashamed of and opposed to this system, but the majority, and this is especially true of the wealthier ones, continue to employ it as a profitable adjunct to their business. The usual defense of such men is that the superior intelligence of their women and the fact that they call only at the homes of the well-to-do insures them against both insult and misinterpretation.

Notwithstanding such excuses the system has been justly exposed to severe criticism—the begging propensities of the canvassers having contributed to this effect—and the more hypocritical Syrian merchants now pretend to deprecate the practice, affecting to speak contemptuously of the hillfolk from the Zahle district as being the principal offenders. The truth is that the poor Zahle folk are in this merely the imitators, when not directly the drudges, of their wealthier compatriots. The real offenders are merchants (so called) whose cupidity and indolence, reenforced by an exaggerated patriarchal authority, enable them to make this use of the pleasing appearance, glib tongues, and insinuating manner of their women. The latter, however naturally disinclined at first, soon become habituated to the work, the younger women especially liking the travel and excitement. Particularly does this class of Syrian realize the worst attributes of the parasite—the man brutally arrogant to the poorer members of his own race and fawningly servile to Americans and all those from whom he considers there is something to be gained; the women mendacious and intriguing, flitting from the White Mountains to Palm Beach, from Mackinac Island to Hot Springs, as the season varies, following as closely as possible the wake of the wealthy.

With the peasant people it is different; the instincts of self-preservation and emulation argue for leniency in judgment toward them. It often happens that the principal asset of a peasant immigrant family consists rather in a claim to kinship with some more prosperous member of their race than in the small amount of cash and belongings they bring along. Such a claim based upon the patriarchal system which retains much of its vigor in Mount Lebanon soon becomes little more than a tradition—and an inconvenient one—in the eyes of Americanized Syrians materially prosperous.

Nevertheless, such claims still force a certain recognition and are apt to be met by the extension of small credits, enabling some member of the family—usually the husband—to commence peddling with an English understanding companion, or else secure transportation for the family to a mill town where they have friends. If the man goes peddling, his wife and children will find shelter with some poor family from their own village, and the woman and girls turn their attention to the manufacture and sale of the lace which all Syrian women and girls can make. Desperately poor—for the making of enough lace to sell on Fourteenth street for 25 cents will take 6 hours, and receiving little or nothing from her wandering husband whose income at the best is very small—the Syrian mother attempts to emulate the example of her wealthier kin and sends her elder girls out with satchels of lace in the hope of realizing better prices by going from door to door in the residential parts of the city. Such a course leads naturally to begging and ultimately to action by the Society for the Prevention of Cruelty to Children.

It is not alone in the matter of begging under the guise of peddling that the poorer Syrian ranks as an imitator—in the matter of the "boarding school"[1] he is as insistent and tricky as his more prosperous relatives. Cases have been known in which

---

[1] Some public or private institution like New York Juvenile Asylum, Catholic Protectory, etc.

Syrian families of this class have applied for the commitment of 4 out of 5 children within 20 days after landing, all details as to alleged residence, widowhood, etc., being carefully "fixed up" by hucksters common to the quarter, and despite many rebuffs have finally succeeded in having the children accepted as charges upon private benevolence prior to departure of parents and elder child to a mill town.

At the present time it is a rare thing to find a young man or woman of the quarter who has not passed several years in the "school." Education is not primarily the benefit sought, a relief from natural responsibilities (rarely justified) is rather the reason, the nomadic life led by so many Syrians and the unfortunate association of institutions with missionary training schools in the Syrian mind influencing the result.

No such anxiety is shown to take advantage of the public day-school system; less than 100 Syrian children are regular pupils at the public and parochial schools of the quarter (Manhattan). As a rule these pupils are regarded as merely "bright" rather than as possessing the application necessary to become scholars. Some years must elapse before the influence of day-school education will have had a chance to make itself felt in the quarter. A Syrian educational society, supported chiefly by American Protestant effort, maintains a day school in which Arabic-speaking children are prepared for entry into the primary grades of the public schools. The attendance is small and irregular.

Throughout the country the same predilection of the Syrian parent for the "boarding school" prevails, though naturally not so strongly expressed outside of New York, and not so apparent in communities in which the Syrian approximates to the industrial rather than to the nomadic type. In so far as morality is concerned, the Syrians in America compare quite favorably with other nationalities. Early marriages are the rule, and the bride of 15 has usually been affianced by her parents for several years previous to the event. Café gossip, an important factor in Syrian social life, acts as a deterrent of flagrant scandal, although when such scandal does occur, public opinion appears to accept the situation complaisantly.

The Syrian in New York has housed himself in the tenements of the old First Ward, from which he has dispossessed an undesirable Irish population, the remnant of which torments him. Hemmed in by the Broadway business district to the east, Battery Park on the south, the North River on the west, and the Cortland street ferry and contiguous business section upon the north, the Syrian quarter in Manhattan covers an area comprising in effect four blocks upon lower Washington street and overflowing into the short side streets.

Long threatened by the invasion of the "skyscraper," this immediate tenement section has remained almost undisturbed for the past 50 years, although surely destined to become a region of "skyscrapers" at a future date. The Syrians appreciate this, and a considerable number of the well-to-do have removed their families within recent years to South Brooklyn, retaining their places of business upon lower Washington street. The poorer immigrants, both because of these business establishments and nearness to the Barge Office, naturally cling to the first established colony.

The tenements of this quarter are, as a rule, old and in bad condition; nor does a Syrian occupancy improve them from a sanitary standpoint. The poor Syrian contracts to pay $5 to $7 for two rooms, and as his family is usually a large one, and the rent out of proportion to his income, he resorts to overcrowding as a relief. Sometimes he is able to get one room for $4 a month, and proceeds to crowd his family of 7 persons into it.

It is not extraordinary to find 6 or 8 women making their headquarters in such a garret, their husbands away peddling and their children in institutions. The entire number seldom occupy the room upon any one night. The Syrian pays his rent, and is accordingly considered a good tenant by agents of a certain class. He at least is sober, and seldom gets into "trouble." The one Syrian who attempted to run a hotel in the quarter was glad to surrender his license and save what rebate he could from the failure.

The American cooking stove is the first new necessity which impresses itself upon the Syrian immigrant's mind. It is often months before the need of a bed makes itself felt; a rug or blanket upon the floor suffices for sleeping purposes. A few chairs and sacred pictures, together with a lamp, are next accumulated, and poor households are not much more ambitious in the way of furnishings. The better class (so called) of Syrians pay from $8 to $20 rent for their living rooms and $20 to $100 rent for their stores. A certain luxury is often apparent in the rugs and curtains found in such homes, but in the furnishings little else that is not American in tone and of a cheap class. In cleanliness and sanitation the homes of supposedly well-to-do Syrians approximate quite too closely to those of the poorer class. In this respect it may be noted that a majority of the wealthy Syrians in New York (of whom there are a score reputed as worth over $10,000 and up to $40,000) are of peasant extraction and have concentrated their energies upon the dollar rather than upon the better aspects of Americanism.

THE SYRIANS. 445

As to citizenship, there are not more than 300 fully naturalized Syrian-American citizens in New York City, but this is rather because of the colony's youth than because of any disinclination for the privileges of citizenship upon the Syrian's part. The younger men become citizens and vote the Republican ticket as a "businessman's" ticket.

It should be borne in mind that the Irish-Americans of the First Ward are Democrats. No strong organization, political or otherwise, may be looked for among the Syrians, the envies and jealousies of these people serving invariably to wreck such attempts, whatever their inception. Such has been the fate of a dozen relief and benevolent societies established in the quarter, as a result of advice that the Syrians look after their own poor, at least to a reasonable extent. The societies in question have generally been as short-lived as ill-managed, and notoriously was this the case with a day nursery subscribed for by Americans and managed by Syrians.

Despite inherent disorganization, a "revolutionary party" exists, and has a local press which immolates the Porte at intervals, but is reputed to savor somewhat of blackmail.

Relatively the quarter has a large number of journals, it being the ambition of every faction to be so represented.

Apart from female and missionary influence, there are Syrians who seek to add to their incomes by "placing" their immigrant countrymen, and were the assertions of these fellows as advocates of Syrian "help" borne out by experience to a reasonable extent we might witness the development of a "padrone" system. Fortunately there are reasons why such a development will not take place, of which "supply and demand" is the principal one.

The Armenian immigrants resemble the Syrians in their inclination to trade rather than industry. The majority of the estimated 15,000 in the country are traders. A large number of them work for large Armenian firms dealing in oriental goods. There are a number of Armenians in New York who are cigarette makers. Some are working in the silk factories, and there are small storekeepers scattered through the country. The poorest of the Armenians do not come here. All who come are former business men who have been persecuted and driven out by the Turks. They come, intending to stay and become American citizens. It is estimated by a leading Armenian that there are 1,500 Armenians in New York, 2,000 in Worcester, Mass., 2,000 in Boston, 400 in Philadelphia, 500 in West Hoboken, 300 in Paterson, and 300 in Chicago. In Worcester, New York, and Philadelphia they have their own churches.

The manufacturing interests of the Syrian in America are confined almost exclusively to one quarter in Manhattan, and are increasing to meet the demands of the Syrian trade throughout the country. Combs, brushes, hat pins, razor strops, bibs, tuckers, aprons, wrappers, garters, suspenders, toothpicks, crucifixes, and small peddling truck generally, is made, and practically for the Syrian peddling trade only. The manufacture of these articles is carried on in lofts, and rarely in tenement houses. The wages paid, mostly upon a piecework basis, average $2 to $3 per week for women and $4 to $6 for men. Occasionally children under age are employed, but as a rule the Syrian is too shrewd to expose himself to possible penalties. The supply of cheap Syrian labor is abundant in the quarter, and none but Syrians are employed by Syrians. While from 15 to 20 per cent. of the Syrian population in America is dependent upon textile-mill work at the present time, the Syrian as a mill worker still remains an experiment. His docility as a proletarian is offset from the managerial standpoint by his fatalism—if driven too hard he simply lies down. Less vigorous than the French Canadians, Poles, and "American-born" mill-workers with whom he competes, he is much less fettered than they. Worked too hard or paid too little in the mill, he becomes a peddler; a member of no "union," he still has at his command in traditions—always retaining their hold longest upon a peasantry—resources which, among his own people, can hardly ever fail to secure for himself and family at least the necessities of existence. Employers claim to pay to Syrian workers the regular scale, and this claim is not seriously disputed by non-Syrian textile workers—the fact appearing to be that the textile wage scale is already as low as the subsistence level, and the Syrian not tending to raise that level. Instances have occurred in which silk-mill owners have used Syrian help in attempts to break strikes, but only rarely and as a war measure. The Syrian does not, as a rule, develop into a valuable mill adjunct, either as a strike breaker or otherwise. Appearances indicate, indeed, that mill owners have been to some extent the victims of cajolery in relation to the value of Syrian help.

In a silk mill in New Jersey where Syrians and Armenians have recently been introduced there are about 25 warpers, about 25 twisters, and about 25 fixers, all German or American, and their wages run from $14 to $18 a week. They were the first to come into the business and have an organization which is protecting the price of their labor. In other mills there is a number of Italians and Jews recently introduced.

There are about 40 winders, American girls for the most part. They begin at $2 a week. The Syrians and Armenians are employed in weaving, the price for which in the last four years has declined about one-third. The work for which formerly 12 cents was paid is now 8 cents. In 1900 occurred a strike in the shop against a reduction in wages. The factory was closed for ten weeks, when Armenian and Syrian labor was brought from New York and other places to replace the former labor. There are now about 250 weavers, 150 of whom are men and 100 are women. The men since the strike are divided as to nationality about as follows: 50 Jews, 25 Armenians, 25 Syrians, 15 Germans, 20 Americans. The 100 girls are divided in about the same proportion, except that there are more Americans among the girls. A large number of the weavers have their wives working with them in the factories, and a number of wives take work home. They receive about 40 cents for 75 yards, and can earn from $3 to $4 per week. Using one loom a weaver can make 15 yards of goods, and using two looms he can make 30 yards a day, at from 6 to 11 cents per yard. On the 11-cent goods he can not make 15 yards, so that he is able to earn about $8 to $12 a week. The majority of the weavers earn $9 a week.

The proprietor states that the Syrians have an instinct for weaving, and learn it very rapidly. They come to the mill, and, as a rule, have to work about a week without pay; then they earn from $3 to $12 per week—men, women, and children. The mill proprietor rents them small frame houses near the mill for $9 per month. A large majority of them live in this settlement. They are apparently clean, thrifty, and fairly temperate; from all reports make quiet, peaceable citizens. The proprietor much prefers them to Armenians or Italians for his purpose, and as his business increases he will be glad to increase his force of Syrian operators. Now and then a Syrian will apply for work, and they will give him an opportunity to learn, but if he finds he is not capable of learning he gives it up, and they never see him again. It is supposed they return to New York.

The problem of labor organization is especially difficult where the Syrians and Armenians are concerned. The other nationalities distrust them. It is claimed by the organizers that they can get along very well with the Germans, Irish, Jews, Italians, and Americans, but not with the "Turks." However, the price of labor has come down to such an extent that the Syrians are now dissatisfied, and have recently made their first overtures to get into line with the other nationalities.

Notwithstanding what is said above, the decline of wages in silk weaving in New Jersey can not be ascribed solely to the influence of immigration of Syrians and Armenians or of other nationalities. The secretary of the Silk Association of America in his report for 1901 (p. 29) speaks of the surprising development of the industry in Pennsylvania, and ascribes it to "the abundant supply of female labor. In New Jersey, for instance," he says, "the percentage of men operators employed in the silk mills is 47, the percentage of women 48, and the percentage of children 5. In Pennsylvania the respective percentages are as follows: Men, 24.4; women, 53.6; children, 22." These factories in Pennsylvania are usually in country districts.

CHAPTER VIII.

IMMIGRATION FROM CANADA.

The position of Canada with reference to immigration into the United States is twofold: First, the movement of Canadians across the border for permanent residence or temporary work in the busy season; second, the rear entrance, whereby European and Asiatic immigrants, who would be barred at the American ports, nevertheless effect an entrance. The latter phase of Canadian immigration properly belongs to a description of the administration of the Bureau of Immigration, and will be found in later pages dealing with that subject. At this point it is proposed to consider only the immigration from Canada proper, and its effect on American labor.

The points at which Canadian immigrants enter the United States are mainly Boston, Buffalo, Detroit, and Sault Ste. Marie. Intermediate railway stations of importance are those along the frontier of Maine, Vermont, and New York. Many immigrants enter the States by way of the Great Lakes. The ferries at Detroit and Buffalo require only 5 to 15 minutes in transit. Consequently large numbers of people making their homes on the Canadian side cross over daily for their regular employment. At Detroit about 500 or 600 Canadians come over every day on the ferries and go back at night, while about 50 Americans work on the Canadian side. Those who come from the Canadian side are usually laborers, but they include also large numbers of stenographers, typewriters, and clerks.

IMMIGRATION FROM CANADA. 447

The cost of living is about the same in Canada, except that rents are cheaper; probably no more so than in the suburbs of Detroit on the American side—Windsor being practically a suburb. The Americans who work on the Canadian side are the higher grade of skilled laborers—foremen and the like—and often their pay is higher than that of Canadians in the same line. On the other hand, the pay of Canadians working on the American side, while it is usually the same as that of Americans, yet in several trades it is claimed that employers prefer them because they are more subservient.

In general, wages on the Canadian side, especially in cities like Toronto, are about the same as in Detroit. Consequently there is not the inducement for immigration that formerly existed. The skilled trades where the greatest complaint is made are those of bricklayers, carpenters, plasterers, and clerks. The bricklayers claim that during the summer season half of the bricklayers in Detroit are Canadians. The wages since 1898 have been $3.60 for 8 hours; prior to that time they were $3.50 for 9 hours. Corresponding wages in Toledo are $4; Chicago, $4; Denver, Omaha, and Kansas City, $6.

Canadians do not cut wages, but by flooding the market they keep them from rising to the standard of other places, such as Toledo and Chicago. Wages in Toronto are about $3 per day of 8 hours.

Formerly the bricklayers' local union charged an initiation fee of $20, which kept out Canadians, but since they have joined the international union an initiation fee paid to the Canadian local permits Canadians to work on the American side, since they belong to the same international. The bricklayers had a strike in 1894 and many Canadians came in as "scabs." The carpenters were similarly affected in 1890, when the strike was weakened by the immigration of "scabs." The plasterers have not been seriously interfered with, not more than 3 or 4 Canadians having come over in the course of a year, and very few scabs. They have had no dispute in 14 years. The plumbers are not affected. Clerks complain more than any other occupation. Pattern makers do not complain to any extent. Wages in the large towns in Canada are equal to those in Detroit.

Shoemakers do not complain, since the organization is growing in Canada faster than in the United States, especially at Hamilton, Toronto, and Montreal.

The increased business prosperity, creating a demand for labor in Canada as well as in the United States, has weakened the pressure of immigration. The main trouble is in the time of strikes, and Detroit has been free from these in recent years, owing to the better organization of the trades council.

It is very generally agreed that the inspection at Detroit under Mr. C. C. McGlogan, who was immigration inspector from May, 1893, to March, 1897, was effective. Formerly large gangs of French-Canadians would cross the border accompanied by the agent of contractors for the lumber fields. Mr. McGlogan put a stop to this. Practically nothing of this kind is now done or has been done for 5 or 6 years. On an average, 200 Canadians were deported each year, but the number has now declined until there were in 1900 only 18 deportations. At the present time nearly all of the laborers who come have been thoroughly coached, and those who have been sent back are only those who have actually stated that they are contract laborers living in Canada.

The law does not give power to send back "birds of passage," and in the opinion of the inspector and local labor representatives it should be amended so that such immigrants who come over during the busy season and then return to Canada during the winter can be deported by the inspectors. Such a law would compel them to move into Michigan and to locate and become local consumers. It is claimed that a serious evil is done to the business of Detroit in that so large a number of Canadians, earning their wages on American soil, spend the money they receive on the Canadian side.

At Buffalo the cost of living on the Canadian side is much less than on the American side. A house and garden at Fort Erie or Berthie renting at $5 or $6 a month would rent in Buffalo at $15 or $16 a month, and rents as cheap as Canadian rents could not be obtained on the American side without going 14 or 15 miles. Quite a number of former Canadians now living in Canada on account of cheapness had lived already on the American side for 5 years in order to obtain their citizenship.

The occupations particularly affected at Buffalo are those of brushmakers, plasterers, lathers, machinists, bricklayers, and stone masons. Carpenters who work for $1 a day in Canada, whose wages were formerly $2.50 in Buffalo, are known to have begun work at $1 per day in order to get a foothold. Employees in the button factory who receive $3.50 to $4 per week at Berlin, Ontario, receive $9 at Buffalo.

The Canadian immigrant at Boston comes by way of steamship from Yarmouth and Halifax, the lines at the present time being the Dominion, the Atlantic Railway and Steamship Company, the Yarmouth Steamship Company, and the Canada Plant Line. In the year ending June 30, 1900, the number of Americans and aliens arriving in Boston from Canadian ports was 26,424, and the number from Europe was

448   THE INDUSTRIAL COMMISSION:—IMMIGRATION.

15,754. In the summer of 1900 the steamship rate from Canadian ports, owing to competition, was reduced from $7.50 to $1.50, which caused an increase of some 6,000 in the arrivals. The following table shows for the port of Boston the arrivals from Canada of Americans and aliens and also the arrivals from Europe:

Arrivals at Boston from Canadian and European ports from date when service was taken over from Massachusetts State board.

Year ending June 30—	Americans from Canada.	Aliens from Canada.	From Europe.
1894		22,888	17,128
1895		18,635	20,377
1896		19,997	21,846
1897		19,258	13,333
1898	12,239	19,602	12,227
1899	13,710	20,522	19,227
1900	18,070	[1] 26,424	15,754

[1] Rate reduced from $7.50 to $1.50 round trip in summer of 1899. Continues same to present time. Competition of Dominion-Atlantic Railway.

Canadian immigration at Boston includes practically the same people every year They come in the fall to look for work on farms and getting in the crops, and in the spring as fishermen and lumbermen. Also large numbers of carpenters come from Nova Scotia. This is the trade most seriously affected by Canadian immigration in Boston. Many Nova Scotian carpenters have moved to Boston and taken up their permanent residence there. Owing to this Canadian immigration the carpenters' union is the weakest of the building organizations, and the least competent to maintain a scale of wages. The following table presents by months from July, 1899, to March, 1901, the arrivals of Americans and aliens from Canada. It will be seen that the arrivals of Americans (mainly tourists) increased in the months of August and September, while the arrivals of Canadians is largest in the spring and fall, owing to the reasons already stated:

Arrivals at Boston from Canadian ports.

Month.	Americans.	Aliens.
1899—July	1,965	1,680
August	5,155	2,738
September	6,779	6,223
October	1,460	4,026
November	315	1,285
December	250	1,243
1900—January	239	760
February	127	736
March	223	1,819
April	298	2,482
May	351	1,723
June	908	1,709
Total 1899–1900	18,070	26,424
1900—July	3,274	2,276
August	10,398	3,059
September	1,996	3,586
November	584	1,492
December	329	1,311
1901—January	334	971
February	207	712
March	225	1,970

At the railway stations along the New England border complaint is made of the immigration of lumbermen and log drivers. In the report of the Immigration Investigating Commission in 1895, during the industrial depression, it was stated that the annual influx of these men was very disastrous to the wages of American lumbermen and a growing menace to their prosperity. Wages had been greatly reduced during the past 10 years and had reached so low a point as to make it well-nigh impossible for American lumbermen who had families to keep them in the ordinary necessities of life. These lumbermen had usually worked in the States before, and all denied coming in under contract.

Large numbers of women and girls cross at these railway points to work in the factory towns of New England. The influence of this immigration is described in the preceding pages dealing with the textile industry.

CHAPTER IX.

THE FOREIGN IMMIGRANT IN NEW YORK CITY.

[Prepared by KATE HOLLADAY CLAGHORN, Ph. D.]

The problems arising from foreign immigration are especially and peculiarly problems of the large cities. In them the immigrants are first received; in them they settle in large proportions, for longer or shorter periods, if not permanently; and in them the pressure of great masses of population throws into situations of unusual stress and strain the incoming peoples subjected to it.

Of all the great cities, New York may be regarded as perhaps the most intimately concerned with these problems, since of the 19 million and odd foreign immigrants who have come to these shores since the beginning of our immigration records no less than 13½ million, or about 71 per cent, have entered at that port, and no inconsiderable proportion of this large number have remained there.

FIRST PERIOD, 1821–1870.

The immigration problem, usually thought to be a comparatively new one, rendered more critical by the newer races now coming in increasing proportions, was outlined in all its features in the period of British, Irish, and German immigration, and at the very beginning of that period, too.

That first notable influx of immigration which caused the Federal Government to make the first regulations as to passenger traffic on the seas, and to establish the first regular record of alien arrivals, promptly called forth general complaints of the evils of immigration, surprisingly such as we hear them to-day.

The managers of the Society for the Prevention of Pauperism in the City of New York speak thus in 1819:

> First, as to the emigrants from foreign countries, the managers are compelled to speak of them in the language of astonishment and apprehension. Through this inlet pauperism threatens us with the most overwhelming consequences. From various causes the city of New York is doomed to be the landing place of a great portion of the European population who are daily flocking to our country for a place of permanent abode. This city is the greatest importing capital of the United States, and a position from which a departure into the interior is generally considered the most easy and practicable. On being possessed of a more extensive and active trade than any other commercial emporium in the Union, it naturally occurs to the minds of emigrants that we possess great means of employment. Our situation is peculiarly healthy, and no local objection, either physical or moral, exists to arrest the approach of foreigners. The present state of Europe contributes in a thousand ways to foster unceasing immigration to the United States. * * * An almost innumerable population beyond the ocean is out of employment, and this has the effect of increasing the usual want of employ. This country is the resort of vast numbers of those needy and wretched beings. Thousands are continually resting their hopes on the refuge which she offers, filled with delusive visions of plenty and luxury. They seize the earliest opportunity to cross the Atlantic and land upon our shores. * * * What has been the destination of this immense accession to our population, and where is it now? Many of these foreigners may have found employment; some may have passed into the interior; but thousands still remain among us. They are frequently found destitute in our streets; they seek employment at our doors; they are found in our almshouse and in our hospitals; they are found at the bar of our criminal tribunals, in our Bridewell, our penitentiary, and our State prison. And we lament to say, that they are too often led by want, by vice, and by habit to form a phalanx of plunder and depredations, rendering our city more liable to increase of crimes and our houses of correction more crowded with convicts and felons.[1]

And, curiously enough, at this same time, when population on this great continent was a mere fringe along the Atlantic seaboard, the same anxiety was felt that is felt to-day to get the immigrant out of the "crowded" cities into the country beyond. It was said in 1817:[2]

> We have room enough yet; let them come. * * * But the emigrants should press into the interior. In the present state of the times we seem too thick on the maritime frontier already. Within there is ample and profitable employment for all, in almost any branch of business, and strangers should be encouraged to seek it there.

---
[1] Second Annual Report of the Managers of the Society for the Prevention of Pauperism in the City of New York, 1819.
[2] Niles's Register, VII, p. 359.

An evil especially felt and directly ascribed to the foreign immigrant was an increase in sickness and the death rate in the city that accompanied the increase in immigration.

The connection between foreign immigration and disease in New York City had been noticed, indeed, before immigration began to be a matter of public record. As far back as 1769 a pesthouse was established in New York, especially "for the reception of diseased emigrants."[1]

In 1795, when yellow fever carried off 730 persons in New York City, at least 500 were foreigners, 452 belonging to one Catholic congregation, some of whom had been so short a time in the country that the pastor, Rev. Mr. O'Brien, did not know them.[2]

The city inspector, in his report for the year 1816, noting the great mortality of the summer of that year, attributes it partly to the excessive heat, but also to the constant influx of immigrants, many of whom were of the poorer class and unaccustomed to the climate.[3]

In 1834 an epidemic of smallpox broke out, which was accounted for by the introduction of it from abroad "among our poor and filthy population."[4]

By 1837 the connection between immigration and the death rate seemed so important that the city inspector, in his report for the year,[5] devoted considerable space to an analysis of deaths and causes of death according to place of nativity, showing the especially high proportion of deaths among the foreign born from two great causes—consumption of the lungs and typhoid fever.

From this time on city inspectors call attention again and again to immigration as the cause of disease, and their reports, taking them year after year, in fact show that nearly one-half the deaths by consumption were of the foreign part of the population, and that more than one-third the whole number of deaths were of foreigners.[6]

Commenting upon the death rate of the period from 1846 through the next 10 or 15 years following, the city inspector, in 1860, points out that in 1851-52 there were 1,639 deaths in the city from typhoid fever; in the same years 590,593 aliens landed at the port; that the largest annual number of deaths ever reported in New York from dysentery and diarrhea were during the period of greatest immigration— 1847-1855; that, in fact, the rate of mortality from these diseases varied directly with the amount of immigration; and that the largest number of deaths in the city in any one year from smallpox were in the period of greatest immigration.[7]

Much of the disease ascribed to foreign immigration was caused by bad conditions on shipboard during the passage. From the very beginning of immigration to this country—from the time of the early explorers and the original colonists—one who embarked for the voyage across the Atlantic did it at serious risk of his life, not so much from pirates and shipwreck (although these were common perils of the deep) as from disease. Accounts of early voyages show that it was quite a matter of course for a ship to lose from 10 to 30 per cent of her passengers by death from disease on the passage, and to land the remainder in a broken-down and enfeebled condition that unfitted them for some time, if not permanently, for active occupation on shore. The disease most common on these voyages was the typhus, "jail," or "ship" fever, the latter familiar title showing how closely the disease was associated with the ocean crossing, and was due to the neglect by shipmasters of the most rudimentary sanitary requirements, of failure to provide for ventilation, cleanliness, and wholesome or sufficient food. And so when immigration was heavy, typhus fever appeared on the voyage as a natural consequence. The severe outbreaks of this disease at the time of the great outpouring in the late forties were partly ascribed to the miserable condition of the emigrants when they left home, but largely to the crowding and bad ventilation of vessels and to the insufficient supply of food provided for passengers. At this time it was said that "scarcely a vessel has arrived with Irish emigrants without having the disease prevailing on board, and in some instances as many as 40 or 50 have died on the vessel, and more than 100 sick have been landed at quarantine from one vessel. Hundreds, too, who have passed the inspection of the health officers and been permitted to land, come up to the city having the seeds of disease already implanted, have sickened within from 1 to 3 weeks, and being frequently kept in town by their friends, contributed to spread the disease and infect the localities in which they sojourned."[8]

These bad conditions led to various United States regulations dealing with passenger traffic, and in 1847 a bureau of immigration was established by the State of

---

[1] J. W. Francis, Historical Discourse, p. 108.
[2] J. H. Griscom, M. D., History of the Visitations of Yellow Fever at New York, p. 7.
[3] City Inspector's Report of Interments in the City and County of New York for the Year 1816, p. 11.
[4] Annual Report of Interments in the City and County of New York for the Year 1834, p. 15.
[5] Annual Report of Interments in the City and County of New York for the Year 1837, p. 480.
[6] Dr. John H. Griscom, Sanitary Condition of the Laboring Population of New York, N. Y., 1845.
[7] Annual Report of Interments for 1860, p. 228.
[8] Annual Report of Interments, 1847, p. 104.

THE IMMIGRANT IN NEW YORK CITY.

New York to provide against sanitary and other evils arising from immigration, but the death rate from diseases caused among immigrants by the passage over continued high.

In 1853 Asiatic cholera broke out in immigrant vessels, and led to demands for further United States legislation to remedy such causes as could "be traced to any state of things on shipboard, such as defective ventilation, bad or insufficient food, or too large a number of passengers crowded together."[1]

Such legislation was enacted in 1855, providing for a limitation of passengers carried, by the tonnage of the vessel—1 passenger being allowed for every 2 tons—providing for space, for ventilation, for stated supplies of food and water to passengers, for cleanliness, and for inspection at the ports to see if all conditions were complied with.

This act seemed to be more effectual, and by 1858 it was said that the sanitary condition of the immigrants had greatly improved,[2] while by 1864 it could be said that the diseases engendered by "confined air, filthy habits, bad fare, and long voyages," which at one period filled the hospitals with the sick and dying, had been so reduced as no longer to be a source of serious apprehension.[3]

Other circumstances than those of the ocean crossing were, however, responsible for the connection made in the public mind between the foreign immigrant and the city's high death rate.

The general situation as regards the health of the city and the foreign-born population at this time was summed up by Dr. John H. Griscom in his report as city inspector in 1842 as follows:

> It will not, it is presumed, be disputed that New York contains a larger proportion of inhabitants of foreign birth than any city in the United States, and this fact assumes, in connection with the mortality of the city, especially with the disease under consideration (consumption), a vital importance as affecting its sanitary reputation.
>
> Here are congregated armies of foreigners drawn from their homes by various causes, and mostly in search of a living, allured by the flattering expectations held out to them of a "free country." They bring with them destitution, misery, and too often disease already taken root. If in good health when living at home, the suffering, privation, and close confinement incidental to the voyage rarely fail to engender disease, especially fevers and diseases of the lungs, from the effects of which they frequently never recover, and their broken constitutions are thus rendered a fertile soil for the germination of seeds of new diseases which future circumstances may plant. Ostracised, they soon experience the depressing effects of being strangers in a strange land. Ignorant of where to look for a support, thousands are cast upon charity for a meager and uncertain subsistence. Living in crowded apartments, in crumbling tenements, and narrow streets, and upon food poor in quality and stinted in quantity, they are peculiarly exposed to inroads of disease.[4]

And later in the report Dr. Griscom announces it as his conclusion that "the first among the more serious causes of diseased general health * * * is the crowded condition, with insufficient ventilation, of a great number of the dwellings of this city."[5]

It is difficult to trace the immigrant to his first dwellings in this city. Enough is known, however, of the general growth of the city to give opportunity for a tolerably close guess as to where he went and what quarters he had.

By the close of the eighteenth century the city was growing rapidly toward the north, streets were being raised and paved, and the dock frontage extended farther into the water. The docks in process of construction became gathering places of all sorts of filth, forming about the city a belt of offensiveness along the river front from which, it may be supposed, the well-to-do were ready to draw back. In the neighborhood of the docks were a large number of old wooden houses, many of which, built before the raising and paving of the streets, had their lower floors 2 or 3 feet below the surface of the pavements.[6] This was particularly the case at the southern end of the island, in the First, Second, and Fourth wards; but in other quarters, too, other offensive neighborhoods had grown up.

In such neighborhoods disease flourished. The outbreak of yellow fever in 1795 "prevailed on the borders of the East River, in the low streets and what was formerly the swamp, and in the narrow alleys."[7] And in such neighborhoods, evidently, the immigrant population found their first homes; for it will be remembered that it was in this epidemic that so large a proportion—500 out of 730—of the victims were immigrants, most of them newly arrived.

By 1820 a cellar population had come into existence in New York, as we know by accounts of a malignant fever that broke out in Bancker street, all cases of which were noted to be of residents in cellars. These, however, were negroes, not foreign immigrants.

---

[1] Report New York Commissioner of Emigration, 1853, p. 140.
[2] Report New York Commissioner of Emigration, 1858, p. 240.
[3] Report of New York Association for Improving the Condition of the Poor, 1864, p. 45.
[4] Annual Report of Interments, 1842, pp. 155-157.
[5] Annual Report of Interments, 1842, pp. 160-161.
[6] Dr. John H. Griscom, History of Yellow Fever, p. 8.
[7] Dr. John H. Griscom, History of Yellow Fever, p. 7.

The yellow-fever epidemic of 1822 drove the well-to-do population uptown to "Greenwich Village," and shortly after that time the growth of the city was so great that builders were taxed to their utmost to provide houses for all who wanted them.

The business district was growing to the north, with Broadway as its main axis, and in the course of this growth, well-to-do residents of the neighborhoods encroached upon moved still farther to the north, leaving their substantial dwellings to be occupied by the poor, who found it desirable to remain near the business district that afforded them a livelihood, and who, to save expense, crowded themselves 4, 5, or 6 families together into a structure adapted to the uses of one family only. And "the poor," as years went on, were more and more exclusively the foreign born and their children.

By 1834 overcrowding was recognized as a serious evil. Gerrett Forbes, city inspector for that year, says that, together with intemperance, the most prominent, cause of the increase of deaths over the increase of the population which he has noted, is "the crowded and filthy state in which a great portion of our population live and apparently without being sensible of their condition."

Former good residence districts that were gradually being changed into crowded quarters of the poor were, notably, along the west side, up toward Greenwich Village, and in the center of the city, the old Fourth Ward, with its many fine old mansions.

North of the city hall, and to the east of Broadway, a neighborhood of evil notoriety had come into being by a somewhat different order of growth from that described above—in the famous Sixth Ward and its little less notorious neighbor on the north, the Fourteenth.

The Sixth Ward was never as good a residence district as some others in the city on account of its peculiar topography. The "Collect," a deep pond in a deep basin, covered a considerable portion of its surface, and while, in its natural state the pond added to the attractiveness of the locality, in 1800 the city began to fill it in, and from that time to 1810, when the work was finished, the spot was a center of offense and filth. The place was made a common dumping ground for garbage, dead animals, and all sorts of trash; a circumstance that would naturally hinder the development of the neighborhood as a good residence district. On the high land above this pond some good houses were probably erected; and an old print showing the "Five Points" in 1827 represents some good and substantial looking dwellings. But a large number of the houses erected in this quarter were shackling frame structures, built on made land; and the famous tenement streets about the "Five Points"—Baxter, Park, and Mulberry—were laid out over the very site of the pond, or along its edges.

By 1830 the Sixth Ward had become notorious for crime and disorder, and by 1834-35 it emerges into especial publicity as a long-settled Irish neighborhood, in the course of the Irish riots that marked those years and that had their center here. In this ward an epidemic of "continued fever" (typhoid) broke out in 1837. A physician, describing this epidemic, said that the cases occurred in the midst of a poor population, "principally Irish and German, whose habits * * * are more or less filthy, and who lived crowded together, with a family in every room in the house, and sometimes more."[1] All cases occured west of the Bowery, where there was far greater crowding than to the east of that street, and all occurred in base ment dwellings, or first floors with no basement or cellar beneath.

A month or two before the outbreak of this epidemic the mayor of the city, Aaron Clark, writing to the common council, on June 5, in regard to the disease likely to be occasioned by immigrants, said that "if they have it not with them on arrival they may generate a plague by collecting in crowds in small tenements and foul hovels."[2]

His prognostication was fulfilled, it is seen, within a very brief period. In the summer of 1842 a number of cases of typhus fever of a severe type occurred in a building in the rear of No. 49 Elizabeth street, in the Sixth Ward, "under circumstances," said the physician reporting on the cases, "which left no doubt of its local origin."[3] The picture he gives of the surroundings of these cases shows us the general features of a housing system for the poor that had developed itself by this time:

The front building, a small two-story frame house, was partly occupied by the proprietor or lessee of the building as a liquor store and partly sublet to several Irish families. A covered alleyway led to the rear building. This was a double frame house 3 stories in height. It stood in the center of the yard, ranged next the fence, where a number of pigstys and stables had surrounded the yard on 3 sides. From the quantity of filth, liquid and otherwise, thus caused, the ground, I suppose, had been rendered almost impassable, and to remedy this the yard had been completely boarded over so

---

[1] Dr. John H. Griscom, Sanitary Condition of the Laboring Population, 1845, p. 15.
[2] Sanderson, Republican Landmarks.
[3] Dr. J. H. Griscom, Sanitary Condition of the Laboring Population, p. 18.

that the earth could nowhere be seen. These boards were partially decayed, and by a little pressure, even in dry weather, a thick, greenish fluid could be forced up through their crevices. The central building was inhabited partly by negroes. In this building there occurred in the course of 6 weeks 9 cases of typhus fever. * * * At my solicitation the alderman of the ward visited the building, the number of pigs about the establishment was reduced to that allowed by law, and chloride of lime, whitewashing, etc., liberally and assiduously employed.

In this example is seen the original "tenement house"—the old-fashioned frame house, once occupied by one family, and now turned over to occupancy by many. In the rear of this, to occupy a part—probably a large part—of the original yard, had been built up a big barrack, expressly for tenement uses. In this a new stage in the development of the tenement-house system is seen. Such barracks were not necessarily erected on lots already occupied along the street line by older buildings, but they were in many cases. Nor was the rear tenement always a barrack building. It was often the original building on the lot—perhaps a one or two story frame shanty, in front of which was erected a barrack building. Sometimes, too, the rear buildings were irregular little frame structures run up in the rear of the lot to fill the space left by a front tenement. But in any case the "rear" tenement was, as a rule, less desirable than the front tenement, and, as in this example, was frequently given over to a different and inferior—that is, less prosperous—race than that which occupied the front tenement. This, too, is a typical feature of the tenement system as it developed. And it will be noticed that the whole tenement was leased and controlled by one man, who sublet the separate apartments occupied by the many families filling the tenements. All of these features played an important part of their own in the development of the tenement system.

The earlier type of tenement house—the old made-over family residence—was responsible for the beginnings of a great "cellar population," whose wretchedness was a continual tax upon the sympathies and conscience of the well-to-do, through a long series of years. The conditions under which they lived are almost incredible to-day. Dr. Griscom says, in 1845:

The most offensive of all places of residence are the cellars. It is almost impossible, when contemplating the circumstances and conditions of the poor beings who inhabit these holes, to maintain the proper degree of calmness requisite for a thorough inspection of their miseries, and sound judgment respecting 1em. You must descend to them; you must feel the blast of foul air as it meets your face on opening the door; you must grope in the dark or hesitate until your eye becomes accustomed to the gloomy place, to enable you to find your way through the entry over the broken floor, the boards of which are protected from your tread by a half inch of hard dirt; you must inhale the suffocating vapor of the heated rooms; and in the dark, dim recesses endeavor to find the inmates by the sound of their voices, or chance to see their figures moving between you and the flickering light of a window, coated with dirt and festooned with cobwebs—or, if in search of an invalid, take care that you do not fall full length upon the bed with her, by stumbling against the bundle of rags and straw dignified by that name, lying upon the floor under the window, if window there is; and all this and much more beyond the reach of my pen must be felt and seen ere you can appreciate in its full force the mournful and disgusting condition in which thousands of the subjects of our Government pass their lives.[1]

The use of cellars, begun in the old single-family residence, occupied by many families, was continued in the tenement house proper; but as the big barracks were built in greater and greater number until the call for houses was more adequately met without recourse to underground apartments, the cellar residences decreased.

From the specially constructed tenant house, placed on the front or rear of the lot, came the "courts" and "alleys" in which tenant houses were crowded upon every available foot of spare ground.

The city inspector, in his report for 1845, said that in comparison with the older type of dwellings, with their crowded cellar apartments, the new "courts" were "luxurious and economical residences." But Dr. Griscom, in his report for 1842, had joined the "courts" with the cellars in their harmful influences upon public health.

These, indeed, were largely responsible for that part of the high death rate among the foreign born which was caused by consumption, as the immigrant ships had been largely responsible for that part caused by typhus. Dr. Griscom says:

The annual reports of the city inspector show that nearly one-half the deaths by consumption are of the foreign part of the population, and that more than one-third the whole number of deaths are of foreigners. Such an immense disproportion can only be accounted for on the supposition that some extraordinary causes of death prevail among the strangers who come to reside among us. Now it is a pretty well ascertained fact that a large majority of the cellar and court population of this city consists of persons of foreign birth and their children; of the dispensary patients about 60 per cent are natives of other countries, and if it were possible to ascertain the parentage of the children receiving aid from these institutions we should find a larger proportion than this directly dependent upon foreigners. There is no doubt that 75 per cent of them are either emigrants or the children of such. Put these facts side by side, then, and we are confirmed in the conclusion that the domiciliary condition of these poor beings, the confined places in which they dwell, the unwholesome air they breathe, and their filth and degradation, are prolific sources of an immense amount of distress and sickness, which in their turn serve by the loss of time, of wages, and of strength, to aggravate the miserableness of their condition, to increase the danger to the public health and the burden of public and private charity.[2]

---

[1] Sanitary Condition of the Laboring Population, pp. 8–9.
[2] Sanitary Condition of the Laboring Population, p. 14.

Further testimony is given to show that it was not so much the original condition of the immigrant as the wretched dwelling he had to live in that caused the high rate of sickness and death among foreigners in the city.

The city inspector says in his report for 1860:

> The further fact should be adduced that most of the children who arrive in this city from foreign ports, although suffering from the effects of a protracted voyage, bad accommodations, and worse fare, do not bring with them any marked disease beyond those which, with proper care, nursing, and wholesome air, could not be easily overcome. The causes, then, of this excessive mortality must be sought for in this city, and are readily traceable to the wretched habitations in which parents and children are forced to take up their abode; in the contracted alleys; the underground, murky, and pestilential cellars; the tenement house, with its hundreds of occupants, where each cooks, eats, and sleeps in a single room without light or ventilation, surrounded with filth, in an atmosphere foul, fetid, and deadly, with none to console with or advise, or to apply to for relief when disease invades them.[1]

Immigration was somewhat checked during the war, but even under those circumstances house building in the city did not keep pace with the population, and the close packing of tenants in confined quarters still brought "disease, demoralization, and death" as their consequences.[2]

Conditions were so bad that in 1864 leading citizens of New York formed themselves into a "citizens' association," for the purpose of investigating and reforming the prevailing evils. A subcommittee, known as the "council of hygiene and public health," undertook a thorough sanitary investigation of the city, and their report affords us one of the most valuable studies of city conditions and a city population that has ever been prepared.

The committee found, as to the tenement system in general, that the—

> tenant houses of this city are unlike the habitations occupied by the poorer classes in any other city, principally in the following respects:
> 1. That the occupants have less personal interest in and control over the character, cleanliness, and surroundings of their domiciles than is usual in other cities.
> 2. That the rate of crowding, both as regards the allowance of area and of air space to each person, far exceeds the ordinary degrees of aggregation of the poorer classes in other cities.
> 3. There is less concern and expenditure for the welfare of the tenants, and at the same time a higher rate of rental for domiciles, than prevails in other cities.
> 4. There is relatively, as well as numerically, a vastly larger population dwelling in crowded tenant houses in New York than in any other great city.[3]

The total population of New York had doubled in 20 years, and the great majority of it—the laboring and poor classes—had "become more and more concentrated upon given areas and in particular streets and districts." In a sanitary survey of the city by the council, completed in December, 1864, it was found that the total number of tenant houses was 15,309, and the average number of families to each was $7\frac{1}{6}$. The number of persons residing in tenant houses and cellars was 495,592, to which should be added those in smaller habitations, attics, stable lofts, etc., where insufficient area and air space were found.[4]

At this time the tenant houses of the city were nearly all found within an area of 4 square miles, and certain parts of the city showed a density of population greater than that of any parts or wards of London or any other European city.

As compared with tenements of former times, those of this period were built to a greater height in stories, there were more rear tenant houses erected back to back with other buildings correspondingly situated on parallel streets, and courts and alleys were more encroached upon and narrowed into unventilated, unlighted, and well-like holes between front and rear tenements.[5]

The accompanying table shows the distribution of the tenant-house population throughout New York at this time, and gives some idea of the relative proportion of tenement-house dwellers to the total population. It must be noticed, however, that the total population given in the table is that for 1860, while the tenement-house population is that of 1864. Consequently the proportion of tenement-house dwellers to total population based on these figures would be somewhat too high. As the population increased only about 16 per cent in the whole decade from 1860 to 1870, however, the disproportion is not so great as it might be.

---

[1] Annual Report of Interments. New York, 1860, Doc. No. 5.
[2] Report of A. I. C. P., 1865, p. 51.
[3] Report of the Council of Hygiene and Public Health of the Citizens' Association of New York, second edition, 1866, p. lxix.
[4] Report Council of Hygiene, p. lxix.
[5] Report Council of Hygiene, p. lxx.

TABLE 2.—*Tenant-house population in 1864.*

[Compiled from Report Council of Hygiene, 1864, p. 349, and Report New York State Tenement-House Commission, 1895, p. 273.]

Wards.	Total population, census 1860.	Total tenant-house and cellar population.	Number tenant houses.	Total population in tenant houses.	Average population to each tenant house.	Total number families in tenant houses.	Average number families to each tenant house.
1	18,148	9,062	250	8,564	$34\frac{1}{4}$	2,181	$8\frac{1}{2}$
2	2,506	....	....	....	....	....	....
3	3,757	1,305	54	1,248	$24\frac{1}{6}$	310	$5\frac{3}{4}$
4	21,994	17,957	486	17,611	$35\frac{1}{4}$	3,636	$7\frac{1}{2}$
5	22,337	11,206	462	10,370	$24\frac{2}{3}$	2,957	$5\frac{1}{2}$
6	26,696	22,897	605	22,401	$34\frac{1}{3}$	4,406	$7\frac{1}{4}$
7	39,982	20,526	627	19,293	$30\frac{4}{5}$	4,586	$7\frac{1}{4}$
8	39,406	16,888	625	15,630	25	3,977	$6\frac{1}{2}$
9	44,385	15,172	596	14,955	$25\frac{1}{10}$	3,836	$6\frac{1}{2}$
10	29,004	18,583	534	18,140	34	4,487	9
11	59,571	65,620	2,049	64,254	$31\frac{1}{3}$	13,433	$6\frac{1}{2}$
12	30,551	....	....	....	....	....	....
13	32,917	15,936	540	14,997	$27\frac{1}{2}$	3,729	$6\frac{3}{4}$
14	28,083	20,425	546	20,008	$36\frac{5}{8}$	4,509	$8\frac{1}{2}$
15	27,587	5,205	197	4,970	25	1,358	7
16	45,176	33,650	1,257	31,500	25	7,088	$5\frac{2}{3}$
17	72,953	66,207	1,890	63,766	$34\frac{2}{3}$	15,974	$8\frac{1}{3}$
18	57,462	36,099	836	35,869	$42\frac{6}{7}$	7,267	$8\frac{3}{4}$
19	32,795	16,272	571	16,067	$28\frac{1}{7}$	3,632	$6\frac{1}{2}$
20	67,519	33,218	1,162	32,205	$27\frac{4}{5}$	8,344	$7\frac{1}{3}$
21	49,017	36,870	1,026	36,675	$35\frac{5}{7}$	7,299	$7\frac{1}{3}$
22	61,725	32,544	996	31,845	32	7,714	7

About this time it was observed not only that poor people were concentrated in certain districts, but that they were more or less segregated according to nationalities. And in 1867 it was noted that the social relations of the foreign to the native population had materially changed; that the foreigners no longer blended with the native stocks to become incorporated with them.[1]

"So large are the aggregations of different foreign nationalities," the report goes on to say, "that they no longer conform to our habits, opinions, and manners, but, on the contrary, create for themselves distinct communities, almost as impervious to American sentiments and influences as are the inhabitants of Dublin or Hamburg. . . . They have their own theaters, recreations, amusements, military and national organizations; to a great extent their own schools, churches, and trade unions; their own newspapers and periodical literature."

These foreigners had at that time in the city 73 churches of their own, 35 newspapers in 5 languages, and many charitable institutions for the benefit of their own people.

The Report of the Council of Hygiene, above referred to, shows more or less in detail how these foreign populations were distributed in 1864.

Beginning at the lower end of the city, where the immigrant first enters it after landing at the immigrant station, it is found that the lower west side, one of the good residential districts mentioned in describing an earlier period, had been wholly converted to a tenement district of peculiar offensiveness.

The inhabitants of the district were largely of foreign birth; about one-half the population were Irish, about one-fourth Germans, the remainder were Americans, Swedes, and Danes. About two-thirds of the population were laborers and mechanics with their families; the remainder were retail shopkeepers and keepers of hotels and sailors' and immigrants' boarding houses. A large element of the population was a floating one, consisting of travelers, immigrants, sailors, and "vagabonds without a habitation and almost without a name."[2]

Many of the tenement houses in this district were the old family residences of a more prosperous time, but many were the big brick barracks built especially for tenement uses; the former mainly along Greenwich street, the latter mainly along Washington street, which, being made ground, had not been built up as Greenwich street was, with buildings of the better class, thus affording opportunities for erecting this other class of buildings.

A marked feature of tenement conditions here was the small size of the apartments, which insured overcrowding.

Throughout all these quarters the utmost neglect of all hygiene laws prevailed. Typhus fever and measles prevailed here, and proved very fatal; and a list of cases

[1] Report A. I. C. P., 1867, p. 42.

[2] Report Council of Hygiene, p. 5.

under the care of the principal charitable society of the city, giving names and addresses, shows that this region was a veritable nest of pauperism.

Following up the west side from Reade street to Fourteenth, different stages of the general process of change characteristic of a great city's growth are to be seen. In the district already described the change was almost complete; as one passed northward, the change was seen in less and less advanced stages.

From Reade to Canal street the greater number of residents were of foreign parentage. The colored population, once very numerous, had almost disappeared. The houses of prostitution—the fringe that an advancing fashionable quarter drags behind it—for which the neighborhood had once been famous, were rapidly disappearing, the former occupants of these houses being replaced by foreigners, who in 'urn were being crowded out by the growth of the business district.[1]

From Canal to Spring street, west of Broadway—a district containing the lower ends of Thompson, Sullivan, Wooster, and Greene streets, of malodorous memory—the inhabitants were about equally divided into Americans, foreigners, and negroes. The majority of the retail stores were kept by foreigners, who were said to be "an industrious and hard-working people."[2] The Americans were well to do, living in their own houses, while the negroes were a poor, lazy class. Houses of ill fame were more numerous here, where the change had not proceeded so far, and the inmates were "composed of nearly all nationalities, not excepting our own."[2] Thieves, pickpockets, and gamblers abounded.

From Spring street to Houston, Irish and Germans comprised a large part of the inhabitants. A few negroes were found here, and many houses of prostitution of the better class, as the district was in the vicinity of the great hotels and the places of public amusement. From Houston street to Christopher street, the inhabitants were mostly of the laboring classes, presumably with a large foreign intermixture.

Between Christopher street and Fourteenth, lay the former "Greenwich Village," and here we catch up with the native born on their journey northward. The population of this district contained, in 1864, probably a larger proportion of native-born residents than any in the city, with the exception of the Fifteenth Ward. Few wealthy families were found here; most of the inhabitants were tradespeople, clerks, mechanics of the better class, and cartmen.

The tenant houses throughout the district from Reade to Fourteenth street were mainly 2 to 4 story brick dwellings, from 20 to 40 years old, built for one family. There were, besides, some of the small, rickety, old frame dwellings, of the type already noted in the Sixth Ward, and a few of the barrack type, mostly in very bad condition. Rear tenements of the lowest grade were to be found in considerable numbers.

From Fourteenth to Fortieth street, the foreign population is seen to have entered the district side by side with the native population in a very literal sense. Passing over Greenwich Village, they had traveled up the western edge of the district above as the native born were traveling up its eastern edge—the center of the island; and, as the foreigners were now coming into a region not already thickly built up, the brick barrack was the prevailing type of tenant house. Here then grew up the characteristic "barrack" evils and here were to be found some of the worst and most extreme types of that class of buildings.

The inspector for the district between Twenty-sixth and Thirty-third streets describes a square almost covered with front and rear tenements, and depicts vividly the terrible sanitary conditions that naturally arise, from lack of ventilation and sanitary conveniences.

He says:

In a majority of rear tenements * * * the apartments are dirty, dark, and uninviting, often reeking with filth, the walls wholly innocent of whitewash, and the atmosphere impregnated with the disagreeable odor so peculiar to tenement houses. In some the sun never shines, and the apartments are so dark that unless seated near the window it is impossible to read ordinary type; and yet the inspector often hears the hackneyed expression, "We have no sickness, thank God," uttered by those whose sunken eyes, pale cheeks, and colorless lips speak more eloquently than words of the anæmic condition inevitably resulting from the absence of pure, fresh air and the general light of the sun. * * * The tenants seem to wholly disregard personal cleanliness, if not the very first principles of decency, their general appearance and actions corresponding with their wretched abodes. * * * This indifference to personal and domiciliary cleanliness is doubtless acquired from a long familiarity with the loathsome surroundings, wholly at variance with all moral or social improvement, as well as the first principles of hygienic science.[3]

The foreign residents of this district were mostly Irish, with a few colored people intermingled.

Going still farther to the north, above Fortieth street, still another phase of foreign life in the city is seen. By this time the foreign population had fairly outrun the native population, and throughout the sparsely settled district of the upper west side, on the broadly stretching vacant lots through which the streets of

---

[1] Report Council Hyg., p. 25. [2] Report Council Hyg., p. 37. [3] Report Council Hyg., p. 245.

a later time had not yet been cut, on the miniature crags and peaks that dotted the ground a foreign squatter population had erected its dwellings.

In the New York Times of November 21, 1864, it was said that there was then—

A population of 20,000 on this island that pay neither rent for the dwellings they occupy nor municipal taxes as holders of real estate. They comprise that portion of the population known as "squatters." In one ward, which we need not name, they combined a year or two ago in sufficient numbers to control the election for alderman and councilmen. We are not altogether sure that they can not control the majority of votes in the same ward to-day.

These 20,000 exempts [says the inspector of the council of hygiene, who gave in his report the above extract from the Times] exercise, by favor of the common council, the right of free pasture for cows and pigs. The public pound has been voted a nuisance; the keepers thereof a double-distilled nuisance. * * * The "freedom of the city" they hold to embrace * * * likewise the right of revising the general municipal surveys. * * * The dwellings of the "exempt" population at frequent intervals hold possession of the public highway. At sundry points they take half the carriage road, the owners no doubt holding to the view that where a dung cart can pass along there is ample accommodation for any other species of vehicle.¹

The squatters' dwellings, which were scattered irregularly around without reference to lot or to street boundaries, were the "shanties" so familiar to an earlier generation of New Yorkers.

The shanty [says an inspector of the council of hygiene] is the cheapest and simplest domicile constructed in civilized communities. The typical shanty is built of rough boards, which form the floor, the sides, and the roof. It is built either on the ground or but little raised above it. It is from 6 to 10 feet high, and its ground area varies much in different cases, but is always of moderate extent. It contains no fireplace or chimney, but a stove, the pipe from which passes through a hole in the roof. It has from 1 to 3 or 4 windows, with single sash, each containing from 4 to 6 panes of small size. Some shanties have but 1 room, others an additional small apartment, used as a bedroom. The better shanties are lathed and plastered. It is evident that to the occupants of the shanty domiciliary and personal cleanliness is almost impossible. In one room are found the family, chairs, usually dirty and broken, cooking utensils, stove, often a bed, a dog or cat, and sometimes more or less poultry. On the outside, by the door in many cases, are pigs and goats and additional poultry. There is no sink or drainage, and the slops are thrown upon the ground.²

It is seen, then, that the shanty could be about as filthy as the tenant house proper, but this advantage, at least, it had over the latter—it housed, usually, only one family, and, standing free on three sides at least, admitted much more fresh air and sunlight.

The shanty population of the upper west side was, in contrast to the lower west side population, largely composed of Germans; but many Irish were found here also. Many were day laborers, employed by contractors in grading, paving, and sewering the streets, and in the removal of rock, or in excavating for public purposes. Some were employed in the stables of the city railroads and stage companies, or in Central Park.

In this district, there were also some brick and wooden tenements, inhabited by mechanics, by drivers and conductors on the city railroads, and by many of those engaged in retail business on the avenues. In the wooden tenements German families preponderated; in the brick, Americans.³

Having traced the progress of the foreign population up the west side, we may return to the lower part of the city.

In 1864 the Fourth Ward could show some of the worst types of the tenement houses in the city. Many of the old residences had been torn down and replaced by the big tenement barracks. One of the most notorious of these, known as "Gotham court" in Cherry street, was 34 feet wide in front and rear, 234 feet long, and 5 stories high. This immense block had at one of the long sides a clear space of 9 feet separating it from a similar structure forming part of the "court;" on the other side a clear space of 7 feet divided it from the rear of the houses on Roosevelt street. Hemmed in, in this way, the "court" could receive the smallest modicum of light and air, and disease was bred here freely. This house represented about the average sanitary condition of the tenant houses in the district, although from its size it was the most notorious among them.

The inhabitants in this district, on Oak, Cherry, and Water streets, on Oliver, James, and Roosevelt, were mainly Irish of the lowest and most degraded class.

The Sixth Ward at this time could lay claim to the most exclusively foreign population of any district in the city. Americans constituted less than 5 per cent of the whole number. Of the foreign population, the Irish constituted 74 per cent; the remaining 26 per cent were mainly German Jews and Italians. The German Jews dealt in old clothing and made Baxter street their headquarters; the Irish kept junk shops, liquor stores, groceries, etc.; the Italians were ragpickers, and organ grinders.⁴ By this time about one-third of the tenant houses in the ward were of the "barrack" type, containing from 10 to 50 families each. The remainder were very old wooden structures, some quite small, containing 4 to 8 families in as many rooms. Many of these houses were used as lodging houses, as many as 30 persons being packed into a single room.

---

¹ Report Council Hyg., p. 293.
² Report Council Hyg., p. 300.
³ Report Council Hyg., p. 303.
⁴ Report Council Hyg., p. 77.

In the Fourteenth Ward, just to the north, one-half of the inhabitants were of the lower orders, mostly Irish and Germans, the former nationality predominating. Here also were to be found the old wooden houses used as tenant houses, and the new brick barracks.

At Houston street, the northern boundary of the Fourteenth Ward, the tenement district of the central part of the city may be said to have ended at this time, the ward above, the Fifteenth, containing a population almost entirely native born and comparatively few tenant houses.

To see the remainder of the tenement-house population we must now turn to the east side.

The Seventh Ward, lying along the East River, and formerly a good residence neighborhood, largely settled by Quakers, was by this time changing to a tenement district. A few of the former well-to-do residents still lived in the central portion, but the population was now made up principally of mechanics, longshoremen, and sailors. In the eastern part of the ward were many crowded tenement houses of the newer type, but most of the tenement population lived in old-fashioned 2 or 3 story dwelling houses, not built for tenements. The population here was mainly Irish, with a sprinkling of other nationalities among the sailors and longshoremen.

The Tenth Ward, just to the north of the Seventh Ward, was at this time the one distinctively and exclusively German district in the city. Here this people had rushed in such numbers as to make it profitable for landlords to erect many new tenement houses, and fewer of the old, dilapidated houses were to be found here than in other quarters. The new tenant houses were said to be of pretty good character.

The Thirteenth Ward, to the east of the Tenth Ward, was densely crowded with the working classes, the majority of whom were Irish; Germans ranked next, and Americans last. Only one-fourth of the buildings were tenant houses. The ward showed a high rate of sickness and mortality, owing to the overcrowded and ill-ventilated dwellings and to the ignorant and careless habits of the people themselves.

To the north, from Rivington to Fourteenth street, in the Seventeenth and Eleventh wards, a German population was pressing in, rather more numerously in the part of the district adjoining the Tenth Ward northward to Seventh street and eastward to First avenue. East and north of here the Irish prevailed. The densely crowded Eleventh Ward contained probably a larger artisan population than any other district in the city. In the whole district old and new tenements were mingled and conditions were bad.

On the upper east side, as in the upper west side, well-to-do native residents were found toward the center of the city, while more foreigners were found in the streets nearer the river. From Fourteenth to Fortieth street the foreign population was mainly Irish or of Irish descent, packed in filthy tenements and of the most unclean and degraded personal habits.

Above Fortieth street squatter colonies, similar to those on the west side, were found, made up of Irish and Germans, and one is noted as far down as Thirty-ninth street and First avenue, where a slight eminence known as "Dutch Hill" sheltered the colony, and by its name indicated their nationality.

It will be observed from this general survey that the Irish were scattered pretty well over the city, while the Germans were largely packed into one or two crowded wards, where they formed a dense settlement of their own nationality, or were to be found in colonies among the squatter population; that in general the Irish were to be found rather more frequently on the west side, the Germans on the east.

Next to be considered are the social and moral aspects of the life of the foreign population thus widely distributed over the city. The tenement houses in which most of them found their homes were certainly little calculated to develop high social and moral types, and indeed brought to bear influences working directly the other way.

Physical devitalization led to moral degeneracy. The general lowering of vitality due to the foul air, darkness, and filth of the tenement is accompanied by a depression of spirits, a reduction of energy and ambition. The tenement dweller is not only incapacitated for work, but loses interest in it and in the progress of his family; resorts to strong drink to stimulate his system, while this in turn reduces his physical health still further and incites him directly to all kinds of vice and crime.

The state of physical and moral degradation brought about in the tenement house became so distinct a type that all observers and investigators remarked it, and some one of them in a flash of genius bestowed upon it the significant, if not elegant, name of "Tenant-house rot."

Dr. Griscom, as early as 1842, had called attention to the "depraved effects which such modes of life exert upon the moral feelings and habits;"[1] and the city inspector in 1851 remarks that "these overpopulated houses are generally, if not always, seminaries of filthiness, indecency, and lawlessness."[2]

---

[1] Annual Report of Interments, New York, 1842, p. 161.
[2] Annual Report of Interments, New York, 1851.

THE IMMIGRANT IN NEW YORK CITY. 459

Overcrowding of itself led to grave evils; and the whole set of influences at work in the tenement were well summed up by the well-known philanthropist, Mr. Charles L. Brace:

> In many quarters of the city family life and the feeling of home are almost unknown; people live in great caravansaries, which are hot and stifling in summer, disagreeable in winter, and where children associate together in the worst way. In many rooms privacy and purity are unattainable, and young girls grow up accustomed to immodesty from their earliest years. Boys herd together in gangs, and learn the practices of crime and vice before they are out of childhood. Even the laborers' families who occupy separate rooms in these buildings have no sense of home. They do not own the house nor any part of it, nor have any interest in it. All that valuable industry which in the country a mechanic or laborer applies in odd hours to his little homestead is here lost. The workman spends his leisure hours in the grogshops or at the corner groceries. The general effect of the system is the existence of a proletaire class, who have no interest in the permanent well-being of the community, who have no sense of home, and who live without any deep root in the soil, the mere tools of demagogues and designing men.[1]

For the existence of the tenement houses themselves, with all their evil influences, the immigrant, the landlord, and the city have to share the responsibility. It is plainly evident that the tenement houses were called into being by the heavy demands for housing made by the constant inpouring of great masses of immigrants, and overcrowding seemed to be an almost inevitable result of this demand, as the immigrants were very poor and land was dear in the city itself, while transportation facilities were not as yet so developed as to permit the city laborer to live in suburban districts where land was cheaper.

But the landlords were especially to blame for the ill consequences arising from the tenement houses, as they were, obviously, the ones who decided in what way and with habitations of what character the immigrants' demand for housing should be met. The immigrant himself was in no position to dictate terms. Poor, ignorant of the country, and with immediate need of shelter, he had to take what was provided for him by the landlord. And the landlord took the utmost advantage of the situation by charging the highest possible prices for the poorest possible accommodations, and disregarding every law of health and decency in erecting the big barracks meant for occupation by the poor.

Successive investigations of the housing system in New York agreed in showing the "greedy and mercenary landlord," rather than the helpless tenant, as the primary cause of tenement evils.

An inspector for the council of hygiene in 1864 thus reports the landlords' methods, with regard to repairs:

> Every expenditure of money which the law does not force them to is refused; and blinds half swung and ready to fall and crash with the first strong wind; doors long off their hinges, which open and shut by being taken up bodily and put out of or in the way; chimneys as apt to conduct the smoke into the room as out of it; stagnant, seething, overflowing privies, left uncleansed through the hot months of summer, though pestilence itself should breed from them; hydrants out of repair and flooding sink and entry; stairs which shake and quiver with every step as you ascend them; and all this day after day, month after month, year in and year out.

But the city, too, must bear a considerable share of the blame for bad tenement conditions, from its neglect to protect the community by adequate legislation against the consequences arising from the greed of landlords and the ignorance and poverty of tenants at a time when, in the first beginnings of the tenement system, legislation could easily have prevented evils which, once having come into being and become vested interests, it could not cure.

In considering the problem of immigration in New York City, another factor, however, has to be taken into consideration besides those already mentioned, namely, the especial characters of the different races represented in our immigration.

The Irish came among us in especially poor physical condition, owing to their miseries and misfortunes at home. This was particularly true of the immigration of the forties and fifties, which spread our tenement-house population beyond its former somewhat narrow quarters, throughout the extent of the city.

One reason why the Irish tenant would submit to crowding in the cities was because he was used to it at home. An architect, writing to the Irish Builder, says:

> The man or woman born in a cabin or garret will much prefer spending their lives in one room with their family, no matter how numerous, to the trouble of adjourning to separate apartments, unless, as I said before, example teaches them better, which is one great advantage in grouping dwellings. I have seen in Ireland a horse, 2 cows, 2 goats, grandmother, father and mother, brothers and sisters, an infant in a cradle, all in one apartment. There was an inner room with 2 bedsteads, one answered as a standing for firkins of butter, the other for seed potatoes. This was in many places in county Cork, and in Erris and Tyrawley. The late Lord George Hill, in his book Facts from Gweedore, mentioned the great difficulty he had in getting the tenantry to give up this gregarious method of living, and at night when the door of the house was shut the effects from want of ventilation on the health of all, man and beast, must be injurious. The disease known as the "head fall," which all but depopulated Tory Island, on the coast of Donegal, about 20 years ago, has been, not without some reason, ascribed to this cause.[2]

---

[1] Report A. I. C. P., 1878, p. 33.   [2] Report A. I. C. P., 1879, p. 53.

While all the foreign population showed a high sickness and death rate in New York City, that for the Irish was exceptionally high in comparison with other peoples, whether from their originally debilitated condition or from their exceptionally intemperate habits or from other causes.

Pauperism, it may be remembered, was the principal evil spoken of in that first complaint against immigration in 1819, which has already been quoted, and at that time the great mass of the paupers were Irish, as indeed has been the case ever since.

Most of the assisted paupers about whom so much complaint was made in the first half of the century just past, were from British and Irish almshouses; and as the Irish immigration was so much larger than the English, the Irish paupers were the most noticeable in their effect upon prevailing conditions. Besides the actual almshouse paupers there was a large class of Irish who, living at home such a hand-to-mouth existence, by irregular and ill-paid employment, were at any moment liable to slip from this precarious footing on the very verge of pauperism into pauperism itself, at any little circumstance of change or misfortune. Such a change did emigration prove to many of them, and the New York almshouses were filled with Irish paupers. It seemed, indeed, as if the burden of pauperism in New York had been transferred directly from Ireland, relieving that country in exact proportion to our additional load. It was pointed out that while the State of New York gave public aid to 346,518 persons in 1856, Ireland, with about double the population, in the same year gave relief to only 304,000 persons, and that the poor rates there were rapidly decreasing.[1]

Reports of the private charitable societies and public institutions show, in conclusive detail, the disproportionately high rate of pauperism shown by the Irish as contrasted with other nationalities.

It was noted in 1860 that—

> The almshouse returns show that about 86 per cent of the persons relieved by charitable aid are of foreign birth, of which 69 per cent were Irish and about 10 per cent German, or nearly 7 Irish to 1 German. As the Irish population, however, is nearly twice that of the German, the actual ratio is about 3½ Irish to 1 German, and 5 Irish to 1 American.[2]

In chronic pauperism, as contrasted with that temporary condition of want requiring relief into which any immigrant might fall while going through the process of industrial adjustment, the Irish were far in the lead. A confidential list published by one charitable society, of cases on their hands for 3 years and over, and giving names and addresses, showed that the great bulk of such cases were Irish. On this list, comprising 650 names, there were only 4 which could be recognized as distinctly German; of the rest, all might, and a great majority must, have belonged to persons of Irish birth or descent.

The Irish were especially hard drinkers, patronizing and conducting the numerous whisky shops in the city, while the Germans confined themselves largely to the milder lager beer.

And the Irish furnished an especially high proportion of the criminal class. The following table[3] shows this, and also the facts about pauperism above stated:

TABLE 3.

Born in—	New York City.		
	Population, 1855.	Relief granted, average of 6 years, 1854-1860.	Arrests for crime, 1859.
	Number.	Per cent.	Per cent.	Per cent.
United States	303,731	48	14.2	23
England, Scotland, and Wales	32,135	5	4.5	7
Ireland	175,775	28	69	55
Germany	95,986	15	10.8	10
All others foreign	22,287	4	1.5	5
	629,914	100	100	100

It will be noted that while the Irish made up only 28 per cent of the total population of the city, they constituted 69 per cent of those receiving charitable aid, and 55 per cent of those arrested for crime. The Germans were 15 per cent of the population, 10.8 per cent of the paupers, 10 per cent of the criminals. The English, Scotch,

---

[1] Report A. I. C. P., 1856, p. 29.
[2] Report A. I. C. P., 1860, p. 49.
[3] Compiled from data in report A. I. C. P., 1860, p. 49.

and Welsh, it is interesting to observe, fell below their proportion in the total population in respect to pauperism, but mounted above it in respect to crime.

It was said in 1864 that "as a class, the Germans and Swiss immigrants are among the most enterprising and prosperous; the English and Scotch rank next; while the Irish are less temperate and self-controlled than either."[1]

The most harrowing pictures of tenement-house life, and the worst conditions, as presented in various reports, were seen in Irish neighborhoods. The Sixth Ward, the worst in the city in the early part of the century, was almost entirely Irish. The one distinctively German ward of the period, the Tenth, adjoining the Sixth Ward, although densely crowded, was quiet, orderly, pleasant, and even in fairly good sanitary condition.

In an account of one example of notable cleanliness in a very dirty neighborhood presented by an inspector of the council of hygiene, it was noted that of the 64 families in the house only 2 were Irish. The rest were German.[2]

The German immigrants, as contrasted with the Irish, came here in good physical condition from healthy country districts, and a large proportion proceeded directly to the country. Those who remained here were industrious and hard-working and orderly, as has been seen—small contributors to the city's pauperism and crime.

There was a type among them, however, that was regarded with a good deal of disfavor by their contemporaries. These were the ragpickers or "chiffoniers," as they were called, and they appear and reappear in the various sanitary reports, from which we get much of our knowledge of tenement-house life. Dr. Griscom called attention to these "chiffoniers" in 1842 as a type introduced within the previous few years " whose persons, like their occupations, were the most degraded imaginable."[3] These were at that time to be found in considerable numbers plying their occupations along the streets, overturning the heaps of rubbish and filth in search of bits of paper, etc., or scraps of food thrown out of houses as garbage, which they either carry home to recook or eat upon the spot. Dr. Griscom seemed to think that these were importations from Paris, London, and other cities; but all indications go to show that most of them were country-bred Germans who had taken to this occupation through their frugal habit of saving and making use of every available bit of material, and had found their opportunity in the general prodigality of refuse dumped in great heaps and piles throughout the city.

Those that he spoke of plied their vocation along the streets; but many found their field in the big dumping grounds that grew up along the outskirts of the city, living in colonies near them. One such colony in the Eleventh Ward is thus described:

It is situated in the rear of Nos. — and — Sheriff street. The houses are of wood, 2 stories with attic and basement. The attic rooms are used to deposit the filthy rags and bones as they are taken from the gutters and slaughterhouses. The yards are filled with dirty rags hung up to dry, sending forth their stench to all the neighborhood and is exceedingly nauseous, operating upon me as an emetic. The tenants are all Germans of the lowest order, having no national or personal pride. They are exceedingly filthy in person and their bedclothes are as dirty as the floors they walk on. Their food is of the poorest quality, with their feet and heads, and doubtless their whole bodies, are anasarcous, suffering from what they call rheumatism, but which is in reality a prostrate nervous system, the result of foul air and inadequate supply of nutritious food. They have a peculiar taste for the association of dogs and cats, there being about 50 of the former and 30 of the latter. The whole number of apartments is 32, occupied by 28 families, numbering 120 in all, 60 adults and 60 children. The yards are all small and the sinks running over with filth. The owner of one-half of this row is ——, and of the other ——. The latter gentleman is a wealthy man and lives with his tenants in the rear, although he owns the front house; he prefers the filth because he thus saves some money. He buys and sells rags—a perfect "chiffonier." Not one decent sleeping apartment can be found on the entire premises and not one stove properly arranged. The carbonic-acid gas, in conjunction with the other emanations from bones, rags, and human filth, defies description. The rooms are 6 by 10 feet; bedrooms 5 by 6 feet. The inhabitants lead a miserable existence, and their children wilt and die in their infancy.[4]

A large part of the "shanty" or squatter population described in preceding pages was made up of this element. By 1860 the ends of streets from Fiftieth street to the Harlem were used as dumping grounds, and chiffoniers gathered along near them. The squatter colony at "Dutch Hill," Thirty-ninth street and First avenue, was one of these.

These people (at "Dutch Hill") find employment in the quarry and manure heap near their homes. They possess cows, swine, goats, and fowls in large numbers. The women, boys, and some of the men are "volunteer assistant to the city inspector." They may be daily seen with their carts drawn by themselves and their dogs; or, if fortune has more signally favored them, a rickety wagon, drawn by a decrepit horse with harness of somewhat primitive construction, facilitates their labors. Going from house to house they ransack the ash barrels and beg the swill and other kitchen refuse to supply food for their cows, pigs, and goats.[5]

But it is pleasant to note that these German ragpickers, though on so low a plane, as to daily habits and mode of life were really on the upward road.

---

[1] Report A. I. C. P., 1864, p. 21. [3] Annual Report of Interments, 1842, p. 377. [5] Report Council Hyg., p. 286.
[2] Report Council Hyg., p. 292. [4] Report Council Hyg., p. 177.

462   THE INDUSTRIAL COMMISSION:—IMMIGRATION.

Dr. Griscom, who had so severely condemned them, speaks of "the perseverance and frugality of this class of operatives," one of whom lately heard of had " by his daily trade   *   *   * amassed $400, which he was about investing in Western lands." "Hundreds of these people," he says further, "derive a good support from the business in this city."[1]

And the legislative committee of 1857, after commenting on the ragpicking colony on Sheriff street, says:

It is said that habits of economy and constant application to their wretched business enable nearly all, sooner or later, to accumulate sufficient funds to enable them to migrate to the West. We are told of a colony of 300 of these people who occupied a single basement,[2] living on offal and scraps, and who saved money enough to purchase a township on one of the Western prairies.[3]

In this circumstance, indeed—the fact that these people removed to the West as soon as they had saved up sufficient money to do so—is indicated one cause of the bad conditions that arise in cities on account of foreign immigration. The city acts like a sieve, letting through the physically sound, the energetic, and ambitious; keeping back the infirm, the very poor, and the lazy.

Many immigrants passed directly through the city to the interior, and these were of the best class; many, like these German chiffoniers, gave the city the benefit of their preparatory period of ignorance, poverty, and low standard of life, but betook themselves elsewhere when they had reached the higher stage of development in which they would have been of more value as citizens. And many more, coming here with debilitated physical constitutions, or without the mental or moral fiber needed for success anywhere, were unable or unwilling to go farther than the |great city they entered.

It had early occurred to those interested in bettering city conditions that one means of relief would be to assist migration to the interior, to country districts.

This means, indeed, was suggested at the very time the immigration problem itself was formulated in the report of the Society for the Prevention of Pauperism for 1819, already quoted from. The managers say:

It would prove a great relief could means of employment be found (for the immigrants) when they enter our city. Many thousands who arrive in this country from Europe have been servants or manufacturers, and do not understand the art of husbandry; yet many arrive in destitute condition who have worked on the soil. A great many others are vigorous, healthy, and capable of learning the art of agriculture. Could some communication be opened with our great farmers and landholders in the interior, and ways and means be provided for the transportation of able-bodied foreigners into the interior and labor be provided for them, it appears to the managers that beneficial consequences might flow from the expedient. Many, very many, foreigners who are honest and industrious and who, for want of employment, are liable to become paupers, would gladly depart into the country and labor upon the soil or in workshops could they thus obtain a bare living. In this case our city would be somewhat relieved, the number on our criminal calendar diminished, and the emigrant now on the brink of pauperism, or begging alms and receiving charitable aid, become useful to himself and to the community. Instead of bringing up his children in idleness, temptation, and crime he would see them amalgamated with the general mass of our population, deriving benefits from our school systems, our moral institutions, and our habits of industry.[4]

In accordance with this thought, many schemes looking to the ruralization of immigrants were tried, one after another.

The Germans, in large proportion, went directly to the interior; but the Irish seemed to find it especially difficult to get away from the seaboard cities or to be got away, and not only from their great numbers, but from their peculiar habits of life— their proneness to intemperance and violence, their improvidence and readiness to depend upon charitable aid—they were the heaviest burden the cities had to carry. It was remarked that—

They had an utter distaste for felling forests and turning up the prairies for themselves. They preferred to stay where another race would furnish them with food, clothing, and labor, and hence were mostly found loitering on the lines of the public works, in villages, and in the worst portions of the large cities, where they competed with the negroes—between whom and themselves there was an inveterate dislike—for the most degrading employments.[5]

By no means all of the Irish in the country were of this helpless, unenterprising class, however, and certain public-spirited men among them formed societies in New York, Philadelphia, and Baltimore early in the century to aid Irish immigrants in every way, but especially in procuring land in and removing to the West. These societies, in a memorial addressed to Congress asking for a grant of land in Illinois for settlement by Irish immigrants, set forth some of the drawbacks hindering the Irishman in his attempts to establish himself here, and urged that some assistance of the sort they asked would transform a class "regarded as burdensome to the settled inhabitants" of great cities into self-respecting, prosperous, and loyal citizens.

---

[1] San. Con. of Lab. Pop. in New York City; Dr. J. H. Griscom, 1845.
[2] Probably an exaggeration.
[3] Report New York State Com., 1857.
[4] Second Annual Report of Managers of Society for Prevention of Pauperism in City of New York, 1819.
[5] A. I. C. P. Report, 1860, p. 50.

This particular scheme was not carried through, owing to the failure of Congress to make the grant. Had it been made, however, it would have been interesting to see how far the natural individualism of the Irishman would have been overcome by such special inducements; to what extent the Irish would have been enticed from the cities by them, and what would have been the effect upon public health, pauperism, and crime in our cities to-day.

The New York State commission of emigration, at its establishment in 1847, opened a labor bureau, which, in their opinion, had considerable success. In 1850 they report finding employment for 8,000 persons. Much of the work of the bureau was done in placing labor in the country upon farms. Agencies were established in several places in New York and other States, by means of which farmers were supplied with laborers of both sexes. Private societies took up this sort of work also, but accomplished little. The experiment was fairly tried; neither friends nor patronage was lacking. The causes of their failure seemed to be, briefly, about as follows: The commissioners of emigration were already providing for the immigrant class—that portion of it, at least, who needed only a little help and direction to find their places in the industrial scheme—as far as this could be done. It was said that 20,000 persons were annually "provided, relieved, and forwarded" by them.[1] Other able-bodied laborers did not seem anxious to leave for the West. It was quite true that work in the city was liable to fail during part of the year. It was inevitable, then, that if the supply of labor was to be kept up during the busy season there must be some unemployed during the dull season. But the laboring classes seemed to prefer remaining in the city to take advantage of the busy times, living upon past earnings in the dull times. It was said—[2]

As a general fact all who are able and willing to work, and are careful to economize their earnings, can here (in New York City) find sufficient remunerative employment to carry them comfortably through the year, and in many cases do much more. Such persons, of course, will not let go a certainty for an uncertainty. Hence they are unwilling to emigrate, and they can not be coerced. And why should they be? Their attachments are centered here, where they can live comfortably; they are needed in the city, and are not likely to become a public charge.

It was also found impossible to send the needy, unemployed poor into the country. In the hard times of 1857 the charitable societies of the city sent out a circular to the unemployed poor, asking those of them who would accept situations out of the city to report their names to the societies; and another circular to employers, which was published widely through the State of New York and the Western States, appealing for employment of any kind for any class of workers.

As a result of these appeals, not an individual offered to go to the country, and not more than a dozen applications for labor were received from the country.

In 1859 a special inquiry into the matter of migration to country districts was made by the Association for Improving the Condition of the Poor, through their visitors and district secretaries, whose close acquaintance with persons and conditions would enable them to secure reliable and valuable information. They were asked to canvass their districts and find how many families having male heads, or how many individuals, both eligible and willing, could be found to go to the West, if means were provided. The inquiry embraced the entire county and city and included 9,281 families, containing 44,557 persons aided by the association; and out of this number not one case was reported by the secretaries as available to send to the country.

Another aspect of difficulty with regard to these schemes was that in drawing off from the city, as they proposed to do, those able to make their way in the country, leaving behind the permanent paupers, they would be increasing the burden of the city instead of lightening it; on the other hand, had they proposed to send the refuse population to the Western States, those States would have been justified in protesting against a scheme of relief for the city that simply meant shifting the burden to them.

The summing up of the whole matter seemed to be that emigration schemes were not likely to have any great effect in reducing pauperism, because those who could make use of the opportunities for labor afforded in the interior could either get there themselves or find work in the city; while those who made up the bulk of the strictly pauper class either would not go or would not be able to care for themselves if they did go.

The net result of all these adjustments and readjustments, this groaning and racking of the social framework in the stress of new conditions, was, after all, a remarkably rapid dispersion of foreign immigrants from the city. Statistical proof of this has to be got at somewhat indirectly for the period before 1850, when no account is given in the censuses of the foreign born in the population. It will be seen by the accompanying table that the immigration to the port for the first decade was larger than the entire growth of the city, including, of course, immigration of

---

[1] A. I. C. P. Report, 1861, p. 34.   [2] A. I. C. P. Report, 1861, p. 35.

the native born from country districts and natural increase by births, so that a considerable proportion of the immigration of this period must have gone elsewhere. It will also be seen, as perhaps is a little surprising, that the rate of dispersion appears to become more and more rapid in each succeeding decade. That is, while immigration in the decade 1820–1830 was not much greater than the total increase of population, in the decade 1830–1840 it was almost 4 times the increase of population, in 1840–1850 it was over 5 times, and in 1850–1860 over 6 times the increase. Dividing the decade 1840–1850, the same tendency is seen.

TABLE 4.—*New York City.*

Years.	Increase in population.	Immigration to the port.
1820–1830	78,883	92,884
1830–1840	110,121	407,716
1840–1850	202,837	1,146,241
1850–1860	298,122	1,994,640

TABLE 5.

Years.	Increase in population.	Immigration.
1840–1845	58,513	305,105
1845–1850	144,324	841,136

That is, immigration for the first half of the decade was a little over 5 times the increase of population; for the second half, almost 6 times.

This change in rate might, at first thought, be attributed to the growing stream of German immigration, the Germans being, as has been noted, more inclined to agricultural pursuits than the Irish, but this can hardly explain the whole matter.

TABLE 6.

Years.	Immigrants from—		Proportion of German to British and Irish.
	Great Britain and Ireland.	Germany and Prussia.	
1820–1830	81,827	7,729	1 : 10½
1831–1840	283,191	152,454	1 : 1¾
1841–1845	267,281	105,188	1 : 2½
1846–1850	750,482	329,438	1 : 2¼
1851–1855	930,664	647,273	1 : 1½

There is a great increase in the proportion of German to Irish immigrants from the decade 1820–1830 to 1830–1840, but there is a decrease in the next decade, and only a very slight increase for the five year periods following. This is not sufficient to account for the change.

The crude impression, then, that the less crowded a country the easier and more rapid is the dispersion of population, would seem to be quite the reverse of the truth. There was, apparently, a greater tendency for immigrants to remain in seaboard cities in 1817, when the interior was an untrodden wilderness, than in 1860. The fact seems to be (within limits and subject to modifications) that as the population increases and becomes more highly organized adjustment to the social framework and dispersion from cities become easier of accomplishment. Thus, in the first half of the nineteenth century the opening of the wilderness, the growth of manufacturing industries in interior towns and cities, the development of transportation and ways of communication by mail and telegraph, were all means of facilitating the passage of the emigrant from the place where his presence was not desired and his labor not especially needed to places where his presence was not particularly objected to and his labor was greatly needed.

SECOND PERIOD, 1871-1900.

It will be remembered (see table, p. 275) that in the decade from 1871-1900 arrivals of each of the three nationalities, Italian, Austro-Hungarian, and Russian, for the first time made up over 1 per cent of the total immigration, and from that time on increased until in the decade just passed (1890-1900) all together constituted about half of all immigrants.

The Austro-Hungarian group, and the Slavonic peoples comprised in the Russian group do not so especially concern New York City, for, while about three-quarters of all immigrants of these races land in New York, a large proportion of them pass directly to the interior. The following table, giving, from the immigration reports for the year 1899-1900, the numbers in the different Slavonic race groups, and of the Magyars, who claimed to be on their way to certain points inland or who were intending to remain in New York, shows to some degree the general tendency of the different groups to settle down at the port of entry. It will be noticed that the number of Bohemians and Moravians arriving in New York, as compared with the number of those races arriving at all ports who gave New York State as their destination is, approximately, as 3 to 1; of Poles as 4 to 1; of Ruthenians and Magyars as 5 to 1; of Lithuanians and Slovaks as 6 to 1; and of Croatians and Slovenians as 9 to 1.

TABLE 7.—*Destinations claimed by immigrants arriving year ending June 30, 1900.*

Races.	Arrivals at all ports.	Arrivals at port of New York.	States given as destinations.						
			New York.	Pennsylvania.	Illinois.	Ohio.	New Jersey.	Massachusetts.	Connecticut.
Magyars	13,777	11,353	2,435	5,198	287	1,583	2,712	117	788
Slavonic races.									
Bohemians and Moravians	3,060	2,329	776	139	841	317	39	42	28
Croatians and Slovenians	17,184	a 9,521	1,183	9,771	1,507	1,505	228	36	111
Lithuanians	10,317	9,170	1,699	3,699	1,658	97	505	1,331	736
Poles	46,938	36,835	9,363	15,671	4,911	1,410	3,977	4,748	2,428
Ruthenians	2,832	2,653	560	1,332	66	54	359	125	111
Slovaks	29,243	25,392	4,055	16,085	1,278	1,683	3,505	289	1,101

a Includes a few Dalmatians.

Of the Hebrew part of the Russian group, and of other Hebrews, not so large a proportion landed at the port of New York in 1899-1900 out of all arrivals as was the case with the Slavs and Magyars, but a very large proportion gave New York State as their destination. To give the exact figures, 73.3 per cent of all Hebrew arrivals at all ports landed at the port of New York, and 72 per cent of all Hebrew arrivals at all ports gave New York State as their destination. This means that a very large number of the Hebrew immigrants settle down at once in the city.

Of the third group—the Italians—no less than 97.4 per cent of the arrivals for 1899-1900 were received at the port of New York, and 54.5 per cent of the arrivals at all ports gave New York as their destination. It is said that many Italians who claim to be coming to New York do not stop in the city, but are reshipped here by bankers and railway ticket agents to distant points, so that the proportion of those who will settle down in the city should be set considerably lower than the number of arrivals for the State would indicate. On the other hand, many Italians who are reshipped in this way return to New York City as their headquarters in their intervals of idleness, and common observation shows a great crowding of Italians throughout the city.

By 1890 these newer peoples had become a considerable element in the city's population. In that year, according to the United States census, the foreign-born population of New York City made up 42.23 per cent of the total population, as compared with 39.68 per cent in 1880, and the numbers contributed by the different nationality groups presented in the chart and table of immigration are shown in the following chart and table for the two decennial periods:

Population in New York City born in leading countries.

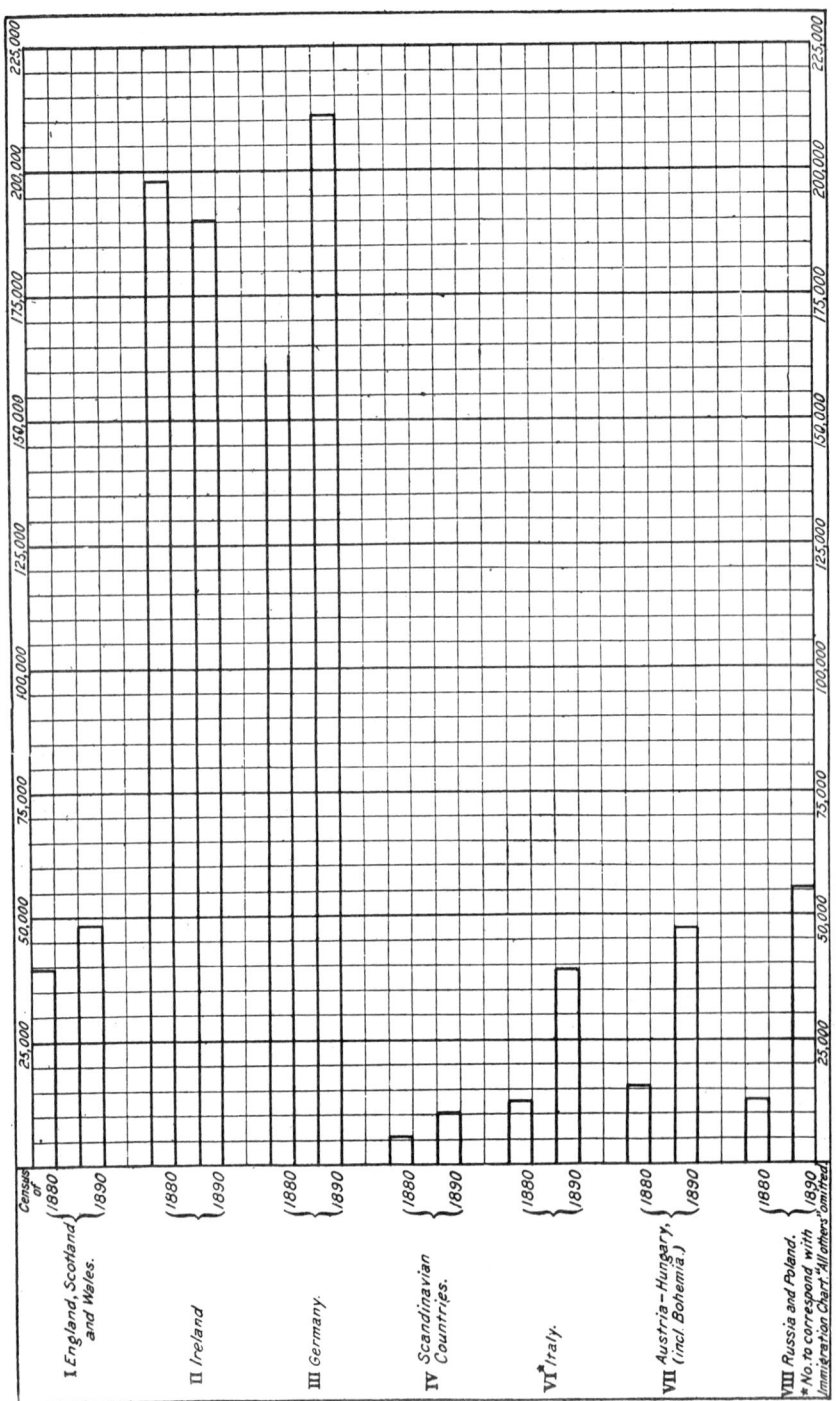

TABLE 8.—*Population in New York City.*

Born in—	Census of—	Population.
I. England, Scotland, and Wales	1880	39,276
	1890	48,114
II. Ireland	1880	198,595
	1890	190,418
III. Germany	1880	163,482
	1890	210,723
IV. Scandinavian countries	1880	5,183
	1890	10,139
VI.[1] Italy	1880	12,223
	1890	39,951
VII. Austria-Hungary (including Bohemia)	1880	16,937
	1890	47,514
VIII. Russia and Poland	1880	13,571
	1890	55,549

[1] Numbered to correspond with Immigration Chart—Class V, "all others," omitted.

It will be noticed that the Irish born have decreased both absolutely and relatively, and that the great German immigration of the eighties has by this time (1890) made the Germans the most numerous element in the foreign population. It will also be noticed how great was the percentage of increase, within the decade, of Italians, Austro-Hungarians, and Russians, and yet how very far any or all of these three groups were from reaching the numbers of either Irish or Germans. It will be noticed, too, how very small a part the Scandinavians played numerically in our foreign population, their energy and other striking characteristics leading us to regard them as more numerous than they really were.

Comparing the proportion each nationality bears to other nationalities in the city with the same proportion for the United States as a whole, it is seen that the city had more than its share of Germans, Irish, Russians, Italians, Austrians, Hungarians, and French, and less than its share of English, Scotch, Scandinavians, Canadians, Bohemians, Poles, Swiss, Chinese, Dutch, and Welsh. (See following table.)

TABLE 9.—*Foreign born, by nationalities, census of 1890.*

Nationalities.	Per cent of foreign born in New York City.	Per cent of foreign born in United States.	Nationalities.	Per cent of foreign born in New York City.	Per cent of foreign born in United States.
All foreign countries	100	100	Scandinavians	1.58	10.09
Germans	32.93	30.11	British-American	1.31	10.61
Irish	29.76	20.23	Bohemians	1.27	1.28
Russians (Hebrews)	7.62	1.97	Poles (Slavs and Hebrews)	1.06	1.59
Italians	6.24	1.98	Swiss	.77	1.13
English	5.64	9.83	Chinese	.32	1.15
Austrians	4.25	1.33	Dutch	.22	.88
Hungarians	1.91	.68	Welsh	.22	1.08
Scotch	1.76	2.62	All others	1.56	2.22
French	1.65	1.22			

To get an idea of the full extent of foreign influence in the city, however, native-born children of foreign parentage must be taken into account. This class shows foreign characteristics to a greater or less degree, from the young child of immigrant parents who came here after marriage—practically a foreigner in all essential respects—to the adult who has been reared in an American community and was born of parents who, perhaps, themselves came here in childhood and were to a great extent Americanized by the time their children were born.

Making this distinction, the population of New York City in 1890 was divided as follows:

TABLE 10.

		Per cent.
Foreign-born whites	636,986 =	42
Native whites of foreign parentage	582,154 =	38
Total foreign element	1,219,140 =	80
Native whites of native parentage	270,487 =	18
Colored (including Chinese)	25,674 =	2
	1,515,301 =	100

The foreign element in New York in 1890, then, made up four-fifths of its population, while the strictly native element was less than one-fifth.

These classes were divided as to age as follows:

TABLE 11.

General nativity.	Per cent under 5 years.	Number under 5 years.	Number 5 years and over.
Total population	11	164,686	1,350,615
Foreign-born whites	.9	6,001	630,985
Native-born whites, one or both parents foreign	19.7	114,808	467,346
Native-born whites, both parents native	15.6	42,185	228,302
Colored (including Chinese)	6.6	1,692	23,982

And by sexes as follows:

TABLE 12.

General nativity.	Per cent of males.	Number of males.	Number of females.
Foreign white	49.4	314,481	322,505
Native white of foreign parents	49.1	285,992	296,162
Native white of native parents	49.8	134,457	136,030

It will be observed that females predominate in all three classes. Among foreign immigrants in general males predominate, and it would be expected that in the foreign population of the city males would also predominate. As a matter of fact, however, not only are females in excess of males for this class, but in greater excess than in the class of native whites of native parentage, which may be assumed to show the normal proportion for a city population of males to females.

This is accounted for, it may be supposed, by the presence of a great army of female domestic servants in the city. An indication that this supposition is the correct one is seen in the fact that when the proportion of males to females in each general nativity class is given by wards, the wards below Fourteenth street, where there is comparatively little employment of domestic servants, and where foreign residents are settled in homes of their own or lodging places, show without exception a surplus of foreign-born males; while the wards above Fourteenth street, where there is, it is true, a considerable foreign resident population, but where the bulk of the domestic service is employed, show equally without exception, until the suburban Twenty-third and Twenty-fourth wards are reached, a surplus of foreign-born females.

The following table shows how all three classes of the population are divided by sexes above and below Fourteenth street, respectively:

TABLE 13.—*Population of New York City. Census of 1890.*

General nativity.	Per cent of males.	Number of males.	Number of females.
Below Fourteenth street.			
Foreign white	52.2	141,326	128,272
Native white, foreign parents	50.7	106,073	103,777
Native white, native parents	52.5	32,091	29,337
Total, excluding colored	51.8	279,490	261,386
Above Fourteenth street.			
Foreign white	46.7	160,515	182,571
Native white, foreign parents	48.3	164,864	176,488
Native white, native parents	48.8	92,806	97,410
Total, excluding colored	47.8	418,185	456,469

It is here seen that in the uptown and downtown groups as well as in the whole city, the other two classes of population show the same preponderance of one sex or the other as the foreign born. For all classes males predominate downtown and females uptown—the downtown districts containing a large working population of single men and also a large "floating element" making their headquarters in lodging houses.

It is also seen, incidentally, how much greater is the proportion of foreign born to the total population in the downtown than in the uptown wards. In the wards below Fourteenth street the foreign born were about one-half of the population, the native born of foreign parentage about three-eighths, and the native born of native parentage about one-eighth; above Fourteenth street, foreigners were a little less than two-fifths, native born of foreign parentage also a little less than two-fifths, and natives of native parentage somewhat more than one-fifth.

Something as to the degree of social assimilation reached by any given race element in the total "foreign element" may be seen from a comparison of the numbers among them of the first generation, of the second generation, and of those of the second generation who have one native and one foreign parent.

The proportion of the second generation to the first is some indication of the length of time that the given nationality-element has been in the country, or of the degree in which they have become permanent settlers here; while the proportion of children arising from marriage between native and foreign parents is an indication of race tendency to amalgamate with the people already in possession of the country.

The following tables give the absolute numbers and percentages of these different classes in New York City in 1890:

TABLE 14.—*Population of New York City, 1890.*

[Numbers.]

	Born in.	Both parents born in.	Born in United States.			Total foreign element.
			Native mothers, fathers born in.	Native fathers, mothers born in.	Total, one or both parents born in.	
England and Scotland	48,114	17,593	11,238	6,144	34,975	83,089
Ireland	190,418	176,176	24,024	15,512	215,712	406,130
Germany	210,723	177,174	31,217	7,586	215,977	426,700
Scandinavian countries	10,139	2,300	580	199	3,079	13,218
Italy	39,951	14,068	752	103	14,923	54,874
Bohemia	8,099	4,060	99	64	4,223	12,322
Hungary	12,222	3,372	220	27	3,619	15,841
Russia	48,790	18,373	808	134	19,315	68,105
Mixed foreign parents		38,321				

TABLE 15.—*Population of New York City, 1890.*

[Percentages.]

	Born in.	Born in United States.				Per cent of those born in United States.		
		Both parents born in.	Native mothers, fathers born in.	Native fathers, mothers born in.	One or both parents born in.	Both parents foreign.	Native mothers, fathers born in.	Native fathers, mothers born in.
England and Scotland	57.9	21.2	13.5	7.4	42.1	50.3	32.1	17.6
Ireland	47	43.4	5.9	3.7	53	81.5	11.2	7.3
Germany	49.5	41.5	7.3	1.7	50.5	82	14.5	3.5
Scandinavian countries	76.7	17.4	4.4	1.5	23.3	74.5	19	6.5
Italy	72.8	25.6	1.4	.2	27.2	94	5.3	.7
Bohemia	65.7	32.9	.8	.6	34.3	96	2.5	1.5
Hungary	77.2	21.3	1.3	.2	22.8	93	6.3	.7
Russia	71.7	27	1.1	.2	28.3	95	4.3	.7

The highest proportion of the first to the second generation is shown by the Hungarians, Scandinavians, Italians, and Russians, in the order named, the first generation being above 70 per cent for all. This is due, obviously, to the newer incoming of these four classes; but it is worthy of notice that the Russians, the very latest arrivals, have the largest proportionate population of any of the four groups, showing that permanent settlement in families begins for them earlier than for the others. The Italians, however, the next latest comers, follow closely in the percentage of the second generation, showing that with them, too, family life begins within a reasonable period of their coming here as immigrants. The Irish and Germans, as our oldest immigrants, show the largest proportion of the second generation, the Irish standing above the Germans in this regard, as coming earlier, and diminishing of late years more rapidly in volume of immigration.

Of the second generation by far the greater proportion for all races had both parents foreign, of the same race. As would be expected, this proportion is high for the newest races, Russians, Italians, and Hungarians, in the order named. The highest proportion of all, however, is shown by the Bohemians, although these people, from longer residence here, show a larger proportion of the second generation than the three peoples just named. This is a curious bit of testimony to the peculiar exclusiveness or clannishness with which these people are charged. Notwithstanding longer acquaintance with the country, Bohemians living here will marry with Bohemians in higher proportion than Russians with Russians or Italians with Italians.

In this table is to be noted the greater proportion of offspring from native mothers and foreign fathers than from native fathers and foreign mothers. The foreigner in general is on a lower social and economic plane than the native, and in general females are less inclined to marry into a lower social plane than are men; but in this case the preponderance of males in foreign immigration has brought a pressure to bear that has broken over that reluctance, and we see marriages of native women and foreign men from twice to nine times as frequent (according to races) as marriages of native men and foreign women. And, naturally, the preponderance of the former class is greater the newer the immigration.

The following table shows how the different nationalities were distributed throughout the city in 1890:

TABLE 16.—*Population of New York City, mother born in specified countries. Census of 1890.*

	Ireland.	Germany.	Italy.	Russia and Poland.	Hungary.	Bohemia.	United States (white).
Total—New York City.	399,348	403,784	54,334	80,235	15,555	12,287	334,725
Ward.							
I	5,911	1,983	66	63	20		1,727
II	384	192	2	2	2		204
III	1,568	819	46	20	5	3	863
IV	8,267	1,847	2,827	580	30	2	2,339
V	6,363	2,445	630	49	16	2	1,823
VI	4,508	2,155	9,863	3,245	32	4	1,219
VII	21,818	6,878	658	16,295	128	16	7,864
VIII	9,625	5,190	6,066	272	42	13	5,905
IX	18,293	7,634	390	202	7	7	19,530
X	2,173	14,402	225	30,476	313	1	2,780
XI	6,668	32,171	373	3,149	7,708	1,102	9,260
XII	58,721	63,291	7,436	1,954	794	843	75,625
XIII	5,396	12,821	139	13,190	1,702	37	4,692
XIV	7,258	3,112	12,821	803	54	14	2,588
XV	4,655	3,472	3,134	281	67	24	6,102
XVI	17,601	6,256	445	185	57	20	14,646
XVII	10,815	58,831	1,665	5,673	2,511	1,021	12,906
XVIII	23,373	15,502	794	267	74	90	15,692
XIX	61,858	80,288	1,939	2,081	1,499	7,944	47,660
XX	28,922	20,018	1,160	373	95	36	17,578
XXI	26,606	9,102	816	402	134	713	16,253
XXII	51,605	33,325	1,499	399	177	34	44,072
XXIII	10,571	19,323	836	189	45	324	16,216
XXIV	6,389	2,724	511	85	43	37	7,181

The accompanying maps [1] show, by different degrees of shading, the different degrees of density reached by the classes of population shown in the above table, but by smaller divisions of area, the sanitary district being taken as the unit in the maps instead of the ward, as in the table.

Of special interest is a comparison between the Irish map, the German map, and the map showing native whites of native parentage. The Irish and German groups are approximately of the same size, the German group being some 4,500 the larger; the group of native whites of native parentage is somewhat smaller than either, falling some 65,000 below the Irish. No other group given, however, approaches the first two so closely in size or can be used as so good a parallel.

---

[1] Map I, population, native white of native parentage; Map II, population born of Irish mothers; Map III, population born of German mothers; Map IV, population born of Italian, Russian, Hungarian, and Bohemian mothers.

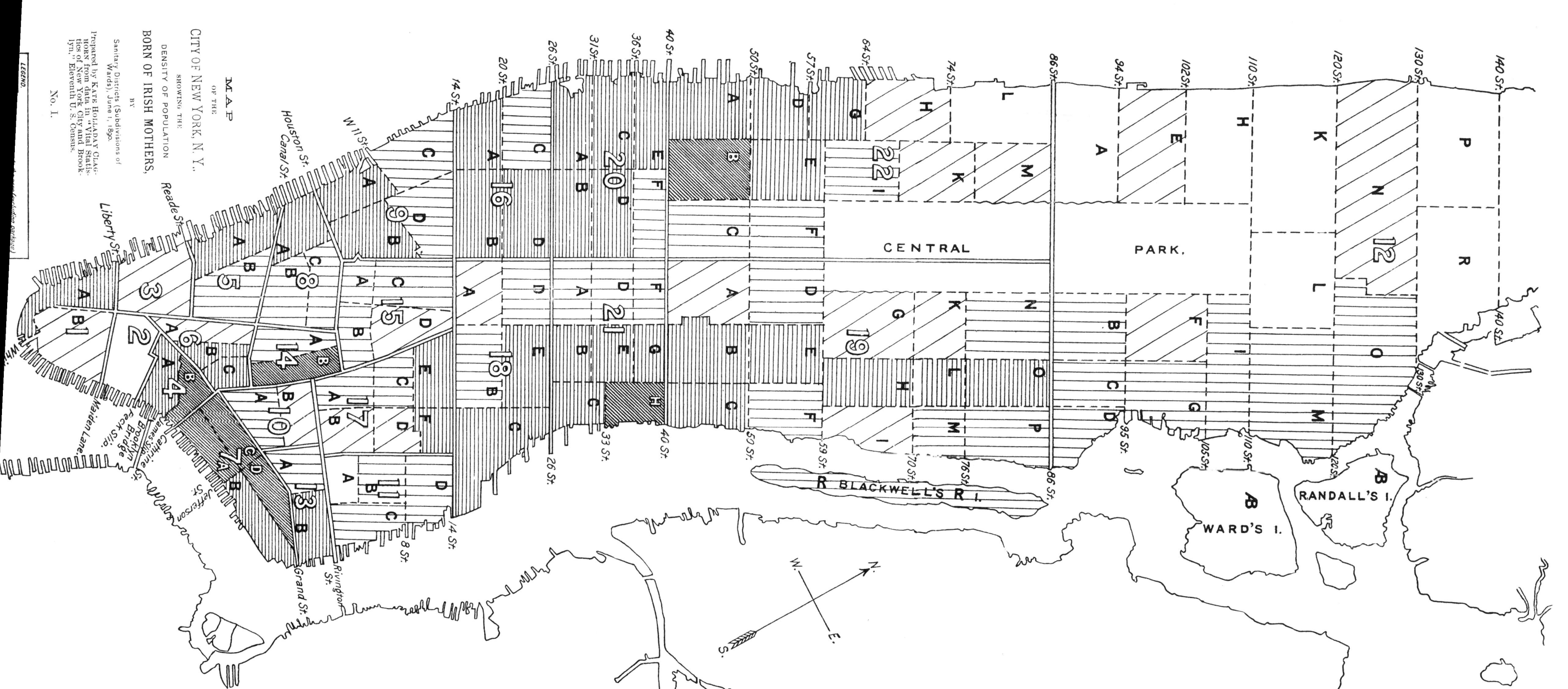

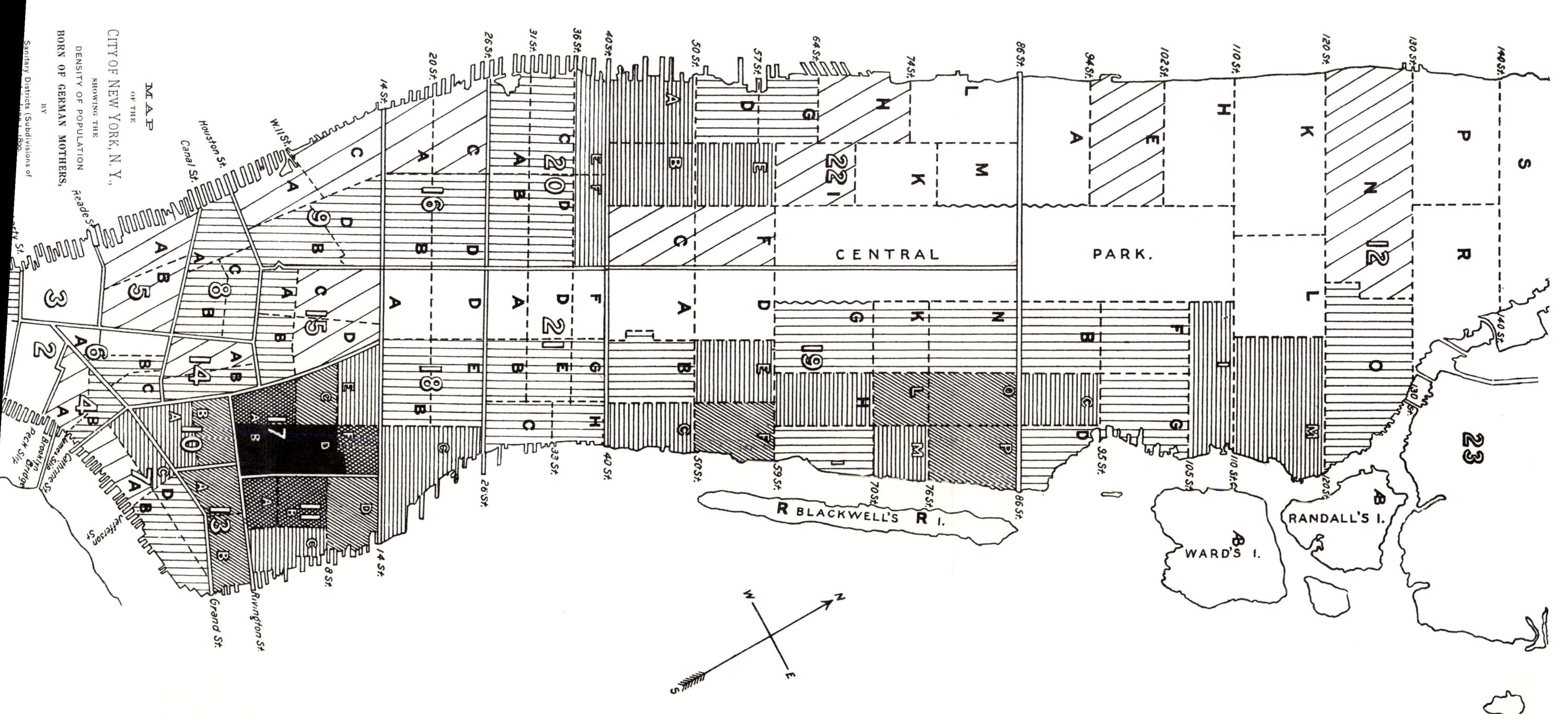

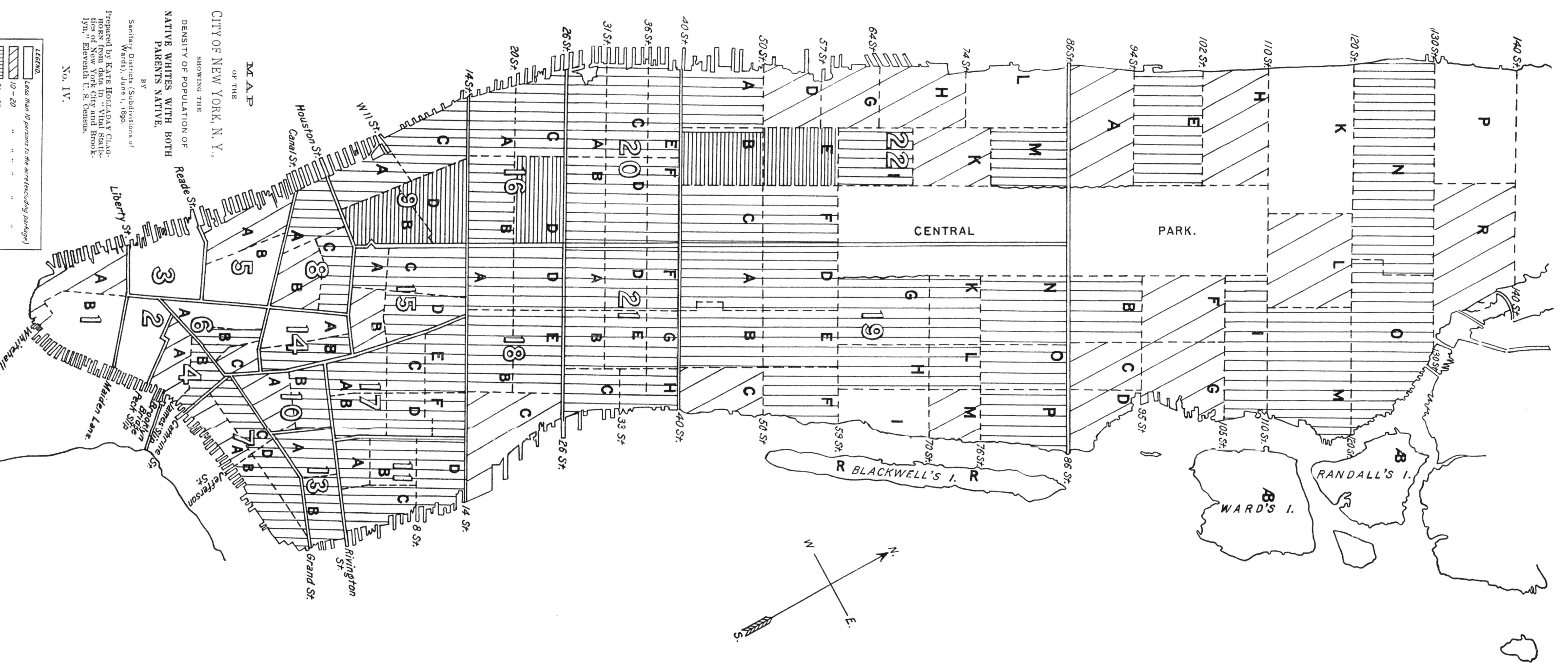

THE IMMIGRANT IN NEW YORK CITY. 471

Turning to the maps it is seen that the native whites of native parentage are distributed over the city with remarkable evenness, and at low degrees of density. In no district are they to be found above the fourth degree of the scale employed (50–100 to the acre). A striking feature of this map is the large proportion of the strictly native element it reveals in the downtown districts, when the heavy overlaying of foreign density, which otherwise conceals them from view, is taken away. In the Seventh, Eleventh, Thirteenth, and Seventeenth wards, even in the densely foreign Tenth Ward, in parts of the Fourth, Sixth, and Fourteenth wards, in the Eighth, Ninth, and Fifteenth, all below Fourteenth street, native whites of native parentage are found as numerously as anywhere uptown.

The Irish element are also distributed quite evenly throughout the city, but, with an additional 65,000 of population to be placed, are found in a larger number of districts in that fourth degree of density which is the highest reached by the native whites of native parentage, and in 6 districts are found in the fifth degree of density employed, showing a population of 100 to 200 to the acre.

The Germans, with a population of about the same size as the Irish, do not nearly so completely cover the map. They are massed closely in certain districts, and in others are scarcely found at all. In certain districts a sixth and even a seventh degree of density (showing a population of over 300 to the acre) has to be employed to represent their congestion.

The table and maps are based upon data given in the Eleventh Census Report, "Vital Statistics of New York City and Brooklyn," and the parts dealing with the foreign element give the separate race elements by birthplaces of mothers, a classification which includes all of the foreign born of a given nationality, all of the native born with both parents foreign, and all of the native born with foreign mothers and native fathers. It thus corresponds to the total foreign element presented in previous tables, with the comparatively small class of native born with native mothers and foreign fathers omitted.

In the Irish and German maps it will be noticed how the Irish and German population has pressed up along the upper East and West Side since 1864, especially up the East Side, and that the German population has taken especial hold in the former district, the Irish in the latter.

It will be noticed also how much less thickly settled the Irish are in their old haunt, the Sixth Ward, than in some other localities, as, for instance, the Tenth, Seventh, and Fourteenth wards, on the West Side just above Fortieth street and on the East Side just below that street. And the Germans are found to be less numerous in their original district, the Tenth Ward, than they are in the Seventeenth, just above, or in the lower part of the ward—their first point of settlement—as in the upper.

Both Irish and Germans, in fact, show the results of pressure by newer people.

Turning to the map showing these newer races, it is seen that the Italians, who were shown in 1864 to have taken up their quarters in the Sixth ward, are by this time more numerous in both the Sixth and the Fourteenth than the Irish. They also fill the upper part of the Fourth Ward (along Roosevelt, James, and Oliver streets, an old Irish neighborhood) almost as numerously as the Irish.

They are found, too, in the West Side tenement district below Fourteenth street, described in preceding pages. Here they form another "quarter," in streets formerly occupied by negroes and Irish, along Thompson, Sullivan, Grand, Broome, and Houston streets. On the map is to be seen the beginnings of a new Italian quarter, in a spot unsettled in 1864, away uptown, in Harlem, that has come to be known as "Little Italy." In this district, which centers about One hundred and tenth street, at this time more Irish and many more Germans than Italians were to be found.

The Russians and Poles—practically all Hebrews—are seen with the lower Tenth Ward—one of their points of first settlement—as a densely packed center, spreading out from there on all sides. They have fairly driven the Germans out of the lower Tenth Ward, and are pressing closely upon them, at this time, to the north. They are also found thickly settled across the Bowery in the Sixth Ward, and across Division street in the Seventh, where in one district they are as numerous as the Irish. No uptown Jewish district is shown on this map, although the table indicates that quite a number, in absolute figures, were to be found in the Nineteenth Ward, on the East Side, between Fortieth and Eighty-sixth streets.

East of Avenue B, in the Eleventh and part of the Thirteenth wards, were to be found many Hungarians, with East Houston street as their center. A considerable proportion of these were Jews, thus adding to the Jewish character of the district.

The only representatives of the Slavonic races that could be represented as distinctly such on the map—on account of the confusion of races in the census classification—were the Bohemians. A few of these are seen on the East Side, above Rivington and Houston streets, mingled with Russian Jews and Hungarians, but their distinctive neighborhood was in the upper East Side.

These maps show clearly the tendency of races to segregation noticed 30 years before. The Italians are seen mainly in former Irish districts, the Hebrews in former German districts; and wherever these newer peoples came the older races began to move out. The Hungarians and Bohemians, too, are gathered into compact groups, and other smaller groups of different nationalities could be shown in like manner.

The Hebrews and Italians, however, of the newer races coming in, are, it may be recalled, the ones especially important with regard to their influence upon city conditions.

The little handful of Italians that made up the immigration from Italy in the earlier decades were mainly a vagabond but harmless class of organ grinders, ragpickers, bear leaders, and the like. Italians of this type were remarked in the Sixth Ward as early as 1864 as noticeable elements of the population, in the report of the council of hygiene, which does not mention their presence in any other district.

This ward and the Fourteenth, just above it, were apparently the first Italian districts. In the latter ward, near its northern boundary, just below Houston street, was a little colony worth glancing at in passing. This was in Jersey street, already described, in 1864,[1] as an exceptionally offensive neighborhood, thickly settled by the very poor, three-fourths of whom were negroes. The houses in the street were then very old, built of wood, and much out of repair.

By 1879 the street was swarming with Italians of the ragpicker class. Their way of life was thus described:[2]

* * * Here (in the yard of No. 5 Jersey street) on lines strung across were thousands of rags hung up to dry; on the ground piled against the board fences rags mixed with bones, bottles, and papers; the middle of the yard covered with every imaginable variety of dirt. * * * We then turned to go into the cellars, in which was a large and a small room. Opposite the door stood a stove, upon which meat was being cooked; to the right stood a bedstead roughly constructed out of boards; in the left-hand corner a similar one. The small room contains another. These board bunks were covered with 3 or 4 army blankets, and would each accommodate 4 men. There was no other furniture in the room, which was so dark that we could only see by waiting till the eyes became accustomed to the light. There was scarcely standing room for the heaps of bags and rags, and right opposite to them stood a large pile of bones, mostly having meat on them, in various stages of decomposition. * * * Notwithstanding the dense tobacco smoke, the smell could be likened only to that of an exhumed body. There were 9 men in the room at the time of our visit, but a larger number occupy the room.

It is a bit of testimony to the sturdy physical constitution of these people that even in such surroundings the inspector "met with no sickness excepting one case of whooping cough and a number afflicted with rheumatism."

Another picture of this colony, as it was in 1884, is as follows:

In Jersey street exist two courtyards. * * * Six 3-story houses are in each. These houses are old and long ago worn out. They are packed with tenants, rotten with age and decay, and so constructed as to have made them very undesirable for dwelling purposes in their earliest infancy. The Italians who chiefly inhabit them are the scum of New York chiffoniers, and as such saturated with the filth inseparable from their business. * * * The courtyard swarms with, in daytime, females in the picturesque attires of Genoa and Piedmont, moving between the dirty children. The abundant rags, paper, sacks, barrows, barrels, washtubs, dogs, and cats are all festooned overhead by clothes-lines weighted with such garments as are only known in Italy. Sorting is chiefly done indoors, but at times a ragpicker may be seen at his work in any convenient spot to be had. * * * In each yard live 24 families (nominally only, because lodgers here as elsewhere are always welcome), paying rents of from $6 to $9 monthly for 2 rooms, the inner one being subdivided by a partition consisting perhaps of a simple curtain, and measuring when so arranged about 5 by 6 feet each.[3]

The surroundings and habits of these people might be filthy, but as to their general character the earlier report says:[4]

Jersey street at first sight looks like a pestilence-breeding, law-breaking colony. A more intimate acquaintance with it, and a few words with one or two white and colored inhabitants, confirmed the first but not the second impression; no more peaceable, thrifty, orderly neighbors could be found than these Italians. They do not beg, are seldom or never arrested for theft, are quiet; though quick to quarrel among themselves, are equally ready to forgive. The officer on duty mentioned that this colony, numbering perhaps 200 Italian families, can not be matched by any similar number of corresponding social condition in New York City for their law-abiding qualities. He seems quite proud of them.

Lower down in the ward, on Crosby street, another colony of Italians was mentioned in 1879. Here will be seen the mingling of the newer Italian immigrants with the older Irish; the Italians, as the economically inferior race, occupying the rear tenements, and the Irish, as the product of longer years of tenement-house living, showing, one would infer from the description, an even deeper degree of filth and certainly of moral degradation than the Italians.

No. — Crosby street is a very low class of tenement house, bearing a bad reputation. The visitor for the section stated that it was the worst house and inhabited by the worst people he had ever met with, and that having refused relief to some of the tenants, he was afraid to enter it. * * * Four buildings, 2 front and 2 rear, each 6 stories high, stood separated by a yard about 20 feet in width. * * *

---

[1] Report of council of hygiene.
[2] Report of New York Association for Improving the Condition of the Poor, 1879, p. 64.
[3] Report of Association for Improving the Condition of the Poor, 1884, p. 43.
[4] Report of Association for Improving the Condition of the Poor, 1879, p. 64.

The rearbuildings are occupied exclusively by Italians, all ragpickers, the front by Irish and a few Germans. An investigation of the front house revealed a shocking amount of dirt; in some instances the floors were invisible under the refuse and garbage. One family represented the mother as out of work, though I afterwards learned she was in her bedroom drunk, while the youngest daughter, half nude, was sitting on the floor, fairly surrounded with dirt, and the eldest, as she answered my questions, held her hand over her nose, which I could see was bruised and bleeding. The odor from the room was sickening. Learning that the cellar was used for ragpickers * * * I made an inspection. The cellar is divided into 21 compartments * * * containing more or less rags, bones, old papers, bottles, placed here before being taken to the rear dwelling to be assorted. * * * Large spaces, not subdivided, contained immense heaps of what even the ragpickers refuse. * * * In summer the stench is unbearable. The cellars in the rear house are also used for ragpickers' stores. I could glean but little information, as scarcely any of the Italians could utter a word of English.

By 1880 the Fourteenth Ward contained so many Italians that it was spoken of familiarly as "New Italy."[1] Italians had also come into the Fourth Ward, in Roosevelt street,[2] and were crowding more and more thickly in the Sixth. A large proportion of these early Italian immigrants were men without their families, and we hear of them most frequently as crowded together in lodgings of the character described in Jersey street.[3] There was little pauperism among these people, if we may judge from the relative infrequency of Italian cases appearing in the reports of private charitable societies. It was noted that they were a class of people who worked and paid their rent.[4]

During these years the itinerant class—ragpickers, organ grinders, and the like— which predominated in the earliest Italian immigration, was being replaced by another class—the stable element of the population in the home country—the steady, industrious peasantry whom only extreme poverty induced to break the bonds attaching them to their native land. Called here by the industrial expansion of the country after the civil war, this class came as unskilled day laborers, were taken charge of in masses by Italian bankers and padroni, and sent hither and thither as occasion was found for their labor. New York City has been and is the headquarters of this class. As has been remarked, 97 per cent of all Italian immigrants to this country now land at the port of New York. Some proceed directly to other parts of the country, but a very large proportion find their agents or employers in New York City, are kept in the city until their services are required in some other part of the country, and return to the city in dull seasons, to be maintained, perhaps, by the contractor until other employment can be found, or at any rate to be on the spot when employment is offered.

The newer immigrants of this class are mainly men without families, either unmarried or having left their families at home, and many of them return year by year to Italy in the dull season with the money they have earned here. But after a few years of this the family is either brought over or the "cafone" marries and settles down here, becoming a permanent member of the community. This statement may seem a little too positive and definite, in view of the fact that the opposite claim is so often made, and that little or no statistical evidence can be offered in proof of the assertion. But too many bits of circumstantial evidence combine to substantiate this to be ignored—the increasing number of women in the immigration record, everyday observation as to the increase of women and children in Italian districts, the personal acquaintance of charitable workers with many family histories, observation by social students of life in Italy itself—all these produce the strongest possible impression that the Italian day laborer after a few years of taking himself most considerately off the hands of the city when he has no work to do, settles down here, when he has enough money to carry him through the year, with wife and family.

There is another class of Italian immigration, not so numerous as the former, but still of considerable importance. This is the class that in this country makes up the great army of barbers, bootblacks, fruiterers, and shoemakers in our cities and towns. These are, some of them, of the "cafone" class at home, but in general they are from cities and small towns in Italy, and have been engaged in some sort of commercial pursuit there. There is absolutely no doubt about this class being a permanent population; and it may be observed that their business success is notable, and that they have brought their trades generally to a higher level than that in which they found them. The Italian fruit peddler bestows a considerable amount of his inherited racial art sense in "composing" his wares to form an attractive picture; the Italian barber pays considerable attention to the attractiveness of his place; the Italian bootblack is not the little ragged urchin of yesterday with battered box and a shrill velocity of motion, but a well-kept looking individual anywhere from 15 to 30 years of age, with a regularly established place of business, ranging from the throne-like arm chair and umbrella to the regular shop as well kept as the barber's. There are bootblacks who make from $10 to $15 a day. The Italian shoemaker lags behind in this list, being of the old-fashioned cobbler type.

---

[1] Report of Association for Improving the Condition of the Poor, 1880, p. 12.
[2] Report of Association for Improving the Condition of the Poor, 1879, p. 67.
[3] Report of Association for Improving the Condition of the Poor, 1884, p. 10 et al.
[4] Report of Association for Improving the Condition of the Poor, 1886, p. 51.

There are, besides, many Italian watchmakers, bakers, confectioners, keepers of cafés and ice-cream saloons, wine dealers, grocers, dry-goods dealers, and many in other businesses. About 400 persons are employed in macaroni factories. There are also many tailors working for Jews, and cigar and cigarette makers. Some are to be found in department stores; and some, having found politics a remunerative calling, are found in the street-cleaning department and on the police force.

Still another element of the Italian population, not a very large one, however, is made up of persons of a higher social grade at home—young men of the upper and lower middle classes who have been either fully or in part prepared to enter some profession, or government office, and who can not find opportunity to do so. Conditions in Italy are such that this class is a large and growing one there. Such young men are not willing to work at anything but professional employment at home, but in a strange land they are willing to turn their hands to anything; even common day labor that will give them daily bread. Individuals of this class are to be found then among those of the two others, and in many cases, after a short period of work in this way, the worker finds his way to a more suitable position. This class, however, is the most difficult to provide for in the city, if they insist upon having the work which they have regarded as corresponding to their social standing. There is abundant opportunity for the unskilled day laborer, or for the tradesman, but the average educated European finds himself at a serious disadvantage in competition with Americans for the better grade of commercial or professional positions.

These are the main elements in the Italian city population. Skilled workmen from the north of Italy in large numbers go directly to the interior as marble-cutters, miners, mill hands, etc. There are, however, some 2,000 workers in marble and mosaic, and many mechanics, masons, stonecutters, bricklayers, carpenters, and cabinetmakers in New York City. Italian cabinetmakers are found largely in the piano factories.

The day laborers and the poorer part of the tradespeople are found with much the same habits as to daily life that were noted in the rag-picking class. They are not distinguished, as a class, for especial neatness and cleanliness. They live in close quarters, with bad air and little light, with 2 to 4 rooms to a family. Sometimes two families will live in 2 or 3 rooms.

All classes are highly industrious, thrifty, and saving. They are strict in keeping to their agreements; always pay their rent, doctors' bills, and lawyers' fees. They are considered very desirable tenants. In an earlier period little money was spent by this people on drink and vicious pursuits; but more lately considerable intemperance, gambling, and vice are to be seen in Italian quarters.

The tradespeople prosper rapidly. The Italian barber enlarges his shop, perhaps finally sells out and becomes a banker; the fruit peddler buys a little shop, then a big one, and may finally become a wealthy importer; and in like manner with the other shopkeepers.

The more ambitious and successful among them move to the suburbs and become property owners in Long Island City, Flushing, Corona, Astoria, etc.

The day laborer can not be said to make notable progress in the first generation. He succeeds well enough, however, it is said, to get out of the clutches of the padroni after 3 or 4 years' residence here.

In all classes the Italian of the first generation is somewhat slower than some other races to take on the habits and customs of the people he has come among. Italians are distrustful of other races and even of those of their own race who are not of their province. Notwithstanding the abuses of the padroni, Italians can not be induced to accept employment through other means. And in their colonies they gather in provincial groups. For instance, in the Mulberry Bend district are to be found Neapolitans and Calabrians mostly; in Baxter street, near the Five Points, is a colony of Genoese; in Elizabeth street, between Houston and Spring, a colony of Sicilians.

The quarter west of Broadway in the Eighth and Fifteenth wards is made up mainly of North Italians who have been longer in New York and are rather more prosperous than the others, although some Neapolitans have come into Sullivan and Thompson streets to work in the flower and feather trades. In "Little Italy," One hundred and tenth to One hundred and fifteenth streets, South Italians predominate. In Sixty-ninth street, near the Hudson River, is to be found a small group of Tyrolese and Austrian Italians.

Both men and women are slow to adopt American ways of dress. The women go unbonneted in peaceful unconsciousness of any need for change. The men may be distinguished from their Irish fellow-workmen a half block away by the characteristic Italian garments that they wear with the characteristic Italian attempt at the ornamental.

In the second generation encouraging signs of social progress are seen. Italian children are brought under the Americanizing influence of the public schools within a brief period after their landing here and before they learn the language, partly through the workings of the compulsory education laws, partly through the double desire of the parents, first to have the children learn English so as to serve as family interpreters, next to get them out of the way in the narrow tenement-house quarters they call home. In school Italian children are found more or less difficult to discipline and irresponsible. They have no fear of authority, but they are good natured and when their confidence is won thoroughly loyal. They are fair students, better than the Irish, but not as good as the Hebrews and Germans at book work. They show, however, great talent for manual work, drawing, etc. One defect they have is lack of application. As one teacher expresses it: "At one moment they will be absorbed in what you are saying, and the next equally interested in a fly on the wall."

Italian parents, under the compulsion of extreme poverty, and also from lack of appreciation of the value of education, are anxious to get their children out of the schools and at work at as early an age as possible. This is the principal cause of the great amount of truancy among Italian children noticed in the large cities.

While the children are in school, however, Italian parents are most friendly to the school and the principal and most respectful of school authority. Sent for upon some question of discipline, they are never resentful toward the principal, as American parents are rather prone to be under like circumstances, and, indeed, show a somewhat terrifying eagerness to add discipline on their own part in the shape of corporal punishment to that already administered by the school.

From the desire or necessity of the parent to have the children go to work not a very great proportion of them go from the grammar school to the high school or college, or even through the grammar grades. The children themselves, however, once started in school, grow interested in their work and would be quite willing to keep on.

Comparing those who have succeeded in keeping on until the higher grammar grades are reached with those in the lower grades, a notable improvement is seen. Pupils in the higher grades are bright, active, alert, and clean. Principals and teachers wage a perpetual warfare against dirt, gaining a substantial victory in the highest grade that is most gratifying.

The boy who drops out of the public school from the lower grammar or primary classes is likely to become a day laborer like his father, but the one who has passed into the higher grades has acquired a desire for something better. Some will make an effort to graduate from the grammar school, will succeed in securing a year or two in the high school or city college, and will become teachers, doctors, and lawyers. Others, with or without this additional training, go into business. Some go into factories or become errand or messenger boys; many are employed in department stores. Boys who have reached this point are more unwilling to take to unskilled labor, it is said by those who are familiar with them, than the second or third generation of the Irish, and it is unfortunately true that their unwillingness goes so far that they will remain unemployed indefinitely, hanging about as corner loungers, if they can not secure the clerkships, factory places, etc., that they want.

It can not, however, be ascribed wholly as a fault to the Italian boy that his aspirations take the shape suggested by the public school itself, which is being criticised more and more freely as time goes on for its exclusive devotion to the bookish side of life, to the exclusion of the manual and industrial element in it.

Italian children who have gone a considerable way through the public schools acquire very definite ideas of social advancement. They begin to be ashamed of the habits and customs of their parents, and bring all the pressure to bear that they can to change these. The child thus becomes an important influence in Americanizing the parents, who are allowed no peace until the peculiar "old-country" customs that mark them off, in the child's mind, as a class apart from the dominant race, the American, are cast aside.

The adult Italian, too, has his opportunity for Americanization in the public schools if he wishes to make use of it. Under the city school system evening classes for instructing adult foreigners in the English language primarily, incidentally in some of the fundamentals of American civic life, are formed as rapidly as there is demand for them.

In all of the principal Italian neighborhoods are evening schools conducting classes for Italians, and Italian evening classes are also found in neighborhoods where they are not considered especially numerous as residents. The schools make especial efforts to bring the advantages they offer to the notice of foreigners. One admirable school in the Fourth Ward issued a circular in the Italian language, announcing three grades of study for Italians, stating that this involves no expense to the pupil, of whom the only requirement made is that he shall attend the school, and urging all in the neighborhood to come. "Taking advantage of this opportunity," the circular concludes, with a touch of Italian rhetoric, "you will deserve well of all men. Despising it, you will incur odium and blame from the Americans and from all those who desire your welfare and who are laboring so diligently for your benefit."

This circular was distributed broadcast in the most populous Italian quarter of the city, but comparatively few pupils were gathered into the school. These were men of various occupations who needed the English language to help them in getting along. They showed little desire for education in general, their attendance was more or less irregular, and when they had learned the English they needed they dropped out. This is largely the case in other evening classes for Italians, but many individual instances of progress and real interest in advancement may be noted. In some cases Italians who were in English classes one year would be found taking bookkeeping and stenography in evening classes the next.

In these evening classes it is hard to keep the attendance up through the 90 nights which make up the year's allowance. This is hardly to be wondered at, however. The pupils in these classes are workingmen and boys, and the wonder is that after a long and hard day's work they have the patience and energy to plod through books at night. The men attending these classes are mechanics of various kinds, cabinet-makers, bricklayers, stonemasons, barbers, and in large proportion common laborers.

Italian girls and young women are also taking advantage of evening classes, and are a remarkably bright, enterprising-looking set. Italian parents generally object to allowing their daughters to go out at night unattended, so that many of the girls appear in the classes with younger sisters as a bodyguard.

In these schools, besides the English classes, are classes in sewing and cooking, in stenography and bookkeeping, and other branches. The proportion of Italian girls who attend these evening schools is comparatively small, but those who do are nearly all aiming to enter the higher classes and to prepare themselves for clerical work in offices and the like.

A probable result of the spread of education among Italian girls will be to lower the birthrate of the Italian population in the city by postponing marriage. The Italian woman in Italy, of the lower classes, marries very young and bears very many children. The Italian woman of the first generation in this country does the same; but the Italian girl of the second generation, seeing other openings before her than matrimony, will marry later, make a better marriage when it is finally made, bear fewer children, and be able to provide for them better. This tendency, indeed, has already been remarked.

The class of Hebrew immigrants that have given most concern to the cities are those from Russia, eastern Austria-Hungary ("Poland"), and Roumania. This class did not begin to come in great numbers until the beginning of the persecutions of the eighties.

German Jews had long been settled in the Fourth and Sixth wards, as the familiar figure of the "old-clothes" man in Chatham (now Park Row) and Baxter streets indicates. And many Hebrew families had removed to the Seventh Ward between 1860 and 1870. Some of the Russian and Polish immigrants appear to have followed their German brethren to the Sixth Ward; but many pressed at once into the Tenth Ward, making the beginning of that settlement, which, every year with a greater circumference, is now known as distinctively the Jewish quarter.

By 1883 we hear of great overcrowding in Essex and York streets among Russian and Polish Jews. It was said that in one house of 16 apartments, of 2 rooms each, about 200 persons were quartered.[1] Like the Italians, the Russian and Polish Jews were poor, were dirty in their habits, but were industrious, and good rent payers. Many of those living in Essex street were peddlers, who traveled about the country during the week and were at home on Saturday nights only, when the overcrowding was exceptionally great.

The legislative commission of 1884 in its report[2] gives some statistics comparing different races as to overcrowding and cleanliness gathered in an inspection of a large number of tenement houses. Referring to the table presented as to comparative cleanliness the report makes the following comment:

It will be seen that the Germans are decidedly in advance, and are followed by the French, English, Americans, Irish, Polish Jews, and Italians in the order named. The low Irish, Germans, and the Polish Jews take very little care of their rooms. * * * The want of cleanliness among the low Irish is very often due to the laziness of the women.

A description of life in the "Big Flat"—a notorious tenement house on Mott street just above Canal—in 1886 gives us a glimpse of the Jews at this time, and of the conditions by which they were surrounded.[3]

In the "Big Flat" were gathered, on a given day in 1886, 478 persons, of whom 368 were Hebrews (156 Roumanians, 198 Poles, and 14 Russians), 31 were Italians, 31 Irish, 30 Germans, and 4 native Americans. On the first floor were rooms for 14 families, and these were mostly occupied by low women and streetwalkers.

Two of the first-floor apartments were occupied at the time the study was made by Jewish people (1 by Poles, 1 by Roumanians), 3 by Irish, 4 by Germans, and 1 by

---

[1] Report of A. I. C. P., 1883, p. 19.
[2] N. Y. State Senate Doc. No. 36, 1885, p. 45.
[3] "The Story of the Big Flat," Report of A. I. C. P., 1886, p. 43 and following.

native Americans. The hallways were "hang outs" for all the hoodlums of the neighborhood, and after nightfall the lower floor was overrun with low women and young men who did not live in the house. None of the tenants living above the second floor were ever to be seen standing around the lower floor or doors. On the upper floors, 47 of the apartments were occupied by Jews, 6 by Italians, 6 by Germans, 5 by Irish, and 1 by native Americans.

The Jews were prin ally engaged in tailoring, but there were some 54 peddlers in the building. Both tailors and peddlers were closely packed in very dirty rooms, and lived upon poor and scanty food.

The children were "very poorly clad, having hardly a stitch on them, nothing but a loose gown, and no underclothing at all."[1] Their food during the day was bread, no butter, and that was eaten by them in the hallway—they did not know what it was to sit at a table.

Some indication of the general character of the different nationalities living in the house is shown by the record of arrests made here from January 1, 1886, to the date of the inspection, September, 1886. The arrests, by nationalities, were as follows:

United States	11	Ireland	1
Poland and Russia	7	China	1
Germany	4		
Italy	1	Total	25

Three of the arrests of Jews were for violations of corporation ordinances, leaving only four offenses of a more serious character corresponding to the offenses committed by the others arrested.

The Hebrew population in the city already dense in 1890, as seen by the map showing their distribution has increased tremendously since then. In 1890 they were seen within certain fairly narrow limits. No figures are as yet at hand to show their exact increase and dispersion, but observation of the different quarters of the city shows that they have extended their limits remarkably within the past 10 years. On the East Side they have pressed up through the Tenth and Thirteenth wards and through the Sixteenth and Eleventh, driving the Germans before them, until it may be said that all of the East Side below Fourteenth street is a Jewish district. As far as observation can tell the tale, the thickly compacted masses of Germans, seen in the map for 1890, are almost wholly dispersed from that region. Some went uptown to the neighborhood of Eighty-seventh street, on the East Side, and elsewhere, but most have gone to Brooklyn and the suburban districts. This fact shows that the city colony, however compact and hard to break it may seem to be, may, by some change in circumstances, be dissolved in a very short period of time, without any apparent effort and almost without public observation. The Germans did not like the proximity of the Jews, and so they left. A like influence may at any time scatter the Jewish and Italian colonies now so hopelessly, it seems, crowded together.

The red crosses on the Italian-Russian map show how continuous, even though slight, was the stream of Jewish population already directed up the East Side in 1890. By this time, 11 years later, the numbers in these neighborhoods are greater, and a large Hebrew colony has formed in the Harlem district, mainly between Ninety-seventh and One hundred and second streets, where the Italians begin, reaching up farther to the north; and here conditions are generally better than in the downtown district. The removal of a Hebrew family up here is usually a token of advancement—in assimilation, at any rate.

The newly arrived Russian Jew is kept in the crowded East Side, not only by his poverty and ignorance, but by his orthodoxy. In this district the rules of his religion can more certainly be followed. Here can be found the lawful food, here the orthodox places of worship, here neighbors and friends can be visited within a "Sabbath day's journey." The young people, however, rapidly shake off such trammels, and in the endeavor to be like Americans urge their parents to move away from this "foreign" district. When they succeed, the Americanizing process may be said to be well under way.

Economic advancement comes to these poverty-stricken Hebrews with surprising rapidity. There is no way of telling definitely what proportion of the very poor eventually rise out of that condition, or how long it takes them to do so. General observation, however, seems to indicate that the proportion is considerable and the rate rapid.

Many tenements in Jewish quarters are owned by persons who formerly lived in crowded corners of others just like them; and from this population comes many and many a Broadway merchant and professional men in plenty. It is a common saying that from Hester street to Lexington avenue is a journey of about 10 years for any given family.

---

[1] Report A. I. C. P., 1886, p. 47.

It is certain that the adult Hebrew immigrant, unlike the Italian, has definite aspirations toward social, economic, and educational advancement.

The poorest among them will make all possible sacrifices to keep his children in school; and one of the most striking social phenomena in New York City to-day is the way in which the Jews have taken possession of the public schools, in the highest as well as the lowest grades.

The city college is practically filled with Jewish pupils, a considerable proportion of them children of Russian or Polish immigrants on the East Side.

In the lower schools Jewish children are the delight of their teachers for cleverness at their books, obedience, and general good conduct; and the vacation schools, night schools, social settlements, libraries, bathing places, parks, and playgrounds of the East Side are fairly besieged with Jewish children eager to take advantage of the opportunities they offer. Jewish boys are especially ambitious to enter professions or go into business, and the complaint is made that they overcrowd such callings, refusing to enter occupations involving hand work as well as head work. But here, too, it must be urged, as in the case of the Italians, that the fault, such as it is, is partly to be ascribed to the ideals of the public school itself. And, furthermore, the Hebrew usually shows such excellence in these special lines that the community probably gains materially rather than loses by having his services offered in this way.

It is not all an upward road for the Italian and Hebrew immigrant, however. As in the case of the Irish and Germans, tenement-house life tends to their physical and moral deterioration.

The Jews, already accustomed to city life, have withstood the physical influences of the tenements most remarkably, keeping the death rate down perceptibly in wards where they predominate; but tuberculosis, a disease they do not bring with them from abroad, is now growing more and more common among them, due to living and working in insanitary conditions and surroundings.

There is considerable sickness among the Italians. The country-bred adult, unused to the confined conditions of the tenements, is liable to tuberculosis. Italian children born and reared in the tenements are anæmic, and to this, as well as to unwise and irregular eating, their high death rate is due.

The moral surroundings, too, are bad. Not only are there, first, the evil moral influences of overcrowding in general, but also the contact with elements of population already deteriorated by a generation of tenement-house life.

The new immigrant, an unsophisticated Italian peasant or a poor Hebrew of quiet family life and moral traditions, is brought into a district where vice has been developed through years of a sifting process which has taken elsewhere the successful of the former generation of immigrants and left the failures where violence and intemperance, especial faults of that earlier generation, are prevalent.

Conditions in the "Big Flat" in Mott street described in preceding pages well illustrate the nature and character of the influences by which the new immigrant is surrounded.

In the Fourth, Sixth, and Fourteenth wards the Italians, and in the Seventh Ward the Hebrews, are thrown in with the corrupt remnants of Irish immigration which now make up the beggars, the drunkards, the thugs, and thieves of those quarters.

The Bowery, running up through the quarters where the newer immigrants—the Italians to the left, the Hebrews to the right—settled in greatest numbers, is the focal line of these evil influences, and the peculiar system of government which allows the conditions prevailing there to continue is to a great extent responsible for the evils seen to be growing in the foreign quarters.

Until within a very few years the Italian laboring population in New York was notably free from glaring vice and intemperance. There were few or no disorderly resorts for Italians, and such a practice as the importation of Italian women for immoral purposes was unknown. Under present city conditions, however, positive inducement having been given for the extension of vice of all kinds, many disorderly resorts have been opened in their most crowded quarters, and it is said that many Italian girls from Naples and other cities have been imported to fill them.

Within the last year or two the Hebrews also have shown tendencies to the grosser vices that have never before characterized them. It can hardly be doubted that a people of their general habits with respect to temperance and the family relation must have fallen under some alien influence to bring about such conditions as are now found to exist on the East Side.

It is in the light of all the above considerations that the records of pauperism and crime for the different races of immigrants of this period should be considered.

Both Italian and Hebrew immigrants are prone to pauperism of the form that consists in placing children out in some institution. This form, though burdensome enough to the community in which it is practiced, can hardly be regarded as so great an indication of the genuine pauper spirit as other forms. Italian or Hebrew parents, in trying to get their children into an institution, are, from their point of view, simply doing their parental duty in getting for their children advantages of education, and so forth, offered by the public that they can not themselves afford to supply. If the free day schools are so good, and attendance there so greatly desired that children are even driven to go to them by compulsory school laws, why should not, they think, the free boarding school (or "college," as they call the public institutions for children) be still more of an advantage, and why should they not secure this for their children? And the parents have no idea of being paupers themselves. Both Italians and Hebrews work unremittingly, and manage to save enough for their own necessities to keep them from the almshouse. The following table from the Eleventh Census shows the number of paupers per million of the population for the first and second generation of certain nationalities. These statistics are for the country at large, but the general race tendency is shown in them.

TABLE 17.—*Ratio of paupers to the million of same nationality or descent, 1890.*

Foreign white.	Ratio to million.	Native white of foreign parentage.	
Total foreign whites	3,031	Total whites of foreign parents	412
Born in—		Of parents born in—	
Ireland	7,550	Ireland	834
France	3,636	France	583
Wales	2,558	England	491
Germany	2,436	Germany	304
Scotland	2,373	Italy	164
Spain	2,326		
England	2,163		
Poland	1,486		
Bohemia	1,439		
Italy	817		
Hungary	785		
Austria	779		
Russia	586		
Greece	533		

Now, as 50 years ago, the pauper population is predominantly Irish, both in the first and in the second generation. Germany is fairly well down in the list, while Italians and Russians (Hebrews) appear in a very favorable light.

With regard to the Hebrews it must be said that a great deal of charitable aid has been given them by fellow-religionists that does not consequently appear on the official records. But this aid is largely temporary in character, to tide the immigrant over his first few months here, and does not imply the existence of a large permanent pauper class.

Even this allowance does not have to be made for the Italians. Less, perhaps, is done for them by private charity than for any other class of people. There are no great Italian hospitals, orphanages, and charitable societies to aid Italians as there are Hebrew institutions for the Hebrews. Consequently the great bulk of Italian pauperism appears on public records, and that is seen to be little.

The census of 1890 gives the following figures as to criminality of different races:

TABLE 18.—*Ratio of foreign white prisoners to the million of foreign whites.*

Total foreign white 1,747

Above average.		Below average.	
Born in—		Born in—	
Greece a	8,524	Austria a	1,404
Spain a	4,485	Belgium a	1,149
Italy b	3,115	Russia	1,144
Ireland	2,971	Germany b	1,065
France	2,468	Poland	1,011
England b	2,114	Wales	889
Hungary	2,083	Denmark	853
Scotland	1,978	Holland a	746
		Sweden	728
		Norway	645
		Portugal a	575
		Bohemia a	305

a Less than 100 prisoners. Numbers too small to give certainty as to ratio.
b More than 1,000 prisoners.

Putting the matter in another way, Italians were 1.98 per cent of the foreign population, while Italian prisoners were 3.7 per cent of the foreign prison population. A like comparison for the Irish is 20.23 per cent to 35 per cent; English, 9.82 per cent to 12 per cent; Russians, 1.97 per cent to 1 per cent; and Germans, 30 per cent to 19 per cent.

Italians, then, are seen almost at the head of this list, and above the Irish; but in modification of this circumstance it must be remembered that the Italian population in general contained a far higher proportion of adult males (the criminal age and sex) than the Irish population, in which females and children were numerous.

From an inquiry made a year or two ago into rates of crime and pauperism in New York City[1] certain results appear that may be embodied in the following table:

TABLE 19.

Persons born in—	Per cent in total population New York City.	Per cent of almshouse paupers.	Per cent of workhouse inmates.	Per cent of penitentiary convicts.
Ireland	12.6	60.4	36.7	15.4
Germany	14	14	6.8	9
England	2.4	4.4	4.4	3.3
Italy	2.6	.68	1.4	2.5
Scotland	.7	2.2	1.4	.9
Hebrews from Russia and Austria-Hungary	3		1	1

In this record it will be noticed that Italy makes a more favorable showing; the figures of total population are those of 1890; the figures of institution population are averages for the ten years, 1885–1895, which affords a fair basis of comparison.

Coming to the second generation, the census of 1890 gives the following ratios of criminality for native whites of foreign parentage:

TABLE 20.—*Ratio of criminals to the million of same nationality class in the general population.*

Total native white of foreign parentage.... 1,400
Parents born in—
Ireland a 3,666
Scotland 1,787
France 1,560

Parents born in—
England 1,207
Italy b 603
Germany a 568
Russia b 229

a More than 1,000 prisoners.   b Less than 100 prisoners.

And the following for juvenile offenders:

TABLE 21.—*Ratio of juvenile offenders to the million of same nationality class in the general population.*

Foreign whites born in—
Italy 784
Spain 332
Poland 285
France 248
England 211
Scotland 186
Ireland 146
Belgium 133
Germany 113

Foreign whites born in—
Hungary 112
Holland 110
Native white, both parents born in—
Ireland 1,069
Italy 840
France 393
England 299
Germany 246

Of the newer immigrants, then, Italy has the most doubtful record as to crime, not so bad as it has been believed, but still bad enough. The crimes most usually committed by Italians are crimes of violence, embracing murder, homicide, and the like; and the crime rate, principally from these causes, in their own country is high. There is reason to believe, however, that conditions there are changing for the better, which will cause a corresponding change in the character of future immigration. It has been claimed, and statistics are given to substantiate the claim, that the part of the crime rate due to homicide is diminishing regularly and continuously in Italy, owing to the general extension of the influences of civilization, such as education, development of commerce, transportation, communication by newspapers, mail, and telegraph. It is said, too, that emigration is helping in this process by, first, the greater prosperity brought to the country through returning emigrants, and, more powerfully, by the more enlightened ideas brought back by them.

---

[1] Byron C. Mathews: "A study in nativities," The Forum, January, 1900, p. 621.

THE IMMIGRANT IN NEW YORK CITY. 481

As the Italian population increases here, moreover, the percentage of females and children increases, and this also will reduce their crime rate.

It is of especial interest to note how all these changes and distributions affected the tenement-house problem, and what tenement-house reform movements and the legislation resulting from them have been able to accomplish in remedying bad tenement conditions.

The agitation in New York City against tenement-house evils, begun by Gerrett Forbes, city inspector, in 1834, did not take effect in legislation especially dealing with tenement houses until 1867, when, as a result of the work of the council of hygiene, 3 years previously, a State tenement-house law was passed.[1]

At this time, as has been noted in preceding pages, tenement houses were made over private residences, the "front and rear" double-barrack or single-barrack buildings extending nearly to the rear of the lot. (See cut, pp. 482–483, types 2, 3, 4, and 5.) In these types will be noticed the unventilated and unlighted inner rooms, and, in the worst examples, the insufficient yard space.

As to yard space, the law of 1867 provided for a distance of from 10 to 25 feet between front and rear tenements, according to their height, and for a "clear, open space" of 10 feet between the rear of any tenement house on the back part of any lot and any other building; but as discretionary power was given to the board of health to modify these distances in special cases, these provisions were largely nullified in practice.[2]

With regard to the ventilation of inner rooms, the law provided that rooms of less than 100 square feet floor area, not communicating with the outer air, or without an open fireplace, should be provided with "special means of ventilation, by a separate air shaft extending to the roof or otherwise, as the board of health may prescribe."[3]

This provision applied to old tenement houses as well as to new ones, and many buildings were fitted with small ventilating flues of about 4 by 6 inches in size; but few were fitted with an "air shaft" in the sense in which the term would now be used.

In all tenement houses—those already erected as well as those to be built—sleeping rooms without external windows were to have transom windows opening into rooms already opening to the external air; and in all tenement houses to be erected every room was to have either an external window or a "ventilator of perfect construction."[4] A minimum area of one-tenth of the superficial area of the room was prescribed for external windows, and the top of one window, at least, in a room was to be not less than 7½ feet above the floor.[5]

The rooms themselves, in new tenement houses, were to be at least 8 feet in height. It was also provided that there should be chimneys running through each set of apartments, giving opportunity for an open fireplace or grate or stove, and that all halls must open directly on the outer air.

These were provisions dealing with light and ventilation. Special sanitary provisions, to meet some of the more glaring sanitary evils noted by the council of hygiene, were as follows:

One of the worst features—perhaps the worst feature—of tenement-house life at this time was the occupancy of cellars for living purposes. The law of 1867 sought to reduce this by providing that no cellar should be occupied unless it was at least 7 feet in height; had its ceiling at least 1 foot higher than the general ground level; had an open space across the front of at least 2 feet 6 inches wide and 6 inches deeper than the level of the cellar floor, and had a window at least 9 feet square.

Another great evil noted in sanitary reports up to this time was the insufficiency of the water supply in tenement houses in general. The law of 1867 provided that all new tenement houses must have water "furnished at one or more places" in the house or yard.[6]

To remedy the appalling general filth, depicted so vividly and variously in successive sanitary reports, the law provided that all tenement houses, new or old, "shall be kept clean," and that the owner should "thoroughly cleanse all the rooms, passages, stairs, floors, windows, doors, walls, ceilings, privies, cesspools and drains," when required to do so by the board of health.[7]

Other sanitary provisions were that yards and areas must be connected with sewers; that receptacles must be provided by the owner of each tenement house for garbage, ashes, and rubbish; that no horses, cows, sheep, goats, or swine should be kept in a tenement house; that contagious diseases must be reported, and that

---
[1] Laws of State of New York, ch. 908, p. 2265, vol. 2: "An act for the regulation of tenement and lodging houses in the cities of New York and Brooklyn." Passed May 14, 1867.
[2] Laws of State of New York, 1867, ch. 908, sec. 13.
[3] Laws of State of New York, 1867, ch. 908, sec. 14.
[4] Laws State of New York, 1867, ch. 908, sec. 14.
[5] Ibid.
[6] Laws, 1867, ch. 908, sec. 15.
[7] Laws, 1867, ch. 908, sec. 9.

TYPES OF DWELLINGS,

(From Report New York State Tenement House Commission, 1896,

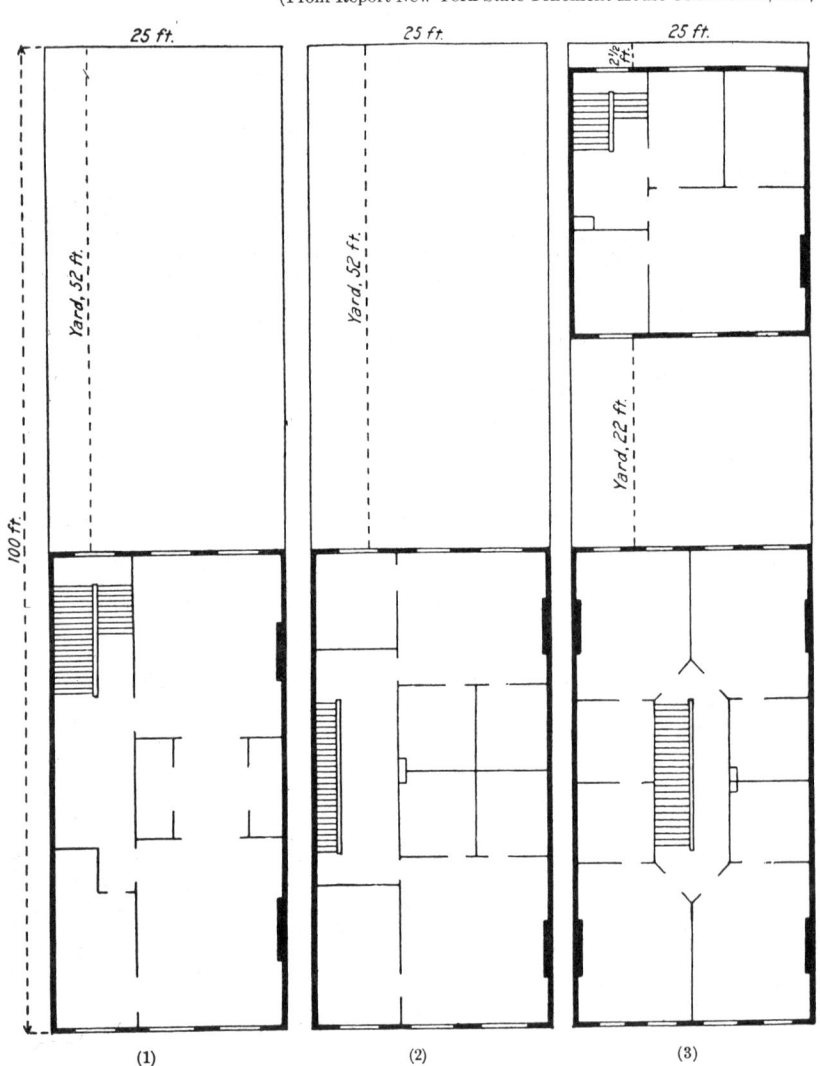

(1) Old-time private residence. (2) Residence converted into a tenement house. (3) "Front-and-rear" tenement.

THE IMMIGRANT IN NEW YORK CITY.

NEW YORK CITY.

and Report New York State Tenement House Commission, 1900.)

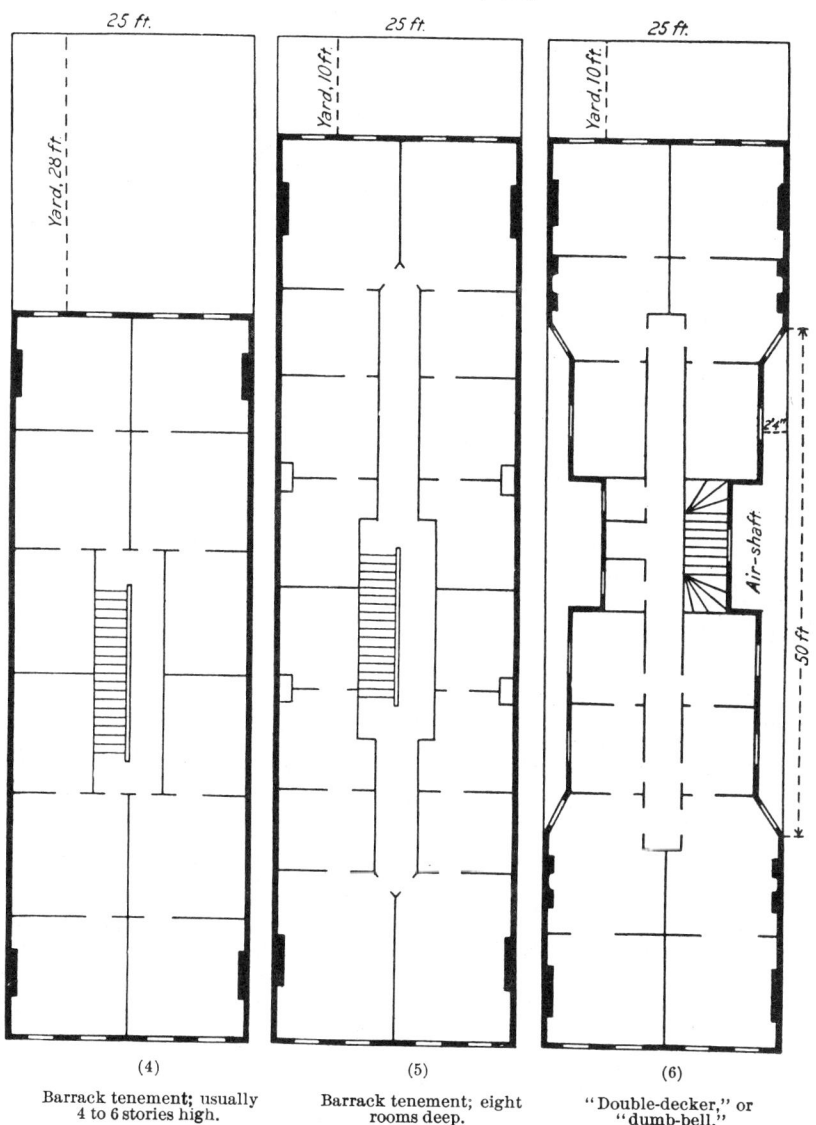

(4) Barrack tenement; usually 4 to 6 stories high.

(5) Barrack tenement; eight rooms deep.

(6) "Double-decker," or "dumb-bell."

every tenement house or lodging house should be provided with "good and sufficient" water-closets or privies, not less than 1 to every 20 occupants of the house, to be connected with the sewers on streets where sewers existed.

No further important legislation was enacted until 1879, when, in consequence of renewed agitation of the tenement-house question from about 1877 on, another State law was passed.[1]

This law remedied two defects in the old law with regard to yard spaces. The old law had provided for minimum spaces between front and rear tenements only in cases where a tenement was built on the front of a lot, at the rear of which a building already stood. The new law made the provisions apply also to cases where a tenement was erected on the rear of a lot at the front of which another building already stood. And with regard to yard room at the back of buildings, the old law had provided simply that the "clear open space of 10 feet" required, should be between the back of the tenement house, and "any other building," thus leaving it possible to build up to the rear line of the lot if the rear of the lot just back of it happened not to be built upon. The new law provided that the 10-foot space should extend between the back of the tenement and the rear line of the lot.[2]

This provision stood directly in the way of building any more rear tenements of the old type, but additional ones may have been erected after this time, under the "discretionary power" which was in this case, as in many others, given to the board of health to modify the provisions of the law.

Up to this time there had been no legal limitation of the proportion of the building lot which might be covered by a tenement building, although the provisions as to distance between buildings had made some practical restriction. The law of 1879 provided that new tenements should not occupy more than 65 per cent of a lot, but as here, once more, discretionary power was given to the board of health to modify the letter of the law, it amounted practically to very little.

For the better ventilating of rooms the law provided that every room used as a bedroom should have an external window. This was a decided step in advance, but this, too, was nullified by giving "discretionary power" to the board of health, which might permit the omission of the external window if "sufficient light and ventilation should be otherwise provided, in a manner and upon a plan approved by" them.[3]

The first definite provision made with regard to overcrowding appears in this law, which requires in each tenement house, new or old, 600 cubic feet of air to each occupant.

The year that this law was enacted was further noteworthy in the history of the tenement house as the year of the invention and introduction of New York's most characteristic tenement house, the "dumb-bell" or "double-decker." (See cut, p. 483, No. 6.) This type of building was introduced as a "model"tenement, and has kept within the provisions of all the tenement-house laws, new and old, enacted before 1900, but it has proved to be one of the worst forms of housing ever employed.

The older types of the tenement house were rarely over 4 stories in height. The double-decker ran up, usually, to 6, often to 7 and 8, stories, thus cutting off more light and air from streets and yards, and gathering a denser population under one roof than the older tenements. Comparing the ground plans of the several types of buildings (see cut), it is seen that the yard spaces themselves are smaller for the double-deckers than was usual for the old "front and rear" buildings. The yard proper of the double-decker occupies only 10 per cent of the lot, as is the case with the worst of the old tenements, the building being kept within the limits of the law as to per cent of lot occupied by the side "air shafts" to be noted in the plan. These are, singly, usually 2 feet 4 inches in width throughout most of their length, or, taken together, as they adjoin one another in adjacent houses, 4 feet 8 inches, and from 50 to 60 feet in length. Surrounded as they are by walls from 60 to 70 feet high and with no intake of air at the bottom, it is plainly to be seen that they can afford very little light and almost no air, to say nothing of the impossibility of using them for the ordinary purposes of a yard.

The usefulness of the air shaft as a means of ventilation is not added to, moreover, by the practice tenants have of using it "as a receptacle for garbage and all sorts of refuse and indescribable filth thrown out of windows" which is "often allowed to remain rotting at the bottom of the shaft without being cleaned out."[4]

It was said in the course of the last tenement-house investigation that the air shaft should be called a "foul air shaft;" that it might be designated as a "culture tube on a gigantic scale," and that it was simply "a stagnant well of foul air emp-

---

[1] Laws of State of New York, 1879, ch. 504, p. 554. An act to amend chapter 908 of the laws of 1867, entitled "An act for the regulation of tenement and lodging houses in the cities of New York and Brooklyn." Passed June 16, 1879.
[2] Ch. 504, sec. 1.
[3] Ch. 504, sec. 2.
[4] Advance sheets of part of the Report of the Tenement House Commission, 1900, printed privately, p. 17.

tied from each one of the rooms opening upon it;" and many people testified that "the air from these shafts was so foul and the odors so vile that they had to close the windows opening into them, and in some cases the windows were permanently nailed up for this reason."[1]

Within the "double-decker" the halls are nearly always totally dark, being lighted only from small windows opening on the stairs or from the front door. Of the 14 rooms usually found on each floor, only 2 receive light and air from the street; 2 from the 10-foot deep yard at the rear, and the remaining 10 from the narrow air shaft only.

The rooms in this type of tenement are usually very small. The front room is about 10 feet 6 inches by 11 feet 3 inches. This is used on hot nights as a sleeping room often by the whole family. The bedrooms proper are about 7 feet by 8 feet 6 inches, and are hardly large enough to contain a bed. These rooms being "lighted" from the air shaft are almost totally dark.

From this time on new tenements in New York City (the present borough of Manhattan) were almost exclusively built upon this plan, and by the present time, 1901, make up about 60 per cent of the total number.

In 1885 the first attempt was made to restrict the height of buildings, the State legislature in that year enacting[2] that tenement houses should not be built higher than from 70 to 80 feet, according to the width of the street. But this provision did not reduce the "double-decker" appreciably from its usual height at that time.

The next important piece of tenement-house legislation was enacted in 1887.[3]

This law remedied certain defects of the law of 1879 with regard to yard space by taking away the discretionary power of the board of health to reduce the 10-foot distance between the rear of buildings and the rear line of the lot, and by extending the provisions of the old law as to the percentage of lot to be occupied to old houses which were to be altered and enlarged. The provision of the law of 1879 on this head applied to new tenement houses only, so that it was quite possible for an owner to alter and enlarge an old tenement house so as to cover the entire lot if he chose.

This law also provided that if halls did not open directly on the external air by means of a window the tenement house could not be used; that water must be supplied "in sufficient quantity at one or more places on each floor;"[4] that water-closets "or other similar receptacles" shall be provided, not less than 1 for every 15 occupants of lodging houses, and not less than 1 for every 2 families in dwelling houses, and that "no privy vault or cesspool shall be allowed," "except when it is unavoidable," the board of health to see to it that no privy vault should remain connected with a tenement house later than January 1 of the following year, except in cases mentioned in the section.[5]

The provision requiring 1 closet for every 2 families was repealed the following year, and the enactment made that 1 closet should be supplied for every 15 occupants in tenement houses as well as lodging houses, and not less than 1 on every floor.[6]

The following tables give some idea of certain general changes in tenement districts and tenement conditions that had been going on in the years since the first tenement-house law was enacted.

The tables show changes in general density of population in the different wards between 1860 and 1890, the character of dwellings in the wards and the percentage of population in them, changes in the average number of tenants to each tenant house between 1864 and 1893, and other data bearing upon the general question.

---

[1] Advance sheets of part of the Report of the Tenément House Commission, 1900, printed privately, p. 17.
[2] Laws of State of New York, ch. 454.
[3] Laws of State of New York, ch. 84 p. 94: An act to amend chapter 410 of the laws of 1882. Passed March 25, 1887.
[4] Ch. 84, sec. 11.
[5] Ch. 84, sec. 6.
[6] Laws of 1888, ch. 422, sec. 1.

486   THE INDUSTRIAL COMMISSION: —IMMIGRATION.

TABLE 22.—*Density of population—New York City.*

	Density, 1860.	Density, 1890.	Per cent of total dwellings containing in 1890—		Per cent of population in dwellings containing in 1890—	
			11 to 20 persons.	21 persons and over.	11 to 20 persons.	21 persons and over.
New York City			20.99	28.83	16.80	66.70
Wards.						
I	117.8	72.2	16.58	21.60	16.60	62.13
II	30.9	11.4	17.02	10.64	25.08	39.18
III	39.5	39.6	21.72	27.27	17.08	68.37
IV	264.9	214.5	22.62	38.62	13.94	76.63
V	132.9	73.7	28.53	29.58	23.30	62.83
VI	310.4	268.8	17.14	46.69	8.50	84.84
VII	201.9	289.7	29.63	43.97	16.56	77.03
VIII	215.3	170.6	37.49	25.76	30.78	55.69
IX	137.8	169	33.63	19.03	31.68	48.40
X	272.7	523.6	17.51	57.49	6.94	89.01
XI	303.9	384.3	25.88	57.75	12.53	83.92
XII	5.5	44.5	16.66	26.76	15.10	63.43
XIII	307.6	428.8	24.18	52.27	11.37	84.04
XIV	295.5	292.6	19.02	49.50	9.10	85.28
XV	139.3	128.3	25.05	16.85	27.66	48.64
XVI	129.4	140.8	32.32	20.24	31.75	48.46
XVII	220.4	311.6	23.45	52.43	12.73	81.80
XVIII	127.7	140.6	23	29.65	18.42	65.45
XIX	22.1	158.5	18.85	30.38	14.50	68.86
XX	152	189.9	28.89	34.72	21.65	67.12
XXI	119.5	153.3	22.33	23.33	21.03	57.81
XXII	40.3	100.6	18.70	33.28	14.17	70.98
XXIII		12.6	14.61	6.17	23.40	22.75
XXIV		2.5	5.62	.70	12.34	6.41

TABLE 23.—*Density of population—New York City.*

	Tenement houses; tenants to house.		Census of 1890.c		
	1864.a	1893.b	Average persons to dwelling.	Families to dwelling.	Persons to family.
New York City			18.52	3.82	4.84
Wards.					
I	34.2	36	15.11	3.09	4.88
II		21.9	9.88	1.34	7.37
III	24.1	32.2	19.02	2.35	8.10
IV	35.2	31.5	24.56	4.92	4.99
V	24.6	29.1	18.60	3.73	4.99
VI	34.3	38.8	31.20	5.50	5.67
VII	30.8	43.4	27.15	5.48	4.95
VIII	25	24.6	17.90	3.85	4.67
IX	25.1	27.4	15.30	3.35	4.57
X	34	57.2	38.50	7.85	4.90
XI	31.3	35.3	31.43	6.73	4.67
XII		32.8	16.18	3.31	4.89
XIII	27.5	41.8	32.06	6.69	4.79
XIV	36.6	40.5	31.25	6.46	4.84
XV	25	27.5	13.54	2.44	5.55
XVI	25	30	15.18	3.21	4.73
XVII	34.6	37.2	27.96	6.43	4.35
XVIII	42.7	30.2	18.76	3.56	5.27
XIX	28.1	36.1	19.15	3.75	5.11
XX	27.8	28.4	20.22	4.57	4.43
XXI	35.7	32.6	15.74	3.03	5.20
XXII	32	33.9	19.81	4.27	4.64
XXIII		22.6	8.64	1.84	4.70
XXIV		12.7	6.15	1.14	5.42

a Report Council of Hygiene, 349.
b Report Tenement House Commission.
c U. S. Census 1890, Population, I, cxcvii.

TABLE 24.

Wards.	Changes in ward density, 1860–1890.		Changes in average tenants to tenement house, 1864–1893.		Number of tenement houses—	
	Per cent of increase.	Per cent of decrease.	Per cent of increase.	Per cent of decrease.	1864.	1893.
Down town:						
I		39	5.3		250	210
II		63.1				8
III	0.3		33.6		54	48
Lower West Side:						
V		44.6	18.3		462	238
VIII		20.8		1.6	625	826
IX	15.4		9.2		596	1,519
Center:						
IV		19		10.5	486	473
VI		13.4	13.1		605	522
XIV		1	10.7		546	636
XV		8	10		197	359
East Side:						
VII	43.4		40.9		627	1,510
X	92		68.2		534	1,196
XIII	39.4		52		540	1,042
XI	26.4		12.8		2,049	2,201
XVII	41.4		7.5		1,890	2,770
Upper West Side:						
XVI	8.8		20		1,257	1,118
XX	25		2.2		1,162	2,830
XXII	149.6		5.9		996	4,146
Upper East Side:						
XVIII	10.1			29.2	836	1,321
XXI	28.3			8.7	1,026	1,458
XIX	617.2		28.4		571	5,450

It is seen here that in the lower West Side wards there has been a considerable decrease of general density, accompanied by an increase in the average density of population in each tenement house; that is, with the growth of business in this part of the city a large number of the old dwelling houses and tenements were torn down. Many of the residents of the neighborhood moved out altogether, decreasing the general density of population; many others of the poorer class, driven out of their former dwellings, crowded themselves into old residences not formerly classed as tenant houses or were accommodated in large tenements built on the sites of smaller ones. A like change is seen in the Sixth, Fourteenth, and Fifteenth wards— increase of business causing decrease of general density and increase of tenement-house density. In the Fourth Ward, in the same district, a decrease in density has been accompanied by a decrease in the average number of tenants to a house, due probably to the falling out of use of some of the more notorious large tenements and the replacing of others by business buildings. In 1864 there were 486 tenements in this ward; in 1893, 473. This is the general region once occupied by the Irish and now by their successors, the Italians. Housing in this region is still largely of the old "barrack" and "front-and-rear" type, although many double-deckers are to be seen.

The Hebrew district across the Bowery—the East Side wards up to Fourteenth street—however, is preeminently the region of the double-decker. Business did not crowd greatly into this district, and as the fast-coming immigrants arrived, one great tenement after another of the "double-decker" type was erected on the sites of old private residences. Scarcely any other type of tenement building is to be seen here, and the capabilities of this type for congesting population are shown by the figures given in the tables for the wards where it flourishes. In Italian districts where the older type of tenement more largely prevails, tenement-house density is less, and also the rate of increase of tenement-house density, between 1864 and 1893; while in Hebrew districts there is high tenement-house density and a tremendous increase of tenement-house density in the same period.

The tenement-house reform movement of 1894 is perhaps the most widely known of any that has been carried through in the city, but the legislation enacted in consequence of this movement in 1895 was not the most radical and effective of any. The law of 1895[1] took away the discretionary power of the board of health to

---

[1] Laws of State of New York, 1895, ch. 567, p. 1099, vol. 2, part 1: An act to amend chapter 410 of the laws of 1882. Took effect May 9, 1895.

reduce the prescribed distances between front and rear buildings, and provided for a 5-foot space at the rear of corner lots.[1]

The discretionary power given to the board of health to increase the percentage of lot to be occupied had been taken away in 1891, except for lodging houses and in the case of corner lots, but the law of 1895 restored it by providing while reenacting the 65 per cent limitation that "where the light and ventilation of such tenement * * * were, in the opinion of the superintendent of buildings, materially improved, he might permit such tenement or lodging house to occupy an area not exceeding 75 per cent of the lot."[1] The law of 1895 made the first provision with regard to air shafts, no previous law having required them or prescribed any minimum size or width therefor. The provisions of this law were that no shaft or court of less area than 25 square feet should be considered as part of the free air space in computing the amount of lot covered by the building, that no air shaft 10 feet square and over should be covered with a roof or skylight, and that the superintendent of buildings might make and modify or change rules and regulations as to air shafts. The Greater New York charter 2 years later took away the power of the superintendent of buildings to alter regulations, although he still might make them, and made the first requirement of a minimum width for air shafts. The minimum width prescribed for these, both in corner and interior lots, was 2 feet 4 inches.[2]

The law of 1895 also took away the discretionary power of the board of health to permit the lighting and ventilating of rooms by other means than the windows prescribed by the law of 1879; it provided that hallways should be kept lighted at night and all day if not lighted by a window; and that ceilings of cellars used as living rooms should be 2 feet instead of 1 foot (as had been before provided) above the general ground level.

A special sanitary provision was that no wall paper should be placed on any wall or ceiling until the old, if there was any, should have been removed.

Laws of 1891 and 1892 had provided that no tenement house should be used for a lodging house, private school, stable, or for the storage and handling of rags, except by permission of the board of health. The law of 1895 made these provisions absolute, except in the case of a private school, which the board of health might, at its discretion, allow. This law reduced the number of cubic feet of air required from 600 feet for each occupant to 400 feet for each adult and 200 feet for each child under 12.

The net result of all this legislation seems to have been a considerable improvement in special sanitary conditions, aside from the general question of light and ventilation.

Cellar dwellings ceased to be a crying evil, due partly, however, to the general increase of housing accommodations as well as to legislation, which, it is seen, was not very drastic as to cellar occupancy.

The general nuisance of foul and stagnant water in yards and cellars, so striking a feature of early tenement-house life, was greatly abated. The visitor of 1900 could go about dry-shod, at least, in tenement yards and courts where 35 years before the accumulation of what should have gone off in sewers and drains made access almost impossible.

But on the whole the tenement-house evil was still so serious in 1900 as to lead to the appointment of a State tenement-house commission to investigate the subject and make recommendations for legislation.

The most serious evils found by this commission in their task of investigation were, in their opinion—

(1) Insufficiency of light and air, due to narrow courts or air shafts, undue height, and to the occupation by the building or by adjacent buildings of too great a proportion of lot area.
(2) Danger from fire.
(3) Lack of separate water closet and washing facilities.
(4) Overcrowding.
(5) Foul cellars and courts, and other like evils, which may be classed as bad housekeeping.[3]

A special and alarming result of the lack of light and air which the commission felt to be the greatest evil of tenement-house conditions at present was "that the dread disease of pulmonary tuberculosis had become practically epidemic in this city." Testimony taken before the commission at its public hearings went to show "that there are over 8,000 deaths a year in New York City due to this disease alone; that there are at least 20,000 cases of well-developed and recognized pulmonary tuberculosis in the city and in addition a large number of obscure or incipient cases," and "that the conditions in the tenement houses were directly responsible for the tremendous extent and spread of this contagious disease."[4]

---

[1] Ch. 567, sec. 8.
[2] Ch. 378, Greater New York Charter, sec. 1318.
[3] Advance sheets of part of the Report of the Tenement House Commission, 1900, p. 7.
[4] Report Tenement House Commission, 1900, p. 15.

THE IMMIGRANT IN NEW YORK CITY. 489

The more noticeable points in the legislation recommended by the commission and enacted in 1901[1] may be briefly summed up as follows:

As to light and ventilation, the new law provides for tenement houses hereafter to be built that not more than 70 per cent of the ground space of interior lots, or 90 per cent of corner lots, shall be occupied, and that there shall be no discretionary power to modify this provision; that the height of a new building shall not "by more than one-third exceed the width of the widest street upon which it stands," and that each must have behind it a yard extending across the entire width of the lot, and varying in depth with the height of the building. A building 60 feet high, except when on a corner lot, must have a rear yard at least 12 feet in depth. One foot of yard space is to be added or may be taken away for every 12 feet above or below 60 feet; but the minimum depth of any yard is to be 10 feet. Buildings upon corner lots must have yards of at least 10 feet in depth.

The above provisions go but a little beyond those of the law that they supersede; the chief advantage arises in the taking away of discretionary power.

The provisions with regard to courts, however, are a long step in advance, and really do away with the necessity of strict provisions as to rear yard space. The fundamental idea of the different sections prescribing in detail the area of courts under different circumstances—whether outer or inner, on the lot line or within the lot—is that courts open to the street on one side (outer courts) shall be, generally, at least, 12 feet in width for buildings 60 feet in height, and that court spaces completely surrounded by the walls of buildings (inner courts) shall, under usual circumstances, have an area of 24 by 24 feet for the same height (60 feet). The dimensions given will be increased or may be decreased wi h the increase and decrease of height of buildings, but outer courts are not, under usual circumstances, to be less than 9 feet wide or inner courts to afford a space less than 21 by 21 feet.

It is also provided that inner courts must have ventilating ducts at the bottom of not less than 5 square feet in area and communicating with the street or yard.

Turning to the plan of the "double-decker," it is seen that this type of building, with its air shaft 4 feet 6 inches wide, having no ventilation from below, is disposed of for the future by the above provisions.

This law forbids in express terms the building of rear tenements, although other of its provisions would practically prevent their erection; and it also prescribes a minimum floor area for rooms. This is a better provision against overcrowding than one with regard to cubic air space in proportion to the number of occupants, which is extremely difficult to enforce. Moreover, as is stated in the commission's report (p. 132), "the rooms in new tenement houses have become so small that it is now necessary to lay down minimum dimensions." The dimensions prescribed are, not less than 120 square feet of floor area for at least one room in each apartment, and at least 70 square feet for each other room. (Sec. 70.)

To remedy special sanitary evils the law of 1901 provides, for new tenements, that no cellar may be occupied for living purposes, and that no basement may be occupied unless the room is 9 feet in height (instead of 7 feet, as in the former law) and has its ceiling 4 feet 6 inches above the surface of the adjoining ground (instead of 2 feet as before); and that in each tenement house there shall be a separate water-closet, in a separate compartment, for every family. This last is an especially useful provision.

For already existing tenement houses the law provides that the provisions applying to new tenement houses with regard to percentage of lot to be occupied and to yard and court spaces must be complied with when any old tenement house is enlarged; and that any new rooms or halls constructed in old tenement houses must meet the requirements of the regulations for rooms and halls in new tenements.

An improvement of conditions such as are seen in tenement houses of types 3 and 4 (see cut, pp. 482–483), and which were untouched by previous legislation, is to be expected from provisions of the present law regarding the light and ventilation of rooms in already existing tenement houses. As is stated in the commission's report "There are in this city a number of old, unsanitary tenement houses containing small dark rooms without any means of light or ventilation to the outer air. In some cases these rooms communicate with an adjoining room which opens to the street or to the yard, and in other cases there are even as many as 3 or 4 rooms in a line, only one of which communicates with the outer air. As the law since 1879 has required that every living room in a tenement house thereafter erected should have a window opening directly to the outer air, it is apparent that these buildings have for more than 20 years been violating fundamental sanitary rules."[2]

To meet this evil the present law provides that each room in already existing tenement houses must have either a window opening on the street or yard, or upon a court of not less than 25 square feet in area, or must have a sash window at least 15 feet square opening into an adjoining room which has an external window. It is further-

---
[1] Laws of the State of New York, 1901, ch. 334.
[2] Report Tenement House Commission, 1900, pp. 137-138.

more provided that an inner room that has to be ventilated by such a sash window must have at least 60 square feet of floor space, 600 cubic feet of air space, and at least 600 cubic feet of air space for each occupant.

The practical result of this provision will be that in houses 4 rooms deep (type 3, cut, p. 482) sash windows will be provided and fairly good ventilation secured, while in tenements of types 4 and 5 one of the dark inner rooms will probably be knocked out to make a court or air shaft of the size required to ventilate the other inner rooms.

The "double-decker," however, which type is seen in about 60 per cent of the tenement houses now on Manhattan Island, is left practically untouched by the present law, except that one finger is laid on the air-shaft evil by providing for a door at the bottom of the shaft giving sufficient access to it to enable it to be properly cleaned out.

A most important provision of the new law is one which requires the absolute removal, by January 1, 1903, of all school sinks and privy vaults. These latter were prohibited, except in special cases, by the law of 1887, and the great majority of those existing at that time have been done away with. But the school sink—a long vault lined with a sort of iron trough, and arranged to be flushed from time to time by running water into the sewer—which came into use in the older type of tenement houses to take the place of the prohibited privy vault, is practically the same thing as the vault, and is as great a nuisance, if not greater, since it admits gases from the sewer to be added to the natural foul emanations of the vault. The commission's report says: "These school sinks were, in nearly every case, found by the commission's sanitary inspectors to be in a horrible condition and a serious menace to the health of the occupants of such houses and the neighboring houses. From their construction it is very difficult to flush them, and the inspectors found many cases where they had not been flushed for weeks. In summer the stench is intolerable, and unquestionably causes a good deal of sickness."[1]

No previous tenement-house law had attempted to deal with the social and moral evils arising from life in the tenements, except indirectly by provisions such as those prescribing that halls should be lighted, and that access to all rooms must be had without passing through bedrooms.

The present law, however, directs a special series of provisions against prostitution in tenement houses. Women carrying on the trade of prostitution in tenement houses are to be considered vagrants, and punished by commitment to the county jail. If a tenement house is used for immoral purposes with the permission of the owner, the tenement building itself shall be subject to a penalty of $1,000; if so used with the consent of the lessee of the whole house, the lease shall be terminable. "Permission of owner or lessee" is to be assumed if proceedings for the removal of the offending tenants be not commenced within 5 days of notice of the unlawful use. The general reputation of the premises in the neighborhood is to be competent evidence. (Secs. 141-145.)

These provisions are thoroughly practical in character, and should bring about considerable improvement in moral conditions if enforced.

The question of enforcement of the laws, indeed, has been all along quite as important as that of the provisions of the laws themselves. That an excellent law is enacted is no indication that the good results expected will arise from it in practice.

The tenement-house commission of 1900, in the course of their investigation, found that of 333 new tenement houses in course of construction which were inspected in the borough of Manhattan, only 15 were found in which there were no violations of law. In the other boroughs there was no such house found in which there was no violation. Of 286 tenements inspected with reference to percentage of lot occupied, 282, or 99 per cent, covered more than 65 per cent of the lot; 274, or 96 per cent, more than 70 per cent of the lot, and 88, or 31 per cent, more than 75 per cent of the lot—the extreme limit of discretion given to the building department. Twenty-nine occupied 80 per cent of lot area or over.

The sanitary provisions of successive laws have not been systematically or fully enforced, the present practice of the department charged with their administration being to take action in regard to sanitary evils only upon complaint of individual citizens—they themselves taking no initiative in the matter.

Such failures of the law are due partly to provisions in the law itself, allowing officials discretionary power to modify its requirements, partly to simple neglect in its enforcement. City officials may not be interested in carrying out the law, or they may be positively unable to do so, owing to the inadequacy of the administrative force at their disposal.

The tenement-house legislation of the present year has endeavored to do away with these hindrances to tenement-house reform by omitting to grant discretionary power as far as possible, by making the desired reforms depend rather upon construction,

---

[1] Report Tenement House Commission, 1900, p. 149.

which if once secured enforces automatically the wished-for change, than upon inspection, which may at any time slacken up or be omitted altogether, and by providing for a separate tenement-house department, which shall stand before the people as solely responsible for the enforcement of the law and shall have a sufficient staff for that purpose.

From the tenement-house legislation of 1901 as a whole may reasonably be expected a material improvement in conditions of lighting and ventilation in new tenement houses and those of the oldest types, but not in the "double-decker." A gradual diminution of tuberculosis and other bad physical conditions arising from insufficient light and air may be expected to follow.

The special sanitary provisions of the law will do away with much of the open offensiveness still remaining and of the disease arising from this cause.

Social and moral evils will be somewhat reduced, directly by the provisions against prostitution, and indirectly by the provisions that make the tenement house a better dwelling generally. The administrative features of the law promise a more adequate enforcement than previous laws have had.

But no radical reduction of overcrowding, the great evil of the tenement, may be looked for. The provisions as to the height of buildings, yard spaces, room spaces, and so forth, will slightly reduce the density of population for separate houses in new tenements, but they leave the already existing density untouched. Furthermore, as new tenement houses replace private residences with the growth of the tenement districts, the general density of population for the city will increase.

All that may be expected from the new law in this regard is that it will check a possible rapid acceleration of the rate of increase of density that seemed impending under the law just superseded, with the pressure of population on housing accommodations.

If the measures adopted in the last tenement-house law, greatly as they improve upon former laws, do not, after all, fully meet the situation, it is an indication that no legislation practically attainable can do so. The commission had the problem plainly and without disguise before them; they also had clearly in mind the measures needed to do away with certain features of the evils noted; they found, however, that the enforcement of these would involve so much expense to owners, both by way of reduction of income from reduction of space to be occupied and by actual outlay for construction, as to put a stop to building operations. It was their conclusion, after thorough study of the conditions, that "adequate light and air, perfect sanitation, even passable home environment, can not be provided by the best tenement house which is commercially possible on Manhattan Island—that is, by the best tenement house which can be built with sufficient prospect of income to warrant its erection;" and that, since "tenement-house reform would not be practical which went so far as to put a stop to building new tenement houses," nor would it "if it compelled such extensive changes in old tenements that owners would turn them to other uses," they must recommend legislation which met the evils only in part. It is hard to see how any future legislation could overcome these difficulties.

On the whole, it does not seem that the newer immigration offers any greater or more serious problems than the old, except in so far as they add to the total numbers and increase the general overcrowding.

In the newer period general health conditions have certainly improved. There is no more of the sickness among immigrants due to unsanitary conditions on the passage over. Under the present immigration regulations only immigrants of fair physical condition are admitted to the country. In the city, notwithstanding bad tenement conditions that might be improved, the general death rate has fallen greatly since the fifties, due to a more enlightened sanitary system.

The newer immigrants arrive here at no lower social level, to say the least, than did their predecessors. Their habits of life, their general morality and intelligence can not be called decidedly inferior. No account of filth in daily surroundings among Italians and Hebrews can outmatch the pictures drawn by observers of the habits of immigrant Irish and even Germans. The Italian ragpicker was astonishingly like his German predecessor, and the Italian laborer is of quite as high a type as the Irish laborer of a generation ago.

In some cases the newer immigrants have brought about positive improvement in the quarters they have entered. Whole blocks have been transformed from nests of pauperism and vice into quiet industrial neighborhoods by the incoming of Italians and Hebrews.

Simple overcrowding, however, is an evil in itself, and when this takes place it becomes desirable to encourage tendencies toward movement out of the cities on the part of immigrants. How far this movement has already proceeded for certain of the newer immigrants may be seen in another part of this volume.

492   THE INDUSTRIAL COMMISSION: —IMMIGRATION.

It should be remembered in making plans for the dispersion of immigrants how strong are certain inducements of real and genuine advantage for them to remain in a large city. That there are advantages offered in cities is shown by the fact that the native born are flocking there as well as the foreign born. The immigrants' journey across the ocean is as much a part of the great general movement from the country to the city going on all over the world for some years as is the journey of the American lad from the country town to the city.

Primarily, the city is the great industrial center. The principal occupation to be found by the immigrant in country districts—agricultural labor—must probably be regarded as, on the whole, less remunerative than any other. Mr. George K. Holmes, Assistant Statistician of the Department of Agriculture, gives the following estimates of actual earnings in 1890 of each large class of workers for hire (the large groups given by the Census Office) made by experts and not hitherto published:[1]

TABLE 25.

Engaged in—	Number.	Earnings (millions of dollars).
Agriculture	8,500,000	
Agricultural labor	3,000,000	645½
Trade and transportation	2,000,000	745
Domestic and personal service	4,000,000	943
Manufacturing and mechanical industries	5,000,000	2,197

The last class, one-third of the wage-earners, received one-half of the earnings of labor; the class of agricultural laborers, one-fifth of the wage-earners, received less than one-seventh of the total earnings.

An allowance of actual yearly earnings for each person in each class (taking count of unemployment) would be, on this basis, as follows:

Agricultural laborers $215
Domestic and personal servants 227
Trade and transportation 340
Lumbermen, quarrymen, etc. 372
Miners 420
Manufacturing and mechanical industries 445

In the cities, mainly, are to be found the opportunities for the higher paid employments, and the larger the city the greater the number of openings. It is quite true that the supply of labor may be greater than the demand in the larger market; but in the larger market each individual sees more chances at least of employment and thinks that he is as likely to be one of those lucky enough to secure them as any other.

Other advantages offered by cities are substantial ones to the immigrant. In the cities are the various institutions for the help and comfort of the poor that provide what they can not easily provide for themselves—the hospitals, dispensaries, charitable societies, schools, libraries, social settlements, and all such things.

Before the immigrant is too severely condemned for lingering in the cities such considerations as these should be taken into account.

CHAPTER X.
AGRICULTURAL DISTRIBUTION OF IMMIGRANTS.

[Tabulation and Text by KATE HOLLADAY CLAGHORN, Ph. D.]

I. INTRODUCTION.

A. DENSITY AND INCREASE OF POPULATION, BY STATES.

The first question to be asked with regard to the agricultural distribution of incoming peoples is, Where is there room for them?

The following tables, compiled from the Twelfth Census (1900), showing the present density of population of the country by States, throw some light on this question:

---
[1] Report of Industrial Commission, Vol. X, p. 152.

AGRICULTURAL DISTRIBUTION OF IMMIGRANTS. 493

NORTH ATLANTIC.

Density of population, 1900.		Increase of population, 1890–1900.	
State.	Persons to the square mile.	State.	Per cent.
Rhode Island	407	New Jersey	30.4
Massachusetts	348.9	Massachusetts	25.3
New Jersey	250.3	Rhode Island	24
Connecticut	187.5	Connecticut	21.7
New York	152.6	New York	21.1
Pennsylvania	140.1	Pennsylvania	19.9
New Hampshire	45.7	New Hampshire	9.3
Vermont	37.6	Maine	5
Maine	23.2	Vermont	3.4

NORTH CENTRAL.

Ohio	102	North Dakota	70.9
Illinois	86.1	Minnesota	33.8
Indiana	70.1	Illinois	26
Missouri	45.2	Wisconsin	22.3
Michigan	42.2	South Dakota	16.8
Iowa	40.2	Iowa	16.7
Wisconsin	38	Missouri	16
Minnesota	22.1	Michigan	15.6
Kansas	18	Indiana	14.8
Nebraska	13.9	Ohio	13.2
South Dakota	5.2	Kansas	2.9
North Dakota	4.5	Nebraska	.7

SOUTH ATLANTIC.

Maryland	120.5	Florida	35
Delaware	94.3	West Virginia	25.7
Virginia	46.2	Georgia	20.6
South Carolina	44.4	North Carolina	17.1
North Carolina	39	South Carolina	16.4
West Virginia	38.9	Maryland	14
Georgia	37.6	Virginia	12
Florida	9.7	Delaware	9.6

SOUTH CENTRAL.

Kentucky	53.7	Texas	36.4
Tennessee	48.4	¹ Louisiana	23.5
Alabama	35.5	Alabama	20.9
Mississippi	33.5	Mississippi	20.3
Louisiana	30.4	Arkansas	16.3
Arkansas	24.7	Kentucky	15.5
Texas	11.6	Tennessee	14.3

WESTERN.

California	9.5	Idaho	91.7
Washington	7.7	Montana	84.1
Colorado	5.2	Arizona	67
Oregon	4.4	Wyoming	52.4
Utah	3.4	Washington	46.4
Idaho	1.9	Utah	32.2
Montana	1.7	Colorado	30.7
New Mexico	1.6	Oregon	30.4
Arizona	1.1	New Mexico	27.2
Wyoming	.9	California	22.7
Nevada	.4	Nevada	¹7.15

¹ Decrease.

The tables give in one column the present density of States, arranged in the order of density; in a parallel column, the rates of increase from the last census period to the present, of the same States, arranged in the order of magnitude of increase. In the relation of these two columns to one another certain features in the general development of these States are indicated.

B. INFLUENCES AFFECTING DENSITY AND INCREASE OF POPULATION.

Leaving modifying circumstances out of account it might be expected that population would have increased most rapidly where it was already least dense. And this expectation is, in great part, confirmed by the tables. Divide the tables for the North Central, the South Atlantic, South Central, and Western States into two portions each, horizontally, and it will be found that, with one or two exceptions, the States standing in the upper half of the density column of each table are to be found in the lower half of the column showing increase. More than that, the order of names in one column, read downward, corresponds closely with the order of names in the other, read upward, thus showing a fairly regular inverse variation of relative density and rate of increase. But turning to the table for the North Atlantic States, it is seen that density and increase are practically parallel; that the States of greatest density are showing the greatest rapidity of increase. This is an indication of different economic conditions prevailing in these different sections.

The number of inhabitants that may be gathered upon a given area depends largely upon the economic activities to be followed.

Manufactures and commerce are able to support populations of a density of indefinite limit; hence the parts of a country where manufacturing interests predominate are able to show a high density accompanied by a high rate of increase for many successive years. This is the case with the North Atlantic States. The industrial pursuits that make up so great a proportion of the economic activities of these States not only absorb and indeed call for a rapidly increasing population, but also concentrate them in already densely populated industrial centers.

In parts of the country given over mainly to the ordinary forms of agriculture, on the other hand, the expanding population must pour out from the fields already occupied into new ones, and increasing density in any given portion will be accompanied by a decreasing rate of increase for that spot. The tables, then, show that only the North Atlantic States may be regarded as predominantly industrial in their character. In all the other sections population is seeking the less densely settled portions.

Other factors, of course, have to be taken into consideration to account for all the variations seen in these tables. A low degree of density may be accompanied by a low rate of increase in certain rural States because for one reason or another the limit of the profitable working of the soil has been reached. This is apparently the case with the three rural States of the North Atlantic division, which follow the order shown in the manufacturing States. This is also apparently the case in Kansas and Nebraska, where certain checks have been given to agricultural development.

The fact that Illinois stands high in the list of density and increase both shows the growth of manufacturing and commercial interests in that State. The Southern States, by their rates of increase and density, show that, notwithstanding their recent activity in industrial pursuits, they are as yet prevailingly agricultural.

The question, then, of finding room for the immigrant seems to depend upon whether he is to be a factory worker or a farmer. If he is to be a farmer, opportunities will naturally be sought for him where population is least dense. Here again, however, a modifying consideration enters. Agriculture has its different phases. The mode in use in this country up to the present day is extensive cultivation—skimming the soil of its first natural richness without returning anything to it. Following this method the cultivator must use much land and new land; and when his sons grow up he must send them farther on to find new land for themselves.

Intensive methods, however, by which careful and thorough cultivation of the soil and the addition of proper fertilizing material give back to it as much as, or more than, it yields up in the form of crops, will, like the manufacturing industries, support populations up to a limit of density continually pushed farther and farther away as new inventions bring greater and greater productive power.

The field for the immigrant is thus widened. If he is able to follow the methods of intensive farming, and if the general development of the country is such as to make such farming profitable by giving a market for the produce he will find opportunity in localities which native farmers, accustomed to the older methods only, consider overcrowded.

C. FOREIGN FARMERS IN INTENSIVE AGRICULTURE.

There are many indications that the foreign peoples now coming among us are especially adapted to carry on intensive farming. Their history at home, their actual success here in those lines show this plainly. In the home countries intensive methods had to be learned as population pressed more and more closely upon the resources of the soil; and in this country the habits acquired at home are not forgotten. The foreign farmer puts his mind on his business, works steadily, and interests himself in keeping up the fertility of the soil and in extracting from it every particle of product it will yield. Testimony was given before the Industrial Commission[1] that "the economic traditions of the European farmer are one of the most valuable assets in American agriculture." The witness, Prof. J. F. Crowell, instances the Scandinavians of the West, the Huguenot colony of North Carolina, the Pennsylvania Germans, and says that such colonies "have been the mainstay and bulwark of progressive agriculture."[2] The chapter on Italian agriculture in this country, just following, shows that the Italians have in a high degree the qualities fitted for successful intensive farming and are largely engaged in it, and scattered references throughout the parts of this report dealing with the separate states confirm the same thing. The chapter on the Bohemians shows that this people is especially skilled in intensive methods and especially tenacious of them. Hungarians also are promising intensive farmers;[3] the Dutch have made a notable success in the Northern States and are now finding their way to the South; and the Germans everywhere are successful in this sort of farming.

The first condition, then, of enlarging the field for the immigrant is met; he is able to engage in intensive farming. The second condition, that such farming should be required to provide for the needs of the community so as to afford a profit to those engaged in it, is also met. The growth of cities and of industries is bringing about just this demand all over the country, as will be seen by the reports from various States following, which indicate that there is no large part of the country, however thickly settled, that has not opportunities for good intensive farmers.

II. DISTRIBUTION OF CERTAIN NATIONALITIES.

A. ITALIANS.[4]

The ever-increasing Italian immigration to this country presents this striking feature, that, although 80 per cent of it is composed of the peasantry of Italy, it does not come to till the American soil, but settles itself in the American cities, where it meets with and causes endless evils. On account of these evils the well-disposed and good-hearted American observer will say that the Italians in not having gone to till the soil have made a mistake, for which they pay dearly. This is, indeed, their original sin, from which they shall be redeemed only by going back to agricultural life on the soil of their new country. The moral of the fable of Anteo, who was strong only as he was united to the soil, ought to be recalled to their vivid and poetic imaginations, because it applies to their case.

In trying to ascertain the causes of this social Italian-American phenomenon, one should consider the conditions under which the Italian peasant leaves Italy and the conditions which he meets in this country. First, he leaves Italy poor, having been there for endless generations—perhaps since the Romans of old had their large estates in Apulia, Campania, Sannium, Lucania, Sicily, and Sardinia, of which Pliny says: "Latifundia Italia perdire"—only a servant of the glebe; that glebe which for a thousand years he has watered with the sweat of his brow. This has been an ungrateful work, through which he has never been able to ameliorate his position, to acquire social standing, nor to attain instruction and education.

In many instances he sold or mortgaged his little holding or borrowed money in order to purchase the passage ticket for himself only, or he obtained it on usurious conditions from one of his relatives or friends in America, some one of whom had already found work for him. In every case he leaves his family at home, the thought of which always fills his heart with pain. The contemporary Italian immigrant, owing to the fact that a great many Italian families have already come to join their relatives, invariably promises his family that he will send for them as soon as his condition will permit; but when families had not yet ventured to come to America, and when only men were emigrating, they left home with the understanding that they would send help to their families, the money to raise the mortgage or pay debts, and at last would return to live the rest of their days in a certain ease with the money saved in America. Undoubtedly there have been a good many cases of this kind, which have given rise to the belief that the Italians come to this country to work, live in abject economy, and at last go back to Italy with their savings. One makes no mistake in saying, however, that those who carried out this plan almost invariably came back to America, unless they were unable to do so, for the reason that during the years of their residence in America they acquired habits and customs which they could not carry out in their native land when they went back to it.

---

[1] Report of Industrial Commission, vol. x, p. 335.
[2] Ibid., p. 334.
[3] "Maryland" p. 554, this report.
[4] Contributed by Alessandro Mastro-Valerio, Chicago, Ill., editor *La Tribuna Italiana*.

Furthermore, the Italian peasants of the central and southern parts of Italy, and of the islands, who are known by the name of "cafoni," and who form the bulk of Italian immigration, are not a rural population (except in the provinces of Naples and Caserta, and the western part of Salerno, which are exclusively agricultural) in the sense in which that term is understood in this country and in the northern part of Italy.[1] There the peasants huddle in towns, which in many cases number as many as 50,000 inhabitants. Those towns are the outgrowths of the burgs of feudal castles, under whose protection they were built. The Italian peasant has lived there for many generations, only to go out early in the morning to the farms, gardens, fields, and vineyards, which sometimes are miles away, and to come back in the evening. Only during harvest time and for certain special duties, do the Italian peasants and farmers and their families sleep in the country. The reason for this habit is found in the insecure protection the open country afforded, on account of wars, barbaric incursions, brigandage, and malaria, to persons and property. This implies the lack of proper and comfortable rural houses for the peasants, who have only rude buildings and huts, except some country villas which look more like strongholds than country places.

One should not wonder, therefore, at the fact that the Italian peasant emigrating to this country with or without his family, does not see his way to go and live the pioneer life in rural districts where his own language is not spoken. The women would object to this more than the men, because they have had less occasion than the men to leave the native burg. But after all, one could not say that this is an insurmountable obstacle which would confront the Italian "cafone" willing to come pioneering or farming in this country, for many Italian "cafoni" of the aforesaid regions of Italy, having emigrated to Brazil and to the Republics of the river Plata, have become as good pioneers and farmers as the English, the French, the Scotch, the Germans and the Scandinavians have proved themselves to be in this country.

My personal experience enables me to affirm that whenever an Italian peasant, after a certain number of years of struggle in an American city, is induced to go back to his old calling, he and his family adapt themselves admirably to the new surroundings, and take up the habits and customs of the American pioneer, farmer, or country gentleman.

One reason for his lingering in the cities is that he has been kept in such subjection on account of his former occupation—agriculture—that he feels ashamed of himself and his work. He comes to this country still detesting it, and here he throws it away with the same pleasure that Hercules had in tearing from his body the shirt of Nessus.

The Italian peasant leaving his burg for America is entirely ignorant of the possibilities of American agriculture, and it never occurs to him that he could earn money and make a position for himself by tilling the American soil, having been accustomed to look with distrust and hate at the soil, not as the alma parens, but as a cruel and ungrateful stepmother. None of his countrymen who are already here and who send money home, or have brought it home themselves, ever write or say that they earn their money by working the soil, first for others, and afterwards for themselves, as farmers. Of the moral and material advantages of American country life, of the comforts and independence it affords, of the rights and duties of the American farmer, as pioneer of civilization and as an exponent and example of the American principles of self-government, which can not be learned in American cities, owing to political corruption, he is totally ignorant, since he has always been a servant of the glebe, with many duties to perform and very few rights to enjoy. He never had the right to vote at home.

These are the conditions under which the Italian peasant lands in this country. Having to work for his living and for the support of his family and to economize whenever he can, he accepts work wherever he can find it or through whoever can find it for him, being too ignorant of the language to ask for it himself. Hence arises the middleman, who hires him to the contractor or to the construction departments of the railroads. The middleman he calls "boss;" but the American calls him "padrone" and the way in which the latter sells him and keeps him the "padrone system."

It is impossible to believe that the Italian working in the country, seeing the splendid American farms, made more beautiful by spring, summer, and fall and a growing crop, does not feel a desire to till the soil in the way in which he sees it done, which seems to give splendid promise of prosperity and comfort. Certainly he must feel the old ingrained instinct, bred in him for thousands of years, awaking in him. I venture to say that there is not an Italian cafone doing unskilled work on a railroad grading, who, at the sight of an American farm, with a white-fenced and red-roofed house, with a revolving windmill, capacious stables and outhouses, with extensive fields where crops are growing and maturing, or of a pair of robet

---

[1] Pasquale Villari, "Lettere Meridionale."

American horses behind a plow, or a well-filled cart of produce, or a herd of cows, sheep, or swine, or of a court well stocked with poultry, does not feel the nostalgia for his old calling and a strong attraction to the soil, which he would like to till again in that diversified and intensive way for which he is so famous.

He does not know, however, how to get the land and the means to work it until it produces. He does not know of any of his countrymen who, by word or example, could show him the possibilities of becoming a farmer in America. He is ignorant of the laws governing the proprietorship of land, and he has no hint at all of the homestead law by which, after a few and easy formalities, he could obtain 160 acres of Government land at once, while for generations, perhaps, he has never possessed a single acre of it.

The Italian immigrants, having settled so largely in the American cities, have formed in them centers of Italian population which are always attracting other immigrants. Considering that the great majority of Italians who compose these centers are country people, they should have been established in the country. If this had been done, the Italians in America in general would have been more respected. Hence the imperative necessity of the establishment of Italian agricultural centers, or nuclei, to attract the Italian peasants who come to this country.

The greater part of the Italians in this country derive their living by working for the American people, but the remainder of them earn it by work necessary to satisfy the needs of their countrymen. These needs Americans or those of other nationalities can not well supply, from lack of a mutual understanding, caused by racial differences which have not yet been overcome. Hence the immigration of certain Italians who come purposely to live upon their countrymen, and in many cases not very honorably. That among this class of people there are a good many individuals who are unprincipled and self-seeking it is useless to deny, because their indifference toward the painful conditions of the Italian cafone in American cities, upon whom they prey meanwhile, is apparent in all the Italian city colonies. These individuals are just those who have helped to make, under other circumstances, the life of the Italian peasant unbearable at home, so much so that he has been compelled to stop working the Italian soil and emigrate to this country, hoping for better thing.

Professor Nitti, of the University of Naples, has words of praise for the Italian cafone, who at last has had and is still having the courage to abandon bad conditions at home and come to America. But he has scathing words for the class of people who have made the condition of the Italian peasant at home quite unbearable, and for those individuals of the same class who are following him over the Atlantic. Living on their countrymen they think that they have no moral or patriotic obligation to elevate their minds or their hearts from their present narrow state. It is to their interest to leave them in this condition, in order that they may make of them tools for the acquisition of mercenary political power, by selling their votes to the political wire pullers and slate makers with whom American cities are infested. This is the most deleterious work they could accomplish, for on account of it the Italian cafone will never acquire civic education, but will despise the idea of true American citizenship, of which he has received the benefits. It seems that in order to foster their own interests, these unscrupulous Italians think they must keep their compatriots in the American towns. It has even occurred that an Italian, while advising a wretched countryman to go to the country, received a mild reprimand from another Italian, a man of some prominence, for giving such advice. It was evident that the advice was against the interests of the prominent Italian. For truth's sake it must be said also that from the class of Italian peasants in American towns bosses or padroni often develop, just as from a group of slaves there sometimes springs a most unhuman overseer, whom the slaveholder employs to look after his human holdings. These nefarious men forget their former condition, and prey upon their old companions in the same way that they themselves were preyed upon. As a swarm of crows, of wolves, and buzzards invariably follows a fighting army to prey upon the dead, these individuals follow the endless stream of Italian immigration wherever it is directed, to prey upon it, and the Italian, although he is compelled to accept their rapacious help, looks at them with the same terror that the wounded on the battlefield look at the cloud of flying crows circling in the air above. If the cafone had come to America alone, and if he had not been followed by these individuals, his condition would not have been as bad as it is now.

In regard to health, city life is most pernicious to the Italian peasant and especially to the children. Putting aside all other considerations, the thought of these poor little creatures ought to inspire well-disposed and generous people to make efforts to induce the cafoni to go to the country.

In my judgment, the children of the Italian townsmen are degenerating. The full-grown children are not nearly so well developed as their parents. A visit to the crowded Italian settlements of any American city would convince the observer. Hardly a child who is not affected with rickets can be found, and those who are bowlegged are so numerous as to excite the deepest amazement and pity. In an Italian family it is an easy matter to distinguish the children born and raised in Italy from those born and raised in this country, because the former bear resemblance in size and health to their parents and the latter do not.

The Italian peasants in our towns do not follow the rules of hygiene and diet which are conducive to perfect health in this country. The long winter compels them to remain much of their time indoors in the single or double room, where a badly constructed stove must be kept always lit and from which poisonous gases often escape. In many cases the domiciles, which are always bad, are under the street level, and therefore damp. Their rooms are not renowned for their cleanliness, and in addition, the washing and drying are done in them. The women and children who on account of the cold are driven inside suffer more than the men who are out working. In regard to diet, the Italians have a marked predilection for certain kinds of food which they must satisfy at all cost. That they satisfy it at the cost of their health is a matter of fact. Farinaceous foods, in the shape of bread and macaroni, vegetables and fruits and olive oil, are most favored by the Italian peasant. In Italy they took to the mill the wheat they raised or bought, and sieved the flour more or less imperfectly. Out of the flour they made a bread, which though not so white as that usually seen here, but rather brown, had all the nutritive elements of the wheat, protein as well as carbo-hydrates; while out of the cheap American flour which they buy now they are getting bread which is white, it is true, but poor in the bone and sinew making protein and rich in the less nutritive carbohydrates. One may safely say that the bran which is given to cows and chickens has more nutritive substance than the white flour the Italian peasants buy at the store, out of which they make large quantities of bread and macaroni. With such a diet the bones of the Italian children do not grow strong enough to support the weight of the body, and therefore, although other causes contribute, so great a number of them are deformed.

When the Italian peasants are not at work on railroad construction or other excavations they live an idle life in the American towns, spending the money they have earned above the amount which has been sent to their families in Italy.

During the long winter months they rarely find anything to do in town. Sometimes they are employed in cleaning the streets of snow whenever extra help is needed. Often they perform vile and disgusting work, such as that of picking rags and all sorts of refuse from garbage boxes—victuals, bones, glass, etc. The sight of an Italian woman, old or young, following this practice is not unusual, while that of Italian children picking cigar stubs from the street gutters is very common.

Almost all this idle time is passed by them in the saloons and in other resorts of their countrymen in the street or in vacant lots playing ball.

One can not help thinking how profitably they could employ their energy during this time if, instead of living in town, they were farming for others or for themselves. They are generally considered as common, unskilled laborers without any special adaptability except that of taking a shovelful of earth from one place to another, because people do not know their ability as intensive farmers, gardeners, vine growers, etc. They do not know what an Italian family can do on a farm.

Lately the "American Agriculturist" published an article from one of its subscribers in Ohio, in which the writer says that if an American farmer wishes to grow rich, as he is doing, he must take, as he has done, an Italian family on his farm. He describes the work of his Italian family and compares it to that of a family of ants or bees. A special characteristic of the Italian is his wonderful capacity for "picking"—anything and everything. An Italian woman working or strolling in the field will fill her turned-up apron with many things which she will find, and even make herself so useful by destroying all insects which she believes are harmful to vegetation that she would be an object of wonder and admiration to the American farmer in general, as she is to the Ohio farmer in particular. And to think that thousands of such Italian families are degenerating in the American towns!

The suffering of the Italian cafone has found a sympathetic echo in the hearts of the Italian people from the Alps to the sea, of the King and Queen in whose hands the government of the kingdom is intrusted, of the representatives of the people, and even of His Holiness the Pope and the whole clergy. Therefore ways and means, public and private, by law and by personal and collective efforts, have been planned and carried into effect to relieve the pitiable conditions. The diplomatic and consular authorities have reported and acted according to the means at their disposition. Often members of Parliament have come to America to investigate for themselves and for the Government. And at last the emigration law, after years of study, discussion, and delay, has been passed and enacted.

But, strange as it may seem, the proper remedy has never been urged, viz, inducing the Italian cafone of the American towns, by any means and at all sacrifices, to establish himself in the country. This should have been recommended by the official investigators or by subsequent legislation as the only radical and

AGRICULTURAL DISTRIBUTION OF IMMIGRANTS.

definitive way to solve the problem, but other less radical and in many instances inefficacious means have been suggested and approved. These measures are inspired by a most watchful state paternalism, which sometimes seems incompatible with the legal position of the Italian in this country, by whose laws he is protected. To protect Italian emigration abroad is the principle which inspires the Italian Government. The establishment of Italian agricultural centers or nuclei with the cafoni of the American towns, around which the incoming cafoni and spostati would be helped to gather, without being compelled to stop in the American cities, as the northern immigrants do, has never been suggested in official or private reports, as far as we know, during the discussions of the emigration law in the Italian Parliament.

The attention of the Italians of the United States, and of the thousands of existing Italian societies, should be called to their duty of redeeming the Italian good name in this country. They should understand that the only means to rebuild the reputation of the Italo-American in general is the plow. It is useless to deny that the better class of Italians are living under the shadow which bad city conditions are casting; and it is easy to understand that unless they wish to be always in the dark they must do something to relieve the situation. This movement to the plow ought to be started by Italians and encouraged by the Americans friendly toward them, and by the Italian Government, as the surest means of following and protecting Italians abroad. But if official paternalism has failed to see such a necessity and provide accordingly, there have been individuals in the United States who have noticed it and carried it out to the best of their capacities and possibilities in ways and to results which are described in the following pages.

ITALIAN AGRICULTURAL COLONIES.

1. Vineland, N. J.

This is the first Italian agricultural colony in the United States, and was founded by an Italian political refugee to this country, Signor Secchi de Casale. He established the first Italian newspaper in New York, "L'Eco d'Italia," with which he kept alive the love for Italy among the few Italians of the United States, Mexico, and Canada. He was a disciple of Mazzini and a friend of Garibaldi, and of the other Italian patriots, with whom he had fought for the independence of Italy In 1849, after the unsuccessful attempt to found a Roman republic, he emigrated to New York with some of his companions. They lived together on Staten Island, in the village of Stapleton, where the house which they occupied, with Garibaldi, still stands, north of Backman's brewery.

Signor Secchi de Casale was very active in this country in behalf of the cause of Italy, both among his countrymen and the American people, who as a whole sympathized with that country in its struggle for liberty. He was a man of heart, who, as the Italian immigration to this country was increasing, made it his duty to help the immigrants to the best of his ability. A good many Italians who now enjoy good positions in New York and elsewhere in the United States were helped by him with advice and protection. His work in favor of the poor little Italian street musicians, who at that time were brought to this country by unscrupulous men, first known to the American people by the name of "padroni," is remarkable. In this connection he was instrumental, with the aid of the Italian consular and diplomatic representatives in this country, in inducing the Italian Parliament to pass, in 1874, an act for the purpose of abating this human exportation from Italy to this and other countries. King Victor Emanuel knighted Signor de Casale, as a recognition of his services toward his country and his countrymen of America.

But the standing monument to his memory is the Italian agricultural colony which he founded at Vineland, N. J., and which is now the most prosperous of the Italian colonies of the Eastern States. The stream of immigration of Italian cafoni had just commenced to set toward New York, when he saw the necessity of inducing them to go to farm the American soil instead of settling in the cities. The evil results of such a practice were evident, even at the first. He therefore proposed to divert the stream of immigration elsewhere. He found in Mr. Charles Landis, of Landisville, N. J., a most valuable helper in his plan. This gentleman being a large landowner, put large tracts of land at the disposition of Chevalier de Casale for his colonization scheme.

The colony was founded in 1878 with a few Italian peasants, and since then it has grown wonderfully—to such an extent that it now counts about 5,000 Italians, engaged at Vineland, Landisville, and Plainfield, all adjoining towns of the State of New Jersey, in highly remunerative agricultural and even manufacturing pursuits. The Italians of Vineland have been able to produce wine from their vineyards since 1881. This was the first Italian wine made in the East. Some wine is still made in the colony, but not in such large quantities as at first. Viticulture has given place to truck farming and to the cultivation of sweet potatoes, which have proved very profitable. The settlements include three Italian societies of mutual help.

Chevalier de Casale foresaw the mistakes which were in store for the Italian peasant if he crowded in the cities, and with his paper, "L'Eco d'Italia," persistently gave loud warning. By the foundation of his Vineland colony he was giving an example of the way to avoid the fulfillment of a future which must cause suffering and shame, worthy of Dante's Inferno. He wished that his colony should be an example for others to follow, and therefore he put all his soul, which was that of a patriot and a philanthropist, into the care of its foundation and management. But he had very few imitators, because indifference, if not greed and selfishness, was in the hearts of those who surrounded him and who came here afterwards.

Chevalier de Casale died in the year 1885, but his noble work as patriot, editor, and colonizer will remain a dear memory in the hearts of the Italians of the United States.

2. Bryan, Brazos County, Tex.

This colony was founded by chance about the year 1880 by some Sicilians who went to work on the main branch of the Houston and Texas Railroad. When the work of the road was finished they found inducement to buy some land on the Brazos River which was good for cotton, but is sometimes subject to inundation. The culture proved profitable, and the first settlers attracted friends and relatives. Now the colony counts about 500 persons, all told. They own a church, of which Father Petillo was once the rector.

Other Italians are engaged in the culture of rice in the rice fields of southeastern Texas, and many more are truck farming around the large Texas towns, particularly Dallas, Houston, and San Antonio.

A settlement of Italians near Dickinson engaged in truck farming and furnishing vegetables to the city of Galveston is noticeable. In Texas there are also many Italian cotton planters, who are scattered all over the State. Worthy of mention is a group of Italian vineyards in the neighborhood of Gunnison, Tex.

3. Asti, Sonoma County, Cal.

In 1881 there were many Italians in San Francisco asking for work. They could not speak the language of the country and found difficulty in obtaining employment. They were generally good, willing, and able farmers. On the other hand, California, containing a larger territory than the Kingdom of Italy, was only inhabited by 1,000,000 population.

The soil and climate of California are similar to those of Italy. The olive, the fig, the orange, the lemon, the flowers, and the grapes thrive in this section of the world as well if not better than in Italy, as in California there is yet a virgin soil which has not been impoverished by centuries of cultivation, and consequently gives luxuriant products without fertilizing.

There one could see on one side farmers asking for work, and on the other, the farm asking for laborers, to whom it would give the richest returns. The question then was: How to unite the elements together.

Mr. A. Sbarboro, an enterprising Italian of San Francisco, spoke to several of his countrymen about the project of forming a cooperative association and engaging in the production of grapes, which were then commanding a high price. He met encouragement on all sides, notably from that eminent surgeon, Dr. Paolo De Vecchi, who has honored the Italian name and his profession in the State of California.

Mr. M. J. Fontana, who, beginning as a poor boy, by energy and activity has succeeded in becoming the head of the largest fruit-canning establishment not only in the United States but of the world, was one of the most fervent supporters of the enterprise.

Pietro C. Rossi, then a bright, energetic young man, who had recently arrived from the district of Asti, Italy, whose ancestors for generations back had been grape growers and wine makers, and who, himself, during the vacations from his college studies, had devoted himself to the practical part of wine making, was the most important acquisition made by the colony. He devoted his immense energy and bright intelligence to the enterprise, was soon elected the president, and contributed largely to the great success eventually attained by it.

Henry Casanova, S. Campodonico, G. B. Cevasco, V. Ravenna, Antonio Daneri, N. Giamboni, M. Perata, Dr. G. Ollino, and other patriotic Italians, assisted in the organization of the colony.

Thus encouraged, Mr. Sbarboro launched what was intended to be a strictly cooperative farming association. The funds were to be raised by the payment of monthly installments of $1 per share, the same as the building and loan associations. Two thousand two hundred and fifty shares were subscribed, which gave an income of $2,250 per month. A board of 9 directors was elected by the stockholders, all serving without any remuneration whatever.

The organizers took good care not to commit the error of many institutions of a like character by falling into the hands of sharpers who have a tract of land for sale that may be worth, say, $10 per acre, and who, by manipulating the directors, saddle it on the company at perhaps $50 to $100 per acre—the beginning of its sure failure.

Avoiding this mistake, they put their money in bank until they had accumulated $10,000, then appointed a committee of 3 directors to seek for a proper location on which to commence work. This committee traversed the State, visiting some 40 different locations, examining minutely not only the quality and richness of the soil, but the salubrity of the climate, its adaptability for growing grapes, which would make not only quantity but quality in wines. Above all, they examined the rain gauge of years past, and finally, fortunately for the colonists, selected a tract of 1,500 acres of rolling hill land, healthy, never having suffered for want of rain, traversed by railroad, with a station which they named "Asti," expecting, as they eventually did, to make as good wine in the new Asti of California, as that which was made in the old Asti of Piemonte, Italy. The station was only 3½ hours by rail from San Francisco.

The first cost of the land was $25,000. They paid the $10,000 that they had in the treasury on account, and every month for fifteen months thereafter, $1,000. The other $1,250 they used in grubbing up the immense oak trees that were situated on what was then a sheep range, and prepared the land for setting out the grape cuttings.

While making the by-laws Mr. Sbarboro inserted an article which read as follows:

All permanent employees on the grounds shall be members of the association. The preference shall be given to Italian-Swiss persons who are either citizens of the United States or have declared their intention to become such.

The article was intended to benefit the laborers. When everything was ready for work, Mr. Sbarboro called a number of laborers to his office and explained what they were expected to do. Their wages would be from $30 to $40 per month, with good board, wine ad libitum, and a house to sleep in. But in order that they should take an interest in the work, each laborer was to subscribe at least five shares of stock, for which $5 per month would be deducted from his wages. He would then be interested in the profits to be made in the enterprise, and when the land became fruitful, he would, if he so desired, be entitled to receive a number of acres of the land which he had helped to cultivate.

But they could not understand the value of cooperation. Notwithstanding much patient explanation of the advantages which they would derive from becoming stock holders, Mr. Sbarboro could not succeed in inducing a single laborer to go to work, if he was to be compelled to take stock in the association.

The organizers were thus obliged to dispose of their stock to intelligent business men of the city and pay the laborers entirely in cash instead of partly in stock.

Whilst the soil was being prepared the colony was enabled to import grape cuttings from all parts of Italy, France, Hungary, and the Rhine, through the kindness of Dr. G. Ollino, of Asti, Italy. These cuttings arrived in good condition and were set out on the rolling hills where the viticulturist in the employ of the company judged they would thrive the best.

The monthly payments continued for five years, each share having paid $60, or a total of about $150,000. When the colony was started, grapes were selling in the market at $30 per ton. When the colony sent the first grapes to market, the price had been reduced to $8 per ton, which was not sufficient to pay for the cost of growing the grapes.

The board then decided to put up a stone winery. An assessment of $10 per share was levied, making $22,500, and a winery, holding 300,000 gallons of wine, with its cooperage, was built. Thus from being farmers only the colonists were compelled to become manufacturers also. As soon as the first wine was made, a sample of it was sent to market, where only 7 cents per gallon was offered for it by the wholesale dealers. Again disaster stared the colony in the face, but fortunately the board of directors and stockholders of the company were men who only became more active when difficulties were to be confronted. Instead of selling the wine to the large San Francisco dealers at ruinous prices, they shipped it in carload lots to New York, New Orleans, Chicago, and all over the United States.

The fine qualities of the wine were immediately appreciated by the dealers and consumers. Instead of being compelled to sacrifice the wine for 7 cents per gallon, they obtained returns of from 30 to 50 cents per gallon, according to the quality. Thus, from being farmers they had become manufacturers, and from manufacturers they were also forced to become dealers, which brought into their control the three branches of the industry.

Year by year sufficient loads of the wines were sold to pay the running expenses and enlarge the plant annually, the balance of the wines being stored in the vaults and kept for aging purposes.

Again the stockholders did not ask for dividends. Every year they issued a report, showing the improving condition of the property, and all were satisfied that the earnings should be added to the improvements, as it was readily seen that the larger the quantity of grapes grown and wine made, the cheaper the wine could be placed on the market and the more successful would be competition with the larger wine houses which had been organized 20 years before them.

They continued improving and adding to the property for 16 years, at the close of which time they not only had the largest dry wine vineyard in California at Asti, with a winery holding 3,000,000 gallons, complete with the best modern machinery and cooperage, but had also acquired at Madera, in the southern part of the State, 1,000 acres of land with vineyard, cooperage, and machinery, where they are making some of the best port, sherry, Muscat, Angelica, and other sweet wines and brandy that are made in the United States.

After 16 years they commenced to pay dividends to the stockholders, thus remunerating them for their long and patient waiting. The value of their shares is now three times over the amount which has been paid, and one can not help but be sorry for the poor laborers who did not embrace the opportunity of deriving a greater benefit from their labors by joining the organizers in taking stock in the company.

As a result of the enterprise the company has during the past 20 years given remunerative employment to over 200 laborers daily. The colony is a settlement with many families, and only yesterday one could count 45 bright children, the oldest being 17 years of age, who were born there. The colony has a school for the children, a post-office, telephone and telegraphic communications, and it is believed to be one of the happiest communities on the face of the earth. Doctors there are none, as they are not required, except in some isolated cases where accidents happen to some of the laborers.

Several of the directors have purchased small tracts of land, where they have erected pleasant country homes and there enjoy the summer vacations, recuperating their health and procuring enjoyment for their families.

In 1897, when the production of grapes by the colony and by the numerous farmers, who had been induced by its example to set their vineyards in the neighborhood, was so large that the cooperage of the colony, although greatly increased, would not contain the juice of this large crop, the directors conceived the happy thought of carving a cistern out of solid rock, measuring 84 feet long, 34 feet wide, and 25 feet high, which was lined with a wall of cement, then made imperforable by a coat of paraffin. This is five times larger than the largest wine vessel which has ever been built in the world, and its fame has been written by the press everywhere.

It takes 2 steam pumps 7 days to fill this enormous wine tank, and, as it stands on an elevation above the winery, it is emptied by gravitation through a tunnel with a 4-inch pipe in 4½ days. This tunnel is connected directly with the smaller cooperage in the winery of the colony.

At the possessions in Madera the colony has also quite a settlement, so large that the railroad company was induced to build a special track from the town of Madera to the winery, 4 miles distant. Here the colony has put up the best machinery for grape crushing and wine and brandy making that there now is in the world. In the city of San Francisco the colony has built and now occupies a 5-story building fronting on Broadway and Battery streets, where 1,000,000 gallons of assorted wines are stored, bottled, and shipped to all parts of the world.

The colony now produces, of superior quality, the wines Chianti, Barolo, Barbera, Grignolino, and Marsala of Italy, and also the red and white wines of France and Germany, such as Burgundy, Zinfandel, Carigan, Cabernet, Medoc, Hock, Chasselas, Riesling, Chablis, Sauterne, and Johannisberger, besides all the sweet wines, such as sherry, port, Muscat, Angelica, Madeira, Malaga, Tokay, together with the sparkling Moscato and extra dry Monte Cristo champagnes.

The colony also produces a very superior quality of brandy and cognac, including the famous Grappa, so much appreciated by the Italian people, which is identical in flavor and taste with that made in the mother country.

The wines of the colony have made California known throughout the world for the production of wines of a superior quality, as the colony now ships daily wines in large quantities to all parts of the South and Central American republics, to China and Japan, and also to England, Germany, Switzerland, Belgium, and even to Nice and Cannes in France, where the wines of California are highly appreciated by the connoisseurs of those countries.

That the Italian-Swiss Agricultural Colony has been successful in making as fine wines as those made in any part of the globe is further attested by the medals it has received at the different expositions—for instance, those held in Paris and Bordeaux, France, and Genoa, Asti, and Turin, Italy. The jury at the Italian-American Exhi-

AGRICULTURAL DISTRIBUTION OF IMMIGRANTS. 503

bition in Genoa, Italy, in 1892, in addition to a gold medal, granted the colony a grand diploma of honor, the same as was granted the colony at the National Exhibition in Turin, Italy, September, 1898, for the excellent quality of its red and white wines, and also for its sparkling champagnes.

4. Italians in other parts of California and the Far West.

The Italian-Swiss Agricultural Colony of Asti is not the only example of what Italians have done in the State of California. There are instances of individuals who have been no less successful. One may say that Italians have shown to the world, more than any other nationality, Americans not excluded, the agricultural possibilities of California, which in climate and soil bears so much resemblance to Italy. Just for this reason Italians have found in it the desideratum to carry out their agricultural ideas. Their colonies, even those of the cities, are conceded to be the best models among the Italian colonies of the other States. The same credit must be given to the Swiss-Italians of Canton Ticino of Switzerland, who have emigrated to California. They are not only successful as farmers, but also as ranchmen and dairymen. The truck farmers around the city of San Francisco and other cities of California are mostly Italians.

There is not a Californian valley where there is not a dozen or more Italian farms, fruit orchards, or vineyards, and Italians are employed in large numbers by American farmers.

The list of vine growers of California in the year 1881, when viticulture was yet in an incipient state, gives 141 Italians. Since that year no new lists have been published, but the census of 1901 will undoubtedly show even more creditable figures in favor of the Italians of California.

The last report of the Italian Chamber of Commerce of San Francisco, published in the year 1897, gives 45,625 Italians living in the 56 counties of California, almost all engaged in agriculture, owning 2,726 farms, orchards, vineyards, ranches, etc., and 837 business concerns, with a capital of $17,908,300. The total capital of agriculturists, ranchers, and business men was reported as $114,325,000.

The groups of Italian truck farmers in the neighborhood of Denver and Pueblo, Colo., of Salt Lake City, Utah, and of Cheyenne, Wyo., are also worthy of mention. They utilize the land of the valleys, where they can get water for irrigating purposes. On the plateau lands, near Denver, they get the water from artesian wells, with windmills and pumps. They form a prosperous lot of people. They are almost all from the southern provinces of Italy, and the number, though now not more than 300, is on the increase. Originally they were miners or laborers on railroad work. They now have the monopoly of furnishing vegetables to the neighboring cities.

5. Italians of Louisiana and Mississippi.

It is safe to say that the Italians of those States are rapidly dislodging the negroes from the sugar-cane plantations. These Italians almost all come from Sicily, and they are yet coming in large numbers. The Italians having been found reliable at first, are now very much sought for by the planters, who employ them extensively, and who would be at a loss without them. In many cases the plantations are divided into parcels, and each is given to a family to cultivate. The cane is bought by the owner of the plantation at market value, and from the amount is deducted the rent of the land, of animals, and of implements, also the bill of provisions advanced from the store. It would be highly desirable that these Italians, who count about 100,000, should become landowners. Owing to the fact that they are almost all Sicilians, who are very much attached to the kind of food of their native land, the importation of Italian produce to New Orleans from Sicily is very brisk. It seems that in their hard work in the cane fields during the very hot season they find great comfort in drinking wine, therefore the importation of Italian and California wine into these States for their use is very great.

The season of cane cutting is known by Italians as "la zuccarata," and each year before la zuccarata thousands of Sicilians go from Italy and also from the Central and Northern States, to Louisiana and Mississippi; so there is a fluctuation of Sicilians from Louisiana and Mississippi the latter part of the winter, when la zuccarata is over, to the railroad and excavation works of the North, and from the North back again, early in the fall, before la zuccarata is begun.

6. The Italian truck farmers of Memphis, Tenn.

In the outskirts of Memphis are located about 50 Italian truck farmers, for whom the community of that town seems to have great respect, judging from reports published by the American and Italian press. They all come from a well-known Italian town of the Valley of the Po, Alessandria, and therefore their settlement is known as

"La Colonia Alessandrina di Memphis." Their pursuit of furnishing Memphis with fruit and vegetables proves profitable, and they are consequently well to do. They have formed among themselves a society of mutual help, known as "La Societa di Mutuo Soccorso dei Giardinieri Italiani di Memphis," which is very prosperous. Certainly this example deserves to be pointed out to the Italian cafoni of the American towns, and to those on whom it is incumbent to do something for them in the way of inducing them to go back to agriculture.

7. Italian agricultural colonies of Daphne, Baldwin County, Ala., and of Lamberth, Mobile County, Ala.

These colonies were established by the writer, the first in the year 1890 and the second in the year 1893. Therefore he will let someone else say something about the first one, which is the more important of the two. On pages 360 and 361 of a voluminous "Relazione d'un viaggio d'istruzione negli Stati Uniti fatto per incarico del Ministero di Agricoltura, Industria e Commercio del Regno d'Italia, dal Prof. Guido Cav. Rossati, Regio enotecnico governativo a New York," and published in Rome in 1900, one reads as follows:

This colony which I visited was founded about the year 1890 by Mr. Alessandro Mastro-Valerio, a worthy Italian newspaper man, now manager of La Tribuna Italiana of Chicago, for the purpose of inducing the Italian peasant who emigrates to this country to till the soil, taking them away from the influence of the great American cities, which is often pernicious and demoralizing, and where they live and practice the lowest trades.

He took there about 20 Italian families, dedicating several years of his life to the progress and welfare of the colony. When I visited the colony, as a guest of Mr. Valerio, in 1897, I was able to notice personally how he exercised with much love his agricultural apostolate among these good and laborious peasants, whom he daily educated in the sound principles of rational agriculture. There, in that shady and invigorating pine forest which our countrymen were reclaiming for agriculture, he was guiding and advising them about the planting and the care of the vineyards, while he was experimenting for the United States Department of Agriculture and the State Experiment Station of Alabama. Meanwhile the culture of sweet and Irish potatoes, wheat, corn, rice, tobacco, cotton, and vegetables was going on. At the same time he was studying the improvement of the soil by fertilizing, and gave courage to the colonists to overcome the inevitable difficulties of the first years. Lastly, he was the soul and brain of the colony, which owes to him its present welfare.

Each family possesses from 25 to 50 acres of land, bought at from $1.50 to $5 per acre. The soil, which is sandy, with a red or yellow subsoil (siliceo-argillous), is not fertile, but can be easily worked, and with the judicious use of fertilizer produces abundantly Irish and sweet potatoes, corn, rice, oats, tobacco, peanuts, and vegetables, even 2 crops, if one wishes. The vines and fruit trees, which the colonists have planted extensively, according to the system of rows and stakes, develop wonderfully and mature fruit very early, so that the vintage is ended by the 10th of July. The early maturing of the fruit is of distinct benefit, because the grapes can be shipped to the Northern markets, where they are sold as high as 15 cents per pound. The medium production per acre in that locality is about 2 tons. Some vines yield a second crop, as abundant as the first, which matures in September or October.

Each colonist has built his own house out of the lumber of the pine forest. The climate is healthy. The air is purified by pine trees. There is very seldom snow in winter, and the summer heat is tempered by the constant breeze (alisei) from the Gulf of Mexico. In order to avoid the damage by frost, which some years happens in March, the colonists use fires during the night of damp leaves and grass on which some petroleum has been sprinkled.

For our countrymen who follow the principle of intensive agriculture—viz, that culture by which one can have the maximum crop of the best quality from a small piece of land—these Southern lands are fitted, though poor. Their low price, the great facility for improvement of their physical and productive condition, the magnificent climate, the very pure water, the diversified culture during the year, the cooperative system of consumption and production for which the colony was preparing itself when I visited it, in order to facilitate the sale of products and the obtaining of credit for the purchase of provisions, implements, fertilizers, etc., are coefficients which point to the definite success of the colony of Daphne, Baldwin County, Ala.

In the vineyards, kept by the colonists with the utmost care, I could note the culture of some varieties of European vines grafted on indigenous stock. These grapes are sold entirely for table use. But some colonists had commenced to make wine, and so I could taste the good quality made by Mr. Rossi and the brothers Latini. The wine production of the colony is not very great, but it will be as soon as the young vineyards produce and new ones are planted. The colony possesses a school and a church at Daphne, the county seat of Baldwin County.

I visited each family, so as to inform myself as to their condition. I noticed a certain welfare, and did not hear any complaint worthy of notice. In order to make my visit useful to the colonists, on the evening of the third day I spent in Daphne I gave them a lecture on viticulture, on wine making, on agriculture in general, cooperation, etc., in the large hall of the court-house, which they attended in full force. The newspapers of Daphne and Mobile published articles on my visit to Daphne.

Owing to the fact that after this favorable report of Prof. Guido Rossati, Margherita of Savoy, then Queen of Italy, sent as a present to the Italian church of Daphne some rich and artistic vestments and an illuminated missal, and the minister of public instruction of Italy, two boxes of books, the writer flatters himself that the establishment of the Italian agricultural colony of Daphne, founded according to the principles set forth in this paper, has been appreciated by the Italian Government and by the Queen, who claimed the title of "the elder sister of Italians, wherever they were, at home or abroad."

The writer, founder of this colony, avails himself of this occasion to express public thanks to the United States Secretary of Agriculture for the invaluable help he has very generously tendered him, in furnishing him with seeds and shrubs, advice,

AGRICULTURAL DISTRIBUTION OF IMMIGRANTS. 505

books, pamphlets and other publications. For the same reasons, he wishes to express no less sincere thanks to the director of the Alabama Experiment Station at Auburn, to the manager of the firm of the German Kali Works, of New York and Germany, to the fertilizer department of the Armour Company, Chicago, and to Miss Jane Addams and Mrs. Mary H. Wilmorth, of Hull House, Chicago.

The colony of Lamberth was established with colonists who wished to settle along the line of the Mobile and Ohio Railway in Mobile County. This colony now counts about 12 families of very prosperous people. They are engaged in viticulture, in which they are very successful, and in truck farming. They have built a church and school, and have a railroad station.

8. Colony at Sunnyside, Ark., and Derivative Colonies.

(a) SUNNYSIDE.

No other Italian colony in the United States was started under better auspices than this, and no other colony had so bad an end. First we should say that an original mistake weighed upon its destiny, for it was not founded for the purpose of taking away from the cities Italian cafoni in order to get them to till the soil, but it was formed with peasants brought from Italy—from the Romagna and the Marche—the provinces of the old Papal States, on the shores of the Adriatic.

About 500 families, in 2 batches and at an interval of 1 year, were brought from Romagna and Marche to Sunnyside via New Orleans and the Mississippi River. The expense of transportation might have been entirely saved if the colonists had been taken from the mass of Italian peasants in the American cities, who would have been greatly benefited. This fact confirms the opinion that the best means which there is at hand for the improvement of the condition of the Italians crowded together in American cities—that of sending them to the country to till the soil—is largely overlooked.

The foundation of this colony came after an understanding between Mr. Austin Corbin, the Eastern railroad magnate, president of the L. T. Railway and Terminal Company, of the Reading Railway, and of the Anchor Line of steamboats on the Mississippi River, and Prince E. Ruspoli, mayor of the city of Rome. Princess Ruspoli was a Miss Curtis, of Boston, and the Prince visited this country several times. He became acquainted with Mr. Corbin, who proposed to him a colonization scheme for Italians on a large tract of very rich Mississippi River land in Chicot County, Arkansas, almost opposite Greenville, Miss., and on a river island known as Sunnyside. The island had before been used as a penal colony, and, as the contract had expired, Mr. Corbin thought in 1894 of forming on it an Italian colony. He made this proposition to Prince Ruspoli, then visiting the United States.

Under the influence of this gentleman the required 500 families were enrolled in Romagna by a special agent, Prof. Alex. Oldrini, of New York, who made the trip there purposely. They were sent to New Orleans under the special protection of the Italian diplomatic and consular authorities, who had interested the American authorities of that port in them, and from there they were sent to Sunnyside, on the steamers of the Anchor Line, owned by Mr. Corbin. During the trip special care was given to the comfort of the colonists. No less care was given to welcome them at Sunnyside, where they found everything ready to commence work at once, in the fall of 1895.

The soil, of fabulous fertility, as is all the soil of the Mississippi Valley, was ready to be planted. Agricultural implements, draft horses, seeds, houses, stores, warehouses, gins, presses, carts, a railroad, a steamer coasting the island, were all ready for the planting, care, and gathering of the cotton crop, its baling and transportation. The cotton was afterwards bought at market price by Mr. Corbin. There was also a school, taught by 12 Selesian nuns, and a church, of which the Rev. Father Bandini, purposely called from Albany, N Y., was the titular. Sunnyside had also a postal and a telegraph office.

Twenty acres of land, with a good house, was allotted to each family at a fair price, and full credit for each was opened at the Sunnyside store, also the property of Mr. Corbin. With such a splendid beginning the colony gave promise of a high prosperity, but unfortunately malaria soon began to decimate its members. Mr. Corbin had promised the Italian diplomatic authorities at Washington, and through them the Italian Government, that he would make the colonists comfortable, and from the vast improvements he commenced at Sunnyside in the line of drainage, sewerage, and sinking of artesian wells to get pure water from the substrata, which undoubtedly would have improved the sanitary condition of the colony, he certainly was keeping his word.

But his death in the year 1896, in his park in the Adirondack Mountains, caused by a fall from his stage coach, put an untimely end to all this. The estate which he left could not undertake the responsibility of continuing his projects until all the affairs pertaining thereto should have been settled, and this required a great deal of time.

The alarming increase of mortality among the colonists (130 deaths occurred in two months) forced a majority of them to abandon the colony in 1897 and 1898. Only 40 small families and single persons remained. Many of the families went back to Italy; others went to Brazil, South America; Alabama, New Orleans, and the North. The remaining families went to form the colonies of Tontitown, Ark.; of Montebello, near St. James, Phelps County, Mo., and of Verdella, also in Missouri. Owing to the fact that there is before the legislature of the State of Arkansas a bill to buy the land at Sunnyside, to make it once more a penal colony, the probability is that the Italian families remaining at Sunnyside will move elsewhere.

If Mr. Corbin had lived his sanitary projects would have been carried out at Sunnyside according to the perfection which science has reached, and we venture to say that what is now done in the Roman Campagna in regard to the prevention of malaria, by guarding against the anophales mosquito, which it has been ascertained spreads malarial fever through germs injected through its bite, would have been done for the colonists at Sunnyside, and this would have been the most prosperous colony of the United States.

(b) TONTITOWN, ARK.

The Rev. Father Bandini, rector of the Sunnyside church, as soon as the exodus of the members of the colony commenced, thought it necessary to found another colony, where they could continue their agricultural pursuits instead of going back to Italy or to live in the towns. Therefore he gathered a certain number of colonists who were ready to follow his advice and with whom he discussed the plan. A committee was appointed to visit land offered to them by the land department of the St. Louis and San Francisco Railway and report. The report was not unanimous as to the adaptability of the land to their use. Some of the committee liked it and others did not. Nevertheless, about 60 families took the favorable side of the report and went there to settle. They formed the colony of Montebello, Mo. Those who took the other side looked for another place, which they found near Springdale, Ark., and settled to the number of 50 families with Father Bandini, founding in the winter of 1898 the colony of Tontitown, named in honor of Henry Tonti, the explorer and companion of La Salle. Tonti founded in 1686 the first Arkansas settlement and military fort, known as Arkansas Post.

There is no doubt that of the three colonies that of Tontitown is the most advanced and prosperous. The land is better than that of the other colonies and the continuous presence of the Rev. Father Bandini, who acts as a religious and civil apostle, on account of the intense interest he takes in the welfare of his countrymen, is a guaranty of success. He directs intelligently the minds and the hearts and the work of the colonists. During the first year he held his people together in spite of adverse circumstances—a most killing frost, a destructive cyclone, and the prejudice of the neighboring Baptists and Adventists. All reports show the colony to be a success, with a splendid future. Father Bandini teaches the school and ministers at the church, both built through the efforts of the colonists. The church, of which we have before us a photogravure, is a very beautiful building.

(c) MONTEBELLO, MO.

In regard to this colony it must be said that the topography and the quality of its soil, the lack of homogeneous direction, and the rather scanty means of the colonists, impaired its progress at first. The men have been compelled each year to go and work elsewhere in order to earn some money and to return to the colony at the end of the work. Nevertheless, it bears marks of decided progress, which gives promise of an increase. The persistence of the Italians, their diversified, intensive ways of agriculture, their frugality and thrift are bearing inevitable fruit.

(d) VERDELLA, MO.

This colony is composed of no more than a dozen families, and it is in the same condition as the colony of Montebello.

These three colonies carry on general farming, though the tendency is toward wine and fruit culture, truck farming, and small grain, for which Italians have special adaptability. Of course, so far to the South, cotton is king, being the staple which brings ready money. The colonists therefore pay to his royal majesty the same homage that Southern people do, by cultivating it as much as possible, especially since during the last few years the price has been highly remunerative to the planters.

9. Miscellaneous.

Questions put to the Italian consuls, consular agents, newspapers, through advertisements, to presidents of Italian societies, business firms, agricultural bureaus of States and Territories, officials of counties where mining camps composed of Italians are located, etc., do not give definite information regarding the number of Italians engaged in agricultural pursuits. All report, however, that in the neighborhood of the American cities and mining camps there are a good many Italians engaged in truck farming and in vine growing. A strong contingent of them are on Long Island, Staten Island, in the State of New Jersey, in the Delaware peach belt, in Pennsylvania, Washington, Baltimore, in the large truck-farming districts of Norfolk, in the wine-producing belt of the States of New York, Pennsylvania, Ohio, and on the southern shore of Lake Erie—even on the islands of that lake where wine is produced.

The advent of the citrus culture in Florida caused some importation of Italians from Sicily for the packing and culture of the fruit for market. A good many of them have become landowners and cultivate on their own account, and are, with the other Florida planters, victims of the frost.

As to Italians in New England, I will quote the following answer to a letter of inquiry: "In answer to your favor of ——, I beg to say that from inquiries made in order to furnish you the requested information, I have found that there are very few Italian farmers in the New England States, owing to the lack of capital, the nature of the soil, and the rigidity of the climate, which makes it hardly remunerative. I do not think that their number is on the increase, for many reasons, among which is that the Italian peasants are not willing again to follow a pursuit which at home has caused them only hardships and privations."

BOHEMIAN SETTLEMENTS IN THE UNITED STATES.[1]

There are proofs that the first Bohemian emigrants must have come soon after the close of the "Thirty years' war" (1618–1648), caused by the revolt of the Bohemians against Ferdinand II, who violated their religious liberties, and finally, with the assistance of nearly all of Catholic Europe, succeeded in crushing the first spark of religious freedom, and forced the Protestant and patriotic elements to seek new homes. Many crossed the "deep waters" and found homes among their Puritan and Huguenot co-religionists in America. The strongest evidence of these early emigrants exists in Cecil County, Maryland, where are to be found many descendants of the well-known Bohemian emigrant, Augustine Herman, the founder of Bohemian Manor, who came to what was then New Netherlands in the year 1633.

Again, after the revolutionary epoch of 1848, exiled patriots and restless students hurried to the shore of this country. The first Bohemian settlements took root as early as 1850 in St. Louis, Milwaukee, New York, Chicago, and in 1855 in some parts of Texas. These people were mostly students, professional men, and wealthy peasants. Having arrived here without knowledge of the English language, they were forced to give up their professions and settle on farms. Wisconsin, Iowa, Missouri, Texas, Minnesota, Illinois, and California claimed the first emigrants. To these new States they brought the knowledge and industry which they were taught in the overcrowded Bohemia. The virgin soil under their cultivation soon began to yield rich harvests; the dugouts and log-cabins made room for fine cottages and luxurious houses; letters describing this prosperity and longed-for freedom were sent to the old home to be read like fairy tales of Hans Andersen, and everybody dreamed of this new Eldorado.

Conditions in Austria were becoming more and more unbearable when the Austro-Prussian war (1866–1871) broke the last thread of patience and endurance, and all those who still cherished any ideals of religious freedom and national independence and who owned any property sold out, usually to the Jews, and migrated westward.

By this time the German element had become more predominant in this country, and the Bohemian skilled laborers usually being able to speak the German, besides their own language, found that the skilled laborer had here a splendid opportunity. The result was a heavy flow of laborers. The cigar makers from Kutna Hora found in New York a great demand for their trade, remained there and formed a settlement renowned as a center of cigar makers. This settlement annually received additions of other unskilled compatriots, who were at once taught the work, which was hard and in constant demand.

After the Chicago fire in 1871 the rebuilding of the city drew another stream of skilled laborers from Bohemia. Tailors found that Chicago was a good location for custom tailoring, and so Chicago became their destination.

---

[1] Contributed by Josefa Humpal-Zeman, editor of Zensky Listy, Chicago, Ill.

The settlements were formed by people from the same city or village, one helping the other until whole families and their relations were over. The oldest son or daughter would often come first and earn enough money to pay the way for another member of the family.

To the luring advertising of steamship and railroad companies can be given a large part of the credit for the emigration in the eighties, almost to the time of the World's Exposition in Chicago in 1893. This caused a great boom, especially to the real-estate interests, where old friends soon found work for the newcomers. The peasants were put to day-labor occupations, the tradesmen taken into shops, and older boys and girls were sent to tailoring, cigar making, and to factories.

In each settlement arose various patriotic, social, and benevolent societies, the most popular among these being the building and loan associations.

The characteristics of the Chicago settlement may also be seen in to the settlements in Cleveland, New York City, Milwaukee, Omaha, St. Louis, Baltimore, and Cedar Rapids, Iowa. Yet each colony has its distinct occupations. The Bohemians of New York are mostly cigar makers. Those of Cleveland are engaged chiefly in building trades, the Standard Oil works, foundries, etc. In Chicago they are engaged in tailoring, lumber work, and building trades; in Cedar Rapids, in building trades; in Sinclair, in the stock yards; in Burlington, in railroad and car shops.

Some Bohemians work with their Slovak neighbors in the mines of Pennsylvania, and a large portion have settled on farms; and here we come to another interesting feature of Bohemian life.

The Bohemians, like all Slavs, are very fond of the soil, and from time immemorial were considered a rural people. They are fond of home life, and one would naturally suppose they would prefer the farm to the city any day. Yet this has not been the case in the United States, and although there are many thousand Bohemians settled on farms the majority prefer the city. The reasons for this are several: First, to settle on a farm requires capital with which to buy farming implements; second, the cost of transportation from the seaports is too great. Then, the life of an American farmer is very lonely in comparison with the ideal village life of Bohemia, where all have grown up from childhood together. In Bohemia are to be had the traditional holidays, feasts, processions, national music, and games, which make the life of a peasant so happy. It is true we have the newspaper, with the rural delivery, to break up the monotony (and Bohemians have over forty newspapers in their language in the United States), but that in itself is one of the elements that sows the seed of discontent, telling as it does with American dash of the life in the large cities. Bohemians love music and they long for friends and society, and that is another reason why they prefer the life of the city day laborer, with the hard toil in lumber yards, to that of a prospering farmer.

There have been several efforts made to form agricultural colonies, but all have failed. The first cooperative colony (Rys) was formed in June, 1897, by a board of energetic and intelligent workmen. It was after the distress of 1894, when so many laboring people suffered from lack of work following the strike of cutters and tailors. The progressive workingmen decided to form a society which was to raise a fund by weekly payments, the first fee being $50, and after that each member was to pay a certain amount per week. They succeeded in raising enough to purchase an old plantation in Virginia. The reason for choosing this State was that it was near the markets, and transportation would not cost much. With the assistance of various friends the first thirteen families left for the colony. Those remaining behind were to send weekly contributions until harvest time. They were all to work as equals, each one considering the good of the other. Soon trouble arose; no one wanted to consider the others' advice; jealousy arose among the women, followed by lack of desire to work by the men. The Chicago friends failed to send their contributions. Soon all grew impatient, and one by one left the colony and moved to Baltimore or New York, and the colony disbanded.

Individually, however, Bohemian farmers have done well. Some in Minnesota and Nebraska have started cooperative mills and cheese factories. The most prosperous farmers are to be found in Iowa, Nebraska, Texas, and Wisconsin. The earliest settlements were in Wisconsin in 1850, in Texas in 1855, in Minnesota in 1854, and in Nebraska in 1868. These settlements were made usually near the rivers, and the majority of those in the Western States had migrated from some other State.

Only in rare instances did the Bohemian farmers come in as farm laborers. The first farmers brought with them from Bohemia money enough to buy land at once. Many of these early settlers had sold large estates in Europe and brought as much as $10,000 with them. These not only bought farms for themselves, but helped others by loaning them money. Those who were not so well-to-do brought at least $1,000, and with this bought cheap lands. As a rule the Bohemians bought uncultivated land, cleared the forests, and by skillful methods of agriculture developed the land into prospering farms. Such instances may be found in Caledonia, Racine County, Wis.; Ely, Iowa; Yankton, S. Dak.; Wilbur, Schuyler, and Abie, Nebr. The

Bohemian settlements grew as the children matured, each son receiving a portion of the land or an entirely new farm.

The people settled mostly in groups, and only in rare instances did they mingle with other nationalities. Where, however, they have come into strange colonies they prosper and soon buy out the others. In exclusively Bohemian localities, as, for instance, in Texas and some parts of Nebraska, like Abie, where the settlements are almost exclusively Bohemian, they retain their Bohemian habits, but where they are near other nationalities they Americanize very rapidly. The Bohemian farmers are good grain and fruit growers and great lovers of trees. Each farm is surrounded by a thriving orchard, and every corner of the land is utilized. They are hard workers, and have little faith in schemes to save work; they give the same amount of energy to the virgin soil of America as they did to the crowded and much-used soil of old historic Bohemia. The result is that their farms prosper and they grow rich.

It must not be inferred that the Bohemian farmer does not believe in machinery, for he does; only he does not believe that the sun and rain alone will do the weeding and cultivating.

There is one new industry in the United States which should afford the Bohemian immigrant a great inducement to leave the overcrowded city, and that is the sugar-beet industry, which, especially in the arid lands of Colorado, is taking strong hold. The sugar beet is one of the great products of Bohemia, and many Bohemian immigrants are expert beet growers. If these could be induced to settle in the neighborhood of Rocky Ford or Holly, Colo., they would help to build up what promises to be a very prospering industry. There are several features of this kind of farming which would be especially advantageous to the Bohemian farmer:

First, he knows how to grow the beet, and as the agriculturists that are teaching the farmer are mostly Europeans, they would teach exactly the same methods as the Bohemian farmer used in Europe.

Secondly, the farms are small, another feature to which the Bohemian farmer is accustomed to from Europe.

Thirdly, on account of the small size of the farms the farmers are brought closer to each other, and so form small villages, with the greater social life to which they were accustomed in Europe.

Fourthly, the factories are in the vicinity, and offer a market and employment to him.

Fifthly, the land is cheap and ample time is given for payments.

At present the tendency of Bohemian immigration is to settle in the large city settlements, and the hard times which we have just survived have checked almost all immigration. Besides, the Austrian Government makes it much harder for a peasant to sell his land and move. The European papers are constantly publishing reports of the "hard times" in America, and so only those come who have relatives here and some prospects. Then also, from the fact that most of the good lands are taken up and farms are much more expensive, there remain fewer inducements for the immigrant to go to the country districts. In the city there is always more opportunity to receive employment and assistance in case of need from the older settlers. If the Government would offer some assistance to immigrants in getting out of the city there is no doubt that many would go.

Bohemians dread to become subjects of public charity, and hence prefer to go where there is some prospect of becoming self-supporting and independent. There is no doubt that fully one-fourth of the city populations would prefer the life of a farmer to that of a day laborer, but have not the means to go the country. It would be better for them and better for the country if the rural people of Europe could locate on farms. City life is extremely dangerous to the second and third generations. The peasant, raised in the open air, hates the close tenements, crowded streets, and filthy alleys. The walls of the house stifle him, and so he is forced to stay outdoors, where he forms his companionships. The saloon becomes his social center, where he can idle away the long and tedious hours of enforced idleness or the long evenings. The children romp in the streets also, and not having playgrounds where they could exercise they find their chief pleasure in reading detective stories and in fighting. They are soon taught that obedience to parents, respect to old age and law, is nonsense. Instead of turning their earnings into one treasury they pay board to the "old folks" and spend the rest as they choose in cheap theatres and music halls. This is the condition of the ordinary peasant class who are the day laborers of the city, and form the lowest stratum in the foreign colony. The professional classes give their children better education, and so throw them into relation with the better class of Americans, which saves them to some extent from the corrupting influences spoken of.

This evil state of affairs would be impossible in the country, where work takes up all the extra energy, and the outdoor life affords conditions to which the people are accustomed. In Europe the laboring classes have their labor unions, and the young apprentices have their Sunday trade schools. The communities are small, and each knows the other. City life, under present conditions, with no playgrounds, no neighborhood centers, no public reading rooms, no manual training schools in the foreign districts, has certainly most distressing effects on the second generation.

If farms were smaller and the houses closer, the towns formed on the style of European villages, with their social aspect, there is no doubt that the country would have the most wholesome influence on the foreign population.

C. FINNISH COLONIZATION.

Political troubles at home, as well as a desire to better their economic condition, have been sending Finns to this country in considerable numbers during the past few years. They are not inclined to linger in cities; a large proportion go directly to country districts, especially to the Northwest, on first arrival. Those who remain in the city are ready at any moment to make their way out of it if work is hard to get.

The following letter from the general agent of a steamship company engaged especially in transporting Finns tells of special efforts he has made to place Finns in agricultural districts, and is of particular interest as showing them in a part of the country which would be supposed to be not particularly well adapted to them. He writes:

I would say, relative to the Tennessee colony of Finns, that it is located in Hickman County and promises satisfactory results.

I have for a long time been much interested in locating Scandinavians advantageously, and have tried several places, giving them up when found lacking in any of the requirements for the happiness and health of settlers. The Hickman County lands I took a little over 2 years ago after very careful examination, and some 8,000 acres have been taken up by settlers, although I had no desire to hurry sales until results of the first settlers' efforts could be seen. The lands are particularly adapted to raising grapes and tobacco, and with cultivation of these, Scandinavians are naturally unfamiliar; but the location is healthy, and the settlers there, all of whom have purchased land, are contented, so that by the fall a good many Scandinavians will know of it and quite a number will no doubt buy farms.

These buyers have all been some time in this country, and the little money they have has been made here. Few of them are from cities; most of them are from the Northwest, where they have been working. Newly arrived Finns and Scandinavians rarely have any money other than that required by the United States laws. Sometimes they bring $50 or $100, but they come here to work, and it is only after they have become familiar with things here and have put by some money that they finally settle down to stay. Of well-to-do farmers in their own country we can not recall any who have come here, and even with political troubles it is doubtful if there will be many of this class coming over. But, as I have said, there are a good many Finns and Scandinavians already in this country who are desirous of settling if they can do so with surety of making money, and I have given much time to looking for healthy suitable places for them, having had lands offered in nearly all the States.

Scandinavians have heretofore preferred the Northwest, but the Central and Southern States to-day, in my opinion, present greater inducements for them to settle, as land is much cheaper, and they can raise almost everything, and many localities are healthy; while land is now high in price in the Northwest, farming there must be conducted on a grand scale to pay, and crops are necessarily limited to cereals. Still, as some Scandinavians will only settle there, I have just arranged for a large tract of land in Wisconsin, so that they might have a choice, and also have gone as far South as South Carolina, where we propose to have a settlement, having found a thoroughly healthy and desirable location for them. From what I have written it will be seen that the class who are buying land have comparatively little money and have to be given plenty of time to pay for the farms they buy, and the Central and Southern States, where the cost of a house is very little and the winters do not demand very much clothing, are advantageous to them, now that the railroads have made it possible for the farmer always to have a market for his produce.

D. DISTRIBUTION OF JEWISH IMMIGRANTS.

To learn what can be or has been done to get this particular class of immigrants out of the cities into country districts is of particular interest and importance, as they show perhaps a stronger tendency than any other class to gather in big cities, and are arriving, year after year, in such numbers as to make that tendency a matter of serious moment to city communities. One reason for this tendency is to be found in the conditions under which emigration takes place. The bulk of Jewish immigration to-day is from Russia, Austria, and Roumania, and, emigration from these countries having been practically forced upon the Jews, they come here in denser and more helpless masses, with less impetus to carry them beyond the port of entry where they are landed than a people set in motion by the economic motive only.

Another reason is that, whether from conditions under which they have been forced to live, or from some inherent characteristic, the Jews are not to-day an agricultural people, but follow, in the main, commercial and industrial pursuits, which are carried on to best advantage in cities or large towns.

Not a little has been done, however, in the way of agricultural settlement by Jews, either on their own initiative as individuals, or in self-sustaining colonies or companies, or with the assistance of more prosperous coreligionists.

Colonization on farms by Russian Jews began as early as 1880, with a group from Odessa who came over with the express intention of going into farming. About 7 families and 45 single men made up the company, the single men being mostly university students imbued with ideas of communism. When they landed in this country they sent about 40 of their people to the different States as farm help, to learn the farming business, leaving a committee in New York to go out and find suitable land. After several months such land was found in Oregon, near Glendale Station, and 25 people—4 families, the rest single men—were sent out as the first settlers. They bought about 760 acres for $7,800. They were aided in the matter of railway fare both by the management of the railway company and by some societies in New York City. They were also aided by the advice and care of a committee. During the first year they met with misfortune. When they first arrived a good market was open for their products. Provisions were very high because a railroad was being built through the place, but after the colony had settled there the building of the railroad was discontinued and the price for provisions fell. For instance, a ton of hay formerly worth $50 fell to $7, so that the immigrants lost a large part of their original investment. The immigrants then made an agreement with the Southern Pacific Railroad Company to chop 2,000 cords of wood at $3.50 a cord. They kept their agreement and made first-class woodchoppers, even though most of them were students. The colony was conducted on a communistic basis. As years went on, though they made encouraging progress, the immigrants felt that farming was not a good business. There were no facilities for education and no communication with civilization, and for the future there was just the hope for making a bare living. After three years 12 families left, and before the fourth year was over all had removed, going in a group to California and finally back to New York. The colonists went into other occupations for the most part. One is now a chemist, one is a druggist in New York City, one is an engineer, two are lawyers, two are dentists, one is superintendent of a hospital, and one returned to Russia, where he is now a merchant.

About the year 1881 a company of about 25 families went to South Carolina and located there. They stayed about a year, but found that the climate did not agree with them. They suffered from fevers and other diseases peculiar to the locality and finally decided to remove to North Dakota, on Government lands. There they remained about four years, but from lack of means could not hold out, and left. It is not known that any remained there. This colony was not a communist colony. There was, however, a communist colony settled in North Dakota, called Baclachin, which was kept up for 3 or 4 years and then disbanded.

In 1882 two colonies were organized in southern Kansas, called Lasker and Montefiore, with about 30 families in each. They worked at a considerable disadvantage because of the dry climate. Up to 2 years ago there were remnants of these colonies left there, but they have since disappeared.

In 1881 a colony of Russian Jews settled in Minnesota, numbering about 50 families. They held their farms for 3 or 4 years and then gradually left, as they had met with ill-success through the ravages of grasshoppers. A few still remained as late as 1889.

In 1887 or 1888 an assisted colony was established in North Dakota at a place called Painted Woods. The assistance given consisted in advancing them money for the purchase of lands at a lower rate of interest and on easier terms than they could have gotten it elsewhere. This colony gave out, but members of the colony went, individually, to another part of North Dakota and are now doing well in agriculture. They are in the Devils Lake region.

Difficulties with agricultural colonization for the Jews in the northwest are that the climate is too severe and the capital required too great. Where the climate is severe and the summer short, enough money has to be made in a brief time to carry the family through the winter. If they are without capital, the failure of a crop in any one season would mean the failure of the entire enterprise.

In 1882 the first of the now well-known Jewish colonies in southern New Jersey[1] was started by the Hebrew Aid Society, of New York—a society formed to give assistance to immigrant Jews. This association purchased about 1,100 acres of land in Salem County, 6 miles from Vineland, and placed there 250 persons, men, women, and children. The society allotted land in tracts of 15 acres to each family, and deeded these farms to the occupants, charging $150 for each, and giving a term of 33 years for payment, without interest. The enterprise was taken over in 2 or 3 years by an organization known as the Alliance Land Trust, and the settlement was named "Alliance."

The families had to be supported through the first winter; but from the time farming operations began the following spring improvement in the general condition of the people was steady.

The Hebrew Aid Society in the same year located 6 Jewish families at the place now known as Rosenhayn.

In 1883 a body of Russian Jewish immigrants formed a settlement on their own account at Carmel, the village near which Rosenhayn was established. This colony

---

[1] For a full account of these colonies see "The Jewish Colonies of South Jersey, Bureau of Statistics of New Jersey, 1901."

was composed of 100 families, comprising about 300 men, women, and children. Each family was allotted 20 acres and went to work to clear the land. The colonists supported themselves, while developing their land, by such day labor as could be obtained in the neighborhood, and by the sale of wood. Houses were built by the aid of a building association, the land being mortgaged as security. None of these colonies were, however, successful as a result of this first start.

The colony at Carmel found the debt they were under too heavy for them to clear. Homestead after homestead was being sold away from them at foreclosure sale, and in 1890 they turned to the Baron de Hirsch for financial aid, which was granted. By 1893, of the 300 families originally in the three colonies, only 200 remained, and by the end of 1896 only 76. The families remaining were heavily in debt. Among the causes of their ill-success were the distance of markets and the amount of labor and capital required to put the land in good condition.[1]

The Jewish Colonization Association, as well as the Baron de Hirsch, came to the aid of these colonies, and they are now fairly prosperous. At Alliance fruit, berries, grapes, and sweet potatoes of excellent quality are raised. The berry and fruit crop of 1899 amounted to $40,000, the sweet-potato crop to $18,000.[2] Rosenhayn now has a population of 800. Of the 1,900 acres comprising the tract about one-fourth is under cultivation. One-half of the farmers own their farms free of incumbrance. Considerable attention is paid to poultry raising. The annual value of crops is between ten and twelve thousand dollars. The aid given the colony at Carmel gave them courage to keep on, and in the decade that followed "they have reached a greatly improved and more comfortable condition."[3] They have not grown wealthy, but have made sure of a footing on the land. This colony has had less outside aid than the others, so that its success is the more praiseworthy.

In addition to the three colonies requiring aid were about 25 Jewish farmers on isolated farms in the surrounding country, who were assisted by the Baron de Hirsch fund.

Other colonies of Jews, which turned out to be utter failures, were started in south Jersey. Among these were Reega, near Mizpah, Malaga and Ziontown in Gloucester County, Alberton, near Manamuskin, and Hebron, near Newfield.

These colonies were all started by speculators for money-making purposes only. It is to be noted that one cause of the rapid break-up of colonies of this class was that very few immigrants could be induced to go into them.

The most important and the best known of the south Jersey colonies is that at Woodbine, established in 1891 by the Baron de Hirsch fund. The policy of the managers of this fund, established especially to aid Russian-Jewish immigrants, is, as is stated in their official announcement in the American-Jewish Yearbook,[4] "to scatter them (the immigrants) throughout the country, so that they will not congest in large cities." In accordance with this idea the agricultural colony at Woodbine was established. The tract selected comprised 5,300 acres, of which 1,800 are now cleared and improved. The first settlers came in the spring of 1892. There were 50 families in all—about 300 persons—from Russia and Roumelia. Each family received 15 acres of land, with the privilege of acquiring 15 acres more if they desired to do so. Each was provided with a house, a horse, and a cow. Payments were to be made on easy installments, perhaps $700 to $800 being the full amount required for one of these farms. The settler agreed to keep a certain proportion of his land under cultivation, but was on his own responsibility as to methods, crops raised, and so on. Agriculture in this colony, however, was no more of a success than it had been found in other colonies. The same difficulties arose—uncleared land, which even after clearing was suitable only for certain crops and needed capital to bring it into good condition even for these, and absence of markets.

It was finally decided to introduce industrial pursuits, to bring a market nearer to the farmer. A town site was laid out in 1897, and manufactories were brought there by the corporation. Factories and houses for operators were erected, and the town now contains a population of over 1,400, comprising 160 Jewish and 34 Gentile families. Fifty per cent of the people own their own homes. Forty per cent of the population is engaged in agriculture and 60 per cent in industrial pursuits.[5]

The factories in town are, a clothing factory employing 168 hands, a lock factory employing 40 hands, and a machine and tool company employing 28 hands. The average earnings of each family on the tract are a little over $500 per year. Of the townspeople employed outside of farming, 50 per cent are in clothing factories, 25 per cent in machine shops, 12 per cent in building trades, 13 per cent are storekeepers, teachers, etc.[6]

---

[1] American-Jewish Yearbook, 1899-1900, p. 48 following.
[2] "Jewish Colonies of South Jersey," p. 6.
[3] Ibid.
[4] 1900-1901, p. 69.
[5] "The Jewish Colonies of South Jersey," p. 20.
[6] Ibid., p. 22.

The historian of the colony says:[1]

The industries are somewhat hampered by the inability of the manufacturers to obtain a sufficient number of operatives to increase their output. The workmen apparently prefer the sweat shops of New York and other large cities with their noisome air, confined quarters, and reeking filth of their surroundings to the commodious, well-lighted, thoroughly ventilated factories and the free air of the open country. One reason why it is so difficult to get these people away from large cities lies in the fact that although the manufacturers have labored earnestly to induce them to come out into the country to work, it has been found impossible to divest their minds of the fear that the employment will not be permanent, and they may be thrown out of employment without means and far from their friends and associates.

It has been found necessary to introduce industrial enterprises into the other colonies also; and it seems to be pretty generally agreed upon that the assisted colony as a purely agricultural affair is not a success. It is said that even of the families still engaged in farming in the south Jersey colonies, one or more members are employed in other occupations; that the farms are not and can not be self-sustaining, and that without constant help from the corporation they could not be kept up in the fine condition in which they now appear. Aside from the question of success in farming, was, however, the question whether these assisted persons were willing to work. The plan was a good test of this and proved successful; they showed their willingness to work very thoroughly.

Another plan tried by the Baron de Hirsch fund for getting immigrants into the country is to assist individuals by offering information and advice as to lands to be purchased and some financial aid in securing them. This work, and also that of conducting the colonies just described, is carried on by a department of the Baron de Hirsch fund known as the "Jewish Agricultural and Industrial Aid Socity." An agent of this society is sent out to examine and report on farm property, which is then, if the report is favorable, brought to the notice of persons wishing to buy farms. When the would-be purchaser has selected his land he is aided by the fund with a loan secured by a second mortgage on the property at low interest and with payments on the principal deferred as may be necessary to make conditions possible for the farmer. The society has found it necessary to require, however, that the colonist himself shall invest sufficient money of his own in the enterprise to have a considerable equity in the property. If the colonist has not invested a fair amount of money of his own he is likely at the first little discouragement to leave the place and default on his payments.

Especially favorable opportunities for the settlement of the persons assisted have been found on the so-called "abandoned farms" of New England. The society has aided two or three hundred families to secure farms in this region. There are a large number of these families in Connecticut, especially around New London.

The Russian-Jewish farmers in Connecticut have succeeded especially well on two accounts. In the first place, the farms that they went to were already in a state of cultivation; what they could produce and the conditions of the market were known beforehand. In the second place, it is a good neighborhood for summer boarders, and thus affords a good market for the farmers' produce. These individual farmers seem to be quite successful. Among those assisted by receiving loans only three cases of default in payment of mortgage in the last 2 years have been recorded.

The general conditions surrounding the Connecticut colony are very favorable. Persons who went there were received very kindly in the neighborhood, mingling freely with the American residents, and receiving considerable friendly advice and assistance from them. There are in all about 200 Jewish families scattered through the State of Connecticut making their living as farmers and being aided considerably by working in tailor shops in their neighborhoods during the winter. Among these are a number of families at Colchester, who moved there of their own initiative, without assistance from the fund. The rubber factory then in operation there gave to the Russian farmers a market for their produce.

There are a few families in Maine. Two years ago some were sent and are fairly successful.

There are also individual Jewish farmers known of in Spring Valley and Suffern, N. Y., and in New Brunswick, N. J. They have been especially successful at dairying. That and truck farming seem to be the best lines of work for them.

It is to be noted that, in general, newly arrived immigrants do not get the advantage of this means of assistance in reaching the country districts. In the first place, they do not come here with money enough. Another difficulty is that very recent arrivals not being able to speak English, could not get along well in rural districts where nothing but English is spoken.

In general, the applicants for these farms are men who have made a little money in the city. A great many of them are tailors, who have saved up from $50 to $1,000 in their occupation, and secure the additional money needed to take up the

---

[1] "The Jewish Colonies of South Jersey," p. 22.

farm on loan from the society. So that when business is unusually prosperous, this class of people are not so likely to stop the work they are engaged in to go into agriculture, and the work of loaning money for the taking up of abandoned farms will slacken, as it has within the past 2 years, on account of the great demand for labor in the cities under the present conditions of business prosperity.

Colonization in New England has been the most successful of any, but for the reasons above mentioned it seems to be about at an end for the present.

The society is now looking into the possibilities of getting newly arrived immigrants into farming, but their plans are not yet sufficiently formulated to be described. They are now trying a plan of sending the newly arrived to Woodbine. These are taking land, not as owners, but as tenants, under the supervision of the superintendent of the agricultural school. They are thus enabled to have some instruction in agriculture as applied under American conditions that could not be given to them elsewhere. Coming into a new country, the newly arrived immigrant has under ordinary circumstances no one to turn to for advice, and this stands in the way of his success.

Both because purely agricultural removal presented such difficulties and because in any group of people there would always be some who could not be provided for in that way, plans for industrial removal have been inaugurated.

This work began in the summer of 1900, when political troubles in Roumania were sending Roumanian Jews to this country in large numbers, and the destitute condition of the Roumanian immigrants stranded in New York was such as to call forth the sympathy and interest of their coreligionists, who formed a private committee to undertake measures for their relief.

The chief means of relief planned for by the committee was to find employment for the Roumanian immigrants in other parts of the country. The secret Order of B'nai B'rith, with the aid of its local chapters throughout the country, assisted in this work, which was found so successful that it seemed well to extend it further. The Baron de Hirsch fund took it up, making it a branch of the Jewish Agricultural and Industrial Aid Society, under the name of the Industrial Removal Society, and has extended its benefits beyond the Roumanian Jews, for whom it was originally intended, to Russian and Polish Jews as well.

Their method of placing immigrants is, briefly, as follows: Persons desiring to remove from the city make a written application, which is kept on file at the office of the society, stating, besides names and addresses, date of arrival in this country and in this city, the language spoken, their ages and occupations. An agent resident in the city investigates as to general reliability and responsibility each case presented. If this report is favorable in any given case, the name is placed on the list of those for whom positions are to be sought. A traveling agent takes these lists and, going through the country, speaks in different towns where there are bodies of Jewish people, to interest them in the work and secure their cooperation in it. The list that the agent has shows the occupation of the applicants for removal, and from this list those who will cooperate in the work are to select the number of persons wanted of the occupations given and to agree to find places for them. For instance, a prominent Hebrew in a Southern town will agree to take 4 blacksmiths; a rabbi will receive and place 2 shoemakers, and so on. The society then sends the number required, paying all expenses of transportation of the persons sent out, but after they reach their destination being under no further responsibility with regard to them.

It is stated at the society's office that about 2,500 persons were assisted in this way from the beginning of the work in August, 1900, to the spring of 1901.

Of those already helped the greater number are men who have left their families in the old country. Only about 30 or 40 families so far have been assisted. When families are to be helped, the head of the family is sent on first to see if he likes the place he is sent to; if he does, the family follows. It is said that little dissatisfaction is expressed either by those who are sent out or by those who receive them, because, in the first place, the persons sending for labor are carefully selected, and, in the next place, the families to be sent are thoroughly investigated.

The following list of occupations of the applicants that happened to be on the roll of the society on the day when the list was copied, by the courtesy of the officers, for presentation in this report is interesting, as showing a greater variety than is usually attributed to the Jew. On the list were: Bakers, barbers, bookkeepers, blacksmiths, brass workers, butchers, buttonhole makers, an egg candler, carpenters, chair makers, cutters, drivers, druggists, a dyer, farmers, finishers, glaziers, hat makers, iron workers, jewelers, locksmiths, machinists, a mason, operators (sewing machine), painters, paper hangers, peddlers, a photographer, a pipe maker, plumbers, pressers, printers, a quilt maker, shoemakers, silversmiths, tanners, tinsmiths, trunk makers, upholsterers, waiters, watchmakers, weavers, a wine maker, a wood turner. Of these perhaps the most numerous were: Barbers, butchers, carpenters, cigar makers, drivers, glaziers, locksmiths, machinists, operators, painters, peddlers, shoemakers, tinsmiths.

The great variety of these occupations, in contrast to the general idea that a Jew

AGRICULTURAL DISTRIBUTION OF IMMIGRANTS.

is always a tailor or a peddler, is accounted for partly by the fact that a large proportion of the Jews who are tailors over here were not tailors in their own country, and in giving their occupations for this list they give those originally followed; partly by the fact that the Roumanian Jews, who have made up the bulk of those helped, differ in their industrial characteristics from the Russian Jews. The Roumanians comprise a merchant and trading class, and a laboring class composed of vigorous, hardy manual workers. They are both skilled and unskilled laborers in occupations requiring physical strength, and are able to adapt themselves more easily than the Russian Jew to the industrial conditions prevailing in the average American community.

Even more interesting than the list of occupations, perhaps, is the list of places to which applicants have already been sent. This list was copied from a map in the office of the society, on which each place which had received applicants was marked in red. The impression to the eye was most vivid, that these newly arrived immigrants had been scattered to practically every part of the country. No corner or section of the map was without its red mark indicating the presence of persons sent by this society.

The list of places is as follows:

Massachusetts: North Adams, Pittsfield, Holyoke, Springfield.
Rhode Island: Providence.
Connecticut: Hartford.
New York: Troy, Albany, Hudson, Syracuse, Rochester, Elmira, Buffalo.
Pennsylvania: Wilkesbarre, Scranton, Stroudsburg, Elizabeth, Amboy, Philadelphia, Pittsburg, Connellsville, Uniontown, Titusville, Erie.
Maryland: Baltimore.
Virginia: Richmond, Petersburg, Norfolk, Newport News, Lynchburg, Roanoke.
West Virginia: Charleston, Wheeling.
North Carolina: Durham, Raleigh, Goldsboro, Winston, Salem, Charlotte, Statesville.
Georgia: Rome, Athens, Atlanta, Macon, Columbus, Albany, Savannah.
Florida: Jacksonville, Tampa.
Alabama: Florence, Decatur, Huntsville, Gadsden, Aniston, Birmingham, Bessemer, Demopolis, Selma, Montgomery, Eufaula.
Mississippi: Columbus, Meridan, Jackson, Vicksburg, Port Gibson, Natchez, Brookhaven.
Tennessee: Knoxville, Chattanooga, Columbia, Lexington, Memphis, Clarksville.
Kentucky: Livingston, Louisville, Paducah.
Ohio: Cleveland, Toledo, Akron, Youngstown, Canton, Bellaire, Zanesville, Columbus, Springfield, Piqua, Dayton, Hamilton, Cincinnati, Portsmouth.
Indiana: Lycurgus, Goshen, Columbia City, Fort Wayne, Logansport, Wabash, Peru, Kokomo, Lafayette, Marion, Indianapolis, Terre Haute, Vincennes, Evansville, Madison, Mount Vernon.
Michigan: Alpena, Grayling, Cadillac, Bay City, Port Huron, Detroit, Grand Rapids, Kalamazoo, Calumet, Hancock.
Wisconsin: Eau Claire, Wausau, Appleton, Manitowoc, Sheboygan, Milwaukee, La Crosse.
Illinois: Elgin, Joliet, Streator, Peoria, Champaign, Springfield, Cairo, Quincy.
Missouri: St. Louis, Kansas City, St. Joseph.
Arkansas: Jonesboro, Fort Smith, Little Rock, Hot Springs, Pine Bluff, Camden, Texarkana.
Louisiana: Monroe, Shreveport, Opelousas, Plaquemine, New Orleans, Baton Rouge.
Iowa: Dubuque, Des Moines, Council Bluffs, Centerville, Keokuk, Davenport, Sioux City.
Minnesota: St. Paul, Minneapolis.
Nebraska: Lincoln, Omaha.
Kansas: Atchison, Leavenworth.
Texas: Gainesville, Greenville, Dallas, Tyler, Marshall, Palestine, Cleburne, Waco, Beaumont, Houston, Halletsville, Victoria, San Antonio, Luling, Austin.
Montana: Helena.
Colorado: Denver.
Arizona: Solomonsville.
Utah: Salt Lake City.
Idaho: Boise City.
California: Sacramento.

With a like thought back of it, but of wider scope than the plan just outlined, was one presented in New York City last winter to relieve the congestion of the city by the removal not simply of the industrial agent—the immigrant, but the industrial opportunity—the big or little factory that gives him employment and is an attractive force keeping him in the city.

The clothing manufacturers in especial were to be urged to remove their factories to other places, where their laborers would naturally follow them, thus drawing off greater masses of the population than the colonization schemes formerly tried were likely to do.

This plan is now being worked out by the Jewish Agricultural and Industrial Aid Society, but as yet there are few definite results to show.

It is meant to place this undertaking on a strictly business basis, by offering to manufacturers solid inducements that shall make them willing to remove. Sometimes offers to manufacturers come from towns that would like to have factories established within their limits, of especially favorable terms of rental of factory buildings. Sometimes the society will give the manufacturer help in removing his plant, and in erecting buildings for employees The inducements to workers are (1) as above mentioned, the removal of the factory which employs them; (2) cheaper house rent; (3) advances of money by the society to help them to move and to establish themselves in the new district; (4) greater possibilities of ownership of land in country districts.

It is claimed that this method of dispersion is particularly practical in that it makes use of existing opportunities. The factories the society propose to remove are already in running order; the towns to which they are to be removed are long-established communities. Settlements made under such conditions do not involve the undue expenditure of effort needed to plant new immigrants in a totally undeveloped place.

In Chicago an association called "The Jewish Agriculturists' Aid Society of America" has for some years been carrying on the work of removing poor Jews from the cities and establishing them on farms. The secretary of the association writes as follows with regard to their work:

> While the activity of our society extends over a period of nearly 13 years, yet the work has been but experimental, and consequently slow of achievement. The purpose of our society is to encourage husbandry among the poor of our people, and in doing this we aim less at colonization, in the common acceptance of the term, than at having individual families take up the work of farming among those who have been at that calling for generations, no matter of what nationality or denomination they be.
> During the years of our activity we have assisted and encouraged nearly 100 families to make farming their sole occupation. One-fifth of that number have been assisted within the last 6 months—since November, 1900. How many of those who have received our aid to settle as farmers have left that avocation we, of course, can not tell; we have, however reason to believe that the percentage is a very small one indeed, if any at all. Besides some of our protégés who have gone West in search of larger farms than what they worked while nearer to us, we are to-day in touch with over 50 of our farmer families who are actually engaged at husbandry and are more or less successful at it.
> All of our protégés are immigrants, though some of them have been in the country for more than 20 years.

Rejecting the colonization principle, this society holds that "individualism * * * has * * * shown itself to be the proper course that must be followed in dealing with the Jewish would-be farmer. * * * The choice of locality and land is left to the prospective farmer. He is to select, purchase, or rent, as the case may be, the land he is to work, and he is to contract the price and the terms of the sale or rental."[1] This method "disposes of much of the overseership so obnoxious to the nature of the Russian Jew," and which has often caused schemes intended for his benefit to fail.

The society began its work in the fall of 1888 by assisting 4 families to purchase 80 acres of virgin prairie land in southwestern Minnesota. Since then from 2 to 10 families have been assisted to remove each year. Up to the present year (1901), 76 families have been helped. Seventy-one of these families are in the middle West, in the States of Illinois, Michigan, Iowa, Wisconsin, Minnesota, and the Dakotas. Eight are working on rented farms, 24 have filed homestead claims on Government land, 39 are located on 30 separate homesteads, aggregating 2,987 acres of land. These homesteads were bought by their owners at a cost of $38,980, and to-day represent a value of $63,970. Five of these homesteads are berry and fruit farms purchased for about $100 per acre; six are cultivated farms purchased for about $20 per acre, 19 were on virgin prairie or wood lands purchased at from $5 to $8 per acre. These latter have been greatly improved by their owners. Over 1,000 of the 2,140 acres comprised in them are under cultivation, and 800 are used for pasturage.

The society encourage their would-be farmers to purchase new, uncultivated soil at reasonably low prices, believing that this is the most advantageous method for them. They will, however, assist those who wish to file claims for homesteads on Government lands.

In the report of the society[2] for 1901 are well set forth some of the benefits expected to arise from life on the farm. The report says:

> Farm life does not permit working at odd and irregular hours. One can not work behind the plow as he may work at the sewing machine, after the hour when the day's work ought to be ended. Nor can the work on the farm be deferred for "later on." The care for the live stock on the farm demands greater punctuality than does the handling of the dead stock in the sweat shop. Mealtime and bedtime come on the farm with more forcible demands for the attention due them than they do in the city. Day and night come and rule on the farm with far more telling effect than they do in the sweat shop or in the factory. The turning of night into day—one of the great curses of the ghetto—is almost an impossibility on the farm. Surely there exists no such opportunity there for this viciousness and disorder as exists in the ghetto. All these conditions have not failed in their good effect on the mind and disposition of our farmers.

Praiseworthy as all of these efforts are, it has to be admitted that they have so far been unable fully to meet the situation. This is especially true of the agricultural work. The removal of 100 or 200 families a year has little effect upon city populations that are added to annually by from 10,000 to 40,000 persons. The assisted colonies are not growing materially. The work of establishing Jewish farmers on abandoned farms seems to have slackened up considerably. Reports of the various societies interested in agricultural removal indicate that individual Jewish farmers once established are fairly successful and remain in farming; but instance after instance of Jewish farmers giving up their farms is given from private sources.

---

[1] Reform Advocate, Chicago, June 8, 1901, p. 532.
[2] Jewish Agriculturists' Aid Society of America, report, Chicago, Ill., 1901, p. 13.

AGRICULTURAL DISTRIBUTION OF IMMIGRANTS.   517

The most successful side of the work seems to be that which places Jewish immigrants in industrial pursuits outside the cities. The numbers sent out within a year by the Industrial Removal Society—the branch of the Jewish Agricultural and Industrial Aid Society already referred to as engaged in this work, are really considerable, and, as has been seen, their beneficiaries have been sent to every State in the Union.

As to the small numbers removed, however, it is claimed that while the results for the present are small, and may be for a number of years to come, yet each family established outside of the city forms a nucleus about which other families will gather. The great mass of Jewish immigrants now coming in who remain in New York City have friends there. If the friends were elsewhere they might go elsewhere.

As to the general fitness of the Jew for agriculture it can not be inferred from the history of Jewish agriculture in this country that the Jew can not succeed in farming. It is claimed that Jewish capital invested in farming is constantly increasing in proportion to the spread of industrial activity in agricultural districts.[1]

In many cases Jews have given up farming, not because they were unsuccessful, but simply because they have found opportunities in other occupations that pay them much better. The American farmer is becoming more or less dissatisfied with his calling, and there is a general idea afloat that farming does not pay as well as industrial pursuits. It is not surprising, then, that the Jewish farmer shares this thought, and will seek to enter those pursuits which he thinks will offer the best chances of a livelihood.

III. IMMIGRATION AND AGRICULTURE IN THE SEPARATE STATES.

NORTH ATLANTIC STATES.

MAINE.

(See table, p. 583.)

With regard to opportunities for immigrants in Maine, the commissioner of the bureau of industrial and labor statistics of that State wrote in 1894 as follows:[2]

Maine, as you well know, being outside of the lines of European immigration, has but a small percentage of foreign-born population. Of the total foreign population of the State in 1890, which was 78,961, 52,076 were from Canada and Newfoundland, leaving but 26,885 as the number from all other countries. Our State is therefore quite free from the influences, good, bad, and indifferent, which come from foreign immigration, and is very well satisfied with this condition of things. In the northern part of our State, Aroostook County, which includes 6,800 square miles of our territory and possesses some of the most fertile soil in New England, is an immense field for agricultural development. A thriving colony of Swedes is established in a township called New Sweden, in the central part of Aroostook County. Commencing with 50 colonists from Sweden in 1870, this settlement now numbers, including those occupying farms in neighboring towns, some 1,500 souls. They are a happy, industrious, and prosperous community, and are universally regarded with great favor throughout the State. There is room in Aroostook County for more of this class of settlers. With some means to start with, they can easily obtain fertile lands for farms, and with the same economy and industry that characterize their countrymen already there, can become independent farmers in a few years.

A brief and comprehensive answer to your questions would be that Scandinavian immigrants to develop and improve our agricultural resources would be welcome and conducive to the good of the State, but that other classes of immigrants from Europe can not be encouraged to come to Maine.

Yours, respectfully,

S. W. MATTHEWS,
Commissioner of Bureau of Industrial and Labor Statistics.

In December, 1900, the secretary of the agricultural department of the State writes:

First. There are greater opportunities in Maine for immigrants at the present time than at any time in the past. This is particularly true in farming, lumbering, and general manufacturing occupations.

Second. Swedes, Acadian and Canadian French, and Finns have proved the most effective as farmers and farm laborers.

Third. The success of foreign farmers appears to be greater in many instances than that of the American born, owing mostly, in my judgment, to the fact that they are willing to live very much cheaper. In many instances, also, they take fuller advantage of the natural resources of the land.

Fourth. I think farmers, as a rule, would oppose the further influx of foreigners into our State.

Fifth. There are no efforts being made at the present time, either by the State, public authorities, or by private persons or corporations, so far as I know, to attract immigrants.

Sixth. About 25 years ago a settlement of Swedes was made in northern Aroostook County, under the auspices of the State. This settlement has rapidly grown until it includes several townships. These people are industrious and honest, and in every way make good citizens. I think the settlement is continually increasing in numbers. Quite a little colony of Jews has settled in one of the poorer towns in a central county of the State, and I know of one or more small colonies of Finns. As a rule these people are industrious and fairly prosperous.

Yours, very truly,

B. WALKER McKEEN.

---

[1] American Jewish Year Book, 1900-01, p. 72.
[2] Report of the Immigration Investigating Commission, Washington, 1895, p. 138.

The colony of Swedes referred to in the letter of the secretary of agriculture is the one in the town of New Sweden, mentioned by the commissioner of labor in the letter first quoted. One of the colonies of Finns is in South Thomaston, and the colony of Jews was in the town of Bowdoinham. This latter colony has, however, left the place, whether on account of nonsuccess there or for some other reason could not be learned.

The statement of the secretary of agriculture that farmers would probably oppose the further influx of foreigners into the State is, in the main, borne out by the statements of representative farmers.[1] All but one reported little or no opportunity for newly arrived immigrants who do not speak English. All thus reporting, however, represented the most densely populated counties of the State—those in the extreme southern and western portion, containing the large cities. And in several cases the statement that there was little or no chance for newly arrived immigrants was modified by some proviso, as "unless they are reliable, intelligent, and will work for less than natives," "unless they are well recommended," and so on. One county heard from (Somerset), much less densely populated than those reporting unfavorably upon the chances for newly arrived immigrants, would welcome them, according to the letter received from a prominent farmer addressed the e. He writes as follows:

I read the communication received from you in regard to farm laborers at several farm gatherings, and it was universally believed that a number of laborers could find profitable employment in this vicinity.

If some plan could be devised by which some proper person should have authority to see that immigrants were protected in their rights, a large number of them could be employed as farm laborers, if capable, to their own advantage, that of the farmer, and the State of Maine as well.

As a matter of fact, farmers are bothered to get laborers. Americans, as a rule, do not like to work on a farm. I have thought for several years that Swedes, Danes, and other good farm laborers could be brought to Maine to good advantage. Employment could be found for men and their wives as well as for single men.

If a number of these people of one nationality or one language could come to one place, so that they could meet on Sundays and in the evening, they would be contented and happy.

It will be noticed in the tables that farm laborers in the counties heard from are as yet mainly native Americans or Canadians. There are a few Swedes noted in Kennebec County, both as farm laborers and as independent farmers, and in York County a few Irish and Germans as farmers.

OPPORTUNITIES FOR TENANCY AND OWNERSHIP.

(Reported by representative farmers.)

YORK COUNTY.—Good chances for renting farms; the tenant to pay half of the crop and half the growth of the stock; owner will furnish tools and stock. Farms can be purchased for about the cost of buildings and the value of the standing wood and timber.

CUMBERLAND COUNTY.—Farms are to let at all times, usually for a cash sum. Farms can be bought for less than the buildings would cost.

OXFORD COUNTY.—No opportunities for renting. As to ownership, a young man without capital should find employment on a well-managed farm, where he can "learn the trade" and earn enough to partly pay for a farm.

KENNEBEC COUNTY.—A few good chances for renting on easy terms, but not many inducements for a poor man to purchase on part payments while hiring out.

LINCOLN COUNTY.—No opportunities for tenancy or purchase on easy terms.

SOMERSET COUNTY.—Good for renting; for purchasing on easy terms, as good as any State in the Union.

NEW HAMPSHIRE.

(See table, p. 584.)

The secretary of the State board of agriculture stated to the immigration investigating commission in 1894 that "the class of immigrants most needed in New Hampshire are men for agricultural laborers and to purchase low-priced farms and women to do general housework. * * * Swedes and Germans would be the most desirable for the purpose named."

Reference to the table for the State, giving reports from representative farmers, shows that of the 7 counties heard from the 5 of greatest density of population afford little or no opportunity for newly arrived immigrants; the 2 least thickly settled would receive them. Foreign farmers are reported in 4 counties. Foreign laborers from European countries—Swedes, Poles, and Irish—are found in the 3 counties of least density of population. Where Swedes and Poles are employed they seem to be liked.

---

[1] See table for Maine.

One correspondent writes from Cheshire County: "Poles are our main reliance," and notes their thrift, and at the same time their desire to improve their condition. He says:

Poles are sharp to ask all they earn, and do not fail to raise their demands as they learn our language. * * * For years I have been a sort of banker for the Poles in this vicinity, and have been surprised at the short time in which they gather from $600 to $1,000.

Some opportunities for starting in independent farming are afforded by the purchase of so-called "abandoned farms." The master of the State grange, Mr. N. J. Bachelder, has stated[1] that as a result of a canvass of the Poles in the State, made about 10 years ago, it was found that there were, out of 32,000 farms in the State, about 1,000 upon which were buildings suitable for occupancy but without occupants. This does not include lands which have been more completely abandoned and upon which no buildings exist. Many of this latter class are growing up to timber, and no use is made of them except for pasturage. Many of these places are unsuited for the use of agricultural machinery, the fertility of the soil is exhausted, and under present circumstances the farms are not profitable to cultivate. Careful, intensive farming, however, would restore fertility, and a growing local market, afforded by the growth of towns and cities and the increase of the summer-boarding business, would offer an inducement to engage in such farming. Farms located near cities and large villages are more productive than they ever were in the past. During the past 10 years 75 per cent of the 1,000 abandoned farms with buildings have been taken up and are now occupied. This has been done mainly by native Americans, but some foreigners have taken up land in this way. There seems to be every reason why industrious foreign farmers should find an opportunity to earn a living on such land by the careful agricultural methods with which they are familiar, in raising truck for boarding-house or summer-residence communities, or for the market in local towns and cities.

OPPORTUNITIES FOR TENANCY AND OWNERSHIP.

(Reported by representative farmers.)

CHESHIRE COUNTY.—(1) Some opportunity for tenancy on farms and by rental. Not many farms for sale in Keene, but there are hill farms within a few miles of Keene for sale. (2) Desirable tenants are always in demand; rent payments or by shares. There are good opportunities for a poor man to establish himself in independent farming.

HILLSBORO COUNTY.—Not any chances of renting, but a man with a few hundred dollars could buy a small farm and pay for it on easy terms.

ROCKINGHAM COUNTY.—Only a few opportunities for tenant farming. No fixed terms; halves is perhaps the most usual arrangement. Some men can manage to purchase land on payments while hiring out. A Canadian Frenchman did near our village.

STRAFFORD COUNTY.—There are a few vacated farms in our locality, and they are often rented or leased to parties for small rentals to hold places together or to hold the old homestead, and also to enable owners to carry insurance. Opportunities for purchase are very slight. With wages as low as they are at present it is all a poor man can do to provide his family's everyday livelihood.

MERRIMACK COUNTY.—There are no opportunities for tenancy, and very limited opportunities for purchase on easy terms.

SULLIVAN COUNTY.—There are some places to be purchased on quite reasonable terms.

CARROLL COUNTY.—There are good opportunities to become a tenant farmer on shares, and very fair opportunities for purchase.

VERMONT.

(See table, p. 585.)

The secretary of the State board of agriculture states, with regard to immigration as related to agriculture in the State at the present time, that no efforts are being made in the State, either by public or private bodies, to attract immigrants. Efforts of this kind in the past have not been very successful, and the farmers as a class would not favor the further influx of foreigners. There are, however, opportunities for immigrants as farm laborers. Farm laborers' wages are from $15 to $20 per month through the year. The secretary writes, further:

Never has farm labor been so scarce since I knew anything about farm work—which has been for full 40 years—as during the season of 1900. It is a general complaint all over the State. Many hundred industrious men could find employment in every county in the State at reasonable compensation.

---

[1] Report of Industrial Commission, vol. x, p. 40, 1899.

Representative farmers speak of the same condition of things. One from Rutland County writes:

> Am much interested in this matter and would like to hear more of it. Just at present there is a marked scarcity of farm help in this immediate vicinity. * * * I have personally been looking for help for months without success.

Another, from Caledonia County, writes:

> Good farm help, both male and female, are wanted, and when found faithful and efficient practically command their own price. I call to mind now several parties who would like help, if it was to be had, both in and out of doors (male and female), at good wages and in good homes.

Testimony before the Industrial Commission[1] shows that there has been a gradual falling off in the number of persons employed on farms in the last 50 years. This is partly due to the general movement to the West and to the cities that has been taking young men from the farms, and partly to the introduction of agricultural machinery, which makes it unnecessary to employ so many men to cultivate a farm as formerly.

The condition of those still employed on farms is, however, materially better than that of the same class in former times, and the tendency to drift away from the farms is at the present time about at a standstill. Employment of labor on Vermont farms is quite constant. There is but little transient labor. Canadian French, Swedes, Norwegians, and Poles come in to do this class of work, such as haying and harvesting—the Swedes, Norwegians, and Poles in increasing proportions of late years. The Scandinavians usually come from Sweden and Norway direct, and are secured as farm laborers at the immigrant station. A farmer, or several joining together, will send to employment agencies at the immigrant station for a certain number of laborers, and these will be shipped to him. They begin at low wages, continue in service until they have commanded better wages and saved up some money, then purchase farms and settle down as permanent residents. They make good help and good citizens.

Those who come are mostly young, unmarried men, but some have families that follow later. Some Scandinavian women are coming as house help, and are well liked. When the Scandinavians settle down as farmers they do not gather in colonies, nor show any disposition to do so; nor do they seem to care to migrate farther west to Scandinavian settlements.

According to the witness giving the above information before the Industrial Commission, there seems no material reason, at least, why they should do so. He gives it as his opinion, after a trip through the West with a view to learning conditions of farming and prices of land, that there is no farm land as productive and cheap as the lands that can be bought in the East, and particularly in Vermont.

There has been a decline of a third or one-half in the prices of land in Vermont, making it, with reference to productive value, some of the cheapest land in the country. Prices range from $5 to $50 per acre. The $5 farms are some distance from town and school; some are rather rough and not adapted, without further improvement, to the use of machinery; a great many are quite fertile and productive. The Scandinavian immigrants, not being so particular about social advantages as the native-born farmers, are willing to take such farms at the low price they are held at, and do well on them.

While the Scandinavians seem to be regarded as the best farm help, Poles are found quite satisfactory. These men also are brought in in considerable numbers every spring, and they, too, show no disposition to colonize or to preserve foreign customs.

The foreign farm laborers so far do not seem to have had any marked influence on agriculture in the State. The greater proportion of farm help is still native born.

The State secretary of agriculture says that of the foreigners the French, Irish, and Norwegians make the best farmers, but Americans are the most successful.

Letters received from representative farmers in six counties confirm the above statements in most points. The kind of farming reported is largely dairying, consequently a large proportion of the labor employed is needed throughout the year. (See table, p. 585.)

Some opportunity for married men as laborers is shown, and a little for women as houseworkers. The farmers are divided as to their preference of nationalities as laborers, but, as in Maine and New Hampshire, it is to be noticed that the greater welcome is given to newly arrived immigrants in the less densely populated counties.

OPPORTUNITIES FOR TENANCY AND OWNERSHIP.

(Reported by representative farmers.)

WINDOM COUNTY.—Few opportunities to become a tenant farmer, but farms are cheap and can be bought on easy terms.

---

[1] Mr. Victor I. Spear: Reports of the Industrial Commission, vol. x, pp. 402 ff.

RUTLAND COUNTY.—Quite a number of farms are let, usually on shares. There are fine opportunities in Vermont for a poor man to undertake sheep farming on cheap land, but dairy farming requires capital and all of a man's time.

WINDSOR COUNTY.—(1) Fair opportunities to become a tenant farmer on shares and opportunities for purchase on easy terms are very good. (2) There are good opportunities to become a tenant farmer on halves, or its equivalent, and good chances for purchase on easy terms.

CALEDONIA COUNTY.—There are farmers that lease farms, with stock and tools; more would do so if they could find reliable tenants. As to purchasing, the best plan is to work out a few years before buying a farm. There are farmers who act as their own foremen, who would furnish a comfortable tenement to a man who would work and board himself.

ORLEANS COUNTY.—There are limited opportunities only for tenancy, but opportunities for purchase are as good as anywhere.

FRANKLIN COUNTY.—Many farms are rented on shares. The tenant furnishes half of seed, half of repairs, etc., half of taxes, and does all the work for half the proceeds. Other farms are rented for cash rental, at from $12.50 to $15 per cow. There are no opportunities for a poor man to establish himself in independent farming while hiring out. Dairy farming requires close attention.

MASSACHUSETTS.

(See table, p. 586.)

The secretary of the State board of agriculture writes as follows:

This State, as is well known, is not an agricultural, but rather a manufacturing, commercial, and residential State, and we have a large population in cities and large towns. Our farming is in the line of specialties rather than general. Dairying, market gardening, and fruit growing are the principal lines, with tobacco growing in the Connecticut Valley as a prominent exception.

Replying to your questions more in detail, would say:

1. Yes, there are greater opportunities for immigrants than in past years, owing to improved business conditions. Probably the conditions in all occupations are better now than in the recent years of industrial depression.

2. In the Connecticut Valley the Poles have come in pretty fast in the past 10 years, and they now constitute a very large proportion of available farm labor. They are generally considered very satisfactory, and nearly every farmer has one or more. In the market gardens around Boston many French Canadians are employed, and appear to give general satisfaction. In the southeastern or cape sections many Portuguese are abandoning fishing and going onto the farms. Of late years considerable farm help in the eastern part of the State has come from Nova Scotia and New Brunswick.

3. We have no reasons for thinking that the foreign farmers (and the proportion of these is small), are any improvement over the native.

4. Farmers favor the coming in of the better classes of foreigners, those who are likely to become useful citizens.

5. No special efforts are being made to attract immigrants. For 10 years or so this office has tried to gather and circulate information concerning available farm property. We have issued several editions of a farm catalogue, and we get many calls for them from New York and States farther south and west.

There are employment agencies in our cities, and, of course, our real estate agents are constantly on the lookout for available farm property which can be handled by them advantageously.

6. No (there are no agricultural colonies of foreigners in the State).

Yours, very respectfully,

J. W. STOCKWELL, *Secretary*.

The "abandoned farms" above referred to, as enumerated in 1890, were 1,461 in number; 772 with buildings, 689 without. The average size of such farms with buildings was 86 acres; without buildings, 87 acres. Much of the abandoned land could be bought for less than $10 per acre. As a result of the movement to bring these abandoned farms to public notice 309 farms were sold up to September, 1900. Judging by the names a large proportion of the purchasers were of American parentage. In one instance reported the original purchaser afterwards sold the property to a Swede. From another report it appears that there are no abandoned farms in the particular town heard from (Bristol County), as the Portuguese are taking all that class of property, and a representative farmer in Hampshire County speaks of Poles settling in their own homes on old farms.

Again the connection is seen between low density of population and the call for foreign immigrants. Representative farmers from counties of population density less than 100 to the square mile agree in saying that there are good chances for immigrants in their respective neighborhoods. (See table, p. 586.) Farmers in crowded counties, of 150 to 700 to the square mile, agree in saying there are few, if any, openings for immigrants. There is general complaint of farm labor drifting to the cities. One farmer writes (from Essex County): "Most of the men who come onto our farms soon leave for positions in some of our manufactories. * * * We are not strictly a farming community, but depend mostly on the shops, where our boys drift as soon as they get out of school." Even the foreigners are more or less temporary on the farms. Another farmer writes (Worcester County): "Poles stay the longest. Swedes stay only until they can speak English." The foreigners, however, do not all or for the most part go from the farms to the factories. Many give up their places as farm laborers to become independent farmers. A farmer in Franklin County writes that French and Irish who came in 50 or 60 years ago are now settled on their own land and among the best citizens. He considers their coming a great benefit to the community as well as to themselves. And now, he reports, the Poles also are settling in homes of their own, some on old farms and others in villages. In onion sections, another farmer writes, Poles have first hired, then bought onion farms. A correspondent from Berkshire County writes that French and Irish farmers in the county "are making very thrifty people. In fact the native farmers are running out."

There is fair encouragement for married farm laborers, and considerable work for women and children. (See table, p. 586.) The table also shows a great variety of nationalities as farmers and farm laborers. Finns are noted in one county (Barnstable) only, and Italians in one county (Plymouth) only.

OPPORTUNITIES FOR TENANCY AND OWNERSHIP

(Reported by representative farmers.)

BARNSTABLE COUNTY.—There are some chances for renting farms. There is plenty of opportunity for thrifty immigrants to establish themselves in independent farming.

PLYMOUTH COUNTY.—There are no opportunities for tenancy here. There is a good chance for an active, intelligent man of good habits to get a good farm in two years. Land is very cheap here, and within 14 miles of Boston. Good land can be purchased for $25 an acre.

BRISTOL COUNTY.—There is not much chance for renting. The opportunities for purchase on easy payments and while hiring out are fair; in some cases it is done.

MIDDLESEX COUNTY.—There is no tenant farming in this vicinity. Several farms are for sale, however. Some are paying for land while hiring out.

ESSEX COUNTY.—(1) Farms can be bought for less than the cost of buildings. (2) Few opportunities for tenant farming, and none to speak of for purchasing land while hiring out.

WORCESTER COUNTY.—(1) There is not much chance for foreigners to become tenant farmers until they learn New England ways. There are many chances for a good laborer to establish himself in independent farming while hiring out. (2) There are good chances to hire farms with or without stock and tools if the tenant is responsible. There are good opportunities for a poor man to purchase if he is industrious, frugal, and provident. (3) There are no opportunities for tenant farming. There are for purchasing farming land cheap and on easy terms of payment. (4) Very few farms are let, but farms can be bought at moderate prices 2 miles out from villages. (5) Few, if any, opportunities for renting; fairly good for purchase on easy terms.

HAMPSHIRE COUNTY.—Not many opportunities for tenant farming; for purchase on easy terms while hiring out the opportunities are good, and there is plenty of work to be had.

FRANKLIN COUNTY.—(1) Considerable land is rented to Polish families to grow onions, in this vicinity; also tobacco and other crops. As to purchasing land while hiring out, the prospect is encouraging for those whom farmers have confidence in. (2) There are some opportunities for renting farms. Purchasing land on payments, while the purchaser was earning a living by hiring out, has been done in numerous cases. In onion and tobacco sections many Poles have hired land by the acre to raise onions, or have taken fields to work on halves, the owner usually furnishing fertilizer and seed. (3) The opportunities for foreigners to become tenants are not good, as they are not accustomed to American methods. Some abandoned farms are to be purchased on easy terms.

BERKSHIRE COUNTY.—In the back towns farms are very low. Price, $10 per acre, including buildings. These are good farms, but back from the centers. Purchaser, by making a small payment down, can take his own time.

RHODE ISLAND.

(See table, p. 588.)

In 1894 the governor of the State wrote to the Immigration Investigating Commission with regard to opportunities for immigrants, as follows:[1]

I do not know of any trade, profession, or occupation at the present time in this State that is not more than supplied with all the labor needed.
Rhode Island is largely a manufacturing State, and I am informed by our commissioner of industrial statistics that scarcely two-thirds of the full force that can be engaged in the factories is now employed regularly.
Yours, very truly, D. RUSSELL BROWN, *Governor*.

---

[1] Report Immigration Investigating Commission, Washington, 1895, p. 150.

AGRICULTURAL DISTRIBUTION OF IMMIGRANTS.

As to present conditions, the secretary of the State board of agriculture reports that there are no greater opportunities for immigrants than in 1894, unless they go to the land. There would seem to be excellent opportunities for the purchase of farming land. Rhode Island, like other New England States, has its "abandoned farms," which the State is interested in bringing again into cultivation. It is stated in the Descriptive Catalogue of such farms, published by the State board of agriculture (p. 3), that "while Rhode Island is not distinctively an agricultural State, yet * * * a large number of inhabitants derive all support directly from the soil." * * *

"Neglected or untilled farms are found in every county of the State," * * * which "were not deserted because they were nonproductive." * * * "Most of these farms, if not every one, will yield a better living than thousands in cities are compelled to accept." There are 349 untilled farms recorded in the catalogue for this small State—251 with buildings, 98 without. The average acreage of these farms is 87, of which 34½ (average) are tillage, 4½ pasture, and 48 are wooded, and the average value is $900 per farm.

There are opportunities not only for those who wish to become farm owners, but for farm laborers. A representative farmer writes that farm wages have increased in recent years because the factories are drawing off the farm laborers, offering them better wages, fewer hours, and more personal liberty.

Farmers would probably favor the influx of foreigners, as "they might not be able to cultivate their farms without them. The American-born farmer of this generation will not work on a farm if he can live—half live—exist—by any other occupation," the Secretary of agriculture states. But no efforts are being made by public or private bodies in the State to attract immigrants.

The secretary of agriculture says further that, of the foreigners, Swedes are most effective as farmers and farm laborers. In reply to the question whether the success of foreign farmers is as great as that of the American born, he also says: "The foreign farmer may have no more than the American farmer, but it is more to him, and makes him more contented."

Replies received from representative farmers were too few to give a general view of conditions.

OPPORTUNITIES FOR TENANCY AND OWNERSHIP.

(Reported by representative farmers.)

BRISTOL COUNTY.—Opportunities for renting are usually on poor and unprofitable farms only. There is about the same chance as elsewhere for a poor man to become an independent farmer while hiring out, but it requires energy and thrift.

KENT COUNTY.—Opportunities for renting are very good, either to run a farm on shares or by hiring it outright. Many farms are sold by installment payments, and many good farms are for sale very cheap.

CONNECTICUT.

(See table, p. 589.)

The secretary of the State board of agriculture writes as follows with regard to present conditions as affected by foreign immigration:

1. There has been a continuous demand at fair wages for agricultural and domestic labor, and good mechanics have been in demand. Some of the factories have been closed or running on short time. Most of the Irish of the second generation are farming for themselves or have gone into other employments, so that Italians, Swedes, and Poles are coming in to perform field labor, while for domestic service we have had to resort to colored help from Virginia and North Carolina. These as a class make good servants, but are uneasy, and spend a large share of their earnings in traveling back and forth. The Swedes and the Poles give good satisfaction, and also the better class of Italians.
3. The foreign farmers live very cheaply. The women assist in field labor. They succeed in making money.
4. There is no objection generally on the part of farmers to the incoming of foreigners of the right sort.
5. There are no efforts to secure immigrants that I know of by public authority, only the publication by the State board of agriculture of a list (descriptive) of farms for sale. These are so often called "abandoned" farms that few of the good farms in the State that are for sale are listed.
6. There are colonies of Russian Jews in Salem, New London County, and perhaps in other towns in that part of the State.
The residents in those parts give differing reports about these people.

Tabulated statistics as to the price, acreage, etc., of the so-called "abandoned farms" are not given in the report referred to. There are 165 listed.

Representative farmers in 3 counties are not enthusiastic as to opportunities for purchase (see reports following). They do not, moreover, seem to agree with the secretary of agriculture, that foreign immigrants are desired, at least those newly arrived who do not speak English. But the number of localities heard from is not sufficient to afford a satisfactory general view.

According to the representative farmers heard from the independent farmers of foreign birth are mainly Irish and Germans, with a few Poles and Swedes in the more thickly settled counties. There is a greater variety of nationalities among foreign laborers. Besides the races just mentioned as farmers, Italians are noted as farm laborers in 2 counties, negroes in 2, Danes, Swiss, and Portuguese in 1.

OPPORTUNITIES FOR TENANCY AND OWNERSHIP.

(Reported by representative farmers.)

MIDDLESEX COUNTY.—Not much chance here for renting farms. Most of the foreigners here are Germans. They buy their land on time and hire out most of the time; work in their own places nights and Sundays.

TOLLAND COUNTY.—There are a few opportunities to rent farms. A poor man might establish himself here as an independent farmer by economy, hard work, and time.

HARTFORD COUNTY.—(1) Practically no chances to rent farms and none to buy on easy terms, as the land is too valuable, being near cities. (2) Only a few chances for renting or for purchase on easy terms. (3) Not many chances for renting. There are opportunities for purchase while hiring out, for first-class men.

NEW YORK.

(See table, p. 590.)

Reports from representative farmers in various parts of the State show that a large proportion of the farm labor employed is kept throughout the year, and there is considerable opportunity for married laborers. The fruit industry and housework give occasion for the employment of women and children; so that an immigrant family wishing to earn a living in a New York farming neighborhood would seem to have especially good chances for doing so.[1] Nine out of the fifteen farmers reporting state definitely, indeed, that there is opportunity for foreign immigrants—those newly arrived, who do not speak English. Four say that the chances are "few," or "moderate;" only one says definitely that there are none. Foreign laborers are, as a matter of fact, reported in nearly every county heard from. Irish and Germans prevail. There are many Dutch (Hollanders) in the western part of the State. According to testimony given before the Industrial Commission,[2] the German and Dutch settlers have been very satisfactory, and make first-class citizens. They seem to be born agriculturists. A German or Dutch immigrant will go to some farmer, stay with him for 10 years or so, and then buy the farm, the former (native-born) owner moving into town to take things easy. This change is made possible by the fact that the natural successors of the former owner—his sons—do not care for farm work, and go off to town, leaving the father, while the foreign farm hand sticks by him.[3] The Germans and Dutch are somewhat inclined to gather in little neighborhood colonies, and are more or less clannish, especially the latter.[3] They are as a rule better and more thorough farmers than the Americans. The Dutch are especially successful in reclaiming and developing muck lands, and are raising considerable quantities of onions and celery. They are bringing as much wealth into the State as the Americans.[3]

Poles, Swedes, Russians, and Hungarians are found in some counties. In one county only (Ontario) are Italians spoken of as farm laborers, and in one county (Schuyler) as independent farmers. Italians have been employed more or less in sugar-beet culture. While the beet-sugar factory at Rome was in operation, Italians, who lived along the canal with their wives and children, were employed to thin the beets. Italians are now employed for the same work on beet farms that supply the factory at Binghamton.

The sugar-beet industry, wherever it is started, offers especially favorable opportunities for foreign farmers and laborers. There are now (according to the Twelfth Census) 3 factories in the State, with a nominal daily capacity of 1,000 tons of beets; but the success of the industry largely depends on securing farmers to raise the beets and laborers to work at their culture. A prominent beet-sugar maker in the State gives it as his opinion that Americans are not suited to this work; that the prevalence of American farmers in a neighborhood is a drawback to success in beet raising, and that the tedious hand culture required for the crop the American

---

[1] One fruit farmer writes: "I have a tenant house that will be vacant (such a date), and want a family with boys and girls large enough to pick berries and pare and trim apples."
[2] Reports, vol. x, p. 323.
[3] Ibid., p. 323.

laborer will not give.[1] For instance, it has been calculated that the laborer must creep 5½ miles to thin one acre of beets, occupying 6 days in the task;[2] but the Americans "do not like to get down on their knees . . . the average man wants to ride."[3] So that beet-sugar makers are perforce obliged to turn to the foreign element who are accustomed to and willing to do this class of work.[3] It will be noticed in accounts of the beet industry in the different States that in all of them foreigners are assisting in carrying on the industry, and are succeeding well.

OPPORTUNITIES FOR TENANCY AND OWNERSHIP.

(Reported by representative farmers.)

DUTCHESS COUNTY.—There is considerable opportunity to rent farms at from $80 to $250 per annum or on half shares. A good many farms are for sale at from $2,000 to $5,000, and good help is scarce, so that probably a purchaser would have no trouble in getting work outside.

RENSSELAER COUNTY.—Good chances for renting. The tenant furnishes all labor, half the seed and taxes for half of the product, or the landlord pays taxes, furnishes stock, horses, implements, and all but labor, the tenant receiving one-third of the product. There are good chances for a man to purchase while hiring out.

ALBANY COUNTY.—Good opportunities for renting for 50 per cent of the net returns. There are good chances for purchase while hiring out, but it all depends on the man.

LEWIS COUNTY.—Many farms are rented, the tenant getting one-half the net proceeds. There are several instances in this locality of purchasing farms while the purchaser was hiring out.

JEFFERSON COUNTY.—Only a few farms are rented. Some farmers furnish everything but the work team and give one-third; others furnish half and give half, except the dairy, which is owned by the landlord. There are no opportunities for purchase on easy terms. The best farms are held at about $50 an acre, and nearly all are unencumbered, and therefore are not for sale.

ONONDAGA COUNTY.—Good men are always in demand to handle farms on shares. Purchasing land while hiring out is not a plan to be encouraged to any great extent, as very few men can divide their attention sufficiently to make this plan a success.

SCHUYLER COUNTY.—Good tenant farmers furnish team and tools and half the live stock and half the seed grain. They receive half of all the crops raised; also live stock. A man with a small capital can find plenty of farms for sale which can easily be paid for by industry, good management, and economy.

WAYNE COUNTY.—(1) Good opportunities for tenant farmers. Many of them already have farms of their own. They can purchase while hiring out, if good managers and economical. (2) There are many farms in the vicinity worked by tenants. There are opportunities for purchase on easy terms, but land values are increasing. (3) There is plenty of opportunity for renting. Many farmers could not get tenants this spring. The usual terms are for the tenant to furnish half the seed, all the tools and the labor, and to receive half the product. The opportunities for purchase while hiring out are good if the party is frugal and reliable. Several in the neighborhood have purchased in this way.

GENESEE COUNTY.—The opportunities for renting are only fair. The land is all occupied and in good demand, either on shares or for a cash rent. The chances for purchase while hiring out are not good. The better plan is to put earnings in savings bank and go where land is cheaper.

NIAGARA COUNTY.—(1) A good many farms are rented and good tenants are in demand. Terms, sometimes money rent, but oftener a share of the products. Farm lands are cheaper here in northwestern New York than in any other part of the United States, considering the advantages. Good farms can be bought for less than cost of buildings. (2) Good opportunities for renting on half shares and good opportunities for purchase on easy terms. Land is worth from $35 to $80 per acre.

NEW JERSEY.

(See table, p. 592.)

With regard to opportunities for immigrants, the State secretary of agriculture writes:

(1) There are opportunities in our State for good immigrants now, particularly such as are able to purchase our farms, which, in many cases, are owned by the old people, the young men having gone into business in the cities. Many of these farms can be bought for the cost of the improvements. If you speak of immigrants as workmen or laborers, if they understand farm work, there is plenty of room for them in our State at better wages than have been paid in previous years.

---

[1] Reports of Industrial Commission, vol. x, p. 555.   [2] Ibid., p. 574.   [3] Ibib., p. 555.

(2) The Germans and Danes are the best farm laborers, although many Hungarians are employed at such labors and some Italians among fruit growers and truck farmers.

(3) I do not know of any instances, circumstances being equal, where the foreign farmers are more successful than the American farmers. Success depends in this, as in other work, upon love for the business and understanding of its requirements.

(4.) I do not think the farmers trouble themselves much about the further influx of foreigners, except that they desire such a class of immigrants as will make good American citizens. They are opposed to making this country a dumping ground for the ignorant, turbulent element from foreign countries.

(5) No efforts are made by public authorities or private persons, so far as I know, to attract immigrants; possibly corporations may do so to some extent, as Italians and some of that class work well in gangs in railroad construction and repairs, sewering of cities, and the like.

(6) There are colonies of Russian Jews in this State, particularly in the southern portion; notably that at Woodbine, founded and sustained largely by the Baron de Hirsch funds appropriated for that purpose. There is another not far from Vineland called Alliance, and still others of smaller numbers.

According to the State secretary of agriculture,[1] foreign immigration to the farms in New Jersey is confined mostly to Hungarians, Swedes, and Germans. Swedes and Germans have had rather more experience in agriculture in the countries they came from than the Hungarians. Foreign laborers are settling and becoming proprietors, in especial, near the large cities, and are going into market gardening on a small scale.[2]

There is apparently no tendency to colonize shown on the part of the foreigners coming into the State, outside of the Jewish settlements, which were started strictly as colonies.

Italian laborers brought in to pick fruit have begun to get hold of the land, for fruit-raising on their own account, and have brought to productivity lands that a few years ago were considered barren and worthless. In the secretary's opinion, when the attempt has been made to form colonies of foreigners with outside aid, the progress has been much less rapid than when they have made a start by their own initiative.

Circumstances are particularly favorable in New Jersey for an immigrant who has some knowledge of agriculture and some means to establish a home there, because lands have so far decreased from former valuations that in many cases the properties can be bought for the value of the improvements on them.

The productive capacity of lands in New Jersey has been increasing steadily of late years until now the State produces more wheat to the acre than any Western State.[3]

A representative farmer[4] says that a great many farms in the State are now occupied by the native born of foreign parentage and that they make very good farmers. The foreign element in his neighborhood are mainly Germans and Irish. Some of the German women work on the farms; a few of the Irish, but not many.

A representative farmer from Mercer County reports that some Italians are employed as laborers in his neighborhood, but the greater part are negroes from southwestern Virginia.[5] They are employed because of the lack of good white help, and are preferred to foreigners because they understand the language and ways of the country.

Reference to the table of returns from representative farmers indicate that there is opportunity for immigrants, even for those who can not speak English, in all the counties heard from. Truck, dairy, and fruit farming, being extensively followed in the State, give a high proportion of employment to farm laborers the year around. Nearly all of the farmers report good opportunities for married laborers and work for women and children.

The foreign farmers reported are mainly Irish and German. In one county Dutch are mentioned. In another, Italian farmers are spoken of. These are undoubtedly connected with the agricultural colony founded by Signor Secchi de Casale in 1878 at Vineland, described in preceding pages.

OPPORTUNITIES FOR TENANCY AND OWNERSHIP.

(Reported by representative farmers.)

CAPE MAY COUNTY.—Opportunities for renting are scarce. Truck farmers own small farms which they cultivate themselves with what help they can hire. A poor man, if enterprising, might purchase while hiring out.

CUMBERLAND COUNTY.—Farms are often rented for a cash rental. There are opportunities for purchasing a farm while the purchaser works on another, as farms are small and not very expensive.

GLOUCESTER COUNTY.—(1) There are many Germans in the neighborhood who are tenant farmers, mostly on shares. (2) The chances for purchase of a farm where the purchaser hires out are not very promising.

---

[1] Reports of Industrial Commission, vol. x, pp. 85, 86.
[2] Ibid.
[3] Ibid., p. 93.
[4] Ibid., p. 124.
[5] Ibid., p. 132.

AGRICULTURAL DISTRIBUTION OF IMMIGRANTS. 527

MONMOUTH COUNTY.—Farms are rented on shares. If the tenant furnishes implements and one-half of the stock he receives one-half the product; if the owner furnishes implements and stock, the tenant receives one-third of the product. There are no instances in this neighborhood where men have purchased land while hiring out.

MIDDLESEX COUNTY.—There are many chances to rent farms. If the landlord furnishes everything, the tenant receives one-third of the produce. If the tenant furnishes crop and implements, he receives one-half of the produce. Chances for purchase of land were never better than at present, on account of the low price, but not by hiring out.

MERCER COUNTY.—Opportunities for renting are fair, but it would be difficult for a poor man to establish himself as a tenant farmer unless he could begin by making a payment of perhaps one-fifth of the price.

PENNSYLVANIA.

(See table, p. 593.)

With regard to immigration in relation to agriculture, the secretary of agriculture for Pennsylvania writes as follows:

The increased demand for manufactured articles and the products of our mines has made a demand for labor. The impetus given business in our towns and cities has also drawn away from the country a considerable portion of those who could have been depended upon for day's work in former years. Most of the immigrants in this State go to the mines and mills, and the demand there has been unusual during the last two years. I am not sufficiently familiar with the exact condition of these industries to be able to definitely answer your question as to the exact state of the demand at this time.

With regard to the second question, very few immigrants have come into Pennsylvania to take up land for agricultural purposes. The most of them pass through to the cheap lands of the West.

Third. The fact that very few immigrants purchase farms in this State makes it impossible for me to state as to their success as compared with our American-born agriculturists.

Fourth. Our farmers do not oppose the incoming of any person who desires to become a citizen and take up residence in the farming districts of the State. Very few, as I have stated, take advantage of our opportunities for locating amongst us.

Fifth. There have been no special efforts made to attract immigrants into this State.

Sixth. We have no agricultural "colonies[" or "settlements" of foreigners in our State.

Very respectfully, JOHN HAMILTON,
Secretary of Agriculture.

Of fifteen representative farmers heard from (see table, p. 593), seven are in counties in the eastern part of the State, four are from the centre, and four from the west. Five of the seven eastern farmers say that there are opportunities in their neighborhoods for foreign immigrants who do not speak English. Farmers from the center of the State are not so encouraging. In the western counties, again, there are more openings. The extent to which immigrants would be taken apparently has nothing to do with density of population.

Among farm laborers are many Germans, some Irish and Swedes. Welsh are found in one county (Montgomery) in a region originally settled by people of their nationality. A few Poles are noted. Little preference as to the nationality of farm laborers is expressed; such as there is, is for German and Swedes.

One farmer writes:

There are about 1,800 farms in this county (Monroe), and I think there are about 10 per cent of the owners that hire help. Nearly all of the farm work is done by the farmer and his family. There is a surplus of young men every spring that seek and secure employment in other counties. The rural population has not increased in 30 years.

Yet, notwithstanding these conditions, there would be an opportunity in almost every community for a sober, industrious German to secure a piece of land for a home and secure work among the farmers by the day at 75 cents and board.

Foreign farmers are found in all counties heard from but three (Luzerne, Center, and Westmoreland), where there were said to be none. Many are Irish and Germans. French are found in Pike and Butler counties, Belgians in Butler County, and a few Poles in Berks.

Not strictly "foreign farmers," but in some ways still representative of the foreign element in agriculture, are the so-called "Pennsylvania Dutch" in Berks, Lebanon, Lancaster, and neighboring counties. The Pennsylvania Dutch are said to be "undoubtedly the finest farmers in the United States to-day," and to have "maintained their industrial enterprises amidst all changes of prices, rates of interest, and so on, so as to increase their wealth, maintain their standard of agriculture, and keep up the standard of living, while other sections of the country have deteriorated and lost ground."[1] Land values in this section are very high—as high as $200 an acre, but the Pennsylvania Dutch have managed to make profit even at this high capitalization. This is because they are frugal, careful of their property, and highly industrious.

---

[1] Testimony of John Franklin Crowell, Reports of Ind. Com., vol. x, p. 333.

OPPORTUNITIES FOR TENANCY AND OWNERSHIP.

(Reported by representative farmers.)

CHESTER COUNTY.—Farms may be rented on thirds and sometimes on halves. Land remote from the railroad may be bought for from $40 to $50 an acre.

BERKS COUNTY.—There are some farms to rent, either for a money rent or a share of the product. There are fair chances for purchase on easy terms.

MONTGOMERY COUNTY.—There are many tenant farmers in this locality. Most of them pay a cash rent; that depends upon the size and condition of the farm. Land is too valuable in this locality for a poor man to attempt to pay for a farm while hiring out.

LEHIGH COUNTY.—Tenant farmers are scarce. Good tenants can rent all the farms they want, usually on shares. There are good opportunities for purchase for the right man.

MONROE COUNTY.—There are good opportunities for renting. The tenant furnishes stock and tools and one-half of the seed, taking one-half of the crop on good farms. On poor farms tenants furnish everything and take two-thirds of the crop. There are good opportunities for purchase for a hard-working and saving man.

PIKE COUNTY.—There are good opportunities for renting, either for money rent or on shares. There are farms here that are now idle for want of good tenants. Our young men seek employment with the railroad, telegraph, and telephone companies, and farm help is scarce. Opportunities for purchasing land while hiring out are good. There are a number of Germans here who have been successful in just that way.

LUZERNE COUNTY.—There are no openings for immigrants to rent farms, and the opportunities for purchase are not good.

CUMBERLAND COUNTY.—Very limited opportunities for renting and for purchase.

BEDFORD COUNTY.—The farms here are all occupied. This would not be a good locality for renting or for purchase.

CENTER COUNTY.—Good, reliable tenant farmers are in demand. Terms are one-third of the product.

CAMERON COUNTY.—Tenant farming does not pay. There is considerable wild mountain land which could be made productive under good management, but not level land.

WESTMORELAND COUNTY.—For good farmers there is plenty of opportunity to rent farms for half of the crops or money rent. There are plenty of opportunities for purchase of land while the purchaser hires out, but only 1 succeeds to 90 who fail.

WASHINGTON COUNTY.—There are very few openings for renting farms.

BUTLER COUNTY.—Opportunities for renting and for purchase on easy terms are not good.

WARREN COUNTY.—Several farms in this section are rented annually. Farms are usually let for a cash rental which is not very high. Land is not bought in this section while the purchaser is hiring out. It is doubtful if this could be done.

NORTH CENTRAL STATES.

OHIO.

(See table, p. 595.)

The State secretary of agriculture writes that there is a greater demand for help on the farm than in former years, that Germans are usually most effective as farmers and farm laborers, that their success as farmers is perhaps greater than that of native farmers, owing rather to greater industry and frugality than to more intensive cultivation, and that farmers, as a class, would probably favor further immigration, but no organized efforts are being made by public or private authorities to encourage it.

Reports from representative farmers (see table, p. 595) indicate that there is a call for immigrants, especially for Germans. The foreign element is not found in the southern part of the State, and in that section there is no call, or very little, for immigrants. In the central and northern counties, however, are many German farmers and farm laborers, and in these counties further additions of foreigners are desired. The correspondent from Henry County writes: "One-quarter of the well-to-do farmers of Henry County came from Germany here with nothing but willing hands. Perseverance and industry was their capital. Still they come, and still we welcome them." Another, from Logan County, writes: "Would be glad to have 50 good German families with growing children, if honest and industrious, come at once to our county."

AGRICULTURAL DISTRIBUTION OF IMMIGRANTS. 529

The German families coming to some of these places are well educated, sometimes better than their American neighbors.[1] Both Germans and French show some tendency to colonize, and in some places insist upon having German and French taught in the district schools. But most of them are growing out of that idea, preferring that their children shall be educated in English.

OPPORTUNITIES FOR TENANCY AND OWNERSHIP.

(Reported by representative farmers.)

ROSS COUNTY.—A great deal of land is let on the tenant system. Tenant finding everything gets one-half the crop; with tools and team furnished, one-third. Opportunities for a poor man to purchase are not very good. Land is high and can not be bought in small plats.

DARKE COUNTY.—Farms rent on shares; one-half is given, and farms are in demand. Purchasers of farms pay a fair amount of cash down.

CHAMPAIGN COUNTY.—Men save their wages, get teams, then rent land for half the crop, or they take the farmers' teams and work the land for a third. Many make enough in this way to buy farms of their own. As to opportunities for a poor man to become an independent farmer, land is from $50 to $100 an acre, "and no one saves much money here. Young farm laborers generally have horses and buggies, dress well, and have a good time. They do not try to save much in the old-fashioned way."

LOGAN COUNTY.—Fair chances for tenancy if tenant is able to equip farm. Better, if able to equip with machines and half the stock. Tenant laborers mostly desired with families. Good chances for purchase.

AUGLAIZE COUNTY.—There are more tenant farmers than places. But little land is for sale and that high.

MARION COUNTY.—Good chances for tenancy. Tenant gets one-third of crop if teams and implements are furnished; one-half if he furnishes these himself. Many have purchased land by saving earnings until able to make a payment.

HANCOCK COUNTY.—Good chances for tenancy. Grain or cash rent. Good chances for purchase by right kind of man.

LICKING COUNTY.—When owner of farm furnishes everything, tenant gets one-third. When tenant has team and tools, he gets one-half. Good chances for purchase.

NOBLE COUNTY.—Many farmers wish tenants. Many farmers have moved to town and have tenants on their farms. Tenant owns half of the stock, pays half of the taxes, and does all the work and a certain amount of repairing. There are some opportunities for a man to secure land and pay for it in small payments; but lands are increasing in demand and prices. Have been very low. Depreciated nearly one-half during panic a few years ago.

TUSCARAWAS COUNTY.—Good opportunities for tenancy on half-crop system. Not much opportunity for a poor man to purchase unless he can pay one-third cash and work in coal mines to pay balance. Land is high.

HENRY COUNTY.—Terms of tenancy: Tenant, three-fifths; landlord, two-fifths of general products and half of hay. Other farms, tenant furnishes one-half teams, tools, seed, and stock (to be fed from farm crops), and receives one-half the crop. As to purchase while hiring out, correspondent says: "That is the way I got my farm. Industrious men are doing the same every year; but they can't do it by patronizing all the saloons and whittling pine sticks."

INDIANA.

(See table, p. 597.)

There are many foreign farm laborers in the State, mostly Swedes and Germans. They have a tendency to colonize, and wherever a German or Swedish settlement has been made, the price of land advances.[2] They make desirable citizens, and most of them are as well educated as the same number of Americans.

The representative farmers heard from do not mention Swedish farmers or laborers. (See table, p. 597.) German farmers are noted in the southern counties. In the same counties the bulk of the farm labor is said to be native white, and there is little call for immigrants. One farmer writes, however: "Send some men here if you can; they can get employment." In the northern counties are apparently fewer German farmers, and in those counties there is little call for immigrants.

---

[1] Testimony of Hon. Joseph H. Brigham, Asst. Sec. U. S. Dept. Agriculture. Reports of Ind. Com., Vol. X, p. 10.
[2] Testimony of Mr. Aaron Jones, master National Grange. Reports of Ind. Com., Vol. X, p. 34.

OPPORTUNITIES FOR TENANCY AND OWNERSHIP.

(Reported by representative farmer)

WARRICK COUNTY.—There are some opportunities for renting, but as a rule general farming is not profitable here. As to purchasing land on payments while hiring out here, this could be done. A good man could get more work than he can do.

GIBSON COUNTY.—Good opportunities for renting. There might be a chance for purchase on payments while the purchaser hired out.

PIKE COUNTY.—There is always room for a few tenant farmers at a rent of from one-third to two-fifths of the produce.

SCOTT COUNTY.—More tenant farmers are not desired. The land rents for one-half the produce in the field. As to purchase of land while the purchaser earned a living by hiring out, there would be little chance of doing so, although land is cheap. It runs from $12 to $25 an acre for upland.

SWITZERLAND COUNTY.—Opportunities for renting are poor, but for purchase are fairly good.

MONROE COUNTY.—Opportunities for renting are very poor. Our county is farmed mostly by the owners themselves, most of whom are small farmers. There might be a few good opportunities for purchase. Land some 5 or 6 miles from Bloomington is not very high, and can be bought on reasonable terms. As to purchase while hiring out, there is still a place for the man who is energetic and honest.

FRANKLIN COUNTY.—As to purchasing land on payments while hiring out, that all depends on the man. The opportunities are all right. The writer began in that way, and to-day is worth $6,000 or $7,000, and is a young man yet.

HENDRICKS COUNTY.—There are very good chances for reliable, competent men to rent farms. Terms vary from one-third to one-half of the whole crop. As to purchase, the opportunities are not very good. Land is too expensive and taxes too heavy.

HENRY COUNTY.—Terms of rental are one-half of product. Opportunities for purchase are not good.

JAY COUNTY.—In renting, landlord receives about one-half, delivered in the bushel. Some farms are for rent, but the farms are mostly occupied by the owners themselves. Land can only be bought by paying seller sufficient to secure against loss in case of foreclosure.

HUNTINGTON COUNTY.—As to tenancy, if a man can get a start, and proves himself to be a good tenant, he has no further trouble, but the supply of poor tenants is in excess of the demand. Usually tenant and landlord each furnish half and receive half, or the tenant furnishes everything and gives the landlord two-fifths. Sometimes the landlord furnishes everything and the tenant gets one-half for doing the work. Sometimes tenants furnish everything and give the landlord one-half, delivered in town, if the land is good. Opportunities for purchase are not very good unless the man has good health and is a good manager. Land is from $30 to $100 an acre; some of it quite poor.

DEKALB COUNTY.—There are plenty of opportunities to rent. Landlord furnishes everything and receives two-thirds of the crop. There is plenty of opportunity to purchase on easy terms if the man is energetic and enterprising.

ILLINOIS.

(See table, p. 599.)

Foreign farm laborers through central Illinois are usually Germans, Danes, and Swedes, and are an intelligent class of people. When they acquire farms of their own, they show a tendency to colonize. It is said that immigration has, in the main, improved the condition of agriculture and has not afforded more labor than there was a demand for, but that it has probably been one cause of the native-born leaving the farms. The manner of farming of German farmers does not appear to depress the price of agricultural products, as they farm like the American farmer, except that they do not perhaps lay out quite so much money for labor, getting more help from wives and children. Their manner of living may, however, depress local markets somewhat. The Germans in Illinois are good farmers, it is said, coming here with a high idea of the necessity of keeping up the fertility of the soil.[1]

The table of reports from representative farmers shows Germans, French, Danes, Swedes, Scotch, and Irish as farmers in the southwestern and central counties of the state, and the same nationalities, with the exception of the French, as farm laborers. The Germans and Swedes appear to be liked as farm laborers, and the call for immigrants is general. From only one county is it reported that there are no openings for them. The large proportion of laborers employed through the year in all the counties heard from is noticeable.

---

[1] Testimony of Mr. Oliver Wilson: Reports of Ind. Com., vol. x, pp. 243, 246, 263.

At Streator, in this State, is a colony of Slovaks. These are not largely employed in agriculture, but some account of them may be of interest here. A leader among them writes about them as follows:

There are about 800 or 900 families of Slovaks here (in and near Streator). Most of the men are working in the coal mines, a few of them in the glass, brick, and tile factories. But very few of them do not own their own homes. In other ways they are doing fairly well. In the town of Kangley, 5 miles from Streator, are about 100 families of Slovaks, and about the same number are at Harwat. Most of these also own their homes. They also work in the coal mines.

South, southwest, and southeast, from 30 to 60 miles, there are Slovaks working in coal mines, but I do not know how they are doing. At Lasalle, 30 miles west, are a few Slovaks, and at Spring Valley and Ladd, 40 to 45 miles away, are some, but I do not know how they are doing.

In and around Streator are only 3 families or so engaged in farming, but about 20 to 25 families have left here for Minnesota within the past 10 years to go into farming. These are doing very well. Some of them are worth about $10,000. Around Streator land is very high, running up to $120 an acre. In the near future about 10 families are expecting to go out West looking for land.

OPPORTUNITIES FOR TENANCY AND OWNERSHIP.

(Reported by representative farmers.)

UNION COUNTY.—Terms for renting are for landlord to furnish teams, tools, and feed for teams, also one-half of the necessary packages for shipping, and to receive one-half of the vegetables or small fruit raised. Opportunities for a poor man to purchase land are not good unless he can pay something down or is able to cultivate the land himself. He can not hire out and pay for a farm.

ST. CLAIR COUNTY.—There are good opportunities to rent, either on shares or for money rent. The rent is generally one-third of the crop. There are no opportunities for a poor man to purchase, as land is too high.

CLINTON COUNTY.—The chances to become tenant farmers are not very good, since there are plenty of tenants equipped to take all the farms to rent. A limited number of men might find opportunities to purchase farms while hiring out.

MENARD COUNTY.—Terms of renting are mostly grain rent, tenant giving one-half of the corn and two-fifths of the small grain. Lands are worth from $25 to $125 an acre. Chances are much against the man who buys on time.

FULTON COUNTY.—Opportunities are good for renting on a cash rent of from $3 to $5 an acre or on equal shares of the product. Opportunities for a poor man to purchase land are decidedly poor, as land is held at from $80 to $100.

KNOX COUNTY.—(1) After men have saved enough money to buy the necessary horses and implements the opportunity to rent is good. Lands are usually $5 to $6 an acre or half the crop in crib or barn. There are no opportunities whatever for a poor man to purchase. Land is too high in this vicinity, ranging from $100 an acre up. (2) There are good chances for renting farms; terms, a cash rent, usually $5 an acre.

MCLEAN COUNTY.—Renters here pay from three-fifths to one-half grain rent or $5 to $5.50 per acre for farm land and $4 for meadow and grass land. There is not much opportunity for a poor man to purchase land here, as it is usually worth $100 an acre.

MICHIGAN.

(See table, p. 600.)

The secretary of state writes, with regard to foreign immigrants and industrial conditions in the State at the present time, as follows:

First. We believe that the opportunities for immigrants were never better than at the present time. Never before has there been such a demand for laborers as we have now. Many farmers have found it difficult to gather their crops on account of the scarcity of labor. This is due to the revival of business along all lines. We have several new industries which have created a demand for laborers, as, for instance, the sugar-beet industry, the Saginaw coal mines, and the manufacture of Portland cement.

There are also splendid opportunities for men to engage in farming of all kinds in northern Michigan. The large fruit crop in western Michigan also gave labor to a great many persons during the summer and fall.

Second. As farmers any wide-awake person can succeed, although some people are better suited for certain lines. In the sugar-beet fields, for weeding, hoeing, etc., the Germans, Polanders, and Russians seem to be the most effective. This will also apply to miners as well, and perhaps to the small settlers who go out to reclaim and build up farms. In the higher grades of farming, such as dairying, fruit growing, or where stock of the various kinds is kept, it needs someone who has had experience in order to succeed. We have many Germans, Scotch, Hollanders, etc., here who are very proficient along their lines and are succeeding nicely.

Third. We find many farmers who succeed are Americans, and vice versa. If the foreign farmers succeed where our people do not, it is because of their thrifty, economical habits. They have great energy and are satisfied to begin at the bottom and grow up, while the Yankee is not built just that way always. We have intensive farmers of all nationalities.

Fourth. Farmers are all glad to see people come here who are willing to work and thus contribute to the upbuilding of the State. We need thousands of them, and those coming can easily get a home for themselves and also be a benefit to those who are here now.

Fifth. Nothing is done by the State to get immigrants. This ought to be done, by all means. Some of the railroads have been engaged in this work and have done much along that line.

There are many colonies of foreigners in the State. Worthy of especial notice is the colony of Hollanders in Ottawa and Allegan counties, on Lake Michigan, near Benton Harbor. They now number about 40,000. The original colonists came over with the Rev. Mr. Van Raalte from Holland in 1847. They came first in large numbers in 1872, but the great influx was in 1880 and 1881. They engaged in agriculture, especially for the factories which put up pickles, canned goods, green corn, tomatoes, and for beet-sugar factories, and in the growing of peaches and fruit. After acquiring a competence they retired from farming, and the village of Holland is made up of retired Dutch farmers. They have their own college—Hope College. The women and children work in the fields the same as the men. They employ only Dutch laborers and very few are coming at the present time from the old country. They are at first slow and do not take up with American ways, but having once become aroused they do the very best work, especially in the farmers' institutes. An off-shoot from this colony is located in Chippewa County, at Rudyard, in the northern peninsula. This was started by advertising at Holland, Mich., and the first Hollander located at Rudyard in February, 1900. Others followed, and they have kept coming until there are now about 5,000 of them in the neighborhood. The Reformed Church has approved the movement, and is aiding the colonists to start a strong church movement there. There is a plan to start an academy there, which would tend to increase the attendance at Hope College, in Holland, Mich. Another colony is located in Sherman township, in Newaygo County. This is not an off-shoot from the Holland colony.

At Rudyard, Finns, Danes, and Norwegians are also located. The account given by a citizen of Rudyard of how the Finns were established there is typical of the way in which such colonies are often started. He writes:

Some 5 years ago I employed some Finlanders as farm laborers at Rudyard. After working for a time some of them took contracts for land for a home. Through their influence others have come from other parts of Michigan and a few from Finland. New immigrants are still coming. There are now about 150 Finlanders there, and they report that we may expect a good number more this spring. This will no doubt become a large settlement.

The writer speaks highly of their character as colonists. He says:

They [the Finns] are very economical and industrious and are successful farmers. They cultivate all of the crops of the country—wheat, oats, barley, rye, pease, timothy, clover, etc., also sell milk to the cheese factory. We do not hesitate to start a Finlander on a new piece of land with or without a cash payment. They improve it quickly and are among the most prompt in payment. They all buy land.

The same correspondent says he:

Can speak as well of the Danes and Norwegians, though our people of these races have not made so much effort to get their friends to join them. The Norwegian families are from other parts of Michigan. The Danes started in this way: a Danish woman married an American living near Rudyard, and induced some of her relatives to come from Denmark. A few more have followed them.

Germans are scattered over the State in somewhat smaller groups than those mentioned especially at Mount Clemens, north of Detroit and southeast of Saginaw, toward Bay City. At Frankenmuth one-third of the citizens are Germans. These Germans have succeeded well in growing sugar beets, while Americans in the State do not take to this kind of farming. American capital, however, puts in the sugar factories. Not many Germans are now coming.

There are many French Canadians in the State, especially in Menominee and Delta counties in the northern peninsula, and in the northern part of the southern peninsula. They came in originally as lumbermen. When the lumber has been cleared off the land has been practically given to them through purchase on tax titles. They live very poorly, as the soil is not advantageous. They are not clannish, as are the Germans and Hollanders, mainly because the distances compel them to mingle with Americans. In Menominee and Delta counties the French Canadians predominate, so that it may be said that this is one great French settlement. They, however, are more eager to send their children to school than is the case in the southern peninsula, where they are scattered. They do not take hold of institute or educational work in agriculture, and do not learn English, but the children are learning English. They continue to come in large numbers from Canada. Menominee and Escanaba high schools are among the best in the State and are supported by French Canadians. The country schools are also good. The parents are grossly ignorant. They get good wages at lumbering in winter and on their own farms in summer.

A prominent resident of Menominee County writes as follows about the growth of the French Canadian colony in his neighborhood:

This section of the northern peninsula of Michigan, Menominee County, was opened up to settlement by the building of the Chicago and Northwestern Railway about 1873-74. About 1876 the timber lands came into market, and I think that nearly 75 per cent of the first settlers were Canadians (French). Their first occupation was cutting and marketing the timber, but in most cases they started in to develop farms, we being among the number in our immediate locality. We find that few remain at this time of the original settlers; the majority of the Canadians get out soon after the timber is off their farms, and either take up new land near by or move further into the woods. There are, however, a few very notable exceptions. We have in our immediate vicinity about a

AGRICULTURAL DISTRIBUTION OF IMMIGRANTS. 533

dozen of them who have developed farms that would do credit to an older country. They in all cases came without money, and now own homes ranging from $2,000 to $10,000. We would say possibly 10 per cent have held their farms and own them. The children of these families are usually settling on farms in the same neighborhood.

Very few new families are coming in. The past season three thrifty families came here from Canada and bought farms. The children of the families that follow up the timber, we find, are inclined pretty much the same way.

These families are being replaced largely by Swedes and Norwegians, who, as a rule, we find more thrifty and better farmers.

A correspondent from Delta County writes as follows about the French Canadians in that neighborhood:

> The French came to this peninsula with the early settlers and have become a part of the population everywhere, being pretty well mixed in with the rest. In the very small settlements, places which have sprung up in consequence of lumbering operations, there is a percentage of about 75, perhaps more. The percentage of French in this city is about 30.
>
> The farmers among them have bought their land, paying for it as they are able, but not usually making purchases outright. Farming is so limited in this vicinity that few of the younger generation have followed their parents in it. More will do so in the future as the industry is developed. In the city few French are merchants. Many are saloon keepers. There are many clerks among the younger French in all lines of business.
>
> Educationally the French are average pupils. Some are very bright and few are very poor. They will not average quite as well as the children of native parentage. They have their own Catholic schools in many places. The railroad interests of the city take some into that calling.

Another correspondent from Delta County writes:

> The first French-Canadian family came to this place from Negaunee, Mich., about 30 years ago. Since that time they have been coming here almost every year up to the present time. Their first occupation was logging and getting out hemlock bark, ties, posts, etc., also wood for charcoal.
>
> Farming is the principal occupation now, except in winter, when most of the young men seek employment with different lumber concerns in this vicinity.
>
> Fully three-fourths of them are engaged in farming and almost all own their own farms. In regard to social improvement, I should say that there has been a change for the better with a few families, but not to any great extent. Having taught school here for a number of years, I can say that the general tendency of most of the French-Canadian parents is to send the children for only a limited period to school, therefore you rarely see one who ever has gone beyond the 8th grade. They hardly ever send them to high school or any college or academy.
>
> The children of these people are not inclined to look for any betterment in their condition, and for the most part follow in the steps of the parents. I am sorry to say that old and young like liquor too well and take things pretty easy. You can judge for yourself when I tell you that there are 8 saloons in this little "neck of the woods," supported mostly by French Canadians and their children.

What is said above about education as a part of the life of these people is confirmed by a correspondent from Menominee, who gives the following general account of the French Canadians in his neighborhood:

> In the city of Menominee there is a settlement of French Canadians of about 2,500 in number. They largely live in one portion of the city which is known as "Frenchtown." So far as their life is concerned it is not essentially different from that of an average citizen. This is a lumbering center, and the occupation of the men is almost entirely that of some part of the lumbering industry. There is not a person in their community of personal influence outside the priest.
>
> These people are almost entirely Catholics, having a large and prosperous church, and well-organized parochial school. The children are keen and bright, but do not remain in school much after the age of 15. Very few of them have a special desire to secure an education. In this respect they fall below the other nationalities here. The boys mainly are engaged in the special work for which this city is famous.
>
> These people are not specially thrifty; they seem to spend their money in dress and in their own special social life.

The sugar-beet industry, now carried on so extensively in Michigan, gives an opportunity for foreign laborers. One factory requires 5,000 acres of beets, and as it takes 1 person a week to thin an acre of beets, 5,000 weeks' work are required in June, and as much in September and October to harvest the beets. It is very difficult to get the labor needed. This is partly due to the fact that this factory was located in a district already given up to peach growing, which requires much labor at the same time that the beet crop requires it. Russian Jews and other foreigners are brought over from Chicago during the two busy seasons.

In the southern tier of counties many farmers have retired and have rented their farms largely to foreigners, themselves locating in villages and cities. Land there is worth from $50 to $60 per acre. This is about the price asked for sugar-beet land.

The fact that these farmers no longer cultivate their own farms is considered a serious obstacle in the way of progressive agriculture. This can hardly be due to the fact that the ex-farmers are Americans and the farmers who replace them are foreigners, since the latter have so abundantly shown their skill at and success in farming. It is probably due rather to the system itself, tenant farming, by whomever carried on, being generally considered less good for the land than direct cultivation by the owner.

Prof. Clinton D. Smith, director of the State agricultural experiment station, says, however, that the owners are less inclined than they would be otherwise to arrange with tenants for raising crops that will improve the land on the ground that "the men on their farms are too ignorant to experiment on any change in methods."

Representative farmers in different parts of the State (see table, p. —) almost unanimously say that there are opportunities in the State for immigrants who do not speak English. Many German farmers are spoken of. In Kent and Charlevoix counties Dutch farmers and farm laborers are mentioned; in Mecosta and Iosco counties mention is made of Swedes and Poles. Two of the farmers express a preference for Germans as farm laborers and 1 for Swedes. On the whole, the opportunities for foreign immigrants in this State seem to be excellent.

OPPORTUNITIES FOR TENANCY AND OWNERSHIP.

(Reported by representative farmers.)

WAYNE COUNTY.—Farms are rented on shares or at about $3 per acre cash. Opportunities for a poor man to establish himself in tenant farming are poor.

JACKSON COUNTY.—Terms of tenancy are as follows: First, equal-share farming, each furnishing half; second, everything furnished, giving tenant one-third; third, tenant furnishing everything and giving one-third; fourth, cash rent. The opportunities for purchasing on shares while hiring out are scarce.

EATON COUNTY.—Opportunities for renting all depend upon ability; steady, sober men who understand farming can find situations here. Purchasing while hiring out is done by thrifty men, but there are better localities for such than this.

KENT COUNTY.—Opportunities for purchase are very good.

LAPEER COUNTY.—Nearly all farms are rented each year. Both cash and crop rent. Opportunities for a poor man to establish himself in independent farming are good for the right kind of a man.

MECOSTA COUNTY.—There are fine opportunities for renting. Renter receives one-third of the crop. Land is cheap here yet, and there is some homestead land. An industrious man with a small family can easily raise his living for the first year on these lands. He can work out on every spare day during the season.

OCEANA COUNTY.—There are good opportunities for renting. One-third goes to the landlord; two-thirds to the tenant, who furnishes all. There are good opportunities for purchase. Land is cheap and there is plenty of work.

IOSCO COUNTY.—Opportunities for renting are limited. A few farms are rented at a cash rental of from $1 to $2.50 an acre. They are generally rented on shares. There are reasonable opportunities for purchase. A few good lands can be secured under the homestead laws of the State and of the United States.

CHARLEVOIX COUNTY.—A few farms can be rented either on shares or for a cash rent. As to purchasing while the purchaser hires out, many are doing so, as stump land can be bought for $5 an acre.

WISCONSIN.

(See table, p. 601.)

The commissioner of labor for the State wrote as follows in 1894 as to the opportunities for immigrants in the State at that time.[1]

> I can state that the northern part of our State has fine timber lands that when improved will make the best of farms, and immigration in that part of the State would be very desirable, providing, first, the persons arriving had a small sum of money to invest in the purchase of land, which is very cheap. In that part of the State, in fact, most any and everything can be raised, including wheat, oats, barley, potatoes, and vegetables of all kinds. * * *
>
> Our State, in my judgment, would prefer the German, for the reason that as a rule they all work and are generally very prosperous with us.

As to the conditions to-day, the secretary of the State board of immigration writes the following:

> Wisconsin, with its diversified industries, offers better opportunities to-day to the immigrant than was offered during the years of industrial depression in our lumber and mining industries. The same is true in practically every line of business; everything so dovetails in together that depression in one line of industry means depression in another.
>
> Second. Germans and Scandinavians are most effective as farmers and farm laborers.
>
> The success of the foreign farmers, if German and Scandinavian, is greater than that of American-born. The Germans or Scandinavians of foreign birth who come here first come from a depleted soil. They grub, dig, and save, and soon put their small farms on a paying basis, and eventually die fairly well to do. Their children do not seem to have the same ambition that the old folks have, and do not work as hard or accomplish as great results. But the grandchildren are more thoroughly Americanized, and seem to do better than the fathers did. American-born children are not content to cultivate small farms, and do not cultivate the large farms to get all out of them that it is possible to get. A part is cultivated and the remainder neglected.
>
> Fourth. We have so much unoccupied land as yet in this State that farmers are glad to see further immigration to the State.
>
> Fifth. The State board of immigration of Wisconsin expends about $5,000 a year in advertising and showing to intending settlers the benefits that can be derived by settling, especially in northern

---

[1] Report Immigration Investigating Commission, p. 151.

Wisconsin. We are not doing anything in the way of trying to attract foreign immigration, but are attempting to draw settlers from older and more thickly settled States. Certain railroads and private land companies are engaged in the work of settling land in northern Wisconsin. There are probably one hundred such firms doing business in northern Wisconsin. There are no agricultural colonies in the State, but there are numerous sections in the State in which Germans, Scandinavians, or Poles prevail as a nationality in such settlements.

The great timber region in the northern part of the State where especial opportunities are offered to settlers is comprised in an area north of a line drawn from Green Bay to the mouth of the St. Croix River, with the counties of Portage, Wood, and Jackson as southern projections, and contains 27 counties occupying about 53 per cent of the area of the entire State. It appears that, considering the whole area from a farmer's standpoint, about 20 per cent is good farming land, about 40 per cent is medium, while 40 per cent is either not suited to farming or only doubtfully so.[1] Of the 18,500,000 acres contained in this tract a little less than 7 per cent is improved. Twenty-four per cent of the total area is held by actual settlers, 5 per cent by the United States (2 per cent being Indian reservations), less than 2 per cent by the State, a little over 5 per cent by the railways, leaving 63 per cent held by private nonresidents. Of the land so held 80 per cent, or about 50 per cent of the total area under consideration, is owned by lumbermen.[2] Of the 17,000,000 acres of unimproved land 8,000,000 are "cut-over" lands, largely burned over and waste.[3] This area is constantly growing.

It is to these lands in especial that attempts are now being made to bring settlers. An interesting experiment has been tried to get foreign residents of cities upon such lands. The following letter from the State commissioner of labor statistics gives some account of this:

The ——— Land Company has been settling Polish people in the northern counties of the State for the past 14 years, and up to the present time has sold land to about 1,000 people, as near as they could estimate it. All of these people have settled in the counties of Shawano, Brown, and Oconto. They came from Chicago, Indiana, and the mining regions of Illinois and Pennsylvania (very few came from Milwaukee). All had accumulated some savings which were made at various occupations in the cities of this country (principally laboring). The land company sold them the land upon payment of a small sum down and the balance to be paid in from 3 to 5 years with interest at 6 and 7 per cent. In every case these people have made a success; so much so that (the manager of the company tells me) most of their sales in the past few years have been to the people who purchased land several years ago and have since paid for it and added more to their holdings. The average price paid for the land was about $11 per acre.

From the ——— Land Company I learned that during the 2½ years they have been in business they have sent 71 families into Marinette County exclusively, with an average of 6 people to a family. These people came principally from the city of Milwaukee, although some of them were from Detroit, Cleveland, Chicago, Hammond, Ind., and the mining regions of Pennsylvania. These people were painters, carpenters, masons, farmers, and laborers, and in every case had saved some money which they had accumulated at these occupations in this country. Their average holding is 80 acres, and the cost $6 per acre, average. The terms of the land company were one-half of purchase price down and the balance in 5 years at 7 per cent. These terms were complied with in every case. From the start these farming ventures seem to have been self-sustaining, for in no case has any of them asked for financial assistance. At the present time there are people on their way from Poland to settle on land in Marinette County.

The following letters from private land companies operating in this region give an idea of how far the opportunities they offer are available for immigrants and what their methods are:

I.

Most of the settlers whom we place on our lands in Wisconsin are farmers from the farming districts of the more improved parts of Wisconsin, Illinois, Indiana, and a few from Ohio. We are getting a large number this year from the State of Iowa, as we have had a few before.
As for foreign immigration, we have had a man in Europe for the past 3 years, our Mr. ———, who is stationed at Copenhagen, Denmark. We have been working on a Russian colony from Odessa. We had a delegation here last summer and they looked over our lands, staying here 4 or 5 weeks. We have brought one German Russian from Odessa and settled him in Clark County. He had plenty of means to buy a good farm. We have not directly handled any foreigners from New York. We can take care of a thousand farmers in two weeks' time by putting them on our lands in Clark, Chippewa, Price, and Sawyer counties, Wis.

Most of the foreigners here are Germans and Norwegians. The Germans and Norwegians are coming steadily, not only from Europe but from the more thickly settled districts in the territory above mentioned. We are selling good agricultural lands at from $5 to $10 per acre, unimproved, in Wisconsin. We have done lots of advertising. We have sent over 200,000 circulars to Europe, and we are using several hundred thousand a year in this country. We have men out on the road taking up renters who want to buy land in the States above mentioned.
The lands we offer are what are called cut-over lands. The lumbermen have taken off the most valuable and merchantable timber and left the land to be cleared and cleaned up and tilled by the farmer, consequently our work is slow and steady and the margin small. We never sell land for more than it is worth; land is enhancing in value all the time.
    Respectfully,   ——— LAND COMPANY.

---

[1] Forestry conditions of northern Wisconsin: Filibert Roth, special agent, U. S. Department Agriculture. Wisconsin Geological and Natural History Surveys, Bulletin No. 1, Econ. series, No. 1, p. 5.
[2] Ibid., p. 6.
[3] Ibid., p. 55.

II.

We inclose circular descriptive of the lands we are offering in this State. In addition to the lands described in this circular we own a number of large bodies of lands that we have not yet placed upon the market. Lands described in the inclosed circular are situated in a well-improved farming portion of the State, and we have made no effort so far to settle them except with farmers from this and surrounding States. There have, however, settled upon our land a number of families of Hollanders, probably 30 or 40 families, some of whom have doubtless come direct from the old country. Should we decide to place some of the other lands which we own upon the market, we will doubtless endeavor to induce newly arrived immigrants to settle upon them.

Yours, truly,

———— & ————.

III.

We have not heretofore dealt with newly arrived immigrants. Our sales have been made altogether to American farmers or to men of foreign birth who have been long settled in the United States and become citizens thereof. We have, of course, a number of Germans and a few Scandinavians among our customers.

We should be pleased to deal with the newly arrived immigrants. Our lands are what are denominated cut-over timber lands. In most instances they were cut-over many years ago, and the process of time and decay has greatly facilitated the work of clearing the land for the plow; fires having kept back the second-growth timber, which in most places is not large enough to be classed as other than underbrush.

The swales are covered with the growth of natural blue-joint grass which makes excellent pasture and hay. The grass crops are par excellence the best for this section, but Indian corn also makes invariably a good crop, ranging from 35 to 90 bushels per acre on the best cultivated farms. Winter wheat is also an excellent crop, as are oats, rye, and vegetables of all kinds.

The expense of clearing the land and putting under plow does not exceed $5 to $7.50 an acre. There is plenty of firewood for fuel. Soil is a sandy loam with clay subsoil. We are prepared, in case an immigrant is a farmer and has some means, to build for him a small comfortable house and barn on each quarter section that may be selected by him. We should require, in such case a cash payment sufficient to cover a little more than the cost of such building, and should expect to carry the balance for such time as might be convenient for the purchaser, provided he proved industrious and self-helpful.

———— Farm Land Company.

IV.

I would say that my land agency does not reach for newly arrived immigrants. We have been dealing thus far with people who have been settled in some adjoining State or in the southern part of this State. We have located a good many of them on improved and unimproved lands in this and adjoining counties. They are mostly German, Norwegian, and some Danes. I have reached my purchasers largely through advertising in the German, Norwegian, and American papers. The price of our lands ranges from $5 to $50 per acre, depending upon the improvements and localities. The unimproved lands we sell at about one-third cash where the buyer moves on to make improvements at once, and the balance of the purchase price to be paid at any future day agreed upon that would be satisfactory to the purchaser. On this land we can raise hay, corn, barley, rye, wheat, oats, sugar beets, tobacco, and most any kind of grain or vegetables that can be grown in the Northwest.

Yours, very truly,

———— ————.

It was stated above that about 5 per cent of the land in the northern part of the State was held by the railway companies. These companies are doing more or less in the way of attracting foreign immigrants, as the following letters will show:

V.

This company has probably been doing more advertising for the past two years than all other landowners put together in this State. Our base of operation has been wholly within the United States, and more particularly in the southern part of this State, northern Iowa, Illinois, Indiana, Ohio, and southern Michigan. We are distributing a large amount of printed matter, doing considerable advertising in newspapers, and have a stereopticon show which gives free entertainments showing pictures of that portion of our line passing through the land grant. The lecturer describes each town of importance, giving views of industries, principal streets, and such other matters of interest as seems best.

We have something over half a million acres of good farm lands which are being offered at from $5 to $7.50 per acre. The crops for which the land is suitable chiefly are wheat, oats, rye, roots, and vegetables. The soil is perhaps better adapted to raising the different grasses than any other part of America. Sheep and cattle breeders are comming to us very rapidly. Our experience teaches us that Germans, Norwegians, Swedes, and Bohemians, and such other foreigners as were farmers in the old country, make the best success of clearing timber lands.

Yours, truly,

W. H. Killen,
Land Commissioner Wisconsin Central Railway.

The pamphlet issued by this company speaks of settlements in given localities of Swedes, Norwegians, Finlanders, Bohemians, and French Canadians, and offers to direct to the proper districts those who desire to take up homes in a settlement of any special nationality.

Another company points out some difficulties in the way of settling foreign immigrants on timber land. The land commissioner of this railway writes as follows:

VI.

Our company owns in the neighborhood of a half a million acres of land in northern Wisconsin and Michigan, which we have just recently commenced to open up for settlement. It is almost entirely heavily timbered hard-wood land, and we have not yet arrived at any systematic method of inducing foreign emigrants to locate. The proposition of locating settlers on timber land is quite a difficult one. Most of the land that is being sold is sold to people who have had some experience in a timber country; and until the lands are cleared, to a certain extent, I presume that this will be their history, and that the method of handling them will be entirely along these lines.

Yours, very truly,
J. F. CLEVELAND,
Land Commissioner Chicago and Northwestern Railway Company.

The land agent of the Chicago, Milwaukee, and St. Paul writes:

Some years ago this company distributed a considerable amount of literature published in English, German, and Norwegian. They were in the form of pamphlets, and were sent broadcast over the various countries. To-day this company is, through an auxiliary known as the Milwaukee Land Company, interested in the development of new towns located on extensions of various lines.

These towns and the territory this company is advertising by means of pamphlets. We also use the press in a general manner as well as a small army of agents.

In these towns there are opportunities for the merchant, the artisan, mechanic, and laborer. The rates of wages are above the average, while living is quite cheap.

As to the manner by which this company induces foreign immigration, I must respectfully refer you to our general passenger and ticket agent, Mr. F. A. Miller, of Chicago. Such matters pertain particularly to his department. I can locate the immigrants after they are brought to me, and between the two departments we have been very successful. We are not confined to any particular nationality. This company owns about 6,600 miles of road, and the foreign element seem to move in squads, and are usually cognizant of the locality in which they are about to settle, seeking information presumably by correspondence with their friends.

Respectfully, yours,
C. A. PADLEY,
General Land Agent.

The general immigration agent of the same road writes as follows:

VII.

Very little effort has been made during the last 12 years to induce immigrants from Europe. They come through the influence of friends mostly. We have an agent (special) in Liverpool. The general European agency was abolished 12 years ago. Our company has colonized over 200,000 people in the Dakotas of different nationalities during the last 18 years, and fully the same number in Minnesota and Iowa. We are colonizing very successfully in northern Wisconsin now of different nationalities as mentioned.[1] I find that they succeed much better in timber country than on prairie land.

Yours, truly,
W. E. POWELL, *G. I. A.*

The Chicago, St. Paul, Minneapolis and Omaha Railway has about 300,000 acres of land remaining unsold, suitable for general crops and diversified farming. The price ranges from $2.50 to $5 per acre. The land commissioner of the road writes:

We are selling our lands to all classes; most of our customers come from the settled portions of southern Wisconsin, northern Illinois, southern Minnesota, Iowa, Nebraska, and Dakota. We have made some sales to foreign immigrants, though not very many; Germans and Scandinavians are the prevailing nationalities.

Yours, respectfully,
G. W. BELL, *Land Commissioner.*

From the point of view of the student of foreign settlements and settlers in the United States, Wisconsin is especially interesting for the number of races represented within its borders, and for the high proportion of the foreign element in its population. Prof. Reuben G. Thwaites, corresponding secretary of the State Historical Society of Wisconsin, has been carrying on an investigation into the history, numbers, etc., of the foreign races represented in the population of the State, and under his direction several monographs on different races have already appeared. These are: "The Cornish in Southwest Wisconsin," by Louis Albert Copeland; "The Belgians of Northwest Wisconsin," by Xavier Martin; "The Planting of the Swiss Colony at New Glarus, Wisconsin," by John Luchsinger; "How Wisconsin Came by its Large German Element," by Kate Asaphine Everest; and "Geographical Origin of German Immigration to Wisconsin," by Kate Everest Levi.[2]

The following briefly summarized account of foreign groups in Wisconsin, and their distribution, is quoted from Professor Thwaites's annual report for 1890, presented as secretary of the historical society after the investigation had been under way about 18 months. Professor Thwaites says:

Wisconsin probably contains a greater variety of foreign groups than any other American State. The principal nationalities now colonized here rank in numbers as follows: Germans, Scandinavians, Irish, natives of Great Britain, Canadians, Bohemians, Dutch, and French. Many of these foreign groups occupy entire townships, and control within them all political, educational, and religious affairs. Here and there we find genuine communities where property is held in common, and from which strangers are carefully excluded; such as the St. Nazianz German Catholic community, in Manitowoc County, where there are men of all essential trades and professions, and where, according to our informants, no communication is held with the outer world if it can be prevented. In considerable districts, particularly among the Germans and Welsh, the English language is reported to be seldom spoken, and public as well as parochial schools are conducted in the foreign tongue. But as a rule the foreign-born people of Wisconsin appear quick to adopt American methods and English speech, and enter with zest into the privileges and duties of citizenship; while no matter

---

[1] Scandinavians, Germans, Bohemians, Poles, and English-speaking people.
[2] All published by the State Historical Society of Wisconsin, Madison, Wisc.

how stoutly the elders may endeavor to perpetuate the foreign ideas which they have brought with them the younger generation can not long be held in leash, complaint being universal in the replies to our circulars that the teachings of the fathers in these matters appear to have but little effect upon youth. The process of assimilation appears to be, as a whole, reasonably rapid and satisfactory. New customs, new manners, new blood are being introduced by the colonists from across sea, and as a rule these are worthy of adoption and absorption.

It is interesting to note the localities where these foreign groups have planted themselves.

Germans.—The Germans number 75 per cent of the population of Taylor County, 65 per cent of Dodge, and 55 per cent of Buffalo. They are also found in especially large groups in Milwaukee, Ozaukee, Washington, Sheboygan, Manitowoc, Jefferson, Outagamie, Fond du Lac, Sauk, Waupaca, Dane, Marathon, Grant, Waushara, Green Lake, Langlade, and Clark counties. There are Germans in every county of the State and numerous isolated German settlements, but in the counties named these people are particularly numerous. Sometimes the groups are of special interest, because the people came for the most part from a particular district in the Fatherland. For instance, Lomira, in Dodge County, was settled almost entirely by Prussians from Brandenburg, who belonged to the Evangelical Association. The neighboring towns of Herman and Theresa, also in Dodge County, were settled principally by natives of Pomerania. In Calumet County, there are Oldenburg, Luxemburg, and New Holstein settlements. St. Kilian, in Washington County, is settled by people from northern Bohemia, just over the German border. The town of Belgium, Ozaukee County, is populated almost exclusively by Luxemburgers, while Oldenburgers occupy the German settlement at Cedarburg. Three-fourths of the population of Farmington, Washington County, are from Saxony. In the same county, Jackson is chiefly settled by Pomeranians, while one-half of the population of Kewaskum are from the same German province. In Dane County there are several interesting groups of German Catholics. Roxbury is nine-tenths German, the people coming mostly from Rheinish Prussia and Bavaria. Germans predominate in Cross Plains, the rest of the population being Irish. The German families of Middletor came from Köln, Rheinish Prussia, and so did those of Berry, a town almost solidly German.

Scandinavians.—The Scandinavians (Norwegians, Swedes, Danes, and Icelanders) of Wisconsin are divided into national groups. The Norwegians are strongest in Dane County, where there are probably not less than 14,000, who were either born in Norway or whose parents were. Other counties having large numbers are Pierce, St. Croix, Eau Claire, Waushara, Waupaca, Washburn, Winnebago, Portage, Buffalo, Trempealeau, Barron, Door, Bayfield, Florence, Lincoln, Rock, Racine, Milwaukee, Grant, and Oneida.

Swedes predominate in Trenton, Isabel. and Maiden Rock, in Pierce County, and are strong in portions of Bayfield, Douglas, Price, Taylor, Door, Jackson, and Portage counties. Danes are found in considerable groups in Adams, Milwaukee, Racine, and Waushara counties. Icelanders practically monopolize Washington Island (Door County), in the waters of Green Bay.

Bohemians.—The Bohemians are settled for the most part in the counties of Kewaunee (where they form three-sevenths of the entire population), Marathon, Adams, Crawford, Grant (towns of Muscoda and Castle Rock), Columbia (Lodi), Trempealeau, Langlade, and Washington (part of Wayne).

Belgians.—We find Belgians closely massed in the towns of Gardiner, Union, and Brussels, in Door County, Red River, and a large part of Lincoln, in Kewaunee County, and in Brown County.

Polanders.—The Polanders are widespread. In the cities of Milwaukee and Manitowoc there are large masses of them. In the city and neighborhood of Beaver Dam, Dodge County, there are 900 Poles, mostly from Posen, Germany. In Berlin and its neighborhood are 1,200 from Danzig, and immigration from thence is still in active progress. There are 2 Polish churches in Berlin, and 1 Polish school in which that language is taught. Other solid Polish groups are found in the townships of Berlin, Seneca, and Princeton. Warren Township, in Waushara County, has a considerable colony of Poles, and others can be found in Trempealeau, Door, Kewaunee, Portage, Marathon, Langlade, and Buffalo counties.

Welsh.—The Welsh are planted upon our soil in large groups. In Waushara County we find the town of Springwater, one-half of the town of Rose, and one-half of Aurora occupied by natives of Wales and their immediate descendants. Spring Green, in Sauk County, has a large colony of them. The whole of Nekimi and the greater part of Utica, in Winnebago Connty, are settled by this people. So are Caledonia and other townships in Columbia County, and the town of Calamus, in Dodge. Monroe County has many solid Welsh neighborhoods, and other compact groups are found in the Third and Sixth wards of Racine.

Italians.—Italian groups are noted in Vernon, Washburn, and Florence counties. In Vernon they hold one-half of Genoa Township.

Russians.—Russians, both Greek Church adherents and Jews, are chiefly found in the city of Milwaukee. Of the Greek Church Russians there are 2,000 in number living on one street in a densely settled neighborhood and said to be mainly engaged in peddling small wares. The Russian Jews are scattered throughout the city; they observe their old social customs with religious tenacity, but are allowing their children to become Americanized.

Dutch.—The Dutch have particularly strong settlements in the northeastern portion of the State, in the city of Milwaukee, and in La Crosse County. The first colony settled in Hollandtown, Sheboygan County, where natives of Holland still own one-fourth of the township. They own one-half of Barton, in Washington County. Alto, Fond du Lac County, is essentially a Dutch town. A considerable stronghold is in the town of Kaukauna, Outagamie County, and the Dutch own much of Depere and Belleville, Brown County. The city of Milwaukee had as early as 1849 a Dutch population of more than 800, which has since greatly increased; they are strongest in the northwest portion of the city, formerly known as "Kilbourntown." There is a large settlement of Frisians in Holland Township, La Crosse County, their village being known as New Amsterdam.

Swiss.—There are between 5,000 and 6,000 Swiss massed in exceptionally prosperous colonies in New Glarus, Washington, Exeter, Mount Pleasant, York, and neighboring townships in Green County. Others may be found in the counties of Buffalo, Pierce (Union), Winnebago (Black Wolf), and Fond du Lac (Ashford).

Irish.—Irish groups are found in Bear Creek, Winfield, and Dellona, in Sauk County; Osceola, Eden, and Byron, in Fond du Lac County; Benton, Darlington, Gratiot, Kendall, Seymour, Shullsburg, and Willow Spring, in Lafayette County; Lebanon, in Waupaca County; Erin, in Washington County; El Paso, in Pierce County; and Emmet, Shields, and Portland, in Dodge County.

English.—Large English setlements, several of them the result of the early immigration of Cornish miners into the lead regions of southwestern Wisconsin, can be found in Iowa, Grant, Lafayette, Columbia, Juneau, and Dane counties.

Scotch.—The Scotch we find in considerable numbers in Columbia, Buffalo. Green Lake, Kenosha, Marathon, and Trempealeau counties.

Finlanders.—Finlanders are quite strongly grouped in Douglas County.

Austrians.—Austrians are numerous in Kewaunee County.

AGRICULTURAL DISTRIBUTION OF IMMIGRANTS.

French.—The principal French-Canadian settlements are in Bayfield, Crawford, Lincoln, St. Croix, and Taylor counties, not counting the French Creoles at Green Bay, Kaukauna, and Prairie du Chien.

The matter of geographical distribution of nationalities and the many changes therein is an interesting one, and the map illustrating this, which is now being prepared, will be of great practical value to the student of colonization. Waupaca, for example, is one of the counties remarkable for its distribution. In the eastern half the Germans now predominate in all the townships except Lebanon and Matteson. In Lebanon the Irish are still strongest although they are being slowly displaced by the Germans, who are indeed gaining all along the line; it is worthy of note that the Germans have frequently displaced large bodies of Irish settlers in the southeastern portions of the State. Matteson Township is held by a mixture of Germans, Norwegians, Irish, and Americans. The western townships of Waupaca County, with the exception of the 3 southwestern—Farmington, Dayton, and Lind, where Americans predominate—are almost exclusively Scandinavian; but even in the American towns there is a large contingent of Danes, and Americans are losing ground.

Enough has been given to exhibit the scope of the inquiry and the progress made. We are slowly building up in America a composite nationality that is neither English nor continental, but partakes of all—it is to be hoped, the best of all. This investigation into the details of the forces at work in a representative State, and the manner of their working is, we believe, of the utmost importance and significance, and when the results are finally presented to the public they are certain to command the general attention of students in history and economic science.

OPPORTUNITIES FOR TENANCY AND OWNERSHIP.

(Reported from representative farmers.)

WAUKESHA COUNTY.—Opportunities to become a tenant farmer here are not very good. Most farmers are working their own land. Opportunities for purchase are not good, as land is very high.

JEFFERSON COUNTY.—Good men, who have proved themselves such, can become tenants. They must be able to furnish tools and some farm implements. Tenant receives half the produce, a house to live in, etc. Land is so high in southern Wisconsin that the opportunities for a poor man are not very good. It would be a life-long struggle to get on a farm.

IOWA COUNTY.—Not many opportunities for renting for new beginners. As soon as they give evidence of ability, good opportunites, especially for those with a small amount of capital. Opportunities for purchase are not as good as farther south.

WAUPACA COUNTY.—Plenty of chances for renting. If tenant and landlord each furnish half, each receive half; if tenant furnishes all, receives two-thirds.

VERNON COUNTY.—There are not many opportunities to rent farms. Tenant furnishes one-half of everything and receives one-half of the crops. As to purchase, many a poor Norwegian boy comes here, works hard, and in a dozen years owns a fine farm. Land is higher here than formerly owing to the tobacco industry.

ADAMS COUNTY.—(1) There are good opportunities for renting farms on crop and cash rent. There are fine opportunities to purchase land in this locality. Unimproved lands, good soil, can be had at from $5 to $10 an acre on easy terms. (2) Not very good opportunities for a poor man to rent. Terms, one-half to one-third of crop as rent to landlord. There is not much land for sale here. There are better opportunities for immigrants to purchase in the middle and northern part of the county. There the land is poorer and many farmers are anxious to sell. A German or Bohemian will get rich on the farm that the American starved and went ragged on.

WOOD COUNTY.—There are some opportunities for renting—generally for half the crops—and very good opportunities for purchase while hiring out. In fact, that is what nearly all have done who have come here in the past.

CLARK COUNTY.—Farming land is rented generally for one-third of the crop, or otherwise, according to agreement. Nearly all of the people now settled in this vicinity acquired their land by purchasing on payments while hiring out, but at present there are few such chances.

EAU CLAIRE COUNTY.—There are good opportunities for renting. Many farms are to be had for from $2 to $4 an acre, or half the crop. There are good chances for purchase. There is much unimproved land that can be bought on terms to suit purchaser, and good chances to work near by.

DUNN COUNTY.—Some very good opportunities for renting, either on cash rent or shares; usually half the crop and increase. There is much good land for sale at reasonable prices. An industrious man who will manage fairly well can get a home in this section.

POLK COUNTY.—Many opportunities for renting, and on easy terms. Many chances for purchase, but they are being taken much faster than formerly. Timber lands as good in quality as any, but stumpy.

TAYLOR COUNTY.—Some chances for renting, on halves. Good opportunities for purchase. Land is cheap, $3 to $10 an acre.

ONEIDA COUNTY.—There are farms to let, and wild or unimproved lands which can be purchased at from $2 to $5 an acre. There are opportunities for winter employment at good wages.

ASHLAND COUNTY.—Not much opportunity for renting, but good opportunities for purchase. Plenty of good land and improved farms on easy terms. Work can be had at any time.

WASHBURN COUNTY.—There is not much chance here for tenant farming, as most of the people are clearing new farms. The chances are good for a man to get a good start to buy land selling the timber off of it. There is a good market for wood. Such wood, dry, is worth $1 a cord.

MINNESOTA.

(See table, p. 603.)

Reports from representative farmers in this State were received from 7 counties only. In all there was said to be opportunity for non-English-speaking immigrants; in two the opportunities were thought not to be great. Scandinavians and Germans, Poles and Bohemians, English, Irish, and Canadians are the foreign farmers and farm laborers noted in these counties, and preferences for Germans, for Scandinavians, and for Canadians are expressed.

These foreigners are found settled in colonies, and also scattered. It is said that the Germans when settled in colonies (especially under semireligious auspices) are inclined to continue the use of the foreign language in the colonies. The Scandinavians drop their language.[1] They are regarded as a good class of citizens and successful farmers.

From an examination made by Mr. LeGrand Powers, chief of the division of agriculture, United States Census, it appears, however, that with reference to the comparative average progress made by the several elements, American born and foreign born, so far as the inquiry shows anything, the American-born farmer is able, on the farms of Minnesota, to make a slightly greater amount of progress than the foreign born.

The State is not densely populated. Government lands are all taken up, but there are school lands in the hands of the State and much uncleared pine land that will ultimately make good farms.[2]

The Duluth and Iron Range Railroad has some land to dispose of. The land commissioner of this railroad writes, with regard to their lands and methods of disposing of it, as follows:

We have about 500,000 acres of land, some of it suitable for stock and dairy farming and some good for timber only. Our prices are from $2.50 to $5 per acre, payable $1 per acre down, balance in five annual payments.

We have no preference as to nationality of purchasers. Our customers have been mostly Scandinavians, Finns, and Poles.

We do not meet immigrants on arrival, nor do we have agents in foreign countries. We have not established any colonies.

Yours truly, B. P. CRANE, *Land Commissioner.*

OPPORTUNITIES FOR TENANCY AND OWNERSHIP.

(Reported by representative farmers.)

FREEBORN COUNTY.—Good opportunities for renting. A good many farms are rented now and there are more to rent, as the well-to-do farmers are retiring. Terms are cash rent or shares of the product. As to purchase, land is very high, but wages are good and work is plenty.

WATONWAN COUNTY.—Not many opportunities for renting. Terms, one-third of the crop. No chances for purchase by a poor man while hiring out, as land is too high.

MCLEOD COUNTY.—Land is rented on shares. Tenant receives two-thirds of crop and furnishes his own seed, tools, etc., or pays $2 an acre cash. No chances for purchase. Land is worth from $25 to $50 an acre.

STEVENS COUNTY.—There are a few opportunities for renting for men with teams and the necessary machinery. Where tenant furnishes the seed, landlord receives one-third of crop. If landlord furnishes the seed, he receives one-half the crop. Land is now worth from $15 to $25 an acre, and when sold on time interest is about 8 per cent. This is not favorable for a poor man to establish himself in independent farming.

PINE COUNTY.—No opportunities for renting, but good land may be purchased cheap.

CLAY COUNTY.—Good opportunities for renting. Tenant receives two-thirds of crop. Good chance to purchase while purchaser hires out if he is industrious and saving.

---

[1] Testimony of LeGrand Powers, Reports of Ind. Com., Vol. X, p. 180. [2] Ibid.

KITTSON COUNTY.—Few opportunities for tenant farming on shares. The landlord often furnishes seed grain and the tenant then only gets one-third of the crop. Land can be purchased on crop shares, but land is too dear and interest too high for a laborer to pay for a farm after deducting his living expenses, which are very high.

IOWA.

[See table, p. 604.]

The commissioner of labor of the State, writing to the Immigration Investigating Commission in 1894,[1] said that the immigration of any class of foreigners to the State at that time was very undesirable. Any foreigner who came there and obtained work would displace a citizen of the State.

The secretary of state writes in December, 1900, that there are present greater opportunities for immigrants, especially in farming and manufactures. Germans are found most effective as farmers and farm laborers, but the success of foreign farmers is no greater than or as great as that of the American born. Farmers as a class would oppose the further influx of foreigners. No efforts are being made by the State to bring in immigrants, but corporations attract them on account of the cheapness of their labor.

The table of replies from representative farmers shows that there is some opportunity for foreign immigrants. Eight of the 15 farmers heard from said such opportunities were open; only 1 said, definitely, that there were none. Foreign farmers and farm laborers were noted in almost every county. These were English, Scotch, Irish, Welsh, Germans, Dutch, Scandinavians, Bohemians, Poles, Slovaks, and Belgians.

OPPORTUNITIES FOR TENANCY AND OWNERSHIP.

(Reported by representative farmers.)

WASHINGTON COUNTY.—A good, reliable man would not find much trouble in getting a farm to rent and on satisfactory terms. As to purchase, this depends altogether upon the man. Occasionally a man will do this very thing (purchase his land while hiring out).

MAHASKA COUNTY.—There are farms to rent, each party furnishing half the stock and farm implements and dividing the profits equally. Opportunities for a poor man to purchase land are not very good, as the land is too valuable.

WARREN COUNTY.—There are good chances for steady, industrious men with families to rent farms, either for cash or grain rents. As to purchase, the best plan is to commence farming by renting on shares for two-fifths or one-half of the crop, house, land, and firewood being furnished. A good man can save enough to make payments on the farm or can hire out and save his wages.

ADAIR COUNTY.—Not very good opportunities for renting. Terms, $2.50 to $3 cash rent an acre, or one-half of the crop. Very good opportunities for a poor man to establish himself as an independent farmer.

STORY COUNTY.—There are fair opportunities to rent farms. Terms, from $2.50 to $4 an acre cash, and for grain from two-fifths to one-half of the grain raised. There are very fair opportunities for purchase, if small cash payments are made.

TAMA COUNTY.—There are plenty of farms to rent on terms of two-fifths of the grain, with $3.50 an acre for grass land or for farm. Good farms sell at from $60 to $100 an acre, with interest at 5 per cent.

BUTLER COUNTY.—There are fair opportunities for renting. Farms rent for cash for from $2.25 to $3 an acre; grain rents, two-fifths of the grain; stock farms, one-half of everything. As to purchase while the purchaser is hiring out, it can be done, but would be rather slow work.

ALLAMAKEE COUNTY.—Not very good opportunities to rent. Terms, one-third of crop or $3 per acre cash. The opportunities for purchase are no longer encouraging, as land is getting too high priced.

CERRO GORDO COUNTY.—There are no opportunities for renting, and none for purchase on easy terms.

CLAYTON COUNTY.—Most tenant farmers pay cash rent. It takes from $500 to $1,000 to get started. Land costs from $75 to $100 an acre for all well-improved farms. This makes it difficult for a poor man to establish himself in farming.

WRIGHT COUNTY.—Farms can be rented by giving two-fifths of the crop or $2.50 to $3 per acre cash. Land is beyond the reach of most poor men with families, prices being $40 to $65 per acre.

O'BRIEN COUNTY.—Some opportunities for renting. Rates, from $2.50 to $3 an acre cash, or from one-third to two-fifths of the crop, delivered in market.

---

[1] Report Immigration Investigating Commission, p. 135.

DICKINSON COUNTY.—There are some chances to work on shares for one-half to two-thirds of the crop, and some on cash rent of $2 an acre. Opportunities for purchase are not very good, as land is high—from $28 to $30 an acre.

GREENE COUNTY.—There are plenty of farms to rent, either at a cash rent of from $2 to $3 an acre or by giving two-fifths of the crop. Land can be bought by paying one-third to one-half cash down, as much time as is desired being given for the balance, at 5 per cent interest.

CRAWFORD COUNTY.—There are many tenant farmers here. They furnish everything, giving the landlord two-fifths to one-third of the crop. Land has reached such a price that there is no opportunity for a man to purchase while he is earning a living at farm labor.

MISSOURI.

(See table, p. 606.)

Returns received from representative farmers in thirteen counties of the State show considerable diversity of opinion as to opportunities for immigrants. Three would welcome them in neighborhoods where negroes and native whites are the only farm laborers reported, indicating a desire to change from that class of labor, or at least to admit another class to supplement them, as in one instance where there are said to be opportunities for immigrants it is also said that native whites are greatly preferred. Foreign farmers—German, Irish, Scandinavian, and French—are found in every county. They seem to be more frequently found than foreign laborers. Where preference is directly expressed, it seems to be for native whites; while three say they have no preference.

OPPORTUNITIES FOR TENANCY AND OWNERSHIP.

(Reported by representative farmers.)

RIPLEY COUNTY.—Terms of renting—landlord receives half the crops and furnishes everything. Good opportunities for purchase while the purchaser hires out.

TANEY COUNTY.—A tenant with team can rent land, giving one-third of the crop for rent. If the landlord furnishes team, feed, etc., he receives one-half the crop as rent. Land is very cheap—$5 to $10 an acre for improved land. There is plenty of Government land. Purchaser can get plenty of work at 50 cents a day.

WRIGHT COUNTY.—There are some good chances for tenant farming. But we don't want tenants; we want home owners; and there is the best opportunity in America here for such. Cheap homes can be purchased on almost any terms, by any man who will work, of from 40 to 160 acres. He can have a home of his own and the most pleasant employment—fruit raising.

LACLEDE COUNTY.—Not much opportunity for renting; fair chances for purchase.

PETTIS COUNTY.—Good opportunities for tenant farming and for purchase.

JOHNSON COUNTY.—Tenant farmers owning their teams, farm implements, etc., receive three-fifths to two-thirds of the produce. There would be poor prospect of success in purchasing land while hiring out here.

SALINE COUNTY.—Good opportunities for renting. Crop rent—corn, one-half; wheat, one-third. Cash rent, $3.50 to $4 per acre. Opportunities for purchase are not especially favorable.

RAY COUNTY.—Good opportunities for renting. Landlord furnishes land and tools, and gets one-third to one-half of the crop. Not very good chances for purchase. Land is from $20 to $75 an acre.

LIVINGSTON COUNTY.—The chances are good for renting. Tenants can get farms for one-half the produce in crib and one-half of the hay in stack. If the farm is well improved tenant will have to pay extra for house and truck patch, say $3 a month. As to purchasing land on payments by earning a living while hiring out, there are a good many farms sold that way. Where a man has a team and a prospect of making a crop, a man can get work most of the time.

HOLT COUNTY.—Few opportunities for renting. Terms, one-half the crops. Farms are usually all cultivated by the owners and their sons. There are no opportunities for a poor man to establish himself in independent farming. Land is from $35 to $75 an acre.

LEWIS COUNTY.—Only a limited number of farms can be rented. There are good chances to buy farms on partial payments, but it is doubtful about getting work to pay for the same.

ADAIR COUNTY.—Very few chances for renting farms or for purchase.

AGRICULTURAL DISTRIBUTION OF IMMIGRANTS.

NORTH DAKOTA.

(See table, p. 607.)

In 1890 the density of population of this State was only 2.7 to the square mile, affording abundant room for immigrants. In 1894 the governor's secretary wrote to the Immigration Investigating Commission:

Would say all portions desire immigration of industrious farmers with means enough to start with—say a few hundred dollars.

Population increased 70 per cent between 1890 and 1900, and is now only 4.5 to the square mile, still offering opportunities for settlers. Representative farmers from all parts of the State express the unreserved opinion that there are openings for non-English speaking immigrants. (See table, p. 607.) In no county heard from does the density reach 20 to the square mile. In all agricultural counties are to be found foreign farmers and farm laborers of many nationalities—Germans, Scandinavians, German-Russians, Austrians, Dutch, Belgians, Bohemians, Poles, Irish, Canadians, English, Scotch, French, and Icelanders.

The proportion of laborers employed through the year is somewhat lower than in some States, owing to the large grain farms; but there is considerable stock farming, also, to keep the proportion higher than it would be otherwise. The wages of farm labor are noticeably high.

OPPORTUNITIES FOR TENANCY AND OWNERSHIP.

(Reported by representative farmers.)

RICHLAND COUNTY.—Scores of farms in every township can be rented, three-fourths of produce going to tenant, or one-half if the landlord finds seed and part of other expenses. First-class opportunities for purchase all about.

RANSOM COUNTY.—Very good chances for tenants who are financially equipped to handle large or fair-sized farms, but no opportunities for purchase on especially easy terms.

LAMOURE COUNTY.—Anyone can get land and work on shares, if he can furnish tools and machinery, by paying one-third of the produce as rent. As to purchase, "Young man, go west," is good advice.

MCINTOSH COUNTY.—Terms of renting, one-fourth of the crop. Land is sold on long-time payments, with interest at 6 per cent per annum, and only a small part down.

STUTSMAN COUNTY.—Land can be leased, where tenant furnishes seed, for one-fourth of the crop. Where owner furnishes seed and pays half the cost of threshing, tenant gives one-half of the crop. Tenant always furnishes tools and machinery. Land can be bought by giving one-half the crop each year, sold by the landlord, and proceeds applied on purchase price of the land. Land can be bought on this plan without any cash payment, at from $8 to $15 an acre, and purchaser can rent near-by land for the first year or two, or he can get work for himself and tools by the day or by the acre.

BARNES COUNTY.—Good opportunities for renting, usually for half the crop. To a family showing themselves honest and industrious, stock and machinery and other assistance will be furnished on time until they are able to pay from the crop. Opportunities to purchase are very good. A large part of the farmers here got their start by purchasing land on payments while hiring out.

CASS COUNTY.—Landlord furnishes everything except stock, machinery, and labor, and receives half the crops. Good opportunities for a poor man to establish himself in independent farming.

GRIGGS COUNTY.—Good, live men can always get land to work and find themselves or found everything. Rather poor opportunities for purchase.

GRAND FORKS COUNTY.—As soon as a man has money to buy 4 horses he can get land on shares. Landlord furnishes seed and pays part of threshing bill. Tenant does the work and receives half the crop. To purchase, a purchaser must have a few hundred dollars to start on, say $500. He would fail otherwise.

WELLS COUNTY.—There are always opportunities for good tenant farmers, on either cash rent or share of the crop—usually the latter. Opportunities for a poor man to establish himself as an independent farmer are good, either by Government land on a homestead claim or buying on crop payments.

BENSON COUNTY.—First-class opportunities for renting. Usually tenant receives half of the proceeds, landlord furnishing seed and paying half of the ordinary expenses aside from the help. First-class opportunities for purchase. Men can take up Government land or buy on a crop payment, turning over one-half the crop to apply on purchase price.

PEMBINA COUNTY.—Many farms are to let, and an industrious man can do well renting. General terms are one-half the crop, owner furnishing seed and paying for half the thrashing. Good opportunities for purchase; no country in the world has greater opportunities. A great many people who own land would part with it on easy terms.

EMMONS COUNTY.—Opportunities for renting are plenty, but poor chances for tenants, as crops average poor. Land is cheap yet, and Government land still vacant, so that anyone can get a piece of land, although comparatively worthless.

BURLEIGH COUNTY.—Good opportunities for renting on terms of about one-third of the crop. The best possible chances for purchase on payments while hiring out.

BOTTINEAU COUNTY.—Good chances for renting. Terms are varied, but the most prevalent are for the tenant to find his own seed and receive two-thirds of the produce.

WARD COUNTY.—Good opportunities for renting and for purchase.

BILLINGS COUNTY.—No general farming is done here.

SOUTH DAKOTA.

(See table, p. 609.)

In this State, as well as in North Dakota, there appears to be abundant room for immigrants. The density of population for the State was 4.5 to the mile in 1890, and 5.2 in 1900, the population having increased 16.8 per cent. Representative farmers in ten of the eastern[1] (farming) counties (see table, p. 609) are practically unanimous in offering encouragement to non-English-speaking immigrants. Only one discourages their coming, saying that there is no chance this year on account of drought. One correspondent from the stock-raising counties west of the Missouri River writes that there are openings for immigrants, especially on sheep ranches, and one correspondent from the Black Hills, also a stock-raising district, writes that opportunities are at hand there.

Foreigners are reported as farmers and farm laborers in all counties where farming is carried on, and are of the usual nationalities found in the Northwest—Germans, Scandinavians, Russians, and Bohemians, with some Belgians, Dutch, Finns, Irish, and Scotch.

The growth of stock-farming is apparently giving rise to a greater demand for labor throughout the year. Opportunities for married laborers are fairly good, but there is little or no work for women and children.

OPPORTUNITIES FOR TENANCY AND OWNERSHIP.

(Reported by representative farmers.)

CLAY COUNTY.—Tenants pay one-third of crop or pay cash, or one-half of the crop and have seed furnished. It is better not to attempt to purchase land without capital.

UNION COUNTY.—Terms of renting are from $300 to $400 for 160 acres, or one-half to two-fifths share rental. Opportunities for a poor man to purchase are not very good, as land is rather high here.

MINNEHAHA COUNTY.—Chances for renting are sometimes very good. Landlord will furnish team and all farming utensils, seed, etc. Opportunities for a poor man to purchase are mainly through renting on shares.

DAVISON COUNTY.—There are opportunities to rent farms for a cash rent or on shares, and also for purchase while the purchaser is hiring out.

CHARLES MIX COUNTY.—There are good opportunities for renting. Terms, one-half the crop delivered in the bin or crib, the landlord furnishing the seed; or one-third to the landlord if the tenant furnishes all the seed. There are good opportunities for a poor man to purchase.

BROOKINGS COUNTY.—Generally the owner furnishes the seed, pays one-half the thrashing bill, and takes one-half the crop. In some cases the renter furnishes the seed and takes two-thirds of the crop. In both cases the renter furnishes all implements, etc., and performs all labor. A man can purchase land on part payments or on time with cash payments. Usually a man can find employment 8 months in the year.

BEADLE COUNTY.—There are good chances to rent farms at from one-fourth to one-third of the crop. Many purchase land while hiring out. Good land can be had for from $7 to $12 an acre.

BUFFALO COUNTY.—Some are renting. They give one-third of the crop. No land is sold on payments.

---

[1] East of the Missouri River.

AGRICULTURAL DISTRIBUTION OF IMMIGRANTS.

SPINK COUNTY.—Farms can be rented by giving one-fourth of the crop, the tenant furnishing everything, or one-half of the crop, the landlord furnishing seed and paying one-half of the thrashing bill. There are fine opportunities for purchase. Land is cheap, costing from $5 to $15 an acre. Chances to labor are plenty, at good wages.

POTTER COUNTY.—Opportunities for a poor man to establish himself in independent farming are numerous.

CAMPBELL COUNTY.—There is little renting in this neighborhood, but there is plenty of land which can be had on terms of from one-fifth to one-fourth of the crop. There are fair chances for purchase, either on crop payment or a fixed price. Land is not very high priced as yet.

MEYER COUNTY.—Land is free, and anyone can homestead and start for himself at once.

WASHABAUGH COUNTY.—Not a farming county. Most of it is Indian reservation.

PENNINGTON COUNTY.—(See table, p. —.)

BUTLER COUNTY.—There are good opportunities for renting for men who can manage the work. Terms, one half to one-third of the crop. There are good opportunities for purchase.

KANSAS.

(See table, p. 611.)

Three out of eight representative farmers heard from in the eastern part of this State report (see table, p. 611) that there are no opportunities for non-English-speaking immigrants in their neighborhoods. Two, however, are from the counties in which are situated the two large cities of Kansas City, Kans., and Wichita, and which may be supposed to have less demand for agricultural labor.

Of the six western counties heard from, five afford openings for immigrants (see table, p. 611). The county where immigrants are said not to be wanted is one which is, apparently, entirely devoted to grain growing, and only 10 per cent of the farm laborers are employed throughout the year.

Foreign farmers and farm laborers are found everywhere (except in the small county of Wyandotte, principally occupied by Kansas City, Kans.). Germans are most prevalent, followed closely by Swedes. Stafford County reports a few Danes as the only foreign farmers. Barton County, in the western part of the State, has many Russian farmers. In Ellis County, also in the western part, it is said that "over half the county are foreigners, mostly from Russia, and prosperous." There are Russians in the eastern part of the State also.

The Union Pacific railroad has about 6,500,000 acres of land for sale in the western part of the State at from 50 cents to $3 per acre for grazing lands and from $3 to $15 per acre for farm lands. The land commissioner of this railroad writes:

We have no preference as to where purchasers may come from. We prefer to make sales to persons who will settle upon and use the land.

A very large proportion of our land sales are made to people of foreign nationalities, particularly English, Swedish, German, and Russian.

The sales to natives of foreign countries are usually made to them after they have spent some years in this country and have gained a considerable insight into the methods of life and farming in the United States.

We have never found it necessary to attempt to colonize on lands according to nationalities.

We maintain traveling agents whose business it is to travel over the country assigned to them and secure purchasers for our lands. We also maintain local agents at nearly all points along the line of road, who look after the sale of lands within their own district.

OPPORTUNITIES FOR TENANCY AND OWNERSHIP.

(Reports from representative farmers.)

MCPHERSON COUNTY.—There are some opportunities for tenant farming. Usual rent is one-third of the crop on upland and half on the bottom land. Very poor chances for purchase.

CHASE COUNTY.—Many farms are rented; terms, one-third to one-half share of crops raised, or the equivalent in cash. Farms are regularly purchased on payments. Those who do so usually farm such purchases themselves, making a living therefrom, and using the surplus to make the payment with.

OSAGE COUNTY.—There is considerable land to rent on terms of one-half the standing corn or its equivalent crop, or one-third harvested and delivered. Cash rent is from $1.50 to $3 an acre. There is small opportunity for purchase on easy terms on account of recent boom in land prices, and at the present rate of interest would not justify time payments.

WABAUNSEE COUNTY.—Not very good opportunities for renting or for purchase.

DOUGLAS COUNTY.—A good man for farming can rent land and give one-half to one-third of the crops as rent on convenient time and payments, and if he understands dairying, can make money. There are some opportunities for purchase on easy terms.

WYANDOTTE COUNTY.—Most of the land in this locality is worked by tenants. In the main it is farmed for a cash rental, an average of $6 or $7 an acre. As to purchasing land on payments while hiring out, it can not be done.

MARSHALL COUNTY.—There are chances to rent good farms at from $2 to $3.25 an acre, or on shares for one-third of the crop as rent.

STAFFORD COUNTY.—There are too many tenants already. No opportunities for purchase while the purchaser is hiring out.

BARTOW COUNTY.—Not many openings for renting at present, but there are some good opportunities for purchase.

FORD COUNTY.—Some have tried to pay for land on the plan of paying so much wheat every year. As to purchasing land on payments while earning a living by hiring out, a few could do this, but many would fail as far west as this. It depends largely on the man and his family as to his success.

KEARNEY COUNTY.—Considerable land in irrigation and set to alfalfa can be rented, but land without improvements. Government land can be homesteaded. School land good for grazing and growing of fodder crops, with an occasional crop of corn, wheat and rye can be had for $1.25 an acre.

ELLIS COUNTY.—Opportunities for renting are good. Tenant can get land with everything furnished him, or he can provide for himself, just as he wishes Some good chances for purchase. A man can buy a farm here and pay for it by shares of crops.

PHILLIPS COUNTY.—Farms are to rent here on shares of grain or stock. There is plenty of cheap land, and it is the easiest place on earth for a man to make a living.

NEBRASKA.

(See table, p. 613.)

The State commissioner of labor, writing to the Immigration Investigating Commission in 1894, says:[1]

Generally speaking, under present industrial conditions there is no demand for labor of any kind, skilled or unskilled, but there is every inducement for foreigners of the right sort seeking homes in the rural districts. * * *

The agricultural resources of the State are still in their infancy, and for years to come there will be room for industrious, self-supporting immigrants who desire to make country homes.

The eastern portion of the State is fairly well populated, though there is still room for immigrants possessing means sufficient to live for one year and purchase needed implements for agricultural pursuits.

The broad prairies of the central and western portion of the State are capable of supporting a much denser population than at present. The drought and consequent failure of crops the present season may seem to contradict this statement, but that is but a temporary misfortune, shared in, to a greater or less extent, by other States farther east which never before lacked moisture for maturing crops. The present dry season has been the means of creating a system of irrigating canals west of the ninety-seventh meridian, which will surely result in cutting up the large tracts of land now in the hands of single owners and converting them into small irrigated farms.

Nebraska produces all the cereals and root crops known to the temperate zone, but corn has been considered the standard crop. The sugar beet is destined to be the most profitable crop in the future.

Nebraska soil has been declared by experts to be equal, if not superior, to any other soil in the world for the production of the sugar beet. There are two large sugar factories in the State, owned by the Oxnard Company—one at Grand Island, in Hall County, and one at Norfolk, Madison County. Irrigated lands and the culture of the sugar beet mean dense population.

As to the nationalities desired, the commissioner writes as follows:

(1) *Scandinavians.*—They are, with the proper restrictions, as pointed out by you, nearly always industrious, consequently prosperous, and more readily adopt our habits and customs. They soon become real American citizens.

(2) *Germans.*—As Germany is a sugar-beet country and many German immigrants are skilled in the culture of the beet, Nebraska can take care of many thousands. There are but few Germans in Nebraska who are not prosperous and contented.

(3) *Irish.*—The tendency of the Irish is to drop into the cities; but as our cities grow, an increasing number of the Irish immigrants can be assimilated.

There are but few other nationalities really desired in this State. All immigrants (restricted as above) from northern or northwestern Europe will be welcome.

The deputy commissioner of labor, writing to the Industrial Commission in the present year, says:

First. I would say that there are splendid opportunities in this State for immigrants to engage in farming and the raising of stock, this being almost purely an agricultural State.

Second. I would say that the nationalities which seem to be most effective in this State are Germans, Bohemians, Swedes, Norwegians, and Danes.

---

[1] Report Imm. Inv. Com., p. 144.

AGRICULTURAL DISTRIBUTION OF IMMIGRANTS. 547

Third. I should say that the success of the foreign farmers in this State is, as a rule, greater than that of native-born farmers. As a general thing their standard of living is lower than that of the American, and by their habits of thrift and saving, which seem very pronounced, they seem on the whole to be more successful farmers than the native born.

Fourth. I would say that so far as I know there is no feeling whatever against foreigners in this State. They seem to be quite welcome among us, and I am not aware of any disposition whatever to oppose the further influx of foreigners into the State.

Fifth. I would say "Yes" (i. e., the State is encouraging immigration). There are several publications issued in this State, one of which is the report of the board of agriculture, and one the report of this bureau, which is in a measure designed to give the resources and industrial condition in the State, for the benefit of intending immigrants. The railroad corporations of this State also are doing a great deal by publication to invite immigration.

Sixth. I would say that there are no regular colonies in this State, although there are quite a number of counties in which will be found settlements of foreigners.

Yours, very truly,

S. J. KENT, *Deputy Commissioner.*

Representative farmers confirm the statement of the deputy commissioner that there are openings for immigrants; only two out of nine heard from saying that there is little or no opportunity for them. (See table, p.613). One correspondent urges, however, that some plan should be devised whereby the wants of the farmer and the terms he offers should be made known, and whereby these wants, in the way of labor, should be met. "Many of the farmers who come here," he says, "are not farmers—know nothing of farming—and would be better elsewhere." English, Irish, Scotch, German, Scandinavian, Bohemian, Russian, and French farmers and farm laborers are spoken of in the different counties, and considerable preference for Germans and Swedes as farm laborers is expressed. As to foreign farmers, one correspondent writes: "Farmers of these nationalities (Germans, English, Irish, Scotch, Swedes, Danes, and Bohemians) have been here from 15 to 40 years, and are among our wealthiest and best farmers."

The Burlington Road has been interested in bringing settlers to the State. The general passenger agent writes:

A limited amount of land, suitable for agricultural purposes, is still owned by this company in Nebraska.

We have no special machinery for reaching foreign emigrants on their arrival in this country; neither have we any agencies in Europe, but depend altogether upon advertising and personal effort in this country to attract farmers of all classes to the trans-Mississippi country, where land is cheap and conditions so favorable.

The assistant land commissioner of the same road gives further information as follows:

The Burlington road has only a small remnant of about 16,000 acres of land now remaining unsold. There is, however, a great deal of excellent land for sale at very reasonable figures all along the lines of this company's road owned by private parties.

The soil and climate of Nebraska are such that all things that grow in this latitude (40 to 42 degrees north) anywhere else in the United States can be raised with success here. Our principal products are corn, wheat, oats, rye, barley, potatoes, grasses, clovers, especially alfalfa, also sugar beets; and, in the way of meat, we produce the best beef, pork, and mutton in the world.

Prices of land vary greatly. In the eastern portions, long settled, prices are higher than most newcomers would be willing to pay. In the central part of the State excellent farming and grazing lands can be purchased at prices varying from $5 to $20 per acre that will produce as much to the acre as $100 land farther east. In the extreme western parts land is very cheap, as it was in the eastern part of the State 25 years ago, so that good grazing lands can be bought in many cases at from $1 to $3 per acre.

The railroad company at one time sold on 10-years' time, with 6 per cent interest on deferred payments. Private owners sell in many cases on 5-years' time, with 6 to 7 per cent on deferred payments.

The railroad company has sold to all classes, people from Eastern States and foreigners. Among people from other States, those living formerly nearest our own borders, in Iowa or Illinois, adapted themselves more quickly to the conditions of a prairie State, and were almost at once very successful while settlers coming from the New England States had to go, more or less, through a school of experience, which, in some cases, delayed final success for a few years.

Foreigners, especially Germans, Swedes, Bohemians, and German Russians, have been, as a rule, very prosperous. Only where strong religious ties were at the bottom of colonization schemes have the latter been successful. There are many such settlements including, among others, German-Catholic, German-Lutheran, Swedish-Lutheran, Irish-Catholic, Holland-Reformed, German-Russian-Reformed, German-Russian-Mennonite, Prussian-Mennonite, Bohemian and Polish Catholic colonies, some of considerable magnitude.

When this railroad company had a large amount of land of its own to sell we maintained an agency at the New York port; also at one time in Liverpool, and we scattered literature abroad in almost every European tongue; but that time has long since passed, and the class of foreign immigrants of late years arriving at our Eastern seaports would not present a profitable field for this kind of work, even if we had the land to sell. We prefer at this date to get our immigration from among the renters or other people who want cheaper land from the States of Iowa, Illinois, Indiana, Wisconsin, Michigan, Ohio, Pennsylvania, or the New England States; in other words, people from the same latitude in the States east of us, and the less the distance they have to move the more likely will they be to understand and adapt themselves to the conditions they find.

Yours, truly,

C. J. ERNST,
Assistant Land Commissioner.

The sugar-beet industry in this State is opening up opportunities for immigrants. One large corporation is making especial efforts to bring to its farm laborers either from rural districts or from cities. This corporation is especially desirous of securing large families. Following are descriptions of their methods, etc.:

We are making a strong effort to bring on to this farm laborers either from rural districts or from cities. We are continually bringing people from cities in this State—for instance, Omaha, Lincoln, and other points—to our farm.

Our principal enterprise is the making of sugar from beets at the factory of the —— Beet Sugar Company, established 2 years ago. The —— Cattle Company has maintained a farm for 15 years at this point. Our success in developing an elaborate agricultural enterprise depends, in my opinion, largely upon our ability to collect these people, and especially those having large families, and giving them profitable employment. I inclose copy of contract which we make with them, which promises to work successfully. It is my plan to give them an opportunity to buy land after they have been here for a while Up to December 31 of last year the —— Cattle Company had paid out in 14 seasons $644,106.90 in wages to laborers. Our pay roll for the last year was $135,773, to which is to be added the pay roll of the —— Beet Sugar Company. I mention this particularly to point out the very great importance of the beet-sugar industry in the matter you are investigating. There is now, although the industry has only made a beginning, a strong and growing demand for farm laborers and tenants, and in a degree to bring factories in competition with one another to secure such labor. For instance, on one or two occasions factories in Colorado have competed strongly with factories in Nebraska for Russian labor, which centers about the city of Lincoln. The Russian labor of which I speak is that of Russian Germans—the people are Teutons, not Slavs.

As you see from a memorandum herewith, wages earned by the largest and most industrious families are very satisfactory. The best of our Russians are good laborers, but as a rule they are naturally more backward than any other, ignorant, under control of leaders, tending to be insubordinate and difficult to please. Russians also when newly arrived have no skill in the handling of animals, and it is necessary to teach them how to handle and drive teams. The best of them, however, are quite satisfactory; and as they know something of beet culture, they are a good deal sought after both in Nebraska and Colorado, and we have also sent some to a beet-growing district in Iowa.

We make so strong a point of getting men with large families that we refuse employment, as a rule, to those with small families. As in the case of farm laborers and contractors under the contract inclosed herewith, with farm tenants who rent land by the acre the opportunity in the culture of beets is the very best. We make special and particular efforts to secure such, and I base the success of beet culture in this State on tenant farmers, as farm proprietors having 160 acres of land or more, well stocked with live stock, do not willingly grow beets as a rule.

Through our large farming operations in summer and the feeding of live stock in winter we are able to provide people more continuous work and subsistence for families than would be possible under any other conditions in a rural district, even under a system of small farms operated by their owners, for the reason that feeding operations would not be on anything like so large a scale, though consisting of the aggregate operations of a very considerable number of farmers.

It was perhaps not your intention to draw out an argument in favor of beet sugar, but the answer to your questions necessarily constitutes such an argument, since the growth of the industry will absorb as farm laborers and tenants all of the classes of people you would like to provide for and as rapidly as they can be supplied; and since beet sugar must necessarily be produced by corporations having considerable financial strength, such people may be more easily, comfortably, and successfully settled in rural districts than if they were to leave the cities for employment in general agriculture.

Yours, truly,

—— ——, *General Manager.*

Additional details are as follows:

(1) About 50 per cent of laborers on farm of the —— Cattle Company are Americans. Other nationalities represented are: Bohemians, Germans, Russians, Scandinavians, Irish, English, and Canadians. Probably Germans are preferred.

(2) During the beet seasons, which constitute about two months in the spring and two in the fall, we are able to employ all the people we can secure, including men, women, and children. Heads of families are, of course, employed for a much longer time, as the beets are not all delivered at the factory until sometime in January; and, in addition to beets, we have a very large acreage of corn to cut, husk, etc. Besides this, our feeding operations are extensive, having fed over 30,000 sheep the past winter, in addition to some cattle and hogs. People who do not speak English may be as valuable to us as those who are conversant with the language.

(3) On our farm of 12,000 acres, in 1900, over 6,000 acres were cultivated by the —— Cattle Company proper, in addition to which tenants of the company planted 625 acres of beets.

(4) During the month of June, 1900, 1,217 people were employed on our farm; this does not mean that so many people were working at one time, but the number on our pay roll. For February, the dullest month of the year at ——, we employed 204 people, which number represents very closely the steady employees and heads of families on our farm.

(5) We encourage men with large families to come here, as every working member can get employment through the beet season. While there is a short period after the crop is laid by until harvest, and again after harvest and delivery of crops, when it is difficult to give steady employment to all heads of families, you will note from a partial list of wages which I inclose herewith that during the month of October, 1900, alone, large families received an amount equal to two-thirds of the average wages per capita paid in the United States. The —— Beet Sugar Company employs about 250 people during the sugar campaign, which period covers a portion of our dull season, and it is part of our plan that the two companies may exchange labor.

(6) During a portion of the beet season in 1900 we paid $1.40 per day, and at harvest time $1.50. During the winter we pay $1.25. These amounts represent wages without board.

(7) The wages paid in summer have increased.

(8) For the season of 1901 we have leased nearly 2,100 acres of land to farm tenants. Of this acreage the largest portion is leased for a given rental, but over 350 acres of beets will·be grown on the shares. The company agrees to furnish land, animals, machinery, and to advance a subsistence, if necessary, for 50 per cent of the proceeds. This is designed for men with large families with limited means, as it enables such to come here and get into a paying business from the start.

(9) There are Germans, Scandinavians, Danes, Irish, and Scotch in the neighborhood as independent farmers.

AGRICULTURAL DISTRIBUTION OF IMMIGRANTS. 549

Partial list of families employed by ——— Cattle Company in beet fields, month of October, 1900, together with amount earned.

G. Adrian	$90.00	S. Munger	$126.71
H. Brehm	98.32	C. Flowers	85.72
J. Cain	92.08	J. Felsing	90.00
A. P. Cook	254.95	J. Fierstein	154.20
J. Cihacek	96.10	F. Headky	99.99
J. M. Cihacek	91.30	E. Higby	195.20
J. Divesh	77.00	L. Hraban	147.00
C. Davison	95.70	A. Hayzler	84.05
J. Deinas	154.18	P. Hulfenstein	91.25
C. Deinas	93.10	Charles Holub	87.40
J. Engelman	85.60	C. Jensen	77.47
George Forbes	143.53	H. Jones	87.44
G. Kercher	155.40	L. Jones	107.47
G. Kastrow	102.85	J. Jacoby	149.00
J. Kohler	105.85	L. Kleich	161.55
Edward Lee	70.85	J. B. Nicholson	80.66
C. Lotway	80.35	A. Pipla	80.36
C. Lehman	90.20	C. Peterson	82.55
G. W. Lee	102.00	A. Pospisil	89.35
J. P. McDonald	119.47	A. W. Shepard	91.20
D. Miller	93.89	J. Stroher	83.00
G. Miller	87.80	P. Schmidt	84.10
Anton Machan	80.80	J. Tremaine	97.39
Joe Mahel	109.50	J. Troutman	123.50
Peter Marcus	155.70	J. Turak	79.55
W. Marten	73.02	H. Milota	74.47
J. W. Mathes	75.00		

(The above list gives some idea of the nationalities employed.)

Memorandum of agreement for growing beets.

This agreement, made this —— day of ———, 190-, between ——— Cattle Company, of ———, Nebr., party of the first part, and ——— ———, party of the second part, witnesseth:
 1. That in consideration of one dollar ($1) in hand paid, receipt of which is hereby acknowledged, and in consideration of agreements by the party of the second part, hereinafter specified, party of first part gives and grants to party of second part, the sum of ——— acres of land described as follows: ——— ——— for the purpose of raising a crop of sugar beets thereon, for and during the season of 190–;
 2. That also in consideration of agreements made by the second party, as hereinafter specified, said party of the first part hereby agrees to give to said second party 50 per cent, or one-half, the net proceeds of the crop of sugar beets grown on said land, said net proceeds being the sum of money paid by the ——— Beet Sugar Company to the ✶——— Cattle Company for the net weight of beets delivered from the land aforesaid at the price paid therefor;
 3. Party of the first part further agrees to furnish to the party of the second part all horses and machinery required in the cultivation of said crop of sugar beets;
 4. Party of the first part agrees to furnish all beet seed required for the said crop of sugar beets, and reserves the privilege of deciding what variety of beet seed shall be used;
 5. Party of the first part agrees to furnish, without cost, manure and lime to be used in fertilization of the said land; said manure and lime to be applied to the land, without cost of labor to the said party of the first part, if applied at the option of the said party of the second part. In case said lime or manure shall be applied by the wish of the party of the first part, said first party shall have the privilege of applying the lime or manure at its own cost;
 6. Party of the first part shall pay to the party of the second part 50 per cent of the proceeds as above, as compensation for all labor of every kind and description necessary for the said crop of sugar beets from the beginning; including clearing of land; plowing and preparation of the soil by harrow, or otherwise; seeding; hand work; hoeing; operation of beet pullers; pulling and topping; placing in piles ready to be loaded on wagons, and assistance in loading in case of immediate delivery;
 7. In case said party of the second part shall himself deliver the sugar beets at the factory, said party of the first part shall pay him for so doing at the rate of twenty-five (25) cents per net ton of beets delivered;
 8. In case it is necessary to put a portion of said crop of sugar beets in silo, the said party of the first part shall pay to the said party of the second part for so doing at the rate of ——— cents per net tons of beets delivered;
 9. The said party of the first part reserves the privilege of such direction or oversight of the labor involved in growing the above crop of sugar beets as it judges necessary, and the said party of the second part shall in such case comply with such directions and instructions;
 10. In case said party of the second part proves to be incompetent or unwilling, or if for any reason, as in case of sickness, he is unable to carry out his part of the agreement, then in that case said party of the first part may, at its option, take entire charge of the growing of the sugar beets on the land mentioned above, giving to said party of the second part due compensation for the work already done, or conducting the work remaining to be done for the account of the second party, as it may be deemed best;
 11. The said party of the first part hereby reserves for its own use all beet tops from beets grown on the above-mentioned land;
 12. The said party of the first part hereby agrees to advance to the said party of the second part such portion of the value of the work done by the said party of the second part, up to any point of time, as may be requested by said party of the second part, it being agreed that a sufficient margin shall remain in the hands of the said party of the first part during the continuance of this contract, as guaranty that it shall be carried out in good faith by said party of the second part;
 13. The said party of the second part on his part hereby agrees to perform all the labor of tillage, cultivation, and harvesting the crop of sugar beets on said land, as specified above, in a thoroughly efficient, honest, and workmanlike manner, and also agrees that his labor shall be continuous and regular, and that he will in no way whatever neglect the work required on said crop;
 14. Said party of the second part also agrees that he will perform all the said labor, as above described, for 50 per cent of the net proceeds, as described above; and
 15. All horses and machinery belonging to the first party in the hands of the second party must be used in the most careful manner. Any loss or damage to either horses or machinery resulting from gross carelessness shall be charged to party of second part.

OPPORTUNITIES FOR TENANCY AND OWNERSHIP.

(Reported by representative farmers.)

NEMAHA COUNTY.—Ninety per cent of our farmers own their farms. Tenant farming is practicable only to a limited extent. Railroad lands are cheap; payments on long time with low interest.

DOUGLAS COUNTY.—(1) Worthy tenants have good opportunities; are sought for and started. They are given two-thirds of the crop usually; often a little less. A good, industrious, honest farmer always succeeds in establishing himself as an independent farmer, and the good land all over Nebraska is rapidly falling into their hands. The saying is they will succeed where a native will starve. (2) Chances for renting farms are by this time mostly taken up. Usually tenant gets one-half to two-thirds of crop. A poor man can establish himself as an independent farmer while hiring out if he is the right man, but he had better buy land where it is cheaper than it is here.

WASHINGTON COUNTY.—Fair opportunity for renting at from $2.75 to $3.50 an acre cash or two-fifths of the crop. Rather poor chance for purchase, as land is worth from $45 to $70 an acre.

DODGE COUNTY.—Good opportunities to become a tenant farmer on reasonable terms and good opportunities for purchase.

FILMORE COUNTY.—Land rents at two-fifths of the crop. Opportunities are good to good, honest farmers. They are being sought for. Farming land is too valuable for a poor man to purchase while hiring out.

BUFFALO COUNTY.—While there is a greater demand for land than the supply, good tenant farmers are scarce and are desired. The terms are usually one-third of the crop, or one-half if seed is furnished. Good opportunities for purchase for the right kind of men. A considerable number of our people are foreigners who came here without means and have established themselves as independent farmers.

PHELPS COUNTY.—Many farms to let; usually for a share of the crop. There are no free lands, but 30 to 60 miles further west good land can be bought on almost any terms at $5 to $10 an acre.

KEITH COUNTY.—Good opportunities for tenant farming. Plenty of land can be leased and can be bought on easy terms.

SOUTHERN STATES.

GENERALLY.

The South Atlantic and South Central States may best be treated as one large group, offering, as they do, certain problems common to each group, and distinctly marked off from those presented by other grand divisions.

The common problems are those arising from the enforced change of agriculture from a system based upon slave labor to one based upon free labor, and are working themselves out through (1) a decline of old kinds of farming; (2) a growth of manufacturing interests; (3) a beginning of new forms of agriculture and of demand for farmers and farm laborers especially fitted to carry these on.

The older form of Southern farming—extensive cultivation of great staple crops, such as cotton, rice, and tobacco, by the aid of cheap labor—is generally regarded as becoming less and less profitable. Extensive cultivation has wasted and exhausted the land. Market conditions for the crops grown are considered generally unsatisfactory. The change from slave to free labor brought about changes in agriculture, the full nature and extent of which are not as yet fully to be traced, but which are, necessarily, more or less serious.

Considerable testimony is brought forward to show that negro labor has deteriorated since the war. The younger generation are said to be roaming off to towns and cities; those who remain are not so faithful and efficient as those of the older generation.

The negro as a farm laborer is generally considered to be at his best in cotton farming. But even here he gives much ground for complaint. A Southern farmer stated before the Industrial Commission:[1]

I think one of the causes of the depression in agriculture in the South is the presence of the negro. The negro does not know how to use improved implements, and does not want to know how, and it is almost impossible to teach him. If a man farming cotton on an extensive scale puts an improved implement in use, every darky says it is impossible to use it, and they do not.

---

[1] Reports of Industrial Commission, vol. x, p. 62.

Furthermore, certain peculiarities of his have given occasion for, and even made necessary, methods of employing labor that are serious drawbacks to agriculture in general.

These methods, especially characteristic of Southern agriculture, are renting, "cropping," and a wage system, in which payment is made by the day rather than by the week or month, and to a considerable extent in provisions instead of money; and all find a support in one idiosyncrasy of the negro—his objection to fixed tasks, close supervision, and continuous labor. Customs vary in detail in different parts of the country, but in general the renting and cropping systems may be described and distinguished as follows:

In "cropping" the landowner furnishes land, team, and tools; the "cropper" furnishes labor. The landowner also furnishes the cropper such supplies as he may want for his family during the year, commonly from a "plantation store," charging usually a price higher than the cash market price. The "cropper" makes the crop, with the aid of his wife's labor and that of his children, and in the fall, when the crop is gathered, the landlord markets it, and the proceeds are divided, the landlord subtracting from the cropper's share sufficient to liquidate his store debt. The landlord is secured for his advance supplies and for his share of the crop by a "crop lien," the terms of which differ in different States. Under the cropping system the landlord usually has some oversight of the "cropper" and his methods.

Renting may be either for a crop or money rent. The crop rent seems to be the one most usually arranged for at present. The chief difference between this and the cropping system seems to be that the renter is on a more independent footing than the "cropper." The renter is, practically, an independent farmer himself, raising his crops as he chooses, marketing them himself, and simply paying to the landlord a stipulated amount of product or of money as the rent of land and house.

The tenant or share system, as a whole, by which transactions between laborer and employer are carried on as far as possible in terms of commodities—shares of crops, goods and supplies from the store bought and sold on credit, tools, teams, etc.— rather than on a cash basis, was originally due, no doubt, to other conditions binding the landlord rather than the preference of his laborers. The landlord had no ready money to pay laborers;[1] he was himself dependent upon credit given by merchants and cotton factors on the basis of the expected crop. Uncertain, besides, as to the price to be realized for the harvested crop, and working upon the narrowest possible margin of expected profit, the landlord could not even make a bargain with his laborers in cash terms. He was obliged to share with them the chances of the market.

The continuance of the system is, however, claimed by the planters to be largely due to the characteristics of the negro laborer. The white farmer is extricating himself to a considerable extent from the credit system, so far as the marketing of his crop is concerned, and is more and more able to pay cash wages to laborers. The tenant system, however, meets the negro laborer's desire for freedom in regulating his work and his working hours more completely than the wage system, and it is the one still most largely in use. A representative Southern farmer testified before the Industrial Commission[2] that while he regarded the tenant plan as "iniquitous," he followed it because he "could not get the labor to work otherwise." The labor thus employed works only about 7 months in the year. The rest of the time is devoted to loafing, fishing, hunting, etc. It seems to be generally agreed that the tenant method is bad for the land. One farmer states: "This ruinous system has done more to impoverish and retard the progress of our farmers than any other combination of circumstances." The renter or cropper takes little pains to keep up repairs or fertility and the land rapidly deteriorates.[3] For instance, the washing away of certain needed elements by rainstorms, freshets, and so forth, may be prevented by terracing up the land; but this the average tenant will not trouble himself to do.[4] Nor will the landowner trouble himself so long as he gets some sort of an income from the land through the rent payable by tenants.

As between renting and "cropping," the latter system is apparently better for the land, as the landlord has some oversight of cultivation; but the tenant prefers the former system because he is freer from restraint, and in many cases the landlord falls in with this desire, to save himself trouble and to get his land tilled at all, labor, under present conditions, being so floating and temporary in its character.

It was said before the Industrial Commission[5] that the disposition to rent land at

---
[1] Report of Ind. Com., vol. x, p —; testimony of Mr. J. E. Nunally, Nunally, Ga.
[2] Ibid., p. 456.
[3] Ibid., p. 504.
[4] Ibid., p. 459.
[5] Reports of Ind. Com., vol. x, p. 486.

so much per acre, instead of on the old cropping system, was likely to prove very injurious to the country.

The tendency is to get rid of the management of the labor, to furnish them cheap stock and cheap utensils, to improve as little for them as possible, and get rid of the worry. The white people as a result will move into the little villages and stations, and it seems to me it will be only a few years until the larger part of the upland section of the country * * * will be occupied by negroes. The lands, of course, under their management as tenants, will wash away and wear out, fences go down, improvements become dilapidated.

This system has its disadvantages for the tenants also. It is generally considered that where the negro is left to himself, in communities solely of his own kind, progress ceases, and even positive deterioration, social and moral, sets in. This is recognized by the progressive negroes themselves, as well as by the whites.

Southern farmers are discouraged with cotton farming under all the conditions above outlined. Labor, although cheap from a money point of view and plenty, is not cheap enough with regard to efficiency and the price of the crop. An instance given before the Industrial Commission illustrates this. A South Carolina farmer and merchant states[1] that when he hired labor by the day he paid 30 cents, one-fourth in cash and three-fourths to be traded out at 50 per cent profit, equalling 19 cents a day actual outlay, " and yet, raising the crops as cheaply as that, the proceeds will not meet the expense of raising."

This farmer, it should be noted, had no complaint to make of the efficiency of the labor employed, and others agree with him in considering the negro a satisfactory cotton laborer. But, however this may be, whether the farmer attributes his failure to labor, to the banks, to the markets, or to the railway companies, the fact remains that cotton farming is generally found unsatisfactory and the farmers are looking about for some means of improvement.

A remedy more and more looked to in all parts of the country is diversified or intensive farming. For this sort of farming the general opinion seems to be that the negro laborer is not suitable. Testimony as to his capability is not all one way, it is true. A prominent and successful fruit grower, testifying before the Industrial Commission,[2] speaks highly of the efficiency, adaptability, and faithfulness of the negro laborer in fruit culture, including such parts of it as require special skill and care.

Others say, however, that the negro can raise cotton and nothing else; that he can not be trusted to care for stock; that he is unable to use farm machinery (as has been noted); that he will not give the care and attention necessary for diversified and intensive farming. It is said that the negro renter will not even cultivate his own garden patch to any great result in providing supplies for his family.

The prevalence of negro labor is, indeed, on the one hand an incentive to go into diversified farming as a relief from the cotton farming, which depends on this inefficient class of labor;[3] and on the other, one of the greatest drawbacks to making the needed change. One farmer testifies[4] " the labor that we have there must be worked some way, and cotton is about the only thing they know how to make."

But, notwithstanding these drawbacks, diversified and intensive farming will undoubtedly gain ground in the South, surely if slowly, the need and advantage are so obvious.

Careful methods of culture will restore fertility to the exhausted soil, the use of improved machinery will reduce the labor cost of crops, diversification of products will supply the wants of the home plantation to greater advantage than purchasing everything with cotton. Supplemented by diversified farming, cotton farming itself is more likely to prosper.

The farmer who is no longer absolutely dependent on the one great crop can cultivate it to better advantage, and by a system of economy and use of hitherto neglected resources, diversified farming need not at all diminish the acreage given to cotton, but may even allow of its increase.

It may be of interest to note the estimated acreage of cotton planted in the last 2 years.

---
[1] Reports of Ind. Com., vol. x, p. 117.
[2] Ibid., p. 382 et al.
[3] A representative farmer writes: "The 'new era' negro from 18 to 30 has become so perfectly unreliable as a field hand that diversified farming is largely forced on the planters."
[4] Reports of Ind. Com., vol. x, p. 76.)

AGRICULTURAL DISTRIBUTION OF IMMIGRANTS.

Estimated acreage of cotton.[1]

States and Territories.	Estimated acreage planted—	
	In 1900.	In 1901.
Virginia	44,000	52,000
North Carolina	1,342,000	1,476,000
South Carolina	2,367,000	2,533,000
Georgia	3,551,000	3,870,000
Florida	169,000	186,000
Alabama	3,085,000	3,362,000
Mississippi	3,063,000	3,124,000
Louisiana	1,285,000	1,401,000
Texas	7,174,000	7,748,000
Arkansas	1,899,000	2,089,000
Tennessee	801,000	913,000
Missouri	53,000	59,000
Oklahoma	246,000	308,000
Indian Territory	344,000	413,000
Total	25,421,000	27,532,000

[1] Crop Reporter, June, 1901 (vol. 3, No. 2).

This presents a general increase for the past year of over 8 per cent, and is due mainly, it may be assumed, to the rise in price of cotton in the markets. It is plain, however, that diversified and intensive farming and the growth of manufactures, so far as they have gone, are not at least restricting the acreage given to cotton.

As an independent industry, too, diversified farming will gain ground. The growth of manufacturing industries in the South is opening a wider and wider home market for dairy, garden, and orchard products, while the North is daily extending its demands for the same commodities, and railroad facilities are bringing these markets nearer to the Southern farms.

All the circumstances above outlined seem especially favorable to the introduction of European farmers and farm laborers with their knowledge of intensive methods and diversified farming into a country that has hitherto known little about them, and that is generally regarded as well—too well—supplied with both farmers and laborers.

As a result of the change going on in the agricultural system much land in the South has fallen altogether out of cultivation.[1] It is "worn out" in the sense that the surface fertility is exhausted, but under intensive methods it is capable of restoration and high cultivation. Other lands now cultivated in large tracts on the extensive system may be broken up into small tracts for cultivation intensively, and will thus sustain a greater population.

Still other lands, held by small farmers. who are at once farmers and laborers, have been left open to settlement by the departure of their owners for the cotton mills, which, employing only white labor, are now drawing heavily upon the small landholding population of the South.

In the cultivation of these lands is a most favorable opening for the foreign farmer, with his traditions of industry and skill in intensive farming. There is in the South, moreover, not only old land to be restored and made profitable by intensive cultivation, but new land yet to be opened up. Texas and Florida are as sparsely settled as the newest States of the Northwest; Louisiana and Arkansas afford thousands of acres of unimproved land to be worked; in Mississippi great tracts of land recently cleared or not yet cleared of timber are ready for the settler.

There has been for some time a decided call for a class of foreign immigrants with capital enough to make initial payments on land and set up as independent farmers. State boards of immigration and private corporations have been, and are now, engaged in trying to attract settlers of this class. There is little express demand for foreigners as farm laborers in comparison. It is as yet generally felt that the negro laborer holds the field, and that the foreign immigrant can not compete with him. But the same qualities that make the foreigner desirable as a farmer make him desirable as a laborer—his industry, his continuous application to his work, his intelligence, and skill. The growing dissatisfaction with the negro laborer is already taking shape in some calls for foreign laborers. (See tables.) Where foreign farmers have settled it is natural to suppose that foreign laborers will find a place, in some cases as a stepping-stone to farming on their own account. Little by little

[1] E. g., Virginia, Maryland, Georgia, Reports of Ind. Com., Vol. X, pp. 104, 109.

farmers will recognize that the cost of labor is not measured by the money paid out for it; and there seems every probability that, under the new system of farming coming in, the foreign farm laborer can compete successfully with the negro in respect to real, as contrasted with nominal, labor cost.

DELAWARE.

(See table, p. 614.)

Representative farmers from the three counties of Delaware report favorably, with one exception, as to opportunities in the State for newly arrived immigrants who do not speak English. Fruit, dairy, and truck farming give employment throughout the year to a large proportion of the farm laborers employed. Married laborers are employed and sometimes preferred, and there is considerable work for women and children. Farm laborers are principally negroes, but there are also Irish, Germans, Swedes, and Poles. In two cases a preference is expressed for Germans and Poles as farm laborers. One farmer says that negroes are employed, but Germans and Swedes would be preferred if they could be had. Germans, English, and Canadians are established as independent farmers in the State. Many of the Germans began as farm laborers. One farmer states that there are no foreign farmers in his neighborhood, but "would like to have them." Another in the same county says, "Our people are very friendly to Germans. They make good 'help' and good citizens. There is a good opening for such people."

As to general conditions, one farmer writes as follows:

I recognize that our wages are much lower than in some sections, but we have advantages in cheaper living for families, and opportunities for women and children to pick berries and other fruits, that largely help to make up the deficiency. I am a landowner and farmer by proxy, living in town and renting the land. I own four farms, which I have made and paid for out of the business of farming and fruit growing. So I think I am in a position to know what has been done, and I do believe there is an opening here for small farmers who are industrious and frugal. I have not a foot of land to sell, so I am not advertising. There is a great call here for house girls at about $2 per week.

OPPORTUNITIES FOR TENANCY AND OWNERSHIP.

(Reported by representative farmers.)

SUSSEX COUNTY.—Very good opportunities for renting, tenant paying share of the crop according to condition of the land. Good opportunities for purchase.

KENT COUNTY.—(1) Terms for renting, half share of the product or a cash rent. Industrious, reliable men can get farms to rent. There are the best opportunities for purchase while the purchaser is hiring out. (2) A large part of the land is worked on the tenant system, always on shares. Tenant does all the work, furnishes a small portion of the fertilizer, and gets half the crop. Land is low in price and easily improved. Many native farm laborers now own their own farms, and are doing well—both white and colored. (3) Good opportunities for renting. Tenant gets all proceeds of poultry and stock and divides grain and fruit. He stocks the farm. As to purchasing while hiring out, this is continually occurring. A man has only to prove his ability and character.

NEWCASTLE COUNTY.—(1) Most of our tenant farmers began as farm hands. (2) The average foreign farm laborer does not seem to wish to become a farmer. Nearly all say when they make $500 they will go back to their own country. There is little chance for purchase in this particular neighborhood.

MARYLAND.

(See table, p. 616.)

In this State a considerable proportion of the agricultural land fell entirely out of cultivation as a result of the change from slave to free labor. Such abandoned lands, in general, are said to be good agricultural lands, abandoned only on account of the difficulty in getting labor to work them properly.

In 1896 the State established a bureau of immigration to call attention to the resources of the State and the advantages offered to settlers, and to assist in the sale of lands. Dutch and German settlers, either direct from the old country or from the Western States, were especially desired as thrifty, industrious farmers, who would be particularly successful in reclaiming marshes and swamps, clearing away land grown up to timber, and improving land that had lost its fertility.

Pamphlets giving full information about the State and its resources were prepared, and an agent sent out to the Western States, to Holland, and to Germany to lecture on those topics. It was claimed that a farmer in Maryland could, on a farm of 40 to 60 acres, make a better and more comfortable living than in the Western and Northwestern States on a 200-acre farm, and that the man who possessed a few thousands of dollars to pay for a farm, cash down, in Maryland, was at once assured of a good future, while a good start could be made with from $400 to $800.

As a result of this activity many families of Germans, Dutch, and Swedes have settled in the State. A German settlement has been established near Preston, in Caroline County. During the autumn of 1898 about 25 families from various places settled throughout the State, mainly in Baltimore, Harford, and Frederick counties, and some on the Eastern Shore. In the spring of 1898 the beginning of a Dutch colony was made at Denton, Caroline County. Within recent years a considerable amount of land was purchased by Germans in Dorchester County. Up to November, 1899, it was estimated that between 400 and 500 families of desirable immigrants had settled in the State and had bought more than 25,000 acres of land.[1]

One obstacle to the work was the difficulty of procuring sufficient land in single tracts, as foreign immigrants preferred to settle in colonies. A tract of 12,000 acres was finally procured in Somerset County, with the idea of making it a Dutch settlement. The Maryland Land and Immigration Company of Baltimore now hold about 3,000 acres of land in this county, as yet unsold, and are planning to settle Dutch families there. About 15 families are already established and doing well. All kinds of crops are grown on these lands, and transportation facilities are good. The prices are from $8 to $25 per acre. The settlers referred to have come mostly from the Western States, and agents are still at work in those States trying to induce immigration. The conditions in Somerset County are considered especially favorable for the Dutch, being so much like those prevailing in Holland. A committee of three farmers from the Dutch colonies of the West, having been sent on to examine and report upon the Maryland lands, declare formally that "According to our best conviction the said lands are especially adapted for a Holland colony," adding naïvely: "It appears to us that these lands are designed by God for our Holland people."

Certain parts of the State appear to offer especial inducements for the better class of Hungarian settlers. An instance is given by the secretary of the bureau of one Hungarian purchaser who bought 400 acres of land in Anne Arundel County for the purpose of raising Tokay grapes, considering that the conditions of climate and soil afforded a remarkable parallel to those in Hungary. Success in this one undertaking probably means the beginning of a Hungarian colony and the development of a new and profitable form of agricultural industry in the country.

For the 12 months ending April 30, 1901, the State board of immigration reports that 249 immigrants came to the State and altogether purchased 4,577 acres of land. Of these immigrants 96 were from other States or Canada, 74 from Germany, 12 from the Netherlands, 23 from Switzerland, 41 from Austria-Hungary, 1 from Denmark, and 2 from South Africa. Descriptive literature and maps had been distributed through shipping and transportation agencies and by advertising in the leading agricultural papers of the Northwestern States and in Europe. Especial efforts appear to have been made to induce immigration from Germany. Of 1,847 pamphlets and maps sent out 1,047 were sent to Germany, as against 284 throughout the other States and Canada, 136 to the Netherlands, 154 to Switzerland, 137 to Austria-Hungary, and less than 25 to any other one country.

The State bureau offers to give to anybody wishing it information as to situation and quality of soil of lands offered for sale in the State or concerning the resources at the command of immigrants, industrial opportunities, routes of travel, etc.

The pamphlet of information issued by the bureau makes the following statement:

The bureau is not connected with any steam navigation company or real-estate syndicate. It is not interested in and does not receive any commission from the sale of land or perform any services in a business line for immigrants; all it is intended for is to furnish information, and this it does gratuitously. It will protect immigrants from imposition by land agents, if such should be attempted. Its office is a public one, and its officials are State officers, but ready to guide and help all intending settlers by furnishing them names of persons or concerns to whom the immigrant safely can apply.

The master of the State grange speaks well of the German farmers who have come into the State.[2] Many, he says, who came as laborers in a few years acquired land of their own, and are now prospering. They were experienced in farming before coming here. Many have settled near the cities and are engaged in truck farming, which requires less capital than some other kinds of farming and is profitable. In his opinion, the incoming of German farmers has been to the improvement of agricultural conditions. They have set a good example of industry and economy, and some are among the best citizens of the State. As farm laborers they are more effective than either the negroes or the class of native whites obtainable in the State.

---

[1] Second Report, State Bureau of Immigration, Baltimore, 1899.
[2] Testimony of Mr. Joseph B. Ager, Reports of Ind. Com., Vol. X, p. 103 (1899).

Reports received from representative farmers (see table, p. —) were from three counties only—two on the Eastern Shore and one in the northwest corner; so they can be taken only as showing conditions in these particular sections.

From the Eastern Shore counties one farmer reports no foreigners as farmers or farm laborers and no opportunity for immigrants. The other speaks of Irish and German farmers and laborers in the neighborhood, and makes note of a colony of Germans brought there in 1870. These people found it hard to learn American ways and the language, he says, and soon left.

OPPORTUNITIES FOR TENANCY AND OWNERSHIP.

(Reported by representative farmers.)

QUEEN ANNE COUNTY.—Land rents here for half of the produce raised. The owner furnishes one-half phosphates, one-half seed wheat, and draws half. Farm lands sell here from $10 to $75 an acre, according to quality and location. To purchase you are required to pay down one-third and give a mortgage at 6 per cent for the balance. The mortgage may usually run as long as the interest is paid.

TALBOT COUNTY.—There are no chances for renting farms. We now have more tenants than there are farms. It is possible for a poor man to establish himself in independent farming while hiring out, but not for the kind of help we are accustomed to.

WASHINGTON COUNTY.—The proportion of tenants to the farms is large. The outfit of a tenant costs from $1,200 to $3,000, and he gets one-half the gross proceeds of the land, paying for one-half of the fertilizer and one-half the seed. It is not practicable for a man to purchase land while hiring out.

VIRGINIA.

(See table, p. 617.)

In 1894, according to the commissioner of agriculture,[1] Virginia desired immigrants able to buy homes, large or small. These were wanted mostly in Southside and Tidewater Virginia, and lands were lower priced in these sections; but the whole State desired an influx of population. English, Scotch, Irish, Germans, and Swedes were the nationalities desired or preferred.

The desire for immigrants still exists. The commissioner of agriculture writes as follows under date of December 17, 1900:

There are fine opportunities for immigrants in this State; greater than heretofore. Owing to the location and climate of this State, intensive farming is becoming very profitable, also stock raising; and there is more demand for labor in all lines of industry.

We have not had enough immigrants to see much difference between the nationalities. The Germans have so far, I believe, made the best class of farmers.

Foreign farmers have been successful, owing to their training in intensive methods of cultivation. Farmers gladly welcome all immigrants who are industrious and law-abiding citizens. There is a wide field and splendid opportunity here for them.

The State has made no effort to secure immigration. The railroads, however, are encouraging them, and also the real-estate agents.

G. W. KOINER, *Commissioner*.

Letters from representative farmers were received from the Blue Ridge region only. Speaking for this locality, 5 of the 8 farmers heard from gave no encouragement as to opening for non-English speaking immigrants. This part of the country is by no means thickly settled, has few large towns, laborers are practically all employed through the year, and there is considerable work for women and children. But almost no foreigners have penetrated to this region. Some Germans and English are noted in Albemarle County, who have done well. One correspondent writes that foreigners would be welcomed as purchasers of land. Farm laborers are exclusively native whites and negroes. Farmers express preference for one or the other of these classes, as they know nothing about foreign labor. Some dissatisfaction with negro labor is expressed. In one case a farmer says Germans would probably suit better. With regard to other parts of the country, Signor Mastro-Valerio notes[2] that Italians are found in the large truck-farming districts near Norfolk.

---

[1] Report of Immigration Investigating Commission, p. 150.
[2] See p. — of this report.

AGRICULTURAL DISTRIBUTION OF IMMIGRANTS. 557

OPPORTUNITIES FOR TENANCY AND OWNERSHIP.

(Reported by representative farmers.)

FRANKLIN COUNTY.—Tenancy on terms of half crop of tobacco and corn and one-third of wheat and oats; owner furnishes teams, tools etc.; tenant finds himself. An industrious, frugal man could buy a little home and pay for it by hiring out or by close work on his farm.

BOTETOURT COUNTY.—A great many farms are rented here (stocked.) Give one-third. Good opportunities for purchase while hiring out.

ROCKBRIDGE COUNTY.—Few opportunities, as renting is not looked upon with favor. A poor man can establish himself in independent farming while hiring out. "The man that is now working for me has done so."

AMHERST COUNTY.—Good parties can become tenant farmers. Can farm on shares, the landowner to furnish land and team and give the renter one-fourth. A poor man can establish himself in independent farming while hiring out. This is being done by many of our laborers.

ALBEMARLE COUNTY.—No answer given.

AUGUSTA COUNTY.—We now have more native tenants than farms. Not a very good chance for a poor man to become an independent farmer while hiring out, though an exceptionally industrious man, a good manager, might succeed.

ALLEGHANY COUNTY.- Good opportunities for renting. Tenant or landlord furnishing teams and seeds gets two-thirds of crop. A man who purchases land on payments will find all of his time needed to cultivate it; but he will have good opportunities to hire out.

WEST VIRGINIA.

(See table, p. 618.)

The table for the State gives reports from representative farmers in (1) the southern part of the State, on the Virginia side, (2) on the Ohio border, (3) in the northeastern part of the State, and (4) in the "Panhandle." The table is not, then, fairly representative of conditions in the State as a whole. In all of the counties heard from but Brooke, the Panhandle county, there are almost no foreign farmers or farm laborers; no desire is expressed for their incoming, and there are said to be no opportunities for non-English speaking immigrants.

Testimony given before the Industrial Commission[1] as to conditions in the extreme northeastern part of the State (the eastern Panhandle) is to about the same effect as that for the above counties.

OPPORTUNITIES FOR TENANCY AND OWNERSHIP.

(Reported by representative farmers.)

MONROE COUNTY.—Not much demand for tenant farmers. They usually get half the produce and are sometimes required to furnish teams. The opportunities for purchase are poor.

RALEIGH COUNTY.—No opportunities for renting, but very good for purchase.

GREENBRIER COUNTY.—Good opportunities for renting either on shares or by lease for a term of years for clearing the land.

PUTNAM COUNTY.—(1) Good land may be rented on halves, the renter furnishing everything but the land and permanent repairs. There is not much chance for a poor man to purchase while hiring out. When he could hire out he would be needed to work his own crops. (2) Not much tenant farming is done here, and there is not much opportunity for purchase on especially easy terms except on the hills and ridges.

MASON COUNTY.—No opportunities for tenancy or for purchase on easy terms.

BARBOUR COUNTY.—There are good opportunities for tenancy; not so good for purchase. Land is high here.

BROOKE COUNTY.—There are good opportunities for renting; not so good for purchase. Land is high.

---

[1] Reports of Ind. Com., Vol. X., p. 591.

558   THE INDUSTRIAL COMMISSION:—IMMIGRATION.

NORTH CAROLINA.

(See table, p. 619.)

The assistant commissioner of agriculture for the State, in reply to a letter of inquiry addressed to him regarding immigration and general agricultural conditions, writes as follows under date of December 29, 1900:

Replying to your inquiries of the 14th instant, I beg to say that there has been but little foreign immigration in North Carolina—not enough to have any perceptible effect upon wages and employment. Relative to your questions I answer as follows:

First. Are there opportunities in your State for immigrants greater than there have been during the recent years of industrial depression? If so, in what occupation?—Answer. Yes, within the past 10 years more than 50,000 negro farm laborers have emigrated from the State—the bulk of them going to the cotton fields of Mississippi and Louisiana. The numerous cotton mills and other manufactories which have recently been erected in North Carolina have secured their laborers mostly from the farms. These causes having almost depleted very many good farms of their laborers, have thrown them upon the market at prices below their real value, hence there are opportunities for foreign farmers of small means to purchase very fine lands at low prices. There is also a better demand for foreign laborers to work in the cotton and trucking fields.

Second. What races or nationalities are most effective as farmers or farm laborers?—Answer. The native population.

Third. Is the success of foreign farmers as great as or greater than that of American born? If it is greater, is this owing to more intensive methods of cultivation?—Answer. There are not sufficient numbers of foreign farmers to make any general comparison. At Valdese, in Burke County, N. C., there is a colony of some 40 families of Waldensian farmers, whose success in farming is greater than their American neighbors, and much of their success is owing to more intensive methods of cultivation.

Fourth. Do farmers as a class oppose or favor the further influx of foreigners in your State?—Answer. Our farmers, as a class, are opposed to pauper immigrants, but welcome farmers who come to buy homes.

Fifth. Are efforts being made in your State, either by public authorities or by private parties or corporations, to attract immigrants?—Answer. Yes; the North Carolina department of agriculture is charged by the legislature with the work of immigration.

Sixth. Please inform me of any agricultural "colonies" or "settlements" of foreigners in your State.—Answer. There is a German settlement of farmers—some 200 people—near Ridgeway, N. C., and a Waldensian settlement—some 50 families—at Valdese, N. C.

Yours, very truly,

JNO. W. THOMPSON, *Assistant Commissioner.*

The German colony at Ridgeway above referred to consists of about 25 persons, brought to its place of settlement direct from Germany about 17 years ago by a German preacher of Brooklyn, N. Y. Most of the colonists are successful in farming, and own their own land in farms of 50, 90, 100, 200, and 300 acres. One family owns a farm of 800 acres. They are engaged in general farming, like other farmers around them, but keep somewhat more stock.

The Waldensian colony is composed of about 40 families from the Italian Alps, province of Turin, and was established 7 years ago. Few families have come in since that time. The colony is prospering. Wheat, corn, and grapes are raised. Two small hosiery mills are about to begin work, and this will be a great help to the place. The present population of the colony is about 250. This colony has become quite widely known for its success, as an instance of what a European farm colony can accomplish.[1]

The immigration work of the State department of agriculture, referred to in the assistant commissioner's letter, was taken up in 1899 under the act of assembly reorganizing the department, which provided that among the duties of the department should be "the inducement of capital and immigration by the dissemination of information relative to the advantages of soil and climate and to the natural resources and industrial opportunities offered in the State; by keeping a land registry, and the publication of descriptions of agricultural, mineral, and forest and trucking lands which may be offered the department for sale," etc.

This work has been carried on as far as the means of the board will allow and the demands of the department seemed to require.

As to the class of immigrants wished for, it is stated in the Annual Report of the Board of Agriculture for 1899-1900, page 12:

The effort of the board, through the assistant commissioner, has been to introduce only such immigration as is desirable in the State, men of means sufficient to enable them to make investments and build homes, no encouragement being given to undesirable steerage immigrants or other undesirable foreigners.

The assistant commissioner, regarding the small German farmers as a highly desirable class of immigrants, attempted to divert some of them from their destination, the Northwest, but was unable to do so because of the fact that "they invariably locate in the State to which they start when they leave the old country."[2]

---

[1] Reports of Ind. Com., Vol. X, p. 335 (Mr. J. F. Crowell); Report North Carolina Board of Agriculture, 1899-1900, p. 90.
[2] Report Dept. of Agriculture, 1899-1900, p. 86.

AGRICULTURAL DISTRIBUTION OF IMMIGRANTS. 559

To reach them in their homes and induce them to make North Carolina the State of their original choice a book of 130 pages in the German language was issued and distributed by the aid of the American consuls throughout Germany, Austria, and Belgium, and also at the Paris Exposition. This resulted in many inquiries and some immigration. One settler who came over is himself now organizing a German-American Land Company with, it is claimed, ample capital. This company will advertise North Carolina's resources, and will have its agents in Germany and Austria to distribute its literature and send farmers of means direct to the State.[1]

The secretary of the State department of agriculture writes in further detail as follows with regard to opportunities for immigrants:

(1) An immigrant may succeed in North Carolina with a very limited capital, provided he is industrious and capable. Our people who have lands to sell are content with a small cash payment and annual payments thereafter from the right people. So that a man with f om $250 to $500 could get a small farm, making an initial payment of from $100 to $200 and time for the rest, using his surplus to maintain himself while his crops are maturing.

(2) The class of farming which may be done in this State is very varied. In the eastern part of the State, with from 25 to 50 acres, an immigrant could make a good living, because there he can grow for the early markets spinach, kale, cabbage, green peas, lettuce, asparagus, onions, beets, string beans, strawberries, dewberries, raspberries, blackberries, cantaloupe, etc. The shipments from this State aggregate 350 train loads per annum from the region described. The strawberry crop alone last year aggregated more than 9,000 tons. In the middle section of the State tobacco and cotton culture together with general farming are the leading industries. In the Piedmont and western or mountain region the cereals, grasses, and winter fruit—apples—are the leading industries. The conditions in the State, both climatic and soil, are extremely favorable for all agricultural and horticultural pursuits, and workers from any part of Europe are generally successful here.

(3) The nationalities sought by North Carolina are the English, Scotch, Germans, and Scandinavians. These more readily assimilate with our people.

(4) Unfortunately we have no facilities for furnishing transportation or even excursion rates for viewing lands; however, both the Seaboard Air Line and Southern Railway systems, two of the largest in the State, conduct land agencies, and furnish those who endeavor to locate along their lines with reduced fares or perhaps free transportation.

(5) This department—the department of agriculture, immigration, and statistics—is authorized by law to keep a land registry wherein are entered all of the lands offered the department for sale. This plan offers the immigrant his lands without commission or the intervention of other agents. The department places the inquirer in communication with the person or persons registering the lands for sale. The size of the tract and its general condition, together with the price, is registered with the department for the inspection of any investor.

(6) In regard to markets will say that this State is most favorably situated, as it is within 18 hours of New York and has excellent facilities for transporting truck and fruits from the trucking fields of the East to the Northern markets. The local markets consume the cotton, tobacco, wheat, corn, oats, etc., while the South Atlantic States afford ample market for the winter cabbage, buckwheat, and apples of the mountain region.

The State has made but small effort to secure foreign immigrants. It has, however, quite an influx from the colder portions of our own country, and these are generally preferred. Many farmers who find the New England, Northern, and Northwestern States almost too cold, and who desire a milder climate, not only for themselves, but to give an open range for 9 or 10 months in the year, and at the same time one not hot enough to be enervating, will find in North Carolina the happy medium.

Very truly, yours,

T. K. BRUNER, Secretary.

Curiously enough, while the State bureau is making these especial efforts to induce immigration, representative farmers heard from (see table, p. 619) are almost unanimous in saying that there are no opportunities in their localities for non-English-speaking immigrants. It is to be noted at the same time, however, that, according to the table, there are as yet almost no foreign farmers or foreign farm laborers in the State and it might be thought there were no opportunities for such people simply through lack of experience with them and their capabilities.

OPPORTUNITIES FOR TENANCY AND OWNERSHIP.

(Reported by representative farmers.)

CRAVEN COUNTY.—Many of the larger farmers and landowners at a distance of 10 to 20 miles from town, where negro labor is scarce (the negroes all want to live in or near towns), are anxious to get tenants, and offer liberal terms that will satisfy any tenant. There are very good opportunities for purchase on easy terms a little distance from towns.

BEAUFORT COUNTY.—Tenant farmers are greatly desired. The opportunities for them are good, if they are of any account. Poor men, if industrious and thrifty, can in a few years buy and pay for a farm of 50 or 100 acres; hundreds have done so all over eastern North Carolina.

PITT COUNTY.—In renting farms the landlord furnishes land, team, farming implements, and feed for the team; the tenant does all the labor and receives half the product. There are first-rate opportunities for purchase to a prudent, saving tenant. Negroes generally spend all they make, be it little or much. I have a white man who has saved $1,000 in 5 years as a tenant.

---

[1] Report State Board of Agriculture, 1899-1900, p. 8.

WAYNE COUNTY.—Only ordinary opportunities to become a tenant farmer; terms generally one-half of the produce, team and tools furnished. Chances very poor for purchase.

WILSON COUNTY.—Very good opportunities for tenancy. The landlord furnishes land, team, farming implements, and feed for team. The tenant furnishes labor and gets one-half of the crop. Fairly good opportunities for purchase, though there is not much land for sale.

EDGECOMBE COUNTY.—Tenants who supply their own team are given half the truck. When the landlord supplies team and feed and farming implements, tenant gets one-third. Cost of fertilizer is divided. There are about the same chances for purchase here as in the greater part of our State. It is better for a poor man to work for wages, save money, and buy for cash. (2) Good men who wish to become tenants can almost always make their own terms. They can always rent for a stated amount or work on shares, the landowner furnishing land, team, and tools, and receiving half the product. There are good opportunities for purchase while the purchaser is hiring out if good economy is used. Very many are now doing this.

WAKE COUNTY.—Tenant farmers are desired. Landlord furnishes land, team, feed for team, tools, etc., and receives half the crop. Some pay one-fourth rent and find everything themselves. Opportunities for purchase are good to a smart working man. Many have bought land while hiring out.[1] (2) Land is rented on halves. Landlord supplies stock and tools. Opportunities for purchase are good here, because land is cheap and laborers are few.

FRANKLIN COUNTY.—There are fair opportunities for renting farms. Terms, one-fourth of the crops as rental, or the same proportion in cash. There are fairly good opportunities for purchase while hiring out if the purchaser is economical and a hard worker.

ALAMANCE COUNTY.—Good opportunities for renting. Tenants furnishing their own stock receive two-thirds of the crops. The local farmers having obtained low prices for their crops for some years past, and demand for labor in mills being very strong, the farmers have gone to factories, and for this reason farms are to be had on easy terms.

BURKE COUNTY.—Conditions would be hard for a tenant farmer, as land here is poor. The opportunities for purchase are unfavorable.

SOUTH CAROLINA.

(See table, p. 621.)

Reports from representative farmers show an almost complete absence of foreign farmers in their neighborhoods. In one county, Greenville, there are mentioned French, Irish, Germans, Swiss, and English. Farm laborers are as yet almost exclusively negroes and native "poor whites," and little or no encouragement is given as to opportunities for non-English speaking immigrants.

Some dissatisfaction with negro labor is expressed, however.

Wages in this State are apparently lower than in any other Southern State, but one farmer writes: "With more efficient labor wages might be increased." Another writes that truck and dairy farming are coming into greater prominence, and that "this change will alter the demand for labor. Negroes can not carry on this sort of farming." Others report the general changes already spoken of in the general survey of agriculture in the Southern States. One says: "Factory work has made labor scarce." Another: "Men going to cotton mills increase the demand on farms." Another: "As cotton mills increase vegetables and fruit are in demand."

It appears, then, that foreign-born labor may, before long, find some opening in this State.

Some interest in the colonization of foreigners as independent farmers is expressed. One correspondent writes as follows from Hampton County:

I would say, in addition to answering your inquiries as well as I could, that this company has some 4,000 acres of very fine farming lands that they are closing the cutting of the pine timber from, for sawmilling purposes, that they would cut up into lots of 25, 50, or 100 acres and sell to a colony on easy terms. It is so situated that they would have plenty of outlet and yet be a community by themselves. The company would want a good, quiet, religious community, and would expect some cash paid in at purchase.

Will take pleasure in answering any inquiries or in showing anyone around the property, and its advantages. It is a good community.

---

[1] Farms range from 5 to 1,000 acres, and are worth from $5 and $10 to $25, on time. Improved land is over $10. Cost of clearing and putting new land into good condition is about $10 an acre. One hundred and sixty-five thousand of the 478,086 acres in the county are under cultivation. The remainder is in field and old field. It costs $5 to $15 per acre to recruit worn-out land.

AGRICULTURAL DISTRIBUTION OF IMMIGRANTS. 561

OPPORTUNITIES FOR TENANCY AND OWNERSHIP.

(Reported by representative farmers.)

HAMPTON COUNTY.—Good opportunities for a tenant farmer. Landlord furnishes work animals, land, house to live in, feed for animals, seed, and plows, and receives half the crop. Laborer cultivates, harvests, etc., about 40 acres for each horse. As to purchase while hiring out, a great many negroes have done this, and there are no reasons why industrious white immigrants could not do better.

DARLINGTON COUNTY.—Good opportunities for tenant farming. There are good opportunities for purchase for a good class of people.

NEWBERRY COUNTY.—In renting land, landowner receives one-fourth of the crops. Sometimes landowner furnishes everything except fertilizer and receives half the crop. There are good opportunities for a poor man to establish himself in independent farming.

CHEROKEE COUNTY.—White men who can run a farm can rent at from one-quarter to one-third of the crops. A poor man can purchase land while hiring out. Land is cheap, living is cheap, and the purchaser can buy on easy terms.

SPARTANBURG COUNTY.—Good tenants get one-half of all crops. Landlord furnishes mule, land, planting seed, house, and wood free. Some lands are sold on long time where yearly payments are made.

GREENVILLE COUNTY.—There are good opportunities to rent farms for reliable people, either on wages or for part of crop. A man can buy land at from $10 to $25 an acre by paying one-quarter down, and can have from 1 to 5 years to pay the balance.

PICKENS COUNTY.—Good tenants will find no trouble in securing farms. One-third of the crop is charged when they have their own stock and tools. If stock and tools are furnished, tenant receives one-half. Farming lands can be bought on reasonable terms and at reasonable prices—from $5 to $30 an acre.

GEORGIA.

(See table, p. 622.)

The managers of the Georgia Industrial and Immigration Bureau stated to the Immigration Investigating Commission in 1894:[1]

> The entire State of Georgia needs and desires a good class of immigrants. * * * We need, very greatly, skilled labor in the factories. We need, most of all, a class of small farmers, gardeners, etc., to divide up the large farms and raise crops that are more profitable than cotton. * * * As to the classes of immigrants, I should say that we prefer Germans, French, Hollanders, Belgians, Scandinavians, Swiss.

At the present time testimony taken before the Industrial Commission seems to indicate that the farmer and farm laborer are less prosperous than formerly,[2] that negro labor, although unsatisfactory, can not be replaced by another class such as the foreign immigrant, because the former is so plenty and so cheap. There are, however, indications that there are still good opportunities for immigrants with intelligence and energy to take advantage of them. There is no "abandoned land" in the strict sense, but agricultural land may be had at from $5 to $10 an acre; near villages and towns for from $20 to $30.[3] Much of the land is exhausted of its first fertility, but fertility may be restored to the land by careful cultivation, and this sort of cultivation is coming more and more into use. The general tendency is to the improvement of farms,[4] and land, in some sections at least, is slowly increasing in value.

Such lands offer opportunities to thrifty foreign purchasers who are familiar with intensive methods of farming. Representative farmers from 14 counties of the State speak of foreign farmers in 4 counties—English, Scotch, Irish, Dutch, and German—and 6 of the 14 say that there are opportunities for foreign immigrants who do not speak English.

On the whole, they confirm the testimony given before the commission as to the difficulties in the way of foreigners as farm laborers. Such laborers are, however, reported in 3 counties at least, and in 1 county, where negroes are entirely employed, a desire is expressed for Protestant Germans or Scotch.

---

[1] Report Immigration Investigating Commission, p. 134.
[2] Reports of Ind. Com., Vol. X, pp. 46, 52, 59, 75.
[3] Ibid., p. 450.
[4] Ibid., pp. 380, 389.

The Central of Georgia Railway is carrying on some work in the way of bringing foreign settlers to this State, and also to Alabama. Their land and industrial agent writes:

> While this company has no regularly employed agents for the purpose of attracting foreign immigrants to this section, yet, through our various freight and passenger representatives throughout the East and the Northwest, we encourage only the thrifty, industrious, and better element of foreign immigrants to locate in this territory; and in connection with this work we are offering lands in tracts to suit the purchasers, aggregating in all about 260,000 acres, in the territory adjacent to the lines of this company in the States of Georgia and Alabama. These lands are adapted to growing all general crops, such as cotton, corn, sugar cane, wheat, rye, and all varieties of vegetables. Fruits, such as peaches, pears, plums, grapes, strawberries, watermelons, cantaloupes, etc., are also grown in large quantities, particularly peaches. These lands vary in price from $1 to $100 an acre, according to location, and, as a rule, can be purchased on easy terms—from 1 to 5 years with interest.
>
> This territory being one of the greatest agricultural sections in the South, we are particularly desirous of locating thrifty German or Swedish immigrants, who, we have found, constitute the best farmers and dairymen. Our work in connection with foreign immigrants commences only after they have been in this country for some time. We have no agents in foreign countries to work this business.
>
> We have no colonies of foreigners established at any point on our line. It is our experience that better results are obtained by distributing the foreign element throughout the agricultural sections rather than colonizing them at some particular point.

There are one or two colonies of Hungarians in the State, who are mainly engaged in viticulture. They were brought to the State by certain Jewish capitalists, who themselves returned to New York. There were about 100 families in all in these colonies, among whom were some Slovaks.

OPPORTUNITIES FOR TENANCY AND OWNERSHIP.

(Reported by representative farmers.)

CHARLTON COUNTY.—Opportunities for renting and for purchase also are very good.

IRWIN COUNTY.—There is some opening for tenant farming, but the best is for settlers, as this is a comparatively new country. The opportunities are good for a man to purchase, as land can be had from $3.50 to $15 per acre, and good time is given to pay for it. In a few years a purchaser could be independent and make a good living. Outside work can be had to make a living outside of the cropping season.

SUMTER COUNTY.—There are good opportunities for tenants. Terms, landlord furnishes house, land, farm stock, and tools; the tenant furnishes balance and gets half of the crop. Land is frequently sold on long time, paid for on installments.

CRAWFORD COUNTY.—There is plenty of land to rent or lease at from $1 to $2.50 an acre. Tenant can get farms, with stock furnished, on shares. There is plenty of land to sell on partial payments on very reasonable terms. No trouble for an industrious man to get along.

WASHINGTON COUNTY.—Good opportunities for becoming a tenant farmer. Tenant can pay a certain proportion of the crop or a stipulated quantity of cotton, usually 1,000 pounds lint cotton for 40 acres cultivable land, with house, garden, and fuel free. The best opportunities for purchase.

WALTON COUNTY.—In renting the landlord furnishes everything—mules, farm horse, wagon, and land—and charges one-half of the crop. The tenant feeds and clothes himself and pays for one-half of the fertilizer used. Land can be bought for $5 to $10 an acre, with all the time wanted to pay for it, at 7 per cent interest, payable annually.

ELBERT COUNTY.—In renting landlord furnishes land, stock, and tools, and receives half of the produce. There are good chances for a poor man to purchase if he is thrifty. Land is cheap, and there is plenty for sale.

GWINNETT COUNTY.—Good opportunities for tenants on halves, with stock and tools furnished, or three-fourths where tenant provides for himself. Small farms can be bought on time.

CARROLL COUNTY—Good opportunities for renting farms. Tenant receives one-half, and landlord furnishes everything, or tenant furnishes everything and receives two-thirds or three-fourths. Good opportunities for purchase to a good man.

BARTOW COUNTY.—Good opportunities to become a tenant farmer. Terms, two-thirds of the grain and three-fourths of the cotton if he furnishes stock; one-half without stock. Opportunities for purchase are not good.

FLOYD COUNTY.—Good opportunities for Americans to rent farms. Terms, one-half, with all expenses paid by landlord. Chances for purchase are fair for an industrious and frugal man.

CATOOSA COUNTY.—In renting tenant pays one-fourth of cotton and one-half of corn if he furnishes his own stock. If the landlord furnishes stock tenant pays one-half of everything. Some men buy land on time and make their living and pay for the land by farming.

AGRICULTURAL DISTRIBUTION OF IMMIGRANTS. 563

FANNIN COUNTY.—Very good opportunities to become a tenant farmer. The tenant furnishes stock and tools, paying one-third of the crop. Good chances for getting work while paying for a farm at Ducktown copper mines.

HABERSHAM COUNTY.—Any sober, steady man can rent as much land as he wants, paying in cereal crops one-third or cotton one-fourth of the produce.

FLORIDA.

(See table, p. 624.)

In 1894, according to the commissioner of agriculture,[1] there was throughout all sections of the State an express desire for immigrants of good character and industrious habits. Wages for unskilled labor in cotton farming were 50 to 75 cents a day, including board. In fruit growing and truck farming on a large scale unskilled labor received from $1 to $1.50 per day and skilled labor from $50 to $60 per month. As to nationalities desired, the preference was given to English-speaking people, although it was thought that Italians would be especially useful in building railroads and canals and in mining, the Germans and French as artisans and mechanics, the Spanish in tobacco manufacture. Further: "Among the European immigrants to this country there are often practical agriculturists and horticulturists who have received instructions in these industries as handed down in their families for generations." To such the State offered great inducements.

By the present time some foreign farmers and farm laborers have found their way into this State. Italians have come in to engage in orange culture. English, Scotch, Irish, Germans, Swedes, Russians, French, and Spanish are reported as independent farmers by representative farmers of the State (see table) and English, Germans, and Swedes (in two counties) as farm laborers. In one county where native whites and negroes only are employed Germans and Swedes are asked for. One correspondent decidedly prefers negro labor, for reasons which he gives in a brief but vivid characterization of the negro laborer. He says:

The negro suits this section best because we do not have to provide houses or food for him. We pay him a stipulated price per day and he finds his own lodging and food, thus giving the housewife no trouble. He comes to work in the morning and leaves at night, sleeps under any kind of shelter, and cooks his own food. If there is no house convenient, he sleeps under a tree. He works about half of his time and is the happiest creature living.

Others are not so well satisfied with negro labor. The following letter from Columbia County shows the need, in that section at least, for some change:

Your letter of inquiry came just at the time I was seeking to get into communication with some one who could assist me in getting a class of reliable and intelligent farm laborers. I am trying to farm with negroes, on half crops, but it is exceedingly unsatisfactory; first, because they are so unreliable and shiftless, and second, because they steal more than half of the crop if given half an opportunity. Within the next 2 years I would like to have 25 families. I have the land and must import the labor if I can find the kind that can do the work of this country. As an experiment I would like to have 2 or 3 families this winter. I would not at present like to try more. I can, however, place several on terms of half croppers, and possibly as tenants. I am very glad to offer my services in any way I can serve you. Trusting that we may be benefited by getting a good class of labor and at the same time help some one into comfortable circumstances, I am,
Yours, etc.,
——— ———.

Another correspondent writes as follows:

West Florida is the agricultural section of the State, and is just being developed. I know of no place where a man of limited means can do better than here. We are sadly in need of good farm labor in the field and house. Sawmills and turpentine farms control the negroes to a large extent and make farm hands very hard to get. Can, intelligent immigrants that would soon learn to speak English would do well. There are a few Germans here, also Swedes, but none of the other nationalities except in the cities. If you could send a colony here that have some means, so they could buy land and make a small payment, they would do well. Wild land can be had from $3 to $5 per acre at present, within 6 or 12 miles from the railroad, and I think our people would lend a helping hand toward getting them located.

OPPORTUNITIES FOR TENANCY AND OWNERSHIP.

(Reported by representative farmers.)

POLK COUNTY.—Excellent opportunities for renting farms. Good farmers can make very satisfactory arrangements. Florida offers exceptional opportunities for the purchase of land on easy terms, as living here is very cheap and land is low.

HILLSBORO COUNTY.—There are but few tenant farmers here and the chances for them are not good. Opportunities for purchase depend upon the man. A few succeed, but not the majority.

PASCO COUNTY.—No place gives better opportunities for renting. Lands, houses, pastures, and fertilizers are furnished by the owner, and the renter gives only half

[1] Report Im. Inv. Com., pp. 131–133.

the net proceeds to the owner; or the renter furnishes team, tools, and three-quarters of the fertilizer, giving the landlord one-fourth of the crop. No country offers such wonderful inducements for purchase on easy terms while the purchaser is earning a living by hiring out.

VOLUSIA COUNTY.—A renter can get all the land he wants, in some cases with good houses, having all the land produces except the oranges, free. There are the best possible opportunities for purchase on easy terms in this country if a man is honest and upright.

PUTNAM COUNTY.—There are no opportunities for renting. Land is cheap and industrious men with small capital would do well. There are opportunities to hire out a part of the year.

ST. JOHN COUNTY.—There is very little done in the way of tenant farming. Many have purchased land by hiring out, and land is cheap.

ALACHUA COUNTY.—Good opportunities for renting. The kind of crop determines the share the tenant gets. It is probably the best way for a man to establish himself in independent farming to hire out while making payments. The opportunities are good for men that will do good work. Land can be bought low and on long time.

COLUMBIA COUNTY.—There are good opportunities to become a tenant farmer for a money rent or half the crops. Land rent is from $1.25 to $1.75 per acre. On halfcropping, horse, land, implements, etc., are furnished by the landlord, and the tenant does all the work, making hay and harvesting. A good man can get all the help he needs in purchasing land if he has any ability to do work and is industrious. Land is cheap and can be bought wholly on time. Living is very cheap.

MADISON COUNTY.—Good opportunities for renting and for purchase on easy terms.

GADSDEN COUNTY.—Tenants have farm and outfit furnished them. Tenant furnishes the labor only and gets half the crop. The opportunities for purchasing land on easy terms are fine for frugal negroes, but they seldom avail themselves of this opportunity. On the other hand, white men could not purchase while hiring out, as this is no country for white laborers. The two races do not work together to advantage.

JACKSON COUNTY.—Opportunities are good for renting land. The landlord furnishes everything but the tenant's board and the tenant receives half the crop; or the tenant furnishes everything and gets two-thirds. An able-bodied man with a healthy wife and growing children can take a homestead and let the family improve it while he works out to support them.

CALHOUN COUNTY.—Good opportunities for tenancy and the very best for purchase to men of energy.

WALTON COUNTY.—Good opportunities for tenancy. There is no standard figure for rental, usually one-third of the crop. There are fairly good opportunities for purchase at present, as favorable, if not more so than in any section of the country.

KENTUCKY.

(See table, p. 626.)

The curator of the geological department, writing to the Immigration Investigating Commission in 1894 said,[1] with reference to a suggestion made that some means be employed whereby immigrants should be given information as to the need or lack of need of labor in various sections of the country:

The suggestion is a good one, provided the work is done by the States, cooperating with the Federal authorities, instead of by land syndicates and colonization companies acting under the sanction, either full or qualified, of Government officials.

He said further:

Kentucky needs not artisans and mechanics so much as agriculturists, fruit growers, etc., although the first-named classes are also desired in many of the counties. Families to settle the more rugged parts of the State, especially what is known (to a large extent incorrectly) as the mountainous part, and who will come expecting to acquire permanent homes, are particularly desired There are already colonies of Swiss, Germans, and Scandinavians planted in the State. More are wanted.

But in Kentucky there is less disposition just now to secure immigrants direct from foreign countries than from other States. It is believed, in the main, such immigration is best for this State at present, though there is ever a welcome for the better class of immigrants coming direct from foreign homes.

At that time a bureau of information and immigration (not a State office) had just been organized and the manager stated to the Immigration Investigating Commission that the State desired immigration in all parts, but had made no organized efforts to induce it beyond a geological survey, with publication of the results. The object of the bureau above named was to collect and publish information about the

---

[1] Report Immigration Investigating Commission, 1895, p. 136.

AGRICULTURAL DISTRIBUTION OF IMMIGRANTS. 565

State for the purpose of bringing in a good class of immigrants and investors, both native and foreign. The nationalities preferred were British, Germans, Swiss, and Scandinavians. Poles, Huns, and the Latin races were not desired, except individuals who came of their own volition.

With regard to present conditions the State commissioner of agriculture writes (January 4, 1901):

First. I do not think the opportunities for immigrants are measurably greater than they were a few years ago unless it be in coal mining. The prices of this product are higher now, and I think the miners and other employees share in the advance.

Second. I think the German farmers are more effective as farm laborers and as farmers, particularly around larger cities and towns where market gardening is practiced.

Third. I think the success of foreign farmers is greater upon the whole and due to intensive methods.

Fourth. Our farmers do not oppose, but favor, the influx of the right kind of foreigners into the State.

Fifth. The Louisville and Nashville Railroad, the Illinois Central Railroad, the Southern Railroad in a general way are encouraging immigrants to settle along their lines. The Commercial Club of Louisville is endeavoring to do the same. There are also private parties and corporations who either own land or are interested in inducing immigration.

Sixth. There is a Swiss colony established at Bernstadt, Laurel County, which seems to have been very satisfactory after some 12 years' experience. The German farmers mentioned in second paragraph above mostly come as individuals and not in colonies.

Very truly, yours, I. B. NALL, *Commissioner.*

The representative farmers heard from (see table) are unanimous in saying that there are no openings for non-English-speaking immigrants in this State. There are no foreign farmers in the counties heard from, except some Swiss in Adair County (not far from Laurel County, where is situated the Swiss colony referred to by the commissioner of agriculture), and no foreign farm laborers. All are negroes or native whites. Out of 9 farmers heard from 3 expressed a decided preference for negroes as laborers, 2 for native whites, and 1 stated there was "no prejudice against foreign labor."

OPPORTUNITIES FOR TENANCY AND OWNERSHIP.

(Reported by representative farmers.)

CHRISTIAN COUNTY.—Good opportunities for tenant if he has energy and pluck. If tenant furnishes team and tools, gets two-thirds of crop; if owner furnishes team and tools, gets one-half of crop. Chances are good for purchase on easy terms.

BARREN COUNTY.—Good chances for tenant. He gets one-third to one-half crop. Good for purchase if tenant can make one payment on land.

ADAIR COUNTY.—Fair opportunity for tenancy, but not much for purchase on easy terms.

CLAY COUNTY.—Very good opportunities to rent. Stock and implements furnished for one-half of crop. If tenant furnishes stock and implements, he gives one-third.

KNOTT COUNTY.—Good opportunity for tenant. He gets one-third of crop. Tolerably easy to purchase.

MADISON COUNTY.—No opportunity for tenancy or purchase; land too expensive.

ANDERSON COUNTY.—Tenant gets one-half crops, house rent free, wood, and stock to work crops. Good chance for purchase if man is economical.

OWEN COUNTY.—There are many tenant farmers, receiving usually one-half crop ready for market, with teams furnished, or grass furnished if tenant furnishes teams. For purchase, best plan is to work on tenant system until enough is accumulated to make payments on land.

ROWAN COUNTY.—Opportunities for renting or for purchase are not good.

TENNESSEE.

(See table, p. 627.)

The Nashville, Chattanooga and St. Louis Railway is interested in securing immigration to the State, and maintains an immigration department for that purpose. The agent of that department writes as follows with regard to opportunities for settlers, and general conditions:

This company has no land for sale, but it has secured a large amount on its lines suitable for colonization. There is no outlay for the maintenance of the agents except myself and one or two assistants. I should think that I have at present some 40.000 acres of land at my disposal. It is suitable for the greatest variety of crops, among others, wheat, corn, oats, barley, rye, buckwheat, tobacco, Irish and sweet potatoes, about 50 kinds of grasses, sorghum, cotton, peanuts, broom corn, cowpeas, beans, tomatoes, strawberries, celery, castor beans, asparagus, Kaffir corn, melons, turnips, onions, fruits and vegetables of every character, including grapes, apples, peaches, pears, quinces, plums, and berries of various kinds. Besides these the land is well adapted to the growing of live stock, poultry, and bees.

These lands are worth from $4 to $10 per acre. We do not care about special classes of purchasers, but would be glad to have good Germans who will enter upon fruit and vegetable culture for the Northern markets. This special branch of agriculture has proved immensely popular. From one section was shipped in a single day 153 carloads of strawberries that caused to be distributed in that locality $40,000 for a single day's shipment.

There are 1 or 2 colonies of foreign immigrants. The Swiss have a very flourishing settlement at Hohenwald, in Lewis County, Tenn. Another colony that has been long settled is at Belvidere, in Franklin County. These were also German-Swiss, and they are accounted the best farmers in the State of Tennessee, making the largest yield of produce and noted for the high character of their farms. Most of the immigrants that come to the State, however, come from the Northwest. Tennessee offers excellent opportunities for industrious farmers. A good deal of manufacturing is also now being carried on which requires a higher class of immigrants.

Yours, truly,
J. B. KILLEBREW,
Industrial and Immigration Agent.

In addition to the colonies noted above may be mentioned the colony of Finns in Hickman County, established by Mr. Hornborg, general agent of the Finland Steam Navigation Company, an account of which, with other colonies planted or proposed by him, will be found on page 510 of this report.

There are, besides, some Italians in the State. Quite a number are engaged in truck farming in the outskirts of Memphis, and are very successful.[1]

A certain "farm company" is now interesting itself in securing immigrants from crowded city districts to cultivate land in northwestern Tennessee. The following circular gives an idea of conditions in a part of the State to which immigration is invited, and of the advantages offered:

We have here a farm of 1,500 acres of cleared land on a tract of 3,000 acres, the same being located in the extreme northeastern corner of this (————) county, and is distant from 2 to 3 miles from ————. This land was cleared from a virgin forest since 1891, since which time all stumps have been removed from 800 acres of land, allowing the use of modern up-to-date farming machinery. This land is as good as can be found in the State; is rolling enough to insure good drainage. The land lies nearly in a square, being intersected by a creek diagonally across its entire length. All of this land is above an overflow from the Mississippi River, and is not subject to its backwater. The principal crops raised are wheat, corn, and hay. Cattle, sheep, hogs, and mules are also raised.

We do not rent, lease, or share crop any of this land, experience teaching us that our best interests require that we have all this work done by daily labor, and for that reason we will not consider any proposition to work any of the land in any other manner.

To this end we seek to settle upon this farm a number of families who are seeking steady employment the year round at a fair price, and we will do all in our power to surround them with a good and comfortable home after they have shown us that they are satisfied to remain, and providing, of course, that they give us satisfaction.

We pay the following prices for able-bodied male labor: 75 cents per day for January to April and October to December; 85 cents per day for May and September; $1 per day for June, July, and August, with a prospect of better wages to the right parties. House and garden spot are free. Wood can be had in abundance, and costs you nothing but the trouble to cut and haul; teams are furnished free of charge for hauling. Settlements in full are made once each month in cash.

We will require references for character and working qualities, and will advance transportation to those furnishing satisfactory references, the amount of same to be refunded in easy monthly payments. We are willing also that you satisfy yourself that you will be fairly treated and that you will work for a responsible concern. This you can do by writing us your religious faith and we will give you the name of our local minister of the same faith, to whom you are at liberty to write.

We are anxious to place on this farm an honest, industrious, and thrifty people, those who know what farm life is and are willing and contented to follow it.

Those to whom this does not apply we say do not come; you will be wasting your time.

Yours, truly,
———— FARM COMPANY.

Of 11 representative farmers heard from in 10 counties (see table, p. 627) 4 were of the opinion that non-English-speaking immigrants could find employment; 3 thought there would be little if any opportunity for them, and 4 thought there would be none. These opinions seem independent of the question whether foreigners had already found their way into the localities mentioned. In 3 of the 4 counties where there were said to be openings for immigrants, there were neither foreign farmers nor farm laborers. In 2 out of the 3 counties where Germans, Irish, and Swiss were found, there was said to be not much chance for immigrants.

OPPORTUNITIES FOR TENANCY AND OWNERSHIP.

(Reported by representative farmers.)

HAMBLEN COUNTY.—There are good opportunities to become tenants. There is always land to rent on a variety of terms. Sometimes renter furnishes everything and gives one-third, or owner may supply seed and stock and take one-half. Land may be bought anywhere in this county on easy terms, but wages are low when it comes to paying for land while hiring out.

GILES COUNTY.—(1) Improvement in methods of farming and in farm implements is calling for a better class of tenants. Those could get land at a reasonable rental. There are good opportunities to purchase for good, honest men who will work.

---

[1] See p. 510 of this report.

AGRICULTURAL DISTRIBUTION OF IMMIGRANTS.

(2) There are good opportunities for rental. The tenant can get one-half of the proceeds of the farm if he furnishes his own tools and farming implements. The prices for produce are very good.

MARSHALL COUNTY.—There is not much chance of renting desirable farms, and no opportunities for purchase on easy terms while purchaser hired out, as wages are very low.

MAURY COUNTY.—Most farms are small, and few are for rent. Where they are leased on shares one-half is usually given to the owner, and in some cases where the tenant stands the expense one third is given to the owner. There is probably no opportunity for a poor man to purchase a farm while earning a living hiring out. A man must have some capital to get started here. Land is high and profits in farming are not large.

WILLIAMSON COUNTY.—There are a few farms to let here. Tenant gives one-third to one-half the crop, according to agreement. The landlord furnishes land, seed, teams, and stock. In portions of our county land can be purchased cheap on yearly payments, near schools and churches. If a man is industrious he can rise right away.

HICKMAN COUNTY.—Land is leased to tenants for one-third of the crop, tenant furnishing stock. Land can be bought at from $5 to $30 an acre.

DAVIDSON COUNTY.—Farms can be had for $10 an acre.

SUMNER COUNTY.—There are no opportunities for tenant farming and none for purchase on easy terms.

LAUDERDALE COUNTY.—Farms can be rented on easy terms provided the intending tenant has small capital. There are very good opportunities for purchase.

OBION COUNTY.—The tenant gets half the crop when furnishing team and tools, and feed for team. If landlord furnishes these in addition to rent, the tenant receives only one-third of the crop. There are good opportunities for good, industrious tenants. Land can be bought unimproved in this county at $5 an acre; one-third cash, the balance in 1 and 2 years.

ALABAMA.

(See table, p. 629.)

The Louisville and Nashville Railroad Company maintains a general immigration and industrial department for the purpose of settling up land in Kentucky, Tennessee, Alabama, Florida, and Mississippi. The general immigration agent writes:

This company has made no special efforts toward inducing foreign immigration (by which I presume you mean newly-landed immigrants) into its territory, and it is only within the last few years that the Scandinavians and other northern Europeans have shown a disposition to locate in the district south of the Tennessee River. However, there is now such a disposition, but mostly on the part of those who have been residents of the United States for some years, and particularly in the Northwestern States. A good Scandinavian settlement has been started at Thorsby, Ala., which is on our main line about halfway between Birmingham and Montgomery. This colony is constantly in receipt of Scandinavian settlers. At Cullman, which is about halfway between Decatur and Birmingham, is a large and prosperous settlement of Germans. Germans, however, are found more or less throughout our territory.

Until the last few years the labor conditions in most parts of the South were such as to not encourage the migration of the great mass of foreign immigrants, who, even while taking up land, must depend largely on the sale of their surplus labor, at least, to insure their living for at least a few years while their lands were being made productive. But the last 2 years has shown a most remarkable advance in the demand for, and in the prices paid for labor, especially in the great coal and iron district of which Birmingham is the center; so that now that district especially presents a most inviting field for that class of people, especially those who are familiar with working in coal mines, coking plants, and iron and steel works. Land can be had very cheap in that district, as the surface is so broken by hills that it is not attractive to the general farmer, though it is productive enough, and can be used profitably in small farms of 20 to 40 acres. All the field, garden, and fruit crops can be grown there most successfully, and over a long season, as also poultry, etc. I think I do not exaggerate when I say that 50,000 families could find advantageous locations in that Birmingham district, where they could get their small tracts of land and where they could find most remunerative employment for their surplus labor, and it seems to me that the various Slavonic peoples would be best adapted to that situation.

As the company itself does not handle lands I would be unable to give specific information on the subject of prices and terms, though I know that in a general way such land can be bought in large lots as low as $2 to $3 per acre, there being one tract in particular of about 140,000 acres which can be bought, I understand, at $2.

This mining and manufacturing district, then, which embraces probably 500 square miles and upward, would be best adapted to the foreigners I have indicated who are more or less familiar with working in mines, coking plants, and iron and steel works; and farther south the Gulf coast district presents a field of vast possibilities for the agricultural immigrants from southern Europe, Italy in particular. The land is cheap and all the conditions most highly favorable for the growing of fruits and garden crops of all sorts; in fact, in normal seasons garden crops can be made throughout the winter, and there is always a remunerative demand for such products.

A few Italians are to be found in our Gulf coast district, but no particular colonies of them.

In brief, it seems to have been the general consensus of opinion of Southern people generally that it was not worth while to make any great effort to attract foreign immigration to that section of the country. This, in my opinion, was a great mistake, as the millions of highly desirable Italian agriculturists who have gone to Argentina in the last 20 years should have been diverted to the Southern

States, where probably they would have succeeded better than they have done in Argentina. I do not know that there will be any decided disposition on the part of any railroad or other interests to make any particular effort to attract foreign immigration to the Southern States, the general belief being that it does not naturally incline in that direction, and much effort and expenditure of money would be necessary to accomplish any substantial results.

Yours, truly,
R. J. WEMYSS,
General Immigration and Industrial Agent.

The "few Italians" spoken of in the above letter are probably certain colonies described in preceding pages of this report.[1] They were located at Daphne, Baldwin County, and at Lamberth, Baldwin County. They are apparently very successful. Representative farmers from 7 counties in this State report no foreign farm laborers in their neighborhoods, and very few foreign farmers. A few Germans and Irish are spoken of in Hale County, and a desire is expressed for Germans, Poles, and Irish to come in as farm laborers. Three of the 7 correspondents are of the opinion that there would be openings for immigrants.

OPPORTUNITIES FOR TENANCY AND OWNERSHIP.

(Reported by representative farmers.)

HENRY COUNTY.—There are good opportunities for renting. Stock is furnished, and house, and the produce is divided. There are fair opportunities for purchase. There are plenty of opportunities to rent farms for the sort of tenants wanted. Terms, one-half the proceeds. A poor man has a good chance to purchase. Land is reasonable, crops plentiful, and the country healthful. The soil is sandy, suitable for white labor, and a workingman can always get help.

BUTLER COUNTY.—There are good opportunities to rent on shares or for cash. In this neighborhood opportunities for purchase are excellent. There are as many as 10,000 to 15,000 acres to be had at from $4 to $10 an acre.

LEE COUNTY.—Good opportunities to rent if tenant is willing to work and will not go too heavily in debt the first year. As for purchase while hiring out, it simply depends on the man.

HALE COUNTY.—In one instance, 3 brothers, Irishmen, took jobs of ditching and well digging, then rented land, a little at a time, saving their money and keeping to their work. They are now merchants and landowners, selling 400 to 500 bales of cotton a year, and are good citizens.

PICKENS COUNTY.—This county has fine opportunities for white tenants. There are good opportunities for purchase. Land is plentiful and can be had at from $1 to $10 an acre.

TALLADEGA COUNTY.—There are good opportunities for renting. A good white man can make satisfactory arrangements by which he can make money. He can find employment for his whole family. Land can be bought on payments.

MISSISSIPPI.

(See table, p. 630.)

The governor of the State wrote, in 1894,[2] that he was doubtful whether foreign immigrants were desired as laborers in Mississippi; but if any came, he thought Germans would be preferred to all others; second, Swedish; then, Italian. As there were no mining interests, and more artisans and skilled labor than could find employment, wages of unskilled labor for ordinary farm work were from $8 to $12 per month.

From reports received from representative farmers in 12 counties of the State, it appears that by this time quite a number of foreign farmers have made their way into the State. These are mainly Germans and Swedes, with a few Irish. In one southern county Germans and Swedes are mentioned as farm laborers; but throughout the State negro farm labor prevails. And there appears to be a decided preference for this class of labor, partly due to the preponderance of cotton farming in the State; partly to unfamiliarity with any other class of labor. One correspondent writes: "Negroes are preferred because no others have been tried; white labor on the large plantations would not be advisable. But on the smaller truck and stock farms a great many could find employment, both men and women." Another writes: "Yes, there are chances for immigrants, but they, as a general rule, do not take to our styles of farming, knowing nothing of cotton work, and no small grains in quantities are sown here except oats."

Another, however, complains of negro labor, saying: "The negro is employed here, but is getting to be worthless. We should like to have some good Germans or

---

[1] Page 504. [2] Report Im. Inv. Com. p. 141.

Swedes. The Germans and Swedes soon learn English and can be employed as carpenters, blacksmiths, brick masons and housebuilders." Another writes that the chances for immigrants are probably good, "although there are none of this class here." In fact, notwithstanding the prevalence of negro labor and the preferences expressed for that class, 6 of the 15 farmers heard from report opportunities for non-English-speaking immigrants in their neighborhoods.

A few Italians seem to have made their way into the Delta country.[1] In testimony taken before the Industrial Commission an instance was given where a large plantation was rented out and subrented in small plots to negroes and Italians. There were about half a dozen families of the Italians. These Italian families made successful cotton farmers, being more energetic than the negroes. They do not stay long, however, as they soon make enough to engage in some other kind of business. On account of their very success in farming, then, they are considered less desirable as renters than the colored people, who stay on the farm. Italians are also found on sugar-cane plantations in the State.[2]

Not many farm hands in the State are hired by the month or day. The tenant system largely prevails.[3] The lands in the State are still owned in large tracts, although not so large as before the war, and the system now prevailing is to let them out in small tracts (especially cotton land) to be worked on shares of the crop, or for a cotton rent.

The Illinois Central Railroad Company is making efforts to induce immigration to the Delta district. The land commissioner writes as follows, under date of June 20, 1901:

We have about 200,000 acres on the Yazoo and Mississippi Valley Railroad in the Yazoo Valley, Mississippi. We have just disposed of 50,000 acres of land grant in southern Illinois. The lands are suitable for all crops, but are specially used for cotton and corn. We have never had any success with foreign immigrants and have no agents for that purpose. All attempts to locate colonies from cities have proven abortive. Greatest success has been in locating individual farmers and sales to local residents.

Yours, truly, EDWARD P. SKENE, *Land Commissioner.*

The Yazoo Valley, to which the Illinois Central is trying to bring settlers, was originally a great forest of hard-wood timber, and up to 1884, when the Yazoo and Mississippi Valley Railroad was completed, there were not over 500,000 acres in cultivation. Since then nearly 1,500,000 acres have been put into cultivation. What the country now needs is thrifty, industrious immigrants with some capital. Cotton is the great staple product in this valley, where a bale to the acre may be grown, an ordinary yield being one-third of a bale to the acre. No fertilizing is needed, the soil being very deep and rich. Diversified farming is recommended, notwithstanding the large yield of cotton, to make cotton raising itself more profitable. Settlers who want to work for cash while improving their land will find abundant opportunity in the many sawmills along the line of the railroad.

A large proportion of the land owned by the railroad is in large tracts, suitable for colonies. One hundred or more families can be located on tracts of 80 or more acres of land which adjoin each other. These lands are sold at from $7 to $9 upward per acre, according to location and number of acres cleared. Terms of sale are, one-fifth cash, the balance payable in 1, 2, 3, 4, and 5 years, with interest at 6 per cent, payable annually.

OPPORTUNITIES FOR TENANCY AND OWNERSHIP.

(Reported by representative farmers.)

WILKINSON COUNTY.—(1) There are the best of opportunities for renting—better than in any other agricultural county in the United States. Land rents from $1.50 to $2.50 an acre, with house, wood, water, garden, and free truck patch free, and often pasturage. There are good opportunities for purchase 4 or 5 miles from the railroad. Lands are cheap there—say from $3 to $7 an acre. These lands will frequently earn their purchase price the first year. (2) There are very good opportunities for tenants. Fair rentals are charged for lands. The share system is used by some. The landlord furnishes team, tools, land, and seed; also, half the fertilizer when used. Tenant furnishes half of all labor and gets half of all crops.

LINCOLN COUNTY.—Land can be bought cheap for cash or on credit. or it can be rented.

COPIAH COUNTY.—There are good opportunities for purchase. Land is usually bought and paid for. This section is pine-ridge land and very healthy.

---

[1] Reports of Ind. Com., vol. x, p. 464-468.
[2] See page 503 of this report. See also some account of them under the heading 'Alabama."
[3] Reports of Ind. Com., vol. x, p. 471.

HINDS COUNTY.—(1) There are unusually favorable opportunities for tenant farmers, either on a lease or as a share worker for the landowner. Tenants that are sober and industrious are needed—as many as can be had. As to purchase, a tenant, if thrifty, can soon own land on very favorable terms. (2) Opportunities for tenant farmers are good. The tenant furnishes nothing but work and his own food and is allowed half the crop.

MADISON COUNTY.—There are plenty of farms to rent at low figures. Some can be had on long lease at $2 an acre annually and some are worked on the share system. The landlord provides the land, teams, and farm implements and the tenant does the work. A great many have purchased land while earning their living by hiring out.

NEWTON COUNTY.—Opportunities for renting are very poor. As to purchase, land is cheap and there is no demand.

LAUDERDALE COUNTY.— (1) There are excellent opportunities for renting. Many a landowner would sell land to a tenant on time, to be paid for in farm labor. Opportunities for purchase are as good as anywhere. (2) In renting, lands can be worked on the share system, the landlord furnishing all the implements, teams, house, and feed for teams. The produce is divided equally. Land may be bought for from $6 to $15 an acre, according to quality of land, and can be paid for on the installment plan.

LOWNDES COUNTY.—Land may be rented for a money rent or a portion of the crop.

OKTIBBEHA COUNTY —There is plenty of land to rent for $2 an acre, the landlord furnishing house, fuel, and water. The tenant gets half the cotton, one-third of the corn, and one-half of other produce, the landlord furnishing everything. There are unsurpassed opportunities for purchase.

CARROLL COUNTY.—There are good opportunities for tenant farmers. At present there is a scarcity of labor. The prevailing rate on the share plan is one-fourth of the cotton or one-third of the corn, or a stated rent of so much cotton or so much money—from $2 to $5 an acre, according to the quality of the land. There are good opportunities for purchase—none better anywhere.

PRENTISS COUNTY.—There are good opportunities for renting. Landowner furnishes land, team, seed, and implements for half the crop, or lets the land for one-third of all grain crops and one-fourth of the cotton crop. There are good opportunities for purchase. Land is cheap and any man here who wants employment can get it at any time.

MARSHALL COUNTY.—The best opportunities that there are, perhaps, in any country, as the labor of women and children is almost as valuable as that of men in the cotton fields. Most of the farming is done on shares. The owner furnishes the land, plows, stock and feed for stock, all tools, wagons, house, and garden spot, receiving one-half of the crop. The laborer puts in his labor only and feeds himself and family, supplies being furnished by the proprietor and paid for when crop is gathered and sold. Garden, potato patch, and melon ground is furnished for laborer's family without rent or cost to them.

As to purchase while the purchaser is hiring out, many negroes are now getting homes for themselves in just this way, and any industrious family could soon have a home. I sold off land to some of my ex-slaves's children, who never left the place when freed, and they have almost finished paying for their land. They will get it paid for in four annual payments.

LOUISIANA.

(See table, p. 632.)

The State maintains an immigration department in connection with the bureau of agriculture. The commissioner of agriculture and immigration writes as follows (December 19, 1900), with regard to opportunities for immigrants at the present time:

First. It is my opinion that there is a greater opportunity for immigrants in our State at this time than has previously existed. The great opportunities are in the manufacturing lines and in farming operations.

Second. From foreign countries, Swedes, Germans, Scandinavians, and Hollanders are preferable. From our own country, farmers from the North and West are desirable.

Third. The foreign farmers, after they become familiar with the soil crops, make equally as good farmers as do the natives. It is through the new and special lines of farming to which they are adapted, more than it is with the native population.

Fourth. Our farmers, as a class, do not oppose the influx of foreigners if they are honest and industrious. On the contrary we welcome them.

Fifth. Efforts are being made through this department to encourage immigration by supplying literature and other information relating to the State's resources. In addition, there are many private corporations, land companies, and real estate agencies.

Very truly, yours,

J. G. LEE, Commissioner.

AGRICULTURAL DISTRIBUTION OF IMMIGRANTS.

The representative of one of the private corporations referred to writes as follows with regard to the methods employed and opportunities offered by his company in the northern part of the State:

Your favor of the 11th instant was received and contents noted carefully. In reply we beg to state that you will please find inclosed under separate cover, of this date, two of our latest pamphlets, which were prepared for the purpose of reaching parties living at a distance. This pamphlet explains fully the conditions of the country surrounding Shreveport, La., and the country along the west shore of the Mississippi River in Louisiana, consisting of the parishes of East Carroll, Madison, Tensas, and Concordia. We were successful in interesting a great many people from the Northwest in diversified farming in a small way around Shreveport; but during the past 2 years we have been giving our entire attention to the development of the country in the parishes of East Carroll, Madison, Tensas, and Concordia, on the west shore of the Mississippi River. This is virtually an undeveloped country, these parishes being practically without railway transportation, and about one-tenth of the land being in cultivation. There is as fine hard-wood timber on these lands as there is to be found in the United States. After the timber is removed they are particularly desirable for farming purposes, for the cultivation of fruits of all kinds, cotton, corn and rice. At this time we have our surveyors in the field and are having arrangements made to build a railroad from Lake Providence—the parish seat of East Carroll Parish—to Vidalia, La., the parish seat of Concordia. This road will run through the center of four parishes and will be the cause of development, in a short time, of this entire country. We control about 300,000 acres of these fine hard-wood and alluvial lands, and are making a specialty of interesting the investor and farmer in this section. We are very anxious to encourage immigration to this country, and nowhere in the South are there such opportunities as there are right here.

Very truly, yours,

—— —— REALTY CO., LTD.

In the southwestern part of the State there is, besides the usual cane, cotton, and corn raised, a considerable production of rice. It is interesting to note, in connection with an inquiry that is dealing with agriculture especially in relation to foreign immigration, that, while rice had been raised for many years in Louisiana in small patches for home consumption, the idea of raising it for market originated with a little band of German farmers who had settled in what is now the northern part of Acadia Parish.[1] This was in 1885. Irrigation was introduced in this district in 1890, to the great improvement of the rice industry.

A private land company operating in this district writes as follows with regard to foreign settlers, prices of land, etc.:

First. We have very few foreigners in southwest Louisiana, the oldest settlers being descendants of Acadians who were driven out of Nova Scotia. They are of French descent. The later arrivals are coming from all of the Northern and Western States, largely from Illinois, Michigan, Indiana, Iowa, Kansas, and Nebraska. We suppose that in the three or four parishes constituting what is known as southwest Louisiana 25,000 Northern and Western people have located during the past 10 or 12 years. With reference to our lists of land we will say, including our own individual lands, we have listed for sale about 1,000 acres. These lands are usually sold on terms of one-third cash, balance in 1 and 2 years. Rice lands located along the irrigating canals, where they are sure of water every year, have a range in price of from $20 to $50 per acre, according to location, nearness to churches, markets, schools, etc. Excellent cotton and corn lands may still be purchased at from $10 to $15 per acre. Twelve years ago these lands were worth from 50 cents to $1.25 an acre.

Yours, very truly, W. W. DUSON & BRO.

Another correspondent interested in the sale of land in this district writes:

We have a very thrifty and rapidly increasing colony of Dunkards between this town and Jennings along the Southern Pacific Railroad. They are engaged principally in raising rice, which is the best money crop for this locality. In nearly every case they own their own land; some of them are entirely out of debt, others owe a balance because they have only purchased recently and have had but one or two crops on their land, but the land is increasing rapidly in value since they purchased and is now worth two or three times what they paid for it.

We still have for sale something like 650,000 acres of land, and of course in such a large body the quality varies. We have good rice land, very fine pasture land, and we have other lands that are too low and wet for agricultural purposes until considerable sums have been expended for drainage, etc. We also have quite a large area that geologists pronounce very promising in the matter of petroleum, but we are not at present engaged in making any investigations or borings for oil.

Very truly, yours, —— ——, *Manager*.

Reports were received from representative farmers in seven parishes of the State, two in the southern portion and five in the northern (see table, p. 632). From one of the southern parishes it is reported that Germans, Italians, and Swedes are found as farmers; Italians as farm laborers (on large sugar plantations only[2]), and that there are good chances for foreign immigrants. From the other parish (Acadia, the rice district) few foreign farmers, no foreign laborers, and few openings for foreigners are reported.

In the northern parishes three correspondents state that there are good chances for foreign immigrants, and at the same time report no foreign immigrants already there except Germans in one parish, and no foreign laborers, while, curiously enough, the two correspondents who state that there are no chances for immigrants report foreign farmers (Germans, Irish, Swedes, and Mexicans) already established in their neighborhood.

---

[1] Crowley Signal, October 6, 1900.
[2] But see statement of Sr. Mastro-Valerio, page 495 of this report.

As in most of the Southern States, there is now more or less effort made to diversify farming, especially in the northern part. This will naturally create opportunities for European immigrant families with dairy work and fruit and vegetable farming.

OPPORTUNITIES FOR TENANCY AND OWNERSHIP.

(Reported by representative farmers.)

IBERIA PARISH.—The opportunities for renting are very good. The tenant may furnish his team and implements and receive half of the crop, or simply furnish his labor and receive one-third of the produce. A poor man who is willing to work can easily buy a small farm on payments of 1, 2, or 3 years, or he can rent the land at a moderate figure, say $2 or $3 an acre.

ACADIA PARISH.—There are good opportunities for renting if a tenant has means to furnish his teams and seed. Lands are on a basis of one-third cash, balance in 1 and 2 years.

WINN PARISH.—There are good opportunities for renting and purchase.

TENSAS PARISH.—There are plenty of opportunities to rent on easy terms and good opportunities to purchase. Land is comparatively cheap, but is rising.

RICHLAND PARISH.—Tenant farmers are what the community needs. The tenant gets one-half. The landlord furnishes stock, implements, etc.; or the tenant furnishes everything and gets three-fourths. There are good opportunities for purchase.

CLAIBORNE PARISH.—There is a first-class chance for renting on very good terms. As to purchasing while purchaser earns a living by hiring out, no better place can be found to do this very thing.

CADDO PARISH.—There are good opportunities for renting on almost any terms. Usually the tenant gets one-half the crop, the owner furnishing tools and farming implements. There are good opportunities for purchase.

TEXAS.

(See table, p. 633.)

The acting commissioner of agriculture wrote, in 1894:[1]

Texas desires immigrants who are sober, industrious, and worthy—who will make good citizens and add to the wealth and prosperity of the State. * * * Unskilled labor is needed in every pursuit in which labor performs the principal agent for developing the resources of the State. But to all of this a word of great caution should be impressed upon each immigrant. None should come into the State without some definite agreement with those who may need and desire their labor, for they can not get employment everywhere in so large an area and might suffer before an employer could be found.

As to present conditions, representative farmers were heard from in the Brazos River region, but in that region only. There was a general agreement among them (with one exception) that chances for foreign immigrants were good. No foreign farm laborers were reported in these counties, but foreign farmers were found in all but one—Germans, Swedes, Danes, Bohemians, Poles, and Italians. One correspondent, indeed, stated that negroes were preferred as laborers in the Brazos River bottoms, on account of their ability to withstand the malarial influences prevalent there, and another seems to think negro labor preferable, as more docile than white. "We do not want any strikers," he says, "and we find the whites are more apt to strike than the negroes."

Several railroads are interested in bringing settlers to Texas.

The land commissioner for the Southern Pacific and Houston and Texas Central writes:

The quantity of land at our disposal is approximately 4,000,000 acres. This land is distributed over 120 counties in the State of Texas, and is therefore adapted to the growth of corn, cotton, wheat, oats, sorghum, rice, and all manner of fruits, vegetables, and melons indigenous to this climate. We have no special preference for purchasers so long as they have sufficient means to make a part payment on the land and work the same after they have bought it. We of course prefer the actual settler to any other class of purchasers.

We reach foreign immigrants through our European agent, who has offices at Hamburg, Antwerp, Rotterdam, London, and Liverpool. We have never established any colonies of foreigners in this State, but there are colonies which have been established in years past which have been remarkably successful, notably the German colonists in the vicinity of New Braunfels and a Scandinavian colony in Travis and Williamson counties. There is a very large German population scattered over the country between Houston and San Antonio, the majority of whom are engaged in agricultural pursuits and are all in a prosperous condition.

[1] Report Immigration Investigating Commission, p. 150.

AGRICULTURAL DISTRIBUTION OF IMMIGRANTS.   573

We maintain agents in the counties in Texas where the lands are upon the market for sale, and advertise throughout the United States and Europe, setting forth the advantages of Texas as an agricultural and grazing country. Our prices range all the way from $2 to $7 per acre, according to the character of the soil, proximity to railroad transportation, water facilities, etc. Our terms on grazing and agricultural lands are one-fifth cash, balance in four equal annual payments at 6 per cent interest per annum deferred payments secured by a lien upon the land.
Yours, truly,
C. C. GIBBS,
Land Commissioner.

The land and tax commissioner of the Gulf, Colorado and Santa Fe writes:

This company having disposed of nearly all their lands are not maintaining agents for the purpose of locating immigrants except what is being done by our general passenger department and in a general way by advising people as to the inducements in this great State for settlers.
Yours, truly,
F. M. GILBOUGH.

The International and Great Northern, the Texas and Pacific, and the Missouri Pacific railways jointly maintain a land and immigration department, and are bringing to the State people of all nationalities, but reach only those who have located somewhere in the United States.

Texas was one of the objective points of the earlier Bohemian immigration, and many of this nationality are now found there. The first settlements here were made in 1855. This is the only Southern State where Bohemian settlers are engaged in agriculture to any appreciable extent. Bohemians are found in the following towns and villages of the State: Ammansville, Antioch, Bartons Creek, Bluff, Bryan, Caldwell, Cistern, Corn Hill, Dubina, Ellinger, Fayetteville, Frelsburg, Freustat, Granger, Halletsville, Industry, Moulton, Plums, Praha, Sealy, Sedan, Shiner, St. John, Schulenburg, St. Mary, Settlement, Sweet Home, Taylor, Nada, Waller, Wallis, Warrenton, Weimar, West, Yoakum, Yneton, and Zee Wee. There are said to be about 57,000 Bohemians in the State, all told.

An account of the Italian settlers in the State will be found on page 500 of this report.

These Italians are engaged in rice culture, in cotton planting, in grape culture, and especially in truck farming near large cities. There is a colony at Bryan, Brazos County, one near Dickinson, and another near Gunnison.

OPPORTUNITIES FOR TENANCY AND OWNERSHIP.

(Reported by representative farmers.)

BRAZORIA COUNTY.—There are good openings for tenants and good opportunities for purchase on payments while earning a living hiring out. The writer started in this way and there are many others.

HARRIS COUNTY.—There are good opportunities for renting, but northern Texas is more desirable. As to purchase on time while hiring out, this is being done here every year. Judgment and industry coupled with economy will succeed here.

BRAZOS COUNTY.—There is plenty of opportunity for tenant farming on shares. The owner furnishes team, tools, etc., and feed for team and receives one-half the product. The landowner will furnish supplies to the tenant to be paid back when the crop is made. There are good opportunities for purchase for an economical, sober, and industrious man. Plenty of them come here without a penny and some of them now own their own little homes.

LIMESTONE COUNTY.—There is a good portion of land worked by tenant farmers. Team and tools are furnished for half the crop, or one-third grain and one-fourth cotton if tenant furnishes team and tools. Opportunities for purchase are good. Lands are reasonable in price and usually can be had on easy terms.

HOOD COUNTY.—There are good opportunities for renting for from one-third to one-fourth of the crop and fine opportunities for purchase.

ARKANSAS.

(See table p. 634.)

In 1894 the governor of the State wrote with regard to immigration and the natural resources of the State as follows:[1]

All portions of our State desire home-seeking immigration. * * * We produce everything in the agricultural line which is produced in this zone. * * * We prefer American, German, and English immigrants (farmers), but welcome all desirable immigrants.

With regard to present conditions and needs, the commissioner of mines, manufactures, and agriculture writes, under date of December 22, 1900:

First. In my judgment there have never been offered opportunities in this State to immigrants equal to those offered at present. The steady increase in the avenues of labor furnish thousands of men

---

[1] Report Immigration Investigating Commission, p. 127.

574   THE INDUSTRIAL COMMISSION:—IMMIGRATION.

employment who were a few years ago entirely cut off from such advantages. These advantages have come principally through the vast increase in mining, manufacturing, and improved methods of agriculture. Not until the last few years have our people interested themselves in cotton mills, while now we have several in operation, and a large number in course of construction. The same is true in our mining districts. The mines that were lying idle a few years ago, principally from a lack of proper railroad facilities, are now in active operation. Cotton pickers have for many years been in demand in Arkansas, but it has only been within the past few years that apple and berry pickers are in the greatest demand during that season of the year. There is still another element, which is especially to the advantage of the permanent homeseeker, and that is the fact that our heretofore unsettled portions of the country are being rapidly taken up, and a man now that wishes to take advantage of the United States homestead law and enter a tract of land is not compelled to isolate himself from all advantages of schools and churches, but may enter the land within a neighborhood already started. We still have about 5,000,000 acres of Government lands subject to entry
 Second. It is my opinion that as a rule the German people are the most effective farmers in this State. However, I have taken notice of the fact that Northern stockmen outgeneral our people in realizing the great advantages offered here for stock raising. Of the gardeners and truck farmers, the German people far surpass all other classes of farmers.
 Third. Their success in my opinion is due to their more intense methods of cultivation. They seem to appreciate what our people have had lying at their door for years, and have never realized the greatness of the opportunities offered. As a general rule, a first-class German farmer will make more truck on 5 acres of good ground than an ordinary American farmer will make on 20 acres. This, however, is being rapidly overcome by the farmers organizing and informing themselves upon questions pertaining to diversified farming. Too many of our American, or I may say in this State, Arkansas farmers, have been taught to depend too much on cotton for everything; but they are fast getting over this idea, and grain, stock, fruits of most all kinds, vegetables, both farm and garden, are now grown and shipped in large quantities.
 Fourth. Our farmers favor the influx of foreigners into this State. We claim that no State in the Union will meet the foreigner with a warmer welcome than the State of Arkansas.
 Fifth. We have several organizations in this State, organized for the express purpose of inviting immigration to our State. Among these may be classed this department of the State. We keep a large amount of immigration literature on hand and at all times take pleasure in answering all inquiries from parties seeking to know more of the advantages this State offers immigrants. There are also other organizations that may be addressed for like information.
 Sixth. Many agricultural colonies have organized in this State, especially of the German race, as this is a great grape and truck farming place. In Johnson County alone there are some four or five colonies. In Prairie, Lonoke, Arkansas, and White counties there are numbers of colonies of Northern people located, and in Drew County there are also colonies of Northern people engaged principally in the raising of stock.
 Very truly, yours, FRANK HILL.

Near Searcy, White County, a tract of 24,000 acres was settled by 20 Hungarian families. The land was sold by the Iron Mountain Railroad. The colony failed, however, and removed to Alabama.
 In Cleburne and Van Buren counties, in the neighborhood of Searcy, efforts are being made to bring settlers to the neighborhood. In these counties alone there are said to be more than 300,000 acres of Government and State lands, subject to homestead and donation, at a cost only of Government and State fees and locating the lands. For a quarter section, Government fees are $14, State fees are $10. These are timber lands, and are situated in the fruit belt of the State.
 Italians were colonized at Sunnyside, in the southeastern part of the State, but were unsuccessful for reasons that were out of their control. Some of the colonists removed to Tontitown, near Springdale, where they now are.[1]
 Returns from representative farmers were too few in number to afford information as to general conditions. Three of the four heard from, however, agree with the commissioner that there are opportunities for immigrants. Few foreigners are noted either as farmers or laborers. In Arkansas County Germans and Swedes are mentioned and a colony of Slovaks.
 Another colony of Slovaks was established near Little Rock, in a settlement called Slovaktown, but it was not successful. The people were disappointed, colonization ceased, and only about 60 families remained.

OPPORTUNITIES FOR TENANCY AND OWNERSHIP.

(Reported by representative farmers.)

OUACHITA COUNTY.—Good opportunities to rent on halves, thirds, or fourths. Very good chances for a poor man with energy to establish himself in independent farming.
 ARKANSAS COUNTY.—There are good opportunities for renting. Farms can be had at from 50 cents to $1 per acre. A man can sometimes get land where the owner furnishes everything. Opportunities could not be better anywhere for a poor man to get a home on long payments or for work. Land sells for from $5 to $10 an acre for farming land; timber land is cheaper.
 CLEBURNE COUNTY.—In renting the tenant gets two-thirds of the corn, three-fourths of the cotton, one-half of the oats and peas. As to purchase, this is a timber country. A man can buy land on time here and find plenty of work to do.
 BENTON COUNTY.—(1) There are good opportunities for renting. Tenants can either rent land for one-third of the crop and furnish everything, or work on halves

---

[1] Page 505 of this report.

AGRICULTURAL DISTRIBUTION OF IMMIGRANTS. 575

with everything furnished. There are fine opportunities for purchase. A man who is of any account can start flat-footed and in 3 or 4 years own his farm. (2) Very poor opportunities for renting. Everyone owns a small farm and does the work himself. There are no chances for a poor man to purchase. A man has no business here unless he has a few thousand dollars to start with.

WESTERN STATES.

GENERAL.

A representative of the Southern Pacific Company writes as follows with regard to the general question of the distribution of foreign immigrants on the Pacific coast:

Permit me to say that our country is much too far from the Atlantic seaboard to attract many European immigrants. Cost and time constitute obstacles to the immediate receipt of immigrants from Europe. Besides, our country is not well known to the common people of Europe; hence people must reside in the United States some time before they become apprised of the desirability of the territory lying west of the Rocky Mountains as a place of residence. Common labor is in very great demand in the Pacific States and Territories in mining, agriculture, horticulture, in lumber enterprises, in commerce, in railroading, and in fact in all industrial and commercial pursuits. If immigrants proceed immediately to the Pacific coast, it is because of some special reason, some friend or some relative who resides there having induced that course, and only the more thrifty and those in better circumstances will ever attempt the trip.

What we do receive, therefore, is of a special class. We have made no special appeal to foreign immigrants, and will not do so because, as a rule, the foreign immigrant is simply capable of common labor, and nearly all the labor of our country is skilled. Horticulture, mining, railroading, and the lumber business are in a measure skilled occupations.

We have projected no colonies upon railroad lands in the Western States because in a very large measure the lands were unsuitable for colonization. The lands were granted in alternate sections, not in solid bodies. Nearly all of the better agricultural land belonging to the companies I represent was disposed of some time ago.

Our country offers inducements to intelligent people, and we are receiving accessions of population, but largely of the class of foreigners who have resided in the country some years, or their children who were born here, or native Americans. We prefer the latter class, and our country, by reason of its remoteness, is receiving perhaps the best class of immigration of any portion of the United States.

I can furnish you no statistics relating to numbers.

Yours, very truly, WILLIAM H. MILLS.

The Northern Pacific Railway has land to dispose of and has done something in the way of attracting settlers, but not especially among foreigners. The land commissioner writes as follows:

The land grant of this company undisposed of amounts to about 20,000,000 acres, but a very large portion of it is unsurveyed and in mountainous districts, and is consequently not suitable for settlement. The lands acquired by this company in eastern North Dakota and Minnesota were chiefly suitable for agriculture, but are all disposed of and are now in the hands of settlers and land companies. The bulk of the lands owned by this company now, aside from lands valuable for their timber, are mostly only suitable for grazing except limited areas in the States of Washington and Montana, which can be utilized for agricultural purposes by irrigation. The cost, however, of putting water upon them is more than the present value of the lands would warrant. This company has an emigration department, but the duties of the head of that department have been mostly confined to furnishing information and advertising the territory tributary to our road. We have done no work among foreign immigrants, chiefly for the reason that we have no lands of suitable character in sufficient quantities to warrant the expenditure.

Yours, truly, WM. H. PHIPPS, Land Commissioner.

The general emigration agent writes in further detail as follows:

This company, during recent years at any rate, has not done any work at all among foreigners abroad, except to send publications in a few cases where persons in Europe or other parts of the world have written requesting the same. We have not, however, had any agents in other countries working up emigration, nor have we any foreign agents especially at work among foreigners in this country. There are colonies of different nationalities at various points along our line, and their fellow-countrymen are joining them all the time. It is also true that persons who have come over from the old country frequently send back for other members of their family to come over to this country to them.

The nearest we have come to the kind of work that I take it you have in mind is our colonizing of Hollanders in the Gallatin Valley in Montana and the Yakima Valley in Washington, but even here our labors have been confined principally to those who were already located in other States, principally Michigan, Iowa, and South Dakota. Some have gone from the cities, but the most part were already engaged in farming.

Yours, truly, C. W. MOTT, General Emigration Agent.

MONTANA.

(See table, p. 635.)

The secretary of the State arid land grant commission writes as follows with regard to opportunities for immigration in the State:

Until there is more done in the way of building irrigation ditches, Montana can not invite immigration. There are no efforts being made to attract the immigrant for the reason that all the land capable of inexpensive irrigation has been taken. With Government aid in the storage of water and construction of the main canals from 8 to 10 million acres of land could be reclaimed, when an immigration bureau would be useful. The majority of the farmers in Montana are Americans, but the Germans and Scandinavians would be encouraged to come when we have irrigated lands to offer them.

Truly, yours, D. A. COBY, Secretary.

Reports from representative farmers show (see table, p. 635) that even now there are thought to be openings for non-English-speaking immigrants. In 6 out of 14 counties heard from there are said to be such openings; in 9 of the 14 foreign farmers are said to have already established themselves, and in 11 counties foreign farm laborers are found. The report of persons naturalized in the State in 1898[1] gives some idea of the different nationalities now there. The number and nationality of persons naturalized was as follows:

Persons born in—		Persons born in—	
Ireland	572	Switzerland	29
Austria	354	Denmark	24
Canada	352	France	22
England	239	Russia	22
Sweden	194	Wales	21
Germany	162	Belgium	9
Italy	127	Bohemia	3
Norway	119	All other	54
Finland	112		
Scotland	84	Total	2,499

OPPORTUNITIES FOR TENANCY AND OWNERSHIP.

(Reported by representative farmers.)

DAWSON COUNTY.—No farming is done here.

PARKER COUNTY.—Opportunities for renting are fair. Usually tenant receives one-half the crop, landlord furnishing everything. Land can be purchased on 5 to 10 years' time.

SWEET GRASS COUNTY.—There is a good chance to establish oneself in independent farming. Government land may be taken up as a homestead.

MEAGHER COUNTY.—Opportunities for renting are not numerous, and the chances for a poor man to establish himself are not good.

FERGUS COUNTY.—There are good chances for renting on all kinds of terms, cash or on shares. Opportunities for purchase are not good in this section.

CASCADE COUNTY.—No renting is done in this county. There are good chances for purchase while the purchaser earns his living by hiring out. Industrious, energetic young men are doing it all the time here.

TETON COUNTY.—There are always opportunities to lease farms. There would be numerous opportunities for a man to purchase land while hiring out, but probably a better plan would be to take up a homestead on Government land and work for wages upon which to improve it. There is plenty of good Government land open for sale here yet.

CHOTEAU COUNTY.—There are very few renters, or farms for rent. There are the best opportunities in the United States, and that is the best in the world, for a poor man to establish himself in independent farming.

MADISON COUNTY.—A man may become a tenant farmer on almost any terms he may want if he is a good man. There are fairly good opportunities for purchase.

JEFFERSON COUNTY.—There are quite good opportunities to rent either for a cash rent or on shares, everything furnished except seed; and there are good opportunities for purchase, especially by a part payment.

SILVERBOW COUNTY.—There are good opportunities for renting; terms, one-half of the produce; and also good opportunities for purchase.

GRANITE COUNTY.—There are not very good opportunities for renting, and none for purchase on easy terms.

MISSOULA COUNTY.—There are good opportunities for renting and purchase.

FLATHEAD COUNTY.—Little farming done here.

COLORADO.

(See table, p. 637.)

The immigration commissioner wrote in 1894 that Colorado then desired first-class immigrants in nearly every portion of the State. Agricultural and horticultural resources needed development, and for horticulture and agriculture Germans and Swedes were preferred.

With regard to present conditions the secretary of the Denver Chamber of Commerce writes as follows:

First. There are better opportunities in Colorado for immigrants than ever before. Farm laborers, ranch hands, miners, smelters, and common laborers are always in demand.

Second. As general farmers or farm laborers Germans or those of German extraction are more effective. For truck gardening in the vicinity of cities Italians seem to take the lead.

Third. Foreign farmers, by reason of their old-country habits of thrift and economy, and by reason of their being accustomed to more intensive methods of cultivation, succeed in many cases where native-born agriculturists fail.

---

[1] Seventh annual report of State bureau of agriculture, labor, and industry, p. 434.

AGRICULTURAL DISTRIBUTION OF IMMIGRANTS.

Fourth. Farmers as a class do not oppose the influx of foreigners into this State.
Fifth. Railways and corporations engaged in the production of beet sugar are making efforts to attract immigrants to various portions of this State.
Sixth. I know of no agricultural colonies or settlements of foreigners in Colorado.
Yours, respectfully,

ARTHUR WILLIAMS, *Secretary.*

The representative of one important beet-sugar company writes as follows with regard to the opportunities open to foreign immigrants in this industry and to inducements offered:

It seems that a solution of the beet-sugar industry in the United States is dependent upon a class of foreign laborers which are at this time only too scarce. Our company is using every endeavor to encourage such immigrants to come here, either from abroad or from some other part of the United States.

This location is a very fortunate one, in that we are, because of our isolated position, enabled to pay such high prices for beets that are grown here. This great valley is surrounded by a still greater mining region which must be supplied with farm products and with sugar, for all of which we receive the very highest prices. Our plans change with our needs, and our procedure of to-day may change for to-morrow, even as the one of to-day is vastly different from those of a few weeks past.

We have been offering our houses, land, and water, free of rent, to people who would grow beets for us. This land, however, will soon be gone, yet we have not reached the capacity of our large factory, and for the coming year we may be in a position to make offers similar to that which we made this spring, but we can not say to-day that we will. Therefore we can only outline in a general way what we can and will do for immigrants.

We have not made an organized effort to bring foreigners to this place.

It would seem to us that in order to formulate and carry out successfully some plan of this sort, it would be necessary for us to purchase a large body of land and hold intact until some definite movement be made to bring here as a whole a great colony. In this respect we would have to determine definitely whence these people would come, what their wishes would be, and their financial ability.

Last year Mr. ———— ————, who was then secretary of this company, went to Germany, his old home, and, so it is understood, attempted to secure a colony. None, however, was brought to this country, and as he has become heavily interested in another plant in this State, and as we have not heard of the German colony coming, the inference is that he did not succeed. Such a plan is far-reaching and hard to work out.

This company started in a small way this year by purchasing about 2,000 acres of the best land in this country and is offering it as per the inclosed circular letter. In a very few days we were flooded with applications from people without means, and it became necessary for us to issue our circular letter of April 6 and to adhere to its terms.

The only people that we have secured are those from Utah and various parts of Colorado and her border States.

We would think that a good plan would be to go into sugar-beet districts of Germany and try to secure settlers.

From the writer's experience of a few months in the business, it is very apparent that the people who grow beets must be taken care of from the very first, and this paternalism is, in all probability, more necessary with foreigners than with our people.

One thing to be considered is that of the wishes of these people relative to the purchase of homes. Abroad they are tenants and the descendants of tenants.

It is observed that after people acquire a small competence growing beets, they leave the arduous work for something lighter, and unless the company owns the land, thereby being able to put upon it other people who must come and start in life, it finds itself without a supply of beets for its factory, and without ground upon which to place people who are willing to grow this supply.

It is not to be assumed that it is our desire that these people should always remain our tenants, for, after being on our land a while, we would expect that they would be free and independent to buy some of the cheap land which is offered for sale, and thereby own their own homes. That is desirable for the general good of the community, and there are splendid opportunities for immigrants in this manner to acquire homes for themselves in a few years. The action of our company would be to bridge over for these people that period of necessity in which they must live, and in which they will doubtless be able to accumulate a little money, and eventually become landowners themselves. We would not be afraid of those few, for, with a colony started, others from the same locality in the old country would be coming continually, and filling the places of the first arrivals who might go upon their own holdings.

The above letter, it will be noted, brings into view very clearly the following points of especial interest with regard to the foreigner in sugar-beet culture: First, the evident necessity of more or less control by the factory of individual growers, to which foreigners are more likely to submit kindly than American farmers; second, the tendency of growers to leave this industry as soon as they have earned a little money at it; third, the consequent dependence by the factory upon a class of tenant laborers, who, like the newly arrived foreign immigrants, are without much money and are making a start in life.

The representative of another company writes that they have not tried to get foreign immigrants as settlers, but have endeavored to induce Eastern farmers to settle on their land and have succeeded fairly well. At least enough families were secured to care for the beets during the present season, and no encouragement could be given to intending settlers until the coming year.

Still another beet-sugar concern heard from reports that, as their factory is located in a well-settled district, it is not their intention to do any colonizing. The representative of the company says:

The only labor we have made any effort to secure thus far has been Russian families who are more or less familiar with beet culture, whom we expect to draw from the western portion of Nebraska in limited numbers.

These families on their arrival here contract with the growers in various localities for doing the hand work on the beet crop. Many of them engage at a stipulated price per acre to do this work, while others hire by the day.

As our company is not planting any considerable acreage of its own, we are only able to bring in this labor to assist the growers in the handling of their crop.

Not directly for the purpose of colonizing foreigners in the rural districts, but indirectly doing so, are the land colonies of the Salvation Army, in Amity, Prowers County, Colo., and Monterey County, Cal. These colonies were founded to make homes for "the worthy poor of our great cities," according to the circular issued by the army, and as many foreigners fall within that class, the colonies will naturally be of considerable assistance to them.

The colony at Amity is established on 1,938 acres of irrigated land, not far from a large beet-sugar factory, which contracts to purchase from the colonists at remunerative prices all the sugar beets they can grow. About 160 colonists are now settled here.

Most of the colonists understand farming. Those who do not are skilled artisans. Schoolhouses, a large orphanage, and a "Workingmen's Sanitarium" are built, or about to be. The colonists are assisted with loans, etc., to purchase implements, stock, etc., and are given time to pay for their land. The enterprise is supported by interest-bearing bonds secured by mortgage on the lands.

Reports from representative farmers in this State are few in numbers (see table, p. 637), but represent the different parts of the State. They show the presence of the sugar-beet industry, and abundant opportunity for married men and their wives and children on the farms. Foreign farmers and farm laborers are noted in all of the counties but 1, and in 3 Swedes or Germans are said to be preferred as laborers.[1] In 3 there are said to be opportunities for immigrants who do not speak English.

OPPORTUNITIES FOR TENANCY AND OWNERSHIP

(Reported by representative farmers.)

PROWERS COUNTY.—Farms may be rented on shares. Tenant pays half crop if landlord furnishes seed; one-third of crop if he furnishes seed himself.

OTERO COUNTY.—There are good opportunities for renting. Farms are usually rented on shares. Alfalfa crop, one-half goes to owner; other crops, one-third to owner. As to purchasing land while hiring out, any man has a chance. I started in that way myself.

ARAPAHOE COUNTY.—There are many good opportunities for tenants if they are good, industrious people. They get one-third to one-half of the crop. The opportunity for purchase while hiring out is good. I got my start in that way.

JEFFERSON COUNTY.—Opportunities for renting are good for practical farmers. The tenant gets one-half the crop with seed furnished, or two-thirds of the crop if he furnishes the seed himself. Good opportunities for purchase for an energetic, practical man; none for drones.

LARIMER COUNTY.—Good opportunities for tenants who are able to furnish their own tools. Terms are usually a share of the crops as rent, one-half to two-thirds. There are reasonably good opportunities for purchase.

ARIZONA.

(See table, p. 638.)

Representative farmers in only 3 counties reported as to agricultural conditions—Cochise, Maricopa, and Yuma. Farming in the 2 latter counties is done with the aid of irrigation. Maricopa County contains the Salt River Valley, where some 200,000 acres are now under cultivation, reclaimed from the desert by means of irrigation. The settlement is about 10 years old. Labor is in great demand, especially in hay and fruit harvest.

In Maricopa County are said to be many Scandinavian farmers, some quite wealthy. In Yuma are a few German farmers. In none of the 3 counties are European farm laborers spoken of, but 2 of the 4 farmers reporting thought there were good openings for immigrants.

Under the desert-land act, land may be entered for $1.25 an acre by citizens of the United States, who also are or intend to become citizens of the State or Territory in which land is entered, on condition that they intend to reclaim the tract of land applied for by conducting water thereon.

---

[1] Groups of Italian truck farmers are found near Denver and Pueblo. See p. — of this report.

AGRICULTURAL DISTRIBUTION OF IMMIGRANTS. 579

OPPORTUNITIES FOR TENANCY AND OWNERSHIP.

(Reported by representative farmers.)

COCHISE COUNTY.—Very good opportunities for a few to rent for a money rent or on shares. If he is a practical farmer, a poor man would probably do well in trying to purchase.

MARICOPA COUNTY.—There are plenty of good opportunities for renting, but some capital is needed, and there are good opportunities for purchase. A good many Scandinavians and Mexicans have bought lands. Other nationalities are fairly well represented. (2) There are good opportunities for renting and good land can be had at all times. This is an irrigated country. Land with water is worth $20 an acre.

YUMA COUNTY.—There is good opportunity for renting. There is plenty of vacant land, with water. As to purchase, there are good chances. Land is worth about $25 an acre, with a water right.

UTAH.

(See table, p. 639.)

Farming in this State is carried on mostly on small farms, worked by the owners and their families. Few laborers are hired. Many of these small farmers are of foreign birth—English, German, Scandinavian, Swiss, and Dutch; and there are also some farm laborers of these nationalities. Italian truck farmers are found near Salt Lake City.[1]

The representative farmers heard from seem to be pretty well agreed that there is little or no opportunity for foreign immigrants who do not speak English.

OPPORTUNITIES FOR TENANCY AND OWNERSHIP.

(Reported by representative farmers.)

WASHINGTON COUNTY.—There is but little, if any, opportunity for renting in this county and few opportunities for purchase on easy terms. (2) Chances for renting are limited. There is a fair opportunity for starting in independent farming for intelligent, active workers by locating on good upland.

GARFIELD COUNTY.—There are opportunities to rent on a variety of terms and good chances for starting independent farming.

WAYNE COUNTY.—Farms are rented on shares from year to year, rarely for any lengthened time.

SEVIER COUNTY.—There are no opportunities for renting here, but the chances for starting independent farming are fairly good.

SANPETE COUNTY.—There are no opportunities for renting and not very good chances for setting up in independent farming. A man would have better facilities in Oregon or Idaho. Some have gone to Idaho from here and others would go if they could sell for any reasonable figure.

MILLARD COUNTY.—There is very little chance to rent. Terms, on shares. There is little opportunity for starting in independent farming.

JUAB COUNTY.—There would be a few opportunities to rent. Each man usually does his own work. There would be no opportunity for starting in independent farming for a man without money.

CARBON COUNTY.—The chances for a poor man to establish himself in independent farming are good.

SALT LAKE COUNTY.—There are very few opportunities for renting in Salt Lake County, as many of our own children have to go to Idaho and Wyoming and other places.

WEBER COUNTY.—There are few opportunities for renting, and terms are about one-half the produce, with seed and team furnished. There are very good opportunities for purchase, however, on easy terms.

BOXELDER COUNTY.—Little opportunity for strangers to rent farms. If tenant furnishes team, tools, and seed he gets two-thirds of the crop. If all is furnished he gets one-third of the crop. The chances for an immigrant to establish himself in independent farming are not very encouraging. Old residents take all the opportunities.

WASHINGTON.

(See table, p. 641.)

The wonderful development of this State has been a work shared in by many foreign settlers. Reports from representative farmers on both sides of the Cascade Mountains show foreign farmers and farm laborers in every county heard from.

---

[1] See p. 503 of this report.

580   THE INDUSTRIAL COMMISSION:—IMMIGRATION.

These are English, Irish, Scotch, Germans, Scandinavians, Finns, Russians, Italians, and French. The Russians are German-Russians, from the Valley of the Volga mainly. Many of these people are to be found in the Northwest. In one county heard from in this State German-Russians make up 25 to 30 per cent of the population. All of the farmers but one say that there are chances for newly arrived immigrants. Labor is scarce in the State and wages high. Mills and camps draw labor from the farms, so that farm labor is always in great demand.

The State is as yet sparsely settled. Population density is as yet only 7.7 to the square mile, and there is Government land to be had.

OPPORTUNITIES FOR TENANCY AND OWNERSHIP.

(Reported by representative farmers.)

KLICKITAT COUNTY.—Grain farms, giving one-third of grain at the thrasher, or one-half when owner furnishes seed and team. Good opportunities to purchase on payments while hiring out. Several have done so. Can take up land and chop and sell cord wood for a start.

WALLAWALLA COUNTY.—Good opportunities to rent, giving one-third of the crop. Good for purchase for man of energy and sound judgment.

ADAMS COUNTY.—Few opportunities for renting. Country is new and persons with means sufficient to own tenant's outfit can do better by taking up new lands for themselves. Easy to purchase. This section of the country has been settled under more adverse conditions than exist to-day.

SPOKANE COUNTY.—Good opportunities for either crop or cash rental. A man who wants to work and farm can do so if he will work at whatever comes up, such as cutting wood.

DOUGLAS COUNTY.—Can rent land for one-third crop, tenant furnishing everything; owner furnishing teams and seed, one-half crop. Land is cheap, $5 to $8 an acre. Can be purchased while purchaser is hiring out if he is energetic.

KITTITAS COUNTY.—Not very good opportunities for renting. Writer knows of no case where a man has purchased a farm while hiring out.

CLARKE COUNTY.—Fairly good for tenancy at one-half crop. Fair for purchase.

THURSTON COUNTY.—What are called "brush ranches" (partly cleared) can be had for a trifle over cost of taxes and repairs. Good farms on halves or at 3 to 5 per cent of value. As to purchase on easy terms, a man of energy and good sense, with a thrifty family, will soon own a good home clear.

OREGON.

(See table, p. 643.)

Oregon is less densely populated than Washington and is growing less rapidly; but representative farmers report good chances for immigrants. Many foreign farmers are settled in the State. From one neighborhood it is reported that about two-thirds of the farmers are Germans. This people seems to predominate; but there are also Scandinavians, Swiss, Dutch, English, Scotch, and Irish. Many of these, now independent farmers, started as very poor men.[1] There are also many foreign farm laborers, although one farmer states that most foreigners in his neighborhood are independent farmers. It is natural to suppose, where land is so cheap, that the foreign immigrant will try rather to work land of his own than hire out, or will hire out only until he has saved enough money to buy land.

OPPORTUNITIES FOR TENANCY AND OWNERSHIP.

(Reported by representative farmers.)

DOUGLAS COUNTY.—Land can be rented for a grain or cash rent. Grain rent, one-third of the product; cash, about $2.50 an acre. There are very favorable opportunities for purchase. A man can find a piece of vacant land and work out enough to make a living while improving and getting started with stock.

MARION COUNTY.—(1) There are good opportunities for renting. Tenant gives one-third of the grain received in the sack, he furnishing all of the seed and doing all of the work. Opportunities are not good for anyone paying for a farm unless he can make a payment of at least one-third down. (2) There are many farms to let. The tenant furnishes seed and team, giving one-third of the crop in bushel or hay in stack or barn, and gets house and garden free. There are many farms for sale on time payments, but one-fourth or one-third must be paid down. The purchaser

---

[1] See note 5, table.

AGRICULTURAL DISTRIBUTION OF IMMIGRANTS.   581

can not depend on hiring out. In fruit neighborhoods a few men can get work with teams.

CLACKAMAS COUNTY.—In renting, if the tenant furnishes team and seed he gives one-third of the crop for rent; if the landlord furnishes everything the tenant pays one-half of the crop or its estimated cash value. As to purchasing land while hiring out, a great many do that. I did myself to begin with. I now have 300 acres adjoining the city of Portland.

YAMHILL COUNTY.—There are not many chances for renting at present. Well-known and good tenants can always get farms to rent at one-third of the crop in field or delivered. Any man of steady, decent habits who can and will work and knows how can always get a start as an independent farmer, as there is much cheap land awaiting improvement. If prices of crops were right, the owners would give a man a show to live. He ought not to come, however, without some ready money.

TILLAMOOK COUNTY.—There are good opportunities to become a tenant farmer at one-third of the crops as rent. As to purchasing land on payments while hiring out, this has not been done here; but I see no reason why a man endeavoring to do this would not have every opportunity now, as farm lands are for sale on time payments.

WASHINGTON COUNTY.—The supply of tenant farmers is small. When grain farming is practiced the owner receives one-third of the grain. Tenants on dairy farms receive one-half of the product and one-half of the increase in stock, the owner furnishing the cows and half of the feed. As to success in establishing one's self in independent farming, it all depends on management, as improved land within 20 miles of Portland is valued at from $30 to $50 an acre.

CALIFORNIA.

(See table, p. 645.)

Representative farmers from 4 southern and 5 northern counties speak of foreign farmers as found in all. There are, as everywhere, Germans and Swedes. There are also English, Scotch, Swiss, and Danes. Mexicans are mentioned in 1 southern county. Portuguese are found in 2 northern counties. In Alameda County (in which Alameda and Oakland are situated) the foreign farmers are mostly Portuguese. There are said to be 35,000 of them in the county. All are independent farmers and fruit growers.

Italians are noted in Santa Barbara County (southern) and Sonoma County (northern). It is said of the Italians in the former location that they select cheap lands on the canyons and foothills. In preceding pages of this report[1] will be found a full description of the wine-making colony of Italians in Sonoma County and an account of Italian agriculture in the State in general.

Farmers in the southern part of the State (see table, p. —) are evenly divided as to chances for immigrants; 2 think there are few or none, 2 think the chances good. Farmers in the northern counties, however, are almost unanimous in claiming that there is at present no room for immigrants.

Some interesting data from the Twelfth Census have been recently presented by advocates of irrigation that may indicate why immigrants are wanted in the south rather more than in the north. It was shown[2] from the census figures that while the State as a whole had increased 22.7 per cent during the last ten years, the thirteen coast counties had gained 25 per cent, the Sacramento Valley 4 per cent, the San Joaquin Valley 25¼ per cent, the mountain districts 9 per cent, and the southern counties 47 per cent. The claim is made that agricultural development is at a standstill except in irrigated regions. The growth of the coast counties, such as it is, is attributed to the growth of cities. The Sacramento Valley, a large farming region, shows only 9 per cent increase, and the increase of the San Joaquin Valley, a fine agricultural region, is unsatisfactorily small. The mountain counties are largely mining and pastoral, which fact accounts for their slow growth. The only high rate of increase is in the seven southern counties, and in the four well-irrigated counties of Los Angeles, Orange, San Bernardino, and Riverside the gain is 67½ per cent.

On irrigated lands, in fruit farming and other sorts of farming, there would evidently be an opening for thrifty foreign farmers and laborers.

The Salvation Army has started a colony at Romie, Monterey County, in the valley of the Salinas, where they own 519 acres of land and have settled 70 colonists. For an account of their plans and methods and the connection of their colonization scheme with foreign immigrants see under "Colorado" in this report. This colony, like the one in Colorado, is situated in the neighborhood of a large sugar-beet factory. The land is irrigated. About $30,000 has already been expended on improvements here.

---

[1] Page 500 following.
[2] Imperial Farmer, Los Angeles, Cal., Vol. I, No. 4, p. 3.

OPPORTUNITIES FOR TENANCY AND OWNERSHIP.

(Reported by representative farmers.)

SAN DIEGO COUNTY.—There are ranches for rent, but a man must understand the fruit business in order to succeed. Managers of ranches get $40 a month. There is plenty of opportunity to purchase land on easy terms and payments.

RIVERSIDE COUNTY.—Many men now own valuable property who commenced with nothing a few years ago, by saving wages, paying on installments, and improving gradually while yet earning wages.

SAN BERNARDINO COUNTY.—Not very good opportunities for renting. Poor men of thrifty and industrious habits can establish themselves in independent farming.

VENTURA COUNTY.—(1) Opportunities for renting and purchase are very poor. (2) Opportunities for renting are not good, but opportunities for purchase are good.

SANTA BARBARA COUNTY.—Very few tenants. Farms are nearly all managed by the owners, whether the farms are large or small. As regards purchase, occasionally a small place can be found at a reasonable price, but all the best land is held at such a high figure that a man can not make the interest by daily labor on the farm.

STANISLAUS COUNTY.—Anyone knowing how to raise sweet potatoes or such crops can rent land with water, giving as rent one-fifth to one-seventh of the crop. Wheat tenants give one-third of the crop. There will be plenty of land for sale, at moderate prices, for several years here and in the adjacent Modesto district. Land here sells for $30 to $40 an acre; half down, usually.

ALAMEDA COUNTY.—There are few opportunities for renting land in this vicinity. It would not be advisable, although many small 4 to 10 acre places are ranched by Portuguese. Opportunities for purchase are good, for farmers can always find work away from their places in the orchards and fields. This is the way the Portuguese have filled up the country here.

SONOMA COUNTY.—Opportunities for renting are good, but no stated terms. Opportunities for purchase are good also.

ELDORADO COUNTY.—There is a little tenant farming done here. Considerable deeded land can be bought cheap and on the installment plan. As to living by hiring out, that is uncertain.

SHASTA COUNTY.—There are no opportunities for renting, and the chances for purchase are not good.

TABLE SHOWING CONDITIONS OF AGRICULTURAL LABOR AND DEMAND FOR IMMIGRANTS.

The matter in these tables referring to density and increase of population was compiled from the Twelfth Census; the remaining matter was compiled from replies received from representative farmers to a circular letter addressed to them. Each line in the tables represents the reply of one farmer. No attempt has been made either to average figures given or to harmonize their statements. The tables, then, can not be taken as giving a strictly statistical exhibit of the matters they deal with, but simply as giving a view of representative opinions in the localities named. The names in brackets following the names of counties in the tables are of the cities of 8,000 inhabitants or over which are situated in those counties.

MAINE.

[Density of population: 1890, 22.1; 1900, 23.2; increase, 5 per cent. Six counties, southwestern part of State.]

Counties.	Density, 1900.	Kinds of farming.	Per cent of laborers employed through the year.	Opportunities for married men as farm laborers.	Work for women and children.	Customary wages, men.			
						Monthly (with board).		Monthly or lump sum (with board), year.	Daily.
						Summer.	Winter.		
York (Biddeford)	67.8	General; dairy	Some [1]	Some	Housework	$15	$15		
Cumberland (Portland)	99.2	General; dairy; fruit	50 per cent [3]	Not for man and wife together.	Washing, cleaning, etc.; corn-canning shop.	20		$18	[2]$1.25–$1.50 [4]1.25
Oxford	16.3	General; dairy	30 per cent	Increasing demand	Housework	16–25	13–23	20	
Kennebec (Augusta, Waterville).	67.2	Dairy; stock	30 per cent	Occasional		[2]12	[2]10	[2]130	
Lincoln	37.8	General; stock; fruit	10 per cent [5]	None for steady employment.		20	15		
Somerset	8.8	General; dairy	50 per cent	Good demand		20–26			

Counties.	Changes in rate of wages, recent years.	Foreign farmers.	Nationality of farm laborers.	Nationality preferred as farm laborers.	Are there chances for immigrants who do not speak English?
York (Biddeford)	Increase	English-Canadians, Irish, Germans	Natives, Canadians	Any faithful acceptable	Not much.
Cumberland (Portland)	No increase		Natives (few), Canadians, Negroes (few).	No preference	Do.
Oxford	$2 to $5 a month increase	Different nationalities (few)	Natives mostly	Native whites	None.
Kennebec (Augusta, Waterville).	No increase	Very few; Swedes	Native whites, Swedes	do	Do.
Lincoln	$5 a month increase	None	Native whites	do	Do.
Somerset	Increase	Some; well to do	Canadian French		Yes; good.

[1] All could get work in winter cutting logs or teaming. Some would be needed on the farms.
[2] Without board.
[3] Remainder can find employment lumbering.
[4] Without board, winter.
[5] Remainder for six months.

NEW HAMPSHIRE.

[Density of population: 1890, 41.8; 1900, 45.7; increase, 9.3 per cent. Seven counties, southern and central parts of the State.]

Counties.	Density, 1900.	Kinds of farming.	Per cent of laborers employed through the year.	Opportunities for married men as farm laborers.	Work for women and children.	Customary wages, men.				
						Monthly (with board).		Monthly or lump sum (with board), year.	Daily.	
						Summer.	Winter.			
Cheshire (Keene):										
1	42.7	Dairy	80 per cent	Yes	Yes	$18-20	$12-15		$1.50 [1.50] 2.00	
2		Grain; dairy	50 per cent [3]	Yes; good	Housework	10-20	15	[2]$15		
Hillsboro (Manchester, Nashua).	129.0	Dairy		Very little		20-22	15-18	18-20		
Rockingham (Portsmouth).	73.8	General	30-50 per cent	Yes	Housework	22		18	1.50-2.00	
Strafford (Dover, Rochester).	99.8	......do	20 per cent	Not many		20	15			
Merrimac (Concord)	56.9	General; dairy	100 per cent	None		[5]15-25				
Sullivan	33.4	......do	50 per cent	For a few		20-22	15-18			
Carroll	18	General	10 per cent	Yes	Yes	20	12			

Counties.	Changes in rate of wages, recent years.	Foreign farmers.	Nationality of farm laborers.	Nationality preferred as farm laborers.	Are there chances for immigrants who do not speak English?
Cheshire (Keene):					
1	Some increase	Swedes (few)	French, Irish, Swedes	Swedes	Yes; Swedes.
2	Increase	Swedes, Irish, English	Poles, Swedes, Irish	Poles	Yes.[4]
Hillsboro (Manchester, Nashua).	No increase	Irish, French Canadians (few)	Native whites		None.
Rockingham (Portsmouth).	Increase	Irish, Canadian French	Native, Irish, Canadian French		Not many.
Strafford (Dover, Rochester).	Slight increase	None	French Canadians	French Canadians	Do.
Merrimac (Concord)	Increase	Irish (few)	Native whites		None.
Sullivan	......do	Not many	......do		For a few, possibly.
Carroll	No increase	None	Swedes		Yes.

[1] Haying.
[2] Poles, first year, $10 a month with board.
[3] More could find work, if they wished to.
[4] Our farms are not half tilled for want of laborers.
[5] Not stated whether summer or winter.

AGRICULTURAL DISTRIBUTION OF IMMIGRANTS. 585

VERMONT.

[Density of population: 1890, 36.4; 1900, 37.6; increase, 3.4 per cent. Six counties, representing all parts of the State.]

Counties.	Density, 1900.	Kinds of farming.	Per cent of laborers employed through the year.	Opportunities for married men as farm laborers.	Work for women and children.	Customary wages, men.				Are there chances for immigrants who do not speak English?
						Monthly (with board).		Monthly or lump sum (with board), year.	Daily.	
						Summer.	Winter.			
Windham	33.8	General; dairy	100 per cent	Single men preferred		$20 18-24	$16 14-20	[1]$18 16-20	[4]$1.50	Yes; for a limited number.
Rutland	48.5	Dairying	50 per cent[3]	Yes	No					Doubtful.
Windsor:	34.6							18-20		
1		do	66 per cent	Yes	Yes; in summer	20-25	15-20	20		None.
2		Dairying; sheep	10 per cent	do	Housework	20	16-18	[5]15-26		
Caledonia	37.4	Dairying	80 per cent	Married preferred	do	17-20	8½-10	13-15		To limited extent; Swedes preferred.
Orleans	30.2	do	50 per cent	Limited extent[6]	Little	14-18	10-15	12-16		Yes.
Franklin	46.8	do	75 per cent							Yes; to some extent. No.

Counties.	Foreign farmers.	Nationality of farm laborers.	Nationality preferred as farm laborers.
Windham	Many Swedes and Poles	Native whites, Swedes, Poles	Foreigners[2]
Rutland	Many Irish; long time here	Natives, Irish, Canadian French, Swedes.	No preference
Windsor:			
1	Canadians, Irish	Mostly natives, French Canadians, and Irish.	Native whites
2	Irish, French Canadians (a few)	Mostly natives	Native whites
Caledonia	French Canadians	Canadians, French, and English	
Orleans	French, Irish	Natives, French Canadians, Irish	
Franklin	French[7]	Natives of French-Canadian and Irish descent.	

[1] Less wages are paid to foreigners just arrived.
[2] The foreigners are liked better than the native born.
[3] Remainder can find work during winter.
[4] Without board in summer.
[5] Difference $5 a month between winter and summer.
[6] Tenant houses furnished for families.
[7] Many who began as day laborers then rented farms and are now owners and prospering.

MASSACHUSETTS.

[Density of population: 1890, 278.5; 1900, 348.9; increase, 25.3 per cent. Nine counties, representing all parts of State.]

Counties.	Density, 1900.	Kinds of farming.	Per cent of laborers employed through the year.	Opportunities for married men as farm laborers.	Work for women and children.	Customary wages, men.				
						Monthly (with board).		Monthly or lump sum (with board) year.	Daily.	
						Summer.	Winter.			
Barnstable	66.4	General; dairying; specialties.	50 per cent [1]	50 per cent are married	Harvesting, berries and vegetables.	$18–$25	$12–$15	$18.00	[2] $1.50 [3] 1.10
Plymouth (Brockton)	169.6	Truck and dairying	50 per cent	Yes	Housework	18	12	15.50	
Bristol (Fall River, New Bedford, etc.).	435.3	Mixed	50 per cent	Laborers mostly single	Factories in Fall River.	15– 20	5– 12	20.00	
Middlesex (Cambridge, Lowell, Malden, Waltham, etc.).	703.6	Dairying; fruit and poultry.	60 per cent	Many prefer married [4]		20– 25	12– 20		1.25–1.75
Essex (Gloucester, Haverhill, Lawrence, Lynn, Salem, etc.):									
1	694.6	Dairying	50 per cent [5]	Only occasionally		15– 25			
2		do	50 per cent	Not many	None	18– 20			
Worcester (Fitchburg, Worcester, etc.):									
1	218.9	do	([6])	Yes [7]	Shoe shops, etc	[8] 10– 20	[8] 6– 8	[9] $40–$50	
2		do	Part	Few	Housework	20– 25	10– 16	250–300	[10] 1.50
3		General and dairying	25 per cent	Very few	Shops and factories		10– 18		
			40 per cent [11]		Children in factories	20	10– 12		
5		Truck and grass	50 per cent	None		18	10	15	
Hampshire	96.1	Dairy and fruit	20 per cent	Yes		16	10		
Franklin:	57.1								
1		General; dairying; tobacco and onions.	75 per cent	Limited—tobacco and onion sections.	Children—onion farming.	20– 25	10– 12	[10] $200	[2] 1.50 [3] 1.00
2		General and mixed	75 per cent	Yes	Yes	[12] 15– 25	10– 18		
Berkshire		Dairy and fruit	50 per cent	Married preferred	do	8– 20	10– 15	12– 20	[13] 1.25
3		Mixed	50 per cent						

[1] Remainder can find employment.
[2] Summer, without board.
[3] Winter, without board.
[4] House is provided where only one man kept; single man preferred.
[5] Many farmers do lumbering in winter.
[6] Foreigners prefer to work 8 months for higher pay, and for very much less during winter. The larger farmers prefer to hire by the year.
[7] Many farmers provide tenant houses.
[8] Inexperienced.
[9] Experienced hands, special price.
[10] Without board.
[11] Remainder chop wood or are idle.
[12] Green hands, $10.
[13] Through year.

MASSACHUSETTS—Continued.

Counties.	Changes in rate of wages, recent years.	Foreign farmers.	Nationality of farm laborers.	Nationali preferred as farm laborers.	Are there chances for immigrants who do not speak English?
Barnstable	Increase	Swedes, Portuguese, Finns	Swedes, Portuguese, Poles, Finns.	Preference as named	Yes.
Plymouth (Brockton)	No increase	Irish	Irish, Canadians, Italians, Swedes.	Swedes	None.
Bristol (Fall River, New Bedford)	Slight increase	Portuguese	90 per cent Portuguese		Not much.
Middlesex (Cambridge, Lowell, Malden, Waltham, etc.)	Increase, day wages; no increase, monthly wages.	Few	Canadians, Irish, Poles	Nova Scotia and New Brunswick.	Do.
Essex (Gloucester, Haverhill, Lawrence, Lynn, Salem):					
1	No increase	Irish (few), Canadian [1]	Natives, English Canadians, Irish.	Native whites	None.
2	No material increase	None	Nova Scotia, New Brunswick	New Brunswick	Do.
Worcester (Fitchburg, Worcester):					
1	Slight increase	Swedes, Canadian French, Irish, Poles.	Poles, Swedes, Danes, Canadian French.		
2	Slight increase in 5 years.	Irish, Poles, Hungarians	Poles mostly, Austrians, Swedes, Irish.	No preference	Yes; at low wages.
3	No material increase	Irish, Canadian, French (few)	Few foreigners		None.
4	No change	Irish, French, German (few)	Irish, Canadian French, Swedes		Very few.
5	No increase	Irish, Swedes	Native whites		Few, if any.
Hampshire	Increase	Poles, Russians, Germans	Poles		Yes.
Franklin:					
1	15 per cent increase	Irish, French, Poles	25 per cent native whites, 75 per cent Poles.	Poles who know English	Yes; at low wages ($10-$15 a month).
2	Increase	Germans, Poles	Poles, Hungarians, Germans, Swedes (numbers in order given).	Swedes	Yes.[2]
3	No increase	French, Germans, Poles (few)	Poles (mostly), Hungarians, Swedes, French Canadians.		Yes; all find employment.
Berkshire	Increase	French and Irish		Americans	Limited extent.

[1] Most who come to farms soon leave for some factory.   [2] Particularly in towns where tobacco and onions are raised.

RHODE ISLAND.

[Density of population: 1890, 318.4; 1900, 407.0; increase, 24 per cent.]

Counties.	Density, 1900.	Kinds of farming.	Per cent of laborers employed through the year.	Opportunities for married men as farm laborers.	Work for women and children.	Customary wages, men.				Are there chances for immigrants who do not speak English?
						Monthly (with board).		Monthly or lump sum (with board) year.	Daily.	
						Summer.	Winter.			
Bristol	525.7	Dairy; onions; celery	10 per cent [1]	None		$15-17	$12-$15		[2]$1.50	
Kent	177.3	General; dairy and truck.	80 to 100 per cent.	Yes; good	Cotton and woolen mills.	25		$15	[3]$1.50-2.00 [4]1.25-1.50	

Counties.	Changes in rate of wages, recent years.	Foreign farmers.	Nationality of farm laborers.	Nationality preferred as farm laborers.
Bristol	Slight increase	Irish, Scotch, Portuguese (a few)	French Canadians, Portuguese	Portuguese	A few.
Kent	No increase	Irish, Canadian French, Swedes, Germans (numerically in order named).	Irish, Canadian French, Swedes	Swedes	Yes; at low wages.

[1] Men are sure to drift into the factories. [2] Without board. [3] Summer, without board. [4] Winter, without board.

CONNECTICUT.

[Density of population: 1890, 154.0; 1900, 187.5; increase, 21.7 per cent. Three counties, center of the State.]

Counties.	Density, 1900.	Kinds of farming.	Per cent of laborers employed through the year.	Opportunities for married men as farm laborers.	Work for women and children.	Customary wages, men.			
						Monthly (with board).		Customary wages, men.	Daily.
						Summer.	Winter.	Monthly or lump sum (with board) year.	
Middlesex (Middletown)	111.9	General; dairying	20 per cent	Married preferred	None	$12–$20	$8–$15	$12–$15	
Tolland	59.1	General	20 per cent	A few	do	20	10	15– 20	
Hartford:	288.6								
1		General	60 per cent	None		20	15	220	
2		Dairy; fruit; tobacco	50 per cent	To a limited extent		20	15	18	
3		Tobacco	50 per cent	Yes	In summer	16– 22	10– 16		

Counties.	Changes in rate of wages, recent years.	Foreign farmers.	Nationality of farm laborers.	Nationality preferred as farm laborers.	Are there chances for immigrants who do not speak English?
Middlesex (Middletown)	No increase	Germans, Irish	Irish, Italians, Germans, Negroes	Germans	Not many.
Tolland	do	Germans	Swedes		None.
Hartford:					
1	do	Germans, Irish	Poles (mostly), Swedes, Swiss, Portuguese, Italians, Danes	No preference	Not many.
2	10–20 per cent increase	Germans, Irish, Swedes	Negroes		If used to farm work.
3	Increase	Irish (many), Poles (a few)	Poles, Irish, Italians, native whites (few).		Yes; at $12–$15 a month.

590   THE INDUSTRIAL COMMISSION:—IMMIGRATION.

NEW YORK.

[Density of population: 1890, 126.0; 1900, 152.6; increase, 21.1 per cent. Twelve counties.]

Counties.	Density, 1900.	Kinds of farming.	Per cent of laborers employed through the year.	Opportunities for married men as farm laborers.	Work for women and children.	Customary wages, men.			
						Monthly (with board).		Monthly or lump sum (with board) year.	Daily.
						Summer.	Winter.		
Dutchess (Poughkeepsie).	102.1	General; dairy; fruit	80 per cent	Yes; but single preferred.	Not much	$16–$20	$10–$18		$1.00–$1.50
Columbia (Hudson)	66.8	...do	50 per cent[2]	Yes	Yes				
Rensselaer (Troy, etc.)	183.3	General; stock; fruit	60 per cent				5– 12		{[3]1.00– 1.25 / [4].75– 1.00}
Albany (Albany, etc.)	313.6	General; dairy; fruit	Dairy all	Married men preferred.	Berries and fruit	18– 20	10		
Lewis	21.7	Dairy	20 per cent	Yes	Children over 15	18– 22	14– 18	$17– 20	
Jefferson (Watertown)	61.3	...do	Few	Yes; on large farms		20– 25	15	10– 20	
Onondaga (Syracuse)	212.5	Fruit; dairy	60 per cent	Yes; good	Housework; fruit farming.	18– 22		10– 22	
Schuyler	46.6	General; fruit; stock; dairy.	All	Very best	Vineyards; housework.	20		16– 18	[5]1.25
Ontario (Geneva)	76.1	Grain; fruit	25 per cent	Yes	Picking and evaporating fruits.				
Wayne:	77.9								
1		General; fruit	Nearly all	...do[7]	Picking and evaporators.	18– 22	10– 15		[6]1.00
2		...do		...do[10]	Plenty; fruits and in evaporators.				[6]1.00
3		...do	Few[9]	...do[11]	Little; housework only.			100– 225	[6]1.00
Genesee (Batavia)	71.4	General; dairy; fruit	80 per cent		On many farms	18– 25	6– 15		
Niagara (Lockport, Niagara Falls, etc.):	143.6								
1		General; fruit	50 per cent	{Yes; for good, steady men.}		16– 20 / [8]20– 25	8– 10	[12]200– 250	
2		...do	60 per cent	Yes		18– 24	5– 10	[12]160– 200	[6].75–1.50

[1] Most men work by the day.
[2] Remainder can find work by cutting ice.
[3] Summer, without board.
[4] Winter; without board.
[5] Without board; 10 cents per hour.
[6] Year around.
[7] Many farmers have tenant houses and employ married men.
[8] Without board.
[9] Good men can get steady employment, but only one out of five care to work in the winter.
[10] Scarcity of married men with families. Many houses are empty.
[11] At good wages; houses and gardens provided.
[12] With house, but without board.

NEW YORK—Continued.

Counties.	Changes in rate of wages, recent years.	Foreign farmers.	Nationality of farm laborers.	Nationality preferred as farm laborers.	Are there chances for immigrants who do not speak English?
Dutchess (Poughkeepsie).	Increase	Few	Native whites	Native whites	Few.
Columbia (Hudson)		Germans	Poles, Irish, Germans, Swedes	Germans	Yes.
Rensselaer (Troy)	No increase		Germans, Russians	...do...	Yes; especially Germans.
Albany	10 per cent increase	Irish, Swedes, Germans	Irish, Germans, Dutch		Few.
Lewis	$2 increase within a year	Germans, Irish	Germans, Irish, native whites		Yes; at low wages.
Jefferson (Watertown)	Monthly, no increase; day, 25 cents increase.	English (a few)	Natives mostly, English, Russians (a few).		None.
Onondaga (Syracuse)	10 to 20 per cent in 5 years	Irish and Germans [1]	Natives of Irish, German, and Scotch descent.		Yes; at low wages.
Schuyler	Increase	English, Irish, a few Germans, Italians	English, Irish, Swedes, Hungarians	Natives	Not much.
Ontario (Geneva)			Irish, Italians	Irish	Moderate.
Wayne:					
1	Increase	Dutch	Dutch, Germans, English		Yes.
2	...do...	Irish, German	Irish, Germans	No preference	
3	$3 a month increase	Germans, Dutch	Dutch, Germans		Yes.[2]
Genesee (Batavia)	10 to 15 per cent increase	Germans, Irish, English, Scotch	Canadians, Scotch, Irish, Germans	Preference in order named	Yes; at moderate wages.
Niagara (Lockport, Niagara Falls):					
1	Increase	Dutch, Irish, English	Dutch (mostly), Irish, Canadians	Canadians, Dutch	Yes; at low wages.
2	...do...	Germans, Irish, Poles	Germans, Irish, Poles	Preference in order named	Yes.

[1] None of recent arrival.   [2] Openings in sugar beet industry and onions.

NEW JERSEY.

[Density of population: 1890, 192.0; 1900, 250.3; increase, 30.4 per cent. Seven counties, south and center of State.]

Counties.	Density, 1900.	Kinds of farming.	Per cent of laborers employed through the year.	Opportunities for married men as farm laborers.	Work for women and children.	Customary wages, men.			
						Monthly (with board).		Monthly or lump sum (with board) year.	Daily.
						Summer.	Winter.		
Cape May	51.6	Truck; dairy	50 per cent	Possible	Housework	$16–$18	$12		
Cumberland (Bridgeton, etc.)	100.2	Truck (fruits and sweet potatoes).	Few		Berries, harvesting, sweet potatoes.	¹15	(²)		
Gloucester:									
1	97.8	General; truck; dairy	80 per cent	Many prefer married	For wives	20	$8–12	$200	
2		General; truck	40 per cent	Very few	Considerable	15–22	5–12		
Monmouth	171.3	General; truck; dairy	50 per cent	Yes	do	9–13	5–10		
Middlesex (New Brunswick, etc.).	255.6	General; dairy	1 or 2 on each farm.						
Mercer (Trenton)	421.9	do	70 per cent	do	In summer			³$8–12	
Union (Elizabeth, Plainfield).	964.6	General; truck; dairy	50 per cent	do				14–18	$1
								10–16	

Counties.	Changes in rate of wages, recent years.	Foreign farmers.	Nationality of farm laborers.	Nationality preferred as farm laborers.	Are there chances for immigrants who do not speak English?
Cape May	No change	None ²	Native whites, negroes, a few Poles.	Poles have proved satisfactory.	Yes; very good.
Cumberland	No increase	Italians	Native whites, Italians		Yes; for Italians.
Gloucester:					
1	Increase in 2 or 3 years	Germans, Irish	Poles	Poles, Swedes	Yes.
2	Increase about $4 a month	Germans (many)	Negroes (mostly), Poles		Very little.
Monmouth	Increase in 3 years	Irish, Germans, Jews (occasional)	Negroes, Poles, Germans, Irish, Swedes.		Yes.
Middlesex	No increase	Germans and Irish (both successful)	Negroes (mostly), Irish, Germans	Swedes and Danes	Yes; of some nationalities.
Mercer (Trenton)	Increase	Irish, Dutch	Negroes, Hungarians, Poles, Swedes, Danes.	Americans	Yes.
Union (Elizabeth, Plainfield).			Every nationality; Americans mostly colored.		Do.

¹ Russian-Jewish farmers in this county, but not mentioned.
² Not stated whether summer only.
³ For newly-arrived foreigners. Experienced men $3 to $5 more per month.

PENNSYLVANIA.

[Density of population: 1890, 116.9; 1900, 140.1; increase, 19.9 per cent. Fifteen counties, first 7 in eastern part; next 4 in central and last 4 in western part.]

Counties.	Density, 1900.	Kinds of farming.	Per cent of laborers employed through the year.	Opportunities for married men as farm laborers.	Work for women and children.	Customary wages, men.			
						Monthly (with board).		Monthly or lump sum (with board) year.	Daily.
						Summer.	Winter.		
Chester (Phoenixville)	125.9	General; dairying	30 per cent	Many prefer married	Yes; dairy farms	$14	$12	$13	
Berks (Reading)	182.6	General; truck	...do	Quite a demand		$10-15	$6-12	$150-175	²$1.00
Montgomery (Norristown, Pottstown)	277.4	General; truck; dairy	50 per cent	Married preferred	Yes			125-30	³.75
Lehigh (Allentown)	286.3	General; dairying	Nearly all	None	Tailoring	10-15	8-12	10-15	
Monroe	33.6	...do	20 per cent	Yes	None	18		12	
Pike	14.1	General; truck; dairy	(4)		Little	12-18	10-15		
Luzerne (Hazelton, Pittston, Wilkesbarre)	282.5	General; dairy	20 per cent	Not for foreigners					
Cumberland (Carlisle)	93.9	General; fruit; dairy	30 per cent	Only for local people		14	10	12	
Bedford	36.9	General; dairy	50 per cent	None		12	8	150	
Center	37.9	General	20 per cent	Yes		15-18	10	15	
Cameron	18.8	Dairy; sheep	13 per cent		For children	15			
Westmoreland	151.1	General	50 per cent	Little		20	10	180	¹1.00-1.50
Washington	111.0	Grain; dairy	Very small	Very limited	Housework	⁷10-17			
Butler	74.4	General; truck; dairy	Majority	Good	Yes	18-20	15-18	15-18	⁵$1.00-1.25
Warren	45.3	Dairy; sheep; fruit	10 per cent						⁶.75-1.00

¹ Without board.
² Summer, with board.
³ Winter, with board.
⁴ Hardly any hiring for year; in winter men work at lumbering by the day.
⁵ Summer.
⁶ Winter.
⁷ Not stated whether summer only.

PENNSYLVANIA—Continued.

Counties.	Changes in rate of wages, recent years.	Foreign farmers.	Nationality of farm laborers.	Nationality preferred as farm laborers.	Are there chances for immigrants who do not speak English?
Chester	Slight increase	Irish (many)	Negroes, Irish, native whites		None.
Berks (Reading)	No change	Poles (a few)	Native whites, Poles (a few)		Yes.
Montgomery (Norristown, Pottstown)	Increase	Germans, Irish (a few)	Negroes, Welsh, German		Yes; for Germans.
Lehigh (Allentown)	...do	Germans[1]	Germans	No preference	Do.
Monroe	Slight increase	Germans, Irish	Natives, mostly; Germans	Germans	Do.
Pike	Increase of 20 per cent	Germans, French	Germans (mostly), Irish (few), Swedes and French.	No preference	Yes; for Germans and French.
Luzerne (Hazelton, Pittston, Wilkesbarre)	No change	None	Few foreigners		None.
Cumberland (Carlisle)	No increase	Very few	Natives		Do.
Bedford	$2 increase last 2 years	Germans	...do		Do.
Center	Slight increase	None	...do		Yes; if used to farm.
Cameron	No increase	Germans (a few)	Germans, Swedes	Swedes	Very few.
Westmoreland	Increase	None	Natives or Germans, native born		Yes; if understand farming.
Washington	Slight increase	Germans (a few)	Natives; a few Germans	Germans	None.
Butler	Increase 50 per cent	Germans, Belgians, French	Few foreigners		Yes; good chances.
Warren	Increase 10 per cent in 2 years.	Swedes	Native whites, Swedes	Natives	A few.

[1] Probably 100 German families that own their farms in the county; a few Irish.

AGRICULTURAL DISTRIBUTION OF IMMIGRANTS. 595

OHIO.

[Density of population: 1890, 90.1; 1900, 102.0; increase, 13.2 per cent. Thirteen counties, representing all sections of the State.]

Counties.	Density, 1900.	Kinds of farming.	Per cent of laborers employed through the year.	Opportunities for married men as farm laborers.	Work for women and children.	Customary wages, men.				
						Monthly (with board).		Monthly or lump sum (with board) year.	Daily.
						Summer.	Winter.		
Athens	73.3	Small; worked by owners.	Little hiring.						
Ross (Chillicothe, Fremont).	63.4	General; stock	Few	Onion growing	Onion growing	$15–$18	$13–$16	[1]$180–$192	
Montgomery (Dayton)	266.1	General; tobacco							
Darke	70.4	...do	80 per cent	None	For strong lads	16– 20			[2]$0.75–$1.00
Champaign	63.6	Grain; stock; dairy;		Married preferred		[3]16– 20			
Logan	64.7	Grain; stock; fruit.	All	...do	Housework				{$1.00– 1.25 [5]$.75– 1.00
Auglaize	79.1	General; stock	50 per cent	Yes	{For women, not children.				$1.25 [5]$1.00
Marion (Marion)	57.1	General	76 per cent		Small fruit	13– 15	10– 15	150– 200	
Hancock (Findlay)	79.8	General; stock	All who wish.[6]	Some prefer married and provide house.		12– 18	8– 15	150– 200	$3.75– 1.25
Licking (Newark)	70.8	General; fruit	80 per cent	Married preferred[1]	Fruit farms	[7]16– 25	[7]16– 25		
Noble	52.7	General; stock	70 per cent[8]	Not many	For boys and girls	12– 20	12– 13	[9]175– 250	.75– 1.00
Tuscarawas	100.8	General; truck	10 per cent[10]			15– 20	12– 13		
Henry	65.7	General; stock; truck.	50 per cent[11]		For German women[11]	13– 18			

[1] Married men are furnished house and garden plat.
[2] Winter, with board.
[3] With board.
[4] Summer, without board.
[5] Winter, without board.
[6] But labor almost impossible to obtain.
[7] With or without board.
[8] Remainder could get work cutting timber, etc.; also in coal mines in winter. They board themselves.
[9] House and garden found; also truck patch, cow pasture, and coal privilege.
[10] Good men are in demand all winter.
[11] Some get $0.75 to $1 per day working on farms.

OHIO—Continued.

Counties.	Changes in rate of wages, recent years.	Foreign farmers.	Nationality of farm laborers.	Nationality preferred as farm laborers.	Are there chances for immigrants who do not speak English?
Athens					
Ross (Chillicothe, Fremont).	$1 to $2 increase in 2 years.	Very few	Native whites and colored		None.
Montgomery (Dayton)					To some extent.
Darke	About same	Germans, here many years	Natives and Germans	Natives and Germans	None.
Champaign	...do		Native whites	Native whites	Yes; if experienced.
			Natives and negroes		
Logan	...do	Germans and Irish	Germans, Swedes, Swiss, Irish	Preference in order named	Yes.[1]
Auglaize	Slight increase	Many Germans	Germans and Irish	Germans	Yes; for Germans.
Marion (Marion)	Increase within 3 years	....do	Germans, Irish, English		Yes.
Hancock (Findlay)	No increase[2]	...do	Germans mostly	Germans	Yes; a few Germans.
Licking (Newark)	Increase	None	Native whites		
Noble	Increase slight	Many Germans; prosperous	Germans	Germans	Yes.
Tuscarawas	Increase	Germans who came many years back and bought land when low.	Native whites	Native whites	None.
Henry	No change	Germans	Germans, native whites	Germans	Yes.

[1] Any who talk German, and others if fairly intelligent. [2] But labor almost impossible to obtain.

AGRICULTURAL DISTRIBUTION OF IMMIGRANTS.

INDIANA.

[Density of population: 1890, 61.1; 1900, 70.1; increase, 14.8 per cent. First eight counties in southern part of State; last four counties, eastern half of northern part.]

Counties.	Density, 1900.	Kinds of farming.	Per cent of laborers employed through the year.	Opportunities for married men as farm laborers.	Work for women and children.	Customary wages, men.				
						Monthly (with board).		Monthly or lump sum (with board) year.	Daily.	
						Summer.	Winter.			
Warrick	56.2	General; stock; dairy	60 per cent	Yes[1]	Picking berries; boys teaming.	$12–$15	$10–$13			
Gibson	61.4	General; stock	..do	..do	Not much			[2]$14–$20		
Pike	61	..do	Very few	Not good	Picking and canning tomatoes.	15			$0.75–$1.00	
Scott	43.7	General; tomatoes	5 per cent			15–18				
Switzerland	52.6	Stock; tobacco; fruit	10 per cent	Yes	Yes	13	10	12	.75	
Monroe	50.4	General; dairy; truck; fruit.	..do	None		15			[4]1.00–1.25	
Franklin	41.6	General; stock	50 per cent	Yes				[2]12–20		
Hendricks (eastern part northern half).	52.2	Stock; grain; fruit	20 per cent	Yes; good	Berry and tomato picking and canning.			18–22 15	41.00–1.50	
Henry	63.5	Grain; stock	50 per cent	Married preferred	Yes	20	15	[2]200		
Jay	72.5	Stock; grain; fruit	Few							
Huntington (Huntington).	75	General; stock	30 per cent	Some		14–18	8–12	12	[5].75–1.00	
Dekalb	69.7	General; stock; dairy	10 per cent	Limited		16–22	12–16		[3]1.25	

[1] The farmers are putting up houses to secure help that will be with them through the year.
[2] Without board; house and truck patch, etc., furnished.
[3] Without board.
[4] Harvest without board.
[5] With board.

598   THE INDUSTRIAL COMMISSION: —IMMIGRATION.

INDIANA—Continued.

Counties.	Changes in rate of wages, recent years.	Foreign farmers.	Nationality of farm laborers.	Nationality preferred as farm laborers.	Are there chances for immigrants who do not speak English?
Warrick	Expected increase [1]	Many, mostly Germans	English, Germans		Yes, especially for Germans.
Gibson	No increase	Germans, Irish	Natives		None.
Pike	Increase	Germans	do		Do.
Scott	Some increase	Germans (a few)	do	Natives	Do.
Switzerland	No increase	Germans	Natives		Do.
Monroe	Some increase	None	Natives		
Franklin	Slight increase		Germans	Germans	Yes.
Hendricks (eastern part, northern half).	No increase	None	Natives		None.
Henry	"Hands are scarcer"	do	Few foreigners		Limited.
Jay	25 cents per day increase	do	Natives		(?)
Huntington (Huntington).	Slight increase	Germans, mostly as owners	Germans, natives	Germans	Yes; German speaking.
Dekalb	Increase	None	Natives		None.

[1] Great scarcity of help.   [2] People here disposed to employ laborers that they can take in and treat as a part of the family.

AGRICULTURAL DISTRIBUTION OF IMMIGRANTS. 599

ILLINOIS.

[Density of population: 1890, 68.3; 1900, 86; increase, 26 per cent. First three counties, southwestern part of State; last four counties, central part of State.]

Counties.	Density, 1900.	Kinds of farming.	Per cent of laborers employed through the year.	Opportunities for married men as farm laborers.	Work for women and children.	Customary wages, men.				Are there chances for immigrants who do not speak English?
						Monthly (with board).		Monthly or lump sum (with board) year.	Daily.	
						Summer.	Winter.			
Union	56.5	Grain; truck; fruit	80 per cent	Yes	Housework, vegetable culture	[1]$13–$16				
St. Clair (Belleville, East St. Louis)	127.5	Grain	...do	...do	Housework	15– 18	$8–$12	$150–$180		Yes.
Clinton	39.8	General; stock and dairy	All if desire	Limited number	Sugar beets	12– 15	8– 12	120– 170		Do.
Menard	45.7	General; fruit and stock	66 per cent	Yes	Sugar beets in future	16– 20	12– 18			Limited numbers.[3]
Fulton	55.8	General; stock	80 per cent	Married preferred						Yes.
Knox (Galesburg):										
1	60.6	Grain; stock	50 per cent[4]	Yes	Fair opportunities	22– 25	17– 20	[5]22– 23		None.
2		...do	60 per cent	...do	A little housework	20	16– 18	25– 30		Yes, Swedes.[3]
McLean (Bloomington)	58.2	...do	75 per cent	...do	Sugar beets	20				Yes.

Counties.	Changes in rate of wages, recent years.	Foreign farmers.	Nationality of farm laborers.	Nationality preferred as farm laborers.
Union	No increase	Germans	Americans, Germans	Americans, Germans.
St. Clair (Belleville, East St. Louis)	Increase	Germans, French, a few others	...do	Germans.
Clinton	$2 to $3[3]	Germans		Germans, but all nationalities accepted.
Menard	Increase	Germans, Danes, Scotch, Irish	Germans, Danes, Swedes, Scotch, Irish.	Americans.
Fulton	No increase	None	Americans	Swedes are acceptable
Knox (Galesburg):				
1	$3 to $5 a month increase in last 3 years	Swedes, mostly Germans, Irish	Swedes	No preference.
2	Not much increase	Swedes, Germans, Irish	...do	Americans, Germans.
McLean (Bloomington)	$2 to $4[2]	Irish, Germans	Americans, Germans	Yes, Germans.

[1] Not stated whether summer only or all year.
[2] Per month increase.
[3] Some find employment with Swedes; some with Americans at low wages.
[4] Plenty of work for remainder in shops.
[5] Without board; house provided.

MICHIGAN.

[Density of population: 1890, 36.5; 1900, 42.2; increase, 15.6 per cent. First eight southern counties; last two northern counties.]

Counties.	Density, 1900.	Kinds of farming.	Per cent of laborers employed through the year.	Opportunities for married men as farm laborers.	Work for women and children.	Customary wages, men.				
						Monthly (with board).		Monthly or lump sum (with board) year.	Daily.	
						Summer.	Winter.			
Wayne (Detroit)	557.2	General; dairy	10 per cent		None	[1]$17–$20	$10	$15		
Jackson (Jackson)	69.4	General; stock; seeds; onions.	15 per cent		Yes; weeding	20– 25	$8– 12	$[2]250–400		
Eaton	57.0	General; stock; sugar beets.	50 per cent	Yes	Housework	20– 26	5– 10	15		
Kent (Grand Rapids)	150.5	General; dairy; truck; sugar beets.	Many	do	Beet raising	22– 26		16– 20		
Lapeer	41.4	Mixed	50 per cent	Yes; labor scarce	do	20– 24		4[1]8– 20		
Bay (Bay City)	142.7	Grain; truck; sugar beets.	10 per cent							
Mecosta	36.5	Grain; stock	30 per cent [3]	Yes	Some—boys and girls				[5]$1.50–$2.00	
Oceana	29.5	General; fruit	50 per cent	do	Fruit	20– 22			[6]1.00	
Iosco	18.3	General	Few [3]		Housework	12– 15				
Charlevoix	33.0	General; stock	All		do	20	16	18		

Counties.	Changes in rate of wages, recent years.	Foreign farmers.	Nationality of farm laborers.	Nationality preferred as farm laborers.	Are there chances for immigrants who do not speak English?
Wayne (Detroit)	$2 per month increase	Germans, Irish	Natives, Germans, Irish	Germans	None.
Jackson (Jackson)	Notable increase, 1901	Germans, English	Germans		Yes.
Eaton	Increase	Germans	Germans, Swedes, Norwegians		Do.
Kent (Grand Rapids)	Decided increase	Dutch, Irish	Dutch		Yes; especially Dutch.
Lapeer	Increase	Germans, many		American born	Not very good.
Bay (Bay City)	25 per cent increase	Swedes, Poles, Germans, Irish	Germans, Poles, French	Germans	Yes.
Mecosta	$5 per month increase	Dutch, Germans	Swedes, Germans, Poles, Irish	Swedes	Yes; good.
Oceana	Fair increase	Canadians, Germans, Poles, Swedes	Native whites		Do.
Iosco				No preference by nationalities.	Yes; Germans, Poles, Swedes.
Charlevoix	Slight increase	Dutch	Native whites, Dutch		Yes.

[1] Without board: tenant house, cow pasture, garden, fuel, etc., provided.   [3] Remainder find employment in lumber camps.   [5] Summer, with board.
[2] With house and garden spot.   [4] Without board.   [6] Winter, with board.

AGRICULTURAL DISTRIBUTION OF IMMIGRANTS. 601

WISCONSIN.

[Density of population: 1890, 31; 1900, 38; increase, 22.3 per cent. Fifteen counties, all parts of State.]

Counties.	Density, 1900.	Kinds of farming.	Per cent of laborers employed through the year.	Opportunities for married men as farm laborers.	Work for women and children.	Customary wages, men.				
						Monthly (with board).		Monthly or lump sum (with board) year.	Daily.	
						Summer.	Winter.			
Waukesha	62.7	General; dairy; stock; fruit.	All	Yes	Yes	$18–$25	$10–$25	$200–$250		
Jefferson	63.5	Dairy; stock; tobacco	..do	..do.[1]	Dairy work and tobacco.	20– 25	20	[2]22		
Iowa	30.3	Dairy; stock	..do	Little	Not steady	20– 25	18– 20	20		
Waupaca	42.2	General; dairy	30 per cent[3]	Yes	Tobacco	20– 20	18– 10	16		
Vernon	35.8	Dairy; tobacco; grain.	70 per cent[4]	..do		20– 22	12– 17		[5]$1.00–$1.50	
Adams:										
1	13.4	General; dairy	40 per cent.	..do	Yes	22	15	18		
2		..do	30 per cent.	..do	Housework	18– 22		15– 18	[6]$1.00	
Wood	32.9	General; stock; dairy	10 per cent.	None	No			20	[7]1.50	
Clark	21.5	General; stock	Very few	Very little		15– 20				
Eau Claire	51.1	..do	50 per cent.	Not good		20– 26	16– 20	225– 250	[7]1.00– 1.50	
Dunn	29.7	Stock; dairy	Few	Yes	Yes	20	20		[5]1.25	
Polk	19.1	Grain; changing to dairy.	Very few			15– 30				
Taylor	11.7	General; dairy	50 per cent.		Very little	20– 30		$1.25	[5]1.50– 1.75	
Oneida	9.9	General	([8])							
Ashland	21.7	..do	60 per cent[9]	Yes				[10]20		
Washburn	6.6	..do		..do	Blueberry picking	22	15			

[1] Married men are preferred by many farmers. Farmer provides tenant house.
[2] Same or less wages paid without board, but with house, firewood, one-half to 1 acre of ground, milk of 1 cow.
[3] Remainder go to pineries.
[4] Remainder can get work in tobacco warehouses.
[5] Without board.
[6] Summer.
[7] A day, haying and harvest.
[8] Logging in winter.
[9] Remainder in woods and factory.
[10] In woods average is $26 to $35.

WISCONSIN—Continued.

Counties.	Changes in rate of wages, recent years.	Foreign farmers.	Nationality of farm laborers.	Nationality preferred as farm laborers.	Are there chances for immigrants who do not speak English?
Waukesha	35 per cent increase	Germans, mostly; Scandinavians, Poles.		Any nationality accepted	Yes.
Jefferson	20 per cent increase	Germans, Scandinavians, Irish	Germans, Scandinavians, some natives.	All acceptable	Do.
Iowa	Increase	All kinds, Swiss	All kinds		Do.
Waupaca	...do	Danes, mostly	Scandinavians, Germans		Do.
Vernon	Increase $3 a month in 2 years.	Norwegians, mostly; Germans, Irish.	Norwegians, native whites	Foreigners	Do.
Adams:					
1	20 per cent increase	Germans, Scandinavians, Bohemians, Poles.	Germans, Scandinavians, Poles	No preference	Do.
2	¼–½ increase	Germans, Irish, Norwegians	Americans, Irish, Germans, Norwegians.		Yes; Germans, Norwegians.
Wood	Slight increase	All classes [1]	Germans, Poles, Americans, Scandinavians.	Germans, Poles	Yes.
Clark	Increase	Germans, Bohemians	Germans, Scandinavians		Do.
Eau Claire		Germans, Norwegians, Poles	Germans, Norwegians		Do.
Dunn	20 per cent increase	Germans, Scandinavians	Germans, Scandinavians		Do.
Polk	Increase	Scandinavians, Germans, Irish	Germans, Scandinavians, Irish, natives.	No preference	Do.
Taylor	Slight increase	Germans, Scandinavians	Germans	...do	Do.
Oneida	Increase 25c–40c per day	Germans, Scandinavians, Poles	Germans, Scandinavians		Do.
Ashland	Increase	Germans, Russians, Danes, Austrians, Swiss.	Germans, German-Russians, Danes, Bohemians.		Do.
Washburn	...do	Germans, Norwegians, Swedes, Bohemians.	All kinds	Germans	Yes; for taking up new farms.

[1] Germans, Poles, Finns, Scandinavians, Irish, Scotch, English, French, Swiss.

MINNESOTA.

[Density of population: 1890, 16.5; 1900, 22.1; increase, 33.8 per cent. Seven counties]

Counties.	Density, 1900.	Kinds of farming.	Per cent of laborers employed through the year.	Opportunities for married men as farm laborers.	Work for women and children.	Customary wages, men.				Are there chances for immigrants who do not speak English?
						Monthly (with board).		Monthly or lump sum (with board) year.	Daily.	
						Summer.	Winter.			
Freeborn	30.3	General; stock; dairy	70 per cent	Very good	Plenty	$23	$12			
Watonwan	26.6	General; stock	10 per cent	None		$18-20				
McLeod	38.9	General; dairy	80 per cent	...do.²		20-25	10-15	$200-$225		
Stevens	15.7	General; dairy and stock	20 per cent	...do				20	$1.25, $1.00	
Pine	8.1	General; stock	None	Some		20-30				
Clay	17.5	Wheat	...do	Yes	None	20				
Kittson	7.4	...do	50 per cent	...do	....do	20	10	200		

Counties.	Changes in rate of wages, recent years.	Foreign farmers.	Nationality of farm laborers.	Nationality preferred as farm laborers.	
Freeborn	Increase	Scandinavians, Germans, Irish¹	Scandinavians, Germans	Germans	Yes; Scandinavians and Germans.
Watonwan	No increase	Germans, Swedes, Norwegians	Germans, Scandinavians		Not much.
McLeod	$2 to $3 a month increase	Germans, Scandinavians, Bohemians, Poles, English.¹		Germans and Scandinavians.	Yes; all classes.
Stevens	Slight increase	Norwegians, Swedes, Germans	Germans, Swedes, Norwegians	Germans	Not much.
Pine	No increase	Germans Scandinavians	Germans, Scandinavians		Yes.
Clay	Increase	Scandinavians, Germans	Scandinavians	Scandinavians	Do.
Kittson	$30 a month, 1892; $25 a month, 1900.	Scandinavians, mostly; Poles; Germans, Canadians.¹	Americans, Scandinavians, Canadians.	Canadians	Do.

¹ Most farmers in the county are foreigners.
² Unless with stock.
³ Without board, summer.
⁴ With board, summer.

IOWA.

[Density of population: 1890, 34.5; 1900, 40.2; increase, 16.7 per cent. Fifteen counties, representing all parts of the State.]

Counties.	Density, 1900.	Kinds of farming.	Per cent of laborers employed through the year.	Opportunities for married men as laborers.	Work for women and children.	Customary wages, men.				
						Monthly (with board).		Winter.	Monthly or lump sum (with board), year.	Daily.
						Summer.	Winter.			
Washington	35.9	Grain; stock; dairy	10 per cent.	Yes	Yes	$20	$15		$18	[1]$1.00–$1.25
Mahaska (Oskaloosa)	59.5	General	70 per cent[2].	Yes; to some extent					[3]{16– 20, [4]30}	
Warren	35.4	General; stock	50 per cent.	Yes	Housework				15– 20	
Adair	28.1	....do	....do	None	None					
Crawford	30.1	Grain; stock	Few	....do		$18– 20	$12– 16			
Greene	37.0	General; stock	10 per cent.	....do		18– 22				[5]$1.50
Story	40.2	Grain; stock	Few	Yes		20– 30	20			
Tama	34.1	....do	30 per cent[6].	Some prefer married	For boys over 14	20– 23	15– 18		[7]220– 250, 250– 300	
Butler	31.1	General	10 per cent.	Yes	Yes	23	19		20	
Wright	31.6	Grain; dairy; stock	....do.[8]	....do.[9]		22	15		240	
O'Brien	29.5	Grain; stock; dairy	40 per cent.						16	
Dickinson	19.6	Grain; stock	20 per cent.	None	Housework	18– 20				1.25–1.50
Cerro Gordo	35.9	Grain	....do	Yes		20				[10]1.50
Clayton	37.2	Grain; stock	80 per cent.	Yes		24				[11]1.00
Allamakee	30.4	General; stock; dairy	All who wish.	Not good.		22	12		225	

[1] Occasionally, in summer wages are higher; without board.
[2] Many work in coal bank in winter.
[3] Not stated whether for summer, winter, or year.
[4] Without board, but with house and garden free.
[5] Summer, with board.
[6] Proportion increasing.
[7] Married men; house, garden, milk of cow free.
[8] More could have work if they wished.
[9] Some farmers now build tenant houses and employ men with families.
[10] Without board.
[11] With board.

AGRICULTURAL DISTRIBUTION OF IMMIGRANTS. 605

IOWA—Continued.

Counties.	Changes in rate of wages, recent years.	Foreign farmers	Nationality of farm laborers.	Nationality preferred as farm laborers.	Are there chances for immigrants who do not speak English?
Washington	25 per cent increase	Bohemians (many), Irish, Germans	Natives, a few foreigners		Not many.
Mahaska (Oskaloosa)	Increase	Dutch, Welsh	Dutch	Dutch	Some.
Warren	10 per cent increase	English, Scotch, Germans	Scotch, English, Swedes, Germans	In order named	Yes.
Adair	Increase from $16, summer	Scotch, Germans, English	All nationalities	No preference	Very few.
Crawford	No increase	Germans, Scandanavians, Irish, Scotch	Natives		
Greene	10 to 20 per cent increase	Scotch, Irish	Natives, Scotch, Germans	Foreigners; steadier	Not many.
Story	Increase	English, Danes, Norwegians	Many nationalities	Native whites	Not good.
Tama	...do	Germans, Irish, Bohemians, Belgians	Natives, Bohemians, Irish	Americans; German are liked.	Some.
Butler	...do	Germans, Irish, Danes, Swedes, English	Germans		Yes; hands very scarce.
Wright	...do	Germans, Irish, Swedes	Natives, Germans, Scandinavians, Irish.	Swedes, Germans	Yes.
O'Brien	...do	Germans, English	Germans, Swedes		Do.
Dickinson	25 per cent increase	Germans, Norwegians, Danes, Poles, Bohemians, Slovaks.	Germans, Norwegians, Danes		Not much.
Cerro Gordo	No increase	Germans, Scandinavians	Germans, Bohemians, Scandinavians.	Americans, Norwegians	None.
Clayton	25 cents a day and $4 a month increase.	Many; mostly Germans		Germans	Yes.
Allamakee	Increase	Germans, Norwegians, Irish	Germans, Norwegians, Irish	Americans, Germans, Norwegians.	Yes; German or Norse.

MISSOURI.

[Density of population: 1890, 39; 1900, 45.2; increase 16 per cent. First 8 counties, south of Missouri River; last 5 counties, north of Missouri River.]

Counties.	Density, 1900.	Kinds of farming.	Per cent of laborers employed through the year.	Opportunities for married men as farm laborers.	Work for women and children.	Customary wages, men.			
						Monthly (with board).		Monthly or lump sum (with board), year.	Daily.
						Summer.	Winter.		
Scott	31.4	General	70 per cent	None		$15	$12	$13.50	
Ripley	21.2	...do	All	Yes				$8–12.00	
Taney	15.5	General; stock; cotton		None		$12–15	$10–12		1$0.50
Wright	26.0	General; fruit; stock	Not many	Not much		15–20			1.00
Laclede	22.7	General; fruit	30 per cent	...do	In fruit	15–13	8	10.00	
Pettis (Sedalia)	47.3	Stock; grain	Almost all	Yes	Yes	15–18		15–18.00	
Johnson	33.2	General				15–18	10–12		1.00
Saline	41.1	General; stock		Yes	Housework			15.00	
Ray	44.2	...do	40 per cent	...do	Yes; women	15–25	12–20	12–20.00	
Livingston	41.9	...do		...do	Yes; housework	15–18		13–15.00	
Holt	37.1	General; stock; fruit	10 per cent	Very little		16–20	16–20		
Lewis	33.4	General; stock; dairying	50 per cent	Limited	Housework	18–20	15–20	116–25.00	
Adair	38.7	Grain and hay	...do	None		14–18	10–15		

Counties.	Changes in rate of wages, recent years.	Foreign farmers.	Nationality of farm laborers.	Nationality preferred as farm laborers.	Are there chances for immigrants who do not speak English?
Scott	No increase	Germans	Germans		Not many.
Ripley	Increase	Irish, Germans chiefly	Americans, Germans, Irish		Yes.
Taney	25 per cent increase	Germans, Irish, Scandinavians	Few foreigners		None.
Wright	No increase	Swedes, Germans, Irish, French, and some others	Americans, Swedes, Germans, Irish	No preference	Yes; Swedes, French, Germans.
Laclede	...do	Not many, if any	Americans		Not much.
Pettis (Sedalia)	Increase	Germans	...do	Americans	Yes.
Johnson	No increase	...do	Germans, Irish		Some.
Saline	...do	Germans (a few)	Negroes, native whites	Native whites greatly preferred.	Yes.
Ray	25 per cent increase	Few	Various nationalities		Very few.
Livingston	$3 to $5 a month increase	Germans	Americans, Germans	Americans	Good.
Holt	No increase	Germans, few Irish	Americans, Germans	No preference	None.
Lewis	...do	Germans, Irish	Germans, Irish	...do	Yes; Germans
Adair	...do		Few foreigners	Natives, Germans, Irish, English (in order named).	Not much.

1 Without board.

AGRICULTURAL DISTRIBUTION OF IMMIGRANTS. 607

NORTH DAKOTA.

[Density of population: 1890, 2.6; 1900, 4.5; increase, 70.9 per cent. First 12 counties, eastern half of State; last 5 counties, western half of State.]

Counties.	Density, 1900.	Kinds of farming.	Per cent of laborers employed through the year.	Opportunities for married men as farm laborers.	Work for women and children.	Customary wages, men.				
						Monthly (with board).		Winter.	Monthly or lump sum (with board), year.	Daily.
						Summer.				
Richland	12.0	Grain; stock	All who desire.	Yes		$25		$10-$13		[1]$2.00
Ransom	8.0	Grain	20 per cent	None		25		10	$20	
Lamoure	5.3	Grain; stock	10 per cent	Yes	Yes	25		15	22	[2]$0.50- 2.00
McIntosh	4.8	...do	Nearly all	Little						
Stutsman	4.0	...do	40 per cent[3]	Yes	Yes	20		10	200	
Barnes	8.7	Grain; flax; stock; dairy.	50 per cent	...do		$20- 25				
Cass (Fargo)	16.3	Grain; stock coming in	30 per cent	...do	Yes	18- 25		14	20	
Griggs	6.5	General	33 per cent	...do	Not for children	20- 22			20	
Grand Forks	17.1	Wheat	20 per cent[3]	Good	Some for children	20- 25		5- 10		[4]1.50- 2.00
Wells	6.4	Grain and stock	60 per cent	...do		25- 30		10- 20		
Benson	6.0	Grain; stock	75 per cent	Yes	Yes; for women	25- 35		15- 20	25	
Pembina	15.8	Grain and potatoes	50 per cent	...do		25- 35		15- 20	$200- 260	[3]2.00- 2.50
Emmons	2.8	Stock	40 per cent	None		20- 25		15- 20	35	
Burleigh	3.6	Grain; stock	66 per cent	Yes ([5])	Yes			20	240	[1]1.50- 2.50
Bottineau	6.6	Grain	All	...do	...do	22		8- 10	20	[5]2.00
Ward	1.2	Grain; stock	All who desire.			25		15		
Billings	.2	No farming done; stock only.								

[1] Summer.
[2] According to season.
[3] Remainder in lumber camps.
[4] August, September, and October.
[5] Harvest.
[6] Most take up farms of their own.

NORTH DAKOTA—Continued.

Counties.	Changes in rate of wages, recent years.	Foreign farmers.	Nationality of farm laborers.	Nationality preferred as farm laborers.	Are there chances for immigrants who do not speak English?
Richland	Little change	Germans, Scandinavians, Bohemians, Poles.	Germans, Scandinavians, Bohemians, natives.	No preference	Yes.
Ransom	No increase	Norwegians, Germans	Scandinavians		Not much.
Lamoure	Possibly slight increase	Norwegians, Swedes, Germans, German-Russians.	Same as farmers	No preference	Yes, at less wages.
McIntosh	No increase	Russians [1]	Russians, Norwegians		Yes; good chances.
Stutsman	do	Germans, Russians, Scandinavians, Poles.	Natives, English, Germans	Germans	Yes, if Germans.
Barnes	Increase	Scandinavians and Germans	Germans, Scandinavians, Austrians, Dutch, Belgians.		Yes.
Cass (Fargo)	5 to 10 per cent increase		Scandinavians, Germans, Canadians, natives.	Preferred in reverse order.	
Griggs	No increase	Scandinavians and Germans	Scandinavians	Scandinavians	Do.
Grand Forks	do	Scandinavians, Canadians, Irish, Germans.	All nationalities	Germans	Do.
Wells	$3 to $5 a month increase	Germans, Russians, Scandinavians, English, Irish.	Same as preceding column	Native whites	Do.
Benson	Some increase	Norwegians mostly, Germans	Scandinavians, Germans	Canadians liked	Do.
Pembina	No change	Germans, Scandinavians, Icelanders, British, Irish, French.	do	Russians	Do.
Emmons	No increase	Russians and Scandinavians	Germans, Russians, Scandinavians.	Preference in order named	Do.
Burleigh	do	Irish, Germans, Scandinavians, Russians, French.	Americans, Germans, Irish, Russians, Scandinavians.		
Bottineau		Norwegians, Swedes, French, Germans.	Swedes, Norwegians	Swedes, Norwegians	Yes, if agricultural.
Ward	Increase	Scandinavians, Germans	Scandinavians		Yes.
Billings					

[1] Make up three-fourths of population.

SOUTH DAKOTA.

[Density of population: 1890, 4.3; 1900, 5.2; increase, 16.8 per cent. First eleven counties east, last five west of Missouri River.]

Counties.	Density, 1900.	Kinds of farming.	Per cent of laborers employed through the year.	Opportunities for married men as farm laborers.	Work for women and children.	Customary wages, men.			
						Monthly (with board).		Monthly or lump sum (with board) year.	Daily.
						Summer.	Winter.		
Clay	22.8	Grain	50 per cent [1]	A few	Yes	$20-$25	$12-$15		
Union	25.0	...do	80 per cent	Fair		20- 25	10- 20	$20	
Minnehaha (Sioux Falls)	29.8	...do	50 per cent	Yes		18- 25		$200-250	
Davison	15.4	General; stock	...do	...do		20	20	15- 20	
Charles Mix	7.6	General; grain; stock	20 per cent [2]	...do		20	10		
Brookings	15.4	Grain; stock	70 per cent	Housework		22- 25	8- 10	3 30- 35	4 $1.50-2.00
Beadle	6.4	...do		Some opportunity	...do	18- 25	10- 12	200-240	
Buffalo	3.7	General					15		
Spink	6.2	General; grain; stock	40 per cent	Yes	Yes	25	10	20	
Potter	3.3	Grain; stock	50 per cent	Few	Few	23	10	200	3 1.00
Campbell	5.9	...do	Very few	None		20	5- 12	200	5 1.00-6 1.50
Meyer [7]		Stock	All; 70 per cent. [8]	Some				10- 40	
Washabaugh [7]		Stock; no farming							
Stanley	.3	...do						9 25- 60	
Pennington (Deadwood)	2.2	Grazing; stock [10]				35			
Butte	.4	Grain; stock	80 per cent	Yes		25	15		11 1.50-12 1.00

[1] Remainder in timber.
[2] Generally plenty of work in the winter by the day or job.
[3] Without board.
[4] Without board, harvest and thrashing.
[5] Haying.
[6] Harvest.
[7] No population returned for part outside of Indian reservation.
[8] Sheep ranches.
[9] Cowboys.
[10] On account of continual drought farming does not pay. Land passing into company's hands. Population decreasing.
[11] Summer, without board.
[12] Winter, without board.

SOUTH DAKOTA—Continued

Counties.	Changes in rate of wages, recent years.	Foreign farmers.	Nationality of farm laborers.	Nationality preferred as farm laborers.	Are there chances for immigrants who do not speak English?
Clay	Increase	Danes, Norse, Germans	Danes, Norse, Germans	No preference	Yes.
Union	...do	Scandinavians, Germans	Scandinavians, Irish, Germans, natives.	Swedes, Norse	Yes; Scandinavians and Germans.
Minnehaha (Sioux Falls)	Slight increase	Irish, Germans, Norwegians, Swedes	Germans, Irish, Scandinavians		Do.
Davison	Some increase	Germans, Russians, Norwegians, Irish, and others.	Many nationalities		Yes.
Charles Mix	$5 a month increase	Scandinavians mostly	All nationalities	No preference	Yes; Dutch, Germans, Scandinavians.
Brookings	No increase	Norwegians, Germans	Native whites; Scandinavians	...do	Yes; good.
Beadle	10 per cent increase	Germans, Belgians	Many nationalities	Germans, Swedes	Yes.
Buffalo	$5 per month increase	Germans, Scandivanians, Bohemians	All nationalities		On Government land.
Spink	30 per cent increase	Germans, Scandinavians	Native whites, Germans	Germans	Yes; Germans and Scandinavians.
Potter	No increase	Many of all nationalities	Germans, Norwegians, Swedes	No preference	Yes.
Campbell	...do	Russians, Norwegians	Scandinavians, Russians	These are liked	
Meyer[1]	Some increase	Germans, Norwegians, Bohemians, Dutch.	Norwegians, Germans, native whites.	Native whites	Yes; especially sheep ranches.
Washabaugh[1]			Indians		
Stanley			Native whites		None.
Pennington (Deadwood)	No increase	Danes and Finns	Russians, Scandinavians, Germans, Irish, Scotch.		Yes.
Butte					

[1] No population returned for part outside of Indian reservation.

AGRICULTURAL DISTRIBUTION OF IMMIGRANTS. 611

KANSAS.

[Density of population: 1890, 17.5; 1900, 18.0; increase, 2.9 per cent. First eight counties, eastern half of State; last six counties, western half of State.]

Counties.	Density, 1900.	Kinds of farming.	Per cent of laborers employed through the year.	Opportunities for married men as farm laborers.	Work for women and children.	Customary wages, men.				
						Monthly (with board).		Monthly (with board).	Monthly or lump sum (with board) year.	Daily.
						Summer.	Winter.			
Sedgwick (Wichita)	43.4	General; stock; dairy	80 per cent		None				$15	
McPherson	23.8	General	30 per cent	Not much	Household	$16–$20	$16–$18		$16– 20	1 $1–2 $2.00
Chase	11.0	Grain; stock		Yes; many prefer						
Osage	32.9	General; stock		To some extent		18– 20	16– 18		18	
Wabaunsee	16.2	Corn; stock	Al			18– 20			3 20– 26	
Douglas (Lawrence)	54.4	Grain; dairy; stock	30 per cent	Yes	Housework					4 1.00– 1.50
Wyandotte (Kansas City)	478.6	General; dairy; stock; fruit		do	Berries, and light farm work.	16			16	5 .75– 1.00
Marshall	27.1	Grain; dairy	66 per cent	None						
Stafford	12.4	Grain	10 per cent	do	Housework	17	15		15– 20	6 1.00
Barton	15.5	Grain; stock; dairy	50 per cent	Yes	Yes; for children	16– 30	12– 20		16– 25	
Ford	5.1	Grain; stock	90 per cent	do	Housework	20				
Kearny	1.3	Grain; stock; poultry (irrigation).	60 per cent	do		20				7 1.25
Ellis	9.6	Grain			Yes				15– 20	1.00– 1.50
Phillips	16.0	Grain; stock	40 per cent	Yes	Housework				16– 18	

1 With board.
2 With board, harvest and haying.
3 For married men, without board, but with house, garden, food for cow, etc., free.
4 Summer, without board.
5 Winter, without board.
6 With board, harvest.
7 Without board.

KANSAS—Continued.

Counties.	Changes in rate of wages, recent years.	Foreign farmers.	Nationality of farm laborers.	Nationality preferred as farm laborers.	Are there chances for immigrants who do not speak English?
Sedgwick (Wichita)			Germans	Germans	None.
McPherson	No increase	Germans	do		Do.[1]
Chase	Slight increase	Germans, Russians, Swedes	Swedes, Germans, Danes, Irish	Germans, Swedes	Yes; good.
Osage	No appreciable change	Germans, Danes, Swedes, Welsh	Germans, Swedes, Welsh, Danes	Germans	Yes; of nationalities named.
Wabaunsee	Increase	Germans, Swedes	Germans, Swedes, negroes		Yes; Germans.
Douglas (Lawrence)	do	Swedes, Germans, Irish	Irish, Swedes, Germans		Some.
Wyandotte (Kansas City)	Not much change	A few Irish	Natives, negroes, few others		None.
Marshall	Increase	Germans	Germans		Yes.
Stafford	No increase	Danes (a few)	Few foreigners		None.
Barton	Increase	Russians (many), Germans, Danes, and Swedes (a few)	Many kinds	Germans	Yes.
Ford	Slight increase	Germans	Natives, Germans		Not many.
Kearny	25 per cent increase	Germans, Swedes	Germans, Swedes, Irish		Yes; of nationalities named.
Ellis	Slight but steady increase	Russians	Russians, mostly		Yes.
Phillips	No increase	Germans	Natives	Germans or Swedes	Do.

[1] Unless Germans, going to a German settlement.

NEBRASKA.

[Density of population: 1890, 13.8 1900, 13.9; increase, 0.7 per cent. Eight counties—first four eastern, last four western.]

Counties.	Density, 1900.	Kinds of farming.	Per cent of laborers employed through the year.	Opportunities for married men as farm laborers.	Work for women and children.	Customary wages, men.				
						Monthly (with board).		Monthly or lump sum (with board) year.	Daily.
						Summer.	Winter.		
Nemaha	36.7	Grain; fruit; sugar beets.	20 per cent	Yes	Sugar beets	$20	$17		
Douglas (Omaha):									
1	412.3	General stock	50 per cent [1]	do	Housework	$10- 22	$5- 22	2$10-$22	
2		General; fruit; sugar beets.	25 per cent		Sugar beets [3]	20	(4)		
Washington	33.4	Grain; stock	50 per cent	Not good	Sugar beets	18- 20	5- 20	16- 20	
Dodge	42.1	General	do	Good	Women, housework	20	15		
Fillmore	26.6	Grain; stock	10 per cent	Yes	Sugar beets; housework.	18- 20		16- 20	
Buffalo	20.6	do	40 per cent	Yes; some prefer married.		16- 20			
Phelps	19.1	General; stock; dairy	30 per cent	Married men preferred	None regular	18	10	16	
Keith	1.8	General; sugar cane	75 per cent	Yes	Yes			18- 25	5$1-1.25

[1] Good hands are never idle.
[2] Without board and washing $10 to $15 more.
[3] A family of six can save $500 in a season.
[4] Board.
[5] Winter.

NEBRASKA—Continued.

Counties.	Changes in rate of wages, recent years.	Foreign farmers.	Nationality of farm laborers.	Nationality preferred as farm laborers.	Are there chances for immigrants who do not speak English?
Nemaha	No change	Germans and French	Irish, Germans, Scandinavians, Poles, French.		But little if any.
Douglas (Omaha):					
1	Increase	Germans, Scandinavians, Bohemians, British, Irish.	Germans	No preference, Germans liked.	Good.
2	$4 a month increase in 5 years.	Germans and Swedes[1]	Germans, Swedes, Danes	No preference if steady	Yes; at low wages.
Washington	Possibly slight increase	Germans, Danes, Swedes, Bohemians, English.	Germans, Americans, Danes, Swedes, Bohemians.	Germans	To limited extent.
Dodge	Increase	All nationalities	All except Irish	Swedes	Yes; in sugar beet industry.
Fillmore	25 to 50 per cent increase	...do	Danes, Swedes, Bohemians, Irish		Yes; with farmers of same nationality.
Buffalo	Slight increase	Germans, Swedes, Bohemians	Germans, Swedes, Bohemians	In order named	None.
Phelps	20 per cent increase	Swedes, Germans, Norwegians, Russians.	Germans, Swedes, Norwegians, Danes.	Germans, Swedes	Yes; especially Scandinavians and Germans.
Keith	10 to 20 per cent increase last 5 years.	Swedes, Irish, Germans	Swedes, Irish, natives	Native whites	Yes.

[1] Came years ago when land was cheap, and now are well off.

AGRICULTURAL DISTRIBUTION OF IMMIGRANTS. 615

DELAWARE.

[Density of population: 1880, 86.0; 1900, 94.3; increase, 9.6 per cent. The three counties of the State.]

Counties.	Density, 1900.	Kinds of farming.	Per cent of laborers employed through the year.	Opportunities for married men as farm laborers.	Work for women and children.	Customary wages, men.				
						Monthly (with board).		Monthly or lump sum (with board) year.	Daily.	
						Summer.	Winter.			
Sussex	46.4	Fruit; truck	Almost all	Yes; preferred	Canning; berry picking.			$10–$13	$0.75	
Kent:										
1	75.5	General; fruit; truck	All who desire.	Yes	do	$12–$14			1.60	
2		General; fruit; dairy	do	do	do	10– 15			$80.75– 1.00	
3		General; fruit; truck; dairy.	(3)	Yes; great demand	do	10– 15			4.50– 1.00	
Newcastle (Wilmington)	178.4	General; fruit; dairy	33 per cent	Preferred	Little	12– 15		$5–$10		
Do			10 per cent	None	None	10– 15				

Counties.	Changes in rate of wages, recent years.	Foreign farmers.	Nationality of farm laborers.	Nationality preferred as farm laborers.	Are there chances for immigrants who do not speak English?
Sussex	Little change	All speak English	English speaking		Doubtful.
Kent:					
1	Slight increase	Germans	Negroes, Germans	Germans	Yes; especially Germans.
2	Monthly; increase $3 to $5.	None	Negroes	Germans and Swedes	Some.
3	No increase	Germans, Canadians	Negroes, natives, Germans, Irish	No preference	Yes; especially Germans.
Newcastle (Wilmington)	Increase	Germans, English	Negroes, native whites	Negroes, native whites	Yes.
Do	No increase	Germans	Poles, Germans	Poles	Do.

[1] Winter, without board.
[2] Without board.
[3] Nine out of ten will be slightly employed two months.
[4] With board.

MARYLAND.

[Density of population, 1890, 105.7; 1900, 120.7; increase, 14 per cent. Three counties.]

Counties.	Density, 1900.	Kinds of farming.	Per cent of laborers employed through the year.	Opportunities for married men as farm laborers.	Work for women and children.	Customary wages, men. Monthly (with board). Summer.	Customary wages, men. Monthly (with board). Winter.	Customary wages, men. Monthly or lump sum (with board) year.	Customary wages, men. Daily.
Queen Anne ("Eastern Shore").	48.8	General; fruit	50 per cent[1]	Yes; plenty	Berry picking, corn thinning, wheat harvest.				²$0.50 [3]$0.75– 1.00
Talbot	71.1	Wheat and corn	66 per cent	A few	Little			$10	4.50– 1.00 [5].50
Washington (Hagerstown).	98.5	Grain; stock	50 per cent	Yes	Fairly good opportunities.			$12– 14	.75– 1.25

Counties.	Changes in rate of wages, recent years.	Foreign farmers.	Nationality of farm laborers.	Nationality preferred as farm laborers.	Are there chances for immigrants who do not speak English?
Queen Anne ("Eastern Shore").	Little change	Irish, Germans	Negroes mostly; Irish and Germans.	Negroes	Slight.[6]
Talbot	No increase	None[7]	Negroes, native whites	Whites	None.
Washington (Hagerstown).	do	Natives of German parentage	do		Yes.

[1] Good laborers can find steady employment.
[2] With board.
[3] Harvest.
[4] Summer.
[5] Winter.
[6] In 1870 Germans were brought here, but found it hard to learn our ways and language, and soon left.
[7] A few in adjoining county—Caroline—Hollanders.

AGRICULTURAL DISTRIBUTION OF IMMIGRANTS. 617

VIRGINIA.

[Density of population: 1890, 41.3; 1900, 46.2; increase, 12 per cent. First six counties along the Blue Ridge; one county along the Allegheny Range.]

Counties.	Density, 1900.	Kinds of farming.	Per cent of laborers employed through the year.	Opportunities for married men as farm laborers.	Work for women and children.	Customary wages, men.			
						Monthly (with board).		Monthly or lump sum (with board) year.	Daily.
						Summer.	Winter.		
Franklin	37.6	General; tobacco	All [1]	Some	Some	[4]$10–$15			[7]$0.50–$0.75 { [3] .35– • .50
Botetourt	31.3	General; tomatoes	do	Yes	Canning industry	20	$12.50	[6]$180	
Rockbridge [5]	36.8	General	do	do	Yes; plenty	8– 12	Less		
Amherst	38.5	General; sorghum; tobacco; fruit.	80 per cent		If they are willing				
Albemarle	37.7	Grain; stock; fruit	All	do	Housework; packing and picking fruit.			[8]120	
Do		Grain; stock; tobacco, truck.							[9]. 50
Augusta	32.0	Grain; stock; fruit	20 per cent	Not many	Very little				
Allegheny	36.1	General; stock	80 per cent		Housework			$10– 12	

Counties.	Changes in rate of wages, recent years.	Foreign farmers.	Nationality of farm laborers.	Nationality preferred as farm laborers.	Are there chances for immigrants who do not speak English?
Franklin	Wages doubled in 3 years	None	Negroes	Negroes	None.
Botetourt	Increase	do	All kinds	No preference	Do.
Rockbridge	do	do	White Americans, negroes	White Americans [7]	Yes; if white.
Amherst	No change	None; but desired as purchasers of land.	Negroes	Germans would probably suit better.	None.
Albemarle	20 per cent increase	Germans, English	Negroes, native whites	Native whites	Yes.
Do	No increase	Pennsylvanians of German descent	do	do	Poor.
Augusta			do		None.
Allegheny	No increase	None	No foreigners; native whites, negroes.		Yes; Germans; Swedish girls for housework.

[1] There are cotton factories not far off, in North Carolina, who get hands from our county, and will hire whole families—men, women, and children—at prices from $1 to $3 a day. Latter price for weavers. [6] To good, competent man house furnished free.
[2] Summer, with board. [7] The negro is too fine a gentleman for a farm hand; they are flocking to the towns. There are a great many empty cabins.
[3] Winter, with board. [8] One hundred and fifty pounds bacon, 18 pounds corn meal, house, garden, and firewood furnished.
[4] Not stated what part of year. [9] With board; harvest and haymaking and corn cutting, $1 a day, with board.
[5] From this and other Virginia counties certain cities have been separated.

WEST VIRGINIA.

[Density of population: 1890, 31.0; 1900, 38.9; increase, 25.7 per cent.]

Counties.	Density, 1900.	Kinds of farming.	Per cent of laborers employed through the year.	Opportunities for married men as farm laborers.	Work for women and children.	Customary wages, men.				
						Monthly (with board.)		Monthly or lump sum (with board) year.	Daily.	
						Summer.	Winter.			
Monroe	28.3	Stock; general	20 per cent	Not much	Very little			$10-$15	$0.75-$0.50	
Raleigh	22.2	General	Few	Good openings	None				3. 75	
Greenbrier	19.7	Grazing	(⁴)	Yes	Housework	⁵$15	⁵$10	⁵150	6. 75- 1.25	
Putnam:										
1	49.1	Stock; general; fruit a growing industry.	30 per cent	do⁷	do				{ 2. 50- .75 / ⁶.75- 1.00 / ⁶.50- .60 }	
2		do	do	do	{ Housework occasionally. }	$12- 18	$8- 16		⁶.65- .85	
Mason	52.6	General; fruit	50 per cent	None	{ Women, housework; children, light work on farm. }			⁶ $13- 19	{ ⁶.85- 1.25 / ².50 / 8. 75 / 9. 75 }	
Barbour	38.7	General; grazing	75 per cent	Good						
Brook	74.4	General; stock; dairying.	100 per cent	do	Good chances					

Counties.	Changes in rate of wages, recent years.	Foreign farmers.	Nationality of farm laborers.	Nationality preferred as farm laborers.	Are there chances for immigrants who do not speak English?
Monroe	Slight increase	None	English, negroes	White labor	None.
Raleigh	Increase	do	No labor employed		Do.
Greenbrier	do	Irish, mostly	Few foreigners; Irish, Germans		
Putnam:					
1	No increase	None	Native whites, Irish (a few)	Native whites	None.
2	No change	do	Native whites, negroes	do	Do.
Mason	No increase	do	Native whites	do	Do.
Barbour	15 per cent increase	do	Native whites, negroes	do	Not many.
Brook	Little increase	German, Irish, English	Germans, Irish, English	Germans	Yes.

¹ Summer.
² Winter.
³ Mine wages, $1.25.
⁴ Farm laborers are scarce. Majority go to lumber camps in the mountains.
⁵ Without board usually.
⁶ Without board.
⁷ Men employed by year are usually married.
⁸ Winter, without board.
⁹ House rent, pasture, garden, and truck patch free.

NORTH CAROLINA.

[Density of population: 1890, 33.3; 1900, 39; increase, 17.1 per cent. Eight counties in eastern and northern part of State; last two in western part.]

Counties.	Density, 1900.	Kinds of farming.	Per cent of laborers employed through the year.	Opportunities for married men as farm laborers.	Work for women and children.	Monthly (with board).		Customary wages, men. Monthly or lump sum (with board) year.	Daily.
						Summer.	Winter.		
Craven (Newbern)	35.3	Truck; cotton	75 per cent	Poor					$0.65
Beaufort	32.2	Corn; cotton; truck	"Many"	Yes	Trucking; cotton	$9–$10	$9–$10	$9–$10	
Pitt	48.0	General; cotton; tobacco; truck.	(¹)	...do	Yes; plenty			²10– 12	
Wayne	52.5	General; truck; cotton	70 per cent	None				13	
Wilson	60.2	Cotton; tobacco; truck	75 per cent	Yes	Yes			³9– 10	
Edgecombe:									
1	51.6	General; truck; cotton	All	Married preferred	Little			8– 10	
2			(¹)	Yes	Yes, plenty			²10– 14	
Wake (Raleigh):									
1	65.0	General; cotton; tobacco.	All	...do	Cotton and tobacco			210	
2		General; truck; cotton	80 per cent	Yes; as teamsters and cowmen.	Berry and vegetable picking.			10	.50– .60
Franklin	53.1	Tobacco; cotton; corn	75 per cent	Not much				8	.60
Alamance	51.9	General; fruit; cotton	All	Married preferred	Yes	8– 10	6– 8	6– 10	
Burke	33.1	Small grain	50 per cent	Not many					

¹ All that desire it can, but only small per cent wish constant employment.
² With board, house rent, firewood.
³ With house, firewood, and garden.

NORTH CAROLINA—Continued.

Counties.	Changes in rate of wages, recent years.	Foreign farmers.	Nationality of farm laborers.	Nationality preferred as farm laborers.	Are there chances for immigrants who do not speak English.
Craven (Newbern)	No change	None	Negroes		None.
Beaufort	do	do	Negroes, native whites (a few)		Do.
Pitt	do	do	Negroes	Negroes	Do.
Wayne	Slight increase	do	"Americans"		Do.
Wilson		do	Natives		Do.
Edgecombe:					
1	Increase	do	do		Do
2	do	do	Negroes, native whites	White on small farms, negroes on large.	Yes.
Wake (Raleigh):					
1	do	do	Negroes	Whites [1]	None
2	10 per cent increase	English, Scotch, Irish	do		Yes.
Franklin	Some increase	None	do		None.
Alamance	No increase	do	No foreigners		Do.
Burke	Slight increase	English, Valdese	Negroes, Italians (a few)		Not many.

[1] "Negroes are of very little account. Politics and schooling have wrought their ruin."

SOUTH CAROLINA.

[Density of population: 1890, 38.2; 1900, 44.4; increase, 16.4 per cent. Eight counties; first two southern, remainder northern.]

Counties.	Density, 1900.	Kinds of farming.	Per cent of laborers employed through the year.	Opportunities for married men as farm laborers.	Work for women and children.	Customary wages, men.				
						Monthly (with board).		Monthly or lump sum (with board) year.	Daily.
						Summer.	Winter.		
Beaufort	37.6	Corn; cotton; truck	All	Yes				$8–$10	$0.40–$0.50
Hampton	25.4	General; cotton; tobacco	50 per cent	do	Cotton			10–12	
Darlington	49.9				Light farm work and cotton.				.75– 1.00
Newberry	50.8	General; cotton	80 per cent	None		$10	$8	5– 6	
Cherokee	59.1	Cotton; changing to truck and dairy.[1]		Yes					
Spartanburg	86.0	General; cotton	90 per cent	None	Cotton	$11–12	$9– 10	10	3.50
Greenville	71.8	Cotton[2]	75 per cent	Yes				8	.50
Pickens	36.5	General; cotton	30 per cent	do [4]					

Counties.	Changes in rate of wages, recent years.	Foreign farmers.	Nationality of farm laborers.	Nationality preferred as farm laborers.	Are there chances for immigrants who do not speak English?
Beaufort	Decrease [5]	Germans (a few)	Negroes		None.
Hampton			Negroes, poor whites, Germans (a few).		Do.
Darlington	Slight increase	Germans, Irish	Negroes, native whites	Negroes, although unsatisfactory.	Limited.
Newberry	No change	None	do		Do.
Cherokee	Increase [4]	do	Negroes	Native whites	None.
Spartanburg	10 per cent increase in two years.		Negroes, native whites		Do.
Greenville	No change	French, Irish, Germans, Swiss, English.	Negroes	More intelligent labor is desired.	Yes; as house servants, gardeners, and truck farmers.
Pickens	No increase	None	do		Some.

[1] This change will alter demand for labor. Negroes can not carry on truck and dairy farming. [4] Factory work has made labor scarce.
[2] Vegetables and fruit will be in demand on account of growth of cotton mills. [5] Owing to low price of cotton.
[3] Summer, without board.

GEORGIA.

[Density of population: 1890, 31.2; 1900, 37.6; increase, 20.6 per cent. Fourteen counties, representing all parts of the State.]

Counties.	Density. 1900.	Kinds of farming.	Per cent of laborers employed through the year.	Opportunities for married men as farm laborers.	Work for women and children.	Customary wages, men.				
						Monthly (with board).		Monthly or lump sum (with board) year.	Daily.	
						Summer.	Winter.			
Charlton	3.4	General; cotton; cane	All who desire.	Yes	Yes			$8–$12		
Irwin	19.9	General; cotton	60 per cent	Yes				8–12	[1] $0.75–$1.00	
Sumter	49.0	General; cotton; sugar cane.	All	Yes					.50	
Crawford	34.0	General	90 per cent	Married preferred	do			8–10	[1] .75	
Washington	41.5	General; cotton	98 per cent	Yes	do			[2] 6–10		
Walton	57.2	do	[3]	do	do	$10–$15	$8	[4] 10–12		
Elbert	50.8	Grain; cotton	All	do	do	12½	8	10		
Gwinnett	50.2	General; cotton	50 per cent	do	do	9	7	8		
Carroll	54.7		All who desire.	do	Hoeing and picking cotton.	12	$8–10			
Bartow	42.9	General; cotton	80 per cent	do	do		8	10		
Floyd	65.5	do	50 per cent	do	do	12	10	10	[1] .60	
Catoosa	34.1		10 per cent	Some	Berry picking		10			
Fannin	28.8	General; fruit	Very few	Not much			10			
Habersham	36.6	General; cotton		Yes; negroes	Yes		12			

[1] Without board.
[2] House, rent, fuel, and garden free.
[3] Demand is great for entire year; negro tenants will not work more than seven months.
[4] With board, house, wood, etc.

GEORGIA—Continued.

Counties.	Changes in rate of wages, recent years.	Foreign farmers.	Nationality of farm laborers.	Nationality preferred as farm laborers.	Are there chances for immigrants who do not speak English?
Charlton	No increase	Irish, Scotch	Few foreigners		Yes; if industrious and honest.
Irwin	Not much increase	None	Negroes, few foreigners	Preference varies with farmer.	Not good as laborers.
Sumter	5 per cent increase	...do	Negroes	Protestant Germans, or Scotch.	Yes.
Crawford	No increase	Very few	...do		None.
Washington	...do	None	"Americans"		Do.
Walton	25 per cent increase	...do	Negroes, native whites	Negroes [2]	Yes.
Elbert	No increase	...do	Native whites, negroes	Native whites	Do.
Gwinnett	Increase	English, Scotch, Germans	English, Germans, Scotch, Chinese, negroes.	Negroes	Not much.
Carroll	Slight increase	Irish, Dutch	Negroes, native whites	No preference	Yes.
Bartow	No increase	None	...do	Native whites	None.
Floyd	Some increase	...do	Native whites		Do.
Catoosa	Very little increase, if any	Germans, Irish	No foreigners		Do.
Fannin	No increase	None	Negroes, a few Irish and Germans		Yes; in colonies.
Habersham	...do	Very few			Very few.

[1] This section is settling up with Northern people.   [2] Although they are getting very unreliable.

FLORIDA.

[Density of population: 1880, 7.2; 1900, 9.7; increase, 35 per cent. Thirteen counties, representing all parts of the State but extreme south.]

Counties.	Density, 1900.	Kinds of farming.	Per cent of laborers employed through the year.	Opportunities for married men as farm laborers.	Work for women and children.	Customary wages, men. Monthly (with board). Summer.	Customary wages, men. Monthly (with board). Winter.	Monthly or lump sum (with board) year.	Daily.
Polk	6.3	General; truck; cassava.	All	Yes	Yes			$15–$20	$1.00
Hillsboro (Tampa)	27.5	Oranges; pineapples	75 per cent						1.25
Pasco	8.1	Truck; fruit; sugar; rice; tobacco.	All		Berries, cotton, tobacco.				[⁷1.75– 1.00 / ³.40– .75
Volusia	7.8	Oranges; truck	...do	Yes; and likely to be more.	Housework				1.00
Putnam	15.1	Oranges; cane; general; stock.	50 per cent	Yes					1.75
St. John	9.5	Truck; fruit	40 per cent						
Alachua	25.1	General; truck; cotton; cassava; cane.	..do⁴						
Columbia	21.6	Cotton; corn; cane	All	Not certain	Plenty			10– 13	¹.75– 1.00
Madison	22.3	General; truck; dairy; stock; cane; cotton.		Married preferred				⁵5– 10	1.65
Gadsden	30.6	General; stock; cotton; cane; tobacco.	All⁶		Tobacco, warehouses, and fields.	⁷$4			¹.75– .80
Jackson	24.3	Cotton; corn	All who desire.	Not many		$8–10			
Calhoun	18.6	General; truck; cassava; cane; cotton.	50 per cent	Yes	Yes			⁸10– 12	
Walton	6.8	Stock; fruit; general	All	None	None			10– 12	

¹ Without board.
² Men.
³ Women and children.
⁴ Good men get steady work; remainder do not want steady work.
⁵ Board and house furnished free to married. Garden and wood free in country.
⁶ "And most of the time we are short of laborers."
⁷ A week.
⁸ Board, wood, and house furnished. Turpentine farms and sawmills pay $1 a day and up.

AGRICULTURAL DISTRIBUTION OF IMMIGRANTS.

FLORIDA—Continued.

Counties.	Changes in rate of wages, recent years.	Foreign farmers.	Nationality of farm laborers.	Nationality preferred as farm laborers.	Are there chances for immigrants who do not speak English?
Polk	Increase	Very few	Native whites, negroes	Germans and Swedes wanted.	Yes; on farms and in phosphate mines.
Hillsboro (Tampa)	No increase	English, Swedes, Germans, Spanish	Native whites, some foreigners	No preference	Poor.
Pasco	...do	Germans, French, Russians, English	English, Germans, negroes		Yes; Germans.
Volusia	Expected increase	Germans, Swedes, French, Irish	Germans, Swedes		None.
Putnam	Decrease[1]	Germans (a few)	Negroes mostly, native whites, English, Germans.	Whites	Germans might get along.
St. John	No increase	None	Negroes, native whites	Negroes	Very few.
Alachua	Before orange freeze $1 a day.	...do	Negroes	...do[2]	Not on farms, but in phosphate or turpentine work.
Columbia	15 to 20 per cent increase	Very few	Negroes, native whites (a few)	Negroes	None.
Madison	No increase	None	Negroes	...do	Yes; but they can not compete with negro labor.
Gadsden	Increase	Germans, Scotch[3]	...do		
Jackson	20 per cent increase	None[4]	...do	...do	A few.
Calhoun	Increase	Germans, Swedes	Few foreigners		Few at full wages.
Walton	No increase	Swedes	Negroes	White labor if could be had.	None.

[1] Owing to freeze of 6 years ago.
[2] "The negro suits this section best because we do not have to provide houses or food for him. If there is no house convenient, he sleeps under a tree, works about half of his time, and is the happiest creature living."
[3] Most new settlers are from southern States and make good citizens. We want more of this class. We do not want foreigners.
[4] We could furnish locations for 25 to 50 families. Norwegians, Swedes, or Germans preferred.

KENTUCKY.

[Density of population: 1890, 46.5; 1900, 53.7; increase, 15.5 per cent.]

Counties.	Density, 1900.	Kinds of farming.	Per cent of laborers employed through the year.	Opportunities for married men as farm laborers.	Work for women and children.	Customary wages, men.				Nationality preferred as farm laborers.	Are there chances for immigrants who do not speak English?
						Monthly (with board).		Monthly or lump sum (with board) year.	Daily.		
						Summer.	Winter.				
Christian	54.7	General; stock; tobacco	All	Very few		[1]$10–$15		$12–$12.50		Negroes	None.
Barren	47.3	...do	75 per cent	Very little		8–10				...do	Do.
Adair	41.1	General	All	None at present		12					
Clay	33.6	General; stock	10 per cent	Not good					[2]$0.50–$0.65 [3]$.40–.60	Americans	Do.
Knott	25.2	General; stock; tobacco	33 per cent	Yes	Plenty	[5]14	$10			...do	Do.
Madison	58.7	General; stock; tobacco	All natives	...do	Yes	[5]12		$12		Negroes, native whites	Do.
Anderson	44.9	General; stock	33 per cent	...do	Housework	10–12	7		.75–1.00	...do	Do.
Owen	43.9	General; stock; tobacco	Nearly all	...do[6]	...do			12–16		"Native born"	Do.
Rowan	34.4	General; tobacco	40 per cent		None	14	12	13		No prejudices against foreign labor.	Very poor.

Counties.	Changes in rate of wages, recent years.	Foreign farmers.	Nationality of farm laborers.
Christian	Little change	None	Negroes
Barren	Little change, if any	...do	...do
Adair	Slight increase	Swiss	Americans
Clay	No increase	None	...do
Knott	...do	...do	...do
Madison	Increase	...do	Negroes, native whites
Anderson	Little change	...do	...do
Owen		Some Germans in parts of the State succeeding well.	"Native born"
Rowan	10 per cent increase	French (a few)	...do

[1] Food furnished families doing cooking.
[2] With board, summer.
[3] Without board, summer.
[4] Winter.
[5] Not stated whether summer or winter.
[6] Large per cent of laborers are married.

TENNESSEE.

[Density of population: 1890, 42.3; 1900, 48.4; increase, 14.3 per cent.]

Counties.	Density, 1900.	Kinds of farming.	Per cent of laborers employed through the year.	Opportunities for married men as farm laborers.	Work for women and children.	Customary wages, men.				
						Monthly (with board).		Monthly or lump sum (with board) year.	Daily.
						Summer.	Winter.		
Hamblen	77.1	General; changing to dairy and stock.	10 per cent	Yes	Picking cowpeas, late summer.	$9–$15	$8–$12		
Giles:								$8–$15	
1	54.6	General; stock		do				[1]12– 20	
2		General; cotton	10 per cent	Yes; good	Housework			13	$0.50
Marshall	59.5	General; stock; a little cotton.	All who wish	Yes	do	10	8	9– 13	
Maury	67.4	General	60 per cent[2]	Married preferred				[3]10– 12	.50
Williamson	52.8	do	90 per cent					10	[4]0.75–1.00
Hickman	25.0	do	All						[5].50– .75
Davidson (Nashville)	236.2	General; dairy; cotton; tobacco.	do						[6].40– .65
Sumner	50.1	General; stock	50 per cent	None	None			10	
Lauderdale	47.8	General; cotton; fruit	do	Yes	A little at housework.			10	
Obion	56.0	General; stock	90 per cent	do[7]	Housework; light farming.			13	

[1] With house rent, garden, wood (no board).
[2] Phosphate mines near by affect employment.
[3] With board, house, and fuel.
[4] Harvest.
[5] Summer.
[6] Winter.
[7] **Farmer will furnish dwelling.**

TENNESSEE—Continued.

Counties.	Changes in rate of wages, recent years.	Foreign farmers.	Nationality of farm laborers.	Nationality preferred as farm laborers.	Are there chances for immigrants who do not speak English?
Hamblen	No change		Native whites and negroes, some Germans and Irish.	Germans and Irish	Not much.[1]
Giles:					
1	do	None	Negroes mostly	Negroes	Little.
2	do	do	Negroes, native whites		Yes.
Marshall	Some increase	do	Americans		None.
Maury	10 per cent increase[2]	Not many[3]	Negroes, native whites	Negroes	Do.
Williamson	No increase		Negroes	do	Yes; good.
Hickman	do		Native whites, negroes	do	None.
Davidson (Nashville)	No increase	None from the Northwest	Negroes	do	Yes.
Sumner	Increase	A few from the Northwest	Negroes, a few Germans and Scandinavians.	Germans	None.
Lauderdale					Not much.
Obion	$3 a month increase	Germans; Irish (prosperous)	Native whites, negroes	Native whites	Yes.

[1] Unless immigrant is specialist in some feature of agriculture.
[2] Since opening of phosphate mines.
[3] Present foreign settlers mostly Jewish merchants. This county was originally settled up by foreigners—Irish, Dutch, and English.

AGRICULTURAL DISTRIBUTION OF IMMIGRANTS. 629

ALABAMA.

[Density of population: 1890, 29.4; 1900, 35.3; increase, 20.9 per cent.]

Counties.	Density, 1900.	Kinds of farming.	Per cent of laborers employed through the year.	Opportunities for married men as farm laborers.	Work for women and children.	Customary wages, men.			
						Monthly (with board).		Monthly or lump sum (with board) year.	Daily.
						Summer.	Winter.		
Henry	36.4	General; cotton; peanuts.	All	Yes	Hoeing and gathering crops.			$6–$8	
Monroe	22.8	General; cotton; cane; rice.	do[1]	None				8–15	
Butler	33.5	General; cotton; cane; truck.	Almost all	Married preferred	Picking cotton and strawberries.			[3]10–15	
Lee	49.6	Cotton	All	Yes; on dairy farms		$10	$8		
Sumter	36.5	Cotton; vegetables							
Hale	42.7	Diversified coming in	All	Yes; under cropping system.		10	8		
Pickens	26.0	Cotton; corn	50 per cent						
Talladega	52.8	Cotton; grain	Almost all					8–10	

Counties.	Changes in rate of wages, recent years.	Foreign farmers.	Nationality of farm laborers.	Nationality preferred as farm laborers.	Are there chances for immigrants who do not speak English?
Henry	Increase	None	No foreigners		None.
Monroe	Decrease	Very few	Negroes[2]		Yes.
Butler	25 per cent increase in 2 years.	None	do		Do.
Lee	Increase	None	do	Negroes of best grade	Think not.
Sumter		Some Germans and Irish	do	Germans and Poles; Irish.	For Germans and Poles.
Hale		None	do		
Pickens	Increase	A few	do		None.
Talladega	No increase		Negroes, native whites		

[1] If they wish. Those we have will not hire by the year.
[2] They have got to be very worthless. We need working people.
[3] Rise to $30 in best of picking season.

MISSISSIPPI.

[Density of population: 1890, 27.8; 1900, 33.5; increase, 20.3 per cent. First seven counties, southern half; last five counties, northern half.]

Counties.	Density, 1900.	Kinds of farming.	Per cent of laborers employed through the year.	Opportunities for married men as farm laborers.	Work for women and children.	Customary wages, men.			
						Monthly (with board).		Monthly or lump sum (with board) year.	Daily.
						Summer.	Winter.		
Wilkinson:									
1	32.3	Cotton; stock (a little)	All	Yes	Yes			$10	[1]$0.50
2		Cotton; stock	75 per cent	do				10	
Lincoln	35.1	Cotton; corn; truck	All[2]	Married preferred	Fruit picking and packing.			$10–20	[3]$0.75–1.25
Copiah	46.0	General; cotton; corn; truck	do						
Hinds:									
1	62.1	Cotton; truck; stock	90 per cent		Yes			10	.60–.75
2		Cotton; corn; truck	All[2]	Yes					[4].75–1.25
Madison	45.5	General; stock; cotton; truck	50 per cent					[5]13	.55
Newton	35.1	Corn; cotton; oats	20 per cent	Not good	Hoeing and corn gathering.	$10	$8	9	
Lauderdale (Meridian):									
1	56.3	Cotton; corn; truck	Few	Yes	Cotton picking			[6]10–15	
2		General; cotton; truck	25 per cent	do	Housework			10	
Lowndes	57.7	General; cotton; stock	Few[6]	None				75–150	
Oktibbeha	46.4	Cotton, changing to dairy and stock.	20 per cent[8]	Yes, to some extent	Dairying and housework.	10–13	8		[7].50–.60
Carroll	36.1	General; cotton; stock	20 per cent[8]	As renters	Light farm work			8–10	
Prentiss	37.6	General; cotton; fruit	All	Yes				10–15	
Marshall	39.1	General; cotton	([9])	As renters	Cotton			10	

[1] With board.
[2] In mills, etc.
[3] Doubtful whether farm labor only.
[4] Without board.
[5] For average negro labor. House supplied, but not board. White labor paid more.
[6] Except in dairy and stock.
[7] Winter.
[8] This represents all who are competent and willing to work.
[9] Employment through year, but crops generally grown on shares.

AGRICULTURAL DISTRIBUTION OF IMMIGRANTS. 631

MISSISSIPPI—Continued.

Counties.	Changes in rate of wages, recent years.	Foreign farmers.	Nationality of farm laborers.	Nationality preferred as farm laborers.	Are there chances for immigrants who do not speak English?
Wilkinson:					
1	No increase [1]	Swedes (a few)	Negroes	Negroes for cotton	None, unless in colonies.
2	Increase	Swedes	...do	Negroes	None.
Lincoln	...do	Many	Negroes, native whites		Yes.
Copiah	Some increase	None	Negroes	No preference	Do.
Hinds:					
1	About the same	Very few	...do	Negroes for cotton	Very slight.
2	15 per cent increase		...do	Negroes	None.
Madison	Little if any increase	German Swedes	Negroes, some Germans and Swedes.	...do	Limited.
Newton	No increase	None	Negroes	...do	None.
Lauderdale (Meridian):					
1	Increase	Few	...do		Do not know, as not tried.
2	$2 a month increase	Germans	...do	Germans and Swedes	Yes; Germans and Swedes.
Lowndes	No increase	None	...do		None.
Oktibbeha	$2 to $5 a month increase	Germans	...do	Negroes	Yes.
Carroll	Some increase	Germans (a few)	Negroes, native whites, few foreigners.	Negroes, Germans	None.
Prentiss	Slight increase	None	Negroes, native whites	Negroes for hard labor	Probably good.[2]
Marshall	No increase	Not many: Irish, Germans, and Swedes	Negroes, native whites, few foreigners.	Of foreigners, Swedes	Yes.[3]

[1] Wages determined by price of cotton. $1 per month for each cent of price. [2] Although none of this class here. [3] Unfamiliarity with cotton farming a drawback.

LOUISIANA.

[Density of population: 1890, 24.6; 1900, 30.4; increase, 23.5 per cent. First two parishes, southern part of State; last five parishes, northern part of State.]

Parishes.	Density, 1900.	Kinds of farming.	Per cent of laborers employed through the year.	Opportunities for married men as farm laborers.	Work for women and children.	Customary wages, men.			
						Monthly (with board).		Monthly or lump sum (with board) year.	Daily.
						Summer.	Winter.		
Iberia	49.8	Cane, cotton, corn	All	Yes	Yes				{1$0.75-$0.85 2 1.25–1.50
Acadia	37.1	Rice, cotton, corn, cane	50 per cent 4	Yes; good					5 1.00
Winn	10.1	General; rice, cotton	All	Yes				$10–$12.80	6 1.00– 7 1.50
Tensas	28.7	Corn, cotton	do	None	Very little				.50– .75
Richland	20.4	do	do	Yes				$10.00	
Claiborne	30.1	do	90 per cent	Yes; good	Yes				7.75–1.00
Caddo (Shreveport)	49.1	do	All	Few				10–15	7.75

Parishes.	Changes in rate of wages, recent years.	Foreign farmers.	Nationality of farm laborers.	Nationality preferred as farm laborers.	Are there chances for immigrants who do not speak English?
Iberia	No appreciable increase	Germans, Italians, Swedes	Negroes, Italians	Negroes 3	Yes; good.
Acadia	Increase	Few	Negroes		Few.
Winn	do	None	Native whites, negroes		Yes.
Tensas	No change	do	Negroes		Do.
Richland	Increase	Germans	do	Germans or Swedes	Do.
Claiborne	do	Few; Germans, Irish, Mexicans	do	Negroes	None.
Caddo (Shreveport)	Little increase	Swedes			Do.

1 Summer, without board; not stated whether for farm labor only.
2 Winter, without board.
3 Italians employed only on large sugar plantations.
4 Remainder go into rice mills in winter.
5 With board.
6 With board; not stated whether for farm laborers only.
7 Without board.

TEXAS.

[Density of population: 1890, 8.5; 1900, 11.6; increase, 36.4 per cent. Five counties on the Brazos River.]

Counties.	Density, 1900.	Kinds of farming.	Per cent of laborers employed through the year.	Opportunities for married men as farm laborers.	Work for women and children.	Customary wages, men.			
						Monthly (with board).		Monthly or lump sum (with board) year.	Daily.
						Summer.	Winter.		
Brazoria	10.3	Truck and fruit	All					$18.00	[1]$1.00
Harris (Houston)	36.2	Corn; cotton; cane; rice; truck.	do						10.75– 1.00
Brazos	37	Grain; cotton; sorghum	90 per cent	Very little		$12–$15	$16–$18	$12–15.00	
Limestone	33	General; stock; cotton		Yes	Cotton	[1]15– 20	[1]19– 23	12–18.00	
								[1]15–23.00	
								12–15.00	
Hood	21	do	All	do				{[3][1]20–22.50}	

Counties.	Changes in rate of wages, recent years.	Foreign farmers.	Nationality of farm laborers.	Nationality preferred as farm laborers.	Are there chances for immigrants who do not speak English?
Brazoria	Increase monthly, not day wages.	Italians (many), Germans, and Swedes.	Native whites from North		Yes.[2]
Harris (Houston)	Increase	Danes and Germans	Negroes	Negroes	Do.[3]
Brazos	No increase	Germans, Bohemians, Poles, Italians.	Negroes, a few whites	Of whites, Germans, and Bohemians.	Yes; Germans, Bohemians.
Limestone	Slight increase	Germans and Poles (a few)	Negroes, native whites, little foreign.	Good foreign labor would be acceptable. Germans would be preferred.	None.
Hood	No increase	None	Americans		Yes; in colonies.

[1] Without board.
[2] In truck farming and small fruit growing. Only 10 acres of land are required and profits are good.
[3] Great opportunities in prairie lands near Houston, especially if acquainted with rice culture.

ARKANSAS.

[Density of population: 1890, 21.3; 1900, 24.7; increase, 16.3 per cent.]

Counties.	Density, 1900.	Kinds of farming.	Per cent of laborers employed through the year.	Opportunities for married men as farm laborers.	Work for women and children.	Customary wages, men. Monthly (with board). Summer.	Customary wages, men. Monthly (with board). Winter.	Monthly or lump sum (with board) year.	Daily.
Ouachita	28.2	General; cotton; sorgtum.		Yes	Hoeing and gathering.			$8–$15	
Arkansas	12.8	Grain; stock; prairie hay.	75 per cent [1]	To some extent		$15			[2]$0.75–$1.00
Cleburne	15.2	Grain; cotton	All who wish	Yes	Cotton and berry picking.				[3].75–1.00
Benton:									
1	35.4	General; cotton	All	Yes; good	Fruit		$10	10	
2		General; fruit	20 per cent	Not good					[6].75–[7]0.50

Counties.	Changes in rate of wages, recent years.	Foreign farmers.	Nationality of farm laborers.	Nationality preferred as farm laborers.	Are there chances for immigrants who do not speak English?
Ouachita	No increase	None	Natives		Yes.
Arkansas	Slight increase	Germans (many), Slovaks	Germans and Swedes	Germans	Yes; limited number.
Cleburne	25 per cent increase	Few [5]	Few foreigners		
Benton:					
1	Increase	Very few	do	No preference	Yes; good.
2	No increase	do	Natives		None.

[1] Hay balers needed all winter.
[2] Winter, with board.
[3] With board.
[4] Without board.
[5] Good chance for a colony of Germans, Irish, or Swedes.
[6] Without board, summer.
[7] Without board, winter.

MONTANA.

[Density of population: 1890, 0.9; 1900, 1.7; increase, 84.1 per cent. First eight counties, eastern and central; last five, western.]

Counties.	Density, 1900.	Kinds of farming.	Per cent of laborers employed through the year.	Opportunities for married men as farm laborers.	Work for women and children.	Customary wages, men.				
						Monthly (with board).			Monthly or lump sum (with board) year.	Daily.
						Summer.	Winter.			
Dawson	0.2	Stock only	Few employed at all.	None	None					
Park	2.6	Grain and hay	50 per cent	Yes						
Sweet Grass	1.1	Hay (irrigation)	70 per cent	do	Housework	$30			$30–$35	
Meagher	.6	Grain; stock	40 per cent	do	Housework	$35– 40	$25–$30		30– 35	
Fergus	.8	Sheep; fodder	90 per cent	do	Children a drawback				35	
Cascade (Great Falls)	9.3	Grain; stock (irrigation)	50 per cent	do [1]		{ [2] 25– 30 [3] 35	[2] 20– 25			
Teton	.7	Stock	60 per cent	do	Housework	30– 40	20– 30			
Chouteau	.7	Stock; sheep; hay	50 per cent	do	do					
Madison	1.7	Grain; sheep	do	do		35	25		30	
Jefferson	3.4	General (irrigation)	80 per cent	Limited		30	25		25	
Silverbow (Butte)	46.8	Irrigated land	50 per cent	Single preferred			25		25	[4] $1.00 [5] 1.50
Granite	2.8	Hay and grain	do	Yes	Yes	30				
Missoula	2.1	General; fruit	do							

[1] But single men preferred.
[2] Farm and ranch hands.
[3] Sheep herders.
[4] Summer.
[5] Haying and harvest.

MONTANA—Continued.

Counties.	Changes in rate of wages, recent years.	Foreign farmers.	Nationality of farm laborers.	Nationality preferred as farm laborers.	Are there chances for immigrants who do not speak English
Dawson	None	None	Very few; stockherders only		None.
Park	20 per cent increase	Very few	Native whites	Native whites	Yes; good.
Sweet Grass	$5 a month decrease	Norwegians, Dutch	Native whites, Norwegians	Scandinavians	None.
Meagher	Increase	Scandinavians mostly	Americans, Scandinavians, Scotch, Canadians		
Fergus	$5 a month increase since 1895.	Many nationalities	Many nationalities	No preference	Yes.
Cascade (Great Falls)	$5 a month increase	Many Austrians, Germans, Scandinavians.	Scandinavians, Germans. Austrians, Canadians, native whites.	Preference in order named	Do.
Teton	15 per cent increase	Many nationalities [1]	Same as farmers	No preference	Do.
Choteau	Decrease	All races, including Chinese	All nationalities	Germans	None.
Madison	No increase	Very few	Americans, Germans		Very little.
Jefferson	About same	Swedes (a few)	Swedes, Irish, Germans		Not much.
Silverbow (Butte)	No increase	Many nationalities	Scandinavians, Germans, English, Irish, Italians, natives.	Swedes, Norwegians	Yes.
Granite	Slight increase		Swedes, native whites		None.
Missoula	No increase	Swedes	do		Yes.

[1] Germans, Scandinavians, British, Irish, Canadians, French.

AGRICULTURAL DISTRIBUTION OF IMMIGRANTS. 637

COLORADO.

[Density of population: 1890, 4.0; 1900, 5.2; increase, 30.7 per cent.]

Counties.	Density, 1900.	Kinds of farming.	Per cent of laborers employed through the year.	Opportunities for married men as farm laborers.	Work for women and children.	Customary wages, men. Monthly (with board). Summer.	Customary wages, men. Monthly (with board). Winter.	Monthly or lump sum (with board) year.	Daily.
Prowers (south)	2.4	Alfalfa; wheat; sugar beets.	50 per cent		Sugar beets	$20–$25	$15–$20		
Otero (south)	55.1	General; truck; alfalfa; sugar beets.	30 per cent	Yes	Children on beet or truck farms.	25	15– 20		
Arapahoe (Denver)	32.4	General; alfalfa; truck.	50 per cent[2]	do	Yes	¹25	15– 20	$20	
Jefferson (center)	10.8	General; alfalfa; fruit.	60 per cent[2]	do	Berries	25	15		
Larimer (north)	2.8	General; stock; sugar beets.	10 per cent	do	Beet farms	25	20	20	

Counties.	Changes in rate of wages, recent years.	Foreign farmers.	Nationality of farm laborers.	Nationality preferred as farm laborers.	Are there chances for immigrants who do not speak English?
Prowers (south)	Increase	None to speak of	Native whites	Native whites	None.
Otero (south)	No increase	Danes, Swedes, Germans	Native whites, Mexicans	Swedes and Germans	Yes.
Arapahoe (Denver)	Increase	Many nationalities[3]	Germans, Swedes, Danes, Irish	Swedes	Yes; many.
Jefferson (center)	20 per cent increase	Many; Swedes mostly	Native whites, Swedes, Germans	Germans	Yes.
Larimer (north)	$5 a month increase in 5 years.	Swedes mostly, Germans, Irish	Swedes, Germans, Irish		None.

[1] Irrigators and extra good men, $30–$40.
[2] All, if competent.
[3] Germans, Scandinavians, British, Irish, Canadians, Italians (many are gardeners).

ARIZONA.

[Density of population: 1890, 0.5; 1900, 1.1; increase, 67 per cent.]

Counties.	Density, 1900.	Kinds of farming.	Per cent of laborers employed through the year.	Opportunities for married men as farm laborers.	Work for women and children.	Customary wages, men. Monthly (with board). Summer.	Customary wages, men. Monthly (with board). Winter.	Monthly or lump sum (with board) year.	Daily.
Coohise	1.5	Alfalfa; grain	40 per cent	Little					$1.00–[3]$1.50
Maricopa: 1	2.4	Alfalfa; grain; fruit; dairy.	30 per cent[3]		Housework			$30	[1]1.00–[2]1.25
2		Alfalfa; grain; stock	80 per cent	Yes	do	$30	$25	[4]35	[5]1.25– 2.50
Yuma	.5	Alfalfa	Almost all[6]		Not much			25	

Counties.	Changes in rate of wages, recent years.	Foreign farmers.	Nationality of farm laborers.	Nationality preferred as farm laborers.	Are there chances for immigrants who do not speak English?
Coohise	No increase	None	Mexicans, native whites		None.
Maricopa: 1	Increase for hay and harvest.	Many Scandinavians	Mexicans, natives, some Scandinavians.		Yes; Scandinavians and Germans.
2	$5 a month increase	Danes (a few)	Americans, Mexicans	Americans	Yes.
Yuma	No increase	Germans (a few)	Mexicans, native whites	White	Not good.

[1] With board.
[2] Without board.
[3] Want is not nearly supplied.
[4] Man with family is given house, pasture for cow, and garden spot.
[5] With board, hay, and harvest.
[6] Owing to cutting of six or seven hay crops per year.

AGRICULTURAL DISTRIBUTION OF IMMIGRANTS. 639

UTAH.

[Density of population: 1890, 2.6; 1900, 3.4; increase, 32.2 per cent.]

Counties.	Density, 1900.	Kinds of farming.	Per cent of laborers employed through the year.	Opportunities for married men as farm laborers.	Work for women and children.	Customary wages, men.				
						Monthly (with board).		Monthly or lump sum (with board) year.	Daily.	
						Summer.	Winter.			
Washington	1.9	Small farming; work by owner and family.	All [1]	Not much		$20–$40	(?)			
Do		Small grain; apples	Very few			20– 40	[3]$25–$35		$1.50–$2.00	
Garfield	.7	General	No steady employment.							
Wayne	.8	Grain; stock	Fluctuating	Not generally						
Grand	.3	Stock						$35	[4]1.00– 1.50	
Sevier	4.5	Grain; hay	Very few	None					[5]1.00– 1.25	
Sanpete	10.4	Wheat; oats	...do	Very little					1.00– 1.00	
Millard	.9	Grain; lucerne		None						
Juab	3.1	Grain	None	Yes	Yes				1.00– 2.00	
Carbon	3.1	Hay (irrigated land)	Nearly all	A few	Very little			$25– 30	[6]1.75–71.00	
Salt Lake (Salt Lake City)	101.2	Grain; stock	40 per cent							
Weber (Ogden City)	46.4	Grain; tomatoes; sugar beets.	None	...do	Sugar beets				[8]1.00–[4]1.50	
Boxelder	1.8	General; fruit; sugar beets.	Few	Very little		25	15	[9]35		

[1] Very few employed, but of those few all are employed by the year.
[2] 30 per cent less than in summer.
[3] Teamsters.
[4] Without board.
[5] Summer.
[6] Without board (summer).
[7] With board (summer).
[8] With board.
[9] Cattle and sheep ranches.

UTAH—Continued.

Counties.	Changes in rate of wages, recent years.	Foreign farmers.	Nationality of farm laborers.	Nationality preferred as farm laborers.	Are there chances for immigrants who do not speak English?
Washington	No increase	Danes, Swedes, Dutch, English	English, Irish, Danes		Limited.
Do	No change	Swiss, Scandinavians, Germans, English	Few; mostly native born		Yes; buying land.
Garfield	No increase	None	Americans	Americans	Not much.
Wayne	do	English, Danes, Swedes			
Grand		All classes	Native whites	Native whites	Not encouraging.[1]
Sevier	No increase			No preference	
Sanpete	Decrease	English, Swedes, Danes	English, Danes, Swedes, Swiss, Germans	Both satisfactory	Very little.
Millard	No increase	do	English, Scandinavians	No preference	Do.
Juab	do	Many Scandinavians	do		Yes.
Carbon	Considerable increase	Swedes, Danes, Germans	Swedes, Danes	No preference	Few only.
Salt Lake (Salt Lake City)	20 per cent increase	English, Scandinavians, Germans	English, Scandinavians		
Weber (Ogden City)	Increase[2]	Many foreigners, different nationalities	Little hired labor employed	English, Swedes, Danes	
Boxelder	do	British, Scandinavians, Swiss, Germans	Native whites, British, Scandinavians	No preference	Very slight.

[1] Farming does not pay.   [2] Since establishment of sugar and canning factories three years ago.

AGRICULTURAL DISTRIBUTION OF IMMIGRANTS. 641

WASHINGTON.

[Density of population: 1890, 5.3; 1900, 7.7; increase, 46.4 per cent. First six counties east of Cascade Mountains; last two west of Cascade Mountains.]

Counties.	Density, 1900.	Kinds of farming.	Per cent of laborers employed through the year.	Opportunities for married men as farm laborers.	Work for women and children.	Customary wages, men.			
						Monthly (with board).		Monthly or lump sum (with board) year.	Daily.
						Summer.	Winter.		
Klickitat	3.1	Grain; fruit; stock	All		Fruit orchards, summer.			[1]$25–$35	[2]$1.00–$1.25
Wallawalla (Wallawalla)	14.6	Grain; fruit; truck	40 per cent[3]	Yes	Housework (a little)			200–300	[2]1.00
Adams	2.9	General	30 per cent	Growing demand	Housework		([4])	[5]25–630	[2]1.00
Spokane (Spokane)	32.4	Grain; dairy; sugar beets.							
Douglas	1.0	Grain; alfalfa; fruit; cane; stock.	Nearly all	Married preferred	Housework	$25–$30	25		
Kittitas	4.0	Grain; dairy; stock	80 per cent	do	do	30	25		[7]1.25– 2.25
Clarke	20.8	Grain; fruit; dairy; stock; hops.	10 per cent	Limited	Fruit gathering	30			[8]1.50
Thurston	13.0	General; fruit; dairy; hops.	All who wish	Yes	Housework, garden, fruit.	26	15–20	[9]25– 30	

[1] Herders.
[2] With board.
[3] 40 per cent on grain farms. Idle time in farm work may be filled in by fruit and hop picking.
[4] Board; to $15–$20.
[5] Teamsters.
[6] Milkers.
[7] Summer.
[8] Without board.
[9] Dairy work.

WASHINGTON—Continued

Counties.	Changes in rate of wages, recent years.	Foreign farmers.	Nationality of farm laborers.	Nationality preferred as farm laborers.	Are there chances for immigrants who do not speak English?
Klickitat	Increase	English, Irish, Germans, Finns	Native whites, Germans, Finns	No preference	Yes; Germans, Finns.
Wallawalla	Slow decrease	Many nationalities [1]	Many nationalities		None.
Adams	10 per cent increase	Germans, Russians	do	Germans, English	Yes.[2]
Spokane	$5 per month increase	Canadians, Swedes, Germans, English.	English, Germans, Swiss, Danes	Germans, English	Do.
Douglas	No increase	Germans, Scandinavians, Russians, Italians.	All nationalities	Germans, Russians, Scandinavians.	Do.
Kittitas	60 to 100 per cent increase [3]	Swedes, Germans, Norwegians	Swedes, Germans, Norwegians	Scandinavians	Yes; good.
Clarke	Slight increase	All nationalities	Scandinavians, Germans		Do.[4]
Thurston	15 per cent increase	do	All nationalities	Swedes, Danes, Germans, Swiss.[5]	Do.

[1] English, Irish, Germans, French, Norwegians, Russians, Chinese.
[2] But English-speaking people preferred.
[3] Impossible to get sufficient competent help at that.
[4] By going on Government land. Capital is needed to clear land of timber.
[5] Italians, Japanese, and Chinese work at contract work and gardening, but employers that use them for other work are under a ban of public opinion.

AGRICULTURAL DISTRIBUTION OF IMMIGRANTS 643

OREGON.

[Density of population: 1890, 3.3; 1900, 4.4; increase, 30.4 per cent. Six counties west of Cascade Mountains.]

Counties.	Density, 1900.	Kinds of farming.	Per cent of laborers employed through the year.	Opportunities for married men as farm laborers.	Work for women and children.	Customary wages, men.				
						Monthly (with board).		Monthly or lump sum (with board) year.	Daily.	
						Summer.	Winter.			
Douglas	3.0	Grain; changing to dairy and fruit.	All	Yes	Hops and fruit	$30–$40	$20–$30			
Marion:										
1	23.7	Grain; general; fruit	All who wish	....do	Strawberries, pease, hops, and prunes.	18– 20	15– 18	$200	[3]$0.75 [4]1.00	
2		General; wheat; stock; dairy.	20 per cent	....do	Little	[1]15–[2]20	10– 20	$15– 30	[5]1.25 [6]1.50	
Clackamas	10.6	General; dairy	80 per cent	....do		[1]20– 25 [2]30– 35	[1]15– 20 [2]25– 30		[7]1.00 [8]2.50	
Yamhill	19.0	Wheat; changing to general.	20 per cent	A few	Hops, prunes			20	[9]2.00	
Tillamook	4.0	Dairy only	All who wish	Yes				20– 30		
Washington	20.2	Grain; stock; dairy; hops; prunes.	75 per cent	....do		25	20			

[1] Farming.
[2] Dairying.
[3] With board (summer).
[4] Haying.
[5] Harvest.
[6] Summer, with board.
[7] Winter, with board.
[8] Summer, without board.
[9] Winter, without board.

OREGON—Continued.

Counties.	Changes in rate of wages, recent years.	Foreign farmers.	Nationality of farm laborers.	Nationality preferred as farm laborers.	Are there chances for immigrants who do not speak English?
Douglas	30 per cent increase	Germans	Germans, English		Yes.
Marion:					
1	25 per cent increase	Many Germans	Native whites, Germans, Chinese.	Native whites, Germans.	Do.
2	10 per cent increase	Germans	Natives, Irish, English	No preference	Not many.
Clackamas	20 per cent increase	Germans mostly, Swedes, British	Germans, Scandinavians, British	British, Germans, Scandinavians.[1]	Yes, at low wages.
Yamhill	No material advance	Scandinavians, British, Germans, Swiss.	Scotch, Germans, Swedes, Swiss, natives.	No preference	Yes; among people of own nationality.
Tillamook	Great increase	Swiss, Swedes, Germans, Irish, Canadians.	Irish, Swiss, Swedes, Germans, natives.	Foreigners and natives	Yes.
Washington	Increase	Germans, Dutch, Swiss	Germans, Scandinavians, Swiss	Swiss as dairy hands	Do.

[1] Most foreigners here are independent farmers.

CALIFORNIA.

[Density of population: 1890, 7.8; 1900, 9.5; increase, 22.7 per cent. First five southern counties; last five northern counties.]

Counties.	Density, 1900.	Kinds of farming.	Per cent of laborers employed through the year.	Opportunities for married men as farm laborers.	Work for women and children.	Monthly (with board). Summer.	Monthly (with board). Winter.	Customary wages, men. Monthly or lump sum (with board) year.	Customary wages, men. Daily.
San Diego (San Diego)	4.1	Fruit		Yes	In berries and vegetables.				1$1.25–$1.65
Riverside	2.4	...do	90 per cent	...do	Picking fruit			$25–$35	²1.50
San Bernardino	1.4	Fruit; general	All	Many prefer married	Picking and packing fruit.			25	³1.50– 2.00 ⁴1.50– 1.75
Ventura: 1	8.3	General; beets	66 per cent	Yes	Fruit				⁴1– 1.50
2		General; walnuts	All	No				25	
Santa Barbara		General; walnuts	(⁶)	Single preferred on ranches.					⁵1.00
Stanislaus	6.6	Wheat; alfalfa; fruit; truck.	(⁷)	A little	Housework			30	⁵1.15
Alameda (Alameda, Oakland).	170.4	General; fruit; sugar beets.	40 per cent	Married best chance	Fruit	$20–$24	$12		⁸1.25– 1.50
Sonoma	23.8	Fruit; poultry; wood	All	Yes	Housework			25	
Eldorado	5	General; truck	10 per cent⁹	No		20– 25			⁴1.50
Shasta	4.5	Fruit	...do	In fruit harvest	In fruit harvest				1.00

¹ Lemon pickers.
² General; without board.
³ Fruit picking done by the box. Pickers can earn $2 to $4 per day.
⁴ Without board.
⁵ With board.
⁶ Great demand in September to November, bean and walnut harvest. In winter for one-half the number to get in crops, plow, etc. Demand during June to August very light.
⁷ Wheat requires few men; the change to diversified farming now going on will require a much larger number of men.
⁸ White labor only. Japanese and Chinese less.
⁹ Remainder drift to cities, cut wood, or mine.

CALIFORNIA—Continued.

Counties.	Changes in rate of wages, recent years.	Foreign farmers.	Nationality of farm laborers.	Nationality preferred as farm laborers.	Are there chances for immigrants who do not speak English?
San Diego	No change	Mexicans	Natives, Chinese	Americans, Germans, English, Swedes.	
Riverside	Somewhat increased	Scandinavians Canadians, English	Natives, Chinese, Japanese		Yes; Germans and Scandinavians.
San Bernardino	Increase	Germans, Swedes	Germans, Swedes, Russians, Mexicans, Chinese, natives.	Germans	Yes; good.
Ventura:					
1	15 per cent increase	None	Native whites, Mexicans, Chinese	All liked	Little.
2	$5 a month increase	Scotch, Germans	All nationalities	Germans	None.
Santa Barbara	No change	Scotch, Italians	Irish, Italian, Spanish	Americans	Very limited.
Stanislaus	No increase	Portuguese	Americans mostly	Of foreigners, Scandinavians and Germans.	Yes; good.
Alameda (Oakland)	Increase	Portuguese (mostly), Danes, Germans	Portuguese, Danes, Germans, Asiatics, natives.	Danes	None; possibly Portuguese.
Sonoma	do	Italians	All nationalities	No preference	None.
Eldorado	No increase	Swiss, Germans, Swedes	Native whites, Germans	do	Not much.
Shasta	Some increase	Very few	Native whites		None.

CHAPTER XI.
IMMIGRATION LEGISLATION AND ITS WORKINGS.
A. THE ALIEN CONTRACT-LABOR LAW.

The Federal legislation restricting immigration is not a single consistent act of legislation, but it is a series of acts added one to another during the past 25 years. It is therefore ambiguous and conflicting at many points, since portions of the earlier laws, without being repealed, have been given a new construction by later laws. This makes the enforcement of the law often a difficult matter. The law, especially as applied to contract laborers, does not accomplish the ends expected by the public and the laboring classes of the country.

It is impossible to understand the weakness of the contract-labor law without understanding first that at the basis of the immigration laws there lies a curious contradiction. The earlier laws enacted by Congress—those of 1875 and 1882—were designed to exclude the vicious, the criminal, and the pauper, those who would not or could not support themselves. The next laws, the anti-contract labor laws of 1885, 1887, and 1888, practically sought to exclude those who had the forethought to provide that on landing here they would find a sure means of supporting themselves. The earlier laws exclude the worst, the later laws exclude the best. The consequence is that the immigrant must summon all his ingenuity and subterfuge to dodge the two extremes. He strives to show that he can support himself, and he strives to show that he does not know of any job by which he can support himself. If he can not support himself he is sent back as liable to become a public charge. If he has provided beforehand for self-support he is sent back as liable to displace American workmen. The immigration inspectors are therefore reduced to a queer predicament. They must discover, first, whether the immigrant is sound in body and mind—that is, whether he can compete successfully for a living with American workmen. If so, they admit him. They must discover, secondly, whether he really has a prospect of finding work, and thereby of competing with American workmen. If so, they exclude him. They exclude him if he can not or will not compete with American workmen, and they exclude him if he gives the best of all evidence that he will compete successfully with American workmen. On the face of the law the contradiction seems inexplicable. But if we look into its history and the conditions surrounding its adoption, we can see a sane explanation. The alien contract-labor law was enacted almost solely at the demand of organized labor. Organized labor meets its test at the critical point of a strike or a lockout. At such a crisis the issue turns solely on the ability of the employer to find workmen who will take the places of his former employees. While the unions may have fortified themselves by controlling the American labor market, they often saw themselves attacked in the rear and utterly routed by a block of immigrants suddenly imported by the employer from abroad or by his agent from Ellis Island. With wages in Europe only one-half or one third of the corresponding grades in America a foreign solicitor would be overrun by applicants on the promise of prepaid transportation and immediate employment. To meet this unfair competition the labor unions, and especially the Knights of Labor, secured through Congress specific legislation known as the alien contract-labor law of 1885, with the amendments of 1886 and 1888. There had already been established by the Chinese exclusion act of 1882 a precedent for the exclusion of immigrants whose amazingly low standard of living and equally amazing industriousness had enabled them wholly to displace American workmen whenever they entered in competition. But in the case of the Chinese there were other considerations not found in dealing with European immigrants. The Chinese were of a distinct race and religion, unacquainted with representative institutions, not bringing their families, expecting to return to their native land, and while temporarily here resorting to low practices and filthy abodes. The excitement and determination of practically the entire population of the Pacific coast left no alternative except absolute exclusion. The case of the Europeans was not so unmitigated. The great majority at that time were coming from countries closely related to our own in ancestry, language, literature, religion, and representative government. Those countries were indeed the fatherland of America. It could not for a moment be considered that, against our own races coming from the lands of our origin, any sweeping exclusion could be adopted. Any restriction which could hope for adoption must be a specific protection against a definite recognized evil. This evil existed and came prominently to view. It was the artificial immigration induced by employers for the purpose of breaking labor organizations. Immigrants of our own race who came here on their own motive or on the representation of friends and relatives were especially exempted from the operation of the law. The first law, that of 1885, applied only to those American employers who induced alien immigration. Section 1 reads as follows:

> It shall be unlawful for any person, company, partnership, or corporation, in any manner whatsoever, to prepay the transportation, or in any way assist or encourage the importation or migration of any alien or aliens, any foreigner or foreigners, into the United States, its Territories, or the District of Columbia, under contract or agreement, parol or special, express or implied, made previous to the importation or migration of such alien or aliens, foreigner or foreigners, to perform labor or service of any kind in the United States, its Territories, or the District of Columbia.

Section 2 declared that such contracts should be "utterly void and of no effect." Section 3 imposed a heavy fine upon the importer or solicitor of immigrants. It declared that—

> every person, partnership, company, or corporation violating the provisions of section 1 shall forfeit and pay for every such offense the sum of one thousand dollars, which may be sued for and recovered by the United States or by any person who shall first bring his action therefor, including any such alien or foreigner who may be a party to any such contract or agreement, as debts of like amount are now recovered in the circuit courts of the United States, the proceeds to be paid into the Treasury of the United States; and separate suits may be brought for each alien or foreigner being a party to such contract or agreement aforesaid.

Section 5 imposed a fine of $500 and imprisonment of six months on the master of any vessel who should knowingly bring to this country a prohibited alien contract laborer.

By an amendment adopted October 19, 1888, it was provided that the "Secretary of the Treasury (should) pay to an informer who furnishes original information that the law has been violated such a share of the penalties recovered as he may deem reasonable and just, not exceeding 50 per centum, where it appears that the recovery was had in consequence of the information thus furnished."

The law as enacted in 1885 was seriously defective. In the first place, it applied only to the importer of contract laborers and not to the immigrant. This defect was attempted to be amended in 1887 by a clause which, liberally interpreted, strikes also at contract laborers, and commanded that they should "be sent back to the nation to which they belong and from whence they came."

In so far as the law has been effective it has been due to this clause which gives power to deport the immigrants. Owing to the strict construction of the law there have been very few cases in which the importer was fined. But there have been over 8,000 deemed contract laborers sent back by the immigrant inspectors. The reasons for the difference are plain. The prosecution and conviction of the importer depends upon district attorneys and judges, who must necessarily follow the strict rules of evidence and must hold themselves to exact definitions of a contract. But the deportation of an immigrant turns upon the circumstantial evidence presented to administrative authorities and the inferences which may be drawn therefrom.

By the law of 1894 (which appeared as a section in the sundry civil appropriation act) the "decision of the appropriate immigration or customs officers," if adverse to the admission of an alien of the excluded classes "shall be final, unless reversed on appeal to the Secretary of the Treasury." Prior to the enactment of this law in 1894 the authority of the Secretary of the Treasury in ordering deportations was not specific. It was only implied in the amendment of 1887, above mentioned, prohibiting the landing of alien contract laborers. Upon the strength of this implied power the courts held that the action of Congress in giving discretionary power to an administrative officer is constitutional.

We have, then, two broad divisions to a discussion of the alien contract-labor law: First, the interpretation placed upon the law by the courts, affecting mainly the importer; second, the administration of the law by the Treasury Department, affecting mainly the exclusion and deportation of alleged contract laborers.

Preliminary to such a discussion we shall find it necessary to discover exactly the classes of aliens who, in the contemplation of the law, are to be excluded, and such other classes as are excepted and are therefore permitted to land and go to work, even though coming under contract.

B. EXCEPTED CLASSES OF ALIEN CONTRACT LABORERS.

In the first place, the courts have interpreted the terms of the laws so as to give to the importer of alien contract labor the benefit of every doubt. By this rule of interpretation the law is not to be construed literally.

> The statute in question is highly penal, and must be so construed as to bring within its condemnation only those who are shown by the direct and positive averments in the declaration to be embraced within the terms of the law. It will not be so construed as to include cases which, although within the letter, are not within the spirit of the law. (U. S. v. Gay, 80 F., 254; 95 F., 227.)

Holding, as the courts have done in certain cases, to what they consider to be the spirit of the law even though contrary to its letter when the contract laborer is involved, and also holding in other cases to the letter of the law when the importer is concerned, we find that the original acts and amendments of Congress are subject to the following exceptions and exemptions:

ALIEN CONTRACT-LABOR LAW. 649

1. **Aliens not immigrants.**—The general law on immigration applied in terms only to "alien immigrants," and consequently prior to 1894 the courts held that other classes of aliens who enter the country, not being immigrants, did not come under the excluding sections. As regards contract laborers, this covers the following classes:

(a) CANADIANS.—All persons who come across the border from Canada to perform daily labor and return at night, even though they be under contract. In United States v. Michigan Central Railroad Company (49 F., 365, Dec. 10, 1891) it was held by Justsce Wallace that a clerk of the railroad company living in Canada but working in the company's office at Suspension Bridge "was not an immigrant because he did not come here intending to acquire a permanent or temporary home. As he did not migrate here the defendant did not encourage his 'migration.' He was not imported, nor did the defendant assist in his 'importation' any more than he was exported and assisted in his 'exportation,' when he went home at night." While the court acknowledged the case in question might be "within the mischief which the promoters of the law intended to remedy," yet it held that it was "not within the ordinary import of the words of the statute."

It was to meet the alleged mischief occasioned by the foregoing interpretation of the law that the workingmen in border towns, like Detroit and Suspension Bridge, secured the adoption by Congress of the so-called "Corliss Amendment," as attached to the "Lodge Immigration Bill" of the Fifty-fourth Congress, vetoed by President Cleveland. This amendment aimed to suppress all day labor by persons retaining their residence in a foreign country, whether under contract or not. The amendment was as follows:

SEC. 4. That it shall hereafter be unlawful for any male alien who has not in good faith made his declaration before the proper court of his intention to become a citizen of the United States to be employed on any public work of the United States, or to come regularly or habitually into the United States by land or water for the purpose of engaging in any mechanical trade or manual labor, for wages or salary, returning from time to time to a foreign country.

SEC. 5. That it shall be unlawful for any person, partnership, company, or corporation knowingly to employ any alien coming into the United States in violation of the next preceding section of this act: *Provided*, That the provisions of this act shall not apply to the employment of sailors, deck hands or other employees of vessels, or railroad train hands, such as conductors, engineers, brakemen, firemen, or baggagemen, whose duties require them to pass over the frontier to reach the termini of their runs, or to boatmen or guides on the lakes and rivers on the northern border of the United States.

SEC. 6. That any violation of the provisions of sections 4 and 5 of this act by any alien or citizen shall be deemed a misdemeanor, punishable by a fine not exceeding $500, or by both such fine and imprisonment, in the discretion of the court: *Provided*, That all persons convicted of a violation of section 4 of this act shall be deported to the country from whence they came.

(b) ALIEN RESIDENTS.—The general immigration laws originally did not apply, as interpreted by the courts, to aliens already resident here, who temporarily depart and return. The terms of the law indicated "alien immigrants," and the courts held that aliens who had formerly resided in this country, though they were unnaturalized, were residents and not immigrants. (In re Martorelli, 63 F., 437, Oct. 13, 1894; in re Maiola, 67 F., 114, Feb. 2, 1895.)

The contract labor law forbids the assisting, encouraging, or soliciting the migration or importation of any alien, making the migration a necessary element on which to ground the deportation of the contract laborer and the penalty on the importer, so that an alien who has resided here did not come under the prohibition.

This defect of the law was amended by act of August 18, 1894 (28 Stat., 390), in so far as the deportation of an alien found to be of the excluded classes was concerned, by making the decision of the Secretary of the Treasury final in the case of all aliens and not merely alien immigrants, but this amendment probably does not affect the importer of alien laborers under contract who might continue to be exempt from penalty in case the imported alien were a former resident of the United States. This is on the assumption that the courts may continue to insist that the element of migration must still form the basis of the liability of the importer, "migration" being interpreted as the first migration to the country.

(c) ALIEN SEAMEN.—The master of a vessel is required by the act of 1891, section 10, to return to the country from whence he came any alien immigrants who have come to this country contrary to the prohibitions of the act. The court held in the case of an alien seaman who had deserted his ship in an American port that the inability of the master to secure his arrest and return to the ship exempted the master from the penalty of the act (U. S., ex rel. Anderson v. Burke, 99 F., 895). The court maintained that—

Immigration laws of the United States must be given a sensible construction having reference to their purpose, and as so construed they apply only to such aliens as enter or are brought to this country with the intention that they shall become residents thereof.

These laws have no application to alien seamen who constitute the bona fide crew of a vessel trading in the ports of the United States and who enter such ports with their ship in the discharge of the duties of their employment, and without any intention of becoming residents of the country, and the master of a vessel can not be subjected to the fine or refusal of his clearance papers provided by the act of March 3, 1891, as a penalty for refusing to return upon his vessel immigrants of the prohibited classes brought into this country, because an alien seaman who is one of the crew escapes from his ship while in port, before the expiration of his term of service without having been discharged or paid, and without the consent or knowledge of the master, and the master is unable to secure his arrest and return to the ship.

At the same time when the court rendered this decision it affirmed, by way of contrast, the action of the Assistant Secretary of the Treasury in deporting certain alien seamen who had shipped to the United States at an absurdly low wage, and to be here discharged, on the ground that they were manifestly working their way to the United States. In this case, where they had stipulated for discharge in the United States, they were plainly immigrants, and were properly deported, "not because bona fide crews of ships fall under the immigration laws, but because they were not a bona fide crew of the ship."

(d) Private servants, secretaries, or domestic servants of citizens and subjects of any foreign country temporarily residing in the United States are not immigrants and are therefore admitted.

2. Alien immigrants.—There are also certain classes of aliens who are immigrants who may be admitted even though they come under contract. This list, as stated in the acts and construed by the courts, is as follows:

(a) PERSONAL OR DOMESTIC SERVANTS.—The meaning of the words "personal or domestic servants" has been tested in re Howard, 63 F., 263, October 19, 1894. In this case the court held that an undercoachman, whose duties are partly to assist in keeping stables, horses, and carriages in good order, but partly to drive the horses when his employer or any of his family go out in the carriages, and to accompany on horseback the younger members of the family when they go on horseback, and who boards with his employer's coachman and sleeps in a room over the coach house, is a "personal or domestic servant," within the meaning of Stat. 1885, ch. 164, prohibiting the immigration of aliens under contracts for labor, and providing that the provisions of the act shall not apply to "persons employed strictly as personal or domestic servants."

Decisions of the Secretary of the Treasury on appeal have held that farm hands are not "domestic servants." The court has also held that a dairyman making butter for his employer, who sells some of the same, is not a domestic or personal servant, and therefore comes under the prohibition. (In re Cummings, 32 F., 75, Syn. Dec., 11014.)

(b) RELATIVES AND FRIENDS.—The act of 1885 contained a proviso that it should not be construed to prohibit any individual from assisting "any member of his family or any relative or personal friend" to immigrate to the United States "for the purpose of settlement here." This, however, does not allow aliens under contract, who are relatives or friends, to be imported.

The significance of this distinction may be judged from the fact that about 65 per cent of the immigrants come on tickets that have been bought and paid for in this country.

By section 5 of the act of 1891 this law was amended by excluding from the second proviso the words "or any relative or personal friend." But the same act, in section 1, expressly provides that it "shall not be held to exclude persons living in the United States from sending for a relative or friend who is not of the excluded classes." These two provisions seem to be conflicting, but on close examination the former, which strikes out the words "relative or personal friend," is found to be of no importance, and the latter simply requires that it should be "affirmatively and satisfactorily shown on special inquiry that such person does not belong to one of the excluded classes or the class of contract laborers excluded by the act of 1885." In other words, when the immigrant comes with his own money the burden is on the Government to show that he belongs to the excluded classes; but when he comes assisted by a relative or friend the burden is on the immigrant to prove that he is not of the excluded classes.

(c) MINISTERS AND COLLEGE PROFESSORS.—The act of 1885 had not specifically exempted from its operations members of the "professional classes" except "actors, artists, lecturers, and singers" (act of February 26, 1885, sec. 5). Shortly after the enactment of the law the corporation of Trinity Church of New York engaged a minister in England to come here and take charge of its church as a pastor. Although the case seems so plainly an oversight in the original enactment of the law, and although Congress itself remedied the oversight in a later amendment, yet the principles laid down by the courts in this case bear so directly on later decisions which are not so plainly exempted from the law that a full résumé of the arguments is here presented. Judge Wallace, in his decision in the Federal court of the southern district of New York (36 F., 303, May 21, 1888), declared that the courts are bound by the "plain, unambiguous, and explicit" terms of a statute, and are "not at liberty to go outside of the language to search for a meaning which it does not reasonably bear in the effort to ascertain and give effect to what may be imagined to have been or not to have been the intention of Congress. Whenever the will of Congress is declared in ample and unequivocal language that will must be completely followed, and it is not admissible to resort to speculations of policy nor even to the view of members of Congress in debate to find reasons to control or modify the statute." (Cited U. S. v. Railroad Co. 91 U. S., 72.) Judge Wallace took this ground even though he admitted that—

it was no doubt primarily the object of the act to prohibit the introduction of assisted immigrants, brought here under contracts previously made by corporations and capitalists to prepay their passage and obtain their services at low wages for limited periods of time. It was a measure introduced and advocated by the trades unions and labor associations, designed to shield the interests represented by such organizations from the effects of the competition in the labor market of foreigners brought here under contracts, having a tendency to stimulate immigration and reduce the rates of wages. Except from the language of the statute there is no reason to suppose a contract like the present to be within the evils which the law was designed to suppress; and it would not be indulging a violent supposition to assume that no legislative body in this country would have advisedly enacted a law framed so as to cover a case like the present.

After laying down the rule above stated relative to the interpretation of the will of Congress, Judge Wallace continued:

The encouragement of migration prohibited by the first section is of aliens under contract or agreement previously made "to perform labor or service of any kind in the United States." The contracts which are declared to be void by the second section are contracts "having reference to the performance of labor or service by any person" in the United States previous to the migration of the alien. The penalty imposed by the third section is imposed on the person or corporation encouraging the migration of the alien under a contract or agreement previously made "to perform labor or service of any kind." No more comprehensive terms could have been employed to include every conceivable kind of labor or avocation, whether of the hand or brain, in the class of prohibited contracts; and as if to emphasize and make more explicit the intention that the words "labor or service" should not be taken in any restricted sense, they are followed by the words "of any kind." Every kind of industry and every employment, manual or intellectual, is embraced within the language used. If it were possible to import the narrower meaning than the natural and ordinary one to the language of these sections, the terms of the fifth section would forbid the attempt. That section has a proviso withdrawing from the operation of the act several classes of persons and contracts. Foreigners residing here temporarily who may engage private secretaries, persons desiring to establish a new industry not then existing in the United States who employ skilled workmen therein, domestic servants, and a limited professional class are thereby exempted from its provisions. The last clause of the proviso is: "Nor shall the provisions of this act apply to professional actors, artists, lecturers, or singers, nor to persons employed strictly as personal or domestic servants." If without this exception the act would apply to this class of persons, because such persons come here under contracts for labor or service, then clearly it must apply to ministers, lawyers, surgeons, architects, and all others who labor in any professional calling. Unless Congress expected the act to apply to the excepted classes, there was no necessity for the proviso. The office of a proviso is generally to restrain an enacting clause and to except something which would otherwise have been within it.

The decision of Judge Wallace, had it been sustained by the higher court, could have been remedied by Congressional action, and this was indeed intended to be done by the act adopted March 3, 1891, where it was provided that in addition to "artists, actors, lecturers," etc., the excluded contract laborers should not include "ministers of any religious denomination, nor persons belonging to any recognized profession, nor professors of colleges and seminaries."

Whether it is preferable to remedy a defective statute by legislative amendment or by judicial interpretation is a question of importance in the enforcement of the alien contract labor law. By successive decisions of the courts the operations of the law have been restricted until its efficiency has been almost extinguished.

The road for this line of judicial restriction was opened by the Supreme Court of the United States in reviewing the foregoing decision of Judge Wallace (148 U. S., 457). While conceding the strength of Judge Wallace's reasoning that the act of the Trinity corporation was "within the letter" of the law of 1885; that "not only are the general words 'labor and service' both used, but also, as it were, to guard against any narrow interpretation and emphasize a breadth of meaning, to them is added 'of any kind;'" and that the "specific exceptions, among them the professional actors, artists, lecturers, singers, and domestic servants, strengthens the idea that every other kind of labor and service was intended to be reached by the first section;" yet the court laid down certain rules for interpretation which have made it possible for the courts in later decisions to greatly restrict the scope of the law.

First, the intention of the lawmakers: The Supreme Court held that "a thing may be within the letter of the statute and yet not within the statute, because not within its spirit, nor within the intention of its makers. * * * Frequently words of general meaning are used in a statute, words broad enough to include an act in question, and yet a consideration of the whole legislation or of the circumstances surrounding its enactment or of the absurd results which follow from giving such broad meaning to the words, makes it unreasonable to believe that the legislators intended to include the particular act."

In its effort to ascertain the intention of Congress the Supreme Court referred to the reports of the Senate and House Committees on Education and Labor recommending the passage of the bill. In the Senate report it was said (Congressional Record, Forty-eighth Congress, p. 6059):

The general facts and considerations which induce the committee to recommend the passage of this bill are set forth in the report of the committee of the House. The committee report the bill back without amendment, although there are certain features thereof which might well be changed or modified in the hope that the bill may not fail of passage during the present session. Especially would the committee have otherwise recommended amendments substituting for the expression "labor and service" wherever it occurs in the body of the bill, the words "manual labor or manual service" as sufficiently broad to accomplish the purpose of the bill, and that such amendment would remove objections which a sharp and perhaps unfriendly criticism may urge to the proposed legislation. The committee, however, believe that the bill in its present form will be construed as including only those whose labor or service is manual in character, and being very desirous that the bill become a law before the adjournment, have reported the bill without change.

In the report of the committee of the House it was said (Congressional Record, Forty-eighth Congress, p. 5359):

It seeks to restrain and prohibit the immigration or importation of laborers who would never have seen our shores but for the inducements and allurements of the men whose only object is to obtain labor at the lowest possible rate, regardless of the social and material well being of our own citizens and regardless of the evil consequences which result to American laborers from such immigration. This class of immigrants care nothing about our institutions, and in many instances never even heard of them. They are men whose passage is paid by the importers. They come here under contract to labor for a certain number of years. They are ignorant of our social condition, and, that they may remain so, they are isolated and prevented from coming into contact with Americans. They are generally from the lowest social stratum, and live upon the coarsest food and in hovels of a character before unknown to the American workman. They, as a rule, do not become citizens and are certainly not a desirable acquisition to the body politic. The inevitable tendency of their presence among us is to degrade American labor and to remove it to the level of the imported pauper labor.

Another test which the court imposed was the circumstances surrounding the enactment of the statute, i. e., the evil which it was designed to remedy. Herein the court indorsed the statement of Justice Brown (U. S. v. Craig, 28 Fed. Rep., 795, 798), who said:

The evil here was "the practice of all large capitalists in this country to contract with their agents abroad for the shipment of great numbers of an ignorant and a servile class of foreign laborers under contracts, by which the employer agreed, on the one hand, to prepay their passage, while, upon the other, the laborers agreed to work after their arrival for a certain time at a low rate of wages. The effect of this was to break down the labor market and reduce other laborers engaged in like occupations to the level of the assisted immigrants, and to discountenance the migration of those who had not sufficient means in their own hands or those of their friends to pay their passage."

The Supreme Court also relied upon the title of the act of 1885, which reads: "An act to prohibit the importation and migration of foreigners and aliens under contract or agreement to perform labor in the United States, or Territories, and the District of Columbia."

The absurdity and inconsistency of enforcing the exclusion of ministers of the gospel under cover of a law designed to benefit American labor appealed strongly to the court. It said:

It appears also from the petitions and in the testimony presented before the committees of Congress that it was this cheap, unskilled labor which was making the trouble, and the influx of which Congress sought to prevent. It was never suggested that we had in this country a surplus of brain toilers, and, least of all, that the market for the service of Christian ministers was depressed by foreign competition. Those were matters to which the attention of Congress or of the people was not directed. So far, then, as the evil which was sought to be remedied interprets the statute, it also guides to an exclusion of this contract from the penalties of the act.

But beyond all these matters no purpose of action against religion can be imputed to any legislation, State or national, because this is a religious people.

SKILLED LABOR (d).—Unquestionably the most sweeping legal decisions affecting the scope of the alien contract labor law is that of United States v. Gay, first decided in the circuit court of the district of Indiana, April 30, 1897 (80 F., 254), and then on appeal in the circuit court of appeals, seventh circuit, June 6, 1899 (95 F., 226). These decisions, following the rule adopted in the Trinity Church case, of inquiry into the intentions of Congress in the discussion of the law, but going far beyond that case, affirmed that the intention of Congress was merely "to stay the influx of cheap, unskilled manual labor;" that Congress wished to shut out only "the cheaper, grosser sort of unskilled and unhoused manual labor;" that the law does not exclude either such professional classes' as surgeons, architects, and physicians, or such skilled occupations as those of engineer, bookkeeper, stenographer, typewriter, clerk, saleswoman, draper, or window dresser;" and, indeed, that "Congress never intended to include in the act skilled labor of any kind."

The leading arguments of the appellate court are given herewith:

Several questions were discussed at the hearing, but there is only one that we think it necessary to consider. The opinion of the court below, printed in the record, shows that the principal ground on which the action was dismissed was that a draper, window dresser, and dry-goods clerk did not come within the prohibition of the statute. The court says in its opinion:

"The statute in question is highly penal and must be so construed as to bring within its condemnation only those who are shown by the direct and positive averments in the declaration to be embraced within the terms of the law. It will not be so construed as to include cases which, although within the letter, are not within the spirit of the law. It must be considered in the light of the evil which it was intended to remedy, which, as is well known, was the importation of manual laborers under contract previously entered into, at rates of wages with which our own laboring classes could not compete without compelling them to submit to conditions of life to which they were unacquainted. (Citing authorities.) It is well settled by these and other cases that the statute must be construed as

ALIEN CONTRACT-LABOR LAW. 653

limited to cases where an assisted immigrant was brought into the country under a contract to perform manual labor or service." (U. S. v. Gay, 80 F., 254.)

We are of the opinion that this ruling is correct, in view of the previous construction placed upon the statute by the Supreme Court in Church of the Holy Trinity v. United States.

Referring to the Trinity case the court continues:

The history of its passage through Congress is given, which shows clearly that Congress never intended to include in the act skilled labor of any kind. The conclusion of the court is that the title of the act, the evil which was intended to be remedied, the circumstances surrounding the appeal to Congress, the reports of the committees of the House and Senate, all concur in affirming that the intent of Congress was simply to stay the influx of cheap, unskilled labor.

Referring to the reports of the Senate and House committees, quoted above in the Trinity case, the court says:

These reports throw strong light upon the intention of Congress and the construction which they expected the courts to place upon the act, notwithstanding the very general terms "labor and service of any kind" employed in the act. To give the act a construction so strict as to include a minister of the gospel or other professional man would exclude any person employed in any calling or service requiring superior skill and intelligence, which would constitute a mischief quite as great as the one intended to be remedied by Congress. At the circuit in the same case Judge Wallace had felt compelled to follow the plain letter of the law and had given judgment for the plaintiff, especially in view of the exceptions which Congress had made of professional actors, artists, lecturers, singers, and persons employed as personal and domestic servants. The reasoning was this: That if, without this exception, the act would apply to this class of persons, because such persons come under contracts for labor or service, then clearly it must apply to ministers, lawyers, surgeons, and architects, and all others who labor in any professional calling. But for these exceptions and the plain language of the statute the circuit court would have reached the same conclusion as to the proper construction of the law as the Supreme Court did, as it says in the opinion:

"The act is entitled 'An act to prohibit the importation and migration of foreigners and aliens under contract to perform labor in the United States.' It was no doubt primarily the object of the act to prohibit the introduction of assisted immigrants, brought here under contracts previously made, by corporations and capitalists, to prepay their passage and obtain their services at low wages for limited periods of time. It was a measure introduced and advocated by the trades unions and labor associations, designed to shield the interests represented by such organizations from the effect of competition in the labor market of foreigners brought here under contracts, having a tendency to stimulate immigration and reduce the rates of wages. Except from the language of the statute, there is no reason to suppose a contract like the present to be within the evils which the law was designed to suppress; and, indeed, it would not be indulging a violent supposition to assume that no legislative body in this country would have advisedly enacted a law framed so as to cover a case like the present."

The statute was again before the Supreme Court, in United States v. Laws (163 U. S., 258; 16 Sup. Ct., 998), and the same liberal construction followed. In this case it was held that a contract made with an alien to come to this country as a chemist on a sugar plantation in Louisiana is not a contract to perform labor and service within the meaning of the act. It is shown by Mr. Justice Peckham, announcing the opinion in that case, that a similar construction had been adopted by the courts in New York in regard to statutes for claims of laborers. (See Ericsson v. Brown, 38 Barb., 390; Aiken v. Wasson, 23 N. Y., 482; Coffin v. Reynolds, 37 N. Y., 640; Wakefield v. Fargo, 90 N. Y., 213.) If construed strictly the act would include every person employed to perform any sort of labor or service except those among the exempted class by Congress. It would include lecturers, lawyers, physicians, surgeons, architects, engineers, bookkeepers, stenographers, typewriters, clerks, salesmen, drapers, and window dressers. But when we once break away from the letter of the law and seek for its true meaning and intent, which was to stay the influx of cheap, unskilled manual labor, then the liberal construction adopted by the Supreme Court furnishes the only safe resting place. Under such a construction it seems quite clear that the employment of a single person to come to this country and engage for a dry-goods house as a draper, window dresser, and clerk does not come within the true intent and meaning of the prohibition. There was no such mischief as that ever complained of, and none such to be remedied. It is not that cheap, uncultivated, unintelligent labor from competition with which our institutions stood in danger. The main purpose of the law, no doubt, was to prevent great corporations and business firms from contracting abroad for common, cheap, unskilled laborers to work in our mines, our mills, our factories, in our lumber woods, in grading canals and railroads, and to work upon other public improvements where a great many manual laborers are required. The practice of employing such laborers and importing them to this country and paying their passage under contracts to work for a stated time at low rates of wages, with which our better-fed and better-housed workmen could not compete, was the mischief Congress had in mind. A silk draper or linen draper is not a common laborer. He may do work with his hands, as does a minister, a lawyer, a surgeon, but to designate him as a common manual laborer would be a misuse of the English language. The habit of working with the hands is not by any means the criterion. All men work with their hands. But in some occupations, like that of working with the spade or shovel or wheelbarrow, or as a common hand in a sawmill, or in the lumber woods with a peavey or crosscut saw, the value of the labor consists principally in the physical results.

The surgeon also works with his hands, but the beneficial results in his case come from the skilled labor of the mind, guided by much study and experience in connection with that of the hand. The stenographer or typewriter works constantly with the hands, and yet the value of his work does not consist mainly in the manual labor done, and it would be a misuse of terms to call him a laborer. He is not such in the ordinary acceptation of the term, no more than is a draper or window dresser. The need of window dressers in large commercial centers like New York to dress out window fronts for the artistic display of silks and woolens is very well known. It has become a favorite way of advertising, and the tradesman who can present the most attractive window is apt to get the best trade. The occupation does not necessarily require any manual labor at all, as that may all be done under the direction and superintendence of the one skilled in that trade or business. It evidently requires experience, with good taste and judgment. He must know the value of perspective, and must be able to arrange and combine light and shade and colors to the best advantage, something as an artist does in a painting. To do this with proper effect requires something more than muscle and a spinal cord. It calls for intelligent skill. So with a skillful salesman of silks and woolens, a mercer, or draper, though he employs the labor of his hands to a certain extent, the principal value of his services comes from a different and more occult source. He must know his wares thoroughly and the best manner of exhibiting them, and have some knowledge and experience in the treatment and management of customers. It was not service of this kind that Congress sought to shut out, but the cheaper, grosser sort of unskilled and unhoused manual labor which was coming from abroad in competition with the common labor in this country, which has ever been on a somewhat higher plane, and where it was the purpose of Congress in the enactment of the law to keep it. Countenance is lent to this construction also by the act of Congress amending the law passed February 23, 1887 (24 Stat., 414, c. 220). Section 8 of this act provides that all persons included in the prohibition of the act shall be sent back to the nations to which they belong and from whence they came. It would be absurd to suppose that Congress intended that persons employed in trade or in any business requiring intelligence and skill, or, indeed any except those from the lowest social stratum engaged in unintelligent and uncultivated labor, should be sent back to the nations from whence they came. It has always been the policy of Congress, as well as the States, to encourage immigration of the better and more intelligent classes. To prohibit the introduction of these was not the purpose of Congress in the enactment of the present law.

(e) NEW INDUSTRIES.—An important exemption from the operation of the law is that of "skilled workmen" imported under contract "to perform labor in the United States in or upon any new industry not at present established in the United States: *Provided*, That skilled labor for that purpose can not be obtained otherwise."

Here are two conditions which in conjunction permit a skilled laborer to be imported under contract, namely, a new industry and the absence of skilled labor for that purpose in the United States. Both conditions are ambiguous. Does the first one mean "not established in 1885, the year when the law was enacted," or does it mean "not established at the time of the importation of the immigrant?" If it means the former, then any industry not established before 1885 would be open to alien contract laborers. If it means the latter, then "how far advanced must an industry be before it is established?" If the object of the alien contract-labor law is to maintain a high standard of wages in the United State through excluding aliens, and if the securing of skilled laborers is only a question of paying high enough wages, "how high must wages be advanced before it can be said that skilled labor can not be obtained?"

Upon the latter point, an early case was decided against the importer on the ground that he had not used "reasonable efforts to discover or to train workmen competent to do the desired work." (U. S. *v.* McCallum, 44 F., 745, Jan. 16, 1891.)

In this case it was decided that the industry in question was a "new" one, not because the kind of article manufactured—"French silk stockings"—had not been successfully produced in this country, but because the particular article, on the particular kind of machine, had not been manufactured. This definition of a "new industry" has been followed in other judicial cases and by the Secretary of the Treasury in the recent Dowie cases.

In the "lace curtain case," decided in 1893 (U. S. *v.* Bromiley, 58 F., 554, Nov. 23, 1893), the court held that prior to 1890 there was no evidence of any manufactory of fine lace in this country, except one establishment at Wilkesbarre, and that since 1890 there had been some eight or ten establishments manufacturing fine lace curtains, as a result of the McKinley tariff law of 1890. The court said:

I have no hesitancy in saying to you that in 1890, 1891, and 1892 it was a new industry. How successful it has been we do not know. It was a new industry, not established, and, according to the testimony, is not established at this date. * * * Even the witnesses called by the Government tell you that skilled menders, such as the defendant required and imported from England, could not have been employed in this country, unless, to use the expressive terms of the witness, they were " stolen from other mills."

The last clause just quoted indicates the second ambiguity above referred to, namely, the absence of skilled labor in the United States. The only way in which employees could be "stolen from other mills" would be through the payment of sufficiently high wages. And while to the employer this might seem like theft, yet to the workmen it would be the very fulfillment of the alien contract-labor law.

As a matter of fact both the courts and the Bureau of Immigration decide the issues solely on the question whether skilled labor can be found in the United States competent for the work desired. They pay little or no attention to the question whether the industry is a new one or an old one. (See "Dowie" case cited below, p. 668.)

(f) PROFESSIONAL ACTORS, ARTISTS, LECTURERS, AND SINGERS.—In a decision rendered by Justice Lacombe in 1899, prior to the decision of the Supreme Court in the Trinity case, the strict interpretation of the statute was insisted upon, and a penalty of $1,000 was imposed upon the importer of a milliner from Paris, notwithstanding the plea that a "milliner" is a "professional artist." (U. S. *v.* Thompson, 41 F., 28, Nov. 26, 1889.) The judge said:

It is well settled by authority that the popular and received import of words furnishes the general rule for the interpretation of public laws. Under this rule the defendant's contention is not sound. Milliners, dressmakers, tailors, cooks, and barbers (some of them no doubt call themselves " artists ") are not " artists " within the popular and received import of that word. In the excepting clause or proviso, therefore, there is nothing to relieve the defendant from the operation of this statute.

It will be inferred from later cases cited above that the rule excluding a milliner would probably not at the present time be sustained.

The question as to whether musicians are artists was decided by the Assistant Secretary of the Treasury in the case of the Straus orchestra in New York by a definition of the word artist.

ALIEN CONTRACT-LABOR LAW.   655

As the accepted definition of the word artists includes musicians who combine science and taste in the manual execution of their art, such musicians of the Straus orchestra may be admitted as artists under the proviso of section 5 as by their skill, taste, and accomplishments as musicians evidently come within the definition. This is not to be interpreted that any combination of musicians would be admitted as artists. (Syn. Dec., 10429.)

(g) RECOGNIZED PROFESSIONS.—The amendment of March 3, 1891, while adding ministers and college professors to the list of exempted classes who are eligible for admission, even though coming under contract, also added the clause "persons belonging to any recognized profession." Under this exception chemists are admitted. In United States v. Laws (163 U. S., 258, May 18, 1896) it was held that a contract made with an alien in a foreign country to come to the United States as a chemist on a sugar plantation in Louisiana, in pursuance of which contract said alien did come to this country and was employed on the sugar plantation, his expenses being paid by the defendant, was not a contract to perform labor or service prohibited under the contract-labor law. The same, after adverting to the general purposes of the act as not to embrace skilled labor, called attention to the fact that by the amendment of 1891 persons belonging to any recognized profession were excepted from its provisions, and said:

We think a chemist would be included in that class. Although the study of chemistry is the study of a science, yet a chemist who occupies himself in the practical use of his knowledge of chemistry as his services may be demanded may certainly at this time be fairly regarded as in the practice of a profession. * * * The fact that the individual in question by this contract had agreed to sell his time, labor, and skill to one employer and in one prescribed branch of the science does not in the least militate against his being a professional chemist; nor does it follow as a bar to the claim that while so employed he is nevertheless practicing a recognized profession.

C. PROSECUTION OF THE IMPORTER.

In considering the enforcement of the law excluding alien contract laborers, there must be kept in mind clearly the distinction already noticed between the penalty imposed upon the importer and the penalty imposed upon the immigrant. The penalty upon the importer is imposed by the Federal courts, with an appeal to the Supreme Court of the United States. The penalty upon the immigrant is imposed by the immigration inspectors, with an appeal to the Secretary of the Treasury. We shall consider first the penalty imposed upon the importer. As stated above, the original law of 1885 applied only to the importer of aliens under contract to perform labor. The penalty section is as follows (sec. 3, act of 1885):

That for every violation of any of the provisions of section one of this act the person, partnership, company, or corporation violating the same, shall forfeit and pay for every such offense the sum of one thousand dollars, which may be sued for and recovered by the United States or by any person who shall first bring his action therefor, including any such alien or foreigner who may be a party to any such contract or agreement, as debts of like amount are now recovered in the circuit courts of the United States; the proceeds to be paid into the Treasury of the United States; and separate suits may be brought for each alien or foreigner being a party to such contract or agreement aforesaid.

1. The proofs of the contract.—The Supreme Court holds, in the first place, that the action to recover a penalty, herein provided for, though it is in the form of a civil contract, is unquestionably criminal in its nature, and the defendant—the importer—can not be compelled to be a witness against himself. (Lees v. U. S., 150 U. S., 476.) The same ground has always been held by the lower courts. In United States v. Mexican National Railway Company (F. 40, 769), the court said:

It is useless to enter upon a critical analysis of the act of February 26, 1885, to demonstrate that the suits thereby authorized are not suits of a civil nature. Suffice it to say that the statute denounces the prohibited act of importation, etc., as an offense; the penalty attached to its commission is the forfeiture of $1,000, and the proceeds are paid into the Treasury, less such share of the penalties, under the amendment of October 19, 1888, as the Secrecary of the Treasury may, in his discretion, pay to the informer. It is apparent that the forfeiture does not arise from any contractual relation between the Government and the offender. It does not accrue from the violation of a private right, but grows out of the commission of an offense against the public. That the mere form of the action is civil is regarded as immaterial, as the courts look beyond that to inquire into the nature of the suit.

Since the importer can not be compelled to be a witness against himself, the prosecution must generally depend for witnesses upon residents of foreign countries, who either were present at the making of the contract in a foreign land, or who could give circumstantial evidence of the contract, or it must depend upon the immigrant himself. The court holds that, according to the terms of the law, the contract or agreement must have been made "previous to the importation or migration." Consequently the only contract that is contemplated is one made in a foreign country outside the jurisdiction of the United States courts. This being the case, the witnesses to the contract continue to be in most cases residents of the foreign country and can not be secured. If they do come to this country it is because they also are immigrants and associates of the alleged contract laborer, and are equally interested with him in concealing the fact of the contract. Consequently, it follows that the only witness to the contract on whom the Government prosecution can usually depend, is the alleged contract laborer himself.

But this witness knows that by confessing the contract he will be punished by deportation, and this threat of deportation is enough to make him conceal the fact that the contract exists. As a matter of experience, it has been found that the circumstance under which an imported laborer can be secured as a witness is usually that when he has had a falling out with his employer, the importer, and thinks that he may be able then both to get revenge and to win the informer's share of 50 per cent of the penalty recovered from the importer.

2. **Elements of violation of the alien contract labor law.**—While the courts have held to a liberal construction of the law as related to the exempted classes who may be admitted, they have held to a strict construction of the terms of the contract.

In one of the earliest decisions (U. S. v. Craig, 28 F. 795, Oct. 11, 1886), which has been followed by all subsequent decisions, the court said:

> To give the right of action under this section, three things are essential: (1) The immigrant must first, previous to his becoming a resident of the United States, have entered into a contract to perform labor or service here; (2) he must have actually emigrated to enter into the United States in pursuance of such contract; (3) the defendant must have prepaid his passage, or otherwise assisted, encouraged, or solicited his migration, knowing that he had entered into this illegal contract.

(a) TIME AND COMPENSATION.—The first of the foregoing essentials named by the court covers the term of the contract. On this point the courts adhere strictly to the rule that a contract to be complete and enforceable, while it may be express or implied, written or parol, must in any case contain the elements of time and compensation—i. e., it must specify the period of time during which the proposed employment is to continue, and must specify the amount of wages to be paid. Says the court in another case (U. S. v. Edgar, 45 F., 44, Jan. 29, 1891):

> It is not unlawful "to prepay the transportation" of an alien, unless at the time of such prepayment the alien is then "under contract or agreement to perform labor or service in the United States." * * A contract that is not enforceable for the reason that it lacks some of the elements of a valid agreement, such as "mutual assent" or a consideration is not a contract. The words "contract or agreement" as used in the statute must be held to mean a complete contract; that is to say, an agreement entered into for a sufficient consideration to perform some kind of labor or service. to the terms of which the parties have mutually assented. If an "implied contract" is counted upon, a state of facts must be alleged from which a court or jury might lawfully draw the inference, as a matter of fact, that the alien had agreed to perform labor or service of some kind and that some other person had agreed to accept such services.

In this case the court held that the letters exchanged between the two parties did not constitute an "express contract," and were insufficient to establish an implied contract, because they omitted to stipulate the amount of compensation to be paid, and the time during which employment was to continue. The letters referred to are as follows:

No. 16 AIKEN STREET,
Barton Hill, Bristol, April 11, 1890.

Mr. GRAY, *Manager.*

DEAR SIR: I have heard that you are in want of men to work on the spelter furnaces. I and one of my fellow workmen would like to come out there as the works here is very slack. If it would be convenient for you to send us a pass each we would come out as soon as possible. We have both worked in the spelter works for many years. Would you oblige us by writing back to let us know, and oblige,
1. BOYCE,
No. 16 Aiken Street, Bristol, England.

The name of my fellow workman, Fred Dorosalski.

[S. C. Edgar, lessee Glendale Zinc Works, manufacturers and refiners of spelter.]

SOUTH ST. LOUIS, *July 1, 1890.*

I. BOYCE,
No. 16 Aiken Street, Barton Hill, Bristol, England.

DEAR SIR: Your letter of April 11 has just been handed me, and I have this day bought two tickets for you and Fred Dorosalski from St. Louis agent of American Line, and all you have to do is to take this letter to Richardson, Spence & Co., No. 17 Water street, Liverpool, and get tickets through to St. Louis. We can give you steady work, and a place for six or eight more smelters, if they want to come. I run fourteen Belgium furnaces. The tickets will not be good after July 18.
Yours, truly,
S. C. EDGAR.

This case was appealed from the eastern judicial district of Missouri to the circuit court of appeals (U. S. v. Edgar, 4 U. S. App., 41), which affirmed the judgment of the lower court for the defendant.

The significance of the strict interpretation of the contract is plainly seen in this case, wherein the counsel for the Government had contended that in construing a measure of public policy we ought not to be critical about the term of the contract for labor mentioned in the contract if there is reason to believe that the act complained of is in violation of the spirit, if not the letter of the law. The court replied:

> We are not disposed to declare what shall be a sufficient contract under the law. The difficulty in supporting the complaint is, that there does not appear to have been any contract or agreement whatever between defendant and the Englishmen "made previous to importation or migration of such alien or aliens, foreigner or foreigners." The letter written by one of the Englishmen, and defend-

ant's answer, did not make a contract or agreement of any kind until something further should be done.

The act of the Englishmen in getting the tickets at Liverpool, and coming to Philadelphia, was necessary to complete the contract or agreement such as it was. In other words, when the defendant prepaid the Englishmen's passage, and thus assisted and encouraged them to come to the United States, there was no contract for labor which had been previously made by them; and so the case is not within the statute.

The foregoing decision makes quite plain the great difficulty imposed upon the Government in securing a conviction under the law, as long as the statute conditions the conviction upon the existence of an enforceable contract.

(b) ACTUAL MIGRATION.—The second essential element in violation of the labor contract law as laid down by the court in United States v. Craig, noted above, is "actual migration to the United States in pursuance to such contract."

Here arises a contradiction in the law. The courts have held from the time of the first cases on the subject, that, in order to make the contract binding, the immigrant must have actually entered into the United States in pursuance of such contract. "Admitting," says the court (U. S. v. Craig, 28 F., 795, decided Oct. 11, 1886), "that the words 'encouraging and soliciting' would seem to indicate an offense in itself, the word 'assisting' in the same connection implies that the immigration shall actually take place before the defendant can be held liable, for a person can not assist in doing that which is never done. In such case the person assisting or advising the immigration could no more be convicted than an accessory before the fact could be, if the crime advised were never committed."

This decision and the others which follow it require that the contract immigrant shall actually have landed, i. e., shall have completed the act of immigration before the contract can be enforced upon the importer. Otherwise the alleged assistance and promise of work given by the person in the United States is only an offer, and the proposition of the laborer is only an offer to come to the United States. There is no contract to employ or be employed.

Now other sections of the law prohibit the landing of contract laborers. Section 6, added to the law in 1887, says:

If in such examination made by immigration inspectors there shall be found among such passengers any person included in the prohibition in this act, they shall report the same in writing to the collector of the port, and such person shall not be permitted to land.

Also section 8 of the act of March 3, 1891, provides that inspection offices, where it is inconvenient to examine aliens on board incoming vessels,

may offer a temporary removal of such aliens for examination at a designated time and place, and then and there detain them until a thorough inspection is made. But such removal shall not be considered a landing during the pending of such examination.

Section 10 provides that—

All aliens who may unlawfully come to the United States shall, if practicable, be immediately sent back on the vessel by which they were brought in.

It is plain that these provisions require the immigration officials not only to send back their only witnesses to the contract but, also, as held by the courts, to prevent the completion of the illegal contract itself. If the immigrant who comes on an illegal contract escapes the vigilance of the inspectors and goes to work for the importer there is of course no punishment because the crime is not detected. But, on the other hand, if the inspectors discover the attempt to commit the crime they are required to step in and save the criminal from completing the last link in his offense. It is as though the law should declare that a man is not a thief who has been discovered by the policeman after he had broken into a house but just before he had actually laid his hands on his intended booty. Technically he is not a thief because he has not stolen anything. The law, therefore, to meet his case, does not charge him with theft but with the crime of burglary. A similar correction is needed in the alien contract labor law if it is to catch the importer.

It has been suggested that this defect of the law could be remedied by making it plain that "encouraging" or "soliciting" immigration is to be considered an offense in itself, apart from the existence of a contract. (Reports of the Industrial Commission, Vol. XV, Ullo, 143.) Judge Brown, in the Craig case, cited above, seems to suggest this view.

(c) ASSISTANCE AND SOLICITATION.—The third element essential to convict the importer is that, knowing the existence of the illegal contract, he should have prepaid the passage or otherwise assisted, encouraged, or solicited the migration of the alien. The contract is not the cause of action, and indeed the defendant need not necessarily have been a party to it. (U. S. v. Craig, 28 F., 795.) But if he assisted or solicited the immigration "in any manner whatsoever," knowing the contract to have been entered upon, he is liable. The law of 1891, which permits a person to prepay the passage of a relative or friend, does not allow such relative or friend to come here under contract, but on the contrary requires that it should be affirmatively and satisfactorily shown that he is not under contract. At the same time, the making of a contract with an alien and his migration into the United States to perform it may of itself be an assistance and solicitation of the employer punishable under the contract-labor law.

In the act of 1891 (§ 3) it is expressly provided that advertisements printed and published in a foreign country promising employment to aliens who may come to the United States shall be deemed a violation of the act of 1885. In this case the actual migration of the alien need not have taken place. The advertisement itself is a violation of the law. The rule herein is different from that which applies to a contract, where, in addition to the contract, there must be actual migration.

D. DEPORTATION OF CONTRACT LABORERS—THE AUTHORITY OF THE TREASURY DEPARTMENT.

Having considered in the foregoing pages the difficulty of securing the conviction of the importer of contract labor, we have now come to consider the other side of the enforcement of the law, namely, the deportation of the immigrant himself.

The law of 1885, it will be remembered, applied solely to the importer. It was not until the act of February 3, 1887, that the immigrant of the excluded classes was prohibited from landing, and was required to be sent back to the nation to which he belonged and from whence he came.

In the act of October 19, 1888, the Secretary of the Treasury was authorized to deport the contract laborer at any time within a year after he had landed.

Again, in the act of 1893 the immigrant was required to state before embarkation whether he was under contract to perform labor in the United States. (Act of March 3, 1893, § 1.)

The question as to whether the authority of the Secretary of the Treasury in deporting immigrants was final in all cases or not was at first decided differently by different Federal judges. It was admitted that "final determination of those facts may be intrusted by Congress to executive officers, and in such a case in which the statute gives a discretionary power to an officer, to be exercised by him upon his own opinion of certain facts, he is made the sole and exclusive judge of the existence of those facts, and no other tribunal, unless expressly authorized by law to do so, is at liberty to reexamine or controvert the sufficiency of the evidence on which he acted." (142 U. S., 660.)

Yet notwithstanding the immigration officials have power to exclude or deport aliens who come within the definition of the excluded classes, the lower courts held, prior to 1894, that they had power to inquire into the fact whether the alien was an immigrant or a resident. If the latter, he did not come under the excluded classes. The discretion of the Secretary, it was held, pertained only to those aliens who were actual immigrants, and who had not previously resided in the country. The judges held that they are immigrants the first time they land, and after the first landing they are no longer immigrants, and are beyond the jurisdiction of the Bureau of Immigration. (In re Howard, 63 F., 263; in re Panzara, 51 F., 275; in re Martorelli, 63 F., 437; in re Maiola, 67 F., 114.)

This defect in the law was remedied in 1894 by the clause already mentioned in the civil appropriation act (28 Stats., p. 390), which made the decisions of the inspectors and Secretary final in the case of all aliens, and not making any distinction between alien immigrants and alien residents. Since that time the courts have recognized that all aliens are within the jurisdiction of the immigration bureau. The decisions fully sustain the right of the immigration officials to decide for the exclusion and deportation of immigrants whom they believe to be contract laborers. There is no appeal to the courts. The only appeal is to the Secretary of the Treasury, an executive official. The court, on habeas corpus proceedings in case of a contract laborer refused permit to land, will not review the action of the immigration official, on the ground that the Secretary of the Treasury is the person who is solely charged with the duty of executing the provisions of the immigration laws, and consequently his decision is final. The court, for the same reason, will also refuse on writ of habeas corpus to review a case of a deportation made within one year after immigration, as provided in the amendment of October 19, 1888, giving authority to the Secretary of the Treasury to arrest and deport aliens illegally landed under the immigration laws within one year. (In re Lifieri, 52 F., 293, July 29, 1892.) The opinion in this case dismissed the writ of habeas corpus, and refused to review the action of the Secretary in deporting the immigrant whose violation of the law was only discovered a few days after he landed.

This recognition of executive discretion goes so far that the courts will refuse to interfere even when they see what they consider serious injustice is being done. In the case of Ota (96 F., 487) the court said:

It appears very clearly from these facts that Ota is not an alien immigrant, and the Commissioner of Immigration and the Secretary of the Treasury, if the same facts were laid before these officers, erred in ordering him to be returned to Japan as such. But, the court continued, under this statute (Aug. 18, 1894, 28 Stats., 390), when the executive officers of the Government upon a hearing such as is contemplated by the law have decided that an alien is not entitled to enter the United States, the courts are without jurisdiction to review that determination upon questions either of law or of fact

In another case the court said that the decision of the Secretary of the Treasury can not be reviewed by courts even though in plain disregard of the statute. (In re Lee Ping, 678; in re Tun Law.)

Another decision affirms that "the statute does not require inspectors to take any testimony at all and allows them to decide on their own inspection and examination the question of the right of any alien immigrant to land." The court is without jurisdiction to discharge upon writ of habeas corpus where the collector undertakes to deport a petitioner without a hearing or pending a hearing." (In re Lee Lung, 102 F., 132, May 12, 1900.) Referring to the opinion in 100 F., 389, that "the power of the court might be properly exerted in such a case to arrest the consequence of the collector's illegal act, but that it could go no further," the court says:

It is not clear as to what is meant by jurisdiction of the courts to "arrest the consequence of the collector's illegal act." If the court is without jurisdiction to inquire, upon writ of habeas corpus, as to the legality of the petitioner's detention, under such circumstances it is without any jurisdiction whatever in the premises. So far as I am advised there is no power in the courts to control the action of the collector of customs, as suggested.

The case established the doctrine that "the collector of customs in determining the right of Chinese persons to land may act upon his own information and discretion, and that such action, however taken, is conclusive of the matter, subject to the right of appeal to the Secretary of the Treasury. That this decision, if he decided not to hear testimony or not to give effect to evidence, which the laws of Congress have provided, shall be sufficient to establish the right of landing in the first instance, or decides not to decide, is conclusive. Under the doctrines of this case it is immaterial, so far as the jurisdiction of this court is concerned, whether the petitioner appealing to the Secretary of the Treasury is heard by the Secretary in person or by a subordinate official in his Department or is heard at all."

It must be remembered, as already stated, that the decision of the Secretary of the Treasury in ordering a deportation is not binding upon the courts in the prosecution of an importer or the steamship company. In United States v. Burke (99 F., 895), it was held that the master of a ship from which a sailor had escaped in an American port should be relieved from the penalty imposed by the collector of customs, because the sailor in question was not an immigrant in the contemplation of the law. In a case of that kind the court held that—

The provisions of the act of August 18, 1894, making the decision of the appropriate immigrant or customs officer excluding an alien from admission to the United States under any law or treaty conclusive upon the courts, does not preclude a court from entertaining jurisdiction to determine the question whether such alien in fact an immigrant within the meaning of such laws.

It should be added to the foregoing that a contract laborer once deported may, nevertheless, return to the United States without a contract, or even with another contract, provided the latter comes under the excepted classes, as, for example, a "personal or domestic servant." But should his work be supplemented by working at the occupation in which the former contract was alleged, he can, upon satisfactory evidence, be arrested and deported. (Syn. Dec. 17893.)

E. THE BUREAU OF IMMIGRATION.

1. **Legislation.**—It will be understood, of course, that the law of 1894 and the decisions thereunder place a large discretion in the hands of the Treasury Department, operating through the Bureau of Immigration. We have to do, here, with both the interpretation of the law by the Department and the administrative machinery of inspection.

The Department, in its interpretation, is, in effect, not bound by the precedents established by the courts. Undoubtedly it was the main object of this amendment to take the matter of enforcing the contract labor law, as far as possible, out of the strict interpretation of the courts and to place it under the informal decisions of officers, who might be able to act upon their impressions and convictions, and to take into account collateral indications not admissible in courts. This may appear to be an undemocratic grant of arbitrary power, in that a large class of people is placed under the pleasure of executive officers without protection in the courts.

This undoubtedly is true, unless within the administrative machinery of the Department is provided an effective substitute for a judicial investigation. Such an attempt has been made, but has not as yet been perfected, as will be shown below.

Acting under the power to inspect and deport immigrants the Secretary of the Treasury was authorized by the act of 1887 to enter into contract with State commissions in any State for the enforcement of the law under rules prescribed by himself. He was also given power to appoint contract-labor inspectors, whose duty it should be to attend to execution of the law of 1885 and 1887. It was not until 1891 that the complete enforcement of the law was taken out of the hands of the State commissioners at the port of New York and the other leading ports and placed under the control of commissioners appointed directly by the Secretary of the Treasury. This authority was included under section 8 of the act of 1891, in these words:

> All duties imposed and powers conferred by the second section of the act of August 3, 1882, upon State commissioners, boards, or officers acting under contract with the Secretary of the Treasury shall be performed and exercised as occasion may arise by the inspection officials of the United States.

The law of 1893, from the standpoint of administration, is the most important legislation on this subject. It was the first to provide for the inspection of immigrants abroad before embarkation. This law requires that the steamship companies shall deliver to the inspector of immigration a list or manifest made out at the place of embarkation of all alien immigrants on board said steamer. These manifests are made in groups of 30 immigrants; the manifest itself, containing 30 names, is given a letter of the alphabet or a number in consecutive order. The questions required to be answered on the manifest are the following: Full name, age, and sex; whether married or single; the calling or occupation; whether able to read or write; the nationality; the last residence; the seaport for landing in the United States; final destination, if any, beyond the seaport of landing; whether having a ticket through to such final destination; whether immigrant has paid his own passage, or whether it has been paid by other persons, or by any corporation, society, or municipality, or government; whether in possession of money, and if so, whether upward of $30, and how much, if $30 or less; whether going to join a relative, and if so, what relative, and his name and address; whether ever before in the United States, and if so, when and where; whether from any prison or almshouse, or supported by charity; whether a polygamist; whether under contract, expressed or implied, to perform labor in the United States; and what is the immigrant's condition of health, mentally and physically, and whether deformed or crippled, and if so, from what cause?

These manifests, filled out, are required to be verified by the master of the vessel before the United States consul or consular agent at the point of departure before the sailing of the vessel. Under this proviso the owner of the vessel is made responsible for the deportation of the immigrant if, at the inspection on the American side, it turns out that he belongs to any of the excluded classes.

Sections 2 and 3 of the law of 1893, providing for verification by the master and surgeon, are as follows:

> Each list or manifest shall be verified by the signature and the oath or affirmation of the master or commanding officer or of the officer first or second below him in command, taken before the United States consul or consular agent at the port of departure before the sailing of said vessel, to the effect that he has made a personal examination of each and all of the passengers named therein, and that he has caused the surgeon of said vessel sailing therewith to make a physical examination of each of said passengers, and that from his personal inspection and the report of said surgeon he believes that no one of said passengers is an idiot or insane person, or a pauper, or likely to become a public charge, or suffering from a loathsome or dangerous contagious disease, or a person who has been convicted of a felony or other infamous crime or misdemeanor involving moral turpitude, or a polygamist, or under a contract or agreement, express or implied, to perform labor in the United States, and that also, according to the best of his knowledge and belief, the information in said list or manifest concerning each of said passengers named therein is correct and true.
>
> That the surgeon of said vessel sailing therewith shall also sign each of said lists or manifests before the departure of said vessel, and make oath or affirmation in like manner before said consul or consular agent, stating his professional experience and qualifications as a physician and surgeon, and that he has made a personal examination of each of the passengers named therein and that said list or manifest, according to the best of his knowledge and belief, is full, correct, and true in all particulars relative to the mental and physical condition of said passengers. If no surgeon sails with any vessel bringing alien immigrants, the mental and physical examinations and the verifications of the lists or manifests may be made by some competent surgeon employed by the owners of the vessel.

2. **Immigration inspectors.**—In the arrangement of floor space at the various ports it is arranged that the immigrants in their groups of 30 shall pass first before the medical inspectors who detain those whom they suspect of physical or mental defects. The others are passed along at once to the immigration inspectors, to be followed later by those who have been detained for medical examination. The immigration inspector has before him the manifest furnished by the master of the vessel, and as the immigrants file past he detains each one long enough to question the immi-

ALIEN CONTRACT-LABOR LAW.   661

grant, to verify the entries on the manifest, and to make up his mind as to the immigrant's eligibility for entrance.

The position of the immigration inspector is the first in importance in the immigration service. These officers are intrusted with the greatest responsibility, and represent to the incoming alien the entire immigration force in so far as 85 per cent to 90 per cent of the incoming aliens are concerned. In other words, the officers in charge of this inspection determine that 8 out of every 10 aliens presenting themselves for admission to the United States shall be landed. These officers can, if they desire, allow undesirable and contract laborers to enter without further recourse. Their decision is final in all cases where they decide affirmatively for admission. The law of 1893 (sec. 5) requires each inspector to hold for special inquiry "every person who may not appear to him to be clearly and beyond doubt entitled to admission." But the law fails to provide for any review of his action or any appeal in case he should admit an immigrant about whom there might be reasonable doubt of his eligibility. This is a serious oversight, when it is considered that these officers are among the lowest paid in all the service, and that they were originally selected merely as interpreters. The question as to whether they were judicially minded and fully understood the principles underlying the immigration laws was not taken into account in their appointment. Men who were originally appointed only as interpreters or registry clerks have been placed on an equality with regular inspectors in their powers of inspection. It can not be expected that such men, themselves immigrants, shall understand the principles and objects which are desired by the American people in adopting exclusive legislation. As a matter of fact this class of inspectors are liberal in admitting people of their own race but captious in admitting other races.

There is at Ellis Island provision for 16 files of immigrants to pass continually before 16 immigration inspectors, and in this way it has been possible to examine 5,000 immigrants in 1 day of 7 hours. It may be observed in this connection, relative to the proposed educational test, that such a test would not at Ellis Island in any way increase the actual time required for passing the inspectors. The lines of immigrants are so long, and the head of the line is being so continually detained by the inspector, that it would be a simple matter to place as many educational inspectors as is necessary at lower points on the line. The educational inspection and the primary inspection could be conducted at the same time at different points along the same line. In this way the apprehension that an educational test would clog the machinery at Ellis Island on busy days, and would detain immigrants beyond the time now consumed, is groundless.

3. **Boards of special inquiry.**—An important innovation in the law of 1893 was the creation of the boards of special inquiry. Prior to the creation of these boards, under the act of 1891, the decision of the inspection officer or of the commissioner of immigration at the ports was final unless appeal was taken to the Superintendent of Immigration, whose action was subject to review by the Secretary of the Treasury. But the law of 1893 introduced the new feature of a jury, or an administrative court, the so-called board of special inquiry. Henceforth the immigration inspector does not pass final decision in case of exclusion, but merely holds the immigrant for a hearing before this new board. For this purpose it is the inspector's duty to detain for special inquiry "every person who may not appear to him to be clearly and beyond doubt entitled to admission."

The members of the board of special inquiry are taken from the existing list of inspectors, but in order that they may have high standing they are designated in writing by the Secretary of the Treasury or the Commissioner General of Immigration. They are 4 in number, and no immigrant is admitted on special inquiry except under a favorable decision made by at least 3 of said inspectors. Furthermore, the commissioner of immigration at the port is deprived of authority in the matter, and appeals are taken directly to the Superintendent of Immigration, whose action is subject to review by the Secretary of the Treasury, as originally provided in the law of 1891. This appeal may be taken either by the immigrant himself or by any dissenting member of the board of special inquiry.

It will be seen that in the board of special inquiry the law contemplates an administrative court, which shall be free, as much as possible, from the personal motives of the individual inspector, and shall be able to establish certain standards for the guidance of the inspection at each port.

On the average it is found that these boards of special inquiry admit 80 to 90 per cent of the immigrants detained for their examination by the primary inspectors. In this way the per cent of immigrants deported ranges from 0.11 of 1 per cent in 1890 to 1.45 per cent in 1898 of all the immigrants who pass before the primary inspectors. The number actually deported has increased from 3,229 in 1898 to 4,602 in 1900, although the ratio to total arrivals has decreased from 1.45 to 1.02 per cent.

This is shown by the following tables, giving for 9 years the deportations for each cause, the total deportations, and the per cent of total deportations to total arrivals.

TABLE 1.—*Number of immigrants arriving, the number excluded, and the percentage of excluded to arrivals, 1890 to 1900.*

Year.	Total number of immigrants.	Total number debarred.	Per cent debarred.
1890	455,302	535	0.11
1891	516,253	1,026	.19
1892	579,773	3,732	.64
1893	439,730	1,630	.36
1894	285,631	2,806	.98
1895	258,536	2,419	.93
1896	343,267	2,799	.81
1897	230,832	1,880	.81
1898	217,786	3,229	1.45
1899	311,715	4,061	1.30
1900	448,572	4,602	1.02

TABLE 2.—*Number of immigrants returned and reasons for their exclusion.*

Year.	Convicts.	Lunatics.	Idiots.	Paupers.	Contract laborers.	Returned within one year.	Diseased.	Assisted.	Other causes.	Total.
1890	3	26	3	503						535
1891	41	36	2	756	123				68	1,026
1892	26	17	4	1,002	1,763				820	3,732
1893	12	8	3	431	518	577	81			1,630
1894	8	5	4	802	1,553	417			2	2,806
1895	4	6		1,714	694	177				2,419
1896		10	1	2,010	776	238	2			2,799
1897	1	6	1	1,277	328	263	1	3		1,889
1898	2	12	1	2,261	417	199	258	79		3,229
1899	8	19	1	2,599	741	263	348	82		4,061
1900	4	32	1	2,974	833	356	393	2	7	4,602

4. Contract labor inspectors.—The method by which the special inspectors, appointed to enforce the contract labor law, perform their duties has been as follows: During the administration of the State commission the contract labor inspector was present at each examination made by the State inspector, and it was his duty, acting under orders of the collector of customs, following the examination made by the State inspectors, to make a separate examination of such cases as he had reason to believe were being imported in violation of the alien contract labor law. To do this, the immigrant was taken to one side with an interpreter and required to make an affidavit under the questioning of the inspector. This affidavit being sworn to was the legal evidence and record upon which his deportation was ordered. This method of examination was continued after 1890, although the Government had undertaken to displace the State inspectors altogether. Congress continued to make separate appropriation for the inspectors of contract labor, and for the other inspectors appointed to enforce the provisions excluding criminals, public charges, and those affected with loathsome and contagious diseases.

The contract labor inspectors were not placed upon the list of immigration inspectors, although they always had places upon the boards of special inquiry, but continued to act as a separate body. This dual system continued until June, 1900, when the commissioner at the port of New York transferred the contract inspectors from their separate and independent positions and placed them upon the list as primary inspectors, or gave them positions upon the board of special inquiry, exactly like other inspectors. Since that date the inspection of immigrants for all causes has been uniform.

Now, the peculiar and striking result of this change in administration has been a remarkable falling off at the port of New York in the number of contract laborers debarred. This is shown by the following table, wherein it appears that the deportations for June, 1900, the last month of the old system, were 38, and for July, 1900, the first month of the new system, were only 1, with an increase as high as 38 in March, 1901, but usually far below the number of the preceding record:

ALIEN CONTRACT-LABOR LAW. 663

TABLE 3.—*Contract laborers debarred, port of New York.*

Month.	Arrivals.	Contract laborers deported.	Month.	Arrivals.	Contract laborers deported.
1899.			April	50,737	16
March	27,795	80	May	60,161	39
April	37,014	75	June	47,005	38
May	48,833	99	July	35,697	1
June	34,183	82	August	27,041	8
July	22,102	30	September	31,706	4
August	24,157	44	October	29,370	15
September	27,540	42	November	23,960	3
October	28,794	30	December	22,131	6
November	26,460	53			
December	20,704	47	1901.		
			January	13,688	8
1900.			February	21,947	6
January			March	34,918	38
February			April	54,216	9
March	33,772	55	May	67,038	22

The explanation of this falling off in deportation of contract laborers is found in the abandonment of the affidavit system formerly practiced by the contract labor inspectors. Upon this important change in method serious differences of opinion exist between the officials of the Bureau at Washington and the commissioner at New York. On the one side it is argued that "there are what may be regarded as two separate systems of legislation in this country relating to the control of alien immigration; the first system proscribing such aliens as are believed by Congress to be detrimental to the welfare of the citizens of the Union, as a whole, if permitted to land; the other class excluding aliens who, it may be confessed, are individually in a high degree acceptable in many instances, but who come under conditions which conflict with the interests and rights of certain classes of American citizens.

"In other words, viewed as to the persons whose well-being they are intended to protect, the "immigration laws" may be regarded as general, while the "contract-labor laws" are specific.

"The general laws provide the means for their own enforcement in what is known as the head tax, or immigration fund; the specific laws, on the other hand, contain no such self-sustaining provision, and Congress distinguishes them broadly from the former by making specific provision for cost of their enforcement in the annual appropriation bills.

"The officials appointed for the administration of the alien contract-labor laws have different duties to perform from those discharged by officials appointed to enforce the "immigration laws," and the distinction between them is emphasized by their payment, respectively, from different funds. As a consequence of the more specific duties of the contract-labor inspectors, more care was used, in their selection and appointment, to secure officers who, either by reason of some special familiarity with labor conditions in the United States or because of their superior intelligence, could detect and prevent attempted violations of the law, than seemed necessary in the appointment of immigrant inspectors, whose work is largely a matter of simple external observation of the individual alien.

"In actual practice at the ports the inspection was made as follows: The aliens arranged in groups filed one after another past an official designated formerly as registry clerk. This official compared the answers in reply to his interrogations of each alien with the description contained of such alien in the ship's manifest on the desk before him. If the answers were satisfactory in all respects, the alien was passed or admitted; if, on the other hand, the replies were contradictory or equivocal, the alien was detained by the registry clerk for an examination by an inspector. These registry clerks were appointed simply for their familiarity with the languages spoken by the aliens, and irrespective of their qualifications in other respects; but grew, in course of time, by a professed application of the principles of civil-service reform, to be "assistant immigrant inspectors," dependent for the removal of the prefix upon their ability to get the raise of pay that would put them a class higher.

"To return to the mode of inspection, after an alien was passed by the registry clerk, a contract-labor inspector, one of whom was stationed at the head of each row or aisle, and in full sight and hearing of the examination, if he suspected the alien of being under a contract to work in this country, took him aside for further examination.

"In this examination, which was made separately and apart from the mass of the immigrants and officials, and before the alien's testimony could be biased by any information as to its effect upon his admission, an interpreter was used. If no facts were elicited to justify the inspector's suspicion, the alien was dismissed without a hearing before a board of special inquiry, thus saving its time for the consideration of other cases. If, on the contrary, the facts disclosed the existence of an agreement to work in the United States as the inducement to the alien's migration, those facts, in the form of replies to the inspector's interrogations, were embodied in a written affidavit, which, upon completion, was read to him by the interpreter, and, if then affirmed by the alien to be true, was acknowledged by him under oath before the inspector. This course was pursued both as a reasonable precaution to prevent his retracting or denying what he had said, if, after the examination, the alien should be apprised by counsel or friends of the effect of his statement, and because the act of March 3, 1891, prior to the establishment of boards of special inquiry, provided that: "The inspection officers and their assistants shall have power to administer oaths, and to take and consider testimony touching the right of any such aliens to land, all of which shall be entered of record." And at that time there was no other means to enter such testimony of record.

"After the establishment of boards of special inquiry, as provided in section 5 of the act approved March 3, 1893, the alien was taken before the board after signing the affidavit and examined by it, the said affidavit being used as the basis of the board's reexamination of the said alien. In order that any injustice to him, arising from a misunderstanding on his part, might be avoided, the commissioner at the port of New York, where the above-described system was in force, was repeatedly directed by the Department to instruct the board that it should inform such alien that it was not necessary for him to prove he had work secured to obtain admission to the United States. If the alien still persisted in the statements contained in the affidavit, to the allegations contained in which the examination of the board was not confined, he was refused a landing, and at the same time notified of his right of appeal to the Department. This right he frequently exercised, the Department sometimes overruling the board, either solely upon the evidence considered by the board or upon that and such other evidence besides as might be submitted, together with argument of counsel in his behalf, and always giving due weight to the recommendation contained in the commissioner's letter transmitting the record to the Department. Sometimes the alien denied the statements contained in the affidavit, and in this case, unless evidence could be secured dehors the affidavit, corroborating it, the alien, if otherwise admissible, would be permitted to land.

"In its workings, as may be reasonably assumed from the above account of it, the affidavit system was entirely satisfactory, both in insuring detection of attempted violations of the law and in preventing injustice to the alien on account of any misapprehension of the law on his part. The agents of the transportation lines and the most experienced and intelligent officers at the New York station are on record as of opinion that a similar system applied in the administration of the immigration laws would expedite the landing of many needlessly detained aliens and avoid the waste of time by the boards of special inquiry in considering the cases of those held for its reexamination upon frivolous or insufficient grounds.

"As might have been anticipated, the existence at the New York station of a separate and more intelligent class of officers, paid on an average 50 per cent larger salaries than the immigrant inspectors, aroused the jealousy of the latter, and was productive of friction. The contract-labor inspectors, too, were men of sufficient good sense to know their duties under the law, and of sufficient strength of will to refuse to submit to any attempt to interfere with the faithful discharge thereof.

"These officers were placed under the immediate administrative management of a supervising inspector, just as the immigrant inspectors and registry clerks were under a chief, and both of these divisions were equally subordinate to the Commissioner of Immigration.

"As a consequence of their superiority, moreover, the contract-labor inspectors were and are specially useful as members of the boards of special inquiry, upon which they continue to serve. All officials who act as board members are empowered so to serve in writing by the Secretary of the Treasury or by the Commissioner-General of Immigration upon the recommendation of the commissioner of the port, who designates such of them from time to time for active duty thereon as he may see fit.

"In the spring of 1900, the commissioner at the port of New York, without authority of the Department so far as the Commissioner-General of Immigration is aware, and despite his orally expressed disapproval of such step, abolished the affidavit system. This placed the two classes of inspectors upon the same footing as far as possible, the distinction becoming one rather of pay than of character of work, so far as actual inspection is concerned. The practical results of the change may be seen by examination of the following table:

Total arrivals July, August, and September, 1899 73,809
Rejected for same period as contract laborers 126
Total arrivals for same period, 1900 94,444
Rejected for same period as contract laborers 13

"During the last-named period under the new system there were detained and sent before the boards of special inquiry for examination under the alien contract-labor laws, out of aggregate arrivals at New York of approximately 95,000, but 115 suspects, less than those rejected during the corresponding period of the next preceding year, out of 25 per cent less arrivals. While this showing may suggest to some minds the inference that the change is an improvement, as showing that the great majority of those formerly denied were entitled to land, the less agreeable but equally reasonable conclusion may be drawn therefrom that the purpose of the law has been practically defeated by the admission of many not entitled to land. In considering which of these two opposing views is correct it would seem but natural for Government officials to lean toward the latter, and thus avoid the damaging admission that they have been rejecting for years so many aliens entitled to admission—a wrong which, if committed, equally involves the officers at the port of New York and those at the Department in Washington, not excepting the Secretary of the Treasury, to whom all can appeal and without whose approval none can be finally refused permission to land."

The commissioner of the port of New York explains the change in administration in the following way:

The modus operandi of making contract labor cases under the affidavit system was simple and deceptive to the alien. In the first place, it must be borne in mind that the meaning of the contract labor law is beyond the comprehension of the ordinary alien coming to this country. On the other hand, the reason for refusing admission to an alien because he was likely to become a public charge is easily understood by the most obtuse. Under the old system the examination of the alien for all other cases except that of contract labor was performed by other immigration officers, and if the alien passed this examination he was turned over to a contract labor inspector, who interrogated him as to this point only. What more natural than that the alien, eager to escape the Scylla of a public charge exclusion, should run into the Charybdis of the contract labor law. Had the alien work promised him? Yes. Brother, cousin, or friend, already in the United States, had written him telling of their success, and, it may be, saying that if he came over here he might find work with them. With this basis of fact, the alien, eager to prove that he would not become a public charge, and the inspector, equally eager to secure a confession of a promise or assurance of work amounting to a contract to perform labor in the United States, were not long in coming to an agreement. The result was an affidavit, written by the inspector and signed by the alien, which generally appeared to be worthless upon its face as a legal document, for the reason that it showed a conclusion and not a statement of the facts necessary to arrive at that conclusion, and in a great many instances the conclusion was that of the writer of the affidavit and not of the alien. The alien and inspector were alone. The alien generally had a wrong conception of the reason why he was being asked these questions, and imagined that this was a part of the process which it was necessary for him to go through in order to obtain admission to the United States. In all cases except English speaking aliens (and these were so few as not to amount to any appreciable per cent) the affidavit was written, not in the language of the alien, but in English. Once this affidavit was obtained, the alien, accompanied by the inspector, proceeded to the board of special inquiry, where the affidavit was read to its members by the inspector. The board caused it to be interpreted back to the alien, and in a large majority of cases the alien confirmed his affidavit, being consequently excluded.

So far as the working of the board of special inquiry is concerned, the affidavit system did not produce satisfactory results. The affidavit of the immigrant, constituting as it did a prepared conclusion of the contract labor inspector, the examination before the board was naturally more or less restricted as to what was contained therein, and any attempt by any member of the board to differ from that conclusion was generally the cause of unpleasant attrition between its members and the then contract labor bureau. If the alien had stated falsely in his affidavit, believing that it would assist him to land, it was only natural that he should persist in corroborating it, especially with the inspector standing at his side; therefore, the full truth concerning such aliens coming to this country was scarcely ever developed under this system. Unless the person named in the alien's affidavit as being the one who had contracted, induced, or assisted him to come to the United States made an application for a rehearing, this was all the trial the alien received before being deported.

There is little doubt that the same percentage of the 115 cases that were tried by the board in the 3 months of July, August, and September, 1900, would, if they had been tried under the old affidavit system, have been excluded and deported, the difference being that in one case the immigrant was convicted on his affidavit only, and the other where all the facts were developed.

Under the present system all the facts connected with the case must, of necessity, be known to the board of special inquiry, while under the former system material facts might have been in the possession of the inspector, or some one in the contract labor bureau, but the board would have remained in total ignorance of them if not thought fit by the contract labor bureau to lay those facts before the board.

5. **Deportation within one year after landing.**—The act of October 19, 1888, added an important amendment to the law by providing that an immigrant who might escape the vigilance of the inspectors at the ports might nevertheless be arrested within 1 year after landing and then deported exactly as he would have been had the inspector debarred him before landing. The law as amended authorizes "the Secretary of the Treasury, in case that he shall be satisfied that an immigrant has been allowed to land contrary to the prohibition of the law, to cause such immigrant, within the period of 1 year after landing or entry, to be taken into custody and returned to the country whence he came, at the expense of the owner of the importing vessel; or, if he entered from an adjoining country, at the expense of the person previously contracting for the service."

The importance of this amendment can readily be understood, and its significance may be judged from the table (Table 2) on page —, where it appears that the immigrants returned within 1 year numbered 356 in 1900, out of a total number returned of 4,602.

It is still questionable whether the period of 1 year is long enough. In New York City there is a serious complaint on the part of the public authorities on account of the large number of aliens who bring their children or dependent relatives to the public institutions at the end of the first year of residence. Under State law 1 year's residence is required to gain legal domicile entitling to the benefits of public charity, and the immigration law of 1891 provides that "any alien who becomes a public charge within one year after his arrival in the United States from causes existing prior to his landing therein shall be deemed to have come in violation of law and shall be returned as aforesaid."

If, now, when alien applicants appear at the end of a year, and by their application for help formally concede that they are paupers, the immigration authorities were legally enabled to arrest and deport them, a large amount of undeserved expense would be saved to the public treasury.

Again, the 1-year period is peculiarly valuable in the case of contract laborers. This class of immigrants now comes to this country admirably "coached" in all the answers which they shall give to the inspectors. It is well known that the business of collecting peasants from the villages of Italy and Austria-Hungary and shipping them to importers in New York, Chicago, and other places has become so highly perfected and developed that it is practically impossible under existing law to discover their true character at the port of landing. The main safeguard, therefore, is in the power of the Bureau of Immigration, through its special agents and detectives, to follow these suspected immigrants to their places of employment where the evidence against them may be secured.

Doubtless, here again, it may seem to be placing a large amount of arbitrary power in the discretion of the Secretary of the Treasury, in that his warrant, without judicial hearing, should be the sole instrument on which aliens are arrested and sent out of the country. This power, however, has been found to be necessary, in order to remove the administration of the law from the delay and formalities of legal procedure.

Since a law of this kind depends for both its interpretation and its energetic enforcement upon executive officers, it may be of interest to trace its operation in a few leading instances where records are available. With this in view, the following recent typical cases have been selected:

F. CASES SHOWING THE OPERATION OF THE CONTRACT LABOR LAWS.

1. **Case of Croatian stave cutters.**—On September 15, 1899, the Bureau of Immigration received confidential information "to the effect that about 200 or 300 Austrian stave cutters are coming to work for the various stave camps in Mississippi, Louisiana, and Texas. These workmen are expected to come secretly in the near future via Baltimore, New Orleans, and Galveston."

One company of 9 Croatians arrived September 24 at New York. They brought with them various sums of money ranging from $30 to $50 each and were provided with railroad tickets to Cincinnati, Ohio, although they had no friends or addresses in that city. They declared that if they were unable to find work at Cincinnati they would go to Memphis, having noticed that place upon the map. They had also the address of one Kronberger, at Ruleville, Miss., said to be the agent of the Austro-American Stave and Lumber Company at that point.

Immigrant Inspector Milton Smiley, at Cincinnati, was ordered to meet these immigrants. On October 5 he reported that 5 Croatians had bought tickets at Columbus, Ohio, for St. Louis and 4 to Memphis, Tenn., all of the same party. They were accompanied by a man who could speak English, but who did not purchase the tickets directly. At Cincinnati he met the 9 people in question, asked where they were going, and they showed him their tickets for Birmingham, Ala., purchased at Washington, Pa., and Columbus, Ohio. He said: "It was at once conclusive in my mind that some one at Pittsburg or along the line was helping them along." Since Washington, Pa., is off the main line of the Pennsylvania Railroad, he inferred that some one had gone there from Pittsburg and gave the tickets to them at Pittsburg. He discovered later on inquiry of the ticket agent at Columbus, Ohio, that 5 tickets had been sold to these foreigners for St. Louis and 4 to Memphis, Tenn., all of the same party. They would give no information as to their work at Memphis, but were going to look for work. The interpreter told them they could get work at Cincinnati, but they preferred to go to Memphis because they had tickets. The leader of the party said that he had been in the United States before, but in Mr. Smiley's opinion he was the agent of the contractor.

In November, 1899, Inspector T. W. Levy was detailed as a detective to the stave-cutters' camp near Greenville, Miss., where he interviewed the boss of the stave-cutters' camp. He learned that there were 130 men, all Slavonians, in camp, being the largest single camp in the United States, under Leopold Kerne Stave Company, of Vienna, Austria, with American headquarters at Memphis, Tenn. Nearly all had been here less than a year. All but a few had landed at New York or Baltimore. Only one had come through Galveston. That there was no trouble to get men, but the companies were now very careful, as the Government was watching them, and heavy penalties would follow if they were caught. But only a short time back 36 men destined to work for his company were sent back to New York. These men had foolishly brought axes and other tools from Austria in their baggage, and got caught in consequence. That over 100 who came at the same time were allowed to land, as they had been smarter and had brought no give-away tools. That the 36 sent back were a part of the others that landed. That there was contract with the men, but all knew and understood that they were to work for his company. That in almost every part of Austria in the stave-cutting districts there are steamship posters telling of the attractiveness of this country, of wages paid for stave cutting, and the stave districts in this country, and that stave men were wanted there. That he did not know for certain, but believed that there were special agents who worked up parties of stave cutters and gave a big discount in passage to the party. That the men who came over in these parties brought very little baggage under advice, and no telltale tools; and all know how to answer questions propounded by Government officers as to their being under contract. That 5 and 6 years ago the stave companies imported men, but there was no need for this now, as matters were "understood," and men who "understood" things could go to work at once on arrival. That men came to Memphis and other places, and from there were distributed to camps. That the foreman kept men's names, but usually "run them by numbers, like a lot of damned convicts." That "it would be no use to show me men's names, as I could not remember or pronounce a single one." That he did not know his men's antecedents, or how or when they came, and did not want to know.

Mr. Levy also says that the names of Karesch and Stolzky, ticket men at Bremen, "which have bobbed up in almost all my investigations, are either themselves or by their agents at the bottom of these importations and assist in them by advice and perhaps work. Certain it is that all men imported through Galveston said that Karesch and Stolzky had told them of localities to which they were going. They no doubt told them of contract laws, of axes and tools as give-aways in baggage and advised leaving them behind, etc. That practically all stave cutters 'understand things' before they leave Austria. That those who do pass inspectors because of lack of sufficient evidence can be followed, and will be found to go to Goebel's Hotel in Memphis, Yielsch Hotel in Shreveport, and a no-name hotel near union depot in Little Rock and from these places at once to the woods, and that once in the woods, unless followed, it is a difficult matter to locate them, as the forests are large in area and the canebrakes in parts almost impenetrable."

In a later communication Mr. Levy wrote that his investigations led him to believe that the contract labor laws have been systematically broken by people connected with the stave business. "In my travels recently I have located a dozen or more camps of stave cutters in which there are many men. I estimate the number at nearly, if not quite, 1,500, three-fourths of whom have been in this country less than 2 years, and the large majority of these less than 1 year, and nearly all of whom came exactly like those off *Köln* came—previously contracted for. * * * Shreveport and Little Rock are the great distributing points. There are dozens of stave factories throughout Arkansas, Louisiana, Mississippi, and Tennessee. The points named are the best for labor-distributing points. I do not believe that there are 2 per cent of the Austrians that go to the above-noted points that are not under contract as stave cutters. I have been painstaking and energetic in my labors, and gone into camps far from the railroad and walked to get into them; have talked with citizens and Slavs and am firmly convinced that the business of stave cutting is done by Austrians systematically imported by interested people and through every port of any consequence on the Atlantic and Gulf seaports, to avoid suspicion, and that positive evidence can never be had, and that the business of importing had reached very large proportions."

Later he wrote: "It appears to me that the importation of Austrians for stave cutting is above all big things of this kind in recent years. The staves these fellows cut are cut by no one in this section of the country, being of a peculiar kind intended for the French and Austrian markets exclusively. No one cuts these staves except Austrians anywhere in the South or Southwest. * * * It is impossible to have direct positive evidence against importers or men. They are too well versed in the laws, but the train of circumstantial evidence against men and importers is sufficiently strong to at least deport, as in the case of our 'farm laborers' off the *Köln*, and other ships."

After the stave cutters had been arrested for deportation, B. Kobler, manager of the Austro-American Stave and Lumber Company, headquarters Shreveport, La., appeared in their behalf and stated that owing to the exhaustion of the forests in Austro-Hungary and Slavonia the stave-cutting industry was compelled to remove to other countries, and was located at districts surrounding Memphis and Shreveport, and naturally the stave cutters, who knew nothing but farming and stave cutting, being thrown out of employment in Austria, came over in large numbers to these American districts. That the 15 men on the steamship *Köln* now under arrest did not have any contract with him or anyone else. But that they had applied to him for work and he had wired to Antone Kronberger, the owner of a stave-cutting concern, asking if he could give employment to these men. They were competent workmen, and the affiant had no interest in them, except that they were countrymen of his in distress, to whom he would like to see justice done.

In January, 1900, Inspector Levy, at Galveston, made the formal and personal tender of the 15 Slavs for deportation by the steamship *Roland*, but the local agent refused to receive them, whereupon he swore out a warrant, upon which the agent was arrested and then released upon a $3,000 bond.

The district attorney recommended dismissal of the agent on the ground that the law does not contemplate criminal prosecutions in cases after landing. The commissioner thereupon dismissed the prosecution. The district attorney thereupon recommended deportation, and the steamship company consented to receive the men, deport them to Germany on a steamship, and to pay the cost of maintenance while in Galveston.

7. **Dr. Dowie's lace makers.**—The lace curtain case reported on page — served as a precedent to the Secretary of the Treasury in the case of the lace makers imported by Dr. Dowie to establish a lace factory at Zion, Ill. Dr. Dowie, through his attorneys, had communicated with the Secretary of the Treasury under date of April 25, 1900, explaining the proposed importation of lace makers from England, and asking to be informed whether he would, in the opinion of the Secretary of the Treasury, be transgressing the law in any particular if he could carry out his plans as at present formulated. Dr. Dowie's attorneys argued that "skilled workmen from foreign countries may be engaged under a valid contract or agreement to perform labor or service in the United States in or upon any new industry, provided such workmen can not be obtained here." They also (U. S. *v.* Bromily, 58 F., 554) held that the alien contract labor law was designed to apply only to the importation in large numbers of foreign unskilled laborers under contract to perform labor or service in the United States.

The Amalgamated Lace Curtain Operatives of America, on May 19, had submitted to the commissioner-general, in reply to his inquiry, a list of the factories at that time established. They were: Tariffville Lace Making Company, established 9 years, 9 machines, 58 operatives, firm recognizes union; Scranton Lace Company, Scranton, Pa., established 9 years, 250 operatives, 17 machines, firm recognizes union; Patchogue Lace Manufacturing Company, Patchogue, L. I., established 9 years, 350 operatives, output 10,000 pairs lace curtains per week, 22 machines, does not recognize the union, but expected to do so in a very short time; Columbia Lace Mills, Campbell & Celand owners, established 8 years, about 60 operatives, does not recognize the union. Wages vary from $10 to $25 per week. The secretary of the union stated:

"I have enough applications already to fill the places of the men that Dr. Dowie wants to import except the last 3 which is mentioned in your letter of the 8th. Sorry that I can not give you any information about those 3, as they are trades that we know very little about at present. * * * Two hundred and twenty-nine machines in the country; 2 men to each machine. A lockout at the Wilkesbarre mill affected 14 men, 49 women, and 26 boys, who could supply Dr. Dowie's mills if needed. At some of the mills we only work three-fourths time."

Dr. Dowie advised the Department from Edinburgh, on November 3, that the first party of his lace makers and families would arrive about November 12 at Philadelphia. He said the party comprised only 3 lace makers, but included also their wives and families, and that the principal party would leave on the return voyage of the steamer in December. The number of actual lace makers, including "draftsmen," will not exceed 35 to 40, all of them going out as practically chiefs of departments, the object being not to import work people in numbers from Great Britain, "but to educate our own people in America, for whose benefit these industries are being established." Dr. Dowie had purchased outright the plant at Beeston, England, and had shipped or was about to ship to this country the machinery of the mill for use in the new establishment. The emigrants, who arrived at Philadelphia, while claiming not to be under contract with Dr. Dowie, all expected to secure employment with him. The board of special inquiry of Philadelphia debarred them on the ground that lace making is an industry fully established in this country and that skilled workmen could readily be obtained in this country at short notice to fully man the new mill about to be started by Dr. Dowie. Dowie's attorneys thereupon appealed to the Secretary of the Treasury, alleging that the manufacture of Lever's fancy lace upon the improved Lever machines is a new industry not established in the United States on February 26, 1885, and not now established here, and skilled labor for this purpose can not be obtained otherwise than from abroad.

The board of special inquiry unanimously voted to debar 5 of the immigrants as coming in violation of the alien contract labor law and the remainder as likely to become public charges.

ALIEN CONTRACT-LABOR LAW. 669

The Secretary of the Treasury decided, on appeal, November 26, 1900, in favor of Dr. Dowie and the immigrants, both those charged with violation of the alien contract labor law, and also those as likely to become public charges. The ground of his decision is stated as follows: "Although lace making with some of its branches has been carried on in this country for some years, heretofore it seems to have been the practice to import the thread used in such establishment. The Department is of the opinion that said industry is a new one, not established, and is within the exception mentioned in the act of February 26, 1885, and as it is not claimed or shown by representatives of the lace makers' union that labor could have been obtained in this country to prosecute the industry, there is apparently no violation of the alien contract labor law."

The decision seemed to turn on the distinction between the old and the new form of the Lever machine. Affidavits were presented maintaining that the modern machine is a great improvement on the old type; that there are only from 7 to 9 of these modern machines in the country, all of them brought here within the last 15 months, and that the firm which brought them (The American Textile Company, of Pawtucket, R. I.) had made many efforts to obtain hands in this country, and that it would be a difficult matter, with the rush of machines now coming to this country, to find sufficient workmen here to handle all these modern Lever machines at once.

8. Buffalo and Pittsburg tailor cases.—The defects in the alien contract-labor law, as shown in the decisions cited in preceding pages, have their main effect in their influence upon the United States district attorneys whose business it is to prosecute the cases. This comes plainly to view in a recent Buffalo case: The immigrant inspector at that port, Mr. J. R. De Barry, reported on August 28, 1900, that a deputation from the tailors' union of Buffalo called on him and stated that Messrs. Fullaytar & Keen, tailors of Buffalo and Pittsburg, were for some time past importing tailors on pauper wages to work for them in Buffalo and Pittsburg at $2 per week and board; that 10 had already arrived, others expected, and that citizens were being discharged and their places filled with this pauper labor; that in the offices of J. W. Klauck, steamship agent, the inspector himself saw stubs on which were the names of the contract laborers, showing that Joseph Keen, of 877 Main street, Buffalo, had paid their passage and sent for them. The inspector stated that copies of the statements of the contract laborers had been made for the district attorney, who had directed him to make complaint against Joseph Keen, under sections 1 and 6 of the laws of 1891. The statement of these tailors showed that they were natives of Hungary and tailors by occupation; that they came to the United States in January to August, 1900; that prior to coming one of them had received letters from a brother which said that he would get him work with Mr. Keen, of Buffalo, at $2 a week. Mr. Keen sent him $25 in a post-office order from Buffalo and is now paying $2 per week and board. No written contract. Had letter from Mr. Keen about September 29. Another, whose son Joseph was working for Mr. Keen, received $32 from his son, and Mr. Keen wrote him and sent him passage ticket from Hungary to Buffalo and 25 florins, to go to work for him. He did not say how much per week he would receive. Another received passage ticket from Mr. Keen through his cousin, who was acting foreman in the shop. Did not say how much per week he would get. Another received a letter from "a kind of foreman in the shop," who wrote and said Mr. Keen would settle the amount he was to receive per week when he came, after the first week. Received 25 florins by letter from Mr. Keen. Is now receiving $10 per week. Another has written to one of the employees of Mr. Keen to get work. The latter spoke to Mr. Keen and then wrote that Mr. Keen would give him work if he came. The five aliens were arrested by the deputy marshal and brought before Commissioner Welman, who let them out on $200 bail, each. So important was the case believed to be that the Attorney-General directed by telegraph United States Attorney Charles H. Brown, of Buffalo, to take charge of the case himself, without leaving it to his assistant. Mr. Brown did so, and then advised the Attorney-General as follows: "I personally examined each of the aliens alleged to have been imported by Joseph Keen in violation of the alien contract-labor law before the grand jury of the Lockport term of the United States district court last week. On such examination it clearly appeared that in no case did Joseph Keen aid or assist in the importation of any of these aliens from Hungary to the United States, who were under contract to perform labor in the United States made previous to such importation. Each of the aliens was examined fully through an interpreter, and no facts could be deduced upon which a charge of violating the statute could be based. A careful consideration revealed the fact that these aliens did not come to the United States under a contract to perform labor in the United States made previous to their importation. * * * The fact that this subject has been a matter of considerable correspondence, in which reference is made to the desire on the part of the Treasury Department that I should give this case my personal attention, inclines me to the opinion that some representative of the Treasury Department has labored under the impression that simple proof of the sending of means of transportation by the defendant to an alien in a foreign country is all that is required to secure a conviction for violation of the alien contract-labor law. I was especially careful and designed to be extremely thorough in a full and complete examination to develop the essential facts upon which to base a prosecution, but no case could be made out and no indictment was found." And in a later communication he added, to enable them to indict the alleged contractors: "For the reason that such evidence did not exist. * * * If any fact can be called to my attention that will establish a contract made by the aliens and the defendant, Keen, prior to their importation, within the terms of the statute itself and as construed by the circuit court of appeals of the eighth circuit in 48 F. R., 91, and the circuit court of appeals for the fifth circuit, 57 F. R., 490, and the case of The United States v. River Spinning Company, 70 F. R., 978, and The United States v. Gay, 80 F. R., 254, I will be only too glad to present it to any future grand jury."

Another example of the hesitation of the law officers of the Government to undertake the prosecution of contract importation cases in view of the decisions of the courts, is that of the same firm of Fullaytar & Keen in the branch at Pittsburg, Pa. The immigrant inspector at that station, Mr. R. D. Layton, secured the affidavit of the alleged imported laborer and of the agent with whom the alleged contract was made, and of the importer himself. The statements are apparently so conclusive that they seem to give proof of a complete contract. They show that the importer advanced the passage money and agreed to the amount of compensation per week. The only link which can be said to have been omitted is that of the period during which employment was to continue. Nevertheless, the United States district attorney did not see his way clear to prosecute the case. The affidavits and correspondence are submitted herewith:

SWORN STATEMENT OF MARTIN HUSCKA.

I am 31 years old. Am a native of Hungary. This is the first time I ever was in this country. came here last March. Arrived in the steamship *Saale*. I am a ladies' tailor by trade. When I was at home I met John Clement, also a ladies' tailor, who told me I could do very much better in America, and that he could get me a job with the firm he worked for in that country. I have known Mr. Clement for about 8 years, and I told him "all right, I would go, but could not afford to pay the passage." He said, "I will fix that all right." He wrote to the firm of Fullaytar & Keen, No. 412 Penn avenue, Pittsburg, about me, and he answered and said all right, he would send the money, and he did send him: $50 money order. I signed the receipt to Mr. Clement and got the money and came over and went to work for Fullaytar & Keen. The letter said he would pay me from $12 a week up, according to my ability. After I had worked a few months he began fussing with me about the $50 which I refused to pay back. He then told the cashier to deduct the money from my pay. He did so, and I quit. After a while he coaxed me to go back, and I went back again and he again held some of my wages for the passage, and I then left for good, and have not worked any place since. I have a wife and children at home, and was doing very well. If I had known I had to repay the $50 I would not have come. I will return as soon as I can earn the money. My friend, A. M. Bushek, who is acting as interpreter, has told me what you have written, and it is true, every word of it, and I so swear.

JOHN CLEMENT, sworn: Am 32 years old; am a native of Hungary; am a ladies' tailor by trade, and understand all you say to me. I first came to this country in 1894, then in 1898 I went back home to Hungary and stayed there until I returned on the 25th of June, 1900, on the steamship *Lacquetaine*. I work for Fullaytar & Keen, at No. 412 Penn avenue, Pittsburg, Pa. I knew Mr. Fullaytar when I was here before, and when I was at home I often wrote to him. Our letters were mostly of a social nature. I wrote Mr. Fullaytar and asked him if he wanted a good man; that I knew one here who might go. He wrote me he did, and I spoke to Mr. Huscka, whom I know very well, and he said he would come out, but not unless his passage was paid. I wrote this to Mr. Fullaytar, who sent me a money order for $50, and I gave it to Mr. Huscka, got his receipt for it, and he came out and went to work for the firm. After that he had some trouble with this firm and he stopped work. I am now working for Fullaytar & Keen. I paid my own passage.

Miss FLORENCE THORN, sworn: I am 17 years old; am cashier for the firm of Fullaytar & Keen; keep their books and assist in the business on this floor; have been there fifteen months. I know Mr. Martin Huscka; he worked here, but he has quit. He quit on the 31st of October, 1900. He worked here from the time he came to this country until he quit. I was ordered to take some money out of his wages and I did so—$15 one time and $15 another. As they talked in a foreign language, I don't know what it was for.

FERDINAND FULLAYTAR, sworn: I am one of the firm of Fullaytar & Keen, at No. 412 Penn avenue. I have been in business for two years and three months. I know John Clement. He is now in my employ as a ladies' tailor. I knew him when he was here before. While he was in Hungary we had a friendly correspondence. He wrote me how bad off they were in the old country and asked me if I wanted a good man. As I had trouble to get a good braider here, I told him "yes," I needed a man, and I sent him $50 money order to pay the passage out of Martin Huscka, who came here and I put him to work. We had trouble with him. for I thought he should pay me the $50 back, but he refused and I ordered my cashier to hold back some of his wages, which she did—about $30—and he stopped work, but after a time I got him to come back. He only worked a short time and he quit again, and I don't know where he is now. I thought I had a right to my money back again.

No. 24002.]
TREASURY DEPARTMENT,
OFFICE OF COMMISSIONER-GENERAL OF IMMIGRATION,
Washington, November 27, 1900.
R. D. LAYTON,
Inmigrant Inspector, Pittsburg, Pa.

SIR: From report contained in your communication of the 26th instant, it appears that the firm of Fullaytar & Keen, of No. 412 Penn avenue, Pittsburg, Pa., has violated the alien contract labor laws by the importation of one Martin Huscka to perform service for them in the United States under contract made prior to his immigration.

CHINESE EXCLUSION LAWS AND TREATIES. 671

In view of this, you are directed to present all the evidence in your possession to the United States district attorney for an expression of his views; and if, in his opinion, action will lie, suit should be instituted to recover penalties prescribed by law.
Respectfully,
T. V. POWDERLY, *Commissioner-General.*

DEPARTMENT OF JUSTICE,
OFFICE OF THE UNITED STATES ATTORNEY, WESTERN DISTRICT OF PENNSYLVANIA,
Pittsburg, January 31, 1901.
R. D. LAYTON,
Immigrant Inspector, Pittsburg, Pa.

SIR: You have submitted evidence to our office of an alleged violation of the alien contract-labor law of February 26, 1885, and its supplements, by the firm of Fullaytar & Keen, of No. 412 Penn avenue, Pittsburg, Pa., by the importation and migration of a certain alien and foreigner into the United States, to wit, one Martin Huscka, then a native of Hungary and a subject of His Majesty the Emperor of Austria and Apostolic King of Hungary, for the purpose of performing labor as a ladies' tailor under agreement made prior to his migration.
After examining the evidence submitted and the law in the case, we are of the opinion that this does not come within the statute as interpreted by the court.
I herewith return all papers in the case.
Very sincerely,
DANIEL B. HEINER, *United States Attorney.*

G. CHINESE EXCLUSION LAWS AND TREATIES.

A COMPLETE LIST OF LAWS AND TREATIES RELATING TO THE EXCLUSION OF THE CHINESE.

Treaty of November 17, 1880, between United States and China. (U. S. Stat. L., vol. 22, p. 826.)
Act to suspend immigration of Chinese laborers to the United States. (Approved May 6, 1882, U. S. Stat. L., vol. 22, p. 58.)
Act amending act of May 6, 1882. (Approved July 5, 1884, U. S. Stat. L., vol. 23, p. 115.)
Act to prohibit coming of Chinese laborers into the United States. (Approved September 13, 1888, U. S. Stat. L., vol. 25, p. 476.)
Act declaring certificates of return for Chinese laborers void. (Approved October 1, 1888, U. S. Stat. L., vol. 25, p. 504.)
Act to prohibit coming of Chinese persons into the United States. (Approved May 5, 1892, U. S. Stat. L., vol. 27, p. 25.)
Act to enforce immigration and contract labor laws of the United States. (Chinese are excepted by section 10 from effects of this law.) (Approved March 3, 1893, U. S. Stat. L., vol. 27, p. 569.)
Act amending act of May 5, 1892. (Approved November 3, 1893, U. S. Stat. L., vol. 28, p. 7.)
Convention between the United States and China of March 17, 1894. (U. S. Stat. L., vol. 28, p. 1210.)
Joint resolution annexing Hawaiian Islands prohibits immigration of Chinese. (Approved July 7, 1898, U. S. Stat. L., vol. 30, p. 751.)
Act providing government for Territory of Hawaii denies Chinese entrance into the United States from Hawaii. (Approved April 30, 1900, Statutes, Fifty-sixth Congress, first session, p. 141.)
Sundry civil appropriation act puts administration of Chinese exclusion acts under Commissioner-General of Immigration. (Approved June 6, 1900, Statutes, Fifty-sixth Congress, first session, p. 588.)
Act providing that United States commissioners may hear questions of illegal entry of Chinese. (Approved March 3, 1901, Statutes, Fifty-sixth Congress, second session, p. 1093.)

CONVENTION OF DECEMBER 8, 1894.

[28 Stat., p. 1210.]

ARTICLE I.

The high contracting parties agree that for a period of ten years, beginning with the date of the exchange of the ratifications of this convention, the coming, except under the conditions hereinafter specified, of Chinese laborers to the United States shall be absolutely prohibited.

ARTICLE II.

The preceding article shall not apply to the return to the United States of any registered Chinese laborer who has a lawful wife, child, or parent in the United States, or property therein of the value of one thousand dollars, or debts of like amount due him and pending settlement. Nevertheless, every such Chinese laborer shall, before leaving the United States, deposit, as a condition of his return, with the collector of customs of the district from which he departs, a full description in writing of his family, or property, or debts, as aforesaid, and shall be furnished by said collector with such certificate of his right to return under this treaty as the laws of the United States may now or hereafter prescribe and not inconsistent with the provisions of this treaty; and should the written description aforesaid be proved to be false, the right of return thereunder, or of continued residence after return, shall in each case be forfeited. And such right of return to the United States shall be exercised within one year from the date of leaving the United States; but such right of return to the United States may be extended for an additional period, not to exceed one year, in cases where by reason of sickness or other cause of disability beyond his control, such Chinese laborer shall be rendered unable sooner to return—which facts shall be fully reported to the Chinese consul at the port of departure, and by him certified, to the satisfaction of the collector of the port at which such Chinese subject shall land in the United States. And no such Chinese laborer shall be permitted to enter the United States by land or sea without producing to the proper officer of the customs the return certificate herein required.

ARTICLE III.

The provisions of this convention shall not affect the right at present enjoyed of Chinese subjects, being officials, teachers, students, merchants, or travellers for curiosity or pleasure, but not laborers, of coming to the United States and residing therein. To entitle such Chinese subjects as are above described to admission into the United States, they may produce a certificate from their Government or the Government where they last resided viséd by the diplomatic or consular representative of the United States in the country or port whence they depart.

It is also agreed that Chinese laborers shall continue to enjoy the privilege of transit across the territory of the United States in the course of their journey to or from other countries, subject to such regulations by the Government of the United States as may be necessary to prevent said privilege of transit from being abused.

ARTICLE IV.

In pursuance of Article III of the immigration treaty between the United States and China, signed at Pekin on the 17th day of November, 1880 (the 15th day of the tenth month of Kwanghsü, sixth year), it is hereby understood and agreed that Chinese laborers or Chinese of any other class, either permanently or temporarily residing in the United States, shall have for the protection of their persons and property all rights that are given by the laws of the United States to citizens of the most favored nation, excepting the right to become naturalized citizens. And the Government of the United States reaffirms its obligation, as stated in said Article III, to exert all its power to secure protection to the persons and property of all Chinese subjects in the United States.

ARTICLE V.

The Government of the United States, having by an act of the Congress, approved May 5, 1892, as amended by an act approved November 3, 1893, required all Chinese laborers lawfully within the limits of the United States before the passage of the first-named act to be registered as in said acts provided, with a view of affording them better protection, the Chinese Government will not object to the enforcement of such acts, and reciprocally the Government of the United States recognizes the right of the Government of China to enact and enforce similar laws or regulations for the registration, free of charge, of all laborers, skilled or unskilled (not merchants as defined by said acts of Congress), citizens of the United States in China, whether residing within or without the treaty ports.

And the Government of the United States agrees that within twelve months from the date of the exchange of the ratifications of this convention, and annually thereafter, it will furnish to the Government of China registers or reports showing the full name, age, occupation, and number or place of residence of all other citizens of the United States, including missionaries, residing both within and without the treaty ports of China, not including, however, diplomatic and other officers of the United States residing or travelling in China upon official business, together with their body and household servants.

ARTICLE VI.

This convention shall remain in force for a period of ten years, beginning with the date of the exchange of ratifications, and, if six months before the expiration of the said period of ten years neither Government shall have formally given notice of its final termination to the other, it shall remain in full force for another like period of ten years.

In faith whereof we, the respective plenipotentiaries, have signed this convention and have hereunto affixed our seals.

Done, in duplicate, at Washington the 17th day of March, A. D. 1894.

                     WALTER Q. GRESHAM. [SEAL.]
                     (Chinese signature.) [SEAL.]

And whereas the said convention has been duly ratified on both parts, and the ratifications of the two Governments were exchanged in the city of Washington on the 7th day of December, one thousand eight hundred and ninety-four:

Now, therefore, be it known that I, GROVER CLEVELAND, President of the United States of America, have caused the said convention to be made public, to the end that the same, and every article and clause thereof, may be observed and fulfilled with good faith by the United States and the citizens thereof.

In witness whereof I have hereunto set my hand and caused the seal of the United States to be affixed.

Done at the City of Washington this 8th day of December, in the year of our Lord, one thousand eight hundred and ninety-four, and of the Independence of the United States the one hundred and nineteenth.

[SEAL.]   GROVER CLEVELAND.

By the President:
  W. Q. GRESHAM,
    Secretary of State.

CHINESE EXCLUSION LAWS AND TREATIES. 673

EXCLUSION ACT OF 1882 CONTINUED UNTIL 1902.[1]

[22 Stat., p. 58.]

AN ACT to execute certain treaty stipulations relating to Chinese.

Whereas, in the opinion of the Government of the United States, the coming of Chinese laborers to this country endangers the good order of certain localities within the territory thereof: Therefore, Be it enacted by the Senate and House of Representatives of the United States of America in Congress assembled, That from and after the expiration of ninety days next after the passage of this act, and until the expiration of ten years next after the passage of this act, the coming of Chinese laborers to the United States be, and the same is hereby, suspended; and during such suspension it shall not be lawful for any Chinese laborer to come, or, having so come after the expiration of said ninety days, to remain within the United States.

SEC. 2. That the master of any vessel who shall knowingly bring within the United States on such vessel, and land or permit to be landed, any Chinese laborer, from any foreign port or place, shall be deemed guilty of a misdemeanor, and on conviction thereof shall be punished by a fine of not more than five hundred dollars for each and every such Chinese laborer so brought, and may be also imprisoned for a term not exceeding one year.

SEC. 3. That the two foregoing sections shall not apply to Chinese laborers who were in the United States on the seventeenth day of November, eighteen hundred and eighty, or who shall have come into the same before the expiration of ninety days next after the passage of this act, and who shall produce to such master before going on board such vessel, and shall produce to the collector of the port in the United States at which such vessel shall arrive, the evidence hereinafter in this act required of his being one of the laborers in this section mentioned; nor shall the two foregoing sections apply to the case of any master whose vessel, being bound to a port not within the United States, shall come within the jurisdiction of the United States by reason of being in distress or in stress of weather, or touching at any port of the United States on its voyage to any foreign port or place: Provided, That all Chinese laborers brought on such vessel shall depart with the vessel on leaving port.

[2]SEC. 4. That for the purpose of properly identifying Chinese laborers who were in the United States on the seventeenth day of November, eighteen hundred and eighty, or who shall have come into the same before the expiration of ninety days next after the passage of this act, and in order to furnish them with the proper evidence of their right to go from and come to the United States of their free will and accord, as provided by the treaty between the United States and China, dated November seventeenth, eighteen hundred and eighty, the collector of customs of the district from which any such Chinese laborer shall depart from the United States shall, in person or by deputy, go on board each vessel having on board any such Chinese laborer and cleared or about to sail from his district for a foreign port, and on such vessel make a list of all such Chinese laborers, which shall be entered in registry books to be kept for that purpose, in which shall be stated the name, age, occupation, last place of residence, physical marks or peculiarities, and all facts necessary for the identification of each of such Chinese laborers, which books shall be safely kept in the customhouse; and every such Chinese laborer so departing from the United States shall be entitled to, and shall receive, free of any charge or cost upon application therefor from the collector or his deputy, at the time such list is taken, a certificate, signed by the collector or his deputy and attested by his seal of office, in such form as the Secretary of the Treasury shall prescribe, which certificate shall contain a statement of the name, age, occupation, last place of residence, personal description, and facts of identification of the Chinese laborer to whom this certificate is issued, corresponding with the said list and registry in all particulars. In case any Chinese laborer after having received such certificate shall leave such vessel before her departure he shall deliver his certificate to the master of the vessel, and if such Chinese laborer shall fail to return to such vessel before her departure from port the certificate shall be delivered by the master to the collector of customs for cancellation.

The certificate herein provided for shall entitle the Chinese laborer to whom the same is issued to return to and reenter the United States upon producing and delivering the same to the collector of customs of the district at which such Chinese laborer shall seek to reenter; and upon delivery of such certificate by such Chinese laborer to the collector of customs at the time of reentry in the United States, said collector shall cause the same to be filed in the custom-house and duly canceled.

SEC. 5. That any Chinese laborer mentioned in section four of this act being in the United States, and desiring to depart from the United States by land, shall have the right to demand and receive, free of charge or cost, a certificate of identification similar to that provided for in section four of this act to be issued to such Chinese laborers as may desire to leave the United States by water; and it is hereby made the duty of the collector of customs of the district next adjoining the foreign country to which said Chinese laborer desires to go to issue such certificate, free of charge or cost, upon application by such Chinese laborer, and to enter the same upon registry books to be kept by him for the purpose, as provided for in section four of this act.

SEC. 6. That in order to the faithful execution of articles one and two of the treaty in this act before mentioned, every Chinese person other than a laborer who may be entitled by said treaty and this act to come within the United States, and who shall be about to come to the United States, shall be identified as so entitled by the Chinese Government in each case, such identity to be evidenced by a certificate issued under the authority of said Government, which certificate shall be in the English language or (if not in the English language) accompanied by a translation into English, stating such right to come, and which certificate shall state the name, title, or official rank, if any, the age, height, and all physical peculiarities, former and present occupation or profession, and place of residence in China of the person to whom the certificate is issued and that such person is entitled conformably to the treaty in this act mentioned to come within the United States.

Such certificate shall be prima facie evidence of the fact set forth therein, and shall be produced to the collector of customs, or his deputy, of the port in the district in the United States at which the person named therein shall arrive.

SEC. 7. That any person who shall knowingly and falsely alter or substitute any name for the name written in such certificate or forge any such certificate, or knowingly utter any forged or fraudulent

---

[1] Sections 2158-2163 of the Revised Statutes and the act of March 3, 1875 (1 Supp. R. S., 86, ch. 141), prohibit the importation of "cooleys" and women for immoral purposes.
[2] See act approved October 1, 1888, which prohibits the issuance of certificates of identity of Chinese laborers and declares void such certificates issued.

certificate, or falsely personate any person named in any such certificate, shall be deemed guilty of a misdemeanor; and upon conviction thereof shall be fined in a sum not exceeding one thousand dollars, and imprisoned in a penitentiary for a term of not more than five years.

SEC. 8. That the master of any vessel arriving in the United States from any foreign port or place shall, at the same time he delivers a manifest of the cargo, and if there be no cargo, then at the time of making a report of the entry of the vessel pursuant to law, in addition to the other matter required to be reported, and before landing, or permitting to land, any Chinese passengers, deliver and report to the collector of customs of the district in which such vessels shall have arrived a separate list of all Chinese passengers taken on board his vessel at any foreign port or place, and all such passengers on board the vessel at that time.

Such lists shall show the names of such passengers (and if accredited officers of the Chinese Government traveling on the business of that Government, or their servants, with a note of such facts), and the names and other particulars, as shown by their respective certificates; and such list shall be sworn to by the master in the manner required by law in relation to the manifest of the cargo.

Any wilful refusal or neglect of any such master to comply with the provisions of this section shall incur the same penalties and forfeiture as are provided for a refusal or neglect to report and deliver a manifest of the cargo

SEC. 9. That before any Chinese passengers are landed from any such vessel, the collector or his deputy shall proceed to examine such passengers, comparing the certificates with the list and with the passengers; and no passenger shall be allowed to land in the United States from such vessel in violation of law.

SEC. 10. That every vessel whose master shall knowingly violate any of the provisions of this act shall be deemed forfeited to the United States, and shall be liable to seizure and condemnation in any district of the United States into which such vessel may enter or in which she may be found.

SEC. 11. That any person who shall knowingly bring into or cause to be brought into the United States by land, or who shall knowingly aid or abet the same, or aid or abet the landing in the United States from any vessel of any Chinese person not lawfully entitled to enter the United States, shall be deemed guilty of a misdemeanor, and shall, on conviction thereof, be fined in a sum not exceeding one thousand dollars, and imprisoned for a term not exceeding one year.

SEC. 12. That no Chinese person shall be permitted to enter the United States by land without producing to the proper officer of customs the certificate in this act required of Chinese persons seeking to land from a vessel.

And any Chinese person found unlawfully within the United States shall be caused to be removed therefrom to the country from whence he came, by direction of the President of the United States, and at the cost of the United States, after being brought before some justice, judge, or commissioner of a court of the United States and found to be one not lawfully entitled to be or remain in the United States.

SEC. 13. That this act shall not apply to diplomatic and other officers of the Chinese Government traveling upon the business ot that Government, whose credentials shall be taken as equivalent to the certificate in this act mentioned, and shall exempt them and their body and household servants from the provisions of this act as to other Chinese persons.

SEC. 14. That hereafter no State court or court of the United States shall admit Chinese to citizenship; and all laws in conflict with this act are hereby repealed.

SEC. 15. That the words "Chinese laborers," wherever used in this act, shall be construed to mean both skilled and unskilled laborers and Chinese employed in mining.

Approved, May 6, 1882.

REGULATIONS BASED ON THE EFFECT OF LAWS.

The most complete view available of the operations of the Chinese exclusion laws is contained in the following regulations, issued by the Commissioner-General of Immigration in the form of instructions to inspectors of immigrants.

REGULATIONS.

1. The provisions of law permitting the admission of Chinese persons to the United States and prescribing the classes of Chinese persons entitled to such admission, and the conditions thereof, are as follows:

[Act of July 5, 1884.] The Chinese exclusion act approved July 5, 1884, provided "that from and after the passage of this act, and until the expiration of ten years after the passage of this act, the coming of Chinese laborers to the United States be, and the same is hereby, suspended, and during such suspension it shall not be lawful for any Chinese laborer to come from any foreign port or place, or having so come to remain in the United States."

[Certificate for exempt classes.] 2. Section 6 of said act provides the course to be pursued by Chinese persons, other than laborers, who by treaty or by said act are entitled to come within the United States, and requires that the certificates therein required "shall be produced to the collector of customs of the port in the district in the United States at which the person named thereon shall arrive, and afterwards produced to the proper authorities of the United States whenever lawfully demanded, and shall be the sole evidence permissible on the part of the person so producing the same to establish a right of entry into the United States; but said certificate may be controverted and the facts therein stated disproved by the United States authorities."

Section 12 of said act provides "that no Chinese person shall be permitted to enter the United States by land without producing to the proper officer of customs the certificate in this act required of Chinese persons seeking to land from a vessel."

[Deportation of Chinese.] And directs that, any Chinese person found unlawfully in the United States shall be removed therefrom to the country from whence he came, and at the cost of the United States.

[Exclusion act continued until 1902.] Section 1 of "An act to prohibit the coming of Chinese persons into the United States," approved May 5, 1892, continued in force for the period of 10 years from the passage of that act all laws then in force prohibiting and regulating the coming of Chinese into this country.

[Chinese merchants.] 3. Section 2 of the amendatory act, approved November 3, 1893, requires a Chinaman making application for entrance into the United States on the ground that he was formerly engaged in this country as a merchant, to establish, by the testimony of two credible witnesses other than Chinese, the fact that he conducted business as a merchant for at least one year before his departure from the United States.

CHINESE EXCLUSION LAWS AND TREATIES. 675

[Decision of immigrant officer final on deportation.] 4. In the act making appropriations for sundry civil expenses approved August 18, 1894, it is enacted "that in every case where an alien is excluded from admission into the United States under any law or treaty now existing or hereafter made the decision of the appropriate immigrant or customs officers, if adverse to the admission of such alien, shall be final, unless reversed on appeal to the Secretary of the Treasury."

[Treaty with China, 1894.] 5. Article 1 of our treaty of 1894 with China provides that for 10 years the coming of Chinese laborers to the United States shall be absolutely prohibited, except under the conditions specified under said treaty; and article 2 of said treaty provides that the preceding article shall not apply to the return to the United States of any registered Chinese laborer who has a lawful wife, child, or parent in the United States, or property therein of the value of $1,000, or debts of like amount due him and pending settlement, and further provides that certain things shall be done by a Chinaman before leaving this country, and that he shall be furnished by the collector with such certificate of his right to return under the treaty as the laws of the United States may prescribe, and said article concludes as follows: "And no such Chinese laborer shall be permitted to enter the United States by land or sea without producing to the proper officer of the customs the return certificates herein required."

* * * * * * *

7. The chief comptrollers of Chinese immigration at Victoria, Vancouver, and New Westminster, British Columbia, have been authorized to issue to Chinese persons of the exempt class the certificates prescribed by section 6 of the act of July 5, 1884. (S. 20571.)

* * * * * * *

12. Chinese persons known as "traders" should not be allowed to land in this country, even though they submit the certificate prescribed by section 6 of the act of July 5, 1884. "The true theory is not that all Chinese persons may enter this country who are not forbidden, but that only those are entitled to enter who are expressly allowed." Collectors of customs are directed to admit only Chinese whose occupation or station clearly indicates that they are members of the exempt class of Chinese named in Article III of the treaty with China, viz: "Chinese subjects, being officials, teachers, students, merchants, or travellers for curiosity or pleasure," and to deny admission to Chinese persons described as salesmen, clerks, buyers, bookkeepers, accountants, managers, storekeepers, apprentices, agents, cashiers, physicians, proprietors of restaurants, etc. (Opinion of Attorney-General, July 15, 1898; S. 19677.)

[Wives and children of Chinese.] 13. The wives and minor children of Chinese persons of the exempt class are not required to present, as a condition precedent to landing, the certificate prescribed by section 6 of the act of July 5, 1884, when the fact is established to the satisfaction of the authorities that the person claiming to enter, either as wife or minor child, is in fact the wife or minor child of one of the members of a class mentioned in the treaty as entitled to enter. (Decision of the Supreme Court of the United States, No. 123, October term, 1899; S. 22056.)

* * * * * * *

[Students.] 15. A Chinese student in China desiring to enter the United States for purposes of study must first obtain the certificate from the Chinese Government, as required by section 6, act of July 5, 1884. (Letter to Mr. E. Van Rensselaer, September 6, 1892.)

* * * * * * *

17. Chinese who were admitted as students, but without the certificates prescribed by section 6 of the act of July 5, 1884, and on their arrival in this country become laborers, are not entitled to remain in the United States, and should be deported. (United States v. Chu Chee, 87 Federal Rep., 312; S. 20868.)

[Merchants.] 18. If a Chinese person secures admission to this country as a merchant and soon ceases to be one but becomes a laborer, such fact ought to have a bearing on the intent with which he came here, and if from all the facts of the case it can be determined that he used the former mercantile occupation as a pretext to come here, with the real intent and purpose of laboring only when here, such former occupation would not shield him, even if his certificate of entry be correct in form and substance, and he is not lawfully entitled to be and remain in the United States. (United States v. Yong Yew, 83 Fed. Rep., 832; S. 18575.)

19. Omission from certificates of any of the statements enumerated in the law would seem to be fatal to the sufficiency of the certificate as evidence of the holder's right to enter the United States. (Letter to Attorney-General, September 6, 1892.)

* * * * * * *

22. A Chinaman claiming to be a merchant and a naturalized citizen of Canada sought admission into the United States without the production of the certificate required by section 6 of the act of July 5, 1884, presenting in lieu thereof, in support of his application for admission, the certificate of naturalization as a British subject and a passport issued by the governor-general of Canada. Upon reference of the subject to the Attorney-General, in an opinion dated January 30, 1895, that officer stated that the certificate before mentioned should be required whether the Chinaman comes direct from China or from some other foreign government of which he may be a subject. He states further that the restrictions and disabilities of the Chinese-exclusion laws are based on moral and racial objections, and not that the Chinese applying for admission to the United States are subjects of the Emperor of China. (Letter to collector at Burlington, February 2, 1895.)

23. A Chinaman, a naturalized citizen of Mexico, who sought admission to this country upon the ground of his affiliation with the Mexican Government was excluded in accordance with the opinion of the Attorney-General dated January 30, 1895. (Letter to Secretary of State, April 20, 1896.)

* * * * * * *

26. The treaty with China promulgated December 8, 1894, does not waive the requirement that Chinese merchants and others of the exempt class shall present at the port of first arrival the certificate provided by section 6 of the act approved July 5, 1884. (Letter of Secretary of State, September 24, 1894.)

* * * * * * *

31. Chinese merchants who desire to enter for the first time the United States must present the certificate required by law. The privilege of entry without certificate is accorded those merchants only who have been formerly merchants resident in the United States. (Letter to Mr. D. McCormick, December 8, 1892.)

32. Section 2 of the act of November 3, 1893, defines a merchant to be "a person engaged in buying and selling merchandise, at a fixed place of business, whose business is conducted in his name."

* * * * * * *

676   THE INDUSTRIAL COMMISSION:—IMMIGRATION.

35. A Chinese person who has clandestinely entered this country can not acquire a right to remain here or to return to the United States by qualifying himself as a merchant. (Opinion of Solicitor of Treasury, March 30, 1899; S. 20943.)
36. The practice of requiring Chinese merchants or other Chinese persons returning to this country to present evidence of their right to enter the United States to the collector or deputy collector of customs in the district to which admission is desired is based upon section 9 of the act of May 6, 1882, and the clause in the act of August 18. 1894, which makes final the decision of the appropriate customs or immigration officer if adverse to the admission of alien, etc., unless reversed on appeal to the Secretary of the Treasury. (Opinion of Solicitor of Treasury, February 6, 1896; letter to collector at Burlington, February 18, 1896.)

*   *   *   *   *   *   *

38. In view of the many cases of hardship due to delays in the investigation and consideration of cases of Chinese persons seeking admission to the United States as alleged returning merchants, and on account of the many fraudulent cases of this character, any Chinese person who may hereafter leave this country with the intention of seeking readmission as an alleged returning merchant under the provisions of section 2 of the act of November 3, 1893, should transmit to the collector of customs at the port from which such Chinese person intends to depart from the United States, at least 30 days before his departure from this country, duplicates of the affidavits of witnesses other than Chinese, setting forth the facts prescribed by the statute referred to upon which he intends to base his application for readmission. Upon the receipt of such duplicates the collector at such port of departure will promptly transmit them to the collector of customs, special agent, or other officer of this Department at or nearest to the place in which such Chinese person claims to have been engaged as merchant, for investigation and report. After the receipt of such report, and upon the personal application and proper identification of such Chinese person, the collector at the point of departure may indorse upon the original papers presented by such Chinese person a statement. over his official signature, to the effect that the right of such Chinese person to return to the United States has been prima facie determined, subject to his proper identification by and the presentation of such original papers to said collector upon his return to this country; and upon the return of such Chinese person to said port of departure, the collector may, in his discretion, admit him to this country without further delay.
While Chinese persons seeking admission as returning merchants can not be excluded upon the ground that they have failed to comply with the foregoing regulations, such failure on the part of those leaving the country after this date would be a fact exciting suspicion and discrediting to the application for readmission, and the regulation heretofore issued will govern the procedure in such cases. (Department Circular No. 28, March 3, 1900.)

*   *   *   *   *   *   *

[Registered Chinese laborers.]—41. A Chinese person claiming the right to be permitted to leave the United States and return thereto as a duly registered laborer shall apply in person to the collector of customs for the district in which he resides at least a month prior to the time of his departure; shall deposit with said collector a certificate of registration from the internal-revenue collector for the district in which he resided at the time of registration; and shall make an oath before the said collector, in writing, a full statement descriptive of his family, or property, or debts, as the case may be, and fully describing himself, giving his name, age, height, local residence, occupation, color of eyes and complexion, and distinguishing marks, if any, and naming the port from which he expects to depart from the United States, which shall be one of those designated in paragraph 42. Such written description shall be filed in duplicate, and to each shall be permanently attached a photograph of the Chinese person referred to therein. The collector of customs, or his deputy, with whom such certificate of registration and written description are filed will make a thorough examination to ascertain whether the applicant is registered and as to the accuracy of the descriptive statement; that the photograph accompanying the latter for the purpose of identification is that of the person described in such certificate and statement, and that his height, weight, and descriptive physical marks are accurately given, and will then write his official signature in part across such photograph and in part upon the adjoining portion of the written descriptive statement to prevent substitution. The collector referred to will then transmit the certificate of registration to the internal-revenue collector by whom the same purports to have been issued for comparison with the record thereof in his office, in respect not only to name and date therein, but in all other particulars. At the same time the collector of customs will in person or through the special agent for the district make thorough investigation as to the facts stated therein. As soon as practicable thereafter the collector of customs referred to will transmit such registration certificate, one copy of the sworn statement, and the reports of investigation to the collector of customs for the district from which such Chinese laborer intends to depart from the United States, and at the same time will transmit to said Chinese laborer the duplicate copy of such sworn statement, with instructions to present the same in person to the collector of customs or his deputy at the port of departure. Upon the receipt of such certificate of registration, the duplicate copies of said sworn statement, and the reports of investigation, the collector of customs or his deputy at said port of departure, after one month from the date of the filing of the original application in the office of the collector of the district in which such Chinese laborer resides, if he finds that the person presenting such duplicate statement is the Chinese person therein described, and is entitled thereto, may sign and give to such person, on his departure from said port, a certificate containing the description referred to in the following form:

CERTIFICATE ISSUED TO CHINESE LABORERS.

UNITED STATES OF AMERICA.

Certificate issued to Chinese laborer departing from the United States with the intention of returning thereto under the treaty between the United States of America and the Empire of China signed March 17, 1894, and proclaimed by the President of the United States December 8, 1894.

This is to certify that ———, a Chinese laborer, described in identification paper numbered ———, port of ———, departed from this port for ——— on this ——— day of ———, 190—, with the intention of returning to the United States via this port within twelve months from said date.
Given under my hand and seal this ——— day of ———, 190—, at ———, State of ———.

[COLLECTOR'S SEAL.]
                          ———————————————,
          Collector of Customs, Port of ———, District of ———.

If the last-named certificate be transferred, it shall become void, and the person to whom it was given by the collector shall forfeit his right to return to the United States.
The certified description should be carefully preserved by the collector at the port of exit as a means of identification of the Chinese person therein mentioned, and who, in order to avail himself of the

privilege conferred by said article 2 of the treaty, must return via the port of departure within one year from the date of his leaving the United States, unless prevented by sickness or other disability beyond his control, in which event the facts shall be officially certified by the Chinese consul at said port of departure to the satisfaction of the collector of the port at which such Chinese subject shall land in the United States.

42. No Chinese person shall be permitted to enter the United States without producing to the collector of customs or his deputy at the port of such entry the return certificate herein required. A Chinese laborer, possessing a return certificate in the form prescribed above, shall be admitted to the United States only at the port from which he departed therefrom, and no Chinese person, except Chinese diplomatic or consular officers and their attendants, shall be permitted to enter the United States except at the ports of San Francisco, Portland, Oreg., Boston, New York, New Orleans, Port Townsend, Richford, St. Albans, Plattsburg, Niagara Falls, Buffalo, Key West, Tampa, Mobile, Eagle Pass, Laredo, El Paso, Nogales, San Diego, Astoria, Pembina, and Honolulu.

43. The collector at the port of departure shall send a copy of the certified description, with photograph of the person therein named attached, and also one of the stubs hereinafter referred to, to the Department; said stub and said copy of the certified description shall be filed together.

Certificates as above described, with a serial number attached, will be issued to collectors of customs at ports from which Chinese depart, upon application therefor to the Department. In all instances collectors will fill out the blanks on the stubs of the certificates. Collectors of customs will submit reports to the Department weekly of Chinese persons departing from and returning to their respective ports under the treaty herein referred to, debiting themselves with the number of certificates received from the Department, crediting themselves with the number used, and reporting the number remaining on hand. The collector shall cancel all certificates presented on admission of returning Chinese, and forward said certificates so canceled to the Department. Collectors will also make weekly report of Chinese persons seeking admission into the United States through their ports, giving the names, description, occupation, and places of destination in the United States of those admitted, including the names of firms to which alleged returning merchants claim to belong, and the evidence upon which such action is based, and also the names, description, and occupation of those to whom admission is refused, and the reason for such refusal; also the names, description, and occupation of such persons permitted to land for transit through the United States. (S. 14186.)

* * * * * * *

[Penalty on master of vessel.]—45. If the master of any vessel shall knowingly bring within the United States on such vessel and land, or attempt to land, or permit to be landed, any Chinese laborer or other Chinese person, in contravention of law, the facts relating thereto shall be promptly reported to the proper United States attorney for the enforcement of the provisions of section 9 of the act of September 13, 1888. Chinese laborers or persons on board such vessel must depart with the vessel on leaving port.

* * * * * * *

48. Three registered Chinese laborers who left the United States for Bluefields, Nicaragua, but who, being shipwrecked on the voyage, decided to return to the United States, were refused the right to readmission for the reason that upon departing from this country they failed to comply with the provisions of article 2 of the treaty with China promulgated December 8, 1894, in that they did not deposit with the collector of customs at the port of departure the papers required by said treaty. (Letter to Representative Meyer, May 27, 1895.)

49. Upon the issuance of the prescribed certificate to a registered Chinese laborer who departs from the United States with the intention of returning thereto, the collector of customs at the place of residence of such laborer, or a special agent of the Department, may be requested to ascertain and report whether or not the statements made by such laborer are true, and if in any instance it should be found that such statements are false, the person to whom the certificate may be issued should be denied admission to this country upon his return. (S. 17532.)

* * * * * * *

54. Certificates of registration granted to Chinese laborers will not be regarded as sufficient evidence of the right of such persons to depart from the United States and return thereto. Such certificates are intended to be issued to Chinese laborers domiciled in the United States, in order that the holders thereof may be protected from arrest and deportation. (Letter to Mr. Hall, April 24, 1893, and to Miss Saunders, April 3, 1893.)

* * * * * * *

This Department has decided that laundrymen are laborers within the meaning of this act, and that the fact that a laundryman has accumulated capital and has become an employer of laborers in the same business does not change his status as a laborer.

* * * * * * *

60. A Chinese barber domiciled in the United States is classified as a laborer. (Letter to Mr. John T. Deweese, November 6, 1893.)

* * * * * * *

62. Chinese laborers who go out of the country under the provisions of the recent treaty with China, promulgated December 8, 1894, can not be permitted upon return to bring their wives with them. The wife partakes of her husband's status as a laborer, and as such is debarred admission by law. (Opinion Solicitor of Treasury, February 7, 1896; letter to collector, Burlington, February 11, 1896.)

63. Registered Chinese laborers who depart from the United States with the intention of returning, but who fail to obtain the certificate prescribed by Article II of the treaty with China for use in such cases, should not be allowed to return to this country. (Opinion of Attorney-General, October 11, 1896; S. 17458.)

* * * * * * *

67. Chinese persons should not be admitted upon the presentation of passports issued by the Secretary of State. (S. 21212; in re Gee Hop, 71 Federal Rep., 274.)

* * * * * * *

69. Under advice of the United States Attorney-General and the Solicitor of the Treasury, Chinese laborers may pass through the United States in transit to foreign countries under certain conditions, viz:

(a) That they have through tickets across the whole territory of the United States;
(b) That the collector of customs at port of arrival is satisfied of their good faith, and prepares and forwards to collector at port of exit descriptive lists; and
(c) That the collector at first port takes a bond in a penal sum of not less than $500 from each person, conditioned for his transit and departure from United States. (S. 21162.)
(d) Bonds given for the transit of Chinese through the United States must require the sureties to produce to the collector of customs to whom such bonds may be given certificates from the collector at

the port of exit, showing that within twenty days from the dates of the arrival the Chinese persons named in the bonds have departed actually from the country. (S. 17201.)

(e) Chinese who apply for admission to the United States, but who are refused such admission, can not pass through the United States in transit under bond, but must be returned to the country whence they came. (Opinion of Solicitor of Treasury, September 21, 1900.)

The privilege of transit under bond of Chinese laborers through the United States is recognized and agreed to in Article III of the treaty with China promulgated December 8, 1894. (See Article III of treaty with China.)

* * * * * * *

71. In the preparation of descriptive lists of Chinese laborers in transit their height should be ascertained with accuracy, and for this purpose the shoes of Chinese should be removed while being measured. (Letter to collector, New York, March 25, 1896.)

* * * * * * *

74. Chinese servants employed in the United States Navy on board war vessels, the same having been enlisted at foreign ports, can not land in the United States. (Letter to the Secretary of the Navy, August 1, 1889; S. 9547.)

75. Chinese cooks and stewards shipped at foreign ports on American vessels can not land in the United States. (Letter to collector, Port Townsend, March 7, 1890; S. 9900.)

* * * * * * *

77. In the case of the United States v. Wong Kim Ark the Supreme Court has decided that children born in this country of Chinese parents are of right citizens of the United States. (S. 19180.)

* * * * * * *

81. State courts have no jurisdiction in the Chinese cases. A United States judge alone has the power, under section 6 of the act of May 5, 1892, to order the deportation to China of a Chinese laborer who has failed to register as required by the acts of May 5, 1892, and November 3, 1893.

A United States commissioner, inter alia, has the power, under section 12 of the act of July 5, 1884, and section 13 of the act of September 13, 1888, to order the deportation of a Chinese prisoner found to be unlawfully within the United States. (Letter to collector, El Paso, September 20, 1893.)

82. Upon refusal of the collector of customs at San Francisco to permit the landing at his port of one Lem Moon Sing, a returning merchant, application for a writ of habeas corpus was made to the Supreme Court. In an opinion of that court rendered May 27, 1895, the application was denied upon the ground that the act of August 18, 1894 (sundry civil appropriation), makes final the decision of the appropriate customs or immigration officer, if adverse to the admission of an alien, unless reversed on appeal to the Secretary of the Treasury. Under this law the right to review the action of collectors of customs in refusing the application of Chinese persons for permission to land is taken away from the court and vested in the Secretary of the Treasury. (Lem Moon Sing v. United States, opinion Supreme Court, May 27, 1895.)

83. The court has not authority, by writ of habeas corpus or otherwise, to review the decision of a collector of customs, sustained on appeal to the Secretary of the Treasury, denying admission to an alleged returning Chinese merchant, and has no jurisdiction to determine the question whether or not the petitioner offered to the collector the proof that he was a merchant. (In re Leong Yong Toug, 90 Federal Rep., 648; S. 20478. See also 143 U. S., 660; 149 U. S., 713.)

84. A decision of the collector, denying the right to enter, affirmed by the Secretary of the Treasury, will not be reviewed by the courts on writ of habeas corpus on the ground of irregularities in taking the testimony. (In re Jew Wong Loy, 91 Federal Rep., 240.)

85. It was held by the Supreme Court that the act of May 5, 1892, obliging all Chinese residents to register under penalty of arrest and deportation was constitutional. (Fong Yue Ting v. United States, 149 U. S., 698.)

* * * * * * *

87. When Chinese are found in this country who are unable to produce the certificate of registration prescribed by law for laborers, or evidence of their status as bona fide merchants engaged in business in this country, or certificates in the form prescribed by section 6 of the act of July 5, 1884, indorsed by a collector of customs with the fact and date of their admission into the United States, they shall be reported to the proper legal authorities for the determination of the right of such persons to remain in the country. (S. 18286.)

* * * * * * *

90. Officers of railroads by which Chinese persons are illegally brought to places in the United States are liable to the penalties imposed by section 11 of the act of July 5, 1884, and should be reported to the United States attorney for prosecution.

Inspection of persons and papers should be made at the border of contiguous foreign territory, so as to prevent the entrance of Chinese persons excluded by law. (Letter to collector, Burlington, Vt., December 10, 1891; S. 12167.)

91. The importation of opium into the United States is forbidden to Chinese subjects under article 2 of the treaty with China, proclaimed October 5, 1881, and all opium so imported should be seized and forfeited. (Letter to collector, San Francisco, April 28, 1892; S. 12616.)

JAPANESE.

The following account is taken from a report issued by Special Agent W. M. Rice, who, under instructions from the Commissioner-General of Immigration, visited Japan in 1899 and reported upon the causes inducing emigration from that country. The following extracts from his report relate mainly to the Japanese emigration companies:

Inasmuch as the Government claims the perpetual allegiance of its subject, it grants a passport, limited to 3 years, and I was informed that a large part of the emigrants who thus go abroad return to their native land sooner or later, and consequently few Japanese, and indeed I may say none, come to the United States with a view to remaining or making homes, the theory of their emigration system being for the promotion of emigration as an educational process and money-making investment for a temporary period. the profits of which accrue jointly to the promoter and to the emigrant, the Japanese Empire being the recipient of what may be described as the unearned increment through its people that thus go abroad, through their contact with more enlightened people and by reason of the accumulated capital, which they return to their native land. It is through the tenacious allegiance which the subjects of Japan yield to their sovereign that the promotion of emigration becomes a reasonably safe business.

CHINESE EXCLUSION LAWS AND TREATIES. 679

It is a feature of the construction of the Japanese law regulating emigration (see regulations, Exhibit No. 1) that in providing the same the Government has acted upon the theory that the character of the Japanese abroad will be taken as an index of the character of the nation at home. Hence these regulations provide for the careful inquiry into the character of those going abroad and also require that provision shall be made for the return of the emigrant, in the event that he becomes sick, or a public charge in a foreign country, before passports are granted. These features of the Japanese law regulating emigration and the granting of passports are very well in themselves, provided they were honestly enforced, and provided the Japanese people stood on an equal footing with the people of the United States in a moral, economical, and educational sense, especially as to the value of their labor. Making the act of emigration, in the nature of things, purely voluntary they would be highly commendable, but there is an abundance of evidence going to show that the average Japanese official and policeman, who practically pass upon the qualifications of emigrants, is but little superior, if any, in point of morals, to the average cooly farmer. Consequently the performance of their duties is at most perfunctory, while the possibility of gain through the emigration companies, of which I shall hereafter treat, renders their investigations and reports of little value.

Upon this point I was informed by various persons it is desirable for the emigrant to go under the auspices of the emigration companies, because these companies smooth the way with the officials and, as some say, are influential. The emigration companies seem to be attached to the system to which I have above alluded by the laws making provision for their organization. They are designated in Japanese "Imin toriatsukinin," and are authorized to make provision for the assisting of the emigrants abroad, provide security for the emigrants' care abroad required by the law, and return in case of sickness or indigence, and in the performance of these services they engage in furnishing contract labor to such countries as permit it, and otherwise contract with the emigrants for the services to be performed by them of a personal character. For such services they receive from the emigrant certain fees, ranging from 10 to 20 yen per capita.

These companies were first organized as ordinary partnerships, but later were brought under the control of the Government, and are now operating under the law described, enacted in the twenty-ninth year of Meijii (1896). (See Exhibit No. 1.) In general these companies, of which there are 12 in all (one new one having been organized while I was in Japan, to wit, the Okayama Emigration Company) are required by the Government to deposit certain moneys as a guaranty that the business transacted shall be strictly in accordance with the provisions of the imperial ordinance, the agents located abroad being subject to the approval of the Government. They have an aggregate capital stock of 558,999 yen ($280,000), distributed as follows:

Name of company.	Place of business.	Capital stock.
		Yen.
Kobe Toko Co	Kobe	30,300
Nippon Kissa Emigration Co	Tokyo	100,000
Kaigwai Toko Co	Hiroshima	60,000
Shin Morioka	Tokyo	8,000
Nippon Emigration Co	Kobe	50,000
Kynshu Emigration Co	Kumamota	50,000
Tokyo Emigration Co	Yokohama	20,000
Do	Tokyo	100,000
Kosei Emigration Co	Wakayama	50,000
Kumamota Emigration Co	Kumamota	40,000
Imperial Colonial Co	Okayama	30,000
Okayama (new company; capital stock unknown)	do	

Six of these companies have agents in the United States and Canada, as follows:

Company.	Agent.	Residence.
Kobe Toko Co	Takijiro Shinobe	San Jose, Cal.
Nippon Emigration Co	Tanichi Takaya	San Francisco, Cal.
Kaigwai Toko Co	Kisuke Hamano	Do.
Shin Morioka	Tanichi Takaya	Do.
Kosei Emigration Co	Tekichi Nishibata	Vancouver, British Columbia (Col. ave.).
Kaigwai Toko Co	do	Do.
Kosei Emigration Co	do	Do.
Kyushu Emigration Co	Kwanichi Kayashi	Vancouver, British Columbia.
Nippon Emigration Co	Massataro Mito	At or in the neighborhood of Victoria, British Columbia.
Horishima Emigration Co	Minama Jinnosuke	San Francisco, Cal., 529½ Geary street.
Kosei Emigration Co	Y. Nishibata	San Francisco, Cal., 260½ Brannan street.

These companies have offices at all important emigration centers, but at the present time Hiroshima seems to be the chief center of operations, I having found 9 branches in that city. The character of the organization maintained by these emigration companies for business and political purposes may be inferred from the fact that in Tokyo they have an association of emigration companies located at Yamashiro cho (street or line) called Kyobashi, which is in the nature of an emigration board of trade. The offices of these companies are well equipped for business purposes, and have the appearance of being well supplied with employees and clerks. The managers and stockholders are among the leading business men and politicians of Japan, and are a formidable power when cooperating together. Among these capitalists and politicians thus interested is Mr. Suguwara, who is a member of the lower House of Parliament and editor of the Jimim, the leading vernacular newspaper of Japan, published at Tokyo. Mr. Suguwara spent several years in Idaho, where he had extensive connection with railway contractors, and, presumably, laid the foundation of his fortune. I met others connected with these companies, whose appearance showed them to be men of position, and I was informed at Hiroshima that the gentlemen I met there were among the leading capitalists of that city.

I find that the emigration companies all advertise, more or less, in the newspapers for contract laborers, designating them to go to Hawaii, Peru, and Mexico, and that in a general way they advertise through circulars, pamphlets, and by means of traveling solicitors for emigrants going to the United States.

* * * * * * *

In fact, the evidence herewith presented, and all circumstances connected therewith and which fell under my observation, tend to show and, in my opinion, establish beyond a reasonable doubt that the capitalists interested in these companies have taken advantage of the law for the protection of emigrants to build thereon a system which has no parallel. The system presents an interesting study in the linking together of money-making enterprises, which must obtain their profit through a common source. Agents of the steamship companies and emigration companies do not occupy offices together. They are, nevertheless, connected very closely through the brokers and hotel keepers, and it is hard to draw a line of separation of interests. Many of the hotel keepers are emigration brokers, and nearly all brokers are intimately connected with the emigration companies, while it is safe to assert that if the steamship companies were to establish and maintain a fixed rate for steerage passage, it would cut the profits of the brokers, hotel keepers, and emigration companies 50 per cent, and it seems to me conclusive that if it were not for the existence of the emigration companies and these agencies for the collection of emigrants to go abroad, the profits of the steamship companies would be materially reduced. By their present methods, the steamship companies, whether intentionally or otherwise, clearly offer inducements for the emigration companies to solicit the emigrants, both being largely capitalized enterprises that have a mutual interest, which is inseparable, as long as they are allowed to exist side by side, the one to obtain fees from emigrants and the other to receive steerage passage.

The emigration company is exploited as a beneficiary institution and a similar argument is made in their favor by high officials of the Japanese Government, but if any number worth mentioning has been returned to Japan by the emigration companies, I have been unable to discover the fact. However, if the term "beneficiary" is made to apply to the filling of the pockets of the stockholders of the emigration companies and others interested in the movements of emigrants, and to the fact that the system affords a splendid means for getting rid of a congested population, then in that sense it is eminently beneficiary, because it is a matter of general repute that they are the most profitable enterprises in Japan. Great stress was laid by Japanese officials with whom I conversed upon the fact that the Japanese Government requires every emigrant to provide sureties to provide for his return to the country in case of need, before granting a passport. This fact is pointed out by a Mr. Shimamura.

The system may be a benefit to Japan, but I deny that it is any advantage to other countries. The aged and decrepit can not emigrate, and the percentage of those who do and become paupers amounts to nothing. This is shown by practical experience, while, on the other hand, their laws are so strict that they defeat their own purposes. It is a well-known fact in Japan, and clearly appears in nearly all the exhibits hereto attached, that it was the difficulty experienced by the coolie class in obtaining sureties and obtaining passports that suggested and built up the emigration companies. There are really no fixed rates of Japanese steerage, so that the steamship companies, if not voluntary parties to the system described, are made involuntary contributors to the emigration companies and emigration brokers. * * *

I talked with many men of long experience in Japan and found but one universal opinion—that not 10 per cent of the emigrants leaving that country could or would go unless they had assistance, or were helped or assisted by some person of influence. Aside from the facts herein presented, the coolie class could find no proper sureties, such as are required by the Government, unless some arrangement was provided for responsible parties for looking after this class of emigration after they land in the United States.

The magnitude of the capital invested, requiring the utmost energy and most aggressive management to make it profitable, which, considered with the zeal, begotten of competition, between the emigration companies, and the influence of wealth and political connection, points to but one conclusion. Consequently, I am forced to the conclusion that the Japanese system of granting passports for a limited period, requiring surety for the welfare of the emigrant abroad, and, in some cases, for the care of his family while absent and his return when sick or disabled, joined with the avarice of organized capital and influence of the emigration companies, is the direct inducing cause of 90 per cent of the emigration from Japan to the United States. * * *

I find, further, owing to the conditions herein described, that the objects and purposes of the laws of the United States regulating immigration are largely defeated so far as related to immigration from Japan. It may readily be perceived that such an organized system, having its feeders among ticket brokers and hotel keepers, joined by ties of interest, and from employment bureaus in Japan and on the Pacific coast, and by reason of its capital and power able to coerce the steamship companies into dividing their profits, with a perfect system of coaching immigrants as to the requirements of the immigration laws of the United States, that the immigration officers here are practically powerless to hold back the influx of pauper and contract labor from Japan, which is increasing year by year.

H. IMMIGRATION THROUGH CANADA.

In proportion to the efficiency of the inspection and deportation of immigrants at the seaports of the United States, immigrants from Europe and Asia, apprehensive of the examination at these ports naturally seek entrance to the United States through the ports of other countries not subject to American jurisdiction. In this way Canada especially has become, as it were, a back door for foreigners who can not find entrance by the more direct route. To a considerable extent Mexico also is a means of ingress for the excluded classes from Asia. Foreigners enter the United States through Canada under two conditions:

First. Those who come to the Canadian ports with tickets through to the United States; second, those manifested to Canadian interior points, intending to cross over to the United States. By either of these methods the immigration through Canada has increased in remarkable proportions, and Canada has come to be understood in foreign countries as an easy route for evading the immigration inspectors of the United States. One of the special agents of the Bureau of Immigration, after inquiry in Europe, makes the following statement (see Report Commissioner-General of Immigration, 1898, p. 38): "It is the popular belief in provincial England that those who are not beyond doubt outside of the prohibited classes can pass muster by evasion and reservation when being examined by the United States immigration inspectors; and when evasion and reservation are not considered quite effective there is always a way open via Canada. Indeed, one energetic agent boldly declared that anyone who really wanted to go to America could scarcely be kept out, no matter how vigilant the United States immigration authorities may be."

The two methods of access to the United States through Canada, above mentioned, present different problems, and may be considered separately:

1. Immigrants to Canadian seaports.—Prior to October 7, 1893, there is no record of the number of immigrants destined for the United States who landed at Canadian ports. The only points of inspection for such immigrants were the stations along the Canadian border, and large numbers of immigrants doubtless escaped inspection by entering clandestinely at the points where inspectors were not stationed. After fruitless negotiations with the Canadian government in order to secure their cooperation in meeting these difficulties, an agreement was finally made in October, 1893, by the Superintendent of Immigration with the steamship companies and the railroad companies. This agreement, though not officially sanctioned by the Canadian government, has nevertheless been allowed to stand without interference or protest. Under its terms the steamship companies agree to admit the inspectors of the United States to their property at those Canadian ports already designated by the Canadian government. The companies agree to give the inspectors facilities in the way of accommodations, access to the immigrants, and to keep the immigrants apart from the public until after inspection shall be completed. The inspectors thereupon furnish a certificate or passport containing a personal description of those immigrants deemed eligible for entrance to the United States, signed by the inspector. This certificate entitles the immigrant to enter the United States without further examination or hindrance, and is accepted on its face by the inspectors at the ports of entry on the American side. Following is a copy of immigrants' certificate:

Certificate granted to immigrant at Canadian port.

This is to certify that —— ——, a native of ——, who arrived at the port of ——, per steamship ——, on the —— day of ——, has been duly inspected and registered and will be admitted into the United States upon presentation and surrender of this certificate to any custom or immigration officer at the ——. His description is as follows: Age, ——; height, ——; color of hair ——; color of eyes, ——.

Remarks: —— ——.

——————————,
Commissioner of Immigration.

The railroad companies, being also parties to this agreement, contract not to sell to any immigrant to any port of the United States a ticket for his transportation or to transport him in cars or vessels from a port of entry until after he has exhibited his certificate or passport; and they agree also not knowingly to transport any rejected or undesirable immigrant, or one who is by law prohibited from entering the United States, into its territory. This provision is largely a dead letter, not through the fault of the railroad companies, but through various subterfuges, such as purchase of tickets by third parties, etc. The steamship companies also agree to pay the inspection officer at the port of landing the head tax for each eligible immigrant. Under this agreement the Secretary of the Treasury designated the ports of Halifax,

Nova Scotia, Quebec, Point Levis, Vancouver, and Victoria as stations for the inspection officers of the immigration service.

The agreement of 1893 was amended May 5, 1896, by supplementary agreement following the legislation of 1894, designating an additional port, St. John, as a landing port for immigrants during the winter, increasing the per capita tax upon aliens from 50 cents to $1 in accordance with the new law on that subject. This amendatory agreement contained also the additional agreement on the part of the railroads and the steamship companies that if any immigrant who has landed at any of the mentioned ports shall apply for admission in the United States within 30 days after arrival at said port without the certificate and shall be debarred from entering the United States, or if it shall be ascertained that the said immigrant has been previously refused admission into the United States by any immigration official of railway and steamship companies, agreed to return the immigrant to the port of landing or to carry him to such place upon his line of travel as he is willing to go most remote from the borders of the United States. The following table shows, since the establishment of the Canadian ports of entry, the extent of immigration by way of Canada:

Immigration through Canada.

Year.	Quebec and Point Levis.	St. John and Halifax.	Vancouver and Victoria.	Total Canada.
1894-95	3,889	817	1,282	5,988
1895-96	5,395	1,508	2,018	8,921
1896-97	4,946	1,596	4,104	10,646
1897-98	5,126	2,218	3,393	10,737
1898-99	8,196	2,354	2,303	13,853
1899-1900	14,556	5,455	3,189	23,200
1900-01	16,771	4,894	3,546	25,211

These figures show an increase in the years 1897 and 1898 of 12 per cent in the immigration by the Canadian route, whereas during the same years there was a small diminution in the aggregate arrivals at the ports of Boston, New York, and Philadelphia amounting, respectively, to 1,800 and 2,500. They also show that from the years 1899 to 1901 the increase (13,853 to 25,211) amounted to 82 per cent. Had the increase in the arrivals at the ports in this country shown a similar proportion of immigration they would have been 515,300 instead of 425,301 in the year 1900. (Report of Commissioner of Immigration, 1899, p. 37; 1900, p. 41.)

2. Immigrants to Canadian interior points.—The foregoing table, showing the large increase of immigration to the recognized ports of entry along the eastern Canadian border, although indicating strongly the growing importance of that line of ingress to the United States, is by no means the most serious aspect of this problem. Unquestionably a large number of immigrants, if not much larger than the foregoing, reach the United States by purchasing tickets to points in the interior of Canada, by which method they escape inspection by the American officers at the Canadian ports and then, having reached their Canadian destination, find means of crossing into the United States as immigrants from Canada. That this method of immigration is used by large numbers is asserted in the reports of the Commissioner-General of Immigration. It is stated (Report, 1899, p. 32) "that Croatian immigrants in one case, who were captured and returned to Europe for violating the provisions of the alien contract-labor laws, alleged that they had adopted this plan to avoid rigid examination, having been informed of the absence of impediments to entry through Canada." The commissioner of immigration at the port of New York reports as a frequent occurrence the recognition of aliens on the streets of that city by the officials who had assisted in their deportation. Repeated instances have occurred of deportation of aliens who, after rejection at a port of this country, have secured entrance by returning through Canada, and, becoming public charges after such entrance, have been returned to their own country at the expense of the immigrant fund. Mr. McSweeney, assistant commissioner of immigration at the port of New York, in his testimony before the Industrial Commission, quoted from the address of Mr. Charlton in the Canadian Parliament February 10, 1890, who estimated that the immigration into Canada from the Old World from the years 1871 to 1881 numbered 342,675 souls, but at the end of that period the total increase in the foreign element of the Canadian population was barely 15,720 souls, there having been in 1871 582,668 persons of foreign birth and in 1881, 599,388. Mr. Charlton estimated, allowing for the normal death rate, that there should have been in Canada in 1881 783,208 persons of foreign birth, showing that during ten years 184,820 immigrants had moved into the United States. Continuing his calculations for the decade of 1881 and 1890, Mr. Charlton estimated by similar calculations that there had passed over

INSPECTION AT EUROPEAN PORTS.

to the United States during these ten years 346,360 foreigners. On the basis of this computation it will be seen that Mr. Charlton estimated that the number of foreigners crossing through Canada into the United States from 1871 to 1881 amounted to an average of 18,482 per year, and the number crossing over from 1881 to 1890 averaged 34,636 per year. This number is largely in excess of the number who come to the ports of Canada manifested openly to the United States.

The character of this surreptitious immigration through Canada is believed to be the worst of all that enters the United States. Mr. Powderly asserts (reports, vol. 15, p. 38) that in his opinion the greater part of the infirm people that come to us, aliens that drift into our institutions, come by way of Canada. Speaking of diseased immigrants, (Report of Commissioner-General, 1900, p. 40) he states that "experience shows that in the past the citizens of this country have not secured the full benefit from this effective physical inspection, because of the practice which has grown up of sending diseased immigrants to Canada manifested to ports in the Dominion, hoping thereby to secure their admittance to the United States. If the Dominion government would undertake such legislation as would prohibit the landing of the diseased, the pauper, and the criminal at Canadian ports, the door would be directly closed against the admission of such aliens to the United States."

The Canadian agreement of May 5, 1896, provided for the identification and collection of head tax upon immigrants who, though actually destined to the United States, attempt to evade payment by purchasing tickets to some point in Canada. The transportation companies agreed in such cases to return to as remote a point from our borders as he is willing to go, any alien who attempts within 30 days after being refused a certificate to enter this country. The essential weakness of this provision lies in the fact that the American Government can not send its officers in company with the immigrant across the territory of Canada, nor can it compel the immigrant to take passage from a Canadian port to European countries whence he came. The willingness of the immigrant is the sole basis of deportation. Consequently, the inspectors along the Canadian border are able only to see that the immigrant is taken back to the Canadian side, whence it is an easy matter for him to find access at some point where inspectors are not stationed. Quite recently the Bureau of Immigration has adopted the new policy of carrying these rejected immigrants directly to the port of New York without going through Canada, and then sending them back to their European countries, and paying the expenses out of the immigrant fund.

INSPECTION AT EUROPEAN PORTS.

So serious has become the evasion of the immigration laws through the Canadian transit that the Bureau of Immigration has in the past 2 or 3 years made special efforts to investigate the conditions under which immigrants embark to this country, and also to provide such consular inspection, and especially medical inspection, at foreign ports as the steamship companies would consent to admit. The reports of these officials to the Bureau of Immigration contain striking testimony to the conclusions already reached in the foregoing pages, and certain of the more detailed communications from these officials are given herewith.

The first is a report made by Special Agent Robert Watchorn, detailed in 1898 to visit Liverpool, Bremen, and Hamburg in order to examine into the methods of embarkation. Following this report is a statement made by the United States consul at Liverpool, explaining the recent attempt of the Bureau of Immigration to provide a medical inspection at Liverpool of immigrants coming to the United States through Canada. Seeing that this inspection depended solely upon the consent and cooperation of the steamship companies and had no legal binding force, it has proven an entire failure and even a disadvantage in the enforcement of the immigration laws, as will be seen in the statements of the letters themselves.

Next is a series of occasional reports made by Dr. Anderson, surgeon in the Marine-Hospital Service, detailed at Liverpool for the examination of immigrants. His reports contain conclusive testimony to the evasions of the United States laws. Finally, a communication is submitted from Dr. Heiser, stationed at Quebec for the inspection of immigrants destined for the United States.

REPORT OF SPECIAL AGENT ROBERT WATCHORN RELATING TO INSPECTION OF EMIGRANTS AT EUROPEAN PORTS.

In June, 1898, the Commissioner of Immigration directed Special Agent Robert Watchorn to make an investigation in Europe on the diversion from United States to Canadian ports of undesirable immigrants and the immigration of paupers and criminals at the expense of foreign charities. The report made by Mr. Watchorn is reproduced herewith in its more important parts:

In June, 1898, the Commissioner of Immigration directed Special Agent Robert Watchorn to make an investigation in Europe on the diversion of undesirable immigrants from United States to Canadian ports and the immigration of paupers and criminals at the expense of foreign charities. The report made by Mr. Watchorn is reproduced herewith in its more important parts:

* * * A call at any of the principal trans-Atlantic ticket offices is quite sufficient to demonstrate that the British "board of trade" compels all ticket agents to acquaint steerage emigrants with the full text of the immigration laws of the respective countries to which emigrants are desirous of going. Not only is a large copy of the immigration laws of the United States prominently displayed in every ticket office, but every intending emigrant is compelled under oath to answer all the questions contained on steerage manifest sheets, and is given solemn warning that if any discovery of inaccurate testimony is found in his answers he may be imprisoned in the United States for perjury. I asked various agents—those of the large trans-Atlantic lines as well as independent agents—what effect this rigid treatment of emigrants had, and in every case was told that they were frequently unable to sell the ticket owing to the unsatisfactory replies of the emigrant, and in the case of the independent agents, it was made quite clear to me that they are compelled to exercise the most diligent care in this respect because in the event of any of their patrons being rejected by the United States Government they have to forfeit the commission on said tickets, and run a great risk of losing the agency for the company returning said emigrant.

What becomes of the rejected emigrant is not so easy to ascertain, but two young men, Welsh striking miners—that is, men who were on strike for higher wages in Wales—were standing near the Princess Landing Stage on the evening of my arrival at Liverpool, and as they looked like men about to go to sea I ventured to engage them in conversation.

I learned, as above stated, that they were striking coal miners, that their names were, respectively, Thos. Williams and James Price, that they had no relatives in America, and had £6 each (borrowed money), and that they had been refused passage to the United States on the ground that they could not be landed at New York. "What are you going to do now?" I said, and they replied, "We are going home. We have been approached by a Dominion Line agent who offers to send us to Canada and to maintain us here until their ship sails. This agent tells us that we can easily work our way across the Canadian line to the American mines, if we are desirous of going there, but we don't like the prospect of a penniless tramp across Canada, hence our determination to return home."

This instance is by no means a singular occurrence at Liverpool and the principal ports at which the board of trade regulations are so energetically enforced. Here, then, is the first cause of the diversion of emigrants from our ports to Canadian ports.

Friday night is always a more or less busy night among the steerage depots at Liverpool, and it may be in order for me to state here that steerage passengers at this port always stop at lodging houses that are licensed to afford accommodations to them. At a certain hour on the day prior to sailing a board of trade physician calls at these boarding houses and carefully inspects the physical condition of all the emigrants therein, and if any are found physically unfit, they are promptly rejected. Mr. Boyle, the United States consul at Liverpool, says, "Rejections by the board of trade physician are by no means uncommon," but at the moment he was unable to give me any exact figures on the question but promised to do so in the near future. The agents shipping to Canadian ports are not permitted to sell tickets to any of the emigrants who have been rejected by the board of trade physician, as their rejection is based solely upon sanitary grounds, and is insisted upon because the health of the ships would be endangered by their presence therein. But all those who are objected to on other than hygienic grounds at once become objects of extreme solicitude to the Canadian ticket agencies.

The United States consul has no power to inspect or pass upon emigrants to Canadian ports even though they are destined to the United States via Canada. In addition to the boarding-house inspection the board of trade physician again inspects all steerage passengers as they board the ship on the day of sailing. I was cordially invited by the United States consul, Mr. Boyle, to witness one or more of these inspections, but I declined his courtesy on the ground that I had not the time to spare. However, I subsequently found that I had sufficient time, but did not accompany the consul, preferring to observe the inspection without the doctor's knowledge of my presence. The inspection to a layman looked like a very rapid affair, the passengers passing the physician at a rate, approximately, of 2,000 an hour.

Only in a few instances were heads uncovered, so that it can not be said to have been a very searching inquiry, although it must be remembered that he had seen most of them at the lodging houses the night previous. This physician, it must be borne in mind, is under no obligation to point out that this or that emigrant is likely to be objectionable to the United States immigration authorities (though it is stated that he has, on many occasions, done so). His sole duty under British laws and regulations is to protect the health of emigrants while on board ship. Mr. Boyle or his assistant are invariably present at the inspection conducted on board ship, though they do not accompany the doctor to the boarding houses.

Mr. Boyle stated that he has such great confidence in the ability, integrity, and faithfulness of the board of trade officials that he practically relies on their inspections and is governed by them. He further states that no examination other than a medical one is ever made, the consul having no authority in matters of emigration other than that of a sanitary nature, including the disinfection of baggage.

It may be opportune to remark, parenthetically, as it were, that whatever may be the result of these sanitary precautions, it can not be denied that the rigid interrogations and lucid explanations at all the large shipping centers serve to nullify the work of the United States contract-labor inspectors, for the emigrant is not only advised that he can not be landed at a United States port, if under contract, but he is made to sign a statement, as has already been pointed out, to the effect that he has no employment, and is then given a printed statement setting forth that he may be called upon to swear to the truth of these statements by the United States immigration commissioners, and if it is found that he has sworn falsely he may be imprisoned for perjury.

After a mechanic or laborer has been subjected to an ordeal of this kind at Liverpool it ought not to be a difficult thing to realize that a week later he will be in prime condition to pass successfully the searching inquiries of the United States contract-labor inspectors. There is such a similarity of action on the part of all the agents and the respective companies doing business at Liverpool that the above account may be said to adequately describe them all. It may be said with equal force that while all who are en route to the United States under contract (either specific or implied) are put through such a course of questioning at Liverpool that they alter their statements on this score and depart for the United States with an intelligent appreciation of the situation they have to face, those who are deemed likely to become a public charge, and are rejected by the agents on that account only, find no difficulty whatever in emigrating to a Canadian port, there being no barrier against them, unless the board of trade physician has objected to them on hygienic grounds. It is a curious fact that England has no quarantine regulations at present against immigrants, but a most rigid one against emigrants. A person may find easy access to England (no matter how badly afflicted), but he can not leave England without passing a satisfactory quarantine examination.

The law expressly requires that the master of any ship departing from an English port to any

INSPECTION AT EUROPEAN PORTS. 685

country (other than those touching the Mediterranean Sea) shall submit a complete manifest of the ship's complement (cabin and steerage), duly and properly authenticated, to the Government emigration or customs officers before sailing, whereas he need not submit the manifests when arriving from any port outside the Mediterranean Sea until 24 hours after his arrival. This manifest must set forth the names and numbers of all the steerage passengers, the ports at which they embarked, whether any were born in the steerage, or if there were any deaths. Cabin passengers are not noted on these manifests. All Mediterranean ports are exempt from this regulation.

After leaving Liverpool for London I stopped at a number of provincial towns, embracing agricultural, mining, and manufacturing industries, but owing to an uncommonly brisk period of trade and an uncommonly good harvest, there was not much emigration spirit among the people; but I deem it worthy of note that at not a single trans-Atlantic ticket agency did I find the slightest hesitancy on the part of the agents to admit that they deem it their duty to advise parties in quest of tickets to the United States how best to effect a lawful (?) landing there. It is the popular belief in provincial England that those who are not beyond doubt outside of the prohibited classes can pass muster, by evasion and reservation, when being examined by the United States immigration inspectors; and when evasion and reservation are not considered quite effective, there is always a way open via Canada. Indeed, one energetic agent boldly declared that anyone who really wanted to go to America could scarcely be kept out, no matter how vigilant the United States immigration authorities may be. * * *

It will be noticed that one of the causes of the diversion from United States ports to Canadian ports is due to the somewhat strict scrutiny on the part of the general agents of the trans-Atlantic lines, and the agility and unscrupulousness of many of the Canadian agents, who make the rounds of all the emigrants' rendezvous in search of the "cast offs," that they may book them to Canada, advising them that the United States is easily entered via Canada. * * *

A casual observer in London would be apt to conclude that the question of immigration was not one that gave the average Briton any undue concern; but how different to the interested investigator! Indeed, it soon impresses itself on such a person that there is no question so vital to the interests of those residing in large cities as immigration, and it is quite within the bounds of moderation to state that the British Government is the best informed in the world as to those who come and go, and also as to the immigration into all other countries, particularly into the United States of America. The board of trade is fully cognizant of the methods in vogue at every immigration station in the United States and Canada, even to the detail of every rejected immigrant, what finally becomes of his case, the decision of the courts in all cases where a prosecution has been undertaken, together with all legislation on the subject enacted and immediately prospective. They have on file the views on immigration of all the American trades unions and many trades unionists, together with the views of leading statesmen and jurists.

It is generally admitted that these investigations carried on by the British Government were intended to serve a humane purpose, and in the main, no doubt, have done so; but whatever the intentions, when one finds these detailed accounts of the examinations of immigrants at New York, Baltimore, Philadelphia, and Boston in the hands of those who are deeply interested in the emigration of those dependent on charitable institutions for support, it is difficult to divest one's self of the opinion that they have served another purpose as well—that of suggesting the easiest point at which to effect an entrance on the part of the less desirable emigrants to the United States.

One agent informed me that he never thought of sending a doubtful case via New York, but preferred Philadelphia or Boston, and as a last resort Quebec or Halifax. I have never been at any of these landing depots other than New York and do not know how he reached this conclusion, except from the reports made by the board of trade experts, who personally inspected all of them and whose reports were laid before Parliament, ordered printed, and put into public circulation. What could be more suggestive to those interested in sending undesirable people to a foreign shore than the following extract from the report of a board of trade expert, Mr. Schloss, pages 41–42, 'Report of the board of trade on alien immigration," 1894?

"The immigration into Boston from Canadian ports—Yarmouth and Halifax—is quite distinct in character from that which takes place from the trans-Atlantic ports and is treated in a widely different manner. Persons found to be ineligible or to have come in violation of the alien contract labor law are debarred from landing; but the examination of passengers coming from the Dominion is of a very slight character. On the occasion when the writer witnessed the landing of passengers brought by a steamer from Yarmouth, Nova Scotia, the doctor and the immigrant inspector stood at the head of the gang plank, the passengers defiling past them. The inspector put questions to the first few who came along. He said he usually put questions to one in ten; the rest he merely glanced at. The entire examination of 24 passengers by the doctor and immigrant inspector occupied 5 minutes.

"Out of 27,641 passengers who arrived at Massachusetts ports from the Dominion of Canada in 1892 only 63 were debarred from landing. * * *

"It is fairly certain that the 5 quarrymen who were sent back to Canada in 1892, as having come in violation of the alien contract labor law, were not the only persons—were, indeed, but a very minute proportion of the persons who came to Boston and minor Massachusetts ports under circumstances making their entry into the United States unlawful. * * *

"What is more, Mr. Colcord, United States immigrant inspector, declared that in his belief every immigrant from Canada whom the inspectors had stopped at Boston had afterwards got into the United States by the land frontier, usually by Vanceboro, Me."

In a footnote the writer says that the United States commissioner of immigration at Boston denied that any European immigrants used Canada as a vantage point for entering the United States, but proceeds to point out that the commissioner was on this point, to some extent at least, in error.

Be that as it may, here stands out the plain incontestable fact that the official expert opinion of the British board of trade is that Canadians find it comparatively easy to enter the United States. It will be noticed that this is part of a report which, taken as a whole, is a compendium of information for the British public on the United States immigration laws and the methods of their enforcement at all the ports of entry on the Atlantic seaboard.

The emigration bureau at 31 Broadway, Westminster, SW., issues a monthly statement to the public advising mechanics, laborers, and domestics where to go and how to get there, also where not to go. This circular is based largely on consular reports, and states the condition of trade in the various industries, and always urges Britons to stay away from undesirable places, leaving the inference to be broadly drawn that those places not included should be selected by persons desirous of emigrating. A special pamphlet setting forth the developments of the tin-plate industry in the United States has been issued very recently, and the emigration bureau urges all persons interested in said industry to secure a copy of it.

It requires no great stretch of the imagination to observe what bearing the various reports have on each other and how they conjointly affect emigration to the United States of America. * * *

The information gathered among the recipients of organized Jewish charity suggested a call on the principal dispenser of said charity. Subsequently a call on the Jewish Colonization Society and also at the headquarters of the Society for the Relief of Destitute Jews. At the former place those in attendance were as silent as the proverbial sphinx, and absolutely refused to impart any information whatever touching emigration or immigration, the means at their disposal, or the manner of its disbursement. Then I called on Mr. Solomon, of the Jewish Colonization Society, at 17 Old Broad street, London. He at once became the questioner, and shortly informed me that if I would bring a letter of introduction from some reputable Hebrew or Hebrew society he would be prepared to discuss the matter with me, but not until then. He said, however, that I might get the information desired by applying at the society's main office at Paris.

I next called on Mrs. E. A. Finn, secretary of the Jewish Relief Sociey, at 41 Parliament street, who appeared to be quite willing to assist me in my search for information, but could not do so officially without the consent of the board of directors of the society. She, however, stated that the chief aim of their society was to colonize Palestine with destitute Jews and sustain them until they could sustain themselves, though when the applicants for charity strongly desired to emigrate to other parts, they sometimes assisted such persons to attain their desired ends. Mr. McLeod, to whom I have already referred, informed me that the board of trade collected returns from all institutions who distributed aid to the poor, and, in view of the fact that none of these societies would disclose any information, that it would be best to get it from a governmental source.

I therefore went again to the board of trade (labor bureau), and there found access to the following data which has a direct bearing on the subject under investigation:

"The Russian and Polish immigrants increased in 1897 by 2,002. Of a total of 12,282 Russian and Polish immigrants 83 per cent went direct to London, and this class of immigrants from Liban is constantly on the increase.

"How many of these Russians and Poles who were not stated to be en route to other countries subsequently left the United Kingdom within the year we have no means of knowing, but that many did so leave is certain, for a great number of persons belonging to these nationalities were certainly included among the 2,700 aliens who, as mentioned above, were ascertained by the customs officers to be proceeding forthwith to other countries, though not so stated in the alien lists.

"There is reason to suppose, moreover, that the above figure is in reality considerably under the mark. Again a certain number of immigrants doubtless left the country subsequently, either through the aid of the Jewish Board of Guardians, or the conjoint committee of that body, and the Russo-Jewish committee, or without such assistance.

"During 1897 the above agencies assisted about 2,000 Jews (mostly Russians and Poles) to emigrate, and while no doubt only a part of these had arrived in this country during the year, this outflow must be taken into account in estimating the growth of the foreign Jewish population of London.

"It is known also that on a smaller scale various Jewish charitable organizations in the provinces (smaller towns) assisted poor Jews to emigrate during the year.

"It is clear, therefore, that there is an appreciable outflow of Russians and Polish Jews other than those described as transmigrants in the alien lists to be set against the immigration, although the data do not exist to enable its magnitude to be estimated. A special report received from Riga again draws attention to the considerable amount of passenger traffic now carried on between the port of Libau and the ports of London and Hull, and mentions that there was an increase of about 2,500 in the number of emigrants by this route to the United Kingdom in 1897, as compared with the preceding year. The consular report adds: The greater number of these were supposed to be en route for South Africa and America."

The number of new cases of destitute aliens who were assisted during the year by the conjoint Jewish aid societies were 1,827.

The number of inmates of the Poor Jews Temporary Shelter (a place which I carefully investigated), Whitechapel, all of them persons who had come from abroad, was 2,811. The majority of these people left the country again within a year, mostly for South Africa and America. The London police report that quite 25 per cent of all those arriving as alien immigrants may be classed as paupers—destitute aliens—and the number of Jews in East London still increases and the area inhabited by them is extending.

The returns show a falling off of 7,000 emigrants to South Africa, and of 22,000 to the United States, but no decline whatever in the emigration to Canada, and in view of the fact that more than 2,000 Russian and Polish Jews were emigrated in 1897 by these charity organizations, it is not to be wondered at that there is no falling off in Canadian immigration.

While the data used in the foregoing report were drawn chiefly from London sources, it must not be overlooked that there are great numbers of destitute aliens, chiefly Russian and Polish Jews, in all the large towns of the United Kingdom, who are in receipt of relief from the various relief societies, including assistance to emigrate.

Satisfying myself after a most patient investigation that many destitute aliens are sent from England to America, I went to Havre to continue my investigations there. Mr. Thackard, United States consul at that place, stated that little or no immigration to France via Havre went thence to London, but that he gathered from the British consul-general that a stream of very undesirable immigration was passing out at Dieppe bound for New Haven, England, many of whom were believed to be en route to Canada; 4,402 aliens left Dieppe for New Haven, England, in 1897, thence to other parts. He says that his inspection of immigrants is confined strictly to a quarantine character, but that it is most searching, and all aliens destined to America via Havre are subjected to a most thorough overhauling and the baggage is all disinfected, the Général Trans-Atlantique Company having erected, at his request, a most complete fumigating apparatus for this purpose.

He regrets that he is not in close touch with the immigration department at Washington, believing that he could occasionally be of service, if he were certain that his views or suggestions would not be regarded as an intrusion by the commissioners of immigration.

He suggested, as a result of a conversation with the British consul, that if destitute aliens arriving in the United States or Canada, giving as their last residence England, that if a passport were demanded by the United States Government it would be an easy matter to distinguish whether they were really British or Canadian, or had merely passed through England or Canada, as a passport can not be acquired by anyone not having resided five years under the British flag. He deems the worst class of people arriving at and departing from Havre to be southern Italians and Orientals, but does not feel that he has any power to object to their shipping to America, except on quarantine grounds, even when he does not think them very desirable * * *

On my way to Bremen I stopped off at Cologne and canvassed the various ticket agencies as to the methods in vogue therein dealing with emigrants, and I learned that under the new German emigration law that they were proceeding with their business on somewhat contracted lines.

Under this new law it is illegal to induce any German or Germans to emigrate from Germany, and all advertising must be confined to the announcement of the proposed sailings, etc. As a result of this all the prospectuses which he formerly distributed setting forth the advantages offered to emigrants in foreign lands have been withdrawn from circulation. I saw huge piles of these circulars and pamphlets on his shelves, but he was not permitted to give them out to German subjects. His principal business is that of booking cabin passengers.

This new law and regulation came into operation on April 1, 1898.

I arrived at Bremen on the day following my inquiries at Cologne, and there found an American vice-consul who not only knows a good deal about emigration and immigration, but who is most willing and anxious to assist the United States Immigration Bureau to the very best of his ability.

Bremen is to Germany what Liverpool is to England, as far as emigration is concerned, and it is here that one comes into close touch with not only the emigration question, but with large numbers of emigrants.

From January 1 to July 1, 1898, 24,209 steerage passengers were emigrated from Bremen and Bremerhaven for the United States. Of this number the United States consul temporarily rejected 623, who were detained for medical treatment; some of whom were subsequently taken to the United States at the risk of the North German Lloyd Company, the manifest sheets bearing the names of these rejected ones being thus marked: "Taken at the risk of the North German Lloyd Company."

The consul also permanently rejected 161 undesirable emigrants.

Now, it is a very interesting thing to note what becomes of these rejected ones. The German emigration commissioner has very great powers in matters touching emigration, and derives them from the new emigration law which went into effect April 1, 1898. It may safely be left to him to see to it that the undesirable stream of emigration through Germany to other countries does not find a lodgment in Germany, and they are compelled to "move on" or return to the country whence they came.

This officer sees to it that no unhealthy person or persons are given passage on any ship leaving Germany—that is, any steerage passenger, as the new law gives him no authority to deal with saloon passengers—and as a result of this distinction an agent at Bremen (who has no connection with the North German Lloyd Company) immediately takes up all the rejected emigrants and ships them to West Hartlepool, or some other English port, as cabin passengers, whence they are sent to America by the process alluded to in the earlier part of this report.

It is a matter of record that the German Government has long taken the precaution to disinfect the baggage of immigrants, and, in some instances, the immigrants themselves, who cross the line into Germany.

Under the "new law" more stringent measures than ever have been taken by the German Government, and a few more stations have been added, viz, Insterburg, Jilsit, and Ruhleben. By way of water these people are not permitted to enter Germany.

A few days prior to my visit to Bremen a steamer smuggled a load of Russian Jews into Stettin. The police at first threatened to return them to Russia, but after much telegraphing, etc., they were permitted to proceed to Bremen, where they were disinfected, and in most cases fell into the hands of Mr. Harry Cohen, the independent agent above referred to, and shipped by him to England and the United States.

The German emigration commissioner made an effort to stop Mr. Harry Cohen from continuing his business as an agent, but he was allowed to continue, because his exclusion would have involved foreign complications, he being the regularly appointed agent of the American Line and Red Star Line. I had a long talk with Mr. Cohen, and learned from him that he gets the bulk of his business direct from his own local agents, who are to be found all through Russia and Galicia. I saw him issue tickets to 27 emigrants who were, for the most part, of the very worst undesirable class; all were sent to Hull, England, thence to Philadelphia, via Liverpool.

To say the least of it, it is a very deplorable thing to see these poor people sent away from Bremen because of a general unfitness to ship thence, and after weeks of additional waiting, and hundreds of miles of additional traveling, to find that they reach their objective point through this devious channel, and it is the general expression of the United States consuls that they regret their inability to successfully cope with this very important question.

The experience of the United States consul at Hamburg (Dr. Hugh Pitcairn) is exactly like unto that of the consul at Bremen, excepting that he has not found it necessary to reject so many emigrants. However, those that have been rejected by him are immediately shipped direct to England, to some one of the 26 English ports, and then reshipped to America.

It appears to me that a quotation from a typewritten statement now before me, being a sort of compendium of the United States consular opinion on emigration from some of the continental European ports, may be used here:

"The disinfection of the undesirable streams of immigration from Armenia and parts of Italy, Galicia, Russia, and Russian Poland is attended to with the greatest diligence by the various countries through whose respective territories they must needs pass before they reach the port at which they intend to take ship to the United States of America; and at the ship's side they are inspected again, all of which signifies, as plainly as anything possibly can, that a large percentage of them is unfit to be absorbed by any self-respecting community.

"The rejection of an undesirable immigrant by a German or a French official is a sufficient thing in itself to guarantee that such an immigrant will not be allowed to remain in either country, but when objected to by a United States official it means that the immigrant will simply be transferred to some other port by the agent already on hand to pick up all the odds and ends of the regular liners and turn their weary and unfortunate feet into the roundabout way which has been made for this refuse class by the ingenuity of the independent and less responsible agents referred to.

"We think it would be a very good thing to visit all the state line control stations and observe the handling of emigrants there. Here, too, are the recruiting stations of the ship companies and emigrant agents, all of whom have local agents at the control stations. We believe that it would be of immense benefit to our country and money well spent to have one or two men, special agents, stationed in that part of the country nearest to these control stations, whose duty it would be to see that the United States alien-contract labor laws are not being infringed upon.

"Such agents should be directed to make frequent trips to the various recruiting stations, gather evidence on the spot, etc. From our point of view such a plan can not fail to work admirably well. Many of the cases arising from the contract-labor laws are dismissed because of an absence of sufficient evidence to convict. Such an officer as herein stated could not only furnish much of the necessary or missing evidence, but actually prevent a great deal of this illicit emigration.

"On the long road of emigration such an officer would be the first hold up, so to speak, or a sort of buffer, the consuls at the seaports the second, and the inspectors at our ports the third.

"Changes in immigration affairs, as in all other vitally important branches of government (dependent upon legislative action), are necessarily made slowly and with much difficulty, but by taking an administrative course these outposts could be established without much difficulty, and an inspection which begins before the too oft deluded emigrant has gotten very far from home can not fail to do a twofold good, i. e., stopping the emigrant from spending his last dollar and of saving our country from his undesirable presence.'"

That our consuls have a patriotic realization of the grave importance of purifying the stream of humanity which constantly flows out to us from the congested and festering quarters of all the old countries, can not be questioned, but they lack the power to check it or divert it from its objective point, and I have no doubt whatever that the consensus of opinion of the United States consuls in Europe (coming in direct contact with the immigrants) is that we need to commence the work of inspection long before the emigrants arrive at our various ports of entry.

It is stated that our Government is represented in Europe by officers of the Navy Department, of the War Department; also by special agents of the customs revenue department, as well as by experts from the Agricultural Department, but hitherto it appears that no one has ever been officially authorized to keep an eye open to the welfare of the United States in the very important matter of passing on the fitness or unfitness of those who come to us and enter into our national life in all its multifarious connections.

Having learned that there were several daily sailings from Hamburg to English ports, I decided to go by one of these routes, with a view to ascertaining how they landed their immigrants in England. Accordingly, I booked on the steamship *Lutterworth* from Hamburg to Grimsby. I did not find any persons in the cabin who might possibly belong to the steerage class, but it was on a Monday night, and I learned that this class of persons is usually carried on the day on which a Hamburg-American liner has departed for America, and they do not depart on Mondays.

The cabin fare, exclusive of food or service, is only $7.50 from Hamburg to Grimsby, while the steerage rate is $5, so that in the event of the German emigration commissioner refusing emigrants steerage shipment out of Germany, it is not at all difficult for them to get out as cabin passengers on the regular liners plying between Germany and England. As I have already pointed out, the German emigration commissioner has no authority to interfere with the emigration of cabin passengers. It is even less of a difficulty to go via Bremen, through the agency of Mr. Cohen at that place. The steerage passengers of the *Lutterworth* went ashore at Grimsby without a single question, except such questions as are asked by the customs officers, and they, of course, pertained only to revenue duties.

On going ashore they went to the several railway stations, destined to various parts of England, chiefly to London and Liverpool.

The new emigration law now in force in Germany compels the shipping companies doing business in Germany to deposit 100,000 marks with the Government as a guaranty that they will return all immigrants rejected by foreign Governments to their native homes (if in Germany) and to the extreme German border line if in any country outside Germany. When rejected immigrants (not German) are returned from America to Germany, the German Government insist on their being forwarded through Germany to their respective homes at once, and if the companies do not act promptly the German emigration commissioner forwards them at Government expense. The Government then appropriates the amount from the deposit made by the company in question, after which the company is prevented from doing any further business until the deposit is made up to the one hundred thousand marks. The operation and enforcement of this law has been most beneficial to the independent agents who send their passengers via England, for they send all kinds and conditions of men without running the slightest risk, because their passengers, if deported from America, are sent to England, where they remain in all their destitution, to be fed and watered by the charity organizations (which abound there), and there they are cultivated, as it were, for a second attempt to enter the desired land. In such cases they are always sent to a different port than that at which they were rejected on their first attempt to obtain a landing.

The social and industrial movements which manifest a remarkable increased interest each succeeding year in all the countries of Europe have one result which is common to all, viz: They emit a certain portion of their population, regardless as to its destination, and it is this very condition which is awakening a sense of danger in all the newer countries of the world and begetting a spirit of vigilance at their thresholds which is intended to keep outside their gates all the undesirable emissions of population from the densely settled sections already alluded to. Indeed, one can not review the trend of recent legislation by any of the European Governments without being deeply impressed with the effect it has on other countries, near and remote.

Nothing, for instance, could have been further from the thoughts of those who originated the plan to compel employers in Great Britain to compensate injured or killed employees than that they would stimulate emigration by its enactment into law, and yet it is morally certain that this will be a characteristic result of this law. * * * This law, together with much recent European legislation, is tending to swell the volume of undesirable emigration from the various countries making said enactments. In contrastive proportion to this activity on the part of the older countries of Europe, I beg to call your special attention to the following laws which have just gone into effect in South Africa (the colony of Natal) and in western Australia, two comparatively new countries. The Natal immigration law went into effect in 1897, and "prohibits the landing in Natal of the following persons (among others), first, of anyone who can not himself write out and sign in the characters of any language of Europe a prescribed application form of admission, giving his name, address, and business; second, of anyone who is a pauper or likely to become a public charge; and third, of anyone not having received a free pardon who has within two years been convicted of a felony or infamous crime or misdemeanor involving moral turpitude, and not being a mere political offense."

The British emigration bureau has publicly announced that this act is intended by the Natal government to keep out Asiatics and such Europeans as are not respectable.

Western Australia passed an act in 1897, that went into effect immediately after its enactment, which provides "that the following persons, among others, are prevented from landing: First, any-one who can not himself write out in the characters of any language of Europe a passage in English of fifty words taken by the appointed officer (immigration inspector) from a British author, and append his name thereto in his own language; second, anyone who is a pauper or who is likely to become a public charge; third, anyone who within 3 years has been convicted of a felony or infamous crime." This act is known as the restriction act of 1897.

It will doubtless be said of these two colonies that even though they were to close their doors entirely it would not affect emigration very much, but this is a great mistake.

It is not necessary to do more than point out that nearly one-third as many of the poorer class of immigrants were admitted in 1896 to these two colonies as were admitted to all North America.

With the narrowing of the channel of admission to these colonies and the absolute certainty of the exclusion of all who are in the prohibited classes (a number which will reach not less than 85 per cent of the whole), it necessarily follows that one of two things must happen: First, either the stream of emigration from the poorer sections of the world must diminish in proportion to the number formerly admitted to the colonies named, or second, those countries keeping "open door" must get an increased immigration from these sections.

A study of the conditions in all of the unhappily congested areas would clearly indicate that there will be no falling off in the number of emigrants so long as the hand of charity contributes to the stream. I have based my calculations as to the decrease of immigration to the colonies under the new law on the first returns furnished since the acts went into operation. The British board of trade reports that after the passage of the "Natal" law a decrease was noticed in the number of foreign immigrants. British and Irish emigrants fell off from 24,594 to 21,109, a decrease of only 14 per cent, while foreign—that is, non-English emigrants—fell off from 11,246 to 7,692, a decrease of 31.6 per cent. The returns from western Australia show a marked increase in the desirable element and an estimated falling off of the undesirable element.

If these significant moves on the part of the government herein named touching immigration are not sufficient t_* awaken a livelier interest in the question among our own people, it may be of further interest to those who favor an unlimited and unrestricted immigration to carefully ponder the following bill, which has successfully passed the House of Lords in the Imperial Parliament of Great Britain, on June 28, 1898:

"A BILL (AS AMENDED BY THE STANDING COMMITTEE) ENTITLED 'AN ACT TO REGULATE THE IMMIGRATION OF ALIENS. A. D. 1898.'

"Be it enacted by the Queen's Most Excellent Majesty, by and with the advice and consent of the lords spiritual and temporal and Commons, in this present Parliament assembled, and by the authority of the same, as follows:

"1. This act may be cited as the aliens act, 1898.

"2. It shall be lawful for Her Majesty from time to time, by order of council, to designate ports in the United Kingdom to which this act shall apply for such period as respects each port as shall be specified in the order. Ports so designated shall be termed regulated ports.

"3. Inspectors and medical officers appointed by the board of trade may board any vessel arriving with immigrant passengers at any regulated port, and may inspect the passengers, and any inspector may, subject to and in accordance with regulations to be made by the board of trade, prohibit the landing of any alien who in his opinion is either an idiot, insane, a person without means of support, or a person likely to become a public charge, or a person suffering from any contagious or infectious disease of a dangerous character, provided that no alien shall be prohibited from landing by an inspector on the ground that he is an idiot, insane, or a person suffering from any contagious or infectious disease of a dangerous character unless with the concurrence of a medical officer of the board of trade.

"4. Any alien prohibited from landing, as aforesaid, shall be sent back, in accordance with regulations to be made by the board of trade, to the port whence he came, and the expense or estimated expense of his return shall be borne by and recoverable in a summary manner from the owner of the vessel in which he arrived.

"5. The board of trade may, with the consent of the treasury as to number and salaries, appoint and may remove inspectors and medical officers for the purposes of this act, and may assign to them their duties, and, subject as aforesaid, fix their remuneration.

"All expenses incurred by the board of trade in or about the execution of this act shall be paid out of moneys to be provided by Parliament.

"The board of trade may make regulations for the execution of the provisions of this act."

No such bill could possibly command the attention of the House of Lords unless it fairly reflected the views of a very large portion of the population of Great Britain, and I am bound to say that though the provisions of the bill are more drastic than our own immigration laws, they in no way do violence to the British conscience as far as my investigations qualify me to estimate the sentiments of the people. If the flash light of an inquiring public mind is ever turned on the noisome, squalid places occupied by the alien immigrants of England, the action of the House of Commons will surely stamp Lord Hardwicke's bill with the seal of public approval, and in that event there remains but one place to which this emitted fragment of the human race can go—America—and unless great care is taken to sift the good and worthy from the vile and loathsome, our leniency will be outraged by the organized charities of Europe, which find it more economical to emigrate its burdens than to perpetuate their measures of relief and sustenance.

In conclusion I dare boldly afirm that thousands of immigrants are landed annually in the United States who are wholly or in part sent by the charity of others, but so thoroughly tutored by their benefactors that their state of destitution and dependence is, to a great extent, concealed; that they are habitually sent to the ports which experience has marked out as the least likely to reject them, New York being shunned by every agent in Europe who has a doubtful case to dispose of. * * *

I am, very sincerely, yours,

ROBERT WATCHORN.

"LETTER FROM THE UNITED STATES CONSUL AT LIVERPOOL DESCRIBING CONSULAR AND MEDICAL INSPECTION OF IMMIGRANTS DESTINED TO THE UNITED STATES THROUGH CANADA.

CONSULAR SERVICE, UNITED STATES OF AMERICA
Liverpool, June 24, 1901.

Hon. W. M. OSBORNE,
Consul-General of the United States,
12 St. Helen's Place, London.

SIR: I beg to reply to your letter of the 20th instant, inquiring whether Dr. Anderson (the United States Government medical officer stationed at this port) or I "exercise under any law the right to refuse permission to any emigrant to sail to the United States, either first, second, or third class, and if so, how many and what restrictions are in force in this regard."

I would first say that at the present time Dr. Anderson's duties relate exclusively to emigrants embarking on ships touching at Canadian ports, and this I will explain further on.

Answering your inquiry in its strict letter I would say that I do not exercise any right to directly refuse permission to any emigrant, irrespective of class, to sail to the United States. It is, however, my duty to see that the various immigration and quarantine laws of the United States applicable to the port of embarkation are carried out. In this connection I would refer to articles 11 and 13 of the "Immigration laws and regulations," of the Treasury Department (last issue, April 9, 1900) and to the "Quarantine laws and regulations," Treasury Department of the United States (revised edition, November 13, 1899).

Every vessel clearing from this port (and the same requirement holds good as to every foreign port) is required to obtain from the consul a bill of health. Practically speaking, the only way in which the consul can exercise direct authority under United States law "to refuse permission to any emigrant to sail to the United States" is by declining to give the bill of health to the ship. Section 2 of the quarantine act of February 15, 1893, requires the consul before granting the bill of health "to be satisfied that the matter and things stated therein are true." If I were not satisfied that such "matters and things" were true I would certainly decline to grant the bill of health, and would also, probably, cable the Department of State to that effect. The "quarantine laws and regulations" of November 13, 1899, give the forms of bills of health (pages 12 and 13). A bill of health sets forth the sanitary history and condition of the vessel, and certifies all the requirements of the United States as to the sanitary condition of the vessel, its cargo, passengers, and crew, have been complied with. Before I sign and grant the bill of health I require the master and surgeon to sign and verify the manifest sheets of emigrants, pursuant to article 13 of the immigration regulations (pages 5 and 6). The signings and verifications on the manifest sheets by the master and surgeon of the ship, and by myself as consul, take place on board ship immediately preceding the sailing, but I require the emigrants' manifest sheets to have been previously presented at the consulate for inspection and sealing, and if I find that any third-class emigrant comes from an infected district I require his clothing, baggage, and personal effects to be disinfected, pursuant to article 11 of the immigration laws and regulations. In accepting the declaration and verification of the master and surgeon of the ship, I take cognizance of the known fact of inspection by the British board of trade officers, and of fulfillment of sanitary regulations both local and as laid down by the American Government, on the part of the ship's management. Occasionally the United States Government details one or more medical officers to this port to act in this matter, and then we jointly sign the bills of health, in that case the practice being for the consul to accept the decision of the United States medical officer so far as sanitary matters are concerned. My experience is that ships' owners accept the suggestions of the medical officer and the consul, and the occasion to object to passengers after they have been inspected by the British officials arises very seldom. I have never felt called upon to refuse to grant the bill of health, but yet the steamship companies understand that if I was not satisfied with the declarations of the master and surgeon as to the good sanitary condition of the passengers and crew and of the cargo I would withhold the document.

For some time Dr. Anderson and another officer of the United States Marine-Hospital Service were on detail here to make observations and inspection of sanitary matters connected with emigration from this port to the United States, with special reference to the plague then existing at certain places on the Continent, and at Glasgow. After the disappearance of the plague these officers were taken off the detail. Subsequently, however, Dr. Anderson was instructed to inspect the emigrants leaving this port for Canadian ports. As is well known, a large number of emigrants embarking at this port enter the United States via Canada. As I understand it, the alternative presented itself of a rigorous and troublesome inspection, involving quarantine stations at the American frontier by officials of the United States Government, or of inspection at Liverpool, the port of embarkation. The latter system, established on the 5th of February, resulted from an agreement or understanding between the Allan, Dominion, and Beaver Lines and the United States Immigration Bureau. But in so acting Dr. Anderson acts purely in an advisory capacity. As a matter of fact, he is not now officially attached to this consulate, he only making the consulate his headquarters as a matter of convenience. He does not claim any legal jurisdiction so far as forbidding any person whatever from embarking on the ships in question; nor does he sign the bills of health of these ships. But he inspects, so far as possible, the emigrants—and that irrespective of whether they are booked only to Canada or through to the United States. If he finds any passenger suffering from a disease which would disqualify him from entering the United States, he so informs the representative of the ship's owners. The understanding is that under these circumstances the passenger will not be allowed to sail if the presumption prevails that his intention is to enter the United States. The rule is for Dr. Anderson to make his examination before the examination by the British board of trade medical officer has been made, and before embarkation; and my information is that on one occasion Dr. Anderson advised the rejection of several passengers who had been passed by the British board of trade official, and the explanation is that there are some diseases which disqualify an alien immigrant from entering the United States, but which do not debar him from embarking from a British port on a British ship.

In conclusion I would say that while Dr. Anderson and myself are satisfied generally with the manner in which the requirements of the United States Government are met at this port, yet that we are strongly of the opinion that improvement should be made in the matter of lodging the emigrants who stay here temporarily, awaiting embarkation; and I am just now exchanging communications with the medical health officer of Liverpool in regard to this matter.

I have the honor to be, your obedient servant,

JAMES BOYLE, *Consul.*

REPORTS TO THE COMMISSIONER-GENERAL OF IMMIGRATION FROM ASSISTANT SURGEON JOHN F. ANDERSON, OF THE UNITED STATES MARINE-HOSPITAL SERVICE, DETAILED TEMPORARILY AT LIVERPOOL FOR THE INSPECTION OF EMIGRANTS GOING TO THE UNITED STATES THROUGH CANADA.

LIVERPOOL, ENGLAND, *April 24, 1901.*

COMMISSIONER-GENERAL OF IMMIGRATION,
Washington, D. C.

SIR: In accordance with instructions in your letter, R. O. D., March 19, 1901, to visit the ports of Queenstown, Londonderry, and Glasgow, to report upon the medical methods of inspection of emigrants from those ports, I have the honor to report the following:

I left here on the evening of the 3d for Queenstown and arrived there the next morning. At present there is only one line carrying passengers to Canada that calls at Queenstown; this line is the Beaver Line. They have one ship each week, leaving here on Sundays and calling at Queenstown the next day. The number of passengers taken on at Queenstown is small, and as far as I was able to learn were exclusively Irish. This statement in regard to nationality, however, must be taken with reserve. While the lack of an inspection at this point leaves a loophole for undesirable emigrants to embark, still I do not think the number justifies the expense of one. Besides I am sure the board of trade will resent it even more than they do here.

On account of ships sailing at short intervals, for some days after my return I was unable to visit Glasgow and Londonderry. I finally left for Glasgow on the 16th and returned on the 17th. There are two lines from Glasgow carrying passengers to Canada, the Allan and the Donaldson, the latter only carrying steerage passengers. The Allan Line have advertised a ship every week for Canada and the Donaldson every fortnight. The number of steerage passengers from Glasgow last year to Canada was under 2,000. I was unable to learn anything in regard to their nationality or in regard to their physical condition. It is quite reasonable to suppose that this number will be largely augmented if there is no inspection at Glasgow and a rigid one. Emigrant agents soon know these things and advertise accordingly. The expense in proportion to the number of passengers would be large if an officer were stationed there, about $1.50 for each emigrant imported.

I left for Londonderry the 18th and returned the 21st.

At present there is only one Canadian line calling at this port. The Allan Line steamers from both Liverpool and Glasgow call there for passengers and mails. I was totally unable to learn anything at all reliable in regard to the number of passengers from this port to Canada. The board of trade said they could not tell me, and the steamship agents said they did not have the numbers. The number must be considerable, for the day I was there I saw about 50 embark on an Allan Line steamer. The facilities for third-class passengers to reach Londonderry from Ireland are good, and they can go from Liverpool for about 10 shillings to Londonderry, if for any reason they can not embark here. The board of trade examination there is useless, as on the day I was present the surgeon was not even there. While it will be easy for passengers to leave there without inspection, for the same reasons as noted in regard to Glasgow, I do not think the expense justifies the results to be obtained.

In regard to Liverpool, I have to say that the Beaver line apparently are trying to assist me, but they are such tricky people that I have little faith in their promises. I have repeatedly caught them attempting to deceive me, and even as late as their last ship I caught 2 passengers whom I had rejected twice before. The success of the inspection here depends so entirely on the sincere cooperation of the steamship companies that unless they do assist in every way possible the inspection is almost useless. I have no way of ever being sure that I see all of the passengers. I am strongly of the opinion that the inspection is a failure, in spite of the fact that my rejections for favus and trachoma have been about 2½ per cent of the total number of passengers examined. I strongly recommend that the work here be discontinued and a rigid inspection be established either on the frontier as at Quebec. for in order to be effective on this side it would be necessary to have an officer at Glasgow, Londonderry, here, and perhaps Queenstown. The expense of this would be considerable, and even if this was done you would have to reckon on the lack of support of the steamship companies. The companies will make many promises, but they make no secret of the fact that they do not want the inspection here, but are kept to it by the Canadian Pacific Railroad, and finally the board of trade resent the inspection of Canadian passengers. They say that it is very presumptive to want to inspect passengers from one part of the British Empire to another. If the inspection is continued I am afraid that when an inspection of American-bound ships is wanted for quarantine purposes some hampering rules may be enforced.

Respectfully,
JOHN F. ANDERSON,
Assistant Surgeon, M. H. S.

LIVERPOOL, ENGLAND, *May 2, 1901.*

COMMISSIONER-GENERAL OF IMMIGRATION,
Washington, D. C.

SIR: In reference to the latter portion of my letter of April 24 in regard to the state of affairs in Liverpool, I further have to inform you of some recent occurrences here: I have been struck recently by the number of passengers of the Beaver line steamers who were booked to points in Canada as contrasted with the number so booked in the beginning of my work here; the Beaver people allow all persons booked to Canadian points, other than Quebec, to embark. I have questioned many of these people, and almost without exception they say that they are going to the States later; that "friends" (probably Shenker & Co.) will meet them and buy tickets for them to the States. On Tuesday I inspected the passengers by the Beaver steamer *Lake Superior*, about 600 in number, and I rejected 19—14 for favus and 5 for trachoma; of these 19, 5 only were refused passage by the steamship company. I protested against this, but to no avail. I called the attention of the agent to the fact that two of the persons allowed to embark who were now booked—one to Sydney, C. B., and the other to Montreal—had been previously rejected by me about one month ago, and now by simply changing their destination were allowed to embark.

On account of the number of persons rejected by me who have been returned to Italy, the Italian Government has withdrawn the licenses of the Beaver Line agents to book passengers from Italy. This being the case, they are making every effort to avoid returning persons to Italy, and by booking their passengers to Canadian points only they allow them to embark even after being rejected by me. I will also inform you that the same line has a ship on the way to the Black Sea to embark passengers from Batoum for Canada. This vessel, I am reliably informed, will stop at Naples or Genoa and fill up her passenger accommodations if not full when she leaves Batoum. The same person informed me that they would very probably have a ship to sail direct from Naples or Genoa about July 1 for Canada with about 2,000 Italians; if so, I will be safe in saying that 4 per cent will be suffering from favus and trachoma, and 75 per cent will be for the United States. The only point at which these persons can be apprehended to prevent their entrance into the United States is on the frontier, and until a frontier inspection is established we will continue to get the riffraff and scum of the European population into the States by way of Canada.

As for the work in Liverpool, in my opinion its usefulness is at an end, in view of the recent moves of the Beaver Line. If persons that I reject can by simply booking to Canadian points be allowed to embark, the quicker it is discontinued the better.

Respectfully,
JOHN F. ANDERSON,
Assistant Surgeon, M. H. S.

LIVERPOOL, ENGLAND, *June 15, 1901.*

UNITED STATES COMMISSIONER-GENERAL OF IMMIGRATION,
Washington, D. C.

SIR: I have the honor to inclose the within letter, which will explain itself. The man, Moses Levi, was rejected by me, with 10 others, on May 7, 1901, and as they have evidently reached the States they lost very little time. The Beaver Line people are quite sore over the continuance of the inspection, as they had hoped it would have been stopped before now. They also blame the decrease in the number of passengers on the number of rejections, which on their line has been about 3 per cent for favus and trachoma alone by me. Ships that formerly carried 800 to 1,000 now rarely have over 400 to 500. They have heard that a frontier inspection will soon be in force, and have notified me that as soon as it is they will refuse to allow my inspection any longer. This being the case, I think it would be decidedly better for us to stop before they make us; so I respectfully suggest that as soon as you mature your plans you notify me by cable when to cease inspections. I request that I be informed, if no objection exists, of the plan of the proposed frontier inspection, for my own information. I will say that shipping men with whom I have talked all agree that a frontier inspection is the only solution of the question, certainly as far as the Beaver people are concerned. I request that the inclosed letter be returned to me.

Respectfully,
JOHN F. ANDERSON,
Assistant Surgeon, M. H. S.

LIVERPOOL, ENGLAND, *July 15, 1901.*
SUPERVISING SURGEON-GENERAL U. S. MARINE-HOSPITAL SERVICE,
Washington, D. C.

SIR: I have the honor to make the usual report for the week ending July 13, 1901. During the week I inspected 650 passengers for Canadian ports. I advised the rejection of 8 persons, 7 of whom were allowed to proceed by the steamship companies, as most of the people I reject are allowed passage by the companies. I do not see that my work here now is worth the cost. All of the persons rejected who were allowed passage were booked to points convenient to the frontier.
Respectfully,
JOHN F. ANDERSON,
Assistant Surgeon, M. H. S.

UNITED STATES CONSULATE,
Liverpool, England, August 14, 1901.
SUPERVISING SURGEON-GENERAL
U. S. MARINE-HOSPITAL SERVICE, *Washington D. C.*

SIR: * * * I received orders from the Bureau on January 15, 1901, detaching me from the United States consulates in London and Liverpool and assigning me to the Immigration Bureau for duty in Liverpool. On the same date I received instructions from the Commissioner-General of Immigration to call on the different Canadian passenger lines and arrange for the inspection of passengers by their lines. At that time there were three lines carrying passengers direct to Canada, viz, the Dominion, Allan, and Beaver. I called on the managers of the different lines and explained my instructions and wishes and requested to know when I should begin work. The Allan line said at once; the Dominion and Beaver people said they would write me next day. After waiting one week I wrote them asking to know their decision; they then wrote saying that I could begin at once. I will here say that the Dominion line soon after discontinued their Canadian service, and so I will not consider them further. The Allan line readily promised me every assistance, a promise that they have kept to the best of their ability. The Beaver people made the same promise, and, in fact, have made it many times, but have often forgotten to keep it. The Beaver people said that they would try it for a while, but did not think they wanted it, as they could not see the necessity, since their passengers were inspected on the Continent when booked, again in Liverpool at the boarding house, then by the ship surgeon, and finally by the board of trade.

The board of trade in an official letter refused to allow me to inspect Canadian passengers at the time of their examination, and added that they thought it rather impertinent for a United States official to inspect passengers by a British ship from one part of the British Empire to another. This difficulty was avoided by inspecting the passengers before embarkation. But, by inspecting the passengers before the board of trade examination a large loophole was left for putting persons aboard whom I had not inspected, a thing that has happened on the Beaver boats often and I believe still occurs. The Beaver people have absolutely refused to be bound by any count I may make, as they claim the right to allow passengers to embark up to the last minute. Several attempts were made by them to put passengers aboard whom I had rejected. I caught them three times, but am sure it occurred many times without my knowledge. The different companies agreed to accept my decision in regard to the rejection of persons who were presumably intended for the United States if suffering from trachoma and favus, but from no other diseases; hence my rejections have been practically for these two diseases alone. On several occasions I have rejected persons who told me that they had previously been rejected in New York or Naples. The Canadian Pacific Railroad manager in Liverpool called to see me soon after I began work and volunteered any assistance possible. I asked him how he was interested in the matter, and he replied to prevent, if possible, their trains being detained on the frontier for inspection of immigrants. I thanked him and told him the Beaver people did not seem to want to act fair. He called on the Beaver people and told them that if they did not render me every assistance possible in the inspection he would refuse to move their passengers on arrival in Canada, a threat that has helped matters some. I will say here that Beaver people are quite down on me and the inspection, and blame the great decrease in steerage Italian passengers directly to the return of rejected persons to Italy. Ships that carried 800 to 1,000 passengers at the corresponding period of last year now have only from 350 to 500; this is in spite of the fact that the other lines are carrying more than last year at the same time. A significant fact in relation to the above is that when I began the inspection, in February, 80 per cent of the steerage passengers were booked direct to United States points; now, only about 40 per cent. Persons booked to the United States are refused passage if rejected; persons booked to Canadian points are allowed passage even if rejected. The Beaver line is not in the passenger conference and carries steerage passengers for about £4 from Liverpool to Canada, which is about 30s. less than the regular rate; consequently the class of passengers is very poor. The Allan line passengers are the usual good class of Liverpool emigrants.

I made my first inspection of Canadian passengers on February 5. Below will be found the numbers, rejection, etc. I have given the two lines separate in order to emphasize the difference in the class of passengers:

Allan line:
Number of ships inspected 19
Number of passengers inspected 4,553
Total number advised rejection 10
Cause of rejection—
   Trachoma 3
   Favus 6
   Other causes 1
Percentage of passengers rejected 0.2
Percentage of rejected persons allowed by company to embark 40
Beaver line:
Number of ships inspected 21
Number of passengers inspected 9,950
Total number advised rejection 230
Cause of rejection—
   Trachoma 79
   Favus 142
   Other causes 9
Percentage of passengers rejected 2.31
Percentage of rejected persons allowed by company to embark 30

INSPECTION AT EUROPEAN PORTS.   693

Summary:
   Total number of passengers examined.. 14,503
   Total number rejected... 240
   Percentage of persons examined rejected.. 1.65

*   *   *   *   *   *   *

In regard to the inspection at foreign ports for the Immigration Bureau, I will say that if all the lines could be made to agree to the inspection and would act fairly, agreeing to refuse passage to all persons rejected, it would be a most excellent thing. The value of the present inspection in Liverpool of Canadian passengers is, in my opinion, small on account of the lack of cooperation of all the lines concerned, and I believe the best interests would be served by a discontinuance of the work.
   Respectfully,
                                                   JOHN F. ANDERSON,
                                                Assistant Surgeon, M. H. S.

REPORT OF DR. VICTOR G. HEISER, DETAILED AT QUEBEC TO EXAMINE EUROPEAN IMMIGRANTS DESTINED FOR THE UNITED STATES.

                                   OFFICE OF COMMISSIONER OF IMMIGRATION,
                                         Port of Quebec, Canada, August 7, 1901.
   DEAR MR. POWDERLY: Through the kindness of Mr. Thomas, I have seen the letter of Dr. Anderson of July 15, ultimo, in which he states that his work in Liverpool scarcely justifies the cost. For your information I would state that we are of the opinion here that the medical inspection at Liverpool does us more harm than good, because it gives the steamship companies the advantage of an expert opinion as to whether a given immigrant can pass the United States inspection. When they are informed that an immigrant will probably not pass they book him to a Canadian point. Of this fact we have ample evidence. We have not yet had an instance of one of these cases presenting themselves at the United States inspection after being rejected by Dr. Anderson, but on several occasions I have gone among the Canadian immigrants and detected cases of trachoma which, upon further investigation, were found to have been rejected (advised) by Dr. Anderson. Upon cross-questioning these cases it was soon learned that the immigrant had no intention of remaining in Canada, but would go to their destination in the United States at the earliest possible opportunity, and that they had only booked to Canada because they had been advised to do so. In view of the foregoing facts it seems reasonable to assume that if there was no inspection at Liverpool, many of the cases would not be forewarned, and consequently would present themselves at the inspection here, and thus give this office a better opportunity to prevent them from going over the border.
   About a week ago I transmitted to the Marine-Hospital Service a report of the transactions of the service here from the commencement of the inspection, on May 20, to the ending of the fiscal year. I thought it well to mention this, because you might want some of the figures in preparing the annual report.
   Yours, sincerely,   VICTOR G. HEISER.

                                   OFFICE OF COMMISSIONER OF IMMIGRATION,
                                         Port of Quebec, Canada, June 30, 1901.
SUPERVISING SURGEON-GENERAL, MARINE-HOSPITAL SERVICE,
                            Washington, D. C.
   SIR: I have the honor to transmit herewith the report of the transactions of the medical division of the immigration service at this port from the commencement of the medical inspection, on May 20, ultimo, to the ending of the fiscal year, June 30, 1901
   During this period there were inspected 3,626 immigrants; passed, 3,575; detained, 51. The cause of the detention and the final disposition of the cases is shown in the medical and surgical report herewith inclosed.
   The conditions under which the inspection must be made are very unsatisfactory and a thorough inspection under the present arrangement is impossible. A new building is under construction and will probably be ready for occupancy about August 1. The Canadian officials kindly consented to make the interior arrangement of the building conform to the ideas of the service here. When the building is completed the facilities for making the inspection will compare favorably with any of those contained at the first-class immigrant stations in the United States.
   Much difficulty has been experienced with the hospital cases—in the first place, to induce hospitals to accept them, and, in the second place, to detain them after they have been accepted. Lately we have not had so much trouble in this direction, and it is believed that as the matter is better understood, the difficulty will disappear.
   Respectfully,   VICTOR G. HEISER,
                                                   Assistant Surgeon, M. H. S.

CHAPTER XII.
LEGISLATION OF FOREIGN COUNTRIES AFFECTING EMIGRATION AND IMMIGRATION.

GERMANY.

In general, European countries, from which the largest number of immigrants come to the United States, have during the past 50 years permitted free and voluntary emigration. Notwithstanding the evident losses to those countries in the fact that emigration takes the more active and productive members and leaves the aged and weaker, yet only in one particular have these governments placed restrictions on emigration, namely, those who attempt to escape their military duties. The German legislation of 1897, however, marks an innovation, if not a reversal of this policy. In the law of June 9, 1897, taking effect April 1, 1898, emigration is looked upon as a matter of national importance and as a means for extending the power of Germany and the influence of German institutions into other lands. Three purposes are sought to be served by this law:[1]

First. Protection for the emigrant in the purchase of his ticket and his transportation to foreign lands.

Second. Additional protection on the part of the fatherland for the emigrant in the country of his settlement.

Third. The maintenance of the German spirit and German institutions among the emigrants, particularly by diverting emigration away from certain countries not suitable, and directing it toward other countries where the circumstances are more favorable.

The latter object takes practical shape in the effort to divert emigration from North America to South America. It is argued that in North America conditions are not suitable for the customs, the spirit, language, and institutions of the fatherland, since the emigrants are rapidly assimilated, and are even transformed into competitors of the agriculture and industry of their native land. On the other hand, in South America, especially in south Brazil and Argentina, the climatic, agricultural, and other conditions are favorable, and there the emigrants even find occupation in branches of German industry, and they continue commercial and political relations with the home country. The practical device of the law whereby this diversion of emigration to South America and to German colonies is effected is through the licensing of companies and persons, who are permitted to solicit emigrants and transport them across the water. This license is granted by the chancellor of the Empire on the ratification of the Bundesrath, and while the law does not designate the countries for which the license is applicable, yet the intention is that the chancellor shall grant licenses only to those companies who conduct emigration to South America and the German colonies. In order that the company which conducts the emigration shall be amenable to the German laws it must have at least one member who is a German subject, and must make deposit of 50,000 marks as a security out of which penalties shall be paid. (Section 5.) The license designates the ports and countries to which the operations of the licensee may be conducted, and countries not mentioned are excluded from the field of operation. All agents of the company or society are required to have a license and to limit their solicitations to the territory designated therein. Licenses can be revoked at any time on proper ground, or in view of violation of their condition. (Section 13.)

Persons prohibited from migration are those between the ages of 17 and 25, who have not completed their military service; persons who are subject to judicial or police proceedings, and all subjects of the Empire for whom a foreign government or a foreign colonization society, or similar enterprise, has paid in whole or in part the cost of passage. To this latter class exceptions may be made by the chancellor in favor of those countries to which it is desired that emigration be diverted. The prohibition against prepaid transportation does not apply to those who have received passage money from Germans residing in a foreign country. (Stoerk, p. 100.) This

---
[1] Stoerk, Das Re' hsgesetz über das Auswanderungswesen vom 9. Juni 1897, Berlin, 1899, p. 28.

permits such emigration to the United States, although licenses are not granted to this country.

There are many provisions in the law protecting the emigrant in the fulfillment of the contract entered into with the transporting agency and providing for safeguards in the transit, for accommodations, and for food supplies.

EMIGRATION LAW OF JUNE 9, 1897.

[Translation.]

I.—*Contractors.*

SECTION 1. Permission is required to forward emigrants.

SEC. 2. Giving or refusing this permission belongs to the chancellor of the Empire, with the consent of the Bundesrath.

SEC. 3. In general, permission is only to be given to—
(*a*) Citizens of, and in business in, the German Empire;
(*b*) Mercantile associations, joint stock companies, etc., whose headquarters are in the Empire; and business firms, branch business firms, and stock companies whose responsible stockholders are citizens of the Empire.

SEC. 4. To foreigners and citizens of the Empire who are established in business outside of the German Empire, permission can only be given—
(*a*) If they empower a German citizen residing in the Empire to represent them judicially in the matter of forwarding emigrants and in dealing with the authorities;
(*b*) If they subject themselves to German law and courts in case of controversies arising from the acceptance and forwarding of emigrants.

SEC. 5. Before permission is given the applicant has to deposit securities for at least 50,000 marks ($11,900), and if intending to undertake a transoceanic forwarding business he must prove that he is a shipowner.

SEC. 6. Permission is to be given only for particular countries, and portions of such, or particular places, and in case of transoceanic forwarding only for particular ports of entry.

SEC. 7. In case permission is requested by German societies whose object it is to procure settlers for lands acquired by them in transoceanic countries, the chancellor of the Empire is not bound by the conditions of section 5; for particular reasons, however, exceptions can be made.

SEC. 8. Permission entitles the grantee to do business throughout the German Empire, with the following restrictions: Outside of the communality of his place of business and that of his branch offices 'he has—as far as concerns more than giving information to inquiries and the publication of conditions and forwarding opportunities—to avail himself of the assistance of agents, as provided in section 11.

SEC. 9. The grantee can have substitutes to transact his business. The appointment of such is necessary for the establishment of branch offices. After the death of a grantee, and in case of guardianship, the carrying on of the business can only be continued by the substitute for six months. The appointment of a substitute has to be approved by the chancellor of the Empire

SEC. 10. The permission given to grantees can, with the consent of the Bundesrath, be revoked at any time by the chancellor. The permission of the appointment of a substitute can be revoked by the chancellor at any time.

II.—*Agencies.*

SEC. 11. Whoever desires to assist in the manner described in section 1 by preparing and contracting the forwarding of emigrants requires permission therefor.

SEC. 12. This permission is given by high administrative authority.

SEC. 13. Permission can only be granted to citizens of the Empire who reside or do business within the district of this high administrative authority (section 12). This permission can not be granted even under compliance with the above requirements—
(*a*) If facts are known which prove the unreliability of the applicant;
(*b*) If permission has already been granted (section 15) to a number of persons considered sufficient for the proportion of the district by the authorities thereof.

SEC. 14. Before permission is granted, the applicant has to give security for at least 1,500 marks ($357).

SEC. 15. Permission to do business in the district of the authority granting the same, if the same is not limited to a part thereof only, can be given; with the consent 'of this authority, the extension of the business into neighboring districts can be granted to the agent by the authorities of such districts.

SEC. 16. Agents can not transact business of the kind mentioned in section 11 for persons other than those mentioned in the instrument of permission, or for their own account.

Sec. 17. Agents can not carry on business in branch offices by substitutes or in traveling about.

Sec. 18. Permission granted to agents can at any time be limited or revoked. Permission must be revoked—

(a) If the requirements of section 13 are not complied with;

(b) When facts exist which prove the unreliability of the agents in regard to business transactions;

(c) If securities, in part or wholly, have been applied to cover claims and are not replaced within four weeks after being called for.

Sec. 19. Complaint against the ordinances of the authorities based on sections 11, 15, and 18, can be entered at the supervising authority within two weeks.

III.—*Ordinances for grantees and their agents.*

Sec. 20. The securities deposited by grantees and their agents serve for all liabilities, fines, and costs arising from their business transactions with emigrants and with the authorities.

Sec. 21. The Bundesrath issues the necessary regulations about the management of the business of principals and agents, particularly—

(a) About the books and registers to be kept, statistics and other records, as well as the blank forms to be used;

(b) About the manner of giving security and the conditions which are to be entered in the bond concerning the liability and supplementing and restoring the securities.

IV.—*Forwarding emigrants.*

Sec. 22. The grantee is permitted to forward emigrants only on the basis of a previously executed written contract. The emigrants can not be placed under obligation to pay or refund the whole or part of the passage money, or to refund or work out any advances made to them, after their arrival at the place of destination; neither can they be restricted in the selection of their occupations or places of residence in the foreign land.

Sec. 23. The forwarding and making contracts to forward—

(a) Of persons owing military duty of the age beginning with 17 and ending with 25 years, before they have procured a certificate of discharge (section 14 of the law, about acquiring and losing German citizenship, of June 1, 1870) or a certificate of the commission for substitutes, showing that their military duty does not interfere with their emigration;

(b) Of persons whose arrest has been ordered by any court or police authority;

(c) Of German citizens for whom the passage money has been paid wholly or in part, or who have received advances from foreign governments or colonial societies or similar agents, are prohibited. (Exceptions to this can be granted by the chancellor of the Empire.)

Sec. 24. Emigrants who do not possess the necessary certificates mentioned in section 23, or who belong to the class of persons mentioned in b and c of the same section, may be prosecuted by the police authorities. The police authorities in the seaports are authorized to prosecute those who ship persons whose forwarding is prohibited by this law.

V.—*Regulations for emigration to trans-European countries.*

Sec. 25. Contracts for forwarding emigrants must include transportation and board to the foreign port of landing. The same is to be extended to the transportation and boarding from the port of landing until the place of destination, as required by the granting of permission (section 1). If the emigrants take passage in a foreign shipping port (not German), or if a change of ships has to take place, these must be mentioned in the contract.

Sec. 26. The sale of passage tickets to emigrants from a transoceanic place is forbidden. This prohibition does not apply, however, to contracts under which the grantee agrees to forward the emigrants from transoceanic ports.

Sec. 27. The contractor is obliged to board and lodge the emigrants at the appointed place of forwarding or shipping, without cost, if the delay of departure is not caused by the emigrants.

Sec. 28. If the delay lasts longer than a week the emigrant has, without prejudicing his claim for damages, the right to withdraw from the contract and to demand the restitution of his passage money.

Sec. 29. The restitution of the passage money can be demanded also if the emigrant or any member of his family accompanying him should die before the beginning of the sea voyage, or if he can prove that by sickness or other circumstances beyond his control he is prevented from undertaking the sea voyage. The same refers to cases concerning the restitution of the corresponding part of the passage money where, according to section 26, the forwarding from a transoceanic port of landing is prevented. One-half of the passage money can be demanded if the emigrant withdraws from the contract for other reasons before the voyage begins.

SEC. 30. Should the ship by accident or any other cause be prevented from continuing the voyage, or by such causes is delayed on the voyage, the contractor (section 1) is bound to furnish the emigrants sufficient lodging and board, and to forward them and their baggage to the place of destination as soon as possible. This ordinance applies also to the forwarding from the transoceanic port of landing (section 26).

SEC. 31. Agreements contrary to the conditions of sections 27–30 have no legal force.

SEC. 32. The contractor can be compelled to insure his obligations arising from the sections 27–30, in a sum exceeding by one-half the amount of the passage money, or to deposit an amount sufficient to cover this sum.

SEC. 33. Contractors are responsible for the seaworthiness of the ships by which the emigrants are conveyed, as well as for their proper provisioning, as prescribed by law. These obligations also rest upon the commanders of the ships.

SEC. 34. Every emigrant ship, before entering upon its voyage, is subject to inspection as to its seaworthiness, outfitting arrangement, and supplies of provisions. This examination is conducted by official inspectors appointed by the respective governments.

SEC. 35. Before leaving port the emigrants and ship's crew must be examined as to their health by a physician appointed by the emigration authorities (section 40).

SEC. 36. The Bundesrath creates ordinances covering the condition, arrangement, outfit, and supplying with provisions of emigrant ships, the official inspection and control of the same, and the sanitary inspection of the passengers and crews before embarkation, the exclusion of sick people, the management of embarkation, and the protection of emigrants in regard to health and morality. The ordinances promulgated by the Bundesrath are to be published in the law paper of the Empire, and to be submitted to the Reichstag at its next sitting.

SEC. 37. As emigrant ships, in the sense of the law, are to be considered all vessels sailing to trans-European seaports and carrying—not considering the cabin passengers—at least twenty-five passengers.

VI.—*Authorities of emigration.*

SEC. 38. For the assistance of the chancellor in executing the duties and rights pertaining to his office in regard to emigration affairs a council of competent persons, consisting of a president and at least fourteen members, is created. The president is appointed by the Emperor, and the members are elected by the Bundesrath. Every two years a new election of members takes place. In general, the organization of the council is regulated by the Bundesrath, and its actions by a self-made order of business.

SEC. 39. This council must be consulted before permission is granted for enterprises the object of which is the settlement of particular parts of transoceanic countries, as well as in limiting or revoking the privileges of a contractor. Besides this, the Reichskanzler may bring before this council, for consideration, proper and important questions about emigration, and motions can be brought by the council before the Reichskanzler.

SEC. 40. For the supervision of emigration and the proper execution of the ordinances thereof, emigration authorities are to be appointed by the respective governments in seaports where contractors have received permission to transact business.

SEC. 41. In the seaport the Reichskanzler causes the supervision of emigration by commissioners appointed by himself. These commissioners are empowered to assist in the inspections provided for in section 34; also to undertake independent inspection of emigrant ships. They have to call the attention of the authorities to discovered discrepancies and offenses and insist upon their being remedied. The commanders of emigrant ships are compelled to give the commissioners, when asked for, a truthful statement about all the circumstances connected with the ship and the voyage, and to permit them at any time to enter the ship's rooms and examine the ship's papers. In foreign countries the duties of the commissioners for the protection of the emigrants are executed by the authorities of the Empire, to whom, if necessary, assistant commissioners can be attached.

VII.—*Forwarding from ports outside of Germany.*

SEC. 42. By order of the Emperor, the Bundesrath concurring, for the regulation of forwarding emigrants and passengers in German vessels sailing from other than German ports, ordinances of the kind mentioned in section 36 can be issued.

LEGISLATION OF FOREIGN COUNTRIES. 699

VIII.—*Fines.*

SEC. 43. Contractors who contravene the ordinances of sections 8, 22, 23, 25, 32, and 33, or the conditions to which the management of their business is subjected by the competent authorities, are liable to a fine of 150 to 6,000 marks ($35.70 to $1,428) or imprisonment up to six months. If the contraventions have been committed by an agent (section 9), the latter is fined; the contractor is also fined if the contravention has been committed with his knowledge, or if he has failed in the necessary care and supervision of his agent as far as it was possible under the circumstances. The same fine is imposed upon commanders of ships who fail in the duties under sections 33 and 41, or who contravene the ordinances issued under section 36, whether the contravention may have been committed in the inland or in foreign countries.

SEC. 44. Agents (section 44) who contravene the ordinances of sections 15, 16, 17, 22, 23, and 25, covering the regulations issued for the management of their business by the competent authorities, are subjected to a fine of from 30 to 3,000 marks ($7.14 to $714) or of imprisonment up to three months.

SEC. 45. Anyone forwarding emigrants without permission under sections 1 and 11, or assisting in such business, is fined with imprisonment up to one year and in the penal sum of 6,000 marks ($1,428), or with either of these fines. The same fine is imposed upon those who make it a business to induce emigration.

SEC. 46. Whoever contravenes the ordinance of section 26 is punished with a fine up to 100 marks ($23.80) or with imprisonment.

SEC. 47. Contravening the ordinances of section 42 is punished with a fine of from 150 to 6,000 marks ($35.70 to $1,428), or with imprisonment up to six months.

SEC. 48. Whoever induces a female to emigrate with a purpose of prostitution, by concealing this purpose, is subject to imprisonment up to five years. Besides the jail punishment, the loss of civil honor and rights is pronounced, at the same time a fine of 150 to 6,000 marks ($37.50 to $1,428). Subjection to police supervision can be imposed. The same punishment is imposed where persons induce female emigration for purposes of prostitution, even where the purposes are made known to such females. Under mitigating circumstances the punishment may be reduced to not less than three months' imprisonment and a fine of 150 to 6,000 marks ($35.70 to $1,428).

Final ordinances.

SEC. 49. The central authority of the Bundesrath will designate the authorities meant by supervising, administrative, and police authorities.

SEC. 50. This law will go into force April 1, 1898, and at the same time all ordinances issued under various laws of states for the permission of forwarding emigrants or assisting in same.

ITALY.

The Italian legislation of January 31, 1901, is modeled closely after that of Germany. It provides for the appointment of a commissioner of emigration and subordinate officers, makes regulations for the protection of the emigrant and his support in case of delay on the part of the steamship company, provides a penalty for false advertisements, and makes provision for the location of employment agencies in the countries to which immigration is most largely attracted. The obligation for military service continues abroad, but may be temporarily suspended during such residence. Italian citizenship is granted by decree to the sons of Italians born abroad or attaining majority abroad (cl. 33). The following is a translation of the Italian law:

ITALIAN LAW OF JANUARY 31, 1901, REGULATING EMIGRATION.

[Translation.]

SEC. I.—*On emigration in general.*

CLAUSE 1. Emigration within the limits prescribed by the existing laws is free.

All men liable to military service having completed or who shall within the year complete their eighteenth year of age, those entered for the naval service, and the soldiers of the corps of royal marines, may emigrate on obtaining due permission, in respect to the first from the prefect or subprefect, to the second from the port captain, and to the last from the commander of the corps.

All military men belonging to the first category of the army, not having completed their twenty-eighth year of age, may emigrate on obtaining permission from the district commandant, to whom proof must be afforded of being within one of the conditions to be specified in the code of regulations.

The emigration of soldiers belonging to the second and third category of the army and navy is free.

The emigration of soldiers of the first category belonging to the army is likewise free, on completing their twenty-eighth year of age, but until the completion of their thirty-second year of age same shall give due notice of their departure to the district commandant. Such notice to be drawn up on unstamped paper, free of charge, as prescribed by the code of regulations.

Such power to emigrate granted to soldiers by the foregoing paragraphs may in exceptional cases be temporarily withdrawn by royal decree on the proposal of the ministers of war and navy.

The minister for foreign affairs, acting in concert with the minister of the interior, has power to suspend all emigration to a given locality on public grounds, or whenever the life, liberty, and property of the emigrant be endangered thereby.

CLAUSE 2. Anyone enrolling, conducting, or sending abroad children under fifteen years of age to be employed in labour, without causing same to be submitted to medical examination and supplied with a mayor's certificate, in accordance with Clause 3 of the regulations on infant labour, September 17, 1886, shall be punishable with a pecuniary fine as prescribed in clause 4 of the act of 11th February, 1886, No. 3657.

CLAUSE 3. Anyone enrolling or receiving in charge within the Kingdom one or more children under fifteen for employment abroad, in itinerant professions or other trades classified in the code of regulations as being injurious to the health or dangerous, shall be punishable with confinement extending to six months, and a fine of one hundred to five hundred lire.

Same penalty shall be inflicted on anyone who shall conduct or send abroad, or consign to third parties for conveyance abroad, children under fifteen years of age for employment as stated in the first part of this clause. In such cases the guardian shall forfeit his guardianship and the parent may be deprived of his paternal rights.

Same provisions shall apply to anyone who shall induce a female under age to emigrate, to lead her to a life of prostitution.

CLAUSE 4. Anyone who in a foreign country shall forsake children under seventeen years of age, committed to their charge within the Kingdom for employment, shall be punishable with a term of confinement extending to one year, and a fine of three hundred to one thousand lire, irrespective of higher penalties in case of ill-treatment and bodily injury.

Should the child not have completed its fourteenth year, the penalty shall be increased by one-half.

The accused, subject or foreigner, shall be prosecuted on demand of the minister of justice or by an action brought by the party; and wheresoever same shall have been previously convicted abroad for the same offence the provisions of clauses 7 and 8 of the penal code shall be applicable.

CLAUSE 5. The competent authorities shall transmit all applications for passports, and deliver same within twenty-four hours from receipt of such application, or voucher, with all documents required by regulations on the delivery of foreign passports.

All passports delivered to emigrants going abroad in search of employment, or to their families, and all deeds required for procuring same, are free from stamp or other dues.

SEC. II.—*On emigration to transoceanic countries.*

CLAUSE 6. Emigrants within the meaning of this present section are all subjects proceeding to countries lying beyond the Suez Canal, exclusive of the colonies and Italian protectorates, or to any country situated beyond the Straits of Gibraltar, the coast of Europe excluded, travelling third class or in such class as the emigrant commissariat shall declare equivalent to our present third class.

Emigrants not being Italian subjects taking passage in any port of the Kingdom are treated as subjects even in respect to provisions of clauses 21, 26, and 27, but same shall not be able to avail themselves of the assistance of the protection offices referred to in clause 12.

No passport is required by such as are not Italian subjects.

All passengers leaving of their own free will, and at their own charge, in third class or its equivalent, on board of Italian or foreign steamers, and journeying beyond the Suez Canal, will not be considered as emigrants unless such as are Italian subjects shall exceed fifty in number. When same shall exceed fifty a special permit of the commissariat will be required before same can be recognized as nonemigrants.

This rule can be suspended by royal decree.

Power is given to the minister for foreign affairs to provide by special arrangements for the protection of emigration which might be effected through the agency of sailing vessels.

Of the commissariat and its subordinate offices.

CLAUSE 7. Subject to the control of the foreign office department, a commissariat shall be appointed, to which all matters pertaining to emigration shall be referred.

Said commissariat of emigration to consist of a commissioner-general chosen among the higher state officials nominated by the minister for foreign affairs with the approval of the council of ministers, three commissioners appointed in accordance with the forms to be fixed in the code of regulations, and such other clerks as the service may require.

The salaries and indemnities of the members of the commissariat will be fixed by royal decree. Should same be chosen from any government office, same shall retain their rank and service rights to which same would be entitled in the department to which same belonged, and to which same can always return with the rank and years of service which same would have attained had they remained therein.

A board of emigration will moreover be formed, to consist of the commissioner-general as delegate of the foreign office department; five delegates of the departments of the interior, treasury, navy, public instruction, and agriculture; three members appointed by royal decree on the proposal of the minister for foreign affairs and chosen among such persons as shall have made the science of geography, statistics, and economy their special study; two members to be chosen in the manner prescribed by the regulations from among Italian subjects resident in Rome, one by the national league of Italian cooperative societies, and the other by the leading mutual aid societies of the chief towns of the Kingdom.

Said council shall be consulted in all matters of importance concerning emigration and in the transaction of business pertaining to various Government departments.

CLAUSE 8. Said commissariat is in correspondence with the authorities of the Kingdom, with emigration departments of other states, and with all other institutions, home or foreign, interested in the protection of emigrants.

Same shall have right to the free posting of its notices in every station or agency, on steamers, vans, and other means of transport by sea or land.

Each year, and not later than the month of April, the minister for foreign affairs shall present to Parliament a general report on emigration, accompanied by a report of the commissioner-general on the state of emigration, permanent or temporary, on the operations of carriers and their agents, on alterations in the existing regulations suggested by experience, and on all other matters concerning emigration.

Such report to be entered in the order of the day of the next sitting for discussion and adoption thereof.

CLAUSE 9. The minister for foreign affairs, in concert with the minister of the interior, shall appoint in the ports of Genoa, Naples, and Palermo, and in such other towns as shall be determined by royal decree, an emigration inspector, invested also with the quality of police officer, and selected from the staff of the department of the interior.

Said inspector shall act in the manner prescribed by the regulations, and shall superintend the care and inspection of passengers' luggage both on their departure and return.

CLAUSE 10. In all places where emigration exists, district or commune committees of emigration, unpaid, may be appointed, to consist of the chief magistrate (prator), or, failing such, of the petty judge, or the mayor or his deputy, of the parish priest or other minister of religion, of a doctor (the three latter to be appointed by the commissariat), and of a representative of the local trade or agricultural societies, chosen by the town council.

All elective members to retain office for three years and to be reeligible.

Said committee to be presided by the chief magistrate or in his absence by the mayor.

CLAUSE 11. On all ships carrying emigrants, the doctor, or one of the doctors on board, shall belong to the royal naval medical staff, on active duty on half pay, same to be appointed by the minister of marine on demand of the commissariat. Such doctors to be likewise charged with the duty of exercising their vigilance on board in the interests of emigration, in accordance with the rules to be enjoined by the code of regulations. Same shall be paid from the emigration fund to which the carrier shall pay in all amounts due to same in such proportion as will be established by the regulations.

The carrier is under obligation to provide such doctors, on the return journey as well, with board and first-class cabin free of charge.

CL. 12. In all States to which Italian emigration is more preferably attracted special offices will be opened by the minister for foreign affairs, and whenever necessary by arrangement with the respective governments for the purpose of affording protection, information, and assistance in procuring employment.

The minister for foreign affairs shall appoint, in accordance with rules to be fixed by regulations, travelling emigration inspectors in all transoceanic countries. Same shall have power to delegate such duty to consular officials as well.

Such inspectors shall report to commissariat on the conditions of Italian emigration the requirements of which same shall duly note and transmit.

In all ports, whether of transit or destination, regular inspections will be made on board of ships conveying emigrants by travelling inspectors or consular officials, in accordance with rules to be fixed by regulations.

On carriers of emigrants and freights.

CL. 13. No one shall enrol or engage with emigrants or promise or sell passage tickets without having first obtained from the commissariat a licence as carrier of emigrants, and a further special licence of said commissariat, subject to required security, in the case of emigrants having a free or partly free ticket, or in whatsoever other manner favoured or enrolled.

Such licences in the case of owners or otherwise of steamers fulfilling all requirements of clause 32 will be granted to—

(a) Italian steamship companies;
(b) Foreign steamship companies duly recognized within the Kingdom, in accordance with clause 230 and following of commercial code;
(c) Italian shipowners trading individually or collectively;
(d) Foreign shipowners and home and foreign freight owners.

All deeds of formation of foreign steamship companies shall, proportionately to the amount of respective capital, shall be subject to a fixed registration fee of five hundred to three thousand lire. Subsequent deeds authorizing increase of capital will be registered on payment of a fixed duty, amount of which shall be in proportion to duty paid on deed of formation, with regard to original capital of the company.

Such licences will be granted to foreign companies, shipowners, and freight owners only on condition that same shall appoint as their agent an Italian subject resident in the Kingdom, or a legally registered Italian firm, and that same shall submit to all laws and regulations of the Kingdom in all that concerns emigration operations and consequent acts.

Such licenses to be valid for one year, and subject on every renewal to a grant fee of one thousand lire, and guaranteed by a deposit in Government shares to the amount of three thousand lire or more of interest value, to be fixed by the minister for foreign affairs in proportion to the importance of the transaction.

All applications for such licenses shall imply full acceptance of all duties devolving on the carrier by effect of this law.

The minister for foreign affairs, under advice of the council of emigration, has power by substantiated decree to refuse, limit, or withdraw such licence.

Such deposit is held primarily as a guarantee for the due fulfilment of all obligations of the carrier or his agent in respect to emigrants and their representatives; and secondly, for due payment of all pecuniary fines incurred by said carrier or his agent by reason of such law. Such deposit to be made up to original amount whenever same shall have undergone any reduction, under pain of forfeiture of licence; same to be restored, saving in the case of pending judgement, six months after such carrier shall have ceased to act as such.

CL. 14. All freight charges which carriers propose to exact from emigrants shall be subject to approval of said commissariat.

Not later than November 15, March 15, and July 15 of each year such carriers shall forward their respective tenders to said commissariat. Same shall duly provide for approval of such freight rates, under advice of the chief department of the mercantile navy, and the boards of trade of the leading Italian maritime cities, with due regard to all information supplied by emigrant inspectors and Italian boards of trade in the principal centres of Italian emigration; as well as of such respecting rate of freights in all leading foreign ports, drawn from periodical reports to be supplied by Italian consular agents.

Whenever a tender is not accepted the commissariat is under obligation to invite the carrier to afford explanations within a reasonable term, upon which same shall forward all documents, together with substantiated proposals, to the higher naval board which shall duly express its opinion on the case. Thereupon the minister for foreign affairs shall fix the freight charges with due reference to the transports to be effected and the class and rate of speed of steamships.

Both in respect to freight rates duly accepted and of such as are by him established the minister for foreign affairs shall give notice to Parliament by means of special report, to which all such opinions and information aforesaid shall be annexed.

As a rule the scale of freight charges shall be fixed every four months, viz, on January 1st, May 1st, and September 1st of each year, and shall remain valid for the ensuing term of four months. Power is reserved, however, whenever necessary, on the proposal of the carriers or at the request of the commissariat to alter such charges, and during such term, with the same forms with which they were originally fixed, and under same form of procedure power is reserved even within such term of four months to fix freight charges to be required of new carriers.

All freight rates to be made public not more than fifteen days prior to their application, and in the case of an extraordinary revision within the shortest time possible.

Said commissariat shall notify such rate of freights thus agreed on to all committees, district and communal, and likewise notifying to same all tenders for transport at lower rates of all carriers so requesting, and to whom in default of local representatives of such carriers. Said committees shall direct all emigrants through the medium of emigration inspectors aforesaid.

All carriers exceeding the freight rates settled and agreed upon, or who shall refuse to carry emigrants at such rate, shall be deprived of their respective licences, which shall not be restored except by decision of the minister for foreign affairs.

Said carriers shall not have power to raise the scale of freights charged to emigrants already publicly notified, or stated on passage ticket, or by equivalent entry.

Whenever a reduction on the rates made public or agreed upon is intended such reduction to be extended to all emigrants shipped for same passage.

CL. 15. In the event of a coalition between carriers to refuse the transport of emigrants at the rate fixed and agreed upon Government is empowered to authorize local committees to act in place of the agents of such carriers; and shall have power, by special concessions to other companies, shipowners, or freight owners, home or foreign, to authorize the shipping of emigrants, and the transshipment in foreign ports on this side of the ocean, and to employ all other suitable means for the protection of emigration.

Such cases occurring the carrier will be deprived of his licence, nor shall same be restored except by duly substantiated decision of the council of ministers. In case of second offence the licence to be finally withdrawn.

CL. 16. All carriers of emigrants may, by letter addressed to the commissariat, who shall take the advice of the competent magistrate, appoint personal agents, for whose actions in matters concerning emigration same shall be civilly responsible. Same to be likewise responsible for all acts of his subordinates, as well as of other carriers or any other person to whom same shall have entrusted, with or without the connivance or consent of the emigrant the transport thereof, wholly or in part. All conditions excluding or restricting such responsibility, even when accompanied by a reduction in the freight charges, shall be void.

Power is given to commissariat to refuse by substantiated decree its assent to the appointment of an agent, and by a similar decree to revoke an assent already granted.

Such agents shall be Italian subjects, and will not be allowed to delegate their power to other persons.

By mutual arrangement, to be notified to commissariat, several carriers may appoint one sole agent.

Agents are strictly forbidden to procure shipment for emigrants on vessels other than those of their own principal or principals.

CL. 17. The carrier and his agents are forbidden to entice emigration in public.

All prescriptions of clause 416 of penal code being maintained, whosoever shall by means of public notices, circulars, or guidebooks concerning emigration, wantonly spread false news or information, or shall distribute within the Kingdom news and information of a like nature published abroad, shall be punished with a term of confinement extending to six months and a fine extensible to one thousand lire.

All circulars and notices of whatsoever kind issued by carriers shall indicate gross and net tonnage and average speed of steamships, date of departure, landing ports, and duration of the entire outward journey.

CL. 18. The minister for foreign affairs in concert with the minister of the interior has power, under special conditions, to allow any private individual to enroll on his sole account any number of persons as he may require for the execution of any given work abroad, or for any colonial undertaking allowed by the laws of the country in which it is to be carried out, on condition that such individual, in the case of emigration to countries referred to in clause 6, shall employ the services of a licensed carrier for the transport and that such carrier shall pay the duty fixed in clause 28.

In the case of journeys to countries unfrequented or slightly visited by Italians, the minister of foreign affairs has power to allow under given conditions, that the shipment be made by shipowner not possessing the qualification of carrier of emigrants.

CL. 19. No carrier or his agent shall deliver passage tickets to Italian emigrants unless same are able to produce passports.

To all emigrants favoured, enrolled, or leaving of their own free will, having arranged for their passage in any place other than the place of abode of such carrier, same or his agent are bound to provide passage tickets not exchangeable for other document until such emigrant has quitted his place of abode for the port of embarcation.

Exception made for carriers authorized by the commissariat: All are forbidden to deliver orders whereby emigrants are to be supplied with railway tickets in their country of destination, unless such tickets be free and deliverable at time and place of departure.

All passage tickets for the use of emigrants, considered as such in accordance with clause 6, are free of stamp and registry duty.

CL. 20. Any ticket sold abroad by any carrier or by others on his account, and made out in the name of any emigrant embarking within the Kingdom, shall entitle such emigrant (on favorable report of emigration inspector of the port of departure) to accommodation on board of the first steamer belonging to such carrier leaving place of destination shown on the ticket, in spite of all contrary declaration contained in such ticket.

All provisions of this present law shall equally apply to all emigrants traveling under the conditions provided for by this clause.

CL. 21. All carriers and their representatives are forbidden to receive from emigrants any gratuities of whatsoever nature over and above the passage money; said emigrants to have right to restitution of double the amounts unduly paid, and compensation for any damages.

All passage money wholly or in part prepaid by any emigrant for himself or his own family shall be refunded, should same be prevented from starting owing to certified illness of self or any member of his family living with or to travel with same; or owing to railway delay, or under any circumstances accidental or otherwise ascribable to carrier or vessel.

In all cases of emigration however favoured or enrolled, and whenever such emigrant for any of above reasons or owing to same not being accepted by party having ordered his enrollment, or because of his rejection by inspection committee, shall be under the necessity of returning from port of embarcation to his home, or to the frontier in the case of foreigners, said carrier to defray all expenses for sheltering, maintaining, and journeying of such persons, as well as transport of baggage, saving all rights of such emigrants to compensation for damages, if any.

Moreover, when for any other reason whatsoever and prior to the departure of the vessel said emigrant shall rescind his contract, all provisions of clause 583, No. 2 of commercial code, being duly observed, same to be entitled with the approval of emigration inspector to the restitution of a moiety of the passage money, besides cost of nourishment for the estimated duration of the journey, wherever same have been included in the passage money.

Finally, should said emigrant, to whatsoever category he may belong, have lost his passage through delay of a train, even when owing to circumstances beyond control, the railway companies to be under obligation to convey same and his baggage back to his station of departure, or frontier station in the case of a foreigner, whenever same shall personally apply for and obtain from the emigration inspector a duly certified order for a pass, to be presented within twenty-four hours at the starting office.

CL. 22. The cost of nourishing and lodging all emigrants on their arrival at their port of embarcation to be chargeable to carrier from midday of the day preceding that fixed for departure as stated on ticket until such day wherein such departure shall take place, whatsoever be the cause of delays.

All emigrants to whom any delay shall have been notified after being supplied with tickets and prior to same leaving place of abode shall be entitled to an indemnity of two lire per diem whenever a full berth has been retained, and in due proportion for the half or quarter, until midnight of the day but one preceding that on which the departure shall occur.

Whenever such delay shall exceed ten days said emigrants are entitled to give up the journey, recover their passage money if already paid, and to claim from board of arbitration referred to in clause 27 compensation for damages, if any.

In all cases in which said emigrants by reason of the vessel or owing to quarantine regulations shall be under the necessity of breaking the journey at any intermediate port, the expense of feeding and, where necessary, of lodging same shall be defrayed by the carrier, who in the event of shipwreck or inability of steamer to proceed, or from stoppage due to accident exceeding fifteen days, shall be under obligation to send another steamer capable of accommodating and conveying said emigrants to the place of destination. Failing which the minister for foreign affairs, after consulting the board of emigration, shall provide accordingly from the deposit.

All agreement by which emigrants shall relinquish their claim to indemnity fixed by present clause is void and of no effect.

CL. 23. The embarcation of emigrants shall be effected by carrier in such ports as are indicated in first section of clause 9.

Reservation made for all cases beyond control: The landing of emigrants in foreign ports not situated on the other side of the ocean is forbidden, as likewise is the sending of emigrants to any non-Italian port for the purpose of embarcation. Infringements of this rule in either case and in the sole exclusive interest of said emigrants are authorized by special permission of commissariat.

CL. 24. All carriers are responsible for any loss sustained by emigrants who are prohibited from landing in the country to which same are bound in consequence of local existing laws on immigration, whenever there be satisfactory proof that such carriers were acquainted before starting with the circumstances giving origin to the prohibition aforesaid.

CL. 25. Whenever the steamer on its return journey shall touch at an Italian port, the carrier, in spite of any agreement to the contrary, is bound to convey at a daily charge of two lire a head per day, board included, all distressed Italian subjects who, to whatsoever cause owing, shall be returning to their home by arrangement and request of a diplomatic or consular agent, to the number of ten (full berths), on steamers of less than a thousand tons, with an increase of one for each additional two hundred or fraction of two hundred tons, the aggregate number of same not to exceed thirty. Children above three years and under twelve to pay one lira a day, and infants under three nothing.

On matters of dispute between carriers and emigrants.

CL. 26. Emigrants have power to institute proceedings for the recovery of sums, claims for damages, and all other matters of dispute arising from the present law, against the carrier or his agent, by application drawn up on unstamped form, addressed to a royal consular official or to any Government office for the protection of emigrants abroad, or, whenever the departure shall not have taken place, to the prefect of the province, to the emigration inspector, or to the committee of such place where the agreement was made or the embarcation was to be effected.

Such application, if abroad, to be made within six months from date of arrival at port of destination, or other port, should said emigrant have been unable to reach same; and if in the Kingdom within three months from date of departure given on the ticket.

In all cases in which said emigrants shall have been compelled to return to Italy, without having been able to communicate with any royal authority or office for protection, said term to begin from date of their landing in the Kingdom.

CL. 27. All matters of dispute arising between carrier and emigrant as per foregoing clause shall be decided, without right of appeal, by a board of arbitration established in the chief provincial town.

Said board to consist of the president of the tribunal or his deputy, who shall preside, of the royal attorney, of a councillor of the prefecture, and of two members appointed by the provincial council.

In case of impediment the president of the tribunal and royal attorney have power to appoint deputies, which in the case of the former shall be a vice-president or one of the judges, and in the case of the latter his substitute.

For the legal requirements of the proceedings the emigrant shall be held as having his abode in the prefecture to which such application shall have been made or forwarded.

Such application to be accompanied by reports and proofs drawn up or collected by consuls, protection offices, traveling commissioners, emigration inspectors, and local committees.

Said board of arbitration of the province wherein said emigrant shall have taken his passage to be competent in spite of all agreement to the contrary; same not to be bound to observance of forms and terms established for preparation of cases to be tried before the judicial authorities, or to notifying of verdict; same to render judgment in accordance with forms of procedure to be indicated in code of regulations, which shall further make provision for notifying of verdict. Thereupon said commissariat shall draw the necessary sums from amount of security and distribute same to whomsoever due in accordance with verdict.

Should such emigrants to be indemnified be abroad at the time, such sums to be delivered to commissariat, by whom same shall be duly remitted at carrier's expense.

All papers and deeds having reference to the case, including verdicts, to be exempted from stamp and registry duties.

Proceedings being concluded, the prefect shall forward all papers pertaining thereto to the royal attorney, in order that same may examine and decide if there be ground for penal prosecution.

All litigation in respect to sums or valuables not exceeding fifty lire, arising at place of embarcation, whether between emigrants and carrier or between emigrants and inn-keepers, or boatmen, or porters, or any other persons whose services shall have been required by said emigrants, to be settled by said emigration inspector, same to provide, without formalities of judgment, on due hearing of the adverse sides, or even in the absence of such one as, though duly summoned, shall have failed to appear.

Same shall draw up a special report on the entire case on the evidence of which decision will be issued having immediate effect. Against such decision no opposition or appeal is allowable.

Emigration fund.

CL. 28. Carriers shall pay to deposit and loan fund of any branch of the royal provincial treasury the sum of eight lire for each whole berth, four for each half and two for each quarter berth. To same fund shall be paid all license fees, pecuniary fines, and all future receipts originating on this bill.

Such payments to be devoted to the constitution of an emigration fund, to be invested in securities issued or guaranteed by government, in respect to such share of same as shall not be required for defraying the ordinary expenditure incurred for the purposes of emigration.

Such share thus reserved to be held by the deposit and loan fund in account current; interest at same rate allowed on voluntary deposits, fixed in accordance with clause 44 of regulations of 9th December, 1875, No. 2802.

All amounts drawn from such current account to be by order of general commissioner with assent of the minister for foreign affairs, same to be expended solely and entirely on behalf of emigration at home or abroad.

The balance sheet of said emigration fund, containing all expenditure on account of said commissariat and sections depending therefrom, in accordance with forms fixed by regulations, shall each year be submitted to Parliament, who shall examine and approve same by special vote.

Said emigration fund is placed under the control of a permanent board composed of three senators and three members of Parliament, to be appointed in each session by respective house. Same to retain their place on the board even during the recess between Parliaments and sessions. Said board to issue every year a report to be presented to Parliament by the minister for foreign affairs.

SEC. III.—*General rules.*

CL. 29. The minister for foreign affairs, in concert with the minister of the interior, has power to impose measures for the protection, and special guarantees for the enrolment, of emigrants not included in Section II of this bill if carried out by commercial agents, companies, private citizens, or foreigners, with stipulated conditions in respect to work, wages, time, or place.

In the case of such enrolments, and provided due claim shall have been made on the part of the emigrant or his agent, pending the execution of a contract, or within ten days from the completion thereof, or within ten days from striking work, the assessment of damages in accordance with arbitration procedure given under clause 27 shall be allowed, the conditions for eventual tender of deposit and recovery of guarantee to be fixed on each occasion in accordance with each separate enrolment.

The minister for foreign affairs has power (under clause 12, paragraph first, of this bill) to appoint emigration inspectors travelling abroad, in all other chief centres of Italian emigration, besides those countries lying across the ocean.

Committees as per clause 10 shall exercise their office equally in favour of emigration not directed towards any country lying across the ocean.

CL. 30. All boards of arbitration as per clause 27 are competent to pronounce judgment in respect to refunding of any amounts claimed by any royal authority, in or without the Kingdom, for expenses incurred by same in the interest of emigrants, whenever the responsibility shall be traceable to carriers, agents, companies, commercial agents, or private individuals, respective security to be available for such repayments.

Penal enactments.

CL. 31. Saving provisions of first paragraph of following clause, the following are punishable:

with term of arrest extending to six months and fine not exceeding one thousand lire, all such as shall incite or favour the emigration of one or more persons, in opposition to laws and regulations, and contrary to prohibition of the minister for foreign affairs as enjoined by clause 1, concluding paragraph;

with fine not exceeding three hundred lire all contravening clause 1;

with term of arrest not exceeding three months and fine not exceeding one thousand lire all acting in contravention to preliminary portion of clause 13;

with fine not exceeding one thousand lire any carrier insinuating, between himself and any emigrant, other brokers than his own duly authorized agents; and with same penalty any carrier or agent of same who shall declare as emigrants of their own free will, travelling with their own money, any person whose passage shall have been entirely or in part paid by foreign governments or private contractors; and in case of second offence with a fine of two thousand lire or under;

with fine not exceeding one thousand lire all acting in contravention to concluding paragraph of clause 16, whom the minister for foreign affairs has power to inhibit, for the time being or altogether, from all part in emigration operations,

with full reservation for any responsibility incurred by such agent in respect to such carrier or carriers by whom same shall have been appointed;
with fine not exceeding two thousand lire all acting in contravention to clause 23;
with fine not exceeding one thousand lire all contraventions to this bill or annexed rules, alike in the case of carriers, agents, contractors, commercial agents, emigrants not included.

Should the carrier be a steamship company, all penalties sanctioned by this bill against carriers shall be applicable to all such as have acted as agents of the company, and the due payment of all pecuniary fines incurred by same shall be guaranteed by security of the company aforesaid.

Copies of all orders and verdicts in respect to offences provided against by this bill shall be forwarded to the minister for foreign affairs, who, in so far as falls within his competence, shall provide accordingly to clause 13 with regard to license.

CL. 32. A code of regulations to be sanctioned, and to be altered whenever necessary by royal decree, with approval of the council of state, shall, besides those already referred to, contain full rules for:

distinguishing with reference to penalties sanctioned by clause 31 temporary from permanent emigration;

distribution of duties enumerated in clause 7 and relative expenditure, and for the regulation choice and salaries of such clerks as are strictly necessary;

preparing balance sheet of emigration fund;

deciding which of the offices depending from said commissariat shall be entitled to postal and telegraphic franchise;

determining standard of capacity and morality of carriers and their agents;

authorizing and regulating committees for protection and other institutions in behalf of emigration due to private enterprise;

appointing of all members by election of all district and communal commissions and establishing the duties thereof;

deciding in which cases and on what conditions the minister for foreign affairs shall have power to oblige carriers to convey missionaries charged with the care of emigrants;

regulating the protection of emigrants in ports of embarcation, even by the establishing of refuge homes, to be erected, as means shall allow, in the ports of Genoa, Naples, and Palermo; for determining mode of admission to such homes, medical inspections, baths, etc.;

enjoining that within two years from date of application of this bill the space now allowed to each emigrant in the dormitories of steamships employed in the conveyance of emigrants be increased to cubic metres 2.75 in the upper gangway and three cubic metres in the lower;

fixing certain rules whereby the average speed of vessels shall not be under ten nautical miles an hour;

arranging for due control of conditions regarding rate of speed and limiting the touching at intermediate ports of such steamers to such stoppages as shall be found absolutely necessary;

settling conditions on which steamers belonging to foreign carriers touching at Italian ports shall be exempted from inspections tending to verify if same are fitted in accordance with prescriptions of the Italian laws and regulations on presenting a document granted by competent authorities and duly authenticated by a royal consular official stating that such steamer shall fill the required conditions;

fixing the number of medical men on board proportionately to the number of emigrants shipped;

fixing the nature and quantity of food and accommodation, or corresponding indemnity in the case of delay in starting, or stoppages of emigrants in all intermediate ports whatsoever, or whenever said emigrants be rejected, on whatsoever grounds, at port of departure or destination; fixing the rations on board and all other matters tending to render the passage more satisfactory;

fixing the amount of luggage to be allowed to each emigrant, carriage free, and indemnity to be paid to same in case of loss or damage;

supervising treatment on board in respect to all Italian passengers, holders of third-class tickets or its equivalent class, returning home;

settling all measures for protecting emigrants journeying to frontier stations or others, whether enrolled, favoured, or travelling of their own free will, with or without previous engagement with carriers or their agents;

calling attention to services rendered by such as, in local committees, arbitration boards, emigrant committees of protection, and other such gratuitous appointments, shall have been instrumental in furthering the aims proposed by this bill;

settling, in conclusion, all matters having reference to the sanitary welfare and due safety of emigrants.

708   THE INDUSTRIAL COMMISSION:—IMMIGRATION.

SEC. IV.—*Special provisions in regard to military service and nationality.*

CL. 33. To clauses 81 and 82 of single code of laws on the recruiting of the army, and 36 of single code on maritime levies, the following to be substituted:

All operations in respect to levies abroad to be entrusted to the royal diplomatic and consular authorities.

All being liable, permanently settled abroad, may undergo inspection in the royal legation or nearest royal consulate, same in accordance with result of such inspection to be enrolled under their proper category or remanded for future inspection, or dismissed, or remanded to a future levy on account of justified impediment.

All being liable, born and residing abroad, or having left their country before having completed their sixteenth year, in America, Australia, Asia (Turkey excepted), Africa (Italian dominions and protectorates, Egypt, Tripoli, Tunis, Algiers, and Morocco excepted), when enrolled, to be temporarily exempted from presentation while such residence abroad shall continue. In case of general mobilization of the army and navy, same to be under obligation to present themselves, saving such exceptions, to be stated in such event, in respect to possibility of same being able to return home within the given time.

All military men as above, on their return to the Kingdom, shall at once notify same to military district if assigned to the land force, or to the office of the commandant of the port if belonging to the navy, and present themselves for fulfilling their military duties. Any contravening to such rules shall be declared deserters.

Same to be able, however, in exceptional cases, to obtain from any royal diplomatic or consular authority leave to return to their native country and remain there for a term not exceeding two months. The war minister has power on each occasion, and in accordance with code of rules, to extend such leave to remain within the Kingdom to all such as shall show proofs of following a regular course of studies.

Such temporary dispensation as per paragraphs 3, 4, and 5 of this present clause to become absolute and final on full attainment of the thirty-second year of age.

CL. 34. Following clause 120 of the code of laws on the recruitment of the army, and corresponding clause 43 of the code of laws for the naval levy, the ensuing clause to be added:

All such as on being called for military service shall be resident students in any college of the Kingdom or Erythrean colony and training for a missionary's calling, or having been enrolled in the first category, shall be entitled to obtain, in time of peace, that such call for service be postponed till full completion of twenty-sixth year, such concession to become void on obtaining such age, or even sooner if such course of training has been abandoned.

Should same be proceeding abroad in the quality of missionaries, to such places and under such conditions as the minister for foreign affairs shall require, same to obtain all facilitations granted to such as, being liable to serve, are born and resident abroad.

CL. 35. Paragraph 3 of first part of clause 11 of civil code is annulled.

CL. 36. The Italian nationality, comprising the acquirement and enjoyment of all political rights possessed by natural-born subjects, may be granted by decree of the minister of the interior in concert with the minister for foreign affairs, to all born within the Kingdom or abroad, having become aliens from the fact of being younger sons of fathers having lost their nationality, or, born within the Kingdom or abroad, whose father shall have lost such nationality prior to birth of same, not having in accordance with clauses 5, 6, or 11 of civil code within a year of attaining their majority declared themselves Italian subjects, or, having expressly chosen to become foreign subjects, provided same shall make declaration to settle in the Kingdom.

SEC. V.—*Transitory rules.*

CL. 37. The date of coming into effect of this bill shall be fixed by successive royal decrees accordingly as the opening of the various branches of the service becomes possible. Said decrees to have for effect the annulment of bill of December 30, 1888, No. 5866, series 3, in respect to such parts of same as shall correspond to present bill, the coming into action of which to be determined by degrees, in such manner that all provisions herein contained shall have taken effect not later than a year from date of issue thereof.

CL. 38. Pending approval of code of regulations and appointment of the emigration commissariat, the minister for foreign affairs is empowered to entrust the temporary discharge of such duties to Government clerks.

T. VILLA,
The Chairman of the Chamber of Deputies.

AGRICULTURAL IMMIGRATION TO BRITISH COLONIES.

Desirable immigration.—Several British colonies have more or less energetic measures in vogue for the encouragement of immigration from the British Isles. The Australasian colonies each maintain agents-general at London, who, in addition to attending to the affairs of the colony, act as immigration agents. Canada maintains not only immigration agencies at London, but agencies throughout England, Scotland, Ireland, and Wales.

In addition to these colonial agencies Her Majesty's Government also has maintained an emigrants' information office at London, established in 1886, "for the purpose of supplying intending emigrants with useful and trustworthy inf rmation respecting emigration chiefly to the British colonies."

This information office issues circulars and handbooks respecting the several colonies of Canada, Australasia, and South Africa. These handbooks describe briefly the conditions in the colonies, demand for labor, cost of labor, wages, and the steamship fares and cost of migration.

The object of the British colonies, rigidly maintained, is only to encourage desirable immigration, and their legislation is strict in excluding undesirable classes. For these desirable immigrants two of the Australasian colonies, namely, Queensland and West Australia, provide free assisted or "nominated" passage. New Zealand provides reduced passage. The other colonies which formerly adopted these devices of encouraging immigration have suspended them.

The nature of this class of free passage may be gathered from the following account in the Australasian circular of the emigrants' information office respecting Queensland:

"*Free and assisted passages.*—The agent-general for the colony of Queensland has been instructed to offer free passages to foreign laborers and female domestic servants from 17 to 35 years of age who have never been otherwise engaged. One pound per adult will have to be paid for ship kit by those accepted. The agent-general is also empowered to entertain application for some assistance toward the total cost of passage of small capitalists, farmers, market gardeners, dairymen, fruit growers, and their families.

"*Nominated passages (important to those who have friends in the colony).*—Persons who have resided in the colony for six months can nominate others who have been duly approved by their relatives or personal friends for free passages upon application to the government immigration agent at Brisbane, Queensland, and upon making the following payments to him there.

"Males from 1 to 12 years of age, £2; from 12 to 40, £4; from 40 to 55, £8; females from 1 to 12, £1; from 12 to 40, £2, and from 40 to 55, £8.

"N. B.—Only female domestic servants, farm laborers, plowmen, and gardeners are eligible for nomination. Neither mechanics nor artisans are eligible to be nominated, nor more than 2 children under 12 years of age of the same family, nor any person above the age of 45 years, unless especially sanctioned by the minister. Nominated emigrants must remain in Queensland for one year, and must not have previously resided in any of the Australian colonies."

Nominated emigrants are met by their friends at the government en igration depots, and may obtain board and lodging for a few days free of expense. They are then forwarded by railway to their respective destinations free of cost. "A bona fide intending selector of an agricultural selection wishing to inspect land before selection may obtain a selector's ticket to the nearest railway station upon payment of the ordinary fare. If he does subsequently select an agricultural selection, the price of his ticket will be refunded to him and free passage will be given him for the carriage of himself and family (if any), ordinary household furniture, agricultural implements, and effects to the railway station nearest to his selection."

There were 895 nominated and full-paying emigrants to Queensland in 1898, two-thirds of whom were farm laborers or domestic servants. In 1900 three-fourths of the entire immigration, numbering 2,161, were free passengers, and only 251 paid full steerage fare. The Government suspended free immigration temporarily in 1900 owing to the drought. The number of "nominated" immigrants is increasing, the nationalities being mainly Irish, English, and Scotch The nominated system is reported by the officials of both Queensland and West Australia as working very satisfactorily. It is also advocated by immigrant agents of Canada as preferable to free and assisted passages. The guarantee given by the nominators, who must be settled residents of the colony, protects the Government against the expense of maintaining the new arrivals, and the classes of people introduced are mostly of a very superior character.

The Australasian colonies maintain employment agencies and labor bureaus, part of whose express duties is the assistance of immigrants and finding employment. New Zealand furnishes no free nominated or assisted passages, but for certain classes provides reduced passages. These are such as have fixed incomes or a capital of at least £100, with £50 additional for each member of the family over 12 years. The regular fare by sailing ships from England to New Zealand for third class is £15 15s. to £19 19s., but the reduced fares to New Zealand are £14 14s. New Zealand does not maintain an immigration depot, but immigrants obtain information as to rates of wages through the Crown land officer. The following is a table showing the fare by sailing vessels and by steamer from England to Sydney, New South Wales. The rates are practically the same to other colonies of Australasia.

	By sailing vessel (about 3 months) occasionally.	By steamer (from 42 to 50 days).
Third class		£14 14s. to £18 18s.
Second class	About £20	£35 to £40.
First class	About £52	£42 to £70.

CANADA.

Of all British colonies Canada at the present time is carrying on the most expensive and systematic agitation in Great Britain for the inducement of immigration to the farming lands of the several provinces. There is maintained at London a high commissioner, with agents in different parts of the country and on the Continent. These agents spend their time in traveling through the country and lecturing on the advantages of Canada, and in advertising through the press. A large number of agencies is also maintained at points in the United States.

During the 6 months, January to June, 1900, the superintendent of immigration distributed through these agencies 1,050,500 pamphlets, circulars, copy books, and newspapers, in English, French, and Hungarian languages. The department of the interior has met the expenses of various delegates from different countries who have visited Manitoba and the Northwest and made reports upon their impressions of the country and its desirability for immigrants. These delegates have included a number of tenant farmers from England, a Russian delegation, and a Finnish delegation.

The immigration agencies in Europe work in cooperation with the steamship agents and with the Canadian Pacific Railway Company. At the same time, it is complained that the expense of migration from England to the northwest of Canada exceeds that to the western part of the United States.

An interesting feature of the educational campaign of the immigration agents in Great Britain is the preparation of "copy books" for use in the schools. It is stated that "the constant use of the copy books by the children can not fail to impress upon their minds facts relating to Canada that they are copying day by day, and we hope also that the introduction of these books into many homes in the different parts of the United Kingdom will be attended with the best results." The present of a brass medal for competition in each school is offered when the schools close for the Christmas holidays to the boy or girl who proves to be the most proficient in the subjects. The Canadian government does not provide free or assisted passages, but directs its energies solely to the educational lines of spreading information throughout Great Britain of the advantages of the country. At the same time the agents make it a part of their duties to personally conduct parties of immigrants across the water to Quebec, whence they are taken in charge by the officers of the railway and the domestic branch of the commission of immigration.

The activity of the latter branch of the bureau of immigration may be inferred from the report of the commissioner for Winnipeg for 1900. This commissioner has under his supervision interpreters in Icelandic, German, French, Finnish, and Ruthenian. He also has traveling agents, who visit the colonies of immigrants and assist them in such ways as is needed. In this way the agencies have located the colonies of Doukhobors, who had migrated from Russia on account of their dislike of military service. These are described as exceedingly desirable colonists. The Galacians or Ruthenians have made satisfactory progress. The agent states that the first 9 Galacians who settled in Canada in 1894 possessed $1,294, and in February, 1900, their total capital was $31,278. The Russian-Moravian, with 25 families, threshed, in 1889, 18,000 bushels of grain and owned 300 cattle. The Russian colony, Burdderfeld, comprising 45 families, threshed 50,000 bushels of grain and owned 500 cattle. A German colony, comprising 125 families, produced 300 bushels of grain and has 40 public schools and 2 churches. The French colony of 100 families and the Swedish colony have also succeeded well.

The vacant lands taken up by these immigrants are partly Government land and partly land of the Canadian Pacific Railway and the Hudson Bay Company. The land entries for the half year ending June 30, for the last 4 years, are as follows: 1897, 1,272; 1898, 2,541; 1899, 4,573; 1900, 4,266. The sales of the Canadian Pacific Railway for the 6 months from January to June, in 1899, were 182,836 acres, or in 1900, 268,628. The Hudson Bay company sold, in the first 6 months of 1900, 34,629 acres for $173,913. The total expenditure of the Dominion Government in behalf of immigration is something like $250,000 per year. It is estimated that 12,000 of these are Americans and that three-fourths of the total immigration is directed to the search of free lands in the Northwest. The following table shows for the first 6 months of 1900 the immigrant arrivals by countries of origin:

United States	8,543
English and Welsh	4,129
Scotch	669
Irish	343
	5,141
Galicians, etc	4,992
Germans	476
Scandinavians	714
French and Belgian	253
Miscellaneous nationalities	3,776
Total	23,895

The Canadian agencies in the United States are the most extensive and energetic of all the agencies under the supervision of the immigration service of Canada. The principal ones are located at Detroit and Saginaw, Mich.; Chicago, Ill.; Stevens Point, Madison, and Milwaukee, Wis.; Columbus, Cleveland, Toledo, and Sandusky, Ohio; Logansport and Indianapolis, Ind.; Louisville, Ky.; St. Louis and Kansas City, Mo.; Omaha, Nebr.; Sioux Falls and Watertown, S. Dak.; Des Moines, Iowa; St. Paul and Duluth, Minn.; Grafton, N. Dak.

The literature published by the department has had the most extensive circulation throughout every State in the American Union. The demand for the atlas of western Canada was so great that the large supply in 1889 became soon exhausted. Circulars and pamphlets which are distributed are entitled "Western Canada," "Settlers' Experiences," "Delegates' Reports," "The Hard Wheat Belt." An extensive system of advertising is carried on throughout the local and foreign papers, using reading notices as well as regularly displayed advertisements, and changing frequently in order to attract public attention. The agents conduct a series of lectures with lantern slides, and visit the individual farmers, explaining to them the advantages of immigration to Canada and the expenses, etc. Their efforts are directed mainly to securing American farmers who have already shown their desirability by the success they have made in their own country. In the spring of 1900 several delegations were provided with free transportation to Canada and return to their localities, and their influence is described as satisfactory. From Missouri more than 80 delegates were sent in the season of 1900. In one train from Kansas and Missouri 200 souls, with 23 cars of settlers' effects, moved to the Canadian Northwest. Another company of families moved from Nebraska overland in "prairie schooners," a trip of 600 miles, to the Canadian Northwest. These colonists were in all cases the direct result of the solicitation of the Canadian immigration agents.

An interesting feature of Canadian immigration is that of dependent children whose migration is assisted by British public or private authorities. The boards of guardians of British poor-law districts are authorized to assist the migration of pauper children at the public expense provided a stated sum be paid to the Canadian minister of interior for the inspection of such children up to the age of 16. This sum ranges from £1 4s. 8d. for each child of 14 and 15 years up to £10 14s. 9d. for each child of 4 and under 5 years. Under these regulations, the following table shows the number of children deported to Canada by the public authorities from the years 1889 to 1898:

Year.	Total numbers.	Number of children included.	Total cost to the guardians.
1889	558	428	£5,266
1890	447	375	4,462
1891	339	296	3,725
1892	381	322	4,035
1893	398	360	4,536
1894	344	299	3,879
1895	292	246	3,154
1896	228	207	2,762
1897	99	85	1,147
1898	90	78	1,169

In addition to the public authorities deporting children there is a large number of private childrens' emigration societies, among which the following are the more important: Childrens' Immigration Homes, Birmingham, founded 1872, forwarded 2,761 children to Canada during 17 years; The Sheltering Home, Liverpool, forwarded 3,700 children in 27 years; Canadian Catholic Immigration Society, London, sends Roman Catholic boys and girls to Canada; Childrens' Home and Refuge, London, forwarded 1,525 children to Canada during 30 years and 49 to other colonies; The Church of England Incorporated Society for Providing Homes for Waifs and Strays, London, forwarded 650 children to Canada; National Waifs' Association, London, otherwise known as Dr. Bernardo's Home, forwarded up to the end of 1899 10,660 children to Canada. The cost of immigration, including outfit and all journeying expenses, is £10 per head. The association has a distributing home at Toronto for boys, at Petersborough for girls, and a small center at Winnipeg, an industrial farm of 10,000 acres at Russell, in Manitoba, to which older lives were sent. The children are placed out with the farmers and others, and a lad who has saved $150 and takes up a free homestead is provided with a house, provisions, and farm machinery, the expense of which he pays back in easy installments.

Manchester and Salford Boys' and Girls' Refuges and Homes and Childrens' Aid Society, Manchester, forwarded 1,300 children to Canada, of whom 40 were sent in 1899.

The Salford Catholic Protection and Rescue Society, Salford, forwarded 707 children in the last 10 years. They are taken to the Province of Quebec and placed out with farmers and others, all of whom are Roman Catholic French-speaking Canadians.

CHINESE EXCLUSION.

The proposed continuation for another ten years of the law excluding Chinese laborers, which expires by limitation in 1902, suggests comparison with legislation on Chinese immigration by the English-speaking colonial provinces of Great Britain, which, like the United States, are open to the influx of that nationality. Following is the text of the Canadian act of 1900 and a summary of legislation in Australian colonies:

CANADIAN ACT RESTRICTING CHINESE IMMIGRATION, 1900.

[63-64 Victoria.]

CHAP. 32.—AN ACT RESPECTING AND RESTRICTING CHINESE IMMIGRATION.

[Assented to July 18, 1900.]

Her Majesty, by and with the advice and consent of the Senate and House of Commons of Canada, enacts as follows:

1. This act may be cited as the Chinese immigration act, 1900.
2. This act shall come into force on the first day of January, one thousand nine hundred and one.
3. The following acts are repealed: Chapter 67 of the Revised Statutes, chapter 35 of the statutes of 1887, and chapter 25 of the statutes of 1892.
4. In this act, unless the context otherwise requires—

(a) The expression "chief controller" means the chief officer who is charged, under the direction of the minister to whom is assigned the administration of this act, with the duty of carrying the provisions of this act into effect and who shall have authority over officers of customs and others appointed for the purpose or charged with the duty of assisting in carrying out the provisions of this act;

(b) The expression "controller" means any customs or other officer at any seaport or frontier customs port, duly appointed as such and charged with the duty of assisting in carrying the provisions of this act into effect;

(c) The expression "master" or "conductor" means any person in command of or in charge of any vessel or vehicle;

(d) The expression "Chinese immigrant" means any person of Chinese origin (including any person whose father was of Chinese origin) entering Canada and not entitled to the privilege of exemption provided by section 6 of this act;

(e) The expression "vessel" means any seagoing craft of any kind or description capable of carrying passengers;

(f) The expression "tonnage" means the gross tonnage according to the measurement fixed by the merchant shipping acts of the Parliament of the United Kingdom;

(g) The expression "vehicle" means any ferryboat, boat, railway car, cart, wagon, carriage, sleigh, or other conveyance whatsoever, however propelled or drawn.

5. The governor in council may—

(a) Appoint one or more persons to carry the provisions of this act into effect;
(b) Assign any duty in connection therewith to any officer or person in the employ of the government of Canada;
(c) Define and prescribe the duties of such officer or person;
(d) Fix the salary or remuneration to be allowed to such officer or person;
(e) Engage and pay interpreters skilled in the English and Chinese languages, at salaries aggregating not more than three thousand dollars a year;
(f) Make regulations for the carrying out of this act.

6. Every person of Chinese origin, irrespective of allegiance, shall pay into the consolidated revenue fund of Canada, on entering Canada, at the port or place of entry, a tax of one hundred dollars, except the following persons, who shall be exempt from such payment, that is to say :

(*a*) Members of the diplomatic corps or other Government representatives, their suites and their servants, and consuls and consular agents;

(*b*) The children born in Canada of parents of Chinese origin and who have left Canada for educational or other purposes, on substantiating their identity to the satisfaction of the controller at the port or place where they seek to enter on their return;

(*c*) Merchants, their wives and children, the wives and children of clergymen, tourists, men of science, and students, who shall substantiate their status to the satisfaction of the controller, subject to the approval of the minister, or who are bearers of certificates of identity, specifying their occupation and their object in coming into Canada, or other similar documents issued by the Government or by a recognized official or representative of the Government whose subjects they are.

(2) Every such certificate or other document shall be in the English or French language, and shall be examined and indorsed (*visé*) by a British consul or chargé d'affaires or other accredited representative of Her Majesty at the place where it is granted or at the port or place of departure.

(3) Persons of Chinese origin claiming on their arrival to be students, but who are unable to produce the requisite certificate as hereinbefore provided for, shall be entitled to a refund of the tax exacted from them on the production, within eighteen months from the date of their arrival in Canada, of certificates from teachers in any school or college in Canada showing that they are and have been for at least one year bona fide students in attendance at such school or college.

(4) Any woman of Chinese origin who is the wife of a person who is not of Chinese origin shall for the purpose of this act be deemed to be of the same nationality as her husband, and the children of the said wife and husband shall be deemed to be of the same nationality as the father.

(5) Nothing in this act shall be construed as embracing within the meaning of the word "merchant" any merchant's clerk or other employee, mechanic, huckster, pedlar, or person engaged in taking, drying, or otherwise preserving fish for home consumption or exportation.

7. No vessel carrying Chinese immigrants to any port in Canada shall carry more than one such immigrant for every fifty tons of tonnage; and the owner of any such vessel who carries any number in excess of the number allowed by this section shall incur a penalty of two hundred dollars for each Chinese immigrant so carried in excess of such number.

(2) No Chinese immigrant shall be allowed to land in or enter Canada coastwise or overland arriving in transit from any port or place in America from any vessel entering at such port or place, in excess of the number which would have been allowed to land from such vessel had it come direct to Canada.

8. No master of any vessel carrying Chinese immigrants shall land any person of Chinese origin, or permit any to land from such vessel, until a permit so to do, stating that the provisions of this act have been complied with, has been granted to the master of such vessel by the controller; and every master of a vessel who violates the provisions of this section shall incur a penalty of two hundred dollars.

(2) The landing of a person of Chinese origin from a vessel, wherever referred to in this act, shall not be held to apply to the landing of such person on the wharf and the placing of him in a proper building where he may remain until the provisions of this act have been complied with and the controller has given his authority for his departure therefrom; and such person, while in such building, shall for the purpose of this act be held to be still on board the vessel by which he arrived. This provision, however, shall not allow the placing of such person in such building until all quarantine requirements have been complied with.

9. No controller at any port shall grant a permit allowing Chinese immigrants to land until the quarantine officer has granted a bill of health and has certified, after due examination, that no leprosy or infectious, contagious, loathsome, or dangerous disease exists on board such vessel; and no permit to land shall be granted to any Chinese immigrant who is suffering from leprosy or from any infectious, contagious, loathsome, or dangerous diseases.

10. Every conductor or other person in charge of any railway train or car bringing Chinese immigrants into Canada shall be personally liable to Her Majesty for the payment of the tax imposed by section 6 of this act in respect of any immigrant brought by or on such railway train or car, and shall deliver, immediately on his arrival, to the controller or other proper officer at the port or place of arrival, a report in the same terms as is required to be made by section 15 of this act, by the master of a vessel, of all persons of Chinese origin arriving by or being on board of the railway train or car of which he is in charge, and shall, unless such persons are in transit through Canada, pay or cause to be paid to the controller the total amount

of the tax payable by Chinese immigrants so arriving by such railway train or car, and he shall not allow any such immigrants to disembark from such train or car until after such report has been made and such tax has been paid.

11. Every Chinese immigrant who enters Canada otherwise than by disembarking from any vessel or vehicle shall forthwith make a statement and declaration of his entry to the controller or other proper officer at the nearest or most convenient port or place, and shall forthwith pay to such controller or officer the tax of one hundred dollars imposed by this act; and if the statement and declaration is made to an officer other than a controller authorized to keep a register, such officer shall report the fact and transmit the tax to the chief controller or to the nearest controller so authorized, and the controller shall make a record thereof in his register and issue the proper certificate of such registration in conformity with the provisions of section 13 of this act.

12. No controller or other officer charged with the duty of assisting in carrying the provisions of this act into effect shall grant a permit allowing to land from any vessel, nor shall any conductor or other person in charge of any vehicle bring into Canada, either as an immigrant or as an exempt, or as in transit, any person of Chinese origin who is—

(a) a pauper or likely to become a public charge;
(b) an idiot or insane;
(c) suffering from any loathsome, infectious, or contagious disease;
(d) a prostitute or living on the prostitution of others.

(2) All such persons are prohibited from entering Canada; and if they enter they shall be liable to imprisonment for a term not exceeding six months, and shall in addition be liable to deportation, and the master, conductor, or other person who knowingly lands or brings or assists or permits to land in Canada any such persons of Chinese origin shall also be liable to a penalty not exceeding two hundred dollars or to imprisonment for a term not exceeding six months.

13. The controller shall deliver to each Chinese immigrant who has been permitted to land or enter, and in respect of whom the tax has been paid as hereinbefore provided, a certificate containing a description of such individual, the date of his arrival, the name of the port of his landing and an acknowledgment that the duty has been duly paid; and such certificate shall be prima facie evidence that the person presenting it has complied with the requirements of this act; but such certificate may be contested by Her Majesty, or by any officer charged with the duty of carrying this act into effect, if there is reason to doubt the validity or authenticity thereof, or of any statement therein contained; and such contestation shall be heard and determined in a summary manner by any judge of a superior court of any province of Canada where such certificate is produced.

14. The chief controller, and such controllers as are by him authorized so to do, shall each keep a register of all persons to whom certificates of entry have been granted.

15. Every master of any vessel bringing Chinese immigrants to any port or place in Canada shall be personally liable to Her Majesty for the payment of the tax imposed by this act in respect of any such immigrant carried by such vessel, and shall deliver, together with the total amount of such tax, to the controller, immediately on his arrival in port and before any of his Chinese crew or passengers disembark, a complete and accurate list of his crew and such passengers, showing their names in full, the country and place of their birth, and the occupation and last place of domicile of each of such immigrant passengers.

16. Every master or conductor of any vessel or vehicle who lands or allows to be landed off or from any vessel or vehicle any Chinese immigrant before the tax payable under this act has been duly paid, or who wilfully makes any false statement respecting the number of persons on board his vessel or vehicle, shall, in addition to the amount of the tax payable under the foregoing provisions of this act, be liable to a penalty not exceeding one thousand dollars and not less than five hundred dollars for every such offence, and in default of payment to imprisonment for a term not exceeding twelve months; and such vessel or vehicle shall be forfeited to Her Majesty, and shall be seized by an officer charged with the duty of carrying this act into effect, and dealt with accordingly.

17. Persons of Chinese origin may pass through Canada by railway, in transit, from one port or place out of Canada to another port or place out of Canada without payment of the tax provided for by section 6 of this act, provided that such passage is made in accordance with and under such regulations as are made for the purpose; and any railway company which undertakes to transport such persons through Canada and fails to comply with such regulations or to take such persons out of Canada at the designated port of exit within a period to be fixed by the chief controller shall be subjected to a penalty equal to double the total amount of the tax payable under the provisions of section 6 of this act.

18. Every person of Chinese origin who wishes to leave Canada, with the declared

intention of returning thereto, shall give written notice of such intention to the controller at the port or place whence he purposes to sail or depart, in which notice shall be stated the foreign port or place which such person wishes to visit, and the route he intends taking both going and returning, and such notice shall be accompanied by a fee of one dollar; and the controller shall thereupon enter in a register to be kept for the purpose the name, residence, occupation, and description of the said person, and such other information regarding him as is deemed necessary, under such regulations as are made for the purpose.

(2) The person so registered shall be entitled on his return, if within twelve months of such registration, and on proof of his identity to the satisfaction of the controller (as to which the decision of the controller shall be final), to free entry as an exempt or to receive from the controller the amount of the tax, if any, paid by him on his return; but if he does not return to Canada within twelve months from the date of such registration, he shall, if returning after that date, be subject to the tax payable under the provisions of section 6 of this act in the same manner as in the case of a first arrival.

19. Every person of Chinese origin who wilfully evades or attempts to evade any of the provisions of this act as respects the payment of the tax by personating any other individual, or who wilfully makes use of any forged or fraudulent certificate to evade the provisions of this act, and every person who wilfully aids or abets any such person of Chinese origin in any evasion or attempt at evasion of any of the provisions of this act, is guilty of an indictable offence, and liable to imprisonment for a term not exceeding twelve months, or to a fine not exceeding five hundred dollars, or to both.

20. Every person who takes part in the organization of any sort of court or tribunal composed of Chinese persons for the hearing and determination of any offence committed by a Chinese person, or in carrying on any such organization, or who takes part in any of its proceedings, or who gives evidence before any such court or tribunal, or assists in carrying into effect any decision, decree, or order of any such court or tribunal, is guilty of an indictable offence and liable to imprisonment for any term not exceeding twelve months, or to a fine not exceeding five hundred dollars, or to both; but nothing in this section shall be construed to prevent Chinese persons from submitting any differences or disputes to arbitration, provided such submission is not contrary to the laws in force in the Province in which such submission is made.

21. Every person who molests, persecutes, or hinders any officer or person appointed to carry the provisions of this act into effect is guilty of an indictable offence, and liable to imprisonment for a term not exceeding twelve months, or to a fine not exceeding five hundred dollars, or to both.

22. Every person who violates any provision of this act for which no special punishment is herein provided is guilty of an indictable offence, and liable to a fine not exceeding five hundred dollars, or to imprisonment for a term not exceeding twelve months.

23. All suits or actions for the recovery of taxes or penalties under this act, and all prosecutions for contraventions of this act which are not herein declared to be indictable offences, shall be tried before one or more justices of the peace, or before the recorder, police magistrate, or stipendiary magistrate having jurisdiction, where the cause of action arose or where the offence was committed.

24. All taxes, pecuniary penalties, and revenues from other sources under this act shall be paid into and form part of the consolidated revenue fund of Canada; but one-fourth part of the net proceeds of all such taxes paid by Chinese immigrants shall, at the end of every fiscal year, be paid out of such fund to the Province wherein they were collected.

25. The governor in council may make such regulations as are necessary to prohibit the entry into Canada of any greater number of persons from any foreign country than the laws of such country permit to emigrate to Canada.

DISABILITIES IMPOSED UPON CHINESE AND JAPANESE PERSONS ON PUBLIC WORKS BY BRITISH COLUMBIA, 1898.

The Province of British Columbia prohibits the employment of Japanese or Chinese persons, either directly or by subcontractors, by any person or corporation to whom any franchise has been granted for the right of erecting a bridge, making a railway, tramway, turnpike road, telegraph or telephone line, the construction or improvement of a harbor, lock, dam, slide, or other like work, the right of ferry, the right of carrying on any trade, business, occupation, or calling, or giving, granting, or offering to such person or body corporate any property rights or privileges whatsoever. The penalty upon conviction before any two justices of the peace or like authority is a penalty not exceeding $25 or less than $10 for every Chinese or Japanese person employed, whether employed directly or by subcontractors.

VICTORIA.

An act of the legislature of Victoria in 1890 was passed, preceded by a preamble, stating that at a meeting of representatives of Australasian governments, held at Sidney in 1888, it was resolved that it was desirable that the laws of the various Australasian colonies for the restriction of Chinese immigration should be assimilated on a basis approved at that meeting, and the act proceeds to enact restriction of Chinese to 1 for every 500 tons; penalty, £500 upon the master for every Chinaman in excess of the number, requiring the master to muster the Chinese before an officer, providing a penalty of £5 to £20 in addition to the head tax upon Chinamen who land without permit, providing against transshipping, giving the governor in council power to make regulations and rendering the vessels liable to seizure for penalties. Chinese residents are prohibited, notwithstanding they hold a miner's license or business license, from voting in any election whatever, unless they are naturalized subjects of the British Empire. The names of all Chinese who had hitherto been voters were stricken from the list.

QUEENSLAND.

The colony of Queensland in 1877, by act of the colonial parliament, imposed a head tax of £10 for every Chinese person entering the colony, the same to be paid by the master of the vessel before landing. Penalty for neglect was fixed at £20 for each Chinese person so landed or permitted to land, in addition to the amount of the head tax, and the vessel should be forfeited and seized and condemned. Chinamen admitted were to be provided with a certificate. Chinamen entering or attempting to enter the colony without paying the head tax were liable to a penalty not exceeding £10. The act applied also to any Chinaman who was one of the crew of any vessel.

By amendment adopted in 1884 the head tax on Chinamen was increased from £10 to £30, and the penalties for violation were increased. Ships were prohibited from importing a greater number of passengers than in the proportion of 1 to every 50 tons of the tonnage, the penalty for violation being £30 or less for each Chinese passenger so carried in excess.

In 1·90 the colony adopted a further act for the restriction of Chinese immigration. This act specially exempted persons duly credited as the representatives of any government, persons born in Queensland, and persons temporarily exempted, such exemptions to be declared by proclamation of the governor in council. By this act no ship shall enter any port or place in the colony having on board a greater number of Chinese passengers than in the proportion of 1 Chinese passenger to every 500 tons of the tonnage of such ship. The master of the ship is required to deliver to the collector the number and names of all Chinese on board the ship, including the crew of the ship. Furthermore, he must muster before the collector or any police officer the whole of the Chinese crew and passengers. The penalty imposed upon Chinamen for unauthorized landing is £50. In default of payment, imprisonment at hard labor from three to six months.

NEW SOUTH WALES.

The legislation of New South Wales relative to Chinese immigration dates from 1881. In that year was enacted a law "to restrict influx of Chinese into New South Wales." This provides that any vessels having on board a greater number of Chinese than in the proportion of one Chinese to every 100 tons of the tonnage shall be liable to a penalty of £100 for each Chinaman carried in excess.

Section 4 provides that the Chinese permitted to land from each vessel shall pay a head tax of £10, to be advanced by the master of the vessel. The same head tax is required by Chinese arriving otherwise than by sea. The penalty on the Chinamen for evasion is £10 in addition to the head tax, and in default thereof imprisonment for twelve months, unless the penalty is sooner paid.

The act of 1881 was repealed in 1888, and the substitute is entitled "An act to provide for the protection of the colony from the disturbances and national dangers of Chinese immigration." It provides especially for the regulation of the Chinese at present resident in the colony, and to indemnify the government for all acts done by the executive or ministerial authority in relation to Chinese immigrants or vessels carrying such immigrants, etc. In this act the number of Chinese is limited to one for every 300 tons of the vessel's tonnage; the head tax is increased to £100; the penalty upon the master of the vessel for violation of the law is £500 for each Chinese landed or suffered to land or escape. Chinamen in the colony not having paid the tax are liable to a penalty of £50, in addition to the head tax, or imprisonment for two years unless the penalty be sooner paid.

No Chinaman is permitted to engage in the work of any gold, silver, or any mine, or any mining pursuit whatever without express authority under the hand and seal of the minister in charge of mines. Chinese who are British subjects are exempted, and regulations for the enforcement of the law are provided.

In 1896 the Chinese restriction act of 1888 is extended so as to apply to "all persons belonging to any colored race inhabiting the continent of Asia or the continent of Africa, or any island adjacent thereto, or any island in the Pacific or Indian oceans," except representatives of foreign Governments.

The act of 1888 is amended by repealing the exception in favor of Chinese by birth a British subject, and therefore, since 1896, not even Chinamen subject to Great Britain can be admitted to the colony unless paying the tax of £100. The law does not apply to ministers of religion, missionaries, native teachers, tourists, merchants, men of science, or students, and the wives and families of such persons, and also their domestic servants, provided they carry a certificate of identification from the British consul at the port of departure.

TASMANIA.

The colony of Tasmania in 1887 limited the number of Chinese to be brought by any vessel to one for every 100 tons of the tonnage. It imposed a penalty of £10 upon the master for each Chinese in excess of the limitation and a head tax of £10 for every Chinese landed. Penalty and exemption similar to those in the other Australasian colonies.

WESTERN AUSTRALIA.

In 1897 the colony of West Australia adopted a stringent law applicable to laborers immigrating from India, China, Africa, or the islands of the Indian and Pacific oceans, or of the Malayan archipelago. The leading features of this act are the restriction of the number of immigrants who may be permitted to land to one for every 500 tons of the tonnage of the vessel. The penalty imposed upon the master or owner for the violation is £100 for each laborer so landing. No laborers of these restricted classes can be imported unless a contract shall have been previously entered into. "Every person who shall cause a laborer to be brought or imported into the colony contrary to this provision of this act shall be liable to a penalty not exceeding £100 for every laborer so brought or imported.". A contract is entered into before the British or colonial authority, and is recorded in proper form. A runaway laborer who attempts to violate the contract shall be arrested, if found, without any other warrant than the act, by any member of the police force, and detained in custody until he is returned to the port or place from which he is shipped, or is otherwise dealt with at the expense of the employer. The employer is also required, under penalty not exceeding £25, to notify a magistrate or police constable of the desertion of any laborer from his employment or disappearance therefrom for a period of three days. The contract for service to which these penalties and provisions apply shall not exceed three years in duration, but may be renewed or may be rescinded by mutual agreement, in which case the employer is required to pay the expenses of the laborer back to the country from which he came.

NEW ZEALAND.

The colony of New Zealand in 1881 limited the number of Chinese to one for every 10 tons of the tonnage of the vessels, and imposed a penalty of £10 for each Chinese in excess. It required a head tax of £10 for all Chinese landed, and imposed penalties, provided for summary jurisdiction by justices of the peace, and provided for certificates similar to those provided by the laws of the other colonies.

IMMIGRATION RESTRICTION ACT, NATAL, 1897.

The immigration restriction act of Natal of 1897 has served as a model for later legislation in New Zealand and New South Wales. The principal sections of this act are as follows:

The immigration into Natal, by land or sea, of any person of any of the classes defined in the following subsections, hereinafter called "prohibited immigrant," is prohibited, namely:

(a) Any person who, when asked to do so by an officer appointed under this act, shall fail to himself write out and sign, in the characters of any language of Europe, an application to the colonial secretary in the form set out in Schedule B of this act.

(b) Any person being a pauper, or likely to become a public charge.

(c) Any idiot or insane person.

(d) Any person suffering from a loathsome or a dangerous contagious disease.

(e) Any person who, not having received a free pardon, has within 2 years been convicted of a felony or other infamous crime or misdemeanor involving moral turpitude, and not being a mere political offense.

(f) Any prostitute, and any person living on the prostitution of others.

4. Any prohibited immigrant making his way into, or being found within, Natal in disregard of the provisions of this act shall be deemed to have contravened this act, and shall be liable, in addition to any other penalty, to be removed from the colony, and upon conviction may be sentenced to imprisonment not exceeding 6 months without hard labor, provided that such imprisonment shall cease for the purpose of deportation of the offender, or if he shall find two approved sureties, each in the sum of £50, that he will leave the colony within 1 month.

5. Any person appearing to be a prohibited immigrant within the meaning of section 3 of this act and not coming within the meaning of any of the subsections (c), (d), (e), (f) of the said section 3 shall be allowed to enter Natal upon the following conditions:

(a) He shall, before landing, deposit with an officer appointed under this act the sum of £100.

(b) If such person shall, within 1 week after entering Natal, obtain from the colonial secretary or a magistrate a certificate that he does not come within the prohibition of this act, the deposit of £100 shall be returned.

(c) If such person shall fail to obtain such certificate within 1 week, the deposit of £100 may be forfeited and he may be treated as a prohibited immigrant, provided that in the case of any person entering Natal under this section no liability shall attach to the vessel or to the owners of the vessel in which he may have arrived at any port of the colony.

6. Any person who shall satisfy an officer appointed under this act that he has been formerly domiciled in Natal and that he does not come within the meaning of any of the subsections (c), (d), (e), (f) of section 3 of this act shall not be regarded as a prohibited immigrant.

7. The wife and any minor child of a person not being a prohibited immigrant shall be free from any rohibition imposed by this act.

8. The master and owners of any vessel from which any prohibited immigrant may be landed shall be jointly and severally liable to a penalty of not less than £100, and such penalty may be increased up to £5,000 by sums of £100 each for every 5 prohibited immigrants after the first 5, and the vessel may be made executable by a decree of the supreme court in satisfaction of any such penalty, and the vessel may be refused a clearance outward until such penalty has been paid and until provision has been made by the master to the satisfaction of an officer appointed under this act for the conveyance out of the colony of each prohibited immigrant who may have been so landed.

9. A prohibited immigrant shall not be entitled to a license to carry on any trade or calling, nor shall he be entitled to acquire land in leasehold, freehold, or otherwise, or to exercise the franchise, or to be enrolled as a burgess of any borough or on the roll of any township; and any license or franchise right which may have been acquired in contravention of this act shall be void.

10. Any officer thereto authorized by Government may make a contract with the master, owners, or agent of any vessel for the conveyance of any prohibited immigrant found in Natal to a port in or near such immigrant's country of birth, and any such immigrant with his personal effects may be placed by a police officer on board such vessel, and shall in such case, if destitute, be supplied with a sufficient sum of money to enable him to live for 1 month according to his circumstances in life after disembarking from such vessel.

11. Any person who shall in any way willfully assist any prohibited immigrant to contravene the provisions of this act shall be deemed to have contravened this act.

12. Any person who shall willfully assist the entry into Natal of any prohibited immigrant of the class (f) in section 3 of this act shall be deemed to have contravened this act, and shall upon conviction be liable to be imprisoned with hard labor for any period not exceeding 12 months.

13. Any person who shall be willfully instrumental in bringing into Natal an idiot or insane person without a written or printed authority, signed by the colonial secretary, shall be deemed to have contravened this act, and, in addition to any other penalty, shall be liable for the cost of the maintenance of such idiot or insane person whilst in the colony.

14. Any police officer or other officer appointed therefor under this act may, subject to the provisions of section 5, prevent any prohibited immigrant from entering Natal by land or sea.

15. The governor may from time to time appoint, and at pleasure remove, officers for the purpose of carrying out the provisions of this act, and may define the duties of such officers, and such officers shall carry out the instructions from time to time given to them by the ministerial head of their department.

16. The governor in council may from time to time make, amend, and repeal rules and regulations for the better carrying out of the provisions of this act.

17. The penalty for any contravention of this act, or of any rule or regulation passed thereunder, where no higher penalty is expressly imposed, shall not exceed a fine of £50, or imprisonment, with or without hard labor, until payment of such fine in or in addition to such fine, but not exceeding in any case 3 months.

18. All contraventions of this act or of rules or regulations thereunder and suits for penalties or other moneys not exceeding £100 shall be cognizable by magistrates

CANADIAN CONTRACT-LABOR LAW OF 1897.

Recommendation for the amendment of the contract-labor law of the United States will be aided by a comparison with the recent legislation of Canada, the only country that has followed the example of the United States in this phase of legislation. The Canadian act of 1897 is not a general act, but is merely in the nature of a retaliatory enactment directed against the United States. An act of 1886 made special provision encouraging the assistance of immigrants as laborers by providing that any moneys advanced to them should be recovered according to the terms of the contract after landing in Canada, and also that "every immigrant who in consideration of money advanced as for said engagements binds himself to enter the service of any employer in Canada on his arrival there in any capacity, and to work for and serve such employer in such capacity during any certain time not exceeding six months and at any named rate of wages, and afterwards refuses and neglects on his arrival in Canada to perform such engagement, shall be liable on summary conviction to a penalty not exceeding $20 and costs, and to imprisonment until such penalty and costs are paid." This law continued in force until 1897, when a statute modeled somewhat after the alien contract labor law of the United States was enacted applicable solely to immigration from the United States under the interpretation of the final clause, as will be seen below. This was amended in 1898 and in 1900, and, together with its amendments, is described as follows by the Canadian Labor Gazette:

The act as originally in force made it unlawful for any person, partner, or corporation in any way to prepay the transportation or in any way to assist or encourage the importation or immigration of any alien or foreigner into Canada, under contract or agreement, parole or special, express or implied, made previous to the importation or immigration of such alien or foreigner, to perform labor or services of any kind in Canada. It was provided, however, that nothing in the act should be so construed as to prevent any citizen or subject of any foreign country temporarily residing in Canada, either in a private or official capacity, from engaging under contract or otherwise persons not residents or citizens of Canada to act as private secretaries or domestics, nor any person, partnership, or corporation from engaging under contract or agreement skilled workmen in foreign countries to perform labor in Canada in or upon any new industry not yet established in Canada, provided that skilled labor for that purpose could not be otherwise obtained. Nor were the provisions of the act to apply to professional actors, artists, lecturers, or singers, or to persons employed strictly as personal or domestic servants. It was also provided that nothing in the act should be construed as prohibiting any person from assisting any member of his family, or any relative or personal friend, to migrate from any foreign country to Canada for the purpose of settling here.

These sections of the act have been allowed to remain as they were, with the exception of that part of the provision which states that the act shall not be construed as "prohibiting any person from assisting any member of his family, or any relative or personal friend, to migrate to Canada for the purpose of settlement here." It was contended that the words "or personal friend" gave unwarranted latitude to persons who might seek to evade the provisions of the act, and for this reason the house in its amendment caused these words to be struck out, thereby restricting the exemptions under this heading to members of the family or relatives.

A very important addition, however, as to what constituted a violation of the act was made in section 8 of the amendment, whereby the promise of employment through advertisements, printed or published in any foreign country to which the act applied, would be regarded as a violation. The exact wording of this section is as follows:

"8. It shall be deemed a violation of this act for any person, partnership, company, or corporation to assist or encourage the importation or immigration of any person who resides in, or is a citizen of, any foreign country to which this act applies, by promise of employment through advertisements printed or published in such foreign country; and any such person coming to this country in consequence of such an advertisement shall be treated as coming under a contract as contemplated by this act, and the penalties by this act imposed shall be applicable in such case: *Provided*, That this section shall not apply to skilled labor not obtainable in Canada, as provided by section 5 of this act."

The original act provided that all contracts or agreements made in violation of the terms of the act should be void and of no effect. This section of the original act has been allowed to remain as it was.

Important changes have been made in the amendment to secure more effective means of enforcing the act in cases of violation. As the act originally stood, the person or company, etc., found guilty of a violation of the act was liable to a penalty of $1,000, and the mode of recovery of this penalty was that the same should be sued for and recovered by the attorney-general of Canada or a person duly authorized thereto by him, but the latter might pay the informer who had furnished the original information that the law had been violated such a share of the penalties recovered as he might deem reasonable and just, not exceeding 50 per cent, where it appeared that the recovery was had in consequence of the information thus furnished; but it was also expressly provided that no proceedings under the act or prosecutions for violations of it could be instituted without the consent of the attorney-general of the Dominion or some person duly authorized by him.

It was contended by those who sought an amendment of these provisions that there were two important obstacles to an effective enforcement of the act under the method of procedure and penalty as set forth. It was maintained that the necessity of obtaining the consent of the attorney-general of Canada for the institution of proceedings was a requirement which made it difficult for parties who believed themselves to be suffering in consequence of a violation of the act from finding the immediate means of redress. The penalty being fixed at $1,000 also had, it was alleged, the tendency to make the courts more conservative in enforcing the provisions of the act, and it was further believed that many cases might arise in which a light penalty would be quite sufficient.

To remove these objections important provisions were made in this session's amendment. The penalty has been changed from one of $1,000 to a penalty not exceeding $1,000 nor less than $50. The mode of recovery of this sum has been greatly simplified. A person may, with the written consent of the judge of the court in which the action is intended to be brought, sue for and recover the amount as a debt in any court of competent jurisdiction in which debts of like amount are now recovered.

This sum may also, with the written consent, to be obtained ex parte, of the attorney-general of the Province in which the prosecution is had, or of a judge of a superior or county court (the section of the old act requiring the consent of the attorney-general of Canada is repealed), be recovered under summary conviction before any judge of a county court (being a justice of the peace) or a magistrate, or stipendiary magistrate, or any functionary, tribunal, or person invested, by the proper legislative authority, with power to do alone such acts as are usually required to be done by two or more justices of the peace, and acting within the local limits of his or its jurisdiction. In these cases the sum recovered shall be paid to the minister of finance and receiver-general.

Thus two methods are provided for the recovery of the penalty. By one it is recovered as a debt to be sued for by any person who first brings an action therefor in a court of competent jurisdiction in the manner provided for; by the other it is recovered on summary conviction before any person or tribunal invested with power to do alone such acts as are usually required to be done by two or more justices of the peace. The receiver-general may in cases where action is brought for the recovery of a penalty, in accordance with these methods, pay, as under the old act, to any informer who furnishes the original information that the law has been violated such share of the penalty as he deems reasonable and just, not to exceed 50 per cent, where it appears that the recovery was consequent upon the information furnished by him.

Separate proceedings may, under this amendment, as in the original act, be instituted for each alien or foreigner who is a party to such contract or agreement.

The provision in the old act making guilty of an indictable offense the master of any vessel who knowingly brings into Canada on such vessel and lands or permits to be landed from any foreign port or place any alien laborer, mechanic, or artisan who, previous to embarkation on such vessel, had entered into contract or agreement, parole or special, express or implied, to perform labor or service in Canada remains as it was. The fine for an offense under this section is not more than $500 for each alien laborer, mechanic, or artisan so brought or landed, or imprisonment for a term not exceeding 6 months.

Section 6 of the original act provided that the attorney-general of Canada, in cases where he was satisfied that an immigrant has been allowed to land in Canada contrary to the provisions of the act, might cause such immigrant, within the period of one year after landing or entry, to be taken into custody and returned to the country whence he came at the expense of the owner of the vessel. This part of section 6 remains as it was, but an additional clause, which provides that if such person enters from an adjoining country he may be returned at the expense of the person previously contracting for his services, has been amended so as to read "at the expense

LEGISLATION OF FOREIGN COUNTRIES. 721

of the person, partnership, company, or corporation violating section 1 of this act," which is that section which sets forth what is to constitute a violation of the act in consequence of a contract entered into with a foreigner to perform labor in Canada.

The act of 1897 contains a special section setting forth that its provisions should apply only to such foreign countries as have enacted and retain in force, or as enact and retain in force, laws or ordinances applying to Canada similar to it. This section was amended by an act passed in June, 1898, which sets forth the method in which evidence may be given as to countries to which the act applied. The amendment of 1898 remains as it was, but the wording of the original section has been changed from "to apply only to such foreign countries" as have enacted, etc., to "shall apply to the importation or immigration of such persons as reside in or are citizens of such foreign countries" as have enacted, etc. Under the original act no violation could be proven if the persons brought to this country from the United States were foreigners and gave satisfactory proof of their not having become citizens of the United States. Under the act as amended it is only necessary to prove that they were at the time of hiring, etc., resident in the United States.

Finally, a new section has been added to the act which provides that nothing in the act shall affect the exercise of the powers of the government of Canada or of any Province in connection with the promotion of immigration.

The text of the Canadian act is as follows:

[60–61 Victoria.]

CHAPTER II.—AN ACT TO RESTRICT THE IMPORTATION AND EMPLOYMENT OF ALIENS.

[Assented to June 29, 1897.]

1. From and after the passing of this act it shall be unlawful for any person, company, partnership, or corporation in any manner to prepay the transportation or in any way to assist or encourage the importation or immigration of any alien or foreigner into Canada under contract or agreement, parole or special, express or implied, made previous to the importation or immigration of such alien or foreigner, to perform labor or service of any kind in Canada.

2. All contracts or agreements, express or implied, parole or special, hereafter made by and between any person, company, partnership, or corporation and any alien or foreigner to perform labor or service, or having reference to the performance of labor or service by any person in Canada, previous to the immigration or importation of the person whose labor or service is contracted for into Canada, shall be void and of no effect.

3. For every violation of any of the provisions of section one of this act the person, partnership, company, or corporation violating it by knowingly assisting, encouraging, or soliciting the immigration or importation of any alien or foreigner into Canada to perform labor or service of any kind under contract or agreement, express or implied, parole or special, with such alien or foreigner previous to his becoming a resident in or a citizen of Canada shall forfeit and pay the sum of one thousand dollars, which may be sued for and recovered by Her Majesty's attorney-general of Canada, or the person duly authorized thereto by him, as debts of like amount are now recovered in any competent court in Canada, the proceeds to be paid into the hands of the receiver-general; and separate suits may be brought for each alien or foreigner who is a party to such contract or agreement.

4. The master of any vessel who knowingly brings into Canada on such vessel and lands or permits to be landed from any foreign port or place any alien laborer, mechanic, or artisan who, previous to embarkation on such vessel, had entered into contract or agreement, parole or special, express or implied, to perform labor or service in Canada shall be deemed guilty of an indictable offense, and on conviction thereof shall be punished by a fine of not more than five hundred dollars for each alien laborer, mechanic, or artisan so brought or landed, and may also be imprisoned for a term not exceeding six months.

5. Nothing in this act shall be so construed as to prevent any citizen or subject of any foreign country temporarily residing in Canada, either in private or official capacity, from engaging, under contract or otherwise, persons not residents or citizens of Canada to act as private secretaries, servants, or domestics for such foreigner temporarily residing in Canada; nor shall this act be so construed as to prevent any person, partnership, or corporation from engaging, under contract or agreement, skilled workmen in foreign countries to perform labor in Canada in or upon any new industry not at present established in Canada, provided that skilled labor for that purpose can not be otherwise obtained; nor shall the provisions of this act apply to professional actors, artists, lecturers, or singers, or to persons employed strictly as personal or domestic servants: *Provided*, That nothing in this act shall be construed as prohibiting any person from assisting any member of his family, or any relative

or personal friend, to migrate from any foreign country to Canada for the purpose of settlement here.

6. The attorney-general of Canada, in case he shall be satisfied that an immigrant has been allowed to land in Canada contrary to the prohibition of this act, may cause such immigrant, within the period of one year after landing or entry, to be taken into custody and returned to the country whence he came, at the expense of the owner of the importing vessel, or, if he entered from the adjoining country, at the expense of the person previously contracting for the services.

7. The receiver-general may pay to any informer who furnishes original information that the law has been violated such a share of the penalties recovered as he deems reasonable and just, not exceeding 50 per cent, where it appears that the recovery was had in consequence of the information thus furnished.

8. No proceedings under this act, or prosecutions for violation thereof, shall be instituted without the consent of the attorney-general of Canada, or some person duly authorized by him.

9. This act shall apply only to such foreign countries as have enacted and retained in force, or as enact and retain in force, laws or ordinances applying to Canada of a character similar to this act.

APPENDIX TO CHAPTER III, PART II.

WAGES OF GARMENT MAKERS IN THE PHILADELPHIA TRADE.

[The following special report, prepared by Miss Helen Marot and Miss Caroline L. Pratt, to accompany the investigation of the clothing trade, was received too late for insertion at the proper place in this volume. It is inserted at this point, and shows especially the influence of country competition upon the wages of garment workers in the city of Philadelphia.]

In general, the same system of manufacture of men's ready-made clothing prevails in Philadelphia as does in Chicago and New York, and in the United States as in England. Ready-made clothing is contracted out and made up in shops of varying sizes, which are classed in the factory inspector's report as "sweat shops."

It is the purpose of this report to deal with wages and other conditions of employment. We shall describe the systems of manufacture and the position of the contractors only so far as these bear upon the former.

In giving the rates of wages paid in Philadelphia to the makers of men's clothing, we present figures which are similar to those of other cities, but the unusual feature of the Philadelphia trade is the effect of the country work (i. e., the manufacture of ready-made clothing in villages and on farms) upon the wages of the town worker, which we undertake to show. As the highest grade of ready-made work is not sent to the country, and as the lower grade is confined to the foreign population in the city, our report deals with this class—that is, the class represented by a $15 suit at retail and all clothing which sells at a price lower than that.

According to the factory inspector's report of 1900, there are 6,774 men and women employed in Philadelphia in the manufacture of coats, vests, and trousers. This total includes ready-made and custom work and summer clothing. The total is greatly in excess of the actual number employed, as the factory inspectors are required to revisit shops whenever the location is changed, and in this way are apt to duplicate the number of employees. Their total is greatly in excess of our estimate, also, because we have considered separately the ready-made and custom work. It is on this basis that the labor unions are organized, makers of ready-made clothing subdividing their unions into Vest makers, Trousers makers, and Coat makers. The tailors, or makers of custom clothing, unite in one body as Journeymen tailors.

It was as difficult to obtain accurate statements as to numbers engaged in the trade from the union officials as from the inspector's report, as their written records do not extend beyond the members of the union. The walking delegate of the Vest Makers' Union had ground for his estimate as the part of the trade he represents is so closely organized. He had upon his books 500 members, and stated that there were not more than 50 outside of the organization. Our observation bore out this testimony, for out of 112 vest makers whom we interrogated as to whether or not they belonged to the union only 5 replied in the negative, although every effort was made to include both union and nonunion shops. The union estimate for the whole trade for 1900 was 3,650, including cutters, while the inspector's estimate was 6,774, exclusive of cutters. Not accepting the union estimate unqualifiedly, and on the other hand not wholly rejecting the factory inspector's figures, but basing our calculations on both and on our observation, it is safe to say roughly that the makers of men's ready-made clothing in shops number between 4,000 and 5,000 people. We accepted the testimony of 261 of these workers relative to their wages.

Unsatisfactory as the above result is as to numbers, we could secure no figures relating to the number of country workers. The manufacturers of Philadelphia repeatedly asserted that they sent 75 per cent of the work to country contractors. We could obtain no other testimony worth considering. The factory inspector's report does not indicate whether the shops reported in country districts are manufacturing for Philadelphia. We accepted the testimony of 73 of these people working in shops and 38 working in their own homes.

We endeavored to make our cases typical, and rejected such statements as were shown to be influenced by conditions peculiar to the persons interviewed. We gave out no printed forms to be filled in by the workers, but each person was carefully questioned.

Besides individual statements, we secured written statements from 50 city contractors. Many of these we found to be incomplete or false when we attempted deductions as to profits, and therefore were obliged to reject all but 15. These 15 statements cover the wages of 227 employees. We accepted also the testimony from 9 country contractors, 4 of whom "farmed out" their work. In these four shops only the wages of the pressers could be used for a comparison, as the wages for operator, baster, and finisher are represented in the price paid to an individual home worker. The remaining 5 shops, including the pressers in the other 4, represent the wages for 129 employees. As will be found upon reference to our tables, we have kept the contractors' statements separate from those of the individual.

The wages varied greatly in the city shops, while in the country they were so nearly identical for the same class of work that we only obtained repetitions beyond a certain point. For example, there were 27 shops in Egg Harbor, all of which were coat shops, all used the same system, and the wages in each class of workers were about the same. After questioning the workers in four shops and talking to their respective employers, we thought the testimony sufficient upon which to base our statement.

The following tables include the shop workers who were employed in the making of coats, vests, and trousers, as operators, pressers, basters, and finishers.

WAGES OF GARMENT MAKERS. 725

Average wage of garment workers.

IN CITY SHOPS TAKEN FROM 261 INDIVIDUAL STATEMENTS OF EMPLOYEES.

Number in class.	Class of workers.	Sex. M.	Sex. F.	Prevailing nationality.	Number of years in United States.	Hours per day.	Week work.	Piece-work.	Average number of pieces per week.	Average price per piece.	Wage per week.	Number of weeks per year.	Average weekly wage throughout the year.	Annual wage.	Trade-union member. Yes.	Trade-union member. No.
25	Operators on coats	25		Jew	12	10	19	6	74	$0.169	$10.72	26	$5.40	$281.10	12	13
58	Operators on vests	52	1	...do	9	10	9	37	121	.087	10.86	28	5.09	303.26	47	3
36	Operators on trousers	36		...do	7	11	1	35	86	.11	9.58	28	5.12	269.33	22	13
9	Basters on coats	9		...do	13	10	9				10.77	26	5.80	302.20	7	2
5	Basters on vests	5		...do	9	10	2	29	120	.06	7.05	30	4.35	226.43		
31	Pressers on coats	31		...do	11	10	3	15	132	.081	8.24	27	4.57	238.07	29	5
18	Pressers on vests	18		...do	9	9	3	12	292	.036	10.90	31	6.57	342.05	12	
15	Pressers on trousers	15		...do	7	13	1	20	319	.027	7.28	25	3.63	189.28	14	7
21	Finishers on coats	21	21	Mixed	9	10	15	9	73	.053	4.74	26	2.35	122.50	11	11
24	Finishers on vests	3	20	Jew	6	10	1	19	265	.027	5.36	25	2.77	144.17	18	1
20	Finishers on trousers		8	Italian	10	10		9	50	.069	3.22	29	1.75	91.30	4	3
9	Average				9	10					8.50	28	4.41	188.10		
261	Total	185	76				63	191							185	58

IN COUNTRY SHOPS, TAKEN FROM 73 INDIVIDUAL STATEMENTS OF EMPLOYEES.

Number in class.	Class of workers.	Sex. M.	Sex. F.	Prevailing nationality.	Number of years in United States.	Hours per day.	Week work.	Piece-work.	Average number of pieces per week.	Average price per piece.	Wage per week.	Number of weeks per year.	Average weekly wage throughout the year.	Annual wage.	Trade-union member. Yes.	Trade-union member. No.
36	Operators on coats	8	28	American		10	36				$5.88	44	$4.93	$256.27		13
12	Operators on trousers	1	11	...do		10	2	10	513	$0.01	5.17	51	5.02	261.40	20	11
12	Basters on coats	11		...do		10	12				7.47	40	5.86	305.02	6	6
13	Pressers on coats	13		...do		10	13				6.90	41	5.62	292.46	8	3
	Finishers *a*										2.98					
	Average					10					5.51	44	5.18	271.72		
73	Total	33	40				63	10							34	33

a In the absence of sufficient individual data, the average made from the statements of the contractors is here inserted for the wage of finishers on all garments.

Average wage of country home workers, taken from 38 individual statements.

Number in class.	Class of workers.	Prevailing nationality.	Sex.		Number of helpers.	Average number of pieces per week.	Average price per piece.	Wage per week.	Trade union.		
			M.	F.					Yes.	No.	
9	Coat makers	American		9		13	$0.226	$2.99		9	
16	Vest makers	...do		16		20	.104	2.10		16	
13	Trouser makers	...do		13		13	.145	1.94		13	
38	Average Total			38				2.26		38	

Comparative wage paid in city and country shops, taken from the testimony of 24 contractors.

City contractors.			Country contractors.		
Class of workers.	Number of employees.	Wage.	Class of workers.	Number of employees.	Wage.
Operators	91	$10.32	Operators	60	$5.18
Pressers	38	11.38	Pressers	16	7.62
Basters	31	6.10	Basters	33	6.13
Finishers	67	4.66	Finishers	20	2.98
	227	8.37		129	5.35

It will be necessary to explain the difference in the organization of shops in town and country. The shops which we visited, and which we believe are typical of the country trade, are located at Egg Harbor, New Jersey, and in Montgomery and Bucks counties, Pa., where the bulk of the work is done. There are 27 shops at Egg Harbor, all coat shops and all organized practically the same way. The others in Pennsylvania are all outgrowths of the "farming out" system. These latter are isolated, and therefore the organization is more independent and often not well worked out; or else it corresponds to town work, which influence can be directly traced, either to one or two employees upon whom the contractor depends, and who had learned their trade in town, or to the contractor himself, who had done the same.

The work of the operator is the same in the country and town shops in that it is confined to machine work, though the division of the work is somewhat different. The city coat operators, working piecework, as they do in some shops, have their work arranged for them in "teams," each member of which confines himself to the stitching on a certain part of the garment. This makes a gain in number produced, but each member of the team is more or less limited in what he can do by what the others in his team can accomplish. This latter consideration is one of those upon which the organized coat makers are basing their demand for week work. They explained that, while the piecework offered opportunities for higher wages to the rapid workers, they were hampered by the inability of the less rapid workers in their team. In week work, however, those classed as first operators, according to the number produced, receive this higher wage. The week-work system throws the responsibility of dividing the work so that everyone is kept busy upon the contractors.

The team work is a more serious consideration with the coat makers than with the vest and trousers makers, because a coat admits of so much finer division of labor. While the teams in vests and trousers number never more than 3, and usually only 2, and many shops organized as piecework without teams at all, the coat operators work in teams of never less than 3.

In the country, week work is the rule, but even where piecework is used the objectionable feature of team work has not troubled the workers.

But the most striking difference between the country and town shops is that the operators in the town shops are invariably men and in the country shops they are women. This latter has been made possible by the introduction of steam or electric power to supersede foot power in the country. At Egg Harbor few shops use foot power, and in Montgomery and Bucks counties, where the shops are younger, foot power is not in use at all. The presence of men in the country shops as operators almost always indicates, in the table, a shop run by foot power. The exceptions to this are to be found in the two American coat operators who gave their wages as $12 per week. These two men were in the same shop, were originally from the city, and the inference was that they furnished, besides their work, the knowledge about the clothing industry necessary to the successful operation of the shop. The shop is organized very much as the city shops are and shows the influence of these two men.

Pressers in the city are exclusively pressers, and the basters, who are usually women, baste. In many of the country shops those who press are the under pressers and basters as well. In these shops when a consignment of goods is ready for shipping all of the men in the shop drop their other work and do the final pressing.

In the country shops all of the "felling" is given to outside women. What finishing must be done during the process of making up the coat is done by the basters and under pressers. All whom we have classified in the country shops as "finishers" are outside workers. In the city shops there are always some women finishers working in the shops. These women do the felling as well as finishing. There are besides many outside finishers who only fell the work as they do in the country.

The "farming-out" system relieves the contractor of all responsibility as to organization. Contractors farm out exclusively or have shops for the better class of work and farm out the cheapest grades. They have a building for handling, storing, and pressing the goods. The coats, vests, and trousers, are distributed about the country among the villagers and farm people and called for later in the week. The worker is expected to finish the garment, except the buttonholes. The pressers retained in the shop are for incidental pressing rather than for pressing the whole garment, except where a different arrangement is made with the workers, and then all of the pressing is done inside.

To understand how and to what extent the country work affects the wages of city garment makers, we must consider, first, wages for the country home workers. The comparison of wages between town and country workers in shops is a fair one, because they are all using the opportunity to make garments as a means of livelihood. On the contrary, the country home workers are usually simply supplementing other earnings. They are farmers' wives and daughters and those of farm laborers. They make clothing in the intervals of housework and farmwork, for most of them help in the haying and harvesting. To show how little a matter of business it is with these farm people, it is possible to make a comparison of output between workers in a shop and the same contractor's employees outside. The weekly output of trousers made by 22 people working inside was 900, while that of 50 families outside was 500; an average of 40.9 per individual for the former and of 10 for the latter—too great a difference to be accounted for on the ground of advantage of factory methods over home work. Our average number of all garments, including coats, vests, and trousers, for each family per week, based upon the testimony of 38 home workers, is 16.3. That of one of the largest country contractors is 12.7 per week per family. Owing to the fact that none of the contractors whom we interviewed made all 3 garments inside the shop, it is impossible to offset these figures by an average output per individual from any one shop. But taking 1 typical coat and 1 vest and 1 trousers shop and averaging the output, we get 31.7 garments per individual for 1 week.

At the most, then, the output is only one-half of that of shop workers. This shows how infrequently the work is the principal occupation of these women. Yet, owing to the immense number engaged in it, the volume of work assumes very large proportions. Isolated as these people are and remote from the contractor, they must accept his rate of payment offered through the driver who delivers the goods.

Where the shop replaces the farming-out system, the employees are drawn from these same farmers' families, and a low standard of wages, influenced by the home earnings, prevails throughout. One would expect these shop earnings to be greater than the home earnings, first, because the grade of work is higher, and, indeed, the contractor's principal reason for bringing the work into shops is the increasing demand for a higher grade of work, hence his closer supervision; and second, because of the better opportunity which a worker has of making a bargain when associated with other workers, whether or not they are joined together through organization.

While collecting the material from the country home workers we foresaw the desirability of making such a comparison. But the country people were so unused to thinking of their work as a regular employment that their answer as to how many garments they could make in a day, working steadily, were mere guesses, and many of them would make no estimate at all. Four trousers makers answered the question as follows: One, with the help of a daughter, actually made 10 pairs per week, but claimed that she could make 4 pairs per day or 24 pairs per week if she gave all her time. She received on an average per pair 13 cents, which is a cent and a half below our average for country home workers on trousers. This would give her and her daughter together a weekly wage of $3.12. Two other women, while making but 6 pairs per week, claimed that each could, without help, make 2 pairs per day, or 12 pairs per week. One of them was paid at the rate of 11 cents and the other at the rate of 19 cents, which represent the extremes of rates given us. Thus the one could make per week $1.32 and the other $2.38. This statement of rates does not by any means represent the difference in grade of work. The 11 cents shows the extreme to which a contractor may go, if he is so disposed, when dealing with isolated people. The statement which puts the best light upon the wages of the country home worker was from a woman who said that, while she made only 11 pairs per week, she could make, unaided, 4 pairs per day, or 24 pairs per week. She received the best grade given out by her contractor, and was paid 18 cents per pair. This would have given her a wage of $4.32. We could not use the few answers which were given us by the coat makers; and while the vest makers gave estimates, we found no vest makers working in shops with whom a comparison could be made. However, answers from 8 vest makers show that they could make on an average 34.8 vests per week. The average rate for all is $0.104, which would give an average weekly wage of $3.62.

The highest wage paid in the country shops to women is $9 per week, and the lowest $2.75, the average being $5.22. This includes coats and trousers shops both in the farming-out districts and at Egg Harbor. A more helpful comparison, perhaps, would be between the statements of country home workers on trousers given above and the wages paid in a trousers shop in the same district. The women operators in this shop are paid by the piece, and the average is $5 per week. They are all skilled operators, 9 in number, with slight variation in wages.

Imperfect as is this material regarding the possible wages of home workers, it is safe to draw the conclusion that there is a slight advantage to those who work in the shop.

The country contractors working in shops save in the cost of production over city contractors in the employment of women operators in the place of men. It is difficult, on account of the different division of labor in the country and city shops, to make in this connection a close comparison of wages.

Average city wages:
   Coat operators, male.................... $10.72
   Vest basters, female................... 6.59

Average country wages:
   Coat operators, female $5.34
   Coat basters, male..................... 7.79

It will be seen, however, that the women coat operators in the country who get the highest wages paid women receive $5.34, and that the city women basters on vests are receiving $6.59. Here we find women in the city engaged in a lower class of work and receiving higher pay than the women in the country who are doing the highest grade of work. If we now take the highest grade of workers among the men, that is, the operators in the city and the basters in the country, we find that the operators in the city receive an advance of nearly $3 over the country coat basters; but part of the advance must be attributed to the greater skill required in operating.

Reference to the above table will show what would be the effect upon rates of wages if women were to enter into competition with men in the city trade. If the vest basters, with an average wage of $6.59, should offer their services even at a considerable increase over their present wages as skilled coat operators the rate of wages for operating coats would be reduced.

So far neither the Jewish women in the trade nor the Americans have come into direct competition with men operators, although American girls are operating in some of the shops in connection with wholesale houses, and in the shops which undertake the highest grades of ready-made garments.

It has become possible for women to enter the trade as operators just so far as the shops have adopted steam or electric power, which has been done with a few exceptions in the country. This has taken place to some extent in the city, and yet the largest manufacturer of ready-made clothing in Philadelphia recently advertised for women operators, having opened a shop which the firm expected would form the nucleus of a larger factory to be built later. Although trade was dull, they had almost no answers, and such as they did have were from girls not sufficiently skilled to be acceptable.

The city contractors, through the year, fill in the deficiencies in seasonal orders sent to the country. The average price paid city contractors is slightly higher than the price paid for country work. If we now take the total wages involved in making a garment, rather than the averages paid the different classes of workers, or the total average for the trade, we can make a clearer comparison in the costs of manufacture so far as wages are concerned.

Average cost in wages per garment.

To city contractors:		To country contractors:	
Coats	$0.395	Coats	$0.287
Vests	.213	Vests	.115
Trousers	.207	Trousers	.138

The largest item of expense, outside of wages, for the city contractor is his rent, which is offset by the freight charges in the expenses of the country contractor. The few other expenses are easily balanced. It is evident that the lower cost of production caused by lower rates of wages has drawn the bulk of what is known as "seasonal work" to the country, leaving only the "rush-order work" for the city contractor, who is near at hand. The effect of dividing the trade between the country and city has been to reduce the annual income of the city garment maker through shortening the working year rather than by altering the rate of wages. It is this short season and irregularity of employment which is alarming to the city worker. It is doubtful whether it is possible to speak at all of a "season" of work at the present time in Philadelphia. During the winter and summer the work is heavier than in the spring and fall months, but even then it is fitful. Unemployment is not peculiar to the Philadelphia trade, but in other cities there is a defined "slack" and "busy" season, which can with some certainty be counted upon. The table on page 711 shows the actual loss in weekly income through irregularity of employment throughout the year. The average rate of weekly wages for all classes in the city is $8.50, the average number of weeks is 28, and the average weekly income throughout the year is $4.41, making a loss of 48 per cent through unemployment.

Contrasting this with the country shop work as given in table on page 711, where the rate of wages is the more serious feature to the employee, the loss in wages through unemployment reaches only a little over 16 per cent. The average wage for all classes, excepting finishers, is $6.20, the weeks 44, and the average weekly income throughout the year is $5.18.

The low-water mark which the annual income of the garment makers has reached in town, taken in conjunction with the rates of wages paid in the country, explains why the city contractor can no longer offer competition successfully. In the United States Special Report on the Slum Districts of Great Cities made in 1893 the average rate for all workers in the Philadelphia district was $8.68. The part of the city reported covered the territory where is found the greatest number of sweat shops, and from where we drew the bulk of the material here reported. The commissioner's report included men and women engaged in "agriculture," the "fisheries and mining," "professional," "domestic and personal service," "trade and transportation," "manufacture and mechanical industries," "housewives and at work," and "scholars and at work." The same report shows for the same district an average loss in time of 2.9 months. A comparison with the wages and time of the garment workers for this locality shows that the income of these people is already below the average in their own neighborhood.

We have not yet spoken of the lower cost of living in the country, which, of course, is fundamental and can not better be shown than through comparative rentals of the same class of workers. The average rent paid by the city worker is $8.96 per month, based upon 180 answers to our question. The families average five persons and occupy three rooms. Out of 84 country garment workers 51 own their own homes, and 33 pay an average monthly rent of $4.59 for a whole house.

The part of the city trade considered here is practically confined to Russian Jews, if we except the cutters and women who "finish" in their homes. The cutters are American and most of the women referred to are Italians. Out of over 100 shops which we visited, we found only 2 owned by Italian contractors. The rest were Jewish. The operators who were working in both of these shops were Italians, the pressers were Jews, and the others were both Jews and Italians.

Of the 261 whom we questioned as to nationality, 237 were Jews, 20 were Italians, and 4 were Americans. Of the 20 Italians, 16 were women finishers. The average number of years these people had lived in the United States, based upon 225 answers, was 9. The lowest time was 1½ years and the highest 30 years. Out of a total of 50 women finishers working in shops, 33 were Jewish, 13 were Italians, and 4 were Americans.

In the country districts of Pennsylvania the garment workers are Americans, some of whom can be further distinguished as "Pennsylvania Dutch." In New Jersey they are Americans and German-Americans. It seems necessary to make this latter distinction as many of them speak German among themselves. Both the Pennsylvania Dutch and these Americans of German parentage are clannish people, but there is no evidence of a lower standard of living than among their American neighbors. In spite of this, it is these people and their American co-workers who are accepting a lower rate of wages than the Jews in the city. In some cases these country people complained bitterly of the wages they received, but we found no such discontent as we did in the city.

It is remarkable in consideration of the foregoing that the influence of the four local Philadelphia unions—the two Coat Makers, Vest Makers, and Pants Makers—has extended so far as it has. They have within the past 2 years shown an increased activity owing to their affiliation with the United Garment Workers of America. The confidence in the label has been of slow growth, because it has not, in theory, appealed to the men as individuals. But a demand for the label has recently come from manufacturers, which has caused a unionizing of shops and increased the membership of the organization. The manufacturers have been forced into this position through what seems to be a growing demand from small towns in Pennsylvania and the West for labeled goods.

Previous to 1900 the coat and trousers makers were hopelessly disorganized. Since then the coat makers have opened an office and are holding regular meetings, and have in some shops effected a change in the system of work. They have not yet, however, been able to increase their rate of wages. The trousers makers have accomplished nothing as a whole, but have prevented in individual shops a reduction in wages. In many of the shops where coats and trousers are made the operators are still obliged to furnish their own sewing machines.

The vest makers, through all discouragements, have held their men together. They have secured steam or electric power in all but a few of the shops, have shortened their day of labor, and are generally maintaining union rates of wages. These rates for vests correspond exactly with the averages obtained in our investigation.

The country shops are also beginning to feel the pressure of the manufacturer, but the workers themselves show little interest in organization. In one section of the country, where a religious sect, the Mennonites, predominate, there is such a strong objection to the union that the contractors have as yet been unable to prevail upon their employees to form one. At Egg Harbor the union has been formed long enough for a few of the workers to realize the value to themselves of organization; that there is a possibility along the line of wages of improving their condition, and that the union need not be entirely for the benefit of the contractor. Although the union is growing, there is little of what is known as labor agitation.

The first consideration of the union in the city has been that of hours. The tendency of the piece-rate system to demoralize hours of labor is as true in the garment trade as in other industries. On the other hand, in week work it is less difficult to maintain a normal working day. It was found that the creation of public sentiment among the workers for shorter hours was a slow process, so that latterly the policy of the unions has been to institute such reforms as would make a long day impossible or unprofitable. The vest makers have made it impossible in the union shops by demanding steam or electric power. Closing off the power at the end of the day prevents operators from working overtime, which in turn ends the day for all others, as they are dependent upon the operator for their supply of work. The coat makers, owing to the greater complexity of a coat, have found it difficult to arrange a piece-rate system which would be applicable to all shops. They are now demanding the week-work system, which besides regulating rates of payment will control the length of the day. The trousers makers have been so far too weak as a body to affect the trade. The piece-rate system, which is universal, is probably due to the will of the contractors rather than to any concerted action of the men themselves.

Although we received unsatisfactory answers to our question as to the length of the day, our figures show in the tables appended that the trousers makers are working on an average 11.5 hours, while the coat and vest makers average only 10. Using the figures relatively, we believe they contain a bit of truth. That is, the trousers makers work longer hours than either of the other two classes.

We have contrasted the systems of city and country work, the rates of wages, and certain influences affecting wages. It remains for us to speak of the most striking contrast between the shops in and outside of the city; the presence of strain in the one and its absence in the other. The difference is not wholly due to the greater intensity of city life, but also to the economic conditions which we have been considering. This strain or intensity which is so marked a feature of the city shop is due to the competition which results from an overfull labor market; to the competition of contractors, who are not only bidding against each other for the rush work, but are constantly striving for the seasonal work, which goes to the country at a lower figure than city wages and rents will permit; and lastly to the piece-rate and "task" systems. These three elements—competition among workers, competition among contractors, and piece-rate and task systems—contribute to a strain which seems to reach the limit of endurance during busy seasons.

There is apparently no dearth of workers in the country, but they are less dependent on their earnings and their expenses are more remote. Nor is there a total lack of competition between country contractors. But that the consignments of goods are larger and much less frequent than those to city contractors, reduces the possibility of bargaining with those who make the consignments, and limits the competition among the country contractors themselves.

The country workers gave us no impression of fighting for the wherewithal to live. It seemed to come with comparative ease and along with it a good time in a mild way. It is hardly necessary to say that the condition and situation of the place of work, which are large factors in the comfort of the employees, add to the balance already placed in favor of the country contractor as an employer. There are no plumbing arrangements, and hence none to get out of order. The pressure of work is never too great to allow for a "cleaning-up" time. There is plenty of space to build in and, therefore, the awful evil of overcrowding is never felt. The shops are usually separated from other buildings, which admits of plenty of fresh air.

HELEN MAROT.
CAROLINE L. PRATT.

PHILADELPHIA, *September 1, 1901.*

CITY SHOPS.

Wages of 25 operators on coats.

Nationality	Number of years in United States	Sex	Hours per day	Week work or piece-work	Average number of pieces per week	Average price per piece	Wage per week	Number of weeks per year	Average weekly wage throughout the year	Annual wage	Trade union Yes	Trade union No
Jew		M	10	P	72	$0.17	$12.44	30½	$7.14	$371.28		1
Do		M	10	P	72	.17	12.44	30½	7.14	371.28		1
Do	16	M		W			14.00	15	4.038	210.00	1	
Do		M	10	P			12.75	27	6.620	344.25		
Do		M	10	P	85	.15	18.00	27	9.346	486.00		
Do		M	11	W	80	.22½	4.00	29	2.230	116.00	1	
Do	10	M	10	W			14.00	39	10.500	546.00		1
Do	12	M	10	W			12.00	25	5.769	300.00		1
Do	10	M	10	W			7.00	26	3.50	182.00		1
Do	14	M	10	W			14.00	34½	9.333	485.333	1	
Do	10	M	10	W			12.00	20	4.615	240.00		
Do	2½	M	10	W			4.50	30½	2.625	136.50		
Italian	9	M		P			10.92		4.80	249.60		
Jew		M	10	P	78	.14	9.60	26	4.307	224.00	1	
Do		M	10	W	60	.16	8.00	28	4.50	234.00		
Do		M	10	W			9.00	26	4.384	228.00		
Do		M	10	W			9.50	24	8.00	416.00	1	
Do		M	8	W			12.00	34½				
Italian	17	M	10	W			12.00	21¾	1.665	86.666	1	
Do	16	M	10	W			4.00	39	3.75	195.00		
Jew	30	M		W			5.00	14	3.903	203.00	1	
Do	14	M	11	W			14.50	21½	5.993	311.75	1	
Do	6	M		W			12.00	26	6.00	312.00		
Do		M		W			10.00	21½	4.166	216.666		
Total		25 M		19 W., 6 P								
Average	12.8		10		74.5	.169	10.726	26.7	5.405	281.101	12	13

Wages of 24 finishers on coats.

Jew	6	F	10	W			$7.50	27	$3.894	$202.50		1
Do	14	F	10	P	60	$0.05	3.00	24	1.384	72.00	1	
Do	14	F		P	60	.05		24	1.384	72.00	1	
Do	10	M	10	W			10.00	30½	5.897	306.666		
Do	3	M	10	W			6.00	27	3.115	162.00		1

WAGES OF GARMENT MAKERS. 733

Italian	20	F.	11	P.	60	.055	3.30	24	1.522	79.20	1	
Do		F.	11	P.	60	.055	3.30	24	1.522	79.20	1	
Do	10	M.	10	W.			7.50	13	1.875	97.50		
Jew	10	F.	10	P.			4.00	12	.923	48.00	1	
Do	14	F.	10	P.	100	.05	5.00	24½	2.371	123.333		1
Do	14	F.	10	P.	108	.05	5.40	23	2.888	124.20		1
Do	11	F.	10	P.	72	.05	3.60	23	1.592	82.80		
Do	3	F.		W.			3.00	15	1.73	90.00	1	
Italian		F.		W.			3.00	41½	2.408	125.00	1	
Jew	2	F.	10	P.	40	.065	2.60	37	1.85	96.20	1	
Italian	9	F.	10	P.	100	.06	6.00					
Jew	9	F.	10	W.			7.00	35½	4.778	248.50	1	1
Do	10	F.	10	W.			8.00	35½	5.461	284.00	1	1
Italian	12	F.		W.			6.50					1
American	2¼	F.		W.			3.50	30½	2.041	106.166	1	1
Italian		F.		W.			2.00	30½	1.16	60.60	1	1
Do	13	F.	10	W.			2.75	30½	1.604	83.416	1	1
Do	6	F.	10	W.			3.00	30½	1.175	91.00	1	1
		F.	10	W.			2.00	30½	1.16	60.666		1
Total		3 M., 21 F.		15 W., 9 P.							9	11
Average	9.6		10.0		73.3	.053	4.747	26.9	2.354	122.50		

Wages of 18 pressers on coats.

Jew	14	M.	10¼	P.	175	$0.08	$14.00	27	$7.269	$378.00		
Do	20	M.	10	P.	120	.08	9.60	26	4.80	249.60	1	
Do	15	M.	10	W.			6.00				1	
Do		M.	10	P.	300	.035	10.50	20¼	4.139	215.25		
Do	17	M.	10	P.	55	.105	5.775	24	2.667	138.60		
Do	12	M.	10	P.	135	.09	12.15	28	6.542	340.20		
Do		M.	10	P.	300	.035	10.50	18½	3.735	194.25		
Do	10	M.	10	P.	180	.065	11.70	43½	9.75	507.00	1	1
Do	13	M.	10	P.	150	.07	10.50	34½	6.932	360.50		
Do	10	M.	10	P.	110	.075	8.25	23	3.649	189.75	1	
Do	10	M.	10	P.	110	.075	8.25	23	3.649	189.75	1	
Do	3	M.		P.	125	.075	9.375	30½	3.468	284.375	1	
Do	11	M.		P.	100	.07	7.000	26	3.50	182.00		1
Italian	2	M.	10	W.	40	.09	3.60	30	2.076	108.00	1	
Jew	16	M.		P.			4.00	26	2.00	104.00		
Do	1	M.		P.	40	.09	3.60	28	2.076	108.00	1	
Do	13	M.	11	W.	40	.09	3.60	30	2.076	108.00		1
Do		M.		W.			10.00		5.00	260.00	1	
Total		18 M.		3 W., 15 P.							12	5
Average	11		10.1		132	.081	8.244	27.2	4.578	238.079		

CITY SHOPS—Continued.

Wages of 9 basters on coats.

Nationality	Number of years in United States	Sex	Hours per day	Week work or piecework	Average number of pieces per week	Average price per piece	Wage per week	Number of weeks per year	Average weekly wage throughout the year	Annual wage	Trade union Yes	Trade union No
Jew	26	M.	10	W.			$12.00	26	$6.00	$312.00	1	
Do	13	M.	10	W.			14.00	26	7.00	364.00	1	
Do	8	M.	10	W.			14.00	30	8.076	420.00	1	
Do	1	M.		W.			6.00	17½	1.656	86.666	1	
Do	13	M.	10	W.			5.00	30½	2.914	151.666	1	
Do	11	M.		W.			14.00	23⅚	6.416	333.666	1	
Do	17	M.	11	W.			16.00	26	8.00	416.000	1	
Do	18	M.	10	W.			11.00	30⅚	6.416	333.666		
Italian	15	M.										1
Total. Average	13.5	9 M.		9 W.			10.777	26.2	5.809	302.208	7	2

Wages of 53 operators on vests.

Nationality	Number of years in United States	Sex	Hours per day	Week work or piecework	Average number of pieces per week	Average price per piece	Wage per week	Number of weeks per year	Average weekly wage throughout the year	Annual wage	Trade union Yes	Trade union No
Jew	4	M.	10	W.			$6.50	26	$3.25	$169.00	1	
Do	12	M.	10	W.			13.00	34⅔	8.667	450.666	1	
Do	9	M.	10	W.			13.00				1	
Do	15	F.	10	P.	135	$0.09	12.15				1	
Do	10	M.		P.	150	.08	12.00				1	
Do	7	M.	12	P.	150	.10	15.00				1	
Do	14	M.		P.			8.00					
Do	10	M.		P.			15.00	37½	8.653	450.00	1	
Do	12	M.	12	P.			12.00	34⅘	10.00	520.00	1	
Do	9	M.					12.50				1	
Do	6	M.					12.50				1	
Do	15	M.					8.00				1	
Do	10	M.					13.00					1
Do	12	M.		P.			17.00	26	8.50	442.00	1	
Do	12	M.	10	P.			15.00	37	10.673	555.00	1	

Do	8	M.	10	P.	....	....	15.00	37	10.673	555.00	1	......
Do	1½	M.	10	W.	....	....	6.00	35⅔	4.115	214.00	1	......
Do	4	M.	10	P.	120	.095	11.40	40	8.769	465.00	1	......
Do	7	M.	10	W.	....	....	5.00	33⅓	3.205	166.666	......	......
Do	10	M.	10	P.	150	.08	12.00	33⅓	7.692	400.00	1	......
Do	12	M.	10	P.	120	.09	10.80	32	6.646	345.60	1	......
Do	4	M.	10	P.	120	.09	10.80	35½	7.373	383.40	1	......
Do	12	M.	10	P.	150	.09	13.50	30⅓	7.875	409.50	1	......
Do	11	M.	10	P.	100	.115	11.50	29⅔	6.558	341.166	1	......
Do	6	M.	10	P.	100	.08	8.00	26	4.00	208.00	1	......
Do	4	M.	10	P.	110	.08	8.80	26	4.40	228.80	1	......
Do	9	M.	10	P.	100	.10	10.00	34⅔	6.666	346.666	1	......
Do	16	M.	10	P.	110	.085	9.35	24	4.315	224.40	1	......
Do	9	M.	10	P.	100	.085	8.50	21⅔	3.541	184.166	1	......
Do	16	M.	10	P.	110	.09	9.90	21⅔	4.125	214.50	1	......
Do	6	M.	10	P.	100	.085	8.50	26	4.25	221.00	1	......
Do	9	M.	10	P.	150	.085	12.75	26	6.375	331.50	1	......
Do	3	M.	10	W.	....	....	9.00	26	4.50	234.00	1	......
Do	10	M.	10	P.	120	.09	10.80	27	5.607	291.60	1	......
Do	4	M.	10	W.	120	.09	10.80	23⅑	4.80	249.60	1	......
Do	12	M.	10	P.	100	.07	7.00	19½	2.625	136.50	1	......
Do	6	M.	10	P.	95	.09	8.55	17⅓	2.85	148.20	1	......
Do	13	M.	10	P.	114	.10	11.40	28⅙	6.173	321.10	1	......
Do	10	M.	10	P.	100	.08	8.00	17⅓	2.666	138.666	1	......
Do	....	M.	10	W.	....	....	10.00	28⅙	5.416	281.666	......	1
Do	....	M.	10	W.	....	....	5.00	28⅙	2.708	140.833	......	1
Do	14	M.	10	P.	150	.08	12.00	30¼	6.980	363.00	1	......
Do	11	M.	10	P.	120	.08	9.60	26	4.80	249.60	1	......
Do	4	M.	10	P.	110	.08	8.80	40⅘	6.844	355.911	1	......
Do	9	M.	10	P.	100	.08	8.00	26	4.00	208.00	1	......
Do	14	M.	10	P.	120	.09	10.80	30⅓	6.30	327.60	1	......
Do	14	M.	10	P.	150	.09	13.50	26	6.75	351.00	1	......
Do	20	M.	10	P.	150	.09	13.50	24⅙	6.274	326.25	1	......
Do	4	M.	10	P.	120	.09	10.80	25⅙	5.226	271.80	1	......
Do	12	M.	10	P.	140	.07	9.80	21⅔	4.083	212.333	1	......
Total	....	52 M., 1 F.	....	9 W., 37 P.	....	....	....	....	....	....	47	3
Average	9.6	....	10	....	121	.087	10.864	28.6	5.095	303.26	......	......

Wages of 31 basters on vests.

Jew	7	F.	10	P.	150	$0.055	$8.25	17⅓	$2.750	$143,00	1	......
Do	11	F.	10	P.	100	.06	6.00	26	3.00	156.00	1	......
Do	13	F.	10	P.	125	.052	6.56	24⅔	3.112	161.868	......	......
Do	7	F.	10	P.	110	.05	5.50	30⅙	3.19	165·916	1	......
Do	3	F.	10	P.	120	.05	6.00	28	3.23	168.00	1	......
Do	13	M.	10	P.	130	.065	8.45	17⅓	2.816	146.466	1	......
Do	5	F.	10	P.	100	.055	5.50	17⅓	1.833	95.333	1	......
Do	7	F.	10	P.	100	.055	5.50	17⅓	1.833	95.333	1	......

CITY SHOPS—Continued.

Wages of 31 basters on vests—Continued.

Nationality.	Number of years in United States.	Sex.	Hours per day.	Week work or piece- work.	Average number of pieces per week.	Average price per piece.	Wage per week.	Number of weeks per year.	Average weekly wage throughout the year.	Annual wage.	Trade union. Yes.	Trade union. No.
Jew	11	F.	10	P.	125	$0.052	$6.562	28½	$3.558	$184.829	1	
Do	7	F.	10	P.	120	.06	7.20	43½	6.00	312.00	1	
Do	7	F.	10	P.	75	.04	3.00	10⅛	.583	30.333	1	
Do	11	F.	10	P.	115	.055	6.325	38	4.615	240.35	1	
Do	6	F.	10	P.	100	.05	5.00	26	2.50	130.00	1	
Do	10	F.	10	P.	120	.055	6.60	30	3.807	198.00	1	
Do	9	F.	10	P.	120	.06	7.20	34½	4.80	249.60	1	
Do	9	F.	10	P.	150	.06	9.00	43½	7.50	390.00	1	
Do	12	F.	10	P.	110	.06	6.60	21⅔	2.748	143.00	1	
Do	9	F.	10	P.	120	.06	7.20	36⅔	5.076	264.00	1	
Do	13	M.	10	P.	130	.05	6.50	30½	3.791	197.166	1	
Do	10	F.	10	P.	100	.12	12.00	38	8.765	456.00	1	
Do	14	F.	10	P.	120	.055	6.60	45	5.711	297.00		
Do	11	M.	10	P.	150	.055	8.25	32	5.076	264.00	1	
Do	2	M.	10	P.	100	.10	10.00	37	7.115	370.00	1	
Do	10	M.	10	P.	100	.12	12.00	37	8.538	444.00	1	
Do	12	F.	10	W.	....	....	....	40	3.846	200.00	1	
Do	12	F.	10	P.	150	.055	8.25	40	6.345	330.00	1	
Do	9	F.	10	P.	160	.055	8.80	32	5.415	281.60	1	
Do	5	F.	10	P.	150	.055	8.25				1	
Do	9	F.	10	P.	120	.055	6.60				1	
Do	10	F.	10	W.	120	.05	4.00				1	
Total		5 M. 26 F.		2 W., 29 P.							29	
Average	9.1		10		120.03	.06	7.054	30.4	4.353	226.436		

Wages of 15 pressers on vests.

Nationality.	Number of years in United States.	Sex.	Hours per day.	Week work or piece- work.	Average number of pieces per week.	Average price per piece.	Wage per week.	Number of weeks per year.	Average weekly wage throughout the year.	Annual wage.	Trade union. Yes.	Trade union. No.
Jew	12	M.	10	P.	240	$0.04	$9.60	33⅓	$6.153	$320.00	1	
Do	15	M.	10	P.	350	.035	12.25	33⅓	7.931	412.416	1	
Do	3	M.	10	P.	350	.035	12.25	33⅓	7.852	408.333	1	
Do	13	M.	8	P.	180	.05	9.00	37	6.403	333.00		
Do	11	M.	10	P.	300	.035	10.50	34⅔	7.00	364.00	1	
Do	12	M.	10	P.	300	.035	10.50	26	5.25	273.00	1	
Do		M.		P.	360	.04	14.40	18⅞	5.20	270.40	1	
Do	10	M.	10	P.	150	.032	4.875	17½	1.625	84.50		

Do	5	M.	9	P.	300	.03	9.00	44 5/12	7.687	399.75	1
Do	11	M.	10	P.	300	.035	10.50				1
Do	11	M.		P.	300	.035	10.50				1
Do	15	M.		P.	375	.035	13.125	36⅔	9.254	481.25	1
Do	9	M.		W.			12.00	34⅔	8.00	416.00	1
Do	5	M.		W.			13.00				1
Do	6	M.		W.			12.00				1
Total		15 M.		3 W., 12 P.							14
Average	9.8		9.7		292	.036	10.90	31.8	6.578	342.059	

Wages of 20 finishers on vests.

Jew	5	F.	10	P.	125	$0.055	$6.875	25	$3.305	$171.875	1	
Do	6	F.	9	P.	250	.02	5.25	25	2.403	125.00	1	
Do	3	F.	10	P.	180	.025	4.50	26	2.25	117.00	1	
Do	10	F.	10	P.	200	.027	5.50	17	1.798	93.50	1	
Do	4	F.	10	P.	100	.05	5.00	52	5.00	260.00	1	
Do		F.	10	P.	60	.02	1.20	21⅔	.50	26.00	1	
Do	11	F.	10	P.	300	.02	6.00	10⅖	1.20	62.40	1	
Do	2	F.	12	P.	200	.017	3.50	26⅙	1.761	91.583		
Do	5	F.	10	P.	300	.02	6.00	26	3.00	156.00	1	
Do	10	F.	10	P.	300	.02	6.00	13	1.50	78.00	1	
Do	9	F.	10	P.			6.50	26	3.25	169.00		1
Do	7	F.	10	P.	200	.012	2.50	17⅓	.833	43.333	1	
American		F.	10	P.			6.00	30⅓	3.50	182.00	1	
Jew	10	F.	10	P.	300	.02	6.00	21⅔	2.50	130.00	1	
Do	7	F.	10	P.	75	.04	3.00				1	
Do	9	F.	10	P.	120	.055	6.00				1	
Do	2	F.	10	W.			5.50				1	
Do	5	F.		P.	400	.02	8.00	39	6.00	312.00	1	
Do	4½	F.	10	P.	400	.02	8.00	34⅔	5.333	277.333	1	
Do	10	F.	10	P.	300	.02	6.00	26	3.00	156.00	1	
Total		20 F.		1 W., 19 P.							18	1
Average	6.6		10		265	.027	5.36	25.7	2.772	144.177		

Wages of 36 operators on trousers.

Jew	15	M.	11	P.	80	$0.11	$8.80	30⅓	$5.133	$266.933	1	
Do	9	M.	11	P.	80	.11	8.80	30⅓	5.133	266.933	1	
Do	15	M.	10	P.	75	.125	9.375	34⅔	6.230	324.00	1	
Do	12	M.	10	P.	65	.125	8.125	39	6.093	316.875	1	
Do	7	M.	10	P.	63	.11	6.93	18	2.398	124.74	1	
Do	14	M.	10	P.	132	.11	14.52	19	5.305	275.88	1	

738   THE INDUSTRIAL COMMISSION:—IMMIGRATION.

CITY SHOPS—Continued.

Wages of 36 operators on trousers—Continued.

Nationality.	Number of years in United States.	Sex.	Hours per day.	Week work or piecework.	Average number of pieces per week.	Average price per piece.	Wage per week.	Number of weeks per year.	Average weekly wage throughout the year.	Annual wage.	Trade union. Yes.	Trade union. No.
Jew	8	M.	10	P.	100	$0.11	$11.00	32	$6.875	$357.50	1	
Do	8	M.	10	P.	70	.115	8.05	32½	5.031	261.625	1	
Italian		M.		P.	102	.115	11.73	26	5.865	304.98		1
Jew	12	M.	10	P.	85	.11	9.35	28	5.034	261.80	1	
Do	11	M.	10	P.	60	.105	6.30	26	3.15	163.80		1
Do	12	M.	10	P.	85	.11	9.35	28	5.034	261.80	1	
Do	11	M.	14	P.	70	.105	7.35	14½	2.025	105.35		1
Do	3	M.	12	P.	100	.11	11.50	41	9.067	471.50	1	
Do	2	M.	10	P.	70	.115	8.05	40	6.192	322.00	1	
Do	9	M.	13	P.	130	.09	11.70	25	5.625	292.50		
Do	5	M.	10	P.	54	.135	7.29	40	5.607	291.60	1	
Do	8	M.	10½	P.	55	.12	6.60	26	3.30	171.60	1	
Do	10	M.	10½	P.	75	.12	9.00	34½	6.00	312.00		
Do	12	M.	18	P.	95	.12	11.40	29½	6.43	334.40	1	
Do	11	M.	9	P.	100	.10	10.00	28	5.384	280.00	1	
Do	11½	M.	11	P.	110	.10	11.00	29½	6.205	322.666	1	
Do	4	M.	10	P.	70	.10	7.00	13	1.75	91.00	1	
Do		M.	12	P.	108	.115	12.42	15	3.582	186.30	1	
Do	3	M.	15½	P.	108	.115	12.42	34½	8.28	430.56	1	
Do	4	M.	10	P.	60	.10	6.00	17½	2.00	104.00	1	
Do	6	M.	14	W.	99	.105	7.39	23	3.267	169.87	1	
Do		M.	14	P.	{Help.		3.00	23	1.326	69.00		
Do	3	M.	12	P.	100	.10	10.00	26	5.00	260.00	1	
Do	5	M.	13½	P.	150	.11	16.50	21½	6.874	357.50	1	
Do	8	M.	13½	P.	150	.11	16.50	21½	6.874	357.50	1	
Do	11	M.	11	P.	110	.10	11.00	28	3.923	308.00	1	
Do	6	M.	12½	P.	100	.12	12.00	32	7.384	384.00		
Do	2½	M.	10	P.	40	.10	4.00	52	4.00	208.00	1	
Do	4	M.	11	P.	75	.125	9.375	34½	6.189	321.875	1	
Do	9½	M.	10	P.	90	.125	11.25	32	6.923	360.00		
Total		36 M.		1 W., 35 P.							22	13
Average	7.9		11.4		86.5	.111	9.585	28.4	5.124	269.335		

WAGES OF GARMENT MAKERS. 739

Wages of 21 pressers on trousers.

Nationality	Age	Sex	Hours	P. or W.	Pieces	Rate	Per week	Weeks	Per piece	Earnings		
Jew	5½	M.	13	P.	300	$0.06	$18.00	21	$7.50	$390.00	1	
Do	12	M.	10	P.	500	.012	7.50	26 2/3	3.846	200.00		
Do	9	M.	10	P.	130	.05	6.50	36 2/3	4.237	220.333	1	
Do	9	M.	16	P.	400	.012	6.00	26	3.00	156.00	1	
Do	9	M.	16	P.	200	.03	6.00	26	3.00	156.00	1	1
Do	7	M.	16	W.	200	.03	6.00	26	3.00	156.00		
Do	8	M.	10	P.			12.00	26	10.00	520.00	1	
Do	9	M.	14½	P.	300	.025	7.50	43½	2.50	130.00		
Do	11½	M.	15	P.	300	.025	7.50	17	1.875	97.50	1	1
Do	2½	M.	14½	P.	350	.015	5.25	13	1.312	68.25	1	
Do	12	M.	14½	P.	300	.015	4.50	13	1.50	78.00	1	
Do	8	M.	14½	P.	200	.04	8.00	17½	3.025	157.333	1	1
Do	6	M.	10	P.	100	.04	4.00	19½	1.511	78.666	1	
Do	11	M.	11½	P.	120	.04	4.80	19 2/3	2.80	145.60	1	
Do	10½	M.	10½	P.	125	.045	5.625	30½	3.274	170.291	1	
Do	5	M.	10	P.	900	.01	9.00	30½	9.00	468.00	1	
Do	5	M.	10	P.	275	.02	5.50	52	4.125	214.50	1	
Do	7	M.		P.	420	.02	8.40	39	3.069	159.60	1	
Do		M.		P.	420	.015	6.30	19	2.301	119.70	1	
Do		M.		P.	420	.02	8.40	19	3.069	159.60		
Do		M.		P.	420	.015	6.30	19	2.301	119.70		
Total		21 M.		1 W., 20 P.	319						11	7
Average	7.4		12.8			.027	7.289	25.4	3.63	189.289		

Wages of 9 finishers on trousers.

Nationality	Age	Sex	Hours	P. or W.	Pieces	Rate	Per week	Weeks	Per piece	Earnings		
Italian	18	F.	10	P.	60	$0.07	$4.20	21	$1.696	$88.20		1
Jew	12	M.	11	P.	45	.09	4.05	26	2.125	105.30	1	
Italian		F.	10	P.	60	.06	3.60	26	1.80	93.60	1	1
Jew		F.	10	P.	50	.06	3.00	26	1.50	78.00	1	1
Italian		F.	10	P.	45	.06	2.70	26	1.35	70.20		
Do	9	F.		P.	100	.035	3.50	19	1.274	66.50	1	
American		F.	11	P.	30	.085	2.55	52	2.55	132.60	1	
Do		F.	11	P.	30	.085	2.55	52	2.55	132.60		
Jew	4	F.	10	P.	36	.08	2.88	19	1.052	54.72	1	
Total		1 M., 8 F.		9 P.							4	3
Average	10.7		10.3		50.6	.069	3.225	29.6	1.755	91.302		

COUNTRY SHOPS.

Wages of 86 operators on coats.

Nationality.	Number of years in United States.	Sex.	Hours per day.	Week work or piece-work.	Average number of pieces per week.	Average price per piece.	Wage per week.	Number of weeks per year.	Average weekly wage throughout the year.	Annual wage.	Trade union. Yes.	Trade union. No.
German-American		F.	10	W.			$8.50	46	$7.519	$391.00		1
Do		F.	10	W.			8.00	46	7.076	368.00		1
Do		F.	10	W.			3.75	30‡	2.187	113.75	1	
Do		F.	10	W.			4.25	46	3.759	195.50		1
Do		F.	10	W.			5.75	46	5.086	264.50		1
Do		F.	10	W.			5.75	46	5.086	264.50		1
Do		F.	10	W.			4.25	46	3.755	195.50		1
Do		F.	10	W.			6.50	46	5.75	299.00		1
Do		F.	10	W.			6.50	46	5.75	299.00		1
German	14	M.	10	W.			3.75	46	3.317	172.50		1
German-American		F.	10	W.			4.50	47	4.067	211.50		1
Do		F.	10	W.			5.00	46	4.423	230.00		1
Do		F.	10	W.			6.50	39	4.875	253.50	1	
Swiss	18	F.	10	W.			7.00	39	5.25	273.00	1	
German-American	25	F.	10	W.			7.50	39	5.625	292.50	1	
Do		F.	10	W.			3.75	26	1.875	97.50	1	
Do		F.	10	W.			2.75	26	1.375	71.50	1	
Do		F.	10	W.			3.25	30‡	1.896	98.583	1	
Do		F.	10	W.			5.50	39	4.125	214.50	1	
Do		F.	10	W.			9.00	30‡	5.25	273.00	1	
Do		M.	10	W.			5.25	49	4.947	257.25	1	
Do		M.	10	W.			6.50	39	4.875	253.50	1	
Do		M.	10	W.			9.00	39	6.75	351.00	1	
Do		M.	10	W.			8.25	39	6.189	321.75	1	
Do		F.	10	W.			7.50	39	5.625	292.50	1	
American		F.	10	W.			4.50	52	4.50	234.00	1	
Do		M.	10	W.			12.00	47‡	11.00	572.00	1	
Do		F.	10	W.			3.50	52	3.50	182.00	1	
Do		F.	10	W.			3.25	52	3.25	169.00	1	
Do		M.	10	W.			4.50	52	4.50	234.00		1
Do		F.	10	W.			4.00	52	4.00	208.00	1	
Do		M.	10	W.			6.60	52	6.60	343.20	1	
Do		F.	10	W.			12.00	45	10.384	540.00	1	
Do		F.	10	W.			4.50	52	4.50	234.00	1	
Do		F.	10	W.			4.50	52	4.50	234.00	1	
Do		F.	10	W.			4.25	52	4.25	221.00	1	
Total	8 M, 28 F.			36 W.							20	13
Average			10				5.884	43.6	4.933	256.278		

WAGES OF GARMENT MAKERS.

Wages of 18 pressers on coats.

American		M.	10	W.		$7.50	52	$7.50	$390.00	1
Do		M.	10	W.		7.50	52	7.50	390.00	1
German		M.	10	W.		6.50	49	6.125	318.50	1
German-American	3	M.	10	W.		6.00	30½	3.50	182.00	1
German	30	M.	10	W.		6.00	26	3.00	156.00	1
Do	20	M.	10	W.		6.00	26	3.00	156.00	1
German-American		M.	10	W.		3.75	46	3.317	172.50	
Do		M.	10	W.		6.00	43	4.961	258.00	
Do		M.	10	W.		9.00	46	7.961	414.00	1
Do		M.	10	W.		9.00	45	7.788	405.00	
American		M.	10	W.		9.00	46	7.961	414.00	1
Do		M.	10	W.		7.50	52	7.50	390.00	
Do		M.	10	W.		6.00	26	3.00	156.00	
Total		13 M.		13 W.						8	3
Average			10			6.903	41.4	5.624	292.46		

Wages of 12 basters on coats.

German-American		M.	10	W.		$9.00	49	$8.48	$441.00	1
Do		M.	10	W.		8.50	49	8.009	416.50	1
Do		M.	10	W.		4.25	39	3.187	165.75	1
Do		M.	10	W.		8.50	28½	4.631	240.833	1
Do		M.	10	W.		4.25	26	2.125	110.50	1
Do		M.	10	W.		9.00	34½	6.00	312.00	
Do		F.	10	W.		9.00	34½	6.00	312.00	1
Do		M.	10	W.		4.00	44	3.384	176.00	1
German-American	2	M.	10	W.		8.50	48	7.846	408.00	1
German-American		M.	10	W.		6.00	48	5.538	288.00	1
Do		M.	10	W.		6.00	39	6.75	351.00	1
German	16	M.	10	W.		9.75	45	8.437	438.75	
Total		11 M., 1 F.		12 W.						6	6
Average			10			7.479	40.3	5.865	305.027		

Wages of 12 operators on trousers.

American		F.		W.		$6.00	52	$6.00	$312.00	1
Do		F.		P.	$0.01	600	47	5.423	282.00	1
Do		F.		P.	.015	411				1
Do		F.		P.	.015	450	52	6.75	351.00	

COUNTRY SHOPS—Continued.

Wages of 12 operators on trousers—Continued.

Nationality.	Number of years in United States.	Sex.	Hours per day.	Week work or piece-work.	Average number of pieces per week.	Average price per piece.	Wage per week.	Number of weeks per year.	Average weekly wage throughout the year.	Annual wage.	Trade union. Yes.	Trade union. No.
American		M.	10	P.	675	$0.005	$3.375	52	$3.375	$175.50		1
Do		F.	10	W.			3.75	52	3.75	195.00		1
Do	} 1 team.	F.	10	P.	500	.01	5.00	52	5.00	260.00		1
Do		F.	10	P.	500	.01	5.00	52	5.00	260.00		1
Do		F.	10	P.	500	.01	5.00	52	5.00	260.00		1
Do		F.	10	P.	500	.01	5.00	52	5.00	260.00		1
Do		F.	10	P.	500	.01	5.00	52	5.00	260.00		1
Total		1 M., 11 F.		2 W., 10 P.								11
Average			10		513.6	.01	5.17	51.5	5.027	261.409		

WAGES OF GARMENT MAKERS.

COUNTRY HOME WORKERS.

Wages of 9 coat makers.

Nationality.	Sex.	Number who help.	Average number of pieces per week.	Average price per piece.	Wage per week.
American	F.	1	11	$0.35	$3.85
Do	F.		5½	.28	1.54
Do	F.	1	33	.19	6.27
Do	F.	2	23	.22	5.06
Do	F.		13	.25	3.25
Do	F.		6	.23	1.38
Do	F.		8	.17	1.36
Do	F.		18	.19	3.42
Do	F.		5	.16	.80
Total	9 F.				
Average			13.6	.226	2.992

Wages of 16 vest makers.

Nationality.	Sex.	Number who help.	Average number of pieces per week.	Average price per piece.	Wage per week.
American	F.		35	$0.10	$3.50
Do	F.		25	.10	2.50
Do	F.		17	.10	1.70
Do	F.		13	.10	1.30
Do	F.		30	.10	3.00
Do	F.	1	30	.10	3.00
Do	F.	1	35	.10	3.50
Do	F.		17	.10	1.70
Do	F.		23	.10	2.30
Do	F.	1	12	.09	1.08
Do	F.		10	.10	1.00
Do	F.		11	.10	1.10
Do	F.		25	.10	2.50
Do	F.		14	.14	1.96
Do	F.		13	.12	1.56
Do	F.	1	17	.12	2.04
Total	16 F.				
Average			20.4	.104	2.108

Wages of 13 trousers makers.

Nationality.	Sex.	Number who help.	Average number of pieces per week.	Average price per piece.	Wage per week.
American	F.	1	13½	$0.135	$1.822
Do	F.	1	10	.13	1.30
Do	F.	1	11	.15	1.65
Do	F.		16	.15	2.40
Do	F.	1	25	.15	3.75
Do	F.		11	.18	1.98
Do	F.	2	33	.14	4.62
Do	F.		9	.14	1.26
Do	F.	1	19	.18	3.42
Do	F.		6	.11	.66
Do	F.		5	.12	.60
Do	F.		6	.11	.66
Do	F.		6	.19	1.14
Total	13 F.				
Average			13.1	.145	1.943

PART IV.

CHINESE AND JAPANESE LABOR IN THE MOUNTAIN AND PACIFIC STATES.

PREPARED UNDER THE DIRECTION OF THE INDUSTRIAL COMMISSION

BY

THOMAS F. TURNER.

ALIEN LABOR IN MOUNTAIN AND PACIFIC STATES.[1]

INTRODUCTION.

The problem of Asiatic competition is one in which the people of the East have felt but little interest. It has been a matter of popular belief that Chinese and Japanese competition affected only the laboring classes of the Pacific coast. The error of this will, I think, conclusively appear from an examination of the data herewith submitted. Every Asiatic who finds employment in the United States, whether on the Pacific or Atlantic coast, displaces an American laborer; and while the baneful influence of coolie competition is more noticeable upon our Western coast, it is certain to have its effect upon the labor of the entire nation.

The Chinese colony in the city of San Francisco is a perfect beehive of busy industry. The problem of cheap living has been solved by this peculiar race. Among the lower and common laboring classes, such as are engaged in agricultural pursuits, the cost of living has been reduced to the minimum and the wages paid are much less than any white laborer can live upon. The Chinese coolie and common laborer seems from instinct to be able to adapt himself to conditions under which no white laborer can live. In many instances, especially in agricultural pursuits, coolie labor has absolutely displaced white labor in the Pacific coast States. Hundreds of factories and workshops in the city of San Francisco are in full operation, employing thousands of Chinese operatives, who are manufacturing boots and shoes, brooms, men's clothing, shirts, shirt waists, ladies' skirts, and, indeed, garments of all kinds, that find their way not only into Western but Eastern markets as well, displacing in many instances the products of our Eastern workshops and factories. So that, as stated, this question is not one which interests the Pacific States alone, but which is of vital concern to the laboring interests of the entire nation.

In discussing the effect upon the white race of Asiatic invasion, the distinguished writer, Sir Henry Wrixon, of Melbourne, says: "The United States, the newest and vastest of nations, where all the social problems of the sons of men are cast in the crucible of experience, has not dealt so effectively, so far, with the question of Mongolian or Asiatic invasion as have Australia and New Zealand." But when it is realized that the displacing of white laborers in California, Oregon, and other Pacific Coast States affects industries as far east as the Atlantic, Congress will learn that the question is not a local one.

MANUFACTURING AND OTHER INDUSTRIES IN CHINATOWN, SAN FRANCISCO.

During my investigations in San Francisco I endeavored to secure information respecting the number of operatives employed in the various lines of manufacture in Chinatown. So far as I could ascertain, no reliable data had been compiled on this subject. One of the chief characteristics of the Chinese race is secretiveness in all affairs pertaining to their business. All inquiries at their stores, manufactories, and places of business were met with the ever-ready response, "Me no sabee."

Through courtesy of the Hon. F. B. Meyers, commissioner of the bureau of labor statistics of the State of California, arrangements were made whereby the heads of the various manufacturing and other industrial establishments in Chinatown were subpœnaed to appear at the labor commissioner's office and give testimony upon the subjects under inquiry. A large number of witnesses were examined, and the data herewith submitted are, I believe, complete and reliable.

In many instances it was impossible to secure accurate information as to the

---

[1] The following report was made in May, 1900, one month before the Chinese inspection service was transferred from the customs service to the Bureau of Immigration. Certain references to the conflict of adthority with customs officers should be read with this correction in view.

number of operatives employed in the various manufacturing establishments, as the operatives would, upon the least signal of the approach of myself and those assisting in the investigations, disappear from the workshops through innumerable doors before we had time to count their number. In a majority of instances, therefore, we simply counted the number of sewing machines in each place, allowing one operative for each machine, which is certainly a conservative basis for the tables submitted below.

Nearly all of these sewing machines are operated by gasoline engines from early morning until a late hour at night. In walking through the streets in Chinatown I have frequently heard the busy hum of hundreds of sewing machines in the crowded basements and factories as late as 9 and 10 o'clock at night.

MANUFACTURE OF CIGARS.

The cigar manufacturing business in San Francisco and other Pacific coast cities is completely monopolized by the Chinese. Many of the wholesale dealers in cigars handle the Chinese-made cigars and put them upon the market as "white-made" and in many instances as "union-made" cigars. In a statement given to me touching this subject by Mr. Fred. W. Wescott, president of the Cigar Makers' Union of San Francisco, that gentleman says that "fully one-third of all Chinese-made cigars are sold to the trade as the product of white labor." Mr. Westcott stated further that "were it not for the Chinese monopoly of this industry, San Francisco, which is now one of the poorest, would be one of the best in the world for cigar makers."

There are to-day about 1,200 Chinese cigar makers in the city of San Francisco. Their shops and factories are scattered all over Chinatown, where these busy toilers may be seen from early morning until late at night turning out cigars by the hundreds of thousands. The scale of prices paid to Chinese cigar makers varies, of course, with the different grades of cigars, and averages from 50 per cent to 33 per cent less than the union prices upon the different grades of cigars. White labor in the cigar manufacturing industry has been driven from the field, and San Francisco, instead of supporting from 2,000 to 3,000 white cigar makers as formerly, has to-day less than 200 union cigar makers, who have remained to struggle against this hopeless competition.

What has been true of the cigar industry has been and will be true of every industry in which American labor is met with Asiatic competition. It is in every instance a *bloodless struggle*, in which the white man must surrender and go down in humiliating defeat.

CHINATOWN INDUSTRIES SUMMARIZED.

The following summary of the industries of Chinatown, in San Francisco, includes only the principal manufacturing establishments. Thousands of Chinese who work for themselves as shoemakers, tailors, cigar makers, and in every line of industry are not included.

Name of industry.	Number of sewing machines.	Number of workmen.	Average hours.	Average wages.
Boots and shoes		251	11 to 12	$1.00
Shirts	195	195	11 to 12	1.00
Men's clothing	335	335	11 to 12	1.00
Overalls	448	430	11 to 12	1.00
Ladies' underclothing	168	168	11 to 12	1.00
Manufacture of cigars		1,200	10 to 14	
Total	1,146	2,579		

THE FRUIT-PACKING INDUSTRY.

The fruit-packing industry has become one of the most important industries in California. Within the last few months a large number of the leading corporations engaged in this business have consolidated under a single management. The testimony of the officers of a number of these companies, which was taken by me, disclosed that during the fruit-packing season a large percentage of the labor employed at the factories is Chinese. It is a fact, however, that is full of significance, that the largest fruit-packing company on the Pacific coast, the

Pacific Fruit Packing Company, owned and controlled by Chinese capitalists, employs more white than Chinese labor.

In the testimony given by Mr. Lew Hing, president of the Pacific Fruit Packing Company, that gentleman says that only about one-third of their help is Chinese; the balance are white women and girls, who are paid from $1.25 to $1.50 per day. When I asked Mr. Lew Hing why it was that a Chinese company should hire American girls and women in preference to Chinese, he replied: "We find that the American girls and women can do the work easier, are quicker and more handy than the Chinese, and can do much more work; so we give it to them."

LABORERS UPON RAILWAY LINES.

The data herewith submitted cover all of the principal railway lines in the West (except those of Washington) i. e., the lines of the Oregon Railway and Navigation Company—the entire Southern Pacific system west of Ogden, Utah; and the Santa Fe lines west of Albuquerque, N. Mex.

While the railway officials were at first disposed to be somewhat reluctant about giving information upon this subject, as soon as assurance was given that no improper use would be made of it and that no newspaper agitation on the subject was contemplated, they gave me their entire coöperation. I was treated with uniform courtesy by the officials of each of the above systems of railway, and without their assistance it would have been impossible to secure the information herewith submitted.

I find that there are employed upon all of the above lines 13,956 common laborers, of whom 9,475 are classified as "Americans;" this number, however, would have been greatly reduced had it been possible to segregate the foreign-born (chiefly alien) whites employed upon the lines of the Southern Pacific Company; the laborers upon the lines of Southern Pacific Company other than Asiatics and Mexicans having been classified as Americans.

As shown in the following tables there are employed upon the above lines 1,776 Asiatics and 2,705 alien whites, Mexicans, and Indians; 33 per cent of the entire number of employees being foreign born. As stated above, the percentage of the foreign-born labor as shown by these tables would be increased from 33 per cent to not less than 45 per cent had it been possible to segregate and classify the alien whites in the employ of the Southern Pacific Company.

Southern Pacific lines within the State of California—Statement showing common laborers employed.

Branch of service.	Common laborers.	Per cent.	Average per day.	Average hours.
Transportation:				
Whites	1,203	100	$2.00	10
Chinese				
Japanese				
Mexicans				
Total	1,203	100	2.00	10
Motive power:				
Whites	1,159	97½	1.50 to 2.00	10
Chinese	29	2½	1.25	10
Japanese				
Mexicans				
Total	1,188	100	1.58	10
Maintenance of way:				
Whites	2,624	76	1.50 to 2.25	10 to 11
Chinese	317	9	1.00	10 to 11
Japanese	137	4	1.00	10 to 11
Mexicans	376	11	1.00	10 to 11
Total	3,454	100	1.35	10¼

Construction.—In the construction department of the Southern Pacific road there is employed a constantly shifting number of laborers; many of this class are Chinese and Japanese; the number ranging all the way from 100 to 1,000 or 1,500 as the exigencies of construction require. They are paid $1.75 per day, for 10 hours' work.

Southern Pacific lines outside the State of California—Statement showing common laborers employed.

Branch of service.	Common laborers.	Per cent.	Average per day.	Average hours.
Transportation:				
Whites	131	100	$2.00	10 to 11
Chinese				
Japanese				
Mexicans				
Total	131	100	2.00	10 to 11
Motive power:				
Whites	177	67	1.50	10
Chinese	44	16½	1.25	10
Japanese	12	4½	1.55	10
Mexicans	32	12	1.50	10
Total	265	100	1.45	10
Maintenance of way:				
Whites	1,366	51½	1.50	10
Chinese	119	4	1.00	10
Japanese	308	11½	1.00	10
Mexicans	851	33	1.00	10
Total	2,644	100	1.12½	10

Southern Pacific system, including all lines west of Ogden—Statement showing common laborers employed.

Branch of service.	Common laborers.	Per cent.	Average per day.	Average hours.
Transportation:				
Whites	1,334	100	$2.00	10
Chinese				
Japanese				
Mexicans				
Total	1,334	100	2.00	10
Motive power:				
Whites	1,336	92	1.50	10
Chinese	73	5	1.25	10
Japanese	12	½	1.55	10
Mexicans	32	2⅜	1.50	10
Total	1,453	100	1.45	10
Maintenance of way:				
Whites	3,990	65	1.50	10 to 11
Chinese	436	7¼	1.00	10 to 11
Japanese	445	7¼	1.00	10 to 11
Mexicans	1,227	20⅜	1.00	10 to 11
Total	6,098	100	1.12½	10¼

SUMMARY OF SOUTHERN PACIFIC LINES.

	Whites.	Chinese.	Japanese.	Mexicans.	Total.	Per cent alien labor.
Within the State of California	4,986	346	137	377	5,846	15
Outside the State of California	1,674	163	320	883	3,040	45
All lines west of Ogden	6,660	509	457	1,260	8,886	25

CHINESE AND JAPANESE IMMIGRATION. 751

The Oregon Railway and Navigation Company, all lines—Statement showing common laborers employed as of February 17, 1900.

Nationality.	Number.	Nationality.	Number.
Americans	1,656	Irish	243
English	146	Swedes	120
Norwegians	69	Chinese	150
Danish	38	French	13
Canadians	81	Germans	198
Scotch	72	Italians	4
Russian Finns	12	Prussians	3
Bavarian	1	Nova Scotians	4
Mexicans	2	Welsh	9
Australians	5	Austrians	2
Swiss	7	West Indians	6
Japanese	313	Cuban	1
Belgian	1	Finlanders	3
Hollanders	7	Russians	11
Portuguese	1	Polanders	2
Bohemian	1		
		Total	3,181

Comparative statement showing number of Americans, as compared with Asiatics and other aliens, employed upon lines of Oregon Railway and Navigation Company.

	Number of common laborers.	Per cent.	Average wages.	Average hours.
Americans	1,656	52	$1.50	10
Asiatics	463	14¾	1.10	10
Mexicans	2		1.10	10
Whites, other than Americans	1,060	33¼	1.25	10
Total	3,181	100	1.24	10

Santa Fe Route, lines west of Albuquerque—Statement showing common laborers employed as of January 31, 1900.

	Common laborers.	Per cent.	Average per day.	Average hours.
Santa Fe Pacific Railroad Company.				
Regular employment:				
Whites	146	21	$2.07	10
Asiatics	317	45	1.10	10
Indians	35	5	1.32	10
Mexicans	199	29	1.37	10
Total	697	100	1.39	10
Construction:				
Whites	64	40	1.73	
Asiatics				
Indians	49	30	1.25	10
Mexicans	48	30	1.67	10
Total	161	100	1.57	
Southern California Railway Company.				
Regular employment:				
Whites	322	81	1.59	10
Asiatics	30	8	1.10	10
Indians				
Mexicans	45	11	1.25	10
Total	397	100	1.51	10
Construction:				
Whites	29	80	1.64	10
Asiatics				
Indians				
Mexicans	7	20	1.25	10
Total	36	100	1.56	10

Santa Fe Route, lines west of Albuquerque—Statement showing common laborers employed as of January 31, 1900—Continued.

	Common laborers.	Per cent.	Average per day.	Average hours.
San Francisco and San Joaquin Valley Railway Company.				
Regular employment:				
Whites	176	100	$1.78	10
Asiatics				
Indians				
Mexicans				
Total	176	100	1.78	10
Construction:				
Whites	422	100	2.04	10
Asiatics				
Indians				
Mexicans				
Total	422	100	2.04	10

SUMMARY—SANTA FE LINES.

	Whites.	Asiatics.	Indians.	Mexicans.	Total.	Average per day.
Santa Fe Pacific Railroad:						
Regular employment	146	317	35	199	697	$1.39
Construction	64		49	48	161	1.57
Southern California Rwy.:						
Regular employment	322	30		45	397	1.51
Construction	29			7	36	1.56
San Francisco and San Joaquin Valley Rwy.:						
Regular employment	176				176	1.78
Construction	422				422	2.04
Total	1,159	347	84	299	1,889	1.62
Per cent	61	18	5	16	100	

	Hours.
Average hours per day	10
Total regular employment	1,270
Total construction	619

Summary showing the number and nationality of common laborers employed on lines of Oregon Railway and Navigation Company, Southern Pacific lines west of Ogden, and Santa Fe lines west of Albuquerque.

	Americans.	Asiatics.	Foreign whites.	Total.	Per cent foreign.
Oregon Railway and Navigation Company	1,656	463	1,062	3,181	48
Southern Pacific lines west of Ogden a	6,660	966	b 1,260	8,886	25
Santa Fe lines west of Albuquerque	1,159	347	c 383	1,889	39
Total	9,475	1,776	2,705	13,956	33

a It was impossible to segregate the white employees on this line according to nationalities There are, no doubt, a large number of white foreigners included among them. As I had no way of segregating them into classes, I have included them all under the head of "Americans."
b Mexican.
c Indians and Mexicans.

A large part of the construction work upon railway lines upon the Pacific coast is let out to contractors, and, so far as I could learn, Asiatic labor is employed very largely upon all such new or construction work.

NUMBER AND NATIONALITY OF ASIATICS EMPLOYED IN MINES.

Much to my surprise, I found that in some of the principal mining States of the West no departments or bureaus of mining have yet been organized, and no attempt has been made to segregate the nationalities of those employed in the mining industry. In order to secure data which I desired, I have resorted to every source from which such information might be obtained. In many instances I have written to the postmasters at or near the various mining camps, and the data herewith submitted on this subject are compiled from information which I believe to be reasonably accurate.

Most of the Chinese are employed at mining work in either gravel or placer. Many Chinese companies buy or lease land, which is worked by Chinese miners. Very few, however, are engaged at quartz mining. Most of the Chinese who are employed about the large mining camps are employed in the capacity of cooks and camp attendants.

The data compiled as of the date of January 1, 1900, indicate that in California there are 16,415 white employees and 3,934 Chinese working in the mines. The wages of the Chinese range from $1 to $1.50 per day, whereas white miners in the same mines receive $2 to $3.50 per day. The hours are from 9¼ to 10 per day. There are also between 3,000 and 4,000 Chinese employed at placer mining for Chinese companies and for themselves throughout the different mining districts of California.

California—Nationality, wages, and hours of miners.

County.	Number white.	Number Chinese.	County.	Number white.	Number Chinese.
Amador	1,000	220	Riverside	225	75
Butte	600	200	Sacramento	140	60
Calaveras	1,186	100	San Bernardino	300	108
Del Norte	45		San Diego	550	50
Eldorado	1,000	110	San Luis Obispo	10	10
Fresno	150	11	Santa Barbara	10	10
Humboldt	105	50	Shasta	1,700	248
Kern	1,000	60	Sierra	500	45
Inyo	277	50	Siskiyou	900	585
Lassen	55	25	Stanislaus	15	
Los Angeles	71		Trinity	1,000	205
Madera	100	48	Tulare	50	25
Mariposa	700	114	Tuolumne	1,500	237
Mono	200	48	Yuba	250	65
Nevada	1,500	600			
Placer	700	550	Total	16,415	3,934
Plumas	576	25			

In addition to the above, there are between 3,000 and 4,000 Chinese employed at placer mining for Chinese companies and for themselves throughout the different mining districts of California.

Oregon.—A letter from the committee on mining and mineral resources of the Portland Chamber of Commerce will explain the situation in that State.

"It is impossible to give the information desired in regard to the number or nationality of laborers employed in the mining industry in Oregon, for the reason that there is no reliable source from which this information can be obtained. Oregon has no State commissioner of mines, or any official whose duty it is to obtain such information. We have not the material at hand from which to make even an approximate estimate of the number of men employed in the mining industries of the State for the years 1897, 1898, or 1899.

"As far as can be ascertained but few Chinese or Japanese miners are employed in the quartz mines, but there are a large number of Chinese who work in gravel and placer ground, most of them on their own account, and, as they keep this up year after year, evidently make fair wages for themselves. The universal practice in the State is to allow 10 hours for a day's work, and wages range from $1.50 to $3.50 per day, according to locality, character of work, and skill of the man. In closing I will state that the number of men employed in the mining industries of Oregon for the present year will be probably double the number employed during the past year, and from present indications the field for good miners will be much greater in this State from now on than ever before.

"Very respectfully,

"J. F. BATCHELDER,
"*Chairman Committee on Mining and Mineral Resources.*"

Arizona.—Most of the Chinese employed in the mining industry in Arizona are employed as cooks, servants, and men of all work about the mining camps. As in Oregon and California, a number of Chinese work at placer mining on their own account, and the number so employed varies considerably from time to time.

In the table given below the number of Chinese in the different towns and settlements in the Territory is given, with an estimated number of those who engage in the mining occupation:

Town.	Chinese population.	Number employed at mining.	Town.	Chinese population.	Number employed at mining.
Clifton	400	75	Maceo	50	20
Globe	300	50	Nogales	100	45
Jerome	200	75	Willcox	100	40
Phoenix	300	100	Solomonsville	75	40
Tucson	800	150	Pierce	50	10
Kingman	100	60	Congress	100	30
Chloride	100	40	Casagrande	100	25
Whitehills	50	18	Morenci	150	63
Flagstaff	200	65	Scattering	700	300
Winslow	75	40			
Holbrook	50	30	Total	4,000	1,276

ASIATIC COOLIE LABOR IN THE AGRICULTURAL INDUSTRIES OF THE PACIFIC COAST.

The agricultural industries of the Pacific coast States, more than the railway, mining, or indeed any other industry, has been made to feel the baneful effect of cheap coolie competition. The passage of the so-called Chinese exclusion law in 1882 stopped, for the time at least, the hordes of coolie laborers who were pouring into the Pacific States.

The Chinese who are already in the United States have shown great enterprise and thrift, and are to-day devoting their attention to the industries in which they have become proprietors, such as mining, truck farming, etc. As a result the Chinese laborer demands and receives fairly remunerative wages; and so long as the exclusion law is honestly enforced this dangerous rival will be removed from the field of destructive competition.

Japanese immigration.—Close upon the retreat of the Chinese coolie, however, came the Japanese, equally menacing to the laboring interests of the country. Almost unnoticed, and without exciting either suspicion or alarm, has Japanese coolie labor crept into the country and established itself in almost every line of industry along our Pacific coast. Every vessel from the Orient that touched at our western ports left large numbers of these little brown toilers upon our shores. They were sent out in gangs to the farming and fruit-growing districts, and almost before the white labor of the coast was aware that this new foe was among them, it found itself displaced by a new rival more dangerous even than the Chinese.

The hop and sugar-beet fields, ranches, orchards, and vineyards are to-day filled with Japanese laborers. Even the Chinese laborer has been driven out by them, and in each of these several important fields of industry the Japanese coolie system is firmly established.

The official records of the immigration office do not show any startling increase in the number of Japanese immigrants to the United States. For the last 5 years they show an average of about 2,000 Japanese arrivals each year. The total number of Japanese immigrants for the fiscal year ending June 1, 1898, was 2,230, about 1,500 of whom were classified as farm hands and gave as their destination California. The total arrivals of Japanese in San Francisco for the fiscal year ending June 30, 1899, were 1,667, of whom 120 were females.

The records of the immigration office fail to account for the great hordes of Japanese coolies who have already secured a monopoly of the labor in the agricultural industries of the Pacific States. In the State of California alone there is to-day a great army of Japanese coolies, numbering upwards of 20,000. They do not colonize as do the Chinese: they are scattered about the State, doing work in the orchards, vineyards, gardens, and hop and sugar-beet fields.

They are more servile than the Chinese, but less obedient and far less desirable. They have most of the vices of the Chinese, with none of their virtues. They underbid the Chinese in everything, and are as a class tricky, unreliable, and dishonest.

The number of Japanese coolie laborers in California to-day is greater than the total number of Japanese arrivals shown by the immigration records at all of the United States ports for the last 10 years. How, then, came they among us? This is another Asiatic mystery. The movements, the motives, the coming and going of these stoical, strange Mongolians are as a closed book to the white races. As with the birds of passage, to-day there may not be one in sight, to-morrow they may be with us in countless thousands.

At the present time they are coming into the United States in constantly increasing numbers. The immigration records for the month of March, 1900, show that nearly 1,000 Japanese immigrants were landed during the month at San Francisco and Seattle. During the week of April 8, 1900, the arrivals reached the startling number of 500 at San Francisco alone, the total for 5 weeks being nearly as great as the entire Japanese immigration for the last fiscal year.

In addition to those who come through our ports, thousands more enter the United States illegally over the border from Canada and British Columbia. Touching this subject, the statement of Mr. Frank C. Schuyler, Chinese inspector at San Francisco, but formerly stationed at Seattle, Tacoma, and Port Townsend, was taken.

Mr. Schuyler says that it is notoriously known that large numbers of Japanese are constantly coming into the United States by the Canadian Pacific Railway from Vancouver, that they are employed as contract laborers upon the railways and in the mines, and that it is a matter of common knowledge that the railway companies operating between British Columbia and the United States encourage and aid such illegal immigration.[1]

In a statement secured from Hon. William Jones, president of the labor commission at Nanamino, British Columbia, that gentleman says: "Nearly all Chinese and Japanese who come to this country (British Columbia) are brought in under contract; but it is extremely difficult to prove the existence of such contracts." Mr. Jones cites an instance where 200 Japanese coolies were imported under contract to work in coal mines. He says further: "There is of course some smuggling done over the border, and large numbers of Chinese and Japanese enter the United States in this way. It is said that the headquarters of those engaged in this illicit business are at Victoria, British Columbia, and Spokane, Wash."

Investigation by State labor bureau of California.—About two years ago the subject of Japanese immigration was investigated by the State labor bureau of California. Through the courtesy of ex-labor commissioner, Hon. E. L. Fitzgerald, and his assistant, Hon. Cleveland L. Damm, of San Francisco, the testimony taken during such investigation was placed at my disposal. A large number of employers of Japanese labor were examined. The testimony of many coolie laborers was also taken. It was shown that in nearly every instance the Japanese immigrants came into the United States in "bands" or "gangs" of 25 and upward.

One very significant fact developed, namely, that nearly all of the coolies who were examined testified that they had not come to San Francisco direct, but had come from the north, most of them having landed at Vancouver, British Columbia.

It was shown that there exists in San Francisco, Seattle, and other Pacific port cities a system of Japanese boarding houses, the keepers of which act as middlemen in the procurement of "gangs" of coolie laborers. It was likewise shown that these boarding-house keepers are in constant communication with their friends and relatives in Japan, also with certain so-called immigration companies in that country. Upon arriving in this country the Japanese immigrants go at once to one of these boarding houses, and within 2 or 3 days after arrival are sent out in gangs, under a boss, into the fields, orchards, and vineyards.

One of the witnesses at this investigation, a Mr. Kolb, a fruit grower of Pleasanton, Cal., stated that nearly all of the labor employed in the hop and sugar-beet industries is Japanese, with some Chinese. Mr. Kolb referred to a notorious Japanese boss by the name of Sato, who, he claimed, had brought a great many Japanese into the country. When asked if he knew where Sato secured the Japanese, he replied, "I do not know exactly, but it looks to me as if he gets them from Japan."

Mr. A. R. Downing, another witness, testified that he is a resident of Pleasanton, Cal.; that "he has made a business of contracting for the cultivation of sugar beets, etc.; that nearly all labor employed is Japanese; that the average wages paid this class of labor was from 85 cents to 90 cents per day, out of which they board themselves."

Mr. A. C. Platt, a former member of the Pleasanton Hop Company, testified

---

[1] See Mr. Schuyler's statement, Exhibit A.

that he was "in favor of employing white labor exclusively: that there is plenty of white labor in California to handle all of the crops, and that he withdrew from the company because the balance of his associates in business insisted on employing Japanese coolie labor."

Mr. Platt also testified that upon one occasion he had a conversation with the Japanese boss—Sato; that "Sato wanted to take hold of the work at the ranch, and wanted me to go in with him and get men from Japan; that the men would get only $4 or $5 a month." Mr. Platt says he told Sato he "didn't want anything to do with that kind of business."

There can be no doubt that there are in this country hundreds of bosses of the Sato type, who make a business of bringing coolie laborers into the country. While it is extremely difficult to prove that such laborers are brought in under specific contract, the methods employed are without question as much a violation of the contract-labor law as if specific contracts were made in each instance.

In this connection reference is made to the affidavit of the Hon. Cleveland L. Damm, former deputy labor commissioner of California, which is attached hereto as Exhibit B.

JAPANESE IMMIGRATION COMPANIES.

As has been stated above, the Japanese bosses and boarding-house keepers in the United States are in constant communication and coöperation with certain so-called immigration companies in Japan. These companies make a business of encouraging and recruiting coolie immigration to the United States. Four of the principal companies of this character are known as the "Kosi Iman Kawaisha," "Nihon Gashi Iman Kawaisha," "Hiroshina Iman Kawaisha," and "Kobe Iman Kawaisha."

A contract is entered into by one of these immigration companies with every Japanese immigrant coming to the United States. By the terms of the contract it is provided that the immigration company shall secure passage for the immigrant to the United States, with necessary passport, and that it shall provide for all his creature comforts while en route, and return him to Japan in case of sickness. Fully 80 per cent of all the Japanese who come to the United States are classified, as shown by the reports of the immigration office, as farmers. The wages of farm hands in Japan are 3 to 4 yen per month, or about $1.50 American money, without board or lodging; yet everyone of this class of immigrants, after paying passage to the United States, is able to show to the immigration officers $30 in gold. It is understood by the immigrants that they must have at least this amount in order to secure landing in the United States.

It is a fact full of significance that of the hundreds of coolies who are constantly coming into the United States every one produces just $30 in gold; no more, and no less.

That the entire system of immigration companies, boarding-house keepers, and Japanese bosses is but an elaborate and ingenious method of avoiding our contract labor laws no one who has investigated the subject can doubt.

The following is an exact translation of one of the immigrant contracts referred to:

Contract.

The Nippon Imin Goshi Company will contract, accepting the request for transportation, of Yoshida Ichitaro, who is a free emigrant, having the purpose to land in San Francisco, North America, and to secure for him work there, within the limitations prescribed by the immigration laws.

1. The emigrant shall perform everything that is needed for getting the passport and must be responsible for all expenses needed for the voyage, and should have the money which is necessary when landing.

2. The maturity of the contract is three years from the date that the emigrant starts.

3. If the emigrant gets sick, or loses the means to get along, Narita Toyashira, agent, will help him and provide him means to get back to Japan in case it is necessary.

4. If the emigrant is sent back at the expense of the Japanese Government the company shall pay all the expenses for the emigrant.

5. The emigrant shall pay 10 yen to the company as its fee. If the emigrant has a child who does not exceed the age of 15 years, the charge for it will be half price, and if the child is not exceeding 10 years of age, he will be carried free of charge.

6. The emigrant shall provide two securities to the company according to acts 3 and 4 hereof, and they will be responsible to pay all of the expenses that have been paid by the company under the provisions of sections 3 and 4.

7. The two securities are responsible in all the matters pertaining to the emigrant.

This contract is made in duplicate, one to the emigrant and one to the company.

Meiji, 31st year (1898), 1st month (January), 31st day.

HAMANAKA HACHITARO,
Special Manager Japan United Immigration Company.

Emigrant:

YOSHIDA ICHITARO,

Securities:

YOSHIDA YOHEI.
YAMAMOTO KUSU.

There is every ground for the belief that the $30 which is exhibited by the immigrant to the United States officials is furnished by the immigration company. The whole scheme is a flagrant violation of our contract labor laws. The class of Japanese immigrants who are thus enabled to come to the United States are of the most objectionable character, and without the assistance of such organizations would be compelled to remain in Japan. The United States Government should take immediate steps to suppress these immigration companies.

The great danger to the laboring interests of the United States of unrestricted Japanese immigration will be better understood after an examination of the following table showing the prevailing rate of wages paid in Japan in the various lines of industry:

Japanese wage rates per day.

	Yen.a	United States money.
Carpenters	0.55	$0.26
Plasterers	.55	.26
Stonecutters	.65	.31
Paper hangers	.50	.24
Joiners	.60	.29
Tailors for Japanese clothing	.50	.24
Tailors for foreign clothing	1.00	.48
Blacksmiths	.75	.36
Printers	.40	.19
Ship carpenters	.60	.29
Compositors	.60	.29
Common laborers	.40	.19
Confectioners	.35	.17
Farm laborers, per month	3.00	1.44

a A yen is valued at 48 cents.

It is little wonder that these strange foreigners, when they come to the United States, are willing to work for 60 and 70 cents a day, which is more than double the wages for which they were compelled to work in Japan. As a result of this unnatural competition the white laborer has been driven from the field wherever the coolie system has found a foothold.

In 1898 California produced 17,229 tons of beet sugar. On account of unexpected drought during the season the total amount of beet sugar produced in the State was about 50 per cent less than the usual annual product. Capitalists who have gone into the beet-sugar industry have brought into the United States hundreds of coolie laborers from Hawaii, China, and Japan. The same system of coolie labor that has been the curse of the Hawaiian Islands for years has been brought to the United States.

California produces annually about 10,000,000 pounds of hops, and fully 75 per cent of the labor employed in this great industry is likewise Chinese and Japanese, principally the latter.

I have asked many of the leading manufacturers and employers of the coast why preference is not given to white labor. The invariable reply has been "because white labor is too independent; it occasions too much trouble to the employer; the gang or boss system is far less troublesome, and besides, the Japanese and Chinese labor is cheaper." Other employers have told me that they would prefer white labor, but that it is unreliable; that most of the common white laborers of the coast are tramps or hoboes.

This is, no doubt, in a measure true. More tramps can be seen traveling along the highways and railways of the Pacific coast States than in any other part of the United States that I have ever visited. The question is, What has made them tramps? That the unequal and unnatural battle which the white laborer of the coast has been compelled to wage against his Asiatic competitor is directly responsible for this deplorable condition I have not the slightest doubt.

The records of the State bureau of labor statistics of California show that during the hard times in 1895-96 over 15,000 white laborers of California were out of employment. The thousands of women and children who were dependent upon them for support were suffering from want and hunger, and yet during all of this distressing period the 36,000 coolie laborers in the State were, for the most part, regularly employed. Cheap labor, like cheap money, is always the last to be out of employment.

RELATION OF ASIATIC IMMIGRATION TO CRIME.

For the purpose of comparison I have secured data from the official records of the cities of San Francisco, Cleveland, and Cincinnati, showing the total number of arrests for crime in each of the cities named for the year ending June 1, 1899. The degrading effect of Asiatic competition upon the white laboring classes of the coast is, it seems to me, forcibly illustrated by a comparison of these figures. Thousands of white laborers, when forced to face the alternative of working side by side with the coolie and receiving a coolie's wage or becoming tramps, have chosen to take to the highways. The population of San Francisco, Cleveland, and Cincinnati is about the same, and yet the number of arrests for crime in the city of San Francisco during the last year was greater than the combined number of arrests in the cities of Cleveland and Cincinnati.

Comparative statement of arrests for drunkenness, burglary, grand and petit larceny, and vagrancy in the cities of San Francisco, Cleveland, and Cincinnati for year ending June 1, 1899.

	Population.	For drunkenness.	For burglary and larceny.	For vagrancy.
San Francisco	350,000	12,183	1,290	2,836
Cleveland	380,000	7,685	1,020	142
Cincinnati	296,000	2,124	853	504

Total arrests for all offenses during year.

San Francisco -- 28,013
Cleveland -- 14,452
Cincinnati --- 10,010

The above figures tell their own story. The appalling number of arrests for vagrancy in the city of San Francisco can be accounted for upon no other theory than that the white toilers of the coast have gone down in hopeless defeat in the unequal struggle with their Asiatic competitors. It has been said that the currency of a nation is always debased to the level of its baser standard coin. It is equally axiomatic that the labor of a community is always degraded to the level of the lowest type of labor with which it must compete. Oil and water will not mix. American laborers may be hoboized; *they will not be coolieized.*

SMUGGLING OVER THE CANADIAN AND MEXICAN FRONTIER.

As already stated large numbers of Chinese and Japanese come into the United States every year from Canada and British Columbia. The line of frontier is so extensive that it is next to impossible to police it effectively. I think, however, that if the Government were to guard more carefully the railway lines operating over the border the number of coolies who enter the United States upon these lines would be greatly reduced.

Hundreds of Chinese immigrants who are denied landing at Seattle and San Francisco secure passage to some Mexican port, usually to Ensanada, from which they work their way over the Mexican border into the United States. Many of them when approaching the border line along the coast wait until low tide and follow the coast line into the United States over the border, the tide water obliterating all marks of the trail behind them. These Chinese are assisted by their countrymen who live at different points along the border, and between them a regular system of signs and communication has been established.

MEXICAN PEON LABOR.

As appears by the tables showing the number and nationality of laborers employed upon the railways of the coast it will be seen that large numbers of Mexicans are employed on some of the lines, notably upon the lines of the Santa Fe company. A large percentage of such Mexicans are aliens who reside on the Mexican side of the line and who come into the United States as laborers.

In the fruit-gathering season hundreds of Mexicans living near the border line are employed annually under contract and come into the United States and work in the orchards, vineyards, and fruit ranches. The American rate of wages is double that of the Mexican. The Mexican peon laborer is little if any better than the Japanese coolie, and the competition of the Mexican is quite as disastrous to white labor as is that of the Chinese and Japanese.

THE CHINESE EXCLUSION ACT.

In 1880 the tide of coolie immigration to the United States from China had attained such alarming proportions that the American people awakened to the fact that unless immediate steps were taken for its suppression the white labor of the Pacific States would be driven back eastward over the mountains and the field abandoned to the Chinese.

A commission was appointed by President Hayes to visit Pekin and present the situation to the Imperial Government, to the end that some agreement might be reached which, while respecting the dignity of the Chinese Government, would secure protection to the laboring interests of the United States. As a result the famous immigration treaty of 1880 was framed, and in 1882 "the Chinese exclusion act," so called, was enacted by Congress.

Class legislation is always objectionable, and legislative discrimination against an individual, class, or nation can be justified only by the most urgent and extraordinary necessity. To the honest toilers of all climes and nations who, tiring of the oppression and limited opportunities which surround them in the Old World, are anxious to avail themselves of the advantages of a free government, the United States has been ever ready to extend a generous welcome. Hundreds of thousands of foreigners have come to our shores, have joined our great army of toilers, and are to-day respected citizens of their adopted country.

The European immigrants are rapidly and easily assimilated. The peculiarities of race yield speedily to new conditions and surroundings. The Irishman, the Englishman, the German, the Frenchman, and Swede of yesterday is to-day an American. Not so with the Asiatic immigrant. There is between the white and Mongolian races an impassable gulf. The two races will not assimilate. The Asiatic immigrant who comes to the United States retains all of his race peculiarities; he remains an Asiatic; he can not be Americanized. The Japanese, while adopting the dress and manners of the American, remains just as much a foreigner as his Mongolian brother, the Chinese. Neither the Japanese nor the Chinese who come to the United States have, as a class, the remotest interest in our Government or our laws. They are no more a part of us than are their countrymen in Yokohama and Hongkong.

It is in the exceptional and extraordinary character of Asiatic immigration that the exclusion law finds its justification. And I predict that the time will come, if indeed it is not already at hand, when the interests of American labor will demand that its provisions be so extended as to prohibit the coming into the United States of the "coolie" classes of all foreign nations.

The purpose of the "Exclusion act" is to exclude only the "coolie" or laboring classes of Chinese immigrants. Chinese merchants, doctors, artists, students, and, in fact, all Chinese other than common laborers, are, by the terms of the treaty and the act, exempt from its provisions.

It is a fact, however, that, as the law is at present administered, the greatest hardships are imposed upon the merchants and others of the exempt classes of Chinese immigrants. A Chinese merchant applying for landing in the United States must establish his identity and standing as a merchant. If he is returning to the United States after a visit to China his papers must be examined by the Government officials, and in many cases they are forwarded to the city in which the merchant claims residence for investigation. Pending such investigation the immigrant is held in detention by the steamship company. The place provided by the Pacific Mail Company at San Francisco for the detention of such immigrants is called the "Detention loft."

It is the duty of this Government in the interest of humanity to see that something is done to compel those who have charge of Chinese immigrants, pending the investigation of their right to land in the United States, to give at least a small measure of consideration to their comfort and creature welfare. The steamship companies who bring these immigrants to our shores receive compensation for the care and keeping of each of them until they are landed, and they should be compelled by the Government to make proper and reasonable provision for their comfort.

I suggested to the officials of the Chinese bureau as early as January last that I saw no valid reason why, in the cases of all Chinese merchants and others of the exempted classes, who desired to visit China with the expectation of returning to the United States, the investigation respecting the business, identity, and status of such Chinese might not be made and his status fixed prior to his departure. Upon his return to the United States the only proof necessary will then be proof of identity. This can be readily furnished, and the further detention of bona fide Chinese merchants for weeks, and in some cases months, in the vile detention lofts will be avoided.

I am much pleased to note that as recently as March last the Treasury Department issued to the officials at the several ports instructions upon this subject, and that hereafter the status of Chinese merchants will be inquired into and established, at least prima facie, prior to their departure from this country, instead of at the time of their return.

FRAUDS COMMITTED BY CHINESE IMMIGRANTS.

The records at the Chinese bureau at San Francisco show that an average of between 3,500 and 4,000 Chinese persons enter the United States at that port each year.

The following tables, compiled from the official records at the Chinese bureau at San Francisco, will give a very correct idea of the extent and character of Chinese immigration at the present time:

The tables given below cover the two last fiscal years, ending June 1, 1898, and June 1, 1899, respectively.

Number of Chinese applying for admission to United States, number admitted and rejected.

JULY 1, 1897, TO JULY 1, 1898.

Month.	Total applying.	Admitted.		Total admitted.	Rejected.		Total rejected.
		Males.	Females.		Males.	Females.	
July	330	323	2	325	11	2	13
August	255	371	3	374	4		4
September	462	370	3	373	4		4
October	397	364	15	379	11	1	12
November	411	306	7	313	16	1	17
December	296	368	11	379	5	3	8
January	115	160	18	178	1	5	6
February	113	92	6	98	1	3	4
March	231	168	12	180	2	2	4
April	218	195	5	200	3		3
May	540	546	10	556	26	1	27
June	438	406	3	409	26	1	27
Total	3,806	3,669	95	3,764	110	19	129

JULY 1, 1898, TO JULY 1, 1899.

Month.	Total applying.	Admitted.		Total admitted.	Rejected.		Total rejected.
		Males.	Females.		Males.	Females.	
July	349	319	19	338	20	4	24
August	694	530	12	542	66	4	70
September	633	272	10	282	108		108
October	250	472	8	480	92	6	98
November	312	284	2	286	72	2	74
December	292	264	10	274	50		50
January	154	205	6	211	37	4	41
February	203	159	1	160	33	2	35
March	82	144	2	146	16	1	17
April	271	184	7	191	25		25
May	420	221	1	222	23		23
June	296	497	6	503	31		31
Total	3,956	3,551	84	3,635	573	23	596

As shown in the above table, there were admitted to the United States at the port of San Francisco for the fiscal year ending June 30, 1898, 3,764 Chinese immigrants, while in the last fiscal year the number was 3,635.

Several classes of Chinese returning, number in transit through the United States, number departing and deported, etc.

JULY 1, 1897, TO JULY 1, 1898.

Month.	Applicants with section 6 certificates admitted. a	Rejected.	Laborers returning under treaty of 1894.	In transit through United States.	Chinese departing from San Francisco.		Returned laborers departing under treaty of 1894.		Deported.
					Males.	Females.	Males.	Females.	
July	38		57	44	245	10	50	1	6
August	102	1	93	113	357	20	99		29
September	157		85	34	427	30	122	2	11
October	122	8	89	55	1,034	50	352	4	35
November	143	11	73	25	838	12	263	1	7
December	164	1	63	35	608	10	105	1	14
January	81		6	14	171	3	35	1	4
February	50		1		219	12	58	1	8
March	67		26	22	208	12	29		4
April	51	1	45	45	189	24	47	1	43
May	144		75	105	249	20	73	1	9
June	74	2	120	59	109	6	16		7
Total	1,193	24	733	551	4,654	209	1,329	13	177

JULY 1, 1898, TO JULY 1, 1899.

July	30	1	112	34	244	12	64	1	40
August	29	12	239	58	191	5	62		6
September	8	50	103	35	336	25	102	1	1
October	102	32	178	42	1,051	31	310		3
November	46	2	90	25	937	37	269	1	9
December	43		74	27	601	8	207	1	6
January	50		22	8	306	12	91	2	22
February	59	5	10	23	149	2	39		37
March	77	3	30	7			66		3
April	52		38	74			52		3
May	58	1	59	111			31		1
June	47	5	130	319			38		4
Total	597	111	985	763	3,815	232	1,331	6	105

a The section 6 certificate is issued only to Chinese immigrants other than laborers; such certificates are issued in compliance with section 6 of the Chinese exclusion act, which provides that all Chinese persons other than laborers who may be entitled by the treaty or act to come within the United States shall, before leaving China, obtain permission from the Chinese Government, with a certificate showing such permission, the name, occupation or profession, etc., of the immigrant.

There has in the past years been a great deal of irregularity at some of the customs districts in the admission of Chinese persons in the exempt classes. Section 6 certificates have in many instances been issued to cooly laborers, who have been allowed to come into the United States as merchants, students, and travelers.

Probably the greatest number of frauds are committed by the class of Chinese laborers who apply for admission on the ground that they were born in the United States, and are therefore "native sons." There has recently been a large increase in the number of arrivals who claim to be "native sons," their claims being supported solely by the unreliable testimony of Chinese witnesses.

The following table contains a comparative statement showing the total number of arrivals of Chinese by months, and number of "native sons" during corresponding months, for the two last fiscal years:

Total number of Chinese admitted at San Francisco under exempt class as "native born" compared with total admissions for fiscal years 1897-98 and 1898-99.

Month.	July 1, 1897, to July 1, 1898.			July 1, 1898, to July 1, 1899.		
	Total admissions, all classes.	Native born.	Per cent native born.	Total admissions, all classes.	Native born.	Per cent native born.
July	325	37	$11\frac{5}{13}$	338	94	$27\frac{7}{8}$
August	374	14	$3\frac{3}{4}$	542	95	$17\frac{7}{2}$
September	373	20	$5\frac{3}{8}$	282	79	28
October	379	45	$11\frac{7}{8}$	480	53	$11\frac{3}{4}$
November	313	35	$11\frac{1}{4}$	286	58	$20\frac{1}{4}$
December	379	51	$13\frac{1}{4}$	274	68	25
January	178	48	27	211	83	$39\frac{1}{4}$
February	98	34	$33\frac{3}{4}$	160	56	35
March	180	48	$26\frac{2}{3}$	146	17	$11\frac{1}{2}$
April	200	62	31	191	18	$9\frac{1}{2}$
May	556	99	$17\frac{7}{8}$	222	39	$17\frac{1}{2}$
June	409	97	$23\frac{3}{4}$	503	60	$11\frac{5}{8}$
Total	3,764	590	$15\frac{3}{4}$	3,635	720	20

At least 75 per cent of the Chinese admitted as "native sons" are common cooly laborers. Many officials with whom I have talked do not hesitate to say that fully 90 per cent of the alleged "native sons" cases are frauds, and that not to exceed 10 per cent of the applicants claiming to be "native sons" are entitled to land as such.

CHINESE LAWYERS.

In every important port there are certain unscrupulous lawyers who devote their entire time to the Chinese business. Some of them, of course, do a perfectly legitimate business. The Chinese merchants in our Western coast cities have important commercial interests, and I have met a few attorneys who have a large and important Chinese clientage, who are an honor to their profession. I speak more particularly of the class of lawyers who are constantly hanging about the Chinese bureau and the customs offices, and whose services are invariably sought in the attempts to secure the landing of coolies and slave girls. It is notorious that some of the lawyers of this class work hand in hand with the worst classes of the Chinese, furnishing false testimony, suborning and intimidating witnesses, and resorting to every means, fair or foul, to secure the landing of their clients.

It is the unquestioned right of every Chinese immigrant to be represented by an attorney if he desires one. The large fees which the Chinese are willing to pay, however, serve as an immense corruption fund, which is constantly used to defeat the objects of the exclusion law. If Congress would fix a maximum fee in each case, commensurate with the services actually rendered, and constitute it an offense for any attorney to ask or receive, directly or indirectly, any further or additional compensation, it would, in my judgment, tend to eliminate one of the principal elements of fraud in connection with Chinese immigration.

HIGHBINDERS AND HIGHBINDERISM.

There exist in the city of San Francisco numerous "tongs," or associations of Chinese of the criminal class, organized for the express purpose of committing crime. They exist on blackmail and pay large sums annually for the protection of gambling houses and other disreputable places which are conducted by the members of these "tongs." The word "tong" is the equivalent of "society," "company," or "organization."

There are in San Francisco at the present time the following highbinder tongs: Chee Kung Tong, Suey On Tong, Bow On Tong, Hop Sing Tong, Hip Sing Tong, Suey Sing Tong, Wa Bing Shoan Tong, Bing Gung Tong, Bow Sin Sere Tong, Gi Sui Sere Tong, Hip Yee Tong, Quong Duck Tong, Jo Lung Sen Tong, Lun On Tong, and Jew Yee Tong.

The tongs or companies of this character must not be confounded with the so-called "Six Companies" or other Chinese organizations which are purely commercial and beneficial in their character.

Among the 25,000 Chinese population of the city of San Francisco about 1,000 represent the worst class of criminals on earth. Many of them have been compelled to flee from their native country on account of crimes committed there. They live without work and fatten upon the prosperity of others of their race. They impose fines arbitrarily and levy blackmail at will. If payment is resisted or refused, they do not hesitate to sentence to death the person who refuses to meet their criminal demands.

The highbinder tongs hold secret sessions, the business of which is to arrange for the collection of tribute. Each tong has its regularly appointed "soldiers," who are commonly known as "Hatchet Men." It is the sworn duty of these Hatchet Men to murder all those who have invoked the displeasure of the tong whenever directed so to do.

These vicious and criminal societies are a constant menace to the peace and good order of society. They exist for the purpose of committing crime. They review and nullify the judgments of our courts with utter disregard for our laws. They have their own tribunals, before which offenders are secretly tried and sentenced to death, and such sentence is executed by their paid assassins, They have no respect whatever for the oath administered in our courts. They even make use of our courts, if necessary, to enforce the arbitrary and secret decisions of their own tribunals. One instance in particular was called to my attention in which an innocent Chinese merchant, as a result of a conspiracy on the part of the highbinder tongs, was accused of murder, tried and convicted in the courts of California, the highbinder societies furnishing all of the witnesses against him. It was afterwards learned that all of the testimony given at this trial was false; that the witnesses had been furnished by the highbinder society which had made use of our courts to take the life of one who had fallen under its displeasure.

It is this criminal class of Chinese members of the several highbinder tongs who make a business of bringing to the United States slave girls and cooly laborers. As high as $3,000 in gold is frequently realized from the sale of a single Chinese slave girl in the city of San Francisco. The hundreds of cooly laborers whom they succeed in bringing into the country are hired out in "gangs," under the direction of a "boss," who collects their wages, the principal part of which is paid over to some company of the highbinders. The condition of this class of laborers is little better than that of slaves. They have little or no personal freedom; they are compelled to work on year after year and receive but a small portion of the fruits of their toil. If any one of them revolts against his masters or seeks to assert his personal liberty he is promptly assassinated.

The power of the highbinder tongs among the Chinese population is almost absolute. So great is the dread inspired among the Chinese by these societies that few have the courage to resist their criminal demands. The State and municipal authorities have been powerless to suppress the crimes of the highbinders, for the reason that no Chinese witness has the courage to appear and give testimony against a highbinder. Every witness who should so appear and testify would be marked for death. The Chinese people as a race is peace-loving; there is little of the warlike spirit among them, and they have not the courage to take a bold stand against this species of outlawry, which is a constant menace, not only to their prosperity but to their lives as well.

I think it a conservative statement when I say that fully 90 per cent of all the frauds committed against the Chinese exclusion act in the bringing into the United States of slave girls and coolie laborers is inspired directly by these highbinder societies. Subornation of witnesses and procurement of false testimony is a part of the business for which they are organized. I have heard of instances in which reputable and highly respected Chinese merchants have, under fear of personal violence from the highbinders, been compelled to give false testimony in cases where these criminal organizations have desired the landing of cooly laborers or slave girls.

Most of these tongs have in their regular employ some attorney of the class heretofore referred to. These attorneys are paid regular annual salaries, in addition to fees in special cases, for their work in behalf of these tongs.

It is my opinion, after a most thorough and careful investigation of this subject, that if the country could be rid of this criminal class of Chinese, and the highbinder societies or tongs permanently suppressed, one of the greatest factors in the commission of fraud in the administration of the Chinese exclusion laws would be eliminated.

In discussing this phase of the Chinese question with Dr. John Endicott Gardner, interpreter at the Chinese bureau, San Francisco, that gentleman said: "Fully 75 per cent of all of the frauds committed at the present time against the exclusion law can be traced directly to the highbinder organizations." Dr. Gardner, in addition to his position as official interpreter for the Government, occupies the chair of Oriental languages at one of the western universities. He is a highly cultured gentleman, and, having spent many years in missionary work in China, has greater familiarity with the language, manners, and customs of the Chinese race than anyone whom I have ever met. The Government is exceedingly fortunate in having as interpreter at such an important port as San Francisco a gentleman of the ability, high standing, and character of Dr. Gardner.

Attached to this report is an extended statement given to me by Dr. Gardner touching many of the points covered in this report. Dr. Gardner's statement is highly interesting and is attached hereto, marked "Exhibit C."

Attached to Dr. Gardner's statement are numerous exhibits, the same being original translations from Chinese documents, as follows:

Exhibit A.—Letter of instructions to a highbinder or salaried "soldier" to kill another.

Exhibit B.—Contract for the sale of a Chinese slave girl, which is in the regular form in constant use among the Chinese who are engaged in this nefarious practice.

Exhibit C.—Coaching paper or catechism furnished by highbinders to Chinese slave girl to be used by her for the purpose of procuring landing in the United States.

Exhibit D.—Voluntary statement of a Chinese slave girl known as "Lee Yow Chun." This statement is made by the slave girl at the Presbyterian Mission Home at San Francisco, to which the girl had fled from her captors. The translation is by Dr. Gardner.

Exhibit E.—Intercepted letter from a highbinder to the officers of his tong.

Exhibit F.—A translation of a letter of warning received by Dr. Gardner from a Chinese friend, advising him that the highbinders had placed a price upon his (Gardner's) head.

An examination of the above exhibits will throw much light upon the methods of the criminal organizations known as the highbinders.

Mr. William Price, lieutenant of police of San Francisco, in speaking of the highbinders, says:

"Their places are finely fitted up, the same as club rooms. There they meet as other organizations do. If a member has anything against another man he places his case before the society and offers so much money to have the man killed. After they have settled on the man to be killed, his head is as good as gone. The societies' rules are so binding that those who are chosen are bound to kill their victim even if there were twenty policemen standing about at the time."

Lieutenant Price says there are about 3,000 Chinese highbinders in San Francisco at the present time, who are nothing but cutthroats and bad men. He styles them "the worst class of people on the face of the earth. They do not molest the white people, as they fear an uprising against their race in the event that any white man was killed." Lieutenant Price states further that "one of the by-laws in all of the highbinder societies is to the effect that every highbinder is obliged to aid in the landing of cooly laborers and Chinese slave girls.

Through the courtesy of United States Commissioner of Immigration North, of San Francisco, who served as one of the commissioners before whom the investigation into the practices of highbinders was heard about 2 years ago, much of the testimony taken at that investigation was placed at my disposal. Some of the important parts of this testimony is submitted herewith as part of my report. They are: Statement of William Price, lieutenant of police, Exhibit D; statement of "Chun Ho," rescued slave girl, Exhibit E; statement of Miss Donaldina Cameron, matron Presbyterian Chinese Rescue Home, Exhibit F.

During my investigations of this subject a number of very prominent and wealthy Chinese merchants in the city of San Francisco visited me at my hotel, most of them coming secretly in the nighttime, as they were fearful that violence would be done them if it became known to the highbinders that they had been to see me. Every one of these men substantiated what Dr. Gardner had said respecting the frauds committed in the landing of coolies and slave girls. They insisted that if the highbinder societies could be broken up that the source of nearly all of the frauds committed against the exclusion act would be removed.

That the State and municipal authorities of California were powerless to break up these organizations all of the Chinese with whom I talked were agreed.

As a result of my investigation I have reached the conclusion that the only way in which this evil can be reached and the country rid of this vicious and disturbing element is for Congress to take the subject in hand.

Ninety-five per cent of all the members of the highbinder societies are aliens and criminals of the worst type. The one thing which they fear above all others, holding it in greater dread than all of our laws, our courts and jails, is deportation to China. The purpose of the highbinder organizations is vicious and criminal. They should be suppressed by law of Congress, and membership therein, or in any society having for its purpose the commission of crime, or the violation of our laws on the part of aliens residing in this country, should render such aliens liable to deportation.

In this connection I take pleasure in referring to the statement of the imperial Chinese consul-general at San Francisco, Ho Yow, marked "Exhibit G," attached to this report.

Also to statement of a Chinese merchant of San Francisco, marked "Exhibit H," and hereto attached.

Exhibit A.

STATEMENT OF FRANK D. SCHUYLER, CHINESE INSPECTOR, SAN FRANCISCO, CAL.

Q. What is your official connection with the Chinese bureau, Mr. Schuyler?—A. At San Francisco, as an inspector.

Q. How long have you acted in such capacity?—A. I think since about the 8th or 9th of last January, during which time I have had about 30 days' leave of absence.

Q. Prior to that time where had you resided and what was your business?—A. Chinese inspector in Seattle, Wash., since the 1st day of September, 1893. I was appointed in New York about the 8th of August, 1893, and proceeded to Seattle, where my official station was designated, arriving there about the 1st day of September, 1893, and have been in actual Government service ever since.

Q. During the time that you were stationed in Seattle, are you able to state approximately the number of Chinese that were landed there annually?—A. I can not, as Port Townsend was the principal landing place.

Q. During your connection with the Government service at Seattle what percentage, if any, of the total admission of Chinese to this country would you think were not entitled to admission, or were admitted upon proofs that you have reason to believe were false?—A. Very few, as it is not a large place; and there are not more than 17 to 20 Chinese firms in Seattle to-day.

Q. What would you estimate the total Chinese population to be in Seattle?—A. It varies; in the summer there are only about 250 to 300, as they go away.

Q. Are there any considerable number of Japanese there?—A. Yes.

Q. From what Japanese ports do they come principally?—A. I can't say. They come to this country via the Canadian Pacific steamers via Vancouver.

Q. Do any considerable proportion of the Japanese immigrants who land in Seattle remain in that country?—A. Prior to my going away it was notoriously known that they came in by the Canadian Pacific Railway from Vancouver to Seattle and from Tacoma to Puyallup, which is between Seattle and Tacoma, where they congregate in large numbers, and went to work for the railroads as contract laborers.

Q. Upon what railroads was it reported that they were employed principally?—A. The Northern Pacific and Great Northern.

Q. Have you any reason to think, through facts that have come to your knowledge, that these Japanese who landed and went at once to work on the railroads came from Japan for that purpose?—A. I think so, as I have seen Japanese come in on the railroad and from a certain mark or peculiarity on their faces we would know that they were the same who went away on the train the next day.

Q. Were they in charge of a boss?—A. Apparently not, although there was always some one who spoke English.

Q. About how many that land in that country go out to work in the mines and on the railroads in the course of a year?—A. All the way from 20 to 50, day after day, for a long time, and then there would be a lapse, so it is hard telling.

Q. Did you ever hear of any Japanese agency or employment bureau through whom these laborers were furnished?—A. Yes; there was a firm there who it was generally supposed had the handling of these Japanese, and the general supposition was that they were the ones who brought them here under contract.

Q. Who would you recommend that I call upon as being the persons most likely to put me in touch as to the details on this subject?—A. Col. F. D. Heustis, collector of customs at Port Townsend, will be able to give all the data on the Japanese immigration question. There is an immigration commissioner at Vancouver who is also well informed.

Q. What do you know upon the subject of wages paid to the Japanese laborers in that country?—A. Only upon representation, which is very much less than any other class of labor.

Q. What do you know upon the subject of Chinese landing in British Columbia and illegally entering this country over the lines?—A. It was a notorious fact that the Chinese landed in this country, coming via the Canadian Pacific Railway via Vancouver and Victoria, large numbers at a time, but that there was no increase in the local population, and the query always remained as to what had become of them. Every man must have $50 when he lands as evidence to the Canadian Government that he is no pauper. This certificate must be renewed every 6 months, and if a man desires to leave the country his head-tax receipt is taken up until he again seeks admission to the United States, when it is returned to him.

Q. Is it not also notorious that the railroads operating between British Columbia and this country encourage rather than discourage the transportation of Chinese to this country?—A. Not Chinese, but the Japanese, I believe.

Q. What have you ever heard of immigration companies located either here or in Japan making a business of furnishing the head money of $25 or $30, as you state they must have, for the purpose of having him exhibit it here?—A. At one time, when two Japanese were rejected for not having the sufficient amount of money, a collection was made up among some Japanese at Victoria, so that they would all have $25 or $30 when they got to San Francisco. They were under the impression that having passed at Victoria they would not be subject to examination at San Francisco. The emigration agent at Vancouver, whose name I can not recall, told me that he had discovered the existence of a company, I think in Kobe, Japan, where they furnished the passage money, and the agents in this country see that the head money is given to the emigrants as they come in; that if a man in Seattle wants 500 men he sends to Kobe, Japan, and they come here by the Canadian Pacific line or the Japanese line.

Q. The general impression then, you would say, is that the greater part of the emigrants that come here come under such an arrangement?—A. Up there, yes; I have no knowledge of what happens here.

Q. What do you know as to the number of Chinese or Japanese who are employed in the principal railways or mines of that vicinity?—A. Japanese are employed on the railroads and Chinese are in the canning business. There are no Chinese employed on the railroads, excepting a few on the Northern Pacific who have been employed on that line for a number of years.

Q. From your knowledge and experience of the situation at Seattle what would you say as to whether the Japanese emigration has been on the increase in the last four or five years?—A. Decidedly on the increase. It has been said that as many as 4,000 to 5,000 have come in in a month. I think that probably 1,200 to 1,500 would be a fair estimate.

Q. Do all of those who come in have to pass through the examination so that the Government is able to have a register?—A. I am not familiar with the form carried out on the Canadian side, but until lately they boldly walked in.

Q. Then the principal number come in over the British Columbia line?—A. I do not know, but would say that the larger number do.

Q. What practical suggestion could you make, from what you know of the situation, as to any reasonable method that might be adopted to check this emigration over the line?—A. The illegal entry over the line is simply a matter of policing the line. It is a matter of legal affairs.

Q. During your entire experience as an officer in the Chinese bureau you have observed, no doubt, that there are quite a percentage who ask admission as a native born?—A. That is practiced more here than at Seattle. We do not admit a Chinese as native born unless he has 2 white people as proof.

Q. I understand that in this city there is a resident Chinese population of about 25,000 to 50,000. About what percentage of that population would you say are women or females?—A. I do not know.

Q. Do you not think that the percentage of females is greater in the native born than the others?—A. Yes, at this place.

Q. What percentage of those who come on the native-born certificate do you think are fraudulent?—A. I can not tell, but at Seattle I do not think there were more than 2 per cent; but here I do not know.

Q. Out of the total admissions at this port in the last fiscal year 1 out of 7 or 8 make application as native born. Don't you think it impossible that this is so?—A. It may be possible, as Chinese came here as early as 1851 and were admitted unlimited.

Q. Why is it necessary to detain a Chinese merchant in the detention loft or any other place for any extended period for the purpose of examining his papers, documents, etc., which on their face appear to be perfectly proper?—A. None, in my opinion. I think that all investigations in cases where no direct information of fraud is brought to the attention of the bureau should be made in the interim of the departure of the subject and his return to this country. It should be investigated upon his departure and filed subject to his return.

Q. Is it not a fact that upon the subject of landing slave girls illegally the highbinder institutions are really the persons who engage in that business principally and in most instances are interested in furnishing false proofs?—A. Yes.

Q. If some measure might be taken by the Government which might rid this country and other Chinese countries of highbinderism, would that not facilitate the law to a great extent?—A. I think the Chinese would work with you hand in hand.

Q. What would you think of a suggestion that a law be passed by Congress making membership proof of either crime or misdemeanor, which would render any member liable to deportation, if alien, and then leave it to the head of the Immigration Bureau as a court?—A. I think that while the consul-general resides here he be made head of this court.

Exhibit C.

AFFIDAVIT OF MR. CLEVELAND L. DAM.

Mr. Cleveland L. Dam, attorney at law, of the city and county of San Francisco, State of California, appeared personally before Special Agent Thomas F. Turner, and in reply to inquiries propounded, testified as follows, to wit:

State of California, *City and County of San Francisco, ss:*

Cleveland L. Dam, being duly sworn, deposes and says: From April, 1895, until October, 1899, I served as deputy labor commissioner of the bureau of labor statistics of the State of California, under the appointment of His Excellency James H. Budd, governor.

Among the first questions considered by the commission was that of the immigration of Japanese. The labor commission made as thorough an investigation as possible, the scenes of investigation being the city of San Francisco, Pleasanton, Vacaville, Solano County, and Sacramento. At Pleasanton we examined Japanese contractors and laborers, merchants from whom the Japanese contractors bought supplies, farmers, and the president of the Pleasanton hop fields; at Vacaville, the orchardists, boarding-house keepers, and Japanese contractors and laborers. The investigation in San Francisco covered the testimony of Japanese boarding-house keepers, officials connected with the United States Immigration Bureau at San Francisco, and merchants who were interested in the production of raisins, hops, and sugar beets in various parts of the State.

As a result of the investigation we could not find any specific contracts between persons of this State and the residents of Japan, but in one particular instance we traced a certain Japanese laborer from Winters, Cal., to his home in Japan, and his return with a number of workmen whom he brought here under his charge and for whom he found employment in the fruit orchards near Vacaville.

We also found evidence and had in our possession certificates of a society having its headquarters in Japan which issued to each emigrant a certificate promising to take care of them while in this country, to find them employment here, to protect them in case of sickness, and to exercise a general supervision over their future welfare.

While we could not find any evidence of existing contracts under which Japanese laborers were brought here, we were satisfied that they were brought here through correspondence with their friends in this country, who held out to them great inducements as far as employment was concerned, and the lucrative pay for that employment. The greatest difficulty had in making these investigations was the proneness of the Japanese to evade the truth. In interrogating them as to why they came here they would at first have nothing to say and then admit that they came here to learn, coming as students, but coming here to work until they had sufficient means to complete their education and study American ways and enterprises.

There are no doubts in my mind but that contracts are made in violation of the laws, but they are possibly made by the boarding-house keeper, who would contract to furnish so much help and rely upon the inducements of the person requiring same to send to Japan and get the men here.

Personally the Japanese laborer who comes here is unreliable and uncertain, and the success that has been attained by Japanese labor in this country has been done by what is known as the "Boarding-house system," where a number of Japanese can always be had. While some are sleeping off the effects of the night's intoxication, others always take their places, so that one need not be without any number of them at all times. This is one of the points relied upon as an excuse for hiring Japanese labor; that under this "boss system" the required number of men could always be had to perform the work, and under these conditions the employer is relieved of the trouble of seeking new hands from day to day.

The evolution of the Japanese is remarkable; after being here a short time and working upon farms, vineyards, etc., he gravitates to the city and seeks some employment of an industrial character which tends to displace mechanics, and in all parts of the city can be seen tailoring, furniture, shoe, restaurant, crockery, and other establishments, showing that the tendency of the Japanese is to engage in profitable employment to the detriment of white labor.

In domestic employment Japanese labor is becoming a very important factor, and to a large extent is taking the place of the diminished number of Chinese domestics, their work, however, not being as satisfactory as that of other domestic help owing to their unreliability.

The influx of Japanese can not be considered otherwise than a serious menace to the welfare of white labor in our State, not only as a competitor of the cheaper class of labor, but of more advanced labor, even to professional spheres, as is now evidenced by his signs and advertisements as physicians, dentists, and even fortune tellers, catering to white trade.

The Japanese stops at nothing, evidently imbued with the idea that he represents a superior civilization; he is here to turn his efforts to profitable account in an open field of competition comprising all avocations.

As he has driven white labor from the orchard, farm, vineyard, beet, and hop fields, and domestic services, there is no limit to which he will not aspire, and the result which must necessarily follow will be a most severe damage to white labor.

C. L. DAM.

Subscribed and sworn to before me this 16th day of February, 1900.

JAMES MASON,
Notary Public in and for the City and County of San Francisco,
State of California.

EXHIBIT D.

STATEMENT OF J. ENDICOTT GARDNER, OF SAN FRANCISCO, CAL.

STATE OF CALIFORNIA, *City and County of San Francisco, ss:*

Personally appeared before the undersigned authority in the above city, county, and State, Dr. J. Endicott Gardner, 37 years of age, and resident of the said city and county, at present occupying the position of United States Chinese inspector and interpreter at the port of San Francisco and professor of Chinese language at the University of California, and missionary.

Q. For how many years were you a resident of China?—A. Sixteen or seventeen.

Q. How was your time occupied during your residence in China?—A. As student in China.

Q. How long have you been connected with the Chinese bureau in the United States?—A. On the Pacific coast 16 or 17 years, from San Francisco to British Columbia, and for short periods at Portland, Port Townsend, Tacoma, Victoria, and Vancouver.

Q. As interpreter it has been your duty, has it not, Doctor, to interrogate Chinese emigrants who desire landing in this country?—A. Yes; both to interrogate and interpret interrogatories put to them by other inspectors.

Q. How extensive can you say your acquaintance and knowledge has been respecting the question, generally, of Chinese immigration and the methods and practices employed in securing admission to this country?—A. Probably on account of being able to read their letters, as well as speaking their language from childhood, I must say that I am as thoroughly familiar with those methods as anyone in California. I have been in the position to be more familiar than anyone else.

Q. What do you say as to whether or not the mode of procedure practiced now at the different Pacific ports is uniform?—A. There is a decided lack of uniformity.

CHINESE AND JAPANESE IMMIGRATION.

Q. In a general way, can you state what has been and what is the effect of this want of uniformity in the mode of procedure and practice?—A. It leads to serious dissatisfaction on the part of the steamship companies, on account of the difficulty at some ports for the Chinese to gain admission, the collectors and officials being more severe and prejudiced, and causing the Chinese to make for ports where admission is gained more easily.

Q. It is a fact, then, that under the present practice and mode of procedure it is more difficult for emigrants at certain ports to gain admission than at others, and it is also a fact that those ports are chosen by the emigrants where they are likely to meet with the least obstruction. This situation, then, you attribute to the lack of uniformity?—A. Yes.

Q. What suggestion could you make that would tend to cure this evil?—A. I would suggest the gathering of data at different points where Chinese enter the United States and have them compared by special agents or with the commission, with the view to bringing about uniformity, so that all collectors, deputy collectors, and Chinese inspectors might act along certain lines. As things are at present, when certain steamship companies find it difficult to get their patrons in the officer at that certain port is made to bear the brunt of all this, and the most honest officer is held up for it.

Q. How long have you been attached to the bureau at this port?—A. I was attached to this bureau first either in 1883 or 1884 until toward the end of 1884. I resigned to go North for a more lucrative post, and returned to this coast when the salary was increased some three years ago, and in the meantime, off and on, I have been in the employ of the United States Government, all the time interpreting and translating between Americans and Chinese.

Q. What do you know, Dr. Gardner, upon the subject of railway and steamship companies being interested in bringing in these Chinese emigrants, and what part do they take in it?—A. So far as the companies themselves are concerned my present knowledge of them enables me to say only that they act in the capacity of being public carriers and wish only as few obstacles as possible to be put in the way of their patrons. I know of only one agent in particular who is directly interested in the coming of Chinese emigrants and furthers their coming to the United States. He is still in the employ of the Pacific Mail Steamship Company and his name is Soo Hoo Fong; and this man now in the employ of the Pacific Mail Company is engaged and has been engaged in furthering Chinese emigrants in coming to this country.

Q. What do you know of the subject generally of men of this kind organizing companies to bring in laborers illegally?—A. I know of some who are banded together for the purpose of aiding Chinese in illegal entrance into the United States; I know that they make that their business. These men are well known to the Chinese community, so well known, and they themselves are so well known, and their business so well known, that they have actually had a word coined for themselves, which is "Bahn Gar," which means "a Chinaman or Chinese who are in the business of importing Chinese coolies or Chinese slaves."

Q. What part, if any, do the highbinders take in promoting this illegal immigration?—A. They furnish false witnesses and frighten off anyone who might feel justified in coming forth and telling the truth.

Q. What do you know, in a general way, about the highbinders, their organizations, etc.?—A. In general they are organized societies for the purpose of committing crime. They exist on blackmail, on pay for protecting gambling houses and disreputable places in general. I know that they take it upon themselves to try cases, to review judgments of our courts with utter disregard for our laws. I know that they nullify our decisions. For instance, if an American court had rendered a decision, they would intimidate the witnesses so that when the cases go into a higher court everything would be changed. They defy our courts by ways and means of their own. I know that they impose their own sentences upon offenders from their own standpoint. They levy fines in some cases and death in others. I know they have in their service paid men to do the killing, and so long have they had this service that the men have a particular name; they are called "hatchet men." I know they control our judicial oaths; that they can say an oath shall or shall not be taken. I know them as organized societies of crime. They distribute revolvers to their members and send them out, and I have noticed in several cases where the revolvers were taken back. Such a notice is now in the possession of Captain Biggy.

Q. It is a fact, Doctor, is it not, that your life has been threatened by these highbinders?—A. Yes. I know they use our courts, if necessary, to enforce their decisions.

Q. In what manner?—A. By laying a charge against a certain Chinaman and having our judge pronounce the sentence. I know that these highbinders furnish witnesses for anything wanted at so much a head. I have had cases in which men have come forward to testify, and when the time came they were spirited away. I know that the headquarters of these societies are in San Francisco, but they have branches in Canada. There are many active members who are able to do a great deal of injury, although many members have joined from fear.

Q. Do you say that these societies named are at all times employed in bringing Chinese labor into this country illegally, and is this a part of their business?—A. It has become a part since the act went into effect.

Q. What proportion of the frauds committed at the present time against the exclusion law could, in your opinion, be traced direct to these organizations?—A. At least 75 per cent.

Q. If some method might be devised whereby the community might be rid of the highbinder organizations, would it then have an effect?—A. It would, decidedly.

Q. How many highbinders of this criminal type would you say are in the city of San Francisco?—A. Speaking approximately, I would say that there are as many as from 1,500 to 2,000.

Q. What proportion of them are alien and what proportion native born?—A. I should not think there are more than 100 or 200 native born, and the rank and file of the population, in my opinion, are aliens.

Q. What do you think would be the effect of such a law, if passed, providing for the deportation of all aliens if found members of such societies?—A. It would break them all up.

Q. What is your opinion of the feasibility of such a law?—A. I think it could be done.

Q. Do you think that deportation is practically the only remedy?—A. Yes.

Q. In a general way, will you state why the Federal and municipal authorities are unable to break up these organizations, or to detect the offender when crime is committed.—A. Because the highbinders furnish witnesses, and terrify witnesses that the State may rely upon.

Q. What would be the result if some honest Chinaman would take the stand and give testimony against him?—A. He would be liable to forfeit his life for it.

Q. And it is the fear of this result which makes it impossible to enforce our laws against them, is it not?—A. That is right.

Q. What part is taken by attorneys in assisting in the illegal landing of Chinese laborers?—A. As it were, the Chinese prepare the cannon balls, and the lawyers fire them.

Q. Are any attorneys regularly employed by these Chinese highbinder societies?—A. Yes; and who have very little legitimate business besides.

Q. What class of lawyers, and about how many of them, are there engaged in this class of business?—A. As a rule, they are of a low grade. Roughly speaking, there are about one dozen in San Francisco.

Q. Do they have any other practice to speak of?—A. Very little.

Q. What do you know as to who compensates these attorneys in this case?—A. As a rule, the middlemen who are allied with the highbinders. These middlemen collect the fees and pay the attorneys.

Q. What fees do these attorneys receive, as a rule?—A. From $25 to $50 for men, and from $100 to $500 for women.

Q. What, in your opinion, would be the effect of a law which would limit the amount of fees or fix a maximum fee which an attorney might charge in all such cases; fixing it at a reasonable amount to the actual and legitimate service rendered?—A. If it can be enforced, and no collecting on the side is done, it would have a very wholesome effect.

Q. What have you to say as to the suggestion that the entire business of the Chinese bureau be transferred from the customs bureau to the immigration bureau?—A. I think very well of it, and think that is where it properly belongs. The reasons are that the very nature of the Chinese business brings it under the head of immigration, and the collector has no officers under him whose duty it is to enforce the Chinese restriction act.

Q. Do you not think that it would be well to enlarge somewhat the power of the inspector of the Chinese bureau to the end that in addition to his present power he might in cases generally have the right of reviewing contested cases?—A. I think well of it. In that connection I would say that the power might be given to a number of inspectors acting collectively as members of a board; then a decision would be given openly.

Q. In what class of Chinese emigrants are the greater amount of frauds committed at present?—A. The so-called Native Sons.

Q. About what percentage of these so-called Native Sons come under fraudulent representations?—A. A very conservative estimate would be about 90 per cent.

Q. Could you suggest any method of procedure or practice which would tend to reduce this?—A. The improvements of the last bill passed requiring white witnesses and also record of birth in our courts.

Q. Your acquaintance, I notice, is very extensive among the upper class of merchants in this city?—A. Yes.

Q. If Congress were to enact a law for the breaking up of these organizations, do you think that the cooperation of these better Chinese could be secured?—A. I think that all we could get from them would be moral support and secret assistance out of fear for the highbinders. That it would meet with approval there is no doubt. The class next to the so-called Native Sons, where there is a large amount of fraud, is that of men who come representing themselves as merchants and who everyone can see are laborers and have every appearance of being laborers and sons of toil. I think our Government ought to have officers in the principal ports of China to cooperate with the Chinese consuls. We should have strict investigation at both ends.

JOHN ENDICOTT GARDNER.

Subscribed and sworn to before the undersigned this February 23, 1900.

C. L. DUNN, *Notary Public.*

[Exhibits attached to statement of J. Endicott Gardner.]

LETTER OF INSTRUCTIONS TO A HIGHBINDER OR SALARIED SOLDIER.

To LUM HIP, *salaried soldier:*

It has been said that to plan schemes and devise methods and to hold the seal is the work of the literary class, while to oppose foes, fight battles, and plant firm government is the work of the military.

Now, this tong appoints salaried soldiers, to be ready to protect ourselves and assist others. This is our object.

All, therefore, who undertake the military service of this tong must obey orders and without orders you must not dare to act. If any of our brethren are suddenly molested it will be necessary for you to act with resolute will.

You shall always work to the interest of the tong and never make your office a means of private revenge.

When orders are given you shall advance valiantly to your assigned task. Never shrink or turn your back upon the battlefield.

When a ship arrives in port with prostitutes on board and the grand master issues an order for you to go down and receive them you must be punctual and use all your ability for the good of the Commonwealth (or State).

If in the discharge of your duty you are slain we will undertake to pay $500 sympathy money to your friends.

If you are wounded a doctor will be engaged to heal your wounds, and if you are laid up for any length of time you will receive $10 per month.

If you are maimed for life and incapacitated for work $250 shall be paid to you and a subscription taken to defray costs of your journey home to China.

This paper is given as proof, as word of mouth may not be believed.

Furthermore, whenever you exert your strength to kill or wound enemies of this tong, and in so doing you are arrested and imprisoned, $100 per year shall be paid to your friends during your imprisonment.

Dated 13th day of 5th month of 14th year Kwong Sui, Victoria, B. C.

[Seal of Chee Kong Tong.]

TRANSLATION OF A BILL OF SALE DRAWN UP IN THE GUISE OF A PROMISSORY NOTE.

I, Ah Kam, being poor and not having anyone on whom to depend, make this agreement, by which to obtain $460 with my person. The middle party in this transaction, Loui Fung, having introduced me to Lang Kui, and having the promise of the latter to pay this debt for me, besides passage money and other expenses, we three are agreed, and to-day the transaction has taken place; not a cent now is owing to Loui Fung. The money having actually changed hands, first into the hands of myself, Ah Kam, and I am this day handed over to Lung Kai, to be taken to California for immoral purposes. The time of service is agreed to be four and one-half years with no pay for the service on the one hand and no interest for the money on the other. Fourteen days of sickness will not be taken notice of, but fifteen days of sickness will have to be made up by serving an additional month. In case of pregnancy an additional year has to be served. As to any expected calamities happening that may happen to anyone, that will be left to the decree of heaven. Should I upon arrival at California attempt to escape, or should refuse to be a prostitute, I agree irrevocably that Lung Kai should sell me to another at pleasure. Lest word of mouth should not be proof, this instrument is drawn up to be such.

Kwong Sui 17th year, 9th month, 1st day (Oct. 1st, 1899).

AH KAM (her mark).

TRANSLATION OF CATECHISM USED IN THE COACHING OF WITNESSES FOR THE LANDING OF A CHINESE SLAVE GIRL.[1]

[Translated by Jno. Endicott Gardner.]

What is your name?—Wong Fook Sing.
How old are you?—61.
How long have you been in the United States?—29 years.
What boat did you take?—Took steamer.
What year, month, and day you came to the United States?—Tung Chi 9th year, 6th month (about July, 1870).
What do you do for a living?—I am at present salesman for Chung Kee & Co., 1107 Dupont street.
What is your occupation?—Working as salesman.
How long have you been with Chung Kee?—4 years.
What is your wife's name?—She was a Miss Lam.
How old is your wife?—47.
Is your wife natural footed or small?—Natural.
Where were you married?—San Francisco.
What year, month, and day were you married?—Kwong Sui 2d year, 5th month, and 1st day. (1876, about June 1.)
How long have you been married?—22 years.
Where is your wife?—In Canton, China.
How many children have you?—Only a girl and no boy.
What is your daughter's name?—Wong Sing You.
How old is your daughter?—22 years old.
Where was your daughter born?—Dupont street, No. 938, third floor.
What year, month, and day was your daughter born?—Kweng Sui 4th year, 6th month, and 1st day. (About July 1, 1878.)
How old was your daughter when she returned to China?—4 years.
What year and month and by what boat did your daughter return to China?—Kwong Sui 7th year, 10th month, 2d day. (About November 2d, 1881.) By Rio.
With whom did your daughter go home to China?—With my wife, who was Miss Lam.
Where did your wife and daughter live after their return to China?—Thirteenth ward, on a straight street.
Is your house in China brick or wood?—Brick.
How many rooms in your house?—One room and one kitchen.
Is there an upstairs in your house?—Yes; it has one room, a bedroom.
Do you recognize your daughter?—Yes.
Have you seen your daughter since her arrival?—Yes.
Did your daughter send over to you her photograph?—My wife this year, 2d month (about March), sent me our daughter's photograph.
Did your daughter write you?—No; only my wife.
Who sent your daughter home?—I did.
Did you ever write to your daughter?—No; only to my wife.
Did you ever send money home?—Yes, the 2d month of this year I sent $200 Mexican by Young Ming to my wife.
What was your former business?—Tinware.
How long were you engaged in that business?—In the tinware store—— (Answer incomplete.)
On what street and under what name was your business?—On Washington street, No. 745, in the basement; named Gung Lung; tinware business.

---

[1] Upon the discovery of the catechism the slave was denied landing by Collector Jackson.

Were you ever back to China?—Kwong Sui 11th year, 10th month, was back. (About October, 1886.)
By what route did you return to China?—By the Portland route.
When you wrote to your daughter to come back did your wife answer the letter?—No.
When did your wife ever write to you?—Afterwards, when she announced that a daughter would be coming over.
Where is your letter now?—Burned up after reading it.
What is your daughter coming back for?—To be married.
Have you brothers or sisters?—No.
Has your wife any brothers?—No.
Where are your parents now?—Dead.
How long have they been dead?—Over twenty years.
What are your parents' name?—Father, Kwong Fook Sun; mother, of the Chun family.
Where are your parents-in-law?—Dead.
How long have your parents-in-law been dead?—27 or 28 years.
What are the names of your parents-in-law?—Lam Ping the name of the father, and Ho the maiden name of the mother.
Did you send any money home this year?—This year in the 2d month I sent $100, Mexican.
How did you send it?—I asked a friend to take it back.
What is that friend's name?—Yeung Ming.
Is your friend back in this country?—He is still in China; he did not return.
How long have you known Chan Chun?—20 years.
Where is he now in business?—Dupont street, No. 1107; Japanese ware business; he is the proprietor.
Where did you become acquainted with him?—On Pacific street, in the Chun Kee cigar store.
Has he ever been back to China?—No.
When your daughter was a month old, did you invite him to the feast?—I did.
Where have you known him?—On Pacific street, No. 741, in the Chun Kee store.
Have you a photograph of yourself at home?—Yes.

TRANSLATION OF MEMORANDUM.

Chun Heung restaurant, 1007.
Quong Cheung Wing basement, 1014.
On Cheung Wo.
Ho Yee.
Madam Choy.
Due from Chan Yeung, $125.
Madam Choy and Chan Yeung are notorious importers of female slaves, associates of Little Pete.—(Note by the interpreter.)

TRANSLATION OF THE PORTLAND SKETCH.

Starting from San Francisco, you go to Portland, taking the boat at the China Mail dock, (this was corrected and "Spear street" was substituted.—Note by translator), the boat starting at 10 o'clock in the morning. Time from here to Portland, 3 days and 2 nights; fare $10. You first get to Astoria and then to Portland. Chinese in Portland are on Second street. The fare from Portland was $48.
(Here follows diagram of the route.)

VOLUNTARY STATEMENT OF LEE YOW CHUN.

PRESBYTERIAN MISSION HOME, *January 17, 1898.*

My name is Lee Yow Chun. I am a native of the Sha Tow village, in the district of Ho Nam, opposite the city of Canton. I have never before been in the United States. I am 16 years old. I reported my age as 20 upon my arrival; that my name was Lee Choy Wan, and that my birthplace was San Francisco. Because we were poor my parents removed to Hongkong, where they could get better wages. My father, whose name was Lee Tsung, died in Hongkong when I was 13. After father's death mother continued to work as household servant. At Hongkong we lived on Kow Yu Fong street. My mother's name is Lum Ah Mui. She is 40 this year. She worked on Kwok Lun street, No. 31. This is where she was working up to my leaving Hongkong. Mother told me one day that a go-between had been to see her on behalf of a wealthy Chinese merchant living in San Francisco, who wanted a wife from China; that she wanted me to go out and take a walk, so that I could be viewed by the go-between, that she could make her report. I did what I was bid, though I knew that mother told me this with some misgiving, as she had declined the offer once and would decline again but for her good nature and her poverty. The go-between having made her a present of $380 as coming from my intended husband, mother said she consented to take so little because I could only marry that merchant as a concubine and also that in 2 or 3 years I could come back to pay her a visit. About a week after, toward evening of the 3d of the 11th month (November 25, 1897), a man whom I had never seen before nor since, and whose name even I do not know, came to our house and took me to a house on a street next to Kwok Lung street. In this house were several women who said they had been to the United States. My mother wanted to accompany me to that house, and I wanted her to go along too, but the man said since we had to part anyway we might as well part then, so that I would not feel so bad when the time came to go on board. So we parted then and there.

When this man had me in that house he took me to a room, after my hair had been dressed, and with no other in the room brought a piece of paper out of which he taught me certain things I was to say when questioned by the customs officer in San Francisco. When he told me what to say in answer to their question "What is your father's name?" I said, "What does that mean. My father has been dead some years." He said, "We have to do that, as that is the law in California. You can not go there to get married unless you follow my instructions." I then listened until he got through with a list of questions and answers. After I had learned my lesson dinner was served, and about 8 o'clock in the evening I was taken down to the water front, where a little boat was in waiting. I was taken on this little boat and the boat people rowed me out alongside steamer *China*, where we passed the night. At 4 o'clock in the morning, when it was yet dark, I was told to go quietly over to the *China*, Shortly after the *China* started for California. I found 8 other girls on board, with 3 more after we left Shanghai. As I was told that my landing depended upon my remembering my story, I went over it every day from the day we started, at times singing it as we would a song, though often weeping as I sang, whenever I thought of mother and of home.

The Chinaman in Hongkong let me have the paper to learn the story from, telling me that when I got its contents well committed to memory I was to throw the paper overboard. The paper was about 18 inches long. I saw that the other girls each had a story to learn also. A day after our arrival at San Francisco we were questioned by the customs officers. I answered as I was told to do by that man in Hongkong. Three or four days after I was told someone was inquiring for me. He pointed to himself and said very hurriedly: "Take a good look at me, so that you can recognize me afterwards as your father." No sooner had he said this than he hurried off to go. I called after him, saying "I could not recognize a person as my father upon seeing him so short a time." He then came back and stood by the vessel a little longer. A pit-marked woman accompanied him. This woman I soon found to be a procuress. This, together with a caution that my mother gave me, as well as some things that the sailors were good enough to tell me, convinced me that all was not right. Several times I told the customs officers, through one of the male passengers as interpreter, that I did not want to be landed. Another girl was of the same mind as myself. Somehow the importers of the girls found out that we did not want to be landed, and some of them came down to frighten us, saying we would be imprisoned at least 5 months before being sent back, and then we could only go as far as Japan, when we would be taken possession of again. This did not swerve us from the course we decided on. When word came from the collector that I could land, not being able to do anything else I fell in a lump on the floor and cried loudly, saying I did not want to be landed by those people; that I would jump into the sea rather than be taken by them. Somehow the fact I cried reached the ears of the official interpreter, who came with another officer and quieted me. Soon after they returned and said the collector had allowed me to go to a rescue home and there to remain until the next returning boat to China.

I am now in that home, happy and contented, enjoying the prospect of soon being restored to my mother.

TRANSLATION OF AN INTERCEPTED LETTER FROM A HIGHBINDER TO THE OFFICERS OF THE CHEE KONG TONG SOCIETY, ONE OF THE LARGEST, IF NOT THE LARGEST, HIGHBINDER SOCIETIES IN THE UNITED STATES.

[Translated by Jno. Endicott Gardner.]

To the officers of the Chee Kong Tong Society.

GENTLEMEN: On the 5th instant Lee Shan came by stage to our store and said that the Chee Kong Tong had deputed him to come here and collect from Chan Tsung, Lieu Ming Chew, and Chew Keuk Min (the last named a woman.—Note by translator). He passed the night in our store. The next day he started out. He then stopped with Szlo Kam until the night of the 10th. Soon after it had turned 1 o'clock Chew Keuk Min died. On the 12th there were certain townsmen of ours who reported that Chew Keuk Min was killed by Lee Shan. Now they are going to arrest Lee Shan. To-day Sz Lo Kam was taken into custody. The trial, however, is not yet commenced. To-day the different brethren held a consultation and decided they would require Lee Shan to make up the sum of $200 for funeral expenses; that they would not be satisfied unless he did make up that amount. How this affair is going to end I don't know. It evidently is going to be quite serious. We hope in some way you brethren will contrive to save him somehow. This is the most important thing to do just now. Furthermore, we have no able person here to attend to the matter. The authorities into custody and yet no trial has taken place. The young woman, when pressed by the authorities, positively identified Lee Shan as the guilty man. We hope you will soon send us word.

Yours, respectfully,   LEE YUET.

JANUARY 21, 1889.

TRANSLATION OF ONE OF THE LETTERS OF WARNING AGAINST HIGHBINDERS SENT TO MR. J. E. GARDNER, NOW OFFICIAL INTERPRETER FOR THE CUSTOMS AT SAN FRANCISCO.

To Mr. JOHN GARDNER.

DEAR SIR: There is a saying that the good will early be within angelic bounds, while the evil will assuredly be punished, while the latter kind would not be long tolerated by heaven. I have long heard of your name in Victoria in connection with the rescue work. Engaging in this good work you of course benefit people. It seems so strange that now there should be one, Lo Tsun, even for a bad man, who has told me, Leung Tsun, to injure you some way, offering as a reward $100. You have done me no harm. How could I bring harm to you. What I am afraid of now is that, with me not willing to injure you, he would find some one else who would be willing. I shall just appear willing. In point of fact, I shall not do anything. I send you word early, so that you may be cautious as you go in or out in order that others may not harm you in some unexpected way. I have long known of your doing good all the time. That is the reason why I am so bold in speaking of this matter as I do. Be sure not to let this go out for fear Lo Tsun should have a design on me for it. It is hard to describe all his wicked ways. Be careful; that is all.

Respectfully, yours,   LEUNG TSUN.

APRIL 2.

EXHIBIT D.

STATEMENT MADE BY LIEUTENANT OF POLICE WILLIAM PRICE TO COMMISSIONER OF IMMIGRATION HART H. NORTH, AT SAN FRANCISCO, CAL., SEPTEMBER 22, 1898.

[Questions put by Commissioner North and answered by Lieutenant Price.]

Q. Lieutenant Price, Chief Lees, the head of the police force of this city, has stated to me that you are probably as well posted as any man here connected with the police force on the subject of so-called Chinese highbinder societies in their various phases, including, among others, the opinion in which they are held by the respectable Chinese element in this city; and in order to get a coherent statement I will start in by asking you how long you have been on the police force in this city.—A. 21 years.

Q. How much of that time have you spent in the Chinatown district?—A. About 2 years, off and on.

Q. Aside from the time that you have been acting as policeman in Chinatown, I suppose, through your connection with the police force, you have known pretty well what has been going on?—A. Oh, yes; all the time. At the time I speak of I had entire charge of the Chinatown squad.

Q. You were at the head of the raids that were conducted under the order of Chief Crowley some 5 or 6 years ago, were you not?—A. Yes.

Q. At that time you demolished the headquarters of a large number of highbinder societies, did you not?—A. 26 societies.

Q. Did that include the headquarters of the Chee Kung Tong?—A. That is the original of all the tongs or societies—what they call among the Chinese the Freemason Society.

Q. Are you a Mason yourself?—A. Yes.

Q. As a matter of fact, the society has no resemblance to our Freemasonry, has it?—A. I have found members in that society; lately it has had Chinese members.

Q. Do they acquire this knowledge through this society, or not?—A. Not through the Chee Kung Tong.

Q. You believe, though, in China or somewhere else, there is a society that resembles in some respects the Freemasonry in the civilized world?—A. Yes.

Q. The Chee Kung Tong is also known as the Triad Society, is it not?—A. Yes.

Q. Are all the other societies offshoots from this society?—A. Yes; the same as other societies organized here and having branches in other places.

Q. What is the purpose of organizing these societies? Are they all organized for the same purpose, or some for one purpose and some for another?—A. All the Chinese highbinder societies are organized for the purpose of murder.

Q. From what do they derive their chief sources of revenue?—A. Through means of blackmail and houses of prostitution.

Q. Do they conduct gambling houses themselves?—A. Yes.

Q. That would be a third source of revenue?—A. Yes.

Q. Are the majority of frequenters of gambling houses in Chinatown members of the highbinder societies?—A. A great many merchants have come to me in the middle of the night to give me information concerning these gambling houses. These merchants are obliged to belong to these societies for the sake of protection; they can not get out of it. Although belonging to the societies, they are always willing to furnish me with information to aid in my breaking them up, but they would not be seen speaking to me on the street.

Q. They are members of the highbinder societies in fact, but not in spirit?—A. Yes; that is the case.

Q. That, I suppose, applies to the majority of the members of the highbinder societies, does it not?—A. Not to the majority, but to a good many of the merchants.

Q. How do they conduct their blackmailing operations?—A. They hire places similar to this office and have their names printed on signboards and hung outside, such as Chee Kung Tong, Suey On Tong, Bow Sing Suey Tong, Suey Sing Tong, Hop Sing Tong, Suey Dong Tong, etc.

Q. Do you know whether all these societies have branches in other cities of the United States?—A. That, of couse, I do not know positively; I have only heard of them. I believe there are branches of these societies in Los Angeles, San Jose, and throughout the East—Chicago, New York, etc.

Q. I am told that the Suey Sing, Hop Sing, and Chee Kung tongs have branches in the principal cities of the United States.—A. They have them wherever there is any number of Chinese.

Q. You were telling about the rooms or offices fitted up by these societies.—A. Their places are finely fitted up, the same as clubrooms. There they meet as other organizations do. If the member has anything against another man he places his case before the society and offers so much money to have the man killed. After they have settled on the man to be killed, his head is as good as gone. They hold a meeting and have something filled with balls, buttons, or beans, or something of that sort. The men are blindfolded and draw. If one draws the certain amount, he is chosen to do the killing. Sometimes there are 2 or 3 chosen, generally 2. As soon as they draw those balls they are in the same fix as a man to be hung. The society's rules are so binding that those chosen are bound to kill that man if there are 20 policemen about when he meets him.

Q. These men who draw the lot go out and hunt up the victim and kill him wherever he may be found?—A. According to the rules of the society, they then go and fix up whatever little business they have, the same as a white man would make his will before going on a journey. Then they go out and hunt their victim. According to their rules, the society hires an attorney for the murderer to defend him in the courts, and does everything possible to aid in his acquittal, furnishing witness, etc. Perhaps the murderer is caught, arrested, tried, and sentenced to death, and executed; then the society has to pay so much money to the relatives in China. If the man is hanged they will probably pay his relatives $500; if he is imprisoned for life, $250; if imprisoned for a shorter time, $100. And this is the same in every case that is brought before the society.

Q. Do you know how much a member of the society pays, as a rule, for having a man killed?—A. All the society can get from him; no certain amount. Some people are willing to pay more and some less. Little Pete, who was killed, was wealthy, and there was about $3,000 or $4,000 on his head.

Q. His enemies had offered that to anybody who would kill him?—A. He was a Sam Yup. The Sam Yups are what you call the aristocracy. There is only 1 Sam Yup to every 15 See Yups. The See Yups are small merchants here, keep laundries, and are people of that class. The Sam Yups own large stores.

Q. They are regularly organized, the Sam Yups and the See Yups, are they not? And are they members of those tongs?—A. Of course they have members in those tongs. They are from different provinces in China—two clans, as it were, the same as in Scotland or England. All these people claim to be cousins.

Q. These classes fight, then, among themselves, do they?—A. They fight all the time. There has been a boycott for 4 or 5 years to prevent a See Yup buying from a Sam Yup, and vice versa. If a See Yup is found buying from a Sam Yup he is taken in the street, his purchase taken from him; he is then conducted to one of these societies and is fined $2, and probably gets a good thrashing besides. Every time a man is brought up the arresting officer of the highbinder society gets $2, so they are very vigilant in consequence.

Q. Little Pete belonged to the Sam Yups, and was one of the richest Chinamen in town, was he not?—A. Not one of the richest, but very rich.

Q. He was supposed to be killed at the instigation of Big Jim, was he not?—A. No; Big Jim was also a Sam Yup.

Q. Why was it that Little Pete was killed? Was it at the instigation of the Sam Yups or the See Yups?—A. The See Yups.

Q. What had he done to the See Yups?—A. Of course, as I say, there are two factions that are all the time fighting. Little Pete was a very intelligent Chinaman, and they accused him of informing the police, on account of raids made by them—which he did, as a matter of fact.

Q. And accordingly there was a price put upon his head?—A. Yes.

Q. He was accompanied by a bodyguard for a great many years, was he not?—A. Oh, yes.

Q. By Lee Chuck, a highbinder, was he not?—A. Yes.

Q. Lee Chuck murdered somebody and was sent to State prison, and Little Pete got somebody else to act as a bodyguard, did he not?—A. He had 4 or 5, at least—3 Chinamen and 2 white men. About 7 o'clock one evening Little Pete came downstairs accompanied by a white man of his bodyguard. Little Pete kept a shoe shop. He entered the barber shop and told his bodyguard (the white man) to go down to the corner of Kearny and Washington streets and get him an evening paper. He sat down on a chair. Chinamen had been watching him, and he was no sooner seated than they came right into the barber shop and shot him.

Q. Did they convict these men?—A. They never got the right parties; I was told that the parties that did the killing went to China on the next steamer.

Q. This is only a fair sample of highbinder methods, is it not?—A. That is an idea of the whole business.

Q. Big Jim was a notorious gambler here for many years, was he not, and was chased out of the city by the See Yup faction?—A. Yes.

Q. He went to China and is there yet and afraid to return, is he not?—A. Yes. You see the merchants are so entirely under the control of these societies and are so dominated by fear that any demand that is made upon them they pay without question. I will tell you of an instance of this: There was a butcher on Washington street. One evening he threw out a little clean water on the street. A Chinese highbinder who was standing near by got the water on the sleeve of his coat. I happened to be there at the time, and when I had passed by, this highbinder went to the butcher and demanded $100 for the offense and said that he would call again. I told the butcher not to pay that money, but to make an arrangement to meet him at a certain place and I would be there. He promised to do so, and would you believe it, before I got back there he had paid the highbinder the $100. This is to show you that anything these highbinders demand they get.

Q. I suppose that the amount of revenue that the highbinder societies exact from these merchants is simply tremendous?—A. I would say that there are about 3,000 Chinese highbinders of this city just living in that way; they do not do anything for a living except levy blackmail.

Q. What do you suppose to be the total population in this city now?—A. About 35,000.

Q. And 3,000 of them are nothing but cutthroats and bad men?—A. The worst class of people on the face of the earth.

Q. They never interfere with white people, do they?—A. Not very often. The Chinese consul talks to them constantly on that point. They are afraid of an uprising of the white people against them, and that they would all be killed, and this fear keeps them from doing so.

Q. Do you know of any instance of their killing white people, or of their levying blackmail on white people?—A. Not very often do they attack white people, and only then when under the influence of liquor.

Q. These highbinders are very much given to securing perjured testimony, are they not—A. It is an impossibility to rely on them. For instance, a man is killed; I am sent to investigate; a man is pointed out to me as the murderer, as positively identified as such, and I have positive evidence that that man was not within 5 blocks of the scene at the time of the murder. I arrested the man, as my duty as a public officer compelled me to do so, but I knew the man to have been in a shop on one street when the other man was murdered on another. However, when taken into court, it was proved that he was not the murderer and was acquitted, and afterwards the right party was secured.

Q. And they are also largely engaged in furnishing perjured testimony to aid in the landing of Chinese girls here, are they not?—A. Yes; one of the by-laws in all of these highbinder societies is to swear to aid in the landing of their people here, especially Chinese women.

Q. I have taken the statements of a number of rescued Chinese girls at the missions, and almost without exception they have told me horrible tales of cruelty inflicted upon these girls in these houses. Most of these girls claim to have seen the killing of some of their number, or to have seen the bodies after they have been killed.—A. I don't know much about the killing of these girls; they are too expensive to kill.

Q. Those who have been killed were generally old girls.—A. When they grow old they are usually placed as cooks. These girls are never seen on the street unless followed by an old hag who keeps the house. These girls are worth about $3,000, and are too valuable to kill.

Q. They are absolute slaves, are they not?—A. Every single one of them.

Q. And were it not for the highbinder societies it would be impossible to keep them in such absolute slavery, would it not?—A. They could not do it at all. The highbinder societies derive their principal source of revenue from protecting these houses.

Q. Can you tell a highbinder from another Chinaman, when you see him? A. I can walk on the streets and pick them out and never make a mistake.

Q. How can you detect them from any other Chinaman?—A. They used to dress differently and wear their hair differently.

Q. Their hair is not so neatly kept—more fluffy—than other Chinamen, is it not?—A. That is right; at the end of the cue where it joins the hair; and then they used to wear different kinds of shoes and different kind of hats (round, stiff-brimmed hats). When they found that I had discovered their mode of dress, they stopped wearing what might designate them as highbinders. Then, again, in searching these men one would invariably find a little piece of red silk in his possession. On that silk was printed what society he was a member of, so that in case of death or accident he could be identified. Then they did away with that and we could not find anything to distinguish them.

Q. I have heard it rumored a good many times that the Chinese consul, the predecessor of the present incumbent, was obliged to leave the city, largely through the threats of the highbinder societies.—A. That is true. I used to know him well, and spent much time with him, seeking information concerning the workings of these societies, which he was always willing to give me. I do not remember his name. Mr. King, the vice-consul, also assisted me greatly in this work.

Q. Mr. Ho Yow is the present Chinese consul, is he not?—A. I do not know this one.

Q. What become of Mr. King?—A. He was also driven out of the city, through the firm of Reddy, Campbell & Metson, attorneys for the highbinder class in Chinatown. Riordan was the attorney for the Chinese consul and Six Companies. The consul-general and Vice-Consul King were always in favor of breaking up these societies, so the highbinder societies had them removed.

Q. Have you any idea as to what laws might be passed by the United States Government which would help to break up these societies?—A. When I was first sent into the Chinatown district in 1888, things were in a very bad condition; there was hardly a day that someone was not killed, even white people, killed by accident, as shot was flying everywhere. One afternoon there were 75 shots fired on the street from cne faction, directed toward another faction. I went to Chief Crowley and told him that I could do nothing; that there were no laws to cover these things. I said to him: "When any of these Chinamen commit deeds of violence they run into the numerous small alleys of Chinatown and get beyond our reach, and after being once lost sight of it is impossible to identify them, unless by some peculiar mark about him. These societies are unlawful and organized for unlawful purposes. They do not recognize our laws, and to compete with them, we have to go beyond our present laws; they are not sufficient. I can put a stop to these societies if you will give me my own way." He said: "I am under bonds here and of course they will sue me if I do as you suggest." I said, "All right." I saw the Chinese consul and he spoke to the chief of police, and also told me to use my own judgment, assuring the chief that if he should be sued, he (the consul), or the Chinese Government, would stand the consequences. The chief sent for me and said that he thought my ideas were all right and gave me permission to carry them out in my own way.

I then went out and got seven or eight strong, healthy officers, and we visited all these places, taking down the numbers and setting out in the right way to get into the workings of these societies. There are a great many different societies in Chinatown, some being organized for charitable purposes, benevolent societies as it were, and in order to be sure that I had the right places and did not make any mistakes, I took plenty of time and care, as I did not want to interfere with any but the genuine highbinder societies. When I had everything arranged I got 16 men in uniform and a surgeon, and supplied them all with axes. We marched from one to another of these societies and literally cut them to pieces; did not leave a bit of furniture 5 inches long in one of them. I suppose we broke up about $180,000 worth of property. Some of these places were fixed up magnificently. Wherever we went we got arms, ammunition, bowie knives 2 feet long in blade, iron bars done up in braided cord, etc.; also chain and steel armor that they wear under their clothing, and which it is utterly impossible to penetrate.

Q. At that time any of the highbinders that you found in these rooms you kicked down stairs, did you not?—A. We did. Of course, by breaking up their meeting places they could not meet. Among the better class of Chinese who belonged to these societies through fear, or for self-protection, we were held in favor for what we had done. Everything they could do to aid me they did. They could not meet me in Chinatown, but came to my home in hacks at night to inform me where I could find these men. I was so well posted in the situation of Chinatown that they could not open their rooms or offices in any place. We broke up their josses—they always have josses in these places. One of them they brought from China and was worth from $700 to $800. I broke up one of these and the friendly Chinese were so superstitious that they feared I would die. One came to me and said he was very sorry; they liked me very much, but I would die in 3 days. One of my men caught cold and his eyes became inflamed. One of these men came to me and said "Soon he will be blind." Three days before the Chinese New Year I met this man and said to him "You see I am not dead yet." He said "New Year surely you die." New Year came and I was not dead, and he said they must get a new joss; that one had been no good.

At the Hop Sing Tong I gave them an hour to remove their fixings and prepare for our coming. This was a building four stories high, an immense place, and I suppose the building and furnishings cost $30,000 or $40,000, and perhaps $100,000. This was owned by the highbinder society. They owned two or three such places, the property and all. I notified them that I would give them 3 hours to move their things out of the building. I went back in 3 hours, at 6 o'clock, and they had nothing moved. They saw I meant business and they tried to save the joss, which was very heavy. In moving it some of the old boards underneath creaked, and they went down those stairs like mad, thinking the joss had spoken; and if you had offered one of those men $10,000 he would not go up those stairs again. There were 7 josses in one building and we tore the whole thing to pieces.

Q. The result of those forrays was to disperse those highbinder societies, was it not?—A. It was done so that they would not have any meeting places. I went around to all the stores, houses of prostitution, and places of that kind in Chinatown and notified these people that if I found out that they were aiding these highbinder societies in any way, manner, or form, by giving them money, I would demolish their places. If they wanted protection, I would furnish it to them; if 1 officer would not do, we would give them 40, but if I found out that any of them had paid any money to these societies I would break up everything they had. In this way several of the societies were driven out of town, and for about 3 years there was not a Chinaman killed in the city. I followed the thing up every day, and if a signboard was put up to denote the meeting place of one of these societies we would split it up in a thousand pieces. This was the means of disbanding them altogether; they then went to other cities. If this method had been kept up, we would not have this trouble at all.

The reason it was not kept up was because suit was commenced in the United State court against the chief of police and raiding officers and everybody who was concerned in these raids, was it not?—The attorneys for the Chinese highbinders raised a large amount of money to carry on these suits, and bothered the chief of police a great deal. It kept us going all the time; the cases were first conducted in our courts then taken to the United States courts. If these people were convicted as gamblers in the lower courts, they were taken into the United States courts and acquitted.

Q. Then in brief, you think that if some laws were passed whereby protection would be granted to the officers in their raids, and power given them to demolish these places as fast as they appeared, it would be the means of completely effacing these highbinder societies, do you not?—A. Yes. You see there are fully 3,000 people who have no visible means of support, and they belong to these societies and meet there for unlawful purposes. I should think there ought to be some law to rid the country of these people.

Q. I suppose if they could be deported if found to be highbinders, and sent back to China, this would have some effect?—A. If they were convicted as thieves and murderers they can be deported, but not otherwise.

Q. These highbinder tongs often fight amongst themselves, do they not?—A. They are fighting all the time among themselves. For instance if one tong is paid higher prices for his work than another; then there is trouble. Or, one tong will want all the patronage and tries to drive out the others. If they hold a meeting of the different societies and one side differs from the other, then the result is a fight between the two, and probably murder.

Q. I suppose, lieutenant, that you keep pretty well posted through the papers, and from information received at headquarters, in regard to the criminal doings in the United States of all kinds?—A. Yes.

Q. You are pretty well posted on the doing of the Clan Na Gael, Mafia, and so on. Now, do you think that any of these societies in the United States, in regard to the strength of organization, number of crimes, and the wealth of the society can in any way compare to the highbinder tongs in San Francisco?—A. Of course in these other societies there are not so many people congregated together as with the Chinese. You see they live all together and apart from the rest of the city.

Q. Is it not a fact that there are five murders among the Chinese to one murder by the Clan Na Gael or Mafia?—A. There are many murders among the Chinese that we have never heard of.

Q. As a rough estimate, since 1880, how many murders would you say have been committed by the highbinder societies in San Francisco?—A. I would say about 30 killed outright—shot down in the streets.

Q. Just tell me what you secured in the way of rules and regulations and other data in regard to the constitution and by-laws and so on.—A. It was a small book, about 1½ inches thick, square, with gilt edges, and illustrated. I took six of them, and did not understand thoroughly what they were, although I had an idea they were the by-laws, and when I got to the office of the chief of police they were eagerly seized. I went back to the place with 4 or 5 men, and from that day to this I have never been able to find another book. There were then about 400 of them.

Q. Were they all the same or different?—A. All the same.

Q. From what tong did you secure these books?—A. The Chee Kung Tong. I have searched Chinatown elsewhere, but have never found another book.

Q. You say there have been only 30 Chinamen killed in this city since 1880? I thought there had been more than that.—A. Of course there have been numbers of Chinamen killed in the houses and such places that we have known nothing about, but in the open streets there have been about 30 shot down alone.

Q. Those killed in the houses would amount to a much larger number, would they not?—A. Of course. One night about 11 o'clock I was on the corner of Spofford alley and Washington street, when the people were coming out of the Chinese theater. A shot was fired, and it struck a woman who was passing in the neck and lodged in the back of her teeth. The shot was intended for a woman, but if it was this one or not I do not know. The man who fired the shot was not more than 1 foot away from me, but there were 2 Chinamen in front of me and 2 or more behind me, and the man turned so quickly and got away into some alley that I could not find him. The woman lived on Sacramento street, and I took her home. I never saw such a brave woman. The bullet was stuck on her back teeth and I pried it off. The doctor saved her, but her tongue was almost cut off. The doctor fixed her tongue as well as he could, and she lived.

Q. In that one battle, at the time you speak of, when there were 75 or 80 shots fired, were there not 5 or 6 men killed?—A. Two killed, 2 or 3 fatally wounded, and several others slightly injured.

Q. I remember reading of 5 or 6 killed at one time. Am I right about that?— A. Their shooting was so terribly wild that they did not kill themselves, but white people were not safe.

Q. They have a common habit, I understand, of carrying the pistol in the hand stuck up in their voluminous sleeve, and going up to a person and shooting him through the sleeve. Is that true?—A. They generally take out the pistol when they shoot, although they carry them very often in their sleeves. Highbinders seldom carry pistols. They are generally accompanied by another person, whom they call "jury," and who belongs to the poorer class of Chinamen. He follows the highbinder and carries the weapon. When caught, we would search the highbinder for a pistol, but would not find anything of the kind on him, and the "jury" would have disappeared with the weapon. The only time the highbinder has a weapon is while leaving his quarters, but on the street you will not find one.

Q. Are they not oftentimes called "hatchetmen?"—A. The hatchet is a great weapon and the blade is about 6 inches long.

Q. A regular cleaver?—A. A good deal like a lather's hatchet.

Q. When you said that there were 30 men killed in the streets, you meant men who were shot; that does not include men who were killed by hatchetmen, does it?—A. They do not use these hatchets very much now; they use knives more, because knives do not make any noise.

Q. At the time you speak of, a number were killed by hatchetmen and others by pistol shots, were they not?—A. They are found dead in the houses; most of them are never found and never will be. They bury themselves.

Q. Then the probabilities are that there have been a vast number of murders committed in Chinatown that have never been heard of?—A. They are the most cruel people in the world. Once I was on the corner of Washington and Dupont streets, about 6 o'clock in the evening. An old merchant came along and was approached by two of these hatchetmen. They at once struck him with the hatchet, driving the blade, 10 inches long, right into him. They knocked him down and continued to stick these things into him.

Q. You saw that yourself?—A. I was standing there looking at them. Just to show you, as I said before, how binding their laws are, they are obliged to kill their man whenever they met him, no matter who was about. I had 2 officers with me at the time and there were 2 more across the street in uniform (we did not usually wear uniform in Chinese quarters). Notwithstanding all this, the murderer walked deliberately out into the middle of the street, and, surrounded as he was by all those officers, when it was impossible for a man to escape, he killed his man. So you see he had no fear of us.

Q. Was he caught red-handed?—A. He had no possible chance for escape and he knew it, but wherever he met his man he was obliged to kill him.

Q. Rev. Mr. Masters has a suggestion that an auxiliary detective force, composed of Chinamen of the respectable class, would be a great aid to the regular police force in stopping the operations of the highbinder organizations. Do you think there is anything in that?—A. It might work if one could come across any Chinamen who are not in fear of these highbinder societies, but I have not found one yet. If you have Chinamen who are afraid to act they would be of no use. The Chinese have 6 men acting in that capacity now; some of them are exconvicts. They are of no use at all. They are supposed to give information concerning these highbinder societies, and they try to get evidence amongst the Chinese, but they have never done anything yet and never will, because they are afraid.

Q. Do any of the white men who are employed by the Chinese as guards and so on, in Chinatown, ever render any aid to the highbinders?—A. They destroy the whole business, because they will never give any information to anybody. They are working for these people and shield them. Of course, the worst houses pay these guards the most money, so naturally they are willing and glad to work for them. This ought to be done away with by all means. Some of them collect $700 or $800 a month and would not give it up. There were the McLaughlin Brothers and a dozen others, who are now all rich. As soon as an officer appears, and these guards do not like him, you can't turn a corner before signals are given, and what can you do?

Q. There has been a great deal of talk about a system of electric bells, and so on, that runs through Chinatown, by means of which warnings are given, etc.— A. You can never catch a Chinaman but once in one way. By the time you are within two blocks of a gambling house, for instance, these signals are given and they know an officer is on their track. Everything is quickly removed, and when the officer enters the place they are sitting there peacefully.

Q. If it were made unlawful to run houses of prostitution, would that help to suppress the highbinder societies?—A. They could not exist then. Sometimes there are 20 or more men interested in one woman.

Q. About what proportion would you say of Chinese women that are landed in this country are destined for immoral lives?—A. Ninety per cent. I would not take one bit off of that. They are sold as fast as they can be brought over. There is not a woman who is brought here who is not sold as soon as she arrives. For every girl who comes here they get about $3,000. They even fool the missions. They get a Chinaman to go up and marry a girl from the mission, then they sell her to some one else.

Q. You have not any suggestions to offer in this matter, have you? There is not anything in connection with highbinders that you have not stated, is there? I do not know just the use the Department will put this to, but they desire to be fully advised on the subject of highbinder organizations.—A. It is impossible to get to the facts of the case on account of the money amongst them. They are impossible to get along with. The condition of things existing among these people is terrible, and persons who are not brought in contact with them would not understand it at all.

Q. The state of affairs as it exists in Chinatown is terrible, is it not?—A. It is a disgrace to the world.

Q. And the respectable Chinese are unable to help it?—A. And they can not do it. The highbinders are assisted by the guides and the attorneys. No decent man can afford to come in contact with these people; he can not afford to get attorneys to defend him in case it is necessary.

Q. And the fact that they do not bother the white people is what has led these societies to pass unnoticed for so many years, is it?—A. That is it. Laws should be made to cope with the Chinese. They have organizations in the nature of clubs, and where gambling was formerly done in open places it is now done under cover of these clubs, which are incorporated under the laws of the State of California.

Q. When accosted by an officer they claim to be playing only lawful games, do they not?—A. An officer has to ring the bell, and by the time he enters the place every evidence of gambling has been put out of sight, and there sits a Chinaman playing a game of casino or some other innocent game, when no sooner has the officer left the place than they go on with their faro, tan games, etc. There is more gambling now in Chinatown than there has been in a great many years, and all under cover of these incorporated clubs.

Q. Are you familiar with the environs of the criminal element of New York?— A. Not very much so. I have been in New York and on Mott street, where I was recognized by a number of Chinamen who had formerly lived in San Francisco.

Q. All the by-laws that have ever been published by white people have never been so binding as these published by the highbinder societies, have they?— A. No; especially in regard to the landing of women.

Q. Some of the laws that you saw had reference to that, had they?—A. Yes.

Q. You are not on the Chinatown force now, are you?—A. No; but whenever they have trouble they send for me.

Q. These Chinese wars break out about once in so often, do they not?—A. Not lately. The last time I was called down there was about a year ago. They have no more respect for our laws than anything in the world. They just laugh at them. I think some law ought to be made to prevent these people from assembling for unlawful purposes. Their places should be kept open, so that passers-by could see into them and know what was going on inside.

Exhibit E.

STATEMENT OF CHUN HO, RESCUED SLAVE GIRL, AT PRESBYTERIAN CHINESE RESCUE HOME, MISS CAMERON, MATRON, TO UNITED STATES COMMISSIONER OF IMMIGRATION HART H. NORTH, AT SAN FRANCISCO, CAL., SEPTEMBER 17, 1898.

[Questions put by Commissioner North and answered by Chun Ho, through Interpreter J. E. Gardner.]

When Chun Ho is told that a statement is wanted from her on this matter she bursts into tears, and says it always makes her cry to think of the ill-treatment she suffered at the hands of the highbinders before she was rescued by the mission.

Q. How old are you?—A. 24.

Q. Where were you born?—A. At Ng Jow, in the province of Kwong Si, the province adjoining that of Kwong Tung.

Q. How did you happen to come to the United States?—A. When I was 19 years old, the mistress No. 3 of a noted procurer by the name of Gwan Lung, who lives in San Francisco, went back to Canton, where my mother happened to be living with me at that time, and gave me glowing accounts of life in California. She painted that life so beautifully that I was seized with an inclination to go there and try my fortune, mother taking $200 Mexican and consenting to my going. I arrived in this country, together with 6 other girls brought by this woman, on the 22d of June, 1893. We all came on fraudulent certificates; the color of those certificates was reddish. (In those days there was such a certificate used, usually known in the customs service as "Red certificates," but they have since been abolished.—J. E. G.) I was told to assume a name to correspond with the name in the fraudulent certificate that was given to me, and I was landed as "Ah Fook." The age in the certificate was 28, and I was told to report my age as 28, which was very much above my true age at the time. The certificate called for a scar on the right temple. As it happened I had no scar. This woman told me to burn my right temple until there should be a mark. The burning was done, but by the time I had arrived in this city the burn had about healed up. The judge had some doubt as to the genuineness of the certificate, and as to my being the party who was entitled to it. I was kept in jail for a few days, but although the burn had healed up, there was some slight mark on my left temple and the judge gave me the benefit of the doubt and I was landed. I was told to claim that I was a married woman; that my husband's name was a Mr. Tsoy, merchant in San Francisco. He was then said to have been a member of the firm of Gum Pun Kee, that was then on Sacramento street, to the best of my recollection. I was also told to claim that my parents were in San Francisco. I was told that if I stuck to those claims I could be landed, and I was landed. The parties interested in my coming over were Quan Lum, his No. 3 mistress, and a noted procurer by the name of May Seen. While I was in jail pending the writ of habeas corpus, these people came frequently to coach me.

When I was first landed I was taken to one of May Seen's houses that were kept by respectable families. They always do that first. From time to time parties came to May Seen's house to see me and to bargain with May Seen as to what price I should be sold at. At the end of two months after my arrival, a Chinaman by the name of Kwan Kay, a highbinder and one who owned some of these houses, came with his woman, Shing Yee, and bought me for $1,950 gold. They gave me a written promise that in four years I should be free. At the end of two years, after taking all my earnings in the meantime, they said I could be redeemed if anyone would pay the sum of $2,100.

I paid my first owners hardly less than $290 a month for the two years; then I was sold for $2,100 to another highbinder by the name of Tsoy Lung Bo. I was in Tsoy Lung Bo's house for about a year when he wanted to take me into the country. I had to promise that I would go, but in the meantime I took steps to get into the Rescue Home, and before he was able to take me to the country the matron of the Rescue Home came with the police and had me rescued. That was about a year ago, and I am still in the home, but I understand Tsoy Lung Bo has ever since, from time to time, been demanding from me the amount he paid for me, threatening to kill me if I should not pay it before going home to China or leaving the mission. Highbinder after highbinder, through men in his employ or members of his own clique, have been going backward and forward in the vicinity of the home, threatening me and saying it would be much better for me to return to this man; that if I valued life at all to go right back, as the matron of the home could not always protect me. I have an aunt living near the home and sometimes I have visited her, thinking they would not know; but they soon found out, and even threatened my aunt, saying that if she would persist in keeping me, if any harm came to her they would not be responsible. These men stood on the street and called these things out to me at the windows.

Q. What steps did you take to be rescued?—A. I had a friend who took pity on me, and it was he who told the matron, and the matron got three police officers. It was by appointment that we met a short distance from the house. I had to pretend that I was going out to the nearest store to make a little purchase, and on the way the police met me, as it were, and took me to the home.

Q. Tell us what kind of treatment you received during your stay in either one of these two places?—A. My owners were never satisfied, no matter how much money I made. When they were angered in any way, they would vent their anger upon me, which they would also do upon the other girls. When they saw that the matrons of the different rescue homes were very much on the alert, they very often removed us from the houses of ill-repute to family dwellings when they wanted to punish us, so that anyone passing by could not hear our cries very well. Those who frequent those places say that they could not report any ill-treatment; I was often punished in that way. The instruments used were wooden clubs and sometimes anything they could lay their hands on; and one time I was threatened with a pistol held at me.

The work of removing myself and the other girls from where we were to family places where we were punished, was done by members of the highbinder societies. That was a part of their work, for which they receive pay.

Q. Before you came to the home, did you ever witness any of the doings of the highbinders?—A. Yes; right on Bakers alley, about 2 years ago. Shortly after daybreak one morning, diagonally opposite my window where I was sitting, I saw one highbinder grab hold of a Chinaman by the name of Yee and shoot at him, hitting him in the forehead, and he shot him again in other parts of his body and ran away. Some other Chinamen coming along and seeing this man there when life was just about extinct, called a policeman. The policeman went toward the other end of the alley and brought up several Chinamen. An interpreter told the dying man if he could not speak to nod his head when the right man was brought before him and that man was tried. What became of the case I don't know, but the man that was brought before him was not the one that shot him. The owners of our house told me that I must close the windows and doors and say nothing, as I might be called upon to testify; and in that way the State was deprived of my evidence.

Q. Do you know the circumstances that led up to the murder?—A. I happen to know some of the circumstances; they were briefly these: The night before both men had two girls in a restaurant drinking and feasting. On returning the girls to the house, one of them—out of fun more than anything else—set his dog on the owner of the house. The dog not only barked, but bit the man; the owner got angry and that led to bitter words, followed by the shooting. The man who was killed was the man who set the dog on the owner of the house, and the owner had a highbinder do the killing.

Q. Have you ever seen a girl killed for any reason?—A. Yes; I saw one after she had been killed by a highbinder. This highbinder wanted money from her; she either did not have it or put him off, but because she did not pay the money he wanted she was shot by him. I saw her after she had been shot. This last murder took place on Church alley. I also know of three other women that have been killed by highbinders. Two of these were shot and one stabbed to death. As a rule, the murderers of girls forced to lead that life are never brought to justice, because no one would dare to testify against the murderers, who are highbinders.

Miss Cameron here produces a photograph of Chun Ho, taken in the costume usually worn by the girls in these houses, and makes the following statement in regard to the persecution of Chun Ho by the highbinders within the past two weeks:

Chun Ho left the home to pay her aunt a short visit, not more than a couple of blocks from this house. Two or three days after she had been at her aunt's house a Chinaman came here and asked us to go down to the aunt's house, saying that there was a great deal of trouble. We went, and found that her former owner had the day before sent a highbinder up to tell her that she must either pay him over $1,000 or else go back and work it out by living that life, and she had sent the highbinder back with a message that she would neither pay the money nor would she go back to that life.

The next evening the owner appeared himself and demanded an interview with her, and the uncle with whom she was staying was afraid to refuse and let him in. He asked Chun Ho if she intended to pay back the price, or if she would go back to him and work it out. She said that she would not do either—that she belonged to the mission now and that the mission ladies would not let her do so. He said that she was not in the mission now and that he would make a great deal of trouble for her if she did not go back. So then she sent up word for one of us to come down.

We went and asked him if it were true that he had been threatening her, and he said that he had lost a great deal of money, over $1,000, by her running into the mission and getting away from him, and now he had come to get it back in some way.

We threatened him with the law and ordered him to leave the house, and so he left. She returned to the mission.

In a few days this man called a meeting of his highbinder society (not being present himself, as he was afraid of being present), but he sent several of the highbinders to her uncle's place of business and forced him to go to the meeting. And there they told him that he would either have to make Chun Ho, his niece, go back to this man's house and work out her own freedom, or else he himself would have to pay over $1,000 for her ransom. He refused to do either, and said that he would appeal to the law and have them arrested if they made him any more trouble; but they still continue to send him threatening messages and to follow her when she goes out on the street to such an extent that, although she is now visiting her aunt, she feels for her own safety she will have to return to the mission.

I will tell you of a case brought to our notice recently in which we were unable to rescue a slave girl through the trickery of these highbinders.

Word was brought to us at the mission that there was a young girl in a house on St. Louis alley, who was very cruelly treated and kept there against her will, and she wished to be rescued and brought to the mission.

We asked for two police officers to go with us to make the rescue and we went down there but on the way we were recognized by some Chinese highbinders and word was sent by their private system of electric bells, warning the different houses of ill-repute that the mission people and two police officers were going down into Chinatown, so when we reached the house where the girl was we found the doors closed and bolted. We demanded entrance, but instead of opening the doors we could hear them putting on more bolts and bars on the inside. We asked the police officers to insist upon their opening the door, but they did not seem to want to do anything in the matter.

Then 3 Chinatown watchmen (white men), hired by the highbinders to protect these houses, appeared and conferred with the police officers, telling them that it was better not to molest the Chinese, and that the mission teachers had no business to force their way into Chinese houses. So we found it impossible to rescue the girl. That night, after returning to the mission, two Christian Chinamen came up and told us that the girl had been watching at the door for us to come and when the alarm was sounded saying that we were near there, the old woman who owned her drew a pistol and holding it at the girl's head, told her to run and hide.

That was the last we heard of her for several weeks, when one day a respectable Chinese woman told us that she had gone into this house on business and saw the girl crying bitterly and asked her what was the matter. The girl said that she was beaten and very cruelly treated and she wanted the mission teachers to come and rescue her. It is useless, however, to attempt to rescue her as the police have no authority to break into the house, and the door is always kept bolted.

Another case of persecution by highbinders is that of a rescued girl who was married from the mission some 8 months ago and she does not dare to leave her husband's house. One day not long ago she was sitting close to a window having her hair dressed and had just left the chair when a bullet came whizzing into the room and just escaped hitting her. I afterwards saw the hole in the wall that the bullet had made where it struck. So that these girls are not safe from the highbinders even after they have married and are under the protection of their husbands.

I am so thankful to make this statement or do anything in my power to assist in placing this matter before the authorities at Washington, and I earnestly trust that some decided steps will be taken to aid the missions in the rescue of these girls and the complete overthrow of these highbinder societies.

Exhibit F.

STATEMENT MADE BY MISS DONALDINA CAMERON, MATRON OF THE PRESBYTERIAN CHINESE RESCUE HOME TO UNITED STATES COMMISSIONER OF IMMIGRATION, HART H. NORTH, AT SAN FRANCISCO, CAL., SEPTEMBER 2, 1898.

[Questions asked by Commissioner North and answered by Miss Cameron.]

Q. What is your full name?—A. Donaldina Cameron.
Q. What is your occupation, Miss Cameron?—A. Assistant superintendent of the Chinese Mission Home.
Q. How long have you been connected with the Chinese rescue work?—A. For over 3 years.
Q. In this city and county?—A. Yes.
Q. In connection with your work, have you ever come in contact with so-called Chinese highbinder tongs or societies, and their members and their workings?—A. I have come in contact with various members of them.
Q. In what connection have you met them?—A. In connection with the rescuing of slave girls.
Q. Can you tell us what their connection with these slave girls is?—A. In one way they buy and sell the girls themselves. That is their principal means of support in a great many cases; in fact, their only means of support is in trading in these girls.
Q. They are the slave owners, are they not?—A. They are slave owners, and they have gone further and threatened, both the missionaries and the Chinese who have assisted in rescuing these girls, with death.
Q. As I understand it, there are two kinds of slave girls—those who are called domestic slaves and who are menials and servants, and those who are placed in the brothels?—A. Yes.
Q. Do the highbinders deal in both kinds?—A. That I am not positive of, but I think they deal principally in putting them in houses of prostitution.
Q. What class of girls have you principally in this home?—A. We have both classes. We have a great many little ones also.
Q. The domestic slaves I suppose are placed from the houses of the highbinders in the families of Chinese?—A. Mostly so I think, but I could not state that positively.
Q. Do these highbinders own the houses of ill fame themselves, or are they merely employed as guards; or what is their connection?—A. I think in some cases they own the houses themselves.
Q. But invariably they are guarding the houses?—A. Yes; and they are employed by the keepers of the houses to wreak vengeance on the girls who escape.
Q. And it is customary for the highbinders to wreak vengeance on the girls themselves, is it not?—A. We know of cases where the highbinders have stolen the girls who have married, from their husbands after they had gone to small country places, out of reach of the protection of the missionaries and rescue people, and have there been kidnaped by the highbinders and returned to the places from which they had been originally rescued. We have been notified in two cases that I think of just now, and we have rescued the girls.
Q. Have you ever heard of the highbinders killing the girls in the houses who tried to escape for any other purpose?—A. I have known of threats, but I have never known of such a thing happening. I have been told by Chinese whom I could depend on that such things have happened.
Q. It is customary, is it not, for these highbinders to coach the girl emigrants before their examination on their arrival here, as to the necessary way to answer questions in order that they may be landed?—A. I think that is invariably done; there can be no doubt about that.
Q. They are constantly engaged in furnishing perjured testimony?—A. Yes.
Q. Is it not customary for highbinders to warn the girls against the missionaries and the rescue home work by preaching horrible stories about them?—A. The girls have frequently told us, after we have rescued them, that they had been told terrible things about the missions before they came here.
Q. They also threaten them with dire results—even going so far as to threaten death—do they not, if they do not tell the stories they are directed to tell by these highbinders?—A. Yes.
Q. You regard the highbinders as an absolute menace to the welfare of all these girls?—A. Most decidedly so.
Q. And against the will and desire of a large number of them?—A. Yes, indeed; I do.

Q. Is it not your experience that at least a larger number of Chinese girls that come to this country are personally desirous of leading virtuous lives?—A. I think the larger proportion of them have no idea of what they are going to do, most emphatically.

Q. What per cent of the girls that are brought to this country do you suppose are destined for bad lives?—A. I was almost going to say 99 per cent.

Q. At least 90 per cent?—A. I should safely say that.

Q. Have you any idea of the earnings of these girls or their owners?—A. I think the average earnings are supposed to be in the region of $5 and $6 a day.

Q. Are these girls purchased as slaves in China and brought here in slavery, or do they come voluntarily in the first instance?—A. I think quite a number come voluntarily, never dreaming what their fate is to be; but I think a great many are landed against their will, especially when it comes to bringing them right here and they get some idea of what they are going to be brought to.

Q. Of the 90 per cent they all come as slaves? As I understand it, these girls are purchased by procurers and others in China, and the agents of the highbinders and their allies bring them here, and they are to all intents and purposes slaves when they leave China.—A. They are bought and paid for in China. They are made to take their own purchase money in their own hand and give it to the person who is selling them, so that it can not come back on the head of the person of the highbinders. That is the Chinese idea, so a girl told me.

Q. Do you know if there are any Chinese women who belong to these highbinder societies—any allies and female brokers?—A. Yes; I think in everyone of these bad houses there is one woman or more who assists in getting the girls.

Q. Do you know whether they are supposed to belong to the highbinder tongs themselves or are they merely working in unison with the highbinders?—A. I really could not say whether they belong to these societies or not, but I know they work in unison and do as much as the men do in getting the girls and in holding them after they have them.

Q. Have you ever come in open conflict with the highbinders since you have been in this mission?—A. In rescuing the girls I have had the men take hold of them and try to drag them away from me, while the girl was holding on to me and trying to come with me. I have had that experience several times.

Q. These Chinese highbinders, as I understand it, never lay hands on a white person?—A. They have never touched me, but often laid hands on my predecessor, Miss Culbertson. On one occasion she had her dress nearly torn off in Fresno in trying to get a girl away on the train at night.

Q. It is a very rare occurrence, is it not, for them to lay violent hands on Americans?—A. Yes; I think it is quite an unusual thing.

Q. But it is customary and ordinary for them to do deeds of violence to Chinese, both men and women, is it not?—A. Yes; indeed it is.

Q. Were it not for the highbinders a large number of these girls would not stay in these houses, would they?—A. I think not. I think there are converts in Chinatown to-day who would gladly leave if not terrified by what would be done to them should they attempt to escape.

Q. Have you ever known head money to be laid on the girls in those houses?—A. In numberless cases.

Q. Do you know how much is offered as a rule?—A. I know hundreds of dollars.

Q. How many hundreds?—A. I do not like to say, as I do not remember exactly, but the last case that I think of now was $500. It is according to the value of the girls.

Q. Do highbinders ever hang around these premises looking for girls?—A. Very frequently. We never receive a girl that the highbinders do not hang around the home more or less for a day or two. We have a chain attached to the inside of the door, so as to prevent the pushing of it open. We always put it on when we open the door.

Q. Would they, in your opinion, come into the house and steal the girls away, should an opportunity occur?—A. Yes; they would. They would even follow us to church. In taking them to church, as we do Sunday evenings, in days gone by they have tried to get them. Only two weeks ago they had a carriage here at the corner to get the girl that we rescued from Sacramento a short time ago. So we do not take her out at night now; just take her out in the morning.

Q. When you go to church, do the highbinders go so far as to slip into church after you?—A. Yes; they have done it. I have no doubt but they frequently do, but I have been positive of it only a few times. Just a few weeks ago some came into the church.

Q. Can you tell a highbinder from one who is not by his appearance?—A. Yes; I generally have a pretty good idea of them.

Q. There are certain characteristics about them that are familiar to the Chinese race, are there not?—A. I have not been long enough identified with them to be able to tell.

Q. Do you know how the highbinders are regarded by the respectable Chinese element?—A. I know they dread them very much indeed; fear them very much. In fact I feel very sure that all the respectable Chinese would wish to have the highbinders banished from the country entirely.

Q. Have you any idea how the highbinder societies could be broken up; by passing what laws?—A. That is too deep for me.

Q. Do you think that if Chinese houses of ill fame were absolutely prohibited it would have any effect in breaking up the association?—Yes, I do; for so many of them depend entirely upon them for support. If the importation of the girls were stopped they would close these houses.

Q. How many Chinese girl inmates of this home are there now, Miss Cameron?—A. We have 39.

Q. How long has this home been in existence?—A. Twenty-three years, I think.

Q. Do you know how many girls have been rescued in that length of time?—A. Over 600; I am not positive of the exact figure.

Q. Do you know about what value is placed on the Chinese slave girl by these highbinder societies and others that are dealing in them?—A. Frequently over $2,000.

Q. Ranging from $1,500 to $3,000, according to the age and appearance of the girl, is it not?—A. Yes.

Q. Have you ever received any threatening letters?—A. Numberless letters have come during the three years that I have been here; slipped in under the door, from Chinese of course. We rescued a very pretty and very young girl who was offered at $2,000. She had only been here a few months, and about a week after we took her into the home there was a great deal of trouble about her, and the highbinders came after her a great deal. One morning when the man came around with the newspaper he found a large dynamite cartridge about a foot long standing up against the front door, placed in such a manner that when the door should be opened the cartridge would fall in and explode.

Q. It was so placed against the door that it was evidently intended to be exploded by the opening of the door?—A. Yes; and when the police were called they found that at all the basement windows similar cartridges had been placed in such a way that when the windows should be pushed up they would be apt to explode.

Q. When was that?—A. Three years ago last April. That is the greatest threatened act of violence that has ever been attempted against the home. Miss Culbertson, my predecessor, was attacked by a Chinaman with a knife; not really attacked, but a Chinaman was coming directly toward her with an open knife when she was rescuing a Chinese girl.

Q. Have you ever yourself seen them draw weapons?—A. No; I never have.

Q. You only attempt rescues, as I understand it, when information is brought you that the girls are desirious of reaching the home?—A. In the cases of grown girls we wait until we hear that they want to come; but where smaller children are concerned we and the officers of the Society for the Protection of Children take them.

Q. What experience have you had with habeas corpus proceedings?—A. They nearly always serve writs of habeas corpus on us when we rescue a girl.

Q. That is, the attorneys for the Chinese highbinders?—A. Yes; the highbinders hire the attorneys.

Q. They try in all ways possible to interfere with the operation of these homes, do they?—A. They go in as witnesses to say that the girl is the wife of some man who is there in court, or the daughter of someone else, and try to claim them in that way.

Q. Try to intimidate the girls all they can, do they not?—A. As we take a girl through the corridors they stand alongside and threaten them, and say that no matter how long it may be they will get them back some way and wreak their vengeance on them.

Q. They oftentimes succeed in terrifying the girls to such an extent that they get them back, do they not?—A. They have done so.

Q. Have you ever rescued girls who have borne evidence upon their persons of scars and other indignities inflicted upon them by the highbinders?—A. Yes; often.

Q. And have they told you that the punishments were inflicted by the highbinders?—A. Yes.

Q. For what purpose?—A. Generally because they did not earn enough money.

Q. Have you any Chinese girls here now who would be willing to relate their experiences, and whose experience might be of interest in this matter?—A. They are very timid when it comes to giving evidence, but still I think I can persuade one or two to do so.

EXHIBIT G

STATEMENT OF GON SING, RESCUED SLAVE GIRL, AT PRESBYTERIAN CHINESE RESCUE HOME, MISS CAMERON, MATRON, TO UNITED STATES COMMISSIONER OF IMMIGRATION HART H. NORTH, SAN FRANCISCO, CAL., SEPTEMBER 2, 1898.

[Questions put by Commissioner North and answered by Gon Sing, through Interpreter J. E. Gardner.]

Q. How old are you?—A. 19.

Q. How long have you lived in this country?—A. Nearly 2 years.

Q. How did you come to leave China?—A. Glowing stories were told me of the life of the Chinese in California, which I believed, and which first led me to come over here. I was bought in China by a Chinaman, acting with a Chinese woman, for $680, Mexican. Then I was sent over here to California by those people. I was told that when I came here I would be married to a respectable, wealthy Chinese merchant. Soon after my arrival, however, I found that was not the intention of all these people. I was resold for $1,680, gold. I was first placed in a house of ill fame in San Francisco, but finding that I was not willing to stay and that I wanted to get into the home, they removed me to Sacramento and placed me in a house of ill fame there. I managed to send word to Miss Cameron, the matron of this home, secretly, and she took steps to have me brought down here, and so I was rescued. This house in which I was kept for a while in Sacramento was kept by a Chinese woman and a Chinese highbinder.

Q. Describe what took place at your rescue.—A. My clothes were nearly snatched off of me at the rescue.

Q. Were you threatened in any way by the highbinders?—A. When in the house in Sacramento I was punished and often struck by the owner of the house because I did not make myself agreeable and because I did not earn enough money for the owners. I had bruises on my person at the time I was rescued. The instruments used were poles and rattans, and I was also threatened that if I ever went to the home when they got me back again they would kill me, but the place was altogether unbearable, and I preferred death to remaining and would take the chances, and so I was rescued.

Q. Did you ever know of any girls being killed by the highbinders?—A. Yes.

Q. Whereabouts?—A. Both in San Francisco and in Sacramento.

Q. Did you ever see with your own eyes a girl killed?—A. Yes.

Q. Where was it; here or in Sacramento?—A. I saw one with my own eyes in Sacramento killed by the highbinders, and I saw one with my own eyes killed in San Francisco.

Q. Will you please describe the killing of the one in San Francisco?—A. The one in San Francisco was shot to death; the one in Sacramento was killed by opium poisoning.

Q. Where in this city was it that the girl was shot?—A. It was in one of the lanes in Chinatown, and took place soon after I arrived here, so that I can not very well remember the English name, but it was in one of the lanes in which these houses are.

Q. Was it during the day or in the night?—A. At night.

Q. Was it in the lane or in the house that faces on the lane?—A. The girl was in the house at the time.

Q. Why was she killed, if you know?—A. I never could get at the bottom of the case, but it was generally believed that there was a little spite about it at the commencement, and then she was one of those who would not earn any money.

Q. How was she shot? Did anyone hold her and someone else shoot her? Describe it.—A. I can not describe how the murder took place.

Q. What was done with the murderer? Did the matter ever become known to the white authorities?—A. I never heard of the murderer being punished.

Q. When a girl grows old and is unable to earn much money, is it not rather customary to kill her?—A. I have heard of their being shot, but I have never seen any old ones.

Q. Do you think they are killed sometimes for the effect it will have on the others?—A. Yes.

Q. Is it not a fact that when a girl has been murdered all the other girls are given a chance to see her body to see that she was killed?—A. Yes.

Q. Why was the girl killed at Sacramento?—A. They were both killed. The one in San Francisco was killed by a pistol shot and the one in Sacramento by opium poisoning, but the one in Sacramento was driven to take poison herself on account of the unbearable position in which she was placed.

Q. Just tell us what you know about the operations of highbinders in connection with these houses.—A. They levy blackmail on the girls in the houses. They undertake to protect the owners against loss, and I have known instances where, after they have undertaken to protect the houses, when a girl or girls would be lost, the highbinders would have to make up the loss, so that they make a regular business of protecting these houses.

Q. Do you know of witnesses being supplied by them to carry out the wishes of the owners of the houses?—A. That is their business. They furnish false witnesses, and fighting or shooting would also be done by the men that they supply. At this very hour I dare not walk the streets of San Francisco alone on account of the highbinders.

Q. Do you know the names of any of the highbinder tongs in Sacramento?—A. Bing Gung Tong and On Yick Tong.

Q. Do you know whether these are branches of tongs existing in this city?—A. They are branches of highbinder tongs in San Francisco.

Q. Have you ever known them to threaten Chinese other than the girls in the houses?—A. Yes, I do know.

Q. You believe, do you not, that the better class of Chinese are in constant fear and terror of the operations of the Chinese highbinder societies?—A. Yes, I know that the better classes of Chinese are in constant fear of them.

Q. Since your rescue have you had any threats or been approached at all by highbinders?—A. Immediately after my rescue a reward of $500 was offered for my recapture. A warning was given me to be careful on my way to church with the other girls, as I might be kidnaped by the highbinders. As a matter of fact, I met four of them on the way to church at the intersection of two streets with a carriage alongside of them. Since then I have not deemed it prudent to go out.

Q. By what method were you landed in this country?—A. I was landed in this country by perjured testimony. A highbinder presented himself at the custom-house claiming that he was my father, and one or two others claiming to have known me in China, and on their testimony I was landed. On the boat on which I came over there were nine other slaves, all imported, and all were landed.

STATEMENT OF GUI NGUN, RESCUED SLAVE GIRL, AT PRESBYTERIAN CHINESE RESCUE HOME, MISS CAMERON, MATRON, TO UNITED STATES COMMISSIONER OF IMMIGRATION HART H. NORTH, SAN FRANCISCO, CAL., SEPTEMBER 2, 1898.

[Questions put by Commissioner North and answered by Qui Ngun in English without the assistance of the interpreter.]

Q. How old are you?—A. 16.
Q. How long have you been in this country?—A. 9 years.
Q. How long have you lived here at the home?—A. Nearly 7 years.
Q. Did you come to this country with your father and mother?—A. No.
Q. How did you come to this country?—A. My father was poor and he sold me to another man.
Q. That was in China?—A. Yes.
Q. How much did he sell you for?—A. $200 Mexican.
Q. Who was the man that he sold you to; a highbinder?—A. No, he was not a highbinder.
Q. Did this man bring you to this country?—A. Yes.
Q. How did he get you here; did he say that you were his daughter, or do you know?—A. I don't know.
Q. What did he do with you?—A. A woman tried to put me in a bad house.
Q. When you were a little girl?—A. Yes; and teach me how to sing. They have a number of girls who are quite young and who sing at feasts.
Q. You were to be put into a house as a "sing song" girl?—A. Yes.
Q. Were you put in such a house?—A. The man that brought me here would not let the woman put me in the house.
Q. What did you do; just stay there with the man and his wife?—A. Yes.
Q. Did they make you work?—A. Yes.

Q. Did they ever beat you?—A. Yes; they took a great big stick and beat me with it.
Q. Why did they do that?—A. He gambled, and if he lost money he came home and beat me.
Q. The woman used to beat you pretty often with a big stick, did she?—A. Yes.
Q. Did you stay with her until you came to this house?—A. Yes.
Q. Were you rescued there?—A. No.
Q. Did you run away and come here?—A. Yes; I ran away and someone told Miss Culbertson, and Miss Culbertson came and got me.
Q. Were you sold more than that once?—A. No.
Q. Did you see the money that you were sold for?—A. She put it on the table for me.
Q. You were about 9 years old at that time, were you?—A. Yes.
Q. That was in China, was it?—A. Yes.
Q. Where in China?—A. In Hongkong.
Q. You came over to this country with the man and his wife, did you not?—A. Yes.
Q. And she would put you in a bad house, but he would not let her, is that it?—A. Yes.
Q. Did you learn to sing?—A. I pretty nearly learned to sing.

Miss Cameron here presents Chun Wui, a Chinese slave girl, whom they had rescued and who had been in the home for 20 years. Chun Wui was blind, made so by being shut up in a chicken coop all night for punishment, and the vermin had destroyed her sight.

EXHIBIT H.

STATEMENT OF THE HON. HO YOW, HIS IMPERIAL CHINESE CONSUL-GENERAL AT SAN FRANCISCO, TO THOMAS F. TURNER.

Q. How long have you filled the office of consul-general at this point?—A. Nearly 3 years; first consul and then consul-general.
Q. During your residence and official station at San Francisco have you had occasion to study the disturbances caused by the so-called highbinder societies?—A. Yes, sir.
Q. Would you be able to state about how many highbinders of the highbinder organizations of the criminal class are in this city?—A. Of the worst kind of them about 400 or 500, but the others are inactive and are forced into it for self-protection.
Q. Is there not some means which might be devised to get rid of them and thus save a lot of trouble?—A. Yes, sir.
Q. Why is it that the State laws are inadequate to reach this evil?—A. In the first place, they can not make any special laws for the Chinese, and innocently to a certain extent protect them. Under the guise of law they can get incorporated and then do all sorts of things.
Q. As I understand, the system under which the highbinders operate and the fear which they inspire in all members of their race makes it impossible to secure testimony?—A. Yes; when any of them testify in such cases they are marked for life.
Q. Is it not a fact that the authorities trace nearly all the misdeeds of the Chinese to these highbinders?—A. Undoubtedly; if we could get rid of the highbinders and disperse them there would be no trouble. There would be better government and the better relations of the American and Chinese would be cultivated. No progress can be made in trade on account of the highbinders.
Q. What would you think of a law of Congress that would provide that mere membership upon the part of any alien in this country in any organization that has for its purpose the commission of crime or violation of law would be felony and any alien found belonging to such organization should be deported?—A. If such a law could be enforced I think it would be an excellent thing, but it is very hard to prove that they are other than what they represent them to be, seemingly innocent organizations, as they are corporated under the State laws.
Q. How would it be to specify the different things which are considered violation of the law, such as blackmail, etc.?—A. I would make this suggestion: Before any organization can be perfected the by-laws must be submitted to the representative of their own country and secure the official indorsement before the organization can be perfected.
Q. I had in mind, Mr. Consul, the organization of a special court or tribunal

before which might be tried all the questions which may arise, such as to deportation, etc., and rather than vest such great power in any one man, I thought it would be wise to have a court of three or four members and the consul or highest official at each port representing each country to act as ex officio member of such court?—A. I think it a very good thing and quite agree with you.

Q. Is there any suggestion with reference to the Chinese exclusion law that you care to make?—A. Yes, sir; take in the first place the so-called native sons—now in the bill pending before the Senate, it says that a native son returning to this country must have one or two white witnesses to swear before the collector as to his birth, and that no other evidence will be accepted. This is very hard for the Chinese; it does not give them their rights. It is all right to prove a certain thing, but to have a certain person to prove it is very hard. It is almost impossible to always have two witnesses to one's birth. Another thing provided in the bill is that those native born who are not registered and whose birth is not certified to in court, can not return. There are two or three thousand native sons in China now who will be excluded if this law is passed.

Q. What would you think of a law which will in the future require all Chinese children to be registered at birth?—A. There could be no objection to that if registered within one or two years.

Q. Have you any idea about how many native sons there are now in this city or State?—A. About 2,000, as far as I know.

Q. Why is it that they do not exercise the right of suffrage and become interested in our laws?—A. They have not had any leaders in that respect; they have had no one to instruct them. They can not read the Constitution, but I believe that the Chinese are working up to that.

Q. Do you not think that it would help to solve the trouble if they took an interest in our local affairs?—A. Yes, sir; our object now is in that direction, to lead them on. They would have gone right on, but have no encouragement.

Q. Has it been brought to your attention that the Japanese are cutting in in competition with the Chinese?—A. Yes; but they can not hurt the Chinese labor, but hurt the white labor more. They can not come up to the standard of the Chinese; they can not be trusted. Their cutting under the wages of the Chinese will affect the market, but not the Chinese. Another point of the exclusion law, no professional can be considered a merchant. There ought to be an extension as to the profession, such as missionaries, students, doctors, lawyers, etc.

Q. Is it not a fact that, under the present administration of the laws here, a great many hardships are placed upon the merchant that should not be placed upon him?—A. Yes; in my opinion a photograph and certificate given to a merchant and then identified upon his return should be sufficient. All investigations should be made before he goes and when he comes back; no trouble should be had. Another point that I would like to bring to your notice: If a merchant wants his wife to come, hitherto all he had to do was to prove that he was a merchant, and the wife and minor child was his wife and child, respectively; but now, since last year, they made a ruling that all children who come here, or the wife of a merchant, must have a certificate of identification. If a merchant has a wife or child in China and wants his wife and children in America, it will be almost impossible for them to prove that they are the wife of this man. All the proofs are on this side, and she can not prove that her husband is a merchant. If a merchant proves his standing and proves her to be his wife, that should be enough. The exclusion act is to prevent cooly labor and not other classes. Another point is that the law allows a laborer to go back to China and limits his time of return to one year. Why not, if he were sick and could not get back within that year, allow us to extend this time? If you allow him to return within one year, you should allow him to return within five years. If the law could be revised and changed to permit return within three years instead of one, I think it would be more reasonable.

Respectfully submitted.

Ho Yow.

SAN FRANCISCO, *April 4, 1900.*

EXHIBIT I.

STATEMENT MADE BY A CHINESE TO THOMAS F. TURNER, AT SAN FRANCISCO, CAL., DECEMBER 23, 1899.

Q. What is your name?—A. My name is ——
Q. Where do you live?—A. San Francisco.
Q. What is your business?—A. Merchandise; importer of rice, tea, oil, and opium.

Q. How long have you been in the United States?—A. Since 1863.
Q. Have you lived all the time in San Francisco?—A. Yes, sir.
Q. How long have you been in business?—A. Since—I think about 30 years.
Q. Can you tell in just a general way about how much business you do in a year?—A. I guess about on an average of from $30,000 to $50,000.
Q. How much do you pay on an average in customs duties to the Government of the United States?—A. During the last 3 years I have averaged about $5,000 a year.
Q. What condition is your business in at the present time?—A. My business is in good condition; I am prosperous and am doing well.
Q. I understand that you are preparing to go back to China; is that true?—A. Yes, sir.
Q. When do you expect to go?—A. On the 17th of this month.
Q. Will you tell me why you are going?—A. Well, 2 years ago I was elected ———. There were 12 highbinder tongs in the city of San Francisco who notified me as ———, that when any member of our society went back to China, they must pay to the highbinders a head tax of $2 each, so in order to defend and protect our members that they would not have to pay this tax to the highbinders, I refused to let them pay it, so they could get nothing from the members. But my time as ——— was up the 1st of last August, and another man took my position as secretary. The next man who was elected was afraid to interfere and did not attempt to prevent the highbinders from collecting the $2 from each member of our society. Some of them paid it and some did not, saying: "We did not pay it during the last 2 years when ——— was secretary, why should we pay you at the present time?" Then the highbinders said ——— has interfered in our business, so the thing to do is to get ——— out of the way, and also the merchants of the ——— society out of the way. So they put a price of $300 on the heads of 8 merchants in my society and upon myself. This is why I thought I would take a trip home until their temper cools off.
Q. What notice did you get that $300 had been placed on your head?—A. Friends came to me and told me to get out of the way and out of danger.
Q. At what time did you get that notice?—A. About a month ago.
Q. Have you, since you have received that notice, been able to go around Chinatown freely, without a guard?—A. No.
Q. What have you done to protect yourself?—A. I have been to the city hall and told Judge D. J. Murphy that my life was in great danger. I said to him: "I do not know what to do; you are a friend of mine, and I will take your advice." He then took me down to Chief of Police Lee, and said to the chief: "This is an old friend of mine and I don't want to see him killed, and I want you to do the best you can for him and protect him." So the chief sends a policeman to guard my place every night since I gave him notice.
Q. Do you have any guard of your own?—A. Yes; my nephew.
Q. What does he do?—A. He stays with me and attends to my business, and whenever I go out around town he goes with me.
Q. Are you afraid to go out alone since you got that notice?—A. I always have a guard. I never go out alone through Chinatown.
Q. Why don't you like to go through that part of town?—A. I am afraid that some highbinder might take my life.
Q. Can you explain to me so that I can tell the authorities in Washington why the police in San Francisco can not break up these highbinders?—A. The law is a little too easy for them. For instance, they want to murder a man; they send a half a dozen highbinders to go together; the one who is do the shooting will wait for his victim while the others stand near by to guard against policemen. As soon as they did the shooting, they throw the gun into an ash barrel, and so have no weapon, and when the policeman comes, all the Chinamen come out together and they can not tell who did the shooting. Unless the policeman saw the man do the shooting, there is no way of catching them.
Q. Why can the officer not find the other Chinamen who saw the killing, who would be willing to go into court and tell what they know?—A. They are afraid to tell.
Q. Why are they afraid?—A. Afraid that the highbinders will go after them.
Q. What will the highbinders do to some good Chinaman who saw the killing and would testify to that in court?—A. He knows that they would kill him if he testified in court.
Q. How many highbinders do you think there are in San Francisco?—A. From 500 to 1,000.
Q. Are all of the members of the highbinder society bad men?—A. Some good ones. Some merchants have to go in to protect themselves from harm. About 100 are very bad; the rest are afraid to kill.

Q. When one of these societies want to kill a man, how do they select the man who is to do the killing?—A. Each highbinder has a number, and they are selected according to their number to do the killing.

Q. Tell me what the highbinder society is organized for?—A. Blackmail and murder, and some of them make it a part of their business to aid in bringing slave girls into the country.

Q. Do the highbinders fear the laws of the State of California?—A. They are not afraid of the laws of this State. They say they are too easy.

Q. Is it not a fact that a great many of the highbinders in Chinatown were criminals in China?—A. Yes, sir; they are not so bad as here. They would not dare in China to do the acts that they would here. They do not dare to murder in China, because they would be beheaded. In China we find out who did the murder. If we can not find him, we arrest his father, brother, or nearest relative and behead him. This makes the Chinamen very much afraid to commit murder. Under the law of the United States it is so hard to convict one that they do not care for the laws.

Q. What do you think would be the best way to break up the highbinders in Chinatown?—A. Some time ago the Chinese consul at this place, with the aid of the police, almost broke it up. The highbinders have lawyers of this city in their employ regularly, who aid them in every way possible, and are paid big fees by the highbinders. They even told me that if the members of our society did not pay the $2 head tax, they would send Lawyer Campbell, their attorney, who would compel us to pay. I told them that I did not fear it, and that if the lawyer tried that I knew we could send him to the penitentiary.

Q. Suppose there was a law that would provide that every member of a highbinder society might be sent back to China, what effect do you think such a law would have?—A. The thing that the highbinder fears most is to be sent back to China, and if a few dozen were sent back I think it would break up the highbinders.

Q. What would happen to the highbinders if they were sent back to China?—A. They would be watched very closely in their native village and would have great difficulty in getting along. They would perhaps be killed by a relative of one who was a victim in this country.

Q. Do you know how many highbinder societies there are in San Francisco?—A. There are any number, some of which are Chee Kung Tong, Suey On Tong, Hop Sing Tong, Hip Sing Tong, Suey Sing Tong, Bing Guing Tong, Hip Yee Tong, Quong Dock Tong, Jo Lum Sen Tong, Jew Yee Tong.

Q. Have these highbinder societies anything to do with the Six Companies?—A. No, sir.

Q. Please explain just what the Six Companies are.—A. For instance, our northern people have a society of their own, the southern people, etc. Each company represents the different neighborhood of China.

Q. What is the purpose of each company?—A. Help the poor, take care of the old and infirm, and when they die provide for having their remains buried.

Q. What kind of a head does your company have?—A. A president.

Q. How is he chosen?—A. By election. Only the business men and merchants of the company have a vote. In my society there are about 80 merchants or representatives of stores, and we choose the president. A member of the company who has no store or interest in a store, and no property, has no vote. The Six Companies are joined together and have another man at the head of all the Six Companies. Acting together, they protect the rights of all their people, take care that their interest is protected, and if they are sick they are taken care of.

Q. Why is it that, with the police protecting you, you do not feel safe to remain in San Francisco?—A. I can not expect an officer to watch me all the time, and know that if an officer were not watching all the time I would be killed by the highbinders.

Q. How many merchants and prominent Chinamen do you think are driven back to China each year by the highbinders?—A. Two or three have been compelled to leave on account of this last trouble, and a great many from time to time are compelled to leave.

Q. The class of Chinese that are compelled to go are the most respectable and better element, are they not?—A. Yes. It is because these men have money and are prosperous that the highbinders get after them, and all those who do not submit are compelled to leave the country.

Q. About what per cent of the merchants who stay here have to pay the highbinders?—A. A very great many of the merchants are compelled to pay the highbinders, but a few of us have refused. I have advised the merchants that if they had any money to give away or spend to give it to the poor and where it will do some good, and not to give it to these men who make their living through blackmail.

Exhibit J.

STATEMENT OF HON. J. P. JACKSON, COLLECTOR OF CUSTOMS, SAN FRANCISCO, CAL.

OFFICE OF THE COLLECTOR OF CUSTOMS,
San Francisco, Cal., December 14, 1899.

Hon. THOMAS F. TURNER,
Special Agent United States Industrial Commission, San Francisco.

DEAR SIR: Referring to our conversation some days since concerning the Chinese exclusion laws and matter in this customs service incident thereto, and your suggestion that I should embody my views thereon in a letter to you, the opportunity now offers to write you as follows:

The number of Chinese resident in this city has materially decreased in late years. Whereas there were about 35,000 of them congregated here some fifteen years ago, I think it doubtful if there are now remaining 20,000 of all classes, male and female. The report of the Treasury Department for the year ending June 30, 1899, shows that there were less than 4,000 new arrivals during the last year through all the ports of the United States.

There is a general misunderstanding in the public mind as to the present status of the exclusion laws. It is not generally known or understood that there is no exclusion law against the coming of all Chinese. The specific interdiction is against "laborers" alone. No Chinese laborer can now come to the United States for the "first time," but such laborers already here can go and come between here and China at will if they have a wife, child, or parent here, or own property or have debts due them of the value of $1,000.

Also all other Chinese who are of the exempt class—that is, who are not laborers—if rightfully in this country can go back to and from China at their pleasure.

The classes of Chinamen who can now come from China to this country for the first time are declared in the treaty to be officials, teachers, students, merchants, and travelers for curiosity or pleasure.

The foregoing classification takes no cognizance of Chinese persons who were born in this country; their right and claim to come and go at their own free will is grounded entirely upon their American citizenship. It is with claimants under this head that the most trouble is experienced and the most fraud perpetrated.

I do not believe that as many as 10 per cent of those coming to this country as merchants are fraudulent, while under the plea of native American born I would not think 20 per cent too high an estimate of the counterfeit claimants.

In the case of those claiming to be native born, Chinese testimony is permitted under the law to establish their nativity, whereas merchants are required to prove their status by witnesses "other than Chinese."

I think it is very doubtful whether under the United States Constitution and laws a different requirement could be enforced in proving nativity here of a Chinaman from that provided for a white man—that is, either may prove it by such witnesses as may know the fact, irrespective of racial distinction.

A requirement that all Chinese births should be registered upon the proof of such birth by father, mother, and midwife would seem to be a safe precaution against future fraudulent claims of this class.

As to merchants who return to this port after visting China, I think their entry here should be facilitated in every way consistent with the treaty between this country and China and the statutes passed in pursuance thereof. I say this because there have been numerous instances where detention of merchants either on shipboard or in the "detention loft" here has been productive of sickness, loss, and damage to health and business. The practice here is to make investigation of the status of merchants at their homes in this country during their absence in China, and thus prevent as far as possible undue detention after their return from their visit. But it often happens that these investigations are not fully satisfactory, needing explanations which only the merchant himself can give, and thus necessitating a new course of inquiry, while he must remain "in durance vile."

I would recommend in case of merchants the same course of procedure that is now required in the case of "returning laborers"—that is, have the status of the merchant determined before he shall leave this country, and then give him a "return permit," which will insure him a landing on presentation.

As it is now a returning laborer can secure a landing immediately on passing quarantine without question or cavil, thus placing him in a much more advantageous position than a merchant.

If I thus seem to favor the "merchant" over the "laborer," it is because I esteem him as a much more desirable denizen.

My experience as collector enables me to judge of the value to the Government of the Chinese mercantile business. The entire amount of duties collected at this port during the month of October last was $603,644.63. Of this sum the Chinese paid $175,836.81, considerably more than one-fourth of the whole. In November (last month) our collections were $508,560.23, of which Chinese paid $156,787.27, nearly one-third of the entire sum.

These two months are not at all peculiar, but are noted as the latest evidences of the business. I have before me a long list of Chinese merchants who pay annually customs duties running from $10,000 to $200,000 each, four of them paying over $100,000 annually and two firms contributing yearly between $150,000 and $200,000 to the Government coffers.

These same merchants subscribed lately over $6,000 to the citizens' fund for welcoming back our soldiers from the Philippines, which was more than one-tenth of the entire amount collected.

Therefore it is that I say they should be fairly treated, especially as the commodities in which they deal are generally of unique character and peculiar to themselves, and thus do not come in any great degree into competition with our own "white traders."

Now, as to laborers, they do come into direct rivalry with our own working population. They have superseded "Bridget" and "Katherine" in the kitchen, and "Annie" and "Nellie" in "upstairs work." The laundry business is almost entirely monopolized by them. As a consequence of this invasion of the household, San Francisco has become conspicuously a city of boarding houses. Families find it easier, if not cheaper, to board rather than to "keep house."

There is still another field in which the Chinese laborer has been utilized, and that is in the vineyard and orchard. While there has been at times a protest on the part of labor organizations against the Chinaman in the harvest field, yet it must be admitted in the busy season his services are welcomed by the vintner and orchardist, and he has shown himself a necessity in this State, where only this season the schools in at least three counties declared a vacation in order to permit the scholars to work in the orchards and canneries.

A new feature in the element of house service has not long since arisen by the advent here of the Japanese. I regard this class of laborers as a decidedly greater menace to our white laborers than are the Chinese.

The qualities that commend the Chinese to favor as laborers are sobriety, industry, and servility. Their vices are gambling and opium eating. These last are indulged generally among themselves,

The Japanese have not the foregoing qualities distinguishing the Chinese, but on the contrary are cunning, shrewd, and crafty. They underbid the Chinaman in his chosen spheres of employment, but unlike him do not nourish or foster their employment, but hold the same only so long as there is anything to be learned thereat, when they will unceremoniously quit the service regardless of obligation or inconvenience to employer. They are at all times self-important and ever ready to resent any imputation against them or their country. They are in no manner naturally servile, but will smother resentment for the time, simply biding the opportunity to vent their revenge. They will work when so necessitated for just so much less than any other laborer as will drive him from the field, and, this done, will then exact the uttermost farthing which the urgency of the work must yield. I think we have much more to fear from Japan than from China.

Now, another matter: I do not know whether it is within the purview of your inquiry to consider the position of the collector of customs with reference to this Chinese business. I will take the liberty, however, of explaining myself thereon.

As you well understand, the entire responsibility of passing upon all Chinese admission papers is placed upon the collector. He examines all laborers' applications for "return permits," all merchants' papers for their return, all certificates from foreign governments for "first comers," and all the evidence in "native-born" cases. Such a draft is this upon my time and attention that when the special agents of the Treasury Department, Messrs. Smith and Linck, investigated the affairs of this custom-house in February last they reported to the Department as follows:

"We find that the greater part of the time of the present collector at this port is devoted to the consideration of Chinese business, hence he has little time to give to the legitimate duties to which he was appointed."

But apart from the fact that my time is thus preoccupied and taken from the duties of the custom-house proper, I hold that the two positions of collector and Chinese inspector, or judge (for such is one of my functions), are totally incompatible. This Chinese business is a parasite that should not be fastened on the custom-house. The duties are not cognate in any manner to those of the collector. My duties as collector are to collect revenue, and while so doing to see to it that the custom-house is not made an obstacle to commerce, a deterrent to trade, and a hindrance to business. It is incongruous that with one hand I encourage the Chinese in trading and business and with the other hand deny them admission to the country. Especially is this true now, when the policy of our country is evidently to foster good-fellowship with China in order to secure a greater measure of her trade. I am fixedly of the opinion that this excrescence should be severed from the customs service.

The proper and fitting place for enforcement of Chinese-exclusion laws is the immigration bureau. It has the control of the contributions of all other nations to our population, and why not the Chinese?

I can see nothing so different or peculiar in the immigrants of China and those of Japan that the same authority should not have jurisdiction over both.

I sincerely trust that the transfer will be made by Congress, and to that end I beg to invoke your favorable, valuable interposition, and remain,
Very truly, yours,

J. P. JACKSON, *Collector.*

EXHIBIT K.

STATEMENT OF J. D. PUTNAM, CHINESE INSPECTOR.

LOS ANGELES, CAL., *March 20, 1900.*
Hon. THOMAS F. TURNER,
Los Angeles, Cal.

SIR: In accordance with your request, as a representative of the Government, for my observations and views in Chinese matters, I would respectfully report upon my observations in regard to the manner in which the Chinese-exclusion act has been enforced, and take the liberty of making some suggestions upon the matter of Chinese exclusion as the subject has presented itself to me after 5 years of careful and constant study.

I have observed that while there is a limited number who work hard to strictly enforce the law in accordance with the Chinese-exclusion act, I believe that there are more Chinese within the limits of the United States at the present time than there were on the 4th day of May, 1894, at the time of the close of the registration.

I believe that the largest number of those entering fraudulently enter through the different ports by connivance with so-called Chinese attorneys, who are allowed to appear and argue cases before the several collectors of customs, presenting Chinese evidence which is wholly unreliable, and often backing such evidence by that of Jews or hangers-on about Chinese quarters, or others seeking the trade of Chinese.

They usually come as one of two classes. Of the first class, I believe the greater number claim to be native-born Americans. Second, those presenting themselves with merchants' papers (which papers they seem to have no difficulty in procuring white men to certify to as Chinese well known to them as merchants). There is not 1 white man in 10 who has made the exclusion act a special study or who knows what constitutes a Chinese merchant. When they wish to procure a signer, merchants will introduce to such person a Chinese whom they state is a partner and a member of their company and who they claim is the party for whom such signer is to certify. After the signer of a certificate sees his name upon said certificate, upon its being returned for investigation, the result universally is that he is ready to make a statement to the inspector to the effect that the photograph represents some party well known to him. Should he state the contrary, a Chinese lawyer will prepare an affidavit and present it to him, which he usually signs. Then the attorney presents the sworn evidence as rebuttal to the inspector's report. The inspector not being authorized to administer an oath (which I believe is an error), he is without power.

I believe that 9 out of every 10 of the Chinese who pass through the United States in bond for Mexican points go with the intention of returning to the United States. I would suggest that Chinese passing in bond be photographed and as accurate a description be taken of them as is taken of a soldier who enlists in the United States Regular Army, and a description and photograph of these passing in bond be forwarded to ports of entry along the Mexican border.

In my opinion the temptation to substitute a prisoner, or person in bond, for one who really wishes to visit China or some point in Mexico, is too great to allow guards appointed by the railroad company to guard the Chinese prisoners or those in bond, as the railroads are opposed to the enforcement of the Chinese-exclusion act, and keep up a constant fight for the Chinese against the Chinese inspector. I have every reason to believe that a large number of the railroad hands, such as conductors, engineers, and brakemen, derive quite a revenue for assisting in the smuggling of Chinese across the desert from border points (after they cross the line). It is almost impossible for Chinese to cross the desert unless by train, except in the winter season.

I believe that there is an organization existing, extending from San Francisco to Hongkong, including the cities where the ports of entry are established, with teachers on board the steamships, whose object is to illegally land Chinese. Further, that they have their schools to teach them a little English, and that by means of maps and charts the applicant is made perfectly familiar with the principal streets, the street-car lines, and principal places of business, parks, etc., about the point in the city in which he claims to have been born.

I believe that there is an organization in this city which landed 3 boat loads of Chinese from Mexico along the coast of this district, of from 19 to 26 each time, during my absence of 5 months from this port. The boat that is suspected of having done the work has been lying in the inner harbor at San Pedro for nearly 3 months, as on their last trip the danger signal was run up, and they returned from Mexico with a few shells on board. I believe that I have learned the signs and signals of this organization, and that I know a part of those so engaged.

The general standing and character of attorneys who represent the Chinese immigrant become very low after a considerable time is devoted to the work in that line. I believe that they, as a rule, become perfectly unscrupulous, and are ready to wink at or connive to introduce perjured evidence of the rankest kind.

I will state that the fees that were paid in the case of Sing Kum, a Chinese slave girl, who was ordered deported during the month of February, 1900, were $250. The attorney asked $150 more to appeal the case from Judge Wellborn's decision. Another attorney stepped in at this point and advised that the woman be allowed to return to China, and that he would make a set of papers for $50, have her return to Mexico, and when she was across the border he was to receive a fee of $50 more. The usual price in the case of men is $75 if released before the commissioner, and an additional $50 if the case goes before the district court.

I would respectfully recommend that in no case should the Government permit the Government's evidence to be divulged until the defense is prepared to complete the case, and if the case is appealed from the decision of the commissioner to come before the district court, it should be upon the evidence taken by the commissioner, and no further evidence should be admitted or considered. My reason for recommending this is that in most cases taken before the district court an entirely new line of defense is set up by defendant's attorney with entire new witnesses who are wholly unknown to the court or the officers thereof.

I believe that the best means of ridding the country of Chinese who have illegally entered would be to allow the commissioner or inspector to offer a reward of $5 for each person, Chinese or others, who will give information leading to the arrest and deportation of Chinese illegally within the United States, to be paid after deportation. I believe that would do more toward detecting frauds than the addition of twenty new inspectors, as Chinese and those engaged in the business make it their business to know the whereabouts of the officers of the Government, and when attempting to cross the line or land a party they have their signs and signals.

Most of the labor on repairs and extensions on the Southern Pacific Railroad between Los Angeles and El Paso, Tex., is performed by Mexican peons, and the work of extension has been done either by Mexicans or the Chinese south of Los Angeles.

While I was in El Paso, Tex., from June until October, 1899, I believe that there were at least 100 per week of these Mexican peons who left El Paso to work on the Southern Pacific, the White Oaks, and the Santa Fe railroads.

I would respectfully suggest that there be a Chinese bureau established, independent of all others (as I look upon the Chinese exclusion act as a political law, which can only be handled upon that theory). All Chinese claiming to be native of the United States should be made to prove the fact of their birth by 2 white witnesses, at least 1 to have known of the fact of birth at time of birth and the other within 1 year after birth, statements to be made upon oath or by a record of birth made at time, with proof from white people that this is the identical person whose birth was recorded at that time.

That the Chinese inspectors be held strictly responsible for their acts and the reports made by them, a record of which reports shall be retained by them, and that there be no appeal except to the Secretary of the Treasury from the decision of the inspector or commissioner, and in no case should the attorney for the defense see or know of the report of the inspector.

I will add that those not acquainted with Chinese and their habits and customs can not realize the demoralizing effect they have upon the young and rising generation. I venture to say that more girls are ruined by the wily Chinese, as few of them as there are, comparatively, than all other criminal classes combined. Stop and think of the Chinese at the washtub, with a young girl's wardrobe, then as her chambermaid, with his head shaved and with his white apron, and with that bland smile on his face, then turn and look at the ladies who visit their places. Can you believe that the Chinese are more than human? The Chinese as a class are a born set of bribers, gamblers, polygamists, and perjurers, and when anyone will show me 1 actually converted Chinamen among them, then it will be one I have not met. You may have evening mission schools for young men of the Chinese for young ladies to teach, and you will have no lack of pupils; but take the ladies away, and put a young man equally capable and religious in their place, and in a short time you will not have a Chinaman attending the school.

I would further recommend that in no case should a Chinese arrested for being illegally in the United States be allowed to give bail for appearance in court, and that the writ of habeas corpus should be denied in all cases.

I would allow Chinese merchants' wives to land only upon positive proof that she was the only living wife and in company with her husband, upon positive proof that he was married prior to his first coming into the United States. I know of several who were landed as wives of merchants who are kept in houses of prostitution.

I would allow Chinese laborers to visit their native land (but no adjacent country, as they usually visit adjacent countries only for the purpose of perfecting plans to illegally bring in contraband Chinese) and remain 2 years, upon depositing their certificates of registration with the proper authority and proving by 2 reliable white witnesses that had known the party for 2 years, that he was an industrious Chinese and not liable to become a public charge. In that manner we would dispose of his labor during his absence. There is not 1 out of 10 Chinese styling themselves as merchants and so registered who are genuine merchants except in name, as many a store or firm claiming to have from $10,000 to $15,000 capital and as having a list filed in the custom-house of from 5 to 15 partners, whose stock could be removed at one time in a single express wagon, and usually 1 or 2 men found about the store, the balance cooking or gardening or running gambling rooms until just before they wish to visit China, and still they have no trouble in procuring signers to their papers as being bona fide merchants. An example should be made of signers of such certificates by bringing them before the grand jury.

I would deport all Chinese prostitutes and Chinese women living in houses of prostitution, as I believe that they are really at the bottom of most of the highbinder troubles.

I would imprison at hard labor for a period of 10 years all Chinese found in the United States after having been once deported or denied landing, as they usually return in bond to Mexico and then return to the United States.

I would not land a Chinese child as the child of a merchant, as it is the custom of the Chinese who go to China as merchants to bring with them upon their return 1 or 2 children purchased by them, and land them as their own. I know of several such cases. I know of several very young children in this city who were brought into the United States in that way, most of them being sent to this city from San Francisco, though it would be impossible to prove it under existing customs.

I believe that only officers of the Government should have charge of Chinese in bond passing through the United States.

I believe that Chinese evidence, unless corroborated by at least 2 white witnesses, should have no weight before a court or jury.

I believe that Chinese inspectors should have authority to administer an oath, and when investigating cases should administer the oath in every instance.

The Chinese and Japanese do nine-tentht of the fruit packing on this coast south of San Francisco and most of the gathering of grapes and small fruit.

Very respectfully,

J. D. PUTNAM, *Chinese Inspector.*

EXHIBIT L.

AFFIDAVIT OF MR. FRED. W. WADHAM RESPECTING ALIEN LABOR AND ASIATIC IMMIGRATION.

STATE OF CALIFORNIA, *County of San Diego, ss:*

Fred. W. Wadham, being first duly sworn according to law, says:

He is now, and for six years last past has been, United States deputy collector, inspector of customs, having his headquarters in said county and State. That during all of said period of time it has been a part of his duty to prevent, so far as possible, the illegal entry of alien Chinese laborers into the United States; that during the said period the said affiant has become familiar with the question of alien immigration, and has become acquainted with the methods employed by Chinese immigrants and those who aid and abet them in procuring the illegal and fraudulent entry into the United States of Chinese laborers; that part of affiant's duty as such deputy collector is to guard and watch the boundary line of the United States and Mexico, and such portion of said boundary line as lies within his jurisdiction; that said boundary line within his jurisdiction covers about 18 miles of exposed coast and boundary line, nearly all of which extends in an uninhabited country; that the entire duty of patrolling, watching, and guarding said boundary line devolves upon this affiant and another deputy collector, and that it is altogether impossible for two men charged with other duties imposed upon them as deputy collectors to properly and effectually guard and watch said boundary line; that to affiant's certain knowledge Chinese laborers are continually coming into the United States over said line in violation of the so-called "exclusion act;" that such immigrants land from the China steamers in Mexico at different points along the coast and enter the United States either from coasting vessels or by following trails along the coast or over the mountains in United States territory; that such immigrants are constantly aided by resident Chinamen and by white and Mexican employers who are interested in bringing them into this country; that despite the most strenuous and vigilant efforts on the part of affiant and his assistant deputy said exclusion law is being continually violated.

Affiant further says that he has positive and definite knowledge that large numbers of indigent Mexicans, who have their homes in Mexico, are constantly coming over the line into the United States and find employment therein; that in affiant's judgment there are at least 150 Mexicans residing just across the line in Mexico who are constantly employed upon this side of the line; that said Mexicans work for a much lower rate of wages than is asked by American laborers, and that as a class they are not only indigent, but many of them are criminals and vicious, and that the effect upon such competition has a demoralizing effect upon the white labor in this vicinity; that to affiant's certain knowledge large numbers of Chinese laborers, who are denied landing at ports north of San Diego, come to Ensenada and ports along the Mexican coast and find their way over the line into the United States in violation of the exclusion laws. Affiant says that as a result of six years of observation and knowledge gained in the public service, coupled with knowledge gained from a residence of 15 years upon the Mexican border, he has no hesitancy in saying that with proper organization, and with adequate powers guaranteed to any inspector, it will be entirely possible to guard said line efficiently and prevent such fraudulent immigration of Chinese laborers into the United States along and over said line; that in order to accomplish such result, in the opinion of affiant, it will be necessary to detail some competent person to such work exclusively.

Affiant says that for a long time past he has had positive information of the existence of an organization, having its representatives at Los Angeles and different points along the coast and in the United States, the object of which is to aid in bringing Chinese laborers illegally into the United States; that the persons interested in such organizations are disreputable, and are even worse to deal with than the Chinese immigrants, their constant practice being the giving of bribes, subornation of witnesses, and the manufacture of false testimony.

Affiant further says not.

FRED. W. WADHAM.

CHINESE AND JAPANESE IMMIGRATION.

EXHIBIT M.

AFFIDAVIT OF MR. P. H. McCARTHY.

Mr. P. H. McCarthy, of the city and county of San Francisco, State of California, appeared personally before Special Agent Thomas F. Turner, and in reply to inquiries propounded testified as follows, to wit:

STATE OF CALIFORNIA, *City and County of San Francisco, ss:*

P. H. McCarthy, being duly sworn, deposes and says: I reside at No. 611 Stockton street, in the city and county of San Francisco. My official position for the past 6½ years has been and is at present president of the Building Trades Council. The Building Trades Council comprises all the trades which may be called upon to erect a building, preparing the material and executing the entire work. The approximate membership of the several branches of the Building Trades Council would number between 10,000 and 12,000 men employed.

I have resided in the State of California for 14 years on the 17th day of next April.

During my connection with the trades of the coast I have had an opportunity of investigating and studying the relations of white labor in connection with that of Asiatic emigration, and in regard to facts having come under my observation respecting the emigration of Chinese and the enforcement of the exclusion law I would state as follows:

The sugar industry was the first to bring to the attention of the people the great injustice being done to the white workmen of this State, and from that point on to the domestic labor employed. Wherever a Chinaman or Japanese is employed it displaces a white man. They are in our factories, they make our clothes; but we do not know it. It is the storekeeper who buys his goods from the Chinaman and sells it to the white man; therefore the storekeeper becomes the middleman. The result of this is that in the city and county of San Francisco, in comparison with the population, we have less white men employed than any city in the United States. It is to this great extent that our people suffer. As regarding the exclusion act, it was the one blessing, but the trouble is that the Chinaman is at liberty to pick out his place of business and do as he pleases. The people of this State decided that the exclusion act was a good thing and hailed it with joy; they are not only willing that it should continue, but will make their claim against its violation more potent. When the sugar fields were investigated and it was found that 95 per cent of the labor employed was Asiatic, how was the white man to maintain himself?

In regard to the idea that Chinese and Japanese labor is necessary in the cultivation in the fields of California, that most of the white labor is tramp and hobo labor, and that good white labor can not be secured to do the work, you will find that this statement is made by interested parties. The fact remains that these men are employing Chinese and Japanese to the exclusion of white help, and try to treat their white help in the same manner, placing them on a level with cooly labor. Should we submit to this? The rancher does not think we have a right to live as he does. We are citizens of the United States, yet he treats us on a level with his cooly help, places us in a shed, and does anything he likes with us. I have known some of the most honest and best citizens of the United States who, in order to accept the labor offered them, were compelled to live on a level with Chinamen and Japanese. They are thus driven to be tramps and hoboes.

I certainly think that it would be possible to secure all the white help necessary to meet the demand in the fruit districts, beet industry, and other departments where Chinamen and Japanese are now employed. If the stock yards of the city of Chicago can employ over 60,000 men, we certainly in this, the best climate in the Union, can have the laborers here. If the fruit grower will pay his white help sufficient and treat them as they should be treated, he will get reliable help and plenty of it.

In San Francisco the factories are filled with Chinese, making it impossible for our people to enter there. They can not go into the fields, for, as I have said before, they are filled with 98 per cent of Asiatic labor. The result of all this is that our people must walk the streets and resort to crime. There are more people driven into the country, sleeping in the haystacks, than we have any idea of. The firm of Miller & Lux have given an order to their several branches that no tramp shall ever be turned away from any of their places on the road, and thus feed over 400 men daily.

There has been a great increase in Japanese since the Geary law. They have not been excluded, and come as they please.

The labor interests of the West, and particularly of the coast, are in accord with the Industrial Commission of Washington to continue the rigid enforcement of the exclusion act, and every laboring man in the State of California will tell you that for the general good Asiatic labor should be kept out of the State of California.

P. H. McCarthy.

Subscribed and sworn to before me this 16th day of February, 1900.

[SEAL.]
James Mason,
Notary Public in and for the City and County of San Francisco, State of California.

LIST OF WITNESSES.

	Page.
Allen, W. H., representative Advance Labor Club, Brooklyn, N. Y.	161–166
Bealin, John J., superintendent New York free employment bureau	223–230
Brown, Geo. W., jr., deputy chief, bureau of licenses, New York City	230–236
Brown, Goodwin, counsel New York State commission in lunacy	202–219
Dobler, Roman, inspector, Immigration Bureau, New York	147–150
Eichler, Chas. G., chief statistical and record division, Bureau of Immigration	133
Fitchie, Thomas, commissioner of immigration at port of New York	70–76
Floyd, Robert, chief clerk Cunard Steamship Line	117–118
Hall, Prescott F., secretary Immigration Restriction League	46–70
Holman, Ed. B., inspector and secretary board special inquiry, Bureau of Immigration	134–137
Hotchkiss, Thomas W., counsel Protective Association of Employment Agencies	236–245
Lederer, Arthur, passenger manager, American Red Star Steamship Lines	118–119
McSweeney, Edward F., assistant commissioner of immigration at port of New York	76–101
Powderly, T. V., Commissioner-General of Immigration	32–46
Quinlan, John J., supervising inspector contract labor bureau, port of New York	120–125
Ritter, Theodore, manager Austro-Hungarian Home	219–223
Rosendale, Jules, special agent department of agriculture of Pennsylvania	187–201
Rossi, Egisto, chief of Italian bureau of immigration	154–160
Safford, Victor M., surgeon, United States Immigration Service	130–132
Schulteis, Herman J., ex-special commissioner of immigration	23–31
Schwab, Gustav H., agent, North German Lloyd Steamship Company	101–114
Senner, Jos. H., former Commissioner of Immigration	166–187
Stucklen, Regina, matron, Immigration Bureau	145–147
Stump, Herman, ex-Commissioner-General of Immigration	3–23
Ter Kuile, Jacob, passenger agent, Fabre Steamship Line	114–116
Ullo, Lorenzo, counsel, Immigration Bureau	137–145
Weihe, William, inspector, Immigration Bureau	150–154
Williams, Louis L., surgeon, Marine-Hospital Service	126–130
Wolf, Simon, attorney at law, Washington, D. C.	245–255

INDEX OF TESTIMONY ON IMMIGRATION.

[References give names of witnesses and pages in testimony—not in digest. For index of special reports see p. 823; index of reviews and digest, p. cxvii.]

Page.
Advertising for immigrants:
    Discontinuance of practice... Schwab, 104
    Effect comparatively slight... Senner, 181
    Existence of practice.. Hall, 49; Senner, 181
Agriculture, effect of immigration, slight............................ Powderly, 41
Aliens, application of immigration law to all.............................. Ullo, 141
American Line.
    Immigration, conditions concerning .... Lederer 118, 119
    Rules for agents as to excluded classes................................ Stump, 20
Anarchism, American workmen opposed to........................... Powderly, 45
Anarchists, instances of exclusion .... Powderly, 37
Anthracite miners, conditions, legislative investigation, unpublished.....
                                                                                                 Rosendale, 188, 192
    Social conditions generally .... Rosendale, 188–192
Anthracite mining, independent operators, relation to railroads... Rosendale, 190
Appeals:
    By immigrant or inspector to higher officers .... Stump, 10
    From board of special inquiry .... Holman, 134
Armenians:
    Character and destination of immigrants....................... McSweeney, 83
    Colonization at Chicago and Lynn...................................... Stump, 10
    Padrone system among .... Stump, 8; McSweeney, 83
Assimilation of foreign born (see also *Colonization; Distribution*):
    Desire for foreign born to become Americanized .... Senner, 183, 185
    Increased possibility of... Senner, 173
Assisted immigrants (see also *Prepaid tickets*):
    Exclusion under law .... McSweeney, 79
    Great Britain, assistance to paupers .... McSweeney, 87
    Insane persons.. Brown, 211
    Paupers, decrease of.. Powderly, 35
    Referred to .... Hall, 60
    Relatives, aid by... Hall, 49
    Russian Jews... Powderly, 33
Austria-Hungary (see also *Huns, Slovaks*):
    Emigration not desired by .... Ritter, 221
    Government assistance to immigrants on landing at New York ....
                                                       McSweeney, 87; Ritter, 219–222
    Immigrants, money sent to Europe by................................ Allen, 163
    Importation of servant girls from............................... McSweeney, 88
    Jews, condition in .... Wolf, 254
Austro-Hungarian Home and Free Employment Bureau, described..
                                                                            Ritter, 219–222
Balance of trade, money sent to Europe by immigrants, relation to .....
                                                                            Allen, 162–164
Board of special inquiry (see also *Inspection*):
    Amendments concerning powers, advocated.................... McSweeney, 99
    Appeals from decisions... Holman, 134
    Constitution and methods of work .... Fitchie, 70; Holman, 134; Weihe, 151
    Discretionary powers as to exclusion and admission, advocated ....
                                                          McSweeney, 99; Holman, 136, 137
    Number of cases considered by...... Holman, 134; Weihe, 150; McSweeney, 90
B'nai B'rith, history and work................................. Wolf, 248–250

806 INDEX TO TESTIMONY ON IMMIGRATION.

Bonding of immigrants (see also *Pauperism*): Page.
    Discussed .... Powderly, 41; Fitchie, 71, 75, 76
    Evasion of liability .... Powderly, 45
    Extension to two years advocated .... McSweeney, 84
    Impossibility of identifying paupers .... Hall, 63, 64
    Impracticability of system .... Hall, 63, 64
    Increased duration discussed .... Schwab, 108
Boot and shoe trade, effect of immigration .... Powderly, 42
Buffalo, Poles, colony of, described .... Senner, 171
Cabin passengers:
    Contract laborers, inspection of .... Dobler, 149, 150
    Evasion of law by .... Powderly, 37
    Inspection on shipboard, methods of .... Dobler, 147–150
    Manifests required from .... Powderly, 37
Canada:
    Assistant immigration from England through .... McSweeney, 87
    Contract labor from, prohibited .... Stump, 16
    Cotton mills, effect of immigration from .... Powderly, 39
    Daily immigration of laborers from .... Stump, 16; Schulteis, 27
    Deportation of prohibited immigrants .... Powderly, 38
    Evasion of law by immigration through .... Schulteis, 28; Powderly, 38
    Government, attitude toward immigration to United States .... Stump, 18
    Head tax largely evaded by immigrants from .... Schulteis, 28
    Immigration of Canadians not restricted .... Stump, 16
    Immigration inspector of United States in, duties .... Stump, 15
    Immigration through, statistics .... McSweeney, 92, 93
    Inspection of immigrants through, insufficient .... Powderly, 38
    Money taken out of country by immigrants, estimated .... Allen, 164
    Number estimated .... Allen, 161 (? 4)
    Number of immigrants from, not counted .... Schulteis, 27
    Opposition of Canadian workingmen to unrestricted immigration .. Schulteis, 28
    Temporary immigration from, and its effects .... Stump, 16; McSweeney, 93
Causes affecting immigration:
    Complexity of .... Senner, 167
    Desire for wider opportunities .... Senner, 182
    Industrial prosperity and depression ... Stump, 3; Hall, 49; Senner, 179, 180, 182
    Particular variations discussed .... Hall, 49
    Railroads and landowners, inducements of .... Schwab, 104
    Relatives—
        Assistance and inducement to immigrate .... Hall, 49
        Letters of .... Stump, 3
    Republican government, desire to enjoy .... Senner, 183
    Solicitation of immigrants by, discussed .... Stump, 7, 19; Schulteis, 23;
        Schwab, 103; Lederer, 119; Rosendale, 189, 200; Ritter, 221
    Steamship companies (see also under *Steamship companies*)—
        Advertisement, effect on immigration ... Hall, 49; Senner, 181; Schwab, 104
        Stimulation by .... Rosendale, 189, 200
    Steerage rates, reduction, influence of .... Hall, 49
Certificates, requirement of immigrants discussed .... Hall, 63
Charitable institutions (see also *Pauperism*):
    Foreign born, large percentage of .... Schulteis, 27
Charitable organizations, immigrants met by .... McSweeney, 85
Child labor, anthracite mines .... Rosendale, 189, 191
Children, immigrant, treatment by matron's department .... Stucklen, 146
Children of foreign parents, prospect of improvement .... Rosendale, 196
Chinese exclusion act:
    Evasion of .... Allen, 162, 165
    Habeas corpus cases, numerous .... Stump, 10
    History of adoption .... Stump, 3
Churches (see also *Religions*):
    Among anthracite miners .... Rosendale, 188
Cities:
    Built up by immigration .... Hall, 59
    Nationalities, respective tendencies of immigrants toward .... Hall, 54, 56
    Slum districts, proportion of immigrants in .... Hall, 56
    Tendency of immigrants toward .... Hall, 54–56
Citizenship (see also *Elective franchise; Naturalization*):
    Anthracite miners .... Rosendale, 188

INDEX TO TESTIMONY ON IMMIGRATION. 807

	Page.
Civil-service law, Immigration Bureau, application to	Fitchie, 72, 73–75
Coal, prices, relation to wages of miners	Rosendale, 190

Coal mines:
  Combinations of producers .... Powderly, 34
  Displacement of American labor by immigrants .... Powderly, 32–34
  Dwelling houses, crowding of .... Powderly, 33
  Effects of immigration, injurious .... Powderly, 32–34
  Foreign-born miners, conditions prevailing among .... Powderly, 44
  Number of immigrants to .... Stump, 19
  Padrone system described .... Powderly, 33, 44
  Standard of living reduced by immigration .... Powderly, 33
  Temporary residence customary .... Powderly, 32
  Unemployed increased by immigration .... Powderly, 32
  Wages—
    Causes of decrease .... Powderly, 34
    Reduced by immigration .... Powderly, 32

Colonies of foreign born:
  Agricultural, unimportance of .... Senner, 182
  Effect discussed .... Schulteis, 31
  Jewish .... Wolf, 246, 247, 254
  New York, location of .... McSweeney, 94
  Temporary in most cases .... Senner, 183, 185
  Tendency of certain nationalities .... Stump, 22
  Unavoidable in certain cases .... Senner, 183

Commissioners of Immigration (see also *Inspection*):
  Appeal from decision of inspector advocated .... Fitchie, 75
  Discretionary power as to admission and exclusion advocated .... Holman, 136; McSweeney, 80
  Increased powers advocated .... Fitchie, 75
  Power to suspend decision of subordinates advocated .... McSweeney, 99

Commission on Immigration, special, appointed by Treasury Department, 1895 .... Stump, 4

Company stores:
  Anthracite regions .... Rosendale, 188, 192
  Legislation proposed .... Rosendale, 192

Connecticut, criminality of foreign born in .... Senner, 175

Consular inspection:
  Advantage in preventing hardships of deportation .... Weihe, 153
  Impracticability, and expensiveness .... Hall, 59, 60; Schwab, 102, 105
  Insufficiency of .... Powderly, 35
  Military service, relation to requirement .... Hall, 62, 64
  Political difficulties .... Hall, 62

Contagious diseases among immigrants:
  Deportation where disease develops after landing .... Safford, 131
  Evasion of law, instances of .... Fitchie, 71
  Favus, character of disease, number of cases, etc .... Williams, 127–129; Safford, 132; Powderly, 35; Fitchie, 71
  Number of cases, exclusions, etc .... Williams, 127
  Parents return with children excluded .... McSweeney, 78
  Quarantine law of 1893, referred to .... Williams, 129
  Return of immigrants deported because of .... Williams, 128
  Steamship companies, character of inspection by .... Williams, 129
  Trachoma, character of disease, number of cases, etc .... Fitchie, 71; Williams, 127–129; Safford, 132
  Treatment in hospital preferable to deportation .... Williams, 127

Contract labor (see also *Inspection*):
  Amendments to law proposed—
    Immigrants, right to sue and collect fines, advocated .... Ullo, 143
    Implied contract or promise, extension to, advocated ...... McSweeney, 79
    Inducements and promises of labor should be held illegal. Quinlan, 121, 122; Ullo, 140, 143; Powderly, 33, 41
    Promise of contract on landing prohibited .... Stump, 6
    Prosecution by any attorney advocated .... Quinlan, 121, 122
    Relatives allowed to furnish employment by contract .... Stump, 21
  Application of law, difficulty concerning .... Ullo, 144
  Arrest and investigation after landing .... Ullo, 144

Contract labor—Continued.   Page.
Cabin passengers, inspection of .... Dobler, 149, 150
Coal mines, beginning of system .... Rosendale, 189
Conviction of employers, difficulty of .... Quinlan, 123; Stump, 5, 6
Convictions, small number of .... Quinlan, 121, 122; McSweeney, 77
Deportation of laborers .... McSweeney, 78, 79
   Contractor can not be punished in case of .... Ullo, 140
   Not originally contemplated .... Weihe, 154
   Power concerning .... Ullo, 140
Desirable immigrants often must be sent back .... Stump, 21
Employer not sufficiently punished .... Schwab, 102
Employer rather than immigrant should be punished. Weihe, 154; Holman, 137
Evasion of inspection in many cases .... Quinlan, 124, 125
Evasion of law, methods of, instances .... Weihe, 151, 152
Evidence—
   Character of .... Weihe, 151
   Contract must be an enforceable one .... Ullo, 140
   Contract must be proved made in foreign country .... Quinlan,
                                                                                                        121, 122; Ullo, 139
     Difficulty of securing evidence of contract .... McSweeney, 77–79;
                                                        Powderly, 33; Schulteis, 31; Ullo, 139, 140
   Immigrant, discussed .... Holman, 135;
                                  Dobler, 150; Weihe, 151; Ullo, 144; McSweeney, 100
Exceptions to exclusion provision .... Ullo, 144, 145
Foremen, invitations sent by .... Weihe, 152
Form of inducement usually offered .... Quinlan, 123, 124
Importation, instances of .... Weihe, 151, 152; Quinlan, 121, 123
Importation, intended to displace American labor .... Quinlan, 124
Inspection and investigation, methods of ...... Holman, 135; Quinlan, 120–125
Inspection department—
   Interpretation of law by .... Quinlan, 124
   New York, increase advocated .... Quinlan, 123, 125
New industries, exception concerning, difficulty from .... Ullo, 140
Organized labor—
   Little assistance in enforcing law from .... Quinlan, 120, 121
   Objection to, based on contract element .... Weihe, 153
Penalty, severer advocated .... Fitchie, 71
Pennsylvania, recent importation to .... Weihe, 152
Relatives, inducements to migrate by, discussed .... Quinlan, 124;
                                                           Powderly, 41; Ullo, 143; Hall, 49
Working of law—
   Discussed .... Schulteis, 31; Stump, 5, 21
   Hardships by separation of families, etc .... Stump, 5, 21
   Importation in large numbers almost exterminated .... Stump, 21
Convicts, exclusion applies only to convicted criminals .... Ullo, 141, 142;
                                                                                               McSweeney, 79, 80
Convict labor:
   Contract system, evils of .... Brown, 217–218
   New York, working of system .... Brown, 216–218
   Relation to free labor discussed .... Brown, 216, 217
   Value of work done .... Brown, 219
Cotton mills, Canada, effect of immigration from .... Powderly, 39
Criminality:
   Foreign born compared with native born .... Powderly, 40; Hall, 50–51
   Illiteracy not connected with .... Schwab, 103; Senner, 171–175
   Immigration, increase through .... Schulteis, 27
   Jews .... Rosendale, 194
   Nationalities compared .... Hall, 51, 64
   Special classes of crimes of certain nationalities .... McSweeney, 100, 101
   Statistics by nationality in certain States .... Senner, 174, 175
Criminals:
   Administration of exclusion law lax .... Schulteis, 26
   Assistance to emigrate by local governments .... Stump, 12, 13
   Deportation, few cases of .... Stump, 12
   England, assisted emigration from .... Schulteis, 26
   Exclusion even though not convicted, advocated .... McSweeney, 79, 80;
                                                                                                    Ullo, 141, 142

INDEX TO TESTIMONY ON IMMIGRATION. 809

Criminals—Continued. Pag..
   Existing laws sufficient protection .... Senner, 185
   Impossibility of ascertaining as basis of exclusion .... Hall, 58
   Power to exclude advocated .... McSweeney, 79, 80
Crimps, kidnapping by, Philadelphia .... Rosendale, 193
Croats, character as immigrants .... Senner, 186
Cunard Steamship Company, immigration conditions on .... Floyd, 117, 118
Customs officers, immigration, duties as to .... Stump, 15
Debarment of immigrants. (See *Deportation; Restriction of immigration.*)
Dependent classes (see also *Insane, Pauperism, Idiots*, etc.):
   Foreign born, expense of maintenance .... Hall, 52
Deportation of immigrants:
   Arrest after landing, lack of authority for .... Stump, 19
   Classes deported .... Stump, 10
   Contract laborers, discussed .... McSweeney, 78, 79; Ullo, 140; Weihe, 154
   Country to which immigrant should be returned .... McSweeney, 99; Ullo; 138
   Denied .... Ter Kuile, 115; Floyd, 117; Lederer, 119
   Extension of time limit discussed .... Stump, 19;
                         Schulteis, 26; Powderly, 40; McSweeney, 97; Brown, 209
   Insane, difficulty of .... Brown, 207–209
   Instances of .... Safford, 131
   Landing, power to deport after, discussed .... Ullo, 144
   Landing, refusal to permit sufficient .... Ullo, 138
   Number and character of immigrants deported 1899 .... Quinlan, 124
   Persons becoming public charges should be deported .... McSweeney, 97
   Practice regarding ....: .... Fitchie, 71
   Proportion at present excluded small .... Hall, 58
   Reduction of immigration by effect .... Stump, 9
   Return of debarred immigrants to United States charged .... Ullo, 142
   Steamship companies—
      Expense borne by .... Stump, 10
      Limited power of United States over .... Ullo, 138
      Penalty for charging passage to deported immigrants advocated ...
                                                         McSweeney, 99
      Penalty for refusal of, to return persons debarred .... McSweeney, 97
Destination of immigrants:
   False statements concerning and their effects .... McSweeney, 91
   Penalty for false statements advocated .... McSweeney, 91
   Unreliability of statistics .... McSweeney, 82, 91; Senner, 173
Detroit, daily immigration of Canadian skilled workmen ... Stump, 16; Schulteis, 28
Distribution of immigrants (see also *Assimilation; Colonization*):
   Cooperation of State bureaus advocated .... Stump, 5; Powderly, 39
   Desirability of more effective .... Senner, 174
   Exhibition of State resources at Ellis Island advocated .... Stump, 5
   Information as to resources, employment, etc .... Powderly, 39
   Northeastern States, tendency toward .... Hall, 55
Divorces, Jewish, by rabbi .... Rosendale, 193
Drunkenness, Jews and others .... Rosendale, 194, 195
Education:
   Compulsory, Pennsylvania, lack of enforcement .... Rosendale, 191
   Jewish institutions .... Wolf, 246, 248, 250, 254
   Manual training, Jewish schools .... Wolf, 248–250
   Relation to industrial efficiency .... Rosendale, 198, 199
Educational test:
   Advocated and discussed .... Hall, 46–69; Rosendale, 196–199
   Delay and vexations in applying .... Senner, 168, 169
   Deprecated .... Stump, 6; Holman, 136; Senner, 168, 169
   Desirable laborers excluded by .... Stump, 6; Schwab, 102
   Effect discussed .... Stump, 21; Powderly, 40
   Favored by States which desire immigrants .... Hall, 66
   Germans, opposition to, due to misunderstanding .... Hall, 61
   Illiteracy—
      Not connected with crime .... Schwab, 103; Senner, 171–175
      Not evidence of unfitness .... Holman, 136, 137
      Should be considered as one criterion .... Holman, 136, 137
      Undesirability of immigrants, proportioned to .... Hall, 51, 54
   Jews, Russian, effect on immigration of .... Schulteis, 29; Powderly, 42

Educational test—Continued. Page.
  Necessity of artificial and strict test............................... Hall, 58
  Opposition of theoretical economists............................... Hall, 67
  Public opinion concerning .... Hall, 66–69
  Roman Catholics, opposition to .... Hall, 67
  School attendance, effect on assimilation.......................... Hall, 54
  Skilled labor, not excluded by................................... Senner, 169
  Steamship companies, opposition stirred up by..................... Hall, 61
  Treaties with foreign countries do not prevent...................... Hall, 65
  Undesirable immigrants best excluded by .... Schulteis, 23; Hall, 51, 58
  Women, injustice in applying to .... Senner, 169
Effects of immigration:
  Advantages of earlier immigration .... Hall, 59
  American industries, value to............................. Rosendale, 198, 199
  Cities built up by .... Hall, 59
  Coal mines, injurious generally............................... Powderly, 32–34
  Country developed by .... Senner, 170
  Dangerous influences decreasing .... Senner, 173
  Evil, generally .... Powderly, 32, 41, 42
  Insanity, prevalence among foreign born .... Brown, 204–207
  Money sent out of country, estimated .... Hall, 52, 53
  Native labor elevated to higher employments .... Stump, 6, 21
  Political effects chief cause for agitation .... Stump, 22, 23
  Unemployment, effect on .... Stump, 16; Schulteis, 23; Powderly, 39
  Wages—
    Depressed by.. Schulteis, 23
    Not depressed by .... Schwab, 103
    Skilled labor, slight .... Stump, 16
    Unskilled labor not affected.................................... Stump, 16
Elective franchise:
  Aliens allowed to vote before naturalization .... Hall, 62
  Question distinct from that of naturalization...................... Stump, 22
Ellis Island (see *Inspection of Immigrants, New York*):
  Cost of buildings.. Stump, 12
Elmira Reformatory, labor of inmates............................... Brown, 217
Emigration:
  European countries, laws recently passed .... Stump, 22
  Opposed by home government, Austria-Hungary.................. Ritter, 221
Employment, political influence in obtaining .... Bealin, 224, 229
Employment agencies:
  Buffalo... Bealin, 224; Hotchkiss, 244
  Character and methods.. Ritter, 222
  Fees charged by... Hotchkiss, 239–243
    New York City .... Brown, 231–235
    Returnable if employment not found, legal requirements... Bealin, 224, 225
  Field for activity... Hotchkiss, 241
  Frauds.. Hotchkiss, 237, 238, 244
  Legal regulation, New York.................................. Bealin, 224–227
  License fees .... Hotchkiss, 238, 244
  Liquor dealers .... Bealin, 224
  New York City, number... Brown, 230
    State bureau .... Bealin, 223, 224
  Private, methods....................... Bealin, 224–228; Brown, 230–235
    New York City .... Brown, 230–235
  State, free, discussed .... Hotchkiss, 242–244
    Need affirmed... Bealin, 229, 230
  State supervision of private................................. Hotchkiss, 238, 242
    New York, methods in .... Brown, 231–235
  State supervision, proposed methods in New York.......... Hotchkiss, 237–242
England (see also *Great Britain*):
  Criminals, assisted immigration from................ Stump, 13; Schulteis, 26
  Illiteracy, percentage low .... Stump, 6
  Pauperism, large proportion of................................. Schulteis, 27
Epileptics, exclusion of immigrants............................ Brown, 210, 211
European countries (see also *Foreign Governments*), separate countries:
  Immigration, restrictive laws in................................. Schulteis, 28
European Immigration Commission, appointment and duties ..... Schulteis, 29

	Page.
Exhibition of State products, hall providing for, advocated	
	Senner, 174, 186; McSweeney, 96
Fabre Steamship Line, immigration business, described	Ter Kuile, 114, 115
Families, amendment concerning admission	McSweeney, 100
Farmers, unskilled not desirable	Hall, 57, 65
Favus, character of disease, number of cases, etc	Williams, 127, 129;
	Safford, 132; Powderly, 35; Fitchie, 71

Fines (see *Contract Labor*):
    Compromise in case of large amount ... Stump, 19
Foreign governments (see also *European Countries*, and separate countries):
    Enforcement of United States laws by, impracticability ... Hall, 60
    Military service, relation to emigration ... Hall, 60, 62
    Undesirable emigrants, assisted by ... Hall, 60; McSweeney, 87
Garment manufacture, conditions ... Rosendale, 196
German-Americans, educational test, favored by ... Schulteis, 25
Germany:
    Desirability of immigration from ... Powderly, 41
    Emigration restricted by ... Stump, 22
    Illiteracy, percentage low ... Stump, 6
    Number of immigrants from, understated ... Schulteis, 30
    Russia, law prohibiting entrance from ... Stump, 14
Glavis, Dr.:
    Lobbying against restrictive legislation ... Schulteis, 25
    Relation to Immigration Bureau ... Stump, 20
Great Britain (see also *England; Ireland*):
    Assisted emigration from ... McSweeney, 87
    Insane, care of ... Brown, 213
    Societies for assisting emigrants ... Hall, 60
    Temporary immigration of skilled labor from ... Quinlan, 122, 123
Greeks:
    Padrone system among immigrants ... Stump, 8
    Undesirability as immigrants ... Schulteis, 23
Hazelton strike referred to ... Powderly, 34
Head tax:
    Applies to all alien passengers ... McSweeney, 81
    Calculated as element of cost ... Schwab, 105
    Canada:
        Immigrants coming through, subject to ... Stump, 18
        Immigrants from, largely evade ... Schulteis, 28
    Description of law ... Stump, 12
    Doubling advocated ... McSweeney, 84
    Evasion slight ... Powderly, 38
    Excessive rate deprecated ... Schwab, 102
    Fund sufficient to defray all expenses ... Stump, 12
    Increase discussed ... Schwab, 105, 108;
        Powderly, 38–40; Schulteis, 24, 31; Hall, 52
    Steamship companies pay, but add to passage money .. Powderly, 40; Stump, 18
Hirsch fund:
    Charities and colonies ... Wolf, 245, 246, 254
    Emigration to United States not assisted by ... Stump, 13
Hirsch Immigration Society, Jews, assistance of immigration by .. Powderly, 36
Hungarians:
    Anthracite miners ... Rosendale, 188, 189, 191
    Care of, in New York, by home government ... Ritter, 219–222
    Coal mines, employment in ... Powderly, 32, 33
    Colonization in Pennsylvania ... Stump, 22
    Illiteracy, percentage ... Stump, 7
    Pennsylvania, reasons for nonassimilation ... Senner, 185, 186
    True nationality of "Huns" ... Senner, 186
    Undesirability as immigrants ... Schulteis, 23
Idiots, exclusion of immigrant ... Brown, 210
Illinois, criminality of foreign-born in ... Senner, 174
Illiteracy of immigrants:
    Coal miners, Pennsylvania ... Rosendale, 189, 191
    Decline in 1897 ... Stump, 7

Illiteracy of immigrants—Continued.
   Northern European countries, percentage low........................ Stump, 6, 7
   Northwestern and southeastern Europe, compared .... Hall, 50
   Questions concerning, not specially authorized by law................ Stump, 17
   Slums of cities, proportion of... Hall, 56
   Southern European countries, percentage high .... Stump, 7
Immigration Bureau (see also *Commissioners of Immigration; Inspection*):
   Civil service law, application to................................. Fitchie, 72, 73, 75
   Customs service, should be entirely distinct from..................... Stump, 15
   New York—
      Officers in charge of... Fitchie, 72
      Organization of... Fitchie, 72
Immigration fund, proposed amendment of law .... McSweeney, 98
Immigration Restriction League:
   Organization and purposes... Hall, 46
   Referred to... Senner, 181
Immigration Protective League, strength and objects.......... Senner, 181, 187
Immoral persons:
   Exclusion advocated .... Ullo, 142
   Women, exclusion advocated............... McSweeney, 79, 97; Stucklen, 146
Indiana, criminality of foreign-born in .... Senner, 175
Inducements to immigration (see also *Causes of Immigration*), railroads and landowners have discontinued .... Schwab, 104
Industrial depression:
   Immigration, relation to... Hall, 58
   Money sent to Europe by immigrants as cause.................... Allen, 162–164
Insane:
   Assisted to emigrate by foreign Governments .... Brown, 211
   Cost of maintenance discussed .... Brown, 205–207
   Cost of support, decrease of, New York............................ Brown, 218
   Deportation of immigrants, difficulty of .... Brown, 207–209
   Diet of .... Brown, 216
   Exclusion of immigrants.. Brown, 210
      Proposed amendments to law .... Brown, 211, 212
   Expense of care, New York................................... Brown, 202, 204
   Farms, employment on..................................... Brown, 215, 216
   Foreign born—
      Expense of care in New York............................... Brown, 205–207
      Prevalence among, New York.................................. Brown, 204
      Proportion compared with native born .... Hall, 51, 52
   Great Britain, care of.. Brown, 214
   Immigrants—
      Difficulty of determining when insanity originated .... Brown, 208
      Insufficient inspection and exclusion .... Brown, 204–207
      Increase in number discussed....................................... Brown, 203
      Inspection of immigrants, possibility of, satisfactory........... Brown, 212, 213
      Japanese, deportation of.. Brown, 208
      Local authorities, abuse in care of................................ Brown, 202
   New York—
      Care of, described.. Brown, 202, 208
      Support by State.. Brown, 214
   Number of, New York .... Brown, 204
   Proportion to total population in different countries........Brown, 211, 214, 215
   Proportion to total population in different sections .... Brown, 213, 214
   State authorities attempt to put expenses upon other States........ Brown, 207
   State care of, advantage .... Brown, 218
   State responsibility for care, advantage discussed............. Brown, 202–204
   Steamship companies, responsibility for deportation................ Brown, 215
   Support of, by private individuals and State .... Brown, 204
   Work of, New York.. Brown, 215
Insanity, age at which manifested .... Brown, 209
   Causes of... Brown, 209, 210
   Irish, prevalence among.. Brown, 213
   Marriage of cousins, relation to .... Brown, 210
Inspection of immigrants (see also *Landing, Manifests; Medical Inspection; Statistics*):
   Board of special inquiry—
      Appeals from decisions.. Holman, 134

INDEX TO TESTIMONY ON IMMIGRATION.

Inspection of immigrants—Continued.
Board of special inquiry—Continued.
Constitution and methods of work........... Holman, 134; Weihe, 150, 151; Fitchie, 70; McSweeney, 90
Discretionary powers as to exclusion and admission advocated.... McSweeney, 99; Holman, 136, 137
Methods of work .... Holman, 134
Proportion of immigrants coming before .... McSweeney, 90
Cabin passengers—
Contract laborers, investigation concerning .... Dobler, 149, 150
Insufficient number of inspectors .... Dobler, 148
Methods of .... Dobler, 147–150
Children, treatment by matron's department .... Stucklen, 146
Contract labor, methods described.............. Quinlan, 120–125; Holman, 135
Courts, no appeal from inspectors to................................. Ullo, 141
Detention, feeding of immigrants during......................... McSweeney, 86
Detention, length of... Weihe, 151
Evasion of, rare... Dobler, 148
False testimony during, should be punished as purjury .... McSweeney, 99
Foreign ports, inspectors at, advocated .... Powderly, 35
History and description of system .... McSweeny, 76, 81
Insane, desirability of more thorough .... Brown, 212, 213
Interpreters, insufficient at present............................. Senner, 180, 181
Matron's department, methods and results .... Stucklen, 145, 146
Medical, at New York, methods and working ..... Stump, 10; Powderly, 35, 38; Fitchie, 71–72; McSweeney, 85; Williams, 126–128; Safford, 130, 131, 132
By steamship companies and foreign authorities. Powderly, 35; Schwab, 105, 106, 107, 113; Ter Kuile, 115; Floyd, 117; Williams, 126, 129, 130; Safford, 132
Methods—
Delay and difficulty... Senner, 168, 169, 180
Described, especially at New York ...... Fitchie, 70–72; McSweeney, 82–85
Immigrants questioned in their own language .... McSweeney, 84, 101
Impossibility of mingling with immigrants pending.............. Rossi, 155
Impossibility of securing accurate answers to questions .... Hall, 58
Inspectors, power to admit final .... McSweeney, 90
Present, satisfactory .... Hall, 63; Ullo, 139
Unsatisfactory .... Schulteis, 27
New York, transfer from State to national authorities .... McSweeney, 76, 85
Number of immigrants, accuracy of count discussed. Schulteis, 27; McSweeney, 81
Oaths, power to administer, advocated .... McSweeney, 97
Pregnant women, number, proportion unmarried and treatment .. Stucklen, 146

Proportion of immigrants detained in different cases........ McSweeney, 95, 96
Registry clerks, character of work .... McSweeney, 82, 84
Steamship companies, few complaints concerning...................... Ullo, 139
Steerage passengers, communication with, pending.............. Dobler, 149, 150
Surgeons of vessels, inspected by....................................... Fitchie, 72
Women, false evidence as to marriage............................. Powderly, 43
Inspectors of immigrants:
Appeal from decision advocated .... Fitchie, 75
Civil-service rules as to appointment .... Fitchie, 72, 73, 75
Contract labor, increase of, advocated .... Quinlan, 123, 125
Foreign languages, need of command by..................... Senner, 169, 170, 181
Incompetency of... Senner, 169, 170
Knowledge of European conditions and character necessary......... Senner, 170
Political influence in appointment .... Fitchie, 73–74
Intelligence offices. (See *Employment agencies.*)
Interpreters, inspection, insufficient at present .... Senner, 180, 181
Ireland, illiteracy in, percentage low .... Stump, 6
Irish:
Anthracite miners .... Rosendale, 188, 189
Insane immigrants .... Brown, 205
Insanity among.. Brown, 213
Italian bureau of immigration:
Character and working.. Powderly, 43; Hall, 64; McSweeney, 86–89; Rossi, 154–160
Efficiency of work.. Rossi, 157

814 INDEX TO TESTIMONY ON IMMIGRATION.

Italian bureau of immigration—Continued. Page.
  Interference with inspection, alleged .... McSweeney, 89; Wiehe; Holman, 135
    Denied .... Rossi, 155
  Maintenance deprecated .... Wiehe, 153
  Padrone system, effect in checking evils .... Rossi, 154-157
  Unnecessary and disadvantageous .... Holman, 135
  Work must be done in barge office .... Rossi, 157
Italians:
  Anthracite miners .... Rosendale, 188, 189, 191
  Cities, tendency toward .... Hall, 54-56
  Coal mines, character and effects of employment .... Powderly, 32, 33
  Convicts furnished with penal certificates by Government .... Rossi, 158
  Decreasing proportion return to Europe .... Ter Kuile, 115
  Desirable character as immigrants .... Senner, 170
  Educational test, effect on immigration of .... Powderly, 40
  Government agency for assisting on landing .... McSweeney, 86-89
  Illiteracy—
    Criminality, pauperism, etc .... Hall, 50-53
    Percentage .... Stump, 7
  Improvement in character, recent .... Ter Kuile, 115
  Increase in immigration due to restriction agitation .... Senner, 167
  Increase in number of immigrants .... Hall, 50, 67
  Money sent back by immigrants .... Rossi, 156, 160; Allen, 162, 163
  Moral character .... Hall, 53
  Naturalization, little inclination toward .... Hall, 57
  Northeastern States, tendency toward, causes .... Hall, 55
  Northern and southern, distinction between .... Hall, 67
  Not desired in any section .... Hall, 57
  Number coming in defiance of law, decreasing .... Ter Kuile, 115
  Number of immigrants, understated .... Schulteis, 30
  Pauperism rare .... Stump, 11
  Permanent immigration increasing .... Senner, 170
  San Raphael Society, work of .... Ter Kuile, 116
  Southern, illiteracy, poverty, etc .... Hall, 67
  Temporary character of immigration .... Hall, 52
    Reasons for .... Rossi, 160
  Temporary immigration from Great Britain .... Quinlan, 122, 123
Italy:
  Emigration law, summarized .... Schwab, 114
  Government—
    Attitude toward emigration .... Ter Kuile, 115, 116
    Encouragement of immigration by .... Stump, 14; McSweeney, 89
      Denied .... Rossi, 154, 158, 160
  Illiteracy in, high .... Stump, 7; Schulteis, 23
  Law prohibits embarkation of excluded emigrants .... Ter Kuile, 116
  Residence of immigrants from, temporary .... Stump, 14
  Steamship agents, punishment by Government .... Rossi, 156, 159
  United States laws, enforcement required by Government ...... Rossi, 158
Jews:
  Agriculture, aversion to, and causes .... Rosendale, 194, 195
  Anthracite miners .... Rosendale, 188, 189
  Antisemitic agitation, effect on immigration .... Hall, 49
  Assimilation and Americanization .... Senner, 185
  Austria, condition in .... Wolf, 254
  Charities .... Wolf, 245-255
  Colonies, agricultural .... Wolf, 246, 247, 254
  Educational work .... Wolf, 248-250, 254
  Hirsch fund aiding emigration to United States denied. Stump, 13; Powderly, 36
    Charities and colonies of .... Wolf, 245, 254
  Illiteracy .... Rosendale, 192, 197
  Immigrants, number and sources .... Wolf, 252, 253
  Immigration of, amount .... Powderly, 36; Wolf, 245-255
  Jewish immigration not encouraged by .... Wolf, 245-247, 249
  Pauperism rare .... Stump, 11
  Pauperism relieved chiefly by private charity .... Hall, 63
  Philadelphia, economic and social conditions .... Rosendale, 192-197
  Population statistics .... Wolf, 250

INDEX TO TESTIMONY ON IMMIGRATION. 815

Jews—Continued. Page.
  Race classification not intended to discriminate against...... McSweeney, 91, 92
  Roumania, condition in... Wolf, 247, 253
  Russia—
    Emigration from, reduced .... Stump, 14
    Persecution in... Wolf, 245, 251–254
    Reasons for severe laws... Stump, 22
  Russian—
    Assisted emigration of........................... Shulteis, 29; Senner, 171
    Character as workingmen.. Schulteis, 29
    Educational test, effect on immigration .... Schulteis, 29; Powderly, 42
    European countries restrict immigration .... Schulteis, 28
    Only Jewish object of charity.. Wolf, 248
    Paupers, supported by wealthy Jews........................... Schulteis, 29
    Undesirability as immigrants..................................... Powderly, 36
  Sweatshop workers... Wolf, 251
  Zionist movement.. Wolf, 254
Labor organizations:
  Contract labor, objection to .... Weihe, 153
  Little assistance in enforcing law......................... Quinlan, 120, 121
  Employment found for members .... Bealin, 223, 224, 229; Hotchkiss, 241
  Immigration, restriction favored by........................ Rosendale, 197, 198
  Information to intending immigrants should be furnished by..... Powderly, 41
  Opposition to immigration due to misinformation.................... Senner, 184
  Skilled labor, opposition to immigration of............................ Hall, 65
Landing of immigrants (see also *Inspection*):
  Certificate of landing advocated; contents......................... Powderly, 45
  Charitable organizations, assistance granted by .... McSweeney, 85
  Description of process .... Stump, 9, 10
  Italian and Austrian agencies for assisting................... McSweeney, 86, 87
Lands, public, advertised as inducement by steamship companies.... Schulteis, 24
Legislation (see also *Inspection; Restriction*):
  Aliens and alien immigrants, distinction between..................... Ullo, 141
  Amendments proposed discussed................................. Fitchie, 71–75
  Amendments proposed by immigration investigating commission ......
                                                                                                             McSweeney, 97, 100
  Amendments suggested by special commission of 1895.................. Stump, 4
  Conflicting and indefinite provisions of laws...... McSweeney, 80; Ullo, 138, 141
  History of.. McSweeney, 76–78; Ullo, 138
  Law of 1893, effect and working .... Stump, 9; McSweeney, 77–80
  Lodge bill .... Stump, 21; Schulteis, 29
  Restrictive effect of existing... Senner, 168
  Revision, general—
    Advocated .... Ullo, 141
    Deprecated .... Senner, 169
  Steamship companies, opposition to.......... Stump, 19; Hall, 61; Schwab, 107
Liquor dealers, employment agencies kept by .... Bealin, 224; Hotchkiss, 237
Liverpool, medical inspection, methods at........................... Williams, 126
Lodge bill:
  History in Congress... Schulteis, 29
  Referred to .... Stump, 21
Manifests of immigrants:
  Additional questions, requirement advocated .... McSweeney, 98
  Cabin passengers, required of .... Powderly, 37
  Causes of discrepancies .... McSweeney, 81
  Certain questions answered carelessly............................ McSweeney, 101
  Evasion of law by steamship companies........................ Powderly, 37, 38
  Impossibility of error and deception .... McSweeney, 92
  Improved paper and ink desired................................. McSweeney, 101
  Manner of preparing and contents .... Stump, 9; McSweeney, 81
  Penalty for failure of company to prepare....................... McSweeney, 99
  Preparation on board vessel advocated .... Powderly, 37
  Questions asked immigrants on buying ticket.................... McSweeney, 77
  Requirement as to outgoing passengers advocated............... McSweeney, 97
  Sworn to in blank.. Hall, 60
  Working of system discussed................................. Powderly, 36, 37
Manufactures, effect of immigration on .... Powderly, 42

Page.
Massachusetts, criminality of foreign born in .... Senner, 174
Matron's department, methods and results of inspection........ Stucklen, 145, 146
Medical inspection:
    Bathing and disinfection on embarkation advocated .... Safford, 132;
                                                                                    Williams, 129, 130
    Cunard Steamship Company... Floyd, 117
    England, insufficiency .... Powderly, 35
    Examination on embarkation by United States physicians advocated..
                                                                                     Powderly, 35
    Insufficiency of present system...................................... Powderly, 35
    Liverpool, methods at... Williams, 126
    Methods of... Stump, 10;
        Fitchie, 71, 72; McSweeney, 85; Williams, 126–128; Safford, 130–132
        Efficiency of... Safford, 132
    Minor defects, record of .... Safford, 131
    Naples, character of .... Ter Kuile, 115
    North German Lloyd Steamship Company, methods....... Schwab, 105, 106, 113
    Number of cases in May, 1899....................................... Safford, 131
    Steamship companies, character of .... Williams, 129
    Thorough, advocated .... Powderly, 38
    Vessels, during passage .... Schwab, 106, 107
Mennonites, immigration due to desire for liberty...................... Senner, 183
Michigan, criminality of foreign born in.............................. Senner, 175
Military service, hinders desirable immigrants from coming........... Hall, 60, 62
Miners. (See *Coal mines.*)
Minnesota, criminality of foreign born in............................. Senner, 175
Missouri, criminality of foreign born in.............................. Senner, 175
Molly Maguires, character of movement .... Powderly, 35
Money brought by immigrants:
    Additional information concerning amount brought, advocated . McSweeney, 98
    Amount, estimated .... Stump, 17
    Incorrectness of statistics... Senner, 173
    Nationalities, comparison by... Hall, 52
    Repeated use of same funds .... Stump, 8
Nationality of foreign-born coal miners, Pennsylvania..... Rosendale, 188–192
Nationality of immigrants (see also separate nationalities, *Huns, Italians, Jews, Poles, etc.*):
    Changes, recent cause of... Senner, 167, 168
    Northern Europe, decrease due to restrictive effect of law........... Senner, 168
    Opinions as to relative desirability....................................... Hall, 57
    Race, substitution for political divisions in statistics discussed..............
        McSweeney, 82, 83, 91, 92; Senner, 187; Safford, 131, 132; Eichler, 133
    Statistics, unreliability of former........... McSweeney, 82, 83, 91; Schulteis, 30
        Denied.. Safford, 130
Naturalization:
    Ability to read advocated... Schwab, 108
    Ability to read and write English advocated...................... Powderly, 108
    Aliens allowed to vote.. Hall, 62
    Anthracite miners .... Rosendale, 188
    Educational test advocated .... Powderly, 45;
                                                                     Holman, 136; Senner, 183
    Evasion of laws .... Powderly, 44, 45
    Landing certificates and records, requirement advocated.......... Powderly, 45
    Proportion among different nationalities.............................. Hall, 57
    Question distinct from that of immigration........................... Stump, 22
    Suffrage before, deprecated .... Senner, 183
New York City (see also *Inspection of immigrants*):
    Chinese landing at.. Allen, 165
    Convict labor, working of system............................... Brown, 216–218
    Criminality of foreign born in .... Senner, 174
    Insane, cost of care .... Brown, 204–207, 218
    Insane, support by State .... Brown, 214
    Russian Jews, settlement in....................................... McSweeney, 94
    Sweating trade, employment of immigrants in.................... McSweeney, 94
    Work of insane .... Brown, 215
New York free employment bureau........................... Bealin, 223, 224

INDEX TO TESTIMONY ON IMMIGRATION. 817

New York State commission in lunacy: Page.
  Powers and work discussed... Brown, 202, 204
  Work of .... Brown, 218
North German Lloyd Steamship Company:
  Control stations, medical examination at......................... Schwab, 105, 113
  Immigration, methods of business, etc .... Schwab, 101, 114
  Medical inspection, methods...................................... Schwab, 105, 106
Northeastern States, tendency of immigration toward, and causes .... Hall, 55
Northwestern States, educational test favored by......................... Hall, 66
Norway, illiteracy, percentage low.. Stump, 6
Number of Immigrants (see also *Statistics of immigration*):
  Canada, immigrants from, not counted............................ Schulteis, 28
    Number coming through, unknown............................... Powderly, 37
  Causes of decrease.. Senner, 167, 168
  Census statistics understate....................................... Schulteis, 30
  Count, numbers too low.. Schulteis, 27, 30
    Accuracy affirmed .... McSweeney, 81; Eichler, 133
  Decrease since 1894, causes.................... Stump, 9; Senner, 167, 168
  Nationality, statistics incorrect.................................... Schulteis, 30;
                                 McSweeney, 82, 91; Senner, 173, 179
    Denied... Safford, 132
    Variations in numbers, by years .... Hall, 50
Occupations of immigrants:
  Classes and number of each..................................... Hall, 48, 50
  Farmers, misleading term....................................... Hall, 50, 65
  Skilled and unskilled labor, relative proportions................. Hall, 50, 54
  Skilled labor, proportion, by nationalities........................ Hall, 54
  Unreliability of statistics.. McSweeney, 82
  Unskilled, undesirability of attempt to exclude................... Hall, 65
Ohio, criminality of foreign born in.................................... Senner, 175
Padrone system:
  Armenians and Greeks .... McSweeney, 83, 88
  Bankers—
    Failures of.. Rossi, 156
    Functions of... Schulteis, 30, 31
    Italian, relation to .... Powderly, 43
  Coal mines—
    Evasion of contract labor law in............................. Powderly, 33
    Prevalence in, and description .... Powderly, 44
  Contract labor law has largely destroyed......................... Stump, 8
  Contracts no longer made in Italy .... McSweeney, 88
  Described generally .... Stump, 8
  Existence of practice... Rossi, 159
    Among Syrians, Turks, Greeks, etc.............................. Stump, 8
    Decreased importance....................................... Ter Kuile, 115, 116
    Suppression only partial...................................... Schulteis, 30, 31
  Italian Immigration Bureau, effort to check abuses.............. Powderly, 43;
                                McSweeney, 86, 87; Rossi, 154–157
  Letters of introduction from correspondents in Italy .... Rossi, 155
  Preferences of Italian immigrants for .... McSweeney, 87
Panic of 1893, money sent to Europe by immigrants as cause...... Allen, 162, 163
Pauperism of foreign born, proportion compared with native born .. Hall, 51, 52
Pauperism of immigrants:
  Assisted emigration decreased................................... Powderly, 35
  Bonding of immigrants—
    Discussed...................................... Powderly, 41; Fitchie, 71, 75, 76
    Evasion of liability.. Powderly, 45
    Extension to two years advocated .... McSweeney, 84
    Impossibility of identifying paupers .... Hall, 63, 64
    Impracticability of system .... Hall 63, 64
    Increased duration discussed................................. Schwab, 108
  Causes, New York City.. Brown, 235
  Deportation—
    Time limit for return of, should be extended.................. Schulteis, 26
    Within one year of landing advocated........... McSweeney, 97; Ullo, 144
  Existing laws, sufficient protection............................... Senner, 184
  Expenses in almshouse borne by immigration bureau............. Stump, 11

Pauperism of immigrants—Continued.
 Jews .... Rosendale, 195, 201
 Landing certificates of applicants for aid .... Powderly, 45
 Small proportion .... Stump, 11
 Steamship companies must return paupers .... Stump, 11
Pennsylvania, criminality of foreign born in.......................... Senner, 174
Perjury, false testimony during inspection should be punished as.. McSweeney, 99
Poles:
 Buffalo, character of population .... Hall, 59
 Buffalo, colony at, described .... Senner, 171
 Character as immigrants .... Hall, 59; Senner, 186
 Coal mines, employment in .... Powderly, 32, 33
 Colonization in Pennsylvania .... Stump, 22
 Desirable character as immigrants .... Senner, 171
Politics, employment controlled by local leaders .... Bealin, 224, 229
Polygamists:
 Impossibility of proving .... McSweeney, 90
 Mormons, immigration of .... McSweeney, 90
Portugal, illiteracy, percentage .... Stump, 7
Pregnant women, number, proportion unmarried, and treatment ... Stucklen, 146
Prepaid tickets:
 Desirable character of immigrants coming on .... Schwab, 104
 Instructions to agents concerning excluded classes .... Schwab, 104
 Limitation to authorized steamship agents, advocated .... McSweeney, 95, 97
 Proportion of immigrants coming on .... McSweeney, 95
 Proportion of steerage passengers coming on .... Schwab, 104;
                   Ter Kuile, 115; Lederer, 118
 Sale by peddlers on installment plan .... McSweeney, 95
 Solicitation of business impossible .... Lederer, 119; Schwab, 107
Prices, coal, relation to wages of miners .... Rosendale, 190
Property test, not satisfactory test of character .... Schwab, 102
Prosecutions. (See *Contract labor.*)
Prosperity, relation of immigration to .... Stump, 3; Hall, 49; Senner, 179, 180, 182
Prostitutes:
 Immigrants .... Ritter, 222
 Power to exclude, advocated .... McSweeney, 79, 97; Stucklen, 146
Public opinion, opposition to restriction of immigration .... Senner, 181
Race classification of immigrants:
 Substitution for nationality .... McSweeney, 82, 83, 91, 92
 Advantages of .... Safford, 131, 132; Eichler, 133
 Errors in methods .... Senner, 187
 Misleading effects of change .... Senner, 187
 Not intended to discriminate, against Jews .... McSweeney, 91, 92
 Questions concerning religion to ascertain .... McSweeney, 92
Race colonies in cities, causes .... Rosendale, 195, 196
Railroads, inducements to immigration by .... Schulteis, 24; Schwab, 104
Rathbun, Iowa, contract laborers going to .... Quinlan, 123
Red Star Steamship Line, immigration, conditions concerning.. Lederer, 118, 119
Relatives of immigrants (see also *Prepaid tickets*):
 Assistance and inducement to immigrate .... Hall, 49
 Inducements to migrate by, relation to contract-labor law .... Quinlan, 124;
                    Powderly, 33, 141; Ullo, 143
Religion, anthracite miners .... Rosendale, 188
Restriction of immigration (see also *Contagious diseases; Educational test; Inspection; Legislation*):
 Austria-Hungary, attitude toward .... Ritter, 222
 Causes, impossibility of controlling .... Senner, 167
 Criminals, exclusion discussed .... Hall, 58;
           McSweeney, 79, 80; Ullo, 141, 142; Senner, 185
 Deprecated .... Senner, 169
 Diseased and insane persons, proposed amendments .... Brown, 212
 Epileptic and weak-minded persons, discussed .... Brown, 210, 211
 Evils existing, not remedied by .... Senner, 180, 184
 Excluded classes—
  Different acts, definition under .... McSweeney, 77, 78
  Discretionary power with immigration officers, advocated .... Holman, 136
  Families, interference with, by exclusion of individuals .... McSweeney, 78
  Hardships in some cases .... McSweeney, 78, 80

Restriction of immigration—Continued. Page.
  Immigrants desired in certain parts of country.................. Senner, 167
  Immoral persons, power to exclude, advocated .... McSweeney, 79, 80, 99;
      Ullo, 142; Stucklen, 146
  Insane, discussed .... Brown, 210
  Inspection, impossibility of accurate............................ Hall, 58
  Jews, attitude toward.. Wolf, 249
  Labor organizations favored by .... Rosendale, 197, 198; Senner, 184
  Laws, enforcement of existing............................. Rosendale, 200, 201
  Laws, restrictive effect of existing.............................. Senner, 168
  Lodge bill.. Stump, 21; Schulteis, 29
  Property test, not satisfactory................................. Schwab, 102
  Races, exclusion of certain, impracticable......................... Hall, 62
  Temporary immigration, restriction advocated .... Rosendale, 198;
      McSweeney, 80; Allen, 161, 162
Roumania, Jews, condition in.............................. Wolf, 247, 253
Russia (see also *Jews*):
  German law prohibiting entrance from .... Stump, 14
  Illiteracy, percentage... Stump, 7
  Jews, emigration from, reduced................................. Stump, 14
  Jews, persecution of .... Wolf, 245, 251–254; Senner, 171
Russians, undesirability as immigrants .... Schulteis, 23
Sailors, kidnaping by crimps........................... Rosendale, 193
St. Bartholmew's Employment Bureau, methods........ Hotchkiss, 236, 240, 241
Sanitary regulations, enforcement of....................... Rosendale, 196, 201
Scandinavians:
  Colonization in Western States................................ Stump, 22
  Desirability as immigrants....................... Powderly, 41; Schulteis, 29
  Northwestern States, settlement in............................. Hall, 54
Schools:
  Attendance, anthracite region, Pennsylvania............. Rosendale, 189, 191
  Attendance in slum districts, Philadelphia .... Rosendale, 192
Senner, J. H.:
  Influence against restrictive legislation......................... Schulteis, 25
  Nationality, attitude toward immigration, etc.................... Senner, 173
Skilled labor:
  Effect of immigration, slight................................... Powderly, 42
  Labor unions, objection to immigration.......................... Hall, 65
  Wages, not affected by unskilled .... Senner, 183
Slums of cities:
  Immigrants in, by nationalties................................. Hall, 56
  Sanitary regulations, enforcement, difficulties.................. Rosendale, 201
Socialism, American workmen, attitude toward .... Powderly, 45, 46
Southeastern Europe, immigration from, statistics and diagrams...... Hall, 48–50
State authorities, opinions as to desirability of immigrants............ Hall, 57
State bureaus of immigration, cooperation in distribution of immigrants
  advocated .... Powderly, 39
States:
  Exhibition of products and assistance to immigration advocated.......
      Senner, 174, 186; McSweeney, 96
  Immigration, impracticability of regulating by.................... Hall, 62
  Immigration bureaus in Europe................................. Senner, 182
Statistics of immigration (see also *Number of Immigrants; Nationality*):
  Accuracy of—
    Existing methods, satisfactory.............................. Eichler, 133
    Former.. Senner, 173, 179
    Unreliability as to various subjects....................... Schulties, 30;
      McSweeney, 82, 91; Safford, 132; Senner, 173, 179
  Destination, incorrectness of .... McSweeney, 82, 91; Senner, 173
    False statements as to.................................... McSweeney, 91
  Ellis Island fire, destruction of records in .... Eichler, 132
  Money brought, incorrectness of .... Senner, 173
  Occupations, unreliability as to............................... McSweeney, 82
  Race, industrial effect of immigration judged by............... McSweeney, 92
  Race classification—
    Advantages of .... Safford, 131, 132; Eichler, 133
    Errors in methods .... Senner, 187

Statistics of immigration—Continued.
  Race classification—Continued.
    Misleading effects of change .... Senner, 187
    Not intended to discriminate against Jews............... McSweeney, 91, 92
    Questions concerning religion, to ascertain .... McSweeney, 92
    Substituted for nationality .... McSweeney, 82, 83, 91, 92
  Ticket agents, cooperation in obtaining............................ Senner, 179
  Variations in numbers and particular years .... Hall, 50
Steamship companies (see also *Steerage traffic; Vessels; Manifests; Tickets*):
  Advertisements, effect on immigration................................ Hall, 49
  Agents—
    Cooperation in obtaining statistics, advocated................... Senner, 179
    Efficient immigration inspectors...................... Stump, 9; Senner, 180
    Instructions concerning excluded classes............. Schwab, 102, 110–113
    License required by European countries .... Schwab, 103
    Responsibility for excluded immigrants....... Schwab, 102, 110; Floyd, 117
  Agreements concerning rates................. Schwab, 103, 107, 109; Floyd, 118
  Canadian, cooperation in enforcing United States law .... Stump, 18
  Capital invested, amount and ownership .... Schulteis, 25, 26
  Contagious diseases, responsibility for return of immigrants having . Fitchie, 71
  Cooperation in enforcing law....................................... Stump, 7–10
  Deportation, liability for.. Schwab, 102
  Deportation of immigrants by, discussed .... Stump, 10; McSweeney, 97, 99;
      Ter Kuile, 115; Floyd, 117; Lederer, 119; Safford, 131; Ullo, 138, 142
  Effort to debar... Weihe, 153
  Excluded classes, care exercised in refusing.. Hall, 61; Schwab, 104; Senner, 168
  Expenses at Ellis Island borne by.................................... Stump, 10
  Expense of detention, dispute as to................................. Stump, 20
  Head tax paid by, but added to passage money .... Stump, 18; Powderly, 40
  Immigrants, right to sue for violation of law, advocated............. Ullo, 143
  Immigrants landed as employees............................... Schulteis, 27, 28
  Immigration legislation laws, attitude toward....................... Stump, 19;
      Schulteis, 24; Schwab, 102, 107; Hall, 61
  Insane immigrants, responsibility for.................... Brown, 208–209, 215
  Inspection of immigrants by agents.................... Floyd, 117; Lederer, 119
    Ineffectiveness of... Schwab, 102, 105
  Manifests prepared by captain and surgeon of vessel .... Stump, 9
  Newspapers influenced by passes and entertainments............. Schulteis, 24
  North German Lloyd, profits of.................................... Schwab, 105
  Penalties on, severer advocated .... Fitchie, 71
  Prepaid tickets, instructions to agents selling .... Schwab, 104
  Profits, excessive.. Schulteis, 25
  Prosecutions conducted before Executive Department............... Stump, 10
  Punishment for willful violation of law, advocated .... Ullo, 142, 143
  Question blanks, form of.. Schwab, 111
  Rates, double passage money charged to doubtful immigrants .... Hall, 61
  Solicitation of immigrants by, discussed .... Stump, 7, 19; Schulteis, 23;
      Schwab, 103; Lederer, 119; Rosendale, 189, 200; Ritter, 221
  Steerage traffic, decreasing importance of .... Schwab, 103
Steerage traffic:
  Air space and sanitary condition .... Williams, 130
  Agreement of steamship company to maintain rates ...... Schwab, 103, 107, 109
  Existing rates stated...... Schwab, 104; Ter Kuile, 115; Floyd, 117; Lederer, 119
  Existing rates higher than in 1880................................. Schwab, 103;
      Ter Kuile, 115; Floyd, 117; Lederer, 119
  Policy in fixing rates .... Schwab, 109
  Reduction of rates and influence in increasing immigration............ Hall, 49
  Relatively decreasing importance................................. Schwab, 103
Stonecutting, effect of immigration................................. Powderly, 42
Suffrage (see also *Naturalization*):
  Aliens allowed to vote before naturalization......................... Hall, 62
  Question distinct from that of naturalization ....Stump, 22
Sweat shops:
  Immigrants, employment in .... McSweeney, 94
  Inspection, difficulties of..................................... Rosendale, 192, 194
  Jews in .... Wolf, 251
  Philadelphia, conditions .... Rosendale, 192, 194

	Page.
Sweden, illiteracy, percentage low	Stump, 6
Switzerland:	
Criminals, assisted immigration from	Stump, 13
Illiteracy, percentage of, low	Stump, 6
Syrians:	
Character and destination of immigrants	McSweeney, 83
Increase of immigrants	Powderly, 36
Padrone system among	Stump, 8; McSweeney, 83, 88
Trachoma common among	Williams, 127, 128
Tariff, relation to restriction of immigration	Rosendale, 197, 200
Temporary immigration:	
Effects not necessarily disadvantageous	Schwab, 108
Evils of, generally	McSweeney, 80; Allen, 161–166
Exclusion of those bringing small amounts of money	Quinlan, 123
Great Britain, skilled labor from	Quinlan, 122, 123
Increasing proportion of	Allen, 166
Italians—	
Character and undesirability of	Quinlan, 122
Decreasing proportion return to Europe	Ter Kuile, 115; Senner, 170
Reasons for	Rossi, 160
Manifests concerning outgoing aliens should be required	McSweeney, 97, 98
Manifests, inquiry concerning, requirement advocated	McSweeney, 98
Money sent out of country by immigrants, evil effects	Allen, 161–166
Amount estimated	Allen, 162
Power to exclude "birds of passage" advocated	McSweeney, 80
Restriction advocated	Allen, 161, 162
Returning passengers, number and causes	Stump, 8
Proportion of immigrants returning	Allen, 161
Theft, employment agencies responsible for	Bealin, 229
Tickets, Steamship (see also *Manifests; Prepaid tickets*):	
Information placed upon, when bought	McSweeney, 77, 92
Question blanks, form of	Schwab, 111
Trachoma:	
Character of disease, number of cases, etc	Fitchie, 71; Williams, 127–129
Instances of evasion of law	Fitchie, 71
Reasons for debarring persons afflicted with	Safford, 132
Turks, padrone system among immigrants	Stump, 8
Unemployment:	
Causes, New York City	Brown, 235
Numbers of unemployed in different cities	Schulteis, 24
Unskilled labor:	
Demand for, large, 1899	McSweeney, 96
Proportion among immigrants	Hall, 54
Undesirability of attempting to exclude	Hall, 65
Vessels (see also *Steamship companies*):	
Air space and condition of steerage	Williams, 130
Inadequate protection of life to immigrants	McSweeney, 94
Wages:	
Anthracite miners, relation to prices of coal	Rosendale, 190
Complexity of influences affecting	Senner, 172
Earning power, increase of	Senner, 172, 176, 177
Increase during the period of greatest immigration	Senner, 172, 176–178
Skilled labor not affected by unskilled	Senner, 183
Statistics regarding	Senner, 176–178
Welsh anthracite miners	Rosendale, 188, 189
Wisconsin, criminality of foreign-born in	Senner, 175
Women:	
Anthracite mines, labor in	Rosendale, 189
Educational test, injustice in applying to	Senner, 169
Evasion of law by	Powderly, 43
Immigrants, false evidence as to marriage	Powderly, 43
Inspection by matron's department	Stump, 10; Stucklen, 145, 146
Prostitutes. (See *Prostitutes.*)	
Unmarried pregnant women, number, etc	Stucklen, 146
Working classes, social condition, slums of Philadelphia	Rosendale, 192–194

INDEX TO SPECIAL REPORTS.

[For index to review of special reports, see p. cxvii; index to testimony, p. 805.]

	Page.
Abandoned farms, settlement by Jews	513
Accidents, coal mining	417–420
Ages of immigrants, relative age distribution:	
Native and foreign born population	295, 296
Various nationalities	296
Agreements between employers and employees:	
Clothing trade	332–334
Coal mining	406
Agricultural distribution of foreign born:	
Adaptability to agricultural life generally	494, 495
Bohemians—	
Colonies, efforts to establish, unsuccessful	508
Success as agriculturists	508, 509
Finns, preference for agricultural life	510
Hollanders	532
Italians, colonies—	
Asti, Cal	500–502
Bryan, Tex	500
Daphne, Ala	504
Lamberth, Ala	504
Memphis, Tenn	503, 504
Montebello, Mo	506
Sunnyside, Ark	505
Tonitown, Ark	506
Verdella, Mo	506
Vineland, N. J	499, 500
Italians—	
Adaptability to agricultural life	498
Aversion to country life, causes	495–497
California	503
Louisiana	503
Mississippi	503
Ruralization, efforts to secure, advantages	498, 499
Japanese and Chinese, Pacific coast	754–758
Jewish Agriculturists' Aid Society of America, objects work	513–516
Jewish colonies—	
Alliance, N. J	511
Carmel, N. J	512
Rosenhayn, N. J	511, 512
Sundry unsuccessful attempts	511, 512
Woodbine, N. J	512, 513
Jews, abandoned farms in New England, settlement on	513
Aversion to country life, reasons for	513
Local distribution by nationalities, separate States	517–646
Opportunities for foreign born as agriculturists, separate States	517–646
Air-space, tenement houses, legislative requirements	374
Alabama	629
Agricultural laborers, wages	629
Foreign-born as agriculturists—	
Nationality of	629
Opportunities	567, 568
Population, density	629

INDEX TO SPECIAL REPORTS.

	Page.
Aliens:	
Employment of—	
Canadians	446
Public works	437–440
Railroads	441, 442
Labor organizations, discrimination against	311–312
Building trades	427–428
Arizona:	
Agricultural laborers, wages	638
Foreign born as agriculturists—	
Nationality of	638
Opportunities	578, 579
Population, density	638
Arkansas:	
Agricultural laborers, wages	634
Foreign born as agriculturists—	
Nationality of	574, 634
Opportunities	573–575
Immigration, attitude of farmers toward	573, 574
Population, density	634
Armenians:	
Distribution, local	445
Number in United States	445
Occupations	445
Assimilation of immigrants:	
Italian, slowness of	474
Sweating system, a means of retarding	321
Bakeries:	
Labor organizations in	428
Machinery, effect	428
Bankers, Italians, relation to the padrone system	433
Basters, wages of, New York City	339
Birds of passage:	
Canadians	448
Permanent settlement of, ultimately	473
Bohemians:	
Agricultural distribution	507–510
Agriculturists, success as	508–509
Cities, tendency toward	508, 509
Clothing trade, characteristics as workers	326
Colonies, efforts to establish	508
Emigration, causes	507, 508
Occupations	508
Boot and shoe trade:	
Chinese, San Francisco	748
Foreign born, percentage of	422
Labor organizations	422
Wages, reduction through introduction of machinery	422
Bricklayers' and Masons' International Union, membership limited to citizens	438
British colonies, immigration to, regulation of	709–722
Building trades:	
Foreign born, employment of, effects	426–428
Hours of labor	426
Labor organizations—	
Discrimination against aliens	427–428
Organized by nationalities	427
Wages	426, 427
Bureau of Immigration, powers extensive	659–661
California:	
Agricultural laborers, wages	645
Foreign-born as agriculturists—	
Nationality of	581, 646
Opportunities	582
Population, density	645
Canada:	
Chinese restriction of immigration	712–715
Clothing, methods of manufacture for public contracts	382–383

INDEX TO SPECIAL REPORTS. 825

	Page.
Canada—Continued.	
Immigration—	
Laws, contract labor	719–722
Regulation of	710–722
Immigration through	681–863
Smuggling of immigrants of	766
Canadians:	
"Birds of passage"	447, 448
Contract laborers, deportation	447
Wages, effect of immigration on	447, 448
Carmel, N. J., colonies of Jews at	512
Carpentry trade labor organizations, organized by nationalities	427
Causes inducing immigration; immigration reflection of the industrial conditions	305, 306
Chicago clothing trade:	
Distribution of workers by nationalities	325
Special-order trade	331, 332
Children, employment in manufacturing establishments	315
Children's clothing, wages of workers on	331
Chinese:	
Canada—	
Immigration through	758
Restriction of immigration	712–715
Criminality	758
Effect on white labor	801–802
Exclusion laws and treaties	671–678, 759–760, 792
Discussion of	795–797, 799
Fruit-packing industry, California	748–749
Highbinders	762–765, 767, 769–771, 775–782, 791, 793–794
Letters of instruction to salaried soldier	771
Letters of warning	775
Letters to officers of Chee Kong Tong Society	775
Illegal immigration	769–771, 800
Lawyers, San Francisco	762
Mining, number employed in, Western States	753–754
Number admitted and rejected, 1897–1899	760–762
Public works, employment prohibited, British Columbia	715
Railroads, employment on, Mountain and Pacific States	749–752
San Francisco, Chinatown, industries in	747–748
Slave girls	767
Bill of sale	771–772
Catechism used in coaching for landing	772
Statement of matron of Chinese Rescue Home	786–789
Testimony of	773–774, 783–785, 789–791
Cigar-making trade:	
Chinese, Pacific coast cities	748
Foreign born, employment of—	
Nationality of	385, 748
Number of	385
Labor organizations, union label	387
Wages—	
Country competition, effect	387, 388
Employment of foreign born, effect of	385, 388
Immigration, effect of	385, 388
Labor organizations, effect of	387
Rates of	386–389
Women, employment of, effect	388
Cities, tendency toward, foreign born:	
Bohemians	508
Early manifestation	449
Reasons for	492
Cloak making:	
Labor organizations in	329
New York City, centered in	329
Wages in	329–342
Clothing cutters, unions of	334
Clothing trade:	
Agreements between employers and employees	332–334

Clothing trade—Continued.   Page.
  Chicago—
    Distribution of workers by nationalities............................ 325
    Special-order trade 331, 332
  Chinese, San Francisco 748
  Cloak making, centered in New York City.............................. 329
  Consumers' League, work of 384
  Contractors' organizations 334
  Employment, average number of days, New York City................. 338–342
  Evolution of 368
  Factory system... 348–367
    Conditions in typical establishments............................ 349–367
    Cost of production reduced by................................... 368
  Foreign born, employment of—
    Distribution by nationality..................................... 317
    Number employed... 316
    Percentage of 319
    Sex distribution.. 317
  Foreign-born workers, characteristics—
    Bohemians 326
    Germans... 326
    Italians... 325, 326, 329
    Jews 325
    Poles... 326
    Scandinavians... 326
  Hours of labor 337, 338
  Labor disputes 328–330
  Labor organizations 327–335, 371, 384
    Cloak makers' unions.. 329
    Clothing cutters' unions 334
    Coat makers' union.. 328
    Custom Clothing Makers' Union of America 332
    Custom Tailors' Union... 334
    Difficulty of forming... 371–372
    Jewish unions... 327, 329, 334, 335
    Knee-pants makers' unions....................................... 330
    Pants makers' union... 328
    Tailors, central and national organizations of.................. 332
    Tenement-house workers, difficulty of forming 371, 372
    Union label... 335, 384
  New York City—
    Development of the trade, history............................... 324
    Nationalities employed.................................... 317, 324, 330
    Product, amount of.. 318
  Philadelphia, wages... 723–743
  Public contracts, restriction on methods of manufacture—
    Canada.. 382, 383
    Great Britain 383
    United States 382
  Sweating system 319–324
    Assimilation of immigrants retarded by.......................... 321
    Cause of system... 322
    Evils inherent 324
    Foreign born, employment of, changes due to 320
    Hours of labor 321
    Responsibility of employer, difficulty of fixing 321, 322
    Subcontracting.. 319, 320
  Tailors, immigrant—
    Number entering the country, 1875–1890.......................... 317–318
    Race distribution... 317
  Task system 345–348
    Contractors' profits.. 347
    Cost of production reduced by 368
    Methods... 345–346
    Wages, generally.. 345–347
    Wages, typical establishments................................... 347, 348

Clothing trade—Continued. Page.
  Tenement-house work.. 369–383
    Air space, regulation..................................... 374
    Articles subject to restrictions........................... 374, 375
    Classes of work.. 369, 370
    Condition of workers..................................... 370
    Contagious diseases, precautions.......................... 378, 379
    Foreign born, employment of............................. 369
    Insanitary conditions..................................... 373
    Labeling of goods.. 377, 378
    Labor organizations, difficulty of forming................. 371, 372
    Landlord, placing of legal responsibility on............... 379, 380
    Legislative restrictions................................... 374–380
      Effects of.. 380
      Penalties.. 379
    Licensing.. 375, 376
    New Zealand, legislative restrictions..................... 378
    Prohibition of—
      Efforts to secure..................................... 381
      Reasons for and against......................... 372, 373, 380, 381
    Registry of tenements and sweat shops................... 375
    Sanitary conditions, regulation........................... 375, 376
    Standard of living reduced by............................ 373
    Subcontract system....................................... 371
    Tenement, legal definition............................... 374
    Wages... 370
  Wages.. 327, 370
    Basters, New York City.................................. 339
    Children's clothing workers.............................. 331
    Cloak makers.. 329, 342
    Clothing cutters... 334, 339
    Coat makers.. 328, 339, 344
    Custom tailors, New York City........................... 342
    Factory system.. 348–367
    Finishers, New York City................................ 340
    Jacket makers, New York City........................... 341
    Knee pants makers...................................... 330, 342
    Massachusetts, average weekly........................... 337
    Movement of, generally.................................. 368
    New York City, General statistics........................ 336–342
    Pants makers.. 328, 341
    Philadelphia... 723–743
    Pressers, New York City................................. 340
    Special order trade...................................... 331, 332
    Task system... 345–348
    Vest makers, New York City............................. 340
Coal mining:
  Accidents—
    Causes.. 418–420
      Nationality of miners injured, Pennsylvania, 1898....... 418
      Number of, by years, Pennsylvania.................... 417
  Agreements between employers and employees............. 406
  Employees, in bituminous mines, total number............. 403
  Employment, amount—
    Average number of days............................ 394, 395–397–415
    Compared with other industries........................ 395, 396
    Irregularity, seasonal.................................... 396
    United States... 394
    Various States..................................... 394, 395, 397, 410
  Foreign-born workers—
    Nationality, various States....................... 391–392, 393, 407, 414
    Number, various States.......................... 391–392, 393, 407
  Labor disputes, strike of 1897............................. 404
  Labor organizations—
    Foreign-born labor, effect of.............................. 407
    History... 405

Coal mining—Continued.
  Labor organizations—Continued.
    Restrictions imposed by... 410, 411
    Wages, effect on.. 404–408
  Machine mining—
    Prices of coal, effect on.. 399–402
    Product, total mined by... 398
    Skill, effect on... 399–402
    Wages, effect on.. 399–402, 404
  Output of coal by years—
    Illinois.. 403
    Indiana... 403
    Ohio.. 403
    Pennsylvania... 397, 403
    United States... 394, 403
    West Virginia.. 403
  Wages—
    Labor organizations, effect of..................................... 404–408
    Machinery, effect of.. 399–402, 404
    Movement of... 412–416
    Rates of, in various States.. 409, 414, 416
    Strike of 1897, effects of.. 408–409
Coat makers, wages of, New York City................................. 328–329–334
Coat Makers Union, clothing trade..................................... 328
Collective bargaining. (See *Agreements between employers and employees.*)
Colonies of foreign born:
  Agricultural—
    Finns... 510
    Italians... 499–506
    Jews.. 510–517
  Bohemians... 508
  Chinese.. 747–748
  Jews... 511–513
Colorado:
  Foreign-born as agriculturists—
    Nationality... 637
    Opportunities.. 576–578
  Immigration, attitude of farmers toward............................ 577
  Population, density.. 636
Competition, country wages, effect on.................................. 316
Conciliation. (See *Agreements between employers and employees.*)
Connecticut:
  Agricultural laborers, wages... 589
  Foreign-born as agriculturists—
    Nationality... 523, 589
    Opportunities.. 523, 524
  Immigration, attitude of farmers toward............................ 523
  Population, density.. 589
Consumers' League, work of... 384
Contagious diseases:
  Clothing trade, legislation... 378, 379
  Tenement-house work, precautions required by law................. 378–379
Contract labor, Japanese.. 755, 765, 766
Contract-labor law:
  Bureau of Immigration, large discretionary powers.................. 659, 660
  Canada.. 719–722
  Deportation—
    Canadians.. 447
    Decision of immigration officials, final........................... 658, 659
    Number deported, New York, 1899–1901......................... 663
  Domestic servants excepted from law................................ 650
  Excepted classes of laborers... 648–654
  Friends of residents excepted.. 650
  Inspection of immigrants, methods.................................. 662–665
  Labor organizations dependent on enforcement of.................. 312
  New industries, labor necessary to establish, excepted.............. 654
  Nonresident aliens, Canadians excepted............................. 649

Contract-labor law—Continued. Page.
  Personal servants excepted... 650
  Proof of contract, essential elements.................................. 656, 658
  Prosecution of importer, difficulties................................... 655
  Professional classes excepted....................................... 650–652, 654
  Provisions, generally 648
  Reasons for enactment... 647
  Relatives of residents excepted....................................... 650
  Resident aliens, excepted.. 649
  Seamen, excepted 649, 650
  Skilled labor, certain classes of, excepted.............................. 652–654
  Specific cases decided under—
    Buffalo and Pittsburg tailor cases................................... 669–671
    Croatian stave cutters... 666–668
    Lace makers, imported by Dr. Dowie............................... 668, 669
Cotton trade. (See *Textile trades*) 420–422
Criminality of foreign born:
  Chinese (see also *Chinese, highbinders*) 758
  Comparative, various nationalities—
    Massachusetts... 289
    United States 286
  Comparative, native and foreign born—
    Generally... 285
    By age groups... 287
    Males 288
  Distribution by nationalities... 479, 480
  Japanese.. 758
  Juvenile offenders, distribution by nationalities 480
  New York City—
    By nationalities, 1854–1860.. 460
    Early complaints 449
    Second generation 480
Custom Clothing Makers' Union of America, organization................... 332
Custom Tailors' Union, organization of 334
Dam, Cleveland L. Testimony regarding Japanese immigration........... 767, 768
Delaware:
  Agricultural laborers, wages.. 615
  Foreign-born as agriculturists—
    Nationality of... 554, 615
    Opportunities... 554
  Population, density... 615
Deportation of immigrants:
  Chinese, San Francisco 760–761
  Contract laborers—
    Canadians 447
    Decision of immigrant officials final................................ 658, 659
    Number deported, New York, 1899–1901........................... 663
  Number deported—
    By races, 1900.. 290
    By years.. 662
  Time within which deportation possible............................... 665, 666
Destination of immigrants, statistics of, 1899–1900........................ 465
Disease (see also *Contagious diseases*):
  Immigration a cause... 450–454
  Regulations, early laws 451
Distribution of foreign-born (see also *Agricultural distribution*):
  Cities, tendency of foreign-born toward............................... 278–280
    An early manifestation 449
    Bohemians 508
    Reasons for 492
  Destinations claimed by immigrants, 1899–1900....................... 465
  Industrial distribution.. 297–299, 311
  Jews, local distribution 515
  Local, generally... 259–261
  Local, by nationalities 261–266
  New York City—
    Local distribution, 1864... 455–458

Distribution of foreign-born—Continued.
  New York City—Continued.   Page.
    Local distribution, 1890... 471, 472
    Nationalities.. 466–469
    Ruralization, early attempts unsuccessful 463
  Earnings, comparative, in various occupations.......................... 492
  Education of foreign born—
    Italians, New York City.. 475, 476
    Jews, New York City 478
Effects of immigration (see also *Labor organizations; Machinery; Occupations of immigrants; Standard of living; Wages*, etc.):
  Social—
    Cities, tendency of foreign-born toward.......................... 278–280, 442
    Criminality of foreign-born 285–289, 449
    Illiteracy of foreign-born, comparison with natives 280–282
      Comparison of races and nationalities........................ 282, 284
Emigration:
  Agencies, Germany, laws 696–697
  Authorities—
    Germany 698
    Italy 701
  Carriers, Italy, laws 702–705
  Contractors, Germany, laws... 696
  Forwarding emigrants, Germany, laws.................................... 697
  Jews, causes of.. 510
  Laws—
    Germany 695–699
    Italy 699–708
  Syrians, causes of... 442
Employment:
  Clothing trade, New York City, average number of days................. 338–342
  Coal mining, amount, average number of working days.. 394, 395–397, 410, 415
  Immigration, effects generally... 428–430
  Wages, factor in considering movement of 309
Employment of aliens. (See *Aliens*.)
European ports inspection 683–693
Factory inspection, tenement-house work.................................. 374–380
Factory system, clothing trade. (See *Clothing trade*.)
Financial condition of immigrants, illiteracy, relation to 284
Finishers, clothing trade, wages of...................................... 340
Finns:
  Agricultural distribution, preference for agricultural life 510
  Emigration, causes 510
Florida:
  Agricultural laborers, wages 624
  Foreign-born as agriculturists—
    Nationality 563, 625
    Opportunities 563–564
    Immigration, attitude of farmers toward.............................. 563
    Population, density 624
Foreign-born labor:
  Efficiency, compared with American 310
  Productiveness of, iron and steel trades 425
Fruit-packing industry, China, employment in............................ 748–749
Gardner, J. Endicott, testimony regarding Chinese 768–775
Georgia:
  Agricultural laborers, wages 622
  Foreign-born as agriculturists—
    Nationality 623
    Opportunities 561–563
    Population, density 622
Germans:
  Characteristics as workers, clothing trade 326
  New York City, standard of living, early conditions 461, 462
Germany, emigration and immigration laws................................. 695–699
Glass-bottle blowers, labor organizations among 426
Glass trade:
  Foreign-born, employment of 426

INDEX TO SPECIAL REPORTS. 831

	Page.
Glass trade—Continued.	
Machinery, effect of introduction	426
Output, limited and unlimited systems	425, 426
Wages	426
Glass workers, labor organizations, discriminations against aliens	425
Great Britain, clothing, methods of manufacture under public contracts	383
Highbinders. (See *Chinese*.)	
Hod carriers, labor organizations formed by nationalities	427
Hollanders, agricultural distribution of	532
Hours of labor:	
Building trades	426
Clothing trade	337, 338
Miners, Western States	753–754
Public works	437–439
Sweating system	321
Housing of foreign-born. (See *Tenement houses*.)	
Illinois:	
Agricultural laborers, wages	599
Coal mining—	
Employment, amount, average number of working days	395, 415
Foreign-born workers, number, nationality	391, 393, 407
Output of coal	403
Wages	409, 413–416
Foreign-born as agriculturists—	
Nationality	530, 531, 599
Opportunities	530, 531
Population, density	599
Illiteracy of foreign-born:	
Comparative, various nationalities	283
Various races	282, 284
Comparison of native and foreign born, by States and cities	280–282
Financial condition, relation to	284
Italians	430, 431
Indiana:	
Agricultural laborers, wages	597
Coal mining—	
Employment, amount, average number of working days	395
Foreign-born workers, number, nationality	391
Output of coal	403
Wages	409
oreign-born as agriculturists—	
Nationality	529, 598
Opportunities	529, 530
Population, density	597
Inspection, European ports	683–693
Inspection of immigrants:	
Methods generally	660–665
Boards of special inquiry, methods	661
Contract laborers, methods	662–665
Inspection of sweat shops, tenement-house work	374–380
Iowa—	
Agricultural laborers, wages	604
Foreign born as agriculturists—	
Nationality	541, 605
Opportunities	541, 542
Immigration, attitude of farmers toward	541
Population, density	604
Irish, New York City, standard of living, early conditions	461
Iron and steel trades:	
Foreign born, employment of	424
Labor disputes, effect of immigration	425
Labor organizations, discriminations against aliens	424
Output, effect of foreign born	425
Italians (see also *Padrone system*):	
Advancement, desire for in second generation	475, 476
Agricultural distribution	495–507
Assimilation slow	474
Characteristics generally	474, 475

Italians—Continued.   Page.
  Characteristics as workers, clothing trade 325, 326–329
  Colonies, agricultural 499–506
  Education of, New York City 475, 476
  Illiteracy 430, 431
  Moral standards 478
  New York City—
    Colonies of 474
    Education of 475, 476
    Occupations 473–474
    Standard of living 472–475
  Occupations 472, 474, 498
    New York City 473–474
  Standard of living 472–475, 498
Italy, emigration laws 699–708
Jacket makers, wages of, New York City 341
Jackson, J. P., testimony regarding Chinese exclusion law 795–797
Japanese:
  California 767–768
  Canada, immigration through 758
  Contract labor 755, 765, 766
  Criminality 758
  Effect on white labor 801–802
  Emigration companies 678–680, 756
  Immigration, general statement 754–755
  Mining, number employed in, Western States 753–754
  Public works, employment prohibited, British Columbia 715
  Railroads, employment on, Mountain and Pacific States ... 749–752
  Wage rates in Japan 757
Jewish Agricultural and Industrial Aid Society, work of 513–516
Jews:
  Agricultural distribution 510–517
  Characteristics as workers, clothing trade 325, 326–329
  Colonies of 511–513
  Education of, New York City 478
  Emigration, causes 510
  Industrial Removal Society, work, methods 514
  Labor organizations 327, 329, 334, 335
  Local distribution 515
  New York City—
    Distribution 476, 477, 487
    Economic advancement 477
    Education, desire for 478
    Standard of living 476–478
  Occupations 325, 514–515
Joint conferences, coal mining 406
Kansas:
  Agricultural laborers, wages 611
  Foreign born as agriculturists—
    Nationality 545, 612
    Opportunities 545, 546
  Population, density 611
Kentucky:
  Agricultural laborers, wages 626
  Foreign born as agriculturists—
    Nationality 626
    Opportunities 564, 565
  Immigration, attitude of farmers toward 565
  Population, density 626
Labels, tenement-made goods 377–378
Labor, efficiency, American and foreign born labor compared ... 310
Labor disputes:
  Coal mining 404, 408, 409
  Clothing trade 328–330
  Effect of immigration on, iron and steel trades 425
Labor organizations:
  Aliens, discriminations against 311, 312, 424, 425, 426, 428
  Bakers 428

Labor organizations—Continued. Page.
 Boot and shoe trade 423
 Building trades 427, 428
 Clothing trade. (See also *Clothing trade.*)
 Coal mining (see also *Coal mining*):
  History and effects 404, 405, 408, 410, 411
 Contract labor law, effectiveness dependent on enforcement of 313
 Foreign born—
  Difficulty in organizing 313
  Effect on coal mines 707
  Ignorance of a menace 312, 313
  Restrictions imposed on, coal mines 410, 411
 Iron and steel trades 424
 Longshoremen 428
 Union labels—
  Cigar trade 387
  Clothing trade 335
 Wages, effect on, cigar making trade 387
 Wood-working trades 423
Landlords, tenement houses, legal responsibility for work in 379–380
Legislation—
 Contract labor law. (See *Contract labor law.*)
 Immigration—
  British colonies 709–722
  Canada 710–715
  Natal 717–719
  New South Wales 716–717
  New Zealand 717
  Queensland 716
  Tasmania 717
  Victoria 716
  Western Australia 717
Tenement houses, New York City. (See *Tenement houses.*)
Tenement-house work, clothing trade, restrictions. (See *Clothing trade.*)
Licenses, tenement-house work 375–376
Longshoremen, labor organizations, organization by races 428
Louisiana:
 Agricultural laborers, wages 632
 Foreign born as agriculturists—
  Nationality 571, 632
  Opportunities 570–572
 Immigration, attitude of farmers toward 570
 Population, density 632
McCarthy, P. H., president Building Trades' Council, San Francisco, affidavit regarding Chinese and Japanese labor 801–802
Machinery:
 Boot and shoe trade, cause of reduction of wages 422
 Coal mines, amount produced by 398
 Glass trades, effect 426
 Introduction due largely to immigration 313, 314
 Skill, effect on 314
 Standard of living, effect on 314
 Textile trades, improvements in 420
 Wages, effect on 314, 399, 402, 404
 Women, employment of, effect on 314
 Wood workers, cause of employment of unskilled labor 424
Machinists, only slightly affected by immigration 425
Maine:
 Agricultural laborers, wages 583
 Foreign born as agriculturists—
  Nationality 517, 583
  Opportunities 517, 518
 Population, density 583
Maryland:
 Agricultural laborers, wages 616
 Foreign born as agriculturists—
  Nationality 554, 555, 616
  Opportunities 554–556

834 INDEX TO SPECIAL REPORTS.

	Page.
Maryland—Continued.	
Immigration, attitude of farmers toward	554, 555
Population, density	616
Massachusetts:	
Agricultural laborers, wages	586
Comparative criminality of different nationalities	289
Foreign born as agriculturists—	
Nationality	521, 587
Opportunities	521, 522
Immigration, attitude of farmers toward	521
Population, density	586
Wages, clothing trade	337
Mexicans:	
Peon labor, Western States	759, 800
Railroads, employment on, Mountain and Pacific States	749–752
Mexico, smuggling of Chinese immigrants from	758
Michigan:	
Agricultural laborers, wages	600
Foreign born as agriculturists—	
Nationality	531–532, 600
Opportunities	531–534
Immigrants, character of	532, 533
Immigration, attitude of farmers	531
Population, density	600
Minnesota:	
Agricultural laborers, wages	603
Foreign born as agriculturists—	
Nationality	540, 603
Opportunities	540, 541
Population, density	603
Mississippi:	
Agricultural laborers, wages	630
Foreign born as agriculturists—	
Nationality	631
Opportunities	569, 570
Immigration, attitude of farmers toward	568, 569
Population, density	630
Missouri:	
Agricultural laborers, wages	606
Foreign born as agriculturists—	
Nationality	606
Opportunities	542
Population, density	606
Montana:	
Agricultural laborers, wages	635
Foreign born as agriculturists—	
Nationality	576, 636
Opportunities	575, 576
Population, density	635
Natal, immigration laws	717–719
Nationality of foreign born:	
Age distribution	296
Distribution of various nationalities	261–266
Nationality of immigrants, successive nationalities, by decades, 1820 to 1900.	268–271
By quinquennial periods, 1875 to 1899	271–274
By years, 1890 to 1899	274, 275
Naturalization of Syrians	445
Nebraska:	
Agricultural laborers, wages	613
Foreign born as agriculturists—	
Nationality	546, 548, 614
Opportunities	546–550
Immigration, attitude of farmers toward	547
Population, density	613
Negroes as farm laborers	550–552
New Hampshire;	
Agricultural laborers, wages	584

INDEX TO SPECIAL REPORTS. 835

New Hampshire—Continued. Page.
  Foreign born as agriculturists—
    Nationality 584
    Opportunities 518, 519
  Population, density 584
New Jersey:
  Agricultural laborers, wages 592
  Colonies of Jews in 511–513
  Foreign born as agriculturists—
    Nationality 526, 592
    Opportunities 525–527
  Immigration, attitude of farmers toward 526
  Population, density 592
New South Wales, immigration laws 716–717
New York:
  Agricultural laborers, wages 590
  Foreign born as agriculturists—
    Nationality 591
    Opportunities 524, 525
  Population, density 590
New York City:
  Clothing trade. (See *Clothing trade.*)
  Criminals, by nationalities, 1854–1860 460
  Distribution of foreign born 466–469
    Jews 476, 477
    Local, 1864 455–458
    Local, 1890 .... 471, 472
  Education of foreign born—
    Italians 475, 476
    Jews 478
  Housing of foreign born—
    Early conditions 451–454, 457–459
    Responsibility for evil conditions 459
  Italians, occupations 473, 474
  Paupers, distribution by nationalities, 1854–1860 460
  Population—
    Age distribution 468
    Density 486, 487
    Foreign born, distribution by nationalities 466, 467, 469
    Increase by decades, 1820–1860 464
    Sex distribution 468
  Standard of living of foreign born—
    Early conditions 461, 462
    Italians and Jews 472–478
  Tenement houses. (See *Tenement houses.*)
New York, port of:
  Number of immigrants entering, 1820–1860 464
  Percentage of immigrants entering 449
New Zealand, immigration laws 717
North Carolina:
  Agricultural laborers, wages 619
  Foreign born as agriculturists—
    Nationality 620
    Opportunities 558–560
  Immigration, attitude of farmers toward 558, 559
  Population, density 619
North Dakota:
  Agricultural laborers, wages 607
  Foreign born as agriculturists—
    Nationality 543, 608
    Opportunities 543, 544
  Population, density 607
Number of immigrants:
  Statistics by decades 267
  Statistics by years, 1820–1900 268
  Armenians 445
  Bohemians 508

Number of immigrants—Continued.   Page.
  By age periods 297
  By sex 297
  Clothing trade, tenement-house work 369
  Coal mining 391–393, 407
  Females 300
  Generally 296, 297
  Italians 472, 474, 498
    New York City 473–474
  Jews 325, 514, 515
  Males 298–300; 301, 302
  Public works, employment of aliens 437–440
  Race distribution 303, 304
  Railroads, employment of aliens 441, 442
  Syrians 442, 445, 446
Ohio:
  Agricultural laborers, wages 595
  Coal mining—
    Employment, amount, average number of working days 395
    Foreign-born workers, number, nationality 391
    Output of coal 403
    Wages 409
  Foreign born as agriculturists—
    Nationality 596
    Opportunities 528, 529
  Immigration, attitude of farmers toward 528
  Population, density 595
Oregon:
  Agricultural laborers, wages 643
  Foreign born as agriculturists—
    Nationality 580, 644
    Opportunities 580, 581
  Population, density 643
Oregon Railway and Navigation Company, nationality of laborers employed. 751
Pacific States, alien labor in 747–802
Padrone system:
  Bankers, Italian, relations with padroni 433
  Cause of system 432
  Commissions exacted by padroni 433
  Conditions existing 432–436
  Employment agent, padrone acts as 433
  History 430–432
  Immigration stimulated by 432
  Labor, character of 435
  Laborers, treatment of 434, 435
  Public work only slightly affected by 440
  Wages 432, 435
Pants makers, wages of 328–341, 330–342
Pants Makers' Union, clothing trade 328
Pauperism:
  Nationalities, comparison of 286, 479, 480
  Native and foreign born, comparative 285
  New York City—
    Distribution by nationalities, 1854–1860 460
    Early complaints 449
Pennsylvania:
  Agricultural laborers, wages 593
  Coal mining—
    Accidents 417–418
    Employment, amount, average number of working days 394, 397
    Foreign-born workers, number, nationality 391, 392
    Output of coal 397, 403
    Wages 409, 412, 413
  Foreign born as agriculturists—
    Nationality 527, 594
    Opportunities 527, 528
  Immigration, attitude of farmers toward 527
  Population, density 593

INDEX TO SPECIAL REPORTS. 837

	Page.
Philadelphia, wages of garment makers	723–743
Poles, characteristics as workers, clothing trade	325–326–329

Population:
  Density—
    Influences affecting ... 494
    New York City ... 486, 487
    Separate States ... 493, 583–646
  Foreign born—
    Immigrants by decades, 1820 to 1900 ... 267
    Immigrants by years, 1820 to 1900 ... 268
    Percentage of, by decades ... 260, 261
  Increase—
    Influences affecting ... 494
    Relation of immigration to ... 277
    Separate States, 1890–1900 ... 493
  New York City—
    Age distribution ... 468
    Density ... 486, 487
    Increase by decades, 1820–1860 ... 464
    Nationalities, distribution by ... 466, 467, 469
    Parentage of residents, nationality ... 467, 469, 470
    Sex distribution ... 468

Pressers wages of, New York City ... 340
Price, William, lieutenant of police, San Francisco. Criminality of Chinese ... 775–782

Prices:
  Immigration, relation to ... 305
  Coal, effect of machine mining ... 399–402

Prosperity, immigration, relation to ... 305, 306
Public contracts, clothing manufacture, restrictions ... 382, 383

Public works:
  Aliens, employment of ... 437–440
  British Columbia, employment of Chinese and Japanese prohibited ... 715
  Hours of labor ... 437–439
  Padrone system, only slightly affected by ... 440
  Wages ... 437–439

Putnam, J. D., Chinese inspector, statement of ... 797–799
Queensland, immigration laws ... 716

Railroads:
  Aliens, employment of ... 441, 442
  Nationality of laborers, Mountain and Pacific States ... 749–752

Religious affiliations of immigrants, nationalities ... 291

Rhode Island:
  Agricultural laborers, wages ... 588
  Foreign born as agriculturists—
    Nationality ... 588
    Opportunities ... 523
  Immigration, attitude of farmers toward ... 523
  Population, density ... 588

Rosenhayn, N. J., colonies of Jews at ... 511–512
Santa Fé, nationality of laborers employed ... 751–752
Scandinavians, characteristics as workers, clothing trade ... 326
Schuyler, Frank D., Chinese inspector, San Francisco, Cal., testimony ... 765–767

Sex of immigrants:
  Distribution by sexes, 1868–1888 ... 432
  Males, predominance of ... 295, 303

Silk trade:
  Syrians, employment of ... 445, 446
  Wages ... 446

Skilled labor, machinery, effect on ... 314

Smuggling of immigrants:
  Canadian frontier ... 681–683, 758, 766
  Mexican frontier ... 758

South Carolina:
  Agricultural laborers, wages ... 621
  Foreign born as agriculturists—
    Nationality ... 560, 621
    Opportunities ... 560, 561
  Population, density ... 621

838 INDEX TO SPECIAL REPORTS.

	Page.
South Dakota:	
Agricultural laborers, wages	609
Foreign born as agriculturists—	
Nationality	544, 610
Opportunities	544, 545
Population, density	609
Southern Pacific Railroad, nationality of laborers employed	749–750
Southern States:	
Agricultural conditions—	
Cotton farming	552
Cropping	551
Intensive farming	552, 553
Renting	551
Tenant system	551, 552
Cotton, estimated acreage	553
Foreign born, agricultural opportunities	553
Negroes as farm laborers	550–552
Standard of living:	
Italians	472–475, 498
Machinery, effect on	314
New York City	461, 462, 472–478
Raised after immigration	327
Syrians	444
Tenement-house work, effect on	373
Textile trades	421
Wages, relation to	310, 311
Stonecutting trade, labor organizations, discriminations against aliens	428
Strikes:	
Coal mining, strike of 1897	404, 408, 409
Clothing trade	328–330
Effect of immigration on, iron and steel trades	425
Sweating system, clothing trade. (See *Clothing trade*.)	
Syrians:	
Character	443, 444
Emigration, causes of	442
Naturalization, extent	445
Number in United States	442
Occupations	442, 445, 446
Standard of living	444
Women, employment of	443
Tailors:	
Labor organizations among	332–334
Race distribution of	317
Wages of, New York City	342
Task system, clothing trade. (See *Clothing trade*.)	
Tasmania immigration laws	717
Temporary immigration. (See "*Birds of passage*.")	
Tenement-house work, clothing trade. (See *Clothing trade*.)	
Tenement houses:	
New York City—	
Early conditions	451–454, 457–459
Insanitary conditions	484, 485
Law of 1867	481, 484
Law of 1885	485
Law of 1895	487
Law of 1901	489, 490
Laws, enforcement of, inefficient	490
Legislation, results of	488, 491
Number of, by wards	487
Report of tenement-house commission, 1900	488
Responsibility for evil conditions	459
Tenants, average number per house	486
Types of tenements	482, 483
Tennessee:	
Agricultural laborers, wages	627
Foreign born as agriculturists—	
Nationality	566, 628
Opportunities	565–567
Population, density	627

INDEX TO SPECIAL REPORTS. 839

	Page.
Texas:	
Agricultural laborers, wages	633
Foreign born as agriculturists—	
Nationality	572, 633
Opportunities	572, 573
Immigration, attitude of farmers toward	572
Population, density	633
Textile trades:	
Machinery, improvements	420
Nationality of operatives	421
Standard of living	421
Wages, cotton mills	420, 422
Turner, Thomas F., statements by Chinese to	791–794
Unemployment, wages, factor in considering movement of	309
Union label:	
Cigar trade, use of	387
Clothing trade, use of	335
United States Government clothing, methods of manufacture under public contracts	383
Utah:	
Agricultural laborers, wages	639
Foreign born as agriculturists—	
Nationality	579, 640
Opportunities	579
Population, density	639
Vermont:	
Agricultural laborers, wages	585
Foreign born as agriculturists—	
Nationality	520, 585
Opportunities	519–521
Population, density	585
Vest makers, wages of, New York City	340
Victoria, immigration laws	716
Virginia:	
Agricultural laborers, wages	617
Foreign born as agriculturists—	
Nationality	617
Opportunities	556, 557
Immigration, attitude of farmers toward	556
Population, density	617
Wadham, Fred. W., affidavit regarding Chinese and Mexican immigration	800
Wages:	
Agricultural laborers, separate States	583–646
Boot and shoe trade, reduction through use of machinery	422
Building trades	426, 427
Canadian immigration, effect of	447, 448
Cigarmaking trade. (See *Cigarmaking trade*.)	
Clothing cutters	334–339
Clothing trade (see also *Clothing trade*)	327–343, 368
Special-order work	331–332
Tenement-house work	370
Coal mining (see also *Coal mining*)	399–402, 404, 408, 409
Comparative earnings in various occupations	492
Cotton mills	420, 422
Country competition, effect of	316
Cigarmaking trade	387, 388
Glass workers	425, 426
Immigration, effect of—	
General discussion	304, 305, 308, 309
Investigation by New York Bureau of Labor Statistics	428, 429
Japan, rates in	757
Labor organizations, effect on—	
Cigar trade	387
Coal mining	404, 408
Machinery, effect on	314
Coal mines	399, 402, 404
Mining, Western States	753–754

Wages—Continued.   Page.
  Movement of, 1870 to 1900 .... 307, 308
  Padrone system 432–435
  Public works 437–439
  Silk trade 446
  Standard of living, relation to 310–311
  Tenement-house work, clothing trade 370
  Textile trades 420–429
  Unemployment, relation to 309
  Unskilled labor in United States and Europe 309–311
  Women—
    Average rates 315
    Effect of employment 388
  Wood workers 424
Washington:
  Agricultural laborers, wages 641
  Foreign born as agriculturists—
    Nationality 580, 642
    Opportunities 580
  Population, density 641
West Virginia:
  Agricultural laborers, wages 618
  Coal mining—
    Employment, amount, average number of working days 395
    Foreign-born workers, number, nationality 391
    Output of coal 403
    Wages 409
  Foreign born as agriculturists—
    Nationality 618
    Opportunities 557
  Population, density 618
Western Australia, immigration laws 717
Wisconsin:
  Agricultural laborers, wages 601
  Foreign born as agriculturists—
    Nationality 537–539, 602
    Opportunities 534–537, 540, 541
  Population, density 601
Women:
  Cigar trade, effect of employment 388
  Employment in factories 315
  Machinery, effect of employment on 314
  Syrians, employment of 443
  Wages—
    Average rates 315
    Effect of employment 388
Woodbine, N. J., Jewish colonies at 512–513
Wood workers:
  Foreign born—
    Nationality of 423, 424
    Percentage of 423
  Labor organizations 423
  Machinery, unskilled labor introduced by 424
  Wages 424

Augsburg College
George Sverdrup Library
Minneapolis, Minnesota 55404